THE
Epicurean

BY
CHARLES RANHOFER
OF
DELMONICO'S

THE EPICUREAN

A COMPLETE TREATISE OF

ANALYTICAL AND PRACTICAL STUDIES

ON THE

CULINARY ART

INCLUDING

Table and Wine Service, How to Prepare and Cook Dishes, an Index for Marketing,
a Great Variety of Bills of Fare for Breakfasts, Luncheons, Dinners,
Suppers, Ambigus, Buffets, etc., and a Selection of
Interesting Bills of Fare of Delmonico's,
from 1862 to 1894.

MAKING A

FRANCO-AMERICAN CULINARY ENCYCLOPEDIA

By CHARLES RANHOFER,

FORMER CHEF OF DELMONICO'S,
Honorary President of the "Société Culinaire Philanthropique" of New York.

———————

ILLUSTRATED WITH 800 PLATES.

———————

Martino Publishing
Mansfield Centre, CT
2011

Martino Publishing
P.O. Box 373,
Mansfield Centre, CT 06250 USA

www.martinopublishing.com

ISBN   978-1-61427-088-1

© *2011 Martino Publishing*

Cover design by T. Matarazzo

Printed in the United States of America On 100% Acid-Free Paper

THE EPICUREAN

A COMPLETE TREATISE OF

ANALYTICAL AND PRACTICAL STUDIES

ON THE

CULINARY ART

INCLUDING

Table and Wine Service, How to Prepare and Cook Dishes, an Index for Marketing,
a Great Variety of Bills of Fare for Breakfasts, Luncheons, Dinners,
Suppers, Ambigus, Buffets, etc., and a Selection of
Interesting Bills of Fare of Delmonico's,
from 1862 to 1894.

MAKING A

FRANCO-AMERICAN CULINARY ENCYCLOPEDIA

By CHARLES RANHOFER,

FORMER CHEF OF DELMONICO'S,

Honorary President of the "Société Culinaire Philanthropique" of New York.

ILLUSTRATED WITH 800 PLATES.

Published by

THE HOTEL MONTHLY PRESS

950 Merchandise Mart
Chicago, Ill.

PREFACE.

N PUBLISHING this work I have endeavored to fill a much needed wan viz:—the best and most effectual manner of preparing healthy and nutritious food.

This edition contains innumerable recipes which I have simplified and explained in a comprehensive manner so as to meet the wants of all. It suggests, also, many useful and important hints to those about entering the profession.

The book is illustrated and contains instructions how to prepare, garnish and serve according to the traditional rules of our most able predecessors, and now followed by the principal chefs of France and the United States.

In some instances, where it was deemed necessary to differ from the standard rules and methods in order to cater to the various tastes, changes have been made.

The book is divided into twenty-four chapters: Table Service, Bills of Fare, Supplies, Elementary Methods, Soups, Stocks, Hot and Cold Sauces, Garnishings, Hot and Cold Side Dishes, Shell Fish, Crustaceans, Fish, Beef, Veal, Mutton, Lamb, Pork, Poultry, Game, Miscellaneous Entrées, Cold Dishes, Vegetables, Cereals, Hot and Cold Desserts, Pastry, Bakery, Confectionery, Ices, Fruit, Wines and Preserves.

Not relying solely on my experience and knowledge, I have quoted from the most illustrious modern author, my much beloved friend and colleague, Urbain Dubois, ex-chef at the Court of Germany, and it gives me sincere pleasure to thank him for his generous assistance.

The profession will acknowledge its indebtedness to the Messrs. Delmonico for the interest shown by them in developing the gastronomic art in this country.

Many will recall the business receptions given to distinguished guests under the supervision and direction of Delmonico.

Mention may be made of the following dinners: to President U. S. Grant, to President A. Johnson, to the Grand Duke Alexis of Russia, to Gen. Prim, to Charles Dickens, to Sir Morton Peto, to Aug. Belmont, to Giraud Foster, to Gen. Cutting, to Luckmeyer, the so-called "Black Swan Dinner," to Admiral Renaud, to Prof. Morse, to Bartholdi, to De Lesseps, to the Comte de Paris, also the ball given to the Russian Admiral and Fleet, and the Greek dinner.

I have entitled this work THE EPICUREAN, and have justly dedicated it to the memory of Messrs. Delmonico, as a token of my gratitude and sincere esteem.

Their world-wide reputation continues to be maintained by Mr. C. C. Delmonico.

In conclusion I feel that my experience will be useful to those seeking information in the gastronomic art.

Hoping the public will appreciate my efforts,

I remain respectfully,

CHARLES RANHOFER.

ESTABLISHED 1827.

Delmonico's

Office Beaver & South Wm Sts

BEAVER & SOUTH W^m STS
22 BROAD STREET
MADISON SQUARE.

New York, Feb'y 24th 1893

Chef

Charles Ranhofer Esq.

Dear Sir:

In my opinion after looking over your work it is very worthy of the reputation you have in my estimation for editing a work of this character, and it is with much pleasure I recommend it to the attention of those to whom it is most directly addressed.

A perusal will I think give one an appetite —

Yours truly

Charles Delmonico —

CONTENTS.

TABLE SERVICE.

TABLE SERVICE.

THE EPICUREAN.

TABLE SERVICE,

AMERICAN, FRENCH, RUSSIAN—FOR BREAKFAST, LUNCH, DINNER, SUPPER, COLLATION OR AMBIGU.

DINNER SERVICE—AMERICAN STYLE—AND BILL OF FARE (Dinner Service à l'Américaine et le Menu).

The success of a dinner depends upon good cooking, the manner in which it is served, and especially on entertaining congenial guests. The American service is copied more or less from the French and Russian, and remodeled to the tastes and customs of this country; as it varies somewhat from all others, a few instructions may be found useful to those desirous of learning the difference existing between them.

THE BILL OF FARE (MENU).

Menus are made for breakfasts, luncheons and suppers, but the most important one is for the dinner; these menus are generally composed a few days in advance to enable the necessary provisions to be purchased, so that on the day of the dinner, there has been ample time to prepare everything necessary, consequently much confusion is avoided and the work better done.

In carrying out the order the menu should be strictly followed, in fact, it must be an obligatory rule to do so.

Making out the bills of fare is the duty of the head cook, who composes and writes them according to the latitude he enjoys and the resources he has at hand.

BILLS OF FARE FOR DINNER.

Should the menu be intended for a dinner including ladies, it must be composed of light, fancy dishes with a pretty dessert; if, on the contrary, it is intended for gentlemen alone, then it must be shorter and more substantial. If the dinner be given in honor of any distinguished foreign guest, then a place must be allowed on the menu to include a dish or several dishes of his own nationality; avoid repeating the same names in the same menu. Let the sauces be of different colors, one following the other.

Also vary the color of the meats as far as possible, from one course to the other. Offer on the menus all foods in their respective seasons, and let the early products be of the finest quality (consult a general market list to find the seasonable produce), and only use preserved articles when no others can be obtained.

If the menus are hand written they must be very legible.

Menus are indispensable for service à l'Américaine; there should be one for each guest, for as no dish served from the kitchen appears on the table, every one must be informed beforehand of what the dinner is composed, and those dishes that are to follow each other.

Menus must be both simple and elegant, and of a size to allow them to be easily placed in the pocket without folding, as it is the general desire to keep the bill of fare of a dinner at which one has assisted.

A few important observations necessary to bills of fare and their classification are here given:

OYSTERS ON THE HALF SHELL.

Oysters appear on the menu the same as in the Russian service; on French bills of fare they do not mention them. Suppress oysters in every month not containing the letter R, such as: May, June, July and August, and serve Little Neck clams instead.

SOUPS.

Soups are served after the oysters. One clear and one thick soup should be selected but if only one is needed, give the preference to the clear soup.

HORS-D'ŒUVRE, SIDE OR LIGHT DISHES.

Hot hors-d'œuvre are, generally, timbales, croustades, cromesquis, palmettes, mousselines, bouchées, cannelons, cassolettes, rissoles, etc. With the same course serve cold side dishes, such as olives, radishes, canapés, caviare, pickled tunny, anchovies, etc.

In the French service, the fish and the solid joints come under the head of relevés or removes. In the American and English service, first comes the fish, then the removes.

FISH.

If the fish be boiled or braized, add potatoes to the menu; if broiled or sautéd, some cucumber salad; and, if fried, serve plain or with a light sauce.

REMOVES OR RELEVÉS.

The relevés or solid joints are composed of saddles, either of veal, mutton, lamb, venison and antelope, or else beef tenderloins or middle short loins. Turkey, goose, capon, pullets, ducks, etc., may be served, accompanied by one or two vegetables.

ENTRÉES.

Place on the bill of fare first the heaviest entrée, and conclude with the lightest; they must be previously cut up so as to avoid carving. No fish figures in the American service as an entrée. but terrapin or crabs may be allowed; also lobsters, shrimps, frogs, croquettes, etc.

Each entrée should be accompanied by a vegetable, served separately, except when it is one of those described above, such as terrapin, etc.

PUNCH OR SHERBETS.

A punch or sherbet is always served after the entrées and before the roast; do not make an extra heading on the menu for these, only placing them on a line by themselves, for instance: Roman punch or American sherbet.

ROASTS.

Roasts are served after the sherbet; a game roast is usually preferred, but poultry, either truffled or not, may be substituted: such as turkey, capon, pullet, duck, guinea-fowl, squabs, etc.; also roasted butcher's meat; but game is usually considered to be more choice.

COLD DISHES.

Cold dishes come after the roast, and before the hot dessert; they are served with green salads; terrines of foies-gras and boned turkey are also served as a second roast. (In the French service these cold dishes are classified as the last entrée.)

HOT SWEET DISHES OR ENTREMETS.

These appear after the roast; they are composed of puddings, crusts, fried creams, fritters, pancakes, borders, omelets, and soufflées, and form a separate course by themselves.

COLD SWEET DISHES OR ENTREMETS.

The cold sweet entremets come after the hot and are composed of jellies, bavarois, creams, blanc-manges, macédoines, charlottes and large cakes, and form another course.

DESSERT.

After the cold entremets come the dessert, composed of cheese, fresh fruits, preserved fruits, cakes, jams, dried fruits, candied fruits, bonbons, mottoes, papillotes, victorias, pyramids, frozen puddings, plombières, ices, ice cream and small fancy cakes, then the coffee and cordials.

SERVICE OF WINES AND CORDIALS (Service des Vins et Liqueurs).

The steward must inform and specify to the butler the wine to be served at each separate course. However important the dinner may be, still decanters of ordinary red and white wine must be placed on the table. The selection of the finer wines is the host's duty, he making his choice when ordering the bill of fare.

The steward's duty is to see that the wines are served at a proper temperature.

All white wines must be served cold.

Sherry and Xeres cool.

Bordeaux between 55 and 60 degrees, Fahrenheit, according to its growth.

Burgundy between 50 and 55 degrees.

Champagnes, cold or iced, or in sherbets.

Dessert wines cool.

For choosing wines consult the table on wines of Delmonico's cellar. (No. 3709.)

Russian Sideboards.—Absinthe, Vermuth Bitters, Kümmel, Mineral Waters, including Apollinaris, Clysmic, St. Galmier and Vichy.

FIRST SERVICE.

With Oysters.—Sauterne, Barsac, Graves, Mont Rachet, Chablis.

After the Soup.—Madeira, Sherry or Xeres.

With Fish.—(Rhine wines) Johannisberger, Marcobrunner, Hochheimer, Laubenheimer, Liebfraumilch, Steinberger. (Moselle) Brauneberger, Zeltinger, Berncasteler.

With Removes.—Côte St. Jacques, Moulin-à-vent, Macon, Clos de Vougeôt, Beaune.

With Entrées.—St. Émilion, Médoc du Bordelais, St. Julien. Dry champagnes for certain countries.

Iced Punches and Sherbets, Rum, Madeira.

SECOND SERVICE.

With Roasts.—(Burgundies) Pommard, Nuits, Corton, Chambertin, Romanée Conti.

Cold Roasts.—Vin de Paille, Steinberger.

With Hot Desserts.—(Bordeaux) Château Margaux, Léoville, Laffitte, Château Larose, Pontet-Canet, St. Pierre, Côtes de Rhone, Hermîtage and Côte-Rôtie. (Red Champague) Bouzy, Verzenay, Porto Première.

THIRD SERVICE.

With Dessert.—(Burgundy) Volnay, Mousseux. (Champagnes) Delmonico, Roederer, Rosé Mousseux, Pommery, Cliquot, Perrier-Jouët, Moët, Mumm.

Wine Liquors.—Muscatel, Malaga, Alicante, Malvoisie of Madeira, Lacryma Christi, red and white Cape, Tokay, Constance, Schiraz.

Cordials.—Curaçoa, Kirsch, Cognac, Chartreuse, Maraschino, Prunelle, Anisette, Bénédictine.

Beers.—Bass' Ales, Porter, Tivoli, Milwaukee.

WINES AND LIQUORS USUALLY CALLED FOR (Vins et Liqueurs Généralement Servis).

A DINNER OF AMERICANS.

RECEPTION-ROOM.

Sherry,   Bitters,   Cocktails.

DINNER WINES.

Haut Sauterne,   Amontillado,   Sherry,   Barsac,   Pontet Canet,
Perrier-Jouet Brut,   Liquors.

A DINNER OF FRENCHMEN.

RECEPTION-ROOM.

Sherry and Bitters,   Vermuth,   Absinthe.

DINNER WINES.

Graves,   Xeres,   Lafaurie,   St. Pierre,   Yellow Cliquot,
Beaujolais,   Liquors.

A DINNER OF GERMANS.

No wines or mineral-waters in the reception-room.

DINNER WINES.

Niersteiner,   Sherry,   Hochheimer,   St. Estèphe,
Pommery Sec.   Beaune,   Liquors.

American service, like the Russian, must be served quickly and hot. As easily understood by the following card, a dinner of ten minute intervals can be served with fourteen courses in two hours and twenty minutes and if at eight minute intervals, in one hour and fifty-two minutes, the same as an eight course dinner of ten minute intervals will take one hour and twenty minutes, so at eight minute intervals it will take one hour and four minutes.

	Figure 1—36 covers. 10 minutes. 2 hours 20. 8 minutes. 1 hour 51.	Figure 2—24 covers. 10 minutes. 2 hours 10. 8 minutes. 1 hour 44.	Figure 3—16 covers. 10 minutes. 2 hours. — 8 minutes. 1 hour 36.	Figure 4—12 covers. 10 minutes. 1 hour 50. 8 minutes. 1 hour 28.
1	Oysters.	Oysters.	Oysters.	Oysters.
2	2 Soups.	2 Soups.	2 Soups.	2 Soups.
3	S. D. hot and cold.	S. D. hot and cold.	S. D. hot and cold.	S. D. hot and cold.
4	2 Fish, potatoes.	1 Fish, potatoes.	1 Fish, potatoes.	1 Fish, potatoes.
5	1 Remove, vegetables.	1 Remove, vegetables.	1 Remove, vegetables.	1 Remove, vegetables.
6	1 Entrée, vegetables.	1 Entrée, vegetables.	1 Entrée, vegetables.	1 Entrée, vegetables.
7	1 Entrée, vegetables.	1 Entrée, vegetables.	1 Entrée, vegetables.	1 Entrée, vegetables.
8	1 Entrée, vegetables.	....	....	....
9	1 Punch.	1 Punch.	1 Punch.	1 Punch.
10	1 or 2 Roasts.	1 Roast.	1 Roast, salad.	1 Roast, salad.
11	1 or 2 Colds, salad.	1 Cold salad.	....	....
12	1 Hot sweet dessert.	1 Hot sweet dessert.	1 Hot sweet dessert.	1 Hot dessert.
13	1 or 2 Cold sweet des'rts	2 Cold sweet desserts.	2 Cold sweet desserts.	....
14	⎰ 1 or 2 Ices. ⎱ Dessert.	⎰ 2 Ices. ⎱ Dessert.	⎰ 2 Ices. ⎱ Dessert.	⎰ 1 Ice. ⎱ Dessert.

	Figure 5—10 covers. 10 minutes. 1 hour 42. 8 minutes. 1 hour 20.	Figure 6—8 covers. 16 minutes. 1 hour 30. 8 minutes. 1 hour 12.	Figure 7—6 covers. 16 minutes. 1 hour 20. 8 minutes. 1 hour 10.	Figure 8—4 covers. 10 minutes. 1 hour 10. 8 minutes. 56.	Figure 9—4 covers. 10 minutes. 1 hour. 8 minutes. 48.
1	Oysters.	Oysters.	Oysters.	Oysters.	Oysters.
2	2 Soups.	2 Soups.	1 Soup.	1 Soup.	1 Soup.
3	S. D. hot and cold.	....	....	....	....
4	1 Fish, potatoes.	1 Fish, potatoes.	1 Fish, potatoes.	1 Fish, potatoes.	1 Fish, potatoes.
5	1 Remove, veg'bles.	....	....	....	....
6	1 Entrée, veg'bles.	1 Entrée, veg'bles.	1 Entrée, veg'bles.	1 Entrée, veg'bles.	2 Entrée, veg'bles.
7	....	1 Entrée, veg'bles.	....	....	....
8	....	....	....	....	....
9	1 Punch.	1 Punch.	1 Punch.	1 Punch.	....
10	1 Roast, salad.	1 Roast, salad.	1 Roast, salad.	1 Roast, salad.	1 Roast, salad.
11	....	....	....	....	....
12	1 Hot sweet dess'rt.	1 Hot sweet dess'rt.	1 Hot sweet dess'rt.	....	....
13	....	....	....	....	....
14	⎰ 1 Ice. ⎱ Dessert.	⎰ 1 Ice. ⎱ Dessert.	⎰ 1 Ice. ⎱ Dessert.	⎰ 1 Ice. ⎱ Dessert.	Dessert.

THE DINNER TABLE, RECEPTION TABLE SERVICE AND WINES. (Le Couvert, Réception, Service de Table et les Vins.)

TABLE SERVICE FOR TWENTY-FOUR PERSONS.

An oblong shaped table is preferable for a large dinner party, the feet being less incommodious: it must at least be six or seven feet wide and twenty-two feet long, with rounded ends. This shaped table is most generally used, although some prefer round, or horse-shoe ones, or an oblong with square ends, and many other fanciful shapes, depending entirely on the size of the room and the taste of the host.

Tables can be lengthened according to the number of seats desired; the space allowed for each guest is, for a square table with square ends, two feet apart between each plate; when the ends are curved, the space for the corners must be twenty-two inches apart, and if entirely round, twenty inches.

Cover a table twenty-two by seven with a felt cover made for the purpose, then over this lay a tablecloth twenty-four feet long and eight or nine feet wide, being careful that it is exceedingly white and smooth, having no creases whatever.

Fold a well starched, large napkin, pinch it triangularly, and place it in the center of the table; have twenty-four smaller napkins also well starched, folded and pinched, and place these at the edge of the table and on each one set a plate with another napkin on top, folded either shaped as a boat, a tulip, or any other pretty design, or else the napkin may be simply folded square.

The bread is placed either under the folds or in the center of the napkin, according to the manner in which it is displayed, or on a small plate to the left of the cover. Another way is to place the bread in front of the napkin.

On the left of each plate, lay a table fork and also a fish fork.

On the right set a table knife, a silver fish knife, a soup spoon, also a small fork for oysters or Little Neck clams

In front, but slightly toward the right of each plate, set a small individual salt-cellar. The double silver pepper castors containing black and red pepper are distributed two on each side, and two at each end of the table, with eight single ones between the double ones.

Glasses are placed in a semi-circle either in front of the plate or else on the right; arrange these according to the courses to be served. First, water glass; second, white wine; third, sherry; fourth, Rhine wine; fifth, champagne; and sixth, Bordeaux.

Before serving the entrées remove the white wine, Sherry and Rhine wine glasses and replace them by fine Bordeaux and Burgundy glasses. Glasses intended for dessert wines and liquors, are only put on the table with the dessert.

THE CENTER LINE OF THE TABLE.

In the center of the table have a large piece of silverware decorated with plants, ferns and natural flowers, or else a high vase or simply a basket of flowers. These baskets or other decorations may be filled with one, or several kinds of variegated flowers, mingling red and white, scarlet and lilac, or Parma violets, or tulips and orchids, these produce a brilliant effect. (The entire house, staircases, halls, etc., may also be decorated with plants, palms, lemon and orange trees, or rubber plants. Mantels and mirrors to be also wreathed with flowers, or else scattered about in clusters, and have hanging baskets tastefully arranged in prominent corners, so as to add to the general beautiful effect.)

On each side of the center piece and on the center line have two prettily arranged baskets containing seasonable or hot-house fruits; on each side of these, set an ornamental piece, either made of nougat, gum-paste or sugar candy, or should these high pieces not be desirable, others may be substituted either of bronze, or else stands covered with flowers, etc.

On each end of these pieces set either candelabras or lamps, and beyond these high stands of graduated tiers filled with bonbons, cornucopias, Victorias, bonbon boxes, etc., all of them forming the center line of the table. Around this line, and at about twenty to twenty-four inches from the edge, draw a line the same shape as the table, and on this place decanter stands for decantered wine; two for sherry, four for white wine, and four for red Bordeaux, making ten in all, and the same quantity of decanter stands for decanters containing water, or instead of ten, twenty-four smaller ones may be substituted, one for each person.

Place at intervening spaces, two compote dishes with stewed fruits, four stands for small fancy cakes, two compote dishes for candied or dried fruits, nuts, etc., or else fresh strawberries, raspberries or mulberries, if in season, a saucerful for each person, and finish by interlacing through these dishes as well as the decanters, strings of smilax or any other pretty creeping vine, following around about twenty-four inches from the edge of the table; set into this verdure at various parts, clusters of natural flowers. A table arranged according to this description will be found to have a most charming and pleasing effect.

The diagram of the table should be obtained, and have the names of each guest tastefully written on fancy cards; lay one of these on the right hand glass of each person, in a prominent manner so that it can be read from a distance which will greatly facilitate the seating of the guests. Procure bouquets of flowers for the ladies, set in fancy vases, tying them with ribbons, and having a pin attached to enable them to fasten them on to their dresses; gentlemen's buttonhole bouquets should also be placed in vases. All these flowers must be in front, but slightly toward the left of each person.

The bills of fare or menus should be placed on the left side, either in silver stands (Fig. 197), or set beside the plate.

The host should always be seated so as to face the door leading into the dining-room. The hostess on the other end of the table directly opposite, their respective seats being at the top and bottom of the table. The seat of honor for a lady is on the right hand of the host, and naturally on the right hand of the hostess for a gentleman. The left hand may also be utilized as seats of honor but of minor importance. A dining room should be kept at a comfortable temperature. The sideboard should be placed at one side of the table, and on this or in the drawers and compartments everything must be arranged in thorough order so as to have them handy, thus avoiding all confusion during dinner.

The entire dessert service including wines to be arranged tastefully on the sideboard, giving a very pretty effect to the room. A service table must either be in the dining-room behind a screen or in a pantry close by; it must contain one or several carving boards, sundry knives and forks, ladles, chafing dishes, etc. The service must be rapid and the dishes served hot; avoid having anything cooked in advance except the large pieces. Entrées and all smaller dishes should be prepared according to their successive order, as the dinner progresses, at an interval of two or three courses, which means about ten or twenty minutes apart. A good steward can always manage to protract the dinner in case the cook is behind time, but it is his duty to inform those in the kitchen at least ten minutes beforehand so as to prevent any possible delay; he must also have a duplicate bill of fare from the kitchen identical with the one on the table, and classified according to the service, so as to be able to consult it in order to know exactly which dish follows the other.

When the dinner is ready, the steward must place his help in their respective positions, and give them final instructions regarding their duties; they should be attired in dress suits, white ties and gloves, and wear no jewelry whatever. In order to serve a ceremonial dinner for twenty-four persons, it will require: a steward, a butler, a carver and six waiters; carefully intrusting the care of the wines to the most intelligent, and the carving to the most expert; the remaining six being for the special table service, they must remain in their respective places to be at the call of the guests should their services be required.

RECEPTION.

The gentlemen are to be received by a waiter, who before introducing them into the reception room, takes their overcoats, canes, hats, umbrellas, etc., leaving these articles in a place set aside for this purpose, near the reception room, then hands each gentleman an envelope addressed to himself in which there will be found a card bearing the name of the lady he is to escort to the dining-room, and who is to be seated on his right hand during dinner.

Two other waiters attired in full dress, introduce the gentlemen into the reception room adjoining the dining-room, the doors to the latter being closed; in the reception room there should be a small Russian buffet, or simply serve some sherry, Xeres, bitters, vermuth and absinthe, to be handed round on trays to each guest as he arrives.

It is absolutely necessary to have a lady's maid to receive the ladies, lay aside their outer garments, or any article they may desire to confide to her care; these must be arranged in such a manner as to be easily returned to their respective owners.

The maid must remain and wait, in order to be continually at the disposal of the lady guests.

When all the invited guests have arrived and been duly introduced, the dinner hour having struck, the steward opens the dining-room doors, bows to the host, this being the signal to announce that dinner is served.

The hostess enters the dining-room first, on the arm of the gentleman in whose honor the dinner is given, followed by the other guests, the host being last. Each one sits down at the seats indicated on the cards, and when all are comfortably seated the dinner begins.

The service must be performed silently, a look alone from the steward sufficing for each man to do his duty. Every article handed round must be on a silver salver.

THE SERVICE.

Oysters.—Little Neck clams are passed around, beginning on one side by the lady on the right and the other side by the gentleman on the right, these being the most distinguished guests ; change this method at each course, those being served last before, being the first now.

The butler will pour out the Chablis, stating the name of each wine he serves.

Soup.—There are usually two soups to select from. While serving green turtle offer at the same time lemon cut in quarters.

Sherry should be served with this course.

Side Dishes.—Pass hot hors-d'œuvre ; these are served on warm plates. Serve the cold hors d'œuvre at the same time, and should the guest prefer the latter, remove the hot plate at once and substitute a cold one for it.

Sherry or Xeres should accompany this course.

Fish.—If there be two kinds of fish, offer the selection, and pass round the one preferred; should it be boiled or braized fish, have potatoes served at the same time; if broiled or sautéd thinly sliced seasoned fresh cucumbers must accompany it, and if fried fish such as whitebait, serve with thin slices of buttered brown bread and quarters of lemon.

Serve Rhine wine or white Bordeaux.

Removes or Solid Joints —The removes may be placed on the table before being taken off for carving; if it be a saddle of venison, it should be cooked rare, passing currant jelly at the same time. A saddle of mutton must also be rare and very hot; it can be cut lengthwise at an angle in thin slices or across, although the first way is preferable; serve both these on very hot plates, and have one or two vegetables accompanying them.

Serve champagne.

Entrées.—The entrées must be served one after the other without placing them on the table beforehand; they must be served on hot plates with one vegetable for each entrée, to be either passed round separately or else carefully laid on the same plate, unless it is desired that they be dressed; in this case dress and present to each guest. Serve Bordeaux at the first entrée, and an extra quality of wine at the last ; continue serving champagne to those who prefer to drink it until the roast.

INTERVAL.—SECOND SERVICE.

Iced Punch or Sherbet.—Should there be no ladies present, cigarettes can be handed round at the same time. Remove the two white wine and sherry glasses, and replace them by those used for Burgundy, also remove the cold side dishes. Ten to fifteen minutes must now be allowed between the courses.

Roasts.—The roast may be displayed on the table before carving, this being frequently requested by epicures; should there be several roasts, carve them all at the same time and pass them round according to desire, adding a little watercress for poultry, and should there be canvas-back duck, let currant jelly and fried hominy be served with also a mayonnaise of celery.

Serve the Burgundy from bottles laid flat in baskets (Fig. 767) holding the basket in the right hand and a white napkin in the left.

Cold.—Serve the cold dishes after the roast, these to be either goose livers (foies-gras) with truffles or boned turkey. The foies-gras must have a spoon to remove it with, and the boned turkey be cut into thin slices, and offer both to the guest at the same time, accompanied by green salads.

Serve Johannisberg or Vin de Paille.

Now remove everything from the table with the exception of the dessert, and to avoid using a brush lift up the extra napkins in front of each person, folding them in two so that the table is neat and clean without being obliged to use a brush or scraper. Lay the dessert plates on the table, and continue the service for the hot dessert.

Hot Sweet Entremets.—Make a distinct service for the hot entremets, then serve the cheese.

Serve a fine Laffitte Bordeaux.

Cold Sweet Entremets.—Make another service for the cold entremets and ices.

Dessert.—Instead of serving the cheese after the hot entremets it may be done now, which is in fact its proper place; pass around the fresh fruits, stewed, candied and dried fruits, bonbon cases, bonbons, mottoes, ices, strawberries and raspberries with cream when in season, passing cakes around at the same time.

Serve Madeira wine, Muscatel and Frontignan, also plates of salted almonds.

CONCLUSION OF THE DINNER.

It is now time for the hostess to bow, push back her chair and prepare to rise, this being a signal for the ladies to retire; after they have returned to the drawing-room, coffee is passed round on a salver containing spoons, hot water, sugar and cream. A few moments later another waiter comes forward with an empty tray to remove the cups the ladies hand him.

The gentlemen partake of their coffee in the dining-room; at the same time serve them Kirsch, brandy, chartreuse, cigars and cigarettes. The doors are closed and the ladies and waiters have retired so as to allow the gentlemen more freedom to talk among themselves, still it will be necessary to enter the drawing room and dining-room occasionally in order to see whether anything be needed so as to avoid being called as much as possible.

After half an hour or so, the gentlemen will rejoin the ladies in the drawing-room and then tea is served. The tea service is accomplished by passing around on trays, tea, sugar, hot water, cream, cups, spoons and slices of lemon. A few moments later another waiter removes the empty cups on a tray.

After the tea the service is considered to be ended.

FRENCH SERVICE (Service à la Française).

There are two different services in use: The French and the Russian.

Although recognizing the priority of both of these services, it will be well to mention the difference existing between them and the English and the American service; first, they differ in the classification of the bills of fare and certain changes in the table service, these alone are sufficient to be interesting.

The old style of French service threatens to disappear entirely and is rarely used, except on very rare occasions.

The three services placed on the table, one after the other, had certainly the advantage of displaying the culinary labor as well as the most variegated and rare products by exhibiting them in all their profuseness. But the great inconvenience is the preparation of dishes beforehand in the kitchen in order to have each service ready at once and to keep them hot in heaters before beginning to serve the dinner.

The dishes for the first course are placed on the table in chafing dishes provided with covers, to be lifted off when the guests are seated, and left on the table till ready to be carved.

Of course this inconvenience is somewhat remedied by keeping the heaters and chafing dishes at a given heat, and there must be placed near the table, either behind a screen in the dining-room or else in an adjoining pantry, a bain-marie with all the necessary sauces required for the dinner, and as soon as the meats are carved, each one is to be covered with its respective sauce before being handed around.

But notwithstanding all possible care and attention the entrées are apt to lose much of their finer qualities by the very act of being cooked and dressed beforehand, then kept hot in these heaters or chafing dishes.

Still this could scarcely have been the sole cause for abandoning the old system, for it continued in usage for several centuries. We are, however, obliged to recognize that first-class families have ceased to make a display of the great luxuriousness indulged in, in the past; to-day they are more restrained, the help less numerous and the chief cook frequently alone with one kitchen assistant, having no longer an extra man for pastry, confectionery and ices. The chef himself must see to the preparation of the pastry, ices and desserts. There is now scarcely to be found any house where for twelve persons they employ a chef, an assistant and a pastry cook and the remainder of the help corresponding to this great amount of luxury.

The bills of fare are simpler; instead of dressing and arranging the service on the table itself, many houses have a mixed service; this is made by presenting the dishes on the table, then removing them to be carved.

The general desire of the day is to dine quicker; taste changes with the fashion. The old French service is fast disappearing, and as it becomes more simple it gradually evolves into a mixed Russian and French service.

FRENCH SERVICE FOR 24 PERSONS (Service à la Française pour 24 Couverts).

The first service is composed of hors-d'œuvre (side dishes), two soups, two removes, four hot entrées, or two cold and two hot entrées.

Remove the cold hors-d'œuvre; serve the punch or sherbet.

The second service is composed of two roasts to take the place of the removes; four entremets, two being of vegetables, one hot sweet entremets and one cold; these to replace the entrées; two entremets cakes to take the place of the cold entrées.

Prepare the table for the dessert.

The third service, or dessert, is composed of two shelved stands filled with bonbons, victorias, bonbon boxes, cossacks, two low stands or drums containing small fancy cakes. two basketfuls of fresh fruits, two assorted compotes, one orange jelly, one Bar-le-Duc jelly and two cheeses; two fancy pieces of nougat or candied sugar to replace the entremets cakes.

The wines should be selected and served as indicated in another chapter, according to the taste and desire of the host.

FRENCH SERVICE, DINNER FOR 24 PERSONS—TO SET THE TABLE (Service à la Française, Dîner de 24 Couverts—Le Couvert).

The table must be sixteen to eighteen feet long and six to seven feet wide, with rounded corners, covered with a table-cloth and having exactly in the center a high stand or epergne, or piece of silverware or bronze, filled with flowers. Continue the middle line with candelabras or lamps; leave a place for the chafing dishes and between these arrange the cold hors-d'œuvre. Set the plates, the glasses to form a semicircle in front; the spoons and knives on the right and the forks on the left.

Commence serving the most honored guest on each right side, and begin each separate service at the person served the last.

All the dishes intended for the table should be dressed tastefully and the edges decorated with open-worked noodle borders; the meats laid symmetrically, the borders to be neither too high nor too much spread so that the dish covers can fit on easily; light bread borders can also be used.

Decorate the meats with trimmed hatelets just before placing them on the table.

NECESSARY MATERIAL FOR 24 PERSONS (Matériel Nécessaire pour 24 Couverts).

Let the china, glassware, silver, cutlery and linen be as much alike as possible, have the glasses all plain or cut of the same pattern and shape; the china either all white, colored or gilt; the linen plain or damasked with large or small designs.

The plates must be changed at each service as well as the knives and forks, they must be washed immediately and used again for the following services, otherwise there will be as many knives and forks needed as plates, consequently far more material.

24 soup plates.	24 dessert knives and forks.
24 side-dish plates.	72 large forks.
72 dinner plates.	72 steel knives.
48 dessert plates.	24 silver or gilt knives.
24 soupspoons.	24 side-dish knives and forks.
24 coffee after-dinner cups.	24 coffeespoons

Small salt cellars and pepper casters, one for each person.

12 radish dishes for 24 persons.	2 shelved stands.
A glass or silver knife rester for each person.	2 silver baskets for fruits.
8 silver toothpick holders.	2 drums for fancy cakes.
24 wine decanters and water bottles.	2 dishes for jellies.
2 soup tureens.	2 dishes for cheese.
2 chafing dishes and covers for removes.	4 compote stands.
4 chafing dishes and covers for entrées.	4 dishes and covers for vegetables.
2 chafing dishes and covers for roasts.	2 dishes for cold entrées.
24 water glasses.	24 sherry glasses.
24 Chablis glasses.	24 Burgundy glasses.
24 Bordeaux glasses.	24 liquor glasses.
24 Frontignan glasses.	24 Champagne flutes or goblets.
24 fine Bordeaux glasses.	24 punch or sherbet glasses.

Fine Baccarat glass is the handsomest; keep in reserve glasses of all kinds in case of an accident.

The oil and vinegar caster, as well as the mustard pot, are to be passed around according to necessity.

RUSSIAN SERVICE (Service à la Russe).

The habit we have of eating everything very hot and very fast comes to us from the " Russian service;" it differs from the French service in the very fact that nothing hot appears on the table, everything is cut up as needed, either in the kitchen or pantry. The carving should be performed very neatly, having all the pieces of even size and placed at once symmetrically either in a circle or straight row on dishes for ten or less persons, then passed round to the guests, who help themselves or are helped, according to their wish.

As for the solid joints, removes or roasts, they can be served precisely the same, or else laid on very hot plates and handed directly to each guest. There must be a sufficiency of every kind of entrée to serve for every person present. Should there be several and a variety of roasts and only one service required, then carve a third part of each one, or more of one than the other if certain dishes seem to be preferred. If there be several removes the same course can be pursued. As soon as one course is being passed around, the following one should be brought from the kitchen so that the dinner can be served uninterruptedly and eaten while hot and palatable.

The cold meat pieces may be dressed and arranged on the table the same as the candelabras, silverware, bronze vases and flower baskets, all of these to be in the center line of the table, leaving eighteen inches of space uncovered between the end of the line and the edge of the table; between this center line and the edge draw a round or oval or any other desirable shape at eighteen inches above the edge. If there be two cold meat pieces lay them on the sides of the table and in the center of the line, and if four, then two at the sides and two at the ends in the center, if eight then have four at the corners between the sides and ends on the eighteen-inch line above the edge; finish to decorate this line with cold sweet dishes, baskets of fresh fruits, shelved stands filled with bonbons, cossacks, Victorias, drums containing small fancy cakes, compoted dried fruits, etc., all these ornaments give the table a charming effect and should be arranged before the guests enter the dining-room.

The straight line alone and the cold meat pieces can be also arranged, finishing at eighteen inches from the edge with garlands of leaves and flowers instead of the dessert, and when ready to serve the cold pieces, take them off and replace them by the taller desserts, shelved stands and drums, ranging the others here and there, half on either side of the table between the middle line and the flowers.

Hot sweet entremets are always served as extras or "flying dishes," after the vegetables.

The service is far less sumptuous and elegant than the French one, yet it pleases many and is very fashionable at the present time. The remainder of the service is exactly like the French.

The old-fashioned bills of fare for the Russian service were classed differently to those of to-day; further on they will be found in great variety, appertaining to different epochs and a selection can be made of those most suitable; the service remains invariably the same, the only change being in the bill of fare.

It is the custom in Russia to serve the iced punches or sherbets after the fish, but it is certainly preferable to wait until the entrées are removed.

SUPPER. (Le Souper.)

"To sleep easily one must sup lightly."

SUPPER BUFFET.

Supper buffets are dressed on tables twelve to twenty feet long by four to five feet wide ; larger or smaller according to the number of guests and the richness of the bill of fare. Be careful that every article on the table shows to the best advantage, arranging each dish in a tasteful manner, yet observing certain indispensable rules so to facilitate the service that the buffet can be replenished and the dishes removed without the slightest confusion. The warm dishes should be served continuously without any delay and only a few at the time. Place a large piece of silverware in the center of the table to contain fruits, following the middle line on the length, then two large baskets of flowers and two pieces either of nougat or sugar, both ornamented with candied fruits, then two large cold-meat pieces and two stands filled with bonbon boxes, mottoes, victorias and bonbons, afterward two candelabras, and two entremets cakes to finish. In the front place a decorated salmon, behind on the other side of the center line stand the tenderloin of beef, and on each side of the fish and tenderloin, two medium-sized meat pieces, then the drums or high stands filled with small cakes. After this the small cold entrées, such as sandwiches and small rolls filled with rillettes; at each end of the table arrange the chicken and lobster salads. On one end of the table have plenty of material handy (according to the importance of the bill of fare), for hot service; have plates, soup tureens and chafing-dishes; behind, near the tenderloin of beef, put the ices, jellies and charlottes.

These suppers are usually served after the first part of the dancing order is finished between eleven o'clock and one in the morning. Frequently small tables are used when there is sufficient room; these are generally reserved for the ladies.

HOT DISHES.

First part.—The soup is either consommé in cups, or barley cream, or rice and almond milk. These must be perfectly clear in order to serve them in cups the same as the consommé.

Oysters prepared in different styles: Fricasseed, Hollandaise, Béchamel, poulette, Viennese, crawfish sauce, etc.; oysters fried or stuffed, small bouchées filled with salpicon, chicken or game croquettes, sweetbreads, lobster, etc., Timbales and mousselines; terrapin, Maryland or Newburg for white, Baltimore and Maryland Club for brown; red-head ducks and canvas-back, also quails and squabs and sometimes deviled crabs, stuffed lobsters, scallops à la Brestoise or frog croquettes.

COLD DISHES.

Second part.—Decorate the table with hors-d'œuvre composed of radishes, olives, celery, anchovy toasts etc.

Large pieces such as a richly decorated salmon, a tenderloin of beef garnished with vegetables, boned turkey and capon, ham stuffed with pistachio nuts and truffles, a suckling pig, a boar's head, large dishes of turkey and capon, truffled or otherwise. Volières of peacock, young swans, pheasants and guinea fowls ornamented with their natural feathers, large terrines of Strasburg foies-gras, woodcock, snipe, reedbirds, quails, leverets, veal kernels and game "pains," en damier; bastions of roast game on croûtons and garnished with fresh water-cress, pyramids of lobsters and crawfish and truffles.

There are a great variety of elegant entrées, and among others the following ones may be selected:

Aspics of all kinds, red beef tongue, foies-gras, fillets of chickens, oysters, etc.; white and brown chaufroids of partridge and chicken, also ravigote ducks, galantines of chicken, cream of pigeons, squabs and quails covered with chaufroid and decorated with black truffles and very green pistachio nuts; smoked and unsmoked tongue well glazed and dressed pyramid form; lamb chops au vert pré, ballotines of quails and squabs, ducklings pear shaped and thrushes à la Périgord; terrines of Nérac and ducks' livers à la Toulouse and young rabbit à la mode de Rouen; pains of chicken or game. Entrées of larks and reedbirds, chicken mayonnaise; lobster, shrimp, crab and salmon salads, also salad à la Russe, and at equal distances have plates of small breads garnished with rillettes and fine sandwiches.

Select from all this gastronomical wealth those dishes liable to satisfy the appetite and at the same time make a beautiful display on the table.

SWEET ENTREMETS AND DESSERTS.

Third part.—Intersperse among the cold dishes, liquor and fruit jellies, bavarois, "pains" of rice puddings, blanc-manges and charlotte russes, assorted creams and crowns, waffles filled with whipped cream, macédoines, assorted large dessert cakes, and timbales of waffles, brisselets and wheelbarrows of small meringues with flowers or fruits, horn of plenty and Sultan vases, cherry baskets, high mounted pieces of gum paste, royal icing, nougat, sugar candy, marchpane and almond paste. Fancy variegated ices, such as virgin cream and biscuit glacé, tutti-frutti, Montelimar, Neapolitan, harlequin, bombs and delicious creams with nuts; parfait with coffee and burnt almond cream, chestnut mousse and soufflés sabayon; sponge and plombière with fruits, Nesselrode puddings and fiori di latte; pineapple water ices and Favart soufflés; fresh, seasonable and hot-house fruits; compotes of fruits, small fancy cakes, Genoese cakes and others iced; bonbons, Victorias, cornucopias, Cossacks, mottoes and bonbon boxes.

This third part of the menu is certainly the prettiest and most coquettish, and with these luxuries ends the selection of dishes from which an elegant table may be set.

Drinks.—Champagne, Bordeaux, Burgundy, wine punches, lemonades, grenadine and syrups of raspberry, currant or orgeat, coffee or tea.

AMBIGU.

A meal usually offered cold without any soup, and set on a table where removes are served at the same time, also entrées, side dishes and sweet desserts, and in which the service is blended into one, for no dishes are to be removed. Certain breakfasts, hunting luncheons, and supper served in the midst of a ball, are also all called ambigu.

SERVICE FOR LUNCHEONS.

SERVICE FOR LUNCHEONS.

Lunch is a small repast indulged in between breakfast and dinner. This meal is called lunch in English, in French goûter or taste, because it is less heavy than the others, and, as generally very little is eaten, it is only tasted. In France this old custom only exists in country towns where breakfast is very matinal; the English and Americans also lunch, for they breakfast early and only dine toward six or seven o'clock, therefore lunch is an indispensable meal with them. Larger and more ceremonious luncheons are frequently served; these are called " dinner luncheons," and many bills of fare for their preparation will be found later on. For family luncheons there are generally served cold meats, light entrées, sandwiches, pastries, ices, preserves, etc.,

LUNCHEON FOR LADIES AND GENTLEMEN, OR FOR LADIES ONLY, OR GENTLEMEN ONLY.

FOR LADIES ONLY.

Although set with more simplicity than the dinner table, nothing elegant must be lacking; in the center of the table place a flower decoration, either a double cornicopia, or a boat, or two dossers set back to back, or a vase, or a temple, etc., according to the reason the lunch was offered to the guests. On each side place a piece made of nougat, one of spun sugar, and at each end a high stand on tiers filled with bonbons, Victorias, mottoes, etc.

At eighteen or twenty-four inches from the edge, according to the width of the table, draw a line the same shape as the table and lay on this decanters of white and sherry wines, also water decanters, one for every two persons; two fruit dishes, four containing small fancy cakes, and two of dried fruits. Set semicircular around each plate as many glasses as there are wines; on the right hand lay a card bearing the name of the guest, and on the left a dress or buttonhole bouquet and the menu standing against the flower vase. Decorate the sideboard with the dessert service; carve the meats near the dining-room, and see that everything is served very hot. Let the wines be of a proper temperature, and specify each one while serving it; as soon as everything is in complete order, open the doors and bow, which means that the lunch is ready, and the guests may assemble in the dining-room to take their places at the seats designated on their cards. The service begins the same as the dinner and continues likewise until the coffee is served, when the ladies retire to the drawing-room to partake of theirs, to listen to music, or to withdraw unceremoniously.

If the lunch should be intended for gentlemen only, suppress all ornamentation except the flowers and fruits; the menu should be more substantial, and if for ladies and gentlemen together, serve the same as for a dinner, observing the same etiquette.

MEAT BREAKFAST (Déjeuner à la Fourchette).

A meat breakfast is composed of broiled meats, cold meat, fish, eggs, croustades, fried dishes, sweets and dessert.

BILL OF FARE.

COLD SIDE DISHES.—MELON.

Radishes, celery, olives, anchovies, caviare, sardines, fresh butter, artichokes poivrade, smoked breasts of goose, canapés of ham, gherkins, shrimps, mortadella, cucumbers, Lyons sausage, mackerel in oil, tomatoes and pickles.

Oysters or Little Neck clams.

FISH.

Broiled—mackerel, shad, smelts, perch, trout, herrings.
Fried—codfish, fillets of flounders, whitebait, frost fish.
Baked—sheepshead, bass, English soles, redsnapper, kingfish.
Boiled—salmon, grouper, halibut, skate, cod's tongues.
Sautéd—weakfish, lobsters, mussels, bluefish, whitefish.

EGGS.

Omelets, scrambled, fried, poached, boiled soft and hard, soft, moulded or on a dish.

ENTRÉES.

Broiled—pig's feet, sausages, blood sausages, sliced venison.
Fried—chicken, tendons of lamb, crawfish cutlets.
Sautéd—tripe, chicken, kidneys, tournedos, calf's liver.

Baked—sweetbreads, lamb chops in papers, quails, pigeons in cases.
Braized—calf's head, sheep's trotters, grenadins of veal.
Broiled—porterhouse steak, sirloin steak, tenderloin of beef, veal, mutton and lamb chops.

COLD.

Game pie, terrine of goose-livers (foies-gras.)
Boned duck, chicken mayonnaise.

ROAST.

Game or broiled or roast poultry, with green salad.

SWEET ENTREMETS AND DESSERT.

If so far no eggs have been mentioned in the bill of fare, then fruit or spirituous omelets of all kinds may be served, or else Celestine omelet, snow soufflé, etc., but in case eggs have already been used, then diversify the bill of fare by giving fritters, crusts, pancakes, pears, apples, peaches, etc. Have also pies, tarts and cakes as well as cheese and fresh fruit.

Coffee and Liquors.

THE BREAKFAST TABLE.

The breakfast table must be laid simpler, although with as much care and taste as for all other meals; naturally there is less ceremony to be observed for a breakfast, the simplicity of the bill of fare and wines rendering it far easier to serve. The hors-d'œuvre and fruit may be placed on the table, and when a dressy appearance is desired, flowers or high cold pieces, such as meat pies, chaufroids, aspics, trout or salmon, may also be added.

The service for the wines and cooking is exactly the same as for a dinner.

SUPPLIES (Approvisionnements).

Good cooking is only obtained by having all the ingredients healthy, appetizing and nutritious; the stomach must not be fatigued, and yet the eye and the palate have to be somewhat flattered. A dish may be more or less simple, more or less difficult, but it must satisfy the taste and to obtain this result a cook should only use the best materials and those of the very freshest.

All the supplies should be of the very first choice; the best cook in the world can fail to work properly unless the provisions are of the best. A cook anxious to perform his duty must pay the strictest attention to the selection of the food; this alone constitutes a science based on a deep knowledge and long practice.

Beef must have light red, marbled meat, the fat being firm to the touch.

Veal meat to be white and firm, also its fat.

Mutton has red meat firm and marbled, the fat to be white.

Pork must be carefully selected from pigs raised on acorns or corn, having firm, white meat, and firm, white, brittle fat.

Chickens to be plump, the breast bone flexible, the ribs easily cracked. Pinch the pinion bones to see whether they are tender; the same of turkeys, other poultry and game. Old fowls can never replace young chickens, therefore use them as little as possible. A fish is to have a clear, fresh eye and must be firm to the touch; mistrust it as soon as the belly flesh becomes soft; the smell will indicate whether it be fresh or stale; the same of crustaceans.

Vegetables to be selected of the very freshest.

Fruits by their appearance and taste.

TABLE OF SUPPLIES.
FISH AND SHELL FISH.

Index for American Fish and when they are in Season.   S indicates when in season.

FISH.	POISSONS.	January	February	March	April	May	June	July	August	September	October	November	December
Angel or moon	....	...	...	...	...	...	...	S	S	...	...	...	...
Bass, lake or black....	Bass de Lac.	...	...	...	...	...	S	S	S	...	...	S	S
" sea....	" de Mer	...	...	...	...	15	S	S	S	S	S	...	...
" striped	" Bar	S	S	S	S	S	S	S	S	S	S	S	S
Blackfish or tautog....	Tautog	...	...	...	S	S	S	S	S	S	S	...	...
Bluefish....	....	...	...	...	...	S	S	S	S	S	S	...	...

FISH AND SHELL FISH.—Continued.

Index for American fish, and when they are in season.   S indicates when in season.

FISH.	POISSONS.	January	February	March	April	May	June	July	August	September	October	November	December
Bonito	Bonite						S	S	S	S	S		S
Butterfish		S	S	S	S						S	S	S
Carp, common & Buffalo	Carpe ordinaire							15	S	S	S		
" German	" miroir	S	S	S	S						S	S	S
Codfish	Morue	S	S	S	S	S	S	S	S	S	S	S	S
Eels	Anguilles	S	S	S	S	S	S	S	S	S	S	S	S
Flounders or flukes	Plie, Limande	S	S	S	S	S	S	S	S	S	S	S	S
Frost fish	Tacaud	S	S	S							15	S	S
Grouper		S	S	S								15	S
Haddock	Aiglefin	S	S	S	S		S	S	S	S	S	S	S
Halibut	Flétan	S	S	S	S		S	S	S	S	S	S	S
Herring	Hareng	S	S	S	S						S	S	S
Kingfish	Umbrine									15	S	S	15
Lafayette													
Lamprey	Lamproie			S	S								
Mackerel	Maquereau					15	S	S	S	S			
" Spanish	" Espagnol					15	S	S	S	15			
Mullet	Mulet						S	S	S	S	S	S	S
Muscalonge	Masque allongé							S	S	S	S	S	S
Perch	Perche	S	S	S	S	S					S	S	S
Pike perch	Sandre	S	S	S	S						S	S	S
" or Pickerel	Brochet ou brocheton						S	S	S			15	S
Pompano								15	S	S	S	15	
Porgy	Sargus	S	S	S	S						S	S	S
Red Snapper		S	S	S	S								
Salmon, Kennebec and Oregon	Saumon du Kennebec et de l'Orégon	S	S	S	S	S	Ken	Ken	Ken	Ken	S	S	S
" trout	Truite saumonée	S	S	S							S	S	S
Shad and roe	Alose et œufs	S	S	S	S	S	15						
Sheepshead							15	S	S	S	S	15	
Skate	Raie	S	S	S	S	S		S			S	S	S
Smelts	Éperlans	S	S	S	15				15	S	S	S	S
Sole, English	Sole Anglaise	S	S								S	S	S
Spot fish		S	S			S				S	S	S	S
Sturgeon	Esturgeon							S	S	S	S	15	
Trout, brook	Truite de ruisseau				S	S	S	S	15				
Turbot, American	Turbot Américain	S	S	S	S	S	S	15					
" English	" Anglais	S	S										
Weakfish							15	S	S	S	S	15	
Whitebait	Blanchaille	S	S	S			S	S	S	S	S	S	S
Whitefish	Lavaret	S	S									S	S

SHELL FISH: CRUSTACÉS ET COQUILLAGES:

FISH.	POISSONS.	January	February	March	April	May	June	July	August	September	October	November	December
Clams, hard	Lucines orangées	S	S	S	S	S	S	S	S	S	S	S	S
" soft	" papillons	S	S	S	S	S	S	S			S	S	S
Crabs, hard	Crabes durs	S	S	S			S	S	S	S	S	S	S
" soft	" moux					S	S	S	S	S	15		
Crawfish	Écrevisses	S	S	S	S					S	S	S	
Lobsters	Homards	S	S	S	S		S	S	S	S	S	S	
Mussels	Moules							S	S	S	S	S	S
Oysters	Huîtres	S	S	S						S	S	S	S
Scallops	Pétoncles	S	S	S							15	S	S
Shrimps, small	Crevettes petites			15	S	S					15	15	

MISCELLANEOUS   DIVERS

FISH.	POISSONS.	January	February	March	April	May	June	July	August	September	October	November	December
Codfish tongues	Langues de morue	S	S	S	S	S					S	S	S
Crabs, oyster	Crabes d'huîtres	S	S	S	S	S					S	S	S
Frogs	Grenouilles	S	S	S	S	S	Best	Best	Best	Best	Best	S	S
Milts	Laitances	S	S	S	S	S	S	S	S	S		S	S
Terrapin	Terrapène	S	S	S	S	S						S	S
Turtle, green	Tortue verte	S	S	S	S	S		S	S	S	S		
Prawns, large	Chevrettes						S	S	S	S	S		

FISH AND SHELL FISH.—CONTINUED.

Index for American Fish, and when they are in season. S indicates when in season.

SALT FISH.	POISSONS SALÉS.	January	February	March	April	May	June	July	August	September	October	November	December
Anchovies	Anchois	S	S	S	S	S	S	S	S	S	S	S	S
Codfish, dried	Morue sèche	S	S	S	S	S	S	S	S	S	S	S	S
Herring	Harengs	S	S	S	S	S	S	S	S	S	S	S	S
" pickled	" marinés	S	S	S	S	S	S	S	S	S	S	S	S
Mackerel	Maquereau	S	S	S	S		S	S	S	S	S	S	S
Prawns	Crevettes	S	S	S						S	S	S	S
Salmon	Saumon	S	S	S		S	S	S	S		S	S	S

SMOKED FISH	POISSONS FUMÉS:	January	February	March	April	May	June	July	August	September	October	November	December
Haddock, smoked or Finnan haddie	Aiglefin	S	S	S							S	S	S
Halibut	Flétan	S	S	S							S	S	S
Herring	Hareng	S	S	S	S	S	S	S	S	S	S	S	S
" bloaters		S	S	S							S	S	S
" kippered		S	S	S	S						S	S	S
Mackerel	Maquereau	S	S	S	S						S	S	S
Salmon	Saumon	S	S	S		S	S	S	S		S	S	S
Shad	Alôse	S	S	S	S						S	S	S
Sturgeon	Esturgeon	S	S	S	S						S	S	S
Whitefish	Lavaret	S	S	S	S						S	S	S

POULTRY.

Index for Poultry and when it is in season. S indicates when in season.
B indicates when the poultry is at its best.

POULTRY.	VOLAILLE.	January	February	March	April	May	June	July	August	September	October	November	December
Capon	Chapon	S	S	S	S	S	S	S					S
Chicken, to broil 1¼ lbs	Poulet à Griller, 1¼ liv's	S	S	S	S	S	S	S	S	S	S	S	S
" Sauter 2½ lbs	" Sauter, 2½ "	S	S	S	S	S	S	S	S	S	S	S	S
" Roast 3 lbs	" Rôtir, 3 "	S	S	S	S	S	S	S	S	S	S	S	S
" Braize 4 lbs	" Braiser, 4 "	S	S	S	S	S	S	S	S	S	S	S	S
Duck, Mongrel	Canards Métis	S	S	S	S					S	S	S	S
" tame	" Domestiques	B	B	B	B	S	S	S	S	S	S	S	B
Duckling	Caneton					S	S	S	S	S	S	S	
Fowl	Poule	S		S	S	S	S	S	S	S	S	S	S
Geese	Oie	S	S	S	S	S	S	S	S	S	S	S	S
" Mongrel	" Métisse	S	S	S	S					S	S	S	S
Gosling	Oison						15	S	S	S	S	S	
Guinea fowl	Pintade	S	S	S	S	S	S	S	S	S	S	S	S
Peacock	Paon	S	S	S	S	S	S	S	S	S	S	S	S
Pigeon	Pigeon	S	S	S	S	S	S	S	S	S	S	S	S
" stall-fed	" engraissé	S	S	S	S	S	S	S	S	S	S	S	S
Pullet	Poularde	S	S	S	S	S	S	S	S	S	S	S	S
Squab	Pigeonneau	S	S	S	S	S	S	S	S	S	S	S	S
Turkey	Dindon	S	S	S	S	S	S	S	S	S	S	S	S
" E. R. I.	" ex Rh'de Is'nd	B	B	S	S	S	S	S	S	B	B	B	B
" Young	Dindonneau	S	S	S	S	S	S	S	S	B	B	B	S
Suckling pig	Cochon de lait	S	S	S	S	S	S	S	S	S	S	S	S

In case no fresh ones are procurable, frozen poultry can be found every day of the year.

FRUITS.

Index for Fruits and when they are in Season.   S indicates when in season.

FRUITS.	FRUITS.	January	February	March	April	May	June	July	August	September	October	November	December
Alligator pears	Avocats							S	S	S			
Apples	Pommes	S	S	S	S	S	S	S	S	S	S	S	S
Apricots	Abricots							15	15				
Bananas	Bananes	S	S	S	S	S	S	S	S	S	S	S	S
Barberries	Epines Vinettes										S	15	
Blackberries	Mûres							S	15				
Cherries	Cerises					S	S	15					
Chestnuts	Marrons	S	S									S	S
Cocoanuts	Noix de Coco	S	S	S	S	S	S			S	S	S	S
Currants, black & red	Groseilles, cassis							S	15				
Figs	Figues										15		
Ginger	Gingembre							15	S	S	S	S	S
Gooseberries	Groseilles vertes dites à maquereau							S					
Grapes, Brighton	Raisins, Brighton							S	S	S	S	S	
" Concord	" Concord							15	S	S	S	15	
" Delaware	" Delaware							S	S	S	15		
" Hautfonds	" Hautfonds							S	S	S	S		
" Hot house	" de serre		S	S	S	S	S	S	S	S	S	S	15
" Ives	" Ives							S	S	S	S		
" Jona	" Jona							S	S	S	S		
" Malaga	" Malaga	S	S							S	S	S	S
" Muscatel	" Muscatelle								S	S	S	S	
" Niagara	" Niagara							S	S	S	S		
" Pokington	" Pokington							S	S	S	S		
" Rebecca	" Rebecca							15	S	S	S	15	
" Tokay	" Tokay							S	S	S	S	S	
Grape fruit or shaddock		S	S	S	S	S	S				S	S	S
Green gages	Reine Claude								S	15			
Huckleberries	Airelles						15	S	S				
Lemons	Citrons	S	S	S	S	S	S	S	S	S	S	S	S
Limes	Poncires												
Mangoes	Mangoes							S	S	S			
Melon, Cantaloup	Melon, Cantaloup							15	S	S	15		
" Musk	" Maraîcher							15	S	S	15		
" Spanish	" Espagnol											S	
" Water	" d'eau pastèque							S	S	S	15		
Nectarines	Brugnons							S	S				
Oranges, Florida	Oranges de Floride	S	S	S								S	S
" Mandarins	" Mandarines	S	S										S
" Spanish	" d'Espagne	S	S	S	S	S	S	S	S	S	15		
Peaches	Pêches							S	S	S	15		
" hot house	" de serre						S	S					
Pears	Poires	S	S	S				15	S	S	S	S	S
Pineapples	Ananas	S	S	S	S	S	S	S	S	S		15	
Plums	Prunes										S	15	
Persimmons													S
Pomegranates	Grenades									S	S	S	
Quinces	Coings									S	S	S	
Raspberries	Framboises						S	S	S				
Strawberries	Fraises				S	S	S	S					
" hot house	" de serre	S	S										
Tamarinds	Tamarins							S	S	S			
Tangerines		S										S	S
Wintergreen								S	S	S	S	S	S

GAME.

Index for Game and when it is in Season.   S indicates when in season.

GAME.	GIBIER.	January	February	March	April	May	June	July	August	September	October	November	December
Antelope and Venison.	Antilope								15	S	S	15	
Bear	Ours	S										S	S
Birds, Doe	Courlis					S	S	S	S				
" Lark	Mauviettes										S	S	S
" Rail-chopper, or Sora.	Râle									S			
" Reed	Mésange Moustache									S	S	S	S
" Rice	Oiseaux de Rizière	S	S	S						S	S	S	S
" Small	Petits Oiseaux	S	S	S						S	S	S	S
Buffalo	Buffle	S										S	S
Ducks, all kinds	Canards de toutes-sortes	3	S	S	S					S	S	S	S
" Blackhead	" à Tête noire	S	S	S	S					S	S	S	S
" Canvas-back		S	S	S	S					S	S	S	S
" Mallard	" Malart	S	S	S	S					3	S	S	S
" Red head	" Tête rouge	S	S	S	S					S	S	S	S
" Teal, bluewing	Sarcelle ailes bleues	S	S	S	S					S	S	S	S
" Teal, green	" ailes vertes	3	S	S	S					S	S	S	S
" Widgeon	Canards siffleurs	S	S	S	S					S	S	S	S
" Wood	" des bois	S	S	S	S					S	S	S	S
Geese, Brant	Oies Barnacles	S	S	S	S					S	S	S	S
" Wild	" sauvages	S	S	S	S					S	S	S	S
Grouse or prairie hen	Tétras ou poule de prairie	S							15	S	S	S	S
" Spruce	Tétras									S	S	S	S
Hare, American	Lièvre, Américain											S	S
" English	" Anglais	S	S							S	S	S	S
Partridge	Perdreau	S							15		S	S	S
Pheasants	Faisans	S									S	S	S
Pigeons	Pigeons					S	S	S	S	S	S	S	
Plovers, Grass	Pluviers									S	S	S	
" Corn, golden	" dorés									S	S	S	S
" Yellow legs	" à pattes jaunes									S	S	S	S
Ptarmigans	Poules de Neige		S	S	S								
Quails	Cailles	S										S	S
Rabbits	Lapins											S	S
Robins	Rouge gorge	Law against selling											
Snipe, Curlew	Bécassines, Courlis									S	S	S	S
" English	" Anglaises									S	S	S	S
" Jersey	" du Jersey									S	S	S	S
" Sand	" de Sable									S	S	S	S
Squabs, wild	Pigeonneaux sauvages									S	S	S	S
Squirrel	Ecureuil	S							S	S	S	S	S
Turkey, wild	Dindon sauvage	S	S	S	S							S	S
Woodcock	Bécasses	S							15	S	S	S	S

Almost everything, not fresh killed, may be found in good condition frozen, nearly every day in the year.

MEATS.

Index for Meats and when they are in season.   S indicates when in season.
B indicates when the meat is at its best.

MEATS.	VIANDES.	January	February	March	April	May	June	July	August	September	October	November	December
Beef	Bœuf	B	B	S	S	S	S	S	S	S	S	B	B
Kid	Chevreau			S	S	S	S	S	S				
Lamb, Spring	Agneau de lait	S	S	S	S	S	S						
Lamb, Yearling	Agneau Tardif	S	S	S	S	S	S	S	B	B	B	S	S
Mutton	Mouton	B	B	S	S	S	S	S	S	S	S	B	B
Pig	Cochon	B	B	B	B	B	B	S	S	S	B	B	B
Veal	Veau	B	B	B	B	B	B	S	S	S	S	B	B

VEGETABLES.

Index of Vegetables and when they are in season.   **M** Indicates the month when in season.
E Indicates when the vegetable comes from Europe; **H** when cultivated in hot-house or hot-beds.

VEGETABLES.	LÉGUMES.	January	February	March	April	May	June	July	August	September	October	November	December
Artichokes	Artichauts	E	E	E	E	E	E	E	E	E	E	E	E
" Jerusalem	Topinambours	M	M	M	M						M	M	M
Asparagus, hot-house	Asperges de serre	M	15										
" Out-door	" en Pleine terre		15	M	M	M							
" Green "	" Vertes		15	M	M	M							
" Tips "	" Pointes		15	M	M	M							
" White "	" Blanches		15	M	M	M							
Beans, Broad	Fèves								M	M	15		
" Lima	Haricots, Lima								M	M	M		
" String	" Verts	M	M	M	M	M	M	M	M	M	M	M	M
" Wax and butter	Mange tout		M	M	M	M	M	M	M	M	M	15	
Beets	Betteraves	M	M	M	new	M	M	M	M	M	M	M	M
Brussels sprouts	Choux de Bruxelles	M	M	15								M	M
Cabbage, Green Kale	" Verts Kale	M	M	M	M								
" Red	" Rouges	M	M	M	M				15	M	M	M	M
" Savoy	" de Savoie	M	M	M	M				15	M	M	M	M
" White	" Blancs	M	new	M	M	M	M	M	M	M	M	M	M
Cardoons	Cardons	M	M										
Carrots	Carottes	M	M	M	new	M	M	M	M	M	M	M	M
Cauliflower	Choux fleurs	E	E	E	H	H	H	M	M	M	M	M	M
Celery knobs, Celeriac	Céleri rave	M	M	M	M				15	M	M	M	M
" Soup	" Vert	M	M	M	M			M	M	M	M	M	15
Corn, green	Maïs frais								M	M	15		
Cranberries	Caneberges	M	M	M	M						M	M	M
Cucumbers	Concombres	H	H	H	H	H	H	M	M	H	H	H	H
" Small pickles	Cornichons								15	M	15		
Egg-plant	Aubergines	M	M	M	M	M	M	M	M	M	M	M	M
Garlic, dry	Ail, sec	M	M	M	M	M	M	new	M	M	M	M	M
Herbs, Basil	Herbes Basilic								M	M	M		
" Bay leaves, dry	" Laurier, sec	M	M	M	M	M	M	M	M	M	M		
" Burnet	" Pimprenelle						M	M	M	M	M		
" Chervil	" Cerfeuil	H	H	H	H	H	H	M	M	M	H	H	H
" Chives	" Ciboulettes	H	H	H	H	H	H	M	M	M	H	H	H
" Fennel	" Fenouil								M	M	M		
" Marjoram	" Marjolaine								M	M	M		
" Mint	" Menthe	H	H	H	H	H	M	M	M	M	H	H	H
" Parsley	" Persil	M	M	M	M	M	M	M	M	M	M	M	M
" Rosemary	" Romarin								M	M	M		
" Savory	" Sarriette								M	M	M		
" Tarragon	" Estragon	H	H	H	H	H	M	M	M	M	H	H	H
" Thyme	" Thym								M	M	M		
Hops	Houblons						15	15					
Kohl-rabi	Choux raves								M	M	M	M	M

VEGETABLES.—CONTINUED.

Index of Vegetables and when they are in season.   **M** Indicates the Month they are in season.

E Indicates when the vegetable comes from Europe; **H** Indicates when the vegetable is cultivated in hot-houses or hot-beds; **S** Indicates when the vegetable comes from the South; **L** Indicates when the vegetable comes from Long Island.

VEGETABLES.	LEGUMES.	January	February	March	April	May	June	July	August	September	October	November	December
Leeks	Poireaux	M	M	M	M	M	M	M	M	M	M	M	M
Mushrooms, cultivated	Champignons cultivés	M	M	M	M	M	M	M	M	M	M	M	M
" Field	" de Prairie				M	M	M			M	M	M	
" Girolles	" Girolles									M	M	15	
" Morils	" Morilles									M	M	15	
Okra or Gumbo	Gombaut	S	S	S	S	S	S	M	M	M	M	M	S
Onions	Oignons	M	M	M	M	M	M	M	M	M	M	M	M
" Bermuda	" de Bermude	15	M	M	M	M	M						
" Small	" Petits	M	M	M	M	M		M	M	M	M	M	M
Oyster-plant	Salsifis	M	M	M	M	M			M	M	M	M	M
Parsnips	Panais	M	M	M	M	M		M	M	M	M	M	M
Peas (South)	Pois		S	S	S	S	S	L	L	L	L		
Peppers	Poivrons	S	S	S	S	S	M	M	M	M	M	M	S
Potatoes	Pommes de terre	M	M	M	S	S	M	M	L	15	M	M	M
" Bermuda	" Bermude	15	M	M	M	M	M						
" Havana	" Havane		15	M	M								
" Sweet	Patates	M	M	M					M	M	M	M	M
Pumpkins	Potirons	M	15							M	M	M	M
Radishes, black	Radis noir				M	M	M	M	M	M	M	M	M
" Horse	Raifort	M	M	M	M	M	M	M	M	M	M	M	M
" Red	Radis rouge	M	M	M	M	M	M	M	M	M	M	M	M
" White or gray	" Blanc ou gris					15	M	M	M	M	M	M	15
Rhubarb	Rhubarbe		M	M	M	M	M						
Salad, Monk's beard	Salade barbe de Capucin	M	M	M									M
" Celery	" de Céleri	M	M	M					M	M		M	M
" Chicory	" de Chicorée	M	M	M				M	M	M		M	M
" Corn	" de Mâches	M	M	M							M	M	M
" Dandelion	" de Pissenlit / Dent-de-lion	M	M	M	M	M							M
" Escarolle	" Escarolle	M	M	M					M	M	M		M
" Lettuce	" de Laitue	M	M	M	M	M	M	M	M	M	M	M	M
" Romaine	" de Romaine						M	M	M	M	M	M	
" Watercress	" Cresson	M	M	M	M	M	M	M	M	M	M	M	M
Shallots	Echalotes	M	M	M	M	M	M	new	M	M	M	M	M
Sorrel	Oseille	H	H	H	H	H	M	M	M	M	M	H	H
Spinach	Épinard	M	M	M	M	M	M	M	M	M	M	M	M
Squash, summer, white	Courge blanche } Été								M	M	M	15	
" " yellow	" Jaune }												
" Winter, Hubbard	" Hubbard Hiver	M	M	M	15					M	M	M	M
" " Marrow	" Moelle "	M	M	M	15					M	M	M	M
Tomatoes	Tomates	H	H	S	S	S	S	S	M	M	M	H	H
Turnips, Rutabaga	Navets Rutabaga	M	M	M	M		M	M	M		M	M	M
" Teltow	" Teltow										M	M	M
" White	" Blancs	M	M	M	M	M	new	new	new	new	M	M	M

MODEL MARKET LIST.

BEEF.

Item	Unit	Recd	On hand	Need
Chuck	pcs.			
Corned, Navel	lbs.			
" Plate	"			
" Rump	"			
Fillets	pcs.			
Heads	"			
Hearts	"			
Kidneys	"			
Legs	"			
Loin, Flat Bone	"			
" Hip	"			
" Short	"			
Marrow Bones	"			
Palates	"			
Ribs	"			
Round	lbs.			
Rump	"			
Tails	pcs.			
Tongues, Fresh	"			
Butt				

LAMB (SPRING).

Item	Unit	Recd	On hand	Need
Legs	pcs.			
Racks, Short Cut	"			
" Twelve Ribs	"			
Saddles, Fore	"			
" Hind	"			
Whole Lamb	"			

LAMB (YEARLING).

Item	Unit	Recd	On hand	Need
Breast	pcs.			
Feet	"			
Fries	"			
Legs	"			
Racks, Short Cut	"			
" Twelve Ribs	"			
Saddles, Fore	"			
" Hind	"			
Shoulders	"			
Sweetbread	"			
Whole Lamb	"			

MUTTON.

Item	Unit	Recd	On hand	Need
Brains	pcs.			
Breast	"			
Feet	"			
Kidneys	"			
Legs	"			
Racks, Short Cut	"			
" Twelve Ribs	"			
Saddles, Fore	"			
" Hind	"			
Shoulders	"			
Whole Mutton	"			

VEAL.

Item	Unit	Recd	On hand	Need
Brains	pcs.			
Breast	lbs.			
Feet	pcs.			
Fore Quarter	"			
Heads	"			
Hind Quarter	"			
Kidneys	"			
Livers	"			
Racks	"			
Shoulders	"			
Spinal Marrow	lbs.			
Sweetbread	pcs.			
Tails	"			
Tongues	"			

PORK AND PROVISIONS.

Item	Unit	Recd	On hand	Need
Bacon	pcs.			
Bologna	lbs.			
Feet, Pigs	pcs.			
Ham, Corned	"			
" Fresh	"			
" Smoked	"			
" Westphalia	"			
Lamb Tongues	"			
Lard	lbs.			
Larding Pork	"			
Loin	pcs.			
Pork Tongues	"			
Salt Pork, Breast	lbs.			
Sausages	"			
" Frankfort	"			
" Meat	"			
Suckling Pig	pcs.			
Smoked Beef	lbs.			
Smoked Beef Tongues	pcs.			
Tenderloin	lbs.			
Tripe	"			

VEGETABLES.

Item	Unit	Recd	On hand	Need
Artichokes	pcs.			
" Jerusalem	peck			
Asparagus	bunch.			
" Tips	"			
Beans, Lima	bushel.			
" String	"			
Beets	"			
Brussels Sprouts	"			
Carrots	bbl.			
Carrots, New	"			
Cabbage	doz.			
Cauliflowers	"			
Celery Knobs or Celeriac	bunch.			
" Soup	"			
Corn, Green	pcs.			
Cranberries	bushel.			
Cucumbers	doz.			
Egg Plant	"			
Garlic	"			
Herbs, Dry	bunch.			
" Chervil	"			
" Chives	"			
" Mint	"			
" Parsley	"			
" Tarragon	"			
Kohl-rabi	"			
Leeks	"			
Melon, Musk	pcs.			
Mushrooms, Cultivated	lbs.			
" Field	"			
Okra	pcs.			
Onions	bbl.			
" Small	peck.			
Oyster Plants	doz.			
Parsnips	peck.			
Peas	bushel			
Peppers	pcs.			
Potatoes	bbl.			
" New	"			
" Sweet	bushel.			
Pumpkin	pcs.			
Radishes	doz.			
Radish, Horse	"			
Rhubarb	"			
Salad, Barbe	"			
" Celery	"			
" Chicory	"			
" Corn	peck.			

MODEL MARKET LIST.—Continued.

Item	Recd	On hand	Need
VEGETABLES—*continued.*			
Salad, Dandelion........peck.			
" Escarolle........doz.			
" Lettuce........ "			
" Romaine........ "			
" Water Cress........basket.			
Shallots........bushel.			
Sorrel........ "			
Spinach			
Squash, Summer (white)........pcs.			
" " (yellow)........ "			
" Winter, Hubbard........ "			
" " Marrow........ "			
Tomatoes........box.			
Turnips........bbl.			
EGGS.			
Fresh........pcs.			
Ordinary........ "			
FISH.			
Bass, Black or Lake........lbs.			
" Rock........ "			
" Sea........ "			
" Striped........ "			
Blackfish........ "			
Bluefish........ "			
Carp, Buffalo........ "			
Clams, Hard........pcs.			
" Soft........ "			
Codfish........lbs.			
" Dry........ "			
" Tongues........ "			
Crabs, Hard........pcs.			
" Meat........lbs.			
" Soft shell........pcs.			
Crawfish........ "			
Eels........lbs.			
Flounders........ "			
Frogs........ "			
Frost Fish........ "			
Grouper........ "			
Haddock........ "			
" Finnan........ "			
Halibut, 6 to 12 lbs........ "			
Herring........pcs.			
" Bloaters........ "			
" Salt........ "			
" Smoked........ "			
Kingfish........lbs.			
Lamprey........ "			
Lobsters........ "			
Mackerel........pcs			
" Salt........bbl			
" Spanish........lbs.			
Mussels........bushel.			
Oyster crabs........quarts.			
Pompano........lbs.			
Perch........ "			
Pike or Pickerel........ "			
" Wall Eyed........ "			
Porgies........ "			
Prawns........ "			
Red Snapper........ "			
Salmon........ "			
" Frozen........ "			
" Kennebec........ "			
" Smoked........ "			
" Trout........ "			
Scallops........quarts.			
Shad........pcs.			

Item	Recd	On hand	Need
Shad Roes........pcs.			
Sheepshead........lbs.			
Shrimp........quarts.			
Skate........lbs.			
Smelts........ "			
Sole. English........ "			
Spot Fish........ "			
Terrapin........doz. or lbs.			
Trout, Brook........ "			
Turbot, American........ "			
" European........ "			
Turtle, Green........ "			
Weakfish........ "			
Whitebait........ "			
Whitefish........ "			
GAME.			
Antelope, S. or L.........lbs.			
Bear........ "			
Birds, Doe........pcs.			
" Lark........ "			
" Rail, Sora........ "			
" Reed, Rice........ "			
Buffalo........lbs.			
Ducks, Black-head........pcs.			
" Brant........ "			
" Canvas-back........ "			
" Mallard........ "			
" Red-head........ "			
" Ruddy........ "			
" Teal B. Wing........ "			
Grouse........ "			
Hare, American........ "			
Hare, European........ "			
Partridges........ "			
Pheasants, English........ "			
Plovers, Bay........ "			
" Grass........ "			
" Yellow legs, large........ "			
" " small........ "			
Ptarmigans........ "			
Quails........ "			
Rabbits........ "			
Snipe........ "			
" English........ "			
" Sand........ "			
Squabs, Wild........ "			
Squirrel........ "			
Turkey, Wild........lbs.			
Venison, L. Saddle........ "			
" S and Legs........ "			
" Whole........ "			
Woodcock........pcs.			
POULTRY.			
Capon........pcs.			
Chickens, B., 1¼ lbs........ "			
" S., 2½ lbs........ "			
" R., 3 lbs........ "			
" Winter........ "			
Ducks, Mongrel........ "			
" Tame........ "			
Ducklings........ "			
Fowl........lbs.			
Geese........pcs.			
" Mongrel........ "			
Goslings........ "			
Guinea Fowl........ "			
Peacock........ "			
Pullets........ "			

MODEL MARKET LIST. —Continued.

	Recd	On hand	Need		Recd	On hand	Need
POULTRY—*continued.*				Grapes, Concord............... lbs.	....	....	....
Pigeons, Stall Fed............. pcs.	....	....	....	" Delaware............. "	....	....	....
Squabs....................... "	....	....	....	" Hot House........... "	....	....	....
Turkeys...................... lbs.	....	....	....	" Malaga.............. "	....	....	....
" Ex. R. I. .... "	....	....	....	" Rebecca.............. "	....	....	....
" Spring................ "	....	....	....	Green Gages .... pcs.	....	....	....
....	....	....	....	Huckleberries........ ......quarts.	....	....	....
....	....	....	....	Lemons...................... pcs.	....	....	....
				Melon, Water................. "	....	...	....
FRUITS.				" Musk.................. "	....	....	....
Apricots........ .... pcs.	....	....	....	Nectarines .... "	....	....	....
Apples....................... "	....	....	....	Oranges...................... "	....	....	....
Bananas...................... "	....	....	....	Peaches...................... "	....	....	....
Barberries.................... lbs.	....	....	....	Pears........................ "	....	....	....
Blackberries.............quarts	....	....	....	Pineapples................ ... "	....	....	....
Cherries..................... lbs.	....	....	....	Plums. Prunes............... "	....	....	....
Chestnuts.................... "	....	....	....	Pomegranates................ "	....	....	....
Currants, Black or Red........ "	....	....	....	Quinces...................... "	....	....	....
Ginger.................quarts	....	....	....	Raspberries.................. quarts	....	....	....
Gooseberries .... "	....	....	....	Strawberries................. "	....	....	....

MISCELLANEOUS.

	Recd	On hand	Need		Recd	On hand	Need
				....			
....	....	....	....	....	....	....	...
....	....	....	....	....	....	....	....
....	....	....	....	....	....	....	....
....	....	....	....	....	....	....	....
....	....	....	....	....	....	....	....
....	....	....	....	....	....	....	....
....	....	....	....	....	....	....	....
....	....	....	....	....	....	....	....
....	....	....	....	....	....	....	....
....	....	....	....	....	....	....	....
....	....	....	....	....	..	....	....
....	....	....	....	....	....	....	.
....	....	....	....	....	....	....	....
....	....	....	....	....	....	....	....
....	....	....	....	....	...	...	....
....	...	...	...	....	....	..	....
....	....	....	....	....	....	..	....

BILLS OF FARE.

The bills of fare are classed as follows: Breakfasts, Luncheons, Dinners, Buffet or standing suppers, Collations, Hunting parties, Garden parties served Ambigu, sit down suppers and dancing parties including the refreshments and supper.

These bills of fare are numbered according to articles and not to pages and every recipe in the book will be found in the Bills of Fare, thus forming a double index, as the table of contents at the end of the book is more conveniently classed by pages.

The breakfast bills of fare include more than one hundred different ways of preparing eggs, fish, minces, chopped meats, broils and sweet dishes.

The luncheons are composed of crustaceans, small entrées, poultry, game, hot entremets and desserts.

The dinners are composed of American, English, Russian and French service: Buffets of the greatest variety and manifold ways of serving them.

At the end of the book is placed a collection of choice bills of fare served by the house of Delmonico, between the years 1862 to 1893.

LIGHT BREAKFAST OF COFFEE, CHOCOLATE, TEA.

Crescents (3414)

Biscuit, plain or with cinnamon { (3266) (3267)

Brioches (3269)

Couques (3277)

Corn bread (3422)

Buns, English and Hot Cross (3270)

Flutes of brioches (3268)

Grissini with sugar and with butter { (3278) (3279)

Muffins (3421)

Rolls (3420)

Échaudés (3282)

Small flutes, finger-rolls (3419)

Flutes or French rolls (3420)

Small rolls, with butter (3420)

Toast dry, buttered (3283)

Toast dipped in milk or cream (3283)

GRIDDLE CAKES.

Buckwheat cakes (with compressed yeast) (3272)

Indian cakes (3274)

Wheat cakes (3276)

Flannel cakes (3273)

Rice cakes (3275)

Polish Blinis (3281)

COOKED CEREALS.

Hominy (3280)   Oatmeal (3280)   Polenta wheaten grits (3280)

BREADS.

Jocko (3416)   Crown (3415)   Graham (3423)   Rye (3423)

American bread (3417)

Pulled bread, bread crumbs pulled out and browned in the oven.

Assorted fruits (3699)   Oranges (3699)   Grape fruit (3699)

Boiled eggs (2856)   Fresh butter (775)

1 — JANVIER.
DÉJEUNER, 12 COUVERTS.
MENU.

Chablis	Huîtres (803)
Madère Sec	Poitrine d'oie fumée (822)
	Radis (808) Olives (800)
	Redsnapper mariné (832)
	Perches à la Polonaise (1208)
Vin de Moselle	Croquettes de pommes de terre en surprise (2782)
	Noisettes de filet de mouton glacées (1610)
	Fedelini Cardinal (2953)
	Poulet sauté Montesquieu (1895)
Beaune	Tomates grillées sauce mayonnaise chaude (2838)
	Œufs moulés en caisses au foie gras (2877)
bntet Canet	Perdreaux rôtis piqués au jus garnis de cresson (2102)
	Salade de mâche (2669)
	Fruits (3699) Fromage (3697)
Alicante	Compotes (3686)
	Salade d'oranges (3690)
	Café (3701)

2 — FÉVRIER.
DÉJEUNER, 10 COUVERTS.
MENU.

Graves	Huîtres (803)
Sherry	Fruits en ravier (793)
	Saucisson à l'ail (818).
	Homard à la Boulognaise (794)
	Œufs des gourmets (2950)
Hochheimer	Alose à la Evers garnie de coquilles d'œufs d'alose (1252)
	Goujons frits au beurre (1163)
	Mignons de filet de bœuf Chéron (1401)
Musigny	Poulet sauté Chasseur (1903)
	Salade Italienne (2635)
St. Emilion	Canvasback grillés (Canards sauvages) (2054)
	Salade de céleri (2660)
	Gâteau d'amandes (3225)
Malaga	Fromage (3697)
	Fruits (3699)
Liqueurs	Café (3701)

3 — MARS.
DÉJEUNER, 24 COUVERTS.
MENU.

	Crabes d'huîtres marinés (805)
	Canapés de langues (777)
Sauterne	Saucisson de Lyon (818)
	Maquereaux fumés (798)
	Pompano Macédoine (1223)
	Pommes Dauphine (2783)
Côte-Rôtie	Tournedos de filet de bœuf Laguipierre (1434)
	Petits pois à l'Anglaise (2742)
	Poulet sauté Diva (1886)
	Pointes d'asperges à la Maintenon (2695).
	Œufs pochés à la Bourguignonne (2926)
Léoville	Faisan truffé rôti (2110)
	Salade de laitue (2672)
	St. Honoré à la Sultane (3261)
Porto	Compotes (3686)
	Fromage (3697) Fruits (3699)
Liqueurs	Café (3701)

4 — AVRIL.
DÉJEUNER. 18 COUVERTS.
MENU.

	Huîtres (803)
Chablis	Harengs marinés (787)
	Œufs de vanneau (784)
	Caviar (778).
	Omelette aux foies de volaille (2884)
Niersteiner	Truites à l'Hôtelière (1292)
	Concombres (2661)
	Tournedos de filet de bœuf Flavignan (1432)
	Lazagnettes à la Philadelphie (2957)
Pontet-Canet	Côtelettes de pigeonneau Signora (2269)
	Pointes d'asperges au fromage (2697)
Chambertin	Sarcelles grillées (2067).
	Salade Russe (2645)
	Gâteaux aux fraises (3262)
	Dessert
Liqueurs	Café (3701)

5   MAI.

DÉJEUNER, 16 COUVERTS.

MENU.

Sherry	Olives Croissants (800)
	Mortadelle (818)
	Sardines (817)
	Canapés de harengs à la Russe (777)
	Consommé tapioca (316)
Haut Sauterne	Maquereau Espagnol farci garni de groseilles vertes (1199)
	Côtelettes d'agneau Gavardi (1675)
	Pommes Gastronome (2789)
Champagne	Filets de poulet à la Mexicaine (1859)
	Petits pois à l'Anglaise (2742)
	Asperges chaudes à la vinaigrette (2692)
	Œufs brouillés en bordure de risot aux foies de canards (2938)
Nuits	Canetons grillés mayonnaise vertes aux fines herbes (1938)
	Salade de laitue (2672)
	Tartelettes aux fruits variés (3337)
Liqueurs	Fromage (3697) Fruits (3699)
	Café (3701)

6   JUIN.

DÉJEUNER, 10 COUVERTS.

MENU.

Niersteiner	Lucines (803)
	Radis (808)
	Beurre (775)
	Olives (800)
	Tranches de saumon grillées sauce Béarnaise (1244)
Champagne	Grenadins de filet de bœuf Beaumarchais (1385)
	Pommes de terre Long Branch (2793)
	Côtelettes de pigeonneaux Lauriston (2265)
	Champignons à la Rivera (2758)
	Œufs frits à la Eugène André (2866)
Château Lagrange	Poulet grillé au jus (1831)
	Salade de romaine (2675)
	Beignets de cerises fraîches (3042)
Liqueurs	Fruits (3699)
	Fromage (3697)
	Café (3701)

7   JUILLET.

DÉJEUNER, 12 COUVERTS.

MENU.

	Lucines (803)
Graves	Concombres en filets (783)
	Harengs saurs (788)
	Haricots verts marinés (824)
	Oranges à la Russe (3613)
Marcobrunner	Kingfish à la Sultane (1185)
	Pommes Viennoise (2812)
	Ris d'agneau Joinville (1761)
	Maïs sauté au beurre (2731)
	Homard à la Bordelaise (1025)
	Œufs durs à la Bennett (2858)
Château Larose	Alouettes grillées (2082)
	Salade de romaine (2675)
	Bordure de riz aux bananes (3005)
	Fruits (3699)
	Fromage (3697)
Liqueurs	Café glacé (3609)

8   AOÛT.

DÉJEUNER, 18 COUVERTS.

MENU.

Xérès	Piments verts (806)
	Avocats (771)
	Olives Espagnoles (800)
	Acharts aux fines herbes (792)
	Omelette aux truffes (2908)
Liebfraumilch	Weakfish à la Pontigny (1309)
	Concombres à l'Anglaise (2661)
	Filets de poulet à la Valençay (1855)
	Macaroni à la mode de Naples (2960)
Champagne	Grenadins de filet de veau aux tomates à l'Argentine (1507)
	Pommes de terre aux truffes émincées (2813)
Château Léoville	Canetons grillés (1938)
	Salade de cresson aux pommes d'arbres (2676)
	Flan d'abricots (3170)
	Poncire à la Madison (3612)
	Fromage (3697)
	Fruits (3699)
Liqueurs	Café à la Turque (3702)

9 — SEPTEMBRE.

DÉJEUNER, 22 COUVERTS.

MENU.

Absinthe, Vermouth, Kümmel.

Concombres marinés (785)
Canapés d'esturgeon (777)
Choux fleurs marinés (776)
Paupiettes de harengs à la Polonaise (789)

Lafaurie
Kingfish Montgolfier (1183)
Salade de concombres (2661)

Mignons de filet de bœuf à la Stanley (1406)
Purée de pois verts (2742)

St. Pierre
Côtelettes de pigeonneaux Provençale (2268)

Œufs au miroir à la Tivolier (2855)

Haut Brion
Perdreaux rôtis au jus garnis de cresson (2102)
Salade d'escarole (2671)

Petites meringues Italiennes au café (3394)

Liqueurs
Fruits (3699)
Fromage (3697)

Café (3701)

10 — OCTOBRE.

DÉJEUNER, 14 COUVERTS.

MENU.

Graves
Huîtres (803)

Cerneaux frais (834)
Choux rouges (776)
Maquereaux à l'huile (797)

Omelette physiologique (2904)

Pompano à la Toulouse (1227)
Moselle
Pommes de terre Gastronome (2789)

Beaune
Côtelettes de chevreuil Buridan (2170)

Petits pois à la Française (2743)
Poulets sautés à la Dodds (1887)

Escargots au beurre de Provence (1016)
Champagne
Râles à la Mareille (2150)
Salade de laitue (2672)

Glace parfait au nougat (3478)

Liqueurs
Confitures de groseilles de Bar (3678)
Fromage (3697)

Café (3701)

11 — NOVEMBRE.

DÉJEUNER, 8 COUVERTS.

MENU.

Hermitage (blanc)
Huîtres et citrons (803)

Cerneaux confits (833)
Saumon fumé (822)

Reltinger
Petit Esturgeon aux quenelles et olives (1289)
Pommes de terre grillées à la chapelure (2776)

St. Estèphe
Filets mignons d'agneau sauce crème (1724)
Nouilles sautées au beurre (2972)

Pain d'écrevisses Chartreuse (2305)

Œufs sur le plat Condé (2912)

Champagne
Outarde en daube (1944)
Salade de céleri (2660)

Pouding soufflé Saxonne (3107)

Fruits (3699)
Fromage (3697)

Liqueurs
Café (3701)

12 — DECEMBRE.

DÉJEUNER, 8 COUVERTS.

MENU.

Montrachet
Huîtres (803)

Saumon fumé (822)
Alose marinée (787)

Piesporter
Tranches de saumon grillées sauce Béarnaise (1244)
Pommes Marquise (2797)

Tournedos de filet de bœuf aux raisins (1439)
Petits pois Ménagère (2744)
Lapereau à la Thieblin (2138)

Chaudfroid de jeunes pintades (2453)

Œufs brouillés aux truffes du Périgord (2947)

Rauzan
Ruddy ducks grillés (2066)
Salade de laitue (2672)

Amandes salées (3696)
Fruits secs (3699)
Compotes (3686)

Liqueurs
Café (3701)

JANUARY—BREAKFAST.

13

Oysters with lemon (803)

Eggs on a dish with cèpes (2922)

Broiled fresh codfish with bacon (1138)

Calf's head vinaigrette (1519)

Hashed pheasant (2299)

Porterhouse steak à la Sanford (1363)

Saratoga potatoes (2803)

Pèlerine tartlets (3335)

Dessert

14

Marinated tunny fish (831)

Omelet, German style (2891)

Grouper à la Franklyn (1162)

Corned beef hash, American style (2291)

Chicken leg cutlets with olives (1875)

Mutton chops plain (1590)

Dauphine potatoes (2783)

Fruits (3699)

15

Eggs on a dish à la Bercy (2910)

Chicken halibut with carrots (1173)

Spinal marrow of veal, Villeroi (1549)

Stewed mutton kidneys à la Burtel (1616)

Chateaubriand Colbert sauce (1381)

Anna potatoes (2770)

Mars cake (3318)

Fruits (3699)

16

Anchovy salad (772)

Eggs Russian style (2865)

Fresh herring paupiettes with milts (1176)

Duck giblets, housekeeper's style (1927)

Edible snails, Bourguignonne (1015)

Veal cutlets à la Seymour (1497)

Demi-glace potatoes (2784)

Triumvirat fritters (3050)

17

Bouillabaisse à la Marengo (1123)

Scrambled eggs with mushrooms (2942)

Oxtail chipolata (1321)

Fried artichoke bottoms (2683)

Broiled chicken à la Delisle (1828)

Mellow potatoes (2799)

Light pancakes with preserves (3079)

Dessert

18

Soft eggs chipolata (2949)

Fried frostfish (1160)

Slices of mutton purée of beans (1635)

Pork cutlets with fine herbs (1780)

Potato and beetroot salad (2652)

Broiled squab, Colbert sauce (2013)

Compote (3686)

Coffee (3701)

19

Palmettes Perrier (922)

Poached eggs with spinach (2933)

Lobster, Dugléré (1031)

Shoulder of mutton marinated with cream sauce (1651)

Fried asparagus tips à la Miranda (2696)

Aspic of foies gras (small) (2412)

Broiled partridge, English style (2085)

Cheese (3697)

20

Marinated smelts (821)

Poached eggs Villeroi (2928)

Lamb's trotters à la Bordelaise (1766)

Turtle stew à la Foster (1093)

Lentils with bacon (2750)

Roasted tenderloin of pork with gravy (1817)

Apples, Portuguese style (2998)

Stewed fruits (3686)

JANUARY—BREAKFAST.

21

Anchovy salad (772)

Ham omelet with green peas (2893)

Small green turtle baked (1092)

Sheep's trotters à la poulette (1659)

Green peas with braised lettuce (2746)

Squabs in earthenware saucepan (2018)

Water-cress salad with apples (2676)

Dessert

22

Radishes (808)

Olives (800)

Crabs, Carolina style (1003)

Gosling stewed with turnips (1954)

Neck of lamb with cabbage (1729)

Oyster plant poulette (2817)

Pork tenderloins, Printanière (1813)

Célestine omelet with whipped cream (3057)

23

Boiled eggs (2856)

Perch stuffed and baked (1210)

Corned beef with cabbage (1315)

Hashed young rabbit (2303)

Celery stalks with velouté sauce (2721)

Truffled pigs' feet, Périgord sauce (1786)

Bavarois with meringues (3133)

Dessert

24

Canapés of anchovies (777)

Salt mackerel with cream horseradish sauce (1195)

Tenderloin of beef pudding with oysters (2322)

Smothered red beans (2700)

Tripe, Lyonnese style (1475)

Broiled quail (2131)

Rum omelet (3059)

Rouen mirlitons (3323)

25

Marinated tunny fish (831)

Soft clams on skewers (999)

Cucumber salad (2661)

Stewed lamb, Parisian style (1756)

Trévise tomatoes (2836)

Pork cutlets, Aurora (1776)

Omelet with russet apples (3071)

Dessert

26

Oysters (803)

Omelet à la Andrews (2898)

Minced tenderloin of pork à la minute (1812)

Lambs' tails, Conti (1763)

String beans à la Pettit (2827)

Edible snails à la Saintonge (1014)

Parisian cakes (3321)

Dessert

27

Shad, Irish style, garnished with croquettes (1254)

Rissoles of mushrooms with marrow (958)

Neck of veal au blanc (1538)

Potatoes à la Bignon (2773)

Lambs' tongues with olives (1765)

Baked stuffed eggplants (2738)

Rum omelet (3059)

Dessert

28

Olives (800)

Westphalian ham (786)

Spotted fish with court bouillon, Calcutta (1287)

Fried oxtails (1323)

Stuffed mushrooms in cases (2762)

Green turtle, Havana style (1091)

Eggs with cream, meringued (3032)

Dessert

FEBRUARY—BREAKFAST.

29

Caviare canapés (777)

Bonvalet omelet (2882)

Codfish tongues with chopped sauce (1141)

Truffled pigs' feet (1785)

Kernel of veal with thickened gravy (1521)

German salad with croûtons (2664)

Broiled ptarmigan (2071)

Dessert

30

Bouillabaisse Parisian (1124)

Eggs on a dish, Bienvenue (2911)

Pork cutlets with mashed potatoes (1782)

Poulpetonnière pigeons (2321)

Broiled bear steak (2046)

Pont-Neuf potatoes (2800)

Stewed or compoted fruits (3686)

Coffee (3701)

31

Oysters and lemons (803)

Eggs miroir à la Provencal (2854)

Chicken halibut baked with Parmesan (1172)

Blanquette of breast of veal à la Jacquart (1490)

Sauerkraut garnished (2819)

Beefsteak with fine herbs (1374)

Celery salad (2661)

Preserved large white currants (3678)

32

Westphalian ham (786)

Bertini omelet (2881)

Salt herring with mashed potatoes (1177)

Lamb carbonade à la Rambuteau (1667)

Broiled pullet, tartar sauce (1991)

Cream of biscuits with kirsch (3011)

Cheese (3697)

Dessert

33

Matelote à la marinière, St. Mandé (1201)

Scrambled eggs with fine herbs (2939)

Lambs' trotters, Chantilly (1767)

Hashed chicken, Ancient style (2292)

Sarah potatoes (2802)

Broiled teal duck (2067)

Corn salad (2669)

Souffléd fritters with lemon peel (3048)

34

Chiffonade potatoes (807)

Hard-boiled eggs, New York style (2864)

Frostfish or whiting baked (1161)

Lamb hash with bananas (2296)

Potatoes à la Parmentier (2811)

Rump steak à la Villageoise (1367)

Apple tartlets (3327)

Coffee (3701)

35

Quenelles of fish, Montglas (2330)

Turkey giblets, salamander (2033)

Beef hash, Sam Ward (2288)

Green peas, English style (2742)

Veal kidneys à l'Anderson (1524)

Broiled ptarmigan (2071)

Rum omelet (3059)

Fruits (3699)

36

Scrambled eggs with tomatoes (2946)

Minced leg of mutton à la Lyonnaise (1632?)

Marchioness potatoes (2797)

Veal kidneys à la Roederer (1525)

Pigs' feet à la St. Menehould (1783)

Mushrooms à la Raynal (2756)

Apples with butter (2999)

Dessert

MARCH—BREAKFAST.

37

Oysters on the half shell (803)

Eggs in cases à la Colbert (2874)

Cisco fish, Castillane sauce (1134)

Kernel of ham, Biarritz (1794)

Veal cutlets maître-d'hôtel (1501)

Dandelion salad (2670)

Compote (3686)

Coffee (3701)

38

Eggs on a dish (2909)

Salt codfish, Spanish style (1142)

Calf's brains, Aurora (1479)

Frogs' legs deviled (1020)

Tournedos of beef, Victorin (1438)

Marshall potatoes (2796)

Apple fritters, Montagnard (3037)

Dessert

39

Fried anchovies (1249)

Eggs à la Gibson (2861)

Kingfish, Princelay (1184)

Minced tenderloin of beef with potato croquettes (1398)

Broiled chicken with tarragon gravy (1831)

Endive salad (2671)

Apple pie (3199)

Dessert

40

Smoked beef (822)

Plain omelet with cream (2886)

Weakfish à la Brighton (1308)

Jugged neck of mutton (1639)

Potato croquettes in surprise (2782)

Lobster mayonnaise (2534)

Pullet legs with new carrots (2005)

Quartered apple fritters (3041)

41

Spanish olives with anchovies (800)

Eggs on a dish à la Monaco (2916)

Smoked herring with cream (1178)

Stewed lamb, Dugléré (1754)

Mussels marinière (1046)

Beefsteak Bordelaise with marrow (1371)

Duchess dariole cakes (3299)

Dessert

42

Shad marinated (787)

Poached eggs à la Mirabeau (2927)

Matelote à la Talabasse (1202)

Sliced kernel of pork à la Cavour (1795)

Potato fritters (2788)

Rib steak à la Bercy (1364)

Omelet stuffed with strawberries (3068)

Dessert

43

Eggs miroir, Jockey Club (2851)

Lambs' kidneys glazed (1702)

Baked beef palate, Chevreuse (1327)

Potatoes persillade (2774)

Chicken legs as cutlets with olives (1875)

Trévise tomatoes (2836)

Lambs' brains with mayonnaise (2446)

Dessert

44

Anchovy salad (772)

Hard-boiled egg croquettes (2863)

Breast of veal stew with roux (1491)

Brussels sprouts sautéd (2704)

Sheep's tongue, Neapolitan style (1658)

Potato shavings (2807)

Baked chicken in shells (2345)

Fruits (3699)

APRIL—BREAKFAST.

45

Broiled sardines (1249)

Omelet Desjardins (2887)

Fried gudgeons (1163)

Rump of beef miroton (1344)

Guinea fowl with sauerkraut (1958)

Mutton chops, Tavern style (1592)

Souffléd potatoes (2808)

Strawberries and cream (3699)

46

Anchovy salad (772)

Eggs on a dish, English style (2914)

Lamprey à la Rabelais (1189)

Baked mashed potatoes (2798)

Calf's brains tomatoed, Béarnaise (1485)

Sirloin steak, Ancient style (1373)

Broiled squabs, Colbert sauce (2013)

Rum omelet (3059)

47

Arles sausage (818)

Canapés of shrimps (777)

Scrambled eggs with tomato purée (2945)

Smelts fried on skewers, tartar sauce (1269)

Kernel of leg of mutton in papers (1631)

Calf's brains à la poulette (1481)

Broiled chicken with bacon, maître-d'hôtel (1830)

Apples with butter (2999)

48

Oysters and lemons (803)

Mackerel in oil (797)

Hard-boiled eggs à la Benoist (2859)

Matelote of canotiers (1203)

Broiled pig's feet (1784)

Cabbage, peasant style (2706)

Roasted wild squabs (2018)

Provençal potatoes (2801)

49

Marinated sardines (817)

Eggs on a dish with tomatoes (2924)

Salmon (salt) à la Bedlow (1247)

Boiled potatoes (2774)

Flat sausages with tomato Soubise (1805)

Broiled tenderloin, anchovy butter (1424)

Endive salad (2671)

Nougat of apricots, cake (3319)

50

Oysters on the half shell (803)

Omelet, Duxelle with fine herbs (2888)

Carp broiled and breaded maître-d'hôtel (1130)

Baked potatoes with cream (2780)

Mutton kidneys on skewers (1618)

Broiled chicken with tarragon sauce (1831)

Lettuce salad (2672)

Apple charlotte (3008)

51

Eggs molded in cocottes à la Bedford (2873)

Lobsters à la Delmonico (1037)

Veal cutlets à la Zingara (1498)

String beans à la Pettit (2827)

Terrine of duck's liver à l'Aquitaine (2596)

Roast squabs (2018)

Cheese (3697)

Strawberry short cake (3262)

52

Small trout fried and marinated with wine (829)

Ham and green pea omelet (2893)

Stuffed lambs' trotters with tarragon gravy (1769)

Squabs à la Crapaudine (2007)

Sausages with truffles (1806)

Cream with lemon peel in pots (3155)

Croustades à la Castillane (895)

Dessert

MAY—BREAKFAST.

53

Clams (803)

Spanish omelet (2907)

Salt codfish à la Villageoise (1144)

Turnips with Béchamel (2848)

Calf's brains with black butter (1484)

Chicken pie à la Rigolo (2371)

Terrine of larks (2601)

Lettuce salad (2672)

54

Eggs à l'Aurora (2857)

Pompano à la Carondelet (1221)

Lamb stew, Irish style (1758)

Macaroni, Parisian style (2961)

Mussels baked with fine herbs (1050)

Minions of tenderloin of beef (1399)

Viennese potatoes (2812)

Hérisson tartlets (3333)

55

Stuffed clams (997)

Fried carp with parsley (1131)

Scrambled eggs with tomatoes and chives (2946)

Baked breast of lamb (1662)

Chicken pie (2554)

Veal kidneys with marrow (1526)

Potato and herring salad (2653)

Frangipane omelet (3058)

56

Canapés Brownson (853)

Porgies à la Manhattan (1229)

Boiled eggs (2856)

Smoked beef with cream (1358)

Lamb kidneys on skewers (1703)

Mashed potatoes in snow (2798)

Roast squabs with water-cress (2018)

Bermuda onion salad (2665)

57

Fried soft shell crabs (1006)

Scrambled eggs with Piedmont truffles (2948)

Matelote of carp, Miroir (1204)

Hashed mutton à la Omer Pacha (2297)

Potatoes in surprise (2809)

Broiled partridge, English style (2085)

Cos lettuce salad (2675)

Francillon cake (3305)

58

Hot potato salad (2654)

Havanese omelet (2894)

Stuffed carp à la Champenoise (1133)

Paupiettes of tripe (1477)

Lamb's head, vinaigrette sauce (1698)

Small sirloin steak à la Bordelaise (1370)

Potato cakes with ham (2779)

Pèlerine tartlets (3335)

59

Cassolettes à la Montholon (861)

Poached eggs à la Boëldieu (2925)

Shoulder of lamb with purée of celery (1753)

Baked cauliflower à la Béchamel (2715)

Calf's brains, peasant style (1483)

Cold asparagus, vinaigrette sauce (2692)

Small Célestine omelet (3056)

Dessert

60

Anchovy salad (772)

Ham omelet with green peas (2893)

Small green turtle baked (1092)

Sheep's trotters à la poulette (1659)

Green peas with braised lettuce (2746)

Roasted squabs (2018)

Water-cress salad with apples (2676)

Dessert

JUNE—BREAKFAST.

61

Omelet à la Andrews (2898)

Bluefish, Havanese style (1118)

Calf's brains in matelote (1482)

Baked potatoes (2771)

Clams, Philadelphia style (994)

Chicken roasted in the saucepan (1881)

Watercress and apple salad (2676)

Baskets filled with oranges (3570)

62

Shrimps with mushrooms and tomatoes, Béarnaise (1081)

Fried eggs with chopped parsley (2871)

Angel fish à la Bahama (1094)

Calf's lights à la Marinière (1529)

Minced lamb à la Rivera (1719)

Cauliflower with fried breadcrumbs (2718)

Hamburg steak à la tartare (1361)

Bordelaise potatoes, new (2775)

63

Shrimps in side dishes (819)

Hard-boiled eggs with noodles à la Carolli (2860)

Bluefish with mayonnaise and tarragon (1121)

Paupiettes of fillet of mutton à la Delussan (1613)

Slices of round of veal with gravy (1547)

Green peas à la Fleurette (2741)

Broiled duckling with green mayonnaise (1938)

Crescents of noodles with cherries (3015)

64

Sweetbread canapés (857)

Scrambled eggs with gravy (2940)

Codfish cakes (1145)

Oxtail, Alsatian style (1322)

Lamb cutlets, Maintenon (1678)

Mussels stuffed, Toulousian (1049)

Roast pullet with water cress (1996)

Dampfnoodles with cream (3030)

65

Cucumber fillets salted, Russian style (783)

Eggs on a dish, Creole style (2913)

Blackfish à la Orly (1114)

Tendon of veal à la Bayeux (1581)

Kidneys of lamb, stewed with Madeira and mushrooms (1704)

Broiled squabs à la Crapaudine (2007)

Potatoes sautéd with artichoke bottoms and truffles (2805)

Border of rice with bananas (3005)

66

Crusts à la Morton (904)

Omelet with caviare à la Stoeckel (2902)

Sea bass with almond butter (1100)

Crépine of lamb's trotters, Périgueux sauce (2242)

Kohl-rabies, housekeeper's style (2708)

Broiled chicken with bacon maître-d'hôtel (1830)

Slices of fillet of veal, Pèlerine potatoes (1514)

Cream pie (3201)

67

Anchovy salad (772)

Perch, Polish style (1208)

Mashed potatoes in snow (2798)

Squab cutlets in papers (2270)

Stuffed tomatoes, Provençal (2835)

Asparagus tips à la Miranda (2696)

Fresh cherry fritters (3042)

Dessert

68

Tunny marinated (831)

Onion and ham omelet (2900)

Turkey wings with turnips (2043)

Green peas, French style (2743)

Baked tripe with parmesan cheese (1474)

Artichoke bottoms à la Mornay (2680)

Crusts with Madeira (3026)

Dessert

JULY -BREAKFAST.

69

Marinated sardines (817)

Cheese omelet (2883)

Pompano à la Duclair (1222)

Anna potatoes (2770)

Sausages with white wine (1807)

Mussels à la poulette (1047)

Duckling, green mayonnaise with fine herbs (1938)

Columbia tartlets (3330)

70

Hard-boiled eggs à la Washburn (2862)

Porgy paupiettes, Hindostan (1230)

Lamb hash, Creole style (2295)

Chicken legs à la Saulnière (1873)

Marchioness potatoes (2797)

Sirloin steak, ancient style (1373)

Genoese cake merigued (3308)

Dessert

71

Radishes (808)

Molded fresh butter (775)

Fried eggs with brown butter (2870)

Blackfish à la Sanford (1115)

Rump of beef, mirotons à la ménagère (1344)

Purée of Jerusalem artichokes (704)

Lamb salad à la Somer (2637)

Chicken legs in papers (1876)

Casino cakes (3293)

72

Scrambled eggs with lobster garnished with Villeroi mussels (2941)

Baked kingfish (1186)

Noisettes of mutton with cooked fine herbs (1612)

Veal kidneys with white wine (1527)

Beef, Chateaubriand maître d'hôtel (1382)

Sarah potatoes (2802)

Mirabeau rice (3213)

Dessert

73

Fried shrimps (1080)

Eggs on a dish, Fermière (2915)

Brandade of salt codfish (1146)

Lambs' crows, ravigote sauce (1668)

Ribs of beef, old style (1332)

Tomatoes à la Boquillon (2833)

Fruits à la Creole (3051)

Dessert

74

Caviare canapés (777)

Green omelet with fine herbs (2892)

Deviled bluefish (1119)

Clam pancakes or fritters (996)

Calf's brains à la Chassaigne (1480)

Mutton tendons with mushrooms (1656)

Roasted squab with watercress (2018)

Small babas with rum (3288)

75

Varenskis polonaise (993)

Shad with sorrel purée (1256)

Eggs au miroir à la Lully (2852)

Lamb stew, Navarin (1755)

Beef and tomato salad (2623)

Baked hash of chicken (2293)

Barigoule artichokes (2689)

Printanier boats (cakes) (3291)

76

Poached eggs with spinach (2933)

Pike perch à la Financière (1214)

Breast of lamb with velouté tomato sauce (1665)

White bean salad (2658)

Sausages Gastronome (1802)

Spare ribs, Parisian style (1808)

Risot à la Ristori (2980)

Fruits (3699)

AUGUST—BREAKFAST.

77

Parsley omelet (2903)

Butterfish marinated and fried (1127)

Sausages with tomato Soubise sauce (1805)

Potted pigeons (1965)

Sliced leg of lamb à la Dordogne (1710)

Cream potatoes baked (2781)

Dessert

78

Canapés of herring, Russian style (777)

Eggs au miroir à la Meyerbeer (2853)

Kingfish on the dish (1187)

Calf's liver à la Claremont (1530)

Plain boiled potatoes (2774)

Broiled squabs (2013)

Madeira crusts (3026)

Dessert

79

Fried eggs à la sole (2869)

Fresh mackerel in papers, Mephisto (1192)

Stewed lamb with turnips (1759)

Calf's liver and bacon (1531)

Provençal potatoes (2801)

Venison fillets à la Lorenzo (2177)

D'Artois cake with apricot marmalade (3302)

Dessert

80

Celery vinaigrette (779)

Eggs on a dish, Venetian style (2920)

Bonito à la Godivier (1122)

Tournedos of beef, Talabasse (1437)

Potatoes, omelet shape (2806)

Broiled reedbirds (2151)

Condé cakes (3297)

Dessert

81

Lobster canapés (777)

Scrambled eggs à la Duxelle with anchovy croustade (2935)

Salt codfish, Faraday crowns (1147)

Minions of veal purée of artichokes (1509)

Lamb hash à la Célestine, baked (2294)

Broiled chicken with tarragon gravy (1831)

Eggplant salad, Provençal (2663)

Gooseberry tart (3309)

82

Omelet with clams (2885)

Porgy with Chablis wine (1231)

Tripe with cooked fine herbs (1478)

Lamb fries, tomato sauce (1696)

Baked cream potatoes (2780)

Roast duck (1921)

Valentine cake with rum (3265)

Dessert

83

Salmon quenelles stuffed (2335)

Tenderloin of beef with Madeira half glaze (1425)

Green peas with braised lettuce (2746)

Frog's legs à la d'Antin (1017)

Chicken roasted in the saucepan (1881)

Omelet stuffed with preserves (glazed) (3067)

Cheese (3697)

Fruits (3699)

84

Anchovy butter canapés (777)

Shrimp omelet (2906)

Pike perch à la Géraldin (1215)

Noisettes of tenderloin à la Berthier (1411)

Chicken quenelles à la Drew (2326)

Broiled duckling (1938)

Gooseberry tart (3309)

Dessert

SEPTEMBER—BREAKFAST.

85

Broiled eels, tartar sauce (1150)

Omelet with mushrooms (2899)

Hashed tenderloin of beef, Sheppler (2289)

Chipolata sausages (1801)

Partridge à la Baudrimont (2093)

Italian salad (2635)

Hollandaise potatoes with melted butter (2790)

Gooseberry flawn (3173)

86

Blackfish à la Villaret (1116)

Scrambled eggs à la Columbus (2934)

Yearling lamb cutlets in crépinette (1691)

Veal, minced Sicilian style (1544)

Parsnip cakes fried in butter (2767)

Beefsteak à la Périgueux (1376)

Baked Biarritz potatoes (2772)

Pancakes with orange-flower water (3078)

87

Sardine canapés (777)

Fried eggs with ham or bacon (2872)

Buffalo fish, cream sauce (1126)

Marshal potatoes (2796)

Partridge with olives (2103)

Slices of fillet of mutton maître-d'hôtel (1614)

Peeled tomato salad (2666)

Pumpkin pie (3203)

88

Shrimps in side dishes (819)

Omelet with sausages (2905)

Picked-up codfish with cream (1148)

Hollandaise potatoes (2790)

Venison cutlets deviled (2173)

Cèpes, Provençal style (2723)

Broiled plovers (2118)

Vanilla Chantilly éclairs (3304)

89

Oysters on half shell (803)

Small trout marinated in wine (829)

Eggs on a dish, Omer Pacha (2917)

Lafayette fish breaded, English style (1188)

Turkey giblets, peasant style (2034)

Calf's brains crépinettes (2244)

Julienne potatoes (2792)

Peach with rice tartlets (3334)

90

Shrimp canapés (777)

Argentine omelet (2878)

Bluefish in papers (1120)

Stewed lamb, Peruvian style (1757)

Partridge with sauerkraut (2104)

Spare ribs, Parisian style (1808)

Potato salad (2654)

Semolina croquettes, pistachio sauce (3019)

91

Eggs cocottes (2873)

Shoulder of mutton with turnips (1654)

Black blood pudding (1772)

Gosling sautéd with tomatoes, Robert sauce (1953)

Baked noodles (2971)

Minced venison (2184)

Broiled grouse (2071)

Dessert

92

Poached eggs, matelote (2930)

Mackerel, with white piquante sauce (1194)

Tripe, Parisian style (1476)

Venison hash, American style (2301)

White beans, maître-d'hôtel (2701)

Broiled reedbirds (2151)

Fresh fruits (3699)

Dessert

OCTOBER—BREAKFAST.

93

Spinal marrow à la Barnave (1548)

Omelet with fine herbs (2889)

Redsnapper à la Chérot (1232)

Gastronome potatoes (2789)

Pork cutlets half glaze and with apples (1777)

Scallops à la Marinière (1076)

Round steak with water-cress (1366)

Cream cakes with whipped cream (3296)

94

Alligator pears (771)

Scrambled eggs à la Jérôme (2936)

Pork chops, Castillane sauce (1778)

Lyonnese potatoes (2794)

Calf's liver with fine herbs (1533)

Red cabbage salad (2659)

Cheese (3697)

Coffee (3701)

95

Fried shrimps (1080)

Omelet with ham and green peas (2893)

Kingfish à la Bordelaise (1181)

Veal hash cakes, Brittany style (2300)

Beetroot fritters with cream (2702)

Yearling lamb cutlets (1669)

Potatoes fried and channeled (2787)

Coffee (3701)

96

Windsor canapés (777)

Omelet with kidneys (2897)

Buffalo fish, cream sauce (1126)

Breast of pork with cabbage (1773)

Calf's liver, Italian style (1532)

Roasted plovers (2119)

Potatoes, housekeeper's style (2791)

Cannelons à la Célestine (3292)

97

Tongue canapés (777)

Eggs on a dish with chopped ham (2923)

Fisherman's Matelote (1205)

Mutton kidneys à la Soubise (1617)

Broiled tripe, tartar sauce (1473)

Ruddy duck roasted (2066)

Creamed potatoes (2781)

Apricot cakes with cream of almonds (3287)

98

Canapés with sliced salmon (777)

Fried eggs, Neapolitan style (2868)

Mullet, D'Antin sauce (1206)

Calf's brains with Venetian sauce (1486)

Pullet legs à la Bayonnaise (2003)

Mutton chops Soyer (1591)

Provençal potatoes (2801)

Biscuits in cases with cream (3289)

99

Poached eggs with gravy (2931)

Cupola of salt codfish, Biscaïenne (2254)

Lamb stewed with turnips (1759)

Broiled plovers (2118)

Corned beef hash (2290)

Omelet soufflé with preserves (3065)

Coffee (3701)

Dessert

100

Soft eggs for epicures (2950)

Oyster patties (939)

Lamb minion fillet pudding à la Gladstone (2323)

String beans with butter (2829)

Salisbury steak (1359)

Mundane fritters (3044)

Fruits (3699)

Dessert

NOVEMBER—BREAKFAST.

101

Crawfish canapés (777)

Omelet with frogs (2890)

Fresh herring à la Calaisienne (1174)

Pork cutlets, gherkin sauce (1781)

Chicken legs, purée of Jerusalem artichokes (1877)

Porterhouse steak (1362)

Potato cakes (2778)

Crescents with preserves (3298)

102

Oysters tartare (804)

Eggs on a dish, Plumerey (2918)

Red snapper à la Princess (1236)

Hashed partridge Clémenceau style (2298)

Kulash à la Finnoise (1318)

Broiled chicken with bacon maître-d'hôtel (1830)

Baked Biarritz potatoes (2772)

D'Artois cake with apricot marmalade (3302)

103

Beets marinated (774)

Soft eggs with purée of sorrel (2951)

Maskinonge à la Providence (1207)

Potato croquettes maïsienne (2782)

Beef palate à la Béchamel (1326)

Minced partridge with rice (2091)

Redhead duck roasted (2063)

Goronflot (3310)

104

Anchovy canapés (777)

Omelet of beef palate (2880)

Fresh mackerel, Bonnefoy (1191)

Jugged venison (2180)

Flat sausage broiled with tomato Soubise sauce (1805)

Delmonico sirloin steak, plain (1375)

Potato tartlets (2810)

Marrow frangipane pie (3088)

105

Fried eels, tartar sauce (1150)

Scrambled eggs with Swiss cheese (2944)

Calf's tails with cabbage (1580)

Zampino, Modena style with string beans (1820)

Mutton cutlets à la Bouchère (1593)

Potatoes half glaze (2784)

Broiled teal duck (2067)

German pancake (3074)

106

Boiled perch, Valois sauce (1209)

Omelet with smoked herring (2895)

Calf's head à la poulette (1516)

Troyes Chitterlings (1775)

Rib steak of beef à la Royer (1365)

Potatoes, housekeeper's style (2791)

Woodcock roasted (2206)

Wells of love (3338)

107

Molded eggs in cases à l'Échiquier (2875)

Pike perch à la Royale (1216)

Breast of mutton (haricot) with turnips (1588)

Jugged rabbit with blood (2141)

Marinated pork tenderloin (1815)

Celery salad (2660)

Puff paste galette (3306)

Stewed fruits (3686)

108

Whitefish à la Gherardi (1311)

Eggs molded à la Parisian (2876)

Mutton kidneys on skewers, Bordelaise sauce (1619)

Tripe à la mode de Caen (1471)

Stuffed tomatoes with fresh mushrooms (2842)

Roast squabs with water-cress (2018)

Cheese (3697)

DECEMBER—BREAKFAST.

109

Bartholomew canapés (852)

Fried eggs à la Montebello (2867)

Wall eyed pike à la Durance (1213)

Hollandaise potatoes (2790)

Young rabbit, Valencia style (2139)

Roast Guinea fowl (1958)

Corn salad (2669)

Darioles with vanilla (3301)

110

Sardine canapés (777)

Omelet with onions and ham (2900)

Fresh herrings mustard sauce (1175)

Woodcock pudding (2325)

Bag sausage fried (1803)

Chicken roasted in the saucepan (1881)

Galettes, half puffed (3306)

111

Oysters on the half shell (803)

Eels fried with butter and fine herbs (1151)

Scrambled eggs à la Martinez (2937)

Oxtail à la Castellane (1320)

Bussy potatoes (2777)

Broiled canvasback duck (2054)

Oyster plant salad (2656)

Lafayette cakes with rum (3313)

112

Onion soup with Parmesan cheese (331)

German carp with sauerkraut (1132)

Omelet with bacon (2879)

Blanquette of tenderloin of pork with mushrooms (1814)

Minion fillets of lamb, shallot sauce with marrow (1727)

Potatoes, housekeeper's style (2791)

Blackhead duck roasted (2052)

Celery salad (2660)

Demonet tartlets (3331)

113

Canapés of herring (777)

Oyster omelet (2901)

Whitefish, pimentade sauce (1312)

Round buttock top of beef baked (1335)

Viennese potatoes (2812)

Roasted pullet with water cress (1996)

Apple fritters, Montagnard (3037)

Mince pie (3089)

114

Frostfish, Cherbourg style (1159)

Eggs on a dish with bacon (2921)

Tripe à la poulette with mushrooms (1472)

Paupiettes of fillets of veal à la Whittier (1511)

Dauphine potatoes (2783)

Roast squabs (2118)

Monk's beard salad (2674)

Madelenes with rum (3316)

115

Rissoles of crawfish à la Béatrice (949)

Hunter's omelet (2896)

Chicken sautéd à la Sherman (2468)

Minced tenderloin of beef, Creole style (1397)

Roast duck (1921)

Lettuce salad (2672)

Cheese (3697)

116

Scrambled eggs with sweetbreads (2943)

Lamb fries, cream horseradish sauce (1696)

Mellow potatoes (2799)

Braised duck with olives (1924)

Cèpes baked with cream (2724)

Cheese (3697)

Dessert

BILL OF FARE FOR INVALIDS

Arrow root, Indian (361)

Bavaroise (362)

Chicken broth, plain (363)

Chicken and mutton broth with barley (364)

Chicken and veal broth (365)

Clam broth and purée (366)

Custard cream of chicken or game (367)

Extract of beef, clarified (369)

Extract of beef, plain (368)

Fish broth with clams (370)

Frog broth and purée (371)

Herb broth (372)

Jelly of chicken and calf's feet (373)

Jelly of meat and calf's feet (374)

Jelly of calf's feet with Madeira wine (374)

Mulled egg and almond milk thickened with rice flour (376)

Mutton broth (375)

Pressed beef juice (377)

Purée of barley with chicken broth (378)

Purée of chicken, partridge, grouse or roebuck (379)

Purée of oatmeal or wheaten grits (380)

Sabayon of chicken or game (381)

Tea of beef, mutton, chicken or veal (382)

Veal broth, refreshing (383)

Wheat, oat or barley broth (384)

117 JANVIER.
LUNCH, 12 COUVERTS.
MENU.

Écrevisses vinaigrette (782)
Caviar garni de citrons (778)

Barsac — Huîtres sur coquilles creuses (803)

Bouillon en tasses (187)

Homard à la crème (1044)

Champagne Perrier Jouët — Tournedos filet de bœuf à la Roqueplan (1436)
Petits pois à l'Anglaise (2742)
Ris de veau à la Parisienne (1576)
Macédoine à la Montigny (2755)
Terrapène à la Maryland (1085)

Château Lagrange — Cailles grillées garnies de cresson (2128)

Mousseline de foies gras à la Dana (2535)
Salade de laitue (2672)

Champagne — Glace soufflée Favart (3534)
Macarons d'angélique (3380)
Fruits (3699)
Bonbons (3642)
Café (3701)

118 FÉVRIER.
LUNCH, 16 COUVERTS.
MENU.

Xérès — Canapés de saumon (777)
Mortadella (818)

Consommé de volaille (190)

Château Yquem — Côtelettes de filet de bœuf à la Babanine (2255)
Tomates à la Trévise (2836)

Champagne Dry Monopole — Poulet sauté à la Marcel (1892)
Petits Pois à la Parisienne (2745)

Champignons sous cloche (2761)

Punch, Favorite (3508)

Château Larose — Bécassines rôties (2159)
Salade de cresson (2676)

Omelette soufflée aux pommes (3063)

Gelée à la Rose (3181)
Charlotte Russe (3145)

Glace pommes de terre farcies sauce marasquin (3575)

Petits fours (3364)
Café (3701)

119 MARS.
LUNCH, 10 COUVERTS.
MENU.

Thon mariné (831)
Céleri rave (779)

Haut Sauterne — Consommé (189)

Canapés Lorenzo (855)

Queues de petites langoustes à la Monte Carlo (1036)

Champagne Perrier Jouet Brut — Côtelettes d'agneau Robinson (1685)
Petits pois aux laitues (2746)

Terrapène Baltimore (1083)

Pontet Canet — Pigeonneaux grillés, sauce Colbert (2013)
Galantine de faisan découpée (2495)
Salade de laitue (2672)
Omelette soufflée à la Vanille (3066)
Glace pouding, Diplomate (3491)
Fruits (3699)
Petits fours (3364)
Café (3701)

120 AVRIL.
LUNCH, 14 COUVERTS.
MENU.

Punch orange à la Russe (3613)

Canapés d'anchois (777)

Graves — Consommé en tasses (189)

Crabes d'huître Salamandre (1005)

St. Estèphe — Côtelettes d'agneau à la Clémentine (1673)
Pommes de terre fondantes (2799)

Asperges à la sauce Hollandaise (2692)

Champagne Mumm Extra — Poulet rôti à la casserole (1881)

Dry — Pâté de jambon (2558)
Salade de romaine (2675)

Mazarine à l'ananas et au kirsch (3053)

Gâteau St. Honoré Sultane (3261)

Plombière Richemont (3481)

Fruits (3699)
Petits fours (3364)
Liqueurs — Café (3701)

121   MAI.

LUNCH, 16 COUVERTS.
MENU.

Lafaurie	Consommé en tasses (189)
	Canapés de caviar (777)
	Coquilles de homard (2348)
Champagne Louis Rœderer	Ailes de poulet à la Génin (1843)
	Petits pois à la Parisienne (2745)
	Ris de veau à la St. Cloud (1566)
	Tomates farcies aux champignons (2842)
Batailly	Poulet grillé au petit salé (1830)
	Galantine de caneton en forme de poire (2487)
	Salade de laitue (2672)
	Omelette fourrée aux fraises (3068)
	Gelée macédoine au champagne (3179)
	Glace mousse Sémiramis (3471)
Liqueurs	Fruits (3699)
	Petits fours (3364)
	Café (3701)

122   JUIN.

LUNCH, 16 COUVERTS.
MENU.

	Fonds d'artichauts printaniers (773)
Chablis	Bouillon (187)
Vieux	Moules à la Villeroi (1048)
St. Pierre	Noisettes de filet de bœuf à la Maire (1415)
	Aubergines à la Duperret (2735)
Champagne Pommery Sec	Ailes de poulet à la Harrison (1844)
	Concombres farcis (2734)
	Asperges sauce Hollandaise (2692)
	Sorbet Tosca (3519)
Nuits	Pigeonneaux rôtis à la casserole (2018)
	Salade de laitue (2672)
	Omelette soufflée aux amandes (3062)
Liqueurs	Fruits (3699)
	Gâteaux japonais (3347)
	Café (3701)

123   JUILLET.

LUNCH, 16 COUVERTS.
MENU.

Xérès et Bitter	Accola (831)
	Betteraves (774)
	Lucines orangées (803)
Chablis	Homards rôtis à la broche (1040)
	Concombres à l'Anglaise (2661)
Champagne Cliquot Sec	Escalopes de ris de veau Carême (2284)
	Maïs bouilli en tige (2730)
	Chaudfroid de poularde (2458)
	Salade de laitue (2672)
	Omelette soufflée légère (3061)
	Gâteau Fleury (3237)
	Framboises à la crème (3699)
	Glace pouding Diplomate (3491)
	Petits fours (3364)
	Fromage (3697)
	Café Granit au cognac glacé (3609)

124   AOÛT.

LUNCH, 12 COUVERTS.
MENU.

Xérès et Bitter	Salade d'anchois (772)
	Cornichons (785)
	Timbales Chevalière (963)
Niesteiner	Crabes moux grillés au beurre ravigote (1006)
	Concombres marinés (2661)
Pontet Canet	Mignons de filet de bœuf Baillard (1400)
	Crème de pommes de terre au gratin (2781)
Champagne Irroy Brut	Ailes de poulet Valerri (1856)
	Petits pois à la française (2743)
Beaune	Canetons rôtis (1938)
	Pâté de foies gras découpé (2563)
	Salade de laitue (2672)
	Beignets de cerises (3042)
	Glace Spongade Parépa (3537)
Liqueurs	Café (3701)
	Claret cup Villars (3712)

125 SEPTEMBRE

LUNCH, 16 COUVERTS.

MENU.

	Éperlans marinés (821)
Haut Sauterne	Olives (800)
	Consommé de volaille (190)
	Homard à la Camille (1028)
Château Couffran	Noisettes de filet de bœuf Triumvir (1419)
	Riz à l'Orientale (2978)
	Filets de poulet à la Gallier (2466)
	Haricots verts sautés (2829)
Champagne Perrier Jouet Spécial	Pâté de cailles à la gelée (2565)
	Salade de romaine (2675)
	Omelette soufflée aux macarons (3064)
	Gelée tunisienne rubanée (3184)
	Fruits (3699)
	Compote (3686)
	Café (3701)

126 OCTOBRE.

LUNCH, 14 COUVERTS.

MENU.

Xérès et Bitter	Rôties Waddington (826)
	Truffes à l'huile (830)
	Consommé (189)
Liebfraumilch	Coquilles de queues d'écrevisses (2341)
	Côtelettes de chevreuil Buridan (2170)
	Petits pois à la ménagère (2744)
Champagne Riunart Brut	Pigeonneaux frits sauce Figaro (2017)
	Cèpes à la Provençale (2723)
	Pluviers grillés, sauce Colbert (2118)
Madère	Chaudfroid de dinde à la Périgord (2462)
	Salade d'Escarole (2671)
Impérial	Gâteau Vacherin à la crème (3264)
	Glace délicieux aux noisettes (3592)
Liqueurs	Petits fours (3364)
	Café (3701)

127 NOVEMBRE.

LUNCH, 18 COUVERTS.

MENU.

Xérès et Bit*er	Piments doux d'Espagne (806)
	Jambon de Westphalie (786)
	Consommé en tasses (189)
	Canapés Martha (856)
	Huîtres à la Béarnaise tomatée (1052)
Château Lagrange	Mignons de filet de bœuf Dumas (1402)
	Pommes de terre fondantes (2799)
	Bécassines farcies Bordelaise (2160)
	Tomates Boquillon (2833)
Champagne Delmonico	Coquilles de ris de veau à la Harper (2357)
	Sorbet Jeune Amérique (3530)
Nuits	Cailles grillées (2128)
	Terrine entière de foies gras en aspic (2413)
	Salade de laitue (2672)
	Glace soufflée à l'Alcazar (3533)
Liqueurs	Fruits (3699)
	Petits fours (3364)
	Café (3701)

128 DÉCEMBRE.

LUNCH, 12 COUVERTS.

MENU.

	Saumon fumé (822)
	Tartelettes de gibier (825)
Sauterne	Huîtres crues (803)
Première	Consommé en tasses (189)
	Homards Provençale (1039)
St. Julien Supérieur	Noisettes de filet de bœuf Berthier (1411)
	Petits pois à l'Anglaise (2742)
	Terrapène au madère (1090)
Clicquot Sec	Perdreaux grillés à l'Anglaise (2085)
	Terrine de mauviettes (2599)
	Salade d'escarole (2671)
	Omelette soufflée à l'Ancienne (3060)
	Flan de pommes Manhattan (3034)
	Riz Mirabeau (3213)
	Glace plombière d'Alençon (3483)
Liqueurs	Fruits (3699)
	Petits fours (3364)
	Café (3701)

JANUARY—LUNCH.

129

Oysters à la Béarnaise tomatoed (1052)

Escalops of fat livers with risot, Périgueux sauce (2281)

Eggs cocottes (2873)

Broiled quails (2128)

Endive salad (2671)

Meringue flawn (3174)

Dessert

130

Scallops Brestoise (1074)

Surtout of chicken livers with mushrooms (2367)

Green peas, French style (2743)

Broiled woodcock (2204)

Water-cress and apple salad (2676)

Mocha cake (3249)

Apples

Dessert

131

Baked scallops on toast (1078)

Loin pork pie, English style (2378)

Broiled ruddy duck (2067)

Celery salad (2660)

Glazed apple marmalade (3125)

Roasted chestnuts

Dessert

132

Baked oysters à la Crane (1057)

Small patties with gravy (2318)

Minced partridge (2090)

Potato croquettes in surprise (2782)

Broiled grouse (2071)

Babas with rum (3288)

Malaga grapes

133

Oysters à la Boucicault (1053)

Veal palates, Epicurean style (1540)

Roasted stuffed squabs (2018)

Lettuce salad (2672)

Banana crusts à la Panama (3023)

Grape fruit

Dessert

134

Scallops Marinière (1076)

Crépinettes of chicken, Turenne (2245)

Broiled canvasback (2054)

Cos lettuce salad (2675)

Fruit flawn (3172)

Florida oranges

Dessert

135

Scallops Havraise (1075)

Skewers of chicken livers, Colbert sauce (2222)

Dauphine potatoes (2783)

Broiled partridges, English style (2085)

Lettuce salad (2672)

Château framboisé (3141)

Pears

136

Curried oysters, Indian style (1071)

Shells of chicken (2345)

Julienne potatoes (2792)

Broiled teal duck (2067)

Endive salad (2671)

Pineapple

Dessert

FEBRUARY—LUNCH.

137

Oyster rissolettes, Pompadour (956)

Beefsteak, Bordelaise with marrow and truffles (1372)

Roast reedbirds with cresses (2152)

Cauliflower salad mayonnaise (2649)

Venetian lemon custard pie (3202)

Chestnut Plombière (3486)

Grape fruit

Dessert

138

Border of risot of lobsters (2213)

Minion fillets of spring lamb à la Benoist (1720)

Brussels sprouts sautéd (2704)

Broiled ptarmigans (2071)

Cucumber salad (2661)

Rice soufflé with maraschino (3121)

Roasted chestnuts

Dessert

139

Lobster à la Bonnefoy (1026)

Minced beef à la Beekman (1396)

Baked cauliflower with cheese (2717)

Roast squabs (2018)

Lettuce salad (2672)

Printanier boats (cakes) (3291)

Apples

Dessert

140

Fried soft clams (998)

Lamb cutlets with string beans (1693)

Marrow squash with Parmesan (2824)

Chicken roasted in the saucepan (1881)

Endive salad (2671)

Small savarin cakes (3324)

Roman bomb (3442)

Bananas

141

Anchovy canapés (777)

Lobster, Paul Bert (1038)

Pork chops with apple croquettes (1779)

Potato and beetroot salad (2652)

Broiled teal ducks (2067)

Jealousy cakes (3311)

Malaga grapes

Dessert

142

Crusts of fat livers (905)

Cromesquis of beef tongue (872)

Baked noodles (2971)

Broiled ptarmigan (2071)

Chicory salad (2668)

Meringued omelet with fruits (3069)

Florida oranges

Dessert

143

Oysters (803)

Cromesquis of striped bass (870)

Broiled breaded lamb cutlets with gravy (1690)

Green peas, French style (2743)

Broiled redhead ducks (2063)

Tomato salad (2666)

Custard in a dish (3159)

Pineapple

Dessert

144

Oysters (803)

Scallops breaded with milk and fried (1077

Veal cutlets with fine herbs (1504)

Roast tame duck (1921)

Water-cress salad (2676)

Floating Islands (eggs) (3163)

Syruped baba (3227)

Pomegranates

Dessert

MARCH—LUNCH.

145

Scallops breaded with eggs and fried (1077)

Veal pie à la Dickens (2380)

Artichoke bottoms, Villars (2682)

Broiled duckling (1938)

Chicory salad (2668)

Rice soufflé with maraschino (3121)

Pineapple

146

Small lobster, Bordelaise (1025)

Fricassee of turkey wings baked (2038)

Tomatoes à la Boquillon (2833)

Broiled reedbirds (2151)

Endive salad (2668)

Meringued apples, Nubian (2996)

Malaga grapes

147

Stuffed oysters, Mornay (1069)

Terrapin, ancient style (1087)

Artichokes, Rachel (2690)

Broiled chicken with tarragon sauce (1831)

Small orange soufflés in cases (3120)

Milk punch iced (3511)

Bananas

148

Lobster with cream (1044)

Squabs roasted in the saucepan (2018)

Eggplant à la Robertson (2737)

Small aspics of foies gras (2412)

Apple flawn, latticed (3169)

Strawberries

Dessert

149

Consommé in cups (189)

Stuffed small lobster tails (1043)

Terrapin, Newberg (1086)

Small "pains" of chicken à l'Écarlate (2543)

Meringued omelet with fruits (3069)

Grape fruit

Dessert

150

Oysters with Parmesan (1073)

Pork cutlets with apples (1777)

Mushrooms sautéd with butter (2760)

Roast English pheasants adorned with their own plumage (2107)

Eggs with coffee cream meringued (3033)

Florida oranges

Dessert

151

Oysters à la Rubino (1055)

Chicken croquettes, Exquisite (877)

Asparagus, vinaigrette (2692)

Roast thrushes (2166)

Lettuce salad (2672)

Custard in a dish (3159)

152

Lobster à la Hervey (1034)

Terrapin à la Crisfield (1084)

Italian salad (2635)

Crépinettes of pigeons, poivrade sauce with truffle essence (No. 2246)

Madeira crusts (3026)

Bavarois with meringues (3133)

Pears

APRIL—LUNCH.

153

Caviare (778)

Scallops à la Brestoise (1074)

Grenadins of beef with sweet peppers (1394)

Noodles with fried bread-crumbs (2973)

Broiled squabs, Colbert sauce (2013)

Stuffed eggs (sweet) (3031)

Grape fruit

Dessert

154

Oysters on the deep shell (803)

Lobster à la Rougemont (1041)

Vienna Schnitzel, German style (1512)

Green peas with braised lettuces (2746)

Timbales of chicken, Parisian style (2382)

Soufflés in cases with vanilla (3120)

Oranges

Dessert

155

Crusts à la Génoise (904)

Deviled lobster (1043)

Lamb steak, maître-d'hôtel (1713)

Baked tomatoes (2837)

Chaudfroid of larks (2454)

Floating island (3163)

Hot-house grapes

156

Radishes (808)

Fresh butter (775)

Croustades of lamb's sweetbreads (2251)

Broiled teal duck (2067)

Potatoes in surprise (2809)

Cake stuffed with apricots (3325)

Cream cakes iced with vanilla (3294)

Bananas

157

Oysters on crusts (1062)

Escalops of beef palates, chestnut purée (2277)

Croustades of chicken livers with Madeira (2250)

Tomatoes à la Trévise (2836)

Squabs Crapaudine (2007)

Cream pie (3201)

Apples

158

Julienne soup, Faubonne (318)

Quenelles of turkey, Providence (2336)

Minion fillets of lamb, Landgrave (1721)

Artichoke bottoms, Florence (2677)

Larks à la Maréchale (2081)

Meringued pancakes, Rossini (3073)

Pineapple

159

Pickled oysters (802)

Lobster tails à la Stanley (1042)

King's pilau of lamb (1709)

Fried frog's legs, cream sauce (1022)

Hot pie, Bontoux style (2314)

Genoese cake (3307)

Strawberries

160

Oysters and lemons (803)

Cream of peas à la St. Germain (260)

Breast of lamb, chopped sauce (1663)

Cromesquis of beef tongue (872)

Boudins of chicken, Soubise (2215)

Baked apples (2992)

Grape fruit

MAY—LUNCH.

161

Clam pancakes or fritters (996)

Small patties, Mazarin (944)

Épigrammes of lamb à la Toulouse (1694)

Broiled squabs (2013)

Lettuce salad (2672)

Surprise of fruits, frothy sauce (3219)

Apples

162

Colombines of chicken liver with ham (865)

Deviled frog's legs (1020)

Patties à l'Andalouse (934)

Slices of lamb, Prévillot (1711)

Broiled ptarmigans (2071)

Chicory salad (2668)

Almondine tartlets (3326)

Hot-house grapes

163

Quenelles of fish, Montglas (2330)

Sweetbread croquettes (893)

Roast tame duck (1921)

Cos lettuce salad (2675)

Cream macaroons in cases (3383)

Spanish oranges

164

Boudins of pickerel à la Walton (844)

Benoîton shells (2339)

Sweetbreads in papers (1573)

Broiled chicken with tarragon sauce (1831)

Water-cress and apple salad (2676)

Apricots with cream of almonds (3287)

Bananas

165

Lobster, Monte Carlo (1036)

Palmettes of ham à l'Aquitaine (927)

Chaudfroid of chicken, Clara Morris (2451)

Ptarmigans (2071)

Lettuce salad (2672)

Crescents with preserves (3298)

Hot-house peaches

166

Brissotins of chicken, supreme sauce (849)

Sweetbreads on skewers (2226)

Parisian green peas (2745)

Roast duck (1921)

Endive salad (2671)

Apple croquettes, Trimalcion (3016)

Pineapple

167

Crusts à la d'Hénin (904)

Célestines with foies-gras and purée of chestnuts (862)

Squab cutlets, Périgueux (2267)

Green peas, housekeeper's style (2744)

Minions of tenderloin of beef, Stanley (1406)

Mellow potatoes (2799)

Lady bouchées with strawberries (3376)

168

Lobster à la Fresne (1032)

Junot palmettes (921)

Minion fillets of lamb in surprise (1725)

String beans à la Pettit (2827)

Strawberry short cake (3262)

Biscuits in cases with cream (3289)

Pears

JUNE—LUNCH.

169

Lobster à la Delmonico (1037)

Timbales Mentana (974)

Mutton cutlets with chicory (1602)

Artichoke bottoms, Montglas (2679)

Croquettes of capon à la Royal (876)

Coffee cream éclairs (3303)

Cherries

170

Lobster, Paul Bert (1038)

Varsovian palmettes (924)

Breast of beef à la Florence (1314)

Stuffed tomatoes baked (2837)

Asparagus, Hollandaise sauce (2692)

Bordelaise tartlets (3328)

Hot-house grapes

171

Clam chowder (300)

Shells of calf's brains (2355)

Noisettes of tenderloin of beef, Berthier (1411)

Broiled duckling (1938)

Macédoine salad (2650)

Strawberries and cream

Peaches

172

Soft shell crabs, sautéd in butter (1006)

Lamb cutlets à la Durand (1674)

Tomatoes à la Boquillon (2833)

Italian salad (2635)

Chicken roasted in the saucepan (1881)

Rice border with bananas (3005)

Grape fruit

173

Frog's legs fried with cream sauce (1022)

Small puff paste salmon patties (945)

Minion fillets of lamb, Lefort (1722)

Roast squabs (2018)

Cos lettuce salad (2675)

Goronflot cakes (3310)

Bananas

174

Cromesquis of mussels (873)

Soft crabs, sautéd (1006)

Tournedos of beef à la Hutching (1433)

Chicken roasted in the saucepan (1881)

Lettuce salad (2672)

Strawberry ice cream (3451)

Pineapple

175

Bressoles of fat livers (848)

Shells of squabs, baked (2356)

Broiled partridges, English style (2085)

Tomatoes stuffed with fresh mushrooms (2842)

Aspics of foies gras (2411)

Strawberry short cake (3262)

Raspberries

176

Clams, Philadelphia style (994)

Cassolettes, Lusigny (860)

Small "pains" of chicken à l'Écarlate (2543)

Ducklings, Rouennaise (1937)

Cos lettuce salad (2675)

Meringued croustades of Venice (3020)

Strawberries

JULY—LUNCH.

177

Shells of lobster (2348)

Squab cutlets, Périgueux (2267)

Potato cakes (2778)

Lamb minion fillet pie à la Manning (2373)

Small vanilla soufflés in cases (3130)

Cream cheese (3698)

178

Pickled alligator pears (771)

Soft clams on skewers (999)

Noisettes of plain tenderloin of beef (1410)

String beans, à la Pettit (2827)

Roasted reedbirds (2152)

Cream cakes iced with chocolate (3294)

Apricots

179

Little Neck clams à la poulette (995)

Sweetbread patties, French style (940)

Grenadins of beef as venison (1388)

Frog's legs fried à la Horly (1021)

Savarin with apricots (3117)

Marly cake (3246)

Blackberries

180

Frog's legs à la Osborn (1018)

Soft shell crabs sautéd in butter (1006)

Chicken cutlets à la Clarence (2258)

Corn cut up (2731)

Potted tenderloin of beef à la Nelson (2320)

Turkish coffee (3702)

Cherries

181

Lobster tart à la Hérault (2374)

Cases of squabs, Umberto (2234)

Boiled corn on the cob (2730)

Small roasted spring chickens as an entrée (1908)

Lettuce salad (2672)

Surprise of fruits (3219)

Gooseberries

182

Croustades of gnocquis, Rivoli (899)

Border of risot of lobster (2213)

Pigeon tart à la Britannia (2377)

Broiled duckling (1938)

Celery salad (2660)

Iced banana pudding (3487)

Currants

183

Stuffed clams (997)

Frog's legs à la d'Antin (1017)

Sweetbreads larded and glazed with gravy (1575)

Surtout of wild pigeons (2368)

Timbale à la Nantaise (2381)

Molded snow eggs (3164)

Bananas

184

Olives stuffed with anchovies (801)

Lobster brochettes (2224)

Cases of sweetbreads, Grammont (2235)

Broiled chickens with tarragon sauce (1831)

Small Quillet cakes (3397)

Muskmelon

Cheese

AUGUST—LUNCH.

185

Lobster, American style (1024)

Pigeons braised with green peas (1969)

Timbales of sweetbreads, modern (2388)

Cream cakes iced with coffee (3294)

Raspberry water-ice (3607)

Peaches.

186

Kulibiac, Russian style (908)

Lobster à la Lawrence (1035)

Beef pie à la Perez (2369)

Shells of mussels (2349)

Raspberry soufflé (3122)

Cheese

187

Frog's legs à la poulette with mushrooms (1019)

Pilau of chicken (1878)

Lobster à la Gambetta (1033)

Tournedos of fillet of beef, Brétigny (1431)

Savarin à la Valence (3259)

Cheese

188

Lobster à la Camille (1028)

Escalops of veal à la Arnold (2285)

Smothered string beans (2828)

Timbale for epicures (2383)

Peach marmalade pancakes macédoine (3075)

Pears

189

" Pain " of pike (2307)

Lobster, mayonnaise (2534)

Squabs, Stanislas (2011)

Green peas, English style (2742)

Noisettes of shoulder of lamb, Epicurean (1730)

Parfait with nougat and with almonds (3478)

Plums

190

Cromesquis of beef palate (867)

Fried sweatbreads, Neapolitan style (1562)

Shells of frog's legs (2347)

Japanese salad (2636)

Cannelons à la Célestine (3292)

Cheese

191

Oysters with fine herbs (1072)

Lobster à la Britannia (1027)

Fried chicken, Médicis (1870)

Small vol-au-vent, Delmontés (2403)

Cream cakes with St. Honoré cream (3296)

Apricots

192

Shells filled with crawfish tails (2341)

Beef palate tourte, Parisian style (2390)

Squabs sautéd à l'Impromptu (2010)

Sarah potatoes (2802)

Sweetbread fritters, cream sauce (1572)

Water melon on ice

Raspberries.

SEPTEMBER—LUNCH.

193

Alligator pears (771)

Boudins of game, Berchoux (2218)

Oysters à la Rubino (1055)

Épigrammes of mutton à la Jardinière (1607)

Timbale of pullet (2386)

Iced soufflés, Favart (3534)

194

Oysters in cases à la Hilton (2231)

Patties with Régence salpicon (943)

Sirloin steak for gourmets (1378)

Squabs roasted in earthenware saucepan (2018)

Fiori di latte à la Bellini (3467)

Apples

195

Shrimp patties (935)

Tournedos of tenderloin of beef à la Roque-plan (1436)

Green peas, housekeeper's style (2744)

Broiled partridges, Colbert sauce (2099)

Francillon cakes (3305)

Cheese

196

Oysters with fine herbs (1072)

Cromesquis of sweetbreads, Babanine (872)

Broiled eggplant, Duperret (2735)

Breasts of grouse à la Czarina (2072)

Marillan cakes (3317)

Bananas

197

Cromesquis of game, Stanislas (871)

Shells of shrimps with oyster crabs (2342)

Chateaubriand, with souffléd potatoes (1383)

Iced pudding, Constance (3490)

Cocoanut

198

Fried soft clams with parsley (998)

Blanquette of pullet with mushrooms (1997)

Slices of kernel of venison à la Hussard (2181)

Small aspics of foies-gras (2412)

Démonet tartlets (3331)

Cheese

199

Consommé (189)

Lobster à la Dugléré (1031)

Timbale of squabs à la Berchoux (2387)

Lamb cutlets, Murillo (1681)

Cream with apples (3014)

Cheese.

200

Strained okra soup (299)

Baked oysters à la Crane (1057)

Cromesquis of beef tongue (872)

Chickens Écarlate à la Derenne (2463)

Apples, Baron de Brisse style (2993)

Concord grapes

OCTOBER—LUNCH.

201
Crawfish tails in shells (2341)

Chicken fricassee (1861)

Venison cutlets, tomato Parisian sauce (2174)

Tomatoes stuffed with fresh mushrooms (2842)

Condé peaches (3081)

Watermelon

202
Stuffed oysters, Mornay (1069)

Crusts of woodcock (906)

Artichoke bottoms à la Florence (2677)

Cream of lobster (2470)

Jelly cake meringued (3243)

Cheese

203
Shells of oysters in their natural shells (2351)

Mutton cutlets with marinade (1604)

String bean salad (2657)

Chicken pie, Australian style (2372)

Alliance fritters (3036)

Barberries

204
Oysters in cases à la Lorenzo (2232)

Venison cutlets with chestnut purée (2175)

Soufflé of chicken à la Delsart (2360)

Broiled teal duck (2067)

Frascati biscuits (3004)

Muskmelon

205
Brissotins of game, Lyonnese (850)

Lobster à la Ravigote (2531)

Green peas, English style (2742)

Noisettes of tenderloin of beef with purée of mushrooms (1420)

Peach ice cream à la Herbster (3453)

Huckleberries

206
Shells of oysters with fried bread (2353)

Salmis of partridge cold (2574)

Croustade à la Périgueux (897)

Italian salad (2635)

Roasted woodcocks (2206)

Souffléd omelet with vanilla (3066)

Cheese

207
Fried soft clams (998)

Patties with purée of game (936)

Shells of terrapin with hazel-nuts (2358)

Broiled snipe (2157)

Frothy purée of apples (3127)

Spanish oranges

208
Shells of oysters baked in their shells (2350)

Épigrammes of lamb, ancient style (1695)

Timbales of pullet (2386)

Plain Delmonico sirloin steak (1375)

Lamb's lettuce salad (2669)

Preserved quinces (3685)

NOVEMBER—LUNCH.

209

Steamed oysters (1064)

Lobster à la Creole (1029)

Rib steak à la Bercy (1364)

Galantine of pheasant, sliced (2495)

Roast chicken garnished with water-cresses (1881).

Rice border with bananas (3005)

Dessert

210

Venison cutlets à la Cauchoise (2171)

Croustades of reedbirds (2252)

Terrapin, Maryland Club (1088)

Redhead duck roasted (2063)

Lettuce salad (2672)

Nesselrode pudding with candied chestnuts (3495)

Dessert

211

Oysters in shells roasted (2352)

Croustades à la Périgueux (897)

Rabbit pie with fine herbs (2379)

Roasted teal ducks (2068)

Peaches à la Stevens (3084)

Dessert

212

Oyster brochettes (2225)

Cromesquis of capon (868)

Breast of veal à la Mondoux (1488)

Young rabbit fillets, currant sauce (2145)

Terrapin à la Philadelphia (1085)

Cream of almond rissoles (3116)

Bananas

213

Scallops, Horly (1077)

Croustades à la Morgan (902)

Veal cutlets, half glaze (1499)

Celery knob salad (2660)

Roasted ruddy ducks (2066)

Genoese Madeleines (3314)

Roast chestnuts

214

Shells of scallops, Parisian style (2354)

Crépine of young rabbit (2249)

Sweetbreads larded and glazed with gravy (1575)

Quenelles of turkey à la Providence (2336)

Roasted woodcock (2206)

Cream cakes with burnt almonds (3295)

Pomegranates

215

White cabbage, English style (776)

Cromesquis à la Rumford (869)

Shells of terrapin with hazel-nuts (2358)

Small vol-au-vent of reedbirds, Diplomate (2407)

Broiled young wild rabbit backs (2149)

Tutti-frutti ice cream (3586)

Stewed quinces

216

Marinated Gurnet (831)

Patties à la Reine (938)

Small sirloin à la Béarnaise (1369)

Frog's legs à la Royer (1023)

Broiled teal duck (2067)

Guanabana water-ice (3603)

Cheese

DECEMBER—LUNCH.

217

Curried oysters, Indian style (1071)

Lobster cutlets à la Shelley (2261)

Baked macaroni (2959)

Cold quail pie (2565)

Asparagus salad (2621)

Croquettes à la Trimalcion (3016)

Cocoanut

218

"Pain" of crawfish, Chartreuse (2305)

Terrapin à la Crisfield (1084)

Timbale of young hare (2389)

Tenderloin of beef with olives (1428)

Chestnut and vanilla soufflé (3118)

Cheese

219

Oyster crab patties (935)

Minion fillets of lamb as venison (1723)

Lobster with mayonnaise (2534)

Loin of pork pie, English style (2378)

Jelly rolled biscuit (3312)

Cheese

220

Stuffed hard shell crabs (1004)

Terrapin cutlets with cream sauce (1089)

Turkey legs with Milanese noodles (2036)

Broiled quails (2128)

Cakes filled with apricot marmalade (3325)

Bananas

221

Small vol-au-vent à la Lucini (2404)

Veal cutlets à la Georgina (1496)

Terrapin stew with Madeira wine (1090)

Apple Charlotte (3008)

Crumbled paste cakes (3345)

Apples

222

Turban of lobsters garnished with shells of lobster (2394)

Marinated pork tenderloin (1815)

Vol-au-vent, Parisian style (2406)

Terrapin, Maryland Club (1088)

Lady's bouchées with strawberries (3376)

Cheese

223

Fresh mushroom patties (937)

Cases of lobster, Ravigote (2447)

Baked stuffed egg-plant (2738)

Gibelotte of rabbits (2147)

Cannelons à la Célestine (3292)

Grape fruit

224

Kulibiac Smolenska (909)

Lobster cutlets à la Lowery (2476)

Chicken pie à la Manhattan (2370)

Sweetbreads à la Montebello (1560)

Africans fancy cakes (3364)

Pomegranates

225   JANUARY.

DINNER, 8 TO 10 PERSONS.

MENU.

Soup

Meissonier (324)

Remove

Sheepshead à la Béchamel (1257)

Dauphine potatoes (2783)

Entrées

Rack of pork, crown shape, with small onions (1798)

Stuffed mushrooms in cases with Madeira (2762)

Pullet à la Dame Blanche (1972)

Green peas with braised lettuces (2746)

Roast.

Woodcock (2206)

Chicory salad (2668)

Hot Entremets

Brioche and cream fritters with sabayon (3040)

Bananas in surprise (3541)

Small fancy cakes (3364)

Nuts and raisins (3699)

Dessert

226   JANUARY.

DINNER, 8 TO 10 PERSONS.

MENU.

Soup

Mutton à la Cowley (329)

Remove

Fresh codfish à la Duxelle—baked (1136)

Mellow potatoes (2799)

Entrées

Corned breast of beef, English style (1315)

Sweet potato croquettes (2831)

Chicken fricassee à la Waleski (1866)

Tomatoes, Queen style (2840)

Roast

Mallard duck (2059)

Cos-lettuce salad (2675)

Hot Entremets

Flawn au lion d'or (3035)

Plombière à la Rochambeau ice cream (3482)

Small fancy cakes (3364)

227   JANUARY.

DINNER 16 TO 20 PERSONS.

MENU.

Soup

Consommé Charmel (224)

Side Dish

Rissoles of partridges à la Waddington (955)

Fish

Chicken halibut baked with parmesan (1172)

Viennese potatoes (2812)

Remove

Braised middle short loin à la Messinoise (1347)

Cardoons with half-glaze (2710)

Entrées

Fillets of chicken à la Bodisco (1835)

Green peas Parisian (2745)

Salmis of canvasback ducks (2056)

Fried eggplant (2739)

Beatrice Punch (3502)

Roast

Quail (2131)

Celery salad (2660)

Hot Entremets

Countess pudding (3097)

Palmyra soufflé ice cream (3535)

Bonbons (3642)

Mottoes (3653)

Black coffee (3701)

228   JANUARY.

DINNER, 16 TO 20 PERSONS.

MENU.

Soup

Consommé Célestine (223)

Side Dish

Palmettes of pheasant à la Torrens (929)

Fish

Red snapper à la Mobile (1235)

Broiled potatoes with fried bread (2776)

Remove

Aitch bone boiled, cream horseradish sauce (1317)

Villeroi celeriac (2722)

Entrées

Chicken à l' Hôtelière (1880)

Fried stuffed lettuce (2752)

Breasts of woodcock à la Diane (2200)

Tomatoes à la Boquillon (2833)

American sherbet (3521)

Roast

Pheasant (2107)

Endive salad (2671)

Hot Entremets

Stuffed pears à la Lombarde (3086)

Plombière à la Richmond ice cream (3481)

Small fancy cakes (3364)

Dessert

Raw oysters or clams (803) may be added to these bills of fare.

229   JANUARY.

DINNER, 8 TO 10 PERSONS.

MENU.

Soup

Bennett (287)

Remove

Smelts, Diplomatic (1268)
Marchioness potatoes (2797)

Entrées

Braised chicken with rice (1914)

Noisettes of beef à la Berthier (1411)
Brussels sprouts à la Baroness (2703)

Roast

Woodcock (2206)
Lettuce salad (2672)

Hot Entremets

Pineapple crusts, apricot sauce (3022)

Iced biscuits à la d'Orléans (3437)

Small cakes (3364)
Stewed fruits (3686)
Dessert

230   JANUARY.

DINNER, 8 TO 10 PERSONS.

MENU.

Soup

Chicken okra (299)

Remove

Fresh codfish slices with Hollandaise sauce
(1140)
Boiled potatoes. English style (2774)

Entrées

Sheep's tongue écarlate with spinach (1657)

Sautéd chicken à la Tunisienne (1901)
Fried oyster plant (2817)

Roast

Ruddy duck (2066)
Celery salad (2660)

Hot Entremets

Apples, Baron de Brisse style (2993)

Orange water-ice (3605)
Small fancy cakes (3364)
Coffee (3701)   Cognac
Dessert

231   JANUARY

DINNER, 16 TO 20 PERSONS.

MENU.

Soup

Consommé à la Rémusat (240)

Side Dish

Chicken croquettes, Hungarian (878)

Fish

Soles à la Lutèce (1272)
Mellow potatoes (2799)

Remove

Ham braised with stuffed tomatoes (1790)

Entrées

Slices of mutton fillet à la Alexandre (1608)
Cauliflower à la Villeroi (2716)
Quails with mushrooms (2134)
Green peas, Parisian style (2745)
Californian sherbet (3523)

Roast

Capon (1826)   Salad

Hot Entremets

Alliance fritters (3036)

Favart soufflé ice cream (3534)
Small fancy cakes (3364)
Nuts and raisins (3699)
Stewed bananas (3687)
Dessert

232   JANUARY.

DINNER, 16 TO 20 PERSONS.

MENU.

Soup

Bisque of crabs à la Stevens (199)

Side Dish

Timbales Chevalière (963)

Fish

English turbot with caper sauce (1307)
Potato croquettes in surprise (2782)

Remove

Saddle of mutton roasted on the spit (1648)

Entrées

Chicken, Vienna style sautéd (1905)
String beans with butter (2829)
Partridges à la Chartreuse (2094)
Gnocquis (2955)

Kirsch punch (3510)

Roast

Mallard duck (2059)
Salad

Hot Entremets

Creamy soufflé with cheese (2982)

Spongade à la Médicis (3536)
Small cakes (3364)
Coffee (3701)   Liquors

Raw oysters or clams (803) may be added to these bills of fare.

233   JANUARY.

DINNER, 8 TO 10 PERSONS.

MENU.

Soup
Fermière style (307)

Remove
Hot eel pie (2315)
Green peas, English style (2742)

Entrées
Breasts of chicken à la Lucullus (1846)
Artichoke (bottoms) with marrow (2687)

Pilau of mutton, French style (1641)
Chicory with cream (2729)

Roast
Grouse with apple sauce (2072)
Escarole salad (2671)

Hot Entremets
Singapore pineapple fritters (3046)

Ice cream with walnuts (3464)
Fancy cakes (3364)
Salted almonds (3696)
Dessert

234   JANUARY.

DINNER, 8 TO 10 PERSONS.

MENU.

Soup
Jérôme with sweet potato quenelles (317)

Remove
Baked stuffed perch (1210)
Mellow potatoes (2799)

Entrées
Sweetbreads à l'Eugénie (1556)
String beans à l'Albani (2825)

Woodcock pudding (2325)
Ballotines of stuffed cabbage (2705)

Roast
Chicken (1881)
Lettuce salad (2672)

Hot Entremets
Apples in surprise (2995)

Maraschino ice cream (3462)
Small cakes (3364)
Fruits (3699)
Dessert

235   JANUARY.

DINNER, 16 TO 20 PERSONS.

MENU.

Soup
Consommé à la Dubarry (229)

Side Dish
Pheasant croquettes (891)

Fish
Sheepshead à la Buena Vista (1259)
Potato cakes (2778)

Remove
Goose stuffed with sausages and chestnuts (1950)

Entrées
Veal cutlets, Milanese (1502)
Green peas, housekeeper's style (2744)

Woodcocks à la Cavour (2198)
Artichoke (bottoms) Jusienne (2678)

Pargny punch (3514)

Roast
Redhead ducks (2063)
Salad

Hot Entremets
Creole fruits (3051)

Coffee mousse ice cream (3473)
Stewed fruits (3686)
Dessert

236   JANUARY.

DINNER, 16 TO 20 PERSONS.

MENU.

Soup
Purée of carrots à la Crécy (268)

Side Dish
Neapolitan timbales (977)

Fish
Fresh codfish à la Norwegian (1137)
Persillade potatoes (2774)

Remove
Tenderloin of beef à la d'Aurelles (1449)

Entrées
Breasts of chicken à la Mirabeau (1849)
Stuffed cauliflower à la Béchamel (2715)

Sweetbreads à la Conti (1554)
Green peas, English style (2742)

Californian sherbet (3523)

Roast
Canvasback ducks with samp (2055)
Salad

Hot Entremets
Franklyn pudding (3098)

Ice cream mousse with maraschino (3476)
Nuts and raisins (3699)
Dessert

Raw oysters or clams may be added to these bills of fare.

237   JANUARY.

DINNER 8 TO 10 PERSONS.

MENU.

Soup

Garbure with lettuce (310)

Remove

Spotted fish, Queen sauce (1285)
Potato fritters (2788)

Entrées

Tenderloin steak with Madeira (1425)
Stuffed tomatoes, Provençal (2835)

California quails à la Monterey (2136)
Green peas, English style (2742)

Roast

Wild turkey, American style (2028)

Hot Entremets

Apples with butter (2999)

Chocolate ice cream (3449)
Small fancy cakes (3364)
Stewed fruits (3686)
Dessert

---

238   JANUARY.

DINNER, 8 TO 10 PERSONS.

MENU.

Soup

Consommé à la Grammont (234)

Remove

Whitefish, Gherardi (1311)
Potato tartlets (2810)

Entrées

Minions of beef tenderloin à la Salvini (1405)
Spinach à la Rougemont (2822)

Sweetbread cutlets, modern style (2271)
Macédoine à la Montigny (2755)

Roast

Pullet with water-cress (1996)

Hot Entremets

Pineapple Carolina (3090)

Lemon water-ice (3604)
Small cakes (3364)
Fruits (3699)
Coffee (3701)

---

239   JANUARY.

DINNER, 16 TO 20 PERSONS

MENU.

Soup
Chamberlain (295)

Side Dish
Godiveau and chives, puff paste patties (944)

Fish
Sole, Venetian style (1278)
Mellow potatoes (2799)

Remove
Sirloin of beef à la Dauphiness (1350)

Entrées
Breasts of partridges à la Jules Verne (2087)
Artichoke (bottoms) with cream béchamel (2686)
Sweetbreads larded and glazed with gravy (1575)
French green peas (2743)
Brandy punch (3510)

Roast
Capon (1826)

Hot Entremets
Pudding à la de Freese (3099)

Excelsior biscuit ice cream (3436)
Fruits (3699)
Dessert

---

240   JANUARY.

DINNER, 16 TO 20 PERSONS.

MENU.

Soup
Consommé à la Daumont (228)

Side Dish
Cannelons of purée of game (859)

Fish
Haddock, Holland style (1165)
Boiled potatoes (2774)

Remove
Mongrel goose à la Royer (1946)

Entrées
Mutton cutlets with cucumbers (1603)
Stuffed tomatoes with mushrooms (2842)

Woodcock salmis à la Sandford (2208)
String beans à l'Albani (2825)
Punch Dolgorouski (3506)

Roast
Teal ducks (2068)

Hot Entremets
Peach fritters with maraschino (3039)

Spongade ice cream à la Parepa (3537)
Stewed fruits (3686)
Dessert

Raw oysters or clams may be added to these bills of fare.

DÎNER, 14 COUVERTS—À L'AMÉRICAINE.

MENU.

Haut Sauterne　　　　　　　　　Huîtres (803)

Sherry　　　　　　　　　　　　POTAGES.

Consommé à la Laguipierre (236)　　Crème de Céleri à la Livingstone (252)

HORS-D'ŒUVRE CHAUDS.

Bouchées de salpicon de foies-gras (943)

Marcobrunner　　　　　　　　　POISSONS.

Sheepshead à la sauce Cardinal (1261)　　Blanchaille frite à la diable (1310)

Pommery Sec　　　　　　　　　RELEVÉ.

Filet de bœuf à la Bernardi (1444)

Pontet-Canet　　　　　　　　ENTRÉES.

Ailes de poulet à la Marceau (1847)　　　Petits pâtés de cailles (2311)

Petits pois à l'Anglaise (2742)　　　　Fonds d'artichauts à la Mornay (2680)

Soufflé de bécasses aux truffes (2366)

Sorbet Andalouse (3322)

Corton　　　　　　　　　　　RÔTS.

Canard à tête rouge (2063)　　　Salade d'escarole (2671)

ENTREMETS DE DOUCEUR.

Munich aux pêches (chaud) (3055)

Gelée aux ananas Californienne (3178)　　Crème bain-marie au café (3162)

Glace Parfait nougat (3478)

Old Port　　　　　　　　　Dessert

───────────── ✚ ─────────────

DÎNER, 60 COUVERTS—SERVICE À L'ANGLAISE.

MENU.

Huîtres (803)

POTAGES.

Consommé à l'Impératrice (231)　　Tortue verte au clair (353)

HORS-D'ŒUVRE FROIDS.

Salade d'anchois (772)　　　Olives Espagnoles farcies (801)　　　Sardines à l'huile(831)

Thon mariné (831)

POISSONS.

Darne de saumon à la Duperré (1240)　　Pompano à la Soya (1226)

RELEVÉS.

Chapon à la Régence (1825)　　Selle d'agneau braisée à la purée de navets (1745`

ENTRÉES.

Côtelettes de veau Pogarski (2273)　　Paupiettes de dindonneau au souvenir (2045)

Canards Mallart au Madère (2061)　　Vol-au-vent de poulet aux champignons (2399

RÔTS.

Faisans rôtis aux truffes (2110)　　Buisson d'écrevisses (2572)

RELEVÉS.

Rissolettes à la Solférino (958)

ENTREMETS.

Asperges sauce mousseline (2692)　　　Petits pois à la Française (2743)

Gelée aux fruits (3187)　　　　　　Crème tutti frutti (3153)

Petites caisses de homards à la ravigote (2447)　　Grosses truffes en serviettes (2843)

RELEVÉS.

Hure de sanglier en surprise garnie d'Africains (3255)　　　Fondue aux truffes du Piémont (2954)

Dessert

DÎNER, 60 COUVERTS—SERVICE À LA RUSSE.

MENU.

Servi par six, dix sur chaque plat.

BUFFET SÉPARÉ.

Vermuth, Absinthe,	Canapés de crevettes (777)	Salade d'anchois (772)
Kümmel, Sherry	Gelée de canneberges (598)	Rhubarbe à la crème (3204)
	Thon mariné (831)	Radis (808)
	Olives (800)	Caviar (778)
Chablis	60 plats d'huîtres sur coquilles (803)	

POTAGES (3 SOUPIÈRES).

Amontillado   Consommé Colbert aux œufs pochés(225)   Bisque de homard (205)

HORS-D'ŒUVRE (3 PLATS DE CHAQUE).

Timbales à la Talleyrand (988)   Palmettes à la Perrier (922)

POISSONS (3 PLATS DE CHAQUE).

Haut Sauterne   Flétan à la Coligny (1168)   Filets de soles, Rochelaise (1276)

RELEVÉS (3 PLATS DE CHAQUE).

Batailly   Dinde à la Française (2029)   Selle d'agneau à la Chancelière (1739)

ENTRÉES (3 PLATS DE CHAQUE).

Champagne   Filets de volaille à la Certosa (1836)   Côtelettes de tétras à la Ségard (2259)
Pommery Sec

        Homard à la Rougemont (1041)   Chaudfroid de cailles à la Baudy (2459)

RÔTS (3 PLATS DE CHAQUE).

Perdreaux truffés (2100)   Poularde au cresson (1996)

LÉGUMES (3 PLATS DE CHAQUE).

Château   Céleri à la moelle (2721)   Petits pois fins à la Parisienne (2745)
La Rose

ENTREMETS SUCRÉS (CHAUDS) (3 PLATS DE CHAQUE).

Brioches St. Marc (3006)   Pouding à la Benvenuto (3092)

ENTREMETS SUCRÉS (FROIDS) (3 PLATS DE CHAQUE).

Vin de Paille   Gelée aux fruits (3 plats) (3187)
            Gaufres brisselets à la crème framboisée (3223)
            60 Glaces variées (3538)

FLANCS.

2 Chariots garnis de pommes d'api (3632)
Une brouette garnie de fleurs sur socle (3638)

CONTRE FLANCS.

Deux étagères garnies de bonbons, marrons glacés et Victorias (3379)
8 Tambours garnis de petits fours (3364)   Macarons (3379)
       Africains (3364)   Bouchées de dames (3376)

SEIZE BOUTS DE TABLE.

4 Corbeilles de fruits frais (3699)   4 Compotiers de fruits secs (3699)
4 Fromages (3697)   4 Compotes de pommes (3686)
      Café (3701)

DÎNER, 20 COUVERTS—SERVICE À LA FRANÇAISE.

MENU.

Premier Service.

On place les hors-d'œuvre sur la table.

Olives (800)   Salade d'anchois (772)   Céleri rave (779)   Beurre (775)
Radis (808)   Melon cantaloup (799)   Mortadelle (818)   Caviar (778)
Huîtres sur coquilles avec citron (803)
Les hors-d'œuvre d'office se servent après le potage

POTAGES.

Consommé souveraine (243)   Purée de volaille à la Dufferin (269)
Marsala
Timbales à la Lagardère (970)

RELEVÉ.

Bass rayé à la Masséna (1106)
Marcobrunner
Selle de mouton à la Duchesse (1644)
Médoc Pomard

ENTRÉES.

Ailes de poulet à la Toulouse (1854)   Côtelettes de filet de bœuf à la Babanine (2255)
Ris de veau à la St. Cloud (1566)   Salmis de bécasses à la Beaumont (2207)
Pichon Longueville

PIÈCES FROIDES SUR SOCLE.

Galantine de dinde à la Berger (2499)   Pâté de foies-gras de Strasbourg (2564)
Château Yquem

Deuxième Service.

Retirer les hors-d'œuvre et les pièces froides et placer le second service, nombre égal de plats du premier service. Salade en même temps que le rôti.

INTERMÈDE.

Punch à l'Impérial (3509)

RÔTS.

Poulardes au cresson (1996)   Canvasbacks rôtis (canards sauvages) (2055)
Chambertin   *Château Laffitte*

ENTREMETS.

Quartiers d'artichauts (2688)   Petits pois à la Française (2743)   Poires à la Ferrière (3085)
Gelée macédoine au champagne (3179)
Xérès

GROS GÂTEAUX (sur socle)

Napolitaine (3250)   Mille-feuilles Pompadour (3247)
Constance

Troisième Service.

Enlever le tout excepté le milieu de table (dormant) qui est garni de fleurs ou de groupes, &c.

DESSERT.

Fromages variés (3697)   Fruits frais en corbeilles (3699)
Tokai
Guéridons garnis de biscuits aux amandes glacées (3369)   de fondants au chocolat (3650)
et de fondants à la vanille (3651)
Alicante
Muscat
Glaces Alaska Florida (3538)   Sabayon à la Denari (3532)   Gelée d'oranges en tasses (3180)
Compote de poires (3692)   La hotte à la Denivelle (3636)
Casque en nougat garni de sucre filé (3598)
Pale ale
Le café et les liqueurs sont servis au salon.

245

DINNER 8 TO 10 PERSONS.
MENU.

Soup
Manestrone Milanese (322)

Remove
Fried soles à la Colbert (1271)
Cucumbers, English style (2661)

Entrées
Boiled leg of mutton with mashed turnips (1629)
Chicken sautéd à la Stanley (1900)
Chicory with cream (2729)
Green peas, housekeeper's style (2744)

Roast
Pullet (1996)
Salad

Hot Entremets
Fruit crusts à la Mirabeau (3025)

Ice cream with white coffee (3460)

Small fancy cakes (3364)

Coffee (3701)

246

DINNER, 8 TO 10 PERSONS.
MENU.

Soup
Oyster soup with ravioles (337)

Remove
Smelts à l'Alexandria (1265)
Persillade potatoes (2774)

Entrées
Roast stuffed chicken with tomato Condé sauce (1883)
Mutton cutlets, Russian style (1600)
Celery stalks half-glaze (2721)
Red cabbage, Montargis (2707)

Roast
Redhead duck (2064)
Salad

Hot Entremets
Cream fritters, Pamela (3013)

Almond ice cream (3461)
Small fancy cakes (3364)

Dessert

247

DINNER, 16 TO 20 PERSONS.
MENU.

Soup
Cream of Brussels sprouts (250)

Side Dish
Rissoles of brains, Princeton (947)

Fish
Shad, Irish style (1254)
Boiled potatoes (2774)

Remove
Goose à la Chipolata (1945)

Entrées
Carbonnade of mutton à la Juvigny (1589)
Salmis of teal duck à la Harrison (2070)
Spinach with cream (2820)
Lima beans (2699)
Tosca punch (3519)

Roast
Truffled turkey garnished with black olives (2031)
Salad

Hot Entremets
Rice border with bananas (3005)

Caramel ice cream (3447)
Small fancy cakes (3364)
Dessert

248

DINNER, 16 TO 20 PERSONS.
MENU.

Soup
Consommé Adelina (215)

Side Dish
Mousseline Waleski (916)

Fish
Redsnapper à la Mobile (1235)
Viennese potatoes (2812)

Remove
Quarter of boar, garnished with cutlets and breasts marinade sauce (2049)

Entrées
Stuffed sweetbreads, Spanish style (1577)
Chicken fricassee, Bouchard (1862)
Cauliflower, white sauce (2719)
Smothered string beans (2828)

Rum punch (3510)

Roast
Blackhead ducks (2052)
Salad

Hot Entremets
Compiègne with sabayon (3009)

Jardinière cutlets ice cream (3555)

Small fancy cakes (3364)

Fruits (3699)
Coffee (3701)

249   FEBRUARY.

DINNER, 8 TO 10 PERSONS.

MENU.

Soup
Purée of potatoes, Benton (278)

Remove
Redsnapper, Demidoff (1234)

Entrées
Leg of mutton, Bourdaloue (1623)
Baked potatoes (2771)

Braised pullet, modern style (1989)
Boiled cauliflower with white sauce (2719)

Roast
Larded English partridges (2102)
Salad

Hot Entremets
Flawn Golden Lion (3035)

Cold Entremets
Strawberry charlotte (3146)
Fruits (3699)
Dessert

---

250   FEBRUARY.

DINNER, 8 TO 10 PERSONS.

MENU.

Soup
Marshall (323)

Remove
Soles à la Normande (1274)
Duchess potatoes (2785)

Entrées
Pullet, English style (1985)
Glazed endive (2740)

Mutton cutlets, macédoine (1594)
Noodles milanese timbales (2988)

Roast
Squabs (2018)
Salad

Hot Entremets
Apple, Nelson (2991)

Cold Entremets
Rice à la Mirabeau (3213)
Small cakes (3364)
Fruits (3699)
Dessert

---

251   FEBRUARY.

DINNER, 16 TO 20 PERSONS.
MENU.

Soup
Julienne faubonne (318)

Side Dishes
Attéreaux of sweetbreads à la moderne (841)
Fried oyster crabs (1005)

Fish
Soles, Venetian style (1278)
Marchioness potatoes (2797)

Remove
Rack of lamb larded and roasted with purée
of split peas (1735)

Entrées
Escalops of pheasant with olives (2283)
Stuffed tomatoes, Provençal (2835)

Sweetbreads, Piedmontese style (1563)
Green peas, English style (2742)

Roman punch (3515)

Roast
Canvasback duck (2055)
Lettuce salad (2672)

Hot Entremets
Spanish pudding (3110)

Pineapple water-ice (3606)
Small cakes (3364)
Dessert

---

252   FEBRUARY.

DINNER, 16 to 20 PERSONS.
MENU.

Soup.
Champêtre (296)

Side Dish
Beef palate croquettes (875)

Fish
Whitefish, pimentade sauce (1312)
Potato cakes (2778)

Remove
Loin of veal à l'Ambassade (1534)

Entrées
Chicken fillets Sadi Carnot (1853)
Green peas with shredded lettuce (2747)

Terrapin à la Newberg (1086)
American sherbet (3521)

Roast
Ptarmigans (2072)
Escarole salad (2671)

Hot Entremets
Chestnut croquettes (3017)

Andalusian ice cream (3446)
Small cakes (3364)
Dessert

253   FEBRUARY.

DINNER, 8 TO 10 PERSONS.
MENU.

Soup
Purée of beans à la Condé (280)

Remove
Fried soles (1280)

Entrées
Leg of mutton, Parisian style (1634)
Celery with béchamel and croûtons (2720)

Reedbirds vol-au-vent, Diplomate (2407)
Green peas, English style (2742)

Roast
Redhead ducks (2063)
Lettuce salad (2672)

Hot Entremets
Golden crusts (3021)

Cold Entremets
Ministerial pudding (3209)

Fresh fruits (3699)
Cheese (3697)
Coffee (3701)

---

254   FEBRUARY.

DINNER, 8 TO 10 PERSONS.
MENU.

Soup
Genoa paste soup (339)

Remove
Porgies with Chablis wine (1231)
Mellow potatoes (2799)

Entrées
Oxtails with glazed vegetables (1325)

Chickens sautéd à la Nantaise (1896)
String beans à l'Albani (2825)

Roast
Leg of mutton (1633)
Water-cress salad (2676)

Hot Entremets
Glazed apple fritters (3037)
Rye bread ice cream (3450)
Fancy cakes (3364)
Coffee (3701)

---

255   FEBRUARY.

DINNER, 16 TO 20 PERSONS.
MENU.

Soup
Consommé Bariatenski (219)

Side Dish
Attéreaux of turkey (842)

Fish
Pompano à l'Anthelme (1220)
Dauphine potatoes (2783)

Remove
Chine of pork à la Parmentier (1774)

Entrées
Chicken épigrammes à la Volnay (1833)
Tomatoes Trévise (2836)

Tournedos of beef à la Marietta (1435)
Green peas, housekeeper's style (2744)
Venetian sherbet

Roast
Brant ducks with cauliflower Villeroi (2053)
Salad

Hot Entremets
Crescents of noodles with cherries (3015)
Coffee mousse ice cream (3473)
Small cakes (3364)
Dessert

---

256   FEBRUARY.

DINNER, 16 TO 20 PERSONS.
MENU.

Soup
Hunter's style (315)

Side Dish
Cassolettes Lusigny (860)

Fish
Sheepshead à la Meissonier (1260)

Remove
Rump of beef, Flemish style (1341)

Entrées
Breast of pullet, Macédoine (2002)
Ravioles à la Bellini (2976)

Mutton cutlets, breaded with purée of truffles (1599)
Artichoke (bottoms) à la Soubise (2681)

Prunelle punch (3510)

Roast
Redhead ducks (2063)
Celery salad (2660)

Hot Entremets
Madeira crusts (3026)

Cold Entremets
Harrison pudding (3207)
Small fancy cakes (3364)
Dessert

257   FEBRUARY.

DINNER, 8 TO 10 PERSONS.

MENU.

Soup

Noodles with Parmesan (330)

Remove

Perch with parsley water (1211)
Boiled potatoes (2774)

Entrées

Suckling pig with sauerkraut (1811)
Spinach à la Rougemont (2822)

Lamb cutlets with mushrooms (1680)
Small bunches of asparagus (2694)

Roast

Squabs (2018)
Water-cress salad (2676)

Hot Entremets

Mundane fritters (3044)

Stewed fruits (3686)
Cheese (3697)
Coffee (3701)

---

258   FEBRUARY.

DINNER, 8 TO 10 PERSONS.

MENU.

Soup

Small individual soup pots (346)

Remove

Baked frostfish (1161)
Potato croquettes, surprise (2782)

Entrées

Leg of mutton à la Bordelaise (1622)
Spaghetti, Queen style (2968)

Breasts of pullets à la Montmorency (1998)
Green peas, English style (2742)

Roast

Ptarmigans (2072)
Celery knob salad (2660)

Hot Entremets

Condé peaches (3081)
Bavarois with Meringues (3133)
Fruits (3699)
Dessert

---

259   FEBRUARY.

DINNER, 16 TO 20 PERSONS.

MENU.

Soup
Shrimps, mignon (345)

Side Dish
Colombines of chicken livers with ham (865)

Fish
Fried oyster crabs (1005)

Remove
Tenderloin of beef, Neapolitan style (1455)

Entrées
Grenades of turkey à la Jules Verne (2035)
String beans à la Pettit (2827)

Salmis of pheasants à la Lorenzo (2106)
Tomatoes à la Boquillon (2833)

Pâquerette sherbet (3527)

Roast
Capon (1826)
Salad

Hot Entremets
Pear crusts (3027)

Ice cream, Ribambelle (3576)
Small cakes (3364)
Dessert

---

260   FEBRUARY

DINNER, 16 TO 20 PERSONS.

MENU.

Soup
Cream of Jerusalem artichokes (257

Side Dish
Attéreaux of game (842)

Fish
Fillets of soles à la Marguery (1273)
Sarah Potatoes (2802)

Remove
Quarter of veal, Scotch style (1541)

Entrées
Grenadins of beef with round potatoes, Valois
sauce (1393)
Chicken quenelles, Bretonne (2328)

Brussels sprouts, Baroness style (2703)
Artichokes à la Rachel (2690)

Mephisto sherbet (3524)

Roast
Redhead ducks (2063)
Chicory salad (2668)

Hot Entremets
Mellow pudding, apricot sauce (3094)

Frozen Entremets
Plombière Montesquieu (3480)
Small cakes (3364)
Dessert

DÎNER 14 COUVERTS—À L'ANGLAISE.

MENU.

POTAGES.
Consommé Comus (226)   Chartreuse (297)

POISSONS.
Black bass à la Narragansett (1095)   Pétoncles à la Brestoise (1074)

GROSSE PIÈCE.
Jambon rôti à la broche sauce madère (1789)

ENTRÉES.
Ailes de poulet à l'Épicurienne (1842)   Côtelettes de mouton à la Nelson (1596)
Filets de faisan aux truffes (2105)   Soufflé de volaille (2359)

RÔTS.
Canvasback duck (canard sauvage) (2055)   Pâté de foies gras découpé (2563)

RELEVÉS.
Charlotte de pommes à la Destrey (3007)   Pouding Lafayette (3208)

ENTREMETS.
Croûtes aux champignons (2759)   Artichauts à la Rachel (2690)
Tartelettes d'abricots (3402)   Gelée au marasquin (3186)
Glace Comtesse Leda (3548)

BUFFET.
Côtes de bœuf rôties à l'Américaine (1331)   Selle de mouton rôtie (1605)   Potage semoule (316)
Os à la moelle sur croûtes de pain grillées (1319)   Tarte de noix de coco (3200)

DÎNER 20 COUVERTS—À LA RUSSE.

MENU.
20 plats d'huîtres et citrons (803)

2 POTAGES.
1 Brunoise aux quenelles (291)   1 Bisque de homard à la Cambridge (207)

2 HORS-D'ŒUVRE CHAUDS.
2 Palmettes de dinde à la Béarnaise (933)

2 ENTRÉES FROIDES.
1 Aspic de crêtes et de rognons de coq à la Mazarin (2410)   1 Salade de poisson (2631)

2 GROSSES PIÈCES.
2 Filets de bœuf à la Godard (1451)

6 ENTRÉES (PAR DEUX).
2 Filets de poularde à la Montmorency (1998)   1 Saumon à la Victoria (1243)
2 Ris de veau à la Montpensier (1561)   1 Faisan à la Montebello (2108)
Sorbet à la prunelle (3510)

2 PLATS DE RÔTI.
1 de canards à tête rouge (2063)   1 de dinde à l'Américaine (2028)   Salade laitue (2672)

4 ENTREMETS DE LÉGUMES.
2 Tomates frites à la Gibbons (2841)   2 Haricots verts étuvés (2828)

6 ENTREMETS DE DOUCEUR.
2 Beignets d'abricots au Marasquin (3039)
1 Gelée à la Russe (3182)   1 Blanc manger Smolenska (3138)
2 Glaces Plombière d'Alençon (3483)

CARÊME—DÎNER 16 COUVERTS—À L'AMÉRICAINE.

Sur le milieu de la table une corbeille de fleurs.

MENU (en maigre).

BUFFET RUSSE.

Huîtres (803)

POTAGES.

Tortue verte au clair (353)   Crème d'asperges St. Vallier (247)

HORS-D'ŒUVRE CHAUDS.

Cromesquis de filet de Bass (870)

RELEVÉS.

Sheepshead au court-bouillon (1262)   Anguille à la maréchale (1149)

Pommes de terre, boules de neige (2798)

4 ENTRÉES.

Terrapène à la Maryland Club (1088)   Redsnapper à la Chérot (1232)

Choux fleurs gratinés (2717)   Bass rayé à la Maintenon (1105)

Vol-au-vent de morue (2400)

Punch à la Tremière (3520)

2 RÔTS.

Sarcelles à la gelée de groseilles (2068)   Grenouilles à la Orly (1021)   Salade de laitue (2672)

Soufflé au fromage de gruyère (2984)

ENTREMETS DE DOUCEUR.

Croûtes aux ananas, sauce abricots (3022)   Pouding Boissy (3205)   Gelée d'orange en tasses (3180)

Glaces, Bombe à la Trobriand (3440)

Dessert

Café (3701)

DÎNER 14 COUVERTS—À L'AMÉRICAINE.

MENU.

Huîtres (803)

POTAGES.

Consommé Franklyn (233)   Tortue verte aux quenelles à la moelle (353)

HORS-D'ŒUVRE

Timbales à la Palermitaine (978)

POISSONS.

Bass rayé à la Mornay (1107)   Crabes d'huîtres frits (1005)

RELEVÉ.

Selle d'agneau à la purée de navets (1745)   Choux de Bruxelles sautés (2704)

ENTRÉES.

Poularde à l'ivoire aux quenelles décorées (1988)   Champignons à la Reynal (2756)

Ris de veau à la Piémontaise (1563)   Tomates à la Reine (2840)

Punch Élisabeth (3507)

RÔT.

Ruddy ducks (2066)   Salade de chicorée (2668)

Soufflé au parmesan (2983)

ENTREMETS DE DOUCEUR.

Compiègne au sabayon (3009)

Gelée macédoine au champagne (3179)   Pouding Valois (3211)

Glaces, Fiori à la vanille (3469)

Fruits (3699)   Fromages (3697)   Compotes (3686)

Café (3701)

265   MARCH.
DINNER, 8 TO 10 PERSONS.
MENU.

Soup
Purée of larks with chestnuts (281)

Remove
Pompano à la Duclair (1222)
Potatoes boiled with fried bread raspings (2776)

Entrées
Breast of veal stuffed and garnished with
tomatoes (1492)

Grenadins of tenderloin of beef (1384)
Timbale of noodles à la Pearsall (2989)

Asparagus in small bunches (2694)

Roast
Blackhead ducks (2052)
Salad

Hot Entremets
Light pancakes with jams (3079)

Alaska Florida ice cream (3538)
Dessert

266   MARCH.
DINNER, 8 TO 10 PERSONS.
MENU.

Soup
Paillettes (339)

Remove
Turbot, caper sauce (1307)
Mashed potatoes (2798)

Entrées
Leg of mutton à la Reglain (1626)
Braised onions (2765)

Chicken cromesquis (868)
Green peas, French style (2743)

Roast
Ptarmigans (2072)
Dandelion salad (2670)

Hot Entremets
Apples à la Giudici (2990)

Parisian ice cream (3573)
Dessert

267   MARCH.
DINNER, 16 TO 20 PERSONS.
MENU.

Soup
Cream of string beans à la Véfour (264)

Side Dish
Colombines of fat liver (866)

Fish
Halibut with fine herbs à la Reynal (1171)
Snow potatoes (2798)

Remove
Rumps of beef à la Chatellier (1339)
Macaroni à la Brignoli (2958)

Entrées
Chicken Championne (1879)
Carrots with cream (2714)

Lamb cutlets, Giralda (1676)
Green peas, English style (2742)
Fine Champagne sherbet (3510)

Roast
Reedbirds (2152)
Salad

Hot Entremets
Italian pudding (3101)

Cold Entremets.
(Ice) Nesselrode pudding with candied chest-
nuts (3495)
Dessert

268   MARCH.
DINNER, 16 TO 20 PERSONS.
MENU.

Soup
Green turtle with marrow quenelles (353)

Side Dish
Palmettes à la Junot (921)

Fish
Salmon, Argentine style (1237)
Potato tartlets (2810)

Remove
Loin of beef à la Norwood (1348)
Fedelini Cardinal (2953)

Entrées
Lamb minions, cream sauce (1724)
Green peas, Parisian style (2745)

Escalops of liver à la Rulli (2280)
Tomatoes, Queen style (2840)
Imperial punch (3509)

Roast
Capon (1826)
Corn salad (2669)

Hot Entremets.
Rice with apples (3115)

Parfait coffee ice cream (3479)
Dessert

269　　MARCH.

DINNER, 8 TO 10 PERSONS.

MENU.

Soup

Tapioca (316)

Remove

Fisherman's Matelote (1205)
Dauphine potatoes (2783)

Entrées

Cases of squabs à la Umberto (2234)
Sweetbreads à la Montpensier (1561)
Stuffed cauliflower béchamel (2715)
Francatelli risot (2979)

Roast

Loin of mutton on the spit (1637)
Lettuce salad (2672)

Hot Entremets

Chocolate soufflé (3119)

Pineapple water ice (3606)
Dessert

270　　MARCH

DINNER, 8 TO 10 PERSONS.

MENU.

Soup

Cream of carrots with Compiègne croûtons
(263)

Remove

Paupiettes of herring with milts (1176)
Duchess potatoes (2785)

Entrées

Leg of mutton, Roederer style (1627)
Mushrooms à la Dumas (2757)
Brant ducks with cauliflower Villeroi (2053)

Roast

Capon with water-cress (1826)
Salad

Hot Entremets

Zephyr of rice with pineapple (3124)

Lemon water ice (3604)
Dessert

271　　MARCH

DINNER, 16 TO 20 PERSONS.

MENU.

Soup
Calf's feet, English style (293)

Side Dish
Chicken rissoles (948)

Fish
Broiled salmon, Bearnaise sauce (1244)
Hollandaise potatoes (2790)

Remove
Tenderloin of beef à la Melinet (1452)
Cèpes with cream (2724)

Entrées
Chicken fillets à l'Impératrice (1841)
String beans à la Bourguignonne (2826)

Sweetbread cutlets, modern style (2271)
Green peas, English style (2742)

Prunelle punch (3510)

Roast
Blackhead ducks (2052)
Escarole salad (2671)

Hot Entremets
Apple charlotte (3008)

Parfait with nougat (3478)
Dessert

272　　MARCH.

DINNER, 16 TO 20 PERSONS.

MENU.

Soup
Hungarian Consommé (235)

Side Dish
Castillane croustades, purée of chestnuts (895)

Fish
Flounders à la Dieppoise (1153)
Potato cakes (2778)

Remove
Hind quarter of lamb with mint sauce (1732)

Entrées
Sweetbreads, Monarch style (1570)
Trévise tomatoes (2836)

Pigeons, printanière style (1966)
Gnocquis timbale à la Choiseul (2987)

Rebecca sherbet (3528)

Roast
Canvasback ducks (2055)
Celery salad (2660)

Hot Entremets
Rice pudding, fruit sauce (3106)

Italian mousse (3475)
Dessert

273   MARCH.

DINNER, 8 TO 10 PERSONS.

MENU.

Soup

Bisque of oysters à la Wilson (210)

Remove

Perch with Valois sauce (1209)
Marchioness potatoes (2797)

Entrées

Shoulder of lamb with purée of celery (1753)
Chicken fricassee à la Bouchard (1862)
Carrots, Colbert style (2711)

Roast

Mongrel ducks (1921)
Monk's beard salad (2674)

Entremets

Strawberry fritters with macaroons (3049)

Fromage glacé ice cream (3553)
Dessert

---

274   MARCH.

DINNER, 8 TO 10 PERSONS.

MENU.

Soup

Cream of rice à la Crémieux (249)

Remove

Salmon, French style (1241)
Cucumber salad (2661)

Entrées

Capon à la Bressoise (1822)
Rack of veal à l'Albani (1542)

String beans à la Pettit (2827)
Mushrooms à la Raynal (2756)

Roast

Teal ducks (2068)
Salad

Hot Entremets

Brioches, St. Mark (3006)

Strawberry ice cream (3607)
Dessert

---

275   MARCH.

DINNER, 16 TO 20 PERSONS.

MENU.

Soup
Velvet (356)

Side Dish
Attéreaux of beef palates (836)

Fish
Canadian turbot à la Houston (1305)
Viennese potatoes (2812)

Remove
Ham à la Benedict (1787)
Stuffed green peppers (2768)

Entrées
Breast of pullet à la Visconti (2001)
Jerusalem artichokes, Salamander (2749)

Small vol-au-vent, Parisian style (2406)
Asparagus, vinaigrette sauce (2692)

Champagne punch (3504)

Roast
Roast saddle of mutton on the spit (1648)
Chicory salad (2668)

Hot Entremets
Meringued apples, Nubian (2996)

Mignon ice cream (3564)
Dessert

---

276   MARCH.

DINNER, 16 TO 20 PERSONS.

MENU.

Soup
Rice à la Rudini (343)

Side Dish
Robertson ham mousseline (915)

Fish
Sheepshead, Cardinal sauce (1261)
Potato fritters (2788)

Remove
Oxtails hochepot (1324)
Stuffed tomatoes, Provençal (2835)

Entrées
Squabs, Carolina (2021))
Fried stuffed lettuce (2752)
Veal cutlets. Pogarski (2273)
Green peas, English style (2742)

Scotch Haggis (1640)

Pâquerette sherbet (3527)

Roast
Canvasback ducks (2055)
Celery salad (2660)

Hot Entremets
Schiller pudding (3109)

Mousse Siraudin ice cream (3472)
Dessert

277

DINNER, 8 TO 10 PERSONS.

MENU.

Soup
Cream of leeks with quenelles (253)

Remove
Flounders à la Jules Janin (1156)
Mellow potatoes (2799)

Entrées
Loin of lamb with sautéd tomatoes (1718)
Baked stuffed eggplant (2738)

Boar saddle with gravy (2050)
Artichoke (bottoms) with cauliflower (2685)

Roast
Chicken (1881)
Salad

Hot Entremets
Rice croquettes with orange raspberry sauce (3018)

Fiori di latte, Bellini ice cream (3467)
Dessert

278

DINNER, 8 TO 10 PERSONS.

MENU.

Soup
Purée of chicken à la Reine (270)

Remove
Pike perch à la Geraldin (1215)
Potato cakes with ham (2779)

Entrées
Capon à la Pondichery (1824)
Kernel of mutton, Milanese (1630)

Green peas with shredded lettuce (2747)
Mushrooms à la Rivera (2758)

Roast
Brant ducks with cauliflower Villeroi (2053)
Celery, Mayonnaise (2660)

Hot Entremets
Mirlitons of pears, bienvenue (3054)

Sicilian pudding ice cream (3499)
Dessert

279

DINNER, 8 TO 10 PERSONS.

MENU.

Soup
Cream of green peas à la St. Germain (260)

Side Dish
Palmettes of fat liver, Delmontés (925)

Fish
Canadian turbot à la Mercier (1306)
Boiled potatoes, English style (2774)

Remove
Tenderloin of beef with vegetables (1466)
Timbales of chicory with cream (2728)

Entrées
Lamb cutlets à la Victor Hugo (1689)
String beans à l'Albani (2825)

Pâté à la Richelieu (2310)

Maraschino punch (3510)

Roast
Redhead ducks (2063)
Salad

Hot Entremets
Coupole Madison (3029)

(Iced) Fleury pudding (3493)
Dessert

280

DINNER, 8 TO 10 PERSONS.

MENU.

Soup
D'Osmont (306)

Side Dish
Turbigo patties (941)

Fish
Pompano à la Carondelet (1221)
Potato croquettes in surprise (2782)

Remove
Saddle of veal with lettuce (1545)
Ravioles à la Bellini (2976)

Entrées
Chicken poêled à la Stuyvesant (1911)
Sweet potatoes with lobster coral (2830)

Thrush pudding (2324)
American sherbet (3521)

Roast
English pheasants (2107)
Lettuce salad with anchovies (2673)

Hot Entremets
Franklyn pudding (3098)

(Iced) Plombière, Havanese style (3484)
Dessert

DÎNER, 12 COUVERTS—À L'AMÉRICAINE.

MENU.

Huîtres (803)

POTAGES.

Consommé Florentine (232)   Crème d'asperges à la St. Vallier (247)

HORS-D'ŒUVRE.

Timbales à l'Arlequin (967)

POISSON.

Filets de bass à la Conti (1102)   Pommes de terre Dauphine (2783)

RELEVÉ.

Selle d'agneau Chancelière (1739)   Fonds d'artichauts à la Villars (2682)

ENTRÉES.

Faisan piqué aux truffes (2111)   Ris de veau à la Théodora (1568)
Macédoine de légumes à la Montigny (2755)   Tomates farcies aux champignons (2842)
Vol-au-vent aux huîtres (2402)

Punch à la Bouquetière (3503)

RÔT.

Poularde truffée (1992)

FROID.

Terrine de foies de canards à l'Aquitaine (2596)   Salade de laitue (2672)

ENTREMETS SUCRÉS.

Gelée aux Reines-Claude (3187)   Bavarois à la vanille (3135)
Gâteau Compiègne (3236)   Cornets à la Crème à l'orange (3148)
Glaces Plombière à la Havanaise (3484)

Fruits (3699)   Petits fours (3364)   Café (3701)

✠

DÎNER, 12 COUVERTS—À L'AMÉRICAINE.

MENU.

Huîtres (803)

POTAGES.

Consommé Andalouse (216)   Bisque d'écrevisses à la Persigny (204)

HORS-D'ŒUVRE.

Bouchées aux crabes d'huîtres (935)

POISSONS.

Pompano à la Mazarin (1224)   Blanchaille frite à la Diable (1310)

RELEVÉ.

Selle d'agneau à la Française (1744)   Choux fleurs au fromage gratinés (2717)

ENTRÉES.

Mignons de filet de bœuf Baillard (1400)   Petits pois aux laitues braisées (2746)
Timbale de volaille Parisienne (2382)
Asperges à la vinaigrette (2692)

Sorbet, jeune Amérique (3530)

RÔTS.

Poules de neige (2072)   Mésanges moustache (2152)

FROID.

Bordure de foies-gras (2483)   Salade de laitue (2672)

ENTREMETS DE DOUCEUR.

Beignets alliance (3036)

Gelée d'orange en tasses (3180)   Brisselets à la crème framboisée (3223)
Glaces, plum pouding (3496)
Dessert   Café (3701)

DÎNER DE 40 COUVERTS—SERVICE À LA RUSSE.

MENU.

Huîtres (803)

POTAGES.

Consommé à la Noailles (237)   Chiffonade aux croûtes (253)

HORS-D'ŒUVRE.

Timbales à la Lombarde (972)   Bressoles de gibier (847)

POISSONS.

Redsnapper à la Créquy (1233)   Aiguillettes de maquereaux à la Bonnefoy (1191)

RELEVÉ.

Selle d'agneau à la Brighton (1738)

ENTRÉES.

Ris de veau à la St. Laurent (1567)   Filets de poulet à la Maréchale (1848)
Terrapène à la Maryland Club (1088)   Soufflé de faisans à la Andrews (2365)

RÔTS.

Poulets rôtis à la casserole (1881)   Mésanges moustache (2152)

LÉGUMES.

Macédoine à la Montigny (2755)   Céleri frit à la Villeroi (2722)

ENTREMETS.

Biscuits Frascati (3004)   Charlotte de pommes Calville (3143)
Gelée aux ananas Californienne (3178)   Couronne à la Choiseuil (3154)

Glaces et Dessert

DÎNER DE 20 COUVERTS—(À LA FRANCAISE).

MENU.

POTAGES.

Consommé Adélina (215)   Purée de lucines à la Hendrick (197)

GROSSES PIÈCES.

Bass rayé à la Rouennaise (1108)   Filet de bœuf à la Baréda (1442)

ENTRÉES.

Côtelettes d'agneau à la Leverrier (1677)
Ailes de poulet à la Villeroi (1857)   Ris de veau à la Binda (1551)
Terrapène à la Crisfield (1084)
Petits vol-au-vent d'huîtres, Maintenon (2405)
Aspic de homards (2414)

RÔTS.

Pigeonneaux rôtis à la casserole (2018)   Canards sauvages (têtes rouges) (2163)

ENTREMETS.

Tomates farcies aux champignons frais (2842)   Epinards à la Rougemont (2822)
Beignets soufflés Médicis (3047)

Gelée a l'orange en tasses (3180)   Bavarois au chocolat (3131)   Flan aux poires (3175)
Dessert

285   APRIL.

DINNER, 8 TO 10 PERSONS.

MENU.

Soup

Fish chowder à la Stebens (301)

Remove

Cutlets of kingfish, Mayonnaise mousseline (2260)

Entrées

Shoulder of lamb à la Benton (1748)
Spaghetti macaroni à la Salvini (2969)

Thrushes in the saucepan (2165)
Okra garnished with barley béchamel croustades (2763)

Roast

Squabs (2018)
Salad

Hot Entremets

Fried cream à la Maintenon (3010)

Vanilla ice cream, Italian meringue (3458)
Stewed fruits (3686)
Nuts and raisins (3699)
Dessert

---

286   APRIL.

DINNER, 8 TO 10 PERSONS.

MENU.

Soup

Pilaff, Turkish style (341)

Removes

Smelts in dauphins à la Hamlin (1270)
Persillade potatoes (2774)

Top round of beef, Parisian style (1336)
Cabbage, Peasant style (2706)

Entrée

Pigeons poêled, Lombardy style (1960)
Quartered artichokes with marrow (2688)

Roast

Ducks (1921)
Salad

Hot Entremets

Pancakes of peach marmalade macédoine (3075)

Small cream biscuits (3137)
Cheese (3697)
Fruits (3699)
Dessert

---

287   APRIL.

DINNER, 16 TO 20 PERSONS.

MENU.

Soup

Noques (358)

Side Dish

Palmettes, Varsovian style (924)

Fish

Pompano, tomato sauce (1228)
Potato fritters (2788)

Remove

Boiled ham à la Leonard (1788)
Spinach à la Noailles (2821)

Entrées

Noisettes of tenderloin of beef à la Bonnefoy (1412)
Artichoke bottoms, Soubise (2681)

English pheasants à la Périgueux (2109)
Smothered string beans (2828)

Siberian punch (3516)

Roast

Ruddy ducks (2066)
Salad

Hot Entremets

Cabinet pudding with sabayon (3096)

(Iced) Mousse with cordials (3476)
Dessert

---

288   APRIL.

DINNER, 16 TO 20 PERSONS.

MENU.

Soup

Rémusat consommé (240)

Side Dish

Renaissance timbales (981)

Fish

Striped bass, Hollandaise sauce (1110)
Boiled potatoes persillade (2774)

Remove

Capons à l'Amphitryon (1821)
Mushrooms with thickened butter (2760)

Entrées

Minions of tenderloin of beef à la Meyerbeer (1404)

Green peas, English style (2742)
Shells of chicken à la Shaw (2344)

Californian sherbet (3523)

Roast

Pullets (1996)
Salad

Hot Entremets

Humboldt pudding (3100)

(Iced) Alençon plombière (3483)
Dessert

289   APRIL,
DINNER, 8 TO 10 PERSONS.
MENU.

Soup
Pot au feu (342)

Remove
Spotted fish with green ravigote sauce (1286)
Mashed potatoes (2798)

Entrées
Braised leg of mutton with rice (1636)
Artichoke bottoms à la Villars (2682)

Baked thrushes (2164)
String beans à la Bourguignonne (2826)

Roast
Chickens (1881)
Tomato salad (2666)

Hot Entremets
Roman Triumvirate fritters (3050)

Strawberry water ice (3607)
Fruits (3699)
Small fancy cakes (3364)
Coffee (3701)

290   APRIL.
DINNER, 8 TO 10 PERSONS.
MENU.

Soup
Champêtre (296)

Remove
Fillets of soles à la Richelieu (1275)
Mellow potatoes (2799)

Entrées
Chicken fricassee with crustacean sauce (1867)
String beans à l'Albani (2825)

Larded veal cutlets with chicory (1500)
Fried oyster-plant (2817)

Roast
Teal ducks (2068)
Salad

Hot Entremets
Apple fritters with kirsch (3038)

Ice cream with orange-flower water (3459)
Fruits (3699)
Cheese (3697)
Coffee (3701)

291   APRIL.
DINNER, 16 TO 20 PERSONS.
MENU.

Soup
Clear mock turtle (354)

Side Dish
Fontage à la Flavignan (907)

Fish
Trout, Joan of Arc (1294)
Snow potatoes (2798)

Remove
Turkey grenades à la Jules Verne (2035)
Turnips with Allemande sauce (2848)

Entrées
Round bottom fricandeau of veal with gravy
(1543)
Spinach with cream (2820)

Artichoke bottoms with cauliflower (2685)

Béatrice Punch (3502)

Roast
Redhead ducks (2063)
Salad

Hot Entremets
Zephyr of rice with pineapple (3124)

(Iced) Cavour pudding (3489)
Dessert

292   APRIL.
DINNER 16 TO 20 PERSONS.
MENU.
Oysters (803)

Soup
Ponsardin fish (308)

Side Dish
La Vallière timbales (971)

Fish
Shad with sorrel purée (1256)
Duchess potatoes (2785)

Remove
Saddle of mutton, German style (1645)
Beets with cream (2702)

Entrées
Duck à la Matignon (1918)
Green peas with shredded lettuce (2747)

Sweetbreads à la St. Cloud (1566)
String beans with butter (2829)

Prunelle punch (3510)

Roast
Pullets with water-cress (1996)
Salad

Hot Entremets
Bananas fried with cherries (3003)

(Iced) Rice à la Ristori (3577)
Dessert

293   APRIL

DINNER, 8 TO 10 PERSONS.

MENU.

Soup

Purée of oatmeal, Toulousaine (275)

Remove

Fillet of salmon trout à l'Antoinette (1302)
Potatoes, Vienna style (2812)

Entrées

Calf's head in tortue (1517)
Chicken sautéd à la Madeleine (1891)
Jerusalem artichokes à la Salamander (2749)
Asparagus à la Maintenon (2695)

Roast

Pheasants (2107)
Salad

Hot Entremets

Mirabeau crusts with fruits (3025)
Custard cream with caramel (3161)
Dessert

294   APRIL.

DINNER, 8 TO 10 PERSONS.

MENU.

Soup

Giblet à la Réglain (311)

Remove

Chicken halibut, carrot sauce (1173)
Potato tartlets (2810)

Entrées

Leg of mutton, Granville (1628)
Ducklings with oronges (1943)

Tomatoes, Queen style (2840)
String beans, with butter (2829)

Roast

Redhead ducks (2063)
Salad

Hot Entremets

Flawn à la Manhattan (3034)

Stewed fruits (3686)
Cheese (3697)
Dessert

295   APRIL.

DINNER, 16 TO 20 PERSONS

MENU.

Oysters (803)

Soup
Vermicelli (339)

Side Dish
Palmettes of Guinea fowl à la Paladio (926)

Fish
Soles à la Trouville (1277)
Dauphine potatoes (2783)

Remove
Breast of veal à la Mondoux (1488)
Sorrel with gravy (2818)

Entrées
Salmis of teal duck à la Harrison (2070)
Oyster-plant, fine herbs (2817)
Coquilles à la Benoiton (2339)

Rum punch (3510)

Roast
Spring turkey with water-cress (2044)
Lettuce salad (2672)

Hot Entremets
Savarin with apricots (3117)

Valence cups with peaches, ice cream (3587)
Small fancy cakes (3364)
Dessert

296   APRIL

DINNER, 16 TO 20 PERSONS.

MENU.

Soup
Lobster, Duke Alexis (321)

Side Dish
Lombardy Timbales (972)

Fish
Shad à la Evers with shad roe croquettes (1252)
Broiled potatoes with fried bread (2776)

Remove
Virginia ham with stringed eggs (1792)
Artichoke bottoms à la Villars (2682)

Entrées
Noisettes of tenderloin of beef à la Magny (1414)
Sautéd sweet peppers (2769)
Chicken boudins à l'Écarlate (2214)

Paradise sherbet (3525)

Roast
Capon (1826)
Salad

Hot Entremets
Pineapple Carolina (3090)

Alaska Florida ice cream (3538)
Dessert

297

DINNER, 8 TO 10 PERSONS.

MENU.

Soup
Sago (316)

Remove
Weakfish à la Brighton (1308)
Potatoes with melted butter (2790)

Entrées
Rack of lamb with sautéd artichokes (1734)
Cutlets of chicken à la Clarence (2258)

Baked stuffed eggplant (2738)
Boquillon tomatoes (2833)

Roast
Turkey (2028)
Chicory salad (2668)

Hot Entremets
Fried bananas, cherry sauce (3003)

Parisian ice cream (3573)
Fruits (3699)
Small fancy cakes (3364)
Coffee (3701)

298

DINNER, 8 TO 10 PERSONS.

MENU.

Soup
Bisque of crabs, Stevens (199)

Remove
Sturgeon with quenelles and olives (1289)
Hollandaise potatoes (2790)

Entrées
Grenadins of tenderloin of beef à la Beau-
marchais (1385)
Red cabbage à la Montargis (2707)

Border of risot of lobster (2213)
Artichokes à la Rachel (2690)

Roast
Mallard ducks (2059)
Salad

Hot Entremets
Orange fritters à la Talleyrand (3045)

(Iced) Pudding Duchess (3492)
Fruits (3699)
Cheese (3697)
Coffee (3701)

299

DINNER, 16 TO 20 PERSONS.

MENU.

Soup
Consommé à la Grammont (234)

Side Dish
Cromesquis of scallops (873)

Fish
Small trout au bleu (1297)
Potato cakes (2778)

Remove
Ham with spinach (1791)
Onions, Hollandaise sauce (2764)

Entrées
Breast of chicken, Mexican style, in papers
(1859)
Carrots, Colbert style (2711)

Tourte of chicken (2391)

Sorbet Young America (3530)

Roast
Ruddy ducks (2066)
Lettuce salad (2672)

Hot Entremets
Pancake sticks Royeaux (3076)

(Iced) Constantine bomb (3439)
Dessert

300

DINNER, 16 TO 20 PERSONS.

MENU.

Soup
Cream of cauliflower, Brisson (251)

Side Dish
Rissoles à la Demidoff (950)

Fish
Stuffed trout (1301)
Marchioness potatoes (2797)

Remove
Turkey with white oyster sauce (2032)
Artichoke bottoms à la Florence (2677)

Entrées
Fillet of lamb, Printanière (1726)
Spaghetti à la Laurence (2966)

Pigeons with crawfish (1968)
Stuffed lettuce with half-glaze sauce (2753)

Punch Elizabeth (3507)

Roast
Canvasback ducks (2055)
Salad

Hot Entremets
Madison Cupola (3029)

(Iced) Vermeil globules à la Damseaux (3588)
Dessert

DÎNER, 14 COUVERTS—SERVICE À L'ANGLAISE.

MENU.

POTAGES.

Consommé Royale (241)   Crème de laitues à la Evers (258)

POISSON.

Bass rayé sauce crevettes aux petoncles frits (1111)   Croquettes de pommes de terre (2782)

GROSSE PIÈCE.

Selle d'agneau à la Française (1744)   Carottes aux fines herbes (2712)

ENTRÉES.

Ailes de poulet à la Harrison (1844)   Ris de veau à la Conti (1554)

Vol-au-vent Delmontés (2403)   Terrapène à la Maryland Club (1088)

RÔTS.

Dinde à l'Américaine (2028)   Salade de cresson et pommes (2676)

RELEVÉS.

Dampfnouilles à la crème (3030)   Soufflé au chocolat (chaud) (3119)

ENTREMETS.

Tomates farcies à la Provençale (2835)   Macaroni au gratin (2959)

Bordure Caroline au champagne (froid) (3140)   Gelée de kirsch aux fruits (3187)

Gaufres roulées, crème au curaçoa (3224)   Tartelettes de Valence (3336)

(BUFFET).

Aloyau à la Norwood (1348)   Selle de mouton rôtie (1648)   Yorkshire pudding (770)

Pommes tartelettes (2810)   Tarte Condé (3220)   Potage d'orge au céleri (285)

AVRIL   302

DÎNER 14 COUVERTS—SERVICE À L'AMÉRICAINE.

MENU.

Haut Sauterne   *Petit Buffet Russe.*

Huîtres (803)

Sherry   **POTAGES.**

Consommé printanier aux qnenelles (239)

Crème d'oseille aux œufs farcis (262)

HORS-D'ŒUVRE CHAUD.

Timbales des Gourmets (966)

Niersteiner   **POISSON.**

Truites à l'Hôtelière (1292)

Champagne Pommery   **RELEVÉ.**

Poularde farcie à la Parisienne (1990)   Céleri à la Villeroi (2722)

St. Julien Supérieur   **ENTRÉES.**

Grenadins de filet de veau, sauce tomate Argentine (1507)

Haricots verts au beurre (2829)

Vol-au-vent à la Financière (2396)

Petits pois à la Française (2743)

Sorbet à la prunelle (3510)

Romanée   **RÔTS.**

Canards à tête rouge (2063)

Petits aspics de foies gras (2412)

Salade de laitue (2672)

ENTREMETS DE DOUCEUR.

Pouding de Cabinet à la Royale (chaud) (3095)

Suédoise de pommes (3218)   Timbale de gaufres (3222)

Charlotte Russe (3145)   Gelée Macédoine au champagne (3179)

Champagne   **PIÈCES MONTÉES.**

Cliquot doux   Bateau Bon Voyage (3631)

Panier de Perrette (3629)

Apollinaris   Glaces Cygne aux roseaux (3597)

Fruits (3699)   Café (3701)   Petits fours (3364)

DÎNER 200 COUVERTS—SERVICE A L'AMÉRICAINE.

Société St. George.

MENU.

Haut Sauterne   Huîtres (803)

POTAGES.

Consommé Souveraine (243)   Crème d'asperges aux pointes d'asperges **(248)**

Amontillado   HORS-D'ŒUVRE.

Timbales à la Sartiges (984)

Johannisberger   POISSONS.

Gold seal   Bass rayé à la Laguipierre (1103)

Blanchaille frite à la mode de Greenwich **(1310)**

Cliquot sec   RELEVÉ.

Baron de bœuf à la St. George (1313)   Pommes rôties (2771)

Château Laffitte   ENTRÉES.

Chapon à la Régence (1825)   Petits pois aux laitues braisées (2746)

Sorbet Rébecca (3528)

Clos Vougeot   RÔT.

Pigeonneaux rôtis à la casserole (2018)   Salade d'escarole (2671)

ENTREMETS DE DOUCEUR.

Plum pudding au rhum (chaud) (3103)
Apollinaris   Charlotte Russe (3145)
Glaces (3538)   Fruits (3699)   Petits fours (3364)   Café (3701)

DÎNER 10 COUVERTS—SERVICE À LA FRANCAISE.

MENU.

DEUX POTAGES.

Le Consommé Balzac (218)   La crème de haricots flageolets (259)

DEUX RELEVÉS DE POISSON.

Les filets de saumon à la d'Artois (1238)   La Matelote des Canotiers (1203)

DEUX GROSSES PIÈCES.

La noix de veau à la Duchesse (1520)   Les filets de poularde à la Varsovienne (2000)

QUATRE ENTRÉES.

Les ris de veau à la Bussy (1552)   La fricassée de poulet au kari (1868)
Les petits pâtés au jus (2318)   Les boudins de kingfish à la Poniatowski (2220)

DEUX PLATS DE RÔTS.

Les faisans Anglais (2107)   Les sarcelles (2068)

DEUX RELEVÉS DU RÔTS.

La Charlotte de pommes à la Destrey (chaud) (3007)   Les Œufs à la crème au café meringués (3033)

QUATRE ENTREMETS.

Les épinards à l'Anglaise (2823)   Les concombres panés et frits (2732)
Les Buissons de meringues (3212)   Les pêches à la Louvoisienne (3198)
Dessert

DÎNER, 100 COUVERTS—SERVICE À L'AMÉRICAINE.

MENU.

Lucines orangées (803)

POTAGES.

Consommé Sévigné (242)

Bisque de crabes orientale (200)

HORS-D'ŒUVRE.

Timbales à la Vénitienne (989)

POISSONS.

Saumon, sauce Marinade (1245)

Soles à la Normande (1274)

Pommes de terre Dauphine (2783)

RELEVÉS.

Filet de bœuf à la Mélinet (1452)

Risot à la Ristori (2980)

ENTRÉES.

Poulet sauté à la Nantaise (1896)

Petits pois à la Française (2743)

Ris de veau à la Piémontaise (1563)

Tomates en caisses gratinées (2839)

Asperges bouillies, sauce crème (2692)

Punch à la Tosca (3519)

RÔTS.

Bécassines (2159)

Pâté de foies-gras découpé (2563)

Salade de laitue (2672)

ENTREMETS SUCRÉS.

Pouding léger aux amandes (3112)

Gelée aux framboises (3183)

Pièces Montées (3628)

Glace Plombière aux cerises (3485)

Fruits (3699)　　Fromages (3697)　　Compote (3686)

Petits fours (3364)　　Café (3701)

MAL.

DÎNER, DE 16 COUVERTS—SERVICE À LA FRANCAISE.

MENU.

Premier Service.

Potage Westmoreland (357)

Consommé à la Daumont (228)

Redsnapper à la Princesse (1236)

Selle d'agneau de printemps à la Chancelière (1739)

Faisan anglais à la Montebello (2108)

Vol-au-vent de grenouilles (2401)

Pigeonneau à la Crispi (2008)

Côtelettes de filet de bœuf Bienville (2256)

Timbales des Gourmets (996)

Pâté chaud de ris de veau à la McAllister (2313)

Deuxième Service.

Mauviettes rôties (2152)

Chapon rôti (1826)

Cardons à la demi-glace (2710)

Petits pois à l'Anglaise (2742)

Pouding à la Franklyn (3098)

Gâteau Mandarin (3245)

Charlotte à la Russe (3145)

Gelée Macédoine au Champagne (3179)

Troisième Service.

Corbeilles de fruits frais (3699)

Compotes de pommes à la gelée (3686)   Bonbons (3640)   Petits fours (3364)

Glace crème pralinée à l'angélique (3455)

Glace orange à l'eau (3605)

DÎNER, DE 20 COUVERTS—SERVICE À LA RUSSE.

MENU.

HORS-D'ŒUVRE.

Radis (808) Olives (800) Caviar (778) Beurre frais moulé (775

Huîtres marinées (802)

Lucines (803)

POTAGES.

Consommé Berry (220) Crème de concombres, Sheppard (254)

HORS-D'ŒUVRE.

Palmettes de jambon à l'Aquitaine (927)

Timbales à la Dumas (965)

POISSONS.

Alose Bruxelloise (1253) Saumon à la Daumont (1239)

RELEVÉS.

Selle d'agneau à la Chancelière (1739)

Canetons à l'Andalouse (1930)

ENTRÉES.

Ris de veau à l'Écarlate (1555) Filets de poulet à la Primatice (1851)

Foie gras de Strasbourg (2562) Turban de homard (2394)

Punch à la Favorite (3508)

RÔTS.

Pigeonneaux (2018) Poulardes truffées (1992)

LÉGUMES.

Asperges Comtesse (2693) Petits pois aux laitues braisées (2746)

ENTREMETS DE DOUCEUR.

Charlotte de pommes (3008) Beignets d'ananas, Singapour (3046)

Gelée aux mirabelles (3187) Bavarois à la Vanille (3135)

FLANCS.

Gâteau à la Reine (3256) Vacherin Sultane (3264)

DESSERT.

Petits fours (3364) Bonbons (3642)

Devises (3653) Fruit confits (3679)

Fruits frais (3699) Compotes de pommes à la gelée (3686)

DÎNER, DE 30 COUVERTS—SERVICE À L'ANGLAISE.

MENU.

POTAGES.

Tortue verte au clair (353)

Crème de maïs à la Hermann (255)

POISSONS.

Tranches de saumon à la Moderne (1242)

Fricandeau d'esturgeon aux petits pois (1288)

RELEVÉS.

Selle d'agneau à la Paganini (1741)

Pointe de culotte de bœuf à la mode bourgeoise (1340)

ENTRÉES.

Épigrammes d'agneau à la Toulouse (1694)

Rissolettes à la Pompadour (956)

Noix de veau au jus lié (1521)

Côtelettes de mouton à la Taverne (1592)

Quenelles de volaille à la Richelieu (2327)

Quenelles de volaille à la Richelieu (2327)

Côtelettes de mouton à la Taverne (1592)

Noix de veau au jus lié (1521)

Rissolettes à la Pompadour (956)

Épigrammes d'agneau à la Toulouse (1694)

RÔTS.

Pigeonneaux rôtis à la casserole (2018)

Salmis de canetons (1940)

ENTREMETS.

Asperges sauce Hollandaise (2692)

Mazarines à l'ananas et au kirsch (3053)

Crèmes frites Paméla (3013)

Gelée macédoine au champagne (3179)

Crème de homard (2470)

Crème de homard (2470)

Gelée macédoine au champagne (3179)

Crèmes frites Paméla (3013)

Mazarines à l'ananas (3653)

Asperges sauce Hollandaise (2692)

PIÈCES MONTÉES.

Le moulin à vent (3639)

Vases en sucre filé (3637)

RELEVÉS.

Gâteau Chamounix (3235)

Jambon au suprême (3255)

309   MAY.

DINNER, 8 TO 10 PERSONS.

MENU.

Soup

Consommé Célestine (223)

Remove

Porgy à la Manhattan (1229)
Persillade potatoes (2774)

Entrées

Duckling à la Grainville, larded (1933)
Grenadins of beef, Prévillot (1391)

Sweet peppers sautéd (2769)
Oyster plant à la poulette (2817

Roast

Chicken (1881)
Water-cress and apple salad (2676)

Hot Entremets

Countess pudding (3097)

Stewed fruits (3686)
Nuts and raisins
Dessert

---

310   MAY.

DINNER, 8 TO 10 PERSONS.

MENU.

Soup

Lazagnette (339)

Remove

Fried brook trout (1299)
Marchioness potatoes (2797)

Entrées

Shoulder of lamb à la Dessaix (1749)
Salpicon of chicken, baked (2338)

Artichoke bottoms with marrow (2687)
Turnips with béchamel (2848)

Roast

Duckling (1938)
Salad

Hot Entremets

Rice with apples (3115)
Burnt almond ice cream with Angelica (3455)
Dessert

---

311   MAY.

DINNER, 16 TO 20 PERSONS.

MENU.

Soup
Bisque of crawfish (201)

Side Dish
Turbigo patties (941)

Fish
Brook trout, Miller style (1295)
Viennese potatoes (2812)

Remove
Pullet, ancient style (1984)
Carrots, Colbert (2711)

Entrées
Blanquette of breast of veal à la **Jacquart**
(1490)
Stuffed cos-lettuce à la Rudini (2816)
Escalops of tenderloin of beef with **truffles**
(2276)
Tomatoes à la Boquillon (2833)

Pargny punch (3514)

Roast
Turkey (2028)
Salad

Hot Entremets
Figaro timbale (3123)

Cold Entremets
Strawberry, Charlotte (3146)
(Iced) Parfait with coffee (3479)
Dessert

---

312   MAY.

DINNER, 16 TO 20 PERSONS.

MENU.

Soup
Montorgueil (326)

Side Dish
Isabella mousseline (912)

Fish
Flounders à la Joinville (1155)
Potato cakes (2778)

Remove
Tenderloin of beef à la Travers (1460)
Stuffed cabbage ballotine (2705)

Entrées
Lamb cutlets à la Giralda (1676)
Mushrooms à la Reynal (2756)

Vol-au-vent of frogs and soubise eggs (2401

Andalouse sherbet (3522)

Roast
Squabs (2018)
Salad

Hot Entremets
Apple pain with vanilla (2997)

Cold Entremets
(Iced) Mousse with chestnuts (3477)
Dessert

313   MAY.

DINNER, 8 TO 10 PERSONS.
MENU.

Soup

Barch, Polish style (286)

Remove

Mackerel, arrowroot mayonnaise sauce (1303)
Cucumbers (2661)

Entrées

Duckling à la Lyonnaise (1934)
Minions of fillets of veal with mushrooms
(1510)

Green peas with lettuce (2746)
Artichoke bottoms à la Montglas (2679)

Roast

Ptarmigan (2072)
Macédoine salad (2650)

Hot Entremets

Pudding soufflé with hazelnuts (3114)

(Iced) Rice with citron garnished with truffles
(3457)
Dessert

314   MAY.

DINNER, 8 TO 10 PERSONS.
MENU.

Soup

Cream of asparagus, croûtons soufflés (248)

Remove

Angel fish à la Bahama (1094)
Hollandaise potatoes (2790)

Entrées

Broiled rack of lamb, Castillane sauce (1733)
Chicken fricassee à la favorite (1864)

Carrots stewed with cream (2714)
Head of asparagus, Countess style (2693)

Roast

Squabs (2018)
Salad

Hot Entremets

Brioches St. Mark (3006)

Vanilla ice cream (3458)
Dessert

315   MAY.

DINNER, 16 TO 20 PERSONS.
MENU.

Soup
Monteille (325)

Side Dish
Timbales à la Duchesse (964)

Fish
Brook trout à la Hussarde (1293)
Potato tartlets (2810)

Remove
Tenderloin of beef à la Bienvenue (1445)
Glazed turnips (2847)

Entrées
Breast of chicken with cucumbers (1860)

Lamb sweetbreads à la financière (1760)
Carrots, Viennese (2713)

Punch Elizabeth (3507)

Roast
Pheasant (2107)
Salad

Hot Entremets
Plumerey pudding (3104)

Cold Entremets.
Bain-marie cream molded (3149)
(Iced) Spongade à la Médicis (3536)
Dessert

316   MAY.

DINNER, 16 TO 20 PERSONS.
MENU.

Soup
Consommé, Dubarry (229)

Side Dish
Bressoles of fat liver (848)

Fish
Pompano à la Toulouse (1227)
Mashed potatoes (2798)

Remove
Squabs à la Crispi (2008)
Fried hops (2748)

Entrées
Timbale of sweetbreads, modern style (2388)
Green peas, housekeeper's style (2744)

Breast of chicken à la Cussy (1838)
Mushrooms in cases with Madeira (2762)

Venetian sherbet (3529)

Roast
Turkey (2028)
Salad

Hot Entremets
Rice pudding à la Bagration (3105)

Cold Entremets
Cream Flamri (3167)
(Iced) Soufflé à l'Alcazar (3533)
Dessert

317 MAY.
DINNER, 8 TO 10 PERSONS.
MENU.

Soup
Bisque of crabs (198)

Remove
Porgy à la Manhattan (1229)
Dauphine potatoes (2783)

Entrées
Tenderloin steak with mushrooms (1427)
Asparagus tips à la Maintenon (2695)

Lobster à la Dugléré (1031)
Risot Francatelli (2979)

Roast
Ptarmigan (2072)
Cabbage salad (2659)

Hot Entremets
Grenades with cherries (3052)

(Iced) Biscuit pudding (3488)
Fresh fruits (3699)
Cheese (3697)

Small fancy cakes (3364)
Bonbons (3640)
Dessert

318 MAY.
DINNER, 8 TO 10 PERSONS.
MENU.

Soup
Bragance (290)

Remove
Halibut à la Kadgiori (1170)
Duchess potatoes (2785)

Entrées
Leg of lamb à la Bercy (1705)
Lettuce braised with gravy (2754)

Breast of pigeons, Hunter's style (1963)
String beans à l'Albani (2825)

Roast
Pullet with water-cress (1996)

Hot Entremets
Apple " pain " with vanilla (2997)
Chocolate ice cream (3449)
Dessert

319 MAY.
DINNER, 16 to 20 PERSONS.
MENU.

Radishes (808)   Fresh butter (775)

Soup.
Consommé Duchess (230)

Side Dish
Chicken quenelles à la Richelieu (2327)

Fish
Striped bass à la Bercy (1101)
Hollandaise potatoes (2790)

Remove
Rump of beef à la Carême (1338)
Beets with butter (2702)

Entrées
Cutlets of chicken à la Adolph Hardy (2257)
Green peas, French style (2743)

Vol-au-vent à la Financière (2396)

Méphisto sherbet (3524)

Roast
Chicken in the saucepan (1881)
Italian salad (2635)

Hot Entremets
Rice pudding with strawberry sauce (3106)

Ice cream corn on cob (3547)
Dessert

320 MAY.
DINNER, 16 TO 20 PERSONS.
MENU.

Olives (800)   Gherkins (785)

Soup
Gumbo with soft shell crabs (314)

Side Dish
Croustades, Perretti (900)

Fish
Bluefish à la Barnave (1117)
Potatoes with melted butter (2790)

Remove
Tenderloin steak with truffles (1429)
Eggplant à la Duperret (2735)

Entrées
Chicken fricassee à la Chevalière (1863)
Cauliflower fried with bread-crumbs (2718)

Lamb cutlets à la Giralda (1676)
Green peas, Parisian style (2745)

Tremière punch (3520)

Roast
Duckling (1938)
Salad

Hot Entremets
Ferrière pears (3085)
Pistachio ice cream (3454)
Dessert

321 MAY.
DINNER 8 TO 10 PERSONS.

MENU.

Soup
Gluten (316)

Remove
Brook trout, Court-bouillon (1298)
Boiled potatoes (2774)

Entrées
Breast of veal, housekeeper's style (1493)
String beans à la Pettit (2827)

Young pigeons, English style (2014)
Onions with soubise sauce (2764)

Roast
Ptarmigan (2072)
Lettuce salad (2672)

Hot Entremets
Mirabeau crusts with fruits (3025)

(Iced) Plombière, Havanese (3484)
Small fancy cakes (3364)
Bonbons (3642)

322 MAY.
DINNER, 8 TO 10 PERSONS.

MENU.

Soup
Consommé Balzac (218)

Remove
Trout à la Beaufort (1290)
Potato croquettes (2782)

Entrées
Duckling fillets à la macédoine (1935)
Parsnip cakes fried in butter (2767)

Lamb cutlets à la Victor Hugo (1689)
Green peas, housekeeper's style (2744)

Roast
Squabs (2018)
Salad

Hot Entremets
Manhattan flawn (3034)

Bain-marie cream with virgin coffee (3162)
Dessert
Assorted salted almonds (3696)

323 MAY.
DINNER, 16 TO 20 PERSONS.

MENU.

Soup
Crawfish à la Renommée (304)

Side Dish
Timbales à la Montgomery (975)

Fish
Fillets of weakfish à la Pontigny (1309)
Mellow potatoes (2799)

Remove
Sirloin of beef with chicory and souffléd sweet
potatoes (1356)
Stuffed peppers (2768)

Entrées
Breasts of chicken à la Lorenzo (1845)
Oyster plant with fine herbs (2817)

Vol-au-vent, ancient style (2398)

Punch Bouquetière (3503)

Roast
English pheasant (2107)
Salad

Hot Entremets
Baba marsala (3002)

(Ices) Fiori di latte Bellini (3467)
Dessert

324 MAY.
DINNER, 16 TO 20 PERSONS.

MENU.

Soup
Quenèfes (358)

Side Dish
Patties with mushrooms (937)

Fish
Baked paupiettes of soles à l'Italienne (1279)
Broiled potatoes with fried bread (2776)

Remove
Pullet à la Arco Valley (1971)
Cucumbers breaded and fried, English style
(2732)

Entrées
Minions of tenderloin of beef with cèpes
Bordelaise (1408)
Stuffed green peppers (2768)

Squabs à la Vestale (2022)
Fried asparagus tips, Miranda (2696)

Montmorency punch (3512)

Roast
Turkey (2028)
Salad

Hot Entremets
Frascati biscuit (3004)

(Iced) Diplomate pudding (3491)
Dessert

DÎNER DE 20 COUVERTS—SERVICE À LA RUSSE.

MENU.

Lucines orangées (803)

POTAGES.

Moselle Berncastle   Consommé Carême (222)

Bisque de homard Portland (208)

HORS-D'ŒUVRE.

Amontillado   Attéreaux de foies gras (838)

POISSON.

Clicquot   Bluefish Barnave (1117)

RELEVÉ.

Tranches de selle d'agneau purée de haricots (1747)

Pontet-Canet   ENTRÉES.

Timbales de pigeonneaux, Berchoux (2387)

Homard Rougemont (1041)

Punch glacé à la prunelle (3510)

RÔTS.

St. Pierre   Canards farcis à l'Américaine (1920)

Soufflés de fromage de gruyère (2985)

LÉGUMES.

Asperges sauce hollandaise (2692)

Petits pois à l'Anglaise (2742)

ENTREMETS.

Old Port   Bananes frites sauce cerises (3003)

Riz aux fraises (3216)

Dessert

DÎNER DE 16 COUVERTS—SERVICE À L'AMÉRICAINE.

MENU.

Lucines orangées (803)

POTAGES.

Haut Sauterne   Consommé Antonelli (217)
Amontillado   Bisque de moules à la Cutting (209)

Piesporter Auslese   HORS-D'ŒUVRE.

Brissotins de homard à l'Indienne (851)

POISSONS.

Kingfish à la Sultane (1185)
Maquereaux espagnols aux petits pois (1200)
Salade de concombres (2661)

RELEVÉ.

Pontet-Canet   Selle d'agneau à la Chancelière (1739)
Aubergines frites (2739)

ENTRÉES.

Clicquot doux   Poulets aux légumes nouveaux (1916)
Petits pois à l'Anglaise (2742)
Pommery   Casseroles de ris d'agneau à la de Luynes (2238)
Tomates farcies (2842)
Têtes d'asperges en petites bottes (2694)

Sorbet parfait amour (3526)

RÔTS.

Nuits   Bécassines (2159)
Pigeonneaux au cresson (2018)

FROID.

Petits aspics de foies-gras (2412)
Salade de laitue (2672)

ENTREMETS SUCRÉS.

Beignets de cerises (3042)
Gelée aux fruits (3187)
Pouding Lafayette (3208)

PIÈCES MONTÉES.

Oporto   Glace Esmeralda (3551)
Liqueurs   Fruits (3699)
Petits fours (3364)
Café (3701)

DÎNER DE 14 COUVERTS—SERVICE À L'ANGLAISE.

MENU.

POTAGES.

Consommé Carême (222)

Crème de patates à la Girard (265)

POISSONS.

Kingfish à la Montgolfier (1183)

Saumon à l'Argentine (1237)

HORS-D'ŒUVRE.

Cassolettes Montholon (861)

RELEVÉS.

Filet de bœuf à la d'Orléans (1450)

Chapon à la Pondichéry (1824)

ENTRÉES.

Bécassines sautées à l'Africaine (2153)	Ailes de poulet à la Bodisco (1835)
Ris de veau à la Napolitaine (1562)	Vol-au-vent à la Financière (2396)
Filets de volaille à la Lucullus (1846)	Côtelettes d'agneau à la Clémence (1673)
Timbales de macaroni (2988)	Pain de volaille à la Villars (2304)
Pigeonneaux à la Crispi (2008)	Homard à la créole (1029)

BUFFET.

Côtes de bœuf rôties au jus (1331)	Selle de mouton rôtie (1648)
Haricots maître-d'hôtel (2829)	Choux à la Paysanne (2706)

RÔTS.

Canetons au cresson (1938)   Mésanges moustache (2152)

RELEVÉS.

Pouding à l'Italienne (3101)   Crèmes frites Paméla (3013)

FLANCS.

Le char des Cygnes (3634))

La Corbeille garnie de fruits en sucre tiré (3628)

CONTRE FLANCS.

Gâteau ananas (3252)   Nougatine (3251)

ENTREMETS.

Petits pois à la Ménagère (2744)	Artichauts à la Rachel (2690)
Gelée à la rose (3181)	Charlotte à la Metternich (3144)
Pain de fraises à la crème (3197)	Tarte à la Rhubarbe (3204)
Fruits (3699)	Petits fours (3364)
Fromage (3697)	Café (3701)

DÎNER DE 12 COUVERTS—SERVICE À LA FRANCAISE.

MENU.

POTAGES.

Consommé Comus (226)

Benoîton (288)

HORS-D'ŒUVRE.

Bouchées à la Reine (938)

RELEVÉS.

Saumon de Kennebec à la d'Artois (1238)

Filet de bœuf au Chasseur (1462)

ENTRÉES.

Caneton aux cèpes (1922)

Pâté chaud de foies gras à l'Alsacienne (2316)

Chaudfroid de poulet à la Clara Morris (2451)

Aspic de homard (2414)

Sorbet Trémière (3520)

RÔTS.

Bécassines (2159)

Selle d'agneau de lait (1743)

ENTREMETS.

Asperges sauce crème (2692)

Petits pois à la Française (2743)

Croûtes de bananes à la Panama (3023)

Blanc manger à la Smolenska (3138)

DESSERT.

Pièces montées (3628)

Glaces, Cartes surprise (3549)

Fruits frais (3699)

Petits fours biscuits aux noisettes (3368)

Fromages variés (3697)

Café (3701)

329   JUNE.

DINNER, 8 TO 10 PERSONS.
MENU.

Soup

Purée of carrots à la Crécy (268)

Remove

Trout à la Beaufort (1290)
Potato fritters (2788)

Entrées

Calves' tongues, Périgueux (1584)
Stuffed artichoke bottoms (2684)

Timbales of fillets of soles à la Gauloise (2384)

Roast

Chicken (1881)
Lettuce salad (2672)

Hot Entremets

Portuguese apples (2998)

Cold Entremets

Spanish custard cream (3152)
Dessert

330   JUNE.

DINNER, 8 TO 10 PERSONS.
MENU.

Soup

Bisque of lobster à la Cambridge (207)

Remove

Fresh mackerel fillets, Bonnefoy (1191)
Broiled potatoes (2776)

Entrées

Beef tongue, macédoine (1470)
Rice, Manhattan style (2977)

Squab cutlets à la Périgueux (2267)
Tomatoes Trévise (2836)

Roast

Pheasants adorned with their own plumage (2107)
Cabbage salad (2659)

Hot Entremets

Apples with burnt almonds (3000)

Mossaganem (3192)
Dessert

331   JUNE.

DINNER, 16 TO 20 PERSONS.
MENU.

Soup
Consommé à la Plumerey (238)

Side Dish
Célestines with foies-gras (862)

Fish
Striped bass à la Conti (1102)
Potato cakes (2778)

Remove
Pullet, Egyptian style, broiled (1986)
Turnips, Spanish sauce (2848)

Entrées
Lamb cutlets à la Signora (1686)
String beans with butter (2829)

Larks with rice (2084)
Asparagus, Hollandaise sauce (2692)

Bouquetière punch (3503)

Roast
Squabs (2018)
Salad

Hot Entremets
Meringued pancakes, Rossini (3073)

Plombière à la Richmond (3481)
Dessert

332   JUNE.

DINNER, 16 TO 20 PERSONS.
MENU.

Soup
Bisque of lobsters (205)

Side Dish
Timbales with red beef tongue (990)

Fish
Salmon à la Béarnaise (1244)
Viennese potatoes (2812)

Remove
Tenderloin of beef braised with roots (1461)

Entrées
Breasts of chicken à la Patti (1850)
Sweet peppers sautéd (2769)

Mutton cutlets à la Savary (1597)
Beet fritters à la Dickens (2702)

Californian sherbet (3523)

Roast
Ducklings à l'Andalouse (1930)
Water cress and apple salad (2676)

Hot Entremets
Tyrolian pudding (3111)
Strawberry ice cream (3438)
Dessert

333   JUNE.

DINNER, 8 TO 10 PERSONS.

MENU.

Soup

Tagliarelli (339)

Remove

Pompano à la Anthelme (1220)
Mellow potatoes (2799)

Entrées

Chicken sautéd, Portuguese style (1898)
Fried eggplants (2739)

Artichoke bottoms and cauliflower baked
(2685)

Roast

Turkey (2028)
Salad

Hot Entremets

Rice croquettes with oranges, raspberry sauce
(3018)

Surprise bananas (3541)
Dessert

---

334   JUNE.

DINNER, 8 TO 10 PERSONS.

MENU.

Soup

Mullagatawny, Indian style (327)

Remove

Kingfish à la Princelay (1184)
Persillade potatoes (2774)

Entrées

Shoulder of lamb with cucumbers (1751)
Green peas, English style (2742)

Border of risot, Valenciennes (2212)

Roast

Duckling (1938)
Salad

Hot Entremets

Alliance fritters (3036)

Ice cream, Malakoff (3150)
Dessert

---

335   JUNE.

DINNER, 16 TO 20 PERSONS.

MENU.

Soup
Consommé à la Sévigné (242)

Side Dish
Croustades Perretti (900)

Fish
Trout cooked in court bouillon (1298)
Boiled potatoes (2774)

Remove
Tenderloin of beef à la Montebello (1454)
Mushrooms à la Rivera (2758)

Entrées
Sweetbreads, Piedmontese style (1563)

Potato and truffle salad in border (2655)

Kirsch punch (3510)

Roast
Squabs (2018)
Salad

Hot Entremets
Crescents of noodles with cherries (3015)

(Ices) Caramel bouchées (3543)
Dessert

---

336   JUNE.

DINNER, 8 TO 10 PERSONS.

MENU.

Soup
Bisque of crawfish à la batelière (202)

Side Dish
Timbales, Mentana (974)

Fish
Bluefish, Havanese style (1118)
Marchioness potatoes (2797)

Remove
Lamb minion fillets, cream sauce (1724)
Eggplant in cases à la Morton (2736)

Entrées
Tournedos of tenderloin of beef à la Marietta
(1435)
Carrots glazed with fine herbs (2712)

Vol-au-vent à la Nesle (2397)

Maraschino punch (3510)

Roast
Chicken (1881)
Salad

Hot Entremets
Fried cream Pamela (3013)

(Ices) Tortoni cups (3584)
Dessert

337   JUNE.
DINNER, 8 TO 10 PERSONS.
MENU.

Soup

Manioca (316)

Remove

Brook trout à la Cambacérès (1291)
Baked potatoes (2798)

Entrées

Loin of veal à la Saintonge (1536)
Okra with barley croustades (2763)

Chicken sautéd à la Marengo (1893)
Rice croquettes with salpicon (2952)

Roast

Squabs (2018)
Salad

Hot Entremets

Apple fritters, Montagnard (3037)

Ice cream à la Cialdini (3445)
Dessert

338   JUNE
DINNER, 8 TO 10 PERSONS.
MENU.

Soup.

Chartreuse (297)

Remove

Kingfish à la Bordelaise (1181)
Cucumbers (2661)

Entrées

Shoulder of mutton with potatoes (1652)
Macaroni à la Cavalotti (2964)

Squabs à la Vestal (2022)
Braised onions (2765)

Roast

Chicken (1881)
Salad

Hot Entremets

Frangipane pie with marrow (3088)

(Iced) Fiori di latte almond milk (3469)
Dessert

339   JUNE.
DINNER, 16 TO 20 PERSONS.
MENU.

Soup.
Bisque of mussels à la Cutting (209)

Side Dish
Rissolettes à la Renan (957)

Fish
Flounders, Genlis style (1154)
Cucumbers, English style (2661)

Remove
Rump of beef, Greek style (1342)
Potatoes with artichokes and truffles (2805)

Entrées
Breasts of chicken à la Chevreuse (1827)
Boquillon tomatoes (2833)

Sweetbreads à la Princess (1565)
Asparagus tips à la Maintenon (2695)

Siberian punch (3516)

Roast
Duckling (1938)
Salad

Hot Entremets
Savarin with apricots (3117)

Rice ice cream, paradise (3456)
Dessert

340   JUNE
DINNER, 16 TO 20 PERSONS.
MENU.

Soup
Benoîton (288)

Side Dish
Canelons of palate of beef (858)

Fish
Sheepshead béchamel (1257)
Dauphine potatoes (2783)

Remove
Loin of veal with gravy (1537)
Eggplant in cases à la Morton (2736)

Entrées
Grenades of chicken à la Ritti (1871)
Fried cucumbers (2732)

Lobster à la Paul Bert (1038)

Californian sherbet (3523)

Roast
Pheasant (2107)
Salad

Hot Entremets
Crust with cherries (3024)

Ceylon with coffee ice cream (3545)
Dessert

341   JUNE.

DINNER, 8 TO 10 PERSONS.

MENU.

Soup

Purée of potatoes à la Benton (278)

Remove

Sea bass à la Villeroi (1099)

Entrées

Grenadins of beef with round potatoes, Valois
sauce (1393)
Artichoke bottoms à la Jussienne (2678)

Vol-au-vent of salmon trout à la Régence
(2408)

Roast

Duckling (1938)
Macédoine salad (2650)

Hot Entremets

Rice border with bananas (3005)

Cream with cherries (3154)
Dessert

342   JUNE

DINNER, 8 TO 10 PERSONS.

MENU.

Soup

Bennett (287)

Remove

Spanish mackerel à la Viennet (1197)
Duchess potatoes (2785)

Entrées

Leg of lamb, onion purée (1716)
Tomatoes à la Gibbons (2841)

Breasts of squab à la Duxelle, stuffed (2019)
Spinach à la Noailles (2821)

Roast

Turkey (2028)
Tomato salad (2666)

Hot Entremets

Strawberry fritters (3049)

Rhubarb pie (3204)
Dessert

343   JUNE.

DINNER, 16 TO 20 PERSONS.

MENU.

Soup
Consommé à la Laguipierre (236)

Side Dish
Timbales à la Beaumarchais (960)

Fish
Brook trout, Montagnarde (1296)

Remove
Chateaubriand, Colbert sauce (1381)
Mellow potatoes (2799)

Entrées
Sweetbreads à la Montebello (1560)
Smothered string beans (2828)

Chicken sautéd à la Sandford (1899)
Fried asparagus à la Miranda (2696)

Elizabeth punch (3507)

Roast
Pheasant (2107)
Italian salad (2635)

Hot Entremets
Strawberry soufflé (3122)

(Ice) Lemons in surprise (3557)
Dessert

344   JUNE

DINNER, 16 TO 20 PERSONS.

MENU.

Soup
Cream of artichokes, Morlaisienne (246)

Side Dish
Capon croquettes à la Royale (876)

Fish
Bass à la Conti (1102)
Hollandaise potatoes (2790)

Remove
Tenderloin of beef, Indian style (1463)
Beets with cream (2702)

Entrées
Pigeons, monarch style (1964)
Asparagus tips with cheese (2697)

Small croustades of sweetbreads (2251)
Cauliflower à la Villeroi (2716)

Mephisto sherbet (3524)

Roast
Chicken (1881)
Salad

Hot Entremets
Munich with peaches (3055)

(Ice) Italian mousse (3475)
Dessert

JUILLET.

DÎNER DE 24 COUVERTS—SERVICE À L'ANGLAISE.   345

MENU.

POTAGES.

Consommé Britannia (221)

Bisque de crevettes à la Veragua (211)

POISSON.

Saumon sauce marinade (1245)

GROSSES PIÈCES.

Selle d'agneau rôtie au jus (1746)

Jambon rôti à la broche sauce madère (1789)

ENTRÉES.

Côtelettes de poulet à la Clarence (2258)

Noisettes de filet de bœuf à la Rossini (1417)

Ris de veau à la Princesse (1565)

Caisses de pigeonneaux Umberto (2234)

RÔTS.

Canetons au cresson (1938)

Perdreaux anglais grillés (2085)

RELEVÉS.

Compiegne au sabayon (3009)

Crème frite Paméla (3013)

ENTREMETS.

Maïs bouilli en tiges (2730)

Fonds d'artichauts béchamel à la crème gratinés (2686)

Moscovite aux fraises (3191)

Pouding glacé à la Fleury (3493)

Punch à la Sibérienne (3516)

BUFFET.

Consommé semoule (316)   Longe de veau au jus (1537)

Noix de bœuf salée Écarlate à l'Anglaise (1316)

Chouxfleurs au fromage gratinés (2717)   Haricots verts étuvés (2828)

Cantaloup (799)

DÎNER DE 16 COUVERTS—SERVICE À L'AMÉRICAINE.

MENU.

POTAGES.

Consommé Andalouse (216)

Crème de maïs Mendocino (256)

HORS-D'ŒUVRE.

Timbales à la Ristori (982)

POISSON.

Kingfish à la Bella (1180)

Pommes de terre fondantes (2799)

Salade de concombres (2661)

RELEVÉ.

Double d'agneau garni de croquettes de pommes (1736)

Tomates à la Boquillon (2833)

ENTRÉES.

Ailes de poulet à la Valerri (1856)

Petits pois à la Française (2743)

Ris de veau à la St. Cloud (1566)

Haricots verts à la Pettit (2827)

Punch à la Béatrice (3502)

RÔT.

Pigeonneaux (2018)

Salade de romaine (2675)

ENTREMETS DE DOUCEUR.

Gelée macédoine au champagne (3179)

Bavarois aux framboises (3134)

Gaufres brisselets à la crème framboisée (3223)

Glaces Manchons Déjazet (3567)

Fruits (3699)   Bonbons (3640)   Petits fours (3364)   Devises (3653)

Café (3701)

347   JULY.
DINNER, 8 TO 10 PERSONS.
MENU.

Soup

Macaroni (339).

Remove

Pompano à la Potentini (1225)
Hollandaise potatoes (2790)

Entrées

Roast duck with cherries (1923)
Tomatoes, Queen style (2840)

Sweetbreads à la Columbus (1553)
Glazed turnips (2847)

Roast

Leg of lamb with gravy (1715)
Lettuce salad (2672)

Hot Entremets

Savarin with apricots (3117)

Renaissance pudding (3210)
Dessert

---

348   JULY.
DINNER, 8 TO 10 PERSONS.
MENU.

Soup

Mussels à la Vigo (328)

Remove

Baked kingfish (1186)
Viennese potatoes (2812)

Entrées

Calf ears, tomato sauce (1505)
Stuffed green peppers (2768)

Stewed pigeons (1967)
Sautéd mushrooms à la Dumas (2757)

Roast

Ptarmigan (2072)
Salad

Hot Entremets

Pancakes with orange-flower water (3078)

White coffee ice cream (3460)
Dessert

---

349   JULY.
DINNER, 16 TO 20 PERSONS.
MENU.

Soup
Consommé printanier with quenelles (239)

Side Dish
Mousseline à la Waleski (916)

Fish
Pike perch, Continental style (1218)
Persillade potatoes (2790)

Remove
Beef tongue à la Soligny (1468)
Stuffed onions (2766)

Entrées
Duckling à la Bordelaise (1931)
Cauliflower with fine herbs (2716)

Mayonnaise of chicken (2625)

Champagne punch (3504)

Roast
Squabs (2018)
Salad

Hot Entremets
Soufflés with raspberries (3122)

(Iced) Romanoff pudding (3497)
Dessert

---

350   JULY.
DINNER 16 TO 20 PERSONS.
MENU.

Soup
Cream of peas, St. Germain (260)

Side Dish
Cromesquis of bass 870)

Fish
Small lobster, Bordelaise (1026)

Remove
Glazed pullet à la printanière (1980)
Marchioness potatoes (2797)

Entrées
Sweetbreads, English style (1571)
Sautéd sweet peppers (2769)

Beef palate tourte, Parisian style (2390)

Parfait amour sherbet (3526)

Roast
Ducklings (1938)
Water-cress salad (2676)

Hot Entremets
Cream with apples (3014)

(Iced) Plombière, Havanese style (3484)
Dessert

351   JULY.

DINNER, 8 TO 10 PERSONS.

MENU.

Soup

Clear mock turtle (354)

Remove

Spanish mackerel with crawfish (1198)
Dauphine potatoes (2783)

Entrées

Loin of lamb with sautéd tomatoes (1718)
Artichoke bottoms à la Mornay (2680)

Timbale of sweetbreads, modern (2388)

Roast

Tame ducks à la Siebrecht (1919)
Cos-lettuce salad (2675)

Hot Entremets

Brioche fritters with sabayon (3040)

(Iced) Bomb, Fifth avenue (3440)
Small fancy cakes (3364)
Dessert

352   JULY.

DINNER, 8 TO 10 PERSONS.

MENU.

Soup

Cold, Russian style (302)

Remove

Bluefish in papers (1120)

Entrées

Leg of lamb, green sauce (1706)
Breaded fried cucumbers (2732)

Chickens sautéd à la Madeleine (1891)
Beet fritters à la Dickens (2702)
Italian salad (2635)

Roast

Stuffed squabs, American style (2012)
Salad

Hot Entremets

Déjazet pancakes (3172)

Melon water-ice (3603)
Dessert

353   JULY.

DINNER, 12 TO 16 PERSONS

MENU.

Soup
Lamb sweetbreads, German style (320)

Side Dish
Mousselines Isabella (912)

Fish
Codfish, Norwegian style (1137)
Mellow potatoes (2799)

Remove
Sirloin of beef à la de Lesseps (1352)
Eggplant à la Robertson (2737)

Entrées
Squabs with Colbert sauce (2013)
Sautéd string beans (2829)

Timbale of Gnocquis à la Choiseul (2987)

Paradise sherbet (3525)

Roast
Pheasant (2107)
Tomato salad (2666)

Hot Entremets
Crusts with bananas à la Panama (3023)

Rice with apricots (3214)
Dessert

354   JULY.

DINNER, 12 TO 16 PERSONS.

MENU.

Soup
Purée of peas with croûtons (282)

Side Dish
Timbales, Périgordine (979)

Fish
Porgies à la Manhattan (1229)
Duchess potatoes (2785)

Remove
Sirloin of beef à la Dégrange (1351)
Cauliflower with fried bread crumbs (2718)

Entrées
Duck with cèpes (1922)
Succotash (2731)

Lamb cutlets à la Périgueux (1683)
Glazed cucumbers (2733)

Imperial punch (3509)

Roast
Chicken (1881)
White cabbage salad (2659)

Hot Entremets
Croustade of Venice meringued (3020)

(Ice) Cherry Plombière (3485)
Dessert

DÎNER DE 30 COUVERTS—SERVICE À L'AMÉRICAINE.

MENU.

Lucines orangées (803)

POTAGE.

Consommé Antonelli (217)

HORS-D'ŒUVRE.

Palmettes Primatice (923)

POISSON.

Bass rayé à la Long Branch (1104)

Pommes de terre duchesse (2785)

RELEVÉ.

Filet de bœuf à la Godard (1451)

Concombres à la Villeroi (2732)

ENTRÉES.

Poulet sauté à la Finnoise (1889)

Petits pois Fleurette (2741)

Ris de veau Zurich (1579)

Haricots de Lima maître-d'hôtel (2699)

Punch à la Romaine (3515)

RÔT.

Selle de Chevreuil (2194)

Salade de céleri mayonnaise (2660)

ENTREMETS DE DOUCEUR.

Pouding soufflé aux amandes pralinées (3113)

Gâteau Chamounix (3235)

Gelée aux fruits (3187)

Glaces Variées

Dessert

DÎNER DE 10 COUVERTS—SERVICE A LA RUSSE.

MENU.

Lucines (803)

POTAGE.

Consommé Bariatenski (219)

HORS-D'ŒUVRE.

Coulibiac à la Russe (908)

POISSON.

Grouper à la Franklyn (1162)

RELEVÉ.

Selle d'agneau à la Chancelière (1739)

ENTRÉES.

Ailes de poulet à la Béranger (1834)

Ris de veau à la La Vallière (1557)

Punch à la Romaine (3515)

RÔT.

Pigeonneaux (2018)

ENTREMETS.

Petits pois à la Francaise (2743)

Beignets de Cerises (3042)

Cornets à la crème à l'orange (3148)

DESSERT.

Pièces montées ou corbeilles de fleurs (3628)

Compotes (3686)   Fruits frais (3699)   Petits fours (3364)

PETIT BUFFET.

Xérès, Absinthe, Vermuth, Kümmel

Caviar (778)   Olives farcies (801)

Tartelettes nonpareil (825)

Canapés de homard (777)   Crevettes en raviers ou en bateaux (819)

357 AUGUST
DINNER, 8 TO 10 PERSONS.
MENU.

Soup

Chamberlain (295)

Remove

Pike perch à la Financière **(1214)**
Boiled potatoes (2774)

Entrées

Lamb cutlets à la Catalane (1671)
Green peas, French style (2743)

Chicken sautéd with fine herbs **(1907)**
Lima beans maître-d'hôtel (2699)

Roast

Woodcock (2206)
Salad

Hot Entremets

Semolina croquettes, pistachio sauce (3019)
(Iced) Semiramis mousse (3471)

358 AUGUST
DINNER, 8 TO 10 PERSONS.
MENU.

Soup

Sorrel, Flemish style (347)

Remove

Black bass with sweet peppers (1097)
Potato croquettes (2782)

Entrées

Stuffed shoulder of lamb with glazed **vegeta-**
bles (1752)

Squab fritters, Oporto sauce **(2020)**
Trévise tomatoes (2836)

Roast

Pheasant (2107)
Salad

Hot Entremets

Venetian meringued croustade (3020)

Cialdini ice cream (3445)

359 AUGUST.
DINNER, 16 TO 20 PERSONS.
MENU.

Soup
Purée of Guinea fowl à la Washburn (279)

Side Dish
Attéreaux of chicken à la d'Antin (837)

Fish
Pompano Mazarin (1224)
Potato croquettes (2782)

Remove
Pullet minion fillets à la Montpensier **(1999)**
Stuffed tomatoes, Trévise (2836)

Entrées
Lamb cutlets, Giralda (1676)
Artichoke bottoms, soubise (2681)

Woodcock hash in a croustade with soft **eggs**
(2302)

Rebecca sherbet (3528)

Roast
Saddle of venison (2194)
Salad

Hot Entremets
Spanish pudding (3110)

Mushrooms, ice cream (3568)
Dessert

360 AUGUST.
DINNER, 16 TO 20 PERSONS.
MENU.

Soup
Bragance (290)

Side Dish
Bondons of pickerel, Walton (844)

Fish
Striped bass à la Rouennaise (1108)
Broiled potatoes with fried bread **raspings**
(2776)

Remove
Sirloin of beef with calf's brain patties (1355)
Stuffed green peppers (2768)

Entrées
Fillet of Guinea fowl à la Gaillardet (1957)
Carrots with cream (2714)

Frog legs à la Royer (1023)

Nenuphar punch (3513)

Roast
Squabs (2018)
Salad

Hot Entremets
Pudding, Scotch style (3108)

(Iced) Parfait with nougat (3478)
Dessert

361　　AUGUST.

DINNER, 8 TO 10 PERSONS.

MENU.

Soup

Cabbage (292)

Remove

Salmon, Daumont (1239)
Gastronome potatoes (2789)

Entrées

Noisettes of mutton à la Provençal (1611)
Carrots, Colbert (2711)

Chicken vol-au-vent with mushrooms (2399)

Roast

Partridges (2102)
Salad

Hot Entremets

Golden crusts (3021)

Cherries with cream (3154)
Dessert

362　　AUGUST.

DINNER, 8 TO 10 PERSONS.

MENU.

Soup

Spaghetti (339)

Remove

Pike perch à la Royale (1216)
Potato cakes with ham (2779)

Entrées

Grenadins of beef, Marc Aurele (1389)
Green peas, housekeeper's style (2744)

Broiled pullet, tartar sauce (1991)
Breaded and fried cucumbers (2732)

Russian salad (2645)

Roast

Reedbirds (2152)

Hot Entremets

Mirlitons of pears à la Bienvenue (3054)

Ice cream with black coffee (3463)
Dessert

363　　AUGUST.

DINNER, 16 TO 20 PERSONS.

MENU.

Soup
Bisque of crawfish à la Humboldt (203)

Side Dish
Scotch Timbales (985)

Fish
Sheepshead, Buena Vista, (1259)
Potato fritters (2788)

Remove
Tenderloin of beef with truffles (1429)
Eggplant, Duperret (2735)

Entrées
Duckling, peasant style (1939)

Glazed and larded sweetbreads with cèpes,
Bordelaise (1574)
Green peas, English style (2742)

Stanley punch (3518)

Roast
Squabs (2018)
Salad

Hot Entremets
Crusts with pineapple and apricot sauce (3022)

Sicilian ice cream (3579)
Dessert

364　　AUGUST.

DINNER, 16 TO 20 PERSONS.

MENU.

Soup
Consommé à la Florentine (232)

Side Dish
Patties, Queen style (938)

Fish
Salmon à la Victoria (1243)
Viennese potatoes (2812)

Remove
Young turkey with turnips (2043)
Baked artichoke bottoms béchamel (2686)

Entrées
Sweetbreads studded, Spanish style (1577)
Stuffed peppers (2768)

Fillet of sole tourte à la Financière (2392)

Pâquerette sherbet (3527)

Roast
Woodcock (2206)
Salad

Hot Entremets
Fried cream, Maintenon (3010)

(Iced) Soufflé Alcazar (3533)
Dessert

DÎNER DE 18 COUVERTS—SERVICE À L'AMÉRICAINF.

MENU.

Lucines orangées (803)

POTAGES.

Consommé à la crème de faisan (227)

Tortue verte liée (853)

HORS-D'ŒUVRE.

Bressoles de foies gras (848)

RELEVÉS.

Bass rayé gratiné au vin blanc (1113)

Pommes marquise (2797)

Cuissot de chevreuil à la Francatelli (2183)

Laitues braisées au jus (2754)

ENTRÉES.

Ailes de poulet au suprême (1858)

Petits pois à la Parisienne (2745)

Timbale de homard à la d'Aumale (2385)

Haricots verts Bourguignonne (2826)

Punch à la Favorite (3508)

RÔT.

Perdreaux sauce au pain (2102)

FROID.

Aspics de foies gras (2411)

Salade de laitues (2672)

ENTREMETS SUCRÉS.

Pommes à la Nelson (2991)

Gaufres brisselets à la crème framboisée (3223)

Gelée aux fruits et au kirsch (3187)   Pièces montées (3628)

Glace Bacchus (3590)   Le puits (3591)

Dessert (3701)

DÎNER DE 200 COUVERTS—À LA RUSSE.

MENU.

HORS-D'ŒUVRE FROIDS.

Estomacs d'oie fumés (822)   Hareng diablé (777)   **Jambon de Westphalie (786)**

Melon cantaloup (799)

Huîtres (803)

POTAGES.

Consommé Franklyn (233)   Bisque d'écrevisses Persigny (204)

HORS-D'ŒUVRE CHAUDS.

Timbales à la Benton (961)   Croquettes de brochet à la Romaine (890)

POISSONS.

Halibut à l'Amiral (1167)   Éperlans Gondolière (1266)

RELEVÉS.

Baron d'agneau tardif à la de Rivas (1661)   Dinde à la Française (2029)

ENTRÉES.

Quenelles de tétras à la Londonderry (2332)

Casseroles de ris d'agneau à la de Luynes (2238)

Chaudfroid de bécassines en buisson (2461)

Salade de homard à l'Américaine (2638)

RÔTS.

Pintades piquées garnies de leur plumages (1956)   Selle de Chevreuil (2194)

LÉGUMES.

Chicorée à la crème (2729)   Choux de Bruxelles sautés (2704)

ENTREMETS SUCRÉS.

Ananas Caroline (3090)

Gelée d'oranges en tasses (3180)

Bavarois en surprise (3132)

FLANCS.

Gâteau Chamounix (3235)   Baba au Marsala 3002)

DESSERT.

Pièces montées (3628)   Compotes (3686)

Petits fours (3364)   Fromages (3697)

Devises (3653)   Glaces variées (3538)

Fruits frais (3699)   Bonbons (3642)

Amandes salées (3696)

Café et liqueurs (3701)

DÎNER DE 20 COUVERTS—SERVICE À L'ANGLAISE.

MENU.

2 POTAGES.

Consommé Britannia (221)

Bisque de homard (205)

2 POISSONS.

Maquereau Espagnol à la Périgord (1196)

Sheepshead au court bouillon (1262)

2 RELEVÉS.

Filet de bœuf Rothschild (1457)

Selle de mouton à l'Allemande (1645)

4 ENTRÉES.

Ailes de poulet à la Génin (1843)

Cèpes farcis (2726)

Palais de veau à la Sévigné (1539)

Haricots verts sautés (2829)

Noisettes de chevreuil à la Thierry (2196)

Croûtes aux champignons (2759)

Soufflés de homard (2363)

2 RÔTS.

Oie à la Royer (1946)

Vanneaux à la Dumanoir (2122)

2 RELEVÉS.

Omelette fourrée aux fraises (3068)

St. Honoré Sultane (3261)

4 ENTREMETS.

Petits pois à la Française (2743)

Croûtes dorées (3021)

Timbale Nantaise (2381)

Rhubarbe à la crème (3204)

BUFFET.

Paillettes au fromage (823)

Marcassin sauce marinade garni de côtelettes et poitrine (2049)

Jambon rôti sauce Madère (1789)

Langues de bœuf à la Romaine (1467)

Épinards bouillis (2823)

SEPTEMBRE.

DÎNER DE 18 COUVERTS—SERVICE À LA FRANCAISE.

MENU.

Huîtres (803)

HORS-D'ŒUVRE FROIDS.

Artichauts poivrade (773)   Olives farcies aux anchois (801)   Bœuf fumé (822)
Canapés d'écrevisses (777)   Cornichons (785)   Thon mariné (831)

POTAGES.

Consommé Colbert aux œufs pochés (225)   Crème de riz Crémieux (249)

HORS-D'ŒUVRE CHAUD.

Timbales Lagardère (970)

RELEVÉS.

Bass rayée Maintenon (1105)   Filet de bœuf à la Richelieu Moderne (1456)

ENTRÉES.

Ailes de poulet à la Lorenzo (1845)

Côtelettes d'agneau à la Talma (1687)

Ris de veau à la Marsilly (1559)

Filet de tétras à la Tzarıne (2073)

ENTRÉES FROIDES SUR SOCLES.

Aspic de poularde à la Cussy (2418)

Pâté de foies gras de Strasbourg (2564)

INTERMÈDE.

Sorbet Californienne (3523)

RÔTS.

Dinde truffée garnie d'olives noires (2031)

Bécassines anglaises au cresson (2159)

ENTREMETS.

Petits pois Parisienne (2745)   Choux de Bruxelles sautes (2704)
Gelée à la rose (3181)   Charlotte de pommes à la Destrey

GROS GATEAUX.

Vacherin (3264)   Nougatine (3251)

DESSERT.

Fruits (3699)   Compotes (3686)   Petits fours (3364)
Café (3701)

369 SEPTEMBER.

DINNER, 8 TO 10 PERSONS.

MENU.

Soup

Monteille (325)

Remove

Blackfish à la Orly (1114)
Boiled potatoes (2774)

Entrées

Squabs, English style (2014)
Tomatoes, Provençal (2835)

Veal tongue, Flemish style (1583)
Fried oyster plant (2817)

Roast

Snipe (2159)
Water-cress and apple salad (2676)

Hot Entremets

Golden Lion flawn (3035)
Iced biscuit, Diplomate (3435)

Stewed fruits (3686)
Coffee (3701)

---

370 SEPTEMBER.

DINNER, 8 TO 10 PERSONS.

MENU.

Soup

Cream of chicory, Evers (258)

Remove

Kingfish, Batelière (1179)
Mashed potatoes (2798)

Entrées

Pullet à la Arco Valley (1971)
Red cabbage, Montargis (2707)

Paupiettes of beef with fine herbs (1421)
Lima beans, maître-d'hôtel (2699)

Roast

Larded partridges with gravy and water-cress
(2102)

Hot Entremets

Light pancakes with jams (3079)

(Iced) Bomb Fifth avenue (3440)
Bonbons (3642)
Mottoes (3653)
Dessert

---

371 SEPTEMBER.

DINNER, 16 TO 20 PERSONS.

MENU.

Soup
Cream of squash (263)

Side Dish
Small patties, Victoria (942)

Fish
Halibut à la Coligny (1168)
Mellow potatoes (2799)

Remove
Beef tenderloin à la printanière (1464)
Tomatoes, Queen style (2840)

Entrées
Partridge fillets à la Véron (2089)
Artichoke bottoms with cauliflower (2685)

Reedbird patty (2312)

Elizabeth punch (3507)

Roast
Saddle of venison (2194)
Salad

Hot Entremets
Apricots with rice à la Jefferson (3001)

Pineapple water ice (3606)
Dessert

---

372 SEPTEMBER

DINNER, 16 TO 20 PERSONS.

MENU.

Soup
Paterson (340)

Side Dish
Rissoles of crawfish, Béatrice (949)

Fish
Striped bass, Bercy (1101)
Persillade potatoes (2774)

Remove
Haunch of roebuck à la Bouchard (2178)
Fried artichokes (2683)

Entrées
Guinea fowl with sauerkraut (1958)
Broiled potatoes (2776)

Braised and stuffed woodcock (2209)
Green peas, Parisian style (2745)

Paradise sherbet (3525)

Roast
Blackhead ducks (2052)
Salad

Hot Entremets
Apples à la Nelson (2991)

Bavarian cream with chocolate (3131)
(Iced) Cavour pudding (3489)
Dessert

373　　SEPTEMBER.

DINNER, 8 TO 10 PERSONS.
MENU.

Soup

Croûte au pot (305)

Remove

Fresh mackerel maître-d'hôtel (1193)
Tomato salad (2666)

Entrées

Grenadins of beef with potatoes, Valois sauce
(1393)
Sautéd string beans (2829)

Timbale of noodles, Milanese (2988)

Roast

Teal ducks (2068)
Macédoine (2650)

Hot Entremets

Soufflé fritters, Médicis (3047)

Biscuit glacé, Diplomate (3435)
Dessert

374　　SEPTEMBER.

DINNER, 8 TO 10 PERSONS.
MENU.

Soup

Purée of wild duck, Van Buren (283)

Remove

Fresh codfish, egg sauce (1139)
Boiled potatoes (2774)

Entrées

Leg of lamb with carrots (1714)
Stuffed artichoke bottoms (2684)

Woodcock stewed à la Dumas (2199)
Beets sautéd in butter (2702)

Roast

Chicken in the pan (1881)
Tomato salad (2666)

Hot Entremets

Custard cream with apples (3014)

Caramel ice cream (3447)
Dessert

375　　SEPTEMBER.

DINNER, 10 TO 14 PERSONS.
MENU.

Soup
Macaronicelli (339)

Side Dish
Kulibiac Smolenska (909)

Fish
Flounders, Dieppoise (1153)
Cucumber salad (2661)

Remove
Sirloin of beef à la Thieblin (1354)
Straw potatoes (2792)

Entrées
Fillets of partridges à la Véron (2089)
Marrow squash with parmesan (2824)

Breasts of woodcock à la Houston (2201)
Smothered string beans (2828)

Golgorouski punch (3506)

Roast
Canvasback ducks (2055)
Salad

Hot Entremets
Peach fritters, Maraschino (3039)

(Iced) Timbales, Algerian style (3580)
Dessert

376　　SEPTEMBER.

DINNER, 10 TO 14 PERSONS.
MENU.

Soup
Bisque of lobster à la Benoist (206)

Side Dish
Andalusian patties (934)

Fish
Salmon trout, Antoinette (1302,
Potato croquettes (2782)

Remove
Hind saddle of lamb, Chancelière (1739)
Lima bean succotash (2731)

Entrées
Fillets of canvasback with orange juice (2058)
Green peas with braised lettuce (2746)

Breasts of chicken, Princière (1852)
Sautéd sweet peppers (2769)

American sherbet (3521)

Roast
Woodcock (2206)
Salad

Hot Entremets
Peaches à la Condé (3081)

(Iced) Plombière Rochambeau (3482)
Dessert

377   SEPTEMBER.

DINNER, 8 TO 10 PERSONS.

MENU.

Soup

Purée of plovers à la Théo (271)

Remove

Blackfish à la Villaret (1116)
Mellow potatoes (2799)

Entrées

Gosling stewed with turnips (1954)
String beans Bourguignonne (2826)

Beef palates à la Béchamel (1326)
Fried eggplants (2739)

Roast

Reedbirds (2152)
Water-cress and apple salad (2676)

Hot Entremets

Chestnut croquettes (3017)

Cold Entremets

Waffle buckets with cream (3128)
Fresh fruits (3699)

378   SEPTEMBER.

DINNER, 8 TO 10 PERSONS.

MENU.

Soup

Mock turtle (355)

Remove

Pike perch, Russian style (1217)
Persillade potatoes (2774)

Entrées

Quarter of lamb with stuffed tomatoes (1731)
Carrots, cream sauce (2714)

Venison grenadins à la royale (2195)
Spinach, Rougemont (2822)

Roast

Young pigeons stuffed (2018)
Lettuce salad (2672)

Hot Entremets

Madeira crusts (3026)

Peach ice cream à la Herbster (3453)
Dessert

379   SEPTEMBER.

DINNER, 16 TO 20 PERSONS.

MENU.

Soup
Florence snow (339)

Side Dish
Richmond mousseline (914)

Fish
Aiguillettes of bass with oyster crabs (1096)
Viennese potatoes (2812)

Remove
Haunch of venison à la Lytton (2179)
Stuffed tomatoes, Trévise (2836)

Entrées
Lamb cutlets, Giralda (1676)
Lima beans, maître-d'hôtel (2699)

Baked snipe (2156)

Rebecca sherbet (3528)

Roast
Grouse, bread sauce (2072)
Chicory salad (2668)

Hot Entremets
Rice with apples (3115)

(Iced) Serano pudding (3498)
Dessert

380   SEPTEMBER.

DINNER, 16 to 20 PERSONS.

MENU.

Soup.
Purée of chicken à la Reine (270)

Side Dish
Bateaux of fat liver, Russian style (843)

Fish
Salmon, Genevoise (1246)
Hollandaise potatoes (2790)

Remove
Ribs of beef, Hindostan (1330)
Cabbage, peasant style (2706)

Entrées
Chicken sautéd, Maryland (1894)
Peas with minced lettuce (2747)

Border of risot, Valenciennes (2212)

Champagne punch (3504)

Roast
Woodcock (2206)
Romaine salad (2675)

Hot Entremets
Mazarine with pineapples (3053)

Plombière d'Alençon (3483)
Dessert

381 SEPTEMBER.

DINNER, 8 TO 10 PERSONS.

MENU.

Soup

Partridge à la Royale (338)

Muskmelon (799)

Remove

Sea bass à la Villeroi (1099)
Cucumber salad (2662)

Entrées

Veal cutlets à la Zingara (1498)
Celeriac knobs, Mirabeau (2722)

Lobster à la Gambetta (1033)

Roast

Chicken in the saucepan (1881)
Escarole salad (2671)

Hot Entremets

Benvenuto pudding (3092)

Brazil nuts ice cream (3464)
Dessert

---

382 SEPTEMBER.

DINNER, 8 TO 10 PERSONS.

MENU.

Soup

Oysters with powdered okra **(336)**

Remove

Salmon à l'Argentine (1237)
Marchioness potatoes (2797)

Entrées

Chicken sautéd, Parisian style **(1904)**
Carrots with cream (2714)

Mushrooms mousserons à la Reynal **(2756)**

Roast

Mallard ducks (2059)
Dandelion salad (2670)

Hot Entremets

Mellow pudding, apricot sauce **(3094)**

St. Jacques cups (3560)

---

383 SEPTEMBER.

DINNER, 16 TO 20 PERSONS.

MENU.

Soup
Purée of grouse à la Manhattan (272)

Side Dish
Cocks' kidneys, Villeroi (864)

Fish
Kingfish fillets, Valençay (2528)
Viennese potatoes (2812)

Remove
Beef tenderloin, Solohub (1459)
Eggplant, Duperret (2735)

Entrées
Pullet with oysters (1994)
Cauliflower, white sauce (2719)

Vol-au-vent Financière (2396)

Pargny punch (3514)

Roast
Redhead ducks (2063)
Celery salad (2660)

Hot Entremets
Peaches à la Colbert (3080)

Bomb with printanier fruits (3441)
Dessert

---

384 SEPTEMBER.

DINNER, 16 TO 20 PERSONS.

MENU.

Soup
Cream of cauliflower à la Brisson (251)

Side Dish
Small patties with shrimps (935)

Fish
Turbot rémoulade sauce (2613)
Potato cakes (2778)

Remove
Braised breast of veal à la Bourdaloue (1487)
Glazed turnips (2847)

Entrées
Venison cutlets, Parisian tomato sauce (2174)
Stuffed cucumbers (2734)

Fillets of partridge à la Véron (2089)
Artichoke bottoms, fried (2683)

Venetian sherbet (3529)

Roast
English snipe (2159)
Salad

Hot Entremets
Cream of rice fritters (3043)

(Iced) Italian mousse (3475)
Dessert

DÎNER DE 24 COUVERTS—SERVICE À L'ANGLAISE.

MENU.

POTAGES.

Consommé Franklyn (233)

Tortue verte (353)

POISSONS.

Carpe à la Chambord (1129)

Filets de soles à la Marguery (1273)

RELEVÉS.

Selle de venaison panée aux cerises noires (2192)

Dindonneau piqué rôti purée d'artichauts (2042)

ENTRÉES.

Boudins de volaille à la Soubise (2215)

Mauviettes à la maréchale (2081)

Attéreaux de palais de bœuf (836)

Petits vol-au-vent à la Lucini (2404)

FROID.

Mousselines de foies gras à la Dana (2535)

Chaudfroid de perdreaux à la Béatrice (2455)

RÔTS.

Canetons à la Rouennaise (1937)

Courlis (2051)

RELEVÉS.

Petites omelettes à la Célestine (3056)

Pommes en surprise (2995)

ENTREMETS.

Laitues farcies demi-glace (2753)	Haricots verts au beurre (2829)
Fonds d artichauts, Montglas (2679)	Salade Italienne (2635)
Gelée Tunisienne rubanée (3184)	Pouding Saxonne (3107)
Flan à la Manhattan (3034)	Gaufres Brisselets crème à la framboise (3223)

BUFFET.

Aloyau bœuf rôti (1346)	Quartier de mouton aux pommes Gastronome (1642)
Moelle sur croûtes grillées (1319)	Salade à la Parisienne (2644)
Compotes (3686)	Tarte à la crème (3201)

Consommé semoule (316)

DÎNER DE 26 COUVERTS—SERVICE À LA FRANCAISE.

MENU.

HORS-D'ŒUVRE.

Caviar (778)   Radis (808)   Anchois (772)   Olives (800)

Huîtres et citrons (803)

2 POTAGES.

Consommé à la Royale (241)   Purée de levraut St. James (274)

2 HORS-D'ŒUVRE CHAUDS.

Timbales à la Talleyrand (988)

Rissoles de palais de bœuf (952)

2 RELEVÉS.

Bass rayé aux fines herbes (1112)

Filet de bœuf à la Bayonnaise (1443)

4 ENTRÉES CHAUDES.

Ailes de poulet à l'Impératrice (1841)

Ris de veau à la parisienne (1576)

Pâté chaud de bécasses (2319)

Côtelettes de faisan Réginald (2262)

2 FLANCS.

Pâté de foies gras découpé (2563)   Ballotines de cailles à la Tivollier (2426)

Punch à la Montmorency (3512)

2 RÔTS.

Selle d'antilope sauce aigrelette (2190)

Poularde au cresson (1996)

2 PLATS VOLANTS.

Soufflé au parmesan (2983)   Tartelettes de crème au fromage (765)

4 ENTREMETS.

Petits pois à l'Anglaise (2742)   Tomates en caisses gratinées (2839)

Croûtes aux poires à la Douglas (3028)   Pouding Castellane (3206)

2 FLANCS.

Gâteau Breton (3232)   Maréchal Ney (3189)

Glace bombe aux fruits printanière (3441)   Ananas en surprise (3595)

Assiettes montées de bonbons (3642)   Compotes (3686)   Fruits (3699)

4 Tambours garnis de petits fours et macarons (3364).

Dessert.

DÎNER DE 20 COUVERTS—SERVICE À LA RUSSE

(*Service par* 10)

MENU.

20 Plats d'huîtres et citrons (803)

2 POTAGES.

1 Soupière de Brunoise aux quenelles (291)

1 Soupière de purée de canards sauvages, **Van Buren (283)**

2 HORS-D'ŒUVRE CHAUDS.

2 Timbales Montgomery (975)

2 POISSONS.

1 Pompano à la Mazarin (1224)

1 Cabillaud à la Duxelle au gratin (1136)

2 RELEVÉS.

2 Dindes cloutées à la Sartiges (2027)

4 ENTRÉES.

1 Epigrammes de chevreuil sauce marinade aux truffes (2176)

1 Ris de veau à la Maltaise (1558)

1 Aspic de foies gras (2411)

1 Côtelettes de homard Lowery (2476)

Punch Trémière (3520)

2 RÔTS.

1 Bécasses sur canapés à la Périgord (2205)

1 Cochon de lait farci et rôti à la broche (1810)

2 LÉGUMES.

1 Céleri sauce Mirabeau (2722)

1 Petits pois aux laitues braisées (2746)

4 ENTREMETS.

1 Pommes à la Portugaise (2998)

1 Munich aux pêches (3055)

1 Buisson de meringues (3212)

1 Gelée aux violettes (3185)

2 FLANCS.

1 Gâteau Mille feuilles Pompadour (3247)

1 Gâteau Napolitain (3250)

Dessert.

DÎNER DE 50 COUVERTS—SERVICE À L'AMÉRICAINE.

MENU.

Huîtres (803)

POTAGES.

Consommé Duchesse (230)

Bisque d'écrevisses (201)

HORS-D'ŒUVRE.

Timbales à la Rothschild (983)

POISSONS.

Sheepshead Bourguignonne (1258)

Plie à la Jules Janin (1156)

RELEVÉS.

Selle de chevreuil à la sauce au vin d'Oporto et gelée de groseille (2193)

Fonds d'artichauts à la Jussienne (2678)

ENTRÉES.

Tournedos de filet de bœuf aux haricots verts (1440)

Ailes de poulet à la Marceau (1847)

Petits pois Parisienne (2745)

Caisses de ris de veau à la Grammont (2235)

Tomates Trévise (2836)

Coquilles de truffes béchamel au gratin (2844)

Sorbet Californienne (3523)

RÔT.

Perdreaux (2102)

FROID.

Terrine de pluviers et mauviettes (2601)

Salade de laitues (2672)

ENTREMETS DE DOUCEUR.

Mazarine à l'ananas au kirsch (3053)

Gelée à l'orange en tasses (3180)

Nid garni d'œufs (3594)

Charlotte Russe (3145)

Pouding à la Waddington (3500)

Fruits (3699)   Petits fours (3364)

Café (3701)

389   OCTOBER.

DINNER, 8 TO 10 PERSONS.

MENU.

Pickled oysters (802)

Soup
Gumbo with hard crabs, creole style (313)

Remove
Sheepshead à la Bourguignonne (1258)
Potato cakes (2779)

Entrées
Beef tongue à la Romaine (1467)
Boiled onions, Hollandaise sauce (2764)

Paupiettes of hare with stuffed olives (2080)
Carrots, cream sauce (2714)

Roast
Reedbirds (2152)
Celery salad (2660)

Hot Entremets
Compiègne cake with sabayon (3009)

(Iced) Caramel bouchées (3543)
Dessert

---

390   OCTOBER.

DINNER, 8 TO 10 PERSONS.

MENU.

Soup
Calf's tail, Rundell (294)

Remove
Smelts à la Norfolk (1267)
Broiled potatoes (2776)

Entrées
Roebuck fillets à la Lorenzo (2177)
Noodles à la Lauer (2970)

Chicken sautéd à la d'Antin (1885)
String beans à l'Albani (2825)

Roast
Squabs (2018)
Lettuce salad (2672)

Hot Entremets
Custard cream of chestnut caramel (3012)

Peach ice cream à la Herbster (3453)

---

391   OCTOBER.

DINNER, 16 TO 20 PERSONS.

MENU.

Soup
Barley with celery (285)

Side Dish
Fat liver croquettes, Dauphine (885)

Fish
Sole à la Normande (1274)
Persillade potatoes (2774)

Remove
Turkey à la Chipolata, stuffed (2024)
Sautéd Brussels sprouts (2704)

Entrées
Palate of beef in tortue (1328)
Fried eggplant (2739)

Plover à la Stoughton (2115)
Oriental rice (2978)

Andalusian sherbet (3522)

Roast
Saddle of venison (2194)
Escarole salad (2671)

Hot Entremets
Peaches à la Stevens (3084)

(Iced) Rabbit in surprise (3596)
Dessert

---

392   OCTOBER.

DINNER, 16 TO 20 PERSONS.

MENU.

Soup
Montorgueil (326)

Side Dish
Timbales à la Marly (973)

Fish
Redsnapper à la Demidoff (1234)
Mellow potatoes (2799)

Remove
Saddle of venison à la Morton (2188)
Baked tomatoes (2837)

Entrées
Pullet à la Mornay (1977)
Smothered string beans (2828)

Salmis of woodcock à la Sanford (2208)
Fried celery (2064)

Nenuphar punch (3513)

Roast
Redhead ducks (2063)
Cos lettuce salad (2675)

Hot Entremets
Peaches, Richelieu (3083)

(Iced) Sicilian pudding (3499)
Dessert

393　　OCTOBER.

DINNER, 8 TO 10 PERSONS.

MENU.

Soup

Oysters, French style (335)

Remove

Frostfish, Cherbourg style (1159)
Dauphine potatoes (2783)

Entrées

Rump of beef, modern style (1345)
Green peas, Parisian style (2745)

Chicken sauté à la Dumas (1888)
Baked stuffed tomatoes (2837)

Roast

Leg of mutton on the spit (1633)
Romaine salad (2675)

Hot Entremets

Baba Marsala (3002)

La Grandina ice cream (3556)
Dessert

394　　OCTOBER.

DINNER, 8 TO 10 PERSONS.

MENU.

Soup.

Purée of woodcock à la Théo (271)

Remove

Flounders à la Madeleine (1157)
Duchess potatoes (2785)

Entrées

Leg of mutton à la Chipolata (1625)
Parsnip cakes fried in butter (2767)

Pigeons garnished with Montglas cases (1962)
Green peas with shedded lettuce (2747)

Roast

Mallard ducks (2059)
Water-cress salad (2676)

Hot Entremets

Orange fritters à la Talleyrand (3045)

(Cold) Printanière crown (3158)
Dessert

395　　OCTOBER.

DINNER, 16 TO 20 PERSONS.

MENU.

Soup.
Cream of rice à la Crémieux (249)

Side Dish
Rissoles of partridge à la Waddington (955)

Fish
Striped bass, Rouen style (1108)
Potato tartlets (2810)

Remove
Saddle of venison larded aigrelette sauce
(2190)
Artichoke bottoms à la Florence (2677)

Entrées
Chicken sautéd, point du jour (1902)
Fedelini Cardinal (2953)

Vol-au-vent à la Nesle (2397)

Young America sherbet (3530)

Roast
Partridges (2102)
Chicory salad (2668)

Hot Entremets
Pudding à la de Freese (3099)

(Ices) Hen and chicks (3594)
Dessert

396　　OCTOBER.

DINNER, 16 TO 20 PERSONS.

MENU.

Soup
Purée of partridge à la d'Henin (276)

Side Dish
Imperial timbales (968)

Fish
Fresh codfish, Norwegian style (1137)
Snow potatoes (2798)

Remove
Sirloin of beef à la Perrin (1353)
Oyster plant with fine herbs (2817)

Entrées
Pullet à la Villars (1982)
Mushrooms with cream (2761)

Lamb cutlets, Giralda (1676)
Baked tomatoes (2837)

Tosca punch (3519)

Roast
English snipe (2159)
Cos lettuce salad (2675)

Hot Entremets
Apples à la Giudici (2990)

Charlotte Corday ice cream (3546)
Dessert

397

DINNER, 8 TO 10 PERSONS.

MENU.

Soup

Purée of wild squabs, Waleski (277)

Remove

Carp à la Chambord (1129)
Viennese potatoes (2812)

Entrées

Snipe à l'Africaine (2153)
Cauliflower with fine herbs (2716)

Chicken sautéd à la Bourguignonne (1884)
Green peas, English style (2742)

Roast

Teal ducks (2068)
Cos lettuce salad (2675)

Hot Entremets

Knob celeriac fritters (3041)

(Iced) Diplomate biscuits (3435)
Dessert

398

DINNER, 8 TO 10 PERSONS.

MENU.

Soup

Chicken and leeks (298)

Remove

Buffalo fish à la Bavaroise (1125)
Potato fritters (2788)

Entrées

Roast goose à la Thieblin (1947)
Macaroni with cream and truffles (2962)

Mutton cutlets with cucumbers (1603)
Fried eggplant (2739)

Roast

Plovers (2119)
Cucumber salad (2661)

Hot Entremets

Crusts of pears, Douglas (3028)

Mousse of fruits with pineapple (3474)
Dessert

399

DINNER, 16 TO 20 PERSONS.

MENU.

Soup
Purée of wild turkey, Sartiges (284)

Side Dish
Mousseline of woodcock (918)

Fish
Blackfish à la Sanford (1115)
Boiled potatoes (2774)

Remove
Suckling pig à la Piedmontese (1809)
Noodles à la Lauer (2970)

Entrées
Pullet à la Seymour (1981)
Glazed endives (2740)

English snipe in papers (2158)
Andalouse sherbet (3522)

Roast
Canvasback ducks (2055)
Lettuce salad (2672)

Hot Entremets
Apples with praslin (3000)

Leona ice cream (3558)
Dessert

400

DINNER, 16 TO 20 PERSONS.

MENU.

Soup
Green turtle (353)

Side Dish
Palmettes of pullet à la Clinton (930)

Fish
Spotted fish, green ravigote sauce (1286)
Potato croquettes (2782)

Remove
Roast goose, German style (1948)
Braised onions (2765)

Entrées
Grenadins of beef with celery béchamel (1392)
Smothered string beans (2828)

Cases of thrushes à la Diana (2237)
Tomatoes Trévise (2836)

Montmorency punch (3512)

Roast
Partridges (2102)
Water-cress and apple salad (2676)

Hot Entremets
Peach pudding, Cleveland (3102)

Burnt almond Angelica ice cream (3455)
Dessert

401   OCTOBER.

DINNER, 8 TO 10 PERSONS.

MENU.

Soup

Oxtail à la Soyer (332)

Remove

Baked finnan haddies (1166)
Viennese potatoes (2812)

Entrées

Turkey wings with celery and chestnuts (2039)
Fried oyster plant (2817)

Slices of kernel of venison in papers (2182)
Tomatoes, Queen style (2840)

Roast

Partridges with gravy (2102)
Lettuce salad (2672)

Hot Entremets

Pancakes à la Déjazet (3072)
(Ice) Fiori di latte with violettes (3470)
Dessert

---

402   OCTOBER.

DINNER 8 TO 10 PERSONS.

MENU.

Soup

Spanish Oilla (349)

Remove

Salmon à la moderne (1242)
Potato croquettes (2782)

Entrées

Boiled chicken, English style (1912)
Lima beans, maître-d'hôtel (2699)

Grenadins of mutton, poivrade sauce (1609)
Red cabbage, Montargis (2707)

Remove

English snipe (2159)
Romaine salad (2675)

Hot Entremets

Timbale Figaro (3123)

Andalusian ice cream (3446)
Dessert

---

403   OCTOBER.

DINNER, 16 TO 20 PERSONS.

MENU.

Soup
Cream of artichokes, Morlaisienne (246)

Side Dish
Rissoles of fat liver à la Ude (951)

Fish
Spanish mackerel à la Viennet (1197)
Hollandaise potatoes (2790)

Remove
Saddle of venison à la MacMahon (2187)
Macaroni, Parisian style (2961)

Entrées
Plovers à la Montauban (2114)
Tomatoes, Provençal style (2835)

Boudins of chicken au Cardinal (2216)
Mushrooms, under bells (2761)

Californian sherbet (3523)

Roast
Squabs (2018)
Celery salad (2660)

Hot Entremets
Tyrolian pudding (3111)

(Iced) Montesquieu plombière (3480)
Dessert

---

404   OCTOBER.

DINNER, 16 TO 20 PERSONS.

MENU.

Soup
Bisque of lobster à la Portland (208)

Side Dish
Timbales à la Marly (973)

Fish
Soles à la Lutèce (1272)
Potatoes with melted butter (2790)

Remove
Pullet à la Mornay (1977)
Fried artichoke bottoms (2683)

Entrées
Lamb cutlets à la Clémentine (1673)
String beans à la Bourguignonne (2826)

Breasts of woodcock à la Vatel (2203)
Green peas, Parisian style (2745)

Trémière punch (3520)

Roast
Blackhead ducks (2052)
Dandelion salad (2670)

Hot Entremets
Apples à la Nelson (2991)
Poupelins (3091)

(Iced) Romanoff pudding (3497)
Dessert

DÎNER DE 24 COUVERTS—SERVICE À LA FRANCAISE.

MENU.

2 POTAGES.

Consommé aux nids d'hirondelles (244)

Tortue verte liée (353)

2 RELEVÉS DE POISSON.

Bass rayé à la Rouennaise (1108)

Crabes d'huîtres frits (1005)

2 GROSSES PIÈCES.

Baron de mouton au four à la purée de pommes (1650)

Filet de bœuf à la Montebello (1454)

8 ENTRÉES.

Ailes de poulet à la Chiselhurst (1837)

Terrapène à la Baltimore (1083)

Ris de veau au chancelier (1569)

Pâté chaud de foies gras à l'Alsacienne (2316)

Poularde braisée Demidoff (1973)

Pain de lapereau à la Maintenon (2308)

Filets de bécasses à la Diane (2200)

Salade de homard à l'Américaine (2638)

2 PLATS DE RÔTS.

Canards ruddy (2066)

Chapon au cresson (1826)

8 ENTREMETS.

Petits pois Parisienne (2745)   Céleri à la moelle (2721)

Fonds d'artichauts Florence (2677)   Choux de Bruxelles Baronne (2703)

Pouding soufflé Saxonne (3107)   Glace asperges sauce au marasquin (3540)

Gelée au kirsch (3187)   Bavarois au chocolat (3131)

2 GROSSES PIÈCES D'ENTREMETS.

La hotte à la Denivelle (3636)

Le Char des Cygnes (3634)

Dessert.

DÎNER DE 25 COUVERTS—SERVICE À L'ANGLAISE.

MENU.

Premier Service.

2 POTAGES.

Consommé Charmel (224)   Crème d'orge Viennoise (249)

2 POISSONS.

Sheepshead sauce Cardinal (1261)   Sandre à la Durance (1213)

2 RELEVÉS.

Selle de mouton rôtie (1648)   Filet de bœuf à la Cauchoise (1446)

6 ENTRÉES.

Ailes de poulet à la Cussy (1838)   Filets de pluvier à la Victor Hugo (2117)

Ris de veau à la Maltaise (1558)   Timbales de levraut (2389)

Mignons de chevreuil à la Lorenzo (2177)   Côtelettes de tétras à la Ségard (2259)

2 FLANCS.

Brissotins de volaille au suprême (849)   Mousseline au Cardinal (910)

Deuxième Service.

2 RÔTS.

Canards à tête rouge (2063)   Poulet à la casserole (1881)

6 ENTREMETS.

Céleri à la moelle (2721)   Haricots verts à la Pettit (2827)

Beignets d'ananas Singapour (3046)   Crème de marrons au caramel (3012)

Bordure Caroline au champagne (3140)   Gelée aux fruits (3187)

2 RELEVÉS.

Glaces Cantaloup en surprise (3591)   Biscuit à l'Hernani (3228)

Dessert.

BUFFET.

Rosbif d'Aloyau à l'Anglaise (1346)   Pommes de terre grillées (2776)

Salade de laitues (2672)   Noix de bœuf salée à l'écarlate (1316)

Potage au riz à la Rudini (343)

NOVEMBRE. 407

DÎNER DE 40 COUVERTS—SERVICE À LA RUSSE.

MENU.

BUFFET SÉPARÉ.

Sherry, Bitters, Canapés d'anchois (777) Radis (808) Olives (800)
Kümmel, Vermouth,   Céleri en branches (779)
Absinthe Saumon fumé (822) Caviar (778) Concombres (2661)

Haut Sauterne   Huîtres (803)

POTAGES.

Xérès Consommé Britannia (221)
    Bisque de crabes (198)

HORS-D'ŒUVRE.

  Attéreaux à la Piémontaise (840)
    Timbale mosaïque (976)

Johannisberg   POISSONS.

  Flétan à la Richmond (1169)
    Redsnapper à la Créquy (1233)

Nuits   RELEVÉS.

  Chapon à la Financière (1823)
    Selle de mouton à la Duchesse (1644)

Léoville   ENTRÉES.

  Cailles farcies aux champignons (2134)
   Côtelettes de chevreuil à la Buridan (2170)
    Quenelles de volaille à la Drew (2326)
    Filets de tétras à la Tzarine (2073)

Champagne   RÔTS.
Ruinart

  Dinde truffée (2031)
   Bécasses sur canapés (2206)

LÉGUMES

  Fonds d'artichauts à la Montglas (2679)
    Choux de Bruxelles à la Baronne (2703)

Château Margaux   ENTREMETS.

  Beignets de brioche à la crème Sabayon (3040)
    Mirlitons de poires Bienvenue (3054)

Lunel Gelée à la Russe (3182)
Liqueurs   Bombe Romaine (3442)
    Dessert

DÎNER DE 16 COUVERTS—SERVICE À L'AMÉRICAINE.

MENU.

Sherry, Bitters,
Vermouth

Huîtres (803)

POTAGES.

Amontillado

Consommé à la Noailles (237)

Purée de chapon Jussienne (267)

HORS-D'ŒUVRE.

Timbales à la Irving (969)

POISSON.

Zeltinger

Soles à la Rochelaise (1276)

Pommes de terre, persillade (2774)

RELEVÉ.

Filet de bœuf à la Montebello (1454)

Quartiers d'artichauts à la Villeroi (2688)

ENTRÉES.

St. Julien

Côtelettes de mouton aux laitues braisées (1601)

Macaroni Brignoli (2958)

Bécassines à la Waleski (2155)

Petits pois à la Parisienne (2745)

Quenelles de foies gras fourrées à la financière (2331)

Punch à la Stanley (3518)

RÔTS.

Batailly

Sarcelles (2068)

Cailles (2131)

Salade d'escarole (2671)

ENTREMETS DE DOUCEUR.

Croûtes de poires à la Douglas (3028)

Pouding de riz à l'Impérial (3494)

Royal Charter   Petits fours (3364)   Fromages (3697)   Fruits (3699)
Liqueurs   Café (3701)

409 NOVEMBER.

DINNER, 8 TO 10 PERSONS.

MENU.

Soup

Oxtail à la Soyer (332)

Remove

Pompano à la Potentini (1225)
Cucumbers (2661)

Entrées

Round buttock top of beef, smothered (1334)
Potatoes à la Parmentier (2811)

Pullet à la Zingara (1983)
Brussels sprouts, baroness (2703)

Roast

Hare backs with cream (2076)
Salad

Hot Entremets

Celeriac fritters (3041)

Parfait with almonds (3478)
Dessert

---

410 NOVEMBER.

DINNER, 8 TO 10 PERSONS.

MENU.

Soup

Oysters, American style (333)

Remove

Striped bass with fine herbs (1112)
Potato fritters (2788)

Entrées

Rump of beef à la Jardinière (1343)
Noodles à la Lauer (2970)

Duck paupiettes with risot (1928)
Tomatoes à la Boquillon (2833)

Roast

Plovers (2119)
Salad

Hot Entremets

Rice croquettes with orange raspberry sauce
(3018)
(Ice) Mousse of fruits with pineapple (3474)
Dessert

---

411 NOVEMBER.

DINNER, 16 TO 20 PERSONS.

MENU.

Soup
Consommé with Lasagnettes (339)

Side Dish
Mousseline of woodcock (918)

Fish
Halibut à la Richmond (1169)
Potato tartlets (2810)

Remove
Saddle of venison à la gastronome (2191)
Cauliflower with fine herbs (2716)

Entrées
Duckling à la Bourguignonne, fried (1932)
Glazed endives (2740)

Sweetbreads à la Marsilly (1559)
String beans à la Pettit (2827)

Stanley punch (3518)

Roast
Plovers (2119)
Fondu with Piedmontese truffles (2954)

Hot Entremets
Apples with burnt almonds (3000)

(Ice) Mokabelle (3565)
Dessert

---

412 NOVEMBER.

DINNER, 16 TO 20 PERSONS.

MENU.

Soup
Cream of lettuce à la Evers (258)

Side Dish
Palmettes à la Périer (922)

Fish
Striped bass à la Whitney (1109)
Persillade potatoes (2774)

Remove
Kernel of veal with half glaze (1522)
Stuffed cucumbers (2734)

Entrées
Fillets of partridge à la Lucullus (2088)
Smothered string beans (2828)

Chicken sautéd à la Maryland (1894)
Eggplants in cases à la Morton (2736)

Venetian sherbet (3529)

Roast
Saddle of venison (2194)
Salad

Hot Entremets
Peach pudding à la Cleveland (3102)

(Ice) Montesquieu plombière (3480)
Dessert

413   NOVEMBER.

DINNER, 8 TO 10 PERSONS.

MENU.

Soup

Purée of young rabbit, St. James (274)

Remove

Baked sole, Italian style (1279)

Entrées

Chicken fricassee (1861)
Creamed macaroni with truffles (2962)

Rack of venison roasted, Colbert sauce (2169)
String beans à la Pettit (2827)

Roast

Teal ducks (2068)
Hot potato salad (2654)

Hot Entremets

Soufflé fritters, Médicis (3047)

(Iced) Biscuit Diplomate (3435)
Dessert

---

414   NOVEMBER.

DINNER, 8 TO 10 PERSONS.

MENU.

Soup

Giblets à la Réglain (311)

Remove

Flounders à la Genlis (1154)
Mashed potatoes (2798)

Entrées

Pullet à la Léondise (1974)
Pumpkin fried in small sticks (2814)

Noisettes of fillet of beef à la fleurette (1413)
Lima beans, maître-d'hôtel (2699)

Roast

Plovers (2119)
Salad

Hot Entremets

Cream with apples (3014)

Macaroon mousse (3477)
Dessert

---

415   NOVEMBER.

DINNER, 16 TO 20 PERSONS.

MENU.

Soup
Consommé, Plumerey (238)

Side Dish
Mousseline, Waleski (916)

Fish
Canadian turbot à la d'Orléans (1304)
Persillade potatoes (2774)

Remove
Loin of deer, cherry sauce (2168)
Brussels sprouts sautéd (2704)

Entrées
Pullet à la Mornay (1977)
Marrow squash with parmesan (2824)

Cases of English snipe à la Carême (2228)
Green peas with shredded lettuce (2747)

Pâquerette sherbet (3527)

Roast
Mallard ducks (2059)
Salad

Hot Entremets
Condé peaches (3081)

(Iced) Timbale, Algerian style (3580)
Dessert

---

416   NOVEMBER.

DINNER, 16 TO 20 PERSONS.

MENU.

Soup
Bisque of crawfish à la Humboldt (203)

Side Dish
Palmettes of quails, African style (931)

Fish
Soles à la Trouville (1277)
Viennese potatoes (2812)

Remove
Sirloin of beef à la Bradford (1349)
Eggplant, Duperret (2735)

Entrées
Paupiettes of young turkey, souvenir (2045)
Green peas with braised lettuce (2746)

Tournedos of venison, St. Hubert (2197)
Smothered string beans (2828)

Pargny punch (3514)

Roast
Woodcock (2206)
Salad

Hot Entremets
Timbale Figaro (3123)

(Iced) Plombière à la Rochambeau (3482)
Dessert

417

DINNER, 8 TO 10 PERSONS.

MENU.

Soup

Mock turtle thickened (355)

Remove

Haddock, Ancient style (1164)
Persillade potatoes (2774)

Entrées

Quarter of pork, Valenciennes (1797)
Chopped lettuce (2751)

Chicken fricassee à la Lucius (1865)
Macaroni spaghetti, Laurence (2966)

Roast

Plovers (2119)
Salad

Hot Entremets

Soufflé of chestnuts with vanilla (3118)

Caramel ice cream (3447)
Dessert

418

DINNER, 8 TO 10 PERSONS.

MENU.

Soup

Spaghetti with cream (348)

Remove

Striped bass, Hollandaise sauce (1110)
Boiled potatoes (2774)

Entrées

Braised chicken with noodles (1913)
Carrots, Viennese style (2713)

" Pains " of young rabbit (2549)
Chestnuts with gravy (2727)

Roast

Brant ducks (2053)
Salad

Hot Entremets

Light pudding with almonds (3112)

Plombière d'Alençon (3483)
Dessert

419

DINNER, 16 TO 20 PERSONS.

MENU.

Oysters (803)

Soup
Clear terrapin (350)

Side Dish
Timbales à la Marly (973)

Fish
Turban of smelts (2393)
Potato croquettes (2782)

Remove
Baron of yearling lamb à la de Rivas (1661)
Okra with barley croustades (2763)

Entrées
Slices of kernel of venison à la Hussarde (2181)
Green peas, Parisian style (2745)

Squab breasts à la Duxelle, stuffed (2019)
String beans à l'Albani (2825)

Montmorency punch (3512)

Roast
Partridge à la Soyer (2097)
Salad

Hot Entremets
Crust of pears, Douglas (3028)

Madrilian ice cream (3562)
Dessert

420

DINNER, 16 TO 20 PERSONS.

MENU.

Soup
Bisque of shrimps, Bretonne (213)

Side Dish
Brissotines of game, Lyonnese (850)

Fish
Sole fillets. Venetian style (1278)
Broiled potatoes (2776)

Remove
Turkey with cèpes (2030)
Tagliarelli in croustade (2986)

Entrées
Young rabbit à la Celtoise (2137)
Sautéd string beans (2829)

Sweetbreads, St. Cloud (1566)
Macédoine à la Montigny (2755)

Mephisto sherbet (3524)

Roast
Ptarmigan (2072)
Salad

Hot Entremets
Biscuits Frascati (3004)

(Ice) Pudding Fleury (3493)
Dessert

421   NOVEMBER.

DINNER, 8 TO 10 PERSONS.

MENU.

Soup

Purée of English snipes à la Théo **(271)**

Remove

Spotted fish, Queen sauce (1285)
Duchess potatoes (2785)

Entrées

Leg of lamb à la Guyane   (1708)
Green peas, housekeeper's style **(2744)**

Duck with sauerkraut (1925)
Beetroot fritters (2702)

Roast

Young rabbits larded and roasted **(2142)**
Salad

Hot Entremets

Noodle crescents with cherries (3015)

(Ices) Mushrooms (3568)
Dessert

---

422   NOVEMBER.

DINNER, 8 TO 10 PERSONS.

MENU.

Soup

Cream of peas with mint (261)

Remove

Stuffed fillets of sole (1281)
Marchioness potatoes (2797)

Entrées

Cutlets of lamb à la Clémence **(1673)**
Artichoke   bottoms, Soubise (2681)

Jugged hare (2075)
Macaroni purée of game (2963)

Roast

Mongrel ducks, stuffed (1929)
Salad

Hot Entremets

Rice pudding. fruit sauce (3106)

(Ices) Tortoni cups (3584)
Dessert

---

423   NOVEMBER.

DINNER, 12 TO 16 PERSONS

MENU.

Soup
Bisque of shrimps à la Veragua (211)

Side Dish
Cromesquis of beef palate (867)

Fish
Canadian turbot à la Houston (1305)
Broiled potatoes (2776)

Remove
Saddle of venison, Tyrolese style (2189)
Stuffed green peppers (2768)

Entrées
Duck with cèpes (1922)
Tomatoes Trévise (2836)

Sweetbreads au Chancelier (1569)
String beans sautéd (2829)
Soufflé of partridges à la Huggins (2364)

Roman punch (3515)

Roast
Capon (1826)
Salad

Hot Entremets
Chestnut croquettes (3017)

(Ices) The marvelous (3563)
Dessert

---

424   NOVEMBER.

DINNER, 16 TO 20 PERSONS.

MENU.

Soup
Cream of cardoons, Livingston (252)

Side Dish
Cassolettes à la Lusigny 360)

Fish
Redsnapper, Mobile (1235)
Viennese potatoes (2812)

Remove
Tenderloin of beef à la Chanzy **(1447)**
Squash with parmesan (2824)

Entrées
Fricasseed turkey (2038)
Sautéd Brussels sprouts (2704)

Quails à la Mirepoix (2125)
Celery béchamel with croûtons (2720)

Paradise sherbet (3525)

Roast
Canvasback ducks garnished with **hominy**
(2055)
Salad

Hot Entremets
Apples. Baron de Brisse (2993)

(Ices) Nest with eggs (3594)
Dessert

DÉCEMBRE. 425

DÎNER DE 16 COUVERTS—SERVICE À LA FRANCAISE.

MENU.

Premier Service.

POTAGES.

Consommé aux nids d'hirondelles (244)

Jarrets de veau à la Briand (319)

HORS-D'ŒUVRE.

Croquettes de crabes Parmentier (879)

Timbales Princesse (980)

RELEVÉS.

Flétan à la Reynal (1171)

Filet de bœuf à la Mélinet (1452)

ENTRÉES.

Épigrammes de levrauts à la Polignac (2078)

Ailes de poulet à la Béranger (1834)

Pâté chaud de ris de veau à la McAllister (2313)

Filets de pigeons aux olives (1970)

Quenelles de volaille à la Drew (2326)

Soufflé de gibier à la Lucie (2362)

Deuxième Service.

Punch Élisabeth (3507)

RÔTS.

Canvasback (Canards sauvages) (2055)   Perdreaux (2102)

ENTREMETS.

Fonds d'artichauts à la Villars (2682)

Pointes d'asperges Miranda (2696)

Pouding Tyrolienne (3111)

Gelée aux ananas Californienne (3178)

Brouette garnie de fleurs sur socles (3638)   Panier de cerises (3630)

Gâteau Reine (3256)   Baba siropé (3227)

Dessert

DÎNER DE 20 COUVERTS—SERVICE A LA RUSSE.

MENU.

Huîtres (803)

POTAGES.

Consommé Impératrice (231)

Bisque de lucines à la Hendrick (197)

HORS-D'ŒUVRE

Crêtes de coq farcies Duxelle (863)

Bouchées à la purée de gibier (936)

RELEVÉS.

Aiguillettes de bass noir aux crabes d'huîtres (1096)

Selle d'antilope à la chasseresse (2185)

ENTRÉES.

Bordure de poulet à la Toulouse (2210)

Vol-au-vent à l'Ancienne (2398)

Ris de veau au chancelier (1569)

Timbale de truffes à la Périgord (2846)

RÔTS.

Ruddy duck (2066)

Cailles au cresson (2131)

LÉGUMES.

Tomates farcies aux champignons frais (2842)

Petits pois Parisienne (2745)

ENTREMETS DE DOUCEUR.

Pêches Richelieu (3083)

Paniers d'oranges à la gelée (3130)

Flamri de semoule (3168)

Bavarois aux marrons (3136)

GLACES.

Poules avec Poussins (3594)

Compotes (3686)　　　　　Bonbons (3642)

Fruits frais (3699)　　　　　Devises (3653)

Petits fours (3364)　　　　　Amandes Salées (3696)

Dessert

DÎNER DE 24 COUVERTS—SERVICE À L'ANGLAISE.

MENU.

POTAGES.

Potage de bécasses (360)

Crème de légumes à la Banville (266)

POISSON.

Turbot Anglais sauce aux câpres (1307)

Pommes de terre Viennoise (2812)

GROSSE PIÈCE.

Filet de bœuf à la d'Orléans (1450)

Haricots verts étuvés (2828)

ENTRÉES.

Ailes de poulet à la Primatice (1851)

Ris de veau Maltaise (1558)

Quenelles de poulet à la Bretonne (2328)

Casserole de ris garnie de poulet Palestine (2239)

RÔT

Dindon farci aux marrons (2041)

FROID.

Terrine de foies de canards à l'Aquitaine (2596)

Salade d'escarole (2671)

RELEVÉS.

Beignets soufflés Médicis (3047)

Compiègne au Sabayon (3009)

ENTREMETS.

Petits pois à l'Anglaise (2742)

Asperges à la Hollandaise (2692)

Pain de bananes Havanaise (3195)

Couronne à la Camper (3156)

Gelée aux violettes (3185)   Éclairs au chocolat (3303)

BUFFET.

Aloyau à la Norwood (1348)   Selle de mouton rôtie à la broche (1648)

Pouding Yorkshire (770)   Pommes rôties (2771)

Tarte aux pommes (3199)   Consommé aux ravioles et aux perles (359)

DÎNER DE 18 COUVERTS—SERVICE À L'AMÉRICAINE.

MENU.

Huîtres (803)

POTAGES.

Consommé à la Berry (220)

Bisque d'écrevisses à la Batelière (202)

HORS-D'ŒUVRE.

Bouchées Andalouse (934)

POISSONS.

Bass rayé à la Whitney (1109)

Blanchaille à la Greenwich (1310)

RELEVÉ.

Filets de bœuf à la Condé (1448)

Céleri à l'Espagnole (2721)

ENTRÉES.

Filets de poulet à la Sadi-Carnot (1853)

Petits pois à l'Anglaise (2742)

Côtelettes de chevreuil Cauchoise (2171)

Épinards Béchamel (2820)

Soufflés de foies gras aux truffes (2361)

Punch Tournesol (3517)

RÔT.

Bécasses (2206)

Salade de laitues (2672)

ENTREMETS SUCRÉS

Baquet de gaufres à la crème (3128)

Gâteau moka (3249)　　　　　　　　　　　　Macaronade (3188)

Palais de dames à la Vanille (3353)

PIÈCES MONTÉES.

Fruits frais (3699)　　　　　　　　　　　　Compotes (3686)

Café (3701)

429 DECEMBER.

DINNER, 8 TO 10 PERSONS.

MENU.

Soup

Westmoreland (357)

Remove

Flounders, Joinville (1155)
Boiled potatoes (2774)

Entrées

Shoulder of lamb à la Garnier (1750)
Cucumbers breaded, English style (2732)

Fillets of Guinea fowl with sauerkraut (1958)

Roast

English snipe (2159)
Salad

Hot Entremets

Meringued pancakes, Rossini (3073)

(Ice) Montélimar with hazel-nut cream (3566)
Dessert

430 DECEMBER.

DINNER, 8 TO 10 PERSONS.

MENU.

Soup

Lentils, Chantilly (273)

Remove

Soles à la Colbert (1271)
Cucumbers (2661)

Entrées

Rack of pork on the spit (1799)
Stuffed turnip cabbage (2709)

Chicken fricassee à la Waleski (1866)
Tomatoes, Queen style (2840)

Roast

Woodcock (2206)
Salad

Hot Entremets

Fritters souffléd, Médicis (3047)

Caramel ice cream (3447)
Dessert

431 DECEMBER.

DINNER, 16 TO 20 PERSONS.

MENU.

Soup

Purée of young rabbit, St. James (274)

Side Dish

Rissoles of sweetbreads (954)

Fish

Spotted fish, Calcutta (1287)
Viennese potatoes (2812)

Remove

Rack of mutton with small roots (1643)
Fried stuffed lettuce (2752)

Entrées

Chicken with oyster sauce (1882)
Green peas, French style (2743)

Salmis of woodcock à la Beaumont (2207)
Minced cèpes in croustades (2725)

Venetian sherbet (3529)

Roast

Turkey stuffed, American style (2028)

Hot Entremets

Apples with burnt almonds (3000)

(Ices) Léona (3558)
Dessert.

432 DECEMBER.

DINNER, 16 TO 20 PERSONS.

MENU.

Soup

Chicken gumbo (299)

Side Dish

Attéreaux of oysters (839)

Fish

Streaked turban of flukes (2393)
Marchioness potatoes (2797)

Remove

Braised turkey à la financière (2026)
Stuffed tomatoes with fresh mushrooms (2842)

Entrées

Sweetbreads à la Marsilly (1559)
Celeriac, Mirabeau (2722)

Salmis of quails à la Morisini (2132)
Mushrooms stuffed in cases (2762)

Siberian punch (3516)

Roast

Canvasback ducks garnished with hominy (2055)

Hot Entremets

Peach pudding à la Cleveland (3102)

Burnt almond angelica ice cream (3455)

433 DECEMBER.
DINNER, 8 TO 10 PERSONS.

MENU.

Soup

Bouillabaisse (289)

Remove

Boudins of salmon with shrimps (2221)
Dauphine potatoes (2783)

Entrées

Stuffed hare à la châtelaine (2074)
Tomatoes, Frossart (2834)

Chicken sautéd à la Diva (1886)
Green peas, Parisian style (2745)

Roast

Squabs (2018)
Salad

Hot Entremets

Crusts with fruit, Mirabeau (3025)

(Ice) Pudding Constance (3490)
Dessert

434 DECEMBER.
DINNER, 8 TO 10 PERSONS.

MENU.

Soup

Gnocquis à la Pagioli (312)

Remove

Flounders à la Dieppoise (1153)
Duchess potatoes (2785)

Entrées

Stuffed chicken with tomato Condé sauce (1883)
Ravioles, Bellini (2976)

Mutton cutlets à la Maréchale (1595)
String beans sautéd with butter (2829)

Roast

Pheasants (2107)
Salad

Hot Entremets

Fritters, Montagnard (3037)

(Ice) Mousse à la Siraudin (3472)
Dessert

435 DECEMBER.
DINNER, 16 TO 20 PERSONS.

MENU.

Soup
Bisque of shrimps, Melville (212)

Side Dish
Croquettes of grouse, Soubise (886)

Fish
Weakfish à la Brighton (1308)
Hollandaise potatoes (2790)

Remove
Ribs of beef à la Bristed (1329)
Fried eggplant (2739)

Entrées
Chicken breasts à la Bodisco (1835)
Carrots, Viennese style (2713)

Young rabbit, hunter's style (2140)
Tomatoes, Trévise (2836)

Sunflower punch (3517)

Roast
Reedbirds (2152)
Salad

Hot Entremets
Meringued peaches (3082)

(Ice) Parfait with coffee (3479)
Dessert

436 DECEMBER.
DINNER, 16 TO 20 PERSONS.

MENU.

Soup
Consommé, Bariatenski (219)

Side Dish
Bondons of woodcock à la Diane (845)

Fish
Striped bass with white wine (1113)
Marchioness potatoes (2797)

Remove
Pullet with ravioles (1995)
String beans sautéd (2829)

Entrées
Noisettes of tenderloin of beef à la Maire (1415)
Glazed cucumbers (2733)

Vol-au-vent of frogs' legs, Soubise (2401)

Parfait amour sherbet (3526)

Roast
Ruddy ducks (2066)
Salad

Hot Entremets
Pudding à la Bradley (3093)
(Ice) Italian mousse (3475)
Dessert

437 DECEMBER.

DINNER, 8 TO 10 PERSONS.

MENU.

Soup

Oysters à la Cruyst (334)

Remove

Turbot à la Mercier (1306)
Boiled potatoes (2774)

Entrées

Pullet with croustades à la Financière (1993)
Artichoke bottoms with marrow (2687)

Noisettes of tenderloin of beef à la Fleurette
(1413)
Green peas, French style (2743)

Roast

Teal ducks (2068)
Salad

Hot Entremets

Rice border with bananas (3005)

(Ices) Fiori di latte à la Orlandini (3468)
Dessert

---

438 DECEMBER.

DINNER, 8 TO 10 PERSONS.

MENU.

Soup

Frogs, garnished with timbales (309)

Remove

Flounders, Madeleine (1157)
Viennese potatoes (2812)

Entrées

Leg of mutton à la Bourgeoise (1624)
Mushrooms à la Reynal (2756)

Chicken broiled à la Delisle (1828)
String beans à la Pettit (2827)

Roast

Woodcock (2206)
Salad

Hot Entremets

Brioche fritters with cream sabayon (3040)

(Ice) Serano pudding (3498)
Dessert

---

439 DECEMBER.

DINNER, 16 to 20 PERSONS.

MENU.

Soup.
Calf's tail à la Rundell (294)

Side Dish
Palmettes à la Périer (922)

Fish
Sole à la Lutèce (1272)
Duchess potatoes (2785)

Remove
Saddle of mutton with glazed roots (1649)
Macaroni Brignoli (2958)

Entrées
Breaded tenderloin of pork, celery purée (1818)
Green peas, English style (2742)

Quails stuffed with mushrooms (2134)
Parisian salad (2644)

Rebecca sherbet (3528)

Roast
Plovers (2119)
Salad

Hot Entremets
Humboldt pudding (3100)

(Ices) Potatoes (3575)
Dessert

---

440 DECEMBER.

DINNER, 16 TO 20 PERSONS.

MENU.

Soup
Hungarian consommé (235)

Side Dish
Ham mousselines, Robertson (915)

Fish
Striped bass, shrimp sauce (1111)
Marchioness potatoes (2797)

Remove
Saddle of venison, hunter's style (2185)
Jerusalem artichokes à la Salamander (2749)

Entrées
Stuffed tame duck à la Britannia (1917)
Trévise tomatoes (2836)

Noisettes of beef, mushroom purée (1420)
Russian salad (2645)

Champagne punch (3504)

Roast
Capon (1826)
Salad

Hot Entremets
Rice pudding, fruit sauce (3106)

(Ice) Cherry plombière (3485)
Dessert

441   DECEMBER.

DINNER, 8 TO 10 PERSONS.

MENU.

Soup

Ravioles with Nizam pearls (359)

Remove

Haddock, Holland style (1165)

Entrées

Loin of pork à la Réglain (1796)
Cucumbers breaded, English style (2732)

Fillets of young rabbit à la Bienvenue, garnished with croquettes (2143)
String beans à la Pettit (2827)

Roast

Squabs in earthenware saucepan (2018)
Salad

Hot Entremets

Peaches à la Condé (3081)

(Ice) Biscuit glacé, Diplomate (3435)
Dessert

---

442   DECEMBER.

DINNER, 8 TO 10 PERSONS.

MENU.

Soup

Crabs à la Loubat (303)

Remove

Black bass with sweet peppers (1097)
Viennese potatoes (2812)

Entrées

Mutton cutlets à la Macédoine (1594)
Baked eggplant (2738)

Mallard duck with celery, half-glaze (2060)

Braised pullet with jelly (2570)

Roast

Partridges with water-cresses (2102)
Salad

Hot Entremets

Custard cream with apples (3014)

(Ice) Plombière d'Alençon (3483)
Dessert

---

443   DECEMBER.

DINNER, 8 TO 10 PERSONS.

MENU.

Soup
Consommé à la Dubarry (229)

Side Dish
Attéreaux of turkey (842)

Fish
Canadian turbot à la d'Orléans (1304)
Potatoes persillade (2774)

Remove
Mutton with Gastronome potatoes (1642)
Asparagus, Countess (2693)

Entrées
Turkey with cèpes (2030)
Risot with Piedmontese truffles (2981)

Young hare, Castiglione (2077)
Teltow turnips with chestnuts (2849)

Champagne punch (3504)

Roast
Redhead ducks (2063)
Salad

Hot Entremets
Peaches à la Colbert (3080)

(Ice) Bomb with prunelle (3443)
Dessert

---

444   DECEMBER.

DINNER, 8 TO 10 PERSONS.

MENU.

Soup
Consommé, Andalouse (216)

Side Dish
Timbales, Soubise (986)

Fish
Striped bass with fine herbs (1112)
Potato tartlets (2810)

Remove
Redhead duck, Baréda (2062)
Artichoke bottoms, Mornay (2686)

Entrées
Veal cutlets, Pogarski (2273)
Green peas, housekeeper's style (2744)

Fillets of young rabbit à la Lavoisier (2144)
Brussels sprouts à la Baroness (2703)

Paradise sherbet (3525)

Roast
Pullets (1996)
Salad

Hot Entremets
Chestnut croquettes (3017)

(Ice) Fiori di latte, Orlandini (3468)

DANCING PARTY OF 100 PERSONS—SERVED FRENCH STYLE.

REFRESHMENTS AND SUPPER.

BILL OF FARE.

First Service, 11 o'clock.

Genoeses with cream meringued (3308)　　Condé cakes (3297)　　Varied fruit tartlets (3337)

Africans (3364)　　　　Macaroons (3379)

Refreshments

Lemonade, Orgeat and Grenadine syrup.

Second Service, 12 o'clock.

Assorted ice creams (3538)　　　　Rolled wafers with Curaçoa cream (3224)

Iced biscuits with vanilla (3438)　　　　Fancy cakes (3364)

Tutti frutti biscuit (3586)　　　　Small cream biscuits (3137)

Hot wine (3715)　　　　*Champagne punch* (3714)

Third Service, 1 o'clock.

SUPPER (HOT).

Consommé (189)　　　　Chicken croquettes exquisite (877)

Victoria patties (942)　　　　Coffee and milk (3701)

Venetian timbales (989)　　　　Escalops of fat livers à la Villeneuve (2279)

COLD.

Roast capon and water cress (1826)

Galantine of pigeons (2496)

Terrine of snipe (2603)

Tenderloin of beef with macédoine croustades (2440)

Small " pain " of capon with tarragon (2542)

Shrimp salad (2647)

Sandwiches of different meats (815)

Small rolls with lobster (809)

SWEET ENTREMETS AND DESSERT.

Thin chocolate wafers (3362)　　　　Fruit jellies (3187)

Fresh fruits (3699)　　　　Varied ice cream (3538)

Assorted fancy cakes (3364)

Champagne.

SOUPER DE 80 COUVERTS—SERVICE À L'AMÉRICAINE.

MENU.

Huîtres (803)

Consommé en tasses (189)

Radis (808)   Olives (800)   Céleri en branches (779)

Homard à la Hervey (1034)

Croquettes de chapon royale (876)

Filet de bœuf à la Milanaise (1453)

Petits pois à l'Anglaise (2742)

Ailes de poulet à la Lucullus (1846)

Fonds d'artichauts à la Soubise (2681)

Terrapène à la Crisfield (1084)

Mousseline de foies gras à la Dana (2535)

Célestine de poularde à la Talleyrand (2450)

Salade d'écrevisses à la Maintenon (2629)

Pigeonneaux rôtis à la casserole (2018)

Truffes en serviette (2843)

Flamri à la crème (3167)

Gelée Tunisienne rubanée (3184)

Gelée au marasquin (3186)

Pouding glacé à la Duchesse (3492)

Ceylan au café (3545)

Fruits (3699)   Petits fours (3364)   Bonbons (3642)   Devises (3653)

Café (3701)

MARS 447

SOUPER DE 80 COUVERTS—SERVICE À L'AMÉRICAINE.

MENU.

Graves Huîtres (803)

Lafaurie Canapés d'écrevisses (777)   Salade d'anchois (772)

Beurre (775)   Radis (808)   Olives (800)

Consommé en tasses (189)
Purée de volaille à la Reine (270)

Niersteiner Croquettes de poulet à la Hongroise (878)
Canapés à la Lorenzo (855)

Côtelettes d'agneau à la Maison d'Or (1679)
Pigeonneaux à la Flourens (2009)

Galantine de faisan découpée (2495)
Pâté de foies gras découpé (2563)

Chambertin Poularde rôtie truffée (1992)
Salade Impériale (2634)

Gelée au marasquin (3186)
Pommery Charlotte Bengalienne (3142)

Glace mousse aux marrons (3477)
Malaga Petites glaces moulées variées (3431)

Café glacé (3609)

Fruits (3699)   Petits fours (3364)
Bonbons (3642)   Devises (3653)

Violettes pralinées (3659)

Dessert

Champagne glacé (3710)

APRIL.

SIDEBOARD SUPPER FOR 300 PERSONS—RUSSIAN SERVICE.

BILL OF FARE.

Consommé (189)   Cream of rice Crémieux (249)

Truffled ham à la Florian (2523)   Chaudfroid of fillets of redhead duck (2460)

Decorated galantines of eels (2488)

Foies gras in border (2483)

Cold chicken fricassee (2467)

Shrimp salad (2647)

Caviare (778)   Lemons and oranges (793)   Small fancy rolls with lobster (809)

Assorted canapés (777)   Assorted sandwiches (811)

ENTREMETS AND DESSERT.

2 Vases of drawn sugar with flowers (3637)

Savoy biscuit (3231)   Baba syruped (3227)

Cream with cherries (3154)   Macédoine champagne jelly (3179)

Bavarois with meringues (3133)   High stands of assorted fancy cakes (3364)

Plates filled with bonbons (3642)   Basket of fresh fruits (3699)

Preserves (3684)

SUPPER, HOT AND COLD FOR 200 PERSONS.

On twenty tables, ten persons to each.

Consommé (189)   Purée of chicken Dufferin (269)

Darne of salmon à la Duperré (1240)   Crab salad (2628)

Chicken fillets au suprême (1858)   Squabs à la Flourens (2009)

Artichoke bottoms à la Villars (2682)   Green peas, French style (2743)

Roast pheasant (2107)

Roast turkey with water-cress (2028)

Fruit jelly with kirsch (3187)   Bengalian Charlotte (3142)

Peaches à la Louvoisienne (3198)

SIDEBOARD FOR TEA, REFRESHMENTS AND ICES.

Tea (3704)   Coffee (3701)   Punch (3501)   Chocolate (3700)

Strawberry mousse (3474)   Small ices (3431)

American sherbet (3521)   Lemonade (3713)   Tea cakes (3339)

MAL

SOUPER ASSIS DE 35 COUVERTS—SERVICE À L'AMÉRICAINE.

MENU.

Canapés de sardines (777)   Anchois (772)   Céleri en branches (779)   Radis (808)

Lucines orangées (803)

Consommé de volaille en tasses (190)

Homard à la Hervey (1034)

Croquettes de palais de bœuf (875)

Petits pois à l'Anglaise (2742)

Côtelettes d'agneau à la Talma (1687)

Haricots verts à la Pettit (2827)

Ailes de poulet à la Lorenzo (1845)

Tomates farcies Provençale (2835)

Chapon rôti (1826)

Salade de pommes de terre en bordure aux truffes (2655)

Gelée au marasquin (3186)

Charlotte Russe (3145)

Glace bombe à la Trobriand (3440)

Glaces moulées variées (3431)

Fruits (3699)   Petits fours (3364)

Café (3701)

JUIN.   450

SOUPER ASSIS 40 COUVERTS.

MENU.

Haut Sauterne   Lucines orangées (803)

Caviar (778)   Salade d'anchois (772)   Olives (800)   **Sardines (831)**

Consommé (189)

Truites de ruisseau à la Carême (2611)

Salade de concombres **(2661)**

Attéreaux de ris de veau à la moderne (841)

Champagne
Perrier-Jouët   Filets de volaille à la Cussy (1838)

Petits pois à l'Anglaise (2742)

Quenelles de volaille Richelieu (2327)

Petits pains de volaille à l'écarlate (2543)

Dôme de homard garni de petites caisses **(2481)**

Chambertin   Canetons rôtis (1921)

Salade de truffes à la Gambetta (2667)

Gelée macédoine au champagne (3179)

Gaufres brisselets à la crème framboisée (3223)

Glaces Délicieux aux noisettes (3592)

Le casque orné de sucre filé (3598)

Fruits cristallisés (3659)   Petits fours (3364)

Bonbons (3642)   Devises (3653)

Fruits frais (3699)

Café (3701)

AMBIGU PICNIC—60 PERSONS.

BILL OF FARE.

HORS-D'ŒUVRE.

Herring salad with potatoes (2633)

Beef sandwiches à la Barlow (812)

Chicken sandwiches (813)

Okra and sweet pepper salad (2651)

Small sturgeon Livonienne style (2594)

Tenderloin of beef with vegetables, mayonnaise (2441)

Smoked red beef tongue (2608)

Pigeon galantines (2496)

Veal and ham pie (2568)

Duckling with Spanish olives (2482)

Leg of mutton à la Garrison (2530)

Broiled chicken (1831)

Frog salad (2632)

Lobster salad, American style (2638)   Bagration salad (2622)

Apricot flawn (3170)

Punch cake with rum (3255)

Charlotte Russe (3145)

Bavarois with meringues (3133)

Raspberries and cream (3699)

Ice Cream.

Vanilla (3458)   Strawberry water ice (3607)   Chocolate (3449)

White coffee (3460)   Iced biscuit with vanilla (3438)

Fruits (3699)   Fancy cakes (3364)

Coffee (3701)

Dessert

AUGUST—GARDEN PARTY—100 PERSONS.

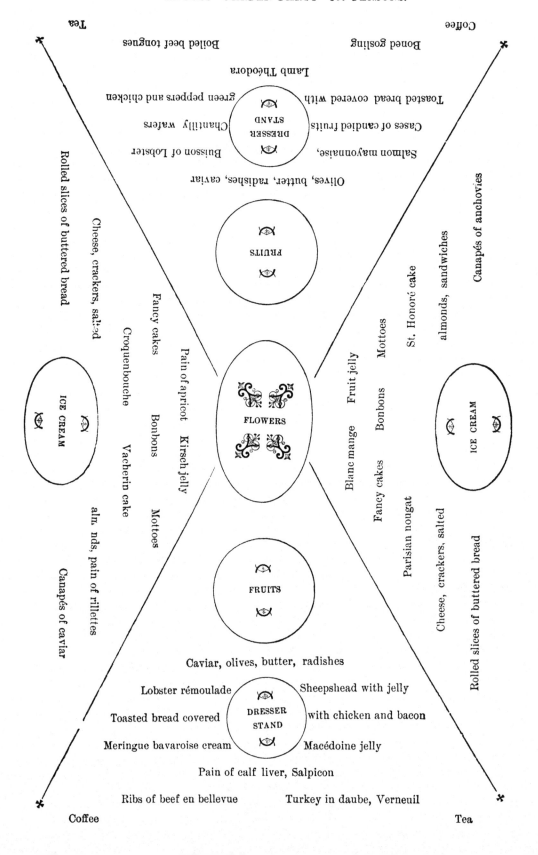

Tea   Coffee

Boiled beef tongues   Boned gosling

Lamb Théodora

green peppers and chicken   Toasted bread covered with

Chantilly wafers   Cases of candied fruits

DRESSER STAND

Buisson of Lobster   Salmon mayonnaise,

Olives, butter, radishes, caviar

FRUITS

Rolled slices of buttered bread

Cheese, crackers, salted

Fancy cakes

Croquenbouche

Pain of apricot   Kirsch jelly

Bonbons   Vacherin cake

FLOWERS

Fruit jelly   Mottoes

St. Honoré cake

almonds, sandwiches

Canapés of anchovies

Blanc mange   Bonbons

Fancy cakes

Parisian nougat

Cheese, crackers, salted

Rolled slices of buttered bread

ICE CREAM   **ICE CREAM**

Bonbons   Mottoes

alm. nds, pain of rillettes

Canapés of caviar

FRUITS

Caviar, olives, butter, radishes

Lobster rémoulade   Sheepshead with jelly

Toasted bread covered   with chicken and bacon

DRESSER STAND

Meringue bavaroise cream   Macédoine jelly

Pain of calf liver, Salpicon

Ribs of beef en bellevue   Turkey in daube, Verneuil

Coffee   Tea

SEPTEMBER. 452

AMBIGU—200 PERSONS.

Radishes (808) Celery (779)

Butter (775) Gherkins (785)

Olives (800) Red cabbage, marinated, English style (778)

Caviar (778) Chow-chow (791)

Salted almonds (3696) Hard-boiled eggs on canapés (777)

Marinated cauliflower (776) Anchovy salad (772)

Potato salad with herring (2653)

Slices of salmon with jelly (2578)

Roasted peacock adorned with its plumage (2552) Galantine of suckling pig (2498)

Kernel of veal with mayonnaise tomatoed sauce (2527) Beef à la mode (2433)

Capon legs with truffles (1826) Cold snipe pie (2567)

Lobster with mayonnaise (2534)

Small "pain" of chicken à la Freycinet (2544) Galantine of gosling, melon shaped (2489)

Pork liver terrine (2551) Japanese salad (2636)

Barlow sandwiches (812) Rillettes (809)

Slices of bread and butter (820) Sandwiches with anchovies (816)

French roll sandwiches, American style (816)

Assorted ice cream (3538)

Fancy cakes (3364) Fruits (3699)

Claret punch (3714) *Lemonade* (3713)

Iced coffee (3609) Iced chocolate (3608)

SUPPER FOR 300 PERSONS—ENGLISH SERVICE.

BILL OF FARE.

LARGE PIECES.

Chicken pie (2554)　　　　　　　　Ribs of beef à la bourgeoise (2431)

　　Ham glazed with sugar (2522)　　　　　　Turkey in daube (2616)

ENTRÉES.

Ballotines of quails à la Tivolier (2426)　　　Decorated darne of salmon (2576)

　Cutlets of pheasant in chaudfroid (2477)　　　Smoked red beef tongues (2608)

　　Lamb cutlets, Imperial (2471)　　　　　Galantine of pullet à la Mozart (2497)

　　　Lobster salad, American style (2638)　　　　Chicken mayonnaise (2625)

RESERVE.

Chickens (2469) and tongues (2608)

　　Terrine of pork liver (2602)

PASTRY PIECES.

　Fleury cake (3237)　　　　　　　Nougatine cake (3251)

　　Savoy biscuit (3231)　　　　　　　Iced baba (3227)

SWEET DISHES OF SMALL PASTRIES AND ICES.

Pear tartlets (3337)　　　　　　　Lozenges (3349)

　　Espagnolettes (3346)　　　　　　Apricot nougat (3319)

　　　Nantes cakes (3352)　　　　　　　Small fancy ices (3538)

　　　　Japanese cakes (3347)

Biscuits glacés (3438)　　　　　　　" Pain" of bananas, Havanese (3195)

　　Malakoff cream (3150)　　　　　　　Surprise Bavarois (3132)

　　　Jelly with fruit and kirsch (3187)

HOT SERVICE ON SIDEBOARD.

Bisque of clams à la Hendrick (197)　　Cream of barley, Vienna style (249)　　Nizam pearls (316)

　　　Roast pullets (1996)

NOVEMBRE. 454

SOUPER BUFFET ET ASSIS DE 400 PERSONNES.

MENU BUFFET.

CHAUD.

Consommé de gibier (192)

Mousseline Isabelle (912)

Huîtres à la Hollandaise (1066)

Huîtres frites à la Orly (1060)

Bouchées à la Victoria (942)

Quenelles de tétras à la Londonderry (2332)

Pétoncles à la Brestoise (1074)

Queues de homard à la Stanley (1042)

Terrapène à la Baltimore (1083)

Café (3701)   Thé (3704)

FROID.

Saumon de l'Orégon à la Vénitienne (2587)

Filet de bœuf aux croustades macédoine (2440)

Galantine de dinde à la Berger (2499)

Langue de bœuf écarlate en arcade (2607)

Bécasses à la Valère (2619)   Aspic de foies gras (2411)

Mousseline de kingfish à la Brière (2536)   Poulet rôti garni de gelée (2469)

Mayonnaise de poulet (2625)   Salade de homard à l'Américaine (2638)

Sandwichs de gibier (814)   Rillettes (809)   Canapés (777)

ENTREMETS SUCRÉS ET DESSERT.

Pouding Valois (3211)   Gelée aux framboises (3183)

Gâteau Vacherin à la crème (3264)   Savarin à la Valence (3259)

GLACES VARIÉES.

Fruits (3699)   Petits fours (3364)   Bonbons (3642)   Devises (3653)

Champagne glacé (3710)

Le souper est dressé en buffet, ensuite servi sur des petites tables de cinq à dix couverts, on découpe le froid que l'on dresse sur des petits plats que l'on place sur chacune des tables ainsi que le hors d'œuvre froid. Avant de servir l'entremet sucré et le dessert on remplace le froid et le hors d'œuvre par les gelées poudings, gâteaux, fruits, etc. Le chaud est au choix des convives.

SOUPER BUFFET ET ASSIS POUR 100 COUVERTS.

MENU BUFFET.

CHAUD.

Consommé de volaille (190)   Crème d'orge à la Viennoise (249)
Huîtres fricassées à la poulette (1067)   Timbales à la Soubise (986)
Coquilles de saumon (2346)   Bouchées Turbigo (941)
Terrapène à la Maryland (1085)   Canvasbacks (canards sauvages) (2055)

Café (3701)   Thé (3704)

FROID.

Chaudfroid de Courlis (2452)   Terrine de lièvre (2598)
Langue de bœuf écarlate à la gelée (2609)   Aspics de filets mignons de perdreaux (2416)
Côtelettes de noix d'agneau mayonnaise (2474)   Filets de poulet à la Gallier (2466)
Salade de céleri mayonnaise (2660)   Salade de homard à l'Américaine (2638)
Sandwichs variées (815)

ENTREMETS DE DOUCEUR FROIDS ET DESSERT.

Gelée au rhum (3186)   Gaufres brisselets à la crème framboisée (3223)
Gâteau noisettes (3241)   Charlotte Bengalienne (3142)
Bombe panachée au café blanc et noir (3444)   Soufflé glacé à la Favart (3534)
Tutti frutti (3586)   Biscuit glacé (3438)   Toronchino Procope (3583)
Fruits (3699)   Petits fours (3364)   Bonbons (3642)   Devises (3653)

———————————✶———————————

Le froid est découpé et servi sur table avant de servir le Souper.

Le Souper assis est servi sur des tables de 5 à 10 Couverts dans l'ordre suivant.

Consommé de volaille   Crème d'orge à la Viennoise
Timbales à la Soubise   Bouchées Turbigo
Huîtres fricassées à la poulette   Coquilles de saumon
Côtelettes de noix d'agneau mayonnaise   Filets de poulet à la Gallier
Terrapène à la Maryland
Chaudfroid de Courlis   Terrine de lièvre
Langue de bœuf écarlate à la gelée   Aspics de filets mignons de perdreaux

Salade de homard à l'Américaine   Sandwichs variées

Canvasbacks (canards sauvages)   Salade de céleri mayonnaise
Gelée au rhum   Gaufres brisselets à la crème framboisée
Gâteau noisettes   Charlotte Bengalienne
Bombe panachée au café blanc et noir   Soufflé glacé à la Favart
Tutti frutti   Biscuit glacé   Toronchino Procope
Fruits   Petits fours   Bonbons   Devises

SUPPER.

JANUARY. 456

Oysters on the half shell (803)
Crawfish marinière (1009)
Breasts of woodcock à la Houston (2201)
Deviled ribs of beef (1331)
Aspic of breast of quail (2419)
(Ice) Croquettes macédoine (3559)
Small fancy cakes (3364)
Dessert

JANUARY. 457

Oysters on the half shell (803)
Lobster on skewers, Colbert (2222)
Game croquettes à la Dauphine (885)
Green peas, English style (2742)
Roast redhead ducks (2063)
Celery mayonnaise salad (2660)
Ice cream (3458)
Dessert

JANUARY. 458

Oysters on the half shell (803)

Woodcock croquettes with truffles (892)

Mutton kidneys on skewers, deviled (1620)

Lobster tails in their shells (2533)

(Ice) Soufflés Palmyra (3535)

Dessert

JANUARY. 459

Oysters (803)
Crusts with Chester cheese (946)
Crawfish with butter (1011)
Lamb sweetbreads, Sévigné (1762)
Roast squabs (2018)
(Ice) Nesselrode pudding with candied chestnuts (3495)
Dessert

FEBRUARY. 460

Oysters (803)
Consommé (189)
Maréchale mousseline (913)
Escalops of fat livers à la Villeneuve (2279)
Green peas, English style (2742)
Doe birds (2051)
(Ice) Stuffed tomatoes (3582)
Dessert

FEBRUARY. 461

Oysters in cases à la Lorenzo (2232)
Fresh mushroom patties (937)
Striped bass à la Manhattan (2428)
Chicken soufflé à la Delsart (2360)
Roast plover (2119)
Salad
Charlotte Russe (3145)

FEBRUARY. 462

Oysters in their natural shells with fried bread (2353)
Lobster, American style (1024)
Chicken salad (2626)
Roasted English snipe (2159)
(Ice) Plombière à la Havanaise (3484)
Dessert

FEBRUARY. 463

Oysters on crusts (1062)
Turkey croquettes (894)
Noisettes of tenderloin of beef, plain (1410)
Sarah potatoes (2802)
Aspic of foies-gras (2411)
Asparagus salad (2621)
Montélimar with hazel-nut ice cream (3566)

SUPPER.

MARCH. 464

Cream of barley, Vienna style (249)

Fried stuffed oysters (1070)

Crépine of reedbirds (2247)

Lobster mayonnaise, Printanière (796)

Roast ptarmigan with gravy (2072)

(Ice) Bomb with kirsch (3443)

Dessert

MARCH. 465

Welsh rarebit (946)

Lamb kidneys on skewers (1703)

Dauphine potatoes (2783)

Roast squabs (2018)

Strawberry water ice (3607)

Sponge cake (3260)

Dessert

MARCH. 466

Clear bouillon (187)

Squab cutlets à la de Luynes (2266)

Green peas, English style (2742)

Broiled chicken (1831)

Norwegian salad (2641)

(Ice) Andalusian cream (3446)

Dessert

MARCH. 467

Consommé (189)

Chicken croquettes, Exquisite (877)

Small green peas, Parisian style (2745)

Lobster à la Newberg (1037)

Pheasant adorned with its own plumage (2107)

(Ice) Fiori di latte à la Bellini (3467)

Dessert

APRIL. 468

Oysters and lemons (803)

Trout marinated in wine (829)

Minions of tenderloin of beef à la Baillard (1400)

English partridges (2102)

Celery salad (2660)

(Ice) Diplomate biscuit (3435)

Dessert

APRIL. 469

Toast with oil and cheese (992)

Croquettes of frogs (884)

Pullet crepine (2243)

Oyster salad (2642)

Roast squabs (2018)

(Ice) Plombière à la Rochambeau (3482)

Dessert

APRIL. 470

Oysters (803)

Crawfish, Maison d'Or (1010)

Sweetbread in cases à la Grammont (2235)

Quartered artichokes (2688)

Roast chicken with jelly and beef tongue (2469)

Strawberry mousse ice cream (3474)

Dessert

APRIL. 471

Bouillon (187)

Toast à la Waddington (862)

Shells of oysters à la Villa (2340)

Breasts of chicken à la Béranger (1834)

Potato shavings (2807)

English snipe (2159)

Mignon salad (2620)

(Ice) Turban with strawberries (3100)

SUPPER.

MAY.   472

Clams (803)

Yorkshire rarebit (946)

Lobster à la Bonnefoy (1026)

Dauphine potatoes (2783)

Broiled chicken (1831)

(Ice) Romanoff pudding (3497)

Dessert

MAY.   473

Consommé (189)

Crusts of clams à la Schenk (903)

Ham mousseline à la Belmont (911)

Ptarmigans, currant jelly (2072)

Romaine salad (2675)

(Ice) Tutti frutti (3586)

Dessert

MAY.   474

Clams (803)

Toast with sardines (992)

Venetian timbales (989)

Lamb cutlets with mayonnaise (2474)

Broiled squabs, Colbert sauce (2013)

(Ice) Bomb with maraschino (3443)

Dessert

MAY.   475

Consommé (189)

Soft clams à la poulette (995)

Lamb cutlets, Signora (1686)

Chicken salad with vegetables (2627)

Broiled duckling (1938)

Salad

(Ice) Parfait with coffee (3479)

Dessert

JUNE.   476

Clams (803)

Brissotins of chicken supreme (849)

Lobsters à la Newberg (1037)

Border of forcemeat à la Duchess (2211)

Roast squabs (2018)

Ice cream parfait nougat (3478)

Salad

Dessert

JUNE.

Clams (803)

Rissoles of lamb (952)

Small green peas, Parisian style (2745)

Duckling à la Rouennaise (1937)

Broiled chicken (1831)

Lettuce salad (2672)

(Ice) Stuffed tomatoes (3582)

Dessert

JULY.   478

Clams (803)

Lobster mayonnaise Printanière (795)

Brissotins of chicken au suprême (849)

Green peas, French style (2743)

Roast squabs (2018)

Salad

(Ice) Bomb streaked with white and black coffee (3444)

Dessert

JULY.   479

Clams (803)

Timbales Calaisienne (962)

Sweetbread cutlets à la Talleyrand (2272)

Green peas, English style (2742)

Roast sand-snipe with water-cress (2161)

(Ice) Vanilla mousse (3458)

Dessert

SUPPER.

AUGUST. 480	AUGUST. 481

AUGUST. 480

Clams (803)

Croustades Parmentier (896)

Chicken quenelles with consommé (2329)

Sautéd mushrooms (2760)

Chaudfroid of lamb cutlets (2475)

Broiled reedbirds (2151)

Salad

Virgin ice cream with orange-flower water (3459)

Dessert

AUGUST. 481

Clams (803)

Quenelles of spring turkey (2336)

Green peas, English style (2742)

Cases of thrush with jelly (2449)

Broiled wild squabs (2112)

Tomato salad (2666)

(Ice) Roman bomb (3442)

Dessert

SEPTEMBER. 482

Oysters (803)

Fish quenelles, Montglas (2330)

Tenderloin of beef with olives (1428)

Artichoke bottoms à la Soubise (2681)

Roast woodcock (2206)

Celery salad (2660)

(Ice) Mousse with peaches (3474)

Dessert

SEPTEMBER. 483

Oysters (803)

Anchovy fritters (835)

Partridge fillets, Giralda (2086)

Roast duckling with green mayonnaise and fine herbs (1938)

Aspics of foies gras (2412)

Salad

(Ice) Fiori di latte à la Bellini (3467)

Dessert

OCTOBER. 484

Consommé (189)

Scallops on toast, baked (1078)

Chicken fillets à la Genin (1843)

Green peas, English style (2742)

Broiled plover (2118)

Salad

(Ice) Biscuit glacés (3438)

OCTOBER. 485

Oysters (803)

Bressoles of fat liver (848)

Minions of tenderloin of beef à la Dumas (1402)

Salad of crawfish with jelly (2630)

Roasted woodcock (2206)

(Ice) Duchess pudding (3492)

Small fancy cakes (3364)

Dessert

OCTOBER. 486

Oysters (803)

Deviled stuffed lobster à la Carlu (1043)

Toasted bread with bacon (827)

Chicken breasts, Empress style (1841)

Broiled snipe (2157)

Cucumber salad (2661)

(Ice) Marvelous (3563)

Dessert

OCTOBER. 487

Consommé (189)

Ham mousseline Virginienne (911)

Small aspics of foies gras (2412)

Roasted ruddy duck (2066)

Lettuce salad (2672)

(Ice) Mokabelle (3565)

Dessert

SUPPER.

NOVEMBER.   **488**   **NOVEMBER.**   **489**

Oysters (803)
Partridge quenelles à la Stuart (2333)
Artichoke bottoms à la Mornay (2680)
Terrapin à la Trenton (1090a)
Roast grouse (2072)
Cos-lettuce salad (2675)
(Ice) Mousse with macaroons (3477)
Dessert

Oysters (803)
Small cases with fat livers (2229)
Lamb cutlets à la Turenne (1688)
Shells of capon with jelly (2590)
Broiled woodcock (2204)
Salad
Parfait with coffee (3479)
Dessert

NOVEMBER.   **490**   **NOVEMBER.**   **491**

Oysters (803)
Toast, Florentine (991)
Cromesquis of crabs, Rumpford (869)
Terrapin, Epicurean style (1090b)
Small aspics of foies gras (2412)
Roast plover (2119)
Celery salad (2660)
(Ice) Toronchino Procope (3583)

Oysters (803)
Consommé (189)
Palmettes of snipe à la Osborn (932)
St. Jacques shells, Parisian style (1079)
Toasted bread with chicken (827)
Roast quails (2131)
Escarole salad (2671)
(Ice) Basket of oranges (3570)

DECEMBER.   **492**   **DECEMBER.**   **493**

Oysters (803)
Consommé (189)
Capon croquettes à la Royale (876)
Peas English style (2742)
Terrapin à la Maryland (1085)
Roast reedbirds with water-cress (2252)
Ice cream with chestnuts (3465)
Dessert

Consommé (189)
Brochettes of oysters with truffles (1058)
Sweetbreads à la Mirabeau (2595)
Fat livers, Toulousaine (2287)
Fried egg-plant (2739)
Roasted grouse (2072)
Salad
(Ice) Biscuit with vanilla, melon shape (3438)
Dessert

DECEMBER.   **494**   **DECEMBER.**   **495**

Welsh rarebit à la Cutting (946)
Lobster à la Bordelaise (1026)
Noisettes of tenderloin of beef Berthier (1411)
Terrapin à la Newberg (1086)
Roast squabs (2018)
Water-cress salad (2676)
(Ice) Harlequin (3554)
Dessert

Consommé (189)
Oysters on toast (1062)
Ham mousseline à la Costa (911)
Terrapin à la Crisfield (1084)
Roast woodcock (2206)
Okra and sweet pepper salad (2651)
(Ice) Potatoes (3575)
Dessert

BUFFET POUR 300 PERSONNES. | BUFFET POUR 200 PERSONNES.

MENU.

CHAUD.

Consommé de gibier (192)

Huîtres à la Villeroi (1056)

Rissolettes à la Renan (957)

Bouchées de ris de veau à la Française (940)

Terrapène, Maryland Club (1088)

Perdreaux piqués rôtis au jus et cresson (2102)

Crabes durs farcis à la diable (1004)

FROID.

Saumon à la Moderne (2582)

Filet de bœuf à la Lucullus (2436)

Volière de faisan à la Waddington (2424)

Jambon décoré à la Gatti (2521)

Ballotines de pigeonneaux à la Madison (2427)

Galantine de faisan à la Lorenzo (2494)

Langues de bœuf, Rochefort (2606)

Salmis froid de perdreaux (2574)

Salade de homard à l'Américaine (2638)

Mayonnaise de volaille (2625)

Tétras rôtis au jus (2072)

Sandwichs (811)

Tartines de pain blanc beurrées (820)

ENTREMETS DE DOUCEUR ET DESSERT.

Paniers d'oranges à la gelée (3130)

Bavarois aux marrons (3136)

Gâteau aux amandes (3225)

Gaufres brisselets à la crème framboisée (3223)

GLACES.

Bacchus (3590)

Le Puits (3599)

Toronchino Procope (3583)

Tutti frutti (3586)

Napolitaine (3569)

Mokabelle (3565)

PIÈCES MONTÉES.

Corne d'Abondance (3635)

Chariot garni de pommes d'api (3632)

Fruits (3699)

Bonbons (3642)

Devises (3653)

Dessert

MENU.

CHAUD.

Consommé (189)

Huîtres frites au beurre (1061)

Rissoles de palais de veau (952)

Bouchées à la Victoria (942)

Terrapène à la Baltimore (1083)

Crabes durs farcis à la Caroline (1003)

Ruddy duck rôti (2066)

Café (3701)

FROID.

Galantine d'anguilles (2488)

Canetons aux olives Espagnole (2482)

Faisan farci à la Prince Orloff (2553)

Chaudfroid de filets de canards à tête rouge (2460)

Filets de poulet Mirebel (2464)

Mousseline de homard (2537)

Aspic de foies gras (2411)

Coquilles de chapon à la gelée (2590)

Tartines de pain de seigle beurrées (820)

Petits pains garnis de rillettes de Tours (809)

ENTREMETS DE DOUCEUR ET DESSERT.

Gâteau Mille feuilles Pompadour (3247)

Gâteau Favart (3263)

Gelée au Madère (3186)

Charlotte Russe (3145)

GLACES.

Ananas en surprise (3595)

Turban à la vanille et aux fraises (3600)

Madrilian (3562)

Pommes de terre (3575)

Pastèque (3589)

Biscuit glacé à la Diplomate (3435)

PIÈCES MONTÉES.

Vase en sucre filé (3637)

Moulin à vent (3639)

Fruits (3699)

Bonbons (3642)

Devises (3653)

Dessert

BUFFET POUR 250 PERSONNES.

MENU.

CHAUD.

Bouillon clair (187)
Brochettes d'huîtres aux truffes (1058)
Rissoles de volaille (948)
Terrapène à la Maryland (1085)
Homard à l'Américaine (1024)
Timbales à la La Vallière (2357)
Café (3701)

FROID.

Saumon à la Farragut (2581)
Filet de bœuf aux légumes mayonnaise (2441)
Buisson de crustacés à la Rochelaise (2572)
Timbale de faisan aux truffes (2605)
Galantine à la Berger (2499)
Langue de bœuf Écarlate en Arcade (2607)
Chaudfroid de mauviettes (2454)
Pâté de longe d'agneau à la gelée (2561)
Cuisses de poulet en forme de caneton ravigote (2529)

ENTREMETS DE DOUCEUR ET DESSERT.

Gâteau Favart (3263)
Biscuit aux amandes (3229)
Gelée prunelle (3186)
Bavarois aux meringues (3133)

GLACES.

Comtesse Léda (3548)
Timbale Chateaubriand (3581)
Panier de Perrette (3629)
Œufs à la Trémontaine (3550)
Mignonne (3564)
Biscuit tutti frutti (3585)

PIÈCES MONTÉES.

Corbeille garnie de fruits (3628)
Panier garni d'oranges (3570)
Fruits (3699)
Bonbons (3642)
Devises (3653)
Dessert

BUFFET POUR 150 PERSONNES.

MENU.

CHAUD.

Consommé (189)
Huîtres à la poulette (1067)
Palmettes à la Varsovienne (924)
Rissoles de palais de bœuf (952)
Bouchées Turbigo (941)
Terrapène à la Crisfield (1084)
Café (3701)

FROID.

Saumon à la Russe (2586)
Filet de bœuf à la Noailles (2437)
Galantine de pigeon (2496)
Jambon truffé à la Florian (2523)
Dinde en daube à la Verneuil (2615)
Côtelettes d'agneau à l'aspic (2473)
Petites caisses de grives à la gelée (2449)
Aspic de faisan (2417)
Salade de homard à l'Américaine (2638)
Mayonnaise de poulet (2625)
Sandwichs de viandes variées (815)

ENTREMETS DE DOUCEUR ET DESSERT.

Gâteau Gênoise (3239)
Gelée à la Russe (3182)
Gaufres brisselets à la crème framboisée (3223)
Gâteau Jamaïque (3242)

GLACES.

Bacchus (3590)
Le Puits (3599)
Bombe à la Romaine (3442)
Fiori di latte fleurs de violettes (3470)
Plombière Montesquieu aux pralines et aux pistaches (3480)
Parfait au café (3479)

PIÈCES MONTÉES.

Le Char des Cygnes (3634)
Bateau bon voyage (3631)
Fruits (3699)
Bonbons (3643)
Devises (3653)
Dessert.

BUFFET POUR 400 PERSONNES.

MENU.

CHAUD.

Bouillon clair (187)

Lucines orangées à la Philadelphie (994)

Moules aux fines herbes gratinées (1050)

Croquettes de canetons à la Muser (881)

Bouchées aux crevettes (935)

Crabes durs farcis aux champignons (1004)

Café (3701)

FROID.

Saumon à la Seymour (2584)

Grenadins filet de bœuf, Rochambeau (2439)

Paon rôti et paré de son plumage (2552)

Pâté de filets d'oie Adolphe Hardy (2557)

Côtelettes d'agneau à l'Impériale (2471)

Terrine de noix de Jambon (2597)

Poulet Écarlate à la Derenne (2463)

Aspic de veau aux artichauts macédoine (2421)

Sandwichs (811)

Rillettes de Tours (809)

ENTREMETS DE DOUCEUR ET DESSERT.

Gâteau à la gelée meringué (3243)

Gelée aux fraises (3183)

Baquets de gaufres à la crème (3128)

Biscuit à l'Hernani (3228)

GLACES.

Melon Cantaloup en surprise (3591)

Nid garni d'œufs (3594)

Pouding à la Constance (3490)

Mousse à l'ananas (3474)

Biscuit glacé à la d'Orléans (3437)

Alexandria (3539)

Petites glaces fantaisie (3431)

PIÈCES MONTÉES.

Le chariot des Colombes (3633)

Le panier de Perrette (3629)

Fruits (3699)

Bonbons (3642)

Devises (3653)

Café (3701)

BUFFET POUR 60 PERSONNES.

MENU.

CHAUD.

Bouillon (187)

Lucines orangées à la poulette (995)

Palmettes à la Périer (922)

Rissoles de poisson (952)

Petits pâtés feuilletés de saumon (945)

Homard rôti à la diable (1030)

FROID.

Truites de ruisseau à la Carême (2611)

Filet de bœuf aux croustades macédoine (2440)

Côtelettes d'agneau au chaudfroid tomaté (2475)

Ris de veau à la Mirabeau (2595)

Célestine de poularde, Talleyrand (2450)

Fricassée de poulet chaudfroid (2467)

" Pain " de foies au salpicon (2547)

Galantine de caneton en forme de poire (2487)

Sandwichs assorties (811)

ENTREMETS DE DOUCEUR ET DESSERT.

Gâteau Moka (3249)

Gelée à la Violette (3185)

Corbeille en Nougat à la Crème (3129)

Pouding Renaissance (3210)

GLACES.

Poule avec poussins (3594)

Lapin en Surprise (3596)

Arlequin (3554)

Mousse aux fraises (3474)

Soufflé glacé à l'Alcazar (3533)

Asperges (3540)

Petites glaces fantaisie (3431)

PIÈCES MONTÉES.

Vase en sucre filé garni de fleurs (3637)

Moulin à vent (3639)

Fruits (3699)

Bonbons (3642)

Devises (3653)

Dessert

BUFFET POUR 80 PERSONNES.	**BUFFET POUR 150 PERSONNES.**

MENU.   **MENU.**

CHAUD.

Bouillon clair (187)
Moules à la Marinière (1046)
Lucines orangées farcies (997)
Brissotins de volaille au suprême (849)
Bouchées à l'Andalouse (934)
Crabes moux grillés beurre ravigote (1006)

FROID.

Truites à la gelée sauce Tartare (2612)
Filet de bœuf aux croustades macédoine (2440)
Ballotine d'agneau en forme de coupole (2425)
Côtelettes de veau à l'Anacréon (2478)
Pâté de foies gras de Strasbourg (2564)
Poularde piquée à la gelée (2571)
Galantine d'oison en forme de melon (2489)
Jambon glacé au sucre (2522)
Sandwichs (811)
Petits pains garnis de rillettes de Tours (809)

ENTREMETS DE DOUCEUR ET DESSERT.

Biscuits à la crème (3137)
Bavarois aux framboises (3134)
Gâteau Napolitain (3250)
Gâteau Reine (3256)

GLACES.

Ananas en Surprise (3595)
Délicieux aux noisettes (3592)
Soufflé glacé Palmyre (3535)
Champignons (3568)
Mousse aux pêches (3474)
Pouding à la Romanoff (3497)
Petites glaces fantaisie (3431)

PIÈCES MONTÉES.

2 Vases en sucre filé garnis de fleurs (3637)
Fruits (3699)
Bonbons (3642)
Devises (3653)
Dessert

CHAUD.

Consommé (189)
Moules à la poulette (1047)
Lucines papillons frites (998)
Croquettes de dinde (894)
Bouchées à la Reine (938)
Crabes moux sautés au beurre (1006)
Café (3701) Thé (3704)

FROID.

Darne de saumon historiée (2576)
Buisson d'écrevisses (2572)
Petits aspics aux crevettes (2422)
Galantine de pintade à la Lytton (2490)
Pâté de caneton à la Rouennaise (2555)
Poulet sauté à la Sherman (2468)
Sandwichs de viandes (811)
Canapés d'anchois (777)

ENTREMETS DE DOUCEUR ET DESSERT.

Gelée aux fruits et au kirsch (3187)
Château framboisé (3141)
Pound cake (3254)
Pouding Harrison (3207)

GLACES.

Cantaloup moulé (3591)
Nid garni d'œufs (3594)
Pouding à la Serano (3498)
Mousse à l'Italienne (3475)
Spongade Médicis (3536)
Petites glaces fantaisie (3431)

PIÈCES MONTÉES.

Le char des Cygnes (3634)
Bateau bon voyage (3631)
Fruits (3699)
Bonbons (3642)
Devises (3653)
Dessert

SEPTEMBRE. 504 ✢ OCTOBRE. 505

BUFFET POUR 300 PERSONNES.

MENU.

CHAUD.

Consommé de volaille (190)

Bouchées à la Victoria (942)

Croquettes de ris de veau (893)

Homard à la Newberg (1037)

Crabes moux frits (1006)

Café (3701)

Thé (3704)

FROID.

Turbot à la Rémoulade (2613)

Chaudfroid de tétras (2457)

Galantine de cochon de lait (2498)

Pain de perdreau à la Montgomery (2548)

Petites caisses de bécassines à la gelée (2448)

Crème de homard (2470)

Pâté froid de cailles (2565)

Perdreaux piqués rôtis (2550)

Salade de chapon (2624)

Sandwichs (811)   Rillettes de Tours (809)

Canapés de caviar (777)

ENTREMETS DE DOUCEUR ET DESSERT.

Gelée au marsala (3186)

Purée de pommes mousseuse (3127)

Gelée aux fruits et au kirsch (3187)

Riz Mirabeau (3213)

GLACES.

Corbeille jardinière aux Colombes (3593)

Cygne aux roseaux (3597)

Crème spongade à la Parépa (3537)

Mousse aux liqueurs (3476)

Bombe aux fruits printanière (3441)

Oranges Posilipo (3571)

PIÈCES MONTÉES.

Arbre prodigieux (3639a)

Moulin à vent (3639)

Fruits (3699)

Bonbons (3642)

Devises (3653)

Dessert

BUFFET POUR 250 PERSONNES.

MENU.

CHAUD.

Bouillon (187)

Huîtres à la Philadelphie (1063)

Croquettes de crabes à la Parmentier (879)

Selle de chevreuil rôtie (2194)

Bouchées de ris de veau à la Française (940)

Café (3701)

Thé (3704)

FROID.

Tranches de sheepshead à la gelée (2589)

Filet de mouton à la Henry Clay (2541)

Jambon de poulet garni de zampino (2525)

Chaudfroid de perdreau Béatrice (2455)

Hure de porc (2570)

Aspic de homard (2414)

Côtelettes de faisan chaudfroid (2477)

Pâté froid de bécasses (2569)

Terrine de mauviettes (2599)

Sandwichs (811)

Pains de rillettes de Tours (809)

ENTREMETS DE DOUCEUR ET DESSERT.

Biscuits de Savoie (3231)

Gelée au champagne (3186)

Crème bain-marie (3160)

Gâteau mandarin (3245)

GLACES.

Ananas en surprise (3595)

Délicieux aux noisettes (3592)

Pouding aux biscuits (3488)

Mousse Sémiramis (3471)

Soufflé glacé à l'Alcazar (3533)

Asperges sauce marasquin (3540)

PIÈCES MONTÉES.

2 Vases en sucre filé (3637)

Fruits (3699)

Bonbons (3642)

Devises (3653)

Dessert

NOVEMBRE.   506 ✦ DÉCEMBRE.   507

BUFFET POUR 200 PERSONNES.

MENU.

CHAUD.

Consommé (189)
Huîtres à la Hollandaise (1066)
Rissoles de ris de veau (954)
Bécassines rôties (2159)
Croquettes de brochet à la Romaine (890)
Café (3701)
Thé (3704)

FROID.

Saumon Vénitienne (2587)
Filet de bœuf à la Evers (2435)
Galantine de perdreau, Élisabeth (2493)
Pâté de lièvre dans un plat (2559)
Côtelettes de homard à la Lowery (2476)
Aspic de filets de caille (2419)
Filets de poulet Renaissance (2465)
Chaudfroid de courlis au fumet (2452)
Estomacs de dinde à la Gustave Doré (2617)
Sandwichs (811)

ENTREMETS DE DOUCEUR ET DESSERT.

Gelée au sherry (3186)
Pouding Castillane (3206)
Bordure Caroline au champagne (3140)
Gâteau de noisettes (3241)
Crème de riz à l'angélique (3151)
Marrons à la crème (3147)

GLACES.

Corbeille jardinière aux colombes (3593)
Le cygne aux roseaux (3597)
Pouding de ris à l'Impérial (3494)
La Grandina (3556)
Fiori di latte à la fleur d'orange (3469)
Sabayon à la Cannetti (3531)

PIÈCES MONTÉES.

Brouette de fleurs (3638)
Chariot de pommes (3632)
2 Corbeilles de fruits (3699)
Glaces (3699)
Bonbons (3642)
Devises (3653)
Dessert

BUFFET POUR 150 PERSONNES.

MENU.

CHAUD.

Bouillon (187)
Huîtres frites au beurre (1061)
Timbales à la Dumas (965)
Bouchées à la Reine (938)
Terrapène Epicurienne (1090)
Poules de neige rôties (2072)
Café (3701)

FROID.

Saumon à la Avelane (2579)
Filet de bœuf à la Violetta (2438)
Galantine de perdreau Clémentine (2491)
Petites caisses de foies gras (2229)
Chaudfroid de cailles Baudy (2459)
Côtelettes de bécasses Sarah Bernhardt (2480)
Terrine de lièvre (2598)
Aspic de crêtes et rognons de coq à la Mazarin
(2410)
Sandwichs assorties (811)

ENTREMETS DE DOUCEUR ET DESSERT.

Gâteau Roederer (3257)
Gelée aux pêches (3187)
Timbales Massillon (3221)
Pouding à la Boissy (3205)

GLACES.

Ananas en surprise (3595)
Délicieux aux noisettes (3592)
Manchon Déjazet à la crème Vénus (3567)
Biscuits glacés (3438)
Glaces assorties (3538)
Punch granit au café (3505)

PIÈCES MONTÉES.

Bateau "Bon Voyage" (3631)
Panier de Cerises (3630)
Fruits (3699)
Bonbons (3642)
Devises (3653)
Dessert

SIDEBOARD FOR 150 PERSONS.

BILL OF FARE.

HOT.

Consommé (189)

Oysters à la poulette (1067)

Sweetbread cutlets à la Talleyrand (2272)

Roast woodcock (2206)

Pullet croquettes à la Wright Sanford (882)

Tenderloin of beef, royale (1458)

COLD.

Salmon with Montpellier butter (2588)

English ham with jelly (2524)

Galantine of partridge, sliced (2492)

Decorated wild boar's head (2618)

Dressed game pie à la Lesage (2556)

Chaudfroid of young Guinea fowl (2453)

Terrine of plover and larks (2601)

Small "pain" of chicken à la Freycinet (2544)

Mousseline of woodcock (2540)

Sandwiches (811)

Small "pains" of Rillettes de Tours (809)

SWEET DISHES AND DESSERT.

Mousseline biscuit (3230)

Greengage jelly 3187)

Chestnuts with cream (3147)

Gugelhopfen cake (3240)

ICES.

Hen and chicks (3594)

Rabbit in surprise (3596)

Excelsior Biscuit (3436)

Printanière fruit Bomb (3441)

Waddington pudding (3500)

Chartreuse mousse (3476).

CENTER PIECES.

Chariot filled with lady apples (3632)

Horn of plenty (3635)

Fruits (3699)

Bonbons (3642)

Mottoes (3653)

Dessert

Lady cake (3244)

SIDEBOARD FOR 350 PERSONS.

BILL OF FARE.

HOT.

Cream of peas, St. Germain (260)

Béchamel oysters with truffles (1065)

Rissoles à la Demidoff (950)

Roast plover (2119)

Patties with mushrooms (937)

Frog croquettes (884)

COLD.

Salmon à la Régence (2583)

Tenderloin of beef on a socle Bouquetière (2434)

Volière galantine of pheasants, Casimir Périer (2423)

Galantine of chicken à la d'Orléans (2486)

Woodcock à la Valère (2619)

Terrine of duck's liver à l'Aquitaine (2596)

Aspic of minion fillets of partridge (2416)

Fillets of sole à la Mazagran (2593)

Assorted sandwiches (815)

SWEET DISHES AND DESSERT.

Plum cake (3253)

Peach jelly (3187)

Cream cornets with orange (3148)

Camper crowns (3156)

ICES.

Bacchus (3590)

The Well (3599)

Banana pudding (3487)

Bomb with maraschino (3443)

Mousse with macaroons (3477)

Apples in surprise (3574)

Waffles with vanilla (3285)

CENTER PIECES.

Basket filled with candied fruits (3628)

Perrette's basket (3629)

Fruits (3699)

Bonbons (3642)

Mottoes (3653)

Dessert

Fruit cake (3238)

NOVEMBER. 510 ✠ DECEMBER. 511

SIDEBOARD FOR 200 PERSONS.

BILL OF FARE.

HOT.

Cream of rice, Crémieux (249)
Oysters Viennaise (1068)
Palmettes of turkey à la Béarnaise (933)
Turbigo patties (941)
Terrapin à la Trenton (1090)
Roast partridges with gravy and water cress
(2102)
Coffee (3701)

COLD.

Decorated slices of salmon (2577)
Saddle of venison à la Harder (2573)
Aspic of oysters (2415)
Chaudfroid of woodcock with fumet (2452)
Red beef tongue with jelly (2609)
Ballotines of quail à la Tivolier (2426)
Terrine of wild rabbit (2604)
Snipe pie (2567)
Sandwiches (811)

SWEET DISHES AND DESSERT.

Breton cake (3232)
Noyau jelly (3186)
Apple Flamri (3166)
Large brioche (3234)

ICES.

Hen with chicks (3594)
Rabbit in surprise (3596)
Plum pudding (3496)
Grandina (3556)
Parisian (3573)
Gramolates with oranges (3610)

CENTER PIECES.

Basket of cherries (3630)
Wheelbarrow filled with flowers (3638)
Fruits (3699)
Bonbons (3642)
Mottoes (3653)
Dessert.

———

Pound cake (3254)

SIDEBOARD FOR 400 PERSONS.

BILL OF FARE.

HOT.

Chicken consommé (190)
Oyster rissolettes à la Pompadour (1054)
Lamb croquettes à la De Rivas (888)
Roast quails (2131)
Crab patties (935)
Timbale à la Renaissance (981)
Coffee (3701)

COLD.

Slices of salmon with jelly (2578)
Ribs of beef in Bellevue (2432)
Galantine of partridge (2492)
" Pain " of partridge à la Montgomery (2548)
Chaudfroid of snipe in pyramid (2461)
Woodcock cutlets, Poniatowski (2479)
Mousseline of pheasant, Princess (2538)
Pâté de foies gras in border (2483)
Chicken legs in the shape of ducklings (2529)
Sandwiches (811)

SWEET DISHES AND DESSERT.

Compiègne cake (3236)
Prunelle jelly (3186)
Apricot rice (3214)
" Pain " of chestnut à la Béotie (3196)

ICES.

Algerian timbale (3580)
Cauliflower with marchioness rice (3544)
Léona (3558)
St. Jacques Cup (3560)
Corn (3547)
Pears in surprise (3574)

CENTER PIECES.

Chariot filled with lady apples (3632)
Horn of plenty (3635)
Fruits (3699)
Bonbons (3642)
Mottoes (3653)
Dessert

———

Pound cake (3254)

SIDEBOARD FOR 300 PERSONS.

BILL OF FARE.

HOT.

Clear bouillon (187)
Fried oysters à la Horly (1060)
Oyster patties (939)
Scallops à la Marinière (1076)
Turkey croquettes (894)
Roast canvasback (2055)
Stuffed lobster tails (1043)

COLD.

Salmon à la Courbet (2585)
Tenderloin of beef à la Noailles (2437)
"Pain" of game Diana (2546)
Bastion, American style (2429)
Chaudfroid of chicken à la Clara Morris (2451)
Cold salmis of quails à la Balzac (2575)
Terrine of partridge de Nérac (2600)
Galantine of pheasant (2495)
Rolls filled with rillettes (809)
Buttered slices of rye bread (820)

SWEET DISHES AND DESSERT.

Macédoine champagne jelly (3179)
"Pain" of apricots (3194)
Pineapple cake (3252)
Ministerial pudding (3209)

ICES.

The helmet (3598)
Delicious with hazelnuts (3592)
Montélimar with hazelnuts (3566)
Ribambelle (3576)
Madeleine (3561)
Rice with maraschino (3578)

CENTER PIECES.

Basket filled with candied fruit (3628)
Basket filled with tortillons (3628)
Fruits (3699)
Bonbons (3642)
Mottoes (3653)
Dessert

———

Wedding cake (3238)

SIDEBOARD FOR 200 PERSONS.

BILL OF FARE.

HOT.

Chicken consommé (190)
Broiled oysters, maître-d'hôtel (1059)
Scallops à la Havraise (1075)
Palmettes à la Périer (922)
Roast redhead ducks (2063)
Coffee (3701)

COLD.

Salmon à la d'Estaing (2580)
Tenderloin of beef à la Violetta (2438)
"Pain" of game à la Bartholdi (2545)
Aspic of tongue à la Picquart (2420)
Chaudfroid of fillets of pheasant (2456)
Cutlets of kernel of lamb in Bellevue (2472)
Galantine of pullet à la Mozart (2497)
Boar's head (2570)
Chicken mayonnaise (2625)
Sandwiches (811)
Small fancy rolls filled with rillettes de Tours
(809)

SWEET DISHES AND DESSERT.

Syruped baba (3227)
Sponge cake (3260)
Californian pineapple jelly (3178)
Blanc mange à la Smolenska (3138)

ICES.

Cantaloup in surprise (3591)
Nest with eggs (3594)
Stuffed tomatoes (3582)
Sicilian (3579)
Ristori rice (3577)
Marvelous (3563)
Granite with currants (3611)

CENTER PIECES.

Cornucopia garnished with fruit (3635)
Wheelbarrow filled with flowers (3638)
Fruits (3699)
Bonbons (3642)
Mottoes (3653)
Dessert

———

Angel cake (3226)

RESTAURANT BILL OF FARE.

BREAKFAST.

JUNE.

Coffee (3701) Chocolate (3700) Arabian racahout (3703)
English breakfast tea (3704)

SIDE DISHES.

Clams (803) Gherkins (785) Sandwiches (811) Radishes (808) Olives (800) Caviare (778)
Anchovies (772) Sardines (817) Lyons sausage (818) Stuffed olives (801) Marinated tunny fish (831)
Mackerel in oil (797) Mortadella (818) Arles sausage (818)

EGGS.

Boiled (2856) Fried à la Eugène André (2866) Scrambled à la Columbus (2934)
On a dish (2909) Fried turned over à la sole (2869) Hard boiled, Russian style (2865)

Omelets: Argentine (2878) With clams (2885) With bacon (2879)
Cocottes (2873) Soft eggs with purée of sorrel (2951) Poached eggs with gravy (2931)

FISH.

Red bass water fish (1098) Pike perch à la Durance (1213) Whitebait (1310)
Black bass à la Narragansett (1095) Mussels à la poulette (1047)
Kingfish à la batelière (1179) Porgy with Chablis wine (1231) Bluefish à la Barnave (1117)

HOT.

Pig's feet à la St. Ménéhould (1783) Veal cutlets (1501) Mutton cutlets (1590) Beefsteak (1368)
Pork chops (1778) Spring lamb cutlets (1669) Roast squabs (2018)
Beef palate à la Béchamel (1326) Chateaubriand (1380)
Escalops of veal à la Habirshaw (2282)
Mutton breast broiled (1585) Stuffed breast of lamb, Velouté tomato sauce (1665)
Frogs' legs à la poulette with mushrooms (1019) Chicken sautéd, half glaze (1906)
Squabs à la Carolina (2021) Delmonico sirloin steak, Spanish style (1377)
Porterhouse steak (1362)

COLD.

Corned beef, pressed (2430) English ham with jelly (2524)
Red beef tongue with jelly (2609) Ribs of beef Bellevue (2432)
Boned turkey (2499) Calf tongue à la Macédoine (2610)
Lamb pie (2561) Beef à la mode (2433)
Aspic de foies gras (2411) Roast chicken with jelly and beef tongue (2469)

SALADS.

Tomato (2666) Water-cress (2676) Celery (2660) Macédoine (2650)
Chicken mayonnaise (2625) Russian (2645)

VEGETABLES.

Potatoes: Fried (2787) Mashed in snow (2798) Broiled sweet potatoes (2832) Saratoga (2803)
Beets with butter and fine herbs (2702) Boiled asparagus with Hollandaise sauce (2692)
Succotash (2731)

BREAKFAST CAKES.

Brioches (3269) Wheaten grits (3280) Hominy (3280) Oat meal (3280) Muffins (3414)
Corn bread (3422) Indian cake (3274) Flannel cake (3273) Waffles (3284)

DESSERT.

Darioles with orange-flower water (3300)
Fresh Fruits: (3699) Apples Oranges Bananas Pears
Watermelon Peaches

Cheese: (2697) American Brie Stilton Roquefort Chester
Glass of cream or milk.

LUNCH.

JULY.

Clams (803)

SOUPS.

Consommé in cup (189)   Pea purée with croûtons (282)   Julienne faubonne (318)
Fish broth with clams (370)   Clam chowder (300)   Chicken okra (299)
Mock turtle thickened (355)   Cream of corn à la Hermann (255)

FISH.

Fresh mackerel maître-d'hôtel (1193)   Fried soft shell crabs (1006)
Striped bass à la Bercy (1101)   Baked codfish Duxelle (1136)
Kingfish à la Batelière (1179)   Fillets of spotted fish English style (1233)
Porgies à la Manhattan (1229)   Eels à la Maréchale (1149)

READY.

Leg of mutton à la Bordelaise (1622)   Sirloin of beef à la Dauphiness (1350)
Sausages with cream potatoes (1804)   Loin of veal with gravy (1537)
Bacon with spinach (1771)   Chicken fricassée à la Bouchard (1862)
Poached eggs with purée of chicken suprême (2932)

TO ORDER.

Veal cutlet maître-d'hôtel (1501)   Small steak plain (1368)
Mutton cutlets with purée of chestnut (1599)   Chicken croquettes exquisite (877)
Lamb cutlets (1669)   Minions of fillet of veal with mushrooms (1510)
Squabs à la Briand (2006)   Chicken cocotte (1832)
Noisettes fillet of beef à la Berthier (1411)   Frog's legs à la d'Antin (1017)
Mutton breast with tomato Andalouse sauce (1586)   Squabs sauté à l'Impromptu (2010)

COLD.

Pickles (785)   Radishes (808)   Olives (800)   Caviare (778)   Celery (779)
English ham with jelly (2524)   Anchovies (772)   Sardines in oil (772)   Lyons sausage (818)
Mortadella (818)   Sandwiches (811)   Mackerel in oil (797)
Stuffed olives with anchovy butter (801)   Marinated tunny (831)   Spring lamb (2561)
Red beef tongue (2609)   Lobster with mayonnaise (2638)   Boned turkey (2499)
Goose liver pie (2562)

SALADS.

Russian (2645)   Tomato (2666)   Chicken mayonnaise (2625)   Potato (2654)   Macédoine (2650)
Water-cress (2676)

VEGETABLES.

POTATOES: Fried (2787)   Saratoga (2803)   Hashed, with cream (2780)   Lyonnese (2794)
String beans à l'Albani (2825)   Boiled asparagus with Hollandaise sauce (2692)
Lima beans maître-d'hôtel (2699)   Green peas, French style (2743)
Green corn on the cob (2730)   Stuffed truffles (2845)
Tomatoes broiled with mayonnaise sauce (2838)

DESSERT.

ICE CREAM: Toronchino, Procope (3583)   Pistachio (3454)   Asparagus (3540)
Nesselrode pudding with chestnuts (3495)   Vanilla (3458)   Chocolate (3449)
Tutti frutti (3586)   Tortoni cups (3584)   Neapolitan (3569)
Banana cream (3451)   White coffee (3460)

WATER ICE: Raspberry (3607)   Orange (3605)   Lemon (3604)
PUNCH: Roman (3515)   Kirsch (3510)   Lalla Rookh (3516)   Maraschino (3510)
Bucket made of Chantilly waffles (3128)   Charlotte russe (3145)

FRUITS: (3699)   Watermelon   Muskmelon   Peaches   Bananas   Apples   Grapes
CHEESE: (3697)   American   Roquefort   Edam   Camembert   Pont l'Évêque

French coffee (3701)   Turkish coffee (3702)

RESTAURANT BILL OF FARE.

DINNER.

MAY.

Clams (803)

SOUPS.

Consommé Carême (222)   Rice à la Rudini (343)   Sherman (344)
Bisque of crawfish à la Batelière (202)   Cream of sorrel with stuffed eggs (262)
Julienne Mogul (318)   Pea purée with croûtons (282)   Croûte au pot (305)
Chicken okra (299)   Chicken okra strained (299)   Small individual soup pots (346)

SIDE DISHES—COLD.

Radishes (808)   Olives (800)   Caviare (778)   Sardines in oil (772)   Lyons sausages (818)
Marinated tunny (831)   Gherkins (785)   Mortadella (818)
Stuffed olives with anchovy butter (801)   Mackerel in oil (797)

SIDE DISH—HOT.

Cromesquis of sweetbread, Babanine (872)

FISH.

Mussels with shallot (1051)   Eels broiled tartar sauce (1150)   Planked shad ravigote butter (1255)
Spotted fish Livournaise (1282)   Weakfish à la Brighton (1308)   Fried soft shell crabs (1006)
Blackfish à la Sandford (1115)   Lobster à la Camille (1028)   Sheepshead, Buena Vista (1259)

REMOVES.

Roast sirloin of beef with brain patties (1355)
Rump of beef Boucicault (1337)   Pullet in surprise (1987)

ENTREES.

Mutton pie Canadian style (2375)   Sautéd chicken florentine style (1890)
Mushrooms crust with truffles (2759)   Minions of tenderloin of beef à la Stanley (1406)
Hot plover pie (2317)   Breasts of turkey Donovan (2037)   Squabs à la Crispi (2008)
Frog shells (2347)   Sweetbread à la St. Cloud (1566)
Sorbets: Lalla Rookh (3516)   Kirsch (3510)   Maraschino (3510)   Rum (3510)

ROAST.

Leg of mutton à la Roederer (1627)   Leg of yearling lamb with gravy (1715)
Beef ribs, American style (1331)   Squabs (2018)
Duckling (1921)   Partridge broiled, English style (2085)   Chicken in the saucepan (1881)

COLD.

Galantine of chicken (2485a)   Trout, tartar sauce (2612)   Terrine of duck livers à l'Aquitaine (2596)
Salads: Lettuce (2672)   Water-cress (2676)   Macédoine (2650)   Chicory (2668)

VEGETABLES.

Purslain à la Brabançon (2815)   Lima beans thickened maître-d'hôtel (2699)
Potatoes Parisienne (2786)   Potatoes, Anna (2770)   Potatoes half glaze (2784)
Green peas, English style (2742)   String beans with butter (2829)
Boiled asparagus with Hollandaise sauce (2692)
Succotash (2731)   Cèpes baked with cream (2724)   Stuffed cauliflower à la béchamel, baked (2715)
Risot à la Francatelli (2979)   Tomatoes à la Boquillon (2833)   Cardoons with half glaze (2710)
Fried eggplant (2739)   Spaghetti macaroni à la Lawrence (2966)
Asparagus tops à la Maintenon (2695)   Corn on the cob (2730)   Spinach with cream (2820)
Macaroni à la Brignoli (2958)   Whole artichoke boiled with white sauce (2691)
Macédoine à la Montigny (2755)   Sweet potatoes roasted (2832)

SWEET ENTREMETS.

Hot: Pancakes with brown sugar (3077)   Glazed apple marmalade (3126)
Cold: Blanc mange with strawberries (3139)   Bain marie cream molded (3149)
Charlotte Russe (3145)   Cream Malakoff (3150)

DESSERT.

Fancy Creams: Biscuit, Excelsior (3436)   Basket filled with oranges (3570)
Nesselrode pudding with candied chestnuts (3495)   Biscuit glacé (3435)
Neapolitan (3569)   Plombière with chestnuts (3486)
Creams: Vanilla (3458)   White coffee (3460)   Pistachio (3454)
Water Ice: Lemon (3604)   Raspberry (3607)   Pineapple (3606)
Assorted cakes (3364)
Preserved fruits (3679) greengages, peaches, pineapple, quinces (3679)
Marmalade (3674) jelly, Dundee, peaches, ginger, Guava, Bar-le-duc (3678)
Stewed fruits (3686) pineapple, peaches, pears, prunes, apples, with jelly, bananas,
cherries, chestnuts, oranges, orange salad, strawberries, raspberries.
Brandy fruits (3660) greengages, pears, oranges, strawberries with cream.
Cheese (3697) Stilton, Brie, Strachino, Gorgonzola, Gruyère, Chester, Gervais, Port Salut, Holland
French coffee (3701)   Turkish coffee (3702)

RESTAURANT BILL OF FARE.

SUPPER.

AUGUST.

Clams (803)

HOT.

Welsh rarebit (946)   Consommé in cups (189)   Golden buck (946)
        Stuffed lobster tails, deviled (1043)   Ramequins (2975)
Deviled mutton kidneys on skewers (1620)   Stuffed hard shell crabs Carolina style (1003)
            Sweetbread croquettes (893)
Chicken legs in papers (1876)   Croustades à la Castillane (895)
Bondons of woodcock à la Diane (845)   Chicken breast à la Chevreuse (1827)
Squab à la Briand (2006)   Minions of tenderloin of beef à la Baillard (1400)

COLD.

Sandwiches (811)   Caviare (778)   Radishes (808)   Mortadella (818)   Anchovies (772)
    Marinated sardines (831)   Celery (779)   Tunny (831)   Lyons sausage (818)
        Boned turkey (2499)   Caviare canapés (777)   Goose liver pie (2562)

SALADS.

Lettuce (2672)   Cucumber (2661)   Water-cress (2676)   Celery (2660)
    Macédoine (2650)   Cos lettuce (2675)   Lobster American style (2638)
            Chicken mayonnaise (2625)
        Russian (2645)   Tomato (2666)

DESSERT.

Ice Cream

SHERBET: Kirsch (3510)   Lalla Rookh (3516)   Prunelle (3510)   Maraschino (3510)

WATER ICE: Raspberry (3607)   Pine apple (3606)   Lemon (3604)   Orange (3605)

FANCY: Pudding Cavour (3489)   Banana in surprise (3541)   Plombière à la Rochambeau (3482)
        Vanilla (3458)   Chocolate (3449)   Coffee (3460)   Pistachio (3454)
            Biscuit glacé (3435)   Neapolitan (3569)
Charlotte russe (3145)   Madeira jelly (3186)   Apricot flawn (3170)

FRESH FRUITS (3699): Bananas, pineapples, apples, oranges, Niagara grapes, huckleberries,
                currants, muskmelon, watermelon

CHEESE (3697): Stilton, Gruyère, Cream, Strachino
French coffee (3701)   Turkish coffee (3702)

------------------------- ✦ -------------------------

All the Epicurean recipes are included in the menus. The heading of each recipe being in English and in French permits any person not thoroughly versed in both these languages to compose his bill of fare in either the one or the other. He has simply to make his selection of the necessary recipe and by referring to the number of the article, write his bill of fare in English or in French as he so chooses. In wording a dinner bill of fare be very careful to denote the fish or shell fish, the butcher's meat, the poultry and game in season, alternating white or brown for each course, also the white or brown sauces. I have as far as practicable replaced the term fillet by breasts for poultry or game and aiguillettes for fish, so that the word fillet need not be too frequently repeated in the same bill of fare. Oysters can be omitted from the bills of fare, also cold side dishes, salads and coffee, besides the details of the dessert following the entremets need only be mentioned by the single word of dessert.

ELEMENTARY METHODS.

(1). BURNT ALMONDS AND FILBERTS (Amandes et Avelines Pralinées).

Split some shelled almonds or filberts in two; if almonds are used mince well and roast lightly in the oven, on a baking sheet without letting them color, then mix in with them half their weight of sugar and enough egg-white, so they be entirely covered by the sugar. When the burnt almonds are spread on cakes, they must be covered over with sugar and glazed in a brisk oven.

(2). CONDÉ ALMOND OR FILBERT PREPARATION (Appareil à Condé aux Amandes ou Aux Avelines).

Put into a vessel three ounces of powdered sugar, one ounce of vanilla sugar, four ounces of icing sugar. Dilute this compound gradually with egg-whites, in such a manner that a smooth running paste is obtained, and beat it well for several minutes, so that it becomes a consistent body. To this add six ounces of dry almonds or filberts, shelled, ground or chopped up very fine.

(3). TO CHOP AND SHRED ALMONDS (Pour Hacher et Effiler les Amandes).

Chopped.—When the almonds are partly dry, chop them up and sift them through a sieve (Fig. 94), chop again all that remains on the sieve and continue until there be no more to pass through.

Shredded Almonds.—Are freshly peeled almonds dried well in a cloth, then cut into thin fillets on their length, or else put them into a special machine that shreds them also, but they never look so well, as the machine cuts them into all sorts of shapes, while with the knife, they are cut into uniform lengths.

(4). ALMOND MILK (Lait d'Amandes).

Pound half a pound of almonds with a few spoonfuls of cold water and two spoonfuls of orange-flower water; prepare a very fine paste with this and dilute with a pint of water; strain the liquid forcibly through a napkin.

(5). TO PEEL ALMONDS, PISTACHIOS OR FILBERTS (Pour Monder les Amandes, Pistaches ou Avelines).

In order to remove the peels from almonds, filberts or pistachio nuts, they must first be plunged into boiling water and left on the fire until the skin detaches easily under the pressure of the finger, then drain and refresh in cold water; now drain and peel them by removing the skins wash in cold water, drain, wipe and dry in the heater or in a well aired place.

For Filberts or Nuts.—To be peeled dry, crack the shells with a nut-cracking machine, being careful not to break the kernel, then peel them dry by putting the nuts on a baking sheet and pushing it into a medium oven, removing them immediately the outer skin detaches when the nut is rubbed between the thumb and first finger; keep them either whole or in halves and use for ice cream and desserts. Those peeled in water are for chopping, or splitting in two for nougats, also for cooked sugar pastes.

(6). TO POUND, CRUSH, AND COLOR ALMONDS (Pour Piler Broyer et Colorer les Amandes).

To Pound.—Almonds are pounded in a mortar or crushed in a machine; in the mortar by wetting a few at the time with either eggs or liquids, then stirring in some sugar. In a machine, by mixing the almonds and sugar together and pouring it into the funnel of the machine; the first time they should be barely crushed, pass through four times, tightening the cylinders slightly for each turn, and the last time the almonds should be reduced to a paste.

To Color Almonds.—Use chopped or shredded almonds for coloring. For pink, dilute a little carmine in some thirty degree syrup with a little kirsch; rub the almonds in this and dry them. For violet, use red, blue and maraschino; for orange, yellow, red and curacao; for lemon color, yellow and noyau; and for green, spinach and orange flower water.

(7). TO BLANCH RICE (Pour Blanchir le Riz).

Before blanching rice it should be picked, washed, then put into a saucepan and moistened with cold water; bring the liquid to boiling point, stirring it frequently with a spoon so it does not adhere to the bottom of the saucepan, and let it boil for seven or eight minutes, pour the rice into a sieve to drain, refresh in cold water and strain.

(8). TO BLANCH VEGETABLES (Pour Blanchir les Légumes).

Vegetables are blanched in more or less time according to their nature, and not only to correct their bitterness, but to soften them as well; the blanching is the prologue of the cooking and is accomplished in boiling, salted water, either in a saucepan, a tinned copper pan, a copper untinned pan, or an untinned saucepan. In the copper and untinned pans, only the green vegetables should be cooked, such as spinach, green peas, string beans, fresh asparagus, in fact all vegetables that must retain a pretty, pale green color. Artichokes should be cooked in a very clean well-tinned saucepan. To blanch parsley, chervil, tarragon, onions, shallots, etc., plunge them in boiling water several times.

(9). TO BONE POULTRY OR GAME (Pour Désosser la Volaille et le Gibier).

Poultry or game are generally boned in order to stuff them properly; they must first be singed lightly, the legs cut off as well as the pinions and neck, keeping the skin of the latter as long as possible ; split the skin right along the back so as to free the carcass on both sides, using a small knife for this purpose, afterward separate the stump from each wing, so as to reach the fillets. When the fore-part of the belly is detached, separate also the thighs by dislocating them at the first joint adhering to the carcass, then bone the fleshy part of the thighs and the drum-sticks. Cut the carcass down as far as the rump, so as to detach it entirely, and if these instructions are strictly followed, the piece of poultry or game will be found to be entirely boned, and the only parts now to be removed are the stumps of the wings and the large nerve found in the flesh of the thighs, and detach from the carcass the two minion fillets from which you remove the nerves.

(10). DISH BORDERS OF NOODLE PASTE, COOKED PASTE, METAL, ENGLISH PASTE OR GUM PASTE, DISH BOTTOMS, FOUNDATIONS, SUPPORTS, TRIANGLE FOR DRESSING TONGUES, HATELETS FOR HOT REMOVES AND ENTREES, FANCY FRILLS, AND FAVOR FRILLS (Bordures de Plat en Nouilles Pâte Cuite, et en Métal, Pâte Anglaise et Pastillage, Fonds de Plats et Supports, Croûton Triangle pour Dresser les Langues, Hâtelets pour Relevés et Entrées Chauds, Bouffettes et Manchettes).

Several kinds of borders are used in the kitchen for the purpose of decorating dishes; those most employed are cut out with a pastry cutter from a band of noodle paste (No. 142.) To make noodle paste borders requires ingenuity, although it is not difficult. First it needs a good noodle paste of a fine color and very smooth; divide it in several parts and roll these into sausage shapes, then flatten down with a rolling pin drawing them out to a sufficient length so the band can reach all around the basin of the dish ; then cut these bands into the desired width keeping them exceedingly straight ; roll them over on themselves without pressing, then unroll slowly on to a paper band to design them with a

FIG. 1.

FIG. 2.

cutter (Fig. 1), rolling up the cut out end as soon as finished to prevent the paste from drying; they may also be molded in molds shown in Fig. 2.

To fasten the border onto the dish, push a string of repère (No. 142) through a cornet around the basin of the dish exactly where the border is to stand upright; place the dish on top of a cool part of the range and unroll the cut-out band speedily onto the repère to fasten it on in an upright position, attach the two ends together, then bend the band outward with the fingers to give it sufficient splay, turning it around all the time until it is dry enough to stand by itself, then cover over to prevent the border from drying.

Another style of border (Fig. 3) greatly admired is made of cooked white paste (No. 131) also carved out with the pastry cutter, but under more simple conditions and is more resisting. These are very appropriate for entrées having an abundance of garnishing or a plentiful supply of gravy, thereby requiring a more resisting substance than noodle paste. This kind can be seen in the different entrées illustrated in this work, but more specially in the figure representing a chicken à la Montesquieu (Fig. 372). But a style even more used and certainly far more practical is a border made of metal (Figs. 4-5-6); they are fit to be served at a family dinner as well as at the most luxurious banquet in which the dishes are invariably handed round to the guests, for

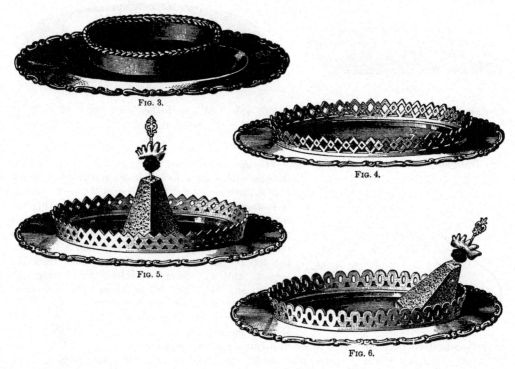

FIG. 3.

FIG. 4.

FIG. 5.

FIG. 6.

instance those viands dressed in the kitchen. These borders are movable and should be made the same size as the basin of the dish for which it is intended. These borders are of sterling silver, but they can be imitated in plated ware; let it be well understood that these borders can only be placed on metal, silver or plated dishes.

For Borders of English Paste or Gum Paste.—Roll out the paste to the desired thickness and with a fancy cutter (Fig. 6A) cut out some pieces and dry them on an even surface covered with paper; when finished place them in closed boxes in a dry place and when ready to use push a string of royal icing on the edge of the basin of the dish or platform and dress the border very evenly around.

FIG. 6 A.

Dish Bottoms, Foundations and Supports.—These foundations or dish bottoms serve for dressing pieces, removes or entrées, so to raise them and give them a more elegant appearance. They are to be made either of bread, rice, hominy, wood or tin. Round

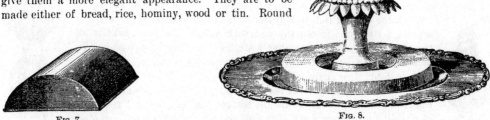

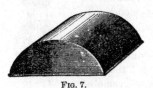

FIG. 7.

FIG. 8.

ones for entrées and ovals for removes or large roasts. The height for entrées is about one and a half inches, while for removes they are to be two inches; those of wood or tin are to be covered with noodle paste, those of rice or hominy are sculptured or carved with a knife.

Molded supports are to be prepared for boned turkeys, capon, pullet, etc.; these are of an oblong shape, rounded at the ends (See Fig. 9 A.); the longest ones intended for turkey's are nine and a quarter inches long by four and three quarters wide and two and a quarter high; for capons

Fig. 9.

Fig 9 A.

they are to be nine inches long, four and a half wide and two inches high; for tenderloins of beef, ten inches long by four wide and two and a half high; for hams, they are oval shaped, twelve by nine and three high.

Triangle for Dressing Tongues, etc.—For the largest ones have the three sides of the triangle each twelve inches long; the thickness at the base is three inches and two inches at the top; they can be made either of rice or hominy in molds having the required dimensions (Fig. 10), or else lower ones with the following proportions: length at the base, twelve inches by eight high; cut off an inch and a half from the top of the smallest and three inches from the largest; this will form a platform for placing the subjects on They can also be made of bread spread over with green butter and then heavily strewn with very finely chopped green parsley. Let it

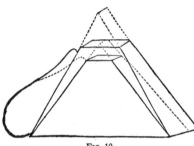

Fig. 10.

be well understood that the socles called dish bottoms are not intended to be eaten. The socle has nothing whatever to do with the dish itself; it represents an accessory made for the purpose of raising the meats, etc., dressed over it, showing off advantageously the surrounding garnishing.

Fig. 11.

Hâtelets (Skewers) for Hot Removes and Entrées.—Hâtelets are employed either as an ornament or else a garnishing; they are applied to removes and entrée dishes. Hâtelets should only be used on ceremonious occasions, for a too prodigal use of them is apt to decrease their value. They are ornamented with unpeeled truffles, mushrooms, or cock's combs, either plain or double hâtelets are also composed of Villeroi quenelles, sweetbread croquettes, or glazed crawfish; they are also made of vegetables, carrots, turnips and artichoke bottoms slightly blanched. Hâtelets intended for garnishing cold pieces are to be found in the chapter on cold dishes (No. 2526).

Fancy Frills for Large Pieces, such as Leg of Mutton, Ham, etc.—Cut a band of paper twelve inches long by three and a half wide; fold it in two on its length and again in two, this making a seven-eighths of an inch wide band, cut it finely on the folded edge, or else pass it through a cutting machine; unfold the band, turn it over so that the cutting detaches better, then twist this band in a spiral around a tin tube; fasten the end with a little mucilage, take it off the tube and place inside either a straight or turned up sconce. To make these sconces, fold a thin sheet of paper six inches square in two, then in four, then again fold in a triangle, beginning at the pointed ends, fold it once more. Cut the paper pointed shaped beginning from the center and rounding toward the bottom; unfold, and with the blade of a small knife, press down each fold so as to have them all come on

Fig. 12.

Fig. 13.

one side and thus form a kind of pointed funnel. Unite the points one on to the other, closing and pressing them together; they should now be the same shape as when cut; place one in the corner of a fine towel, fold it over, press down heavily with the palm of the left hand, then pull the napkin quickly away with the right hand; by this operation, and the pressure, the paper is both folded and goffered at once; the sconce is now made and it only requires to have the bottom cut off to fit it into the frill. (See Fig. 13 and 14.)

Fancy Frills for Cutlets, Chicken Legs or Wings. —Cut some sheets of paper five inches long by three inches wide, fold in two across the length; fold once more in two; cut them by clipping in slits one thirty-second of an inch apart, or else use the machine. Fold this band, twining it in such a manner that the slits are rounded, then fasten with a little mucilage; roll the frill spiralwise on a column-tube or a piece of round wood three-eighths of an inch in diameter. Attach the end of the paper with a little mucilage and when the frill is properly fastened, cut the ends off straight so that they are all of one length (Fig. 12).

FIG. 14.

FIG. 15.

Favor Frills.—Have a small piece of rounded wood an eighth of an inch in diameter and an inch and three-quarters long, tapered on one end; roll on this spiralwise, some prepared paper a third smaller than for the other frills; fasten the two ends together on the stick and trim the paper adhering to the stick with a small ribbon fastened on in the shape of a little rosette. These favors are for chicken-breasts, lobster cutlets, etc.

(11). TO PREPARE BOUCHÉES (Pour Préparer les Bouchées).

Roll out on a floured table some six turned puff paste (No. 146), keeping it one quarter of an inch in thickness; let this paste rest, and then cut from it a dozen round pieces, using a channeled pastry cutter, from two, to two and a quarter inches in diameter (Fig. 16).   Turn these over on to a wet baking sheet, leaving them a short distance apart, and egg over the surfaces with a brush.   Trace on them quickly a ring using a smooth, well heated pastry

FIG. 16.

FIG. 17.

FIG. 18.

cutter (Fig. 17), so that the incision is clear, and with a small knife trace three lines in the inside of this ring (Fig. 18); put the baking sheet into an oven, not excessively hot, and cook the bouchées for eighteen to twenty minutes: detach them from the baking-sheet, slipping a knife underneath each one, open at once to empty them, save the covers, and keep warm until needed.

(12). TO BRAIZE OR POÊLER, SMOTHER OR SAUTER (Pour Braiser, Poêler, Étuver ou Sauter).

Braizing meat is to cook a piece of meat in a saucepan, lining the bottom with bardes or slices of fat pork, slices of veal, carrots and onions cut in slices, a bunch of parsley garnished with bay leaves, a little thyme, chives and one onion with cloves in it. Arrange the meat, fowl or game on top of these and moisten with some broth, then re-cover the meat with more bardes of fat pork : these meats must be cooked slowly in a slack oven, or by placing hot coals on the cover.

Poêler.—Cut up one pound of breast of pork and half a pound of raw ham, into half inch squares; six ounces of carrot, four ounces of onion in half inch squares, two bay leaves, the same quantity of thyme, a bit of mace, two cloves and some basil, the whole of these aromatics tied inside a bunch of parsley. Melt the pork with the vegetables and bouquet, not letting it color, then place on top a fat pullet prepared and trussed as for an entrée, covering the breasts with slices of peeled lemon, and bardes of fat pork tied on with a string; pour over some fat broth from the stock-pot and also some white broth to moisten to half the height, being careful to renew the moistening at times so that the same quantity always remains.

Smothering meat is to cook it slowly in a good stock without evaporation taking place, so that it cooks entirely and retains its natural flavor. Smothered meats must always be thoroughly cooked.

Sauter.—Either in a sauteuse or in a pan; let the article cook rapidly on a quick fire tossing backward, forward, and frequently. We sauté potatoes, etc. Chickens or tenderloin are sautéd either in fat or oil on a moderate, but well regulated fire, turning the meats over when they are a fine color.

(13). TO BREAD WITH BREAD CRUMBS, ENGLISH, FLOUR, MILANESE CRACKERS AND DEVILED (Pour Paner à la Panure, à l'Anglaise, à la Farine, à la Milanaise, à la Poudre de Cracker et à la Diable).

Bread Crumbs.—We generally bread crumb all substances that are to be broiled or fried; if for broiling, they must first be coated with oil or melted butter, then laid in bread crumbs, or white breading, or else in bread raspings, or brown crumbs as explained below.

For substances to be fried, such as croquettes, roll them first in white bread crumbs, then dip them in beaten eggs strained through a Chinese strainer, or else put four eggs in a bowl with salt, pepper, a tablespoonful of oil, the same quantity of water, and strain all through a strainer.

Drain quickly and roll them again in white bread crumbs, and smooth the surfaces either by rolling them on a table or else use the blade of a knife.

To Bread Crumb, English Style.—Use only the yolk of the eggs instead of whole ones, mixing for each ten yolks, ten ounces of melted butter.

White Bread Crumb.—Is used for breading meats, fish and all substances to be fried; this breading is prepared with slightly stale bread, cutting off the crusts, and grating or rubbing the crumbs in a cloth, then passing it through a sieve (Fig. 95.), it must be kept in a cool, dry place, spreading it out and stirring at times.

Brown Bread Crumbs.—Is prepared with white bread dried in a heater and slightly browned in a very slack oven and afterward pounded and sifted through a sieve (Fig. 95).

To Bread with Flour.—Dip the articles such as fish, etc., in seasoned milk, then roll them in flour. For egg-plant, roll them merely in flour, omitting the milk.

To Bread Crumb à la Milanaise.—Mix bread crumbs and grated parmesan cheese, half and half; dip the substances to be breaded, in melted butter, then lay them in the cheese and bread-crumb mixture, equalizing well the crumbs with the blade of a knife.

To Bread with Powdered Crackers.—Dip the substance in beaten egg and its equal quantity of milk and then roll them in powdered crackers.

To Bread à la Diable (deviled).—Season first the substances, then coat them over with mustard and dip them in beaten eggs and roll them lastly in bread-crumbs.

(14). BREASTS OF PORK SALTED AND SMOKED, ENGLISH BACON (Lard de Poitrine Salé et Fumé. Petit salé à l'Anglaise).

If needed for summer use, begin toward the end of March to dry-salt some breasts of pork for four days, then pack them tight in a salting tub and cover over with a thin layer of salt. Pour over them a freshly made, and highly salted brine, place on top a perforated cover, and lay over some heavy stones, so that the breasts are entirely submerged, and leave them in this state until needed, setting the tub in a cool well-aired place.

This salt pork will keep well until the fall, although it will be much saltier than if prepared in the usual way. The usual way is to wash the breasts and put them in brine in a special salting tub without any other meat; use a fork to remove them from the brine, as the hands cause fermentation, and when the salt pork is needed for use, it can be unsalted in cold water for several hours or till sufficiently done. Bacon or smoked salt pork is prepared the same, putting it in a brine half as strong and keeping it in a 50 degree Fahrenheit temperature, but no more. Drain and dry in an aired place, then smoke for three days in the cold.

(15). BRINE (Saumure).

Brine is used for the preservation of meats and at the same time to give them the taste of any preferred aroma; for this reason we select among the many ways that are employed in different countries, one that we are sure will answer for our present needs.

Boil in a large kettle twenty-five quarts of water, twenty-four pounds of salt, two pounds of saltpetre, three pounds of brown sugar and two ounces of carbonate of soda. Into a bag put a mixture weighing ten ounces, including thyme, bayleaf, sage, rosemary, juniper berries, savory, having more of each as desired, or less, if a certain taste displeases. After the salt is dissolved, leave the liquid to cool and then weigh it with a salt weight; with this it should be twelve degrees.

To salt the meats, be careful to accomplish this when dry, by rubbing the meat with salt and a little saltpetre, and then let rest for twenty-four hours before putting it in brine. Strain the brine and cover all the salted parts and leave it in a cool place during the operation. The time needed for salting is according to the size of the pieces.

A ham weighing seventeen pounds requires twenty-five days; a breast weighing twelve pounds requires fifteen days; a shoulder weighing fifteen pounds requires twenty days.

These indications are for meats to be eaten unsmoked. In case they should be smoked leave them ten days longer. Soak for twelve hours in cold water and then hang them in a smoking room or else in a big chimney, having them smoke slowly with oak shavings mixed with thyme, bayleaf, sage, etc.

To Salt Hams.—Put into a large kettle one pound of salt, four ounces of saltpetre, six ounces of brown sugar, thyme, bayleaf, basil, two ounces of juniper berries, a quarter of an ounce of botanic calament, all tied up in a bag, and when the salt has dissolved by boiling, remove from the fire, let cool to settle the brine and then pour off the clear part. Burn some aromatic herbs in a barrel, put in the hams, pour the brine, already strained through a sieve, over, close the barrel and leave it for eighteen days; drain out the hams, hang them up for twelve days in a well-aired cool place, then hang them in the chimney for twenty days. Wrap them in sheets of paper and hang in a dry place.

For Winter Hams.—These hams can only be kept during the winter. Have two hundred pounds of small corn-fed hams; rub over well with salt, then put them into a barrel and leave them for three days in a very cool place. Three days later put them into another barrel, cover over with salt brine, having sufficient salt to allow a potato to float on the surface; the hams must be entirely immersed in the brine, cover with a board and a weight atop. Twelve days after change them into another barrel and pour the brine again over, this is so that they change positions and salt easier.

After another lapse of twelve days, drain and put them to soak in cold water for twelve hours; drain once more, leave to dry in the open air for eight days, then smoke them in a smoke house for two days with hickory wood.

(16). CLARIFIED AND PURIFIED BUTTER (Beurre Clarifié et Épuré).

Clarified.—To clarify butter it should first be melted so as to extract all the buttermilk, letting it cook slowly; skim and when well despumated from all its impurities and it begins to smoke then it is ready; strain it through a fine piece of linen and keep to use when needed.

Purified.—Melt some butter in a deep saucepan, boil it for two or three minutes, remove, let stand to settle, then skim and pass it through a fine sieve pouring off the top only so to leave the sediment on the bottom.

(17). BUTTER FOR BUTTERING MOLDS (Beurre Pour Beurrer les Moules).

Melt one pound of veal kidney suet by chopping it up finely, then putting it into a saucepan with half a pint of water on a slow fire, stir occasionally to prevent its fastening on to the bottom of the saucepan and when the fat is limpid, add the same weight of fresh, saltless butter; stir until the butter and fat are perfectly clear.

Cold Butter for Buttering Molds.—It suffices only to knead some unsalted butter on the table to extract all its moisture and give it body, then put it into a cloth, sponge it off, put it in a pan in a warm temperature and work it until it becomes soft as cream.

(18). TO PREPARE LIQUID CARAMEL (Caramel Liquide).

Liquid caramel is most necessary; it is used for coloring broths, gravies and even sauces, when their tints are found to be too light, still caramel should be used with discretion, for it is apt to give a bitter taste to the colored liquids into which it is added. Put a few spoonfuls of powdered sugar into a copper pan, stir it over a slow fire, then remove it on to a slower one to let cook until it becomes quite brown, and the smoke arising from it is whitish, this is a sign that it is thoroughly done. Take the pan from off the fire, moisten the sugar proportionately with hot water, and allow the liquid to boil while stirring, and cook till the consistence of a light syrup is obtained. Caramel should be kept in a small, well-closed bottle, having a cork perforated lengthwise, so that when the bottle is turned over, the liquid can drop out slowly without it being necessary to uncork it.

(19). TO CARVE ON THE TABLE (Pour Découper à Table).

Carving should be done with ease and dexterity. It is a simple operation, yet to be a perfect carver one must have a few ideas of the natural construction of the various pieces to be cut up. The meat to be carved must be laid on a dish without any sauce or garnishing, so as to be able to turn it around to the most convenient position. The tools indispensable for carving consist of a solid two or three-pronged fork, a good, keen, sharp-bladed knife and a pair of carving

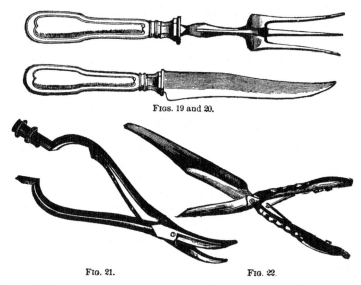

FIGS. 19 and 20.

FIG. 21.   FIG. 22.

scissors. It is essential to begin on the most practical side, and also to be able to distinguish all of the best parts so as to carve without deteriorating from their appearance or without injuring their gastronomical qualities.

It is an easy study, but one that ought not to be neglected, for what embarrasses and confuses a carver is when he is unable to find the different joints, or else when he begins cutting a piece of meat against the grain. It is to facilitate this operation that we deem it necessary to give a few hints and suggestions, and as almost each piece is accompanied by a design, it will be easy to learn how to carve those meats usually served whole on the table.

(20). FISH; HOW TO CARVE (Pour Découper le Poisson).

A general rule almost always observed for cutting up fish at table, is to use only silver implements; this to be specially followed for boiled and braised fish. Fried fish is the only kind where knives are allowable. To carve boiled fish, use either a silver fish slice, spoon or fork. The lines

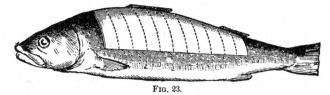

FIG. 23.

traced on the back of the fish (Fig. 23) denote in what direction it must be cut, observing, as the figure indicates, that it should be on the opposite side to the belly, for on this part the fleshiest meat is found. To cut up a bass, salmon, etc., or any fish of a long shape, first trace a line following the course of the bone, beginning at the head and finishing at the tail, then divide this back piece into slices and lay each one on a separate plate. All meats taken from the back and sides of a fish are fleshier and preferable to those found on the belly.

Fish slice.—A name given to a certain utensil with which fish is cut at the table to serve it on plates. These slices are made of silver or silver-plate; the blade is broad and sharpened

Fɪɢ. 24.

on one side, fastened to a handle. Smaller slicers are also placed on the table to facilitate serving flat cakes, flawns and tarts that are difficult to lift with a spoon or a knife.

(21). PARTRIDGES; HOW TO CARVE (Pour Découper les Perdreaux).

There are various ways of carving partridges; when young, simply divide them in two lengthwise; when large, either detach the hind part from the breast or divide each one in three on their length, that is, cut a part of the breast with the leg on, so to leave the upper breast adhere to a part of the carcass; then detach with a pair of carving scissors; this is demonstrated in the

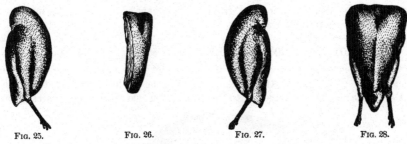

| Fɪɢ. 25. | Fɪɢ. 26. | Fɪɢ. 27. | Fɪɢ. 28. |

drawing. If the hind part is detached with the breast, then this should be divided into three parts and returned to their original position; in this manner it is difficult to perceive that the partridge has been cut, for it is given its natural form. Large partridges need simply cutting in four.

(22). PHEASANT AND GROUSE OR PRAIRIE CHICKEN; HOW TO CARVE (Pour Découper un Faisan une Grouse ou un Tétras).

A pheasant can be carved the same way as a large chicken (Fig. 35), which means to cut it in five pieces, but should it be extra large two fillets can be taken from each side of the breast, leaving an upper or central part of the breast. The legs are generally dry and tough, yet should they have to be served, cut each one in two.

Grouse or prairie chicken can be carved exactly the same.

(23). ROAST BEEF; HOW TO CARVE RIBS (Pour Découper une Pièce de Côtes de Bœuf Rôti).

Fɪɢ. 29.

American roast beef is taken from the ribs; sometimes seven ribs are served, but the piece containing only six is far more advantageous, while the four rib piece, cut from the short loin is better still. Roast beef must be carved on the table, or else on the dining-room sideboard, for when cut beforehand it becomes dry and loses the best part of its juices. Roast beef is to be cut in thin slices, leaving a small piece of fat adhering to each one; at once place them on hot plates and be careful to baste with a little of the gravy flowing from the meat on to the dish.

(24). TENDERLOIN OF BEEF; HOW TO CARVE (Pour Découper un Filet de Bœuf).

Whether the tenderloin be roasted or braized, when cutting off slices for the guests, do not let them be too thick or too thin; remove half an inch of the sole from the tenderloin (Fig. 30) and

FIG. 30.

cut the meat into even thin slices, crosswise if the tenderloin be large; if thin, have the slices cut on the bias, but do not penetrate through the sole piece; pare the bottom free of fat. Serve these slices on very hot plates with a little of its gravy, independent of the accompanying sauce or garnishing, which must be served separately.

(25). HOT HAM; HOW TO CARVE (Pour Découper un Jambon Chaud).

Ham served hot is better when carved at the table, for it retains its essential juices. The most delicate part of a ham is the kernel, it being the fleshiest: this is to be cut in not too thick slices, leaving the fat adhering to the meat, then placed on hot plates; serve a good

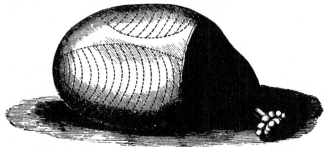

FIG. 31.

sauce separately in a sauceboat. When the ham is accompanied by a garnishing, it must also be served separately and offered to the guests. In order to have a ham prepared for handing round, it should first be cut up, then reconstructed the same as should a leg of mutton.

(26). LEG OF MUTTON; HOW TO CARVE (Pour Découper un Gigot de Mouton).

If the leg be roasted, carve it at the table or in the dining-room. It must be served on a dish without gravy, sauce or garnishing. Seize the end bone of the leg, having the kernel uppermost, for this is to be cut first, it being the fleshiest and the best part of the leg. The slices must be

FIG. 32.

broad and thin, to be served on very hot plates, each one accompanied by a little of the good gravy flowing from the meat. Should the leg have a garnishing this must be served apart.

Lamb is carved the same way. The bone end of the leg to be trimmed with a specially made handle, or else a fancy favor frill. When the leg is to be presented at the table, it should be previously carved and reconstructed to its original shape.

(27). SADDLE OF MUTTON, SADDLE OF LAMB, AND SADDLE OF VENISON, ROASTED; HOW TO CARVE (Pour Découper une Selle de Mouton, d'Agneau, et de Chevreuil Rôti).

The dish containing these roasts must be placed on the table before the person who is to carve; the loin end to be turned to the left, for from this end is the saddle begun. There are two ways of carving the roasted saddle; the first way is to cut the slices on the length of the meat, slightly bias; see braized saddle, Fig. 33. They to be neither too long nor too thin. For the second way, the slices are cut the entire length of the meat, but in every case serve on very hot plates, adding a little of the good gravy from the meat and serving another gravy separately in a sauceboat.

(28). BRAIZED SADDLE OF MUTTON; HOW TO CARVE (Pour Découper une Selle de Mouton Braisée).

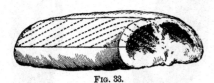

FIG. 33.

To have a braized saddle of mutton carved on the table, it should be placed on a hot dish without any gravy or garnishing; first make two incisions, one on each side, just between the fat of the flank or the kernel, then cut the large fillets across in rather thick slices; avoid having too much fat on any of them. A saddle of mutton can be carved in the kitchen without deteriorating from its good qualities; in this case, remove the fillets entirely, pare free of all fat and cut them across in half inch thick slices; return them to their original position, and when serving, hand around at the same time, both garnishing and a sauceboatful of gravy or sauce.

(29). LOIN AND KERNEL OF VEAL; HOW TO CARVE (Pour Découper une Longe ou une Noix de Veau).

Before carving a loin of veal, first detach the tenderloin and kidney; cut the loin into crosswise slices, not too thin, and place each one on a hot plate, adding a slice of the kidney or minion fillet, also a little good gravy or any sauce accompanying this remove, only serving it separately.

On Fig. 327 will be found a larded kernel of veal, served as an entrée on a round dish. In order to cut the kernel, it requires to be held firmly by the fork on the udder side, enabling the larded meat to be cut in not too thick slices. Serve on hot plates with a little gravy, independent of the sauce or garnishing that accompanies it.

(30). GOOSE OR DUCK; HOW TO CARVE (Pour Découper une Oie ou un Canard).

Geese and ducks are carved the same as other poultry; when young, their legs can be served, but if large and older it were better to leave them undetached on the carcass. To carve a goose with ease, the breast must be turned toward the carver, as shown in Fig. 34. The meats of each side of the breast are to be cut in not too thin fillets and immediately placed on hot plates, then basted over with a little good gravy. When the geese are stuffed, add to each plateful a small piece of the dressing. If serving the legs of a young goose or duck it is obligatory, first to detach them from the carcass and divide in medium-sized pieces with the carving scissors. Large tame ducks are carved the same as geese, and young ducklings can be separated in four parts. The breast alone of wild ducks is used, lifting one fillet from off each side or both fillets may be divided lengthwise in two; serve these on a little good gravy taken from the carcasses, after breaking them up and pressing out all the juice; heat this gravy slightly with lemon juice, salt, mignonette and finely chopped blanched shallot.

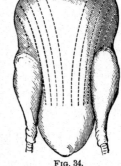

FIG. 34.

(31). PIGEONS; HOW TO CARVE (Pour Découper des Pigeons).

Young pigeons are served whole or simply cut lengthwise in two; when very large, separate the hind part from the breast part and make two pieces of each of these.

(32). PULLET OR CAPON; HOW TO CARVE (Pour Découper une Poularde ou un Chapon).

A large piece of poultry that requires to be carved at table, calls for the greatest care in order to have all the pieces neat, even and of a proper size, neither too large nor too small. A pair of carving scissors will be found indispensable. To proceed with ease have the pieces laid on a dish in front of the carver; should the pinions be left on the wings, cut them off with the scissors, then cut from the breast one small slice, taking the minion fillet along; from the remainder of the breast cut another pretty slice through the entire length. If the breast of the chicken be very large cut from it another slice without encroaching on the top part of the breast; after one side is finished cut the other without changing its position and as soon as the fillets are all removed, detach the thighs from the carcass by disjointing them, but first cut away the skin from the carcass just where the thigh begins; in this way it can be lifted off with a fork assisting with the blade of a knife. As soon as one thigh is detached, separate the leg at the knee bone with the scissors and divide the thigh in two, either across or on the length.

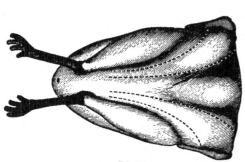

FIG. 35.   FIG. 36.   FIG. 37.

The carcass can also be divided transversely in two or three pieces. The whole operation must be dexterous and speedy as all eyes are apt to be watching the carver, therefore he must not hesitate, but proceed bravely to the end. When a medium-sized fowl is to be carved, it can first be divided into four parts, detaching the legs from the carcass, then the breasts without making any upper breast. With these four parts eight pieces can be secured, two from each leg and two from each breast, cutting these on their length according to the lines marked in the figures.

(33). ROAST TURKEY; HOW TO CARVE (Pour Découper une Dinde Rôtie).

To be able to carve a turkey at table it requires a certain amount of self-possession, for they are frequently very fat, and, therefore, more difficult to manipulate than a pullet. Unless it cannot be avoided, the legs of a roast turkey should not be detached, serving only the breast part: this is done in two distinct ways: the first consists of cutting the breast pieces in crosswise slices slightly on the bias as shown in the figure; the second by cutting the fillets lengthwise from the breasts with-

FIG. 38.

out having any upper breast part; in either case it is proper before beginning to detach the wings from both sides with a part of the breast adhering. When the thighs are wanted, detach them one after the other; clip off the drum sticks at the knee joint and then divide the second joint meats in pieces, leaving the drum stick whole. The gravy that is to be served with a roast turkey should always be in a separate sauceboat.

(34). CHOPPED PARSLEY, TRUFFLES, ONIONS, SHALLOTS, MUSHROOMS, TONGUE AND CORAL (Pour Hacher le Persil, les Truffes, les Oignons, les Échalotes, les Champignons, la Langue et le Corail).

For Chopped Parsley see No. 123.

For Truffles.—Slice them and wipe off all the adhering moisture, then chop them up fine, spread them on a tin sheet covered with a sheet of paper, dry in the air and keep them in a cool place till needed.

For Onions.—Cut them in two, suppress the end stalk, and slice them perpendicularly, then cut them horizontally into squares more or less large; they may afterward be chopped up so as to loosen them, and have them finer; wash them in cold water, drain on a cloth to extract all the liquid; proceed the same for shallots, without cutting them in two and put them on a plate in a cool place.

For Mushrooms.—If they are already cooked, drain them well, slice, then chop them up; if raw, peel off the skin, wash them nicely, cut in squares, then chop; use them immediately.

For Red Beef Tongue.—Use only the thin end of the tongue, slice, chop and lay it on a tin sheet covered with a sheet of paper, expose them to a draught to dry, chop once more until very fine, then pass them through a sieve, and keep in a cool place till needed.

For Lobster Coral.—Take out the red part found inside of a boiled lobster, wash it nicely, changing the water frequently, dry it in the air, then chop it up very fine to pass through a sieve (Fig. 96); spread it on a tin sheet over a sheet of paper, dry it in the air, and keep it for use in a cool place.

(35). TO COAT JELLY MOLDS AND MOLD JELLIES (Pour Chemiser les Moules à Gelée et Mouler les Gelées).

If the mold need be only lightly coated, it is sufficient just to cool it on ice, then pour into it the cold liquid jelly and move it around so that it reaches all the sides; put the mold back on to the ice, and begin the operation again a quarter of an hour later, but should the coating of jelly be required thick, then glue over the top of the mold a heavy paper, and when the gum is dry, cut a ring in the surface of the paper with the tip of a small knife, leaving all around a margin a quarter of an inch, then pour some jelly into the mold, and turn it round on the ice inclining it in such a way that the coat acquires the necessary thickness on all its sides.

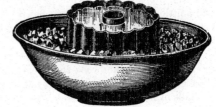

FIG. 39.

To Mold Jellies.—Put some ice into a small vessel, add its equal quantity of water, and set it in a cylindrical fancy mold; fill this up with some cold liquid jelly, lay on top and half an inch higher than the mold a tin sheet or plate, cover this with broken ice without any salt and after the jelly is thoroughly cold and firm, unmold it. In order to accomplish this, dip the mold quickly into hot water at one hundred and fifteen to one hundred and twenty degrees Fahrenheit; wipe it briskly and overturn it on to a cold dish as soon as the jelly detaches, and then remove the mold.

(36). TO PREPARE COCOANUT (Préparation de la Noix de Coco).

Break a cocoanut across in two, exactly in the center; slip the blade of a thin round-tipped knife between the nut and the shell, push it in with the right hand and turn the cocoa with the left; detach and take out the entire half nut; remove the outer skin covering the nut with a vegetable knife (Fig. 156), and when it is all peeled, throw the nut into cold water; drain and scrape it on a coarse grater. Use a part of it for roasting by putting the grated nut on a sheet of paper into a moderate oven and keep the remainder into a stone jar in the ice-box mixing it with an equal weight of sugar.

(37). VEGETABLE COLORS (Couleurs Végétales).

Spinach green is frequently used for coloring purées, soups, butters, sauces and sugar. It is the healthiest coloring matter, and if possible use no other. Spinach green is prepared with very green, fresh spinach, well washed, pounded in a mortar and when well reduced to a paste, extract all the juice through a coarse cloth, and place this in an untinned copper sugar pan, and heat it till it decomposes, then pour it over a fine sieve so the pulp or coloring matter remains on top; the strained liquid is colorless and useless. For yellow, use a decoction of saffron or dandelion flowers; for red, employed for coloring bisques, orchanet dissolved in butter is used. The roucou annotto also gives a yellowish red and is much used. Vegetable colors, and clarified carmine, Breton Landrin, are those mostly employed. Breton Landrin green is beautiful for coloring sugar cooked to crack, as it is not detrimental to its transparency.

Colorings : Carmine and Cochineal Red.—Take two ounces of No. 42 carmine, broken in pieces; wet with a little cold water; crush in a small mortar and dilute with a little twenty-five degree syrup. Besides this, boil two quarts of syrup also to twenty-five degrees, mix in the carmine, boil up once, strain through a napkin and leave to cool, then add a few coffeespoonfuls of liquid ammonia and pour into bottles.

For Red Cochineal.—Finely pound five ounces of fine cochineal; place it in a copper pan and moisten with a quart of water, adding three ounces of cream of tartar, three ounces of alum and six ounces of sugar; set the pan on the fire and let the liquid reduce to half; now put in two gills of spirit of wine; boil up once, strain through a napkin and pour into bottles.

(38), COURT-BOUILLON, PLAIN. (Court-Bouillon Simple).

Plain court-bouillon is used for cooking large fishes, such as salmon, halibut, bass and lobsters.

This court-bouillon is prepared with vinegar, roots and sliced onions, a large bunch of parsley, salt and water. If the fish has to be plunged into boiling water, cook the court-bouillon for seven or eight minutes previous to putting it in, and if on the contrary, then pour the liquid over the fish, and bring it to a boil.

(39), COURT BOUILLON WITH WINE (Court Bouillon au Vin).

The court bouillon is a most necessary auxiliary in all kitchens, where it plays an important part; it is prepared fresh every day, and special care is taken to have it good, for in it the principal fishes are cooked, and with it the sauce Normande is made, so useful for hurried work.

First prepare a broth with the heads of large, fresh fish, some roots, onions, a bunch of parsley and a little salt; let it boil very slowly for half an hour, then strain and skim off the fat, and leave it to settle until clear. From the bones and heads of bass, sheepshead, blackfish, etc., the best fish stock is obtained.

Cook a mirepoix composed of sliced roots, shallots and onions, add to it the fragments of fish as explained above and cook these together for a few moments on a good fire; moisten with two or three gills of white wine and let it fall to a glaze over a brisk fire; moisten it again at once with two gills of fish broth and also let this fall to a glaze, then remoisten to their height with good fish broth and a little white wine, add a bunch of aromatic herbs, a bunch of parsley, and some fresh mushroom peelings, boil the liquid while skimming and set it on one side of the range to despumate for a quarter of an hour, skimming it carefully. Strain the stock through a sieve, let it settle, and pour off the top into a glazed vessel, and if it be not succulent enough, then reduce it again; keep it in a cool place.

This stock may be easily kept from one day to another, if care be taken to keep the vessel and its contents incrusted on ice. This court bouillon may also be moistened with red wine; in either case, it must be prepared with the greatest care possible.

(40), ALMOND CREAM (Crème d'Amandes).

Pound one pound of almonds with one pound of loaf sugar, slowly adding four small eggs and some orange flower water. When the almonds have become a fine paste, take them from the mortar and transfer to a vessel, incorporating in six eggs, one at the time and one pound of fresh butter softened and divided in small pats.

(41), ENGLISH CREAM WITH COFFEE (Crème Anglaise au Café).

Boil a quart of milk, add to it four ounces of freshly roasted coffee beans, cover the saucepan and leave to infuse for half an hour. Beat eight egg-yolks with half a pound of sugar, dilute with the boiling coffee milk strained through a fine colander; stand the saucepan on a slow fire, stir the cream until it becomes quite thick, without allowing it to boil, then take it off, strain through a sieve and pour it into a vessel, stir frequently till cold.

(42), ENGLISH CREAM WITH VANILLA, LEMON OR ORANGE ZEST (Crème Anglaise à la Vanille ou aux Zestes de Citron ou d'Orange).

Beat in a saucepan half a pound of sugar with ten raw egg-yolks; mingle both well together and dilute with a quart of boiling milk, having had half a vanilla stick broken in pieces infused therein. Cook the cream on a moderate fire, stirring with a spoon

dry for a few minutes; they are now to be placed in larger buttered rings, or surrounded with bands of buttered paper to support the paste while cooking; line the inside with buttered paper and fill with raw rice; cook in a moderate oven; when done remove from the rings, empty out the rice, brush the crusts with an egg-wash and put in the oven to color nicely.

To Make Puff Paste Crusts Plain or with Fluted Cutter.—Cut the paste round or oval shaped in any desired size, arrange them on a moist baking sheet, a short distance apart, and prick them; moisten the edges with a brush and apply around this a band of the same paste three-sixteenths of an inch in thickness by five-sixteenths of an inch in width; fasten the ends of the band together, egg the surface and bake these crusts in a moderate oven the same as small bouchées.

(53). EGGING AND MOISTENING (Dorer et Mouiller).

Egging With Whole Eggs.—Beat the eggs with half as much water and run them through a sieve.

Egg-yolks Alone.—Stir the yolks with the same volume of water and strain.

With Milk.—Mix as much milk as yolks, beat well together and strain.

Moistening.—Moisten lightly with water, baking sheets or else flats of paste on which another is to be laid in order to fasten the two together.

For both egging and moistening use a feather or a very soft hair brush (Fig. 184).

(54). TO BEAT UP THE WHITE OF EGGS (Pour Fouetter les Blancs d'Œufs).

FIG. 46.

Although the eggs intended for beating up the white should be perfectly fresh, still they must not be newly laid, for when these are used they are liable to become a greenish color, while baking. Procure an egg-beater or a whip made for this purpose, and a small untinned basin, separate most carefully the yolks from the whites, and put these into the basin with a very little salt, then begin to whip, slowly at the beginning but proceed gradually to increase the velocity of the motion as the volume increases so as to allow them to absorb all the air possible, which gives them their consistency. Should the whites threaten to turn, they must be whipped again until smooth, adding to them a handful of powdered sugar or a few drops of citric acid.

(55). FAT PREPARED FOR FRYING (Graisse Préparée Pour la Friture).

The preference is generally given to beef kidney suet; cut it in half inch pieces and place these in an untinned iron pan with one gill of water for every pound of fat; cook on a slow fire stirring carefully from time to time so that it cannot adhere to the bottom. When very clear and it ceases to froth it is a sign that it is done, then strain through a sieve or cloth.

(56). FAT FOR SOCLES AND FLOWERS (Graisse Pour Socles et pour Fleurs).

Fat for Socles.—Remove the skin and all the membranes from twenty pounds of mutton kidney suet, cut it up in half inch squares, and put this grease into twenty-five quarts of cold water with one pound of carbonate of soda, wash well the fat, change the water frequently, drain, then melt it on a slow fire, being careful to stir it so that it does not adhere to the bottom of the pan, nor brown in the slightest, add to it eight ounces of Siam benzoin and as soon as it is thoroughly rendered out, mix in the same quantity of lard, strain through a fine towel, and put it aside to cool slightly; then add a little ultra-marine blue. Stir with a whisk until cool, and having body enough to be worked; fasten a mandrel on a round or oval board, begin working at the bottom of the foundation with a profile, previously soaked in cold water and kept wet, and when the base is very firm, continue coating the mandrel with the fat, and profiling it until the whole socle is finished. Decorate with natural or grease flowers as below forming a wreath around the top of the mandrel, or if preferred festoon it, leaving a few inches of the decoration fall in scallops gracefully around.

To Make Grease Flowers.—Have half as much fat prepared for socles as virgin wax, melting both together; color them in various colors while the fat is still hot and place in vessels keeping each color separate; have for instance: white, pink, red, green, brown, etc., let cool. Twelve hours later unmold the fat on to a wet napkin and scrape into fine shavings with a strong knife, then gather all of these in a damp cloth so as to soften and have it get smooth by kneading it till it becomes ductile as clay; roll into small balls and place these between two wet cloths; rub the top of each ball with a piece of smooth ice until it is very thin so that it resembles the petal of a real flower for example, to make a rose arrange some pink fat around a small stick to imitate the center of the flower, fasten on the petals all around as quickly as they are prepared and when there are sufficient, pull out the stick and begin another until enough flowers are obtained. Fasten them on to the upper border of a socle. This same grease can be used for modeling.

(57). TO SCALE AND CLEAN FISH; TO SKIN EELS (Pour Écailler le Poisson, le Nettoyer et Dépouiller les Anguilles).

For English Soles.—Remove the black skin, starting at the tail with a knife, then pulling it off. If trout be required for boiling, they must be cooked with the scales on. German carp should not be scaled.

For Salmon, Turbot, Bass or Mullets.—Scrape the outside with a strong knife in order to remove the scales. All fish must be emptied either by the gills or by an opening made in the belly; cut away the fins with a pair of strong scissors.

To Skin Eels.—They must be hung up by the head on a hook, remove a little piece of the skin all around below the fins so as to be able to catch hold of it, then grasp it with a cloth, and pull it down the whole length of the body, turning it inside out. Shave the spinal bone with a sharp knife, and in a contrary direction from the bone, or else the entire bone may be removed by detaching it from the flesh, beginning at the extreme thin end of the tail, and pulling it out entirely, the same for the ventral.

(58). FONDANT (Fondant).

Put into a small untinned copper basin two pounds of loaf sugar, moisten it with sufficient water to melt it, about one pint, and put the basin on a good fire to bring the sugar to a boil; skim it carefully and so long as the impurities rise to the surface and continue boiling till the sugar is cooked to the degree of ball; then pour it on to a marble table or slab and keep it in position by four bars of iron, an inch square, and the length needed; when it is thoroughly cold work it with a spatula until it becomes a white and creamy paste; set it in an earthen vessel, and keep it in a cool place to use when needed. This fondant can be flavored and colored according to taste.

(59). FORCEMEATS; REMARKS ON (Observations sur les Farces).

Forcemeats are indispensable for performing fine work and are liked by good livers; they are principally used for hors-d'œuvre, garnishings, removes and entrées; for stuffing breasts or shoulders of veal, poultry, game and fish. They are also necessary to form borders, for holding the garnishing and for large timbales; they must always be prepared in advance with the very freshest meats, otherwise they are likely to be of little good and liable to spoil, this being of the greatest importance to observe, and be sure to keep them on ice until needed. Always be careful when composing a menu, not to have too many dishes containing forcemeats, for they will detract from the simplicity and natural plainness of a dinner.

(60). TO PREPARE AND MAKE FORCEMEATS AND TO RECTIFY THEM (Pour Préparer et Faire les Farces et les Rectifier).

Fig. 47.   Fig. 48.

Chicken.—Use only the lean and well pared meats of poultry or game, some panada, fresh butter, or cooked and cold veal udder, raw egg-yolks or else the whites, or sometimes whole eggs, salt and spices, also cold sauces or else raw cream. Pass the meat once or twice through a machine to remove the nerves (Fig. 47); afterward pound it to a pulp so it can readily pass through a metal sieve fitting on to the mortar (Fig. 48); pound the meat once more, then add the panada, the butter or udder, continuing to pound all the time, and then add the eggs singly without ceasing to pound and the seasonings; pass through a strong hair sieve. Put this into a thin tin vessel, set it on ice and stir for a few moments with a spoon in order to have it perfectly smooth, keep in a cool place until needed.

FIG. 49.

Game.—To make game quenelle forcemeat, proceed the same as for the chicken; to have it delicate, use brown sauce or melted meat glaze, and pass the meat once more after all the ingredients are mixed in. For this it requires a strong hair sieve, or one of fine tinned wire; stand this sieve on a round dish, slightly larger than itself, so it can receive the force-meat as it falls through; put only a small quantity on the sieve at the time; press it forcibly with a large wooden spoon to have it pass through rapidly, and when all is finished, place it in a tin vessel and stir it for a few moments with a spoon to render it smooth and keep it in a cool place until needed.

To Rectify Forcemeats.—Try a little piece, formed into a half inch ball, in boiling water or in the oven, and if too consistent add some cream or velouté, for white forcemeats, and espagnole or melted glaze for brown game. If too weak, a little pounded panada is to be added, mixing it in gradually with some egg-yolks, whites or whole eggs.

(61). TO PREPARE BREAD STUFFING, AMERICAN AND ENGLISH STYLE (Pour Préparer la Farce au Pain à l'Américaine et à l'Anglaise).

Bread stuffing is used to stuff poultry and game and sometimes fish. Soak in water or milk a quarter of a pound of bread-crumbs, squeeze out all the liquid and put the bread into a saucepan; beat it up with a spoon and add to it a little boiled milk or broth, so as to form a paste the same as for a panada, remove it from the fire and set it aside to cool, season and mix in five or six table-spoonfuls of chopped-up onions, either raw or cooked in butter, some chopped parsley and three or four raw egg-yolks. Bread stuffing may also be prepared without cooking, only mixing white bread-crumbs with butter or chopped suet, raw egg-yolks, parsley and chopped onions.

American Style.—Steep half a pound of bread-crumbs in milk and when well soaked extract all the liquid; put it over a slow fire in a saucepan and stir up with a spoon, to have it dry; add two ounces of onions, cut in dice, and fried colorless in butter, and when the stuffing is cold, add four ounces either of butter or beef marrow chopped fine, salt, pepper, sage, thyme, parsley, minced green celery leaves and four raw egg-yolks.

English.—Have half a pound of bread-crumbs steeped in white broth and all the liquid extracted; put it on the fire to dry, then add four ounces of beef suet well skinned and chopped up fine; season with salt, pepper, nutmeg and add three ounces of chopped onions fried and lightly colored, one whole egg and four raw egg-yolks.

(62). CHICKEN OR GAME FORCEMEAT WITHOUT PANADA (Farce de Volaille ou de Gibier Sans Panade).

Ingredients.—One pound of breast of chicken or game, raw and free of sinews; eight egg-yolks, half a pound of butter, salt, red pepper, nutmeg and two gills of well reduced velouté (No. 415). Pass twice through the machine (Fig. 47). One pound of raw and nerveless chicken or game fillets, or else chop the pieces very fine and pound them to reduce to a fine paste; rub this through a round quenelle sieve (Fig. 142). Incorporate into it eight egg-yolks one by one, also half a pound of butter divided into small pieces; season with salt, red pepper and nutmeg, and add two gills of well reduced velouté (No. 415). Work the forcemeat well in a mortar, so that it acquires a good consistence; test it and if necessary to rectify (see No. 60). This forcemeat is used to make either red, white or green quenelles.

(63). FORCEMEAT OF CHICKEN, FISH OR GAME WITH WHIPPED CREAM AND BUTTER
(Farce de Volaille, Poisson ou Gibier avec Crème Fouettée et Beurre).

Pound half a pound of chicken fillets after passing them twice through the machine (Fig. 47), then press this pulp through a sieve and return it to the mortar to pound once more, mixing in with it little by little, five ounces of butter, one whole egg and four yolks, or instead of the egg and yolks substitute four egg-whites. Season with salt, nutmeg and red pepper, then take out the forcemeat and set it into a thin metal vessel; lay this on the ice, beat up the forcemeat well for a few minutes, incorporating slowly into it the volume of one pint of very firm, well drained whipped cream, one pint of cream before being whipped will produce about three pints after being whipped; use the same preparation for forcemeats of game and fish, increasing or decreasing the panada and eggs according to the consistency of the viands employed.

(64). CHICKEN LIVER, FINE BAKING FORCEMEAT (Farce Fine de Foies de Volaille à Gratin).

Heat four ounces of grated lard, add to it one pound of sautéd cold chicken livers; pound well half a pound of bread-crumb panada (No. 121), add the livers a little at the time, pounding continually, fry in butter one tablespoonful of shallots, adding to them two tablespoonfuls of mushrooms, half a tablespoonful of truffles, both chopped, and a teaspoonful of chopped parsley; when all these ingredients have fried lightly add to them two gills of espagnole sauce (No. 414); let get slightly cold, then stir in one whole egg and three yolks; season with salt, pepper and nutmeg, add the chicken livers, rub all forcibly through a sieve and mix this preparation with one pound of quenelle forcemeat.

(65). CHOPPED FORCEMEAT FOR CHICKEN GALANTINES (Farce Hachis pour Galantines de Volaille).

To prepare chopped farces or sausage-meat only lean meats without any skin or nerves are to be used, and fresh fat pork. Chop up both meat and pork and in some special cases they require to be pounded after being chopped.

Farce or chopped meats for galantines of poultry is prepared with one pound of chicken or other poultry meat, and one pound of fat pork. The chicken may be replaced by lean veal, or half pork and half veal; chop all up very fine, and season with three quarters to one ounce of spiced salt (No. 168); pound well for a few minutes, then add two whole eggs, and one gill of water or cream; chopped truffles or cooked fine herbs may also be added if desired.

(66) CHOPPED FORCEMEAT FOR GAME GALANTINES (Farce Hachis pour Galantines de Gibier).

This is prepared with half game meat, either from the shoulder or thighs of hare or young rabbits, or the thighs of partridges or pheasants, and half fat pork, having a pound of each. Season with an ounce of spiced salt (No. 168). When it is well chopped mix in with it half a pound of foies gras. Strain galantine farces, but when the galantine farces of game or poultry are well chopped this is rarely required.

(67). CHOPPED FORCEMEAT FOR GAME PIE (Farce Hachis pour Pâté de Gibier).

Prepare a pound of lean veal or pork forcemeat without nerves or skin, a pound of fat pork, and season with salt, white pepper and red pepper; mince finely one ounce of onions and two ounces of carrots; fry them both in butter with thyme and bayleaf, adding the parings and carcasses of some game; moisten with a pint of white wine, and reduce till dry, then moisten once more with a pint of broth and reduce again till dry; now take out the bones, thyme and bayleaf, and pound up all the meat as well as the vegetables; rub this through a sieve and mix it in with the farce

(68). CHOPPED FORCEMEAT FOR ORDINARY SAUSAGES (Farce Hachis pour Saucisses Ordinaires).

Prepare a pound of lean, nerveless pork-meat and a pound of fat from the pig's throat; chop them up very fine, and season with three-quarters of an ounce of salt, black pepper and red pepper; when thoroughly chopped and a compact paste is formed, then mix in half a gill of water.

Another Way.—Remove the sinews from four pounds of lean fresh pork, taken from the shoulder or neck; add the same weight of not too mellow fat, from under the chine; chop together, season with a third of an ounce of salt for each pound, black pepper and red pepper to taste.

(69). CHOPPED FORCEMEAT FOR COUNTRY SAUSAGES WITH SAGE (Farce Hachis pour Saucisses de Campagne à la Sauge).

Have three pounds of corn-fed lean pork, free of all its sinews, and one pound of fat pork; cut them both into inch squares, then chop them up finely together, and season with an ounce of salt and a teaspoonful of ground black pepper, a quarter of an ounce of powdered sage, the sixth part of a teaspoonful of cayenne pepper, a bit of powdered saltpetre and a gill of water. Work well together so as to mix thoroughly.

(70). COOKED CHOPPED FORCEMEAT WITH CHESTNUTS AND WITH CHESTNUTS AND TRUFFLES (Farce Hachis Cuite aux Marrons et aux Marrons et Truffes).

For each pound of forcemeat, chop up one medium shallot; fry it colorless in butter, then add to it one pound of chopped ordinary sausage-meat (No. 68); let it cook for a few minutes, and add four ounces of chopped chicken liver for every pound of the sausage-meat; season with pepper, salt and nutmeg, and let cook for a few minutes longer, then add some chopped parsley and two pounds of cooked whole chestnuts.

With Chestnuts and Truffles.—Mix one-half truffles and one-half chestnuts with this forcemeat.

(71). CHOPPED FORCEMEAT WITH TRUFFLES (Farce Hachis aux Truffes).

Add to the chopped forcemeat for ordinary sausage-meat (No. 68), one-half pound of raw or preserved black truffles cut in slices, and mix in also half a gill of Madeira wine for every pound of sausage-meat. In winter the truffles may be added two or three days in advance, not in summer, as they are liable to mold.

(72). CODFISH FORCEMEAT FOR STUFFING FISH (Farce de Morue Fraiche Pour Farcir les Poissons).

Chop up finely one pound of codfish free of bone and skin. Break three eggs in a saucepan, season with salt and pepper and add one gill of cream and a teaspoonful of butter, cook on the fire stirring the same as for scrambled eggs, let this cool, have also two ounces of bread crumbs soaked in milk and well squeezed. Put four ounces of butter in a sautoire with two finely chopped shallots, fry without coloring, then add the fish, four ounces of mushrooms and an ounce of truffles both to be finely chopped; season with half an ounce of spiced salt (No. 168), and into it stir the scrambled eggs and the bread crumbs. Cover the saucepan and cook in the oven for an hour, after removing beat in a spoonful of chopped parsley and four raw egg-yolks. This preparation can also be used for rissoles and coulibiacs.

(73). COOKED AND RAW GAME OR CHICKEN FORCEMEAT FOR LINING CASES FOR SWEETBREADS, CHICKEN, ETC. (Farce Cuite et Crue de Gibier ou de Volaille pour Garnir les Caisses de Ris de Veau, de Volaille, etc.).

Have one pound of raw chicken or game fillets cut in dice, fry them in four ounces of butter, seasoning with salt, pepper and nutmeg, and let cook for a few minutes, then set away to cool. Begin by pounding the meat, then add gradually to it eight ounces of butter, or calf's udder in small bits, and remove the whole from the mortar. Pound ten ounces of flour and milk panada, (No. 121), add to it eight egg-yolks one by one, and then the cooked meat, and continue pounding for ten minutes longer; rub all through a fine sieve, and mix to this forcemeat one pound of raw quenelle forcemeat (No. 89); either of chicken or game. Poach one of the quenelles and rectify if necessary as explained (No. 60); four spoonfuls of cooked fine herbs may be added to this forcemeat.

(74). CREAM CHICKEN FORCEMEAT WITH BÉCHAMEL AND MUSHROOM PURÉE (Farce de Volaille à la Crème à la Béchamel et Purée de Champignons).

For this forcemeat obtain one pound of chicken or game meat without any nerves or skin, pass this twice through the machine (Fig. 47), or else chop it up and pound to pulp; season with salt, red pepper and nutmeg, and mix in with one egg-white and two gills of cream béchamel (No. 411), and two gills of mushroom purée. For the purée of mushrooms, chop up one pound of peeled fresh mushrooms, cook them in butter till they have rendered all their moisture, then season and pound them with a third of their quantity of good béchamel reduced and thickened. When cold mix the mushrooms in gradually with the forcemeat in the mortar, rub all through a fine sieve, and try it to see whether it be too solid, if so, add some sweet cream by working it in with a whip, so as to have it consistent and smooth.

(75). CHICKEN OR GAME CREAM FORCEMEAT (Farce à la Crème de Volaille ou de Gibier).

Have one pound of chicken or game meat (the breast), free of nerves or skin, pass them twice through the machine (Fig. 47); or else chop and pound to a pulp, then press through a sieve, return to the mortar and mix in one egg-white, half an ounce of salt, red pepper and nutmeg, the equal quantity of six or eight gills of cream, before whipping; mixing it in gradually with a whip and working it well. Should the forcemeat be too thick add cream, and if it lacks consistency, more egg-white.

(76). CREAM FORCEMEAT OF FISH (Farce de Poisson à la Crème).

Take one pound of boned and skinned bass or any other firm fish; pound and rub it through a fine sieve; return it to the mortar, season with an ounce of salt, some nutmeg and red pepper and mix in while still stirring with a whip, two egg-whites and from six to eight gills of cream, measured before whipping; pass the whole through a very fine sieve. Try a small piece in order to rectify if not correct, and if found to be too firm add more cream, and if too soft some more egg-whites.

(77). BAKED FISH FORCEMEAT (Farce à Gratin pour Poisson).

Put six ounces of butter into a sautoire and when hot add half a pound of finely chopped mushrooms and two ounces of chopped truffle parings. After the mushrooms have rendered their moisture, add one pound of cooked firm fish broken into fragments; as the whole becomes hot, remove it from the fire, cool partly, then add five egg-yolks and five whole eggs, seasoning with salt, pepper and nutmeg; pass it through a medium sized sieve (Fig. 98), return to the vessel and beat it well with a spoon, incorporating in two spoonfuls of tomato purée, strained through a fine sieve (Fig. 100) and half a pound of raw fish quenelle forcemeat.

(78). FOIES GRAS FORCEMEAT (Farce de Foies Gras).

Pound half a pound of frangipane panada (No. 120) with six ounces of butter and half a pound of raw and very white fat livers; season with salt, pepper and nutmeg and when the whole is well pounded, strain through a sieve, then add six raw egg-yolks and two well beaten whites while continuing to work the forcemeat.

(79). CHICKEN OR GAME FORCEMEAT WITH RICE FOR BORDERS, BOTTOMS OF DISHES AND SURTOUTS (Farce de Volaille ou de Gibier au Riz pour Bordures, Fonds de Plats et Surtouts).

Prepare and unnerve one pound either of chicken or game; pass it twice through the machine (Fig. 47) to suppress all the nerves and pound it to a pulp, take it from the mortar. Put eight ounces of pâte à choux, cream panada (No. 121) into the mortar, pound it thoroughly with the same weight of cooked veal udder, add the game or chicken meat, season with salt, pepper and nutmeg, two gills of well reduced cold velouté (No. 415), six egg-whites and a little cream, then add half a pound of well picked, washed and blanched rice, cooked in white broth and cooled. Mix together and keep it in a cool place. This forcemeat is used for borders, surtouts and dish bottoms.

(80). FOIES-GRAS AND CHICKEN FORCEMEAT FOR BORDERS, BOTTOMS OF DISHES AND SURTOUTS (Farce de Foies-Gras et de Volaille pour Bordures, Fonds de Plat et Surtouts).

Pound well one pound of raw fat livers; season with salt, pepper and nutmeg, then add eight egg-yolks, one at a time, continuing to pound the forcemeat; put in three pounds of chicken quenelle forcemeat (No. 89) and when all is well blended stand it on ice to use as needed. Forcemeat borders are made in special molds of a crown form, lightly hollowed on top, an inch and a half to two inches high. The bottoms of dishes and the surtouts are not as high, being only one inch generally and two inches in diameter narrower than the basin of the dish.

(81). BAKING FORCEMEAT FOR ORDINARY USE (Farce a Gratin Ordinaire).

Fry in four ounces of melted lard, one bayleaf, two ounces of carrots and two ounces of celery, both cut in dice, one shallot and two ounces of onions, both finely chopped, also one ounce of truffles, the same of mushrooms and one tablespoonful of chopped parsley; add its equal quantity of calf's liver and two gills of espagnole sauce (No. 414). When the meats are cooked, let the preparation first get cold, then pound and rub it through a sieve; lay this forcemeat into a bowl, cover it with buttered paper and keep it in a cool place; mix with this three tablespoonfuls of raw quenelle forcemeat, either of veal, chicken or game, in order to thicken it, but only just when ready to use. The liver may be replaced by the same quantity of cooked or raw meat, either lamb, veal, chicken or game chopped up very fine and seasoned with salt, pepper and nutmeg.

(82). CHICKEN GODIVEAU (Godiveau de Volaille).

One pound of the white meat from a tender young chicken; three quarters of a pound of dry, brittle beef kidney suet, without skin or fibres; three quarters of an ounce of spiced salt (No. 168) two whole eggs; three quarters of a pound of cream panada, (No. 120); moisten and finish exactly the same as the veal godiveau (No. 85).

(83). GODIVEAU OF PIKE (Godiveau de Brochet).

A pound of skinless and boneless pike meat, chopped and pounded fine; two pounds of dry and brittle beef kidney suet free of fat and nerves, also chopped up fine; mix the two together, chop once more and season with an ounce of spiced salt; pound to a pulp to obtain a fine paste, and incorporate into it gradually, one pound and a half of cream panada (No. 120), and afterward twelve beaten up egg-whites. Try the forcemeat to see whether it be too hard, if so add some cream, and if too soft, more egg-whites.

(84). GODIVEAU OF RABBIT OR OTHER GAME (Godiveau de Lapereau ou Autres Gibiers).

Take one pound of rabbit meat or any other game, one pound of dry, brittle beef kidney suet without skin or fibres, one ounce of spiced salt (general spices, No. 168), six eggs and four ounces of pâte à choux panada (No. 121). Moisten and finish the same as the veal godiveau (No. 85).

(85). VEAL GODIVEAU (Godiveau de Veau).

Veal godiveau frequently takes the place of forcemeat and is excellent if well prepared.

Have a pound of fresh veal meat cut off from the kernel without any fat or nerves whatever; cut it up into inch pieces, and pass them twice through the machine (Fig. 47), or in case there be no machine, chop them up very finely. Have also a pound and a quarter of beef kidney suet, perfectly dry and brittle, remove all its skin and fibres, and chop it up very finely, seasoning with one ounce of general spices (No. 168). Pound well the veal, add to it the suet, and pound all together to a pulp, so as to form a smooth paste, then stir in four whole eggs singly, as well as four ounces of frangipane panada (No. 120), in small quantities at the time. After the godiveau is well pounded, put it away for two hours in a cool place, then pound it over again, moistening it gradually with ice-water or else small pieces of very clear and clean ice. When the godiveau becomes sufficiently soft, try its consistency, by poaching a quenelle of it in boiling water, and if found to be too firm, add a little more ice-water, but if not sufficiently consistent, pound one ounce more panada with one egg, and incorporate the farce slowly to the panada, or even the egg alone will answer.

(86). CHICKEN FORCEMEAT FOR MOUSSELINE (Farce de Volaille pour Mousselines).

Ingredients.—One pound of chicken breast-meat, one egg-white, two gills of béchamel, four tablespoonfuls of cream forcemeat, and the value of one quart of whipped cream.

Have one pound of chicken breast-meat free of nerves; pass it twice through the machine (Fig. 47), pound it to a pulp and rub through a sieve, season with half an ounce of salt, red pepper and nutmeg, and incorporate gradually into it one egg-white and two gills of béchamel (No. 409).

Strain all this through a sieve, and put it in a metal vessel on the ice for fifteen minutes, then work it well with a whip, incorporating gradually into it four tablespoonfuls of cream forcemeat (No. 74) and the value of a quart of whipped cream thoroughly drained. Try a little of it in a mold and if too consistent add a little more of the whipped cream.

(87). GAME FORCEMEAT FOR MOUSSELINE (Farce de Gibier pour Mousselines).

Take one pound of the breast-meat of some raw game suppressing the skin and nerves, pound and pass it through a sieve. Place this purée in a tin vessel and mix in one egg-white slowly working it gradually so that it attains body, then incorporate, always slowly, two or three gills of raw cream without once ceasing to mix the preparation. When mellow add four or five tablespoonfuls of purée of cooked foies gras, pounded and pressed through a sieve, season, and when very smooth poach a small piece in a small timbale in a bain-marie so to judge of its consistency; it must be firm, although mellow; if found necessary add a few egg yolks.

(88). SALMON FORCEMEAT FOR MOUSSELINE (Farce de Saumon pour Mousselines).

One pound of pared fish pounded and seasoned with half an ounce of salt, cayenne pepper and nutmeg, then rub through the sieve the same as the cream chicken forcemeat. Return it to the mortar and work into it one raw egg-white, half a pint of béchamel (No. 409) and two tablespoonfuls of cream forcemeat (No. 76). Put it on to the ice, work vigorously and when very cold incorporate gradually into it equal quantity of well drained whipped cream. Serve this in timbales as hors-d'œuvre or garnishing.

(89). CHICKEN QUENELLE FORCEMEAT, WITH SOUBISE OR TOMATO (Farce à Quenelle de Volaille, Soubisée ou Tomatée).

Ingredients for these Quenelles.—One pound of chicken, half a pound of pâte à chou panada (No. 121); a quarter of a pound of butter, half an ounce of salt and nutmeg, six egg-yolks, one whole egg, one pint of chicken cream forcemeat. In order to make chicken or game forcemeats only the breasts are used, having them well pared, cut in pieces and pass through the machine (Fig. 47). Put this into a mortar, and pound it to a pulp, rub it through a sieve, pound it once more, and add to it the panada, putting it in gradually, then the butter or udder, without stopping the pounding process, and afterward the egg-yolks one by one, season with salt and nutmeg, rub the forcemeat again through the sieve, and then lay it in a thin metal vessel on the ice, and beat it up again for a few minutes so as to render it smooth. Poach a small piece of it, and if found to be too consistent, then thin it with a little cold sauce or raw cream, and keep it in a cool place until needed. Instead of using velouté or cream, one pint of chicken cream forcemeat (No. 75), may be added, made of chicken, egg-whites and cream. Quenelle forcemeats made of chicken can be used with soubise or tomatoes by mixing in either some soubise (No. 543), or fine consistent tomato purée (No. 730), instead of the cream or velouté.

(90) FISH QUENELLE FORCEMEAT (Farce à Quenelle de Poisson).

Fish forcemeats are prepared with the raw meats of either pike, bass or sheepshead, increasing the weight with panada for those fishes requiring more consistence, such as cod, etc. Any fish lacking body, such as whiting, etc., can be mixed with sheepshead, bass or others. Pike meat is renowned as having plenty of consistence and is easy to procure. Prepare one pound of pike meat free of bones and skin, pound it well and when reduced to a paste take it out of the mortar. Pound one pound of cream panada (No. 120), with eight ounces of lobster butter, add the pike meat, pound again all together, then mix in slowly six raw egg-yolks, salt, nutmeg, sweet peppers and Hungarian paprika pepper; press the forcemeat through a sieve and put it in a thin metal vessel on ice, beat it well to have it smooth. Poach a small piece to try its consistence and rectify if needed, either by adding cream or panada, mixing the farce to the latter, a little at the time. To this forcemeat is frequently added some tomatoed soubise or mushroom purée and if required to be very light beat in two well whipped egg-whites.

(91). GAME QUENELLE FORCEMEAT (Farce à Quenelle de Gibier).

Ingredients.—One pound of game, half a pound of calf's udder, half a pound of bread-crumbs soaked in hot milk, salt, red pepper, nutmeg, four egg-yolks and one whole egg.

Pass one pound of the breast of game twice through the machine (Fig. 47), pound it to a pulp and rub it through a sieve, then set it in a cool place or on the ice. Soak some bread-crumbs in milk, extract from them all the liquid, let them dry and get cool; pound the bread-crumbs with calf's udder in four different parts and continue the process until all is done, then season with salt, red pepper and nutmeg, half an ounce in all; add to this the game pulp, and continue pounding for ten minutes, then mix in four egg-yolks, singly, and one whole egg. Poach one of the quenelles in boiling water to discover its consistency, and if found necessary to rectify refer to No. 60.

(92). LAMB OR VEAL QUENELLE FORCEMEAT (Farce à Quenelle d'Agneau ou de Veau).

Procure one pound of either lean fillet, or kernel of lamb or veal; ten ounces of cooked calf's udder; four egg-yolks, two whole eggs, ten ounces of panada with flour (No. 121), three quarters of an ounce of salt, nutmeg and red pepper: suppress the fat and skin from the meat, cut it into half inch squares, put this twice through the machine (Fig. 47), then pound the meat, and when converted into a paste rub it forcibly through a round sieve (Fig. 142), or any other one not too fine; take it out of the mortar, lay in the panada, pound it fine, add to it the calf's udder, a little at the time, then the seasonings and strained meat, also the egg-yolks singly, and the whole eggs; pound again and after the preparation is thoroughly blended, rub it through a fine sieve. Set this forcemeat into a bowl, and stir it up a few moments with a spoon; poach one quenelle in boiling water to judge of its consistency, and if too hard, mix into it a few spoonfuls of cold velouté (No. 415), or raw cream; if, on the contrary, it is too thin, pound a little panada to smooth it down, and mix it in gradually with the forcemeat, by so doing it assumes a greater consistency.

(93). DIFFERENT FORCEMEATS FOR RAVIOLES OF BEEF, CHICKEN AND VEAL (Différentes Farces pour Ravioles de Bœuf, Volaille et Veau).

For Beef.—Half a pound of cooked chopped tenderloin of beef, quarter of a pound of brains in small one-eighth squares, two ounces of cooked and chopped ham, two ounces of chopped spinach. Two ounces of grated parmesan; salt, pepper, nutmeg, three egg-yolks and two table-spoonfuls of cream. All these ingredients well mixed and to be used for square ravioles.

Chicken.—Half a pound of chopped white or black poultry meat, and half a pound of chopped veal udder; pound well together with four egg-yolks and a gill of velouté; season with salt, pepper and nutmeg; mix into this preparation four ounces of parmesan cheese; this is for round ravioles.

Veal.—Fry two ounces of onions in four ounces of butter without allowing it to take color; moisten with broth, reduce to a glaze and put in the veal, seasoning with salt, pepper and nutmeg; add four egg-yolks and chopped parsley. Make triangular shaped ravioles with this.

(94). TO PREPARE GELATINE FROM CALF'S FEET (Pour Préparer la Colle de Pieds de Veau).

Calf's feet gelatine is more especially used for preparing jelly and gelatineous sweet dishes. Soak seven or eight very fresh calve's feet, split in two, having the bones all extracted, put them into a small soup-pot with water and let the liquid boil for ten minutes; then drain it off, also the feet; cool these off and return them to the clean soup-pot with two spoonfuls of sugar, the juice of four lemons, and half a bottleful of white wine. Cover with water, then heat the liquid while skimming, and at the first boil set it on the stove to obtain a regular and continuous ebullition for four to five hours, strain the liquid into a bowl and let it get very cold. When the gelatine is firm, remove all the fat from the top, then wash the surface with warm water so that not a vestige of grease remains. Lift out the jelly without disturbing the sediment at the bottom of the bowl, and put it back, either all or part into a saucepan to melt.

For one quart of gelatine, mix in three quarters of a pound of broken sugar and the juice of four lemons; when the sugar is dissolved, test the consistency so as to rectify it if necessary, by adding either more water or more gelatine, according to its strength or weakness. Beat four egg-whites without getting them frothy, put these into one gill of cold water and pour it over the dissolved gelatine, place the saucepan on a moderate fire, beat the liquid slowly till it is about reaching boiling point, then remove the saucepan to a slower fire, so that the liquid quivers, but does not boil; now add the juice of four lemons, cover the saucepan and keep it near the boiling point for thirty minutes, the gelatine should now be limpid. Filter it through a bag or strain it through a napkin fastened to the four feet of a filtering stool (Fig. 51) and pour it back into the filter until it becomes perfectly clear; this operation must be performed in a very warm place.

(95). TO PREPARE PIG'S SKIN GELATINE (Pour Préparer la Colle de Cauenne).

Soak in cold water for five or six hours, six pounds of fresh pork skin; put it into a saucepan with cold water to double its height, and blanch it in this water until it boils, then drain and refresh it; scrape off the pieces one by one, wash them well, and return them to the saucepan with more clean, cold water and boil the liquid while skimming it; set it on one side of the range or on the gas stove, and add half a bottleful of white wine, then continue boiling for seven hours, skimming it frequently. Pass the liquid through a sieve into a basin, let it get cold and firm on ice, then remove all the fat from the top and wash the surface off with very hot water; melt it once more to mix it in with the necessary broth and clarify it with meat and eggs or white of eggs, proceeding the same as for aspic-jelly (No. 103).

(96). GHERKINS (Cornichons).

Cut off the stalks and ends from small gherkin cucumbers; put a few handfuls in a coarse towel or bag, with a heavy handful of kitchen salt, shake them in this bag to cleanse well and remove all the outer roughness and then toss them on a large sieve to free them of the salt; range in a barrel, pour over a brine made with sufficient salt to float an egg or a potato on its surface, cover, and on top lay a heavy weight to keep them under water; leave them so for six days. Now drain off the brine and return to the barrel more fresh brine, it containing as much salt as the first one; put back both cover and weight to keep them submerged under the liquid and leave stand in a cool place. After a short time a scum will form on the surface; this must in no ways be disturbed until the gherkins are needed, for it acts as a protector, preventing any air from penetrating into the liquid. When the gherkins are wanted for use, take them from the brine; unsalt by putting them in fresh water for twelve hours. Pour half water and half vinegar in an untinned copper basin, throw into it a small bagful of spices, such as cloves, peppers, mustard seeds and mace. Place on the fire and at the first boil, plunge in the well drained gherkins and leave to bubble for a few moments, then remove the basin from the fire and put both gherkins and vinegar into a large jar or barrel to cool off; put in with them a handful of tarragon, some small blanched onions and shallots and a few red peppers; stand this in a well aired place for a few days and the gherkins will be then ready for use.

(97). GRATED PARMESAN AND SWISS CHEESE (Fromage Parmesan et Fromage de Gruyère râpé).

Cut off all the rind from the cheese, leaving no black part on whatever; grate by rubbing the cheese against a sufficiently coarse grater (Fig. 177) until it is all consumed; keep in a cool but not too damp place.

(98). GRATED HORSERADISH AND HORSERADISH RIBBONS (Raifort Râpé et en Rubans).

Grated horseradish should be made of clean, fresh horseradish root, peeled or scraped, washed and dried, then rubbed against a large grater; it can either be served fresh or put into a stone jar with salt and vinegar, corking it well to preserve till needed. For horseradish ribbons, peel the root the same as for grating, and scrape it with the sharp blade of a knife, held at an angle from the top to the bottom; by this method fine ribbons of the root are obtained; let them be as long as it is possible to have them. Long horseradish should be used for this purpose.

(99). COOKED CHOCOLATE ICING (Glace Cuite au Chocolat).

Put into a sugar-pan a quarter of a pound of unsweetened chocolate; let it soften at the oven door, and dilute it with two gills of warm syrup at sixteen degrees, or simply with water, then add to the liquid some icing sugar, so as to obtain a smooth preparation neither too soft nor too thin.

(100). COOKED COCOA ICING (Glace Cuite au Cacao).

Dissolve a quarter of a pound of cocoa or unsweetened chocolate in a sugar-pan; cook three quarters of a pound of sugar in another pan with one pint of water till it reaches the degree of small thread, mash the cocoa with a spoon, dilute it gradually with the cooked sugar, then cook all together until it reaches small thread again; remove it from the fire, rub it against the sides of the pan with a spoon in order to mass it well; this icing is used to ice Genoese, éclairs and a variety of small cakes.

(101). ROYAL ICING, AND ROYAL ICING FLAVORED WITH ZESTS (Glace Royale et Glace Royale Parfumée aux Zestes.)

Royal Icing.—Put into a vessel the whites of one or several eggs (those not too fresh are preferable), and add to them some icing sugar, sifted through a very fine sieve, sufficient to have the eggs and sugar combined; form into a running paste, add several drops, either of lemon juice or acetic acid, according to the quantity of icing. With a wooden spatula beat up slowly to begin, then continue the action more briskly, always turning it in such a way that the air may enter, which helps to make the icing lighter and firmer. Beat it until the spoon, being lifted from the icing, it stands on it upright, without falling off. This royal icing is excellent for decorating pieces, cakes, etc., but for flowers or decorations to be made entirely of royal icing, then after beating, add more icing sugar, but do not get it too hard. Royal icing can be made any color by using vegetable colors.

Royal Icing flavored with Zests.—Put into a basin, half a pound of sugar, add a few spoonfuls of sugar flavored either with orange or lemon zest, adding gradually sufficient white of egg to allow it to flow; this icing is used for covering cakes.

(102). ICING WITH SYRUP FOR CAKES FLAVORED WITH VANILLA, ORANGE, LEMON OR FRUIT JUICES (Glace au Sirop pour Gâteaux Parfumée soit à la Vanille, à l'Orange, au Citron ou au Jus de Fruits).

Put one pint of water and a pound of sugar in a saucepan, adding half a vanilla bean or else some orange or lemon peel; stand it on the fire, let boil up a few times to obtain a syrup, then remove the saucepan from the range immediately, suppress the vanilla or peels and incorporate sufficient sugar to form a very smooth flowing paste.

For Uncooked Fruit Juice Icing.—Prepare it with strawberry, raspberry, currant or pineapple juice. Simply crush the ripe, fresh fruits, pour them on a sieve to collect all the liquid. Put some icing sugar in a vessel, dissolve it with a little thirty-degree syrup, and the fruit juice, incorporating the liquid slowly; just before using this icing warm it in an untinned copper vessel, stirring it during the operation. The icing sugars are colored according to taste and are used for icing Genoeses, pouring it over or else dipping in all kinds of small cakes, such as éclairs, etc.

(103). TO PREPARE, CLARIFY AND FILTER ASPIC JELLY (Pour Préparer la Gelée d'Aspic, la Clarifier et la Filtrer).

Aspic or meat jelly is prepared with chicken or game broth, obtaining it as clear as possible, and mixing it with a certain quantity of gelatine made either with calf's feet or pig skin, or even with isinglass. Aspics are also prepared with special stocks made under the following conditions: brown in a saucepan half a pound of breast of veal, one knuckle, and two fowls, suppressing the breasts; when the meats are lightly colored moisten them amply with some light broth, free of all fat, and add to it four or five boned and blanched calf's feet, also some roots and onions, a garnished bouquet, but no salt, boil the liquid while skimming, remove it to the side of the range, and finish cooking the meats, lifting them out as soon as they are done. Strain the liquid through a sieve, skim off all the fat, try a little of it on ice to judge of its consistency, and should it not be sufficiently firm, then heat it up once more, and stir into it a few gelatine leaves softened in cold water and dissolved in a small separate saucepan. The aspic should never be reduced with the idea of rendering it firmer, because the boiling only wastes it without thick-

Fig. 50.

Fig. 51.

ening it; chop one pound of lean beef, one pound for two quarts of liquid, add to it **four** egg-whites or two whole eggs and one pint of white wine, dilute it gradually with the aspic jelly, put it into a saucepan on the fire, stir the liquid with a whisk until the instant boiling point is reached, then remove it to one side, and let it simmer very slowly, till it becomes perfectly clear, then strain it through a flannel bag (Fig. 50); or moisten a clean napkin and arrange it on a kitchen filtering stool as shown in Fig. 51; should the jelly not be sufficiently limpid, **pour it** through again until perfectly clear.

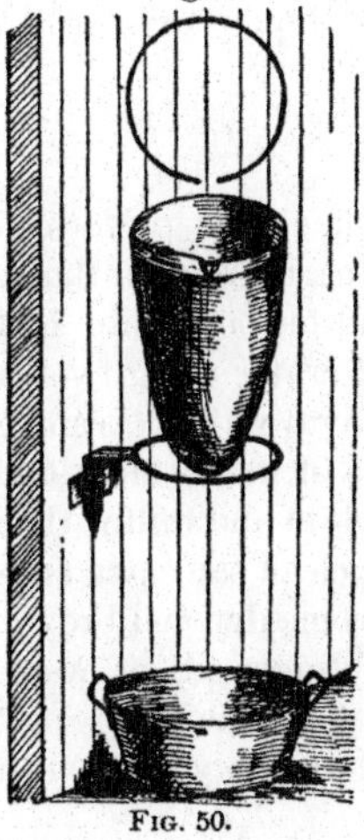

(104). CALF'S FOOT JELLY WITH MADEIRA WINE (Gelée de Pieds de Veau au vin de Madère).

Take the value of one quart of calf's foot gelatine and mix into it three quarters of a pound of sugar and the juice of four lemons. After the sugar is dissolved try its consistency to rectify it if necessary, adding more water or more gelatine according to whether it be too soft or too hard. Beat up four egg-whites without letting them come to a froth, mix in a gill of cold water and pour this over the dissolved gelatine; set the untinned basin on a moderate fire, whip the liquid slowly until on the verge of boiling, then withdraw it to a slower heat and keep the liquid simmering without boiling; now add the juice of four lemons; cover and leave stand for thirty minutes. The jelly should now be limpid; filter it through a flannel bag or a napkin fastened to the four feet of a filtering stool (Fig. 51), return the jelly to the bag and continue the operation until it passes through clearly; this should be done in a warm place. As soon as the jelly is properly filtered let it stand until cold and then add one gill of good Madeira, pour it into a mold previously imbedded in ice and leave it for one hour and a half to set.

(105). MEAT JELLY WITH GELATINE (Gelée de Viande à la Gélatine).

Put four quarts of good broth with one pound of gelatine into a saucepan, adding a quarter of an ounce of pepper-corns, two cloves, a few branches of celery and a little mace, put it on to the fire and stir continuously with a whip until the liquid boils; season to taste. Break six eggs, put them with their shells into a bowl and beat them up a little mixing in with them, half a bottle of white wine or a quarter of a bottle of Madeira, one gill of tarragon vinegar, and a quart of small pieces of clean ice, dilute this with a quart of the liquid jelly, and pour the clarification into the remainder of the jelly, stirring it constantly, then return the saucepan to the fire and continue the beating. When the jelly has reached the boiling degree, remove it from the fire, and keep it very warm for half an hour, but it must not boil again; filter as indicated (No. 103).

(106). SWEET JELLY WITH GELATINE, OR FISH ISINGLASS (Gelée Douce à la Gélatine ou à la Colle de Poisson).

Put into a basin four quarts of water, three pounds of sugar, half a pound of gelatine or ten ounces of fish isinglass and the peel of eight lemons, stir the whole well together until the sugar is melted, then set the basin on a slow fire and beat well with a whip; as soon as it begins to boil put in twelve partly beaten egg-whites into which has been added the juice of twelve lemons; mix the whole well together stirring unceasingly and allowing it to boil slowly from fifteen to twenty minutes, then withdraw the basin from the fire and let the jelly rest for a few moments; now pour it through a flannel bag upheld by a ring (Fig. 50); return it several times until it acquires a perfect limpidity. The lemon-peel can be suppressed, flavoring it with any kind of liquor or clarified fruit juice.

(107). LARD (Saindoux).

Lard is the produce of leaf lard melted with fat pork; this operation should be performed rapidly, especially in summer time. Remove the membranes and sanguineous parts from all that is required for making the lard—say about twenty pounds; cut the leaf lard and fat pork into half inch squares and steep them separately for two hours in an abundance of cold water using twelve quarts for each and two ounces of crystal soda also for each; wash both in several waters, keeping them separated; drain and lay first the fat pork in a saucepan with four quarts of water, melt it on a slow fire being careful to stir the bottom frequently; as it melts it becomes white and milky, then transparent, when in this state, strain it through a colander and return it to a clean saucepan adding the leaf lard; set it on a good fire and stir incessantly until the squares become dry and brown, then strain the fat, press well the squares, leave to cool slightly, afterward adding a gill of water for every two pounds of the fat. Beat the whole vigorously, let cool and draw off the clear part before the fat has had time to congeal, just when it begins to set, beat thoroughly to have it smooth.

(108). AXUNGE (Axonge).

Axunge is exclusively obtained by melting leaf lard without using any other material; axunge is finer than lard and is also employed for kitchen and pastry purposes. The leaf lard is melted in a bain-marie or by steam, this latter method being preferable. Remove the skin and fibers from ten pounds of leaf lard, cut it up in squares about half an inch each and bathe them in eighteen quarts of water with half a pound of crystal soda; wash in several waters, drain and pound in a mortar, then put it into a well tinned copper basin in a bain-marie and steam by keeping the water boiling all the time until the lard is all melted, now strain it through a fine colander and leave to cool slightly, adding one pint of cold water, stir well, let it rest, then pour off the clear part when it begins to set, beat well to have it smooth.

(109). VEAL UDDER (Tétine de Veau).

Veal Udder is the fatty part covering a kernel of veal; remove it entirely, tie it up and cook in plenty of white broth; when done take it out, pull off the string and press it lightly under a weight. Pare and cut it either into strips, squares or bands, etc. It is used in forcemeats instead of butter, pass it twice through the machine, pound well and then pass through a sieve. The way to keep it is to leave it covered in a cool place or else cover over entirely with salt.

(110). TO PREPARE LARDING PORK (Pour Préparer le Lard à Piquer).

Lift the bands of pork leaving as little meat on as possible, from the first rib to the end of the loin; lay them in brine for three months, then drain off, and put them on a table to rub one by one and cover with salt. Set them one on top of the other in a cool, dry place and range a board over with a weight on top; turn them over, and throw on some salt, and at the end of a month change those from the bottom to the top, and three months after, fasten a strong twine to each piece, and hang them up separately in a cold, dark room to dry.

Another Way.—The piece of pork taken from the back is the only one to use for larding purposes, as it is firm and not liable to crack. Remove all the meat from it, and cut it into an oblong piece, this being called a band; salt it dry with fine salt for three or four weeks, and if it be necessary to use it shortly after its salting, then rub it with very fine salt, and hang it up in a dry and cool place. This pork must be salted toward the end of the winter; fat pork never receives more salt than it needs, whichever way it may be employed, or however long the operation may last.

(111). TO CUT FAT PORK FOR LARDING (Manière de Tailler le Lard Pour Piquer).

The larding pork must be white and firm, perfectly dry and cooled on ice, specially in summer so to make it harder and to be enabled to cut it more evenly. Divide the pork into the required length leaving on the rind; remove a slice from the top of the necessary thickness to have the pork of the same thickness throughout, paring the two ends square, then divide it into lardons at equal distances cutting them perpendicularly as far down as the rind, for this use a thin knife, called a lard slicer, and cut the lard the size designated by Fig. 52, then cut them horizontally to obtain very square lardons of the desired size.

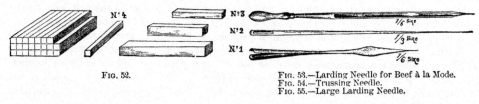

FIG. 52.

FIG. 53.—Larding Needle for Beef à la Mode.
FIG. 54.—Trussing Needle.
FIG. 55.—Large Larding Needle.

No. 1, lardons as represented in the figure are from three to four-eighths of an inch square, by three and one-quarter to four inches long. This size is for larding beef à la mode, braised tongue, kernel of veal, leg of mutton, etc.

No. 2, are three-sixteenths of an inch square by two and one quarter inches long; this size is convenient for saddles of venison, fricandeaux, tenderloins of beef, etc.

No. 3, these are five-thirty-seconds of an inch square, by two inches in length; this size is for poultry, large game, fish, sweetbreads, veal cutlets, etc.

No. 4, lardons of one-eighth of an inch square, by one and three-quarter inches long; this size is for small game, pigeons, chickens, etc.

The lardons as shown in the figures are represented one quarter their actual size.

(112). TO LARD MEAT, POULTRY AND GAME (Pour Piquer les Viandes la Volaille et le Gibier).

If it be butcher's meat, pare it properly by removing in strips the skin covering the meat, then all the superfluous fat.

The way to lard a tenderloin is to pare a fine tenderloin of beef, weighing six pounds after it is trimmed; remove the fat, slide the blade of a thin knife between the skin and the meat, and press it on the skin so as to avoid injuring the flesh; remove also the superfluous fat on the side, then cut the two ends round shaped. Choose a larding needle of suitable size to hold the larding pork that should be cut into pieces of three-sixteenths by two and a quarter inches long; lay the tenderloin lengthwise on a heavy towel, place this over the left arm, then proceed to lard the meat with the larding needle threaded with a piece of the pork, boring the meat from right to left. The needle containing the pork must be stuck in the flesh to a depth depending upon its length, but the needle must be withdrawn with one stroke, so that the pork remains in the meat visible of

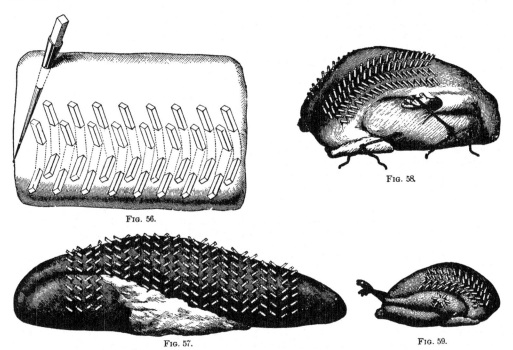

FIG. 56.

FIG. 58.

FIG. 57.

FIG. 59.

an equal length on both sides. After the first row is larded, the next one should be slipped exactly between those of the first row; then instead of larding between the two lards of the last row, begin the operation from the start, which means lard two more rows the same as the first, observing that the second ones are arranged contrarywise to the first two, then continue until the whole tenderloin is filled. Proceed exactly the same for fricandeau, racks of veal, grenadins or sweetbreads.

When a piece of poultry or game is required to be larded, it must first be drawn, singed and trussed, then singe the breast once more, or else dip this part into boiling water to harden the meat; after this is cold, lard with lardons adapted to their size. This in fact is the whole theory of larding, and by examining various larded pieces, one can easily become an adept in the art.

(113). LEMONS; TO CUT THEM IN VARIOUS MANNERS (Citrons Taillés de Différentes Manières).

FIG. 60.

First wash and wipe the lemons, then cut them lengthwise in four, to serve either with oysters or fried fish.

Channeled slices of lemon are made by cutting small notches on the lemon lengthways of the peel, then cutting the lemon in crosswise slices an eighth of an inch thick. These are used for garnishing broiled fish. Slices of lemon cut the same way without being channeled, are frequently served with tea.

Halved lemons are prepared by paring off the two ends and then make sixteen notches in the center, the third of the length of the lemon with the tip of a small knife; these gashes should be very regular; run the knife through as far as the center, having eight cuts to the right and eight to the left, this makes eight long triangles;

FIG. 61.

detach the lemon in two parts (Fig. 60). These are used also for cold fish and hâtelets or skewers (Fig. 61).

Shells of lemon can also be made, making two shells from one lemon. Cut from the center of the lemon, beginning at the stalk, as far as the middle of one side and from the other end of the lemon as far as the middle of the other side, about one half inch of the peel, without detaching it; cut across the lemon, keeping the ribbon of the peel intact, thus producing two identical pieces; these halved shells are used for garnishing fried fishes such as sole à la Colbert, etc.

(114). COOKED MARINADE (Marinade Cuite).

Mince one pound of carrots, as much onions and half a pound of celery root; fry all these vegetables in a quarter of a pound of lard without letting them attain color, and moisten with two quarts of vinegar and one quart of water or more according to the strength of the vinegar. Add an ounce of parsley leaves, three bayleaves and as much thyme, half an ounce of basil, garlic, cloves, a bit of mace, a tablespoonful of crushed whole peppers and the same quantity of allspice, and some salt. Boil the whole for half an hour, put it aside to get cold and use this marinade for marinating venison, mutton, hare, etc.

(115). RAW MARINADE (Marinade Crue).

There are two kinds of raw marinade; *the first* one is made of oil, minced onions, branches of parsley, thyme, bayleaf, slices of lemon, salt, mignonette, garlic and basil. *The second* one is made of two quarts of vinegar, four quarts of water, minced carrots and onions, bayleaf, a clove of garlic, thyme, basil, mace, whole peppers and sprigs of parsley.

(116). HOW TO DRESS MERINGUES (Pour Dresser les Meringues).

Fig 62.

Prepare a meringue paste as in No. 140. Pour the preparation into a pocket furnished with a socket and push it into rounds on to white paper bands; dust them over with fine sugar and press down the middle lightly, so as to efface the tip, formed by the socket, then range these paper bands on top of some wet boards. Cook the meringues on these boards in a very slack oven, leaving them in for fifty minutes; they must be of a fine golden color and well-dried; after taking them from the oven, detach them carefully from the paper, and remove all the soft parts from the insides, using a teaspoon for this purpose, then lay them immediately on a raised edged tin sheet, one beside the other, the hollow part uppermost, and keep them in a warm heater for twelve hours.

(117). MINCE MEAT (Mince Meat).

Suppress all fibers and skin from half a pound of beef kidney suet, chop it up very finely; have also chopped half a pound of cooked ox heart; seed and pick half a pound of Malaga raisins, half a pound of Smyrna raisins, half a pound of currants, chop up three ounces of citron, cut three ounces of candied orange peel into three-sixteenth of an inch squares, peel and chop finely two pounds of apples. Have two ounces of brown sugar, half an ounce of ground cinnamon, a quarter of an ounce of grated nutmeg, a quarter of an ounce of allspice and ground ginger, and a quarter of an ounce of powdered coriander seeds, one pint of cider, one gill of rum, quarter of a gill of brandy and the peels and juice of two lemons. Mix all the ingredients together and put them into a stone crock leaving it in a cool place for at least fifteen days before using.

(118). TO TURN, CHANNEL AND FLUTE MUSHROOMS (Pour Tourner et Canneler les Champignons).

Choose the freshest mushrooms and those of equal size, cut off the stems, wipe well the heads, and take them one by one in the left hand, the hollow side underneath, then with the tip of a small pointed knife cut away the peel in regular rings without destroying the mushroom, and turn from right to left pressing all the time against the tip of the small knife; this must be done quickly and let us observe that it is not on the first trial that a mushroom can be properly turned, it takes practice to accomplish this properly. As quickly as each one is done, throw it into a saucepan containing cold, acidulated water, just sufficient to cover, then drain off the water, and cook the mushrooms for seven or eight minutes with the lid on, adding salt, butter and lemon juice, to keep them as white as possible. As for fluting mushrooms, this art is only learned after long experience. Mushroom fluting has become almost a profession, and the difficulties to be overcome can be better understood on examining those pretty mushroom heads so delicately carved, we see displayed by all preserve manufacturers.

(119). TO STONE OLIVES (Pour Énucléer les Olives).

If the olives are plump, large and contain small stones, these can be removed with a machine made for the purpose (Fig. 63) or with a tube from a column box, but generally the meat is cut off in spirals around the stone by means of a small knife. After the stone is removed, the olives resume their former shape, then plunge them into boiling water, and take them out again at once; they must be blanched without boiling.

(120). PANADA CREAM FRANGIPANE (Panade Crème Frangipane).

Boil four gills of cream; put into another saucepan, four eggs, an ounce and a half of flour and some salt; mix and dilute with the cream, set it on the fire, and stir it with a spoon, bearing on the bottom of the saucepan, and when thickened and well worked remove it from the fire at the first boil and then set it away to cool with a buttered paper over it.

FIG. 63.

(121). PANADA OF FLOUR AND MILK, BREAD-CRUMBS, AND PÂTE À CHOUX (Panade de Farine et de Lait, Mie de Pain et Pâte à Choux).

Flour and Milk.—Put in a saucepan half pound of flour, also four eggs and work well together adding some salt, and dilute with six to eight gills of milk; stir it over the fire and remove at the first boil, pour it into a bowl, cover with a buttered paper and let get cold.

Bread-crumbs.—Soak four ounces of bread-crumbs in a pint of water, squeeze out all the liquid and put it into a saucepan with a little salt and three gills of milk; thicken it on the fire without ceasing to beat, and stir it up with a spoon until it detaches itself from the pan, then set it in a bowl, cover with buttered paper and put away to cool.

Pâte à Choux.—Put one pint of water or broth in a saucepan with two ounces of butter, set it on the fire, remove it aside at the first boil, and incorporate into it three quarters of a pound of sifted flour, mix well and dry on a slow fire till the paste detaches itself from the saucepan and let cool slightly, then stir into it gradually two whole eggs and four yolks, set it away in a cool place with a buttered paper over, for further use.

(122). WHEAT AND RICE FLOUR PANADA (Panade de Farine de Gruau et de Riz).

Wheat Flour.—Boil half a pint of broth with half an ounce of butter, remove it to the side of the fire, and add to it four or five ounces of flour, or as much as it can absorb, stir the paste quickly, return it to a slow fire to dry, do not cease stirring until it detaches from the saucepan. Pour it into a bowl, cover with a round piece of buttered paper, and set it away to cool.

Rice Flour.—Have one pint of white broth or milk and half an ounce of butter; boil together and add sufficient rice flour to form a paste, let it dry, then set it away with a buttered paper cover to get cool.

(123). PARSLEY BOUQUET, IN BRANCHES, FRIED OR CHOPPED (Persil en Bouquet, en Branches, Frit ou Haché).

Plain Bouquet or Bunch of Parsley.—Take about one ounce of parsley branches, including the leaves, wash them nicely and fold them in such a manner that they form a small bundle or fagot, to be tied with a piece of string.

The Garnished Bouquet of Parsley.—Make it exactly the same as the plain bouquet the only difference being that it envelopes various aromatics, such as thyme, bayleaf, clove of garlic, basil, marjoram, chives. green celery, etc. When we speak of a garnished bunch of parsley without any specification, we mean garnished with a bayleaf and a small twig of thyme.

Parsley in Branches for garnishing should be taken from well washed, very green parsley, from which the coarser stalks have been removed; keep it in fresh water and use when needed, draining it first: for garnishing fish, boiled beef, etc.

Fried Parsley is used as an accessory to fried dishes; it is not a garnishing, but simply a decoration; detach some leaves from some very green parsley, wash them in cold water, drain, press them in the hand or in a cloth to extract all the water, and when dry, lay them in a wire basket to plunge into boiling fat; drain as soon as they stiffen.

Chopped Parsley.—Choose very green parsley, wash, drain and press it so as to extract all the water, then cut it up as finely as possible, afterward chopping it well; wash it again, drain and squeeze it thoroughly to remove all the water; lay it on a cloth sieve and leave it in a cool place till needed.

(124). ALMOND PASTE FOR FANCY CAKES (Pâte d'Amandes à Petits Fours).

Take one pound of peeled and well dried almonds; one pound of powdered sugar, and five whites of eggs. Pound the almonds and the sugar, either in a machine or mortar, and when well reduced to a powder, pass it forcibly through a twelve mesh sieve (Fig. 96); return it to the mortar, and mix in with the almonds the five egg-whites little by little, so as to make a paste, which can be now beaten and worked until a good body is obtained, having it as fine as possible.

(125). ALMOND PASTE WITH COOKED SUGAR AND FILBERT PASTE (Pâte d'Amandes et Pâte d'Avelines au Sucre Cuit).

Almond Paste.—Shell and skin one pound of almonds; pound them with half a pound of powdered sugar and a little water to make into a very fine paste, the same consistency as a macaroon paste. Cook three pounds of sugar to small crack, and as soon as ready pour it in small strings on to the paste, stirring constantly with a spatula and leave stand till cold. When this paste is thoroughly cooled off, return it to the mortar and pound it once more with liquors or vanilla syrup, to have it obtain a body and make it into a fine paste, then put it in a stone jar and leave it in a cool place.

Filbert Paste with Cooked Sugar.—Have one pound of shelled filberts pounded to a pulp with a pound of powdered sugar and a gill of water; lay this paste in a basin. Cook in a copper pan two pounds and a half of sugar to small crack, pour it slowly over the paste mixing it so that it mingles in well, then leave to cool and pound again, stirring in half a gill of liquor, either kirsch, maraschino or any other. Color the paste green or pink according to taste.

(126). ALMOND PASTE WITH EGG-YOLKS (Pâte d'amandes aux jaunes d'œufs).

Have one pound of almonds, one pound of sugar, and eight egg-yolks; pound or mash the almonds in a machine with the sugar so as to reduce them to a fine powder, then strain through a twelve mesh sieve (Fig. 96), put them into the mortar, and mix in well the yolks adding them little by little; pound all up together so as to obtain a very fine paste, having it quite thick.

(127). ALMOND PASTE WITH GUM TRAGACANTH (Pâte d'Amandes à la Gomme Adragante).

Put three ounces of gum tragacanth to steep in two gills of water for twenty-four hours, then strain forcibly through a piece of linen. Pour this gum on a marble slab and work with the hand to have it acquire a body, incorporating in slowly two pounds of icing sugar, then add one pound of pounded almonds and the juice of a lemon strained through a sieve; beat the paste well and pour it into a vessel or stone pot; closing hermetically; keep in a very cool place to use when needed. This paste may be colored red, green, orange or any other color.

(128). ALMOND PASTE WITH PISTACHIOS (Pâte d'Amandes aux Pistaches).

Have three quarters of a pound of almonds, half a pound of pistachio nuts, a pound and a half of sugar, two tablespoonfuls of orange flower-water and five egg-whites. Peel the almonds and pistachio nuts; dry and pound them with the sugar, egg-whites and orange flower-water till they become a fine paste, then add to it a little vegetable green, so as to give it a soft, green color.

(129). BABA PASTE (Pâte à Baba).

Sift a pound of flour on the table, divide it in four even parts and use one of these to make the leaven by forming it in a circle and placing three quarters of an ounce of yeast in the center, diluting with a little warm milk to obtain a soft paste; roll this into a ball, cut it crosswise on the top with two cuts of the knife and lay it in a floured vessel; cover with a cloth and leave to rise in a mild temperature to double its size. Pile the remainder of the flour into a hillock, make a hole in the center to form a hollow and in it lay an ounce of sugar, a spare half ounce of salt (according to the saltness of the butter), six ounces of butter and six eggs. Mix all the ingredients well together and work the flour in slowly, then begin to knead the paste so that it becomes smooth and acquires a body slowly adding three more eggs and four ounces of butter; continue to knead until again quite smooth with plenty of body, then mix in the leaven, wrapping it lightly in the paste and cutting the whole in every direction until thoroughly mingled and the paste is finished, then add to it two ounces of seeded Malaga raisins, two ounces of Sultana or Smyrna currants softened in water, two ounces of cherries cut in four and two ounces of finely cut up citron. Lay the paste in a vessel, cover with a cloth and let rise to a third more than its size, then break it up with a spoon; the paste is now ready to be used.

(130). BRIOCHE PASTE (Pâte à Brioche).

Take one pound of flour, three quarters of a pound of butter, seven to eight eggs, half an ounce of yeast, two pinches of salt, four pinches of sugar, two spoonfuls of brandy and some water. Dissolve the yeast in half a pint of tepid water, and with this liquid and a quarter of a pound of the flour, make a rather thick paste, put it into a small saucepan with a little luke-warm water at the bottom, and let it rise in a slack heater. Sift the remainder of the flour on the table, form a hollow and put in the center, the salt, sugar, brandy, two spoonfuls of water, three of the eggs and the butter; mix together thoroughly with the hand, and incorporate gradually the flour so as to obtain a smooth paste, then beat sharply with the hands for a quarter of an hour, adding the rest of the eggs one at the time. Beat it well against the table to let it acquire a body; then lay out the paste and spread the yeast over, fold it up to enclose the yeast and break it into small pieces with the hands; pile up the broken pieces, cut the paste once more, and put the pieces as quickly as they are cut into a floured vessel, cover it and set it to rise in a moderate temperature, until it will be raised to twice its original size; this will take at least six hours. Set the paste again on the floured table, break it up and refold it several times with the hands, return it to the vessel, cover and put it back once more in the same place to rise. Break the paste up again three hours later, put it back into the vessel, and this time set it either in a cool place or on the ice to become firm. It should now be left at least three hours before using.

(131). COOKED PASTE FOR FANCIFUL BORDERS (Pâte Cuite pour Bordures de Fantaisie).

Boil one pint of water with a quarter of a pound of butter and a grain of salt; as soon as the liquid boils remove it from the fire, and incorporate in one pound of flour so as to obtain a good paste, then replace it on to a moderate fire and stir vigorously until it detaches from the bottom of the saucepan, then remove it entirely and pour it on to a floured table; as soon as it cools off slightly, knead it with the hands, adding to it slowly one pound more flour; by this time the paste should be perfectly smooth; after it has obtained a consistency, turn it the same as puff paste (No. 146), giving it seven or eight turns, having the paste remarkably smooth; it must be used at once.

(132). CREAM CAKE PASTE (Pâte à Chou).

Put into a saucepan half a pint of water, a grain of salt, one ounce of sugar and two ounces of butter; set the saucepan on the fire and when the butter floats, remove the pan from off the range, and incorporate into it a quarter of a pound of fine flour, stir vigorously not to have it the least lumpy, and put it back on to a slow fire to dry until it detaches easily from the bottom, then take it off once more, and mix in a tablespoonful of orange flower-water; four or five minutes later stir in four or five eggs, add... m one at the time; it must now be more consistent than otherwise, and if a little of it should be dropped from the spoon, it must retain its shape and not spread.

(133). DRESSING PASTE (Pâte à Dresser).

Sift a pound of flour on the table, arrange it in a circle and in the center lay half an ounce of salt, four ounces of butter and a gill of water; mix thoroughly, working the flour in as fast as possible. When the paste begins to attain a body, knead it thoroughly twice, mold it round, form, and leave in a cool place.

(134). ENGLISH PASTE FOR BORDERS (Pâte Anglaise Pour Bordures).

One pound of fecula, one pound of sugar, six egg-whites. Lay the fecula on the table, forming a hollow in the center, into this put the sugar, a little tepid water and six egg-whites, lightly whisked; make a very hard paste, set it in a cool place hermetically closed in a bag for about two hours.

(135). FINE FOUNDATION, ORDINARY FOUNDATION OR SHORT AND FLAWN PASTES
(Pâte à Foncer, Fine, Ordinaire ou Brisée et à Flans).

Fine Foundation Paste.—Have one pound of flour, three quarters of a pound of butter, half a pint of cold water and half an ounce of salt. Sift the flour on a table, bring it all together and make a hollow in the center, spreading it with the hand, and in this space lay the butter, divided into small bits, half of the water and the salt; make a dough by mixing first the butter with the water, then drawing the flour into this wet part, a very little at the time, so as to obtain a paste neither lumpy nor too firm; if necessary, add the rest of the water, a very little at the time, mass it together, and knead it briskly two or three times. To knead dough is to put it in front of one, and push it little by little with the palms of both hands and pressing it hard against the table so as to get it smooth; after this is finished, bring it together again, detach carefully all the bits adhering to the table, and roll it into a ball with the hands, turning it in the left hand. Let the paste rest in the ice-box a quarter of an hour before using it.

Ordinary Foundation or Short Paste is made with one pound of flour, half a pound of butter, half a pint of water and a third of an ounce of salt. Make a hollow in the center of the flour, put into this the butter, salt and half of the water; work well the paste, adding more water, knead it properly, then roll it into a ball on a floured table; cover and let rest for one hour.

Flawn Paste.—One and one-quarter pounds of flour, three-quarters pound of butter, a little salt, two tablespoonfuls of sugar, three or four egg-yolks; make the paste on the table, adding enough water so the paste will not be too firm; knead, bring together and leave to rest, being careful to cover it.

(136). FROLLE PASTE OR SWEET (Pâte à Frolle ou pâte Sucrée).

Arrange one pound of sifted flour in a circle on the table; in the center lay half a pound of butter, half a pound of sugar, the peel of a lemon, chopped very fine, a pinch of salt, one whole egg and four to five yolks. Work the whole well together to obtain a smooth paste, kneading it twice; form into a ball and put aside in the icebox to rest.

(137). FRYING BATTERS (Pâtes à Frire).

No. 1.—Put into a vessel, half a pound of flour, a little salt, four tablespoonfuls of oil and three egg-yolks; dilute these with sufficient water at once, so as not to have to add any more, and the size of half an inch ball of compressed yeast dissolved in a little tepid water; mix till it becomes smooth and flows without being stringy; it should well cover the spoon. Lay a cloth over the vessel, and keep it in a moderate temperature. At the last moment add to it three beaten egg-whites.

No. 2.—Place in a vessel half a pound of flour, a little salt, two tablespoonfuls of oil, diluted in tepid water, and then add a piece of compressed yeast the size of a half an inch ball, dissolved in a little water. Set the batter in a moderate temperature, and when it begins to ferment, add a handful of flour, salt, oil and water. The batter should be renewed every day without adding yeast; the fermentation produced by the batter will be sufficient to keep it light, and avoid the use of any more yeast.

No. 3.—This is a finer preparation, intended for sweet dishes, etc. Take half a pound of flour, dilute it with tepid water, into which an ounce of butter has been melted, also salt; make a soft, very smooth batter and when it has cooled off, add to it half a gill of brandy, two egg-yolks and two whites, beaten to a stiff froth.

No. 4.—This is frying batter with baking powder. Put five ounces of flour into a vessel, diluting it with two gills of tepid water, one tablespoonful of brandy, two of oil, a pinch of salt and one egg-yolk. When ready to use, add a small coffeespoonful of baking-powder and one egg-white, beaten to a stiff froth.

(138). MACAROON PASTE (Pâte à Macarons).

Made with one pound of peeled and well dried almonds, three quarters of a pound of powdered sugar, a quarter of a pound of vanilla sugar and eight egg-whites. Pound the almonds with the sugar and part of the whites, so as to obtain a not too fine paste, then gradually add the remainder of the whites; work the paste well to have it obtain plenty of consistence.

(139). MARCHPANE PASTE WITH ORANGE-FLOWER WATER (Pâte Massepain à l'eau de Fleur d'Oranger).

One pound of almonds, one pound of sugar, one gill of orange flower-water and the juice of one lemon. Peel the almonds, wash them in cold water, drain on a cloth and pound them with the orange flower-water, adding the sugar and the lemon-juice; obtain a very fine paste and put it into a small saucepan to dry on a slow fire, turning it steadily until all the moisture evaporates and it detaches from the sides and bottom of the pan. A round bottomed saucepan or basin is far preferable to the flat ones, which are in general use.

(140). PLAIN MERINGUE PREPARATION AND ITALIAN MERINGUE WITH COOKED SUGAR
(Pâte à Meringue Ordinaire et Pâte à Meringue Italienne Avec Sucre Cuit).

The preparation for meringues is composed of twelve or fifteen egg-whites for each pound of powdered sugar; set these whites in a basin with a grain of salt and beat up with a whip, very slowly at first, but increasing the velocity of the movement as the quantity becomes greater. The beaten whites should be stiff and remarkably smooth; then mix in the sugar a little at a time, using a wooden spoon for the purpose.

Italian Meringue with Cooked Sugar.—Cook one pound of sugar to "ball" (No. 171); incorporate a very little of it at a time into six beaten whites, without ceasing to stir; when all the sugar is absorbed work it for two minutes longer on a slow fire to have it very smooth.

(141). MILAN PASTE (Pâte à Milan).

Form a hollow in the center of a pound of flour on the table, lay in it half a pound of butter, half a pound of sugar, a little salt and three eggs; mix well and knead the dough twice, then put it aside to rest in a cool place.

(142). NOODLE PASTE, NOODLE PASTE FOR BORDERS AND REPÈRE PASTE FOR FASTENING
(Pâte à Nouilles, Pâte à Nouilles pour Bordures et à Repère pour Coller).

Noodle Paste.—Make a ring on the table with a pound of sifted flour, in the center lay a pinch of salt, a tablespoonful of tepid water and five beaten eggs; mix the eggs in slowly with the flour and then wrap the paste in a cloth, leave it to rest for fifteen minutes and afterward knead it well to have it smooth; this requires some time to do.

Noodle Paste for Borders.—The same preparation as for the above, the only difference being that the five whole eggs are replaced by ten yolks. This paste can also be used for covering dish bottoms.

Paste for Fastening on Borders (Repère).—This is simply sifted flour diluted with beaten egg and passed through a fine wire sieve to obtain a sufficiently liquid paste that can be pushed through a cornet. It should be consistent enough not to run.

(143). OFFICE PASTE (Pâte d'office).

Sift one pound of flour on the table, make a hollow in the center, and in this lay half a pound of sugar, two whole eggs and four yolks. Mix all together to form a smooth paste, knead it twice, and let it rest in a cool place before using it.

(144). PIE PASTE (COLD) (Pâte à Pâté) (froid).

This is prepared with melted butter as follows: Sift a pound of flour, form a hollow in the center and in it lay four egg-yolks and the third of an ounce of salt dissolved in a little water. Melt eight ounces of butter, pour the clear part slowly into the hollow, then work the flour gradually into it, adding the necessary water and knead the paste at once, roll it into a ball and leave to cool. This paste is far mellower than when made with cold butter.

Another proportion for cold pie paste is to have one pound of flour, four ounces of butter, four eggs, tepid water and salt; prepare and finish as above.

(145). PASTES FOR HOT PIES (Pâtes à Pâtés Chauds).

Lay in a circle on the table one pound of sifted flour; make a hollow in the center and into this put a third of an ounce of salt dissolved in a little water, eight ounces of butter, two egg-yolks and two gills of water. Mix first the butter with the eggs and water, add the flour working it in a little at the time, also pour in a little water as it becomes necessary, being careful not to get the paste too thin, and still avoid being too dry, otherwise it will not hold together well; knead the dough twice, detach it from the table and form it into a ball on the floured table, and when smooth, cover and let it rest.

Another recipe is: one pound of flour, eight ounces of butter, half a pint of water, four egg-yolks, and a third of an ounce of salt dissolved in water; to be prepared the same as the above.

(146). PUFF PASTE AND HALF PUFF PASTE (Pâte Feuilletée et demi Feuilletée).

This paste is actually not so very difficult to make, only it requires particular attention. Weigh one pound of the very best quality, not too fresh, but well dried flour; one pound of butter, well drained and cooled on the ice, then kneaded in a cloth to make it become flexible. Sift the flour on to the table, arrange it in a circle, and put into this one teaspoonful of salt and a glassful of water. With the right hand mix gradually the liquid with the flour,

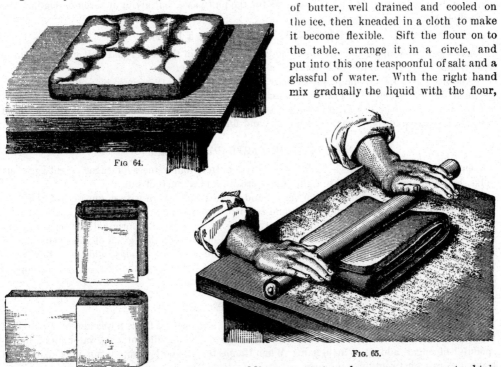

FIG 64.

FIG. 65.

FIG 66.

adding more water when necessary, so as to obtain a smooth, even paste, soft in preference to hard, and of a consistency neither stringy nor ropy; as soon as the dough is made, knead it well for two minutes, detaching all the small particles from the table, but if the paste be well made it should adhere neither to the table nor to the hand; cover it with a cloth and let it rest for twelve minutes. Dredge the table lightly with flour, lay the paste on top, and roll it out square shaped, roll out the butter likewise, lay it in the center of the paste, on top, then bring the four outer edges back on to the butter so as to inclose it well (Fig. 64); take a pastry rolling pin, apply it on the paste, and using the two hands push the paste and butter forward, rolling it out to the thickness of three-sixteenths of an inch or thereabout, keeping it straight on both sides as represented in the following design (Fig. 65). Fold this band into three, press it down with the rolling pin to compress it, the accompanying design will show how to fold it (Fig 66). The paste has now only received one turn; to fold it once more, give it a half turn so as to lengthen it to the same thickness, but in a contrary direction, as thin as before; then fold the paste in three, cover it and let it rest for ten or twelve minutes; the paste will now have received two turns; then give it two turns more, exactly the same as the others, and let it rest each time for ten minutes. Before giving the last two necessary turns to fine puff paste, it must have already had six, if more are given it will be found detrimental to its delicacy.

One special obstacle to be absolutely avoided during the operation is not to let any butter whatever escape from the folds of the paste, which might easily occur if the paste happens to be too soft, if rolled out too thin, if not rolled out regularly in smooth layers, and if it is thicker on one side than the other. In summer it is very difficult to obtain good puff paste without the use of ice or at least without a cold cellar; in any way this inconvenience can be obviated by substituting good beef kidney suet for butter. This fat must first be skinned, then soaked in cold water, well drained, and pounded in a mortar, so as to convert it to a smooth paste, and then made supple by working it with the hands for a few minutes while wrapped in a cloth. If the paste should be made in moist, summer weather it must be laid on a cold baking sheet dredged with flour, and put aside in the ice box.

For Half Puff Paste.—The parings from puff paste make an excellent half paste. If this paste should have to be made, prepare a dough of three-quarters of a pound of butter for one pound of flour, operating exactly the same as for the puff paste, but giving it seven or eight turns instead of six.

(147). RAVIOLE PASTE (Pâte à Raviole).

Lay a pound of sifted flour on the table, form a hollow in the center and in it place one ounce of salt, four eggs, two ounces of butter and a little tepid water.

Another proportion is one pound of flour, one ounce of salt, two eggs, one ounce of butter, two heaping tablespoonfuls of grated parmesan and a little tepid water. The paste should be soft, yet not too firm, knead it well to have it smooth, lay it on a board, cover with a cloth and let it rest in a cool place for one hour, then roll out and finish making the ravioles.

(148). SAVARIN PASTE (Pâte à Savarin).

One pound of flour, half a pound of melted butter, four ounces of sugar, eight eggs, six yolks, half an ounce of yeast, half a gill of raw cream, and a pinch of salt.

Sift some of the flour into a warm vessel, and make a soft leaven with a quarter of the flour and the yeast, dilute it with tepid water, and cover it with some more of the flour, then leave it to rise in a warm temperature. When the leaven has risen to half its original size, break up the dough with the hands, and work into it gradually, and one by one the eggs and the remainder of the flour, then knead the dough vigorously for ten minutes to give it a body, add to it slowly the melted butter, afterward the sugar and salt, and lastly the raw cream; the zest of lemon chopped or grated may be added if desired.

(149). TART PASTE (Pâte à Tarte).

Make a paste on the table with three-quarters of a pound of flour, a quarter of a pound of arrowroot or fecula, half a pound of butter, three egg-yolks, two gills of cold water and a tablespoonful of sugar, adding a little salt. When the paste is smooth, wrap it up in a cloth, and leave it to rest for twenty-five minutes.

(150). TIMBALE PASTE (Pâte à Timbale).

Mix one pound of flour, three-quarters of a pound of butter, four or five egg-yolks, one grain of salt, and one gill of water. Form a paste, reserving a little of the water. Knead it well, then add slowly the rest of the water, roll it out, and set it aside to rest under a cover.

(151). SMALL PUFF PATTIES (Petits Pâtés Feuilletés).

Make a puff paste the same as for puff paste (No. 146), giving it six turns, roll out the paste to three-sixteenths of an inch in thickness, let it rest awhile, then from it cut about fifteen round

FIG. 67.   FIG. 68.   FIG. 69.

pieces, using a smooth **pastry** cutter one and three-quarters to two inches in diameter; collect the parings together at once, roll them out with the rolling pin to one-eighth of an inch thick, and cut the same quantity of round pieces with the same cutter, turn them over on to a wet baking sheet in straight rows, a small distance apart, and lay on each one, a one to one and a quarter inch ball of veal Godiveau forcemeat, or one of fish, chicken, game, with or without chives. Moisten the paste around the garnishing, cover each one with the pieces that were cut first, pressing them down to make the two layers of paste adhere together all around the garnishing; flatten the paste with the back of a small one and a half inch pastry cutter, egg the tops using a soft brush, and cook these small patties in a well heated oven.

(152). TO POACH QUENELLES, SMALL TIMBALES AND MOUSSELINES (Pour Pocher les Quenelles les Petites Timbales et les Mousselines).

Quenelles.—Quenelles are poached by pouring hot (nearly boiling) water into a sautoire by the side of the quenelles, set the sautoire on the fire to bring the liquid to a boiling point, and at the first boil, cover the sautoire, remove it to the side of the range so that the water only quivers, and take out the quenelles with a skimmer as soon as they are firm. The length of time to poach quenelles depends upon their size; either ten or fifteen minutes. Dry them on a cloth before dressing.

Small Timbales.—Range the timbales in a sautoire; fifteen minutes before serving, fill it to half the height of the molds with boiling water, and set the sautoire on the fire; when the water is ready to boil, remove and place it in a slack oven for ten or fifteen minutes; after a lapse of ten minutes touch the forcemeat in the center, and if firm, take them out, let stand for a little and invert the molds into a cloth to drain off all the liquid. Unmold.

Mousselines.—Put these into a flat sautoire furnished with a perforated grater having the holes at regular spaces apart so that each one can receive a mold. The molds being rounded at the bottom, these holes are to keep them standing upright. Pour boiling water into the saucepan nearly sufficient to cover the height of the molds and stand it on the fire; when the water boils, remove and push it gently into a slack oven for ten or fifteen minutes, sufficient time to poach them slowly; they will be found done when touched in the center, they resist to the pressure of the finger, then take them from the water, stand them on one side to drain and unmold. If the oven be too hot the timbales rise, which must be avoided otherwise they lose their quality.

(153). TO PRESS MEATS, GALANTINES, BREASTS, SWEETBREADS, ETC. (Pour Presser les Viandes, Galantines, Poitrines, Ris de veau, etc.).

For Meat Juices.—Have a press as shown in Fig. 70. The meats intended for pressing should be done rare, but cooked through, so that all the juice can be extracted. There is also a press for pressing galantines, sweetbreads, etc. This one is made as represented in Fig. 71; besides, there should be a double series of strips of wood, five inches across; the thinnest being a quarter of an inch thick, and the thickest are five inches; these are for the purpose of receiving the movable shelf belonging to the press so that all the pressed articles will be even throughout. For galantines it is also necessary to have a dozen tinned, sheet-iron sheets, a sixteenth of an inch thick, twelve inches long and six inches wide. These sheets are to be used when there are several galantines to equalize their thickness so that they are all pressed uniformly. The size of the press is thirty-eight inches high, twenty-eight inches wide and sixteen inches deep; the screw to be twenty-six inches long, and the wheel one foot in diameter. Press to the required thickness by arranging the strips either higher or lower;

FIG. 71.

FIG. 70.

for galantines they are put an inch lower than the galantine itself; turn the screw slowly until the movable shelf rests on the two strips which are the thickness required.

Sweetbreads are pressed either in round or oval molds, proportionate to the size of the sweetbreads; place these molds, one beside the other, on a shelf of the same dimension as the movable one and fill each one with a piece of unlarded, braised sweetbread just sufficiently large enough to fill up the mold when pressed.

For Breast of Mutton or Lamb, Braised and Cooked.—Range them on a board and press with a half inch thick strip on both sides to receive the movable shelf the same as the sweetbreads.

Beef Tongues are placed in a mold the shape of the tongue, it being two inches thick, eight and a half inches long and three and a half inches on its widest part. Molds containing two, four, or six tongues can be had.

Boned Hams are pressed in oval timbale molds.

Corned Beef in square molds, two and a half inches deep.

(154). TO PREPARE DECORATED QUENELLES, MOLDED QUENELLES AND POCKET QUENELLES (Pour Préparer les Quenelles Décorées, Moulées et à la Poche).

Large decorated quenelles are used as a garnishing or to complete relevé garnishings: they can be prepared with chicken, game or fish forcemeat. These quenelles are made on pieces of buttered white paper, shaping them to any desired form with a small knife while smoothing the surfaces neatly. Large quenelles are usually decorated with truffles or red beef tongue, the

FIG. 72.

FIG. 73.

FIG. 74.

former being preferable. The truffle decoration can be applied on to the quenelles either before or after poaching; in the first case the decorations are slightly incrusted into the forcemeat after wetting them with egg-white; the quenelles are then plunged into boiling water with the paper they have been molded on. If the quenelles are to be decorated after poaching then the pieces must be simply applied on, but first cover, or, better still, dampen one side with soft forcemeat so that they can adhere. Quenelles are poached in salted water without allowing it to boil.

Molded.—Butter some plain, oval-shaped, quenelle molds, using slightly melted butter; decorate the bottom of the mold the same as shown in the design. If required to be stuffed, then

FIG. 75.

FIG. 76.

FIG. 76 A.

place a layer of forcemeat on the decoration and over this any salpicon whatever (see salpicons, No. 165), and finish to fill the mold; smooth the tops, stand the molds on a baking pan, pour enough boiling water in to fill the pan to half the height of the molds and then poach in a slack oven. These molds are simply buttered, filled with forcemeat, smoothed on top and poached.

Pocket Quenelles.—Mix together half as much quenelle forcemeat (No. 89), as cream forcemeat (No. 75), incorporating the latter gradually into the former, pass it all once more through a fine sieve, and fill a strong paper cornet with a third part of this forcemeat, push small quarter inch quenelles the shape of beads on to a buttered sheet, and then poach them in boiling, salted

FIG. 77.

FIG. 78.

FIG. 79.

water. Color half of the remaining forcemeat with a little vegetal carmine, of a fine, light red color, and put this also into a paper cornet, and force them through on to another buttered sheet, letting these quenelles be channeled shaped, poach in salted, boiling water. Color the remainder of the forcemeat with spinach green or vegetal green to obtain a light pistachio color, and set them into a paper cornet also, and with it form oval shaped quenelles on to a buttered sheet, pour over some boiling, salted water, and let them poach for a few minutes. These quenelles are used as garnishings for soups, and for a variety of entrées.

(155). TO MOLD QUENELLES WITH A SPOON, EITHER PLAIN, FILLED OR ROLLED IN FLOUR (Pour Mouler les Quenelles à la Cuillère, Simples, Fourrées ou Roulées à la Farine).

Select two common, large and very thin iron soup spoons, put one of these into a small panful of hot water, and taking the other in the left hand fill the hollow center with the forcemeat, smooth the top with the blade of a small knife dipped in tepid water, arranging it in such a manner that there is as much forcemeat above as below the level of the spoon, then remove the quenelles with the hot spoon sliding it beneath the forcemeat, then slip it at once on to the bottom of a buttered sautéing pan, without turning it over, so that the same side is on top. If the quenelles are wanted filled, prepare a montglas composed of mushrooms, tongue, truffles or foies-gras; thicken it with some very compact reduced, good brown sauce, so that when cold the preparation can be divided into small parts, and rolled into olive shaped pieces in the hand; in this case, when the

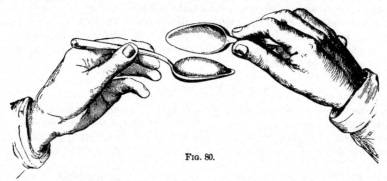

FIG. 80.

spoon is filled with forcemeat, make a small hole with the finger on the surface so as to insert the montglas, salpicon or purée, cover over with more forcemeat, being careful that it is the same thickness all over the filling, smooth it down nicely, and remove the quenelle with the hot spoon to slip it on to the bottom of a buttered sautéing pan without turning it over. Generally for one pound it will take eight large soup-spoonfuls, or sixteen dessert-spoons, or thirty-two tea-spoons, or sixty-four coffee-spoons. Poach these quenelles by pouring hot water into the sautéing pan beside the quenelles, and set the pan on the fire to bring it to boiling point; at the first boil, move it on one side, so that the water only simmers for six to fourteen minutes, according to their size. Lift the quenelles with a skimmer, and drain them on a cloth before using them.

FIG. 81.   FIG. 82.   FIG. 83.   FIG. 84.

To Prepare Quenelles Rolled in Flour.—Divide some game, chicken or fish forcemeat into pieces; roll each one on a flour dredged table into strings three-quarters of an inch in diameter; cut these into pieces three-quarters of an inch long; roll them on the table to give each one the shape of an olive or small egg half an inch in thickness and one inch in length. Larger ones can be made of Godiveau an inch and three-quarters long by five-eighths in thickness. Poach the quenelles in boiling water with salt added to it. The Godiveau quenelles are poached by ranging them at equal distances on a baking tin covered with a sheet of paper, then placing it in a very slack oven.

(156). TO RAISE, PARE AND POACH BREASTS OF POULTRY AND GAME (Pour Lever, Parer et Pocher les Filets de Volaille et de Gibier).

Cut off the pinions from a clean, singed chicken, split the breast skin from one end to the other in the center, open it so as to disclose the flesh, then detach the breasts with a small knife following the breast-bone, and leaving the minion fillets adhering to them, removing them later if not needed. Take these breasts one by one, lay them the smoothest side uppermost on a table, press them down with the left hand and slip the blade of a knife between the flesh and the skin, so as to remove the latter at one pull without breaking it. Beat the breasts lightly with a damp knife handle, trim them in round half hearts on one end, and pointed on the other; remove the inside nerve, and the fine skin from the minion fillet, beat these lightly and lay them on the inside surface of the breasts, if found necessary to enlarge them, but unless the breasts are very small, they are not added. They can be interlarded either with slices of truffle or tongue, by cutting five or six incisions across the minion-fillet and garnishing them with either of these. Proceed exactly in the same manner for breasts of game.

To Poach.—Place the breasts of poultry or game in a buttered sauteing pan; turn all the points toward the center and on them, place a sheet of buttered paper, put on the cover and set the pan in a slack oven leaving it in long enough to poach according to their size and quality.

(157). TO CLEAN CURRANTS, MALAGA AND SMYRNA RAISINS (Pour Nettoyer les Raisins de Corinthe, les Raisins de Malaga et de Smyrne).

Lay the currants on a table mixing in with them some flour, rub well together, then shake them through a coarse sieve, (No. 95) having eight meshes so that the small currant stalks pass through; wash well and dry them, then pick them over to free them of all the gravel stones which are generally to be found in these fruits, as well as the large stalks adhering to them.

Smyrna (Sultana) raisins are cleaned the same as currants; abstain from washing them. Seed Malaga raisins and pick off the stalks.

(158). RAVIOLES (Ravioles).

Roll out some raviole paste (No. 147), very thin and in a perfect square; lay on top half an inch from the edge and one inch apart some chicken raviole forcemeat balls (No. 93), three-quarters of an inch in diameter, after the entire flat is covered, moisten it lightly by passing a brush around the forcemeat balls and then place another flat of paste on top, it to be the same thickness as the

 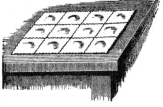 

FIG. 85. FIG. 86. FIG. 87.

under one and about four inches wider. Press on to this upper paste between the balls of forcemeat with a ruler and the whole length of the flat and then across so that every one of the balls is enclosed in a small square; cut each of these out with a channeled wheel or jagger (Fig. 87). The jaggers are used for cutting lattice work bands for pies, or else replace it by a round channeled pastry cutter. Lay the cut pieces on a flour dredged saucepan lid and then drop them into boiling water to poach for about twelve minutes.

(159). TO REDUCE AND STRAIN SAUCES THROUGH A TAMMY (Pour Réduire les Sauces et les Passer à l'Étamine).

FIG. 88.

The reason sauces are reduced is to give them the delicacy and succulence necessary to their finish, by incorporating into them fumets, stocks and the required condiments. The stocks that are to be added to the sauces in order to reduce them should be as concentrated as possible so as to avoid any superfluous labor. In order to reduce a strained, despumated sauce, pour it into a flat saucepan having a thick bottom, set it on a brisk fire and let the sauce boil while stirring it well with a spatula, and pressing it down in a way that the sauce will fail to adhere to the bottom, and therefore burn. Mix in gradually the stock needed for its improvement, and continue to boil until it has acquired the necessary consistency and succulence, then take it off, and strain it through a tammy.

(160). RICE FOR CROUSTADES AND RICE WITH CREAM (Riz Pour Croustades et riz à la Crème).

Pick well four pounds of Carolina rice, put it into a newly tinned saucepan without washing it, adding a half pound piece of fresh pork, moisten it to three times its height with some water: heat the liquid on a moderate fire, and at the first boil, remove it to a slower one; twenty minutes after when the liquid is nearly all absorbed, cover the rice with a heavy buttered paper, close the saucepan, and set it at the opening of a slack oven, finish cooking the rice, drying it thoroughly, then remove the saucepan from the oven, take out the piece of pork, and work the rice while still in the saucepan, using a spatula for the purpose, then pound it again in a mortar so as to reduce it to a smooth paste. Lay this rice on a dampened marble slab, or a thick baking sheet, knead it with the hands so that it becomes smooth, mold it round shaped, and set it in a saucepan, buttered over with a brush, or else a mold proportionate to the size needed for the croustade. Press the rice down well, cover the top with a round sheet of buttered paper, and set it in the ice box for seven or eight hours, but not allowing the saucepan or mold to touch the ice. Unmold the rice after dipping the saucepan in hot water, cutting it out with a knife.

Rice with Cream.—Blanch for a few moments half a pound of fine, picked and washed rice; drain and refresh, then put it back into the saucepan and moisten it with one quart of boiled milk in which a stick of vanilla has been infused. Let the liquid come again to a boil, cover the saucepan, and finish cooking the whole very slowly for forty minutes. When the rice is tender and has absorbed all the liquid, add to it a pinch of salt, three ounces of sugar, two ounces of fresh butter and a few spoonfuls of whipped cream. Sometimes a few egg-yolks are added to this rice, if so, they must be put in before any other of the ingredients, while the rice has all its heat, so that the eggs can cook while in the act of stirring them.

(161). TO PREPARE RISSOLES (Pour Préparer les Rissoles).

Rissoles are prepared in two different ways, the first, by rolling out some fine paste or clippings of puff paste, into a long, thin piece from ten to fourteen inches wide; wet the bottom edges of this paste, then lay on it four balls of an inch and a quarter in diameter for the two and three-quarter inch rissoles made of rissole preparation, and from two and three-eighths inches distance apart from each other, and two inches from the edges; refold the paste forward, so as to cover up the prepared balls, and fasten the paste down to six-eighths of an inch around the balls;

Fig. 89.

Fig. 90.

press on the two layers of paste to adhere them together, then cut out the rissoles half circular with a channeled pastry-cutter either two and one-quarter, two and one-half or two and three-quarters inches in diameter. As soon as the rissoles of the first row are cut, lay them aside; pare the edges of the paste and begin the operation again; reduce the height of the cut out rissoles by pressing them down with the finger without misshaping them. These rissoles may now be breaded and dipped in egg, or left white; in the first case, lay them simply on a tin sheet covered with a white paper till ready to fry. In the second, place them at some distance apart on a floured cloth so that the paste cannot adhere to it. To prepare rissoles differently, roll out a thin flat, cut it into small round pieces with a channeled pastry-cutter either two and one-quarter, two and one-half or two and three-quarters inches in diameter, and on each one of these, lay a prepared rissole ball; wet the paste all round, and fold the piece of paste over the ball fastening the two edges together. Press the tops lightly with the fingers, keeping them a good shape, and lay the unbreaded ones on a floured cloth, and the breaded ones on white paper.

(162). TO CUT ROOTS WITH A SPOON AND A VEGETABLE CUTTER (Manière de Couper les Racines à la Cuillère et à la Machine).

Peel or scrape carrots, peel turnips, celery roots, turnip-cabbage or kohl-rabi, sweet potatoes or common potatoes; wash and keep them in cold water until needed; all of these vegetables including peeled truffles can be cut olive shaped or in rounds large or small according to require-ments (Fig. 91). The rounds should be from a quarter of an inch to one inch in diameter; the long ovals from half an inch to one and a quarter inches. The oval spoons for this purpose may be either plain or channeled. When cutting vegetables with a spoon into either balls or olives dip the sharp end of the spoon into the thickest part of the root all through the depth and endeavor to remove the pieces as whole and perfect as possible.

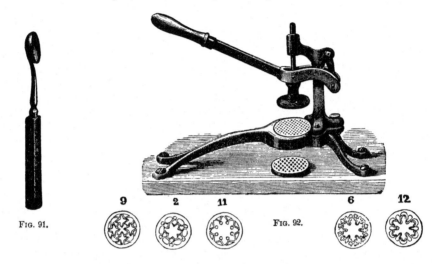

FIG. 91.   FIG. 92.

Vegetable Cutter.—(Fig. 92). This utensil is simple, practical and useful. It is used for cutting vegetables and roots into various shapes for soups or garnishing; having them pass by pressure through the deep cutters made of steel and movable so they can be easily changed when so desired. To proceed, first cut the roots into thin slices, all of equal thickness; place one of these on any one of the selected cutters; put this under the press and bear heavily on it. The pieces will fall through; pick out the imperfect ones; the others are ready for use.

(163). BLONDE AND BROWN ROUX (Roux blond et brun).

Roux is flour fried in butter and allowed to attain more or less color; it is used for thickening gravies, soup stocks and sauces; there are two kinds of roux, the blonde and the brown; the blonde is made as follows: Put into a saucepan to melt, one pound and two ounces of butter, add to it one pound of sifted flour and place the saucepan on a moderate fire to let it cook slowly while stir-ring until it becomes of a light blonde; this is used for velouté. For the brown, leave it on the fire or in a slack oven until it assumes a darker color; should it not be necessary to use it at once, pour it into a vessel, and employ it as needed, but when required for immediate use, take it from the fire, leave it in the pan and let it lose a few degrees of its heat before moistening it. For a velouté, dilute it with a white velouté stock, and a brown espagnole stock if needed for brown; the proportions for both velouté and espagnole being: one pound and two ounces of butter, one pound of flour and four quarts of either white or brown stock.

(164). RUM FLAVORED WITH VANILLA; SPIRIT OF STRAWBERRIES, RASPBERRIES AND APRICOTS (Rhum Vanillé; Esprit de Fraises, Framboises et Abricots).

Rum flavored with Vanilla.—Put twelve vanilla beans cut in pieces in a quart bottle with a quarter of a pint of boiling water, twelve hours later fill up the bottle with good rum and leave it for ten days; it will then be ready for use.

Spirit of Strawberries, etc.—Crush thirty pounds of strawberries or raspberries; to this pulp add three quarts of spirits of wine, put into an earthen crock, cover and leave to infuse for fif-teen days. Distill the fruits in an alembic in a bain-marie and continue the distillation until the liquor reaches twenty degrees. Spirit of apricots is made the same way only taking twenty pounds of fruit instead of thirty for each three quarts of spirit. The fruits are pressed through a sieve and the kernels broken and crushed in a mortar, then mixed in with the apricots.

(165). SALPICON; HOW TO PREPARE (Salpicon; Manière de le Préparer).

Salpicons are prepared with cooked and cold meats and fish, red beef tongue, sweetbreads or beef palates; they are also made of chicken or game fillets, foies-gras, also with truffles, mushrooms. cèpes, and besides these, oysters, lobsters, crawfish, etc.

The characteristic of salpicon is that it is cut into small squares; they may be prepared with one kind of substance alone, but are generally mixed, for example: chickens, with red beef tongue, truffles or mushrooms; game, with foies-gras or truffles, and fish, with mushrooms and truffles. Salpicons are always thickened with a sauce corresponding to the nature of the meat, and in all cases it must be succulent and condensed.

(166). TO SCALD (Échauder).

In an analogous sense, scalding means to dip, to plunge in boiling water. A pig, a suckling pig, calf's head and feet of either the calf or sheep, chicken's legs and even whole poultry is scalded.

To scald a pig is to detach the bristles adhering to its back by means of hot water, done by dipping it once or twice in hot water to facilitate pulling them out more readily, then scrape the surface with a knife; this operation must be performed as quickly as possible. The same to be done for calf's feet and head, also for sheep and lamb's trotters. Poultry is sometimes scalded, but this system of treatment should be completely abandoned and the feathers picked off dry, this being far superior to the scalding process; for by scalding poultry, especially young chickens they become partially cooked and the skin is apt to tear when being trussed; they also contract a bad taste and decompose quicker than those that are dry picked.

(167). SIEVE-CLOTH OF DIFFERENT SIZE MESHES (Toile à Tamis de Différentes Grosseurs).

Fig. 93 (four mesh) is used for broken and coarsely chopped almonds; Fig. 94 (six mesh) is used for Mocha sugar, finely chopped almonds and raisins; Fig. 95 (eight mesh) is used for bread

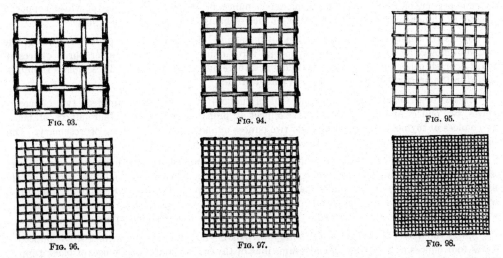

FIG. 93.   FIG. 94.   FIG. 95.

FIG. 96.   FIG. 97.   FIG. 98.

crumbs; Fig. 96 (twelve mesh) is used for powdered macaroons, purées and marmalades; Fig. 97 (sixteen mesh) is used for sugar, flour and purées; Fig. 98 (twenty-eight mesh) is used for icing sugar. A mesh indicates the number of holes to each linear inch.

(168). SPICES, AROMATICS, AND SEASONINGS FOR COOKING PURPOSES (Épices, Aromates et Assaisonnements pour la Cuisine).

The different articles employed as seasonings in kitchen work are comprised of salt, spices, aromatics, butter, fat, vinegar, oil and mustard. Salt is without exception the most indispensable seasoning; it removes the insipid taste from meats, vegetables and all other eatables. It excites the appetite and helps digestion, but of course must be used with judgment, for too much is apt to make it unhealthy. Coarse salt is the one to be used for cooking boiled meats and vegetables. Finely pulverized white salt is for table use and the one used in kitchens for seasoning is merely crushed and sifted purified salt. Spices are of different kinds; they are void of nutritious properties and are only for the purpose of improving the taste of various foods. They are composed of common black and white pepper, cayenne pepper; then come the weaker spices such as nutmeg, cinnamon, cloves and coriander. For seasoning, common raw pepper, ground only when ready to use is both agreeable and a tonic, but as much cannot be said for pepper cooked in stews, sauces or soups, for it loses its aroma while cooking and therefore only the acridity remains. Peppers that do not deteriorate while cooking are paprika (a Hungarian product), and red pepper; these both give a most agreeable flavor to stews and sauces, increasing as the cooking proceeds, and either of them are agreeable to the taste and a tonic without producing any irritating results.

Aromatics.—Among the most aromatic plants used in the kitchen must be mentioned bay leaf, marjoram, chives, sage, thyme, wild thyme, savory, tarragon, pimpernel, chervil, pepper-cress, parsley, onion, shallot, garlic and horseradish root. Some of these are used in a dry state, others in a fresh, and both are employed in numerous preparations. They can be used in sautés, braizés, in sauces and even in soups. The action of these aromatics on the general health is only injurious when indulged in injudiciously or in too large quantities, but when employed with a certain reserve, they are both healthy, stimulating and agreeable.

Curry, the Best, comes from India.—An imitation curry is made of one ounce of coriander seeds, two ounces of cayenne, a quarter of an ounce of cardamon seeds, one ounce salt, two ounces of tumeric, one ounce ginger, half an ounce of mace and a third of an ounce of saffron.

Prepared Red Pepper is made with paprika (Hungarian red pepper), and Spanish sweet pimentos mixed in equal quantities. In case paprika cannot be had use quarter cayenne pepper and three-quarters Spanish pimentos.

Spices.—Before grinding spices be careful that they are the freshest; grind each kind separately and sift them through a silk sieve, then mix thoroughly and put them into hermetically closed bottles, and set these in a cool place (they are only to be mixed when ready to use).

Spices for Bread Stuffing.—Two ounces of sage, one ounce of marjoram, half an ounce of cayenne pepper, half an ounce of allspice, one ounce of thyme, two ounces of white pepper, a quarter of an ounce of nutmeg, and half an ounce of finely minced green celery leaf.

Spices for Game Pies and Galantines.—One pound of cinnamon, one pound of nutmeg, one pound of cloves, one pound of whole peppers, three ounces of cayenne pepper, three ounces of sweet Spanish pepper, three ounces of thyme and three ounces of bay leaf. These spices should be mixed in the proportion of one ounce to a pound of salt.

Spices for General Use.—Two ounces of cinnamon, two ounces of nutmeg, two ounces of cloves, two ounces of white pepper, twelve ounces of prepared red pepper, four ounces of mace, two ounces of thyme, two ounces of sage, two ounces of marjoram, two ounces of rosemary. One ounce of spices to two pounds of salt.

Spices for Turtle Soup.—Two ounces of curry, half an ounce of thyme, two ounces dry mushrooms, half an ounce of sage, a quarter of an ounce of mace, half an ounce garden citron, half an ounce of basil, half an ounce marjoram, half of the peel of a chopped lemon, two ounces of white pepper. These aromatics and spices are used when there is no time to prepare a stock, or when preserved turtle has to be used. Two ounces of spices to one pound of salt.

Spices for Goose Liver Patties (Pâté de foies gras).—Four ounces of nutmeg, four ounces of cloves, four ounces of basil, four of marjoram, four of thyme, two and a half ounces of black pepper, three ounces of white pepper, two and one-third ounces of bay leaf, two and a half ounces of mace, two and a half ounces of ginger, two and a third of coriander seeds, one and two-thirds ounce of sweet pepper. One ounce of these mixed spices to every two pounds of salt.

(169). STEARINE; HOW TO CAST AND COLOR IT (Stéarine; Manière de la Couler et de la Colorer).

Casting stearine in plaster molds is most simple and only requires a little attention. Tinned copper molds should be smooth in the inside and even polished. Put all the plaster molds in a vessel after separating each piece and leave them in tepid water for half an hour or longer according to their size. For tinned copper molds coat them first with a thin layer of stearine, then place another layer on this first one and continue until the stearine be sufficiently thick. The stearine must be melted in a bain-marie or on a slow fire, being careful to keep it stirred and also not to heat it too violently so that it remains white, for if too greatly heated it turns yellow and thereby looses its beautiful white appearance; if this should happen it should only be used to coat the inside of large pieces or else for pads for filling the inside of borders. To cast stearine in plaster molds, take the molds from the water, drain them out for a moment and then fit each piece into its respective place ; tie around firmly, fill up with the melted stearine and when a light crust has formed on the surface, break it and empty out the mold ; let rest for one minute, put it back into the water, remove and unmold with the greatest care. Should the unmolded pieces fail to be smooth or else be creased, this is caused by the stearine not being sufficiently warm and the molds too cold, and that the stearine was cast too slowly. This is of great importance to observe and is most essential when perfection is required. When the objects intended for casting are frail, such as rings, arms, figures or other thin pieces, it will be advisable to insert thin wires into these parts before casting the stearine in the mold. After unmolding the subjects, wash the mold well, being careful that no particles of stearine remain in the joints. so that it can be thoroughly closed and the stearine cannot escape through these joints. Scrape the seams or moldings carefully. Stearine subjects can be colored with one or more colors; for this purpose use water paints (tubes in preference). This kind is mostly employed for this work and to it add a little beef gall to enable the paint to adhere on to the greasy surface. Use a soft badger brush and proceed with care; always wait until the first coat be dry before applying another. With a little taste and skill subjects can be painted so that a great effect is produced, especially for the larger ones. When required to be bronzed, mix a few drops of gum arab with a little of the gall, add bronze powder and a little water ; stir well, keeping it the consistency of honey. Paint over the subject with a camel's hair brush and if one coat be not sufficient then give another, adding a little more water.

(170). TO STRAIN PURÉES (Pour passer les purées).

FIG. 99.

FIG. 99a.

FIG. 99b.

Vegetable, chicken, crustacean, and game purées are strained through a tammy (Fig. 99) in order to obtain them as fine as possible. To accomplish this it will require the service of two persons : take hold of the tammy on both sides, pour the purée into its hollow center, then have two wooden spoons one laying in the other, and press them vigorously against the tammy, allowing the purée to fall into a deep dish set underneath; this is easily accomplished and depends entirely upon the regular motion of the two spoons, as they must advance backward and forward without getting separated, or use either one of the machines shown in Figs. 99a and 99b.

(171). TO COOK SUGAR (Pour cuire le sucre).

In former days sugars were less refined than in our time, therefore it was most important that they should undergo the operation of clarification, or, as the very word implies rid them of their impurities and make them perfectly clear. To-day this operation is almost useless, however, in case of necessity we will give the exact manner of proceeding, for it may sometimes be found useful. Put twenty pounds of sugar into a copper basin, melt it with two-thirds of its quantity of water, or one-half pint of water to each pound of sugar, set it on the fire, and when the scum begins to rise, throw in some egg-whites beaten up with water, the proportions being one white for each quart of water; do not stir it again, but let it rise to the surface twice, then pour in half a pint of clear water without eggs; let it rise a third time, and as it does so, remove from off the fire and skim it. Return it to one side of the fire to let it boil and drive the scum on one side of the basin, skim this off as quickly as it gathers. Soon the sugar will become very fine, clear and transparent, but if otherwise, then let it boil till it clarifies thoroughly and pass it through the flannel bag. Sugar clarified by this process is ready to be submitted to all kinds of cooking which we explain further on. The cooking of sugar is easily measured by a thermometer, but a clever workman will quickly find it out by the mere touch. These various cookings take different names which we will now endeavor to explain.

First—Lissé ou Petit Filet or Small Thread.—Cook the sugar, and in order to be sure that it has reached the first cooking, take out a little of the sugar with a spoon, dip the index finger in it and apply the finger to the thumb; separate the two fingers immediately, the sugar should then form a small thread, the thermometer marking two hundred and fifteen degrees Fahrenheit, (one hundred and one degrees Centigrade).

Second—Grand Lissé or Large Thread.—At two hundred and seventeen degrees, the sugar stretches a little more between the fingers, it is now cooked to large thread (one hundred and two degrees Centigrade).

Third—Petit Perlé or Little Pearl.—The sugar reaches this cooking when between the two fingers it stretches and forms a thread that breaks. The thermometer is then two hundred and twenty degrees (one hundred and five degrees Centigrade).

Fourth—Grand Perlé or Large Pearl.—As soon as the sugar extends from one finger to the other without breaking it has reached large pearl, two hundred and twenty-two degrees Fahrenheit (one hundred and six Centigrade).

Fifth—Au soufflé ou Glue, or the Blow.—Dip a skimmer into the sugar, knock it at once against the edges of the basin, blow through the skimmer so as to make the small bubbles fly out, and when they do so properly, the sugar has reached its degree of cooking. The thermometer now marks two hundred and thirty degrees Fahrenheit (one hundred and ten degrees Centigrade).

Sixth—Petit Boulé or Small Ball.—Dip the finger first into cold water, then in the sugar, and immediately into water; if the sugar has reached to proper cooking or small ball, it can be rolled into a soft ball between the fingers, two hundred and thirty-six to two hundred and thirty-eight degrees Fahrenheit (one hundred and fourteen to one hundred and fifteen degrees Centigrade).

Seventh—Grand Boulé or Large Ball.—When the thermometer reaches two hundred and forty-six to two hundred and forty-eight degrees Fahrenheit or one hundred and nineteen to one hundred and twenty degrees Centigrade, then the ball instead of remaining soft when rolled between the fingers, becomes solid and hard, the sugar has now reached large ball.

Eighth—Petit Cassé or Small Crack.—Dip the tip of the finger into cold water, then into the sugar and rapidly into cold water again, so as to detach it from the finger; if it has reached its proper cooking it should break. The thermometer is now two hundred and ninety degrees Fahrenheit (one hundred and forty-three degrees Centigrade).

Ninth—Cassé or Crack.—Letting the sugar boil a few minutes longer, it will reach the crack; now dip the finger into cold water, then into the sugar, and again into the water, the sugar must break between the teeth without adhering to them. It reaches this degree when the thermometer is at three hundred and ten degrees Fahrenheit (or one hundred and fifty-four degrees Centigrade).

Tenth. Grand Cassé or Large Crack or Caramel.—This last cooking is exceedingly delicate and requires the most particular care, so as to avoid having the sugar turn black which it is apt to do very easily. When reaching this last cooking, the sugar slightly loses its whiteness and assumes a shade scarcely perceptible to the eye; this is when the thermometer reaches three hundred degrees Farenheit, and it is now time to add to each twenty pounds of sugar, a teaspoonful of lemon juice. Continue the cooking and when the thermometer reaches three hundred and forty-five to three hundred and fifty degrees Fahrenheit, then remove the basin quickly from the fire, and instantly pour its contents on a marble to get cold.

These are the various degrees the cooking of sugar undergoes, practice alone makes perfect in this particular work, which can only be acquired after much study and attention.

(172). SUGARS OF DIFFERENT COLORS, AND ICING SUGAR (Sucres de Différentes Couleurs et Sucre à glace Impalpable).

For Pink, have powdered sugar from which icing sugar has been sifted, spread it on a baking-sheet covered with white paper, lay the tin on top of a very moderate fire, and pour into it sufficient carmine to give it the necessary color; mix and rub it slowly between the hands until the moisture contained in the carmine be entirely evaporated, then sift it through a sixteen mesh sieve (Fig. 97).

For Yellow.—Prepare the sugar the same as for the pink, using Breton vegetal yellow.

For Orange.—The same as the pink, coloring with Breton vegetal orange, or yellow and red mixed to imitate orange.

Lilac and Violet.—The same as the pink, coloring it with red and ultramarine blue, or else with Breton vegetal lilac or violet.

Blue—Breton vegetal blue and ultramarine blue.

Green.—Breton vegetal green, or else spinach green or watercress green.

Icing Sugar.—There are very few cities where powdered sugar is unobtainable, also icing sugar (confectionery sugar), but in case it has to be prepared at home the following remarks will be found useful. Pound some lump sugar to the finest powder, pass it through an ordinary sieve, then through an icing sieve called a drum; this latter includes two sieves, one for passing ordinary sugar and another much finer for passing the icing sugar, meaning exceedingly fine powdered sugar almost impalpable.

(173). BAND TART (Tourte à bande).

Roll out on a floured table, a layer of foundation paste (No. 135), cut in this a round, eight inches in diameter, lay this round on a small baking-sheet, moisten the border with a brush, and apply on this wet part, a puff-paste border having received six turns, five-eighths of an inch in thickness, one and one-half inches wide and twenty-six inches long; cut the two ends bias, fasten

Fig. 100.

them together after slightly dampening them and set the tart aside in a cool place for fifteen minutes. Prepare an egg wash of well beaten whole eggs, or the yolks alone diluted in a little cold water, apply it to the border, prick the inside or else put in a small mold, to prevent it inflating, then set the tart in a hot oven the same as for a vol-au-vent for thirty or forty minutes. After removing it from the fire, detach it from the sheet, and lay it on a dish to keep warm.

(174). EMPTY TARTS, ANCIENT STYLE (Tourtes à l'Ancienne).

Spread on a baking-sheet a layer of foundation paste eight inches in diameter; wet the edges of this crust using a brush, and lay on the center a spherical shaped pad, four and three-quarters in diameter and two and one-half high, made of paper and wrapped in slices of fat pork. Cover this pad with an upper layer of paste made with puff-paste clippings, fasten the upper and lower crusts together by pressing them down with the thumb, and cut away the surplus paste with the tip of a small knife, following the outlines of the lower crust. Moisten the edges of the crust and place it on a band of six-turn puff paste (No. 147), an inch and a half wide by twenty-six inches long, and three-eighths of an inch thick; cut off the ends on the bias, wet them slightly and fasten

FIG. 101.

them together with the finger; channel the band lightly, decorate the dome with leaves cut from the paste, egg the surface, also the band, and bake the tart for thirty to forty minutes in a well heated, but not too hot oven. After removing the tart from the fire, cut the dome at the base so as to remove the pad; it is now ready to fill.

(175). THICKENINGS FOR SOUPS, SAUCES AND STEWS (Liaisons pour Potages, Sauces et Ragoûts).

Thickening for Soups.—Put some egg-yolks into a bowl, beat them up with a wooden spoon and dilute with a few spoonfuls of good raw cream; some broth, or cold sauce; pass this through a sieve or tammy, add a dash of grated nutmeg and a few bits of fine butter. Boil well the soup, remove it to one side of the range and mix in the strained thickening; return it to the hot fire, to let cook without ceasing to stir and especially without letting it boil.

For Sauces.—This thickening is composed of egg-yolks beaten and diluted with some cold broth or raw cream. In order to thicken the sauce, it should necessarily be boiling, then remove it from the hot fire and stir a spoonful or more of it into the thickening, then pour the rest of the thickening into the sauce and cook it while stirring over a slow fire, without permitting it to boil. All sauces thickened with eggs must afterward be strained through a tammy.

Thickening or Liaison Prepared Ready to Use.—Twenty-five egg-yolks for one quart of cream; mix well together, pass it through a fine strainer and keep it in a pot (Fig. 171) in order to thicken sauces and stews as they are needed.

Butter and Cream Thickening.—Incorporate some butter and cream, and just when ready to serve, stir it vigorously (do not heat it again), and serve it at once.

Blood Thickening.—Reserve the blood of poultry or game, adding to it a little vinegar to prevent it from coagulating, then strain it through a sieve and stir it in gradually when needed to thicken a sauce.

Arrowroot, Fecula and Cornstarch Thickening.—Dilute one or the other of these with some water, broth or cold milk; strain through a sieve, and pour it into the liquid, stirring it continuously.

Thickening of Kneaded Butter.—Incorporate as much flour into butter as it will absorb to form a soft paste; mix it in small parts in the sauce, stirring constantly until all the butter is melted.

(176). TO LINE AND BAKE TIMBALE CRUSTS (Pour Foncer et Cuire les Croûtes à Timbales).

Butter a plain timbale mold, five inches in diameter at the bottom, five and a quarter across the top and five and a half inches deep. If the timbale is to be decorated, apply some bits of sweetened noodle paste against the sides and bottom of the mold, dampen them with a brush dipped in water and then line the timbale with a paste not rolled out too thin. With a pastry cutter, two inches in diameter narrower than the mold, cut the paste from the bottom, but do not remove it; cover the whole surface of the paste with buttered white paper and fill in the empty space with common flour; dampen the edges, and cover the top first with a round piece of buttered paper, and then with a layer of the same paste, fastening it down to the dampened sides. Egg over the surface, and let it rest for fifteen minutes in a cool place, then set the timbale on a round baking sheet and cook it for fifty minutes in a hot oven. After removing it, unmold, open the top (the end which before was the bottom), and lift up the round piece previously cut with the pastry cutter, and which can easily be removed, then take out all the flour through this opening, also the paper, and brush the inside twice over with egg-yolks, then lay the timbale for a very few moments in a very hot oven so that it browns nicely, and range it on a dish to be garnished.

(177). TO BRUSH AND PEEL TRUFFLES (Pour Brosser et Peler les Truffes).

Put some raw, fresh truffles into cold water; wash them well, changing the water, then take them out one by one, and rub the surfaces over strongly with a hard brush, and throw them as fast as they are done into clean water, drain; take them out again one by one, and remove with a small knife all those parts the brush failed to touch, then refresh them leaving them as little as possible in the water. Wipe the truffles on a cloth, and with the tip of a knife detach all the skin covering them, cutting it away as thinly as possible, put the truffles as fast as they are done into a saucepan with a well-fitting lid; put also the peelings into a saucepan, and keep them in a cool place while waiting to be used.

(178). TO DRESS, SINGE AND TRUSS POULTRY AND GAME FOR ENTREES (Pour Habiller, Flamber et Brider la Volaille et le Gibier à Plumes pour Entrées).

After having dressed (drawn) and singed the pieces of poultry or game, remove the fork and breastbone, lifting it out through the neck without injuring the breasts; cut the legs below the

FIG. 102.

FIG. 103.

joint, suppress the drumstick bones, and slip the leg into its place, having previously burned the top of the leg with alcohol so as to remove the outer skin. To truss either capon, young turkey, pullet, chicken or guinea-fowl: first, have a trussing needle threaded with some strong string, pass it through one thigh to the other and in the joint of the thick part of the leg, then cross through the wing directing the needle toward the neck, and take up the skin of the neck while passing through it, fastening it down to the back; pass through the other wing, tighten the string so that the wings and thigh are well attached to the body of the fowl, and the breasts are quite prominent. Secondly, with the needle cross through the back near the rump, direct the needle so that it passes the thickest part of the two legs, fasten the string strongly so that the thigh is well attached to the side, thrust the posterior inside, and tie it down with a few turns of a string. To prepare geese and tame ducks for entrées, suppress the wings and neck, singe and pick them, cut off the claws, truss the legs inside, and fasten them down by crossing through with the needle at the joints of the thighs and the stumps of the wings; give them a rounded appear-

FIG. 104.

ance, and push the posterior into the inside, and tie it firmly in place. For squabs, partridges and quails: pluck the feathers, singe and lightly pick them and draw them through the pouch; then truss them by making an incision in the rump, and tie them the same as the chickens.

(179). TO DRESS, SINGE AND TRUSS POULTRY AND GAME FOR ROASTING. (Pour Habiller, Flamber et Brider la Volaille et le Gibier à Plumes pour Rôtir).

Dressing poultry and feathered game consists of first bleeding, then plucking out the feathers, drawing, singeing and trussing them. To dress a chicken it must first be singed lightly all over with spirits of wine set afire, or over a gas-jet, in order to remove every vestige of feathers. When the poultry or game is singed, then pick out all the feather-stumps remaining in the skin. Burn off the skin from the legs to enable it to be taken off with a cloth. To singe small birds stick them simply on small skewers four or six at a time and pass them over a flame. For drawing a chicken cut on the back of the neck making a long aperture through which the pouch and wind pipe can be removed; put the index finger into the interior following the neck to detach the lungs adhering to the inside; make a small opening next to the rump to empty the chicken entirely and then wipe out the insides, cut the skin below the head, chop the neck off on a level with the breast chop off the feet and the end of the pinions and cross the wings over the back of the chicken. Thread a long piece of string into a large trussing needle, lay the chicken on the table, pressing it down on its back, then with the open left hand take hold of the two thighs, so as to keep them held up at an equal height, pass through the flesh with the needle just below the drum-sticks, turn the chicken over on its side to thread it through the wings, running the needle through the breast skin; pull the string tight tie it on the side with a knot, and lay the chicken once more on its back, press the thighs down again with the left hand and run the needle through above the drum-

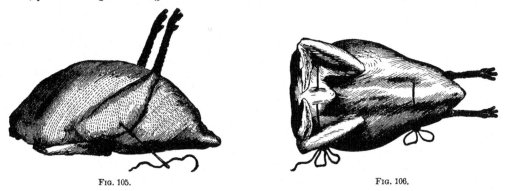

FIG. 105.   FIG. 106.

sticks, then turn the chicken over on its side, and introduce the needle across the carcass, and at a quarter of the length of the bird near the rump to the other side, to meet the other end of the string and then tie it into a knot (Fig. 106). In this manner the chicken is properly trussed, and both knots being on the same side, they are easily cut and the string pulled out when the chicken is cooked. Pheasants, partridges and pigeons are to be trussed the same way when intended for roasting. After the poultry or game is trussed, lard it with thin slices of fresh pork,

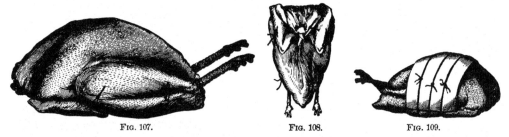

FIG. 107.   FIG. 108.   FIG. 109.

sufficiently large to cover the whole breast, pare them square shaped, score them lightly on one side, and lay them over the breast, fastening them on with a string as shown in Fig. 109.

Wild Ducks (Canvas Backs, Red Heads, Black Heads, Mallard, Ruddy, Teal, etc.).—Select two fine red head ducks, pick them as far up as one inch from the head, being very careful not to tear the skin; singe and draw. In order to accomplish this, the skin must be cut the whole length of the neck from its beginning until the back of the head is reached, remove the pouch and windpipe, stick the finger in the neck far down in the inside to detach the lights from the bones

FIG. 110.

FIG. 111.

and all adhering to the breast, make an incision above the rump and take out the gizzard drawing up the whole of the insides; cut the neck where it begins at the carcass, cutting the skin as far up as it is picked. Wipe the duck carefully, thrust the feet inside and season it interiorly with salt and mignonette. Should the duck be gamy it must have the inside washed out. Pick the feathers from the head and separate it where the neck finishes ; pick out the eyes and place the head in the opening that was used for drawing the bird; truss the duck bringing the feet toward the front and passing the trussing needle threaded with string near the first joint of the thigh next to the feet. Run the needle through the duck under the breast and then across the other thigh, pressing the duck down well so as to round well the breast, bring the neck skin down on the back and run the needle on the bias through the pinion-bone at the same time through the neck skin to pass it through the other pinion and return from whence it started, pull the string tight and push the rump inward, running the needle through to keep it in place, and bringing it back to one inch from its starting point, passing it through the skin and through the head by the eyes, fasten the two ends of string together tying them firmly.

(180). VOL-AU-VENT CRUST (Croûte de vol-au-vent).

Prepare a puff paste with one pound of fine, dry flour and one pound of good butter, proceeding as for No. 146; give it six and a half turns, and when the paste is made, lay it on a floured baking tin, and set on top of it a model of tin or heavy cardboard having the exact dimensions desired for the vol-au-vent, cut the paste all around this with a small, heated knife. following the outlines of the model, but keeping the knife slightly inclined outward. As soon as the vol-au-vent is cut, turn it with one stroke upside down on to another dampened round baking sheet, being

FIG. 112.

careful not to injure its shape; groove the edges lightly with the back of a knife as represented in in the plate (Fig. 112); egg the surfaces over, and trace a ring, using the tip of a small knife an inch and a half from the edge, then in the center of this ring trace four or five light incisions to form lozenges. Bake the vol-au-vent in a hot oven for thirty minutes or more according to its size, opening the oven as little as possible. When the paste is dry and a fine color, take it out, open it by lifting up the center cover, and empty it of all the uncooked paste within, lay the vol-au-vent on to a dish, and keep it warm in the heater, not allowing the crust to get cold before using it. Small vol-au-vent crusts may be prepared the same way, using a three and a half inch pastry cutter to cut them with.

(181). SMALL VOL-AU-VENT CRUST IN TWO PIECES (Petites croûtes de vol-au-vent en deux pièces).

Roll out with the rolling pin on a floured table, one pound of six-turn puff paste (No. 146), one quarter of an inch to three-eighths in thickness, let it rest for fifteen minutes, then cut from its surface six channeled or plain round pieces three and a half inches in diameter; as soon as this is done, remove the centers with a smooth pastry cutter two and a half inches in diameter; dipping it each time into hot water so as to make a clean cut, but it must be wiped dry

FIG. 113.

before using. Cut up the clippings of paste, roll them to an eighth of an inch thick, and from this piece cut six round channeled or plain round under crusts three and a half inches in diameter, range these at regular distances on a wet baking sheet, moisten the edges of the paste with a brush, and lay on top of each one, one of the prepared rings, taking them up

FIG. 114.

delicately so as not to break them, and press lightly on them to fasten the edges together; egg the surfaces of the rings, and let them rest for ten minutes, then push the baking sheet into a well heated, but moderate oven to bake from twenty to twenty-five minutes; after removing, detach them from the tin, press the center of the paste down with the finger, and keep them warm for garnishing. Small vol-au-vents may be prepared the same way making them of one piece only.

(182). WHITE STOCK FOR MEATS AND VEGETABLES (Blanc pour cuisson de Viandes et Légumes).

Have half a pound of chopped beef suet or marrow, and as much fresh fat pork, melt the whole in a saucepan, adding to it two minced carrots, two onions and one onion with six cloves in it, a bunch of parsley garnished with a bayleaf and as much thyme and a bit of mace. Add to it a teaspoonful of whole peppers, and put this on the fire to fry without coloring. Mix in well one ounce of flour, and dilute with three quarts of water, and four quarts of broth, salt, and the pulp of two lemons. This stock is used for cooking calf's heads, lamb trotters and also for artichoke bottoms, cardoons and oyster plants.

KITCHEN UTENSILS.

ROASTER AND SPITS (Rôtissoire et broches).

In large kitchens the only roaster possible is the one shown in Fig. 115 with its broad hearth, long spits, long hanging chains and wheels; an endless chain with a weight sufficiently heavy to rotate it,

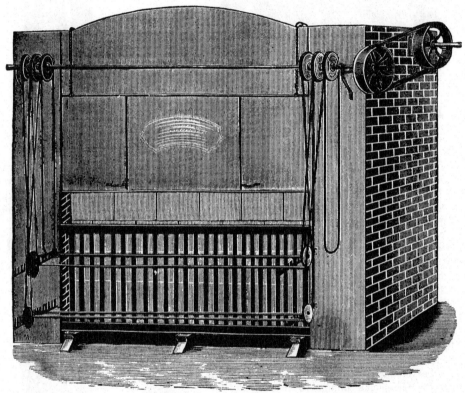

Fig. 115.

steam, electricity or hydraulic pressure can to be used advantageously to attain the same end. Fig.117, represents a roasting spit for small game, quails, woodcocks, thrush, etc. It is provided with six skewers; run the game on to one of these through the two leg bones; use as much as possible the different sides for different games, for instance one side for quails, partridges or thrush and the other three skewers for snipe, woodcock, plovers, bustards, etc. These spits are very useful for large dinners, for eight quails can be put on each skewer or forty-eight quails can be roasted at once without having them too

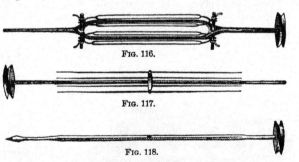

Fig. 116.

Fig. 117.

Fig. 118.

crowded. The length of the spit is sixty-eight inches and the length of each one of the six skewers is twenty inches. For cradle spit No. 116, the cut of meat to be roasted such as loin, the saddle is placed exactly in the center to regulate the weight evenly.   The simple spit for poultry, game. turkey, etc. is shown in Fig. 118.   A spit being at times an impossibility, one is frequently obliged to have resource to the more simple roasters.   The greatest objection to the old fashioned shell roaster is that the spit did not turn alone, it had to be everlastingly

FIG. 119.

FIG. 120.

turned for if left the meat would certainly spoil; a great improvement on this is the turning spring spit to be wound up like a clock and strikes an alarm when slackening by the movable balls of the fan striking on a gong (Fig. 119).   There are other roasters having two spoons turning at the same time as the spit feeding a small reservoir found on the top of the spit and through

a shallow furrow perforated by small holes, the meat is continuously basted.   The three pieces composing this oven are movable and can therefore be transported to any desirable place; the shell can easily be fastened on to the wall.   There are also English spits adapted for all hearths (Fig. 120); it is easy to fasten it to a movable hearth fitting with the spit.   These are run by clock work placed on top; the roasts are suspended perpendicularly and always turn in the same direction.

Fig. 121 represents a wrought or sheet iron pan; the interior has a basket which is used for frying small fish, potatoes, croquettes, etc.   Place inside the objects intended for frying and plunge the basket into the frying fat after it has attained the required heat; the articles being cooked and of a fine color, withdraw the basket to drain them properly.

FIG. 121.

Fig. 122 represents a copper case containing four high saucepans called bain-maries. A bain-marie consists of a vessel filled with boiling water into which is placed another vessel containing the substances that are required to be heated.   The materials placed in the second vessel

FIG. 122.

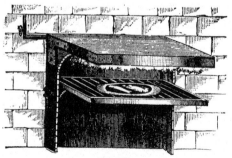

FIG. 123.

can only acquire the temperature of the boiling water and heat gradually and progressively and therefore can be stopped at any time.   Each saucepan should be ticketed with the name of the sauce it contains so that any sauce or soup can be selected without wasting time in searching for it.

Fig. 123. The salamander and oven hithertofore used in kitchens to glaze or brown dishes presented difficulties on account of the attention and watchful care it necessarily required. By means of the new gas salamander, fish can be almost instantaneously glazed when covered with a well thickened or buttered sauce without any danger whatever of having the sauce curdle. This salamander is lighted by gas and can be fastened to the wall at the back of the range. It consists of two platforms, the upper one fixed and the lower one movable and sufficiently big to place the largest dishes on it. Naturally the gas comes from the top

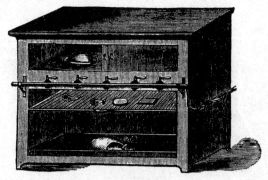

FIG. 124.

and it is easy to regulate its intensity by a stop cock. Two minutes suffice to obtain a perfect glazing without having the bottom of the dish attain the slightest heat, thus the sauce cannot deteriorate whatever. It is an indispensable utensil and assists the cook greatly both as regards its usefulness and speed.

Fig. 124 is the reproduction of a very useful broiler, offering numerous facilities for various purposes. The broiling takes place in a metal case, it being provided with five gas tubes, having the sides bored with small holes, the gas projects into small bells to have it purified and then can be used for broiling without the annoyance of smell nor smoke. It is principally used for broiling toasts, canapés, or toasts for sandwiches; meats can also be broiled thereon such as cutlets, chops and beefsteaks. When the bottom is closed with a movable door, it can be used for roasting chickens, legs of mutton, beef, etc. The top part is useful for keeping things hot. All gas stoves can be regulated and moderated, according to the work, by modifying or increasing the volume of gas.

FIG. 125.

Fig. 125 shows a singeing apparatus shaped like a horn; the largest part, from whence issues the flame is covered with a very fine metallic cloth which causes the flame to become enlarged. There is an opening on the other or thin end about an inch in diameter for the purpose of combining the air with the gas, forming a Bunsen burner. Poultry and game can be singed without blackening the skin whatever.

FIG. 126.

Fig. 126 is a steam table with covered dishes, cases and bain-maries. The square boxes are used for soups, stews, etc.; the covered dishes for large pieces of meat to be carved and for entrées; the small steamers are for keeping the sauces and gravies. Instead of a dish on the right, place a carving-board with a knife and fork. The inside is used for keeping the dishes hot before and after they are dressed. These steam tables are heated by steam or gas, and are advantageously used either as a hot closet or as a substitute for a chafing dish.

BROILER AND RANGE (Grillade et Fourneau).

The broiler shown below is most useful, for on it can be cooked all meats, either using charcoal, or embers, or gas.   In olden times meats were broiled on the embers of a chimney hearth, fanning

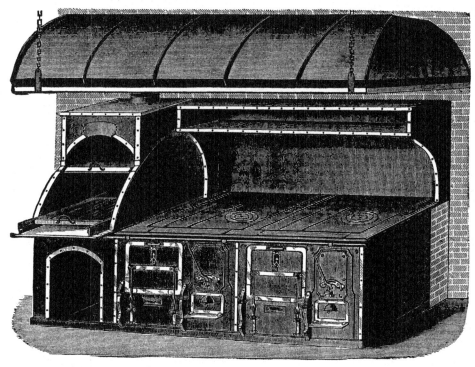

FIG. 127.

continuously to keep the fire alive.   For many years sliding broilers have been used and charcoal. With gas the broiling is done in a metal case, by a gas tube having the sides pierced with small

FIG. 128.

holes.   Although gas is very little used in kitchens still it deserves to be encouraged ; for not only does this style of broiling interest amateurs by its ingenuity, but it also has its particular advantages which are manifold, as the operation takes place without the slightest trouble and without having the meats give forth any smoke or disagreable smell, for the heat attains the meat from the top and all the escaping fat falls into a receptacle Fig. 127 shows an improved range an explanation of which is unnecessary.

PORTABLE HEATER (Étuve Portative).

This heater is used for transporting meats out-outside or keeping hot dishes to be served.   It is heated with small cakes of prepared coal, made red-hot in the hearth of the range, then put into a small sheet-iron box placed at the bottom of the heater. The heaters are made of tin and provided with two gratings inside; they can be of any size (Fig. 128).

FIG 129

It can also be heated with an alcohol lamp.

STEAM KETTLE WITH DOUBLE JACKET (Marmite à Vapeur avec Double Fond.

Fig. 129. A steam double bottom kettle either having a ball in the center or else a winding pipe. In this same shaped pot all systems can be employed. The one shown on the figure has a double jacket; on top place a ring and in this a tinned basin; fill it half full of boiling water and use it for cooking ices; stocks, broths and consommés are cooked in those having a ball in the center, or else a winding pipe, but the ball is preferable. For cooking potatoes, lobsters, terrapin, etc., iron pots with rounded corners are used; on the bottom is an iron winding pipe furnished with holes: at the bottom is a hole for letting the water from the condensed stream run out, on top a hinged cover sufficiently heavy to close it hermetically, specially required for these kinds of pots.

SAUTOIR, SAUCEPAN, SOUP POT, BRAZIERE (Sautoir, Casserole, Marmite, Braisière).

Fig. 130 represents a flat, thick copper saucepan, generally called a sautoir; they are also made of a thinner copper and are intended for sautéing fillets of chickens, escalops, cutlets, etc. It is necessary to have these of all sizes, large as well as small.

Fig. 131 represents a copper saucepan tinned in the interior and furnished with a cover fitting inwardly. These also must be of all sizes according to the importance of the work to be executed.

FIG 130.   FIG. 131.

Fig. 132 represents a glazing saucepan; the edges of this one are only half as high as the ordinary saucepan; it is covered with a hollow cover fitting outside the pan; this is for the purpose of holding red hot coals or ember so to glaze and color the meats.

FIG. 132.   FIG. 133.   FIG. 134.

Fig. 133 represents a soup pot for broths with side handles, with or without a faucet, serving to draw off the liquid. Copper pots are preferable to iron or earthen ones, the first give the broth or soup a dark color and the latter in time acquire a bad taste.

Fig. 134 represents a braizière or long stew pan having rounded ends and handles. Its deep cover is made to hold hot embers, but this is not necessary if the braizing is done in the oven, then a well fitting cover will be found sufficient.

FISH KETTLE (Poissonnière).

Fig. 135 represents a fish kettle, these are either of copper or tin. The fish is placed on a metal sheet perforated with half inch holes, this has handles on both sides, it is put down into the bottom of the fish kettle and lifted again when the fish is cooked, thus avoiding the breaking of it.

Fig. 136 represents oblong shaped, deep baking pans having handles on each end. These pans are furnished with a perforated metal grate. Their raised edge cover (Fig. 136), can when turned upside down, also serve for a deep pan suitable for cooking flat fishes, fricandeaux, sweetbreads, etc.

Fig. 137 represents a series of six small timbales with flat bottoms ranging from No. 1 to No. 6. These timbales as shown in the figures are just half their actual size.

Fig. 138 shows a series of convex molds for mousselines, No. 1 to No. 6. These molds like the flat bottomed ones are drawn half their proper size. They are to be placed on metal sheets perforated according to the size of the molds, supported by half inch high feet.

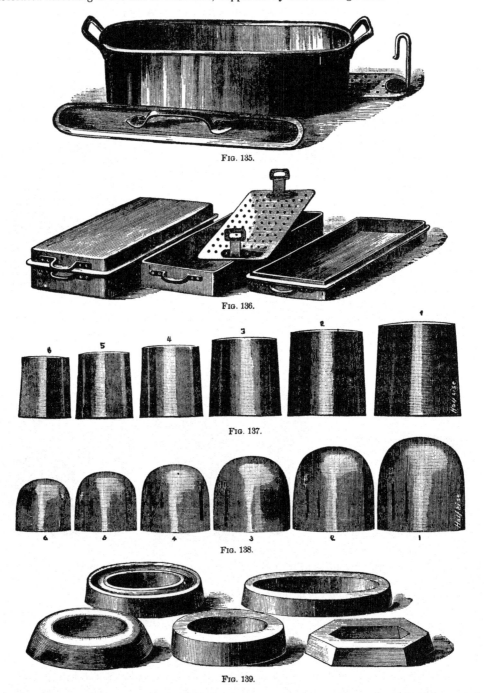

FIG. 135.

FIG. 136.

FIG. 137.

FIG. 138.

FIG. 139.

Fig. 139 are various border molds, the first has a concave bottom and is specially used for dressing entrées of chicken and game fillets, quenelles, etc. The second is an oval mold with a flat bottom useful for large relevé borders. The third is a round bomb shaped mold with flaring sides, used for molding rice or forcemeat borders. The fourth is a plain bottom mold and the fifth is of an octagon shape with a flat bottom.

BASIN (Bassine).

Basins are made of copper; as a general rule they are not tinned. In large kitchens there are some that are tinned and others that are not. If untinned they can also be used not only for

FIG. 140.

beating up egg whites, cooking fruits, and jellies, but also for blanching and cooking green vegetables, such as spinach, green peas, string beans, etc., thereby retaining their natural color, giving them a more appetizing appearance.

KITCHEN SIEVES (Tamis de Cuisine).

FIG. 141.

FIG. 142.

FIG. 143.

It is impossible to perform any kitchen work without the use of large and small sieves. Sieves and colanders are indispensable either for straining purées, forcemeats, gravies and broths, for draining purposes or when required to be laid aside for further use.

MOLDS (Les Moules).

The Figs. 144 and 145 represent two fancy jelly molds; they are cylindrical shaped, having a cover of the same size, hollow on top so that it can hold chopped ice. Many dessert molds are to be found in the market unprovided with covers, thereby making them useless and inconvenient. The Fig. 146 shows the cover of the mold seen upside down having a small piece adjusted to the center which fits into the cylinder of the mold.

FIG 144.   FIG. 145.   FIG. 146.

FIG. 147.

Fig. 147 is a copper macédoine mold with a tinned double copper bottom. This double bottom is movable and is kept at an even distance from the sides and bottom of the mold by three catches attached to it. If the double bottom be removed it then can be used for aspics of foies gras, unmolding it on to a jelly border having a support placed in the center.

JUICE PRESS (Presse Sucs).

These presses are for extracting all the liquid parts of fruits needed for preparing syrups and fruit jellies, such as currants, raspberries, blackberries, strawberries and barberries, in fact all fruits. This utensil should be made of wood for all red fruits lose their natural color when brought in contact with any metal.

CREAM MOLDS (Moules à Crème).

Made of tin or copper; they are fancy and cylindrical. Used for molding cold creams, pains of fruits, blanc manges, etc. (Fig. 148).

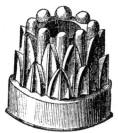

FIG. 148.   FIG. 149.

JELLY AND BABA MOLDS (Moules à Gelée et Moules à Baba).

Jelly molds are made both of copper, tinned in the inside, fancy and cylindrical, and are used for thick creams, blanc manges, flamris, etc. Three or four are not too many to have in a kitchen. Baba molds are of copper, tin and earthen-ware ᵣ they are cylindrical shaped and generally have deep furrows in them, but can be of any shape (Fig. 149).

"PAIN" AND PUDDING CYLINDRICAL MOLDS (Moules Cylindriques à Pain et à Pouding).

These are cylindrical shaped, tinned on the inside. Generally puddings are cooked in these molds, but they can also be used for rice or fruit pains, besides they are very useful in a kitchen either for hot entrées or else molding hot or cold sweet dishes. Dome shaped molds can also be used to poach pains and puddings (Fig. 150).

FIG. 150.   FIG. 151.   FIG. 152.

Fig. 151 is a copper mold, tinned inside and outside, the double bottom is removable and is kept at an even distance from the edges and bottom by three catches fastened to it. It can be used for cold dessert creams; the same mold without the double bottom, but having a cover fitted on the outside can be utilized for hot or cold puddings.

Fig. 152 represents a tin mold for making paste croustades and can also be used for molding rice or hominy.

FIG. 153.

PIE MOLDS (Moules à Pâté).

Hot pie molds are shallow and round; for cold pies they are round, oval or oblong; made of tin or copper, but the tin ones answer the purpose. The round or oval ones are hinged (Fig. 153).

WHIPS OR WHISKS USED FOR KITCHEN AND PASTRY (Fouets de Cuisine et de pâtisserie).

Whips or whisks are made of wicker or tinned wire, several of them should be kept on hand as they are frequently used. The wicker ones are the best, especially for beating creams, but for whipping hot liquids, such as consommé, sweet or meat jellies, the wire ones are preferable. When beating the white of eggs be careful to observe that the tin on the whisks is partly worn off, for the contact of egg-white with new tin causes it to curdle (Fig. 154). Some use whisks made of untinned brass wire, the wire not being as heavy as the other.

FIG. 154.

KITCHEN KNIVES, CLEAVER, CAN-OPENER (Couteaux de Cuisine, Couperet, Ouvre-boîte).

Have one large, strong knife for chops, one large carving knife for cooked meats, one smaller one for the same purpose and one kitchen knife. It is always advisable to keep a few

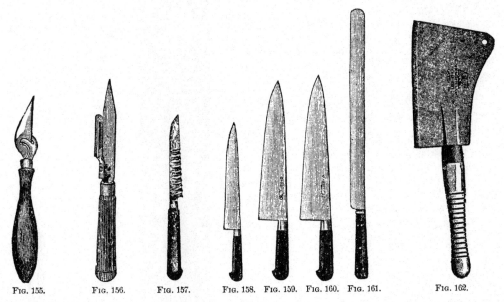

FIG. 155.   FIG. 156.   FIG. 157.   FIG. 158. FIG. 159. FIG. 160. FIG. 161.   FIG. 162.

well sharpened ones in reserve, either for carving or any other unforeseen occasion. Besides these there must be a channeled knife for turning vegetables and fruits. A knife for peeling and also a can-opener; it is most necessary to have a large and strong cleaver for splitting bones, also to be used instead of a mallet for beating meats to flatten them according to one's wants (Figs. 155 to 162).

SUGAR DREDGER (Poudrière).

Fig. 163 represents a sugar dredger containing about a pint. It is to be filled three-quarters full with powdered sugar and is used for sweetening pastry, fritters, omelets, etc.

FIG. 163.

LEG OF MUTTON HANDLE (Manche à Gigot).

FIG. 164.

These handles are made of metal fitting on to the bone of a leg of mutton, lamb or ham; they assist the carver to turn around and cut the meat according to necessity. The old style ones are silver plated and screwed on to the bone, but the new style are made of steel and are fitted on by means of a rubber ring placed inside which grasps the bone tightly without breaking it (Fig. 164).

THERMOMETER (Thermomètre).

Fig. 165, a thermometer used for cooking sugar. These can be used for all kitchen purposes, cold chambers, refrigerators, etc.

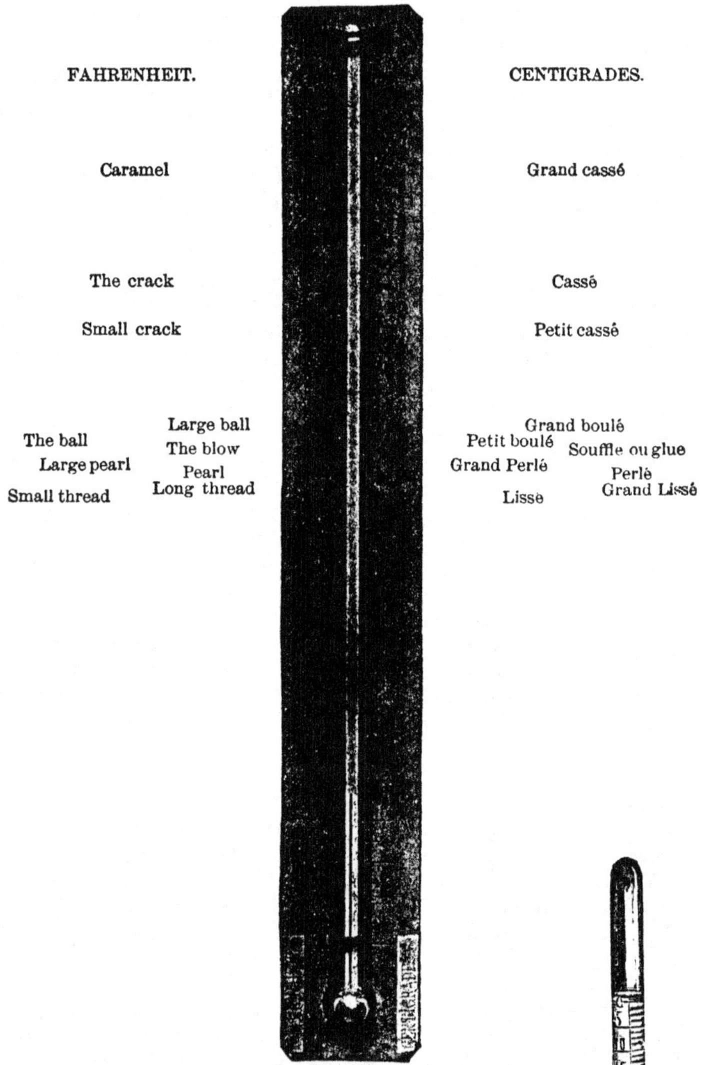

FAHRENHEIT.

CENTIGRADES.

FAHRENHEIT.

Caramel

Grand cassé

Ice..................... 32 degrees

Burgundy Wine........ 45   "

The crack

Cassé

Ice Refrigerator........ 50   "

Small crack

Petit cassé

Bordeaux Wine........ 55   "

Water for unmolding
     ice cream........... 40   "

Dining Room.......... 62   "

The ball   Large ball

Grand boulé

Senegal Heat..........182   "

Large pearl   The blow

Petit boulé   Souffle ou glue

Grand Perlé   Perlé

Boiling Water.........212   "

Small thread   Pearl
               Long thread

Lisse   Grand Lissé

Sugar Small Thread....215   "

"   Long Thread....217   "

"   Pearl...........220   "

"   Large Pearl......222   "

"   The Blow.......230   "

"   The Ball........236   "

"   Large Ball......246   "

"   Small Crack.....290   "

"   The Crack......310   "

"   Caramel........345   "

FIG. 165.

COPPER BASIN FOR COOKING SUGAR WITH THERMOMETER (Bassine pour Cuire le Sucre au Thermomètre).

Fig. 166 is a small copper basin with a tin cover having a hole in its top sufficiently large to allow the thermometer to be inserted. The steam that condenses on the side of the cover is continually cleansing the sides of the basin, so that when the sugar is well stirred there is no necessity to watch it, only see that it continues to cook to the desired heat.

FIG. 166.

SYRUP GAUGE (Pèse Sirop).

After a person has the habit of cooking sugar he rarely requires a syrup gauge; the degree of cooking can be judged by simply touching it with the fingers, but those who have not yet attained this proficiency need always use the syrup gauge. Place in a bottle and then plunge into the syrup this glass instrument which rises or falls according to the thickness or thinness of the liquid thereby giving the exact degree of its cooking by the numbers marked on it (Fig. 167).

FIG. 167.

COLUMN BOX (Boîte à Colonnes).

Fig. 168 represents a column box. These tubes are for removing fanciful cuts of truffles, tongues, egg white, etc. The medium sized ones can be utilized for stoning Spanish olives; they are also used for coring apples and for rolling paper frills, for cutting vegetables, jardiniere, macédoine or Chartreuse, for bread croûtons, etc.

LEMON SQUEEZER (Presse Citron).

Fig. 169 represents a lemon-squeezer. This kind is in common use and is used for squeezing lemons for ices, jellies, etc.

FIG. 168.

FIG. 169.

STRAINER (CHINESE), AND MIXING POT FOR THICKENING (Passoire Chinois et Mélangeur pour Liaisons).

Fig. 170 represents a sauce strainer commonly called Chinese; they are made of tin or metallic tammy. It is necessary to have several sizes more or less fine ; they are either pointed or flat as shown in the design and are in constant use for sauces and gravies.

Fig. 171 is a kind of pot containing a mixer. This is to stir egg-yolks and cream together for pouring it into sauces and ragouts for thickening; this is found especially handy for Hollandaise sauce.

FIG. 170.   FIG. 171.

GRIDIRON (Gril).

Fig. 172 represents a thin wire double gridiron; it is useful for toasting bread, crackers, broiling oysters, tomatoes, and sliced potatoes. Stronger and thicker gridirons are used for meats and fish, having just sufficient room to hold the articles.

FIG. 172.

MEAT CHOPPER (Pour Hacher les Viandes).

Fig. 173 is a perpendicular machine used for chopping meats; these are excellent, and are

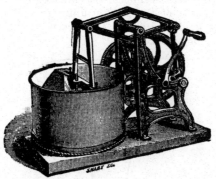

FIG. 173.

well adapted for making Salisbury steaks or Hamburg steaks. They have this advantage that they cut the meats without cutting the nerves, so that the meat comes to the top lightly chopped and nerveless.

FONTAGE CROUSTADE MOLD (Moule à Croustade Fontage).

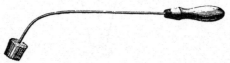

FIG. 174

Fig. 174 represents an iron in imitation of a small channeled timbale mold; it has a handle fourteen inches long, bent at the end and is furnished with a wooden handle. This mold is for the purpose of making fontage croustades (see Fontage, No. 907).

KITCHEN FORK (Fourchette de Cuisine).

Fig. 175 represents a kitchen fork, used for turning over any broiled articles, sautés or else for tossing rice, etc.

Fig. 175.

SKEWERS AND HATELETS (Brochettes et Hâtelets).

Fig. 176.

Kitchen skewers are of iron, used for supporting large pieces of meat when laid on the spit. Small game

Fig. 176a.

are run on to skewers; the blade is flat, rounded on one end and pointed on the other. Table skewers are of white metal, silver or plated ware; they are used when broiling kidneys or other meats which are thrust on them (Fig. 176). **Fig. 176a** represents a hatelet and should not be confounded with a skewer.

KITCHEN GRATER (Râpe de Cuisine).

Fig. 177.

An utensil made of tin having a semi-circular surface bored with projecting holes on which is to be grated either bread, cheese or various kinds of roots. There should always be two small graters in every spice box, one for grating nutmeg, the other for orange, lemon or Seville orange peel. The two latter ought to be enclosed in small separate boxes (Fig. 177).

PASTE PINCHER (Pince à Pâte).

With this small pincher the crest of pies are pinched; it will be better to have two; one large and one small (Fig. 178).

Fig. 178.

PASTRY BAG OR POCKET AND SOCKETS (Poche et Poche avec Douilles).

These pockets are made of unbleached duck; they are used for laying out meringues, choux, or else quenelle forcemeat; they are of the greatest utility in kitchen and pastry work and it is advisable to have them of graduated sizes. The sockets are movable and are fitted in the bottom of the pocket before filling them.

Fig. 179.

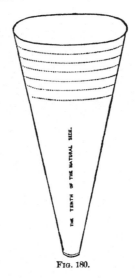

Fig. 180.

Fig. 181.

Fig. 180 shows us the graduated different sizes reduced to the tenth of their proper dimensions; these are the ones most generally used for kitchen work and pastry.

Fig. 181 is half the natural size and represents a section of a series of sockets the most used for all work.

SOUFFLÉ PAN, AND PIE DISH (Casserole à Soufflé, et Plat à Tarte).

These vessels are of plated ware or sterling silver, made in different shapes and different sizes; they are indispensable in a kitchen and are used principally for cooking soufflés, but they can also be used for baking purposes, for poaching creams by bain marie and in fact for serving vegetables or garnishings on the table (Fig. 182).

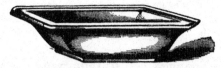

FIG. 182.   FIG. 183.

Pie Dish.—Made of English china that can be placed in the oven without any danger of cracking; they are most useful. In these dishes one can cook meat, chicken, game or fish pies, fruit pies, or puddings, or creams, they can also be used for soufflés. There is no end to their utility in a kitchen and there should always be plenty of different sizes. What makes them more useful and convenient is that they can very well be placed on the table with their contents as they were taken from the oven; for instance, anything baked, creams, puddings, etc. (Fig. 183).

KITCHEN BRUSHES (Pinceaux de Cuisine).

Brushes will be found very useful in a kitchen; it is better to have several; they can be made by any one; merely tying turkeys' tail feathers firmly together. Take the feathers, one by one, remove the feathers on each side, leaving only the end, then put about fifteen of these

FIG. 184.   FIG. 184a.

together, tie with rows of strings, beginning on the feathered end and girding tightly; fasten at the other or upper end, tying the string firmly; now cut the lower end to equalize the quills; they do not last very long. Brushes can be purchased made of hair with a tin handle, much neater, stronger and easier to keep clean; these are shown in the Figs. 184 and 184a.

OMELET, AND OYSTER STEW PAN (Poêle à Omelette, et Casserole pour les Huîtres).

Omelet Pan.—A black, iron pan, polished on the inside. These pans are used principally for omelets; they should never be washed; when coated or burned on the inside, scrape with a flexible knife all that sticks to the bottom, heat well and then rub with a cloth and some salt until perfectly clean. The French omelet pans are the best, both for shape and strength (Fig. 185).

FIG. 185.   FIG. 186.

Oyster Stew Pan.—This saucepan is made of various sizes in tin with a copper bottom. It is furnished with a rounded cover perforated in the center with several small holes. The handle is very long. This saucepan is used for oysters and their liquor placed on the hot fire and when the steam escapes through the holes then remove it at once (Fig. 186).

SPOONS (Cuillères).

Fig. 187, represents four spoons, soup or table, dessert, tea and coffee.

The approximative liquid capacity is: six soup or tablespoonfuls of liquid make a gill or forty-eight a quart.

Twelve dessertspoonfuls of liquid for a gill; eighteen teaspoonfuls and thirty-six coffeespoonfuls. For sugar it requires eight tablespoonfuls of powdered sugar for a pound, sixteen dessertspoonfuls, twenty-four teaspoonfuls and forty-eight coffeespoonfuls. For flour it takes ten tablepoonfuls for a pound, twenty dessertspoonfuls, thirty teaspoonfuls and sixty coffeespoonfuls.

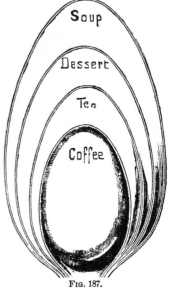

FIG. 187.

WEIGHTS AND MEASURES (Poids et Mesures).

Various ways of obtaining weights and measures.

Weight by Quarts.—One quart of water weighs two pounds and four ounces; one quart of milk two pounds and an ounce and a half; cream two pounds and one ounce; oil one pound and fourteen ounces; melted butter the same weight as oil; powdered sugar one pound nine ounces; rice one pound three ounces; flour one pound two ounces; breadcrumbs eleven ounces; horseradish or cocoanut twelve ounces; wheaten grits or Indian meal fifteen ounces; oatmeal thirteen ounces; semolina one pound seven ounces.

Weight by Handfuls.—A handful of sugar weighs six ounces; flour four ounces; bread-crumbs two ounces; rice three ounces; herbs, parsley, etc., one ounce.

Weight by Coffeecups.—Six cupfuls of sugar weigh one pound; nine of flour one pound; eight of Indian meal, one pound; six of rice one pound. Ten black coffeecupfuls of water make one quart. Six teacupfuls of water make one quart. Four breakfast cupfuls of water make one quart.

REFRIGERATOR, ICE-BOX AND COLD ROOM (Réfrigérateur, Glacière Timbre et Chambre froide).

These refrigerators are to be kept full of ice so to reduce the temperature inwardly and to avoid inconvenience arising from the excessive heat of the atmosphere. A refrigerator as shown

FIG. 188.

in the accompanying design is all that is necessary for a restaurant, etc. At a third of its height are placed wooden gratings to uphold the ice, underneath is to be found a sheet of zinc or galvanized sheet iron with a small gutter, at the end, between this and the sheet of iron is a space of six inches. The bottom parts of these ice-boxes are used for keeping either beef palates, calf's heads, sheep's trotters, croquette preparations of all kinds, etc.; each compartment should be entirely separate from one another, having a special one for fish, one for poultry, one for game, one for cold meats, one for garnishings, etc.

The Ice box is simply a box of an oblong shape sufficiently thick to be filled with a non-conducting material such as charcoal, sawdust, tow, or simply an hermetically empty space not to allow the air to pass through the box; they are lined inside with galvanized sheet iron or zinc.

The cold room is of a more modern invention, the meats being hung up in the inside. Cooked meats, also different provisions requiring a cold temperature of forty-five to fifty degrees Fahrenheit, such as butter, milk or cream, rest on shelves or in drawers, without being in direct contact with the ice, for it is evident that the cold air surrounding these provisions does not contain the slightest moisture that might destroy their properties. Another advantage the cold room has is that a quantity of cold entrées or sweet dishes already decorated with the jellies that are to be served will keep in perfect condition for a few days, while those placed directly on the ice do not afford the same security; however, each one has its own peculiar advantages and one must not be sacrificed for the other, on the contrary in all large kitchens each one has its own place and both have become indispensable.

MEAT-SAFE (Garde-Manger).

This is a kind of round or square cage composed of metallic cloth on a framework of iron or wood, provided inside with several shelves; also hanging hooks to which can be hung meats, poultry and game. On the shelves are placed all the provisions that should be exposed to the air without incurring any danger of contact with flies. These meat-safes are either suspended from the ceiling of the pantry by a pulley or else fastened to the wall outside a window; in both cases in order to have them accomplish their purpose they must be exposed to a thorough draught of air in as cool a place as possible. If the meat safe is hung in a room it can be entirely open on top, if on the contrary it is fastened outside then the upper part must certainly have a slightly inclining roof so that no rain can penetrate the inside. These meat-safes are only useful where ice is scarce for ice-boxes, are far preferable under all circumstances.

CENTIMETERS AND INCHES (Centimètres et Pouces).

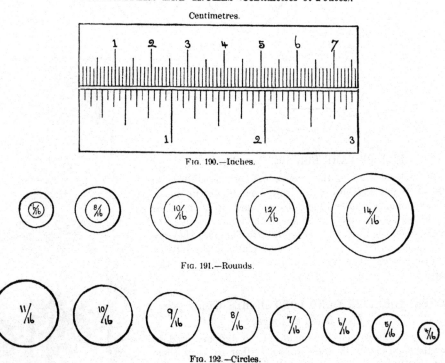

Centimetres.

Fig. 190.—Inches.

Fig. 191.—Rounds.

Fig. 192.—Circles.

Figs. 190 to 196 indicate the difference between the centimeter and the inch; the dimensions of circles, triangles, lozenges, ovals, rounds or squares all measured by the sixteenth of an inch across the diameter, or on the length for ovals and lozenges. These figures will at once give an exact idea of the proportions as they are explained in the different recipes, either for garnishings or salpicons or else for the diameter of sockets, column tubes, etc.

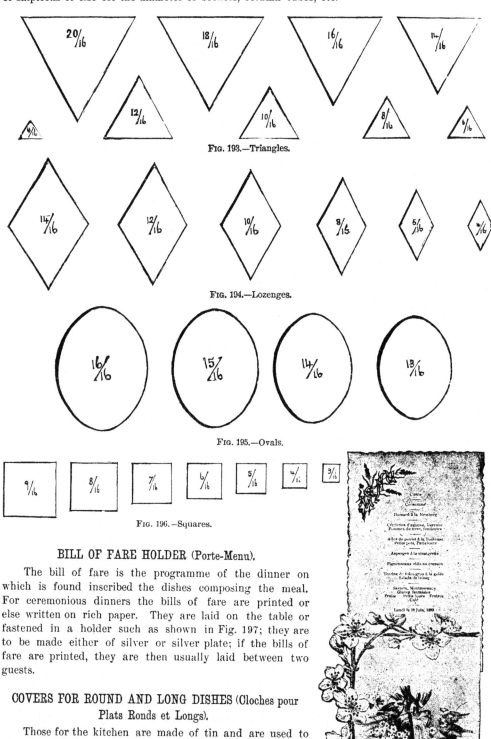

FIG. 193.—Triangles.

FIG. 194.—Lozenges.

FIG. 195.—Ovals.

FIG. 196.—Squares.

BILL OF FARE HOLDER (Porte-Menu).

The bill of fare is the programme of the dinner on which is found inscribed the dishes composing the meal. For ceremonious dinners the bills of fare are printed or else written on rich paper. They are laid on the table or fastened in a holder such as shown in Fig. 197; they are to be made either of silver or silver plate; if the bills of fare are printed, they are then usually laid between two guests.

COVERS FOR ROUND AND LONG DISHES (Cloches pour Plats Ronds et Longs).

Those for the kitchen are made of tin and are used to cover the dishes after they are dressed, either to keep them in the hot closet or to carry to the dining-room; have always round and long ones for both large and small dishes. These require to be kept very clean and bright.

FIG. 197.

SOUPS (Potages).

Soup is the prelude of the dinner; it is a healthy, light and stimulating food, agreeing with every one, especially children and old people. The basis of soup is broth, and therefore it is on this article that one's whole attention must be borne. There are two kinds of soup, fat and lean; they are divided into clear and thick; the garnishings for these soups are either composed of crusts, vegetables, creams of game or poultry, eggs, fish, quenelles, timbales, chiffonades, finely minced herbs, crustacean, farinaceous, etc. These two kinds of soups are divided into six chapters: First, Bisques; second, Consommés and Garnishings; third, Creams; fourth, Cosmopolitan or Mixed; fifth, Fish; sixth, Purées. Purées may be made into creams by using less butter and adding instead cream and egg-yolks, while creams can be turned into purées by suppressing the cream and egg-yolks, and stirring in, when ready to serve, a piece of fresh, fine butter.

(184). FAT (La Graisse).

Fat is insoluble in water, but melts by heat and floats on the surface of a liquid. As it is enveloped in the cells of a very fine indissoluble membrane, one part of the fat adheres always to the fibers, unless the cooking be too long and the cells are broken by the force of the boiling. Fat exists either separately in certain parts of animals, and in other parts it is interposed between the fibers; these last parts are always the most digestible and the most nourishing.

Albumen (*L'Albumine*).—Is of the same nature as the white of egg which contains scarcely anything else than albumen; it is soluble in cold or tepid water and coagulates between one hundred and fifty to two hundred and ten degrees Fahrenheit. Albumen abounds in the blood and it is found in every part of the flesh; it coagulates after being dissolved, and in broth forms what is called scum, rising to the surface of liquids in which meats are cooked. The less blood the animal has lost, the more albumen there is, and as the blood contains much osmazome, the result will be that meat having the most blood will produce a more savory soup than that which has lost a larger quantity.

When a piece of either beef or mutton is needed rare, it must be plunged into boiling liquid, and being at once seized by the action of the heat, the albumen coagulates and encloses the osmazome inside. Allow fifteen minutes for each pound of meat for a leg of mutton weighing six to eight pounds; if boiled according to this time the meat will be found rare, unless the boiling has been too long. If on the contrary, this same piece of meat be put into cold water and is allowed to cook slowly, the albumen not coagulating at once, will let the osmazome escape into the liquid and the meats will be white and less juicy, but as nothing is lost, the broth will have gained by it in quality.

Bones (*Les os*).—Are inorganic parts having much solidity besides being of a gelatineous nature; they contain considerable fat substance analogous to marrow, but this is but a part of their matter. Bones contain eight times more gelatin than meat. They are generally split into smaller pieces.

(185). FIBRINE (La Fibrine).

Fibrine is insoluble; it forms the base of the muscles or flesh. After meat has been very much cooked, after it has boiled a long time, the remainder of it is almost pure fibrine. Fibrine is not very nutritious, and when it has thoroughly exhausted its soluble qualities, it becomes difficult to digest. Pure fibrine has no savor, it is insipid or flavorless and becomes yellow and brittle after drying.

Gelatin (*La Gélatine*).—Gelatin is soluble in very hot or boiling water, in tepid water it swells and dissolves only partially, and in cold water it softens without dissolving. It is colorless, insipid, inodorous and is susceptible to pass rapidly into a state of acetic fermentation. There is very little nutrition in gelatin; when in sufficient quantity it gives the broth the peculiar quality of forming into a jelly when cold. Gelatin exists in all parts of the meat, but more profusely in gristle and bone. In a pure state it is insipid.

Osmazome (*L'Osmazôme*).—Soluble even when cold, this is a part of the flesh of the beef, of the brain and of certain mushrooms. It is osmazome which gives to the broth its savor, its aroma and its sapidity. It is supplied with an exceedingly stimulating property, exciting the appetite and helping considerably to facilitate digestion; it seems to exist only in the flesh and blood, and more abundantly in old cattle and in dark meats, than in young animals and white meat. The properties of osmazome are more perceptible when the meats are broiled or roasted; then the sapidity is stronger and the aroma more exhilarating. Poultry gives very little sapidity to broths unless they be old and very fat, for their grease has a more pronounced flavor than that found in quadrupeds. Gristle, fat and bones are entirely free of osmazome; in broths there is one part osmazome to seven parts gelatin.

(186). CARE TO BE TAKEN WHILE PREPARING BROTH (Des Soins à Prendre pour Préparer le Bouillon).

First.—Select the freshest meats procurable; do not wash, but remove all that is not of the very freshest; bone and tie up each piece separately leaving them as large as possible; split the bones and put them into a soup-pot with cold water and the meat.

Second.—Heat and boil it up slowly to give the albumen time to dissolve in the liquid; it coagulates as soon as the liquid reaches one hundred and fifty degrees Fahrenheit, and rising to the surface brings with it all the impurities contained therein, which is called scum.

Third.—Carefully remove this scum as quickly as it rises to the surface, and before the liquid boils, for after that the scum partly dissolves and the rest of it precipitates and destroys the transparency of the broth. When the broth is well skimmed, add salt, allspice, and vegetables; then keep it boiling as continuously and slowly as possible to prevent too much evaporation.

(187). CLEAR BOUILLON (Bouillon Clair).

There is nothing that resembles consommé more than clarified bouillon, and if it does not entirely take its place as regards quality, still it is often used instead. Clarified bouillon is in reality only an imitation of consommé, it is equally true that with care it can easily be prepared in excellent conditions, the principal one being to operate with good bouillon, either of chicken, beef or game, etc. To obtain clear bouillon, only lean meats must be used for clarification: in order to obtain four quarts of bouillon, have one pound of lean beef free of all fat and nerves, chop it finely, and mix in with it, two raw eggs and one pint of cold bouillon; place the strained bouillon on the fire, skimmed free of all its fat, and when it reaches boiling point, pour into it the clarification, beating it well with a whip. As soon as the bouillon boils, keep it to the same degree of heat without allowing it to boil, for one hour; skim the fat off, season with salt and a little sugar, and color it with caramel (No. 18), then remove and strain through a wet napkin stretched and fastened to the four legs of a kitchen stool (Fig. 99), or else a silk sieve. These bouillons are to be served with garnishings of Italian pastes and farinas, also garnishings of vegetables, etc., for various soups.

(188). WHITE CHICKEN BOUILLON OR BROTH (Bouillon Blanc de Volaille).

Have ten quarts of water in a soup pot; add to it three pounds of knuckle of veal, and trimmings, seven pounds of very fresh poultry. Boil, skim, and put in three quarters of a pound of carrots, half a pound of turnips, twelve ounces of leeks, two onions, one stuck with two cloves, two ounces of celery, one ounce of parsley roots, two bay leaves, salt, sixty grains of whole peppers; boil slowly and continuously for four hours, then strain through a silk sieve. If needed in a great hurry, boil six quarts of ordinary stock, have two fowls of three pounds each, after removing the breasts, chop the remainder of the fowls coarsely, put them in the stock, add four ounces of minced carrots and six ounces of leeks also minced, boil slowly for one hour; skim off the fat, season with salt, strain through a fine sieve or moistened napkin, and serve. The breasts are used for forcemeat or to clarify broth.

(189). CLARIFIED CONSOMMÉ (Consommé Clarifié).

Proportions.—When the stock (No. 194a) is ready put five quarts of it into a soup pot, adding two pounds of lean meat and three pounds of cleansed and washed fowls. Boil it up slowly, and just when ready to come to a boil, carefully remove the scum arising on the surface and then add half a pound of roasted veal. Simmer slowly until the fowl is cooked, which will take from two and a half to three hours, lifting it out as soon as it is done so as to save the breasts which will be found useful for garnishings, purées, salads, sandwiches, etc.; return what remains of the fowls to the broth once again and continue boiling for half an hour longer, skim the fat off very carefully and mix in the clarification.

Clarification.—Trim off the fat, remove the nerves from a piece of beef sufficient to obtain two pounds after it is chopped up, and mix in with this chopped meat half a quart of cold stock (or water); pour this clarification into the broth, add two ounces of minced carrots, and two ounces of minced leeks; season with salt and color the soup with caramel (No. 18); keep the liquid in a boiling state for one hour. The consommé should be perfectly clear, sapid and tasty; strain it through a silk sieve or a fine napkin and use when needed, serve in cups, or in a soup tureen with any garnishing desired.

Remoistening.—After the stock or consommé has been taken out of the pot, pour in sufficient water to have the meats entirely re-covered and boil again for three hours; remove all the fat and strain it through a napkin; do not salt this. This remoistening is used for diluting certain soups, and to moisten veal or chicken stock with which meat extract is made (see meat extract, No. 368).

(190). CLARIFIED CHICKEN CONSOMMÉ, (Consommé de Volaille Clarifié).

Put into a soup pot eight quarts of white chicken broth (No. 188), add two pounds of knuckle of veal, one pound of chicken legs and pinions, then boil, skim, and put in four pounds of roasted, unbrowned chicken, two minced leeks, one medium sized minced carrot, one onion stuck with one clove, a little parsley and celery roots. Boil continually for four hours. Chop up very fine two pounds of veal, mix in with it two whole eggs, dilute with one quart of cold broth and stir this into the consommé, using a whip, adding two broken up chicken carcasses. Boil on a slow fire for one hour, salt it according to taste, and strain it through a silk sieve.

(191). CLARIFIED FISH CONSOMMÉ (Consommé de Poisson Clarifié).

Butter the bottom of a saucepan, garnishing it with sliced onions, and place on top six pounds of fish bones, such as bass, perch or any other gelatinous fish, a bunch of celery, parsley, bay leaf, thyme, one pound of minced carrots, a pound and a half of leeks, and dilute with one quart of water. Cover the saucepan, set it over a slow fire, and let fall to a colorless glaze, then moisten with four quarts of hot water, boil, skim and let simmer for one hour, then strain through a sieve, and clarify the broth with the whites of four eggs and half a bottleful of white wine.

(192). CLARIFIED GAME CONSOMMÉ (Consommé de Gibier Clarifié).

Butter the inside of a very thick saucepan, cover the bottom with sliced onions, and lay on top three pounds of broken knuckle of veal and eight pounds of game, such as partridges, quails, pheasants and young rabbit, also half a pound of legs and pinions or bits of poultry, moisten with a pint of stock, place it on a moderate fire, and cover the saucepan; let steam and fall to a glaze, then dilute with half bottle of white wine, and ten quarts of stock or water. Boil, then skim and season with salt and two pepper corns for each quart of liquid, two cloves, also half a pound of carrots, one ounce of parsley roots, half a pound of leeks, two ounces of celery, the whole minced. Remove all the bones from two very fresh young rabbits; put these in with the stock and boil all for four hours; strain through a sieve and put it back into the saucepan; chop up fine the flesh from the rabbits with as much lean beef meat, mix in with it two whole eggs and dilute with half a bottleful of white wine. Skim off all the fat from the broth and stir in the chopped rabbits, continuing stirring for one minute, then let come to a boil, move it from the hot fire, and boil slowly and unceasingly for one half hour more; after the consommé is very clear, strain it through a silk sieve or through a napkin.

(193). CLARIFIED LENT VEGETABLE CONSOMMÉ (Consommé maigre de Légumes Clarifié).

Mince about three pounds of carrots and three pounds of turnips, one pound of the white of celery, one pound of onions, half a pound of parsley roots, a quarter of a pound of parsnips and a pound and a half of leeks. Put half a pound of butter into a saucepan, warm it and fry the vegetables, then moisten with two quarts of water and reduce slowly until they fall into a glaze. Dilute it with ten quarts of water, season with salt, pepper, half an ounce of sugar and cloves, adding one pound of mushroom stalks, then boil slowly until the vegetables are well done without mashing, and strain through a sieve. Return it to the fire and clarify the broth with the whites of four eggs and half a bottle of white wine. After it is very clear, strain it through a silk sieve or a napkin.

(194a). BEEF STOCK OR BROTH (Bouillon de Bœuf).

Proportion of Ingredients.—Ten quarts of water, a quarter of a pound of chicken legs, one and one quarter ounces of salt, six ounces of leeks, half ounce of soup celery, eight pounds of meat with bone, twenty grains or cloves of black pepper, six ounces of carrots, one half ounce of parsnip, one half clove of garlic (if desired), two whole cloves, three ounces turnips, four ounces of onions, one of which stuck with two cloves.

Put ten quarts of water into a stockpot, add eight pounds of beef meat (trimmings and bone), let there be at least two-thirds meat, being careful to have both meat and trimmings well freed of fat; and a quarter of a pound of scalded chicken legs, after removing the outer skin. Heat this up slowly so that it comes gradually to a boil, then skim carefully and add twenty grains of whole black peppers and one and one quarter ounces of salt. Put into a net six ounces of carrots, three ounces of turnips, six ounces of leeks, half an ounce of parsnips, one half an ounce of soup celery, and two ounces of onions in which two cloves should be stuck. Close the net and set it in the pot; after the vegetables have cooked for two hours, remove the net containing the vegetables and continue boiling the soup for two hours longer, making four hours in all. Take off all the fat from the surface and strain the soup either through a silk tammy or a napkin; pour it into another pot to make consommé; and in case it should be needed the following day only, pour it into vessels and set it to cool; the following is an economical way of doing so: set the vessels in a water reservoir supplied continually with cold water from melting ice in the refrigerators and brought through a pipe in the bottom of the tank, have a larger overflow pipe placed near the top so as to allow the water as it heats to flow off.

(194b). PARTS OF BEEF USED FOR PREPARING BOUILLONS AND STOCKS, SEE FIG. 302
(Parties du Bœuf Servant à Faire les Bouillons et les Fonds, Voir Fig. 302).

These various pieces are No. 2, the cheek jowl; No. 3, the neck: No. 4, the brisket; No. 5, the cross-ribs; No. 6, the shin; No. 8, the plate; No. 9, the navel; No. 10, the inside flank; No. 11, the thick flank; No. 17, the round bottom; No. 18, the leg. The shin is the bottom part of the hind quarter the nearest to the ankle bone. The gelatinous flesh of the shin renders it suitable for the preparation of stock, broths and jellies.

(195). GAME, VEGETABLE, FISH AND CHICKEN STOCK, FOR THICK SOUPS (Fonds de Gibier, Légumes, Poisson et Volaille pour Potages Liés).

In order to make thick stock use consommé of game, vegetables, fish or chicken before they are clarified. Place half a pound of butter in a saucepan with half a pound of sifted flour of the best quality, let cook well on a slow fire without coloring when needed for vegetables, fish or chicken, but for game make a brown roux; for either one or the other dilute this roux with boiling broth (if the soup should be a chicken soup, chicken broth should be used to dilute the roux, if game soup then game broth should be used, fish with fish broth, for vegetable, vegetable broth). Use a whisk turning it rapidly, so as to avoid having lumps; stocks for soups should be kept rather thin, that is to say but little thickened and should be well despumated, the fat removed before passing through the tammy; return the saucepan to the fire, and stir continuously with a spatula from the bottom until the broth boils. Remove the saucepan and place it so that only one side of the contents cook slowly for one hour; skim and take off all the matter that swims on the surface until the stock be entirely free from fat, and other impurities floating on top arising from the clarification, then strain through a tammy or fine sieve, and use this stock for thick soups either of game, vegetables, fish or poultry.

(196). BISQUES (Bisques).

An exquisite and delicious bisque. The ancient bisques made between the years 1700 and 1750, differed greatly from our modern bisques. They were more like stews than soups or potages and were prepared with squabs, quails, pullets and fish, the crawfish only serving as a garnish, and were basted over with a crawfish gravy. Bisques as they are made to-day, are simply a purée, thickened with rice, or thick stock, or wet crusts and accompanied by various garnishings. Bisques are divided into five classes: First, those made of clams, oysters or mussels; Second, crabs; Third, shrimps, Fourth, crawfish; Fifth, lobsters. They must be highly seasoned, although not containing much red pepper, rather clear than thick, slightly colored, and accompanied by small, simple garnishings.

(197). BISQUE OR PUREÉ OF CLAMS À LA HENDRICK (Bisque ou Purée de Lucines à la Hendrick).

Put sixty medium-sized opened clams into a pan, with their own juice; set it on the fire, and when they are very firm to the touch drain and pound the clams with their equal weight of cooked hominy; after all is well pounded and reduced to a paste, wet it with the clam juice poured off gently from the top, and some water in case the bisque be too thick, then pass it through a sieve or tammy and season with red pepper and very little salt if necessary, warm the bisque without boiling it, and just when ready to serve incorporate therein some fine butter and a little cream, garnish with sippets of bread fried in butter and some small pike quenelles (No. 90).

(198). BISQUE OF CRABS (Bisque de Crabes).

Put twenty-four live crabs in cold water with a little salt, and leave them to soak for one hour, mince four ounces of carrot and the same quantity of onion, fry them in butter in a saucepan sufficiently large to contain all the crabs, add some parsley sprigs, thyme and bay leaf, season with salt, half a bottle of white wine and some white stock, then cover and cook for fifteen minutes; lift out the crabs, strain the broth, and set it aside to rest, pouring off the top twenty-five minutes later. Remove the shells from the crabs; pick out the lungs from both sides, wash each one separately in tepid water and suppress the small legs, then drain well and pound them to a paste with half their quantity of cooked rice, dilute this purée with some of the juice they were cooked in, drain through a sieve and then a tammy and mix in one pint of bechamel (No. 409). Season with salt and red pepper, heat up without boiling and just when ready to serve, incorporate therein a quarter of a pound of fine butter, stirring it well with a spoon until it be completely melted. Pour the very hot bisque into a soup tureen and serve separately a garnishing of pieces of bread cut into one quarter of an inch squares and fried in butter; divide them by putting six or eight in each separate soup-plate when serving.

(199). BISQUE OF CRABS À LA STEVENS (Bisque de Crabes à la Stevens).

Wash twenty-four live crabs in several waters; then drain them, fry half a pound minced onions in butter, adding a quarter of a pound of rice flour and then the crabs; moisten with half a bottleful of white wine and two quarts of broth; cook slowly in a covered saucepan for fifteen minutes, then lift out the crabs only, and strain the broth into another vessel, and leave it to deposit its sediment. Remove the large shells from the crabs, also the small legs and lungs, then wash the crabs well in warm water, moving them around in the pan so as to free them of all adhering sand; after draining them well, pound them in a mortar with the addition of a little butter; moisten them with the decanted stock and some other broth, should it be too thick; strain through a sieve or tammy, and return them to the saucepan. Heat to a boiling degree without actually letting it boil, warm it, then add some egg-yolks, cream and fine butter; strain again through a tammy and serve the soup very hot with crusts of bread cut dice shaped, a quarter of an inch in size.

(200). BISQUE OF CRABS, ORIENTAL (Bisque de Crabes à l'Orientale).

Prepare and cook the crabs the same as for bisque of crabs (No. 198), have one pound of onions, cut them in halves through the center of the root and stalk, remove from each side of the halved onion, and on the bias, one quarter of an inch of the root and stalk; mince this up very fine, blanch, then drain and fry the pieces in butter, moistening them with one part of cream. Pound well the crabs to reduce them to a paste and add six quarts of oatmeal previously cooked for thirty minutes in one quart of water. Add the onions, and when all is well mingled together, increase the quantity of bisque with the decanted crab juice and more broth, if the purée be too thick; strain through a sieve or tammy, return it to the fire, and heat it without boiling, and just when ready to serve, stir in a quarter of a pound of fresh butter. Pour the soup into a very hot soup tureen and add a garnishing of crescent shaped quenelles, made of sweet potatoes (No. 317).

(201). BISQUE OF CRAWFISH (Bisque d'Écrevisses).

Wash in several waters four dozen crawfish after removing the fins, the same as for bisque Persigny (No. 204); put the crawfish into a saucepan, pouring over half a bottleful of white wine, four ounces of minced onions, the same quantity of finely minced carrots, a few sprigs of parsley, one bay leaf, as much thyme, salt, mignonette, a little red pepper and half a pint of broth; cook all together for ten minutes with the cover on, tossing them several times in the meanwhile, then take them from off the fire and leave them standing for ten minutes longer in their broth; pour them into a colander to drain, and afterward select half of the finest, medium and equal sized ones; remove the tail ends from these, and the shells, and keep the meats aside for the garnishing, also half of the finest, but smallest shells from the head; stuff these with a red pike forcemeat finished with crawfish butter (for this see crawfish butter, No. 573), and with the remainder of the crawfish and the fragments make a bisque, pounding them with their equal quantity of rice; when all is well pounded, moisten with the broth they were cooked in and more plain broth, then strain through a sieve and a tammy. Warm it well without boiling, and incorporate into it when ready to serve, a piece of crawfish butter; pour the soup into the tureen and garnish with the tails and bodies both cut lengthwise in two. Crawfish bisque should be colored slightly more than the shrimp bisque. Use for coloring bisques some orchanet warmed in clarified butter or any other greasy substance, or clear vegetal carmine. Breton makes an excellent coloring for bisques.

(202). BISQUE OF CRAWFISH À LA BATELIÈRE (Bisque d'Écrevisses à la Batelière).

After removing the fins from the middle of the tails as for à la Persigny (No. 204), wash forty-eight crawfish in several waters, drain them, mince some carrots, leeks, onions and celery root, fry them in butter and just on the eve of browning, mix in a quarter of a pound of flour; cook the flour for a few minutes, and then add the crawfish, some sprigs of parsley, two bay leaves, salt and mignonette, cover the saucepan and cook for fifteen minutes, tossing them several times, then drain. Pick out the meat from the tails, cut them in two and reserve them for the garnishing; pound the shells as well as the claws with twelve hard boiled egg-yolks, and when a good paste is obtained, moisten it with the thick stock, strained first through a sieve not too fine, and afterward through a tammy; moisten again with fat or lean broth. Should the bisque be required for a lean dinner; warm it up without boiling and incorporate in half a pound of crawfish butter with cayenne and half a gill of Madeira wine. Set the crawfish tails into a soup tureen and pour the bisque over, and when serving the soup put into each plate six pieces of bread a quarter of an inch square, fried in butter.

(203). BISQUE OF CRAWFISH À LA HUMBOLDT (Bisque d'Écrevisses à la Humboldt).

Wash thoroughly in several waters, four dozen crawfish, after removing the fins from the middle of the tail (see bisque Persigny, No. 204), drain them, then fry in butter, some carrots, onions, leeks, celery and parsley roots all cut into small squares; moisten with half a bottleful of Rhine wine, the same quantity of broth, and season with salt, mignonette and cayenne, and a gill of tomato purée (No. 730), put this with the crawfish on the fire in a well covered saucepan and cook for fifteen minutes, tossing them frequently while cooking; then drain them, and pick out the meat from the tails. Pound the shells with double their quantity of rice and when all forms a paste, moisten with the broth strained through a fine sieve; season and warm up without boiling, and when ready to serve, mix in a quarter of a pound of crawfish butter. Place the crawfish tails with small pancakes, cut round, five-eighths of an inch in diameter, in the soup tureen and pour the bisque over.

(204). BISQUE OF CRAWFISH À LA PERSIGNY (Bisque d'Écrevisses à la Persigny).

Remove the small black vein found in the center of the tail from forty-eight crawfish, using for this purpose either the tip of a knife, or else by twisting it round to the right, and pulling the fin away from the middle of the tail, and the vein attached to this will come off at the same time; it is most necessary to abstract this as it is always filled with sand. Wash the crawfish well; put them into a saucepan with a pint of broth, and the same quantity of white wine, salt, black pepper, two ounces of butter, two minced shallots, parsley and bay-leaf; boil for fifteen minutes, then drain and empty the bodies of twelve of the finest among them; pound the others to a fine paste, adding one quart of velouté sauce (No. 415), and one quart of broth; let boil again for fifteen minutes, then add to the bisque, half a pound of sliced bread, buttered and browned in the oven; simmer for fifteen minutes longer; then strain first through a sieve, and then through a tammy. Heat it up once more, and just when ready to serve, incorporate into it a quarter of a pound of fine butter, with a little red pepper added; fill the empty bodies with chicken forcemeat (No. 62) and lobster or crawfish butter mixed; poach them in boiling water, and when done cut them lengthwise in two; have also a garnishing of crusts made with savarin, a quarter of an inch square, dried in the oven, and served separate.

(205). BISQUE OF LOBSTER (Bisque de Homard).

Plunge into boiling, salted water, twelve pounds of small, live, well washed lobsters; cook them for twenty-five minutes, then drain; break their shells, and extract all the meat. Pound the lobster meat with its equal quantity of boiled rice; season with salt and red pepper, then dilute it with fat broth or lean, should the bisque be desired lean, strain through a sieve, and again through a tammy. Heat it up without allowing it to boil, add a pint of béchamel (No. 409), and half a pound of lobster butter (No. 580); stir well the bisque until the butter is thoroughly melted. Color a lobster bisque a deeper red than the crawfish. Crusts of brioche, a quarter of an inch square, and dried in the oven may be served at the same time.

(206). BISQUE OF LOBSTER À LA BENOIST (Bisque de Homard à la Benoist).

Mince very fine one medium carrots, one leek and two onions, fry them in butter and moisten with fat broth, or lean, some parsley sprigs, thyme, bay leaf, garlic, salt and black pepper. At the first boil, put in with this, twelve pounds of raw, live, and washed lobsters, continue to boil for thirty minutes, then drain them, break the shells, remove all the meat, reserve that from the claws, and pound the remainder with its equal quantity of wheaten grits. Make a light roux with four ounces of butter and five ounces of flour, moisten it with some of the broth the lobsters were cooked in, boil, skim, add this to the lobster preparation. Heat it up all together, then strain through a sieve and afterward through a tammy, warm it up again and just when ready to serve and very hot, stir into the bisque a piece of lobster butter (No. 580), and a quart of double cream. Put a garnishing into the soup tureen and pour the soup over; serve as a garnishing the lobster meat from the claws cut into small Julienne (No. 318), and small cream forcemeat quenelles, laid through a cornet on a buttered tin, and poached in a little boiling water.

(207). BISQUE OF LOBSTER À LA CAMBRIDGE (Bisque de Homard à la Cambridge).

Select twelve pounds of small, live lobsters, eight of them in all; remove the claws and cook them apart in boiling, salted water for twenty-five minutes. Cut in slices crosswise the remainder of the lobsters, fry these pieces in butter on a hot fire, adding four tablespoonfuls of flour; when slightly colored, moisten with half a bottleful of white wine and two and a half quarts of broth, half a gill of brandy, salt and pepper. Cook all for fifteen minutes, then remove the meat from the shells, pound it to a paste, and dilute it with its own broth; strain through a sieve, and afterward through a tammy; mix in one quart of béchamel (No. 409); warm up without boiling, and just when ready to serve, thicken the soup with twelve raw egg-yolks diluted in a quart of cream, and when the soup thickens, incorporate into it a quarter of a pound of lobster butter (No. 580). Put the following garnishing into a soup tureen, and pour the soup over. Remove the meat from the boiled lobster claws, cut the red part of it in slices an eighth of an inch thick, and from these punch out rounds three-quarters of an inch in diameter, using a column tube for the purpose; also have small, round quenelles, half an inch in diameter, made from the fillets of a pike or whiting in the shape of round beads.

(208). BISQUE OF LOBSTER À LA PORTLAND (Bisque de Homard à la Portland).

Cut twelve pounds of lobster lengthwise in two, break the claws, sprinkle over some butter, and cook them on a baking-sheet in a hot oven for twenty-five minutes. Remove them, and suppress the largest shells, pound the meat with its equal quantity of plain boiled rice, seasoned with salt, pepper, and curry, and when all is well reduced to a paste, dilute it with broth; strain through a sieve and then a tammy, and warm up the soup without boiling; thicken it with twelve hard boiled egg-yolks pounded with four ounces of butter, and mix in also a pint of double cream, and serve as garnishing some mushrooms cut into fine Julienne and lobster quenelles. Put the soup into a tureen.

Lobster Quenelles.—Cut one pound of cooked lobster meat in thin slices, add the coral and two ounces of butter; pound well and when reduced to a paste, take it from the mortar. Pound three quarters of a pound of panada, add gradually to it half a pound of butter, then the lobster paste, three eggs, one after the other, salt, pepper, nutmeg, and two tablespoons of Allemande sauce, test and rectify if necessary (No. 60). Roll this forcemeat to use for lobster quenelles, or else fill some sheeps' casings with it to make lobster boudins.

(209). BISQUE OR PURÉE OF MUSSELS À LA CUTTING (Bisque ou Purée de Moules à la Cutting.

Clean well three gallons of raw mussels, scraping them with a knife; wash them several times in clean waters, and take them out with the hand so as not to disturb the sand settling at the bottom. Put them into a saucepan with minced onions, sprigs of parsley, pepper (no salt), and one pint of water; set the saucepan on the fire, and when they begin to get warm, toss them and return them to the fire; cover the pot, and toss them again frequently, until the mussels open and are well cooked, then take them off, and pick them from the shells, reserving about thirty of the smallest for the garnishing. Strain the juice, and let it rest so as to be able to pour off the top and avoid the sediment at the bottom, pound the mussels with as much pearl barley (half a pound) cooked in water, salt and butter, for three hours; moisten with the mussel gravy and water in case the soup be too thick; season with salt and red pepper, then strain all through a fine sieve or tammy; warm it without letting it boil, and just when ready to serve put in a piece of fresh butter, stirring it well into the soup with a spoon until it be melted. Garnish the soup with the thirty small mussels laid aside, and savarin croûtons, a quarter of an inch square and dried in the oven. All lean bisques are made exactly the same as the fat ones, only substituting fish broth for meat, and garnishing with milts, scallops of sauted eel fillets, pike, quenelles with crawfish butter, crawfish tails, and the hearts of oysters. The sieve used for the bisque or purée is a round strainer made so as to fit in the mortar having a flange on the edge to fit the outside of it, the pestle is used to force the substance to be passed through it.

(210). BISQUE OR PURÉE OF OYSTERS À LA WILSON (Bisque ou Purée d'Huîtres à la Wilson).

Put sixty medium sized oysters in a saucepan with their own juice, set it on a hot fire to poach them; then drain. Fry colorless in some butter, two medium shallots and the same quantity of onions; dredge some curry over, and moisten with some of the oyster juice, season with salt and red pepper. Pound the oysters, and when they are a firm paste, wet them with some of their juice, and strain them through a fine sieve or tammy, warm them without boiling, adding a thickening of potato flour diluted in cold water, one tablespoonful for each quart, and when ready to serve, mix in some cream and fine butter; make a garnishing of chopped oysters and mushrooms, mixing some bread-crumbs and fine herbs with these, and seasoning with salt, pepper and nutmeg; add some raw egg-yolks and roll this mixture into balls; lay them on a buttered baking sheet, and poach them in a slack oven.

(211). BISQUE OF SHRIMPS À LA VERAGUA (Bisque de Crevettes à la Veragua).

Cut into small three-sixteenth of an inch squares, two ounces of carrots, four ounces of onions and two ounces of celery root; put into a saucepan six ounces of butter, fry therein the vegetables without browning and add three pounds of fresh, well washed shrimps, one bay leaf and several sprigs of parsley, also a bottleful of white wine and half a pound of chopped mushrooms. Boil for ten minutes, drain, remove the parsley and bay leaf, then shell a quarter of the shrimps, suppressing the tails, which must be laid aside for the garnishing, pound the rest of the shrimps with the shells of those the tails were taken from, add one-fourth of the same quantity of rice and moisten with the stock and broth; strain this purée through a sieve or tammy, add one pint of béchamel, season with salt and cayenne pepper; warm without boiling, and just when ready to serve, add to it a piece of fine butter and some cream. Serve the soup very hot, with Savarin crusts, five-eighths by one-eighth of an inch thick, and dried in the oven, also the shrimp tails cut into small squares.

(212). BISQUE OF SHRIMPS À LA MELVILLE (Bisque de Crevettes à la Melville).

Throw one pound of shrimps into boiling, unsalted water and cook them for five minutes, drain, then dredge them over with salt and toss in a colander to mix the salt in well; when cold, shell the tails and keep them for garnishing. Mince one carrot, one onion, a celery stalk and two leeks, fry these in butter with one bay leaf and moisten with three quarts of either fish or vegetable stock and half a bottleful of wine; boil for twenty-five minutes, then put into this broth two pounds of raw shrimps and the shells of the tails reserved for the garnishing; boil for five minutes longer, then drain. Put into a stewpan two pounds of sliced bread. cover it with broth and let simmer for twenty minutes, then drain it on a sieve, pound the shrimps, add the moistened bread, and continue pounding until all is reduced to a paste, then dilute with the shrimp broth, and press all through a fine sieve, season and strain through a tammy. Heat it up till near the boiling point, but do not allow it to boil, then thicken with eight egg-yolks diluted with two gills of cream and a quarter of a pound of good butter, incorporating it vigorously into the bisque with a spoon, then pour it into a very hot tureen, with the shrimp tails cut into three or four pieces as a garnishing.

(213). BISQUE OF SHRIMPS, BRETONNE (Bisque de Crevettes, Bretonne).

Have three pounds of very fresh shrimps, throw them into boiling salted water and boil them for a few minutes, then drain and remove the shells from the largest ones, allowing three for each person; stuff these with pike forcemeat (No. 90), mixed with fine herbs; then poach them in boiling salted water, drain and keep them aside for garnishing the soup. Pound the remainder of the shrimps with a quarter of their quantity of crushed wheaten grits, previously cooked in water for thirty minutes, also twelve ounces of minced onion blanched and fried colorless in butter, adding to it six spoonfuls of flour diluted with milk, and cook all very slowly. Moisten the purée with broth. pass it through a sieve or tammy, put the purée into a saucepan, heat it to near the boiling point, then season with salt and cayenne pepper; when ready to serve add a piece of butter. Place the stuffed shrimp shells in the soup tureen, pour the soup over the purée and serve.

(214). CONSOMMÉ, GARNISHINGS OF (Consommé, garnitures pour).

Garnishings of Consommés.—Consommé garnishings are served separately, by placing them in a tureen and pouring over sufficient of the soup to cover them; having only a little consommé in the tureen it is easier to serve the garnishing without breaking; divide equally into each plate and pour over some clear consommé; in case the garnishing is to be served in the same tureen as the soup (to be avoided as much as possible) first put the consommé into the tureen, and then the garnishing that all may be very hot. The garnishings we are about to describe may be served with either beef, chicken, game or fish consommé, for the fish using the lean garnishings. Consommés can also be thickened with potato fecula or arrowroot, by diluting these substances in a little cold water or broth, pour it into the consommé, stirring it all the time with a whip, boil, skim and then add a little Madeira or Xeres wine. These soups are called clear thick soups when they are thickened either with fecula or arrowroot.

(215). CONSOMMÉ À L'ADÉLINA (Consommé à l'Adélina).

The admitted rule for all soups is one quart of soup for four persons. The garnishing consists of round chicken quenelles, three-sixteenths of an inch, poached in boiling water; green peas cooked in boiling, salted water, and carrots cut into balls the same size and shape, and cooked in white broth with a little sugar. Also timbales, twelve pieces in all. Dilute one-quarter of a pint of purée of chestnuts with a quarter of a pint of cream and four egg-yolks, salt, and nutmeg; butter some dome-shaped tartlet molds, put a round piece of truffle at the bottom, and then fill the molds with the above preparation; set one beside the other in a stewpan with boiling water reaching to half their height, and poach them in a slack oven; when firm to the touch, unmold and place them in a vegetable dish with the quenelles, carrots and green peas; pour over a little consommé, just sufficient to cover, and serve separately a tureen of consommé, having all very hot. Into each plate put some of the contents of the vegetable dish and tureen; this rule stands for all consommé garnishings, that is, one timbale, and a dozen and a half carrots, peas, and quenelles, inclusive.

(216). CONSOMMÉ À L'ANDALOUSE (Consommé à l'Andalouse).

For this consommé prepare a garnishing composed of timbales, cucumber crescents, and small quenelles. The timbales are made with a pint of tomato purée strained through a very fine sieve; mix into this ten raw egg-yolks and a gill of cream; season with salt and nutmeg. With this preparation fill some No. 2 timbale molds (Fig. 137), stand them in a sautoire containing boiling water to reach to half their height and push into a slack oven; remove as soon as they are firm to the touch and let them rest for fifteen minutes, then divide each timbale into three parts. Place them in a vegetable dish with a little consommé. Pare some cucumbers to resemble crescent olives, blanch, drain, and cook in consommé. Have small quenelles made with chicken quenelle forcemeat (No. 89), and cream forcemeat (No. 75), half of each; push them through a pocket into rounds in a buttered sautoire and poach in a little boiling salted water; add the cucumbers and quenelles to the timbales, and serve at the same time with a tureen full of consommé.

(217). CONSOMMÉ ANTONELLI, LEAN OR FAT (Consommé Antonelli, en Maigre ou en Gras)

Use consommé of either chicken or fish, the following quantity being for twelve persons. Keep on the side of the range, three quarts of chicken consommé for fat, or fish broth for lean; thicken one or the other with three spoonfuls of tapioca, and cook for twenty-five minutes, skimming it nicely. Choose sixteen raw truffles, having all of them, if possible, one inch in diameter; peel them and mark with a column tube of five-eighths of an inch, a place for a cover; cut off the round cover using the tip of a small knife, and keep the piece aside; scoop out the insides with a vegetable spoon, leaving the surface as thin as possible, then salt them, and fill the empty space with a purée of goose livers (foies-gras) mixed with cream and egg-yolks, or if intended for lean, with a purée of salmon, béchamel, cream and egg-yolks. Close the opening with the piece laid aside, and arrange one beside the other in the bottom of a stewpan, just large enough to contain them; moisten them to half their height with consommé and Madeira, cover with buttered paper, and let the water boil, then place it in a slack oven for fifteen minutes, so as to poach the preparation inside the truffles. Serve these truffles in a vegetable dish with sixteen fine cocks' kidneys if for fat, or if for lean, sixteen pike quenelles the same shape as the kidneys; serve also a garnishing of small stars cut from noodle paste, blanched and cooked in consommé.

(218). CONSOMMÉ BALZAC (Consommé Balzac).

The garnishing for this consommé is composed of three kinds of timbales, chicken, shrimps, and green peas, and turnip balls.

For the Chicken Timbales have half a pint of chicken purée, two spoonfuls of béchamel, six egg-yolks, salt, pepper, and nutmeg.

For the Shrimp Timbales, half a pint of shrimp purée, two spoonfuls of béchamel, six egg-yolks, salt, pepper, and nutmeg.

For the Green Pea Timbales, half a pint of purée of green peas (No. 261), two spoonfuls of béchamel, six yolks, salt, pepper, and nutmeg. Butter twenty-four timbale molds (Fig. 137, No. 2) fill each eight with a different one of the compositions; stand them on a baking tin with boiling water, reaching to half their height and poach in a slack oven. When partly cooled off, unmold, pare and divide in three parts, cutting them across. Put them into a vegetable dish with a garnishing of turnip balls, blanched, and cooked in consommé till they have fallen to a glaze; send this garnishing to the table with a soup tureen full of consommé.

(219). CONSOMMÉ À LA BARIATENSKI (Consommé à la Bariatenski).

Make a pancake preparation (No. 3072), without sugar, and with it cook some very thin pan-cakes; when done cut from them pieces one and five-eighths inches long, by one and a half wide; spread over each piece a layer of chicken forcemeat, mixed with chopped mushrooms and parsley and a little anchovy paste; roll them up and lay them on a buttered baking pan; then poach them in a slack oven; prepare some marrow quenelles (No. 252), roll them into balls, five-eighths of an inch in diameter, and poach them in boiling water; have also a pluche of chervil (No. 448). Serve the same as for à l'Adelina (No. 215), using chicken consommé.

(220). CONSOMMÉ À LA BERRY (Consommé à la Berry).

Prepare for this consommé a garnishing composed of small soft eggs (No. 2949), and lozenges prepared as follows: Take a pint of purée of asparagus, beat in twelve egg-yolks, a little raw cream and seasoning; pour the preparation into buttered baking tins, the bottoms to be covered with a sheet of paper; poach in a slack oven and when cold turn them over on a napkin; remove the paper and cut up into small lozenges, one inch long, by half an inch wide; have also the same sized lozenges cut from both carrots and turnips, keeping them an eighth of an inch thick; blanch and cook separately in consommé and when done the liquid should be reduced to a glaze. Serve the garnishings in a separate tureen, accompanied by a tureen full of consommé.

(221). CONSOMMÉ À LA BRITANNIA (Consommé à la Britannia).

Put on to boil three quarts of fish consommé, or chicken if needed for fat; thicken it with three spoonfuls of arrowroot diluted with cold broth, and remove it to one side. Pound the meat from a cooked lobster by breaking the shells and removing about three-quarters of a pound of its meat, and add to it half a pint of velouté (No. 415). Season and strain through a fine sieve, mix this with some chicken and cream forcemeat (No. 75), divide it into two parts, and color one of them delicate red; butter some long eight inch molds, by one and one-eighth square; fill half of each so as to form a triangle with the white forcemeat and the other half with the red, place the molds in a sautoire with water to half their height and poach them in a slack oven, then cut them in slices, a quarter of an inch wide. Have some asparagus tops, and serve the garnishing in a vege-table dish with a little consommé added, and a soup tureen of consommé separate.

(222). CONSOMMÉ CARÊME, LEAN OR FAT (Consommé Carême en Maigre ou en Gras).

For Fat.—Have chicken consommé, thickened with arrowroot, allowing one spoonful for each quart, and diluted in half a gill of Madeira wine. Spread over a sheet of buttered paper, a layer of cream forcemeat (No. 75), one-eighth of an inch thick, poach it in a slack oven, then let get cold, and cut it in lozenge-shaped pieces; prepare crusts half an inch square, or else round shaped six by one-eighth high, and fried in butter. A printanier composed of small vegetables, trimmed either with a column, or else a vegetable spoon, using carrots, turnips, and string-beans, blanch and cook them in white broth.

For Lean.—Serve a fish consommé thickened with arrowroot and a garnishing composed of frog quenelles; a small printanier trimmed into squares, and each vegetable blanched separately and then cooked in fish consommé; crusts of bread cut round shaped, three-quarters of an inch in diameter, by an eighth of an inch in thickness, laid over with butter and browned in the oven.

Frog Quenelles.—Pound one pound of frog's meat and rub it through a sieve; lay it aside; pound also five ounces of rice flour panada (No. 122) with five ounces butter, adding it in three different parts. While still continuing to pound, season with salt, red pepper and nutmeg; add the frog meat, pound again, then rub it all forcibly through a sieve. Mix in with it one whole egg, and two yolks, working them in well, then try the forcemeat and rectify it if necessary (see No. 60). With this forcemeat make some olive shaped quenelles, poach and add them to the rest of the garnishing.

(223). CONSOMMÉ CÉLESTINE (Consommé à la Célestine).

A garnishing of thin pancakes without sugar; spread over each pancake a layer of chicken force-meat and fine herbs; set on top and press down another pancake, add another layer of forcemeat and one more pancake, and press the whole lightly, then with a column tube cut out round pieces one and three-quarters inches in diameter; lay these on a buttered baking tin, one beside the other, and leave them in a slack oven for about ten minutes, just allowing them time enough to poac . Place the garnishing in a tureen with some lettuce cut in very fine thread-like fillets, blanched and cooked in consommé and a pluche of parsley (a few leaves of young, blanched parsley); serve at the same time a soup tureen of consommé.

(224). CONSOMMÉ CHARMEL (Consommé Charmel).

A garnishing of small timbales the shape of half an egg, and one inch in diameter, have some molds of this shape and size; butter the insides and set them on a tin sheet having inch high feet attached to it, place this on to a larger pan, the smaller one having holes bored in seven-eighths of an inch in diameter, and a space of a quarter of an inch between each. Prepare one pint of pigeon purée, adding to it half a pint of éspagnole sauce (No. 414), reduced with Madeira, season with salt, pepper and nutmeg, and mingle all well together. Fill the molds with this preparation, pour water into the lower pan, a sufficient quantity to half the height of the molds, when set in the holes, and then poach them in a slow oven, unmold, and serve at the same time some braised sweetbreads pressed under a weight, cooled off and cut into three-eighth squares, then rewarmed in a little consommé; have also a few Julienne cut mushrooms. Serve this garnishing in a vegetable dish with a little consommé. Serve a soup tureen of consommé separate.

(225). CONSOMMÉ COLBERT, WITH POACHED EGGS (Consommé Colbert, aux œufs pochés).

A garnishing of carrots and turnips cut into quarter of an inch balls, then blanched and cooked separately in white consommé. Green peas, lozenge-shaped string beans, and small sprigs of cauliflower, and some very small eggs poached in water, salted and acidulated with vinegar, crusts of bread-crumbs, six-eighths of an inch in diameter by one-eighth in thickness, masked with butter and browned in the oven.

(226). CONSOMMÉ COMUS (Consommé Comus.).

A garnishing of small round rolls one and a quarter inches in diameter, made of ordinary bread dough; in these make an incision around the flat side and empty out the insides completely. Blanch some white cabbage leaves, suppressing the cores, drain them and cut them up very fine, then fry them in butter with quarter of its quantity of cooked ham cut in one eighth inch squares; moisten with a little white wine, add half its quantity of cooked, skinned and chopped up sausages; set this into the rolls, cover the tops with a layer of chicken quenelle forcemeat (No. 89), and poach them in a slack oven. Lay them on a vegetable dish round side up; and moisten with a little good consommé, then let simmer for a few minutes in the oven; add some cooked foies-gras (goose livers) cut in three-sixteenth of an inch squares, and some round five-eighth inch slices of lettuce, blanched and cooked in consommé. Serve this with a soup tureen of consommé at the same time.

(227). CONSOMMÉ CREAM OF PHEASANTS OR GAME (Consommé Crème de Faisans ou Gibier).

Choose small, fresh pullet eggs; boil them for four minutes in boiling water, then lay them in water to cool off and remove the shells; open them on one end with a tube half an inch in diameter from a column-box (Fig. 168), take out the yolks with a root-spoon, and empty them very carefully, slightly decreasing the thickness of the white: then fill each egg separately; using a cornet for the purpose, with cream pheasant forcemeat (No. 75), or other game forcemeat, as soon as each one is done, close the opening with the piece taken off, and set each one in an egg cup. Arrange these on the bottom of a deep stewpan containing a little boiling water, close the vessel, and poach the forcemeat, by putting the pan for fifteen minutes in a slack oven; dress the egg in a vegetable dish with a little consommé added, and serve at the same time a soup tureen of game consommé.

(228). CONSOMMÉ À LA DAUMONT (Consommé à la Daumont).

A garnishing of dome-shaped timbales decorated with truffles and filled with a maréchale mousseline (No. 912); then poach in a slow oven and serve separately, some blanched turnips and cut into balls three-eighths of an inch in diameter, and cooked in white consommé; small pâte à chou (No. 132) balls, with parmesan cheese, the size of green peas, and fried a fine color; some blanched chervil (pluche), and rice cooked in white broth. Serve all the garnishing in a vegetable dish, and a tureen of chicken consommé at the same time.

(229). CONSOMMÉ À LA DUBARRY (Consommé à la Dubarry).

A garnishing of timbales of mushrooms prepared as follows: half a pint of mushroom purée, half a pint of béchamel sauce (No. 409), eight egg-yolks and one whole egg; season with salt and nutmeg and fill with this some low and plain, buttered tartlet molds, poach them in a slow oven, unmold, and set them in a vegetable dish with some semolina quenelles, serve the garnishing separately with a soup tureen full of game consommé and crusts of bread, five-eighths by one-eighth of an inch, sprinkled over with butter and browned in the oven.

Semolina Quenelles.—Take a quarter of a pound of butter, beaten to a cream with eight raw egg-yolks, mixing them in gradually, add to it seven ounces of semolina, salt, pepper and nutmeg, and with this preparation make some small quenelles with coffeespoons; poach them slowly for thirty minutes. They should swell up to twice their original size.

(230). CONSOMMÉ À LA DUCHESS (Consommé à la Duchesse).

The garnishing for this consommé is composed as follows: prepare some bread-crumb croûtons half an inch thick by five-eighths in length, slit them with the tip of a small knife at one-eighth of an inch from the edge all around; stand them on a baking sheet, pour over some melted butter and brown in a hot oven, remove, lift off the covers, scoop out the inside crumbs. Fry a little finely chopped onion in butter, dilute with some béchamel and season with salt, pepper and nutmeg; add the same amount of finely chopped lobster meat, thicken with egg-yolks, cream, and a little nutmeg; with this preparation fill the crusts, cover the tops with quenelle forcemeat finished with lobster butter and poach in a slack oven, then dress. Serve some consommé in a separate soup tureen containing rice, blanched and cooked in consommé, and small green peas, cooked English style (No. 2742). The croustades to be served separately at the same time as the consommé.

(231). CONSOMMÉ À L'IMPÉRATRICE (Consommé à l'Impératrice).

For garnishing, have quenelles half-spherical shape, decorated with truffles and filled with a cream forcemeat, then poached in a slow oven; as soon as they are firm to the touch, unmold and set them in a vegetable dish with a little consommé and some rice cooked in white broth, some very small fresh green peas and rounds of red carrots, blanched and cooked in broth; serve separately a soup tureen of chicken consommé.

(232). CONSOMMÉ À LA FLORENTINE (Consommé à la Florentine).

Make a garnishing of small stars cut from carrots each one an inch and a quarter in diameter by one-sixteenth of an inch in thickness; blanch them in boiling, salted water, then finish to cook in consommé; have also inch diameter rings made of chicken forcemeat (No. 62), colored with spinach green laid through a pocket on buttered tins, then poached in boiling, salted water; some rounds cut from turnips three-sixteenths of an inch in thickness by three-quarters of an inch in diameter, blanched, cooked in consommé and reduced to a glaze; when the liquid has all evaporated the turnips should be done. Serve these garnishings with a little consommé and at the same time a soup tureen of hot consommé.

(233). CONSOMMÉ À LA FRANKLYN (Consommé à la Franklyn).

The Garnishing.—Cut out some rounds with a three-sixteenth inch tube from some slices of carrots a quarter of an inch thick, and from the reddest part. Trim some slices of turnip the same, and punch out the same quantity of pieces as of carrot, using the same tube, and cook them in consommé with a little sugar; also cook some string beans cut lozenge-shape in salted water and afterward drain all well. Butter some timbale molds (No. 5, Fig. 137); garnish them to three-quarters of their height with the vegetables, blending well the colors, and fill up the molds with a preparation made from a pint of cream, eight egg-yolks, two whole eggs, salt and nutmeg, strained through a sieve. Set these molds in a stewpan, with boiling water to cover half their height, and push them into a slack oven; when the preparation is poached remove them from the oven and set them away to cool. Unmold them and trim off the tops; then cut them through the center crosswise, and place them in a vegetable dish with a little consommé; also have pearl barley blanched and cooked in consommé; make some stars with bits of rolled-out puffed paste, a sixteenth of an inch in thickness, and baked in an almost cold oven, so that they remain white, these to be served on a plate apart. Serve a soup tureen of consommé at the same time as the garnishing, and allow three stars to each plate of soup.

(234) CONSOMMÉ À LA GRAMMONT (Consommé à la Grammont).

For the Garnishing.—A quarter of a pound of filbert nuts, pounded with half a pint of cream, when reduced to a paste, place this purée into a bowl with half a pint of suprême sauce (No.547), and ten whites of eggs; season, press through a sieve and then set the preparation into buttered timbale molds (No. 5, Fig. 137), lay them in a stewpan, one beside the other, with sufficient boiling water to cover half the height of the mold, then poach them in a slack oven, unmold, and cut them in two across the center; arrange them in a deep dish or vegetable dish; besprinkle them with a little consommé and have also game quenelles molded in molds, the size and shape of half a bird's egg cut lengthwise; in order to make these quenelles, mix an equal quantity of quenelle forcemeat (No. 89), with game and cream forcemeat (No. 75), and turnips cut into three-eighths of an inch balls, using either a vegetable or root spoon, then blanch and cook them ir white consommé.

(235). CONSOMMÉ À LA HONGROISE (Consommé à la Hongroise).

For this consommé make some of the following biscuits: beat twelve egg-yolks in a vessel, whip the whites to a stiff froth and mix them lightly with the yolks; also four ounces of sifted flour and two ounces of grated parmesan; season with pepper, nutmeg and powdered parmesan; spread this evenly on a sheet of paper, keeping it three-sixteenths of an inch in thickness and cook in a slack oven. Detach the paper, and cut the biscuit up into lozenges an inch and a half long by three-quarters of an inch in width. Besides this, prepare another garnishing with half a pint of onion purée and the same quantity of cream, six egg-whites, salt, paprika and nutmeg; with this fill some timbale molds (No. 4, Fig. 137), stand them in a sautoire, with boiling water, to half their height and poach in a slack oven; unmold, and divide in two, longitudinally. Make some small potato quenelles in the shape of a three-eighth of an inch ball; poach them in boiling salted water. Place the timbales and the quenelles in a vegetable dish, cover with consommé and serve the biscuits separately the same time as the soup.

Potato Quenelles.—Put ten ounces of purée of potatoes in a saucepan and dry thoroughly, working continuously to avoid burning. When it detaches from the pan, add to it two ounces of butter; season with salt and nutmeg, add four raw egg-yolks and mix in gradually two ounces of pâte à chou (No. 132).

(236). CONSOMMÉ À LA LAGUIPIERRE (Consommé à la Laguipierre).

For Garnishing.—Butter some small molds, shaped like small half pigeon's eggs; fill these with a game mousse, made of any seasonable game; set them on tin sheets; poach in a slack oven, unmold, and serve them in a separate vegetable dish, adding some oval shaped chicken quenelles, laid on a buttered tin through a bag, and poached in a little boiling water in a slow oven. Serve separately small one-quarter inch square crusts made of twelve turns of puff paste or trimmings and baked white in a very slow oven.

(237). CONSOMMÉ À LA NOAILLES (Consommé à la Noailles).

A garnishing made of artichoke bottoms, two inches in diameter; remove the centers, using a half inch tube for the purpose, then divide the rest into sixteen equal sized pieces, and pare them nicely; put them into a vegetable dish with a little consommé, also some consistent Royal garnishing (No. 241), cut into quarter of an inch squares. Have also round timbales made of game, hare, or leveret, or any other seasonable game; half a pint of game purée, half a pint of éspagnole sauce with tomatoes (No. 414); salt, pepper, nutmeg, and five whole or twelve yolks; butter the insides of the molds, fill them with the preparation, and poach them in a slow oven; when firm to the touch, unmold and set them in a vegetable dish with the royal cream cut in squares, and the artichoke bottoms. Serve very hot, and at the same time send a soup tureen of game consommé slightly thickened with arrowroot; adding just when ready to serve a little good Xeres or Madeira wine.

(238). CONSOMMÉ À LA PLUMEREY (Consommé à la Plumerey).

For the Garnishing.—Have some lettuce soaked in cold water, then washed in several waters to remove all the adhering sand, blanch in plenty of water, cool off, and press out all the liquid, bend the leaves over, one third of their length at the top, trim the stalks nicely, braize them for one hour and serve them in a vegetable dish after dividing them in two, lengthwise. Have half a pint of purée of duck; the same quantity of suprême sauce (No. 547), half a pint of bouillon, twelve raw egg-yolks, and two whole eggs, season with salt, pepper, and nutmeg, then press it through a tammy, and fill some buttered timbale molds (No. 5, Fig. 137,), with this preparation; poach them in a slack oven, unmold, cut in two crosswise, and add them to the lettuce. Crusts of bread five-eighths of an inch square by one-eighth of an inch thick, sprinkled over with butter, and browned in the oven; serve these separately; send to the table at the same time a tureen of chicken consommé; serve in each plate, half a lettuce, and one slice or half a timbale, pour over some consommé and add three croûtons for each person.

(239). CONSOMMÉ PRINTANIER WITH QUENELLES (Consommé Printanier aux Quenelles).

Put two quarts of clarified consommé on to boil. Prepare a garnishing composed of tender carrots, turnips, celery roots, cucumbers, asparagus tops, string beans cut lozenge-shape, also small flowerets of cauliflower; cut the roots either olive or ball-shape, using a vegetable-spoon, blanch them in salted water, then let fall to a glaze several times in a little broth until they are cooked, then put them as soon as done into the soup tureen, adding the cauliflower, asparagus and some green peas previously boiled in salted water. Besprinkle this garnishing with a pinch of sugar, pour the broth over, and finish with small quenelles, three-eighths of an inch in diameter, having a quarter of the quantity of the other garnishing. Serve the soup with slices of toasted bread instead of the quenelles; when needed for a plain printanièr, and for a consommé printanièr royale, employ the same garnishings, adding slices of timbales royale (No. 241).

(240). CONSOMMÉ À LA RÉMUSAT (Consommé à la Rémusat).

Mince up fine one small white onion, one carrot and one turnip, half a celery-knob, and the white part of a leek; fry these very slowly with some butter, season, and moisten with a little broth, then cook them covered, letting the liquid fall several times to a glaze, and until the vegetables are well done; press them through a tammy, and put this purée into a bowl. For one pint, add ten raw egg-yolks and one whole one, half a pint of cream, a pinch of sugar, salt and nutmeg; pour this preparation into buttered timbale molds (No. 4, Fig. 137) and poach by putting them into a stewpan with boiling water to half their height. When done cut each timbale in two through the center crossways and place them in a vegetable dish with some small chicken forcemeat quenelles, colored white, red and green, and pushed through a cornet on a baking sheet into the shape of beads, a quarter of an inch in diameter, having the same quantity of each color, and poach them in boiling salted water; drain them, and add them to the slices of timbale; serve separately and at the same time a soup tureen of chicken consommé.

(241). CONSOMMÉ À LA ROYAL (Consommé à la Royale).

Butter some timbale molds (No. 5, Fig. 137), then fill them with the following preparation, mix well one pint of cream, eight egg-yolks, two whole eggs, salt and nutmeg; strain it through a sieve, and fill up the timbales, put them into a stewpan with boiling water reaching to half their height, and poach them in a slack oven, until firm to the touch. Remove them from the oven, let get partially cold, then unmold, and cut them crosswise through the center; put them into a separate vegetable dish with some white of chicken, mushrooms and truffles cut into small pieces an eighth of an inch square by five-eighths long. Serve at the same time a soup tureen of chicken consommé.

(242). CONSOMMÉ À LA SÉVIGNÉ (Consommé à la Sévigné).

For the garnishing, butter some timbale molds (No. 3, Fig. 137), and fill them with the following preparation: one pint of the purée of the white of chicken made with equal parts of chicken and rice, cooked in consommé, the whole passed through a sieve, and moistened with one gill of suprême sauce (No. 547), eight egg-yolks, and one gill of cream, seasoning with salt and nutmeg. Set the timbales in a sautoire with boiling water reaching to half their height, and poach them in a slack oven; then let get partially cold, and unmold; and cut them crosswise through the center. Lay them in a vegetable dish with a little good consommé and some boiled green peas, serve separately, but at the same time, a soup tureen of chicken consommé.

(243). CONSOMMÉ À LA SOUVERAINE (Consommé à la Souveraine).

A garnishing of timbales. Make a preparation with one pint of mushroom purée, two gills of éspagnole sauce with essence of game (No. 414), ten egg-yolks, salt, red pepper, and nutmeg; fill some dome-shaped molds with this, and poach them in a slack oven, placing the molds in a stewpan with boiling water reaching to half their height; when done, which means firm to the touch, unmold them, and put them into a vegetable dish with some consommé, also some turnips cut into triangles, half an inch by an eighth of an inch thick, blanched and cooked in consommé, squares of the red part of carrot cut the same thickness, blanched and cooked with consommé; some artichoke bottoms cut into quarter of an inch squares, and half inch round pieces of blanched lettuce leaves.

(244). CONSOMMÉ WITH SWALLOWS' NESTS AND CHINESE BIRDS' NEST SOUP (Consommé aux nids d'Hirondelles de Chine, et Potage aux nids d'Hirondelles).

A Garnishing.—Salanga from the Philippine Islands; these swallows build their nests in the rocks on the seashore. The nests greatly resemble shells and are formed of a transparent, yellowish material; certain naturalists affirm that they are the spawn of fish picked up from the ocean. For twelve persons, put six swallows' nests to soak in cold water for twelve hours; drain them and clean them carefully, removing with a coarse needle all the bits of feathers, and small, almost imperceptible black spots found adhering to the nest. Wash them well in several waters, then lay them in a saucepan and cover them with white broth; let it come to a boil, then set it on one side, and leave it in the same degree of heat, only it should not boil; drain the nests, put them in a soup tureen, and pour over an excellent chicken consommé. Swallows' nests can be obtained all the year round, the price varying according to their rarity.

Chinese Bird's Nest Soup.—The Chinese in New York prepare this soup in the following way: For each person soak about half an ounce of swallows' nests for four hours in cold water, then drain. Place a young fowl in a soup pot, cover with water and let boil, add a few sprigs of parsley and salt, boil slowly and when the fowl is done, take it out and strain the broth, skimming off all the fat. Cook the birds' nests in some of this broth, take it from the fire at the first boil, cover well and keep it in a bain-marie, to it add some lean ham cut in thin strips. Remove all the fat from the broth, strain it over the nests and put it back on the fire until it almost attains boiling point, now add the cooked chicken meat, free of fat, nerves or skin and cut up into quarter inch dice; season to taste and serve.

(245). CREAM SOUPS (Potages Crème.).

I believe it to be more advisable to select fresh vegetables for making cream soups, and to thicken them with raw egg yolks, butter and cream. The flavor of the fresh vegetables combined with the velvety liaison, helps to make these thick soups highly estimated, even were the cream and eggs to be suppressed. Purées can be made of these creams, by finishing them as indicated in the purée soups. For Lenten cream soups, moisten them with a vegetable stock instead of broth, and use lean béchamel, in the place of velouté. Cream soups will be improved by passing them through a tammy.

(246). CREAM OF ARTICHOKES, MORLAISIAN (Crème d' Artichauts Morlaisienne.)

Trim well some artichoke bottoms so that all the green part of the leaves be removed; mince up two pounds of this, blanch and drain them. Put two ounces of butter in a saucepan, and when very hot, set in the artichokes and fry them without browning; moisten with two quarts of broth; cover the saucepan, and let boil slowly until the artichokes are done, then drain and mash them in a mortar; and pass the purée through a fine sieve; put it back into a saucepan, and dilute it with its own broth, adding one pint of velouté sauce (No. 415). Set it on the fire and stir constantly, bearing on the bottom of the saucepan with a spatula; let boil up once, then remove all the fat; season with salt, sugar, and nutmeg, and thicken the soup with raw egg-yolks, cream and butter. The quantity of liaison for each quart of this soup, is two egg-yolks, one gill of cream, and two ounces of butter. Serve separately some Savarin croûtons, a quarter of an inch square, and dried in the oven.

(247). CREAM OF ASPARAGUS À LA ST. VALLIER (Crème d'Asperges à la St. Vallier).

Mince up fine, five medium-sized onions, throw them into boiling salted water, and let them boil for five minutes, then drain, and fry them in a quarter of a pound of butter without coloring; add four heaping tablespoonfuls of flour, and let fry slowly for several minutes, then put in with them two pounds of green and tender asparagus, cut in one-inch length pieces, washed several times, and blanched for ten minutes in boiling, salted water. Moisten with two quarts of broth, and when the asparagus is done, drain it off, and mash it in a mortar diluting it with its own broth; pass all through a fine sieve, and put the purée into a saucepan, to heat; season with salt, sugar and nutmeg, and after it begins to boil, remove all the fat arising to the surface; just when ready to serve, thicken the soup with raw egg-yolks, diluted in cream, and incorporate therein some fine butter. Serve in a soup tureen with a garnishing of green peas and small quenelles, three-sixteenths of an inch in diameter, laid through a cornet on a buttered pan, and poached in some boiling salted water, poured into the pan; when done, drain them, and add them to the soup.

(248). CREAM OF ASPARAGUS WITH CROÛTONS SOUFFLÉS OR ASPARAGUS TOPS (Crème d'Asperges aux Croûtons Soufflés ou aux pointes d'Asperges).

Bend some small green asparagus, beginning at the root end, so as to break it off, keeping only the tender parts (two pounds); cut into one inch length pieces, wash well, changing the water several times, then drain and throw into boiling, salted water, continue the boiling for ten minutes, then drain. Put four ounces of butter into a saucepan; when very hot add the asparagus, and fry colorless on a quick fire; moisten with two quarts of broth, and when done, drain and mash; then pass through a fine sieve. Add one pint of velouté (No. 415) to the broth, color it with some spinach green or Breton vegetable coloring, season with salt, sugar and nutmeg, and just when serving thicken the soup with raw egg-yolks diluted in cream, and work in two ounces of butter (No. 175). Serve separately some croûtons soufflés made with pâte a chou (No. 132) rolled in strings and cut in three-sixteenth of an inch lengths; these pieces to be rolled in flour, then rolled around in a sieve to make them round. Fry in hot fat; or asparagus tops may be served as a garnishing instead of the croûtons.

(249). CREAM OF BARLEY, VIENNA STYLE, OR OF RICE À LA CRÉMIEUX (Crème d'Orge à la Viennoise, ou de Riz à la Crémieux).

Put into a saucepan two ounces of butter, and when very hot, add four ounces of well cleaned pearl barley; heat it, then moisten with four quarts of broth; cover the saucepan, and cook the barley slowly for three hours, or more, until it yields easily to the pressure of the finger, then drain and pound in a mortar, diluting it with its own stock, afterward straining through a sieve or tammy. Return it to the fire, and in case it should be too thick add more of the broth; stir continually with a spatula, bearing on to the bottom of the saucepan, until the soup is ready to boil; season with salt, sugar and nutmeg, and add the thickening to the soup, stirring it in well until all the butter is melted (No. 175).

For Cream of Rice à la Crémieux.—Pound or mash well in a mortar, half a pound of fresh bread-crumbs, mixing in gradually two whole eggs, and the third of its quantity of fine butter; form this into small, round cakes, seven-eighths of an inch in diameter and one-eighth of an inch thick; bake them in a hot oven. and serve the same time as the soup. The cream of rice is prepared exactly the same way as the barley, the only difference being that this requires less cooking than the barley.

(250). CREAM OF BRUSSELS SPROUTS (Crème de Choux de Bruxelles).

Blanch in boiling, salted water for ten minutes, two pounds of well cleaned Brussels sprouts, drain and fry them in butter, then moisten with two quarts of white broth, and when cooked, drain them into a mortar, and mash them to a paste; dilute this purée with its own broth, and should it be too thick, add some more white broth, then strain through a sieve or tammy, and add one pint of velouté (No. 415); heat all up without boiling and thicken with two egg-yolks, one gill of cream and two ounces of butter, this being the quantity to use for every quart of soup. Serve separately a garnishing of brioche croûtons (No. 51), one quarter of an inch square, and dried in the oven.

(251). CREAM OF CAULIFLOWER, BRISSON (Crème de Choux fleurs à la Brisson).

Divide the cauliflower into several parts, clean them well, pare nicely, and remove the hearts; it will require two pounds for the soup. Cook them until half done in boiling, salted water, then drain and fry in four ounces of butter, moistening with two quarts of white broth; season with salt, sugar and nutmeg, and when the cauliflowers are done, drain off the broth, and mash in a mortar to reduce to a paste; dilute this with its own broth, add one pint of velouté (No. 415), and if the purée be too thick, then add more white broth. Set it on the fire to heat without boiling, and just when ready to serve, thicken it with cream, raw egg-yolks and butter (No. 175). Serve a garnishing of croûtons soufflés, with parmesan cheese made as explained (No. 248), having added grated parmesan cheese to the paste.

(252). CREAM OF CELERY OR CARDOONS À LA LIVINGSTONE (Crème de Celeri ou Cardons à la Livingstone).

For the Celery, remove the threads covering the stalks; have two pounds of very white, cut-up celery, blanch it in plenty of water, and cook in two quarts of white broth; when done, drain and mash it well to reduce it to a paste, diluting it with its own broth; press it through a fine sieve or tammy, add one pint of velouté (No. 415), and some more broth should the purée be too thick; then heat the soup without letting it boil, seasoning with salt, sugar and nutmeg. Thicken it with egg-yolks, cream and butter (No. 175). Serve in a separate tureen a marrow quenelle garnishing.

Marrow Quenelles.—Melt half a pound of well cleansed marrow; strain into a cool bowl through a fine muslin; beat it till it becomes a cream, then add eight egg-yolks one by one, and beat again until thoroughly incorporated, season with salt, pepper, nutmeg, add half a pound of white and very fresh bread-crumbs; divide this into four parts and form these into strings half an inch thick, then cut them across to have each one-half an inch long; roll in flour and poach in boiling water; serve with the soup. The cream of cardoons is made in exactly the same way as the cream of celery.

(253). CREAM CHIFFONNADE WITH CRUSTS OR OF LEEKS WITH QUENELLES (Crème Chiffonnade aux Croûtes ou de Poireaux aux Quenelles).

Prepare one pound and a quarter of lettuce leaves, eight ounces of sorrel leaves, three ounces of water-cress, and one ounce of chervil leaves, all well washed in several waters, and cut up very fine. Put half a pound of butter into a saucepan, and when very hot, add the herbs, and allow them to fry without attaining a color, then moisten with two quarts of veal stock or white broth, and boil for one-half hour, adding a quart of velouté (No. 415), and a thickening of four egg-yolks, one gill of cream and two ounces of butter for each quart of soup; strain through a sieve, and season with salt, red pepper and nutmeg. Serve a garnishing of round shaped bread crusts seven-eighths by one-eighth of an inch, sprinkled over with butter and browned in the oven.

For the Cream of Leeks, have two pounds of the white part of leeks, prepared and finished as for the chiffonnade, but instead of round bread croûtons, replace these by a garnishing of chicken quenelles (No. 89).

(254). CREAM OF CUCUMBERS À LA SHEPPARD (Crème de Concombres à la Sheppard).

Peel or remove the green skin from the cucumbers, mince up two pounds of them, blanch them in boiling, salted water for ten minutes, then drain. Heat four ounces of butter in a saucepan; when very hot, add the cucumbers, and fry them colorless, moistening with two quarts of white broth; boil all slowly until the cucumbers are thoroughly done, and then drain and mash them in a mortar; thin out this purée with its own broth, and if still too thick, add some more white broth, and strain the whole through a tammy. Add one quart of velouté (No. 415), season with salt, sugar and nutmeg, and heat it up without boiling; remove all the white particles arising to the surface, and thicken the soup with egg-yolks, cream and fine butter (No. 175). Pour the soup very hot into a tureen with a good white of chicken garnishing allowing one ounce for each quart, and cut up into three-sixteenths of an inch squares.

(255). CREAM OF GREEN CORN À LA HERMANN (Crème de Maïs Vertes à la Hermann).

Boil some corn on the cob in water having salt and butter added to it; drain, then cut off the tender part of the corn; about two pounds in all. Pound this in a mortar with thick béchamel sauce and dilute this purée with white broth. Place a pound of chicken forcemeat (No. 60) in a deep buttered dish; stand it in a sautoire with water reaching to half the height of the dish, let boil and then put it in a slack oven to poach the forcemeat; leave it to cool, then pound in a mortar adding the corn purée, and enough broth to obtain a not too thick purée; strain through a tammy, heat up without boiling, and just when ready to serve add, to thicken the soup, egg-yolk and cream; work in a piece of fresh butter. Serve separately some Compiègne croûtons browned in the oven.

(256). CREAM OF GREEN CORN À LA MENDOCINO (Crème de Maïs Vertes à la Mendocino).

Cook the corn on the cob in salted water, adding a piece of butter; when done, remove the grains, mash them in a mortar, and dilute the purée with a quart and a half of broth; strain through a sieve or tammy, and set it into a saucepan; heat it up without allowing it to boil, and season with salt, sugar and nutmeg. Just when ready to serve, thicken the soup with egg-yolks, cream and fine crawfish butter (No. 573), with lemon juice added. Serve with a garnishing composed of shrimp tails, cut in small pieces.

(257). CREAM OF JERUSALEM ARTICHOKES (Crème de Topinambours).

Peel the artichokes, and afterward weigh two pounds of them, and mince them well. (Jerusalem artichokes can be imitated by using half artichoke bottoms, and half sweet potatoes.) Mince up one-quarter of a pound or two medium onions; fry them in butter, and then add the artichokes; fry also. Add two tablespoonfuls of flour, season with salt, sugar, and nutmeg, and moisten with two quarts of white broth. Boil and cook slowly until the artichokes are easily crushed; then drain and mash them; increase the volume of the purée with the broth the artichokes have been cooked in, strain through a sieve or tammy, and heat up without boiling; just when ready to serve thicken the soup with egg-yolks, cream and fresh butter (No 175). A garnishing is made of artichoke bottoms, cut into one-quarter of inch squares.

(258). CREAM OF LETTUCE, ROMAINE OR CHICCORY À LA EVERS (Crème de Laitue, Romaine ou Chicorée à la Evers).

Procure two pounds of lettuce, romaine or chiccory, and proceed exactly the same for either. Wash them in several waters after removing the greenish leaves, then cook them in boiling, salted water, until the hardest parts yield under the pressure of the finger, then drain and cool them off; squeeze out all the water, and chop them up coarsely. Put into a saucepan four ounces of butter, and when very hot, add the lettuce and let fry for a few minutes; moisten with two quarts of broth, then boil and simmer for fifteen minutes, adding one quart of velouté (No. 415), strain through a sieve or tammy, heat it up again, and when the soup is near boiling point, thicken with egg-yolks, cream and butter (No. 175), seasoning with salt, sugar, and nutmeg.

Garnishing.—Pound in a mortar, one-half pound of bread-crumbs with two whole eggs, adding them in gradually, and half of the same quantity of pâte-à-choux (No. 132), roll it out to three-sixteenths of an inch in thickness, and cut in squares, then fry in clarified butter.

(259). CREAM OF LIMA, KIDNEY OR HORSE BEANS (Crème de Haricots de Lima, Flageolets ou Fèves de Marais).

The manner for preparing either of these creams is exactly the same; cook till half done in salted water, two pounds of lima beans. Drain them and fry them colorless in two ounces of butter; moisten with two quarts of white broth, season with salt, sugar, and nutmeg, then cook slowly until thoroughly done; drain them and mash them in a mortar, moistening with two and a half quarts of white broth, then strain this purée either through a fine sieve or tammy, adding to it one pint of velouté (No. 415), return it to the fire, let heat to near boiling, then despumate well all the scum and grease arising to the surface, and thicken it with egg-yolks, cream, and fresh butter (No. 175). A garnishing of bread croûtons of five-eighths of an inch square by one-eighth of an inch in thickness, sprinkled over with butter and browned in the oven.

(260). CREAM OF PEAS À LA ST. GERMAIN (Crème de pois à la St. Germain).

Throw into boiling, salted water, two pounds of medium-sized peas, and boil them for ten minutes with a little piece of mint; drain them, then put four ounces of butter into a saucepan, and when warm, throw in the peas, and let them fry for a few minutes; moisten with white broth, adding a few lettuce leaves, about four ounces, and two ounces of onions; the lettuce to be cut up fine, and the onions minced; season with salt, sugar, and nutmeg, and boil until the peas are thoroughly cooked, then drain, suppress the mint, and mash them in a mortar, moistening them with two and a half quarts of white broth. Press through a sieve or tammy, and return them to the saucepan with a pint of velouté (No. 415); should the purée be too thick, then add more broth; warm it well without boiling, and thicken the soup with egg-yolks, cream and butter, (No. 175). Pour the soup into a soup tureen with some chopped up chervil, and a garnishing of extra fine peas.

(261). CREAM OF PEAS WITH MINT (Crème de pois à la Menthe).

Parboil two pounds of shelled green peas until partly cooked; then drain and put them on to fry with half a pound of fresh butter; moisten with white broth and add half a pound of minced white onions. When the peas are entirely cooked drain and pound them, diluting with velouté and the same broth they were cooked in; rub the whole through a tammy and return to the saucepan; put it on the fire and heat without boiling. Just when prepared to serve, thicken with egg-yolks, butter, and cream, adding a few mint leaves finely chopped and as garnishing some small chicken quenelles made with half chicken quenelle forcemeat, and half cream forcemeat laid through a pocket on a buttered baking tin.

(262). CREAM OF SORREL WITH STUFFED EGGS (Crème d'oseille aux Œufs Farcis).

Pick the hard stalks from the sorrel, wash it in several waters to free it from all the adhering sand, then drain and press it. Weigh two pounds of this, and chop it up fine; put four ounces of butter into a saucepan, and when hot, add the chopped sorrel and fry it colorless; moisten with a quart and a half of white broth, and one quart of velouté (No. 415); season with salt, sugar, and nutmeg; then put it on the fire to boil slowly, removing the butter floating on the top. Strain it through a sieve or tammy, and put it back to come to a boiling point without letting it boil, and thicken with raw egg-yolks, cream and fine butter (No. 175), adding to it at the last moment some lettuce chopped up and cooked in consommé. Pour the soup into a tureen, and serve separately a garnishing of hard boiled, stuffed half eggs.

A Garnishing of Stuffed Half Eggs.—Cut lengthwise in two, some small hard boiled eggs; remove the yolks, and fill the whites with chicken forcemeat and cream, mixing in with it chopped mushrooms, hard boiled egg-yolks and fine herbs; let the stuffing be dome-shaped, then dust over with grated parmesan; lay these eggs on a dish, and brown them nicely in the oven. Place them in a vegetable dish, and pass it around the same time as the soup.

(263). CREAM OF SQUASH, TURNIPS OR CARROTS WITH COMPIÈGNE CROÛTONS (Crème de Courges, de Navets ou de Carottes aux Croûtons de Compiègne).

Peel the squash and mince two pounds of the inside, with four ounces of onions, or else select young, tender turnips, peel and mince two pounds of these, or, cut some carrots so as to have two pounds of the reddest part; the turnips and carrots should be parboiled. Put six ounces of butter into a saucepan, and when hot, add one of the above vegetables chopped very fine, and after it is lightly fried without coloring, then moisten with two quarts of white broth, skim and continue to boil until thoroughly cooked, then drain, mash the vegetable to reduce it to a paste, and dilute with the stock it was boiled in; season with salt, sugar and nutmeg, and if too thick use more broth; thicken with egg-yolks, cream and fine butter. Compiègne croûtons (No. 51), cut in quarter of inch squares, and dried in the oven, should be served as a garnishing.

Garnishing for Turnips.—Three ounces of butter worked with a small whip until perfectly white, then incorporate slowly into it two egg-yolks, two spoonfuls of sifted flour, salt, sugar and nutmeg; mix in with this three whites of eggs, beaten to a stiff froth, and poach in a slow oven, in some buttered dome-shaped molds; unmold and serve separately the same time as the soup.

Garnishing for Carrots.—Small chicken forcemeat and cream quenelles, laid through a cornet on a buttered pan and poached in boiling water, then drained and served with the soup.

(264). CREAM OF STRING BEANS À LA VÉFOUR (Crème de Haricots Verts à la Véfour).

Clean and blanch some beans in boiling, salted water, then drain them; put four ounces of butter into a saucepan on the fire, and after the butter is warm, throw in the beans, and fry them for a few moments. Moisten with two quarts of broth, and let the beans cook, then drain, and pound them in a mortar, dilute them with some of their own broth, and should the purée be too thick, then add more broth, put the purée back into a saucepan adding one quart of velouté (No. 415); season with salt, sugar and nutmeg, and stir well while bearing the spoon on to the bottom till it reaches boiling point, but be careful that it does not boil. Thicken with egg-yolks, butter and cream. Serve separately a royal cream prepared as follows:

A royal cream (No. 241), garnishing poached in a buttered baking pan, let stand till cold, then cut it into small three-eighths of an inch squares and serve with the soup.

(265). CREAM OF SWEET POTATOES À LA GÉRARD (Crème de Patates à la Gérard).

Have two pounds of sweet potatoes previously steamed; peel, mince and fry them in four ounces of butter, moistening with two and a half quarts of white broth; cook until done, then strain and pound them in a mortar, diluting the purée with its own broth, and in case it be too thick, add some more white broth and a pint of velouté (No. 415); strain the soup through a sieve or tammy, then return it to the saucepan, and heat it to boiling point without allowing it to boil. Thicken with egg-yolks, cream and butter, using two egg-yolks, two gills of cream and two ounces of butter for each quart.

The Garnishing to be of one-quarter of a pound of bread-crumbs pounded in a mortar, and mingling with it gradually two eggs and a third of its volume of pâte-à-choux (No. 132); roll it into small balls, three-sixteenths of a inch in size, and fry them in clarified butter, serving them the same time as the soup.

(266). CREAM OF VEGETABLES À LA BANVILLE (Crème de Légumes à la Banville).

Mince four ounces of leeks, six ounces of carrots, four ounces of turnip-cabbage, two ounces of celery, four ounces of turnips, and four ounces of onions. Place four ounces of butter into a saucepan on the fire, and when hot, add to it the finely minced vegetables and moisten with two quarts of white broth; boil, skim and cook slowly. As soon as the vegetables are well done, drain them, and pound them in a mortar, diluting the purée with some of its broth; strain through a sieve or tammy, heat it to a boiling point without letting it boil, then thicken with egg-yolks, cream and fine butter (No. 175.)

Garnishing, Small Buttered Timbales (No. 6, Fig. 137) filled with one layer of finely cooked chestnuts and one layer of cooked rice, filling them up with royal cream (No. 241), and poach in a slack oven; unmold and serve these in a separate tureen with a little consommé poured over.

(267). PURÉE OF CAPON À LA JUSSIENNE (Purée de chapon à la Jussienne).

Prepare a delicate quenelle forcemeat as for No. 89; put a pound of this into a buttered mold furnished with a socket, and let poach by placing the mold in a saucepan containing boiling water, to half its height, and placing it on the fire; at the first boil take it off, and set it in a very slack oven until poached; then unmold, and let get cold. Pound this preparation in a mortar, diluting it with two quarts of broth and one quart of velouté (No. 415); strain through a sieve or tammy, and heat up without boiling; just when ready to serve, stir the broth well, and season it with salt and nutmeg, adding three ounces of butter, working it in until it is all melted. Pour the soup into a soup tureen. For garnishing have some rice blanched and cooked in white consommé, also some croûtons made of fragments of puff paste (No. 146), cut a quarter of an inch square; they should be cooked in a very slack oven, and when done, served separately.

(268). PURÉE OF CARROTS À LA CRÉCY (Purée de Carottes à la Crécy).

Only use the red part of the carrot for this soup; mince up two pounds of red carrots, cutting them with a knife into thin lengthwise slices. Put two ounces of butter into a saucepan on the fire, and when it begins to heat, add to it two ounces of onions, and fry for one instant; then add the red carrots, and continue to fry slowly without letting it attain a color; moisten with three quarts of broth, salt; add a bunch of parsley, celery, and bay leaf, and boil until the carrots are entirely done; then put in half a pound of rice previously blanched, and cooked in consommé; drain, and mash the carrots and rice. Moisten this purée with the broth, and if it be too thick add some white broth to it; strain through a sieve or tammy, and return it to a clean saucepan; heat it to a boiling point, stirring continually, and bearing on the bottom of the saucepan with the spoon, to prevent the purée from adhering; let to boil slowly on one side of the saucepan only, for twenty minutes, removing all the scum and fat from the surface as quickly as it appears; season with salt, and sugar and when ready to serve incorporate gradually into it two ounces of fine butter, stirring the soup with a spoon until all the butter melts, and serve at the same time small quarter inch squares of bread-crumbs fried in butter. Rice, noodles, and Japanese pearls can also be served as garnishings for Crécy soup.

(269). PURÉE OF CHICKEN À LA DUFFERIN (Purée de poulet à la Dufferin).

Take a good three pound chicken; raise the fillets, break up the bones and put them into a saucepan, with three quarts of broth; leave to boil for an hour, then strain the liquid through a fine sieve. Sauté the removed fillets, then pound them with four hard boiled egg-yolks, and mix in slowly a pint of velouté; also two quarts of stock. Strain the purée through a tammy, heat up without letting it boil, and just when ready to serve incorporate in two ounces of fresh butter, working it well into the soup. Serve separately a garnishing of pearl barley, and puff paste croûtons cooked white, meaning cooked in a very slack oven.

(270). PURÉE OF CHICKEN À LA REINE (Purée de Poulet à la Reine).

For Twelve Persons.—Garnish the bottom of a braziere with slices of fat pork, minced carrots and onions, and a bunch of parsley garnished with a little thyme and bay leaf; place on top one chicken, moisten with a pint of broth, and let it reduce slowly but entirely; moisten again with two quarts of broth, let the liquid come to a boil, then skim it off and continue boiling until the chicken is thoroughly cooked. Remove all the meat from the chicken without any skin or fat, and pound this with half a pound of very fresh bread-crumbs, season it with salt and nutmeg, then moisten with the stock, rub this through a tammy, and heat it up without boiling, adding to it an almond-milk prepared as follows: Pound one ounce of freshly peeled almonds, add gradually to it one pint of milk and press this forcibly through a napkin. Just when ready to serve, put into the soup three ounces of fine butter, stirring it continually until thoroughly melted. Serve the soup with a garnishing of small quenelles, bead-shaped, of three-sixteenths of an inch in size, made of quenelle and cream forcemeats (Nos. 75, 89), half and half of each, and laid through a cornet on a buttered baking sheet, then poached in boiling water.

(271). PURÉE OF ENGLISH SNIPE, PLOVER OR WOODCOCK À LA THÉO (Purée de Bécassines, Pluviers ou bécasses à la Théo).

Remove the fillets from eight English snipe; with half of them make a quenelle forcemeat the same as explained for game forcemeat (No. 62), let the quenelles be made either with a tea-spoon or else pushed through a pocket on a buttered sheet, in shapes of oval olives, and then poach them in boiling salted water; these quenelles are to be used for the garnishing. Put two ounces of butter into a saucepan with two ounces of chopped onions; fry them colorless, add the remaining fillets and carcasses, and when all is well browned, moisten with three quarts of broth and a quart of espagnole sauce (No. 414), let cook for thirty minutes, and despumate, which means to boil only on one side of the saucepan, and remove with a spoon all the fat and scum arising to the surface; then drain and remove most of the bones. Pound the carcasses and meats, dilute them with the broth, season and strain through a colander and afterward through a tammy; thicken when ready to serve with four ounces of butter divided into small pats, incorporating them in with a whip, until they are entirely melted; lay the quenelles in a soup tureen, and pour the very hot purée over.

(272). PURÉE OF GROUSE À LA MANHATTAN (Purée de Tétras à la Manhattan).

Roast three grouse for twenty minutes; cut off the fillets and break up the bones, putting them into a saucepan with four quarts of broth, adding a bunch of parsley garnished with bay leaf, half a pound of carrots, quarter of a pound of onions, and let simmer for one hour. Pound the fillets, add to it the same quantity of purée of sweet potatoes, and dilute all with the broth strained through a fine tammy, then return it to the fire in a saucepan to heat without boiling; season and stir into it just when ready to serve four ounces of fine butter. Make a garnishing with one pint of the soup; mix into a half a pint of cream, eight yolks and two whole eggs, and poach this in small buttered timbale molds (No. 5, Fig. 137), and cut crosswise before being put into the purée.

(273). PURÉE OF LENTILS, CHANTILLY (Purée de Lentilles Chantilly).

Unsalt a pig's head for twelve hours, partially cook it; put into a saucepan one and a half quarts of picked and washed lentils, add the half pig's head, and moisten with four quarts of cold water to cover all well, then add two carrots cut in four lengthwise, four onions, one with two cloves in it, half a pound of well pared raw ham, and boil slowly until all be thoroughly cooked, then take out the half head, bone it, remove all the fat, and put it under a weight to reduce it to three-eighths of an inch thick; drain the lentils, suppress the vegetables and ham, and pound the lentils, diluting them with their own broth. Strain all through a sieve, add two quarts of béchamel (No. 409), and heat it up without boiling; skim and when ready to serve, incorporate into it a good piece of fine butter. Cut the gelatinous parts of the head into dice, and serve them with the soup as a garnishing, also some croûtons of bread fried in butter.

(274). PURÉE OF LEVERET OR YOUNG RABBIT, ST. JAMES (Purée de Levraut ou Lapereau St. James).

Remove all the bones from the leverets or young rabbits, break up the carcasses, and fry them in butter with minced onions, carrots and a bunch of parsley garnished with thyme, bay leaf and celery, moisten with four quarts of broth, let the liquid boil up, then skim, and season with salt, pepper and cloves, continue to boil for one hour, then strain through a sieve. Cut up the meat in three quarter inch squares; fry these in butter with two ounces of lean ham, adding four table-spoonfuls of flour, and mix all well together, then moisten with the above stock, let boil and finish cooking. When the meats are well done, drain them off, and pound them in a mortar, diluting this purée with the stock, then press it through a sieve or tammy, the latter being preferable, for all purées are improved by being pressed through a tammy, as it removes any grains that may be in them. Heat the soup without boiling, season to taste, and incorporate into it a piece of good butter weighing a quarter of a pound, stirring it sharply with a spoon till thoroughly melted. Add a garnishing composed of small game and cream forcemeat (No. 75) timbales, the size and shape of half a pigeon's egg, poached in a slack oven and served in the soup.

(275). PURÉE OF OATMEAL TOULOUSAINE (Purée d'Avenas Toulousaine).

Put three pints of water into a saucepan; when it boils, drop into it like rain, six ounces of oatmeal coarsely ground, salt and one ounce of butter, let cook for three hours, dilute it with three pints of white broth, and pass it through a tammy, return it to the fire stirring it continually, and at the first boil remove it to the side of the fire, and let boil and despumate for twenty-five minutes; skim all the fat, season with salt, nutmeg and sugar, and just when ready to serve, incorporate into it a piece of fine butter; pour the soup into a soup tureen with a garnishing of bread croûtons an inch in diameter sprinkled over with butter and browned in the oven, also croûtons made of firm Royal cream (No. 241), using whites of eggs instead of yolks, poached in a slack oven, and cut into squares.

(276). PURÉE OF PARTRIDGES OR QUAILS À LA D'HÉNIN (Purée de Perdreaux ou de Cailles à la d'Hénin).

Roast some partridges; suppress the skin and bones, and pound the meat with one ounce of butter and two gills of velouté (No. 415) for each partridge; press this through a sieve and put it into a bowl with one raw egg-yolk and a litttle nutmeg. Put on the fire to boil, two quarts of thickened game stock; add to it the fragments of birds and a garnished bouquet, some minced carrots and onions, salt and nutmeg; boil on one side of the saucepan only in order to despumate for one hour, then remove all the fat, strain, and return it to the saucepan; at the first boil add the prepared purée, season to taste, then pour the soup into a soup tureen, after straining it through a fine colander, adding a garnishing of hulled barley and some small game quenelles.

(277). PURÉE OF PIGEONS OR WILD SQUABS À LA WALESKI (Purée de Pigeons ou de Pigeons Ramiers à la Waleski).

Infuse in half a pint of boiling Madeira wine, some thyme, marjoram, basil, cloves, mace, and pepper corns. Roast four pigeons, remove all their meat, and break up the carcasses, putting them into a saucepan with two quarts of broth, adding a quarter of a pound of onions, quarter of a pound of carrots, and two ounces of celery, all finely minced; salt properly, and let boil for one hour, then strain through a napkin, and return it to a clean saucepan to boil and thicken with two tablespoonfuls of fecula diluted in a little cold water. Pound the meat from the birds with eight hard boiled egg-yolks and one ounce of butter, add some of the broth to this purée to dissolve it, then strain it through a tammy, heat it up without boiling, and add to it the Madeira wine infusion after straining it through a napkin; stir in when ready to serve, two ounces of good butter, then pour it into the soup tureen and serve as garnishing, small cream forcemeat (No. 75) timbales No. 5, cut in two crosswise.

(278). PURÉE OF POTATOES À LA BENTON (Purée de Pommes de Terre à la Benton).

Mince up three pounds of peeled potatoes; put half a pound of butter into a saucepan, and when warm, add one pound of the white part of leeks minced, and fry them colorless; then add the potatoes, and moisten with six quarts of white broth, and continue to boil until the potatoes are done, and break easily under the pressure of the finger; drain and rub through a sieve with the broth, and some white broth added: season with salt and nutmeg, and put in one pint of velouté (No. 415); return this to the fire, and stir continually till boiling point is reached, then skim and just when ready to serve work into it four ounces of fine butter, stirring well the soup until all the butter is melted. Serve separately round croûtons three quarters of an inch, and an eighth of an inch thick, buttered and browned in the oven.

(279). PURÉE OF PULLET OR GUINEA FOWL À LA WASHBURN (Purée de Poularde ou Pintade à la Washburn).

Roast some small pullets or guinea fowls, remove all the meat, and suppress from this the fat and skin; break up the carcasses and put them into a saucepan with some minced carrots, leeks, a bunch of parsley and bayleaf. Cut half a pound of breast of pork; put two ounces of butter into a saucepan with the pork and fry together for a few minutes, then add the leeks, carrots and bunch of parsley, also the carcasses; moisten with six quarts of beef stock, season with salt, pepper-corns and two cloves, and boil up the liquid, skim off the fat and continue boiling for one hour, then strain through a sieve. Pound the meat taken from the pullets or guinea fowl with twelve hard boiled egg-yolks and two ounces of butter, diluting it with the stock, heat it up and have it boil for a few minutes, season, and stir in four ounces of butter, working it in the soup with a spoon until it is entirely melted, then pour it into the soup tureen and serve the following garnishing separate:

Garnishing.—Sauté four ounces of chicken livers; pound and press them forcibly through a sieve, adding four egg-yolks and some cooked fine herbs. With this preparation make small half inch diameter balls, roll them in egg and bread-crumbs, and fry them in clarified butter.

(280). PURÉE OF RED BEANS À LA CONDÉ (Purée de Haricots rouges à la Condé).

Soak for twelve hours in tepid water, one quart of red beans; drain them, then put them into a saucepan with six quarts of water, one carrot cut in pieces, one onion and a bunch of ungarnished parsley, and let cook slowly for three hours, seasoning with salt, pepper and cloves. When the beans are sufficiently done, drain them and mash them in a mortar; dilute this purée with its own broth, giving it a proper consistency, then incorporate into it, when ready to serve, a quarter of a pound of good butter. Serve separately small croûtons of bread a quarter of an inch square, fried in butter.

(281). PURÉE OF REEDBIRDS OR LARKS WITH CHESTNUTS (Purée d'Ortolans ou d'Alouettes aux Marrons).

Procure three dozen larks, pick them, remove the pouches and gizzards, and take off the fillets, laying them aside. Fry the carcasses in a quarter of a pound of fine butter, with half a pound of smoked, lean, raw ham, cut in quarter inch squares, and moisten with three quarts of game consommé (No. 192), and one quart of espagnole sauce (No. 414). Boil slowly and despumate for one hour, then drain and pound the carcasses and ham with one quarter of a pound of blanched rice cooked in consommé, and one pound of chestnuts; moisten this with the broth and strain all through a sieve, and afterward through a tammy, add some Madeira wine, a pinch of cayenne pepper, and when ready to serve, work into it a three ounce piece of fine butter, stirring it in vigorously till thoroughly melted. Sauté the fillets when ready, and serve them with the soup.

(282). PURÉE OF PEAS WITH CROÛTONS OR RICE (Purée de Pois aux Croûtons ou au Riz).

Have one pound of dry peas (green split peas), wash them well changing the water until it is perfectly clear, then put them into a saucepan with three quarts of beef stock or water, one carrot cut lengthwise in four, two large onions with four cloves, salt and pepper. Boil and let cook slowly on the range or in a slack oven, then remove the carrots and cloves, and pass the peas through a fine sieve with the onions. Season properly and moisten as required, then let the soup boil up again, skim it and work in about four ounces of butter. Serve a garnishing of bread croûtons cut in quarter inch dice and fried in butter, or else some rice boiled in consommé.

(283). PURÉE OF WILD DUCKS, [CANVASBACK, REDHEAD OR MALLARD] À LA VAN BUREN (Purée de Canards Sauvages [Canvasback Tête Rouge ou Mallard] à la Van Buren).

Roast two ducks for eighteen or twenty minutes, remove the fillets, and break up the bones, putting them into a saucepan with a split knuckle of veal and a quarter of a pound of ham, also two cut up tomatoes, and one onion with four cloves in it. Moisten with four quarts of broth, cook for two hours and strain the broth; pound the fillets after removing all the skin, with the same quantity of cooked hominy, and two ounces of butter, dilute this with the broth, season with salt and nutmeg, and heat it up without boiling. Just when ready to serve incorporate into it, four ounces of good butter. and beat the broth up well with a spoon, until all the butter is melted; then pour it into a soup tureen with a garnishing of celery cut in dice, and blanched and cooked in some consommé, also quarter inch squares of brioche dried in the oven.

(284). PURÉE OF WILD TURKEY À LA SARTIGES (Purée de Dinde Sauvage à la Sartiges).

Twenty-four Persons.—Braise a wild turkey in a braising pan, garnishing the bottom of it with slices of fat pork, and slices of onions and carrots, and on top lay the turkey; moisten with a quart of broth, let fall to a glaze, then moisten again to its height with more broth, adding a bunch of parsley, garnished with thyme, bay leaf, one clove of garlic and a split knuckle of veal, also two celery stalks, and let cook slowly; when the turkey is done, remove it, and strain the broth through a fine sieve. As soon as the turkey is nearly cold, cut away all its skin, and detach the meat adhering to the bones, about four pounds in all; pound this with four ounces of freshly peeled almonds, and dilute with four quarts of broth and two quarts of velouté (No. 415), strain it through a sieve, and then incorporate into it half a pound of fresh butter. A garnishing of green peas cooked in salted water and some pearl barley boiled three hours in white broth to be added to the soup tureen.

(285) BARLEY SOUP WITH CELERY (Potage d'Orge au Céleri).

Put half a pound of butter in a saucepan on the fire, and when it begins to heat, dredge in ten ounces of small pearl barley, well freed of all dust and impurities; let cook for a few minutes, then moisten with three quarts of white broth, and stir continually until it comes to a boil; salt, and cook for two hours and a half, till the barley be thoroughly done; adding three-quarters of a pound of celery roots cut in quarter inch squares, and blanched in boiling salted water for ten minutes. After the celery is well cooked; and just when serving the soup, taste it to see whether the seasoning be correct, then add a thickening of egg-yolks, cream and fine butter (No. 175).

(286). BARSCH POLISH STYLE (Barsch à la Polonaise).

Wash and peel ten red and sweet beet roots, cut them in slices of one eighth of an inch in thickness; put them into an earthen pot, or a wooden bucket; wet them plentifully with luke warm water, mix a handful of bread-crumbs (the addition of bread-crumbs is to hasten fermentation), cover with a linen and leave it thus stand for a few days. When the barsch is well acidulated, take off the crust of fermentation which lies at the surface; strain the liquid, put it into an earthen pan or into an enameled iron saucepan; garnish it with a piece of fresh pork, knuckles of veal, breast of beef, a chicken or a duck; put it on the fire, and as soon as it commences to boil, skim it, and garnish with a few celery roots, parsley, onions, leeks, salt and whole pepper, dry mushrooms (Gribouis). Cover and boil slowly as for a pot-au-feu; take out the meat when cooked. Cut the beet roots which have been used to make the sour juice, in the shape of Julienne, and an equal quantity of onions, leeks and carrots; fry them in butter and wet with the broth of the barsch. Then add finely shredded cabbage and the mushrooms, and let all cook slowly. When all is cooked cut the breast of beef in squares of three quarters of an inch, put some Frankfort sausages in boiling water for ten minutes, take off the skin, cut them in squares of three-eighths of an inch add them to the soup, as well as some small round raviolles. These raviolles are made with chopped cooked meat, well seasone , and to which has been added a little brown sauce. When ready to serve this soup, put a littl broth into a saucepan, add to it some well colored and grated beet roots, and let boil, remove it then from the fire as soon as it boils, pass it through a linen into the soup: add to this soup some fennel or chopped parsley, salt and black pepper. This soup must be a little acid; should it not be acid enough, add a little vinegar. If this soup is to be served at fine dinners, you may add garnishing of marrow quenelles (No. 252), of the size of an olive, some hard boiled eggs, cut lengthwise in two, and stuffed with the yolks which have been removed, crushed fine and seasoned with salt, pepper, grated horseradish and chopped parsley, and after being stuffed sprinkle them with melted butter, bestrew on them some bread-crumbs and put into an oven to color. This soup can be thickened with sour cream (the Russian smitane), to suit the taste. The barsch can also be served in cups at receptions and evening parties, in preparing it in the following manner: Take off the grease of the barsch and strain it, and then clarify it by adding to each gallon one pound of lean meat of beef chopped and mix with a bottle of good Bordeaux wine, and leave it at the corner of the stove, without letting it boil; strain it through a napkin and serve very hot in cups.

(287). BENNETT SOUP (Soupe à la Bennett).

This soup as made renowned by an article that appeared in the New York *Herald*, March, 1874.

Put into a soup pot six gallons of water, take a piece of the shoulder of beef (the chuck), weighing ten pounds; cut off all the fat and remove the bones; divide the meat into inch squares; set the bones and trimmings into a net, and place all into a pot with the water. Set the pot on the fire, and let boil; at the first boil remove all the scum arising to the surface, then add salt, a spoonful of whole peppers tied in a small bag with three cloves, one pound of carrots, and three-quaarters of a pound of turnips, cut in half inch squares; half a pound of celery cut in quarter of an inch pieces, four ounces of onion, three-sixteenth inch squares, four pounds of cabbage, suppressing all the hard parts, and one pint of well washed barley. Cook for three hours, taste to see whether the seasoning be correct, stir in a tablespoonful of chopped parsley, and serve hot.

If this soup should be made with dry beans, they need to be soaked in cold water twelve hours previous, and added to the soup, after it has boiled one hour.

With dried whole peas.—Soak them the previous evening, and add them to the soup, after it has boiled one hour.

With lentils.— Add them after one hour.

With rice.—Add it after two hours and a half.

With split peas.—Add them after one hour.

With potatoes.—Add them after two hours.

Three hours cooking will be sufficiently long to boil this soup, no matter which garnishing is used. Put in the vegetables according to the time designated for their cooking, so that the soup be always ready after three hours boiling, and see that the vegetables are not too well done. Remove the net containing the bones and trimmings, take out the meat and the gelatinous parts adhering to the bones, cut them up into small pieces, and serve them with the soup.

(288). BENOITON SOUP (Potage à la Benoiton).

Have half a pound of carrots, a quarter of a pound of turnips, a quarter of a pound of celery, half a pound of leeks, half an ounce of parsnips, and a quarter of a pound of onions; blanch separately the carrots, turnips, celery, and parsnips cut into three-sixteenth inch squares, and mince the leeks and onions. Put six ounces of butter into a saucepan on the fire, and when the butter is warm, throw in the onions, afterward the leeks, letting them fry for two minutes, and then the remainder of the vegetables; fry all together without attaining a color, and moisten with four quarts of broth, adding bouquet of parsley garnished with thyme, garlic, and bay leaf, and boil all slowly for one hour; remove the bouquet, and add to the soup half a pound of peeled tomatoes cut in two, squeezed out, and divided into small half inch squares. Season and continue cooking for another half hour, then add a quart of purée of fresh peas, one ounce of rice, blanched and cooked in consommé, string beans cut lozenge-shaped, some asparagus tops and a pluche of chervil.

(289). BOUILLABAISSE (Bouillabaisse).

Prepare one-half pound of red snapper, one-half pound of lobster, one-half pound of perch, one-half pound of sea bass, one-half pound of blackfish, one-half pound of sheepshead, one-half pound of cod, one-half pound of mackerel. Cut all of these fish into two and a quarter inch squares. Mince a fine Julienne of a quarter of a pound of carrots, two ounces of chopped onions, and two ounces of leeks; have also two cloves of garlic. Heat in a saucepan, one gill of sweet oil, add to it the vegetables and garlic, fry them without allowing to color, then add one tablespoonful of flour, mix all together, and put in the fish; moisten to its height with half white wine and half water, adding two medium sized peeled tomatoes, cut in two, pressed out, and chopped up coarsely; let boil for fifteen minutes on a quick fire to reduce the moistening, then add one clove of crushed and chopped garlic, some saffron, salt, pepper, the pulp of a lemon pared to the quick, and chopped parsley; remove the two whole cloves of garlic. Serve the broth or stock in a soup tureen, the fish separately as well as thin slices of toasted bread; should the moistening not be sufficient for the soup, then add some fish broth to it.

Another Way.—Have one pound of codfish, one of sea bass, and one of chicken halibut; cut these in two and a quarter inch diameter pieces. Put into a saucepan three pounds of fish bones and parings with some carrots and onions finely minced, white wine, parsley, garlic, thyme, bay leaf, salt, and pepper. Moisten with half a bottleful of white wine and sufficient water to cover the fish entirely, then boil for twenty minutes and strain. Mince up a quarter of a pound of leeks, a quarter of a pound of onions, add three whole cloves of garlic, and fry these in a gill of oil without letting the mattain a color; then put in the fish, and two pounds of live lobster cut in half inch slices from the tail. Moisten with a fish stock and white wine, a pinch of saffron, and lemon juice. Boil on a brisk fire for fifteen minutes, then remove the garlic; put some pieces of toasted bread into the soup tureen, pour the broth over, and serve the fish in a separate tureen.

(290). BRAGANCE SOUP (Potage à la Bragance).

Blanch half a pound of rice, drain, and put it into two quarts and half of boiling white broth, then set the saucepan on the side of the range. Roast a chicken, cut it up, break the carcass, and put the pieces into the soup, with the severed thighs, a few slices of raw celery root and some mushroom parings; cook the soup for one hour; skim off the fat, strain it without pressing, then return it to the saucepan to let boil on the side of the fire, and season with salt. Pound the white chicken meat with the addition of a piece of butter, press it through a tammy, and add to this preparation: one whole egg, eight yolks, two tablespoonfuls of velouté (No. 415), and as much raw cream, season and poach these in timbale molds No. 5, Fig. 137), buttered; at the last minute, pour the soup into the tureen, adding to it a few spoonfuls of green peas, and serving the timbales cut crosswise in a separate vegetable dish.

(291). BRUNOISE SOUP WITH QUENELLES (Potage à la Brunoise aux Quenelles).

Brunoise is made with half a pound of the red part of carrots, a quarter of a pound of turnips, quarter of a pound of celery, quarter of a pound of leeks, quarter of a pound of onions, and a quarter of a pound of cabbage. Trim or cut the vegetables into quarter inch squares, the leeks to be prepared Julienne shape; mince the onions and blanch each of the vegetables in separate waters, except the onions and leeks. Put four ounces of butter into a saucepan on the fire, and when it is very hot, throw in the onions, and the leeks a few moments later; cook a little longer, then add all the vegetables, and fry colorless. Dilute with one pint of broth, adding a good pinch of sugar, and reduce slowly till the moistening is entirely evaporated, and the vegetables adhere to the bottom of the saucepan; moisten again with four quarts of broth, then boil, skim and continue the cooking for one hour and a half more. Season with salt and pepper, pour the very hot soup into a tureen over a garnishing of small chicken quenelles three-sixteenths of an inch in diameter laid with a cornet on to a buttered sheet and poached in boiling salted water, and then well drained.

(292). CABBAGE SOUP (Potage aux Choux).

Remove the outer leaves from a medium three pound cabbage, and divide it into four parts: wash well in plenty of water, then blanch in boiling water for ten minutes, with the addition of half a pound of salt pork, cut lengthwise in two; drain the cabbage and pork, refresh them thoroughly in cold water for half an hour, then drain and squeeze out all the water from the cabbage. Put the cabbage into a saucepan, season with a little salt and pepper and lay on top one pound of brisket of beef, a bunch of parsley garnished with bay leaf, two medium carrots cut in four, two large onions with two cloves in them, and the lard that was blanched with the cabbage. Moisten with three quarts of boiling water, skim, close the lid hermetically and boil slowly for three hours. Drain and cut the cabbage into small pieces, set them into a soup tureen, with some sliced bread dried in the oven, pour the soup over and serve.

(293). CALF'S FEET SOUP, ENGLISH STYLE (Potage Pieds de veau à l'Anglaise).

Cut in two lengthwise, and remove the bones from four calf's feet; blanch them, then braise them so that they are entirely cooked, taking about four or five hours. Strain the feet, and set them under a weight to reduce them to a quarter of an inch in thickness, and, when thoroughly cold, cut them up into inch squares. Prepare a pound of carrots, half a pound of turnips, half a pound of celery cut quarter inch squares, quarter of a pound of onions in three-sixteenth inch squares. Put four ounces of butter in a saucepan on the fire, and when hot, add the onions and let fry for a few minutes, then the carrots, turnips and celery; fry all colorless, and moisten with the broth from the calf's feet, increasing its quantity with broth so as to obtain four quarts. Boil, remove the fat, season with salt and pepper and thicken the soup with two heaping tablespoonfuls of fecula diluted in a quarter of a bottle of white wine, one gill of Madeira and a pint of tomato purée; then boil again, and despumate the broth. Blanch and cook for three hours in white broth, two ounces of pearl barley, add it to the soup, also the prepared calf's feet. Lay on a buttered pan through a cornet some chicken quenelles three-eighths of an inch in diameter, colored with spinach green, pour boiling salted water over, and when poached, drain and add to the soup; when the whole is very hot, pour it into a soup tureen and serve.

(294). CALF'S TAIL À LA RUNDELL (Queue de Veau à la Rundell).

Parboil twelve calves' tails, cut them into pieces about one inch long, and fry them in butter with a quarter of a pound of onions, and adding one pound of carrots cut in quarter inch squares, a bunch of parsley garnished with thyme, bay leaf and a clove of garlic. Moisten with four quarts of broth, and allow the liquid to boil and to continue boiling slowly till the tails and vegetables are thoroughly cooked, then remove the bunch of parsley. Cut two medium cabbages in four, plunge them into boiling, salted water, let boil for ten minutes, then drain and cut out the cores and other hard parts; divide each quarter into eight pieces, put them in a saucepan, pour the broth the tails were cooked in over it, let the cabbages boil up once, then finish the cooking in a slack oven for two hours. When ready to serve, lay the cabbages in a soup tureen, add the tails and vegetables, and pour some consommé over; season to taste and serve the soup with thin slices of buttered bread, browned in the oven.

(295). CHAMBERLAIN SOUP (Potage à la Chamberlain.).

Keep boiling on the side of the range, two quarts of thickened soup (No. 195); boil and skim it well. Have four ounces of minced onions, Bermuda ones in preference, blanch them in plenty of water, then drain and fry them in butter; moisten them with one quart of broth, adding a pinch of sugar. When done, press them forcibly through a fine sieve, and mix this purée to the thick stock; boil, then skim, and when ready to serve, thicken the soup with a thickening of four egg-yolks, one gill of cream, and two ounces of fine butter. Serve separately a garnishing of small cream chicken forcemeat timbales molded in timbale molds (No. 5, Fig. 137), poached and cut in two crosswise, putting them into a vegetable dish with a little consommé added, and serve.

(296). CHAMPÊTRE SOUP (Potage Champêtre).

Despumate for twenty-five minutes on the side of the range, two quarts of thick white soup stock (No. 195), with a handful of mushroom parings added. Take some long French rolls called "flutes," each one being one inch and a half in diameter; scrape off the superficial upper crust, and cut them transversely into a quarter of an inch thick slices; brown these on one side with clarified butter, then drain them off, leaving the butter in the pan. Cover the toasted sides of these slices with a paste made of fresh Swiss, Chestershire, and Parmesan cheeses, pounded and moistened with a little beer and Marsala wine, finishing with a pinch of cayenne pepper; dust this paste over with grated parmesan, return the bread to the pan, and put it into a hot oven to glaze the cheese, then range them on plates. Skim all the fat from the soup, strain and put it back into the saucepan, add half a gill of soubise purée (No. 723), mingled with four egg-yolks, butter and grated nutmeg; pour it into a soup tureen and serve at the same time as the cheese crusts.

(297). CHARTREUSE SOUP (Potage à la Chartreuse).

Boil up two quarts of clarified veal broth; put into it four or five spoonfuls of French tapioca, and let cook together for twenty-five or thirty minutes; strain, and return it to the saucepan on the side of the range. Prepare with some thinly rolled out raviole paste (No. 147), four or five dozen small ravioles, filling them with three different preparations: one-third of them with a good purée of spinach, one-third with a purée or cooked foies-gras combined with a little melted beef extract, and the other third with finely chopped up fresh oronge-agaric, thickened with a little reduced sauce, or should there be no oronge-agaric then use cèpes or peeled mushrooms. Plunge into boiling water four or five not over ripe tomatoes; drain them as soon as the skin peels off, and press them through a tammy, and if the purée be too thin, then let it drain on a fine sieve, reserving the liquid, and putting it into a saucepan with some good veal stock and reduce it to a half glaze. Cook the ravioles slowly in salted water for twelve to fifteen minutes with the cover on, then drain, and lay them in the soup tureen. Remove the soup from off the fire, mix it in with the purée of raw tomatoes, season, and pour it over the ravioles.

(298). CHICKEN AND LEEK SOUP (Potage à la Volaille et aux Poireaux).

Put into a saucepan one chicken, weighing three pounds. Let it be very fresh, drawn and singed; add a small split knuckle of veal, moisten with four quarts of good broth, and boil up the liquid: skim and let simmer uninterruptedly for three hours. After the chicken is three-quarters done, remove it and lift off the skin; mince up the flesh, and put this into a saucepan, with the white part of twelve leeks, cut in two inch lengths, then lengthwise in four, and blanched in boiling salted water, drain them and put them on to cook with the minced chicken. After all is well done, pour it into the soup tureen; season the broth properly, and strain it through a fine, damp napkin; add this to the tureen and serve. Have a separate garnishing of small timbales, made with eight egg-yolks, one pint of cream, salt, sugar, and nutmeg, strained through a sieve; fill some buttered timbale molds (No. 4, Fig. 137), with this preparation, poach them (No. 152), then unmold, cut them in two crosswise, and lay them in a vegetable dish with a little broth added. Serve the garnishing separately at the same time as the soup.

(299). CHICKEN OKRA SOUP (Gombo de Volaille).

Prepare two pounds of the breast of chicken cut into half inch squares, half a pound of salted raw ham cut in quarter inch squares, half a pound of onions cut in eighth inch squares and two pounds or eight fine tomatoes plunged into boiling water to remove their skins; then cut in four, and slightly pressed to extract the seeds; four ounces of rice, picked, washed and cooked in salted water with half an ounce of butter, one pound of okras cut crosswise in pieces a quarter or three-eighths of an inch, according to their size, four ounces of finely cut up green peppers, four quarts of broth and four ounces of butter. Put the butter into the saucepan on the fire, and when it is very hot, throw in the onions to fry colorless, add the ham and let all fry together ; then add the chicken meat; fry again slowly while stirring, till the butter is entirely clarified; then moisten with chicken broth made from the bones of the chicken, and four pounds of leg of veal, adding some beef stock. Remove all the fat from the soup, and boil for twenty minutes; put in the okras and green peppers, then continue cooking until the gumbo or okras are entirely done; add the tomatoes, boil a few minutes longer and season with salt, Worcestershire sauce and mushroom catsup. Place the rice in a soup tureen, and pour the soup over. This soup is frequently strained and served in consommé cups.

(300). CLAM CHOWDER (Chowder de Lucines).

Prepare a quarter of a pound of well chopped fat pork, a small bunch of parsley chopped not too fine, four ounces of chopped onions, one and a half quarts of potatoes cut in seven-sixteenth of an inch squares; two quarts of clams retaining all the juice possible; one quart of tomatoes peeled, pressed and cut in half inch squares. Put the fat pork into a saucepan, and when fried, add the onions to fry for one minute, then the potatoes, the clams and the tomatoes; should there not be sufficient moistening, pour in a little water and boil the whole until the potatoes are well done. Add five pilot crackers broken up into very small bits; one soup spoonful of thyme leaves, two ounces of butter, a very little pepper and salt to taste. This quantity will make four gallons, sufficient for sixty persons.

Another way. — Chop up a quarter of a pound of fat pork, melt it down, adding four ounces of onions cut in quarter inch dice, and fry them with the pork, without coloring, then add one and a half pounds of potatoes cut in half inch squares, a pound of peeled and halved tomatoes, pressed out and cut in five-eighth inch squares, one ounce of coarsely chopped parsley, seventy-five medium sized clams, removing the hard parts and chopping them up very fine, the clam juice, a little salt if found necessary, pepper and thyme leaves. Boil the whole till the potatoes are cooked (the green part of celery chopped fine) and should the clam juice not be sufficient, then add a little water.

(301). CHOWDER OF FRESH AND SALT WATER FISH À LA STEBENS (Chowder de Poisson d'Eau Douce et d'Eau de Mer à la Stebens).

Fresh Water Fish.—Prepare a pound and a half of fresh water fish, such as eels, pike perch or wall-eyed perch (sandre), and cut in one and a half inch squares; also one pound of potatoes cut in half inch dice, three-quarters of a pound of minced onions, half a pound of chopped fat pork, and three green peppers chopped fine. Melt the pork, add to it the onions fry without coloring, then the add squares of potatoes and the fish, moisten to the height of the fish with water, season with salt and black pepper and let boil until the potatoes are cooked. This chowder must be thick and appear more like a stew, still, some broth can be added to it, to thin it out according to taste.

Salt Water Fish.—Prepare two pounds of sea bass, sheepshead, blackfish and kingfish, cut them in one and a half to two inch squares, have also three-quarters of a pound of minced potatoes, three ounces of salt pork, and three ounces of onions. Put the salt pork into a saucepan with one ounce of butter, fry lightly with the onions, then add the potatoes and the fish, also a bunch of parsley garnished with thyme and summer savory; season with salt, black and red pepper, and moisten to the height of the fish with some water. Cook on a quick fire for twenty minutes, or until the potatoes are done, then remove the parsley, add two broken and soaked pilot crackers and serve.

(302). COLD SOUP, RUSSIAN STYLE (Potage Froid à la Russe).

Cut into quarter inch squares, one salted cucumber and two fresh ones, free of their peel and seeds, (one pound in all), put these into a soup tureen on the ice; add the meat from sixty crawfish, or one pound of the meat from a lobster's claws, cut in quarter inch squares of the same dimension as the cucumbers; and half a pound of braized sturgeon or salmon cut in quarter inch squares; put all these on ice until ready to serve. Have one quart of sour cream, strain it through a tammy, also two quarts of kwass, and stir into it a few pieces of very clean ice, also the cucumbers and lobster laid aside; season with salt and a pinch of powdered sugar, and serve separately on a plate some hard boiled eggs, cut in four and sprinkled over with chervil and fennel.

Kwass.—In order to make twelve bottles of kwass, procure two pounds of rye, two pounds of wheat, and one pound of hulled barley; pour tepid water over all, and when these grains are swollen, add four pounds of rye flour, and mix well together with tepid water, so as to form a paste neither too thin nor too thick. Put this into a large earthen pot, into a hot oven, and let it brown. After this has cooked five hours, pour it into a pail or barrel and mix in with it twelve bottlefuls of cold water; let rest for twenty-four hours, then decant the liquid and clarify it with a quarter of a pound of yeast mixed with a third of a bottleful of Madeira wine; rest again for five hours, and remove the clear part, and with this liquid fill up the bottles, setting one dry Malaga raisin into each one, then cork, tie, and keep the bottles in a cool place.

(303). CRAB AND SHRIMP SOUP À LA LOUBAT (Potage aux Crabes et aux Crevettes à la Loubat).

Wash well twenty-four hard crabs; boil them, and remove all the shells as well as the lungs; cleanse them in water changing it frequently, then remove all the meat contained therein, and pound it while diluting with three pints of thickened fish soup stock (No. 195). Allow to despumate for half an hour, then skim off the fat and strain it through a sieve, returning it to a clean saucepan; place this on the fire, and stir continually, and at the first boil, skim it carefully; adding some red pepper; thicken the soup with six egg-yolks, half a pint of cream and three ounces of butter; make a garnishing of quenelles as follows: Have a pike quenelle forcemeat (No. 90), pushed through a cornet to form three-sixteenths of an inch beads, on a buttered tin sheet, and poach them in boiling, salted water; have also three-eighths inch ball of potatoes cooked in a very little white broth, and some shrimp tails cut into two or three pieces.

(304). CRAWFISH SOUP À LA RENOMMÉE (Potage d'Écrevisses à la Renommée).

Boil a few dozen crawfish in a court bouillon with white wine; drain them, and detach the tails from the bodies, suppressing the tail shells. Keep boiling on the side of the fire, one and a half quarts of thickened white soup stock; put into it the crawfish shells after pounding them, and let the soup despumate for thirty-five minutes, remove all the fat, strain and return it to the saucepan; boil it up again, and stir in cayenne pepper to taste. Take all the meat from the tails and claws of the crawfish, chop up the claws with the parings of the tails and claws, mixing in a little bread panada, red butter, a few raw egg-yolks and red pepper; prepare a small forcemeat with this, and shape it into tiny quenelles, rolling them on a floured table; poach them, then drain and put them in the soup tureen with the crawfish tails cut in two lengthwise. Skim the fat from the soup, thicken it with four egg-yolks and two spoonfuls of purée of white asparagus tops, and also a little raw cream; let the thickening cook without boiling, and finish the soup with a piece of good butter working it vigorously with a whip.

(305). CROÛTE AU POT (Croûte au Pot).

Put into an earthen pot (a pipkin) twelve quarts of stock, adding a piece of the rump of beef, which must weigh eight pounds when trimmed and free from part of its fat, and a fowl weighing four pounds, drawn, singed and well washed; then add one pound of carrots, half a pound of onions with four cloves in them, two ounces of celery, and twenty-four whole peppers. Let boil up, salt it, and continue boiling very slowly for three hours and a half to four hours. Remove the vegetables as soon as each one is done, pare the carrots cork shaped one inch in diameter, and cut them into three-sixteenth inch thick pieces; the turnips shaped like a clove of garlic. Cut lengthwise in two some small French rolls, make them into pieces two inches long, scoop out the crumbs, and on this side besprinkle them with some good chicken fat, brown them in a hot oven. Lay them on a dish, the rounded side uppermost, and one beside the other; sprinkle them over again with chicken fat, and brown them in the oven. Cut a cabbage into four parts, wash these in plenty of water, and blanch in salted water for ten minutes, then drain, and refresh for half an hour; press well, and put it in a saucepan with a carrot cut in four, and one onion with cloves in it; season with salt and pepper, and moisten with stock and half a pint of chicken fat; the cabbage must be covered two inches above its height, then cook for two hours. When the cabbage is done, drain, and serve it in a vegetable dish with the rolls around, and lay the carrots and turnips on top; send the soup to the table in a separate soup tureen.

(306). D'OSMONT SOUP (Potage à la D'Osmont).

Mince up four ounces of carrot, two ounces of onions, and one ounce of celery, fry these in four ounces of butter, adding four pounds of fresh tomatoes cut in two and pressed. Moisten with two quarts of broth, and let cook for half an hour, then press the whole through a fine sieve; put this into a saucepan, adding one quart of thick soup stock (No. 195), boil, skim, and when ready to serve, taste the soup to see whether it be seasoned properly, if it should be too thick add some bouillon to it, and then pour it into a soup tureen with a garnishing of rice blanched and cooked in white consommé, also some small chicken forcemeat quenelles (No. 89) colored with spinach green.

(307). FERMIÈRE STYLE SOUP (Potage à la Fermière).

Have four medium sized onions, four ounces of leeks, half a cabbage, suppressing the core, three-quarters of a pound of potatoes, four ounces of turnips, half a pound of carrots and four ounces of celery, all minced up very fine, also some minced lettuce. Put one pound of scraped fat pork into a saucepan on the fire, and when hot, add the minced onions and leeks; fry for two minutes, and throw in the other vegetables and cook them without letting them get brown. Sprinkle over four spoonfuls of flour, let cook and a few minutes after, dilute with four quarts of stock; stir the whole until it boils, then add a bunch of parsley garnished with bay leaf, four ounces of string beans cut lozenge shape, and two ounces of raw ham cut in one-eighth inch squares; boil again for three-quarters of an hour, and then add a handful of chopped up sorrel, and a little minced chervil; season with salt and pepper, remove the parsley, season to taste, and pour the soup into a soup tureen over slices of toasted bread or else slices of buttered bread browned in the oven.

(308). FISH SOUP À LA PONSARDIN (Potage de Poisson à la Ponsardin).

Cut one pound of fillet of bass into slices a quarter of an inch thick, and one inch and a quarter in diameter; fry these in some butter, and set them under a weight; when cold pare them. Take the tails from one pound of shrimps, peel them, and keep the meat aside. Put into a saucepan, one very fresh bass head, also the parings cut from the fillets and the shrimps, add half a pound of stalks or parings of mushrooms, a quarter of a bottleful of white wine, and three quarts of water, also a bunch of parsley, thyme, bay leaf, carrots and minced onions; boil for thirty minutes, then strain. Make a blond roux with quarter of a pound of butter, and quarter of a pound of flour; moisten it with the fish broth, boil, despumate, and thicken it with egg-yolks, cream and lobster butter, with Kari; serve as a garnishing the shrimp tails and the small prepared fillets of bass.

(309). FROG SOUP AND FROG SOUP WITH TIMBALES (Potage aux Grenouilles et aux Timbales de Grenouilles).

Mince well a quarter of a pound of the white part of leeks, wet them with two quarts of fish broth, let boil slowly for half an hour, then press them forcibly through a sieve, returning this to the saucepan. Have one pound and a half of frogs, suppress half a pound from the thighs (the thick part of the thigh); put the balance in with the broth, and four ounces of fresh bread-crumbs; boil for ten minutes, then drain and pound all well. Dilute with the broth, strain it through a sieve, heat it up without boiling, and thicken with egg-yolks, cream and fine butter, the proportions being four yolks, one gill of cream, and two ounces of butter. Cook separate in some broth, the half pound of frogs kept aside; remove all the bones, and put them into the soup with a pinche of chervil (No. 448).

Frog Timbales.—Use the same soup, but instead of the garnishing of boned frog thighs, substitute small timbales the shape of half a pigeon egg; butter and fill them with frog forcemeat (No. 222), and cream; then poach them (No. 152) in a slack oven. Unmold, and serve separately in a vegetable dish with a little consommé; put a timbale into each plate when serving the soup.

(310). GARBURE WITH LETTUCE (Garbure aux Laitues).

First wash sixteen small lettuce heads several times, changing the water each time; blanch them for ten minutes, then refresh and press out all the liquid from them; lay them on a cloth, season them with a little salt and pepper, and place on each a chicken forcemeat ball of an inch and a quarter in diameter, mixing in with it a little chopped chervil. Wrap up the forcemeat in the lettuce, fold them over, giving them a long appearance; then tie three times round with a fine string (lettuce for soup must not be wrapped in lard), and put them in a stewpan lined with carrots, onions, and a garnished bouquet. Cover with some veal stock, protect with a sheet of buttered paper, boil, and let the lettuce simmer for two hours, then drain, untie, and trim them slightly; put them into a vegetable dish, moistening them with consommé, and keep them in a warm place until needed. Trim off some small rye rolls, the same as for croûte-au-pot (No. 305); range them in a deep dish, baste them over with chicken fat, and brown them in the oven; drain off the fat, and when colored, moisten them with good broth, season with a little mignonette, and send to the table at the same time a soup tureen of consommé. Serve grated parmesan cheese separately. Put into each plate one of the crusts, also one lettuce and cover with consommé.

(311). GIBLET SOUP À LA REGLAIN (Abatis à la Reglain).

Prepare the giblets taken from three ducks or two geese, the necks, pinions and gizzards; remove the skin from the necks, cutting them off near the head, pluck the pinions and singe them; make a cut on the side of the gizzards to remove the inside without breaking the pouch, suppress the interior white skin, also the outside tough part, retaining only the soft meat, cut this into quarter inch squares, then divide the neck and pinions into small pieces; as well as the unblanched hearts. Fry slowly in four ounces of butter, the white part of six leeks cut into inch long pieces, then blanch, add the giblets and fry all together for fifteen minutes, then dilute with half a gill of Madeira wine, and one gill of broth, and let fall slowly to a glaze. Moisten again with three quarts of broth and boil, then simmer slowly until thoroughly cooked; strain the liquid through a sieve, and thicken it by working into it two heaping spoonfuls of arrowroot or potato fecula, diluted in a little cold water. Add to the soup, the livers braized and cooled off, cut into quarter of inch squares, and some blanched chervil leaves; season with salt and cayenne pepper and serve with a garnishing of carrots, turnips and celery cut in squares of a quarter of an inch, blanched and cooked separately in white broth.

(312). GNOCQUIS SOUP À LA PAGIOLI (Potage aux Gnocquis à la Pagioli).

To Make the Gnocquis.—Put a pint of milk into a saucepan on the fire with two ounces of butter, salt, nutmeg and a pinch of cayenne pepper. At the first boil remove the saucepan and add to its contents sufficient flour to make a thin paste; dry this paste on a slow fire, stirring constantly until it no longer adheres to the pan, then remove it from the fire to allow the paste to cool off a little, and then incorporate into it seven or eight eggs. Pour this paste into a linen bag furnished with a socket having an opening of an eighth of an inch, boil some water in a saucepan, add to it a little salt, and force the paste through the socket in the form of strings into it in order to poach it, and when firm, drain them and range them in a vegetable dish, alternating layers of gnocquis with grated parmesan cheese, then brown the whole in the oven. Serve with a separate tureen full of consommé.

(313). GUMBO OR OKRA WITH HARD CRABS, CREOLE STYLE (Gombo aux Crabes durs à la Créole).

Chop up a quarter of a pound of fat pork, put it into a saucepan on the fire, adding half a pound of onions cut in dice, and a pound of lean beef in squares; fry all together, then add six peeled tomatoes cut in two, two pounds of minced young okras, twelve small cooked crabs, suppressing the shells and lungs, wash them thoroughly and split them in four, one clove of garlic, three green peppers minced up fine, six quarts of broth, salt, pepper and a little curry; boil all up till well cooked, then thicken with six tablespoonfuls of arrowroot dissolved in cold water. Serve separately some rice cooked in twice its quantity of water, with salt; fill some buttered molds (No. 5, Fig. 137), with this, set it in a slow oven, unmold and serve at the same time as the soup.

(314). GUMBO OR OKRA WITH SOFT SHELL CRABS (Gombo aux Crabes Moux).

Set into a saucepan four ounces of butter to heat, add to it two ounces of shallots, four ounces of lean raw ham, and fry without letting attain a color; pour in four quarts of thickened fish stock, a quarter of a pound of finely cut up green peppers and let the whole simmer for twenty minutes, then add sixteen soft shell crabs cut in two or four, according to their size, and well cleansed; boil again for fifteen minutes and drain off the crabs; pare them nicely and return them to the saucepan with the liquid, and thicken this with eight spoonfuls of ground gumbo or okra, and some good butter. Prepare a separate garnishing of rice cooked with twice its quantity of water, salt and lard, boiling all together for ten minutes; fill a buttered one quart charlotte mold with this, and set it in a slack oven for fifteen minutes; unmold, and serve the same time as the soup.

(315). HUNTERS' STYLE SOUP (Potage à la Chasseur).

Roast three partridges and one young wild rabbit, all barded with slices of fat pork; when done, remove the fillets from the partridges as well as from the rabbit, doing this very carefully. Put the rest, meat and bones, into a saucepan or stock pot, with a fowl split into pieces, and two pounds of small, half inch squares of beef. Moisten with four quarts of beef stock (No. 194a),let it boil, then skim and add some carrots, turnips, onions and two cloves; cook slowly for two hours, salt properly, then cut into squares the fillets taken from the partridges and rabbit. Have some small, round rolls, an inch and a quarter in diameter; after completely emptying them with a knife, fill the insides with a delicate young rabbit godiveau (No. 84), mixing in with it some chopped up mushrooms and truffles. Lay the rolls on a buttered pan, one beside the other, besprinkle them over with butter or broth, and dredge some grated parmesan cheese on top; set them in a slack oven for fifteen minutes, then lay them in a vegetable dish; strain the rest of the broth through a napkin, clarify it and boil it up again, thickening with a spoonful of tapioca for each quart and adding half a gill of Madeira wine.

(316). JAPANESE OR NIZAM PEARLS. TAPIOCA, MANIOC, SAGO OR SALEP, SEMOLINO, CASSAVA, GLUTEN (Perles de Japon ou de Nizam, Tapioca Manioc, Sagou Salep, Semoule, Cassave et Gluten).

It takes from twenty to forty minutes to cook these farinaceous foods. Let drop like rain into the boiling consommé, the proportion of one spoonful for each pint of liquid; boil slowly, and skim the surface carefully. The length of time to cook Japanese or nizam pearls, is to boil them for ten minutes, and finish cooking in a bain-marie, for thirty minutes longer.

For sago and salep, boil for ten minutes, and finish cooking in a bain-marie for twenty minutes longer.

French tapioca needs boiling five to ten minutes.

Manioc tapioca which is generally used in this country requires longer cooking; it will take twenty minutes; it may be kept in a bain-marie for ten minutes longer.

Gluten takes twenty minutes to cook.

Semolino and farina, ten minutes.

Cassava, twenty-five minutes.

(317). JEROME SOUP WITH SWEET POTATO QUENELLES (Potage à la Jérôme aux Quenelles de Patates).

Pour some game broth (No. 195), into a soup tureen; serve separately sweet potato quenelles as a garnishing, also some blanched tarragon leaves. Have croûtons of bread one and a quarter inches in diameter, covered with butter and browned in the oven; serve them at the same time as the soup and garnishings.

Sweet Potato Quenelles.—Bake some sweet potatoes in the oven, remove their insides when they are done so as to obtain a half pound of potato; and add while mashing them one ounce of butter, one ounce of grated parmesan, one whole egg, one yolk, salt, pepper, and nutmeg, also one tablespoonful of potato fecula. Make some flattened oval shaped quenelles, poach and serve when done with the soup.

(318). JULIENNE SOUP FAUBONNE AND MOGUL (Potage à la Julienne Faubonne et Mogol).

To Cut the Vegetables.—Cutting vegetables Julienne, is the act of dividing them into slices either long or short, thick or thin. There is fine, medium and large Julienne.

In order to accomplish this, cut first the roots or meats into thin slices, then divide them into bands of an equal width, so as to cut them transversely into fillets as wide as they are thick, or in other words square; the fine Julienne is five-eighths of an inch long by little over one-sixteenth of an inch square; the medium is seven eighths of an inch long by one-eighth of an inch square, and the large Julienne is cut one and three-quarters to two inches long by three-sixteenths of an inch square. The vegetables cut in Julienne are usually intended for soups, while chicken, game, foies-gras, truffles, tongue and mushrooms are used for garnishings.

For Julienne.—Put into a saucepan containing six quarts, four ounces of butter, add a vegetable Julienne cut one and three-quarter inches by three-sixteenths of an inch square, six ounces of the red part of carrots, four ounces of turnips, two ounces of leeks, two ounces of celery root and two ounces of minced onion. Blanch the carrots, turnips and celery separately, should they be hard; place the saucepan on a slow fire to simmer the roots without browning them, then moisten with two gills of broth, let fall slowly to a glaze and begin again, until the vegetables are nearly cooked, being careful to stir them occasionally. Moisten with three quarts more of boiling broth, let boil, skim, remove the fat, and add four ounces of cabbage leaves, suppressing the hard part and cutting them up fine and blanching them, boil all together till the vegetables are cooked, then add a chiffonnade composed of a handful of sorrel, the leaves of a lettuce head and a little chervil, all well cleaned, washed, pressed and cut up fine. Boil again for fifteen minutes, then skim and season with salt and sugar. Serve the Julienne with green peas cooked in salted water; slices of bread croûtons may also be served separately, with the Julienne or else poached eggs or quenelles.

For Julienne Faubonne.—Have two quarts of Julienne and one quart of purée of peas mixed.

For Julienne Mogul.—One quart of Julienne, one quart of purée of peas and one quart of purée of tomatoes.

(319). KNUCKLE OF VEAL À LA BRIAND (Jarrets de Veau à la Briand).

Put into a stockpot eight quarts of broth with eight pounds of knuckle of veal; boil the liquid, skim, and then add to it six leeks, two celery roots, a bunch of parsley, and a freshly roasted young pullet weighing three pounds, continue to boil till the meat is all cooked. After the knuckles are done, bone them and set the meat under a weight to flatten it down to one quarter of an inch in thickness, and when cold cut it up into quarter of an inch squares. Take the chicken out of the soup as soon as it is cooked, and set it away to cool, then cut off all the meat, omitting the skin and bones, and cut this meat into quarter of inch squares. Skim the fat from the stock, strain it through a sieve, and return it to the saucepan, having previously washed it, add the squares of chicken and veal to this, and let the whole simmer for half an hour, with the addition of four ounces of rice, blanched and cooked in consommé, half a pound of lean, cooked ham, cut into quarter of inch squares, and eight tomatoes, plunged into boiling water; peel off the skin then cut into four, and squeezed lightly so as to remove the seeds; boil again for twenty minutes, skim and season the soup to taste and serve very hot. Braised lettuce as explained for Garbure soup (No. 310) to be served in a separate vegetable dish.

(320). LAMB OR VEAL SWEETBREAD SOUP, GERMAN STYLE (Potage de ris d'Agneau ou de Veau à l'Allemande).

Blanch some lamb or veal sweetbreads, by placing them in a saucepan with sufficient water to cover them; let the liquid boil, then remove from the hot fire, until they are firm to the touch; set them under a weight to reduce them to one half of an inch thick, when cold cut them up in squares, two pounds in all. Put four ounces of butter into a saucepan, and when very hot, lay in the sweetbreads and fry them slowly without coloring, moisten with three pints of broth, and three pints of velouté (No. 415), let come to a boil while stirring continually, and then cook slowly until the sweetbreads are thoroughly done; thicken the soup just when about serving, with two egg-yolks, one gill of cream, and two ounces of fine butter; these proportions being for one quart of soup. For garnishing fry in butter all the fragments, drain off the butter, set them aside to cool, and chop them up very fine, with as much cooked mushrooms, and mix with this half its quantity of veal quenelle forcemeat (No. 92) and chopped parsley; season with salt, pepper, and nutmeg, then divide this preparation into equal parts, so as to make small balls five-eighths of an inch in diameter, lay them on a tin sheet, and poach them in a slow oven. Have some noodles (No. 142) cooked in salted water; pour the soup into a soup-tureen, and add to it the quenelles, the sweetbreads, the noodles and some finely chopped parsley.

(321). LOBSTER AND CRAWFISH SOUP, DUKE ALEXIS (Potage de Homard et d'Écrevisses au Duc Alexis).

Mince finely some carrots, onions and celery; fry them in butter, and moisten with one quart of white wine and two quarts of broth, adding four peeled tomatoes cut in two and pressed. Put into this stock, eighteen crawfish, let them boil for five minutes, then lift them out, and put in four pounds of live lobsters, selecting the smallest ones procurable, and cook them for half an hour, then drain them, and pick out all their meats, keeping aside only the meat from the claws, and pounding the rest; dilute this with the above stock, adding one quart of thickened fish soup stock (No. 195); strain through a sieve and heat up to boiling point, but do not allow it to boil; thicken it with raw egg-yolks, cream and fine butter, the proportion being two raw egg-yolks, one gill of cream and two ounces of fine butter for each quart of soup. Detach the tails from the bodies of the crawfish; suppress the belly side so as to keep only the thin shells of the bodies, and stuff these with the crawfish meat, chopped up fine and mixed in with an equal quantity of fish forcemeat made with crawfish, butter (No. 573), season well, and poach them in boiling, salted water. Put these stuffed bodies into the soup as garnishing, and if too large cut them in two lengthwise.

(322). MENESTRONE MILANESE SOUP (Potage Menestrone à la Milanaise).

Chop up half a pound of fat fresh pork, put it into a saucepan with a clove of garlic, half a pound of raw ham cut in dice, three-sixteenths of an inch square, half a pound of string beans, cut lozenge shape, half a pound of small flageolet beans and half a pound of Kohl sprouts cut in quarter inch squares. Fry all these vegetables with the ham in the chopped up fat pork, moisten with six quarts of broth, boil, skim, then add one pint of green peas, one pound of asparagus tops, and half a pound of broad or lima beans, after removing their outer skins, and also eight medium peeled and quartered tomatoes. Boil the whole, and when these vegetables are nearly done, twenty minutes before serving, add a quarter of a pound of blanched rice. Cook some smoked sausages, by soaking them for ten minutes in boiling water, then lift them out and peel them; cut into slices, and put them into the soup; suppress the clove of garlic, and serve with grated parmesan separate.

(323). MARSHALL SOUP (Potage à la Marshall).

Make a garnishing of stuffed cucumbers, by peeling three small cucumbers, divide them cross-ways into parts each a quarter of an inch high, and blanch the pieces for fifteen minutes in salted water, then drain, cut out the center with a three-quarter inch column tube, so as to remove the seeds; fill the insides with a raw fine herb quenelle forcemeat (No. 89), and range them in a saucepan garnished with salt pork; moisten them with broth, add some salt, cover with buttered paper, and leave them to cook slowly. Despumate on the side of the fire two quarts of consommé, thickening it with two dessertspoonfuls of fecula diluted in two gills of Madeira wine; pour the soup into a soup tureen and serve the cucumbers at the same time, but in a separate vegetable dish.

(324). MEISSONIER SOUP (Potage à la Meissonier).

Despumate on the side of the range, about three quarts of thickened soup, prepared with mutton broth. Remove the fat and hard parts from a cold, braised saddle of mutton; then take one pound of lean meat and pound it, mixing with it when cold, three minced white onions fried in butter and cooked in consommé. Pound all well together, and rub it forcibly through a fine sieve, and put this purée into a bowl with a little cayenne pepper and from four to eight raw egg-yolks, diluting with two gills of cream. At the last moment skim the fat from the soup, strain, and return it to the saucepan to let boil up, then set it aside and thicken it at once with the above preparation; heat it once more without boiling, and finish the soup with a piece of butter; pour it into a soup tureen and serve with a plateful of hot, small, round pieces of toasted bread.

(325). MONTEILLE SOUP (Potage à la Monteille).

Serve a chicken consommé (No. 190), garnished with stuffed lettuces (No. 2752), and cucumbers prepared as follows: Cut off the ends of the cucumbers, peel them nicely, and divide them length-wise into inch pieces; remove the seeds, pare them to resemble cloves of garlic, then fry them in butter in a saucepan, season, and finish cooking them in a little white broth, in such a way that they are thoroughly done when the liquid is entirely reduced. Serve separately the lettuce and cucumbers in a vegetable dish, and at the same time a tureen of chicken consommé.

(326). MONTORGUEIL SOUP (Potage à la Montorgueil).

Keep boiling on the side of the fire, one and a half quarts of thickened chicken soup stock (No. 195), despumating it for forty minutes. Prepare a garnishing of tender vegetables, composed of green peas, string beans, green or white asparagus tops, small Brussels sprouts, small new carrots whole or cut up, some of the tender leaves picked from a cabbage, and some well minced lettuce and sorrel leaves. These vegetables must be blanched separately according to their nature, only the sorrel leaves remaining raw. One hour before serving, skim off the fat from the soup, strain the broth, and return it to the saucepan; boil the liquid on the side of the range, add the vegetables according to their tenderness, the hardest ones first, and finally the cut up leaves. Now put into an earthern bowl, five or six egg-yolks, dilute them with a little cream, add some grated nutmeg and a few small pats of butter; thicken the soup with this, and finish with a small piece more butter, mixed with some spinach green. Pour it into a soup tureen and serve.

(327). MULLAGATAWNY SOUP, INDIAN STYLE (Potage Mullagatawny à l'Indienne).

Put eight quarts of broth into a saucepan with two knuckles of veal, sawed crosswise into four pieces, and some fragments of chicken; boil, skim and add a bunch of parsley garnished with bay leaf and a clove of garlic; season with salt, pepper, mace and cloves; boil slowly for three hours, then remove the veal knuckles and cut off all the meat adhering to the bones, and set it under a weight to press it to a quarter of an inch thick and let get cool and cut up into quarter of inch squares. Strain the broth through a sieve, and skim off the fat. Have half a pound of carrots, half a pound of turnips, half a pound of onions, two ounces of knob celery, six apples and four ounces of ham, all well minced, adding one pound of boneless chicken meat, after removing the skin and fat, and cutting it in five-eighths inch squares. Put six ounces of butter into a saucepan, heat it well, then begin first by frying the onions, afterward the carrots, turnips, ham, knob celery, apples and chicken. When all are fried and slightly colored, add to them six tablespoonfuls of flour, mixing it in well, then dilute with the broth, let boil and continue to boil until every article is well cooked; season and add three teaspoonfuls of curry, and a little sugar, drain, remove the pieces of chicken and press the vegetables through a sieve. Put this purée back into the saucepan, return it to the fire with the veal and chicken, and stir from the bottom of the saucepan until boiling point. Let simmer for twenty-five minutes, taste and see if the seasoning be correct, then serve. Send to the table at the same time, some rice boiled in salted water, mixing in some lard or butter.

(328). MUSSEL SOUP À LA VIGO (Potage de Moules à la Vigo).

For Ten Persons.—Take two ounces or one medium sized onion, cut it in one-eighth of an inch squares, and fry brownless in some butter, add to this sixty medium mussels previously cooked in very little water and white wine (no salt), parsley, thyme and bay leaf; when the shells open they are done, remove them from the shells; from each one remove the black and nervous part, being careful not to break them while doing so. Strain the broth, let it settle so as to be able to pour off the clear top, put a little of the broth with the mussels and keep them warm. Put the rest of the broth in a saucepan with two quarts of thickened lean fish stock (No. 195). Boil and despumate for ten minutes, then thicken with six egg-yolks, diluted in half a pint of cream and four ounces of fine butter. Put into the soup tureen four ounces of mushrooms cut in small Julienne, also the mussels; pour the boiling soup over and serve.

(329). MUTTON À LA COWLEY AND MUTTON HOCHEPOT (Mouton à la Cowley et Mouton à la Hochepot).

Bone and remove carefully the skin, nerves, and fat from three necks of mutton, cutting the meat into three-eighth inch squares. Put into a saucepan the fragments, bones and parings taken from the necks, also a split knuckle of veal; moisten with eight quarts of broth, and put it on the fire in order to boil the liquid; skim, and add some carrots, turnips, bunch of celery, leeks, and onions, all minced up fine, seasoning with pepper, salt, and cloves. Boil slowly and uninterruptedly for two hours; then skim off the fat, and strain the broth through a sieve. Put six ounces of butter into a saucepan, with four ounces of one-eighth inch squares of onions; add four ounces of leeks cut Julienne shape, half a pound of carrots, half a pound of turnips, two ounces of celery, all being cut in three-sixteenth inch squares, and the meat from the necks previously prepared;

moistening the whole with the broth, and cook for two hours. Then free it from fat, season and add a garnishing of small chicken quenelles (No. 154), shaped as large peas and a pluche of chervil. A supplementary garnishing may be added of rice, or of pearl barley.

For Mutton Hochepot, use the mutton the same as explained for the above, adding for each quart of broth, one pint of the purée of dried peas, and half a pint of purée of spinach. For all mixed clear soups, the consistency should be approximately after the soup is drained, two-thirds of liquid to one-third of solid matter, while for thick soups, three-quarters liquid to one-quarter solid.

(330). NOODLE SOUP WITH PARMESAN CHEESE (Potage aux Nouilles au Parmesan).

For the Paste.—Sift through a fine sieve, half a pound of flour, moisten it with four egg-yolks and one whole egg, adding a little salt and water; work well together and knead it till the paste is thoroughly well mixed, roll it down to one-sixteenth inch in thickness; let it dry in the open air; then fold it up, one inch and a half wide, and cut this into fine strips, dredging them over with flour, to prevent them sticking together; blanch them in boiling, salted water for one minute, then drain and put them into a saucepan with some consommé to simmer for five minutes; remove all the fat from the top, and serve in a soup tureen with some good consommé. Serve separately some grated parmesan cheese.

(331). ONION SOUP WITH PARMESAN CHEESE BROWNED, AND THICKENED ONION SOUP (Soupe à l'Oignon et au Parmesan Gratiné et Soupe à l'Oignon liée).

Cut into small eighth of an inch squares, two medium or four ounces of onions, fry them in butter and moisten with two quarts of broth, adding a bunch of parsley garnished with chervil, bay leaf and a clove of garlic; season with a little salt, pepper and some meat extract; boil for twenty minutes, then remove the bouquet, and pour the soup over very thin slices of bread placed in a metal soup tureen, in intervening layers of bread and cheese, parmesan, finishing with the parmesan, and sprinkle a little over the top of the soup. Bake in a hot oven.

Onion Soup Thickened.—To prepare onion soup cut up two medium onions, mince them finely, and fry them colorless in butter, adding two dessertspoonfuls of flour, and cooking it a few moments with the onions, then dilute with two quarts of broth. Season with pepper and a little salt, boil for ten minutes, and just when ready to serve thicken the soup with raw egg-yolks diluted in cream, and a little fine butter. Pour the soup over round, thin slices of bread, about one inch and a quarter in diameter, dried in the oven.

(332). OXTAIL SOUP À LA SOYER (Potage de Queue de Bœuf à la Soyer).

Cut three oxtails into small pieces from the thin end, stopping at the third joint from the thick end, and keep this large piece aside for braising (No. 1324). Put four ounces of butter into a saucepan; cut four ounces of the red part of a carrot, and the same quantity of turnip into quarter inch squares, add these to the butter after it is hot, also a bunch of parsley, garnished with one bay leaf, and fry without letting attain a color, then add three tablespoonfuls of flour and the tails; cook all together to a light brown, afterward moistening with four quarts of broth, and adding a quarter of a pound of blanched onions, cut in squares. Season with salt and Worcestershire sauce, boil slowly and continuously until the meat is done. Have cooked separately for three hours in some white broth, two ounces of pearl barley, add this to the soup, also one gill of sherry when serving. If clear oxtail be needed, suppress the flour and barley, and thicken with three spoonfuls of arrowroot diluted in a little cold water.

(333). OYSTER SOUP, AMERICAN STYLE (Soupe aux Huîtres à l'Américaine).

For Ten Persons.—Put sixty medium oysters including their juice, and as much water, into a tin saucepan with a perforated cover (Fig. 186), specially made for this soup; season with salt and pepper, and set them on a quick fire; as soon as the steam escapes through the holes on the cover, remove the saucepan from the fire, and pour into it two and a half gills of milk, and two and a half ounces of butter, then serve. In those establishments whose specialty is oysters, before serving oyster soup, they place before each person a plateful of finely minced raw cabbage (cold slaw); this cabbage is to be seasoned with salt, pepper, vinegar, and tomato catsup.

(334). OYSTER SOUP À LA CRUYST (Soupe aux Huîtres à la Cruyst).

For Ten Persons.—Mince up the white part of a small leek, and cut one small onion into one-eighth inch squares; fry these colorless in two ounces of butter, add two ounces of bread-crumbs, frying it in with the onion, and also sixty oysters with their own juice and a quart and a half of fish broth. Set the saucepan over a quick fire, and stir vigorously to prevent the oysters from sticking to the bottom, then skim, and season with salt, pepper and nutmeg; when ready to serve thicken the soup with raw egg-yolks, cream and fine butter, the proportions for each quart being, two egg-yolks, one gill of cream and two ounces of butter. Stir in also, when serving, a little chopped parsley.

(335). OYSTER SOUP, FRENCH STYLE (Soupe aux Huîtres à la Française).

Cut two ounces of onions into eighth of an inch squares; fry them without coloring in some butter, and add sixty medium oysters with as much water as there is oyster juice; then season with salt, pepper and nutmeg. Place the saucepan on the fire, and remove again at the first boil, lay the oysters into a soup tureen and strain the broth through a fine sieve, returning it to the fire to add to it half a pint of béchamel (No. 409), and thicken it with egg-yolks, cream and butter, the proportions for each quart being, three raw egg-yolks, one gill of cream and two ounces of good butter. Make a garnishing of pike quenelles (No. 90), adding to it some cooked fine herbs; another garnishing may also be used, composed of round bread croûtons, each one inch in diameter, sprinkled over with butter and browned in the oven; serve these separately, but at the same time as the soup.

(336). OYSTER SOUP WITH POWDERED OKRA OR GUMBO (Soupe aux Huîtres au Gombo en poudre).

Mince a two ounce onion finely, fry it in two ounces of butter without letting it attain a color, then add sixty medium oysters with their juice, and the same quantity of water, season with salt and red pepper, then place the saucepan on a quick fire and remove at the first boil; skim and thicken with two spoonfuls of powdered gumbo for each quart of soup. Have some rice boiled in salted water; when done, mix in with it a little butter and set it in a buttered mold, place it in a hot oven for ten minutes and serve this separately, but at the same time as the soup, after unmolding it.

(337). SOUP WITH OYSTER RAVIOLES (Soupe aux Ravioles d'Huîtres).

Poach in white wine three or four dozen large oysters, drain them, and keep the broth; cut the oysters into small dice, and thicken this salpicon with three spoonfuls of pike forcemeat (No. 90), and as much reduced béchamel (No. 409). With this salpicon and some raviole paste (No. 147), rolled out very thin, prepare some small round ravioles, cutting them out with a pastry cutter one inch and a quarter in diameter. Put to boil on the side of the fire, three quarts of thickened fish stock (No. 195); add to this the oyster broth, and despumate the whole for twenty-five minutes; at the last moment remove all the fat, and thicken the soup with a thickening of four or five egg-yolks, cream, butter, season to taste with salt, and a pinch of cayenne. Pour the soup into a tureen, add to it the ravioles, previously cooked for twelve minutes in salted water.

(338). PARTRIDGE SOUP À LA ROYALE (Potage de Perdreau à la Royale).

Put to boil on the side of the fire, two quarts of thickened game stock (No. 195). Pound the meat taken from the breasts of two cooked and cold partridges; press them forcibly through a sieve, and put this purée into a bowl to dilute with seven or eight egg-yolks, and a few spoonfuls of raw cream; season it to taste. Fill small buttered timbale molds (No. 2, Fig. 137) with this preparation, poach them (No. 152). Break up the partridge bones, add them to the soup, also a bunch of aromatic herbs, and some mushroom parings. Twenty minutes later skim off the fat, season and strain the soup through a tammy, and return it again to the saucepan; boil it up twice, and then stir in four spoonfuls of Madeira wine, meanwhile keeping it very hot. At the last moment unmold the small poached timbales; put in the soup tureen, and gently pour the soup over them.

(339). ITALIAN OR GENOA PASTES; LASAGNE, LASAGNETTE, TAGLIARELLI, MACCARONI, VERMICELLI, SPAGHETTI, PAILLETTES, MACCARONCELLI, FLORENCE SNOW

(Pâte d'Italie ou de Gênes; Lasagne, Lasagnette, Tagliarelli, Maccaroni, Vermicelli, Spaghetti, Paillettes, Maccaroncelli et Neige de Florence).

All these various pastes are to be previously blanched by throwing them into boiling water for five or ten minutes according to their respective thickness. When blanched, drain them, and finish cooking in broth or consommé, the proportion being half a pound of paste to three or four quarts of liquid. Put the paste into a soup tureen and pour the soup over, serving at the same time on a separate plate, some grated parmesan cheese.

Lasagne, Lasagnette and Tagliarelli.—Blanch of these one half pound for five minutes, cook them in a quart of broth, and serve in a tureen with consommé.

Maccaroni, Spaghetti, Vermicelli, Paillettes, Maccaroncelli.—For the large macaroni, blanch half a pound for twelve minutes or less in proportion to their thickness, when done, drain, and cook them in a quart of broth. Serve in a soup tureen with consommé.

Italian or Genoa Pastes and Vermicelli.—Blanch half a pound of these for five minutes, drain and cook them in a quart of broth, serve in a soup tureen with consommé.

Florence Snow.—Florence snow is made of fine gluten paste, extremely white and distributed into very fine shavings. This paste does not require any cooking; range it on plates and pass it round to the guests, after serving the soup, when each one takes some if so desired. This paste dissolves as soon as it comes in contact with a hot liquid.

(340). PATERSON SOUP (Potage à la Paterson).

Put into a saucepan on the fire three quarts of broth, and when boiling, dredge into it five spoonfuls of tapioca; let it cook for twenty-five minutes, being careful to remove all the scum arising on the surface, then strain and keep it warm. Have a garnishing of timbales of purée of green peas made as follows: One pint of purée of green peas, into which mix one whole egg and four yolks, salt, sugar and nutmeg; pour this into buttered timbale molds (No. 3, Fig. 137), place the molds in a pan with water to half their height, and poach them in a slack oven, unmold and cut them in two crosswise; have also small three-eighths of an inch pearl quenelles (No. 154), also some mushrooms cut in three-sixteenth inch squares.

(341). PILAU, TURKISH STYLE (Pilau à la Turque).

Put two knuckles of veal into a saucepan with eight quarts of broth, a few slices of raw ham, one chicken, and a roasted shoulder of lamb; boil up the liquid, skim, and add to it three carrots, two turnips, one celery stalk, six leeks, two onions, and two cloves; continue to boil slowly, till each one of the meats is done, then take them out as fast as cooked; strain the broth, remove all the fat, and clarify it, then reduce it one-quarter. Cut the chicken into small pieces, and put them into the soup; mince the shoulder of lamb, cut the ham into small dice, and after placing the knuckle of veal under a weight to get cool, cut it up into squares, and add all these to the soup, with some salt, red pepper, a slight infusion of saffron, and half a pound of blanched Sultana raisins. Parboil a quarter of a pound of rice for ten minutes in boiling, salted water, drain, and put it into three pints of boiling white broth; at the first boil, remove it from the fire, cover, and finish cooking in a cool oven for twenty-five minutes; when done, put it into the soup and serve.

(342). POT-AU-FEU (Pot-au-feu).

For Sixteen Persons.—Have a soup-pot of enameled or lined cast-iron containing sixteen quarts of liquid; put into it a piece of boned, rolled and tied up, rump of beef weighing eight pounds and eight quarts of water or beef stock. Put the pot on the fire; heat it so as to bring the liquid to a boil, then skim it off carefully at the first boil, and set the pot back from the hot fire. Roast the bones taken from the meat, also one pound of knuckle of veal and some chicken giblets, add them to the soup, and leave it on one side or on a gas stove, watching it well to see that it boils slowly and continuously, on one side only, so as to obtain a very clear broth; let the meats cook for four or five hours, more or less according to their thickness and tenderness, and when the beef is half done, strain slowly the liquid through a sieve without disturbing it. Remove the piece of rump empty the pot, clean it well, and return to it the meat and the broth, after having partially removed the fat, then put the saucepan back on the fire, and at the first boil mix to it a pound and a half of the white part of leeks tied together, a pound and a half of large carrots, three-quarters of a pound of turnips, half a pound of celery-knob or root, one medium onion with two cloves and one ounce of parsnips, then add one or two young chickens weighing three pounds each, trussed and browned in the oven. Continue to boil all very slowly, being careful to remove the chicken and meat as fast as they are done; also the vegetables, keeping them warm. Saw sixteen pieces from a marrow-bone each one inch long, wrap them up in separate pieces of linen, tie them, and poach them for eight minutes in the boiling broth. At the last moment salt and color the broth properly, and strain it through a silk sieve or a damp napkin, keeping it warm. Have two vegetable dishes of braised cabbage, the leeks, carrots, turnips, and celery arranged in clusters, and neatly trimmed so that every person may be able to help himself to one or the other as desired. Toast, or butter, and then color in the oven, thirty-two croûtons of bread three-sixteenths of an inch thick, by one and a half inches in diameter, also have the sixteen pieces of prepared marrow. Pour the soup into the soup tureen, and send the vegetables to the table, separately, also the croûtons and marrow. When serving the soup, put into each plate a piece of marrow bone, two croûtons and some soup, and pass the dishes containing the vegetables around separate. The boiled beef can be served at the same time, dressing it on to a dish, and surrounding it with the chicken cut in pieces, and branches of parsley; serve at the same time a sauceboat of tomato sauce (No. 549).

(343). RICE SOUP À LA RUDINI (Potage au riz à la Rudini).

Put a quarter of a pound of picked and washed rice into a saucepan, with two quarts of cold water, set it on the fire, and stir occasionally to prevent the rice from sticking to the bottom; let it boil up once, then refresh it, finish cooking it in consommé with a piece of fine butter, and a pinch of black pepper; mingle in with it when done, three ounces of grated parmesan cheese, four raw egg-yolks, and set it away to get cold. Divide this preparation into small five-eighth inch diameter balls; a few moments before serving roll them on to a dish containing two beaten eggs, drain them and put them one by one into new frying fat not too hot, and let them assume a nice golden color; then drain them again, and dry them in a napkin. Have two quarts of thickened chicken broth (No. 195), bring it to a boil, and remove it from the fire. Place four egg-yolks in a bowl, dilute them with one gill of cold broth, add four ounces of fine butter divided in small pieces, pour slowly into this thickening a quarter of the stock while stirring continually; return it to the rest of the stock, working it in briskly with a whisk, season to taste; pass it through a fine sieve or tammy. Pour this into a soup tureen, and serve separate a garnishing of the rice balls, and a plateful of grated Parmesan cheese.

(344). SHERMAN SOUP (Potage à la Sherman).

Have a garnishing of stuffed cabbage leaves, prepared as follows: Blanch some cabbage leaves, drain and trim them nicely, then fill the insides with a quenelle and cooked fine herb force-meat (No. 89), roll them up and lay them one beside the other, cover them with bouillon and a sheet of buttered paper, cook in a slack oven for two hours, being careful to add some moistening when they become too reduced. Cut some carrots into three-eighth inch balls, blanch and cook them in broth; prepare a pluche of chervil; chervil leaves free of stalks, thrown into boiling water for one minute, then drained. Cut the cooked cabbage in slices of a quarter of an inch leaves, lay them on a deep dish, and dust over some grated parmesan cheese, over this place some thin slices of buttered bread browned in the oven, then another layer of cabbage, cheese and bread; pour over some very fat broth, besprinkle grated parmesan on top, and bake in the oven. Pour some consommé into a soup tureen, add the carrots and chervil, and serve the baked cabbage apart.

(345). SHRIMP SOUP, MIGNON (Potage aux Crevettes Mignon).

Keep boiling on the side of the fire one quart and a half of thickened fish stock (No. 195). Break off the tails from a hundred cooked red shrimps, pick the meat from the shells, trim them and pound the parings with one-third of the picked tails, selecting the smallest ones for this; also a piece of butter and four egg-yolks, then press all through a sieve; keep the purée in a cool place, also the remainder of the picked tails cut in small dice. Put into the boiling soup half of the pounded shells; with a smallest size root spoon, five-sixteenth of an inch, cut out some very small cooked truffle balls, and set these into another small saucepan; divide into two equal parts the value of four or five spoonfuls of raw fish quenelle forcemeat (No. 90); into one mix some Breton carmine, leaving the other half white ; place these two forcemeats separately into a paper cornet, and push them through on to a buttered baking sheet to form beads; poach them separately in salted water, drain and lay them in the soup tureen. From one quart of shelled green peas select one to two gills of the smallest and tenderest, and boil them in water; when drained, add them to the quenelles in the soup tureen. After the soup is well despumated, remove all its grease and strain it through a tammy; return it to a clean saucepan, let it boil, adding to it three spoonfuls of Madeira wine; two minutes later, thicken it with the shrimp purée and cook this thickening without letting it boil. Remove, and finish with a dash of cayenne pepper and a piece of red butter. Pour the soup into the tureen, add to it the shrimp tails, butter and truffles, and serve at once.

(346). SMALL INDIVIDUAL SOUP-POTS (Petites Marmites Individuelles).

There are two different ways of serving these. The first by making the soup in small soup-pots each one containing one-half a quart or more. diminishing the proportions of meat, vegetables and liquid, either of water or broth, after the proportions indicated in the pot-au-feu (No. 342). The

Fig. 198.

second is to serve the pot-au-feu when it is ready, with the contents, dividing it into small individual pots, making an equal division of the meats, vegetables and liquid, into as many parts as there are half quarts of soup; and divide as well the meats, vegetables, and liquid into small two quart pots, having the meats and vegetables the same size as for the pint ones; for the one or the other use only half the beef meat well pared; the carrots, turnips, and celery cut into cylindricals, and divided into small parts, and each chicken into sixteen pieces; (Before using the small stone pots, they should be lined with the fragments of the chickens and vegetables, aromatics and spices, and cooked in the oven for twelve hours, pouring at intervals boiling water into them, so that they remain always full, then washed well out before using.) After the pots are filled, pour over the very hot broth, adding a tablespoonful of braised cabbage and the leeks divided, then boil the contents for a few minutes, and just when ready to serve, add for each pint four marrow bones sawed into inch thick pieces. Dress them over napkins on a plate. Each guest should have his individual soup-pot containing a little over a pint, and serve at the same time slices of toasted bread or bread buttered and browned in the oven, the size being three-sixteenths by one and one-half inches in diameter.

(347). SORREL, SORREL WITH HERBS, AND SORREL FLEMISH STYLE (Oseille, Oseille aux Herbes et Oseille à la Flamande).

Remove the stalks from a good handful of sorrel, mince it up fine, then fry it in two ounces of good butter, and moisten with two quarts of broth or water; season with salt and a dash of sugar, and let boil for fifteen minutes. Cut thin slices from some French rolls, butter them, and put them in the hot oven to brown; set them in the soup tureen and pour the soup over.

Sorrel with Herbs.—Sorrel soup may also be made by mincing fine a small handful of sorrel, half as much lettuce, and quarter as much chervil as lettuce. Melt and heat two ounces of butter in a saucepan, put in the herbs, fry them, and then moisten with two quarts and a half of broth or water, boil slowly for half an hour, and just before serving pour in gradually a thickening of four egg-yolks, a gill of cream, and one ounce of fine butter. A garnishing may be served of croûtons dried in the oven, or some vermicelli.

Flemish Style.—For sorrel, Flemish style, prepare the soup as in the first article above; the only difference to observe is, that before putting in the sorrel, fry some leeks, onions, potatoes and artichoke bottoms, all minced up very fine; add the sorrel, and finish as for the above. Serve with a garnishing of rice cooked in white broth, and some green peas.

(348). SPAGHETTI WITH CREAM (Spaghetti à la Crème).

Melt four ounces of butter in a saucepan, adding two dessert spoonfuls of flour; cook the flour slowly, so as to make a blond roux, then dilute with two quarts of consommé, stir the liquid until it boils, move it aside at once, and continue to boil slowly and uninterruptedly for twenty-five minutes, strain through a fine strainer, and put it back into a clean saucepan. Cook in salted water, some spaghetti macaroni, drain it and cut it up in one inch length pieces, having about one pound, and put this in with the consommé. Place in a bowl four raw egg-yolks, with two ounces of grated parmesan, dilute it with two gills of raw cream, and one ounce of butter; pour this thickening into the soup, and let heat without boiling; season, and serve it in a soup tureen. The spaghetti can be replaced by any of the Italian pastes.

(349). SPANISH OILLA (Oilla à l'Espagnole).

Put to soak in tepid water for twelve hours, half a pound of chick peas (Garbanzos). Set in an earthen pot, or any other kind, six pounds of lean breast of beef, three pounds of leg of mutton cut near the knee bone, half a pound of unsmoked salt pork, cut in one piece and then blanched, and half a pound of smoked ham, well pared and blanched. Cover with water, add the garbonzos boil and skim, maintaining a slow ebullition. Two hours after, put in the broth, one fowl, two partridges, a piece of squash weighing one pound, half a pound of carrots, half a pound of onions, a bunch of parsley with a bay leaf, and clove of garlic, and one pound of chorissos sausages (garlic sausage). Blanch twelve lettuce heads, also two cabbages cut in four. After removing the cores (the hard part), take out the meats as soon as they are severally done, cool them partially, and then cut them into half inch squares. Strain the broth through a napkin, pour it in a soup tureen with rice cooked in fat broth, and if the meats should not be added to the soup, serve them separately as a garnishing, by cutting them up in slices, and arranging them in a circle on a dish. The chicken in the center, a partridge on each side, the lettuces on one side, the chick peas on the other, the cabbages on the ends, and the sausages cut into slices and laid on top of the cabbage. A tomato sauce served separately, also a green sauce à l'éspagnole (No. 473).

(350). TERRAPIN, CLEAR, THICK OR WHITE (Terrapène au Clair, Liée ou à Blanc).

Prepare and cook the terrapin as told in No. 1082, observing all the instructions given for the preparation of these turtles.

For Clear Terrapin.—When the terrapins are cooked, select the largest ones, bone them entirely, and cut up the pieces found to be too large, and being more than one inch; it will require one pound and a half. Prepare a stock the same as for clear turtle (No. 353), thicken with arrowroot or else fecula, when the stock is ready and nicely seasoned, add the terrapin to it, boil it up for a few minutes and finish the soup with some brandy and Madeira wine. Serve separately the pulp of two lemons, two hard boiled, chopped up eggs, and some chopped parsley, the whole on one or several plates, together or each article separate.

For Thick Terrapin Soup.—Make it exactly the same as the clear terrapin, with the exception of using the same stock as for thick green turtle soup (No. 353).

For Terrapin Soup, White.—Prepare it as for the above, only thickening it with velouté (No. 415); diluting it with chicken broth (for lean use lean velouté and fish broth). Boil, skim, season properly, then add when ready to serve, some raw egg-yolks, cream and fine butter, the proportions being two raw egg-yolks, one gill of cream and two ounces of fine butter for each quart.

(351). DRIED TURTLE, THICK AND CLEAR (Tortue Sèche Liée et Claire).

Dry.—This green turtle comes from South America; it is raw and dried in pieces; the only parts being used for drying are the cutaneous ones. When the dried turtle is needed put it first to soak in cold water for two or three days, changing the water frequently. Half a pound of dry turtle suffices to make soup for eight persons; when the pieces have softened, put them into a small stock-pot with six quarts of water, adding to it a piece of shin of beef, weighing two pounds; a two pound piece of neck of veal, a three pound chicken, two or three chicken giblets, a bone of cooked ham, carrots, celery, a bunch of marjoram, savory, parsley, thyme, and bay leaf. Cook the meats the same as for a pot-à-feu (No. 342), either on the gas, or on the back of the range, and as soon as the pieces of turtle are done, remove them and plunge them into cold water; then cut them into one inch and a quarter squares, and lay them in a saucepan with a little consommé; skim off the fat from the soup, strain, and set about two quarts of it into a saucepan; thicken it with blond roux (No. 163), despumate the soup while allowing it to boil slowly, remove all the fat, and season with salt and cayenne pepper, also two gills of good Madeira wine. Put the pieces of turtle into a soup tureen, and pour the soup over. Should the turtle be needed clear, then suppress the roux, clarify the broth, and thicken it with arrowroot or potato fecula. Serve slices of lemon at the same time.

(352.) PREPARATION OF A GREEN TURTLE WEIGHING ONE HUNDRED POUNDS (Préparation d'une Tortue pesant cent livres).

Lay the turtle on its back, and when it stretches out his head, seize it with one hand, and holding a knife in the other, cut its neck, leave it to bleed, then lay it again on its back, pass the knife along the flat shell, about one inch from the edge. Detach the flat shell and remove all the meat from the inside, doing exactly the same for the back, then saw them into six or eight pieces, plunge them into boiling water to remove the scales, doing the same for the four fins. Put the turtle meat into a soup pot with two knuckles of veal, moisten it with broth, let boil, then skim and add sprigs of parsley, celery, sage, marjoram, basil, thyme, bay leaf, mace, cloves, whole peppers and salt, cook for one hour, add the pieces of shell and fins and let boil again until all are cooked, then take them out and put them into cold water. Remove the gelatinous parts of the turtle, cut them into one and a half inch squares, strain the broth through a fine sieve and reduce it to a half glaze, add the green parts and let boil very slowly until the turtle be thoroughly cooked and the stock well reduced. If wanted for further use pour it into tin boxes, surround them with ice, and when perfectly cold cover the tops with hot fat and lay them aside in the ice box.

(353). GREEN TURTLE SOUP, CLEAR À LA ROYAL OR THICK WITH MARROW QUENELLES (Soupe Tortue Verte, Claire à la Royale ou liée aux Quenelles à la Moelle).

Clear.—Put eight quarts of beef stock into a soup-pot with four pounds of leg of veal, and four pounds of fowl or chicken wings, thyme, bay leaf, parsley, basil, marjoram, mushroom trimmings, and celery; boil all for three hours, then strain through a sieve, and afterward through a napkin. Clarify this stock the same as consommé with chopped beef. Cook separately the prepared turtle, and keep it warm in a steamer (bain-marie); add to the soup a dessertspoonful of arrowroot for each quart, diluted with a little water, and add it to the boiling broth, stirring it in with a whip; boil and despumate the soup for twenty minutes, then season. When ready to serve, drain the turtle, lay it in a soup tureen, and pour over the stock, seasoning with cayenne pepper and half a gill of Xérès for each quart.

For Clear Turtle à la Royal.—Add some royale timbales (No. 241).

Thick Turtle with Marrow Quenelles.—Proceed exactly the same as for clear turtle, but instead of thickening it with arrowroot, thicken the soup with a little brown roux, moistened with the turtle stock, boil and despumate, and strain through a fine sieve Garnish with marrow quenelles (No. 252), or if preferred, use turtle fat instead of marrow. Quenelles may also be made with a quarter of a pound of hard boiled egg-yolks pounded with one ounce of butter and four raw egg-yolks, seasoning with salt, nutmeg, and chopped parsley; divide this into pieces, roll them into balls half an inch in diameter, and poach them in boiling water; drain, and serve with the soup.

(354). MOCK TURTLE OR CALF'S HEAD, CLEAR SOUP (Soupe Fausse Tortue ou Tête de Veau au Clair).

Bone a calf's head the same as described for plain calf's head (No. 1519); put it into cold water in a saucepan on the fire, boil up the liquid and let it continue boiling for half an hour, then drain, refresh and singe it. Butter the bottom of a saucepan, cover it with slices of ham, a carrot and some onions, a bunch of parsley garnished with sage, chives, thyme and bay leaf. Split the bones taken from the head, lay them on this bed of vegetables and add two pounds of knuckle of veal, and a pound and a half of chicken, or else some chicken thighs, either of these being partially roasted; moisten with a quart of water, and let boil on a moderate fire until the liquid is reduced and fallen to a glaze, and the vegetables slightly colored. Moisten again with six quarts or either broth or water, add the blanched calf's head, boil up the liquid again, then skim and throw in one onion with a clove in it, a little mace and a quarter of a pound of mushroom trimmings; continue to boil slowly and when the head is cooked, remove it from the stock; cover it over with broth, and leave it till cold. Now cut away the white skin near the snout, divide the meat into equal sized half inch square pieces, taking only the cutaneous parts. Remove the chicken when done, season the stock, skim off the fat and strain it through a sieve, clarify it with two pounds of chopped beef and one whole egg, proceeding the same as for a consommé. Strain the liquid through a napkin or a silk sieve, and thicken it with a spoonful of fecula for each quart, diluting the fecula with half a gill of sherry and a little water, and then pouring it into the soup, stirring it vigorously until all is well mixed, then return it to the fire and stir again until it boils. Pound the meat from the chickens free of all fat, bones and skin, add to them when well pounded, four hard boiled egg-yolks, salt, nutmeg and four raw egg-yolks, rubbing all through a sieve, mix in some chopped parsley and with this preparation make some small half inch diameter quenelles; poach them in boiling and salted water, drain and put them into a saucepan with the pieces of calf's head, moisten with the stock, boil and skim, then add half a gill of Madeira or extra sherrry wine for each quart of soup, and the juice of half a lemon for each quart; pour it into a soup tureen and serve very hot.

(355). MOCK TURTLE SOUP, THICKENED (Soupe Fausse tortue Liée).

It needs one gallon of soup for twelve persons. Proceed exactly the same as for the clear mock turtle only leaving out the fecula thickening. Put four ounces of butter into a saucepan on a slow fire, and when melted, mix in with it a quarter of a pound of flour, cook it slowly to obtain a blond roux, which then moisten with clear turtle stock, until it becomes the consistency of a light sauce, cook it slowly and keep despumating it for half an hour, then strain it through a sieve or tammy, and return it to the fire in a very clean saucepan, and after bringing the liquid up to a boil, despumate it again. Add the quenelles, the calf's head cut in pieces, and the pulp of a lemon without any peel or pips, also half a gill of sherry wine for each quart of soup.

(356). VELVET SOUP (Potage Velours).

Mince up fine the red part of a few good carrots; stew them with butter, salt, sugar and a little broth, and when done strain through a sieve and afterward through a tammy (Fig. 88). Put two quarts of good clear broth on to boil, mix in with it four tablespoonfuls of tapioca, let it despumate for twenty-five minutes on the side of the fire, skimming it off well. At the last moment add the carrot purée, season boil up once or twice more, and serve in a soup tureen.

(357). WESTMORELAND SOUP (Potage à la Westmoreland).

For sixteen persons.—Prepare two quarts of reduced and well-seasoned chicken consommé (No. 190); boil it, then thicken it with arrowroot, colored with a little roucou (Annotto); dilute the arrowroot and roucou in cold water, and add it slowly with the soup, stirring it in continually with a whip or spoon; then boil and skim.

Prepare three-quarters of a pound of cooked calf's head the gelatinous, cutaneous parts, free of all fat and meat, press to three-eighths of an inch, cut this into three-eighth inch squares, and keep them warm in a quart of consommé. Have half a pound of round chicken quenelles (No. 154), half an inch in diameter laid through a bag on to a buttered tin pan, and poached in boiling salted water, and add them to the calf's head. Braised sweetbreads set under a weight, having half a pound in all, and pressed down to three-eighths of an inch in thickness, then cut in squares when cold, and put them to keep hot with the quenelles and calf's head; have also some celery cut in quarter inch squares, blanched and cooked in consommé, a quarter of a pound in all, and when done, add them to the other garnishings. Just when about serving, taste the soup, season it accordingly, and pour it over the garnishings in a soup tureen.

(358). NOQUES OR QUENÈFES SOUP (Potage aux Noques et aux Quenèfes).

Melt in a saucepan three ounces of butter, dredge in the same weight of flour and stir this over a moderate fire so as to obtain a light roux (No. 163); moisten with two quarts of broth, and stir again until it boils slowly and on one side only; despumate the soup by removing all the scum and fat arising to the surface.

Noques.—Beat up with a spoon five ounces of partially melted butter placed in a bowl, and when it is creamed, then incorporate into it three egg-yolks and one whole egg; as the compound becomes frothy, add to it four ounces of flour and two beaten egg-whites, season with salt and nutmeg, and try the preparation by taking up a teaspoonful and letting it fall, detaching it with another teaspoon, into boiling, salted water, and if it be too light and requires more consistency, then add a little more flour mixed with a little hot water, but if it be too consistent, then more butter is needed. Keep the noques in boiling water without letting them boil until they are well poached and firm, then drain, and range them in a soup tureen; remove the fat once more from the soup and thicken it with four egg-yolks and two gills of cream and a little butter; pour it over the noques after straining it through a fine sieve.

Quenèfes.—Put into a bowl four yolks and two whole eggs, salt, and nutmeg; mix well, then add six ounces of flour, and to test whether the paste is sufficiently thick, take up some of it in a teaspoon, detach it with another spoon moistened with hot water, and let it drop into boiling water to cook for half an hour without boiling. Drain and use these quenèfes instead of noques for the above soup.

(359). RAVIOLE AND PEARL SOUP (Potage aux Ravioles et aux Perles).

Place four quarts of good consommé into a saucepan, and after it boils skim it well. Blanch in boiling water for five minutes, two ounces of Nizam pearls, drain, and add them to the boiling consommé; cook until they become transparent, which will take about twenty minutes, pour the soup into the soup tureen, adding some poached ravioles (No. 158), and serve at the same time a plateful of grated parmesan cheese.

(360). WOODCOCK SOUP (Potage de Bécasses).

Remove the four fillets from two cold roasted woodcocks; pound two of these fillets with the livers and a few slices of cooked foies-gras; press through a sieve, and put this purée into a mortar, mixing in with it a third of its quantity of raw game quenelle forcemeat (No. 91); two whole eggs, a pinch of nutmeg, and half a gill of cold éspagnole sauce. Poach this preparation in small buttered timbale molds (No. 1, Fig. 137). Despumate on the side of the fire, two quarts of game stock (No. 195), add to it the carcasses, necks, and heads of the woodcocks, all chopped up and a few aromatic herbs and twenty minutes later, skim off the fat, strain it through a tammy, and put it back into a clean saucepan, to heat, stirring it with a spatula continually to prevent the soup adhering to the bottom of the pan, finish by incorporating into it a small piece of butter, having previously removed the soup from the fire. Pour the soup into a tureen, adding the two breasts kept aside, mincing them up in Julienne, also the poached timbales.

SOUPS AND DIFFERENT PREPARATIONS FOR INVALIDS.

---

(361). INDIAN ARROWROOT (Arrowroot de l'Inde).

Prepare a plain chicken broth as indicated in No. 188; for each quart of this dilute a tablespoonful of arrowroot with a little of the cold broth, so as to form a smooth and liquid paste, add to it gradually the boiling broth, then boil all, stirring unceasingly with a spatula. After the first boil, simmer it gently for half an hour, carefully stirring it at times to prevent it from sticking to the bottom of the pan; then serve.

(362). BAVAROISE (Bavaroise).

An infusion of tea sweetened with gum syrup and orange flower-water with milk. Have half as much boiling milk as tea; sweeten it with gum syrup, and flavor with orange flower-water; the latter can be replaced by a small glassful of good brandy. Bavaroise is taken at night before retiring.

(363). CHICKEN BROTH PLAIN (Bouillon de Poulet Simple).

Chop up three pounds of chicken carcasses; put them in a saucepan with two quarts and a half of water, and a little salt; boil, then skim, add a well washed lettuce head, and half an ounce of chervil. Let boil for an hour and a half, remove all the fat and pass through a fine sieve; serve in cups. This preparation should produce about a quart of liquid.

(364). CHICKEN AND MUTTON BROTH WITH BARLEY (Bouillon de Poulet et Mouton à l'Orge).

Break up three pounds of chicken carcasses and place them in a saucepan with a pound of lean mutton cut in squares and an ounce of pearl hulled barley washed in several waters, half a pound of minced and blanched turnips; moisten with three quarts of water, boil, skim, and reboil all gently for three hours; skim again, season and strain through a fine sieve; serve in cups.

(365). CHICKEN AND VEAL BROTH (Bouillon de Poulet et de Veau).

Place in a saucepan a pound and a half of broken up chicken carcasses and as much lean veal cut up in half inch squares; add three quarts of water, two ounces of carrots and an ounce of cut up turnips, both blanched in plenty of water and besides these two ounces of celery. Boil the whole for an hour and a half, skim off the fat, season with a little salt and strain through a fine sieve; serve in cups.

(366). CLAM BROTH AND PURÉE (Bouillon de Lucines Orangées et Purée)

Put one pint of clams into a saucepan with their own juice and a little water; cover the saucepan and set it on the fire, removing it after the first boil, then drain, and strain the liquor through either a fine sieve or else a napkin; serve it in cups. The clam purée to be prepared as follows: Pound the clams; after they are reduced to a paste, then moisten them with their own liquor, and as much water. and strain through a sieve. For either plain broth or purée, a little milk and butter may be added.

(367). CUSTARD CREAM OF CHICKEN OR GAME (Crème Bain-Marie de Volaille ou de Gibier).

Cut either a three pound chicken, or two grouse, or two partridges into four parts, remove the lights and kidneys, wash well and cook them in two quarts of water seasoned with salt, a few parsley stalks, half an ounce of chervil, six ounces of turnips, and four ounces of minced celery; boil, skim, and let simmer until the chicken or game be cooked, then strain the broth through a napkin. With twelve raw egg-yolks mix one quart of this broth, adding a very little at the time, and strain through a sieve; fill up some small cups to an eighth of an inch from the top; place these cups in a low saucepan with boiling water sufficient to reach to half their heighth, then set them on the fire and as soon as the water is ready to boil, push the saucepan into the oven; when firm to the touch, remove them, and serve them either hot or cold as required.

(368). PLAIN EXTRACT OF BEEF (Extrait de Bœuf Simple).

Chop up very fine one pound of lean beef, put it into a saucepan and dilute it gradually with three pints of cold bouillon (No. 187); set it on a slow fire, and stir until it comes to a boil, then place it on the back of the stove where it will not boil, leave it there for half an hour, and strain it through a fine sieve or napkin.

(369). EXTRACT OF BEEF, CLARIFIED (Extrait de Bœuf Clarifié).

Remove the fat and nerves from five pounds of lean beef, either from the leg or rump, chop it up very fine and divide it equally into three empty and well washed champagne bottles, adding to each bottle, one gill of broth or water, or not any should a more concentrated extract be desired; cork and tie them well. Place these bottles in a high bain-marie, wrapping each bottle up in a cloth, and fill to five-sixths of their heighth with water; boil continually for two hours, and leave the bottles in the water one half hour after removing the saucepan from the fire, then uncork carefully. Fold two sheets of filtering paper together, lay them in a glass funnel and set these over high gallon glass jars, pour the liquid slowly through the paper and when all is strained, fill a well washed and clean champagne bottle with it; cork it up, letting the liquid reach nearly as far up as the cork, and put it on ice to keep.

(370). FISH BROTH WITH CLAMS (Bouillon de Poisson aux Lucines Orangées).

Heat two ounces of butter in a saucepan, add to it two ounces of minced onions, an ounce of carrots, two ounces of turnips and two leeks. Fry colorless, then put in two pounds of the heads and bones of fish and moisten it to its height with water, adding an ounce of celery, one tomato, a little thyme, bay leaf, parsley and salt. Cover and cook for twenty-five minutes, then strain through a sieve, return it once more to the saucepan adding a quart of clams and their juice; boil, strain again through a fine sieve, taste and serve in cups.

(371). FROG BROTH AND PURÉE (Bouillon de Grenouilles et Purée de Grenouilles).

Mince half a pound of celery, carrots, turnips, and leeks; fry them without letting them acquire a color in two ounces of butter, then moisten with two quarts of chicken broth or water, and add a pound of frog's legs and hind parts, half an ounce of chervil, and two ounces of lettuce, both cut very fine. Boil all slowly for three quarters of an hour, season with a little salt and sugar, then strain through a napkin and serve in cups.

For the Purée, pound the frog meat and add to it four ounces of bread-crumbs soaked in milk and then squeezed out. When all is well pounded, dilute with the same quantity of broth as above, and strain through a tammy; a little butter and milk may be added to advantage; this purée should be served in a clear state in cups.

(372). HERB BROTH (Bouillon aux Herbes).

Four ounces of lettuce, one ounce of chervil, one and a half ounces of sorrel, all well washed, and cut up fine. Put these into a saucepan on the fire, with a little butter, stirring occasionally; when lightly cooked moisten with two quarts of white chicken broth (No. 188), or its equal volume of water. Let cook for fifteen minutes, adding one and a half ounces of butter and a little salt. Serve this in cups, either plain or with sippets of toasted bread or else with rice, semolina, etc.

(373). CHICKEN AND CALF'S FOOT JELLY (Gelée de Volaille et de Pieds de Veau).

Bone six calves' feet, blanch, and refresh them in cold water; put them in a saucepan with six pounds of round bottom of veal, four large fowls, after removing the breasts, two knuckles of veal and sixteen quarts of water. Boil, then skim, and season with salt and pepper, adding a bunch of parsley, garnished with thyme, bay leaf, and two cloves of garlic, a little celery, three onions, one having two cloves in it, four carrots, and eight leeks; boil constantly until perfectly cooked from six to eight hours, and test the jelly to see whether it be firm enough, by putting a little on a plate on ice; if too gelatinous, then add a little water. Strain through a fine sieve, and remove the fat.

For Clarification.—Chop fine the chicken breasts, mix in with eight egg-whites, diluted with a little white broth, or half a bottleful of white wine; mix in the jelly gradually with the eggs, and put it back on the fire, stirring it constantly with a whisk, and when on the point of boiling remove it from the range, and strain through a flannel bag, restraining until it flows clear.

(374). MEAT AND CALF'S FOOT JELLY (Gelée de Viandes et de Pieds de Veau).

Bone eight calves' feet, blanch, cool, and put them into a saucepan with six pounds of round bottom or shoulder of veal, six pounds of legs of beef, two veal knuckles and sixteen quarts of water. Boil, skim and add salt, whole pepper, a bunch of parsley, garnished with thyme, garlic, bay leaf and celery, three onions, one with four cloves in it, some medium carrots and eight leeks. Boil unceasingly until the meats are well done, (from six to eight hours), then strain through a sieve and skim off the fat. Set a little of it on some ice to see whether it is sufficiently gelatinous, and if too consistent add a little veal broth, then proceed to clarify the jelly as follows: Chop up very fine two pounds of lean veal, mixing with it half a pint of egg-white, diluted with half a bottle of white wine or a little water, and mix the jelly stock gradually with this meat, put it back on the fire, stir continually with a whip and when ready to boil, remove and add half a bottleful of Madeira wine, pour the jelly into a flannel jelly bag, restraining it until it be perfectly clear.

For calves' foot jelly and Madeira wine (*gelée de pieds de veau au madère*) see No. 104.

(375). MUTTON BROTH (Bouillon de Mouton).

Cut into pieces four pounds of very fresh neck of mutton free of fat; put these into a saucepan. Prepare two ounces of carrots, four ounces of turnips, two ounces of celery, four ounces of leeks, a few sprigs of parsley, and a little thyme; fry colorless, the turnips, celery, carrots, and leeks in a quarter of a pound of butter; moisten with four quarts of water or stock, season well and let boil slowly during one hour and a half; remove all the fat from the surface, strain it through a napkin and serve it in cups. Another way is to wash in cold water three pounds of very fresh neck of mutton, cut into pieces; put this into a saucepan with two and a half quarts of water, boil, skim, then add three quarters of a pound of minced turnips, a few parsley stalks, and a few thyme leaves, seasoning with salt. Boil slowly for two hours, remove all the fat, strain it through a fine sieve and serve. Some pearl barley cooked separately in water or broth may be added to either. If the broth needs to be clarified, then chop up half a pound of lean mutton and mix in with it one raw egg; dilute with a little broth or water, and put it into the mutton broth, stir it up quickly, and place the whole on the fire so that it barely simmers, and when clear, strain through a napkin.

(376). MULLED EGG AND ALMOND MILK THICKENED WITH RICE FLOUR (Lait de Poule et Lait d'Amandes, Lié à la Farine de riz).

Break two very fresh eggs into a bowl, dilute them gradually with two gills of boiling water, adding some powdered sugar and a little orange flower-water; mix thoroughly and drink very hot.

Thickened Almond Milk.—A quarter of a pound of peeled fresh almonds and four bitter ones; pound them in a mortar, adding gradually half a pint of water, sugar, and one pint of milk. Press this well through a napkin, warm it up without boiling and thicken it with half an ounce of rice-flour diluted with half a pint of cold water; return it to the fire and remove at the first boil.

(377). BEEF JUICE (Jus de Bœuf).

In order to obtain a pint of beef juice it will take about five pounds of meat free from all fat and nerves; cut it into about five-eighth of an inch thick slices; broil them nicely, not too rare or too well done, and after taking them from the broiler, cut them up into five-eighth inch squares, and press them well in the press shown in Fig. 70, to extract all their juice; when it is all well pressed out, strain it through a fine sieve or napkin, remove all the fat from the surface and serve in small cups.

(378). PURÉE OF BARLEY WITH CHICKEN BROTH (Purée d'Orge au Bouillon de Volaille).

Soak two ounces of pearl or other barley in cold water for twelve hours; wash it, then lay it in a saucepan and cover it well with four quarts of chicken bouillon (No. 188); boil and add more as the broth diminishes, boil until the barley bursts; continue to cook until the broth is thickened by the soluble parts of the barley, it takes about three hours to cook the barley; then strain forcibly and serve. A little butter and milk may be added if desired; serve in cups.

(379). PURÉE OF CHICKEN, PARTRIDGE, GROUSE OR ROEBUCK (Purée de Poulet, Perdreau, Tétras ou Chevreuil).

Raise the fillets from a roast chicken or from either two partridges or two grouse, or else one pound of the saddle of roasted venison, pound them, add four ounces of bread-crumbs, previously soaked in chicken or game broth and squeezed thoroughly, pound again and dilute this purée with simply lightly salted chicken or game broth, free of any spices, aromatics or vegetables. Strain through a sieve and warm it up without boiling, adding two ounces of butter, stirring it in well; moisten with either chicken or game broth, letting it remain sufficiently liquid so as to be easily drank from cups.

(380). PURÉE OF OATMEAL OR WHEATEN GRITS (Purée d'Avenas ou de Blé).

Put four quarts of water or broth into a saucepan, let boil, and dredge in a shower while stirring one pound either of oatmeal or wheaten grits; let cook for thirty minutes, pass it through a tammy, and add either more water or some broth, so as to obtain a clear purée fit to be drank easily from a cup, without using a spoon; a little salt and butter may be added.

(381). SABAYON OF CHICKEN OR GAME (Sabayon de Volaille ou de Gibier).

Put eight egg-yolks into a high and narrow bain-marie; dilute them with one pint of chicken or game broth, and place the bain-marie saucepan on a slow fire or in boiling water, then stir well with a whip or wooden beater until the sabayon becomes thick and frothy; as soon as it is done serve it very hot in cups. A little sherry added to the broth is considered an improvement by some.

(382). BEEF, MUTTON, CHICKEN, OR VEAL TEA (Thé de Bœuf, Mouton, Poulet ou Veau).

Two pounds of lean meat free from nerves and skin, either beef, mutton, chicken, or veal, taken from the thighs or any other juicy parts. Cut the meat into small quarter of inch squares, set them in a saucepan and pour over three pints of cold water, with a little salt added. Boil, skim, and keep near boiling point for one hour, then strain through a sieve or napkin and serve in cups. Another way is to fill up champagne bottles with the meat, put half a gill of water in each, tie down the cork with a string or wire, boil for three hours, uncork and pass through a napkin.

(383). VEAL BROTH, REFRESHING (Bouillon de Veau Rafraîchissant).

Mince up four ounces of carrots, four ounces of turnips, four leeks, and two celery roots; fry them in two ounces of butter, letting them attain a light color, then add ten pounds of split knuckle of veal, and moisten it all with water until well covered, then boil and skim; add salt and let boil continually for two hours. Chop very fine two pounds of bottom round of veal, free of fat, sinews and skin; to this add one whole egg diluted with a little water or cold broth, pour it gradually into the veal broth and clarify it by beating with a whip; return to the fire to boil slowly and continuously for three-quarters of an hour, adding one ounce of chervil, two ounces of lettuce, and two ounces of wild chiccory, all well washed and cut up fine. Boil again for twenty or thirty minutes, then strain either through a fine sieve or napkin.

(384). WHEAT, OATS, OR BARLEY BROTH (Bouillon de Blé, d'Avoine ou d'Orge).

Wash half a pound of either of these in several waters, then leave to soak for twelve hours; parboil them in plenty of water, and afterward cook them slowly in white chicken bouillon (No. 188). When done and the grain crushes easily between the fingers, strain and press it well to extract all the insides. Half a pound of wheat should produce two quarts of liquid. To be served in cups.

SAUCES.

STOCKS, ESSENCES, AND AUXILIARIES.

(385). DUXELLE, OR COOKED FINE HERBS (Duxelle ou Fines Herbes Cuites).

Put four ounces of scraped fat pork and butter into a saucepan, and when well melted add to it six ounces of either chopped or one-eighth of inch pieces of shallot, a clove of crushed and chopped garlic, let these ingredients fry without coloring, adding half a pound of raw, finely chopped mushrooms; set it on the fire, and reduce while stirring continuously until the moisture from the mushrooms be entirely evaporated, then add an ounce of chopped parsley washed and pressed out; an ounce of chopped truffles may be added, but this is optional. If it needs to be thickened add to it half a pint of demi-glaze sauce (No. 413), and reduce until it acquires a consistency.

(386). ESSENCES AND FUMET (Essences et Fumet).

A sauce is thick, essence is not. Essence is an extract from the most nutritious parts of meat. Fumet, or flavor, is a steam which rises from certain cooked or raw meats, imparting a most agreeable smell and taste, it is the same preparation as essences, but less watery and reduced with Madeira.

(387). CHICKEN ESSENCE (Essence de Volaille).

Fry one pound of sliced kernel of veal and a pound and a half of broken chicken bones in some butter without coloring them, adding two minced shallots, half a pound of minced carrots, and four ounces of onions. Moisten with one quart of white chicken bouillon (No. 188) and reduce to glaze; moisten again and reduce once more, then add a bunch of parsley garnished with two bay leaves and as much thyme, four cloves and half a bottleful of white wine; boil, skim, and cook slowly for half an hour, then strain through a napkin or silk sieve.

(388). FISH ESSENCE (Essence de Poisson).

Cut in slices two pounds of bass, porgies or any other bony, and very fresh fish; put them into a saucepan and season with salt, whole peppers and half a pint of white wine. Fry lightly in butter without attaining a color, three ounces of minced onions, three ounces of carrots, a bunch of parsley garnished with two bay leaves and the same of thyme, two cloves and two shallots; add all these to the fish with one quart of water, and cook slowly for forty minutes, then strain through a fine sieve.

(389). GAME ESSENCE (Essence de Gibier).

Have two pounds of young rabbit and the same quantity of raw pheasant, and put them into a saucepan with two chopped shallots, two ounces of mushrooms and two ounces of carrots, the mushrooms and carrots being either cut in quarter inch squares or minced; a bunch of parsley garnished with thyme and bay leaf, a clove of garlic and six cloves. Moisten with one quart of veal blond (No. 423), and half a bottle of white wine, also a quart and a half of broth; boil all slowly, skim and let simmer for one hour, then strain the essence through a silk sieve.

(390). HAM ESSENCE (Essence de Jambon).

Fry in butter and color lightly, one pound of sliced, smoked or unsmoked ham, add to it two ounces of minced onions, and four ounces of carrots, a bunch of parsley garnished with the same quantity of bay leaf as thyme, and moisten with half a pint of white wine; reduce this in a covered saucepan, moisten again with one quart of veal blond (No. 423), and let boil and simmer for forty minutes, then skim and strain through a napkin or fine silk sieve.

(391). HOT ASPIC ESSENCE, CLEAR AND THICKENED (Essence d'Aspic Chaude Claire et liée)

Put into a saucepan, half a gill of vinegar, a few bits of tarragon, a bunch of parsley, a quarter of a pound of minced ham and a coffeespoonful of mignonette, a little mace; let all simmer for fifteen minutes, then moisten with half a pint of veal blond (No. 423), and a pint and a half of consommé (No. 189); reduce it all to half, strain it through a sieve and clarify with one egg-white; press the aspic through a napkin and use it for roast poultry.

Thickened Aspic.—Before clarifying, add its equal quantity of espagnole, and reduce it to the consistency of a sauce, despumate the surface and strain through a tammy.

(392). MUSHROOM ESSENCE (Essence de Champignons).

Put one pound of mushrooms previously washed and cut in four into a saucepan with the juice of half a lemon, salt, and a pint of broth; let boil together for ten minutes; cover the saucepan hermetically and let stand till cold; strain through a fine sieve.

(393). ROOT ESSENCE (Essence de Racines).

Have half a pound each of vegetables such as carrots, onions, turnips, parsnips, parsley root and celery; wash them well, and mince them up very fine, then fry them lightly in three ounces of butter and moisten with a quart and a half of water and half a bottle of white wine; let cook slowly for one hour, remove all the fat and scum, then strain through a napkin or silk sieve.

(394). ESSENCE OF TAME OR WILD DUCKS (Essence de Canards Domestiques ou Sauvages).

This is made with the fragments of six roasted duck bones, broken up and put into a saucepan with one pint of mirepoix stock, one quart of veal blond (No. 423), a bunch of parsley garnished with bay leaf and thyme, mignonette and nutmeg. Let simmer for one hour, then add the juice of an orange and a lemon, also their peels; strain through a napkin or a silk sieve.

(395). TRUFFLE ESSENCE (Essence de Truffes).

Brush and peel two pounds of fresh truffles; put them into a saucepan with half a bottle of Madeira wine and a pint of broth (No. 187), add two ounces of celery, as much carrots and as much onions, all minced up very fine, a bunch of parsley, thyme, bay leaf, salt and ground pepper. Cover the saucepan and allow the truffles to boil slowly for twenty minutes. Then let them get cold in their broth, keeping the cover hermetically closed. Strain through a napkin or fine sieve.

(396). RAW FINE HERBS (Fines Herbes Crues).

Composed of parsley, chervil, tarragon, fennel, chives and pimpernel, picked, washed, thoroughly drained and each one chopped up separately; onions and shallots cut in very small dice or else chopped are considered the same as fine herbs. (The parsley, onions and shallot may be blanched by tying them in a small muslin bag, and plunging into boiling water, then refreshing them several times, afterward extracting all the water they contain.)

(397). FUMET OF PARTRIDGE OR OTHER GAME (Fumet de Perdreaux ou d'autres Gibiers).

Cut four ounces of onions into slices, put them into a well buttered saucepan with four ounces of sliced carrots, and lay on top eight ounces of sliced ham, four ounces of mushroom parings, two pounds of young rabbit and two pounds of partridge, add a pint of white wine and reduce to a glaze; moisten with a quart of broth (No. 187), cover the saucepan, and let boil and reduce on a brisk fire, moderating the heat when the liquid is reduced to three-quarters, then continue reducing until it has fallen again to a glaze. Add four quarts of game broth (No. 195), a tablespoonful of allspice (whole), a bunch of parsley garnished with celery, bay leaf, and thyme, and let cook for an hour and a half. Strain this through a napkin, put it back on the fire to clarify with two partridge breasts and one pound of lean veal, both well chopped; dilute it with half a bottle of white wine, stir well, and take it off the fire at the first boil; as soon as the fumet is very clear, strain it through a napkin.

(398). CHICKEN OR GAME GLAZE (Glace de Volaille ou de Gibier).

To the chicken stock, set apart to prepare a glaze, some good veal stock (No. 423) may be added, operating the same for a game stock, to which put in parts of both veal and chicken; the process is always the same; it is especially during the shooting season that excellent game glaze can be prepared with all the smaller parts and bones of large game. Prepare an ordinary broth, obtaining it as clear as possible, strain, skim off the fat and let it deposit its sediment. Collect all the good meat from the large game, such as thighs, shoulders or breasts of hare or deer, also from old partridges, and the pinions and giblets from the pheasants or partridges. Make a mirepoix of roots, and minced onions, put with it all the above meats, also a piece of the shoulder, breast of veal; their white fragments, or those of chickens, and fry them for a few minutes; moisten them moderately with some broth (No. 187), and let this fall to a glaze, then moisten again abundantly with the prepared game broth, adding a few boned and parboiled calves' feet; as soon as the meat is done, drain well; strain and skim the liquid; let it settle so as to be able to pour off the clear top and reduce this once more.

(399). FISH GLAZE (Glace de Poisson).

Put into a saucepan six pounds of bass, four of soles, and two of codfish; moisten with fourteen quarts of water and one quart of white wine; boil, skim, and season with salt, cloves, whole allspice, two cloves of garlic, half a pound of onions, and a bunch of parsley garnished with two bay leaves and as much thyme. Let simmer for one hour, then strain through a napkin, and redue to a quarter of its quantity, then set it away in a bowl to get cold; turn it out, and cut off the top, leaving the sediment at the bottom, then put it back on the fire, and reduce to the consistency of a thick syrup.

(400). CLEAR HALF GLAZE (Demi-Glace Claire).

This demi-glaze must not be confused with demi-glaze sauce. The demi-glaze is not a sauce but simply good, clarified gelatinous gravy reduced to half the consistency of a glaze; which means only slightly thickened; it must be bright, clear, and succulent. Before taking it from the fire mix in with it a spoonful of Madeira wine for each two quarts of liquid.

(401). MEAT GLAZE, CLEAR (Glace de Viande Claire).

Have a stockpot sufficiently large to contain four pounds of knuckle of veal, eight pounds of shoulder of veal, six pounds of shin or leg of beef, and add to these sixteen quarts of water and a very little salt; boil, skim, and garnish with a pound and a half of onions, one of them containing four cloves, two pounds of carrots cut in quarters, a bunch of eight medium sized leeks, with a few branches of celery, and a bouquet made of two ounces of parsley leaves, three bay leaves and as much thyme; bring to a boil, skim as fast as the fat and white particles rise to the surface, and boil in this manner for eight hours, then strain it through a sieve, and reduce down to two quarts. Put this into a tin can having a tube half an inch in diameter, a quarter of its height from the bottom, and plugged with a tight cork; cork well and tie it firmly down, then put it on to boil in water for one hour, remove it from the water, and keep it in a warm place for three days to settle, then take out the top, then the lower cork, and receive the glaze as it falls in an earthern vessel. This glaze should be very clear; suppress the bottom, and use it in sauces etc., or else add it to the spanish sauce stocks.

(402). MEAT GLAZE, PLAIN (Glace de Viande Simple).

To Prepare Meat Glaze.—In the every day work of a kitchen, the meat glaze is always prepared either with the superfluous stocks or remoistening broths; it is a very easy matter to accomplish this. Skim off the fat from all surplus stocks, and then strain them; should they be troubled, clarify with a little lean beef operating the sauce as for consommé. After the liquid is once strained, set it into one or several saucepans, pouring it off steadily from the sediment, and reduce the liquid quickly, while stirring it in the saucepan with a ladle, until it becomes slightly thick; now pour it into a smaller saucepan, and leave it to boil on one side of the fire, while skimming, until the glaze is quite thick, then pour it into cans and let it get cold in a cool place to use when needed.

(403). ROOT GLAZE (Glace de Racines).

Put into a saucepan two pounds of carrots cut in big squares, as many onions, one pound of celery roots, and three pounds of turnips; season with a little salt, four cloves, one teaspoonful of whole allspice, and moisten with twelve quarts of water, adding four pounds of split knuckle of veal, and two pounds of the kernel, also a bunch of parsley, garnished with thyme and bay leaf; let cook slowly for four hours, then strain the whole through a fine sieve; return it to the fire, despumate well all the white and fat particles from the surface; let it continue to boil till the consistency of a thick syrup is obtained, then put it away to use when needed.

(404). CLEAR GRAVY (Jus Clair).

Butter the interior of a saucepan, cover the bottom with slices of onions, and lay on top some slices of unsmoked ham, add six pounds of split knuckle of veal, four pounds of beef and its bones, two pounds of parings of a roasted leg of mutton, with its bones broken, and four pounds of roasted chicken carcasses. Moisten with one quart of broth (No. 421), set it on the range, cover, and reduce on a moderate fire until the gravy becomes perfectly clear and falls to a glaze, remoisten with eight quarts of remoistening (No. 189), so that all the ingredients are covered, then boil, skim and season with salt, whole peppers, a bunch of parsley garnished with a bay leaf and as much thyme, a clove of garlic and four cloves, let the whole cook for four hours, then strain through a fine sieve, skim off the fat and reduce to half, and then clarify it with one pound each of veal and beef chopped up together. After the gravy is clear, strain it through a napkin and it is now ready for use.

A gravy may be made by remoistening espagnole sauce stock (No. 421), and adding to it some roast beef bones, chicken carcasses, etc.

(405). THICK GRAVY (Jus Lié).

Cut into square pieces, six pounds of a shoulder of veal, put them into a saucepan with half a pound of melted lard to fry on a moderate fire, turning over repeatedly with a spoon; a quarter of an hour later put in one pound of cut up carrots and four ounces of onions; continue to fry the meats from twelve to fifteen minutes longer. Now moisten them with the value of one pint of remoistening (No. 189), cover the saucepan and let the liquid reduce until it has fallen to a glaze without allowing it to burn; moisten the meats again with eight quarts of hot broth and half a bottleful of white wine; skim the liquid at the first boil, then remove it to the side of the range and throw in a ham bone, a partly roasted chicken weighing four pounds, also a few chicken giblets, add a few whole spices and a bunch of parsley garnished with aromatic herbs. When the meats are about three-quarters done, skim the fat from the gravy and thicken with flour dissolved in cold water, two tablespoonfuls for each quart of liquid; continue to boil while skimming off more fat, and half an hour after, pour it through a sieve into another saucepan, let it come to a boil, then set it on one side of the fire to despumate for twenty-five minutes, stirring in at intervals a few spoonfuls of broth. Skim, remove the fat once more, and strain the gravy into a vessel leaving it to get cold, while stirring it from time to time.

(406). MATIGNON (Matignon).

Cut half a pound of carrots, half a pound of onions, half a pound of celery root and two ounces of parsley root into either three-sixteenth inch squares or small Julienne; fry them lightly without coloring in half a pound of chopped up fat pork, and add to them half a pound of ham cut either in squares or Julienne shape, also a quarter of a pound of mushrooms, a few branches of parsley (about half an ounce), two bay leaves, as much thyme and a teaspoonful of mignonette; moisten with a pint of white wine and a pint of veal blond (No. 423); boil and reduce the moisture to a glaze.

(407). ALLEMANDE SAUCE (Sauce Allemande).

Allemande sauce is made by reducing some velouté (No. 415), incorporating a little good raw cream slowly into it. When the sauce is succulent and creamy thicken it with a thickening of several raw egg-yolks, then boil the sauce for one minute to cook the eggs, pressing against the bottom of the pan with a spatula, strain it through a tammy into a vessel. Stir it from time to time until cold.

(408). ALLEMANDE SAUCE WITH MUSHROOM ESSENCE (Sauce Allemande à l'Essence de Champignons).

After the velouté (No. 415) sauce is reduced in a flat saucepan with a fifth part of mushroom essence (No. 392), thicken with twelve egg-yolks, some nutmeg and two ounces of butter, incorporate slowly a part of the sauce into the thickening, then pour the whole into the sauce, adding the juice of one lemon. Set the saucepan on the fire, stir at the bottom with a spatula, boil the sauce for one minute, then strain through a tammy; pour it in a high saucepan and set it in a bain-marie, and cover it with a little white stock (No. 422) to prevent the surface from drying or set it away in a vessel for further use.

(409). BÉCHAMEL SAUCE (Sauce Béchamel.)

This is made by preparing a roux of butter and flour, and letting it cook for a few minutes while stirring, not allowing it to color in the slightest; remove it to a slower fire and leave it to continue cooking for a quarter of an hour, then dilute it gradually with half boiled milk, and half veal blond (No. 423). Stir the liquid on the fire until it boils, then mingle in with it a mirepoix of roots and onions (No. 419), fried separately in butter, some mushroom peelings and a bunch of parsley; set it on a slower fire and let cook for twenty-five minutes without ceasing to stir so as to avoid its adhering to the bottom; it must be rather more consistent than light. Strain it through a fine sieve then through a tammy into a vessel, and allow it to cool off while continuing to stir; set it aside for further use.

(410) CHICKEN BÉCHAMEL (Béchamel de Volaille).

Lift the breasts from two chickens, bone the rest of them and cut the meats into three-eighth inch squares; cut up also one pound of lean veal the same size. Put half a pound of butter into a saucepan with four ounces of onions cut into three-sixteenth inch squares; fry slowly without letting them attain a color, then add the chicken and veal, and when all are well fried, throw in half a pound of flour; stir well and let the flour cook for a few minutes, then moisten with four quarts of chicken bouillon (No. 188); season with salt, mignonette, a bunch of parsley garnished with two bay leaves and as much thyme, then let boil and simmer for one hour and a half, skim off the fat and scum carefully. Strain the béchamel through a fine sieve and then a tammy, and, to reduce it, add one quart of cream, and when the sauce covers the spoon, pass again through the tammy into a vessel; stir from time to time until it gets cold.

(411). LEAN BÉCHAMEL WITH CREAM (Béchamel Maigre à la Crème).

Put ten ounces of butter in a saucepan with half a pound of onions cut in three-sixteenth inch squares, half a pound of carrots cut in quarter inch squares and a quarter of a pound of celery root cut the same; fry the whole on a slow fire, adding a quarter of a pound of flour. Let cook for a few minutes, then moisten with two quarts of boiled milk; stir with a spatula until boiling point; add a bunch of parsley garnished with two bay leaves and as much thyme, season with salt and whole peppers, and let cook slowly for one hour, then skim off the fat and reduce the sauce by adding to it gradually one pint of cream; strain the whole into a high saucepan through a tammy (No. 159) and keep warm in a bain-marie, setting a few pats of fresh butter on top.

(412). BÉCHAMEL WITH MUSHROOM ESSENCE (Béchamel à l'Essence de Champignons).

Put a quarter of a pound of butter into a saucepan, add to it two ounces of onions cut in three-sixteenth inch squares, a quarter of a pound of lean veal cut in three-eighth inch squares, two ounces of carrots cut in one-quarter inch squares and two ounces of unsmoked ham cut in one-quarter inch squares, also a bunch of parsley garnished with two bay leaves and as much thyme, and let these fry on a moderate fire; drain off the butter, and add four quarts of velouté (No. 415), seasoning with salt, pepper and grated nutmeg, then cook the whole for one hour, afterward straining it through a tammy, and reduce it with one quart of essence of mushrooms (No. 392). Strain it again through the tammy and just when ready to use, incorporate into it half a pound of fine, fresh butter.

(413). HALF-GLAZE SAUCE, CLEAR AND THICKENED (Sauce demi-glace Claire et liée).

A half glaze sauce only differs from an espagnole by its lightness. This sauce is generally made in large quantities at the time, so as not to begin it so frequently, as it requires the utmost care in its preparation. Heat in a saucepan one pound of clarified butter, and when it is very hot fill it up with flour so as to obtain a paste rather too light than otherwise; thicken it well while stirring for a few minutes on the fire, and then set it aside in a warm part to cook and brown very slowly, without adhering to the bottom of the pan, and without letting it get black. Five or six hours after, pour it into a vessel, cover it with paper, and let this roux stand to get cool.

To make the Sauce : dilute the roux very slowly, with some beef stock (No. 194a), having it only slightly warm, and prepared for this purpose, and finish it exactly like the espagnole; it must be as clear as possible and of a light color; strain and skim it well. Stir the liquid over the fire to thicken the sauce, managing not to have any lumps in it, and should it not be perfectly smooth, then strain it through a fine colander Put four ounces of butter in a saucepan, add to it four ounces each of sliced carrots, onions and celery root; the same quantity of lean ham cut in quarter inch squares, a bunch of parsley garnished with bay leaves, thyme and allspice, fry without coloring, pour the sauce over the whole, add four gills of good white, dry wine, and a quarter of a pound of mushroom parings, and let all boil while stirring, then remove it at once to the side of the range, and continue boiling on one side only, so as to be able to despumate it properly for several hours. Strain and put as much of this as is needed into a reducing saucepan with two gills of meat glaze (No. 401); boil, reduce it to the necessary degree, using a spatula to stir it from the bottom, without leaving it for one instant, incorporate slowly into it a little good veal blond (No. 423) and a small quantity of good white wine. When the sauce is succulent without being too thick, strain it through a tammy and pour it into a vessel, or else into a saucepan to keep warm in a bain-marie.

Clear Half-Glaze Thickened.—Have a quart of well-reduced clear gravy (No. 404); put it on the fire to boil, add six tablespoonfuls and skim it carefully, adding two tablespoonfuls of fecula, arrowroot, or cornstarch, diluted in a little cold water, pouring it slowly into the stock while stirring it with a whip; boil again, skim and strain through a fine sieve; set it in a bain-marie and cover the top with some Madeira wine.

(414). BROWN, ESPAGNOLE OR SPANISH SAUCE (Sauce Brune Espagnole).

Espagnole or Spanish sauce is a leading sauce from which many smaller ones are made. To obtain a good espagnole, it is necessary to have good stock (No. 421); in case there be no stock specially prepared for this purpose, use good clear broth. For four quarts of stock, melt in a saucepan one pound of butter, stir into it the same weight of very dry, good flour, so as to obtain a clear paste; then let it cook for four or five minutes on the fire, without ceasing to stir, and afterward set it back on to a very slow fire, or in a slack oven, to let it get a good dark brown color, being careful to move it about often. When the roux is cooked, take it from the oven and dilute with the prepared stock, not having it too hot, and stir the liquid again over the fire to bring it to a boil. Should the sauce not be sufficiently smooth—should any lumps appear in it, then strain it through a fine sieve, and put it back into the saucepan; and at the first boil, set it on one side so that it only boils partially, and let it despumate in this way for two or three hours. Skim off well the fat, and strain the broth into a vessel to let get cold, meanwhile stirring frequently.

(415). VELOUTÉ SAUCE (Sauce Veloutée).

The velouté like the espagnole is also a leading sauce used for making secondary sauces. Melt three-fourths of a pound of butter in a small saucepan; stir into it three-fourths of a pound of good flour, and let the roux cook for a few minutes, then set the saucepan on a slower fire without letting it color; in order to obtain a well thickened sauce, the flour must be well cooked. When the roux is sufficiently done dilute it gradually with four quarts of good stock (No. 423). In case there be no special stock prepared for this sauce then use some good clear chicken stock (No. 195). Stir the liquid over the fire until it comes to a boil, then move it aside to let it cook on one side only; despumate the sauce for one hour, skimming off all the white particles arising to the surface; remove all the fat, and strain the velouté through a sieve into a vessel and let it get cool while lifting off the scum that forms on the top.

(416) VELOUTÉ AND BROWN, ESPAGNOLE OR SPANISH SAUCE FOR LEAN (Sauce Veloutée et Espagnole en Maigre).

The lean veloute or the lean Spanish sauce are made the same way as the fat (Nos. 414 and 415), or using fish stock (No. 417); for lean velouté the stock must be reduced to a glaze without coloring.

(417). FISH STOCK FOR LEAN ESPAGNOLE AND VELOUTÉ SAUCE (Fond de Poisson pour Sauce Espagnole et Sauce Veloutée en Maigre).

Butter the bottom of a sixteen-quart thick bottomed saucepan, and cover it with a layer of sliced onions, and on top of these four pounds of bony fish or else fish bones cut into pieces; moisten with one pint of water and set it on a brisk fire, covering the saucepan, and let it reduce to a glaze. Moisten again with one pint of white wine and four quarts of boiling water; skim off the fat and add a bunch of parsley garnished with two bay leaves, as much thyme, and half a pound of minced carrots and four ounces of celery, two cloves of garlic, and then let cook slowly for two hours; strain the whole through a fine sieve and use this stock for diluting the roux.

(418). BRAISE STOCK FOR BRAISING MEATS (Fond de Braise).

Cover the bottom of a saucepan with bardes of fat pork, one pound of minced onions, one pound of minced carrots, and on top place either a leg of mutton, a piece of poultry, a tenderloin of beef or a kernel of veal. Moisten to the height of the meat with some beef stock (No. 194), add a bunch of parsley containing a bay leaf and as much thyme, a clove of garlic and two cloves; season with salt and whole peppers, and after it has cooked, strain it through a fine sieve, and return the stock to the braised meats to simmer until it is reduced to half. This braise may be replaced by a mirepoix stock for braising meats.

(419). MIREPOIX STOCK AND DRY MIREPOIX (Fond de Mirepoix et Mirepoix Sèche).

This is the essence of meats and vegetables. Put into a saucepan half a pound of chopped fat pork, fry it until melted, and then add half a pound of butter, one pound of lean veal cut in three-eighths of an inch squares, and one pound of unsmoked ham, also a pound of carrots and six ounces of onions cut in quarter inch squares, and a bunch of parsley garnished with a bay leaf and as much thyme, some basil, a clove of garlic, two cloves, and mace. Add to this a few mushroom parings, season with a little salt and mignonette, and when all the ingredients are well fried and of a fine golden color, moisten them with three quarts of remoistening (No. 189), and one pint of white wine, and a pint of Madeira wine; boil the whole slowly for two hours, then strain it forcibly through a tammy (No. 159) without removing the fat. Mirepoix is used for moistening meats, fishes, etc.

Dry Mirepoix is made of minced, raw vegetables, and roots which are fried in lard and moistened with some good stock and white wine, and allowed to reduce to dryness. It is employed to cover the breasts of fowl, game, and also meats that are to be roasted on the spit.

(420). POÊLER STOCK FOR COOKING FOWL OR WHITE GAME MEAT (Fond de Poêle pour Cuire la Volaille et le Gibier Blanc).

Poêler.—Consists in cooking fowls or white game meat, the breasts of which are covered with slices of peeled lemon, then barded and cooked in a rich stock having it reach to half their heighth. To make the stock cut up one pound of fat pork, and half a pound of unsmoked ham into quarter inch squares; one pound of carrots and as many onions, both minced, a garnished bouquet of bay leaf and as much thyme, fry the whole lightly in half a pound of butter, adding a bunch of basil garnished with two cloves, mace, and a clove of garlic; moisten all with two quarts of veal blond (No. 423), add salt, ground pepper.

(421). BROWN, ESPAGNOLE OR SPANISH SAUCE STOCK (Fond pour Sauce Brune Espagnole).

Butter the bottom of a thick bottomed saucepan and garnish it with slices of onions, placing on top half a pound of ham, some slices or parings of fat pork, twelve pounds of knuckle of veal, shoulder, and trimmings, six pounds of beef or parings, and moisten with one quart of beef stock (No. 194a); leave the saucepan on the fire until the broth is half reduced, then cover the saucepan and moderate the fire, continue to boil till all the moisture is reduced and falls to a glaze, which is easily perceived as the grease then becomes clear; moisten it once more with eighteen quarts of beef stock; boil, skim off the fat, and add a bunch of parsley, garnished with two bay leaves and as much thyme, basil, celery, and two cloves of garlic, also one pound of carrots cut lengthwise in four, salt, ground pepper, and a little sugar. Cook all together for six hours, skim off the fat and strain through a sieve to keep for further use. This stock is used for moistening brown roux.

(422). VELOUTÉ STOCK (Fond pour Velouté).

Butter the bottom of a sixteen quart saucepan, having a thick bottom, cover it with sliced onions and on top of these lay four pounds of knuckle of veal and shoulder, half of each, four pounds of fowl without the breast, and moisten with one pint of remoistening (No. 189), put it on a brisk fire and cover the saucepan, as soon as the liquid is reduced to half, moderate the fire and let the sauce fall slowly to a glaze without browning, then moisten with six quarts more of white broth, skim off the fat and scum and season with salt, crushed whole peppers and a little sugar, add a bunch of parsley and celery green, garnished with two bay leaves and as much thyme, also half an ounce of basil, besides four ounces of mushroom parings or stalks and half a pound of minced carrots, then let cook for six hours, remove all the fat, add from time to time a little remoistening (No. 189), salt it to taste and strain through a sieve or a napkin. Use when needed.

(423). VEAL BLOND STOCK (Fond de Blond de Veau).

Butter the bottom of a saucepan capable of containing sixteen quarts; set in four sliced onions, and on top of these four pounds of split knuckle of veal and four pounds of shoulder of veal, two fowls, after removing the breasts, and moisten all with one quart of beef stock (No. 194a). Place the saucepan on a brisk fire, keeping the lid on, and reduce the moisture by moderating the heat of the fire, and letting the liquid fall slowly to a glaze; now moisten again with six quarts more of beef stock, season with salt and whole peppers, and add four leeks, two carrots, cut in pieces, a bunch of parsley, some celery, one bay leaf and as much thyme. Cook all slowly for six hours, then skim off the fat and strain through a fine sieve. Chop up the breasts taken from the two fowls with the same quantity of lean beef, and mix this in a little cold water, and with this meat clarify the veal blond the same as consommé; then strain it through a napkin.

Veal blond should be clear, succulent and of a nice color, the grease should be thoroughly removed from it; added to clear soups it greatly improves them; it is also used in reducing sauces.

HOT SAUCES.

(424). AFRICAN SAUCE (Sauce à l'Africaine).

Put two ounces of butter into a sautoire and when hot add two ounces of chopped up onions and fry without coloring; moisten with a pint of broth and a pint of espagnole sauce (No. 414), add a small bunch of parsley garnished with half a bay leaf and as much thyme. Bring the whole to a boil, skim, remove the fat and let cook for half an hour; strain through a tammy and incorporate slowly into the sauce, two ounces of butter, a pinch of cayenne and the juice of a lemon, also a gill of Madeira wine and two ounces of exceedingly fine cut up truffles.

(425). ALLEMANDE WITH RED WINE AND FRUITS (Allemande au Vin Rouge et aux Fruits).

Cook six ounces of dry black cherries or prunes, cut in four, in two gills of red wine and as much water, add a bit of cinnamon stick, three cloves, and the peel from one lemon; let simmer for twenty minutes on a slow fire, then drain and add to the juice the same quantity of espagnole (No. 414) as there is sauce; reduce, skim, and after the liquid is well reduced, take out the lemon peel, cinnamon, and cloves, then put the cherries back into the sauce and serve. Cherries and prunes may both be used together, half of each.

(426). AMERICAN SAUCE (Sauce Américaine).

Split open the bodies of two cooked lobsters, take out all the creamy parts, rub them through a sieve, and keep them aside for further use. Wipe well the shells, break them into pieces and chop them up coarsely on the table with the thick end of a knife. Fry in some oil, carrots, celery, parsley, shallots, and minced onions, add to these the chopped shells and let cook all together until their moisture is reduced, then moisten slightly above their height with white wine and mirepoix (No. 419); let this liquid boil up for two minutes, then move it on a more moderate fire, and add some thyme, bay leaf, and basil. Let the whole cook from twenty to twenty-five minutes, then strain it forcibly through a sieve into a bowl, and leave it to settle for a quarter of an hour, afterward removing all the fat, pour off the top gently into a sautoire, pressing it through a fine sieve, and let it reduce to a half-glaze. Mix in with it about a third of its quantity of tomato sauce, reduce it once more without ceasing to stir until it becomes short and succulent, by mixing in three or four spoonfuls of sherry wine. Strain it now into another saucepan, work in the butter, and finish with a dash of cayenne pepper, and two spoonfuls of the creamy part from the bodies already strained. This sauce should be served as quickly as it is made; in any way it must be kept stirred until the very last moment.

(427). ANCHOVY SAUCES (Sauce aux Anchois).

Anchovy Fat Sauce.—Set into a saucepan half a pint of brown poivrade sauce (No. 522); the same quantity of espagnole (No. 414), and half a pint of veal blond (No. 423). Allow the liquid to boil up while stirring continuously, then despumate; just when ready to serve incorporate in two ounces of anchovy butter (No. 569).

For Lean Anchovy Sauce.—Clean twelve anchovies, by removing their skin and tails; wash and pound in a mortar; to this pulp add double their quantity of butter, rub through a fine sieve, and incorporate two ounces of this butter into one quart of white sauce (No. 562); season, and add a little lemon juice and nutmeg, then strain the whole through a tammy. The anchovy butter can be replaced by essence of anchovies, already prepared in bottles; in this case incorporate in just when prepared to serve, two ounces of fresh butter.

(428). APPLE SAUCES (Sauce aux Pommes).

Hot with Butter and Gravy.—Peel a pound of sour apples, cut them in quarter inch thick slices, and remove the cores. Put a quarter of a pound of butter into a sautéing pan and when hot, throw in the apples and let them fry on both sides until they are a fine color, then moisten with four gills of veal blond (No. 423), and two ounces of brown sugar (or cayenne pepper) if preferred, and a little grated nutmeg, press the apples through a sieve and serve hot.

For Hot or Cold.—Peel and core one pound of sour apples, put them into a saucepan with a pint of water and when done, drain and pass them through a sieve; now add sugar, nutmeg, and an ounce of butter and serve the sauce hot; for the cold suppress the butter.

(429). ARGENTINE SAUCE (Sauce Argentine).

Put into a sautoir, four tablespoonfuls of oil; set it on the fire and when hot, add two ounces of chopped onions, and a finely shredded green pepper, a crushed and chopped clove of garlic, a bunch of parsley garnished with a bay leaf, and as much thyme; fry the whole without attaining color; then drain off the oil and moisten with one gill of white wine, and two gills of tomato purée (No. 730); season, and add a pint of espagnole sauce (No. 414), and three tablespoonfuls of meat glaze; boil the whole, skim carefully, and reduce to a proper consistency; pass through a tammy and serve.

(430). AURORA SAUCE, FAT AND LEAN (Sauce à l'Aurore, en Gras et en Maigre).

For Fat.—Put into a saucepan half a pint of velouté (No. 415), with essence of mushrooms (No. 392), and half a pint of veal blond (No. 423); reduce to half, strain through a tammy, heat it up once more and when ready to serve incorporate two ounces of crawfish butter (No. 573) into the sauce.

For Lean.—Have in a saucepan one quart of béchamel sauce (No. 409); pound four hard boiled egg-yolks with four ounces of lobster butter (No. 580); press through a fine sieve, mix the two together adding the juice of a lemon, strain through a tammy and serve hot.

(431). BARNAVE SAUCE (Sauce à la Barnave).

Put four ounces of butter into a saucepan and when hot add a quarter of a pound of red carrots blanched and the same quantity of onions, both cut into three-sixteenth inch pieces. First fry the onions, then add the carrots and fry together a little, add a garnished bunch of parsley with thyme, a clove of garlic, a pound of game carcasses and when a good color add half a bottle of red wine and a pint of broth. Let all cook for three-quarters of an hour, skim it carefully, strain the sauce through a tammy or sieve, dilute it again with another pint of broth and throw in an ounce of very fresh bread raspings, an ounce of butter and the juice of one orange.

(432). BAVAROISE SAUCE (Sauce Bavaroise).

Reduce to half its volume one gill of vinegar; take it from the fire and let get cold, then add one gill of béchamel (No. 409), four raw egg-yolks and four ounces of butter divided into small pats, a gill of water, salt and nutmeg. Stir the preparation over a moderate fire until it thickens, then incorporate into it three ounces of butter, a small bit at a time, working it in well with a whip so as to have it light, add to finish, three ounces of crawfish butter (No. 573) and a tablespoonful of grated horseradish.

(433). BÉARNAISE SAUCE, HOT MAYONNAISE, AND WITH TOMATOES (Sauces Béarnaise, Mayonnaise Chaude et aux Tomates).

Put into a saucepan one gill of vinegar with two ounces of chopped shallots, also a few tarragon leaves; cover the saucepan with its lid, and reduce the liquid almost completely, then take it from off the fire. Let the vinegar get slightly cold, and afterward mix in with it four raw egg-yolks, season with salt and mignonette, and return it to a slow fire, and then incorporate into it slowly three ounces of clarified butter, stirring it continually in the meanwhile with a small whip; now strain it through a tammy; whip it well, and mix in with it a coffeespoonful of chopped tarragon, and the same quantity of chopped parsley. This sauce should have the consistency of a mayonnaise, and can also be made the same as the above, with half butter and half oil.

Hot Mayonnaise.—Is made the same as a béarnaise, only using oil and suppressing the tarragon.

Hot Mayonnaise with Tomatoes.—Pour one quart of hot mayonnaise in a deep saucepan, set it either on a slow fire or in a bain-marie, and when it begins to curdle, take it off and beat it up quickly, adding a little cold water; continue the beating process until perfectly smooth, then heat it again stirring vigorously without allowing it to boil, and finish by adding eight tablespoonfuls of well reduced tomato purée (No. 730), four tablespoonfuls of melted meat glaze (No. 401), and some lemon juice. Strain through a fine sieve, then mix in a teaspoonful of chopped parsley and a little cold water.

(434). BERCHOUX SAUCE (Sauce à la Berchoux).

Put into a sautoire one pint of milk and let boil, then add two ounces of fresh bread-crumbs; season with salt, nutmeg, and red pepper and moisten with the quarter of a bottleful of champagne. Now pound a pinch of tarragon with two pinches of chervil, and a quarter of a clove of garlic; when it becomes a pulp add four ounces of fresh butter and a little spinach green to color. Incorporate this butter into the sauce, strain through a fine tammy; if the sauce should be too thick add a little cream.

(435). BIGARADE SAUCE (Sauce à la Bigarade).

A bigarade orange is a sour orange before it changes to an orange color; peel it without touching the white parts, using a peeling knife (Fig. 156), cut the peel up into small fine Julienne, plunge it into boiling water, and cook it until it is tender; drain and enclose it in a covered saucepan with four gills of espagnole (No. 414) or velouté (No. 415) if needed for a white sauce. Just when ready to serve, finish the sauce with a dash of cayenne pepper, meat glaze, the orange juice and the juice of a lemon; strained through a tammy, adding two ounces of fine butter. The bigarade can be replaced by an orange and a lemon, using the peel and juice of both fruits.

(436). BORDELAISE SAUCE, WITH MARROW AND MAÎTRE D'HÔTEL WITH MARROW
(Sauce Bordelaise, à la Moelle et Maître d'Hôtel à la Moelle).

Bordelaise Sauce.—Put into a saucepan half a bottleful of Bordeaux wine, adding a small garnished bouquet containing a little garlic, half a bay leaf, and two cloves; a quarter of a pound of the peelings and stalks of some chopped mushrooms, one tablespoonful of blanched shallots lightly fried in three spoonfuls of oil, one pint of espagnole sauce (No. 414), half a pint of veal blond (No. 423), and season with salt, mignonette and cayenne, boil, skim off the fat and then pour in half a bottleful of white wine, and when the sauce is reduced, strain it through a tammy and stir in a teaspoonful of chopped parsley; a pound of beef marrow cut in either squares or slices may be added to the bordelaise just when ready to serve. A simpler way is to brown some minced shallots in oil with a clove of crushed garlic, adding red wine and gravy, then reduce it to half, pour in the espagnole, boil, skim off the fat and serve.

Bordelaise Sauce with Marrow.—Fry minced shallots in oil with a clove of garlic (crushed); moisten with red wine and reduced gravy, add some espagnole; boil and despumate, then put in squares of beef marrow or else have them cut in slices and plunged into boiling water and drained; add only when ready to serve.

Maître d'Hôtel with Marrow.—Have some maître d'hôtel butter (No. 581), slightly melted, into which add four ounces of shallots for each pound of butter, the shallots being cut into one-eighth inch squares, eight tablespoonfuls of meat glaze or chicken glaze, and add just when ready to serve, slices of marrow previously thrown into boiling water and drained.

(437). BOURGUIGNOTTE SAUCE—LEAN (Sauce à la Bourguignotte—Maigre).

Cut a pound of eels into slices being careful that they are very fresh; put these into a saucepan with two quarts of water, two ounces of minced onions and two ounces of mushroom parings, a bunch of parsley garnished with bay leaf and as much thyme, two minced shallots, pepper and allspice. Set the saucepan on the fire, let it come to a boil, and continue the boiling for twenty minutes, then strain the liquid and reduce it, adding one pint of lean espagnole sauce (No. 416), and a little lean broth (No. 417); let boil once again, despumate it, pour in a quarter of a bottleful of good white wine; boil and despumate again for half an hour, then add another quarter of a bottle of white wine, making half a bottleful in all; Volnay wine is excellent for this sauce. After it is reduced to a proper consistency, and just when ready to serve, incorporate into it a quarter of a pound of crawfish butter (No. 573).

(438). BREAD SAUCES, AMERICAN, ENGLISH, FRENCH, REGLAIN AND GERMAN FRIED (Sauces au Pain, Américaine, Anglaise, Française, Reglain et Frite à l'Allemande).

American.—Put into a saucepan one ounce of butter with one ounce of finely chopped onions, fry them lightly without coloring and moisten with a pint of boiling milk, add two ounces of bread-crumbs, salt, cayenne pepper and cloves, and just when ready to serve, add a little cream to finish. This sauce should be consistent and hot without boiling.

English is made exactly the same, only replacing the fried onions by a raw onion cut in four, and whole peppers instead of the cayenne.

French.—Chop up a shallot and a quarter of a clove of garlic, putting them in a saucepan with two gills of white wine; let simmer and reduce, adding two tablespoonfuls of very fine bread-crumbs, a little fresh butter, a dash of mignonette and grated nutmeg and two gills of broth, let reduce to half, then squeeze in some lemon juice and a teaspoonful of chopped parsley.

A la Reglain.—Set four gills of milk into a saucepan, adding two ounces of bread-crumbs and one shallot cut in small eighth inch squares, a whole clove of garlic, and let heat without boiling for a few minutes, seasoning with salt, a little cayenne and nutmeg, two ounces of butter, a teaspoonful of raw fine herbs, one gill of white wine and the juice of an orange.

Fried German.—Melt and heat gradually half a pound of butter so as to obtain a hazel-nut butter, incorporate into it three ounces of white bread-crumbs, cook it over a slow fire for a few minutes without ceasing to stir, salt it lightly and take off the fire to pour into a hot sauce boat.

(439). BRETONNE SAUCE (Sauce à la Bretonne).

Mince up four ounces of onions, fry them in two ounces of clarified butter, and when fried without attaining a color, drain them and moisten with one gill of veal blond (No. 423); reduce and let fall to a glaze. Add one gill of velouté (No. 415) if for white, and espagnole (No. 414) if for brown; season with salt and pepper, and meat glaze; strain it forcibly through a sieve, and incorporate into the sauce just when ready to serve, half an ounce of fresh butter. For a lean sauce, moisten with some fish stock (No. 417), and lean velouté or espagnole (No. 416) and fish glaze (No. 399).

(440). BUTTER SAUCE (Sauce au Beurre).

Put into a saucepan, two heaping tablespoonfuls of flour, dilute it with half a pint of cold water, add some salt and whole peppers, one clove, grated nutmeg, and half an ounce of butter. Set it on the fire, and stir well until it boils; then allow it to cook slowly for fifteen minutes; remove it from the fire, and incorporate into it by degrees, one pound of fresh butter, and the juice of two lemons. If the sauce should become too thick, add a little more water, then strain it through a tammy. With this sauce a quantity of other sauces may be made such as caper, egg, oyster, horse-radish, etc.

(441). CAPER SAUCE (Sauce aux Câpres).

Set into a saucepan two ounces of butter, mix it with one and a half ounces of flour; beat the flour and butter well together with a spoon, so as to obtain a smooth paste; now moisten it with two gills of water, add a pinch of salt, stir the liquid on the fire until the sauce becomes thick. At the first boil, remove it to the side of the range. It should be somewhat more consistent than thin. Incorporate into it gradually, two ounces of butter divided into small pats, the sauce should now be creamy; remove it and finish by adding some small nonpareil capers, and the juice of a lemon; then serve.

(442). CARDINAL SAUCE, FAT AND LEAN (Sauce Cardinal en Gras et en Maigre).

For Fat.—Reduce one pint of velouté (No. 415), with two gills of mushroom essence (No. 392), or else veal blond (No. 423), season with salt, pepper, and nutmeg; add a tablespoonful of meat, chicken, or game glaze (No. 401), two ounces of fresh butter, and the juice of one lemon. Serve in a sauce-boat, and dredge over the top chopped-up lobster coral.

For Lean.—Soak six carp milts in cold water, cook them for ten minutes in white broth (No.
195) with the juice of one lemon, salt, and half an ounce of fine butter, then drain; put into a
saucepan six tablespoonfuls of thick béchamel (No. 409), add to it a gill of cream; boil, season
with salt and cayenne pepper, and beat in one ounce of fresh butter, strain through a tammy, add
the milts, and heat them up rolling them in the sauce. Serve in a sauce-boat, dredging the top
with some very finely chopped lobster coral.

(443), CASTILLANE SAUCE (Sauce à la Castillane).

Pour into a saucepan six gills of espagnole sauce (No. 414) and two gills of veal blond (No.
423), reduce it to a third, then add a tablespoonful of powdered sweet Spanish peppers, a very
finely shreded green pepper, and a quarter of a pound of raw lean ham cut into small three-
sixteenth inch squares, boil all slowly, despumate the sauce, and just when ready to serve squeeze
in the juice of a lemon.

(444), CELERY SAUCE (Sauce au Céleri).

Have half a pound of white celery stalks cut in quarter inch pieces, put them in boiling and
salted water for five minutes, drain and place them in a saucepan with a pint of white stock (No.
422), then reduce it to half, adding a pint of well-reduced velouté (No. 415), and just when ready
to serve, incorporate into it two ounces of fine butter and half a gill of fresh cream, seasoning
with salt, nutmeg and red pepper.

(445), CHAMPAGNE SAUCE, ALSO WITH CHABLIS, RHINE WINE, SAUTERNE OR GRAVE-
WINE (Sauce au Champagne, Chablis, Vin du Rhin, Sauterne ou Grave).

The sauces may be made white or brown for a base; for white, using velouté (No. 415), for
the brown, having a brown espagnole (No. 414). Reduce one quart of espagnole with half a pint of
mushroom essence (No. 392), or the liquor in which they have been cooked, also a pint of mirepoix
stock (No. 419), add a pint of champagne or any other wine and reduce once more until the
sauce be sufficiently consistent. If made with velouté thicken it with egg-yolks, cream and small
pats of butter.

(446), CHATEAUBRIAND SAUCE (Sauce Chateaubriand).

Put into a saucepan one pint of espagnole sauce (No. 414), with two tablespoonfuls of meat
glaze (No. 401), one pint of veal blond (No. 423), and reduce it all to half, then strain through a
tammy, and just when ready to serve, stir in half a pound of fine butter, the strained juice of a
lemon and a teaspoonful of chopped parsley. To make it with tarragon put into a saucepan two
gills of dry white wine with some chopped shallots and mushroom peelings, and reduce it all to
half. Mix in with it six tablespoonfuls of meat glaze (No. 401), and finish with three gills of
reduced velouté (No. 415), let it boil for two minutes, then strain; at the last moment mingle in
with it three ounces of butter in small pats, working it in well with a small tinned wire whisk; add
the strained juice of a lemon and a few finely shreded tarragon leaves.

(447), CHERRY SAUCE (Sauce aux Cerises).

Lay in a saucepan, half a pound of currant jelly with six cloves, a small stick of cinnamon,
two orange peels, one ounce of meat glaze. (No. 401), half a pint of veal blond (No. 423), one pint
of espagnole sauce (No. 414), one gill of Burgundy, and four ounces of dried and pounded cherries,
let all boil together for a few minutes, then add the strained juice of two oranges, mix all together
well, and serve.

Another way is to have a quarter of a pound of dried black cherries with their pits; soften
them in cold water, and pound them in a mortar with three gills of red wine; pour the preparation into an untinned copper vessel, add a small stick of cinnamon, and two cloves, also a piece
of lemon peel; let the liquid boil for two minutes, then thicken it with a teaspoonful of fecula
diluted with a little cold water; remove it to the side of the fire, cover, and keep it warm without
boiling for fifteen minutes, then strain through a sieve and serve.

(448), CHERVIL OR PARSLEY PLUCHE SAUCE (Sauce à la Pluche de Cerfeuil ou de Persil).

A pluche is the leaves of either parsley or chervil blanched and combined with a sauce or soup.
Reduce one pint of velouté (No. 415) with two gills of white wine; season with salt, pepper,
nutmeg and the juice of a lemon, and just when serving incorporate into it four ounces of fresh
butter. Should the sauce be too thick add a little broth (No. 187), and then put in a heavy
pinch of blanched chervil or parsley leaves.

(449). CHIVRY SAUCE (Sauce à la Chivry).

Blanch in a red copper untinned vessel a handful of herbs composed of parsley leaves a third; chervil a third; pimpernel a sixth, and tarragon a sixth; drain them and extract well all their moisture, then put them into a mortar with a pinch of chives, pound them finely, adding a piece of butter, and after removing the preparation from the mortar rub it through a sieve, and add to it three gills of reduced velouté (No. 415) and a pinch of cayenne pepper. Color the sauce with a little spinach green or green vegetal coloring.

(450). CLERMONT SAUCE (Sauce à la Clermont).

Cut six medium onions in two; then remove the stalk and root from both ends giving a sharp slanting blow with the knife, so when they are removed the onions easily fall apart; then mince them up finely. Put four ounces of butter into a saucepan on the fire, and when it is hot, add the onions, and fry them slowly so that they become a nice golden color, then drain off the butter, and finish cooking with a quart of remoistening (No. 189); season with salt, pepper, and sugar, and when the onions are well done, and the stock reduced to half, add to it a pint of espagnole sauce (No. 414) with two tablespoonfuls of meat glaze (No. 401); season nicely and serve.

(451). COLBERT, ENGLISH AND TARRAGON SAUCES (Sauce à la Colbert, à l'Anglaise et à l'Estragon).

Colbert.—Boil up one gill of meat glaze (No. 401) in a saucepan, remove it from the fire, and then incorporate into it four ounces of fresh butter, working them well together with an egg-whisk, until the butter is thoroughly melted; then add the juice of two lemons, some grated nutmeg, and two tablespoonfuls of good sherry wine; strain through a tammy, add a teaspoonful of chopped parsley, and serve.

English.—Put a saucepan on the fire, containing two tablespoonfuls of Worcestershire sauce, and two of mushroom catsup, the same quantity of melted meat glaze (No. 401); take it off when it bubbles, then work slowly into it two ounces of anchovy butter, the juice of one lemon, and a little grated nutmeg; strain through a tammy and serve.

With Tarragon or Chervil.—Pour a gill of melted meat glaze (No. 401) into a saucepan; at the first boil take it off the fire, and whip in with it a quarter of a pound of butter divided into small pats; finish the sauce with the juice of two lemons, and half a spoonful of tarragon leaves, or else a spoonful of chervil leaves, one or the other finely cut up.

(452). CRAB SAUCE (Sauce aux Crabes).

Have a pint of white sauce (No. 562), in a saucepan, add to it a pinch of cayenne pepper and the same quantity of ground mace, also two ounces of crab meat cut in dice, or if possible some oyster crabs blanched in their own oyster juice, and drained.

(453). CRAWFISH SAUCE (Sauce aux Écrevisses).

Fry in two ounces of butter, one ounce of carrots, one ounce of celery root, one ounce of onions, and one ounce of shallot, a few parsley leaves, thyme, one bay leaf, and one clove of garlic. Moisten with half a bottleful of white wine, and let the whole cook for ten minutes, adding to it twenty-four well washed crawfish, a little salt and mignonette. Cook all together for five minutes, while tossing them up frequently, then take out the crawfish and let the stock settle; pour off gently the top, straining it through a very fine sieve; then reduce it to half and add a pint of velouté sauce (No. 415) and half a pint of white wine, and reduce it once more. Shell the crawfish, take the meat from the tails and lay them on one side; pound the remainder with five ounces of butter, heat it, and then pass it through a sieve into a bowl filled with ice water; lift up the butter, wipe it, and incorporate this butter into the sauce; color it with orchanet or else vegetable carmine, and strain it through a sieve. Add the crawfish meat cut in small dice to the sauce, and serve at once.

(454). CREAM SAUCE (Sauce à la Crème).

Put into a small saucepan, one pint of béchamel (No. 409), reduce it with two gills of cream; when ready, incorporate into it a quarter of a pound of fresh butter; season with salt and a dash of cayenne pepper.

(455). CURRANT SAUCE, WITH RED WINE, PORT WINE, CALIFORNIA WINE, WHITE WINE AND WHITE CURRANTS (Sauce Groseilles au vin de Bordeaux, au vin de Porto, au vin de Californie, au vin Blanc et aux Groseilles Blanches).

Plain currant jelly without being heated may be served with canvasback duck and saddle of venison. But if some people prefer sauce, the following will be found good:

Currant Sauce with Red Bordeaux Wine.—Put half a bottle of Bordeaux wine into a saucepan on the fire, and when the wine begins to simmer take it off, and put into it, to infuse, ten cloves, the peel of a lemon and a bit of cinnamon; leave them in for twenty minutes, and then add to it half a pound of currant jelly and two ounces of sugar, more or less, according to taste; dissolve and mix well, and when thoroughly melted, strain the sauce through a sieve and serve it hot.

Currant Sauce with Port Wine.—Put half a pound of currant jelly in a saucepan on the fire, dilute it with half a bottleful of port wine and one pint of brown espagnole sauce (No. 414), and when well dissolved strain through a sieve and serve hot.

Currant Sauce with California Wine.—Melt half a pound of currant jelly with half a pint of red California wine, and when well dissolved strain it through a tammy and serve hot.

Currant Sauce with White Wine.—Made with half a pound of currant jelly, a pinch of cinnamon, the same of ground cloves, half a bottle of white wine, and a pint of velouté (No. 415), besides the pulp of one lemon; strain through a sieve and serve hot.

White Currant Sauce.—Blanch and strain a pint of picked white currants, mix in with them half a pound of apple with orange jelly, the juice of two lemons and half a pint of velouté (No. 415). Dissolve with half a pint of white wine; strain through a tammy and serve hot.

(456). CURRY SAUCES, INDIAN AND WITH APPLES (Sauces au Kari, à l'Indienne et aux Pommes).

Curry.—Brown in some butter four ounces of minced onions, adding to it one teaspoonful of curry; two minutes later moisten with two gills of velouté (No. 415), two ounces of mushroom peelings, and a bunch of parsley garnished with a bay leaf. Reduce the sauce, and pour into it slowly about two gills of chicken broth (No. 188), and at the very last moment two spoonfuls of good raw cream. Pass the sauce through a tammy, and incorporate into it a piece of fresh butter, then heat it up without boiling.

Curry, Indian.—Put into a saucepan four ounces of ham, two ounces of onions, two ounces of mushrooms, all minced up very fine, a bunch of parsley garnished with as much bayleaf as thyme, one onion with three cloves in it, one teaspoonful of ground sweet Spanish pepper, a dash of cayenne pepper, a dessertspoonful of curry, a pinch of mace and one quart of chicken broth (No. 188). Let simmer and reduce to half; add one quart of allemande sauce (No. 407), and a pinch of saffron, pass it through a tammy and just when ready to serve incorporate into it two ounces of fresh butter.

Curry with Apples.—Put four ounces of butter into a saucepan, adding to it four ounces of apples, four ounces of onions, two ounces of ham, all finely shredded, a pinch of mace, a teaspoonful of pepper-corns, a bay leaf and as much thyme. Set the saucepan on a moderate fire, and let all fry till the onions begin to brown, being careful to stir it constantly, and add a tablespoonful of curry, the same of vinegar, a teaspoonful of sugar, one quart of velouté (No. 415), two gills of veal blond (No. 423) and one teaspoonful of meat glaze (No. 401). Pass all through a tammy and add two gills of cream.

(457). DANISH SAUCE (Sauce à la Danoise).

Put two ounces of butter in a saucepan, with four ounces of thinly sliced ham, and when lightly fried and a fine color, drain off the butter; detach the glaze with a gill of broth, add a clove of garlic, a bay leaf, as much thyme and a pint of espagnole (No. 414); cook slowly, despumate, season well, and pass the sauce through either a sieve or a tammy. Cut four ounces of chicken fillets, eight of mushrooms, and four of ham, into three-sixteenth inch squares; put them into the sauce with a small teaspoonful of chopped parsley.

(458). D'ANTIN SAUCE (Sauce à la d'Antin).

Put into a saucepan two ounces of butter, add two ounces of onions cut in one-eighth inch squares, and fry them without letting them attain color; moisten with one pint of espagnole (No. 414), one gill of Madeira, and one gill of tomato purée (No. 730); add half an ounce of chopped truffles, two ounces of mushrooms cut in eighth of an inch squares, a teaspoonful of chopped parsley, and a small pinch of tarragon leaves; and also one coffeespoonful of chopped chives.

(459). DEVILED SAUCE (Sauce à la Diable).

Lay in a saucepan three tablespoonfuls of vinegar, two ounces of one-eighth inch squares of shallot, a few parsley leaves, one bay leaf, as much thyme, and a clove of garlic crushed and chopped; let the whole boil for a few minutes, then add a pint of espagnole (No. 414), a pinch of mignonette, a very little cayenne pepper, a gill of red wine, and two tablespoonfuls of diluted mustard, also two tablespoonfuls of tomato sauce.

(460). DIANA SAUCE (Sauce à la Diane).

Into a saucepan put a quarter of a pound of butter; when hot add to it one medium onion, two shallots, one ounce of celery, all cut up very finely, and a bay leaf, and when these ingredients are well fried, add to them one pound of raw game carcass, and let the whole color nicely, adding three tablespoonfuls of flour, to make a roux, brown it slightly and then moisten with one pint of velouté stock (No. 422) and a pint of cream. Let the sauce cook and despumate for half an hour, seasoning it with salt, pepper, and nutmeg; then strain it through a sieve, and afterward through a tammy, return it to the saucepan, and reduce it properly, incorporating into it two ounces of butter.

(461). DUXELLE SAUCE WITH COOKED FINE HERBS AND TRUFFLES (Sauce à la Duxelle aux Fines Herbes Cuites et aux Truffes).

Set into a saucepan two ounces of grated salt pork, and two ounces of butter, six shallots cut in squares; one clove of crushed and chopped garlic; when all these are fried without coloring add one quarter of a pound of chopped mushrooms, a bay leaf, as much thyme and two cloves. Moisten the whole with half a pint of white wine, and the same quantity of broth, one pint of espagnole (No. 414) or velouté (No. 415), if for white and let cook for fifteen minutes. Add one tablespoonful of chopped truffles and a half a teaspoonful of chopped parsley; take out the bayleaf, thyme and cloves.

(462). EGG SAUCE, ENGLISH AND POLISH (Sauce aux œufs, à l'Anglaise et à la Polonaise).

For English Egg Sauce.—Put a pint of velouté (No. 415) in a saucepan with some pepper, nutmeg, the juice of a lemon, and four hard boiled eggs chopped up over a white cloth, and then added to the sauce with a tablespoonful of chopped parsley. Should the sauce be too thick dilute it with some mushroom broth and white broth.

For Polish Egg Sauce.—Have six small hard boiled eggs; chop up the whites and yolks separately; put into a sufficiently large frying pan half a pound of clarified butter, let it heat until it becomes hazel-nut butter, then season with salt, a tablespoonful or chopped parsley, a tablespoonful of diluted mustard and the chopped eggs; mix all without boiling and pour into a sauce-boat to be served separately.

(463). FENNEL SAUCE (Sauce au Fenouil).

Put one pint of velouté (No. 415) and a spoonful of meat glaze (No. 401) into a saucepan, and let them come to a boil, then thicken with one egg-yolk and some fresh butter, adding the juice of one lemon, and a tablespoonful of very finely chopped fennel.

(464). FINANCIÈRE SAUCE FOR FAT AND FOR LEAN AND WITH GAME AND CHICKEN (Sauce à la Financière en gras et en Maigre et au Gibier et à la Volaille).

Put four ounces of butter in a saucepan, add four ounces of cooked lean ham cut in three-sixteenth inch squares, fry without coloring and then throw in four ounces of mushrooms or their parings, two bay leaves, as much thyme, one ounce of truffle parings and two gills of dry Madeira or sherry, let simmer and reduce over a slow fire. Moisten with one pint of veal blond (No. 423), and one pint of espagnole (No. 414), then let boil and despumate, adding a gill more Madeira, and when the suce is done, strain it through a tammy.

For Lean.—Replace the ham by smoked salmon or sturgeon, the sherry by sauterne, the **veal** blond by fish stock (No. 417), and use lean espagnole, and then finish the same as for the fat.

For Financière Sauce with Game or Chicken.—Infuse in a quarter of a bottleful of warm white wine or champagne, two ounces of mushrooms and one of truffles. Place two ounces of butter in a saucepan with two ounces of finely minced raw ham, and when it is fried, drain off the butter and moisten with one pint either of chicken or game stock (No. 195), one pint of espagnole (No. 414), and the infused mushrooms and truffles; season with a dash of cayenne pepper, and let boil, skim and reduce it to a proper degree. Strain the sauce and keep it warm in a bain marie.

(465). FINNOISE SAUCE (Sauce à la Finnoise).

Put two gills of velouté (No. 415) into a saucepan with six tablespoonfuls of melted meat glaze (No. 401), a pinch of paprika and a pinch of sweet Spanish pepper and salt; mix all well together, let boil, and incorporate slowly into it six ounces of butter, working it in with a wire whisk, and then add a coffeespoonful of chopped up parsley just when prepared to serve.

(466). FLAVIGNAN SAUCE (Sauce à la Flavignan).

Pound half a pound of very fat chicken livers, two ounces of butter, one tablespoonful of chopped parsley and a pinch of finely cut tarragon; have three gills of port wine in a saucepan with one pint of espagnole (No. 414), add to it salt, pepper, coriander seeds, cinnamon and sugar, boil it for a few minutes, and then mix in the pounded livers, stirring them in well; boil again for a few minutes longer and strain through a tammy; finish with two ounces of butter before serving.

(467). FRENCH SAUCE (Sauce à la Française).

Reduce one pint of béchamel (No. 409), with two gills of mushroom essence (No. 392) in a saucepan, season with mignonette and nutmeg and half a small clove of crushed and chopped garlic, as well as a tablespoonful of meat glaze. Just when ready to serve incorporate into the sauce four ounces of crawfish butter (No. 573), strain through a tammy, then add a teaspoonful of vinegar and chopped parsley.

(468). GASCOGNE SAUCE AND WITH TOMATOES (Sauce Gascogne et aux Tomates).

Heat one gill of oil in a saucepan with two cloves of crushed and chopped garlic; add to this one teaspoonful of chopped parsley, the same quantity of chives. two ounces of chopped mushrooms, one ounce of chopped truffles, nutmeg, and mignonette, when all these ingredients are fried without coloring, add half a pint of white wine and one pint of velouté (No. 415). Boil, skim off the surface, reduce and pour in two gills of white wine; thicken with four egg-yolks diluted with half a gill of cream, and just when ready to serve incorporate into the sauce one ounce of anchovy butter (No. 569).

Gascogne and Tomato Sauce.—Add to the above sauce two gills of tomato purée (No. 730), previously strained through a very fine sieve.

(469). GENEVOISE SAUCE (Sauce Genevoise).

Place in a saucepan one pound of the head of salmon, moisten it with a bottleful of red wine, and a pint of fish broth or water; add four ounces of mushroom parings, a bunch of parsley garnished with bay leaf, as much thyme, and a clove of garlic, two shallots, and one minced onion, a teaspoonful of pepper corns, and half a teaspoonful of whole allspice; set it on the fire to boil and continue boiling slowly for half an hour. Strain the liquid through a fine sieve; reduce it with a pint of espagnole sauce (No. 414) and half a gill of Madeira wine; when the sauce is well reduced and despumated, work into it just when ready to serve, two ounces of anchovy butter (No. 569).

(470). GÉNOISE SAUCE (Sauce à la Génoise).

This sauce must not be confused with genevoise. Put into a saucepan two gills of vinegar, and two chopped shallots, let reduce till dry, then add a pint of espagnole (No. 414) and two gills of chicken essence (No. 387) or else fish essence (No. 388), according if needed for fat or lean; one ounce of chopped gherkins, two tablespoonfuls of small nonpareil capers, half an ounce of Sultana raisins and half an ounce of currants, a coffeespoonful of sugar, a dash of cayenne, mignonette, and nutmeg; reduce the whole to a proper consistency and add one gill of tomato purée; boil, despumate and reduce to the consistency of a light sauce. Serve this sauce with roasted or broiled poultry.

(471). GOOSEBERRY SAUCE (Sauce aux Groseilles Vertes à Maquereau).

Cut off the stalks and remove the black spots from half a pound of gooseberries; blanch them in an untinned copper vessel for two minutes, drain and add them to a pint of Hollandaise sauce (No. 477) or instead of using them whole they may be rubbed through a sieve and the pulp mixed with the Hollandaise sauce.

(472). GOURMETS SAUCE (Sauce des Gourmets).

Cut four tomatoes in two across, press out the seed and put them in a saucepan with parsley, thyme, bay leaf, salt, mignonette, and one small minced onion; boil for twenty minutes, drain and strain through a sieve; keep the liquid; then put a pint of the pulp into a saucepan with two gills of meat glaze (No. 401), beat them well together with a wire whisk, and stir in a quarter of a pound of lobster butter, adding a tablespoonful of wine vinegar, one pinch of minced tarragon and a tablespoonful of finely chopped and blanched shallots slightly fried in butter.

(473). GREEN SAUCE (Sauce Verte).

Pour into a saucepan one pint of white wine; add a tablespoonful of vinegar, two well chopped shallots, also the quarter of one bay leaf, two stalks of chives, two sprigs of thyme, and four branches of chervil; reduce the whole thoroughly, and then add to it one pint of velouté sauce (No. 415), a little cayenne pepper, and some spinach green; strain through a tammy, incorporate a few pieces of good butter and serve.

(474). GREEN HOLLANDAISE SAUCE (Sauce Hollandaise Verte).

Set into a saucepan five tablespoonfuls of flour, one tablespoonful of pepper corns, some thyme and bay leaves. Dilute this with a pint of water and boil while stirring so as to make a thick but smooth paste; cook it on a very slow fire for fifteen minutes, then take it off, let it get slightly cold, and add ten egg-yolks, afterward the butter and water, a very little at the time; using in all about two pounds of fresh butter and half a pound of ravigote butter, the juice of three lemons or simply a spoonful of vinegar; color with spinach green, and if too thick, thin it out with water, then strain through a tammy and keep it in a bain-marie at a moderate heat.

(475). GRIMOD SAUCE (Sauce à la Grimod).

Set in a bain-marie two raw egg-yolks, the juice of one lemon, salt, pepper, nutmeg, and mignonette, also a quarter of a pound of butter; beat the eggs and butter together over a slow fire using a small egg-beater; add a little cayenne pepper, a pinch of saffron leaves infused in half a gill of water; and when the sauce begins to get warm, strain it through a tammy, and keep it in a moderate temperature until needed to serve.

(476). HAM SAUCE AND HARLEQUIN SAUCE (Sauce au Jambon et à l'Arlequin).

Ham Sauce.—Place in a saucepan on the fire two ounces of butter, add to it two ounces of lean ham either scraped or finely chopped, and then fry it without letting it attain color, and moisten with a pint of cream ; reduce and add one pint of béchamel (No. 409); boil it again and thicken the sauce with six raw egg-yolks and half a pint more cream; and just when ready to serve throw in a teaspoonful of chopped parsley.

Harlequin Sauce.—Heat three ounces of butter in a saucepan, add half a pound of raw ham cut in three-sixteenth inch squares; fry without coloring, drain off the butter, take out the ham and detach the glaze with a little broth, adding four gills of espagnole sauce (No. 414), two of champagne, and two of veal blond (No. 423); reduce and despumate; strain through a tammy, add the ham, four ounces of gherkins cut in three-sixteenth inch squares, and four ounces of egg-white cut the same; also four ounces of carrots cut in same size squares, blanched and cooked in consommé with a little sugar, four ounces of cooked truffles cut the same as the carrots, and a heavy pinch of blanched parsley leaves.

(477). HOLLANDAISE SAUCE AND HOLLANDAISE MOUSSELINE SAUCE (Sauce Hollandaise et Sauce Hollandaise Mousseline).

Reduce half a gill of vinegar into which a coffeespoonful of white pepper corns has been added; remove it from the fire, and pour in about half a gill of cold water, five egg-yolks, two ounces of butter, salt, and grated nutmeg; set this saucepan into a larger one containing boiling water, or simply on a very slow fire; stir the contents constantly with a wire-egg beater, and as soon as the sauce becomes consistent add fresh butter divided into small pats, until six ounces have been consumed; squeeze in the juice of one lemon, more or less, according to taste, and if the sauce be too thick add a little more water to it; then strain it through a tammy (No. 159), pour it in the vessel described in Fig. 171, put it in a bain-marie not too hot, then stir it again constantly for a few minutes and serve.

Hollandaise Mousseline.—Reduce one gill of vinegar, with a few grains of pepper; take it off the fire, and when the liquid is nearly cold mix in with it five egg-yolks, beating them well with a wire whip, then add five ounces of fresh butter, salt, and nutmeg; set the saucepan over a slow fire, stir the preparation rapidly until the butter is melted, then strain the sauce through a sieve or tammy into another saucepan; set this one into another containing boiling water and keep it on the side of the range, working the sauce incessantly until it is thick and frothy, adding little by little a quarter of a pound of butter, and one pint of well-drained whipped cream; it is now ready to be served.

(478). HORSERADISH SAUCES WITH BREAD-CRUMBS, BÉCHAMEL OR CREAM (Sauces au Raifort à la mie de Pain, Béchamel ou Crème).

The horseradish needed for making sauces should be first scraped, then grated on a coarse grater. For plain horseradish, white sauce (No. 562), butter (No. 440) or Hollandaise sauces (No. 477) are used. The horseradish should never be cooked in the sauce, it must only be put in, in order to heat it.

Horseradish Sauce with Bread-crumbs.—Soak two ounces of bread-crumbs in hot water, then squeeze. Cook with broth in a saucepan for a few minutes, finishing with an ounce of butter, two spoonfuls of raw cream, salt, and a pinch of sugar. At the last moment add the grated horseradish to the sauce. This sauce is also frequently prepared with plain velouté (No. 415), lightly reduced and finished with three spoonfuls of raw cream. This sauce must be passed through a tammy (No. 159) and then the grated horseradish added.

Horseradish Sauce Béchamel, is made by pouring a pint of well seasoned béchamel into a saucepan; season with salt, cayenne, and sugar; take it off at the first boil, and add one gill of cream, and one ounce of fresh butter, also six ounces of grated horseradish; warm the sauce without boiling.

Horseradish and Cream.—Reduce a pint of cream to one-third, add to it salt, nutmeg, sugar and eight ounces of grated horseradish; warm it up and thicken with half a gill more of cream, two egg-yolks, and two ounces of butter.

(479). HUNGARIAN SAUCE (Sauce à la Hongroise).

Pour into a saucepan, the value of half a pint of tomato purée (No. 730) cooked plain, which means drained, but not thickened, also the same quantity of onion purée (No. 723), a gill of melted meat glaze (No. 401), and a pinch of paprika; let it all boil while stirring for two minutes, then remove it to the side of the range, and incorporate slowly into it, five ounces of butter, divided into small pats, without ceasing to stir.

(480). HUNTER'S SAUCE (Sauce au Chasseur).

Put two ounces of butter into a saucepan, with two shallots cut in one-eighth inch dice; fry them a light golden color, and then moisten with one pint of espagnole (No. 414), and one pint of game stock; season, and boil on one side only, to despumate, then add half a bottle of Bordeaux, one ounce of cooked lean ham cut into small three-sixteenth inch squares, and two ounces of mushrooms. This sauce may be thickened with two gills of liquid game blood mixed with a tablespoonful of good vinegar; thicken it without boiling, strain the sauce through a tammy and serve.

(481). HUNTRESS SAUCE (Sauce à la Chasseresse).

Put into a saucepan on the fire, two ounces of butter with two spoonfuls of chopped onions; fry these for a few minutes, then add two ounces of chopped fresh mushrooms and two ounces of unsmoked, salted beef tongue cut into dice pieces three-sixteenths of an inch. After the humidity from the mushrooms has evaporated, let them fry together without coloring. Moisten with a quart of game stock (No. 195), and half a bottle of champagne, add a bunch of parsley garnished with a bay leaf and as much thyme, and then continue to boil slowly for half an hour; strain the sauce through a fine sieve, and thicken it with four tablespoonfuls of bread-crumbs, adding one ounce of butter, a teaspoonful of chopped parsley and the juice of a lemon.

(482). HUSSARDE SAUCE (Sauce à la Hussarde).

Fry in a saucepan two ounces of lean ham with two ounces of butter, adding two ounces of onions, two cut-up, blanched celery roots, all cut in squares, moisten with half a pint of broth (No. 194a) and half a pint of white wine; add a bunch of parsley garnished with a bay leaf and as much thyme, a clove of garlic and a pinch of tarragon; let the whole boil for half an hour, and then thicken it with two ounces of butter kneaded with one ounce of flour, squeeze in the juice of a lemon, strain the sauce through a tammy and mingle in with it two ounces of grated fresh horseradish.

(483). INDIAN SAUCE (Sauce à l'Indienne).

Put two ounces of butter into a saucepan with two ounces of onions, two ounces of lean unsmoked ham, one ounce of celery and a bunch of parsley garnished with thyme and two cloves of garlic. Moisten with two gills of veal blond (No. 423), one quart of espagnole (No. 414) or velouté (No. 415) (if velouté is used thicken with four egg-yolks and half a gill of cream), add one tablespoonful of pepper corns, three cloves, one pinch of saffron, and one teaspoonful of curry. Reduce all this and then strain it through a tammy (Fig. 88), and just when ready to serve incorporate into it two ounces of fresh butter.

(484). ITALIAN SAUCE (Sauce à l'Italienne).

Place a tablespoonful of olive oil and two ounces of butter in a saucepan with two ounces of onions, and four shallots, all chopped up; a bunch of parsley garnished with a bay leaf and the same quantity of thyme, two cloves and one clove of garlic, two ounces of ham cut in squares, fry all these without letting them attain color, add a quarter of a pound of chopped mushrooms; moisten with one gill of white wine and three gills of veal blond (No. 423), salt, red pepper and nutmeg to season, add a quart of espagnole (No. 414), or velouté (No. 415), skim off and reduce the sauce; suppress the parsley, just when ready to serve add the juice of a lemon and a teaspoonful of chopped parsley. For Italian sauce with truffles add two ounces of chopped truffles.

(485). JUVIGNY SAUCE (Sauce Juvigny).

This sauce is made by putting a teaspoonful of chives and the same quantity of parsley, both finely chopped, into a saucepan with two ounces of butter, set it on the fire and add to it one tablespoonful of shallots; fry all lightly without coloring, then put in one pint of velouté (No. 415), one gill of white wine, some salt, pepper, and nutmeg, let boil up for a few minutes; despumate well, and just when serving stir in a tablespoonful of small capers.

(486). LAGUIPIERRE SAUCE (Sauce à la Laguipierre).

Pour into a saucepan a quarter of a bottleful of white wine or champagne, add to it two ounces of chopped mushrooms, one tablespoonful of chopped and blanched shallots, half a clove of garlic, one bay leaf, six grains of allspice, eighteen grains of pepper, and let all these simmer together with two gills of veal blond (No. 423) for fifteen minutes, then add one pint of velouté (No. 415), and one gill of reduced mushroom essence (No. 392); thicken the sauce with four egg-yolks and one gill of cream, strain the whole through a tammy (No. 159), and then beat into it two ounces of fresh butter and the juice of one lemon.

(487). LITHUANIAN SAUCE (Sauce à la Lithuanienne).

Knead together in a saucepan four ounces of butter with one and a half ounces of fresh bread-crumbs, add the juice of one lemon; two spoonfuls of meat glaze (No. 401), some nutmeg and mignonette. Set this on a moderate fire, and stir the preparation without letting it boil; just when ready to serve, add one tablespoonful of chopped parsley, dilute it with stock (No. 423); see that the sauce is not too thick.

(488). LOBSTER SAUCE, LOBSTER SAUCE WITH MADEIRA WINE AND LOBSTER SAUCE WITH LOBSTER BUTTER (Sauce Homard, Sauce Homard au Vin de Madère et Sauce au Beurre de Homard).

Lobster Sauce.—Place a pint of velouté sauce (No. 415), in a saucepan with pepper corns, thyme, bay leaf and a tablespoonful of chopped and blanched onions, cook all together, then strain through a tammy (No. 159); just when ready to serve incorporate in a piece of lobster butter (No. 580), and a dash of vinegar.

Lobster Sauce with Madeira Wine.—Put into a saucepan two gills of dry Madeira wine, one chopped shallot a pinch of parsley leaves, mignonette and grated nutmeg, reduce with two gills of broth, and when well reduced add one pint of allemande sauce (No. 407) and two ounces of very red lobster butter (No. 580), strain through a tammy and drop in one ounce of lobster meat cut in three-sixteenth of an inch squares.

Lobster Sauce with Lobster Butter.—Have in a saucepan half velouté sauce (No. 415) and half Hollandaise (No. 477), a little water, salt, mignonette and nutmeg. When the sauce is very hot incorporate in a piece of lobster butter and some chopped parsley.

(489). LOMBARDE SAUCE (Sauce Lombarde).

Have in a saucepan half a bottleful of white wine, add to it two ounces of butter, one teaspoonful of chopped parsley, two finely chopped and blanched shallots and a quarter of a pound of chopped mushrooms. Let all simmer till the liquid is reduced, then add a pint of béchamel (No. 409), and a gill of cream, also the juice of a lemon and a pinch of mignonette.

(490). SAUCE À LA LUCULLUS (Sauce à la Lucullus).

Garnish the bottom of a thick bottomed buttered saucepan with four onions cut in slices, four ounces of sliced ham, one pound of sliced veal and half a pound of game fragments, moisten with one pint of veal blond (No. 423). Set this on a slow fire and let reduce to a glaze, then remoisten with two and a half quarts more broth, adding a bunch of parsley, as much celery, and two bay leaves, with an equal quantity of thyme, four cloves, two ounces of truffle parings and four ounces of mushrooms, let it boil until perfectly cooked, then strain through a tammy and reduce it to the consistency of a thick syrup, and add one quart of velouté (No. 415) or espagnole (No. 414); for either one or the other have two spoonfuls of meat glaze (No. 401), then put in four ounces of truffles cut in balls and four ounces of channeled mushrooms; mix well with the sauce and serve.

(491). LYONNESE SAUCE WITH TARRAGON (Sauce Lyonnaise à l'Estragon).

Cut up eight ounces of onions into three-sixteenth inch squares; blanch, then drain and fry them in two gills of oil or else six ounces of butter; when nearly done, put them into a saucepan with one pint of veal blond (No. 423), one pint of espagnole (No. 414) or velouté sauce (No. 415), and one tablespoonful of meat glaze (No. 401); reduce it, then add the juice of a lemon, some nutmeg, and mignonette. Strain the sauce through a tammy (No. 159), then incorporate into it four ounces of butter and a teaspoonful of tarragon leaves finely shredded and blanched.

(492). MADEIRA SAUCE, OR SHERRY, MARSALA, ETC. (Sauce au vin de Madère, au Xérès, ou au Marsala, etc.).

Reduce well one pint of espagnole (No. 414), adding slowly to it one gill of veal blond (No. 423), or chicken stock (No. 195) and a few truffle parings; when the sauce is well reduced, incorporate into it by degrees, two gills of Madeira wine or any other preferred. As soon as the sauce is finished, pass through a tammy and keep warm in a bain-marie.

(493). MAÎTRE D'HÔTEL SAUCE, THICKENED (Sauce à la Maître d'Hôtel, Liée).

Put into a high saucepan three gills of velouté (No. 415) or béchamel (No. 409) with two gills of water; let it warm up and then add to it slowly half a pound of butter, working it in well, pass through a tammy; season with the juice of a lemon, some salt and pepper, and should the sauce be too thick then add a little more water; strain again through a tammy, add one teaspoonful of chopped parsley.

(494). SAUCE À LA MANTAISE (Sauce à la Mantaise).

Pound four ounces of chicken fat livers with two ounces of beef marrow; fry in two ounces of butter, two ounces of mushrooms, one teaspoonful of chopped parsley, two chopped shallots, and one crushed clove of garlic; let this get cold, and then pound it well adding to it the pounded livers and marrow; with this preparation fill a mold well lined with bardes of fat pork, and cook it in the oven for an hour, then unmold it over a sieve to drain. Dilute this mixture with a pint of espagnole (No. 414) or velouté (No. 415), and one or two gills of chicken essence (No. 387); strain it through a tammy, and beat up the sauce well before serving.

(495). SAUCE À LA MARCEAU (Sauce à la Marceau).

Keep in a bain-marie, three pints of espagnole (No. 414) reduced with some game fumet (No. 397) and Madeira wine. Cook in plenty of salted water, in a covered vessel, one dozen peeled cloves of garlic, until very tender, then drain them; wipe them dry on a cloth, and fry them for a few minutes in a pan, with some melted butter till the moisture is thoroughly evaporated, then rub them through a sieve and afterward through a tammy (No. 159), and add this purée slowly into the sauce; stir well, and pour it into a sauceboat.

(496). MARINADE SAUCE (Sauce Marinade).

Cut into thin slices a quarter of a pound of carrots and as many onions; lay them in a sauce-pan with two ounces of butter, and a bunch of parsley garnished with a bay leaf, as much thyme, basil, and a clove of garlic, two minced shallots, and four cloves. Fry the whole lightly without coloring in the butter, and then moisten with two quarts of water, and one pint of vinegar or more according to strength, and a tablespoonful of peppercorns; let cook for one hour, then strain through a sieve, return it to the fire, and reduce to half; add one quart of espagnole (No. 414) and reduce again to the consistency of a sauce.

(497). MARINIÈRE SAUCE (Sauce Marinière).

Have two ounces of onions cut into small three-sixteenth inch squares; fry them colorless in two ounces of butter, then moisten them with a gill of white wine, adding one tablespoonful of brandy, two ounces of finely chopped mushrooms, one pint of velouté (No. 415), two gills of veal blond (No. 423) or fish stock (No. 195) (if for lean), salt, pepper, nutmeg, one clove of garlic, one bay leaf, and as much thyme. Let cook, despumate for half an hour, skim well the surface, and add another gill of white wine, then strain the sauce through a tammy (No. 159), and just when ready to serve, throw in a teaspoonful of chopped parsley.

(498). MATELOTTE SAUCE (Sauce Matelotte).

Cut in slices one pound of pike, half a pound of eels, and half a pound of carp; put these into a saucepan with minced carrots and onions, two ounces of each, half a handful of parsley and basil, two small cloves of garlic, bay leaf, thyme, salt and allspice; pour in half a bottleful of Bordeaux wine, and half a pint of fish broth or water; let boil for ten minutes, then drain and add to the liquid either half a pint of espagnole sauce (No. 414), or some kneaded butter; reduce, dilute with a gill of Bordeaux wine, and finally incorporate into it, two ounces of fresh butter. Just when ready to serve throw into the sauce, half a pound of mushrooms, and twenty-four small white onions lightly browned in a pan and cooked in broth.

A More Simple Way, is to fry a little minced onions and shallot in butter, and when a nice color drain off the butter and moisten the onions with two gills of Burgundy wine; let the liquid reduce to half and then incorporate four gills of espagnole sauce (No. 414); let reduce once more, and after the sauce is properly done, strain it through a sieve, and keep it warm.

(499). SAUCE À LA MILANESE (Sauce à la Milanaise).

Have two ounces of butter in a saucepan with one ounce of minced, raw ham and two table spoonfuls of chopped shallot; fry them without coloring, and then add a small handful of parsley and basil, a bay leaf and as much thyme, one ounce of chopped mushrooms, a pinch of cayenne, a bit of mace, two cloves, one coffeespoonful of sugar, the juice of a lemon, half a gill of dry Madeira, and a pint of consommé (No 189). Boil all and reduce it to half, then add one pint of allemande sauce (No. 407), and strain the whole through a tammy (No. 159), afterward incorporating into it two ounces of fine butter. A garnishing should be added to this sauce of pignolas, cooked spaghetti cut in half inch lengths, cooked ham and mushrooms cut in half inch sticks and an eighth of an inch square.

(500). SAUCE À LA MIRABEAU (Sauce à la Mirabeau).

Pound three hard boiled egg-yolks with a handful of chervil and two tablespoonfuls of capers, adding a quarter of a pound of butter, a clove of garlic chopped and crushed; then rub the mixture through a sieve. Put into a saucepan a quart of velouté (No. 415) and two gills of chicken stock (No. 195); let it boil up; despumate the surface and reduce the whole, afterward adding very slowly the prepared butter, working it in the sauce with a whisk, season highly and strain through a tammy, heating it again before using.

(501). MODERN HOLLANDAISE SAUCE (Sauce Hollandaise Moderne).

Modern Hollandaise is made as follows: Melt two pounds of butter in a saucepan without heat-ing it too much, then let it settle, and pour off the top. Beat twelve egg-yolks in a saucepan with half a pint of water. Set the saucepan on a slow fire, and stir the contents continuously with a whisk; and as soon as the eggs become consistent incorporate into them the butter previously melted, little by little, some salt and mignonette; or else a dash of cayenne instead of the mi-gnonette, and besides this the juice of four lemons. If the sauce be too thick add a little water, and then pass it through a tammy (No. 159). Put the sauce in the mixing pot (Fig. 171); keep it in a bain-marie, not too hot, until needed.

(502). SAUCE À LA MONTEBELLO (Sauce à la Montebello).

Prepare one pint of thick bearnaise sauce (No. 433). and incorporate into it three gills of well reduced tomato sauce (No. 549), then strain the whole through a very fine sieve, and dilute it with two gills of champagne.

(503). SAUCE À LA MONTIGNY AND TOMATO EXTRACT (Sauce à la Montigny et à l'Extrait de Tomates).

Put into a saucepan two ounces of fresh butter and two teaspoonfuls of chopped shallots; let fry colorless with a bunch of parsley garnished with thyme and bay leaf; cook together for five minutes, then moisten with two gills of tomato extract, a gill of meat glaze (No. 401), three gills of espagnole sauce (No. 414), a pinch of powdered sugar, a pint of velouté (No. 415), chopped parsley and lemon juice.

Tomato Extract.—Cook some tomatoes for half an hour; strain them through a coarse sieve, put them on a piece of muslin over a vessel to retain all the falling liquid, and reduce this liquid to a thick syrup.

(504). SAUCE À LA MORNAY (Sauce à la Mornay).

After reducing a good béchamel sauce (No. 409), stir into it incessantly a few spoonfuls of mushroom sauce (No. 392) and some raw cream, also essence of fish (No. 388), should this sauce be needed for fish; but if otherwise then use a few spoonfuls of good chicken stock (No. 195) reduced to a half-glaze. When the sauce becomes succulent and creamy, pour it into a small saucepan, beat it smooth while heating it, and finish it off of the fire with some butter and grated parmesan cheese. This sauce is used for dishes that are bread-crumbed and for meats baked by a salamander. Its delicacy forbids it being boiled.

(505). MUSHROOM SAUCE (Sauce aux Champignons).

Turn and wash half a pound of small mushroom heads (No. 118); put them into a saucepan with the juice of a lemon, and a piece of butter the size of a walnut, some salt and a gill of water. When they are cooked, after three minutes, drain, and put the liquid back into a saucepan with a pint of velouté (No. 415) or espagnole (No. 414), either fat or lean according to its requirements, then reduce and despumate the sauce. Just when ready to serve incorporate into it two ounces of butter and the cooked mushrooms.

(506). MUSSEL SAUCE (Sauce aux Moules).

Scrape eighteen mussels, wash them clean in several waters, and put them into a saucepan with half a gill of water, some vinegar and pepper, but no salt, sprigs of parsley and minced onions; cover the saucepan, set it on the fire, and toss it several times until they open, then take them from their shells, cut off their black parts, and strain the broth after it has well settled; pour off the clear part, leaving the sediment at the bottom, and strain this through a sieve. Put one pint of velouté (No. 415) into a saucepan, also two gills of the mussel broth; reduce, and thicken with four raw egg-yolks, a little nutmeg, half a gill of cream, two ounces of butter, and the juice of a lemon; strain the whole through a tammy (No. 159), and finish by adding a small coffeespoonful of chopped parsley and the eighteen cooked mussels; warm well and serve.

(507). NEAPOLITAN SAUCE (Sauce Napolitaine).

Put two ounces of cooked, lean, and well chopped ham into a saucepan with a bunch of parsley garnished with a bay leaf, and as much thyme, some mignonette, nutmeg and cayenne, two gills of Madeira wine, and two gills of broth; let reduce to half on a slow fire, then suppress the bunch of parsley, and add one pint of espagnole (No. 414); boil it up again, despumate, and strain it through a tammy (No. 159), put it back to reduce once more, adding to it two gills of Malaga wine, and a quarter of a pound of current jelly, dissolving the latter slowly by degrees, and two spoonfuls of grated horseradish.

(508). NONPAREIL SAUCE (Sauce Nonpareille).

Reduce one pint of velouté (No. 415), with two gills of cream, incorporating in two ounces of fresh butter; strain it through a tammy (No. 159), and set in one ounce of truffles, two ounces of mushrooms, two ounces of cooked egg-whites cut in squares, two tablespoonfuls of chopped coral, one teaspoonful of chopped parsley, one tablespoonful of small capers, and three ounces of red beef tongue or ham cut into three-sixteenths of an inch pieces.

(509). SAUCE À LA NORMANDE (Sauce à la Normande).

Cut three pounds of bony fish into pieces, such as sheepshead, bass, blackfish, redsnapper, etc., let the pieces be of a quarter of a pound each; put them into a saucepan with two minced onions, two ounces of mushroom parings, some parsley, a bay leaf, the same quantity of thyme and two cloves of garlic, moisten with a quarter of a bottle of white wine, three pints of water, two gills of oyster liquor and let the whole cook slowly for thirty minutes, then strain the sauce through a fine sieve, and add to it one quart of velouté (No. 415), another quarter of a bottle of white wine, and reduce it all; just when ready to serve, thicken the sauce with four egg-yolks and incorporate into it two ounces of butter and the juice of a lemon; season well and finish by straining once more through a tammy (No. 159).

(510). OLIVE SAUCE (Sauce aux Olives).

Verdal or Spanish' Olives, Stuffed or Not Stuffed.—Remove the stones from two ounces of olives without injuring their shape, then throw them into boiling, salted water, drain them after they have boiled up once or twice, and put them into a pint of reduced and clear espagnole (No. 414). The empty spaces in the olives may be filled with a chicken quenelle forcemeat (No. 89), mixed with anchovy butter (No. 569); poach and drain, and stir them into the sauce.

(511). ORANGE SAUCE (Sauce à l'Orange).

Shred the peel of an orange as finely as possible, throw the pieces into boiling water, and let them cook for five minutes, then drain and put them into a saucepan with two gills of beef juice, three gills of espagnole (No. 414), the juice of two oranges and of one lemon, and a pinch of cayenne pepper.

(512). SAUCE À LA D'ORLÉANS (Sauce à la d'Orléans).

Fry lightly in one ounce of butter three chopped shallots; add a tablespoonful of meat glaze (No. 401), and one pint of allemande sauce (No. 407), and incorporate into it half a pound of crawfish butter (No. 573) and a pinch of cayenne pepper; strain through a tammy and serve.

(513). OYSTER SAUCE (Sauce aux Huîtres).

Poach in white wine one dozen small oysters; strain the juice and leave it to settle. Put on the fire to reduce three gills of velouté sauce (No. 415), and stir into it slowly one gill of good fish stock (No. 195) and the oyster juice, thickening the whole with half a gill of cream, and two egg-yolks; season with salt, pepper, nutmeg, and the juice of a lemon; then strain the sauce, add a little butter to it, also the oysters and some chopped parsley.

(514). SAUCE À LA PALERMITAINE (Sauce à la Palermitaine).

Place all together in a saucepan one ounce of cooked, minced ham, one ounce of chopped pignolas, one clove of garlic, one gill of oil, eight tomatoes washed, cut across in two and well pressed, a bunch of parsley garnished with as much bay leaf as thyme, mignonette, nutmeg and two cloves. Let all cook, then drain, and strain forcibly through a fine sieve, reduce together both the broth and purée, adding to it two gills of white wine, a teaspoonful of sugar, three gills of broth, one quart of allemande (No. 407), four ounces of butter, and the pulp of a lemon.

(515). PARISIAN SAUCE (Sauce Parisienne).

To make the essence, cook two ounces of truffle parings in three gills of boiling dry white wine with some parsley, bay leaf, and a small minced shallot, then leave it for half an hour in a high covered saucepan in a bain-marie before draining it over a sieve. Pour this essence into a pint of velouté (No. 415); reduce and add two spoonfuls of meat or chicken glaze (No. 398), a pinch of cayenne, and stir in just when ready to serve two ounces of butter and the juice of a lemon.

(516). PÉRIGORD SAUCE (Sauce Périgord).

Peel eight ounces of medium sized fresh Périgord truffles; cook them for five minutes with salt and Madeira wine, then remove them from the fire and keep them in the covered saucepan. Make an infusion with two gills of Madeira wine, one ounce of raw ham, the truffle peelings, thyme and bay leaf, and a few sprigs of parsley. Put on the fire to reduce, four gills of good velouté (No. 415), and incorporate into it slowly, one gill of cream, and the same quantity of the Madeira wine infusion already prepared. When the sauce is succulent and sufficiently consistent, strain and pour it into a saucepan, mixing in with it the cooked truffles cut into thin slices; keep the sauce warm in a bain-marie.

(517). PÉRIGUEUX SAUCE (Sauce Périgueux).

Peel three ounces of fresh truffles; cook them with some salt and Madeira wine; remove them from the fire and keep them in a covered vessel. Infuse in two gills of boiling Madeira wine, one ounce of raw ham cut into dices, the truffle peelings, some thyme, bay leaf, and sprigs of parsley. Put on the fire to reduce, one pint of espagnole (No. 414), stir slowly into it, one gill of veal blond (No. 423), and the same quantity of Madeira infusion. When the sauce is succulent and sufficiently consistent, strain it, and set it into a saucepan with a few spoonfuls of the cooked truffles cut into eighth of an inch squares.

Another way is to infuse in two gills of Madeira wine, one ounce of truffle peelings with a little thyme and bay leaf, leaving them in for thirty minutes. Pour into a saucepan a pint of espagnole sauce (No. 414) with essence of ham (No. 390), a little mignonette, and two gills of chicken or game stock (No. 195), then reduce and strain the sauce through a tammy (No. 159). Place in another saucepan two ounces of truffles cut in small one-eighth inch squares with two gills of Madeira wine, reduce it until dry, and incorporate into the sauce just when ready to serve one ounce of fresh butter.

(518). PICKLE SAUCE (Sauce aux Cornichons).

Slice two ounces of pickles into thin pieces, and lay them in a saucepan with one gill of vinegar and a pinch of mignonette; let it boil up quickly and reduce it to half its quantity, then add one pint of espagnole (No 414), two gills of veal blond (No. 423), a bay leaf, and as much thyme. Despumate the sauce for fifteen minutes, then suppress the bay leaf and thyme, and serve.

(519). PIEDMONTESE SAUCE (Sauce Piémontaise).

Fry lightly without coloring in two ounces of clarified butter, four ounces of onions, when done, drain the butter, and finish cooking them in one pint of veal blond (No. 423). Skim off all the fat, and then pour in a pint of béchamel (No. 409) or espagnole (No. 414), reduce and add two ounces of white Piemont truffles cut in squares; just when ready to serve, stir in an ounce of garlic butter (No. 576) mixed with anchovy butter (No. 569); then add a dash of cayenne pepper and the juice of a lemon.

(520). PIGNOLA SAUCE, ITALIAN STYLE (Sauce aux Pignons à l'Italienne).

Put two ounces of brown sugar in a saucepan with three gills of good vinegar, three gills of veal blond (No. 423), and a bunch of parsley garnished with a bay leaf and thyme, some mignonette and nutmeg. Let the whole simmer over a slow fire, and reduce it to half. Then add a pint of espagnole (No. 414) and two gills of red wine; reduce again and put in four ounces of pignolas, let them boil in the sauce and serve.

(521). PIMENTADE SAUCE (Sauce Pimentade).

Cut up into quarter inch squares a quarter of a pound of lean veal and two ounces of onions, a quarter of a pound of raw, lean ham, then add a small clove of crushed garlic, put all these into a saucepan with some butter and let cook slowly. Fry some sweet Spanish peppers in oil after removing the skins; also some green peppers having both finely chopped, add these to the ham, veal and onions and then add a little good gravy and espagnole sauce (No. 414), also a little tomato purée (No. 730). Boil all together, season properly, skim off the fat and serve.

(522). POIVRADE SAUCE (Sauce Poivrade).

For Fat Poivrade à l'Espagnole.—Have a pint of poivrade (No. 523), half a pint of espagnole (No. 414), half a pint of veal blond (No. 423), and reduce all till properly done, season well.

For Lean Poivrade.—Suppress the ham from the poivrade (No. 523), and replace it by sturgeon, and the fat stock by some lean stock (No. 195).

For White Poivrade with Velouté.—Reduce two gills of white wine to half, adding some white peppers, aromatic herbs and mushroom parings. Put into this reduced stock three gills of velouté sauce (No. 415), with a little glaze (No. 401), and then stir in slowly a few spoonfuls of good stock (No. 423); when the sauce becomes succulent, set it into a deep saucepan, and if not used at once in a bain-marie.

(523). POIVRADE FOR SAUCES (Poivrade pour Sauces).

Not to be mistaken for poivrade sauce. Put into a saucepan four ounces of butter with half a pound of onions and six shallots, both cut into one-eighth inch squares, also a pound of carrots, half a pound of lean ham cut in three-sixteenth inch squares, a tablespoonful of pepper corns or else a teaspoonful of mignonette, a bunch of parsley garnished with two bay leaves, a clove of garlic and four cloves. Fry the whole slowly without coloring; then moisten with one pint of vinegar and a pint of veal blond (No. 423), reduce all until dry, and moisten once more with a pint of veal blond and two gills of white wine, also three pints of espagnole (No. 414). Boil slowly, despumate for an hour, and strain through a sieve.

(524). POLISH SAUCE (Sauce à la Polonaise).

Place in a deep saucepan, two tablespoonfuls of grated fresh horseradish, one coffeespoonful of powdered sugar, with one tablespoonful of meat glaze (No. 401), and a pint of velouté (No. 415); squeeze in the juice of a lemon, add the chopped peel of a quarter of a lemon with a teaspoonful of chopped parsley or fennel, season with salt, pepper and nutmeg, set the saucepan in a bain-marie and when ready to serve incorporate two ounces of fresh butter into the sauce.

(525). POMPADOUR SAUCE (Sauce Pompadour).

Fry lightly in two ounces of butter two finely chopped shallots, do not let them color; add to them four ounces of minced mushrooms; stir with a spoon until they have exhausted all their moisture; now pour in five gills of velouté (No. 415) and let the whole boil, with three gills of veal blond (No. 423), despumating it well. Thicken the sauce with six raw egg-yolks diluted in a gill of cream, add two ounces of butter, salt, pepper, and nutmeg, also a spoonful of chopped and blanched parsley.

(526). PORTUGUESE SAUCE (Sauce à la Portugaise).

Rub on a loaf of sugar, the peel of one lemon and one orange; scrape the sugar off with a spoon to obtain the part colored by the peels, then put this in a saucepan with a coffeespoonful of coriander seeds and two gills of port wine; set the pan on the fire and when a white foam rises to the top, remove it at once and cover. Half an hour later pour the wine through a fine sieve and add to it three gills of béchamel sauce (No. 409), and two of tomato purée (No. 730); let the sauce boil up once then strain it through a tammy; add to it the juices of both the lemon and orange, besides a spoonful of chopped parsley.

(527). POULETTE SAUCE (Sauce à la Poulette).

Pour a pint of velouté (No. 415) into a saucepan; let it boil, then thicken it with four raw egg-yolks diluted with a little cream; add at the last moment two ounces of butter, the juice of a lemon and some chopped parsley.

(528). PRINCESS SAUCE (Sauce à la Princesse).

Put one pint of béchamel (No. 409) into a saucepan, adding to it two tablespoonfuls of chicken glaze (No. 398), one gill of cream, and some grated nutmeg; stir in just when ready to serve, four ounces of fresh butter, a teaspoonful of chopped parsley, and the juice of one lemon.

(529). PROVENÇAL SAUCE, FAT OR LEAN (Sauce à la Provençale en Gras ou en Maigre).

Fry lightly in two gills of oil, half a pound of minced onions, two ounces of ham (or smoked salmon, if for lean), a pinch of parsley leaves, a crushed and chopped clove of garlic, thyme, bay leaf, mignonette, nutmeg, a pinch of ground cloves; dilute with a pint of fish stock (No.195), if for lean, or veal blond (No. 423) if for fat; let cook, despumate, and when the broth is reduced to a third, add a pint of espagnole (No. 414), if for brown or allemande (No. 407) if for white; one or the other, for fat or lean. Stir in two ounces of fresh butter and the juice of a lemon to finish.

(530). QUEEN SAUCE (Sauce à la Reine).

Set into a saucepan, an ounce and a half of fresh bread-crumbs, and one pint of chicken essence (No. 387); pound two ounces of sweet almonds freshly peeled with two gills of cream, and press this forcibly through a napkin. Pound two hard boiled egg-yolks, with two ounces of fresh butter; season with salt, cayenne, and nutmeg, rub it through a sieve, then add this to the bread-crumbs, seasoning with salt, cayenne, and nutmeg, and also the cream almond milk, besides three gills of fresh cream. Chopped truffles may also be added to this sauce.

(531). RAVIGOTE SAUCES, AROMATIC, WHITE, WITH OIL AND GREEN PRINTANIÈRE (Sauces Ravigote, Aromatique, Blanche, à l'Huile et Printanière Verte).

Aromatic Ravigote.—Fry in one ounce of butter, two ounces of onions, moisten with two gills of Chablis wine, three gills of consommé, (No 189) and the juice of a lemon; add a piece of garlic the size of a pea, two chopped shallots, one ounce of chopped, pickled cucumbers, half an ounce of capers, some parsley roots cut in Julienne and blanched, branches of tarragon leaves, four cloves, two bay leaves, as much thyme, and some nutmeg; boil the whole slowly for half an hour, then strain it through a fine sieve; add this to one quart of espagnole (No. 414). Reduce and add two spoonfuls of mustard; strain the whole through a tammy (No. 159) and incorporate into it two ounces of fresh butter, a teaspoonful of chopped chervil and half a teaspoonful of tarragon leaves, finely cut-up.

White Ravigote.—Infuse in one gill of vinegar, a quarter of an ounce of chervil, a quarter of an ounce of tarragon, and a quarter of an ounce of pimpernel; add to the infusion one pint of velouté (No. 415) and one gill of white wine, then boil together for ten minutes; strain through a tammy (No. 159) and beat into the sauce two ounces of butter and a teaspoonful of chopped parsley.

Hot Ravigote with Oil.—Set into a saucepan three tablespoonfuls of chopped shallots with one gill of vinegar and three gills of white wine, reduce the liquid to half, then add to it a quart of velouté (No. 415), beat it up with a wire whisk and stir into it three gills of oil, putting in a very little at a time and continuing to beat, then add a teaspoonful of mustard, a pinch of tarragon and the same of chopped chervil.

Green Ravigote Printanière.—After picking and washing half an ounce each of chervil, tarragon, chives and pimpernel, blanch them all in a copper vessel containing boiling, salted water, leave them to boil for a few minutes, then drain and refresh them; drain once more, and press out all the water. Pound these herbs well, and mingle with them four ounces of butter, color with spinach green (No. 37) then rub the whole through a sieve, stir well this butter into a pint of velouté, (No. 415) add to it a spoonful of good vinegar some pepper and nutmeg; pass this sauce through a tammy (No. 159).

(532). RÉGENCE SAUCE (Sauce à la Régence).

For Fat.—Set four ounces of butter in a saucepan, add four ounces of chopped onions; fry lightly and add two ounces of ham cut in three-sixteenth inch squares, eight ounces of minced mushrooms or their parings, branches of parsley, two bay leaves, as much thyme, two cloves and mignonette; fry all these ingredients together without coloring, moisten with two quarts of espagnole (No. 414) and a pint of chicken stock (No. 195), cook the whole for forty-five minutes, skim and pass through a tammy (No. 159). Put in a saucepan on the fire, three gills of white Bordeaux; when reduced to half, add a quarter of a pound of peeled truffles; heat well and put this in with the above sauce.

For Lean.—Use fish stock (No.195) instead of fat chicken stock, suppress the ham and replace it by sturgeon or carp.

(533). ROBERT SAUCE (Sauce à la Robert).

Fry slowly in a saucepan two white onions weighing six ounces, and cut into small squares, with two ounces of butter, in such a way that they are half cooked without browning, then drain off the butter, and moisten the onions with two gills of consommé (No. 189), and one gill of white wine; reduce the sauce to a glaze, then moisten once more with three gills of espagnole sauce (No. 414), reduced with one gill of veal blond (No. 423); add a coffeespoonful of sugar, a teaspoonful of vinegar, a tablespoonful of mustard, and a pinch of cayenne; let boil for a few minutes to enable the fat to be skimmed off, and keep the sauce warm in a bain-marie.

(534). ROMAN SAUCE (Sauce Romaine).

Mince two ounces of celery root and put it into a saucepan with a coffeespoonful of coriander seeds, the same quantity of powdered sugar, a small clove of garlic crushed and chopped, a bunch of parsley and basil garnished with two bay leaves, and a quarter of a bottleful of champagne; let simmer for thirty minutes, then add one pint of espagnole (No. 414), and one gill of veal blond (No. 423); strain the whole through a tammy, and stir in two ounces of fresh butter and the juice of a lemon, also two ounces of Sultana raisins washed and boiled in half a gill of Madeira wine.

(535). RUSSIAN SAUCE (Sauce à la Russe).

Have two tablespoonfuls of grated horseradish in a saucepan with one pint of velouté (No. 415), a teaspoonful of chopped chives, a coffeespoonful of finely cut tarragon, a tablespoonful of mustard, and one gill of cream; season with salt and pepper, and add one teaspoonful of sugar, the juice of a lemon, and a heavy pinch of finely minced fennel, heat the sauce without boiling.

(536). SALMIS SAUCE, WITH WHITE WINE, WITH CHAMPAGNE, WITH RED WINE AND TRUFFLES (Sauce Salmis, au vin Blanc au Champagne, au vin Rouge et aux Truffes).

With White Wine.—Fry in butter without coloring the broken carcasses of six quails or three partridges; add to this half a bottleful of white wine and some broth, a garnished bunch of parsley and a few mushroom parings, then let boil slowly for one hour. Make an espagnole sauce (No. 414) with this fumet, and when properly reduced add to it the pounded meats and fragments previously cut off from the carcasses; pass all through a tammy, and then pour in some game glaze (No. 398) and butter, just when ready to serve.

With Champagne—Lay in a saucepan one pound of game carcasses, such as pheasants or grouse, after breaking them in pieces; to them add a quarter of a bottleful of champagne, two bay leaves, two minced shallots and one pint of broth; let all these simmer for half an hour before straining through a fine sieve, then reduce it to half with a pint of espagnole, adding another quarter bottleful of champagne and reduce it once more. Season with salt, black and red pepper, also grated nutmeg, and strain through a tammy, and just when ready to serve mix in two ounces of fresh butter.

With Red Wine and Truffles.—Break up the carcasses of six snipes, or plovers, or woodcocks; fry them in some butter with their intestines, suppressing the gizzards and pouches, two bay leaves, as much thyme and as much basil, some truffle peelings, one pint of espagnole (No. 414), and two gills of red wine. Boil, skim, and when prepared to serve squeeze in the juice of a lemon; strain the sauce through a tammy, (No. 159), and add to it one or two ounces of peeled and minced truffles.

(537). SHALLOT SAUCE AND SHALLOT GRAVY (Sauce à l'Échalote et Jus à l'Échalote).

Blanch in boiling salted water three finely chopped shallots, placing them in the corner of a napkin; afterward cook them in a gill of consommé (No. 189); reduce this latter until dry, then add to it one gill of velouté (No. 415). Now pound four hard boiled egg-yolks with six ounces of butter; put the preparation into a saucepan, and stir it while heating till it becomes very hot, then season with salt, mignonette and lemon juice; if too thick add a little water and then strain it through a tammy (No. 159), and mix in a coffeespoonful of chopped parsley; stir it into the above prepared sauce.

Shallot Gravy.—Put eight minced shallots, a small bay leaf, some thyme and branches of parsley in a saucepan, moisten with two gills of clear gravy (No. 404) and let all cook for ten minutes on the corner of the range; strain through a napkin, and keep the sauce warm in a bain-marie until needed.

(538). SHARP SAUCE WITH CAPERS AND ONION PURÉE (Sauce Piquante aux Câpres et à la Purée d'Oignons).

Sharp Sauce.—Reduce to one-half, five or six spoonfuls of tarragon vinegar, with some shallots, cut in one-eighth of an inch squares. Put on the fire to reduce, three or four gills of sauce espagnole (No. 414) free from all fat, one gill of veal blond, (No. 423) and then the above infusion, pouring it in slowly, and when the sauce is sufficiently succulent and thick, strain it into a saucepan and keep it warm in a bain-marie.

Sharp with Capers, and Onion Purée—Add a pint of espagnole (No. 414) to a tablespoonful of good vinegar, and set them in a saucepan with a bay leaf, a clove of garlic, a little thyme, two cloves, and two gills of broth, also a pinch of powdered sugar; let the whole boil for fifteen minutes, then skim off the fat; strain through a tammy, and finish by adding two spoonfuls of capers, and two of onion purée.

(539). CHOPPED SAUCE (Sauce Hachée).

Add one tablespoonful of chopped shallots to one gill of vinegar; put them in a saucepan with one chopped and crushed clove of garlic; let boil slowly until thoroughly reduced then moisten with a gill of broth, and one pint of espagnole sauce (No. 414); add two ounces of chopped mushrooms, one tablespoonful of parsley, one of pickles, and one of small capers, all chopped separately, and just when serving, incorporate into the sauce two ounces of butter, salt, pepper, and nutmeg.

(540). SHRIMP SAUCE, SHRIMP AND CREAM SAUCE (Sauce aux Crevettes, Sauce aux Crevettes à la Crème).

Shrimp Sauce.— Skin half a pound of cooked shrimps; pound their shells with a quarter of a pound of butter, and the juice of one lemon; pass this through a sieve. Cut the shrimps into dice shaped pieces. Boil one pint of white poivrade sauce (No. 522), thicken it with two egg-yolks, and half a gill of fresh cream, and finish with a quarter of a pound of shrimp butter (No. 586), adding a pinch of cayenne pepper, a coffeespoonful of fine herbs, and the pieces of shrimp.

Shrimp and Cream Sauce.—Reduce one pint of béchamel (No. 409) with one gill of mushroom essence (No. 392), and incorporate into this, two ounces of shrimp butter (No. 586), a gill of cream, and two ounces of small dice pieces of shrimps; season with cayenne pepper and serve.

(541). SHRIMP AND CRAB SAUCE (Sauce aux Crevettes et aux Crabes).

Pour into a flat saucepan about one pint of béchamel sauce (No. 409), let it reduce, and incorporate into it six tablespoonfuls of mushroom essence (No. 392) and the same quantity of raw cream. When the sauce is very creamy, take it off the fire, and whisk into it gradually with a wire whip three ounces of fresh butter, and at the very last moment two ounces of shrimp butter (No. 586). Season and serve it in a separate sauce-boat with the shrimp tails, cut up into small pieces if they are large, but if small, leave them whole. Add the same quantity of crab meat cut the same size.

(542). SICILIAN SAUCE (Sauce Sicilienne).

Pour two gills of Marsala wine into a saucepan, adding to it one ounce of truffles and two ounces of mushrooms, both chopped; also two shallots, chopped, blanched and lightly fried in an ounce of butter; and also one teaspoonful of chopped parsley, a clove of crushed and chopped garlic, a bunch of parsley garnished with a bay leaf, and the same of thyme, pepper and some grated nutmeg. Let all these simmer and reduce on a slow fire, then remove the parsley, and add four gills of allemande (No. 407), and two of game (No. 389), or chicken essence (No. 387), the juice of half a lemon, the same quantity of orange, besides the peel of the latter finely cut up and blanched, and a coffeespoonful of powdered sugar.

(543). SOUBISE SAUCE (Sauce Soubise).

Cut off the stalks and roots from twelve onions after having divided them in two, throw them into boiling salted water for a few minutes, then drain, refresh, and drain them again. Heat a half a pound of butter in a saucepan, add to it the onions and fry them without coloring until well done, then pour in a pint of velouté (No. 415) and half a pint of stock (No. 422), some peppercorns and grated nutmeg. When the onions are sufficiently cooked, press them forcibly through a tammy (No. 170) and return the sauce to the saucepan on the fire, and add to it six gills of fresh cream; season properly, and incorporate in at the last moment a small piece of fresh butter.

(544). SOUR SAUCE (Sauce Aigrelette).

Put into a saucepan one pint of allemande sauce (No. 407) with one ounce of meat glaze (No. 401), some white pepper and nutmeg; beat the sauce well and stir in one gill of lemon juice, the same quantity of gooseberries or verjuice, also two ounces of fresh butter; strain through a tammy and serve.

(545). SOYA SAUCE (Sauce Soya).

Reduce one pint of velouté (No. 415) or espagnole (No. 414) with two gills of essence of either chicken, game or fish, and when the sauce is of a sufficient consistency, add to it two tablespoonfuls of soya sauce, and two ounces of fresh butter; beat in slowly with a whip.

(546). PRINTANIÈRE SAUCE (Sauce à la Printanière).

Pick and wash half an ounce of chervil, half an ounce of chives, a quarter of an ounce of tarragon, and a quarter of an ounce of burnet. Throw these herbs into boiling salted water, to blanch for two minutes in an untinned copper vessel, drain, refresh, and drain once more to press out all the water; pound and add four ounces of butter, a tablespoonful of good vinegar and sufficient spinach green to color nicely; press this butter through a fine sieve and when prepared to use it, add it to a pint of hot allemande sauce (No. 407); season to taste and serve.

(547). SUPREME SAUCE (Sauce Suprême).

Remove the breasts from five chickens, break up the carcasses and second joints. Cut two pounds of kernel of veal into large squares, and cook them with the chicken bones, in half a pound of butter without allowing them to color, then moisten with seven quarts of velouté stock (No. 422); let boil, skim well, and season with salt, pepper, and a bunch of parsley garnished with basil and bay leaf, and continue to boil for two hours, being careful to skim off the top when necessary; then strain the whole through a fine sieve. Place a saucepan on a slow fire, containing one quarter of a pound of butter and as much flour; when cooked without coloring, moisten it with one and a half quarts of the above stock, and let it boil on one side of the stove only, so as to be able to skim it properly, now add a quarter of a bottleful of Sauterne wine, cook again, and despumate for two hours; strain the sauce through a tammy, and reduce with one pint of cream, and just when ready to serve, beat in a piece of fresh butter.

(548). TARRAGON SAUCE (Sauce à l'Estragon).

Reduce one pint of velouté (No. 415), or espagnole (No. 414) with half a pint of chicken essence (No. 387). Infuse a pinch of tarragon leaves in a gill of chicken essence, and add this infusion to the velouté or espagnole; strain all through a tammy, and just when serving throw in a tablespoonful of tarragon leaves cut in lozenges, and blanched in boiling water in an untinned copper pan.

(549). TOMATO SAUCE (Sauce aux Tomates).

Put a quarter of a pound of butter in a saucepan, with half a pound of carrots, half a pound of onions, half a pound of bacon or unsmoked ham, all cut in quarter inch squares, a bunch of parsley garnished with thyme and bay leaf, and four cloves; when fried colorless, add eight pounds of tomatoes cut in two and well pressed; season with salt and mignonette, and moisten with a quart of moistening (No. 189), then cook it all slowly for forty minutes. Make a blond roux (No. 163) with a quarter of a pound of butter, and a quarter of a pound of flour; dilute it with one quart of white stock (No. 422), and the tomatoes; then strain the whole through a fine sieve or tammy (No. 159), let it boil again, despumate the surface, and reduce it until it becomes the consistency of a sauce.

(550). TOMATO SAUCE ANDALOUSE, À LA CONDÉ, À LA PARISIENNE (Sauce aux Tomates à l'Andalouse, à la Condé, à la Parisienne).

Wash and cut in halves, four pounds of tomatoes, press them well to extract all their juice and seeds, then put the pulps into a saucepan with four ounces of minced onions, three bay leaves and as much thyme, four ounces of green peppers finely shredded, two ounces of mushroom parings, one clove of garlic, four ounces of ham, one pinch of saffron leaves, one small coffeespoonful of mignonette and one pint of espagnole (No. 414); let the whole cook for twenty minutes; then strain the sauce through a tammy (No. 159), and stir into it at the last moment two ounces of fresh butter.

A la Condé.—Fry eight ounces of minced onions in two ounces of butter, add four pounds of very ripe tomatoes cut in halves, and the juice and seeds extracted, three bay leaves and as much thyme; also some cayenne pepper. Let the whole cook on a slow fire, then drain and strain through a sieve, return the sauce to the saucepan, adding one pint of espagnole (No. 414), reduce it to a proper consistency, and stir into it two tablespoonfuls of meat glaze (No. 401) just before serving.

Parisienne.—Have in a saucepan two ounces of chopped mushrooms with a teaspoonful of chopped parsley, a small crushed clove of garlic and two shallots, both finely minced, two ounces of bacon cut in dice, three bay leaves, the same quantity of thyme, a teaspoonful of whole peppers, salt, and four pounds of tomatoes, cut in halves, and their juice and seeds well extracted; also one pint of moistening (No. 189). Let this all cook for twenty minutes, drain and strain through a sieve, add to the purée one pint of velouté (No. 415), one pint of onion purée (No. 723), four tablespoonfuls of meat glaze (No. 401) and two ounces of fine butter. Before serving be assured that the sauce is seasoned properly.

(551). TRUFFLE SAUCE (Sauce aux Truffes).

Moisten one pound of chicken parings with three pints of velouté stock (No. 422) and a quarter of a bottleful of white wine; add to it a bunch of parsley garnished with a bay leaf, and as much thyme, a quarter of a pound of minced carrots, four ounces of onions, one branch of celery and one coffeespoonful of whole peppers; let it all simmer for two hours, then strain through a sieve and reduce the sauce to half, skimming it well in the meanwhile; now add one quart of allemande sauce (No. 407), and reduce again with a quarter of a bottleful of white wine. Strain the whole through a tammy, and just when serving incorporate into the sauce four ounces of fresh butter and three ounces of peeled and minced truffles.

(552). TURTLE SAUCE, FAT AND LEAN (Sauce Tortue Grasse et Maigre).

Fat.—Pour into a saucepan three gills of dry Madeira wine, add two ounces of minced, lean ham, one pinch of mignonette, a bunch of parsley garnished with a bay leaf, the same quantity of thyme and basil, two small green peppers, one chopped shallot, one ounce of truffles and two of mushrooms chopped separately. Let all these ingredients simmer and reduce on a low fire adding to them four gills of espagnole (No. 414), two gills of concentrated veal blond (No. 423), two gills of tomatoes (No. 730), and add two more gills of Madeira wine; strain the sauce through a tammy and beat in when ready to serve two ounces of fresh butter.

Lean.—Cut into slices half a pound each of carp, eels and pike; put them into a saucepan with a quarter of a bottle of white wine, one quart of water, one clove of garlic, four ounces of onions cut in four, two ounces of mushroom parings, a bunch of parsley containing basil, marjoram, thyme and bay leaf, some mace, mignonette and a pinch of cayenne. Let simmer and reduce the stock to half on a very slow fire, then strain it forcibly through a tammy, return it to the fire and add one pint of espagnole (No. 414), and one gill of tomato purée (No. 730); reduce once more, pour in a quarter of a bottleful of champagne, squeeze in the juice of a lemon, and when ready to use incorporate into the sauce two ounces of lobster butter (No. 580).

(553). LA VALLIÈRE SAUCE (Sauce à la La Vallière).

Reduce one quart of velouté (No. 415) with one quart of veal blond (No. 423), and the broth obtained from cooking eight ounces of mushrooms, add one tablespoonful of meat glaze (No. 401) and thicken the sauce with four egg-yolks diluted in half a gill of cream and two ounces of fresh butter. Strain through a tammy and add half a pound of channeled mushrooms (No. 118).

(554). VALOIS SAUCE (Sauce à la Valois).

Boil two gills of white wine with one gill of vinegar and add two tablespoonfuls of chopped shallots, let the liquid reduce thoroughly, then remove it from the fire, let partly cool and stir in six egg-yolks, beat them up with an egg-beater and finish the sauce with four ounces of fine fresh butter slowly incorporated; strain and after returning it to the saucepan stir into it two ounces more of butter and mix in one spoonful of chopped parsley, or replace half the parsley by chopped tarragon leaves if preferred.

(555). VENETIAN SAUCE (Sauce à la Vénitienne).

Have ready in a steamer or bain-marie saucepan one pint of velouté sauce (No. 415), and just when about serving add to it one gill of chicken (No. 398) or fish glaze (No. 399), some salt, pepper, and nutmeg, and a teaspoonful of good vinegar; thicken the sauce with egg-yolks and cream, then add two ounces of fresh butter, and a coffeespoonful of fresh parsley, also a pinch of finely shredded tarragon leaves.

(556). VENISON SAUCE (Sauce Venaison).

Dilute in a saucepan five gills of poivrade sauce (No. 522), and four ounces of currant jelly with half a bottleful of Burgundy wine, adding two tablespoonfuls of vinegar and the same quantity of sugar, also the pulp of a lemon; reduce for a few minutes, then strain through a tammy.

(557). VICTORIA SAUCE (Sauce à la Victoria).

Cover a saucepan containing one tablespoonful of finely chopped shallots and the juice of two lemons; let boil together, then add two ounces of well chopped mushrooms and boil again until these have evaporated all their moisture, then put in two gills of melted meat glaze. When ready to serve finish the sauce by mixing in a quarter of a pound of butter, a teaspoonful of vinegar, the same of soya sauce (No. 545), a pinch of tarragon leaves and one of parsley, besides two tablespoonsfuls of chopped up pickles.

(558). VIENNESE SAUCE (Sauce à la Viennoise).

This sauce is prepared with one pint of allemande sauce (No. 407), seasoned with nutmeg, red pepper, and the juice of a lemon; finish it with four ounces of crawfish butter (No. 573), and just before serving, throw in a teaspoonful of chopped parsley.

(559). VILLARS SAUCE (Sauce à la Villars).

Into a pint of chicken essence (No. 387) add two tablespoonfuls of rice flour diluted in a gill of cold milk, also some salt, pepper and lemon juice, two ounces of cooked chicken cut in small squares and four chopped hard-boiled egg-yolks; work the sauce steadily, reduce properly, and add one gill of double cream, and two ounces of fresh butter.

(560). VILLEROI SAUCE (Sauce à la Villeroi).

Put into a sautoire with some butter two ounces of lean ham; fry for a few minutes, then drain off the butter and moisten the ham with one gill of white wine; reduce it until dry, then pour in a pint of velouté (No. 415) and season the sauce with mignonette and nutmeg; reduce again and then thicken with four egg-yolks diluted in a gill of cream; let the sauce boil up once or twice while stirring it at the bottom of the sautoire with a reducing spatula, then strain it through a tammy (No. 159), and mix in with it some chopped and drained mushrooms, also a teaspoonful of chopped parsley or fine herbs. This sauce should be more consistent than allemande sauce and it is used only when beginning to cool, to coat cold meats. It can also be soubised by adding to it a few tablespoonfuls of soubise sauce (No. 543).

(561). WESTPHALIAN SAUCE (Sauce Westphalienne).

Put three gills of white wine and half a pound of minced, lean Westphalia ham into a saucepan with a bunch of parsley garnished with one bay leaf and the same quantity of thyme, some mignonette, salt and nutmeg. Moisten the whole with two gills of veal blond stock (No. 423), then reduce and finish with four gills of espagnole (No. 414), reduce again to the proper consistency, then strain through a tammy, and just when ready to serve stir in two ounces of butter and the juice of a lemon; pass through a tammy and serve.

(562). WHITE SAUCE; WHITE ENGLISH SAUCE AND WHITE SAUCE WITHOUT BUTTER
(Sauce Blanche, Anglaise et Sauce Blanche sans Beurre).

Melt some butter in a saucepan and beat it with the same weight of flour; season with salt, pepper, and nutmeg, and moisten with water. Set it on the fire and stir constantly until it begins to bubble, then thicken it just before serving with egg-yolks, cream and fresh butter, adding the juice of a lemon; strain the sauce through a tammy and serve.

White Sauce, English Style.—Infuse in a pint of boiling cream, the peel of one lemon, a cof-feespoonful of white pepper corns, some thyme and a bay leaf, leaving them in for half an hour. Melt three ounces of butter, and stir in it two ounces of flour, fried without coloring, add the pre-pared infusion, straining it first through a fine sieve, also the juice of a lemon. Set the saucepan on the fire, and stir well till it boils, then leave it for a few minutes and incorporate into it three ounces of fine butter.

White Sauce, Without Butter.—Break into a saucepan four raw egg-yolks, add to them one gill of olive oil, salt, pepper and nutmeg. Heat some water in a saucepan larger than the one con-taining the eggs and oil, set the smaller into the larger one, and as soon as the water is sufficiently hot that the hand cannot bear the heat then begin to stir it so as to mix the eggs with the oil; as quickly as the sauce is well thickened, take it from the saucepan and serve it at once, adding the juice of a lemon. This sauce should only be tepid, for if a degree warmer the egg-yolks coagu-late and the oil separates from them. This sauce is excellent for artichokes and plain boiled aspar-agus.

(563). YORK SAUCE (Sauce d'York).

Made by reducing some vinegar with shallots, cut in eighth of an inch squares, and adding to it two or three spoonfuls of white bread-crumbs lightly fried in butter and some good gravy. Let the sauce cook for ten minutes on the side of the range, season to taste, and finish with some chopped parsley and lemon juice.

(564). ZUCHETTE SAUCE (Sauce à la Zuchette).

Reduce some brown espagnole sauce with the liquid part of drained tomatoes, add some dry mushrooms that have been previously soaked, moisten from time to time with a little veal blond stock (No. 423). Pare some cucumbers in either clove of garlic or olive shape, blanch and cook these in white broth having just sufficient to moisten, so that when the cucumbers are done the stock will be thoroughly reduced. Strain the sauce through a tammy, put in the cucumbers and serve.

HOT BUTTERS.

---

(565). BLACK BUTTER (Beurre Noir).

This butter is used for eggs, brains or fish. Put four ounces of butter in an omelet pan over a slow fire, and when it falls after raising, skim it off, and set it again on the fire; as soon as it is black, but not burned, season it with salt and mignonette. Strain it through a fine strainer over the eggs, etc. Throw a dash of vinegar in a hot pan, and pour it over the eggs through a fine strainer.

(566). MELTED BUTTER (Beurre Fondu).

Set four ounces of butter in a saucepan, season it with salt, pepper, mignonette, and the juice of a lemon; let it melt sufficiently to liquify it, or else melt it thoroughly, and let it settle, pouring off the top carefully, refraining from disturbing the sediment at the bottom.

(567). HAZEL-NUT BUTTER (Beurre Noisette).

Place four ounces of butter in a pan on the fire, and as soon as the froth falls, skim it care-fully, and leave it on the fire until it begins to brown slightly, then let it settle and pour off the clear part; season with salt, pepper, and lemon-juice, and throw this over fish or any other article, after straining it through a fine strainer.

COLD BUTTERS.

(568). ALMOND BUTTER (Beurre d'Amandes).

Pound in a mortar, one ounce of peeled sweet almonds mixed with a few bitter ones; add four ounces of sugar, and moisten with a little milk, then stir in eight ounces of fresh butter, and beat it all well together, then press the whole through a fine sieve.

(569). ANCHOVY BUTTER (Beurre d'Anchois).

Wash an ounce of anchovies, wipe them well to remove the silver scales covering them, then pound them thoroughly, adding a quarter of a pound of butter, and a little cayenne pepper. Rub through a sieve and use when needed.

(570). CAMBRIDGE BUTTER (Beurre Cambridge.)

Lay in a mortar and pound well, six hard boiled egg-yolks, with four well cleansed anchovies and a spoonful of chopped capers, also some tarragon and chives; when the whole is reduced to a paste, add to it one spoonful of English mustard, and the same quantity of French mustard, some salt, pepper, and vinegar, and one pound of fresh butter. Rub the compound through a sieve, and then mix in with it a tablespoonful of chopped parsley.

(571). CAYENNE, CHILI, PAPRIKA AND SWEET SPANISH PEPPER BUTTER (Beurre de Cayenne, Chili, Paprika, Piments doux d'Espagne).

Mix into half a pound of fresh butter, either a full teaspoonful of cayenne pepper or Chili pepper, and two teaspoonfuls Hungary paprika pepper; add to it some salt, lemon juice and sweet Spanish pimentos.

(572). CRAB BUTTER (Beurre de Crabes).

Wash well some crab coral, then pound it in a mortar, adding double its quantity of butter, a dash of cayenne pepper and the juice of two lemons; press it through a sieve.

(573). CRAWFISH BUTTER (Beurre d'Écrevisses).

Have one pound of very red crawfish shells, pound them with two pounds of butter and when they are reduced to a paste, then put it into a saucepan and cook slowly until the butter be thoroughly clarified; strain it through a piece of muslin into a bowl, and as soon as the greatest heat has passed off, beat it up with a spoon till it becomes cold. If needed to be colored a deeper red, add a little orchanet melted in a little butter, or else some vegetal carmine.

(574). FINE HERB BUTTER, COOKED (Beurre aux Fines Herbes Cuites).

Fry in some butter a few blanched and finely chopped shallots, add to them a few well chopped truffles and fresh mushrooms, and let the whole get quite cold, then add to it some fresh butter, salt, pepper, chopped parsley and lemon juice.

(575). RAW FINE HERB BUTTER, (Beurre aux Fines Herbes Crues).

Wash some parsley, chervil, tarragon, pimpernel, chives and water-cress leaves, and then cut them up finely. Wipe off a piece of fresh butter in a cloth, and beat it up in a warm basin until it becomes slightly creamy, then mix in with it gradually the raw fine herbs; season this butter with cayenne, salt and lemon juice.

(576). GARLIC BUTTER (Beurre d'Ail).

Blanch one ounce of garlic in plenty of water, drain and pound it well, adding half a pound of butter and seasoning with salt and red pepper.

(577). BUTTER WITH GREEN GOOSEBERRIES (Beurre aux Groseilles à Maquereau).

Have a pound of well picked green gooseberries; pound them well and then add to them one pound of fresh butter, pound again together and season with salt, pepper and fine herbs.

(578). HORSERADISH BUTTER (Beurre de Raifort).

Pound four ounces of scraped horseradish with eight ounces of butter, some salt and red pepper; then rub it through a sieve. If this butter be needed to add to a sauce, only put it in at the last moment. Horseradish should not be allowed to boil; neither should it be prepared too long in advance.

(579). KNEADED BUTTER (Beurre Manié).

Kneaded butter is frequently used at the last moment to thicken sauces and cooked small vegetables. In order to prepare this auxillary, it is necessary to lay a piece of butter on a plate or in a small vessel, and incorporate into it slowly with a wooden spoon, a sufficient quantity of flour to form a smooth paste, but not too consistent, so that it can easily be dissolved by the heat.

(580). LOBSTER AND SPINY LOBSTER CORAL BUTTER (Beurre au Corail de Homard ou de Langouste).

Lobster Butter.—Pound one pound of very red spiny lobster shells with two pounds of butter until they are reduced to a paste; put this into a saucepan till the butter be cooked and clarified, then strain it through a piece of muslin into a bowl. As soon as the butter has thrown off its first heat, begin beating it with a spoon till it gets cold, and if needed to be dyed a deeper red shade, then add to it a little orchanet, melted in a small quantity of butter, or clear vegetal carmine.

Coral Butter.—Take some lobster eggs, also the red parts found in the interior of the body and crush them very finely in a mortar; mix in a piece of fresh butter four times the volume of the eggs; pass the whole through a Venice sieve and serve.

(581). MAÎTRE D'HÔTEL BUTTER (Beurre Maître d'Hôtel).

Mix in with some fresh butter, chopped parsley, salt, pepper, and lemon juice.

(582). MONTPELLIER BUTTER (Beurre Montpellier).

Pick, wash, and blanch one pound of chervil, chives, tarragon, pimpernel, and water-cress; drain and refresh them, then press them well to extract all the water, and pound them in a mortar with six hard boiled egg-yolks, six well washed anchovies, five ounces of pickled gherkins, five ounces of dry capers, and add salt, pepper, and a piece of garlic the size of a pea; pound all together and rub the whole through a fine sieve, and when it has all passed, put two pounds of butter into the mortar, add the strained ravigote, two tablespoonfuls of oil, and one of tarragon vinegar; and mix it all thoroughly together. Montpellier butter should be a pretty, light green color.

(583). RAVIGOTE OR GREEN BUTTER (Beurre à la Ravigote ou Beurre Vert).

Made with one ounce of tarragon, two ounces of chervil, one ounce of chives, well washed, half an ounce of blanched parsley leaves, and one ounce of chopped and blanched shallot; pound all these herbs with half a pound of butter, and color it with some spinach green strained through a sieve.

(584). SAFFRON BUTTER (Beurre de Safran).

Lay a pinch of saffron on a plate and work it in a nut of butter with a spatula; it is then ready to use.

(585). SHALLOT BUTTER (Beurre d'Échalotes).

Peel and mince finely twelve shallots, then pound them, afterward adding half a pound of butter; rub the compound through a sieve.

(586). SHRIMP BUTTER (Beurre de Crevettes).

Pound one pound of shrimps without removing their skins, also two ounces of lobster coral; add to this one pound of fresh butter, some salt, cayenne pepper and the juice of a lemon, then press the whole through a sieve.

COLD SAUCES.

(587). APPLE SAUCE (Sauce aux Pommes).

Apple Sauce.—Peel a pound of sound apples, suppress the cores and seeds and place them in a saucepan with a little water; when cooked drain and press through a sieve; reduce and add a little brown sugar and the juice of two oranges and their finely shredded peels that have been previously cooked in salted water.

(588). CHANTILLY APPLE SAUCE WITH HORSERADISH À LA SANFORD (Sauce Chantilly aux Pommes et au Raifort à la Sanford).

Core a pound of sour apples, lay them in a saucepan with a little water; when done drain out and press through a very fine sieve. Add to the pulp one ounce of powdered sugar and two ounces of grated horseradish; stir well and beat in lightly the value of one pint of well-drained whipped cream. Serve this sauce separately with young ducks or goslings.

(589). APPLE SAUCE, ENGLISH STYLE, (Sauce aux Pommes à l'Anglaise).

Cut up one pound of peeled apples, small, cook them with a little water and a grain of salt; when dry mix in four spoonfuls of grated fresh horseradish; remove from the fire at once, and press through a sieve; mix into the pulp a spoonful of sugar and the juice of two oranges. Heat up without boiling, and remove as soon as the sugar is dissolved. This sauce can be served with all salted and smoked meats.

(590). APPLE SAUCE FOR GOURMETS, APPLE SAUCE WITH HORSERADISH AND ORANGE JUICE (Sauce aux Pommes des Gourmets, Sauce aux Pommes au Raifort et jus d'Orange).

Gourmets.—Take one pound of peeled apples, remove the seeds and put them in a saucepan with a little water, when cooked, drain and strain through a sieve, reduce and add a little brown sugar, the juice of two oranges and their peels finely cut up and boiled in salted water.

With Horseradish and Orange Juice.—The same preparation as for apple sauce (No. 587), adding the juice of two oranges and six tablespoonfuls of grated fresh horseradish.

(591). SWEDISH APPLE SAUCE (Sauce aux Pommes Suédoise).

Cut five or six apples into four quarters, peel and cook them in a little white wine, reduce all of their moisture, then press them through a sieve. Place this purée in a bowl and mix in with it about an equal quantity of finely chopped horseradish, thicken this preparation with a few spoonfuls of mayonnaise (No. 606). This sauce is excellent for roast geese or roast pork, as well as for cold meats.

(592). BOAR SAUCE (Sauce Sanglier).

Grate half a pound of fresh horseradish, then lay it in a bowl with four ounces of cranberry jelly (No. 598), adding a spoonful of mustard, the well chopped peel of one lemon and one orange, two ounces of powdered sugar and one tablespoonful of sweet oil, mix all the ingredients well together and serve.

(593). CHAUDFROID, BÉCHAMEL CREAM SAUCE, WITH TOMATO PURÉE AND WITH FECULA (Sauces Chaudfroid, Béchamel à la Crème, Béchamel à la Purée de Tomates et à la Fécule).

Béchamel Cream Chaudfroid.—Is made with béchamel reduced with fowl or fish essence well despumated, and half its quantity of white chicken or fish jelly added.

Béchamel Tomato Purée Chaudfroid.—Is a chaudfroid prepared the same as for the cream, adding to it a quarter of its quantity of red tomato purée strained through a very fine sieve.

With Fecula.—Boil a quart and a half of chicken broth with six gelatine leaves and when well dissolved thicken with four ounces of fecula previously diluted in cold water. Mix with this chaud-froid half a pint of cream, strain it through a tammy (No. 159), stir up well and dip into this chaudfroid once or several times the whole pieces of meat required to be glazed.

(594). CHAUDFROID BROWN AND GAME (Chaudfroid Brun et Chaudfroid de Gibier).

Put into a saucepan, one pint of very clear well-colored espagnole sauce (No. 414), reduce it with some veal blond (No. 423), and dilute with half its quantity of aspic jelly (No. 103). Boil up the sauce and remove it at once to the side of the fire, in order to despumate it for ten minutes, skimming it well in the meantime; then take it off entirely and pass through a tammy. Before using try a little to find out whether it coats properly; if not strong enough add some gelatine.

Game Chaudfroid.—Add one pint of game essence (No. 389) to half a pint of sauterne wine, moisten with game stock (No. 195), and add one quart of well-reduced espagnole sauce (No. 414), despumate and stir in one pint of jelly. The white wine may be replaced by Madeira.

(595). CHAUDFROID GREEN OR RAVIGOTE (Chaudfroid Vert ou Chaudfroid Ravigote).

Blanch in boiling and salted water, one handful of chervil, parsley, tarragon and pimpernel; drain and pound these with a few capers; press through a sieve and mix this purée with a velouté sauce (No. 415), then reduce and despumate, adding some chicken stock (No. 195); reduce once more, and now add the juice of one lemon and some spinach green, also half its quantity of either meat, chicken, or game jelly.

(596). CHAUDFROID WHITE WITH VELOUTÉ AND BLOND CHAUDFROID (Chaudfroid Blanc au Velouté et Chaudfroid Blond).

Pour into a saucepan, one pint of velouté (No. 415) (for lean, use fish velouté); reduce it with half a pint of chicken broth (No. 188), or veal stock (No. 423), then add one pint of aspic jelly (No. 103); boil up this sauce, remove it to the side of the fire to be able to despumate for fifteen minutes, skimming it carefully in the meanwhile, then take it off the fire, strain, and try a little before using, to see whether it is sufficiently thick to cover the meats. For blond chaudfroid, add chicken glaze (No. 398) to white velouté (No. 415).

Thickened with Egg-yolks à l'Allemande.—Velouté (No. 415) reduced with essence of chicken (No. 387) well despumated, and thickened with egg-yolks, mixed with half as much melted white jelly.

Blond Chaudfroid.—Is made with half brown and half white chaudfroid.

(597). CHICKEN AND GAME SAUCE (Sauce pour Volaille et Gibier).

This sauce is prepared with some sweet oil, the juice of a lemon, chicken or game gravy, chopped fine herbs, garlic, shallots, salt and pepper.

(598). CRANBERRY SAUCE (Sauce aux Caneberges).

Wash five pounds of cranberries, lay them in an untinned saucepan on the fire, with one quart of water, let cook slowly while stirring frequently, and when they are done add to them five pounds of sugar; pass them through a coarse colander, put in jars and set the jelly away in a cool closet.

(599). CUMBERLAND SAUCE (Sauce à la Cumberland).

Cook in salted water the finely shreded peels of two oranges and two lemons, and when they are tender put them into a vessel with one tablespoonful of mustard, a pinch of ground ginger, a pinch of cayenne pepper, a gill of Madeira wine, the juice of one orange and one lemon, some salt, and two tablespoonfuls of vinegar, and mix in with these ingredients half a pound of currant jelly.

(600). CURRANT OR GOOSEBERRY SAUCE WITH SUGAR (Sauce aux Groseilles Blanches ou Vertes au Sucre).

Pick one pound of white currants from their stalks, or pick off the stems from one pound of gooseberries; blanch either one or the other, and then drain them on a sieve. Have cooked half a pound of sugar to the small crack, lay in the currants, let it boil up once, and then pour it into glasses to serve cold with meats, game or poultry.

(601). CURRANT SAUCE WITH ORANGE (Sauce aux Groseilles à l'Orange).

This is prepared with currant jelly diluted with port wine; add to it the rind of one orange grated on sugar and pressed through a sieve. Peel another orange and after shredding the peel very finely cook it in water, drain and then add it to the sauce, with the juice of the two oranges.

(602). FINE HERBS SAUCE AND SHALLOTS WITH OIL (Sauce aux Fines Herbes, et aux Échalotes à l'Huile).

This sauce is prepared with chervil, parsley, chives, and small squares of blanched shallots, also some tarragon leaves. Dilute a little mustard in oil and vinegar, season well, and stir in the above chopped fine herbs. Shallots with fine herbs and oil is made by mixing in with fine herbs, and oil is made by mixing in with one gill of vinegar, some salt, pepper, and two gills of sweet oil, chopped and blanched shallots, chopped tarragon and English mustard.

(603). GREEN SAUCE (Sauce Verte).

Wash some parsley leaves, chervil, tarragon, and burnet; plunge them into boiling water in a copper vessel, and blanch them for three minutes: drain, press out all the liquid, and then pound the herbs in a small mortar with a few chives added; press them through a sieve, and put into the same mortar a few hard boiled egg-yolks and some anchovy fillets; pound them also, and stir in gradually the green purée; dilute the preparation with some oil, vinegar and mustard, and finish the sauce with a spoonful of finely chopped pickled gherkins.

(604). GREEN SPANISH SAUCE (Sauce Espagnole Verte).

Pound to a paste one ounce of chervil and one ounce of parsley; add to it four ounces of bread-crumbs soaked in water and then squeezed out, six anchovy fillets, two ounces of chopped pickled gherkins, two ounces of capers, and one small chopped up onion; pound well the whole and then rub it through a sieve into a bowl, beat it well with some sweet oil, the same as for a mayonnaise, adding salt, pepper, and spinach green to color; soften the sauce with a little water.

(605). HORSERADISH AND CREAM SAUCE, AND WITH OIL (Sauce Raifort à la Crème, et à l'Huile).

Put into a bowl a quarter of a pound of grated horseradish with an equal quantity of fresh bread-crumbs, a little sugar, some salt, the juice of two lemons, a tablespoonful of vinegar and a little white stock (No. 422), also adding a pint of cream. This sauce is used with cold meats.

With Oil.—Cut some slices of lemon after suppressing the yellow and white rind; put them into a vessel with oil, vinegar, salt and pepper, some chopped parsley, tarragon, grated horseradish and a little ground pepper; mix all well together. Broiled fish may be served with this sauce.

(606). MAYONNAISE SAUCE (Sauce Mayonnaise).

In order to obtain a quick and certain mayonnaise sauce, it must be worked simply with a small wire whisk. Put five egg-yolks into a bowl suppressing every particle of the white, add some salt, white or red pepper, and ground mustard; after these are thoroughly mixed pour in slowly a quart of sweet oil and one gill of vinegar, alternating them without once stopping to work vigorously. In a few minutes the sauce becomes voluminous, consistent, smooth and firm.

(607). MAYONNAISE SAUCE À LA BAYONNAISE (Sauce Mayonnaise à la Bayonnaise).

Lay five egg-yolks in a bowl with a quarter of a gill of water, half an ounce of salt, a little pepper and a little cayenne, then beat it up and incorporate slowly into it two and one-half pints of oil and one gill of vinegar, stirring it unceasingly, and when the sauce thickens add to it more vinegar, and continue pouring in the oil and vinegar till they are both consumed. It must be of a high consistency, of a white color, and of a good flavor; it is preferable to use a wire whisk in place of a wooden spoon for this purpose. Add to this mayonnaise half a pound of lean Bayonne ham, cut in squares, some powdered Spanish peppers, and some chopped parsley.

(608). MAYONNAISE CARDINAL (Sauce Mayonnaise Cardinal).

Pound one ounce of lobster coral with a little vegetal carmine, a teaspoonful of English mustard, some salt, cayenne pepper, and the juice of two lemons; pass all this through a fine sieve, and mix in with it slowly a pint of mayonnaise sauce (No. 606); this sauce should be a nice light red color.

(609). MAYONNAISE FIGARO (Sauce Mayonnaise Figaro).

Strain some cooked tomatoes through a very fine sieve, then let them drain well for several hours in a napkin, and mix this pulp in slowly with very firm mayonnaise sauce (No. 606); add to it some powdered cayenne, very finely chopped, and blanched shallots and anchovy essence.

(610). MAYONNAISE SAUCE PROVENÇAL WITH SWEET PEPPERS (Sauce Mayonnaise Provençale aux Poivrons doux).

Mash four medium sized cloves of garlic with two tablespoonfuls of English mustard, two cooked egg-yolks, two tablespoonfuls of bread-crumbs soaked in milk and all the liquid pressed out; beat the whole with two raw egg yolks, half a coffeespoonful of pepper, some salt and a teaspoonful of sweet Spanish peppers; incorporate in a pint of oil, dropping it in slowly, and a few spoonfuls of tarragon vinegar, also a little water. Just when serving mix in the sweet Spanish peppers, previously broiled so their skin can be removed, then cut them up in squares. The sweet peppers can be replaced by those that come in cans, which are very well prepared.

(611). MAYONNAISE SAUCE WITH ARROWROOT (Sauce Mayonnaise à l'Arrowroot).

In case any difficulty be found to raise a mayonnaise either on account of defective oil, or on account of the weather, the following manner will explain how always to obtain a good result: Dilute in cold water in a small saucepan, a heaping spoonful of arrowroot or simply fecula; be careful there are no lumps in it, then heat it over a slow fire, stirring well with a spoon, until it forms a smooth paste, having it hard, in preference to soft. As soon as this is done, pour it into a vessel, and beat it with a spoon until it loses its greatest heat, then mix in a pinch of salt, a little red pepper, and a pinch of ground mustard. and three or four raw egg-yolks. Work well the preparation while pouring in very slowly, two or three gills of good sweet oil, alternating it with a dash of vinegar.

(612). MAYONNAISE SAUCE, GREEN WITH FINE HERBS, PRINTANIÈRE, AND RAVIGOTE (Sauce Mayonnaise Verte aux Fines Herbes Printanière et Ravigote).

Pick and wash a handful of chervil, tarragon, chives, burnet and garden water-cress. Blanch them in boiling, salted water for five minutes, then drain, refresh and press well to extract all the water. Pound this thoroughly, adding the juice of one lemon and some ground mustard. Mix this ravigote into a pint of mayonnaise sauce (No. 606), and color it a fine pistache green with some spinach green.

(613). MAYONNAISE SAUCE WITH JELLY AND JELLIED (Sauce Mayonnaise à la Gelée et Collée).

In order to make this mayonnaise set a thin tin salad bowl on chopped ice containing one pint of white jelly (No. 103), add to it a pint of oil, a gill of tarragon vinegar, a little salt, and some white or red pepper. Stir the mixture well with an egg-beater being careful to remove all that adheres to the sides, then add little by little the juice of one lemon; also some chopped and blanched chervil may be advantageously added to the sauce.

Mayonnaise Sauce Jellied.—Use an ordinary mayonnaise (No. 606) with oil, pouring into it slowly some cold liquid jelly (No. 103). A jellied mayonnaise may also be prepared by whipping the jelly on ice and incorporating into it at the same time some oil and vinegar, exactly the same as for the egg mayonnaise.

(614). MAYONNAISE SAUCE WITH FRUIT JELLY (Sauce Mayonnaise à la Gelée de Fruits).

Break four raw egg-yolks into a vessel; mix in with them two tablespoonfuls of water, salt and a little white and red pepper, stir well and incorporate slowly, especially at first, one quart of sweet oil and eight spoonfuls of vinegar at different intervals. To make the fruit jelly mayonnaise, add for one pint of mayonnaise sauce (No. 606), one spoonful of English mustard, and a quarter of a pound either of currant, grape, apple, quince or cranberry jelly.

(615). MAYONNAISE MOUSSELINE SAUCE (Sauce Mayonnaise Mousseline).

Made with a jelly mayonnaise the same as explained in No. 613, leaving out the chervil, and stirring in the same quantity of unsweetened whipped cream, well drained and very firm. An ordinary mayonnaise without being jellied can also be used.

(616). MINT SAUCE (Sauce à la Menthe).

Put into a sauce-boat half a glassful of good vinegar, a strong pinch of powdered sugar, a little cayenne pepper, and two heavy pinches of finely chopped fresh mint leaves; let them infuse for half an hour.

Another way.—Mix in a saucepan one gill of good vinegar with the same quantity of water; add to it two spoonfuls of powdered or brown sugar; boil it up once, and then set it away to get cold; put in some finely shredded fresh mint leaves.

(617). ORANGE SAUCE (Sauce à l'Orange).

Have half a pound of currant jelly (No. 3670), two gills of port wine, the juice of three oranges and of two lemons, and the peel of two oranges grated into sugar. Dissolve the currant jelly and the flavored orange sugar with the liquids, add a grain of salt, and a dash of cayenne, then strain the sauce; it should be more light than consistent. This sauce is excellent for either cold or hot game.

(618). PEACH OR APPLE MARMALADE (Marmelade de Pêches ou de Pommes).

Peaches.—Peel and remove the stones from one pound of peaches, cook in a little water, drain and press through a sieve, sweeten with an ounce of brown sugar. These marmalades are for roast meats and poultry.

Apples.—A pound of peeled apples cooked in a little water, pressed through a sieve and sweetened with an ounce of brown sugar.

(619). PERSILLADE SAUCE (Sauce Persillade).

Place in a small bowl one tablespoonful of mustard and four pounded hard boiled egg-yolks. dilute this gradually with two gills of oil and four tablespoonfuls of vinegar, or the juice of four lemons ; add to it salt, pepper and mignonette, some parsley leaves, chervil and tarragon, all finely chopped, and serve the sauce separately. Chopped hard boiled egg-whites are frequently added to this sauce.

(620). POIVRADE SAUCE (Sauce Poivrade).

Put into a bowl one gill of espagnole sauce (No. 414), add to it twice its quantity of oil, some Chili and tarragon vinegar, pepper and salt; beat the whole together with a whisk and throw in a teaspoonful of chopped parsley and some finely chopped blanched shallots.

(621). POLISH SAUCE (Sauce à la Polonaise).

Squeeze into a sauce boat the juice of four lemons and of two oranges; add to them a heavy pinch of mignonette, two teaspoonfuls of mustard, and six tablespoonfuls of pulverized sugar; mix well and dilute this preparation sufficiently to have it the consistency of a syrup.

(622). RAISIN SAUCE (Sauce aux Raisins).

Pour two gills of good vinegar into a saucepan, add a bunch of parsley, garnished with two bay leaves and as much thyme, pepper corns and cloves; reduce the liquid to half; then add four gills of good gravy (No. 404). Boil the whole, dissolve a tablespoonful of fecula in two gills of cold broth, mix in with the sauce, then boil, skim and add a quarter of a pound of Smyrna raisins and the same quantity of currants, also half a pound of currant jelly (No. 3670), dissolving it slowly; let the sauce get cold and serve it up with game.

(623). RAVIGOTE SAUCE WITH OIL (Sauce Ravigote à l'Huile).

Pound a handful of chervil, burnet, tarragon and chives, also a little garlic and shallot; add to them a spoonful of béchamel sauce (No. 409), some salt, white and red pepper, ground mustard and grated horseradish root; pass all through a tammy (No. 159), and mix in with it sufficient oil and vinegar to obtain a sauce that will not be too thick.

(624). RÉMOULADE SAUCE (Sauce Rémoulade).

Chop up well one blanched shallot, have a handful of parsley leaves, chervil, tarragon and burnet; pound the whole in a small marble mortar; **add four** nicely cleaned anchovy fillets, five or six hard boiled egg-yolks, rub all the ingredients through a sieve, then mix in three or four raw yolks, stir into this preparation one pint of oil, half a gill of vinegar and mustard, the same as for mayonnaise (No. 606) and finish the sauce with capers, finely chopped pickled gherkins and a dash of cayenne pepper.

(625). RÉMOULADE SAUCE, INDIAN STYLE (Sauce Rémoulade, à l'Indienne).

Pound in a mortar four hard boiled egg-yolks, add to them two raw yolks, one spoonful of mustard, salt, pepper and the juice of two lemons, and a quarter of a gill of water in which a few saffron leaves have been infused and a quarter of a coffeespoonful of curry; strain all through a sieve and put the preparation into a bowl to stir and work in slowly one pint of sweet oil, and half a gill of vinegar, adding a teaspoonful of powdered sugar, some parsley, chervil, tarragon, chives and two shallots chopped and blanched, besides the hard boiled egg-whites cut into small squares.

(626). RÉMOULADE SAUCE VERT-PRÉ (Sauce Rémoulade Vert-Pré).

Place in a mortar four hard boiled egg-yolks with two raw yolks, two spoonfuls of mustard, salt, pepper and a smack of garlic; pound them well together and then press through a sieve and lay the compound in a bowl; work it well, incorporating into it one pint of oil and half a gill of vinegar, till it becomes the consistency of a mayonnaise. Cut three shallots in small squares and blanch them in boiling water, drain and add them to the mayonnaise; chop separately a handful of parsley, chervil and half as much tarragon, burnet, water-cress and chives; mix together all these herbs, and put in three heaping tablespoonfuls to the prepared mayonnaise, color it a pretty pistache color with spinach green, and throw in when finished two spoonfuls of chopped up capers.

(627). RÉMOULADE SAUCE WITH ANCHOVIES (Sauce Rémoulade aux Anchois).

Pound four hard boiled egg-yolks; add to them four raw egg-yolks, two spoonfuls of mustard and eight anchovies; rub all through a sieve, and put the mixture into a vessel to work and stir in gradually one pint of oil and a half gill of vinegar, season with very little salt and pepper, and then add three chopped and blanched shallots, some parsley and two ounces of chopped capers.

(628). RÉMOULADE SAUCE WITH FINE HERBS (Sauce Rémoulade aux Fines Herbes).

Put into a bowl one tablespoonful of mustard, salt, pepper and a raw egg-yolk; beat this up with a wooden spatula and pour very slowly into it from six to eight spoonfuls of oil, also two of vinegar and one tablespoonful of Chili vinegar; add finely chopped parsley, chervil and tarragon.

(629). ROSSEBERRY SAUCE (Sauce à la Rosseberry).

This sauce is made with one tablespoonful of English mustard diluted in a gill of good vinegar, adding a coffeespoonful of powdered sugar and two tablespoonfuls of grated fresh horseradish, then adding some salt and chopped parsley.

(630). ROUGEMONT SAUCE (Sauce à la Rougemont).

Procure four ounces of lobster coral or eggs, the creamy parts of the bodies of two lobsters, and pound these together with six hard boiled egg-yolks, then press the whole through a sieve into a bowl; dilute and incorporate into it five gills of oil and half a gill of vinegar, two chopped and blanched shallots, a dash of cayenne, a tablespoonful of tarragon and chervil, and half as much chopped parsley, as well as one ounce of chopped pickled gherkins.

(631). TARTAR SAUCE (Sauce Tartare).

Deposit in a bowl one gill of velouté sauce (No. 415), two tablespoonfuls of mustard, four fresh egg-yolks, salt and pepper; stir well together and incorporate into it five gills of oil and half a gill of tarragon vinegar, two chopped and blanched shallots, a dash of cayenne pepper, and a tablespoonful of tarragon and chervil, also half the quantity of chopped parsley, and an ounce of chopped up pickled gherkins.

(632). TARTAR SAUCE, ENGLISH STYLE (Sauce Tartare, à l'Anglaise).

Make a mayonnaise with three hard boiled egg-yolks, one gill of velouté, (No. 415) a pinch of ground mustard, salt, and sweet oil; stir into it gradually two spoonfuls of English anchovy essence; the same of Harvey sauce, and the same of Worcestershire sauce, so as to give the tartar a fine dark color.

(633). TOMATO CATSUP (Catsup de Tomates).

Boil one quart of vinegar in a saucepan, adding a quarter of an ounce of capsicum peppers, one ounce of garlic, half an ounce of shallot, all nicely peeled, and half an ounce of white ground pepper, also a coffeespoonful of red pepper, and let boil for ten minutes, then strain through a fine sieve. Mix in with this vinegar, one and a half pounds of tomatoes, reduce all together and then add the juice of three lemons, and salt to taste. Should this sauce be too thick, add more vinegar or some water; fill up the bottles, let stand till cold, then put them in a very cool place to use when needed. This sauce is excellent as a relish for cold meats fish, oysters, etc.

(634). VINEGAR SAUCE WITH FINE HERBS (Vinaigrette aux Fines Herbes).

Chop up finely the following herbs: chives, chervil, tarragon, and parsley; put them into a bowl with some salt, pepper, a little cayenne pepper, three spoonfuls of vinegar, and six of olive oil; stir all well together and serve.

(635). VINEGAR SAUCE WITH SHALLOTS AND MUSTARD (Vinaigrette aux Échalotes et à la Moutarde).

Cut a shallot in one-eight inch squares, blanch and drain it. Put one gill of vinegar in a bowl, add to it salt and two gills of sweet oil, some mustard, and the blanched shallots.

(636). ZISKA SAUCE, PARISIAN SAUCE FOR ALL FOODS (Sauce Ziska, Sauce Parisienne pour tous Mets).

Put into a bowl two teaspoonfuls of English mustard with a little salt and some sugar; beat it all well together, then pour in slowly the value of three gills of sweet oil, and half a gill of good vinegar, also a few finely chopped pickled gherkins.

Parisian Sauce for all Foods.—Put into an earthen vessel, either over hot cinders or in a heater for twenty-four hours, two gills of water, two gills of vinegar, one gill of verjuice, two gills of white wine, one ounce of ground mustard seeds, half an ounce of black pepper, half a teaspoonful of ground ginger, half a teaspoonful of mace, a quarter of a teaspoonful of cloves, four ounces of salt, a few branches of basil, four bay leaves, two ounces of pounded shallots, one dried bitter orange peel, and half a gill of lemon juice. After all these have infused for two days, strain the sauce through a fine sieve, put it into bottles, and keep it to use for cold meats.

GARNISHINGS.

All the following garnishings may be served for removes by arranging them in clusters and making them either larger or smaller, according to the dishes required to be garnished. For large pieces of meat that are intended for removes they must be larger than for those intended for entrées; in the latter case they should be mixed together instead of being dressed in separate groups.

(637). ADMIRAL GARNISHING (Garniture à l'Amiral).

Take eight mussels à la Villeroi (No. 698), sixteen fluted mushrooms (No. 118), half a pound of skinned and sautéd shrimps; eight trussed crawfish, the tail shell removed. Parsley leaves to be arranged in bunches at both ends. Serve with Normande sauce (No. 509). For an entrée mix the mushrooms and shrimps with the sauce, add chopped parsley and oranges around the Villeroi mussels and crawfish.

(638). À LA REINE GARNISHING (Garniture à la Reine).

Is composed of the white meat cut from a cooked chicken, truffles and mushrooms, all being cut into three-sixteenths of an inch squares. This garnishing is used with bouchées of the same name, or else inside small patties à la Reine; in this case mingle the ingredients with a velouté sauce (No. 415) thickened with egg-yolks and leave it to get cool before filling the patties.

(639). ANDALOUSE GARNISHING (Garniture à l'Andalouse).

Made with eight braised lettuce, eight small Chorisos (smoked sausages) cooked with the cabbage, two pounds of cabbage, half a pound of chick peas; one pound of braised ham; one pint of espagnole sauce (No. 414) reduced with two gills of tomatoes (No. 730). Dress the lettuce, the cabbage and the chick peas in clusters, range the sausages on one end and the ham on the other.

(640). AQUITAINE GARNISHING (Garniture à l'Aquitaine).

Have a pound of escaloped duck livers sautéd in butter; half a pound of small button mushrooms cooked with butter, lemon juice, salt and water; a quarter of a pound of small whole truffles, cooked in Madeira wine; half a pound of pressed beef palate cut cock's-comb shape, warmed in meat glaze (No. 401) and butter. Infuse a stick of Ceylon cinnamon for ten minutes in a gill of Madeira wine; strain this through a napkin into a quart of reduced espagnole sauce (No. 414). Dress the garnishing in clusters, pour over half the sauce and serve the remainder in a separate sauce-boat. This garnishing can be used for entrées; if this be the case, mix the ingredients composing it together in a sautoire with the sauce, and dress them.

(641). BARLEY À LA REINE GARNISHING (Garniture d'Orge à la Reine)

Wash in several waters four ounces of pearl barley; cook it in salted water for three hours until thoroughly done, and it crushes easily when pressed between the fingers; drain and let it simmer in a little good, fresh cream. Just when ready to serve, stir in an equal quantity of chicken purée (No. 713) with almond milk (No. 4), and with this garnish some croustades (hollow tartlets made of fine paste (No. 135) rolled out very thin).

(642). BEEF TONGUE GARNISHING, ANDALUSIAN TOMATO SAUCE (Garniture de Langue de Bœuf, Sauce Tomates Andalouse).

Cut twelve slices, each one three-sixteenths of an inch thick from the thick end of a cooked beef tongue; pare them neatly either into rounds, ovals, or half hearts; heat them in a little half glaze (No. 413), and dress them around a remove covering with a Andalusian tomato sauce (No. 550).

(643). BOUCHÉES OF PURÉE OF PHEASANTS GARNISHING (Garniture de Bouchées à la Purée de Faisans).

Prepare a dozen puff paste bouchées (No. 11), cook them only a short time before they are needed so as not to be obliged to heat them over again. After they are emptied, keep them warm. Put into a saucepan a few spoonfuls of good pheasant purée (No. 716); press through a tammy (No. 170), and heat it while stirring well on a slow fire and incorporate into it a few spoonfuls of good game fumet (No. 397), reduced to a half-glaze, but be careful it does not boil; season highly and finish by stirring in a small piece of butter. Fill the bouchées with this purée, baste over with a little sauce and cover either with their own covers, or else with a round piece of cooked truffle cut out with a column tube (Fig. 168). Dress pyramidically on a folded napkin.

(644). BOURGEOISE GARNISHING (Garniture à la Bourgeoise).

Have two pounds of cabbage, parboiled and cooked with half a pound of salt pork, blanched for fifteen minutes, moisten with a quart of strained broth (No. 194a), and its fat. Twenty pieces of small cork shaped turnips, blanched and cooked in broth, reduced to a glaze just when cooked. Twenty small pear-shaped carrots, blanched, cooked in broth, and reduced to a glaze just as they are finished. Twenty small, blanched, braised and glazed onions. Dress the cabbage on both ends of the meat, garnishing the former with the salt pork cut in slices, and group the carrots, turnips. and onions around in alternate clusters. Serve separately a gravy (No. 404) thickened with espagnole sauce (No. 414), and well reduced.

(645). BRÉTIGNY GARNISHING (Garniture à la Brétigny).

Remove the breasts from sixteen reedbirds, roll them in a sauce made with some gravy (No. 404), to which has been added meat glaze (No. 401), the carcasses and a little Madeira wine, the whole allowed to reduce and then strained. Have sixteen pieces of channeled mushrooms (No. 118) cooked in butter, and seasoned with salt, pepper, and chopped truffles; sixteen slices of sweetbread of one ounce each, blanched and sautéd in butter and seasoned with salt, pepper and chopped parsley. Sixteen pieces of potato cut into one inch diameter balls, then blanched and sautéd in butter. Range the potato balls on the ends of the dish, and place the sweetbreads, mushrooms, and reedbird breasts around in alternate clusters. Serve with this garnishing a separate sauce-boat of Madeira sauce with truffle essence (No. 395).

(646). PARMA BROCHETTES GARNISHING (Garniture Brochettes de Parme).

Made with semolino cooked in light broth and a grain of salt. Prepare a well cooked and thick mush; remove it from the fire, and finish it with some grated parmesan and butter, seasoning it to taste. Spread this preparation in layers on baking sheets dampened with cold water, having each one an eighth of an inch thick; as soon as they are cold and stiff, cut them into one inch rounds; prepare half as many rounds of the very best fresh Swiss cheese. Take some small wooden skewers, and pass on each three rounds, one of cheese and two of semolino, placing the cheese one in the center; dip them in beaten eggs, and roll them in white bread-crumbs. A few minutes before serving plunge them into hot fat, a few at the time, to heat and get a nice color, then drain and serve them separately on a folded napkin, or else around the piece to be garnished.

(647). BRUSSELS GARNISHING (Garniture Bruxelloise).

One pound of Brussells sprouts, blanched and cooked in consommé (No. 189). Half a pound of salt pork cut in slices and broiled. Half a pound of carrot balls three quarters of an inch in diameter, blanched, cooked in consommé (No. 189) and reduced to a glaze. Half a pound of small blanched onions braised and glazed. One pound of Chipolata sausages cut in two lengthwise. Dress all these garnishings in different groups around the remove, and serve separately a sauce-boat of half-glaze sauce (No. 413) with ham essence (No. 390) added.

(648). FRIED CALVES' BRAIN GARNISHING (Garniture de Cervelles Frites).

Calves and lambs' brains are those most generally used for garnishings. They are first soaked so as to be able to scrape and cleanse them properly, then cooked in water with some salt, vinegar, thyme, bay leaf, sliced onions, branches of parsley and pepper corns. Let the brains get cold in a vessel containing their own strained broth, and then divide the calves' brains into six pieces, and lambs' brains into two rounds or ovals. Dip them in beaten eggs, roll them in white bread-crumbs and fry them a fine golden color in hot fat. Serve separately a Chateaubriand sauce (No. 446).

(649). CARDINAL GARNISHING (Garniture Cardinal).

The cardinal garnishing is composed of twelve ounces of lobster quenelles made with a teaspoon (No. 155), twelve ounces of sautéd shrimps, twelve ounces of small onions blanched and then cooked in fish stock (No. 417) and let fall to a glaze, six ounces of small whole truffles rolled in a little fish glaze (No. 399) and fresh butter, then arranged pyramidically, the onions dressed the same. Dress the quenelles in clusters and cover them lightly with a Cardinal sauce (No. 442), and the shrimps sautéd in butter with fine herbs and lemon juice. Some Cardinal sauce to be served separately.

(650). CÈPES OR MUSHROOMS STUFFED À LA DUXELLE, PROVENÇAL OR MINCED WITH BÉCHAMEL GARNISHING (Garniture de Cèpes ou de Champignons Farcis à la Duxelle, Provençale Emincés à la Béchamel).

Remove the stalks from two pounds of young cèpes or mushrooms, wash them well and cook them with lemon juice, some butter and salt. (In case no fresh cèpes can be obtained then use preserved ones.) For garnishings, the heads alone are employed. Drain them, and fry them in some sweet oil with a finely chopped shallot and a crushed and chopped clove of garlic, one tablespoonful of chopped parsley and a gill of brown espagnole (No. 414), also a tablespoonful of meat glaze (No. 401) and some chopped-up truffles. Cèpes or mushrooms are also used as a garnishing when stuffed with a Duxelle (No. 385), thickened with a little raw lamb quenelle forcemeat (No. 92) or else a baked liver forcemeat (No. 64). In both cases they are to be placed in a baking-sheet and sprinkled over with either oil or melted butter, putting them into the oven to bake. Sliced cèpes or mushrooms are also to be used as a garnishing, cutting them up finely and sautéing them in butter or oil, then thickened with béchamel (No. 409), reduced with a little meat glaze (No. 401). These minced cèpes are served either on hollow crusts or in a vegetable dish.

(651). CHAMBORD GARNISHING (Garniture Chambord).

The Chambord garnishing is composed of eighteen pieces of truffles cut the shape of a clove of garlic and cooked in Madeira wine and afterward rolled in a little fish glaze (No. 399) and fine butter. Eighteen crawfish tails from which the shells have been removed and the bodies glazed. Eighteen heads of fluted mushrooms (No. 118) cooked in a little water, butter and lemon juice. Ten pieces of fish quenelles decorated with truffles. Eighteen small pieces of milt à la Villeroi (No. 698), or fillets of striped bass; a lean Spanish sauce (No. 414) reduced with Madeira and white wine, or else a lean velouté sauce (No. 415), reduced with fish broth, mushrooms and champagne wine, and buttered at the last moment. Dress the truffles, the mushroom heads and the crawfish in alternate clusters, and cover them either with the white or brown sauce; arrange around this garnishing the quenelles decorated with truffles, the Villeroi milts or fillets of striped bass, and send a third part of the sauce to the table in a separate sauce-boat.

(652). EGGS WITH CHEESE GARNISHING (Garniture d'œufs au Fromage).

This garnishing is composed of two ounces of butter, six whole eggs, four ounces of Swiss and parmesan cheese, both grated, a pinch of sugar and nutmeg. Beat up the eggs for two minutes, add to them the cheese, sugar, nutmeg, and half of the butter; melt the remainder of the butter in a saucepan, pour into it the eggs, and stir the liquid over a slow fire using a spoon for this purpose, until the compound thickens to the consistency of cream. Take it off the fire, keep stirring it again for two minutes, then mix in with it two spoonfuls of raw cream or velouté (No. 415). Pour the melted cheese in some boat shaped tartlet crusts, made with very thin foundation paste; bake them in a hot oven and serve.

(653). CHEESE CRUST GARNISHING (Garniture de Croûtes au Fromage).

First cut some slices three-eighths of an inch thick from a kitchen loaf; divide them into long squares, two and a half inches by one and a quarter. Grate some Swiss and parmesan cheese, a quarter of a pound of each, and put it into a vessel with three soupspoonfuls of Stilton cheese, and mash them together with a spoon in order to obtain a smooth paste, then work into it slowly a few spoonfuls of sherry wine or ale, without letting it get too soft, season with red pepper, and cayenne. Moisten lightly with melted butter the prepared slices of bread, toast them on both sides cover one side with a layer of the cheese preparation; dredge over them some grated parmesan, and lay the slices on a dish to push it in the oven so as to color the tops, or else use a salamander (Fig. 123) for the purpose; arrange these toasts around a remove or else serve them separately on a folded napkin or simply on a plate.

For Chester Cheese.—Use the same slices of bread, only instead of toasting them, lay them in a sautoire with hot clarified butter; brown them on one side only, then drain, and leave the butter in the sautoire. Cover the fried sides with a layer of grated cheese (Chester), sprinkle over a dash of cayenne pepper, and return the crusts to the sautoire containing the butter, then push it into a moderately heated oven. When the cheese has become creamy, take out the sautoire, and dress the crusts either on folded napkins or around a remove.

(654). CHESTNUT WITH GRAVY GARNISHING (Garniture de Marrons au jus).

Peel two pounds of chestnuts; scald them so as to be able to remove their red skins, then lay them in a buttered flat saucepan. Moisten them to their height with broth (No. 194a) and let the liquid come to a boil, then remove the saucepan to a slower fire while cooking the chestnuts, being careful to keep them whole. After they are tender the moistening should be reduced to a glaze, and then glaze them over with a brush before serving them. Another way is to split the shells on the side of each chestnut, plunge them into very hot frying fat, drain, and peel off the shells and red skins; cook them in boiling water with two ounces of butter, one ounce of celery, a little sugar and salt; simmer the whole and reduce the moisture entirely, then add a little meat glaze (No. 402) and some good gravy (No. 404); reduce and roll the chestnuts around so as to glaze them thoroughly and dress them either around a remove or in the center of an entrée.

(655). CHEVREUSE GARNISHING (Garniture Chevreuse).

Eight ounces of truffles cut in small slices, heated in Madeira wine and some meat glaze (No. 401). Sixteen ounces of foies-gras of either duck or goose, weighing in all about a pound. Thirty-two pieces of stuffed Spanish olives. Mingle these garnishings together in a sautoire, and add one quart of supreme sauce (No. 547), and at the very last moment add two ounces of very fine butter.

(656). CHICKEN MINION FILLETS GARNISHING (Garniture de Filets Mignons de Poulet).

Pare the minion fillets by removing the inside nerve, and the fine skin which covers them, have them all the same shape and size, then cut on each minion five or six small crosswise incisions dividing them in equal spaces, and in these incisions lay small, round slices of truffles, half an inch in diameter and cut very thin. Lay the minions on buttered sheets, giving them the shape either of a crescent or else laying them straight without bending them, but they can also be rolled around a column mold and laid one beside the other, streak half of them with truffles and the others with tongue, and fill the inside of them with quenelle forcemeat (No. 89), place on each of those streaked with truffles an olive, and on those streaked with tongue a ball of truffles, half an inch in diameter, put them in a buttered sautoire, moisten with a little mushroon essence (No. 392), cover them with buttered paper, and let them poach in a slow oven. Use these minions for improving garnishings.

(657). CHIPOLATA GARNISHING (Garniture à la Chipolata).

This garnishing is composed of eighteen small whole carrots or else cut into balls and glazed, eighteen small glazed onions, eighteen cooked mushrooms, fluted (No. 118) eighteen whole chestnuts moistened with broth and cooked until they fall to a glaze, and small broiled Chipolata sausages (No. 754). Set these various garnishings into a sautoire, and pour over when ready to serve some espagnole sauce (No. 414) reduced with Madeira wine, add half a pound of half inch squares of salt pork, fried in butter and cooked in consommé; arrange the garnishing in clusters for removes, or mingled for entrées.

(658). CHOUX WITH CHEESE GARNISHING (Garniture de Choux au Fromage).

Prepare a pâte-a-chou with three gills of water, half a pound of flour, a quarter of a pound of butter, a pinch of salt and a pinch of sugar, when dry mix into the paste five or six eggs one after the other and finish with a handful of grated cheese. Make round choux laying them on a baking tin a short distance apart, either with a pocket or a spoon, egg the surfaces and dredge over with parmesan; bake in a good but slackened oven. When dry, remove and leave till partly cold, then open the sides and fill each one with a spoonful of cheese fondue (No. 2954). Dress on a napkin or around a remove.

(659). COCKS'-COMBS GARNISHING À LA COLBERT (Garniture de Crêtes de coq à la Colbert).

Select one pound of cock's-combs of equal size; put them into a colander and plunge it by degrees into some water a little warmer than tepid, then heat it gradually, in the meanwhile watching them attentively until they are done, or when by rubbing them with a cloth, the skin detaches. Drain at once, and put them in a cloth with a little fine salt, and rub them thoroughly till they are clean; finish cleansing by rubbing them with salt between the fingers, and in case the skin should not peel off, plunge them once more into boiling water, and finish by skinning properly. Now put them into warm water to soak for twenty-four hours, changing the water several times, and then cut off the tip of the points and the roots of the combs; lay them once more in plenty of salted, tepid water, and squeeze them well to make them disgorge their blood; change the water several times, and finish by cooking them very slowly in acidulated water, then drain dry, and roll them in meat glaze (No. 401), fine butter and chopped parsley.

(660). CONNÉTABLE GARNISHING (Garniture Connétable).

Prepare sixteen minion fillets of chicken well freed of all sinews and skin; streak eight of them with tongue and dress them in a circle, shaping them around a three-quarter inch column cutter, put them on small square pieces of buttered paper; fill the interiors of each with chicken quenelle forcemeat (No. 89) laid through a pocket, and on top of the forcemeat set small half inch balls of truffles. The other eight minion fillets are to be also laid in a circle on squares of buttered paper, filling the interiors with the same forcemeat as the others, but on the top of each set a stoned olive stuffed with anchovies; place them all on a buttered baking-pan, cover over with a buttered paper, moisten with mushroom essence (No. 392) and poach in a slack oven. Have sixteen small game quenelles made with a teaspoon (No. 155) and laid in a buttered sautoire, after decorating them with pistachio nuts, and poached in boiling salted water. Sixteen escalops of ducks' liver, covered on both sides with a villeroy sauce (No. 560) containing mushrooms and raw fine herbs; let these get cold, then dip them in beaten eggs, and bread-crumbs, and fry them to fine golden color. Garnish the remove with the quenelles, minions and Villeroi ducks' livers. Serve a financière sauce (No. 464) separately.

(661). CRAWFISH GARNISHING (Garniture d'Écrevisses).

Whole crawfish are sometimes used combined with other garnishings, but they are considered more as decorations than otherwise; in any case they must first be cooked in a court-bouillon (No. 38), and the shells removed from the tails, without detaching the meat from the bodies, or leave the shells on.

How to Cook Them.—Wash the crawfish, changing the water several times during the operation; suppress the small vein found in the middle underneath the fins, at the tail end, then lay the fish in a saucepan, and season with salt, mignonette, vinegar, or white wine, sliced onions, branches of parsley, thyme, and bay leaf. When they are cooked, break off the small side claws, and remove the shell or not as desired. They can now be trussed as shown in Fig. 506, for skewers. The crawfish tails after being picked out of their shells, are used as garnishings, sautéing them in butter and seasoning with salt, pepper, fine herbs and fish glaze (No. 399). The body shells stuffed with forcemeat (No. 90) are used for soups.

(662). DEMIDOFF GARNISHING (Garniture à la Demidoff).

Sixteen pieces of small, flat lobster croquettes (No. 880), sixteen pieces of risolletes of pancakes with forcemeat or hashed fish, sixteen pieces of large drained oysters, rolled in powdered crackers and fried in clarified butter, drained and dredged over with chopped parsley. Dress this garnishing around a remove and serve separately a lean velouté sauce (No. 415) reduced with some of the oyster liquor.

(663). DOLPHETTES OF CHICKEN GARNISHING (Garniture de Dolphettes de Poulet).

Brown two shallots in two ounces of butter; add one pound of cooked white chicken meat cut in one-eight inch squares, and four ounces of ham cut the same; season with salt, pepper, and nutmeg, and cover the whole with a pint of espagnole sauce (No. 414), and a gill of tomato sauce (No. 549). Let the whole boil up once, then remove it, and set it aside to get cold, and with this preparation make crescent shaped croquettes; dip them in beaten eggs, and bread-crumbs, and fry them nicely.

(664). DOLPHETTES OF TENDERLOINS OF BEEF GARNISHING (Garniture de Dolphettes de Filet de Bœuf).

Fry colorless, in two ounces of butter, one ounce and a half of chopped shallot; add to it a pound and a half of cooked and finely hashed tenderloin of beef, three ounces of fresh bread-crumbs, three ounces of grated parmesan, and eight egg-yolks or two to three whole eggs. Let this preparation cool off, then divide it into eight parts, forming each one into a ball; roll these in fresh bread-crumbs and grated parmesan, mixed well together and fry them to a fine color.

(665). DUCHESS GARNISHING (Garniture Duchesse).

Lay on the table a quarter of a pound of flour; two ounces of parmesan, and two ounces of Chester cheese, both finely grated; a grain of salt and a pinch of cayenne pepper; dilute with a little water and one egg so as to obtain a smooth and firm paste. Roll this out on the floured table to one-eighth of an inch in thickness; cut it into inch and a half diameter round pieces, and lay these on buttered sheets; cook in a hot oven, not having them brown. Beat up some fresh butter in a bowl; mix in with it double its quantity of grated Chester cheese, and a dash of cayenne pepper. Lay the round pieces of cooked paste two by two, one on top of the other, after spreading them all thickly with the cheese preparation; range them once more on the sheet, and heat for a few minutes in a moderate oven, then dress on a napkin or around the remove.

(666). FERMIÈRE GARNISHING (Garniture à la Fermière).

Sixteen persons.—One pound and a half of braised cabbage (No. 2706), arranged in clusters. Eighteen small braised lettuce (No. 2754), eighteen potatoes, cut olive shaped, blanched, cooked afterward in broth, and let fall to a glaze. Eighteen pear shaped carrots, blanched, and cooked in white broth, then let fall to a glaze. Dress all these garnishings in clusters, being careful to alternate tastefully the different colors. Serve separately thickened gravy (No. 405).

(667). FINANCIÈRE GARNISHING (Garniture à la Financière).

Sixteen Persons. For Removes.—Should the garnishing be required for dressing around a large piece, then it can be composed of whole peeled truffles of quenelles, molded in a dessert-spoon (No. 155), escalops of foies-gras, mushroom heads, cock's-combs and kidneys, lamb sweet-breads or small veal sweetbreads larded and glazed. This garnishing is used for garnishing removes of poultry, game and meats, dressing it in groups around and serving a financière sauce (No. 464), separately.

For Entrées.—Cooked, peeled and minced truffles; small mushroom button heads, slices of sweetbreads a quarter of an inch thick, pared with a cutter to an inch in diameter, quarter inch thick slices of foies-gras pared with an inch diameter, round cutter, and oblong quenelles. Put the garnishings into a sautoire and cover with financière sauce (No. 464). Use this garnishing for covering or surrounding entrées.

(668). FLEMISH GARNISHING (Garniture à la Flamande).

Blanch and drain a pound and a half of cabbage, put it into a saucepan with half a pound of salt pork, pepper, one onion with two cloves in it, and sufficient unskimmed broth (No. 194a) to cover the cabbage, then let cook all together for two hours. Cut sixteen carrots into pear-shaped pieces, parboil them first, and then finish cooking them in some broth with sugar, until they fall to a glaze. Have sixteen cork-shaped pieces of turnips, parboil and cook them also in consommé with sugar, till they fall to a glaze. Drain the cabbage when it is done, and lay them on the ends of the remove to be garnished, being careful to suppress the onion containing the cloves. Cut the salt pork into slices, and lay these on top of the cabbage, then set the carrots and turnips in clusters on the sides. Serve separately a half-glaze sauce (No. 413) or else a white sauce (No. 562).

(669). FRENCH GARNISHING (Garniture à la Française).

Twenty-four pieces of truffles, the size and shape of a crescent olive, in a good half-glaze sauce (No. 413) with Madeira. Six ounces of cooked cock's-combs and four ounces of cooked cock's-kidneys. Twenty-four small mushroom heads, turned (No. 118), sautéd, drained and rolled in meat glaze (No. 401) and fresh butter, twenty-four pieces of small chicken quenelles (No. 89) poached in a small pointed mold decorated with truffles, twenty-four crawfish tails, shelled and sautéd in butter, seasoned with salt, lemon juice, chopped parsley, meat glaze (No. 401) and fresh butter. A French sauce (No. 467), to be served separately.

(670). FRITADELLES OF VEAL GARNISHING (Garniture de Fritadelles de Veau).

Dip a pound and a half of bread-crumbs in some milk, and when well soaked, extract all the liquid; have a pound of pared and well chopped roast veal, also two ounces of finely chopped beef marrow. Put two ounces of chopped up onions in a saucepan to fry in two ounces of butter, but do not let it attain a color, then add the veal, the pressed bread-crumbs and the beef marrow, salt, pepper and nutmeg, also a finely chopped lemon peel; reduce and beat in two eggs. After the preparation has cooled off, divide it into small parts so as to be able to make flat croquettes, dip them in egg, then in bread-crumbs and fry to a good color.

(671). FRITADELLES OF ROAST BEEF GARNISHING (Garniture de Fritadelles de Rosbif).

Cut into three sixteenth inch squares, one pound of lean roast beef, chop up two ounces of onions, fry in two ounces of butter, dredge over with two spoonfuls of flour, moisten with broth and reduce; then add the beef, salt, pepper, nutmeg, chopped parsley and two ounces of cooked lean ham cut as small as the beef, heat the whole without boiling; set it aside to get cold and then roll it into balls one inch and a quarter in diameter, flatten down, dip in beaten eggs, bread-crumbs, and fry them nicely in butter.

(672). GODARD GARNISHING (Garniture à la Godard).

Make twelve quenelles, in an entremet spoon (No. 155), decorate richly. Twelve small sweetbreads larded and glazed, the throat sweetbreads if possible. Twelve large cock's-combs, and twelve cock's-kidneys. Twelve pieces of escalops of foies-gras, cut half heart shaped; twelve fluted mushrooms (No. 118) and twelve medium whole truffles, all rolled in a little half-glaze sauce (No. 413). Six very small squabs may be added if desired, but it is apt to make the garnishing too large. Dress around the dish in clusters, serve a half-glaze sauce (No. 413), separately.

(673). GRIBOULETTE GARNISHING (Garniture de Griboulettes).

Have ten ounces of chopped raw beef free of nerves, half a pound of kidney suet, the skin and fibers suppressed; chop each of these separately, then mix in with them five ounces of fresh bread-crumbs, three tablespoonfuls of onions, chopped and fried in butter, one tablespoonful of chopped parsley, salt, and pepper. Divide this preparation into flat balls, flatten them down to an inch and a half in diameter, dip them in beaten egg, then in the bread-crumbs and fry in clarified butter until a fine color.

(674). GRIMOD GARNISHING (Garniture à la Grimod).

Ten ounces of cooked cock's-combs warmed in a little dry Madeira and half-glaze sauce (No. 413). Twenty ounces of cock's-kidneys poached the same as quenelles, drained and thickened with meat glaze (No. 401) and butter. Twenty ounces of foies-gras quenelles, mixed in and thickened with a half-glaze sauce and Madeira. Arrange all of these in clusters around a remove, and serve separately a Grimod sauce (No. 475).

(675). HENRION GARNISHING (Garniture à la Henrion).

Raise the fillets from six snipes, remove all the nerves and skin, pare, season them with salt, and pepper, and sauté them in butter a few minutes before serving. Trim twelve slices of un-smoked red beef tongue into half heart-shaped pieces the same size as the snipe fillets, and heat them in a little half-glaze sauce (No. 413) with Madeira wine. Have twelve croquettes made of blanched chicken livers, the finely chopped insides of the snipes, and the meat cut from the thighs, also some mushrooms; the livers, thighs, and mushrooms to be cut into three-sixteenths of an inch square; mix the whole with a brown sauce (No. 414), and use this preparation for making round croquettes one and a half inches wide by one quarter of an inch thick, dip them in beaten egg, then bread-crumbs, and fry them a nice color. Serve separately a financière sauce (No. 464), finished with the snipe carcasses.

(676). IMPERIAL GARNISHING (Garniture à l'Impériale).

Have a half pound or eight whole truffles peeled and cooked in champagne; eight escalops of foies-gras, breaded à la Villeroi, and fried; sixteen pieces of fluted mushroom heads (No. 118) cooked in butter. lemon juice and water; eight cocks'-combs and eight cocks'-kidneys, sixteen chicken quenelles made with a teaspoon (No. 155). Arrange the foies-gras at the end of the dish and the remainder of the garnishing in clusters around, and cover with a little half-glaze sauce (No. 413) and Madeira. Serve in a separate sauce-boat a financière sauce (No. 464).

(677). JARDINIÈRE GARNISHING (Garniture à la Jardinière).

The jardinière is composed of whole roots and vegetables, or else cut into distinct pieces, such as carrots, turnips, string beans, cauliflower, small glazed onions, Brussels sprouts, asparagus tops or cucumbers cut in the shape of cloves of garlic. The carrots and turnips are to be blanched, but not refreshed, then sautéd in butter with a little sugar, and finished cooking in beef broth (No. 194a), just sufficient so that when the roots are done the moistening is reduced to a glaze. The small onions to be sautéd in butter with a little sugar and let fall to a glaze; the string beans cut in lozenges and cooked first in salted water, then refreshed and drained and sautéd in butter. The cauliflowers to be cooked in water and cut into small flowerets, the Brussels sprouts, asparagus tops and cucumbers cooked in salted water, then sautéd in butter. The green vegetables should be cooked in a copper vessel, the others in a tinned one. This garnishing is usually arranged in clusters and served with a separate brown Madeira sauce (No. 492). For entrées mix all the vegetables together and add to them a brown sauce (No. 414) and some fine butter.

(678). LIVERS À LA VINCELAS GARNISHING (Garniture de Foies-Gras à la Vincelas).

For this garnishing use fat duck or geese livers, weighing from a half pound to a pound. Périgueux foies-gras preserved plain may be substituted in case no fresh livers are on hand, but when the latter can be procured, then blanch and braise them in a mirepoix with Madeira stock (No. 419), let them get cold in it, then cut them up into quarter inch slices, and trim them either round shaped or into ovals or hearts. In the meanwhile prepare four ounces of peeled truffles, eight ounces of salt, unsmoked red beef tongue, and six ounces of cooked mushrooms, cut all these three into eighth of an inch squares, and lay them in a Madeira sauce reduced with some good white wine, and after the preparation is cooked, let it get cold, and with it cover one side of the livers, and over this lay chicken cream forcemeat (No. 75); dredge finely chopped pistachios over the top. Garnish the bottom of a dish with slices of fat pork, lay the livers on top, and cover the whole with buttered paper, set it into a moderate oven for ten minutes, and serve separately a champagne sauce (No. 445).

(679). CHICKEN LIVER GARNISHING IN CASES OR CROUSTADES (Garniture de Foies de Volaille en Caisses ou en Croustades.)

Choose a pound of very white, fine, and fat chicken livers, mince them well and fry them briskly in butter, moisten with half a gill of Madeira wine and half a pint of espagnole sauce (No. 414); season with salt, pepper and the juice of a lemon. With these prepared livers fill some croustades made with puff paste fragments, or else oiled cases previously dried in the oven, garnishing the bottoms with chicken and fine herb forcemeat (No. 75). Serve a half-glaze sauce (No. 413) with Madeira separate.

(680). MACÉDOINE GARNISHING (Garniture Macédoine).

Cut into small quarter of an inch squares, eight ounces of carrots, selecting only the very red part, or else use a round or oval vegetable spoon, two to three-eighths of an inch in diameter; have eight ounces of string beans cut into small lozenges, also six ounces of very tender turnips, prepared exactly the same as the carrots; blanch these separately in salted water, keeping them slightly hard, then lay them with a piece of butter in a sautoire, and season with salt and sugar; toss them for a few minutes on a brisk fire to dry well the moisture, then drain off the butter. Put on, to reduce, two or three gills of béchamel (No. 409), stir into it a few spoonfuls of raw cream, and finally a few spoonfuls of root glaze (No. 403); remove it from the fire, and add to it the vegetables already cooked, as well as six ounces of green peas, and six ounces of asparagus tops, both previously boiled in salted water. Finish the macédoine by incorporating into it three ounces of fresh butter broken up into small bits.

(681). MARROW AND CHIVES CANAPÉS GARNISHING (Garniture Canapés à la Moelle et à la Ciboulette).

Have sixteen oval shaped bread croûtons, slit them all around a quarter of an inch from the edge, and fry them in clarified butter. Empty out the centers, and garnish the insides with slices of marrow previously plunged into boiling water, drained, and seasoned with salt and cayenne pepper; dredge over the top some finely shred chives, and set them for one minute into a warm oven; before serving cover with a Madeira sauce (No. 492).

(682). MARROW FRITTERS GARNISHING (Garniture de Beignets de Moelle).

Cut some beef marrow in thick slices, and plunge them into boiling water, then drain and leave them to get cold. Dip each separate piece into bread-crumbs, then in beaten egg, and again in bread-crumbs, and fry them a fine golden color in very hot frying-fat. A separate sauce-boat of half-glaze sauce (No. 413) should be served at the same time.

(683). MARROW FRITTERS WITH TRUFFLES GARNISHING (Garniture de Beignets de Moelle aux Truffes).

Cook in white velouté stock (No. 422) for ten minutes, six marrow bones cut in six inch lengths; let them get cold, then take out the inside marrow. Prepare a half-glaze, with an equal quantity of jelly, or simply put a gelatine leaf in the half-glaze, and to it add some chopped truffles; put a little of this half glaze into the bottom of timbale molds (No. 3, Fig. 137) set on top a piece of the marrow sufficient to fill it half, and over the marrow a slice of truffle, and again a piece of marrow, so as to fill the mold to within an eighth of an inch from the top; finish with some of the sauce, then unmold, and dip each one in beaten egg, roll in bread-crumbs, and fry, or else simply cover the marrow with an espagnole sauce (No. 414), containing chopped truffles, having it almost cold, then dip them in frying paste (No. 2, No. 137), and fry them a fine color; serve a half-glaze sauce separate (No. 413).

(684). MATELOTE GARNISHINGS (Garnitures Matelote).

These garnishings are composed of roe, milt, crawfish tails, small glazed onions, whole mushrooms, and even truffles; they are to be dressed either in clusters or mixed together; if the latter be desired, then cover them with a matelote sauce (No. 498), and if the former, arrange them in distinct groups, and serve the sauce separately.

(685). MATELOTE BOURGUIGNOTTE GARNISHING (Garniture Matelote Bourguignotte).

Eighteen crawfish cooked in a court bouillon (No. 38). Eighteen croûtons of bread cut into half heart-shape and fried in butter. Eight ounces of small mushroom heads, eight ounces of small onions blanched, then cooked in consommé and glazed. Eight ounces of crawfish tails, a pint and a half of bourguignotte sauce (No. 437). Put into this sauce the mushrooms, small onions, and crawfish tails; dress this garnishing around the remove, and decorate the dish with crawfish and the bread croûtons fried in butter.

(686). MATELOTE MARINIÈRE GARNISHING (Garniture Matelote Marinière).

This garnishing is to be made with thirty-six small quenelles of pike (No. 90) seasoned with cayenne pepper, thirty-six cooked mussels, after removing the small black appendage found attached to them, thirty-six crawfish tails, and six ounces of minced truffles. Mingle all these ingredients in a sautoire, and cover them with a marinière sauce (No. 497), reduced with a part of the mussel broth. Add butter to the sauce just before serving.

(687). MATELOTE NORMANDE GARNISHING (Garniture Matelote Normande).

To be made with eighteen cooked mussels out of their shells, eighteen medium sized blanched oysters, eighteen pieces of milt à la villeroi (No. 698), to be the same size as the oysters; eighteen medium sized cooked mushroom heads, eighteen trussed crawfish cooked in a mirepoix (No. 419), eighteen round crusts one inch in diameter, cut from the crusty part of small rolls, buttered and colored in the oven. Mix in a sautoire with some Normande sauce (No. 509), the mussels, oysters, and mushroom heads, then dress them around a remove, and garnish the outside edge with the croûtons, the crawfish, and the milt à la Villeroi (No. 698).

(688). MILT GARNISHING (Garniture de Laitances).

Select very fresh milts, and suppress all the sanguineous parts; soak them for one hour, then lay them in a saucepan with some water, salt, vinegar, and parsley. Boil up the liquid, and remove it to the side of the range, and keep it thus for twelve to fifteen minutes in order to have them poached. They are to be served either with a Colbert sauce (No. 451), or else milt à la Villeroi (No. 698).

(689). MIRMIDONS WITH PARMESAN GARNISHING (Garniture de Mirmidons au Parmesan).

A mirmidon is a small canelon. They are made thin and short and are filled with a special preparation. Pound two raw chicken fillets with an equal quantity of cooked fat livers; two or three raw peeled truffles, and two raw egg-yolks; season this forcemeat and press it through a sieve. Prepare a noodle paste (No. 142), roll it out into a thin, long, three inch wide band, and cut this band transversely into three inch length pieces; plunge them into boiling, salted water, and let them cook for eight minutes, then remove the saucepan to the side of the fire, to keep the water bubbling for two minutes longer; the paste should now be done. Drain the pieces with a skimmer, and set them in a vessel containing tepid, salted water, then lift them out one by one to wipe dry, and spread on the table; cover each separate piece with a layer of the prepared forcemeat, rolled so that the edges of the paste meet, and arrange these mirmidons on the bottom of a buttered sautoire (Fig. 130), keeping them close together, the edges of paste underneath; moisten to their heighth with a tomato sauce (No. 549) and half-glaze sauce (No. 413), reduced with two or three spoonfuls of Madeira wine; boil the sauce, cover the saucepan and set it on a very slow fire to allow the mirmidons to simmer from fifteen to twenty minutes; drain, trim the ends nicely, then range them in layers in a vegetable dish, dusting over each layer with grated parmesan, and besprinkling the top with a little Madeira sauce (No. 492).

(690). MORIL AND GIROLLE GARNISHING (Garniture de Morilles ou de Girolles).

Wash in several waters one pound of morils; cut off half of their stalks, then throw them into boiling water, and leave them to soak awhile; change the water, then drain them by lifting them up with the hand and laying them on a sieve, afterward sauté them in four ounces of butter, adding the juice of a lemon, and let them cook for ten minutes. Moisten them with one pint of consommé (No 189), adding a bunch of parsley garnished with thyme and a bay leaf; boil the whole for twenty minutes, then suppress the parsley and drain off the broth; now add some espagnole sauce (No. 414), and fine herbs, and reduce it to the consistency of a light sauce, to which add the morils and serve very hot.

Girolle.—Cut off the stalks from two pounds of girolles and then divide them into two or four pieces, according to their size. Wash well in several waters, then drain. Heat four ounces of butter in a sautoire, adding the girolles and some lemon juice; moisten with a pint of bouillon (No. 187,) season with salt and let boil slowly for a few moments, then drain and put them back into the saucepan. Reduce a pint of espagnole sauce (No. 414) with the clear part of the stock, add it to the girolles just when serving and finish the sauce with a little chicken glaze (No. 398) and two ounces of fresh butter.

(691). MOUSSERON GARNISHING, PRINCESS SAUCE (Garniture de Mousserons, Sauce Princesse).

An eatable mushroom growing under moss, found in woods. Cook two pounds of mousserons under a cover, by placing them on a buttered dish, and seasoning with salt, pepper, and two gills of white wine; cover with a bell cover, begin to cook on the fire, then finish for twenty minutes in a moderate oven; drain and place the liquid in a pint of princess sauce (No. 528), reduce and when done to perfection, add a tablespoonful of chicken glaze (No. 398), and two ounces of butter. Roll the mousserons in the sautoire and serve.

(692). MUSHROOMS À LA DELSART GARNISHING (Garniture de Champignons à la Delsart).

Select twelve fine, large mushrooms, cut off the stalks and empty them partly with a vegetable spoon, being careful not to break them, then throw them gently into fresh acidulated water. Chop up finely two ounces of the mushroom parings, one ounce of onions, one clove of crushed garlic, and one teaspoonful of chopped parsley, heat well two ounces of butter in a saucepan, add the onions to fry colorless, then the garlic, and parsley, and finally the mushroom parings after these have reduced their moisture, put in two ounces of bread-crumbs, a pint of béchamel (No. 409), salt, pepper, and nutmeg, stirring in four raw egg-yolks, drain the mushrooms, and fill them with this preparation, having it slightly bomb-shaped on top, bestrew with bread-raspings, and pour over a little butter. Lay them on a baking-tin covered with slices of fat pork, place this in a hot oven to brown the forcemeat, and serve with a half-glaze sauce (No. 413) and Madeira.

(693). MUSSELS BORDELAISE GARNISHING (Garniture de Moules à la Bordelaise).

Poached mussels are frequently used with other garnishings but they can also be served alone around small fish.

For Mussels Bordelaise.—Procure five dozen mussels, clean them well, washing them in several waters and then cook them with some mignonette, parsley, and sliced onions, but no salt, adding a little water. Set them on a slow fire, and when the mussels are opened, take them out of their shells, remove the black appendage, drain, and roll them in a Bordelaise sauce with marrow (No. 436); do not let them come to a boil, and use them for a garnishing.

(694). NOISETTES OF VEAL AND LAMBS' FRIES GARNISHING (Garniture de Noisettes de Veau et d'Animelles d'Agneau).

Noisettes of Veal, are found in the shoulder of either veal or lamb; soak and blanch them, then cook them in a saucepan lined with bardes of fat pork and some good mirepoix stock (No. 419), let them get cold in this, and then pare them by removing all the fat parts; mix them in with a fleurette sauce.

Fleurette Sauce is made with béchamel (No. 409) reduced with cream, into which mix finely cut up chives and finished at the last moment with a piece of fresh butter.

For the Lamb's Fries Garnishing.—Split them in two lengthwise, take them out of their skin season each piece with salt and pepper, and roll them in flour, and afterward dip them in beaten eggs and bread-crumbs, and fry them a fine color. Garnish with the veal noisettes the sides of a remove, and at the ends set the lamb's fries.

(695). OLIVES PLAIN OR STUFFED GARNISHING (Garniture d'Olives Simples ou Farcies).

Spanish olives are the best for garnishing; select the largest, and stone them with the assistance of a small knife, cutting the meat around in spirals, and then removing the stone. Throw them as quickly as they are done into cold water; heat this up without boiling it; refresh them, and add them to any desired hot sauce, being careful that they do not boil and break.

For Stuffed Olives.—They must be first blanched, and allowed to cool; they can either be stuffed with a plain quenelle forcemeat (No. 89) or with a baking forcemeat (No. 81) mingled with a little raw chicken forcemeat (No. 62), then thrown immediately into a saucepan containing hot broth, and leave them in until the forcemeat is well poached; they are then to be added to any sauce they are required to accompany.

(696). ORONGES À LA LIVOURNAISE GARNISHING (Garniture d'Oronges à la Livournaise).

Have sixteen medium sized oronges, suppress the stalks, empty out half of the inside of the oronges with a vegetable spoon and chop up the stalks and insides just removed; fry this in two ounces of butter until all the moisture is evaporated and it is perfectly dry, then add the juice of one lemon and three tablespoonfuls of mushroom catsup. Let this now get cold, and then add to it half its quantity of chicken forcemeat (No. 89), a tablespoonful of chopped parsley and two tablespoonfuls of tomato sauce (No. 549); season well. Mix together and fill the oronges with this preparation, giving them a dome-shape. Lay them on a dish garnished with a few bardes of fat pork and sprinkle over some bread raspings and grated parmesan cheese; pour over a little good sweet oil, a little broth, and place it in a slack oven for twenty to thirty minutes. A half-glaze sauce (No. 413), accompanies this garnishing.

(697). OYSTER GARNISHING À LA TYKOPF (Garniture d'Huîtres à la Tykopf).

First blanch thirty-six small oysters, then drain and wipe them on a napkin, cut away the muscles or hard parts and fill in this space with a crab croquette preparation (No. 879), cover the oysters with a light coating of béchamel sauce (No. 409), with finely chopped truffles added, and leave them in till they are very cold, then dip them in bread-crumbs and beaten eggs and fry them in clarified butter.

(698). OYSTERS, MUSSELS OR MILTS À LA VILLEROI GARNISHING (Garniture d'Huîtres de Moules ou de Laitances à la Villeroi).

Blanch, drain and wipe thirty-six oysters; reduce an allemande sauce (No. 407), with the oyster liquor, adding two tablespoonfuls of cooked fine herbs, let get cold and coat the oysters with it, leave them till very cold, and then dip them into eggs and fry them a fine golden color. For mussels proceed the same, only first removing the black piece adhering to them; milts are to be cooked also the same.

(699). OYSTER GARNISHING FOR SHELLS AND FOR PATTIES WITH MUSHROOMS (Garniture d'Huîtres pour Coquilles et pour Bouchées aux Champignons).

The first step to take is to open the oysters, detach them from their shells, and poach them in their own juice, after this is done, drain them off. They can be bread-crumbed and baked in their own shells if needed whole, or in small scollop shells if they are in salpicon (No. 165), or else they are used to garnish bouchées. To prepare them for the patties proceed as follows: Blanch thirty-two medium sized oysters in their own juice in a saucepan, drain and dry them on a napkin. Fry a finely chopped shallot in two ounces of butter, moisten with the oyster juice, add a pint of béchamel sauce (No. 409), reduce and then strain the whole through a tammy (No. 159), cut the oysters into small squares and fry them in two ounces of butter over a brisk fire, and add them to the prepared béchamel, also two tablespoonfuls of chopped mushrooms

(700). PALATE OF BEEF GARNISHING À LA MANCELLE IN CASES (Garniture de Palais de Bœuf à la Mancelle en Caisses).

After the palates of beef (No. 1326) are cooked, put them under a weight to get cold, then cut out of them round pieces an inch in diameter, sufficient to have a pound. Set these into a saucepan with half a pound of mushrooms and four ounces of truffles both sliced and of the same diameter as the palates, add six gills of espagnole (No. 414), one of tomato sauce (No. 549), the juice of a lemon and one tablespoonful of meat glaze (No. 401). With this preparation fill some small china cases, or else oiled paper ones dried in the oven, dredge bread-crumbs over the tops, also grated parmesan cheese, pour on a little melted butter and set them in the oven to brown.

(701). POLPETTE GARNISHING (Garniture de Polpettes).

Pare well one pound of lean, raw mutton, then chop it up fine, also half a pound of pork fat or calf's udder. Mix well the mutton and udder together, season with salt, pepper and nutmeg and add three whole eggs, then divide this into eighteen parts and with them make balls, roll them in flour, dip them in beaten egg and roll them once more in bread-crumbs, smooth neatly and fry them in clarified butter. Range them nicely around a remove.

(702). PRAWNS, CRAWFISH, CRABS OR LOBSTERS WITH RAW FINE HERBS GARNISHING (Garniture de Crevettes, Écrevisses, Crabes ou Homards aux Fines Herbes Crues).

After the prawns are cooked, refresh and shell them; leave them whole and sauté them in butter, seasoning with salt, pepper, and raw fine herbs, also the juice of a lemon. Crawfish tails may be left whole. For crabs, take out the largest piece, from the crab, and for lobsters cut them in escalops or slices, three-sixteenths of an inch in thickness; finish them the same as for the above.

(703). PROVENÇAL GARNISHING (Garniture à la Provençale).

Prepare for this garnishing eighteen small stuffed tomatoes à la Provençal (No. 2835), eighteen stuffed mushrooms (No. 692), adding to them a bit of garlic, and eighteen croquettes, made with half a pound of minced onions blanched for ten minutes in plenty of water, then fried colorless in butter with their same weight of minced cooked artichoke bottoms, add an allemande sauce (No. 407), and when cold make small croquettes with this preparation, letting them be round and flat; bread-crumb and then dip them in egg, bread-crumb again and fry them a fine color. Garnish around the remove, with these, alternating the tomatoes, the stuffed mushrooms, and the croquettes.

(704). PURÉE OF ARTICHOKE BOTTOMS AND JERUSALEM ARTICHOKES (Purée de Fonds d'Artichauts et de Topinambours).

Cut out two pounds of artichoke bottoms, and blanch them in salted water, drain and mince up fine; lay this into four ounces of butter, but do not let color, then drain off the butter, and moisten with a quart of broth (No. 189); let cook slowly until the bottoms are done, and when the moisture is reduced, add one pint of béchamel (No. 409), and reduce the preparation once more, but without ceasing to stir for an instant until it becomes consistent. Season, rub through a sieve and put this purée into a saucepan to heat while stirring, but it must not boil. Just when ready to serve add four ounces of fine butter. Prepare the Jerusalem artichokes exactly the same, the only difference being that they are peeled and minced raw before frying them in butter, then finish exactly the same as for the artichoke bottoms; all purées for garnishing, should be of such consistency as not to spread.

(705). PURÉE OF ASPARAGUS (Purée d'Asperges).

Break off the tender ends of sufficient green asparagus to obtain a pound of tops. Blanch these in boiling, salted water in a copper basin, then drain them well and fry in a saucepan with four ounces of butter. Moisten with a pint of broth (No. 189), and let them cook until this is entirely reduced, then pound the asparagus in a mortar, adding a pint of very thick béchamel sauce (No. 409), season with salt and sugar, reduce the whole, press through a fine sieve, and return the purée to the saucepan, to heat without boiling; stir in at the last moment two ounces of fine butter.

(706). PURÉE OF BEANS BRETONNE (Purée de Haricots Bretonne).

Mince half a pound of onions; set them in a saucepan with four ounces of butter, a bunch of parsley garnished with bay leaf, garlic, thyme and salt; let fry slowly, browning the onions slightly. Let one pound of white beans soak for twelve hours, then boil them with two ounces of butter added, and when nearly done, drain and pound them in a mortar with the onions, suppressing the parsley; add a pint of béchamel (No. 409), two gills of double cream, and two tablespoonfuls of chicken glaze (No. 398); press through a tammy (No. 170) and add two ounces of butter at the very last moment.

(707). PURÉE OF BRUSSELS SPROUTS (Purée de Choux de Bruxelles).

Blanch in boiling salted water in an untinned vessel, two pounds of well cleaned Brussels sprouts; drain and put them into a saucepan, with one quart of broth (No. 189), two ounces of butter, some salt and sugar; boil slowly until done and the moisture entirely reduced, then mash them and press them through a sieve. Put the purée back into the saucepan with a pint of either velouté (No. 415), or espagnole (No. 414), and a tablespoonful of meat glaze (No. 401); heat it well and finish with two ounces of fine butter just when serving.

(708). PURÉE OF MILAN OR SAVOY CABBAGE (Purée de Choux de Milan ou de Savoie).

Divide a cabbage into four parts; remove the core, then blanch, drain, refresh and shred it finely; fry two tablespoonfuls of chopped shallot in four ounces of butter, add four ounces of minced mushrooms, a tablespoonful of chopped parsley, and some salt to season, then the cabbage, one quart of broth (No. 194a), and two ounces of butter; let simmer until done to perfection, and when the liquid is entirely reduced, add two pints of béchamel sauce (No. 409), press through a sieve, and keep it very warm until serving; then add two ounces of fresh butter.

(709). PURÉE OF CARROTS (Purée de Carottes).

Made with two pounds of the red part of minced carrots; blanch and then finish cooking them in four ounces of butter without browning; moisten with a quart of velouté stock (No. 422), season with salt and a little sugar, and let cook slowly until the carrots are tender, and the broth reduced.

In case they should not be sufficiently moistened, add a little more beef stock (No. 194a), then pound the whole in a mortar; press them through a sieve, and return this purée to the saucepan with a pint of thick béchamel (No. 409); stir briskly, and just when ready to serve, add two ounces of fine butter.

(710). PURÉE OF CAULIFLOWER OR SEA-KALE (Purée de Choux-fleurs ou de Choux de Mer).

Cut a cauliflower weighing two pounds into four parts, clean well, and set on to cook in a tinned vessel with salted water and two ounces of butter; when done, drain, and put the pieces into the saucepan to finish cooking with one quart of beef stock (No. 194a), four ounces of bread-crumbs, salt and sugar, reduce till dry, then mash well the cauliflower, adding half a quart of allemande sauce (No. 407); press through a sieve and keep the purée warm, stirring in two ounces of butter just before serving.

Sea-kale is to be prepared exactly the same.

(711). PURÉE OF CELERY, CELERY KNOBS AND CARDOONS (Purée de Céleri Céleris-raves et Cardons).

For Celery.—Blanch two pounds of white celery stalks, after washing and scraping them, drain and mince them up. Put four ounces of butter into a saucepan and when warm, add the minced celery and let fry without coloring, then moisten with a quart of stock (No. 189), seasoning with salt and sugar, cook and reduce this to nothing, then pound and press it through a sieve, heat it once more, add to it a pint of béchamel (No. 409), and lastly two ounces of fresh butter.

For the Celery Knobs.—Have two pounds of celery knobs, cut each in four pieces, after peeling them; blanch them in hot water, drain, return them to the saucepan with salt, sugar and two ounces of butter, and reduce till dry, pound and rub through a sieve, add a gill of allemande (No. 407), and just before serving, stir in two ounces of fine butter.

Cardoons.—Mince some cooked cardoons; reduce a béchamel (No. 409) with meat glaze (No. 401), add the cardoons and reduce the whole together for twelve minutes; season with salt and sugar; rub through a fine sieve and return the pulp to the saucepan to heat without boiling and finish at the last moment with a piece of fresh butter.

(712). PURÉE OF CHESTNUTS (Purée de Marrons).

Peel one pound of chestnuts, plunge them into boiling water so as to remove the inner skin, then lay them in a saucepan, and moisten them to their height with white broth (No. 189), adding a stalk of celery. Cook them with the lid on over a moderate fire, and when soft, and the broth entirely reduced, pound them in a mortar with two ounces of butter, seasoning with a little salt and sugar; pass this purée through a hair or tinned brass sieve (iron sieve should not be used for passing purées) and return it to the saucepan to heat without ceasing to stir, but at the same time watching that it does not boil, beat in a little velouté (No. 415) and cream.

(713). PURÉE OF CHICKEN (Purée de Volaille).

Cut off two pounds of meat from a cooked chicken, suppress all the skin and nerves, and pound the remainder with a piece of butter and two-thirds of its quantity of very consistent boiled rice. Strain through a tammy (No. 170), and set this purée in a saucepan, season, add to it two spoonfuls of good, well reduced and thick velouté (No. 415), and heat it without allowing it to boil, and without ceasing to stir; incorporate into it at the last moment two ounces of fine butter.

(714). PURÉE OF CUCUMBERS (Purée de Concombres).

Peel the cucumbers and suppress the seeds; weigh two pounds of them after they are pared, blanch them for a few minutes in boiling, salted water, drain well, mince and fry them in four ounces of butter, then moisten with sufficient stock (No. 189), to cover, and let them cook and reduce until all the broth is absorbed. Pound them in a mortar adding a pint of very thick béchamel (No. 409), press through the sieve and heat the purée, adding two ounces of fine butter just before serving.

(715). PURÉE OF FLAGEOLET, LIMA OR BROAD BEANS (Purée de Haricots Flageolets ou de Lima, Fèves de Marais).

Wash two pounds of flageolet beans, and then cook them in six quarts of salted water to which has been previously added two ounces of butter; when done, drain and pound the beans in the mortar, then put them into a saucepan with one pint of very thick béchamel sauce (No. 409), and two tablespoonfuls of meat glaze (No. 401); season with salt, sugar, and red pepper, pass the whole through a sieve, and heat it again without boiling. Should the purée be too thick, add a little cream, and just before serving, two ounces of fine butter.

Lima beans, broad beans and fresh white beans, are to be prepared and finished exactly the same.

(716). PURÉE OF GAME (Purée de Gibier).

Remove one pound of cooked meat from either partridge, snipe, hare, grouse or wild duck, suppress all the skin and nerves, and pound the rest with a piece of butter, then rub it through a sieve. Put this pulp into a saucepan, season it with salt, red pepper, and nutmeg, and mix in half a pint of reduced and very thick velouté (No. 415), if for white game, or a brown sauce (No. 414) for brown game; heat it without ceasing to stir and without letting it boil, and just when ready to serve, add two ounces of fine butter. Should a very thick purée be required, then pound the meats with a quarter of its quantity of boiled and very consistent rice, or else with some cooked game forcemeat (No. 62).

(717). PURÉE OF GARLIC (Purée d'Ail).

Peel half a pound of garlic; cook it in plenty of salted water in a covered vessel, then drain and wipe off the moisture. Fry it for a few minutes over a brisk fire in a pan, with two ounces of butter, season with salt and pepper, and take it off and pound it; mix in a few spoonfuls of good, consistent bechamel (No. 409), and set this purée into a saucepan; heat it well without boiling; just before serving stir in a piece of butter and a little melted glaze (No. 401).

(718). PURÉE OF KOHL-RABIS (Purée de Choux-Raves).

Cut these vegetables in four, peel and blanch them for ten minutes, and finish cooking them in one quart of broth (No. 189); season with salt, and when the moistening is reduced, pound the kohl-rabis, adding to the pulp two pints of reduced velouté (No. 415), and two gills of cream; press well through a tammy (No. 170), and just when serving stir in two ounces of fresh butter.

(719). PURÉE OF LENTILS WITH CREAM (Purée de Lentilles à la Crème).

Pick over and wash a pound and a half of lentils; place them in a saucepan with one quart of broth (No. 194a), a bunch of parsley garnished with thyme and bay leaf, two ounces of blanched salt pork, one onion with a clove in it, and a few sliced carrots; when done, remove the pork, parsley, and carrots, and drain the lentils; pound them in a mortar, season with salt and nutmeg, and dilute the pulp with a gill of béchamel (No. 409) and cream, and add an ounce of butter when ready to serve.

(720). PURÉE OF LETTUCE (Purée de Laitues).

Clean and remove the greenest leaves, and use the whitest of six lettuce heads (having two pounds after this is accomplished); blanch them in boiling salted water, then drain, and press them well to extract all the liquid; put them into a saucepan with one quart of broth (No. 194a), some salt and sugar, and two ounces of bread-crumbs; let the lettuce cook, reduce the liquid entirely, then pound it in a mortar, adding one pint of velouté (No. 415), and one tablespoonful of meat glaze (No. 401). Pass all through a tammy (No. 170), heat the purée and just when prepared to serve, incorporate into it two ounces of fresh butter.

(721). PURÉE OF LOBSTER (Purée de Homard).

Have two pounds of cooked lobster meat; pound it in a mortar with four ounces of butter, season with salt and red pepper, and rub through a sieve, stirring into the pulp six gills of well reduced béchamel (No. 409), heat it well, and just when about serving beat in two ounces of fine lobster butter (No. 580); color it a pale red.

(722). PURÉE OF CULTIVATED AND WILD MUSHROOMS AND MORILS (Purée de Champignons Cultivés et de Prairies et de Morilles).

For the Cultivated Mushroom Purée.—Peel a pound of mushrooms, wash them properly, and mince them finely, then put them into a saucepan with four ounces of butter, let them cook on a slow fire, and when nearly done, moisten them with two gills of velouté (No. 415), and the juice of a lemon. Pound and pass them through a sieve, return them to the saucepan to heat without boiling, and finish with two ounces of fine butter.

Purée of Wild Mushrooms.—Peel a pound of wild mushrooms, cut them up into squares and cook them in water, butter and lemon juice, in a saucepan closed hermetically; drain and pound to convert them to a paste, mixing in half their quantity of poached quenelle forcemeat (No. 89). Add a few spoonfuls of very thick béchamel (No. 409), and season with salt and sugar; press through a tammy, set the purée into a saucepan, and heat it well without boiling, and before serving stir in a little fine butter, and some cream should the purée be too thick.

For the Morils.—Have two pounds of them; cut off the stalks and divide them in two; wash them in tepid water changing it several times, and when clean, drain, and mince them well. Wash them again in tepid water, and drain once more. Heat four ounces of butter in a sautoire, add the morils with lemon juice, and moisten with one pint of broth (No. 189), salt, and pepper; let boil for ten minutes, drain and pour off the top of the broth. Pound the morils, moisten them with this broth, adding a pint of béchamel (No. 409), a spoonful of meat glaze (No. 401), and heat it well without boiling, finishing with two ounces of butter.

(723). PURÉE OF WHITE ONIONS SOUBISE AND PURÉE OF ONIONS, BROWN (Purée d'Oignons Blancs Soubise et Purée d'Oignons Brune).

For the first purée, mince a pound and a half of white onions, plunge them into boiling, salted water and let them parboil for ten minutes, drain them well and put them into a saucepan over a slow fire to allow the moisture to evaporate, add a little good stock and let reduce till dry, then pour in a pint of well thickened béchamel (No. 409), and reduce the preparation over a brisk fire until it becomes consistent. Season with salt and sugar, pass through a sieve and return it to the saucepan and heat the purée without letting it boil, adding a little melted meat glaze (No. 402).

To make the brown purée, abstain from parboiling the onions, but instead, fry them very slowly until they assume a fine color, then mingle in a little espagnole (No. 414), and reduce till consistent; strain the purée, heat it once more and add to it a little melted glaze (No. 400).

(724). PURÉE OF SPLIT PEAS (Purée de Pois Secs).

Wash well and drain one pound of dry split peas, set them in a saucepan with two quarts of velouté stock (No. 422), seasoning with salt and sugar, and adding half a pound of onions, a bunch of parsley garnished with a bay leaf, and two ounces of butter. Cook slowly, suppress the parsley, then drain and pound the peas in a mortar with a pint of béchamel (No. 409) added, press the whole through a tammy (No. 170), heat it well again, and just before serving incorporate into the purée two ounces of fine butter.

(725). PURÉE OF POTATOES (Purée de Pommes de Terre).

Peel and wash two pounds of medium sized potatoes, put them into a saucepan with sufficient water to cover, and a little salt, let them boil till soft, then drain off the water and cover them with a wet cloth, set the lid on the saucepan and put them into a slack oven for twelve minutes to steam. (They may be cooked by steam for half an hour, which is always preferable to boiling in water.) Rub them either through a sieve or pass them through the machine (Fig. 99a), and put this purée back into the saucepan; season, add a little sugar, then heat it up without boiling, stirring in half a pint of cream and two ounces of fine butter.

(726). PURÉE OF SWEET POTATOES (Purée de Patates).

Suppress the ends of a pound and a half of small sweet potatoes, peel and cut them into pieces and fry them in some butter, moisten them to their height with stock (No. 189), and when the potatoes are done and the moistening reduced, pound them in the mortar, seasoning with salt and nutmeg, and adding a gill of cream. Pass this purée through a tammy (No. 170), heat it up well, and before serving, stir in two ounces of fine butter.

(727). PURÉE OF PUMPKIN (Purée de Courge).

Peel and cut a pound of pumpkin into three-quarter inch squares; fry them in four ounces of butter, then moisten them to their height with some stock (No. 194a), adding salt and sugar, and when thoroughly done and reduced, mash them well with half a pint of allemande sauce (No. 407), pass through a sieve, return to the saucepan, heat well, and just before serving, stir in two ounces of fine butter.

(728). PURÉE OF SORREL (Purée d'Oseille).

Pick and clean well one pound of sorrel leaves, and put them into a saucepan with a gill of water and some salt; dissolve while stirring with a spoon, and then pour it into a colander so as to drain it properly; now rub it through a sieve. Prepare a little blond roux (No. 163) with one ounce of butter and the same of flour, add to it the sorrel, and let it cook in this for a few moments without ceasing to stir; moisten with a little good gravy; let the purée reduce, and just when ready to serve, mix in a little fine butter and some meat glaze (No. 402).

(729). PURÉE OF SPINACH OR OF CHICCORY (Purée d'Épinards ou de Chicorée).

Pick and wash the spinach leaves until very clean, having two pounds after this is done; cook them in boiling, salted water, and when they crush easily between the fingers, drain, refresh and drain them once more by pressing them well so as to extract all the water. Pound them thoroughly in a mortar, set them in a saucepan to heat, and season with salt, nutmeg, and sugar; stir in a pint of velouté (No. 415), and two spoonfuls of meat glaze (No. 402), and strain through a fine sieve; return them to the saucepan to heat well and just when ready to serve incorporate into the purée four ounces of fine butter.

The chiccory is to be prepared exactly the same as the spinach.

(730). PURÉE OF TOMATOES (Purée de Tomates).

Cut in halves and press well, half a pound of tomatoes; fry two ounces of minced onions in two ounces of butter without browning, then add the tomatoes, and cook till done, drain them well on a hair sieve, press them through, and put this purée into a saucepan to heat again, stirring in three ounces of kneaded butter (No. 579). Just before serving add two ounces of fresh butter.

(731). PURÉE OF TRUFFLES AND PURÉE OF TRUFFLES WITH RICE (Purée de truffes et Purée de Truffes au Riz).

Peel a few good, raw truffles, half a pound in all; put the peelings into a saucepan with some Madeira wine, cook them for a few minutes to extract the essence, then strain. Grate the truffles and set them in a saucepan with a pint of béchamel (No. 409), and let them cook for five minutes, adding four ounces of poached quenelle forcemeat (No. 89). Pound and rub the whole through a sieve; reduce the truffle essence with half a pint of half-glaze sauce (No. 413), incorporating into it slowly a few spoonfuls of melted glaze (No. 402), and when sufficiently succulent and thick, pour it into the purée, heat this without allowing it to boil, remove it from the fire when ready to serve and stir in two ounces of fine butter.

Purée of Truffles with Rice.—Mince half a pound of cooked truffles, and then pound them with a quarter of a pound of rice boiled in white broth until very dry; season with salt, cayenne, and nutmeg, and pound this in a mortar adding one gill of velouté (No. 415), and a little cream. Press through a tammy (No. 170), heat, and finish with two ounces of fine butter.

(732). PURÉE OF TURNIPS (Purée de Navets).

Peel, wash and mince two pounds of turnips; parboil them for ten minutes in boiling salted water, drain, and fry them colorless in four ounces of butter; moisten with a quart of white stock (No. 422), seasoning with salt and sugar, and let cook slowly until the moistening be entirely reduced, when they are done pound them, adding two pints of thick béchamel (No. 409); pass through a sieve, and warm the purée again, incorporating into it, two ounces of fine butter just before serving.

(733). CHICKEN OR GAME QUENELLES MOLDED IN A SPOON (Quenelles de Volaille et de Gibier Moulées à la Cuillère).

To make these quenelles use either chicken or game quenelle forcemeat (No. 89); prepare them as described in No. 155. Dress them around a remove, and cover with either a half-glaze sauce (No. 413) made with the essence of game or else with velouté (No. 415). These quenelles can also be used by covering them with Villeroi sauce (No. 560), then bread-crumb and fry them to a fine color.

(734). FISH QUENELLES MOLDED, POCKET CHICKEN QUENELLES, CHEESE QUENELLES (Quenelles de Poisson Moulées, Quenelles de Volaille à la Poche, Quenelles au Fromage).

Use fish cream forcemeat (No. 76), finish exactly as quenelles in molds (No. 154), filling the center with a salpicon (No. 165) composed of mushrooms, truffles or shrimps mingled with allemande sauce (No. 407), serving allemande with mushroom essence (No. 408) apart.

Decorated Quenelles, can be prepared in another manner; for these see decorated quenelles in Elementary Methods (No. 154), using a salpicon as for the above and serving the sauce separately.

Pocket Quenelles or else with a Cornet.—Mix half fish quenelle forcemeat (No. 90), and half fish cream forcemeat (No. 76), then make the quenelles which are used generally for soups (No. 239). These can also be made of game (No. 91) or chicken forcemeat (No. 89).

Cheese Quenelles.—Pour into a saucepan three gills of water, three ounces of butter, a little salt and sugar; boil, then incorporate seven ounces of sifted flour, work it well until dry, add enough eggs to bring the preparation to the consistency of forcemeat, two ounces of grated parmesan, and six ounces of lean ham cut in small eighth of inch squares; roll this paste on a floured table into half inch diameter strings and cut them into half inch lengths; roll each one olive shaped, flatten to half, plunge them into boiling water, and poach for ten minutes without boiling; drain in a colander, then on a cloth. Range them in a vegetable dish in layers, bestrewing each one with grated parmesan, and basting with not too thick béchamel (No. 409), reduced with cream; cover and dredge the top with grated parmesan, then bake for fifteen minutes in a slack oven. Serve this garnishing with a remove of roast beef or mutton only leaving it in the vegetable dish.

(735). GODIVEAU OF VEAL, OF PIKE, CHICKEN OR GAME QUENELLES (Quenelles de Godiveau de Veau, de Brochet, de Volaille ou de Gibier).

Prepare the quenelles either with veal (No. 85) pike (No. 83) or else of chicken godiveau (No. 82), young rabbit or any other game. Divide it into several parts, then roll into strings three-quarters of an inch thick on to a table dredged with flour and cut them into inch lengths, roll and lengthen to the shape of a quenelle an inch and a half long. Poach in boiling, salted water. Veal godiveau quenelles are covered with Madeira Spanish sauce (No. 414), those of pike with béchamel (No. 409), those of chicken with suprême (No. 547) and those of game with demi-glaze (No. 413).

(736). RAMISOLLE GARNISHING (Garniture de Ramisolles).

Soak fourteen ounces of fresh bread-crumbs in some milk for one-half hour, then extract well all the liquid. Remove the skin from eight ounces of cooked chicken meat, eight ounces of raw chicken livers and three ounces of truffles; all being finely chopped up. Fry in one ounce of butter, a tablespoonful of chopped shallots or onions, before they attain a color, add to them the raw chicken livers and fry both together, then throw in the chicken and truffles, seasoning with salt, pepper and nutmeg, and lastly add the bread-crumbs, let it all get very hot, then cool it off slightly and beat in six egg-yolks. Lay this preparation between two pancakes, cut into desirable pieces, dip them each in beaten egg, roll in bread-crumbs and fry. A Madeira sauce (No. 492) accompanies this garnishing.

(737). RICE GARNISHING INDIAN STYLE AND WITH BUTTER (Garniture de Riz à l'Indienne et au Beurre).

Rice makes an excellent garnishing, and is adapted for the use of many meats, fish, poultry and game. Fat rice is served with poultry, and is merely rice cooked in chicken broth or soup stock (No. 194a), slightly fat; it should be rather more consistent than otherwise, but at the same time tender or soft; it is finished with a little nutmeg, and sometimes with a handful of grated parmesan cheese.

Rice, Indian Style, is served likewise as a garnishing for chicken or veal, and is prepared with fine Indian rice, its grains being long, white and whole; in case none of this can be procured, then take Carolina rice. Plunge it into a bountiful supply of boiling water after picking and washing it, and as soon as it no longer cracks between the teeth, then drain it through a colander, and wash it off with salted tepid water, spread it over a large sieve, cover with a cloth, and leave it to dry for a few moments at the oven door, then dress it in a vegetable dish, cover and serve.

Rice with Butter.—Blanch some rice for five or six minutes, drain and wash it off with tepid water, then leave it to dry on a cloth. Put two spoonfuls of chopped onion into a saucepan, leave it to fry in some butter, and then add to it the rice; when it is very hot, moisten with white stock (No. 194a), and leave it to finish cooking on a good fire, keeping it slightly firm, set it to smother for a few moments at the oven door, then remove it, and beat up into it with a fork a good sized piece of butter. Dress the rice in a vegetable dish, cover it with a small napkin previously dampened in hot water, put the cover on the dish and serve.

(738). RICHELIEU GARNISHING, ANCIENT AND MODERN (Garniture Richelieu, Ancienne et Moderne).

Ancient.—Eighteen medium sized onions (each one weighing an ounce), stuffed with chicken forcemeat à la Soubise (No. 89). Six ounces of cock's-combs, eight ounces of escalops of foies-gras (No. 2279). To be served with champagne sauce separate (No. 445).

Modern.—Six ounces of pear-shaped blanched carrots, six ounces of cauliflower, six ounces of green peas, six ounces of string beans, six ounces of asparagus tops, six ounces of potato balls, six ounces of mushrooms, eight stuffed lettuces and eight stuffed tomatoes. Dress these in separate groups and serve separately a demi-glaze sauce (No. 413).

(739). PIEDMONTESE RISOT GARNISHING (Garniture de Risot Piémontaise).

Risot can be employed either as a soup or a garnishing; the manner to prepare it is most simple. Put into a saucepan two spoonfuls of chopped up onion, let it fry to a nice golden color in some butter, and add to it a pint of clean but unwashed Piedmont rice; cook it for two minutes while stirring, and then moisten with three pints of broth, cook it again for twenty minutes without touching it; by this time the rice ought not to be too much done, but the liquid nearly all absorbed; remove it from the fire, and finish simply by incorporating into it about a quarter of a pound of good butter, a very little at the time, using a two pronged fork (Fig. 175) for stirring, and two handfuls of grated parmesan cheese, also some cayenne pepper. If the rice be of good quality and properly cooked, it requires no further seasoning; cover it for five or six minutes, and then dress it in a vegetable dish, and dredge over some more parmesan. Risot prepared in this way may be placed in large timbale molds, or else in a border mold, first brushing the inside over with some melted glaze. If desired the cheese may be served separately instead of mixed with the rice.

(740). ROTHSCHILD GARNISHING AND COCKS'-KIDNEYS VILLEROI (Garniture Rothschild et Rognons de coq à la Villeroi).

This garnishing is composed of eighteen kidneys à la Villeroi, nine game quenelles made in a dessertspoon (No. 155), nine escalops of sweetbreads, nine escalops of smoked ham cut from the lean part and pared into half-hearts, nine escalops of foies-gras the same shape and size as the ham, and eighteen small whole truffles. Dress these ingredients in clusters, and serve with a brown Madeira sauce (No. 492), to which has been added a little game glaze (No. 398), one-half to be poured over the garnishing, and the rest to be served separately. Serve the cocks'-kidneys apart.

Cocks'-Kidneys Villeroi.—Simply poach the kidneys by putting them into a colander, and plunging into boiling water until they are poached and firm, then drain and cover with a Villeroi sauce (No. 560), let get cold, dip them in beaten eggs and bread-crumbs, and then fry to a fine color, and serve on a folded napkin with a bunch of fried parsley on top, and quartered lemons around.

(741). SALPICON GARNISHING (Garniture Salpicon).

A salpicon is composed of several meats cut in three-sixteenths to one-quarter inch dice, and combined with truffles and mushrooms trimmed exactly the same. It is used either with a brown espagnole sauce (No. 414), or if a white sauce is desired, with a velouté (No. 415), or an allemande (No. 407). The salpicon should be mixed with the sauces mentioned in each recipe.

(742). SALPICON GARNISHING, COLUMBIAN (Garniture Salpicon, Colombienne).

Is composed of sixteen ounces of mushrooms, four ounces of roast game fillets, six ounces of lambs' fries. and if for fat, a fat financière sauce (No. 464), and if required for lean, use twelve blanched and well drained oysters cut in pieces and sautéd in butter, with six ounces of mushrooms, six ounces of salmon sautéd in butter, and with these use a lean financière sauce.

(743). FAT LIVER SALPICON (Salpicon de Foies-Gras).

Braise fourteen ounces of fat duck's or geese livers in a matignon (No. 406) (this is their weight after being cooked), leave them to get cold, and then cut them up into small dice, also four ounces of truffles, and two of ham. Serve with a half-glaze sauce (No. 413).

(744). FLAVIGNAN SALPICON (Salpicon à la Flavignan).

Stir into a pint of Flavignan sauce (No. 466), two ounces of spinal marrow and three ounces of brains cooked in acidulated water, seasoned with salt and whole peppers and garnished with aromatic herbs, thyme, bay leaf, parsley leaves, and onions. Boil together for fifteen minutes, then let them get cold in this broth, afterward cutting them in quarter of an inch squares. Have also four ounces of braised sweetbreads cut in squares; four ounces of cooked ham, and four ounces of cocked mushrooms, all prepared the same.

(745). HUNTER'S SALPICON (Salpicon au Chasseur).

Is composed of roasted game breasts cut in three-sixteenth inch dice pieces, truffles cut the same, as well as mushrooms and tongue, and chicken livers cut up in one-quarter inch pieces, mixed with a Hunter's sauce (No. 480).

(746). LOBSTER, SHRIMP OR CRAWFISH, WITH MUSHROOM OR TRUFFLE SALPICON

(Salpicon de Homard, d'Écrevisses ou de Crevettes, aux Champignons ou aux Truffes).

Take from the thickest part of the tails, sixteen ounces of cooked lobster meat, or shrimps, or crawfish, and four ounces of mushrooms, both cut in small three-sixteenths of an inch dice; have one pint of béchamel sauce (No. 409), reduced with cream and thickened at the last moment with two ounces of fresh butter.

With Truffles.—Suppress the mushrooms and add two ounces of truffles cut the size and shape as the mushrooms.

(747). MONTGLAS SALPICON (Salpicon à la Montglas).

Made with four ounces of truffles, eight ounces of mushrooms, eight ounces of red beef tongue and eight ounces of chicken or game livers, all cut into small sticks; if needed for a white salpicon garnishing, then mix these with either a velouté (No. 415), or suprême sauce (No. 547), or allemande (No. 407), and if for brown then use espagnole (No. 414), or chicken glaze (No. 398), with essence of mushroom (No. 392).

(748). PALERMITAINE SALPICON (Salpicon à la Palermitaine).

To be prepared with five ounces of small macaroni cut in half inch lengths, five ounces of partridge breast, five ounces of artichokes in quarter inch squares, and three of ham in three-sixteenth inch squares; all these ingredients to be mixed with a turtle sauce (No. 552).

(749). PRÉVILLOT SALPICON (Salpicon à la Prévillot).

Have eight ounces of fresh raw mushrooms, twelve ounces of egg-plant and one ounce of onions all cut into small squares; place three ounces of butter in a saucepan to heat, then lay in the onions to fry lightly first, add the egg-plant and later the mushrooms with a mite of garlic. Moisten with a half-glaze sauce (No. 413) and white wine, despumate, reduce and lastly add some chopped parsley.

(750). RÉGENCE SALPICON (Salpicon à la Régence).

For Lean.—Use four ounces of truffles cut in three sixteenth inch squares, six ounces of mushrooms cut the same, six ounces of crawfish tails likewise cut in three-sixteenth inch pieces, four ounces of milt, and four ounces of very small bead-shaped fish quenelles, all to be combined with a lean régence sauce (No. 532).

For Fat.—Five ounces of braised sweetbreads, five ounces of chicken livers and five ounces of mushrooms, all these to be cut in three-sixteenth inch squares, five ounces of small bead-shaped chicken quenelles (No. 154), and four ounces of truffles cut the same as the other ingredients; to be used with a fat régence sauce (No. 532).

(751). ROYAL SALPICON (Salpicon à la Royale).

For Fat.—Ten ounces of mushrooms cut in three-sixteenth inch squares, ten ounces of white chicken meat cut the same, and four ounces of truffles cut the same. To be used with a fat suprême sauce (No. 547).

For Lean.—Ten ounces of lobster, ten ounces of mushrooms and four of truffles, all cut up in three-sixteenth inch squares, mixed with a lean béchamel sauce (No. 411), finished at the last moment with crawfish (No. 573) or lobster butter (No. 580) and cream.

(752). TURBIGO SALPICON (Salpicon à la Turbigo).

Have eight ounces of artichoke bottoms cut in one-quarter inch squares and the same of braised ducks' livers cut the same size, and cooked in a mirepoix (No. 419) with four ounces of three-sixteenth inch squares of truffles. A fine strained tomato sauce (No. 549) mixed with twice its quantity of velouté (No. 415) and thickened with cream and egg-yolks.

(753). TURTLE SALPICON (Salpicon Tortue).

For Fat.—Four ounces of truffles cut in three-sixteenth inch squares; ten ounces of the gelatinous part of calf's head cut in quarter inch squares, six of sweetbreads the same, and four of tongue also cut in three-sixteenth inch squares. Mix with a turtle sauce (No. 552).

For lean.—Four ounces of truffles cut in three-sixteenth inch squares, ten of green turtle cut in one-quarter inch squares, six of mushrooms cut in three-sixteenth inch squares, and four ounces of hard boiled egg-yolk quenelles, in the shape of small beads, a turtle sauce (No. 552) with tomatoes sauce (No. 549) prepared lean.

(754). SAUSAGE GARNISHINGS (Garnitures de Saucisses).

Large broiled sausages one and a quarter inches in diameter are served as a garnishing, after removing their skins and cutting them across into quarter inch thick slices.

For Chipolata Garnishing use small thin sausages an inch and a half long sautéd and served with Madeira wine.

For Lubeck Garnishing, fry them in the pan with some chicken fat and use with a thick gravy (No. 405).

Strasburg Smoked Sausages are small smoked ones poached for a few minutes in boiling water and served without any sauce whatever.

(755). SCALLOP SHELLS FOR RELEVÉS GARNISHING (Garniture de Coquilles de Pétoncles ou Coquilles St. Jacques Pélerines Pour Relevés).

These shells must be chosen the smallest kind and of equal size. They may be filled with a preparation for shells, St. Jacques (No. 1079), or havraise (1075), or brestoise (1874); smooth well the tops, dust over with white bread-crumbs and a little grated cheese, besprinkle with a little butter and bake them in a hot oven. This garnishing is easy to serve, and has one great advantage; that of being able to prepare it in advance.

(756). SPANISH SWEET PEPPERS SAUTÉD, GARNISHING (Garniture de Piments Doux d'Espagne Sautés).

These peppers are imported from Spain or Havana; select those that are fresh and with thick meat. Put them on the broiler or in the oven, until they soften, and the skin peels off, remove, and open them; suppress all the hard parts and skin; sauté them in oil with some chopped onions and mushrooms, seasoning with salt, pepper, and fine herbs. If fresh Spanish sweet peppers cannot be procured, then take the preserved ones; they are already prepared in cans and only need draining to have them ready for use.

(757). SPINAL MARROW GARNISHING (Garniture d'Amourettes).

Calf's spinal marrow is preferable to beef's. Put three pounds of calf's spinal marrow to soak in cold water for three hours, changing the water each hour; then remove the thin sanguineous skin covering them and trim them. Cook them for a few minutes in a little salted water with some vinegar, parsley leaves, thyme, bay leaf, whole peppers, and sliced onions; pour it all into a bowl and let the marrow get cold in the stock, then cut them up into pieces two inches long. Bread-crumb half of these, dip them in egg, and fry them until they acquire a good color. Drain and wipe well the other half, sauté them in butter, seasoning with salt, pepper, and fine herbs. A Colbert sauce (No. 451), accompanies this garnishing served in a separate sauce-boat.

(758). STRAWS CHEESE GARNISHING (Garniture de Pailles au Fromage).

Prepare seven ounces of flour, four ounces of butter, and four ounces of grated cheese, four tablespoonfuls of raw cream, two egg-yolks, a dash of cayenne, and a grain of salt. First rub well between the two hands, the butter and flour, so as to have them sandy; then lay this in a ring on the table, and into the center pour the cream, egg-yolks, cheese, pepper, and salt; make the dough using for this purpose the blade of a knife so as not to heat the paste, and when well mingled, roll it out into a square piece the thickness of one-eighth of an inch. Cut this into bands two and three-quarter inches wide, and cut these again across into ribbons as wide as their thickness; roll them with the hands on the floured table to give each one a round shape, then range them at once on to a buttered baking sheet, clip off their ends together so as to have them all of equal length, and egg the surfaces. Cook these straws for seven or eight minutes in a slack oven, then take them out and detach them from the sheet with the blade of a knife, and return them at once to the oven to finish cooking, a few minutes being sufficient for this purpose. Serve them on folded napkins.

(759). SMALL SWISS CHEESE SOUFFLÉ GARNISHING (Garniture de Petits Soufflés au Fromage Suisse).

Butter twelve hollow tartlet molds; fill them to almost their height with a cheese soufflé preparation (No. 2984) not too light. Range these molds in a sautoire with a little hot water, and let them poach in a slack oven for sixteen to eighteen minutes without allowing the water to boil. After removing them from the oven, unmold on a deep buttered silver dish; dredge over some grated parmesan cheese in such a way that the tops of all the small loaves are well covered; a quarter of an hour before serving, pour over some good raw cream so that they float in the liquid to about half their height, then place them in a moderate oven to let them absorb the cream, souffléing them slightly and coloring them at the same time. Serve the instant they leave the oven.

(760). TARTLETS À LA PARMENTIER (Tartelettes à la Parmentier).

Roll out thin some timbale paste (No. 150), and line some small hollow tartlet molds. Pre-pare a little purée of potatoes the same as for Duchess potatoes (No. 2785), keeping it rather stiff, and mix with it egg-yolks, butter, and parmesan cheese; with this fill the tartlet molds, having previously pricked the paste with the tip of a small knife, press the potatoes down well and smooth the top; butter it over, and besprinkle with grated parmesan, then put them into a moderate oven to cook. Unmold and serve.

(761). TARTLETS OF NOQUES WITH PARMESAN GARNISHING (Garniture de Tartelettes de Noques au Parmesan).

Line some large tartlet molds with fine paste (No. 135) and prick the paste. Prepare a pate-à-chou with cheese (No. 132), lay it on a floured table and divide it into several pieces; roll them with the hands into strings the thickness of macaroni, then cut them across into pieces the same length as their thickness; place them on a sieve containing a little flour, and toss them so that they form into small balls, then plunge these balls into boiling, salted water. Let the water boil up twice, set them on one side of the range until the paste is well poached, and then drain them through a colander. Put on the fire to reduce two or three gills of good béchamel (No. 409), incorporating into it slowly a few spoonfuls of mushroom broth and some raw cream; when well thickened finish with few spoonfuls of melted glaze (No. 402), take it from the fire and throw in the noques; let simmer for five minutes on a very slow fire, and then add butter and parmesan cheese, and a little grated nutmeg, fill the tartlet molds with this preparation; smooth the surface neatly and dredge a little parmesan on top, bake them in the oven for a quarter of an hour, unmold the tartlets and serve them exceedingly hot.

(762). POLENTA TARTLETS (Tartelettes de Polenta).

Boil a quart of water, then add to it three-quarters of a quart of polenta letting it fall like rain into the boiling liquid. Cook it on the fire while stirring unceasingly, and incorporate into it, three ounces of butter, three ounces of parmesan and six egg-yolks. Fill small tartlet molds lined with fine paste (No. 135) with this preparation, leaving a hole in the center and filling it in with salpicon Previllot (No. 749); cover the whole with polenta, smooth the top, besprinkle with butter and dredge over grated parmesan, and then cook them nicely in a moderate oven.

(763). SEMOLINO TARTLETS (Tartelettes à la Semoule).

Line some tartlet molds with fine paste (No. 135), cook in a pint and a half of bouillon (No. 187), half a pound of semolino, with two ounces of butter, the same of grated parmesan and two whole eggs, and fill the molds with this preparation, leaving an empty space in the center to fill in with a Columbian salpicon (No. 742), cover over with some semolino preparation, pour over some butter, bestrew grated parmesan on top and cook in a slow oven.

(764). SPINACH TARTLETS (Tartelettes aux Épinards).

Line the small tartlet molds with a thin foundation paste (No. 135), prick the bottom, pick and wash one pound of spinach, parboil it in salted water in an untinned copper vessel, and when the leaves crush easily between the fingers, drain, refresh and drain it once more, press it well between the hands to extract all the water, and weigh one pound of it, then chop it up finely, and put it into a saucepan over a quick fire with four ounces of butter added, leave it to dry for a few minutes, then thicken it with one tablespoonful of flour, moistening with two gills of cream. When cold add two ounces of parmesan, two ounces of butter, eight egg-yolks and four whites beaten to a stiff froth; mix together thoroughly and fill up the molds; finish cooking them in a slack oven.

(765). TARTLETS WITH CREAM AND PARMESAN CHEESE GARNISHING (Garniture de Tartelettes à la Crème au Parmesan).

Roll out a timbale paste (No. 150), very thin, and with it line some large, flat tartlet molds; prick the bottom paste and strew over some grated parmesan cheese, and in the center of each one lay a small pat of butter. Beat up in a bowl, five raw egg-yolks, dilute with one pint of raw cream, add a grain of salt, a pinch of flour, a pinch of sugar, some pepper, strain, and add a handful of grated parmesan; then pour it into the lined molds so as to fill them up, set these molds on a baking sheet, and push them carefully into a slack oven to let cook for fifteen minutes, more or less according to the size of the molds; leave them at the warm oven door for five minutes, then unmold quickly and dress them on folded napkins or around a remove.

(766). TOULOUSE GARNISHING (Garniture Toulouse).

Have eight ounces of truffles cut either into balls or else minced, and cooked in a little Madeira wine; add to these truffles, sixteen mushroom heads, eight turned and the other eight fluted (No. 118) twelve pretty cocks'-combs, and twelve cocks-kidneys. Dress in clusters both the truffles and the other ingredients, and cover the whole with a buttered velouté sauce (No. 415) or clear chicken half-glaze (No. 389). Serve separately some of the same sauce.

(767). TRUFFLE GARNISHING (Garniture de Truffes).

Raw truffles to be used whole for garnishings should be first peeled, then cooked for eight or ten minutes in some good Madeira. In case there be no fresh truffles on hand, then use the preserved ones which are considered excellent. For garnishing with truffles, cut them in slices, or olive shaped, or in quarters, or in small sticks, or else left whole; minced truffles are also used, prepared by cutting them into thin slices and sautéing them in butter and oil over a brisk fire; season and finish with a little Madeira or suprême sauce, or even chicken glaze (No. 398) or half-glaze (No. 400) well reduced and buttered.

(768). TURTLE GARNISHING (Garniture Tortue).

The turtle garnishing for meat removes is composed of lamb's sweetbreads or else small calf's sweetbreads, larded and braised; of brains cut into three-quarter inch pieces, bread-crumbed and fried; small peeled truffles cooked in Madeira wine, mushroom heads, quenelles made with a teaspoon (No. 155), egg quenelles composed of hard boiled egg-yolks, pounded with a little butter, some fine herbs and raw yolks, pickled gherkins cut into small balls, stoned and blanched olives, calves' palates, and crawfish á la Bordelaise (No. 1008).

Put into a saucepan some turtle sauce (No. 552), add the peeled truffles, mushrooms, quenelles pickles, olives, egg-quenelles, and palates; mix well together and dress this garnishing, decorating around with the crawfish, brains, and the larded and glazed sweetbreads. Serve a turtle sauce (No. 552) with Madeira separately.

For a Lean Turtle Garnishing.—Make it of fish quenelles (No. 90), hard-boiled egg quenelles, mushroom heads, pickled gherkins cut in balls, stoned and blanched olives, and large crawfish. The lean turtle sauce to accompany it should be reduced with fish essence (No. 388).

(769). WINGS OF TURKEY OR PULLET À LA VILLEROI GARNISHING (Garniture d'Ailerons de Dinde ou de Poularde à la Villeroi).

Singe turkey or pullet wings and bone them as far as the joint, season with salt and pepper, and fill in the empty space with a little quenelle forcemeat (No. 89) and fine herbs, laying it in through a cornet and pushing the skin into the cut side so as to well enclose the forcemeat. They may be sewn with coarse thread, and then blanched and drained. Remove the feather stubs carefully and put the wings into a saucepan lined with bardes of salt pork, and covered with some mirepoix stock (No. 419). Lay more slices of pork on top of the wings and let them cook slowly for one hour or more; drain, pare, lay them in a bowl, pour the mirepoix stock over, and leave to get cold; then take them out and cover them with a villeroi sauce No. 560), with some chopped mushrooms added. Dip in beaten egg, and bread-crumbs, and fry a fine color.

(770). YORKSHIRE PUDDING GARNISHING (Garniture de Pouding Yorkshire).

Dilute in a bowl, half a pound of flour with one pint of milk, and five whole eggs, salt, and four ounces of melted butter, keeping the paste liquid; strain it through a sieve. Cover a raised edged baking pan with a layer of melted butter or fat, pour in the preparation, having it a quarter of an inch high, set it in a slow oven, and half an hour after turn it over, and cook the other side for another half hour. When done cut it into squares or lozenges and serve it as a garnishing. A thickened gravy (No. 405) should be served at the same time.

SIDE DISHES.

COLD SIDE DISHES (Hors-d'Œuvre Froids).

Hors-d'œuvre, or side dishes, signifies out of the work, they having no place on the bill of fare. They are certain appetizing dishes placed on the table before dinner, remaining on in the Russian service, until the dessert; in the French service they pass round a few hors-d'œuvre after the soup, such as melons, olives, radishes, celery, figs, artichokes, canapés,etc.

In Russia the hors-d'œuvre is highly appreciated, and as in the Russian service the removes, entrées and roasts do not appear on the table, which should be handsomely decorated with all kinds of hors-d'œuvre so as to make an elegant display. In formal dinners they serve in another apartment close to the dining-room, a table spread with a variety of side dishes; they also serve at the same time kümmel, brandy, vermouth, absinthe, gin, etc.

(771). ALLIGATOR PEARS (Avocats).

Originally from South America. Select the fruit when very ripe, peel off the outer green skin, and cut the pear in slices, range them on a side dish, season with salt, pepper and vinegar, and garnish around with slices of lemon cut in halves.

(772). ANCHOVIES—SARDELS—ANCHOVY SALAD AND ANCHOVIES WITH OLIVES, (Anchois et Salade d'Anchois, Anchois aux Olives).

Anchovies from Marseilles and Italy are considered very fine, their meat being red and of an exquisite taste, yet, in New York, the white meat anchovies imported from Holland called Sardels are preferred. Wash them well, changing the water frequently, then let them soak; afterward drain and wipe well with a dry cloth to remove the fine white skin covering these fishes, divide them in two lengthwise, remove the middle bone, and pare well the fillets, cut off their ends square, having them all of equal length, and then lay them in small jars and cover over with oil, to use when needed. Drain and arrange them symmetrically on side dishes, and garnish either with parsley, chervil or chopped tarragon, sprinkle over a dash of vinegar and some good oil, garnish with chopped hard boiled eggs, or else quartered eggs and slices of green lemon cut in halves.

Anchovies with Olives.—When the anchovies are prepared as for the above, pare them on one side, and remove a little of the ends, then roll them over a round stick of wood five-eighths of an inch in diameter, so that an olive can be inserted in the center. The olives should be stoned with a small cylindrical cutter, and the empty space filled with hard boiled egg-yolks rubbed through a fine sieve, or else some anchovy butter (No. 569). Range them symmetrically and sprinkle over a little good sweet oil.

(773). ARTICHOKE BOTTOMS PRINTANIER, SMALL APPETITE, SMALL RAW POIVRADE (Fonds d'Artichauts Printaniers, Petit Appétit, Petits crus Poivrade).

It is necessary to have small artichoke bottoms; remove the green part covering the bottoms and all the leaves until the stringy core is reached; pare the bottoms to have them very round and even, and rub them as quickly as they are done with half a lemon, then throw them into cold water. Blanch them until the core or choke can be easily removed, then cook them in water, butter, lemon juice, and salt; drain and make incisions in the bottom, and marinate them for one hour in a seasoning of salt, pepper, oil, and vinegar, then drain them. Garnish them with a small vegetable macédoine (No. 680), well seasoned with salt, pepper, vinegar, and mayonnaise, then dress them on a side dish.

For Small Appetite, instead of the macédoine, take some small green chiccory, wash it well and add to it some chopped chervil and tarragon; season with sa't, pepper, oil, and vinegar, dress and decorate the tops with small anchovy fillets.

Small Artichokes, Poivrade.—Choose small, freshly gathered artichokes, green and tender; trim the bottoms, rub them with lemon, and remove two or three rows of the hardest leaves, place the artichokes at once into cold acidulated water, and when ready to serve, drain and lay them on a side dish with clean pieces of ice set around. Serve in a separate sauce-boat, a French dressing made with salt, pepper, vinegar, oil, and mustard.

(774). BEETS (Betteraves).

Select very red beets without being stringy; cook them either in water, or by steam, or else in the oven; do not cut off either the stalk or root until ready to use. Peel and put them into an earthen or stone crock, and cover them over with vinegar. They may also be seasoned with salt and cloves, or else salt and carraway seeds. Cut them in slices and arrange on a side dish, pouring a little vinegar over.

(775). BUTTER FRESH MOLDED (Beurre Frais Moulé).

The butter must be of the very best quality, without a particle of salt, and used the same day it is made.

For Shells.—Grate with a table knife a piece of firm but not too hard butter; when there is sufficient on the blade of the knife, remove it with the finger to place it immediately on a butter dish or in ice water.

Fig. 199.

For Pats.—Divide a pound of butter into sixteen equal parts, or one ounce for each. The butter must be well worked, neither too soft nor too hard; set it into cold water, with two grooved wooden pallets lift out a piece of butter the size of a ball half an inch in diameter, press the butter between the two pallets, turn it round lightly, and remove the surplus with the first finger of the right hand; when a pat is formed, take it out and throw it into cold water.

For Vermicelli Butter.—Put butter not too hard into a machine called a butter syringe, having a tin perforated sheet with holes three thirty-seconds of an inch in diameter; push the butter through these so that it falls into the water.

To Serve it in Small Stone Pots.—Fill some small gray stone pots with butter and cover with pieces of fine muslin; these are placed as they are on the table. Butter is often served, drained, and laid on grape leaves, or simply in butter dishes with small pieces of very clean ice around.

(776). RED AND WHITE CABBAGE, ENGLISH STYLE, AND MARINATED CAULIFLOWER
(Choux Rouges et Choux Blancs à l'Anglaise et Choux-Fleurs Marinés).

Cut either a white or red cabbage in four, remove the core and hard parts of the leaves, cut the latter up very fine, and lay them in a vessel with a handful of salt for each cabbage; turn them over every day, and at the end of four days, drain them, and put them into a stone jar, pouring over the cabbage some good, boiling vinegar, add a few cloves, some ginger, small blanched onions, red peppers; and grated horseradish root; a few days later the cabbage may be served as a hors-d'œuvre, laying it in side dishes.

For Marinated Cauliflower.—Choose white and hard cauliflowers, cut off all the leaves and divide the flower into small clusters; remove the core, pare them nicely, and range them into a very clean tinned saucepan. Cover with cold water, boil up the liquid, then add salt, and let them boil for ten minutes; now remove the cauliflowers, lay them in cold water, drain, and set in glass jars or else stone crocks; cover them with white vinegar, add cloves, salt, red peppers, tarragon, mace, and mustard seed, all of these tied in a small bag, and leave to marinate for about four days; when needed, range them on side dishes, and pour over a little of the vinegar in which they marinated. A mayonnaise sauce (No. 606), may be passed round the same time as the cauliflower.

(777). CANAPÉS, WINDSOR, ANCHOVY, SARDINES, CAVIARE, RUSSIAN HERRING, SMOKED SALMON OR STURGEON, DEVILED HERRING, SHRIMP, CRAWFISH, LOBSTER, ANCHOVY BUTTER, RED BEEF TONGUE OR HAM, CARÊME AND HARD-BOILED EGGS (Canapés Windsor, aux Anchois, aux Sardines, aux Caviar, aux Harengs à la Russe, de Saumon ou d'Esturgeon, de Harengs à la Diable, de Crevettes d'Écrevisses, de Homards, au Beurre d'Anchois, à la Langue Écarlate ou au Jambon, à la Carême et d'Œufs Durs).

These canapés can be arranged on grape leaves or a folded napkin. Cut slices of bread from the crumb of a dense loaf of bread containing no holes, having them all of uniform size, the same as when preparing sandwiches; the oblong ones three and one-half by one and one-half inches and three-sixteenths of an inch thick; the round ones two and

FIG. 200.

FIG. 201.

one-half inches in diameter and the same thickness; the oval ones three inches long by two and one-fourth inches wide, and the same thickness as the round and oblong ones. Toast lightly, and butter over either with butter mixed with anchovy essence or simply with plain butter; season with salt, mustard and red pepper, and push through a cornet on to the borders, a string of anchovy butter, or any other kind, such as lobster (No. 580), Montpellier (No. 582), etc. Garnish or cover the empty space in the center.

FIG. 202.

FIG. 203.

FIG. 204.

FIG. 205.

For Windsor Canapés.—Have half a pound of cold chicken white meat; pound it with a quarter of a pound of cooked ham, and a quarter of a pound of cooked tongue; when the meats are reduced to a paste, add to it one pound of butter, two ounces of grated Chester cheese, a spoonful of English mustard, and a dash of cayenne pepper. Cut oval-shaped slices of bread (Fig. 200), toast them on both sides, let get cold, and then cover them with the above preparation; smooth the surface and decorate with fillets of gherkins, and beets to form lozenges; lay capers in the intersections, and on top some half-set jelly, and dress the canapés on folded napkins.

For Anchovy Canapés.—These are made round-shaped; butter them over with fresh butter, season with salt, pepper and mustard, and arrange the anchovy fillets, in the form of a rosette with a border around; garnish between the anchovies with chopped parsley and egg-yolks rubbed through a sieve, and hard boiled egg-whites chopped up very fine (Fig. 201).

For Sardine Canapés.—Spread on one side of an oblong toast, Montpellier butter (No. 582), garnish the top with sardines, first removing the skin and bones, and then garnish between these with chopped yolks and whites of egg, and some chopped parsley. Decorate by placing a piece of sardine lengthwise on the canapé and six smaller pieces set at an angle (Fig. 202).

For Caviare Canapés.—Make the canapés oblong shape as explained above; the border to be of fresh butter. If the caviare should be too hard, work in with it some oil and lemon juice; fill the empty center with this caviare, and around the inside border, and on top of the caviare lay a row of very finely chopped raw onions (Fig. 203).

For Russian Herring Canapés.—Remove the fillets from unsalted herrings; wipe off the white skin with a cloth and suppress the middle bone, then cut them into small fillets. Have a sour apple peeled and chopped finely, mix it in with some sour cream, butter some oblong slices of bread with fresh butter, garnish the tops with a layer of the chopped apple, and on this arrange the herring fillets, one row around the edge and two lengthwise of the canapés, garnish between the fillets with capers and chopped egg whites and yolks (Fig. 204).

For Smoked Salmon or Sturgeon Canapés.—Cut either of these fish into thin fillets; have oblong canapés buttered on one side with anchovy butter (No. 569), range the fillets of salmon or sturgeon on top, lay five crossbars from side to side (Fig. 205) and around the edge, garnish the interstices with parsley and yolks and whites of eggs chopped up separately.

For Deviled Herring Canapés.—These are made of oval slices of bread buttered with anchovy butter (No. 569). Remove the fillets from some Yarmouth bloaters, roll them in mustard and red pepper, and dip them in bread-crumbs; broil these, then garnish the canapés with them, decorating the surface with the yolk and white of egg, and chopped up parsley.

For Shrimp Canapés.—Have round slices of bread buttered on one side with shrimp butter (No. 586), lay a string of the shrimp butter around the edge, and on top marinated shrimp tails, sprinkle over chopped parsley.

For Crawfish Canapés.—Have round slices of bread buttered over with crawfish butter (No. 573), and a string of crawfish butter on the edge; cut the crawfish in two, lengthwise, season them with salt, pepper, oil and vinegar, arrange them in the form of a rosette and garnish the center with very green chervil leaves.

For Lobster Canapés.—Round slices of bread buttered over with lobster butter (No. 580), and a string of the same butter around the edge; cut the lobster meat into three-sixteenth inch squares, season them with salt, pepper, oil and vinegar or lemon-juice, and garnish the top of the canapés with these.

For Anchovy Butter Canapés.—Butter the canapés on one side with anchovy butter (No. 569), mixing with it butter, mustard and hard boiled egg-yolks, rubbed through a sieve. Dredge chopped hard boiled egg-whites over the top.

For Red Beef Tongue or Ham Canapés.—Cut some slices of tongue or ham an eighth of an inch thick; pare round-shaped slices of bread two and a half inches in diameter, toast them and let them get cold, then butter them over with butter; season with salt, cayenne, and mustard; then trim the tongue or ham round shaped exactly the same size as the toasts; put them on the toasts and lay in the center a three-quarter inch diameter ball of grated ham or tongue, the ham ball on top of the ham, and the tongue ball on top of the tongue; cover with jelly and sprinkle over chopped parsley, serving them on a folded napkin, arranged in the form of a rosette; garnish with green parsley leaves.

For Carême Canapés.—Cut in Julienne some truffles and pickled gherkins, and mix them in a béchamel chaufroid (No. 593); have also some fillets of sole and smoked salmon. Toast oval-shaped canapés, cover them with anchovy butter (No. 569), lay the salmon or sole on top and cover with the chaufroid of truffles and gherkins; sprinkle over some chopped parsley and serve on a folded napkin.

Hard Boiled Egg Canapés.—Boil a few eggs till hard, when very cold, shell and chop the yolks and whites separately. Cut some oblong pieces from a kitchen loaf having them slightly wider than for sandwiches, cover one side with a thin layer of ravigote butter (No. 583) and surround the edges with thin fillets of anchovies. Decorate the tops with marinated tanny fillets, forming them into distinct compartments and fill these in with the chopped eggs, being careful to separate well the colors, dress the canapés on napkins.

(778). CAVIARE (Caviar).

The best caviare comes from the northern part of Europe. It is composed of sturgeon's roe preserved in salt, pepper, and onions, and then left to ferment. It is a very heavy article of food and difficult to digest. When the caviare is too hard, it can be softened by working it with olive oil and lemon juice. Lay it on a side dish with slices of lemon around; the caviare can also be garnished with finely chopped raw onions.

(779). CELERY STALKS, CELERY, FENNEL, CELERY HEARTS, CELERY KNOBS, WITH VINAIGRETTE MAYONNAISE (Céleri en Branches, Céleri, Fenouil, Céleri Rave, Vinaigrette Mayonnaise).

For Celery Stalks.—Have some good heads seven inches long; remove the outer leaves until the the fine, tender, yellow ones are reached, then clean them by cutting off all the hard parts; split the stalks into four, and make a few slight incisions on their length; throw them at once into cold water, and all those parts that are notched will curl outward, giving the celery a beautiful appearance. They are either served in side dishes or else in high glass stands.

For Celery, Fennel, Celery Hearts.—Pare these well, wipe them on a cloth, and lay them on side dishes; serve at the same time, anchovies pounded and pressed through a sieve diluted with warm oil. English people eat celery with the cheese, the Italians eat fennel at the end of the repast.

For Celery Knobs, with Vinaigrette Mayonnaise.—For vinaigrette, wash the knob, and put it to cook in boiling, salted water, refresh it, and cut it up into slices, from these remove some round pieces with a vegetable cutter one and three-quarters to two inches in diameter, and lay them on a deep dish to marinate in oil, vinegar, salt, and pepper. Two hours later, drain them off, and mix them in some mayonnaise; lay them in a line on a side dish and surround them with anchovy fillets. Decorate with pounded hard boiled egg-yolks rubbed through a sieve, mixing in half the same quantity of mayonnaise, and push this through a cornet; lay tarragon leaves on the outside, and throw over some finely chopped chervil. If very tender cut in thin slices after being peeled; season with salt, pepper, oil, and vinegar, and cover with a mayonnaise sauce.

(780). CHEESE CRUSTS (Croûtes au Fromage).

Cut slices of bread three-eighths of an inch thick, three and a half inches long, and one and three-quarters inch wide; fry them on one side only in butter, drain, and let get cold. Spread them over with fresh butter on the side they were not fried, mixing in with it some pepper and mustard. Cover the butter with slices of Chedder, Swiss, or Chestershire cheese, place on top another piece of buttered bread, and serve on folded napkins.

(781). CLAMS OR RAW OYSTERS ON THE HALF SHELL (Lucines Orangées ou Huîtres sur Coquilles).

Clams are prepared and served the same as raw oysters on the half shell (No. 803).

(782). CRAWFISH À LA VINAIGRETTE (Écrevisses à la Vinaigrette).

Prepare the crawfish as explained (No. 1009); cook them in a white wine mirepoix (No. 419), and when cold shell them by suppressing the tail carapace without detaching them from the bodies. Dress in a circle on a side dish, pour over a vinaigrette sauce (No. 634) and garnish the center with very green fresh parsley leaves.

(783). CUCUMBERS, FRESH SLICED, IN FILLETS OR SALTED RUSSIAN STYLE (Concombres Frais en Tranches, en Filets ou Salés à la Russe).

Sliced Fresh Cucumbers.—If the cucumbers be green, small and seedless, peel and cut off the ends; then pare the inside into thin slices. If large divide them into two or four parts lengthwise before slicing; in either case they should macerate for fifteen minutes, sprinkled over with salt; when they have thrown off the water, drain and season with pepper or mignonette, vinegar, oil and chopped parsley; the same quantity of finely chopped onions may also be added.

Another way of preparing them is to peel and slice them simply, then season with salt, pepper, oil and vinegar, and serve on side dishes.

Cucumbers in Fillets.—Peel a cucumber and cut it crosswise into quarter inch lengths, roll each piece separately to form a long, thin ribbon and season all of these with salt, mignonette, pepper, oil and vinegar. Roll them up into cork-shaped pieces and mince them across so as to obtain long fillets, then serve on a side dish, pouring more oil and vinegar over.

Salted Russian Style.—(Agoursis). Dress them on side dishes in their own brine.

(784). EGGS, BUSTARD, PLOVER AND SEA-GULL (Œufs de Vanneaux, de Pluviers et de Mouettes).

Oil over some small crimped paper cases, one inch in diameter, lay them upside down on a grater and push in the oven to stiffen without coloring, set them away to cool, then fill as high as the top through a pocket garnished with fresh butter, or else lobster butter (No. 580), or even half of each. Lay in the middle of each case a bustard's egg, after boiling it and removing the shell. In order to cook these eggs, they must be put in cold water and boiled for eight minutes, then cooled off, and the shell broken gently, remove and wash the egg well. Dress the cases crown-shaped on a dish, and garnish the center either with water-cress or else very green parsley stalks.

FIG. 206.

(785). GHERKINS (Cornichons).

Have some gherkins prepared as explained in elementary methods (No. 96); dress them on a side dish with a few shallots, onions and hot peppers, adding a little tarragon and vinegar.

(786). HAM, BOILED AND RAW WESTPHALIAN (Jambon Bouilli ou cru de Westphalie).

FIG. 207.

Boiled Ham is served cut in thin slices, pared and dressed crown-shaped, garnishing the center of the dish with parsley branches, and decorating with chopped jelly around; serve fresh butter at the same time as the ham.

Westphalia Ham is a raw ham from Westphalia. Slice as finely as possible; roll each piece into small cornets, the fat part on the outer edge, and garnish the inside of these cornets with small sprigs of very green parsley.

(787). HERRING, SHAD OR MACKEREL, MARINATED (Harengs Alose ou Maquereau Marinés.)

Clean twelve fat very fresh and soft-roed herrings, or any other of the above fishes; put them into a vessel between layers of salt and leave in a cool place for twelve hours; drain off. These may be served whole, or else cut off their heads and tails. Mince four ounces of carrots, two ounces of onions, and fry colorless in two ounces of butter, adding a bunch of parsley garnished with two bay leaves, as much thyme, two cloves of garlic, a teaspoonful of whole pepper and a few bits of mace. Moisten the whole with a bottleful of white wine and a pint of water, then let cook slowly for one hour. Lay the herrings in a deep, covered vessel, strain the stock and pour it over; boil before setting it in a slack oven for fifteen minutes; let the herrings get half cold, then arrange them on to a dish, strain the gravy over, adding to it whole peppers, bay leaf, cloves and round slices of blanched onions, and dress them on separate side dishes, pour some of the pickle over, and garnish with the slices of onions and half slices of finely cut lemons.

(788). SMOKED HERRINGS (Harengs Saurs).

Suppress the heads and tails from a few nice herring; range them in a flat saucepan, moisten them to their height in tepid water, and set the saucepan on the fire, leaving it there till the liquid is very hot, then remove them back. Thirty minutes after drain the herrings, lift off the skin, and wipe them well with a cloth; take out the middle bone; pare the fillets, coat them over with oil and broil them lightly, then range them nicely on a side dish; squeeze over the juice of a lemon, sprinkle them with some good oil, and decorate with branches or chopped parsley at each end, and half slices of lemon around.

(789). PAUPIETTES OF DUTCH HERRINGS, POLONAISE (Paupiettes de Harengs de Hollande à la Polonaise).

Unsalt some herrings for a few hours, remove their white skin, and serve them after cutting them across in four, and reshaping them again, or else split them in two lengthwise, and pare them into oblongs. Pound the trimmings in a mortar with a few anchovy fillets, as much butter as fish but no salt, add lemon juice, then rub through a sieve, and add some finely chopped chervil, tarragon and chives; spread a layer of this preparation inside each herring fillet, roll them up cylindrical shape, and dip the ends in hard boiled chopped up eggs, one in the white and the other in the yolk, and dress them on a side dish, garnishing with fine herbs, and around with beets and capers.

(790). HORSERADISH (Raifort).

Scrape with a knife a fine horseradish root. Wash it well and let it soak for a few minutes then dry and grate it. Put it into a vessel with a little cream, not making it too liquid; it should be thick enough to lift with a fork, or it may be served simply grated, and laid on a side dish.

(791). CHOW-CHOW (Chow-Chow).

This is a combination of different vegetables, preserved in vinegar with mustard and many strong spices. The vegetables composing the chow-chow are cauliflowers, small onions, gherkins, string beans, and small carrots. It can be purchased already prepared. Lay it simply on side dishes.

(792). INDIAN PICKLE WITH FINE HERBS (Acharts aux Fines Herbes).

This is a product of East India. The way to prepare it is as follows: Mince finely slices of pumpkin and some small onions, cooking partly in boiling water; then trim some cauliflower, and small corn two inches long, and only half ripe; let these vegetables lay in salt for fifteen days in an hermetically closed jar, then unsalt them for six hours; pour over strong wine vinegar, add some ginger-root, saffron and small red peppers, and keep in a cool place for one month. When ready to use, lay them on side dishes, pour a little oil over, and sprinkle them over with chervil, chives and shallot all finely chopped.

(793). LEMONS, ORANGES, FIGS, BLACKBERRIES (Citrons, Oranges, Figues, Mûres).

Fresh Fruits Considered as Side Dishes.—Arrange any of these fruits on grape leaves or else on side dishes. The oranges and lemons may be cut into quarters.

(794). LOBSTER À LA BOULOGNAISE (Homard à la Boulognaise).

Cut up some cooked lobster meat into small quarter inch squares, the same quantity of celery and finely chopped beet root. Mix all these with a little mayonnaise sauce (No. 606), adding to it chopped up chervil and tarragon and some red pepper. Range this on side dishes and sprinkle over the lobster coral finely chopped, or else the lobster sprawn and some chopped parsley.

(795). LOBSTER MAYONNAISE PRINTANIÈRE (Homard Mayonnaise Printanière).

Select a freshly cooked and heavy lobster, cut up the meat taken from the tail and claws into slices, and dress them crown shaped on a side dish, and garnish the center with the green creamy part from the body. Prepare a mayonnaise sauce (No. 606) with some chervil, tarragon and lobster coral, all chopped up finely, cover the whole of the lobster with the mayonnaise and serve.

(796). RUSSIAN MACÉDOINE (Macédoine Russe).

This is composed of anchovies, marinated tunny fish, cucumbers, shrimps, beets, a few olives and some red herring fillets, all cut into quarter of an inch dice. Mix all in a mayonnaise with finely chopped tarragon, and arrange it on side dishes, garnishing with thin slices of pickled lobsters, some capers and chopped parsley.

(797). MACKEREL IN OIL (Maquereaux à l'Huile).

These mackerel come already prepared like sardines in oil; open the cans, remove the mackerel and dress them on a side dish with chopped parsley around and surround with slices of lemon.

(798). SMOKED MACKEREL (Maquereaux Fumés).

Raise the fillets from the mackerel, remove the skin, and trim them into thin slices, lay these on a dish, and between each, set a slice of cold boiled potatoes. Sprinkle over a vinaigrette of oil, vinegar and pepper, dredge over some chopped chervil, very tiny squares of shallot and some chopped fennel and tarragon leaves.

(799). MUSKMELON AND CANTALOUPE (Melon Vert Maraîcher et Cantaloup).

The cantaloupe melon is certainly the finest and best; if good the fruit is a handsome orange-red, the sides very prominent and covered with a rough exterior coat. The muskmelon outside is green, covered with a rough gray rind, the inside of a green and yellow color. To serve either one or the other, set them in a cool place for at least twelve hours before using them, have them very cold and cut either in halves or slices, and lay them on top of a grape leaf or any other kind. Do not serve the side that laid on the ground. They are eaten plain, seasoned with salt and pepper, or else sugar.

(800). OLIVES CRESCENT OR LUCQUES, SPANISH QUEEN, BLACK, VERDALES (Olives Croissant ou Lucques, Espagnoles, Noires, Verdales).

Wash the olives in fresh water and serve them covered with slightly salted water. The crescent, black and verdal olives come from the south of France, the Spanish from Seville. Black olives are served dry without any brine; they come also from France and Italy, and are for sale in New York.

FIG. 208.

801). OLIVES STUFFED WITH ANCHOVY BUTTER AND WITH ANCHOVIES (Olives Farcies au Beurre d'Anchois et aux Anchois).

Remove the stones from some large verdal olives, using for this purpose a column punch five-sixteenths of an inch diameter, or the machine (Fig. 63); throw them at once into cold water, drain, and garnish them through a cornet with anchovy butter (No. 569). Close up the openings with hard boiled egg-white, or else a piece of truffle, either one cut with the same cutter, or capers may be used instead.

Olives Stuffed with Anchovies.—Remove the stones the same as for olives with anchovy butter, garnish the insides with fillets of anchovies, arrange them on a side dish, and pour over a little fine oil and lemon juice, then serve.

(802). PICKLED OYSTERS (Huîtres Marinées).

Blanch some large oysters, drain them after the first boil and keep the liquor; boil some vinegar with cloves, whole pepper, whole allspice, half an ounce of each for every quart of vinegar, and add a little mace; put two-thirds of the oyster liquor with one-third of the vinegar, and also the oysters into hermetically closed glass bottles, and keep them in a cool place. Serve on side dishes with sliced lemon and sprigs of parsley set around.

(803). RAW OYSTERS ON THE HALF SHELL OR LITTLE NECK CLAMS (Huîtres Crues sur Coquilles ou Lucines Orangées).

Open the oysters carefully by inserting the blade of the knife between the shells and prying them open so as to avoid breaking and leave them in their deep shells with the liquor. Serve six or eight according to their size with a quarter of a lemon for each guest. Crackers or slices of very thin bread and butter can be served at the same time. The clams are to be treated exactly the same. A hot sauce or a shallot sauce made with finely chopped shallots mixed with salt, pepper and vinegar, or else a pimentade sauce (No. 521), can also be eaten with the oysters. They should only be opened when ready to serve and sent to the table on finely broken ice.

(804). OYSTERS TARTARE (Huîtres Tartare).

Blanch some large oysters, drain them well, and season with salt, pepper, fine herbs, shallots cut into very small dice and blanched, capers, minced pickled cucumbers, and lobster coral chopped up very fine. Have some thin slices of bread cut oval shaped the size of an oyster, fry in butter, place one oyster on each and cover every one of these with the chopped garnishing, finish by covering all with a mayonnaise jelly (No. 613).

(805). OYSTER CRABS, PICKLED (Crabes d'Huîtres Marinés).

These crabs are very plentiful in certain Virginia oysters. Boil some vinegar, season it with salt, whole peppers, spices, mace, cloves and bay leaf, throw the crabs into this vinegar with an equal quantity of oyster liquor, skim it carefully and remove it at the first boil, then set it away in bottles and keep them in a cool place. Serve on side dishes with slices of lemon around, and a little of their own pickle poured over.

(806). GREEN OR RED PEPPERS (Piments Verts ou Rouges).

Divide them into four parts, or else cut them up fine; they may be boiled once in boiling water, refreshed and seasoned as a salad, or eaten simply raw without blanching. If they are previously pickled in vinegar, squeeze the vinegar from them, and season them with oil, salt and pepper, surrounding the dish with small white onions.

Red and sweet peppers are plunged into hot frying fat to remove the first skin, then cut them in two to broil over a slow fire, seasoning with salt, mignonette, pepper, oil and vinegar.

(807). POTATOES, CHIFFONNADE (Pommes de Terre Chiffonnade).

Cut some cold cooked potatoes into three-sixteenth inch slices, also some cooked and pickled beets; take twenty rounds from each of these, using a cutter an inch and a quarter in diameter; dress them in a circle overlapping each other, alternating the potatoes and beets and garnish the center with cut up chiccory, or any other cut up salad; seasoned with salt, pepper, fine herbs, oil and vinegar; cover the latter with some thick, ravigote mayonnaise (No. 612), and decorate the top with a few anchovy fillets, tarragon leaves and chopped parsley.

(808). RADISHES, BLACK, AND RED (Radis Noirs et Roses).

For the Black Radishes.—Choose very tender ones being careful that they are not hollow, peel them by removing the black rind, then cut in fine slices across, and lay them in a soup plate with a little salt; cover with another plate, and toss the radishes between the two; fifteen minutes after, drain off the water and season with a little oil, vinegar and pepper, and toss them again between the two plates; range them on side dishes. After the radishes are sliced, pieces as large as can be obtained may be cut from them with a round vegetable cutter; this gives them a finer and more even appearance.

For Red Radishes.—Cut off the roots, and also the outside leaves, leaving on two or three of the prettiest, smallest, and greenest. Lay the radishes in cold water, taking them out half an hour later, and wash carefully, so that no earth adheres to them. Imitation tulips can be cut from radishes using the longer ones for this purpose. Have a small, sharp knife, divide the red peel from the radish into five or six thin pieces, beginning to cut from the bottom, and slipping the knife behind the skin as far as the stem;

FIG. 209.

shape each piece on the tip into a point, at the stalk of the radish; then lay them on a side dish with a few pieces of ice, and serve fresh butter at the same time.

(809). ROLLS, SMALL FANCY WITH LOBSTER, SHRIMP, CRAWFISH, FILLETS OF SOLE, CHICKEN SALPICON, FOIES-GRAS OR RILLETTES DE TOURS (Petits Pains Garnis de Homard, Crevettes, Écrevisses, Filets de Soles, Filets de Volaille ou Salpicon, Foies-gras ou Rillettes de Tours).

Have small plain rolls three and one-quarter inches long by one and three-quarter inches wide. These rolls must not be split on the side, but make an opening on the top, reserving the cover. Empty them of their crumb, and fill the entire insides with either lobster, crawfish, shrimp, or pressed cold fried soles, cutting them in three-sixteenth inch squares, season with salt, pepper, oil, vinegar, tarragon, chervil, and parsley, thickening with a little mayonnaise. After the rolls are filled with this, lay the cover on top, and arrange them pyramidically over a folded napkin.

For Chicken or Salpicon.—Cut the chicken into three-sixteenth inch squares, also some mushrooms, and the same quantity of unsmoked red beef tongue, all the same size pieces; add half as much one-eighth of an inch squares of truffles, season with a mayonnaise mixing in with it a very fine tomato purée (No. 730), and seasoning it all highly, garnish and serve the same as the lobsters.

For Fancy Small Rolls Garnished Either with Chopped Ham, Foies-Gras from the Terrine, or Rillettes de Tours.—Make these rolls smaller than the others having them two and a quarter inches long by one and a quarter inches wide, fill them by making an incision on the side, and in this lay the garnishing of chopped ham, foies-gras, or rillettes. They can also be served plain arranged on a folded napkin.

(810). SALMON WITH SAUTERNE WINE (Saumon au vin de Sauterne).

Mince some onions, put them in a flat saucepan, with butter, add a bunch of parsley garnished with thyme, bay leaves, and a few cloves of garlic, fry the whole slightly in butter, add whole pepper, grated nutmeg, ground pepper, salt, moisten it with Sauterne wine, boil and let simmer during one hour; pass through a fine sieve, put this stock in a saucepan, add the salmon, cover the saucepan tightly, put in the oven for about thirty minutes, arrange them on a deep dish, pour the stock over so as the fish will be entirely covered and let it cool off.

(811). SANDWICHES (Sandwichs).

To prepare the butters for these sandwiches mix it well with salt, red pepper and mustard, if needed for mustard butter; for the anchovy butter add a little essence of anchovy to it, and for foies-gras butter have half foies-gras and half butter pounded and pressed through a sieve. Cut some slices of bread-crumb from a compact loaf without any holes, having each one five-sixteenths of an inch in thickness, and four inches square. These slices of bread may be toasted and allowed to cool, instead of using them direct from the loaf; in both cases, spread over them some mustard butter, as explained above, when used for meats and poultry; use foies-gras butter for game and anchovy butter (No. 569) for fish and crustaceans, but either one or the other can be used, except foies-gras, as there is no special rule to follow for buttering sandwiches. Garnish the bread with thin slices of meat well pared and free of all fat; on top of this meat lay

FIG. 210.

FIG. 211.

FIG. 212.

another slice of buttered bread, then press them down flat one on top of the other; for the oblongs cut them four inches square then straight through the center, and for the triangles across from the two opposite corners. Dress them in pyramids; for the oblong ones cut away the corners, and bevel the edges, but for the triangles merely bevel them.

(812). BARLOW SANDWICHES (Sandwichs à la Barlow).

Spread some slices of bread, crumb over with mustard butter (No. 811), lay on this butter some pickled cucumbers, and on these some finely shred and seasoned lettuce hearts, on top of this slices of chicken the same size as the bread, then more shred lettuce hearts, and the chopped yolks and whites of hard boiled eggs over; set another slice of buttered bread on top, and arrange the sandwiches in a pyramid on a folded napkin.

(813). SANDWICHES OF CHOPPED OR THIN SLICED CHICKEN (Sandwichs de Volaille Hachée ou en Tranches Fines).

Scrape some chicken breasts or else chop them up finely; mix this with som well seasoned mayonnaise (No. 606); spread this over slices of buttered bread and cover with another slice; press down, pare the corners as explained in No. 811, and dress on a folded napkin.

(814). GAME SANDWICHES (Sandwichs de Gibier).

Spread over the bread with foies-gras butter; on top lay some thinly sliced or chopped up game, cover over with another slice of bread also buttered with foies-gras butter, press them both together and pare neatly, then dress on a folded napkin.

(815). SANDWICHES OF DIFFERENT MEATS (Sandwichs de Viandes Variées).

Use roast beef or roast tenderloins, cut the bread in quarter inch thick slices, coat one side with a layer of butter prepared with English mustard and on these lay the meats; cover with another slice of buttered bread, pare and dress on napkins. The roast beef may be replaced by beef tongue or lamb, corned beef, chopped raw lean beef, veal, grated ham or foies-gras. Grated horseradish can be strewn over the butter if liked.

(816). FRENCH ROLL SANDWICHES, AMERICAN STYLE AND WITH ANCHOVIES (Sandwichs de Flûtes à l'Américaine et aux Anchois).

Have some French rolls, four inches long and one and a half inches in diameter, make an opening on the top, empty them, removing all the crumbs possible and keeping the covers. Cut up some roast chicken, the same quantity of fresh red beef tongue and half the quantity of ham, all into one-eighth of an inch squares, a few minced pickles and green peppers, then season with salt, pepper, a little tarragon and finely shred chervil. Mix the whole with just sufficient mayonnaise sauce (No. 606), to bind the ingredients together. The chicken, tongue and ham may be replaced by shrimps cut in two or into small squares, fill the rolls, set on the covers and serve on napkins.

French Roll Sandwiches with Anchovies.—Prepare the rolls as for above; chop up four hard boiled eggs, the yolks and whites separately; put them into a bowl with a pinch of chopped tarragon, one of chervil and one of chives all cut up very fine, season with salt, pepper, a table-spoonful of vinegar and four tablespoonfuls of oil, fill the rolls with alternate rows of anchovies and eggs, until entirely filled, then replace the covers, and serve on napkins.

(817). SARDINES MARINATED (Sardines Marinées).

Range in layers in a big stone vessel about six pounds of large fresh sardines besprinkling each layer with salt, cover the sardines with a cloth and let macerate for two hours in a cold place; wipe them off one by one and return to the same washed vessel, then roll them in a little oil and place on a broiler; cook on a slow fire; they should be just singed, neither dry nor brown. Remove the fish and lay them one beside the other in the same vessel without tearing the skin; cover over with vinegar cooked with salt and aromatics but have it cold for use and strained; let macerate in this for one or two hours according to its strength. Take the sardines out again and lay them on a sieve; when well drained, range in layers either in a large crock or any other glazed vessel, having a cover to fit, alternating each layer by one of minced onions, bay leaves and peppercorns. These sardines can be kept in excellent condition for several weeks.

(818). SAUSAGES SMOKED; WITH OR WITHOUT GARLIC, D'ARLES, LYONS, MORTADELLA
(Saucissons Fumés à l'Ail ou Sans Ail, d'Arles, de Lyon, et Mortadelle).

Remove the skin covering the sausage, slice it up finely, and range it crown-shaped on a side dish with a sprig of parsley in the middle and chopped parsley around.

For Arles and Lyons Sausage.—Cut in very thin slices, do not remove the skin. Slice Mortadella very thin and cut each round into two or four.

(819). SHRIMPS IN SIDE DISHES (Crevettes en Raviers ou en Bateaux).

Fig. 213.

Throw some fine shrimps into boiling and unsalted water remove at the first boil and place in a bowl, sprinkle with salt; leave them an hour or two to become marinated with the salt, drain, then dress them in a pyramid or crown-shaped on side dishes, garnishing with sprigs of parsley and throw over very small pieces of clear ice.

(820). SLICED AND BUTTERED WHITE OR RYE BREAD, SLICED AND ROLLED BREAD
(Tartines de Pain Blanc ou de Seigle Beurrées, Tartines Roulées).

Cut thin slices from the crumb of a loaf of white or brown bread, cover one side with butter and put one on top of the other, the buttered sides together; pare them into oblong or three cornered pieces.

Sliced and Rolled Bread.—These are slices of bread cut very thin, buttered on one side, and rolled up; cover each roll with a sheet of waxed paper, and twist the ends so that the bread is well enclosed. Bread done up in this way will remain fresh quite awhile.

(821). MARINATED SMELTS (Éperlans Marinés).

Wipe the smelts, empty them through the gills, then salt and flour them over; fry in oil, and drain on a grate until cold. Range them in a flat vessel one closely beside the other. Put some vinegar into a frying pan with a little water and oil, salt, whole peppers, bay leaves, and minced onions; boil the liquid up twice, then remove and when cold pour it over the smelts and leave to macerate for a few hours before using.

(822). SMOKED BEEF, SALMON, STURGEON, GOOSE BREAST, OR TONGUE (Bœuf Fumé, Saumon, Esturgeon, Poitrine d'oie et Langue.)

Cut the beef into very thin slices, and serve with sprigs of parsley around.

Smoked Salmon or Sturgeon.—Cut thin slices of smoked salmon or smoked sturgeon three-sixteenths of an inch thick; broil them on a gridiron for one minute on each side, and when they are cold, arrange them on a side dish, pour a little sweet oil over, and serve with chopped parsley and slices of lemon around, or to be served raw cut in thin slices, and dressed either in a circle or straight row with chopped parsley around.

Smoked Breast of Goose.—Cut the meat off the breasts lengthwise into very thin slices; range in straight rows with parsley around the dish.

Red Beef Tongue.—Cut the tongue in thin equal sized slices, suppressing the fibrous parts and fat; range them in a circle in the center of a small side dish, one on top of the other; garnish around with parsley and chopped jelly in the center.

(823). STRAW CHEESE (Paillettes au Fromage).

These are made with parings of a puff paste giving it six turns (No. 146); and dredging over the paste at each turn some grated parmesan cheese and red pepper, after it is rolled out. Then roll them very thin, let them rest and cut from the pieces bands an eighth of an inch wide, and seven inches long; place them on a floured baking sheet close together but not touching each other; bake them in a slack oven so that they become dry and crisp.

(824). MARINATED STRING BEANS (Haricots Verts Marinés).

Blanch lightly a sufficient quantity of large string beans, drain, refresh, and set them in a stone crock, and pour over some boiling water and vinegar, mixed by halves, some salt, cloves, and tarragon leaves added; the next day drain off the vinegar, boil it once more, and pour it again over the beans, with some English mustard diluted in Chili vinegar; serve on side dishes with a little of the vinegar in which they have marinated.

(825). TARTLETS OF GAME, LOBSTER, SALMON OR NONPAREIL (Tartelettes de Gibier, Homard, Saumon ou Nonpareil).

These are small round or oval tartlets, made of a very thin foundation paste (No. 135), and the insides garnished with buttered paper, and filled in with rice. Cook them in a slack oven, empty them, egg over the edge, and set them in a quick oven to color. Cut some roast game in small dice, with an equal quantity of mushrooms, and bind with a little light chaufroid, season well and serve the tartlets on folded napkins.

Lobster and Salmon Tartlets.—Use either round or oval tartlet crusts, the same as for the above, garnish the insides with either salmon or lobster cut in dice, and some mushrooms, capers, fine herbs, salt, pepper, lemon juice and olive oil; dress them on folded napkins.

Nonpareil Tartlets.—Have either round or oval tartlet crusts; cut some tunny fish and anchovies in three-sixteenth inch dice, also some beetroot, lobster and pickled cucumbers the same size, stoned olives cut across in thin slices, shrimp tails, three-sixteenth inch dice of celery knob; season and fill the tartlets with this; dredge over the tops with truffles, parsley, lobster coral, and pistachio nuts, all chopped up separately and minutely, and cover over with partly thickened jelly.

(826). TOASTS À LA WADDINGTON (Rôties à la Waddington).

Trim some slices of bread-crumbs three-eighths of an inch thick, oval shaped, two and a half inches long by two inches wide; toast them lightly and cover one side with chopped ham and butter mixed. Remove the stones from some large verdal olives, cut off the ends, and then slice them into three pieces, so as to make rings each three-sixteenths of an inch high; lay them in a circle on the toast, on the outer edge, and fill each alternate olive ring with chopped up hard boiled egg-white, and the rest of them with the yolks prepared the same. Make a turban with one or two anchovies inside of these, fill this with chopped beetroot and cover the whole with jelly having the consistency of syrup. Serve them very cold, arranging them in form of a crown on a folded napkin, with sprigs of parsley in the center.

(827). TOASTED BREAD GARNISHED WITH CHICKEN, BACON, CHOPPED CHICKEN, AND PEPPERS (Tranches de Pain Grillées Garnies de Poulet, Petit Salé, Poulet Haché et Piments).

These are slices of bread toasted on both sides, and left to get cold. They are generally buttered with mustard or anchovy butter (No. 569), and on one side over the butter lay the necessary garnishing without covering it again. They can be made with roast-beef and horseradish, or caviare, foies-gras, anchovies, sardines, hot roast beef with gravy, chicken, bacon, and lettuce, chopped chicken and green peppers, also broiled sardines.

(828). TROUT FRIED AND MARINATED—SMALL (Petites Truites Frites et Marinées).

Select some fresh trout, empty and wipe well; salt over, dip in flour and fry in oil a few at a time, then drain and lay them in a deep dish. Heat some oil in a saucepan, mix with it a quarter as much vinegar as water, thyme, bay leaf, basil, sliced onions and cloves; cook this marinade half an hour on a very slow fire and let it get partly cold, then pour it over the fish and leave to marinate for six hours before serving. Dress them on a dish with a little of their marinade and some slices of lemon.

(829). TROUT MARINATED IN WINE—SMALL (Marinade de Petites Truites au Vin).

After the fish are cleaned, salt them over for one hour, cook them in strongly acidulated water, drain and range them in a deep vessel or a small barrel covered with slices of lemon. Prepare a court bouillon without water, using only white wine and vinegar, rings of white onions, a sprig of parsley, salt, spices and aromatics; put it on to boil and when the onions become soft, lift them out with a skimmer and lay them on the trout and pour into the stock an equal quantity of aspic jelly (No. 103), strain this over the fish and let cool off on ice. Serve the trout on a dish with the slices of lemon and onion around and at the same time a sauce-boatful of persillade sauce (No. 619).

(830). TRUFFLES (Truffes).

Select those that are small and very round, brush over, and peel. Set them in a saucepan with two ounces of butter, salt and nutmeg, and place them on the fire for a quarter of an hour, being careful to watch that they do not boil; a little fire can also be placed on the cover; then drain and arrange them in a glass bottle filling it with Aix oil, and closing hermetically. To serve truffles, drain them off, dress, and to the oil add a little lemon juice.

(831). MARINATED TUNNY FISH, SARDINES, GURNET AND ACCOLA (Thon Mariné, Sardines, Grondins et Accola).

Red gurnet and accola are smaller than the tunny fish, the meat being very white and delicate. Tunny fish comes already prepared in boxes the same as sardines; open them, drain them from the oil, either one or the other, but from the sardines wipe off their skin. Lay them on side dishes, sprinkling over some fresh oil, and garnish around with chopped parsley, capers, sliced lemon or Séville oranges; serve slices of buttered bread at the same time.

For Gurnet or Accola.—Cut it in slices, season, cover with oil and broil the pieces; when cold dress them crown-shaped or lengthwise, sprinkle over some more oil, and garnish around with parsley, chopped eggs and slices of lemon.

(832). TURBOT OR RED SNAPPER MARINATED (Turbot ou Red Snapper Mariné).

Mince up some onions, put them in a sautoire with a piece of butter, adding a bunch of parsley garnished with thyme and bay leaf, a few cloves of garlic, white pepper, grated nutmeg, ground pepper and salt. Fry them slightly in the butter, then add some Sauterne wine, and let simmer for one hour; pass the liquid through a fine sieve, then return to the sautéing-pan; add to it either some turbot or red snapper, cover well, and set it in the oven for thirty minutes; remove from the saucepan to cool in a deep dish, with the liquid covering the fish, then drain and dress the fish, pour some of the liquid over and garnish with sliced lemon.

(833). GREEN WALNUTS (Cerneaux).

When the juice is in the almond state, break them in two, detach the white parts with a circular movement, then throw them into cold water in which a little powdered alum has been dissolved; drain through a colander, and throw over a handful of white salt, two finely cut up shallots, and put them into a salad bowl, adding the juice of two lemons; roll them in their seasoning, and serve on side dishes.

(834). PICKLED GREEN WALNUTS (Cerneaux Confits).

These walnuts come ready prepared; serve on side dishes with a little of their liquor.

Walnuts preserved in sugar and drained, then laid in a vessel with vinegar, cloves and ginger make an excellent hors-d'œuvre.

HOT SIDE DISHES (Hors-d'Œuvre Chauds).

The hors-d'œuvre is composed of certain dishes served after the soup, somewhat taking the place of those formerly called "flying dishes," for they did not appear on the table, but were passed directly to the guests.

(835). ANCHOVY FRITTERS (Beignets d'Anchois).

Prepare some very thin pancakes, cut them into narrow strips, three-quarters of an inch wide, by three inches long, cover them with a layer of chicken quenelle forcemeat (No. 89), with raw fine herbs added, set on top half of a well cleaned anchovy, then roll them over, dip in eggs and bread-crumbs, and fry to a fine color. The anchovy fillets may be prepared by arranging them crown-shaped and filling the centers with a quenelle, then dipping them in frying paste to cover well, and fry them immediately in frying fat over a hot fire, drain, wipe and salt. Dress the fritters on folded napkins and garnish the tops with a bunch of fried parsley.

Fig. 214.

(836). ATTÉREAUX OF BEEF PALATE (Attéreaux de Palais de Bœuf).

Obtain some round tin cases, two and one-quarter inches deep, the bottom being one and three-eighths inches in diameter, while the top is an inch and five-eighths; the bottom must be perforated with a hole so as to allow the skewer to pass through and fasten on to a piece of bread. Cut some rounds of well pressed beef palate, one inch and a quarter in diameter by three-sixteenths of an inch in thickness; have as many pieces of truffles and mushrooms, both of them an eighth of an inch thick, and seven-eighths of an inch in diameter. Reduce an allemande sauce (No. 407), with some jelly. Run on to small silver skewers, first a piece of palate, then alternate with a piece of mushroom, then another round of palate and truffle; set each skewer into a round case, and fill them up with the partly cold prepared sauce; when cold, unmold by dipping in hot water, dip in beaten eggs, then roll them in bread-crumbs, and fry to a fine color; serve on folded napkins.

(837). ATTÉREAUX OF CHICKEN À LA D'ANTIN (Attéreaux de Poulet à la d'Antin).

Braise the chickens and leave them to cool in their stock; remove the fillets, pare them of their fat, and take away all the skin and bones; cut them up into three-sixteenths of an inch thick slices, and then into one inch squares. Cut up some mushrooms the same size and thickness, and as much truffles; put all of these in a dish and cover with allemande sauce (No. 407), having it well reduced; mix into this sauce some chervil chopped finely and cooked colorless in butter, also some fresh mushrooms, truffles, and a little chopped parsley and tarragon. When the ingredients are almost cold, thread first a square of chicken, then one of mushroom, and one of truffle; cover evenly with the remainder of the sauce, having it nearly cold; let cool off completely, pare them of uniform shape then roll in bread-crumbs, dip in beaten egg smoothing the bread-crumbs neatly with the blade of a knife, and fry in hot frying fat until they attain a fine color, and the heat has penetrated them throughout. Dress on a folded napkin with fried parsley on top.

(838). ATTÉREAUX OF FAT LIVERS (Attéreaux de Foies-Gras).

Cook some foies-gras cut into one-inch squares and three-eighths of an inch thick pieces, lay them in a vessel. and add an equal quantity of the same sized squares of cooked red beef tongue; season with paprika, meat glaze (No. 402), and finely chopped truffles; sprinkle over a few spoonfuls of Villeroi sauce (No. 560), sufficient to cover, and run through these pieces of liver and tongue small wooden or metal skewers; when cold pare and roll them in bread-crumbs, dip in beaten eggs, and bread-crumb them once more, smoothing the bread-crumbs, then plunge them into hot frying fat and fry them a fine color; dress on folded napkins and surround with slices of lemon.

(839). ATTÉREAUX OF OYSTERS (Attéreaux d'Huîtres).

Blanch medium-sized oysters; drain, wipe and run small wooden skewers through them, alternating each oyster with a slice of mushroom; cover with a Villeroi sauce (No. 560), let get cold, and then roll them in bread-crumbs, and dip in beaten eggs; bread-crumb again, smooth the breading, and fry the attéreaux into hot frying fat, drain and replace the wooden skewers by metal ones, and finish by dressing them pyramidically on a napkin with fried parsley on top.

(840). ATTÉREAUX PIEDMONTESE (Attéreaux Piémontaise).

Make a preparation of consistent cooked polenta, finished with butter and grated parmesan; spreading it a quarter of an inch thick. Cut from this round pieces an inch and a quarter in diameter, also some white Piemont truffles an inch across and an eighth of an inch in thickness; pieces of fresh Swiss cheese, three-quarters by one-eighth of an inch, and run these alterately on skewers, first the polenta, then the cheese and truffles; dip them in beaten eggs and bread-crumbs, and fry to a fine golden color.

(841). ATTÉREAUX OF SWEETBREADS À LA MODERNE (Attéreaux de Ris de Veau à la Moderne).

It requires for the preparation of these attéreaux, some cylindrical shaped tin molds, each one being two and a quarter inches deep, the bottom one and a quarter inches, having a perforated hole to pass the skewer through; the top of the mold must measure an inch in diameter. Cut some cold sweetbreads into slices, three-sixteenths of an inch thick, and from these remove, with a round cutter, pieces one inch in diameter. Have also rounds of truffles, and the same of tongue, seven-eighths of an inch across, and an eighth of an inch thick. Mix all these together in a vessel with a few spoonfuls of cooked fine herbs, thickening with a little meat glaze (No. 402); let get cold, then run them on to small silver skewers, alternating the truffles with tongue and sweetbreads; lay the molds on a large piece of buttered bread-crumbs (Fig. 490), set the skewers into the molds, and let them penetrate through the holes into the bread to keep them upright, and fill the empty space in the cases with a Villeroi sauce (No. 560); set them aside on the ice to get perfectly cold; unmold by dipping them into hot water; bread-crumb the attéreaux, dip them in beaten eggs and bread-crumbs, and fry them a fine color in hot frying fat; drain on a cloth, and dress on a folded napkin.

(842). ATTÉREAUX OF TURKEY OR GAME (Attéreaux de Dindon ou de Gibier).

Take the white meat from a roast turkey or some game, and cut it into slices three-sixteenths of an inch in thickness; with a round cutter remove pieces three-quarters of an inch in diameter. Prepare some truffles and mushrooms half an inch in diameter, by an eighth in thickness; mix all these with an allemande sauce (No. 407), with cooked fine herbs added, and run them alternately on to small silver skewers; bread-crumb them as above and fry.

(843). BATEAUX OF FAT LIVERS, RUSSIAN STYLE (Bateaux de Foies-Gras à la Russe).

Butter some boat-shaped tartlet molds, and line them with chicken forcemeat (No. 62), leaving an empty space in the center which fill with a cooked and pounded foies-gras preparation rubbed through a sieve, and mixed with a quarter of its quantity of chopped mushrooms, also a few spoonfuls of Madeira sauce (No. 492). Cover this preparation with a layer of the forcemeat, and put the molds to poach in a slow oven in a baking pan, with a little boiling water poured into the bottom. Cool them off slightly before unmolding, then bread-crumb them, English style (No. 13), plunge them in hot fat to heat well while coloring, drain and dress on napkins.

(844). BONDONS OF PICKEREL À LA WALTON (Bondons de Brochet à la Walton).

Butter some cylindrical molds the shape of a cask bung, one and three-quarter inches high, one and three-eighths inches wide at the bottom, and one and five-eighths inches at the top or opening. Prepare a pike quenelle forcemeat as follows: Half a pound of pickerel, six ounces of butter, four egg-yolks, a quarter of a pound of cream cake paste (No. 132), salt, pepper, nutmeg, and two egg-whites beaten to a stiff froth. Fill the molds with this forcemeat, and finish as explained in No. 884. Serve separately a salpicon made of oysters or mussels, and crawfish or lobster, cut in dice, and some mushrooms; mix with as much Hollandaise sauce (No. 477) as béchamel (No. 409).

(845). BONDONS OF WOODCOCK À LA DIANE (Bondons de Bécasses à la Diane).

Butter some cylindrical molds the same size and shape as those for No. 844. Fill them with a woodcock and cream forcemeat (No. 75), and finish exactly as for timbales; unmold and dress. Serve separately a sherry sauce (No. 492), with small three-sixteenth inch dice of ham and truffles added.

(846). BRESSOLES OF CHICKEN (Bressoles de Volaille).

Have some oval molds buttered the same as for the foies-gras (No. 848) they should be a quarter of an inch high; cover the bottoms and sides with quenelle forcemeat either of chicken or game (No. 62). For chicken bressoles mix in with chicken quenelle forcemeat a third as much purée of foies-gras and in the center place a salpicon of chicken à la Reine (No. 938).

(847). BRESSOLES OF GAME (Bressoles de Gibier).

Take game quenelle forcemeat (No. 91) not too solid and fill the center of the bressole with a salpicon of foies-gras, truffles and mushrooms combined with a brown Madeira sauce (No. 492); finish and serve as the foies-gras bréssoles.

(848). BRESSOLES OF FAT LIVERS Bressoles de Foies-gras).

Butter some quarter-inch high, oval shaped molds; fill the bottoms and sides with foies-gras forcemeat (No. 78).

For the Foies-Gras Bressoles.—After covering the bottoms and sides with the foies-gras quenelle forcemeat, lay over a slice of foies-gras, and cover this with a little montglas salpicon (No. 747); set one mold on top of the other, so as to enclose the foies-gras and montglas, and plunge them into boiling water to poach the contents; unmold, drain on a cloth, and leave them stand until they are cold, then pare and dip them in beaten eggs; roll them in fresh bread-crumbs, smooth the surfaces with the blade of a knife, and just previous to serving, fry them a fine golden color; drain, and dress them crown-shaped on a folded napkin with a bunch of fried parsley in the center.

(849). BRISSOTINS OF CHICKEN, SUPREME (Brissotins de Volaille au Suprême).

Proceed exactly the same as for brissotins of game Lyonnese (No. 850) only replacing the game salpicon by a chicken à la Reine salpicon (No. 938) and the game forcemeat by a chicken and cream forcemeat (No. 75). Use a supreme sauce (No. 547) with these.

(850). BRISSOTINS OF GAME, LYONNESE (Brissotins de Gibier à la Lyonnaise).

Butter some timbale molds (No. 2, Fig. 137), fill them with game and cream forcemeat (No. 75), and poach in a slow oven, laying them in a baking pan and pouring boiling water around to half the height of the molds; when firm to the touch, remove from the oven, and let them get thoroughly cold. With a tube measuring five-eighths of an inch in diameter, less than the bottom of the mold, remove the center of the forcemeat, and from this piece cut two slices three-sixteenths of an inch in thickness; put one of these slices into the empty space in the timbale, cover with a game chasseur salpicon (No. 745), and lay the other slice on top, as shown in the accompanying figure dip them in beaten eggs, and bread-crumbs, smooth the surfaces nicely, and mark the end with the tube that has been used to remove the center and fry a nice color, now lift off the marked slices or rounds, fill the inside with a Madeira sauce (No. 492), put the piece back again in place of a cover and serve.

FIG. 215.

(851). BRISSOTINS OF LOBSTER, INDIAN STYLE (Brissotins de Homard à l'Indienne).

To be made precisely the same as the game Lyonnese (No. 850), only replacing the game salpicon by a lobster and mushroom salpicon (No. 746), thickened with velouté sauce (No. 415) and curry, and use pike forcemeat (No. 76), instead of game forcemeat. Finish with an Indian sauce (No. 483).

(852). CANAPÉS BARTHOLOMEW (Canapés Barthélemy).

Cut slices of bread five-sixteenths of an inch thick; pare them by shaping them into three and one-eighth of an inch lengths, and have them two inches and an eighth wide. Cut off from the four corners, quarter inch triangles, and dip the bread into melted butter, roll them in grated parmesan and set them on a dish that can be placed in the oven, lay on top thin slices of cooked ham, and cover the whole with melted Stilton cheese, season with red pepper, and put the dish into a hot oven for one minute; serve them either on the same dish or else on a napkin.

(853). CANAPÉS BROWNSON (Canapés à la Brownson).

Pare some slices of bread the same as for the Bartholomew (No. 852), then toast them, cover one side with a fine purée of potatoes (No. 725), and set on top thin slices of interlarded corned beef fried in butter, and over another layer of the potato purée, trim them neatly and dip them in beaten egg, roll them in bread-crumbs, smooth the surfaces with the blade of a knife, and lay them on a baking sheet; sprinkle over some butter, dust the tops with grated parmesan cheese, and brown them in a hot oven; serve on folded napkins.

(854). CANAPÉS OF GAME (Canapés de Gibier).

Prepare slices of bread three-eighths of an inch thick, cutting them three inches long and two inches wide, pare them into ovals, make an incision all around by sinking the knife down to half the depth of the bread, fry them in butter, and empty them out. Have one ounce of cooked game, either snipe, plover, or partridge; one ounce of cooked mushrooms and one ounce of truffles, all cut in fillets one-eighth of an inch by one-half of an inch. Break up the game carcasses moisten them with Madeira wine and espagnole sauce (No. 414), and let it reduce well, then strain through a tammy (No. 170). Put it into a saucepan with the prepared salpicon, mix it, and fill the bread crusts with this preparation; lay over a few thin slices of foies-gras, cover these dome-shaped with game forcemeat (No. 75), and set them into a moderate oven, when done, brush over the tops a little glaze (No. 402), and put in the oven an instant to harden, then serve.

Fig. 216.

(855). CANAPÉS LORENZO (Canapés à la Lorenzo).

Fry colorless two ounces of onions cut in one-eighth of an inch squares, and when done add a tablespoonful of flour; let this cook for a few minutes without browning, then moisten with a pint of fresh cream; season with salt, cayenne pepper and nutmeg, and reduce it to the consistency of a well thickened sauce; now throw in one pound of crab meat sautéd in butter over a brisk fire in a pan, letting it boil up once and then set it away to cool. Cut slices of bread a quarter of an inch thick; from it cut round pieces four inches in diameter, using a cutter for this purpose; divide them straight through the center to make two even-sized pieces of each, toast them on one side only; cover this side with two ounces of the crab preparation for each half round, and lay the following preparation on top: with the hands work in a tin basin half a pound of butter, add to it grated parmesan cheese, cayenne and white pepper, and knead these together, adding grated parmesan so as to form a thick paste; cover the entire canapé with a layer of this butter and cheese, and set them on a buttered baking-sheet in the hot oven so they attain a fine color, then serve them as quickly as they are removed from the oven. They may be made round shaped two and a half inches in diameter if preferred.

(856). CANAPÉS MARTHA (Canapés à la Martha).

Muffins three inches in diameter are used for these canapés: cut them through the center and toast them without burning, then cover with two ounces of lobster croquette preparation (No. 880); spread it on flat, lay over each a thin slice of Swiss cheese exactly the same size as the muffins, dust over with bread raspings and grated parmesam and brown them in the oven.

(857). CANAPÉS OF SWEETBREADS (Canapés de ris de Veau).

Cut into three-sixteenths of an inch squares one-half pound of braised sweetbreads, a quarter of a pound of cooked mushrooms and two ounces of lean cooked ham; fry all with four ounces of butter, adding a bunch of parsley garnished with thyme and bay leaf; moisten with a little broth (No. 189) thickened with espagnole sauce (No. 414); skim off the fat and reduce the sauce till nearly dry, then stir in three egg-yolks and a piece of fresh butter. Prepare some slices of bread three-sixteenths of an inch thick and one and a half inches by two and three-quarters; toast them, cover with the preparation the same thickness as the bread, smooth the surfaces and dip them in beaten eggs, then roll them in bread-crumbs, and fry them in very hot fat; serve on a folded napkin.

(858). CANNELONS OE BEEF PALATE OR LAMBS' SWEETBREADS AND CELERY
(Cannelons de Palais de Bœuf ou de Ris d'Agneau et Céleri).

Cut eighth of an inch square pieces from a cold braised and pressed beef palate, add to it an equal quantity of mushrooms and half as many truffles, then mix this salpicon with a well reduced allemande sauce (No. 407). Roll out some eight-turn puff paste to the thickness of one six-teenth of an inch, wet this paste slightly and cut it into half inch wide bands. Butter the exterior of some cylindrical molds, one and a quarter inches in diameter by two and a half inches long; apply the bands on to these, turning them around so that half the paste of one row overlaps half of the last one, and continue until the cylinder is well covered; egg them over twice and cook them in a hot oven, remove, unmold and place each on a square of buttered paper, fill with some chicken quenelle forcemeat (No. 89), garnish the center with the above prepared salpicon, and finish the

bottom and top with more forcemeat, then set them in a moderate oven for ten minutes. Range them on folded napkins and serve. Instead of beef palates, lamb sweetbreads and celery mixed with an allemande sauce, may be substituted and finished exactly the same.

(859). CANNELONS WITH PURÉE OF CHICKEN OR GAME (Cannelons à la Purée
de Volaille ou de Gibier).

Butter the outsides of some tin cornets, two and a half inches by one and a half inches, roll around them a thinly rolled out half inch band made of puff paste trimmings, overlapping half of the paste at each round, lay them on a slightly

FIG. 217.

dampened baking sheet, egg over twice, and cook them lying flat in a hot oven, when done, pull out the tin cornets, and set the cannelons upright, the wide opening at the top, and the point pared in such a manner that they are all of an exact height, keep them in this position by placing them in a paupiette mold; and fill the insides of the cannelons either with a game purée (No. 716), or a chicken purée (No. 713). Cover the wide opening with game or chicken forcemeat (No. 89) according to its contents, and set them in a slow oven for ten minutes, then serve on folded napkins.

(860). CASSOLETTES LUSIGNY (Cassolettes à la Lusigny).

Fill some timbale molds (No. 2, Fig. 137) with butter melted to the consistency of cream, leave to cool, then dip them into very hot water and unmold, roll them in cracker dust, dip in beaten eggs, then in bread-crumbs, and again in beaten eggs and bread-crumbs; smooth neatly with a knife and slit around the top with a pastry cutter dipped in hot water, this should be a quarter of an inch in diameter smaller than the timbale itself; fry a few at the time in very hot frying fat, and when of a fine color, remove the covers, stand them on a grate, at the oven door and let all the butter drain out. Cut up some un-smoked, salted tongue, mushrooms, truffles, and chicken, into small quarter inch squares, combine this salpicon with buttered allemande sauce (No. 407), fill the cassolettes, and place on top a round of truffle the size of the opening to take the place of a cover; it should be a quarter of an inch in thickness.

FIG. 218.

(861). CASSOLETTES, MONTHOLON (Cassolettes à la Montholon).

Procure timbale molds (No. 3, Fig. 137), fill these with butter melted to a cream, and let get very cold; unmold by dipping them into hot water, and stand them away on the ice until hard, then dip them into powdered crackers, and in beaten eggs, also in bread-crumbs, again in the eggs, then roll them in bread-crumbs once more, smooth the surfaces with the blade of a knife, and form an incision on the top with a round pastry cutter three-quarters of an inch in diameter; plunge them into very hot frying fat, lift off the cover, and turn them over on to a grate placed over a tin pan, and set them at the oven door; when the butter has entirely melted, fill the insides with a salpicon of truffles, beef palates, and sweetbreads, mixed with suprême sauce (No. 547), lay on top a cover made of a fluted and glazed mushroom, and serve hot.

(862). CÉLESTINES WITH FOIES-GRAS AND PURÉE OF CHESTNUTS (Célestines au Foies-Gras à la Purée de Marrons).

Put on the fire to reduce about two or three gills of Madeira sauce (No. 492) incorporating into it slowly, a few spoonfuls of good glaze (No. 402); when succulent and thick the same as a montglas, add a few spoonfuls of chopped truffles, then withdraw the saucepan from the fire. Cut from half of a cooked foies-gras, ten or twelve crosswise slices not having them too thin, pare these into drawn out half inches all of the same size; season, glaze over with a brush, and cover one side with the truffle preparation mixed with the parings of foies-gras pounded and strained, smooth and cover with a thin layer of raw forcemeat, then roll the célestines in bread-crumbs, dip in egg, and plunge a few at the time into hot fat so as to color as well as heat them. Drain and dress in a circle on a hot dish with a chestnut purée (No. 712), in the center.

(863). COCKS'-COMBS STUFFED, DUXELLE (Crêtes de Coqs Farcies à la Duxelle).

Prepare and cook the cocks'-combs the same as cocks'-kidneys (No. 864), cool, drain, and cut an incision in them filling it in with Duxelle (No. 385), mingled with a little chicken forcemeat (No. 89), cover them with a well reduced allemande sauce (No. 407), to which has been added a little jelly, let these get very cold, and then dip them into eggs and bread-crumbs, plunge in very hot frying fat, and fry till a fine color. Dress on folded napkins, and decorate with a bunch of parsley on top.

(864). COCKS'-KIDNEYS VILLEROI (Rognons de Coq à la Villeroi).

Cook some cocks'-kidneys in a mirepoix (No. 419) moistened with mushroom broth; when cold, drain, and dip them in a well reduced and thick allemande sauce (No. 407), into which has been added a little jelly and finely chopped mushrooms, and some chopped parsley; when cold dip in beaten eggs, bread-crumb, and fry to a fine color; dress on a folded napkin in a pyramid form, and decorate with a bunch of fried parsley.

(865). COLOMBINES OF CHICKEN LIVERS WITH HAM (Colombines de Foies de Volaille au Jambon).

Put on to reduce one pint of béchamel sauce (No. 409), incorporating into it one gill of mushroom broth and one spoonful of chicken glaze (No. 398), one ounce of butter, and a little red pepper; take off the fire, and add to it half a pound of chicken livers, and as much cooked ham, both cut in three-sixteenth inch squares. Have a pound of boiled rice that has had a little butter and parmesan stirred into it, and with this line some hollow tartlet molds, leaving an empty space in the middle; fill this in with the above preparation, and cover over with a thin layer of the same rice, then let them get quite cold. Unmold, and lay them first in grated parmesan, then in beaten eggs, and lastly in white bread-crumbs; smooth them nicely with the blade of a knife, plunge them into boiling frying fat, a few at the time, in order that they attain a good color, then drain and range them on folded napkins.

(866). COLOMBINES OF FOIES-GRAS (Colombines de Foies-Gras).

Have a piece of cooked foies-gras cut into small dice, mix in with it half as much cooked chopped truffles. Reduce a little good brown sauce (No. 414), incorporating slowly into it a few spoonfuls of melted glaze (No. 402), and the truffle broth; when properly thickened add the salpicon, remove the saucepan at once from the fire, and let stand till cold. Prepare a rather consistent semolino preparation with broth, and after it is finished, reduce for two minutes to obtain a body, then withdraw and add butter, parmesan and two diluted egg-yolks. With this line some buttered tartlet molds, leaving a hollow space in the center; fill this up with a part of the foies-gras preparation, and cover with more of the semolino, then let the tartlets get quite cold; unmold, roll in grated parmesan, dip in beaten egg, then in bread-crumbs and fry nicely. When done, drain and dress on a napkin.

(867). CROMESQUIS OF BEEF PALATES (Cromesquis de Palais de Bœuf).

Prepare and cook a beef palate as explained in No. 1326; put it under a weight. Cut it in lozenge-shaped pieces, two inches by three inches; heat these in a half-glaze (No. 400), set them under a weight, lay on each side a slice of foies-gras (goose livers) and cover this with raw chicken forcemeat (No. 89). Roll them in grated bread-crumbs, dip in beaten eggs, roll again in the bread-crumbs and fry until a good light color. Serve on a folded napkin, with a bunch of parsley on top.

(868). CROMESQUIS OF CHICKEN, CAPON, FAT PULLET OR DUCK (Cromesquis de Volaille, de Chapon, Poularde ou de Canard).

Cook a calf's udder as described in No. 109, and when finished cut it up into very thin slices from the widest part, then beat it down to decrease the thickness. Fry in two ounces of butter, one small finely chopped up shallot, add to it three ounces of flour and let cook slowly, then moisten with a quart of chicken broth (No. 188); season with salt, pepper and nutmeg; reduce, and add a pound of white poultry meat, either of chicken, capon, fat pullet, duck or other, and one pound of well drained mushrooms and four ounces of truffles; all three cut into three-sixteenths of an inch squares; let boil up once or twice while stirring from the bottom of the sautoire with a reducing spatula (Fig. 601), and incorporate into it some good chicken jelly (No. 103); lay this preparation aside to become cold, having it spread on a flat dish to half an inch in thickness, and leave it until it is quite hard, then cut it up into equal sized oblongs one and a quarter inches by two and a half inches; cover each one with a slice of udder so as to completely enwrap it, and just when ready to serve, dip the cromesquis into a frying batter (No. 2, Fig. 137), and plunge them into boiling fat to color; drain, and dress them pyramidically on a napkin with a bunch of fried parsley to decorate.

(869). CROMESQUIS OF CRABS, SHRIMPS, CRAWFISH OR LOBSTER À LA RUMPFORD (Cromesquis de Crabes, de Crevettes, d'Écrevisses ou de Homard à la Rumpford).

For the cromesquis use either crabs, shrimps, crawfish or lobsters; cut a pound of the one desired into three-sixteenth inch squares, also half a pound of mushrooms the same, and add them to a quart of velouté sauce (No. 415); let it boil, season and reduce, then thicken with six egg-yolks, one gill of cream and two ounces of lobster butter (No. 580), pour out the preparation and set it aside to get cold. Dampen two napkins, press out every particle of water, and place between them some white wafers to soften. Roll the cold preparation into balls, flatten them down and wrap them in the white wafers or else the preparation can be merely laid between the two wafers, pressed down well and cut into lozenges. Dip them in frying paste (No. 2, Fig. 137), plunge them into hot fat, and fry them a fine color, drain, wipe off and dress them on folded napkins, with fried parsley on top.

(870). CROMESQUIS OF FILLETS OF STRIPED BASS OR OTHER FISH (Cromesquis de Filets de Bass Rayé ou Autre Poisson).

Put into a bowl a small cut, cold striped bass salpicon, having about half a pound of it, and add to it half its quantity of blanched oysters, and as many mushrooms, the two latter being cut into quarter of an inch dice pieces. Put on to reduce a few spoonfuls of béchamel (No. 409), stirring into it the oyster broth and a little melted glaze (No. 402), let it reduce until very thick, then pour in the salpicon, being careful not to have too much of the sauce; finish the preparation with a dash of grated nutmeg, and leave it to get thoroughly cold. Divide it into parts, each one the size of a ball an inch and a half in diameter, and give them an oblong shape; wrap each one of these in some white waffles softened between two damp cloths. Dip the cromesquis one by one into frying paste (No. 2, Fig. 137), drain them well and plunge them at once, but only a few at the time, into plenty of hot frying fat to heat them through, and let get a very fine color. Drain and dress them on folded napkins.

(871). CROMESQUIS OF GAME STANISLAS (Cromesquis de Gibier à la Stanislas).

Made with either snipe, grouse, young rabbit, partridge or plover with truffles. Remove the skin and nervous parts from some roast game, prepare a pound of the meat and cut it into three-sixteenths of an inch squares, and cut up four ounces of truffles exactly the same. Reduce a quart of espagnole sauce (No. 414), with some game fumet made with the carcasses and a little meat glaze (No. 402), season, add the game and truffles, let boil and cool off. Prepare a few exceedingly thin, small bands of fat pork, seven inches in length and three-quarters of an inch wide, also some round pieces two and a quarter inches in diameter. Divide and roll the preparation into one and a half inch diameter balls, flatten them down to three-quarters of an inch in thickness, and roll the band around the edge, lay the round pieces on top and bottom, then dip the cromesquis into a frying pâste (No. 137, No. 2), and plunge them into very hot fat to attain a fine color, drain and dress them pyramidically on a folded napkin with a bunch of fried parsley on top.

(872). CROMESQUIS OF LAMB, BEEF TONGUE OR SWEETBREADS, BABANINE (Cromesquis d'Agneau, de Bœuf de Langue ou de Ris de Veau à la Babanine).

Prepare a few bands of fat pork a sixteenth of an inch in thickness; have some crépinette or dressing of pork, well cleaned and well drained, spread it on a cloth, and cover over with the bands of pork. Cut into three-sixteenths of an inch squares, one pound of either lamb sweetbreads or beef tenderloin, or lamb or calf tongues, half a pound of mushrooms cut the same size, half a pound of lamb brains, cut the same, half a pound of onions cut into three-sixteenth inch squares, blanched and cooked in broth (No. 194a). Put all these ingredients into a pint of allemande sauce (No. 407) with four ounces of cooked ham, and four ounces of foies-gras cut into dice; let the preparation get cold, then divide it into an inch and a half balls, wrap them up in the crépinette and after they are all prepared, bread-crumb them English style (No. 13), butter over, and broil them on a slow fire, dress on hot dishes, and serve separately a well buttered velouté sauce (No. 415), to which has been added some lemon juice and chopped parsley.

(873). CROMESQUIS OF OYSTERS, MUSSELS, SCALLOPS OR CLAMS, BÉCHAMEL (Cromesquis d'Huîtres, de Moules, de Pétoncles ou de Lucines à la Béchamel).

Blanch lightly either some oysters, mussels, scallops or clams in their own juice, and a little water; drain and cut up one pound into large three-eighths of an inch dice pieces. Reduce three pints of béchamel sauce (No. 409), with the above broth, sauté in butter over a brisk fire the blanched pieces of oysters or others, with half their quantity of minced fresh mushrooms, add these to the béchamel sauce, after carefully draining off the butter, then let it get cold, and divide it into parts; roll each one into a ball an inch and a half in diameter, flatten them down to three-quarters of an inch in thickness, and garnish around with a band of very thin prepared pancake; lay a round piece both on top and bottom to cover the entire surface, and then dip the cromesquis into frying batter (No. 137, No. 2), plunge them into very hot fat and let fry a fine color; dress them on folded napkins, placing a bunch of fried parsley in the center.

(874). CROQUETTES (Croquettes).

There are certain preparations called croquettes made either of meat, fish, crustaceans, vegetables, or eggs, cut up into small dice, and frequently mixed with mushrooms cut the same size as the meats, and then mingled with certain sauces. Croquettes are made of various shapes such as pear, cylindricals, balls, or cakes. These croquettes are breaded in eggs and bread-crumbs, and are fried in very hot frying fat until they attain a fine golden color, they must be served as soon as done. Dress on folded napkins decorating with a bunch of parsley on top; to be served without any sauce, therefore the preparation should be mingled with a light, gelatinous or else well buttered sauce.

Fig. 219.

(875). CROQUETTES OF BEEF PALATES (Croquettes de Palais de Bœuf).

Made with braised beef palate pressed under a weight reducing it to three-sixteenths of an inch in thickness; cut a pound of this into small squares, and half a pound of mushrooms cut into the same sized pieces; cover this salpicon with a pint and a half of well seasoned allemande sauce (407), and finish the same as the sweetbread croquettes (No. 893).

(876). CROQUETTES OF CAPON À LA ROYAL (Croquettes de Chapon à la Royale).

Cut a pound of white capon meat into three-sixteenth inch squares, also half a pound of mushrooms, a quarter of a pound of sweetbreads, and the same of truffles, all cut alike. Mix together and fill some buttered timbale molds (No. 2, Fig. 137). Put six egg-yolks into a basin, beat them up with a pint of cream, some salt, pepper, and nutmeg; strain this through a sieve, and finish filling up the molds with it; poach them in a slow oven, and as soon as they become hard, unmold, and dip them in beaten eggs, bread-crumb and fry them to attain a good color, drain and dress them on a napkin garnishing around with fried parsley.

(877). CHICKEN CROQUETTES, EXQUISITE (Croquettes de Volaille Exquises). •

Place two ounces of butter in a saucepan with two ounces of rice flour, stir well and let it cook slowly until slightly brown, then moisten with a quart of veal blond stock (No. 423), and stir continuously till it comes to a boil; set it on one side to boil slowly, and despumate; reduce the sauce and thicken it with egg-yolks, cream and fresh butter. Now add to this sauce, a pound of the white meat taken from a fat pullet, and cut into three-sixteenths of an inch squares, half a pound of cooked mushrooms, four ounces of artichoke bottoms, all being cut the same size as the pullet, and season with salt, pepper, and nutmeg; then pour it out, and let it get perfectly cold. Pound in a mortar, one ounce of truffles with one ounce of cooked rice, and three tablespoonfuls of béchamel (No. 409), press it through a sieve, and let get cold, then divide this into half inch balls. Make some balls, an inch and a half in diameter, of the chicken croquette preparation, and in the center of each insert a truffle ball, flatten them to three-quarters of an inch; dip them in beaten eggs and bread-crumbs, fry nicely and dress them in pyramids over a folded napkin, garnishing the top with fried parsley.

(878). CHICKEN CROQUETTES, HUNGARIAN (Croquettes de Poulets à la Hongroise).

These are made with one pound of the white meat from a roast chicken, half a pound of mushrooms, and a quarter of a pound of unsmoked red beef tongue, each article cut into one-sixteenth of an inch squares. Put into a sautoire a pint and a half of Hungarian sauce (No. 479), thickened with egg-yolks and cream; when it nearly boils, stir in the chicken, mushrooms, and tongue; allow to boil a minute then cool; with this preparation form cork-shaped croquettes, dip them in beaten eggs and roll them in bread-crumbs, and then fry to a nice color. Dress on napkins and garnish with fried parsley.

(879). CRAB CROQUETTES, PARMENTIER (Croquettes de Crabes à la Parmentier).

Line some buttered paupiette molds with a thin lining of duchess potato preparation (No. 2785), finished with parmesan cheese; fill the space with a crab and cooked mushroom salpicon mixed with a reduced thick béchamel (No. 409), the same as for a croquette preparation; let it become hard while in a cool place, and finish filling the molds with more of the potato purée. Dip the molds into hot water in order to unmold the croquettes, then roll these in flour, afterward in beaten eggs, and lastly in white bread-crumbs, then plunge them into very hot frying fat to color; drain, and serve on folded napkins and garnish with fried parsley.

(880). CRAB, CRAWFISH, LOBSTER OR SHRIMP CROQUETTES, VICTORIA (Croquettes de Crabes d'Écrevisses, de Homard ou Crevettes à la Victoria).

These croquettes are made with any of the above crustaceans. Cut a pound of any of these meats into dice shapes, and have also one-quarter of a pound of truffles cut the same size as the meat. Put a quart of velouté (No. 415), into a sautoire, season with salt, white, and red pepper, and add half a pint of celery purée (No. 711), let reduce and moisten with cream; and incorporate into it two ounces of lobster butter (No. 580) for each pound; then add the meat, let this preparation get quite cold, then divide it into balls an inch and a half in diameter, forming these into cork shaped croquettes, two inches in length, roll them in beaten egg and then in bread-crumbs, and fry a fine color; dress on folded napkins, arranging a bunch of fried parsley on top.

(881). DUCKLING CROQUETTES À LA MUSER (Croquettes de Canetons à la Muser).

Have a pound of the meat taken from the breast of a duckling, without any fat or skin, and cut it into three-sixteenths of an inch squares, fry lightly without coloring, one ounce of chopped onions in two ounces of butter, add the duckling, and fry for a minute longer, then season with salt, pepper, and nutmeg, drain off the butter and add half a pound of potato purée (No. 725), four raw egg-yolks, and two tablespoonfuls of grated parmesan; mix well and with this preparation form cork-shaped croquettes, two inches in length, dip them in eggs and bread-crumbs, and fry them a fine golden color, dress them on folded napkins and set on top a bunch of fried parsley.

(882). PULLET CROQUETTES, WRIGHT SANFORD (Croquettes de Poularde à la Wright Sanford).

Mince two ounces of peeled truffles, cut them into small three-sixteenths of an inch squares, suppress the skin from several fat pullets and all the hard parts so as to obtain one pound of meat, and cut it up the same as the truffles. Put the bones and parings from the pullets into a saucepan with the peelings from the truffles, three gills of veal blond stock (No. 423), and a garnished bunch of parsley; cover and set it on a brisk fire to reduce the liquid to half, then strain through a tammy (Fig. 88).

Pour into a flat saucepan, one pint of béchamel (No. 409), mix into it a few pieces of raw ham, reduce the sauce while stirring it well from the bottom of the saucepan with a reducing spatula (Fig. 601), and incorporate into it gradually the above stock; continue to reduce until the sauce becomes thick and succulent, then take out the ham, and replace it by the truffles, and afterward the pullet; season with salt if deemed necessary, and a little nutmeg. Spread this preparation on a baking sheet covered with a piece of paper, having it an inch in thickness, and when it is cold and stiff, overturn it on the table previously dredged with bread-crumbs; remove the paper, and cut the preparation into oblongs, three inches long by one inch wide; dip these in beaten eggs, roll them in fresh bread-crumbs, and throw them into hot fat; as soon as they are nicely colored, take them out and drain. Dress them pyramidically on folded napkins, and garnish around with fried parsley.

(883). FISH CROQUETTES (Croquettes de Poisson).

The Fish Croquettes may be prepared with either salmon, trout, sole, bass, kingfish sheepshead, or red snapper. Simply cut up the meat into small three-sixteenths of an inch squares; lay them in a vessel and mix in a third of their quantity of cooked mushrooms, and half as many truffles as there are mushrooms, all cut into the same sized pieces. Put on the fire to boil a few gills of good, consistent béchamel (No. 409); mix into it slowly the mushroom liquor and a few spoonfuls of good melted glaze (No. 402), and when the sauce has become succulent, add the salpicon in the saucepan; heat it without boiling, and spread it over a tin sheet to become hard, leaving it for a few hours in a cool place or on the ice. Divide the preparation into balls, an inch and a half in diameter, lay them on a table bestrewn with white bread-crumbs, and roll them either in the shape of corks or balls; dip them in beaten eggs and roll them in the bread-crumbs; smooth well the surfaces with the blade of a knife, then range them on a tin sheet; put them in hot frying fat; cook only a few at a time and let them get a nice color. After the croquettes are finished and well drained from the fat, range them in pyramid-form over a folded napkin, and garnish around with fried parsley.

(884). FROG OR OYSTER CROQUETTES (Croquettes de Grenouilles ou d'Huîtres).

Sauté some frogs' legs with butter in a pan over a brisk fire; season, take off all the meat from the bones to obtain one pound; cut in small squares, have half a pound of cooked and well-dried mushrooms, cut them into quarter inch squares, and mix them with a quart of well seasoned and reduced béchamel and cream sauce (No. 411); incorporate two ounces of butter, and toss the salpicon in the sautoire. Let the preparation get thoroughly cold, and then form it into balls an inch and a half in diameter; flatten them down to half an inch in thickness, dip them in eggs and bread-crumbs, and fry them a fine golden color, then drain and serve on folded napkins with fried parsley.

Oyster Croquettes.—Instead of frogs blanched oysters may be substituted after removing the hard parts, and dividing them into squares; sauté them, drain off the butter and finish the same as the frogs.

(885). GAME, CHICKEN OR FAT LIVER CROQUETTES, DAUPHINE (Croquettes de Gibier, de Volaille ou de Foies-gras à la Dauphine).

Remove the fillets either from some game or chicken (or replace them by some fat livers), suppress all skin and nerves and chop them up finely, then pound in a mortar and add one pint of velouté (No. 415), and one ounce of butter with some essence of mushrooms (No. 392) worked into it, pass it through a tammy being careful to have the purée more consistent than liquid. Break separately in a bowl, eight egg-yolks and one whole egg for each quart of purée, add this and season with salt, pepper and nutmeg. Butter some molds (No. 2, Fig. 137), fill them with the preparation, and poach them in a slow oven; let get cold, then unmold, and roll them in beaten eggs and bread-crumbs, and fry to a good color, dress, range them on folded napkins and garnish with fried parsley. These croquettes may be made by mixing half foies-gras with either the chicken or game.

(886). GROUSE CROQUETTES WITH TOMATOED SOUBISE SAUCE (Croquettes de Tétras Sauce Soubise Tomatée).

Cut the meat from roasted grouse into three-sixteenth inch squares removing all the skin, bones and nerves; cut the same quantity of cooked mushrooms the same size; mingle the two with some well reduced Madeira sauce (No. 492), season with salt, pepper and nutmeg, let boil up once, then pour it into a vessel to incorporate in a little fresh butter; let this preparation get cool. Divide it into equal parts and shape each one into a cylindrical croquette, two inches long by one inch in diamater, dip in beaten eggs, roll in bread-crumbs and fry to a fine golden brown, drain, wipe and dress on folded napkins; serve separately a soubise sauce (No. 543), with tomato sauce (No. 549) added.

(887). GUINEA FOWL OR PULLET CROQUETTES IN SURPRISE (Croquettes de Pintade ou Poularde en Surprise).

Have one pound of the white meat from a roasted Guinea fowl; suppress all the fat and nerves, and cut it up into small three-sixteenth inch squares; add to these a quarter of a pound of truffles cut the same size, and put all into a pint and a half of a well buttered, cold supreme sauce (No. 547). Form the preparation into balls an inch and three-quarter in diameter, flatten them down to half an inch in thickness, and remove the center of each with a half inch tube; fill this empty space with a foies-gras ball, then dip them into beaten eggs and roll them in bread-crumbs, then fry them till a nice color. Serve on folded napkins, garnished with fried parsley.

(888). LAMB CROQUETTES À LA DE RIVAS (Croquettes d'Agneau à la de Rivas).

Take a pound of lean meat, free of nerves, from a tenderloin or leg of lamb, half a pound of mushrooms, and a quarter of a pound of red beef tongue; mingle these well with a pint of velouté (No. 415), and half a pint of fine tomato purée (No. 730); reduce well together, season, and set it aside to get cold; finish precisely the same as sweetbread croquettes (No. 893).

(889). PARTRIDGE CROQUETTES WITH GAME FUMET (Croquettes de Perdreaux au Fumet de Gibier).

Cut half a pound of three-sixteenth inch squares from the breasts of some roast partridges, after suppressing the skin and nerves; spread half a pound of partridge quenelle forcemeat (No. 91), on a buttered paper to the thickness of three-sixteenths of an inch; poach this in a slow oven, and when cold cut it up into three-sixteenth inch squares. Have also eight ounces of mushrooms cut the same. Reduce a quart of velouté (No. 415), with a pint of game fumet (No. 397), and a pint of mushroom essence (No. 392); when the sauce is well reduced add to it the salpicon; put it back on to the fire, and stir to bring it to a boil, and just when on the eve of boiling, set it aside to get cold. Divide this into balls each an inch and a half in size, roll them on a table dredged with bread-crumbs, and form them into cork shaped pieces, then dip them in beaten egg and in bread-crumbs, fry in hot fat until a good color, and dress the croquettes on a folded napkin, garnishing them with fried parsley.

(890). PIKE CROQUETTES À LA ROMAINE (Croquettes de Brochet à la Romaine).

Cut into three-sixteenth inch squares, half a pound of mushrooms, and one pound of pike fillets, sautéd in butter, and cut into the same size pieces as the mushrooms, also two ounces of truffles, and mix these together with an espagnole (No. 414) reduced with Marsala wine. Have some cream cake paste (No. 132); put it with an equal amount of pike quenelle forcemeat (No. 90); butter some timbale molds (No. 2, Fig. 137), cover the bottoms and sides with a thin layer of this forcemeat, and garnish the centers with a salpicon; cover over with more forcemeat, and poach them in a very slow oven for twenty minutes, then unmold, dip them in eggs, roll in bread-crumbs and fry till a good color; drain, dress on folded napkins, and garnish with fried parsley.

(891). PHEASANT CROQUETTES (Croquettes de Faisans).

Cut in three-sixteenth of an inch dice the cooked and cold breast meats taken from pheasants; put these into a small bowl with half their quantity of cooked truffles and mushrooms, a few spoonfuls of red beef tongue also cut up. Set a little béchamel (No. 409) on the fire to reduce, and incorporate into it a few spoonfuls of pheasant fumet prepared with the game bones and parings, also the same quantity of mushroom essence (No. 392). After the sauce is thickened, add to it the salpicon, and season the whole to taste; when cold divide it into small parts and with them make pear or cork-shaped croquettes, fry them when needed and dress, garnishing with fried parsley. These croquettes can also be made with partridge or quail.

(892). WOODCOCK CROQUETTES WITH TRUFFLES (Croquettes de Bécasses aux Truffes).

Suppress the skin and nerves from one pound of woodcock fillets; cut them into three-sixteenth inch dice, and add a quarter of a pound of truffles; reduce one quart of espagnole (No. 414) and velouté (No. 415) combined, and when well reduced thicken it with four raw egg-yolks, and two ounces of fresh butter; add to it the game meats and truffles, and return it to the fire, stir incessantly until the first boil, then take it off and set it away to cool. Divide this preparation into one and three-quarter inch sized balls; roll them on a table dredged with bread-crumbs to give them the shape of a pear, and dip these into beaten eggs, and afterward roll them in bread-crumbs; smooth the surfaces with the blade of a knife, and plunge them into hot fat; when done drain on folded napkins, imitate the stalks with bits of parsley, range them crown shaped garnishing the center with fried parsley. The game may be replaced by a salpicon of foies-gras.

FIG. 220.

(893). SWEETBREAD CROQUETTES (Croquettes de ris de Veau).

Braise, then set aside to cool, one pound of sweetbreads, cut them into three-sixteenths inch squares, have also three-quarters of a pound of cooked mushrooms cut the same. Put into a sautoir one quart of velouté (No. 415) well seasoned with salt, black and red pepper and nutmeg, and thicken the sauce with four raw egg-yolks diluted with half a gill of cream and two ounces of fine butter; add the sweetbreads and mushrooms, set it on the fire and continue to stir until it boils, then pour this preparation into a vessel to get thoroughly cold. Divide it so as to make it into cork-shaped pieces, which roll in beaten eggs, and fry a fine color; drain; dress them pyramidically on folded napkins and decorate with fried parsley.

(894). TURKEY CROQUETTES (Croquettes de Dinde).

Put three ounces of butter into a saucepan with three ounces of flour; make a light blond roux, and dilute it with a quart of cream and a pint of milk, add salt, red pepper and nutmeg, then reduce and despumate this sauce. Add two pounds of white turkey meat, and a pound of mushrooms, all cut into three-sixteenths of an inch squares, and the mushrooms pressed free of all moisture; bring to a boil while stirring briskly with a reducing spatula, and incorporate slowly two ounces of fresh butter. Another way is to use twelve ounces of cooked chicken, eight ounces of mushrooms, two ounces of butter and two ounces of flour; moisten with five gills of white chicken broth (No. 188). And still another way is to employ two pounds of chicken, two pounds of chopped mushrooms, and a quart of velouté sauce (No. 415) reduced with cream.

(895). CROUSTADES À LA CASTILLANE (Croustades à la Castillane).

Prepare a very thick chestnut purée as already described in the garnishings (No. 712), with it fill some six-sided molds previously cooled in ice-water and drained before filling, when perfectly cool dip them into very hot water to unmold. Bread-crumb them in cracker dust, beaten eggs and bread-crumbs, smooth the surfaces, and mark an incision with a pastry cutter three-quarters of an inch in diameter; fry them to a fine color, remove the cover and empty out the insides to refill with beef tenderloin cut in quarter inch dice pieces and sautéd in butter with some mushrooms cut exactly the same, and a brown and Marsala wine sauce (No. 492). Instead of replacing the lid, cover the aperture with a small round celery croquette three-quarters of an inch across, that has been made with braised celery cut in small squares and mixed with velouté sauce (No. 415), and when cold bread-crumbed and fried.

FIG. 221.

(896). CROUSTADES À LA PARMENTIER (Croustades à la Parmentier).

Prepare a potato purée (No. 725); rub it through a very fine sieve as described in the purée and with it fill some buttered six-sided molds; let them get thoroughly cold on ice, then unmold and dip them in beaten eggs and bread-crumbs, mark an incision on top with a three-quarters of an inch in diameter pastry cutter, and fry them in hot frying fat till a nice color is attained, then remove the lid, empty out the insides and refill with a salpicon of crawfish for one-half, and mushrooms and truffles for the other half; mingled with an allemande sauce (No. 407). Serve very hot on folded napkins.

(897). CROUSTADES À LA PÉRIGUEUX (Croustades à la Périgueux).

Cook half a pound of hulled barley in two quarts of beef stock (No. 194a) for three hours, and when well done, and the liquid entirely reduced, then beat it with a spatula to make it attain a body, while adding two ounces of butter, salt, nutmeg and red pepper. Lay some six-sided molds into cold water, take them out one by one, drain and fill with the prepared barley; leave them to cool on the ice, then unmold and bread-crumb them, mark the top with a three-quarter inch pastry cutter, fry them, empty their insides, and fill them with a salpicon composed of truffles cut in small one-eighth inch squares, and small quarter of an inch bead quenelles with a brown Madeira sauce (No. 492). Instead of covering the aperture with its own cover, have one made of a round piece of glazed truffle, three-quarters of an inch in diameter, by one-eighth in thickness. Dress them in a pyramid on a folded napkin.

(898). CROUSTADES, CAROLINA STYLE (Croustades à la Caroline).

Pick well half a pound of rice, wash and put it into a saucepan, moistening with some fat, beef stock (No. 194a) to three times its height, then boil, cover the saucepan and continue the boiling for thirty minutes; by this time the moisture should be entirely evaporated. Mix in with this rice, four ounces of butter, beating it in well, then fill up some six-sided molds after they have been dipped in ice water and drained; let the rice get cold, unmold, roll them in fine cracker dust, then in beaten eggs, and finish by rolling them in fresh bread-crumbs, smooth the surfaces with a knife, and mark an incision on top with a three-quarters of an inch pastry cutter, then fry them to a fine color; remove the covers, empty out the insides and fill them with the following garnishing: Cut some shrimps and mushrooms into three-sixteenths of an inch squares; put them into a sautoir with a cream sauce (No. 454), season and bring it to a boil while stirring steadily, thicken well with egg-yolks, fresh butter and cream, and fill the croustades with this; lay on top of each one a round piece of truffle instead of a cover, and dress these croustades on a folded napkin.

(899). CROUSTADES OF GNOCQUIS À LA RIVOLI (Croustades de Gnocquis à la Rivoli).

Prepare a gnocquis paste with half a pound of flour, half a pound of fecula, one quart of milk, five ounces of butter, fifteen raw egg-yolks and one whole egg, some salt, sugar, nutmeg and four tablespoonfuls of grated parmesan cheese. Put into a bowl the flour, fecula, cheese, salt, sugar and nutmeg, and incorporate in slowly two and a half ounces of butter, eight egg-yolks and the whole egg, work them well together, then add the remainder of the butter and eggs; butter some six-sided molds two and a quarter inches in diameter, two inches wide at the bottom, and one inch and an eighth in height, fill with the gnocquis paste and then poach them; when cold unmold, dip them in eggs and bread-crumbs, and mark a place on top for a cover, fry them a fine color and empty the insides to fill with a salpicon of truffles, mushrooms and unsmoked red beef tongue, small delicate chicken quenelle balls, serve with a brown sauce (No. 414), reduced with meat juice and tomato essence. Dress them on a folded napkin.

(900). CROUSTADES PERRETTI (Croustades à la Perretti).

Have ready two pounds of noodles (No. 142), cook this for four minutes in boiling, salted water, drain well and return it to the saucepan; season, and finish with six ounces of butter and four ounces of parmesan in such a way as to obtain a compact preparation. With this fill some buttered six sided molds, cool them on ice, unmold, dip them in beaten eggs, roll them in white bread-crumbs, and smooth the surfaces with the blade of a knife. mark them on one side with a pastry cutter, three-quarters of an inch in diameter, and ten minutes before serving plunge them into hot fat to attain a golden color, drain, and empty them, then fill the insides with a salpicon of chicken and mushrooms, mingled with some supreme sauce (No. 547), and chicken glaze (No. 398); put back the cover previously removed, and dress them to serve.

For Talliarines proceed the same as for the noodles, only use a salpicon of olives cut in small three-sixteenth inch squares, some mushrooms, foies-gras, brown sauce (No. 414) and tomato sauce (No. 549).

(901). CROUSTADES À LA PIEDMONTESE (Croustades à la Piémontaise).

Set a quart of broth or water on the fire, and when it boils, drip into it like rain, six ounces of semolino, let it cook slowly for twenty minutes, then incorporate into it one ounce of butter and four spoonfuls of grated parmesan, also a little salt and nutmeg. Lay in cold ice water some six-sided molds (Fig. 221), take them out one by one, and fill them with the above preparation; leave them to stand on ice till cold, then unmold, dip them in beaten eggs, and roll in powdered crackers, then again in beaten eggs and afterward in bread-crumbs, smooth the surfaces with the blade of a knife, and mark on top with a round three-quarter of an inch pastry cutter; fry them a fine color, remove the covers, and empty out the insides; fill these with a salpicon of truffles, mushrooms, beef palates, duck livers, small quenelles and a little brown Madeira sauce (No. 492). Replace the covers, and serve them dressed on folded napkins.

For Polenta Croustades proceed exactly as for the semolino, finishing them the same; fill the insides with white truffles and quarter inch squares of sweetbreads, and cover with an espagnole sauce (No. 414) reduced with dry mushrooms and tomato essence added.

(902). CROUSTADES À LA MORGAN OR WITH SCRAMBLED EGGS AND TRUFFLES
(Croustade à la Morgan ou aux Œufs Brouillés aux Truffes).

Peel and steam some sweet potatoes, then pound them with a little butter and a few egg-yolks; fill some six sided molds (Fig. 221) previously laid in ice water and drained, press in well the potato, and set them on the ice to become cold, unmold and roll them in cracker dust, dip them in eggs and bread-crumbs, and mark an incision on top with a pastry cutter three-quarters of an inch in diameter; fry them a fine color, remove the cover, empty out the insides, and fill them with some mushrooms, artichokes, and fat livers cut in three-sixteenths of an inch squares, and mixed in a saucepan with a sufficient quantity of poulette sauce (No. 527). When all are filled, range them on a folded napkin.

For Scrambled Eggs and Truffles.—Fill the empty spaces with a preparation of eggs scrambled with truffles and grated cheese.

(903). CRUSTS OF CLAMS À LA SCHENK (Croûtes de Lucines Orangées à la Schenk).

Cut a few slices of bread so as to obtain eight crusts, having them half an inch thick; pare them into ovals, and slit them on the surface of one side, by making a slight incision a short distance from the edge, following the oval with the tip of a small knife, then fry them in clarified butter; drain as quickly as they get a nice color, and empty out the insides. Fill them with fish forcemeat (No. 90), poach for a few minutes. Blanch thirty-two medium-sized clams; drain, and cut them up into pieces, but should they be very small then leave them whole; add them to a little allemande sauce (No. 407), season with pepper, mignonette, nutmeg and lemon juice, and, if desired, a very little salt, besides a few cooked fine herbs. Cover the crusts with this preparation, and bestrew over the tops bread-crumbs and grated parmesan; set them into a very hot oven, and when a fine color and hot, dress them on folded napkins.

Crusts à la Schenk.—Remove all the hard parts from twenty-four clams, using only the soft pieces; chop these up and season with black and red pepper but no salt; put them into a saucepan with half an ounce of butter, a teaspoonful of very finely minced onion, the clam juice and two tablespoonfuls of cream; place the saucepan on the fire, and remove it on one side before the contents come to a boil. Lay slices of toasted bread on a chafing-dish, pour over the clams and serve. Slices of buttered brown bread may accompany this hors-d'œuvre.

(904). CRUSTS D'HENIN, MORTON, CHAMBERLAIN, OR À LA GÉNOISE (Croûtes à la d'Henin, à la Morton, à la Chamberlain, ou à la Génoise).

If cut round shaped à la d'Henin they are two and one-quarter inches across; if oval shaped à la Morton, two inches by three; if oblongs, Chamberlain, two and three-quarters inches by one and three-quarters inches; if lozenge shape à la Genoise, four inches by two and one-quarter inches all of these to be cut half an inch in thickness.

For Round Shaped à la d'Henin.—Made with foies-gras; mark an incision all around the crusts a quarter of an inch from the edge, fry them in butter, and empty out the insides to fill in with a cream forcemeat (No. 75), poach for a few minutes. Mince some foies-gras, garnish the crusts with this, and cover with a Toulouse garnishing (No. 766), lay over a chicken and cream forcemeat (No. 75), bestrew over some chopped truffles and besprinkle with clarified butter; poach them in the oven without browning for twenty minutes, and serve on napkins without any sauce whatever.

Oval Crusts à la Morton.—Fill the insides with a chicken quenelle forcemeat (No. 89), poach them in the oven, and garnish with slices of truffles, slices of hard boiled eggs, and slices of mushrooms. Cover with a béchamel sauce (No. 409) to which some chopped chives have been added, dredge bread crumbs and grated parmesan on top, and set them in a slow oven for twenty minutes before serving.

Oblong Crusts à la Chamberlain.—Fill the insides with a godiveau forcemeat (No. 82), poach them, then mince some raw chicken or game fillets, sauté them in butter over a brisk fire, add some velouté (No. 415), truffles and mushrooms; cover the crusts with this, bestrew the tops with grated cheese and bread-crumbs, pour over some butter, and place them for twenty minutes in the oven, and serve hot on folded napkins.

Lozenge-shaped Crusts à la Génoise.—Fill the insides with a pike quenelle forcemeat (No. 90); lay over some oysters and slices of lobsters or crabs, sauté a few mushrooms in butter, seasoning with salt and pepper, moisten with cream, and let boil for a few seconds, then add a little béchamel sauce (No. 409), and with this cover the whole; besprinkle with bread-crumbs and parmesan, and brown the crusts in the oven.

(905). CRUSTS WITH FOIES-GRAS (Croûtes au Foies-Gras).

From a kitchen loaf (Fig. 210) cut quarter inch thick slices and from these obtain twenty oval-shaped crusts, each three inches long by two and a quarter inches wide; prepare a baking liver forcemeat (No. 64) with fat pork and aromatic herbs; when cold pound it with a few parings of cooked foies-gras; rub this through a sieve. Put into a vessel about two gills of this purée, beat it with a spoon incorporating slowly into it three or four spoonfuls of good brown sauce (No. 414) reduced with Madeira till succulent and thick; add to the preparation a third as much cooked foies-gras cut in small dice and two chopped truffles. Take up the crusts one by one, dip them into a mixture of egg-yolks and raw cream that has been strained through a sieve and steep without deforming them, then cover the surfaces with a part of the above preparation, smooth it into a dome-shape, and take up the crusts with a palette to dip them entirely in beaten eggs; let drain and immerse in white bread-crumbs, and plunge a few at the time into plenty of hot frying fat to attain a fine color; drain, dress on a folded napkin and serve.

(906). CRUSTS OF WOODCOCK (Croûtes de Bécasses).

Have a kitchen loaf of bread (Fig. 210) and from it cut seven or eight oblong slices, each one three-eighths of an inch thick; brown lightly in clarified butter on one side only, then remove them leaving the butter in the sautoire. Fry on a brisk fire the intestines of two woodcock with melted fat pork and a few good chicken livers, also two or three slices of calf's liver, aromatic herbs and seasoning. Pound this preparation, rub it through a sieve and put the pulp into a vessel to stir in with it a few spoonfuls of good, reduced and well thickened Madeira sauce (No. 492), adding also four raw egg-yolks and a dash of nutmeg. With this cover the browned sides of the crusts, smoothing the surfaces bomb-shaped. Return the crusts to the sautoire then set the pan on the oven to fry the bread underneath, and poach the preparation. Glaze the surface with a little meat glaze laid on with a brush, remove from the pan, place them on a napkin to drain, then dress them on hot plates, and serve very hot.

FIG. 222.

(907). FONTAGE CROUSTADES À LA FLAVIGNAN (Croustades Fontage à la Flavignan).

Into a vessel put four ounces of sifted flour, two or three egg-yolks, a little salt, and four tablespoonfuls of olive oil; mix all well together with a gill and a half of tepid water, adding a little beer or a little compressed yeast the size of a three-eighths of an inch ball, diluting it in a little luke warm water. Cover the vessel and place it in a mild temperature of eighty degrees for about two hours. Heat some lard on the fire, place in it a fontage iron (Fig. 174). As soon as the iron is hot, dip it almost entirely in the paste, take it out at once and plunge it into the hot frying fat and keep it there until the paste is cooked and can be detached from the iron, then remove and invert it on a grate to keep warm, while continuing the operation until a sufficient number are prepared, and just when serving fill them with a Flavignan salpicon (No. 744).

(908). KULIBIAC, RUSSIAN (Coulibiac à la Russe).

Dilute in a pint of warm milk, the third of an ounce of yeast; fill it up with half a pound of flour, and beat well with a spatula to form a very smooth leaven; let it rise to double in a mild temperature, then add to it half a pound of flour, half a pound of butter, six eggs, some cream and a little salt; beat it well with the spatula to obtain a smooth paste, then lay it on the table, make a hole in the middle and fill this with sufficient sifted flour that when mixing it with the hands it does not adhere, and set it away in a warm place for one hour. Break up the paste and bring it together again, and lay it aside in the ice-box. Roll it out to three-sixteenths of an inch in thickness, set this layer on a floured cloth, and place on it one inch and a quarter apart, round balls, an inch in diameter, made of the following preparation: Have a pound of salmon and bass cut in quarter inch squares; half a pound of mushrooms in three-sixteenth inch squares, fry them in butter and moisten with Madeira, then add the fish and some espagnole sauce (No. 414), two chopped hard boiled eggs, and four ounces of rice cooked in consommé (No. 189), salt, pepper, nutmeg, and chives. Dampen slightly with a brush around the forcemeat, and cover over with another layer of paste. Prepare a buttered baking sheet, cut out the kulibiacs with a small wheel if for squares, or else with a pastry cutter if for rounds, turn them over and lay them on a baking sheet and set them aside in a warm temperature, egg the surfaces twice, dredge a little bread-crumbs over, besprinkle with butter and cook. They can be made in one entire piece, turning it over on a buttered sheet, egg the surface, dredge bread-crumbs over, besprinkle with butter, and when done cut them out with a knife; in either case dress them on folded napkins.

(909). KULIBIAC SMOLENSKA (Coulibiac à la Smolenska).

Fry a chopped shallot in butter without letting it attain a color, add a quarter of a pound of raw mushrooms cut in quarter inch squares, and when the moisture has evaporated, add carrots, turnips, and celery roots, all blanched and fried in butter, also some cabbage; season with salt, black and red pepper, and moisten with some remoistening (No. 189), then let cook slowly in such a way that the moisture becomes thoroughly reduced when the vegetables are done; thicken it with half velouté (No. 415), and half espagnole (No. 414), and set it aside to get cold. Roll out some foundation paste (No. 135), to an eighth of an inch in thickness; cut from this round pieces three and a half inches in diameter, and fill the centers with the above preparation, shaping it into one and a half inch balls, wet the edges of the paste, and raise them up to join the opposite corners, pinch them well together to make them fasten, and range on a baking sheet; egg over the surfaces, and let them cook in a hot oven; serve on folded napkins.

(910). CARDINAL MOUSSELINE (Mousseline au Cardinal).

Fig. 223.

Forcemeats for mousselines are prepared either with chicken, game, or fish, the same as explained in the Elementary Methods (No. 86). Butter some mousseline molds (No. 2, Fig. 138) with cold butter, and decorate with fanciful cuts of truffles; at the bottom of each mold place a thin slice of truffle, then dredge all over with very finely chopped lobster coral so as to cover the sides completely. Fill with salmon mousseline forcemeat, poach the same as described in the Elementary Methods (No. 152), and dress on to a dish containing a little consommé; serve a cardinal sauce (No. 442) separately.

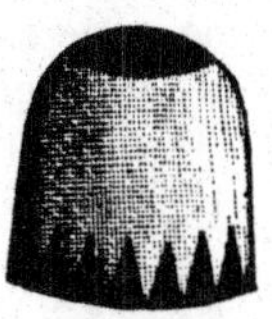

(911). HAM MOUSSELINE OR MOUSSE À LA BELMONT, COSTA, VIRGINIENNE (Mousseline ou Mousse de Jambon à la Belmont, à la Costa et à la Virginienne).

A la Belmont.—Chop very fine a pound of cooked ham, and a quarter of a pound of breast of chicken freed from nerves and fat. Add two dessertspoonfuls of cold béchamel sauce (No. 409), thickened with cream and eight egg-yolks, and pour in slowly three spoonfuls of good cream and one of Madeira. Add the same volume of well drained whipped cream as there is forcemeat, and finish the same as mousseline à la Costa. Serve separately a chicken essence (No. 387), thickened with rice flour, to which a little tomato purée (No. 730) is added, and some lean ham cut in very small dice.

A la Costa.—Take one pound of raw, lean ham previously cut in small dice soaked in cold water for three hours, drain and pound with one-quarter of a pound of chicken breasts previously run through the machine (Fig. 147), then press the meat through a fine sieve and put this in a metal pan on the ice, work and add gradually the volume of one pint of well drained not sweetened whipped cream and a teaspoonful of fecula. Butter some mousseline molds (No. 2, Fig. 138), dredge over some finely chopped, cooked, lean ham, fill the molds with preparation and poached as explained (No. 152), dress on a dish having a little consommé in it. Serve separately a Westphalian sauce (No. 561).

A la Virginienne.—Chop finely a quarter of a pound of raw or cooked, lean Virginia ham, also a quarter of a pound of chicken breasts, mix the two together and pound, add béchamel sauce (No. 409), pass through a fine sieve, adding two soupspoonfuls of tomato purée (No. 730), and one teaspoonful of fecula; mix with this the same volume of chicken cream forcemeat (No. 75), put in a thin basin on ice and add to it the volume of one pint of well drained unsweetened whipped cream, finish the same as à la Costa. Serve separately a champagne sauce (No. 445).

(912). ISABELLA MOUSSELINE (Mousseline Isabelle).

FIG. 224.

Decorate mousseline molds (No. 2, Fig. 138) with red beef tongue and truffles; fill them with mousseline game forcemeat (No. 87), made either with snipe, plovers, doe-birds, or woodcock, finish them precisely the same as for the cardinal (No. 910); dress and serve separately a marsala sauce (No. 492), with chopped truffles.

(913). MARÉCHALE MOUSSELINE (Mousseline à la Maréchale).

FIG. 225.

Decorate mousseline molds (No. 2, Fig. 138) with truffles and tongue, as in the accompanying design (Fig. 225), garnish them with a poultry mousseline forcemeat (No. 86), made with turkey, and finish exactly the same as for the cardinal (No. 910), serve separately a well buttered allemande sauce (No. 407), with finely minced oronges or mushrooms added.

(914). RICHMOND MOUSSELINE (Mousseline à la Richmond).

FIG. 226.

Decorate the molds with tongue and truffles as shown in Fig. 226, fill them with a game mousseline forcemeat (No. 87), made either with hare, rabbit, or grouse, and finish as described for cardinal (No. 910). Dress, and serve with a separate sauce-boat of a well buttered financière sauce (No. 464).

(915). ROBERTSON HAM MOUSSELINE (Mousseline de Jambon à la Robertson).

FIG. 227.

Chop up finely or grate a quarter of a pound of lean ham; put it into a saucepan with half a pint of tomato purée (No. 730), and half a pint of béchamel (No. 409), strain through a fine sieve and let get cold. Pound in a mortar one pound of chicken fillets after passing them twice through the machine (Fig. 47); mix in with this two egg-whites, and the above prepared sauce, press through a fine sieve, and stir in four tablespoonfuls of cream forcemeat (No. 63), and the value of one quart of whipped cream. Fill some molds (No. 2, Fig. 138) previously decorated with truffles as shown in the plate with this preparation, and finish them the same as for the cardinal (No. 910), and send to the table with a separate sauce-boat of half-glaze sauce (No. 413), with ham added.

(916). MOUSSELINE À LA WALESKY (Mousseline à la Walesky).

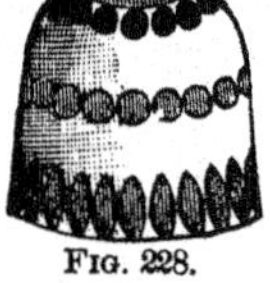

FIG. 228.

Decorate the mousselines with truffles, tongue, and pistachios, as shown in Fig. 228, fill half the molds with duck mousseline prepared the same as chicken mousseline (No. 86), and half with Guinea fowl mousseline (No. 87), and finish the same as for the cardinal (No. 910). Serve separately a Colbert sauce (No. 451), buttered just when ready to use.

(917). MOUSSELINE OF WHITE GAME À LA MÉDICIS (Mousseline de Gibier Blanc à la Médicis).

FIG. 229.

Prepare a game mousseline forcemeat as described in the Elementary Methods (No. 87), made either with pheasants, partridges, or quails. Decorate some molds with truffles the same as shown in Fig. 229, and fill them with the mousseline (No. 2, Fig. 138) forcemeat made of any of the above or other white game; finish exactly as for the cardinal (No. 910), and serve with a buttered allemande sauce (No. 407), containing mushrooms cut into small Julienne (No. 318).

(918). WOODCOCK MOUSSELINE (Mousseline de Bécasses).

FIG. 230.

Prepare a mousseline forcemeat made with the meats from woodcock as indicated in Elementary Methods (No. 87); mix in with it a few spoonfuls of truffles cut in small squares an eighth of an inch in size; with this forcemeat fill some mousseline molds (No. 2, Fig. 138) decorated with truffles and red beef tongue as shown in Fig. 230; smooth the tops and poach as explained (No. 152). At the last moment take out the mousselines, cover the bottom of the dish with a little consommé (No. 189), unmold and dress them in a circle. Serve separately an éspagnole sauce (No. 414), reduced with game fumet (No. 397), having prepared it with the woodcock parings.

(919). MOUSSELINE OF YOUNG RABBIT (Mousseline de Lapereau).

Pound three-quarters of a pound of the fillet meat taken from a raw young rabbit, rub it through a sieve, and return it to the mortar to mix in six egg-yolks, one by one, and a quarter of a pound of fresh butter divided in pieces. Put this preparation into a thin iron vessel and heat it up for ten minutes incorporating into it slowly a quart and a half in volume of unsweetened whipped cream. Butter and decorate the mousseline molds (No. 2, Fig. 138) with truffles; fill them with the preparation and poach in a bain-marie in a very slack oven. After removing the mousseline from the oven, let it rest two minutes before unmolding on a hot dish containing a little consommé (No. 189). Serve separately some good velouté sauce (No. 415), reduced with the fumet of young rabbit (No. 397).

(920). PALMETTES (Palmettes).

Palmettes are molded in bottomless molds, made of tin bands three-eighths of an inch in height, and heart-shape, from three to three and a half inches on the longest side by two and a half on its widest, and being three inches long in the center of the heart. These molds are to be buttered and laid on sheets of very strong paper, cut three inches by four, and buttered on one side; place the molds on this buttered side and fill them with a mousseline force-meat (No. 86), made either of fish, chicken or game, to which has been added various salpicons. Instead of the mousseline forcemeat, a quenelle forcemeat (No. 89) and a cream forcemeat (No. 74) (an equal quantity of each), may be substituted. The palmettes should only be slightly poached, having them of a sufficient consistency to allow them to be bread-crumbed without breaking; they must first be dipped in eggs and then in bread-crumbs, and fried in white and very hot fat; when a fine color they are to be dressed crown-shaped, and garnished with small frill favors (No. 10). The pointed ends of these trimmed handles are inserted into the point ends of the palmettes. Serve at the same time as the palmettes, but separately, a light sauce.

FIG. 231.

(921). JUNOT PALMETTES (Palmettes à la Junot).

Prepare a plover or woodcock mousseline (No. 87), adding to it some finely minced mushrooms and velouté sauce (No. 415); fill the molds, poach, and finish them exactly the same as for (No. 920); fry them in clarified butter, dress them crown shaped on a napkin and garnish with favor frills (No. 10). Serve separately a salmis sauce (No. 536), with some truffles cut in three-sixteenths of an inch squares.

(922). PÉRIER PALMETTES (Palmettes à la Périer).

Mix half pike quenelle forcemeat (No. 90) with half chicken cream forcemeat (No. 75), and garnish the centers of the palmettes with a salpicon of shrimps mingled with a well buttered béchamel (No. 409) cover with more forcemeat, then poach, bread-crumb and fry them in clarified butter. Fill with chicken forcemeat some dome-shaped molds an inch and a quarter in diameter, previously buttered and decorated with truffles; poach, unmold and lay them on the widest part of the palmettes; garnish with a favor frill (No. 10), and serve with a separate sauce-boat of a buttered half-glaze sauce (No. 413) with chopped mushrooms and truffles added.

(923). PRIMATICE PALMETTES (Palmettes à la Primatice).

Fill some palmette molds with a doe-bird or plover quenelle forcemeat (No. 91) finished with an espagnole sauce (No. 414) and game fumet (No. 397): add to it some chopped truffles, and poach the forcemeat in a moderate oven; unmold, and dip the palmettes into eggs, and roll them in bread-crumbs mixed with finely chopped ham, fry them in clarified butter till a fine color. Then drain and dress them, garnishing with favor frills (No. 10). Serve separately a half-glaze sauce (No. 413) with tongue. mushrooms. and truffles. cut into very small squares, added to it.

(924). VARSOVIAN PALMETTES (Palmettes à la Varsovienne).

To be made with a chicken mousseline forcemeat (No. 86), mixed with a salpicon of truffles, tongue, and mushrooms, cut in eighth of an inch squares, having two ounces of each for every pound of forcemeat; fill the molds, poach, unmold, and bread-crumb them, then fry in clarified butter. Garnish with favor frills (No. 10), range them on a napkin, and send to the table with a sauce boat of velouté sauce (No. 415), with raw fine herbs added.

(925). PALMETTES OF FAT LIVERS DELMONTÉS (Palmettes de Foies-Gras à la Delmontés).

Pound well together half a pound of game quenelle forcemeat (No. 91), a quarter of a pound of foies-gras, and half a pound of cream forcemeat (No. 75). Butter some palmette molds, fill them with this preparation, poach, unmold, then bread-crumb, and fry them nicely; dress them on folded napkins, garnish each one with a favor frill (No. 10) and serve with a separate sauce-boat of sherry or Madeira sauce (No. 492), with truffles and lean ham, both cut in eighth of an inch squares, added.

(926). PALMETTES OF GUINEA FOWL AND WILD DUCK, PALADIO (Palmettes de Pintade ou de Canard Sauvage à la Paladio).

Make a game mousseline forcemeat with Guinea fowl, and as much redhead duck (No. 87), mixing in some cooked fine herbs; fill the molds, poach, unmold, bread-crumb and fry them exactly the same as for No. 920. Dress them crown-shaped and serve separately a Parisian tomato sauce (No. 550), strained through a very fine sieve, trimming the palmettes with favor frills (No. 10).

(927). PALMETTES OF HAM À L'AQUITAINE (Palmettes de Jambon à l'Aquitaine).

Make with ham mousseline (No. 911), and finish the same as for No. 920, only frying the palmettes in oil. Infuse a small stick of cinnamon in Madeira wine, reduce it with half-glaze sauce (No. 413), strain, and add mushrooms, truffles, and beef palate all cut in small two-sixteenth inch squares; serve this separately.

(928). PALMETTES OF HARE AND YOUNG RABBIT, POLISH (Palmettes de Lièvre ou de Lapereau à la Polonaise)

Have a mousseline forcemeat made with hare or young rabbit (No. 87), adding to it truffles and mushrooms cut in eighth of an inch squares; fill the molds, poach, unmold, egg and bread-crumb, then fry them a fine color in clarified butter. Garnish with favor frills (No. 10), and serve on napkins. A velouté sauce (No. 415) with essence of mushrooms (No. 392) to be served separately.

(929). PALMETTES OF PHEASANTS À LA TORRENS (Palmettes de Faisans à la Torrens).

Have ready a game mousseline forcemeat (No. 87) prepared with pheasant's meat; add to it some finely shred, cooked lean ham, and fill the molds with this, poach, unmold and fry the palmettes the same as for No. 920. Serve with a hunter's sauce (No. 480) separate, after decorating with favor frills (No. 10).

(930). PALMETTES OF PULLET OR CAPON, CLINTON (Palmettes de Poularde ou de Chapon à la Clinton).

Prepare the palmette molds as indicated in No. 920; fill them only half full, and in the center place a foies-gras purée made from some Strasburg paté of foies-gras pressed through a sieve; finish filling the molds, poach, unmold, bread-crumb and fry them in clarified butter; trim with favor frills (No. 10), and serve with a separate sauce-boatful of white Colbert sauce (No. 451) with chopped truffles.

(931). PALMETTES OF QUAILS OR PARTRIDGES, AFRICAN (Palmettes de Cailles ou de Perdreaux à l'Africaine).

Have ready some heart-shaped molds as already described in No. 920; fill them with a quail or partridge mousseline forcemeat (No. 87), with a quarter of its quantity of foies-gras cut in one-eighth inch squares; poach them very slightly, just sufficient to allow them to be bread-crumbed after dipping in eggs, and fry them to a fine color; trim with favor frills (No. 10); serve them crown-shaped on a folded napkin, and send to the table with a separate sauce-boat of African sauce (No. 424).

(932). PALMETTES OF SNIPE WITH TRUFFLES À LA OSBORN (Palmettes de Bécassines aux Truffes à la Osborn).

Have half a pound of snipe or game quenelle forcemeat (No. 91), diluted with two gills of espagnole (No. 414); let it get cold on the ice, and beat into it the value of a pint of whipped cream, adding two ounces of truffles cut into one-eighth inch squares. Fill the molds described in article No. 920, poach, unmold, egg and bread-crumb the palmettes, then fry them a fine color, drain, dress and trim with favor frills (No. 10). Serve separately an espagnole sauce (No. 414), reduced with a snipe fumet sauce (No. 397) with chopped truffles added.

(933). PALMETTES OF TURKEY À LA BÉARNAISE (Palmettes de Dinde à la Béarnaise).

Mix with a cream and turkey forcemeat (No. 75), a quarter of its quantity of soubise (No. 723), fill the palmette molds with this, laying slices of foies-gras in the center, poach, and finish them exactly the same as described in No. 920, serve separately a béarnaise sauce (No. 433).

(934). PATTIES À L'ANDALOUSE (Bouchées à l'Andalouse).

Prepare puff paste bouchées as already explained in the Elementary Methods (No. 11). Cook them only shortly before they are needed, so as not to be obliged to heat them over again, and when done, remove the covers and empty out the insides, fill these with a salpicon of cooked, smoked ham, artichoke bottoms, chicken quenelles, and mushrooms, all cut into three-sixteenths of an inch squares, and mingled with Marsala wine sauce (No. 492). Dress them pyramidically on a napkin and serve.

(935). CRAWFISH, CRAB, OYSTER CRAB, SHRIMP OR LOBSTER PATTIES

(Bouchées d'Écrevisses, de Crabes, de Crabes d'Huîtres, de Crevettes ou de Homard). FIG. 232.

Make a dozen small puff paste patties the same as for No. 934. Cut a salpicon of cooked crawfish tails; put it into a bowl and mix in half as many cooked mushrooms, both being cut into three-sixteenths of an inch squares. Set on the fire to reduce a few spoonfuls of velouté (No. 415), incorporating slowly into it the mushroom liquor, and a few spoonfuls of the broth the crawfish tails were cooked in, finishing with a piece of lobster butter (No. 580), thicken the salpicon with this sauce, and use it to fill the patties; cover them with their own lids, and dress on folded napkins. By following this method cooked and firm fish meat can be used for filling bouchées, besides crabs, oyster crabs, lobsters, or shrimps, etc.

(936). PURÉE OF GAME PATTIES (Bouchées de Purée de Gibier).

Prepare them exactly as for à l'Andalouse (No. 934), put into a saucepan some game purée (No. 716), either of snipe, partridge, quail, pheasant or young rabbit; heat it without boiling over a slow fire, incorporating into it a few spoonsfuls of half-glaze (No. 400); season, finish with a small piece of fine butter, garnish the patties, dress and serve very hot.

(937). FRESH MUSHROOM PATTIES (Bouchées de Champignons Frais).

Cut some raw fresh mushrooms in squares, fry them in butter, and add to them some cream and béchamel sauce (No. 409), thickened with egg-yolks, and fresh butter, add some chopped parsley. Finish exactly the same as for No. 934.

(938). PATTIES À LA REINE (Bouchées à la Reine).

Pound well half a pound of white meat taken from the breast of a cooked chicken, using the same quantity of rice; press through a sieve, and set the purée into a saucepan to heat without boiling, incorporating into it one ounce of fine butter, and season with a little salt; if it should be too thick, add some cream. The chicken purée may be replaced by a small salpicon of white chicken meat cut in eighth of an inch squares, and added to a velouté sauce (No. 415) reduced with cream. Instead of using the puff paste lid, lay on top a round piece of truffle, three-quarters of an inch in diameter, and an eighth of an inch in thickness, glazed with a little meat glaze (No. 402).

(939). SOOLLOP, OYSTER, OLAM, OR MUSSEL PATTIES (Bouchées de Pétoncles, d'Huîtres, Luci-nes ou Moules).

Blanch oysters or clams in their own juice. Cook mussels in white wine with pepper and a few drops of vinegar; scollops in a little white wine. Drain and cut either of these into quarter inch squares, fry them in some butter on a hot fire, and cover with a velouté sauce (No. 415) thickening the sauce with egg-yolks, and fresh butter. Fill the patties and serve them very hot.

(940). SWEETBREAD PATTIES, FRENOH STYLE (Bouchées de Ris de Veau à la Fran-çaise).

Soak and blanch some sweetbreads in hot water, then refresh and let get cold before cutting them up into thin slices; season, cook or fry on both sides in oil, without browning, then press to a quarter inch thick when cool, and cut them into small quarter inch dice. Lay this salpicon in a small saucepan, and add to it half its quantity of cooked mushrooms, and a quarter as much salted but unsmoked red beef tongue cut the same size, dilute this salpicon with a sauce made of broth (No. 194a), and fecula which has previously been diluted with cold broth; let simmer for a few moments, season and use it to fill some puff paste bouchées made with beef suet instead of butter (No. 146); range and dress them pyramidically on folded napkins, heating them for a few seconds at the oven door before sending to the table.

(941). TURBIGO PATTIES (Bouchées Turbigo).

These are made with three-sixteenths of an inch dice of duck's livers, truffles and artichoke bottoms, mixed with a tomato purée (No. 730), pressed through a very fine sieve, adding the same quantity of well reduced velouté sauce (No. 415). Heat well and thicken with egg-yolks and cream; fill the patties with this garnishing, and replace the covers by a small half inch ball of foies-gras taken from the terrine and passed through a fine sieve, dipped in eggs, bread-crumbed and fried.

(942). VIOTORIA PATTIES (Bouchées à la Victoria).

Cut in three-sixteenths inch dice, some lobster meat and truffles; cover them with a lobster sauce (No. 488), adding a dash of cayenne pepper, heat well without boiling, and fill the prepared patties (No. 934). Range them on folded napkins and serve hot.

(943). SALPIOON OF FOIES-GRAS, MONTGLAS, RÉGENOE, ROYAL PATTIES (Bouchées de Salpicon de Foies-gras, Montglas, Régence, Royale).

Either of foies-gras salpicon (No. 743), montglas (No. 747), régence (No. 750), or royal (No. 751). After the patties (No. 934) are cooked, remove the covers, empty the insides, and fill with either of the above salpicons. Dress them very hot on napkins, and serve at once.

(944). PUFF PASTE PATTIES OF VEAL GODIVEAU WITH OHIVES, ORAOOVIAN, MAZARIN OR ST. HUBERT (Petits Pâtés Feuilletés de Godiveau, aux Ciboulettes Oracovienne, Mazarin ou St. Hubert).

Small patties are frequently served as a hot hors-d'œuvre; they should be cooked only while the oysters are being eaten, so to have them ready to send to the table after the soup.

Fig. 233.

Small Patties of Veal Godiveau.—Roll out thin some fragments of puff paste; remove from it round pieces two and a half inches in diameter, turn them over on to a baking sheet slightly wetted with water, using a brush for the purpose, and lay in the center of each a veal godiveau (No. 85) ball, one inch and a quarter in diameter. Moisten the paste around the godiveau with a brush slightly wetted with water, and place on top another puff paste round, three-sixteenths of an inch in thickness; turn them over, and fasten the two edges together. Mark some lines on the top of the paste with the back of the pastry cutter an inch and a half in diameter, egg the surfaces twice, and cook them in a brisk oven for fifteen minutes.

Small Patties of Godiveau with Chives.—Fill the patties with some veal godiveau (No. 85), to which has been mixed some chopped chives and parsley.

Small Patties of Godiveau Cracovian are made with pike godiveau (No. 83), and cooked fine herbs, and garnished and finished like patties of godiveau of veal.

Small Patties Mazarin.—Take chicken godiveau (No. 82) and mix with it truffles, tongue and mushrooms cut in eighth of an inch squares, also some raw fine herbs; finish the same as for the veal godiveau (No. 85).

Small Patties à la St. Hubert, are to be made with game godiveau (No. 84), mixing in with it truffles, mushrooms, tongue cut in squares and some glaze (No. 402), and finishing exactly the same as the veal godiveau (No. 85).

(945). PUFF PASTE SALMON PATTIES—SMALL (Petits Pâtés Feuilletés de Saumon).

Prepare a fish forcemeat (No. 83) with salmon meat, and a third part of pike; after being pressed through a sieve, put it in a bowl, and render it smooth, mixing in with it two or three spoonfuls of chopped up cooked truffles and a small piece of anchovy butter (No. 569). With this preparation and some puff paste make about fifteen small patties the same as described in No. 934, egg the surfaces and cook them in a good oven; when done remove them from the baking sheet and serve on folded napkins.

(946). GOLDEN BUCK, WELSH RAREBIT À LA CUTTING OR YORKSHIRE (Golden Buck, Welsh Rarebit à la Cutting ou Yorkshire).

Golden Buck.—Cut some best quality American cheese; not too fresh, into five-eighths of an inch squares, put these into a sautéing pan with half a gill of beer, and a pinch of red pepper, place the pan on a hot fire, and stir well the mixture with a small wire whisk until the cheese is melted and flowing. Lay on a serving dish two slices of toasted bread, each three and a half inches wide, and three-eighths of an inch thick; cut them slanting into four parts so as to obtain four triangles, then lay them together again to form the original square, and pour over the melted cheese; on each of the triangles place a well drained poached egg, and serve immediately.

Welsh Rarebit.—Is made exactly the same as the golden buck, suppressing the poached eggs.

Welsh Rarebit à la Cutting.—Use exactly the same preparation as the ordinary Welsh rarebit, only the cheese to be a little thinner, and add to it just when ready to serve a well beaten egg, stirring it thoroughly with the cheese, but at the same time watch well that it does not boil; pour this preparation on to the prepared toasts.

Yorkshire Rarebit.—Is finished by having two poached eggs, and two slices of bacon for each slice of toast.

(946a). CHESTER CRUSTS (Croûtes au Chester).

Cut some slices from a kitchen loaf, not too thin, fry them in butter on one side only in a flat saucepan or frying-pan; drain and cover the fried side with a thick layer of Chester cheese, sprinkle over with a pinch of cayenne pepper. Lay the crust again in the pan with more butter and push into a hot oven. When the cheese becomes creamy, the under part of the crusts should be dry, then remove from the oven and serve.

(947). RISSOLES OF BRAIN, PRINCETOWN (Rissoles de Cervelles à la Princetown).

Roll out a thin layer of brioche paste (No. 130), cut round pieces from it with a three inch in diameter pastry cutter. Stir into two ounces of butter, one tablespoonful of very finely chopped onions, and add to it a pint and a half of reduced allemande sauce (No. 407). Cut half a pound of brains into quarter inch dice pieces; wipe them dry, and fry them in butter on a hot fire with half their quantity of mushrooms, season and add this to the prepared sauce, then lay it aside to get cold. With this preparation garnish the pieces, forming it into balls each an inch and a half in diameter; moisten around, and fold the paste over in two, then set it aside to rise in a moderately warm place; when double the original size, fry the rissoles slowly until they are cooked and of a nice color, then dress them on folded napkins, and serve.

Fig. 234.

(948). RISSOLES OF CHICKEN (Rissoles de Volaille).

Slice half a pound of chicken and cut it into Julienne (No. 318), as well as four ounces of mushrooms and two ounces of peeled truffles; mix them in with five gills of velouté sauce (No. 415) previously thickened with raw egg-yolks, cream and butter; set it on the fire, and stir steadily until it boils, then remove and set the preparation aside to cool. With this preparation make some rissoles; bread-crumb them the same as explained in No. 161 and fry in very hot white frying fat; dress on a folded napkin and decorate the top with fried parsley. All rissoles are dressed and decorated the same.

(949). RISSOLES OF CRAWFISH À LA BÉATRICE (Rissoles d'Écrevisses à la Béatrice).

Poach some pike forcemeat (No. 76) three-sixteenths of an inch in thickness, then cut it up into squares; add to these half as much crawfish cut into the same sized pieces, half the quantity of forcemeat as mushrooms and half the quantity of mushrooms as truffles. Reduce this salpicon down with cream béchamel (No. 411) thickened with egg-yolks, cream and fine butter, and with this preparation proceed to make rissoles the same as explained in No. 947. Serve on folded napkins.

(950). RISSOLES À LA DEMIDOFF (Rissoles à la Demidoff).

Roll out some brioche paste (No. 130) to one-eighth of an inch in thickness; divide it into rounds with a channelled three and a half inch in diameter pastry cutter, and lay in the center of each a ball of preparation an inch and a half in diameter. Wet around these, fold over, and fasten the two edges together, then lay them on a floured cloth, and leave them to rise in a mild temperature until double their height; fry them slowly in very hot fat so that the paste be thoroughly cooked and serve when done on folded napkins. For the preparation cut about two ounces of mushrooms, two ounces of truffles and two ounces of breast of pheasant; heat well with velouté sauce (No. 415) until boiling point; allow to cool; use this preparation to garnish the rissoles.

(951). RISSOLES OF FAT LIVERS À LA UDE (Rissoles de Foies-Gras à la Ude).

Take out the contents of a pound terrine of foies-gras; remove all the grease from the forcemeat, and cut the liver into three-sixteenths inch squares, and put them aside in a very cool place. Pound the forcemeat found around the liver without any of the grease, add to it nine raw egg-yolks, season to taste, and put in with it two tablespoonfuls of chicken glaze (No. 398), and the fat liver cut in pieces. Roll out very thin some fragments of puff paste, having it only an eighth of an inch in thickness; cut with a channeled pastry cutter round pieces, three inches in diameter, and lay in the center of each, an inch and a quarter sized ball. Moisten around with a brush slightly wetted with cold water, fold them over, fasten well the edges so that the interior is hermetically enclosed, then dip them in beaten eggs and bread-crumbs, and fry them in hot fat for a sufficient length of time, to allow the paste to cook properly; dress them on a dish over a folded napkin.

(952). RISSOLES OF GAME, CHICKEN OR FISH FORCEMEAT, BEEF OR VEAL PALATE OR LAMB (Rissoles de Farce de Gibier, de Volaille, ou de Poisson de Palais de Bœuf ou de Veau, ou d'Agneau).

For the rissoles of game, chicken, or fish forcemeat see No. 63. Mix in with either of these some raw fine herbs; prepare and finish the same as for the rissoles in Elementary Methods (No. 161).

Beef or Veal Palate.—Cut a pound of beef or veal palate into three-sixteenth inch squares; have also six ounces of cooked lean ham cut the same and put them with some béchamel (No. 409) and melted meat-glaze (No. 402); set aside to get quite cold. Roll out fragments of puff paste and finish the rissoles as for No. 161. Serve on folded napkins.

Lamb.—Chop up finely one medium sized shallot; fry it in butter and add to it both velouté (No. 415) and tomato sauce (No. 549); stir in a pound of cold lean roast lamb cut in three-sixteenth inch squares, season to taste, transfer it to a vessel to set aside until perfectly cold, then form it into rissoles the same as for No. 161, and serve on folded napkins.

(953). RISSOLES OF MUSHROOM AND MARROW (Rissoles de Champignons à la Moelle).

Cut half a pound of mushrooms into dice shaped pieces, and fry them on the fire with two ounces of butter, adding a bunch of parsley garnished with thyme and a bay leaf, two ounces of sliced raw ham, and a teaspoonful of flour, also two spoonfuls of brown sauce (No. 414), a little broth, and some salt; let these all cook slowly, skim off the fat, and when done add the juice of a lemon, and set the preparation aside to get cold; finish them the same as explained à la Ude (No. 951).

For Marrow.—Cut in half inch slices and soak for three hours, changing the water several times; throw them into boiling broth, and when done, drain and coat over with some well reduced half-glaze (No. 400) with red pepper, and finish the same as the mushroom rissoles. Serve very hot on napkins.

(954). RISSOLES OF RED TONGUE OR OF SWEETBREADS (Rissoles de Langue Écarlate ou de Ris de Veau).

Red Tongue.—Reduce one pint and a half of espagnole sauce (No. 414), with a little meat glaze (No. 402), and two spoonfuls of Madeira wine, add to it one pound of red veal tongue cooked and cooled under a weight, then cut into three-sixteenth inch squares, eight ounces of mushrooms and two ounces of truffles, the two latter articles being cut into eighth of inch pieces; heat the mixture well until boiling point is reached, then set it aside to get cold. Use this preparation for making the rissoles the same as No. 161, and serve them on folded napkins.

Sweetbreads.—Fry one ounce of chopped up onions in butter with one pound of braised sweet-breads previously pressed under a weight to reduce it to three-sixteenths of an inch in thickness, then cut into Julienne; add some cooked and well drained mushrooms, diluting the whole with velouté sauce (No. 415), thicken properly with egg-yolks, cream and fresh butter, add chopped parsley, salt, pepper and nutmeg, set this preparation aside to cool and finish the rissoles as for No. 161. Serve on folded napkins.

(955). RISSOLES OF PARTRIDGE À LA WADDINGTON (Rissoles de Perdreaux à la Waddington).

Chop up very fine one pound of raw partridge meat free of nerves, with five ounces of blanched fat pork, and five ounces of beef marrow; season with salt, pepper and nutmeg, then add two ounces of chopped up truffles, one whole egg, and a tablespoonful of half-glaze (No. 400); make rissole balls with this preparation the same way as explained for No. 947; dress them when finished in pyramids on a napkin, garnishing with a bunch of fried parsley.

(956). RISSOLETTES À LA POMPADOUR (Rissolettes à la Pompadour).

Rissolettes are made with very thin pancakes, cutting them into round pieces two and a half inches in diameter; the salpicon ball to be an inch; they are fastened together by a string of chicken forcemeat (No. 89), a quarter of an inch thick, and laid on one-half of the circles. The paste for the pancakes is composed of half a pound of flour, stirring gradually into it, five eggs, a little milk, salt and two ounces of melted butter; the paste must be liquid. Put some clarified butter into small frying pans, add a little of the paste and spread it around so as to form very thin pancakes; when done lay them on a cloth, and cut from them with a round two and a half inch in diameter pastry cutter, pieces for the rissolettes.

Rissolettes à la Pompadour.—Have a small Julienne salpicon of beef palate and mushrooms mixed with a little well-reduced and well-seasoned béchamel (No. 409), set into a vessel to get cold. Make a ball of this preparation one inch in diameter, and lay it on the center of one of the pancake rounds, two and a half inches wide; fold the pancake and fasten the two edges together with a string of chicken quenelle forcemeat (No. 89); dip them in eggs and bread-crumbs and fry them to a fine color. Serve on folded napkins.

(957). RISSOLETTES À LA RENAN (Rissolettes à la Renan).

Prepare a chicken purée by pounding together half a pound of chicken and half a pound of rice cooked in white broth, adding half a pint of béchamel (No. 409), two ounces of fresh butter and some meat glaze (No. 402); season, press through a tammy, let get thoroughly cold, then finish making the rissolettes the same as for à la pompadour (No. 956).

(958). RISSOLETTES À LA SOLFÉRINO (Rissolettes à la Solférino).

Cut some foies-gras, truffles, mushrooms, quenelles and sweetbreads into small three-sixteenth inch squares; put this salpicon into a well-reduced allemande sauce (No. 407), and when cold make the rissolettes with this salpicon, the same as for à la pompadour (No. 956).

(959). TIMBALES, REMARKS ON (Observations sur les Timbales).

There are several kinds of timbales; those made with a very thin timbale paste; those of quenelle forcemeat and those of cream forcemeat, either of chicken, game or fish. The name timbale should only be applied to those made of paste cylindrical-shaped like a footless goblet, or a silver mug, or else half spherical-shaped in imitation of the kettle-drum used in an orchestra and filled with a garnishing of some kind. A "bung" would better represent the idea of what is commonly called timbale, and I would suggest the adoption of the French of bung "bondon," for I scarcely believe that the elegance of the bill of fare would be marred by reading: "Bondons of Pickerel à la Walton," or "Bondons of Chicken à la Reine," or "Bondons of Woodcock à la Diane," or "Bondons of Pheasants à la Benois." I have not the slightest intention of changing the conventional name. I only suggest an idea that might be advantageously followed if so desired. For making timbales cylindrical molds (No. 2, Fig. 137) two and five-eighths inches wide by two and one-eighth inches high are generally used; butter the insides with fresh unmelted butter and decorate with fanciful cuts of truffles, tongue, pistachios, etc. They may also be strewn with truffles, tongue, lobster coral and pistachios, all these being chopped up finely and separately, then dried in the air. Fill with forcemeat either with or without a salpicon, then poach; for this consult Elementary Methods (No. 152). Invert on to a dish containing a little consommé and serve the sauce that accompanies the timbales separately.

(960). TIMBALES À LA BEAUMARCHAIS (Timbales à la Beaumarchais).

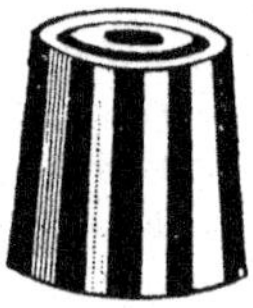

Make a salpicon with mushrooms and foies-gras cut in three-sixteenths of an inch squares; mix them in an espagnole sauce (No. 414), reduced with game essence (No. 389) and let get cold. Butter and decorate the molds (No. 2, Fig. 137) with a large truffle ring at the bottom, and a small piece of truffle in the center of this; ornament the sides with eight perpendicular thin slices of truffles each three-sixteenths of an inch wide, laid at equal distances apart around the mold; cover the bottom and sides with a game quenelle forcemeat (No. 91); in the middle place a half inch in diameter ball of the salpicon, lay over more forcemeat, and poach the timbales as in No. 152. Serve separately a half-glaze sauce (No. 413), with essence of game (No. 389) and Rhine wine added.

FIG. 235.

(961). TIMBALES À LA BENTON (Timbales à la Benton).

Line some buttered timbale molds (No. 2, Fig. 137) with some timbale paste (No. 150), having it rolled out as thinly as possible; fill up the interior with buttered paper stuffed with flour, cover the top with a layer of the paste and pinch the edges with a pastry tong; egg over the surface twice, and cook it in a moderate oven; when done uncover, empty out, unmold, and brush the timbales with eggs and set them in the oven to color nicely. Fill them with a salpicon of truffles, tongue, mushrooms and chicken mingled with a buttered allemande sauce (No. 407).

FIG. 236.

(962). TIMBALES À LA CALAISIENNE (Timbales à la Calaisienne).

Prepare the timbales the same as for à la Benton (No. 961). Have a garnishing of either poached oysters or mussels, or else of both, and crawfish, or shrimps cooked and shelled. Cut the mussels into five-eighths of an inch squares, and the crawfish or shrimps into quarter of an inch pieces; reduce a normande sauce (No. 509), with the oyster juice or some mushroom broth, and add to it a little fish glaze (No. 399); put the garnishing and sauce together, heat well, and fill the timbales with it. Place on top a cover composed of three rolled out layers of puff paste, each one-eighth of an inch in thickness, the bottom one measuring an inch and a half across, the next one an inch and a quarter, and the top one three-quarters of an inch.

FIG. 237.

(963). TIMBALES À LA CHEVALIÈRE (Timbales à la Chevalière).

Butter some timbale molds (No. 2, Fig. 137) using kneaded butter, but neither melted nor wet. Decorate the sides with pieces of sweet noodle paste (No. 142), executed by cutting out fanciful pieces and laying them on the sides in a design formed of two back to back crescents, divided by three rounds of different sizes, the largest one on the top and decreasing in size to the bottom, moisten the noodle paste. Line the molds with a thin timbale paste (No. 150) without disturbing the decoration. Fill inside with some buttered paper and flour, cover over with a layer of thin paste, cut it evenly around the top, and pinch the edges with a pastry tong. Cook the timbales in a moderate oven; remove the lid and the insides, and brush over the paste with some glaze, then garnish with foies-gras, mushrooms, and balls of truffles, the whole combined with a Madeira sauce (No. 492). Lay on top some cocks'-combs and kidneys rolled in a little meat glaze (No. 402), arranging them tastefully.

FIG. 238.

(964). DUCHESS TIMBALES (Timbales à la Duchesse).

FIG. 239.

Prepare a salpicon of truffles, foies-gras, artichoke bottoms, and rings of olives, made by removing the stones with a tin tube, and cutting them in slices across; mix with a well reduced financière sauce (No. 464), and let get cold. Decorate the bottom of the mold (No. 2, Fig. 137) with a ring of truffle, and fill in the empty space of this with some chopped up pistachios; lay at equal distances at lower edge of the side of the mold, ten small round pieces of beef tongue, each one three-sixteenths of an inch in circumference; and from these set bands of truffle perpendicularly reaching to the top of the mold, each one being three-sixteenths of an inch in width; garnish the bottom and sides with a layer of quenelle chicken forcemeat (No. 89), and place in the center a half inch diameter ball of the salpicon; cover with more forcemeat, then poach and finish the same as for No. 959. Serve a Madeira sauce (No. 492) separately.

(965). TIMBALES À LA DUMAS (Timbales à la Dumas).

For the salpicon have some well reduced Duxelle, and mix in truffles with raw egg-yolks. Decorate the molds (No. 2, Fig. 137) by placing in the center of the bottom a round piece of tongue, and at equal distances, around this four round bits of truffles; make four triangles the length of the mold from slices of tongue, each one being an eighth of an inch wide, lay them on symmetrically, and place eight round bits of truffle inside of each triangle near the bottom, and eight more near the top, intersecting them alternately. Garnish the bottom and sides with chicken cream forcemeat (No. 75), lay a half inch ball of the salpicon in the center, and cover with more forcemeat, poach, unmold, and serve with a light ravigote sauce (No. 531).

FIG. 240.

(966). TIMBALES FOR GOURMETS (Timbales des Gourmets).

FIG. 241.

The salpicon for these is composed of a reduced Madeira sauce (No. 492), to which is added some ducks' livers and truffles cut in one-eighth inch dice; leave till cold. Lay on the bottom of the molds (No. 2, Fig. 137) a three-quarters of an inch in diameter slice of truffle, and arrange the sides in panels, made by placing eight perpendicular bands of of truffles an eighth of an inch wide all around at intervals, and between each two arrange narrow strips to connect them, three in one, and two in the other, so that they alternate and form distinct oblongs, and in each one of these oblongs— there being two on one row, and one and two halves on the other—lay oval pieces of red beef tongue. Cover the bottom and sides with chicken cream forcemeat (No. 75), and place a half inch ball of the salpicon in the center; fill with more forcemeat, and finish the same as timbales (No. 959). Serve separately a gourmet sauce (No. 472).

(967). HARLEQUIN TIMBALES (Timbales à l'Arlequin).

Prepare a salpicon of artichoke bottoms cut into three-sixteenth inch squares; mix them in with a well buttered cold supreme sauce (No. 547). Decorate the timbale molds (No. 2, Fig. 137) by placing a ring cut from a truffle in the center of the bottom, one-eighth of an inch narrower than the bottom itself, and in the center of this ring lay a round piece of tongue; ornament the sides with alternate lozenges of truffles, red beef tongue, and some royal (No. 241) cut thin; also lozenges of forcemeat prepared as follows: Have two ounces of quenelle forcemeat (No. 89) with chopped truffles added, and the same quantity of forcemeat with chopped pistachios; spread a layer one-sixteenth of an inch of each preparation of forcemeat on sheets of paper; poach till firm to the touch, let cool and cut in lozenges to use for decorating the timbales. Cover the decoration with a coating of chicken quenelle forcemeat (No. 89),

FIG. 242.

place in the center a half inch diameter ball of the prepared salpicon, cover over with more forcemeat, then poach and unmold the timbales as described in No. 959. Serve separately a velouté sauce (No. 415), reduced with a purée of onions (No. 723) and cream, and thicken it at the last moment with a piece of fresh butter.

(968). IMPERIAL TIMBALES (Timbales Impérial).

Fig. 243.

The salpicon to be made of a well reduced supreme sauce (No. 547), adding to it tongue, truffles and mushrooms cut in small Julienne. Cut some narrow bands of truffles, a sixteenth of an inch wide, and six-eighths of an inch long; butter the molds (No. 2, Fig. 137), set a five-eighths of an inch round of truffle at the bottom and on the side close to the bottom a row of quarter inch in diameter rounds of truffles at the top opening of the mold, lay these bands in long triangles around the edge; on the top of each triangle set a three-sixteenth inch round piece truffle; cover the insides of the molds with cream forcemeat (No. 74), and in the center lay a half inch ball of the salpicon, finish filling the mold, poach and dress it the same as for No. 959. A lucullus sauce (No. 490) to be served separately.

(969). IRVING TIMBALES (Timbales à la Irving).

FIG. 244.

Pound some cooked game or young rabbit, free of all sinews and skin with an equal quantity of rice, half as much béchamel (No. 409) and a little fresh butter, rub through a fine sieve, and set it away to get cold. Butter some cold molds (No 2, Fig. 137) and decorate the bottom with a three-quarters of an inch in diameter slice of truffle, and the sides with triangles cut from truffles, one and five-eighths of an inch long, by three-eighths of an inch wide at the widest part. Set them round the narrow ends reaching to the bottom, the widest ends meeting together at the opening of the timbale. Fill the bottom and inner sides with game cream forcemeat (No. 75) and place a ball of the prepared game purée in the center, and fill it up with game forcemeat; finish cooking and serve same as No. 959. Serve separately a champagne sauce (No. 445), with some essence of game (No. 389).

(970). LAGARDÈRE TIMBALES (Timbales à la Lagardère).

FIG. 245.

Make a salpicon of mushrooms and beef palates combined with an allemande sauce (No. 407) reduced with mushroom essence (No. 392), the pieces for the salpicon to be cut into three-sixteenths of inch squares. Have round molds an inch and a half in diameter, having at the bottom an indent a quarter of an inch deep by one inch in diameter, the molds to be one and five-eighths of an inch high, and two inches and one-eighth wide at the opening. Decorate the molds after buttering them when cold with triangles of truffles, three-quarters of an inch long by three-eighths of an inch wide; lay them close together around the opening of the mold, and on the top of each point set a round bit of tongue, three-sixteenths of an inch; garnish the bottom and sides with chicken cream forcemeat (No. 75) and fill the center of the inside with a salpicon ball half an inch in diameter; fill up the mold with more of the forcemeat, finishing it the same as for No. 950. Set on top in the indent a three-quarters of an inch ball of very fine chestnut purée (No. 712) quite thick, bread-crumb and fry in very hot fat, and serve a supreme sauce (No. 547), with essence of mushrooms (No. 392) separately.

(971). LA VALLIÈRE TIMBALES (Timbales à la La Vallière).

FIG. 246.

The molds are to be dome-shaped, with an indent a quarter of an inch deep, and one inch in diameter; the molds themselves being an inch and three-quarters high and one and five-eighths wide. Decorate the sides with bands of truffle each one inch long, and lay them on like the letter V, meeting together both top and bottom and thus forming zigzags; at each place where they join, put a small round bit of truffle; fill the round part of the mold with a red cream forcemeat (No. 74) and the rest with a quail and cream forcemeat (No. 75). Remove with a tube the stone from a large Spanish olive, cut off a sixteenth part of its top and bottom and fill it with chicken quenelle forcemeat (No. 89), and place on top a fine caper; poach and set one on the indents of the timbales, they having been previously poached and dished, and serve with a separate sauce-boat of well buttered velouté sauce (No. 415) with lemon juice added.

(972). LOMBARDY TIMBALES (Timbales à la Lombarde).

FIG. 247.

Line buttered timbale molds (No. 2, Fig. 137) with thin timbale paste (No. 150), garnish the sides with buttered paper, and fill the center with rice; cover over with a small piece of buttered paper, moisten lightly the inside border of the timbales, and cover with a layer of paste; fasten the two together, pinch the border with a channeled pastry tong, egg over the top and place on it three small layers of thin puff paste, the lowest one being an inch and a half in diameter, the second, one and a quarter, and the last or top one, one inch, all three being cut out with a channeled pastry cutter. Cook the timbales in a moderate oven, remove the lids, empty out the rice and paper, unmold and egg over the outside, then set them in a quick oven; garnish the insides with pieces of chestnuts, sweetbreads and truffles cut into quarter inch squares, and mixed with an allemande sauce (No. 407); replace the covers and serve on a Lombard sauce (No. 489).

(973). MARLY TIMBALES (Timbales à la Marly).

FIG. 248.

Garnish the bottom of a buttered timbale mold (No. 2, Fig. 137) with a round piece of truffle, and the entire sides with thin truffle crescents intercalated to resemble fish scales; in the center of each scale, lay a small one-eighth of an inch round bit of tongue. Fill them with a partridge and cream forcemeat (No. 75), and set in the center a ball of salpicon made as follows: Mingle some partridge fumet (No. 397) with a reduced espagnole (No. 414), and add to it some foies-gras and mushrooms, both cut into one-eighth inch squares, and left till cold before using. Poach the timbales in a moderate oven, when done, dress and serve separately a sauce composed of one-third of espagnole sauce (No. 414), one-third of tomato sauce (No. 549), and one-third of veal blond (No. 423) reduced together.

(974). MENTANA TIMBALES (Timbales à la Mentana).

FIG. 249.

The salpicon to be made of chicken livers à la Duxelle, (see below), thickened with egg-yolks, to be used when cold. Butter some timbale molds (No. 2, Fig. 137), and place on the bottom a one inch in diameter slice of truffle, cut away the center with a three-quarters of an inch vegetable cutter, and replace the truffle by a piece of red beef tongue. Decorate the sides of the mold with thin, eighth of an inch wide strips of tongue, laid on slanting, having ten strips in all, and in the center between every one, a round bit of truffle measuring three-sixteenths of an inch across, with a smaller one one-eighth of an inch on the top and bottom, also laid on slanting, making three round bits of truffle between the two strips of tongue. Fill the insides and bottom with a chicken and cream forcemeat (No. 75), and in the center lay a ball of the prepared salpicon; then more forcemeat, and finish them as for No. 959. Serve separately a périgueux (No. 517) and tomato sauce (No. 549) mixed.

For salpicon of chicken livers à la Duxelle, cut some chicken livers in quarter inch squares; fry them in butter with a little shallot, mushroom, and truffles, all chopped finely, and mingle with a little well reduced half-glaze (No. 400).

(975). MONTGOMERY TIMBALES (Timbales à la Montgomery).

FIG. 250.

Prepare a pheasant salpicon with truffles and mushrooms added, mixing them in with a velouté sauce (No. 415), add a little meat glaze (No. 402), and leave till cold. Butter a round timbale mold, having a round identation at the bottom; decorate the whole length of the flat side with strips of tongue, and place a dot of truffle an eighth of an inch in diameter on the top of each strip, having eight in all; dredge over the sides with finely chopped pistachios, and cover the bottom and sides with a delicate pheasant game quenelle forcemeat (No. 91), and set in the center a ball of the salpicon; fill the mold with some more of the same forcemeat, poach and dress (No. 959), place on top a small round croquette three-quarters of an inch in diameter made of the salpicon. Serve separately a velouté sauce (No. 415), finished with essence of game (No. 389).

(976). MOSAIC TIMBALES (Timbales Mosaïque).

FIG. 251.

The timbale molds (No. 2, Fig. 137) are to be entirely decorated with small lozenges of tongue, truffle and hard boiled egg-whites, to represent a mosaic ground work. Begin by placing a ring of truffle at the bottom of the mold, inside of this a smaller ring of egg-whites, and in the center to fit in a half inch round of beef tongue; this fills the entire bottom. Decorate the sides with alternate lozenges to form squares or boxes, having all the red on one side, the black on the other, and the white on top of each square; the upper and lower row should be divided in two lengthwise; by following these directions they will form perfect mosaic squares, taking care that the points are directed outward; support this decoration with a snipe quenelle forcemeat (No. 91); set in the center a ball made of royal cream (No. 241), and finish filling the molds; poach and serve them as for No. 959. Serve a white Colbert sauce (No. 451) separately.

(977). NEAPOLITAN TIMBALES (Timbales Napolitaine).

The salpicon is composed of tongue, truffles and mushrooms, cut in three-sixteenth of an inch squares and combined with espagnole sauce (No. 414), meat glaze (No. 402) and tomato sauce (No. 549); let cool, cut some macaroni into pieces a sixteenth of an inch long, fill the empty places in each macaroni half of them with a round piece of truffle to fit it exactly, and the other half with beef tongue instead of truffles. Butter the timbale molds (No. 2, Fig. 137), lay a round piece of truffle on the bottom, and around it set the bits of macaroni, one row filled with tongue, and over this, one filled with truffles; one laid symmetrically above the other until the mold is filled. Garnish the bottom and sides with chicken quenelle forcemeat (No. 89), and a half inch ball of the salpicon in the center, fill up with more forcemeat and finish them exactly the same as for No. 959. Serve a separate sauce-boat of Neapolitan sauce (No. 507).

FIG. 252.

(978). PALERMITAINE TIMBALES (Timbales à la Palermitaine).

FIG. 253.

The salpicon to be composed of red beef tongue, mushrooms and foies-gras, mingled with a tomatoed half-glaze sauce (No. 413). Butter the interior of the timbale molds (No. 2, Fig. 137) with some well kneaded, softened butter that has not been melted, and set on the flat bottoms a thin round piece of truffle measuring three-quarters of an inch across. Cook till slightly firm some small spaghetti macaroni; drain it well, dry, and turn it in a spiral around the entire inside of the mold beginning at the bottom and continuing until the mold is completely full; it is better to use a single piece of macaroni for this. Support the macaroni with a layer of chicken quenelle forcemeat (No. 89), and set a half inch ball of the salpicon in the center; cover with more forcemeat and finish the same as for the timbales (No. 959). Serve separately a Palermitaine sauce (No. 514).

(979). PÉRIGORDINE TIMBALES (Timbales Périgordine).

Prepare a very consistent chestnut purée (No. 712), adding to it a little meat glaze (No. 402), some fresh butter and raw egg-yolks; let this get thoroughly cold. Garnish the bottom of the timbale molds (No. 2, Fig. 137) with a thin slice of truffle, cut out the center with a half inch vegetable cutter, and replace the piece with a round cut of tongue exactly the same size; fill up the bottom and sides with a chicken and cream forcemeat (No. 75), and set in the center a half inch ball of the chestnut purée; cover over with more forcemeat and finish the same as for timbales (No. 959). Have a separate sauce-boat of half-glaze sauce (No. 413), finished with essence of truffles (No. 395).

FIG. 254.

(980). PRINCESS TIMBALES (Timbales à la Princesse).

FIG. 255.

Butter some timbale molds (No. 2, Fig. 137), and roll close together around the inside strings of short paste (No. 135), an eighth of an inch in diameter, keeping them as long as possible; begin at the bottom in the center and continue in spirals till the top is reached, then coat the bottom and sides with a chicken quenelle forcemeat (No. 89), laying a ball of white montglas salpicon (No. 747) in the center. Cover the top with a thin lid of the paste and cook in a slow oven for about half an hour; remove the lid, and fill the timbales with a Madeira wine sauce (No. 492); substitute for the cover a half spherical quenelle decorated with truffles cut fancifully; dredged with chopped pistachios, made of chicken cream forcemeat and poached in a slack oven. Serve on a napkin.

(981). TIMBALES À LA RENAISSANCE (Timbales à la Renaissance).

FIG. 256.

Have ready a salpicon of truffles, chicken and artichoke bottoms, all cut into three-sixteenth inch squares; mix them with an espagnole sauce (No. 414), well reduced with meat glaze (No. 402) and tomato sauce (No. 549). Butter the insides of timbale molds (No. 2, Fig. 137), lay on the bottom a round piece of red beet-root cut very thin, an inch and a quarter in diameter; cut from the center a round piece a quarter of an inch across, and replace it by a very green cooked pea. Garnish the mold with a layer of chicken cream forcemeat (No. 75), both on the bottom and sides, and set in the center a ball of the prepared salpicon, then finish exactly the same as for No. 959. Serve a Chateaubriand sauce (No. 446) separately.

(982). RISTORI TIMBALES (Timbales à la Ristori).

FIG. 257.

Prepare a salpicon of truffles, mushrooms and artichoke bottoms cut into three-sixteenth inch squares, and mingled with an allemande sauce (No. 407), then put away to get cold. Butter the inside of timbale molds (No. 2, Fig. 137), decorate the bottoms with a thin round of truffle, three-quarters of an inch in diameter, and on the top and bottom of the sides lay inverted triangles of tongue, or the red part of lobster, having twenty-four in all, twelve on the top, and twelve on the bottom; and in the center of the side range symmetrically twelve small rounds of truffle to form a circle. Fill the bottom and sides with a chicken and cream forcemeat (No. 75), well mixed, and in the middle set a half inch ball of the salpicon; finish with more forcemeat, then poach and unmold as explained in No. 959. A velouté sauce (No. 415) with finely chopped truffle sauce (No. 551), to be served separately.

(983). ROTHSCHILD TIMBALES (Timbales à la Rothschild).

FIG. 258.

Decorate the bottom of each buttered timbale mold (No. 2, Fig. 137) with a thin round slice of truffle measuring three-quarters of an inch in diameter; around the sides range six lozenge shaped pieces of the truffle, each one divided by a round bit of truffle an eighth of an inch across, and more of the same sized and shaped pieces at both tips of the lozenges, making eighteen small rounds in all. Fill the bottom and sides with a chicken cream forcemeat (No. 75), and lay in the center a ball, half an inch in diameter, composed of foies-gras taken from a terrine and rubbed through a sieve; fill the mold with more forcemeat then poach and finish the same as for No. 959. Serve separately a purée of chestnuts (No. 712), diluted with velouté sauce (No. 415) and cream to the consistency of a sauce, incorporating into it at the last moment, a piece of melted fresh butter.

(984). SARTIGES TIMBALES (Timbales à la Sartiges).

FIG. 259.

Butter some timbale molds (No. 2, Fig. 137), decorate the center of the bottom with a rosette design made of truffles, and around the top and bottom of the sides of the mold, lay a detached row of round pieces of truffle, having those at the bottom somewhat smaller than those at the top. In the center on each side make a truffle cross-shaped like an X, one inch high, and in the middle of it, lay a small eighth of an inch round of tongue, and on each side rings of tongue, three-eighths of an inch in diameter. Fill the bottoms and sides with a grouse cream forcemeat (No. 75), and set in the center of this a salpicon composed of squares of truffle cut in three-sixteenths of an inch, and mingled with a well reduced half-glaze sauce (No. 413); fill up with more of the forcemeat, and finish the same as the timbales (No. 959). Serve separately an espagnole sauce (No. 414) with game essence (No. 389).

(985). SCOTCH TIMBALES (Timbales à l'Écossaise).

FIG. 260.

Prepare some very thin pancakes the same as for rissolettes (No. 956). Butter timbale molds (No. 2, Fig. 137) and line the inner sides with these pancakes; prepare a salpicon with four ounces of white chicken meat, the same quantity of mushrooms, and two ounces of rice; combine these ingredients with a buttered béchamel (No. 409) and let get cold. Fill the molds half full with chicken quenelle forcemeat (No. 89), and cream forcemeat (No. 75), the same quantity of each well mixed together; in the center lay a half inch ball of the salpicon, and finish filling the mold with more forcemeat, poach and finish the same as for No. 959. After they are unmolded, lay them in the oven for one minute, then serve separately a Spanish sauce (No. 414) reduced with mushroom essence (No. 392).

(986). SOUBISE TIMBALES (Timbales à la Soubise).

FIG. 261.

Butter some timbale molds (No. 2, Fig. 137), and lay on the bottom a round piece of truffle, three-quarters of an inch in diameter; on the sides place truffle bands an eighth of an inch wide, by half an inch long, having twenty-five of these pieces for each mold; lay them on in five lines, one above the other, the bottom corner of one joining the opposite top corner of the next one; between these lines place rounds of truffles. Fill with chicken cream forcemeat (No. 75), mixing in with it a third of its quantity of soubise purée (No. 723), cook and finish the same as for the timbales (No. 959). Serve separately a velouté sauce (No. 415), reduced and finished by adding to it a piece of fresh butter.

(987). SOYER TIMBALES (Timbales à la Soyer).

FIG. 262.

Prepare a timbale of foundation paste the same as for Lombardy (No. 972). Fill it with a garnishing of game and cream quenelles (No. 733), small mushroom heads, truffles cut into five-sixteenths of an inch pieces, and sweetbreads cut the same; mix with it a lucullus sauce (No. 490); after the timbales are filled, replace the covers, dress them on a folded napkin and serve hot.

(988). TALLEYRAND TIMBALES (Timbales à la Talleyrand).

FIG. 263.

Make a salpicon of foies-gras and mushrooms, mixed with a half-glaze sauce (No. 413), and finished with raw egg-yolks. Butter some timbale molds (No. 2, Fig. 137), and throw indiscriminately into the insides small sticks of tongue, truffles and chicken five-sixteenths of an inch wide by one-sixteenth of an inch square; letting them assume any fancy shape into which they may fall. Cover the bottom and sides with a cream forcemeat (No. 75), and lay in the center a salpicon ball half an inch in diameter; cover with more of the forcemeat and finish cooking and serving the same as for No. 959. Have a buttered allemande sauce (No. 407), adding to it a dash of cayenne pepper, and the juice of a lemon.

(989). VENETIAN TIMBALES (Timbales à la Vénitienne).

FIG. 264.

Make a salpicon of ducks' livers cut up into one-eighth of an inch pieces, cut the same of some truffles, mushrooms, and red beef tongue, and mix all with a well reduced allemande sauce (No. 407). Butter some timbale molds (No. 2, Fig. 137), lay at the bottom a round slice of truffle, and from the center of it cut out with a vegetable cutter, a piece half an inch in diameter, and place in its stead a round piece of tongue; dust over the sides with very finely chopped pistachios shaken through a sieve, and fill up the molds with chicken cream forcemeat (No. 75), laying a ball of the salpicon in the middle; finish as in No. 959. Serve separately a béchamel sauce (No. 409), reduced with mushroom liquor and some chopped parsley added.

(990). TIMBALES WITH RED BEEF TONGUE (Timbales à l'Écarlate).

FIG. 265.

Butter some timbale molds (No. 2, Fig. 137) and throw in some very finely chopped unsmoked beef tongue to make it adhere well to the bottom and sides, then fill with a chicken cream forcemeat (No. 75); poach and unmold the same as for No. 959. Send to the table with a separate sauce-boat of sauce prepared as follows: Cut some chicken livers into three-sixteenth inch squares; sauté them in butter, moisten with white wine and espagnole sauce (No. 414), and strain through a tammy; add to the sauce a garnishing of truffles cut in three-sixteenth inch squares. These timbales contain no salpicon.

(991). FLORENTINE TOASTS (Rôties Florentine).

Roll out a layer of fancy roll paste (No. 3418) form raised edges around it, having it three inches wide, by twelve inches long; besprinkle with oil, and garnish with anchovy or sardine fillets; season with chives, garlic, and chopped onions, and lay on top slices of peeled and pressed tomatoes, also thin slices of American cheese. Cook them in a hot oven, and when done strew over chopped parsley and savory, cut them into pieces an inch and a half wide, having eight of them in all, or if preferred they may be made of slices of toasted bread three inches long, by one and a half wide, instead of paste.

(992). TOAST WITH OIL AND CHEESE, SARDINES À LA SEVILLE (Rôtie à l'Huile et au Fromage, aux Sardines et à la Séville).

Toast some slices of bread three inches by one and a half; dip them in fine olive oil, and lay them on a dish; strew over some grated parmesan, pepper and lemon juice, set them for a few seconds into the oven, giving them just sufficient time to melt the cheese, and serve the instant they leave the oven.

For Sardine Toast.—Instead of the cheese, pound a few anchovies with an equal quantity of fresh butter and a pinch of parsley; with this butter cover some slices of toasted bread. Wipe off gently with a cloth the skins from a few sardines, lay them on top of the toast, then set them in the oven for a few minutes, and serve very hot.

Toast à la Seville.—Chop up separately some anchovies, parsley, chives, shallots and garlic, then mix them together in a bowl with oil, spread this mixture on toasted slices of bread three-eighths of an inch thick by three inches square; divide these slices through the center; lay some anchovy fillets on top. Dress the toast on a dish, pour over a little oil, and sprinkle with mignonette; push them into the oven for two minutes, then squeeze over the juice of an orange, and serve.

(993). VARENIKIS—POLISH SIDE DISH (Varenikis—Hors-d'Œuvre Polonais).

The day before the varenikis are needed for use put some pot cheese in a cloth, wrap it up and tie with a string; lay it on a colander, place a weight on top and leave it without further pressure until the next day so that all the buttermilk drains off. Take it out of the cloth, put it in a mortar, seasoning with salt, pepper and a dash of nutmeg, then pound well to have it a very smooth paste. Now add gradually two ounces of fresh butter then a heaping tablespoonful of marrow frangipane and as much cream cake paste (No. 132) and lastly four egg-yolks; continue to pound and mix until the paste is exceedingly smooth, then rub it through a sieve; lay it in a vessel and let rest in the ice-box. Prepare a raviole paste (No. 147) and after half an hour roll it very thin and from this cut out some strips; cover each band with a small part of the preparation the size and shape of a nut and form them into small rissoles the same as for ordinary rissoles (No. 161); lay each one as soon as prepared on a slightly floured tin and stand them in a cool place. Ten minutes before serving throw them into a saucepanful of lightly salted boiling water. As soon as poached drain them on a cloth and then arrange them in a silver dish; pour a few spoonsfuls of sweet cream over, serving more separately. In Russia they substitute melted butter for cream and serve sour cream apart.

MOLLUSKS and CRUSTACEANS.

THE QUAHAUG OR LITTLE NECK CLAMS (Lucines Orangées ou Clovis).

There are many kinds of these bivalves, but these of which we speak are greatly appreciated as an article of food. Small ones an inch to an inch and three-quarters in diameter are served raw, in the months of May, June, July and August, entirely replacing the oyster. Little neck clams are the most remarkable of their kind, their principal characteristic being the uniting to the hinge of cardinal and lateral teeth; beside these they possess three other teeth, two being diverging. They are far preferable to the large clams for all culinary preparations, being more tender, of a finer flavor and their taste less strong than the others.

FIG. 266.

(994). CLAMS, PHILADELPHIA STYLE (Lucines Orangées à la Philadelphie).

Procure two dozen medium sized clams; poach them in their own juice with as much water, and as soon as they are firm to the touch, drain them off. Fry two finely cut-up shallots in butter without letting them attain color, add the clams, and heat them with a little sherry and brandy, seasoning with mignonette and a very little salt; just when prepared to serve thicken the gravy with cream, egg-yolks and a small quantity of butter. Serve the clams in a vegetable or deep dish, and lay on top and around some small round three-quarters of an inch rice croquettes.

(995). CLAMS À LA POULETTE (Lucines Orangées à la Poulette).

Poach twenty-four clams, suppressing the hard parts, put them into a sautoir with a pint of poulette sauce (No. 527) and heat them thoroughly; season with pepper, mignonette, nutmeg and lemon juice, and thicken the whole with egg-yolks and fresh butter, adding chopped parsley.

(996). CLAM PANCAKES AND FRITTERS (Crêpes et Beignets de Lucines Orangées).

Break two whole eggs into a bowl, and add a pinch of white pepper; beat them thoroughly with a tablespoonful of flour and a tablespoonful of cream; stir briskly, and put into the mixture ten medium sized raw clams chopped up very fine, and with this preparation make some rather thick pancakes.

Fritters.—Place in a saucepan one gill of milk, half an ounce of butter, some cayenne pepper and nutmeg; boil the whole and add three ounces of flour; dry the paste, then remove it from the fire, incorporating slowly into it two whole eggs, and finish with four spoonfuls of double cream; now add to the paste six ounces of small sized clams, drained and chopped; mix well and then take up some of the preparation with a spoon held in the right hand and using the first finger of the left hand, detach it from the spoon, and let it fall into hot frying fat; when done, drain and range the fritters on napkins.

(997). STUFFED CLAMS (Lucines Orangées Farcies).

Fry colorless two ounces of finely chopped onions in two ounces of butter, dredge over two spoonfuls of flour, stir well, then add the liquor from ten raw clams, two ounces of chopped mushrooms, and one gill of white wine; boil up the whole, skim off the foam arising to the top, and reduce to half, seasoning with red pepper and nutmeg. Chop up the raw clams, and set them into the prepared sauce; place it on a brisk fire and stir steadily, and when the clams are poached, add some chopped parsley, and thicken with egg-yolks and cream. Lay this preparation aside for further use, but if it is to be used at once, fill up some well rounded buttered clam shells, dust over with bread-crumbs and lay a small pat of butter on top of each; place them on a baking pan in the oven to heat and color nicely, then arrange them crown-shaped on a folded napkin, garnishing the center with very green parsley branches.

LONG OR SOFT CLAMS (Lucines).

Long or soft clams resemble somewhat the Venus clam, however, they have no exterior tube. These mollusks live in both sand and mud.

(998). SOFT CLAMS FRIED, GARNISHED WITH FRIED PARSLEY (Lucines Papillons Frites Garnies au Persil Frit).

Drain some medium sized soft clams; immerse them in milk, drain them once more, then roll them in flour and fry. After being rolled in the flour, they may be dipped in beaten eggs, then in bread-crumbs and fried until a fine color is assumed; dress them on a napkin, garnishing with fried parsley.

(999). SOFT CLAMS ON SKEWERS OR HATELETS (Lucines Papillons en Brochette ou Hatelets).

FIG. 267.

Run some silver skewers through the soft clams, alternating each piece with a three-quarters of an inch square of lean, unsmoked bacon; dip the whole into melted butter, and roll them in bread-crumbs, broil them over a slow fire, and when done dress on a hot dish and cover with maître-d'hôtel butter (No. 581). They may be prepared exactly the same only omitting the bread-crumbs.

(1000) SOFT CLAMS À LA NEWBERG (Lucines Papillons à la Newberg).

Warm in a sautoire two ounces of butter, add to it one dozen very fresh soft clams, a little salt, black and cayenne pepper, boil for a few minutes, moving them with care so as to avoid breaking them, moisten with a gill of Madeira and a little velouté sauce (No. 415), add two egg-yolks and a little cream, also a little butter. Warm without boiling, and serve.

CRABS (Crabes).

FIG. 268.

A species of amphibious crustacean, oblong and wide or broad according to its kind; there is the sea, the fresh water, and the land crab. Generally the tail is bent under the belly, and the head not separated from the body. The body is covered with a hard shell frequently blackish in color; the meat is difficult to digest. The ordinary crabs that are used in New York, either hard or soft shelled are sea crabs.

(1001). HARD SHELL CRABS BAKED ON A DISH (Crabes Durs au Gratin dans un Plat).

After some large crabs have been cooked in a court bouillon, as for No. 1002, pick out all their meat, keeping it as whole as possible; put it into a sautoir with some allemande sauce (No. 407), and sliced mushrooms, also chopped parsley; mix well. Butter a silver dish, besprinkle it with bread-crumbs, and fill with the crab preparation, dredge bread-crumbs fried in butter on top, and lay the dish in the oven; when nicely browned, serve on a folded napkin.

(1002). HARD SHELL CRABS, IN COURT BOUILLON (Crabes Durs au Court Bouillon).

Soak the crabs for a quarter of an hour in cold water containing a handful of salt; wash them nicely. Fry in butter some minced carrots, onions, and celery, with pepper-corns, thyme, bay leaf, and branches of parsley. Moisten with white wine and broth, throw in the crabs, and let boil for fifteen minutes, then dress them on a napkin and range branches of parsley around; pour the top of the stock from its sediment, reduce it with velouté sauce (No. 415), when ready to serve, work in some fine butter, and serve it separately.

(1003). HARD SHELL CRABS, STUFFED, CAROLINA STYLE (Crabes Durs Farcis à la Caroline).

Fry colorless in butter some finely choppped onions; sprinkle over a little rice flour, fry again for a few minutes and moisten with milk; season with salt, red pepper, nutmeg, thyme, and powdered basil; add the crab meat, and half of its quantity of rice previously boiled in plenty of water, "Creole rice" (No. 1251); fill some clean crab shells with this preparation, until they are quite full and dome-shaped; dredge over with bread-crumbs, besprinkle with butter and brown in a hot oven, or the preparation may be dipped in beaten eggs, rolled in bread-crumbs and fried in hot fat.

(1004). HARD SHELL CRABS, STUFFED WITH MUSHROOMS AND DEVILED (Crabes Durs Farcis aux Champignons et à la Diable).

To obtain one pound of crab meat it is necessary to have twenty crabs; soak them for a quarter of an hour in water with a handful of salt added, wash them and boil for fifteen minutes; let get cold and remove the shells which are to be well washed and dried. Take off all the small legs and the lungs; wash the crabs singly, and pick out all the meat obtainable; chop up either two onions or one ounce of shallot for every pound of crab meat; fry them colorless in butter; add a quart of béchamel (No. 409) reduced with cream, the crab meat, salt, red pepper and nutmeg; do not have the preparation too soft, and with it fill the shells dome-shaped, about four ounces in each; dip them entirely into bread-crumbs, sprinkle over melted butter, and lay them on tin rings to avoid the crabs touching the bottom of the pan; brown in a hot oven, and dress on napkins with parsley around.

With Mushrooms.—Prepare the crabs as the above. Fry a little shallot in butter, mix in as much flour as the butter can absorb and cook to obtain a light roux; moisten this with half cream and half milk, seasoning properly, then add the crab meat and half the same quantity of mushrooms cut in small three-sixteenths of an inch squares; boil up once; set it in a vessel and use this preparation for stuffing the crabs; finish and serve the same sauce as with the other crabs. This cream sauce can be replaced by reduced velouté (No. 415) and thickened whith egg-yolks and cream.

Deviled and Stuffed.—The crabs are to be prepared as above. Before sprinkling with crumbs, cover the top of the crab preparation with mustard; cover with bread-crumbs, and sprinkle butter on top; brown in a hot oven, and dress on napkins, garnishing with green parsley.

(1005). OYSTER CRABS FRIED À LA NEWBERG OR À LA SALAMANDER (Crabes d'Huîtres Frits à la Newber et à la Salamandre).

Oyster crabs are generally found in great quantities the Virginia oysters.

Fried.—Drain and dip the crabs in milk, roll them in cracker-dust, and toss them in a coarse sieve to remove the surplus cracker, then fry them in very hot, fresh lard. Butter some channeled oval tartlet molds three and seven-eighths inches by two and three-eighths inches wide, line them with a very thin puff paste made from parings, and fill up the insides with fine sheets of buttered paper and rice; cook them in a hot oven, empty them well of the paper and rice, and finish by filling them with as many of the fried crabs as they will hold, dress them on folded napkins and serve them while still very hot. The scarcity of these crabs bring their price as high as two dollars and a half a pound.

Oyster Crabs à la Newberg.—Put some oyster crabs in a sautoire with a little butter, salt, and red pepper; toss them well and moisten with a little cream; remove from the fire at the first boil, thicken with raw egg-yolks diluted in cream, pour over a little good Madeira wine and serve.

À la Salamander.—Wash some medium sized prettily shaped deep oyster shells; set them on a very straight baking sheet. Drain very fresh oyster crabs, season them with salt, black and red pepper, and fill the shells full of these; strew over bread-crumbs, and grated parmesan cheese, besprinkle with butter, and brown in a quick oven, serve the shells as soon as they are done. (These crabs should be put in the shells without any sauce.)

(1006). SOFT SHELL CRABS, BROILED, RAVIGOTE BUTTER, FRIED, SAUTÉD IN BUTTER (Crabes Moux Grillés, Beurre Ravigote, Frits, Sautés au Beurre).

Wash the crabs, being careful to pick off all the seaweed, and pull out the lungs; wipe dry. Lay them on a double broiler, salt over and baste with butter, broil them on a slow fire, and when done, dress on a hot dish and cover with ravigote butter (No. 583).

Fried.—Wash the crabs, remove the lungs from both sides and dip into milk, then roll in flour and fry in plenty of very hot frying fat. When of a fine color, drain and dress on a folded napkin, and on top arrange a bunch of fried parsley.

Sautéd in Butter.—After the crabs have been well washed, remove the lungs from each side, roll them in flour, and sauté them in very hot purified butter (No. 16); when done and of a fine color, dress and to the butter in which they were cooked, add some lemon juice; strain this butter through a strainer over the crabs, and strew chopped parsley on them.

CRAWFISH OR CRAYFISH (Écrevisses).

This crustacean has the head and the corselet blended in one single piece, having attached five pairs of feet; the tail is more or less apparent. Crawfish are aquatic and turn red when cooked. Persons suffering from a weak stomach should avoid partaking of them, as they are very indigestible, but they are delicious for those who are able to indulge in them. They are useful for decorating cold dishes and entrées, and are used by themselves in the form of pyramids.

FIG. 269.

(1007). CRAWFISH À LA BATELIÈRE (Écrevisses à la Batelière).

Procure three dozen live crawfish, wash them thoroughly, place them in a net, and plunge them for two minutes into plenty of boiling water in order to kill them, then remove and break off the small legs. Fry three very finely chopped shallots in butter with six ounces of minced mushrooms, thyme and bay leaf, add the crawfish and moisten with white wine; let cook for ten minutes, suppress the thyme and bay leaf, season with salt and red pepper, and just when prepared to serve add half an ounce of fresh butter and some chopped parsley.

(1008). CRAWFISH À LA BORDELAISE (Écrevisses à la Bordelaise).

Choose live crawfish; set them inside a net, wash them well, and plunge them rapidly into boiling water, leaving them in only sufficiently long to kill, then drain and pick off the small legs. Fry a mirepoix of roots and minced onions in oil, moisten with white wine, season, and add aromatic herbs, a bunch of parsley and a few spoonfuls of brandy; let the whole boil for several minutes, then throw in the crawfish and cook them from ten to fourteen minutes according to their size, while tossing steadily. Take them off the fire, strain the broth through a sieve, leaving the crawfish in the saucepan. Cut in small three-sixteenth of an inch squares or in Julienne, some red part of carrots, and tender celery roots, parboil both in salted water, and then drain, fry without coloring in some butter, onions, cut in three-sixteenths of an inch squares, add to it the roots, and fry together for a few minutes, then moisten with two or three spoonfuls of broth and the crawfish stock; let the liquid fall twice to a glaze so that the vegetables are well cooked, and moisten again with the stock of the crawfish reduced to a half-glaze. Cook together for five or six minutes, then thicken with small pieces of butter kneaded with flour, adding also two or three spoonfuls of Madeira wine and a dash of cayenne pepper; remove the sauce to the side of the fire in order to add butter to it. Dress the crawfish on a deep dish with a little of their own broth, and serve the sauce in a separate sauce-boat.

(1009). CRAWFISH AU COURT BOUILLON AND MARINIÈRE (Écrevisses au Court Bouillon et à la Marinière).

To prepare the court bouillon, mince up two ounces of onions, two ounces of celery root and two ounces of carrots, and put them into a saucepan with a bunch of parsley, thyme and bay leaf, also one pint of water, some salt and a pint of white wine; let boil for ten minutes. Put three dozen live crawfish into a net, plunge this into boiling water and leave it until the shells turn red, then take it out, and break off the small legs, and finish cooking the fish in the court bouillon for about ten minutes, tossing them well in the meanwhile; remove them with a skimmer and dress them. Strain the broth or court bouillon, reduce it to half, add a piece of fresh butter and pour it over the crawfish.

Marinière.—After the three dozen crawfish have been cooked in the court bouillon, dress them in a silver tureen; strain the court bouillon, reduce it to half with a little brandy and thicken it with kneaded butter and bread-crumbs, season with salt and a dash of cayenne, and incorporate into it a little piece of fresh butter; pour this over the crawfish, toss them well, and strew over some chopped parsley.

(1010), CRAWFISH, MAISON D'OR (Écrevisses Maison d'Or).

After three dozen crawfish have been cooked in the court-bouillon (No. 1009), dress them in a silver tureen. Fry in butter some pieces of raw lean ham cut in one-eighth inch squares, moisten with the court bouillon and the same quantity of champagne, adding fish-glaze (No. 399); reduce and incorporate in a little fresh butter; pour this over the crawfish, and strew over a little chopped parsley.

(1011), CRAWFISH WITH BUTTER (Écrevisses au Beurre).

Select four or five dozen large, live, and well cleaned crawfish; put them inside a net and plunge this into a large vessel containing boiling water, in order to kill the crawfish at once. Drain them well, then break off all their small legs; melt some butter, having a sufficiency of it, according to the quantity of crawfish; pour off the top of it only into a saucepan, and cook it un-til it becomes nut brown, then add to it the crawfish, a bunch of parsley, aromatic herbs, some cut up onions and pepper corns; let cook while tossing for ten minutes, drain and put them back in the saucepan besprinkle with a handful of white and fresh bread-crumbs; pour over two or three gills of mirepoix stock (No. 419); remove the saucepan to a slower fire to let the crawfish cook for a few moments longer, but without ceasing to toss. Take them from the fire, trim them and add to the sauce some sherry and small bits of butter for the purpose of thickening it. Dress the crawfish on a deep dish, and pour the sauce over.

(1012), CRAWFISH WITH CREAM (Écrevisses à la Crème).

After having prepared and washed three dozen crawfish as No. 1007, place them in a sauce-pan with a good sized piece of very fresh butter, a bunch of chives and parsley garnished with thyme, bay leaf and basil, a minced onion, two cloves, mushroom parings, a little salt and pepper; moisten with a small ladleful of vegetable stock (No. 195), and set the covered saucepan on a very hot fire for ten minutes, tossing the contents frequently; after this is done, take them from the fire and drain in a colander. Break off all the small legs and the shell from the tails, then lay the crawfish in a saucepan with their own strained stock, to keep hot without boiling. Just when ready to serve, drain, and set them into a silver tureen, one on top of the other, the tails inward, and the heads reclining against the sides of the tureen, and cover over with a lean unctuous béchamel sauce (No. 409), reduced with the broth in which the crawfish were cooked.

EDIBLE SNAILS (Escargots).

A shelled snail. The snails intended for eating are those that feed on aromatic plants. They are nourishing, but difficult to digest, are unsuitable for weak stomachs, and always require to be well seasoned. Broths are made from snails and are found to be very soothing for any irritability of the stomach.

(1013), EDIBLE SNAILS, TO PREPARE (Escargots, Préparation).

Should the snails be taken from grape vines, either in the spring time or autumn, they must be put into a cage, and starved for eight days. If they be purchased in the winter in the markets, they are then closed

FIG. 270.

and ready to cook; in the latter case, wash them well in tepid water to break the openings and remove the glue, then put them into a vessel with fresh water and salt, and let them disgorge for twelve hours (the vessel to be covered with a grater to prevent the snails escaping); afterward wash them again in several waters. Put the snails into a stock pot with water and a pinch of potash; cook until the meats can be removed from the shells—half an hour will suffice for this, then drain and pick them out of the shells. Wash the meats in several waters, suppressing the green vein found in the thinnest part of the snail, then range them in a small earthen pot lined with fat pork; add an onion, a bunch of aromatic herbs, a clove of garlic, a few spoonfuls of brandy, and moisten to their heighth with broth and white wine; close the pot, fasten the cover down with paste, and let cook over a slow fire or gas stove for six hours. When the snails are well done remove, and let them cool off in their own broth. Wash well the shells and let them dry before using.

(1014). EDIBLE SNAILS, BORDELAISE AND SAINTONGE (Escargots à la Bordelaise et à la Saintonge).

Bordelaise.—Cook the snails as explained in No. 1013; fry in butter some onions, carrots and celery root; cut in three-eights of an inch squares, sprinkle over some flour, and moisten with white wine and fish stock (No. 195), add the cooked snails without the shells, and when hot, thicken with kneaded butter and finish with fine herbs and lemon juice.

À la Saintonge.—(Small snails.) After they are cooked as above, put them back into their shells, and fry them in butter, shells and all, adding a crushed and chopped clove of garlic, salt and pepper; moisten with white wine, thicken with an allemande sauce (No. 407), bread-crumbs, butter and parsley.

(1015). EDIBLE SNAILS À LA BOURGUIGNONNE (Escargots à la Bourguignonne).

After the snails have been prepared according to No. 1013 put a little clear gravy (No. 404) into each shell, then one or two snails from which suppress the thin and pointed end; close the opening with a thick layer of fresh butter, mixing in with it salt, black pepper, parsley and chives both chopped, lemon juice and a little fresh bread-crumbs. Arrange the shells on a metal dish provided with a grater for the purpose of upholding the snails, let cook for a few moments and serve them very hot accompanied with a silver skewer to remove the snail from its shell. Metal or earthen dishes are expressly made having the bottom indented to receive the snails.

(1016). EDIBLE SNAILS, PROVENÇAL, AND WITH PROVENÇAL BUTTER (Escargots à la Provençale et au Beurre de Provence).

Prepare and cook the snails as for No. 1013, fry in oil without browning, some shallots, mushrooms, garlic, and parsley, all to be finely chopped and seasoned with salt, pepper, and nutmeg, add a little flour, stir well and moisten with white wine and fish stock (No. 195), reduce thoroughly to the consistency of a sauce. Fill the shells by putting into each one, one or two snails according to their size, finish filling with the sauce, and cover with bread-crumbs, besprinkle with butter, and heat them in a hot oven.

With Provençal Butter.—Cook and prepare the snails as for No. 1013, set at the bottom of each shell a little of the following butter: Stir into some butter finely chopped parsley, onions, and crushed garlic, and finely cut up thyme and bay leaf, season with salt, black and red pepper, pound and press through a sieve. Set the snails on this butter and finish filling the shells with the same and some fresh bread-crumbs, range them on a dish, and place them in the hot oven; serve when the butter boils in the shell. Accompany these snails with a small silver pick to remove the insides.

FROGS (Grenouilles).

A small quadruped of the Rana family, having a smooth skin, flat head, large mouth, and bulging eyes; it lives in the water. The under part of the stomach is white, dotted with brown. Frogs' meat contains a gelatinous principle, more fluid and less nourishing than any other animal; it is considered quite a delicacy, and is healthy and agreeable to the taste. Refreshing broths are made with frogs' legs, analogous to those composed of chicken or veal.

FIG. 729.

(1017). FROGS' LEGS À LA D'ANTIN (Cuisses de Grenouilles à la d'Antin).

Have a pound of very fresh frogs' legs, season them with salt, pepper and nutmeg, then fry them in butter with a teaspoonful of finely chopped onions; add some chives, minced mushrooms, capers, and chopped truffles; moisten with half a pint of white wine, reduce till dry, then pour in a little espagnole sauce (No. 414), dress and dredge over chopped parsley, chervil, and a few tarragon leaves.

(1018). FROGS' LEGS À LA OSBORN (Cuisses de Grenouilles à la Osborn).

Cut a pound of thighs in two to divide them, then each leg in two at the joint; season with salt and pepper and fry them in some butter with a teaspoonful of chopped up onions, a finely shred green pepper, two peeled tomatoes cut into eight pieces, four ounces of finely minced mushrooms and one gill of espagnole sauce (No. 414), cover and set the pan in the oven for fifteen minutes, then dress the frogs' legs, reduce the sauce and pour it over, sprinkling the top plentifully with chopped parsley, then serve.

(1019). FROGS' LEGS À LA POULETTE WITH MUSHROOMS (Cuisses de Grenouilles à la Poulette aux Champignons).

Cut the frogs' thighs in two to divide them, and the legs at the joint; should they be small, leave the legs whole only suppressing the feet, having one pound in all after they are trimmed. Fry them in butter with six ounces of fresh, minced mushrooms, add half a pint of velouté sauce (No. 415), and let simmer for a few minutes, then thicken the sauce with three raw egg-yolks diluted in half a gill of cream; season with salt, cayenne pepper, nutmeg, lemon juice and chopped parsley.

(1020). FROGS' LEGS DEVILED (Cuisses de Grenouilles à la Diable.)

Have one pound of well-pared frogs' legs; season them with salt, pepper, nutmeg, lemon juice and mustard, and immerse them in melted butter, then roll them in bread-crumbs, and range them on a double broiler; besprinkle with butter, and broil over a slow fire, then dress them on a deviled sauce (No. 459).

(1021). FROGS' LEGS FRIED À LA ORLY (Cuisses de Grenouilles Frites à la Orly).

Divide medium-sized frogs legs by cutting them apart at each joint; put them into a vessel with minced onions, branches of parsley, salt, pepper, nutmeg, lemon juice and sweet oil; let them marinate for two hours, then roll them in flour and fry till a good color; drain, and besprinkle with salt; dress them on folded napkins with fried parsley on top. Serve in a separate sauce-boat a tomato sauce (No. 549).

(1022). FROGS' LEGS FRIED WITH CREAM SAUCE (Cuisses de Grenouilles Frites Sauce Crème).

Should the frogs' legs be large, cut them in two by separating them at each joint; season with salt and pepper, and wet them over with a little milk, roll them in flour and fry them till a good color. First take out the small pieces, then the larger ones, and dress them on a napkin with a bunch of parsley on top; serve a cream sauce (No. 454) in a separate sauce-boat.

(1023). FROGS' LEGS ROYER (Cuisses de Grenouilles à la Royer).

Fry in two ounces of butter, one pound of trimmed frogs' legs with a teaspoonful of chopped onions added; when done, cover them with an espagnole sauce (No. 414) and half as much tomato sauce (No. 549); reduce and season to taste. Broil some slices of bacon, cut them up into squares; dress the frogs' legs, dredge over with chopped parsley and surround with the pieces of bacon to form a border.

LOBSTER (Homard).

A large sea crawfish, the cuirass being strewn with blue spots more or less big on a reddish

foundation which covers a white tissue. This crustacean is not very fleshy, feeds but little and is very difficult to digest; when cooked it turns red. Its claws and tails are the only meaty parts and are excellent for food.

Spiny Lobster (Langouste), Palinurus Locusta.—The spiny lobster has two large horns in front of its eyes, two others underneath and it is with these it catches and draws toward it the fish on which it feeds. Its back is covered with prickles and very rough. During the winter this crustacean lives in the deep ocean and is very common in the Mediterranean sea. Its meat can only be digested by robust stomachs and it always requires to be highly seasoned.

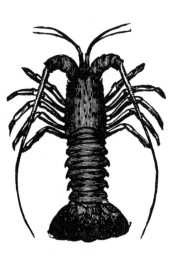

FIG. 272.

FIG. 273.

(1024). LOBSTER OR SPINY LOBSTER, AMERICAN STYLE (Homard ou Langouste à l'Américaine).

Cook in a court bouillon some medium sized lobsters, proceeding exactly as described in crawfish au court bouillon (No. 1009); drain and then split them lengthwise in two. Cover with sweet oil in a sautoire, some onions and shallots both finely minced, also thyme and bay leaf; lay the lobsters over, the cut side on top, heat for a few minutes, season, and pour into the bottom of the sautoire, two gills of white wine, and the same quantity of court bouillon stock; cover closely and boil over a good fire for twelve minutes, then keep it warm without boiling for ten minutes longer. Drain, strain off the liquid, put it back to reduce to a half-glaze, then thicken it with tomato sauce (No. 549), mingling in a few spoonfuls of Madeira wine. When the sauce is finished, take it from the fire and butter it with fresh butter, adding a dash of cayenne pepper, and half a gill of burned brandy; dress and pour the sauce over the whole.

(1025). SMALL LOBSTERS À LA BORDELAISE (Petits Homards à la Bordelaise).

Take four small lobsters weighing one pound each and kill them in boiling water, drain, and break off the large claws, put them together in a narrow saucepan, and moisten to three quarters of their height with a court bouillon made with white wine (No. 39); let cook for twelve minutes, then set aside, and leave them for ten minutes longer in their stock. Cut up into three-sixteenth of an inch squares, half a pound of carrots, a quarter of a pound of onions, and a quarter of a pound of celery root; parboil them separately and finish cooking them in broth for three-quarters of an hour, letting the liquid fall to a glaze until they are done, then add some tomatoes cut up in dice; keep this on one side. Drain the lobsters, split them each in two lengthwise, and detach the half tails from the bodies; suppress the claw shells and return the tails to their shells, also the bodies; place again in the saucepan, cover and keep warm. Strain their broth and free it of fat, let it reduce to a half-glaze, and thicken with a few spoonfuls of brown sauce (No. 414) reduced with Madeira and a little tomato sauce (No. 549). Finish with two spoonfuls of burnt brandy, and a pinch of cayenne; take it from the fire to stir in some butter and the vegetable stock; range in vegetable dishes the half bodies, and half tails in their shells, set the shelless claws on top, and cover over with a part of the sauce, serving the remainder in a sauce-boat.

(1026). LOBSTER À LA BONNEFOY (Homard à la Bonnefoy).

Chop up two ounces of onions and two shallots, fry them in oil without letting attain a color, and add to them two live lobsters' tails cut in pieces across three-eighths of an inch thick with their shells. Sauté them for a few moments over a brisk fire, and season with salt, cayenne, a bunch of parsley, garnished with thyme, and a clove of garlic, moisten with a pint of white or red wine; cover the sautoire, and cook the lobsters for fifteen minutes, then drain off the pieces, dress them in a pyramidal form on a dish, and add to the broth a few tablespoonfuls of tomato sauce (No. 549), and espagnole sauce (No. 414). Pound the creamy parts picked from the bodies with a little cayenne pepper, press it through a sieve, and stir it into the sauce with some minced mushrooms; pour this over the lobsters, and finish by sprinkling the surface with chopped parsley; add a little finely shredded tarragon leaves.

(1027). LOBSTER À LA BRITANNIA (Homard à la Britannia).

Boil two lobsters of two pounds each in boiling water with some cut up carrots and onions, parsley, thyme, bay leaf, and vinegar; cook for twenty to thirty minutes, then let the stock settle, and pour off the top steadily from the sediment; divide the bodies from the tails, take out the meat from the latter, also from the claws, and keep it warm in a little of the stock; take also the creamy parts from the bodies and rub them through a sieve. Reduce a pint of mushroom broth or essence (No. 392) with half a pint of velouté sauce (No. 415), and half a gill of meat glaze (No. 402), also one gill of Madeira wine; thicken it with four tablespoonfuls of bread-crumbs, and season with salt, red pepper, and nutmeg; add half a pound of mushroom heads, and half a pound of small artichoke bottoms cut in four. Escalop the lobster tails, dress them in a crown shape, and place the rest of the meats in the center, on top lay the mushrooms and artichoke bottoms, then finish the sauce by thickening with egg-yolks, butter, and cream, add some lemon juice, and chopped parsley, also the creamy parts from the bodies; pour the sauce over the lobster, and serve very hot.

(1028). LOBSTER À LA CAMILLE (Homard à la Camille).

Heat in a sautoir some good sweet oil, and throw into it live lobsters, each one cut across into twelve pieces; season with salt, pepper, mignonette, thyme, bay leaf and cayenne pepper; toss them over a brisk fire for twelve minutes, then add three medium fresh tomatoes, peeled, seeded and cut in dice, a few parsley leaves and a clove of crushed garlic; let reduce for ten minutes, then pour in a gill of brandy, set it on fire, and as soon as it is extinguished pour in two gills of white wine, reduce to half, and just when ready to serve, add some meat glaze (No. 402) and lemon juice.

(1029). LOBSTER À LA CREOLE (Homard à la Créole).

Take two medium lobsters each one weighing about two pounds; cut them up into twelve pieces and sauté them over a quick fire with half as much butter as oil; add two ounces of onions and one ounce of chopped shallot, salt, pepper, and a garnished bunch of parsley, then moisten with four gills of consommé (No. 189), and one gill of Madeira wine, add four medium, peeled, pressed and halved tomatoes, one green pepper, cut into small bits, and a little curry. Let this simmer for fifteen minutes, add fine herbs and serve. Boil some rice in water with salt and butter, drain, set it into a buttered mold, and leave it in the oven for ten minutes, then unmold and serve the rice separately but at the same time as the lobsters.

(1030). DEVILED, ROASTED LOBSTER (Homard Rôti à la Diable).

Kill the lobster in hot water; split in two lengthwise, and range it on a baking pan; season with salt and cayenne, and pour over some melted butter. Bake it in a moderate oven for twenty minutes, cover over with maître d'hôtel butter containing plenty of diluted mustard. Serve on a very hot dish, break the shells with pincers made for this purpose, remove the meat and serve them directly on the plates.

(1031). LOBSTER À LA DUGLÈRE (Homard à la Duglère).

Cut live lobsters into pieces, heat some butter in a sautoir, and when hot range the pieces of lobster one beside the other; fry them over a quick fire, then moisten with brandy, set it on fire, add Madeira and white wine, seasoning with salt, pepper and a little cayenne pepper; add to it some peeled, pressed and cut up tomatoes, a clove of crushed garlic, and a good, cooked mirepoix (No. 419). As soon as the lobsters are done, lay them in a dish, reduce the sauce with velouté (No. 415), and incorporate into it just when ready to serve, some butter and lemon juice; pour this over the lobster, and dredge the surface with a pinch of chopped chervil and chives.

(1032) LOBSTER À LA FRESNE (Homard à la Fresne).

Take two lobsters each weighing two and a half pounds, and cook them by steam for one half hour. Detach the tails from the bodies; take the meats out of the former whole, and set it aside to get cool, and from them obtain one pound to cut up into slices; put these into a vessel with half as much mushrooms, and half as much truffles as mushrooms, moisten the whole with a pint of velouté sauce (No. 415), reduced with cream and thickened with egg-yolks and butter, not having too much, only just sufficient to envelop the garnishing; dress the lobsters, arranging them dome-shape, smooth the surface nicely, and decorate with large fanciful cuts of truffles; garnish around with some cream quenelles (No. 76) without decorations.

(1033). LOBSTER À LA GAMBETTA (Homard à la Gambetta).

Cut about four pounds of raw lobster tails into transversal pieces three-eighths of an inch thick. Fry in four ounces of butter, two ounces of leeks, the same quantity of onions, the same of carrots, and the same of celery, a branch of parsley, thyme and bay leaf, add the remaining part of the lobsters and moisten with half a bottleful of white wine and a quart of fish stock (No. 195); let all cook for half an hour, then strain the stock through a sieve, add to it some velouté sauce (No. 415), and reduce all together, pass through a tammy into a saucepan previously rubbed with a little garlic. Sauté the slices of lobster tails in some clarified butter over a brisk fire, add a teaspoonful of shallots, salt and red pepper, then moisten with white wine; reduce quickly and pour in the reduced velouté, and a little tomato sauce (No. 549); thicken with four egg-yolks, butter and cream; dress the whole into a dish and garnish around with croûtons fried in oil and croquettes of rice cooked and seasoned with hazelnut butter (No. 567), salt, saffron and cayenne pepper; when cold make this into small balls three-quarters of an inch in size, dip them in eggs, then in bread-crumbs and fry to a fine color. On top lay some trussed crawfish.

(1034). LOBSTER À LA HERVEY (Homard à la Hervey).

Prepare a court bouillon (No. 38), and in it cook two lobsters each of two pounds; drain them for a few minutes; detach the tails from the bodies, and keep them warm in a little of their broth. Cut some peeled truffles into thin slices an eighth of an inch thick, and three-quarters to one inch in diameter; set them in a bain-marie with a little melted glaze (No. 402) and Madeira wine. Slice the lobsters' tails and claw meat, and fry the pieces in butter; moisten with a pint of cream, reduce and season highly, then thicken with egg-yolks, cream and butter. Dress and garnish the dish with round apple croquettes one inch in diameter, and cover the entire top with the prepared truffles.

(1035). LOBSTER À LA LAWRENCE AND MARYLAND (Homard à la Lawrence et à la Maryland).

Cut into twenty-four pieces the tail parts of four cooked lobsters; season them with salt and mignonette. Heat well in a sautoire four ounces of butter, and two gills of oil, add to it the pieces of lobster, and sauté them over a brisk fire, adding four ounces of onions, and two small bunches of parsley garnished with garlic, cloves, and bay leaf; moisten with half a bottleful of red wine, and two gills of espagnole sauce (No. 414); put in some chopped mushrooms, and the pulp of one lemon; suppress the parsley and bay leaf, and serve the remainder in a dish with finely shred chives strewn over the top.

Maryland Style.—Cut cooked lobsters in slices one-quarter inch in thickness, sauté in fresh butter, moisten with cream, let simmer for a few minutes, and before serving, thicken the lobster with cooked yolks of eggs, crushed with double the amount of butter, then press through a fine sieve, seasoning with red and white pepper and add a little good sherry.

(1036). SMALL SPINY LOBSTER TAILS À LA MONTE CARLO (Queues de Petites Langoustes à la Monte Carlo.

Cut a few fresh mushrooms into large dice, and cook them with butter and lemon-juice; poach a few dozen large oysters, cut them up into three-eighths of an inch squares, and strain their broth. Cook twelve ounces of picked rice in some fish stock (No. 195), mixed with the oyster and mushroom broths, and a coffeespoonful of red pepper (No. 168); have it when done, the consistence of a Creole rice. Keep in boiling water seven or eight small spiny lobsters, each one weighing ten ounces; drain, and detach the tails from the bodies; put the latter back into the water to cook for ten minutes longer, then drain and pick out all the creamy parts. Split each tail in two lengthwise, both meat and shells, keep all the water running off from the meat, and fry these halved tails in a sautoire for five or six minutes with some oil and chopped shallots; season, and dredge over a little red pepper; moisten them to their height with good court bouillon (No. 38) and white wine, add some mushroom peelings, a garnished bunch of parsley, a lemon pulp, and two chopped tomatoes, and allow the liquid to boil rapidly for five or six minutes, then drain off the halved tails, so as to take out the meats and keep them warm. Strain the lobster broth, stir into it the water reserved from the meats, and reduce it to a half-glaze, then thicken it, first with a little velouté sauce (No. 415), and afterward with a thickening of egg-yolks, cream, and two or three spoonfuls of the creamy parts; butter the sauce off the fire without ceasing to stir. After the rice is done to perfection, pour over it a few spoonfuls of hazelnut butter (No. 567), and let it smother for five or six minutes; stir in the oysters and mushrooms; dress this rice into a vegetable dish, smooth the surface dome-shaped, and in the center stick standing three or four large crawfish; around these dress the half tails almost upright, and cover over with a little of the sauce, serving the surplus in a sauce-boat. Should the spiny lobsters have to be replaced by small ordinary lobsters, then the lobster claws must be substituted for the crawfish and be stuck into the summit of the dome.

(1037). LOBSTER À LA NEWBERG OR DELMONICO (Homard à la Newberg ou à la Delmonico).

Cook six lobsters each weighing about two pounds in boiling salted water for twenty-five minutes. Twelve pounds of live lobster when cooked yields from two to two and a half pounds of meat and three to four ounces of lobster coral. When cold detach the bodies from the tails and cut the latter into slices, put them into a sautoir, each piece lying flat and add hot clarified butter; season with salt and fry lightly on both sides without coloring; moisten to their height with good raw cream; reduce quickly to half and then add two or three spoonfuls of Madeira wine; boil the liquid once more only, then remove and thicken with a thickening of egg-yolks and raw cream (No. 175). Cook without boiling, incorporating a little cayenne and butter; warm it up again without boiling, tossing the lobster lightly, then arrange the pieces in a vegetable dish and pour the sauce over.

(1038). LOBSTER À LA PAUL BERT (Homard à la Paul Bert).

Take eight one-pound lobsters and plunge them into boiling water into which has been added a bunch of parsley, sliced onions, salt, pepper and vinegar; let them boil steadily twenty minutes, then remove; detach the bodies from the tails; take the meat out whole from the latter by breaking the inside of the shell only; then wash and dry the shells. Cut up the tail meat into transversal slices; put four ounces of butter into a sautoire, range the lobster escalops on top, and sauté them, adding a small finely chopped up shallot, half as much shrimps as lobster, and half as much fresh, peeled walnuts as shrimps. (Should there be no fresh walnuts procurable, take dry ones and soak them for twelve hours in salt and water, then peel.) Drain off the butter and replace it by a reduced béchamel sauce (No. 409) thickened with egg-yolks, cream and fresh butter, with lemon juice and chopped parsley, being careful to have the sauce quite thick. Fill the lobster shells with this preparation, dress them crown-shaped on a bed of parsley, and arrange a bunch of parsley leaves on top.

(1039). LOBSTER, PROVENÇAL STYLE (Homard à la Provençale).

Divide into equal pieces two medium sized raw lobster tails, season them with salt and mignonette, and sauté them in oil over a very hot fire, turning them round so that they color nicely on both sides. Mince up very finely eight ounces of onions, cutting them first in halves, and suppressing the root and stalk, put them in with the lobster with salt, pepper, mignonette, a bunch of parsley, garnished with thyme and bay leaf, half a pint of tomato sauce (No. 549), and four spoonfuls of burnt brandy, boil a few minutes; take out the pieces of lobster, strain the sauce through a sieve, and reduce it over a brisk fire with half a bottleful of white wine, despumate the sauce, and when nearly reduced, put back the lobster, season to taste, and serve.

(1040). LOBSTER ROASTED ON THE SPIT (Homard Rôti à la Broche).

Kill a large six-pound lobster by plunging it into boiling water for three minutes, lay it on the spit without trussing, only fastening the claws together with an iron skewer, or else attach it to the spit cradle and lay it in front of a good fire, turning it around while besprinkling with a brush dipped in butter and lemon juice; salt it while it is very hot; pour over a good mirepoix with wine (No. 419) and aromatics. A lobster weighing six pounds requires forty minutes cooking, and must be besprinkled quite frequently; when the meat is done, the shell should be softened. Remove the lobster from the spit, dress it on a dish and serve separately a shallot sauce finished with some butter; serve it in a sauce-boat, or replace it by a half-glaze reduced with white wine, into which has been added the juice of a lemon or orange.

(1041). LOBSTER À LA ROUGEMONT (Homard à la Rougemont).

Kill three lobsters each weighing two pounds by plunging them for two minutes into boiling water; when well drained, break off the claws from the bodies so that they occupy less room in cooking, and put the whole into a saucepan; moisten with half a bottleful of white wine, and the same quantity of water, and add cut up carrots, celery, leeks and onions, thyme, bay leaf, parsley branches and pepper corns, let all boil for twenty-five minutes, and drain off the lobsters. Detach the tails from the bodies, split the latter lengthwise to obtain all the creamy parts, which must be pressed through a sieve and laid aside. Cut the tail meat into slices, keeping all the water issuing from it; fry in either two ounces of butter or oil, the body shells after chopping them up coarsely on the table, add minced carrots, celery, onions, leeks, shallots and paprika, half of the lobster stock, and the water from the meat; let all boil for fifteen minutes, then strain through a sieve. Suppress the shells from the claws, cut up the meat the same as the tails, season with salt and fry them both with butter for two minutes over a brisk fire, then moisten with the stock, adding half a pint of velouté sauce (No. 415), and one gill of tomato purée (No. 730); let simmer for twelve minutes. Add half the quantity of cooked mushroom heads, and the creamy parts of the lobsters, thicken with egg-yolks, one gill of cream and two ounces of butter, pour over a little burnt brandy, and less than half as much Madeira wine; dress this on a chafing dish, and serve at the same time some rice cooked in milk, seasoned with salt and lemon peel.

(1042). LOBSTER TAILS À LA STANLEY (Queues de Homards à la Stanley).

Wash, blanch, and cook in a white broth (No. 194a), twelve ounces of good Carolina rice, keeping it quite consistent; twenty to twenty-five minutes will suffice to have it done; keep it warm. Suppress the tail shell of a large, freshly cooked lobster; cut the meat into slices, and lay them in a sautoire; sauté these, when done add the same quantity of fish quenelles (No. 90) molded in a small coffeespoon (No. 155), five or six whole hard boiled egg-yolks, a few dozen crawfish tails, and the same amount of poached and trimmed oysters. Put on to reduce five gills of velouté sauce (No. 415), pour into it slowly a few spoonfuls of fish court-bouillon (No. 38), a part of the broth from the oysters, the crawfish, a coffeespoonful of powdered curry dissolved in two spoonfuls of broth. When the sauce has become thick and succulent, strain it, and return it to the saucepan to heat once more, then cover the garnishings with a small part of it, keeping it in a bain-marie, while the remainder is to be set on the side of the range, and butter worked into it. Dress the lobster, in a chafing dish dome-shape, with the garnishing around, and on top lay symmetrically four cooked crawfish, having their tails shelled, and pour a little of the sauce over the lobster; lay a round truffle on the summit of the dome, and send to the table at once with a sauce-boat of the buttered sauce. The rice to be served separately.

(1043) SMALL LOBSTERS À LA CARLU, STUFFED LOBSTER TAILS, DEVILED (Petits Homards à la Carlu, Queues de Homards Farcies et à la Diable).

Split in two lengthwise three or four small, cooked and cold lobsters, and pick the meat from the bodies, cut it into half inch square pieces, and set in a saucepan with half its quantity of cooked mushrooms, cut in quarter inch dice. Put on to reduce three gills of good béchamel sauce (No. 409), incorporating slowly into it the broth from the mushrooms. With this sauce cover the prepared salpicon and use it to fill the half lobster shells that have been well cleaned; smooth the tops and cover over with a thin layer of cream fish forcemeat (No. 76), having it slightly dome-shaped; sift over white bread-crumbs and sprinkle the surface with melted butter, then range the shells on a buttered baking sheet, and brown the tops in a moderate oven for ten minutes, then dress them on napkins.

To Stuff Lobster Tails.—Cut in three-sixteenth of an inch squares, one pound of lobster meat cooked in a court bouillon (No. 38), add to these half the same quantity of cooked mushrooms cut up the same size. Fry colorless in butter, two tablespoonfuls of onions, add two ounces of flour, and fry without browning; dilute with a pint of milk and cook again for a few minutes, then add the lobster and mushrooms, mix well, boil up once, remove, and cool off. Fill the half tail shells, well cleaned and dried, with this preparation, dredge over bread-crumbs, besprinkle with butter and brown them in a hot oven.

For Deviled.—Clean and dry the half body shells; fill them with the same preparation as above, having it dome-shaped, smooth the surface, and coat over with mustard; dredge bread-crumbs on top, besprinkle with butter, and brown nicely in the oven.

(1044). LOBSTER WITH CREAM (Homard à la Crème).

Plunge two lobsters each weighing two pounds into boiling water, so as to kill them quickly; break off the large claws, and lay them in a narrow saucepan with the bodies; moisten them to their height with white wine and water, add branches of parsley, bay leaf, onions, finely shred carrots and salt; let boil for twenty minutes, drain and detach the tails from the bodies. Take out the creamy part from the bodies, press through a sieve, and keep this aside. Fry in some butter, four finely chopped, blanched shallots, moisten them with the lobster stock, and boil for fifteen minutes, strain, remove the fat, and reduce to a half-glaze, then thicken with two spoonfuls of velouté sauce (No. 415); continue to reduce while pouring in two gills of good raw cream, strain this sauce and add to it the creamy parts of the lobster, a dash of cayenne pepper and half a gill of burnt brandy; butter it without ceasing to stir so that the butter is thoroughly incorporated. Cut across in slices the tail meat and shells; cut the remaining bodies in two, and dress the two halves one beside the other in the center of a dish; range around the slices of tail, alternating each piece with a fine slice of cooked truffle, and on top of the body shells lay the claw meat; cover the lobsters with a part of the sauce, and serve the rest in a separate sauce-boat.

MUSSELS (Moules).

This bivalvular shell-fish is without any distinct head, or eyes, or organs of mastication; there are sea and river mussels. The shells from the sea kind are oval shaped, convex on the outside, and concave inside, black, bluish, smoothly polished, and varying from two to three inches in length. Mussels must be chosen very fresh. Be careful after having washed them to place them in a vessel with salted water and leave them for several hours.

FIG. 274.

(1045). MUSSELS, HOW TO PREPARE (Moules, pour Préparer).

Obtain four quarts of medium sized mussels; tear off the grass, scrape them well, and wash them several times, changing the water constantly. Put them when clean into a saucepan with half a pint of water or white wine, a few sprigs of parsley, thyme, and bay leaf; set the saucepan over a brisk fire, cover it well, and open the mussels by tossing them frequently, then take them out with a skimmer to transfer them into another saucepan. Strain the broth, leaving all sediment at the bottom, pouring it off gently not to disturb the sand; take out all the empty shells, cut off the foot (the black appendage) from the mussels with a pair of scissors, and put them back on their half shells into their own broth.

(1046). MUSSELS À LA MARINIÈRE (Moules à la Marinière).

The mussels should be prepared as for No. 1045. Cook in butter one shallot with the same quantity of very finely chopped onions; moisten with white wine, add the mussels and a little velouté sauce (No. 415), and mussel broth; keep this warm and just when ready to serve, stir in a piece of fresh butter and chopped parsley.

(1047). MUSSELS À LA POULETTE (Moules à la Poulette).

Prepare the mussels as for No. 1045; cut two ounces of onions into one-eighth of an inch pieces and cook them in a saucepan with two ounces of butter, not letting them attain a color, moisten with a pint and a half of velouté sauce (No. 415), and a small part of the mussel broth; reduce this sauce with mushroom parings added, strain it through a tammy, and thicken with a thickening of egg-yolks diluted with a little of the broth, and fine butter; cook this thickening without allowing it to boil, stirring it steadily; season to taste and serve.

(1048). MUSSELS À LA VILLEROI (Moules à la Villeroi).

These must be prepared as for No. 1045. Take the mussels from their shells; cut off the foot without injuring the mussel, then dip them into an allemande sauce (No. 407) with cooked fine herbs, well reduced and partially cold; dip them in for the second time when very cold, then put them aside in the ice-box for one hour; lift them up with a thin knife, immerse them in beaten eggs, then in bread-crumbs and fry them of a fine color; serve on folded napkins.

(1049). MUSSELS STUFFED À LA TOULOUSAINE (Moules Farcies à la Toulousaine).

To be prepared the same as for No. 1045. Take them out of their shells after draining, cut off the foot, and divide the mussels up into half inch pieces. Fry in oil a cut up onion, and a whole clove of garlic; add to it fresh bread-crumbs, and moisten with mussel broth and milk; boil and stir in a little finely chopped, cooked spinach, suppress the garlic, and add the mussels. Fill the shells with this; range them on a dish, strew bread-crumbs and parmesan on top, besprinkle with fine oil, and brown them nicely in a quick oven. Serve on a folded napkin.

(1050). MUSSELS WITH FINE HERBS, BAKED (Moules aux Fines Herbes Gratinées).

Prepare and cook the mussels as for No. 1045. Take them entirely out of their shells; cut off the foot with scissors, and range them one beside the other on a buttered dish; sprinkle the top over with finely and separately chopped up shallots, onions, mushrooms, and parsley; lay bread-crumbs and grated parmesan over, pour in some melted butter, and set the dish in the oven for eight or ten minutes.

(1051). MUSSELS WITH SHALLOT (Moules à l'Échalote).

Set into a saucepan a few dozen, medium sized mussels; let them open over a brisk fire, with a bunch of parsley added, and toss them about until the meats get firm. Drain them through a colander laid over a bowl, in order to collect all their broth, then remove the empty shells from each, and put the mussels back into the saucepan to keep warm. Put into another sauce-pan two spoonfuls of chopped shallot, and one of onions; add a gill of white wine, and two spoonfuls of tarragon vinegar; reduce the liquid slowly to half, remove the saucepan from the fire, and let the contents get partially cold, then stir in three or four raw egg-yolks. Beat with a spoon, and thicken the liquid slightly by stirring it on the fire, then take it off, and incorporate into it slowly, five ounces of butter divided into small pats, without ceasing to stir; finish the sauce with two spoonfuls of shallot juice, chopped parsley and lemon juice. Dress the mussels into a vegetable dish, pour over the sauce and serve.

OYSTERS (Huitres).

Fig. 275.

Fig. 276.

A bivalve having an irregular shell attached by hinges, and having an oblong, grooved indent across. It is headless, toothless and sexless; it cannot live out of water, and is specially fond of the mouths of rivers. The fishing begins in September, and finishes in the latter part of April; in all the intervening months, or those containing no letter R in their names, the oysters are replaced by Little Neck clams. Fresh oysters are easier digested in the raw state than when cooked, for the heat hardens them while the sea water in the raw ones facilitates digestion. Oysters contain plenty of water, very little solid animal matter, a great deal of lime and sulphate of iron, osmazome and gelatin. These bivalves agree with worn-out constitutions, but should be eaten very fresh. Like certain fishes, oysters contain phosphorus.

(1052). OYSTERS À LA BÉARNAISE, TOMATOED (Huîtres à la Béarnaise Tomatée).

Place some large oysters in a saucepan on the fire; poach them slightly in their own liquor, drain and suppress the hard parts, then roll them in a sautoir containing cooked fine herbs. Butter some boat-shaped tartlet molds, line them with a delicate chicken forcemeat (No. 62); and lay one oyster and some of the fine herbs in every mold; cover over with more forcemeat, so that it is well filled and rounded on the top, then poach, unmold, and dip them in beaten eggs; roll in bread-crumbs, and fry in clarified butter. Serve a separate sauce-boat of tomato béarnaise sauce (No. 433).

(1053). OYSTERS À LA BOUCICAULT (Huîtres à la Boucicault).

Butter a deep dish; pour into it some oysters with their own liquor; season with salt, pepper, tomato catsup and tobasco sauce; scatter over a few bits of butter, here and there, and then set the dish into a hot oven; serve as soon as the oysters are poached, that is as soon as they are firm to the touch.

(1054). OYSTERS RISSOLETTES À LA POMPADOUR (Rissolettes d'Huîtres à la Pompadour).

After blanching medium-sized oysters, drain and suppress the hard parts; prepare some round pieces of thin pancake, two and a half inches in diameter; fill half of each with a little thick Italian sauce (No. 484); lay an oyster on top with more sauce over, then force a quarter inch cord of fish quenelle forcemeat (No. 90) through a cornet on one half of the pancake; fold over and fasten the edges together; dip them in beaten eggs, then in bread-crumbs, and fry a fine color; then dress on a folded napkin and garnish with a bunch of fried parsley.

(1055). OYSTERS À LA RUBINO (Huîtres à la Rubino).

Butter a deep dish and pour into it the oysters with their own liquor; season with salt and black pepper, and add the heart stalks of a head of celery cut into thin lengthwise slices, and a few small pieces of fresh butter; cover it over with another dish and set it into a moderate oven for fifteen minutes, then serve.

(1056). OYSTERS À LA VILLEROI (Huîtres à la Villeroi).

Poach some large oysters in their own liquor; drain and wipe them dry. Reduce some velouté sauce (No. 415), with the oyster liquor and a little jelly, thicken it with egg-yolks, and leave it to get nearly cold; cover the oysters with one or two layers of this sauce, range them on a baking sheet, one beside the other, and put them away until thoroughly cold, pare them, then dip in beaten eggs, roll them in bread-crumbs, and fry in plenty of hot fat to a golden color; drain and dress them on a folded napkin; lay on top a bunch of fried parsley, and serve with a sauce-boat of Madeira sauce (No. 492).

(1057). OYSTERS BAKED, À LA CRANE (Huîtres au Gratin à la Crane).

Lay in a deep dish fit to be placed in the oven, a bed of medium sized drained oysters; season with salt, pepper, and a few small pieces of butter; sift over some fresh bread-crumbs, and pour in a little sherry wine and some of the oyster liquor; repeat the same operation until the dish is full, then besprinkle the whole with bread-crumbs; scatter small pats of butter here and there, and set the dish into a hot oven for ten to fifteen minutes to bake them a fine color, then serve.

(1058). OYSTER BROCHETTES WITH TRUFFLES (Huîtres en Brochettes aux Truffes).

Poach in their liquor three dozen large oysters; when they are cold, pare and season, run a small wooden skewer through their centers, alternating each oyster with a round slice of cooked truffle. Dip these brochettes into a well reduced allemande sauce (No. 407), into which has been added chopped mushrooms and fine herbs. Range them at once on a baking sheet, and leave them in the ice-box till the sauce is thoroughly cold; three hours later, detach them from the sheet, remove the superflous sauce, and shape them nicely, roll them in white bread-crumbs, dip them in beaten eggs, and again in bread-crumbs, smooth the surfaces, and plunge the brochettes into very hot fat, until they attain a golden color; then withdraw the skewers and dress them at once on a folded napkin. Garnish with fried parsley.

(1059). BROILED OYSTERS, MAÎTRE D'HÔTEL AND ON SKEWERS (Huîtres Grillées Maître d'Hôtel et en Brochettes).

Drain some large oysters; wipe dry, and season with salt and pepper; range them on a hinged broiler, coat over either with melted butter or oil (but no bread-crumbs), broil them over a quick fire without coloring, then dress them on pieces of toast, and pour over a little slightly melted maître-d'hôtel butter (No. 581); or, they may be bread-crumbed after dipping in butter, and then broiled over a slow fire, covering with the maître d'hôtel butter.

For Brochettes or Skewers.—Blanch some large oysters, run a skewer through them twining around with a band of very thin and fat bacon, cut sufficiently long that one alone answers for a brochette; sprinkle over some butter, and broil them over a quick fire, then dress them on a hot dish, and cover with maître d'hôtel butter (No. 581).

(1060). FRIED OYSTERS À LA HORLY (Huîtres Frites à la Horly).

Poach some medium sized oysters in their own liquor, drain and suppress the hard parts; wipe them in a cloth, and lay them in a vessel to season with salt and pepper, adding parsley, chopped mushrooms, lemon juice and a little oil; let marinate for two hours; now dip them in fine frying batter (No. 137), into which has been mixed well beaten egg-whites; immerse each oyster into this paste and plunge them at once into very hot fat; fry them a fine color, drain, salt, and dress them on a folded napkin. Set a bunch of fried parsley on top and quartered lemons around; to be served with a separate sauce-boat of light tomato sauce (No. 549).

(1061). OYSTERS FRIED WITH BUTTER OR LARD (Huîtres Frites au Beurre ou au Saindoux)

Fried Oysters With Butter.—Poach the oysters lightly in their own liquor, then drain and roll them in pulverized cracker-dust, dip them in beaten egg that has been mixed with a little milk seasoned with salt and pepper and strained through a strainer; roll them in bread-crumbs. Put some butter into a sautoire or frying-pan; when very hot lay in the oysters one beside the other, and as soon as they are fried nicely on one side, turn them over on the other when done; drain, and pile them on a folded napkin, and serve very hot.

Fried Oysters with Lard.—Drain medium-sized oysters; roll them in pulverized cracker-dust, then dip them in eggs to which have been added an equal quantity of oyster liquor and seasoned with salt and pepper, beaten well with a whisk and strained through a strainer. Roll them once more in the cracker-dust, shape them nicely, and plunge them into very hot lard; when a fine color, drain, besprinkle with a little table salt and dress on folded napkins.

(1062). OYSTERS ON CRUSTS (Huîtres sur Croûtes).

Blanch in their liquor, three dozen large oysters; pare and cut them up into five-eighths inch squares. Put on to reduce a few spoonfuls of good béchamel sauce (No. 409), mix in with it two or three spoonfuls of raw, chopped, peeled mushrooms, continue to reduce the sauce without ceasing to stir, and incorporate into it slowly a few spoonfuls of the oyster broth, and a little cream. Use this sauce to mingle with the oyster salpicon, being careful to keep the mixture of a good consistency, and use it to cover seven or eight hollow bread-crusts (No. 52), prepared the same as for poached eggs browned and emptied just when ready to serve. Smooth the surfaces, bestrew with bread-crumbs and sprinkle over with a little melted butter; brown them with a hot shovel or else a gas salamander, and serve.

Another Way.—Prepare some oysters the same as oysters à la poulette (No. 1067). Cut the tops from some rolls, empty them by removing all the crumbs, rub fresh butter over the inside and outside of the rolls, color nicely in the oven; when the crust is crisp, fill it with the prepared oysters, put the cover on, and serve on a folded napkin.

(1063). OYSTERS, PHILADELPHIA STYLE (Huîtres à la Philadelphie).

Put two ounces of butter into a pan and let it cook till nut brown, then add to it twenty oysters well drained and wiped; fry them till they assume a light color on both sides, then pour in a quarter of a pint of oyster liquor, salt and pepper. Serve at the same time thin slices of toasted bread, or else pour the oysters over slices of toast laid in a deep dish.

(1064). STEAMED OYSTERS AND ON TOAST (Huîtres à la Vapeur et Sur Croûtes Grillées).

Wash very carefully some medium sized unopened oysters; lay them on a wire grater provided with a handle so that they can easily be removed when done; set this grater into a steamer, cover it as hermetically as possible, and when the oysters are opened, lift them out, take off the flat shell, and serve them in the deep ones. Each guest seasons his oysters according to his individual taste, with salt, black or red pepper or tomato catsup. Serve some melted butter separately.

Steamed Oysters on Toast.—They must be steamed as for the above; open and put them into a sautoire with their own juice; season with salt, pepper and add a little fine butter, and serve them in a deep dish over slices of toasted bread.

(1065). OYSTERS, BÉCHAMEL WITH TRUFFLES (Huîtres Béchamel aux Truffes).

Reduce a cream béchamel sauce (No. 411) with the oyster liquor; season with salt, cayenne and nutmeg; add the poached oysters (No. 1067) and just when ready to serve, stir in a piece of fresh butter and very finely chopped truffles.

(1066). OYSTERS À LA HOLLANDAISE (Huîtres à la Hollandaise).

Poach the oysters (No. 1067), then drain them, dress them into a deep dish and cover them with a Hollandaise sauce (No. 477).

(1067). FRICASSEED OYSTERS OR À LA POULETTE (Huîtres Fricassées ou à la Poulette).

To Poach Oysters.—Set a saucepan on the hot fire, and place the oysters in it with their own liquor, being careful to stir them about at times to prevent them adhering to the bottom; when firm to the touch, drain them from their liquor. They can also be poached by placing a few at the time between two tin sheets, the top one or cover being smaller than the bottom one, so that the ridge of the top sheet be the same size as the bottom of the lower one. Put the oysters in the bottom buttered sheet with their own liquor, salt, pepper and fresh butter, cover with the smaller sheet turned over, set this on the fire and at the first boil, place it in a slow oven for about ten minutes or until poached, then drain off the liquor.

Oysters Fricasseed or à la Poulette.—Reduce some velouté sauce (No. 415) with oyster liquor, season with salt, pepper and nutmeg, and thicken with egg-yolks diluted in a little cream; incorporate into it a piece of fresh butter, some strained lemon juice and chopped parsley.

(1068). OYSTERS, VIENNAISE (Huîtres Fricassées à la Viennaise).

Reduce some velouté sauce (No. 415) with oyster liquor, and just when prepared to serve, thicken it with raw egg-yolks and cream; stir in a piece of lobster butter (No. 580), and some finely chopped parsley, mix the oysters with the sauce and serve.

(1069). OYSTERS STUFFED À LA MORNAY (Huîtres Farcies à la Mornay).

Poach about thirty medium oysters in their liquor, pare and split them through the center, then stuff this opening with a fine hash made of half lobster, half mushrooms and a little parsley mixed with a little béchamel sauce (No. 409), reduced until it becomes thick; garnish a buttered baking dish with these oysters, cover with a layer of cold Mornay sauce (No. 504), smooth the top nicely and strew over some grated parmesan cheese; and color in a very hot oven or under the gas salamander (Fig. 123).

(1070). OYSTERS STUFFED AND FRIED (Huîtres Farcies et Frites).

Poach large oysters in their own liquor; when cold, trim them and cut them through their thickest part without separating the pieces, then stuff this opening with a preparation of cooked fine herbs mingled with a reduced and thick béchamel sauce (No. 409); press down the top part so as to attach them together, then season. Just when ready to serve bread-crumb them English style (No. 13), and fry them in clarified butter, and after they have attained a fine color, drain and serve them at once on folded napkins.

(1071). OYSTERS WITH CURRY—INDIAN STYLE (Huîtres au Kari à l'Indienne).

Have some large oysters placing them in a saucepan with their own liquor, put on the fire and when slightly firm to the touch, drain and suppress the hard parts. Cut up two ounces of onions into very small squares; fry without coloring, besprinkle with a little flour, and stir well, then moisten with the oyster liquor and white wine, season with salt, pepper and curry, let boil, and despumate; add the oysters and keep warm until ready to serve. In the meantime cook some rice in water with salt and a piece of butter; when done and dry, add to it a very little béchamel sauce (No. 409), also a small pinch of saffron; heat it thoroughly and lay it in a plain border mold (Fig. 139) dipped in cold water; unmold it on the serving dish; lay the oysters inside this border, and send to the table while very hot.

(1072). OYSTERS WITH FINE HERBS (Huîtres aux Fines Herbes).

Drain medium-sized oysters; dry them on a cloth and roll them in flour, then sauté them in very warm butter, and dress them on a hot dish; squeeze over the juice of a lemon, and bestrew the top with chervil, parsley and chives, all finely and separately chopped up.

(1073). OYSTERS WITH PARMESAN FRIED IN OIL (Huîtres au Parmesan Frites à l'Huile).

Take medium sized oysters that have not been poached; drain and dry them in a cloth; then roll them in grated parmesan cheese. Beat up some eggs in a vessel; add the same quantity of cream, stir well, and strain through a strainer, dip the oysters in this, roll them in cracker dust, and smooth them nicely, plunge them into very hot oil, and fry them to a nice golden color, drain, salt, wipe and dress them on folded napkins.

SCALLOPS, ST. JACQUES SHELLS (Pétoncles, Coquilles St. Jacques ou Coquilles des Pélerins).

Testaceous bivalvular mollusks, having a semi-circular shell grooved on the sides forming rays on each valve toward the edges. They are eaten, although of a tough nature.

FIG. 277.

(1074). SCALLOPS À LA BRESTOISE (Pétoncles à la Brestoise).

Cook the scallops in a sautoir with white wine and half as much mushroom liquor, drain and chop them well. Fry in butter without coloring, finely cut up onions, moisten with the scallop broth, add fresh breadcrumbs, and let cook slowly for ten minutes, then add well-chopped lobster coral, fine herbs, salt, nutmeg, a dash of cayenne, a piece of butter and the chopped scallops; mix thoroughly and with this preparation garnish the scallop shells full and rounded on top; besprinkle with fresh bread-crumbs, pour over a little butter, and set them in a moderate oven; when a fine color, dress crown-shaped on folded napkins with sprigs of parsley in the center.

(1075). SCALLOPS À LA HAVRAISE (Pétoncles à la Havraise).

Pour white wine into a saucepan; add the scallops and take them off at the first boil; drain and mince them finely. Fry without coloring some chopped shallots, dredge over a little flour, add the minced scallops and their broth reduced; lobster coral and chopped up parsley. Fill well buttered scallop shells with this preparation, having them rounded on the top, strew over bread-crumbs, besprinkle with butter and color in a hot oven, then dress them on a napkin in a straight row, and garnish with sprigs of parsley.

FIG. 278.

(1076). SCALLOPS À LA MARINIÈRE (Pétoncles à la Marinière).

This simple dish is highly appreciated by amateurs of shell-fish. Cut the scallops up into quarter-inch squares; put them back on their deep shells; season with salt and pepper, dredge over some finely chopped fresh mushrooms, parsley and bread-crumbs, and lay on each a small piece of butter, also a teaspoonful of white wine. Cook in a hot oven from ten to twelve minutes, and after removing them, pour over a little lemon juice, then dress on folded napkins garnishing with sprigs of parsley.

(1077). SCALLOPS, ORLY (Pétoncles à la Orly).

Put the scallops into a bowl with salt, pepper, nutmeg, shallots, oil and lemon juice, let marinate for one hour, then roll them in cracker-dust and plunge them into hot, white frying fat to fry a fine color. They are to be dressed on a folded napkin and garnished with fried parsley, serving a tomato sauce (No. 549) separately.

With Milk and Flour.—Season with salt and pepper; moisten with a little milk, roll them in flour and fry a golden brown; drain, wipe and dress the scallops on a folded napkin.

With Eggs and Bread-crumbs.—Season the scallops with salt and pepper, immerse in beaten eggs, roll in bread-crumbs and fry to a nice color; drain, wipe and dress on a napkin.

(1078). SCALLOPS ON TOAST, BAKED (Croûtes de Pétoncles au Gratin.)

Toast some slices of Jocko bread (No. 3416), and lay them on a well buttered dish. Blanch the scallops in a little white wine, salt and pepper, range them on the toast, one beside the other, very close together. Mix the scallop broth with some béchamel sauce (No. 409), and with this cover all the scallops and toast; besprinkle with bread raspings, grated cheese and butter, and brown them in a hot oven.

(1079). ST. JACQUES SHELLS, PARISIAN STYLE—LARGE SPECIES OF SCALLOPS (Coquilles St. Jacques à la Parisienne—Grands Pétoncles).

Open eight or ten large, fresh St. Jacques shells (Fig. 277—large species of scallops), detach the meats, also the white and red milts, poach with a little white wine, drain and cut them into dice pieces; keep this salpicon aside. Fry some chopped onions and shallots in butter, add raw mushrooms cut in small squares and let cook until they have reduced their moisture, then put in the prepared salpicon five or six minutes later. Season the stew, thickening with freshly reduced béchamel (No. 409), boil again for a few moments without ceasing to stir; it should now be quite consistent; finish off of the fire with a dash of cayenne pepper, a piece of fresh butter and a piece of red butter (No. 580). Take the stew up with a spoon and fill the shells, bestrew the preparation with bread-crumbs, sprinkled over with melted butter and then bake in a moderate oven for ten minutes, take out and dress.

SHRIMPS (Crevettes de Mer).

A small crustacean with a long body, the tail is about as long as the body itself. The two first feet end in a claw shape; only after being cooked or dipped in alcohol does its meat turn red.

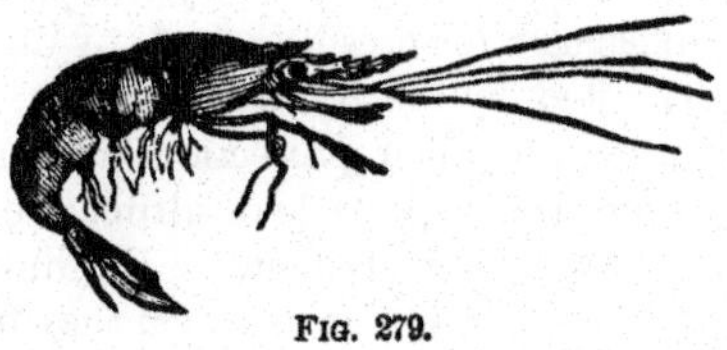

(1080). FRIED SHRIMPS (Crevettes Frites).

Take half a pound of shrimps; they should be alive; wipe them in a cloth. Melt a quarter of a pound of butter in a saucepan, let it settle and pour off the top into a pan; when very hot, add to it the shrimps, season, and fry

FIG. 279.

them over a good fire from eight to ten minutes or until they become a good red color, then serve.

(1081). SHRIMPS WITH MUSHROOMS AND TOMATOED BÉARNAISE (Crevettes aux Champignons à la Béarnaise Tomatée).

Drain some large shrimps; fry them in butter with raw minced mushrooms; season with salt, nutmeg, pepper and lemon juice; add some chopped parsley and a little fish glaze (No. 399). Fill the bottom of a dish with some tomatoed béarnaise (No. 433), and dress the fried shrimps on top, strewing over a little chopped parsley.

TERRAPIN (Terrapène).

Diamond-back or salt water terrapin are found all along the Atlantic coast, but more especially in the Chesapeake bay and its tributaries; other salt water species from Massachusetts to Texas are quite numerous, and as a substitute for those of the Chesapeake are extensively used by houses of ordinary reputation. The scarcity of Chesapeake diamond-back terrapin grows more apparent each year, and even now it frequently requires many days of laborious and tedious work and many

FIG. 280.

miles of walking over soft boggy marshes, of prodding in deep narrow channels with long shafted tongs by men skilled and familiar with all their cunning habits before one is taken from a hiding place, just below the surface, sufficiently deep for protection against the winter frosts. The favorite place for the hibernation of the very largest size is a few inches below the soft oozy mud at the bed

of a three or four fathom V-shaped channel in the bed of a creek of about the same distance from shore to shore. Thousands of such creeks penetrate the shores and islands of the Chesapeake, and those less frequented by man are instinctively selected by the terrapin for its haunts. At least ninety per cent. of those taken from the beds of deep creeks will measure six and one-half to eight and one-half inches with an average weight of nearly two and three-fourths pounds, are females; while eighty per cent. of those bedded in the marshes have an average weight of three-fourths of a pound and measure less than five inches. The males invariably bed in the marshes and among the rushes of very shallow ponds, only venturing in cold water during the summer and the warmest spring and fall months. in which time they lead a migratory life in search of food, consisting principally of small shell fish and the soft-shell crabs. About ninety-eight per cent. of the male terrapin never exceed five inches in length on the bottom shell, while the female has been known to measure nine inches and weigh seven and one-half pounds. In the month of December, 1885, Delmonico received from Baltimore a Chesapeake Maryland terrapin measuring eight and three-fourths inches, weighing nine and one-half pounds and containing fifty-six eggs; this must be accepted as one of the finest specimens ever found of the diamond-back Chesapeake bay terrapin. The standard length for those who buy and sell terrapin is six inches; when of this dimension they are called "counts." Both the male and female are very shy and active, swim well and run (though awkwardly) with considerable speed. Prior to about 1870 the salt and brackish waters of the bay literally teemed with this now nearly exterminated and hence valuable reptile; they could be taken by the dozen at a single haul of a long net, but the market value was so small as to render them almost worthless except for local use, and in consequence thousands of large egg terrapin were fed away to swine or cooked for fattening fowls. The people, thoughtless and unprincipled, have robbed themselves by trapping incalculable quantities of terrapin before they had matured sufficiently for breeding and by digging eggs from beneath the sand shores where they had been deposited by the females to hatch. While the laws enacted by the legislatures of Maryland and Virginia for their protection differ somewhat they are both excellent, and had they been rigidly enforced this spectacle of ultimate extermination would not exist. The time for hibernation usually lasts about six months, beginning with approaching frosty weather in the fall and continuing till the warm spring weather; they bury a few inches deep in the mud and leave, at the spot where they disappear, a mound in the middle of which a hole can be discerned. It is this mound and its hole which first attracts the attention of the fisherman; during this period an enormous quantity of terrapin are caught in their torpid state. They take no nourishment whatever while in this condition. They hatch their young toward the end of June and the beginning of July. The terrapin season is from the month of November to May; they are at their best during December, January, February and March. Very often terrapin are sent to market in October and November, also penned terrapin of the year before.

Penned Terrapin.—Are those caught beforehand and kept in an enclosed place; they are fed on oysters, crabs or fish; these terrapin are never so good as those freshly caught. The small species of terrapin are divided into two classes: heifers, the under shell of these never measuring more than five inches in length, and bulls five to five and a half. Terrapin begin to hatch their eggs at the age of four years; while growing their shell lengthens one inch every year, so their age may be approximately judged by their length, for example: a six-inch terrapin is supposed to be six years old.

TABLE LIST NO. 1.

	Number.	Size.	Pound.	Ounce.	Accord'g to No.	Price per Pound.	Price per Dozen.	Total.
A	12	5	9¾	13	No. 6	$0.90	$ 8.77	
Gross.....................102	12	5¼	15	20	No. 1	1.30	19.50	
Waste 20	12	5½	13½	18	No. 5	1.10	14.85	
—	12	5¾	15¼	21	No. 5	1.15	17.54	
Net......................... 82	12	5¼	14¼	19	No. 2	1.20	17.10	
	12	5½	14¼	19	No.4-5	1.12	15.96	
Average dozen 15.70.							$93.72	
Average weight of each terrapin 18 ounces.								
	12	6¼	22½	30	No. 3	1.60	$36.00	
B	12	6¾	25½	34	No. 5	1.60	40.80	
Gross.....................156	12	6	20	24	No. 6	1.30	23.40	
Waste..................... 20	12	6¼	26	26	No. 6	1.35	27.00	
—	12	6¾	28	34	No. 5	1.60	41.60	
Net.........................136	12	6½	24	32	No. 3	1.65	39.60	
Average dozen 35.15.							$208.40	
Average weight of each 30 ounces.								
	12	7	30	40	No. 4	1.70	$51.00	
C	12	7¼	36	48	No. 3	1.80	64.80	
Gross.....................214	12	7½	34¼	46	No. 5	1.75	59.94	
Waste..................... 20	12	7¾	36¾	49	No. 5	1.80	66.15	
—	12	7	26¼	36	No. 6	1.60	42.00	
Net 194	12	7¼	30¾	42	No. 5	1.70	52.26	
Average dozen 53.72.							$336.15	
Average weight of each 43 ounces.								
	12	8¼	38¼	52	No. 6	1.85	$ 70.76	
D	12	8¼	41¼	55	No. 5	1.90	78.83	
Gross.....................273	12	8	39	52	No. 5	1.85	72.15	
Waste..................... 20	12	8¼	49	65	No. 3	2.05	100.45	
—	12	8	42	56	No. 4	1.90	79.80	
Net.........................253	12	8	44½	59	No. 3	2.00	89.00	
Average dozen 81.08.							$490.54	$1,128.81
Average weight of each 56 ounces.								

The average weight of the dozen for the whole list is 27¾ pounds. The average price of the whole list is $1.70. The average price of the dozen for the whole list is $47.00.

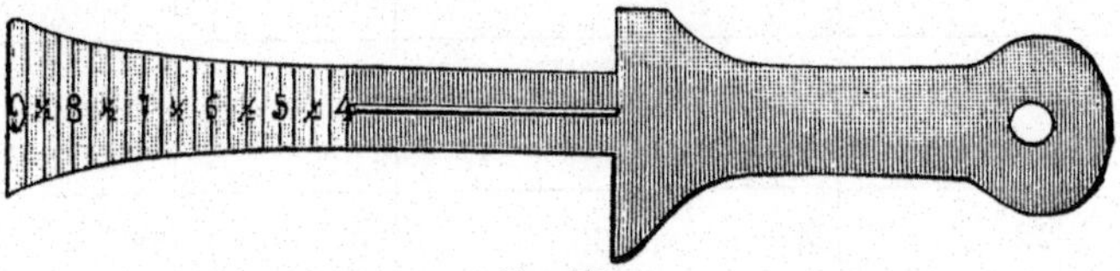

FIG. 281.

The prices quoted above are the actual prices of terrapins in New York, Baltimore and Crisfield, and are liable to fluctuate according to the market supply; this can be overcome by diminishing or augmenting the price per pound.

The letters in the four divisions of the table No. 1, refer to sizes of the terrapins. A. denotes terrapins from five to six inches; B. from six to seven, etc.

To make use of these tables: Weigh the terrapins and barrel as received, deduct weight of barrel, grass, etc., which will leave the net weight. Sort the terrapins by sizes in differences of a quarter of an inch, using the measure shown in Fig. 281. Weigh the terrapins of each size by ounces, then find the average weight of each, refer to table No. 2, looking in the first column for the corresponding length, then find in what column their average weight in ounces is found; in this same section will be found their price by the pound; for instance: a seven and three-quarter inch terrapin weighing 64 ounces at $2.05 cents a pound will cost $8.20, or one dozen will cost $98.40.

TABLE LIST NO. 2.

Length of Under Shell and approximate weight.	No. 1. Price per lb.		No. 2. Price per lb.		No. 3. Price per lb.		No. 4. Price per lb.		No. 5. Price per lb.		No. 6. Price per lb.
5 inches 1 pound	18 oz.	$1.20	17 oz.	$1.15	16 oz.	$1.10	15 oz.	$1 05	14 oz.	$1.00	13 oz.	90c
5¼ inches 1 pound 2 ounces	20	1.30	19	1.20	18	1.15	17	1.10	16	1.05	15	1.00
5½ inches 1 pound 5 ounces	24	1.35	23	1.30	22	1.20	20	1.15	18	1.10	16	1.05
5¾ inches 1 pound 7 ounces	26	1.40	25	1.35	24	1.30	23	1.20	21	1.15	19	1.10
6 inches 1 pound 11 ounces	30	1.65	29	1.60	28	1.50	27	1.40	26	1.35	24	1.30
6¼ inches 1 pound 14 ounces	32	1.70	31	1.65	30	1.60	29	1.50	28	1.40	26	1.35
6½ inches 2 pounds 1 ounce	36	1.75	34	1.70	32	1.65	31	1.60	30	1.50	28	1.40
6¾ inches 2 pounds 5 ounces	42	1.80	40	1.75	38	1.70	36	1.65	34	1.60	32	1.50
7 inches 2 pounds 9 ounces	48	1.85	46	1.80	42	1.75	40	1.70	58	1.65	36	1.60
7¼ inches 2 pounds 14 ounces	52	1.90	50	1.85	48	1.80	46	1.75	42	1.70	40	1.65
7½ inches 3 pounds 1 ounce	56	2.00	52	1.90	50	1 85	48	1.80	46	1.75	44	1.70
7¾ inches 3 pounds 3 ounces	64	2.05	60	2.00	58	1.90	51	1.85	50	1.80	46	1.75
8 inches 3 pounds 8 ounces	72	2.10	64	2.05	60	2.00	56	1.90	52	1.85	48	1.80
8¼ inches 3 pounds 12 ounces	74	2.15	72	2.10	64	2.05	60	2.00	54	1.90	52	1.85
8½ inches 4 pounds	76	2.25	74	2.15	72	2.10	64	2.05	58	2.00	54	1.90

This list is only for the best Chesapeake Maryland terrapins.

To Select Terrapin.—To buy terrapin See Schedules or Tables Nos. 1 and 2. When buying terrapin be careful to observe that the extreme tip or muzzle of the head is not injured, that the bottom of the feet are not worn off, that the head is prettily shaped, small thin and pointed, the eyes brilliant and the feet small and slender. The superiority of their race is made apparent by their fine appearance. There is no doubt that the diamond-back Chesapeake bay terrapin are far better than any other kind found in the markets. Their price is very high, they being sold on an average of the five to six inch ones or over at a $1.25 a pound or $15.00 to $17.00 a dozen; the six to seven inch ones bring $1.50 a pound or $35.00 to $40.00 a dozen; the seven to eight inch ones bring $1.75 a pound or $55.00 to $60.00 a dozen; the eight to nine inches bring $1.90 a pound or $80.00 to $85.00 a dozen. They should be procured before the extreme cold weather sets in to avoid freezing during the trip, for once frost bitten they die easily.

To Keep the Terrapin.—In order to keep them properly they must be left in a cold place forty to forty-five degrees Fahrenheit; it should also be clean, well aired, dark and better be too damp than too dry. They must be placed in large or small boxes according to the quantity; range the terrapin in the boxes, pressing them down one beside the other so that they cannot possibly move, and between each bed lay damp sea grass. When packed like this they may be kept for several months. Examine the terrapin now and then. Should there be any dead ones take them out. They must be handled with care, laid one next to the other, not thrown, as they are very tender and delicate and are liable to die easily, incurring a heavy loss, as a dead terrapin is a ruined one and ought to be thrown away at once. No eggs are found in terrapin of less than six inches long.

(1082). TO PREPARE AND COOK TERRAPIN (Pour Préparer et Cuire la Terrapène).

Drop the terrapin in sufficient tepid water to allow it to swim, and leave them thus for half an hour, then change the water several times and wash them well. Scald, by plunging them into boiling water, and take out as quickly as the skin (a small white skin on the head and feet) can be removed with a cloth, put them on to cook in water without any salt or seasoning, or else in a steam vessel leaving them for thirty to forty-five minutes, and lift them out as quickly as they are done. In order to be sure of this, press the feet meat between the fingers, and if it yields easily under the pressure, they are ready. Those that cannot be cooked in forty-five minutes are considered of an inferior quality, and those that are not done after one hour (unless they are very large), should be rejected as worthless, for although the meat may eventually become tender, it will be stringy and not have the same delicate taste of a good terrapin. Let them get cold, cut off the nails, then break the shell on the flat side, on both sides near the upper or top one; detach this shell from the meats, empty out all the insides found in this upper shell, suppressing the entrails and lights, and carefully removing the gall bladder from the liver, being very particular not to break it, also cutting away with the tip of a small knife any gall spots to be found thereon, then place the liver in cold water. Remove the white inside muscles, as well as the head and tail; separate the legs at their joints and divide into an inch and a quarter pieces; do not break the bones; the lights, entrails, head, tail, claws, heart, muscles and gall bladder to be thrown away. Lay the terrapin in a saucepan with the eggs and liver cut in thin slices, season with salt, black pepper and cayenne, and cover with sufficient water to attain to the heighth of the terrapin, then let boil and finish the cooking in a slow oven for twenty to thirty minutes; the terrapin is now ready to be used, and can easily be finished by following the recipes found later on. Should it only be required for the next day, place in tin molds or else small China pots, the proportions being at the inside bottom two and three-eighths inches, on top, three inches in diameter, and two and three-eighth inches high. Allow four or six eggs to each, fill them up with terrapin, about six ounces for each, and finish filling with the broth; each mold will contain one portion. When unmolded each one should weigh seven ounces. This quantity will be sufficient for two or three persons for a dinner and for five persons for a buffet.

(1083). TERRAPIN À LA BALTIMORE (Terrapène à la Baltimore).

Have one quart of prepared terrapin as explained in No. 1082; drain it off. Cook four ounces of butter in a saucepan till it becomes hazelnut butter (No. 567), but watch carefully that it does not blacken; add to it the terrapin with some salt, freshly ground black pepper and a pinch of cayenne, fry for few moments, then moisten with the broth. Dilute one tablespoonful of fecula, arrowroot or cornstarch in a little cold water, pour it in with the terrapin, toss well to thicken nicely, and just when ready to serve add half a gill of good sherry wine. After the terrapin has been prepared it is served in chafing dishes kept warm by water boiling continuously by means of an alcohol lamp,

FIG. 282.

FIG. 283.

or else in small silver plated saucepans (Fig. 282) or in China terrapins (Fig. 283), the backs of which are loose and are used as covers; whichever way may be chosen, be most particular that the terrapin is always served very hot.

(1084). TERRAPIN À LA CRISFIELD (Terrapène à la Crisfield).

Heat well four ounces of butter in a sautoir, and place a quart of cooked and drained terrapin into it, season with salt and cayenne, and fry the terrapin for a few minutes, then add one pint of good fresh cream. Reduce this cream to half, thickening with a tablespoonful of rice flour diluted with half a gill of sweet cream; pour in when ready to serve, half a gill of good sherry wine.

(1085). TERRAPIN À LA MARYLAND OR PHILADELPHIA (Terrapène à la Maryland ou à la Philadelphie).

Pound eight hard egg-yolks, with four ounces of butter; then pass through a sieve. Prepare and cook one quart of terrapin as explained for No. 1082, add a pint of cream, let boil for five minutes, then thicken it with the prepared egg-yolks and butter, and let simmer for ten minutes, seasoning with salt, and white or cayenne pepper; just when serving mix in half a gill of good sherry or Madeira wine.

(1086). TERRAPIN À LA NEWBERG OR DELMONICO (Terrapène à la Newberg ou à la Delmonico).

Prepare and cook the terrapin the same as No. 1082. For each quart, add a half a pint of cream, reduce to half, season with salt and cayenne pepper, thicken with five raw egg-yolks diluted with half a pint of cream, and two ounces of fresh butter, toss the terrapin while adding the thickening; this must not boil, finishing with half a gill of very good sherry wine or Madeira. The sauce should be thick and served very hot.

(1087). TERRAPIN, ANCIENT STYLE (Terrapène à l'Ancienne).

Choose a six and a half inch terrapin, scald to remove the skin, and wrap it in several sheets of buttered paper; put it on a baking sheet and set it into a slow oven; it will take about an hour to cook; unwrap, and break the shell; remove the meats, suppress the gall-bag attached to the liver, also any spots found on the same, and cut it up into slices; take away the head, tail, claws, and white muscles on the four members, and then warm the terrapin in a good thick gravy (No. 405), season with salt, freshly ground pepper, cayenne, butter, adding some good sherry wine. Serve on a chafing dish.

(1088). TERRAPIN, MARYLAND CLUB (Terrapène, Maryland Club).

Have the terrapin ready and cooked as for No. 1082. For one quart of it, place four ounces of butter in a sautoir on the fire; let it heat and skim it well until it begins to become (nut butter); add to it the terrapin, and season with salt, cayenne and black pepper, also half a gill of good sherry. It can also be prepared by placing it in a chafing dish with salt, cayenne, fresh butter, and half a gill of good sherry.

(1089). CUTLETS OF TERRAPIN AND CROQUETTES, CREAM SAUCE (Côtelettes de Terrapène et Croquettes Sauce Crème).

Have a pound and a half of cooked and boneless terrapin, cut in half inch squares; put these on the fire in a stewpan, seasoning with salt and red pepper; heat well and thicken with egg-yolks, butter, and cream moistened with a little good sherry; let get partially cold and then mold in cutlet-shaped bottomless molds laid on a sheet of heavy buttered paper slightly larger than the mold itself, and set on level baking tins. Fill the molds to the top with terrapin, lay them on ice, and when the preparation is perfectly cold, unmold and dip the cutlets into beaten eggs, roll in bread-crumbs, then fry them in clarified butter; wipe and dress crown-shaped on folded napkins, garnishing the center with fried green parsley. If for croquettes mold the terrapin in timbale molds (No. 2, Fig. 137) and finish the same as the cutlets; serve a cream sauce (No. 545) separately.

(1090). STEWED TERRAPIN WITH MADEIRA WINE (Ragoût de Terrapène au Madère).

After the terrapin have been cut up, fry them in butter, then dredge over a little flour that has been browned in the oven. Fry once more for a few minutes, moisten with half white wine and half broth (No. 194a), season with salt and pepper, and let simmer and despumate for twenty minutes; finish cooking in the oven for thirty or forty minutes longer, and just when prepared to serve, add a little good Sherry or Madeira wine.

(1090a). TERRAPIN À LA TRENTON (Terrapène à la Trenton).

Prepare two terrapins, each weighing three pounds; when cooked and ready, as explained in No. 1082, add one pint of cream and reduce to half; then thicken with three hard-boiled eggs reduced to a paste with three ounces of butter and three coffeespoonfuls of fecula diluted in three spoonfuls of good sherry. Season with salt, freshly ground black pepper, a teaspoonful of paprika and a teaspoonful of powdered sweet Spanish peppers; finish with a little good sherry.

(1090b). TERRAPIN, EPICUREAN STYLE (Terrapène à l'Épicurienne).

The diamond-back Chesapeake, Maryland terrapins are considered the best. They must be freshly caught. Long Island terrapins are also much liked by epicures, some averring that they are as fine as the Chesapeake, but this is not a fact, and I do not hesitate to class them according to the following order: First, the Chesapeake, then the Long Island, Virginia, Charleston and Savannah, North Carolina, Florida, Mississippi and Texas, the Gulf, Mobile, etc. Take two terrapins, each one of three pounds weight, and prepare them as described in No. 1082. Fry in two ounces of butter, adding two ounces of rice flour well mingled in; moisten with water as high as the terrapin and let boil until thoroughly cooked, seasoning with salt and pepper; add a pint of cream and reduce; finish with three hard-boiled egg-yolks, pounded and formed into a paste with three tablespoonfuls of good sherry wine. Serve separately on a folded napkin some very small oysters, drained and rolled in cracker dust, then fried in butter; surround these with quartered lemons.

TURTLE (Tortue).

An amphibious quadruped, having all its body, except the head, feet, and tail, covered with a very hard shell. It is enclosed in a cuirass composed of two pieces; the one covering the back is

FIG. 284.

called the carapace; this is convex shaped; the vertebra are attached to it. The underneath one is attached to the breast; this is flat and is called the plastron. The choicest and most delicate part of the turtle is that attached to the upper shell.

(1091). TURTLE, HAVANA STYLE (Tortue à la Havanaise).

Lard the fins of a turtle with calf's udder, braise them in a mirepoix stock (No. 419), moistened with Madeira, and when the turtle is cooked, take out the stock and put it into a flat saucepan with an equal quantity of espagnole sauce (No. 414); reduce and despumate; add some finely shredded green peppers, peeled and quartered tomatoes, Spanish olives stuffed with anchovies and fish quenelles (No. 90); glaze the turtle with meat glaze (No. 402), dress with the garnishing around, and serve.

(1092). GREEN TURTLE BAKED—SMALL (Petite Tortue Verte au Gratin).

Obtain a young turtle weighing ten pounds; remove and lard the meat with small lardons; clean well the carapace; braise the meats in a mirepoix stock (No. 419) with the belly shells, letting the meats be well cooked, and the braise stock reduced to half; transfer the meats to a vessel, strain the stock over and let it get cold. Cut the meats up into quarter inch squares, as well as the cutaneous parts from the belly. Fry in butter four ounces of onions cut in squares; sift over some flour, and moisten with the stock; add the turtle meat; stir the preparation until it comes to a boil, season and thicken with hard boiled egg-yolks mixed with an equal quantity of butter, and press through a fine sieve. Add some parsley and finely chopped raw mushrooms; then use this stew to fill up the carapace or deep shell; bestrew over with bread-raspings, besprinkle with butter and brown a nice color in a slow oven; serve when very hot.

(1093). TURTLE STEWED À LA FOSTER (Ragoût de Tortue à la Foster).

Cut the turtle meat into one inch and a quarter squares; fry them in butter, and sprinkle over with flour, stir well, then moisten with broth, adding a bunch of parsley garnished with thyme and bay leaf, small onions, a piece of bacon cut into three-sixteenth inch squares, and mushrooms cut the same; season with salt, black and red pepper, this should not be confused with cayenne pepper, they are entirely different (No. 168); when the stew is done and ready to serve, pour in a little Madeira wine, suppress the parsley, reduce it properly and serve.

FISH (Poisson).

(1094). ANGEL FISH À LA BAHAMA (Poisson Ange à la Bahama).

Prepare a wine court bouillon (No. 39), dress an angel or moon fish, tying down the head. Place this fish on a fish kettle grate; just cover it with the cold court bouillon, and allow the liquid to come to a boil, then set it on one side of the range; cover the top with a buttered paper and let cook without boiling; the time it will take depends entirely upon the size of the fish; if it weighs six to eight pounds, it will certainly take from one hour to one hour and a quarter. When finished, drain, and slide it on a dish; surround with clusters of cooked shrimps and cooked mushrooms and cover the garnishing with a lean velouté sauce (No. 416) with white wine, the court bouillon and two cloves of garlic added; reduce this to the consistency of a sauce, then take out the garlic and add some powdered sweet Spanish peppers and curry; serve the remainder of the sauce separately.

(1095). BLACK BASS À LA NARRAGANSETT (Bass Noir à la Narragansett).

Cut the bass through its entire length in two; suppress the fillet skin and remove the back bone; divide each fillet in two lengthwise pieces, then into slices, half an inch thick; have twelve of these paring them all into half-hearts; range them in a well buttered sautoir, one beside the other, moistening to their height with a mirepoix stock (No. 419). Cover over with a sheet of buttered paper, and set this into a slow oven to cook, then transfer the fillets on a dish, and strain the broth over the fillets; when cold remove them entirely from what now should be a jelly; reduce some velouté sauce (No. 415) with this jelly and mushroom essence (No. 392); when reduced quite thick, add chopped mushrooms and fine herbs and set it aside to get partially cold; cover the entire fillets with this, leave them until perfectly cold, then pare nicely and dip in beaten eggs, roll in bread-crumbs and fry to a fine color in clarified butter; dress crown shaped on a folded napkin with fried parsley in the center and quartered lemon around. Serve a separate sauce-boat of the following sauce: Chop up one shallot, fry it in butter, add to it twelve small finely minced clams without any liquor, and moisten with a pint of unsalted béchamel (No. 409). Season to taste; when ready to serve thicken with egg-yolks and cream, incorporating a good sized piece of fresh butter, lemon juice and chopped parsley.

(1096). BLACK BASS AIGUILLETTES WITH OYSTER CRABS (Aiguillettes de Bass Noir aux Crabes d'Huîtres).

Pare twelve fillets of black bass free of skin, shaping into aiguillettes; season with salt and pepper, then put them into a sautoir, and moisten with fish stock (No. 195) and the oyster crab broth; cook in a slow oven, basting them frequently while they are cooking, then drain off the liquid and reduce it with the same quantity of velouté sauce (No. 415). Just when prepared to serve, incorporate into it a good sized piece of butter, then strain through a tammy. Put the oyster crabs into a sautoir with a little white wine, set it on the fire, and at the first boil drain them well. Dress the fish in two straight rows on a long dish; set the oyster crabs between these two rows, and cover the whole with half of the sauce, serving the other half separately.

(1097). BLACK BASS WITH SWEET PEPPERS (Bass Noir aux Poivrons Doux).

Split the bass lengthwise on the belly side to the back, but do not separate the pieces; take out the backbone; season with salt, baste with a little oil, besprinkle with fresh bread-crumbs, and broil over a slow fire, turning it once only; when done dress on a hot dish. Garnish around with sweet peppers fried in oil with a little crushed and chopped garlic, salt, black and prepared red pepper (No. 168), fine herbs and lemon juice.

(1098). RED BASS. WATER FISH (Bass Rouge. "Water Fish").

Cut into short Julienne some carrots, leeks, parsley root and celery root; slice or cut some onions into squares, and put all into a saucepan to moisten with fish broth (No. 195); boil and reduce to a glaze; moisten again with water, add salt and the fish whole, cooking it in this court bouillon. Drain, reduce the stock, thickening it with a little velouté sauce (No. 415), the juice of a lemon, and butter; mix in with it blanched parsley leaves. Dress the fish on a folded napkin, surround with sprigs of parsley and serve the sauce separate.

(1099). SEA BASS À LA VILLEROI (Bass de Mer à la Villeroi).

Remove the fillets, bones, and skin from a sea bass; pare the fillets into half-heart shapes and season each piece with salt and pepper; sauté these in butter with lemon juice, and take them out singly to place on a baking sheet; set a light weight on top; when cold pare them exactly alike and cover over with a well reduced allemande sauce (No. 407) and a little jelly, into which has been added finely chopped mushrooms and parsley; let get very cold, then bread-crumb them by rolling them first in bread-crumbs, afterward in beaten eggs, and once more in the bread-crumbs; smooth the surfaces with the blade of a knife, and lay them at the bottom of a wire basket; plunge it in very hot frying fat, taking them out when a fine color; dress on napkins and serve with fried parsley as a garnishing.

(1100). SEA BASS WITH ALMOND BUTTER (Bass de Mer au Beurre d'Amandes).

Remove the fillets from the fish; season them with salt and pepper, saturate with oil, and broil over a slow fire without browing; dress and surround the fillets with potato balls three-quarters of an inch in diameter, first boiled, then sautéd in butter. Cover the surface of the fish with slightly melted almond butter (No. 568), and besprinkle the potatoes with finely chopped parsley.

(1101). STRIPED OR ROCK BASS À LA BERCY (Bass Rayé ou de Roches à la Bercy).

Prepare two small bass each of two pounds, and when very clean cut the heads into pieces, adding a few large bones from other fish; put all these into a small saucepan and moisten to their height with a good fish court bouillon, prepared with white wine (No. 39); season, let the liquid boil for a quarter of an hour so as to extract all the essence from the bones, then strain and skim

FIG. 285.

off the fat. Have a small oval baking-tin with raised edges, just large enough to hold the fillets of fish; sprinkle over with chopped up onions, shallots, and mushroom parings; lay the fillets of fish on top and moisten to its heighth with some of the above court bouillon; after the liquid has come to a boil, set the pan into a moderate oven so that the fish cooks for fifteen minutes, then drain and dress the fillets on a medium sized dish covering it with a smaller one to keep it hot.

Strain the broth, free it from fat, and pour into it two spoonfuls of good white wine, then let it reduce to the consistency of a half-glaze; take it off, stir in a piece of butter, finishing with lemon juice; pour this sauce over the fish. Glaze this sauce immediately with an iron or gas salamander for two minutes, or if there be neither, lay the dish on a thick baking sheet and set it in a brisk oven, being careful not to disturb the sauce. The delicacy of this preparation depends entirely upon the excellence of the court bouillon.

(1102). STRIPED BASS À LA CONTI (Bass Rayé à la Conti).

Lift the fillets of bass; suppress the skin and trim them into half inch thick slices, paring them into half-hearts, two inches by two and a half; season. Cut also from the fish small strips three inches long, and three-quarters of an inch wide, sloping the ends down to points; make five or six bias incisions through half their thickness and fill each one with a slice of very green pickled gherkin; lay these strips on the largest end of the fillet, shaping them like a horseshoe, and place the fillets in a buttered sautoir; moisten with a good white wine court-bouillon (No. 39), and cover over with a sheet of strong buttered paper; bring the liquid to a boil and finish cooking in a slow oven for ten to fifteen minutes. Dress and garnish with three-quarters of an inch ball-shaped potato croquettes (No. 2782), strain the broth and reduce it to the consistency of a glaze, finishing the sauce with a good sized piece of butter, stirring it in with a wire whisk, also the juice of a lemon and chopped parsley.

(1103). STRIPED BASS À LA LAGUIPIERRE (Bass Rayé à la Laguipierre).

Lift off the fillets from several bass, three-quarters of a pound each; suppress the skin and beat them down with the handle of a knife, fold them in two in the center, and trim them half heart-shaped, then lay them in a buttered sautoir and moisten with a good court bouillon (No. 38). Prepare small pike quenelles (No. 90), some oysters or mussels and mushrooms; have a velouté sauce (No. 415), reduced with some of the court bouillon and thickened with egg-yolks and cream; strain through a sieve and keep half of it aside; to the other half add the quenelles, mushrooms and oysters. Dress the well-drained fish crown-shaped, fill the center with the stew, and cover the fish with half of the remaining sauce, sending the other half to the table in a sauce-boat. Do not garnish the fish with potatoes, when the sauce is poured over it, serve them separately.

(1104). STRIPED BASS À LA LONG BRANCH (Bass Rayé à la Long Branch).

After the bass has been dressed and cleaned remove the fillets and meats adhering to the skin, trimming them into half inch thick slices shaped like half-hearts, three and a half inches by two; place on a baking sheet, cover with buttered paper, and poach them in butter and a court bouillon (No. 38); let get slightly cold under the pressure of a weight; drain and pare them again. Prepare a good essence (No. 388), with the heads and bones of the fish; skim off the fat and strain, then slowly incorporate into it one quart of reduced velouté (No. 415); add a little oyster liquor and mushroom essence (No. 392), and when the sauce is properly reduced and of a sufficient succulence, thicken it with egg-yolks and finish with a piece of crawfish butter (No. 573); when partly cold cover the fillets with a thick layer of this sauce, and set them aside to get cold. Dip each piece of fish into beaten eggs, bread-crumbs, and fry of a good color in clarified butter, drain and dress on folded napkins.

(1105). STRIPED BASS À LA MAINTENON (Bass Rayé à la Maintenon).

Procure small bass weighing from four to six ounces; cleanse and wash them well; wipe dry and remove the skin on each side; season with salt and coat over with butter; wrap them up in heavy oiled paper, then broil them for fifteen or twenty minutes; unwrap and dress them on a dish; glaze over with lobster butter (No. 580), and surround with oyster bellies and pike quenelles (No. 734). Cover these garnishings with lobster sauce (No. 488), and serve at the same time a separate bowl of the sauce.

(1106). STRIPED BASS À LA MASSENA—WHOLE (Bass Rayé à la Masséna—Entier).

Fry colorless in butter, two ounces of onions cut in one-eighth of an inch squares, as much carrots cut the same, as much minced mushrooms, one bay leaf, the same quantity of thyme and parsley leaves, moistening with white wine and broth, half and half; cook together for twenty minutes and let get cold. Clean and dress a bass of six pounds, place it in the fish kettle, and pour over the prepared court-bouillon; boil and skim the liquid when required, then remove it from the hot fire and continue boiling slowly for forty-five minutes, drain, and strain the stock, and add part of this to an allemande sauce (No. 407), reduce the two together. When ready to serve dress the bass, glaze it with fish glaze (No. 399), mingled with lobster butter (No. 580), garnish around with sautéd mushrooms and lobster escalops sautéd with fine herbs. Incorporate into the sauce a large piece of lobster butter, pour two-thirds over the lobster and mushrooms, surround these with oysters à la villeroi (No. 698), and serve the rest of the sauce in a separate sauce-boat.

(1107). STRIPED BASS À LA MORNAY (Bass Rayé à la Mornay).

Remove the fillets from a bass, skin and pare nicely, then lay them one beside the other (the side the skin was on being uppermost) on an oval-shaped raised edge baking pan, covering the bottom with butter and finely sliced onions and carrots; moisten to their heighth with a white wine court bouillon (No. 39), season with salt, and cover the top with a buttered paper; cook in a slow oven basting the fillets frequently. When the fish is done, drain it off and dress the pieces on a dish, covering it with another smaller one to keep it warm. Strain and reduce the gravy, incorporating into it a few spoonfuls of good béchamel (No. 409); when it appears rich and succulent, finish with some parmesan cheese, butter, and a pinch of cayenne pepper; pour this sauce over the fish, dredge grated parmesan on top, and let it bake slightly in a very hot oven or brown the surface with an iron or gas salamander (Fig. 123).

(1108). STRIPED BASS À LA ROUENNAISE (Bass Rayé à la Rouennaise).

Dress the fish and put it into a fish kettle, moistening with a mirepoix (No. 419), and white wine, adding to it a few branches of parsley; when the fish is done, drain the stock, and reduce it; mingle it with a Normande sauce (No. 509), finished with lobster butter (No. 580). Dish up the fish and garnish around with blanched oysters, mushroom heads, and pike quenelles (No. 90), molded with a teaspoon (No. 155), the whole arranged in clusters. Cover over with half of the sauce, and serve the remainder in a sauce-boat. Besides these garnishings an outside row of trussed crawfish should be added.

(1109). STRIPED BASS À LA WHITNEY (Bass Rayé à la Whitney).

Remove the fillets from a striped bass; lift off the skin and pare them half heart-shaped; lay them in a buttered sautoir, season with salt, red pepper, and finely chopped shallots; moisten exactly to their height with a court bouillon and white wine (No. 39); cover with buttered paper, then set it on the fire to cook slowly for twenty-five minutes; drain the liquid from the fish, and reduce it with as much velouté sauce (No. 415) to the consistency of a light sauce, thickening with raw egg-yolks and cream, incorporating also into it a piece of fresh butter. Pare the fillets, dress them crown shaped and garnish the center with lobster escalops, minced truffles and mushrooms. Cover the whole with two-thirds of the sauce, sending the rest to the table in a separate sauce-boat.

(1110). STRIPED BASS BOILED WITH HOLLANDAISE MODERN SAUCE (Bass Rayé bouilli, Sauce Hollandaise Moderne).

Wash and clean well a six pound bass, tie down the head and put it into a fish-boiler with plenty of salt and a large bunch of parsley garnished with a clove of garlic; cover it entirely with cold water containing a little vinegar. Set the kettle on a brisk fire, boil the liquid, skimming off the scum at the first boil, then place it on one side of the range to keep bubbling while covered for three-quarters of an hour; drain and dress it on a folded napkin, garnishing one side with boiled potato balls and the other with small potato croquettes (No. 2782), shaped either as balls or olives, and at the ends lay very green sprigs of parsley. Accompany this with a sauce-boat of modern hollandaise sauce (No. 501).

(1111). STRIPED BASS, SHRIMP SAUCE WITH FRIED SCALLOPS (Bass Rayé Sauce Crevette aux Pétoncles Frits).

Lift the fillets from a three pound bass, pare them neatly, removing the skin, and lay them on a buttered dish, seasoning with salt and pepper; moisten with white wine and court bouillon, (No. 39), and let cook in a slow oven without attaining a color, then dress on a hot dish. Roll some scallops in flour, fry them in very hot fat without browning, drain and put them into a frying pan containing a piece of butter; color slightly, besprinkle with salt and chopped parsley. Cover the fish, with a shrimp sauce (No. 540), lay the scallops around and send some of the sauce to the table in a separate sauce-boat.

(1112). STRIPED BASS WITH FINE HERBS (Bass Rayé aux Fines Herbes).

Pare some boneless and skinless fillets of bass in the shape of half hearts; put them in a sautoir after buttering it well, and moisten them with wine and mushroom liquor; cover and put to cook in a slack oven; drain off the liquid, pour it into a sautéing pan with as much velouté sauce (No. 415); reduce well and finish by incorporating a large piece of butter and some lemon juice; taste to judge of its seasoning and add more accordingly. Strain this sauce through a tammy (No. 159), add some chopped blanched parsley and dress the fish in a circle or a straight row, then cover with the sauce and serve immediately.

(1113). STRIPED BASS WITH WHITE WINE—BAKED (Bass Rayé Gratiné au Vin Blanc).

Take off the fillets from a medium sized bass weighing about two pounds, remove the skin from these and lay each whole fillet on the dish intended for serving, and that can be placed in the oven; cover the fish with white wine, and strew over some onions cut in thin slices, sprigs of parsley, thyme, bay leaf, mushroom parings, salt, pepper, and a few small bits of butter. Cover with another dish of the same shape, only smaller and put it in the oven for fifteen to twenty minutes; now drain off the liquid, reduce it with as much velouté sauce (No. 415), and when very well reduced, strain through a tammy (No. 159), and incorporate in two ounces of butter, working it thoroughly with a small wire whip. Pour this all over the fish to cover it entirely, strew the top with grated parmesan or fine bread-raspings, and let it attain a fine color in the hot oven or salamander (Fig. 123); serve as soon as it is browned.

(1114). BLACKFISH À LA ORLY (Blackfish à la Orly).

Lift the fillets from a blackfish; remove the skin by laying the black side on a very level table or board; press down on the fish with the left hand, while with the right pass a knife between the skin and flesh. Divide the fillets into thin, lengthwise slices; marinate them in salt, sweet oil with minced onions, lemon juice, and tarragon leaves; two hours later drain them on a cloth, flour over, and dip in a good frying batter (No. 133); plunge them into hot fat, and cook slowly till a fine color, then drain, salt, and dress them on napkins with sliced lemon around; serve a tomato sauce (No. 549) separately.

(1115). BLACKFISH A LA SANFORD (Blackfish à la Sanford).

Remove the fillets from sufficient blackfish leaving on the black skin; divide each fillet into two pieces. Cover the bottom of a sautoir with butter, chopped shallots, and onions, and chopped mushrooms; lay on top the pieces of blackfish, and a branch of parsley, and moisten with a court bouillon (No. 38), let boil slowly for six minutes, then remove the sautoir on a very slow fire; when done lift out the fish with a spatula, suppress the black skin, and dress it on a dish. Garnish with handsome mushroom heads, oysters, and parsley sprigs; strain the broth, reduce it to a half-glaze, and thicken it with a pint of reduced velouté sauce (No. 415). Finish it away from the fire with butter, lemon juice, and a very little finely shredded chives.

(1116). BLACKFISH À LA VILLARET (Blackfish à la Villaret).

Cook a whole blackfish in a mirepoix stock with white wine (No. 419), drain the stock after the fish is done, strain, and reduce it with the same quantity of velouté sauce (No. 415), adding chopped up shallots; thicken the sauce with raw egg-yolks, cream, fresh butter, and fish glaze (No. 399); strain it again through a tammy and finish with chopped parsley. Range the fish on a dish, garnish around with potato croquettes (No. 2782), and branches of parsley, sending the sauce to the table in a separate sauce-boat.

(1117). BLUEFISH À LA BARNAVE (Bluefish à la Barnave).

Select very small bluefish weighing half a pound; clean, wash, and wipe them dry. Fill the insides with a pike quenelle forcemeat (No. 90), into which has been mixed a quarter of the same quantity of cooked fine herbs (No. 385). Range the fish on a buttered baking dish, sprinkle over some butter and cook in a moderate oven; when done dress them on a mushroom purée (No. 722), and serve a separate barnave sauce (No. 431), at the same time as the fish.

(1118). BLUEFISH, HAVANESE STYLE (Bluefish à la Havanaise).

Clean a bluefish weighing six pounds; wash and wipe it nicely; raise the fillets, suppress the skin and pare them half heart-shaped. Put some clarified butter into a sautoir on a brisk fire and when hot, lay in the pieces of fish; sauté, then drain and dry them, afterward dress them crown shaped on a baking dish. Have already prepared a good tomato sauce made from peeled tomatoes cut into five-eighths inch squares, minced mushrooms and four ounces of onions cut into three sixteenth inch pieces; half a pound of sweet peppers, half a pint of espagnole sauce (No. 414), two pints of fish broth (No. 195); reduce the whole properly and cover the fish thickly with this preparation, then set it into the oven and serve after a few moments, dredging over some chopped up parsley.

(1119). BLUEFISH DEVILED (Bluefish à la Diable).

Have well cleansed, washed and dried bluefish; split them open on the belly side without separating the parts, dredge over salt and pepper and besprinkle with oil; broil them till half done then cover over with diluted mustard, strew bread-crumbs on top and finish broiling the fish over a slow fire. Serve the following sauce in a sauce-boat: Chop up two shallots; place them in a saucepan with a gill of vinegar, a crushed and chopped clove of garlic, whole black peppers, green peppers, bay leaf, espagnole sauce (No. 414), and gravy. Let simmer, despumate and strain through a tammy (No. 159), finishing with a little chopped parsley when serving.

(1120). BLUEFISH IN PAPERS (Bluefish en Papillotes).

Fry colorless in butter one ounce of shallots and the same quantity of mushrooms and half as many truffles as mushrooms, chopping each one finely and separately; moisten with a half-glaze sauce (No. 413), and some gravy, then reduce this sauce, add to it a little chopped parsley and let get partially cold. Oil some pieces of paper cut heart-shaped; pour some of the sauce on one of their sides, lay the fish on top with more sauce over and fold the paper in such a manner that it thoroughly encloses the fish, and is air tight, range the papers on a serving dish, sprinkle over a little oil, and set it into a hot oven and when they swell and are of a fine color send them to the table at once.

(1121). BLUEFISH WITH MAYONNAISE AND TARRAGON (Bluefish à la Mayonnaise et à l'Estragon).

Lift the fillets from very fresh bluefish, also the skin covering the meats by placing the fish on a very even board and pressing down on the fish with one hand, while using the other to slip a thin, straight knife between the skin and meat. Cut the fish into slices, season, and bread them by first dipping them in eggs and then in bread-crumbs; put the pieces on to cook in a sautoir with clarified butter, being careful to turn them over when nicely browned on one side; when done equally well on both sides, drain and serve them on a hot dish surrounded with quartered lemons. Serve separately at the same time a mayonnaise sauce with tarragon (No. 612).

(1122). BONITO OR TUNNY FISH À LA GODIVIER (Bonite ou Thon à la Godivier).

Raise the fillets from a young bonito or tunny fish after having washed and cleansed it well; place it in a buttered sautoir and moisten to its height with a mirepoix stock (No. 419). Cover with heavy buttered paper, let boil, and finish cooking in a slack oven. Fry one shallot in butter, dilute it with some of the fish stock and the same quantity of espagnole sauce (No. 414); after the sauce is well reduced mix in with it a little tomato sauce (No. 549), a little crushed garlic and some chopped parsley. Dress the bonito, lift off its skin and pour the sauce over.

(1123). BOUILLABAISSE MARENGO (Bouillabaisse à la Marengo).

Procure several fishes of medium size, and firm meats, such as sheepshead, blackfish and bass, and two small live lobsters; all these fish must be of the very freshest. Cut off the fins and projecting bones from the fish, suppress the heads and thin tail ends, then cut them into pieces about two inches in size; break off the lobster tails after killing them in boiling water, then place all these pieces of fish in a tureen to salt, laying a piece of ice on top. Finish cooking the two lobster bodies in the same water, drain and split open; remove all the creamy parts, rub them through a sieve, and chop up the remaining parts of the bodies. Have a sauce-pan containing a little oil, fry in it a mirepoix (No. 419), and minced onions, add two cloves of garlic, a bunch of parsley, aromatic herbs, peelings of fresh mushrooms, the two chopped bodies, the heads and trimmings of all the fish, also a few cut up small bony fishes. Moisten to their heighth with hot fish broth (No. 195); cook for fifteen to twenty minutes on a good fire, letting the liquid reduce to one third; strain and remove the fat. Line the bottom of a deep sautoir with two cut up seedless tomatoes, onions, and shallots; range the pieces of fish and lobster on top, one beside the other, and moisten to their heighth with the prepared stock; it should just be sufficient to cover, otherwise reduce it. Cook the fish in this for fifteen to eighteen minutes over a brisk fire, then remove the pan on one side, and strain a part of the liquid into another saucepan; thicken this with a few spoonfuls of tomato sauce (No. 549), and when succulent and thick, take it off, pour in some burnt brandy, and the creamy parts of lobster, adding a dash of cayenne pepper; finish it with butter. Dress the pieces of fish in a pyramid form, surround this with a crown of thin crusts of kitchen bread browned nicely in butter, and cover the fish and crusts with some of the sauce, serving the surplus in a bowl.

(1124). PARISIAN BOUILLABAISSE (Bouillabaisse à la Parisienne).

For eight persons this dish requires ten pounds of fish such as bass, angel fish groupper or any other fish having firm flesh, the tail of a small lobster and a few large crawfish; all this fish must be of a superior quality and of the very freshest. Suppress the heads and thin tail ends from all the fish after cleaning well, and with the bones, head and parings prepare a good broth. Cut the bodies of the largest ones into steaks or squares; chop up a white onions, and a piece of the white of leek; with these bestrew the bottom of a saucepan wider than its heighth, add two small seeded and chopped tomatoes, two cloves of garlic, a bay leaf, a bit of saffron, the pulp of a peeled and seeded lemon, two small peppers, a bunch of parsley and salt; in case no fresh tomatoes are on hand, use a tomato purée (No. 730), but not a sauce; lay in the pieces of fish with two gills of good olive oil, and three gills of white wine, then cover with the prepared broth, after straining and skimming it. Set the saucepan on a hot fire, boil the liquid rapidly for fifteen to eighteen minutes—the fish should by this time be thoroughly cooked and the broth succulent and slightly thickened by the reduction; season to taste, and finish with a pinch of chopped parsley, and a small piece of grated garlic. Have a deep dish, lay in it fifteen slices of plain, white bread three-quarters of an inch thick and slightly buttered; sprinkle them with a portion of the broth, turn them over and pour on the remainder. Dress the pieces of fish on another dish with a little of the broth; suppress the parsley, garlic and bay leaf, and send the two dishes to the table at the same time.

(1125). BUFFALO FISH À LA BAVAROISE (Buffalo Fish à la Bavaroise).

Scale and dress two Buffalo fish; raise the fillets without removing the skin; season and dip them in flour. Melt some butter in a pan pouring off the top while hot, put the fish into the pan, and fry very slowly, turning the pieces over when done; drain and dress them on a dish; put some melted butter into that already in the pan, cook it to hazelnut butter (No. 567) and take it from the hot fire; pour in a spoonful of cooked vinegar and a pinch of chopped parsley and chives, pour this butter over the fried fillets and serve.

(1126). BUFFALO FISH, CREAM SAUCE (Buffalo Fish à la Crème).

Cut off the head and thin parts of the tails from three Buffalo fish; scale, drain, suppress the gills, wash and dry, raise the fillets and lay them in a buttered sautoir, moistening with a white wine mirepoix stock (No. 419), and let cook for fifteen to twenty minutes; drain off the fish and strain the stock. Prepare a good béchamel with cream (No. 411) and add to it a part of the strained fish broth; strain the whole and put it on to reduce, incorporating gradually into it some mushroom broth and fresh cream. Pour this sauce over the fish fillets and let them simmer in it for fifteen minutes on a very slow fire. Dress the fish and pour over a cream sauce (No. 454).

(1127). BUTTER-FISH, MARINATED AND FRIED (Butter-fish Marinés et Frits).

Make an incision an eighth of an inch in depth on both sides of the fillets, lay them on a dish and let marinate in salt, pepper, lemon juice and oil. Two hours later, drain them off, roll in flour and fry firm to a fine golden color.

(1128). CARP (Carpe).

Common Carp is a fresh water fish of the family of the "gymnopones." It is used on our tables, its meat being considered a most excellent food.

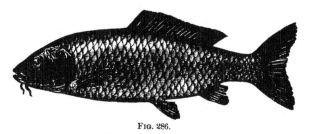

FIG. 286.

German Carp.—A species of carp partially bare, the back and belly being the only parts covered with two or three rows of golden scales, half as large again as the common carp.

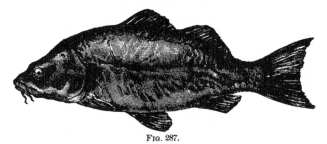

FIG. 287.

Salmon Carp.—A common carp, the meats having acquired through local circumstances a reddish tint and a taste analogous to the salmon.

(1129). CARP À LA CHAMBORD—COMMON CARP (Carpe à la Chambord—Carpe Ordinaire).

Procure common carp; scale it by slipping the blade of a knife between the scales and the skin, empty it out, cut off the gills, wash and wipe dry. Remove the skin from one side of the fish so that the meat is exposed, and stud this side with truffles; fill the inside with a fish quenelle forcemeat (No. 90), into which has been mixed a quarter as much cooked fine herbs (No. 385); cover with thin slices of fat pork. Braise the carp in a white wine court bouillon (No. 39). Instead of studding the carp on one side, after it is cooked, the whole body may be covered with a light layer of the forcemeat then brushed over twice with egg-yolks, allow to dry and imitate fish scales, using for this the tip of a soupspoon; beginning at the head. Cover over with thin slices of fat pork and in either case lay the carp in a fish kettle moistening it to half its heighth with a white wine mirepoix stock (No. 419), adding more moistening as fast as it evaporates; when the fish is done let it acquire a good color, then dress with the garnishings around in clusters, composed of mushroom heads, glazed truffles, trussed and glazed crawfish tails, smelt quenelles decorated with truffles and milts à la villeroi (No. 698), with the third part of a genevoise sauce (No. 469), to which the broth has been added and the whole reduced; pour over the mushrooms and send the remainder to the table in a sauce-boat.

(1130). CARP BREADED AND BROILED, MAÎTRE D'HÔTEL (Carpe Panée et Grillée, Maître d'Hôtel).

After the carp is prepared and split in two lengthwise, remove the spinal bone, season with salt and dip the fish first in melted butter, then in bread-crumbs and broil it over a slow fire; when finished bring the two halves together; dress it as if it were whole. Surround with potato balls sautéd in butter, seasoned with salt, fine herbs and lemon juice well stirred in.

(1131). CARP FRIED, GARNISHED WITH PARSLEY (Carpe Frite Garnie de Persil).

Scale one or several carps; cut off the gills and remove the entrails, then split them in two lengthwise through the belly without separating the parts; take out the spinal bone and the one found in the head. (Soak the milts for a few minutes in milk, drain, salt, roll in flour and fry.) Fry the carp until it becomes firm and of a fine golden color, then drain and range it on a folded napkin, lay on top a bunch of fried parsley and surround with the fried milts and lemons cut in four.

(1132). GERMAN CARP WITH SAUERKRAUT (Carpe Miroir à la Choucroûte).

Select a German carp of medium size, cleanse it well, wipe dry, tie down the head and lay the fish in a deep and narrow baking pan covered with fragments of fat pork, roots and sliced onions bay leaf, branches of parsley and basil. Moisten with half broth (No. 194a) and half white wine, seasoning with salt, cloves and whole peppers; cover over with a heavy sheet of buttered paper, then let it boil and finish cooking it in a moderate oven, basting frequently. When done, dress the fish on a thick layer of cooked sauerkraut (No. 2819), and surround with small, round, one inch in diameter lobster croquettes breaded and fried (No. 880). Strain and skim the fat from the gravy, thicken it with a few pieces of kneaded butter (No. 579), pass it again through a tammy and serve it in a separate sauce-boat.

(1133). CARP STUFFED À LA CHAMPENOISE—SALMON (Carpe Saumonée Farcie à la Champenoise).

Scale and clean two carps each of two pounds; prepare a pike quenelle forcemeat (No. 90), adding to it a quarter as much cooked fine herbs (No. 385). Stuff both the fish with this forcemeat and wrap them up separately in slices of fat pork, or in buttered paper, braise them in a mirepoix (No. 419); moisten with white wine and broth, and when the fish is cooked, strain, and skim the fat from the gravy, then reduce it with an equal quantity of espagnole sauce (No. 414). Boil it on one side only, despumating well; add some champagne wine, and reduce once more. Just when ready to serve, dress a garnishing around the fish, composed of mushrooms, quenelles, and small onions; cover over with a part of the sauce, and send the rest to the table in a separate sauce-boat, arranging around the edge of the dish trussed crawfish, and fried carps' milts.

(1134). CISCO, CASTILLANE SAUCE (Cisco à la Sauce Castillane).

Raise the fillets from both sides of the cisco, remove the skin, and place the fillets when well pared into a bowl or dish, seasoning with salt, pepper, sweet oil, lemon juice, sliced onions, and branches of parsley; let marinate in this for two hours, turning them over occasionally; drain them from the marinade leaving in the vegetables, and dip the fillets into beaten egg, then into bread-crumbs; plunge them in hot frying fat, and fry to a fine color, drain, salt, and dress them on a folded napkin, garnishing with fried parsley. Serve a castillane sauce (No. 443) in a separate sauce-boat

(1135). CODFISH (Morue ou Cabillaud).

The cod is a species of sea fish of the Gadus family, caught principally on the banks of New foundland. Salt or dry codfish keeps a very long time without deteriorating.

FIG. 288.

The meat is not the only part used for the table, as the tongue either fresh or salted, is considered a very delicate morsel.

(1136). FRESH CODFISH, À LA DUXELLE, BAKED (Morue Fraîche ou Cabillaud à la Duxelle au Gratin).

Fill the empty gill holes and the inside of the belly with a pike forcemeat (No. 90), into which has been mixed a quarter of the same quantity of cooked fine herbs (No. 385); season the fish with salt, pepper, and chopped up shallots, and moisten lightly with Madeira wine; cover over with an espagnole sauce (No. 414), dredge bread-raspings on top, and pour melted butter over all, then place the fish in a moderate oven to brown, and cook for about forty-five minutes according to its size. When the fish is thoroughly done, squeeze over the juice of a lemon, and bestrew the surface with chopped parsley.

(1137). FRESH CODFISH, NORWEGIAN STYLE (Morue Fraîche à la Norvégienne).

Raise the fillets from a very fresh codfish; cut and pare them into half heart-shaped pieces, season with salt, pepper, parsley, lemon juice, and chopped shallots. Lay them in a straight row on a baking dish with their seasoning, sprinkle liberally with bread-crumbs, and on top a little parmesan cheese, pour over melted butter, and cook the fish in a hot oven. Serve a separate sauce-boat of white wine sauce (No. 445), thickened with egg-yolks, and cream, and finished with a little nutmeg.

1138). FRESH CODFISH, BROILED WITH BACON OR HAM (Morue Fraîche Grillée au Petit Salé ou Jambon).

Cut the codfish into transversal slices; season each with salt and pepper, and saturate with oil, then broil them over a slow fire; dress the pieces on a very hot dish, garnish around with thin slices of broiled ham or bacon, and sprinkle over butter mixed with fine herbs, lemon juice, capers, and finely chopped pickled gherkins.

(1139). FRESH COD'S HEAD, EGG SAUCE (Tête de Morue Fraîche Sauce aux Œufs).

After cleaning, washing, and tying the head of a codfish weighing about ten pounds, place it in a fish kettle, and cover with salted water; add parsley branches, sliced onions, whole peppers and vinegar, boil and leave it on the side of the fire for half an hour, keeping it near the boiling point. When the fish is done, dress it on a long dish covered with a napkin, and garnish the ends with parsley leaves, laying boiled potatoes pared olive-shaped on each side. Serve a separate sauceboat of egg sauce (No. 462).

(1140). FRESH CODFISH, SLICES À LA HOLLANDAISE (Morue Fraîche Tranches à la Hollandaise.)

Have some slices of codfish, cook them by throwing over them some very salty boiling water and keeping it near the boiling point for half an hour; when done, drain and dress in the center

Fig. 289.

Fig. 290.

of a dish over a folded napkin, surrounding the fish with branches of parsley. Serve separately small three-quarters of an inch in diameter balls of potatoes, cooked in salted water, drained and laid in a vegetable dish with sufficient melted butter poured over to cover.

(1141). FRESH COD'S TONGUES WITH BLACK BUTTER OR CHOPPED SAUCE (Langues de Morue Fraîche au Beurre noir ou à la Sauce Hachée).

Pour two quarts of water into a saucepan, let boil, then add half a pound of carrots, and a quarter of a pound of onions, both finely minced, a few sprigs of parsley, and two gills of vinegar. Let the whole boil for fifteen minutes, then throw in the cods' tongues; cover the saucepan; at the first boil remove it from the hot fire to keep the liquid at the same heat, but without boiling for fifteen minutes; then remove and drain the tongues, wipe them on a cloth to dry all the moisture, and dress them on a very hot dish; season with salt, pepper, and chopped parsley, then pour over a liberal quantity of black butter passed through a fine sieve; set the dish for a few moments in the oven before serving. Instead of black butter a chopped sauce (No. 539) can be substituted.

(1142). SALT CODFISH, SPANISH STYLE (Morue Salée à l'Espagnole).

Cut pieces of salt codfish two inches long by one wide; soak them for eighteen hours, changing the water three times. Fry in one gill of oil to a golden color, three cloves of garlic, and three tablespoonfuls of chopped onions; drain off the oil, and add two bay leaves, thyme, whole pepper, two gills of vinegar and one gill of water, also some sweet Spanish peppers, the codfish and half a bottle of white wine; have this remain near the boiling point until thoroughly cooked, pass the stock through a sieve, put it back with the codfish, season to taste with nutmeg and pepper, then thicken with bread-crumbs soaked in water and well pressed out. Have prepared small stuffed tomatoes and round, hollow croûtons of bread fried in oil; dress the fish in the center of a dish, and surround with the tomatoes placed on top of the croûtons.

(1143). SALT CODFISH LYONNESE STYLE (Morue Salée à la Lyonnaise)).

Put two pounds of codfish to soak for eighteen hours after paring well the surface; change the water every six hours, then place the fish in a saucepanful of cold water, bring to boiling point and set it on one side of the range to let bubble only without boiling for half an hour, then drain it off. Mince finely half a pound of white onions; fry them slowly in four ounces of butter and half a gill of olive oil on a very slack fire so that the onions cook while acquiring a golden color; add to it the well drained and shredded fish removing all the bones and skin, toss the whole for ten minutes over a brisk fire, adding at the last moment a pinch of pepper, and a crushed and chopped clove of garlic, also a spoonful of mustard and a dash of vinegar. Dress and surround with boiled potatoes cut in slices and fried in butter.

(1144). SALT CODFISH À LA VILLAGEOISE—BAKED (Morue Salée au Gratin à la Villageoise).

Cut and pare the codfish into two inch square pieces, soak them for eighteen hours, then lay them in a saucepan and cover with enough water to bathe them; heat the liquid without boiling and keep it in this state for half an hour, drain and remove the skin and bones from the fish, shred it well and set it in a saucepan to pound with a wooden spoon, and when mashed to a paste dilute with a few spoonfuls of béchamel (No. 409), reduced and thickened; season to taste; add two ounces of butter divided into small parts and the third of its quantity of chopped potatoes; finish with cream. Season the preparation nicely, adding a pinch of cayenne pepper, then pour it all into a pie dish, smooth the surface and dust over with grated parmesan; sprinkle with melted butter and bake in a moderate oven.

(1145). CODFISH CAKES AND BALLS (Morue Salée en Galettes et en Boulettes).

Pare well the salt codfish and put it to soak; shred it while raw and set it into a saucepan with the same quantity of raw potatoes and sufficient cold water to cover, let boil from twenty-five to thirty minutes, or until the potatoes are done, then drain off the water and cover with a damp towel, set them in the oven a few moments to dry. Pound the whole in a mortar, adding pepper and butter, and when the preparation is reduced to a pulp, form it into two-inch diameter cakes, roll them in flour and flatten to three-quarters of an inch in thickness, fry these in clarified butter, dress on napkins or else on a very hot dish.

For the Codfish Balls use the same preparation, making balls of it one inch in diameter; dip in milk, roll in flour, fry them in very hot fat.

(1146). BRANDADE OF SALT COD (Brandade de Morue Salée).

Soak salt codfish for fourteen hours, changing the water several times, put it on to cook in cold water, set it on one side at the first boil and let it bubble for twenty-five minutes, then shred half a pound of this fish. Fry in oil two tablepoonfuls of chopped onion and one clove of garlic, let attain a good golden color, then put in the codfish to warm; pound and convert it into a paste, working it well with a whip, and then incorporate into it slowly one pint of oil, a little well thickened béchamel (No. 409), some double raw cream, pepper, nutmeg, salt if found necessary, and chopped parsley; dress it pyramid form and garnish around with oyster patties (No. 939), oysters à la villeroi (No. 698) and trussed crawfish. Serve separately a hot béarnaise mayonnaise sauce (No. 433).

(1147). SALT CODFISH, FARADAY CROWNS (Morue Salée, Couronnes à la Faraday).

Soak some salt codfish cut in two inch squares and well pared, for twelve hours; six hours in cold water, and six in tepid water; change this and put the fish into a saucepan containing fresh cold water. Let the liquid reach boiling point, then set it on one side of the range without allowing it to boil for twenty-five minutes; take out the codfish, refresh and suppress the skin, shred and return it to a saucepan with an equal amount of potatoes prepared for duchess (No. 2785), and mixed with béchamel sauce (No. 409) until reduced and consistent, then add a pinch of cayenne pepper. Divide this preparation into parts the size of an egg, roll them into balls on a floured table, and mold in Savarin crown-shaped molds; unmold and draw them out to an oval form and fill the insides with a little of the same preparation, so as to fill up half the empty space, then fry in clarified butter. Serve with a poached egg in the center of each. Broil some thin slices of bacon, cut them into inch and a half lengths and with these surround the crowns.

(1148). PICKED UP CODFISH WITH CREAM (Morue Salée à la Crème).

Shred the codfish while raw, suppressing all skin and bone; wash it several times in cold water until properly unsalted, then blanch in an abundance of water; drain, and put the fish into a sautoir covering it with cream and let boil until sufficiently reduced thicken with some béchamel (No. 409); season with prepared red pepper (No. 168) and nutmeg. It can either be thickened with the béchamel or else reduce the cream until of a correct consistency. Serve in a deep dish.

(1149). EELS À LA MARÉCHALE (Anguilles à la Maréchale).

Skin an eel as described in No. 57, suppress the second blueish skin by first laying the eel over a bright charcoal fire, then hold the head in one hand in a cloth, and with another cloth in the other hand, pull off the skin all at once; shave the spinal bone and ventrals with a very keen

FIG. 291.

knife, contrary ways from the bone. Empty out the insides and the blood adhering to the spinal bone, and cut the fish up into three inch lengths; braise in a mirepoix, and white wine stock (No. 419), and fish stock (No. 195). When the fish is cooked, drain, and lay it on a dish, pouring the strained stock over; let get cold, then drain off the pieces, and bread them English style (No. 13), and broil over a slow fire. Add to a suprême sauce (No. 547), reduced with the above stock, some minced truffles, olive shaped quenelles, and small shrimps; serve the eels on a hot dish, and the garnishing separate.

(1150). EELS, BROILED OR FRIED, TARTAR SAUCE (Anguilles Grillées ou Frites, Sauce Tartare).

Cut slices of eel three inches long, and cook them in white wine mirepoix (No. 419), and fish stock (No. 195). When done, range the pieces in a tureen, and pour their stock over, strained through a sieve; let them cool off, then drain and dip each piece in melted butter, roll them in bread-crumbs, and broil over a slow fire; dress them on a hot dish, or else bread the eels by dipping in eggs and rolling in bread-crumbs, smooth this nicely, and fry in plenty of hot fat; drain, dress on a folded napkin, and decorate the top with fried parsley; serve separately a plain tartar sauce (No. 631).

(1151). EELS, FRIED WITH BUTTER AND FINE HERBS (Anguilles Frites au Beurre et aux Fines Herbs).

Having cleaned some small eels, season with salt and pepper; roll them in flour, and fry slowly in butter; when done, dress and pour over the butter in which they were cooked. Bestrew over with finely cut-up chives and chopped parsley, squeeze over the juice of a lemon, and surround with a border of very thin slices of lemon, laying a bunch of parsley on top.

(1152). FLOUNDERS (Plies Carrelets ou Limandes).

A fish of the genus Platessa, allied to the halibut. Both eyes are on the side of the head, corresponding to the dorsal sides of the fish; its body is covered with small, almost imperceptible scales; its meat is very delicate and delicious if they be caught on a sandy bottom.

(1153). FLOUNDERS À LA DIEPPOISE (Plies Carrelets ou Limandes à la Dieppoise).

Season and fold in two the fillets removed from the flounders; place them in a buttered sautoir, laying on each one a small piece of butter; garnish the pointed ones with a crawfish claw, removing the small claw tip, and put them to cook in a slack oven, basting frequently until done. Squeeze the juice of a lemon into a buttered allemande sauce (No. 407); range the fish crown-shaped on a dish and fill up the middle either with oysters or mussels after cutting off the feet, also small channeled mushroom heads (No. 118); strain the sauce and pour it over the whole.

(1154). FLOUNDERS À LA GENLIS (Plies Carrelets ou Limandes à la Genlis.)

Remove the fillets from the flounders; pare them neatly, season and cover one side (the skin side) with fish forcemeat (No. 76), fold them in two. Butter a baking dish, throw chopped mushrooms on the bottom and besprinkle with a few spoonfuls of white wine; lay the fillets on top and on each one a small piece of butter and a little fish stock (No. 195). Set the dish into a slack oven and when cooked, remove and drain off the liquid; strain and reduce it with a béchamel sauce (No. 409), cover the fillets with this, dredge over with bread-crumbs and grated cheese, pour over a little melted butter and brown in a hot oven.

(1155). FLOUNDERS À LA JOINVILLE (Plies Carrelets ou Limandes à la Joinville).

Remove the fillets and the skin on one side; flatten with the handle of a knife and season; cover this side with a fish forcemeat (No. 76) with raw fine herbs, and fold in two; pare and range in a buttered sautoir and stick into each tip a crawfish claw without the smallest end claw; pour over some white wine and a small bit of butter on the top of each fillet; cook in a slack oven, being careful to baste several times while cooking, and as soon as the fish is done, drain them off, dress in a circle and reduce the liquid, adding to it an allemande sauce (No. 407), thickened with shrimp butter (No. 586). Fill the center of the circle made of the fish with a salpicon of shrimp tails and truffles cut in dice; cover the whole (except the crawfish claws) with the sauce and garnish each claw with a paper frill, then serve.

(1156). FLOUNDERS À LA JULES JANIN (Plies Carrelets ou Limandes à la Jules Janin).

Remove the fillets from the flounders, from these remove the black skin, season, cover with a quenelle forcemeat (No. 90), pare, and fold them in two; lay these fillets on a buttered dish, moisten with white wine, pour over some butter, and set the dish in the oven. When they are done drain them into a sautoir, straining the liquid; reduce this with an espagnole sauce (No. 414) and Madeira; garnish the fish ranged in a circle with oysters, sliced truffles, and crawfish tails. Butter the sauce, pass it through a tammy, and pour it over the whole.

(1157). FLOUNDERS À LA MADELEINE (Plies Carrelets ou Limandes à la Madeleine).

Remove the fillets and skin from the fish; season and cover the side the skin was taken from, with a fish quenelle forcemeat (No. 90) with cooked fine herbs (No. 385) mixed in it; roll them up cork-shaped, and set them in buttered tin paupiette rings; place these on sheets of buttered paper, then in a sautoir, moisten with mirepoix stock (No. 419), and cook in the oven until properly done, then unmold and dip each one in beaten eggs, then in bread-crumbs; fry a fine color and dress on napkins with a bunch of fried parsley on top. The sauce to accompany these is made with one shallot, a medium sized onion, as much celery root and carrots, all cut up into three-sixteenth inch squares; blanch the carrots and celery in salted water, then set them into a little white broth to let fall to a glaze; fry lightly the shallots and onions, add to them the carrots and celery, and moisten with broth, throw in a little sugar, then cook in such a way that the vegetables are done when the liquid is entirely reduced. Moisten again with cream, reduce once more, thicken with egg-yolks and fresh butter, add a little powdered sweet pepper, and serve.

(1158). FLOUNDERS, PROVENÇAL STYLE (Plies Carrelets ou Limandes à la Provençale).

First lift off the fillets from the flounders, and season them with salt, pepper, and nutmeg, beat to flatten with the handle of a knife, then fold in two; trim the pointed edge of each with a crawfish claw, after removing the movable small end attached to it; range the fillets in a buttered sautoir, moisten with mushroom liquor and white wine, seasoning with salt and pepper; cover over with buttered paper, and leave to cook. Reduce some provençale sauce (No. 529), prepared with velouté sauce (No. 415) and the fish stock, and when well reduced incorporate in a small piece of maître-d'hôtel butter (No. 581). Dress the fillets either in a circle or a straight row, and cover over with a part of the prepared sauce. Decorate every one of the claws with a fancy frill, and serve with the remainder of the sauce separately. The fish can be surrounded by small stuffed halved tomatoes (No. 2835).

(1159). FROSTFISH OR WHITING, CHERBOURG STYLE (Tacaud ou Merlan à la Mode de Cherbourg).

Have a medium sized frostfish or whiting; butter a sautoir, sprinkle it over with chopped up mushrooms, and lay the fish on top with parsley, thyme, and bay leaf; moisten with oyster liquor, cover and boil; when the fish is cooked drain off the stock and reduce. Dress the fish in the center of a hot dish and when the stock is reduced to half, thicken it with kneaded butter (No. 579); strain through a tammy, and surround the fish with blanched oysters, pouring the sauce over all. Put in the oven for a few minutes; when ready to serve, sprinkle over chopped parsley.

(1160). FROSTFISH OR WHITING, FRIED (Tacaud ou Merlan Frit).

Make a slight incision on each side of the fish; season with salt and roll them briskly in flour; plunge them in small quantities into hot frying fat and let acquire a color while cooking. The smaller the fish, the hotter the fat must be. When fried, salt and dress them at once. All fried articles should be served very hot, and garnished with fried parsley or simply sliced lemon. The smaller fish such as gudgeons, etc., are dipped in milk and flour, then fried on a hot fire; dress them in pyramid form on a napkin with fried parsley on top and quartered lemon around.

(1161). FROST FISH OR WHITING BAKED (Tacaud ou Merlan Gratiné).

Make incisions on both sides of the fish and season. Butter the bottom of a baking dish, sprinkle over with finely chopped onions and mushrooms, and on this bottom range the fish, pressing them down all on the same side; cover over with more chopped onions and mushrooms and besprinkle with bread-crumbs, pour over melted butter and cook in a moderate oven, basting them at times. Take out the dish, put a gill of half-glaze sauce (No. 413) reduced with white wine into the bottom, return to the oven to cook for ten minutes longer, when ready to serve squeeze over the juice of a lemon, bestrew chopped parsley over the top and serve in the same dish they were cooked in.

(1162). GROUPER À LA FRANKLYN (Grouper à la Franklyn).

A fish of the perch family of the genus Serranus. Raise the two fillets of the fish on each side of the main bone, remove the skin; cut the meat up into bias half inch slices, paring them oval shaped; put into a vessel to season with salt, pepper, thyme, bay leaf, sliced onions, lemon juice and oil; one hour after range these escalops in a sautoir with their marinade; moisten with broth and mushroom liquor and allow the whole to cook slowly. When done strain the stock and reduce half of it with a lean financière sauce (No. 464). When ready to serve incorporate into it a piece of fresh butter, reduce the rest of the stock to a glaze, glaze the dressed escalops, using a brush for the purpose after adding to it some lobster coral butter (No. 580), pour a little of the sauce around the fish and serve the rest of it separately.

(1163). GUDGEONS OR WHITEBAIT FRIED IN BUTTER (Goujons ou Blanchaille Frits au Beurre).

After having cleaned, prepared, and salted the fish, roll them in flour; set them in a coarse sieve and sift off rapidly the superfluous flour, then plunge them into hot frying lard. Melt clarified butter in a pan, when hot lay in the gudgeons that are nearly finished frying, or any other small fish; toss them about, adding small bits of butter, lemon juice, and chopped parsley; dress on a hot dish, and pour the hot butter over.

(1164). HADDOCK, ANCIENT STYLE (Aiglefin à l'Ancienne).

Cut the fish across in sufficiently thick slices to part each joint of the spinal bone; cook them in boiling, salted water, to which has been added branches of parsley, sliced onions, and vinegar; when the fish is done, drain, and remove the bones and skin, and lay the slices on a buttered dish, cover over with velouté sauce (No. 415) containing cooked fine herbs (No. 385); besprinkle with bread-crumbs, and grated parmesan, and brown the surface nicely in the oven. Serve a velouté sauce separately having it well buttered.

(1165). HADDOCK, HOLLAND STYLE (Aiglefin à la Mode de Hollande).

Cut slices from a haddock of a sufficient thickness to strike each joint of the spinal bone; put these into a glazed vessel for twenty-four hours with some fine salt; two hours before serving lay them in a fish kettle and pour over boiling water; keep it on the side of the range at a boiling degree until thoroughly cooked; dress, and garnish around with branches of parsley, and boiled potatoes; serve separately some melted butter.

(1166). FINNAN HADDIES, BROILED MAÎTRE D'HÔTEL AND BAKED WITH CREAM (Aiglefin Fumé Grillé, Maître d'Hôtel et à la Crème au Gratin).

Finnan haddies is haddock slightly salted and smoked; brush it over with oil; broil on a slow fire; dress and pour over a maître d'hôtel butter (No. 581).

Baked with Cream.—Put in a saucepan a little cream to which add a piece of butter kneaded with a little fecula, add a bay leaf, some thyme, basil, mignonette and pepper. Boil, add the haddock and let cook, when done, strain the sauce, add chopped parsley and shredded chives, put the finnan haddies in a buttered dish, cover with the sauce, bestrew with bread-crumbs, sprinkle with butter and bake; serve as soon as it is a fine color.

(1167). HALIBUT, ADMIRAL (Flétan ou Holibut à l'Amiral).

Trim a chicken halibut weighing about six pounds, split the fish through the dark side, detach the fillets and season the inside; lay it on a buttered baking pan, the white side uppermost; moisten with court bouillon stock with white wine (No. 39), and cover over with several sheets

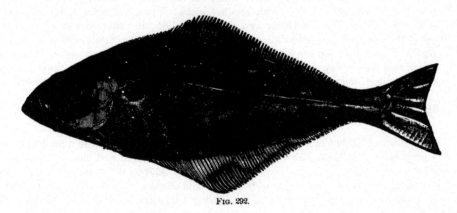

Fig. 292.

of buttered paper; cook the fish in a slow oven, drain the stock and reduce it to a half-glaze adding double its quantity of reduced velouté sauce (No. 415); just when ready to serve incorporate lobster butter (No. 580) into this sauce. Dress the halibut and garnish around with crawfish tails, mushroom heads and fanciful cuts of gherkins; cover over all with a third part of the sauce and arrange another garnishing around the border of the dish either of mussels or oysters à la villeroi (No. 698). Serve the remainder of the sauce in a separate sauce-boat.

(1168). HALIBUT À LA COLIGNY (Flétan à la Coligny).

Have a young halibut weighing two to four pounds; detach the meat from the bones on each side by making a gash in the center and on the whole length of the dark side of the fish; break the dorsal bone at a quarter of its length on the head side and proceed the same on the tail side, so as to be able to remove half of the bone when the fish is fried. Marinate it in a dish for two hours with salt, pepper, oil, lemon juice, thyme and bay leaf, then roll it in flour, beaten eggs and bread-crumbs; fry the fish in an oval pan with frying fat, not too hot, increasing the degree of heat as fast as it cooks; when done and of a fine color, drain and wipe; take out the middle bone the same as for soles à la Colbert (No. 1271), and fill the interior with lobster coral butter (No. 580). Garnish both ends with fried parsley and cut lemons as explained in No. 113, and serve at the same time, but separately, a dish of dressed cucumbers (No. 2661).

(1169). HALIBUT À LA RICHMOND (Flétan à la Richmond).

Butter the inside of a dish that can be placed in the oven, lay on it the halibut fillets after suppressing the skin, but leaving the fillets whole; season with salt, pepper and onions and place small pieces of butter on top; let cook in the oven for twenty to thirty minutes, basting frequently, then drain off the liquid and reduce with an equal quantity of velouté sauce (No. 415), thickening it at the last moment with lobster butter (No. 580); garnish around the fish with shelled shrimp tails and cover over with half of the sauce, serving the remainder in a separate sauce-boat. Range neatly on top sliced truffles warmed in Madeira wine and fish glaze (No. 399).

(1170). HALIBUT KADGIORI (Flétan Kadgiori).

Fry in butter, one ounce of chopped onions with half a pound of rice; heat together and moisten with fish stock (No. 195) to three times its heighth, then cook for twenty minutes; afterward pour it into a plain border mold (Fig. 139) rounded on the top. Cut a young chicken halibut into five-eighths of an inch square pieces, having about two pounds in all; fry these in butter in a frying pan with salt and cayenne pepper, add to it three chopped up hard boiled eggs, a pint of velouté sauce (No. 415), and two ounces of butter; mix well, and dress this fish inside the unmolded rice border, besprinkling the rice with hazelnut butter (No. 567).

(1171). HALIBUT, WITH FINE HERBS À LA REYNAL (Flétan aux Fines Herbes à la Reynal).

Dress a halibut by cutting off the fins and scraping the scales from the dark side; split it lengthwise in two on this side, and lay the fish on a small oval baking-pan with raised edges or on oval silver dishes; moisten it to its heighth with wine court bouillon (No. 39), and cover over with buttered paper; let the liquid boil for ten to twelve minutes, then remove from the hot fire and put it in the oven for thirty minutes longer; drain the fish, and let it dry thoroughly; dress it on a dish, keeping it hot, covered over with another plate. Strain and skim the liquid; reduce half of it to a half-glaze. Fry in butter two chopped shallots, and four ounces of mushrooms also chopped, thicken with two spoonfuls of velouté sauce (No. 415); dilute this sauce with the reduced liquid, and let cook for five minutes, then set it on one side to cook slowly, finish with butter, adding chopped parsley, and lemon juice. Wipe off all the humidity from the halibut, and cover it with the sauce; lay on top of the fish a straight row of very white cooked mushrooms.

(1172). CHICKEN HALIBUT BAKED AND WITH PARMESAN (Jeune Flétan au Gratin et au Parmesan).

Boil some slices of halibut in a court bouillon (No. 38); lay in a baking dish a border of potato croquette preparation (No. 2782), either hard and shaped with the hand and channeled, or else soft and pushed through a pocket. Have a layer of béchamel (No. 409) on the bottom of the dish, then one of the shredded fish, another layer of béchamel, and one more of the fish, finishing with the béchamel; sprinkle over with bread-crumbs, and grated parmesan, pour over a little butter, and brown in a hot oven.

With Parmesan.—Prepare the same and make a solid paste by mixing together butter and parmesan cheese with a pinch of cayenne pepper, work it well and roll it out to an eighth of an inch in thickness; cover the last layer of béchamel with this, and brown nicely in the hot oven.

(1173). CHICKEN HALIBUT WITH CARROT SAUCE (Jeune Flétan à la sauce aux Carottes).

Cut a well-cleaned eight pound chicken halibut in two lengthwise, and cut each part up into eight ounce pieces; place them in cold water for half an hour, drain and cook in water containing a quarter of the same quantity of milk; season with salt, and remove it from the hot fire at the first boil, leaving it to simmer without boiling, for fifteen minutes. Dress on a folded napkin and surround with very green parsley leaves. Serve at the same time a separate sauce-boat of béchamel sauce (No. 409), mixing in with it grated red carrot previously cooked in butter.

(1174). HERRINGS, FRESH, À LA CALAISIENNE (Harengs Frais à la Calaisienne).

A sea fish of the genus Clupea. Split as many herrings as needed through the entire back, and take out the middle bone. Stir into some fresh butter, salt, parsley, chopped up mushrooms, and lemon juice; stuff all the herrings with this butter, and lay the milts with the eggs already fried in the center; close up the herrings, and wrap them in a double sheet of paper; broil them over a slow fire, unwrap and serve very hot.

(1175). HERRINGS, FRESH, MUSTARD OR THICKENED MAÎTRE D'HÔTEL SAUCE (Harengs Frais, Sauce Moutarde ou Maître d'Hôtel Liée).

Choose very full herrings, clip off the fins, cut incisions on the backs, and lay the fish on a dish; season, sprinkle with oil, then range them on a hot broiler, and broil them over a good fire, turning them round; eight or ten minutes suffices to cook them. Dress them on a dish, and serve a mustard sauce separately, prepared as follows: Put some lean velouté (No. 416) into a saucepan, season well, and butter profusely; into this mix a quarter as much common mustard. Pour the sauce into a sauce-boat and serve with the herrings, or else serve a thickened mâitre d'hôtel sauce (No. 493).

(1176). HERRINGS, FRESH, PAUPIETTES WITH MILTS (Harengs Frais, Paupiettes aux Laitances).

Suppress the skin, head, and thin tail parts of the herrings; open them to remove the main back bone, then remove the two fillets and pare them oblong; cover the side the skin was taken from with a layer of fish quenelle forcemeat (No. 90), with cooked fine herbs (No. 385), and roll them into cork-shaped pieces; range these in buttered tin rings any size that may be convenient, having them the shape of a bung; set them on a dish, pour over a little butter and court bouillon (No. 38), and cook in a moderate oven for fifteen to twenty minutes. When done dress them in the center of a dish and surround with small cases of milts prepared as follows: Fry a shallot in butter with chopped parsley and fresh mushrooms likewise chopped; season with salt, pepper, and lemon juice; let get cold, then mix in with these the same quantity of fish forcemeat (No. 90). Cover the bottom and sides of some previously oiled paper cases stiffened in the oven, fill the centers with herring milts, and cover with the remainder of the preparation; on each one place a channeled mushroom head (No. 118), and then cook in a slow oven; cover the paupiettes with crawfish butter sauce (No. 573), and serve with a sauce-boat of the same.

(1177). HERRINGS, SALT, WITH MASHED POTATOES (Harengs Salés à la Purée de Pommes de Terre).

Soak the herrings in cold water for six hours, changing the water frequently; split them in two the whole length of the back, and unsalt them in milk for two hours; drain, wipe dry, and fry them in fresh butter; dress on a dish over potatoes mashed with cream (No. 2798).

(1178). HERRINGS—SMOKED AND SALTED—WITH CREAM (Harengs Fumés à la Crème).

Split the smoked herrings in two the entire length of the back; close them up and lay them in a saucepan with half milk and half cream, just sufficient to cover; boil them slowly until thoroughly done, then serve on a very hot dish with branches of green parsley around, and send to the table with a separate sauce-boat of cold, thick cream.

(1179). KINGFISH À LA BATELIÈRE (Kingfish à la Batelière).

Cut a half pound kingfish crosswise into two pieces; range them in a low saucepan moistening with red wine; season with salt, pepper, cloves, garlic, mushroom parings, and add one gill of

FIG. 293.

brandy, pouring it slowly over the other ingredients, set it on the fire and throw in some small onions fried and previously blanched; leave them in for ten minutes on a hot fire. Dress the fish and garnish the intersections with the small onions, strain the sauce through a tammy, add to it butter, and pour it over all; surround with heart-shaped croûtons of bread fried in butter and crawfish.

Some kingfish weigh as much as three pounds.

(1180). KINGFISH À LA BELLA (Kingfish à la Bella).

Lift off the fillets of a kingfish; remove the skin and pare the pieces into half hearts; season and cover each one with a quenelle forcemeat (No. 90), decorate the top with a circle made of very green halved pistachio nuts, laying channeled mushrooms (No. 118) in the center; dust over the remainder of the forcemeat with finely chopped coral. Place the fillets in a buttered sautoir, moisten with a little court bouillon, and lay a heavy piece of buttered paper on top; cook them in a slow oven, and then dress them with a ravigote sauce (No. 531), sending more of the sauce in a separate sauce-boat.

(1181). KINGFISH À LA BORDELAISE (Kingfish à la Bordelaise).

Raise the fillets from each side of the large inside bone; remove the skin, pare nicely and season. Bestrew a buttered baking dish with chopped up raw shallots, mushrooms and a little garlic; fold the fillets over and trim them pointed on one end; lay them in the dish and moisten with wine court-bouillon (No. 39), let cook slowly in the oven for fifteen to twenty minutes, then drain, strain off the liquid, skin off the fat and reduce to a half-glaze, incorporating into it two gills of reduced velouté sauce (No. 415), and a few spoonfuls of mushroon broth. Dress the fish either in a straight row or a circle and cover with the well-reduced sauce, garnishing around with trussed crawfish prepared à la Bordelaise (No. 1008).

(1182). KINGFISH À LA FIGARO (Kingfish à la Figaro).

Raise the fillets from the fish, remove the skin, pare and cut them lengthwise in two; season each piece with salt, pepper and lemon juice, let marinate for one hour then dip them in beaten eggs, bread-crumbs and fry to a fine color. Dress on a napkin and garnish the top with fried parsley and around with lemon. Serve separately mayonnaise sauce (No. 606) with tomato purée (No. 730) strained through a very fine sieve and thoroughly drained, then add to it very finely cut up chervil.

(1183). KINGFISH À LA MONTGOLFIER (Kingfish à la Montgolfier).

Have six fine kingfish weighing half a pound each; lift off the fillets, skin, and from two fillets cut ten long small slices; make five or six incisions crosswise on them, and fill them in with slices of truffles; turn these fillets round into crowns and range them on a buttered baking sheet, cover over with a heavy piece of buttered paper, then moisten with a little court bouillon (No. 38). Pare the other fillets of kingfish into half hearts after having folded them in two across, macerate with salt, pepper and lemon juice for half an hour, drain and lay them in a buttered sautoir garnished with chopped mushrooms, shallots and onions; moisten with white wine and mushroom liquor, then cook slowly in the oven; drain off the liquid, reduce and incorporate into it two gills of velouté sauce (No. 415). Besprinkle the bottom of an oval shaped buttered baking dish with chopped truffles, lay the cooked fillets on top, surround them with medium sized fresh mushrooms heads previously peeled and cooked in a little water, salt, butter and lemon juice; pour the sauce over, bestrew with bread-crumbs, grated parmesan and melted butter and color slightly. Place the small prepared truffled slices in the oven and when done use them to garnish the whole fillets, ranging between each one a trussed crawfish.

(1184). KINGFISH À LA PRINCELAY (Kingfish à la Princelay).

Pare into ovals some fillets taken from a fish, season with salt and pepper; fry them in oil and when done, dress either in a row or in a circle. Fry a little flour in oil without browning, add chopped onions, and one bay leaf, moisten with good court bouillon (No. 38) to obtain a rather light sauce, reduce it well, pass it through a tammy, throw in small capers and cover the fish with this sprinkle.

(1185). KINGFISH À LA SULTANA (Kingfish à la Sultane).

Lift off the fillets and remove the skin, pare them to the shape of a half heart, season with salt and cover one side with fish quenelle forcemeat (No. 90); range them in a buttered sautoir, the pointed end toward the center of the pan. On the round end place a crescent made of the red meat found in the lobster claws having it an eighth of an inch in thickness; between the pointed end of the fillet and the crescent imitate a rosette with five halved pistachios. Moisten with a little court bouillon (No. 38), cover over with a buttered paper and place to cook in a slack oven. When done, dress them flat in a circle and fill the center with a garnishing composed of truffles, mushrooms and escalops of lobster mingled with some lean espagnole sauce (No. 416) made with Madeira, reduced properly and thickened; finish with fresh butter. At the tip of each fillet attach a fancy favor frill (No. 10) and serve with a separate sauce-boat of the same sauce.

(1186). KINGFISH, BAKED (Kingfish au Gratin).

Select a good fresh kingfish, take off the fillets, suppressing the skin; season with salt, pepper, and nutmeg, then fold them in two and pare nicely; butter the bottom of a baking dish, bestrew it with chopped onions and mushrooms; range the fillets over, laying a fluted mushroom (No. 118) on each fillet. Pour over a cold half-glaze sauce (No. 413), pour into the bottom of the dish, three or four tablespoonfuls of white wine; bestrew bread-crumbs over, and sprinkle the surface with a brush dipped in melted butter. Set the dish into a moderately heated oven, and let the fillets cook for fifteen to eighteen minutes; after removing the dish lay it on another to be sent to the table.

Another Way.—Butter a baking dish, and place in it the fish folded in two, nicely pared; pour over some white wine, lay mushroom heads on top, and mask with a brown sauce (No. 416), into which a quarter as much tomato sauce (No. 549) has been mixed. Bestrew the surface with bread raspings, pour melted butter over all, and bake and cook in a hot oven; when serving press the juice of a lemon on it, and besprinkle with chopped parsley.

(1187). KINGFISH ON THE DISH—GASTRITE (Kingfish sur le Plat—Gastrite).

Cut off the fins from well cleaned fish, split them from head to tail on the belly side, in order to take out the dorsal bone; season with salt and pepper. Butter the bottom of a small baking dish, cover it over with chopped mushrooms and onions, and lay the open kingfish on top upside down, the skin side underneath; pour half a gill of white wine in the bottom of the dish, and besprinkle the top with gastrite; pour over a little melted butter, and bake in a moderate oven for twelve to fifteen minutes. After taking the fish from the fire, slip into the bottom a few spoonfuls of half-glaze sauce (No. 413) finished with lemon juice.

For the Gastrite.—Take the crumb part of a stale loaf of bread, put it in a towel with a little flour, close the towel and work the bread so it will crumble, then pass it through a fine sieve, and mix it with a little chopped up parsley and grated parmesan or Swiss cheese.

(1188). LAFAYETTE FISH, BREADED ENGLISH STYLE (Poisson Lafayette Pané à l'Anglaise).

Score the fish on both sides on the thick fillets; season with salt and pepper. Melt lightly two ounces of fresh butter, stir into it six raw egg-yolks, salt, pepper, and nutmeg; dip the fish into this mixture, then roll it in bread-crumbs, smooth the surface nicely, and fry a fine color in very hot clarified butter; drain, wipe and salt the fish, then dress it on a folded napkin and garnish with fried parsley and quartered lemons.

(1189). LAMPREY À LA RABELAIS (Lamproie à la Rabelais).

Bleed the lamprey, reserving the blood, and mix it in with a little vinegar; cut the fish into slices, fry them in butter adding chopped onions, salt, sugar, and allspice; dredge over with a little flour, moisten with white wine, and lay in a bunch of parsley garnished with thyme and bay leaf, also small glazed onions; let cook from twelve to fifteen minutes. Dress the lampreys and the small onions, thicken the sauce with the blood and then strain it through a tammy (No. 159); cover the fish with this sauce, and surround the lampreys with fluted mushroom heads (No. 118) fried in butter, and seasoned with salt, pepper, and fine herbs; range round the whole very thin sliced lemon.

(1190). FRESH MACKEREL (Maquereau Frais).

Of the genus Scomber, of the family of Scomberoïds. They are distinguished by five small fins attached above and below the tail (Spanish mackerel have eight of these), also by an elongated head, a largely opened mouth and brilliant coloring. This fish is bare of scales; its length attains from fifteen to twenty inches for fresh mackerel, and from fifteen to thirty for Spanish mackerel; the meat of the latter is much whiter and firmer than the former.

(1191). FRESH MACKEREL, BONNEFOY—FILLETS (Filets de Maquereau Frais à la Bonnefoy).

Cut off the head and thin tail part of three or four fresh and clean mackerel; detach the fillets, season, roll in flour and cook them in clarified butter, turning them when done over on one side. Put into a small saucepan one gill of melted glaze (No. 399) and four to five spoonfuls of thickened tomato sauce (No. 549) and a teaspoonful of chopped shallot cooked in butter; let the sauce boil, then remove it to one side to finish with butter, chopped parsley and lemon juice. Drain the fillets, dress them on a dish and cover with the sauce; serve at the same time small potato balls plainly cooked in salted water and steamed for five or six minutes.

(1192). FRESH MACKEREL IN PAPERS, MÉPHISTO (Maquereau Frais en Papillotes, Méphisto).

Split the mackerel lengthwise in two; suppress the middle bone, pare, season with salt, pepper and nutmeg, then coat the surface with oil and broil over a slow fire (the milts and roe to be cooked apart in the oven). Cut some sheets of paper into long hearts, oil them over and lay on one of their sides a little deviled sauce (No. 459), on top range the fish with either the milts or roe and cover over with more of the sauce; fold the paper over and twist it well around so as to enclose the fish hermetically; range them on the same dish intended for the table, pour over a little oil and lay them in a hot oven. When the paper has swollen and is a fine color, place the dish on top of another and serve.

(1193). FRESH MACKEREL, MAÎTRE D'HÔTEL (Maquereau Frais, Maître d'Hôtel).

Split very fresh and well cleansed mackerel lengthwise through the back; remove the dorsal bone, season with salt, and roll in melted butter, or else in oil; broil them for fifteen to twenty minutes on a slow fire turning them and brushing over with a brush dipped in butter or oil. Dress them on a very hot dish and cover with a layer of maître d'hôtel butter (No. 581). After rolling them in melted butter or oil, they may be dipped in bread-crumbs.

(1194). FRESH MACKEREL, WITH WHITE PIQUANTE SAUCE (Maquereau Frais à la Sauce Piquante Blanche).

Suppress the heads and the thin tail parts of four fresh, well cleansed mackerel; remove the skins and pare the meat into half hearts, lay these on a dish, season with salt, pepper, thyme, bay leaf, cut up onions, oil and lemon juice, turning them over at intervals. One hour later take the pieces from their pickle, dip them in flour and cook in clarified butter; when done and of a fine color, drain and dress them either in a straight row or in a circle on a dish and pour around a white sharp (piquante) sauce (No. 538).

(1195). MACKEREL, CREAM HORSERADISH SAUCE—SALT AND SMOKED (Maquereau Salé et Fumé Sauce à la Crème au Raifort).

Soak salt mackerel for twelve hours, changing the water several times; cook the fish in an abundance of water into which has been added a dash of vinegar, thyme, bay leaf, branches of parsley, and sliced onions; remove the saucepan at the first boil, and leave the fish in the water without allowing it to boil any more for fifteen minutes; drain, dress the mackerel on a folded napkin, and surround with parsley leaves. Serve at the same time a sauce-boat of cream sauce (No. 454), into which has been incorporated half its quantity of grated horseradish heated in the sauce without boiling.

For Smoked Mackerel.—Instead of boiling the fish, broil it over a slow fire, and serve it on a horseradish sauce with cream (No. 478).

(1196). SPANISH MACKEREL À LA PÉRIGORD (Maquereau Espagnol à la Périgord).

Pare the fillets removed from the mackerel into half heart-shapes; lay them in a buttered sautoir, decorating the thickest part of each fillet with a rose-shaped ornament of truffles dipped in egg-whites. Baste over with melted butter, lemon juice, white wine, and salt; cover with a buttered paper, and let cook in a slow oven. Dress the fillets, reduce their liquid, adding velouté sauce (No. 415) and slices of truffles fried in butter. Cover the truffles with a third part of this sauce, and glaze the fillets with fish glaze (No. 399) combined with lobster coral butter (No. 580). Serve the remainder of the sauce separately.

(1197). SPANISH MACKEREL À LA VIENNET (Maquereau Espagnol à la Viennet).

Chop up separately some onions, shallots, and mushrooms; fry the onions and shallots in butter then add the chopped mushrooms; lay on top mackerel fillets pared half heart-shaped season

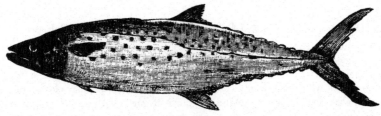

Fig. 294.

with salt, mignonette, and nutmeg; place over a liberal piece of butter, cover with a strong buttered paper, and set the pan in the oven for fifteen minutes, then drain off the butter. and add a little white wine, espagnole sauce (No. 414). and tomato sauce (No. 549). Dress the fish, reduce the sauce, and when ready pass through a tammy and pour it over the fillets.

(1198). SPANISH MACKEREL WITH CRAWFISH—FILLETS (Filets de Maquereau Espagnol aux Écrevisses).

Lift up the fillets from six small and very fresh mackerel, season and cover the surfaces of the cut sides with a layer of pike forcemeat (No. 90), and fine herbs finished with a piece of red butter (No. 573); flatten the surfaces with the blade of a knife, range them as fast as they are done one beside the other on a well buttered baking pan, dredging fine herbs on top; put them to cook in a moderate oven from ten to twelve minutes, basting them over with butter; remove and dress them on a dish, cover over with a little velouté sauce (No. 415) reduced with crawfish broth and finished with red butter (No. 573), and lemon-juice. Range a cluster of crawfish tails at each end of the dish and serve the remainder of the sauce separately.

(1199). SPANISH MACKEREL WITH GOOSEBERRIES—STUFFED (Maquereau Espagnol Farci Garni de Groseilles Vertes).

Split well-cleaned mackerel down the back; take out the bone just below the head and two inches above the tail; season the inside and fill the empty space with a fish forcemeat (No. 76), into which has been added some allemande sauce (No. 407), and a third of its quantity of cooked fine herbs, give the fish its original shape, roll it tightly in two sheets of paper and tie it at both ends, in the center and once again between these, making in all five rows of string; place the fish on a baking pan, set it in the oven for twenty to thirty minutes, remove, unwrap and dress, serving with a garnishing of gooseberries around the fish.

For a Gooseberry Garnishing take half a pound of gooseberries; suppress the stalks and ends, then blanch them for two minutes in boiling water in an untinned copper vessel or until they crush between the fingers, drain and then mix them in a thickened maître d'hôtel sauce (No. 493); pour over the fish and garnish.

(1200). SPANISH MACKEREL WITH GREEN PEAS (Maquereau Espagnol aux Petits Pois).

Fry two tablespoonfuls of chopped onions in two ounces of butter, lay in the mackerel cut up into four ounce slices and when well fried, moisten with water, add a garnished bunch of parsley and salt and let the fish cook; when ready to serve add cooked peas (No. 2742); finish by thickening with a little velouté sauce (No. 415), egg-yolks and butter. Dress the fish, pour the peas over and serve.

(1201). MATELOTE À LA MARINIÈRE, ST. MANDÉ (Matelote à la Marinière St. Mandé).

Cut into four ounce slices, one pound of eels and one pound of carp, salt and marinate for two hours, then wash and drain. Put one quart of red wine into a saucepan sufficiently large to contain three quarts; add a large bunch of parsley garnished with one bay leaf, as much thyme and one clove of garlic. one coffeespoonful of whole allspice, pepper and the necessary salt, one ounce of butter and half a pound of mushrooms; let all cook for fifteen minutes, then put in the eels, cork for ten minutes longer before adding the carp and a pint of small white onions blanched for about ten minutes, drained, then fried in butter to a good golden color with a little sugar; thicken the whole with kneaded butter (No. 579) and strain through a sieve. Dress the fish, cover it with the sauce and garnish around with fried croûtons of bread, some trussed crawfish and fried egg-yolks and milts.

(1202). MATELOTE À LA TALABASSE (Matelote à la Talabasse).

Mince two ounces of onions, two ounces of leeks, add two crushed cloves of garlic; fry these in some good oil, besprinkle with flour and add half a pound of mackerel, half a pound of sheepshead, half a pound of bass and half a pound of blackfish, all cut up in steaks; moisten to cover with white wine and water, half of each, salt, pepper, cloves and a garnished bunch of parsley; cook on a brisk fire; pound one clove of garlic with a little saffron and two ounces of butter, rub it through a sieve, drain the stock, reduce and thicken it with the garlic butter, adding the juice of a lemon and chopped parsley; dress the fish, pour the sauce over and garnish around with crawfish and croûtons of bread fried in butter.

(1203). MATELOTE OF CANOTIERS (Matelote des Canotiers).

Cut up into steaks one medium carp, a pike and a small eel, all being fresh and clean, with the heads and parings of the fish, some roots, aromatic herbs and mushroom parings; prepare a good broth, strain and free it from fat; put the slices of fish in a saucepan or earthen vessel, with a few mushroom heads, a bunch of parsley garnished with garlic, whole peppers and salt, and small fried and browned onions; moisten to its height with the prepared broth, and let it boil on a brisk fire in such a way that the liquid reduces to half while the fish cooks, then thicken the sauce moderately with kneaded butter (No 579), boil the sauce up twice, then remove it on one side to add a piece of butter. Dress the slices of fish on flat crusts of bread browned in butter, surround them with the garnishing, and pour the sauce over the whole.

(1204). MATELOTE OF CARP, MIROIR (Matelote de Carpe, Miroir).

Scale the carp, draw it by the stomach, tie down the head and place it in a narrow low-bordered baking tin, lined with fat pork, minced roots and onions, mushroom peelings and a bunch of parsley; salt the fish, moisten it to half its height with white wine and fish broth, let it come quickly to a boil, and ten minutes after cover the fish over with a strong buttered paper, set it in a moderate oven, to finish cooking slowly without turning it over, but basting frequently. When done remove the fish from the pan with a large perforated skimmer, and dress it on a dish, surround it with a garnishing of very white peeled mushrooms and keep it warm. Strain the liquid into a sautoir, remove the fat and pour in a glassful of red wine; reduce it over a slow fire, and when very succulent, thicken with kneaded butter (No. 579); cover the fish with some of the sauce and serve the remainder separately.

(1205). MATELOTE OF FISHERMEN (Matelote des Pêcheurs.)

Clean well a small eel, a carp, a pike, and a tench; cut them up into slices after suppressing the heads and thin parts, then salt them. Cook in a saucepan some minced onions, add the heads and bones from the fish, and two minutes after moisten with white wine; put in a bunch of parsley garnished with garlic, mushroom peelings and salt, then cook this broth for twenty minutes; strain, remove the fat, and pour it into a saucepan to thicken with kneaded butter (No. 579); let cook for seven or eight minutes. Wipe well the pieces of fish, put them into a saucepan wider than its height, cover with the sauce, adding two dozen uncooked mushrooms and let all boil for fifteen minutes on a brisk fire, being careful to remove each piece of fish as soon as it is done. Dress these pieces on a deep dish over thin flat crusts of bread browned in butter, surrounded with the mushrooms, then reduce the sauce without ceasing to stir; butter it off from the fire and finish by adding to the sauce pieces of four ounces each, and the juice of a lemon; pour this over the fish.

(1206). MULLETS WITH D'ANTIN SAUCE (Mulets à la Sauce d'Antin).

Raise the fillets from the mullets and suppress the skin; cut them each lengthwise in two and season with salt, mignonette, thyme, bay leaf, sliced onions, branches of parsley, tarragon, vinegar and oil; let marinate for one hour, turning them over frequently, then drain and roll them in flour; form them crescent-shaped on a wire basket and fry in hot fat till a fine color. Serve in a sauce-boat a d'Antin sauce (No. 458).

(1207). MASKINONGE À LA PROVIDENCE (Maskinongé à la Providence).

Stud slices of the fish with anchovy fillets; plunge these slices in boiling water to which a little vinegar has been added, for two minutes, take them out and lay them in a saucepan; cover the entire fish with a velouté sauce (No. 415), with white wine and mushroom parings, adding a garnished bunch of parsley; let simmer until the fish is cooked, then drain off the liquid; reduce and thicken it with egg-yolks, butter and cream; pass it through a tammy, and incorporate into it a piece more butter and chopped parsley. Dress the slices of fish, covering over with a third part of the sauce, and serve the remainder of the sauce separately.

(1208). PERCH, POLISH STYLE (Perche à la Polonaise).

A species of bony fish "Thoracic," characterized by a very powerful prickly crest placed on the back. River perch have very white, firm and fine meat of an exquisite savor; it is one of the best fresh water fishes.

FIG. 295.

Select medium sized perch, clean and scale; boil them in salted water for two or three minutes until the skin detaches easily, then take from the fire and carefully lift off the skin. Roll the fish in beaten eggs into which has been mixed a little melted butter, salt, and pepper, then in bread-crumbs, and lay them on a baking tin; brown in a hot oven to finish cooking, and when a good color, serve on a tomato sauce (No. 549), adding a little grated horseradish to it.

(1209). PERCH, SAUCE VALOIS—BOILED (Perche Bouillie à la Sauce Valois).

Scale and clean two or three medium sized perch; boil sufficient water in a flat saucepan to cover the fish, adding to it salt, parsley roots with the green leaves, minced onions, and celery; after this has boiled for a few moments, plunge in the fish, and let boil merely for a few times, then set it on one side of the range to finish cooking. If the perch be required hot, serve them on a folded napkin with boiled potatoes on each side of the fish and green parsley at the ends. Serve a Valois and tarragon sauce (No. 554) separately.

(1210). PERCH, STUFFED AND BAKED (Perche Farcie au Four).

Split the perch through the whole length of the back, keeping on the head and tail bone; suppress the large spinal bone and fins. Season the inside and fill the space with a fish forcemeat (No. 76) and cooked fine herbs (No. 385). Set the perch on a buttered dish, season with salt and pepper, and pour over white wine and mushroom essence (No. 392); let it cook for twenty minutes in a moderately heated oven, then drain and reduce the gravy, mixing it in with a Spanish sauce (No. 414), when the sauce is ready, incorporate into it some butter, lemon-juice and chopped parsley; dress the fish and cover with the sauce.

(1211). PERCH, WITH PARSLEY WATER, CELERY ROOT AND PARSNIPS (Perche à l'Eau de Persil, de Céleri et de Panais).

Scrape four ounces of parsley roots, and the same quantity of parsnips and the same of celery roots; cut them up into very fine shreds. Cook these separately in salted water for twenty minutes, then drain off the water. Cook the perch in this water, and when done and dressed, surround with boiled potato balls made three-quarters of an inch in size and the roots. Serve a part of the well reduced liquid in a separate sauce-boat at the same time as the fish.

(1212). PICKEREL, TOMATO ANDALOUSE SAUCE (Brocheton, Sauce Tomate Andalouse)

Score both sides of the fillets taken from the fish; put them in a tureen with salt, pepper, chopped up onions, parsley, oil, and vinegar; one hour later drain them from their marinade,

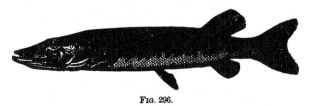

Fig. 296.

roll them in flour, and fry to a fine color, and when firm dress with a tomato Andalouse sauce (No. 550) served separately.

(1213). PIKE PERCH OR WALL EYED PIKE À LA DURANCE (Sandre à la Durance).

Split a one-pound pike perch in two, through the middle of the back, and take out the spinal bone lay this boned fish on a buttered dish and moisten with mushroom stock, and white wine; season with salt and pepper, laying small pieces of butter on top; let boil up once, then place the dish in the oven covered with another smaller one, and cook for fifteen minutes; drain off the stock, thicken it with a little butter mixed with an equal quantity of flour (kneaded butter). Dress the fish, strain the sauce through a tammy, and when ready to serve add to it a good sized piece of butter, the juice of a lemon, and fine herbs. Cover over with a third part of the sauce, and garnish around with the following smelt fillets: Place fillets of smelts on a table to season; cover the cut sides with a layer of raw fish forcemeat (No. 76), mixed with chopped mushrooms, fold over the fillets so that the forcemeat is enclosed, then roll them in flour and dip in beaten eggs; plunge a few at the time into very hot frying fat to become a fine color, while cooking, then drain and salt. Dress these around the fish, serving the remainder of the sauce in a separate sauce-boat.

(1214). PIKE PERCH OR WALL EYED PIKE À LA FINANCIÈRE (Sandre à la Financière).

Braise the fish whole in a white wine mirepoix stock (No. 419), remove the skin, dress the fish on a dish and glaze with fish glaze (No. 399) and lobster butter (No. 580) mixed. Reduce the stock and put it with a lean financière sauce (No. 464); strain it through a tammy, and finish with butter. Garnish around the fish with fish quenelles (No. 90), made in a teaspoon (No. 155), whole truffles, and mushroom heads; pour a third of the sauce over, and serve the remainder in a separate sauce-boat.

(1215). PIKE PERCH OR WALL EYED PIKE À LA GERALDIN (Sandre à la Geraldin).

Cut the fish in quarter pound slices, cook in salted water into which vinegar has been added; range the slices on a long dish over a folded napkin, serve separately a garnishing of lightly blanched oysters, drained, dipped in eggs, rolled in fresh bread-crumbs, and fried in lard or oil. The sauce to accompany this fish is a half-glaze sauce (No. 413), into which has been stirred cayenne pepper, and small mushroom heads.

(1216). PIKE PERCH OR WALL EYED PIKE À LA ROYAL (Sandre à la Royale).

Raise the fillets from the fish; season, and fold in two; trim them the size and shape of medium chicken fillets, then range them in a buttered sautoir; besprinkle with butter and white wine, and place it in the oven covered over with buttered paper; when done, reduce some velouté sauce (No. 415), to which has been added the stock; work up with butter, and reserve a third of this; to the other two-thirds add truffles, lobster and mushrooms, all finely shredded; stick a frill favor (No. 10) into the top of each fillet, dress crown-shaped, and pour the garnishing in the center, serve the reserved sauce in a separate sauce-boat.

(1217). PIKE PERCH OR WALL-EYED PIKE, RUSSIAN STYLE (Sandre à la Russe).

Fry in butter some minced carrots, small onions and a garnished bunch of parsley, add to these some fish steaks each one weighing a quarter of a pound and previously marinated in salt for two hours; moisten with white wine court bouillon (No. 39), and as soon as the fish is cooked, drain and dress it. Garnish with the small onions, strain the broth through a sieve, reduce, skin and add to it some butter kneaded with flour, strain again through a tammy, put in a few capers, pour the sauce over the fish and garnish around with sippets of bread fried in butter.

(1218). PIKE PERCH OR WALL-EYED PIKE, CONTINENTAL STYLE—FILLETS (Filets de Sandre au Continental).

Raise the fillets from four medium sized fish, flatten and pare them oval-shape leaving on the skin, then season. Range them in a sautoir containing hot butter, placing them on their cut sides, then poach slightly, drain them and set them under a weight to keep them flat, leaving the butter in the sautoir. Cover the cut side of the fillets with a layer of fish forcemeat (No. 90) finished with red butter (No. 580); smooth this rounded on the top and strew over finely chopped lobster coral. Return the fillets to the sautoir containing the butter, cover over with buttered paper and finish cooking in a slow oven; thicken some good velouté sauce (No. 415) with cream, egg-yolks and butter, strain it through a tammy and add to it some oysters and shrimps. Dress the fillets in a circle, lay the oysters and shrimps in the center, and pour the sauce over the whole.

(1219). PIKE WITH HAZELNUT BUTTER SAUCE (Brochet au Beurre Noisette).

Cut in half pound slices and marinate for one hour in salt a medium sized scalded and cleaned pike, drain and put the pieces into a saucepan with water, salt, vinegar, cut up roots and onions, also a bunch of parsley. Put the saucepan on a good fire letting the liquid boil for five minutes then remove it on one side to keep quivering for a quarter of an hour in such a way that the fish cooks in the meantime. Put eight ounces of melted butter in a saucepan, pouring it off from its sediment, heat it to reach the degree of hazelnut butter (No. 567), then throw in an ounce of chopped parsley. Dress the fish; surround with fresh parsley leaves and send the butter to the table in a sauce-boat.

(1220). POMPANO À LA ANTHELME (Pompano à la Anthelme).

Raise the fillets from four fresh fish, leaving on the skin; cut with a small vegetable spoon, half inch diameter balls of potatoes, obtaining a quart when finished, boil them in salted water, and as soon as they are done, drain, return them to the saucepan, cover with a cloth, and set them in a slack oven for a few minutes. Boil up a pint of fresh cream, then add to it the potatoes. Season the fish fillets with salt, flour them over and cook them in a frying pan with clarified butter, when done range them in the center of a dish. Thicken the potatoes with shrimp butter (No. 586) and dress them around the fish besprinkling the whole with very green chopped parsley.

(1221). POMPANO À LA CARONDELET (Pompano à la Carondelet).

Cut four fish into quarter of a pound slices, boil them in salted water containing thyme, bay leaf, parsley branches and vinegar; at the first boil remove them from the hot fire to let quiver on one side of the range for fifteen minutes; when finished, drain and suppress the skins, keeping the meat as whole as possible. Fry a medium sized onion in butter, dust with curry powder and moisten with court bouillon and white wine (No. 39); thicken this stock with thick béchamel (No. 409), and reduce it properly; stir in egg-yolks and fresh butter, then strain the whole through a tammy. Dress the fish; pour the sauce over and surround either with fried milts or mussels à la villeroi (No. 698).

(1222). POMPANO À LA DUCLAIR (Pompano à la Duclair).

Lift the fillets from the fish, pare them into half hearts and marinate with salt, pepper, oil and lemon juice; lay them in a sautoir containing clarified butter and cook in the oven. Mince up very finely one medium raw onion, a small bit of garlic and two ounces of celery root; fry them in butter and moisten with fish stock (No. 195), adding a few cloves, let this cook for twenty minutes, then pass it through a sieve and incorporate into it some velouté, reduced to the consistency of a sauce, when ready for serving incorporate therein chopped parsley and a piece of fresh butter. Dress the fillets either in a circle or a straight row, cover over with one-half of the sauce, and serve the other half in a separate sauce-boat.

(1223). POMPANO À LA MACÉDOINE (Pompano à la Macédoine).

Have several fresh fish; lift off the fillets, suppress the skin and cut them into thin slices; lay these in a buttered sautoir one beside the other, and season with salt, pepper and nutmeg; when they are cooked set them under a weight to get cold, mask over with a well reduced allemande sauce (No. 407), into which has been stirred some mushroom purée (No. 722). Bread-crumb them English style (No. 13), and lay each fillet close, one beside the other, in the sautoir, pour over some butter and brown them in a brisk oven; when removed dress them in a circle, garnish the center with a vegetable macédoine (No. 2755), thickened with fresh butter just when ready to serve.

(1224). POMPANO À LA MAZARIN (Pompano à la Mazarin).

Pare the fillets taken from the fish, suppress the skin and season with salt, pepper and nutmeg; lay them in a buttered sautoir, moisten with white wine and court bouillon (No. 39), basting them several times while cooking; when done, drain off the liquid and reduce it with the same quantity of velouté sauce (No. 415) thickened with egg-yolks and cream, finishing the sauce with lobster butter (No. 580); strain all this through a tammy and pour it over the fish; range round the latter pike quenelles (No. 90) decorated with truffles (No. 154) and fried breaded oysters from which the heart has been removed.

(1225). POMPANO À LA POTENTINI (Pompano à la Potentini).

Split three fish, each weighing a pound and a half, lengthwise down the spinal bone; leave the skin on the meats, season with salt, coat over with oil, and roll them in white bread-crumbs; broil for fifteen to twenty minutes over a slow fire, turning them over when half done. Dress them on a dish, pour over slightly melted lobster butter (No. 580) thickened with velouté sauce (No. 415); add the juice of a lemon and chopped parsley; garnish around the fish with sliced fresh cucumbers, laid in salt for fifteen minutes, and all the liquid extracted, then seasoned with pepper, vinegar, and oil, as well as some finely chopped chervil.

(1226). POMPANO À LA SOYA (Pompano à la Soya).

Suppress the heads and thin tail parts from three fish weighing three quarters of a pound each; cut the meat into steaks, and sprinkle over with salt. Cut in fine shreds, half a pound of leeks, and a quarter of a pound of celery, the same of carrots; fry them in butter over a slow fire without coloring, then add the pieces of fish, and moisten to their heighth with broth and white wine; season with pepper, parsley, thyme, and bay leaf. When the fish is done, remove from the fire and dress. Lay around the dish mellow potatoes (No. 2799), and thin slices of blackfish à la Orly (No. 1114). Serve with a sauce-boat of horseradish and cream sauce (No. 478).

(1227). POMPANO À LA TOULOUSE (Pompano à la Toulouse).

Split the fish through the middle at both ends through their entire length; braise these in a mirepoix stock with white wine (No. 39), and when the fish is done, drain the stock, and reduce it with the same quantity of velouté sauce (No. 415); thicken it with egg-yolks, and fresh butter, and put it on the back of the fire to keep it near the boiling point, then strain it through a tammy. Dress the fish, garnish around with mushrooms, truffles, fish quenelles, crawfish tails, or else shrimps. Cover the garnishing with the sauce, and lay on top small breaded smelts fried in oil, or these may be replaced by gudgeons or thin slices of perch fillets, place around a border of crusts of bread, buttered and browned in the oven.

(1228). POMPANO FILLETS FRIED WITH TOMATO SAUCE (Filets de Pompano Frits à la Sauce Tomate).

Remove the fillets from several fresh fish, also the skins; cut them across diagonally, and lay them on a dish to season; marinate the slices for a quarter of an hour in sweet oil, lemon juice and chopped parsley. Take up the pieces, one by one, dip them into a frying batter (No. 137), and plunge them in hot frying fat; let them slowly attain a good color while cooking, and when done drain and salt. Dress the fillets in a pyramid form on a napkin, and garnish with fried parsley and cut lemons, or else serve with a sauce-boat of tomato sauce (No. 549).

(1229). PORGIES À LA MANHATTAN (Porgies à la Manhattan).

Cut the fish into quarter of a pound slices and boil them in a court-bouillon, moistened with white wine (No. 39); drain and remove the skin carefully, then dress on the center of a hot dish. Dip two ounces of cracker-dust and as much bread-crumbs into a little milk; press out all the liquid and put this paste into a saucepan with fish stock (No. 417) and a little milk, in order to have the sauce not too thick; season with salt, nutmeg and pepper, and rub through a sieve, then finish with fresh butter just when prepared to serve. Shell some fresh green corn by splitting the grains through the center, and pressing on them with the back of a knife to extract all the inside part, chop this up finely, and add to it the sauce, also some hashed lobster coral and chopped parsley; pour the whole over the fish.

(1230). PORGIES, PAUPIETTES HINDOSTAN (Paupiettes de Porgies à l'Indostan.

Remove the fillets and skin from the fish; pare to the size of one and three-quarters inches to four inches, and season with salt, nutmeg and pepper; then coat the flesh side with a thin layer of fish quenelle forcemeat (No. 90), to which has been added cooked fine herbs (No. 385). Roll them up into cork-shaped pieces and set them in buttered tin cylinders; lay these in a sautoir, moisten with mirepoix stock (No. 419), sprinkle over with butter, and set them in the oven for a few moments simply to stiffen the fish; remove, unmold, dip in egg, and roll in white bread-crumbs, then run an iron skewer through, and dip each one in melted butter, and broil them for fifteen to twenty minutes over a very low fire. Dress them on a stand made with rice and saffron, surround with sliced lemon, each slice being cut across in two, and serve separately an espagnole sauce (No. 414), mixed with curry and buttered with cayenne butter (No. 571).

(1231). PORGIES WITH CHABLIS WINE (Porgies au vin de Chablis).

Prepare enough court bouillon (No. 39) with white Chablis wine to cover the fish; range some well cleansed fish on the grate of a fish kettle, boil the court bouillon in the kettle, and replace the grate containing the fish into the boiling liquid. Give a few boils, then remove to the side of the range, keeping the kettle covered for a few minutes; when the fish is cooked, drain it off and dress it on a napkin laid over a long dish; surround it with sprigs of parsley. Drain the broth, skim off the fat, reduce, and thicken it with small pieces of kneaded butter (No. 579); boil it once or twice, then remove, and finish with a few pats of fresh butter, chopped parsley, and lemon juice.

(1232). RED SNAPPER À LA CHÉROT (Red Snapper à la Chérot).

Raise the fillets from the fish, pare them into half hearts, lard half of them with anchovies, and the other half with lardons of eel; put them in a buttered sautoir and moisten to their height with a mirepoix stock (No. 419) and champagne wine; baste frequently, and when the fish is done, drain it off and reduce the stock. Fry a finely chopped onion in butter, dilute it with the stock and a tomato purée (No. 730), boil, despumate, and just when ready to serve work in a piece of fresh butter, a little sugar, and some chopped parsley. Dress the fish crown-shaped, pour some of the sauce over and garnish the center with some villeroi quenelles; serve the rest of the sauce separate.

(1233). RED SNAPPER À LA CRÉQUY (Red Snapper à la Créquy).

Serve the fillets taken from a fish either whole, or else divided into quarter pound pieces; cook them in a mirepoix (No. 419), moistened with Madeira wine; when cooked reduce this to half, adding its equivalent of espagnole sauce (No. 414). Continue to reduce, incorporating into the sauce some lobster butter (No. 580), a pinch of cayenne, and lemon juice. Prepare a garnishing of gherkins, carrots, quenelles, and truffles, the carrots to be cut in half inch balls blanched and cooked in white broth, the quenelles made with a coffeespoon (No. 155) and poached, and the gherkins cut olive-shaped, and the truffles, cut in the shape of cloves of garlic and heated with a little glaze (No. 402) and Madeira. Dress the fish in the center of a dish, and surround with the garnishings arranged in groups; pour some sauce over, and serve the rest separately.

(1234). RED SNAPPER À LA DEMIDOFF (Red Snapper à la Demidoff).

Keep the fillets whole while taking them from the fish; remove the skin, pare and cut them up into bias slices, trim these giving them an oval shape, then season and cover the surface with a cream forcemeat (No. 76). Decorate the tops with truffles, range them in a buttered sautoir, and moisten with fish stock (No. 195); cover over with buttered paper, and let cook in a slack oven. Reduce the stock with an equal quantity of velouté sauce (No. 415); garnish around the fish with oysters from which the hard parts have been removed, small lobster rissolettes made as in No 956, and very green parsley leaves on each end. Serve the sauce in a separate sauce-boat.

(1235). RED SNAPPER À LA MOBILE (Red Snapper à la Mobile.

Pare the fillets lifted from a fish, suppress the skin, and cut them up into half heart-shaped pieces; make an incision on one side, and fill this with a forcemeat prepared as follows: Fry colorless in butter some shallots, mushrooms, chives, and parsley; add to it a tomato purée (No. 730), season with salt, pepper, and nutmeg, and mix in a little béchamel sauce (No. 409). Lay the fish on a buttered dish, and cover with a Chivry sauce (No. 449).

(1236). RED SNAPPER À LA PRINCESS (Red Snapper à la Princesse).

Remove the skin from fillets of fish and cut them up into half inch thick slices; pare these into ovals, three and a half inches long by two and a quarter wide, season with salt and pepper. Lay on each oval a bed of mushroom purée (No. 722), and cover the whole with quenelle forcemeat (No. 90). Egg the surfaces, bestrew with bread-crumbs and a little parmesan, then set them in a lightly buttered sautoir; place this in the oven and when the fish is done, serve it with a separate princess sauce (No. 528).

SALMON (Saumon).

The salmon is a large fish, its weight reaching thirty pounds. The body is covered with scales, the meat is tender, thick, red colored and delicate, of an exquisite taste, but very difficult to digest.

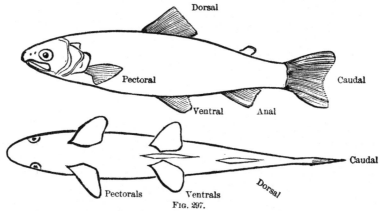

FIG. 297.

No fish has more than two pectorals, or two ventrals; may have several anals, and several dorsals; none, unless deformed or monstrous, has more than one caudal.

(1237). SALMON À L'ARGENTINE (Saumon à l'Argentine).

Remove the meats from the fillets of a fish, also the skin; trim them into half inch bias slices, then pare them the shape of a half heart. Range these pieces in a buttered sautoir, season with salt and pepper, and moisten with white wine and a court bouillon (No. 39) or else some mirepoix stock (No. 419). Cover over with a strong buttered paper and set them to cook in a slow oven. As soon as the fish is done, drain off the liquid and reduce it with espagnole sauce (No. 414), to a half-glaze; dress the fillets, pour the sauce over and garnish the center with a very consistent argentine sauce (No. 429).

(1238). SALMON À LA D'ARTOIS—FILLETS (Filets de Saumon à la d'Artois).

Select a piece from the tail end of an uncooked fish, remove the meat from each flat side of the bone, suppress the skin and cut the fish into half inch thick slices, pare them the shape of a chicken fillet, season and cover both sides with a forcemeat (No. 90) wet with beaten egg-whites and sprinkle over with finely chopped truffles, lay them in a buttered sautoir, baste the fish with melted butter and cook in a moderate oven. When done dress the pieces in a circle and garnish the center with cooked minced truffles and mushrooms. Cover over with a béarnaise sauce (No. 433) made with lobster butter (No. 580) and finished with meat glaze (No. 402).

(1239). SALMON À LA DAUMONT (Saumon à la Daumont).

Cut slices of fish half an inch thick, more or less, so as to strike the exact joints of the large dorsal bone so that it can be cut through without any resistance, otherwise the fish will be torn and spoiled. Put these slices into a buttered sautoir, season them with salt, whole peppers, branches of parsley, thyme, bay leaf and minced onions; cover with cold water and let cook slowly; suppress the skin and bones, dress the fish and garnish around with mussels, shrimp tails and blanched oysters. Cover the whole with a well buttered Normande sauce (No. 509), and decorate the top with minced truffles heated in a little half-glaze (No. 400) and Madeira, and around with fluted and glazed mushrooms and trussed crawfish.

(1240). SALMON À LA DUPERRÉ—DARNE (Darne de Saumon à la Duperré).

A darne means a large slice of salmon, four to six inches thick, cut from the middle of the fish; after it is scaled, put it into an earthen vessel and cover with fine salt, leaving it thus for one hour, then take it out and lay it in a fish kettle; cover with cold water and a gill of vinegar, salt, minced carrots and onions, thyme, bay leaf and a bunch of parsley; let the liquid come to a boil, then skim and remove it to the side of the range so that it quivers only for forty to sixty minutes. Drain off the darne, suppress the skin and sanguineous parts covering the flesh, and dress it on a dish; glaze it over with fish glaze (No. 399) mixed with lobster butter (No. 580); garnish around with the tender part of oysters, mushroom heads turned and channeled (No. 218) and arranged in clusters; cover with a pint of matelotte sauce (No. 498) buttered when prepared to serve with lobster butter (No. 580), and fill a sauce-boat with the same sauce; lay a row of bread croûtons fried in butter around the edge of the dish.

(1241). SALMON, FRENCH STYLE (Saumon à la Française).

Dress a small salmon, put it into a fish kettle and moisten with mirepoix stock and white wine (No. 419); set it on the hot fire and as soon as it reaches the boiling degree, skim and put it aside, keeping it at the same degree of heat, but without boiling for an hour or more, according to

FIG. 298.

the size of the fish. When done suppress the skin and sanguineous parts covering the flesh, glaze it over with fish glaze (No. 399) and lobster butter (No. 580) mixed, dress on a dish and garnish around with mushroom heads, small truffles and milts cooked in a marinade. Cover over with financière sauce (No. 464) and lay around the garnishing small slices of eel fried in butter, glazed crawfish and bread croûtons fried in butter; serve a financière sauce (No. 464) separately.

(1242). SALMON À LA MODERNE (Saumon à la Moderne).

Prepare a garnishing composed of blackfish fillets à la orly (No. 1114), small onions, milts, and mushrooms, also a champagne sauce (No. 445). Cut from a medium sized salmon, two inch thick slices; macerate them for one hour in fine salt, drain, and range them on the grate of a small fish kettle to plunge them into a boiling plain court bouillon (No. 38). Let it boil once more, and keep it at the same degree of heat but without boiling for twenty-five to thirty minutes; when done drain the slices on a cloth to wipe off all the moisture; suppress the skin, then dress them one over-lapping the other on a long dish; around the fish range the small onions, mushrooms, and milts; pour some of the sauce over, and garnish both ends with the fillets. Send the champagne sauce to the table in a sauce-boat.

(1243). SALMON À LA VICTORIA (Saumon à la Victoria).

Trim slices of fish, each about half an inch in thickness; cook them in a mirepoix stock (No. 419), moistened with red wine, and when done, which will take from eight to ten minutes, drain them off, and strain the stock; reduce this, and despumate it; just when ready to serve stir in a piece of lobster butter (No. 580). Serve the fish, surrounding it with sautéd lobster escalops, and small anchovy tartlets; cover the lobster with half of the sauce, and pour the remainder in a sauce-boat to be served at the same time.

(1244). SALMON—BROILED SLICES—BÉARNAISE SAUCE. (Tranches de Saumon Grillées à la Sauce Béarnaise).

Cut off two slices from the fish, each half an inch thick; lay them on a dish to sprinkle with salt, adding sweet oil, minced onions, and parsley leaves; let them marinate for one hour. Set them on a broiler and broil them for thirty minutes, basting them over with oil or melted butter. When done, remove the skin, dress them on a dish and pour over a little oil mingled with lemon juice and chopped parsley. Send to the table with a sauce-boat of béarnaise sauce (No. 433).

(1245). SALMON MARINADE SAUCE (Saumon à la Sauce Marinade).

Cut any desired width slices from a medium sized salmon, in a manner to separate the bone at the joint, or about every half inch. Range them on a dish, besprinkle with vinegar and oil. season with salt, peppercorns, thyme, bay leaf, parsley leaves, cloves, mace, and a clove of garlic. Let them marinate in this for two hours, then range the slices on a fish kettle grater, and cover liberally with salt and the marinade; moisten with sufficient cold water to immerse the fish and thirty minutes before serving time, place it on the hot fire to bring the liquid to a boil, then move it aside and keep it at the same degree of heat, but without boiling for eighteen to twenty minutes. Dress the slices on a folded napkin with parsley leaves around; serve a separate sauce-boat of lean marinade sauce (No. 496).

(1246). SALMON—QUARTER—GENEVOISE SAUCE (Quart de Saumon à la Sauce Génevoise).

The illustration (Fig. 299), represents this remove of salmon as it should be dresssed.

Choose a fresh salmon weighing from twelve to sixteen pounds, suppress the head and about eight inches of meat from the thin tail end; divide the remainder into two equal parts cutting it through the thickness in the center, split each part in two lengthwise pieces leaving half of the large bone adhering to each part; it is one of these half slices that is shown in the illustration. Tie these four halves together to give them their primitive shape; lay the fish on a grater of

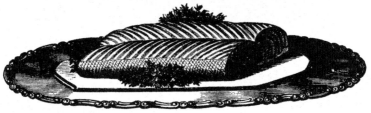

FIG. 299.

a small fish kettle with an abundance of salt, let macerate for one hour, then cover with cold water and two gills of vinegar, add simply a large bunch of parsley, then heat the liquid while skimming, and at the first boil remove the kettle to the side of the fire so that the liquid quivers only for thirty to forty minutes. A quarter of an hour before serving, drain off the fish on the grater and with the tip of a knife cut a slit in the middle of each quarter of the width of three inches on the whole length of the skin, in a straight line, so as to remove all the central part, suppress also the sanguineous crust covering the flesh, leaving them bare. Wash the fish in its own broth, then rub the surfaces with a piece of fresh butter or red butter (No. 580). Slide the fish on a long dish, the bottom being supplied with a perforated board, and covered over with a folded napkin. Send to the table with a dishful of three-quarter inch potato balls boiled in salted water and a sauce-boat of genevoise sauce (No. 469).

(1247). SALMON SALTED, À LA BEDLOW (Saumon Salé à la Bedlow).

Soak some salt salmon for twelve hours, changing the water several times, then boil it in acidulated water adding a handful of parsley branches. Have a béchamel sauce (No. 409), and just when ready to serve incorporate into it pats of fresh butter; add some nasturtiums and garnish around with small crab croquettes (No. 879).

(1248). SALMON—SMOKED AMERICAN STYLE (Saumon Fumé à l'Américaine).

Boil over a slow fire some fresh, mellow smoked salmon, then dress it with the following sauce: Chop up finely two shallots, place them in a saucepan with half a pint of fish essence (No. 388), and one gill of vinegar, reduce with a pint of lean velouté (No. 415); stir in the juice of a lemon, two ounces of anchovy butter (No. 569) and four finely chopped hard boiled egg-yolks; strew a little chopped parsley over and serve.

(1249). SARDINES BROILED. ANCHOVIES FRIED. SILVER FISH IN PAPERS (Sardines Grillées. Anchois Frits. Silver Fish en Papillotes).

Broiled Sardines.—If the sardines be fresh, empty and scrape on each side, then wipe well. Put them on a plate, pour oil over, and place them on a double hinged broiler; broil, dress and baste with maître d'hôtel butter (No. 581). Serve at the same time some slices of toast. In case there be no fresh sardines then use those in tins; take them out of the box, suppress the skin, and cut off both ends, finish them the same as the fresh ones.

Fried Anchovies.—If no fresh anchovies be handy, then use unsalted ones, splitting them in two and soak in fresh water for three hours. Drain, clean, and put them on a deep plate pouring over vinegar, oil, adding mignonette pepper. Dip them in frying paste, then plunge into very hot oil to fry them to a fine color; drain and dress on a folded napkin in a pyramidical form, arranging a bunch of fried parsley on top. Serve with anchovy sauce (No. 427).

Silver Fish in Papers.—After cleaning the fish, slightly detach the fillets in order to remove the middle bone; salt and coat over with oil, broil them but little. Oil some sheets of paper, cut into heart-shapes; on one side place a little Duxelle (No. 385), over this the fish, and finish with a little more Duxelle, then fold the paper all around to enclose them hermetically; when they are two-thirds folded pour in some Madeira sauce (No. 492), and finish to close. Butter the dish on which they are to be served, put on the papers and set it in the oven. Serve when the papers have swollen and they are of a fine color.

(1250). SHAD BROILED, RAVIGOTE BUTTER (Alose Grillée, Beurre Ravigote).

The shad is a fish of the Clupeidæ family, found in North America and Europe. It is an excellent fish with a toothless mouth, and a large veined head. Select a very fresh shad; split it down the

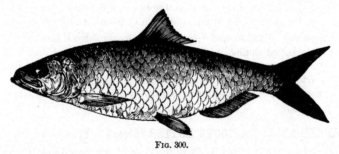

FIG. 300.

entire back, remove the spinal bone, and season with salt, and place it on a dish with some oil, afterward broil it with the flesh side on the broiler, having a low but well maintained fire; turn it over when a fine color to finish cooking. Dress the fish on a hot dish; besprinkle with ravigote butter (No. 583), partially melted to the consistency of thick cream, and serve.

(1251). SHAD À LA CREOLE (Alose à la Créole).

Raise the fillets from a shad, remove the skin, and cut the fish into half inch thick slices; pare them half heart-shape (each one should weigh four ounces after being pared). Cook them in a mirepoix stock with white wine (No. 419), and when done drain off the stock to reduce it with velouté sauce (No. 416). Dress the fillets of shad in a circle, and fill in the empty space with rice à la créole, and surround the fish with fried shad milts or broiled shad roe.

To Prepare Créole Rice.—Have half a pound of washed rice for every shad; set it in a saucepan, moisten with twice as much water, adding two ounces of butter; let boil, and then finish cooking in the oven for twenty minutes; stir into it a little saffron, butter, and lemon juice.

(1252). SHAD À LA EVERS GARNISHED WITH SHAD ROE SHELLS (Alose à la Evers, Garnie de Coquilles d'Œuf d'Alose).

Split a shad through the back, remove the middle bone; fry in butter very finely hashed onions, shallots, and fresh mushrooms; add to this some bread-crumbs after soaking and pressing them, also chopped parsley, butter, and egg-yolks, salt, pepper, and nutmeg. Fill the inside of the shad with this preparation, lay it on a buttered pan, pouring over a little white wine and velouté sauce (No. 415); besprinkle with bread-crumbs, parmesan, and butter, then set it into the oven so that the fish cooks well and browns nicely. When done squeeze over the juice of a lemon, and dredge with chopped parsley. Cover the tops of the shells in the oven, and serve them on napkins the same time as the shad.

For the garnishing use shells of shad's roe, prepared by wrapping the roes in strong buttered paper, and cooking them in a slow oven; remove the paper and adhering skins, and use them to fill well some cleaned scollop shells. Fry a little bread-raspings in butter with the addition of chopped up mushrooms and onions; moisten with a little white wine, add some béchamel (No. 409), and pour this over the filled shells; bestrew the top with bread-crumbs and grated parmesan, besprinkle over a little butter, color them and serve on a dish over a folded napkin.

(1253). SHAD, BRUSSELS STYLE (Alose à la Bruxelloise).

Raise the fillets from a shad and remove the skin, then lay the fish on a buttered dish. Mix with two ounces of fresh butter, one ounce of finely chopped fresh mushrooms, pepper, salt, nutmeg, lemon juice and a clove of crushed garlic; cover the fish with this preparation, dredge over bread-crumbs and grated parmesan and pour over a little melted butter. Cook the shad in a hot oven and when done, press over the juice of a lemon; besprinkle with chopped parsley, and cover with a rather light brown sauce (No. 414) made with white wine.

(1254). SHAD, IRISH STYLE, GARNISHED WITH SHAD ROE CROQUETTES (Alose à l'Irlandaise Garnie de Croquettes d'Œufs d'Alose).

Split a medium sized shad through the entire length of the back; take out the spinal bone, then season the fish with salt; coat it over with sweet oil and broil it to a fine color, having it at the same time well cooked, then dress it on a hot dish. Garnish around with potato balls five-eighths of an inch in diameter, cooked in salted water, well drained, and covered with a green ravigote sauce (No. 531), sending a sauce-boat of the same to the table. Around the potatoes lay croquettes made of shad's roe, round and flat, the same as below, and serve the whole very hot.

Shad's Roe Croquettes.—Boil a shad's roe in a little mushroom broth, then skin it. Fry in melted butter a little chopped shallot, add to it the roe, some béchamel cream, salt and prepared red pepper (No. 168), reduce and stir in a piece of fresh butter; when this preparation is cold make it into one and a quarter inch croquette balls, flattening them down to half an inch in thickness; dip them in beaten eggs, then in bread-crumbs and fry to a fine golden color, then drain, wipe and dress around the potatoes.

(1255). PLANKED SHAD, RAVIGOTE BUTTER (Alose à la Planche, au Beurre Ravigote).

Procure a very dry cherrywood plank, three-quarters of an inch thick, fourteen inches long, and ten inches wide; it should be beveled on the bottom edge with two crosspieces of wood which should be screwed on underneath. Open the shad by splitting it down the back, remove the spinal bone and season with salt; cut off the head and thin tail part, and fasten the shad on the plank; set it in front of the fire to cook, or better still underneath a gas salamander (Fig. 123.) When the fish is done—which will be in about thirty minutes—lay both the plank and shad on a dish, and cover the top of the fish with ravigote butter (No. 583); serve it immediately.

(1256). SHAD, WITH SORREL PURÉE AND SORREL LEAVES (Alose à la Purée d'Oseille et aux Feuilles d'Oseille).

With Sorrel Purée.—Trim the fillets of shad into half hearts, cook them as in No. 1253, and then dress in a circle; garnish the center with some sorrel purée (No. 728).

With Sorrel Leaves.—Fry two ounces of chopped onions, moisten with fish broth, and add half a pound of sorrel leaves; lay the whole shad on top of this with two ounces of butter put on the cover, closing it hermetically with a little dough made with flour and water, and cook it in a moderate oven for five hours. Serve the fish whole with the broth reduced.

(1257). SHEEPSHEAD À LA BÉCHAMEL (Sheepshead à la Béchamel).

Cook two pounds of peeled mushroom heads with butter and lemon juice, then cut them up into transverse slices. Butter a border mold (Fig. 139) either oval or round according to the shape of the dish it is intended for; bestrew the inside with bread-crumbs and fill in the empty space with duchess potato preparation (No. 2785); press down the potatoes well, butter over with a brush, then set it on a baking sheet to brown nicely in the oven. Cut a six-pound sheepshead into square pieces, cook them in salted water, and as soon as done, drain; shred the fish suppressing all the bones, skin, etc., and put it into a sautoir; pour over some good, reduced, thick béchamel (No. 409), raw cream and mushroom broth, adding butter piece by piece after it is taken from the fire. Invert the border on a dish—garnish the center with the shredded sheepshead alternating with layers of the sliced mushrooms; pour over a little of the sauce and shape it into a dome; cover the summit with a layer of Mornay sauce (No. 504), smooth nicely, then besprinkle with grated parmesan and melted butter, glaze in a very hot oven or else a gas salamander (Fig. 123). Decorate the dome with four or six trussed crawfish and serve separately a reduced béchamel sauce (No. 409) finished with red butter (No. 580).

(1258). SHEEPSHEAD À LA BOURGUIGNONNE (Sheepshead à la Bourguignonne).

Mince four ounces of onions, and fry in two ounces of butter, moistening with a bottle of Burgundy wine; season, and add a garnished bunch of parsley, then continue to cook for fifteen minutes. Remove the fillets from a fine sheepshead, suppress the skin, and cut the fish into half inch thick slices, pare them half heart-shaped; these slices should each weigh four ounces; lay them one beside the other in a baking dish and pour over the strained wine. Cook the fish in a moderate oven for fifteen minutes, basting occasionally; when done drain the fish on a dish, strain the stock through a sieve, skim off its fat, and thicken it with a few bits of kneaded butter (No. 579), then pour it over the slices of sheepshead and serve.

(1259). SHEEPSHEAD À LA BUENA VISTA (Sheepshead à la Buena Vista).

Put a well cleansed sheepshead into the fish kettle and cook it in mirepoix stock (No. 419); when the fish is done, dress and garnish around with sauted shrimp and the soft part of some oysters. The sauce to accompany this is made with béchamel (No. 409) mixed with a tomato purée (No. 730), seasoned with salt, cayenne pepper, and lemon juice; strain this sauce and add to it a few blanched tarragon leaves, pour half of this over the fish and garnishing. Place around some fried porgy paupiettes (No. 1230), and potato cakes (No. 2778). Serve the remainder of the sauce in a sauce tureen.

(1260). SHEEPSHEAD À LA MEISSONIER (Sheepshead à la Meissonier).

Blanch separately one ounce of parsley root, one ounce of celery knob root, two ounces of mushrooms, two ounces of the white of leeks, all cut in fine strips, and minced onions, also blanched separately. Put three ounces of butter into a saucepan on the fire, and when hot place therein the onions, leeks, mushroom, parsley and celery roots, and fry without browning. Moisten with white wine and fish stock (No. 417). Lift the fillets from the fish, pare them neatly, and lay them in a deep buttered dish, the skin part downward; pour over the prepared stock, and cover over with another dish, then cook in the oven for fifteen to twenty minutes. Put into a saucepan, one pint of velouté (No. 415), boil, and reduce it with the stock to the consistency of a light sauce, add the vegetables, dress the fish, pour the sauce and the roots over, and bestrew the whole with very green, chopped parsley.

(1261). SHEEPSHEAD, CARDINAL SAUCE (Sheepshead à la Sauce Cardinal).

Clean and prepare a sheepshead, tying down the head, then place it on the grate; plunge this into cold salted water in a fish kettle; place on the fire, and at the first boil, cover the kettle and remove it to one side so that the liquid only quivers; keep it thus for forty-five to sixty minutes, then drain and rub the surface over with a piece of butter; dress the sheepshead and garnish it around with very green parsley branches and olive-shaped potatoes boiled in salted water. Serve at the same time a cardinal sauce (No. 442) in a separate sauce-boat.

(1262). SHEEPSHEAD WITH THICKENED COURT BOUILLON (Sheepshead au Court Bouillon Lié)

Clean well a very fresh sheepshead weighing about six pounds, and place it on a grate of a fish kettle; pour over just sufficient court bouillon (No. 38) to cover. Set the fish kettle on the fire and let the liquid come to a boil while skimming, then remove it at once to the side of the range to keep quivering without boiling for half an hour. Melt some butter in a pan, add to it a finely chopped shallot and fry it colorless, also eight ounces of minced mushrooms; moisten with some of the court bouillon and let reduce. Lay the sheepshead on a buttered dish; season with salt and mignonette and pour the sauce over; cover with another dish and finish cooking in the oven for fifteen to twenty minutes. Just when ready to serve, dress the fish, reduce the stock and thicken it with some velouté sauce (No. 415) and a little tomato sauce (No. 549); pour it over the fish after removing the skin from both ends. This sauce should be rather light than otherwise. Sprinkle chopped parsley over all.

(1263). SKATE À LA LECHARTIER (Raie à la Lechartier).

Suppress the fins and wash a medium-sized skate, after having emptied it, divide it into three parts, the two wings and the body; lay these in cold water of a sufficient quantity to cover entirely, then add salt, pepper, vinegar, sliced onions and parsley leaves. Set the fish boiler on the fire removing it at the first boil, put in the liver and keep it on one side without letting it boil for full half an hour, drain off the fish, scrape it well on both sides in order to remove the skin properly. Put into the bottom of a baking dish a bed of cooked fine herbs (No 385), on this the skate with the sliced liver around; cover all with a well reduced béchamel (No. 409), into which has been stirred a little melted fish glaze (No. 399); besprinkle with grated parmesan, bread-crumbs or raspings and chopped parsley, the whole well mixed together; pour over a little butter and bake in the oven. When serving squeeze on the juice of a lemon.

(1264). SKATE, WITH HAZELNUT OR BLACK BUTTER (Raie au Beurre Noisette ou Noir).

Cut the fish up into three parts, the two wings and the body; each wing into three parts and the body into two, making eight parts in all. Suppress the head and tail, empty it from the belly side, reserving the liver. Plunge the pieces of skate into boiling water until the skin will detach when scraping it off with a knife. After all the pieces are well cleansed soak them for one hour in cold water. Boil some water in a saucepan, add to it minced roots and onions, aromatic herbs, a bunch of parsley, salt and three gills of vinegar; let this boil for ten minutes, then throw in the skate and the liver, cover over when it begins to boil, set it on one side to poach merely, without boiling; a quarter of an hour later drain and dry all the moisture on a cloth. Dress the fish on a dish with the liver sliced, cover it liberally with hazelnut butter (No. 567) or else black butter (No. 565), or a sharp sauce (No. 538).

(1265). SMELTS À l'ALEXANDRIA (Éperlans à l'Alexandrie).

A genus of fish of the Malacapterigian order of the salmon family, being five to six inches long. This fish is remarkable for its silvery coloring, and the delicacy of its meat, which has a slight fragrance of the violet or cucumber.

Smelts à l'Alexandria.—For twelve smelts mince finely four medium leeks, and fry them in butter. Cut the heads and tails from the smelts, and fry the fish with the leeks; besprinkle with flour and moisten with tomato gravy, adding whole peppers and a garnished bunch of parsley containing bay leaf and garlic. When the fish is done, dress and reduce the sauce, thickening it with egg-yolks and butter, then strain it through a tammy (Fig. 88); garnish round the dish with the smelt's milts or roe fried in butter, cover with a part of the sauce and serve the remainder in a sauce-boat.

(1266). SMELTS À LA GONDOLIÈRE (Éperlans à la Gondolière).

Bone medium sized smelts after cleaning nicely; split them down through the back, remove the bone, and season with salt, pepper, and nutmeg; stuff their insides with a pike quenelle forcemeat (No. 90), into which a quarter as much cooked fine herbs (No. 385) have been added, and softened with a little good cream; fill the smelts with this, close to give them their original shape, and wrap them up in a double sheet of buttered paper. Braise the fish in a mirepoix stock with white wine (No. 419), and as soon as they are done, strain the liquid and reduce, adding to it a Venetian sauce (No. 555); unwrap the smelts, range them in the center of a dish and pour the sauce over, garnishing the ends with trussed crawfish.

(1267). SMELTS À LA NORFOLK (Éperlans à la Norfolk).

Cut off the heads and thin tail parts from some large smelts; bone, and stuff them with a pike queneile forcemeat (No. 90) containing raw fine herbs; range them on a buttered baking dish, season with salt, pepper, and nutmeg, and dredge over chopped shallots fried in butter; moisten with white wine, put to cook in a slow oven basting frequently with its own stock; when done drain off the fish, reduce the liquid with velouté (No. 415), skim and season well. Just when ready to serve incorporate into the sauce a little fresh butter and cut up mush-rooms.

(1268). SMELTS, DIPLOMATIC (Éperlans Diplomate).

Have large fresh smelts cut off the fins, the dorsal, remove the eyes, split the fish open through the back, suppress the gills and sever the spinal bone a little below the head, and just above the tail, then detach and remove it. Salt the insides and fill them through a cornet with fish forcemeat (No. 90) mixed with cooked fine herbs (No. 385) and chopped truffles; shape them into rings by slip-ping the tail through the gill and mouth so that they bite their tails; tie to keep well together, then flour them lightly; dip each one into raw egg-yolks beaten up with melted butter, drain, and then roll them in white bread-crumbs. Heat some butter in a raised-edged baking pan, range the fish in this butter, one beside the other, and push it into a moderate oven to cook on both sides; the but-ter should be plentiful and very hot. Drain the smelts as soon as they are done, untie, and dress them on a long dish with a bunch of fried parsley at each end. Serve a separate lobster sauce (No. 488).

(1269). FRIED SMELTS, ON SKEWERS, TARTAR TRUFFLE SAUCE (Éperlans Frits en Brochettes; Sauce Tartare aux Truffes).

Choose the smelts of a medium size; empty, clean, and wipe dry, then season and dip a few at the time into milk, then roll quickly in flour, and sift through a very coarse sieve. Take them up by the heads, and run small metal skewers through the eyes, either four or six on each one; plunge them at once into hot frying fat in order to have them a nice color, then drain and salt. Dress the smelts on a folded napkin, garnish with fried parsley and quartered lemons, and serve with a sauce-boat of tartar sauce (No. 631), with chopped truffles added.

(1270). SMELTS IN DAUPHIN À LA HAMLIN (Éperlans en Dauphin à la Hamlin).

Prepare some very thin pancakes; cover each one with a thick layer of pike forcemeat (No. 90), into which raw fine herbs have been mingled; place another thin pancake on top, then pare them into half hearts. Bone some smelts leaving on the head, remove the eyes, replace by a small bit of forcemeat, and a dot of truffle, roll them up with the fillets inside and fill the empty space in the center of each side with some of the same forcemeat; set on top a small fluted mushroom head (No. 118). Cover the half hearts with the forcemeat, and lay a smelt over; place in its mouth a small piece of red lobster cut from one of the claws. Set these on a buttered baking sheet, pour over some butter, and cover with a sheet of buttered paper, then cook them in a slack oven; dress crown-shaped, and serve with a ravigote sauce (No. 531), separately.

(1271). FRIED SOLES À LA COLBERT (Soles Frites à la Colbert).

The sole is an excellent tasting fish, its meat being delicate and choice. It is found in almost every sea. The shape is nearly oblong, and its mouth long and projecting.

Fried Soles à la Colbert.—Dress a medium sized sole, paring off the black skin; detach the fillets from the bone on the same side, two inches from the head, and three from the tail; break the bone with the dull edge of a knife, three inches from the head and four from the tail; dip the fish into salted milk, roll it in flour, then immerse entirely in beaten eggs, and roll in fresh bread-crumbs; let the sole fry slowly so that it cooks, and is of a fine color, and when done, remove the piece of spinal bone, and fill the inside with maître d'hôtel butter (No. 581). Dress on a hot dish and garnish with cut lemons (No. 113).

(1272). SOLES À LA LUTÈCE (Soles à la Lutèce).

Cut off straight the heads from three well cleaned soles; remove the black skin; shorten them greatly with a pair of scissors, split them through the middle of the skinned side, and season with salt and pepper; dip in flour, then in beaten egg, and lastly in bread-crumbs; fry in clarified butter, dress on a very hot oval-shaped dish, and garnish around with five-eighths of an inch in diameter potato balls, fried and afterward rolled in fresh butter; season with salt, lemon juice, and chopped parsley. Serve a Parisian sauce (No. 515), at the same time, but separately.

(1273). SOLES À LA MARGUERY—FILLETS (Filets de Soles à la Marguery).

Raise the fillets from two clean, skinned soles; fold in two, pare nicely and season, range them on a buttered baking dish and bestrew the surface with shallots and mushroom peelings: moisten to cover with a white wine court bouillon (No. 39) and allow the liquid to come to a boil, then finish cooking the fillets in a slow oven. Drain them off singly, and dress on a dish; garnish one side with shrimp tails, and the other with blanched oysters, from which the hard parts have been removed, or mussels. Keep the whole very warm. Strain the broth the soles were cooked in, reduce it to a half-glaze, thicken with a mere spoonful of Normande sauce (No. 509) and finish with a piece of fresh lobster butter (No. 580); pour this over the fillets and garnishings, then glaze the sauce with a gas salamander (Fig. 123); two minutes will suffice for this. When the fish is ready to be served, brush the surface with thin lines of red butter (No. 580).

(1274). SOLES À LA NORMANDE (Filets de Soles Normande).

Raise the fillets from four medium sized soles weighing about a pound each; remove the skin, pare them neatly and fold in two. Put them on a buttered baking sheet, season with salt, pepper and chopped onions and moisten to their height with white wine and mushroom broth or else court boullion (No. 39), let the liquid come to a boil, then set the pan in a moderate oven to leave until the fish is well cooked, basting frequently with the stock; drain off the fish and strain the stock, then reduce it with some velouté (No. 415) and thicken with raw egg-yolks, cream and fresh butter. Dress the sole fillets in a circle on a dish and garnish the inside border with half circular-shaped croûtons three-sixteenth of an inch thick and an inch and a quarter in diameter; heat the dish slightly, dip the flat side of the croûton in beaten eggs, stick it to the plate, besprinkle with melted butter and color in a hot oven. Around the fillets of sole arrange some quenelles molded in a coffeespoon (No. 155), some mussels or oysters from which the hard parts have been removed and channeled and turned mushroom heads (No. 118), then cover the whole with the sauce. Garnish the inside of the circle with fillets of smelts or milts à la villeroi, drip over the surface thin lines of meat glaze (No. 402), using a brush for the purpose, and lay trussed crawfish on top.

(1275). SOLES À LA RICHELIEU—FILLETS (Filets de Soles à la Richelieu).

Raise twelve fillets from the soles; pare them their whole length and flatten; season and lay them on a buttered raised-edged baking tin with the parings and bones, half a bottle of white wine, sprigs of parsley, bay leaf, salt, and whole peppers; make a court bouillon by boiling twenty minutes; strain it, and cover the fillets, and poach them partially only; a few moments will suffice for this. Drain and range them on another clean baking sheet, covering over with a buttered paper, and let get cold under a weight, then pare them once more; strain the above stock, skim off the fat, and reduce it to a half-glaze, incorporating it slowly into a little espagnole sauce (No. 414) with the oyster and mushroom broth. When the sauce is of a sufficient succulence strain and keep it in a bain-marie. Make a pike forcemeat (No. 76). Butter some oval rings three and one-half inches by one and three-quarter inches, and a quarter of an inch thick, lay these on sheets of buttered paper, fill them with pike forcemeat; smooth nicely, and range on top the pared fillets; set the rings on a baking sheet one beside another, cover with buttered paper cut in the desirable size. This operation may be performed a few hours before dinner time, that is if the baking sheets can be kept on ice to prevent the forcemeat from souring. Fifteen minutes before serving set the sheets in a slow oven to heat the fillets, and poach the forcemeat. After taking them out lift off the paper, then with a fish skimmer remove each bed of forcemeat and fillets without disarranging them whatever, remove the rings and the paper, dress at once on a dish and surround with very hot garnishing of twelve quenelles, godiveau of pike (No. 83), and two dozen channeled mushrooms (No. 118) on the other; as soon as the dishes are garnished set them into the heater. At the very last moment heat the sauce while stirring, adding butter in moderation; remove the dish from the heater, drain off the liquid and lightly cover the fish garnishings with the sauce. Send a sauce-boat of the sauce into which has been added two dozen oysters, from which the hard parts have been removed, trimmed and cut in large dice.

(1276). SOLES À LA ROCHELAISE (Soles à la Rochelaise).

Remove the black skin from a fine sole; insert the knife on each side to separate the fillets without detaching them; lay the fish on a buttered dish, the black skin side underneath; moisten with white wine and oyster broth, season and set on top some small pieces of butter; place it in the oven to cook without coloring. Drain off the stock, add a minced onion, and reduce it to half, pouring in a little espagnole sauce (No. 414), and thickening with butter and lemon juice; strain this through a tammy; garnish around the sole with mushroom heads and the soft part of oysters; add chopped parsley, pour part of the sauce over the whole, serve the rest separately.

(1277). SOLES À LA TROUVILLE (Soles à la Trouville).

Suppress the heads and skin from two well cleaned soles; split them down on the dark side in order to remove the large bone; season the fish, and fill in the empty space with a fish farce (No. 90) with cooked fine herbs (No. 387), mixed with a salpicon of blanched oysters. Range the soles on a baking dish or sheet, moisten them with a court bouillon with white wine (No. 39); season, and let the liquid reach boiling point, then finish cooking the soles in a moderate oven. After they are done, strain their stock and reduce it to a half-glaze; incorporate into it slowly some reduced velouté (No. 415), also a few spoonfuls of oyster broth. Dress the soles on a dish, cover them over with the sauce, and surround the sides with small quenelles (No. 90) made with red butter (No. 580), and the ends with a cluster of fried oysters. Send a surplus of the sauce to the table in a sauce-boat.

(1278). SOLES, VENETIAN STYLE—FILLETS (Filets de Soles à la Vénitienne).

Detach entirely the fillets from six fine, very thick soles; remove the black skin, beat to flatten lightly and fold each one in two, pare and place them in a sautéing pan, having it well buttered, the pointed ends laid toward the center; add a little salt and lemon juice, sauté without coloring, and when done dish up in a crown-shape, cover with a Venetian sauce (No. 555), and garnish the pointed end with a crawfish claw from which the smaller movable claw has been removed, garnish with a paper frill (No. 10); serve.

(1279). SOLES BAKED ITALIAN STYLE (Soles au Gratin à l'Italienne).

For this dish select medium sized soles, lay them on the table the white side underneath, then proceed to cut off the heads on the bias; from this side suppress the gills and empty the sole thoroughly; cut off the thin tail end and scrape the surface with the dull edge of a knife to detach slightly the skin covering the tail, keeping the tail bone in position with the same side of the knife; seize the skin with a towel, and tear it off violently with one stroke. Use a pair of large scissors to remove the small bones found on the outside, and scrape the white skin, then wash, wipe, and make a straight incision on the skinned side to the middle bone, then detach the fillets half an inch on each side. Butter a baking dish, lay in it the soles, having the skinned side down, and pour over two gills of white wine, salt and pepper; lay a few pieces of butter on top, and let the stock come to a boil, then set the dish into the oven for five minutes; when through lay six channeled mushroom heads (No. 118) in a straight row on top, cover with an Italian sauce (No. 484), and dredge over a thin layer of bread-raspings; pour over melted butter, and color in a hot oven for twelve to fifteen minutes; then serve.

(1280). FRIED SOLES (Soles Frites).

Fried soles are prepared the same as à la Colbert (No. 1271), by slightly detaching the fillets without breaking the bone; dip them in milk and flour, and plunge in hot frying fat to cook; when done and of a fine color, drain, wipe, salt, and dress the fish on a napkin; garnish with fried parsley and quartered lemons.

(1281). STUFFED SOLES—FILLETS (Filets de Soles Farcis).

Spread on a raised-edged buttered baking sheet a layer of quenelle forcemeat (No. 90) to the thickness of half an inch, smoothing well the surface. Take twelve fillets of soles, not too large, pare and season them properly, poach these slightly in a sautoir with melted butter; drain and let get partially cold under a light weight; pare them once more and range them at short distances from each other on the layer of forcemeat, placing them on the poached side. Brush over with melted butter and finish cooking in a slack oven as well as the forcemeat. After removing the pan from the oven, cut the forcemeat all around the fillets with the tip of a small knife, lift one after the other up with a palette, forcemeat and all, and dress them in two rows on a long dish, one overlapping the other; garnish between the rows with poached oysters and the ends with a bunch of crawfish tails. Cover the bottom of the dish and the oysters with a normande sauce (No. 509) serving more in a separate sauce-boat.

(1282). SPOTTED FISH À LA LIVOURNAISE (Spotted Fish à la Livournaise.

Carefully pare some fillets taken from the fish into half hearts; lay them on a buttered dish and cover over with tomato sauce (No. 549), gravy (No. 405) and a brown sauce (No. 414), the whole reduced to the consistency of a very succulent sauce, but thin. Besprinkle with bread-crumbs, sprinkle over with oil, and bake the fish in a hot oven; when ready to serve, bestrew the surface with chopped parsley and a few pounded fennel seeds.

(1283). SPOTTED FISH, ENGLISH STYLE—FILLETS (Filets de Spotted Fish à l'Anglaise).

Raise the fillets from three small spotted fish, each one weighing from three-quarters to one pound; pare and season them with salt, oil, lemon juice and branches of parsley, leaving them marinate in this for half an hour. Drain, cut shapely, and dip them in beaten eggs, roll in fresh bread-crumbs and finally immerse in melted butter; broil the fillets a quarter of an hour, turning them over when done. Serve with a hot horseradish sauce (No. 478) or a melted maître d'hôtel (No. 581).

(1284). SPOTTED FISH, MUSSEL SAUCE—WHOLE (Spotted Fish Entier Sauce aux Moules).

Spotted fish weighing from three to five pounds are usually excellent. Empty, scale and tie down the heads; cooks them in a plain court bouillon (No. 38), and at the first boil, remove the kettle on one side to allow the liquid to bubble only for thirty to forty-five minutes. Drain out the fish, dress it on a napkin, surround with parsley, also balls of boiled potatoes three-quarter inch in diameter and Villeroi mussels (No. 698), also a sauce-boat of normande sauce (No. 509). The fish can also be cut in pieces, simply cooked in a wine court bouillon (No. 39) and served the same as above.

(1285). SPOTTED FISH, QUEEN SAUCE—FILLETS (Filets de Spotted Fish Sauce à la Reine).

Procure a very fresh, well cleaned fish weighing four pounds; remove the fillets, skin, pare, and flatten them with the handle of a knife, lay them on a dish, season with salt, oil and lemon juice, and one hour after, besprinkle with chopped parsley, roll in flour. Dip them in eggs beaten up with melted butter, then in bread-crumbs and broil them for a quarter of an hour, turning them over when done on one side. Serve a hot queen sauce (No. 530) separately.

(1286). SPOTTED FISH, WITH GREEN RAVIGOTE SAUCE (Spotted Fish à la Sauce Ravigote Verte).

Cut from twenty to twenty-four aiguillettes from the spotted fish; put these into a tureen with salt, mignonette, branches of parsley, a bit of thyme, bay leaf, basil, a little tarragon vinegar, a little good oil, six shallots and two cloves of garlic both finely minced, toss them about frequently in their seasoning so that they become thoroughly impregnated. Just when ready to serve, drain and roll them in flour. Have sufficient sweet oil poured into a frying pan to bathe the entire fish, let it get very hot, then plunge into it the slices to let attain a fine color and become quite crusty; drain and dress them in a pyramid form. Serve separately a green ravigote sauce (No. 531).

(1287). SPOTTED FISH, WITH COURT BOUILLON, CALCUTTA (Spotted Fish au Court-Bouillon, Calcutta).

Cut in medium size Julienne four ounces of the red part of a carrot, and half as much celery root; cut up as many mushrooms as there is celery, but keep them aside; blanch the carrots and celery separately, and when done, drain, and lay them in a saucepan to cook in a little broth, (No. 194a) letting it fall to a glaze several times and eventually mix in the cut up mushrooms. Lay well cleaned fish in a narrow fish kettle, cover with partially cold fish court bouillon and white wine

(No. 39) heat this to boiling degree, then set it on one side to keep the liquid quivering for twenty to thirty minutes, according to the size of the fish. Strain the liquid through a sieve, skim off the fat, and reduce it to a half-glaze, thickening it with Indian curry sauce (No. 456), boil it up once or twice; dress the fish on a dish, surround it with the vegetables and cover with a part of the sauce, serving the remainder separately.

(1288). STURGEON FRICANDEAU, WITH SORREL OR WITH GREEN PEAS (Fricandeau d'Esturgeon à l'oseille ou aux Petits Pois).

Cut a fillet of sturgeon from the middle part of the fish; remove the skin, pare, and if too thick, split it in two without detaching the parts; flatten down the meat and lard it the same as for a veal fricandeau, then season. Line a flat saucepan with fragments of fat pork, minced roots and onions, lay the fricandeau on top, and moisten to half its height with some veal blond stock (No. 423); set the saucepan on a moderate fire and let the liquid fall very slowly to a glaze, then moisten it once more, and again reduce it to a glaze, and finish the cooking by adding a very little broth at a time, while basting it constantly; finally glaze the fricandeau in the oven. Drain, dress it on a dish, pour its own stock over after straining and skimming it. Serve a separate garnishing of either sorrel or green peas.

(1289). STURGEON OR STERLET WITH QUENELLES AND OLIVES—SMALL (Petit Esturgeon ou Sterlet aux Quenelles et Olives).

Take a small sturgeon or sterlet weighing eight to ten pounds; scale, suppress all the large scales from the back and sides; open it on the belly side in order to empty and notch the inside ligament, taking the place of the spinal bone, at equal distances, with the tip of a knife, then tie the head down with a string. Place the fish in a small narrow fish kettle, sufficiently long, garnish with fat pork, minced roots and onions, salt, and cover over with thin slices of pork, keeping them down in their place with some string. Moisten to half the height with white wine and very rich veal blond (No. 423); boil the liquid for ten minutes, remove it on one side so as to cook the fish slowly while covered, for about an hour. Drain the sturgeon, untie, then strain and skim the stock, reducing it to a half-glaze, and incorporating into it slowly a few gills of a good, reduced brown sauce (No. 414), finishing with a few spoonfuls of Madeira wine, then strain once more. At the very last moment, drain the fish, place on a dish, and surround it with garnishing of quenelles and stuffed olives; cover with some of the sauce, sending the rest to the table in a sauce-boat.

(1290). TROUT À LA BEAUFORT (Truite à la Beaufort).

A genus of fish of the salmon family, all their species being carnivorous; they live a greater part of the time in fresh water, generally that which is the purest and the most rapid. They are very highly esteemed.

FIG. 301.

Trout à la Beaufort.—Draw the fish through the gills without scaling or opening the belly; put it into a fish boiler with two gills of vinegar, cold water and half a bottleful of white wine, salt, sliced carrots and onions and a bunch of parsley, set it on the fire and bring the liquid to a boil while removing the scum, and at the first boil set it on one side to keep the liquid at the same degree, but without boiling from twenty to thirty minutes; at the last moment drain off the fish and slide it on a dish covered with a folded napkin, dressing it on its side and not on the belly, so that the handsome shading of its skin may be entirely revealed; rub the surface over with a piece of butter to prevent the skin from drying; garnish around with small pike quenelles (No. 90) made with lobster butter (No. 580), decorated with truffles; lay a milt or roe fried in butter on the sides and garnish the ends with fillets of flounders scored with slices of truffles and stoned olives. Cover with a matelote sauce (No. 498) and send to the table a separate sauce-boat of the same sauce.

(1291). TROUT À LA CAMBACÉRÈS (Truites à la Cambacérès).

Dress four trout each one weighing three-quarters of a pound, suppressing the gills and entrails, put them into a small fish boiler (Fig. 135), moisten just to their heighth with a mirepoix stock with white wine (No. 419) and cover the kettle, let come to a boil, and when cooked drain off the liquid and reduce it to the consistency of a syrup, add to it some espagnole sauce (No. 414), half inch balls of truffles, green olives and small mushroom heads, also Madeira wine, a pinch of cayenne and a little tomato sauce (No. 549) passed through a very fine sieve. At the last moment stir in a piece of fresh butter, dress the trout, surround with the garnishing, cover over with a part of the sauce, serving the remainder separately.

(1292). TROUT À l'HÔTELIÈRE (Truites à l'Hôtelière).

Have one fish weighing a quarter of a pound for each person, split it through the entire length of the back; take out the middle bone and lay it on the flesh side on a buttered dish, pour over some oil, season, and set into a quick oven; when done put inside each trout a spoonful of maître d'hôtel butter (No. 581), close, dress and garnish with potatoes, English style. (These English potatoes are potatoes cut the same size and shape as a pigeon's egg, then steamed for about fifteen minutes.) Serve a separate sauce made of espagnole (No. 414) and meat glaze (No. 402), finishing it at the last moment with a piece of good butter and lemon juice; run it through a tammy, then add chopped parsley.

(1293). TROUT À LA HUSSARDE (Truites à la Hussarde).

Each trout to weigh a quarter of a pound; split them through the entire back, take out the middle bone and lay them on a dish, season with salt, mignonette, thyme, bay leaf, oil and lemon juice; two hours later lift them out of their marinade. Mix into some fresh butter a quarter as much cooked fine herbs (No. 385), garnish the inside of the fish with this, and wrap them up in a sheet of buttered double paper, put them to cook in a slow oven for twenty minutes, then unwrap and dress over a white poivrade sauce (No. 522).

(1294). TROUT À LA JOAN OF ARC (Truites à la Jeanne d'Arc).

Remove the fillets and skin from several quarter of a pound trout, put them in a dish, seasoning with salt, pepper, oil, vinegar, bay leaf, parsley and minced onions, let marinate for two hours, then take out and dip into melted butter, roll them in bread-crumbs and broil over the fire, dress, sprinkle with cayenne butter (No. 571) and serve separately a velouté sauce (No. 415), finished with crawfish butter (No. 573) and lemon juice; strain through a tammy.

(1295). TROUT À LA MEUNIÈRE (Truites à la Meunière).

Procure several four-ounce trout, scale, draw and season, cut an incision on the thickest part of the fillet, roll the fish in flour. Heat some butter in a frying pan over a moderate fire, lay in the trout and cook while turning them over, drain and dress on a dish leaving the butter in the pan, and to it add a few spoonfuls of melted butter; cook this to hazelnut (No. 567), then remove the pan from the fire, put into it a coffeespoonful of anchovy essence or a piece of anchovy butter (No. 569) to let it froth, then gradually add two or three teaspoonfuls of vinegar; when hot throw in a pinch of chopped parsley, and pour this butter over the very hot fish.

(1296). TROUT À LA MONTAGNARDE (Truites à la Montagnarde).

Score some fine trout, lay them in salt for one hour, then shake them out, put the fish into a fish boiler, moisten with white wine and a little water, add branches of parsley, thyme, bay leaf, cloves, garlic and basil. Let cook and when done, drain the fish and strain the stock, reduce and thicken with kneaded butter (No. 579), skim the surface and strain it again through a tammy, add some blanched parsley leaves, then pour this sauce over the trout.

(1297). TROUT AU BLEU—SMALL (Petites Truites au Bleu).

Small brook trout live where the water is rapid and pure. There exist certain reservoirs, for instance at the Saratoga Club, where each day the fisherman bring the product of their catch, so that amateurs of good fish may always have on hand trout to be killed just when ready to use; this is an excellent method to bring out all the good qualities of its meat.

The various ways of cooking this fish are most simple kill the trout by knocking their heads against a hard substance, open the belly to draw, clip off the gills and wash out the inside. Plunge into boiling water, salted and acidulated with vinegar, and as soon as it reboils, remove the saucepan to the side of the fire to keep the liquid in a bubbling state only for fifteen minutes. Drain the trout, dress it on a napkin, and garnish with parsley and potatoes. Serve at the same time fresh and melted butter. Cooked in this manner the trout may become twisted and broken, but this does not interfere with its good quality.

(1298). TROUT, COOKED IN COURT BOUILLON AND SERVED WITH DIFFERENT SAUCES
(Truites Cuites au Court Bouillon et Servies avec Différentes Sauces).

Prepare a stock with white wine and carrots, onions, celery root, all well shredded, salt, peppercorns, and a bunch of parsley, garnished with half a clove of garlic. Let the liquid boil until the roots are pretty nearly done, then strain it. Lay in a narrow saucepan four medium sized clean trout, moisten them to just their height with the strained stock, cover and cook slowly; when done dress them on a dish, strain the stock, remove the fat, and reduce it to a half-glaze adding to it an equal quantity of Vallière sauce (No. 553), or a Genoise sauce (No. 470) or a Génevoise sauce (No. 469), or gourmets sauce (No. 472), or a well buttered béchamel cream sauce (No. 409), into which has been added a little anchovy essence. Cover the trout with a part of the sauce and serve the rest in a sauce-boat.

(1299). TROUT, FRIED—SMALL (Petites Truites Frites).

Have some small two ounce trout, split open the bellies to empty, scrape lightly and wipe them on a cloth; season with salt, score and roll them in flour. Shape them into rings by passing the tails through the gills and tying; plunge a few at the time into hot frying fat, let cook for eight to ten minutes, then salt, remove the strings, and dress them on napkins with fried parsley on top, and slices of lemon around.

(1300). TROUT, LAUSANNE STYLE (Truites à la Mode de Lausanne).

Clean well twelve small trout each weighing four ounces. Fry in butter two ounces of onions and four ounces of mushrooms both finely but separately chopped up; put this into a baking dish lay the fish on top and moisten with white wine; sprinkle over with fresh butter and let cook in a hot oven; as soon as they are done, strain the stock into a saucepan, reduce it with velouté sauce (No. 415) and just when ready to serve, incorporate into the sauce some butter and lemon-juice; strain through a tammy and add chopped parsley; pour it over the trout previously dressed on a dish.

(1301). TROUT, STUFFED (Truites Farcies).

Draw four trout by the gills, each fish to weigh half a pound; wipe well the insides, and fill the belly with a paste made of fresh butter, white bread-crumbs, parsley, onion, and mushrooms, all finely chopped. Season, then roll each one in a separate sheet of oiled paper; lay them on a baking dish containing melted butter, and let cook for fifteen to twenty minutes in a moderate oven, turning and basting them frequently. Wrap and dress them on a dish; serve with their own butter, and slices of lemon ranged around in a circle.

(1302). SALMON TROUT—À L'ANTOINETTE (Truite Saumonée —à l'Antoinette).

This fish has the color and taste of the salmon. Toward the middle of spring it leaves the ocean to ascend the rivers; this trout is easily digested and is of an exquisite flavor. Our American species is very inferior in quality to those of Europe; they are much larger, and their meat not as red, nor can the taste be compared; therefore epicures are generally disappointed when eating our salmon trout.

À l'Antoinette.—Score the fish and marinate it in salt, mignonette, lemon juice, chopped onions, parsley, thyme, and bay leaf. Drain and roll it in flour, then in beaten eggs, and finally in bread-crumbs; fry in clarified butter, and serve with a separate sauce made as follows. Have one pint of velouté (No. 415), incorporate into it two ounces of anchovy butter (No. 569), salt, pepper, and nutmeg; heat and thicken with two egg-yolks and cream; pass it through a tammy, and serve with capers and shrimp tails.

(1303), TUNNY FISH OR HORSE MACKEREL—FRIED—WITH ARROWROOT MAYONNAISE SAUCE (Thon Frit à la Sauce Mayonnaise à l'Arrowroot).

Lift the fillets from a young tunny fish or from a horse mackerel, suppress the skin and from the meats cut some lenthwise slices or aiguillettes, lay these on a dish to season with salt, mignonette, slices of onions, sprigs of parsley, thyme, bay leaf, oil and vinegar. Leave to marinate for two hours, then drain and wipe dry, dip them in eggs, then in bread-crumbs, fry to a good color; drain and dress on a folded napkin placing a bunch of fried parsley on top. Serve separately arrowroot mayonnaise sauce (No. 611).

(1304) CANADIAN TURBOT À LA D'ORLÉANS (Turbot Canadien à la d'Orléans).

Raise the fillets and skin from the fish; trim and pare into half hearts, then lay them in a buttered sautoir; season with salt, pepper, lemon juice, adding butter and white wine, then cook it over a hot fire, basting frequently while cooking. Dress on a decorated forcemeat border and fill in the inside with mushroom heads, crawfish tails and slices of truffle between each fillet. Make a velouté sauce (No. 415) with the stock and cream, run it through a tammy and pour half of it over the fish, serving the other half in a sauce-boat.

(1305), CANADIAN TURBOT À LA HOUSTON (Turbot Canadien à la Houston).

Pare the fillets cut from a turbot into half hearts; range them in a buttered sautoir seasoning with salt, pepper, nutmeg, finely chopped shallots and butter; moisten with white wine, then cook in a slow oven, drain the stock, reduce and add it to a reduced velouté sauce (No. 415) thickened with egg-yolks, cream and butter. Dress the fish on a buttered baking dish, pour over the sauce and dredge over grated Swiss cheese; besprinkle with melted butter and brown in a brisk oven, then serve.

(1306). CANADIAN TURBOT À LA MERCIER (Turbot Canadien à la Mercier).

A turbot having a dark skin on both sides and the shape of chicken halibut; when dressed and clean, split it through the back, butter a small raised-edged dish, a little larger than the fish; cover the bottom with shallots, mushrooms and parsley, all finely chopped, and lay the fish on top, season and moisten to its height with a good cold court bouillon with white wine (No. 39); let the liquid boil for ten minutes over a moderate fire; cover it with a sheet of buttered paper, and finish cooking in a slack oven, basting it frequently. After removing besprinkle with chopped parsley, and serve it on the same dish surrounded with oysters à la Villeroi (No. 698).

(1307). ENGLISH TURBOT WITH CAPER SAUCE (Turbot Anglais Sauce aux Câpres).

Select a very fresh turbot with thick and white meat, scale and draw, then soak it for one hour in cold water containing a quarter as much milk. Lay it on the drainer of a fish kettle with some salt, and moisten with fresh water mixed with white wine or vinegar; let boil very slowly for three-quarters of an hour. Drain the turbot, rub the white surface with a piece of butter and dress, surrounding it with branches of parsley and balls of boiled potatoes three quarters of an inch in diameter. Serve separately a white sauce (No. 562); finished just when ready to serve with a piece of fresh butter and capers, or else serve a mussel sauce instead of caper (No. 506).

(1308). WEAKFISH À LA BRIGHTON (Weakfish à la Brighton).

Pare some fillets of weakfish, after suppressing their bones and skin, trim them heart-shaped, lay them in a buttered dish with finely shredded chives, truffles and mushrooms; moisten with white wine and oyster liquor, adding a liberal piece of butter. When the fish is done, strain, reduce the stock with well-seasoned velouté sauce (No. 415), and just when serving stir in some fresh butter, lemon juice and a sufficient quantity of small blanched oysters. Dress the fish, garnish with the oysters and pour the sauce over.

(1309). WEAKFISH À LA PONTIGNY (Weakfish à la Pontigny).

Raise the fillets from weakfish; pare them into oval shaped slices and lay in a buttered sautoir; moisten with mirepoix stock (No. 419) with red wine, and let come to a boil, then set the pan into the oven; when the fish is cooked, drain off the stock, and reduce it with an equal quanity of espagnole sauce (No. 414), adding a garnishing of mushrooms, round soubise quenelles, crawfish tails or else shrimps. Dress the slices overlapping with the garnishing around and reduce well the sauce; stir into it some maître d'hôtel butter (No. 581), pour it over, and surround the whole with crotûons of bread fried in butter.

(1310). WHITEBAIT FRIED GREENWICH STYLE AND DEVILED (Blanchaille Frite à la Mode de Greenwich et à la Diable).

The season for whitebait is June, July, and August; it somewhat resembles the small coalfish.

Whitebait Fried.—Lay the fish on ice for twenty minutes previous to serving; roll them in a towel with a handful of flour; shake and then toss them in a very coarse sieve to remove the superfluous flour; plunge them into very hot frying fat. One minute will suffice to cook them; drain and sprinkle over with salt and serve.

Whitebait, Greenwich Style.—To fry whitebait is to dry them in a towel to absorb all their moisture, then roll them in flour, and fry in very hot frying fat; when crisp, drain on a napkin and dress on a very hot dish. Send to the table accompanied with slices of brown or white bread cut very thin and buttered, also quartered lemons; serve at the same time a pepper-caster containing cayenne pepper.

Deviled Whitebait.—Dip them in milk, lay them on a dish containing mustard and cayenne pepper, then in cracker dust, and fry in very white beef kidney suet, drain, and salt. Dress on a napkin with fried parsley on top. Serve separately, slices of brown or fresh graham bread cut exceedingly thin and buttered.

(1311). WHITEFISH A LA GERHARDI (Lavaret à la Gerhardi).

Split a whitefish in two along the spinal bone; remove this, then season. Lay the fish on a buttered dish, moisten with white wine, add chopped up onions, then let cook to reduce the liquid to the consistency of a half-glaze; mix into it a Hollandaise sauce (No. 477). Dress the fish and surround it with blanched oysters, mushrooms and shrimp tails; pour two-thirds of the sauce over, and serve the remainder in a sauce-boat.

(1312). WHITEFISH, PIMENTADE SAUCE (Lavaret Sauce Pimentade).

Raise the fillets from the whitefish, pare and season with salt, pepper, and nutmeg. Coat them over with sweet oil, and broil on a slow fire; dress on a hot dish, and surround with slices of lemon. Serve a separate pimentade sauce (No. 521).

BEEF (Bœuf).

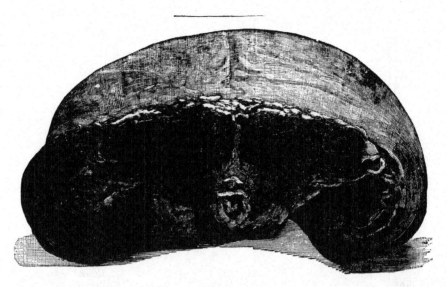

(1313). BARON OF BEEF À LA ST. GEORGE (Selle de Bœuf à la St. George).

The baron of beef weighs about one hundred and fifty pounds. It is the saddle of beef cut from the hip of a young and tender ox as far down as the second rib, this being pared and the thinnest part covered with slices of fat so as to have the meat of uniform thickness and cooked alike throughout. It takes about five hours to cook a baron of beef in a baker's brick oven, the best to use for large pieces of this description, after being cooked they should be put in a heater or warm place, for about two hours, to finish cooking slowly. When cooked arrange it on a large dish, garnishing on the edges with shavings of horseradish (No. 98) and the ends with Yorkshire pudding (No. 770). Serve thickened gravy (No. 405) well skimmed and strained through a fine sieve, in a separate sauce-boat, also some baked potatoes.

(1314). BREAST OR BRISKET OF BEEF À LA FLORENCE (Poitrine ou Bavette de Bœuf à la Florence).

The name of brisket is applied to the part of the beef adjoining the cross ribs, and the neck. If the beef be of a good quality, the plate or brisket makes an excellent and economical boil, the meat being juicy and interlarded with fat giving it a very good flavor.

Put a quarter of a pound of butter in a saucepan, and when warm, add half a pound of lean bacon and half a pound of ham cut into squares of a half of an inch. When the bacon and ham are well browned, add four ounces of onions cut into an eighth of an inch squares, and two pounds of brisket of beef well freed from fat, boned and cut into one inch squares. Add a bunch of parsley, also thyme, bay leaf and a small clove of garlic, two cloves, two celery heads cut in quarters and trimmed and some stewed tomatoes. Moisten with a little broth (No. 194a), cook for two hours and a half, adding a little more broth at times, and serve on a dish garnished around with gastronome potatoes (No. 2789).

(1315). CORNED BREAST OF BEEF WITH CABBAGE (Poitrine de Bœuf Salé aux Choux).

Lay a breast of beef in a brine of half salt, and set it in a cold room, leaving it for twelve days. Unsalt it for two hours, then put the meat in a saucepan with cold water. Let it boil, skimming it occasionally, and place it on one side of the fire to simmer for several hours, or until the meat be thoroughly cooked. Blanch two or three cabbages, cut them in quarters, remove the hard centers, called the core, and two hours before serving put the cabbage in with the beef. When the meat is done properly, drain, and arrange it on a dish, garnishing it round with the cabbage, put some boiled potatoes at either end, and serve a little good gravy separately.

BEEF, AMERICAN CUTS (Bœuf Coupe à l'Américaine).

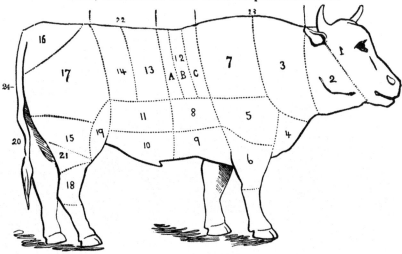

(Fig. 302.)

1. Head.	9. Navel.	17. Round bottom.
2. Beef jowl.	10. Inside flank.	18. Leg of beef.
3. Neck.	11. Thick flank.	19. Butt.
4. Brisket.	12. Six Prime ribs, A first cut,	20. Oxtail.
5. Cross ribs.	B second cut, C third.	21. Horseshoe legs.
6. Shin.	13. Short loin.	22. Hip and loin.
7. Chuck ribs.	14. Hip.	23. Whole chuck.
8. Plates.	15. Round.	24. Round top.
	16. Aitchbone rump.	

BEEF FRENCH CUTS (Bœuf Coupe à la Française).

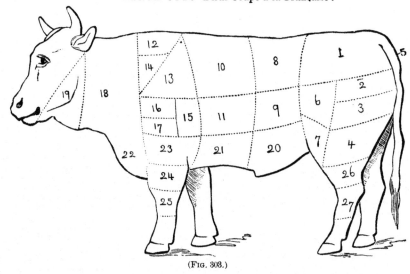

(Fig. 303.)

1. Culotte.	10. Côtes Couvertes, à la noix.	19. Plat de joue.
2. Tranches petit os.	11. Plat de Côtes.	20. Flanchet.
3. Milieu du gîte à la noix.	12. Surlonge partie intérieure.	21. Milieu de poitrine.
4. Derrière du gîte à la noix.	13. Derrière de paleron.	22. Cros bout.
5. Tendre de tranches inté-	14. Talon de Collier.	23. Queue de gîte.
rieure.	15. Bande de Macreuse.	24. Gîte de devant.
6. Tranche grasse intérieure.	16. Milieu de Macreuse dans le	25. Cros du gîte de devant.
7. Pièce ronde partie intérieure.	paleron.	26. Gîte de derrière.
8. Aloyau avec filet.	17. Boite a molele.	27. Cros du gîte de derrière.
9. Bavette d'Aloyau.	18. Collier.	

BEEF AMERICAN CUTS.

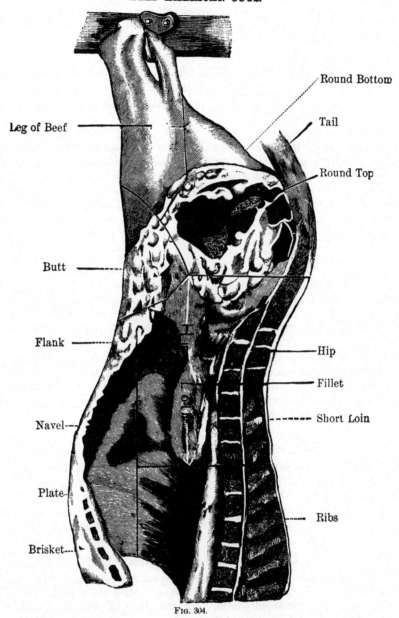

Round Bottom

Tail

Round Top

Leg of Beef

Butt

Flank

Hip

Fillet

Navel

Short Loin

Plate

Brisket

Ribs

Fig. 304.

(1316). CORNED ROUND BOTTOM, TOP, ENGLISH STYLE (Noix de Boeuf Salée Écarlate à l'Anglaise).

Bone and prick the meat with a larding needle, rub it over with pulverized saltpetre, salt, and brown sugar, then put it in an earthern vessel or a wooden tub, pouring over a brine prepared as follows: Throw a potato into salted water; when it rises to the surface it is an indication that the brine is sufficiently strong; pour enough of this over the meat to cover entirely and set it in a cool place where the thermometer does not register above forty degrees, leaving it for fifteen days, and carefully turning the meat over at various intervals. When ready to be used, drain the corned beef, wash, then boil in plenty of water. For a six-pound piece it will take about two hours and a half. After cooking for one hour, add to it a pudding made of flour and beef suet, also cabbage, onions, and pared carrots and turnips. Three-quarters of an hour before serving, throw in some medium sized peeled potatoes; range the corned meat on a dish, garnish around with the cabbage, carrots, turnips, and onions arranged in clusters, and at the ends place the pudding cut into slices. Pour into the bottom of the dish a clear gravy (No. 404). The quantity of water requisite to cook the corned beef depends entirely upon the quantity of salt used, and the length of time the beef was in the brine; if the beef is very salty, it will require more water than otherwise, and it is even advisable to change it after the first boil.

(1317). EDGEBONE OR AITCHBONE, BOILED CREAM HORSERADISH SAUCE (Quasi de Bœuf bouilli Sauce Raifort à la Crème).

Edgebone or aitchbone, is a bone of the rump which in dressed beef presents itself in view edgewise; it is also called aitchbone.

Have a piece of the edgebone weighing twelve pounds; put it in a soup pot capable of holding twice the quantity the size of the meat. Cover with some good broth (No. 194a), place it on the hot fire to bring to a boil, salt to taste, skim well, and add two pounds of carrots, or four medium sized ones, two fine turnips, a four ounce onion stuck with two cloves, six leeks, half a medium sized parsnip, a small handful of celery and one cabbage. Simmer slowly for three or four hours, and when the meat is cooked, drain and dish it up, laying the carrots and turnips cut into pieces, also the cabbage nicely trimmed, around the sides, and green sprigs of parsley at the ends. Serve separately a cream horseradish sauce (No. 478).

(1318). KULASH À LA FINNOISE (Guylas à la Finnoise).

Cut a pound of trimmed tenderloin of beef in inch squares, also two ounces of one-eighth of an inch squares of onions. Put four ounces of butter into a sauté-pan, and when hot, add first the onions and then the beef; season with salt and paprika (a Hungarian pepper), moisten with a little good gravy (No. 404), and cook for one hour and a half, adding a little espagnole sauce (No. 414).

Another way is to use a pound of lean tenderloin, cut in inch squares, half a pound of the breast of bacon cut in half inch squares, a pound of potatoes cut in half inch squares, a quarter of a pound of onions in one-eighth of an inch squares, frying them in half a pound of butter. Put in first the beef, then the potatoes, salt, pepper, and spice, add a pint of good gravy (No. 404), cover hermetically, and cook slowly for one hour and a half.

(1319). MARROW BONES ON TOAST (Moelle sur Croûtes Grillées).

Scrape and clean well some marrow bones (the best marrow bones are found in the round, the second best in the hind legs). Saw them off in three and a half inch length pieces; wrap them in a cloth, and plunge them in boiling broth; let it continue to boil for twenty minutes, then drain and serve the bones containing the marrow on a folded napkin, and slices of toasted bread separately, or take out the marrow, and serve it on slices of toast without the bones.

(1320). OXTAILS À LA CASTELLANE (Queues de Bœuf à la Castellane).

Cut some large oxtails in three inch lengths, soak for an hour, drain, and blanch the pieces for half an hour, then throw them into cold water. Mask the bottom of a saucepan with fragments of bacon, roots, and sliced onions. Put the pieces of tails on top, and moisten with sufficient broth to cover them entirely; boil the liquid, skim, and let simmer slowly for three hours. Drain them, trim, and return to the saucepan; strain and remove the fat from the broth, pour it over the tails, and finish cooking slowly for one hour. Braise some whole chestnuts (No. 654), and when done, arrange the oxtails pyramid form on a dish, surround by the braised chestnuts, reduce the stock with a little espagnole sauce (No. 414), and some blanched celery cut into quarter of an inch squares; when it is cooked pour the sauce over and serve.

(1321)) OXTAILS À LA CHIPOLATA (Queues de Bœuf à la Chipolata).

Prepare and cook the oxtails the same as indicated in oxtails à la castellane (No. 1320), glaze them with meat glaze, dish them, garnishing around with broiled sausages à la Chipolata (No. 754), some braised salt pork cut in squares, some small glazed onions (No. 2765), balls of carrots, whole chestnuts, celery roots cut in cloves of garlic form, and some mushroom heads; the vegetables blanched and cooked separately in the oxtail broth. Pour over this same broth free of all its fat, and reduced with espagnole sauce (No. 414), and Madeira.

(1322). OXTAILS ALSATIAN STYLE (Queues de Bœuf à l'Alsacienne).

Cut the oxtail at a joint of the bone in three inch lengths. Soak them in lukewarm water for one hour, changing the water twice during the time, then throw them in cold water, and drain. Mask the bottom of a saucepan with fragments of ham and bacon, roots and sliced onions; set the pieces of oxtail on top, and cover them up entirely with broth leaving the fat on, and a little brandy. Four hours before dinner boil the liquid, skim, then set the pot in the oven to finish. When ready, strain the broth through a very fine sieve, remove all the fat, and let it rest quietly without stirring. Decant it carefully, pouring it over the oxtails, and leave it until nearly cold, then lift them out; trim the pieces and dip them in melted butter. Roll them in fresh bread-crumbs and broil them on a very slow fire. Arrange them over some cooked sauerkraut (No. 2819), garnishing the dish, and serving a good gravy separate.

(1323). FRIED OXTAILS (Queues de Bœuf Frites).

Select in preference the thickest end of six oxtails, cut them in pieces three inches long, so as to strike the joints. Soak them for one hour, drain, then throw them into boiling, salted water, and let cook for half an hour. Drain again, and set them in a saucepan with a pound of onions, and two pounds of carrots, all cut into slices, three quarts of broth, two garnished bouquets, salt and pepper; let boil slowly for three hours and a half; by that time they should be well done, if not, let them continue boiling longer. When cooked, put them in an earthen dish, strain the broth over the meat; and when three quarters cold, drain, dip them in eggs, then in bread-crumbs and fry them in very hot fat until they attain a good color. Serve a tomato sauce (No. 549), at the same time but separately.

(1324). OXTAILS HOCHEPOT (Queues de Bœuf Hochepot).

Divide the oxtails at the joints of the bone on the thick end, while at the thin end leave two joints together. Soak them in warm water for one hour, changing it several times, then drain and wipe them, and lay them in a brazier lined with slices of bacon and ham. Moisten with sufficient mirepoix stock (No. 419) to cover them entirely, adding a gill of brandy, an onion, a carrot, a garnished bouquet, salt, pepper, and grated nutmeg. Four hours before serving let it come to a boil on a very hot fire, then cover and let simmer on one side for three hours. Strain the broth through a fine sieve, skim off the fat, and reduce it to the consistency of a light half-glaze, then pour it in a stewpan with the pieces of well trimmed oxtails. Simmer, then turn it on a dish, arranging it high, and garnish it round with clusters of pear-shaped pieces of glazed carrots, the same of turnips, some small onions, chestnuts, celery root, all cooked separately in a little broth, and left to glaze. Add to the garnish some green pickles cut and shaped like olives.

(1325). OXTAILS WITH VEGETABLES (Queues de Bœuf aux Légumes).

Prepare and cook the oxtails as explained in à la Hochepot (No. 1324), only adding half a pound more of salt pork. When the meat is cooked, dish it up with the salt pork as garnishing, also carrots, turnips, celery knobs, all blanched and cooked in the broth, and two clusters of braised cabbage. Strain, skim, and reduce the broth so as to have it succulent, then pour some of it over the dish, and send the rest to the table in a sauce-boat.

(1326). BEEF PALATES À LA BÉCHAMEL (Palais de Bœuf à la Béchamel).

Remove the black parts from twelve beef palates; soak them in warm water, adding a little salt. Place them on a slow fire and when the white skin can be detached, then drain and scrape them with a knife in order to remove properly the skin adhering to the palate. Throw them as soon as done into cold water, then drain them, and put them to cook in some broth (No. 194a), adding a bunch of parsley, finely minced carrots, onions stuck with cloves. Leave them to cook for five or six hours, then drain and lay them under a weight. Cut them in one and a quarter inch squares, then prepare a béchamel sauce (No. 409), neither too thick nor too thin, warm the palates in the sauce, season with salt and ground pepper, and stir in a piece of butter just wnen ready to serve.

(1327). BEEF PALATES BAKED, CHEVREUSE (Palais de Bœuf au Gratin à la Chevreuse).

Prepare and cook the palates the same as for à la béchamel (No. 1326); put under a weight, when cold cut them into squares four by two and one-half inches. Cover each piece with a layer of quenelle forcemeat (No. 89) and fine herbs (No. 385), roll them up, and arrange them in buttered tin rings two and one-half inches high by one and three-quarters inches in diameter. Put them in a sautoir moistened with veal blond (No. 423). Set them in a slow oven for twenty minutes, unmold and dress crown-shaped on a dish; cover with a quenelle forcemeat (No. 90), leaving an opening in the center, smooth the surface with a knife, pour over some melted butter, and sprinkle grated parmesan cheese on top. Put this into a slow oven to brown well, and just when sending it to the table pour into the center a garnishing à la Chevreuse (No. 655).

(1328). BEEF PALATES IN TORTUE (Palais de Bœuf en Tortue).

Prepare the beef palates as explained in à la béchamel (No. 1326), lay them under a weight, then cut in oval-shaped pieces three and one-half by two inches, either with a knife or a pastry cutter. Cover one side with a dome-shaped layer of quenelle forcemeat (No. 89), mixing in with it a fourth of its quantity of cooked fine herbs (No. 385). Lay them in a stewpan one beside the other, the forcemeat side on top, and pour into the bottom of the pan a good half-glaze (No. 400) with Madeira, and heat slowly in a mild oven. When the forcemeat is hard to the touch, cover the surface with some Madeira sauce, return the palates to the oven for one moment to glaze, then arrange them crown-shaped round the bottom of a dish hollow in the center and raised edges. Fill the center with a garnishing made as follows: To some Madeira sauce (No. 492), add a pinch of cayenne pepper, some forcemeat quenelles, a few pickled gherkins cut olive-shaped, turned mushrooms heads (No. 118), slices of cooked veal tongue one inch in diameter by an eighth of an inch in thickness. Garnish the edge of the dish with fried egg-yolks and small larded and glazed sweet-breads (No. 1575).

(1329). RIBS OF BEEF À LA BRISTED (Côtes de Bœuf à la Bristed).

Choose a piece of rib, the meat of it being a pink color and well mortified. Remove the flesh from the spine, saw off the bone at the end of each rib, bone these at the side of the breast, being careful not to injure the layer of fat covering it, then saw off the bones six inches from the spine; now fold the boned piece over the other one, and in order to keep it in shape, tie firmly with twelve rounds of string, knotting it each time it goes round the meat. Garnish the bottom of a brazier with bardes of fat pork, and slices of ham, and lay the ribs on top. Moisten with four quarts of broth (No. 194a), and half a pint of Madeira wine; set around it two carrots cut lengthwise in four, two stalks of celery, two medium sized onions with two cloves in each, one bunch of parsley garnished with thyme and bay leaf, mace, salt and whole peppers. Let boil slowly for three and a half to four hours, basting frequently with its own juice, and glaze a fine color. Strain the gravy, skim off the fat and reduce it with the same quantity of brown Spanish sauce (No. 414), and half a pint of Madeira wine. Lay the piece of meat on a dish, garnish around with stuffed tomatoes (No. 2842), and stuffed mushrooms (No. 650), and slip into the bottom of the dish one-third of its own sauce. Serve at the same time the rest of it in a sauce-bowl, after having mingled in a piece of good butter.

(1330). RIBS OF BEEF À L'HINDOSTAN (Côtes de Bœuf à l'Indostan).

Prepare the piece of beef exactly the same as for the beef American style (No. 1331); set it in a dish with round slices of onions, sprigs of parsley, thyme, bay leaf, salt, mignonette, a glassful of sweet oil and a little vinegar. Leave it to marinate for two hours, turning the meat over several times in its pickle, then wrap the marinade up in several sheets of strong buttered paper, also the meat, and cook as explained in the American beef (No. 1331). Wash two pounds of rice in tepid water, blanch for one minute in boiling water, and put it into a saucepan; moisten with three pints of broth (No. 194a), add three-quarters of a pound of butter, an infusion of saffron, salt, and cayenne pepper; boil and finish cooking for three-quarters of an hour in the oven; when the rice is done, take away the sixth part, which must be put in a saucepan, adding to it some allemande sauce (No. 407), and then let it get cool. Use this rice to make small croquettes for garnishing. Lay the balance of the rice on the dish with the ribs, surrounding it with the small croquettes. Serve at the same time a sauce-boat full of thickened gravy (No. 405).

(1331). RIBS OF BEEF OF THIRTY-TWO POUNDS, AMERICAN STYLE (Côtes de Bœuf de trente deux livres, à l'Américaine).

These ribs lay next to the short loin, on the side near the neck; in veal and mutton this part is called the rack; the ribs are the most desirable part of the beef, and are either roasted or braised. Choose the ribs from a tender, well mortified piece of meat, saw off the projecting part of the spine. To roast on the spit, it must be wrapped up or packed in several sheets of strong, greased paper; tie with several turns of string, lay it in a cradle spit (Fig. 116) to cook, which will take about three hours and a half before a good, regular fire. Half an hour before removing from the spit, remove the paper, let brown nicely, then put it on a heater to keep warm for forty-five minutes before serving. To roast in the oven, place the ribs in a baking pan, pour on some fat, and roast it for four hours, carefully basting several times during the cooking; salt and set it on a heater to keep warm three-quarters of an hour before serving. When sending the roast to table serve with it a sauce-bowl of good thickened gravy (No. 405) and a dish of mellow potatoes, prepared as follows: Cook some potatoes in salted water for thirty minutes, drain and press them through a colander, adding half an ounce of butter for each pound of potatoes. Form this purée into balls an inch and a half in diameter, lay them on a buttered pan, pour over some more butter, and brown them in the oven. Serve them at the same time as the roast beef. The time for cooking different sizes is: For a cut of five pounds, forty minutes, then keep in hot closet for fifteen minutes longer; for a cut of ten pounds one hour, keep in hot closet twenty minutes; for a cut of fifteen pound one hour and three-quarters, keep in hot closet twenty-five minutes; for a cut of twenty pounds, two hours and one-quarter, then keep in a hot closet thirty minutes; for twenty-five pounds, two hours and a half, then keep in a hot closet thirty-five minutes; for a cut of thirty pounds, three hours, then keep in a hot closet forty minutes.

(1332). RIBS OF BEEF, OLD STYLE (Côtes de Bœuf à la Vieille Mode).

Cut a rib of beef with the bone, one rib to the piece, the same as a veal or mutton cutlet, lard the lean part of the meat with small strips of fat pork; season with salt, pepper, spices and chopped parsley. Put a quarter of a pound of butter into a saucepan on the fire; when the butter is hot set in the rib of beef and let it color on one side then on the other. When half done place the lid on the saucepan, and push into the oven; as soon as cooked dish up the rib, strain and skim off the fat from the gravy in the saucepan, then pour it over the meat garnished around with potatoes à la Française.

(1333). DEVILED SPARE RIBS OF BEEF (Côtes de Bœuf à la Diable).

Use the spare bones of a piece of a cold roast rib of beef. Take out the bones without removing too much of the meat around them, then season with salt and pepper, rubbing the surface over with mustard. Roll them in fresh bread raspings, drop some butter over, and broil on a slow fire; lay them on a dish, pouring over a little thickened gravy (No. 405).

(1334). ROUND BUTTOCK TOP SMOTHERED (Tendre de Tranches à l'Estouffade).

Lard a buttock-top of ten to twelve pounds, with large slices of larding pork, season it with salt, pepper and nutmeg. Line a brazier with slices of fat pork, some raw, lean ham, sliced carrots and onions, and a bunch of parsley garnished with thyme and bay leaf. Place the meat on top of this garnishing, and set around it three calves' feet, split lengthwise through the center, moisten with a pint of white wine and broth (No. 194a), boil, cover the stewpan, and reduce the stock to a glaze, which degree can easily be told when the fat becomes clarified, and the vegetables begin to attach themselves to the pan. Moisten again slowly with some more broth, cover the brazier hermetically and let simmer in a slow oven for five or six hours, according to the size of the buttock; when cooked, strain the gravy, remove the fat from it and reduce. Glaze well the meat, bone the calves' feet, set them under a weight, after filling them with cooked fine herbs (No. 385). When cold, cut them up into square pieces, season with salt and pepper, oil and vinegar, dip them into a frying batter (No.137), and fry to a fine color, lay the meat on a dish, garnish around with the fried pieces of calves' feet, and serve the gravy separately in a sauce-bowl.

(1335). ROUND BUTTOCK TOP BAKED (Noix de Bœuf Gratinée).

Have a piece of the round top braized and cold, weighing two pounds; cut it into equal sized slices, not having them too thin; put in a stewpan or on a dish, piece by piece, the slices one on top of the other, and baste with a half-glaze sauce (No. 413); cover with a second dish, and set to warm in a slow oven. Mince half a pound of cooked mushrooms, fry them in butter, drain off the latter, and add a pint of half-glaze sauce (No. 413), four heaping tablespoonfuls of grated horseradish, and two tablespoonfuls of bread-crumbs, also a large pinch of chopped parsley. After the meat is warm, lift out the slices one by one, lay them on a long dish one beside the other, covering each separate slice with a part of the above preparation. When the meat has been replaced into its natural shape, cover it entirely with the remainder, besprinkle over with rasped bread-crumbs, and put to bake in a moderate oven, basting it frequently with the gravy the meat was warmed in. Garnish the border with potato croquettes (No. 2782), ball-shaped, and each one an inch in diameter.

(1336). ROUND BUTTOCK TOP, PARISIAN STYLE (Noix de Bœuf à la Mode de Paris).

Lard a round top of beef of from ten to twelve pounds with large lardings of pork, season with pepper, nutmeg and chopped parsley; line a brazier (stewpan) with slices of pork, set the meat on top, and put the pot without its cover into a hot oven. When the meat is well colored, moisten with some broth (No. 194a), adding a garnished bunch of parsley with thyme, bay leaf, and a clove of garlic. It will take from five to six hours to cook, according to the size of the piece of meat, and after it is well done, drain off the gravy, strain it through a fine sieve, remove all the fat, and reduce it in order to obtain a rich gravy; take away one third of this. Add to the remaining two-thirds, a purée of tomatoes (No. 730), also some espagnole sauce (No. 414). Dress the beef on a dish, surround it with small carrots cut pear-shaped, and previously blanched and cooked in a very little white broth (No. 194a), so that they are reduced to a glaze, also some small glazed onions. Pour some of the gravy over the meat, and serve the rest in a separate sauce-bowl. A sirloin of beef can be used instead of the round top.

(1337). RUMP OF BEEF À LA BOUCICAULT (Pointe de Culotte à la Boucicault).

The rump or hip of beef is placed on the exterior side of the spine, at the lower extremity; it commences where the loin ends and finishes at the beginning of the tail. The rump of beef is the most delicate part of the hind quarter; it is excellent for boiling or braising purposes, also for corning.

Bone a sixteen pound piece of the rump of beef, trim off the fat, season with salt and mignonette, roll it lengthwise and tie, then set it in a brazier, and moisten to twice its height with some broth (No. 194a); heat the liquid, skim it carefully; at the first boil, remove the brazier, so that the broth only simmers gently, adding six medium carrots, three turnips, two onions, six leeks, and two stalks of celery. Let continue to cook for five hours; after three hours add two pieces of salt bacon, of one pound each, parboiled for twenty minutes; let the whole simmer for two hours or more until the meat is perfectly cooked, then strain the liquor, skim off the fat, add a little espagnole sauce (No. 414), and reduce to the consistency of thick gravy. Glaze the piece of meat; dress on a large dish, and garnish the side with knob celery braised and glazed, sautéd Brussels sprouts, the bacon cut in slices dressed on each side of the sprouts, and celery; at the end slices of beef tongue (unsmoked) coated on both sides with thick soubise sauce (No. 543), breaded and fried; pour over part of the gravy, send the rest of the gravy in one or two separate sauce-boats.

(1338). RUMP À LA CARÊME (Pointe de Culotte à la Carême).

Bone and pare a piece of rump of beef weighing twenty pounds; remove the fat, and trim it so that it is much longer than its width; cover it with suet, roll lengthwise and tie it with fourteen rounds of the string, making a knot at each round. Put the rump of beef into a saucepan with half a pound of melted fat pork; brown slowly, turning it over frequently. Remove the meat after it is a nice color, drain off the grease, and cover the bottom of the sauce-pan with a thin layer of chopped onions and carrots, set the meat on top, moisten with a pint of broth (No. 194a) and half a bottle of sauterne wine, reduce the moisture to a glaze, and moisten again to the height of the meat with some good broth. Boil up the liquid, skim, and add a bunch of parsley garnished with thyme, bay leaf and a clove of garlic; season with salt, pepper and cloves. Cook slowly for five hours, carefully moistening it at times with hot broth so as to keep the liquor half of the heighth of the meat; drain off the gravy, skim off the fat, and add a pint of Madeira sauce (No. 492) reduced and strained. Untie, pare, glaze and dish up the piece of meat, pour around it one-third of the sauce, garnish around with stuffed mushroom heads (No. 650), sautéd lamb's sweetbreads, and rice croquettes with parmesan. Serve the remainder of the sauce in a sauce boat.

(1339). RUMP OF BEEF À LA CHATELLIER (Pointe de Culotte de Bœuf à la Chatellier).

Pieces of boiled beef are only to be served at family dinners. Select a rump of beef weighing twenty pounds, having it exceedingly fresh; bone, roll up, and tie. Lay it in a stock pot, and moisten plentifully with broth (No. 194a); boil, skim carefully, then continue to boil slowly and regularly for five hours. After it has cooked three hours, put into a net four pounds of carrots, and two pounds of turnips (both pared and cooked cork-shaped), also one onion with five cloves in it, eight leeks, a stalk of celery, and half a parsnip; set the net containing these vegetables into the stock pot, and let cook with the beef. Blanch separately a quartered cabbage, drain, put it into a separate saucepan and moisten with some very fat broth taken from the pot; let cook for an hour, and just when ready to serve, drain the meat, untie, brush over with meat glaze (No. 402) and glaze in the oven to a fine color; garnish the ends with the drained cabbage, arrange the carrots and turnips in clusters on both sides, and at one side set some mellow potatoes (No. 2799), and at the other side some stuffed peppers (No. 2768); have a horseradish sauce (No. 478) served separately; glaze the meat once more, and serve very hot.

(1340). RUMP OF BEEF, BOURGEOISE STYLE (Pointe de Culotte de Bœuf à la Mode Bourgeoise)

Have six pounds of rump of beef, or use instead a piece of sirloin; remove all the fat and sinews, lard it, following the grain of the meat, with fat pork, and season with salt, pepper, nutmeg and chopped parsley. Place the meat in an earthen bowl, with sliced carrots and onions, pour over half a pint of brandy, and let macerate eight hours in a cool place, turning it over frequently. Drain and wipe off any moisture adhering thereon, then tie, and set it in a saucepan with some melted pork. Roast it until the meat is well seized and browned, then moisten with half a bottle of white wine; reduce to half and add sufficient broth (No. 194a) to cover the meat, set round it two boned and blanched calf's feet, a bunch of parsley garnished with thyme and bay leaf, mace, whole peppers, three carrots and two medium onions, with four cloves in them and the brandy. Boil up, then skim, continue to boil slowly or else put in the oven to simmer for two hours and a half. Drain the meat, untie and trim it, straining the gravy through a tammy, replace the meat in the saucepan with an abundant quantity of carrots cut into three-quarter of an inch balls, then blanched, and some glazed onions; pour over the stock. also some broth, so that they be entirely covered at the bottom. Boil and finish cooking slowly in the oven, drain, glaze the meat, and set it on a dish; garnish around with the small glazed onions and the carrots; strain the juice, free it from fat, and reduce until it becomes thoroughly succulent, then pour a part of it over the meat, and serve the rest separately in a sauce-boat.

(1341). RUMP OF BEEF, FLEMISH STYLE (Pointe de Culotte de Bœuf à la Flamande).

Have the meat prepared and cooked the same as for à la Boucicault (No. 1337), using the pork, but no vegetables. Cut up some carrots pear-shaped, about four pounds in all, as many turnips cut into one inch in diameter balls; also a four-pound cabbage cut in four, blanch each sepaately and divide it into twenty small parts, tying each one together with a coarse thread. Lay the cabbages in a row in the center of a low saucepan, through its entire length, set in the turnips on one side and the carrots on the other, dilute with just sufficient stock from the meat to cover the vegetables, and one hour and a half before serving, place over them a heavy piece of buttered paper. Boil on a very slow fire, or in the oven, and when the vegetables are cooked, serve up the piece of meat, and set on one side of it half of the carrots and turnips, laying the other half on the other side, alternating them so as to vary the colors. Place the cabbages at the two ends, and lay on them the salt pork cut into slices. Reduce the gravy to the consistency of a light half-glaze, moisten the meat with a part of it, and serve the rest in two sauce-boats.

(1342). RUMP OF BEEF, GREEK STYLE (Pointe de Culotte de boeuf à la Grecque).

Prepare and cook a piece of beef as explained for à la Carême (No. 1338); glaze and place around it a garnishing of tomatoes, Greek style, prepared as explained below; serve at the same time the braise stock, strained, skimmed and reduced.

Stuffed Tomatoes, Greek Style.—Chop very fine one pound of lean beef, veal or lamb with two ounces of beef suet; bake two large onions till quite brown, chop them up with the meat, adding pepper, salt and a little water; cook the whole in a deep pan for two hours, then add a little butter and a lump of sugar, and continue cooking until quite dry, stirring it occasionally. Cut a piece off the top of some tomatoes, scoop out the centers, fill with the preparation, put back the covers, and rub them over with a little flour and powdered sugar. Place the tomatoes in a pan with small bits of butter spread over each. Pass the insides removed from the tomatoes through a sieve, add to this a little butter and a tablespoonful of oil, pour this into the pan, and bake the tomatoes slowly; they must be slightly browned when done. This same meat dressing can be utilized for stuffing cabbages or egg-plant.

(1343). RUMP OF BEEF, JARDINIÈRE (Pointe de Culotte de Bœuf Jardinière).

Braise a rump aitchbone of beef, after it is done drain it to pare, decreasing the thickness of the layer of fat covering the meat and cut it away underneath so that the slices will not be too wide; now divide it into uniform slices not too thin; reshape the piece to its original form and lay it on a baking dish with a part of its stock strained, skimmed and mingled with a few spoonfuls of Madeira, then reduced to a half-glaze; stand it in a mild oven and glaze while basting frequently. Apart from this prepare a garnishing of braised lettuce, small braised carrots, small flowerets of cauliflower all of one size and cut up string beans, besides some thick slices of cucumbers lightly scooped out on one side; then blanched, stuffed and glazed. At the last moment remove the rump, stand it on a long dish arranging it in a half circle, then dress the garnishings symmetrically in the hollow of the half circle. Place the stuffed cucumbers the whole length on the outside of the meat, forming them into a chain; glaze the slices of beef with a brush, slip a few spoonfuls of the reduced stock in the bottom of the dish and serve the surplus well reduced separately.

(1344). RUMP OF BEEF, MIROTONS À LA MÉNAGÈRE (Pointe de Bœuf Mirotons à la Ménagère).

For mirotons take six ounces of either cold braised or cold boiled beef. Mince two ounces of onions, or one medium-sized onion, also a small shallot; fry them in butter with a whole clove of garlic and a bunch of parsley garnished with thyme and bay leaf. Dilute with a little white wine and some brown sauce (No. 414), boil for twenty minutes, then remove the bunch of herbs and garlic. Season and place the sliced beef in a stewpan; pour the prepared sauce over, and let simmer for fifteen minutes, then lay it on a dish and cover the meat with the sauce and sprinkle chopped parsley over.

(1345). RUMP OF BEEF, MODERN STYLE—BRAISED (Pointe de Bœuf Braisé à la Moderne).

Pare an aitchbone of beef, suppressing all the bones; roll lengthwise, tie and lay it in a long saucepan with melted fat pork; let it fry slowly for half an hour, turning it over frequently; season, then take the meat from the pan, spread on the bottom of this same saucepan a thick layer of minced vegetables and onions and replace the meat over, moisten with three or four gills of broth; let reduce very slowly and wet it again with as much white wine, then reduce to a glaze. Now

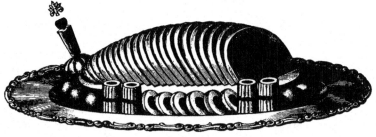

Fig. 305.

moisten the meat to its height with broth, boil up the liquid, skimming well the fat from the surface and cover the saucepan; stand it in a slack oven and have the meat cook until well done which will take at least five hours. Put the meat on a baking dish to truss and pare; strain the stock, suppress its fat and add broth to it should there not be sufficient and reduce it if there be too much. Return the meat to a narrower saucepan, pour the stock over and add a glassful of Madeira or Marsala wine; finish to cook in a slack oven basting it at times so that it assumes a glaze; it should be tender and finely colored. When prepared to serve, drain the meat and cut it into well formed transversal slices of even thickness, dress these on a foundation of rice fastened on a long dish and surround with a garnishing prepared beforehand and having it symmetrically arranged. At the end of the dish where the narrow slices of the beef begin fasten a small fried bread support and in it stick a skewer garnished with cut vegetables and a round truffle. The garnishing around the meat consists of eight small chartreuses of vegetables, a dozen ball-shaped croquettes and a dozen thick slices of cucumbers hollowed out and stuffed, each one to be decorated with a slice of truffle cut out with a vegetable cutter. Serve at the same time as the remove a sauce-boatful of the strained, skimmed and reduced stock in which the beef was cooked. This dish is prepared to have served to the guests at a dinner party.

(1346). ROAST BEEF—MIDDLE SHORT LOIN—ENGLISH STYLE (Rosbif d'Aloyau à l'Anglaise).

Cut along the vertebra and toward the top of the back a piece containing the greater part of the tenderloin, from the end rib to the hip; this part called the middle short loin, and is the choice piece for roasting; it is used in the best houses in England and France. The meat must be selected from a young and tender beef of deep crimson color and veined with slices of fat. Cut from the center a piece weighing, ten, twenty, or thirty pounds, more or less, according to the number of guests to be supplied, cut away the fat, and a piece of the flank seasoning with salt and pepper, and fold the flank over; the meat should be the same thickness throughout. Tie it well, making a knot at each turn of the string. It can be wrapped up in several sheets of buttered paper. A piece of beef roasted on the spit is far preferable to one cooked in the oven. It suffices to place it in the middle of an English cradle spit (Fig. 116), but sometimes

Fig. 306.

it is impossible to cook it in this way. Therefore the most practical manner is to cook it as follows: Set it in a deep pan with raised edges, and furnished with a grate slightly raised on four feet an inch and a half high (Fig. 306). Pour into the pan a few spoonfuls of fat, put the meat on the grate, and roast it in a moderate oven allowing for a short loin weighing fifteen pounds one and a half hours, one of twenty, two hours, and one of thirty, two and a half hours, forty pounds, three and a half hours, the time always to be calculated according to the regularity of the fire and the thickness of the meat; roast the meat, basting and turning it over frequently, add a little water in case the grease threatens to burn. When nearly done salt. When the short loin is nearly cooked untie, and keep in a hot closet from fifteen to forty minutes according to the size, then serve it in a large dish; it must be cut in slices lengthwise of the meat, beginning at the sirloin and then the tenderloin. Serve on very hot plates with a sauce-boat of clear gravy (No. 404) passed around at the same time.

(1347). MIDDLE SHORT LOIN BRAISED À LA MESSINOISE (Aloyau Braisé à la Messinoise).

Select a short loin weighing about thirty pounds; taken from a young and tender beef, and prepare it as follows: remove all the fat surrounding the tenderloin, detach the tenderloin from the chine-bone sufficiently so as to be able to saw off the chine-bone. Cut away the aitch bone from the sirloin. Prick the thick flank with the tip of a small knife; flatten it; remove the skin from the tenderloin, also the large nerve on the sirloin, trim the loin well, leaving the flank wider on the thin side of the tenderloin. Season with salt and pepper, lard the meat with larding pork and seasoned raw ham, roll the flank over the tenderloin, covering the latter with slices of fat an inch or more in thickness; tie it up, making a knot at each turn of the string, which must be about three-quarters of an inch apart. Cover the bottom of a buttered braising pan with cut slices of carrots and onions, lay the loin on top, moisten to a quarter of its height with broth, (No. 194a) and a quarter of a bottleful of Marsala wine, adding a quarter of a pound of sliced mushrooms. Reduce to a glaze, then moisten again to three-quarters of its heighth with the same quantity of broth and Marsala wine as before. Cook slowly for four hours, basting it frequently with its own gravy, and when the meat is cooked, trim and lay it on a long dish, garnishing the sides with small macaroni Milanese timbales (No. 2988), and the ends with small round ravioles (No. 158). Strain the gravy, skim it carefully, reduce to the consistency of a quarter-glaze, then pour over the meat one-third of it, serving the rest at the same time in a sauce-boat.

(1348). MIDDLE SHORT LOIN À LA NORWOOD (Aloyau à la Norwood).

For thirty pounds, prepare the middle short loin the same as for No. 1347, but remove most of the fat adhering to the flank, season with salt and pepper. Put the meat in an earthen dish with some carrots, onions, thyme, bay leaf and sprigs of parsley, olive oil and lemon juice. Macerate the whole for two hours, then remove the meat without the vegetables, tie the flank over the tenderloin, making a knot at each turn of the string, leaving an interval of three-quarters of an inch between each; wrap up the marinade with the short loin in several sheets of buttered paper, place it on a roast pan. with some grease at the bottom of the pan, and some minced carrots and onions, adding a little water; roast in the oven; when the meat is nearly done, remove the paper, salt it and glaze, return to the oven to attain a nice color, then set it in a warm closet for about twenty minutes; it will take about two and a half hours to cook it. Dish the meat up, glaze it again, and garnish with quartered and peeled apples, previously placed in a buttered plate, lightly dredged with sugar and cooked in a hot oven. Add a garnishing of small potatoes cut olive-shaped, blanched and cooked in butter; add the vegetables from the marinade, to one quart of espagnole sauce (No. 414), and some good gravy (No. 404), reduce and skim free of fat, pass through a sieve and serve in a separate sauce-boat.

(1349). SIRLOIN OF BEEF À LA BRADFORD (Contrefilet de Bœuf à la Bradford).

Have a sirloin prepared and cooked as explained for chiccory and sweet souffled potatoes (No. 1356); garnish the sides with small corn fritters, and decorate the ends with corn and potato croquettes. Serve separately some good gravy (No. 404) thickened with a little brown sauce (No. 414), also a sauce-boatful of horseradish cream sauce (No. 478).

Corn Fritters.—Cut the grain through the center the whole length of the cob, and by pressing on it with the dull edge of the knife, the interior of the grains can be removed without the skins; chop the corn up fine and mingle it with a very delicate pancake batter (No. 3072), and cook it in small pancakes each two inches and a half in diameter; garnish the sides of the sirloin with them, having one overlapping the other.

Corn Croquettes.—Cut the corn as for corn fritters; mix the corn with two-thirds of its quantity of finely mashed potatoes and cream, to which add a piece of good butter, set it in a dish to get cold and then form it into cylinder-shaped croquettes one inch in diameter by two and one-quarter inches in length, dip them in beaten eggs, then in bread-crumbs and fry a fine color in hot fat, garnish the ends of the dish with these croquettes.

(1350). SIRLOIN OF BEEF À LA DAUPHINESS (Contrefilet de Bœuf à la Dauphine).

Remove the sirloin from a piece of middle short loin, suppress the fat and nerves, and pare to an oblong shape keeping on the flank, lard the meats with lardons of fat pork (No. 1, Fig. 52); season and roll the sirloin over on itself so that the meats are enveloped; tie firmly, making a knot at each round of the string. Cover the bottom of a braziere (Fig. 134), with slices of fat pork and sliced carrots and onions; over these place the sirloin. Crack two knuckles of veal, lay them around the meat and moisten with some good stock (No. 194a) as high as the meats; boil, skim and set it on one side to boil slowly, put the cover on the braziere and some lighted charcoal on this. It will take about three hours to cook; keep basting frequently. When the sirloin is done, untie and strain the stock which should be reduced to two-thirds; lay the sirloin on a baking sheet and cover it with a Soubise sauce (No. 543), well reduced and thickened with raw egg-yolks diluted with a little cream. Strew the top with bread-crumbs and grated parmesan, then brown in the oven to a fine color, dress and decorate the ends with stuffed tomatoes (No. 2842) and the sides with Dauphine potatoes (No. 2783). Serve separately the stock reduced with espagnole sauce (No. 414) and Madeira wine.

(1351). SIRLOIN OF BEEF À LA DÉGRANGE (Contrefilet de Bœuf à la Dégrange).

Prepare and cook the sirloin the same as for à la de Lesseps (No. 1352); untie, glaze and lay it on a dish, garnishing both sides with carrots and green peas, and the ends with fried celery, strain and skim off the fat from the gravy, slip a part of it under the sirloin, serving the rest in a separate sauce-bowl.

Carrots and Peas, Garnishing.—Cut some carrots with a vegetable cutter into balls of three-eighths of an inch in diameter; blanch and cook them in white broth (No. 194a) with a little butter and sugar; when the carrots are done, and the juice well reduced, mix in an equal quantity of peas, thickening the whole with a little half-glaze (No. 400) and fresh butter.

Fried Celery.—Pick out the most tender leaves in the heart of a raw celery head; cut them into thin strips the whole length of the stalk; they may be either blanched or used raw. Dip each piece in a good frying batter (No. 137), and fry to a fine color in hot fat.

(1352). SIRLOIN OF BEEF À LA DE LESSEPS (Contrefilet de Bœuf à la de Lesseps).

Prepare a piece of sirloin as follows: Remove the sirloin from a middle short rib, remove also the fat and nerves, pare it to an oblong shape, roll it over on itself as shown in Fig. 307, after larding it with large lardons of fat pork (No. 1, Fig. 52).

FIG. 307.

Cover the bottom of a braziere with slices of fat pork, lay the meat on top and moisten to three-quarters of its hight with mirepoix stock (No. 419). Boil, then push the braziere into the oven to let cook for about three hours, basting it several times in the meanwhile, also turning it around while cooking. After the sirloin is cooked, glaze it over and strain the stock through a very fine sieve; skim off the fat carefully and reduce the stock with a little espagnole sauce (No. 414) and Madeira wine. Dish up the sirloin and garnish around with one pound of rice, sauté it in a quarter of a pound of butter; moisten to two-thirds higher than the rice itself with unskimmed broth strained through a silk sieve; season well with salt, a dash of cayenne, powdered saffron, nutmeg and sweet Spanish pepper. Leave the rice in the oven to cook for twenty minutes, and just when ready to serve toss it up thoroughly with a fork; now dress it on each side of the sirloin and garnish the ends with stuffed tomatoes (No. 2842). Serve the reduced stock in a separate sauce-boat.

(1353). SIRLOIN OF BEEF À LA PERRIN (Contrefilet de Bœuf à la Perrin).

Prepare and cook the sirloin as explained in sirloin with Jerusalem artichokes (No. 1357); glaze and dress it on a very hot dish, garnish each side with marrow canapés, prepared as follows: Have slices of toasted bread three and a half by one and three-quarter inches; lay on them several slices of blanched marrow, sprinkle over with very finely chopped chives, and set them in the oven for one minute. Garnish the sides of the dish with these, and pour over a Madeira sauce (No. 492); arrange at the two ends tomatoes prepared as follows: Plunge very ripe and firm tomatoes into boiling water, remove the skins, cut them into four parts, squeeze them slightly and lay them in a saucepan with some good butter, salt and ground pepper; cook them on a quick fire, garnish the sirloin and serve.

(1354). SIRLOIN OF BEEF À LA THIEBLIN (Contrefilet de Bœuf à la Thieblin).

Have the sirloin prepared and cooked as explained in the de Lesseps (No. 1352). Dress and glaze it, garnishing each side with red cabbage, prepared as explained below, and the ends with Sarah potatoes (No. 2802). Strain and skim the fat from the gravy, reduce it and serve it in a separate sauce-boat. Cut a red cabbage into quarters, remove the hard center, and shave the balance fine; blanch, then drain and put it into a saucepan with butter, salt, pepper, bay leaf and a medium sized onion cut in one-eighth of an inch squares; let cook slowly for three hours, stirring it several times in the meanwhile with a spoon. Take out the bay leaf and add a piece of butter and some slices of apples previously cooked in butter.

(1355). SIRLOIN OF BEEF WITH BRAIN PATTIES (Contrefilet de Bœuf aux Bouchées de Cervelles).

Prepare and cook a sirloin as mentioned in (No. 1357), glaze and lay it on a very hot dish, and pour a little good gravy over. Serve separately some patties filled with brains cut in small squares combined with as much mushrooms cut the same, sautéing both in butter, season with salt, pepper, chopped parsley and finish with well buttered velouté sauce (No. 415). Serve also at the same time a sauce-boat of half-glaze with Madeira (No. 400), having it well buttered.

(1356). SIRLOIN OF BEEF WITH CHICORY AND SOUFFLÉD SWEET POTATOES (Contrefilet de Bœuf aux Endives et aux Patates Soufflées).

Take the sirloin from a short loin, remove a part of the flank so as to give it an oblong shape; also a part of the fat, and all the sinews from the covered part. Lard it nicely with pieces of larding pork (No. 1, Fig. 52); cover the bottom of a baking pan with sliced fat pork, minced onions and carrots, and lay the sirloin on top, pouring over some good fat (clarified drippings), and add a little broth, set it in a hot oven and baste frequently while cooking; a few minutes before dishing up, salt the meat. When done arrange it on a dish, pour over some thick gravy (No. 405) and garnish it around with souffléd sweet potatos (No. 2831), serve separately a dishful of chiccory with cream (No. 2729), also some thick gravy (No. 405) in a sauce-boat.

(1357). SIRLOIN OF BEEF WITH JERUSALEM ARTICHOKES (Contrefilet de Bœuf aux Topinambours).

Lift the tenderloin from the short loin, saw the ribs from the beginning of the spine from the sirloin and remove the flat bone. Trim the sirloin into a long square shape and cook it either on an English spit, a cradle spit or else in the oven. For the latter, set the sirloin on a baking pan having a grater (Fig. 306), pour over some fat and for a sirloin weighing ten pounds allow sixty minutes for its cooking, when nearly done, salt, dress it on a dish, garnishing all around with some stewed Jerusalem artichokes (No. 2749); serve a separate sauce-boat of good thickened gravy (No. 405).

(1358). SMOKED ROUND TOP OF BEEF WITH CREAM (Noix de Bœuf Fumé à la Crème).

Cut up as finely as possible one-half pound of smoked beef taken from a piece of the round top; set it in a saucepan on the fire with cold water, at the first boil, drain off all the water, but should the meat still be too salty, then set it in boiling water, and drain it well a few moments after. Put the well drained meat into another saucepan, with the addition of some cream, let simmer for a few minutes, then thicken it with a little fecula or corn starch diluted in cold water or milk. Cook again for a few minutes, season with salt, a dash of cayenne pepper, and finish with a little fresh butter. To thicken smoked beef with cream a little béchamel sauce (No. 409) may be used instead of fecula.

(1359). SALISBURY STEAK (Bifteck à la Salisbury).

Put two pounds of tenderloin of beef in the chopping machine (Fig. 173); this machine is far superior to any other, for in chopping the meats the sinews and other hard parts collect at the bottom of the machine, on the shelf; the meat arising to the surface is the best part; take this out, leaving the hard, fibrous pieces at the bottom. Mold the Salisbury steak in a ring three-quarters of an inch high by three inches in diameter or else in a small empty goose-liver terrine (No. 10). These raw steaks are frequently served without any seasoning or else seasoned and broiled very rare.

(1360) BEEF STEAK, HAMBURG STYLE (Bifteck à la Hambourgeoise).

One pound of tenderloin of beef free of sinews and fat; chop it up on a chopping block with four ounces of beef kidney suet, free of nerves and skin or else the same quantity of marrow; add one ounce of chopped onions fried in butter without attaining color; season all with salt, pepper and nutmeg, and divide the preparation into balls, each one weighing four ounces; flatten them down, roll them in bread-crumbs and fry them in a sauté pan in butter. When of a fine color on both sides, dish them up pouring a good thickened gravy (No. 405) over.

(1361). HAMBURG STEAK À LA TARTARE (Bifteck de Hambourg à la Tartare).

Hamburg steaks are made with lean and tender beef, either the tenderloin or sirloin. Chop up with a knife on a chopping block twelve ounces of raw beef free of all fat and nerves; season with salt and pepper, add half a medium onion cut in small one-eighth of an inch squares or else have it finely chopped; form it into a ball and flatten. These steaks are generally eaten raw. For cooked see the Hamburg steak No. 1360. For steaks à la Tartare, add half a finely cut up green pepper or else it can be cut in small squares. After the steak is formed into a flattened ball make a hole in the center and break into it one very fresh egg, or else the yolk only.

(1362). PORTERHOUSE STEAK (Bifteck d'Aloyau).

Select a good, fleshy middle short loin, the meat being pink and very tender.   Cut slices an inch and three-quarters thick, in the tenderloin and sirloin, sawing away the spine bone from the rib.   Cut off the fat and sinews, and trim it nicely to the shape of the accompanying plate; after trimming it should weigh two pounds and a quarter.   Season with salt and pepper, and baste over with oil or clarified butter, then broil on a slow, well sustained fire for fifteen minutes if desired rare, eighteen minutes if properly done, and well cooked, twenty minutes, only turning it over once in the middle of cooking.   When finished, lay the steak on a very hot dish, covering it with maître d'hôtel butter (No. 581).

Fig. 308.

It is easy to find out when the meat is done.   Press lightly in the center with the first finger, and if the meat be soft, and offering a slight resistance, then it is cooked rare; to have it done properly it must be firm, without resisting as much to the touch; and to be well done, it must be firm, and offer resistance.   Practice alone can teach how to cook by the touch, which differs according to the quality of the meat.

(1363). DOUBLE PORTERHOUSE STEAK À LA SANFORD (Bifteck d'Aloyau Double à la Sanford)

Mr. Wright Sanford, one of the most fervent disciples of the house of Delmonico, and an acknowledged epicurean, was specially fond of ordering this dish.   Much care should be given to its cooking which must operate slowly, while maintaining the same degree of heat throughout, so that it thoroughly reaches the steak.

Cut through all the thickness of the short loin a slice two and a quarter inches thick; it should weigh after being trimmed, four pounds and a half.   Season with salt, cover with oil, and broil the steak on a slow, but well sustained fire for twenty-four minutes if needed rare, twenty-eight minutes to be properly done, and thirty-two minutes if desired well done. Turn the meat over when half cooked, dress the steak on a very hot dish, garnish the top with ribbons of horseradish (No. 98), and pour around a Madeira sauce (No. 492), well buttered with some maître d'hôtel butter (No. 581).

(1364). RIB STEAK À LA BERCY (Entrecôte à la Bercy).

Take the chuck-ribs of prime beef, these lying under the shoulder.   Bone and cut in slices an inch and a half in thickness.   This meat requires to be beaten in order to be made tender, then lay it either in oil or melted butter; season with salt and mignonette pepper, and broil on a very slow fire for twenty or twenty-five minutes.   When the meat is done, set it on a very hot dish, and pour over the following sauce: Put into a saucepan two medium sized finely chopped shallots, some finely chopped marrow, the same quantity of butter and as much meat glaze (No. 402), salt, pepper, lemon juice and chopped parsley. Let cook rapidly on a very hot fire for one minute, place the steak on a very warm dish, and pour the Bercy sauce over.

(1365). RIB STEAK À LA ROYER (Entrecôte à la Royer).

Cut from the thin covered part of a rib piece slices which when pared will weigh one pound and a quarter; season them with salt, rub them over with oil, and broil them over a rather quick fire from eighteen to twenty-two minutes.   Dress them on a dish, and cover with a half-glaze sauce (No. 413), into which incorporate a piece of good butter and some chopped up truffles.   Garnish around the steak with stuffed mushroom heads (No. 650).

Fig. 309.

(1366). ROUND STEAK WITH WATER-CRESS (Bifteck de Noix de Bœuf au Cresson).

Cut from the round top of a young beef, the meat being pink and tender slices of three-quarters of an inch thick.   Season them with salt and peppers, coat them over with sweet oil, and broil on a moderate, well sustained fire for eight or ten minutes; as soon as they are done set them on a very hot dish, and pour over a layer of maître-d'hôtel butter (No. 581). Wash well some fresh water-cress, drain, and season it with salt and vinegar, garnish round the dish with it.

(1367). RUMP STEAK À LA VILLAGEOISE (Bifteck de Pointe Culotte à la Villageoise).

Only *young beef that have never performed any labor can supply tender* rump steaks. Cut transverse slices of three-quarters of an inch thickness from a rump of beef; season them with salt and pepper, and baste over with oil or melted butter; lay them on the grid-iron and broil over a brisk fire from twelve to fourteen minutes. Chop up some boiled, peeled, and cold potatoes, put them in a saucepan with butter, salt, pepper, nutmeg and sweet cream; boil them once, then let simmer until the ingredients have sufficient consistency. Butter the inside of a baking dish, line it with a layer of these potatoes, besprinkle over with bread crumbs and grated parmesan cheese, and put to bake in a very hot oven. Glaze the rump steak with meat glaze (No. 402), and serve it on top of the potatoes.

(1368). SMALL SIRLOIN STEAK OF TWELVE OUNCES, PLAIN (Bifteck de Contrefilet de douze Onces, Nature).

Fig. 310.

Cut slices an inch and a quarter thick from a sirloin; beat them to flatten them down to one inch, trim nicely, after which they should weigh twelve ounces; salt on both sides, spread them over with oil or melted butter, and broil them on a steady fire; it will take about eight minutes to have them very rare, ten to have them properly done, and twelve if desired well done; set them on a hot dish with a little clear gravy (No. 404) or maître-d'hôtel butter (No. 581).

(1369). SMALL SIRLOIN STEAK À LA BÉARNAISE (Bifteck de Contrefilet à la Béarnaise).

Prepare and cook the beefsteak as for the plain (No. 1368); apart from the cooking described by minutes in that number, the time for broiling depends entirely upon the thickness of the meat, and the intensity of the fire. In order to judge whether the meat be done to the touch when it offers a certain resistance; this can easily be learned after once being accustomed to broiling. Dress the beefsteak over a Béarnaise sauce (No. 433); glaze the top with meat glaze (No. 402) using a brush for the purpose.

(1370). SMALL SIRLOIN STEAK À LA BORDELAISE (Bifteck de Contrefilet à la Bordelaise).

When the beefsteak has been cooked as described in the plain (No. 1368) lay it on a dish and cover with Bordelaise sauce (No. 436).

(1371). SMALL SIRLOIN STEAK À LA BORDELAISE WITH MARROW (Bifteck de Contrefilet à la Bordelaise et à la Moelle).

Cook a small sirloin steak as for No. 1368, then arrange it on a very hot dish and cover with a sauce prepared as follows: Cut four ounces of beef marrow into quarter-inch thick slices, plunge them into boiling water, then drain. Dress them on the steak and cover with a Bordelaise sauce (No. 436).

(1372). SMALL SIRLOIN STEAK À LA BORDELAISE WITH MARROW AND TRUFFLES (Bifteck de Contrefilet à la Bordelaise à la Moelle et aux Truffes).

After cooking the steak the same as a plain one (No. 1368) lay it on a very hot dish and cover with the following sauce: Cut three ounces of marrow into quarter inch thick slices, and one ounce of truffles in thin slices. Parboil the marrow and drain it off; heat the truffles in a little Madeira and half-glaze (No. 400). Over the steak arrange the marrow and truffles one intercalated with the other; cover with Bordelaise sauce (No. 436) and serve.

(1373). SMALL SIRLOIN STEAK, ANCIENT STYLE (Bifteck de Contrefilet à l'Ancienne).

After the sirloin is cooked as in the plain (No. 1368) lay it on a dish, besprinkling it over with some anchovy butter (No. 569). Form on top a crown of anchovy fillets garnishing the interior with capers, and set round the steak a garnishing of potato balls, each an inch in diameter, fried three quarters in hot fat, and finishing cooking in the oven with some butter; when done drain off the butter, and season with salt, chopped parsley and lemon juice.

(1374). SMALL SIRLOIN STEAK, WITH BUTTER AND COOKED FINE HERBS (Bifteck de Contrefilet au Beurre aux et Fine Herbes Cuites).

After the beefsteak is cooked as explained in plain (No. 1368) dish it up and cover the top with a layer of butter and cooked fine herbs (No. 385). Garnish around with fresh green water-cresses, seasoning it with salt and vinegar.

(1375). DELMONICO SIRLOIN STEAK OF TWENTY OUNCES, PLAIN (Bifteck de Contrefilet Delmonico de Vingt Onces, Nature).

Cut from a sirloin slices two inches in thickness; beat them to flatten them to an inch and a half thick, trim nicely; they should now weigh twenty ounces each; salt them on both sides, baste them over with oil or melted butter, and broil them on a moderate fire for fourteen minutes if desired very rare; eighteen to be done properly, and twenty-two to be well done. Set them on a hot dish with a little clear gravy (No. 404) or maître d'hôtel butter (No. 581).

(1376). DELMONICO SIRLOIN STEAK À LA PÉRIGUEUX (Bifteck de Contrefilet Delmonico à la Périgueux).

After cooking the steak the same as for plain (No. 1375), lay it over a Périgueux sauce (No. 517), into which mix the third of its quantity of small chicken quenelles, forced through a cornet to three-eighths of an inch in diameter, glazing it with meat glaze.

(1377). DELMONICO SIRLOIN STEAK, SPANISH STYLE (Bifteck de Contrefilet Delmonico à l'Espagnole).

Prepare and cook the sirloin steak as described for plain (No. 1375). Chop up separately a quarter of a pound of lean beef free of sinews, and the same quantity of fresh pork. Mix these together with a tablespoonful of cooked fine herbs (No. 385), and one egg-yolk; season with salt, pepper, and nutmeg, then divide the preparation into four parts; roll it on a floured table into balls, flatten them to half an inch thick, then dip them in beaten eggs, and roll them

FIG. 311.

in bread-crumbs; smooth this with the blade of a knife; plunge them into very hot fat for two minutes to brown the outsides. Drain and lay them one beside the other in a sautoir moistening them to their height with half-glaze sauce (No. 413), and let simmer for three-quarters of an hour, basting them frequently. Brown in oil four ounces of minced onions, add to it four ounces of finely minced green peppers, one clove of garlic, half a pound of peeled tomatoes cut in four and pressed; let cook together and reduce with a little brown sauce (No. 414) and gravy (No. 404). Lay the garnishing on the bottom of a dish, the glazed steak on top, and the hash balls over, one overlapping the other.

(1378). SIRLOIN STEAK FOR GOURMETS; EXTRA FORTY OUNCES (Bifteck de Contrefilet des Gourmets; Extra Quarante Onces).

Cut from a good thick sirloin of beef, slices, each one being four to five inches thick; beat to flatten them down to three inches, then trim them carefully, salt them on both sides, cover with either clarified butter or melted marrow, and place in a double gridiron and broil them over a moderate fire for twenty minutes if desired rare, twenty-six minutes to have them properly done, and thirty minutes when needed to be well done. Lay them on top of a gravy prepared as follows: Have two tablespoonfuls of finely chopped shallot, fry it colorless in three ounces of butter, add some

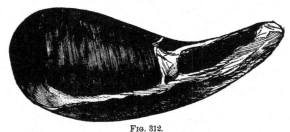

FIG. 312.

melted glaze (No. 402), stir in four ounces of fine butter, a teaspoonful of the best tarragon vinegar, chopped parsley, a dash of cayenne pepper, and two ounces of beef marrow cut into half inch squares. When the marrow is warm, pour it on the dish, lay the extra size steak on top, glaze it with meat glaze (No. 402), and garnish around with gastronome potatoes (No. 2789).

(1379). TENDERLOIN OF BEEF. HOW TO PREPARE (Pour Préparer le Filet de Bœuf).

The tenderloin is found in the inside of the short loin in the hollow formed under the spinal bone. Detach the tenderloin from the spinal bone of a middle short loin by following the bone with the knife; then displace it from the flat bone and from the spinal bone, scraping it off so that no meat remains on the bones. Remove the fat and large nerves and with a thin knife remove the hard skin covering the tenderloin. It is to be served whole or else cut up. Use the middle slices for Chateaubriands; for ten ounce tenderloin steaks use on each side of the Chateaubriand, for mignons, noisettes and tournedos the thin end and the other end for grenadins; the head part is also used for mincing, for Salisbury steaks, Hamburg steaks, etc.

(1380). CHATEAUBRIAND, PLAIN TWENTY OUNCES (Chateaubriand Nature Vingt Onces).

The name of Chateaubriand is given to the piece of meat taken from the middle of a large tenderloin. After it has been nicely trimmed, the Chateaubriand should weigh twenty ounces, or a pound and a quarter. Flatten it down to the thickness of an inch and a quarters, put it to cook on a broiler over a slow but regular fire for sixteen minutes if needed exceptionally rare, eigthteen minutes when properly done, and twenty for well done. Serve on a hot dish with maître d'hôtel butter or gravy.

FIG. 313.

(1381). CHATEAUBRIAND, COLBERT SAUCE (Chateaubriand Sauce Colbert).

Season a Chateaubriand with some salt, brush it over with oil, and broil on a slow, regular fire. Lay it on a dish, and garnish the two ends with potatoes cut olive-shaped and fried in butter, and cover with the following sauce: Reduce half a pint of white wine with a teaspoonful of meat glaze (No. 402), and half a pint of espagnole (No. 414). When well reduced, strain it through a sieve, boil again, and when ready to serve, incorporate therein a quarter of a pound of butter, some chopped parsley, and the strained juice of a lemon.

(1382). CHATEAUBRIAND MAÎTRE D'HÔTEL SAUCE, THICKENED (Chateaubriand Sauce Maître d'Hôtel Liée).

Prepare and cook a Chateaubriand as for No. 1380, lay it on a dish; reduce some velouté (No. 415) with white wine; add a little meat glaze (No. 402), and incorporate into it when ready to serve some maître d'hôtel butter (No. 581). Cover the whole Chateaubriand with this, and garnish the dish with potatoes prepared as follows: Cut up some potatoes into large six-sided olive shapes; first blanch, then finish to cook in clarified butter or else in lard over a good fire, keeping them covered until they become soft and browned; drain off the fat and put in some small pieces of fresh butter, salt and chopped parsley, serve as a garnishing.

(1353). DOUBLE CHATEAUBRIAND, TWO AND A HALF POUNDS WITH SOUFFLÉD POTATOES
(Chateaubriand Double de Deux Livres et Demie aux Pommes Soufflées).

Season well the meat with salt, rub sweet oil over both sides, and broil on a slow, regular fire; for rare, twenty minutes; properly done, twenty-six minutes, and well done, thirty minutes. It is preferable to broil it on a double-hinged broiler without pressing it down, and turning over when half cooked. When done, set it on a large hot dish, spread over some maître d'hôtel butter (No. 581), letting the dish be sufficiently large to contain a quantity of souffléd potatoes (No. 2808). It is better to serve a single Chateaubriand, for the excessive thickness of a double one renders the cooking of it doubtful, yet it is a dish epicureans frequently call for.

(1384). GRENADINS OF TENDERLOIN PLAIN FIVE OUNCES (Grenadins de Filet de Bœuf Nature de cinq onces Chaque).

From a raw and well trimmed tenderloin of beef, cut lengthwise of the meat, half heart-shaped slices, five inches long by two and a half inches wide, and half an inch thick. Beat them lightly, trim evenly, and lard them on one side with rows of fine larding pork (No. 4, Fig. 52). Season with salt and pepper. Put some fat or clarified butter in a sauté-pan, and when very hot, lay in the grenadins on their larded side; four minutes later when a fine color, turn them over; it will take about eight or ten minutes to cook them rare. Serve on a hot dish, and pour some clear gravy over (No. 404).

FIG. 314.

(1385). GRENADINS OF TENDERLOIN À LA BEAUMARCHAIS (Grenadins de Filet de Bœuf à la Beaumarchais).

Cook the prepared grenadins the same as for plain (No. 1384); drain off half the butter, and to the remainder add a coffeespoonful of finely chopped, blanched, and drained shallot, fry this colorless, then put in a little velouté (No. 415), and thicken with egg-yolks; butter well with good, fresh butter, and add some meat glaze (No. 402), and lemon juice; strain through a tammy; now mix into the sauce a little chopped parsley. Pour the sauce on the dish intended for serving the grenadins, and arrange them either in a straight row or in a circle; surround with as many croûstades as there are grenadins, these croûstades to be filled with mushrooms stewed in cream. Serve a slightly thickened half-glaze sauce (No. 413) separately.

(1386). GRENADINS OF TENDERLOIN À LA BONIFACE (Grenadins de Filet de Bœuf à la Boniface).

Prepare and cook the grenadins as explained in plain grenadins (No. 1384), drain them on a cloth, lay them on a dish, and cover them with a bordelaise sauce with mushrooms (No. 436), garnishing the dish with marrow fritters (No. 682).

(1387). GRENADINS OF TENDERLOIN À LA HALÉVY (Grenadins de Filet de Bœuf à la Halévy).

Prepare and cook the grenadins as for No. 1384. Plunge some good, sound tomatoes in boiling water, peel them, cut them crosswise in two, squeeze them without injuring their shape, and season them with pepper and salt. Heat some oil in an omelet pan, and when very hot, put in the halved tomatoes; cook them, then arrange them crown-shaped on a dish, lay a grenadin on each tomato and garnish around with stuffed mushrooms (No. 650). Serve a well reduced and well buttered half-glaze sauce separately (No. 413).

(1388). GRENADINS OF TENDERLOIN AS VENISON, POIVRADE SAUCE (Grenadins de Filet de Bœuf en Chevreuil, Sauce Poivrade).

Trim some slices of tenderloin, cut lengthwise, and shape them in half-heart forms. Marinate them for three days in a cooked and cold marinade (No. 114). Drain and dry them, then fry in an omelet pan in hot clarified fat on a very quick fire. When done rare, drain and lay them on slices of bread fried in butter, cut the same size and shape. Pour over a poivrade sauce (No. 522.)

(1389). GRENADINS OF TENDERLOIN MARC AURELE (Grenadins de Filet de Bœuf à la Marc Aurèle).

Prepare a pate-à-chou (No. 132); spread from a pocket on a baking sheet pieces an inch and a quarter in diameter; when they are cooked they should be about two inches in diameter. Egg them twice with a soft brush and dredge over the half of them some grated parmesan cheese, and the other half finely chopped truffles. Bake them in a slow oven until dry. Remove them from the baking sheet, and cut off all the bottoms. Fill those covered with cheese, with small macaroni cut in quarter inch lengths mixed with tongue cut in quarter inch squares, season and add a litttle velouté (No. 415), some butter. mignonette pepper and nutmeg, then toss in a saucepan without using a spoon. Fill those covered with truffles with a little macédoine of vegetables cut ball-shaped, each a quarter of an inch in diameter. Push through a cornet at the edge of the opening of the choux a row of chicken forcemeat (No. 89). Restore the bottoms and fasten them on with chicken forcemeat, lay them on a plate in the oven for one minute to poach the forcemeat. Cook the grenadins the same as for plain (No. 1384); when done, drain and arrange them in a row, garnishing one side of the dish with maccaroni and parmesan choux, and the other with the macédoine and truffles. Serve a Colbert sauce (No. 451) at the same time.

(1390). GRENADINS OF TENDERLOIN, PALADIO (Grenadins de Filet de Bœuf à la Paladio).

Cut lengthwise from a tenderloin some slices half an inch in thickness, and shape them like half hearts, then lard them with small pieces of larding pork (No. 4, Fig. 52). Garnish the bottom of a sautoir with slices of bacon, place on top finely cut onions and carrots, and set the grenadins above. Moisten with Beef stock (No. 194a), cover the saucepan, and reduce until dry. Moisten again, cover with a sheet of buttered paper, then set it in the oven to cook, basting it frequently during the time. Glaze them a fine color, then have pieces of cooked ham the same shape, fry them in butter with sliced apples. Arrange the cooked ham on a dish, put grenadins on top, reduce the gravy, strain, and remove the fat, mixing in some espagnole (No. 414) reduced with Madeira wine, and pour it over the grenadins. Garnish the dish with the slices of fried apples.

(1391). GRENADINS OF TENDERLOIN, PRÉVILLOT (Grenadins de Filet de Bœuf à la Prévillot).

Prepare and cook the grenadins as for plain grenadins (No. 1384); arrange them on top of some half heart-shaped croûtons of bread fried in butter, the same shape and size as the grenadins, and cover them with a Prévillot salpicon (No. 749).

(1392). GRENADINS OF TENDERLOIN WITH CELERY, BECHAMEL (Grenadins de Filet de Bœuf au Céleri, Béchamel).

Prepare and cook the grenadins, as for plain (No. 1384). Cut in quarter of an inch squares some tender and white celery; blanch it in plenty of salted water, drain and dry well; then fry them in butter without browning. Moisten with broth (No. 194a), and when cooked, mix in a little béchamel (No. 409), and fresh cream. Reduce, pour it on a dish, and arrange the glazed grenadins on top.

(1393). GRENADINS OF TENDERLOIN WITH ROUND POTATOES, VALOIS SAUCE (Grenadins de Filet de Bœuf aux Pommes de Terre en Boules à la Sauce Valois).

Arrange and cook the grenadins as for plain (No. 1384), glaze and lay them on a piece of poached quenelle forcemeat shaped like a half heart. Cover with a Valois sauce (No. 554), surround the grenadins with round potatoes seven-eighths of an inch in diameter, previously fried in butter and seasoned with salt, pepper, chopped parsley and lemon juice.

(1394). GRENADINS OF TENDERLOIN WITH SWEET PEPPERS (Grenadins de Filet de Bœuf aux Piments Doux).

Proceed and cook the grenadins as for plain (No. 1384), glaze and lay them on a dish, garnishing it with sautéd sweet peppers prepared as follows: Plunge the peppers in hot frying fat, remove the peel covering the outside by rubbing with a dry cloth; cut them in two lengthwise, and fry them in oil, turning them over carefully while cooking. When done season with salt, pepper and a clove of garlic crushed, drain them from the oil, and finish with a little meat glaze (No. 402), butter, lemon juice and fine herbs. Preserved sweet peppers can always be obtained; it is only necessary to drain them, fry them in butter or oil, adding a little garlic, lemon juice and fine herbs.

(1395). MINCED TENDERLOIN OF BEEF À LA ANDREWS (Émincé de Filet de Bœuf à la Andrews).

Pare and trim well all the fat from off a tenderloin, cut it lengthwise to obtain escalops or small slices an inch and a half in diameter by an eighth of an inch in thickness, the weight to be one ounce. Prepare the same quantity of veal kidney; cut it in pieces of the same thickness and one inch in diameter. Put an ounce of butter in a sautoir and when very hot and slightly browned, add the tenderloin and afterward the veal kidney. Cook them on a quick fire, seasoning with salt, pepper and lemon juice; serve on a very hot dish.

(1396). MINCED TENDERLOIN À LA BEEKMAN (Émincé de Filet de Bœuf à la Beekman).

Cut into thin slices six ounces of cold tenderloin of beef, either roasted or braised. Place in a saucepan a few spoonfuls of brown sauce (No. 414), boil and skim; add a pinch of cayenne pepper, a little Worcestershire sauce, half as much mushroom catsup, then the slices of beef. Cover the saucepan, set it in the oven, but do not allow the liquid to boil, as it hardens the meat, then when the tenderloin is quite warm, serve it lengthwise on a dish. Strain the sauce through a fine strainer, covering the meat with it.

(1397). MINCED TENDERLOIN, CREOLE STYLE, (Émincé de Filet de Bœuf à la Créole).

Cut six ounces of tenderloin of beef lengthwise, shape the slices into escalops an inch and a half in diameter, by an eighth of an inch in thickness. Sauté them in butter, when ready take the meat out and keep it warm between two dishes, adding beef stock (No. 194a) with part of its fat, some halved tomatoes peeled, pressed and fried in butter, also some green peppers sliced fine and fried in butter. Season highly, arrange the minced meat in a border of rice boiled in salted water to which half an ounce of butter has been added, and serve.

(1398). MINCED TENDERLOIN OF BEEF WITH POTATO CROQUETTES (Émincé de Filet de Bœuf aux Croquettes de Pommes).

Cut into thin slices the best part of a cold roast tenderloin, to weigh about four ounces, then pare them to make them of an even size. Heat some butter in a small saucepan, add to it two teaspoonfuls of finely chopped onions, also four spoonfuls of chopped mushrooms. When the moisture from the mushrooms has evaporated wet them with four spoonfuls of Marsala wine, reduce again to half, then thicken with a half-glaze sauce (No. 413). Heat the slices of beef between two dishes with the addition of a little clear gravy (No. 404), not allowing it to boil. If the tenderloin was previously braised instead of roasted, then the meat should be cut thicker, and heated in the sauce for twenty five minutes without boiling; arrange it on a dish either in one or two rows, and cover with the sauce. Surround the meat with potato croquettes (No. 2782), formed into balls of an inch in diameter and flattened.

(1399). MINIONS OF TENDERLOIN OF BEEF—PLAIN (Mignons de Filet de Bœuf Nature).

Trim carefully a tenderloin of beef, remove all the fat and nerves, then cut it into slices each one weighing five ounces; beat them lightly to have them all of the same thickness, then pare and cut them into round shapes. Salt on both sides, dip them in melted butter or sweet oil, and broil on a moderate, well-sustained fire; they should take six minutes if desired rare, eight minutes to have them properly done, and ten minutes if required well done. When half cooked turn them over and finish on the other side. Dress on a hot dish and pour some clear gravy (No. 404) over.

FIG. 315.

(1400). MINIONS OF TENDERLOIN OF BEEF À LA BAILLARD (Mignons de Filet de Bœuf à la Baillard).

First cook the minions the same as for the plain (No. 1399); dress them flat on a very hot dish; on each minion lay a piece of foies-gras removing it from the terrine with a spoon. Cover the whole with good Madeira sauce (No. 492) to which has been added truffles cut in fine Julienne and fresh mushrooms.

(1401). MINIONS OF TENDERLOIN OF BEEF À LA CHÉRON (Mignons de Filet de Bœuf à la Chéron).

Prepare and cook the minions as explained in the plain (No. 1399). Cover the bottom of a dish with a béarnaise sauce (No. 433), sprinkle over with some chopped parsley, and lay the minions on top, and on each one set an artichoke bottom slightly smaller than the minion, and previously cooked and sautéd in butter. Garnish with a little macédoine thickened with velouté (No. 415), and fine butter, and season well.

(1402), MINIONS OF TENDERLOIN OF BEEF À LA DUMAS (Mignons de Filet de Bœuf à la Dumas).

When the minions are prepared and cooked as for plain (No. 1399), lay each one on a round slice of unsmoked but cooked beef tongue; let these be the same diameter as the minion and three-sixteenths of an inch in thickness. Reduce a velouté (No. 415) and soubise sauce (No. 543) to half, and when ready to serve thicken it with egg-yolks, raw cream, and a piece of fresh butter. Cover the minions with this sauce, strew over grated fresh bread-crumbs and grated parmesan cheese, and sprinkle with clarified butter; brown in a very hot oven or under a gas salamander (Fig. 123), and garnish the dish with ham croquettes shaped like small crescents, then serve.

Ham Croquettes.—Have a quarter of a pound of cooked ham cut in one-eighth squares. A quarter of a pound of mushrooms cut the same dimensions from which you will have pressed out all the moisture, add a little reduced béchamel (No. 409), and season with pepper and nutmeg (no salt). Put on the fire, and when cooked lay them on a dish to get cold, then divide the preparation into balls each an inch in diameter; roll them longways and shape them into crescents, dip them in beaten eggs, roll them in grated bread-crumbs and fry them in hot fat a fine color.

(1403), MINIONS OF TENDERLOIN OF BEEF À LA FEARING (Mignons de Filet de Bœuf à la Fearing).

After the minions are prepared and cooked the same as for plain (No. 1399), lay them on round flat poached quenelles of chicken forcemeat mixed with cooked fine herbs (No. 385), the same size as the minions, and a quarter of an inch thick. Glaze the minions with meat glaze (No. 402), and garnish around with a garnishing prepared as follows: Put some financière sauce (No. 464) into a saucepan, add balls of game forcemeat half an inch in diameter, some olives, mushrooms, artichoke bottoms divided into six pieces, a few cocks'-combs, or beef palates cut the same shape as the cocks'-combs, cock's-kidneys, and whole truffles.

(1404), MINIONS OF TENDERLOIN OF BEEF À LA MEYERBEER (Mignons de Filet de Bœuf à la Meyerbeer).

The tenderloin is to be prepared and cooked the same as for plain (No. 1399), and when done properly prepare a Piedmontese risot (No. 2981). Garnish the center of a dish with this, piling it high and dome-shaped; then glaze the minions, and arrange them around the rice. Divide some lamb or mutton kidneys in two, having half a kidney for each minion; season these with salt and pepper, then sauté them in some butter on a hot fire. When done, drain off the butter, add a little fresh butter and some meat glaze (No. 402), and toss the kidneys in this. Lay half a kidney on top of each minion, serving at the same time, but separately, a sauce-boatful of sauce Périgueux (No. 517).

(1405), MINIONS OF TENDERLOIN OF BEEF À LA SALVINI (Mignons de Filet de Bœuf à la Salvini).

Prepare and cook the minions as for plain (No. 1399), lay them on a dish, glaze them, and place on top of each minion a slice of plainly cooked duck's liver the same shape, but smaller than the minion, and on top of each piece of liver, a slice of black truffle. Cover the minions with an allemande sauce (No. 407), with parmesan cheese, adding to it some minced mushrooms and chopped parsley. Brown in a very hot oven or under a gas salamander (Fig. 123).

(1406), MINIONS OF TENDERLOIN OF BEEF À LA STANLEY (Mignons de Filet de Bœuf à la Stanley).

After preparing and cooking the minions as described in plain minions (No. 1399), glaze them with a brush, and lay them on a dish. Remove the peel from several bananas, cut them lengthwise in two, and cut each half across; roll the pieces in flour, and plunge them to fry in very hot oil. Fry in butter without browning, one small onion weighing an ounce and chopped up very fine; moisten this with one gill of cream, reduce and strain through a sieve, then thicken it with egg-yolks stirred up in cream. Add some freshly grated horseradish, until the preparation thickens well, then season with salt. Warm this without boiling, garnish the minions with it, having it an inch deep and bomb-shaped. Sprinkle chopped parsley over the top, and set on each one, a quarter of a fried banana.

(1407). MINIONS OF TENDERLOIN OF BEEF À LA VERNON (Mignons de Filet de Bœuf à la Vernon).

To be prepared and cooked the same as for plain (No. 1399). Set them on a dish on top of slices of bread cut the same size, and fried in butter. Garnish around with cucumbers cut into olive-shaped pieces, blanched, drained, and put in a saucepan with some velouté (No. 415), and quarter inch squares of celery, blanched until nearly cooked. Boil slowly till the cucumbers are done, and when ready to serve, stir into it a piece of fresh butter, spread this over each minion, and on each one lay a slice of crawfish butter (No. 573) or lobster butter (No. 580), seasoned with a little cayenne pepper; throw a little chopped parsley over the red butter.

(1408). MINIONS OF TENDERLOIN OF BEEF WITH CÈPES À LA BORDELAISE (Mignons de Filet de Bœuf aux Cèpes à la Bordelaise).

Prepare and cook the minions as indicated in plain minions (No. 1399). Glaze and garnish them around with a garnishing of cèpes à la bordelaise made as follows: Choose medium sized cèpes, not too large, remove the stalks, and trim them without altering their shape. Pour some oil in a pan, and when hot, throw in the cèpes, color, season, and reduce the moisture. Finish cooking them with a Madeira sauce (No. 492), some chopped parsley, and a little garlic crushed and chopped fine. Serve at the same time a sauce-boat of Madeira sauce.

(1409). MINIONS OF TENDERLOIN OF BEEF WITH CHESTNUTS, MARSALA SAUCE (Mignons de Filet de Bœuf aux Marrons, Sauce Marsala).

Have the minions prepared and cooked the same as for plain (No. 1399). Split open the sides of some chestnuts, plunge them into very hot fat, or roast them in the oven; remove the outside peel, also the inside skin, blanch them in plenty of water, then cook them in broth (No. 194a) with a little butter added, and a stalk of celery. When thoroughly done, drain, and use only those which have remained whole and intact; return these to the saucepan adding a little half-glaze sauce (No. 413), and some Marsala wine. Dress the glazed minions on a bread croûton fried in butter, and garnish them with the chestnuts either around or inside should they be arranged crown-shaped. Pour the sauce over and serve.

(1410). NOISETTES OF TENDERLOIN OF BEEF, PLAIN (Noisettes de Filet de Bœuf Nature).

Trim a tenderloin of beef, cut it in slices and beat lightly to flatten to three-eighths of an inch in thickness, then trim them again round-shaped; each one should weigh three ounces. Salt them on both sides; put half oil and half butter in a saucepan and set it on a hot fire, place therein the meat, and let cook quickly. It will take about five minutes to have them rare, seven minutes to cook them properly, and eight minutes if desired well done. When finished, remove, lay them on a plate, glaze and serve on a dish with a little clear gravy (No. 404) poured around.

FIG. 316.

(1411). NOISETTES OF TENDERLOIN OF BEEF À LA BERTHIER (Noisettes de Filet de Bœuf à la Berthier).

Prepare the noisettes as for No. 1410, set them in an earthen dish, then season them with salt and mignonette, oil, vinegar, thyme, bay leaf, sprigs of parsley and sliced onions. Leave them in this pickle for three hours, then drain the pieces, wipe dry, and sauté them with butter on a hot fire. When done dress them over a tomato sauce (No. 549) with horseradish, stirring in a little finely chopped blanched and lightly fried shallots. Stuff some Spanish olives with anchovies, put them in sheets of buttered paper, warm them in a slow oven, remove the papers, glaze the olives, and garnish the noisettes with these. Three olives are sufficient for each noisette.

(1412). NOISETTES OF TENDERLOIN OF BEEF À LA BONNEFOY (Noisettes de Filet de Bœuf à la Bonnefoy).

Arrange, prepare and cook the noisettes as explained for plain (No. 1410). Dish them and pour over a sauce prepared as follows: Put some half-glaze sauce (No. 413) into a small saucepan, stir it well with a whip and mixing in with it the same quantity of butter; season with mignonette, lemon juice and chopped parsley. Cut some pieces of beef marrow, a quarter of an inch thick, throw them into boiling water, and drain them. Have double the quantity of thin slices of mushrooms; lay the mushrooms and marrow intercalated in some tartlet molds, dressing them dome-shape fill up with sauce; put them on ice. When cold unmould them by dipping the molds in hot water; dip them in beaten eggs, then in bread-crumbs and fry to a good color. Dress them crowned-shaped around the noisettes, allowing two pieces of fritter for each noisette.

(1413). NOISETTES OF TENDERLOIN OF BEEF À LA FLEURETTE (Noisettes de Filet de Bœuf à la Fleurette).

Prepare the noisettes as explained in noisettes plain (No. 1410), season them and lay them on a dish, pour over them a little cold cooked marinade (No. 114), and some Madeira wine. Let macerate for three hours, then drain and dry them on a cloth. Sauté them in butter, and when properly done, after seven minutes, remove and glaze them. Drain the butter from the stewpan, put in a little half-glaze (No. 413), reduce, while adding the marinade, a very little at the time, and when nicely reduced, finish with a little good cream. Strain the whole through a tammy (No. 159) and mix in some finely minced chives. Place each noisette on a thin slice of bread, browned in butter, lay them on a dish and cover each with the gravy.

(1414). NOISETTES OF TENDERLOIN OF BEEF À LA MAGNY (Noisettes de Filet de Bœuf à la Magny).

Prepare and cook the noisettes of tenderloins the same way as explained in No. 1410; when done lay them on a dish, and place on top of each noisette a thin slice of fattened goose liver (foies-gras d'oie). Pour over a sauce allemande (No. 407), mixing in with it a quarter of its quantity of grated parmesan cheese. Besprinkle with more grated cheese, baste over with a little melted butter and brown in a quick oven or under a gas salamander (Fig. 123).

(1415). NOISETTES OF TENDERLOIN OF BEEF À LA MAIRE (Noisettes de Filet de Bœuf à la Maire).

The noisettes of tenderloin of beef are to be prepared and cooked as for plain noisettes (No. 1410); glaze them, and lay them over a garnishing of potatoes maître d'hôtel (No. 2795). Serve separately a half-glaze (No. 400) with tomato sauce (No. 549) with chopped fine herbs added, and stir in a piece of fresh butter just when ready to serve.

(1416). NOISETTES OF TENDERLOIN OF BEEF À LA NIÇOISE (Noisettes de Filet de Bœuf à la Niçoise).

When the noisettes are prepared and cooked the same as for plain noisettes (No. 1410), dress them on a layer of tomatoes previously skinned, halved, squeezed and fried in hot oil mixed with eighth of an inch squares of cut ham; season with salt, pepper, nutmeg, and a taste of garlic. Lay these tomatoes inside a border made of risot Piemontaise (No. 2981). Glaze the noisettes, set them inside the border and garnish around the outside with small potato balls half an inch in size, and cooked in butter with chopped parsley strewed over.

(1417). NOISETTES OF TENDERLOIN OF BEEF À LA ROSSINI (Noisettes de Filet de Bœuf à la Rossini).

These noisettes are prepared and cooked the same as for plain noisettes (No. 1410). Glaze and lay them on small slices of bread, a quarter of an inch thick, and the same diameter as the noisettes fried in butter. Choose some very large white, chicken livers, cut them into thick slices, sauté them in some butter, and set a slice on each noisette, and on top of this a fine round slice of truffle. Mask the whole with a Madeira sauce (No. 492), with essence of truffle (No. 395) added to it.

(1418). NOISETTES OF TENDERLOIN OF BEEF IN SURPRISE (Noisettes de Filet de Bœuf en Surprise).

Fry in butter without browning, a finely chopped, blanched shallot; add to it half a pint of tomato sauce (No. 549), and a pint and a half of espagnole sauce (No. 414). Boil and skim well, then add half a pound of chopped mushrooms, a quarter of a pound of chopped truffles, two ounces of chopped ham and some raw chopped fine herbs. Season properly, let get cold, and then prepare eighteen noisettes plain as for No. 1410. Make an incision on the side of each, fill these with the cold preparation, season, and dip the pieces in beaten eggs, then roll in bread-crumbs, and fry them in clarified butter. Remove from the fire, set them on a plate, glaze, and dish them over a tomato sauce (No. 549), having some meat glaze (No. 402) added.

(1419). NOISETTES OF TENDERLOIN OF BEEF, TRIUMVIR (Noisettes de Filet de Bœuf Triumvir).

From the heart of a small tenderloin of beef beaten until excessively tender, cut some slices which after being flattened and pared should weigh three ounces each, and be three-eighths of an inch thick, and all trimmed to equal size; season with salt and pepper, then cook them on a quick fire for three minutes; turn over, and cook them for three minutes more. Glaze and cover with a white béarnaise sauce (No. 433); place in the center of each noisette a triangle of very black truffle warmed in some good gravy with a few tarragon leaves, and some meat glaze (No. 402). Pour this gravy round the béarnaise.

(1420). NOISETTES OF TENDERLOIN OF BEEF WITH PURÉE OF MUSHROOMS (Noisettes de Filet de Bœuf à la Purée de Champignons).

These are prepared and cooked the same as for plain noisettes (No. 1410). Glaze and lay them in round, flat croustades made with either foundation paste (No. 135) or very fine parings of puff paste, and garnished with a mushroom purée (No. 722).

(1421). PAUPIETTES OF TENDERLOIN OF BEEF WITH COOKED FINE HERBS (Paupiettes de Filet de Bœuf aux Fines Herbes Cuites).

Cut lengthwise from a pared tenderloin ten slices five inches long by two and a quarter wide and three-sixteenths of an inch in thickness; beat them lightly, season with salt, pepper and nutmeg; cover one side with a layer of cooked fine herbs (No. 385), thickened with a little well reduced half-glaze (No. 400). Roll the paupiettes into cylindrical forms one and three-quarters in diameter; roll them inside a barde of fat pork, maintain them in shape with two turns of string; range the paupiettes in a sautoir lined with bardes of fat pork, wet with mirepoix stock (No. 419), to half their heighth and then reduce the moistening entirely. Remoisten and finish to cook slowly in the oven; when done pare and dress them on a dish; strain and skim the fat from the stock, reduce it with a little white wine and espagnole sauce (No. 414), and pour it over the paupiettes.

FIG. 317.

(1422). PILAU À LA REGLAIN (Pilau à la Reglain.)

Put a quarter of a pound of butter into a saucepan on the fire; when the butter is melted, add a quarter of a pound of blanched salt pork cut into half inch squares, two ounces of chopped medium-sized onions, and a pound of tenderloin of beef cut into inch squares, a garnished bouquet of thyme, bay leaf and a clove of garlic. Moisten with a pint of stock (No. 194a), reduce the liquid entirely, then moisten again with another pint of stock, and let reduce to a glaze. Now add half a pound of rice, cover to double its heighth with stock, then season with some saffron, salt and cayenne pepper. Simmer until it is all done, and the liquid entirely evaporated; dress it on to the middle of a dish, and surround the pilaff with peeled tomatoes, split in halves and slightly squeezed free from their juice, and cooked in half butter and half oil, seasoned with salt and pepper. Sprinkle parsley over all and serve.

(1423). TENDERLOIN—STEAK OF TEN OUNCES, PLAIN, BROILED OR SAUTÉD (Filet de Bœuf de dix Onces Grillé ou Sauté Nature).

Select the tenderloin of a good red color and nicely streaked with fat. Pare it carefully, remove all the fibrous parts, cut it into slices, each weighing eleven ounces, and beat lightly to flat-

FIG. 318.

ten them to an inch and a quarter in thickness. Trim well in order to give them a round-shaped appearance. Each tenderloin after being trimmed should weigh ten ounces; season them with salt, baste over with oil or melted butter, lay them on a gridiron, and broil them on a moderate well-sustained fire, turning them over only once during the time they take to cook, which is ten minutes to have them rare, twelve minutes to have them properly done, and fourteen minutes well cooked. Lay them on a hot dish. Prepare the tenderloin steaks as for the above, season and sauté in clarified butter over a bright fire. Turn them over after they have been on the fire for about six minutes and again after another six minutes, making twelve in all. When the gravy from the meat can be seen on the surface, then remove the steak and lay it on a dish; drain out the fat completely from the pan, detach the glaze with a little clear gravy (No. 404), reduce, strain and pour it over the meat; serve.

(1424). TENDERLOIN STEAK WITH ANCHOVY BUTTER (Filet de Bœuf au Beurre d'Anchois).

Trim and cook the tenderloin as for the plain (No. 1423); lay it on a very hot dish, and cover the surface with some anchovy butter (No. 569).

(1425). TENDERLOIN STEAK WITH MADEIRA, HALF-GLAZE (Filet de Bœuf au Madère, Demi-glace).

Have the tenderloin prepared exactly as for plain (No. 1423), seasoning it with salt. Put some clarified butter in a sauté pan (Fig. 130), when very hot add the tenderloin to cook it slowly, turning it over six minutes after it has been on the fire, then finish cooking, which will take about twelve minutes in all; drain off the fat and pour into the bottom of the saucepan, half a gill of half-glaze sauce (No. 413), and a quarter of a gill of good Madeira wine. Reduce quickly, turning the meat over, then dress the tenderloin. Pour into the stewpan a quarter of a gill more Madeira wine, reduce the whole to half, strain the gravy, put it back into a saucepan, stir in some very good butter, then pour the whole over the steak.

(1426). TENDERLOIN STEAK WITH MARROW (Filet de Bœuf à la Moelle).

Cook the steak, after preparing it the same as for plain (No. 1423). Have four ounces of marrow for each steak, cut in quarter of an inch thick slices, plunge them into boiling water for one minute, drain, and then arrange them symmetrically over the tenderloin, covering the whole with a Madeira sauce (No. 492), sprinkle some chopped parsley on top.

(1427). TENDERLOIN STEAK WITH MUSHROOMS (Filet de Bœuf aux Champignons).

Prepare and cook as explained in tenderloin with olives (No. 1428), dress it on a dish and garnish the top with cooked, channeled mushrooms (No. 418), heated in a reduced half-glaze sauce (No. 413), with some mushroom essence (No. 392); pour this over the meat and serve.

(1428). TENDERLOIN STEAK WITH OLIVES (Filet de Bœuf aux Olives).

Have the tenderloin prepared and cooked as described in plain (No. 1423). Detach the glaze from the pan with a little Madeira wine and clear gravy (No. 404) reduced. When reduced sufficiently to cover a spoon, strain and replace it on the fire in a low saucepan; add ten stoned olives for each tenderloin having previously thrown them into boiling water to blanch them and let them boil up once. Dress the meat, cover with the sauce and arrange the olives around.

(1429). TENDERLOIN STEAK WITH TRUFFLES (Filet de Bœuf aux Truffes).

Prepare the tenderloin and cook it the same as for tenderloin with olives (No. 1428). For each ten ounce tenderloin, have about one ounces of truffles, peeled and cooked in Madeira wine. Mince them, that is cut them into very thin slices, and arrange them either over the tenderloin or else around it, crown-shaped one overlapping the other. Cover the whole with a half-glaze sauce (No. 413) and Madeira.

(1430). TOURNEDOS OF TENDERLOIN OF BEEF, PLAIN (Tournedos de Filet de Bœuf Nature).

Cut some slices about two and a half ounces, from a well trimmed tenderloin of beef; beat them lightly to flatten to a quarter of an inch thick, pare them round shaped two and a quarter inches in diameter. Each piece of tournedos after being trimmed should weigh two ounces; season with salt and pepper, then warm some fat in a sautéing pan, lay in the tournedos one beside the other and cook them on a brisk fire, being careful to turn them over only once during that time. Drain, wipe and glaze them with some meat glaze (No. 402), using a brush for the purpose; dress, and pour a little clear gravy (No. 404), into the bottom of the dish. It will take about four minutes to have them rare, five to have them properly done, and six to have them well done.

FIG. 319.

(1431). TOURNEDOS OF TENDERLOIN OF BEEF À LA BRÉTIGNY (Tournedos de Filet de Bœuf à la Brétigny).

Prepare and cook the tournedos as for plain (No. 1430); glaze them, then lay them on a dish, one slice overlapping the other. Split through the back as many reedbirds as there are tournedos, preparing them as follows: Bone them, season with salt, pepper, sauté them on a quick fire while the tournedos are being prepared. Garnish one side of the meat with sweetbread minced and fried in butter with fine herbs and lemon juice, and the other side with sliced mushrooms, fried in butter with fine herbs (No. 385) and lemon juice, dress the reedbirds on both ends. Pour a little Madeira sauce (No. 492), with truffle essence (No. 395) into the bottom of the dish, and serve some of the same sauce in a separate sauce-boat.

(1432). TOURNEDOS OF TENDERLOIN OF BEEF À LA FLAVIGNAN, WITH SMALL STUFFED TOMATOES (Tournedos de Filet de Bœuf à la Flavignan, avec Petites Tomates Farcies).

Prepare the tournedos exactly the same as for the plain (No. 1430), glaze and dress them in a straight row one overlapping the other; garnish the sides of the dish with as many small tomatoes as there are pieces of meat, and serve a Colbert sauce (No. 451) separate.

Small Stuffed Tomatoes.—Cut off the tops half an inch in diameter, and scoop out the interiors; squeeze them without misshaping them, and remove the insides with a small vegetable scoop. Rub lightly the bottom of a bowl with some garlic, and for half a pound of chicken forcemeat (No. 89), placed in the bowl, mix in the same quantity of foies-gras taken from a terrine; add a quarter of a pound of mushrooms and two ounces of chopped truffles, salt, pepper, nutmeg, chopped parsley, a little Madeira wine, and grated parmesan cheese. Fill the tomatoes with this preparation and bake them in a moderate oven for twenty minutes.

(1433). TOURNEDOS OF TENDERLOIN OF BEEF À LA HUTCHING (Tournedos de Filet de Bœuf à la Hutching).

To be prepared and cooked exactly the same as plain tournedos (No. 1430); after being glazed, set them on a dish over croquettes of horseradish and cream made the same size as the tournedos.

For Croquettes of Horseradish.—Reduce some good cream to half its quantity, add two ounces of butter, season it with salt and nutmeg, and stir in it sufficient grated fresh horseradish to form a consistent paste; let cool, then shape them into inch and a half balls, flatten them down to a third of their diameter, dip in eggs, roll in bread-crumbs and fry in clarified butter. Place on each tournedo a slice of apple fried in butter, and in the center of this lay a round slice of cooked ham an inch in diameter by a quarter of an inch thick, also fried in butter; drain off the butter; and detach the glaze from the pan with a clear gravy (No. 404), half-glaze (No. 400) and some Madeira; strain the sauce through a fine sieve, and pour it on to the dish around the tournedos.

(1434). TOURNEDOS OF TENDERLOIN OF BEEF À LA LAGUIPIERRE (Tournedos de Filet de Bœuf à la Laguipierre).

Cut off slices from a nice small tenderloin of beef, pare well, and beat lightly to flatten to a quarter of an inch thick, trim them round-shaped two and a quarter inches in diameter; they should weigh after being pared two ounces each; season them with salt and pepper, then lay them on a dish and pour over some Madeira wine, letting them macerate for one hour turning them over several times; drain and wipe them nicely. Put some clarified butter into a saucepan, when very hot set in the tournedos one beside the other, place the pan on a hot fire, and cook them the same as the plain tournedos (No. 1430). Drain off the butter, put in a little clear gravy (No. 404) and meat glaze (No. 402), reduce the liquid quickly, turning the tournedos over to glaze them. Prepare beforehand slices of unsmoked red beef tongue, two inches in diameter by a quarter of an inch thick, also some round slices of foies-gras, one and a half inches in diameter by three-sixteenths of an inch, and rounds of truffles one inch by an eighth of an inch in thickness. Dress the tournedos on slices of bread a quarter of an inch thick, and two and a half inches in diameter; these slices to be fried in butter; lay on top of each one a tournedos, and on these the foies-gras, and finally the round slice of truffle. Pour over a Laguipierre sauce (No. 486).

(1435). TOURNEDOS OF TENDERLOIN OF BEEF À LA MARIETTA (Tournedos de Filet de Bœuf à la Marietta).

Have the tournedos prepared the same as for à la Laguipierre (No. 1434); set them on a dish over round slices of bread cut the same diameter as the tournedos, fried in butter, and a quarter of an inch thick. Cover them with port wine sauce (No. 492) into which mix some finely chopped up shallots previously blanched, some finely cut and chopped oronge mushrooms, nutmeg, espagnole sauce (No. 414), lemon juice, and pistachio nuts cut in fillets. Garnish around with timbales made of short paste (No. 135), filling them either with noodles or parboiled macaroni, drained and reduced with broth (No. 194a), seasoning with pepper, nutmeg and parmesan cheese, also some butter and velouté (No. 415). Between each timbale lay slices of tongue cut the shape of cock's-combs, and warmed in butter, then glazed.

(1436). TOURNEDOS OF TENDERLOIN OF BEEF À LA ROQUEPLAN (Tournedos de Filet de Bœuf à la Roqueplan).

Prepare some tournedos the same as for à la Laguipierre (No. 1434); lard one of them with salt pork (No. 3, Fig. 52), one with cooked tongue, one with cooked ham, and one with truffles cut the same size as the pork. When the tournedos are done, glaze, then dress them on a dish, intercalating each one with a fried egg-yolk; place on top game quenelles (No. 91) shaped in a hollow tartlet mold, and decorated with truffles. Pour into the bottom of the dish, a tomato sauce (No. 549) mixed with half-glaze (No. 413) with clear gravy (No. 404), and garnish around with fried potatoes Julienne (No. 2792), just when ready to serve.

1437). TOURNEDOS OF TENDERLOIN OF BEEF À LA TALABASSE (Tournedos de Filet de Bœuf à la Talabasse).

Cook very rare some plain tournedos (No. 1430); lay them over sippets of bread fried in butter, and place around them slices of marrow, and on top of each tournedos a little horseradish butter (No. 578), mingled with chopped up and parboiled shallot, also some chopped parsley. Set the dish for one moment in the oven, and serve very hot.

(1438). TOURNEDOS OF TENDERLOIN OF BEEF À LA VICTORIN (Tournedos de Filet de Bœuf à la Victorin).

Prepare and cook the tournedos exactly the same as for Laguipierre (No. 1434). lay them on top of pieces of thin bread, cut the same diameter as the tournedos, and cover them with a thick celery purée (No. 711); place on top a ring cut from a carrot, two inches in diameter, and a quarter of an inch thick, with an empty space in the center of an inch and a quarter, blanched, braised, and reduced to a glaze; set on a top large mushroom stuffed with fine cooked herbs (No. 385) thickened with allemande sauce (No. 407), and baked in the oven till a fine color. Pour around an espagnole sauce (No. 414), reduced with sherry wine, and when ready to serve incorporate into it a piece of good butter, working it in well with a whisk (Fig. 154).

(1439). TOURNEDOS OF TENDERLOIN OF BEEF WITH RAISINS (Tournedos de Filet de Bœuf aux Raisins).

These are to be prepared and cooked as for tournedos Laguipierre (No. 1434); reduce a gill of tomato sauce (No. 549), with one gill of espagnole (No. 414), and half a gill of Madeira wine; when all is well reduced, strain it through a very fine sieve, put it back into the saucepan, and add to it eight fresh Malaga raisins for each piece of meat, or in case there are none fresh, then use dried ones, seeded and softened in a little Malaga wine. Dress the tournedos on slices of bread their same diameter, and a quarter of an inch thick, fried in butter, set the raisins around, and serve with the sauce poured over.

(1440). TOURNEDOS OF TENDERLOIN OF BEEF WITH STRING BEANS (Tournedos de Filet de Bœuf aux Haricots Verts).

These are to be prepared the same as for tournedos à la Laguipierre (No. 1434); cook them very rare, glaze them with meat glaze, and dress. Surround with a garnishing of string beans à la Pettit (No. 2827), around the bean garnishing, place sippets of bread, one and a quarter inches by three-sixteenths inches, fried in butter; dress them one overlapping the other.

(1441). TENDERLOIN OF BEEF À L'AMBASSADE—WHOLE (Filet de Bœuf à l'Ambassade—Entier).

Pare a fine tenderloin using the same care as if intended for larding (No. 112); cover it with thin slices of fat pork, tie it well so as to keep the latter in position; fill the bottom of a narrow baking pan with slices of pork, laying minced carrots and onions on top, pour over some good, melted fat, set the tenderloin over, and put it in the oven for forty to forty-five minutes, basting it several times while it is cooking, and turning the baking pan frequently so that the meat cooks evenly and colors well, letting it be done rare. A few minutes before serving salt it; when ready untie and glaze it, dress the tenderloin on a small rice foundation, two inches high and of the same shape and size as the tenderloin. On each side arrange a garnishing of small croustades filled with baked béchamel cauliflower (No. 2715), at each end place potato balls, fried in butter, three-quarters of an inch in diameter; stick five silver skewers into the top of the tenderloin, each one made of a fine truffle and sweetbreads; the truffles to be glazed in meat glaze (No. 402). Serve a Madeira sauce (No. 492) in a separate sauce-bowl.

Should the tenderloin be needed for a plain dinner, and it were necessary to carve it in the kitchen or dining-room, or even in an adjoining pantry, then proceed as follows: Cut the two ends of the tenderloin, remove the chain (the chain is the irregular portion partly detached from the tenderloin), one-half inch from the bottom; cut the end triangle-shaped, then continue cutting very fine bias slices. Place each slice on a hot plate with a little good gravy (No. 404) and some of the garnishing; serve the Madeira sauce apart.

(1442). TENDERLOIN OF BEEF À LA BAREDA—WHOLE (Filet de Bœuf à la Bareda—Entier).

Trim nicely a fine tenderloin weighing about six pounds. After it is pared the same as Bernardi (No. 1444), lard the top of it with medium sized lardings (No. 2, Fig. 52) and raw ham; lay in an earthen dish, season with salt and mignonette, and sprinkle it over with sweet oil. Cut in slices two medium onions and one lemon, add them to the tenderloin with a few sprigs of parsley, two bay leaves, some thyme, and a clove of garlic; let remain in this for two hours, turning the meat constantly while in the marinade. Two hours before ready to serve place the tenderloin in an oval saucepan with the ingredients around it, moisten it with half a pint of Madeira wine, and one pint of beef stock (No. 194a); let it reduce slowly and when the liquor comes to a glaze, moisten again with more stock to half the heighth of the meat; boil up, then cover the saucepan and set it in the oven. When the tenderloin is nearly done strain the gravy, free it from its fat, and reduce it to a half-glaze; trim the tenderloin, lay it on a pan, and glaze it, then dress the meat on a bed of risot à la Piemontaise (No. 2981), set around the fillets a fine garnishing made of sixteen artichoke bottoms two and a quarter inches in diameter, eight of which to be filled with tongue cut in three-sixteenths inch squares, and mixed with half-glaze sauce (No. 413), the other eight to be garnished with chicken breast cut in three-sixteenths inch squares and mixed with velouté sauce (No. 415). Place over the garnishing sixteen small grooved mushroom heads (No. 118), and decorate the tenderloin with five truffle and Villeroi quenelle skewers. Serve in a separate sauce-boat a velouté (No. 415) and espagnole sauce (No. 414), half of each reduced with the stock from the meat, and a little tomato purée (No. 730) added to it.

(1443). TENDERLOIN OF BEEF À LA BAYONNAISE—WHOLE (Filet de Bœuf a la Bayonnaise—Entier).

Select a fine tenderloin of beef, pare it as for à la Bernardi (No. 1444); lard it with small pieces of larding pork (No. 2, Fig. 52). Lay the tenderloin on an oval dish, pour over a gill of olive oil, one sliced onion, a few sprigs of parsley, one bay leaf broken into several pieces, and twelve pounded whole peppers. After three hours, drain the meat from the marinade, then roast it either on the spit or in the oven, and glaze it a fine color. Fry in butter some thin slices an eighth of an inch thick of ham, cutting them half heart-shaped; arrange them on each end of the tenderloin, garnishing the sides with macaroni prepared as follows: Blanch some macaroni, drain, and return it to the saucepan with some stock (No. 194a); let boil, and reduce for twenty minutes, so that the stock is entirely evaporated, then season with pepper, nutmeg, and grated parmesan. Toss the macaroni and cheese in the saucepan so that it will be thoroughly stirred without using a spoon. Serve separately a half-glaze (No. 413) and tomato sauce (No. 549), not too thick.

(1444). TENDERLOIN OF BEEF À LA BERNARDI—WHOLE (Filet de Bœuf à la Bernardi—Entier)

Prepare and lard a fine tenderloin as already explained (No. 112). Garnish the bottom of a pan with slices of pork, minced carrots and onions, and place the tenderloin on top; cover it with some good fat and put it in a very hot oven to roast; the time for accomplishing this is thirty minutes for a four pound tenderloin, then let it rest on a heater or in any warm place for ten minutes or longer; five pounds will take thirty-five minutes, and twelve minutes to rest, while six pounds will take forty-five minutes and fifteen minutes to rest. As soon as the tenderloin is nearly done, salt it properly, before serving pare both ends, remove the chain, give it a good appearance, glaze, then dress it on a grooved rice foundation, previously browned in the oven. Dress around the tenderloin, small croustades made of fine foundation paste (No. 135) laid into deep tartlet molds: fill these croustades with a little macédoine thickened with butter and a little béchamel (No. 409), over this macédoine set a round game forcemeat quenelle, (No. 91) forced through a cornet on a buttered tin sheet quenelle, being the same in diameter as the croustades; put in the center of each a ring of thinly sliced truffle, then poach them in a slow oven serve separately a sauce Périgueux (No. 517), adding to it some small one-eighth inch squares of cooked ham.

(1445). TENDERLOIN OF BEEF À LA BIENVENUE—WHOLE (Filet de Bœuf à la Bienvenue—Entier).

Tenderloins intended for braising purposes should be chosen fat, for the lengthy cooking they have to undergo diminishes their size considerably. Raise the tenderloin, remove all the fat, and separate the skin from the meat; have ready large lardings of pork (No. 1, Fig. 52), season them with thyme, chopped and finely pounded bay leaf, salt, pepper and allspice.   Lard the inside of the tenderloin with these, cover with thin bardes of fat pork and tie it well.   Garnish the bottom of a braziere with slices of pork, moistening with a mirepoix stock (No. 419), put in the meat, warm it, then push the pan into the oven to simmer for three or four hours according to the size of the tenderloin.   Strain the gravy through a fine sieve, skim off the fat, reduce it, then drain the tenderloin, glaze and set it on a dish or on a rice foundation.   Skim and reduce the stock from the meat with an espagnole and marsala sauce (No. 492), strain it through a sieve, garnish around the tenderloin with pieces of unsmoked red beef tongue cut heart-shaped, also some minced truffles, and quenelles à la Villeroi, add some fine butter to the sauce, and serve in a separate sauce-boat.

(1446). TENDERLOIN OF BEEF À LA CAUCHOISE—WHOLE (Filet de Bœuf à la Cauchoise—Entier).

Have prepared and cooked a tenderloin as explained in à la Bernardi (No. 1444); when done and glazed, dress it and garnish it around with cabbage.   Lay on top of the cabbage, slices of sausage, decorate the ends with turnips cut cork-shaped, blanched and cooked in beef stock (No. 194a) with butter and sugar, and then reduced to a glaze; serve a separate espagnole sauce (No. 414), reduced with some clear gravy (No. 404).

How to Prepare the Cabbage.—Mince two cabbages, blanch them for ten minutes, drain and place them in a saucepan covering them with some beef stock (No. 194a) with one third of the volume of fat taken from the stock pot; add one pound of sausage, a carrot cut lengthwise in four, and two medium onions with two cloves in them, also a bunch of parsley garnished with bay leaf.   Season with salt and pepper, cook slowly, remove all the fat and let reduce to a half-glaze.

(1447). TENDERLOIN OF BEEF À LA CHANZY—WHOLE (Filet de Bœuf à la Chanzy—Entier).

Pare and lard a fine tenderloin of beef; lay it in a deep baking pan lined with sliced onions, carrots and fat bacon and baste over with butter; salt and cover with buttered paper.   Roast it for

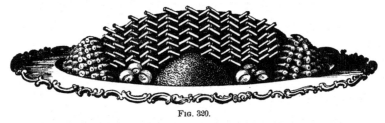

FIG. 320.

one hour in a moderate oven basting frequently and adding a gill of hot broth from time to time; lastly, drain off the tenderloin, pare it neatly and dress on a long dish, surround with a handsome garnishing composed of two pretty groups of turned and glazed carrots, two clusters of fine green peas cooked English style (No. 2742), alternated with a few very white mushroom heads, etc., at the same time serve a boatful of good thick gravy (No. 405).

(1448). TENDERLOIN OF BEEF À LA CONDÉ—WHOLE (Filet de Bœuf à la Condé—Entier).

Arrange the tenderloin and cook it the same as for à la Bayonnaise (No. 1443); glaze it, then lay it on a rice foundation, garnishing it around with game croquettes (No. 885); intercalating them with small chicken timbales.   Decorate the meat with three or five skewers made of truffles and cocks'-combs; serve a tomato sauce à la Condé (No. 550) separately.   This dish is prepared to figure at a dinner party, but not being carved, it cannot be conveniently handed round, so after being shown on the table, it should be removed and cut into slices, placing one on each plate with some of the garnishing and sauce, then handed to the guests.

(1449). TENDERLOIN OF BEEF BREADED AND BROWNED IN THE OVEN À LA D'AURELLES
(Filet de Bœuf Pané et Coloré au Four à la d'Aurelles).

This tenderloin should be prepared the same as for à l'Ambassade (No. 1441); when done, trim, drain and cover it with four egg-yolks mixed with two ounces of melted butter, salt and ground nutmeg.   Besprinkle over with bread-crumbs in which mingle a little grated parmesan cheese; press the bread-crumbs down slightly with the blade of a knife. and pour over some melted fresh butter. Set the meat in a hot oven so as to brown quickly; serve it up and garnish the dish with veal kernels (or small sweetbreads). Pour a Périgueux sauce (No. 517), over the garnishing and finish with small quenelles. A half-glaze sauce (No. 413) is to be served separately.

(1450). TENDERLOIN OF BEEF À LA D'ORLEANS—WHOLE (Filet de Bœuf à la d'Orléans—Entier).

Have a fine tenderloin larded with strips of cooked red beef tongue and truffles, cook it the same as for à la Bienvenue (No. 1445); glaze, then dress it, garnishing one side with small chicken quenelles molded with a teaspoon (No. 155), and the other side with some small peeled truffles previously warmed in Madeira sauce and meat-glaze. Place at both ends rounds or slices of cooked ham, cut one and a half inches wide by an eighth of an inch thick, and warmed in a little butter and meat glaze (No. 402). Decorate with skewers made of game quenelles à la Villeroi and cocks'-combs. Served separately an Orléans sauce (No. 512).

(1451). TENDERLOIN OF BEEF À LA GODARD—WHOLE (Filet de Bœuf à la Godard—Entier).

After cooking a tenderloin of beef the same as for à la Bienvenue (No. 1445) pare and glaze it. Make a foundation of rice, two inches high, and from ten to twelve inches long and five inches wide, egg the surface, flute it symmetrically and color it in a hot oven. Lay this on the middle of a hot dish, set the tenderloin on top and garnish around with twelve truffles cooked in Madeira wine, twelve fine mushroom heads grooved and turned round (No. 118), and twelve cock's-combs. Moisten with a little half-glaze (No. 400). Set around twelve oval quenelles decorated with red beef tongue, decorate the top with five skewers made of truffles and double cocks'-combs, and serve with a half-glaze (No. 413) separately.

(1452). TENDERLOIN OF BEEF À LA MELINET—WHOLE (Filet de Bœuf à la Melinet—Entier).

Have a fine tenderloin prepared and cooked as for à la Bayonnaise (No. 1443), pare, glaze and dish it, garnishing it with the following preparation made in advance. Cut some round pieces of unsmoked red beef tongue two inches in diameter by three-sixteenths of an inch in thickness; prepare a macédoine, thickened with béchamel (No. 409), well buttered and set away to cool; place on each slice of tongue a lump of this macédoine an inch and a half in diameter, flatten it down slightly, and cover it entirely with chicken quenelle forcemeat (No. 89). Baste over with melted butter, and sprinkle grated parmesan cheese on top, place on a well-buttered baking pan, set them in a slow oven and as soon as they are a fine color remove and arrange them on each side of the tenderloin; place a glazed mushroom on each piece of garnishing and serve separately a marinade sauce (No. 496), with chopped up truffles added.

(1453). TENDERLOIN OF BEEF À LA MILANESE—WHOLE (Filet de Bœuf à la Milanaise—Entier).

The tenderloin is to be prepared and cooked the same as for à l'Ambassade (No. 1441). When done remove it from the fire, wipe away all the fat and moisture adhering to it, brush it over with beaten eggs and cover with fresh bread crumbs and parmesan cheese; besprinkle with butter and brown it nicely in the oven. Arrange it on a foundation made of short paste (No. 135), garnishing around with small spaghetti macaroni blanched, then drained and cooked in some consommé (No. 189). Season with salt and mix in some parmesan cheese and a little brown sauce; add the macaroni, tongue, truffles and mushrooms, all cut Julienne shape. Serve separately an espagnole sauce (No. 414) reduced with some good gravy.

(1454). TENDERLOIN OF BEEF À LA MONTEBELLO—WHOLE (Filet de Bœuf à la Montebello—Entier).

To be prepared and cooked the same as explained for à la Bayonnaise (No. 1443); after it is done, pared and glazed, dress it on a symmetrically trimmed rice foundation, and garnish it with a preparation made beforehand, composed of sixteen artichoke bottoms two inches in diameter. Fill with a salpicon made of sweetbreads, truffles, and mushrooms, to which has been added some well reduced allmande sauce (No. 407); have it slightly bomb-shaped and cover the whole with a cream forcemeat (No 74); sprinkle over very finely chopped tongue, pour over some butter, and poach the whole in the oven for fifteen minutes or more; have some mushroom heads fried in butter, and seasoned, finished with some meat glaze (No. 402) and fine herbs. Dress the artichoke bottoms on each side of the tenderloin, the cooked mushrooms at the end; pour some well-seasoned thickened gravy (No. 405) over, and serve a Montebello sauce (No. 502) separate.

(1455). TENDERLOIN OF BEEF, NEAPOLITAN STYLE—WHOLE (Filet de Bœuf à la Napolitaine —Entier).

Have a fine tenderloin cooked and prepared as described in à la Bienvenue (No. 1445); only lard it with pork and ham, cut the size shown in No. 2, Fig. 52; when done, pare, glaze, and lay it on a trimmed rice foundation, garnishing around with macaroni croquettes. Strain the braise, skim off the fat, and reduce it with some broken game bones and half a pint of Malaga wine; strain again, keep back one-third without adding anything to it to put with the meat, and divide; to one add some citron cut in fine Julienne shape, and to the other some sultana raisins; serve the remainder into two equal parts; the citron sauce in one sauce-boat, and the raisin sauce in another, or the two may be mingled together.

(1456). TENDERLOIN OF BEEF À LA RICHELIEU, MODERN—WHOLE (Filet de Bœuf à la Richelieu, Moderne—Entier).

Arrange the tenderloin and cook it the same as for à la Bernardi (No. 1444) a few moments before serving, glaze it and lay it on a rice foundation on a dish sufficiently large to garnish one side with stuffed tomatoes (No. 2842), and a bunch of glazed lettuce (No. 2753); the other side with stuffed mushrooms (No. 650), and some braised celery (No. 2721), and at each end a cluster of potatoes trimmed to the size of a small egg, and boiled in salted water for twenty minutes; drain off the water, and crush each potato separately in a cloth, then reshape them and range them on a buttered pan, pour some more butter over, and brown nicely in the oven, then add more butter, simply melted, neither cleared nor clarified. This meat may be ornamented by setting five skewers into it garnishing them with finely cut up vegetables. A Madeira sauce (No. 492) in a sauce-boat to be served separately.

(1457). TENDERLOIN OF BEEF À LA ROTHSCHILD—WHOLE (Filet de Bœuf à la Rothschild— Entier).

Pare a tenderloin and cook it the same as for à la Bienvenue (No. 1445); after it is done drain off the gravy, free it from fat, and reduce it to a half-glaze. Fry in butter some half heart-shaped slices of Westphalia ham, drain off the butter, remove the ham, and add half as much half-glaze (No. 400) as espagnole (No. 414), then reduce it to a proper consistency, and when ready to serve work in a small piece of butter; serve part of this sauce separately. Dress the tenderloin on a rice foundation (No. 10), garnish with some breasts of quail sautéd in butter, the ham, also fried scallops of foies-gras; cover this garnishing with the reserved sauce espagnole and half-glaze; lay on top the tenderloin, eight Villeroi quenelles and between each quenelle a double and curled cock's-comb.

(1458). TENDERLOIN OF BEEF À LA ROYAL—WHOLE (Filet de Bœuf à la Royale—Entier).

Prepare tenderloin as described à l'Ambassade in No. 1441; lard the interior with pork, ham and truffles, each cut into lardings three-eighths of an inch square. When the fillet is cooked, drain the gravy skim off the fat, and set it into another saucepan with some broken game bones; simmer for one hour, then strain and add to it its equal quantity of espagnole (No. 414); reduce this sauce to proper consistency, being careful to remove all the grease and scum arising to the surface; put aside a third part of it, and add to the two-thirds remaining some grooved or turned mushrooms (No. 118); forcemeat quenelles round-shape and truffles cut olive-shaped. Pare and glaze the tenderloin, and dress it on a rice foundation; place the garnishing around in clusters and decorate the tenderloin with five skewers, made of cocks'-combs and truffles. Sauté a little minced raw ham in butter, moisten with a gill of Madeira wine and the third part of the gravy kept back from the rest; boil, skim, drain through a sieve and serve in a separate sauce-boat.

(1459). TENDERLOIN OF BEEF À LA SOLOHUB—WHOLE (Filet de Bœuf à la Solohub-—Entier).

Prepare a tenderloin of beef in the following manner: After it has been well pared stud with truffles the third part of it (the center), and the narrow end third, lard with pork lardons (Fig. 52,

No. 2), leaving the other end unlarded. Cover the studded part with a band of fat pork, line a long, narrow braziere with slices of fat pork, carrots, onions, and a garnished bunch of parsley; place the fillet on this; braise the meat with a very little moisture, only adding stock when it becomes too reduced; when almost done take out the meat and place it on a baking sheet; egg and bread-crumb the unlarded end, bestrew with grated cheese, pour melted butter over and brown in a hot oven. Dress on a rice foundation into which has been mixed some quarter inch squares of foies-gras. Garnish the sides of the tenderloin with minced cèpes à la Bordelaise (No. 1574) and the ends with small patties filled with tomato purée (No. 730), strained through a very fine sieve and to which has been added some meat glaze (No. 402), thickening at the last moment with cream and egg-yolks. Serve a Russian sauce (No. 535) separately.

(1460). TENDERLOIN OF BEEF À LA TRAVERS—WHOLE (Filet de Bœuf à la Travers—Entier).

To be prepared exactly as for à la Bayonnaise (No. 1443), and when cooked glaze it after paring it nicely and set it on a rice foundation. Garnish around with artichoke bottoms filled with a sweetbread croquette preparation (No. 893), dip them in eggs, bread-crumb them and fry, have also a garnishing of small timbales made of timbale paste (No. 150), filled with spinach and cream, and covered with small puff paste tops. Pour a little good gravy (No. 404) into the bottom of the dish, and serve separately a marinade sauce (No. 496) well buttered with chopped mushrooms added.

(1461). TENDERLOIN OF BEEF BRAISED WITH ROOTS—WHOLE (Filet de Bœuf Braisé aux Racines—Entier).

The tenderloin for this must be prepared and cooked the same as for à la Bienvenue (1445); glaze, then dress it and garnish around with small olive-shaped carrots first blanched, then cooked in broth (No. 194a), butter and sugar; when done the broth will be reduced to a glaze; also have turnips cut ball-shaped, blanched, then cooked in broth, butter and sugar and reduced the same as the carrots; some small glazed onions, and celery roots cooked in gravy (No. 404). Serve separately the braise stock reduced with espagnole (No. 414); when ready to serve add some Madeira wine.

(1462). TENDERLOIN OF BEEF, HUNTER'S STYLE—WHOLE (Filet de Bœuf au Chasseur—Entier).

This tenderloin is to be cooked and prepared exactly the same as for à la Bayonnaise (No. 1443); pare it, glaze, and dress it on a rice or short paste (No. 135) foundation, garnishing around and on each side with game quenelles (No. 91), molded in a tablespoon (Fig. 80), and laying them one beside the other on a buttered tin sheet; pour into this sheet some boiling salted water, and keep the water continually boiling while poaching the quenelles until they are thoroughly done. Raise the tenderloins and sirloin from four young rabbits or any other kind of game, paring them to the same shape as the rabbit tenderloin; remove all the nerves with the tip of a knife, then lay them on a dish, and season with salt, pepper, nutmeg, thyme, bay leaf, branches of parsley, minced carrots and onions, lemon juice, and two tablespoonfuls of oil; let them marinate in this for one hour, being careful to turn them over several times, then take them from the dish without the vegetables and after dipping them into a frying batter (No. 137); fry them a fine color and garnish with these. Have a half-glaze sauce (No. 413), add to it some game carcasses and Madeira wine, when the same is ready strain either through a sieve or tammy, and mix in with the sauce some eighth of an inch square pieces of cooked ham. Pour a third of this around the tenderloin, and send the rest to the table in a separate sauce-boat.

(1463). TENDERLOIN OF BEEF, INDIAN STYLE—WHOLE (Filet de Bœuf à l'Indienne—Entier).

Have a fine tenderloin prepared and cooked as for à la Bayonnaise (No. 1443), then glaze and dish it, garnishing the sides with rice timbales, and the ends with small rice croquettes the size and shape of Spanish olives. Serve in a separate sauce-boat a light poivrade sauce (No. 522) with curry.

Indian Rice.—How to prepare the rice for the timbales and croquettes: Pick one pound of rice, wash well, blanch and drain it; set it in a saucepan with half a pound of butter, and the decoction of a pinch of saffron infused in half a gill of water, salt and cayenne pepper. Cover the rice with beef stock (No. 194a), boil and let finish cooking in a slow oven for half an hour, then remove a quarter of it and put it into a bowl, mixing in with it sufficient allemande sauce (No. 407) to give it consistency, then let get cool, and afterward form it into croquettes the size and shape of a Spanish olive, fill some timbale molds with the balance of the rice.

(1464). TENDERLOIN OF BEEF À LA PRINTANIÈRE—WHOLE (Filet de Bœuf à la Printanière—Entier).

Pare a tenderloin, lard it with fat salt pork cut in the shape of lardons (No. 2, Fig. 52); garnish the bottom of a long narrow braziere with fragments of fat pork, minced vegetables, onions and aromatics: moisten the meat with a pint of stock (No. 194a); reduce this liquid slowly to a glaze, then remoisten to three-quarters of its heighth. Boil the liquid for seven to eight minutes and cover the tenderloin with buttered paper; close the braziere, put it back on a slower fire and continue to cook with fire over and under for a couple of hours basting it oftentimes with its stock. The meat ought now to be perfectly well done; drain it off to pare; strain

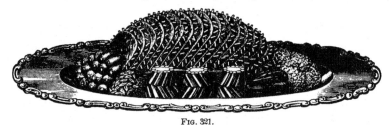

FIG. 321.

and free the stock from fat, pour into it one glassful of Marsala wine and reduce to a half-glaze. Place the tenderloin on a deep baking pan, pour the stock over and glaze while basting frequently; drain off and strain the stock once more, suppress all of its fat and thicken with a few spoonfuls of brown sauce (No. 414) or tomato sauce (No. 549); keep it in a bain-marie. Fasten a wooden foundation covered with cooked paste on the bottom of a long dish, glaze with a brush. Carve the tenderloin into slices, reshape as before and dress it on this foundation; surround with a fine variegated garnishing divided in groups composed of braised lettuce, small timbales of vegetables, small glazed carrots, flowerets of cauliflower and lozenge-shaped string beans. Glaze the meat and cover the bottom of the dish with a small part of the sauce having the rest served in a sauce-boat.

(1465). TENDERLOIN OF BEEF WITH TRUFFLES—WHOLE (Filet de Bœuf aux Truffes—Entier).

To be prepared as for l'Ambassade (No. 1441); stud the tenderloin with raw truffles cut to represent nails, drive them in the surface of the meat one inch apart from each other, using a wooden peg for the purpose a little smaller than the nail. Cover the tenderloin with slices of fat pork, and tie them on; finish cooking exactly the same as tenderloin à la Bayonnaise (No. 1443), and when the meat is done, drain, trim and dress it on a long dish, garnish on each side with small peeled truffles, covering with clear half-glaze (No. 400). Serve separately a Madeira sauce with essence of truffles (No. 395).

(1466). TENDERLOIN OF BEEF WITH VEGETABLES—WHOLE (Filet de Bœuf aux Légumes—Entier).

Prepare and cook the tenderloin exactly as for à la Bienvenue (No. 1445); after having it pared and glazed, set it on a small rice foundation, garnishing it around with the following vegetables arranged in separate groups in order to vary their different colors. This dish can be decorated with pear-shaped carrots, small clusters of cauliflower, turnips cut into balls, artichoke bottoms garnished with Brussels sprouts, small glazed onions or any other vegetable in season, being careful to suppress any kind that will be served at the same dinner, and which has intentionally been avoided in this, such as asparagus tops, for there is seldom a dinner when this vegetable is not served in some way or the other, either as cream soup, or plain boiled. Also green peas, string beans and flageolets, these all being generally used as vegetables served with the entrées. Mushrooms are also employed largely for garnishing, and boiled potatoes are invariably served with fish. Send a sauce-boat of half-glaze sauce (No. 413) to the table, the same time as the tenderloin.

(1467). BEEF TONGUE À LA ROMAINE (Langue de Bœuf à la Romaine).

Remove from a beef tongue, the fat and cartilaginous part lying near the end. Soak it for one hour and a half in cold water, then put it into a saucepan sufficiently large to contain a gallon of water, adding salt, pepper and one onion with two cloves; let cook for three hours. Remove the skin covering the tongue, and place the latter on a dish, garnishing around it with small ravioles (No. 2976), mingled with gravy (No. 404), tomato purée (No. 730), and parmesan cheese; serve separately a Roman sauce (No. 534).

(1468). BEEF TONGUE À LA SOLIGNY (Langue de Bœuf à la Soligny).

Prepare and cook a beef tongue the same as beef tongue Roman (No. 1467); cut it into quarter of an inch thick slices; and from these cut circles of one and three-quarter inches in diameter, also as many slices of truffles as there are circles of tongue; keep them warm in a little meat glaze (No. 402) and Madeira wine. Mince a two-ounce onion, fry it in oil with four ounces of artichoke bottoms cut into eight pieces, season with salt, pepper and a little garlic, adding the truffles and tongue, some lemon juice and chopped parsley, and serve all on a dish surrounded by sippets of bread fried in butter.

(1469). TONGUE, ITALIAN, BAKED (Langue à l'Italienne au Gratin).

Cold braised tongue may be used for this, or else unsmoked boiled red beef tongue. Cut into thin and pared slices, put inside a drill pocket furnished with a grooved socket, some potato croquette preparation (No. 2782), not too firm; force a border of this on the extreme edge of the inside of a dish, garnishing the interior of the border with sliced tongue. Fry in butter one shallot, some chives, and a few mushrooms all finely chopped, thicken with a thin béchamel sauce (No. 409), stirring in some grated parmesan cheese, cover the tongue with this, sprinkle grated bread raspings and parmesan cheese on top, pour over some butter, and put it in the oven to acquire a good color.

(1470). BEEF TONGUE, MACÉDOINE (Langue de Bœuf Macédoine).

Pare and remove from a beef tongue the fat and cartilaginous part, lying near the thick end; blanch it for fifteen minutes and lard it with small lardings (No. 3, Fig. 52); seasoned with pepper, salt, and chopped parsley. Line a saucepan with slices of fat pork, place the tongue on top, and moisten with a mirepoix stock (No. 419), and white wine, then let cook for two and a half to three hours according to its size. Remove the skin, strain the stock through a sieve, then skim off all the fat and reduce it one third. Glaze the tongue nicely with this, dish it up, and garnish around with a vegetable macédoine (No. 2755) thickened with velouté (No. 415) and some good butter. A Madeira sauce (No. 492), should be served separately.

(1471). TRIPE À LA MODE DE CAEN (Gras-double à la Mode de Caen).

In order to be successful with this recipe, it will be necessary to have a large earthen pot and a brick oven with hermetically closed cast iron doors; it will take for a pot containing thirty-five pounds, from twelve to fourteen hours; beside the tripe as ordinarily used, include also the "franchmule" the fourth stomach properly called the reed (Abomasum) and "feuillet" the third stomach properly called the manyplies (Omasum) and two boned ox feet. The tripe must be raw, well cleansed, and extremely fresh. Divide it into pieces two inches square; cover the bottom of the pot with slices of pork, lay the tripe on top and season with salt, mignonette, five onions, one of them having five cloves in it, a boned ox foot, a bunch of parsley garnished with thyme and bay leaf, a clove of garlic, and some quartered carrots, and above this set another layer of tripe, and ox foot, seasoned with salt and mignonette, and so on until the pot is full, besides adding a quart of water. The last layer must be the "feuillet." When the tripe is taken from the oven, remove the "feuillet" and skim off all the fat, take out the vegetables and parsley, then serve very hot.

(1472). TRIPE À LA POULETTE WITH MUSHROOMS (Gras-double à la Poulette aux Champignons).

Select previously well cleansed raw, fat and very fresh tripe, blanch it for ten minutes and when drained cool it off, cut it into large pieces and put them into a stock-pot with water, salt, allspice, carrots, onion with two cloves, and a bunch of parsley garnished with thyme and bay leaf; let boil very gently on a slow fire for eight hours keeping the cover on close, then put the tripe aside to cool in its own water. Drain and wipe it off, and cut it into two inch by one-half inch pieces, then fry them in butter without attaining a color; drain off the butter, cover the tripe with an allemande sauce (No. 407), and just when ready to serve incorporate into it a piece of fine butter, some chopped parsley and minced mushrooms, and a little lemon juice.

(1473). TRIPE À LA TARTARE (Gras-double à la Tartare).

Have some well cooked honey-combed tripe; cut it into two-inch squares, put it in a bowl, seasoning it with salt, pepper, parsley and chopped onions; sprinkle over some oil and lemon juice, and let the tripe macerate in a cool place for one hour. Drain it off, and dip each piece in melted butter and fresh bread-crumbs, then broil them on a slow fire. Dress the tripe on a very hot dish, and serve at the same time, but separately, a sauce-bowl of tartar sauce (No. 631).

(1474) TRIPE BAKED WITH PARMESAN CHEESE (Gras-double Parmesan au Gratin).

Have some very fresh cooked tripe; cut it into one and a quarter inch squares arrange them on a buttered dish in layers, besprinkle each layer with pepper and grated parmesan cheese, and pour over a tomato sauce (No. 549) mixed with an espagnole sauce (No. 414) and a little good gravy, dredge over the top some bread-crumbs and more grated parmesan, pour over some butter and brown in a hot oven.

(1475). TRIPE LYONNAISE (Gras-double Lyonnaise).

Have some fresh tripe, white and well cooked; cut it into strips two inches long by a quarter of an inch wide; mince four ounces of white onions, fry them slowly in a pan with half oil and half butter, in the meanwhile frying the tripe in another pan; when the contents of both have attained a nice color, mix them together and continue frying for ten minutes, tossing them constantly, when brown, season with salt, pepper, lemon juice or good vinegar and chopped parsley. Drain off the butter well and serve on a very hot dish.

(1476). TRIPE, PARISIAN STYLE (Gras-double à la Parisienne).

Cut Julienne-shaped (No. 318) some carrots and celery roots, blanch them, drain and fry them in lard with minced onions and leeks; add the quarter of the same quantity of mushrooms cut into three-sixteenth inch squares, and two pounds of tripe cut into strips one inch and a half by one-quarter of an inch, and season with salt, pepper, a bunch of parsley garnished with thyme, bay leaf and a clove of garlic. Moisten to the height of the tripe with broth (No. 194a), boil up once, and then place it in the oven for one hour; skim off the fat, reduce the stock with a tomato sauce (No. 549) and soubise sauce (No. 543); serve up the tripe, pouring the reduced sauce over.

(1477). TRIPE PAUPIETTES (Paupiettes de Gras-double).

Cut strips of cooked tripe four inches long by two inches wide; cover one side of these with a layer of cream forcemeat (No. 75) mingled with some chopped ham, cooked fine herbs (No. 385); roll the strips up, and lay them in buttered tin rings; line a saucepan with slices of fat pork and slices of raw ham, carrots, celery, and minced onions, also a garnished bouquet; then place the paupiettes on top. Dilute it to the heighth of the rings with broth (No. 194a). Cover with a round piece of buttered paper, and put it to cook in a slack oven for two hours, adding a very small quantity of broth each time the gravy becomes too much reduced; when the paupiettes are well done, drain them, lay them in a sauté pan, pour over them their own gravy reduced to a half-glaze, and put them back into the oven; glaze and dress them on a very hot dish pouring over the gravy to which has been added a tomato sauce (No. 549) and a dash of cayenne pepper, straining the whole through a very fine sieve.

(1478). TRIPE WITH COOKED FINE HERBS (Gras-double aux Fines Herbes Cuites).

Take some white, fresh, and well-cooked tripe; cut it into strips of one and a half by one inch, and fry them in butter. Fry separately in butter some chopped onions and shallots, some chopped fresh mushrooms, and when the latter have evaporated their moisture, add half as much chopped truffles as there are mushrooms, then put in the tripe, seasoning it all with salt, pepper, a little lemon juice, some meat glaze (No. 402) and a very little tomato purée (No. 730), sprinkle over some chopped parsley.

VEAL (Veau).

(1479). BRAINS À L'AURORA (Cervelles à l'Aurore).

Remove the thin skin covering the brains also the fibres. Lay the brains in fresh water for several hours, carefully changing it at intervals, then put them in a saucepan, cover with water, and season with salt, whole pepper, chopped onions, thyme, bay leaf, and a little vinegar. Boil, then let simmer for twenty minutes; drain, and cut each one into twelve equal-sized pieces. Arrange them on a buttered and bread-crumbed dish, cover with an aurora sauce (No. 430), adding to it for each brain the chopped whites of four hard boiled eggs; and some chopped up parsley. Set the four hard yolks on a sieve, and with a spoon press them through over the brains. Spread some butter on top, and brown in a hot oven.

(1480). BRAINS À LA CHASSAIGNE (Cervelles à la Chassaigne).

Prepare the brains the same as for the poulette (No. 1481); drain and dress them on a hot dish and cover with the following sauce: Have a pint of velouté (No. 415), four hard boiled egg-yolks pounded with six ounces of butter, a tablespoonful of English mustard; pass the whole through a fine sieve, and add chopped and blanched chervil, chives, tarragon, and shallot, also a little spinach or vegetal green. Season properly, then add just when serving, a few chopped gherkins; pour this sauce over the brains.

(1481). BRAINS À LA POULETTE WITH MUSHROOMS (Cervelles à la Poulette aux Champignons).

Soak some brains in cold water for two hours, remove the sangineous skin enveloping them, and lay them in a saucepan to cook; cover with water, add a dash of vinegar, some sliced carrots and onions, a bunch of parsley garnished with thyme and bay leaf, a clove of garlic, and whole peppers; cook without boiling, letting them barely simmer on the side of the range half an hour; drain on a napkin and cut them lengthwise in four, range in a circle on a dish, and fill up the empty space with mushrooms added to a poulette sauce (No. 527), pouring a part of it over the brains. Garnish around with triangle-shaped croûtons of bread fried in clarified butter, and serve the remainder of the sauce separately.

(1482). BRAINS IN MATELOTE (Cervelles en Matelote).

Have the brains prepared and cooked as for the aurora (No. 1479). Brown in a pan either with butter or lard, three dozen small raw onions, seasoning with salt and a pinch of sugar; when of a fine color, put them into a small sautoir with some broth (No. 194a), and finish cooking, letting the liquid fall several times to a glaze; drain the brains, wipe dry, and dress them triangle-shaped on a dish; between each brain set a few of the onions, a cluster of stoned and stuffed olives, and one of small mushroom heads. Cover the brains with a brown sauce (No. 414) reduced with red wine, and finished with a little anchovy butter (No. 569); garnish around with trussed crawfish.

(1483). BRAINS, PEASANT STYLE (Cervelles à la Paysanne).

Cook the brains and finish them the same as for aurora (No. 1479); drain, wipe, and cut them in thick slices; roll each of these in flour. Put some melted butter into a sautoir, let boil and purify well, and when it begins to blacken, add the pieces of brain; as soon as they are colored on one side, turn them over, and let them do likewise on the other, then lift them out without breaking and lay them on a napkin; wipe and then dress the slices on a well buttered white sauce (No. 562) into which has been mixed lemon juice and chopped parsley.

(1484). BRAINS WITH BLACK OR HAZELNUT BUTTER (Cervelles au Beurre Noir ou au beurre Noisette).

Have the brains prepared and cooked the same as for the poulette (No. 1481); when done drain and dress them in the center of a very hot dish; strew over with chopped parsley, salt and pepper and baste with black butter (No. 565); put a dash of vinegar into the pan and pour it over the brains with the butter; both butter and vinegar must be strained through a fine sieve.

(1485). BRAINS WITH TOMATOED BÉARNAISE SAUCE (Cervelles à la sauce Béarnaise (Tomatée).

Skin some brains, that is, remove carefully the membrane that covers them without break-ing the brain; soak them in cold water for two hours, then plunge them into boiling water only to stiffen; drain and cook them for twelve minutes in a good white wine mirepoix (No. 419) and arrange them on a dish. Cover with a tomatoed Béarnaise sauce (No. 433).

(1486). BRAINS WITH VENETIAN OR GREEN HOLANDAISE SAUCE (Cervelles à la Sauce Vénetienne ou à la Sauce Hollandaise Verte).

Blanch the calves' brains the same as for the poulette (No. 1481); divide each one in four parts and dress every piece on a separate oval-shaped slice of bread that has been fried in butter; place them on a hot dish and cover either with Venetian sauce (No. 555), or Hollandaise vert pré sauce (No. 477).

(1487). BREAST OF VEAL À LA BOURDALOUE (Poitrine de Veau à la Bourdaloue).

Remove the bones from a breast of veal without touching the gristle; pick the skin with a trussing needle to extract all the air, and season it on the boned side; roll it up lengthwise and tie. Cover the bottom of a saucepan with a few minced vegetables, lay the breast on top, salt lightly and moisten to half its height with some unskimmed stock (No. 194a); add a bunch of aromatic herbs, put on the lid and let the liquid reduce to a glaze; remoisten to half its height and finish cooking the meat in a moderate oven, turning it over frequently during the time so that it gets a fine color all over. Before serving drain, untie, and keep it warm, while stirring into its gravy half a glassful of white wine; let boil, strain through a sieve, free it of its fat and thicken with a brown sauce (No. 414). Dress the meat on a long dish and garnish around with veal quenelles, and small canapés garnished with chopped up ham, serving the sauce separately.

(1488). BREAST OF VEAL À LA MONDOUX (Poitrine de Veau à la Mondoux).

Procure a white and fat breast of veal; cover a baking pan with minced carrots and onions, fragments of fat pork and a garnished bouquet; lay the breast on top, moistening to its heighth with stock (No. 194a); first boil then cook it in a slack oven for three hours, being careful to turn it over several times during this period. When the breast is well done, remove the hard ribs, leaving on the gristle; set it under a weight, and when nearly cold bread-crumb them English style (No. 13). Butter liberally a baking sheet, lay the meat on top, sprinkle over with more but-ter, then brown it nicely in a slow oven. Dress on a long dish and range around a garnishing composed of tomatoes cut in halves and the moisture extracted, shredded green peppers, chopped onions and a clove of garlic, the whole fried in butter and diluted with a little velouté (No. 415), nicely seasoned and besprinkled with chopped parsley.

(1489). BREAST OF VEAL AU GASTRONOME (Poitrine de Veau au Gastronome).

Select a fine breast of veal as long and wide as possible; remove the red bones covering the gristle, prick the skin with a needle, and lay a towel over the meat, then with a cleaver strike the top with a few blows so as to expel the air; slip the blade of a knife between the skin and ribs, as far as the gristle and the ends, and fill the space in with a veal quenelle forcemeat (No. 92) to which has been added very finely chopped chives and red beef tongue; sew up the skin quite close to the rib bones to give it its original shape. Butter the bottom of a roasting pan; cover it with minced carrots and onions and a garnished bunch of parsley, lay the breast on top, spread it over with good fat and pour in a pint of stock (No. 194a) or water. Two and a half hours before serv-ing put the breast into a moderate oven, baste it occasionally, glaze it of a fine color and serve it with the half-glaze (No. 400) poured over and gastronome potatoes (No. 2789) around.

VEAL, AMERICAN CUTS (Veau, Coupe à l'Américaine).

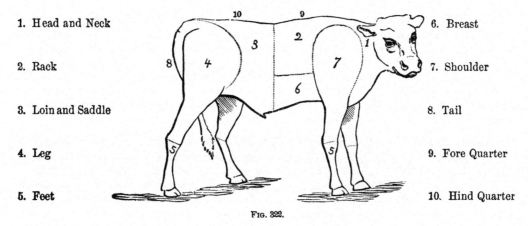

1. Head and Neck	6. Breast
2. Rack	7. Shoulder
3. Loin and Saddle	8. Tail
4. Leg	9. Fore Quarter
5. Feet	10. Hind Quarter

FIG. 322.

VEAL, AMERICAN AND FRENCH CUTS.

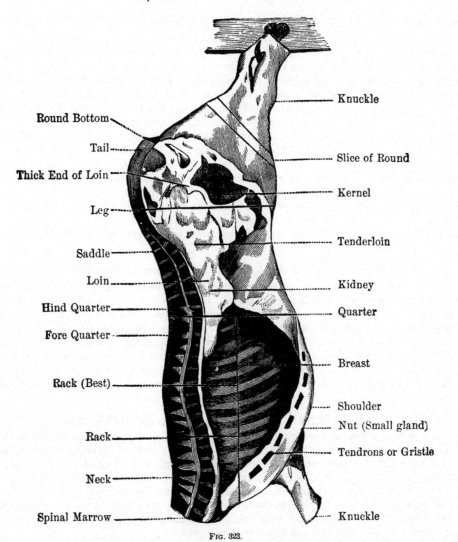

FIG. 323.

(1490). BLANQUETTE OF BREAST OF VEAL À LA JACQUART (Blanquette de Poitrine de Veau à la Jacquart.

Have two pounds of breast of veal cut into half inch pieces; lay them in tepid water for two hours, then drain and fry colorless in butter; moisten with remoistening (No. 189) add salt, a garnished bunch of parsley, one onion, two cloves and pieces of carrots; let all boil for one hour, or until finished cooking; drain, and make a velouté (No. 415) with the stock; after this sauce is well skimmed, thicken it with six egg-yolks, butter, and lemon juice; run it through a tammy. Pare the pieces of meat, put them back into the sauce, also the onions and some turned and channeled mushrooms (No. 118); stir and toss well together in the saucepan, then dress with braized chestnuts (No. 654) around.

(1491). BREAST OF VEAL STEWED WITH ROUX (Ragoût de Portrine Veau au Roux).

Cut a breast of veal into pieces an inch and a half square; fry them without browning in some butter; then drain this butter off and moisten with a quart of stock (No. 194a). Make a roux (No. 163) not too dark; dilute it with a part of the stock, then throw in the veal, one carrot, two onions (one of them having two cloves in it) and a bunch of parsley garnished with thyme and bay leaf; season with salt, pepper and a pinch of sugar, and let boil slowly for one hour, then add forty small onions fried to a fine color in butter and twenty turned mushroom heads (No. 118). When the meat is done, the sauce should be reduced to a proper consistency; dress the veal, lay the small onions around with the turned mushrooms; season the sauce, strain it through a sieve and pour it over the stew.

(1492). BREAST OF VEAL WITH TOMATOES, QUEEN STYLE—STUFFED (Poitrine de Veau Farcie aux Tomates Reine).

Select the breast of veal as long and wide as it can be had; split it open its entire length on the straight side without separating the two parts, or even the ends; season the inside with salt, pepper, and nutmeg, then proceed to fill the empty space with a forcemeat prepared as follows: have one pound of lean veal, the same of fat pork, and half a pound of panada (No. 121); chop the veal and pork up separataly, add to it the panada, then pound the whole well together with some salt, pepper, and nutmeg, two whole eggs, two spoonfuls of parsley, half a pound of mushrooms, and half a pound of ham both chopped. Mix well this preparation, and fill the breast with it; sew up the aperture with coarse thread, then lay the meat in a brazière lined with slices of fat pork, minced carrots and onions; moisten with a pint of stock (No. 194a), and after letting it fall to a glaze, moisten it once more with a quart of stock; when this comes to a boil, set the pan in a moderate oven for two hours and a half to three hours, basting it over frequently, and when done glaze it to a fine color. Strain and skim off the fat from the gravy, and reduce it to a half-glaze; dress the meat on a long dish, pour part of the gravy over, and garnish the dish with queen tomatoes (No. 2840), serve a separate sauce-boat of the same stock reduced with the same quantity of espagnole sauce (No. 414).

(1493). BREAST OF VEAL À LA MÉNAGÈRE (Poitrine de Veau à la Ménagère).

Have a fine fat breast of veal; prick the skin with a needle, cover over with a cloth; strike it several blows with a cleaver, then fry it lightly in butter, and when nicely browned, remove and trim it into an oval-shape; return it to the saucepan, add small bits of bacon, carrot, and turnip in the shape of balls; moisten with white wine and stock (No. 194a), then let fall to a glaze. Remoisten again and cook the meat in a slow oven while moistening frequently until thoroughly done, then dress it with the carrots on one side and the turnips on the other, the pieces of bacon on the ends; strain the gravy, free it of its fat, and reduce it to a half-glaze. Just when ready to serve, add to half of the gravy a liberal piece of fresh butter, lemon juice, and chopped parsley, serve it in a sauce-boat; pour over the breast the remaining gravy.

(1494). CALF'S CROW À LA NORMANDE (Fraise de Veau à la Normande).

After soaking a fine calf's crow, cut it up into quarter pound pieces. Lay on the bottom of the vessel intended for cooking this dish, first a layer of calf's feet cut in two lengthwise and the crow, on top a bed of minced onions and shallots, a little garlic and chopped parsley; season each layer with salt and mignonette, continuing until the vessel is full; then cover over with a piece of fat pork and add a bunch of thyme, bay leaf and parsley; pour over two bottlefuls of cider with a glass of brandy. Hermetically close the vessel by rubbing a little paste between it and the lid, and set it in a slack baker's oven for six hours; skim off the grease; remove the meat, free it from bones, place it on a chafing dish and strain the stock over.

(1495). VEAL CUTLETS À LA CHIPOLATA (Côtelettes de Veau à la Chipolata).

Pare some veal cutlets and lard them with cooked unsmoked red beef tongue. Cover the bottom of a buttered sautoir with round slices of onions, carrots, thyme, bay leaf, and branches of parsley; lay the cutlets on top and moisten to the heighth of the vegetables with stock (No. 194a); cover with a buttered paper, let boil and cook on a moderate fire basting them frequently. Dress the cutlets when done, strain the stock, skim off the fat and reduce it to a half-glaze, add as much brown sauce (No. 414) and garnish with braised chestnuts (No. 654), braised carrots and turnips, also some mushrooms and small boiled chipolata sausages (No. 754).

(1496). VEAL CUTLETS PLAIN AND À LA GEORGINA (Côtelettes de Veau Nature et à la Georgina).

Have a rack of very white veal containing four covered ribs; bone the chain of the spine and saw off the rib bones from the beginning of the spine; trim the chops thus obtained, flatten them lightly and pare them rounded at the angles: season with salt, lay them in melted butter. Twenty minutes before serving broil them on a slow, well maintained fire to let them acquire a good color; it will require from sixteen to eighteen minutes to cook them to perfection, turning them over after they have been on eight or nine minutes. Dress them on hot dishes, pour some clear gravy (No. 404) over and serve.

À la Georgina.—Dress the cutlets crown-shape and garnish around or in the center with risot and parmesan cheese (No. 739), and minced mushrooms in the center. Around the risot place artichoke bottoms cut in two and fried in butter. Pour into the bottom of the dish some light gravy (No. 404), and serve a tomato sauce (No. 549) and half-glaze sauce (No. 413) mixed separately.

(1497). VEAL CUTLETS À LA SEYMOUR (Côtelettes de Veau à la Seymour).

Prepare the cutlets the same as when cooked plain (No. 1496), season and dip in eggs, roll them in chopped up truffles and bread-crumbs and fry in clarified butter. Dress and garnish around with flowerets of cauliflower and cromesquis of sweetbreads (No. 872). Pour part of a ravigote sauce (No. 531) over the cutlets, serving the remainder separately.

(1498). VEAL CUTLETS À LA ZINGARA OR SINGARA (Côtelettes de Veau à la Zingara ou Singara).

Prepare the cutlets exactly as for the plain ones (No. 1496); lay them in a sautéing dish with some butter, and cook them quickly, adding a garnished bunch of parsley and half a pint of white wine; reduce this to a glaze, moisten once more with a pint of stock (No. 194a) and let smother for fifteen minutes; turn them over and finish cooking taking from fifteen to twenty minutes longer. Cut some Westphalia ham in slices, pare them like half hearts, and just when ready to serve fry them in butter and lay one between each cutlet when dressed; detach the ham glaze in the pan with some white wine and add to it the half-glaze of the cutlets, also a pinch of cayenne and lemon juice; strain the sauce and pour it over the cutlets and ham.

(1499). VEAL CUTLETS, HALF-GLAZE (Côtelettes de Veau, Demi-glace).

After preparing six cutlets as for maître d'hôtel (No. 1501) without any larding, put them into a heavily buttered sautéing pan with a garnished bunch of parsley, a quarter of a pint of Madeira wine and half a pint of good veal blond stock (No. 423). Let come to a boil, then place it in a slow oven; at the end of fifteen minutes turn them over so that they do not cook too rapidly, and after another fifteen minutes they should be sufficiently glazed. Dress them on a dish; strain and skim the fat from the stock adding to it a spoonful of half-glaze (No. 400); pour this over the cutlets and garnish them with paper frills (No. 10); then serve.

(1500). VEAL CUTLETS WITH CHICORY—LARDED (Côtelettes de Veau Piquées à la Chicorée).

Pare six small veal cutlets, keeping the bone end rather short and the meat not too thick; lard them in the center all on the same side. Cover the bottom of a sautoir with fragments of fat pork and cut up onions and carrots, on this range the cutlets, season and moisten to their heighth with stock (No. 194a); stand the sautoir on a hot fire, reduce the liquid to half, then cover the cutlets with buttered paper; cook while covered on a slow fire or in a very slack oven increasing the moistening from time to time, lastly, glaze the cutlets at the oven door having them uncovered and basting with their own stock. Dress them, in a straight row on a long dish, the handle bone placed underneath; surround both sides with a garnishing of chiccory cream (No. 2729); detach the glaze from the sautoir with a little broth and baste the meats with this after it has been skimmed and strained.

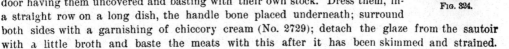

Fig. 324.

(1501). VEAL CUTLETS, MAÎTRE D'HÔTEL (Côtelettes de Veau Maître d'Hôtel).

Cut six cutlets from a rack rather thick and straight, each one having one rib bone; cut the chain bone so as to detach the meat; suppress all the skin covering the fat and shorten the bone on the spine end, beat down the cutlets, not too thin, with a damp cleaver on a slightly wet table; scrape the rib bone toward the top where the frill is placed; round and pare the meat of the cutlet; season with salt, coat over with oil or melted butter; range them on a broiler, and broil them on a moderate fire for sixteen to eighteen minutes, turning them over at the end of eight or nine minutes. Lay them on a dish, glaze over with a brush, trim the handles with a paper frill (No. 10) and dress them crown-shaped on the serving dish with a layer of maître d'hôtel butter (No. 581) between each one. For plain serve the above with a clear gravy (No. 404).

(1502). VEAL CUTLETS, MILANESE (Côtelettes de Veau Milanaise).

FIG. 325.

Have six pared veal cutlets; dip them in clarified butter, then in breadcrumbs and immerse them in strained and beaten eggs; then again in breadcrumbs mixed with half the quantity of grated parmesan, and smooth this second breading carefully with the blade of a knife so as to have it level and even. Twenty minutes before serving put into a sautéing-pan sufficiently large to contain the cutlets without squeezing them, enough clarified butter to allow them to swim; fry them to a fine golden color, being careful to turn them over once only, then drain, ornament with a paper frill (No. 10) and dress; pour around a tomato sauce (No. 549) mixed with half-glaze sauce (No. 413), and surround with tomato or macaroni Milanaise timbales (No. 2988).

(1503). VEAL CUTLETS STUDDED WITH TRUFFLES (Côtelettes de Veau Cloutée aux Truffes).

Pare six covered veal cutlets keeping the rib bones rather short, and the meats seven-eighths of an inch thick; stud them rosette-shaped all on the same side with pieces of truffles square on one end, and pointed on the other. Cover the bottom of a sautoir with scraps of fat pork, minced carrots and onions; on this range the cutlets, season, and moisten to their heighth with beef stock (No. 194a); set the saucepan on a brisk fire, reduce the liquid to half, cover the chops with buttered paper, and let cook with the lid on over a slow fire, or else in the oven, increasing the moistening at frequent intervals. At the very last moment allow them to glaze while uncovered, basting with their own stock; lift them out, pare them slightly, garnish the handles with paper frills (No. 10), and dress over a Madeira sauce (No. 492) reduced with essence of truffles (No. 395).

FIG. 326.

(1504). VEAL CUTLETS WITH FINE HERBS (Côtelettes de Veau aux Fines Herbes).

Cut, pare, beat, and season six or eight veal cutlets; put them into a sautoir containing butter, fry them on both sides over a brisk fire, and when well browned, drain off the fat into another small saucepan, and lay it on one side. Moisten the meat with a little stock (No. 194a), let the liquid fall slowly to a glaze in such a way as to finish the cooking, and lastly add a few spoonfuls of white wine. In the fat put aside, fry colorless two or three spoonfuls of chopped shallots and onions, with five or six spoonfuls of chopped up raw mushrooms, and continue frying until these have lost all their humidity, then thicken with a half-glaze sauce (No. 413). Let this cook for a few minutes, and pour it over the cutlets in the sautoir; besprinkle with a few spoonfuls of chopped truffles and cooked ham, and let simmer together for seven or eight minutes. Dress the cutlets garnished with frills (No. 10) on a long dish; add to the sauce a pinch of chopped and blanched parsley leaves, pour it over the meat.

(1505). STUFFED EARS, TOMATO SAUCE (Oreilles Farcies à la Sauce Tomate).

Cook three or four small and very clean calves' ears in stock (No. 182); drain and leave them till nearly cold, and when properly wiped, shorten and divide each ear into two parts; pare nicely, season and stuff these halves by covering them over with a thick baking forcemeat (No. 81), mixed with a third of its quantity of veal quenelle forcemeat (No. 92), and a few spoonfuls of cooked fine herbs (No. 385); smooth them down nicely and roll the half ears into white bread-crumbs, dip them in beaten eggs, bread-crumb once more, and plunge into very hot frying fat to brown while heating; drain, salt, and dress them on a folded napkin with fried parsley. A tomato sauce (No. 549), should be served separately.

(1506). CALVES' FEET, AMERICAN STYLE (Pieds de Veau à l'Américaine).

Dry and singe six calves' feet; split them in two to suppress the middle bone, return them to their original shape, and tie them together, then parboil for ten minutes; remove, drain, and put them back into a saucepan with water, salt, carrots, and onions, a bunch of parsley garnished with thyme and bay leaf, whole peppers, and cloves; let this cook on a moderate fire for one hour and a half. Fry in some lard, a few celery roots, onions, and ham cut in dice; moisten with the above stock and white wine, add to it the feet, and when well cooked, which will take about three hours, drain and bone them; season over with salt, mignonette, and nutmeg, and place them under a weight; when cold, pare, besprinkle with finely chopped parsley and shallots, then dip them in eggs, then in bread-crumbs and fry over a slow fire for fifteen minutes, basting them with melted butter. Dress and serve with a separate sauce-boat of espagnole sauce (No. 414) and velouté sauce (No. 415), half of each, seasoned with curry, and thickened with egg-yolks.

(1507). GRENADINS OF FILLET OF VEAL, TOMATOED ARGENTINE SAUCE (Grenadins de Filet de Veau Sauce Tomates Argentine).

If fine grenadins are required, they should be cut either from the minion fillet or from the large saddle fillet or from the kernel; in either case beat the meat with a cleaver, having the blade dampened, flatten to three-eighths of an inch in thickness; pare them into half hearts or ovals, all of the same size; season and lard with fat pork. Place these grenadins in a sautoir lined with scraps of fat pork, roots and sliced onions; moisten to half their height with stock (No. 194a), and cook, letting the liquid fall to a glaze several times, and finally finish glazing it in the oven, basting with its own stock. Just when ready to serve, lift them out, drain and lay them on a long dish, one overlapping the other in a single row, and around pour an Argentine tomato sauce (No. 429); sprinkle the meat over with the stock, strained free of fat and well reduced.

(1508). MINCED FILLET OF VEAL, PORTUGUESE (Émincé de Filet de Veau à la Portugaise).

Chop up one shallot very finely and put it into a saucepan with half a pint of port wine and a finely shredded orange peel, a pint of cayenne pepper, lemon juice and half a pint of espagnole sauce (No. 414); boil and reduce the whole to the consistency of sauce. Heat some cooked veal fillets cut up into slices, dress them in the center of a circle of poached eggs laid on oval-shaped croûtons, and place on top of each egg a piece of tongue cut the shape of a croûton; pour the sauce over all.

(1509). MINION FILLETS OF VEAL, WITH PURÉE OF ARTICHOKES (Filets Mignons de Veau à la Purée d'Artichauts).

From the thickest part of an uncooked, pared minion fillet of veal, cut off slices each half an inch, having them slightly biased so as to obtain them wider; flatten with the cleaver, pare into rounds two and a quarter inches in diameter or in ovals, then season. Heat some clarified butter in a sautoir, range the minions on the bottom and fry them quickly on both sides, turning them over as fast as they are glazed; drain off the butter and moisten to half of their height with some good veal blond (No. 423); let fall two or three times slowly to a glaze always adding more of the same stock. When the minions are well glazed and cooked, lift them up one by one with a fork, and dress each on a flat crust of bread browned in the oven; range these on a long dish in two straight rows, and at both sides lay some artichoke purée (No. 704) pushed through a pocket; pour over part of the stock from the fillets after it has been reduced with a spoonful of Madeira wine. Serve the remainder in a sauce turren.

(1510). MINIONS OF FILLET OF VEAL WITH MUSHROOMS (Mignons de Filet de Veau aux Champignons).

From a good fillet of a saddle of veal cut eight or ten bias slices half an inch in thickness and weighing six ounces; beat to flatten and pare slightly oval-shape, lard them on one side with thin lardons (No. 4, Fig. 52). Season these minions and range them one beside the other in a sautoir having the bottom coverered with fragments of fat pork and a few slices of onion; moisten to their heighth with veal blond (No. 423) and let this fall slowly to a glaze; moisten again and cook them in this manner, allowing the liquid to fall two or three times; now drain out the minions, pare them neatly and strain the stock, skim off its fat and reduce it well. Put the minions back into the sautoir, pour their stock over and glaze to a fine color in a slack oven keeping them well basted. On the center of an entrée dish fasten a very thin wooden bottom covering it with

Fig. 327.

cooked paste (No. 131); dry this and glaze it over with a brush. Have some quenelle forcemeat prepared with the veal parings, fill a small timbale mold four inches in diameter by two inches in heighth; cover this forcemeat with buttered paper and poach in a bain-marie. At the last moment invert this forcemeat "pain" on the center of the foundation, range the minions around one overlapping the other; on the top dress some mushroom heads in a pyramid, having them cooked very white and coated with velouté (No. 415); add to the stock in the sautoir some half-glaze (No. 400), pour some of this sauce into the bottom of the dish and serve what remains apart.

(1511). PAUPIETTES OF FILLET OF VEAL À LA WHITTIER (Paupiettes de Filet de Veau à la Whittier.)

Blanch some small heart sweetbreads; cut them up into inch squares. Pare three fillets of veal, cut them into eighth of an inch lengthwise slices, flatten them slightly and pare into oblongs, four by two and a quarter; lay them on the table, season and spread over with a forcemeat prepared as follows; Chop up the parings of the meat with the same weight of fat pork; mix in cooked fine herbs (No. 385), bread-crumbs, egg-yolks and chopped up ham, season, roll up each paupiette, wrap them in sheets of buttered paper and tie them at both ends the same as a boned turkey, braise these for one hour and a half, unwrap, glaze and dress on a well-buttered béchamel sauce (No. 409). Fry the sweetbreads on a brisk fire, add to them some raw fine herbs, meat glaze (No. 402) and the juice of a lemon, dress them in the middle of the paupiettes.

(1512). SCHNITZEL, GERMAN STYLE (Schnitzel à l'Allemande).

Pare neatly a tenderloin or a round bottom of veal and cut in thin slices across the grain of the meat, beat these with the blade of a cleaver to thin them considerably, then season with salt and pepper; dip them first in beaten eggs, then roll in bread-crumbs and fry in clarified butter (No. 16) on a brisk fire, when cooked and of a fine color, dress them flat in a circle on a buttered espagnole sauce (No. 414), into which some lemon juice has been stirred; on each slice of veal place one egg fried in butter in a frying pan, and on these eggs range lozenge-shaped and symmetrically some fillets of anchovies, and in the center of each lozenge lay a few nonpareil capers; surround the dish with a border of gherkins and sliced lemon having the peel notched.

(1513). SCHNITZEL, VIENNA STYLE (Schnitzel à la Viennoise).

Select some good tenderloins of veal; suppress the nervous parts and then cut them into slightly bias slices; beat this with the blade of a cleaver, and chop lightly with the back of the blade of a knife; pare and season with salt and pepper, roll them in flour, and dip each piece separately in beaten eggs, roll in bread-crumbs, sauté and cook them in clarified butter, then dress them in a circle on a hot dish. Serve separately a tomato sauce (No. 549) or thickened gravy (No. 405)

(1514). FILLET OF VEAL SLICED WITH PELERINE POTATOES (Tranches de Filet de Veau aux Pommes Pèlerine).

Slices of veal should bear no resemblance either to cutlets or minions. Slices of veal breaded and fried are often called cutlets which is an error, the name of cutlets should only be applied to a piece of meat cut from the rack having a rib bone ("côte," from which it derives its name) attached to it; sometimes the word is used for imitation cutlets, but as veal, mutton, or lamb the name should not be given to any part excepting to one containing a rib. They must be thin and pared oval-shaped; nor are they to be taken from the fillet or kernel, but from the large part of the minion fillet. Trim the meat, cutting it transversely into three-eighths of an inch thick slices; beat them well with a moistened cleaver to flatten, pare in ovals and season. Pour some clarified butter into a large sautoir, and cook the sliced meat in this over a good fire, turning them when done on one side; drain on a napkin, and glaze with a brush; dress them one overlapping the other on a long dish in one straight row, and surround with Pelerine potatoes. Serve a sauce-boatful of a tomato sauce (No. 549) and half-glaze sauce (No. 413) mixed, at the same time.

Pelerine Potatoes.—Have one-third of pate-à-chou (No. 132), and two-thirds of potato purée (No. 725); mix thoroughly together and form into balls three quarters of an inch in diameter; roll in flour, dip in eggs, roll once more in cracker-dust, then fry in hot fat to a fine color.

(1515). CALF'S HEAD À LA RENAISSANCE (Tête de Veau à la Renaissance).

Prepare and cook the calf's head exactly as for the plain (No. 1519); when cold cut one pound of it into inch squares and lay them in a saucepan with an espagnole sauce (No. 414) and Madeira. Heat it up slowly adding a quarter of a pound of mushrooms, a quarter of a pound of square pieces of sweetbread, two ounces of cut up truffles, and twenty-four olives. Dress the calf's head in shallow china dishes, each one containing sufficient for one person; lay on a slice of brain Villeroi, and cover with a layer of puff paste (No. 146) and bake in a good oven. This entrée may be served in a large dish, the size being in proportion to the number of guests.

(1516). CALF'S HEAD À LA POULETTE (Tête de Veau à la Poulette).

Prepare and cook the calf's head as for the plain (No. 1519); when cold select the cheek pieces and snout free of all fat, and cut them up into one and three-quarter inch squares; put these in a sautoir with some velouté sauce (No. 415), heat it up slowly and thicken just when ready to serve with egg-yolks and butter, seasoning with salt, pepper, nutmeg, lemon juice and fine herbs. Serve very hot.

(1517). CALF'S HEAD IN TORTUE (Tête de Veau en Tortue).

Prepare and cook the head the same as for No. 1519; reduce some espagnole sauce (No. 414) with Madeira and cayenne pepper; add to it veal quenelles (No. 92), sweetbreads sliced a quarter of an inch thick cut from round pieces an inch and a quarter in diameter, mushrooms, olives, veal palates, balls of gherkins and trussed and glazed crawfish. Drain the head, wipe dry on a napkin, dress and surround it with the garnishing well and symmetrically arranged; pour the sauce over, and set the glazed crawfish around the whole.

(1518). CALF'S HEAD EN TORTUE, DRESSED (Tête de Veau Dressée en Tortue).

Bone half of a very white calf's head, put it into boiling water for fifteen minutes, then cut it up and finish cooking it in a white stock (No. 182) acidulated with lemon juice; it will take three

FIG. 328.

hours to boil slowly. Have a silver plated dish with a border of the same; in the center of this fasten a fried bread pyramid covered with raw forcemeat and then poached in the heater or slack oven;

prepare a garnishing composed of small quenelles molded with a coffeespoon (No. 155) and poached, large cocks'-combs, olives, fresh mushroom heads, round truffles and green pickles cut into small half-inch diameter balls. Keep in a bain-marie a slightly tomatoed Madeira sauce (No. 492) with a little truffle moistening. Half an hour before serving drain the pieces of head on a cloth, pare them rounded, and slit the outside gristle of the ear in order to be able to turn it backward, then lay them in a saucepan with half of the sauce, let simmer over a gentle fire and just when prepared to serve set the ear on the top of the pyramid, fastening it down with a small skewer, and surround this support with the remainder of the head and garnishings; cover over lightly with the sauce and pour the rest into a sauce-bowl to be served at the same time as the entrée.

(1519). CALF'S HEAD PLAIN OR VINAIGRETTE (Tête de Veau au Naturel ou à la Vinaigrette).

Choose a very white, fat and well cleaned calf's head, bone it entirely; split it in two to par-boil and when done, dry, singe and scrape it; remove the tongue, then lay it in cold water to steep for one hour. Suppress the sanguineous skin found on the brain and soak this for one hour; place in a saucepan with a quart of water, salt and vinegar, let boil slowly for fifteen minutes to cook it. Cut each half head into five pieces, namely: the ear cut off largely from the base, the eye, the snout and two cheek pieces; put one pound of chopped suet into a saucepan able to hold twelve quarts of water; add to it a quarter of a pound of flour and stir together on the fire for a few moments, then lay in quartered carrots and onions, a bunch of parsley garnished with thyme, bay leaf, a clove of garlic and two cloves, a dessertspoonful of whole peppers, salt and half a gill of vinegar, mix well and add five quarts of water; set this on the fire, stir till it boils, then put in the pieces of head and the tongue; let cook for two hours, and when it softens between the two fingers, remove the white skin covering both tongue and inside of the snout, drain off the pieces and wipe them dry. Dress the head simply on a dish or folded napkin, lay the slit ears in the center hav-ing turned them backward with the other pieces around the tongue and brains split lengthwise in two; garnish around with branches of parsley; and serve at the same time a sauce-boat of vinai-grette sauce (No. 634), also a saucerful of onions and parsley, both finely chopped, whole capers and vinegar pickles.

(1520). KERNEL OF VEAL À LA DUCHESS (Noix de Veau à la Duchesse).

Select a good kernel from a fat calf, retain the udder and pare the fleshy part of the kernel which is not covered; trim nicely and remove the skin that covers the meat and stud it over with square pieces of truffles one inch long and pointed on one end; salt the meat lightly and cover the studded part with some slices of fat pork, tying them down. Lay the kernel in a deep sautoir lined with fragments of suet or fat pork, and pour over a little melted butter and a little stock (No. 194a), let cook in a moderate oven for two or three hours according to its size, basting it with the drippings in the pan. When done, untie and dress it on an oval dish, surrounding the meat with duchess potatoes (No. 2785), laying them in a long square; glaze over with a brush and serve separately a sauce-boat of brown sauce (No. 414), reduced with a part of the stock, Madeira, white wine and chopped up truffles.

(1521). KERNEL OF VEAL WITH THICKENED GRAVY (Noix de Veau au jus lié).

Take a kernel of veal, keep the udder whole and set it between two white cloths to beat it down with a cleaver; pare a third of the kernel by removing the fat and sinewy skin, then lard the meat with lardons (No. 2, Fig. 52). Line a saucepan with slices or fragments of veal, place the kernel on top with a few onions and sliced carrots, and lay at the side a bunch of parsley and

FIG. 329.

chives; moisten with stock (No. 194a), cover with buttered paper and let boil, then put on its lid and set it in the oven for an hour and a half to two hours basting it often—the time for its cook-ing depends on the quality and the size. When done, drain and strain the stock. Skim off the fat, reduce it to a glaze; use some of it to glaze the kernel, and to the remaining part add one pint of espagnole (No. 414). Dress the kernel, pour some of the sauce around and serve the balance in a sauce-tureen. Serve separately a sorrel garnishing (No. 2818), a Romaine garnishing (No. 2816), a chiccory garnishing (No. 2729) or a spinach garnishing (No. 2820).

(1522). KERNEL OF VEAL WITH HALF-GLAZE (Noix de Veau à la Demi-glace).

Select a kernel of veal as white and fat as procurable; raise carefully with the tip of a knife the swollen skin covering a part of it, then lay it on the table and press the meat down with the left hand while slipping the blade of a very sharp knife between it and the skin, pressing the knife slightly against this skin; pare the meat all around into an oval shape, and lard the entire surface with medium-sized lardons (No. 2, Fig. 52). Three and a half hours before serving put some minced carrots, onions and slices of lean ham into a buttered deep sautoir, the kernel of veal on top and a pint of stock (No. 194a), let this come to a boil and reduce to a glaze; moisten again to two-thirds of its heighth with stock, cover with buttered paper, boil and place it in the oven, basting over occasionally; three-quarters of an hour before serving, remove the lid and paper covering the meat and glaze the latter. Dress the kernel and serve in a sauce-boat the stock passed through a silk sieve, the fat removed and reduced to a half-glaze.

(1523). SMALL KERNELS OR NUTS WITH MACÉDOINE (Noisettes de Veau à la Macédoine).

Small Kernels.—A small gland enveloped in fat, found in the shoulder of veal near the joint of the two large bones, on the left of the plate bone. This kernel is the size of an ordinary walnut, and is considered a tidbit morsel. Procure sixteen of these kernels, soak them on the corner of the range for two hours, without boiling, then parboil, refresh and drain well; lay them under a weight, pare them oval-shaped, and put them into a sautoir lined with slices of fat pork and moistened with a mirepoix stock (No. 419) made with either white wine or Madeira; let cook for three-quarters of an hour; a quarter of an hour before serving, drain off, strain and skim the stock; pour it back over the kernels and reduce the whole to a half-glaze; dress in a circle, filling the center with a macédoine of vegetables (No. 680); pour the half-glaze over the kernels and serve.

(1524). VEAL KIDNEYS À L'ANDERSON (Rognons de Veau à l'Anderson).

For six persons have three small or two large very fresh kidneys; suppress the fat and fibrous parts, then cut them up into small slices. Fry in butter in a sautoir one ounce of chopped onion, add the pieces of kidney, and toss them over a quick fire while seasoning; as soon as the meats are cooked, pour all into a sauce pan; remove them with a skimmer on a dish leaving the liquid in the pan, and into it pour one gill of veal blond (No. 423), and one gill of red wine; stir well with the kidney juice, and thicken with a small piece of kneaded butter (No. 579), boil and pass through a tammy; add the kidneys, and finish seasoning with salt, pepper, nutmeg, and chopped parsley. Cut some potatoes into three-sixteenths of an inch thick slices, then with a round vegetable cutter an inch and a quarter in diameter, remove some pieces; fry these of a fine golden color in butter, drain off the latter and add a little meat glaze (No. 402), a little salt, parsley, and lemon juice; dress these potatoes in a circle, filling the middle with the kidneys and their gravy.

(1525). VEAL KIDNEYS À LA ROEDERER (Rognons de Veau à la Roederer).

Mince three small kidneys after suppressing the fat and fibrous parts; fry them in butter in a sautoir on a hot fire, season and as soon as the meats are seized, pour into a sautoir; remove the kidneys with a skimmer, and lay them on a dish, leaving their liquid in the pan; into this add a little espagnole sauce (No. 414), some champagne, cooked and turned mushrooms (No. 118), meat glaze (No. 402), chopped and blanched parsley, and lemon juice; pour the sauce over the kidneys, and garnish around with small Milanaise macaroni croquettes made by cooking one pound of macaroni in salted water for fifteen minutes, then drain and cut into quarter inch lengths; put them back into the saucepan with grated parmesan and Swiss cheese, half of each, a little salt, pepper, nutmeg, béchamel (No. 409), and a large piece of butter; mix well, then let get cold. With this preparation make croquettes, either cylinder-shaped or any other form; dip in eggs, bread-crumb, and fry to a golden brown.

(1526). VEAL KIDNEYS WITH MARROW (Rognons de Veau à la Moelle).

Split a fine veal kidney through its widest part, pare, and suppress the fat and fibers, then season; run a skewer through the length, coat over with melted butter, roll in bread-crumbs, and broil over a slow fire; dress and cover with slices of blanched beef marrow, pour a Colbert sauce (No. 451) over, and serve very hot.

(1527). VEAL KIDNEYS WITH WHITE WINE (Rognons de Veau au Vin Blanc).

For six persons take three small fresh veal kidneys, pare off the fat and fibers and cut them up into small slices; fry these with some butter in a sautoir or frying pan and toss them over a very brisk fire; season and as soon as the meats are seized, remove them with a skimmer on a dish, leaving the liquid in the pan; stir into this one gill of stock (No. 194a), as much white wine and four ounces of mushroom heads cut in four, cook while covered for five minutes, thicken the sauce with a little butter kneaded in flour, or else use some thick brown sauce (No. 414); let the sauce cook and reduce with it the kidney liquor that is in the pan, and when reduced and consistent, put back the kidneys with some chopped parsley, heat without boiling and serve. These kidneys may be garnished with triangular croûtons of bread-crumbs fried in butter.

(1528). LEG OR HAUNCH OF VEAL, À LA MIRIBEL (Ouissot de Veau à la Miribel).

Bone as far as the joint, a medium sized haunch of veal; sew it up oval-shaped, and lay it in a braziere lined with fat pork and vegetables; moisten with a pint of broth (No. 194a), let fall to a glaze and moisten again to half its heighth with broth or water, season, cover with a buttered paper and let the liquid come to a boil, then reduce it to half, and set it in the oven to cook slowly while basting and turning it over every half hour; it will take three hours to cook properly. Dress, glaze it nicely and pour into the dish half of the reduced gravy serving the remainder in a sauce-tureen, having it added to the same quantity of tomato sauce (No. 549) and then reduced. Send to the table at the same time a dish of vegetables composed of fried cauliflower, fried egg-plant, fried potatoes and rice croquettes.

(1529). CALF'S LIGHT À LA MARINIÈRE (Mou de Veau à la Marinière).

Fry one pound of small squares of bacon in butter, add a calf's light cut into two inch pieces and marinated for eight hours previously in salt, pepper, thyme, bay leaf, white wine, sweet oil, minced onions, slices of lemon, garlic and parsley leaves. After the light is well fried, dredge over with some flour, toss well, then moisten with white wine and stock (No. 194a), half an hour before serving, add small onions fried in clarified butter; and a little sugar, and ten minutes before sending to the table, put in some mushrooms; finish cooking the whole, dress and garnish with croûtons of bread fried in butter, laid all around the stew.

(1530). CALF'S LIVER À LA CLERMONT (Foie de Veau à la Clermont).

Cut up finely one pound of white onions and fry in butter to have them a nice golden color. Drain this off, and moisten the onions with sufficient stock (No. 194a) to allow them to swim; set it on a slow fire to cook and fall to a glaze, moisten with one and a half pints of espagnole (No. 414), reduce to half. Cut slices from a calf's liver three-eighths of an inch in thickness; pare each one the shape of a large chicken fillet, and lay them in a sautéing pan with clarified butter, season with salt and pepper, and fry on both sides till they are firm to the touch, then drain off the butter and add the above Clermont, finishing with chopped parsley. Remove at the first boil, dress the liver and pour the Clermont over.

(1531). CALF'S LIVER AND BACON (Foie de Veau au Petit Salé).

Cut quarter of an inch thick slices of liver, season with pepper and a little salt, dredge over with flour, and fry with some butter in a pan. When the liver is cooked, dress, pour over the butter and garnish with very thin slices of broiled bacon.

(1532). CALF'S LIVER. ITALIAN STYLE (Foie de Veau à l'Italienne).

From a fine calf's liver cut six transversal slices, each three-eighths of an inch thick; season with salt and pepper. Melt some clarified butter in a sautoir, and when hot range in the slices of liver to cook rather slowly for five minutes on one side, then turn them over to cook as long on the other—ten minutes in all—lay them on a plate, leaving the butter in the sautoir, and glaze them over. Add to the butter in the sautoir one tablespoonful of chopped shallot and two of onions; fry very slowly, then put in double the same quantity of chopped up mushrooms and let cook until they have exhausted all their moisture; dilute with a little velouté and reduce for a few moments, slowly adding one gill of white wine and three teaspoonfuls of essence of truffles (No. 395); take from the fire, and replace the liver leaving it to heat without boiling. Dress the slices in a circle on a dish, and finish the sauce with a pinch of chopped parsley, and pour the whole over the liver.

(1533). CALF'S LIVER WITH FINE HERBS—FRIED (Foie de Veau Sauté aux Fines Herbes).

Cut from a fine calf's liver three-eighths of an inch thick slices; season them with salt and pepper, and roll in flour, then fry in butter, keeping them rare; it will take about four minutes for each side. Add to the butter some shallots, mushrooms, chives, parsley, and chervil all finely chopped; dress the liver, pour over the chopped preparation and finish with the juice of a lemon.

(1534). LOIN OF VEAL À L'AMBASSADE (Longe de Veau à l'Ambassade).

Have a loin of veal leaving on the two ribs; bone it entirely, prick the flap and beat it. Remove the kidneys and all their surrounding fat, and lay the kidneys inside the loin, then season with salt and pepper, and fold over the flap so that it incloses both kidney and minion fillet; roll and tie it with twelve rows of string, making a knot at each row while keeping the meat an equal oblong shape. Cover the bottom of a braziere with slices of fat pork, sliced carrots and onions, and a garnished bunch of parsley; lay the meat on top and moisten with a pint of stock (No. 194a); let fall to a glaze, moisten again with a quart of the stock, and cover over with a sheet of buttered paper; set the pan in a slow oven and keep basting and moistening several times until thoroughly cooked, which will take about two hours. Untie the meat, dip it in eggs and bread-crumbs, dredge over with grated parmesan, besprinkle with fresh butter, and brown it in a quick oven; garnish around with fried halved tomatoes and stuffed mushrooms (No. 650), reduce the stock to half, and serve at the same time as the meat.

(1535). LOIN OF VEAL À LA PRINTANIÈRE (Longe de Veau à la Printanière).

Remove the fat from the kidney side of a loin of veal; bone it entirely, flatten the flap after pricking it with the tip of a knife; season lightly with salt and pepper, and then roll the flap over, bringing it on the kidney side; tie it into an oblong-shape. Line a saucepan with slices of fat pork, a few sliced onions and carrots, two split calves' feet, a knuckle of veal, and a little ham; lay the loin of veal on top, and moisten the whole with a pint of stock (No. 194a). Set the saucepan on a brisk fire, then let the liquid fall to a glaze and get a fine golden color, then moisten again with a pint of stock; cover the meat with a sheet of buttered paper, place the lid on the saucepan and let cook slowly for two hours, basting and remoistening frequently. Remove the paper and glaze the meat; skim the fat from the stock, pass it through a fine strainer, and reduce it with an equal amount of brown espagnole sauce (No. 414). Dress the loin on an oval dish; garnish around with a printanière of carrots and turnips cut round, cooked and glazed separately, some braised lettuce, cauliflowers, glazed onions, and string beans.

(1536). LOIN OF VEAL À LA SAINTONGE (Longe de Veau à la Saintonge).

Procure a good loin of veal; remove the fat, also the kidneys, taking a part of their fat away; break the spine bone at the joints, and put the kidneys back near the ribs; cover over with the flap; pare the meat into an oblong-shape nearly the same dimensions throughout, tie and roast it in the oven, not having it too hot after placing some good fat on top; leave it in for two hours, then salt, glaze and brown to a fine color. Dress the meat garnishing around with green peas Parisian style (No. 2745), and the ends with cork-shaped turnips, blanched and cooked in beef broth (No. 194a) with a little sugar and butter, sufficiently moistened that when they are cooked they have fallen to a glaze. Serve a separate sauce-boat of a buttered velouté sauce (No. 415), seasoned with nutmeg.

(1537). LOIN OF VEAL WITH GRAVY (Longe de Veau au Jus).

The veal should be white and fat. Remove all fat and kidneys from a loin, detach the minion fillets entirely; separate half the meat from the bones beginning at the spinal bone, then give one cut of the saw on each bone joint remaining against the sirloin; bone the flat bone and the ends of a few of the ribs which must be cut off to give it a good appearance; prick the flap or flank with the tip of a knife to extract the air which swells it up, and relay the minion fillets on the opposite side they were originally taken from, also a slice of meat removed from the flat bone so that the loin be of an equal size throughout; then roll the flap over and tie the meat with twelve rounds of string; wrap it in sheets of buttered paper and tie this up with ten rounds of string; lay the loin on a baking pan on top of a grate, set one inch above the bottom; sprinkle with good fat and leave it to cook in the oven for two to two and a half hours. Fifteen minutes before serving the loin, untie and lay it on another baking pan to leave in the oven to become a fine golden color; dress, glaze with a light glaze and serve with clear gravy (No. 404) thickened with half-glaze sauce (No. 413).

(1538). NECK OF VEAL AU BLANC (Cou de Veau au Blanc).

Have three pounds of the neck of veal, without sinews, cut in pieces three inches long by one and a quarter wide, parboil, drain, then throw them into cold water; when cool, drain again and pare them into equal sized pieces. Put a quarter of a pound of butter into a saucepan with a quarter of a pound of unsmoked bacon; let this fry lightly, then add the veal and fry together to a fine color; besprinkle with four spoonfuls of flour, and brown it slightly with the meat, then moisten with stock (No. 194a), season with salt, whole peppers, a garnished bunch of parsley with thyme and bay leaf and two cloves; cook for two hours before adding sixty small onions, and continue the cooking until both the onions and meat are done; now transfer the onions and meat into another saucepan with about thirty medium-sized cooked mushrooms. Skim the fat from the sauce; reduce and season it properly, thicken it with three egg-yolks diluted in a little cream, and finish with fresh butter and lemon juice; strain through a tammy, pour it over the meat, kept warm in a bain-marie until needed. Dress the meat, with the onions and mushrooms around and pour the sauce over the whole.

(1539). VEAL PALATES À LA SÉVIGNÉ (Palais de Veau à la Sévigné).

Soak well six veal palates for six hours, then parboil them in boiling water, afterward throwing them into cold water. Scrape the palates with the dull edge of a knife, carefully removing all the white skin from the top as well as the black one found underneath, and wash again in several waters. Braise them in a mirepoix stock (No. 419) for two hours; set them under a weight, pare them oval-shaped and cover with a quenelle forcemeat (No. 92) dredging the surface with chopped truffles. Place the palates in a buttered sautoir and heat them on a moderate fire; dress in a circle around an empty croustade and fill the croustade with a preparation of suprême sauce, escalops of foies-gras, truffles and mushrooms. Serve more of the suprême sauce (No. 547) separately.

(1540). VEAL PALATES, EPICUREAN STYLE (Palais de Veau à l'Épicurienne).

Fry one coffeespoonful of finely chopped blanched shallots in very hot butter; add to it a few mushroom heads and braised lamb's noisettes free from fat; fry together for a minute, seasoning with salt and prepared red pepper (No. 168). Moisten with cream and a little béchamel (No. 409) then lay in the veal palates prepared as for à la Sévigné (No. 1539) and cut round-shape an inch and a quarter in diameter and let simmer for five minutes; finish with a little butter and serve very hot.

(1541). QUARTER OF VEAL, SCOTCH STYLE (Quartier de Veau à l'Écossaise).

Choose a haunch of veal from a very white calf; pare and saw off a piece of the shine bone and trim like a leg of mutton, then wrap the meat up in several sheets of paper; lay it in an English cradle spit (Fig. 116), and let cook before a moderate fire from one hour and a half to two hours; unwrap and finish cooking until a fine color; salt it over, remove it from the spit and pare the end bone. Dress the meat on a large oval dish, decorate it with a paper frill cut out and curled, pour over some clear gravy (No. 404), and garnish around with boiled carrots, turnips, and string beans; serve gravy in a sauce-boat separately.

(1542). RACK OF VEAL À L'ALBANI (Carré de Veau à l'Albani).

Take the covered ribs of a rack of veal, cut the spine out entirely, bone the ribs to within two and a half inches of the spine, and saw them off. Pare the top of the rack, lard it with salt fat pork lardons (No. 2, Fig. 52), then roll the flap over, tie and wrap it in buttered paper; put it in the oven to roast; a little before serving time unwrap the rack, glaze, brown, and dress it, garnishing around with Dauphine potatoes (No. 2783). Serve a cream béchamel sauce separately (No. 411).

(1543). ROUND BOTTOM FRICANDEAU OF VEAL GLAZED WITH GRAVY (Sous-noix Fricandeau Glacée au Jus).

A fricandeau is to be prepared either with the kernel, or round bottom; under all circumstances the meat must not be cut too thick, then beat it with a damp cleaver in order to flatten it even more while breaking the fibers. Lard the meat with larding pork (No. 2, Fig. 52) on its smoothest side; cover the bottom of a deep sautoir with fragments of the pork, sliced vegetables and onions, and aromatic herbs; lay the meat on top of this stock, baste it over with melted butter or good dripping, salt, and let cook on a moderate fire while watching carefully; moisten it by degrees with stock (No. 194a), allowing it to fall slowly to a glaze but without letting it brown; then moisten to the height of the larded side, and at the first boil cover the sautoir, and push it into a slow oven to finish cooking the meat, while basting it frequently, which will take an hour and a half to two hours, drain off the gravy and lay the meat on a hot dish; strain the gravy, free from all its fat, reduce properly and pour it over the meat.

(1544). ROUND BOTTOM OF VEAL, MINCED, SICILIAN (Sous-noix de Veau Émincé à la Sicilienne).

Minces are made with cold meats cut in slices a quarter of an inch thick; pare them either round or oval, suppressing the fat and trimming them neatly. Dress either in a circle or in a straight line, pour over some clear gravy (No. 404) and cover over with another smaller dish, then heat the whole in a slack oven. The meat must be thoroughly warmed without allowing the liquid to boil; drain this off and serve with a Sicilian sauce (No. 542).

(1545). SADDLE OF VEAL AND CHOPPED LETTUCE—LARDED (Selle de Veau Piquée aux Laitues Hachées).

To prepare this dish choose a fine saddle not too fat; pare by removing the skin from the large fillet or loin; shorten the flap and suppress the minion fillets. Lard the large fillet or loin with larding pork (No. 2, Fig. 52) and lay it in a deep baking pan, the bottom covered with

FIG. 330.

pork and veal fat; besprinkle the saddle plentifully with butter, cover it with a buttered paper and place it in a moderate oven to cook for an hour and a quarter to an hour and a half, basting it frequently with the fat from the pan; should this fat threaten to burn, add to it a few spoonfuls of good veal blond (No. 423). When the meat is of a fine color and well seized, drain, pare the edges and dress it on a long dish; dissolve the glaze in the pan with a little water or stock, let it boil for two minutes, then strain; free it from fat and reduce once more to a glaze. Surround the saddle with a garnishing composed of croustades garnished with chopped lettuce and cream (No. 2751), pour over it a part of the reduced sauce, serving the remainder separately.

(1546). SHOULDER OF VEAL À LA BOURGUIGNOTTE (Épaule de Veau à la Bourguignotte).

Bone the shoulder by splitting it on the side of the plate as far down as the handle without injuring the skin; when the bones are all removed, cut away all the sinews and fat; equalize the thickness of the meat; season it with salt and spices, and spread over it a layer of farce prepared with one pound of chopped veal, and one pound of fat pork, seasoned with salt, pepper, allspice, and bits of garlic. Roll it to an even thickness, tie it with ten rows of string making a separate knot at each turn, then wrap it up in several sheets of buttered paper, tie this well and roast the meat either in the oven or on a cradle spit. Unwrap it twenty minutes before serving to let attain a fine color; dress and garnish around with stuffed mushrooms (No. 650), serving with a sauce-boat of brown sauce (No. 414), and tarragon into which squeeze the juice of four lemons.

(1547). SLICE OF ROUND OF VEAL WITH GRAVY (Rouelle de Veau au Jus).

The round is a piece of veal cut across through the thickness of the thigh, having it about two to three inches thick; lard it with lardons (No. 2, Fig. 52). Put a quarter of a pound of butter in a low saucepan, then the slice of veal, and fry it till it attains a fine golden color, then moisten with a gill of stock (No. 194a) and the same quantity of white wine; add a bunch of parsley garnished with bay leaf, half a pound of minced carrots, an onion with two cloves, whole peppers, and salt, set it in the oven to bake slowly for an hour and a quarter, basting it over frequently, then glaze the meat and strain the juice; free it from fat, reduce it to a proper degree and pour it around the dressed slice, serving it very hot.

(1548). SPINAL MARROW OF VEAL À LA BARNAVE (Amourettes de Veau à la Barnave).

The spinal marrow is the marrow taken from the vertebral column of the calf and with which very delicious dishes are prepared. Suppress the sinewy skin surrounding them and soak them for three hours in cold water, changing it every hour, cut them up into two inch lengths and lay them in a saucepan with some water, adding vinegar, salt, thyme, pepper corns and bay leaf. Put this on the fire and let boil for three minutes. When cold, drain and marinate the marrow in oil, lemon juice, salt and pepper, dip each separate piece into a fine light frying batter (No. 137), plunge them into very hot fat, drain, salt and dress on folded napkins garnishing the top with a bunch of fried parsley. Serve a Barnave sauce (No. 431) separately. Spinal marrow prepared as above may also be served with black butter (No. 565) or hazelnut butter (No. 567).

(1549). SPINAL MARROW OF VEAL À LA VILLEROI (Amourettes de Veau à la Villeroi).

Lay some very fresh spinal marrow for one hour in cold water; scrape off or remove the covering and the sanguineous parts over-spreading the marrow, then put them back into cold water for another hour. Drain and lay them in a saucepan, cover them with water, season with salt, whole peppers, vinegar, sprigs of parsley, thyme and bay leaf. Boil slowly for fifteen minutes, then drain and cut them in two inch length slices; season them with salt and mignonette. Cover each piece with a little Villeroi sauce (No. 560), lay them on a plate, and when very cold detach each one with a knife; roll them in eggs and bread-crumbs, smooth the surfaces with a knife, then plunge them into very hot fat, a few at the time, until they assume a nice golden color. Drain and arrange them on a folded napkin, garnishing the tops with fried parsley.

(1550). THE WAY TO PREPARE SWEETBREADS (Manière de Préparer Les Ris de Veau).

Sweetbread is a glandulous substance found below the calf's throat and is considered a most delicate morsel. Separate the throat sweetbreads from the hearts; the throat part is the largest of the two, the heart is whiter, of a round shape and more delicate and tender than the throat. place them in cold water to disgorge for several hours changing it each hour so as to have them very white; lay them in a saucepan with an abundant supply of cold water, set it on the fire and when the sweetbreads are firm to the touch or poached, or more properly speaking parboiled, then refresh and suppress all the wind-pipes, fibers and fatty parts, afterward lay them under a very light weight. This blanching is for the purpose of hardening the sweetbreads so as to be able to lard them more easily. Blanched sweetbreads are used for sautéing by cutting them in two through their thickness. For brochettes they are cut in slices and for garnishing in the shape of salpicon.

(1551). SWEETBREADS À LA BINDA (Ris de Veau à la Binda).

Prepare and cook the sweetbreads as for those larded and glazed with gravy (No. 1575). Have some round two inch diameter croûtons of tongue, and some of forcemeat the same size and shape. Make a low croustade of foundation paste (No. 135), fasten it to the center of a round dish and dress in a circle around it, alternate croûtons of the tongue and forcemeat; fill the croustade with Neapolitan paillettes and dress the glazed sweetbreads on top. A half-glaze sauce (No. 413) to be served separately.

Paillettes.—A kind of small macaroni three-thirty-seconds of an inch in diameter without any hole in the center.

(1552). SWEETBREADS À LA BUSSY (Ris de Veau à la Bussy).

Prepare and cook the sweetbreads exactly as for à la Montebello (No. 1560), prepare a salpicon with sweetbreads cut in square pieces, also some truffles and mushrooms, all cut in three-sixteenths inch squares, lay these in an allemande sauce (No. 407), and let get cold. Cover one side of each sweetbread with this preparation, giving it a dome-shape, and lay over the salpicon a cream forcemeat (No. 75), dredging chopped truffles over all; besprinkle with butter and set them into a slack oven to heat without browning. A brown Madeira sauce (No. 492) is to be served at the same time, but separately.

(1553). SWEETBREADS À LA COLUMBUS (Ris de Veau à la Columbus).

Stud and braise the sweetbreads the same as for No. 1554, dress them on small croûtons of foies-gras forcemeat (No. 78) dipped in eggs and fried in butter; in the center lay some cock's-combs and kidneys and cover the whole with a Colbert sauce (No. 451) made with the braise stock from the sweetbreads and reduced to the consistency of a half-glaze.

(1554). SWEETBREADS À LA CONTI (Ris de Veau à la Conti).

Soak well and blanch six medium sized sweetbreads; stud them each in seven places with truffles wrap them up in a thin slice of fat pork, tie it on securely, then lay them in a sautoir lined more slices of pork, minced carrots and onions, and a garnished bunch of parsley. Moisten one pint of beef-stock (No. 194a), let it fall to a glaze, and then add a quart more stock; con- ue the cooking for half an hour longer. Reduce the stock and glaze the sweetbreads, then dress in the center of the dish, and lay around them in clusters or else in the center some cocks'-combs, kidneys, and mushrooms. Pour over the garnishing a well buttered velouté sauce (No. 415), and serve in a sauce-boat some of the same reduced with the stock passed through a tammy, and finish with a piece of butter. Have a trussed and glazed crawfish on top of each sweetbread. Serve separately a sauce-boat of velouté sauce reduced with the braise stock strained through a sieve and incorporate in a piece of fresh butter just when ready to serve.

(1555). SWEETBREADS À L'ÉCARLATE (Ris de Veau à l'Écarlate).

Select eight medium very white heart sweetbreads, after they are soaked and blanched, press them slightly in the press (Fig. 71), and lard afterward with fat salt pork, cook them in a pan with very little moistening, basting them frequently with their own juice, so as to glaze them a fine color. Boil a quarter of a pound of coarse macaroni in salted water, and when tender, drain and refresh it in tepid salted water; spread it out lengthwise on a towel and cut it up into a quarter of an inch lengths; as quickly as they are cut set them upright on to a buttered sheet and with a cornet filled with quenelle forcemeat (No. 89,) stuff the empty space to half its heighth, and lay small round bits of truffle cut the same size on top, then cover the whole with a buttered paper, heat the bottom of the sheet lightly, then set it into a slow oven for one minute to poach the forcemeat; detach the pieces from the pan taking them up one by one and lay them on the truffle side against the bottom and sides of a buttered plain border mold; fill in the empty space of the mold with some of the same forcemeat, covering over all with a buttered paper; poach this border for twenty-five to thirty minutes in a bain-marie, so that the forcemeat hardens to the touch. When prepared to use, un- mold the border on a dish and fill the center with the sweetbreads. Have sixteen round pieces of unsmoked beef tongue, and sixteen rounds of truffles, all an inch and a quarter in diameter, by one- eighth of an inch in thickness; heat them in a little meat glaze (No. 402) and Madeira. Dress them in a ring around the sweetbreads on the crest of the border, alternating the colors; cover the bot- tom of the dish with half-glaze sauce (No. 413), and serve some of the same sauce separately, reduced with a purée of tomatoes (No. 730), butter, grated parmesan, and minced mushrooms.

(1556). SWEETBREADS À L'EUGÉNIE (Ris de Veau à l'Eugénie).

Prepare and stud the sweetbreads (No. 1550), braise and glaze them the same as for à la conti (No. 1554); dress them either in a circle or in a straight row, if the latter, garnish the sides, but if the former fill the interior with a risot finished at the last moment with fresh butter the braise stock reduced to the consistency of a light glaze. Serve a béchamel cream sauce (No. 411), separately.

(1557). SWEETBREADS À LA LA VALLIÈRE (Ris de Veau à la La Vallière).

Prepare, cook, and glaze the sweetbreads the same as for those larded with gravy (No. 1575); dress them in a circle filling in the center with a garnishing of small mushroom heads stirred into a buttered allemande sauce (No. 407), adding to it lemon juice and chopped parsley; arrange out- side the circle twelve small croustades, six of them filled with green peas, and the six others with soubise purée (No. 723). Lay on each croustade a slice of glazed truffle, and a small trussed and glazed crawfish between every one.

(1558). SWEETBREADS À LA MALTESE (Ris de Veau à la Maltaise).

In order to succeed with this dish it will be found necessary to have two tin rings for each sweetbread; one two inches in diameter by three-eighths of an inch high used for pressing the sweetbreads, and another two and a half inches in diameter by five-eighths of an inch high. Pre- pare and cook the sweetbreads as for à la conti (No. 1554); set them under a weight in the smallest ring for fifteen minutes. Butter two pieces of paper slightly larger than the largest ring, butter the inside of this ring and lay it on top of one of the papers, then cover the paper and ring with a layer of cream forcemeat (No. 75), press down in the ring on this an unmolded sweetbread, and finish filling the ring with another layer of forcemeat; smooth the surface nicely and on top imitate a Maltese cross with four long lozenges of red beef tongue, one and one-eighth inch long; cut down the center and turned over so that the opposite sides come together; in the middle of these four reversed lozenges place a small round of tongue a quarter of an inch in diameter and decorate between with little bits of truffle; lay the second sheet of buttered paper over this decoration, turn the buttered side down, and proceed the same for all the sweetbreads and rings. Turn the rings over and range them on a level buttered baking sheet in such a way that the decoration is underneath; place it in a slow oven for fifteen to twenty minutes, being careful that the forcemeat does not brown. Unmold and dress; prepare a tomato sauce (No. 549) mixed with béarnaise sauce (No. 433), into which incorporate a little meat glaze (No. 402), pour a part of it over the bottom of the dish and serve what remains in a separate sauce-boat.

(1559). SWEETBREADS À LA MARSILLY (Ris de Veau à la Marsilly).

Place in the center of a dish a cut out rice croustade foundation. Choose eight medium-sized throat sweetbreads, blanch and cool them in the press (No. 71), lard them with fine larding pork (No. 3, Fig. 52), and range in the bottom of a narrow saucepan lined with a braise; season and moisten to half their height with beef-stock (No. 194a); let this fall very slowly to a glaze, then remoisten to half their height with more of the same broth, reduce again, and pour a gill of Madeira or Marsala wine over the sweetbreads; allow the liquid to boil up twice before setting the saucepan in a slack oven to finish cooking the sweetbreads while basting and having them attain a nice color. Fry eight small and pared artichoke bottoms; drain and range them dome-shaped with small fresh green peas cooked English style (No. 2742) thickened with a well-buttered béchamel (No. 409). Dress the sweetbreads on the rice foundation with the artichoke bottoms around; send to the table accompanied by a sauce-boat of velouté (No. 415), reduced with the sweetbread stock.

(1560). SWEETBREADS À LA MONTEBELLO (Ris de Veau à la Montebello).

Blanch until firm to the touch some medium-sized sweetbreads that have been in soak for a few hours, then drain, refresh and pare by suppressing all the sinews and fat. Lay them in a sautoir lined with slices of fat pork, sliced onions and carrots and a bunch of parsley, moisten to half their height with beef-stock (No. 194a), let this liquid fall to a glaze and then remoisten; cover with a buttered paper and finish cooking in a slack oven. After they are done, pare and set them in oval tin rings, two and a half by five-eighths of an inch in diameter and half an inch high; let them cool off in these under the pressure of a weight. Cut up the parings into small three-sixteenths inch dice; also some mushrooms and truffles; fry a chopped shallot in butter, add to it the mushrooms, the truffles and the sweetbreads, also a little velouté (No. 415), then season; when this preparation is cold, use it to cover one side of the sweetbreads, having it well rounded on the top, cover over with a layer of cream forcemeat (No. 75), and dredge the surface with finely chopped red tongue; place the sweetbreads on a buttered baking pan, pour melted butter over and the sweetbreads in a slack oven for twenty minutes; serve a Montebello sauce (No. 502) separately.

(1561). SWEETBREADS À LA MONTPENSIER (Ris de Veau à la Montpensier).

Have six heart sweetbreads of equal size; soak them in cold water and afterward lay them in a saucepan containing cold water and parboil until they harden, pare and let cool in the press (Fig. 71). Lard three of them with fine salt pork (No. 3, Fig. 52) and the other three with truffles cut the same size; braise them as for à la Conti (No. 1554), and when cooked and glazed, strain off the stock, free it from its fat and reduce it to a half-glaze. Dress the sweetbreads around a rice croustade garnished with small quenelles and mushrooms thickened with velouté (No. 415) and between each sweetbread lay a whole peeled and glazed truffle; dress on top of the garnishing a pyramid of truffles and surround the base with a circle of mushroom heads; glaze the truffles and sweetbreads. Serve with a separate tureen of velouté sauce (No. 415) reduced with the sweetbread stock, passed through a tammy.

(1562). SWEETBREADS, NEAPOLITAN STYLE (Ris de Veau à la Napolitaine).

Prepare and cook some throat sweetbreads the same as for à la Montebello (No. 1560); lay them under a weight in oval rings, and when cold cover one side of each, having it rounded on top, with cooked fine herbs (No. 385) mingled with a little half glaze (No. 413); covering this over with a layer of chicken quenelle forcemeat (No. 89). Dip them in beaten eggs and fry in clarified butter. Dress the sweetbreads and lay around a garnishing composed of macaroni cut in two-inch lengths, a quarter as much unsmoked red beef tongue, shredded finely, and the same volume of cooked mushrooms cut into small fillets; add tomato sauce (No. 549), velouté sauce (No. 415) and meat glaze (No. 402).

(1563). SWEETBREADS, PIEDMONTESE STYLE (Ris de Veau à la Piémontaise).

Lay the sweetbreads to cool under a weight or in the press (Fig. 71) after they are blanched; then cut them across through their thickness into slices, season and range these in a sautoir with melted butter, cook them nicely and moisten with white wine; reduce and add a little velouté sauce (No. 415). A few minutes later put in some white Piedmontese truffles, half an ounce for each sweetbread. Dress this inside a border of Piedmontese risot (No. 739).

(1564). SWEETBREADS, PORTUGUESE STYLE (Ris de Veau à la Portugaise).

Blanch and dress the sweetbreads as told in No. 1550; trim them into quarter inch thick slices and sauté colorless in butter; when almost done finish cooking in a half-glaze sauce (No. 413), work in a little fresh butter and Madeira; just when ready add as much Portuguese sauce (No. 526) and let reduce till this becomes of a sufficient consistency, then add some olives stuffed with quenelle forcemeat (No. 89) containing anchovy butter (No. 569). Poach in the sauce then dress the olives on the bottom of a dish, lay the sweet-breads on top and cover with a part of the sauce, serving the remainder apart.

(1565). SWEETBREADS À LA PRINCESSE (Ris de Veau à la Princesse).

Prepare and cook the sweetbreads the same as for larded and glazed with gravy (No. 1575). Lay each kernel of sweetbread on an artichoke bottom cooked in white stock (No. 182), and pour over some half-glaze sauce (No. 413). Dress them in a circle and garnish the inside with small braised veal noisettes and cover with a well-buttered velouté sauce (No. 415); reduced with the braise stock.

(1566). SWEETBREADS À LA ST. CLOUD (Ris de Veau à la St. Cloud).

Prepare and stud each sweetbread with five studs, four of truffles and the center one of tongue; braise and cook them as for à la Conti (No. 1554). Dress in a circle and garnish the center with a purée of mushrooms (No. 722). Pour a light allemande sauce (No. 407) around, and send to the table with a sauce-boat of the same sauce.

(1567). SWEETBREADS À LA ST. LAURENT (Ris de Veau à la St. Laurent).

Blanch sufficient sweetbreads, then put them to cool under a weight; cut them up into quarter inch thick slices then into one inch squares, also some veal kidneys the same size and shape, and slices of mushroom heads. Run small silver skewers (Fig. 176) through a piece of sweetbread, a piece of kidney and mushroom; dip them in melted butter, then in bread-crumbs and broil over a slow fire. Pour over an Italian sauce (No. 484) with a little chopped truffle added.

(1568). SWEETBREADS À LA THÉODORA (Ris de Veau à la Théodora).

The sweetbreads are to be prepared and cooked exactly the same as for Montebello (No. 1560); put them under a weight in round rings. Fry a shallot in butter, add to it some fresh mushrooms, unsmoked beef tongue, truffles, fine herb,s all finely chopped, and a little meat glaze (No. 402). Butter some silver cases, fill them half full with this preparation, lay the sweetbreads on top and set them in a slow oven to cook for fifteen to twenty minutes; when ready to serve put on each one a half spherical quenelle decorated with truffles, over this a Spanish olive stuffed with quenelle forcemeat (No. 89), and on top of all a whole pistachio nut stuck in the forcemeat,

FIG. 331.

Serve separately a champagne sauce (No. 445) reduced with the stock the sweetbreads have been braised in.

(1569). SWEETBREADS AU CHANCELIER (Ris de Veau au Chancelier).

Soak and blanch the needed quantity of sweetbreads, then cut them across in two; fry these pieces in butter with a little fine shallot and parsley, adding lemon-juice, salt, pepper and nutmeg; when done lay them under a weight or in the press (Fig. 71); pare oval-shaped when cold. Reduce some chicken purée (No. 713) with an allemande sauce (No. 407). When it has cooled off cover one side of the sweetbreads with it, having the tops well rounded, then smooth the surface, dip in eggs, roll in bread-crumbs, level the bread-crumbs with the blade of a knife and fry them all to a fine color. Serve a supreme sauce (No. 547) separately into which chopped truffles have been added.

(1570). SWEETBREADS AU MONARCH (Ris de Veau au Monarque).

Prepare and cook the sweetbreads precisely the same as for larded and glazed (No. 1575); dress in a circle on round crusts of bread two and a half inches in diameter by one quarter of an inch in thickness, and fried in butter; lay on top of every sweetbread a crown-shaped quenelle two inches in diameter and streaked with truffles, on this set a crawfish; in the center pour a garnishing composed of a salpicon of square pieces of mushroom, artichoke bottoms, truffles, and foies-gras all cut the same size and mixed with Madeira sauce (No. 492); serve separately some of the same sauce.

(1571). SWEETBREADS, ENGLISH STYLE (Ris de Veau à l'Anglaise).

Blanch six medium size unlarded sweetbreads; lay them in a sautoir garnished with slices of fat pork, minced carrots and onions, thyme, bay leaf and whole peppers; moisten to three-quarters of their height with beef stock (No. 194a), and after it comes to a boil finish cooking in a moderate oven, when done, remove and put them under a press in oval tin rings; when cold unmold them and cut them crosswise through the center. Cover one side of each sweetbread with cooked fine herbs (No. 385), laying it on a quarter of an inch thick; set the other half belonging to it on top and remove all the superfluous preparation oozing from the sides. Beat up well one-quarter of a pound of melted butter with six egg-yolks, dip the sweetbreads into this, then roll them in freshly grated bread-crumbs; bread-crumb them twice before laying them on a baking tin, pour a little butter over and cook them in a moderate oven; serve a brown English sauce separately.

Brown English Sauce.—Reduce espagnole sauce (No. 414) with meat-glaze (No. 402) adding just before serving some Worcestershire sauce, butter, lemon juice and fine herbs.

(1572). SWEETBREAD FRITTERS, CREAM SAUCE (Beignets de Ris de Veau, Sauce Crème).

Soak and blanch a sufficient quantity of sweetbreads; suppress the windpipes and fat, and cut them in two across through their thickness, then lay them in a tureen with finely shredded chives and shallots, salt, pepper, allspice, lemon juice and a little oil; keep them in a cool place for one hour turning them over occasionally, then drain them on a cloth carefully removing every vestige of herbs; dip the pieces into a frying paste (No. 137) not having it too thick, and fry them slowly until they are cooked and have acquired a fine color, then drain and dress on folded napkins, garnish the top with fried parsley. Serve with a cream sauce (No. 454) in a sauce-boat.

(1573). SWEETBREADS IN PAPERS (Ris de Veau en Papillotes).

Split some blanched, cold and pressed sweetbreads in two through their thickness; sauté them in butter seasoning with salt and pepper. Chop up one small onion and one shallot, lay them in a saucepan with melted fat pork to fry colorless, adding six ounces of chopped fresh mushrooms; reduce the moisture of these, season, and add six ounces of cooked ham cut in small one-eighth inch dice; heat the whole well, then add chopped parsley. Cut heart-shaped pieces from a sheet of paper, nine inches long by five wide; oil and lay them on the table; cover one side with thin slices of fat pork or cooked ham, lay a little of the preparation on top, then a piece of sweetbread, and finish with another layer of the preparation; fold the paper three-quarters around and pour a little Madeira sauce (No. 492) through the opening and finish folding so as to enclose all hermetically; range these "papillotes" in the serving-dish, place it in the oven, basting over carefully with a little sweet oil. They should be browned, but not blackened and swollen to double their original size.

(1574). SWEETBREADS LARDED AND GLAZED WITH CEPES BORDELAISE (Ris de Veau Piqués Glacés aux Cèpes Bordelaise).

Lard with larding pork (No. 3, Fig. 52) some equal-sized sweetbreads; blanch and cool them off under a weight; range them very close to one another in a sautoir lined with salt pork, vegetables and minced onions; moisten to half the heighth with beef stock (No. 194a) and let the liquid fall to a glaze; moisten once more and finish cooking in a moderate oven, or else with hot fire underneath and on top of the cover; basting the sweetbreads frequently in order to glaze them nicely. When done drain, dress on a garnishing of cèpes à la Bordelaise.

Cèpes à la Bordelaise.—Sauté in oil some cèpes, when partly done add some finely chopped shallots, season with salt and pepper, add chopped parsley and lemon juice. Serve the stock, well reduced and thickened with brown sauce (No. 414), in a sauce tureen.

(1575). SWEETBREADS LARDED AND GLAZED WITH GRAVY (Ris de Veau Piqués et Glacés au Jus).

Prepare the sweetbreads as explained in No. 1550; when blanched and stiffened lard them in two sections as shown in Fig. 332, with medium lardons (No. 3, Fig. 52). Line a saucepan with slices of fat pork, cut up onions and carrots, a bunch of parsley garnished with thyme and bay leaf and some veal parings, lay the sweetbreads over and moisten with stock (No. 194a); season with salt and whole peppers then cover with a buttered paper. Boil up and finish to cook in a slack oven for forty-five minutes, basting frequently during the time; glaze and let assume a good color. Strain the stock through a fine sieve, skim off

FIG. 332.

its fat and reduce it to the consistency of a light syrup. Dish up the sweetbreads and pour the gravy around.

(1576). SWEETBREADS, PARISIAN STYLE (Ris de Veau à la Parisienne).

Stud one-half of the sweetbreads with truffles, envelope them in thin bardes of fat pork, and lard the other half; braise them as for larded and glazed chicken with gravy (No. 1575). Decorate a flat border mold with fanciful cuts of truffles, fill it up with forcemeat (No. 80) and poach it in a bain-marie. When ready to serve, invert the mold on a dish, unmold and lay the sweetbreads on the border, filling in the empty space with minced truffles and mushrooms mixed with a brown sauce (No. 414) reduced with Madeira and lay around the outside of the border some whole mushrooms and truffles glazed with meat glaze (No. 402). Serve a separate sauce-boat of brown sauce reduced with the stock and Madeira wine and the truffle and mushroom parings, strained through a tammy.

(1577). SWEETBREADS STUDDED, SPANISH STYLE (Ris de Veau Cloutés à l'Espagnole).

Stud with truffles eight medium sweetbreads previously blanched; then wrap them up in small pieces of clean white linen giving them an oval-shape; cook them in some well seasoned mirepoix stock (No. 419), drain, unwrap and wring the cloths out in cold water, then wrap them up again and let get cold one beside the other under the pressure of a light weight; unwrap once more and lay them in a baking tin with some of their own stock partly reduced to a half-glaze; warm them at the oven door while basting. Dress these sweetbreads on an oblong-shaped cut out rice foundation, decorate around the outside with clusters of small cooked mushroom heads and poached quenelles; cover over with some béchamel sauce (No. 409) reduced with cream and seasoned with prepared red pepper (No. 168). Serve separately an espagnole sauce (No. 414), reduced with the remainder of the stock, adding to it some stuffed Spanish olives (No. 695).

(1578). SWEETBREADS, WITH QUENELLES, (Ris de Veau aux Quenelles).

The sweetbreads are to be prepared and cooked as for à la Conti (No. 1554); when done range them in a circle and garnish the middle with small bead-shaped quarter inch quenelles; cover with a half-glaze sauce (No. 413) so as to glaze the sweetbreads, and serve a Madeira sauce (No. 492) in a separate sauce-boat.

(1579). SWEETBREADS, ZURICH (Ris de Veau Zurich).

Lard the edges of six heart sweetbreads with fillets of tongue, and stud the centers with truffles; braise and glaze them the same as for à la Conti (No. 1554), dress them on small croustades filled with a garnishing composed of veal palate, truffles, mushrooms, all cut in quarter inch squares, and a brown sauce (No. 414), reduced with the stock used for braising the sweetbreads (part of this sauce should be reserved to serve in a separate sauce-boat). Range around these some round-shaped quenelles made with chicken quenelle forcemeat mixed with soubise (No. 89) and decorated with truffles.

(1580). CALVES' TAILS WITH CABBAGE (Queues de Veau aux Choux).

Take twelve calves' tails, cut the thick ends into four pieces two inches long and parboil them with a pound of sliced bacon; cut a large cabbage in four, blanch it for fifteen minutes, drain, refresh, suppress the core and press out all the water; tie the pieces together. Put the parboiled tails into a stock pot, the bacon, the cabbage and a garnished bunch of parsley; moisten with one pint of stock (No. 194a) season with nutmeg, pepper, and a little salt, and let boil slowly until the tails are done and the stock reduced, then take all from the pot, drain, and dress the tails intercalated with the cabbage and the bacon laid on top; cover with an espagnole sauce (No. 414) reduced with some clear gravy (No. 404).

(1581). TENDON OR GRISTLE OF VEAL À LA BAYEUX (Tendon de Veau à la Bayeux).

Cut some tendons three inches long by two and a quarter wide; place them in a sautoir with butter and square pieces of unsmoked bacon, small onions, dice-shaped pieces of ham, small pear-shaped carrots, and a bunch of parsley; fry slowly, moisten with stock (No. 194a), season and let cook for two hours and a half, being careful to remove the grease; remoisten frequently till the stock is reduced to the third of a glaze. Dress the tendons, place the garnishings around, pour the sauce over the meat and serve.

(1582). TENDON OR GRISTLE OF VEAL À LA BIARRITZ (Tendon de Veau à la Biarritz).

Pare and cut the tendon into pieces measuring three inches long fry them in clarified butter, drain off the butter and add to the meat some white wine, a little espagnole sauce (No. 414), and meat glaze (No. 402). Heat some clarified butter and add to it well cleansed Piedmontese rice; when very hot moisten with broth (No. 194a), boil and let cook in a moderate oven for twenty minutes, then add to it the meats and leave it in the oven for fifteen minutes longer. Dress the tendons and rice and surround with veal kidneys, fried in butter, and fine herbs.

(1583). CALVES' TONGUES À LA FLAMANDE (Langues de Veau à la Flamande).

To Salt the Calves' Tongues.—Take out the pipes from twelve tongues; prick them all over with a coarse trussing needle and put them into a stone vessel containing sixteen quarts. Dissolve a sufficiency of salt in ten quarts of water so that when an egg is dropped in, it will float on the top; add four ounces of saltpetre, and when all is thoroughly dissolved, pour it over the tongues. Set them in a cool place, and leave them there for twelve days, turning them over every third one. Drain and cook them plainly in water with some chopped beef suet, and when done, peel off the skins and keep the tongue warm in a light half-glaze sauce (No. 413); dress and surround them with a Flemish garnishing (No. 668), pouring over a clear gravy (No. 404).

(1584). CALVES' TONGUES À LA PÉRIGUEUX (Langues de Veau à la Périgueux).

On the center of a round dish fasten a wooden bottom covered with cooked paste (No. 131) and having a six inch high pyramidal support in the center, also covered with paste; brush the whole

FIG. 333.

with meat glaze (No. 402). Cook six or seven large calves' tongues in water, selecting those which have been in brine for twelve days. Roll out on a floured table a thin band of half puff paste (No. 146), three and a half to four inches wide; roll it on a roller to unroll on a baking sheet slightly wetted with water, then with a cardboard pattern cut from this band large pieces, straight on one side and rounded on the other, one end being pointed while the other is straight, and on the rounded side cut it into small sharp points; prick the surfaces, egg over with a brush without touching with the hands, and cook them in a slow oven until they become a light golden color; after removing let get partially cold under a very light weight. Drain the tongues, peel and keep them for ten minutes under a weight to flatten lightly; pare and cut each one in two or three pieces from top to bottom, then reconstruct them as they were before, and cover the cut sides with a layer of soubise (No. 723), reduced and thickened with a little meat glaze (No. 402), and slightly cool; keep them their correct shape, afterward glaze them over with a brush; cover the wooden bottom and surround the central support on the dish with a thick bed of good risot (No. 739), and stick on top of this support a small skewer garnished with truffles. Dress the tongues upright leaning them against the rice, lay between each one of the bands of paste to separate the tongues, letting them project slightly beyond. Cover over with a Madeira sauce (No. 492), reduced with truffle parings, and send a separate Périgueux sauce (No. 517), to the table at the same time as the tongues.

MUTTON (Mouton).

AMERICAN CUTS.

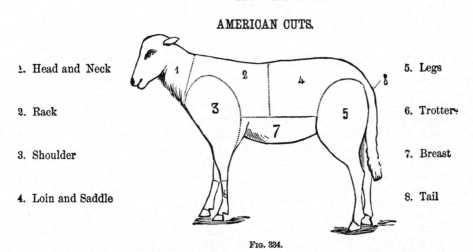

1. Head and Neck

2. Rack

3. Shoulder

4. Loin and Saddle

5. Legs

6. Trotters

7. Breast

8. Tail

Fig. 334.

(1585). BREAST OF MUTTON PLAIN (Poitrine de Mouton au Naturel).

Take three fine well covered breasts of mutton; remove with a blow of the knife the bone part covering the tendons, tie up the breasts and put them into a baking tin, having the bottom covered with slices of fat pork, carrots, onions and a bunch of garnished parsley; moisten with sufficient stock (No. 194a) to allow them to swim, bring to a boil on the top of the fire, skim, then place in the oven to cook for two hours and a half, turning the meats over during the time. When the bones can be easily detached drain off the breasts and suppress all the rib bones leaving the tendons on; lay the meats under a weight or in the press (No. 71) to reduce them to half an inch in thickness, and when cold pare off the skin without touching the fat; trim them into half hearts, dip in melted butter and stick a piece of the bone in the pointed end; broil over a slow fire to a fine color, then dress, glaze and pour a clear gravy (No. 404) over; garnish each bone end with a frill (No. 10).

(1586). BREAST OF MUTTON STUFFED—TOMATO ANDALOUSE SAUCE (Poitrine de Mouton Farcie Sauce Tomate à l'Andalouse).

Remove the bony part of a breast of mutton over the tendons open on the straight edge in such a way as to form a pocket and fill this with some of the following stuffing; sew it up and braise the meat in a mirepoix stock (No, 419); when cooked dress glaze and cover with part of the stock reduced to the consistency of half-glaze; serve a tomato Andalouse sauce (No. 550) separately.

For the Stuffing.—Chop up finely half a pound of lean, sinewless pork with half a pound of bacon, add to it half a pound of soaked and well pressed bread-crumbs. Season with salt, pepper, nutmeg, chopped onion and a bit of garlic, both of these lightly fried in butter and finish with chopped parsley and two whole eggs.

(1587). BREAST, TENDON AND SHOULDER OF MUTTON, NAVARIN (Poitrine, Tendon et Épaule de Mouton Navarin).

Cut into half inch pieces one pound of breast, one pound of tendon and one pound of shoulder of mutton. Lay these meats in a vessel, season them with salt, pepper, two cloves, nutmeg, thyme, bay leaf and a bunch of parsley containing a clove of garlic; pour on a quarter of a bottleful of Madeira wine and let marinate for six hours, then drain off the meats, wipe dry and fry them with chopped up fat pork and half a pound of three-quarter inch dice pieces of blanched lean bacon; add to this the Madeira and aromatics with some brown sauce (No. 414) and let cook on a moderate fire while skimming off the fat thoroughly. In the meantime prepare some turnips cut out with a

(531)

one-inch vegetable spoon, fry them in lard and when they begin to brown, sprinkle over some pow-dered sugar and after they are of a fine color, remove with a skimmer, place in a saucepan and finish cooking in a little of the brown sauce taken from the stew, and wetting with some stock (No. 194a). Dress the stew, range the turnips around and pour over the gravy from both the meat and turnips reduced together with half a pint of white wine and strained through a tammy (No. 159).

(1588). HARICOT OF BREAST OF MUTTON WITH TURNIPS (Haricot de Mouton aux Navets).

Have three pounds of breast of mutton cut up into two inches pieces; fry them in six ounces of butter letting them get a fine color, then drain them through a colander; trim and cut the bones, pare square, add one ounce of flour to the butter and when slightly browned, moisten with the three pints of broth, (No. 194a) boil, skim off the fat and strain through a tammy. Set all this into a clean saucepan and add to it the well-pared pieces of meat, add two carrots, two onions, one with three cloves in it, a bunch of parsley garnished with bay leaf, thyme and a clove of garlic, salt and pepper; let boil until the meat is well cooked and the sauce properly reduced. Pare two pounds of turnips the same shape as pigeon's eggs, fry them in butter and as they first begin to brown, sprinkle over with powdered sugar, and when they have attained a very fine color, put them into the stew removing the fat pieces an hour before serving allowing them all to cook together After the meat is done, which can easily be perceived if the bones detach easily, remove the carrots, onions and parsley, then dress the meat and garnish with the turnips; strain the sauce and pour it over; in case the sauce be too thin reduce it until it acquires proper con-sistency.

(1589). CARBONADE À LA JUVIGNY (Carbonade à la Juvigny).

The piece from the end of the last chop to the beginning of the leg is called carbonade. The bones are first extracted from the loin and it is then pared on all its length

FIG. 335.

and width and larded with medium lardons (No. 3, Fig. 52), season, roll and tie it up into an oblong square (Fig. 335). Line the bottom of a saucepan or braziere with slices of fat pork, slices of veal, carrots, onions, bay leaf and thyme; lay the carbonade over, set a heavy buttered paper on top and pour in a quart of stock (No. 194a); let simmer for two hours and a half. Fifteen minutes before serving time, glaze the carbonade letting it become a fine color, dress it and garnish around with small pear-shaped carrots cooked in broth (No. 194a), small blanched onions cooked the same, small turnip balls blanched and browned in the pan with a little sugar and finished cooking in broth, and celery knobs the size of a clove of garlic, blanched and cooked likewise in broth. All these vegetables should be only sufficiently moistened so that when they are done the liquid is reduced to a glaze; strain the meat stock, remove its fat and finish by reducing it to the consistency of a half-glaze and add Juvigny sauce (No. 485).

(1590). PLAIN MUTTON CUTLETS AND MUTTON CHOPS (Côtelettes de Mouton Nature et Côtelettes de Filet Nature).

For plain cutlets use racks of mutton, having the meat tender and well-matured, suppress the skin covering the fat, shorten the rib bones and divide into equal-sized cutlets make a handle to the cutlets by removing the fat from about one inch of the end and scraping the bone clean, when nicely pared they should each weigh about four ounces. Salt the cutlets, baste with oil and range them all on the same side on the broiler; they take from eight to ten minutes to cook. When done, dress them on a dish, pour over a clear gravy (No. 404) and trim each chop with a paper frill (No. 10).

Mutton Chops are cut either from a loin or half saddle of a sheep split lengthwise in two. These chops should be cut rather thick, each one about an inch and a half and then flattened to an inch. Pare and season with salt, baste with oil and broil for about twelve minutes, dress and serve very hot.

FIG. 336.

(1591). MUTTON CHOPS SOYER (Côtelettes de Mouton Soyer).

Soyer chops are cut from the saddle dividing it into one and a half inch thick slices cut the full width of the saddle; they should each weigh twelve ounces after being pared and are to be cooked for twelve minutes; when they are done they can be split through the center so that one chop will answer for two persons; serve them very hot with a half-glaze sauce (No. 413) into which Worces-

FIG. 337.

tershire sauce has been added, and buttered at the last moment, with the addition of fine raw herbs and nonpareil capers.

(1592). MUTTON CHOPS, TAVERN STYLE (Côtelettes de Mouton à la Taverne).

FIG. 338.

Cut the chops from the saddle, lengthwise having them an inch and a half thick; flatten, pare and garnish each one with a kidney fastened on with a skewer thrust into the fat part of the chop above the minion fillet; sprinkle with salt, baste with oil, and broil until of a fine color on one side, then turn over to finish cooking on the other. ten to twelve minutes in all; serve very hot surrounding them with water-cress.

(1593). MUTTON CUTLETS À LA BOUCHÈRE (Côtelettes de Mouton à la Bouchère).

Have a good fleshy rack of mutton with fine, tender pink meat; suppress the superficial skin covering the fat, and cut five cutlets from each rack; remove the spinal bone and round the tops; they should be thick and pared very little without handles, as they are not garnished with frills; salt over and dip them in melted butter, then roll in fine bread-crumbs. Eight or ten minutes before serving, range them on the broiler all on the same side, and when partially done and a fine color, turn them over to finish the cooking; when they are finished, dress in a circle garnishing the middle with the following: Cut four ounces of gherkins in small fillets like a small Julienne, (No. 318); four ounces of mushrooms, and four ounces of tongue, cut exactly the same as the gherkins; thicken this garnishing with a brown English sauce (No. 1571), finishing with a dash of cayenne pepper.

(1594). MUTTON CUTLETS À LA MACÉDOINE (Côtelettes de Mouton à la Macédoine).

Cut off fine cutlets from a fine rack; pare them the same as if cooked plain (No. 1590), and ten minutes before serving, put them on the fire in a sautoir with clarified butter; when they are done, drain off the butter and replace it by a little clear gravy (No. 404), and white wine; reduce, then roll the cutlets in this glaze to give them a nice gloss; dress in a circle and garnish the center with a macédoine (No. 680). Detach the sauce with a little broth and white wine, and strain it through a tammy over the cutlets.

(1595). MUTTON CUTLETS À LA MARÉCHALE (Côtelettes de Mouton à la Maréchale).

Prepare and trim some mutton cutlets, as for plain cutlets (No. 1590), season and sauté them quite rare in clarified butter; let cool off under a weight pressed lightly on them, then pare and cover both sides of the cutlets with a thin layer of cooked fine herbs (No. 385); place on top of this another thin layer of chicken quenelle forcemeat (No. 89), bread-crumb them English style and range them on a baking tin; pour clarified butter over and brown in the oven; remove, drain, garnish with paper frills (No. 10). Dress them on a crown-shaped trimmed rice croustade, fill the center with some turned truffles rolled in a little meat glaze (No. 402) and butter and serve separately a half-glaze sauce (No. 413) with essence of truffles (No. 395).

(1596). MUTTON CUTLETS À LA NELSON (Côtelettes de Mouton à la Nelson).

FIG. 339.

Chop up separately and thoroughly some cooked ham and truffles. Pare a few cutlets, season and dip them in beaten eggs, cover one of their sides with the ham and the other with the truffles, dredging bread-crumbs on both sides, dip them again in the eggs, roll them in the bread-crumbs, and range them in a sautoir with clarified butter; fry over a very brisk fire; when cooked, drain, wipe, garnish the handles with paper frills (No. 10), and dress them in a circle. Pour a little Victoria sauce (No. 557) into the center of the crown and serve more of it in a sauce-boat.

(1597). MUTTON CUTLETS À LA SAVARY (Côtelettes de Mouton à la Savary).

Obtain a rack of mutton of tender meat, take off all the skin, shorten the rib bones and cut the rack into even thick cutlets. (The cutlets are to be cut more or less thick according to the thickness of the meat.) Suppress the hard skin covering the fillets, round the meat neatly cutting the tops into a point, and remove all superfluous fat. Make a handle to the cutlets by removing the fat from about one inch of the end and scraping the bone clean. Macerate these cutlets in a cooked marinade (No. 114), drain, wipe dry and fry them in clarified butter; pour off the fat and moisten with meat glaze (No. 402) and Madeira, roll the cutlets in this to glaze them, then dress them in a circle; garnish the handles with frills and fill in the center with a purée of Jerusalem artichokes (No. 704). Serve separately a half-glaze sauce (No. 413) with lemon-juice added and surround with one inch potato balls cooked in the oven with clarified butter, drained, salted, and dressed.

(1598). MUTTON CUTLETS BREADED, ENGLISH SAUCE (Côtelettes de Mouton Panées, Sauce Anglaise).

Season some well pared cutlets, dip them in melted butter, roll in fine white bread-crumbs, and lay them on the broiler to cook while turning them over—about eight minutes will suffice—when done, of a fine color on both sides, dress and decorate with paper frills (No. 10); serve at the same time a brown English sauce (No. 1571) either separately or underneath the cutlets.

(1599). MUTTON CUTLETS BREADED WITH PURÉE OF TRUFFLES OR WITH PURÉE OF CHESTNUTS (Côtelettes de Mouton Panées à la Purée de Truffes ou à la Purée de Marrons).

Pare several outlets all of the same thickness, salt and dip them in clarified butter, then roll them in fine bread-crumbs and broil over a slow fire until they are cooked and attain a good color then trim the handle with a paper frill (No. 10), and dress in a circle around a croustade filling this with a purée of truffles (No. 731). Serve a half-glaze sauce (No. 413) apart.

With Chestnuts.—Prepare the cutlets as for the above with the only difference that they should not be breaded and the purée of truffles replaced by a purée of chestnuts (No. 712).

(1600). MUTTON CUTLETS, RUSSIAN STYLE WITH HORSERADISH (Côtelettes de Mouton à la Russe au Raifort).

Have some well pared cutlets; lard them with cooked ham, then lay them in a sautoir with clarified butter, fry over a brisk fire, moistening with a little Madeira and meat glaze (No. 402). Pour some well reduced velouté (No.415) into a saucepan, and add to it some freshly grated horseradish, thickening with a few egg-yolks, then put in the whites of the eggs beaten stiff; use this preparation to cover over the larded side of the cutlets; smooth them nicely with a knife, and bestrew with bread-crumbs fried in butter; pour melted butter over and brown in a hot oven, then serve after having trimmed the handles with paper frills and dressed the cutlets flat on a well acidulated Colbert sauce (No. 451), with minced cèpes added.

(1601). MUTTON CUTLETS WITH BRAISED LETTUCE (Côtelettes de Mouton aux Laitues Braisées).

Pare the cutlets as indicated for plain (No. 1590), larding them with medium lardons (No. 2, Fig. 52). Butter the bottom of a sautoir, and cover it with slices of fat pork, slices of veal, carrots, onions, a bunch of parsley garnished with thyme and bay leaf, and a few cloves; lay in the cutlets and moisten to half their height with a mirepoix stock (No. 419), then cover over with buttered paper, let cook to reduce in the oven, being careful to baste frequently, and to add more liquid as quickly as it evaporates, they will take about two hours. Have some lettuce blanched and braised (No. 2754); when done and well drained, dress them in the center of a dish placing the cutlets around after glazing them and trimming the handles with paper frills (No. 10). Strain, remove the fat from the stock and reduce with a little brown sauce (No. 414) and white wine; pass through a tammy and pour a part of it over the meat serving the remainder in a sauce boat with the cutlets.

(1602). MUTTON OUTLETS WITH CHICCORY, TRUFFLES OR FRIED POTATOES (Côtelettes de Mouton à la Chicorée, aux Truffes ou aux Pommes Frites).

With Chiccory.—Dress them in a circle when prepared the same as for the marinade (No. 1604), fill the empty space with a chiccory garnishing (No. 2729), serving a half-glaze sauce (No. 413) separately.

With Truffles.—Prepare, cook, and dress the cutlets the same as for the above; fill the inside of the circle with finely shredded truffles added to a half-glaze sauce (No. 413) and Madeira wine.

With Fried Potatoes.—After they are prepared, cooked, dressed, and glazed, fill in the inside of the circle with half inch balls of potatoes sautéd in butter, and seasoned with salt, parsley, and lemon juice.

(1603). MUTTON OUTLETS WITH CUCUMBERS (Côtelettes de Mouton aux Concombres).

Prepare and cook the cutlets the same as with braised lettuce (No. 1601); when done dress them crown-shaped, and fill the inside of the circle with cucumbers cut the shape of a clove of garlic, cooked in stock (No. 194a), drained, and mingled with cream béchamel sauce (No. 411).

(1604). MUTTON OUTLETS WITH MARINADE (Côtelettes de Mouton à la Marinade).

Select two racks of mutton having the meats tender and well matured, remove the remainder of the breast leaving the cutlet bones only four inches long, also remove the neck as far down as the third cutlet; saw off the spinal bone without injuring the fillet as far as the joints of the cutlets, then cut from each rack either five, six, or even seven cutlets according to the thickness of the meat, each one when pared ought to weigh four ounces. Pare the meat from the end of the bone, about one inch deep to make a handle, then flatten each cutlet lightly and suppress the fibrous skin on the fat, also the skin adhering to the inside of the bone; salt over and dip the cutlets in melted butter, and broil them on a bright fire, only turning them over once to have them retain their blood and be juicy. Glaze, garnish the handles with frills (No. 10), and dress; pour a little clear gravy (No. 404) into the bottom of the dish, and serve with a separate marinade sauce (No. 496).

(1605). DOUBLE BARON OR SADDLE, ROASTED (Double Baron ou Selle Rôtis).

The double of mutton is the back hip part with the leg on which the saddle with about seven of the ribs is left adhering (Fig. 340). Select a good sheep not too large, but young and fat, remove the skin and suppress the fat; cut several incisions on the fat to facilitate and equalize the cooking,

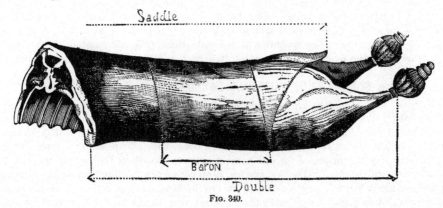

FIG. 340.

then lay it in a copper pan and cook in a moderate oven; the meat must be left rare, then salt it over. Dress and decorate the leg bone with paper frills (No. 10), pouring a clear gravy (No. 404), on the bottom of the dish. The baron and saddle are to be cooked the same way and served the same; they differ only in cut. The baron is taken from the loin end as far as the first rib (Fig. 340). The saddle is the whole hind part of the mutton without the legs.

(1606). SHEEP'S EARS À LA WESTPHALIAN (Oreilles de Mouton à la Westphalienne).

Blanch and braise some sheep's ears after having thoroughly cleansed them in a mirepoix stock (No. 419); when cooked put them in a vessel with the stock strained over, and let get cold. Cut out the inside of the ears with a column tube, then reheat them in the braise stock. Dress on a baking dish and fill the interiors with veal quenelle forcemeat (No. 92), to which add chopped truffles and some velouté sauce (No. 415), thickened with egg-yolks; dredge over some bread-crumbs and grated parmesan cheese; sprinkle over a little melted butter and place in the oven to color slightly. Dress them in a circle and fill the center with thin slices of ham fried in butter over a brisk fire; dilute the glaze in the pan with white wine and brown sauce (No. 414), reduce and pour it over the ham; sprinkle chopped parsley over the whole.

(1607). ÉPIGRAMMES OF MUTTON À LA JARDINIÈRE (Epigrammes de Mouton à la Jardinière).

Have eight mutton cutlets prepared as for plain (No. 1590), season, dip in eggs and bread-crumbs, equalize the bread-crumbs and fry in clarified butter or if preferred omit the breading and simply sauté the cutlets plain. Braise some breast of mutton the same as for plain (No. 1585), then put them under a weight and when cold pare them into half hearts; dip these in Villeroi sauce (No. 560), and after this is cold dip them in eggs, then in bread-crumbs, immerse them in plenty of hot frying fat; when of a nice color, drain. Decorate the top of a hollow border mold with all kinds of cut up vegetables, fill the inside with quenelle forcemeat (No. 92), poach, unmold on hot dishes. Range the breasts and cutlets alternately in a circle on top of this and fill the empty center with a jardinière (No. 677); serve an espagnole sauce (No. 414) separately after it has been reduced with the braise stock which has been strained and freed from fat, and some mushroom essence (No. 392).

(1608). MUTTON FILLETS À L'ALEXANDRE (Filets de Mouton à l'Alexandre).

Pare the mutton fillets, cut them up into thin slices a quarter of an inch thick and cover each one with a cooked fine herb preparation (No. 385), seasoning first with salt and pepper, dip in beaten eggs, roll in fine bread-crumbs, giving each a horseshoe-shape and fry in clarified butter. Slice six mutton kidneys, as many raw mushrooms and half as many truffles, fry the kidneys in butter, add to them the mushrooms and truffles, drain off the butter and replace it by a little espagnole sauce (No. 414), lemon juice and fresh butter, pour this stew into a dish and dress the cooked fillets over in straight rows, one overlapping the other.

(1609). FILLETS OF MUTTON GRENADINS, POIVRADE SAUCE (Filets de Mouton Grenadins, Sauce Poivrade).

Pare the small minion fillets; beat them into half hearts, season, range them in a tureen and cover with a cooked but cold marinade (No. 114), leaving them in for twenty-four hours, drain off the fillets, wipe well and lard with fine larding pork (No. 4, Fig. 52). Set them into a buttered sautoir, besprinkling over with more butter and push them into a brisk oven so that the larding cooks at the same time as the meat; after removing drain off the fat and moisten with a little gravy (No. 404), let this fall to a glaze over a hot fire, then lift out the fillets and dress them in two straight rows on a large dish, garnish around with triangular croûtons of bread fried in butter; pour into the same sautoir a few spoonfuls of poivrade sauce (No. 523), and at the first boil pour the sauce through a fine strainer, pour part of it over the fillets and serve the remainder in a sauce-boat.

(1610). NOISETTES OF MUTTON, GLAZED (Noisettes de Mouton Glacées).

Noisettes of fillet of mutton are cut from the large fillet or tenderloin of a saddle, or else from the minion fillet. Cut them up into slanting four ounce pieces or thereabouts, beat lightly, then pare them round-shaped about two inches in diameter; after they are trimmed they should each weigh three ounces; season and place them in a deep vessel with a little Madeira wine, thyme, and bay leaf, leaving them to marinate for one hour; drain and wipe them thoroughly dry, then range them in a sautoir with hot clarified butter, and let fry on both sides, turning them over. Drain off the butter and replace it by two spoonfuls of clear gravy (No. 404), and the Madeira from the marinade; let the liquid fall to a glaze while turning the noisettes over, then take them out and pare them of equal size. Cover one side of each with a layer of consistent soubise purée (No. 723), smooth them dome-form, and range on a buttered baking sheet; coat them over with a layer of reduced and nearly cold espagnole sauce (No. 414), and then push them into a slow oven to glaze. Lay each separate noisette on a thin slice of fried bread also covered with soubise and dress on a very hot dish.

(1611). NOISETTES OF MUTTON, PROVENÇAL STYLE (Noisettes de Mouton à la Provençale).

Select large mutton fillets; remove the fat and skin, then cut them up on the bias into four-ounce slices; flatten and pare them round-shaped (after they are pared they should weigh three ounces each), then salt over. Chop up the parings very finely, have an equal quantity of salt pork and cut-up ham, each chopped separately and mixed after, and a handful of soaked and pressed bread-crumbs; season with salt, pepper, and nutmeg. With this preparation make some small cakes the same size as the noisettes; dip them in beaten eggs and roll in fine bread-crumbs; fry them in butter the same time as the noisettes, drain, dry and lay the noisettes on top of the forcemeat cakes; glaze them over and pour some Provençal sauce (No. 529) around and serve.

(1612). NOISETTES OF MUTTON WITH COOKED FINE HERBS (Noisettes de Mouton aux Fines Herbes Cuites).

Pare some mutton fillets, remove all sinews and fat, then cut them up into slices; pare them round: fry in butter, season, drain off the butter and add some cooked fine herbs (No. 385), and half-glaze sauce (No. 413). Dress the meat on round slices of bread cut a quarter of an inch thick by two inches across, fried in butter and laid on a dish; pour the sauce over and serve.

(1613). PAUPIETTES OF FILLET OF MUTTON À LA DELUSSAN (Paupiettes de Filets de Mouton à la Delussan).

Cut the mutton fillets when well pared in eighth of an inch thick slices lengthways of the meat; flatten down these small bands and season each with salt and pepper; cover one side with chicken forcemeat (No. 62) into which has been added an equal quantity of cooked fine herbs (No. 385); roll them up cylinder-shape and run them on a skewer; pour over some melted butter and broil them over the fire; dress and cover over with a reduced espagnole sauce (No. 414), to which sliced mushrooms have been added; incorporating into it at the last moment some chopped parsley.

(1614). SLICES OF FILLET OF MUTTON, MAÎTRE-D'HÔTEL (Tranches de Filets de Mouton à la Maître-d'Hôtel).

Pare well the minion fillets from the mutton; cut them lengthwise through their thickness, pare and season with salt, then bread-crumb them English style (No. 13), and broil to a fine color. Dress these on a hot dish and sprinkle over with either maître-d'hôtel butter (No. 581) or else a thickened maître-d'hôtel sauce (No. 493).

(1615). FILLETS OF MUTTON LARDED, WITH GREEK RAVIOLES—WHOLE (Filets de Mouton Entiers Piqués aux Ravioles à la Grecque).

Raise, pare, and remove the sinews from some mutton fillets; lard them with fine larding pork (No. 3, Fig. 52) and roast them in a hot oven; when done, dress on a garnishing of Greek ravioles.

Greek Ravioles.—Chop fine and pound one pound of fillet or loin of mutton, add to this a sheep's brain, cooked, well drained, and pounded, and two ounces of rice previously boiled in water; season with salt, pepper, nutmeg, and add one ounce of chopped onions fried in butter, some chopped parsley, a little béchamel (No. 409) half an ounce of fresh butter, and four raw egg-yolks; taste this forcemeat, to see whether the seasoning be correct, then use it to make square ravioles as described in No. 158, when poached and drained, place them in some clear gravy (No. 404) to simmer for a few moments until it is absorbed, bestrewing the ravioles with grated cheese; pour over a thin tomato purée (No. 730) serving a clear gravy (No. 404) separately.

(1616). MUTTON KIDNEYS À LA BURTEL (Rognons de Mouton à la Burtel).

Suppress both the skin and fatty parts from eight kidneys; separate each one into two and lay them in a pan with melted butter, and a pinch of shallot; toss quickly and when well seized, season with salt, pepper, and a dash of cayenne pepper; as fast as their humidity is reduced lift them up with a skimmer and lay in a small vessel. Pour a quarter of a pint of Madeira wine into the pan, let reduce to half, then add as much melted glaze (No. 402); boil the liquid, and thicken it at once with small bits of kneaded butter (No. 579); at the first boil stir in the kidneys, and at the same time two tablespoonfuls of cooked ham cut in small dice, and a pinch of chopped up tarragon. Remove the stew from the fire, pour it into a dish and surround with fried bread croûtons glazed with a brush.

(1617). MUTTON KIDNEYS À LA SOUBISE (Rognons de Mouton à la Soubise).

There is a certain way of splitting the kidneys and running them on skewers so that when cooked they form a very distinct hollow in the center; for this it requires that they be split deeply on the hollow side, opened, and two skewers thrust through the entire thickness, each side of the fat so that the meats come together again while cooking, the center forming a pocket; season and roll them in melted butter, broil over a good fire, then withdraw the skewers, and glaze the kidneys with a brush. Dress them on a dish and fill in the hollow with a slightly consistent soubise purée (No. 723), laid on through a small pocket or paper cornet. Serve them at once; the soubise may be replaced by a béarnaise sauce (No. 433).

(1618). MUTTON KIDNEYS ON SKEWERS (Rognons de Mouton en Brochettes).

Select fine chocolate colored mutton kidneys, for those either black or pale yellow are of a poorer quality. Split them three-quarters through the round part, so as to open without separating the pieces; suppress the light skin that covers the surfaces, spread them out, and stick a metal skewer

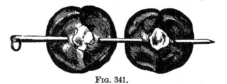

Fig. 341.

through their thickness, to keep them entirely opened; season with salt, coat with oil or melted butter, and roll them in bread-crumbs, then broil with the open side toward the fire; five or six minutes after turn them over and lay a piece of maître d'hôtel butter (No. 581), the size of a small hickory nut, on top of each, and after they are done, dress. The skewers may be removed before serving, and a little of the maître d'hôtel butter laid on top of each kidney.

(1619). MUTTON KIDNEYS ON SKEWERS, BORDELAISE SAUCE (Brochettes de Rognons de Mouton à la Sauce Bordelaise).

Cut the kidneys across in six pieces; have small inch squares of bacon an eighth of an inch thick, place an alternate piece of kidney and bacon on the skewers, season, dip in oil, and roll in bread-crumbs; broil over a brisk fire, serving with a separate bordelaise sauce (No. 436).

(1620). MUTTON KIDNEYS ON SKEWERS, DEVILED (Rognons de Mouton en Brochettes à la Diable).

Split the kidneys through on the round side, opening without separating the parts; spread open and thrust a metal skewer through; season with salt, and coat over with mustard and prepared red pepper (No. 168), roll in bread-crumbs, besprinkle with oil and broil, then dress them on a deviled sauce (No. 459).

(1621). MUTTON KIDNEYS SAUTÉD WITH FLEURONS (Rognons de Mouton Sautés aux Fleurons).

To obtain good sautéd kidneys it should be well understood that they must be tossed over a brisk fire and fried, not cooked in their sauce; split eight mutton kidneys in two, obtaining sixteen, halves. Put three ounces of butter in a sautéing pan, and when hot add the kidneys laying them on their flat side; season with salt and pepper, then toss them over a bright fire until they are sized, but very rare, meaning that the meats are browned without drying. In another pan, fry two tablespoonfuls of chopped onions, and when of a good color moisten with a little gravy (No. 404), brown sauce (No. 414) and white wine; boil this sauce quickly, stirring it for a few moments and when nicely thickened, add to it some cooked fine herbs (No. 385), lemon juice and the kidneys, heat well without boiling, dress and pour the sauce over. Garnish with some fanciful fleurons cut from puff paste parings (No. 146) made as follows: Cut the paste in the shape of minion filets of chicken; cut these through from the edge half way across the width, bring the two ends toward each other to form a half circle, this will open the cuttings, place on a baking sheet and cook in a mild oven.

(1622). LEG OF MUTTON À LA BORDELAISE (Gigot de Mouton à la Bordelaise).

Bone a leg of mutton without opening it, lard the inside of the meat with medium shreds of raw ham seasoned with salt, pepper and fine spices; fill in the hollow space with a few spoonfuls of veal and fat pork chopped up with fine herbs; sew up the opening. Saw the handle bone off short and lay the leg in a braziere with melted salt pork and let fry on a slow fire for fifteen minutes, turning it so that it acquires a good color all over. Moisten with a pint of stock (No. 194a), then cover the saucepan and let the liquid fall slowly to a glaze; remoisten to about the heighth of the meat and continue cooking on a slow fire for an hour and a half, add to the meat a half pound of blanched bacon cut in half inch squares, and boil moderately for an hour longer, then surround the meat with a garnishing of large carrots and turnips cut in three-quarter inch balls; twelve medium white onions browned in a pan with lard, salt and a pinch of sugar, two cloves of garlic and a bunch of parsley garnished with thyme and bay leaf—the meat and vegetables must both be done at the same time. Drain the leg, dress and range around the vegetables; strain and free the gravy from fat, thicken it with a little tomato sauce (No. 549) and serve in a sauce-boat.

(1623). LEG OF MUTTON À LA BOURDALOUE (Gigot de Mouton à la Bourdaloue).

Bone the leg without opening it, and lard the meat with raw ham, seasoned with salt, pepper, fine spices and chopped parsley. Tie up the leg and fry it in butter, then moisten with red wine and beef stock (No. 194a), and add small half inch blanched carrot balls, small onions and a garnished bunch of parsley, having the moistening to three-quarters the height of the leg, season and set it in a slow oven for three or four hours. After the leg is cooked, dress it on a dish, strain the stock, free it of its fat and reduce it with some brown sauce (No. 414). Garnish one side with the carrots and the other with the onions and at both ends place some mushrooms sautéd in butter (No. 2760). Pour a part of the sauce over the onions and carrots and serve the rest in a sauce-boat.

(1624). LEG OF MUTTON À LA BOURGEOISE (Gigot de Mouton à la Bourgeoise).

Bone a leg of mutton without opening it, lard it with large pieces of salt pork seasoned with salt, pepper, allspice and chopped parsley; cover the bottom of a braziere (Fig. 134) with slices of the same pork, lay the leg on top with a gill of Madeira wine and a little beef stock (194a), let fall to a glaze, then pour over more broth and a gill of brandy, and add a bunch of parsley garnished with thyme and bay leaf, carrots and onions cut in four, one clove of garlic and a few peppers, moisten with some more stock and cook slowly allowing half an hour for each pound of meat. In the meanwhile prepare a garnishing of turned carrots and small onions, blanch and cook them separately till half done, then finish cooking in the leg of mutton braise strained for the purpose; in order to accomplish this, place the leg in another braziere and strain the stock over, when the meat is cooked and glazed surround it with clusters of the vegetables, reduce the liquid, pour half of it over the meat, and serve the other half in a sauce-boat.

(1625). LEG OF MUTTON À LA CHIPOLATA (Gigot de Mouton à la Chipolata).

Select an eight pound leg of mutton, saw the handle off two inches below the joint, bone the loin end and pare well the fat; trim and round the end around the loin. Line a braziere (Fig. 134) with a layer of carrots and minced onions, adding the bones and parings from the meat, also a garnished bouquet; lay in the meat and moisten with beef stock (No. 194a) then cover the braziere and reduce till the liquid falls to a glaze; remoisten to three-quarters its height with more broth, let come to a boil, skim and set it in the oven to cook for three to three hours and a half, being careful to baste it constantly during this time. Remove the leg, strain the stock and return both it and the leg to the braziere with some square pieces of breast of pork fried in butter, mushroom heads, small onions fried in butter, roasted chestnuts and fried sausages (No. 754) having their skin suppressed; let the whole simmer slowly for one hour, skim off the fat, dress the leg ranging the garnishings tastefully around; pour the sauce over and serve.

(1626). LEG OF MUTTON À LA REGLAIN (Gigot de Mouton à la Reglain).

Bone a leg of mutton without opening, place it in an earthen vessel and pour over a cold cooked marinade (No. 114); marinate it for twelve hours, then lard the meat with medium-lardons (No. 2, Fig. 52) and lay it on a dish to coat over with lard; roast it and when it has attained a fine color, pour over its strained marinade and finish the cooking, keeping it basted at short intervals. Prepare some slices of tongue and cover each one with a croquette preparation made with sheep's brains, minced mushrooms, velouté sauce (No. 415), chopped parsley, egg-yolks and fresh butter; dust with bread-crumbs, dip in eggs and fry. Dress and garnish the leg around with the slices of tongue, and serve with a separate marinade sauce (No. 496).

(1627). LEG OF MUTTON À LA ROEDERER (Gigot de Mouton à la Roederer).

Prepare and cook a leg of mutton on the spit, reserve carefully the dripping pan stock; half an hour before serving blanch half a pound of small macaroni for ten minutes, drain, and lay it in the dripping pan under the meat. Prick the leg with a trussing needle to let its blood fall on the macaroni. When the leg is cooked, drain and dress on a vegetable dish layers of the macaroni alternated with grated parmesan, and so on until finished; pour some clear gravy (No. 404) over into which a little tomato purée (No. 730) has been added. Dress the meat, garnish the handles with a frill (No. 10) and serve a little clear gravy separately.

(1628). BOILED LEG OF MUTTON, GRANVILLE (Gigot de Mouton Bouilli à la Granville).

Saw off short the end bone of a leg of mutton, suppress all surperfluous fat, and weigh it. plunge it into a large soup-pot containing boiling, salted water, cover, and continue to boil until the leg is cooked, which will require fifteen minutes for every pound of meat. Boiled legs of mutton should always be cooked rare. Have already prepared a garnishing of carrot balls, three-quarters of an inch in diameter, blanched and cooked in beef stock (No. 194a); small boiled onions; olive shaped potatoes, boiled, drained and then rolled in a little fresh butter with chopped parsley and lemon juice, and cork-shaped turnips, blanched and cooked in beef stock; form a handle about two inches long by scraping the end bone clean. Dress the leg, glaze the surface and garnish around with clusters of the vegetables. Serve at the same time a buttered tomatoed velouté sauce (No. 415). Just when ready to send to table, arrange a paper frill (No. 10) on the end bone and serve.

(1629). BOILED LEG OF MUTTON WITH MASHED TURNIPS AND CAPER SAUCE (Gigot de Mouton Bouilli à la Purée de Navets et à la Sauce aux Câpres).

With Mashed Turnips.—Have a leg of mutton prepared and cooked as explained à la **Granville** (No. 1628). Put to boil with the leg after it has been in the water for half an hour, two pounds of turnips cut in four; when done mash them to a pulp and pass through a sieve, season with salt, nutmeg and a little sugar and add four ounces of butter, lay this around the meat, serving some clear gravy separately.

With Caper Sauce.—Garnish around the leg with boiled potatoes, and serve with a butter sauce (No. 440) into which nonpareil capers have been added.

(1630). LEG OF MUTTON À LA MILANAISE—KERNEL (Noix de Gigot de Mouton à la Milanaise).

Remove the kernels from four legs of mutton, the same as the kernel of veal; free the top from fat and sinews and lard it with lardons (No. 3, Fig. 52); line a braziere with slices of fat pork, set the kernels on top and wet with one pint of mirepoix (No. 419); reduce the liquid to a mere nothing, then remoisten to three-quarters of their heighth adding two gills of brandy. Cook it in the oven until done, being careful to baste frequently; prepare a rice socle, lay the kernel on top, glaze and garnish around with small macaroni timbales Milanaise (No. 2988). Serve the stock reduced with espagnole sauce (No. 414) separately.

(1631). LEG OF MUTTON IN PAPERS—KERNELS (Noix de Gigot de Mouton en Papillotes).

Remove the kernel from a leg of mutton the same as for a kernel of veal; pare it nicely, take off all the fat and lard it with small lardons (No. 3, Fig. 52), then roast it quite rare, cut it in quarter inch thick slices. Have a sufficiently large sheet of paper, cut it into heart-shape, butter over and lay a little finely sliced ham on top of one side; over this place some Duxelle (No. 385) well reduced with a clove of garlic and chopped parsley, and set the slices of mutton on top, cover the whole with more Duxelle, then fold the paper, crimp the edges around; before finishing the crimping pour a little Madeira sauce (No. 492), and finish plaiting the paper to enclose hermetically, lay the paper on the dish intended for the table, pour over a little oil and push it into a moderate oven, when nicely browned, serve separately with a very hot Duxelle sauce (No. 461) to which some Madeira wine has been added.

(1632). LEG OF MUTTON À LA LYONNAISE—MINCED (Émincé de Gigot de Mouton à la Lyonnaise).

Pare and suppress all the fat from a cold cooked leg of mutton, cut it in slices and fry these in a little butter, season with salt and pepper, parsley and lemon juice, and just when ready to serve pour off the butter and add a piece of meat glaze (No. 402). Dress the meat crown-shaped on a dish.

Fry some minced and blanched onions in butter; when a fine golden color, drain off the butter and add some velouté sauce (No. 415) and cream; reduce well and then pour it over the slices, bestrew chopped parsley over and serve very hot.

(1633). LEG OF MUTTON ON THE SPIT (Gigot de Mouton à la Broche).

Pick out a leg with a short handle bone, and very rounded at its thickest part, having a thin transparent skin and covered with white fat near the tail. Let it hang as long as possible to be tender. When it is required for use, pare nicely, remove the aitchbone, saw off the knuckle and make a handle two inches long; scrape the bone very white. Lay the leg on the spit thrusting the split in near the end bone, letting it come out at the loin bone, then cover over with sheets of well buttered paper. One hour and twenty minutes before serving, lay it in front of the fire, baste often, when nearly cooked salt over. Just when ready to serve withdraw the spit, dress and pour over some clear gravy (No. 404); trim the end bone with a paper frill (No. 10). Serve separately a sauce-boatful of clear gravy (No. 404).

(1634). LEG OF MUTTON, PARISIAN STYLE, IN THE OVEN (Gigot de Mouton à la Parisienne au Four).

Saw off the handle of the leg below the knuckle bone; insert a piece of garlic near the handle, then lay the meat in a baking pan: pour some good drippings and water over and roast it in the oven, adding a little more water every time the fat clarifies in order to prevent it burning; when cooked, dress the leg, surrounding it with large olive-shaped potatoes cooked with butter in a slow oven and baste the leg with the gravy, serving the remainder in a sauce-boat. Trim the handle (Fig. 164) with a paper frill (No. 10) or one of silver used for this purpose.

(1635). LEG OF MUTTON WITH PURÉE OF BEANS (Gigot de Mouton à la Purée de Haricots).

Pound half a pound of chopped fat salt pork with an equal quantity of cooked ham, bread-crumbs, two eggs, a finely shredded shallot, previously fried in butter, parsley, and a tiny bit of crushed garlic; cut some thin slices of a leg of mutton, flatten to three-sixteenths of an inch, pare to two inch squares, season them with salt, pepper, and nutmeg, and cover one side with the prepared forcemeat, roll them up and run a skewer through each; dip them into melted butter, roll in bread-crumbs, and broil over a slow fire to attain a good color, then dress them on a purée of white beans (No. 706), with a little clear gravy (No. 404) poured over the whole.

(1636). LEG OF MUTTON WITH RICE (Gigot de Mouton au Riz).

Bone a leg of mutton; remove the aitchbone and the large bone as far as the joint; season with salt, pepper, and nutmeg, and fill the inside with a pork stuffing as in No. 68, mixing with it half its quantity of boiled and finely chopped ham, as much bread-crumbs as ham, an ounce of chopped onion, a clove of crushed and chopped garlic, and two egg-yolks. Sew up the leg so as to secure the forcemeat enclosed therein. Melt half a pound of fat pork, fry the leg in it, drain off the fat, season, and moisten to three quarters its height with stock (No. 194a), adding to the liquid two medium onions, stuck with two cloves, and four peeled and quartered tomatoes: allow the leg to cook slowly for three hours, then strain off the stock, free it of its fat and take away a third part, returning this to the leg after having untied it. Add to the other two parts, half a pound of Carolina rice and let cook for twenty minutes, then put in some butter and grated cheese, stirring it in with a fork. Dress the leg, glaze it over and decorate the handle bone with a paper frill (No. 10); garnish around with the rice, strain the stock from the leg once more, skim off its fat, reduce to half and serve it in a separate sauce-boat.

(1637). LOIN OF MUTTON ROASTED, ON THE SPIT OR IN THE OVEN (Longe de Mouton Rôtie à la Broche ou au Four).

Have a three pound loin of mutton; bone it entirely without detaching the minion fillet; remove the skin covering the fat and roll the flank over on itself as far as the minion fillet, then tie it firmly with five rounds of string, making a knot in each round, giving the loin the shape of a long square. Set it to roast either on the spit or in the oven; if for the former it will take from thirty to forty minutes, and a few more if for the latter. When the loin is cooked and of a fine color, untie, dress, and glaze it, strain the gravy, free it of its fat, and serve a part of it under the meat and the remainder separately.

(1638). LOIN WITH PURÉE OF CARROTS (Longe à la Purée de Carottes).

Suppress part of the fat without uncovering the meat from a loin of mutton; beat and flatten the flap, bone the loin without separating the tenderloin from the fillet, then season with salt, mignonette and nutmeg; roll it up in the shape of a muff and tie it well, lay the meat in a saucepan with some grated fat pork and let fry to a fine golden color; drain off the fat and moisten with a pint of stock (No. 194a) and a gill of brandy, adding a bunch of parsley garnished with thyme and bay leaf; cover over with a strong sheet of buttered paper, set it on the fire and when it comes to a boil push it into a moderate oven until thoroughly cooked, then untie, glaze and dress on a purée of carrots (No. 709).

(1639). NECK OF MUTTON JUGGED AND MARINATED, THICKENED WITH BLOOD (Collet de Mouton Civet Marinade Lié au Sang).

Bone a neck of mutton, remove all the sinews and fat and then cut it up into one and a quarter inch square pieces; lay them in a vessel to season with salt, pepper, nutmeg, sprigs of parsley, minced onions, oil, a little vinegar, bay leaf and thyme; let marinate for two hours, then drain and wipe off the pieces. Heat four ounces of butter in a saucepan, add to it the meat and fry them well, dredge in two spoonfuls of flour and moisten with one pint of red or white wine and stock (No.194a) in a way that the meat is covered; add a garnished bunch of parsley and leave to cook for an hour and a half, putting in half an hour before serving, some small glazed white onions and cooked mushrooms. The meat being now well done and properly seasoned, take out the parsley and thicken the sauce either with some pig's or chicken's blood, then serve.

(1640). SCOTCH HAGGIS (Panse Caillette).

In a quart of water boil one pound of calf's liver until throughly done; chop it up finely with one pound of beef suet, free of skin and fibres, one pound of lean beef from the rump, one pound of onions and add an ounce of salt, an ounce of ground pepper, one pound of oatmeal and the water the liver was boiled in. With this preparation fill a well-cleaned sheep's paunch, sew it up with strong thread and wrap it in a buttered cloth; plunge it into boiling water and let cook gently for four hours; prick it several times while cooking with a trussing needle; drain, unwrap a few moments later and turn it over on a hot dish. Serve at the same time cakes made with three pounds of oatmeal, one pound of wheat flour, an ounce of lard and salt. These cakes are eight inches in diameter and one-eighth of an inch thick; bake them in a slow oven.

(1641). MUTTON PILAU, FRENCH STYLE (Pilau de Mouton à la Française).

Remove the fat and bones from the thick end of a loin of mutton; divide the meats into regular one and a half inch pieces and fry them in butter for ten minutes; add sliced carrots and

FIG. 342.

onions, mushroom peelings and salt; moisten to three-quarters of the height with mutton broth made with the bones and trimmings; reduce the moisture slowly to a glaze, then moisten and reduce once more; remoisten for the third time to the full height and continue to boil slowly until the meats are very nearly done, now lift them out one by one, pare nicely, and place them in a charlotte mold or a special tinned copper saucepan, provided with a hermetically fitted lid (Fig. 342), strain the liquid over the meats, letting it reach slightly above their height and add three spoonfuls of tomato purée (No. 730), a tablespoonful of powdered sweet Spanish peppers and a little cayenne pepper. Boil, then add half a pound of well-picked and washed Carolina rice, dried for an hour on a sieve; close the saucepan hermetically and set it in the oven to cook the contents for twenty minutes without touching it—the rice should be kept quite whole. Serve this stew in a tureen or vegetable dish or else in the saucepan itself.

(1642). QUARTER OF MUTTON WITH GASTRONOME POTATOES (Quartier de Mouton aux Pommes Gastronome).

Suppress and trim the end bone of the leg by sawing it off two inches from the shank bone; cut the meat away evenly two inches deep, and scrape the bone free from meat. Bone the spine as far as the beginning of the ribs and saw it through its whole length; roll the flap over and tie it down; put the quarter on the spit, passing the bar alongside the handle, letting it come out at the loin bone, and follow along the minion fillet; maintain the meat in position with skewers, equalize the weight well, so that the spit turns evenly and fasten the handles firmly. Cover the quarter over with a buttered paper, and one hour and a quarter before serving, put the spit in front of the fire; fifteen minutes before dinner, unwrap and let it brown nicely; withdraw it from the spit, glaze, dress and garnish around with gastronome potatoes (No. 2789), and trim the end bone with a fluted paper frill (No. 10); pour over a rather thin half-glaze sauce (No. 413), and serve.

(1643). RACK OF MUTTON WITH SMALL ROOTS (Carré de Mouton aux Petites Racines).

Have two racks of six ribs each and five inches wide; beginning at the fillet, bone the loin on the spine end, and saw through the spinal bone, pare the racks and lard it with medium lardons (No. 3, Fig. 52), then place the two racks in a sautoir containing slices of fat pork, carrots, onions, cloves, a garnished bunch of parsley (No. 123), moisten with a pint of water, reduce entirely and re-moisten to three-quarters of its heighth with beef stock (No. 194a); let cook for one hour, basting frequently in such a way that they become both cooked and glazed at the same time. Dress the racks on a garnishing of small roots cut in balls, or else on a garnishing of cream chiccory purée (No. 729).

Fig. 343.

(1644). SADDLE OF MUTTON, DUCHESS STYLE (Selle de Mouton, à la Duchesse).

Pare and shorter the rib bones above the flaps; cut these off straight and with the tip of a knife, separate the rings of the spinal bones at equal distances apart; tie it firmly and lay it on a spit to cook for one hour to one hour and a quarter according to its size; baste frequently while cooking, untie, salt, brown and glaze the meat. Dress and garnish around with duchess potatoes (No. 2785) and the ends with spinach rissoles prepared as explained (No. 161), filling them with spinach (No. 2820). A separate half-glaze sauce (No. 413) is to be served at the same time.

(1645). SADDLE OF MUTTON, GERMAN STYLE (Selle de Mouton à l'Allemande).

Braise a saddle exactly as explained for the saddle with glazed roots (No. 1649). Half an hour before serving, drain and cover the surface with a lamb forcemeat (No. 92), and raw fine herbs that have been mingled with some allemande sauce (No. 407). Finish cooking in a moderate oven and when done, glaze and dress the meat on an oval dish, garnishing around with carrots and green peas sautéd together.

(1646). SADDLE OF MUTTON. PIEDMONTESE STYLE (Selle de Mouton à la Piémontaise).

Have a good saddle of mutton, hang it in a cool place for eight days to have it tender; pare the two fillets, suppress all the fat and skin adhering to the meat so as to be able to lard it with larding pork, then roll the flanks under. Tie up the saddle, lay it in an English cradle spit (Fig. 344), after it has been wrapped in a buttered paper, and let roast in front of a moderate fire for an hour and a quarter, basting it frequently during the time; remove the paper to let attain a good color, then untie it on a baking pan, detach the two fillets, leaving on some of the fat; cut them up slanting and replace them from whence they were taken. In the meantime prepare a Piedmontese risot (No. 739), and just when ready to serve dress the saddle on a relevé dish with the risot; be-sprinkle over with a few handfuls of chopped white Piedmontese truffles, glaze it over and send to the table accompanied by a sauce-boat of thickened gravy (No. 405).

(1647). SADDLE OF MUTTON, PRINTANIÈRE (Selle de Mouton Printanière).

Prepare and braise a saddle the same as for the one with glazed roots (No. 1649), half an hour before serving, glaze the surface of the meat, strain the stock and reduce with Madeira sauce (No. 492). Dress the saddle on a long dish with a macédoine garnishing (No. 680) around it alter-nating the colors. Pour a little of the sauce under the saddle; glaze it properly and serve the remainder of the sauce-boat apart.

(1648). SADDLE OF MUTTON ROASTED ON THE SPIT (Selle de Mouton Rôtie à la Broche).

The saddle is the whole loin and first rib; cut off the two legs below the tail in a round-shape, direct-ing the knife toward the flanks (Fig 340). Carefully remove the fat both on the top and the under toward the loin end, and part of the kidney fat. Roll the flanks of the meat over on themselves.

make incisions in the fat on the top of the saddle, more or less deep according to its thickness, and keep the saddle in position with four or five rounds of string. Place the saddle on the spit, hold it in place with skewers run through the flanks of the meat and the holes in the spit; thrust a fork into the meat of the sirloin near the bone, and place on the top a long skewer, tying it firmly

Fig. 344.

at the two ends. Cover the meat with several sheets of buttered paper, tie them on, and one hour and a quarter before serving roast the saddle before a good, clear and well regulated fire. Fifteen minutes before serving, unwrap, glaze over and let it acquire a fine color; dress it on a very hot long dish, pour over some clear gravy (No. 404), and serve at the same time a sauce-boatful of clear gravy (No. 404), and half-glaze sauce (No. 413), half of each.

(1649). SADDLE OF MUTTON WITH GLAZED ROOTS—BRAISED (Selle de Mouton Braisée aux Racines Glacées).

Cut the loin parts beginning at the first rib; cut off the two legs below the tail, in a round direction going toward the flank, remove the thin skin covering the fat, and roll the flank over, keeping it in position with six rounds of string, tying a knot at each round. Place the meat in a braziere having the grater or leaf covered with sliced pork, moisten with two quarts of stock (No. 194a) adding half a pound of grated fat pork, two carrots, two onions, two bunches of parsley garnished with thyme and bay leaf, and one gill of brandy; three hours before serving let it come to a boil on a brisk fire, baste the meat covered with a heavy and strongly buttered paper, then set it in the oven being careful to watch that it simmers slowly until it is cooked; ten minutes before serving drain it on a baking pan, untie carefully, coat it over with glaze, and glaze it in the oven. Dress the saddle, glaze it afresh and group around clusters of glazed new carrots, glazed onions and celery root. Strain the stock, remove the fat and reduce with brown sauce (No. 413) and Madeira, this sauce to be served separately.

(1650). SADDLE OR BARON—IN THE OVEN—WITH MASHED POTATOES (Selle ou Baron au Four à la Purée de Pommes).

Prepare a saddle or baron of mutton the same as for No. 1648; after it has been pared and tied, wrap it up and lay it in a deep baking pan coated over with fat; add a little water, then put it in the oven to cook for an hour to an hour and a quarter, unwrap fifteen minutes before serving;

Fig. 345.

glaze, color nicely, then dress it on a hot long dish; pour some clear gravy (No. 404) over and serve at the same time a sauce-boat of clear gravy reduced to a half-glaze, also a vegetable dish full of mashed potatoes (No. 2798), or else olive-shaped potatoes cooked in butter.

(1651). SHOULDER OF MUTTON, MARINATED WITH CREAM SAUCE (Épaule de Mouton Marinée Sauce à la Crème).

Bone the shoulder as far as half way down the shank bone; lard the inside of the meat with small lardons (No. 2, Fig. 52), seasoned with salt and pepper, then set it into a vessel and pour over a cooked and cold marinade (No. 114), leaving it in for twelve hours. Line a saucepan with bards of fat pork and sliced carrots and onions; roll and tie the shoulder and lay it on top; moisten with a pint of stock (No. 194a), and when reduced to a glaze, remoisten and cook the meat to a fine color in the oven for three hours and a half; remove the shoulder, skim the fat from the stock, add one pint of cream to the stock, and let simmer for a few minutes; strain through a sieve and reduce to the consistency of a good sauce, adding to it a very little bread-crumbs; serve this at the same time as the shoulder.

(1652). SHOULDER OF MUTTON WITH POTATOES (Épaule de Mouton aux Pommes de Terre).

Bone two shoulders of mutton leaving on the handles only; suppress the sinews and skin from the inside meats, season and roll up lengthwise, sewing them well; put them into a small roasting-pan lined with fragments of salt pork, and pour melted butter over, and cook them till three-quarters done in a moderate oven, turning them over and adding a little water, should the fat threaten to burn. A few minutes before serving season with salt. Cut into medium slices some raw peeled potatoes; mince three or four white onions, and fry them with butter in a sautoir over a slow fire; when they begin to brown add the potatoes, season and fry together for seven or eight minutes. Remove the meat to lay it on a long earthen dish capable of going in the oven, set the potatoes around, aud baste them, also the meat with the strained fat from the pan; let the shoulders cook in a moderate oven for twenty-five minutes longer, then dress and garnish the handles with paper frills (No. 10) and lay the potatoes around them.

(1653). SHOULDER OF MUTTON WITH RICE (Épaule de Mouton au Riz).

Cut into small two inch squares a shoulder of young mutton; put them into a saucepan with hot butter, and let fry on a brisk fire until they take a color: season, and add a few spoonfuls of raw ham cut in dice, and a bunch of parsley garnished with one bay leaf, as much thyme and a clove of garlic. Fry all together fcr a few moments, then moisten to their heighth with stock (No. 194a), and half a pint of tomato sauce (No. 549); when the liquid has boiled for five minutes remove the saucepan on a more moderate fire, and when the meats are partially or three-quarters done, put in a sufficient quantity of rice corresponding to the volume of the third of the liquid; cook this rice for fifteen minutes, then set the saucepan into a slow oven to finish cooking both rice and meat. Pour the stew into a vegetable dish and serve.

(1654). SHOULDER OF MUTTON WITH TURNIPS (Épaule de Mouton aux Navets).

Bone a shoulder of mutton keeping the shank bone on; remove all sinews from the inside meats as weii as the fat, and lard with medium lardons (No. 2, Fig. 52); season with salt, pepper, and nutmeg, then roll it up and tie. Put some clarified butter in a saucepan with the shoulder, fry it to a fine color, then moisten with stock (No. 194a) or water, adding some medium-sized carrots cut in four, and two medium onions, a bunch of parsley garnished with thyme, bay leaf, and a clove of garlic, let sim-mer for two hours. Withdraw the carrots, onions, and parsley, and replace them by some turnips pared into olive or clove of garlic shape, and fried in butter with a little sugar; let the whole cook slowly for an hour and a half, making three and a half hours in all, skim off the fat, season to taste, and dress the shoulder with the turnips around, then reduce the stock, strain, pour part of it over the meat and serve what remains in a sauce-boat.

(1655). SHEEP'S TAILS WITH OLIVES (Queues de Mouton aux Olives).

Suppress the thin ends of eight tails previously parboiled; put them into a saucepan with half a pound of lard, two onions and a half minced carrot; fry the whole together, seasoning well, and when they are a nice color, dredge over with two ounces of flour; moisten with hot stock (No. 194a) and white wine. Boil the liquid for ten minutes, then remove it to the side of the range or else set it in the oven until the tails are cooked; strain the sauce through a sieve, skim the fat off carefully, and add to it a quarter of a pint of white wine; reduce until properly thickened. Pare the tails, lay them in the sauce to heat and add some stoned Spanish olives; a few minutes later, serve on a very hot dish and surround with the garnishing of olives, purée of potatoes (No. 725) or risot (No. 739).

(1656). MUTTON TENDONS WITH MUSHROOMS (Tendrons de Mouton aux Champignons).

Cut the tendons from the end of the breast; braise. then lay them under a weight, and when cold cut them up into escalops, and dip in Villeroi sauce (No. 560), fry in clarified butter; dress crown-shaped with stewed mushrooms and cream in the middle.

(1657). SHEEP'S TONGUES, ÉCARLATE WITH SPINACH (Langues de Mouton Écarlate aux Épinards).

Have several sheep's tongues; prick them with a trussing needle, and rub over with a little powdered saltpetre; keep them in a cool place until the following day; then prepare a brine of salt water, stir it to dissolve the salt, having enough of it to enable a potato to float on the surface. Lay the tongues in an earthen crock, pour the salted water over, and a few days after when sufficiently red, soak them for twelve hours, and then blanch in plenty of water. Braise the tongues in a mirepoix stock (No. 419) moistened with white wine, and let boil; when cooked set them under a weight, pare and keep warm; dress and garnish with cooked spinach (No. 2820). Serve a half-glaze sauce (No. 413) apart.

(1658). SHEEP'S TONGUES, NEAPOLITAN STYLE (Langues de Mouton à la Napolitaine).

Blanch and then braise the tongues for two hours in a mirepoix stock (No. 419) with white wine; when cooked pull off the white skin that covers them and lay them under a weight. Split the tongues lengthwise in two, cover the flat side with some Duxelle (No. 385), dip them in beaten eggs and fry; dress in a circle filling in the center with some Neapolitan macaroni (No. 2960), and serve with a tomato sauce (No. 549) mixed with half-glaze sauce (No. 413).

(1659). SHEEP'S TROTTERS À LA POULETTE (Pieds de Mouton à la Poulette).

Prepare and cook them as for the vinaigrette (No. 1660); then drain. Put some velouté sauce (No. 415) reduced with mushroom liquor into a saucepan, add the trotters and some turned or channeled mushrooms (No. 118) previously cooked. Boil, season with salt and pepper, and thicken with egg-yolks diluted in cream, and just when ready to serve incorporate fresh butter, lemon juice and chopped parsley.

(1660). SHEEP'S TROTTERS À LA VINAIGRETTE (Pieds de Mouton à la Vinaigrette).

Should they have to be prepared at home they would need scalding and scraping with a knife in order to remove all the hairs; cut the soles from the hoofs so as to suppress a part of the woolly tuft found thereon; cut the ends of the ergots, tie the feet, four of them together, and blanch until they boil; then drain and refresh, place them in a soup-pot, covering them over with cold water, adding salt, pepper, spices, a garnished bunch of parsley (No. 123), onions, carrots and one ounce of flour diluted in cold water. Bring the liquid to a boil, cover the vessel and cook the feet for five hours, when done take out the shank bone which easily detaches without the slightest effort. Just when ready to serve untie and drain; remove the leg bone and wipe the feet on a cloth; dress them on a hot dish with a napkin under, and surround with green parsley leaves. Serve a vinaigrette sauce (No. 634) separately.

LAMB (Agneau).

(1661). BARON OF YEARLING LAMB À LA DE RIVAS (Baron d'Agneau Tardif à la de Rivas).

Cut a baron from the hind part of the lamb from the first rib to the loin bone (Fig. 340). Roast it on the spit or in the oven, and when done trim and dress on a dish; glaze with meat glaze (No. 402) and garnish around with twelve stuffed tomatoes (No. 2842) and twelve stuffed mushrooms (No. 692) and outside of these set small bouchées filled with cream spinach (No. 2820), place on top a ball of potato croquette (No. 2782) one inch in diameter. An aromatic tomato sauce (No. 549) to be served apart.

(1662). BREASTS OF LAMB, BAKED (Poitrines d'Agneau au Gratin).

Prepare and cook the breasts the same as for chopped sauce (No. 1663); put them under a weight or in the press (Fig. 71) and press to five-eighths of an inch thick, and when cold pare by removing the skin and part of the fat; cut into an oblong shape, then cover with a baking forcemeat (No. 81); lay on top of each three mushrooms, one large and two small ones; place them on a well-buttered baking dish, pour over an Italian sauce (No. 484), bestrew with bread raspings and besprinkle with butter, then brown in the oven; serve on the same dish and garnish the sides with round cuts of red beef tongue warmed in a little meat glaze (No. 402), with butter and lemon juice.

(1663). BREASTS OF LAMB, CHOPPED SAUCE (Poitrine d'Agneau à la Sauce Hachée).

Have two fine breasts of yearling lamb or young mutton; suppress the bone part covering the gristle; lay the meats in a low saucepan lined with bardes of fat pork, cut up carrots and onions, and a garnished bouquet; moisten with stock (No. 194a) cover over with buttered paper and set it into a moderate oven to cook for two to two hours and a half, until the bones can be easily removed. Drain and place the meats under the pressure of a weight to reduce to five-eighths of an inch, and when quite cold, pare and remove the skin carefully without touching the fat, and cut the meat up into half hearts, trim them, nicely rounding the angles, and dip them in melted butter, roll in bread-crumbs, and broil over a slow fire till they attain a fine color and are very hot, then dress them either in a straight row or in a circle. Garnish around with olive-shaped pieces of potato cooked in fresh butter, and when done, and the butter is drained off, add some salt and the juice of a lemon, dredging over with chopped parsley. Serve a chopped sauce (No. 539) separately.

(1664). BREAST OF LAMB WITH TURNIPS (Poitrine d'Agneau aux Navets).

Remove the skin covering the breast, also the gristle bone from two breasts of lamb; cut them up into three-quarters of an inch square pieces and fry them till brown in butter, then drain off the fat and moisten with a pint of stock (No. 194a); boil and reduce to a glaze; remoisten a very little at the time, repeating this several times while cooking, and three-quarters of an hour before serving, drain off the meats, pare and return them to the saucepan; strain the sauce over and add some turned turnips fried in butter, and continue the cooking, season properly. When the meats and turnips are well done and fallen to a glaze, dress the turnips around.

(1665). BREAST OF LAMB WITH VELOUTÉ TOMATO SAUCE—STUFFED (Poitrine d'Agneau Farcie à la Sauce Tomate Veloutée).

Split open one or several yearling lamb breasts on the rib sides, by slipping the blade of a knife between the bone and the meat so as to make a pocket, season the inside and fill the empty space with forcemeat (No. 65), seasoned highly and to which add a handful of soaked and pressed out bread-crumbs, also some raw onions chopped and parboiled, cooked minced mushrooms and chopped parsley, each of them chopped up separately, and also stir in two whole eggs. Sew up the opening in the breast, cook it in beef stock (No. 194a) and when done properly, which will take about two hours and a half, drain and untie, then serve with a tomato sauce (No. 549) reduced with velouté sauce (No. 415).

(1666). CARBONADE OF LAMB À LA JARDINIÈRE (Carbonade d'Agneau à la Jardinière).

A carbonade or loin is the end of the rack (Fig. 335), from where the cutlets begin as far down as where the tail begins. Chop off entirely the chine bone without detaching the minion fillet, remove the skin covering the large fillet over its entire outside surface, and lard the meat with medium lardons (No. 3, Fig. 52). Roll over the flap, tie it with six rounds of string, forming a knot at each round, and then lay the meat in a saucepan lined with slices of fat pork, veal, ham, cut up vegetables, a garnished bunch of parsley and allspice, salt it over lightly and wet it with a beef stock (No. 194a); let fall to a glaze, then remoisten to its height with white wine and stock; allow the boiling to continue for five minutes, then uncover the saucepan and place it in a moderate oven to finish cooking, being careful to baste it frequently with its own stock, having it finally assume a fine color. Glaze, untie, dress and strain and skim the liquid, reduce and serve it in a sauce-boat; garnish around the meat with a jardinière garnishing (No. 677).

(1667). CARBONADE OF LAMB À LA RAMBUTEAU (Carbonade d'Agneau à la Rambuteau).

Bone entirely, or else remove the aitchbone only, from a loin of lamb: suppress all the fat and sinews, also the skin that covers the sirloin and lard with medium-sized larding pork (No. 3, Fig. 52) and season with salt, pepper and fine herbs; roll the flap over and tie. Line a saucepan with bardes of fat pork, lay the carbonade on top and moisten to its height with mirepoix stock (No. 419); and white wine boil, then simmer in the oven for two and a half to three hours; glaze, untie, dress on a long dish and garnish around with small glazed onions, mushroom heads and potato balls. Strain the stock, free it of fat and reduce it with as much velouté (No. 415), thicken with raw egg-yolks, fresh butter and lemon juice; strain it once more through a tammy, and use part of it to cover the garnishings, sending the remainder to the table separately.

(1668). LAMB'S CROWS, RAVIGOTE SAUCE (Fraises d'Agneau à la Sauce Ravigote).

Select two very white and clean lamb's crows. Line an earthen crock with slices of fat pork, range the crows on top and add to them two medium onions one having four cloves in it, a bunch of parsley garnished with thyme and bay leaf, salt and pepper; moisten with white wine and beef stock (No. 194a), cover the top with more slices of the pork, then place a deep plate over, filling it with water, and let cook slowly in a moderate oven for four hours, drain, and dress on a hot dish, surround the crows with sprigs of parsley and serve with ravigote sauce (No. 531).

(1669). LAMB OUTLETS, PLAIN—YEARLING (Côtelettes d'Agneau Tardif Nature).

FIG. 346.

Five or six cutlets can be taken from a rack of yearling lamb, four or five from a spring lamb; remove the skin, cut them into any desired thickness, and should the rack be too thin, then cut them off on the bias. Remove and pare the bone from each chop, then beat down to flatten to half an inch in thickness, and trim them all around, removing the skin from each side of the rib bone; scrape about an inch of the end of the bone, clean off the meat and fat to enable it to be decorated with a paper frill; when cooked season with salt, coat over with butter or oil, place on the gridiron all on the same side and broil on a slow but well maintained fire. When cooked on one side, turn over and finish cooking on the other; the entire operation should take about six minutes; trim the handles with paper frills (No. 10), dress and serve with a little clear gravy (No. 404).

(1670). LAMB OUTLETS À LA BUSSY (Côtelettes d'Agneau à la Bussy).

Pare eight yearling lamb cutlets; season with salt, mask over with oil and broil quite rare on a brisk fire. Prepare beforehand a salpicon of truffles, sweetbreads and mushrooms all cut up into quarter inch pieces and mixed with a well reduced allemande sauce (No. 407); as soon as it becomes quite cold, add to it dice pieces of duck's liver cut the same size. Spread this salpicon on the chops all on the same side rounding it well on top; cover over with a cream forcemeat (No. 75), besprinkle with finely chopped truffles and pour over a little melted butter. Place the chops in a slack oven to heat the salpicon, trim the bone handles, dress the chops flat on a light béchamel and cream sauce (No. 411). Serve with some of the same sauce in a separate sauce-boat.

(1671). LAMB CUTLETS À LA CATALANE (Côtelettes d'Agneau à la Catalane).

Cut off twelve lamb cutlets; pare them with the bones quite short, beat them flat, salt over and roll in oil, range them on a broiler all one way, and broil the chops on a brisk fire on one side only. Reduce one pint of béchamel (No. 409) adding to it a few spoonfuls of mushroom broth, and when nicely thickened stir in some prepared red pepper (No. 168), four spoonfuls of cooked mushrooms, the same quantity of cooked lean ham, both well chopped separately, and let this preparation become cold. Cover the cooked sides with a layer of the preparation, having it dome-shaped on top; bestrew with grated parmesan, then lay them on a buttered sautoir and pour butter over; set this for one instant on top of the range, then finish cooking the cutlets in a hot oven and have the preparation well browned; remove them at once to garnish the handles with frills (No. 10) and dress with a half-glaze (No. 413) and tomato sauce (No. 549) containing shredded sweet peppers.

(1672). LAMB CUTLETS À LA CHARLEROI (Côtelettes d'Agneau à la Charleroi).

Sauté sufficient trimmed and seasoned lamb cutlets in butter; when done, drain and arrange them on a baking sheet one beside the other; cover over with a buttered paper and let get cold under the pressure of a light weight. Pare the cutlets once more and lay on one of their sides a reduced and thick soubise purée (No. 723); smooth and let harden for an hour, then lift up the cutlets one by one, and dip them in a Villeroi sauce (No. 560), allow the surplus of this to drain off, then range them on a baking sheet, apart from one another so that they do not touch and keep this in a cool place to harden the sauce. Detach the cutlets from the sheet, trim off any surplus of sauce, and roll the chops in grated parmesan, dip them at once into beaten eggs, and cover over with white bread-crumbs; smooth the surfaces nicely and range them in a frying-basket (Fig. 121), plunge this into hot frying-fat, drain, trim the handles and serve on a folded napkin.

(1673). LAMB CUTLETS À LA CLÉMENCE (Côtelettes d'Agneau à la Clémence).

Have ten well-pared fine cutlets seasoned with salt and pepper; sauté them in butter, dress crown-shaped and fill the inside with a ragoût made as follows: To a velouté sauce (No. 415) add some meat glaze, (No. 402) good Madeira wine and lemon juice, also escalops of lamb's sweetbreads fried in butter with minced mushrooms. Between each cutlet lay a round slice of salted, unsmoked red beef tongue cut three-sixteenths of an inch in thickness and one inch and a half in diameter; garnish around with fine Julienne potatoes (No. 2792); trim the cutlet handles with frills, and serve very hot.

(1674). LAMB CUTLETS À LA DURAND (Côtelettes d'Agneau à la Durand).

Pare eight lamb cutlets chosen from the covered sides of the rack; suppress the spinal bone and fibrous skin from the rib bones, flatten them slightly, season and sauté them in butter, turning them over when they are half done, and finish cooking them properly. Prepare some very thin pancakes (No. 3078), cut them into heart-shapes, having them slightly smaller than papers would be, as there is no necessity to plait them; push a string of quenelle forcemeat (No. 92) through a pocket on the edges and on half the hearts only, put a little cooked fine herb sauce (No. 461), in the center, lay a cutlet over this, with some more of the sauce above; close and fasten the pancake hermetically together, and range them all on a buttered dish, set it in a slack oven for ten minutes, sprinkle butter over and serve on the same dish with a half-glaze sauce (No. 413) poured around.

(1675). LAMB CUTLETS À LA GAVARDI (Côtelettes d'Agneau à la Gavardi).

Season eight fine lamb cutlets; range them in a sautoir lined with fragments of salt pork; roots and sliced onions; moisten to their height with stock (No. 194a) and cover with another piece of the pork; reduce the liquid slowly, remoisten once more, and finish to cook while glazing. Braise separately some rings of blanched carrot, and the same quantity of medium-sized onions each one weighing about an ounce, have also some braised lettuces (No. 2754), dress the cutlets on a dish in a circle, garnish the center with as many of the lettuces as there are cutlets and on each cutlet lay one of the carrot rings with an onion in the center, glaze the whole with meat glaze (No. 402). Reduce the braise stock after it has been strained and freed of fat, with a little espagnole (No. 414) and Marsala wine; serve this in a sauce-boat.

(1676). LAMB CUTLETS, GIRALDA (Côtelettes d'Agneau à la Giralda).

First sauté ten fine cutlets, then set them under a weight and pare them when cold. Cut some sweet Spanish onions into three-sixteenth of an inch square pieces, blanch and cook them in butter, not allowing them to attain color, then add the same quantity of cooked sweet Spanish peppers and thicken the whole with a well-seasoned and reduced velouté (No. 415), allow it to cool, mask the cutlets with this preparation, smooth nicely dome-shaped and cover over with a well-reduced allemande sauce (No. 407); bestrew grated parmesan over and brown in the oven. Pour a supreme sauce (No. 547), finished with shrimp butter (No. 587) in the bottom of the dish, garnish the cutlet handles with frills (No. 10) and range them on top of the sauce.

(1677). LAMB CUTLETS, LEVERRIER (Côtelettes d'Agneau à la Leverrier).

Broil some well pared, first cut cutlets; have as many one and three-quarter inch diameter tin rounds with slightly raised edges; butter and decorate the bottoms with a star each point of which should be formed one half of tongue and the other half of truffle. Cover the cutlets with a layer of forcemeat and place them in buttered bottomless cutlet shaped molds, so that the cutlet is enveloped in forcemeat and fills them up entirely; smooth well the surface and then turn over on the widest part, the star decorated tin round, so that the decoration is exactly on the kernel. Put them for a few moments into a moderate oven and after the forcemeat is poached, lift off both the tin round and the mold molding the chop. Pare some artichoke bottoms two inches in diameter, season and fry them in butter, then dress them flat in a circle and lay a cutlet on top of each; trim the handles with frills (No. 10), pour a little half-glaze (No. 400) in the bottom of the dish and serve separately a half-glaze sauce (No. 413) with orange juice and butter added at the last moment.

(1678). LAMB CUTLETS À LA MAINTENON (Côtelettes d'Agneau à la Maintenon).

Trim, pare and season twelve lamb cutlets; sauté them over a brisk fire, having them rare, then drain, wipe and cover both sides with a well-reduced soubise sauce (No. 543), into which some cooked fine herbs (No. 385) and chopped parsley have been added; when cold dip in beaten eggs, then roll in bread-crumbs and grated parmesan, smooth the surfaces with the blade of a knife and sauté them in clarified butter; dress each cutlet on a peeled, halved and pressed out tomato already fried in butter, and surround the whole with three-quarters of an inch in diameter balls of potatoes, blanched and fried in butter; a half-glaze sauce (No. 413) to be served in a sauce-boat.

(1679). LAMB CUTLETS À LA MAISON D'OR (Côtelettes d'Agneau à la Maison d'Or).

Trim some slices of bread cut three-sixteenths of an inch in thickness, into half heart shapes; fry them in butter and when cold cover the surfaces with some foies-gras in terrine, rounding it on the tops and set them in the oven for one instant to heat only. Dress in a circle and place a cooked cutlet on each slice of bread and lay some minced truffles in the center, cover the whole with Madeira sauce (No. 492) and garnish the handles with a frill (No. 10), then serve.

(1680). LAMB CUTLETS À LA MINUTE, WITH MUSHROOMS, SAUTÉD (Côtelettes d'Agneau Sautées à la Minute aux Champignons).

Pare a dozen lamb cutlets; season, then cook over a brisk fire in a sautoir with clarified butter, turning them round when a fine color on one side; brown both sides alike and cook them till done, then drain off the butter and baste them with a little melted light meat glaze (No. 402) and Madeira, reduce on a quick fire to dry the meat on both sides. Lay the cutlets on a dish, trim the handles with a frill (No. 10) and dress them crown-shaped, have Madeira sauce (No. 492), add to it some minced mushrooms, and pour the whole into the center of the crown or else in a croustade.

(1681). LAMB CUTLETS, MURILLO (Côtelettes d'Agneau à la Murillo).

Pare twelve lamb cutlets having them both wide and thin; range them in a sautoir with hot butter, laying them all one way; cook on one side only, then drain and cover this cooked side with slightly cold minced mushrooms reduced and thickened with some good béchamel (No. 409) finishing with a dash of cayenne pepper, smooth the surface of these mushrooms nicely, dredge over with grated parmesan, sprinkle with melted butter. Return the chops to the sautoir, and set it in the hot oven to finish cooking and brown. Dress them at once on separate plates with a little half-glaze (No. 400) on the bottom and hand them to the guests.

(1682). LAMB CUTLETS À LA NUBIAN (Côtelettes d'Agneau à la Nubienne).

Cook and dress them the same as cutlets à la minute (No. 1680), garnish the center of the circle with minced truffles minced mushrooms, rounds of red beef tongue cut one inch across, and an eighth of an inch thick, the whole mingled with velouté sauce (No. 415) and essence of mushrooms (No. 392). Place around the edge of the dish a few ball-shaped rice croquettes an inch and a quarter in diameter and serve the whole very hot.

(1683). LAMB CUTLETS À LA PÉRIGUEUX (Côtelettes d'Agneau à la Périgueux).

Prepare one pound of chopped forcemeat (No. 65), season highly and add four ounces of finely chopped truffles. Pare twelve lamb cutlets, keeping the end bones quite short and only leaving the kernel meat on; beat them down thin, then lay in a sautoir with hot butter, simply to stiffen the meat, remove at once on a baking sheet; cover with a buttered paper and let get partially cold under the pressure of a weight, or in the press (Fig. 71), afterward covering both sides of the meat with a layer of the above forcemeat; enclose them separately in square pieces of pork "crepinette" or kall fat, broil nicely over a slow fire and dress on a very hot dish, pouring a little clear gravy (No. 404) into the bottom of it. Serve with a sauce-boat of Périgueux sauce (No. 517), to which is mixed some pearl chicken forcemeat quenelles (No. 154).

(1684). LAMB CUTLETS À LA POMPADOUR (Côtelettes d'Agneau à la Pompadour).

Prepare this dish with twelve fine well pared lamb cutlets seasoned with salt and pepper, then fried in butter; set them under a weight, wipe dry and cover both sides with a thoroughly reduced cold soubise (No. 723); dip them in beaten eggs and bread-crumbs, then fry again slowly in clarified butter and dress on a garnishing composed of flageolet beans, quarter inch balls of carrots and turnips. The whole mingled with Pompadour sauce (No. 525).

(1685). LAMB CUTLETS À LA ROBINSON Côtelettes d'Agneau à la Robinson).

Season eight fine cutlets with salt and pepper, then fry them in butter. Apart from this cut up some chicken livers into three-eighths of an inch squares, cook them briskly in butter for a few minutes, and dress the chops in a circle, garnish the handles with frills (No. 10) and lay the drained livers in the center; pour over a Madeira half-glaze sauce (No. 413) with fine herbs.

(1686). LAMB CUTLETS À LA SIGNORA (Côtelettes d'Agneau à la Signora).

Pare twelve lamb cutlets leaving on only the kernel and the bone; spilt them in two through their thickness, season and stuff each one with a slice of truffle an eighth of an inch thick; substitute quenelle forcemeat (No. 92) for the fat that has been removed so as to give the chop its original shape. Dip them in beaten eggs, roll in bread-crumbs, smooth the surfaces with the blade of a knife, then fry the cutlets in clarified butter (No. 16); drain and place paper frills (No. 10) on the handles. Dress in a circle and pour into the center a well buttered supreme sauce (No. 547) into which chopped truffles have been added.

(1687). LAMB CUTLETS À LA TALMA (Côtelettes d'Agneau à la Talma).

Fry twelve lamb cutlets, keeping them quite rare; lay them under a light weight or in the press (No. 71) and when partly cold, pare and dip them in a rather thick, nearly cold béchamel sauce (No. 409); range them on a sheet of buttered paper and on every cutlet place a slice of foies-gras, cover this over with more béchamel and when partly cold, dredge over with bread-crumbs and trim well the cutlets, removing the excess of sauce, strew with a little parmesan cheese, pour on a little butter and brown to a fine golden color in the oven, trim the handles with a frill (No. 10) and dress in a circle filling the center with minced fresh mushrooms mingled with supreme sauce (No. 547) and lay around thin round slices of truffle pouring a little half-glaze sauce (No. 413) over these, and serve.

(1688). LAMB CUTLETS À LA TURENNE (Côtelettes d'Agneau à la Turenne).

Pare a dozen nice cutlets taken from the covered ribs of the racks and suppress the spinal bone and fibrous skin from the ribs; make a gash across the middle of the kernel and fill it up with a cooked fine herb preparation (No. 385), mingled with a little half-glaze (No. 400) and thickened with egg-yolks. Bread-crumb and fry them in butter, trim the handles with a frill (No. 10), dress the cutlets crown-shaped and cover with a buttered half-glaze sauce (No. 413) into which has been added some mushrooms and stuffed olives (No. 695).

(1689). LAMB CUTLETS À LA VICTOR HUGO (Côtelettes d'Agneau à la Victor Hugo).

Season the cutlets with salt and pepper, coat them over with oil and broil nicely till done; cover each one with well-buttered and consistent béarnaise sauce (No. 433), into which has been added some grated fresh and very white horseradish, lay on every cutlet a round slice of truffle warmed in a little meat glaze (No. 402) and Madeira wine, dress the cutlets in a circle, pour a little half-glaze sauce (No. 413) around the cutlets; trim the handles with a frill (No. 10) and serve.

(1690). LAMB CUTLETS BREADED, SAUTÉD AND BROILED (Côtelettes d'Agneau Panées Sautées ou Grillées).

Sautéd.—Pare ten lamb cutlets into good shape, flatten, season and dip them in beaten eggs to roll after in bread-crumbs; smooth the surfaces with the blade of a knife and then put them in a sautoir with hot purified butter (No. 16), cook on both sides turning them over only once, drain and trim with fancy frills (No. 10), dress on a very hot dish and serve.

Broiled.—Bread-crumb the cutlets the same as when sautéing them; eight minutes before serving, roll them in melted butter, broil over a slow fire turning them on both sides; take them off when done and lay them on a plate, trim with fancy frills, then dress them in a circle on a very hot dish pouring a little clear gravy (No. 404) into the bottom.

(1691). LAMB CUTLETS IN CRÉPINETTE (Côtelettes d'Agneau en Crépinette).

Prepare twelve rather thick but well-trimmed lamb cutlets, leaving the kernel only, and suppressing all the fat and sinews; chop the meats without cutting through, then season with salt, pepper and nutmeg. Make a forcemeat with half a pound of chopped fat pork, half a pound of cooked fine herbs (No. 385), and two ounces of fresh bread-crumbs; mix thoroughly and lay it on both sides of the cutlets; wrap each one separately in a square piece of "crépinette" or caul fat well fattened; butter them over with a brush dipped in butter, and broil for twenty-five minutes on a slow fire, turning them round when done on one side; then lay them on a small baking tin; trim the handles with frills (No. 10); dress in a circle on a dish, adding some reduced clear gravy (No. 404.)

(1692). LAMB CUTLETS IN PAPERS (Côtelettes d'Agneau en Papillotes).

Lamb cutlets from their peculiar tenderness and delicacy are well adapted to be prepared in papers. Trim eight spring lamb cutlets pared most carefully and keeping them as wide as possible, season and fry in a sautoir with some melted fat pork, turning them over while cooking; let them remain quite rare; remove the cutlets leaving the pork in the pan and to it add finely chopped onions,

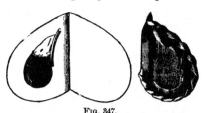

FIG. 347.

shallots, mushrooms, and truffles; after these have rendered their moisture take them out and mix in with some chopped parsley, and lean, cooked, and finely shredded ham combined with two spoonfuls of baking forcemeat (No. 81). Divide this preparation into as many parts as there are cutlets and cover each one with a layer of it, cut some sheets of strong paper into heart-shapes, oil over on one-half the right side, pour a little sauce, with a cutlet on top, then a little more of the sauce and fold over the paper; plait the two edges together in such a way as to enclose the meat completely, then lay them on a buttered dish that can stand the heat of the oven, and on which they are to be served; set it in the oven, and when they have acquired a fine color serve; or they may be broiled over a very slow fire in their papers and then dressed on a very hot dish.

(1693). LAMB CUTLETS WITH STRING BEANS (Côtelettes d'Agneau aux Haricots Verts).

Pare the breast bones four inches long, cut off the neck to the third rib, saw off the spinal bone without spoiling the fillets as far as the rib, then cut from each rack five, six, or seven chops according to the thickness of the meat and the purpose they are intended for. Remove the meat from the end bones of each chop an inch deep, and flatten the meat lightly; suppress the fibrous skin adhering to the kernel, also the one attached to the bone; season with salt, and dip in melted butter; roll them in fresh bread-crumbs, then broil over a brisk fire, turning them only once during the operation. Trim the handles with frills (No. 10), dress and garnish with sautéd string beans (No. 2829), pour around some clear gravy (No. 404) having had a blanched and chopped shallot boiled in with it and serve.

(1694). ÉPIGRAMMES OF LAMB À LA TOULOUSE (Épigrammes d'Agneau à la Toulouse).

Saw off the breasts from two racks of lamb, remove the bone covering the gristle and put the breasts in a saucepan lined with fat pork, carrots, onions and a garnished bouquet (No. 123); cook them just long enough to be able to remove the bones easily, and when this is done drain and range on a baking sheet and set a weight on top. From each rack make five covered cutlets, pare them nicely, season and fry to a fine color, dress and detach the stock from the pan with a little clear gravy (No. 404), with a little half-glaze sauce (No. 413). Pare the breasts into half hearts and when very cold round the angles and insert a bone into each pointed end of the meat; return these to the sautoir, and pour over the stock reduced to a half-glaze. Range the cutlets and breasts alternately or else in straight rows, one of cutlets and one of breasts, or if in a round have one half breasts and the other half cutlets; garnish the center with a Toulouse garnishing (No. 766) either laid in the center or else in a croustade, or should the epigrammes be dressed in a straight row, then place it around. Serve separately the stock strained through a sieve. A cutlet may be set on top a piece of breast which will serve as a croûton, and dress them crown-shaped with the garnishing in the center.

(1695). ÉPIGRAMMES OF LAMB, ANCIENT STYLE (Épigrammes d'Agneau à l'Ancienne).

Braise two breasts of lamb (No. 1694); drain and take out the bones reserving them to use later for imitating handles; let the meat get cold under a weight to reduce to half an inch, then pare nicely by suppressing the skin and cutting them up into half heart-shapes, season with salt and pepper and cover over entirely with Duxelle sauce (No. 461). When cold bread-crumb them in eggs. Scrape the reserve bones, sharpen one end and insert one in each half heart. For eight pieces of breast have eight covered cutlets, pare them nicely, season and broil or fry, then glaze them over with a brush. Brown the breasts in a sautoir with very hot clarified butter, when done drain and decorate the handles with frills (No. 10), also those of the cutlets and dress them in a circle, intercalating the breasts with the cutlets. Reduce some white wine velouté (No. 415) with mushroom broth and add to it a garnishing of quenelles and mushrooms; range this garnishing in the middle of the circle and decorate around with small glazed lamb's sweetbreads.

(1696). LAMB FRIES, CREAM HORSERADISH OR TOMATO SAUCE (Animelles d'Agneau à la Sauce Raifort à la Crème ou à la Sauce Tomate).

Skin and then cut them up either in two or four, according to their size; lay them in a vessel to season with salt, pepper, oil and lemon-juice, and leave to marinate for one hour; roll them in flour, immerse in beaten eggs and roll again in bread-crumbs, then fry them to a fine golden color and drain. Dress them on a napkin in a pyramid; garnish the top with a bunch of fried parsley, and around with quartered lemon. Serve separately either a cream horseradish sauce (No. 478) or a tomato sauce (No. 549).

(1697). LAMB HASLETS MARINATED (Fraissure d'Agneau à la Marinade).

Blanch the lights, drain and cut them up into inch and a half squares; melt some chopped fat pork in a saucepan and when very hot lay in the lights and fry them for a few minutes over a very brisk fire; add the heart cut into eight pieces and the liver in inch and a quarter pieces; season with salt, pepper, mignonette and a bunch of parsley garnished with thyme and bay leaf, sprinkle over with flour, then moisten with stock (No. 194a) and half white wine; let the whole cook till done to three-quarters, then lay in sixty small fried onions and a pound of small mushrooms; as soon as these are cooked, suppress the parsley, season nicely and notice whether the sauce is not too thin; when right, dress, pour the liquid over and garnish around with croûtons fried in butter.

Another Way.—This dish may also be made by placing the haslets cut up in an earthen crock with minced carrots, onions, thyme, bay leaves, sprigs of parsley, salt pepper, mace, vinegar and oil and allowing it to marinate for twelve hours, being careful to turn the meat several times so that it all reaches the marinade; drain and fry in butter, besprinkle over with flour, moisten with white or red wine and stock (No. 194a) season and boil slowly till thoroughly cooked, then serve.

(1698). LAMB HEAD, GÉNOISE OR VINAIGRETTE SAUCE (Tête d'Agneau Sauce Génoise ou Vinaigrette).

Bone the head as far as the eye, remove both the lower and upper jaw and the eyes, leaving on the crown only with the brain; steep and blanch the head for fifteen minutes, then refresh, wipe, singe and tie it up. Dilute some flour in cold water, adding to it some salt, pepper, onions, carrots, a garnished bouquet and vinegar; boil the head in this for two hours, then drain and untie it and dress on a napkin with parsley ranged around. Serve separately a well-buttered and acidulated génoise sauce (No. 470) or else a vinaigrette sauce (No. 634).

(1699). LAMB KIDNEYS À LA LULLY (Rognons d'Agneau à la Lully).

Cut eight skinned kidneys lengthwise; fry them in butter over a hot fire, season and add some finely chopped blanched shallots fried in butter, some minced mushrooms, chopped parsley and lemon juice. Just when prepared to serve, stir in a piece of fresh butter, dress the kidneys and pour the sauce over, garnishing around with small one inch in diameter potato croquettes (No. 2782) and then serve.

(1700). BROCHETTES OF LAMB KIDNEYS (Brochettes de Rognons d'Agneau).

Peel off the thin skin covering the kidneys, cut them across into three-sixteenth of an inch slices, season with salt and pepper, and baste with sweet oil. Thread these on skewers alternating each piece with a bit of bacon one inch square and an eighth of an inch thick; dip the whole into oil and roll in fresh bread-crumbs, broil them over a slow fire, dress and sprinkle with maître d'hôtel butter (No. 581).

(1701). LAMB KIDNEYS, FLEMISH STYLE (Rognons d'Agneau à la Flamande).

Fry colorless in butter one tablespoonful of chopped onions, one small chopped shallot, one whole clove of garlic, half a pound of fresh cut up mushrooms, salt, pepper, and cayenne; moisten with a gill of Madeira wine adding a little melted meat glaze (No. 402), some cream and a small piece of kneaded butter (No. 579); when ready remove the garlic. Skin eight lambs' kidneys, split each one lengthwise in two and fry them in butter; season as soon as they evaporate their moisture and are cooked; dress and pour the above sauce over.

(1702). LAMB KIDNEYS, GLAZED (Rognons d'Agneau Glacés).

Peel the skin from twelve kidneys, split each one into two parts; put a piece of butter in a pan with a tablespoonful of chopped shallot, fry without browning then add the kidneys; season with salt and pepper and as soon as they are well sized besprinkle with a few tablespoonfuls of melted glaze (No. 402); roll them in this off the fire and bestrew with chopped parsley, finishing with the juice of a lemon; dress on a very hot dish and surround with fried croûtons glazed over with a brush.

(1703). LAMB KIDNEYS ON SKEWERS (Rognons d'Agneau en Brochettes).

Split open the kidneys on the round side three-quarters through without separating the parts; run skewers through, having two kidneys to each metal skewer (Fig. 341); season with salt and pepper and cover over with oil, broil them first on the open side and when sufficiently done, turn them over on the other; dress them the open side uppermost, and lay on every kidney a little maître d'hôtel butter (No. 582). Squeeze a little lemon juice over and serve very hot.

(1704). STEWED LAMB KIDNEYS WITH MADEIRA AND WITH MUSHROOMS (Rognons d'Agneau Sautés au Madère et aux Champignons).

To obtain fine stewed kidneys it must be perfectly well understood that they should be sautéd over a quick fire in order to seize them rapidly and ought never to be allowed to boil or cook in their sauce. Suppress the skin from eight fresh lambs' kidneys; mince them up, removing all the hard parts. Heat some butter in a pan and when hot, put in the kidneys and fry them over a brisk fire; season with salt and pepper, and when the meats are sized without being dry, take them out with a skimmer, leaving the liquid in the pan. Fry a tablespoonful of chopped onions in butter in a sautoir, pour into it the reduced kidney gravy, and let the whole cook with a little half-glaze sauce (No. 413), and half a gill of Madeira wine, strain and skim the fat from the sauce, and pour it over the kidneys, heat them without boiling, and finish the stew with lemon juice and chopped parsley.

With Mushrooms.—Instead of using Madeira, reduce the sauce with mushroom essence (No. 392), and add some sliced mushrooms.

(1705). LEG OF LAMB À LA BERCY (Gigot d'Agneau à la Bercy).

Remove the thick loin and bone from a leg of yearling lamb and saw off the knuckle, remove about five inches of the meat to form a handle. Line a saucepan with fragments of fat pork, raw suet, roots, minced onions, and aromatics; lay in the meat, salt it over, and place on the fire for a few moments, turning it round; moisten to its height with light broth (No. 194a), and let boil; continue the boiling process while skimming well the surface, then close the saucepan and remove it back to a slower fire in order that it continue to cook but much more moderately; it will take from three to four hours, and the liquid should then be reduced to two-thirds; drain the leg, lay it in a small, deep, narrow baking pan, also its strained and skimmed stock reduced to a half-glaze (No. 400) with Madeira and gravy (No. 404); put it in the oven to become a fine color while basting frequently with its own stock, then strain this off, remove all its fat and reduce; pour a third of it over the dressed leg, garnish it with a frill (No. 10), and serve separately a bordelaise sauce (No. 436), stirred into the remainder of the stock.

(1706). LEG OF LAMB À LA BRITANNIA, OR GREEN SAUCE OR CAPER SAUCE (Gigot d'Agneau à la Britannia ou Sauce Verte ou Sauce aux Câpres).

Pare nicely a leg of yearling lamb, cut off the knuckle bone at the handle, remove about two inches of the meat from this to make a handle, scraping the bone clean, weigh the meat and plunge it into boiling water; let it boil for fifteen minutes for each pound and add to it salt, pepper a bunch of parsley garnished with thyme, bay leaf, clove of garlic, two cut carrots and four onions. After the leg is done, dress on a long dish, and trim it with a paper frill (No. 10), glaze the meat. Serve separately a well buttered espagnole sauce (No. 414), into which add lemon juice, mignonette and chopped parsley; garnish around with cauliflower boiled in salted water.

With Green Sauce.—Prepare it exactly the same as for the above, and when the leg is dressed serve without garnishing and with a green sauce (No. 473) served separately.

With Caper Sauce.—Prepare, cook and dress it as for the above; serve separately a caper sauce (No. 441).

(1707). LEG OF LAMB À LA FEARING, KERNEL (Noix de Gigot d'Agneau à la Fearing).

Lift the kernel from a leg of yearling lamb, pare it exactly the same as a kernel of veal and then fry it in clarified butter, drain this off and moisten with Madeira wine and some veal blond stock (No. 423), putting in very little at the time, only adding it as fast as it becomes reduced. Dress, strain the gravy, and reduce it with brown sauce (No. 414) and Madeira. For the garnishing have medium-sized whole truffles, cooked fresh mushrooms, cocks'-combs and kidneys, all being cooked separately. Dress these in separate and distinct clusters, and cover them all with part of the sauce, serving the rest of it in a sauce-bowl.

(1708). LEG OF LAMB, À LA GUYANE (Gigot d'Agneau à la Guyane).

Bone a leg of yearling lamb reserving the bone for the handle; fill the hollow space with a dressing made of fresh pork, bacon, cooked ham, chopped mushrooms and soaked and pressed out breadcrumbs, adding to it eggs and season with salt, pepper and nutmeg. Sew up the leg and then brown it in some fat pork; wet it with white wine and put in with it some roots, carrots, turnips, celery and onions; season, boil, skim and continue the boiling for three to four hours, then strain the stock, free it of its fat and keep back half of it, reduce the other half with espagnole sauce (No. 414) and a little tomato purée (No. 730) with a dash of cayenne added. Dress the leg, pare the handle nicely and range an Indian risot (No. 737) around; cover with the stock after it has been well reduced and place a paper frill (No. 10) on the handle bone. Pour the prepared sauce in a sauce-bowl and serve it at the same time.

(1709). LEG OF LAMB, KING'S PILAU (Gigot d'Agneau Pilau du Roi).

Have one pound of boned leg of lamb; pare off all the fat and sinews and then divide it into three-quarters of an inch pieces; have also a quarter of a pound of three-eighth inch dice of raw ham, fry all these in butter over a bright fire with a garnished bunch of parsley (No. 123); moisten with half a pint of stock (No. 194a), season and reduce to a glaze, then remoisten once more with another half pint and so on until the pilau is done and very rich; season with a dash of cayenne pepper and salt. Fry colorless a chopped onion in butter, add to it a quarter of a pound of washed and dried rice; when this is quite hot, wet it with twice its volume of the stock from the pilau and stock (No. 194a), cover, bring to a boil and place it in the oven for twenty minutes and as soon as done, add butter and parmesan. Fill a border mold (Fig. 139) with this, unmold on a dish, remove the bunch of parsley from the pilau and pour it into the center of the border, cover over with a layer of the same rice; reserved for the purpose, smooth it neatly with a knife, strew parmesan cheese on top, besprinkle with butter and brown in a hot oven.

(1710). SLICES OF LEG OF LAMB À LA DORDOGNE (Tranches de Gigot d'Agneau à la Dordogne).

These are slices of meat cut from a leg of raw spring lamb, free of all fat and sinews and should be three-sixteenths of an inch in thickness; season and cover them all with a chicken or forcemeat into which as much fine cooked herbs (No. 385) have been mixed; roll them up into cylinder shapes, run on small metal skewers (Fig. 176), then dip in melted butter and bread-crumbs; broil them over a slow fire till done, dress and pour over a half-glaze sauce (No. 413) buttered at the last moment with maître d'hôtel butter (No. 581).

(1711). SLICES OF LEG OF LAMB À LA PRÉVILLOT (Tranches de Gigot d'Agneau à la Prévillot).

Cut some three-sixteenths of an inch thick slices from the kernel of a raw leg of lamb, pare them into rounds, two inches in diameter, season with salt and fry in clarified butter. Fry colorless in butter, one ounce of onions cut in three-sixteenth inch squares, half a pound of mushrooms in quarter inch pieces, some peeled egg-plant cut in three-eighth inch squares and a little piece of garlic; moisten with clear gravy (No. 404) and half-glaze (No. 400) and reduce, then pour it into a dish, bestrew with chopped parsley and lay the slices of lamb over.

FIG. 348.

(1712). BLANQUETTE OF LEG OF LAMB (Blanquette de Gigot d'Agneau).

Take some cold leg of lamb, suppress from it all the fat and sinews, remove the skin and cut the meat into quarter-inch thick slices; pare them rounded and range the pieces in a sautoir, add to it some velouté sauce (No. 415) finished with a little mushroom liquor—enough to cover the meat—stir in salt, mignonette and leave the stew on the fire for a few moments before serving, but it must not be allowed to boil. Dress the blanquette either in a circle or a straight row, and thicken the sauce with four egg-yolks diluted in a little milk, fresh butter, vinegar or lemon juice; strain the sauce through a tammy and add to it some minced mushrooms, heat without boiling, pour it over the meat and garnish around with bread croûtons fried in butter.

(1713). LAMB OR MUTTON STEAK PLAIN, MAÎTRE D'HÔTEL (Steak d'Agneau ou de Mouton Nature, Maître d'Hôtel).

The steak is a slice either of lamb or mutton cut through the entire thickness of the leg; for

FIG. 349.

this a two-pronged steel fork is used (Fig. 349) thrust into a hole bored for the purpose in the butcher's

FIG. 350.

table, having it the same diameter as the handle of the fork; the leg is placed on the fork in such a way that the shank bone passes between the two prongs, then cut off slices from five to six-eighths of an inch thick; saw through the bone the same thickness as the meat. The fork is for the purpose of upholding the bone so that it can be sawed through more easily. Season the steak with salt, coat it over with oil and broil, serve on a very hot dish either plain or with a maître d'hôtel butter (No. 581).

(1714). LEG OF LAMB WITH CARROTS (Gigot d'Agneau aux Carottes).

Prepare the leg exactly the same as for gravy (No. 1715), only serve at the same time, but separately a garnishing of carrots made by parboiling about two pounds of new carrots cut into pear shapes and then cook them in a little stock (No. 194a) with salt and sugar added; finish cooking them very slowly tossing at times to have them all done alike, then thicken with four raw egg-yolks diluted with a gill of cream and a little fine butter; add some chopped parsley and serve with a thickened gravy (No. 405) in a separate sauce-boat the same time as the leg.

(1715). LEG OF YEARLING LAMB WITH GRAVY ROASTED (Gigot d'Agneau Tardif Rôti au jus).

Pare and beat a leg of yearling lamb to soften it, then run the spit skewer through to bring it out at the kernel without injuring the meat, allowing it to follow the course of the bone. Tie the bone tightly to the spit, place a long skewer over it and fasten firmly at each end. It will take from an hour to an hour and a quarter to cook. When done, dress and trim the handle with a frill, (No.10) and serve the dripping pan gravy at the same time as the meat, stirring into it a little clear gravy (No. 404); skim the fat from the top and pass it through a fine sieve.

To Roast in the Oven.—Lay the leg in a baking pan, besmear it with good fat and cook it for one hour to an hour and a quarter according to its size. It will take a few moments longer to roast it in the oven than on the spit.

(1716). LEG OF LAMB WITH PURÉE OF ONIONS WITH CREAM (Gigot d'Agneau à la Purée d'Oignons à la Crème).

Cut off the end of the shank bone of a leg of lamb; pare the leg to shape and remove the superfluous fat; roast it on the spit or else in a baking pan in a moderate oven, pouring over some melted fat, and basting it frequently; salt it over fifteen minutes before serving. Dress and trim the handle bone with a paper frill (No.10), and serve separately a purée of onions with cream prepared as follows: Mince two pounds of white onions, plunge them into boiling, salted water and let cook for five minutes, then drain very dry, and place them in a saucepan with four ounces of butter; cook the onions colorless, season and stir in two tablespoonfuls of flour; wet with cream in such a manner as to keep the mixture consistent, then set it into a slack oven, and when the onions have finished cooking, rub them through a sieve. Pour the purée back into the saucepan, mix well, heat and serve.

(1717). LOIN OF YEARLING LAMB, GERMAN STYLE (Longe d'Agneau Tardif à l'Allemande)

Take a loin of yearling lamb, or the part beginning from the top of the leg and extending as far as the first rib on the rack; remove the aitchbone without injuring the minion fillet, pare carefully the fat from the interior, and remove the tough skin from the sirloin, season with pepper, salt and nutmeg. Roll this loin up, tie it firmly and then braise it in a mirepoix stock (No. 419) with a little brandy added. It will take two hours and a half to three hours to cook; drain, untie and set it under a light weight or under the press (No. 71) and when cold cut the meat into half heart-shaped slices and dress them in a circle on a baking dish, cover over with an allemande sauce (No. 407), besprinkle with bread-crumbs and a little grated parmesan cheese, pour butter over and set the dish in a moderate oven. When it has attained a fine color, withdraw from the oven and drain off the butter, garnish the center with minced truffles and mushrooms mixed with some lighter allemande sauce (No. 407).

(1718). LOIN OF LAMB WITH SAUTÉD TOMATOES (Longe d'Agneau aux Tomates Sautées).

Proceed exactly as for German style (No. 1717), and when cold and the slices are pared heart-shaped, cover each piece with cooked fine herbs (No. 385), eggs and bread-crumbs and fry to a nice color; dress in a circle and fill the inside empty space with split and peeled tomatoes that have been pressed and fried in butter with shallots and seasoned with salt, pepper and chopped parsley. Serve a tomato sauce (No. 549) and half-glaze (No. 400) separately.

(1719). MINCED LAMB À LA RIVERA (Émincé d'Agneau à la Rivera).

Minces are generally made with cooked meats; cut quarter inch thick slices from the kernel part of a cold roast leg of lamb, pare them into rounds two and a half inches in diameter, range them in a sautoir pouring over a few spoonfuls of half-glaze sauce (No. 413), clear gravy (No. 404), and port wine, heating it all without boiling. Cut some sour apples into quarters, peel and remove the cores and seeds; lay them in a sautoir, besprinkle with sugar and cook them in a slack oven till done. Dress the minced meat in a circle with the apples in the center, and pour the port wine sauce over.

(1720). MINION FILLETS OF LAMB À LA BENOIST (Filets Mignons d'Agneau à la Benoist).

Pare the minion fillets, suppressing all fat and sinews; cut the meats transversely into small slices, flatten, pare them into rounds, and when ready season with salt; sauté them in half butter and half oil, drain on a plate, and glaze over with a brush. Lay each piece of meat on a thin crust of bread cut the same size as the noisettes, and on top of every one place a slice of cooked foies-gras cut also the same dimension; cover the whole quickly with a pretty thick white wine sauce (No. 492), in which grated parmesan has been added; bestrew with grated parmesan, and glaze the surface under a gas salamander (Fig. 123) or a very hot oven. Dress on a hot dish and set a fine slice of truffle on each; serve immediately.

(1721). MINION FILLETS OF LAMB À LA LANDGRAVE (Filets Mignons d'Agneau à la Landgrave).

Remove all the sinews from one or more minion fillets; season with salt, sweet oil, and lemon juice, then fry them in butter, and dress on slices of bread cut one and a quarter inches across by five inches long. Pour over a velouté sauce (No. 415) or allemande sauce (No. 407), having it well buttered and seasoned with Worcestershire sauce, and either mignonette or cayenne pepper.

(1722). MINION FILLETS OF LAMB À LA LEFORT (Filets Mignons d'Agneau à la Lefort).

Prepare the meats as for the Benoist (No. 1720), lay them on a dish, pour over a cold cooked marinade (No. 114) and let macerate for one hour, then drain and wipe. Roll them in oil to broil over a brisk fire turning them, and when done lay on a hot dish over slices of bread trimmed to the same shape and size as the noisettes and three-sixteenth of an inch in thickness, fried in clarified butter and glazed over. Set into a sauce-pan half a pint of tomato sauce (No. 549) and half a pint of gravy (No. 404), some branches of parsley, thyme, bay leaf and garlic; reduce this to a third, then strain and return it to the saucepan; at the very first boil take it from the fire and stir in two ounces of minced cèpes; pour this over the minion fillets.

(1723). MINION FILLETS OF LAMB AS VENISON (Filets Mignons d'Agneau en Chevreuil).

Pare six or eight yearling lamb fillets or else those of a young sheep, by suppressing all the fat and skin; cut them up through their length and on the bias, then beat the pieces and trim them into half hearts; lard with fine lardons (No. 1, Fig 52), and lay them in a deep china dish to cover with cooked and cold marinade (No. 114); macerate in this for a few hours, then drain and range them on the bottom of a sautoir into which put half butter and half oil; sauté them briskly and when done drain; glaze the surfaces and keep them for a few moments at the oven door. Dress on half heart-shaped bread croûtons fried in butter and arranged in a circle on a dish; pour over a poivrade sauce (No. 522).

(1724). MINION FILLETS OF LAMB CREAM SAUCE (Filets Mignons d'Agneau Sauce à la Crème).

Raise the minion fillets from three or four saddles of lamb, free them of their fat and sinews, pare and lard with small lardons (No. 3, Fig. 52), lay them in a vessel to season with salt, pepper, thyme, bay leaf, minced onions and nutmeg, let marinate for twelve hours turning them about occasionally, then drain and wipe dry. Fry these meats in some good hot fat, and when done drain it all off and detach the glaze with some fresh cream thickening with a little well buttered béchamel (No. 409). Dress in a circle and pour the sauce over.

(1725). MINION FILLETS OF LAMB IN SURPRISE (Filets Mignons d'Agneau en Surprise).

Pare and suppress all the fat from some lamb minion fillets, trim them into half hearts and make an incision on one side and flat across the thickness and almost through the entire width, but without separating the parts. Fry in butter a chopped shallot and four ounces of finely chopped truffles; moisten with four tablespoonfuls of Madeira wine, reduce this to a mere nothing, then stir in two spoonfuls of chopped parsley, a tablespoonful of meat glaze (No. 402) and a thickening of two raw egg-yolks; fill the incisions with this mixture, egg and bread crumb the meats and fry them in clarified butter. Pour a half-glaze sauce (No. 413), with Madeira over after dressing them in a circle.

(1726). MINION FILLETS OF LAMB PRINTANIÈRE (Filets Mignons d'Agneau Printanière).

Remove the fillets from a saddle of lamb, free them from sinews and fat. Make sufficient lamb quenelle forcemeat (No. 92) to fill a border mold indented slightly on the top (Fig. 139), buttered and decorated with truffles; then fill with the forcemeat and lay it in a saucepan with boiling water to reach to half its heighth, place in a slack oven till firm to the touch. Cut up the meat into bias slices, each one weighing about four ounces when pared; salt and fry them in butter over a brisk fire, when done, take them out, wipe and roll in a sautoir with a very little hot meat glaze (No. 402), then dress them at once crown-shaped on the border of poached forcemeat, fill in the center with a garnishing of spring vegetables and pour a little half-glaze sauce (No. 413) to which is added some tomato sauce (No. 549) on the dish and serve some separately.

(1727). MINION FILLETS OF LAMB WITH SHALLOT SAUCE AND MARROW, ROASTED AND LARDED (Filets Mignons Piqués et Rôtis à la Sauce Échalote et Moelle).

Lift some minion fillets and suppress from them all the fat and sinews, then lard them with very fine lardons (No. 3, Fig. 52), lay them in a baking pan, salt over and baste with drippings, then roast them in a very hot oven. Eight or ten minutes should suffice to have them done properly, dress on oblong slices of toast and cover with some clear gravy (No. 404) and serve separately a shallot sauce with marrow.

Shallot Sauce with Marrow.—Place in a saucepan one ounce of butter with two shallots, cut in one-eighth of an inch squares as much meat glaze (No. 402) as butter, salt, pepper, lemon juice and chopped parsley, place on the fire for two minutes, then add some marrow, cut in quarter inch squares and previously blanched by dipping in boiling water.

(1728). MINION FILLETS OF LAMB WITH TRUFFLES—SAUTÉD (Filets Mignons d'Agneau Sautés aux Truffes).

Suppress the fat and trim neatly two lamb fillets half heart-shape, cut incisions on one side to a third of their depth and season with salt, nutmeg and pepper, stuff with cooked fine herbs (No. 385), and close the opening with a little lamb quenelle forcemeat (No. 92); fry them quickly in butter and when they are stiffened drain off the fat and replace it by a tablespoonful of melted meat glaze (No. 402); roll the fillets in this, dress them on a dish and put a little espagnole sauce (No. 414) in with the glaze remaining in the pan, let this cook and reduce, then add a piece of butter and some lemon juice to the sauce. Pour over the fillets range around slices of truffles that have been moistened with Madeira sauce (No. 492).

(1729). NECK OF LAMB WITH CABBAGE (Collet d'Agneau aux Choux).

Cut the neck a little long on the rib side; leave four rib bones on it; bone it all thoroughly, remove the sinewy and fat parts, then season with salt and pepper, stuff with lamb forcemeat made of cold finely chopped lamb, an equal quantity of soaked and pressed out bread-crumbs, fried, chopped onions, minced cooked mushrooms, chopped parsley, chopped up cooked ham and raw eggs. Fill the neck with this, sew up the meat so as to enclose well the stuffing and braise it in a very little stock (No.194a) for three hours; remove the threads, glaze, dress and surround with cabbage. Strain the stock, add to it a little brown sauce (No. 414), bring it to a boil, skim off the fat carefully and when reduced serve in a sauce-boat.

(1730). NOISETTES OF SHOULDER OF LAMB, EPICUREAN (Noisettes d'Épaule d'Agneau Épicurienne).

These noisettes or glands are found in the fatty part of the shoulder near the shoulder blade; remove all the skin which envelops them. Fill the bottom of a flat saucepan with thin slices of fat pork, lay the noisettes on top, and moisten with a mirepoix stock (No. 419); cover over with more slices of the pork, and let cook in a slow oven from three-quarters to one hour according to their size. When the noisettes are done, strain the stock through a fine tammy and skim well the fat. Decorate a low border mold (Fig. 139) with fanciful cuts of truffles, fill it with chicken and cream forcemeat (No. 75), and poach in a bain-marie, the same as a timbale; then unmold it on a dish and garnish the interior of the border with mushrooms stewed and moistened with reduced cream and a little béchamel (No. 409). Range on top the noisettes from which the fat has been removed and then glazed in their own stock after it has been thoroughly reduced.

(1731). FORE QUARTER OF LAMB WITH STUFFED TOMATOES—ON THE SPIT (Quartier de Devant d'Agneau à la Broche aux Tomates Farcies).

Detach the shoulder from the rack on the covered rib side and leave the neck side without removing it; bone the shoulder, leaving only the end bone, and pass a skewer through the shoulder and the breast; adjust or lay it on the spit, fastening the two ends with a strong string; run a skewer through the meat near the shoulder, having it run through the hole in the spit to prevent the meat from slipping while cooking. Cook in front of a brisk fire basting frequently; it will take from thirty to forty-five minutes; when nearly done, salt it over. Dress the meat on a very hot dish and serve clear gravy (No. 404) separately; garnish the end bone with a frill (No. 10), and set around baked stuffed tomatoes (No. 2842).

(1732). HIND QUARTER OF LAMB WITH MINT SAUCE OR COLBERT SAUCE (Quartier de Derrière d'Agneau à la Sauce Menthe ou à la Sauce Colbert).

Pare very carefully a good hind quarter of lamb; suppress and pare the end bone or handle bone after sawing it two inches below the joint of the leg; cut away the meat two inches down, then scrape the bone clean; now lay the quarter in a baking-pan (Fig. 136), salt it evenly, and baste with dripping fat; set it in a moderate oven and let cook for three-quarters to one hour. Dress on a long hot dish, trim the handle with a frill (No. 10), pour a little of its gravy over, and serve with a separate mint sauce (No. 616) or Colbert sauce (No. 451).

(1733). RACK OF LAMB, CASTILLANE SAUCE—BROILED (Carré d'Agneau Grillé à la Sauce Castillane).

Have a good, tender rack of lamb; remove the chine bone, cut the ribs very short, and pare the fillets to the bone without taking any meat from the ribs; separate all these ribs by giving sharp blows with the dull edge of a knife on the chine bone, to break the bones, but without cutting through the meats; pass a skewer between the middle of the rack, and the rib bones in such a way as to uphold the rack in its original shape; dip it into melted butter, season with salt and pepper, and roll it in white bread-crumbs, then broil over a slow fire for twenty-five to thirty minutes. Dress, withdraw the skewer, and serve with a separate Castillane sauce (No. 443), or any other suitable one, such as bordelaise (No. 436), or Périgueux (No. 517).

(1734) RACK OF LAMB WITH ARTICHOKES—SAUTÉD (Carré d'Agneau Sauté aux Artichauts).

Cut short the breasts of two racks of lamb; take out the chine bones and put the meats into a sautéing-pan with melted fat pork and a bunch of parsley containing aromatics and a clove of garlic, season and fry over a brisk fire. Aside from this cut eight small, slightly pared, tender and raw artichoke bottoms in two; lay them in another sauté pan with some oil, then season and fry them over a moderate fire. As soon as the lamb is nicely done, drain off the fat, pour over half a bottleful of white wine and let reduce to a glaze; baste the meats with a little half-glaze sauce, (No. 413) and take them from the fire to lay on a hot dish; suppress the garnished parsley and surround the meats with the artichokes.

(1735). RACK OF LAMB WITH PURÉE OF SPLIT PEAS—LARDED AND ROASTED (Carré d'Agneau Piqué et Rôti à la Purée de Pois Secs).

Select a good tender rack of lamb; suppress the chine bone, cut the rib bones short and straight and pare the fillet meats without taking any from the ribs; lard the meat lengthwise with medium sized lardons (No. 3, Fig. 52), then wrap the rack in a sheet of oiled paper and attach it on the spit fastening it with a skewer; let it roast for twenty or thirty-five minutes while basting frequently; a few moments before serving unwrap to brown it nicely, then salt it over, withdraw the skewers and serve with a little clear gravy (No. 404) poured over, and some more in a sauce-boat to be served at the same time. The above dish is to be served with a garnishing of purée of split peas (No. 724) in a vegetable dish.

(1736). DOUBLE OR SADDLE OF LAMB WITH THE LEGS AND POTATO CROQUETTES
(Double ou Selle d'Agneau avec les Gigots aux Croquettes de Pommes).

Cut half a lamb crosswise that is the entire saddle with the two legs, leaving one of the ribs attached to the saddle, saw off the knuckle of the leg bones, make a handle two inches long by removing the meat and scraping the bone well; roll the flanks under, tie the loin with three rounds of string having a knot at each round, then wrap the meat in a very heavy buttered paper and let roast either on the spit or in the oven. Unwrap it fifteen minutes before serving so as to brown it nicely, then dress and glaze, garnish around the dish with potato croquettes (No. 2782) and decorate both legs with paper frills (No. 10); serve separately a rather light half-glaze sauce (No. 413).

(1737). FORE SADDLE OF LAMB WITH CHESTNUTS (Selle d'Agneau de Devant aux Marrons).

Select a fore saddle of lamb with the two racks, lift off the shoulders and cut the rack bones in such a way that the saddle is not more than four inches high through its entire length; suppress the skin covering the fat and then roast it in a pan in the oven; this will take about twenty minutes. When done dress on a long dish, glaze and garnish around the meat with peeled chestnuts braised with branches of celery, and pour over some gravy (No. 404) or else serve it separately.

(1738). HIND SADDLE OF LAMB, À LA BRIGHTON (Selle d'Agneau à la Brighton).

Prepare and trim a saddle of lamb as explained for the braised saddle (No. 1745); cover it over with "crepruette," (caul fat) or thin slices of fat pork. Boil twelve to fifteen quarts of soup stock in a saucepan, season it with salt, pepper, mignonette, a bunch of parsley garnished with thyme and bay leaf, two quartered carrots and two onions, one of them having two cloves in it, then boil and skim. About one hour and a quarter before serving put in the saddle and let boil unceasingly for an hour to an hour and a half according to its size; when done drain it off, untie, glaze and dress; garnish around with Villeroi cauliflower (No. 2716), and serve a Viennese sauce (No. 558) separately.

(1739). HIND SADDLE OF LAMB À LA CHANCELIÈRE (Selle d'Agneau à la Chancelière).

Prepare the saddle the same as for the turnips (No. 1745), and when nearly cooked drain, and pare nicely and evenly; place in a baking pan, cover the top with a coating of beaten eggs, and dredge fine bread-crumbs over, pour on some melted butter and brown in a hot oven. Strain the broth, reduce it to a half-glaze and add to this a little tomato sauce (No. 549) and béchamel (No. 409); serve this with the saddle. Line some tartlet molds with fragments of very thin puff paste (No. 146), fill them with well-cooked fat rice stirred in with some béchamel (No. 409) and seasoned with salt and nutmeg and the well-beaten egg-whites; fifteen minutes before serving the meat set these in the oven and when they are cooked range them around the saddle and serve.

(1740). HIND SADDLE OF LAMB À LA FLORENTINE (Selle d'Agneau à la Florentine).

Roast a saddle of yearling lamb in the oven having it laid in a baking pan; salt and baste with dripping. It will take from an hour to an hour and a half to have it properly roasted if the oven be very hot. When done, dress and glaze the meat, surround it with a garnishing of artichoke bottoms à la Florence (No. 2677), and serve with a separate white Colbert sauce (No. 451).

(1741). HIND SADDLE OF LAMB À LA PAGANINI (Selle d'Agneau à la Paganini).

Have the saddle prepared and cooked the same as for Florentine (No. 1740); dress the meat and garnish around with slices of foies-gras intercalated with slices of truffles; cover these with a suprême sauce (No. 547) and lay on top partridge quenelles decorated with truffles. The saddle may be garnished with skewers thrust into it composed of double cocks'-combs and glazed truffles. Serve a sauce-bowl of suprême sauce at the same time as the saddle.

(1742). HIND SADDLE OF LAMB À LA SANFORD (Selle d'Agneau à la Sanford).

Prepare and cook the meat the same as for Florentine (No. 1740), but instead of artichoke bottoms have a garnishing of croustades made of puff paste parings (No. 146) and filled with a Sanford apple sauce (No. 588) pushed in through a pocket, lay on top of each a paste cover made by having three thin flats of paste of different dimensions the smallest one on top, serve separately some rich gravy (No. 404).

(1743). HIND SADDLE OF LAMB, AMERICAN STYLE (Selle d'Agneau à l'Américaine).

Cut off the hind saddle between the first and second ribs, remove both legs, cutting them away in a round from off the loin and toward the flanks; suppress also a thin peel covering the skin and some of the loin and kidney fat; roll the flanks over on themselves, keep them in position with four turns of twine, then run the spit between the twine and saddle; hold the latter in position with several skewers which should run through both the saddle and spit (Fig. 344), then have a sufficiently strong skewer to run into the loin marrow bone fastening it securely on the spit with a string, place over the saddle a long skewer held to the spit with two rings—one at each end of the saddle or instead of rings strong twine may be used; cover the meat with heavy buttered paper and maintain it in position with four rows of string. The cradle spit (Fig. 116) is better adapted for roasting this cut of meat; all that is necessary is to place the saddle in the middle. One hour before serving, put the saddle in the spit and ten minutes before needed, unwrap, glaze, and dress on a dish; serve with a separate half-glaze sauce (No. 413).

(1744). HIND SADDLE OF LAMB, FRENCH STYLE (Selle d'Agneau à la Française).

Pare a saddle suppressing the skin and superfluous fat, roll the flaps or flanks under; truss and braise it in a brazière (Fig. 134) with bits of fat pork, minced carrots and onions; season and let the meat smother while turning it over; cover with a pint of stock (No. 194a) and reduce it slowly to a glaze, then recover to its exact heighth with hot broth, and let cook with the lid on over a slow fire or in a moderate oven, basting and turning frequently; should it be insufficiently moistened, add more hot broth. When the saddle is almost done, drain and trim it; strain the stock, skim off the fat carefully, and return the meat to the braziere to finish cooking, and glaze in a moderate oven.

Dressing.—Drain the saddle, detach both fillets from the top, and cut them into even slices, then return them to their original position; lay the saddle on a dish that can be placed in the oven. Have three quarts of béchamel sauce (No. 409), reduced with cream and mushroom broth; when sufficiently reduced take it from the fire and stir into it a quarter of a pound of grated parmesan, three ounces of butter, and a little cayenne pepper; beat it thoroughly until partially cold, then cover the saddle with it smoothing the surface neatly; bestrew with grated parmesan, and finish baking in a hot oven. Pour a little of the stock around the meat, serving the remainder separately, and send to the table accompanied by a vegetable dish of glazed cucumbers (No. 2733).

(1745). HIND SADDLE OF LAMB WITH MASHED TURNIPS—BRAISED (Selle d'Agneau Braisée à la Purée de Navets).

Trim a saddle of yearling lamb, suppress the skin that covers it and the surplus of fat near the tail; take away very little of the kidney fat; roll the flanks under and tie the saddle with four rows of string making a knot at each row; lay it in a low braziere lined with fragments of fat pork, sliced onions and carrots, celery roots and a bunch of parsley garnished with thyme and bay leaf, and let the meat smother while turning it over; moisten with one pint of hot stock (No. 194a); after it has slowly fallen to a glaze cover it to its height with more hot stock and let it fall very slowly to a glaze once more, then remoisten to its full height and cook while covered on a slow fire, turning it over and basting it frequently. Should the stock reduce too freely then add more hot stock. Two hours and a half will suffice for the cooking, then drain and pare the meat, strain the stock, and remove the fat and return it once more to the braziere with the saddle and let this cook for half an hour longer, glazing it in a moderate oven; then dress and surround with mashed turnips pushed through a pocket into round tartlet crusts and laid one beside the other; pour one-third of the stock over the meat and thicken the remainder with reduced espagnole sauce (No. 414) and Madeira, serving it in a sauce-boat.

(1746). HIND SADDLE OF LAMB WITH GRAVY—ROASTED (Selle d'Agneau Rôtie au Jus).

Trim a saddle of lamb by removing the legs and skin that covers it, also a little of the fat on the thick loin end and kidneys; roll the flaps over on themselves and tie the saddle firmly with four rows of string making a knot at each row; lay it in a baking pan, sprinkle over with salt, pour some fat on top and set it in a moderate oven; it will take from an hour to an hour and a quarter to roast a saddle without the legs. Serve the meat with some good clear gravy (No. 404).

(1747) SLICES OF SADDLE OF LAMB WITH PURÉE OF BEANS (Tranches de Selle d'Agneau à la Purée de Haricots).

Cut transversal slices three-quarters of an inch in thickness from a small saddle of lamb; season with salt and fry till done in clarified butter. Dress them in a straight row on a long dish, one piece overlapping the other; surround with a purée of white beans (No. 706) pushed through a pastry bag (Fig. 179). Cover the meats with a half-glaze sauce (No. 413) having some chopped fresh mushrooms added to it, and serve some of the same sauce in a sauce-boat.

(1748). SHOULDER OF LAMB À LA BENTON (Épaule d'Agneau à la Benton).

Bone a shoulder of lamb retaining the end or the handle bone; saw off the knuckle an inch from the handle and season the meat with salt, pepper and nutmeg, roll it into an elongated shape, tie it round with six rows of string making a knot at each row. Fry the shoulder lightly in a saucepan containing butter and melted fat pork and when lightly browned, drain off the butter and moisten to three-quarters of an inch of its height with stock (No. 194a), add a bunch of parsley garnished with bay leaf, as much thyme and a clove of garlic, boil and skim, then cook in a slow oven for about two hours, basting the meat frequently with its own broth. Twenty minutes before serving, put in four ounces of minced onions fried to a light color in butter and finish to cook and glaze the shoulder. Have two pounds of medium-sized, peeled, quartered and cored apples, range them on a buttered sautéing pan, pour over a little butter and sprinkle with sugar, then cook them in a slack oven. Prepare and fry two pounds of potatoes cut in cylinders one inch in circumference, and cut across three-sixteenths of an inch thick; soak them in cold water for an hour, then drain, wipe and fry in white frying lard until they assume a nice color, then salt over. Drain the shoulder, lay it in the center of a dish and glaze it over; strain and skim the fat from the stock, reduce it to the consistency of a light syrup and pour a little of it in the bottom of the dish; set the apples at both ends and arrange the fried potatoes at the sides; serve the reduced gravy at the same time, but separately.

(1749). SHOULDER OF LAMB, À LA DESSAIX (Épaule d'Agneau à la Dessaix).

Bone two shoulders of lamb leaving on only the end or handle bones; remove all the sinews and fat, have some chopped farce (No. 68) put the whole into a mortar to pound, season, and add a handful of soaked and pressed bread-crumbs, one whole egg and a few spoonfuls of cooked fine herbs (No. 385); use this forcemeat for stuffing the shoulders, then sew them up so as to enclose the stuffing, and lay them in a narrow saucepan lined with bits of fat pork and minced roots; season, moisten the meats with a little stock (No. 194a), and when they are cooked, and of a fine color, drain them off, untie, and remove from the end bone the meat so as to be able to trim them with paper frills (No. 10). Dress on a dish, pour over some of their own stock, and reduce the remainder with as much espagnole (No. 414), until the consistency of a half-glaze sauce is obtained; garnish around with half heart-shaped croustades made of mashed potatoes, dipped in eggs, then in bread-crumbs, the surfaces smoothed nicely, and then slit them all round a quarter of an inch from the edge; and fry; when finished, drain, remove the covers, empty and refill the insides with a small vegetable macédoine (No. 680) combined with béchamel (No. 409), serving a sauce-boatful of half-glaze sauce (No. 413) at the same time.

(1750). SHOULDER OF LAMB À LA GARNIER (Épaule d'Agneau à la Garnier).

After boning two shoulders of lamb, leaving on only the end or handle bones, stuff the insides with lamb forcemeat (No. 92); braise them the same as for à la Benton (No. 1748); then drain, skim, and reduce the stock with an equal quantity of espagnole sauce (No. 414). Dress and glaze the shoulders, then garnish around with whole chestnuts (No. 654); braised celery (No. 2721); cover the garnishing with a part of the sauce and serve what remains separately.

(1751). SHOULDER OF LAMB WITH CUCUMBERS (Épaule d'Agneau aux Concombres).

Prepare and braise two shoulders of spring lamb as explained for à la Benton (No. 1748), when done, untie and glaze; dress them either on a garnishing of cucumbers with Danish sauce (No. 457), or else on a macédoine garnishing (No. 680), or a jardinière (No. 677). Strain the stock, remove all its fat, and reduce it to the consistency of a light syrup, serving it in a sauce-boat the same time as the shoulders.

These shoulders may be dressed in the shape of ducks or hornpipes, dishing them upon the same garnishings.

(1752). SHOULDER OF LAMB WITH GLAZED VEGETABLES—STUFFED (Épaule d'Agneau Farcie aux Légumes Glacés).

Boil an unsmoked red beef tongue in water for three hours before serving, cut it up into quarter inch thick slices and from these remove two and half inch diameter pieces with a round cutter, keep them warm in a sautoir with a little stock (No. 194a). Bone thoroughly two shoulders of spring lamb, suppress the fat and sinews, then season the inside, cover the surfaces with a thin layer of lamb forcemeat (No. 92) and bestrew with fine cooked herbs (No. 385). Roll the shoulders lengthwise, tie them firmly so to keep them in proper shape, then braise in a little moistening without browning. Drain and trim the ends, then cut the remainder of the meat into half inch thick slices, pare them rounded two and a half inches in diameter, and dress them in a straight row on a circle intercalating each slice with one of tongue; arrange either around or in the center, according to the way they are dressed with glazed carrots, turnips and small onions; strain the stock, skim off its fat and reduce it with espagnole (No. 414) to the consistency of a half-glaze sauce (No. 413); serve this separately.

(1753). SHOULDERS OF LAMB WITH PURÉE OF CELERY—STUFFED (Épaules d'Agneau Farcies à la Purée de Céleri).

Bone two shoulders of lamb keeping on the handle bone and sawing the knuckle one inch from it; free the meat of fat and sinews, pare nicely, then season with salt, pepper, and nutmeg.

Dressing for Stuffing the Shoulders.—Take one pound of sausage meat, half a pound of finely chopped raw ham, four tablespoonfuls of finely chopped onions, half a pound of minced mushrooms, two tablespoonfuls of chopped parsley, a quarter of a pound of dry bread-crumbs, two whole eggs and a seasoning of salt, pepper and nutmeg. Fill the two shoulders with this dressing, roll them up and sew them in such a way that none of it can escape, garnish the bottom of a saucepan with slices of fat pork, set the shoulders on top and moisten with a white wine mirepoix stock (No. 419); boil and simmer slowly for two hours and a half. As soon as the shoulders are done glaze and strain the stock, remove all its fat and reduce it to the consistency of a syrup. Dress the shoulder either on a celery purée (No. 711) or a tomato purée (No. 730), or one of artichokes (No. 704), or else of cucumbers (No. 714), macédoine (No. 680), or jardinière (No. 677); trim the handle bones with frills (No. 10) and serve the gravy apart.

(1754). STEWED LAMB, DUGLÉRÉ (Ragoût d'Agneau à la Dugléré).

Have an equal weight of the rack, breast, and loin of lamb; suppress the skin from the rack, also the chine bone, and cut the ribs quite short nearly level with the large fillet, then divide these meat across in even pieces each one being an inch and a quarter wide. Cut the breast into inch and a half squares after paring and suppressing the skin; cut off all the fat from the loin and remove the skin and chine bone, then divide it into inch and a quarter wide pieces. Fry these meats colorless in either lard or butter with two medium onions, one small carrot cut lengthwise in four and a pinch of sugar; when they begin to brown drain off the fat and moisten to half the heighth with stock (No. 194a) adding a garnished bouquet (No. 123) ;let the liquid fall to a glaze not allowing it at any time to cook too fast, and keeping it well covered; have the meats brown nicely, then remoisten to their heighth and reduce this liquid. When half cooked drain off the piece to pare and return them again to the saucepan with the broth and half a bottleful of white wine; when the meat is thoroughly done and the liquid reduced to half, throw in some fresh green peas, young carrots, small onions, small new potatoes and new flageolet beans, first putting in those taking the longest to cook, having previously browned the onions in a frying pan. Finish cooking. Dress the meats around the vegetables, skim the fat from the stock and strain it over all.

(1755). STEWED LAMB, NAVARIN (Ragoût d'Agneau Navarin).

Suppress all the bones of a leg of lamb, remove the fat and sinews, then cut it up into squares an inch and a half in size; put these pieces into a bowl to season with salt and pepper, adding a bunch of parsley garnished with thyme, bay leaf, garlic and cloves, also some Madeira wine, let marinate for seven hours; after the lapse of this time drain the meat and fry with grated fat pork and half a pound of small dice pieces of blanched bacon; moisten with the Madeira from the marinade adding also the aromatics and some brown sauce (No. 414); cook the whole over a slow fire for two and a half hours skimming and adding half a bottleful of white wine. After the stew has been cooking for one hour put in with it a quart of fried and slightly browned turnip balls. Three-quarters of an hour later both meat and turnips should be done, skim nicely, season to taste and serve, dressing the meat in the center of the dish, the turnips around and the strained sauce over all.

(1756). STEWED LAMB, PARISIAN STYLE (Ragoût d'Agneau à la Parisienne).

Bone and cut off all fat and sinews from a shoulder of lamb; divide it into one inch and three-quarters pieces and fry these either in butter or good fat; when the meat is a golden color, drain off all the fat and moisten with one quart of brown sauce (No. 414), a pint of stock (No. 194a) and a pint of white wine; add a bunch of parsley garnished with thyme, bay leaf and garlic, salt and pepper. Boil, skim and simmer, and after it has been cooking for three-quarters of an hour put in forty small onions fried in butter and as many potato balls, three-quarters of an inch in circumference, half a pint of tomato purée (No. 730), and a pound of small, cooked mushroom heads; it takes about an hour and a half to cook this stew properly. When cooked remove the bunch of parsley, skim off the fat from the stew and dress in the center of a dish, surround it with the vegetables and pour the strained sauce over all.

(1757). STEWED LAMB, PERUVIAN STYLE (Ragoût d'Agneau à la Péruvienne).

Cut up into inch and a half squares one leg of raw yearling lamb; season the pieces with salt, pepper, allspice, two ounces of minced onions and squeeze the juice of a lemon over; let macerate in this for two hours, then drain them off and fry in butter; moisten with stock (No. 194a) and espagnole sauce (No. 414)—half of each—to three-quarters of the height of the meats, then cook in a slow oven. After the meat is done, skim the fat from the stock and add to the stew one quart of cooked Lima beans (No. 2699); let the whole simmer on the range for fifteen minutes, then dress with the sauce and garnish around with sweet peppers fried in oil.

(1758). STEWED LAMB, IRISH STYLE (Ragoût d'Agneau à l' Irlandaise).

Cut some lamb tendrons into squares: shorten the rib bones of a rack, cutting it about level with the large fillet, suppress the skin and chine bone, and with the parings of both these meats, prepare a mutton broth. Plunge the tendrons into boiling water placed in a saucepan, put it on the fire, skim, then drain and pare the pieces and return them to the same saucepan with two small onions, one garnished bouquet, two finely shredded raw potatoes and proper seasoning; moisten to the height of the meat with the prepared broth, strained and free of fat. Cook the stew over a moderate fire in such a way that when the lamb is nearly done, the liquid is found reduced to half and slightly thickened, and the potatoes well dissolved, pass the sauce through a tammy; now add to it a garnishing of raw potatoes pared like olives and about the size of a walnut; and small blanched onions, also the meat; season with salt and pepper and continue to cook, both the meat and potatoes and onions should be done at the same time. Dress the lamb in a deep dish with the potatoes and onions around and strain the sauce over.

(1759). STEWED LAMB WITH TURNIPS (Ragoût d'Agneau aux Navets).

To be made with two pounds of shoulder and one pound of breast of lamb. Cut up into one and three-quarters to two inch pieces, the best part of a shoulder and breast, having two-thirds of the shoulder to one-third of the breast. Heat some lard in a saucepan, put in the meat and brown while stirring, season with salt and a pinch of sugar, and when of a nice reddish brown, dredge over a spoonful of flour, five minutes later, drain off the fat and moisten to a little more than the heighth of the meat with broth (No. 194a), adding a bunch of parsley garnished with thyme and bay leaf and a few grains of pepper. Boil together for five minutes, then withdraw the saucepan to a slower fire in order to cook the lamb without reducing the liquid too rapidly; pour in at intervals a few spoonfuls of broth and when the meat is three-quarters done, mix into the stew a garnishing of turnips shaped into balls or else quartered, browned in a pan with butter. Finish to cook the turnips in the stew. Just when ready to serve rub a piece of garlic on an iron spoon and let it steep in the stew for a few moments, dress the meat on to a dish, garnish around with the turnips and pour the strained sauce over.

(1760). LAMB SWEETBREADS À LA FINANCIÈRE (Ris d'Agneau à la Financière).

Lard with lardons (No. 4, Fig. 52) some even-sized lamb sweetbreads previously parboiled, refreshed and put to cool under a weight, range them closely together in a sautoir lined with fat pork, roots and minced onions; moisten to half their heighth with stock (No. 194a), and let this liquid fall to a glaze; moisten once more and finish cooking in a moderate oven, basting over frequently in order to glaze them well. Prepare a rice border, shaping it by hand and channeling with a piece of wet turnip, or else a molded one may be used, pour some butter over this, and brown it in the oven. Range in the center of the border a financière garnishing composed of truffles, quenelles, escalops of foies-gras, mushrooms, and cock's-combs, pouring over a financière sauce (No. 464), place the glazed sweetbreads on top of this garnishing.

(1761). LAMB SWEETBREADS À LA JOINVILLE (Ris d'Agneau à la Joinville).

Braise some lambs' sweetbreads as indicated for the financière (No. 1760). Prepare and pound a border made of forcemeat (No. 79), place it on a dish; lay a croustade made either of bread or paste in the center of the border; place the sweetbreads after they are well glazed around, and fill the croustade with a garnishing composed of quenelles, mushrooms, truffles, and a suprême sauce (No. 547) into which lobster butter (No. 580) has been added. Between every sweetbread lay a slice of tongue cut out to imitate a cocks'-comb and glazed with meat glaze (No. 402) and on the summit of the garnishing place some round chicken quenelles decorated with truffles (No. 154).

(1762). LAMB SWEETBREADS À LA SÉVIGNÉ (Ris d'Agneau à la Sévigné).

Soak and parboil some hearts of lamb's sweetbreads, lay them in a sautoir lined with bardes of fat pork, sliced carrots and onions and a garnished bunch of parsley (No. 123); moisten to their heighth with some stock (No.194a), boil, skim and finish cooking in a slow oven. Put them to press in round rings; when cold take them out, cover with a thick Villeroi (No. 560), let get cold and then dip in beaten eggs, then in bread-crumbs. Poach some quenelle forcemeat (No. 92) in Savarin molds decorated with truffles, unmold and fill the hollow centers with a salpicon of truffles and mushrooms, cover over with a suprême sauce (No. 547). Have the sweetbreads fried in clarified butter and laid around the garnishing.

(1763). LAMBS' TAILS À LA CONTI (Queues d'Agneau à la Conti).

Parboil twelve yearling lambs' tails cut from the saddle at the beginning of the tail. Cover the bottom of a sautoir (Fig. 130) with fragments of fat pork, minced carrots and onions and a garnished bouquet (No. 123); put in the tails and moisten to their entire height with broth (No. 194a), then let them cook slowly in the oven. When done, drain them on a baking sheet, besprinkle with salt and set a weight on top, strain the stock, remove the fat and reduce it to half; when the tails are cold, pare them by cutting off the ends so that they remain only three and a half inches long, dip in melted butter, then in bread-crumbs and broil on a slow fire, dress on a dish in a circle, glaze well and fill the inside space with a thick lentil purée (No. 719). A thick half-glaze sauce (No. 413) accompanies these tails having it served separately.

(1764). TENDRONS OR GRISTLE OF LAMB WITH ROBERT SAUCE—BROILED (Tendrons d'Agneau Grillés à la Sauce Robert).

Raise the cartilaginous parts from the breast which are called the tendrons or gristle, remove the breast bones keeping on only the tendrons, season with salt, pare into half hearts and lay them in a double broiler after brushing over with oil, and then broil them on a slow fire; when done dress on a Robert sauce (No. 533), insert a small bone into each piece to represent a handle and trim it with a paper frill (No. 10).

(1765). LAMBS' TONGUES WITH OLIVES (Langues d'Agneau aux Olives).

Steep and parboil twelve lambs' tongues, then cook them in stock (No. 194a) drain and suppress the white skin that covers them. Line a saucepan with slices of fat pork, range the tongues on top one beside the other, and braise them in a mirepoix stock (No. 419) with Madeira. After they are cooked place them under the pressure of a light weight to cool, then divide them laterally in two; pare nicely and heat in some clear gravy (No. 404), glaze and dress them in a circle, filling the interior with a garnishing of blanched olives combined with Madeira sauce (No. 492) reduced with the stock.

(1766). LAMBS' TROTTERS À LA BORDELAISE AND À LA BORDELAISE WENBERG (Pieds d'Agneau à la Bordelaise et à la Bordelaise Wenberg).

Scald, scrape and singe twenty-four lambs' feet, split them underneath through the thickness of the meat their whole length, remove the pointed hoof bones leaving the foot whole. Dilute a small handful of flour with cold water in a saucepan able to hold three gallons, add to it salt, whole peppers, parsley leaves, thyme, bay leaf, cloves, garlic and carrots cut in four; put in the feet and let cook for five hours; when done, drain. Fry six shallots colorless in butter, moisten them with red wine, a little espagnole sauce (No. 414), brandy and meat glaze (No. 402); season with salt and pepper, add the feet, simmer and serve them in a very little sauce.

A la Bordelaise Wenberg.—Prepare as for the above adding finely minced hot peppers, plenty of brandy and red wine, and when ready to serve, a little freshly ground black pepper.

(1767). LAMBS' TROTTERS À LA CHANTILLY (Pieds d'Agneau à la Chantilly).

Prepare the feet the same as indicated for poulette (No. 1768), placing them in a saucepan with two spoonfuls of chopped onions and shallots; moisten with two gills of white wine, and reduce to half, adding two gills of velouté sauce (No. 415), a garnished bouquet (No. 123), and a few fresh mushroom peelings; boil and reduce the sauce without ceasing to stir, incorporating slowly in it a few spoonfuls of mushroom broth, and when it is well reduced and succulent, strain and add to it the lambs' trotters; let them simmer in the sauce for twelve minutes over a very slow fire; at the last moment thicken the sauce with two raw egg-yolks diluted in cream. Take the stew from the fire and finish it with a few pieces of butter, a pinch of chopped parsley and lemon juice. Dress the feet on a hot dish, strain the sauce over, and surround with a string of small stuffed mushrooms (No. 650), or should they be too large cut them in two.

(1768). LAMBS' TROTTERS À LA POULETTE AND À LA DIDIER (Pieds d'Agneau à la Poulette et à la Didier).

Singe with alcohol about two dozen well cleaned lambs' trotters, cook them in white stock (No. 182); suppress the hairy tuft found between the two divisions of the forked hoofs; shorten the bones of these hoofs and then split each foot in two lengthwise, and take out the large shank bone. Put some flour into a saucepan, dilute it with cold water and add salt, whole peppers, vinegar, and a bunch of parsley garnished with thyme and bay leaf; moisten with more water then put in the feet either singly or else three bunched firmly together; boil, skim, and continue the boiling slowly for five or six hours either on the corner of the range or else in a slack oven. Drain the feet and place them in a flat saucepan with mushrooms and velouté sauce (No. 415); season, boil, and thicken with egg-yolks, cream, fresh butter, lemon juice, and chopped parsley.

À la Didier.—Prepare and cook twenty-four feet as indicated for the above. Fry two tablespoonfuls of chopped onions in butter; when a light golden color, besprinkle with flour, and allow it to cook a few moments without browning; dilute this with some stock (No. 194a), adding a bunch of parsley and some mushroom parings; after it has cooked some time, skim off the fat and run the sauce through a sieve, then add to it the feet and some turned and channeled mushroom heads (No. 118); thicken with egg-yolks and fresh butter, and finish with strained lemon juice, and chopped parsley; serve very hot.

(1769). LAMBS' TROTTERS WITH TARRAGON GRAVY—STUFFED AND BROILED (Pieds d'Agneau au jus d'Estragon—Farcis et Grillés).

Prepare and cook the trotters the same as for the Poulette (No. 1768); (do not remove the shank bone before cooking); drain them from their stock and while yet hot suppress this bone without deforming the foot; fill the empty space made by abstracting the bone with a fine quenelle forcemeat (No. 92) containing half its quantity of foies-gras from a terrine and chopped up truffles, seasoning very highly. Beat up two raw eggs, add salt and two spoonfuls of cooked fine herbs (No. 385); dip the lamb trotters in this egg mixture one by one, drain well, then roll them in white bread-crumbs, afterward steeping them in melted butter; range them as fast as they are completed on a broiler and broil for twenty minutes over a slow fire, turning them over. Dress on a hot dish, pouring some clear gravy (No. 404) on the bottom of the dish to which has been added some blanched tarragon leaves.

(1770). WHOLE LAMB À LA THÉODORA—HOT AND COLD (Agneau Entier à la Théodora—Chaud et Froid).

Bone the neck as far down as the third rib, break the rib bones in the middle of the breast, disconnect the sinews at the joints of each shoulder, and run an iron skewer through them; fasten the thigh bones well on this skewer, then break the kernel leg bone and sever the two leg bones; cross over the two handle bones, then wrap the meat in strong buttered paper and lay it in a cradle spit (Fig. 116) to cook for one hour and a half, basting it frequently during this time. Unwrap and let it acquire a fine color, then dress it on a large dish and lay around plenty of Sarah potatoes (No. 2802). Serve some clear gravy (No. 404) separately, pouring part of it over.

Cold.—After the lamb has been prepared and cooked the same as the above, let it get cold, then glaze it over several times with meat glaze (No. 402); garnish around with chopped jelly. On this jelly and all around arrange five kinds of egg garnishings, for instance eggs glazed with chaufroid (No. 2509); eggs à la Justine (No. 2505); eggs with salpicon (No. 2514), eggs à la Rouennaise (No. 2506) and eggs Juliet (No. 2504). Serve separately a tartar sauce (No. 631).

PORK (Porc).

(1771). BACON—SMOKED—WITH SPINACH, ENGLISH STYLE (Petit Salé Fumé aux Épinards à l'Anglaise).

Cut from a side of smoked bacon some pieces weighing about a pound each; boil them in unsalted water. Clean some spinach, cook it in separate salted water, drain but do not chop. Put it into a sautoir with a piece of butter divided in small pats, and when prepared to serve place it in the center of a dish, remove the rind from the bacon, cut it in slices, and lay them overlapping one another on top of the spinach.

(1772). BLACK BLOOD PUDDING (Boudins Noirs).

Blood puddings are made with the pig's blood collected in a receptacle, and well stirred while hot to prevent coagulation.

Composition.—In blood puddings there is to be found, blood, leaf lard, onions, apple marmalade, cream, salt, pepper, allspice, nutmeg, celery, savory, and parsley.

Proportions.—For twelve pounds of black pudding have three pounds of blood, three pounds of onions, three pounds of leaf lard, two pounds of apple marmalade, and a pint of cream.

Chop up fine three pounds of onions, selecting the yellow ones in preference; put two ounces of lard in a saucepan with the onions, and leave to cook on a slow fire about two hours; stir from time to time. Have three pounds of leaf lard, take off the skin and cut up into quarter inch squares; put these into a colander and plunge it for five minutes in boiling water, being careful to keep the pieces detached; drain for a few moments without pressing. Put this lard in with the onions, when the latter are well cooked, and stir until thoroughly mixed; this should be done on a very slow fire; now pour in the blood straining it through a fine wire sieve (Fig. 170) to suppress any coagulated parts; mix all well, adding the apple marmalade; season with a third of an ounce of salt for each pound of preparation, a third of an ounce of pepper, allspice, chopped parsley, nutmeg, celery, and savory to taste. Keep these ingredients in a bain-marie at a seventy degree temperature, while the puddings are being stuffed. Soak eight yards of pigs' casings for half an hour in tepid water; run the water through them; be assured that there are no holes. Push a pudding cornet down the casing to the length of four inches, and fill by pouring in the preparation; close up the filled end with a tight knot after letting about two ounces of the preparation run out, thus avoiding the too fatty part. Divide the length of the filled casing into five inch pieces, beginning at the tied end and twisting the first division from left to right, and the second from right to left, and so on consecutively, alternating the twists. Make a knot at the other end and then lay this prepared part in a dry receptacle. Keep twenty quarts of water steadily boiling, and when all the puddings are finished, plunge them all together into this boiling water; take from off the fire and leave them about twenty-five minutes so they become cooked. To find out when they are done to perfection no blood must be seen issuing through a hole to be perforated in the skin with a coarse pin.

To Cook.—Score the pudding on both sides and boil on a moderate fire. Serve on a hot dish accompanying it with either French or English mustard seed separately.

(1773). BREAST OF SALT PORK WITH CABBAGE (Poitrine de Porc salé aux Choux).

Have a two-pound piece of the breast of bacon, unsalt it for two hours, scrape and parboil for ten minutes, then lay it in a saucepan full of boiling water to let cook very slowly for one hour; add to it two small and very clean curled cabbages cut in four and finish cooking the bacon and cabbages together; drain off and press the cabbages in a colander to extract all their water, then lay it on a long dish. Remove the rind from the bacon, cut it up into slices and dress them symmetrically over the cabbage, pouring a little clear gravy (No. 404) into the bottom of the dish.

(1774). CHINE OF PORK À LA PARMENTIER (Échinée de Porc à la Parmentier).

The chine comprises the loin and a few of the rack chops; decrease the thickness of the fat, leaving it only half an inch in depth on its entire surface; beat down the projecting chine bone;

score the fat into lozenges and wrap the meat in an oiled paper; cook it either on the spit or in the oven. The time it will take will be from an hour and a quarter to an hour and a half; before serving unwrap the chine, sprinkle over with salt and brown it nicely; glaze and remove from the spit or oven. Dress and garnish around with potato balls cooked in broth and fried in butter; serve a Bretonne sauce (No. 439) separately.

(1775). CHITTERLINGS OF TROYES (Andouillettes de Troyes).

Chitterlings require a great deal of care in their preparation; in fact it must be remarked that the quality depends entirely upon the proper cleansing of the bowels.

Ingredients.—Pork bowels, calf's crow, throat fat taken from the pig, salt, pepper, allspice, nutmeg, onion, shallot, mignonette and parsley. Take some pork bowels, removing the stomach and the casing, only using the large intestine, wash this in cold water. Turn it inside out in such a way that the fatty part is inside; in order to accomplish this easily, take a stick a yard long, place the end of it in three inches of the narrowest end of the pipe and run the pipe entirely on the stick, keeping it all the time in its original place; when it is all on let slide by pulling it slowly on the first part, that is on the stick, and the pipe will turn over all alone. Now clean it in lukewarm water acidulated with vinegar, changing it three times and leave to soak for three hours; rub it once more through the hands so as to remove all the remaining gluey parts. Put aside the uncrimped part of the pipe which will answer for wrapping purposes and set the remainder in a pot full of cold water; heat until the pipe becomes a little hard, not letting it boil. Afterward cut the pipe lengthwise, lay it perfectly flat spread it out and clean it thoroughly; cut it into thin strips as long as possible without separating the parts. Cut also into the same lengths the crimped part of a calf's crow suppressing the fat center. Cut up about a pound and a half of salt pork into strips. Now lay all these out on a table in the proportion of two-thirds of the bowels and the other third composed of crow and throat fat; dress in oblong shape, being careful that the left side has the least possible loose ends; the size to be about eight to nine strips. Season this laid out part with a minced seasoning composed of three onions, three shallots, half a handful of very finely chopped parsley, pepper, allspice, nutmeg and mignonette, strewing it over the whole. Pass a strap made of two six inch lengths of birchwood fastened together with an inch length of string through the opening on the left end, and turn it in such a way that the chitterling has the appearance of a twisted cable. Cut the pipes laid aside for wrapping purposes into sixteen inch lengths, have the fatty part outside, operating the same as when turning over the gut itself, placing the gut one inch below the hole; run the chitterling through, being careful to keep the first end at the extremity of the chitterling; tie both ends. Although this may appear very easy, yet it is a difficult operation to perform for the first time and requires a certain practice.

To Cook the Chitterlings.—To have them very white, cook in a stock of half milk, half water, one onion, thyme, bay leaf, salt and lemon; leave to boil slowly for about three hours. In order to give a finer appearance, restuff the chitterling after the first cooking in an uncrimped pipe and leave on a slow fire for fifteen minutes, keeping it near boiling point. Now lay it in a napkin and press between two boards with weights on top or else in the press (Fig. 71); the chitterlings will be square-shaped.

To Broil.—Score the chitterlings on both sides about three-sixteenths of an inch in depth, baste with oil or butter, broil on a slow fire and dress on a dish over a little clear gravy (No. 404).

(1776). PORK CUTLETS À L'AURORA (Côtelettes de Porc à l'Aurore).

Cut off six covered cutlets from a rack of pork, beat to flatten to half an inch in thickness, then season with salt and pepper; fry them in butter and when done range them on a dish capable of being placed in the oven; cover over with well-seasoned béchamel cream sauce (No. 411) thickened with raw egg-yolks and adding some very finely cut up chives. Press a few hard-boiled egg-yolks through a sieve holding it over the chops, and when the top is well covered, pour on some butter and brown in a brisk oven.

(1777). PORK CUTLETS HALF-GLAZE AND WITH APPLES (Côtelettes de Porc à la Sauce Demi-Glace aux Pommes d'Arbre).

Cut off and pare twelve cutlets from two racks of a young pig—they should weigh about five ounces each after being nicely trimmed, range them in a sautéing pan covered with a layer of melted butter, add a bunch of parsley garnished with a clove, thyme, bay leaf, and season with salt and pepper. Pour over half a gill of Madeira wine, cover with buttered paper, put on the lid, and

PORK AMERICAN CUTS. (Porc Coupe à l'Américaine).

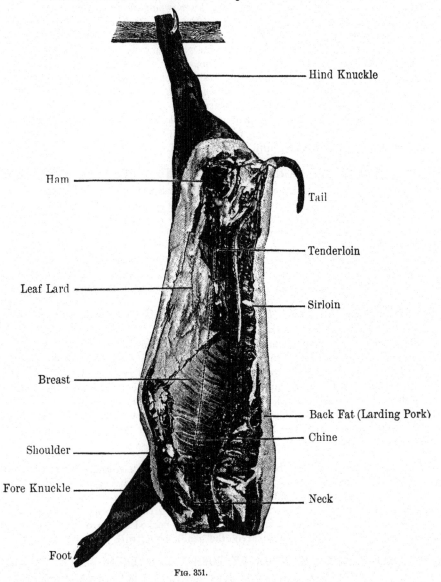

Hind Knuckle

Ham

Tail

Tenderloin

Leaf Lard

Sirloin

Breast

Back Fat (Larding Pork)

Chine

Shoulder

Fore Knuckle

Neck

Foot

FIG. 351.

DIVISION OF PORK (Division du Porc).

A pork is divided in two parts called halves, and each of these in thirteen, making twenty-six in all, exclusive of the head, which forms the twenty-seventh:

1. Feet—(Pieds)
2. Chine—(Échine)
3. Tenderloin—(Filet)
4. Back Fat—(Lard)
5. Shoulder—(Épaule)
6. Ham—(Jambon)
7. Leaf Lard—(Panne)
8. Fore Knuckle—(Jarret de Devant)
9. Hind Knuckle—(Jarret de Derrière)
10. Breast—(Poitrine)
11. Tail—(Queue)
12. Sirloin—(Longe)
13. Neck—(Cou)

The intestines not included in these are composed of:

1. Gut—(Chaudin)
2. Casing—(Menu)
3. Stomach—(Panse)
4. Liver—(Foie)
5. Lights—(Mou)
6. Caul Fat—(Crépine)
7. Crow—(Fraise)

when the liquid reaches boiling point place it in a slack oven so that the chops cook slowly and brown slightly without attaching to the dish; after twenty minutes turn them over. Should the butter become too hot add a little broth (No. 194a) until thoroughly cooked, and when assured of this fact, remove the chops from the fire, drain off the butter and detach the glaze found adhering to the bottom of the dish with a little Madeira wine; now add a pint of espagnole sauce (No. 414), suppress the parsley and drain well the chops, trim their handles and dress. Strain the sauce through a tammy finishing it with a little fresh butter and lemon juice; cover over the chops with half of this sauce, serving the other half in a separate sauce-boat.

With Apples.—Have the cutlets prepared and cooked the same as No. 1777, only garnish around with apples cut in one-quarter of an inch thick slices by two and a half inches in diameter; remove the seeds with an apple corer, fry them in lard and when nearly done sprinkle over some sugar and continue the cooking until they are glazed.

(1778). PORK CUTLETS AND CHOPS, PLAIN AND CASTILLANE—BROILED (Côtelettes de Porc Grillées Nature à la Castillane et Côtelettes de Filet).

Certainly the best way to prepare pork cutlets is to broil them; when fried they lose their finest qualities. From a small rack cut off six cutlets beat, pare, season and roll them in a little oil, then broil over a good fire for twelve to fourteen minutes, being careful to turn them; trim the handles with paper frills (No. 10), and dress on a very hot dish.

Castillane.—After the cutlets have been prepared and cooked as for the above, dress them on a hot dish and serve with a sauce-boatful of Castillane sauce (No. 443). Prepare chops the same as cutlets, they should be cut from a loin instead of from the rack.

(1779). PORK CUTLETS WITH APPLE CROQUETTES (Côtelettes de Porc aux Croquettes de Pommes d'Arbre).

Prepare and cook the cutlets the same as for cooked fine herbs (No. 1780), trim the handle bones and dress in a circle; fill the center with apple croquettes (No. 3016) in the form of inch balls, and serve separately a brown sauce (No. 414), with essence of ham (No. 390.) To make apple croquettes, mince some apples very small and cook them slowly in fresh butter; when nearly done add a little sugar and finish the cooking. Let this preparation get quite cold, then divide it into small parts of a sufficient size to make inch in diameter balls; roll these in bread-crumbs, beaten eggs and then more bread-crumbs, smooth this over neatly with a knife and fry the croquettes in very hot fat.

(1780). PORK CUTLETS WITH COOKED FINE HERBS (Côtelettes de Porc aux Fines Herbes Cuites).

After the cutlets have been pared and seasoned, fry them very slowly in butter turning them over when a fine color on one side; fourteen minutes will suffice to cook them. Lay the cutlets on a dish, keep it warm while detaching the glaze in the pan with a little gravy (No. 404), and reducing it with some half-glaze sauce (No. 413); add cooked fine herbs (No. 385), and lemon juice, then pour the whole over the cutlets; trim the handle bones with paper frills (No. 10), and serve.

(1781). PORK CUTLETS WITH GRAVY, ROBERT OR GHERKIN SAUCE—BREADED (Côtelettes de Porc Panées au Jus, à la Sauce Robert, ou à la Sauce aux Cornichons).

Prepare four cutlets with their rib bones beginning at the third rib from the neck; the meat should be white and firm; beat down to flatten to half an inch in thickness, then pare evenly and season with salt and pepper, dip the cutlets in melted butter, then in white bread-crumbs and broil over a slow fire for fifteen minutes; when cooked and nicely browned, trim the handles with frills (No. 10), dress in a circle and pour some clear gravy (No. 404), into the dish.

With Robert Sauce.—Prepare and cook as above and serve with Robert sauce (No. 533).

For Gherkin Sauce.—Pour one gill of vinegar into a saucepan with two chopped up shallots and a pinch of pepper; reduce completely, then add some brown sauce (No. 414), and a little gravy (No. 404), reduce. despumate and just when ready to serve, throw in chopped up pickled gherkins, or else have a pickle sauce as described in No. 518.

(1782). PORK CUTLETS WITH MASHED POTATOES—HASHED (Côtelettes de Porc Hachées à la Purée de Pommes).

From the rack of a young pig cut off six cutlets; pare and remove all the meat from the bones, keeping the rib bones for further use. Chop up the meats with half as much cooked udder and add to this hash, a third of its quantity of raw truffles in one-eighth of an inch dice-shaped pieces; season highly and divide the preparation into eight even parts; shape each one similar to a cutlet using the reserved bones for handles, and wrap in squares of "crepinette" or caul fat; dip in beaten eggs, bread-crumb well, and lay them in a sautoir containing melted butter; heat simply to stiffen both sides, then moisten to their heighth with gravy (No. 404); boil the liquid, cover the sautoir and set it in a slack oven for an hour and a half; trim them with paper frills (No. 10). Dress and pour the reduced stock into the bottom of the dish and serve with a vegetable dishful of mashed potatoes (No. 2798).

(1783). PIGS' FEET À LA ST. MÉNÉHOULD (Pieds de Cochon à la St. Ménéhould).

Have eight scalded and clean pigs' feet; soak them for several hours in water, drain, and place them in a saucepan with cold water; bring this to a boil, and continue simmering slowly for three-quarters of an hour; then drain, refresh, wipe and singe the feet; tie them together with a tape and range them in a stock pot having the bottom covered with large vegetables; pour over plenty of water and a bottleful of white wine, adding salt and aromatics, then boil again while skimming; now paste on the lid with a paste made of flour and water, and continue cooking the feet for twelve hours in the oven, allowing them to cool off in their own stock; drain, untie, and split each one in two lengthwise; season over with salt and mignonette, bread-crumb them English style, or with egg-yolks beaten up with melted butter (No. 13), then roll in bread-crumbs, broil of a nice color over a moderate fire, serve very hot.

(1784). PIGS' FEET—BROILED (Pieds de Cochon Grillés).

If the feet have to be cooked at home, then clean them well and tie them together in pairs; boil them in a stock in which salted meats have been cooked, or else in a broth fragrant with vegetables, onions, carrots, a bunch of parsley garnished with thyme, basil etc., peppercorns, cloves and allspice; four or five hours will suffice to have them done properly, then let them cool off in the same liquid; unwrap and cut each foot into two parts; wet the surfaces with a brush dipped in butter or melted lard, pare and roll in bread-crumbs; broil them for fifteen to twenty minutes over a moderate fire.

(1785). PIGS FEET TRUFFLED (Pieds de Cochon Truffés).

This is one of the best, at the same time the easiest way of utilizing the pigs' feet. Make two pounds of forcemeat composed of one pound of fat pork taken from under the spine and a pound and a quarter of lean taken from the end of the tenderloin. Peel five good sized truffles, cut one of them up in slices to lay over the "crépinette" or caul fat, and the other four in small three-sixteenths of an inch squares. Mix the forcemeat with the small bits of truffle, two eggs, two pinches of flour, and a few drops of orange flower water; season with a third of an ounce of salt for every pound, white pepper and nutmeg; mix well together and leave stand for half an hour. Bone four pigs' feet cooked in a white stock, cut the meat into small pieces and put them into a saucepan with good broth (No. 194a) just sufficient to cover, add the truffle peelings and a little sherry wine. After this has been boiling ten minutes pour the whole into a flat square vessel to make a layer half an inch thick, then leave it to get cold. Soak a "crépinette" or caul fat in cold water, wipe it perfectly dry and then spread it out; lay on this three slices of truffle placed lozenge form. Roll out a ball of the forcemeat of two ounces, flatten to an oval form. Cut some of the feet now formed into a jelly the same shape only a little smaller; and lay it on the forcemeat, cover with another piece exactly the size and shape of the first then wrap around the "crépinette" giving it while rolling it in the hands the shape of an oval.

To Cook the Feet.—Butter these with a brush, dip them in white bread-raspings, and then broil them over a slow fire; turn four times while cooking to allow the juice of the feet to penetrate the forcemeat. At the last moment increase the heat; they should be of a fine golden color all over.

(1786). PIGS' FEET WITH TRUFFLES, PÉRIGORD (Pieds de Cochon aux Truffes du Périgord)

Cook the feet the same as when prepared for broiled (No. 1784), let them get partially cold in their stock, then drain, unwrap and cut each one in two lengthwise; bone every one of the halves properly, season with salt and mignonette and fill all their insides with a stuffing of pork and chopped truffles, with a quarter as much fine liver baking forcemeat (No. 81). Smooth the surface of this dressing and cover it over with slices of raw truffles; wrap each half foot in a square of soaked and well dried "crepinette" or caul fat, brush over with butter or melted lard, and dip them in bread-crumbs; broil for twenty minutes over a moderate fire, then dress on a hot dish with a little gravy (No. 404) added.

(1787). HAM À LA BENEDICT OR WITH JARDINIÈRE ROASTED (Jambon Rôti à la Benedict ou à la Jardinière).

Steep the smoked ham in cold water for twenty-four hours; wash, pare and remove the hip bone; put it in an earthen dish, pour over some Madeira wine and season with whole peppers, cloves, thyme, bay leaf, mace, garlic, sliced carrots and onions and lemon juice; keep it in a cool place for twelve hours turning the ham round several times in this marinade. Five hours before serving, wrap the ham up with its strained marinade fried in butter and moistened and reduced with white wine and the moistening of the marinade, in sheets of strong oiled paper; cover the paper with a flour and water paste so that the ham is hermetically enclosed, then cover this paste with another sheet of very thin oiled paper; lay it either on the spit or in the oven, pour oil over and roast for three hours; remove from the fire and make a small hole on the top to penetrate the paste and papers, set a funnel into this, and pour in a gill of good Madeira, the same quantity of malaga and half a gill of brandy. Cover the hole with a round piece of paper, and paste it over to concentrate all the steam which is essential to obtain success. An hour after, take the ham from the oven or spit, unwrap, pare carefully and glaze with meat glaze (No. 402); dress and garnish around with escalops of foies-gras, cocks'-combs and kidneys, and slices of red beef tongue three-sixteenths of an inch thick, and one inch and a quarter in diameter, quenelles and channeled mushrooms; cover the whole with a well-buttered suprême sauce (No. 547), and trim the handle with a paper frill (No. 10), insert a few skewers in the top garnished with cocks'-combs and channeled mushrooms (No. 118).

This ham may be served with a jardinière garnishing (No. 677) and a half-glaze sauce (No. 413) served separately.

(1788). HAM À LA LEONARD—BOILED (Jambon Bouilli à la Léonard).

Immerse in cold water for twelve hours a fresh, smoked ham, after cutting off the end of the handle bone and shortening the hip bone; suppress the part of the meat and the smoked fat and lay the ham in a large saucepan covering it over abundantly with cold water; set it on the fire, bring the liquid gradually to a boil, then drain off this water and replace it with tepid water, adding carrots, onions, a bunch of parsley garnished with thyme, bay leaf, sage and basil; season with peppercorns, cloves and mace. At the first boil remove it on one side so that it simmers only (the length of time for its cooking will be a quarter of an hour for each pound); when the ham is nearly done, take the saucepan from the fire and leave it to cool off in the water for one hour longer. Just when prepared to serve drain the ham, suppress the rind and aitchbone, pare the fat and meat around and underneath and cut off all the meat from the handle. Lay the ham on dish and slice a piece off from the bottom so that it will stand plumb; glaze it over with a brush and place it in a deep baking tin with a little clear gravy (No. 404) and as much Madeira wine; boil this up and keep it in a slack oven for fifteen minutes, basting frequently with the gravy. Dress on a long dish on a three-inch high rice socle, trimmed like a croustade and colored in the oven; pour half the gravy over, trim the handle bone with a frill (No. 10) and surround with twenty-four croustades, eight filled with green peas, eight with asparagus tops, and eight with quarter-inch squares of mushrooms. Serve at the same time but separately a sauce-boat of Madeira sauce (No. 492). This ham may also be served with a garnishing of Italian macaroni or lazagnes and a tomato sauce (No. 549) and half-glaze sauce (No. 413) instead of the Madeira.

(1789). HAM, ROASTED ON THE SPIT, MADEIRA SAUCE, OR MARINATED AND ROASTED, WHITE WINE SAUCE (Jambon Rôti à la Broche Sauce Madère, ou Mariné Rôti au Four à la Sauce au Vin Blanc).

On the Spit.—Select a small raw unsmoked ham, remove the aitchbone, saw off the handle joint and suppress the rind and part of the fat, leaving only a layer half an inch in thickness; pare the ham into a round shape, then lay it in brine from two to eight days, and later when needed for use, wash it in plenty of cold water; wipe and envelop the lean parts in a large slice of fat pork tie up the ham and roast it on the spit, basting it frequently with white wine; serve hot with a sauce-boat of Madeira sauce (No. 492).

Marinated and Roasted in the Oven—White Wine Sauce.—Prepare the ham the same as for the above, only instead of salting it, place it in a vessel to marinate for two days with white wine and a seasoning of salt, pepper, sliced onions, cloves, minced carrots, parsley leaves, thyme, bay leaf, a little sugar and sweet oil; turn the meat over every three hours. Wrap the ham up with its marinade in several sheets of strong paper and roast it in a moderate oven for three hours and a half. Thirty minutes before serving, unwrap and glaze the surface, strain the stock, remove its fat and thicken it with a little brown sauce (No. 414) and white wine; boil for half an hour remove the fat, dress the ham, have it nicely glazed and pour a little of the sauce under, while serving the remainder in a sauce-boat.

(1790). HAM, WITH CARROTS, STUFFED TOMATOES OR MUSHROOMS—BRAISED AND GLAZED (Jambon Braisé et Glacé aux Carottes, Tomates ou Champignons Farcis).

Have the ham of a young pig freshly salted and smoked; saw off the handle straight, also the hip bone; pare the meats and fat slightly, and lay it to soak in cold water for twelve hours, then drain, scrape well, wash and wrap it in a cloth; lay it in a soup-pot with four times its heighth of water, let it come to a boil, then set it on one side to simmer slowly; add to it carrots, onions, cloves, a bunch of parsley garnished with thyme and bay leaf, and half a bottleful of white wine; allow it to boil for three hours, then drain, remove the cloth and cut off the rind. Lay the ham in a low braziere (Fig. 134) with half a bottleful of Madeira wine, a little brandy, and four tablespoonfuls of meat glaze (No. 402); finish cooking it in a slack oven, basting it often, and when the ham is of a fine color, and the liquid reduced, dress and decorate with a frill (No. 10). Strain and reduce the stock with some espagnole sauce (No. 414); cover the bottom of the dish with a third part of this sauce, serve seperately the other two-thirds in a sauce-boat.

After the ham has been dressed, surround it with a garnishing of carrots cut into small pear-shape, blanched and cooked in stock (No. 194a), then a little sugar added and fallen to a glaze; pour in a little half-glaze sauce (No. 413), add a piece of butter just when ready to serve.

Stuffed tomatoes (No. 2842), stuffed mushrooms (No. 692), or any other garnishing may be substituted, serving with a separate half-glaze sauce (No. 413) with Madeira.

(1791). HAM WITH SPINACH—BOILED (Jambon Bouilli aux Épinards).

Take a fine freshly salted, smoked ham, pare the meats also the fat, which should be exceedingly white; suppress the hip bone, saw off the knuckle bone and then unsalt the ham in a plentiful supply of water for twenty-four hours. If it should have been dried and salted for some time prior to the day of using, then it will require thirty-six hours of unsalting. Wash, drain and tie it in a towel. Five hours before serving lay it in a large braziere or soup pot with four times its volume of cold water, adding four quartered carrots, two onions containing six cloves, a bunch of parsley garnished with thyme, bay leaf, basil and mace, then let it boil and simmer slowly for four hours more or less, according to the weight and size of the ham, calculating a quarter of an hour for each pound. To be assured that it is properly cooked, run the tip of a skewer into the flesh and if it can be withdrawn at once the ham is sufficiently done. Remove the braziere or pot from the fire half an hour before serving; drain the ham on a dish, take off the towel and pare the rind and fat tastefully; clean the handle bone thoroughly cutting off the meat for about two and a half inches from the end, then set it in the oven to dry the surface. Garnish the top of the fat with a thin layer of quenelle forcemeat (No. 92), containing lobster butter, and arrange in the center of this a fanciful decoration of pistachioes, truffles, etc., cover with buttered paper. Set the ham in the oven to poach the forcemeat, or if preferred glazed, then replace it by a glaze made by besprinkling the fat with sugar and glazing it of a fine reddish color. Dress the ham on a garnishing of spinach (No. 2821), trim the handle with a frill (No. 10) and lay around some triangle-shaped croûtons fried in butter; serve with a Madeira sauce (No. 492). Instead of chopped spinach, English spinach (No. 2823) may be used. Serve a half-glaze sauce (No. 413) separately.

(1792). VIRGINIA HAM WITH STRINGED EGGS (Jambon de Virginie aux Œufs Filés).

This dish is a favorite one among Spanish people. Select the ham from a young pig, pare and cook it the same as the boiled ham with spinach (No. 1791); when done, drain and cut off the rind, pare the upper surface evenly, and wipe the fat over with a cloth, besprinkle with a thin layer of powdered sugar and glaze it either under a salamander (Fig. 123) or in a very hot oven. Trim the handle with a frill (No. 10) and dress on a low, carved rice socle, placed on a long dish. Break sixteen fresh eggs, place the yolks in a bowl and pound them without beating, then rub them through a strainer, and to poach them resemble coarse vermicelli; for this result it is necessary to have an oblong, wide-mouthed strainer, its aperture being six inches long by three wide and two inches and a half deep; the bottom must be furnished with six tin tubes shaped like a socket, having an opening at the bottom an eighth of an inch or less wide and soldered on the outside. Have a sugar pan of sufficient size and half full of twelve degrees hot syrup; keep the strainer on top of this boiling syrup, and pour the strained eggs into it, letting them fall through into the syrup; as quickly as they harden lift them out and spread in a sieve dampened with water, so that these strings do not adhere to one another, then dress them around the ham. Madeira sauce (No. 492) may be served separately.

(1793). PIGS' HEADS WITH PURÉE OF SPLIT GREEN PEAS (Tête de Cochon à la Purée de Pois Verts Secs).

Cut a pig's head into pieces, bone, singe and parboil; refresh and finish cooking it in white stock (No. 182); when done and ready to serve, drain out the meats, wipe them dry, and dress on a rather consistent purée of split green peas (No. 724) having it well seasoned and finished with a piece of good butter. Send to the table with a sauce-boat of half-glaze sauce (No. 413). This dish can also be served with a piquante sauce (No. 538), or else a Robert sauce (No. 533).

(1794). KERNEL OF HAM À LA BIARRITZ (Noix de Jambon à la Biarritz).

A kernel of ham is sufficient for eight persons. Soak it for eight hours in cold water, pare lightly and wrap up in a small cloth; put it into a saucepan with plenty of cold water and bring the liquid slowly to a boil; remove the saucepan to the corner of the range, so that the liquid simmers on one side only, it taking in all about two to three hours according to the size. Leave it in the water half an hour before serving, then drain, suppress the rind, trim the meat and fat carefully, and dress it on a risot prepared as follows: Fry colorless two spoonfuls of onions, add a quarter of a pound of unwashed but clean rice, and warm it with the onions; wet it to three times its heighth with stock (No. 194a), boil and let cook in the oven without disturbing whatever until all the liquid is absorbed, then stir in a coffeespoonful of prepared red pepper (No. 168). Have six scalded tomatoes, twenty-four cooked mushroom heads, and sixteen small Chipolata sausages fried in butter (No. 657). When the rice becomes dry, pour over it four ounces of hazelnut butter (No. 567). Drain the ham, pare and glaze it over with a brush; lay the rice on the bottom of a dish, the ham on top and surround with the sausages and mushroom heads stewed in cream, placing santéd sweet Spanish peppers, and the scalded tomatoes cut in two, pressed and fried in butter at the ends. A Madeira sauce (No. 492), should be served separately.

(1795). KERNEL OF PORK À LA CAVOUR AND WITH NOODLES—SLICED (Tranches de Noix de Porc à la Cavour et aux Nouilles).

Cut from the kernel part of a young, fresh pig, some slices to weigh four ounces each, beat to flatten to half an inch in thickness, then trim them round-shaped; they should now weigh three ounces each; season with salt, pepper, and nutmeg, sauté them rare. Reduce some thick espagnole (No. 414); add to it fine cooked herbs (No. 385), and let it get cold; cover both sides of the slices with this and roll them in bread-crumbs, then immerse in beaten eggs and roll in bread-crumbs for the second time; smooth the breading nicely and fry in clarified butter. Have a spaghetti garnishing containing shredded mushrooms, clear gravy (No. 414), and ready prepared tomato paste, to be found at Italian grocers, and grated parmesan; pour this macaroni on a dish and dress the slices of pork on top. These slices may also be dressed on top of a garnishing of noodles fried in butter, and serve a tomato sauce (No. 549) and half-glaze sauce (No. 413) separately.

(1796). LOIN OF PORK À LA REGLAIN (Longe de Porc à la Reglain).

Trim a loin of pork cut off from the first rib as far down as the ham, leaving but a quarter of an inch of fat on its surface; rub this over with salt and leave it so for twenty-four hours; wash, drain and wipe, then set it in a saucepan with melted fat, minced onions and garnished parsley. Place the saucepan on the fire to brown the meat slowly, and when a fine color moisten to a quarter of its height with stock (No 194a), bring to a boil and finish cooking in the oven. Half an hour before serving plunge one pound of rice in boiling water; set it on the fire and at the first boil take it off to pour in some cold water to stop the boiling, then return it to the fire and remove again at the first boil, now cover the saucepan and leave the liquid to simmer without letting it actually boil for ten minutes longer. Pour the rice on a sieve, drain it well and put it back into the saucepan with half the meat stock; boil it up then set it in a moderate oven; the rice ought to absorb the stock, and when well cooked press it into a border mold (Fig. 139) previously dipped in cold water, then unmold it. Cut the loin up into about two ounce pieces without any bones and scarcely any fat; pare them into quarter inch squares; reduce the remaining stock with as much velouté (No. 415), add the meat, season with a dash of prepared red pepper (No. 168), heat well then dish the meat up inside a border and pour the sauce over; dredge with chopped parsley and serve.

(1797). QUARTER OF PORK VALENCIENNES (Quartier de Porc à la Valenciennes).

Have a quarter of a young pork, salted for eight days without any saltpetre, and when ready for use wash it well in cold water; remove the hip bone, tie it up and cook it in water; when three-quarters done drain, suppress the rind and finish cooking in the oven, and glaze with some clear gravy (No. 402) and white wine. Dress it on a long dish, trim the handle with a frill or ruffle (No. 10) and garnish around with risot (No. 739) in which two pounds of sausages have been boiled, finishing with a pinch of Spanish red pepper; at each end lay stuffed tomatoes (No. 2842), the rice on the sides, the slices of sausages on top. Cover the meat with an espagnole sauce (No. 414) well reduced with tomato sauce (No. 549) and seasoned with prepared red pepper; (No. 168); serve at the same time a sauce-boat of the same sauce.

(1798). RACK OF PORK CROWN-SHAPED WITH SMALL ONIONS (Carré de Porc en Couronne aux Petits Oignons).

Cut off two racks containing six cutlets each, both the same length and height, leaving on a part of the loin; suppress the chine bone as far as the beginning of the ribs and lay the meats in a round or oval deep dish so that the kernel of the chops be inside and the ends of the cutlets outside; tie the ends together with a piece of string and fill the inside of the crown thus obtained with sausage forcemeat into which has been mixed eggs and bread-crumbs, then cook in the oven for an hour and a half. Fry sixty small onions or more in butter, having them only slightly browned, then finish cooking in stock (No. 194a) till they fall to a glaze; dress and glaze the crown, garnish the center with onions and pour a Robert sauce (No. 533) over the whole, or a Provençal sauce (No. 529) to which add a little tomato sauce (No. 549).

(1799). RACK OF PORK ON THE SPIT (Carré de Porc à la Broche).

Cut a rack of fresh pork containing six to eight ribs; leave it covered a quarter of an inch thick with its own fat and pare the chine bone; saw it off as far as the edges of the ribs, separate the adhering meat on top of the ribs and cut them so they are only two and a half inches long; score the top into lozenges, roll over the flap and tie up the rack with eight rows of string; lay it on the spit and leave it to cook for about an hour, basting it occasionally. Glaze, dress and serve over some clear gravy No. (404).

(1800). RACK OF PORK WITH STUFFED PEPPERS (Carré de Porc aux Piments Farcis).

Obtain a rack of pork containing eight ribs with the breast; remove the chine bone, and saw it off at the beginning of the ribs, bone also the breast leaving on only two and a half inches of the ribs; remove the fat all but a quarter of an inch and score this into lozenges. Roll over the flap, tie and set the meat in a china dish, season with salt, pepper, thyme, bay leaf, parsley and round slices of onion, pouring over some sweet oil and lemon juice. Wrap the rack and its marinade in several sheets of buttered paper, lay it in a baking pan, besprinkle with fat and cook it in a sufficiently hot oven for one hour. Twenty minutes before serving unwrap and leave the meat in the oven to brown and glaze to a fine color. Place the vegetables in a saucepan with some espagnole sauce (No. 414) and white wine; skim off the fat and reduce. Dress the rack, surround it with stuffed peppers (No. 2768), and pour some of the sauce over, serving the remainder at the same time but separately.

(1801). SAUSAGES CHIPOLATA (Saucisses à la Chipolata).

Push some sausage meat (No. 68) into a sheep's casing being careful not to fill it too much; twist it into small inch to inch and a half lengths, turning each sausage in a contrary direction, the first to the right, the second to the left, and so on to the end; in this way the sausages keep together better while cooking. Prick the casing with a larding or any other needle. Cook on a slow fire and dress on a chipolata garnishing (No. 657).

(1802). SAUSAGES GASTRONOME (Saucisses au Gastronome.

Garnish the inside edge of a pie-dish with a border of quenelle forcemeat (No. 92) laid on through a cornet; set on the bottom a layer of cooked fine herbs (No. 385), over this long sausages prepared with chopped truffles after pricking them, and cover the whole with an Italian sauce (No. 484) containing truffles; bestrew the surface with bread raspings and a pinch of grated parmesan, pour butter over and cook in the oven for fifteen to twenty minutes, until the sausages be well done and browned.

(1803). SAUSAGES IN BAGS (Saucisses en Sac).

Make some muslin bags twelve inches long by two and a half inches in diameter; fill them up with cold American sausage meat (No. 68), then cut them across bag and forcemeat together in half inch thick slices; remove the muslin, bread-crumb the pieces and broil or fry them in butter in the pan or else place in a little water in a frying pan and boil, then finish cooking in a moderate oven or on a slow fire.

(1804). SAUSAGES WITH CREAM POTATOES, BAKED (Saucisses aux Pommes de Terre Hachées à la Crème Gratinées).

Have some pork forcemeat the same as sausage forcemeat (No. 69); for each pound of this forcemeat mix in four ounces of cooked fine herbs (No. 385) and half a pint of béchamel (No. 409), also a little meat glaze (No. 402); thicken the whole with six egg-yolks; use this forcemeat to fill small sheep's casings previously salted, being careful not to have them too full, then twist the sausages into five inch lengths. Garnish the bottom of a deep baking dish with chopped potatoes and cream (No. 2780); lay the sausages on top after frying them for one minute in hot frying fat, pour over some thick velouté sauce (No. 415) and bestrew with bread-crumbs and grated cheese; baste with melted butter and set the dish in a very hot oven to bake for fifteen to twenty minutes, or until browned to a fine color.

(1805). SAUSAGES—FLAT—WITH TOMATO SOUBISE SAUCE (Saucisses Plates à la Sauce Tomate Soubise).

Roll some sausage meat into four ounce balls and wrap these up in "crepinette" or caul fat; shape them into slightly lengthened flat pieces. There can be some parsley, tarragon or other herbs added to the sausage meat according to taste. Dip them in melted butter, then roll in bread-crumbs, and broil over a slow fire, afterward dress on a purée of tomatoes (No. 730), mingled with soubise sauce (No. 543).

(1806). SAUSAGES WITH TRUFFLES (Saucisses aux Truffes).

Take two pounds of fresh pork meat from the neck; remove carefully all the fibrous parts retaining as much meat as fat; season with an ounce and a half of salt, a teaspoonful of freshly ground allspice, and add four ounces of truffles cut in small dice or finely chopped. Make sausages of this preparation, broil and dress them on a garnishing of minced truffles mingled with supreme sauce (No. 547).

(1807). SAUSAGES LONG—WITH WHITE WINE (Saucisses Longues au vin Blanc).

Prepare some five or six inch length sausages the same as the Chipolata (No. 1801), prick them with a small larding needle, fry in fresh butter, and when cooked dress on a dish; drain the butter from the sautoir and replace it by white wine, chablis, sauterne or champagne, one or the other, extending the sauce with velouté sauce (No. 415); boil it up once, strain through a tammy, and finish with lemon juice and fresh butter; pour it over the sausages.

(1808). SPARE RIBS, PARISIAN STYLE (Petit Salé à la Parisienne).

Take some of the breast ribs of a pig and salt them for twelve hours in a light eight degree brine; remove and wash off in cold water. To cook them it is better to take an already salted broth, one in which a ham or any other meat has been boiled. When this reaches boiling point, throw in the ribs and leave to cook without boiling.

(1809). SUCKLING PIG, PIEDMONTESE STYLE (Cochon de Lait à la Piémontaise).

Pick and wash two pounds of rice; parboil and lay aside a third part, then put it into a saucepan with strained unskimmed stock (No. 194a) reaching to more than twice its heighth, season with a little salt, pepper and nutmeg, and when the rice is cooked which will take about half an hour, stir in with a fork, four tablespoonfuls of grated parmesan. Stuff the inside of the pig with this, sew it up and cook it on a cradle spit or in the oven, basting it over frequently with sweet oil. Three-quarters of an hour before serving, set the other two-thirds of rice in a saucepan, moisten it with stock (No. 194a) and half a pound of chicken fat, adding also a bunch of parsley garnished with thyme, bay leaf and a clove of garlic, bring to a boil, place in the oven and when the rice is cooked, remove the parsley and stir in with a fork, fresh butter, meat glaze, grated parmesan and mignonette. Dress this rice around the suckling pig and serve a Colbert sauce (No. 451) separately.

(1810). SUCKLING PIG, ROASTED ON THE SPIT, OR STUFFED AND ROASTED (Cochon de Lait Rôti à la Broche ou Farci).

Empty well a scalded pig, truss the limbs and head, run it on the spit and roast before a good fire, basting it over with a large brush wet with oil. The great difficulty is to have it a beautiful color while cooking to perfection. It should take from an hour and a half to two hours, having the skin crackling browned and crisp. When the pig is cooked dress on a large dish and surround with water-cresses seasoned with salt and vinegar, serve at the same time a sauce-boatful of clear gravy (No. 404), or one of mint sauce (No. 616) or else both, and a vegetable dish of Naples style macaroni (No. 2959).

Suckling Pig Stuffed and Roasted.—The pig may be stuffed with an American bread stuffing (No. 61), in this case it will be necessary to cook it for half an hour longer.

(1811). SUCKLING PIG, SALTED AND SMOKED WITH SAUERKRAUT (Cochon de Lait Salé et Fumé à la Choucroute).

Empty and scald a suckling pig and keep it for ten days in plenty of brine containing four ounces of sage, four ounces of thyme, and half an ounce of bay leaf; drain dry and smoke it to a yellow color with sawdust into which mix a little sage. Boil the pig in water a quarter of an hour for every pound, dress when well drained on a bed of sauerkraut (No. 2819); garnish with the bacon, sausages, sliced carrots, and Chipolata sausages. A very rich clear gravy (No. 404) is to be served separately.

(1812). TENDERLOIN OF PORK À LA MINUTE—MINCED (Émincé de Filet de Porc à la Minute).

Have some cooked, cold, and well trimmed tenderloins of pork, cut in half heart-shapes; put them in a sautoir with a little gravy (No. 404) and heat up without boiling. Cover either of these meats with the following sauce: Fry a finely chopped shallot in butter, add to it some bread-crumbs and raw fine herbs; moisten with a little gravy, season with salt and pepper, and thicken with kneaded butter (No. 579). Just when prepared to serve, pour in a little diluted mustard; dress the mince, and pour the sauce over.

(1813). TENDERLOIN OF PORK À LA PRINTANIÈRE (Filet de Porc à la Printanière).

The tenderloin is the long, narrow plump piece of meat laying under the kidney along the spinal bone; it is a part of the loin; it weighs from half a pound to a pound. Have four fine whole pork tenderloins; pare, remove the sinews and lard them with medium lardons (No. 3, Fig. 52), line a sautoir with bardes of fat pork, sliced carrots and onions, and a bunch of parsley garnished with thyme and bay leaf. Lay the larded tenderloins on top, moisten with a pint of stock (No. 194a) and a gill of Madeira, cover with a round piece of buttered paper, reduce and let the liquid fall to a glaze; moisten once more until it reaches half the heighth of the meat, then cook for one hour or more in the slow oven; glaze and dress on a rice foundation an inch and a half high, garnish around with small carrots cut in the shape of cylinders or pears, balls of turnips, both blanched and cooked in broth, olive form potatoes, green peas and asparagus tops. Skim the fat from the surface of the stock, strain and reduce it with some espagnole sauce (No. 414), strain it once more through a tammy and cover the meat with a part of this, serving the remainder in a sauce-boat.

(1814). TENDERLOIN OF PORK, BLANQUETTE OR ESCALOPED, WITH MUSHROOMS OR TRUFFLES (Blanquette de Filet de Porc, ou Escalopes aux Champignons ou aux Truffes).

Have two pounds of the tenderloin of fresh pork; pare in order to remove the sinewy skin covering it, also the fat, cut up into one and a quarter inches in diameter escalops, an eighth of an inch thick; place them as soon as ready in a liberally buttered sauté-pan, and season over with salt. Cut across in slices one pound and a half of large mushroom heads; add to the meat and cover entirely with melted butter, and a round piece of paper, and when prepared to serve, place them on a brisk fire to stiffen only, turning them over to finish cooking; drain off the butter, and add in its place, a few spoonfuls of velouté sauce (No. 415) a little chicken glaze (No. 398) and lemon juice, finally thickening with egg-yolks, butter, and cream. Dress the whole on a rice border.

With Truffles.—Replace the mushrooms by fresh truffles if procurable.

(1815). TENDERLOIN OF PORK, MARINATED (Filet de Porc Mariné).

Pare several pork tenderloins; split them in two lengthwise, then beat and trim; lard them with fine larding pork (No. 3, Fig. 52), salt over, and range in a deep dish; cover with a cooked cold marinade (No. 114), and leave the tenderloins in this for twenty-four hours, being careful to turn them over at frequent intervals, then drain, wipe dry, and lay them in a sautoir lined with fragments of fat pork, minced carrots and onions; moisten slowly with stock (No. 194a), and reduce the liquid gently to a glaze; remoisten several times, putting in very little at the time, until the meats are done, and then finish glazing in the oven. Dress the tenderloins, detach the glaze from the sautoir with a little clear gravy (No. 404) and two spoonfuls of the above marinade; thicken the whole with some brown sauce (No. 414), reduce, and strain it over the tenderloins. Surround with half heart-shaped croûtons fried in butter.

(1816). PORK TENDERLOINS, PIMENTADE SAUCE (Filets de Porc Sauce Pimentade).

Pare the tenderloins and lard them with medium lardons (No. 3, Fig. 52). Fry some mirepoix (No. 419) in butter, moisten it with Madeira wine and let get cold; cover the tenderloins with this and wrap them up in several sheets of buttered paper, then roast in a hot oven for twenty minutes; unwrap, glaze, and let attain a good color. Prepare a pimentade sauce (No. 521) reduced with the mirepoix; pour some of this sauce under the tenderloins and serve some separately.

(1817). TENDERLOINS OF PORK, ROASTED, BROILED OR SAUTÉD (Filets de Porc Rôtis, Grillés ou Sautés).

Roasted.—Take small pork tenderloins; pare them nicely and lard with fine lardons (No. 3, Fig. 52); marinate them while raw for two hours, then roast for twenty minutes in a quick oven. Dress and pour their own gravy over, after straining and skimming it, surround with watercresses.

Broiled, Maître-d'Hôtel Butter.—Pare the tenderloins, then split them lengthways in two without detaching the pieces; season with salt and mask with butter; roll them in bread-crumbs, and broil over a moderate fire, then cover with maître-d'hôtel butter (No. 581).

Sautéd Half-Glaze.—Cut them whistle-shaped in two lengthwise, beat and pare into half-hearts, season with salt and sauté on a moderate even fire; drain off the fat, detach the glaze with a little Madeira and half-glaze sauce (No. 413), reduce, dress the tenderloins and pour the gravy over.

(1818). PORK TENDERLOINS WITH PURÉE OF CELERY—BREADED (Filets de Porc Panés à la Purée de Céleri).

Pare some pork tenderloins suppressing all fat and sinews, then cut them into lengthwise bias slices and trim into half hearts; season each piece with salt, dip into melted butter and roll in white bread-crumbs; broil over a bright fire and when done dress them over a purée of celery (No. 711).

(1819). PIGS' TONGUES, PROVENÇAL STYLE (Langues de Cochon à la Provençale).

Prepare and cook some salted tongues; when they are cold cut them lengthwise in two. Pare eight peeled onions by cutting off the roots and stalks on the slant; mince them up finely and fry colorless in oil, moisten with stock (No. 194a) and white wine, add salt, pepper, a clove of garlic and a garnished bunch of parsley (No. 123); boil and cook on a slow fire for one hour then remove all the fat and the parsley, and reduce with some thick béchamel (No. 409), pass through a tammy. When this is cold cover each half tongue on the flat side with a part of this preparation after paring them all one size; besprinkle with some gastrite (No. 1187), heat and brown in the oven to a fine color, then dress in a circle and fill the inside with sautéd sweet peppers (No. 2769), and around with stuffed onions (No. 2766). A tomato sauce (No. 549) and half-glaze sauce (No. 413) reduced together is to be served separately.

(1820). ZAMPINO, MODENA STYLE, WITH STRING BEANS—STUFFED (Zampino Farci à la Modène aux Haricots Verts).

Zampino is the foot of a young pig, including a part of the leg stuffed (Fig. 352). Let this salt for twelve days in brine, and when needed for use soak it for three or four hours; scrape the rind and

Fig. 352.

prick it with a larding needle to prevent breaking while cooking; wrap it up in a thin cloth, tie it at both ends and in the middle, and lay the leg in a braziere covering over with cold water; let it simmer for two hours or more and when the pointed end is done take out the leg, unwrap and serve over a garnishing of string beans. Serve separately a half-glaze sauce (No. 413) reduced with white wine. For the preparation of the Zampino see hams of chicken with Zampino (No. 2525).

POULTRY (Volaille).

(1821). CAPON À L'AMPHITRYON (Chapon à l'Amphitryon).

A capon is a castrated cock fattened for the table; truss a good capon as for an entrée (No. 178) selecting it white and very fat, fill the inside with a delicate quenelle forcemeat (No. 89) with truffles into which mix some chestnuts roasted in the oven and broiled Chipolata sausages after removing their skins, and stoned verdal olives; rub the breast over with half a lemon, then cover with bards of fat pork. Cook the capon as for poêler (No. 12) and when done, dress on a rice foundation and garnish around with clusters of channeled mushrooms (No. 118) with half-glaze stuffed tomatoes, and whole truffles with glaze (No. 402), a little Madeira and butter, strain the stock, free it of its fat and reduce with the same quantity of velouté (No. 415). Insert three skewers garnished with glazed truffles and crawfish on top and serve the sauce separately.

(1822). CAPON À LA BRESSOISE (Chapon à la Bressoise).

Singe, draw and clean well a fine capon; make a forcemeat by soaking a pound of bread-crumbs in milk, then pressing out all the liquid and adding seasoning and eight ounces of very finely chopped beef marrow and three whole eggs. Stuff, truss and tie up the capon as for an entrée (No. 178). Place in a saucepan a quarter of a pound of lard and half a pound of fresh fat pork cut up in quarter inch squares, lay the capon on top and brown it slowly, then wet with some stock (No. 194a) and simmer, adding more liquid when needed until thoroughly cooked. Strain the gravy, free it of fat and untie the capon, dressing it in the middle of an oval dish, pour the well-reduced gravy over, serving a poulette sauce (No. 527) separately.

(1823). CAPON À LA FINANCIÈRE (Chapon à la Financière).

This relevé is dressed on an oval wooden bottom having in the center a four-sided tin support made hollow so that it be lighter. This wooden bottom and support must both be covered with a cooked paste or else of noodle paste (No. 142) dried in the air. Fasten a string of noodle paste of about three-eighths of an inch in diameter on the edge of the socle; this is intended for upholding the capons and garnishing. On the edge of the bowl of the plate, place a noodle paste border (No. 10). Prepare the capons as for an entrée (No. 178) having them stuffed with a stuffing made of cooked chicken livers, grated fresh lard, truffle parings, bread-crumbs, salt and cayenne pepper. Cover over with bards of fat pork placed in a narrow braziere (Fig. 134) moisten with sufficient stock (No. 194a) to cover the capons, add aromatic herbs and lemon pulp free of seeds and peel, then cook on a good fire, having the liquid reduce to one-third, at the last moment drain off the capons, untie and dress one on each side of the support inserting a garnished skewer on top; fill in the sides between the capons with a varied garnishing composed of mushrooms, cocks'-combs and quenelles; cover over either with a velouté sauce (No. 415) if needed for white or a financière sauce (No. 464) if for brown; surround the base with a row of peeled truffles cooked in wine and glazed over with a brush, and serve apart a velouté sauce reduced with mushroom broth if for the white or else a brown financière sauce with Madeira.

(1824). CAPON À LA PONDICHÉRY (Chapon à la Pondichéry).

Draw, singe and truss a capon for an entrée (No. 178), chop up finely a few onions, fry them colorless in butter, add to it some rice and moisten to three times its height with beef stock (No. 194a) seasoning with cayenne pepper, salt and butter; let boil then cook in the oven for twenty minutes. Line a buttered saucepan with carrots, onions and slices of fat pork, lay the capon on top and moisten with a little stock (No. 194a); let this reduce entirely then add more moistening and a bunch of parsley garnished with thyme and bay leaf. When the capon is done strain the stock, remove the fat and add it to the capon to keep it warm. Reduce the skimmed stock with velouté sauce (No. 415), curry, saffron and powdered sweet Spanish peppers; dress the rice on the bottom of a dish, lay the capon on top and cover it with a third of the sauce, serving the other two-thirds in a separate sauce-boat.

(1825). CAPON À LA RÉGENCE (Chapon à la Régence).

Singe, draw, and remove the breast bones from two capons; fill the breasts with seasoned butter, then truss as for an entrée (No. 178); lard the breasts with fine lardons (No. 3, Fig. 52), and cover the unlarded parts with slices of fat pork. Put the capons in a covered braziere (Fig. 154), and moisten them with mirepoix (No. 419), to a little above their wings; cover over with buttered paper, and leave to simmer slowly for one hour. Uncover the braziere, take off the paper, and glaze all the larded parts. Have four larded sweetbreads, ten large truffles, twelve fine cocks'-combs, and eight big crawfish. Make a garnishing with chicken quenelles and mushrooms, combining these with some régence sauce (No. 532). Cut a piece of bread-crumb ten and a half inches long by four and a quarter wide, and three and a half inches high, it to be conical-formed; fry this, then attach it to the center of a dish with repère paste (No. 142), so that it can support the two capons; have these well drained and arrange them to rest against the bread, the rump parts uppermost. Pour the prepared garnishing into the bottom of the dish; place two large sweetbreads below the two breasts, and two more in the middle intersections, then two crawfish on each side of the sweetbreads; glaze the sweetbreads and the larded parts of the capon and serve with a régence sauce apart. Make six hatelets with the cocks'-combs and the truffles (Fig. 11), and fasten them in tastefully.

(1826). CAPON LEGS WITH TRUFFLES. ROAST CAPON (Cuisses de Chapon aux Truffes. Chapon Rôti).

Bone entirely six legs taken from medium-sized and very tender capons; remove carefully the sinews, then season with salt, pepper, and nutmeg; stuff them with quenelle forcemeat (No. 89), into which mix half as much small squares of foies-gras; sew them up and braise in a mirepoix and white wine stock (No. 419); moisten slowly, being most careful to baste frequently, and when done, withdraw the threads, glaze and dress the legs on the strained and skimmed stock. Serve separately a supreme sauce (No. 547), with sliced truffles added.

Roast Capon.—Stand the capon on the grate fitting in the roasting pan; for this see the plate in roasted sirloin of beef (Fig. 306); have the bird trussed for roasting (No. 179). The grater is used so that the meat does not lie in the dripping, this being the best way to attain perfect results in roasting, but attention must be paid to keep turning it over and basting frequently with the dripping fat; care must also be observed not to allow this fat to burn, and in order to avoid this pour a little hot water from time to time into the pan. After the capon is nicely done, withdraw untruss, and serve it on a very hot dish; drain off all the fat so that only the glaze remains in the pan, detach this with a clear gravy (No. 404), strain the gravy, remove the fat and pour a part of it over the capon, serving the remainder in a sauce-boat.

CHICKEN (Poulet).

(1827). CHICKEN BREASTS À LA CHEVREUSE (Estomacs de Poulet à la Chevreuse).

Dip the breasts of two or three chickens in boiling water, lard them with some fillets of ham, and truffles cut the size shown (No. 4, Fig. 52), braise and as soon as cooked drain and arrange them against a triangle-shaped bread support; between each chicken lay a group of truffles, one of olives and another of quenelles; pour some suprême sauce (No. 547) around them and serve more in a sauce-boat.

(1828). CHICKEN À LA DELISLE—BROILED (Poulet Grillé à la Delisle).

Split a chicken in two through the back after having drawn, singed and cleansed it well; trim it nicely, remove the lights and season with salt and prepared red pepper (No. 168), dip in melted butter, then roll in bread-crumbs and broil over a slow fire; serve on a garnishing prepared as follows: Peel four medium tomatoes, cut them in four, press out the seeds and fry in butter with finely shredded green peppers, adding a little kneaded butter (No. 579), let simmer until thoroughly done. Prepare a low oval border of Piedmontese risot (No. 739) with parmesan; unmold on a dish and lay the tomatoes in the center with the broiled chicken on top; trim the drum sticks with frills (No. 10), and serve very hot.

FIG. 353.

(1829). CHICKEN À LA IRVING—BROILED AND STUFFED (Poulet Farci et Grillé à la Irving).

Procure very young chickens each one to weigh a pound and a quarter; draw, singe and clean them well picking out all the pin feathers; split them in two through the back, and take off the meat from the legs without injuring the skin; chop up this meat with the same quantity of fresh fat pork, a few spoonfuls of cooked fine herbs (No. 385), and half as much bread-crumbs; season with salt, pepper and nutmeg, adding one whole egg; lay this dressing in the inside part of the chickens, cover with melted butter and besprinkle with bread-crumbs; lay them on a double hinged broiler to broil very slowly but to a fine color. Fry colorless one tablespoonful of onions with as much small squares of raw ham; moisten with a gill of veal blond (No. 423), a gill of espagnole sauce (No. 414), and a gill of tomato purée (No. 730); let the whole simmer for ten minutes, then strain the sauce through a fine sieve and pour it into the bottom of the dish; sprinkle over with chopped parsley and lay the stuffed chickens on top.

(1830). CHICKEN WITH BACON, MAÎTRE-D'HÔTEL—BROILED (Poulet Grillé au Petit Salé à la Maître-d'Hôtel).

Singe a good small chicken, draw and clean it well plucking out all the feathers; leave the pinions on; cut off the legs one inch below the joint and split the chicken down through the back to open it entirely; take out the breast bone and lights, clean the insides properly decreasing the bones of the carcass; beat the chicken in order to flatten it, and pare (Fig. 353), then lay it in a dish and baste with melted butter or oil; season with salt and place it in a double broiler to broil over a slow fire for fifteen to twenty minutes; after the chicken has acquired a fine color and is properly done, dress it on an oval hot dish and cover with some maître-d'hôtel butter (No. 581), surround with slices of bacon and serve.

(1831). CHICKEN WITH TARRAGON GRAVY OR SAUCE—BROILED (Poulet Grillé au Jus à l'Estragon ou à la Sauce à l'Estragon).

Draw a young pound and a half chicken, cut off the legs at the first joint, cut a slit in the chicken near the pope's nose and pass the stump bone through the slit; split the chicken in two lengthwise, pare each part, beat down to flatten, season and roll in melted butter, then in white bread-crumbs and broil on both sides turning over when the meats are found to be done. Dress the two half chickens on a hot dish garnish the leg bones with frills (No. 10), and serve with some good tarragon gravy or else with tarragon sauce (No. 548).

(1832). CHICKEN COCOTTE (Poulet en Cocotte).

Cut up one small pound and a quarter to pound and a half chicken; season with pepper, only divide it into four parts, the two legs and the breast part cut in two; put the pieces in the bottom of a cocotte (small earthen saucepan, Fig. 354) with a little piece of butter the size of a nut, placing the legs underneath and the breasts on top, add a small bunch of parsley garnished with thyme and bay leaf and over lay two ounces of unsmoked bacon cut in five-eighths inch squares blanched, then fried in butter, also a dozen and half pieces of potato-shaped like cloves of garlic and as many small raw onions fried to a light color in butter; lay here and there half an ounce more butter, put on the lid and push into a moder-

FIG. 354.

ate oven for half an hour. The cocotte should stand directly on the bottom of the oven; turn the ingredients over carefully ranging the meat on top of the vegetables; let cook for another ten to fifteen minutes, then add a little clear gravy (No. 404) and chopped parsley; toss and serve in the cocotte itself.

(1833). ÉPIGRAMMES OF CHICKEN À LA VOLNAY (Épigrammes de Poulet à la Volnay).

Raise the fillets from four chickens, remove the minion fillets and skin, bone thoroughly and stuff the thighs, then put them into half heart-shaped bottomless molds three-eighths of an inch high, braise and leave to cool under the pressure of a weight; pare, dip in eggs and bread-crumbs and fry nicely. Sauté the breasts on a moderate fire, drain and dress them in a circle alternate with the thighs, decorate with fancy favor frills (No. 10); and fill the center with a garnishing of whole chestnuts, truffles, mushrooms and cover with velouté sauce (No. 415) that has been thickened at the last moment with egg-yolks and raw cream.

(1834). CHICKEN FILLETS OR BREASTS À LA BÉRANGER (Filets ou Ailes de Poulet à la Béranger).

Raise the fillets or wings with the pinions attached from six roasted chickens of two pounds each, having them well larded and not too much cooked; pare nicely, suppressing the skin and lay them in a sautoir with well buttered cream béchamel (No. 411). Dress them in a circle with a croûton of unsmoked red beef tongue between each piece. Add some mushroom heads to the béchamel and use them to fill in the center of the circle; lay on top half-spherical decorated chicken quenelles and garnish around with small half heart bread croûtons fried in butter and having their pointed ends dipped first in meat glaze (No. 402), then in chopped parsley. The word "ailes" should be used in preference to the word "filets" in making French menus, to avoid the repetition of this word which appears so often in French.

(1835). CHICKEN FILLETS OR BREASTS À LA BODISKO (Filets ou Ailes de Poulet à la Bodisko).

Raise the large fillets from six two pound chickens; suppress the skin and split them in two through their thickness without detaching the parts; season with salt, pepper, and nutmeg, and fill up the opened space with cooked fine herbs (No. 385) mixed with quenelle forcemeat (No. 89). Break six egg-yolks in a dish, add two gills of melted butter and beat them together; dip the fillets into this and then roll them in bread-crumbs; lay them on a buttered baking pan, pour butter over and cook in a hot oven, then drain. Trim the pointed ends with favor frills (No. 10), and dress the fillets in a circle filling the center with cèpes fried in butter, moistened with sour cream and reduced. Serve separately a well buttered white bordelaise sauce (No. 436), thickening it with egg-yolks and butter, straining it through a tammy.

(1836). CHICKEN FILLETS OR BREASTS À LA CÉRTOSA (Filets ou Ailes de Poulet à la Cértosa).

Clean well six good fleshy chickens; raise the fillets covered with their skin and sauté them in butter. Prepare a fine Julienne (No. 318) with the red part of carrots blanched in an abundance of water, drained and fried in butter with mushrooms, cut the same shape and size, and also some truffles cut likewise. Add the Julienne to the chickens, moisten with very little broth (No. 194a), and Marsala wine, cover the saucepan and let cook in a slack oven; baste and moisten the chicken slowly, and as soon as the sauce is found to be sufficiently reduced, thicken it with velouté sauce (No. 415), egg-yolks, and cream, then dress the fillets in a pyramid, and pour the sauce over; garnish around with bread-crumb croûtons cut heart-shaped, and fried in butter.

(1837). CHICKEN FILLETS OR BREASTS À LA CHISELHURST (Filets ou Ailes de Poulet à la Chiselhurst).

Raise the fillets from six two pound chickens; pare, suppress the skin, and lard six of them with small shreds of larding pork (No. 3, Fig 52) and the other six with slices of truffles the same size as the pork; pare the minion fillets and lard six with smaller pork lardons than those used for the fillets, and the other six with small pieces of truffles cut the same size. Lay them in two separate buttered sautoirs, the truffles in one and the larding pork in the other, having previously given the minion fillets the shape of a crescent. Cover over the truffled fillets with thin lardon of fat pork, and cook those larded with pork on a brisk fire while those with truffles are to be cooked more slowly. Dress in a circle alternating the two kinds, and fill the center with balls of truffle mingled with supreme sauce (No. 547). Place the truffled minions on top of the larded fillets and the larded minions on top of the truffled fillets; cover with a light suprême sauce, serving some of the sauce in a sauce-boat.

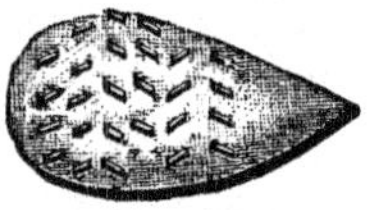

FIG. 355.

FIG. 356.

(1838). CHICKEN FILLETS OR BREASTS À LA CUSSY (Filets ou Ailes de Poulet à la Cussy).

Pare twelve chicken fillets being careful to keep the minion fillets aside, beat these large fillets to flatten them, then pare into half hearts, rounded on one side and pointed on the other, season with salt and white pepper. Take the minion fillets, the parings and as much raw chicken meat and with it prepare a cream forcemeat (No. 75), adding to it a quarter as much very fine mushroom purée (No. 722). Pour clarified butter into a sautoir, heat it well and range the chicken fillets on top simply to stiffen on one side only; drain them off leaving the butter in the pan and place the fillets on a baking sheet, one beside the other, cover with buttered paper and let get cold without

FIG. 357.

any pressure, then pare. Cover these fillets with the cream forcemeat, smooth them well rounded on the top and range them once more in the sautoir containing the butter, place them in the oven to finish cooking and to poach the forcemeat; brush them over with butter as soon as the forcemeat becomes sufficiently solid not to have them spoiled, then dress them rosette-shaped on a dish, garnishing each pointed end with a favor frill (No. 10). Serve with a well buttered supreme sauce (No. 547), part of it poured under the fillets and the other part served separately.

(1839). CHICKEN FILLETS OR BREASTS À L'ÉCARLATE (Filets ou Ailes de Poulet à l'Écarlate).

Take the fillets from six medium chickens, remove all the skin and epidermis, detach the minion fillets and free them of the sinew and skin which covers them, streak them with pieces of beef tongue and form into rings and place in a buttered sautoir. Sauté the large fillets over a brisk fire with butter. Cut twelve slices of very red beef tongue into half hearts the size of the fillets and three-sixteenths of an inch thick; warm them in stock (No. 194a) and just when ready to serve, drain and decorate each fillet with a favor frill (No. 10), dress in a circle having them intercalated with the half-hearts of tongue. Poach the minion fillet rings, fill the inside of the circle with a garnishing composed of small mushroom heads, truffle balls and quenelles all mixed with velouté sauce (No. 415), reduced with cream, and range the minion fillets around the whole; serve a well buttered velouté sauce separately.

(1840). CHICKEN FILLETS OR BREASTS, CHEVALET À L'ÉCUYÈRE (Filets ou Ailes de Poulet Chevalet à l'Écuyère).

FIG. 358.

Prepare the large fillets and minion fillets the same as for Harrison (No. 1844), lay them on sheets of tin bent into semicircles three inches by one and a half high, well buttered and maintain both fillets on this mold with wooden skewers run through holes bored in the tin, laying the streaked minion fillets on top of the larger fillets underneath (Fig. 358) baste over with butter and cook in a slow oven. Truss some fine crawfish cooked à la bordelaise, dress them crown-shaped on a dish garnished with a tomato purée (No. 730) and lay the fillets of chickens on top of the crawfish; serve separately a bordelaise sauce (No. 436) made with white wine and having three-sixteenths inch squares of mushrooms added.

(1841). CHICKEN FILLETS OR BREASTS À L'IMPÉRATRICE (Filets ou Ailes de Poulet Impératrice).

Procure six young chickens each one weighing about a pound and a half; lift off the breasts with the pinions and large fillets attached and suppress all sinews and skin. Chop the fillets on both sides without penetrating through the flesh and season with salt, pepper and nutmeg; dampen the surfaces with egg-white, besprinkle with very finely chopped truffles and over these spread a very thin layer of cream forcemeat (No. 75); dip in fresh bread-crumbs and lay them on a buttered sheet, pour butter over and cook in a hot oven. Make some croustades in half heart-shaped buttered bottomless molds lined with puff paste fragments (No. 149) rolled out thin; line them with buttered paper and fill them with rice and then cook in a moderate oven; when done empty out and fill up with bits of celery cut in quarter-inch dice blanched, cooked in broth and fallen to a glaze, then mingled with velouté sauce (No. 415) and thickened; when ready to use with egg-yolks diluted in cream and a few small pats of butter. Lay the breasts on top of these croustades, trim the pinions with paper frills (No. 10) and serve very hot.

(1842). CHICKEN FILLETS OR BREASTS, EPICUREAN (Filets ou Ailes de Poulet à l'Épicurienne).

Prepare the fillets of six young two-pound chickens, observing that they be white and tender; remove the skin and epidermis and lard them with fine larding pork (No. 4, Fig. 52), place them in a buttered sautoir and let cook to attain color in a very hot oven, then drain and decorate with

FIG. 359.

frills (No. 10). Streak each minion fillet with six round thin slices of truffles, roll them into rings and place them in a buttered sautoir to poach in the oven without coloring. Dress the large fillets on a forcemeat ring and decorate the outside with the minion fillets. Detach the glaze from the bottom of the sautoir with a little sherry wine, free it of all fat and add a little velouté sauce (No. 415); thicken just when ready to serve with raw egg-yolks diluted with cream and fresh butter; run the sauce through a tammy and pour a part over the breasts and minions and the balance in a sauce-boat. Make twelve five-eighths of an inch diameter balls with foies-gras taken direct from a terrine, rubbed through a sieve; dip them in eggs, roll in bread-crumbs and fry in very hot frying fat; place one of these balls in the center of each minion fillet ring and serve at once.

(1843). CHICKEN FILLETS OR WINGS À LA GÉNIN (Filets ou Ailes de Poulets à la Génin).

Take the skin covered fillets from six chickens with the wings, and after paring them neatly, sauté them in butter over a good fire, seasoning with salt and pepper; when done and a fine color, add a little finely chopped shallots and let these fry with the chicken fillets, then add some finely minced fresh mushrooms; when these have evaporated their humidity, moisten with white wine and finish with a little chicken glaze(No. 398). Dress the wings on half heart-shaped bread croûtons fried in butter; add a little velouté sauce (No. 415) to the sauce, reduce and season properly, finishing it with a little foies-gras; pass through a fine sieve, pour over the fillets, sprinkle chopped parsley over and serve very hot.

(1844). CHICKEN FILLETS OR BREASTS À LA HARRISON (Filets ou Ailes de Poulet à la Harrison)

Pare twelve raw chicken fillets to the shape of half hearts; lift off the minion fillets and remove the sinews and fine skin which covers, then cut six bias incisions through half of the thickness of these minions and in each of them lay a thin round slice of truffle. Place the fillets in a buttered sautoir and the scored minions on top lengthwise, pour butter over and cover with a strong buttered paper; cook for ten to twelve minutes on a slow fire. Prepare some boned terrapin à la Maryland (No. 1085); spread a quarter inch thick layer of this on a baking sheet and when cold cut it up into oblong pieces, one and three-quarters wide by three and a half long; dip these

FIG. 360.

pieces in eggs and bread-crumbs, and fry to a fine color; drain, wipe and dress the fillets flat on these terrapin crusts. Pour a little half-glaze (No. 400) with Madeira in the bottom of the dish and serve with a separate sauce-boat of espagnole sauce (No. 414) into which squeeze the juice of an orange, adding a dash of cayenne pepper, meat glaze (No. 402) and plenty of butter.

(1845). CHICKEN FILLETS AND BREASTS À LA LORENZO (Filets et Ailes de Poulets à la Lorenzo).

Raise the breasts with the fillets from six young, one pound and three-quarters to two pound chickens; lift off the skin and epidermis, also the minion fillets; place the breasts on a buttered baking sheet with the minions scored with truffles on top, laying them along

FIG. 361.

the thick edge of the breasts; pour over butter and cover with buttered paper, then cook in a moderate oven; garnish the minions with paper frills (No. 10). Dress crown-shaped and fill the inside with a Lorenzo garnishing made as follows:

Lorenzo Garnishing.—Have espagnole sauce (No. 414) with a few tarragon leaves added, celery cut in one inch pieces, blanched and cooked in broth (194a); blanched olives stoned and filled with quenelle forcemeat (No. 89) containing ancho-vies, whole chestnuts cooked in broth; artichoke bottoms pared into half hearts, five-six-teenths inch squares of truffles and some large capers. The border for chicken breasts à la Lorenzo, are made oval and in the following manner: Butter a mold (Fig. 139) with butter softened without being melted; decorate the sides either with fanciful cuts of truffles, or tongue, or even both; fill it up with cream forcemeat (No. 75) or quenelle forcemeat (No. 89) and lay this border in a sautoir; pour boiling water around, set it in a slow oven and when poached, meaning when firm to the touch, unmold and dress the breasts on top and the garnishing in the center.

(1846) CHICKEN FILLETS OR BREASTS À LA LUCULLUS (Filets ou Ailes de Poulet à la Lucullus).

The large and the minion fillets are to be prepared as described in the Harrison fillets (No. 1844), lay them in a buttered sautoir, twisting slightly so as to have them assume the shape of a chop; lay the minion fillets on the outside edge of the large fillet, mask with melted butter, cover with a strong buttered paper and cook in a slack oven for twelve to fifteen minutes; trim the pointed ends with favor frills (No. 10); dress the fillets in a circle filling up the inside with a garnishing of truffles and tongue balls half an inch in diameter, also capon kidneys, all to be mixed with béarnaise sauce (No. 433) into which has been stirred a few spoonfuls of meat-glaze (No. 402).

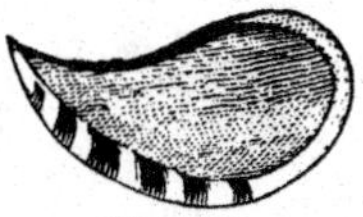

FIG. 362.

(1847). CHICKEN FILLETS OR BREASTS À LA MARCEAU (Filets ou Ailes de Poulet à la Marceau).

FIG. 363.

Remove the breasts from six chickens each one of them to weigh from a pound and a half to two pounds; suppress the skin and sinews and lift off the minion fillets to streak with truffles; pare the large fillets into half heart-shapes, and lay them in a buttered sautoir; place the minion fillets on the outer edges, pour over butter, cover with buttered paper and cook in a moderate oven. Fill with cream chicken forcemeat (No. 75) some flat quarter inch thick half heart-shaped molds, placed on a sheet of buttered paper and poach very lightly, then sauté on both sides in butter and dress unmolded in a circle with the chicken fillets on top. Prepare a Marceau sauce (No. 495); when ready to serve add a little fresh butter; fill the middle of the circle with small mushroom heads fried in butter, cover over with a part of the sauce and send the remainder to accompany the dish poured into a separate sauce-boat.

(1848). CHICKEN FILLETS OR BREASTS À LA MARÉCHALE (Filets ou Ailes de Poulet à la Maréchale).

Pare twelve raw chicken fillets; remove the minion fillets, and suppress the senews and skin which covers them, then marinate in salt, pepper, parsley leaves, and lemon juice. Make an incision on one side of these large fillets, and fill it in with a Duxelle (No. 385), or else fine herbs cooked with truffles; dip in beaten eggs, then roll in bread-crumbs, and baste with clarified butter; immerse them once more in the bread-crumbs, and put on them a buttered baking sheet; pour melted butter over, and brown in a brisk oven, or else broil over a slow fire, or even sauté them in clarified butter; trim with favors (No. 10) and dress in a circle filling in the inside with a Toulouse garnishing (No. 766). Dip the minion fillets in a fine light frying batter (No. 137), roll them up into rings, and when fried and have attained a fine color, drain and dress pyramidically over the Toulouse garnishing. A suprême sauce (No. 547) to be served separately.

(1849). CHICKEN FILLETS OR BREASTS À LA MIRABEAU (Filets ou Ailes de Poulet à la Mirabeau).

Keep the minion fillets when removing the fillets or wings from the chickens; suppress all the skin and sinews from the large fillets, take off the minion fillets and marinate the larger ones for two hours in a vessel containing salt, pepper, nutmeg, lemon juice, thyme, bay leaf, and parsley leaves, turning them over frequently; remove, drain, and roll in flour, then in beaten eggs, and lastly in bread-crumbs; fry in clarified butter. Pare the minion fillets into oblongs, spread over a layer of chicken quenelle forcemeat (No. 89), with cooked fine herbs (No. 385), and roll them into cylinder shapes, now range them inside a buttered timbale mold and let cook in a slow oven. Dress the chicken breasts in the center of a dish on top of a little Mirabeau sauce (No. 500), surround them with the prepared paupiettes, and on every one of these lay a channeled mushroom (No. 118) cooked and glazed in chicken glaze (No. 398). Serve with a sauce-boatful of the same sauce.

(1850). CHICKEN FILLETS OR BREASTS À LA PATTI (Filets ou Ailes de Poulet à la Patti).

Raise the large fillets from six young, two pound chickens that are quite fleshy, suppress the skin and epidermis; remove the minion fillets and from them the nerves and skin; streak these with red beef tongue. Cut an incision through one side of the large fillets without detaching the parts;

FIG. 364.

turn over so that the cut part is now outside; fill in the inside with quenelle forcemeat (No. 89), into which incorporate some foies-gras pressed through a sieve; make the fillet oval-shape like an egg, and lay the streaked minion fillet along the top of it. Place in a buttered sautoir, cover each fillet with a thin slice of fat pork, and cook in a moderate oven. Prepare a cream forcemeat (No. 75) border decorated with pistachios; poach, unmold, and dress with the fillets or breasts over, garnishing with favor frills (No 10); fill the inside of this border with very thick, well buttered chicken purée (No. 713), into which add half the same quantity of rice boiled in almond milk (No. 4). Garnish around with sliced truffles heated in a little meat glaze (No. 402), butter and Madeira, and serve with a sauce-boatful of supreme sauce (No. 547).

(1851). CHICKEN FILLETS OR BREASTS À LA PRIMATICE (Filets ou Ailes de Poulet à la Primatice).

Clean and singe six two pound chickens; lift off the large fillets and detach the minions, remove the skin and epidermis from the large fillets and lay them in a buttered sautoir. Suppress the sinews from the minion fillets, also the fine skin which covers and cut six incisions at equal distances on their length; insert an oblong piece of truffle into the first incision beginning at the smallest end; an oblong of tongue into the second incision, and so on, alternating them until the entire six are filled, then twist the minions into a round-shape and place them in a buttered sautoir; use a cornet to push into the centers some forcemeat having half quenelle (No. 89) and half cream (No. 75), both well mixed together and set a round piece of truffle on top, having it an eighth of an inch thick by three-quarters of an inch in diameter, pour over melted butter, cover over with strong buttered paper and cook in a slack oven for six to eight minutes. Sauté the large fillets on a quick fire, then dress them in a flat circle over croûtons of bread cut the same shape, but slightly narrower. On each fillet lay one minion fillet and fill the inside of the circle with a garnishing of fillets of mushrooms an eighth of an inch wide by five-eighths of an inch long; green peas, lozenge-shaped string beans, the red part of a carrot cut in triangles, quarter of an inch squares of turnips, truffles cut olive-shaped, and semi-circular pieces of tongue, all of those being added to a little velouté (No. 415) and fresh butter. Have a half-glaze sauce (No. 413) with truffle essence (No. 395) served at the same time, but separately.

(1852). CHICKEN FILLETS OR BREASTS À LA PRINCIÈRE (Filets ou Ailes de Poulet à la Princière).

Choose six well-cleansed chickens, each one to weigh a pound and three-quarters to two pounds; remove the large fillets leaving the pinion on, with the bone kept rather long; lift off the minion fillets, also suppress the large fillets' skin and the thin skin covering the minions; dip the latter in egg-whites, then roll in very finely chopped pistachios, previously run through a sieve; twist them around the finger to form a circle and place them in a buttered sautoir; cover with a sheet of buttered paper and poach just when ready to serve only; this will take but five minutes on a moderate fire. Chop the surface of the large fillet without misshaping it whatever, season with salt, pepper, and nutmeg, then cover over with chicken forcemeat and dredge or throw over finely chopped truffles, lay these in a buttered sautoir, shaping them all alike, six with the pinions on the right and six with the pinions on the left, then cook in a slack

FIG. 365.

oven. When done remove and run a ring cut from beef tongue a quarter of an inch thick on the pinion bone and decorate this also with a frill (No. 10). Dress crown-shaped filling in the interior with a garnishing composed of cocks'-combs and kidneys, also slices of foies-gras, the whole combined with supreme sauce (No. 547). Poach the minion fillets and dress them around, serving with a sauce-boatful of the supreme sauce.

(1853). CHICKEN FILLETS OR BREASTS À LA SADI-CARNOT (Filets ou Ailes de Poulet à la Sadi-Carnot).

To be made with twelve breasts. Fry a chopped shallot in butter keeping it quite colorless and add to it two tablespoonfuls of finely minced truffles, three tablespoonfuls of minced fresh mushrooms and a teaspoonful of chopped parsley; fry the whole for a few moments on the fire, then add a little chicken glaze (No. 398), season and let get partially cold before stirring in three raw egg-yolks. Remove the skin and epidermis from the breasts and cut five gashes on the top of the minion fillets; introduce in each gash a thin round of truffle half an inch in diameter form the fillets into rings and lay them in a buttered sautoir, filling their interiors with quenelle forcemeat (No. 89) and on top of this set a five-eighths of an inch round of truffle. Split the large fillets through their sides and fill them with the above preparation, then range them in a sautoir with clarified butter and lemon juice; sauté, drain, garnish with favor frills (No. 10) and dress in a circle on half heart-shaped croûtons of bread-crumbs fried in butter, cover with a tomato sauce (No. 549) and Béarnaise sauce (No. 433), mixed and garnish around the large fillets with the minion fillets, glazing the slices of truffles with meat glaze.

(1854). CHICKEN FILLETS OR BREASTS À LA TOULOUSE (Filets ou Ailes de Poulet à la Toulouse).

Pare twelve raw chicken fillets; take off the minion fillets, cut in the large fillet a deep gash lengthwise without separating the pieces, turn the meat over so that the gashed part is now outside and fill in the inside with a well mixed quenelle forcemeat (No. 89) and foies-gras that has been passed through a sieve half of each, having as much as would make an inch and a half diameter ball; envelop well this dressing in the flesh of the fillet, shaping them into pretty ovals and well rounded on the top (Fig. 364); put in more or less forcemeat, according to the size of the fillet so that when they are finished they look all alike; lay on top of each of these a small minion fillet streaked by cutting six incisions and placing in each one a thin slice of truffle proportioned to the size of the minion fillet. Cover the bottom of a sautoir with clarified butter, lay over the chicken fillets at equal distances apart, pour over more melted butter and cover with a strong buttered paper; cook them in a slow oven for twelve to fifteen minutes, drain, trim with favor frills (No. 10) and dress in a circle; pour into the center a Toulouse garnishing (No. 766).

(1855). CHICKEN FILLETS OR BREASTS À LA VALENÇAY (Filets ou Ailes de Poulet à la Valençay).

Pare twelve raw chicken fillets without detaching the minion fillet; cut a gash down the whole length and in the middle of each fillet without separating the parts; turn the meat inside out fill the inside space with a preparation of chopped truffles fried in butter and thickened with meat glaze then allowed to cool off and mix with one egg-yolk. Dip each one of the fillets in velouté sauce (No. 415) reduced with cream and when they are quite cold, immerse them in beaten eggs and roll in fresh white bread-crumbs; smooth them shapely with the blade of a knife. At the last moment range the fillets in a sautoir with clarified butter and brown them on both sides over a

FIG. 366.

moderate fire; drain and trim with favor frills (No. 10). Dress in a circle filling the inside space with tomatoes prepared as follows: Cut medium-sized sound and peeled tomatoes into quarters, press out the juice and seeds, then fry them in butter seasoning with a little salt and sugar. Serve a half-glaze sauce (No. 413) with Madeira separately.

(1856). CHICKEN FILLETS OR BREASTS À LA VALERRI (Filets ou Ailes de Poulet à la Valerri).

Prepare twelve fillets by removing the thin skin covering them; remove the minion fillets to streak with red beef tongue; turn each one of these around a large Spanish olive, replacing its

FIG. 367.

stone by quenelle forcemeat (No. 89), pushed through a cornet; on top of this forcemeat set a small truffle ball. Lay these in a buttered sautoir, cover with a sheet of buttered paper, and poach them in a slow oven, just when ready to use. Sauté the large fillets lightly with butter and lemon juice, and lay them under a weight, then divide them in two through their entire thickness. Range half of them very closely

FIG. 368.

together, and pour over a layer of soubise (No. 723), having it a quarter of an inch thick, set the other twelve halves on top of these halves, and leave till cold, then pare them all evenly into half heart-shapes; dip each separate double piece in well reduced but partially cold allemande sauce (No. 407), and let cool off again, then dip in eggs, roll in bread-crumbs, and fry in clarified butter; drain, trim with favor frills (No. 10), and dress in a circle; fill up the center with mushrooms sautéd in butter and fine herbs, pour over some half-glaze (No. 400) and Madeira, and set the minion fillets on top of these mushrooms. Serve separately a sauce-boat of half-glaze sauce (No. 413).

(1857). CHICKEN À LA VILLEROI (Poulet à la Villeroi).

An entrée of chicken à la Villeroi arranged and dressed as in Fig. 369 can be served at the most elegant dinners. This entrée is dressed on a wooden foundation with a round and slightly conical support in the center, both being covered with cooked or noodle paste (No. 142). Cook about fifteen fine, turned, very white, even sized mushroom heads. Select three good, tender chickens, not too large, but quite fleshy; when well cleaned, truss and cover over with thin slices of fat pork and "poêlé" them in some good stock (No. 12), keeping them quite rare; drain, untruss and cut each chicken into five pieces; first take the legs while still very hot, and quickly remove the large second joint bone; cut off the stump at two-thirds of its length and range them on a small baking tin, one beside the other, letting them cool off under a weight. Detach the upper part of the breasts from the bodies, suppress the breast bones, pare them into oblongs and also leave to cool. Remove the

FIG. 369.

skin from the fillets, pare them prettily, detaching the pinion bone and cutting away the flesh from around. Trim the legs the same shape as the fillets and imitate the minion bone by the shortened stump. Dip each one of these pieces separately into a well seasoned, succulent and thick tomato sauce (No. 549) and Villeroi sauce (No. 560) mixed; return them at once to the same tin they were taken from, and leave to cool for a couple of hours; now take up the pieces one by one, detach any surplus of sauce and roll them immediately in fresh white bread-crumbs, then dip them in beaten eggs and bread-crumb once more; shake them nicely without handling them too much, and place them in a frying basket (Fig. 121); fry in very hot fat till a good color is acquired, then drain and dress the legs and fillets against the support almost upright one piece slightly overlapping the other; on the summit of the support lay a bed of fried parsley and over this the breasts pyramidically arranged; set the mushroom heads in a row around the bottom of the dish, cover over with a little of the velouté and serve the entrée at once.

(1858). CHICKEN FILLETS OR BREASTS AU SUPRÊME (Filets ou Ailes de Poulet au Suprême).

Select six medium chickens of two pounds each, remove the large fillets, also their skin and 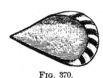 epidermis; pare these into half hearts and range in a buttered sautoir; on top of the thickest part of these lay the minion fillet in a half circle after it has been scored; pour over butter and the juice of a lemon, cover with a buttered paper and cook in a hot oven. Set some supême sauce (No. 547) and chicken glaze (No. 389) in a sautoir and just when ready to serve stir in fresh butter, cream and six ounces of peeled and sliced truffles. Trim all the fillets with favor frills (No. 10) and dress them in a circle filling in the inside with the sliced truffles and sauce. Serve a sauce-boat of supreme sauce (No. 547) at the same time.

FIG. 370.

(1859). CHICKEN FILLETS OR BREASTS, MEXICAN STYLE, IN PAPERS (Filets ou Ailes de Poulet à la Mexicaine en Papillotes).

Remove the fillets from six fine medium-sized chickens; pare them leaving on the pinions and skin, then sauté them, and when done wrap them up in a matignon with white wine (No. 406), adding peeled tomatoes cut in eight pieces, fried in butter and seasoned with salt, pepper, and chopped parsley. Prepare some sheets of paper heart-shaped and well oiled; place on one half a little of the cooked matignon, the tomatoes, some risot (No. 739) and fried sweet peppers; lay one of the breasts or fillets on top and cover with more of the ingredients, then close by pinching the two edges together all around and lay them on a buttered dish; place in a hot oven to heat the contents and color the paper; serve immediately.

(1860). CHICKEN FILLETS OR BREASTS WITH CUCUMBERS (Filets ou Ailes de Poulet aux Concombres).

Obtain some very small clean chickens, raise the fillets and remove the minion fillets; pare the large fillets, suppress the skin and lard the tops with fine lardons (No. 4, Fig. 52) of larding pork, season and range them in a sautoir with butter, place this on a hot fire and two minutes later, remove and put them into a hot oven to let cook rare, but of a fine color, then glaze over with a brush, remove, drain and garnish the ends with favor frills (No. 10). Dress into the middle of a hot dish a garnishing of purée of cucumbers (No. 714), smooth the surface with the blade of a knife and dress the chicken fillets on the outside, pouring some supreme sauce (No. 547) around and serving more in a sauce boat.

FIG. 371.

(1861). CHICKEN FRICASSEE (Fricassée de Poulet).

Take a well cleansed chicken of two and a half to three pounds; cut the two fillets, the legs, the breast in one, back in two and two wings retaining all the skin. Fill a saucepan with cold water, and soak the pieces of chicken in it for one hour, then throw this off and replace it by one quart of cold water adding to it two medium onions, one containing a clove, a bunch of parsley garnished with a bay leaf and thyme, salt and pepper. Cook the chickens, skim and let simmer gently, be sure that the chicken is cooked before taking them out, and when done, drain on a colander, then lay the pieces in cold water; make a roux with three ounces of butter and three ounces of flour, cook for a few moments without browning, then put in the chicken stock and the liquid from a pound of mushroom heads, as soon as the sauce comes to a boil, remove it to the corner of the range for half an hour. Pare and clean the pieces of chicken carefully, lay them in a low saucepan, remove all the fat from the sauce and pour it through a wire sieve on the chicken, cover and heat it over a slow fire, thicken with four egg-yolks and one ounce of butter by first diluting the yolks with a little of the sauce and increasing gradually until half the sauce is combined with the eggs, then stir it all together, set it on the fire and roll the pieces in; after the sauce thickens, strain it again through a tammy, add the mushrooms to the sauce. Dress the chicken by forming a high square with the two back pieces and the two wings, in the center of the dish; place the two fillets and two legs against the square and the piece of breast on top, cover with the sauce, putting the mushrooms on the four corners, pour the sauce over and garnish around with small round rice croquettes made with almond milk.

(1862). CHICKEN FRICASSEE À LA BOUCHARD (Fricassée de Poulet à la Bouchard).

Singe and cut up the chickens as for a plain fricassee (No. 1861), fry them without letting attain a color in some butter, and add a heaping tablespoonful of flour, mix well and pour in a pint of chablis wine, some broth (No. 194a), and a garnished bunch of parsley (No. 123); cook very slowly and when done, take out the pieces of chicken; thicken the sauce with four egg-yolks and a little butter, pass the sauce through a tammy and just when ready to serve add two chopped blanched shallots; some tarragon leaves and chopped parsley. Pour this over the chicken, garnishing around with Villeroi oysters (No. 698), and mushroom heads fried in butter, then tossed in meat-glaze (No. 402), butter and lemon juice; serve immediately.

(1863). CHICKEN FRICASSEE À LA CHEVALIÈRE (Fricassée de Poulet à la Chevalière).

After the chickens are singed, remove the pouch and raise the fillets whole, with the pinions; slide the blade of a keen, thin knife between the meat and skin covering the fillets, lard them over with fine shreds of pork and lay them in a lightly buttered sautéing pan. Pare the minion fillets and lard them with either truffles or tongue, then shape them into rounds, two and a quarter inches in diameter; place them in a buttered sautoir on thin slices of fat pork. Cut up the remainder of the chickens and cook them the same as for the plain chicken fricassee (No. 1861). Trim the legs and bread-crumb them. Prepare and cook a croustade the same width as the serving dish, having it three inches high, glaze the larded fillets; cook the minion fillets, and fry the legs to a nice golden color. Dress the backs and wings in the center of the croustade; cover lightly with allemande sauce (No. 407), then range the legs leaving them against the backs; place the larded fillets between these legs, and the minion fillets around; in each of the latter set a fine glazed truffle, then glaze the fillets. Serve with a velouté sauce (No. 415), thickened when ready, with egg-yolks, butter, and cream; heat well without boiling, and throw in some chopped mushrooms.

(1864). CHICKEN FRICASSEE À LA FAVORITE (Fricassée de Poulet à la Favorite).

Prepare and cut up the chickens the same as for the plain fricassee (No. 1861); soak the pieces for half an hour, then drain and return them to the saucepan to moisten with white broth (No. 194a); cook the chicken, drain it in a colander, and run the liquid through a napkin; put it back on the fire to reduce to half adding eight gills of velouté sauce (No. 415), then reduce once more until the sauce adheres to the spoon, afterward finish with egg-yolks and butter. Strain through a tammy, and keep hot in a bain-marie. Wash thoroughly the pieces of cooked chicken in cold water; pare nicely, and place them in the sauce; after they are well heated, dress and garnish around with a cluster of carrot balls half an inch in diameter, blanched and cooked in white stock (No. 194a) and a little sugar, also small white onions cooked in white broth. Decorate the outside with small flat egg-plant croquettes containing mushrooms and truffles, and use also trussed crawfish for the ornamentation.

(1865). CHICKEN FRICASSEE À LA LUCIUS (Fricassée de Poulet à la Lucius).

Draw and singe a clean, white meat three pound chicken, cut it up into eight pieces and split the carcass in two, also the neck and legs, wash these pieces in tepid water, place them in a sauce-pan containing water to heat, simply to stiffen the meat, then drain, refresh and wipe well on a cloth. Boil half a pound of blanched rice in broth for twenty minutes, keeping it white and consistent; when ready pour it into a plain buttered border mold (Fig. 139), pressing it down well and keep it in a warm heater for eight minutes. Melt some butter in a saucepan, add to it the pieces of chicken with a garnished bouquet (No. 123), two quartered onions, salt and pepper corns, fry the chicken over a good fire without browning, dredge over a heaping spoonful of flour and continue cooking two minutes while stirring, take the saucepan from the fire, and pour in gradually some hot stock (No. 194a), stirring until it reaches boiling point; let cook for eight minutes on a moderate fire, then remove it to a slower fire to finish cooking the chicken; as fast as each of the pieces are done; the tenderest ones first, take them out, suppressing the legs and carcasses, then pare the remainder and lay them in another saucepan, strain the sauce, reduce it for a few moments to thicken, pour it over the chicken and finally finish the fricassee with a thickening of two raw egg-yolks, half a gill of cream and an ounce of butter divided in small pats; cook this thickening without letting it boil, and squeeze in the juice of a lemon. Dress the fricassee inside the rice border, unmold it on a hot dish, cover it moderately with the sauce and send the remainder to the table in a sauce-boat.

(1866). CHICKEN FRICASSEE À LA WALESKI (Fricassée de Poulet à la Waleski).

Take three medium chickens each one to weigh two pound and a half; cut both up into seven pieces each, the two legs, two fillets, two from the back and one breast bone; steep them in cold water for an hour, then drain and range in a saucepan; moisten to cover with broth (No. 194a) adding a medium carrot cut in four, a middle-sized onion, a bunch of parsley garnished with thyme and bay leaf, one clove, and peppercorns; allow the chickens to cook for fifteen minutes, then drain and reserve the broth; refresh and sponge the pieces on a cloth, paring them neatly. Melt three ounces of butter in a saucepan, lay in the pieces of chicken and fry rapidly without browning; a few moments later cover with some clear velouté sauce (No. 415), prepared with the chicken broth and a glassful of white wine; boil up this liquid once, then set the saucepan on one side of the fire to finish cooking the contents; when done, free the sauce of all its fat before straining it through a sieve into a sautoir, adding to it a few spoonfuls of mushroom broth. Reduce while stirring from the bottom of the sautoir until a thick, succulent sauce is obtained, then put in a thickening of six egg-yolks, and an ounce and a half of lobster butter (No. 580). Strain this through a tammy over the pieces of chicken, remaining in the saucepan. Just when serving squeeze in the juice of a lemon. Dress in a thin border of cream forcemeat (No. 75), decorated with truffles; surround this border with a circle of sautéd sweet peppers (No. 2769), with mushroom heads on top, and a trussed crawfish between every one. Serve the surplus of sauce in a sauce-boat.

(1867). CHICKEN FRICASSEE WITH CRUSTACEAN SAUCE (Fricassée de Poulet au Coulis de Crustacés).

Wash in plenty of water, then cook four dozen crawfish with white wine, an onion, parsley roots, thyme, bay leaf, a grain of pepper and salt; let cook over a brisk fire for five minutes, and after the first boil strain the broth through a fine sieve, then through a napkin; let it settle and pour the top off gently. Detach the tails from the crawfish bodies, pick out the meats, trim and keep them hot while covered. Chop up the tail parings and the claw meats, mix with an equal quantity of cooked chopped mushrooms, season and add a very thick béchamel (No. 409) reduced with a little chicken glaze (No. 398) so as to have a consistent preparation, then season with a coffeespoon of prepared red paper (No. 168); keep this in a bain-marie. Fasten a fried bread support on a dish. Put into a sautoir containing butter, two two-pound chickens each one divided into five pieces and parboiled in water, removing them at the first broil to drain, and fry in butter, keeping them white; season, dredge over a tablespoonful of flour for each chicken, moisten gradually with hot broth (No. 194a) and boil the liquid without ceasing to stir, letting it be in this state for eight to ten minutes; finish cooking the chickens over a slow fire. Use the crawfish hash to fill some hollow semicircular crusts; cover this with a layer of the reduced thick béchamel (No. 409) bestrew with grated parmesan and glaze under a salamander (Fig. 123); when the chickens are ready dress them on the dish leaning against the prepared support intercalating them with the crawfish tails; reduce the sauce by incorporating into it a few spoonfuls of the crawfish liquor and thicken with four egg-yolks and half a gill of cream, finishing with red butter (No. 580). Strain some of this over the chickens and serve the remainder in a sauce-boat; surround the chickens with the filled crusts after they are baked and browned.

(1868). CHICKEN FRICASSEE WITH CURRY (Fricassée de Poulet au Kari).

Divide two small chickens of a pound and a half each after cleaning well into four distinct parts; pare them well. Put two or three spoonfuls of chopped onions in a saucepan and fry with butter till of a fine color; add the pieces of chicken, toss them for two minutes and season, sprinkling two dessertspoonfuls of powdered curry over. Moisten to their height with stock (No. 194a), put in a bunch of parsley garnished with thyme and bay leaf. Peel and chop up a small sour apple, add it to the chicken and let cook over a slow fire, taking out the fillets as soon as they are done; then remove the legs and place them in another saucepan with the fillets. Strain the sauce and reduce it with a few spoonfuls of good raw cream and as much mushroom broth; take it off the fire, thicken with three egg-yolks diluted with cream and a piece of butter divided into small pats. Dress the chickens, cover over with the sauce and serve a vegetable dishful of Indian rice.

(1869). CHICKEN, MARINADE SAUCE—FRIED (Poulet Friteau à la Sauce Marinade).

Cut off the stumps and pinions from two chickens each one a pound and a half in weight, singe, draw and free them well of their pin feathers, cut them both into five pieces, two legs, two wings and the breast, suppress the second joint bones from the legs and the wish bone from the breast. Lay the pieces in a vessel to season and marinate in oil and lemon juice with sliced onions and parsley leaves; a quarter of an hour before serving, drain off the chickens, wipe them nicely on a cloth, dip in cold milk, roll in flour and plunge one piece at the time in hot frying fat, observing that those taking the longest to cook must be the first ones to be put in; fry them to a nice color, but not too rapidly, as fast as one piece is done, take it out and drain it on a cloth, salt over and dress in a pyramid on a folded napkin. Send to the table accompanied by a sauce-boatful of marinade sauce (No. 496), or else a poivrade sauce (No. 522), or a green sauce (No. 473).

(1870). CHICKEN, MÉDICIS—FRIED (Poulet Friteau Médicis).

Lard two two and a half pound very white chickens with truffles after they have been singed, drawn and well cleaned. Braise them in a saucepan lined with bardes of fat pork and moistened with mirepoix stock (No. 419) and two gills of white wine, when done, lay them in an earthenware vessel and cover with their own strained broth, leaving them thus until thoroughly cold, then cut them up into ten medium-sized pieces each, making two of each fillet, two of each leg and two of the breastbone. Place these in a vessel with two tablespoonfuls of vinegar, pepper and salt, leave them in this pickle for two hours. Heat about three pounds of good fresh lard, when very hot, dip each separate piece of chicken in frying batter (No. 137), and then in the fat to fry to a fine color, having them thoroughly warmed throughout. Drain, salt over and dress in a pyramidical form on a dish covered with a folded napkin, garnishing the top with a bunch of fried parsley. Serve a cream béchamel sauce with chopped truffles (No. 411), separately.

(1871). GRENADES OF CHICKEN À LA RITTI (Grenades de Poulet à la Ritti).

Pare some chicken fillets, remove the skin and lard with the smallest sized lardons (No. 4, Fig. 52), place them in a sautoir, the bottom covered with thin bardes of fat pork, keeping the pointed ends lying toward the center of the pan; moisten with mirepoix stock (No. 419) and mushroom liquor, then cook on a hot fire and glaze, drain and dress them on croûtons the same size and shape. Put the minion fillets in a buttered sautoir after twisting them into rings, fill the centers through a cornet with quenelle forcemeat (No. 89) and on this lay a ball of truffle; cover with a sheet of buttered paper, poach in a slack oven. Dress the grenades in a circle and the minions around, fill the middle with some foies-gras, mixed with allemande sauce (No. 407), glaze the grenades with meat glaze (No. 402).

(1872). JAMBALAIA OF CHICKEN (Jambalaia de Poulet).

Cook a quarter of a pound of rice the same as explained below, having the grains swollen but not broken and keep it dry at the oven door. Cut three ounces of cooked lean ham in three-eighths inch dice, also six ounces of cooked chicken meat, suppressing all bones and skin and having them one size. Warm the ham in a sauté-pan with butter, add to it the pieces of chicken to heat while tossing, season and sprinkle over lightly with prepared red pepper (No. 168), then put in the well drained rice, toss it with the meats and pour the whole into a vegetable dish.

Indian Rice, which is generally served as a garnishing for chicken or veal is prepared with Indian rice, it having long, white and very perfect grains; plunge a sufficiency of this into a liberal supply of boiling water, after it has been washed and picked, and as soon as it ceases to crack between the teeth, drain it on a colander; wash it in tepid salted water, spread it on a large sieve covered with a white cloth and dry for a few moments at the oven door or else in a hot steamer. Dress on a vegetable dish, cover over and serve. This is the most simple and effectual method.

(1873). CHICKENS LEGS À LA SAULNIÈRE—BIGARRURES (Bigarrures de Cuisses de Poulet à la Saulnière).

Bone the legs of some young chickens leaving on only half of the drumstick, season with salt and pepper, and fill the insides with chicken forcemeat (No. 89), mixing in with it one-third of cooked forcemeat (No. 73), and some chopped parsley; lard those taken from the right with medium lardons (No. 3, Fig. 52), and stud those taken from the left with truffles, covering these with thin slices of fat pork. Cook them in two low saucepans lined with fat pork and moistened with a mirepoix and white wine stock (No. 419); cover over with sheets of buttered paper, and cook in the oven. Glaze those that are larded, and when done drain and decorate with paper frills (No. 10). Dress in a circle filling up the interior space with a financière garnishing (No. 667).

(1874). CHICKENS' LEGS, AMERICAN STYLE—DEVILED (Cuisses de Poulet à l'Américaine à la Diable).

Broil slowly some chicken legs and when well done, dip them in English mustard diluted with mushroom catsup, salt, and cayenne, then roll them in bread-crumbs, and broil again over a slow fire until they acquire a fine color. Dress, pour lightly melted maître d'hôtel butter (No. 581) over, or else a deviled sauce (No. 459) into the bottom of the dish.

(1875). CHICKENS' LEGS AS CUTLETS WITH OLIVES (Cuisses de Poulet en Côtelettes aux Olives).

Take the legs of six young chickens; bone them keeping on part of the drumsticks, but do not open; suppress well the sinews, season and stuff with chicken quenelle forcemeat (No. 89) and fine herbs (No. 385); sew them up with coarse thread, leaving them in their original shape, range them in a flat saucepan one beside the other, salt over lightly, moisten just to cover with stock (No. 194a) and lay a piece of buttered paper on top, then cook the whole very slowly. Drain off the legs, and let cool between two boards or in the press (Fig. 71), pressing them down lightly; unsew and pare all around and on the ends, season and then dip in beaten eggs and bread-crumbs

Range them one beside the other in a flat sauce-pan with melted butter, return them to a hot fire and brown slightly on one side, then reverse them and brown them on the other. Drain and trim each drumstick with a small paper frill (No. 10); dress in a circle on a hot dish and fill the inside with an olive garnishing (No. 695), made with either verdal or Lucques olives, and serve with a sauce-boat of Colbert sauce (No. 451).

(1876). CHICKENS' LEGS IN PAPERS (Cuisses de Poulets en Papillotes).

Take out the bones from some chicken legs, leaving on half the drumstick, season, lay them in a sautoir containing bardes of fat pork and moistened with a white wine mirepoix stock (No. 419); when they are well cooked set them under the pressure of a light weight; pare all around, also the ends. Cut some sheets of strong paper into heart-shapes, oil them over and lay a very thin slice of fat fresh pork on top of one of the halves, cover this with a layer of reduced duxelle (No. 385) and a chicken leg above; cover with more of the duxelle and a very thin slice of cooked ham; enclose them in the papers, plaiting it all around, lay these on a silver dish, place them in a slack oven and when the papers have acquired a fine color and are considerably swollen, serve them immediately.

(1877). CHICKENS' LEGS, PURÉE OF JERUSALEM ARTICHOKES—FRIED (Cuisses de Poulets Frites à la Purée de Topinambours).

Remove the first joint bones, season and fry the legs in butter with finely shredded carrots, onions and leeks, adding parsley, thyme and bay leaf. Moisten with stock (No. 194a) and white wine and let simmer slowly until thoroughly done, then turn them on a deep dish, covering them entirely with their stock and leave them to cool off in this; dip each piece in beaten eggs, then roll in bread-crumbs and fry to a fine color. Dress them in a circle over a purée of Jerusalem artichokes (No. 704) serving with a separate half-glaze sauce (No. 413).

(1878). PILAU OF CHICKENS (Pilau de Poulets).

Cut up in four pieces each, two small chickens weighing no more than a pound and three-quarters apiece, obtaining two legs, two breasts, fry them for a few moments in butter, then moisten to their height with stock (No. 194a), adding a bunch of parsley garnished with aromatics, and seasoning with salt, pepper, and spices; cook the whole slowly, being most particular to remove the tenderest pieces as rapidly as they are done and transfer them into another saucepan; strain the stock, remove its fat, and pour the liquid over the meats with four gills of boiling stock added, and then throw in half a pint of Carolina rice for every quart of broth, and a little powdered saffron; cook the rice for ten minutes on a good fire then withdraw it to the corner of the stove to continue cooking for ten minutes longer; the rice should now be dry and tender; finish by taking it off the fire, and incorporating into it two ounces of fresh butter divided in small pats. Dress the stew in a deep dish or else a vegetable dish.

(1879). CHICKENS À LA CHAMPIONNE—ROASTED (Poulets Rôtis à la Championne).

Select two very fleshy chickens of two pounds each; singe, draw and clean them, picking out all the pin feathers; truss them as for an entrée, explained in the Elementary Methods (No. 178); cover the breasts with dry mirepoix (No. 419) and wrap up in a thin slice of fat pork; roast them on a spit before a slow but well-regulated fire, basting over frequently. Cut up quite fine one pound of cooked and peeled mushrooms; combine them with reduced béchamel sauce (No. 409) and finish with a little paprika and melted meat glaze (No. 402); with this preparation fill some hollow, round or semi-circular crusts (No. 52), smooth the surfaces and bestrew the tops with parmesan, then glaze them in a brisk oven or under a salamander (Fig. 123). As soon as the chickens are taken from the spit, unwrap and cut them up into five pieces each, suppressing the drumsticks; range them inside a cooked paste border (No. 10) fastened on at some distance from the edge of the dish as shown in Fig. 3; around this border lay the garnished crusts and cover the chickens lightly with a little tomato sauce (No. 549) sending a sauce-boat of the same to the table to be handed round the same time as the chicken.

(1880). CHICKENS À L'HÔTELIÈRE—ROASTED (Poulets Rôtis à l'Hôtelière).

Peel twenty medium fresh mushroom heads, empty out the insides and stuff them as explained in No. 650. Roast two tender chickens on the spit before a good fire, basting them over with butter. Chop up the mushroom ends and put them in a saucepan with thyme and bay leaf, minced shallots, two gills of white wine and two gills of gravy (No. 404); cover the pan and cook over a slow fire for ten minutes, then strain the liquid through a sieve and reduce it to the consistency of a half-glaze, adding four tablespoonfuls of melted glaze (No. 402) and two of Madeira wine; boil up the sauce for two minutes and remove it on one side to finish with butter. Salt and untruss the chickens, cut each one into five pieces and dress them pyramidically on a dish; surround with the stuffed mushrooms and pour the sauce over the chickens.

(1881). CHICKEN IN THE SAUCEPAN—ROASTED (Poulet Rôti à la Casserole).

Brown a fine, small, whole chicken trussed for roasting (No. 179) in any kind of earthen saucepan with a little butter. After the chicken has attained a light golden color, moisten it with a spoonful of clear gravy (No. 404) and half a glassful of white wine; cover over and let the liquid fall to a half-glaze. When ready to serve dish up the chicken after untrussing it. A few small whole onions may be added as a garnishing after blanching them in boiling water and then frying them. Cover the whole with a half-glaze sauce (No. 413).

(1882). CHICKENS WITH OYSTER SAUCE (Poulets à la Sauce aux Huîtres).

Blanch four dozen medium-sized oysters in their own liquor. Bard two small chickens weighing a pound and a half each, after having them singed and trussed; run them one at the time on a slender spit, fasten well by tying the legs with twine and roast in front of a good fire basting over with melted butter; untruss, untie and cut each one either in four or five parts, pare the pieces, dress them pyramid form on a dish and cover with velouté sauce (No. 415), reduced with the oyster liquor and then with fresh cream, buttering the sauce well when off of the fire, add to it the oysters, warm them, and pour the whole over the chickens besprinkling the top with chopped parsley.

(1883). CHICKENS, TOMATO CONDÉ SAUCE—STUFFED (Poulets Farcis à la Sauce Tomate Condé).

Roast some chickens, when cooked and cold, remove the breast meat, carefully leaving the other part of the chicken intact, cut these breasts into dice, also half as much mushrooms as there is chicken and half as many truffles as mushrooms, all cut in three-sixteenths of an inch squares. Put this salpicon into a béchamel sauce (No. 409), well reduced with the mushroom broth, then use it to replace the breasts in the chickens, rounding it well on the top; cover the whole with béchamel sauce (No. 409), besprinkle with bread-crumbs and a little grated parmesan cheese, pour on some clarified butter and set the chickens in a slack oven to brown slightly. Dress them on a garnishing of noodles sautéd in butter (No. 2972), and well browned, and serve at the same time a sauce-boat of clear tomato condé sauce (No. 550).

(1884). CHICKENS À LA BOURGUIGNONNE—SAUTÉD (Poulets Sautés à la Bourguignonne).

Clean and singe two small chickens, then cut them up into five parts; range these in a sautoir with melted butter and oil, some shallots and mushroom peelings; season and fry to a good color on both sides; finish to cook in a slow oven being careful to withdraw the fillets and breasts as quickly as they are done, take out all the pieces from the sautoir, unglaze its bottom with a gill of Madeira and a pint of half-glaze sauce (No. 413), strain and reduce by incorporating into it slowly two gills of Burgundy wine, previously boiled in a red copper untinned pan with aromatics and mushroom peelings. When the sauce becomes succulent, pour it over the dressed chickens and surround them with a circle of round, flat croûtons of bread fried in butter and having one side covered with a layer of baking forcemeat (No. 81), glazed over with a brush and kept warm at the oven door.

(1885). CHICKENS À LA D'ANTIN—SAUTÉD (Poulets Sautés à la d'Antin).

Prepare two small chickens of two pounds each, by cutting each one into five parts and tossing them in a sautoir with clarified butter over a moderate fire; cook when needed four artichoke bottoms, drain and mince, then put them in with the chicken, also two chopped, blanched shallots, two ounces of finely shredded cooked ham and some minced truffles and mushrooms. Pour off the fat and replace it by velouté sauce (No. 415) and meat glaze (No. 402), adding chervil, chives and a little finely cut up tarragon leaves, white wine and Madeira, reduce to a proper degree, then dress the chickens and cover with a part of the sauce, trim the drumsticks with paper frills (No. 10) and serve the remainder of the sauce separately.

(1886). CHICKENS À LA DIVA—SAUTÉD (Poulets Sautés à la Diva).

Choose good, medium-sized chickens of about two pounds each; draw, singe, and suppress well all the adhering feathers; detach the legs and wings leaving on the pinions and sufficient meat on the breast bones so that they are of the same size as the other four pieces. Put some butter to melt in a sautoir, and when a light brown, lay in the pieces of chicken, seasoning with salt, pepper, and powdered sweet peppers: toss without browning, and moisten with about a gill of veal blond (No. 423) to detach the glaze, and then finish cooking the chickens, moistening as quickly as the stock reduces, and when sufficiently done, dress. Add to the sauce some béchamel (No. 409) and tomato sauce (No. 549), a little tarragon vinegar, and some chopped, blanched shallot; just when ready to serve, thicken with egg-yolks, and butter; strain through a tammy, and pour it over the chickens, bestrewing the top with very green chopped parsley; garnish around with small flat chicken croquettes (No. 877), an inch and a quarter in diameter by half an inch in thickness, and between each of these lay a bordelaise crawfish (No. 1008), placing a channeled mushroom (No. 118) on top of every croquette.

(1887). CHICKEN À LA DODDS—SAUTÉD (Poulet Sauté à la Dodds).

Cut up the chicken as explained for sautéing chicken (No. 1906), and put the pieces in a sautoir with four ounces of butter, cook without browning, and add four ounces of small squares of onions; place it on the fire for a few seconds to cook the onions without letting attain color; then add two teaspoonfuls of curry, and two tablespoonfuls of flour; season with salt and pepper, moisten with a pint and a half of stock (No. 194a), and let boil and simmer quite slowly; when done, drain, pare well the pieces, and place them in a saucepan. Strain the sauce and reduce it with some good cream; pour this over the chicken. At the first boil dress in the shape of a pyramid and cover with a part of the sauce, reserving the remainder for the sauce-boat. Boil some rice in water for ten minutes, drain and press it into a buttered mold furnished with a cover; place it in a slack oven for fifteen minutes, and just when ready to serve, unmold it on a dish, and send it to the table with the chicken.

(1888). CHICKENS À LA DUMAS—SAUTÉD (Poulets Sautés à la Dumas).

Cut three chickens into five pieces each, having two legs, two wings and one breastbone piece; season with salt and pepper and toss them in butter with three small chopped shallots; remove the wings and breasts as rapidly as they are cooked and finish the legs, which take longer. Pare all the pieces and return them to a sautoir on the fire with a clear top part of the butter and three-quarters of a pound of minced mushrooms, pour over a few spoonfuls of thin béchamel (No. 409), roll them in the sauce without allowing it to boil. Detach the glaze from the other sautoir with a little Madeira, and add it to the sauce. Blanch three-quarters of a pound of rice, drain and place it in a saucepan and moisten it to three times its height, meaning if there be two inches high of rice, put in six inches high of unskimmed broth (No. 194a); boil, cover the saucepan and finish in the oven; it will take about twenty minutes. When the rice is sufficiently done, add to it three-quarters of a pound of very red beef tongue cut in small three-sixteenths of an inch squares, also three ounces of butter and the same quantity of grated parmesan cheese, a teaspoonful of powdered sweet peppers and a bit of cayenne pepper. Fill a plain buttered border mold (Fig. 139) with this prepared rice, keep it warm and when ready to serve invert it on a dish; dress the chickens pyramid-form in the center and cover the whole with the sauce thickened with egg-yolks, cream and butter, finishing with a pinch of prepared red pepper (No. 168). Garnish around with breaded and fried spinal marrow of veal, and send a sauce-boat of the same sauce to the table with the chicken.

(1889). CHICKENS À LA FINNOISE—SAUTÉD (Poulets Sautés à la Finnoise).

Prepare and cook three chickens the same as for the chicken hunter's style (No. 1903); when three-quarters done, put in three ounces of chopped and blanched onion, and three ounces of small squares of ham, moisten with half a pint of stock (No. 194a) in order to detach the glaze and finish cooking the chickens; in case this moisture should be found insufficient, add a little more stock to it; season with sweet Spanish peppers, salt and paprika. Just when ready to serve pour in a pint and a half of velouté (No. 415) and half a pint of cream; reduce slowly until the chicken is thoroughly cooked, thicken with egg-yolks, cream, fresh butter and lemon juice. Dress the chickens inside a border of rice boiled in stock (No. 194a) and finished with a little fine butter; strain the sauce through a tammy, pour it over the chickens and trim the wings and legs with paper frills (No 10), or serve the chickens simply with a Finnoise sauce (No. 465).

(1890). CHICKENS À LA FLORENTINE—SAUTÉD (Poulets Sautés à la Florentine).

Cut up three one and a half pound chickens in four pieces each, season with salt, pepper, ground cloves and a teaspoonful of powdered sweet Spanish peppers; sauté them in half oil and half butter, and add six ounces of raw, unsmoked ham cut in quarter inch dice; turn over to color evenly and keep sautéing on the fire, or else set the pan in a slow oven and when done drain off the pieces; add to these two gills of Malaga wine, a pint of espagnole sauce (No. 414), three table-spoonfuls of meat-glaze (No. 402), and six tablespoonfuls of tomato sauce (No. 549), also three dozen small onions that have been blanched and cooked in white broth (No. 194a), six dozen carrot balls each five-eighths of an inch in diameter, blanched for ten minutes then finished with white broth and a little sugar; three dozen turned and channeled mushroom heads (No. 118) cooked in a little water, butter, salt, lemon juice and six ounces of minced truffles. Boil up the whole, dress the chicken with the garnishing around; reduce the sauce to perfection, pouring half of it over the chicken, and trim the legs and wings with frills (No. 10); strain the remainder of the sauce and serve it separately.

(1891). CHICKENS À LA MADELEINE—SAUTÉD (Poulets Sautés à la Madeleine).

Cut in quarters two small one and three-quarter pound chickens after cleaning them well; season with salt, pepper, paprika, and sweet Spanish peppers; put them into a liberally buttered sautoir, and when they commence to brown add half a pound of bacon cut up in quarter inch squares, having it previously blanched, four ounces of carrots and the same quantity of turnips cut in three-sixteenth inch squares and blanched separately, four ounces of onions in one-eighth inch squares also blanched, and a small garnished bunch of parsley (No. 123). Moisten with a little stock (No. 194a) and velouté (No. 415), cover the sautoir and finish cooking in a slack oven until cooked; when ready to serve thicken the sauce with egg-yolks, cream, butter and lemon juice; pour this over the chickens trim the handle bones and serve.

(1892). CHICKENS À LA MARCEL—SAUTÉD (Poulets Sautés à la Marcel).

Prepare a sufficient number of chickens the same as for sautéing (No. 1906); season with salt and pepper; pour some oil into a sautoir and when very hot add the pieces of chicken and sauté them colorless; when nearly done put in one small chopped up shallot for every chicken, also a clove of garlic. Scoop out some potatoes olive-shaped, with a large oval vegetable spoon; cook them slowly in butter as well as some small artichoke bottoms after having them blanched, then finish cooking in butter; dress the chickens, garnish the artichoke bottoms with a consistent, mellow chestnut purée (No. 712) pushed through a pocket, and lay on top of this medium-sized channeled and glazed mushroom heads (No. 118); range these around the chicken and the potato olives between every one; trim the handles with frills (No. 10) and serve with a separate Colbert sauce (No. 451).

(1893). CHICKENS À LA MARENGO—SAUTÉD (Poulets Sautés à la Marengo).

Take two chickens and prepare them exactly as for the sautéd chickens (No. 1906); heat some oil in a sautoir, range in the pieces one beside the other, and set it on a brisk fire tossing them until they are of a fine color, then add a clove of crushed and chopped garlic and some mignonette. Just when prepared to serve drain off three quarters of the fat and replace it by half a pint of white wine, detaching the glaze from the pan, then add a pound of mushroom buttons, and four ounces of thickly sliced truffles. espagnole sauce (No. 414), a little meat-glaze (No. 402), a little fine tomato purée (No. 730) and lemon-juice. Dress the chickens in a pyramid form, cover over with the garnishing and trim the drumsticks and pinions with paper frills (No. 10); decorate the edges of the dish with egg-yolks fried in a small frying pan with a little oil, some half-heart small bread croûtons and middling-sized trussed crawfish.

(1894). CHICKENS À LA MARYLAND—SAUTÉD (Poulets Sautés à la Maryland).

For this dish choose small one pound chickens, split them open through the back, pare nicely (Fig. 353) and season, rub over with flour, then immerse in beaten eggs and bread-crumbs. Heat some clarified butter in a sautoir, fry the chickens in it very slowly to cook and attain a fine color, then finish cooking them in a slack oven for ten minutes. Dress the chickens on a béchamel sauce (No. 409), reduced with cream, and garnish the top with small corn fritters (No. 1349) and slices of broiled bacon, decorate the legs with paper frills (No. 10).

(1895). CHICKENS À LA MONTESQUIEU—SAUTÉD (Poulets Sautés à la Montesquieu).

By observing the drawing for this entrée the elegance of this new style of dressing can easily be perceived. On an entrée dish one inch from the edge fasten a standing openwork border made of cooked paste (Fig. 3), spreading it out slightly; brush this over with egg-yolks and dry it in the air. In the center of this border, fasten a wooden bottom to be covered with the same paste rolled out very thin. Singe three clean chickens, detach the legs, leaving on as much skin as possible, then lift off the large fillets with the pinions leaving the minion fillets adhere to the breasts, remove the skin from four of the large fillets, pare and lard with fine larding pork (No. 4, Fig. 52), range them in a sautoir lined with fat pork, salt and pour butter over. Detach the minion fillets from the breasts, trim four of them, cut five gashes on their top, into these place rounds of truffles,

FIG. 372.

laying them in a buttered sautoir. Bone the legs, pare the meats evenly, salt and stuff them with a rather firm quenelle forcemeat (No. 89) into which mix some truffled Duxelle (No. 385); sew them up and range them in a sautoir, covering over with fat pork and basting with some stock (No. 194a); cook very slowly, then drain and let to get cold under the pressure of a light weight. With the remaining large fillets and the minion fillets prepare a little cream forcemeat (No. 75) and with it fill a small, plain pyramidical mold flat on top; poach this in a bainmarie for ten minutes; cut the stuffed legs in two and return them to the sautoir with their stock reduced to a half-glaze, heat up slowly while basting at the oven door; glaze the larded fillets in a hot oven and poach the streaked minion fillets. At the last moment unmold the croûton of forcemeat on the paste-covered dish; dress the legs around, one overlapping the other, pour over a little good reduced velouté sauce (No. 415), and then range the four large fillets intercalating them with the streaked fillets; on top of the pyramid insert a small skewer garnished with truffles (Fig. 11). Surround the border with a chain of round, peeled truffles cooked just when needed with glaze (No. 402) and Madeira and send with the entrée a sauce boatful of velouté sauce reduced with the truffle broth.

(1896). CHICKENS À LA NANTAISE—SAUTÉD (Poulets Sautés à la Nantaise).

Prepare three chickens the same as for hunter's style (No. 1903,) sauté them in butter without browning and remove each piece as fast as cooked; drain off the grease, detach the glaze with a little mushroom broth and Madeira wine, add some béchamel and cream (No. 411) and let simmer slowly, pouring in a little more cream if necessary; strain the sauce and keep it boiling hot. Make a croquette preparation with artichoke bottoms and cooked lean ham, the former cut in three-sixteenth inch squares and the latter in one-eighth pieces; mingle with some thick cold béchamel (No. 409) and form it into pear-shaped croquettes, dip in eggs and bread-crumbs and fry to a fine color in clean, white, and very hot frying fat. Fry some shrimps in butter, season with salt, pepper, fine herbs and lemon juice. Dress the chickens, pass the sauce through a tammy and pour part of it over the chickens; dress the shrimps in clusters and artichoke bottom croquettes between each; serve the rest of the sauce separately.

(1897). CHICKENS À LA PARMENTIER—SAUTÉD (Poulets Sautés à la Parmentier).

Draw and singe three two pounds chickens, clean them well, suppressing all the pin feathers, cut them up in to five pieces, namely: two legs, two wings and a breastbone piece; sauté in butter and when three-quarters done add potatoes cut cylindrical shape an inch in diameter then sliced three-eights of an inch thick, or else cut in five-eighths squares; cook them partially in a frying pan with clarified butter. Finish cooking the chicken and potatoes together in the oven, being careful to remove the breasts as soon as they are done. Dress the chickens on a dish with the potatoes around, detach the glaze from the sautoir with a little clear gravy (No. 404), Madeira and half-glaze sauce (No. 413), reduce the liquid for two minutes, pass through a tammy and pour it over the chickens.

(1898). CHICKENS À LA PORTUGAISE—SAUTÉD (Poulets Sautés à la Portugaise).

Have three chickens prepared the same as for hunter's style (No. 1903), sauté them in half oil and half butter, season with salt and pepper, and when they are three-quarters done add three pounds of peeled tomatoes, halved through the center and the seeds and juice pressed out, a little finely cut up chives and three tablespoonfuls of melted glaze (No. 402); boil and simmer until thoroughly cooked. Prepare eighteen small very sound halved tomatoes; press lightly to extract the juice and fill them with a dressing prepared as follows: Put four ounces of bread-crumbs into a bowl with a tablespoonful of chopped parsley, a crushed and chopped clove of garlic, the chopped livers of three chickens, salt, pepper and nutmeg; mix the whole well together and fill each half tomato with some of this; besprinkle with bread-crumbs and grated parmesan, and lay a small piece of butter on top of every one, set them in a hot oven and when nicely browned take out and dress in a circle on a dish with the chickens in the center, dredge over with chopped parsley and decorate the leg and wing bones with paper frills (No. 10).

(1899). CHICKENS À LA SANFORD—SAUTÉD (Poulets Sautés à la Sanford).

Draw and singe small one pound and a quarter to one pound and a half chickens, divide them into four pieces, suppressing the legs above the joint, also the pinion of the wings; season with salt and pepper, and rub over with flour; they may now be if so desired dipped in eggs and in bread-crumbs; sauté them slowly in clarified butter, and when well done drain and dress; pour a little good gravy (No. 404) in the dish and garnish around with hollow tartlets filled up with Chantilly sauce à la Sanford (No. 588).

(1900). CHICKENS À LA STANLEY—SAUTÉD (Poulets Sautés à la Stanley).

Select three chickens each one weighing two pounds and a half; draw, singe, and detach the legs from the bodies, cut the carcasses on a level with the breasts and plunge these for a few moments in hot water to stiffen them, then dip them at once in cold water to refresh, lard them with lardons (No. 3, Fig. 52). With the meat taken from the legs and all the parings prepare a quenelle forcemeat (No. 89), finishing it with a dash of cayenne pepper, and two tablespoonfuls of béchamel (No. 409). Butter eighteen hollow tartlet molds with rounded bottoms, besprinkle the insides with finely chopped raw truffles, and fill them up with the prepared forcemeat; range these in a sautoir having boiling water around and reaching up to half their height, then poach the forcemeat slowly. Besides this, poach a layer of the same forcemeat on an entrée dish and keep it warm. Cut the breasts of the chickens into three pieces, two fillets and the upper part of the breast; suppress the pinions. Mince ten ounces of white onions, and fry them slowly with butter in a sautoir, and when a good color, add the chickens; season with salt and pepper, and moisten with three gills of chicken broth prepared with the carcasses and bones of these chickens; cover the sautoir and allow the liquid to fall to a glaze, then begin the operation again until the fillets and breasts are thoroughly done; remove and transfer to a flat saucepan; increase the chicken stock with a few spoonfuls of good velouté (No. 415), reduce this sauce without ceasing to stir, incorporating more of the broth into it, and lastly a gill of good raw cream; the sauce should now be succulent and of a medium consistency; thicken it with a liaison of two egg-yolks, and cook this without boiling, then strain it through a tammy into another saucepan to work it vigorously while adding butter; finish with a dash of cayenne pepper, and the juice of a lemon. At the last moment dress the fillets in a circle on the bed of forcemeat laying on the dish; fill the center of this with cut up cooked mushrooms, and place the breast pieces on top; cover over with a part of the sauce, pouring the remainder into a sauce-boat to be served separately. Unmold the small forcemeat molds, dress them around the fillets and glaze over with a brush, then serve.

(1901). CHICKENS À LA TUNISIAN—SAUTÉD (Poulets Sautés à la Tunisienne).

Divide two two-pound chickens into five pieces each, range the pieces in a sautoir with half melted butter and half oil, sauté on a moderate fire and then in the oven. When they are three-quarters cooked, season and finish, being careful to remove the fillets and other tender pieces as quickly as they get done; drain them all off, leaving only the fat in the sautoir, then pare the chickens piece by piece and range them at once in a low saucepan with a little clear gravy (No. 404) and meat glaze (No.402); keep this in a warm place; fry two ounces of finely chopped onions in butter left from the chickens with the gizzards cooked and cut in small squares, the chopped up livers and four ounces of cold tenderloin of beef or lamb cut also into one-eighth inch squares, add salt, pepper and bread-crumbs and cool this off before breaking in a few raw egg-yolks. Form this preparation into five-eighths inch diameter balls and put them in with the chicken, also a quart of velouté (No. 415) and two gills of Madeira wine. let simmer and reduce the sauce, skimming off the fat. Dress the chickens in a pyramid form with the quenelles around, and cover over with a part of the sauce passed through a tammy, serving the remainder separately. Trim the pinion bones and drumsticks with paper frills (No. 10) and lay trussed crawfish all around.

(1902). CHICKENS POINT DU JOUR—SAUTÉD (Poulets Sautés au Point du Jour).

Take two chickens and prepare them exactly as for bourguignonne (No. 1884), range them in a sautoir with melted butter. Fry colorless in butter, four ounces of chopped onions, dredge over with a tablespoonful of flour and make a small light roux; moisten this with red wine and stock (No. 194a) add a bunch of parsley garnished with thyme and bay leaf and a few mushroom parings, despumate and reduce well the sauce. Sauté the chickens in the butter and when well browned add two dozen small glazed onions, as many cooked mushroom heads and as many olives as mushrooms; strain the above sauce, pour it over the chickens and at the first boil, take out the chickens and dress. Reduce the sauce, add to it a handful of small nonpareil capers and pour it over the chickens, garnish around with tiny round crusts an inch and a half in diameter, toasted and covered on one side with anchovy butter (No. 569).

(1903). CHICKENS, HUNTER'S STYLE—SAUTÉD (Poulets Sautés au Chasseur).

Pick out three good chickens of about two and a half pounds each, draw, singe, then clean well and extract all the small pin feathers, cut them each up into seven pieces, the two wings, two legs, two pieces of the back and one of the breast bone; season with salt and pepper; melt six ounces of butter in a sautoir until it becomes a fine golden color, then lay in the pieces of chicken and toss them well; when they acquire a fine light brown on one side, turn them over to brown likewise on the other, cover the sautoir and finish cooking on a very slow fire or in the oven. When the meats are well done, drain off the butter and detach the glaze with a little stock (No.194a). Fry colorless in butter a large pinch of chopped shallot, moisten with half a bottleful of red or white Burgundy wine, reduce to half, then add a pint of espagnole sauce (No. 414) and simmer the whole for a few moments, season well, and when the sauce is properly reduced, return the chickens to it, put it back on the fire to remove at the first boil and add three ounces of cooked, lean ham cut up in one-eighth of an inch squares, slice three onions across, having them two inches in diameter by three-sixteenths of an inch in thickness, remove the largest rings and roll them in flour, then fry a few at the time in plenty of fat; dress the chickens and use these rings to garnish the top, decorate the stumps of the legs and the pinions with paper frills (No. 10) and serve immediately.

(1904). CHICKENS, PARISIAN STYLE—SAUTÉD (Poulets Sautés à la Parisienne).

Peel a few medium-sized truffles, lay them in a saucepan with a little salt and Madeira wine; cook them slightly; cook also as many mushrooms with a piece of butter and the juice of a lemon. Take two singed, drawn chickens, cut off the pinions and drumsticks, detach the thighs, and divide the breasts into three pieces, the two fillets and the upper breast part; cut the carcasses in two; crack the thigh bones in order to remove them, then place the thighs in a buttered flat saucepan; add the pinions, necks, and carcasses, season and cook on a moderate fire stirring them about at times; when partly done, add the fillets and upper breast parts, a bunch of parsley garnished with aromatic herbs, and a clove of garlic. After all the meats are well sized lift them out with a skimmer, and transfer to another saucepan, adding the truffles. Drain off the fat from the contents of the first saucepan, put in the truffle parings, and moisten with half a glassful of Madeira; boil up once or twice, then mix in double as much brown sauce

(No. 414) and the truffle stock; let cook on a brisk fire for ten minutes: skim off the fat, and strain this sauce over the chickens; heat without allowing the liquid to boil. Fasten a small fried bread pyramid in the center of a dish, around it dress first the carcasses and pinions, then the thighs and breasts, placing the upper breast pieces on top; surround the chickens with the truffles and mushrooms, place a few cocks'-combs here and there, and free the sauce once more of its fat; pour it over the chicken and serve.

(1905). CHICKENS, VIENNA STYLE—SAUTÉD (Poulets Sautés à la Viennoise).

Select chickens that weigh from a pound to a pound and a quarter; bleed them just when ready to use, and pluck them quickly, then cut them up into four pieces, performing all this operation most speedily so that the chickens have no time to become cold; season over with a mixture of salt, pepper, thyme, powdered bay leaf, and lemon juice, then dip in flour, afterward in beaten eggs, and bread-crumb them only once. Cook in a sautéing pan with clarified butter over a very hot fire, drain, sponge, and season; dress them dry with a bunch of fried parsley on the top.

(1906). SAUTÉD CHICKENS WITH HALF-GLAZE (Poulets Sautés Demi-Glace).

Sautéd chickens are cooked various ways, either with a plain sauce or garnishing.

How to Sauté.—Cut up two chickens each of two pound weight, having them well cleaned and singed, into seven pieces, viz: two legs, the breastbone, whole breasts, and the backbone, split in two, suppressing the pinions and giblets. Break the second joint bone of the legs and remove it. Heat some butter and oil in a sautoir, range the pieces of chicken in this,

| FIG. 373. | FIG. 374. | FIG. 375. |

and cook over a good but not too fierce fire, turning them over when of a nice color and well browned; remove the saucepan from off the fire and place it in the oven to finish cooking the chickens, taking out the pieces as fast as they are done, and when the legs are sufficiently cooked, drain the fat from the sautoir and return to it the pieces previously removed, then pour over a pint of half-glaze sauce (No. 413), boil up for a minute, turning the pieces over so that they are thoroughly covered with the sauce on all sides. Dress these pieces of chicken on a dish, cover and keep hot. Pour a gill of Madeira or white wine, or else half of each, into the sautoir, reduce to half, add another half pint of half-glaze sauce and some mushroom and truffle parings; boil up for a minute while stirring incessantly with a spoon, strain the sauce through a fine strainer pour it over the chickens and serve.

(1907). CHICKENS WITH FINE HERBS, TOMATO GARNISHING—SAUTÉD (Poulets Sautés aux Fines Herbes, Garnis de Tomates).

Fry chopped parsley and mushrooms and four blanched chopped shallots in butter: add two young two-pound chickens, both cut up into five pieces and a garnished bunch of parsley (No. 123); season with salt and pepper; let all cook without adhering to the pan, skim off the fat and add a pint of espagnole sauce (No. 414), some clear gravy (No. 404) and the juice of a lemon. Put some butter and oil in a pan and when hot range one beside the other, some halved tomatoes having the seeds pressed out; season with salt and pepper, add a whole clove of garlic; fry these over a hot fire keeping them whole, and when their moisture has evaporated suppress the garlic and besprinkle with a little prepared red pepper (No. 168). Dress the chickens in a pyramid form, surround with the tomatoes and pour over the chicken gravy just as it is; dredge the surface with chopped parsley and serve with a separate half-glaze sauce (No. 413) mixed with tomato sauce (No. 549).

(1908). SPRING CHICKENS AS AN ENTRÉE, ROASTED—SMALL (Poulets Reine Rôtis en Entrée de Broche).

Singe three small chickens weighing three-quarters of a pound each; draw, and clean well; truss as for an entrée (No. 178), cover the breasts with a dry matignon with Madeira (No. 406) and tie on this thin slices of fat pork to keep it in place, tying the pork with three rows of string; run iron skewers lengthwise of the chickens and fasten them on the spit; three-quarters of an hour before serving roast them in front of a bright fire basting over with butter and the fat from the dripping pan. When done, remove, unwrap and untruss. Invert on a dish a decorated and poached quenelle forcemeat (No. 80) border; lay in the center of the dish and on this a triangular center of fried bread covered with the same forcemeat, poach in the oven and range the chickens in a triangle on this border, leaning them up against the fried bread center. Dress between each one small clusters of round and peeled truffles rolled in meat glaze (No. 402), insert a garnished skewer in the bread center and the chickens. Pour some Madeira sauce (No. 492) reduced with truffle parings into the bottom of the dish after straining it through a tammy and serve more of it in a sauce-boat.

(1909). CHICKEN À L'AQUITAINE—BRAISED (Poulet Braisé à l'Aquitaine).

Draw and singe a fine corn-fed chicken weighing two and a half to three pounds; break the breastbone and fill the inside with a good dressing composed of beef marrow and raw ham combined with a handful of bread-crumbs, one egg-yolk, salt and nutmeg; sew up the stomach skin at the vent and truss with the legs inside; cover with slices of fat pork and then lay it in a narrow saucepan garnished with a bunch of parsley containing two cloves, some ham trimmings and an onion; moisten to half the height of the chicken with broth and allow the liquid to boil for a few moments, then set the saucepan on a slower fire to have it cook from half to three-quarters of an hour, basting it over frequently and letting it acquire a fine color. Strain off the stock, remove its fat and reduce it with espagnole sauce (No. 414) to the consistency of a half-glaze sauce. Infuse a piece of cinnamon in a gill of Madeira wine for fifteen minutes, strain it through a napkin and add it to the sauce. Place in a saucepan some round and well-pared slices of duck's liver, some cocks'-combs and kidneys, truffles and mushrooms; pour two-thirds of the above sauce over these, then untruss the chicken and dress it with the garnishing distributed around and the remainder of the sauce served in a separate sauce-boat.

(1910). CHICKENS À LA LÉONIA—BOILED (Poulets Bouillis à la Léonia).

Have very tender two-pound chickens, prepare and truss them as for an entrée and range them in a saucepan with stock (No. 194a) to cook slowly; when done cut each chicken into five pieces; two legs, two wings, and one of the breast bones. Fry lightly in butter one shallot or half a medium onion, add four ounces of dried mushrooms, softened in water and chopped up finely, also a bunch of parsley garnished with thyme and bay leaf, moisten with two gills of white wine and a pint of velouté sauce (No. 415); skim the top properly for fifteen to twenty minutes, then take out the parsley and pour in a pint of tomato sauce (No. 549) and a quarter of a pound of lean ham cut in three-sixteenths inch squares, let the sauce reduce until quite thick, add the pieces of chicken and when thoroughly warm, dress with the sauce, bestrewing the surface with chopped parsley.

(1911). CHICKENS À LA STUYVESANT—POÊLÉ (Poulets Poêlés à la Stuyvesant).

Have two good chickens weighing three pounds each; truss them for entrée (No. 178) and cook them as explained under the heading to poêler (No. 12); when done properly, drain, untruss and cut them up into five or six pieces, dress them in a pyramid form on a layer of forcemeat three-quarters of an inch thick, poached on the same dish intended for the table, and surround with a circle of channeled mushrooms (No. 118), new carrots cut pear-shaped and blanched, then cooked in stock (No. 194a) with a little sugar; throw some very small cooked green peas over the whole, also a printanière sauce (No. 546) and send to the table with some of the same sauce served separately.

(1912). CHICKENS, ENGLISH STYLE—BOILED (Poulets Bouillis à l'Anglaise).

Prepare and truss some young two-pound chickens as for an entrée (No. 178), boil them in stock (No. 194a) and drain when done ; dress and cover with a well buttered velouté sauce (No. 415), adding to it chopped parsley and lemon juice.

(1913). CHICKEN WITH NOODLES, MACARONI, RAVIOLES, OR MIRMIDONS—BRAISED
(Poulet Braisé Soit aux Nouilles, Macaroni, Ravioles, ou Mirmidons).

Cook a chicken the same as with rice (No. 1914), roll out thin, some noodle paste bands (No. 142) two inches wide, cut it into fine shreds, plunge them into boiling, salted water and let cook for eight to ten minutes while covered; remove from the fire to drain on a sieve. Return these noodles when dry to the saucepan and add two or three spoonfuls of good béchamel (No. 409), fresh butter, grated parmesan, a bit of nutmeg and salt and pepper, then dress on a hot dish; lay the chicken on top either whole or neatly cut up, pour over its liquid reduced to a half-glaze and thickened with a little tomato sauce (No. 549). This chicken can be served exactly the same only substituting macaroni (No. 2960), ravioles (No. 2976), or mirmidons (No. 689).

(1914). CHICKEN WITH RICE—BRAISED (Poulet Braisé au riz).

Draw a chicken weighing three pounds, break the breastbone and fill the inside with a good dressing composed of beef marrow and raw ham, a handful of bread-crumbs, one egg-yolk, salt, pepper, and nutmeg. Sew up the opening on top and truss with the legs inside; bard nicely, and lay it in a saucepan proportionate to its size, with the giblets, a garnished bunch of parsley, (No. 123) two cloves, and some ham parings. Moisten to about its height with stock (No. 194a) from the stock pot retaining all the fat and let boil up briskly for five to six minutes; remove the saucepan on one side of the range to finish boiling the liquid slowly for half to three-quarters of an hour. Place half a pound of well-washed and lightly blanched rice into another saucepan, wet it with two-thirds of the chicken broth after straining it through a fine sieve; in case there be not sufficient add a little broth; cook eighteen to twenty minutes on a hot fire; it should be softened and sufficiently dried; remove and finish by stirring in with a fork, a piece of butter, also a dash of nutmeg. Dress the rice on a dish, lay the chicken on top after draining and untrussing it, then serve. A small handful of grated parmesan cheese may be added to the rice if desired. Serve separately the remaining third of the stock reduced to a half-glaze.

(1915). CHICKEN WITH TARRAGON—BRAISED (Poulet Braisé à l'Estragon).

Choose a good three-pound, very white chicken; singe and draw it well; clean and free it from pin feathers; slip between the skin and breast meat a six ounce piece of butter mingling it with a heavy pinch of tarragon leaves; truss for an entrée (No. 178), and cover with bards of fat pork; place it in a saucepan, also the neck, gizzard, and a few veal parings; moisten just sufficiently to cover the chicken having three-quarters of unskimmed broth (No. 194a), and one-quarter of white wine. Boil up this liquid, then remove the saucepan to a more moderate fire to allow the chicken to cook for forty-five to sixty minutes; when properly done, strain the liquid, free it of fat, and put this latter in with the chicken to keep it warm. Throw a few tarragon leaves into a little boiling water; take the saucepan from the fire at the first boil, and drain these leaves on a sieve. Clarify the chicken stock, reduce, and afterward add to it a piece of chicken glaze (No. 398), and the juice of one lemon; untruss the chicken, dress and decorate the breast with the blanched tarragon leaves; pour a part of the gravy around, serving the remainder in a sauce-boat.

(1916). CHICKENS WITH NEW VEGETABLES—SMALL—BRAISED (Petits Poulets Braisés aux Légumes Nouveaux).

Procure two small tender chickens each one to weigh a pound and a half; singe and draw, truss for an entrée (No. 178), then lay them in a saucepan with melted butter and fry over a slow fire for ten to twelve minutes, turning them around and not letting them brown; moisten with a pint of stock (No. 194a); season and add a garnishing composed of small new blanched carrots and uncooked fresh green peas. Cover the saucepan and finish cooking the vegetables together with the chickens in a slack oven, occasionally adding a little hot stock (No. 194a). As soon as they are nicely done, drain, untruss and cut each one into four pieces; dress them in a pyramid form in the center of a long dish. Strain the vegetables, thicken them with butter and add a pinch of sugar; range them around the pyramid of chickens, and on both ends of the dish lay a cluster of mushrooms and one of small glazed onions.

(1917). DUCK À LA BRITANNIA—STUFFED (Canard Farci à la Britannia).

Chop up a little green sage also one shallot, put them into a vessel and season with salt and pepper, add three hard-boiled egg-yolks, two dozen chestnuts and two tablespoonfuls of bread-crumbs; work the whole well together and with it fill the duck; truss and roast for three-quarters of an hour to one hour, then dress on a croûton of fried bread, pour over a poulette sauce (No. 527), and serve more in another sauce-boat.

(1918). DUCK À LA MATIGNON (Canard à la Matignon).

Select a fine young duck and truss it after singeing and drawing. Cut up some carrots, bacon and onions into three-sixteenth inch squares; have also sprigs of parsley, thyme and bay leaf. Put the bacon into a sautoir with two ounces of butter, fry, put in the onions without coloring them, then add the carrots, herbs and seasoning; moisten with Madeira wine and let fall to a glaze. When cold wrap the duck with this matignon in strong sheets of buttered paper, and roast either on the spit or in the oven from three-quarters of an hour to one hour. Unwrap and add the vegetables to half a pint of espagnole sauce (No. 414) and as much broth (No. 194a); boil and despumate for half an hour reducing to the consistency of a light sauce; strain this through a tammy (No. 159) and pour a part of it over the dressed duck, serving the remainder in a sauce-boat.

(1919). DUCK À LA SIEBRECHT (Canard à la Siebrecht).

Have a duck prepared and cooked the same as for roasting (No. 1921), dress and serve at the same time a sauce prepared as follows: Peel and cook some sour apples, and when done strain off the liquid part collecting the pulp in a vessel; mix into this a quarter as much grated fresh horseradish and as much unsweetened well drained whipped cream; pour this sauce into a sauce-boat and serve it to accompany the duck.

(1920). DUCK, AMERICAN STYLE—STUFFED (Canard Farci à l'Américaine).

Singe, draw, and clean well a young duck, fill the insides with an American bread stuffing (No. 61); truss for roasting (No. 179) and roast it either on the spit or in the oven, three-quarters of an hour should be allowed. Dress it on a hot dish and pour a little gravy (No. 404) around, serving more in a separate sauce-boat.

(1921). ROAST DUCK (Canard Rôti).

Singe and draw a nice fat duck, chop up the liver with the same quantity of fresh fat pork, season and mix in a small finely chopped onion, some chopped parsley, a handful of breadcrumbs passed through a sieve and one egg-yolk; with this dressing stuff the duck's stomach; truss for roasting and cook either on the spit or in the oven for thirty to forty-five minutes, according to its size; baste over several times with butter, salt, and then take it from the spit; untruss and dress it on a dish garnishing around with slices of lemon. Send at the same time a sauce-boat of good gravy taken from the dripping pan, adding a little good stock (No. 194a) to it. This duck may be served plain without dressing if desired.

(1922). DUCK WITH CÈPES (Canard aux Cèpes).

Put a good clean, trussed duck into a saucepan with melted fat pork and two minced onions, fry, season and moisten with two to three gills of gravy (No. 404), then cook smothered, turning it over. When three-quarters cooked, add two to three dozen small fresh and peeled cèpes free of stalks; finish cooking together with the duck, and when done, drain off the latter to untruss and dress on a dish with the cèpes grouped around. Strain the gravy stock, thicken it with a little tomato sauce (No. 549) and pour it over the duck and garnishing, then serve.

(1923). DUCK WITH CHERRIES (Canard aux Cerises).

Prepare a duck for an entrée (No. 178) after cleaning and singeing it; lay it in a saucepan lined with slices of fat pork and moisten to half its height with a mirepoix white wine stock (No. 419) bring the liquid to a boil and finish cooking in a slow oven. Suppress the stones and stalks from one pound of sour cherries, set them into an untinned copper pan with a little water, lemon peel, cinnamon and sugar, and let boil for a few moments, in case there should be no fresh cherries at hand take candied cherries or dried black ones; these should be soaked for an hour in tepid water, drained and put into a pan with a little fresh water, lemon juice and its peel, also cinnamon. Boil the cherries, then keep it at the same degree of heat, but discontinue the boiling for half an hour; the liquid should now be entirely absorbed. After the duck is ready, remove it from the saucepan and untruss, strain its stock, free it of fat and let reduce with some good brown sauce (No. 414), and after it attains a sufficient succulence and is well-reduced, run it through a tammy over the cherries. Dress the duck in the center of a dish, pour half the gravy over, lay the cherries around and serve the remainder of the sauce in a sauce-boat.

(1924). DUCKS WITH OLIVES—BRAISED (Canards Braisés aux Olives).

Dress two ducks for entrées (No. 178) and lay them in a saucepan lined with bardes of fat pork; moisten to half their height with a mirepoix white wine stock (No. 419) and let boil, skim and simmer slowly for three-quarters to one hour. Stone about one pound of verdal olives, blanch, drain and add them to a brown sauce (No. 414) stirred in the mirepoix stock from the ducks after it has been strained and skimmed. Dress the ducks, cover lightly with sauce and garnish around with the olives.

(1925). DUCKS WITH SAUERKRAUT (Canards à la Choucroute).

Dress two nice ducks; place them in a saucepan lined with bards of fat pork, some carrots and onions and a garnished bunch of parsley (No. 123); moisten with stock (No.194a), boil; skim and cook in a moderate oven for an hour to an hour a half. Put two pounds of well washed sauerkraut in a saucepan, add two onions, one containing two cloves, half a pound of sliced carrots, half a pound of blanched breast of bacon and half a pound of raw sausage (with or without garlic according to taste). Moisten with half broth and half fat taken from the stock-pot, boil and cook slowly for two hours, then drain and dish it around the duck with the sausage and bacon cut in slices dressed intercalated. Stir a poivrade sauce (No. 522) into the duck stock, pour a third of it over the ducks, serving the other two-thirds separately.

(1926). DUCKS WITH TURNIPS (Canards aux Navets).

Truss a good, clean singed duck, lay it in a saucepan with melted fat pork or else lard, and fry very slowly until it acquires a fine color, then season and fry for a few moments longer, draining it off afterward. Pour into the same fat a tablespoonful of flour, cook slowly together for a few moments, moistening gradually with a pint of stock (No.194a); stir the sauce while it keeps boiling for fifteen minutes on the side of the range. Skim off the fat, strain, and add this strained sauce to the duck with a garnishing of good, sound turnips cut in clove of garlic-shapes or else in balls, and browned in a pan with butter, salt, and a little sugar; finish cooking the duck and turnips on a very slow fire, and when both are ready, lift out the bird, untruss, and dress it in the center of a dish, surrounding it with the turnips; strain the stock, skim and reduce, if there should be too much, and when correct, pour it over the duck, and serve.

(1927). DUCKS' GIBLETS, HOUSEKEEPERS' STYLE (Abatis de Canards à la Ménagère).

After a duck has been drawn and singed, chop off the neck as far down as the back, and divide this neck into two or three pieces. Remove the gall from the liver, being careful not to break it, and cut the liver in two or three pieces according to its size. Clean the wings well. Put four ounces of butter into a saucepan with the wings, the neck, and four ounces of lean salt pork blanched and cut in quarter inch squares; when these are nicely fried, add the liver, dredge in for every set of giblets a heaping tablespoonful of flour; stir well and let the flour cook for one second, then moisten with stock (No. 194a) and white wine; season with salt and pepper, and add one dozen small onions, and as many carrots cut pear-shape; let simmer for one hour and a half, remove the fat from the surface and put in a pint of uncooked green peas, then boil together for half an hour longer. When well done and properly seasoned, dress the meats in the middle of a dish with the vegetables arranged around, pour the sauce over and serve.

(1928). DUCKS' PAUPIETTES WITH RISOT (Paupiettes de Canards au Risot).

Singe some young ducks; bone them entirely, removing all the meat and use this to make a well seasoned quenelle forcemeat into which mix finely cut up chives, truffles, and mushrooms, both chopped and three-sixteenth of an inch squares of cooked ham. With this forcemeat cover pieces of the duck's skin cut in four or six parts, and roll them up into paupiettes, covering each one with a slice of fat pork; lay these in buttered paupiette rings, and place them in a sautoir covered with bardes of fat pork, and moisten with some good stock (No. 194a); cover over with a buttered paper, and then a round baking dish which will fit into the saucepan. Cook in a moderate oven, and when done and glazed to a fine color, take from the rings and dress them in a circle; garnish the center with risot (No. 739), and place a channeled mushroom head (No. 118) on top of each paupiette; serve with a sauce prepared as follows: Fry some minced onions in oil, drain, place it in a saucepan with lemon juice, mignonette, and Spanish sauce (No. 414), also the skimmed duck stock reduced to a half-glaze, and then strained through a tammy; serve it in a sauce-boat at the same time as the paupiettes.

(1929). MONGREL DUCK—ROASTED AND STUFFED (Carnard Métis Farci et Rôti).

A mongrel duck is the mixed breed of the wild and the domestic duck; it is generally larger than the domestic, and is usually served stuffed with a dressing made of soaked and pressed bread-crumbs, into which mingle chopped and blanched onions, chopped parsley, butter or chopped up marrow, salt pepper and nutmeg. Put the duck in a baking pan, cover with fat and roast in the oven, basting over at frequent intervals while cooking. A mongrel duck will take from an hour and a quarter to an hour and a half, and a goose from two and a half to three hours. Dress on a long dish; pour some clear gravy (No. 404) into the roasting pan, strain off the fat and reduce, pour a little of this over the bird and serve the remainder apart.

(1930). DUCKLING À L'ANDALOUSE (Caneton à l'Andalouse).

Procure a young duck; singe, draw and clean it well, then truss it as for an entrée (No. 178); fry it very slowly with chopped up leaf lard and when it assumes a fine color, remove it from the saucepan, drain off the fat and cover the bottom with slices of ham, cut up carrots and onions, a bunch of parsley garnished with thyme and bay leaf and the duck; moisten with a little white wine and let this fall quickly to a glaze, then remoisten with a little stock (No. 194a), and let fall to a glaze twice more. After the duck is half cooked pour in two gills of Malaga wine and finish cooking slowly for about three-quarters of an hour; transfer the duck to another saucepan and keep it hot. Strain the stock and reduce it with the same amount of espagnole sauce (No. 414), to the consistency of a succulent sauce, and add to it a garnishing of small mushroom buttons, stoned Spanish olives, and small ball-shaped chicken quenelles; dress the duck, garnishing with part of the sauce, and serve the remainder separately.

(1931). DUCKLINGS À LA BORDELAISE—SAUTÉD (Canetons Sautés à la Bordelaise).

Cut up two ducklings into five pieces each, obtaining the two legs, the two wings and one piece from the breastbone; pare them nicely, leaving on the pinions, but suppressing the bone from the legs, sauté in half clarified butter and half oil with the addition of four ounces of bacon cut in three-sixteenth of an inch squares, the well-chopped livers, two teaspoonfuls of chopped shallot, the same of parsley and a soupçon of garlic; moisten with white wine, add half a pound of finely chopped cèpes, four ounces of cooked ham cut in eighth of inch squares, espagnole sauce (No. 414), and some tomato purée (No. 730). Remove at the first boil, dress the duck, pour the sauce over, garnish the extremities with paper frills (No. 10), and serve immediately.

(1932). DUCKLING À LA BOURGUIGNONNE—FRIED (Caneton Frit à la Bourguignonne).

Divide a young tender duck into five pieces; two legs, two wings and a breast piece; pare nicely leaving the pinion bones on the wings and suppressing the leg bones; lay these pieces in a vessel to season with salt, pepper, lemon juice, chopped parsley, very little pulverized thyme and bay leaf and olive oil. Break up the carcass, fry it in butter, until well colored, adding mushroom parings, shallots, cloves, mignonette and nutmeg, then moisten with red wine and cook the whole slowly for half an hour, strain through a sieve and add this stock gradually to an espagnole sauce (No. 414), that is being reduced, and boil both together to the consistency of a light gravy. Roll the pieces of drained duck in flour, immerse them in eggs and fry in a very white frying fat over a moderate fire, allowing them to attain a fine golden brown while cooking, serve on a folded napkin with the sauce in a sauce-boat.

(1933). DUCKLINGS À LA GRAINVILLE—LARDED (Canetons Piqués à la Grainville).

Have two ducklings, draw, singe and lard them with medium lardons (No. 3, Fig. 52), having previously plunged them in boiling water to render the meat firm. Line a saucepan with some slices of ham, place the ducklings on top and set around carrots, onions and a bunch of parsley garnished with bay leaf and thyme. Moisten to half their height with stock (No. 194a) and finish cooking, basting over frequently and glazing them in such a way that they attain a nice color; strain the stock free of its fat and reduce it to the consistency of a light syrup, mix in some blanched chopped up shallots, then remove from the fire and squeeze in the juice of two oranges. Dress and garnish around with slices of apple besprinkled with sugar and cooked in the oven; serve the sauce in a sauce boat separately.

(1934). DUCKLING À LA LYONNAISE (Caneton à la Lyonnaise).

Bone the breast of a large duckling, singed and well cleaned. Fill up the empty space with a liver baking forcemeat (No. 64), mixed with a few spoonfuls of lean cooked ham cut in dice-shapes, and bread-crumbs, sew the breast skin, truss the duck, wrap it up in larding pork and let braise in a narrow saucepan slightly moistened with some stock (No. 194a), and a little white wine. Drain the duck, untie and untruss, then dress it on a dish and surround with clusters of small glazed onions alternated with clusters of whole chestnuts, first cooked, then fallen to a glaze with a little gravy (No. 404). Strain the stock, remove its fat and reduce it to a half-glaze, thicken it with a little brown sauce (No. 414), and serve it separately.

(1935). DUCKLINGS' FILLETS À LA MACÉDOINE OR GREEN PEAS (Filets de Canetons à la Macédoine ou aux petits pois).

Singe, drain, and clean two young ducklings trussed for entrée (No. 178); lay them in a saucepan lined with bardes of fat pork, moisten to half their height with good mirepoix wine stock (No. 419), let boil, then skim or simmer over a slow fire or in the oven until done, basting over at frequent intervals, and glazing to a fine color; it will take from three-quarters of an hour to one hour to cook them. When the ducks are thoroughly done, remove the fillets, strain, skim, and reduce the stock with espagnole sauce (No. 414), and when it becomes succulent and properly reduced, add it to the fillets with a piece of fine butter, rolling all the while to mix well. Dress the fillets in a circle, filling the inside with a macédoine of vegetables (No. 680), or small fresh peas with bacon prepared as follows: Have half a pound of bacon cut in half inch dice, unsalt by parboiling, drain and fry in butter with some small onions; moisten with brown sauce (No. 414), and some of the duck stock, let simmer until the onions and bacon are cooked, then throw in three pints of peas cooked French style (No. 2743). Mix all together and pour it into the center of the fillets, or else serve with a garnishing of cucumbers and Villeroi (No. 2732).

(1936). DUCKLINGS' FILLETS À LA PÉRIGUEUX (Filets de Canetons à la Périgueux).

This entrée is to be dressed on a wooden foundation covered with cooked or noodle paste (No. 142). Have a small pyramidal mold, smooth and well rounded, and poach in it a loaf of chicken or veal forcemeat mingled with an equal quantity of liver baking forcemeat (No. 64); keep this mold in water until needed. Cook six ducklings in a good mirepoix stock (No. 419), having only very little

Fig. 376.

liquid, and when done drain them out to untruss; detach the two fillets from each breast retaining both skin and wing bones, then pare. Quickly unmold the small forcemeat loaf on the center of the paste-covered foundation; mask it over with velouté (No. 415), reduced with the duck stock, and dress the fillets in a detruncated circle around, that is the six fillets on the right side are to incline one way, while the six on the left the other. On the summit of the support, in the hollow formed by the points of the fillets, dress a tasteful cluster of small, round truffles peeled and cooked when required with Madeira sauce, and glazed over with a brush. Lightly cover over the fillets and the bottom of the dish with more of the same sauce, and send a sauce-boatful of it at the same time as the fillets.

(1937). DUCKLING À LA ROUENNAISE (Caneton à la Rouennaise).

Chop up half a pound of onions, blanch, then fry in butter; chop up also half a pound of chicken livers, and half a pound of leaf lard, each one separately; mingle all together, and when very hot thicken with six egg-yolks; add four ounces of bread-crumbs to this preparation, some chopped parsley, and finely cut up chives. Remove the breastbone from a duck and fill the empty space with the above; truss for roasting and wrap it up in buttered paper, and roast for about half an hour. Serve it on a little clear gravy (No. 404), and have a sauce-boatful of the following sauce: Cut up two ounces of onions in one-eighth of an inch squares; cook them in salted water, drain and return them to a saucepan to moisten with red wine; when this has fallen to a glaze dilute it with espagnole sauce (No. 414).

(1938). DUCKLING WITH GREEN MAYONNAISE AND FINE HERBS—BROILED AND ROASTED—(Caneton Grillé et Rôti à la Mayonnaise Verte aux Fines Herbes).

Broiled.—Split a singed, clean young duckling through the back, open it entirely and flatten well, trim neatly cutting off the legs at the first joint, salt and cover with oil; put it in a hinged double broiler, close and broil over a moderate even fire for about eighteen minutes; when done and of a fine color, dress on a hot dish, serve separately a sauce-boat of green mayonnaise fine herb sauce (No. 612).

Roasted.—After singing and drawing the duckling, truss it for roasting (No. 179) and cook either on the spit or in the oven for twenty-five to thirty-five minutes; baste frequently, salt only when cooked, then untruss and dress on a very hot dish, pour some clear gravy (No. 404), over and garnish around with water-cress seasoned with salt and vinegar.

(1939). DUCKLING, PEASANT STYLE (Caneton à la Paysanne).

Blanch and braise a small curled cabbage after cutting it in quarters and taking out the core, blanch separately some trimmed carrots and turnips, and celery root cut like cloves of garlic. Fry six ounces of half inch pieces of bacon in a saucepan, remove it with the skimmer leaving the fat in the sauce-pan, and in this fry very slowly a clean duckling trussed—as for an entrée (No. 178); when of a fine color moisten it with a little white wine and let this fall quickly to a glaze, then remoisten with a very little stock (No. 194a), and bring it twice to a glaze. After the duckling is partly cooked, put in the bacon and vegetables, moisten with broth to half the height finish cooking the whole very slowly on the fire or else in the oven. At the last moment untruss the duck and dress it on a dish, surrounding it with the garnishings and the quartered cabbage; lengthen the stock with a little more gravy, strain and thicken it with either some sauce or kneaded butter (No. 579); boil for two minutes, strain and pour it over the duck.

(1940). SALMIS OF DUCKLING (Salmis de Caneton).

To Roast.—Select a young and very tender duck, prepare and truss it for roasting the same as explained in No. 179; it should be roasted on the spit or in the oven for fifteen to twenty-five minutes according to its size and the heat of the fire. A domestic duck ought to be served quite rare, and should be killed without bleeding. Dish it after untrussing and pour over a little of its gravy, garnish around with water-cress and serve the remainder of the gravy in a sauce-boat.

For the Salmis.—Cut the roasted duck up in two or three slices from each breast. Chop up the legs and carcasses and fry them in butter with an ounce of onions and as much shallot, both minced very finely; add the parings, pepper and mignonette, then moisten with red wine and some brown sauce (No. 414); reduce this to half, strain it through a tammy and pour it over the pieces of dressed duck; surround with heart-shaped bread croûtons and serve very hot.

(1941). DUCKLING, WITH BIGARADE SAUCE (Caneton à la Sauce Bigarade).

Make a small hash with some fresh pork, the duck's liver and two cooked chicken livers; mix into it a handful of white bread-crumbs, one egg-yolk and two or three spoonfuls of mushrooms, onions and parsley all minced very fine. With this preparation fill a duck's stomach; sew up the apertures, truss and roast it on the spit or in the oven, basting liberally with butter. Drain and dress it on a dish with some clear gravy (No. 404), and serve a bigarade sauce (No. 435) separately.

(1942). DUCKLING, WITH JERUSALEM ARTICHOKES (Caneton aux Topinambours).

Cook the duckling the same as for Andalouse (No. 1930), and when done dress and surround it with a garnishing of glazed and peeled Jerusalem artichokes; serve with a separate sauce-boat of half-glaze sauce (No. 413) worked with butter and finished with parsley and lemon juice.

(1943). DUCKLINGS, WITH ORANGES (Canetons aux Oranges).

Prepare two ducklings as for an entrée (No. 178). Line a saucepan or a braziere (Fig. 134) with carrots, onions, fragments of fat pork, slices of ham and raw veal, a bunch of parsley garnished with thyme and bay leaf, mushroom peelings and melted fat pork. Lay the ducklings over, the breasts upper-most and pour on a pint of stock (No. 194a); cover and reduce the liquid slowly and completely, then remoisten with half stock and half champagne or white wine, and let simmer until thoroughly cooked. Strain the stock, remove its fat, despumate and reduce it to a half-glaze; take out a fourth part of it and to the remainder, add the blanched and shredded peels of two oranges; let cook again for fifteen minutes. Peel two oranges, free of all pith, remove the pulp between each section and take out the seeds, then add this to the sauce; dish the ducklings, cover with a quarter of the sauce kept aside and surround with two medium oranges cut in four. Serve the sauce separately at the same time as the ducks, or else substitute an orange sauce (No. 511).

(1944). BUSTARD EN DAUBE—WILD GOOSE (Outarde en Daube—Oie Sauvage).

As a bustard is nearly always tough, it is necessary to hang it up for several days. Pick, singe, draw and clean it well; cut off the pinions, neck and drumsticks; detach the legs from the body as well as the breasts, and lard all these meats with large shreds of raw ham, then season; lay them in a vessel with a pint of vinegar and as much water, let macerate for twenty-four hours. Cover the bottom and sides of a large stone stock pot with thin slices of fat pork, range in the bottom a few small carrots and turnips in the shape of three-fourth inch balls, a few onions, a bunch of aromatic herbs and two boned and blanched calf's feet, dredge over whole peppers and cloves then put in the carcass, legs and breast pieces after draining them from their marinade. Moisten to half the height of the meats with white wine, cover over with bards of fat pork, and reduce the liquid for a few moments. Close the vessel hermetically with a piece of paper and a common plate half filled with water and let it cook very slowly in the oven for six to seven hours, according to its tenderness; remove carefully and dress on a large dish with the calf's feet and vegetables; skim the fat from the strained liquid and strain it again over the meat.

(1945). GOOSE À LA CHIPOLATA (Oie à la Chipolata).

A whole goose can either be served as a relevé or as a roast; the slices, legs and giblets as an entrée. A goose is usually served at unceremonious dinners. Draw and singe a goose, clean it well and truss it as for an entrée (No. 178); fill the inside with a sausage forcemeat (No. 68) into which mix a handful of bread-crumbs, several eggs and cooked fine herbs (No. 385); season highly. Line a braziere with bards of fat pork, cut up carrots and onions and a bunch of parsley garnished with chervil; lay the goose on top of these, surround it with bits of veal and moisten with Madeira wine, broth and white wine to half its height; boil, skim and simmer for three to four hours until properly cooked. Strain the stock, remove all its fat and reduce to half, then pour it into some brown sauce (No. 414) in the act of being reduced, adding more of the Madeira. Dress the goose and garnish around with clusters of small braised and glazed onions, blanched carrots cooked in stock (No. 194a), braised chestnuts fallen to a glaze, and mushroom heads cooked, turned and channeled (No. 118); cover over with a part of the sauce and serve the remainder in a sauce-boat.

(1946). GOOSE À LA ROYER (Oie à la Royer).

Prepare the same as for the chipolata (No. 1945) and after the stock has been strained, skimmed and reduced to a half-glaze, add to it the juice of one orange, some currant jelly and finely shredded cooked orange peel, pour a part of this sauce over the goose, and garnish around with sour apple tartlets (No. 3327); serve the rest of the sauce separately.

(1947). GOOSE À LA THIÉBLIN—ROASTED (Oie Rôtie à la Thiéblin).

Pick out a fine goose, draw, singe and clean it thoroughly, then truss it for roasting. Boil fifty peeled chestnuts in some stock (No 194a) with a few shredded celery stalks, adding only sufficient of the moisture just to allow them to cook, and when done, drain. Put two pounds of pork forcemeat in a sautoir over a brisk fire, cook, stir occasionally and season with salt, mignonette, nutmeg, chopped parsley, a handful of bread-crumbs and two whole eggs, add the chestnuts and use this dressing to fill the insides of the goose, wrap it up in several sheets of buttered paper and roast it for two and a half hours, basting it over frequently. Twenty-five minutes before serving, unwrap the goose and return it to the spit in order to have it acquire a fine color, dress and serve with Zuchette sauce (No. 564). Garnish around the goose with croustades filled with gooseberries preparing them in the following way: Have two pounds of gooseberries, cut off the tops and stalks, blanch for two minutes, then drain. Cook in a saucepan a quarter of a pound of sugar to small crack, add the gooseberries, toss them gently, then cool off, stir in as much whipped cream as there are gooseberries, having it unsweetened and well drained; serve a sauce-boat of gravy (No. 404) at the same time.

(1948). GOOSE, GERMAN STYLE—ROASTED (Oie Rôtie à l'Allemande).

Prepare and cook the goose the same as for stuffed with chestnuts (No. 1950), but instead of filling with chestnut forcemeat, substitute ten apples, peeled, quartered, cored and cooked in a vessel with six ounces of dried currants and four ounces of seeded raisins, half a pound of bread-crumbs, cinnamon and two whole eggs. Mince well a red cabbage after carefully removing all the hard parts and lay it in a saucepan with stock (No. 194a), from which the fat has not been removed, and salt, cook slowly until ready to serve, then put in a tablespoonful of vinegar, garnish around the goose with this cabbage and outside of it set a string of small broiled sausages (No. 754).

(1949). GEESE GIBLETS WITH TURNIPS (Abatis d'Oie aux Navets).

Put half a pound of unsalted bacon into a saucepan with a little butter and let fry for a few moments, then add the giblets prepared as for No. 1927 and the seasoning, also two dozen small onions and four dozen turnips cut the size and shape of large Spanish olives, having previously fried them in butter with a pinch of sugar. Drain them and add them to the stew with a bunch of parsley garnished with thyme and bay leaf, and pour in some espagnole sauce (No. 414) and stock (No. 194a), boil, skim and simmer for half an hour; season to taste with salt and pepper. When the giblets are cooked, remove the parsley and serve the meat in the center of a dish with the vegetables around and the sauce poured over the whole.

(1950). GOOSE STUFFED WITH CHESTNUTS AND WITH SAUSAGES AND CHESTNUTS— ROASTED (Oie Rôtie Farcie aux Marrons et aux Saucisses et Marrons).

Select a fine goose: singe and reserve the fat and giblets, then wipe out the insides and fill it, also the breast with a dressing prepared as follows: Take one pound of chopped veal, and two pounds of chopped fat pork, only mixing them together afterward, and season with salt, pepper, nutmeg, and allspice; add two gills of stock (No. 149a) or water, and pound the whole together; then mix

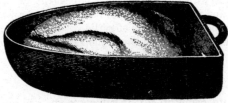

Fɪɢ. 377.

in sixty chestnuts that have been roasted in the oven and freed of skins. Truss the goose and lay it in a roasting-pan with its own fat and half a pint of hot water, sprinkle fine salt over it, and cover with a buttered paper; then place it in the oven to cook for three hours, being careful to baste it occasionally; it should be well done; salt over, untruss, and dress on a dish; skim the fat from the surface of its liquid, pour in a little gravy (No. 404), boil, and then strain through a sieve. Throw a little of this over the goose and serve the remainder separately.

With Sausages and Chestnuts.—Prepare and cook the goose exactly the same only omit putting the chestnuts in the dressing; but braise them and use them for garnishing both sides of the goose and arrange small broiled Chipolata sausages (No. 754) on the ends.

(1951). GOSLING À LA SOYER (Oison à la Soyer).

Draw, singe, and clean well a young goose; truss, filling the inside with a dressing made of a pound of finely chopped beef suet, a pound of soaked bread-crumbs, having all the water extracted, half a pound of butter, some onions fried in butter with the goose liver cut in small squares, sage, thyme, basil, marjoram, parsley, salt, pepper, and nutmeg. Roast the goose either on the spit or in the oven for an hour and a half to two hours, basting it frequently. When done, dish it up on top of a purée of apples seasoned with sugar and nutmeg. Peel some apples cut in four; range on a generously buttered dish, sprinkled over with sugar, and cook for ten minutes in the hot oven, and lay around the goose. Serve separate a sauce prepared with the glaze from the dripping pan detaching it with a little gravy (No. 404), strain and skim; mix in gradually some espagnole sauce (No. 414) in which currant jelly has been dissolved; strain the whole through a sieve, and serve it in a sauce-boat to accompany the goose.

(1952). ROAST GOSLING OR MONGREL GOOSE (Oison ou Oie Métisse Rôtis).

A gosling roasted on the spit makes an excellent dish. It can also be cooked in a slow oven laid in a narrow earthenware (Fig. 377) or iron pan with plenty of fat; generally both these birds are stuffed before being roasted. A mongrel goose may be filled with partly broiled chestnuts lightly fried in butter or fat pork; it can also be stuffed with small apples after removing the core with a tube five-eighths of an inch in diameter, or both chestnuts and apples can be replaced by a fresh pork hash into which fine herbs and bread crumbs have been mixed, or even by small sausages roasted partially in fat pork or grease. If the goose be large it will take two to three hours to have it tender; when a gosling is cooked on the spit it must first be trussed, then wrapped in buttered paper and roasted for one hour, being careful to baste frequently and to remove the paper after it has been in three-quarters of an hour to let it acquire a fine brown color, and it is then served simply with good reduced gravy (No. 404). A kind of thick pancake can be served at the same time made with bread-crumbs soaked, pressed, then pounded in a bowl and diluted with whole eggs and milk, seasoning with salt, pepper, pulverized thyme and marjoram and chopped blanched onions. Lay this preparation on a well-greased tin sheet and cook in the oven basting it bountifully with goose grease, after cutting it into inch and a half squares.

(1953). GOSLING SAUTÉD WITH TOMATOES, ROBERT SAUCE (Oison Sauté aux Tomates à la Sauce Robert).

Have a good gosling, singe, draw and cut it up into seven pieces—the two legs and five pieces taken from the breast; season with salt and pepper and fry slowly in lard. Drain off the fat and detach the glaze from the pan with a little clear gravy (No. 404). Cut twelve peeled tomatoes across in two, press out the juice and seeds and fry them in a frying pan with very hot oil; season with salt, pepper and a crushed and chopped clove of garlic. When the pieces are cooked, dish up and dress the fried tomatoes over; sprinkle very green chopped parsley on top, pour the gravy around and serve separately some Robert sauce (No. 533).

(1954). GOSLING STEWED WITH TURNIPS (Ragoût d'Oison aux Navets).

Cut up a small tender and well cleaned gosling into medium-sized pieces, suppressing the pinions, drumsticks and neck; cut also half a pound of lean bacon into half inch squares; fry them for a few moments in butter, and remove with the skimmer, leaving the fat in the saucepan; lay the pieces of goose into this fat, fry over a hot fire while stirring, season and add one onion and a bunch of parsley garnished with thyme and bay leaf. When the meats are browned, drain off the fat and dredge the goose with flour, moisten to its height with hot stock (No. 194a), and boil up this liquid while stirring, letting it remain in this state for ten minutes; the sauce should now be slightly thickened. Cover well the saucepan with its lid and continue to cook moderately. Take raw turnips and cut them into balls three-quarters of an inch in diameter, place them in a pan with the strained fat from the goose, season with salt and a pinch of sugar, and color them briskly; when half cooked lift out the pieces of goose to trim neatly, strain its stock and return it to a clean saucepan with a gill of Marsala wine, the pieces of goose, the bacon and the turnips; boil together for ten minutes and finish cooking in a slack oven. The gosling and turnips should both be found done at the same time; dress all in a deep dish with very little sauce.

(1955). GUINEA FOWL (Pintade).

The guinea fowl is a pretty bird the same size as an ordinary fowl, having slate-colored

Fig. 378.

feathers covered with small round white spots; it is raised in the poultry yard; when young its meat is most agreeable to eat. The fecundity of a guinea fowl is most remarkable.

(1956). GUINEA FOWLS LARDED AND DECORATED WITH THEIR OWN FEATHERS—ROASTED (Pintades Piquées Rôties Garnies de Leur Plumage).

Guinea fowls are frequently disguised with their own or with pheasants' feathers, for their resemblance is almost similar. Select young guinea fowls, dress and truss them as if intended for roasting (No. 179); plunge the breasts in boiling water to stiffen the skin and lard them with very fine shreds of larding pork (No. 3, Fig. 52); wrap them up in several sheets of buttered paper, then roast them either on the spit or in the oven; when they are three-quarters done, unwrap and brown a fine color; salt and dress on croûtons of bread fried in butter, and decorate with either their own feathers; serve a separate sauce-boat of clear gravy (No. 404).

(1957). GUINEA FOWLS FILLETS À LA GAILLARDET (Filets de Pintades à la Gaillardet).

Raise the fillets from half a dozen young guinea fowls, remove the skin and epidermis, and sauté them over a brisk fire, but without coloring. Set them under a weight and when partly cold pare them into half hearts, cover with some well-reduced Villeroi sauce (No. 560) and range them as quickly as they are ready on a tin sheet to cool thoroughly. Detach them from this sheet, roll them in bread-crumbs, dip in eggs and again in bread-crumbs, smoothing the breading with the blade of a knife. Fry them in clarified butter to a fine golden brown, drain on a napkin and trim the pointed ends with favor frills (No. 10), then dress in a circle and garnish the center of the dish with tomatoes fried in oil with finely chopped shallots and mushrooms, also some chopped parsley, serve with a separate Colbert sauce (No. 451).

(1958). GUINEA FOWLS WITH SAUERKRAUT (Pintades à la Choucroute).

Cook two pounds of good sauerkraut perfectly plain with a piece of smoked bacon and half a pound of sausages. Bard two young guinea fowls and cook them smothered in a saucepan; when nearly done, add them to the sauerkraut, which is not thoroughly cooked yet, and finish both together. Drain off the fowls and meat and reduce the liquid remaining in the sauerkraut, thickening it with a piece of kneaded butter (No. 579); finish off the fire with a piece of plain butter. Dress on a dish, form a hollow in the center and lay in it the cut up fowls glazing them over simply with a brush; serve a clear gravy (No. 404) separately.

(1959). PIGEONS À LA CHARTREUSE (Pigeons à la Chartreuse).

Blanch half a cabbage and cut it up into two parts, remove the core, then braise these with half a pound of bacon. Place some melted fat pork in a saucepan and fry in it three pigeons; when colored range them over the cabbage and garnish the spaces between the pigeons with turnips and carrots each blanched separately, and small onions browned in a pan; season and then withdraw the saucepan, pushing it into a moderate oven. A quarter of an hour later moisten with a gill of hot stock (No. 194a). Finish cooking the pigeons and vegetables very slowly; untruss the birds and dress them over the braised cabbage laid in the center of the dish; between each pigeon place a cluster of of onions, turnips and carrots, separating each one of these by a thick slice of the bacon standing upright. Increase the quantity of pigeon stock with a little clear gravy (No. 404), suppress all the fat and thicken lightly with a little brown sauce (No. 414); strain this, pour part over the pigeons, cut the causages in slices and dress them around the pigeons one overlapping the other. Serve the rest of the sauce separately.

(1960). PIGEONS À LA LOMBARDY—POÊLED (Pigeonneaux à la Lombarde—Poêlés).

Prepare eight pigeons; singe, draw and truss for an entrée (No. 178); wrap them up in a dry matignon (No. 406), with slices of fat pork and then in strong buttered paper. Butter and garnish the bottom of a saucepan with sliced carrots and onions, thyme, bay leaf and sprigs of parsley, add the pigeons, half a pint of white wine and as much stock (No. 194a), boil until there is no more moisture, then remoisten to half the height of the birds and let simmer gently until they are cooked, which will take from thirty to forty-five minutes, drain and strain the stock, skim off all its fat and reduce. Dish the pigeons in a circle over artichoke bottoms fried in butter and fill up the middle with a garnishing of escaloped sweetbreads also fried in butler, and on top lay small squares of cooked lean ham half an inch in diameter and fried in butter, and over these cooked channeled mushroom (No. 118) heads. Cover these garnishings with velouté sauce (No. 415) stirred into the pigeon stock and serve also a sauce-boatful of the same sauce.

(1961). PIGEONS À LA VALENCIENNES (Pigeons à la Valenciennes).

Cut six ounces of bacon into small dice; fry them for a few moments in butter. then lift out, leaving the fat in the saucepan, and into this put three fine, clean and trussed pigeons, also a few small onions and a garnished bunch of parsley (No. 123). Fry and moisten to half their height with broth, let fall to a glaze and remoisten once more to half the height of the pigeons and finish cooking over a moderate fire. When they are almost done strain the stock and return it to the saucepan without the onions and parsley and let boil up; now add four gills of good rice for each quart of liquid; put back the bacon and a coffeespoonful of prepared red pepper (No. 168) and finish all together. Dish up the rice. untruss the pigeons and dress them on top, surround the whole with small chipolata sausages and the small onions.

(1962). PIGEONS GARNISHED WITH MONTGLAS CASES—STUFFED (Pigeons Farcis Garnis de Caisses Montglas).

Fasten a wooden foundation on a dish, it to be one inch high and not too wide; cover with cooked paste (No. 131) or noodle paste (No. 142) decorated on the top with a piping in relief and having a wooden or tin triangle or conical-shaped support in the center, also covered with paste and bored on

FIG 379.

top so that a skewer can be inserted. Bone the breasts of three young, clean pigeons by splitting them lightly through the back, but leaving the legs and thighs attached to the bodies; season the inside meats and fill the breasts with baking liver forcemeat (No. 81) combined with a third as much raw forcemeat (No. 89), a few spoonfuls of cooked lean ham and as much cooked truffles, all to be well chopped; sew up the back, truss as for an entrée (No. 178) with the legs thrust inside the body, bard over and wrap each one in a small buttered cloth, then cook in a good poêler stock. As soon as the pigeons are done, drain, unwrap and retighten the cloth more firmly; put them back into their stock to leave cool, then drain again and when unwrapped, wipe them carefully with a cloth. Now detach the breasts from the rump of each pigeon to cut into lengthwise slices, return them to their original position and then place the birds in a sautoir with a part of their stock reduced to a half-glaze warm them in the open oven basting frequently. Remove the pigeons to a small baking sheet, smooth the cut parts nicely and cover the breasts with a not too thick Mornay sauce (No. 504), so the form of the pigeons remain intact; place them for a moment in the hot oven to have the sauce adhere, then dress them at once in a triangle almost standing upright against the support; on top of this insert a small skewer garnished with truffles; surround the bottom of the dish with a chain of small china cases filled with montglas (No. 747), then covered with a layer of forcemeat and poached in a bain-marie; when serving this entrée send also a sauce-boatful of the reduced pigeon stock thickened with a little sauce.

(1963). PIGEONS, HUNTRESS STYLE—BREASTS (Filets de Pigeons Chasseresse).

Raise the fillets from six pigeons leaving the minion fillet adhere, pare and suppress the skin, then salt and lay them in a sautoir with butter and lemon juice; place this on a hot fire and as soon as they are firm to the touch, remove to place under a weight; then pare again and cover one side only with a salpicon of sweetbreads, truffles and mushrooms mingled with well-reduced allemande sauce (No. 407). Cover this salpicon with chicken quenelle forcemeat (No. 89) diluted with a little cream. Dust the tops with bread-crumbs and grated parmesan cheese, mask with butter and lay the breasts in a sautoir, having the bottom covered with thin slices of fat pork, set it in the hot oven and when the breasts are of a fine color and very warm, dress them in a circle, pouring a Diana sauce (No. 460) in the middle.

(1964). PIGEONS, MONARCH STYLE—SMOTHERED (Pigeons au Monarque—à l'Étuvée).

Choose six good squabs; draw, singe, and clean them well; dip the breasts into boiling water to harden the skin and facilitate the larding process, then lard them with small lardons of fat pork (No. 4, Fig. 54), and braise them in a mirepoix stock (No. 419); glaze and let them get a fine color; when done, drain and dress. Garnish around with stuffed olives, truffles, mushrooms, quenelles, cocks'-combs, and kidneys, or the combs may be imitated by pieces of veal palate removed with a cutter into comb-shapes. Cover with a velouté sauce (No. 415) reduced with mushroom essence (No. 398), and thickened with raw egg-yolks and fresh butter, sending some of the sauce to the table separately. Surround these garnishings with trussed crawfish, and between these lay slices of foies-gras an inch and a quarter in diameter by three-sixteenths of an inch in thickness, breaded à la Villeroi and fried.

(1965). POTTED PIGEONS (Ragoût de Pigeons au Four).

After cleaning and singeing six pigeons, cut them up into four pieces; lay three ounces of butter in a saucepan with six ounces of bacon cut in quarter inch squares; when this begins to brown put in four ounces of onions cut in slices. Range the pigeons in an earthen pot or deep dish with a bed of the bacon on the bottom, the pigeons on top, and more bacon over; add salt, pepper, and sprigs of thyme; moisten with thin brown sauce (No. 414), placing here and there a few pieces of pilot cracker dipped in water. Boil and then let simmer or push in the oven until thoroughly done, and serve in the same crock they have been cooked in.

(1966). PIGEONS, PRINTANIÈRE STYLE (Pigeons à la Printanière).

Prepare a garnishing composed of carrots and turnip balls formed with a half inch vegetable-spoon, and some large green peas; have the carrots and turnips blanched separately, and the peas simply cooked in an untinned copper pan. Break the breastbones of three tender pigeons, remove these bones and fill the breasts with a dressing made of fresh fat pork, chicken livers cooked, chopped, and pounded with a little panada and two egg-yolks. Truss the pigeons with the legs thrust inside for entrée (No. 178), and lay them in a saucepan lined with fat pork, roots, and minced onions; cook them almost dry, only having a very little stock (No. 194a), reduce it to a glaze, and repeat this several times, when finished; drain them off, untruss and cut each one in two lengthwise, then reconstruct them into their former shape. Dress them on a dish leaning them against a triangle-shaped fried bread support fastened on the center of the dish, and between each pigeon set a different garnishing namely; the carrots, turnips, and peas. Increase the quantity of stock with a little stock (No. 194a), strain, skim, and reduce it, thicken it with brown sauce (No. 414), and serve it in a sauce-boat.

(1967). STEWED PIGEONS (Pigeons en Compote).

Bleed six young pigeons in order to kill them, reserving the blood in a bowl; mix with it a spoonful of vinegar to prevent its coagulating. After the pigeons are drawn, singed and well cleansed, truss them with the legs thrust inside. Glaze four dozen small, raw onions, cut eight ounces of bacon into half inch pieces and fry them for a few moments in a saucepan with butter; remove them with a skimmer leaving in the fat, and to this add the pigeons, fry them on all their sides, and season when they have acquired a fine color, then dredge over a spoonful of flour and cook together for two minutes while tossing them about, now moisten the pigeons gradually to their height with white wine and hot stock (No. 194a), stir the liquid till it boils rapidly, then leave it in this state for five minutes, afterward removing the saucepan to a more moderate fire; now add a garnished bunch of parsley (No. 123) and some mushroom peelings. When the pigeons are three-quarters done, put in both the glazed onions and the bacon and finish cooking together. At the last moment, drain out the pigeons, untruss and range them on a dish surrounded by the garnishings. Strain the sauce, free it of fat and thicken it with the blood mixed with two raw egg-yolks, cook this thickening without boiling it and finish the sauce with a piece of butter, then strain it over the pigeons.

(1968). PIGEONS WITH CRAWFISH (Pigeons aux Écrevisses).

Cook some small crawfish with salt, white wine and parsley; break off the tails and suppress their shells in order to be able to pare them, chop up the fragments and add them to a little bread forcemeat finished with fine herbs and egg-yolks. Break the breastbones of two or three pigeons so as to remove the bone, fill up the empty space with the prepared forcemeat, truss and braise them with very little moisture, then strain off the stock, free it of fat and add to it a few spoonfuls of the crawfish stock, thickening with raw egg-yolks diluted with cream, then put in the crawfish tails, untruss the pigeons, dish them and pour the sauce over.

(1969). PIGEONS WITH GREEN PEAS (Pigeons aux Petits Pois).

Truss six pigeons as for an entrée (No. 178), returning the livers to their original place. Melt some chopped fat pork in a saucepan, add to it a quarter of a pound of small five-eighths inch squares of bacon and fry for a few moments, then remove them with a skimmer. Put the pigeons into this saucepan with five or six small onions for each bird, brown slightly and slowly, then add one and a half quarts of green peas, a bunch of parsley and the bacon. Two minutes later moisten with two gills of stock (No. 194a), boil for five minutes and withdraw the saucepan to a slower fire, push into the oven, and finish cooking the peas and pigeons, then drain out the birds, untruss and dress them on a dish; thicken the peas with kneaded butter (No. 579), and place them around the pigeons.

(1970). PIGEONS WITH OLIVES—BREASTS (Filets de Pigeons aux Olives).

This entrée is dressed in the hollow of a cooked paste border (No. 10) cut into points and open-worked with a pastry cutter. The band intended for making the border should be cut out on a floured table as soon as it has been rolled; fasten it on a dish a quarter of an inch from the inside edge,

Fig. 380.

spreading it slightly; egg it over with a brush and dry for a few hours. After this paste is dried, lay inside of it a wooden foundation covered with more of the same paste rolled out thin. Besides this, prepare a little raw chicken forcemeat (No. 89) mixed with an equal quantity of baked liver forcemeat (No. 80) pounded and passed through a tammy. Poach this forcemeat in a pyramidical mold rounded and smooth an inch and a half high, placed in a bain-marie; unmold this pyramid in the center of the dish, for it is intended to uphold the entrée. Select a few dozen of the finest and largest Spanish olives procurable; stone and blanch them to stuff with foies-gras forcemeat (No. 78). Singe six young but large pigeons quite fleshy, fill the breasts with a spoonful of grated fat pork and fresh chopped truffle peelings; truss and cover with fat pork, then cook in some good stock; as soon as done remove to untruss; detach the breasts from the back, remove the two fillets from both breasts, suppress the skin, pare and take off the minions. Lay the six fillets from the left side in a small sautoir, mask them with a little espagnole sauce (No. 414) reduced with the pigeon stock and Madeira; cover and keep them hot. Pare the other six fillets, mask them also on the inside with a layer of baking forcemeat thickened with a little raw forcemeat, smooth well, and range these fillets in another small sautoir having a little half-glaze on the bottom to heat the forcemeat; warm it while glazing over with a brush. At the last moment unmold the pyramid, lay the fillets around alternating them, and all turned in the same direction standing almost upright. Dress a part of the olives in the center space formed by the circle on top of the pyramid, and range the others around the open-worked border. Cover the fillets lightly with the sauce, also the garnishings and serve more separately.

(1971). PULLET À LA ARCO VALLEY (Poularde à la Arco Valley).

Prepare, cook, and dress the pullet the same as for à la Seymour (No. 1981); serve at the same time but separately a velouté sauce (No. 415) reduced with mushroom broth and thickened when ready to serve with egg-yolks, cream and fresh butter, adding chopped parsley, small mushroom buttons and small chicken quenelles. Garnish around with cassolettes (No. 860) of oysters poached, drained and mingled with allemande sauce (No. 407).

(1972). PULLET À LA DAME BLANCHE (Poularde à la Dame Blanche).

Truss a pullet to be served as an entrée (No. 178), rub over the breast with half a lemon, and cover with slices of fat pork. Poêler the pullet in some good stock, as explained in No. 12, adding to it a piece of bacon previously blanched. When the pullet is cooked, strain the stock, free it of fat, and keep the chicken hot in this. Place on the fire to reduce four gills of velouté sauce (No. 415), incorporating a part of the reduced stock slowly into it with a coffeespoonful of prepared red pepper (No. 168); when succulent, strain. Dress the pullet on a thin layer of forcemeat (No. 79) poached on a dish, surround it with small clusters of potatoes cut in balls with a large vegetable scoop, and simply cooked first in salted water, then steamed. Cover the pullet with a part of the sauce, serving the remainder separately. Pullets or capons may be handed round to the guests after being cut up, and they can also be carved on the dining-room sideboard, and served on hot plates with some of the garnishing, and a little of the sauce.

(1973). PULLET À LA DEMIDOFF (Poularde à la Demidoff).

Draw a pullet through the side; crack the breastbone so as to be able to draw it out and fill the empty space with quenelle forcemeat (No. 89), containing cooked fine herbs (No. 385) and chopped truffles, sew up the skin underneath, also the side opening, and truss the pullet to be served as an entrée (No. 178). Cover over with fat pork, and cook it for an hour and a half in some good mirepoix stock (No. 419). When done to perfection, drain, untruss, and dress it on a dish having a bottom of croustade rice fastened to it and surround with a garnishing dressed in groups composed of small truffle balls cut out with a three-eighths vegetablespoon, small balls from the red part of carrots, and small balls of white turnips, also clusters of fresh green peas cooked English style in an untinned pan. Cover the pullet with a little velouté sauce (No. 415) strained and reduced with the pullet stock, and finished with two spoonfuls of good raw cream, serving a sauce-boat of velouté sauce (No. 415) separately.

(1974). PULLET À LA LÉONDISE (Poularde à la Léondise).

Roast the pullet the same as No. 1996 and range it on a layer of macaroni into which has been mixed crawfish or shrimp tails, mushrooms, and quenelles. Serve with a sauce-boat of financière sauce (No. 464).

(1975). PULLET À LA LESTER WALLACK (Poularde à la Lester Wallack).

Break and remove the breastbone of a clean pullet, fill in the empty breast space with a dressing made of grated fat pork, chopped mushrooms, and bread steeped in milk and this liquid squeezed out; truss as for an entrée (No. 178), cover with bards of fat pork, and poêler it quite white (No. 12), then untie and dress on a rice croustade foundation fastened on a dish; surround it simply with turned and channeled mushroom heads (No. 118), cooked artichoke bottoms about two and a half inches in diameter, removing the center with a five-eighths of an inch cutter, then divide into eight pieces, and small chicken quenelles poached in salted water; all these garnishings to be arranged in separate groups. Cover the pullet with some good velouté sauce (No. 415), reduced and thickened with egg-yolks and cream, and finished at the last moment with a salpicon of foies-gras (No. 743), passed through a fine sieve; serve more of the sauce in a sauce-boat.

(1976). PULLET À LA MARTINIÈRE (Poularde à la Martinière).

Poêler a pullet very white (No. 12); drain and cut it up into eight pieces; dress them simply on a force-meat ring poached on the dish; surround with a circle of medium-sized poached spoon quenelles (No. 155), and cover the chicken and quenelles with good velouté sauce (No. 415), reduced with mushroom peelings, and finished with a little good cream. Serve the remainder of the sauce separately with very small and very white mushrooms added.

(1977). PULLET À LA MORNAY (Poularde à la Mornay).

Select a good clean pullet and truss it for entrée (No. 178); poêler it in a stock (No. 194a), keeping it very white, then drain, and when half cold detach the bread so as to be able to dress a garnishing in the empty spaces of the remaining carcass. Escalop these breast fillets and lay them in a sautoir with a garnishing composed of cocks'-combs and kidneys, mushrooms and foies-gras, and moisten this stew rather sparingly with reduced thick allemande sauce (No. 407). Range this in the cleaned out empty space, having them reassume their former shape, smooth them nicely and cover with a layer of Mornay sauce (No. 504), smooth this also and besprinkle over with a grated parmesan cheese, then glaze the surface under a salamander (Fig. 123) or in a hot oven. After finishing the pullet dress it on a long dish containing a layer of poached forcemeat, cover the breasts with a row of slices of truffles and surround the base with clusters of chicken croquettes.

(1978). PULLET À LA NANTUA (Poularde à la Nantua).

Split down the back of a singed and very clean pullet; bone the breast and legs, leaving on the wing bones; season the inside meats and fill the empty space with quenelle forcemeat (No. 89) combined with crawfish butter (No. 573) and prepared red pepper (No. 168) also the crawfish tails cut lengthwise in two. Sew up the pullet, truss and have the breast well rounded, then cover over with slices of fat pork and lay it in a narrow saucepan, cover three-quarters of its height with skimmed stock (No. 194a), adding aromatic herbs and mushroom peelings; cook it in this alone for one hour; it should really only be poached; then drain off the pullet, untie and dress it on a thin layer of forcemeat poached on a dish; cover lightly with velouté sauce (No. 415) reduced with a part of the stock and finished with red butter (No. 580). Surround with small timbales of fat rice made in timbale molds (No. 6) letting it be quite white; serve the remainder of the sauce in a sauce-boat.

(1979). PULLET À LA PÉRIGORD (Poularde à la Périgord).

After the pullet has been singed stuff the breast with pounded veal suet seasoned with salt, prepared red pepper (No. 168) and a clove of garlic, adding to it some chopped up truffles. Insert thick slices of truffles between the fat and skin, then wrap the fowl in a matignon (No. 406) and roast it on the spit or oven; unwrap and reduce the matignon with espagnole sauce (No. 414) and Madeira; dress the pullet with some clear gravy (No. 404) and serve the sauce separately.

(1980). PULLET À LA PRINTANIÈRE—GLAZED (Poularde Glacée à la Printanière).

Have a clean, singed pullet; break the breast bone and stuff the breast with grated fat pork mingled with truffle peelings, truss for entrée (No. 178). Scald the breast in boiling water to harden the meat, then dip these scalded parts at once into cold water, wipe dry and lard with fine lardons of larding pork (No. 3, Fig. 52). Lay the pullet in a saucepan containing fragments of fat pork, roots and minced onions, salt over and steam for fifteen to twenty minutes, then moisten with two or three gills of stock (No. 194a) and allow it to fall to a glaze. Remoisten to half its height with stock and reduce the liquid slowly to half, finish cooking the pullet in this manner, basting it over frequently; when done it should be glazed to a fine color; drain it off to untruss and dress on a dish, surrounding it on both sides with clusters of new cooked carrots and small glazed onions. Strain and skim the pullet stock, reduce it until it becomes succulent, then thicken with a little good brown sauce (No. 414), serving it in a sauce-boat.

(1981). PULLET À LA SEYMOUR (Poularde à la Seymour).

Soak a pound and a half of bread in milk, then press out all the liquid and add it to half a pound of very finely chopped beef suet taken from around the kidneys and a seasoning of shallots, chopped parsley, salt, pepper, cream and egg-yolks; use this to stuff the inside and the breast of a pullet, prepared for roasting (No. 179), tie it up and cover with fat pork then roast it before a good fire basting it over frequently, remove, dress and pour on some clear gravy (No. 404), then serve.

(1982). PULLET À LA VILLARS (Poularde à la Villars).

Truss a pullet as for an entrée (No. 178) with the legs inside; rub over the breasts with half a lemon, cover with bards of fat pork, tie well and poêler it in some good stock (No 12) keeping it very white. Just when prepared to serve, drain out the pullet, untie and dress it on a trimmed rice croustade foundation fastened on a dish, and surround it with a white garnishing composed of lamb's sweetbreads, cocks'-kidneys and mushroom heads, dressed in clusters and these alternated with fire slices of red beef tongue cut in points to resemble cocks'-combs. Cover the pullet and garnishings with a little Villars sauce (No. 559) and serve more of it separately.

(1983). PULLET À LA ZINGARA (Poularde à la Zingara).

Draw two pullets, singe and truss with the legs inside, then tie, stiffen the breast meats and lard them with lardons of tongue and fat pork (No. 3, Fig. 52). Line the bottom of a saucepan with bards of the same pork and slices of veal, round slices of carrots and onions, one whole onion containing a clove and a bunch of parsley garnished with thyme and bay leaf; lay the pullets on top, cover over with strong buttered paper and moisten with one quart of stock (No. 194a); boil, skim and cook slowly for an hour to an hour and a half, and thirty minutes before serving allow it to brown to a nice color. Pound four ounces of unsmoked red beef tongue with the same amount of butter, season with pepper and grated nutmeg and dissolve this in a quarter of a pint of meat glaze (No. 402), heat it up and add a little espagnole (No. 414); rub the whole through a tammy and lay this purée on the bottom of a dish with the pullets on top.

(1984). PULLET, ANCIENT STYLE (Poularde à l'Ancienne).

Draw and singe a pullet, trim and insert slices of truffle between the skin and flesh, truss as for an entrée (No. 178), and lard the legs with rosettes of truffles, bard it nicely and cook in stock (No. 194a) then drain and dress garnishing around with cauliflower and serving a separate well-buttered velouté sauce (No. 415) into which mingle some chopped up truffles.

(1985). PULLET, ENGLISH STYLE (Poularde à l'Anglaise).

After the pullet is cooked as for ancient style (No. 1984), dress it the same, only changing the garnishing to one of potatoes, carrots, turnips, Brussels sprouts and green peas, the whole cooked in salted water; serve a cream béchamel (No. 411) separately.

(1986). PULLET, EGYPTIAN STYLE—BROILED (Poularde Grillée à l'Égyptienne).

First braise the pullet and when cold cut it up and place it in a vessel with salt, pepper, oil and lemon juice, drain, then immerse in bread-crumbs, saturate with oil and broil over a slow fire. When very hot and of a fine color dress on a layer of rice oriental style (No. 2978). Serve with a separate espagnole sauce (No. 414) into which has been added prepared red pepper (No. 168).

(1987). PULLET IN SURPRISE (Poularde en Surprise).

Dress a pullet leaving the neck skin very long; break the breast bone in order to remove it and fill the empty breast space with rather firm quenelle forcemeat (No. 89). Truss the pullet with the legs thrust under the skin and wrap the breast around with thin slices of fat pork, braise (No. 12) it the same time as a chicken and then let both get cold. Untruss the pullet, divide the breasts from the carcass, leaving on the legs and a part of the breast, so that it forms a long hollow case; lay it erect on a small baking sheet and fill the bottom of the hollow case with a layer of chicken cream forcemeat (No. 75); poach this for two minutes in a slack oven. Cut the two pullet fillets into large Julienne, also those taken from the cooked chicken; put them in a saucepan with the same quantity of cooked foies-gras and as many cooked truffles both cut up the same size as the chicken meat, mingling some good reduced velouté sauce (No. 415) with the whole; it should

FIG. 381.

remain quite consistent. Dress this on the top of the cream forcemeat in the hollow case, smooth it well rounded on top, and cover with a thick layer of the same forcemeat; smooth this carefully to the shape of the original breast in order to have the pullet served whole. Decorate both sides of the breast with graduated truffle crescents; butter the forcemeat lightly with a brush and poach in a very slack oven. After removing the pullet, dress it on a dish having its bottom covered with a layer of foundation rice (No. 160) to maintain it in position, and lay on the outer edge a fancy silver border (Fig. 6); keep the whole hot for ten minutes, then remove and dress on each side a cluster of very white mushrooms; cover them as well as the breast with a little suprême sauce (No. 547) prepared with the stock and serve with a sauce-boatful of the same.

(1988). PULLET IVORY WITH DECORATED QUENELLES (Poularde à l'Ivoire aux Quenelles Décorées).

Break the breast bone of a cleaned and singed pullet, tie it up as for an entrée (No. 178) and insert a piece of butter into the breast; cover over with bards of fat pork and set it in a saucepan of its own dimensions; moisten to its height with stock (No. 194a), boil the liquid over a hot fire then remove the saucepan on a slower one, cover and finish cooking the pullet for forty-five to sixty minutes. As soon as done to perfection, strain the stock through a napkin into another vessel leaving the pullet to keep warm. Skim the fat from the stock and pour the top gently into another saucepan, then reduce it with some velouté sauce (No. 415) and cream; strain this through a tammy. Dress the pullet, pour the sauce over, and garnish around with chicken quenelles decorated with truffles (No. 154).

(1989). PULLET, MODERN STYLE (Poularde à la Moderne).

Peel two pounds of fresh truffles and chop up the peelings; pound them with one pound of panada, adding half as much raw foies-gras; continue to pound, putting in eight ounces of grated fat pork, a few eggs and seasoning, then rub the whole through a sieve. Fill the breasts of a pullet with a part of this dressing, using the remainder for the insides; braise (No. 12) with a very little moistening; dress when cooked, and garnish around with cocks'-combs, and the peeled truffles sautéd in butter, and cooked in Madeira. Reduce the braise stock with velouté sauce (No. 415), and just when ready to serve incorporate a few pats of fine butter; pour it over the pullet and garnishings, and serve some well-buttered chicken purée (No. 713) separately.

(1990). PULLET, PARISIAN STYLE—STUFFED (Poularde Farcie à la Parisienne).

This entrée is dressed on a dish decorated with an open-work border made of cooked paste (No. 10), having the empty space in the center covered with a wooden foundation masked over with noodle paste (No. 142), dried in the air. Draw a pullet through the side, break the breastbone to be able to draw it out, and stuff the breast with quenelle forcemeat (No. 89), finished with a few spoonfuls of cooked fine herbs (No. 385), and a foies-gras salpicon cut in three-eighths of an inch dice, and truffles of the same size; sew the breast skin underneath, and truss the pullet as for entrée (No. 178); cover with slices of fat pork and cook in a good stock (No. 194a), keeping it white, and when done properly, drain, untie, and untruss. Lay it on the foundation already placed on the dish; surround

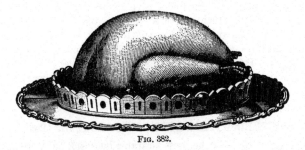

FIG. 382.

it with a garnishing of round truffles cooked at the last moment with Madeira and melted glaze (No. 402). Cover the pullet with some good velouté sauce (No. 415), reduced with its own stock and the Madeira and glaze in which the truffles have been cooked, and serve a sauce-boat of the sauce at the same time.

(1991). PULLET TARTAR SAUCE—BROILED (Poularde Grillée à la Sauce Tartare).

Draw and truss a pullet as for an entrée (No. 178), then split it down the center of the back, flatten and bread-crumb it English style with egg-yolks and butter beaten together; broil on a slow fire, and serve on a very hot dish; pour a little good gravy (No. 404) under, and send to the table with a separate tartar sauce (No. 631).

(1992). TRUFFLED ROASTED PULLET (Poularde Truffée Rôtie).

A few days before this is needed draw the pullet through the side and wipe the inside well. Peel twelve to sixteen ounces of fine, fresh truffles, leaving them either whole or cut in two or four according to their size. Melt two ounces of grated fat pork in a saucepan, add to it the truffles and season with fine allspice; fry for two minutes, remove and use this to stuff the breast of the pullet. Sew up the openings and truss, then lay it aside in a cool place. When needed wrap it in buttered paper, run it on a spit (No. 118) or else lay it in a small cradle spit (No. 116) without boring any hole through it whatever, and roast it for one hour, basting frequently. Unwrap it ten minutes before serving to salt over and allow to attain a fine color; take it out, untie and send it to the table with a sauce-boat of good reduced gravy (No. 404) into which has been added the chopped up truffle peelings.

(1993). PULLET WITH CROUSTADES FINANCIÈRE (Poularde aux Croustades Financière).

Draw a pullet, singe and free it well of all the pin feathers adhering to the flesh; truss as for an entrée (No. 178) and rub over with lemon juice; wrap it up in thin slices of fat pork, tying it on firmly. Cover the bottom of a saucepan with bards of fat pork, slices of veal, two slices of raw, smoked ham, a few cut up carrots, two onions, two cloves, a bunch of parsley garnished with thyme and bay leaf, and season with salt and whole peppers; place it on the fire and let simmer for an hour or more and when done, strain the stock through a napkin, remove its fat and reduce it with two gills of espagnole (No. 414). Drain the pullet, untruss and lay it on a dish, garnishing around with some croustades made in molds (No. 3, Fig. 137) and filled with financière salpicon (No. 667).

(1994). PULLET WITH MUSSELS OR OYSTERS (Poularde aux Moules ou aux Huîtres).

Truss and cook a pullet exactly as with the ravioles (No. 1995), wash some mussels in several waters and place them in a covered saucepan over a brisk fire to open; when this occurs remove from their shells, transfer them to another vessel. Fry colorless in butter a little parsley and chives, add two gills of either béchamel (No. 409) or velouté (No. 415), a little stock (No. 194a) and grated nutmeg; boil this sauce up once or twice, then put in either the mussels or else some prepared oysters; just when ready to serve, drain the pullet, untruss and dress. Thicken the sauce with a few raw egg-yolks and fine butter, heat it up without boiling and range the garnishings around the pullet, cover over with a part of the sauce and serve what remains separately.

(1995). PULLET WITH RAVIOLES (Poularde aux Ravioles).

Draw a fine pullet, singe and clean it well, truss it for an entrée, (No. 178), and cover over with slices of fat pork. Butter the bottom of a braziere (Fig. 134), lay over some sliced onions and carrots, a bunch of parsley garnished with thyme and bay leaf, a clove of garlic and two cloves. Moisten with stock (No. 194a) to three-quarters its height, then boil, skim and cook slowly for one hour and a half to two hours; drain off the stock, free it of fat and return this to the braziere to keep the pullet warm. Reduce the stock with velouté (No. 415) if for white, or espagnole (No. 414) if for brown. Dress the pullet on a layer of ravioles (No. 2976) mingled with some velouté or espagnole and parmesan cheese, and serve a separate sauce-boat of the sauce with cooked fine herbs (No. 385) and chopped parsley added.

(1996). PULLET GARNISHED WITH WATER-CRESS—ROASTED (Poularde Rôtie au Cresson).

Six to nine months old pullets are the most desirable ones especially when quite fat. Roasted poultry should be treated with extreme care, for the roast is the most essential part of a dinner and is partaken of by almost every one. Should the fowl not be barded, then it must be enveloped in a buttered paper and basted frequently while cooking, either with butter or else good poultry fat. Draw and singe a good pullet, truss it for roasting (No. 179) and place it on the spit or in the oven, although roasting on the spit is far the most preferable. When the pullet is nicely done dress and surround with water-cress, serving its own gravy strained and free of fat separately.

(1997). BLANQUETTE OF PULLET WITH MUSHROOMS (Blanquette de Poularde aux Champignons).

Begin by detaching the legs from a trussed and singed pullet, cut each of these in two, then lay them in a vessel containing water; divide the breast in two and cut each piece into three parts; plunge them also into the cold water with the cut up carcass; let soak for fifteen to twenty minutes then drain and lay them in a saucepan with an onion and a bunch of parsley, and cover plentifully with white chicken broth (No.188); boil and skim this liquid for twelve minutes then take it off the fire. Prepare a white roux (No.163) with flour and butter, dilute it with the strained and skimmed pullet broth when partially cold and stir this sauce well until it boils; let it despumate for a quarter of an hour on the side of the fire while removing the fat from the surface. Pare and wipe the pieces of pullet, return them to the saucepan with two dozen turned mushrooms (No. 118); strain the sauce over and finish cooking, finally dressing the pieces of pullet in a deep dish with the mushrooms. Reduce the sauce for a few minutes, thicken with two egg-yolks finishing it off the fire with a piece of butter worked in, also some lemon juice; strain and pour it over the pullet.

(1998). PULLETS À LA MONTMORENCY—BREASTS (Filets de Poularde à la Montmorency).

Fasten to a dish a plain or ring-shaped bottom covered with cooked paste (No. 131) or noodle paste (No. 142), having in its center a tin cup equally covered with ornamental pieces of paste, egg it all over and dry in the air. Pare the fillets of five small pullets, suppressing the superficial

Fig. 383.

skin, remove the minion fillets and streak them with truffles, also suppress the pinion bones, trimming them into half hearts rounded on one end and pointed on the other. Place the minion fillets on the larger ones, both slightly bent: Range the fillets on the bottom of a sautoir with a layer of cold clarified butter, being careful to have them all lie in one direction, so that the pointed ends extend toward the center. With the cut up pullet carcasses, prepare a little chicken essence (No. 387) and when done and nicely seasoned, strain and skim off the fat and incorporate into it a few gills of good velouté (No. 415) in the act of being reduced. When this sauce is perfect and succulent, finish it with a few spoonfuls of good, raw cream and afterward a piece of fresh butter; keep it in a bain-marie till needed. Just when ready to serve, sprinkle the fillets over with salt and poach them lightly, drain and dress in a circle on the foundation prepared on the dish. Fill the center cup with a garnishing of peeled truffles cooked in Madeira; cover the fillets lightly with the sauce, serving the rest in a sauce-boat.

(1999). PULLET À LA MONTPENSIER—MINION FILLETS (Filets Mignons de Poularde à la Montpensier).

Streak twelve minion fillets with truffles, shape them into rings two inches in diameter and poach them with butter in a small sautoir. Cut twelve quarter inch thick slices from the middle part of freshly cooked red beef tongue and from each of these slices cut out a round piece the same size as the minion fillet rings; lay these tongue rounds on thin crusts of bread fried in butter and covered with a layer of consistent soubise (No. 723), then mask the tongue rounds with a layer of reduced thick Madeira sauce (No. 492), and on top set the minion fillet rings, one on each, filling in their hollow spaces with a large stuffed Spanish olive standing upright and covered with more of the same Madeira sauce. Dress the hot fillets in a circle and in the center place a garnishing of green asparagus tops (No. 2693).

(2000). PULLETS' BREASTS À LA VARSOVIAN (Filets de Poularde à la Varsovienne).

Prepare and cook the pullet fillets as for Montmorency (No. 1998), poach them in butter and dish in a circle intercalating with a croûton of bread fried in butter; fill the center with cèpes sauted with fine herbs and garnish around with small chicken croquettes (No. 877) made crescent-shaped and fried in hot and very white frying fat. Cover the fillets with béchamel (No. 409) into which has been mixed a little meat glaze (No. 402) and lemon juice; have a sauce-boat of the same sauce served at the same time as the fillets.

(2001). PULLETS' BREASTS À LA VISCONTI (Filets de Poularde à la Visconti).

Pare the fillets of three pullets each one weighing from three to four pounds; suppress the superficial skin covering the minions, also the pinion bones; beat them lightly, giving them the shape of a half heart on one end and pointed on the other; range these fillets on the bottom of a sautoir covered with a layer of clarified, and cold butter being careful to place them all in such a way that the sharp ends point toward the center. Just when ready to serve, salt them over and cook slowly on both sides while turning, then drain and dress in a circle on a ring of poached force-meat laid on a dish. Serve them with a garnishing in the center composed of cocks'-combs and kidneys, mushrooms and truffles, mingled with suprême sauce (No. 547), into which has been added half its quantity of mushroom purée (No. 722).

(2002). PULLETS' MINION FILLETS WITH MACÉDOINE (Filets Mignons de Poularde à la Macédoine).

Pare twelve pullets' minion fillets, remove the outer skin and inside sinew; pare and streak with three-quarter circles of red beef tongue cut into graduated sizes; range them on the bottom of a sautoir and cover with clarified butter, forming each one into the shape of a crescent, salt, sprinkle with butter, and cook in a slow oven, then drain off. Cover a dish with a garnishing of macédoine vegetables mixed with béchamel (No. 680), and finished with a few spoonfuls of melted glaze (No. 402) and several small pats of fresh butter; surround this with the minion fillets. Fill some crescent-shaped bottomless molds placed on a sheet of buttered paper with quenelle forcemeat (No. 89) leveled to the height of the mold with the blade of a knife. Place a sautoir on the fire containing clarified butter, set in the molds having the paper on top, push in the oven to detach the paper; remove this and lay the sautoir on the fire to color the crescent to a fine color on both sides; unmold, drain, and dress the minion fillets on these, and around arrange the macédoine garnishing (No. 680).

(2003). PULLETS' LEGS À LA BAYONNAISE (Cuisses de Poularde à la Bayonnaise).

Remove the legs from three singed pullets retaining the skin covering the back as far down as the rump; bone them entirely with the exception of the drumstick; put them in a vessel with salt, mignonette, lemon juice and a broken bay leaf; let marinate for three hours, being careful to turn them over several times. Twenty-five minutes before serving, drain and roll each one in flour, fry them in grated fat pork and when they attain a fine color and are well cooked, remove. Slice four medium onions three-sixteenths of an inch in thickness; detach the pieces so they form rings, flour over and fry these to a golden brown. Dress the legs in the middle of a dish, cover over with brown poivrade sauce (No. 522) with some grated Bayonne ham added to it, and garnish the whole with the fried onions; trim the stump bones with paper frills (No. 10) and serve immediately.

(2004). PULLETS' LEGS DEVILED (Cuisses de Poulardes à la Diable).

Generally this dish is prepared with pullets' legs already cooked and then broiled, but raw ones can also be used. Score and season well—pepper should predominate—then roll them in mustard diluted with oil; besprinkle with bread-crumbs and broil on a slow fire, turning them over. Serve with a deviled sauce (No. 459).

(2005). PULLETS' LEGS WITH NEW CARROTS (Cuisses de Poulardes aux Carottes Nouvelles).

Have three singed pullets and from them remove the legs and the skin covering the back, bone them entirely, retaining the drum sticks; stuff them with quenelle forcemeat (No. 89) and cooked fine herbs (No. 385), shaping them like a cutlet; cover with slices of fat pork and braise them in a little mirepoix stock with white wine (No. 419) into which add six dozen small new blanched carrots, but in case there be no new ones procurable use others, cutting them up to represent the new ones. When these are cooked, lift them out and place them in a saucepan with a little butter, chicken glaze (No. 398) and fine herbs. Strain the stock, free it of fat and reduce it with espagnole sauce (No. 414) to the consistency of half-glaze; skim well the surface of the sauce; dress the legs in the center of a dish with the new or other carrots around, pour over some of the sauce and serve the remainder of it separately.

(2006). SQUABS À LA BRIAND (Pigeonneaux à la Briand).

Soak bread-crumbs in a little broth; press it to extract well the moisture, then lay it in a bowl with a quarter as much good butter, a few egg-yolks and one whole egg; work this preparation well, seasoning with salt, pepper, parsley and onions chopped and blanched; use this for filling the squabs, then truss them for an entrée (No. 178) and run them on the spit to roast, being careful to baste over occasionally with butter; untie them, remove the larding pork covering the breasts and lay them on a bed of sautéd tomatoes (No. 2841). Serve a brown sauce (No. 414) separately into which mix Worcestershire sauce, meat glaze (No. 402), chopped parsley and tarragon vinegar.

(2007). SQUABS CRAPAUDINE—BROILED (Pigeonneaux Grillés Crapaudine).

After a squab has been well drawn, singed and thoroughly cleaned, cut each side from the pinion of the wing to the tip of the breast; open without detaching the parts, having the legs and back on one end, and the breast on the other; beat well to flatten, season and dip in melted butter; roll them in bread-crumbs and broil slowly While this is progressing chop up one shallot exceedingly fine, blanch, drain and fry it colorless in butter, add to it some clear gravy (No. 404) and a little espagnole sauce (No. 414) and white wine; season and then pour this sauce into a dish, dress the squabs on it and surround with slices of lemon cut in halves.

FIG. 384.

(2008). SQUABS À LA CRISPI (Pigeonneaux à la Crispi).

Bone the backs of some small squabs, fill the insides with quenelle forcemeat (No. 89), containing mushrooms, ham and truffles cut in three-sixteenths of an inch squares, enclosing it well in the birds. Lay some rings in a sautoir already garnished with slices of fat pork, and place the squabs inside these rings, cover with more slices of the pork and moisten with a very little mirepoix stock (No. 419) with Madeira wine, and when cooked place a round tin plate on the squabs with a weight on top to flatten the birds slightly. Dress them crown-shaped and cover over with green ravigote sauce (No. 531); lay a cooked trussed crawfish and serve more of the sauce separately.

(2009). SQUABS À LA FLOURENS (Pigeonneaux à la Flourens).

Procure eight squabs, draw, singe and truss as for an entrée (No. 178), or one squab for each guest Chop up very fine eight ounces of beef marrow, mix with it eight ounces of butter, some chopped parsley, finely cut up chives, eight chopped tarragon leaves, a little crushed and chopped garlic, salt, pepper, four ounces of lean ham cut into one-eighth inch squares, four ounces of bread-crumbs and two whole eggs. Fill the squabs with this dressing and roast them either on the spit or in the oven for thirty minutes, basting them frequently. When done, untruss, dress in a circle and pour in a garnishing of sweetbreads and artichoke bottoms cut in three-sixteenth inch squares to which has been added some espagnole sauce (No. 414). Serve some of this sauce separately.

(2010). SQUABS À L'IMPROMPTU—SAUTÉD (Pigeonneaux Sautés à l'Impromptu).

After the squabs are prepared the same as for broiling, fry them in clarified butter, and when done, dress. Fry and cook colorless a teaspoonful of chopped shallots for each pigeon, add to it a little flour, moisten lightly with stock (No. 194a) and white wine, boil and skim; reduce this rapidly over a hot fire and just when ready to serve, incorporate a little fine butter, lemon juice and chopped parsley; pour this over the squabs and serve at once.

(2011). SQUABS À LA STANISLAS—STUFFED (Pigeonneaux Farcis à la Stanislas).

Fry eight ounces of bacon cut in three-sixteenth of an inch squares in butter, also as much fresh mushrooms sliced the same size, with a little chopped shallot and parsley. Fill the pigeons with this preparation and roast them. Have as many round truffles as there are pigeons, each one inch in circumference, peel and use the parings to pound with quenelle forcemeat (No. 89), and with this make some quenelles the shape and size of large verdal olives; poach and put them into an allemande sauce (No. 407) with a little meat glaze (No. 402), also the peeled truffles and some channeled mushrooms (No. 118). When the squabs are roasted untruss and dish up with the garnishings ranged around.

(2012). SQUABS, AMERICAN STYLE—STUFFED (Pigeonneaux Farcis à l'Américaine).

Have six squabs, draw, singe lightly and truss as for roasting (No. 179); fill the insides with an American bread dressing (No. 61), and cover the breasts with thin slices of fat pork; roast them either in the oven or on the spit; they take about twenty minutes when stuffed and fifteen when not. Dress and surround with slices of broiled bacon, pouring a little clear gravy (No. 404) around.

(2013). SQUABS, COLBERT SAUCE—BROILED (Pigeonneaux Grillés Sauce Colbert).

Select small squabs and after they have been plucked, drawn and singed, clean them nicely and cut the necks from the bodies; truss with the legs thrust inside and split them down through the back the whole length as far as the rump; beat the breasts to have them quite flat, pare, then season with salt and mignonette; immerse them in melted butter and roll in bread-crumbs; then broil over a slow fire for about ten minutes, laying them with the breast side downward and turning them over as fast as they attain a good color, finish cooking and dress with some gravy (No. 404) poured over or else serve them on a Colbert sauce (No. 451); garnish around with slices of lemon cut in halves.

(2014). SQUABS, ENGLISH STYLE (Pigeonneaux à l'Anglaise).

Truss eight squabs as for an entrée (No. 178), wrap them up in bards of fat pork. Lay them in a saucepan lined with thin slices of ham and moisten to their height with white wine mirepoix stock (No. 419); cover with a round sheet of buttered paper and place the lid on tight. Boil and simmer until the squabs are thoroughly done; which will take about twenty-five minutes. Prepare eight oval-shaped bread croûtons, three inches long by two wide, make an incision all around a quarter of an inch from the edge and to half their depth, then fry in clarified butter, and empty out the center. Dress the squabs on these croûtons, range on a dish and place between each a vegetable garnishing composed of carrots trimmed to imitate new ones, then blanched and cooked in broth; turnips shaped like corks with the edges rounded, then blanched and cooked in white stock (No. 194a), small green peas boiled in salted water with fresh mint, tossing with butter after draining, and string beans boiled in salted water and finished with butter, fill in the center with a fine cauliflower boiled in salted water and having butter poured over. Serve a York sauce (No. 563) separately.

(2015). SQUABS, NEW YORK STYLE (Pigeonneaux à la New Yorkaise).

Have some squabs drawn, singed, cleaned, and trussed for an entrée (No. 178); fry them white in butter and dredge over a little flour; fry for a few moments longer without browning, then moisten with beef stock (No. 194a); add a bunch of parsley garnished with thyme and bay leaf, small onions, potato balls made five-eighths of an inch in circumference, and small half inch dice of bacon fried in butter. A few moments before serving, add some quenelles shaped to represent large verdal olives either of godiveau or else of chicken quenelle forcemeat (No. 89), into which mingle chopped sweetbreads and parsley; poach these in boiling water. Just when ready to serve, remove the parsley, thicken the stew with raw egg-yolks diluted with cream, and incorporate a piece of fresh butter, and dress the squabs in the middle of a dish with the garnishing around.

(2016). SQUABS WITH TARRAGON (Pigeonneaux à l'Estragon).

After the squabs have been drawn and singed, split them lengthwise in two down the back, but do not separate the parts; beat lightly, and season with pepper and salt. Put two ounces of butter into a sauté pan, and after it begins to heat, lay in the squabs, the breast side downward, and set it on a brisk fire; when browned on one side, turn them to do likewise on the other; they take about twelve minutes to cook. Dress and pour off half the butter in the pan, and to the remainder add a pinch of flour, stir well, pour in some clear gravy (No. 404), two tablespoonfuls of good tarragon vinegar, and salt; let the sauce give one or two boils, season it nicely, and pour it over the squabs.

(2017). SQUABS WITH FIGARO SAUCE—FRIED (Pigeonneaux Frits à la Sauce Figaro).

Singe and draw some young, tender pigeons; truss as for an entrée (No. 178), then wrap them in slices of fat pork. Butter a saucepan, line it with sliced carrots and onions, and a garnished bunch of parsley (No. 123); lay the squabs on top. Moisten to half their height and let the liquid fall to a glaze, then remoisten and boil very slowly until cooked to perfection, adding half a bottleful of white wine, pouring it in at two or three different intervals. Let the squabs become cold, then split them in two, pare nicely and dip them in frying batter (No. 137), and fry to a fine color, having the birds well heated throughout. Drain, wipe off, and salt; dress them on a folded napkin with a bunch of parsley on top. Serve at the same time but separately a figaro mayonnaise sauce (No. 609).

(2018). SQUABS IN EARTHENWARE SAUCEPAN OR STUFFED—ROASTED (Pigeonneaux Rôtis à la Casserole ou Pigeonneaux Farcis Rôtis au Four).

In Earthenware Saucepan.—Procure six squabs, draw, singe and truss ,well with the legs thrust inside, keeping them a pretty shape. Put two ounces of butter into a small earthenware saucepan and when hot, add the squabs and roast them in this over a good fire or in the oven; when done, drain and pour off the fat, detach the glaze with a little gravy (No. 404), untruss the squabs, put them back in the pan, dress, strain the sauce over them and serve in the earthen ware pan.

Stuffed.—Steep a piece of bread in broth and at once squeeze out all the moisture; lay it in a saucepan and add to it as much chopped beef suet, a few egg-yolks and one whole egg; stir this preparation with a spoon and season with salt, pepper, chopped parsley and onions. Break the breastbones of three young, drawn and clean squabs, fill the empty space with the prepared dressing and roast them quickly on the spit, basting over with melted butter. Salt over when ready to take out, untruss and dress on a dish, garnishing them if so desired with a little very green water-cress seasoned with salt and vinegar, and serve some gravy (No. 404) separately.

2019). SQUABS, BREASTS À LA DUXELLE—STUFFED (Filets de Pigeonneaux Farcis à la Duxelle).

Pare eight to ten breasts of squabs; split them in two through their thickness without detaching the parts, but simply to form a pocket, fill this in with a little duxelle with raw truffles (No. 461), close the opening, season the breasts, dip them in beaten eggs mixed with cooked fine herbs, (No. 385) roll in fresh bread-crumbs and then in melted butter and broil over a slow fire. Dress the breasts crown-shaped on a dish with a little half-glaze sauce (No. 413) to which has been added butter, lemon juice and chopped parsley.

(2020). SQUAB FRITTERS, OPORTO SAUCE (Beignets de Pigeonneaux, Sauce Oporto).

Pluck, draw and singe some nice squabs, free them of all their feathers, cut off the stumps and pinions, then divide them in two lengthwise and afterward split them across on the bias to obtain two pieces from each, one from the legs and from the wings; lay them in a vessel and season with salt, whole peppers, nutmeg, thyme, bay leaf, sliced onions, lemon juice and a little oil, leave to marinate for two hours, turning them over occasionally, take each piece out and dip it in frying batter (No. 137), then plunge into very hot frying fat, drain, salt and dress them in a pyramid form on a folded napkin; serve separately a currant sauce (No. 455) with Port wine.

(2021). SQUABS À LA CAROLINA (Pigeonneaux à la Caroline).

Cut up some squabs after being dressed in six pieces each; have the same quantity of blanched terrapin of the same size; place them in a saucepan and moisten with half Madeira and half stock (No. 194a); season with salt and pepper and boil up once, then finish cooking in a slack oven for about thirty minutes; when done thicken the sauce with hard boiled egg-yolks pounded with as much butter and then passed through a sieve, add a little white wine and season highly. Roll well the meat in the sauce to have it thick, and serve the whole inside a border made of rice boiled in salted water, and fresh butter added, for ten minutes or until it ceases to crackle between the teeth, then drain and mingle it with a little béchamel (No. 409). Mold this rice in a liberally buttered plain border mold (Fig. 139), push it into the oven for a few moments, invert it on a dish, remove the mold and fill in the center with the stew.

(2022). SQUABS À LA VESTAL (Pigeonneaux à la Vestale).

Mix in with some veal godiveau (No 85) truffles, chives and parsley all well chopped; range this forcemeat in a plain well-buttered border mold (No. 139) and poach in a slack oven. Cut some squabs in four, fry them in butter to a nice color, drain off the grease, add allemande sauce (No. 407) and small mushroom heads; fill the inside of the unmolded border with this stew; bestrew over with bread-crumbs and grated parmesan; pour melted butter on it and brown the whole in a hot oven serving when of a fine color.

(2023). TURKEY HEN (Dinde).

The hen turkey is the female of the gobbler; it hatches on the ground and is very prolific. The meat of the hen turkey is far more delicate than that of the male, therefore it is more frequently selected for stuffing with truffles or chestnuts. In order to have it good it must be young and raised in the barn-yard. Its meat is better in winter time after leaving it hang for a certain period; it can be roasted or else cooked in its own gravy, both ways are excellent, but if old then it should be boiled. Wild turkeys abound principally in North America and feed on fruits and green acorns; their meat is far more delicate and succulent than that of the domestic turkey. The eggs are much liked either boiled or cooked in an omelet.

(2024). TURKEY À LA CHIPOLATA—STUFFED (Dinde Farcie à la Chipolata).

Select a small turkey not too fat but quite fleshy; bone the entire front part leaving the breast-skin as long as possible, also the thighs; diminish the thickness of the fillets and place these pieces where there is no meat so as to equalize the thickness of the meat. Season the inside of the breasts. Cut lengthwise two veal minion fillets and fry them in butter, season and throw over some cooked fine herbs (No. 385), then let get cold; mix in with these a few fillets of veal udder, and of cooked ham and truffles, also an equal quantity of chicken quenelle forcemeat (No. 89). Fill the empty space with the garnishing and forcemeat mixed; press the forcemeat into the skin of the turkey and let it assume its original shape; braise it for an hour and a quarter to an hour and a half on a very slow fire, and at the last moment glaze, drain off and untruss the turkey. Dress it on a rice croustade foundation (Fig. 9a) and surround with a chipolata garnishing (No. 657) into which a good espagnole sauce (No. 414) with Madeira wine has been added reduced with the braise stock; pour a part of this sauce over the turkey, and serve the remainder separately.

(2025). WILD TURKEY À LA DELAGRANGE—STUFFED (Dinde Sauvage Farcie à la Delagrange).

Singe and draw a young wild turkey, then truss for an entrée (No. 178). Prepare a dressing composed of bread-crumbs soaked in warm water and the liquid entirely extracted, season with salt, fine spices, sage, chopped onions fried in butter, and finely chopped beef marrow; add some roasted chestnuts, and broiled sausages free of skin, and cut into slices. When all the ingredients are thoroughly mixed, fill the turkey with it and braise in a saucepan garnished with bards of pork, and moistened with a white wine mirepoix stock (No. 419); when nearly done, glaze, drain, untruss, and dress on a layer of Piedmontese risot (No. 739); serve with béchamel sauce (No. 409) reduced with the mirepoix stock, thickening with raw egg-yolks and cream; when ready to serve incorporate a little chicken glaze (No. 398), and a piece of fine butter. Pour part of this sauce over the turkey serving the rest in a sauce-boat.

(2026). SMALL TURKEY À LA FINANCIÈRE—LARDED (Petite Dinde Piquée à la Financière).

The turkey represented in Fig. 385, the recipe of which is given below, is simply dressed on a rice croustade foundation (Fig. 9a), cut an inch and a quarter thick. Prepare a financière garnishing composed of whole truffles, mushroom heads, large cocks'-combs and four large chicken quenelles molded on buttered paper and decorated with truffles; keep them warm. Select a good, small fleshy turkey not too fat, break the breastbone in order to draw it out, and fill up the empty space

FIG. 385.

with grated fat pork pounded with fresh truffle peelings; sew up the skin, truss it with the legs inside and lard the fillets and thighs with fine shreds of larding pork (No. 3, Fig. 52). Put the turkey in a small braziere lined with fragments of fat pork, roots and minced onions; moisten to half its height with good broth (No. 194a) and reduce the liquid quickly to half, finish cooking the turkey quite slowly while basting frequently; at the last moment allow it to brown nicely in the oven. Strain and skim the stock, reduce it to a half-glaze, incorporating into it slowly some good espagnole (No. 414) that is in the act of being reduced, adding at the same time a few spoonfuls of good dry white wine. Untruss the turkey, dress it on the foundation and surround it with the prepared garnishings dressed according to the illustration; glaze the truffles and pour a little of the sauce over the cocks'-combs and mushrooms. Serve the prepared sauce at the same time as the relevé which is intended to be placed on the table.

(2027). TURKEY À LA SARTIGES—STUDDED (Dinde Cloutée à la Sartiges).

Singe, draw and truss a ten pound turkey as for an entrée (No. 178), stuff the insides with a quenelle forcemeat (No. 89) mixed with cooked fine herbs (No. 385); dip the breasts in boiling water to stretch the skin, drive twelve truffle nails into each fillet at equal distances apart and arranged symmetrically in rows of six each, then wrap the turkey in slices of fat pork fastening them on with a string. Cover the bottom of a saucepan with fat pork, lay in the turkey and moisten to a little above its height with a mirepoix stock (No. 419), boil, skim and cook in a moderate oven. When the bird is done drain it off and dress it on a rice foundation. Have a garnishing of cocks'-combs truffles, quenelles, and cèpes dressed in clusters around the turkey; strain and skim off all the fat from the stock, reduce it to a succulent sauce with some espagnole

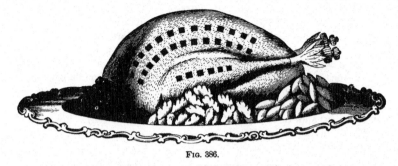

Fig. 386.

(No. 414) added; pour a part of this over the garnishings and the remainder to be served separately with Spanish olives stuffed and minced mushrooms.

(2028). TURKEY, AMERICAN STYLE—ROASTED (Dinde Rôtie à l'Américaine).

Draw, singe and truss a turkey weighing from eight to twelve pounds, selecting a very fresh one.   Clean the insides thoroughly, having it well washed and dried, then fill with a bread stuffing (No. 61); wrap it well in strong buttered paper and lay it on the spit, running the iron rod of the spit between the loins and the string that is used for trussing the turkey; fasten the legs firmly to this rod and roast before a good fire for about an hour to an hour and a half.   Fifteen minutes before serving, unwrap the turkey, that is to remove the paper and let it assume a fine color while continuing to baste; it should be a golden brown and cooked to perfection.   Dress and pour around a little gravy (No. 404) and then garnish with very green water cress; serve with a sauce-boat of cranberry sauce (No. 598).

(2029). TURKEY, FRENCH STYLE (Dinde à la Française).

Choose a small fat turkey; draw, singe and clean it well, extracting all the pin feathers; break the breastbone, remove it and fill the breast with an English bread dressing (No. 61); sew up the skin underneath and truss it for an entrée (No. 178); lay it in a braziere of the same dimensions as the turkey, having it lined with slices of fat pork, moisten to half its height with mirepoix stock

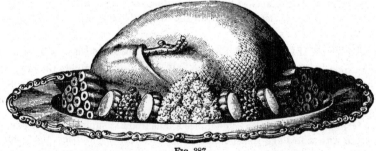

Fig. 387.

(No. 419) and let the liquid come to a boil; then cover the turkey with a thick buttered paper and cook for an hour and a half to two hours with the braziere well closed; simmer slowly while basting frequently.   At the last moment drain off the turkey, untruss and dress on a rice foundation (Fig. 9a) surrounding it with clusters of cauliflower, mushroom heads, braised celery, glazed carrots and stuffed cucumbers, or else both, all being arranged in separate groups.   Cover the breasts with some velouté sauce (No. 415) reduced with the stock already strained and skimmed, serving at the same time a sauce-boat of the same sauce.

(2030). TURKEY WITH CÈPES (Dinde aux Cèpes).

Pick out four dozen good unopened cèpes weighing about four pounds, having them fresh, sound, and of equal size; cut off and peel the stalks, chop them up and cook in butter with a little chopped onion.   Prepare a fine hash with one pound of veal, and one pound of fresh fat pork, seasoning it highly, add the chopped cèpes and a handful of soaked and pressed out bread-crumbs. Crack the breastbone of a fat turkey, remove the bone and fill in the empty space with the prepared dressing, sew the skin underneath and truss for entrée (No. 178). Lay the bird in a buttered stew-pan covering the bottom with small squares of bacon; surround it with the peeled and seasoned cèpes heads, and a bunch of parsley; season and moisten with a quart of stock (No. 194a); baste the turkey with butter, salt well, and place it in the oven to leave until the moistening is entirely reduced, then moisten again to half its height with more stock; boil, close the pan, and keep it cooking in the oven for three hours, pouring in a little broth at times while basting it occasionally. At the last moment drain off the turkey to untruss and dress on a dish surrounding it with the cèpes and bacon. Strain the stock, skim it free of fat, then thicken and reduce with some good béchamel, (No. 409) and a few spoonfuls of half-glaze (No. 400). Pour a part of this over the turkey and the surplus in a sauce-boat.

(2031). TURKEY TRUFFLED AND GARNISHED WITH BLACK OLIVES (Dinde Truffée et Garnie d'Olives Noires).

Have a fine fat tender turkey weighing about eight or ten pounds; truffle it three days before-hand with two pounds of leaf lard, three bay leaves, thyme, salt, pepper, a very little crushed and chopped garlic, and two chopped up shallots. Peel three pounds of truffles, chop up the parings, and place all together in a vessel, cutting the large truffles into pieces. Strain the melted lard over these and let get cold, stirring the whole well together with a gill of brandy, and season. Fill up the turkey with this and insert a slice of thin fat pork between the breast skin and the meat; place on this fat pork slices of truffle. Truss for roasting (No. 179) and wrap in buttered paper; lay it on a cradle spit(Fig. 116), and cook for an hour and a half to two hours, basting frequently; unwrap it fifteen minutes before serving; salt and let acquire a good color. Dress on a long dish, garnish around with black olives, and serve separately some clear gravy (No. 404) taken from the drippings well skimmed and strained.

(2032). TURKEY WITH WHITE OYSTER SAUCE (Dinde à la Sauce Blanche aux Huîtres).

Truss an eight pound turkey to serve for an entrée (No. 178), put it into a saucepan, moisten to cover and two inches higher with stock (No. 194a) and let boil; skim, season with salt, whole peppers, and a bunch of parsley garnished with bay leaf; boil this slowly for one hour or more until thoroughly cooked; when done, drain, untruss, and dress it either whole on an oval rice border, or cut up and placed inside a rice border. Serve the turkey with a white sauce (No. 562), or the same sauce containing small lightly blanched and well drained oysters and raw fine herbs. A part of the sauce should be poured over the turkey, and the remainder served in a sauce-boat.

(2033). TURKEY GIBLETS À LA SALAMANDER (Abatis de Dinde à la Salamandre).

Bone the cleaned pinions and cut them into half inch squares; divide the neck at every joint and put all the pieces into a saucepan with clarified butter (No. 16); fry and besprinkle with flour, and cook again for a few moments; moisten with stock (No. 194a) and season with salt, pepper, a garnished bunch of parsley (No. 123), and some small onions. When the meats are done add the liver after frying it in butter, also some minced mushrooms; suppress the parsley and onions, thicken the sauce with a few egg-yolks, cream and butter, then put back the onions. Butter a baking dish, bestrew over with bread-crumbs and fill it with the stewed giblets; dredge bread-raspings and grated parmesan on top, pour over butter and brown under a salamander (Fig. 123), then serve.

(2034). TURKEY GIBLETS, PEASANT STYLE (Abatis de Dinde à la Paysanne).

These are composed of the pinions, liver, neck, legs, heart, gizzard and head. Prepare a gar-nishing of turnips, carrots and onions; cut the turnips into clove of garlic shapes; the carrots are to be cut with a root spoon into three-quarter inch balls, and the small onions pared to the same size as the carrots, the three to be blanched separately for a few moments in salted water; drain the turnips and brown them in the pan over a good fire with butter, salt and a pinch of sugar; drain the carrots, cook them again in stock (No. 194a) and let fall to a glaze as well as the onions. Take the giblets from two fresh turkeys, put the livers aside and clean the remaining parts; scald them sim-ply to stiffen, pare and wipe on a cloth. Cut in three eighths of an inch squares six ounces of bacon without the rind, fry colorless in butter and when melted remove the bacon, leaving the fat in the saucepan, then put in the giblets and fry over a good fire while stirring with a spoon; season, and after the meats are nicely browned, besprinkle with a heaping spoonful of flour and let cook for a few moments, continuing to stir. Remove the saucepan from the fire and moisten the meats with a little stock (No. 194a) and a little white wine; stir the sauce until it comes to a boil and cover the saucepan; cook the stew over a good fire for six minutes adding a garnished bunch of parsley (No. 123) and an onion. Pare the pieces, strain the sauce and return them to the saucepan with the sauce poured over; let cook for one hour then put in the carrots, turnips, onions and bacon. Finish cooking the whole together, and a quarter of an hour before taking from the fire put in the turkey livers without the gall, and finally skim the fat from the sauce; strain it into a saucepan, let reduce, season to taste and dress the pieces of giblet in a deep dish; surround with the turnips, carrots, onions and bacon, pour the sauce over and serve.

(2035). TURKEY—GRENADES—À LA JULES VERNE (Grenades de Dinde à la Jules Verne).

Raise and pare the fillets from one or two turkeys weighing eight pounds each; shape them into half hearts rounded on one side and pointed on the other; remove the skin and lard the tops with small lardons of larding pork (No. 3, Fig. 52), and then braise in mirepoix stock (No. 419) being careful to baste occasionally and to glaze toward the end so that they assume a fine color. Dress them on a rice socle placed in the center of a dish, pour over the strained and reduced stock, lay on top croustades made of thin foundation paste (No. 135), having them one inch and three quarters in diameter and filled with a fresh mushroom salpicon cut in quarter inch squares and fried in butter; then moisten with a little Madeira and let fall to a glaze; garnish around with half-spherical quenelles the same circumference as the croustade, having it decorated with truffles. Serve in a sauce-boat a velouté sauce (No. 415) reduced with cream and butter just at the last moment.

(2036). TURKEY LEGS WITH NOODLES, MILANESE (Cuisses de Dinde aux Nouilles à la Milanaise).

Bone the legs of a young turkey, leaving half of the drumstick bone to use for a handle; fill up the boned parts with chicken forcemeat (No. 62) into which mingle finely chopped truffles and mushrooms; sew up to inclose well the dressing. Line a sautoir with bards of fat pork and lay the stuffed legs on top; moisten with white wine mirepoix stock (No. 419), and braise slowly, basting and glazing until a fine color is obtained. Dress the legs on a garnishing prepared with noodles (No. 142) velouté sauce (No. 415), tomatoes, parmesan cheese and strips of red beef tongue and mushrooms added. A half-glaze sauce (No. 413) with tomato essence accompanies this dish, but it is served separately.

(2037). TURKEY—BREASTS OR FILLETS—À LA DONOVAN (Ailes ou Filets de Dinde à la Donovan).

Raise the fillets or breasts from two turkeys, retaining the upper skin; fry them in butter and moisten with a little mirepoix stock (No. 419), then allow it to fall to a glaze; moisten once more and cook very slowly, barely moistened, so that when done the liquid is reduced to a mere glaze. Range the fillets in the center of a dish on a rice socle and garnish around with clusters of quenelles molded with a coffeespoon (No. 155), mushroom heads and small croustades filled with Montglas (No. 747). A half-glaze sauce (No. 413) with Madeira sauce to be served separately.

(2038). TURKEY WINGS FRICASSED AND BAKED (Fricassée d'Ailerons de Dinde au Gratin).

Select a dozen and a half large young turkey wings; singe, bone as far as the first joint and remove the second joint; stuff them with quenelle forcemeat (No. 89) with fine cooked herbs (No. 385) and sew them up. Line a flat buttered saucepan with onions and carrots, slices of fat pork and a garnished bunch of parsley (No. 123), range the wings on top larded across with two rows of larding pork (No. 4, Fig. 52) or else leave them unlarded, and then moisten with stock (No. 194a), seasoning with salt and whole peppers, cover over with buttered paper and let boil. Push the saucepan into a slack oven and three-quarters of an hour after add six small onions for each wing, previously blanched in boiling water. When the whole is cooked take out both the onions and wings, strain the stock through a sieve, add to it some velouté sauce (No. 415), and reduce together; thicken the sauce with raw egg-yolks and fresh butter, pass it through a tammy, season to taste. Put a part of this sauce into a deep china dish capable of being placed in the oven, lay the wings and onions on top, and pour over the remainder of the sauce; bestrew with bread-crumbs and parmesan and let acquire a good color while in the oven; drain and serve the dish on another covered with a folded napkin.

(2039). TURKEY WINGS WITH CELERY AND CHESTNUTS (Ailerons de Dinde au Céleri et aux Marrons).

Take twelve scalded and very white wings without any pin feathers whatever, singe and bone all the fleshy first part, then soak them. Line a saucepan with slices of fat pork, lay on the wings and moisten with mirepoix stock (No. 419) placing more fat pork on top. For young turkey wings it will take three-quarters of an hour, but when the birds begin to get harder the wings require one hour or more cooking. Just when ready to serve, drain well and range them in a dish, strain, skim and reduce the stock, clarify, strain once more through a napkin. Have some chestnuts braised with celery prepared as follows: Put some skinned chestnuts into a saucepan with as much celery stalks cut in inch and a quarter squares, having it already well blanched; moisten with stock (No. 194a) and cook on a slow fire until both chestnuts and celery can crush easily under a pressure. Reduce in a sautior a little espagnole sauce (No. 414) with the stock and pour it over the chestnuts, then finish cooking slowly, season to taste, and pour over the wings when ready.

(2040.) TURKEY WINGS WITH RISOT—STUFFED (Ailerons de Dinde Farcis au Risot).

Choose two dozen large turkey wings; singe and bone as far as the second joint, leaving on the tip; fill up the empty space with quenelle forcemeat (No. 89) with fine herbs and sew up the opening with thread; scald them in boiling water to stiffen the skin and refresh to pare; range them in a sautoir lined with fragments of salt pork, onions and roots, salt over and moisten to half their height with stock (No. 194a); let fall to a glaze and remoisten to their height with more broth and a little white wine, cover with fat pork and finish to cook very slowly. Apart from this prepare a good risot with half a pound of rice and some stock (No. 194a); when done remove and finish with butter, parmesan cheese and two spoonfuls of tomato sauce (No. 549). Drain the wings, untruss and cut off the tips; dress the risot in a vegetable dish and the wings on top, pour some of their own stock over after skimming and reducing it well and serve remainder in a sauce-boat.

(2041). TURKEY GOBBLER STUFFED WITH CHESTNUTS (Dindon Farci aux Marrons).

The gobbler turkey is a large-sized bird having a medium convex shaped beak and is specially known by the erectile mammilated carnucle or fleshy membrane covering its head and extending over a part of the beak and neck. The turkey's tail is provided with fourteen distinct feathers that can be raised in such a manner as to form a semi-wheel. Its plumage is of a fine black or greenish color mingled with gray and white; they usually weigh from six to eighteen pounds. Draw, singe, pare, truss and remove the breastbone from a young gobbler turkey, the same as for roasting. Chop up ten ounces of kernel of veal and sixteen ounces of pig's leaf lard, both to be chopped separately then mixed together; season with salt and spice, adding a little shallot and the liver both well chopped. Put this into a mortar with a gill of stock (No. 194a), pound well, remove and place in a sautoir to cook for fifteen minutes, let cool and stir in sixty cooked chestnuts; stuff the turkey with this roast, dress and pour over a little good gravy (No. 404).

(2042). SPRING OR YOUNG TURKEY, PURÉE OF ARTICHOKES—LARDED AND ROASTED (Dindonneau Piqué et Rôti à la Purée d'Artichauts).

A spring turkey by its delicate flesh is considered one of the most desirable meats, especially if stuffed with peeled Perigord truffles. The spit (Fig. 118) is the only manner worthy of cooking this bird; it is at its best when two or three months old. Dress two young turkeys, each one to weigh about six pounds; truss for roasting (No. 179) and singe them and lard the breasts with two rows of larding pork on each fillet and two rows on each leg (No. 3, Fig. 52). Three-quarters of an hour to one hour before serving roast them either on the spit or in the oven, basting frequently with butter; when done and of a fine color, salt them over and remove on a dish to untruss and carve, first detaching the two legs and fillet pieces; cut each of these in pieces, then glaze and dress. Serve with a separate sauce-boat of good gravy and a vegetable dish of purée of artichokes (No. 704).

(2043). SPRING TURKEY WITH TURNIPS—WINGS (Filets ou Ailes de Dindonneau aux Navets).

Procure a spring turkey of about eight pounds; draw, singe and clean it well, suppressing all its pin feathers, remove the breasts with the skin and pinion bone attached; fry in butter some carrots, onions, lean salt pork, thyme and bay leaf, then moisten with stock (No. 194a). Line a flat saucepan or sautoir with bards of fat pork, strain the above stock and pour in a third part of it, add the fillets, and let the liquid reduce to a glaze, then add another third part and set the pan in the oven to cook while basting plentifully and adding more stock as fast as it reduces, finally glazing to a beautiful color. Aside from this blanch and cook some turnips in stock and sugar having just sufficient moisture that when done they have fallen to a glaze; they should first be cut into cork-shaped pieces with square angles. After they are finished cooking, put in a little meat glaze (No. 402) and fresh butter; strain the stock, remove its fat and reduce it with as much velouté sauce (No. 415), thickening just when ready with raw egg-yolks diluted in stock, and finishing by stirring in a piece of fresh butter. Lay the breasts in the center of a dish, with the turnips around and cover the whole with the sauce.

(2044). SPRING TURKEY WITH WATER-CRESS—ROASTED OR BROILED (Dindonneau Rôti ou Grillé au Cresson).

Draw a young spring turkey, singe and truss, bard it with thin slices of fat pork and let roast for half to three-quarters of an hour at a moderate, but well regulated fire, basting it over frequently with butter, at the last moment salt it over, remove, untruss and lay it on an oval dish pouring over a little of the dripping-pan fat well skimmed and strained through a sieve. Surround it with water-cress seasoned with salt and vinegar.

Broiled Spring Turkey.—Should it be a small young one, then prepare it the same as a chicken, the time of cooking depending upon its size; when done and of a fine color, dress on a hot dish and pour over some lightly melted maître d'hôtel butter (No. 581).

(2045). PAUPIETTES OF YOUNG TURKEY, SOUVENIR (Paupiettes de Dindonneau au Souvenir).

Remove the nerves from the minion fillets, beat them lightly and cut into oblongs, season and spread over the surface a layer of well seasoned quenelle forcemeat (No. 89) into which has been mixed some chopped truffles, roll them cork-shaped and place in buttered tin paupiette rings ranged on a buttered baking sheet having the bottoms of the rings covered with croûtons of bread fried on one side only and of the same dimensions as the rings, the unfried side resting on the buttered sheet; on top of each place a channeled mushroom head (No. 118) and cover this with a bard of fat pork, then cook in a slack oven. Have braised as many turkey legs as there are paupiettes and when done to perfection, drain and cut them

FIG. 388.

into small pieces; enclose each one of these in some quenelle forcemeat with cooked fine herbs (No. 385); bread-crumb, dip in eggs and fry to a fine color, then glaze. Dress the paupiettes in a circle, fill the center with the fried legs and serve with a separate cream soubise sauce (No. 543).

GAME (Gibier).

(2046). BEAR STEAKS BROILED (Tranches d'Ours Grillées).

Bear's meat when young can be broiled and after it is cooked, has much the same flavor as beef. Cut some slices from off the thigh, season with salt and coat over with oil, then broil; when done dress on a sharp sauce (No. 538) with grated horseradish added.

(2047). BLACKBIRDS À LA DEGRANGE (Merles à la Degrange).

Procure eight blackbirds, draw and singe, suppress the feet and necks. Fry in butter some carrots, onions, ham and fat pork cut in three-sixteenth inch squares, also parsley, thyme, bay leaf and six chicken livers; when well cooked, lay aside to cool, then pound into a pulp with a little bread-crumb and seasoning; press this through a sieve and use this forcemeat for filling the blackbirds; fry them in butter, drain it off and replace it by a little glaze (No. 402), lemon juice, chopped truffles, parsley and a little half-glaze sauce (No. 413). Dress the birds inside a rice border finished with butter and parmesan cheese, and pour the sauce over the birds.

(2048). BOAR (WILD PIG) TENDERLOINS ROASTED, HAUNCH, ROBERT SAUCE, CUTLETS SAUTÉD (Sanglier (Cochon Sauvage) Cuissot Sauce Robert, Filets Rôtis Côtelettes Sautées).

Only young ones can be used. They can be roasted without marinating, and as the meats are covered with fat it is useless to lard them. Roasted pieces are served from the haunch, saddle, tenderloin or loin, basted with its own gravy or else a very highly seasoned sauce.

For the Haunch.—After the boar is singed and well trimmed, scald it in boiling water, then saw off the end or handle bone an inch and a half from the knuckle bone and marinate in a cooked cold marinade (No. 114) or eight days; drain, wipe and wrap it in strong sheets of buttered paper, including the vegetables and marinade; lay it on a cradle spit (No. 116) or in the oven to roast for one hour and a half, more or less according to the size of the haunch or leg, being careful to baste every twenty minutes with the grease from the dripping pan. Ten minutes before serving unwrap and remove the buttered paper, also the cracknel; glaze the haunch in the oven and place it on a dish to trim with a fancy frill (No. 10), pour gravy (No. 404) around and serve a Robert sauce (No. 533) in a sauce-boat.

Boar's Tenderloins are prepared by paring, larding, marinating and roasting, then dressing on croûtons and serving with shallot and fine herb sauce (No. 537).

The Cutlets are pared and sautéd drained and trimmed with frills (No. 10), afterward dressed in a circle; drain the fat from the pan, detach the glaze with white wine and espagnole sauce (No. 414), reduce; then strain it through a tammy and pour it in the middle of the cutlets.

(2049). YOUNG WILD BOAR—QUARTER—GARNISHED WITH CUTLETS AND BREASTS MARINADE SAUCE (Quartier de Marcassin Garni de Côtelettes et de Poitrines, Sauce Marinade).

Have a quarter of young wild boar very tender; suppress the rind and marinate in a cooked cold marinade (No. 114) for twenty-four hours; drain and wrap in several sheets of strong buttered paper. Put it in a roasting pan and cook it in the oven. Have the breasts braised, and when done bone and lay them under a light weight to get cold, then cut them into eight pieces paring each one to the shape of a half heart, then dip in eggs and bread-crumbs, and fry till hot and of a fine golden color. Trim eight cutlets, marinate them for twenty-four hours, drain, wipe and sauté with clarified butter. Dress the breasts on one side of the quarter and the cutlets on the other, glaze them with meat glaze (No. 402) and cover the quarter with a little marinade sauce (No. 496), serve more of it separately with the boar, trimming the handle of the leg with a paper frill (No. 10).

(2050). BOAR SADDLE AND QUARTER—ROASTED (Selles et Quartiers de Sanglier Rôtis).

Before roasting a saddle or quarter of boar is better to be sure that the animal is a very young one. The saddle tenderloin must not be pared as for venison, neither are the quarters pared; simply steep the pieces of meat for twenty-four hours in a cooked and cold marinade (No. 114). They are to be roasted in a very deep pan lined with fragments of salt pork and cut up roots, then basted over with butter. For a young boar it will take from an hour and a quarter to an hour and a half in a moderate oven. After removing it from the fire, dress it on a dish and unglaze the bottom of the pan with a few spoonfuls of the marinade; reduce the liquid for a few moments, then strain, skim off the fat and thicken the sauce either with some sauce or kneaded butter (No. 579); serve it in a sauce-boat. With roast boar a light acidulated sauce is usually served, prepared with a little of its marinade; a saucerful of currant jelly is also its usual accompaniment.

(2051). DOE BIRDS ROASTED AND BROILED (Courlis Rôtis et Grillés).

Small doe birds are the size of a large plover, having a long bent beak. It is a delicate game being slightly analagous to the plover; let set till tender then pick, singe and suppress the gizzard and crop without emptying out the insides. Truss them bent under like the plovers (No. 2119) bard over with very thin slices of fat pork and cook either on the spit or in the oven, or else broil; serve on canapés with clear gravy (No. 404) separate. Doe birds can be prepared in several ways, proceeding exactly the same as for the plovers.

(2052) BLACKHEAD DUCKS ROASTED OR BROILED (Canards Sauvages à Tête Noire Rôtis ou Grillés).

Pick the feathers from two blackhead ducks, and truss as described (No. 179); fasten them on the spit then cook the ducks, if fine and large for fourteen or eighteen minutes before a bright fire. Untruss and serve them to the guests after cutting them up on very hot plates; serve currant jelly at the same time. For broiled blackheads see broiled canvasback ducks (No. 2054).

(2053). BRANT DUCKS WITH CAULIFLOWER VILLEROI—ROASTED (Canards Sauvages Brant Rôtis aux Chouxfleurs Villeroi).

Brant ducks are prepared the same as blackhead ducks and when roasted, dress them on a long dish; garnish around with cauliflowers à la Villeroi (No. 2716), serving a separate poivrade sauce (No. 522) into which incorporate half as much fresh butter.

(2054). CANVASBACK DUCKS BROILED (Canards Sauvages Canvasback Grillés).

Clean nicely and split through the whole length of the back, open entirely to have them perfectly flat, wipe, trim and season with salt and pepper; coat over with oil and put them inside a double boiler sufficiently thick not to have them squeezed too tight; broil over a brisk fire for eight or ten minutes and as soon as done, dress on a buttered half-glaze sauce (No. 413) into which has been added butter, lemon juice and chopped parsley.

(2055). CANVASBACK DUCKS ROASTED GARNISHED WITH HOMINY OR SAMP (Canards Sauvages Canvas Back Rôtis Garnis Avec Hominy ou Samp).

Pick the feathers from some nice Havre-de-Grace canvasback ducks, each one to weigh three pounds, prepare them for roasting as described (No. 179), lay them on a spit to roast before a

Fig. 389.

brisk fire for sixteen to twenty minutes, more or less according to their size; untruss and dress on to a very hot dish, surround with squares of hominy dipped in eggs and bread-crumbs, then fried, present them whole to the guests, remove to carve and place on very hot plates with a piece of hominy for each person.

Fig. 390.

Woodcock—(Bécasse).

Fig. 391.

Quail—(Caille).

Fig. 392.

Plover—(Pluvier).

Fig. 393.

English Snipe—(Bécassine Anglaise).

Fig. 394.

Prairie Hen (Grouse)—(Tétras).

Fig. 395.

Ptarmigan—(Poule de Neige).

Hominy and Samp (*Crushed Corn*).—Cook some hominy in boiling salted water, spread it on a baking sheet in a five-eighths of an inch thick layer and when cold cut it into oblongs one inch wide by two and a half inches long, dip them in eggs and bread-crumbs and fry to a fine color, then drain, salt and dress on folded napkins. Samp is a species of Indian corn crushed to the size of small peas; it should be soaked in cold water for several hours, then cooked in a covered saucepan with water, salt and butter for three hours, placed in a slack oven after it has boiled up once. Put it to cool on a dish, divide it into inch and three-quarters balls, flatten, keeping them thin on the edges and thick in the center, dip in eggs and bread-crumbs and fry nicely to a fine color

(2056). SALMIS OF CANVASBACK DUCKS (Salmis de Canards Sauvages, Canvasback).

Cook either on the spit or in the oven two ducks prepared for roasting (No. 179); when nearly done, untruss and divide each one into six pieces, cutting the breast in four and legs in two. (The legs are generally fibrous and tough.) Put all the pieces in a saucepan with their own blood and keep them warm in a bain-marie, having a lid on top. Put the fragments of the ducks, broken in pieces into another saucepan with a pint of red Bordeaux wine, half a shallot and a pinch of mignonette, let boil slowly until the liquid is reduced to half, then pass it through a colander into a sautéing dish, adding the same quantity of thick espagnole sauce (No. 414); reduce the whole until consistent, pass it once more through a tammy and finish by incorporating therein a tablespoonful of sweet oil and the strained juice of half a lemon. Pour this sauce over the cut up ducks and dress on the center of a dish, garnish around with half heart croûtons hollowed out in the center and filled with minced celery parboiled and cooked in consommé (No. 189), cover with half-glaze and Madeira sauce (No. 413).

(2057). CANVASBACK DUCKS, BIGARADE SAUCE—BREASTS (Filets de Canard Sauvages, Canvasback, Sauce Bigarade).

Prepare and cook the canvasback ducks the same as roasted (No. 2055); when still very rare, remove and raise the two fillets and divide each one into three pieces. Put them in a chafing dish with a little melted game glaze (No. 398), as much butter and the juice of half a lemon, roll them well in this to glaze and dress on a bigarade sauce (No. 435).

(2058). CANVASBACK DUCKS WITH ORANGE JUICE, PORT WINE AND CURRANT SAUCE —BREASTS (Filets de Canards Sauvages, Canvasback, au Jus d'Orange à la Sauce Porto et à la Gelée de Groseilles).

Roast the ducks the same as for roasting (No. 2055) keeping them very rare; raise the two fillets, one from each side of the breast and cut each one into two lengthwise pieces; put them in a chafing dish, pour over some bitter orange juice, also a little game glaze (No. 398) and brown poivrade sauce (No. 522); serve separately a sauce made with currant jelly dissolved in port wine, heating it in a bain-marie, then strained through a fine wire sieve, surround with half-heart-shaped croûtons of bread fried in butter.

(2059). MALLARD DUCKS ROASTED AND BROILED—(Canards Sauvages, Mallard Rôtis et Grillés).

Draw two singed and clean Mallard ducks, wipe out the insides with a cloth and fill the empty space with some bread dressing combined with butter or chopped suet, thyme, bay leaf, parsley, and a few finely sliced green celery leaves, adding egg-yolks; truss (No. 179), and run a skewer through to fasten them on the spit, then roast basting over with melted butter or oil. The fire should be quite brisk, and if so, twenty minutes will be sufficient to cook them. Dish them up with sliced lemons around, and serve the gravy separately.

Broiled.—Mallard ducks are broiled and dressed the same as canvasback, the only difference to be observed is perhaps a modification in the time of cooking.

(2060). MALLARD DUCKS WITH CELERY HALF-GLAZE—ROASTED (Canards Sauvages, Mallard Rôtis au Céleri Demi-Glace).

Truss some mallard ducks for roasting (No. 179), and when cooked dish up as the others. They may be served either whole or else cut up into six pieces or the fillets only if they be whole; place the garnishing around; should they be dressed in a circle then fill in the center with a garnishing composed of cardoons or celery cut in half inch squares, blanched and cooked with chopped beef marrow also blanched, and afterward drained; put them into a little half-glaze sauce (No. 413), and let simmer for a few moments.

(2061). SALMIS OF MALLARD DUCKS WITH MADEIRA (Salmis de Canards Sauvages, Mallard au Madère).

Cut two roasted wild ducks into six pieces; remove the skin and part of the bones, then divide the breasts and legs, suppressing the feet, and range them in a sautoir keeping it covered. Chop up the carcass, bones, and parings; fry a mirepoix (No. 419), and minced shallots with aromatic herbs, add to this the chopped carcasses and moisten with two or three gills of red wine previously boiled in a copper pan, and reduce it to three-quarters; again moisten to their height with stock (No. 194a) and continue to cook for twenty minutes; strain this through a tammy, remove the fat and return it to the fire and reduce, thickening with half-glaze sauce (No. 413), and finishing with two spoonfuls of Madeira wine. As soon as it is completed, strain it over the pieces of duck, and heat in a bain-marie for a quarter of an hour. Dress the pieces on a dish, cover over with a part of the sauce and serve the remainder separately; surround with thin round crusts masked on one side with baked liver forcemeat (No. 81), and serve.

(2062). REDHEAD DUCKS À LA BARÉDA (Canards Sauvages à Tête Rouge à la Baréda).

These ducks are first to be prepared the same as for roasting; put them in a pan, cover with good fat and roast them in the oven; add one gill of vinegar, a spoonful of powdered sugar, and mignonette pepper; baste the birds several times while cooking and salt over a few moments

Fig. 396.

before removing from the oven. Untruss and strain the stock, suppress all the fat, and place it in a sauce-pan with some espagnole sauce (No. 414) currant jelly, mixing the whole well together, pass through a sieve. Make a sour apple marmalade, drain properly and press it through a very fine sieve, stir in some unsweetened whipped cream; serve these two sauces separately at the same time as the birds.

(2063). REDHEAD DUCKS, ROASTED AND BROILED (Canards Sauvages à Tête Rouge Rôtis ou Grillés).

Prepare the ducks as for No. 2059, lay them on the spit to roast for fourteen to eighteen minutes, more or less according to their weight; salt over, remove from the spit and untruss and serve on a very hot dish, or they can be roasted in the oven, putting them into a baking pan; pour a little fat over and set them in a hot oven; they will take a few minutes longer to cook this way, then serve on a very hot dish. Hand round separately on a folded napkin some hominy or samp the same as for canvasback ducks (No. 2055). Cut up the ducks and serve on very hot plates. Four slices can be taken from each duck, two on each fillet and one or two of these served to one guest.

Broiled.—Have them prepared the same as the canvasback duck (No. 2054), then cook and dress exactly the same.

(2064). REDHEAD DUCKS WITH FRIED CELERY(Canards Sauvages à Tête Rouge au Céleri Frit).

Prepare and cook two redhead ducks the same as for roasting (No. 2063); dress and garnish around with celery prepared in two different ways. From four celery stalks, remove the outer branches, using only the white and tender ones; cut into four inch lengths half of the largest branches and blanch them as well as the four roots, peeled and cut in eight pieces then nicely pared; drain and put into a saucepan and cover to their height with a light ten degree syrup; cook on a slow fire, drain through a strainer and dip each separate piece into frying batter (No. 137) and fry to a fine golden color, ranging them afterward on each side of the ducks. Cut the remainder or tender stalks lengthwise into fillets the size of a straw, dip them in frying batter, then fry slowly to a fine color; drain, salt over and use them for decorating the ends of the dish. Serve separately a brown sauce (No. 414) reduced with white wine pressing into it the strained juice of an orange.

(2065). RUDDY DUCKS À LA HAMILTON (Canards Sauvages, Ruddy à la Hamilton).

Prepare and cook the ducks the same as for roasted (No. 2066); detach the fillets without taking off the skin and range them at once in a sautoir, pour over some reduced espagnole sauce (No. 414) and a little good sherry; roll them in this off the fire and strain the juice of a lemon over. Dress the fillets in a circle on a poached and unmolded forcemeat border placed on a dish, and fill the insides with a garnishing of truffles, mushrooms, olives and cut up foies-gras; cover both fillets and garnishing lightly with the sauce and serve more of it separately after straining it.

(2066). RUDDY DUCKS, ROASTED (Canards Sauvages, Ruddy Rôtis).

This duck is roasted either on the spit or in the oven. Pick and take off all the down; singe, wipe and draw, then cut off the wings near the body, suppress the necks, turn in the feet and truss, the same as canvasback (No. 179). Put them to roast on the spit or in the oven for twelve to fifteen minutes according to the heat of the fire and the size of the duck, keeping them rare; take them off and serve with a little clear gravy (No. 404) poured over and garnish with quartered lemons; serve.

(2067). TEAL DUCKS, BROILED (Canards Sauvages, Sarcelles Grillées).

Split the teal duck, lengthwise in two through the back after cleaning well; pare and season with salt and mignonette; coat over with oil and place in a double broiler without pressing too tight. Broil over a brisk fire and serve on a good, rich gravy (No. 404) surrounded by slices of lemon.

(2068). TEAL DUCKS, ROASTED (Canards Sauvages, Sarcelles Rôtis).

This is a small kind of wild duck, the meat being quite nutritious and of an excellent flavor the blue wings are preferred to the green. Prepare the teal (No. 179), roast before a brisk fire for ten

Fig. 397.

to fifteen, minutes either on the spit or allow the same time in the oven. When done to perfection salt over, untruss and serve on a hot dish either whole or carved, each one to be divided in four pieces. Dress the legs on the bottom of the dish with the breasts over, glaze, then pour into the bottom a little good gravy (No. 404); surround the birds with slices of lemon cut in two through the center.

(2069). TEAL DUCKS À LA PONTCHARTRAIN, BREASTS (Filets de Canards Sauvages, Sarcelles à la Pontchartrain).

Lift the breasts from four very plump raw teal ducks; keep on the skin and score this lightly; marinate these in oil with cut up chives, parsley leaves, salt, mignonette and lemon juice; let them remain in this for two hours and just when ready to serve, pour two tablespoonfuls of oil in a sautoir, heat it up and put in the breasts; place it on a good fire, turning the pieces over when done on one side; drain and dress in a circle with half heart-shaped croutons between each piece, having them the same size as the breasts; cover the whole with a well-reduced buttered espagnole sauce, (No. 414) straining into it the juice of an orange. They can also be broiled, after scoring, seasoning and coating over with oil, then put into a double broiler without pressing and when cooked dress in a circle with croûtons between each fillet and the same sauce as above poured over the whole.

(2070). SALMIS OF TEAL DUCKS À LA HARRISON (Salmis de Canards Sauvages, Sarcelles à la Harrison).

Roast some teal ducks as for No. 2068. Fry a shallot lightly in butter without acquiring color; add some raw chopped mushrooms, salt, pepper and nutmeg, then moisten with champagne and reduce with the following fumet and espagnole sauce (No. 414) to a proper consistency. Break up the carcasses of the birds, moisten these with broth (No. 194a) and cook for fifteen minutes, then strain forcibly; add to it some cooked ham cut in one-eighth of an inch squares and chopped parsley. The ducks must be cut in four pieces each, namely: two legs, two wings, each of these to be cut lengthwise: dress, mix the gravy and sauce together, pour it over and surround with heart-shaped croûtons, then serve.

(2071). GROUSE, PRAIRIE HENS OR PTARMIGAN, BROILED (Tétras, Poules de Prairie ou de Neige Grillés).

There are two ways of preparing these birds for broiling; the first, or the one most generally employed is to cut off the feet at the first joint, also the neck, leaving the throat skin on as long as possible: split the grouse lengthwise through the back to open it entirely; remove the breastbones, flatten lightly and season with salt; dip them in oil and broil over a moderate fire, then dress on toast with clear gravy (No. 404).

Another Way is after the grouse is picked, drawn and singed, truss with the legs thrust inside, and cut them lengthwise in two, beat lightly, pare neatly, season and dip in melted butter, then in bread-crumbs and broil in a double broiler on a moderate fire, turning them when well done on one side; dressed grouse can be cooked in either of these ways, being careful not to have the broiler too tight, and when dressed they may be covered with maître d'hôtel butter (No. 581) or else have a cold tartar sauce (No. 631) served separately.

(2072). GROUSE OR PRAIRIE HENS ROASTED WITH GRAVY, FRIED BREAD-CRUMBS OR APPLE SAUCE (Tétras ou Poules de Prairie Rôtis au Jus, Mie de Pain Frite ou Sauce aux Pommes).

Select some grouse and after picking, singeing and drawing, truss them without barding for roasting (No. 179), run a skewer through and fasten this firmly to the spit, then roast before a good fire or they may be put in a baking pan, smeared over with fat and roasted in the oven, but in either case they need basting frequently with melted butter. When almost done, salt them over and as soon as they are finished (which will take from twenty to twenty-five minutes), like all black meats these should be cooked rare, untruss and dress on a croûton of bread cut so that they stand plumb on it, and serve some clear gravy (No. 404) separately or replace it by apple sauce (No. 428), served the same, or a bread sauce (No. 438), may be substituted or surround with fried bread-crumbs prepared as follows: Brown some slices of bread in the oven and when of a good color and very dry, pound and pass through a fine wire sieve, mix these crumbs with a little butter, put it into a sautoir and set in the oven to fry until of a nice color.

(2073). GROUSE OR PRAIRIE HENS À LA TZARINA—BREASTS (Filets de Tétras ou de Gelinottes à la Tzarine).

Remove the breasts from six fresh grouse or prairie hens, suppress the minion fillets and pare the larger ones prettily the same as chicken fillets, taking off all the skin; beat down to flatten and season with salt, lay them in a sautoir with cold clarified butter and cover with a buttered paper. With the minion fillets, and the breast parings, prepare game cream forcemeat (No. 75), have it nice and smooth and keep it cold. Butter a plain border mold (Fig. 139), decorate the sides with fanciful bits of truffle and lay it aside on ice. Prepare a garnishing composed only of fine and very white cocks'-combs, not having them too much cooked and place them in a bain-marie. With the carcasses of the breasts without the legs prepare a good fumet, and strain it. Put on to reduce a few gills of good béchamel (No. 409) with a small bunch of green fennel, mushroom peelings and a spoonful of prepared red pepper (No. 168) and incorporate the fumet slowly into this; when this sauce becomes rich, but not too thick, strain and keep it in a bain-marie stirring it up occasionally. Fill the decorated mold with the cream forcemeat pressing it in carefully, cover it over with a buttered paper and poach it for fifteen to twenty minutes in a bain-marie. At the last moment poach the fillets

FIG. 398.

over a brisk fire, turning them around and keeping them rare; two minutes will suffice for their cooking drain them off at once to pare and pour into this same sautoir one gill and a half of good game stock (No. 195), reduce the liquid to half with the butter and incorporate this slowly into the sauce. On the rounded end of each of the fillets lay an oval piece of cooked truffle covered with a thin layer of raw forcemeat to help fasten it on. Unmold the border on a dish, fill the interior with the well-drained combs and dress the fillets in a circle on the border. Cover them as well as the combs with a part of the sauce and serve the rest apart.

(2074). HARE À LA CHÂTELAINE—STUFFED (Lièvre Farci à la Châtelaine).

Skin and draw a good hare, not having it too young, lard it with shreds of larding pork (No. 3, Fig. 52), make a hash with its minion fillets, the heart, liver and a few good cooked chicken livers, put this into a vessel and mix in an equal quantity of chopped fat pork, bread-crumb raspings, chopped onions, one egg, salt and thyme. With this dressing fill the hare's stomach, sew up the opening, truss the shoulders, head and legs, then put it into a long braziere, having the bottom covered with fragments of fat pork, minced onions and roots, aromatic herbs and mushroom peelings, add two or three gills of white wine and cover with buttered paper; cover the pan and allow the hare to cook very slowly for two or three hours with fire over, and under or in the oven, adding a little broth or gravy from time to time. When the hare is three-quarters done, lift it out, strain the stock, skim it free of fat and thicken with a little brown sauce (No. 414), then boil again for five minutes. Pour this into the braziere, replace the hare and add two or three dozen fresh peeled mushrooms, then finish cooking all together. Dish up the hare, untruss and surround it with the garnishing and a part of the sauce, serving the remainder separately.

(2075). JUGGED HARE (Civet de Lièvre).

To prepare this dish the hare should not be too tender; those are only desirable when eaten roasted. Skin the hare, draw it well reserving the blood in a small bowl with a dash of vinegar added. Separate the four limbs from the back, cut them up into medium-sized pieces and split the head in two, then cut the back across. Lay these parts in a vessel to season and marinate with a few spoonfuls of brandy, aromatic herbs and sprigs of parsley; leave them in this for five to six hours. Melt in a saucepan half a pound of chopped fat pork, add to it half a pound of bacon cut in flat squares, and as soon as these are browned, remove them with a skimmer, leaving the fat in the saucepan, and to it add the well drained pieces of hare. Fry over a very brisk fire stirring at times, and when the meats are well browned, besprinkle with two spoonfuls of flour; cook this while turning for a few minutes, then moisten the stew to its height, with a third part of good red wine previously boiled in an untinned copper vessel, and two-thirds of broth (No.194a), adding both very slowly. Stir the liquid until it boils and let it continue thus for ten minutes; withdraw the saucepan to a slower fire, put in a bunch of aromatic herbs, two or three small onions and mushroom parings. Continue the cooking until the meats are partly done, then set a large colander on top of a vessel and pour into it the stew; return the sauce to a sautoir, adding to it a few spoonfuls of red wine, boil the same as before, add a few spoonfuls of gravy (No. 404) to enrich it, reduce for a few moments, skimming off the fat and put it back into the first saucepan. Take up the pieces of hare one by one, pare them free of all superfluous bone and return them to the sauce, all except the head, and add the bacon and the marinade the hare was in. Place the saucepan on the fire to finish cooking the meats very slowly; twenty minutes before taking off the stew, mix in with it two dozen mushrooms and finish cooking all together. At the last moment thicken the gravy with the blood laid aside, being careful that once this is added not to let it boil again. Dress the meats and bacon on a dish, strain the sauce over and surround with clusters of mushrooms and the same of small onions glazed separately.

(2076). HARE'S BACK ROASTED WITH CREAM (Râble de Lièvre Rôti à la Crème).

The hares used for roasting should be chosen particularly tender. Suppress the shoulders, legs, and neck, leaving the back whole; remove the fillet skin delicately so as to be able to lard the meats with larding pork (No. 3, Fig. 52); season and lay the back in a small baking pan to mask over with

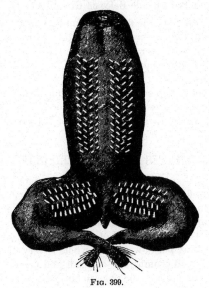

Fig. 399.

butter and roast in the oven for twenty-five to thirty minutes while basting at times. Drain off the back and dress it on a dish, pour off half the fat and put into the pan a few spoonfuls of half-glaze (No. 400); boil up for five minutes to detach the glaze from the bottom of the pan, then strain and let reduce for a few moments, adding a gill of raw cream; finish the sauce with a dash of vinegar.

(2077). YOUNG HARE À LA CASTIGLIONE—SAUTÉD (Levraut Sauté à la Castiglione).

Cut a young hare into twelve parts; two shoulder pieces, four from the legs and six from the back and ribs, put these in a sautéing pan and fry on a good fire with plenty of fresh butter; throw over some chopped parsley and mushrooms, two blanched and very finely chopped shallots, a little cooked ham either cut very small or in eighth of an inch squares, salt, pepper, and nutmeg; moisten with a pint of broth (No. 194a) adding a bunch of parsley garnished with thyme, bay leaf, a little garlic, and a clove; cook on a slow fire, then finish in a slack oven in a hermetically closed saucepan, allowing it to be in for twenty to thirty minutes; remoisten as fast as the liquid becomes reduced, adding only a very little at the time so that when done there remains very little of the stock, and that has fallen to a glaze without adhering to the pan. After the hare is done, pour in two gills of espagnole sauce (No. 414), and half a gill of Madeira at the same time, suppressing the parsley, and finish with the juice of a lemon. Garnish around with heart-shaped croûtons fried in butter.

(2078). ÉPIGRAMMES OF YOUNG HARES À LA POLIGNAC (Épigrammes de Levrauts à la Polignac).

Raise the fillets and minion fillets from two young hares; suppress the skin and nerves and cut the fillets slanting into two pieces each; beat lightly and pare them all into cutlet form; season with salt, pepper, fine spices and truffles cut in thin shreds. Mince the fragments of the meat, add a third as much pork tenderloin and chop the two well together with as much chopped fat pork as fresh pork; season with salt, pepper and nutmeg, adding some reduced espagnole sauce (No. 414). Divide this preparation into twelve parts, have as many squares of "crépine" or caul fat four inches by five spread out on a cloth, on each one lay half of its intended forcemeat, on top the pared cutlet-form fillet and then the remainder of the forcemeat; fold the "crépine" or caul fat into an oval shape, lay them on a baking sheet, baste over with butter, bestrew with bread-crumbs and cook in the oven. Dish them up in a circle intercalated with cutlets made of very delicate hare quenelle forcemeat (No. 91) made with the parings, dip in eggs, bread-crumb over and then fry in olive oil. Pour into the center of the circle a little marinade sauce (No. 496) with chopped truffles added. The quenelle forcemeat cutlets can be replaced by others made of hare croquette preparation (No. 885).

(2079). YOUNG HARES' FILLETS WITH CURRANT JELLY AND RAISIN SAUCE (Filets de Levrauts à la Sauce de Gelée de Groseilles et aux Raisins).

Pare and suppress the nerves from the fillets and minion fillets of two young hares; cut the larger ones on the bias to obtain two or three slices, flatten, pare into half hearts, season and put them in a buttered sautoir sprinkle over with butter. With the bones and fragments make a fumet (No. 397) and moisten it with skimmed broth (No. 194a), and when ready pass this through a sieve and pour it into a saucepan with a gill of vinegar, then reduce the liquid to a half-glaze, stir in some currant jelly, a piece of lemon peel and a handful of well-washed dry raisins softened in hot water. Push the fillets into a brisk oven and as soon as cooked add them to the sauce; dress, pass the sauce through a tammy and pour part of it over the meats, serving the rest in a sauce-boat.

(2080). YOUNG HARES' PAUPIETTES WITH STUFFED OLIVES (Paupiettes de Levrauts aux Olives Farcies).

Take the fillets and minion fillets from two young hares, suppress the nerves and separate them lengthwise in two; flatten all the pieces and then cut them up into twelve bands or strips an inch and a half wide by two and a half long; season with salt, pepper and nutmeg. Pass twice through the chopping machine (Fig. 47) a pound of the lean meats, cut from the legs and shoulders of the hare with as much fresh fat pork; when the whole is very fine add to it some cooked fine herbs (No. 385), two ounces of bread crumbs, one egg, salt and pepper. Spread a layer of this hash on each strip, roll them over on themselves and place in buttered paupiette rings. Make a fumet (No. 397) with the carcasses and fragments moistening it with white wine; reduce some espagnole sauce (No. 414) with this fumet, despumate it free of all fat and scum that arises to the surface. Cook the paupiettes in a sautoir lined with bards of fat pork, and moisten with white wine mirepoix stock (No. 419); when done, drain off and strain the stock, reduce it with the espagnole and fumet. Stuff some Spanish olives with anchovies, heat them in a little gravy (No. 404); dress the paupiettes in a circle, fill the center with the stuffed olives and place a channeled mushroom (No. 118) on each paupiette; cover with a part of the sauce, serving the rest in a sauce-boat.

(2081). LARKS À LA MARÉCHALE (Mauviettes à la Maréchale).

Bone and stuff about fifteen larks with a baking forcemeat (No. 81) mixed with a little raw forcemeat (No. 91) and chopped truffles. Form these into ball-shapes and wrap each one in a small piece of cloth; tie them up tight and cook in a very little clear stock (No. 194a); drain off to tighten the cloth. When cold, unwrap the birds and pare; lay each one inside of a large head of cèpes or fresh mushrooms previously scooped out with a vegetable spoon. Lay these in a sautoir, pour over some hot butter and cook for ten minutes on a bright fire while covered, then baste with a few spoonfuls of half-glaze sauce (No. 413), cook again for seven or eight minutes on a slow fire, remove them with a pallet and dress on a dish; add two spoonfuls of Madeira wine to their broth and thicken it with a little half-glaze sauce (No. 413), reduce for two minutes and then pour into the dish.

(2082). LARKS BROILED (Alouettes Grillées).

Take the larks well cleaned and picked, split them lengthways through the back, season and broil; three to five minutes suffice to cook them. Dress on canapés made of toasted oblongs of bread-crumbs, cover with game fumet (No. 397) made with quail and espagnole sauce (No. 414) that has been liberally buttered, then serve.

(2083). LARKS, PÉRIGUEUX SAUCE—ROASTED (Alouettes Rôties Sauce Périgueux).

Roast without drawing, only removing the gizzard, singe and cover with very thin bards of fat pork and run a metal skewer through four of them, keeping them slightly apart so that the heat can penetrate between each one. They only require to be cooked from five to six minutes, then dress them on croûtons of bread covered with liver forcemeat; remove the larding and pour over a Périgueux sauce with Madeira (No. 517).

(2084). LARKS WITH RICE (Mauviettes au Riz).

Singe, draw and bone about fifteen fine larks; spread them out on the table to season and lay in each one a ball of game quenelle forcemeat (No. 91) mixed with baking forcemeat (No. 81) and a part of their own intestines, cooked, pounded and rubbed through a sieve; form the birds into ball-shapes and sew them up, then lay them in a saucepan with butter or melted fat pork; season and fry quickly for seven or eight minutes while turning them over; now remove them from the pan, leaving in the fat, and into this add two spoonfuls of chopped onions; fry and mix with it three or four spoonfuls of chopped raw ham; fry together for two minutes longer, then put in three gills of good picked rice without previously washing it; heat well while stirring and moisten with a quart of good unskimmed broth (No. 194a). After this has boiled for fifteen minutes, or when the rice begins to soften add the untrussed larks, a pinch of prepared red pepper (No. 168), a garnished bunch of parsley (No. 123) and two spoonfuls of tomato purée (No. 730); cook both rice and larks moderately and finish by incorporating into it a generous piece of butter divided into small pats. Dress in a deep dish and pour over two spoonfuls of half-glaze sauce (No. 413) and tomato sauce (No. 549).

(2085). PARTRIDGES, BROILED ENGLISH STYLE (Perdreaux Grillés à l'Anglaise).

Cut two tender partridges in two after they have been drawn and singed; cut off the legs to the height of the knee to slip them under the skin; beat lightly, suppress the surplus of bone, season and bread-crumb them English style, rolling them in oil or melted butter, then in fresh bread-crumbs. Range these half partridges on a broiler, and broil for eighteen minutes over a moderate fire, turning them from one side to the other; serve with a sauce-boat of half-glaze sauce (No. 413) and sliced lemon around.

(2086). PARTRIDGES, GIRALDA—BREASTS OR FILLETS (Ailes ou Filets de Perdreaux à la Giralda).

Raise the breasts from four partridges; remove the skin and sinews and lift off the minion fillets; streak these with five slices of truffle cut the shape of a cock's-comb. Lay the large fillets in a buttered sautoir and the minion fillets formed into rings in another, filling the centers with quenelle forcemeat (No. 91) pushed through a cornet and on each one lay a small channeled mushroom (No. 118). Butter and decorate with cooked beef tongue, a plain border mold hollowed out on top (Fig. 139), fill it with partridge quenelle forcemeat (No. 91); poach in a bain-marie for half an hour first on top of the range and then in the oven. Prepare a fumet with the carcasses as in No. 397, strain and reduce with the same quantity of espagnole sauce (No. 414) and a little Madeira; skim to free it well from fat, removing all the impurities arising on the surface. Sauté the fillets, poach the minion fillets, drain off the butter from the former and replace it by a few spoonfuls of Madeira to detach the glaze. Make a partridge purée with the meats picked from the birds, some rice and béchamel; rub it through a sieve and place it in a saucepan to season with salt, prepared red pepper (No. 168) and nutmeg, adding plenty of butter. Invert the mold on the center of a dish, lift it up and place the fillets on the border with a fried croûton of bread to separate each one and pour the purée in the center; serve more of the sauce separately.

(2087). PARTRIDGES À LA JULES VERNE—BREASTS OR FILLETS (Ailes ou Filets de Perdreaux à la Jules Verne).

Fasten a wooden foundation on a dish having it slightly sloped and channeled all around, then cover it entirely with cooked paste (No. 131). On the center of this foundation attach a tin basket covered over with more of the same paste, embossed and decorated with a pretty hanging border; the empty space in the basket is filled with a croûton of fried bread covered with a layer of the same paste. The three partridge heads must retain their own feathers and should be selected as fresh as possible; to keep them in a proper position, penetrate the necks with a wire

sufficiently thick to uphold them thrusting the other end of the wire into the piece of bread prepared for this purpose in the basket; between each head is also fastened a small paper case filled
with a truffle. Raise the breasts from five or six partridges without the minion fillets; suppress the
skin, beat them to flatten and pare with the same care as is bestowed on a chicken fillet, then
season and place them at once in a sautoir with clarified butter, at the last moment poach the

FIG. 400.

breasts over a good fire turning them around, they should be kept rare, then drained, wiped free of
butter and on each wide end place a round piece of truffle cut out with a round cutter and covered on
one side with a very thin layer of raw forcemeat to make it adhere. Dress these breasts in a circle the
pointed ends downward on the paste-covered foundation cover them lightly with a little good
velouté sauce (No. 415), reduced with partridge fumet (No. 397) and serve with a sauce-boatful
of the same.

(2088). PARTRIDGES À LA LUCULLUS—BREASTS OR FILLETS (Ailes ou Filets de Perdreaux à la Lucullus).

Roast some partridges that have been wrapped up exactly as explained for à la Matignon (No.
2096); when done remove the breasts, pare and lay them in a sautoir with a little half-glaze (No.
400). Prepare a fumet (No. 397) with the parings and carcasses. Butter a plain border mold
deep on the top (Fig. 139), decorate the sides with fanciful cuts of truffles and fill it entirely with
partridge cream forcemeat (No. 75). Cut some raw artichoke bottoms into small squares, then
blanch, cut some carrots into half inch diameter balls, and blanch them likewise, some turnips
the same, blanching them as well, some small cooked mushroom heads and truffles shaped like a
clove of garlic. First put the artichokes with some butter, add the carrots and turnips, and
moisten with a little Madeira and the fumet; let cook slowly and when these three vegetables are
done, then add the mushrooms and truffles; as soon as the liquid reduces entirely pour in some
velouté sauce (No. 415) and toss the garnishings in it, adding small pieces of fresh butter; with this
fill the hollow in the center of the unmolded border; glaze the breasts or fillets, trim them with
favor frills (No. 10) and lay them on top of the garnishings; surround the border with small three-
quarters of an inch balls made of foies-gras from a terrine pressed through a sieve, bread-crumbed,
egged, then fried.

(2089). PARTRIDGES À LA VÉRON—BREASTS OR FILLETS (Ailes ou Filets de Perdreaux à la Véron).

Trim the breasts of four partridges, then range them in a sautoir with clarified butter,
and salt over. Cook the legs in a small saucepan with some stock (No. 194a), let them get quite cold
and then cut off the tenderest parts of the meats; pound these with the cooked partridge livers,
two or three spoonfuls of cooked truffles and two spoonfuls of velouté sauce (No. 415); then press
the whole through a sieve. Put this pulp into a saucepan with an equal amount of chestnut purée
(No. 712), and two spoonfuls of good melted glaze (No. 398); season and heat without ceasing to
stir and without letting it boil; finish with a piece of butter. Poach the partridge breasts, drain
off the butter and pour a little sauce over; dress them in a circle on a dish alternating each
one with a croûton of bread cut cock's-comb-shaped and browned in clarified butter; lay the purée
in the center of the circle, and cover over the fillets with a melted glaze applied with a brush.

(2090). PARTRIDGES—MINCED (Émincé de Perdreaux).

Remove the best parts from two breasts of roasted partridges, pare and suppress the skin and bones; cut the meat up into small, thin slices and range them in a small sautoir. Reduce a few spoonfuls of half-glaze sauce (No. 413) with a little tomato sauce (No. 549) and a little Madeira, adding a bunch of parsley garnished with aromatic herbs; when of a good succulence, strain it over the meats and heat them up without boiling. At the last moment dress the slices on a small, long dish and cover with the sauce; surround with a row of large, stuffed Spanish olives heated in a little of the sauce, but they should not boil.

Minced Pheasant Woodcock or Duckling may be prepared exactly the same. The olive garnishing can be replaced by a row of small slices of red beef tongue, or else stuffed and baked artichoke bottoms, each one cut in two.

(2091). PARTRIDGE MINCED WITH RICE (Émincé de Perdreaux au Riz).

Cut in slices the breasts of two roast partridges; if very tender take also the thick thigh part and pare the slices neatly; range them in a sautoir with two or three minced truffles and cover with half-glaze sauce (No. 413); keep the meats warm in a bain-marie. At the last moment dress the mince and truffles in the center of a risot border inverted on a dish, or else the stew can be served alone and surrounded with a row of oval game quenelles, poached, cut in half across, breaded and fried, and set on the flat end. Even these quenelles can be replaced by small hollow bread crusts cut either into triangles or half circles and covered with a salpicon of truffles.

(2092). SALMIS OF PARTRIDGES (Salmis de Perdreaux).

Pick, singe, draw and truss four partridges as for an entrée (No. 178); roast them either on the spit or in the oven; they will require half an hour to cook, remove, untruss and let get partly cold, then cut them up into five pieces each; the two legs, two fillets and one breast piece; suppress all the skin covering each member and put them into a saucepan with buttered paper over and cover with the lid; keep either in a bain-marie or else at a moderate heat. Break up the bones, put them into another saucepan and moisten with a pint of broth (No. 194a) and a pint of Chablis, leave it on the range until it boils, then add a pint more broth and let cook very slowly for half an hour, being careful to skim off all the fat as it arises to the top, then strain through a napkin. Fry in butter a little chopped shallot, thyme, bay leaf and whole peppers, moisten with the stock and reduce with as much espagnole sauce (No. 414) stirring well from the bottom with a spatula to prevent it adhering thereto. After this sauce is well reduced, pour it through a tammy and put one-third of it with the pieces of partridge. Fry sixteen half heart-shaped croûtons in butter; dish up the salmis putting the legs at the bottom on top of bread croûtons, cover these lightly with the sauce and lay the wings and breasts between intermingling in the other croûtons and in the intersections formed by them, dress some turned and channeled mushroom heads (No. 118) and cut up truffles. Incorporate a few spoonfuls of good oil into the remainder of the sauce and pour it over the salmis.

(2093). PARTRIDGES À LA BAUDRIMONT (Perdreaux à la Baudrimont).

Roast two partridges; untruss and set aside to cool, remove breast meats in a way to form a hollow in the shape of a case, cut the meats into three-eighths of inch squares; prepare an equal quantity of mushrooms cut the same, as much ducks' livers and some small partridge quenelles made with a coffeespoon (No. 155). Put a gill of Madeira into a saucepan, heat it well without boiling and let a piece of Ceylon cinnamon infuse therein for half an hour, take this out, then add some espagnole sauce (No. 414) and reduce the whole; throw in the salpicon and when all is cold, use it to fill the partridges, having the breasts nicely rounded; cover over with quenelle forcemeat (No. 91), smooth neatly and cover the whole with melted butter; bestrew bread-crumbs and parmesan over and brown in a moderate oven, being careful to baste occasionally while cooking. Arrange the partridges on a dish, glaze with a little half-glaze sauce (No. 413) and serve a financière sauce (No. 464) apart.

(2094). PARTRIDGES À LA CHARTREUSE (Perdreaux à la Chartreuse).

Blanch two cabbages each cut in four and the core removed; drain and divide them into small clusters, press out all the water and braise them with a piece of bacon of about ten ounces that has been previously parboiled. Prepare a garnishing of carrots and turnips, blanch and then cook them in broth to allow finally to fall to a glaze; have also some quenelles made with a coffee-spoon (No. 155). Fry in butter or melted fat pork, two trussed partridges, season and when of a fine color, drain them off, make a hollow in the middle of the cabbage in the saucepan and lay the partridges in, and finish cooking all together. As soon as the birds are done, drain them off and keep them warm in a saucepan with a little half-glaze (No. 400), drain off also the bacon and cabbage, extract all the fat from the latter and dress half of it in the center of a dish, lay the partridges on top and surround with the rest of the cabbage, the carrots, the turnips and the que-nelles all in separate clusters. Glaze the partridges over with a brush and serve with a sauce-boatful of the half-glaze from the saucepan.

Another Way.—Decorate a timbale mold with carrots and turnips, upholding the decorations with a layer of thick game quenelle forcemeat (No. 91). Cut up the partridges and fill the mold with the cabbage, the bacon and the partridges, place it in a sautoir containing water and put in the oven for half an hour; unmold, pour part of the sauce around the chartreuse and serve. A half-glaze sauce (No. 413) should be served separately at the same time.

(2095). PARTRIDGES À LA MARLY (Perdreaux à la Marly).

Have two partridges, truss them as for an entrée (No. 178), and fill them with well seasoned partridge quenelle forcemeat (No. 91), into which mix truffles and cooked beef tongue cut in three-sixteenth of an inch squares; tie thin slices of fat pork over and braise in a white wine mirepoix stock (No. 419); strain this and put the fat back into the saucepan to keep the birds warm therein. Raise the fillets from the breast of a raw partridge, remove the sinews and cut the meats into escal-ops; sauté them in butter without browning, drain off the butter, remove the meats and keep them warm in this. Put half a pint of the stock used for cooking the partridges into a sautoir with as much allemande sauce (No. 407), reduce and add some cut up truffles and mushrooms; the sautéd part-ridge escalops, a little fresh butter and lemon juice. Dress the partridges on the bottom of a dish, place the garnishing around, and outside of it lay some crescent-shaped game croquettes (No. 885).

(2096). PARTRIDGES À LA MATIGNON, GARNISHED WITH "PAINS" À LA MONTGLAS—
(Perdreaux à la Matignon Garnis de Pains à la Montglas).

Prepare and truss two partridges as for an entrée as in No. 178. Wrap the two partridges with dry matignon (No. 406) in several sheets of paper; roast and when done, unwrap and place the matignon in a saucepan with some clear gravy (No. 404) and espagnole sauce (No. 414); reduce, despumate and strain through a tammy. Butter twelve mousseline molds (No. 1, Fig. 138), deco-rate them with fanciful cuts of truffles, and cover the entire inside with a layer of partridge que-nelle forcemeat (No. 91), filling the center as far up as the edges with a montglas prepared as follows: Cut off the white meats from half of a roasted partridge; have as many mushrooms heads cut the same size, and half as many truffles as mushrooms, also as much cooked beef tongue as truffles; mingle these with a little supreme sauce (No. 547), when the molds are full finish with more forcemeat. Put some boiling water in a saucepan to reach to a third of the height of the molds and poach these in a slack oven for fifteen to twenty minutes. Dress the partridges, glaze and lay them on top of an oval rice foundation (Fig. 9a); unmold the montglas pains around, and cover over with some of the sauce having the rest served apart.

(2097). PARTRIDGES À LA SOYER (Perdreaux à la Soyer).

Make a forcemeat with the partridge livers and a few chopped chicken livers; knead in a piece of butter, pepper, salt, a little shallot previously fried lightly in butter and chopped parsley. Have two trussed partridges (No. 179); put about two ounces of this prepared forcemeat into each one, and cook them on the spit for half an hour; dress on canapés, and pour some clear gravy (No. 404) under. Serve separately the same time as the partridges an English bread sauce (No. 438).

(2098). PARTRIDGES BRAISED À LA MOLIÈRE (Perdreaux Braisés à la Molière).

Truss three partridges as for an entrée (No. 178); cover the breasts with slices of lemon and these with bards of fat pork. Line a flat saucepan with the fragments of pork, some ham, cut up vegetables and a bunch of parsley garnished with thyme and bay leaf: lay the partridges on top and moisten with half a pint of dry white wine and half a pint of stock (No. 194a); boil this liquid, skim and continue to boil slowly either on the side of the range or in the oven until the partridges are cooked then drain and untruss. Cut each one up into five parts and arrange them in a saucepan to keep warm in a bain-marie with the fat drained from the first saucepan; in the stock place the broken carcasses, moisten with half a pint of clear gravy (No. 404) and half a glassful of Madeira, boil up, then strain through a sieve and reduce again to half, thickening it with some velouté sauce (No. 415); pour this over the cut up partridges and keep the whole warm. Prepare a partridge quenelle forcemeat (No. 91) mold it with a tablespoon the same as explained in No. 733, and range these quenelles in a buttered sautoir, decorate with truffles and poach. Dress the partridges on a forcemeat foundation (Fig. 8) without the central support and garnish around with the quenelles, cover with a little supreme sauce (No. 547) serving a sauce-boatful of it separately.

(2099. PARTRIDGES BROILED—COLBERT SAUCE (Perdreaux Grillés Sauce Colbert).

After the partridges have been well cleaned, split them lengthwise through their backs; cut off the feet and slip the legs under the skin; beat, pare carefully, season with salt and pepper and dip them in melted butter and broil over a slow fire; serve when done either on a Colbert sauce (No. 451) or a hunter's sauce (No. 480) or else a tartar sauce (No. 631).

(2100). PARTRIDGES TRUFFLED AND ROASTED (Perdreaux Truffés et Rôtis).

Draw two young partridges, wipe them well and singe. Peel five or six raw truffles, cut them in four and season; chop up the peelings and pound them with fresh fat pork, adding to it the cooked partridge livers with two or three pullet livers; season the preparation and press it through a sieve. Melt a quarter of a pound of grated fat pork, add to it the cut up truffles, season and warm up for a few seconds while tossing over the fire, then mix them in with the forcemeat. After this preparation has cooled off, use it to fill the partridge breasts and bodies; sew up the openings, truss and cover or else lard them with fine larding pork (No. 3, Fig. 52), fasten them on the spit and roast for fifteen to twenty minutes in front of a good fire, basting over with butter. As soon as they are done sprinkle salt over and remove from the spit; untruss and dress each one on a large crust of bread browned in butter and laid on an oval dish; surround the partridges with sliced lemons only, serving water-cress separately, also some clear gravy (No. 404).

(2101). PARTRIDGES WITH CABBAGE (Perdreaux aux Choux).

Dress four partridges, truss them for an entrée as in No. 178, and plunge the breasts in boiling water to stiffen the skin, then lard with medium lardons (No. 3, Fig. 52). Blanch for fifteen minutes four medium cabbages after removing the heart or core, and part of the green leaves; refresh, drain and press out every particle of water, then divide each quarter into two, remove the thick stalks, season lightly with salt and pepper, roll in thin slices of fat pork, tie with a string; put them into a braziere (Fig. 134) with the partridges and a pound of bacon cut in two equal-sized pieces and blanched for ten minutes; add also a one pound sausage, four medium carrots cut lengthwise in four, two onions, one having two cloves stuck in it, and a bunch of parsley garnished with thyme and bay leaf. Moisten with some stock (No. 194a) adding a little chicken fat; let cook, and after it comes to a boil finish in a slack oven for thirty to forty minutes. If the partridges be old ones they require one hour and a half to cook; remove them from the braziere, also the sausages and bacon which must be put under a light weight to cool off; it will take fully three hours to cook the cabbages. Have four dozen small carrots cut in pear-shapes and as many turnips of cylindrical form, two inches long by half an inch in diameter, round the ends neatly, then blanch, cook and let fall to a glaze separately. Half an hour before serving return the partridges to the cabbages and keep the whole warm. Cut the bacon into large three-fourths of an inch squares, the sausages into slices, and put both these into a sautoir with a few spoonfuls of the cabbage stock so that they keep hot until ready to serve; drain the cabbages through a colander, pressing it lightly to form into a socle on the bottom of the dish, laying the four untrussed partridges on top in a square, placing two clusters of carrots and two of turnips, alternated with the slices of sausages between the partridges, having the bacon in the center on top. Cover the partridges only with a half-glaze sauce (No. 413), and serve some of the same sauce separately.

(2102). PARTRIDGES LARDED AND ROASTED WITH GRAVY AND WATER-CRESSES
(Perdreaux Piqués Rôtis au Jus Garnis de Cresson).

Prepare and truss the partridges for roasting as explained in No. 179; dip the breasts into boiling water to stiffen the skin, and lard with small lardons (No. 3, Fig. 52). Lay them on the spit to roast, salt over and untruss a few moments before serving; glaze and dress on a canapé and surround with water-cress, serving at the same time a sauce-boatful of partridge fumet (No. 397) or clear gravy (No. 404). They can be barded instead of larded by covering their breasts with a thin slice of fat pork, tying it on with three rounds of string; roast and dress the same as the others. An ounce of good butter may be placed inside of each bird before cooking.

(2103). PARTRIDGES WITH OLIVES (Perdreaux aux Olives).

Lard two good-sized partridges with fine larding pork (No. 3, Fig. 52), and put them into a narrow saucepan lined with fragments of the same pork, minced roots and onions; season and moisten with a little white wine, then reduce to a glaze. Cook the partridges in very little moisture with stock (No. 194a), having it fall several times to a glaze. After the partridges are nicely done, drain them off to untruss. Strain the stock, skim off its fat and reduce, then incorporate it into brown sauce (No. 414) in the act of being reduced with two spoonfuls of Madeira added at the same time. Dress the partridges on a dish, surround with a garnishing of olives stuffed with baked forcemeat (No. 81), then poached and covered over with some of the sauce; serve the rest in a sauce-boat.

(2104). PARTRIDGE WITH SAUERKRAUT (Perdreau à la Choucroute).

Cut a roast partridge into small pieces and lay them aside. With the game bones and parings some aromatic herbs and white wine, prepare a small quantity of concentrated fumet (No. 397); thicken it with very little half-glaze sauce (No. 413) and keep it in a bain-marie. Cook some good sauerkraut with a small piece of bacon, proceeding as for garnished sauerkraut (No. 2819), adding a piece of butter divided into small pats, dish it up and form a hollow in the center; into this dress the pieces of game, pour over the sauce, cover with the sauerkraut and surround this with the bacon cut in slices.

FIG. 401.

(2105). BREASTS OR FILLETS OF PHEASANTS WITH TRUFFLES (Ailes ou Filets de Faisans aux Truffes).

Raise the breasts from six pheasants; remove the minion fillets, pare the large ones into half hearts after suppressing the skin and lay them in a thickly buttered sauté pan and *cover over with melted butter*; place the minion fillets in a smaller sauté pan after removing *the thin skin* that covers them also the sinews; streak them by cutting six bias incisions on the surface and filling these with half circles of channeled truffles and finish by giving them the shape of a ring; cover over with very thin bards of fat pork or else buttered paper. Make a fumet (No. 397) with the parings and legs, suppressing the rump, and add to it carrots, onions and a garished bunch of parsley (No. 123), moisten with a pint of stock (No. 194a) and two gills of Madeira and let this come to a boil and continue the ebullition process very slowly for one hour and a half, strain through a napkin and separate it into two parts, reduce one of these to the consistency of a light glaze and to the other add as much velouté sauce (No. 415) that is being reduced. Escalop one pound of fine truffles, put them in a bain-marie with a little meat glaze (No. 402), Madeira and as much fine butter, close the receptacle well and keep hot for at least fifteen minutes. Just when prepared to serve, sauté the pheasants' breasts; finish cooking them in a slack oven and when the larger fillets are done drain off the butter, being careful to retain the glaze, detach this with a little Madeira and add some velouté sauce (No. 415) and fresh butter; dress the large fillets in a circle, cover with half of the above sauce and on the large ones lay the smaller ones, brush over with meat glaze (No. 402), pouring the truffles in the center; serve the other half of the sauce separately.

(2106). SALMIS OF PHEASANT À LA LORENZO (Salmis de Faisan à la Lorenzo).

After the pheasant has been roasted the same as for No. 2107, cut it up into six or eight pieces; pare these nicely, removing all the skin, put them into a saucepan with half a pint of red or white wine, two shallots cut in three-eighths inch squares, the peel of a bitter or an ordinary orange and that of a lemon, all cut in small fillets and then blanched; add a pint of espagnole (No. 414) and a few spoonfuls of game glaze (No. 398). Pound the parings, rub through a sieve and add this pulp to the sauce, heat it up without boiling and keep it warm in the same way in a bain-marie. Dish up the pheasants, squeeze the juice of a bitter orange into the sauce and pour it over the dressed birds, garnish around with bread-crumb croûtons cut in heart-shapes and fried in butter and small game croquettes prepared as for No. 885.

(2107). PHEASANTS ADORNED WITH THEIR OWN PLUMAGE—ROASTED (Faisans Rôtis Garnis de Leur Plumage).

The pheasant's head can be preserved in advance and also keep carefully the wings and tail intact. Pick the pheasants, singe, draw and truss for roasting (No. 179); bard them over and roast either on the spit or in the oven, basting frequently while cooking; when done, take off, untruss and dress on top of trimmed croûtons hollowed out in such a way that the pheasants can stand well on them; glaze over and decorate with their own plumage, keeping it in place with metal skewers and letting them appear natural and lifelike; surround with clusters of water-cress. Strain and skim the fat from the dripping-pan stock and dilute it with some clear gravy (No. 404); pour a third of it over the pheasants and the other two-thirds serve in a sauce-boat.

(2108). PHEASANTS À LA MONTEBELLO (Faisans à la Montebello).

Cut into quarter inch squares, three-quarters of a pound of cooked duck's livers, and a quarter of a pound of truffles, season with salt and pepper, add half a pound of butter and put this equally inside of two pheasants; truss them for an entrée (No. 178), and cover with bards of fat pork; place them in an oval braziere saucepan (Fig. 134), and moisten with half a pint of champagne and a pint of mirepoix stock (No. 419). Cook on a slow fire or in the oven for three-quarters of an hour. Prepare a garnishing to be composed of escaloped and braised foies-gras, eighteen large truffles, fourteen double cocks'-combs, and fourteen fine cocks'-kidneys. Just when ready to serve drain off the pheasants and untruss. Have already prepared a conical-shaped piece of bread-crumbs, four and a half inches long by three inches wide, and eight inches high; made for the purpose of upholding the birds; form a hollow on each side near the top to enable the pheasants to be placed therein; fry this piece of bread to a fine color, and paste it on the dish. Place the birds in an incline inside this hollow space with the breasts uppermost, and then garnish all around with the truffles, livers, and kidneys, so that the bread is completely covered; trim five skewers with some of the truffles and the cocks'-combs (Fig. 11); stick two of them in each pheasant, and one on the summit of the bread; cover the whole with espagnole sauce (No. 414) reduced with the essence of truffles, and serve more of it in a separate sauce-boat.

(2109). PHEASANT À LA PÉRIGUEUX (Faisan à la Périgueux).

Have a good pheasant not too gamey; break the breastbone and fill the empty breast with liver baking forcemeat (No. 64), mixed with a salpicon of cooked truffles. Truss it with the legs thrust inside and cover the breast with a dry mirepoix (No. 419) wrap it in a half sheet of buttered paper tied on with a string. Fasten the pheasant on the spit and let roast for fifty to sixty minutes before a good fire while basting, then take it off, untie and dish it up, covering it with a Périgueux sauce (No. 517). Serve some of the same sauce separately.

(2110). PHEASANT TRUFFLED—ROASTED (Faisan Truffé Rôti).

Choose a good, fat, well set, and tender pheasant; after it has been drawn and well cleaned, fill its inside and breast with raw, peeled truffles, slightly fried in melted fat pork, and seasoned, proceeding the same as for truffled pullet (No. 1992). Lard the pheasant or else wrap it up in fat pork; thrust a small skewer through in order to fasten it to the spit and roast for fifty to sixty minutes according to its tenderness, basting it over with butter. As soon as it is done, detach the bird, untruss it on a dish or else on a thick oval slice of bread browned in butter. Serve with a separate sauce-boat of clear gravy (No. 404) and some water-cress.

(2111). PHEASANT WITH TRUFFLES—LARDED (Faisan Piqué aux Truffes).

Break the breastbone of a clean pheasant to facilitate the removal of the bone, and fill up the empty space with baking forcemeat (No. 81) mixed with a little raw forcemeat (No. 91), and raw, chopped truffles added; sew the skin underneath the breast and truss with the legs pushed in the thigh; this is done by removing the drumstick and pushing the leg bone back into this space; put the pheasant in a narrow saucepan lined with fat pork, salt over and besprinkle with melted butter. Cook for forty-five minutes while covered, basting over frequently, and lastly glaze it, then drain. Untruss it on a rice foundation (Fig. 9a) poached on a dish and surround this with round, peeled truffles cooked in wine; pour into the bottom of the dish a few spoonfuls of brown sauce (No. 414) reduced with the truffle liquid and a few spoonfuls of Madeira wine. Accompany this entrée with a sauce-boatful of the same sauce.

(2112). WILD PIGEON OR SQUABS POUPETON, ANCIENT STYLE (Poupeton de Pigeons Ramier ou de Ramereaux à l'Ancienne).

Chop up half a pound of veal with half a pound of beef marrow and half a pound of fat pork; season with salt, pepper and nutmeg; pound all together, mixing in four ounces of soaked and well pressed bread-crumbs, two whole eggs, some chopped mushrooms fried in butter and chopped pars-ley. Lay a buttered flawn ring eight inches in diameter on a sheet of buttered paper; fill the bottom and sides with the forcemeat (No. 81) and in the center lay a stew made of six wild pigeons prepared as explained below. Cover the top with more of the forcemeat, having it bomb-shaped, egg over and cook in a moderate oven. For the wild pigeon stew, truss the pigeons as for an entrée (No. 178); brown them in butter with escalops of uncooked sweetbreads, some ham or bacon cut in five-eighths squares and blanched mushrooms, also a garnished bunch of parsley (No. 123). Dredge three tablespoonfuls of butter over the whole and let it attain a fine color; then moisten with white wine and stock (No. 194a). When the birds are cooked suppress the parsley, reduce and thicken the sauce, adding the juice of a lemon; put it into a vessel to get cold and then cut the birds lengthwise in two, pare neatly and use for filling the inside of the poupeton.

Wild Squabs are roasted or broiled the same as tame squabs. See No. 2018.

(2113). GOLDEN PLOVER OR GRASS PLOVER AND BUSTARD PLOVER (Le Pluvier ou le Vanneau).

Plover's meat is of a very delicate taste; it excites the appetite and digests easily. Plover are eaten larded or barded after being drawn and then cooked on a brisk fire. The golden and the bustard plover are very much alike, living in the same localities, eating the same food, and their meats are almost similar. Golden plover's eggs are used the same as bustard plover, but are considered much inferior.

(2114). PLOVERS À LA MONTAUBAN (Pluviers à la Montauban).

Draw, singe and clean the plovers, thrust the legs inside and split them lengthways through the back; open, beat and season with salt and pepper; sauté them in clarified butter, drain this off and moisten with a little champagne and brown sauce (No. 414), adding some peeled and sliced or whole truffles. Dress the plovers in a straight row, surround them with the truffles and strain the sauce through a tammy, pour part of it over and serve the rest in a sauce-boat.

(2115). PLOVERS À LA STOUGHTON (Pluviers à la Stoughton).

Draw the plovers, singe, clean and poêler them as for No. 12; after wrapping them in thin bards of fresh fat pork tying each one on with three rows of string. Fry the intestines in butter, carefully suppressing the gizzard and stomach pouch, drain off the butter and replace it by Madeira and brown sauce (No. 414). Then simmer for a few minutes; pass it through a tammy and add to it some foies-gras escalops, truffles and cocks'-combs; dress the plovers in a low croustade made of tart paste (No. 149) and pour over the garnishing.

(2116). PLOVERS À LA PARNY—BREASTS (Filets de Pluviers à la Parny).

Raise the breasts from six plovers; pare, beat, salt and sauté them lightly on the side that adheres to the bones; cover this side with a salpicon of fresh mushrooms mixed with a reduced, thick half-glaze sauce (No. 413); spread a layer of quenelle forcemeat (No. 91) on top and bestrew with finely chopped truffles; range them in a sautoir, pour melted butter over and ten minutes before serving, set them in a hot oven and baste at times with melted clarified butter. Drain as soon as they are done and dress in a circle on the edge of a low, carved rice foundation (Fig. 9a); fill the inside of the circle with small turned mushroom heads (No. 118) mingled with espagnole sauce (No. 414), reduced mushroom essence (No. 392) and Marsala wine. Serve a sauce-boat of this brown sauce at the same time as the fillets.

(2117). PLOVERS À LA VICTOR HUGO—BREASTS (Filets de Pluviers à la Victor Hugo).

Remove all the skin from the breasts taken from seven plovers; streak the minion fillets rounds of truffles, pare the larger ones into half hearts rounded on one end and pointed on the other; place a minion fillet twisted into a half-circle on the edge of the round end of the fillet itself, and range these in a sautoir, cover with butter and cook in a hot oven, basting frequently while cooking. Prepare fourteen half heart-shaped croustades the same size as the fillets, made with very thin foundation paste (No. 135) and fill with paper and rice; empty them as soon as done and egg over the outside, return them for an instant to the oven to color, and then fill them with a purée of mushroons (No. 722); lay one of the fillets in each and glaze over. Serve separately a brown sauce (No. 414) with game fumet (No. 397) and Madeira.

(2118). PLOVERS BROILED (Pluviers Grillés).

Split them lengthwise in two through the back, open and flatten (see broiled woodcock, No. 2204); season with salt and pepper, coat them with oil and broil in a double gridiron; dress on croûtons of basted bread, cover with maître-d'hôtel butter (No. 581) and serve.

(2119). PLOVERS ROASTED (Pluviers Rôtis).

Singe and draw half a dozen of either golden or grass plovers. With their intestines and some grated fat pork make a dressing seasoned with salt, pepper, parsley and finely chopped shallot fried in butter; fill the insides of the birds, bard them over tying on the pork. Turn the feet and maintain them by passing one through the other; run the under part of the throat on the leg to keep it in this position; thrust a skewer through, fastening it on the spit, and when cooked remove, untruss and dress on top of croûtons (No. 51), pour over some good gravy into which mix game glaze (No. 398); surround with water-cress seasoned with vinegar and salt.

(2120). PLOVERS ROASTED À LA MARTEL—LARDED (Pluviers Piqués Rôtis à la Martel).

After being drawn, or simply after removing the gizzard, for they are frequently roasted the same as woodcock without drawing, only trussed and larded with fine lardings of pork (No. 4, Fig. 52); fry their intestines with melted fat pork and a few good chicken livers, chopped truffles and cognac to make a preparation the same as described for woodcock canapés (No. 2205), and with it cover some oblong crusts. Glaze and heat them at the oven door and serve with the birds on these. Have a separate colbert sauce (No. 451) finished with cayenne butter (No. 571).

(2121). SALMIS OF YELLOW-LEG PLOVERS À LA DUCLAIR (Salmis de Pluviers à Pattes Jaunes à la Duclair).

Roast six yellow-leg plovers very rare either on the spit or in the oven; cut them up for a salmis retaining only the breasts, cut these in two through the center; pound the remainder of the meats with the same quantity of rice to obtain a purée; with the broken up carcass make a white wine fumet (No. 397); dress the fillets in a circle and fill the center with the purée, lay on top of it some slices of truffle warmed up in half-glaze (No. 400) with Madeira and fresh butter. Prepare some forcemeat as follows: Fry the intestines in butter with chopped shallots and chicken livers, season and rub through a sieve. Make some oblong crusts two and a half inches long, two wide and half an inch in thickness, slit them all around and fry to a fine color in clarified butter, remove the upper part and empty out the centers, then fill them with the prepared forcemeat, rounding it slightly on top and poach in a slack oven. Range these crusts around the dressed salmis and serve with a sauce-boat of espagnole sauce (No. 414) reduced with the fumet and Madeira wine.

(2122). BUSTARD PLOVERS À LA DUMANOIR (Vanneaux à la Dumanoir).

Chop up the intestines of several bustard plovers with as much grated fat pork, pound and press through a sieve, add fine spices and chopped truffle parings, mixing in a little brandy and a soupçon of garlic. Truss the plovers as for roasting (No. 179), stuff them with the above preparation and roast in a hot oven. Dress them when done on hollow oval bread croûtons. Glaze them over with game glaze (No. 398), pour a little gravy in the bottom of the dish and serve separately a small quantity of half-glaze sauce (No. 413) with Madeira.

(2123). QUAILS À LA CAPRÉA (Cailles à la Capréa).

Truss eight quails as for entrée (No. 178), after picking, singeing, drawing, and cleaning them well; stuff them with butter into which has been mingled salt, pepper, and lemon juice, then sauté them in some butter; transfer to a saucepan lined with bards of fat pork, and cook with a very little white wine mirepoix stock (No. 419); place around a bunch of parsley garnished with a bay leaf, eight ounces of lean bacon cut in quarter inch squares, and eight ounces of lean ham cut the same, also eight ounces of artichoke bottoms, the whole blanched separately, and four ounces of truffles cut as cloves of garlic. When the quails are cooked, untruss and transfer them to another saucepan, skim the stock, and pour the strained fat over the quails to keep them hot; now strain the stock itself, remove all the fat that is left, and add it to some espagnole sauce (No. 414), and a little Madeira; season and boil it down to the consistency of a succulent sauce. Blanch four ounces of rice, cook it with very little unskimmed stock (No. 194a), and when done place it in a flat bottomed border mold (Fig. 139) having it carefully buttered, or if to unmold at once dip it merely into cold water; fill it very tight, unmold on a dish and on top of the border lay oval pieces of tongue, a quarter of an inch thick by three inches long and two inches wide; remove the centers, making the same shape oval only two inches long and one inch wide; on these lay the quails, glaze over with game glaze (No. 398), and inside the center of the border dress the bacon, ham, artichoke bottoms, and truffles; cover with some of the sauce, serving more apart.

(2124). QUAILS À LA MACÉDOINE—LARDED (Cailles Piquées à la Macédoine).

Truss eight quails after they have been picked, drawn, and singed, proceeding the same as for an entrée (No. 178); dip the breasts in boiling water and lard them with small lardons (No. 4, Fig. 52). Line a low saucepan with bards of fat pork, lay the quails on top, and moisten with a white wine mirepoix stock (No. 419); braise in a slack oven and when almost done, glaze over. Untruss and dress in a circle with a garnishing of macédoine vegetables (No. 680), in the center; strain the stock, free it of its fat, and reduce to the consistency of half-glaze, serving it separately. The quails may be barded instead of larded, and the macédoine replaced by green peas Parisian style (No. 2745), or else cucumbers cut as cloves of garlic, blanched and cooked in consommé (No. 189), then thickened with bechamel (No. 409), etc.

(2125). QUAILS À LA MIREPOIX (Cailles à la Mirepoix).

Bone the breasts from the inside of six small and singed quails. Shred finely into small Julienne, some onions, red part of carrots, tender celery stalks, and fresh mushrooms; fry all these very slowly with butter in a small saucepan, stirring occasionally until cooked; season and remove. Leave these ingredients to cool off partially in the saucepan, then put in two or three spoonfuls of glaze (No. 398) barely melted so as to have a thick preparation of a proper consistency to roll into balls. Insert one of these balls into the breast of every quail, sew up the skin, truss and fry them for two minutes in a saucepan; season and moisten with a gill of Madeira wine; glaze over with a brush, and finish cooking them smothered. When the quails are properly done, drain off to untruss; lay each one in an oval china case with a part of their stock; cover with a little good, reduced, thick brown sauce (No. 414) having it almost cold, and let this sauce become glossy for two minutes at the oven door; serve the quails at once.

(2126). QUAILS, PIEDMONTESE STYLE (Cailles à la Piémontaise).

Bone the breasts of four or five clean quails, fill in the empty space with a baked forcemeat (No. 81) and truffles, mingled with a little raw forcemeat (No. 91); truss and cook smothered with Madeira wine and gravy. Have one quart of water, half a pound of polenta, and a piece of butter and some salt and with it prepare a mush; as soon as done, finish with a handful of parmesan and another piece of butter. With this preparation fill a buttered border mold (Fig. 139) and keep it warm. Fry quickly in butter about fifteen small Chipolata sausages (No. 754), drain, cut them apart and glaze over with a brush. At the last moment, lift up the quails and cut each one in two, unmold the polenta border on a hot dish, dress the quails pyramidically in the center and lay the halved sausages in a circle on top of the border, cover the border and sausages with Piedmontese brown sauce (No. 519).

(2127). QUAILS À LA TALLEYRAND—BREASTS (Filets de Cailles à la Talleyrand).

Raise the fillets, suppress the skin and nerves and pare them into half hearts, season and sauté with slices of raw truffles add a half-glaze sauce with Madeira (No. 413). Lay them on half heart-shaped bread croûtons the same size as the fillets and hollowed out, then filled with a salpicon of mushrooms mingled with half-glaze sauce made of game essence (No. 389). Dress in a circle on a dish, put truffles in the center and pour the sauce over all.

(2128). QUAILS BROILED (Cailles Grillées).

Have the birds very clean and truss with the legs thrust inside; split them through the back without separating, open, trim, beat and season, then coat them over with butter or oil and broil. Dress on well pared toasted slices of bread and cover with maître-d'hôtel butter (No. 581).

(2129). QUAIL CUTLETS, GIRONDINS (Côtelettes de Cailles aux Girondins).

Prepare the same as the above, split them in two equal parts, the legs to form a handle and trim with a fancy frill (No. 10). Sauté on a brisk fire, keeping them rare, then place under a light weight, cover over with Villeroi sauce (No. 560), let get cold, then dip in eggs and bread-crumbs and fry in clarified butter, dress on croûtons of cooked red beef tongue, filling the center with minced cèpes fried in oil, seasoned with salt, pepper and chopped parsley; drain and mix in with the cèpes a little game glaze (No. 398) and lemon juice. Serve a sauce-boat of Bordelaise sauce (No. 436) at same time.

(2130). QUAILS IN PAPERS (Cailles en Papillotes).

Prepare eight cleaned quails by removing the bones beginning at the back and leave on one leg only, then stuff with game forcemeat (No. 91) into which has been added cooked fine herbs (No. 385) and a little glaze (No. 402); put them into half heart-shaped bottomless molds, having them laid on a baking sheet covered with thin bards of fat pork, pour butter over and cook in a moderate oven for half an hour; leave them in their molds and set a weight on top. Fry in butter chopped shallot, mushrooms, truffles and parsley, add a quart of velouté sauc (No. 415), reduce and thicken with four egg-yolks, a little cream and the juice of two strained lemons. Cut out six sheets of strong paper into heart-shapes, coat them with oil; on the right side of the heart and near the center having the point toward you, place on a layer of the cooked fine herb sauce (No. 385), over this a quail, and on top another layer of the sauce; fold the paper in two forming a half heart, crimp the two edges together to enclose hermetically and then set each one on a small silver dish; place them in a slack oven for fifteen to twenty minutes and when a fine color serve, placing the hot dish from the oven on a second plate.

(2131). QUAILS ROASTED (Cailles Rôties).

After they have been plucked and drawn, singe and cut off the end of the claws; truss and cover the breasts, first with a grape leaf buttered over with a brush, and then with a thin slice of fat pork; run them on small skewers and fasten them to the spit; baste over with melted butter and let cook for fourteen to sixteen minutes then salt; take off and untruss, or they may be put in a baking pan sprinkled with butter and cooked in a hot oven. Dress each one on a crust covered with a layer of baking forcemeat with foies-gras (No. 78), and serve at the same time some clear gravy (No. 404).

(2132). QUAILS, SALMIS OF, À LA MORISINI (Salmis de Cailles à la Morisini).

Prepare six quails the same as for roasting (No. 2131), divide them in two splitting through the center of the breast, suppress the legs and pare the remainder of the birds. Mince two shallots finely, break the legs and put them into a saucepan with the fragments of quail and the shallots; moisten with red or white Bordeaux wine (either will answer), and as much mirepoix stock (No. 419) and espagnole sauce (No. 414). Let boil slowly for fifteen minutes, then strain through a sieve, put in the quails, heat up without boiling and dish up in a circle. Add some finely cut up mushrooms and truffles to the sauce and pour it over the quails; surround the salmis with heart-shaped bread croûtons fried in butter.

(2133). QUAILS WITH BAY LEAF (Cailles au Laurier).

Pick, draw and singe six quails, truss for roasting (No. 179). Chop up the livers, the same quantity of chicken liver and as much grated fat pork as liver; add chopped parsley, pepper, a tablespoonful of chopped shallot, a handful of bread-crumbs and one small beaten egg. Mix the ingredients well together and fill the quails with it; roast them in a moderate oven, basting over frequently with lard; drain this into a saucepan and add to it some bread-crumbs, raw ham cut in one-eighth squares, fry nicely and put in two bay leaves, moisten with thickened, gravy (No. 405) and game-glaze (No. 398); skim off the fat, add the juice of a lemon and also a little butter; mix well with a wire whisk, dress, and pour the sauce over the quails.

(2134). QUAILS WITH MUSHROOMS—STUFFED (Cailles Farcies aux Champignons).

This entrée is dressed on a foundation covered with cooked paste (No. 131) having a low support fastened to the center, also covered with the same cooked paste and decorated on the upper edge with a raised border, it being spread out and open-worked (Fig. 8). Bone the breasts of ten quails, fill up the empty space with a baking forcemeat (No. 81), mixed with a little raw forcemeat

FIG. 402.

(No. 73), and a few spoonfuls of raw truffles cut in small dice; sew up the skin, truss and cover with bards of salt pork. Lay them in a deep sautoir lined with salt pork, roots and minced onions, moisten with a glassful of white wine and let reduce, then remoisten with unskimmed stock (No. 194a). Boil the liquid, withdraw the pan to a slower fire to finish cooking the quails, drain them off, untruss and untie. Cut each one lengthwise in two and dress them to imitate a rosette on the foundation, standing almost upright without injuring their shapes and leaning them against the support. Fill up the empty border with a garnishing of pretty white mushrooms all of the same size; cover them as well as the quails with a little good velouté sauce (No. 415), reduced with the quail stock and that of the mushrooms.

(2135). QUAILS WITH RISOT (Cailles au Risot).

Draw four or five singed quails, bone the breasts from the inside of the birds and fill in the empty space with baked forcemeat (No. 81), mingled with a little raw quenelle forcemeat (No. 91) and having chopped truffles added. Truss the quails, fry in a sautoir with butter, season and moisten with Madeira wine and gravy (No. 404), reduce this liquid to half and finish cooking them smothered. At the last moment drain off, untruss and split each one lengthwise in two, then dress on a risot (No. 739). Strain the stock, remove its fat and pour it over the birds.

(2136). CALIFORNIA QUAILS À LA MONTEREY (Cailles de Californie à la Monterey).

Having drawn and singed six California quails leave the breast skin as long as possible without breaking it. Peel half a pound of truffles, chop up the peelings and cut the truffles in half inch square pieces, season with No. 1 spices (No. 168), then add the livers, a few chicken livers, a little brandy, a soupçon of garlic and four ounces of fresh butter; stuff the quails with this and truss them for an entrée (No. 178), cover with thin bards of fat pork tying it on with three rows of string, run a skewer through and range them on the spit; put to the fire for about three-quarters of an hour, then unwrap and dress on hollow crusts forming them into a circle; cover with half-glaze sauce (No. 413) finished with essence of truffles (No. 395) and fill the center with cooked and turned small mushroom heads, turned olives and small game quenelles made with a coffeespoon (No. 155); pour some sauce into this garnishing, serving more separately.

(2137). YOUNG RABBIT À LA CELTOISE (Lapereau à la Celtoise).

Divide a young rabbit into twelve pieces after skinning and drawing it; put these to steep in a raw marinade for six hours, then drain and wipe, lay the pieces in a sautoir with fat pork cut in half inch squares and blanched; set the sautoir on a good fire and fry the rabbit with the addition of some small onions and a bunch of parsley garnished with thyme, bay leaf and a clove of garlic; when the meats are done, baste them over with white wine and some clear gravy (No. 404), adding six peeled tomatoes cut across in two and the seeds well extracted, also half a pound of lean cooked ham cut in three-sixteenths inch squares and a pint of brown sauce (No. 414). Remove the parsley, skim off the fat and season highly with salt, pepper and prepared red pepper (No. 168); dress the rabbits inside a risot à la piemontese border (No. 2981), pour very little of the sauce over and serve.

(2138). YOUNG RABBITS À LA THIÉBLIN (Lapereaux à la Thiéblin).

Skin, empty, and trim two young rabbits; put the livers aside, and divide each rabbit into twelve pieces; heat some oil and butter, half of each, in a sautoir, put in the pieces of rabbit, and season well with salt, pepper, a crushed clove of garlic, and a bunch of parsley garnished with thyme and bay leaf; fry them quickly, moisten with espagnole sauce (No. 414), white wine, a little clear gravy (No. 404), and tomatoes; let simmer till thoroughly cooked, and add the sautéd livers, and some mushrooms. Dress the rabbit and mushrooms, covering over with the sauce. Prepare a rabbit forcemeat (No. 84), mix with it a little espagnole sauce reduced and stirred with some half-glaze made of game fumet (No. 397); place it in small oval molds and poach in the oven; cut them in two lengthways, bread-crumb them first without any eggs, then again with eggs, and fry to a fine color in clarified butter; drain, wipe, and dress them around the rabbit. Serve separately an espagnole sauce (No. 414) made with game fumet (No. 397).

(2139). YOUNG RABBITS, VALENCIA STYLE (Lapereaux à la Valence).

Cut up in twelve pieces each, two skinned and drawn young rabbits; put half a pound of chopped fat pork in a sautoir, adding the rabbits when it is very hot and fry over a brisk fire, season with salt and pepper, and add also half a pound of blanched bacon cut in quarter inch squares, one medium onion cut the same size, four quartered, peeled and pressed tomatoes, and a bunch of parsley garnished with thyme, bay leaf, and a clove of garlic. Cover the saucepan and cook on a moderate fire; just when ready to serve, skim off the fat, suppress the parsley, and put in a little game glaze (No. 398); dress and dredge chopped parsley over the top. Stiffen some small oiled cases in the oven, fill them with rabbit forcemeat (No. 84), into which cooked fine herbs (No. 385) have been added; place on top the minion fillet scored with truffles removed from the rabbit, and over these thin slices of fat pork; bake in a slow oven, drain off the fat, and lay a small glazed truffle in the center of each fillet; range these cases around the dish, and serve.

(2140). YOUNG RABBITS, HUNTER'S STYLE (Lapereaux au Chasseur).

Skin and draw two young rabbits; wash, wipe, and cut each one into twelve pieces; put them into a sautoir on a brisk fire to fry and color the meats lightly, adding half a pound of raw ham cut in one-eighth of an inch squares, four ounces of onions cut exactly the same size, a bunch of parsley garnished with thyme, bay leaf, garlic, and a clove. Drain off the fat, and season with salt and pepper, putting in a pint of espagnole sauce (No. 414), and as much Burgundy wine; simmer, reduce, and add a pint of cooked minced mushrooms and half as many truffles. Dish it up and garnish with the mushrooms and truffles, pour a third of the sauce over, and range croûtons of bread fried in butter all around; serve the remainder of the sauce in a sauce-boat.

(2141). WILD RABBIT JUGGED WITH BLOOD (Civet de Lapin de Garenne au Sang).

Procure a good, young, fleshy wild rabbit, preserve all the blood in a bowl, stirring into it a little vinegar to keep it liquid. Skin and prepare it, and cut it up into equal-sized pieces. Put the meats into a vessel to season and let marinate for two hours with a little boiled vinegar, a little white wine and a tied bunch of fresh and wild thyme. Chop up some fat pork, melt it in a frying pan and add to it half a pound of small squares of bacon; after these are well sized, remove them with a skimmer and add to the fat the well-drained pieces of rabbit and cut up onions; fry over a good fire until the meats are nicely browned and have evaporated their moisture, then put them into a fireproof stone vessel with a glassful of red wine; reduce this over a brisk fire and moisten the meats at once to their height with white wine and stock (No. 194a); let this liquid come to a boil, then remove the vessel on one side to boil gently until partly done; strain the liquid through a sieve, pare the surplus bones from the meats and return the latter to the saucepan with the cut up bacon, the marinade, a bunch of parsley and a peeled clove of garlic. Put the stew back on the fire and thicken it with a little cooked roux or diluted flour, finish cooking slowly. A few moments before serving, transfer all the pieces of rabbit and bacon into another saucepan, strain the sauce over and boil up once or twice thickening it off the fire with the reserved blood; let cook again but without boiling. Dress the stew on a dish and surround it with small clusters of onions glazed separately, if intended for a more ceremonious dish, a few clusters of fresh, peeled mushrooms cooked in butter may be added.

(2142). YOUNG RABBIT ROASTED AND LARDED (Levraut Piqué et Rôti).

Suppress the skin from the back and hind legs of a good, trimmed rabbit; fill the body with a bread forcemeat (No. 61), with cooked fine herbs (No. 385) and chopped truffles mixed with a third as much liver baking forcemeat (No. 64); sew up the opening. Break the bone of the thick thigh

Fig 403.

part so as to be able to bend the legs under and keep them in position while trussing; truss also the fore legs and the head, keeping the latter upright. Lard the back and thighs with larding pork (No. 3, Fig. 52). Lay the rabbit on a spit, maintaining it in position with skewers, and roast it for thirty to forty minutes, basting over frequently with butter, and when done salt it over. Remove, untruss, and dress on a dish; serve separately some clear gravy (No. 404), also a light sharp sauce (No. 538).

(2143). FILLETS OF YOUNG RABBITS À LA BIENVENU, GARNISHED WITH CROQUETTES
(Filets de Lapereaux à la Bienvenu, Garnis de Croquettes).

Remove and lard both the fillets and minion fillets from four young rabbits, having the lardons exceedingly small (No. 4, Fig. 52); place them in a sauté pan with clarified butter, place on a brisk fire, let cook and drain off the butter, detaching the glaze with a little white wine. Dress them in the center of a dish and serve with a separate marinade sauce (No. 496), garnishing around with prepared croquettes as follows:

Hare Croquettes.—Fry colorless in butter, one ounce of finely chopped onions adding four ounces of chopped mushrooms and eight ounces of cold roast rabbit taken from the legs and shoulders, mix with a well reduced brown sauce (No. 414), also a little meat glaze (No. 402) and fresh butter, add salt, pepper and chopped parsley; when this preparation is cold divide it into inch and a half balls, flatten them to three-quarters of an inch thick, dip in eggs, roll in bread-crumbs and fry to a fine golden color; drain, wipe and lay them around the dressed rabbit, resting one against the other; serve with the sauce as explained above.

(2144). FILLETS OF YOUNG RABBITS À LA LAVOISIER (Filets de Lapereaux à la Lavoisier).

Raise the fillets and minion fillets from four young rabbits, suppress all the nerves and cut them into bias slices; flatten and shape into half hearts, split them through their thickness to form a pocket and season this with salted spices (No. 168), stuff the cavity with reduced duxelle (No. 385) and cover over with very consistent allemande sauce (No. 407); when cold, dip in eggs and bread-crumbs, then sauté in butter, draining this off when done, decorate with fancy favor frills (No. 10) and dress in two rows, trim the sides with cèpes sautéd à la Provençale (No. 2723) and the ends with oval shaped rabbit croquettes decorated with truffles; a separate half-glaze sauce (No. 413) with Madeira should be served in a tureen.

(2145). FILLETS OF YOUNG RABBITS WITH CURRANT SAUCE (Filets de Lapereaux Sauce aux Groseilles).

Remove the nerves and pare two young rabbit fillets, also the minion fillets; lard them with small lardons (No. 4, Fig. 52) and marinate for two hours, then strain the marinade and put its vegetables on the fire to fry in butter, braise the fillets in this, glaze and dress in a circle. Break up the bones and cook them in butter, adding a little flour; with this make a small roux (No. 163), season it with pepper and salt, adding an onion and a bunch of garnished parsley, moisten with boiling port wine, reduce and strain through a sieve, boil it up again and despumate well adding some currant jelly, dissolving it slowly in the sauce; strain the whole through a tammy and pour a part of it under the meats, serving the remainder separately. The fillets can be roasted instead of braised if so desired.

(2146). FILLETS OF YOUNG RABBITS WITH ARTICHOKE OR MUSHROOM PURÉE (Filets de Lapereaux à la Purée d'Artichauts ou de Champignons).

Raise the fillets and minion fillets; divide the larger ones in two or three pieces, then pare each one and make a deep incision on one side; season this and stuff it with cooked fine herbs (No. 385) mingled with a well-reduced half-glaze sauce (No. 413); bread them English style (No. 13), and broil over a slack fire. Dress in a circle filling the center with a purée of mushrooms (No. 722) or artichokes bottoms (No. 704) and serve separately an espagnole sauce (No. 414) reduced with fumet of rabbit (No. 397). Instead of stuffing the whole inside, one side only need be filled, after sautéing the fillet on one side, mask it with raw game quenelle forcemeat (No. 91), then dip in eggs and bread-crumbs and fry in clarified butter to a fine color; serve the same as the above.

(2147). GIBELOTTE OF RABBITS (Gibelotte de Lapins).

Cut clean fine tame rabbits in pieces, put them into a vessel to season and marinate for a couple of hours with onions, parsley, and vinegar. Melt some chopped up fat pork in a pan; add to it a quarter of a pound of cut up bacon, fry and drain this off. Put the rabbit meats into the same pan and fry over a good fire, bestrew with a spoonful of flour, and moisten to their height with one-third of white wine, and two-thirds of stock (No. 194a); boil up the liquid, then transfer the stew into a saucepan to let cook slowly until partly done; strain the sauce, pare the meats and return them to the same saucepan with the bacon, a clove of garlic, a garnished bunch of parsley, and two dozen small onions browned in a pan; continue to boil all together. At the expiration of a quarter of an hour, put in fifteen to twenty fresh mushrooms, and seven or eight minutes later, dress the meats on a dish with the garnishings around, if there be too much sauce, reduce it; strain it over the stew, and surround with plain bread-crusts cut into triangles, and browned in butter.

(2148). GIBELOTTE OF YOUNG RABBITS, PARMENTIER (Gibelotte de Lapereaux Parmentier).

After disjointing two young rabbits, wash them in plenty of cold water to extract all the blood, wipe on a cloth drying them at the same time, then fry in butter to stiffen; add two tablespoonfuls of flour, salt, pepper, grated nutmeg, and half a clove of crushed garlic; moisten with half a bottle-ful of white wine, and some stock (No. 194a), keeping the sauce rather thick, now throw in a garnished bunch of parsley (No. 123), and some mushroom parings. Let cook for three-quarters of an hour, skim the fat from the top, drain off the pieces of rabbit, and pare each one, then put them aside in a saucepan to keep hot with a few spoonfuls of the sauce. Now reduce the remainder of it to re-semble a thick velouté sauce (No. 415), and thicken it with a liaison of four egg-yolks; strain it through a tammy, and place it in a bain-marie. When prepared to serve, dish up the pieces of rabbit, and garnish around with olive-shaped potatoes cooked in stock (No. 194a) and a pound of cooked mushrooms; add to the sauce kept warm, a heavy pinch of chopped parsley, and two shallots blanched and chopped; also two spoonfuls of olive oil and the juice of a lemon; pour it over the rabbit.

(2149). WILD RABBIT BACKS, BROILED (Râbles de Lapins de Garenne Grillés).

Pare the backs of three field rabbits, skinned and cleaned; suppress the breasts, then season; dip them in beaten eggs, roll in bread-crumbs, and immerse in melted butter; broil for twenty minutes over a moderate fire while turning. Dress on a dish and serve with a separate sharp sauce (No. 538), or else a tartar sauce (No. 631).

(2150). RAIL À LA MAREILLE—ROASTED AND BROILED (Râle Rôti et Grillé à la Mareille)

A species of bird belonging to the grallic order; they are in great demand on account of the delicacy of their meats, especially in the fall season. There are two kinds, the water rail and the land rail; the latter being the best.

À la Mareille.—Pick, draw, singe, and truss six rails, carefully remove all their pin feathers, then stuff them with the following dressing: Chop six ounces of chicken livers with as much fresh fat pork, both to be chopped separately; mix all together, then season with salt, pepper, nutmeg, and chopped truffles, mushrooms, and parsley; cook in a brisk oven, and afterward dress on hollow crusts fried in butter garnished with forcemeat and poached in the oven; serve a Bigarade sauce (No. 435) separately.

Roasted.—Prepared the same as the above without any dressing; roast in a hot oven, and dress on croûtons of bread fried in butter, and covered with foies-gras forcemeat (No. 78); pour clear gravy (No. 404) over, and serve with currant jelly.

Broiled.—Split the rails, cook and dress the same as the English snipe (No. 2157).

(2151). REED BIRDS, BROILED (Mésanges Moustaches Grillées).

Split them through the back, remove the intestines, pare and season; place them in a hinged broiler, cook lightly on the opened side and finish cooking on the other side; a few moments should suffice. Dress one resting on the other intercalated with toasts; spread over a little maître d'hôtel butter (No. 581).

(2152). REED BIRDS, ROASTED (Mésanges Moustaches Rôties).

Remove the gizzards and the pouch from the birds; cut off the legs halfway, singe and cover with bards of fat pork pared very thin; thrust small skewers through, and spread the birds with

FIG. 404.

a spare layer of softened butter; roast them for seven to eight minutes at a brisk fire, salt over when unwrapping and dress on buttered and browned crusts. Serve with sliced lemon.

(2153). SNIPE—ENGLISH—AFRICAN STYLE (Bécassines Anglaises à l'Africaine).

Divide six snipe in two parts, beat, pare and place them in a sautoir with melted butter; cook the intestines and some chicken livers in butter with half as much grated fat pork, two ounces of bread-crumbs and half a pint of half-glaze sauce (No. 413), pass it through a sieve and incorporate into it a few spoonfuls of chopped truffles; fill some hollowed out half heart-shaped croûtons with this preparation, cover with slices of fat pork and poach in the oven. Sauté the snipe and when done lay on top of the croûtons and cover with espagnole sauce (No. 414), reduced with game fumet (No. 397); serve an African sauce (No. 424) separately.

Dowich snipe are prepared the same as English snipe.

(2154). SNIPE—ENGLISH—À LA MONTALAND (Bécassines Anglaises à la Montaland).

Truss twelve very clean snipe, roast them on the spit or in the oven, leaving them quite rare; lift off the breasts. Fry the intestines and livers in butter, season with salt and pepper; cut off all the leg meats and pound them with the fried intestines, then press through a sieve. Reduce half a pint of champagne with two finely minced shallots, also some truffles, mushrooms, chopped parsley, mignonette and a pint of espagnole sauce (No. 414), add to it the pounded meats, a spoonful of olive oil and the juice of a lemon. Dress the snipe on half heart croûtons covered with foies-gras, and pour the sauce over.

(2155). SNIPE—ENGLISH—À LA WALESKI (Bécassines Anglaises à la Waleski).

Bone the backs of twelve snipe. Put into a basin three ounces of bread-crumbs, half a pound of unmelted butter, two chopped and blanched shallots, some chopped mushrooms, finely cut up chives, salt, pepper, nutmeg and brandy; stuff the birds with this dressing and lay them in buttered bottomless oval molds the same size as themselves, then cook in a brisk oven. Prepare some foundation paste (No. 135), croustades the same shape and size as the snipe, and when baked and emptied fill them with delicate game cream forcemeat (No. 75); poach in a slack oven and dress in a circle on a hot dish; lay a snipe on every croustade, glaze over and fasten on one end a well cleaned head, the eyes formed of forcemeat and a round of truffles; cover with brown Madeira sauce (No. 492) and game glaze (No. 389).

(2156). BAKED SNIPE (Bécassines au Gratin).

Singe and bone twelve snipe leaving on the feet only as far as the phalanges, add a few chicken livers to the livers and intestines. Fry in butter, also one shallot, mushrooms, truffles and parsley all finely chopped, season with salt, pepper and nutmeg, set this aside to cool, then pound thoroughly. Pound a third as much panada (No. 121), add little by little six raw egg-yolks and the preparation; when thoroughly pounded, press the whole through a sieve and use half of it to fill the snipes, sew them up, truss and cover with fat pork; wrap them in paper and cook in the oven from ten to twelve minutes; when done, untie, untruss and lay them in a circle on a dish covered with the remainder of the forcemeat; fill the center with truffles, olives and mushrooms, cover with thick allemande sauce (No. 407), bestrew bread-crumbs and grated cheese on top and brown in a moderate oven.

(2157). BROILED SNIPE (Bécassines Grillées).

Split the snipe lengthwise through the back, cut off the legs, pare nicely and thrust the beak through one of the breasts (see broiled woodcock No. 2204), season, coat with oil and broil over a good fire, dress on slices of toast and pour some maitre-d'hôtel butter (No. 581) over; serve very hot.

(2158). ENGLISH SNIPE IN PAPERS (Bécassines Anglaises en Papillotes).

Cut six snipe in two lengthways, pare, beat lightly, season and toss them to stiffen both sides. Fry in butter some shallots, raw mushrooms, truffles and parsley all finely chopped, add a few spoonfuls of espagnole sauce (No. 414), besides this fry the intestines with a few chicken livers, season, pound and press through a sieve; put this pulp in with the cooled off fine herbs and divide the preparation in twenty-four parts using one of them to cover the inside of each half snipe. Cut some sheets of paper into hearts, oil, and on one side lay a half snipe, over a layer of grated fat pork and cover with the remainder of the preparation, fold the paper, crimp it all around to enclose properly the birds and dress each one on a small oval dish intended for the table, heating and browning them on this. When of a fine color and swollen considerably, remove from the oven; serve separately an espagnole sauce (No. 414) reduced with game fumet (No. 397).

(2159). SNIPE, ENGLISH, ROASTED (Bécassines Anglaises Rôties).

Pick, singe, remove the gizzard and pouch and truss the snipe thrusting the feet inside; cover the breast with a very thin slice of fat pork and cross over this as well as the joint of the thick part of the leg with the beak. Roast them from six to eight minutes, dress on slices of toast, pour the gravy over and garnish with water-cress.

(2160). SNIPE STUFFED, BORDELAISE (Bécassines Farcies, Bordelaise).

Clean the birds well, draw, remove the gizzard and pouch and chop up the intestines, mix in with them as much grated fat pork, some parsley, chives, salt and pepper; fill the snipe with this dressing and roast them in the oven; dress them on hollowed out bread crusts fried in butter and filled with marrow Bordelaise (No. 436).

(2161). SAND SNIPE ROASTED WITH WATER-CRESS (Petites Bécassines de Sable Rôties au Cresson).

Pick and singe a dozen sand snipe without drawing them; cover with very thin small slices of fat pork, and run a thin hatelet or skewer into them one after the other. Lay them on a baking sheet, pour good fat over and roast in a quick oven; when done salt and dress in pairs on bread croûtons, three inches long by one and a half wide covered over with butter; pour over some clear gravy (No. 404) and decorate with water-cress. Serve.

(2162). THRUSHES ANDRIEUX (Grives Andrieux).

A bird similar to the blackbird with speckled plumage; its meat is very succulent. Bone the the backs of eight well-cleaned thrushes, leaving on the breastbone and legs; season the meats and fill the insides with game quenelle forcemeat (No. 91), and cooked fine herbs (No. 385). Enclose the dressing, sew and truss the birds for an entrée (No. 178). Line a low saucepan with bards of fat pork, put over bottomless oval molds three inches long, two wide and half an inch high, place a thrush in each of these rings. Cut up some ham, veal, carrots and onions in three-eighths of an inch squares, place them around the birds, also a bunch of parsley garnished with thyme and bay leaf, cover with a round piece of strong buttered paper, moisten with a little stock (No. 194a) and Madeira and reduce the liquid till dry, then remoisten with broth and let boil. Close well the saucepan and push it into a moderate oven, leaving it there until the birds are nearly done, then untruss and glaze to a fine color; return them to another saucepan with a little braise stock to keep hot until ready to serve. Prepare some croustades with foundation paste (No. 135); in oval molds three and a quarter inches long, two and an eighth wide and three-quarters of an inch high. Strain the stock, skim off the fat and reduce with the same quantity of espagnole sauce (No. 414), and a gill of good Madeira into which has been infused a piece of Ceylon cinnamon; take a third part of this sauce to serve separately at the same time as the thrush and to the other two-thirds add some truffles and escalops of cooked duck's liver; fill the croustades with this, drain the birds, glaze over and lay them on top, then serve.

(2163). THRUSHES À LA BIANCA (Grives à la Bianca).

Have as many birds as guests; pick, singe and remove the gizzard, pouch and intestines and fill the inside of each one with Spanish olives stuffed with anchovies, finishing to fill up the empty space with lightly melted fresh butter. Cut as many oval croûtons as there are birds, having them three inches long by one and three-quarters wide and half an inch thick; slit them all around a quarter of an inch high and three-sixteenths of an inch from the edge; take out the inside and place a bird in this hollow; lay them in a sautéing pan the bottom covered with a bed of clarified butter and put it on the hot fire; as soon as the butter is well heated push it into the oven and after the croûtons are colored and the thrushes well cooked, take them out and drain them from the butter on a cloth, then range in a circle on a dish and fill the inside with a garnishing made of minced mushrooms and truffles mingled with half-glaze (No. 400), a tablespoonful of good olive oil and the juice of half a lemon; pour this sauce over all and serve.

(2164). BAKED THRUSHES (Grives au Gratin).

Have some well-cleaned thrushes, bone keeping on the legs; season the meats, and in each bird set a ball of forcemeat made with quenelle forcemeat (No. 91), and foies-gras from a terrine, half of each. Truss and fry in butter with a bunch of parsley garnished with thyme and bay leaf; drain off the butter, moisten with a little Madeira and stock (No. 194a), and reduce the moisture entirely while cooking slowly. Range a layer of game quenelle forcemeat mixed with cooked fine herbs (No. 385) on a dish; this layer should be seven inches in diameter by three-quarters of an inch high; place the dish on a baking-pan containing a little boiling water and poach the forcemeat in a slack oven. Dress the thrushes on this forcemeat, the breasts lying toward the outer edge and the legs in the center; cover the birds with well reduced velouté sauce (No. 415) into which mix a little game glaze (No. 398), and cooked fine herbs (No. 385); bestrew with parmesan, pour over melted butter, and brown in a hot oven or salamander (Fig. 123). Serve separately a velouté sauce (No. 415) reduced with white wine and mushroom essence (No. 392).

(2165). THRUSHES IN THE SAUCEPAN (Grives à la Casserole).

Pick and singe one dozen thrushes; remove the gizzard and pouch without drawing them, truss for roasting and fry in butter in an earthenware saucepan over a brisk fire. When done remove them from the saucepan, untruss and dress in a circle on a hot dish, the legs lying inwards; add to their stock a little game glaze (No. 398), some clear gravy (No. 404), the juice of a lemon, and a small pinch of chopped parsley. Pour the sauce over the birds, and serve.

(2166). THRUSHES AND ROBINS, ROASTED AND BROILED (Grives ou Rouges Gorges Rôtis ou Grillés).

Pick, draw, and singe six thrushes or robins; stuff them with forcemeat made of four ounces of lean cooked ham cut in dice, and as much finely chopped sausage meat; put this into a sautoir on a bright fire to cook, when cool add four ounces of truffles, and the same of foies-gras, cut in three-sixteenths of an inch squares; mix in six ounces of thick and well-reduced allemande sauce (No. 407). Truss the bird as for an entrée (No. 178), cover the breast with a grape leaf, and on this place a thin layer of fat pork; cook on the spit or in a quick oven, untruss and dress on canapés with the following gravy poured around: Fry two bay leaves in butter with one chopped shallot, salt, pepper, and fine herbs, add half a pint of white wine, and a little stock (No. 194a); let boil and simmer, then put in some game glaze (No. 398), and minced mushrooms; when ready the bay leaves should be removed.

For Broiling.—Prepare and broil the thrushes the same as quails (No. 2128), only not allowing them to cook quite as long; dress and serve the same.

(2167). VENISON. ANTELOPE. DEER (Chevreuil. Antilope. Daim).

The animal should be chosen at the age of eighteen months to two years and a half, in order to have it savory and tender. The flesh is then excellent, however its quality depends principally upon its place of abode. Those with brown hair are better than those with red. Males over three years of age are unfit to eat in certain months of the year.

The meats of the kid or doe are also excellent after they have attained the age of nine or ten months. The parts generally used are those from the saddle, leg, baron (see mutton, Fig. 334, for the cuts), quarter, haunch, hip, cutlets and the racks from the fifth rib by the neck as far down as the tenderloin, the shoulders, tenderloins and breast. The saddle tenderloin and rack are larded. The haunch and quarters are marinated from two to ten days and are also larded, but if very fresh and tender venison is eaten without being marinated.

(2168). LOIN OF DEER, CHERRY SAUCE (Longe de Daim, Sauce aux Cerises).

The loin is the part of the deer beginning at the thick loin end and reaching as far as the first rib; remove the skin from the sirloin and put the meat into an earthen dish with a quart of vinegar and two gills of water, should the vinegar be too strong; adding whole peppers, salt, bay leaf, thyme and parsley leaves. Leave it to marinate for several days, then lard with medium lardons (No. 2, Fig. 52); lay it in a baking pan, and pour over some fat; cook in a hot oven and when three-quarters done season with pepper, salt, pour over vinegar, a little broth and gravy; when done dress and cover with the skimmed stock serving a cherry sauce (No. 447) apart.

(2169). RACK OF VENISON, ROASTED COLBERT SAUCE (Carré de Chevreuil Rôti, Sauce Colbert).

Have two racks of venison of seven ribs each, bone, suppress the shine bone (see drawing for rack of mutton Fig. 343); remove the skin covering the meat and lard with lardons (No. 3, Fig. 52); put them into a cold cooked marinade (No. 114) for six hours. Roast, dress on a hot dish, pour over the well-skimmed gravy from the dripping pan, to which clear gravy (No. 404) has been added, and surround with Marchioness potatoes (No. 2797) serving a Colbert sauce (No. 451) separately.

(2170). VENISON CUTLETS À LA BURIDAN (Côtelettes de Chevreuil à la Buridan).

Have some well-pared cutlets (see mutton cutlets, No. 1590), lard them on one side only with fine larding pork (No. 4, Fig. 52), all on the same side so that the handle is on the right; put them in cold marinade for three hours. Make some coffeespoon quenelles (No. 155) with young rabbit and game quenelle forcemeat (No. 91), poach in boiling water and drain. Sauté the cutlets in butter, drain it off and replace it by a little game glaze (No. 398) and a gill of vinegar to detach the glaze from the pan, adding a little brown sauce (No. 414); allow it to boil up once or twice and then strain through a sieve and add the quenelles; glaze the cutlets and garnish with paper frills (No. 10). Dish up the cutlets in a circle, fill the center with the quenelles, and serve the sauce separately. Garnish around with small round croquettes made like croquettes à la trimalcion (No. 3016).

(2171). VENISON CUTLETS À LA CAUCHOISE (Côtelettes de Chevreuil à la Cauchoise).

Cut and pare some venison cutlets and lay them in a sautéing pan with clarified butter; sauté on a brisk fire, then remove from the pan, keeping them warm; detach the glaze with a little white wine and poivrade sauce (No. 523), roll the cutlets in this to have them well covered, take out and trim the handles; range them in a circle and fill the center with some cream of game (No. 2240), and all around with a garnishing made of cabbage purée, mingled with egg-yolks and velouté sauce, then poached in mousseline mold (No. 4, Fig. 138).

(2172). VENISON CUTLETS À LA FINANCIÈRE (Côtelettes de Chevreuil à la Financière).

Prepare some venison cutlets the same size as those of mutton (No. 1590); lard them on one side only, but all on the same side, with the handles on the right; put them into a buttered sautoir with the larded side uppermost and cook them in a hot oven; finally drain off the butter from the sautoir, glaze the cutlets with a brush, trim them with paper frills (No. 10) and dress in a circle on a low venison quenelle forcemeat border; fill the center with a financiere garnishing (No. 667).

(2173). VENISON CUTLETS, DEVILED (Côtelettes de Chevreuil à la Diable).

Coat some cutlets with mustard and immerse them in melted butter; roll in bread-crumbs and broil. Have some shallots fried in butter and moisten them with a light poivrade sauce (No. 522) and game glaze (No. 398), adding mushrooms, lean cooked ham cut in small squares and chopped parsley. Dress the cutlets crown shape, pour the sauce over and decorate the handle bones with frills (No. 10).

(2174). VENISON CUTLETS, TOMATO PARISIAN SAUCE (Côtelettes de Chevreuil, Sauce Tomate Parisienne).

Pare some venison cutlets, season with salt and pepper and sauté in clarified butter or oil over a brisk fire; when of a fine color and sufficiently done, drain off the fat and detach the glaze from the pan with a little white wine, adding a little brown sauce (No. 414) and meat glaze (No. 402). Dress the cutlets after trimming them with paper frills (No. 10) intercalating them with half heart-shaped croûtons and pour the sauce in the center; serve a tomato Parisian sauce (No. 550) separately.

(2175). VENISON CUTLETS WITH CHESTNUT PURÉE (Côtelettes de Chevreuil à la Purée de Marrons).

Pare some venison cutlets the same as mutton cutlet No. 1590, season with salt and dip in oil or melted butter, roll in bread-crumbs, equalize the surfaces and broil to a fine color, trim the handles and dress in a circle, filling the center with a consistent and mellow chestnut purée (No. 712); serve with a half-glaze sauce (No. 413) reduced with Madeira and game fumet (No. 397).

(2176). ÉPIGRAMMES OF ROEBUCK, MARINADE SAUCE WITH TRUFFLES (Épigrammes de Chevreuil, Sauce Marinade aux Truffes).

Pare some roebuck cutlets, put them into a deep dish and season with salt, pepper, mignonette, thyme, bay leaf, parsley leaves, olive oil and lemon juice. Prepare a game quenelle forcemeat (No. 91) with half venison and half rabbit meat, lay eight half heart-shaped bottomless molds, they being three and a half inches long by two wide and half an inch high, on sheets of buttered paper, fill them with the quenelle forcemeat and poach lightly in a slack oven; as soon as sufficiently done to bread-crumb, remove, unmold and dip in beaten eggs, then in bread-crumbs, smoothing this with the blade of a knife. Just when prepared to serve, drain the cutlets, wipe and sauté them in butter, fry the quenelles to a fine color, then drain off the cutlets, trim them with paper frills (No. 10) and dress in a circle on a hot dish, alternating them with the quenelles (they to be arranged with the pointed ends uppermost), pour a little marinade sauce (No. 496) with Madeira into the bottom of the dish and serve a sauce-boat of the same, mingling into it three tablespoonfuls of truffles cut in one-eighth inch squares.

(2177). DEER OR ROEBUCK FILLETS À LA LORENZO (Filets de Daim ou de Chevreuil à la Lorenzo).

Pare two minion fillets of a deer or a roebuck; suppress the superficial skin covering them and marinate for five or six hours in a little cooked marinade (No. 114), drain, lard the entire upper surface with lardons (No. 4, Fig. 52), range them on a small buttered baking pan, one beside the other, cover with buttered paper and cook in a moderate oven for half an hour, until well done. Remove and cut them into slightly bias slices, and dress either in a straight row or else in a circle, and fill the sides or inside with braised chestnuts (No. 654), stuffed Spanish olives (No. 695), mushroom heads, round, medium truffles and large capers; cover with a Pignola Italian sauce (No. 520) and game glaze (No. 398) and trim around with potato croquettes (No. 2782).

(2178). ROEBUCK—HAUNCH OR QUARTER—À LA BOUCHARD (Hanche ou Quartier de Chevreuil à la Bouchard).

Suppress all the nerves from a good haunch of venison; lay it in a cold cooked marinade (No. 114), for two days, then drain, pare it on the kernel end and lard with lardons (No. 2, Fig. 52), range it on the cradle spit (No. 116) and let roast before a good fire from three-quarters of an hour to an hour. Dress and garnish around with stuffed peppers and rissoles of brain, Princetown (No. 947), mixed with a chopped sauce (No. 539), serving pimentade sauce (No. 521) separately.

(2179). ROEBUCK—HAUNCH OR QUARTER—À LA LYTTON (Hanche ou Quartier de Chevreuil à la Lytton).

Choose a very fat haunch of roebuck; bone the thick loin end, sprinkle salt over, and coat the surfaces with butter: wrap it up in buttered paper, then in a flat of paste made with three pounds of flour into which is added an ounce of salt, three eggs, and just sufficient water to form a very firm dough; place this in a wet cloth, and leave it for several hours, then roll it out to an eighth of an inch in thickness; wrap it all around the meat; fasten the two ends and sides by wetting them both and have one overlap the other to prevent any fissure whatever, then cover it all with buttered paper; lay it on a cradle spit (Fig. 116), or else in a moderate oven in a baking-pan. The length of time to cook it depends upon its size; for a medium haunch of venison it will take two hours; deer require three hours. Remove the paper, brown the paste nicely, and serve with a poivrade sauce (No. 522), finished with currant jelly and cold sour apple marmalade (No. 3674).

(2180). JUGGED VENISON (Civet de Chevreuil)

To jug venison use the breasts, neck, shoulder, and thick loin end (the shoulder and loin ends are to be larded through the meat with seasoned lardons (No. 2, Fig. 52). Cut the meats into pieces an inch and a half to two inches square, and for three pounds of it allow six ounces of unsmoked bacon cut in quarter-inch dice; fry the whole in butter, and when stiffened dredge with three table-spoonfuls of flour; let brown slightly, then moisten with six gills of red wine, and three gills of stock (No. 194a), adding a bunch of parsley garnished with thyme and bay leaf, some dry orange peel, a whole clove of garlic, and a seasoning of pepper and salt; cook slowly for one hour and a half, then put in three dozen small onions fried in butter, and three-quarters of a pound of small mushrooms; skim the fat from the surface, and add two gills of brandy, one gill of Madeira, and the strained juice of two lemons, or else three tablespoonfuls of good vinegar. Pile up the meats on a dish; season and reduce the sauce, suppress the parsley, and pour it over the meats; surround with heart-shaped bread croûtons fried in oil, then serve.

(2181). VENISON—SLICES OF KERNEL—À LA HUSSARDE (Tranches de Noix de Chevreuil à la Hussarde).

Cut off some slices from the kernel of a haunch, five-eighths of an inch thick; pare into ovals each one to weigh about half a pound, and marinate in cold cooked marinade (No. 114) for two hours; sauté them rare in butter, and dress on a hussarde sauce (No. 482).

(2182). VENISON—SLICES OF KERNEL—IN PAPERS (Tranches de Noix de Chevreuil en Papillotes).

Pare oval-shaped some slices half an inch thick cut from the kernel of the haunch; they should each weigh five ounces after being trimmed; broil them rare, and then wrap in heart-shaped sheets of oiled paper; on top of each slice lay a thin slice of fat pork, and over this some well seasoned and thick Duxelle (No. 385), then close the paper, crimp it all around, and lay them on a buttered dish that can be placed in the oven; and on which they should be served; push it in the oven for a few moments to serve when a fine color.

(2183). ROEBUCK, LEG OF, À LA FRANCATELLI (Cuissot de Chevreuil à la Francatelli).

Have a leg of roebuck weighing about ten pounds; pare and lard it with lardons (No. 2, Fig. 52), and marinate for six hours in cold cooked marinade (No. 114); then roast in the oven, bast-

Fig. 405.

ing frequently with melted butter while cooking, this operation taking about an hour and a half to an hour and three-quarters; salt. Dress, garnish around with bouchées (No. 11) filled with chestnut purée (No. 712). Serve a venison sauce (No. 556) in a sauce-boat. Hand around currant jelly the same time as the meat.

(2184). MINCED VENISON (Emincé de Chevreuil).

Cut a piece of cooked saddle of venison into even-sized slices; pare and range them in a small sautoir. Reduce the value of two gills of half-glaze sauce (No. 413), incorporating into it a few spoonfuls of the venison gravy and a few spoonfuls of raw cream; when this sauce becomes succulent, finish it with a dash of good vinegar and pour it over the slices of venison. Heat these meats well over a slow fire without allowing the sauce to boil and baste frequently with the same. Dress the stew the same as for minced partridge (No. 2090), either inside a border or else on a dish, and surround with fried Villeroi quenelles (No. 733) or crusts of bread hollowed out and filled in with a cooked salpicon of truffles; strain the sauce over. This mince may also be surrounded with stuffed Spanish olives (No. 695).

(2185). SADDLE OF ANTELOPE, HUNTRESS STYLE (Selle d'Antilope à la Chasseresse).

Procure a fine thick saddle of antelope; raise the sirloin from one part, remove the skin and lard with small lardons (No.3, Fig.52); lift up the minion fillets, suppress their sinews and score with large slices of truffles; pare the remainder of the meat and chop it up with as much fat pork, season with mixed spices (No. 168) and add two eggs. Make a stock with the parings and bones of the antelope. Marinate the sirloin and minion fillets and cook them in a brisk oven. Make small balls with the chopped meats; bread-crumb, English style (No. 13), and bake them in a slow oven; reduce some espagnole sauce (No. 414) and Madeira with the prepared stock, and when a consistent sauce is obtained, put in the meat balls, whole chestnuts and stuffed olives (No. 395). Prepare a bread croûton five inches wide, eight long and two and a half high; hollow it out lengthways on both ends and on each side form semicircles two inches in diameter; carve the croûtons nicely, fry in butter, and fasten firmly to a dish. Cut the sirloin up lengthwise on the bias, lay the pieces in the hollow and the minion fillets in the center. Fasten a skewer garnished with cocks'-combs and kidneys and crawfish in the middle, and one on each of the two ends, and around with croustades garnished with the above prepared garnishing. Serve a huntress sauce (No. 481) with the meat.

(2186). SADDLE OF VENISON À L'ATHALIN (Selle de Chevreuil à l'Athalin).

For cutting up a venison saddle see Fig. 322. Pare a saddle of venison, removing the skin covering the sirloin; lard it with lardons (No. 2, Fig. 52) across the grain of the meat and marinate for twelve hours in cold cooked marinade (No. 114). Put it in a baking pan with bards of fat pork on top and the marinade; pour butter over and when half cooked baste with more butter and besprinkle with flour. Set the parings into a sautoir with a stalk of celery, onions containing cloves and a bunch of parsley garnished with garlic, thyme and bay leaf; moisten with red wine and stock (No. 194a), boil and simmer for one hour, then thicken lightly with a little kneaded butter (No. 579); remove the saddle from the roasting pan and pour in some gravy (No. 404) to detach the glaze, then add it to the sauce and strain the whole through a tammy, skim off the fat and place a third of the sauce on a dish, dressing the saddle on top; serve the remainder separately in a sauce-boat and some currant jelly on a plate.

(2187). SADDLE OF VENISON À LA MACMAHON (Selle de Chevreuil à la MacMahon).

Pare and marinate a saddle the same as for à l'Athalin (No. 2186). One hour before dinner drain and roast it in the oven, and when done skim off the fat and put in half a pint of the marinade and as much raw cream; reduce the sauce, cut some medium-sized apples in quarters, range them in a liberally buttered sautoir, bestrew with a little powdered sugar and pour butter over, place in the oven, and when cooked dress the saddle, glaze and pour over a little gravy (No. 404); range the apples on each side and serve the sauce separately.

(2188). SADDLE OF VENISON À LA MORTON (Selle de Chevreuil à la Morton).

Pare, lard and roast a saddle of venison; as soon as it is done cut off the tenderloin and replace it without deforming the meat, then pour over a little gravy (No. 404) and garnish around with macaroni croquettes, glazed turnips, fried Jerusalem artichokes, boiled white beans and boiled potato balls three-quarters of an inch in size; serve currant jelly apart, also a poivrade sauce (No. 522) having a little Worcestershire added and the whole stirred with some maître d'hôtel butter (No. 581), when ready to serve.

(2189). SADDLE OF VENISON, TYROLESE STYLE (Selle de Chevreuil à la Tyrolienne).

Prepare and roast the saddle the same as the one with currant jelly (No. 2193); detach the glaze from the pan with a little port wine, a small quantity of espagnole sauce (No. 414), and into it put as much currant jelly, then strain through a fine sieve. Lay the meat on a long dish, pour some good gravy (No. 404) over and surround with tartlets of sour apple marmalade covered with puff paste parings (No. 146); serve the sauce apart.

(2190). SADDLE OF VENISON—LARDED—AIGRELETTE SAUCE (Selle de Chevreuil à la Sauce Aigrelette).

Lard the saddle the same as explained for saddle with currant sauce (No. 2193), put it in a dish, the minion fillet side uppermost and the larded side underneath, season with mignonette, cloves, garlic, vinegar, onions, thyme, bay leaf and lemon juice; after it has been steeping for six hours, remove and roast it in the oven or on a spit and dress on a hot oval dish; serve an aigrelette sauce (No. 544) separately.

(2191). SADDLE OF VENISON, GASTRONOME (Selle de Chevreuil, Gastronome).

Trim and lard a saddle of venison; lay it in a baking pan covered with slices of fat pork, carrots, onions and a bunch of parsley garnished with thyme and bay leaf; moisten with white wine and stock (No. 194a) and cook in the oven, basting at frequent intervals with white melted butter; when done and of a fine color cut it up lengthways of the meat and reconstruct it as before, strain the stock, remove all the fat and reduce, add Marsala wine, serve the sauce separately. Garnish the ends with mushrooms or cèpes and olives stuffed with anchovies, and gastronome potatoes (No. 2789) at the ends. Serve also a Colbert sauce (No. 451) with the meat.

(2192). SADDLE OF VENISON—BREADED—BLACK CHERRY SAUCE (Selle de Chevreuil Panée Sauce aux Cerises Noires).

Instead of larding the saddle, it can be breaded when three-quarters cooked by sprinkling over with white bread-crumbs or pumpernickel; pour on some butter and brown in a hot oven. A black cherry sauce (No. 447) seasoned with cinnamon accompanies this.

(2193). SADDLE OF VENISON, PORT WINE SAUCE AND CURRANT JELLY (Selle de Chevreuil à la Sauce Oporto et à la Gelée de Groseilles).

Cut the saddle from a roebuck the same as a saddle of mutton, leaving one rib adhere to the end of the loin on both sides; remove the haunch, cutting it off rounded or straight, while crossing the thick loin end; pare the surplus fat and remove the skin carefully that covers the sirloin: lard it with two rows of lardons (No. 3, Fig. 52) inserting them into the meat across the saddle, and the entire length of the sirloin. Roast it either on the spit or in the oven, detach the pan, glaze with a little gravy (No. 404), strain this through a sieve, skim off the fat and pour it over the saddle. Serve separately, but at the same time some currant jelly or port wine, and jelly sauce made by dissolving the jelly in port wine and thickening it with brown sauce (No. 414).

(2194). SADDLE OF VENISON—ROASTED (Selle de Chevreuil Rôtie).

FIG. 406.

Unless the meat is far advanced it is unnecessary to marinate it; simply pare the pieces and suppress the skin so as to be able to lard the flesh with larding pork, either crosswise or lengthwise, with lardons. Saddles and quarters of venison are roasted either on the spit or in the oven, basting over with butter. A small saddle of venison takes forty minutes to cook. Roasted venison is served either with a clear gravy (No. 404), a brown sauce (No. 414) with lemon juice added, or else a sauce prepared with the stock it was cooked in, mingled with half-glaze (No. 400), then reduced with raw cream and finished with lemon juice or a dash of vinegar. Or it can also be served with currant jelly dissolved in espagnole sauce (No. 414) and port wine.

(2195). VENISON GRENADINS À LA ROYALE—TENDERLOIN (Grenadins de Filet de Chevreuil à la Royale).

Trim off some grenadins from the minion fillets, each one to weigh five ounces, and pare into half hearts; after removing the sinews lard with fine larding pork (No. 4, Fig. 52), and marinate for twelve hours; dry, wipe and sauté in good hot fat; drain, glaze and dress in a circle, filling the center with potato quenelles breaded and fried in clarified butter; serve a Colbert sauce (No. 451) separately.

(2196). VENISON NOISETTES À LA THIERRY—TENDERLOIN (Noisettes de Filet de Chevreuil à la Thierry).

Cut the tenderloin into slices, each to weigh four ounces when pared and rounded; lay them in a sautoir with melted butter, season with salt, mignonette, a whole clove of garlic and a bay leaf. Just before serving place the saucepan on a hot fire and sauté them quickly; lay each noisette on a bread croûton fried in butter of the same diameter and a quarter of an inch thick; dress them in a circle and in the center have a garnishing of game quenelles made with a coffeespoon (No. 155), truffles cut in the shape of crescent olives mixed with espagnole sauce (No. 414), reduced with game essence (No. 389) and Madeira wine.

(2197). VENISON TOURNEDOS ST. HUBERT—TENDERLOIN (Tournedos de Filet de Chevreuil St. Hubert).

Pare some slices to weigh three ounces each, season and sauté them briskly in a sauté pan with butter; drain, wipe, glaze and dress on a bed of soubise purée (No. 723); garnish around with Spanish olives stuffed with anchovies. Serve separately a tomato sauce (No. 549), mixed with grated horseradish.

(2198). WOODCOCKS À LA CAVOUR (Bécasses à la Cavour).

Cut six woodcocks in four each and withdraw the intestines, discarding the pouch and gizzard. Fry the quartered birds in butter with some truffles, mushrooms and escaloped sweetbreads; moisten with a little white wine and season with salt, pepper and finely cut-up chives. Fry also the intestines in butter, with the parings, some minced ham, carrots and onions, mushroom parings, all well chopped, thyme and bay leaf; wet with a little white wine when cooked, press through a tammy and add this pulp to the woodcocks; moisten once more with white wine and a little brown sauce (No. 414), despumate well and reduce to a proper degree; dress the meat in a border made of risot (No. 739) and pour the sauce over.

(2199). WOODCOCKS À LA DUMAS (Bécasses à la Dumas).

Pick, singe and truss eight woodcocks, put them into a saucepan with fresh butter and fry over a brisk fire, adding chopped shallots, salt, pepper and nutmeg. When the birds are cooked drain off the fat, add to their stock the juice of one lemon, a quarter of a bottleful of champagne and half a pint of espagnole sauce (No. 414); reduce and put in some whole truffles, cocks'-combs and kidneys. Dress the woodcocks on some stuffed crusts (No. 51) and place the garnishing around.

(2200). BREASTS OF WOODCOCKS À LA DIANE (Ailes ou Filets de Bécasses à la Diane).

Raise the breasts from six well-cleaned woodcocks, remove all the sinews and skin and stiffen them while heating in a little butter; place them under a light weight. Make a dressing with the intestines, removing the gizzard and pouch, adding a little chicken liver and grated fat pork, chopped parsley and seasoning; fill some hollow crusts with this, pour butter over and poach in a slack oven; on each crust lay a woodcock breast brushed with game glaze (No. 398), then dress them in a circle, stick either a whole or half head in each croûton and fill the center with olive-shaped game quenelles (Fig. 83); cover with brown Périgord sauce (No. 516).

(2201). BREASTS OF WOODCOCKS À LA HOUSTON (Ailes ou Filets de Bécasses à la Houston).

Fry quickly in butter six breasts of woodcocks previously cleaned, singed, and seasoned; as soon as cooked, drain them off. Cook the small part of the intestines before pounding and rubbing them through a sieve. Prepare a little game quenelle forcemeat (No. 91), mix in with it an equal quantity of liver baking forcemeat (No. 64), and the pounded intestines. With this preparation fill a smooth buttered border mold (Fig 139), having the bottom rounded, and poach it in a bain-marie. Take a part of the woodcock carcasses, to make a good fumet (No. 397), and after it has been strained and the fat removed, incorporate it into a good brown sauce (No. 414) while reducing, also a few spoonfuls of Madeira. When the sauce has attained succulence, strain it over the woodcock breasts, and keep them in a bain-marie. Fry quickly in a frying-pan, with oil and melted butter, half a pound of peeled truffles cut in slices or in large shreds, season and drain off the fat, pour over a few spoonfuls of Madeira wine, and reduce; then add it to the prepared breasts, and dress the whole in the inside of the border, unmolded, on a hot dish.

(2202). BREASTS OF WOODCOCKS A LA MANCELLE (Ailes ou Filets de Bécasses à la Mancelle).

First clean and singe six woodcocks, then roast them; remove all the breast part, and cut off the remainder of the meat to pound with the same quantity of rice; obtain a purée, and combine it with a little espagnole (No. 414) reduced with game fumet (No. 397). Cut some thin slices of foies-gras, pare them into ovals, and dip in flour, then fry in butter; dress the fillets alternating them with the slices of foies-gras; pour into the bottom of the dish a little espagnole sauce (No. 414) reduced with woodcock fumet (No. 397) and Madeira wine, and to the remainder of the sauce add truffles and mushrooms cut in one-eighth inch squares, serving this separately.

(2203). BREASTS OF WOODCOCKS À LA VATEL (Ailes ou Filets de Bécasses à la Vatel).

Raise the breasts from six fine woodcocks, remove the skin and sinews, and fry them in butter over a brisk fire. Fill some heart-shaped bottomless molds with a game quenelle forcemeat made from the woodcocks' legs and parings and young rabbit meat; poach them slowly in a slack oven, unmold, cool off, and lay on buttered paper, coat the tops with woodcock cream forcemeat, made as game cream forcemeat (No. 75), and dress the breasts two on each croûton; cover entirely with woodcock cream forcemeat, smooth with a knife, shaping them into hearts, run the beak through from side to side between the forcemeat and fillet. Bestrew with finely chopped coral sifted through a sieve and imitate a flame with yellow tinted game quenelle forcemeat pushed through a cornet, on which place thin fillets of tongue. Pour butter over the whole and push into a moderate oven; when removed lay them on top of a sauce made with game fumet (No. 397) and essence of truffles (No. 395), serving a financière garnishing (No. 667), cut in salpicon (No. 741) apart.

FIG. 407.

(2204). BROILED WOODCOCKS (Bécasses Grillées).

Split the woodcocks lengthwise through the back; open entirely, beat lightly, pare, salt, and coat over with oil; broil them over a brisk fire (for they must be served quite rare) and when done dress them on oval toasts (No. 51); cover entirely with maître d'hôtel butter (No. 581), and serve very hot, surrounding the toast with sliced lemon (No. 113).

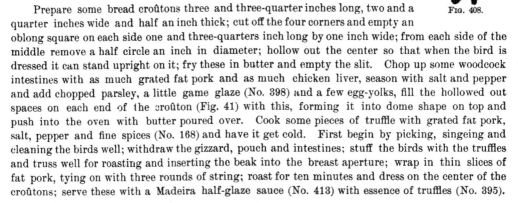

FIG. 408.

(2205). WOODCOCKS ON CANAPÉS À LA PÉRIGORD (Bécasses sur Canapés à la Périgord).

Prepare some bread croûtons three and three-quarter inches long, two and a quarter inches wide and half an inch thick; cut off the four corners and empty an oblong square on each side one and three-quarters inch long by one inch wide; from each side of the middle remove a half circle an inch in diameter; hollow out the center so that when the bird is dressed it can stand upright on it; fry these in butter and empty the slit. Chop up some woodcock intestines with as much grated fat pork and as much chicken liver, season with salt and pepper and add chopped parsley, a little game glaze (No. 398) and a few egg-yolks, fill the hollowed out spaces on each end of the croûton (Fig. 41) with this, forming it into dome shape on top and push into the oven with butter poured over. Cook some pieces of truffle with grated fat pork, salt, pepper and fine spices (No. 168) and have it get cold. First begin by picking, singeing and cleaning the birds well; withdraw the gizzard, pouch and intestines; stuff the birds with the truffles and truss well for roasting and inserting the beak into the breast aperture; wrap in thin slices of fat pork, tying on with three rounds of string; roast for ten minutes and dress on the center of the croûtons; serve these with a Madeira half-glaze sauce (No. 413) with essence of truffles (No. 395).

(2206). WOODCOCKS ROASTED (Bécasses Rôties).

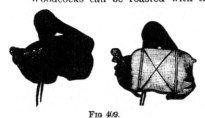

Woodcocks can be roasted with their intestines or else drawn; the gizzard and pouch must always be removed, but the necks left on. Singe the birds, truss by inserting the beaks through the legs (Fig. 409); lard over and lay them on the spit, roast for twelve to sixteen minutes before a bright fire, basting over with butter and laying pieces of bread in the dripping pan, that is if the birds are not drawn; if they are, then cook their intestines separately with melted fat pork and a few good chicken livers, finishing them the same as the woodcocks on canapés à la Périgord (No. 2205). After removing the birds from the spit, salt them over, dress on a dish with the crusts and sliced lemon placed around; serve some gravy separately. The beak may be stuck in the stomach in front so that in case the bird is cut in two the head will be divided equally.

FIG 409.

(2207). SALMIS OF WOODCOCKS À LA BEAUMONT (Salmis de Bécasses à la Beaumont).

Roast five whole woodcocks, remove the intestines and cut each bird into five pieces, suppress all the skin and lay them in a sautoir. Pound the parings and carcasses, place the purée in a saucepan with three finely cut up shallots and a bunch of parsley garnished with a bay leaf. Moisten with a pint and a half of red or white wine or else champagne according to taste; reduce to half, then add a pint of espagnole (No. 414); let simmer on the side of the range for half an hour, being careful to remove all vestige of fat and scum as fast as it arises to the surface; pass the sauce through a tammy and reduce it to the consistency of a light one, adding some peeled and cut up truffles or mushrooms, or even both. Dress the woodcock on a dish and surround with the truffles or mushrooms; garnish around with hollow crusts filled with the intestines, as much chicken liver and half as much grated fat pork seasoned with salt, pepper and chopped parsley; then poach in the oven.

(2208). SALMIS OF WOODCOCKS À LA SANDFORD (Salmis de Bécasses à la Sandford).

Roast six woodcocks very rare; cut them in four, lift off all the skin and place the birds in an alcohol chafing dish; season with salt, pepper, add a little blanched shallot, three gills of wine, the juice of a lemon, a little fresh bread raspings and an ounce and a half of butter; simmer for a few moments, then serve.

(2209). WOODCOCKS STUFFED (Bécasses Farcies).

Bone three woodcocks, remove the best part of their breast meat and cut these into large dice; lay them in a vessel and add an equal quantity of truffles and as much foies-gras; season these meats, and pour over two tablespoonfuls of Madeira. Pound the leg meats with those of three wild pigeons or as much of rabbit, adding a third as much panada (No. 121), and four egg-yolks; season and strain this forcemeat. Melt four tablespoonfuls of grated fat pork, add to it the woodcock intestines, also five or six good chicken livers, season highly and leave stand till cold, then strain and mix the forcemeat with this, also the meats and truffles laid away in the vessel. Fill the woodcock with this preparation, shaping each one to resemble a boned turkey, and wrap a piece of fat pork around; attach them firmly in separate pieces of thin muslin, tying it on tight to keep them in proper shape, then cook in some good stock on a moderate fire for one hour; leave them in this partly cold, then drain, unwrap. and tie them up again tight until thoroughly cold, keeping them in shape, but not under the pressure of any weight. Unwrap them half an hour before serving, stand them upright in a saucepan with a little of their own stock, reduced to a half glaze; heat them in a very slack oven, basting over frequently, then dress them in a triangle on a forcemeat border, poached in the oven and turned out on a dish, having fastened to the center a portion of bread covered with some of the forcemeat. Place in the angles the three birds' heads, slightly cooked and glazed over with a brush; fasten three skewers garnished with truffles in the summit of the pad and cover the woodcock, and border lightly over with a brown sauce (No. 414) prepared with the stock and the truffle parings.

MISCELLANEOUS ENTRÉES

(2210). BORDER OF CHICKEN FORCEMEAT FILLED WITH CHICKEN BLANQUETTE À LA TOULOUSE (Bordure de Farce de Volaille Garnie d'une Blanquette de Poulet à la Toulouse).

Raise the fillets from six young, fat chickens; roll them in a buttered sautoir. With the leg meats prepare a chicken and rice quenelle forcemeat (No. 79). Have a fancy border mold, butter it and fill it up with the forcemeat, place this border in a sautoir and poach for half an hour.

FIG. 410.

Pare the fillet pieces, sauté them in butter, drain this off and replace it by fat béchamel (No. 409), and minced truffles added to it; keep it warm in a bain-marie. Trim a dozen truffles into round shapes an inch and a quarter in diameter, cook them in a little Madeira, add some meat glaze (No. 402), and put into a bain-marie. Unmold the border, dress the chicken blanquette in the center. Cover with a Toulouse garnishing (No. 766), and on the top of the garnishing arrange the prepared truffles.

(2211). BORDER OF FISH FORCEMEAT À LA DUCHESS WITH CRAWFISH TAILS AND MORILS (Bordure de Farce de Poisson à la Duchesse aux Queues d'Ecrevisses et Morilles).

Prepare a not too light cream fish forcemeat (No. 76) with some pike meat; also prepare a plentiful garnishing with good morils blanched and cooked, unshelled crawfish tails, slices from the tails of small freshly cooked lobsters, and poached oysters; lay all of these in a flat saucepan, and keep covered. Half an hour before serving fill a fancy border mold with the prepared forcemeat, and

FIG. 411.

poach for twenty-five minutes in a bain-marie. Besides this put on to reduce three gills of velouté sauce (No. 415), incorporating into it slowly a few spoonfuls of good court bouillon (No. 38), and the oyster and crawfish broth; when this sauce becomes succulent, strain it over the garnishing, heat up without boiling, and finish with a piece of red butter (No. 580). At the last moment turn the border over on a hot dish and fill the center with the garnishings, dressing them in a dome without any sauce; on this lay four pretty cooked crawfish, having them whole, only the tails being shelled; place a small round truffle on the summit, and serve the sauce apart.

(2212). BORDER OF RISOT VALENCIENNES (Bordure de Risot Valenciennes).

Blanch and cook six beef palates in a good mirepoix stock (No. 419), drain and leave them to cool under a weight, pare and cut up into large Julienne; lay these in a sautoir with three gills of Madeira sauce, simmer on a slow fire for a quarter of an hour, and when very tender add half the quantity

Fig. 412.

of freshly cooked truffles cut like the fillets. Have a good risot prepared with about a half pound of Piedmontese rice (No. 739); as soon as done remove and mix in one spoonful of sweet Spanish pepper reduced to a pulp; cover the saucepan and keep it for five to six minutes on the side of the range and then finish with butter and grated parmesan; season to taste. With this rice fill a buttered border mold, as shown in the cut, place it for a few moments in the heater to harden, then unmold it on a dish and fill the center with beef palate preparation; serve at once.

(2213). BORDER OF RISOT OF LOBSTERS OR SPINY LOBSTERS (Bordure de Risot de Homards ou de Langoustes).

Boil two good lobsters or spiny lobsters in a white wine court-bouillon (No. 419), drain, and five to six minutes later detach the tails from the body and keep them warm in a few spoonfuls of their liquor. Cook four or five uniform-sized peeled truffles in Madeira wine, cut them up in broad slices of an inch thickness and keep them warm in a saucepan with their own broth that has been strained and mixed with a little melted meat glaze (No. 402). With half a pound of good Piedmontese rice prepare a risot (No. 739) cooked with plain fish broth (No. 195) and a small spoonful of prepared red pepper (No. 168); as soon as done finish with fine butter and fresh parmesan; mold

Fig. 413.

it in a buttered border mold, as shown in the cut, and keep it slightly warm. Split two lobster bodies, take out all the creamy parts, press through a sieve and lay it aside. Chop half of the shells, fry them in oil for a few moments and sprinkle with a pinch of prepared red pepper (No. 168), then moisten with two or three gills of good court-bouillon and white wine (No. 419); cook slowly for ten to twelve minutes, strain the liquid, free it of fat and reduce to a half-glaze; thicken with a gill and a half of good tomato sauce (No. 549), and reduce it once more for a few moments, then remove from the fire and finish with two spoonfuls of the creamy parts from the bodies, add some butter, stir vigorously and lastly put in two or three spoonfuls of the reduced truffle broth. Suppress the tail shells hastily, pare the meats, trim off the thin ends and cut all the pieces in not too thick slices; lay them in a sautoir and cover with a few spoonfuls of the sauce buttered at the very last mome... Unmold the border on a hot dish and in the center place the slices of lobster and the truffles in a pyramidical form; pour part of the sauce over, serving what remains in a separate sauce-boat.

(2214). ROUDINS OF CHICKEN À L'ÉCARLATE (Boudins de Volaille à l'Écarlate).

This entrée is dressed on a low rice croustade (Fig. 9a) slightly hollowed on top. First cook two small red beef tongues in boiling water with the pared meats taken from a large raw chicken, prepare a quenelle forcemeat (No. 89), keeping it rather firm; season tastily and smooth by working it with a spoon, then finish by incorporating in slowly some béchamel sauce (No. 409) reduced with chopped fresh mushrooms until it becomes succulent and thick, but do not pass it through a sieve. After the sauce is well mixed with the forcemeat divide it into seven or eight equal parts and roll these into pieces, two and a half inches long and three-quarters of an inch thick, on a floured table, press them down a little with the blade of a knife to decrease their thickness. Range these boudins as soon as done one beside the other on a lightly buttered raised-edge baking tin and cover with salted hot water, then heat the liquid until the forcemeat hardens. Drain the boudins on a cloth, pare them evenly and dip them in beaten egg-whites, then in white bread-crumbs. Now drain the tongues, cut them into lengthwise slices not too thin, and pare them at once, giving them an oval shape, then cutting them lengthwise through the center; roll them in a sautoir with half-glaze (No. 400) so as to cover them lightly and dress them in a row, alternating each one with a boudin; cover these with a little good reduced velouté (No. 415) mixed with a montglas composed of chicken with half as many truffles and mushrooms cut in fillets. Surround the base with a chain of small round truffles glazed over with a brush. Send to the table at the same time a sauce-boat of velouté sauce.

(2215). BOUDINS OF CHICKEN À LA SOUBISE (Boudins de Volaille à la Soubise).

Have half a pound of leaf lard chopped up very finely, add to it one ounce of soaked and pressed bread-crumbs, pound the two together, then press through a sieve. Put this into a bowl with half a pound of raw chicken meat minced very finely, mingle well together and gradually add half a pint of soubise onion purée (No. 723), nine raw egg-yolks, a quarter of a pound of raw truffles (if obtainable), cut in three-sixteenths inch squares, and with this preparation fill some ready prepared sheep's casings three inches long and one inch in diameter, not too full, throw them into boiling water, remove them almost immediately and prick them with a larding needle, then broil them over a very slow fire; serve a soubise sauce (No. 543) in a separate sauce-boat.

(2216). BOUDINS OF CHICKEN AU CARDINAL (Boudins de Volaille au Cardinal).

Prepare a consistent chicken forcemeat (No. 75), cut half of a medium-sized onion into small one-eighth inch squares, blanch, refresh and drain, then fry them colorless in butter, stirring continuously; drain well and mix this with the forcemeat. Butter sixteen molds the shape of the half of a small boudin (this shape is well shown in the quenelles, Fig. 81), three and five-eighths inches long by one and three-eighths inches wide. Scatter some finely chopped lobster coral over the insides of these molds and fill them up with the forcemeat, leaving an empty space in the center; fill this with a salpicon composed of truffles, red beef tongue and mushrooms cut in three-sixteenths inch squares and mingled with some well-reduced allemande sauce (No. 407). After they are ready place eight on top of the other eight, the salpicon to be in the center; twenty minutes before serving lay them in a flat saucepan one beside the other, pour some boiling water over and poach without boiling, then drain and unmold on a napkin. Dress them in a row on a dish, one close to the other, on a lobster sauce (No. 488), buttered with lobster butter (No. 580); serve some of the same sauce in a sauce-boat and throw over some chopped lobster coral.

(2217). BOUDINS OF CHICKEN WITH MONTEBELLO SAUCE (Boudins de Volaille à la Sauce Montebello).

Put a pound and a quarter of chicken quenelle forcemeat (No. 89) into a vessel; smooth and mix in a quarter as much salpicon of truffles and cooked foies-gras. Lift the forcemeat with a tablespoon and push it with the finger to have it fall on a floured table; roll these pieces into sausage shapes, flatten a little on both sides with the blade of a knife, then range them at once in small quantities on a smooth and floured saucepan lid without once handling them. Place a sauté pan on the fire with water, salt it when it reaches boiling point, then slide in the boudins, boil up once and remove to the side of the range, leaving in the boudins until the forcemeat hardens, then lift them out with a skimmer and lay them on a cloth, one next to the other, to wipe and pare lightly. Dip them into beaten egg, roll in fresh white bread-crumbs and place them on the bottom of a sautoir with clarified butter to brown both sides while turning them over carefully; drain and dish in a circle on a Montebello sauce (No. 502).

(2218). BOUDINS OF GAME À LA BERCHOUX (Boudins de Gibier à la Berchoux).

Cook on a slow fire half a pound of chopped leaf lard with a quarter of a pound of chopped onions, and let get cold. Have half a pound of cooked and finely chopped game meat and seven ounces of soaked and well-pressed bread-crumbs; pound both of these together and pass through a sieve; put it into a bowl and mix in gradually the onions and lard. also two gills of béchamel sauce (No. 409), seven raw egg-yolks, a quarter of a pound of chopped mushrooms, and truffles, some salt, prepared red pepper (No. 168) and nutmeg. Fill some ready prepared sheep's casings, three inches long and one inch wide, with this preparation—not too full—and plunge them into boiling water; prick them with a larding needle, and then broil them over a slow fire. Serve a Berchoux sauce (No. 434) separately.

(2219). BOUDINS OF GAME OR CHICKEN BLOOD À LA VICTORIN (Boudins de Sang de Gibier ou de Sang de Volaille à la Victorin).

Collect a pint of blood either from a hare, rabbit or chicken, stir into it a little vinegar to prevent coagulation; cut half as much breast of fat pork as there is blood into three-sixteenths of an inch squares, fry these in butter with a little chopped onion and mix in the blood, or else fry the onion in butter and stir into the blood some cooked veal udder instead of the fat pork, a little apple marmalade, and mix together; season well with salt, pepper, a little sugar and cream. With this preparation fill some sheep's casings one inch in diameter; when filled, but not too tight, divide them in three-inch lengths, tying the ends; poach, drain and when cold rub them over with lard; prick and broil them on a slow fire and serve plain without any sauce.

(2220). BOUDINS OF KINGFISH À LA PONIATOWSKI (Boudins de Kingfish à la Poniatowski).

Prepare a quenelle forcemeat of kingfish (No. 90), into which add an eighth of its quantity of chopped truffles; roll them into round pieces three-quarters of an inch in diameter and two and a half inches long; wrap each one separately in buttered paper, then poach in boiling salted water; drain, dip in beaten egg, and fry in clarified butter. Drain and dress on a folded napkin; serve a separate sauce-boat of Polish sauce (No. 524).

(2221). BOUDINS OF SALMON WITH SHRIMPS (Boudins de Saumon aux Crevettes).

Prepare one pound of fish quenelle forcemeat made with salmon (No. 90). Butter some boudin molds the same as for boudins of chicken au cardinal (No. 2216) and garnish the sides with the delicately prepared salmon forcemeat, adding to it four ounces of fresh mushrooms, and two ounces of truffles, both cut into eighth of an inch square bits; lay one mold on top of the other, and set them in a sautoir close together; pour over boiling water, and put them to poach in a slack oven; unmold and dress them on a well-buttered Normande sauce (No. 509).

(2222). SKEWERS OF CHICKEN LIVERS, COLBERT SAUCE (Brochettes de Foies de Poulet, Sauce Colbert).

Cut up into one-inch squares some chicken livers; season with salt and pepper and run them on to metal skewers (Fig. 176), intercalating each piece with a thin one-inch square of bacon; coat over with oil or melted butter, roll in bread-crumbs and broil over a slow fire; dress them on a Colbert sauce (No. 451).

(2223). SKEWERS OF LAMPREYS, MARINADE SAUCE (Brochettes de Lamproies, Sauce Marinade).

Skin a fine lamprey, clean well and cut off the head, also the thin tail end, then divide it into quarter-inch pieces; lay these in a tureen with sliced onions, parsley, a clove of garlic, truffle peelings, aromatic herbs, allspice, salt and a little brandy, and let macerate for a few hours in a cool place, tossing them about at short intervals; when sufficiently steeped drain them off and wipe dry; run an iron skewer (Fig. 176) through, alternating each slice with one of fresh, fat salt pork. Set these brochettes on a baking sheet. pour a little butter over and cook them in the oven, basting frequently with more melted butter. Add to the marinade two gills of brown sauce (No. 414), as well as half a pint of stock (No. 194a); remove all scum rising for a quarter of an hour while standing it on the side of the range; remove all its fat and afterward strain the sauce, pour into it half a glassful of Marsala wine, reduce again for ten minutes, keeping it in a bain-marie (Fig. 122). When the pieces of fish are cooked, take them from the oven, sprinkle them liberally with salt and dress on a dish, surrounding them with cut-up lemons, and serve the sauce separately.

(2224). BROCHETTES OF LOBSTERS (Brochettes de Homard).

Plunge some live lobsters in boiling water just sufficiently long to easily detach the meat from the shells; drain them, and break the tail shells so as to obtain all the meat contained therein; cut this up into transversal slices three-sixteenths of an inch thick, season them highly with salt and prepared red pepper (No. 168), immerse them in melted butter, and run skewers (Fig. 176) through the pieces, alternating each one with slices of cooked mushrooms; lay them again in butter, and broil them over a steady fire for twelve to fourteen minutes. Dress them on a dish, pour over some Colbert sauce (No. 451); serve very hot.

(2225). OYSTER BROCHETTES (Brochettes aux Huîtres).

Poach lightly some large oysters in their own liquor, dry them on a cloth, pare, and lay them in a deep plate, season and mix them with some fine herbs cooked with truffles (No. 385) and a pinch of sweet peppers; cover the oysters with oil, and roll them in this seasoning. Run them one by one on small skewers (Fig. 176), alternating each with slices of cooked mushrooms; brush them over with melted butter, roll them in bread-crumbs and broil them for six or seven minutes, turning them frequently, then dress them at once.

Brochettes the same as the above are prepared by wrapping each seasoned oyster in a thin slice of bacon, or else alternating each oyster with a square of bacon; run the skewers through both and cook them over a hot fire.

(2226). BROCHETTES OF SWEETBREADS (Brochettes de Ris de Veau).

Blanch the sweetbreads, suppress the windpipes and fat and place them under a weight to reduce to the thickness of an inch; when cold cut them lengthwise into slices an inch square; cut these into pieces three-eighths of an inch thick; season with salt, pepper, oil and chopped parsley; run each square on small silver skewers (Fig. 176), alternating them

FIG. 414.

with a thin piece of bacon cut an inch square; besprinkle with white bread-crumbs and broil over a slow fire for fifteen to eighteen minutes, having all four sides equally cooked. Dress on a hot dish, pour maître d'hôtel butter over (No. 581) and garnish with slices of lemon.

(2227). CASES À LA MONTGLAS—SMALL (Petites Caisses à la Montglas).

Cut some chicken fillets into fine Julienne, also truffles and red beef tongue; put on the fire to reduce two gills of good espagnole (No. 414), incorporating into it slowly the truffle broth, and a few spoonfuls of Madeira and meat glaze (No. 402); it should be succulent and thick, then throw in the Julienne, and remove the saucepan at once from the fire, to allow the contents to cool off. With some liver baking forcemeat (No. 73), mingled with a little raw quenelle forcemeat (No. 89), line the bottom and sides of about fifteen china cases, making a hole in the center of each; into this place a little of the prepared montglas, and cover with more of the forcemeat, smoothing it down with the blade of a small knife. Range the cases on a baking sheet containing a little hot water and keep them in a slack oven for fifteen to eighteen minutes in order to poach the forcemeat and montglas. After removing the cases cover the tops with a layer of Madeira sauce (No. 492), and return them to the oven for two minutes to have them attain a glossy appearance. Dress in a circle on a folded napkin, garnishing the center with a layer of very green parsley leaves.

(2228). CASES OF ENGLISH SNIPE À LA CARÊME (Caisses de Bécassines Anglaises à la Carême).

Bone nine snipe thoroughly after they have been well-singed and cleaned; fill them with game quenelle forcemeat (No. 91) into which mix a little Madeira and cooked fine herbs (No. 385); lay them in oval molds the size of the inside of the paper cases in which they are to be served, and cover with slices of fat pork; cook them in the oven for twenty minutes. Oil a sufficient number of paper cases, turn them over on to a grater and stiffen in the oven; cover the bottom and sides with delicate game forcemeat (No. 75), into which mix some chopped truffles. Lay the unmolded snipe in the center, reconstruct the heads naturally, imitating the eyes with a little white forcemeat, and a small round of truffle; push the beak on the neck end leaving only the head protrude, then place the cases in a buttered sautoir, cover with a round of buttered paper, and push into the oven to poach the forcemeat; drain off all the fat, and cover with a brown sauce (No. 414) made with a game essence (No. 389) extracted from the carcasses, and some Madeira wine.

(2229). CASES WITH FAT LIVERS--SMALL (Petites Caisses de Foies-Gras).

Cut into small escalops half of a large cooked fat liver; put it into a small sautoir with an equal bulk of escalops of cooked truffles cut the same size as the livers; moisten these with a little good, thick sauce reduced with Madeira; let simmer without boiling for seven or eight minutes, then

FIG. 415.

take it off and leave to cool partly. With this stew fill eight or ten china cases, cover the tops quickly with a thick layer of chicken forcemeat (No. 89), smooth nicely, and then range the cases on a small baking sheet. Poach the forcemeat in a slack oven, warming the stew at the same time, and finally cover the surface of the forcemeat with a little cold Madeira sauce (No. 492) applied with a brush; return to the oven for two minutes to gloss the sauce, and then dress the cases pyramidically on a folded napkin.

(2230). CASES OF LARKS OR SNOW BIRDS (Caisses d'Alouettes).

Bone thoroughly one dozen snow birds or larks; put the intestines into a pan with grated fat pork, a few chicken livers and a few foies-gras parings, fry over a quick fire, season and mix in some mushroom peelings. When this preparation is cold, pound and press it through a sieve, then mix in with it twelve ounces of chopped and pounded fat pork, four ounces of chopped and pounded lean pork, pound all together and pass through a sieve. Take out a third part and divide the other two-thirds into twelve parts and fill the birds with them; roll them up into balls, range them on the bottom of a saucepan and brush over with a little melted game glaze (No. 398) and Madeira wine, cook them quickly for a few minutes to stiffen, then remove. Oil twelve small oval paper cases, having them an inch and a quarter wide by two inches long; drain and set them on the grater to stiffen in the oven; cover the bottoms and sides with a layer of the forcemeat (No. 73), set a bird on top of each case, range them on a small baking sheet, push into a slack oven and a few moments later baste the birds with a little melted game glaze (No. 398); remove them five minutes after, dress on a dish and brush over with some good reduced sauce.

(2231). CASES OF OYSTERS À LA HILTON (Caisses d'Huîtres à la Hilton).

Prepare and line the cases exactly as for Lorenzo (No. 2232); fill them with small oysters after removing the muscle or ligament, cover over fine herbs cooked dry (No. 385), and finish with a béchamel sauce (No. 409), reduced with the oyster liquor, well seasoned; besprinkle with fried breadcrumbs, brown in a hot oven and serve on folded napkins.

(2232). CASES OF OYSTERS À LA LORENZO (Caisses d'Huîtres à la Lorenzo).

Either buttered metal or china cases may be used for these, or else buttered paper ones stiffened in the oven; cover their bottoms and sides with a thin layer of fish quenelle forcemeat (No. 90), mixed with some soubise purée (No. 723). Poach medium-sized oysters in their own liquor and white wine; drain and pare them, cut them up into pieces half an inch in size, and use these to fill in the cases; set on top some mushrooms that have been chopped up raw, fried in butter, then covered with velouté sauce (No. 415) reduced with the oyster liquor and finished with

Fig. 416.

a piece of lobster butter (No. 580) and a dash of cayenne; cover over with a layer of the same forcemeat, smooth and moisten the tops with a brush dipped in melted butter; range the cases on a baking sheet, and set them in a slack oven from twelve to fifteen minutes, then serve.

(2233). CASES OF QUAILS À LA DÉJAZET (Caisses de Cailles à la Déjazet).

Bone thoroughly some well-cleaned quails, open them on a cloth, season with salt, pepper and nutmeg, cover the inside meats with a layer of game forcemeat (No. 91) with chopped truffles added and envelop the forcemeat, forming them in the shape of an egg, and lay them inside of bottomless oval molds of the same size as the paper cases in which they are to be served; set the molds on a baking sheet, cover with thin slices of fat pork, moisten with white wine mirepoix stock (No. 419) and cook in a hot oven. Mask the bottom and sides of the paper cases previously oiled and stiffened with a thin layer of quenelle forcemeat (No. 91) and the same quantity of cooked forcemeat (No. 73), both well mixed together; put the quails in the center and push into the oven for about twenty minutes, then cover with a salmis sauce (No. 536), mixed with the strained and skimmed braise stock.

(2234). CASES OF SQUABS À LA FOLSOM AND CASES OF SQUABS À LA UMBERTO (Caisses de Pigeonneaux à la Folsom et Caisses de Pigeonneaux à la Umberto).

Pluck well all the pin feathers from some drawn, singed and cleaned squabs; bone them entirely, beginning by making an incision in the meat on the back and following the line down on each side with the help of a small knife; remove the breast and wing bones, then fill the inside with chicken forcemeat (No. 89) into which has been mingled mushrooms and truffles chopped up fine, fried in butter and wetted with a little Madeira. Oil the insides of some paper cases, turn them upside down on a baking pan, push them into the oven to stiffen and then cover the bottoms and sides with a layer of the same forcemeat; set the squabs on top, one on each, and cover with a slice of fat pork; cook them in a slack oven for half an hour. Drain off the fat and dress the cases in a circle, having on top of each one a channeled mushroom head (No. 118); pour a Madeira sauce (No. 492) over that has been reduced with some mushroom essence (No. 392).

Cases of Squabs à la Umberto.—Butter or oil as many oval paper cases as there are squabs to be prepared; place them in the oven to stiffen and brown, then drain. Bone the birds, stuff them with a delicate quenelle forcemeat (No. 89), into which mix chopped truffles and mushrooms; lay them in a sautoir in oval rings of the same diameter as the cases, moisten with a little mirepoix stock (No. 419), reduce it to a glaze, then remoisten to half the height of the squabs, and when done the stock ought to be well reduced; lay them in the cases and cover over with African sauce (No. 424), dress and serve.

(2235). CASES OF SWEETBREADS À LA GRAMMONT (Caisses de Ris de Veau à la Grammont).

Blanch and braise the sweetbreads as indicated in la Montebello (No. 1560), then put them in round rings under the pressure of a weight. Melt some butter; fry in it a little shallot, parsley, mushrooms and truffles, all finely chopped, season and moisten with Madeira wine; let fall to a half-glaze, then thicken with egg-yolks. Fill some cases half full of these herbs, lay the sweet-

Fig. 417.

breads on top and cover each one with a slice of fat pork; place them in the oven, and when cooked remove the pork and drain; pour the stock over the sweetbreads; when cooked reduce to a half-glaze.

(2236). CASES OF THRUSHES (Caisses de Grives).

Select six good, fat thrushes, not taking those that are too large; singe and split them down the back to bone the breasts and draw the insides; season the interior meats and lay in each one a ball of game quenelle forcemeat (No. 91), mixed with a third as much of the intestines from the birds, cooked, pounded and rubbed through a sieve. Sew up the opening on the top, truss the legs and shorten the stumps. Melt some grated fat pork in a saucepan, range the birds in this, season and fry while turning them over until partly cooked, then drain and draw out the sewing thread without disturbing the legs. Add to the fat in the saucepan two or three spoonfuls of cooked fine herbs (No. 385), a pinch of bread-crumbs and some grated fat pork, obtaining a light paste. Oil over with a brush six oval paper cases, and on the bottom of each spread a layer of this paste and over place a thrush; set the cases on a buttered sheet, cover with buttered paper and push into a slack oven to finish cooking the birds. At the last moment remove, untruss the legs, glaze over with a brush and set each case inside another white one in order to serve them neatly.

(2237). CASES OF THRUSHES À LA DIANA (Caisses de Grives à la Diane).

Split eight thrushes through the back, leaving on the breastbone and legs; stuff them with chicken quenelle forcemeat (No. 89), add to this forcemeat a third of its volume of foies-gras from a terrine, mix well together and inclose a ball of the forcemeat an inch and a half in size in a bird, and place them in buttered oval tin rings, covering over with thin layers of fat pork, and cook them in a slack oven. Oil some oval paper cases, turn them on to a grater and lay this on a baking sheet, stiffen them in the oven, remove and line them with a light layer of the same forcemeat; place a thrush inside of each and push them into a slow oven for twelve minutes; as soon as done remove the pork, drain off the fat and cover with a half-glaze sauce (No. 413) and game fumet (No. 397); set the case inside of another cleaner and larger one, then serve.

(2238). CASSEROLES OF LAMB SWEETBREADS À LA DE LUYNES (Casseroles de Ris d'Agneau à la de Luynes).

Braise twelve unlarded lamb sweetbreads as for la Montebello (No. 1560); when cooked place under a weight to reduce to half an inch thick, and when cold cut them up into squares, as well as a quarter as many cooked truffles into one-quarter of an inch squares. Put on to reduce some béchamel sauce (No. 409), stirring into it some truffle essence and a little good melted game glaze (No. 398); when the sauce is properly reduced, add to it the salpicon of sweetbreads and truffles. Fill some small porcelain or silver casseroles (flat saucepans) with this preparation, having them quite full and rounded on the top; smooth the surfaces dome-shaped with a knife, let get cold and then cover over with a thin layer of forcemeat, besprinkle with parmesan and bread-crumbs, pour a little melted butter over, then bake lightly in a slack oven.

(2239). CASSEROLE OF RICE WITH CHICKEN OR YOUNG GUINEA FOWL À LA PALESTINE (Casserole de Riz Garnie de Poulet ou Pintade à la Palestine).

Pick and wash in several waters, one pound of rice, more or less according to the size of the casserole that is to be made. Place it in a saucepan, moisten with double its quantity of water and cover entirely with slices of fat pork, salt over and allow to cook, then drain and pound, moistening with a little water. Put this into a saucepan on the fire and let get dry, then turn it over on to a baking sheet or a marble slab and taking in the hands a little less than half, mold it to the shape of a mushroom head, proceeding exactly the same with the other half, keeping back a piece to roll into a round form, then flatten it down to half its thickness. Dress the croustade, laying the flat side of one of the small mushroom pieces on a sheet of paper, then fasten the flattened ball in the center and place the other large mushroom on top of this, only having it reversed, the widest part uppermost. Carve the croustade all around and cover it with clarified butter, then brown in a brisk oven and empty out the inside; fill it with fillets or breasts of chicken sautéd in clarified butter and small artichoke bottoms cut in four, also some truffles; when these ingredients are well done dress them inside the croustade; drain the fat from the sautoir, moisten with a little Madeira to detach the glaze, then add some half-glaze sauce (No. 413), reduce, and pour it over the chickens; garnish around the top with hatelets of chicken Villeroi.

A Potato Casserole can be prepared the same as the one of rice, having a very dry mashed potato preparation moistened with raw egg-yolks, then molded; baste butter over and brown in the oven; empty it out and fill up with chicken livers sautéd in butter with cooked fine herbs (No. 385) and Madeira sauce (No. 492).

(2240). CREAM OF PARTRIDGE OR CHICKEN (Crème de Perdreau ou de Poulet).

Pound the meats taken from two roast partridges or chickens, with a piece of butter, a few parings of cooked foies-gras and two or three spoonfuls of reduced velouté sauce (No. 415); pass the whole through a sieve. Dilute this pulp with ten egg-yolks and one whole one, two gills of good raw cream and two gills of very concentrated game fumet (No. 397) prepared with the partridge bones or those of the chickens. Pour this preparation into a small vegetable dish or small buttered timbale molds (No. 1, Fig. 137), and poach in a bain-marie, done by placing the dish in a saucepan containing hot water, having this water quiver only and not boil. As soon as the cream is set, remove to serve.

(2241). CREAM OF PHEASANT, CHANTILLY (Crème de Faisan, Chantilly).

Pound the meats of a raw pheasant; season and pass them through a sieve; return to the mortar and pound again with four egg-yolks, and three-quarters as much butter; put this into a thin metal bowl, and beat on ice to render it smooth and acquire a body, mixing in about a gill of raw cream; try a little piece in the oven in a very small mold to discover its consistency, and rectify when necessary. Prepare a montglas composed of uncooked foies-gras, truffles, and recently cooked tender red beef tongue; place it in a small sautoir to mingle with two or three spoonfuls of velouté sauce (No. 415) reduced with pheasant fumet (No. 397); keep it in a bain-marie. Butter a mold (Fig. 139) with clarified butter; fill with the forcemeat, smooth the top, then poach in a bain-marie for twenty minutes, with a white paper laid on top; wipe the mold neatly after it has been removed, and turn the contents over on to a rice croustade foundation (Fig. 9a) fastened on to a dish; this to be an inch thick, and slightly wider than the mold; fill the hollow at once with the montglas; brush the forcemeat lightly with a little of the velouté sauce, serving more separately.

(2242). CRÉPINE OF LAMBS' TROTTERS, PÉRIGUEUX SAUCE (Crépine de Pieds d'Agneau, Sauce Périgueux).

Prepare and cook the lambs' trotters the same as for the poulette (No. 1768), drain and wipe; open them lengthways, and bone them entirely, using the utmost precaution not to tear the flesh; divide each one into two parts, season and fill the hollow place in each half foot with a salpicon composed of truffles, veal udder and cooked foies-gras, combined with raw quenelle forcemeat (No. 92), and a little baking forcemeat (No. 81); place on each four slices of truffle; wrap each half foot in a band of "crépine" or caul fat, previously well dried and beaten between two cloths to reduce its thickness; roll these crépines in melted butter. then in bread-crumbs, smooth and equalize the surfaces with the blade of a knife, and boil them for twenty to thirty minutes over a very slow fire, turning them during the operation. Dress them on a very hot dish, and serve with a sauce-boat of Périgueux sauce (No. 517).

(2243). CRÉPINE OF PULLET (Crépine de Poularde).

Put half a pound of grated fat pork in a saucepan with as much butter and oil, set it on the fire with the pullet, and brown this to a fine color, then take out and untruss. Brown in butter some finely chopped shallot and mushrooms, season with salt, pepper and chopped parsley, let cool off, and use it to mask the surface of the pullet, then lay over a layer of not too hard quenelle forcemeat (No. 89), and wrap the whole up in a piece of "crépine" or caul fat; baste with butter, bestrew with bread-crumbs, and place it in a hot oven to finish cooking the pullet; dress and pour around a buttered half-glaze sauce (No. 413), with lemon juice added.

(2244). CRÉPINE OF BRAINS (Crépine de Cervelles).

Prepare and cook some brains as for the poulette (No. 1481); when well drained, split them in four through the thickest part. Blanch one pound of onions, cut in eighth of an inch dice pieces, in salted water for ten minutes; drain them off, then fry these in butter to cook without coloring; season with salt, pepper, nutmeg, thyme and bay leaf; add a quart of velouté sauce (No. 415), reduce well, suppress the thyme and bay leaf, and thicken with six egg-yolks and a little butter; let this preparation cool off partially, then envelop the slices of brains in plenty of it, and then wrap them in "crépine" or caul fat, giving each one a flat oval-shape; dip in butter and roll in bread-crumbs, broil over a slow fire, and serve on a slightly thickened aspic gravy (No. 391).

(2245). CRÉPINE OF CHICKEN À LA TURENNE—BREASTS (Crépine de Filets de Poulet à la Turenne).

Fig. 418.

Pare and chop up finely half a pound of raw chicken fillets, and one pound of chopped fresh fat pork; season with an ounce of spiced salt (No. 168), and two tablespoonfuls of chopped truffles. Pound the chopped chicken, add to it the pork. Spread some pieces of "crépine" or caul fat on a napkin; divide half of the prepared forcemeat into inch and a half diameter balls, and lay on top of the crépine a fine slice of truffle, over this a forcemeat ball; flatten down to half, and place on top some minced mushrooms previously fried in butter with fine herbs, and on this lay another slice of truffle. Wrap the crépines into oval-shapes, and dip each in butter, then roll in bread-crumbs to broil over a slow fire; serve on a half-glaze sauce (No. 413) finished with mushroom essence (No. 392).

(2246). CRÉPINE OF PIGEONS, POIVRADE SAUCE WITH TRUFFLE ESSENCE (Crépine de Pigeons, Sauce Poivrade à l'Essence de Truffes).

Truss six pigeons as for an entrée (No. 178); braise them in a mirepoix stock (No. 419) and when done transfer them to a vessel, straining the mirepoix stock over and then let get thoroughly cold. Spread some pieces of "crépine" or caul fat on the table; split the pigeons in two, pare nicely and cover with a forcemeat made of half a pound of veal and half a pound of veal suet, both being finely chopped and pounded to a pulp, then mix in two ounces of bread crumbs, salt, pepper, nutmeg, finely shredded chives, chopped up mushrooms and a few egg-yolks; when this forcemeat is of a sufficient smoothness, and has acquired a firmness, use it to cover over both sides of the pigeons, laying it on rather thick; place a few slices of truffles on top and wrap the whole in pieces of crépine; baste over with melted butter and roll in bread-crumbs, then put them in a slow oven to get very warm, and serve on a poivrade sauce (No. 522) with essence of truffle (No. 395) added.

(2247). CRÉPINE OF REEDBIRDS (Crépine de Mauviettes).

Take one dozen well cleaned and boned reedbirds, remove the breasts and put the leg meats and intestines into a sautoir, fry them in butter with some truffle parings and let get cold; season with salt and pepper, pound to a pulp and press through a sieve; mix in with this as much game quenelle forcemeat (No. 91), and later add an equal quantity of fine herbs. Pare the breasts, remove the skin without extracting the minion fillets, season and cover both sides with a part of the forcemeat. Have some fresh and well soaked " crépine " or caul fat; remove the fattest parts with a knife and wrap the breasts in, dip them once in butter, then in bread-crumbs, smoothing this nicely with the blade of a knife, fry in clarified butter, drain and dress in a circle with a bread croûton between each of the breasts. Fry some chopped mushroom, shallot and parsley, moisten with a little white wine and good stock; reduce the stock, add to it a little meat glaze (No. 402) and parsley and finish with a piece of fresh butter; cover the crépines with this and serve at once.

(2248). CRÉPINE AND SAUSAGES OF VENISON (Crépine et Saucisses de Chevreuil).

Crépine.—Take a pound of venison minion fillets, suppress all the sinews and cut it up into medium quarter-inch squares, place these in a vessel with half as many raw truffles cut in three-sixteenths inch squares, and season with salt and spices, pour a little Madeira over and marinate for one hour. Mix in with some prepared pork farce (No. 68), three ounces of foies-gras braised and cut in three-sixteenths inch squares; after it is cold, pound the parings with a few truffle parings and put the whole together, season highly and divide the preparation into even parts each the size of an egg and shape them into flat ovals, wrap up in fresh pork " crépine " or caul fat, brush over with butter, dip in bread-crumbs and broil on a moderate fire for fifteen minutes while turning over; range them on a dish, pouring a little reduced gravy (No. 404) in the bottom, or add some Westphalian sauce (No. 561) to this.

Sausages.—Chop up three pounds of lean and sinewless venison with the same weight of fresh pork, a coffeespoonful of fine spices or else powdered sage, two coffeespoonfuls of pepper, three of salt, and three gills of water; when the whole is well chopped fill some mutton casings so as to form sausages five to six inches long; prick them and broil.

(2249). CRÉPINE OF YOUNG RABBITS (Crépine de Lapereaux).

Remove all the meats from two raw young rabbits after they have been properly cleaned; suppress all the skin and sinews and chop up finely, then mix in an equal quantity of chopped fresh pork and season highly. Chop all this once more together, adding one-sixth of the same quantity of cooked fine herbs (No. 385) such as onions, shallots, mushrooms, truffles and parsley. Lay this hash on a large piece of " crépine " or caul fat and roll it up oval shape, flatten to half an inch in thickness, butter over with a brush and place it in a deep, narrow, but long baking pan; cook for thirty or forty minutes in a slack oven while basting occasionally. Drain and dress on a dish, serving at the same time a sauce-boatful of good gravy reduced with game glaze (No. 398).

(2250). CROUSTADES OF CHICKEN LIVERS WITH MADEIRA (Croustades de Foies de Volaille au Madère).

Prepare some croustades in channeled molds, buttered while cold and lined with fine foundation paste (No. 135), fill them up with buttered paper and rice, over this a round of buttered paper, cover and fasten on a flat of the same paste; pinch the edges and lay on the center a puff paste cover made in three layers an eighth of an inch thick and two inches in diameter for the lower one, an inch and a half for the second and an inch for the upper one; egg over and bake in a hot oven, take off the lid and empty out the insides. Fry some chicken livers in a sautoir over a brisk fire, drain off the fat and moisten with a little Madeira or Marsala wine, adding some small cooked mushroom heads and half-glaze sauce (No. 413). Fill the croustades with these livers and mushrooms, sauce over, replace the covers and serve.

(2251). CROUSTADES OF LAMB SWEETBREADS—SMALL (Petites Croustades de Ris d'Agneau).

Keep warm eight to ten small channeled croustades made of astruc, each to be provided with

FIG 419.

a channeled and pointed cover. Cut into dice some recently glazed lamb's sweetbreads: put this salpicon into a small saucepan with half the quantity of cooked truffles cut the same as the sweetbreads. Put a few spoonfuls of good béchamel (No. 409) on to reduce, incorporating in the truffle broth and a little melted meat glaze (No. 402); when succulent and thick mix it with the salpicon, then remove it at once from the fire and fill up the small croustades, smoothing the preparation to a dome; leave to cool, cover with a thin layer of raw forcemeat (No. 89), bestrew with parmesan and bread-crumbs, pour melted butter over and warm slightly in a slow oven.

(2252). CROUSTADES OF REEDBIRDS (Croustades de Mauviettes).

Cut ten to twelve crusts of bread; slit them all around and simply brown the surfaces in a sautoir with clarified butter to open and empty them out. Bone ten to twelve fine reedbirds, season and fill them with a little baking forcemeat (No. 81), besprinkled with chopped truffles; lay a piece of foies-gras in the center, and return them to their original shape; run a thin skewer through the legs. After the crusts have been emptied and are nearly cold, cover them over quickly with a thin layer of the same forcemeat, and in the hollow space in each lay one of the birds, sinking it down in such a way that it will not be deformed while cooking. Butter them over with a brush, season and cover with a thin slice of fat pork. Place the crusts on a buttered baking sheet, and this on a thick baking-pan so that the heat reaches the top more than the bottom. Cook the birds for twelve to fifteen minutes in a slack oven, and after removing them cover over with a good, reduced, thick and cold brown sauce (No. 414); let them attain a gloss at the oven door, then dress the crusts on a folded napkin.

(2253). CROUSTADES OF THRUSHES (Croustades de Grives).

Bone five or six thrushes, leaving on the thighs and two-thirds of the stumps; season them on the opened side and fill with baking forcemeat (No. 81), mingled with a spoonful of plain, raw pork forcemeat (No. 73); bestrew this dressing with a pinch of chopped truffles, and lay in the center a small slice of cooked foies-gras or half a good pullet's liver, seasoned and partly cooked with melted fat pork. Reconstruct the birds to their original shape, but do not sew them, only uphold the legs with a slender wooden skewer; cover over with a small band of buttered paper, and range them in a narrow sautoir lined with fat pork, moistening to half their height with good unskimmed fat. Boil for two minutes, salt over, and remove the sautoir on one side, keeping them for ten to twelve minutes without boiling. These thrushes should merely poach; leave them till partly cold in their liquid, then drain off to pare. Cut six hollow crusts (Fig. 42), slit them around, and fry lightly in butter, then empty out the centers and cover the hollow with a layer of forcemeat. In the middle of each of these crusts lay one thrush, cover over with a very thin slice of fat pork, and place these on a small, lightly buttered baking sheet and put this one inside another, so as not to have the crusts brown too rapidly. Cook the thrushes in a slack oven for ten to twelve minutes, and as soon as they are nicely done remove and cover them at once with a thin coating of brown sauce (No. 414) reduced with game fumet (No. 397) and Madeira. Glaze the surface of the sauce to let it acquire a brilliancy and luster, then dress and serve.

(2254). CUPOLA OF CODFISH À LA BISCAYAN (Coupole de Morue à la Biscayenne).

Butter a cupola-shaped mold, coat the inside with a layer of butter and dust over with white bread-crumbs, then pour into the mold three well-beaten eggs, shuffle them around so they moisten the entire surface, drain off the surplus egg and bread-crumb the mold once more; with this double breading it will be found easy to cover the mold with a layer of rice prepared as follows: Cook half a pound of rice with just sufficient fish stock (No. 195) to cover, and when dry finish it with butter and grated parmesan; beat it up vigorously and lay it aside to get cold, then use it to spread half an inch thick over the entire interior surface of the mold. Soak two inch-square pieces of salt codfish for eighteen hours, changing the water three times in the meanwhile. Fry four ounces of onions cut into three-sixteenths inch dice in two gills of oil, add to this four crushed and chopped cloves of garlic, a pint of thick tomato purée (No. 730), a pint of broth (No. 194a) and six ounces of capers; cook the codfish in this preparation, and when done and the stock quite consistent let it become cold, afterward using it to fill the cupola, finishing the top with another layer of the rice. Place the mold on a small baking sheet for half an hour in the oven, then detach the rice with the blade of a knife and invert it on a hot dish; surround the cupola with sweet peppers sautéd in oil and bestrew the whole with chopped parsley.

(2255). OUTLETS OF TENDERLOIN OF BEEF À LA BABANINE (Côtelettes de Filet de Bœuf à la Babanine).

Cut up in squares a pound of raw tenderloin of beef, well-trimmed and free of all fat and sinews, then chop it up very fine. Chop separately a quarter of a pound of beef-marrow, then chop the two together. Season with salt, pepper and nutmeg; mix in slowly half a pint of cream while continuing to chop; roll out and flatten a small ball of this hash, place it in the oven to try its consistency; if the preparation be too firm add a little more cream, if too soft a few raw egg-yolks. Divide the preparation into eight equal parts, roll each one separately on a table dredged with rice flour, shape them like cutlets, arrange them on a buttered pan, pour over a little melted butter, and cook in a quick oven for six or eight minutes. Serve separately a Lithuanian sauce (No. 487).

(2256). OUTLETS OF TENDERLOIN OF BEEF À LA BIENVILLE (Côtelettes de Filet de Bœuf à la Bienville).

Cold roast or braised tenderloin of beef is used to make these cutlets; trim one pound of beef free from fat or sinews; cut it into three-sixteenths of an inch squares, and the same quantity of cooked mushrooms cut the same size. Reduce some brown Madeira sauce (No. 492) in a saucepan, add to it some raw egg-yolks, and a little good butter, then mix in the beef fillet, also the mushrooms. Heat the preparation well, and when boiling pour it in a dish to let it become perfectly cold, then divide it into twelve equal parts. Roll them out on a table dredged with grated bread-crumbs; shape them in form of cutlets, dip them in beaten egg and then roll them in bread-crumbs; flatten the tops with the blade of a knife, so as to make them smooth and equal-sized, then fry them in very hot fat until they have assumed a good color, and serve them with well-buttered gourmets sauce (No. 472).

(2257). CHICKEN OUTLETS À LA ADOLPHE HARDY (Côtelettes de Poulet à la Adolphe Hardy)

Chop up finely one pound of raw chicken fillets after suppressing all the sinews and fat; add half the same quantity of fresh butter, season and mix the whole well together. Divide the preparation into two inch in diameter balls and shape them like a cutlet; dip in beaten eggs and bread-crumbs and fry in clarified butter; drain and decorate with favor frills (No. 10). Range them in a circle, filling the center with a garnishing of minced cèpes fried in butter, drained and moistened with cream reduced with the cèpes, season and just when ready to serve finish with a piece of butter, lemon juice and chives minced very fine.

FIG. 420.

(2258). CHICKEN OUTLETS À LA CLARENCE (Côtelettes de Poulet à la Clarence).

Fry lightly in butter and lemon juice six well-pared chicken fillets cut into half hearts; place them under a weight to press lightly and divide each one into halves through the thickest part and trim neatly again. Bone the legs, suppress the nerves and fat and fry them in butter, then allow to cool; pound these with the same quantity of foies-gras from a terrine, adding about six egg-yolks and proper seasoning; pass this through a sieve and then mix in four tablespoonfuls of chopped truffles, a little melted glaze (No. 402) and a dash of cayenne and nutmeg. With this preparation cover both surfaces of each fillet, range them on a lightly buttered baking sheet and let get cold on ice; detach them from the sheet, heating it underneath, then roll each separate one in bread-crumbs, dip in beaten egg, roll once more in the crumbs, and smooth the breading with the blade of a knife. Plunge a few chops at a time into hot frying fat to brown nicely, then drain and insert a small favor frill (No. 10). Dress them in a circle on a forcemeat ring poached in a plain border mold (Fig. 139), hollowed on the top; in the center of the ring range minced fresh mushrooms thickened with well-reduced béchamel sauce (No. 409).

(2259). GROUSE OR PRAIRIE HEN OUTLETS À LA SÉGARD (Côtelettes de Tétras ou de Poulet de Prairie à la Ségard).

Braise the fillets from the breast of a grouse, remove the skin and nerves and chop up finely; add six ounces of butter, season with fine spices and mix in three tablespoonfuls of game cream forcemeat (No. 75); with this preparation shape some cutlets, dip them in beaten egg and bread-crumbs and fry in clarified butter over a good fire. Serve separately, but at the same time a tomato sauce (No. 549) mixed with half-glaze sauce (No. 413).

(2260). CUTLETS OF KINGFISH, MAYONNAISE MOUSSELINE (Côtelettes de Kingfish, Mayonnaise Mousseline).

Make a very delicate fish quenelle forcemeat (No. 90); mold this into cutlet-shaped molds, and poach until sufficiently consistent to be able to egg and bread-crumb; fry in clarified butter, and when a fine color dress on napkins. Garnish the ends with paper favor frills (No. 10) and serve with a mayonnaise mousseline sauce (No. 615) separately.

(2261). LOBSTER CUTLETS À LA SHELLEY, OR WITH CREAM SAUCE (Côtelettes de Homard à la Shelley, ou à la Sauce à la Crème).

Cook in a court bouillon (No. 38) one lobster of two and a half pounds, take out all the meat, cut one pound of this into three-sixteenths inch squares, add to it half a pound of cooked mushrooms cut the same as the lobster, and mix this salpicon with a velouté sauce (No. 415), reduced with mushroom essence (No. 392), and into which has been added a little meat glaze (No. 402); season, stir well over the fire, and when the preparation reaches boiling point, pour it into a vessel to get cold. Have a bottomless cutlet mold five-eighths of an inch high by three and three-quarters inches long and two inches wide; butter and lay it on a piece of buttered paper slightly larger than the mold, garnish the bottom and sides with a light layer of pike forcemeat (No. 90), set the salpicon in the center and cover with more forcemeat; poach this lightly, unmold and set it aside till cold, then dip it in beaten eggs, then in bread-crumbs; fry in clarified butter, drain and serve on napkins with favor frills (No. 10) and a separate lobster sauce (No. 488) containing chopped truffles.

With Cream Sauce.—Have a lobster croquette preparation (No. 880), mold it to the shape of a cutlet, bread-crumb and fry the sauce as for the above; when a fine color, dress the cutlets and garnish with favor frills (No. 10), serving them with a separate cream sauce (No. 454).

(2262). CUTLETS OF PHEASANT À LA REGINALD (Côtelettes de Faisan à la Réginald).

Cut up a pound of the white meat of a cooked pheasant free of fat and skin into three-sixteenths inch squares, also four ounces of truffles; mingle these with reduced béchamel (No. 409) and meat glaze (No. 402), season properly and let get cold. Divide the preparation into one and three-quarters inch in diameter balls, roll and lengthen them on one end in the shape of a cutlet and lay them in bread-crumbs; then dip in beaten eggs and again in the bread-crumbs, flatten them down to half an inch in thickness and mold them into cutlet-shaped bottomless molds; unmold and fry in very hot white fat or clarified butter, drain and trim with fancy favor frills (No. 10). Dress either in a circle or in a straight row, and serve at the same time a well buttered velouté sauce (No. 415), into which squeeze the juice of a lemon; strain it through a tammy and then add chopped parsley and small three-sixteenths of an inch pieces of cooked mushrooms and red beef tongue.

(2263). CUTLETS OF SQUABS À L'ALBUFÉRA (Côtelettes de Pigeonneaux à l'Albuféra).

To be prepared the same as the signora (No. 2269); replace the slice of truffle by a braised cock's-comb, having it fall to a glaze in Madeira and half-glaze (No. 400). Serve separately a poivrade sauce (No. 522) with truffles.

(2264). CUTLETS OF SQUABS À LA JARDINIÈRE (Côtelettes de Pigeonneaux à la Jardinière).

Thrust the legs inside as many young pigeons as needed, and split them in two lengthwise, flatten, then trim each half cutlet-shaped, the leg bone to take the place of the handle, season and roll in butter after breading them over, broil and dress on a jardinière garnishing (No. 677), decorating the leg with a paper frill (No. 10); serve.

(2265). CUTLETS OF SQUABS À LA LAURISTON (Côtelettes de Pigeonneaux à la Lauriston).

Truss the legs inside of six prepared squabs; split them in two lengthwise, beat down to flatten, season and pare into cutlet shapes. Lay them in a sauté-pan with butter, shallots, mushrooms and truffles, all finely chopped, and cut up chives; cook together for half an hour without browning, then drain off the butter and place the cutlets under the pressure of a weight; let the herbs get quite cold, then mix them with some chicken quenelle forcemeat (No. 89), and with this preparation cover each inner side of half a squab; dip them in beaten eggs and roll them in bread-crumbs, smooth well the breading and fry in clarified butter. Dress the birds in a circle, garnish the handle with a frill (No. 10) and fill the inside with a purée of green peas (No. 2742). Serve a half-glaze sauce (No. 413) with Marsala wine separately, adding to it a dash of cayenne pepper.

(2266). CUTLETS OF SQUABS À LA DE LUYNES (Côtelettes de Pigeonneaux à la de Luynes).

Prepare the cutlets the same as for the Lauriston, only replace the forcemeat by a well-reduced allemande sauce (No. 407) with lemon juice added. Cover the cutlets with this and when cold dip them in eggs, roll in bread-crumbs, and fry in clarified butter; dish up and fill the hollow of the circle with asparagus tops. Serve separately a well-buttered half-glaze sauce (No. 413) into which mingle lemon juice and chopped parsley.

(2267). CUTLETS OF SQUABS À LA PÉRIGUEUX (Côtelettes de Pigeonneaux à la Périgueux).

After dressing the pigeons as for jardinière (No. 2264), pour over a Périgueux sauce (No. 517), to which add a garnishing of small chicken quenelles, laid through a cornet on to a buttered baking sheet into bead shapes a quarter of an inch in diameter, then poached in boiling water and drained.

(2268). CUTLETS OF SQUABS À LA PROVENÇAL (Côtelettes de Pigeonneaux à la Provençale).

Prepared the same as the jardinière (No. 2264), then fried in oil with minced onion, and a clove of garlic; drain off the oil and replace it by white wine, espagnole sauce (No. 414) and tomatoes. Cover the saucepan and finish to cook; just when ready to serve, add minced mushrooms and chopped parsley.

(2269). CUTLETS OF SQUABS À LA SIGNORA (Côtelettes de Pigeonneaux à la Signora).

Have some well-cleaned and singed young pigeons; make an incision down the entire length of the backs and bone them by beginning at this incision and following the line of the carcass on both sides, then take out all the bones leaving a drumstick on the same side of each pigeon; season. Mix well together some chicken quenelle forcemeat (No. 89), with as much cooked forcemeat (No. 73); spread out a layer of it on the inside of the squab, and in the center on the back place a fine slice of peeled truffle, having it three-sixteenths of an inch in thickness; cover this over with another layer of the forcemeat, and wrap this in the boned pigeon, shaping it like a cutlet; dip in melted butter, then in bread-crumbs. Butter a baking sheet, and range either buttered molds or rings shaped like cutlets on top, set the pigeons in these, sprinkle butter over, then place them in a moderate oven, and let cook for twenty minutes. Remove the sheet from the fire, drain off the pigeons and decorate the legs with paper frills (No. 10); dress them in a circle, and serve separately a queen sauce (No. 530).

(2270). CUTLETS OF SQUABS IN PAPERS (Côtelettes de Pigeonneaux en Papillotes).

Draw, singe and clean nicely some young pigeons, cut an incision in the skin between the rump and the breast; thrust the legs inside, split the pigeons in two lengthwise and pare them to resemble cutlets, then fry lightly in butter with lemon juice without letting acquire a color; set them under a weight and trim them again into the required shape. Place some oil, grated fat pork, chopped shallot, mushrooms, parsley, salt, allspice and eighth-inch squares of ham into a sautoir; when these ingredients are well fried, but not browned, add some half-glaze sauce (No. 413) and Madeira wine. Coat some heart-shaped sheets of paper with oil, on one of the halves lay a thin slice of fat pork, over this some of the above prepared sauce and then a pigeon cutlet on top, finishing with more of the sauce and a thin slice of cooked ham; fold the empty half of paper over on the full one, pinch the edges well together to enfold all and enclose hermetically, then lay them on a well-buttered dish intended for the table; set it in the oven to brown the paper and heat the cutlet. The paper should swell up; serve as soon as done.

(2271). SWEETBREAD CUTLETS, MODERN STYLE (Côtelettes de Ris de Veau à la Moderne).

Cut one pound of sweetbreads into slices; season and cook with some butter in a sautoir, turning them over when done on one side; drain, let get cold under a weight, then cut up into small quarter-inch dice pieces; lay them in a tureen with half a pound of cooked mushrooms cut the same size, and a quarter of a pound of unsmoked beef tongue cut in three-sixteenths inch dice; mix this salpicon with some allemande sauce (No. 407), bring to a boil, stir well with a reducing spatula and set it away to cool in a dish; when cold shape it into cutlets, dip them in beaten eggs, then in bread-crumbs and fry; then dress in a circle, garnish with favor frills (No. 10) and pour a financière sauce (No. 464) into the bottom of the dish.

(2272). SWEETBREAD CUTLETS À LA TALLEYRAND (Côtelettes de Ris de Veau à la Talleyrand).

Braise some unlarded sweetbreads and set under a weight to get cold; cut one pound of these into quarter-inch dice-shaped pieces with the same quantity of artichoke bottoms, and mushrooms cut the same, and four ounces of truffles cut in three-sixteenths inch dice and mingled with a béchamel sauce (No. 409) thickened with egg-yolks and fine butter. After this preparation is cold divide it into equal parts and shape them as cutlets; dip in egg and bread-crumbs, fry to a fine color; dress in a circle, garnish with favor frills (No. 10), pouring a cream of soubise sauce (No. 543) in the center.

(2273). VEAL CUTLETS, POGARSKI (Côtelettes de Veau Pogarski).

Chop up one pound of fillet of veal free of all sinews, mix it in with ten ounces of butter, two ounces of bread-crumbs, half an ounce of salt, and nutmeg; roll about three ounces of this on a table, besprinkle with rice flour and shape them into the form of cutlets; dip in beaten eggs, roll in bread-crumbs and fry in clarified butter; glaze each cutlet over with a brush and dress them in a circle with paper favor frills (No. 10) on the ends. Garnish with fried potatoes cut in five-eighths inch balls and serve separately a tomato sauce (No. 549) mixed with half-glaze sauce (No. 413).

(2274). CUTLETS OF YOUNG HARE À LA FAVORITE (Côtelettes de Levraut à la Favorite).

Take both fillet and minion fillets, suppress the sinews and cut the meat lengthwise in two or three pieces; flatten and pare into half hearts, salt and lay them on a buttered baking sheet; bend them all to the right and give them the shape of a cutlet. Cut each minion fillet in three equal pieces, streak them on their length with truffles and place on the outside edge of the cutlets, cover over with bards of fat pork or else melted butter and cook in a brisk oven; drain and decorate with fancy favor frills (No. 10). Lay these cutlets on bread-crumb croûtons cut the same size, dressing them in a circle, and fill the center with a stew composed of quenelles made with the leg and shoulder meats, truffles, mushrooms and espagnole sauce (No. 414), well reduced and beaten with some fumet (No. 397) made of the hare's carcasses and bones; serve more of this sauce apart at the same time.

(2275). YOUNG RABBIT CUTLETS À LA PRÉVILLOT (Côtelettes de Lapereaux à la Prévillot).

Take four very tender young rabbits, remove the hind part of them and cut them in two lengthways through the center, bone the thighs leaving on the leg bone; remove all the sinews, then season and stuff them with godiveau of rabbit (No. 84), made with the minion fillets and fillets, mixing into it some cooked fine herbs (No. 385); sew them up and shape them into cutlets, stiffen and color these lightly in butter on both sides, then set them under a light weight and when cold pull out the threads and pare them all alike into cutlet form; dip them in egg and bread-crumbs. Prepare a fumet (No. 397) with the rabbit parings; when ready to serve have some hot clarified butter in a sautoir, put in the cutlets and cook to a fine color; drain, wipe and trim the handles, dress and pour around a Prévillot salpicon (No. 749), and serve the fumet separately, reduced with a little espagnole (No. 414).

(2276). ESCALOPS OF TENDERLOIN OF BEEF WITH TRUFFLES (Escalopes de Filet de Bœuf aux Truffes).

After paring a medium-sized tenderloin, cut it lengthwise in two, then across in pieces three-sixteenths of an inch in thickness; trim them round-shaped an inch and a quarter in diameter. Place them one beside the other in a well-buttered stewpan, add some slices of the truffle of the same dimensions; cover with melted butter and when ready to serve put the stewpan on a moderate fire for a few moments. Drain off the butter, and finish with a reduced Madeira sauce (No. 492).

FIG. 421.

(2277). ESCALOPS OF BEEF PALATES WITH PURÉE OF CHESTNUTS (Escalopes de Palais de Bœuf Purée de Marrons).

Prepare and cook the beef palates the same as for palates à la béchamel (No. 1326); when cold and pressed cut them into oblongs two and three-quarters inches by one and one-half inches.

Cover both sides of the pieces with a layer of delicate chicken quenelle forcemeat (No. 89), mixing in with it an equal quantity of cooked fine herbs (No. 385). Dip in eggs and fresh bread-crumbs,

Fig. 422.

and fry them to a fine color. Dress them crown-shaped, and garnish the center of the crown with a consistent purée of chestnuts (No. 712).

(2278). ESCALOPS OF CHICKEN, FINANCIÈRE (Escalopes de Poulet Financière).

Lift off the breasts from four fine chickens; remove the minion fillets, and suppress the skin; cut the breasts crosswise into three-sixteenths of an inch thick slices, pare these lightly to ovals and range them in a sautoir with clarified butter. Streak the minions with truffles, form them into circles, and place in a buttered sautoir. Sauté the prepared escalops on a hot fire, drain off the butter, and add quenelles, mushrooms, truffles, and some financière sauce (No. 464). Poach the minion fillets; dress the escalops inside a decorated chicken cream forcemeat border, or else in a croustade, and serve separately a half-glaze sauce (No. 413) with Madeira, or if for white, replace this by some good velouté sauce (No. 415).

(2279). ESCALOPS OF FAT LIVERS À LA VILLENEUVE (Escalopes de Foies-Gras à la Villeneuve).

From a good fresh and firm raw fat goose liver cut seven or eight escalops one and a quarter inches in diameter by three-sixteenths of an inch thick; pare them into ovals or rounds, season and range on a sautoir; surround with fine slices of raw truffles, cut the same diameter, season and sauté them, pour over the whole some good half-glaze (No. 400) and Madeira. Boil up the liquid, then push the dish into a slack oven, basting them with their liquid. Twelve to fifteen minutes will suffice to poach the liver in this stock. At the last moment, dress the escalops on a dish in a close circle, and dress the slices of truffles around, one overlapping the other; thicken the stock with a little good sauce, pour it over the liver and truffles, and serve immediately.

(2280). ESCALOPS OF FAT LIVERS À LA RULLI (Escalopes de Foies-Gras à la Rulli).

Braise for forty minutes in a mirepoix (No. 419) with Madeira some duck's or geese livers, wrapped in thin slices of fat pork or caul fat and buttered paper; put them into a small vessel, and pour the stock over, then let get cold in this; remove them from the stock and cut them into slices a quarter of an inch thick; pare them into rounds an inch and a quarter, and have the same quantity of truffles and mushrooms sautéd in butter. Fry some shallots in butter, add chopped up parsley, meat glaze (No. 402) and some well-reduced allemande sauce (No. 407), and with this cover over the livers, mushrooms and truffles. Have small sheets of buttered paper, lay on the livers, partly overlapping the livers lay a slice of truffle, and partly overlapping the truffle lay a slice of mushroom; cover again with a little more of the sauce, and leave to get very cold; remove from the paper, then roll the escalops in bread-crumbs, afterward dip them in beaten egg, again in bread-crumbs, again in the egg, and in the bread-crumbs once more; smooth the crumbs with the blade of a knife, and fry them a fine color; dress on a folded napkin with a bunch of fried parsley to decorate.

(2281). ESCALOPS OF FAT LIVERS WITH RISOT, PÉRIGUEUX SAUCE (Escalopes de Foies-Gras au Risot, Sauce Périgueux).

Prepare three-quarters of a pound of Piedmontese rice into a risot (No. 739). Cut up the quarter of a fat liver cooked and cold into small escalops; put them in a sautoir with half as many cooked truffles also cut up; add three spoonfuls of Madeira sauce and as much melted meat glaze (No. 402). Keep the stew hot. Lastly finish the risot with fresh parmesan, fine butter, and prepared red pepper (No. 168). Pour half of this into a large buttered plain dome-shaped mold, press it well on the sides in such a way that a hollow is formed in the center; fill this with the foies-gras stew and cover with the remainder of the rice; keep it in a heater for seven to eight minutes, then turn it out on a dish, covering the bottom of it with a little Périgueux sauce (No. 517).

(2282). ESCALOPS OF LAMB OR VEAL À LA HABIRSHAW (Escalopes d'Agneau ou de Veau à la Habirshaw).

Lift off the fillet from a loin of lamb or veal, remove all fat and sinews, cut it up into small slices three-sixteenths of an inch thick, flatten, pare and shape them into rounds; they should each weigh one ounce after being trimmed; fry these in butter over a brisk fire, drain off the butter and add salt, pepper, minced cèpes, meat glaze (No. 402), a spoonful of Madeira wine and chopped parsley. Cut some cucumbers across into an inch and a quarter thick slices, and remove from them pieces with a column tube an inch and a half in diameter, pare and take out the insides with a smaller tube, three-quarters of an inch in diameter; line a baking sheet with thin slices of fat pork, lay the cucumbers on top and fill in the insides with cooked fine herbs (No. 385), into which mix a little chicken quenelle forcemeat (No. 89); cover over with more slices of pork and cook them slowly in the oven; when the cucumbers are sufficiently done dress them in a circle which will form a border and fill the inside with the escalops.

(2283). ESCALOPS OF PHEASANTS WITH OLIVES (Escalopes de Faisans aux Olives).

Raise the breasts of two raw pheasants, cut them in twelve thin escalops of equal thickness, oval-shaped and rather large, season and range them in a sautoir with clarified butter to stiffen them simply on one side, drain them on to a baking sheet covered with buttered paper and lay another sheet of the same on top; then let them cool under the pressure of a light weight. With the pheasant parings prepare a good forcemeat (No. 91), fasten on a round dish a rice croustade foundation cut into a ring, having it half an inch thick; take up the escalops one by one and with an oval pastry cutter slightly narrower than they themselves pare so as to have them all of even size. Cover the stiffened side with a thin layer of a preparation made with half purée of truffles and half purée of foies-gras mingled with a little melted glaze (No. 402) and a sixth of its quantity of the above raw pheasant forcemeat. Smooth the surfaces neatly and replace the escalops in the same sautoir as the butter; push this into a slack oven to poach the preparation and the escalops. Drain them off and dress in a circle on the rice ring fastened on to the dish, fill in the hollow center with a garnishing of large Spanish olives, glaze the escalops lightly with a brush and pour over the garnishing a little good Madeira sauce (No. 492) reduced with pheasant fumet (No. 397); serve a sauce-boatful of the sauce at the same time.

(2284). ESCALOPS OF SWEETBREADS À LA CARÊME (Escalopes de Ris de Veau à la Carême).

Braise some unlarded sweetbreads; when cold cut them into slices three-eighths of an inch thick and shape them into rounds an inch and a quarter in diameter; add to them half their quantity of mushrooms sliced thick and a quarter as many sliced truffles, mix with an allemande sauce (No. 407), season correctly and dress inside a border of rice, prepared as in No. 737.

(2285). ESCALOPS OF KERNEL OF VEAL À L'ARNOLD (Escalopes de Noix de Veau à l'Arnold).

Cut some thin slices from the round bottom of veal, pare them shapely an eighth of an inch thick by one and three-quarters inches in diameter, range in a buttered sautoir on a brisk fire and fry both sides to a fine color, then drain off the butter and replace it by some sherry wine, mushroom catsup, anchovy essence, finely shredded lemon peel, cream and velouté sauce (No. 415); heat the whole, removing the sautoir at the first boil. Dress the slices of veal, reduce the sauce and pour it over; garnish around with small triangle croûtons of bread fried in butter.

(2286). ESCALOPS OF YOUNG HARE À LA ROEDERER, GARNISHED WITH QUENELLES
(Escalopes de Levraut à la Roederer, Garnies de Quenelles).

Prepare the escalops in the following manner: raise the fillets and minion fillets from a young hare, remove all the sinews, and cut them up into escalops; fry in butter with sliced fresh truffles, drain off the butter and detach the glaze with white wine; slice some ham thinly, and from these remove small rounds with a tin tube, adding them to the other ingredients, then heat up the whole without boiling. Drain off the escalops, and dress in a circle of game quenelles (Fig. 75). Reduce the white wine with as much half-glaze sauce (No. 413), and when this becomes rich and succulent season properly, strain and pour it over the whole.

(2287). FAT LIVERS À LA TOULOUSAINE—WHOLE (Foies-Gras Entier à la Toulousaine).

Select a fine, raw, fresh and white fat liver that has not yet been put in water or milk; remove the gall, and stud each side with a row of raw truffles; season and butter over with a brush; wrap it first in thin bards of fat pork, then in a flat of pie paste (No. 144), closing all the apertures carefully.

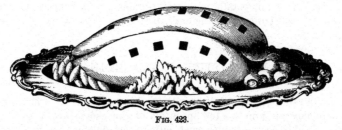

Fig. 423.

Lay it on a baking sheet and cook for an hour and a quarter in a slack oven. After it has been removed, unwrap, take away the fat pork and dress the liver on a long dish, garnishing around with small molded quenelles, cocks'-combs and mushrooms; serve at the same time an espagnole sauce (No. 414) reduced with Madeira and an infusion of Ceylon cinnamon.

(2288). HASH À LA SAM WARD—TENDERLOIN OF BEEF (Hachis de Filet de Bœuf à la Sam Ward).

Have a pound and a half of cold braised or roasted tenderloin of beef; three ounces of cooked mushrooms, three ounces of cooked potatoes, all cut in three-sixteenths of an inch squares, and one ounce of cooked ham cut in one-eighth of an inch squares. Fry in butter without browning an ounce of chopped shallot, then add the ham, mushrooms, meat and potatoes; mix in a little velouté sauce (No. 415) and purée of tomatoes (No. 730); do not allow to boil. Season to taste and arrange the hash on a very hot dish; surround it with pieces of bread fried in butter.

(2289). HASH À LA SHEPPLER—TENDERLOIN OF BEEF (Hachis de Filet de Bœuf à la Sheppler).

Half a pound of cold tenderloin of beef cut in small three-sixteenths of an inch squares, half a pound of mushrooms cut the same size, an ounce of finely chopped shallots; fry these in butter, then add the tenderloin and the mushrooms, also a little espagnole sauce (No. 414), salt, pepper and chopped parsley. Dish this hash in a circle of noodles cooked and finished with parmesan cheese, and serve.

(2290). CORNED BEEF HASH (Hachis de Bœuf Salé).

Have four ounces of boiled potatoes cut in three-sixteenths of an inch squares, put them in a saucepan, and moisten with sufficient beef stock (No. 194a) to cover them entirely. Season with pepper and nutmeg, and half an ounce of butter; simmer until the stock is reduced; add six ounces of corned beef cut the same size as the potatoes; warm without boiling, and serve when the meat is very hot.

(2291). CORNED BEEF HASH, AMERICAN STYLE (Hachis de Bœuf Salé à l'Américaine).

Put in a large frying-pan one ounce of butter; when hot add four ounces of potatoes, and six ounces of corned beef, both cut in three-sixteenths of an inch squares. Season with pepper and nutmeg, and fry, slowly inclining the pan so that the hash assumes the shape of an omelet. When a fine color drain off the butter, and turn it on to a long dish the same as an omelet.

(2292). HASHED CHICKEN, ANCIENT STYLE (Hachis de Volaille à l'Ancienne).

Raise the breasts of a roast chicken, remove the skin and sinewy parts and cut the meat into three-sixteenths of an inch squares; also cut a shallot into one-eighth inch squares; fry all lightly in butter without coloring, then add chervil, parsley and mushrooms, all well chopped; fry once more and mix with velouté sauce (No. 415); warm the preparation thoroughly and thicken with egg-yolks, cream, butter and lemon juice. Dress and garnish around with heart-shaped bread croûtons fried in butter. An equal quantity of potatoes cut the same size as the chicken may be added, and when the whole is dressed strew the top with chopped parsley.

(2293). HASHED CHICKEN, BAKED (Hachis de Volaille au Gratin).

Cut a pound of the white meat of a chicken into three-sixteenths inch squares. Fry one shallot in butter without allowing it to brown, add some reduced béchamel sauce (No. 412) and the chicken, seasoning with salt, prepared red pepper (No. 168) and nutmeg. Place on the edges of the basin of a dish a border of potato, pushing it through a pocket furnished with a star-shaped socket; fill the inside of this border with the hash, bestrew with bread-crumbs, pour butter over and bake in a hot oven.

(2294). HASHED LAMB À LA CÉLESTINE—BAKED (Hachis d'Agneau à la Célestine au Gratin).

Pare a kernel of a raw leg of lamb, make with it a little quenelle forcemeat (No. 92) and when passed through a tammy mix into it a few spoonfuls of raw chopped truffles. Suppress the skin and sinews from a pound of cooked lamb's meat, either the saddle or leg; chop it up and add to it a quarter of a pound of chopped mushrooms and two ounces of ham chopped the same. Reduce a few spoonfuls of half-glaze sauce (No. 413), incorporating into it slowly the mushroom broth and two tablespoonfuls of Madeira wine; when well reduced and thick withdraw it from the fire to stir in the prepared hash; heat this without boiling, season, and let it get slightly cold. Use half of the prepared forcemeat to cover the bottom and sides of a pie dish (Fig. 183); fill in the hollow center with hash, cover it over at once with the remainder of the forcemeat, smooth the surface and bestrew with bread-crumbs; pour some melted butter over and bake lightly in a slow oven.

(2295). HASHED LAMB, CREOLE STYLE (Hachis d'Agneau à la Créole).

Have one pound of lean, cold leg of lamb without skin, fat or sinews; chop it up finely and place it in a high saucepan in a bain-marie (Fig. 122) with a little brown sauce (No. 414), a few peeled and quartered tomatoes, fried in butter, some finely shredded green peppers and plenty of seasoning. Dress the whole in a rice border, made by boiling some rice in slightly salted water with some butter; when dry place it in a plain border mold (Fig. 139), liberally buttered, and set it in the oven covered over for ten minutes to dry more thoroughly. Invert it on the center of a dish, and dress the hash in the middle.

(2296). HASHED LAMB WITH BANANAS (Hachis d'Agneau aux Bananes).

Take six ounces of lean, skinless and nerveless cold lamb cut in one-eighth of an inch squares; fry a tablespoonful of finely chopped onion in butter and when done, but not browned, add to it a quarter of a pound of cooked and finely minced potatoes; moisten with a little stock (No. 194a), reduce for a few moments to the consistency of a sauce, and add the lamb cut into squares; heat up all without boiling and dress on a dish, surrounding the hash with slices of bread cut in triangles and fried in butter. Decorate the top of the hash with two bananas peeled and cut lengthwise in two, roll in flour, fry them in very hot oil, drain and cut them across in two and with these quartered fruits garnish the top of the hash.

(2297). HASHED MUTTON À LA OMER PACHA (Hachis de Mouton à la Omer Pacha).

Suppress all the fat, sinews and skin in order to obtain one pound of lean, cold leg of mutton; chop it up finely and place it in a bain-marie (Fig. 122) with four tablespoonfuls of reduced sauce; add to this some cooked fine herbs (No. 385) and chopped parsley, seasoning with salt, pepper and nutmeg; add meat-glaze (No. 402) and a piece of fresh butter. Fry in hot clarified butter some peeled tomatoes, cut across in two and slightly pressed out; season them with salt, mignonette and chopped parsley, and dress these halved fried tomatoes in a ring with the hash laid in the center; decorate the top with fried croûtons of bread cut in the shape of crescents.

(2298). PARTRIDGE HASH À LA CLÉMENCEAU (Hachis de Perdreaux à la Clémenceau).

Roast two partridges on the spit; lay them aside to cool, then lift off the breasts, suppressing the skin, bones and sinews; cut these meats into eighth of an inch squares, having half as much mushrooms cut the same size, and as many peeled truffles as mushrooms; add to it the cooked livers, cut exactly a like size. Make a light roux (No. 163), add to it the gizzards and broken up carcasses, one bay leaf, sage, cloves and minced shallot; fry together with the roux, moisten with a quart of stock (No. 194a), reduce to half and pass it through a tammy without pressure, then again reduce well and add the salpicon; heat up without boiling, season properly and dress the hash inside a potato border; bestrew the top with bread-crumbs and parmesan, pour over butter and brown under the salmander (Fig. 123). This hash may be accompanied by poached eggs laid on round slices of toasted bread to be handed around at the same time, and it may also be served without the border, surrounding it simply with croûtons of bread fried in oil.

(2299). HASHED PHEASANT (Hachis de Faisan).

Chop up the best parts of a cooked and pared pheasant; put the hash into a small saucepan; chop up also three peeled truffles. With the pheasant bones prepare a small game fumet (No. 397) and thicken it with a little half-glaze sauce (No. 413); reduce this with two spoonfuls of Madeira and when very hot pour it over the hash, mixing in the truffles, and heat up the whole without boiling. Dress on a dish and surround with oval game quenelles, cut in two across, bread-crumbed and fried.

(2300). HASHED VEAL CAKES, BRITTANY STYLE (Hachis de Veau en Galettes à la Bretonne).

Have one pound of lean leg of veal without any fat or sinews whatever, chop it up and mingle with it half a pound of fresh fat pork, equally chopped, and season with salt, prepared red pepper (No. 168) and mignonette; chop again for a few minutes, then put this hash into a vessel and stir well into it two egg-yolks and a quarter of a pound of mushrooms fried in butter and minced very fine; roll this preparation on a floured table into one inch and three-quarters in diameter balls, then flatten them down to three-eighths of an inch in thickness with the blade of a knife; dip them in beaten eggs, roll in bread-crumbs and smooth the surfaces nicely. Heat some melted butter in a sautoir, range the cakes in this merely to stiffen them on both sides, then drain off half of the fat and moisten to their height with some gravy (No. 404); boil up the liquid and place the saucepan in the oven for one hour, keeping it well covered and basting frequently with their own liquid; remove them from the sautoir with a skimmer, dress them in a deep dish and cover over with minced white onions prepared beforehand, but having half of the strained stock from the cakes added at the last moment.

(2301). VENISON HASH, AMERICAN STYLE AND WITH POACHED EGGS (Hachis de Chevreuil à l'Américaine et aux Œufs Pochés).

Fry in a sautoir some shallots, parsley and chives; do not color them; moisten with half white wine and half stock (No. 194a), add as much espagnole sauce (No. 414), reduce, then put in two-thirds of venison and one-third of mushrooms, both cut up in quarter-inch squares. Prepare a border with potato croquette preparation softened with eggs, push it through a cornet on to the edge of the inside basin of the dish, using a channeled socket; then fill the border with the hash, bestrew it with bread raspings, pour over butter and brown in a hot oven.

A more simple hash can be prepared with cold roasted venison and cooked potatoes, equal quantities of both cut in quarter-inch squares. Heat without boiling in a poivrade sauce (No. 522), seasoned to taste. Dish it up very hot and surround with croûtons fried in butter.

(2302). HASHED WOODCOCK IN A CROUSTADE WITH SOFT EGGS (Hachis de Bécasses en Croustade aux Œufs Mollets).

Line a low croustade mold (Fig. 152) with fine foundation paste (No. 135), form an outer edge and egg it over twice; cover the bottom and sides with buttered paper and fill it with uncooked rice, bake in a moderate oven and then empty of its contents. Take the meats from six cooked woodcock and cut them into small three-sixteenths inch squares, after suppressing all the bones, skin and sinews. Fry the intestines in butter, pound these with the meat from the legs, etc., and make of it a purée to place in a saucepan with the fragments and parings; add a few minced shallots and boil up for some moments, then put in some espagnole sauce (No. 414), pass the whole through a tammy and reduce to the consistency of a half-glaze sauce (No. 413); now add the woodcock meats and season properly. Fill the croustades with this hash and on top of it range either well drained poached eggs (No. 2931) or soft eggs (No. 2949). This hash can also be dressed in a bread croustade fried in butter.

(2303). YOUNG RABBIT HASH GARNISHED WITH CROQUETTES (Hachis de Lapereaux Garni de Croquettes).

Trim nicely the meats of one or several cold roasted young rabbits, cut them up into quarter-inch squares. Reduce some espagnole sauce (No. 414) in a sautoir, either with champagne or good white wine, to the consistency of half-glaze, add to it the meats and season well; heat it up without boiling in a bain-marie for one hour, dish up the hash and surround it with small round and flat young rabbit croquettes, made with cold rabbit free of bones, sinews or fat, and cut up into three-sixteenths inch squares, with the same of truffles and mushrooms; mix all these together with espagnole sauce (No. 414), finished with rabbit fumet. Fry, wipe, salt and dress them around the hash, scattering chopped parsley over the whole.

(2304). "PAIN" OF CHICKEN À LA VILLARS (Pain de Volaille à la Villars).

Prepare a chicken quenelle forcemeat (No. 89); dilute with a little Madeira sauce (No. 492). Butter a cylindrical-shaped low mold, decorate it with a few fanciful cuts of truffles and fill it with the forcemeat; poach by putting it in a saucepan with water to half its height; bring the water to the boiling point and poach in a slack oven; when firm to the touch in the center remove from the oven and unmold. Have the breasts and minion fillets well pared and free of sinews, then cut into escalops; sauté them on a brisk fire with some minced truffles, season and drain off the butter, replacing it by a little Madeira and half-glaze (No. 400), adding two dozen small channeled mushroom heads (No. 118); when the whole is very hot dress the mushrooms around the "pain" and the escalops and truffles in the center of it. Serve a Madeira sauce (No. 492) at the same time.

(2305). "PAIN" OF CRAWFISH, CHARTREUSE (Pain d'Écrevisses, Chartreuse).

With some raw salmon and pike meats prepare a cream forcemeat of fish (No. 76); prepare also a fine montglas with truffles, mushrooms and lobster-claw meat, cut in small Julienne; mingle all with some good thick brown sauce (No. 414) reduced with Madeira and the truffle broth. Take a part of this montglas and use it to fill seven or eight scallop shells, smooth and round the preparation on top in the shape of a dome and cover with a thin layer of fish cream forcemeat (No. 76). Butter a small, narrow, pyramidical mold, keep it on ice for a few moments and then line

Fig. 424.

the sides and bottom with fish cream forcemeat (No. 76), leaving a hollow space in the center; fill this in with the montglas and close the opening with a layer of the same forcemeat. Poach the "pain" for twenty-five minutes in a bain-marie, or until it is firm to the touch in the center, keeping it covered with a round piece of paper; stand the shells steadily on a baking sheet, push into a slack oven for ten to twelve minutes, and before taking them out cover the tops with a little good velouté sauce (No. 415) reduced and finished with red butter (No. 580); take out at once and keep them warm for two minutes at the oven door, then remove and on each one lay a slice of lobster. Invert the "pain" on a small cooked noodle paste (No. 142) foundation an inch and a quarter high, it being slightly wider than the mold; coat the forcemeat with a little velouté sauce and place a slice of lobster exactly on the center of the "pain." Dress the shells around its base and serve at the same time a sauce-boatful of velouté sauce finished with red butter.

(2306). "PAIN" OF PHEASANT WITH CREAM (Pain de Faisan à la Crème).

Pound the raw meats taken from a pheasant; season and rub through a sieve; return this to the mortar to pound again with four egg-yolks and three-quarters as much butter as there is pulp. Put this preparation into a thin iron vessel and beat it on ice to have it smooth and acquire a body, mixing in gradually about a gill of raw cream. Fry a small part of this in the oven in a diminu tive mold to judge of its consistency and rectify it if found necessary. Prepare a montglas of cooked foies-gras, truffles and very red freshly cooked and tender beef tongue; put all into a small sautoir to thicken with two or three spoonfuls of good velouté sauce (No. 415) reduced with pheasant fumet (No. 397) and keep it warm in a bain-marie. Butter the inside of mold (Fig. 150), using a brush dipped in clarified butter, and fill it up with the forcemeat; smooth the top, cover with a round of buttered paper, and poach it in a bain marie for twenty minutes or until firm to the touch. After removing it from the oven wipe dry and invert it on a rice croustade foundation (Fig. 9a) fastened on a dish; it should be an inch thick and a very little wider than the mold; fill the hollow in the twist with the montglas and cover the forcemeat lightly with a brush dipped in the same velouté sauce (No. 415). Send a sauce-boat of this same sauce to the table with the "pain."

(2307). "PAIN" OF PIKE (Pain de Brochet).

Pound to a pulp half a pound of pike meat, and press it through a sieve; work it in a mortar with half a pound of fresh butter, two ounces of sifted flour, salt and allspice; mix in gradually four eggs, and a pint of cream, and set this preparation into small buttered molds, cover over with a buttered paper, and close the lid; but should the molds not be provided with covers, then lay over a sheet of buttered paper, on top set a tray with a weight on it, and cook them in a bain-marie kept at the boiling point for an hour and a half. Unmold, dress, and serve separately either a Madeira sauce (No. 492) or else a lobster sauce (No. 488), but to either one or the other add some mushrooms, lobster cut in fillets and small nonpareil capers. The "pains" may be sur rounded by crawfish tails or carp's milts sautéd in butter with fine herbs.

(2308). "PAIN" OF YOUNG RABBITS À LA MAINTENON (Pain de Lapereaux à la Maintenon).

Bone four young rabbits, reserving the minion fillets; suppress the sinews from the meats and cut them into dice; also cut exactly similar a third as much fat pork; fry both these in butter with parsley, truffles and mushrooms, all finely chopped, salt, pepper, nutmeg and fine spices; when cold pound and press through a sieve, adding half as much panada, first pounding it, then mixing it in gradually with the forcemeat until well incorporated, then put in twelve egg-yolks singly, and one pint of espagnole sauce (No. 414) well reduced with game fumet (No. 397). Grease a cylindrical mold with sponged and softened butter, decorate it with fanciful cuts of truffles, and fill with the prepared forcemeat; cover with bards of fat pork, and then poach; unmold, glaze and fill the center with a stew composed of truffles and mushrooms. Cut the minion fillets on the bias in three lengthwise pieces, pare them evenly, score and streak with truffles; turn them into a ring form, and lay them into a generously buttered sautoir, cover over with buttered paper, and cook in a brisk oven; glaze and dress them on top of the "pain." Cut quarter-inch thick slices of brain, and from them remove twelve rounds with an inch and a quarter tin tube, dip in egg and bread-crumbs, and fry; garnish the "pain" around with these and serve with a sauce-boat of half-glaze sauce (No. 413) with game fumet (No. 397).

(2309). PATTY À LA PALMERSTON—LARGE, HOT (Gros Pâté Chaud à la Palmerston).

Prepare a hot pie crust as indicated for hot pie à la Bontoux (No. 2314), but do not fill it. Make a forcemeat with four ounces of chicken chopped up very fine, four ounces of chopped lean veal and a pound of beef kidney suet well skinned and chopped; mix the whole well together and chop once more, seasoning with salt, spices and nutmeg. Pound well in the mortar with two ounces of pâté-à-chou panada (No. 121), add to the forcemeat a little at a time, and one whole egg; pound well together until it becomes exceedingly smooth, then moisten with a little water to soften; cover the bottom and sides of the pie with this forcemeat. Have some escalops of sweet bread fried in butter, with chicken livers and bacon cut in quarter-inch squares and blanched, some lean cooked ham cut the same size, and minced veal kidney briskly fried in butter. With this preparation fill up the hot pie and cover with a layer of the above forcemeat and over this place a flat of foundation paste (No. 135), fastening it on the sides; cut away all the surplus paste around, pinch the edges and egg over. Decorate the top with designs cut out of puff paste, egg these twice and bake the pie in a slack oven; when ready to serve raise up the cover and pour in a half-glaze sauce (No. 413) mingled with a little tomato sauce (No. 549).

(2310), PATTY À LA RICHELIEU—HOT, LARGE (Gros Pâté Chaud à la Richelieu).

Butter a hot pie mold, lay it on a small baking sheet covered with a round piece of buttered paper, and line the mold with paste (No. 135); let it reach half an inch above the mold, cover the bottom and sides with buttered paper, then fill it up with rice and cover with a sheet of buttered paper. Dampen the inside paste and place a layer of the same on top, flatten the two layers together, cut off the surplus paste around the edge, pinch the top crest and the edges, egg it over and bake for one hour. Cut the cover inside of the border, empty the patty, egg over inside and outside, return to the oven, without the cover, until it assumes a nice color. Put into a buttered

Fig. 425.

sautoir twelve blanched lambs' sweetbreads, season and moisten with stock (No. 194a), let fall to a glaze and remoisten; allow the liquid to reduce once more, and continue until the sweetbreads are moderately cooked; drain, trim and divide into slices three-eighths of an inch thick by one and a quarter inches in diameter, add to them a half a pound of mushroom heads cut transversely into thick slices, and an equal amount of rounds of red beef tongue the same size. Mingle these garnishings with a little velouté sauce (No. 415) reduced with the mushroom broth and a few spoonfuls of glaze (No. 402). Arrange this inside the pie, forming into a dome on top, and around it dress a chain of halved quenelles of veal molded with a soupspoon (No. 155) and poached; in the center range a pyramid of small round peeled truffles cooked when needed with Marsala wine. Cover the quenelles lightly with the velouté sauce. Serve the pie with the remainder of the velouté in a sauce-boat.

(2311), QUAIL PATTIES—SMALL (Petits Pâtés de Cailles).

Bone thoroughly three or four quails; divide each one in two parts, season and cover the inside with forcemeat (No. 81) in which has been added half as much raw game forcemeat (No. 91) and chopped truffles, and season with game pie spices (No. 168); envelop, giving the quail an oval shape. Cut some layers of pie paste (No. 145) into ovals seven inches by four inches; on the center of one put a thin slice of fat pork (No. 110); over this spread a thin layer of chopped game forcemeat (No. 66), place half a quail on top and moisten the paste all around; wrapping with this paste, fold over the side, then roll out the paste on each end, moisten the top of the paste and bring the two ends together on the top; cover the paste with a thin oval layer of puff paste (No. 145). Make a small opening in the top, range the patties on a baking sheet, egg them over, make fanciful cuts with the tip of a knife, and cook for forty minutes in a moderate oven. Pour into the opening a little half-glaze sauce (No. 413) and Madeira.

(2312), REEDBIRD PATTY—LARGE, HOT (Gros Pâté Chaud de Mauviettes).

Butter a hot pie mold (Fig. 153) and line it with pie paste (No. 145). Bone the breasts of about thirty reed-birds; fill them with game forcemeat (No. 91) and an equal quantity of foies-gras mixed together, having some chopped truffles added. Heat some melted fat pork in a sautoir; when very hot range the birds on it simply to stiffen them, season and let get cold. Fill the mold with the reedbirds and game forcemeat (No. 91), alternating one and the other and intermingling in slices of raw truffles; have it dome-shaped, then cover with thin slices of fat pork and this with a flat of the same paste, fastening the edges together; cut a small hole in the center, decorate it, egg over, and cook the pie for an hour and a quarter in a moderate oven; after it has been ten minutes from the fire, take off the mold and open and suppress the pork. Pour in a few spoonfuls of brown sauce reduced with a fumet (No. 397), and mix with it a little Madeira; put back the cover and serve.

(2313). SWEETBREAD PATTY À LA McALLISTER—LARGE, HOT (Gros Pâté Chaud de Ris de Veau à la McAllister).

First blanch the sweetbreads, then set them under a weight, and when cold escalop and fry them in butter with raw ham cut in dice-shaped pieces and peeled truffles; moisten with Madeira wine and let it fall to a glaze. Line a plain hinged pie mold (Fig. 153) with foundation paste (No. 135); fill the bottom and sides with a layer of chicken quenelle forcemeat (No. 89), mixed with half as much foies-gras forcemeat (No. 78) and chopped truffles; finish filling the mold with the sweetbreads, lay a bed of forcemeat on top, rounding it slightly; moisten the edges of the paste and cover with a flat of paste, cut flush with the mold and pinched all around; decorate the top with lozenges made of puff paste fragments (No. 146); egg over twice, and cook in a moderate oven for two hours and a quarter. When done, unmold and fill the pie with Madeira sauce (No. 492).

(2314). PATTY À LA BONTOUX—LARGE, HOT (Gros Pâté Chaud à la Bontoux).

Make a pie crust in a mold, imitating the pinchings of a Strasburg pâté de foies-gras pie with a pâté de foies-gras pie paste (No. 135). Cover the inside with buttered paper and fill it with rice, cover with a round of paper, moisten the edges, and cover with a lid of the same paste, fasten to the crust of paste, cut off the surplus around, pinch the edges, decorate the dome with leaves of noodle paste (No. 142), and in the center place an imitation artichoke made of the same paste; set it in a moderate oven after egging over twice, and when done remove the lid, empty and egg the exterior surfaces, then let attain a fine golden color. In case there be an empty foies-gras pie crust on hand it can be utilized. Fill either one or the other with a bed of macaroni mingled with reduced velouté sauce (No. 415) and tomatoes, finished with butter, parmesan, and meat glaze (No. 402); mix in also with the macaroni an escalop of foies-gras, truffles and hare quenelles made with hare forcemeat. This is made like game forcemeat, substituting hare for game (No. 91). Roll in sheets of buttered paper, three-quarters of an inch in diameter, and when poached remove the paper and cut into thick slices. Heat the garnishing well without boiling, and with it fill the crust.

(2315). EEL PIE—HOT (Pâté Chaud d'Anguilles).

Cut into slices two pounds of skinned eels (No. 57), having it well cleaned, suppressing the head and thin parts; cut the remainder into three-inch pieces, and be careful to abstract all the blood; wash, wipe dry, then bone the pieces and separate the meats; lard each one with thin slices of truffle; lay the fish in a tureen, season and pour over a few spoonfuls of brandy or Madeira wine; let macerate for a couple of hours. Fry in a sautoir with some butter a few spoonfuls of shallots and mushrooms; lay in the eel fillets and let them simply harden while turning them over, then

FIG. 426.

add the Madeira marinade and two spoonfuls of brown sauce (No. 414); at the first boil remove the sautoir from the fire and bestrew the fish with chopped parsley. Prepare a fish forcemeat (No. 90), finishing it with four spoonfuls of chopped truffles. Cover the bottom of a small baking sheet with a round sheet of heavy paper; on it set a buttered hot pie mold with hinges (Fig. 153); cover the bottom and sides with foundation paste (No. 135), and cover the paste with a layer of the fish forcemeat, then fill up the empty center with the eel fillets and fine herbs, alternating them with layers of forcemeat; fill till dome-shaped on top above the edge of the mold, then smooth it neatly and lay over another flat of the same paste, attaching it to the sides of the mold; fasten it to the projecting borders of the inside paste previously dampened with a brush; cut it away evenly, press it down and pinch it tastefully through its thickness. Make a small aperture on the summit of the dome; moisten the surface and decorate with imitation paste leaves, or any other fanciful design of the same, then brush over the entire top and border with egg; set the pie into a moderate oven to cook for an hour and a half, being careful to cover with a sheet of paper as soon as the paste is well dried. After taking the pie from the oven, lay it on a dish, unmold and pour into the inside through the aperture on top, a few spoonfuls of good half-glaze sauce (No. 413) reduced with Madeira wine.

(2316). FAT LIVER PIE, ALSATIAN—LARGE, HOT (Gros Pâté Chaud de Foies-Gras à l'Alsacienne).

Line a hot pie mold (Fig. 152) with foundation paste (No. 135) made with egg-yolks, not having it too fine; pinch the edges prettily and fill it three-quarters full with baking forcemeat (No. 81) mingled with half as much raw game quenelle forcemeat (No. 91); cover this forcemeat with a round of buttered paper, egg the edges of the pie and cook it in a slow oven for one hour, then take it out and suppress a part of the forcemeat; keep the pie warm. Select two fine halves of fat liver of equal size, season with salt, then butter them with a brush, cover with thin bards of fat pork and inclose in an envelope of paste pie (No. 144), fastening them on tightly so that the liver can

FIG. 427.

thoroughly poach smothered; place them on a baking sheet and cook for an hour in a slack oven. Prepare a garnishing of coarse macaroni one and a quarter inches long; mix in some large Julienne of cooked beef tongue; also have eighteen uniform-sized peeled mushroom heads. After the livers have been taken out of the oven, unwrap and cut each half into crosswise slices slightly on the bias; between each one of these lay a fine slice of peeled truffle freshly cooked in Madeira. Arrange the livers to give them a nice shape, heat them in a slack oven, glazing with a brush. Take the pie from the heater and fill the empty space with the macaroni garnishing; lift up the slices of liver one by one with the aid of a palette, and dress them one beside the other on top of the garnishing; coat with a little Madeira sauce (No. 492) reduced with the truffle stock and then surround the base with the mushroom heads. Serve at the same time a sauce-boatful of Madeira sauce (No. 492).

(2317). PLOVER PIE—LARGE, HOT (Gros Pâté Chaud de Pluviers).

Make a hot pie crust the same as for Bontoux (No. 2314). Bone one dozen plovers or more according to the size of pie; stuff them with game quenelle forcemeat (No. 91), into which incorporate one-eighth of an inch squares of truffles and range them in a sautoir one beside the other; moisten with a little mirepoix stock (No. 419) prepared with white wine and cook on a moderate fire until done; then lay them in another sautoir with espagnole sauce (No. 414) reduced with game fumet (No. 397), and a garnishing of mushroom heads and medium-sized peeled truffles; when all the ingredients are very hot fill the hot pie crust and serve.

(2318). PATTIES WITH GRAVY—SMALL (Petits Pâtés au Jus).

Take one pound of lean meat from the thick loin end and free it of fat and sinews; chop and pound it with five ounces of chopped fat salt pork, and two ounces of bread crumbs; season with salt and pepper, and chopped parsley. Line some round channeled tartlet molds with fine foundation paste (No. 135); cover the bottoms with a layer of the above forcemeat, set in the middle a ball of salpicon à la financière with truffles (No. 667), and finish with another layer of the forcemeat; cover

FIG. 428.

with a flat of foundation paste (No. 135), place on this a round flat of thin puff paste (No. 146) one inch in diameter, egg over, and with the point of a knife make a fanciful rosette on the top. Let cook for half an hour in a slack oven; remove, lift off the covers, and pour in some half-glaze sauce (No. 413) with Madeira wine; unmold and serve.

(2319). WOODCOCK PIE—HOT (Pâté Chaud de Bécasses).

Bone six very clean, singed woodcock, keeping the heads which should be cleaned, the eyes imitated with quenelle forcemeat, and a round piece of truffle for the pupil; cook the intestines in butter, and when cold pass through a sieve and mix them with some game quenelle forcemeat (No. 91), seasoned highly with salt, pepper, duxelle, and chopped parsley; stuff the birds with this, enclose well the dressing, and lay them in bottomless oval molds the same size as themselves; cover with bards of fat pork, and cook in a moderate oven. Make a fumet (No. 397) with the bones, adding to it some espagnole sauce (No. 414) in the act of being reduced; take away a third, and to the remaining two-thirds add some truffles and mushrooms; let both garnishing and birds be cold. Line a hot pie mold (Fig. 152) with foundation paste (No. 135), leaving it reach above the top; fill the center with the birds and garnishing alternated, then wet the top part of the paste, and cover over with a flat of the same; make an edge reaching half an inch above the level of the mold, pinch it on the side and top, and decorate the summit either with noodle paste '(No. 142), forming an aperture in the center, or puff paste parings; egg over twice; bake in a hot oven for an hour and a quarter to an hour and a half; add a gill of Madeira wine to the remaining two-thirds of sauce and pour it into the hot pie, then serve.

(2320). POTTED TENDERLOIN OF BEEF À LA NELSON (Terrine de Filet de Bœuf à la Nelson).

To prepare this dish it will require a covered pie dish which can stand the heat of the oven. Cut slices from a well-trimmed tenderloin of beef free of sinews, and season them with pepper and salt; cover the bottom of the pie dish with a layer of good butter, spread over this some minced onions, and on the onions a bed of minced potatoes. Season with salt and pepper, and set the slices of tenderloin on top. Place the pie dish over a hot fire for a few minutes, then put it into a moderate oven for forty-five minutes; add a tablespoonful of clear gravy (No. 404), and the same quantity of meat glaze (No. 402), Worcestershire sauce, and mushroom catsup; sprinkle over the surface chopped hard-boiled eggs and parsley. Serve it on a dish over a folded napkin.

(2321). POULPETONNIÈRE OF PIGEONS (Poulpetonnière de Pigeons).

To be made with two pigeons. Line a bottomless oval mold two inches high by six inches long and four inches wide with thin slices of fat pork, place over an eighth of an inch thick layer of godiveau (No. 82). Mix in a bowl two spoonfuls of cooked fine herbs (No. 385) and two spoonfuls of sweetbread parings or roast veal, either of these to be chopped up, mixing it in well; season with salt and pepper, and add some reduced velouté sauce (No. 415). Lay a layer of this in the oval mold, over this lay two pigeons cut in four pieces, fried in butter, then drained and moistened with a little gravy (No. 404) and brown sauce (No. 414), cooked for half an hour and cooled. Spread over some fine herbs, finishing with another layer of godiveau; cook in a slack oven, remove the mold, dress and pour over the remainder of the potted pigeon sauce after it has been strained and thickened with butter.

(2322). TENDERLOIN OF BEEF PUDDING WITH OYSTERS (Pouding de Filet de Bœuf aux Huîtres).

Pour a pound of sifted flour on the table, make a hole in the center, so that the flour forms a crown, and in the hollow of the crown set three-quarters of a pound of beef kidney suet, after removing the skin and fibers, and chopping it up well; add half an ounce of salt, half a pint of water, more or less, according to the quantity the paste can absorb, and in order to obtain a firm paste without its crumbling; let it repose for one hour or more, then roll it out to three-sixteenths of an inch in thickness; butter the inside of a dome-shaped mold, line it nicely with the above paste, then cut some slices of tenderloin, about two ounces in weight each, trim them and season them with salt and pepper. Fry in butter without browning two ounces of chopped onions, add to it the slices of tenderloin, leaving them in just time enough to stiffen, then remove them and lay them in an earthen bowl; add to the butter one teaspoonful of flour and let cook for a few minutes; moisten with stock (No. 194a) and white wine, and with this make a little stiff sauce; pour it over the tenderloin, and when all is nearly cold fill the mold with layers of the tenderloin, the sauce and some raw oysters, drained and well dried, removing the hard parts of the oyster. When the mold is nearly full, wet the edges of the paste, and cover with an upper crust, pressing it down on to the lower crust; cover it over with a damp, buttered and floured cloth, fastening it on tight, then plunge it into hot water to boil for one hour and a half to two hours. Unmold and serve with an English brown sauce (No. 1571).

(2323). LAMB PUDDING—MINION FILLETS À LA GLADSTONE (Pouding de Filets Mignons d'Agneau à la Gladstone).

Fry lightly in butter one ounce of chopped onions and shallots, fry separately some yearling lamb minion fillets, then mingle the two together, adding espagnole sauce (No. 414), some Harvey sauce, gravy, salt and pepper. Line a mold (Fig. 151), from which the inside has been removed, with beef suet paste, made as explained in woodcock pudding (No. 2325), fill it up with alternate layers of the meat and minced potatoes; pour the sauce over, moisten the edges of the paste and cover over with a flat of the same paste, lay on a buttered, floured soft towel and tie it all around with a string, then plunge the pudding in boiling water and leave it to cook for two hours; remove the towel, unmold, glaze with meat glaze (No. 402), spread on with a brush and serve.

(2324). THRUSH PUDDING (Pouding de Grives).

Butter and line a dome-form mold with a woodcock pudding paste (No. 2325), made with beef suet, butter, salt and flour. Fry in butter over a quick fire, some fat pork, ham and twenty-four boneless thrushes; as soon as done, drain off the fat and add salt, pepper, chopped parsley, Madeira sauce and half-glaze (No. 400). Place all of this in the dome and cover with a flat of the same paste; lay a wet and buttered cloth over and fasten it strongly underneath on the rounded side, set this in boiling water and let cook for an hour and a half, unwrap and turn it out of the mold on a hot dish and pour over a good Madeira sauce (No. 492) with game essence added (No. 389), serving a part of it separately.

(2325). WOODCOCK PUDDING (Pouding de Bécasses).

Cut up two clean raw woodcocks, dividing each one into five or six pieces, then season. Prepare a paste with a pound of flour, three-quarters of a pound of finely chopped beef suet, a little water and salt; give it two turns like a puff paste, roll it out and use it to line a half spherical-shaped mold; bestrew the bottom with raw onions, shallot, fresh mushrooms and parsley all finely chopped, and on this range the pieces of woodcock, dredging them over with chopped parsley. Cook the intestines taken from the birds with grated fat pork, press through a sieve and dissolve with a little half-glaze (No. 400), then pour it over the woodcocks. Close the opening with a layer of the same paste, fastening it well to the edges, and place the large part of the mold on the middle of a wet towel and tie the ends firmly on the top or round part of the mold. Cook the pudding for two hours in boiling water, then drain off the mold, untie the towel and turn the pudding over on a dish, remove the mold and cover the bottom of the dish with a little sauce reduced with game fumet (No. 397) and truffle peelings; glaze the paste with a brush and serve with a separate sauce reduced with game fumet.

(2326). CHICKEN QUENELLES À LA DREW (Quenelles de Volaille à la Drew).

Butter some oval molds three inches long by two wide and two and a quarter inches deep; decorate them with cuts of truffles and cover this with a layer of chicken quenelle forcemeat (No. 89), then poach in a slack oven. Prepare some forcemeat croûtons so that when they are trimmed and fried they will be exactly the same size as the quenelles and each a quarter of an inch thick; these are to be made of chicken quenelle forcemeat (No. 89) and foies-gras forcemeat (No. 78), half of each, mixed well and rubbed through a sieve. Spread this on sheets of strong buttered paper and poach in a slack oven; when cold dip in beaten eggs and bread-crumbs, and fry to a fine color; drain, wipe and dress these around a croustade (Fig. 8) made of fine foundation paste (No. 135), fastened with paste on to the center of a dish, pouring a little suprême sauce (No. 547) around. Unmold the quenelles and lay them on the forcemeat croûtons; fill the croustade with whole peeled truffles and channeled fresh mushrooms (No. 118); cover these garnishings with suprême sauce (No. 547); finish when ready with raw egg-yolks, cream and fresh butter, range some trussed crawfish on top of the garnishing, then serve.

(2327). CHICKEN QUENELLES À LA RICHELIEU (Quenelles de Volaille à la Richelieu).

FIG. 429.

Decorate some oval-shaped molds with fanciful cuts of very black truffles. Pound one ounce of truffles with the same quantity of cooked rice and half as much fresh butter, adding one or two spoonfuls of béchamel sauce (No. 409), pass all through a sieve and let get very cold. Garnish half of the molds with chicken quenelle forcemeat (No. 89), lay the prepared truffle purée in the center, cover over with more forcemeat and poach them in a slack oven; as soon as they are firm to the touch, unmold and dress them crown-shaped; serve separately a Périgueux sauce (No. 517).

(2328). CHICKEN QUENELLES, BRETONNE (Quenelles de Poulet Bretonne).

This entrée is to be dressed on a paste foundation that covers the bottom of a dish, the sides of it to be decorated, and it should have a round flat support in the center, shaped rather on a slope and two inches high; this support is to be made of fried bread covered with forcemeat and poached in a slack oven. In this manner the quenelles will have a firm foundation to stand against, and the mushrooms being supported by this prop cannot impair the solidity of the circle, but in order to be perfectly safe it were better that the bottom of the dish be provided with an out-

FIG. 430.

standing ledge, thus giving more strength to the circle. Prepare a pretty garnishing of turned mushrooms (No. 118) of even size, and cooked very white; have some minced onions also prepared, reduced with good béchamel sauce (No. 409), and thickened off the fire with two egg-yolks, finishing with a dash of cayenne. Pound the raw meats of a large chicken, mixing in a third as much pâte-à-choux panada (No. 121), adding it very slowly so that the meats will take some time to pound, then put in about four or five spoonfuls of the minced onions. When all is well mingled add two or three raw yolks; pass this forcemeat through a sieve, lay it aside in a metal bowl, smooth it on ice, and mold it into about fifteen handsome quenelles (No. 154); poach and remove carefully with a skimmer; drain on a cloth, and dress them at once in a uniform circle, slightly spreading outward; arrange the mushrooms on top of the support, and cover them with a little good velouté sauce (No. 415), reduced with the mushroom broth and parings; serve more of this sauce apart.

(2329). QUENELLES OF CHICKEN WITH CONSOMMÉ (Quenelles de Poulet au Consommé).

Prepare a quenelle forcemeat with the breasts of two chickens the same as for No. 89; form a small quenelle and throw it into a little boiling broth; remove it from the fire and poach it for about ten minutes, cut it in two to be assured of its delicacy, and if found too hard add two or three spoonfuls of allemande sauce (No. 407) to the forcemeat, and if too soft a little panada (No. 121), pounding it well and adding only a small quantity at a time; then place the forcemeat in a tin vessel and lay it on ice. Put the four well-roasted legs and all the fragments of the chickens into a saucepan, with the exception of the livers and gizzards, moisten to the height of the meats with some good stock (No. 194a), then boil and skim; add an onion stuck with a clove, a minced carrot and a bunch of parsley garnished with a bay leaf; let cook for one hour on a very slow fire, then strain, skim off the fat, clarify and pour it through a napkin; it should be of a fine color. An hour and a quarter before serving butter a sautéing pan liberally, having it large enough to hold twelve soupspoon quenelles, and mold them as explained in No. 155. Twenty minutes before serving put this sautéing pan on the range and moisten the quenelles with some of the boiling broth (No. 194a); cover and set it on one side to poach without boiling; as soon as they feel hard under the pressure of the finger, and have risen to the surface of the broth, drain them on to a white cloth and lay them either in a vegetable dish or a silver one and pour the boiling prepared consommé over.

(2330). QUENELLES OF FISH, MONTGLAS (Quenelles de Poisson à la Montglas).

This entrée is to be dressed in the center of a carved border made of rice croustade (No. 160). Prepare a fish quenelle forcemeat (No. 90) with pike perch; when strained put it into a thin metal vessel, and with a spoon incorporate in, while working it on ice, two spoonfuls of good béchamel sauce (No. 409) reduced with a coffeespoonful of powdered curry, diluting with the mushroom liquor; keep the forcemeat on ice. With the head and parings of the pike perch make a good white wine court-bouillon (No. 39); strain, free it of fat, and reduce to a half-glaze. Put on to reduce three gills of velouté sauce (No. 415), and incorporate the court-bouillon slowly into it, also a few spoonfuls of the reduced mushroom broth. Strain the sauce when succulent and sufficiently thickened; pour it into a small saucepan and stir it occasionally on the side of the range. Prepare a plentiful montglas, composed of truffles, mushrooms, and cooked lobster-claw meat; mingle in a few spoonfuls of reduced velouté sauce (No. 415), and keep it in a bain-marie; prepare also a fine salpicon of trimmed and poached oysters, add a few spoonfuls of good reduced velouté sauce and the oyster liquor, finishing with a coffeespoonful of anchovy essence, paste or purée; let this preparation get cool, then divide it into small parts, and roll each one to the shape of a long olive. With the fish forcemeat mold some quenelles with a soupspoon (No. 155);

FIG. 431.

stuff them with the salpicon rolled in olive-shapes, and cover with more of the forcemeat; smooth the surfaces nicely; poach these quenelles in salted water without allowing the liquid to boil, and as soon as the forcemeat stiffens drain on to a cloth. Dress the montglas in the center of the rice border, and between the latter and the montglas range the quenelles stand-ing almost upright; cover them lightly with the prepared sauce, and serve at the same time a bowl-ful of the same, buttering it well, and finishing it at the last moment with a piece of lobster butter (No. 580).

(2331). QUENELLES OF FOIES-GRAS, STUFFED À LA FINANCIÈRE (Quenelles de Foies-Gras Fourrées à la Financière).

Fasten a bread or rice croustade on a dish as shown in Fig. 431, hollowing it one inch only on the top; in the center place a rice support slightly conical in shape and two inches high. Have this croustade fastened on a dish and keep it covered. Prepare a montglas of truffles; mix it with a very thick brown sauce (No. 414), leave to cool, then divide it into small parts and roll each of these into long olives. Pound a raw foies-gras, season and pass it through a sieve; pound also half as much breast of raw chicken and add slowly to it half the same quantity of bread panada (No. 121); press this forcemeat through a sieve and return it to the mortar, season and pound once more, incorporating in gradually the pounded foies-gras and three or four egg-yolks; season

FIG. 432.

highly; smooth by beating on ice, then try a small piece to judge of its consistency. With the bones, fragments of chicken and broth prepare a suprême sauce (No. 547); keep it in a bain-marie. Butter a dozen quenelle molds, decorate them with truffles (Fig. 75), fill them full of forcemeat, form a depression in the center, place in one of the montglas olives and cover with more force-meat so that it lies exactly in the center of the quenelle; smooth dome-form with the blade of a small wet knife to have it a perfect shaped quenelle. Range these molds on a deep baking pan containing a little hot water, cover with buttered paper and poach in a slack oven. Remove and dress them almost upright on the croustade, leaning them against the support, and finally cover with a little of the suprême sauce. Fill the empty space in the center with a tastefully arranged cluster of mushrooms and imitation cocks'-combs made of veal palates, masking them with more of the sauce, and in the middle lay a fine glazed truffle; cover very lightly with the sauce and serve what remains in a sauce-boat.

(2332). QUENELLES OF GROUSE, LONDONDERRY (Quenelles de Tétras Londonderry).

Obtain some oval-shaped molds three inches long by two and a quarter wide, they being half an inch thick; butter them over with cold fresh butter and decorate with fanciful cuts of very black truffles (Fig. 75); cover the bottoms with grouse quenelle forcemeat (No. 91) and fill up the center with a salpicon of grouse and mushrooms, half of each, thickened with Madeira sauce (No. 492), then let stand till cold. Cover over with more of the forcemeat, smooth the surface and poach in boiling water, having just sufficient to reach halfway up the molds. When firm to the touch unmold, drain and dress on a dish bottom having a support on top filled with truffles; cover the quenelles with Madeira sauce (No. 492) and game fumet (No. 397), and also serve a sauce-boatful of the sauce.

(2333). QUENELLES OF PARTRIDGE À LA STUART (Quenelles de Perdreau à la Stuart).

Have oval-shaped molds, and decorate them with fanciful cuts of very black truffles and red beef tongue; garnish half of each mold with a delicate partridge cream forcemeat (No. 75); lay in the center some cold cooked fine herbs (No. 385) reduced with velouté sauce (No. 415), and cover with more of the forcemeat; poach them in a slack oven, and serve with a separate sauce-boat of béchamel sauce (No. 409) finished with essence of truffles (No. 395).

FIG. 433.

(2334). QUENELLES OF PHEASANT—FRIED (Quenelles de Faisan Frites).

With some raw pheasant meat taken from the breasts prepare a quenelle forcemeat (No. 91), and when passed through a sieve put it in a tin vessel and cook until smooth; mix in with it two spoonfuls of chopped truffles; use this to fill a dozen quenelle molds (Fig. 75); have the tops quite high and smooth. Range these molds on a raised-edge baking tin containing a little hot water; boil the liquid up twice, then cover the molds with buttered paper and poach uncovered in a slack oven; when firm to the touch remove. Cool them off partly before unmolding, then dip in eggs, then in bread-crumbs, fry and serve on a folded napkin with fried parsley on top.

(2335). QUENELLES OF SALMON—STUFFED (Quenelles de Saumon Fourrées).

Fasten on to the center of an entrée dish a wooden bottom an inch and a half in thickness; cover it with a thin flat of noodle paste (No. 142); in the middle of this fasten a small round support cut sloping, and on top set a small basket, all of these being covered with noodle paste; the

FIG. 434.

inside must also be covered, and the outside with ornamental leaves cut from the same paste. Egg over this paste and dry it for a few hours. Prepare a forcemeat with ten ounces of salmon, eight ounces of panada (No. 121), eight ounces of lobster butter (No. 580) and four egg-yolks; rub it through a sieve and when very smooth try a small piece to rectify if necessary; let this harden on the ice for twenty minutes, stirring it frequently. Make a fine truffled montglas with mushrooms and truffles thickened with a good velouté sauce (No. 415), reduced and finished with a few tablespoonfuls of fish glaze (No. 399); let this preparation get cold and divide into small parts and roll into long-shaped olives. Have the forcemeat very smooth and form it into quenelles with a spoon (No. 155), and stuffing each one with a little montglas poach them in salted water, drain on a cloth and decorate the smoothest side with a truffle lozenge, fastening it on with a little of the uncooked forcemeat. Dress these quenelles in a circle around the base on the dish, inclining them somewhat; fill the basket with small truffles, cover the quenelles lightly with a little good lean velouté sauce (No. 416) reduced with fish court-bouillon (No. 38) and mushroom broth, having a separate sauce-boat of the same sauce. The truffles in the basket may be replaced by mushrooms or a small pyramid of crawfish tails or shrimps dressed around a bed of fresh parsley.

(2336). SPRING TURKEY QUENELLES À LA PROVIDENCE (Quenelles de Dindonneau à la Providence).

FIG. 435.

Decorate some oval-shaped molds (Fig. 75) with red tongue, truffles and pistachios; fill them half full with some very mellow turkey quenelle forcemeat (No. 89), and lay in the center a royal salpicon (No. 751); cover with more forcemeat and poach them in a slow oven; unmold and dress them crown-shaped, filling the well with shrimps rolled in a little chicken glaze (No. 398), lemon juice and lobster butter (No. 580). Dress over a printanière sauce (No. 546) and serve a separate sauce-boat of the same sauce.

(2337). WOODCOCK QUENELLES À LA D'ARTOIS (Quenelles de Bécasses à la d'Artois).

FIG. 436.

Butter some pieces of strong paper three inches by four, spread on them a layer of woodcock quenelle forcemeat (No. 91), oval-shaped, two and a half inches long by one and a half wide and a quarter of an inch thick; garnish the centers with a brown montglas (No. 747), and cover with another layer of the quenelle forcemeat, having it dome-shaped, and smoothing with a knife. Decorate the top with truffles and red tongue; cover with thin slices of fat pork and a strong buttered paper, then poach them in a slack oven until they are firm to the touch; dress them crown-shaped in a dish, cover them with half-glaze (No. 400) and Madeira sauce (No. 492); serve separately a sauce-boat of the same sauce.

(2338). SALPICON OF CHICKEN, BAKED (Salpicon de Volaille au Gratin).

Take one pound of white meat of a cooked chicken, cut it into small dice and put the pieces in a saucepan with four spoonfuls of cooked lean ham, and as much mushrooms, all to be cut alike, and mingle in a few spoonfuls of good reduced béchamel sauce (No. 409), finishing the preparation with a small piece of melted chicken glaze (No. 398). Pour the whole into a small pie dish (Fig. 183), smooth it to a dome and cover with a layer of duchess potato preparation (No. 2785), smooth again, butter over the top and bestrew with bread-crumbs and grated parmesan; bake for a quarter of an hour in a slack oven and serve in the same dish.

(2339). SHELLS BENOÎTON (Coquilles Benoîton).

Prepare the same sauce as for à la Villa (No. 2340), mixing into it a third each of whole braised chestnuts (No. 654), fine mushroom heads and whole small truffles; strew the tops with unsmoked beef tongue and green pistachios, both cut up in small one-eighth inch squares; then dredge with bread-crumbs and butter. Brown in a moderate oven for ten to fifteen minutes and serve.

(2340). SHELLS OF OYSTERS À LA VILLA (Coquilles d'Huîtres à la Villa).

Poach the oysters, drain and suppress the hearts. Sauté in butter half as much escalops of cooked lobster, and half as much white part of cooked chicken as lobster. Cut the poached oysters in five-eighths of an inch squares, mingle with the lobster, chicken and béchamel sauce (No. 409), thickening with egg-yolks, cream and fresh butter; use this preparation to fill up some buttered and bread-crumbed clean oyster shells; when very full sift over each a little fried bread-crumbs, and set them in the oven a few minutes before serving.

(2341). SHELLS FILLED WITH CRAWFISH TAILS (Coquilles Garnies de Queues d'Écrevisses).

Prepare a salpicon with the meats picked from the large claws and the tails of crawfish; add to it a third as much cooked mushrooms, cut in dice shape, and mingle with some good reduced thick béchamel sauce (No. 409); with this fill eight or ten silver or china table shells (Fig. 438); smooth

FIG. 437.

the preparation to a dome and cover with a layer of the cream fish forcemeat (No. 76). Range the shells on a small baking sheet, dredge the forcemeat with grated parmesan and brown for five minutes under the salamander (Fig. 123); keep the shells hot at the oven door for five minutes longer, then dress them symmetrically on a wooden foundation covered with white paper; surround this foundation with green parsley leaves.

(2342). SHELLS FILLED WITH SHRIMPS AND OYSTER CRABS (Coquilles Garnies de Crevettes et de Crabes d'Huîtres).

FIG. 438.

Put the oyster crabs into a saucepan on the fire, with a little white wine, and when poached drain and lay them in a sautoir with the same amount of cooked and shelled shrimps fried in butter; add lean béchamel cream sauce (No. 411) that has been well seasoned; with this fill some buttered and breaded silver shells (Fig. 438) or else clean clam shells; throw bread-crumbs over, baste with butter and brown in a hot oven.

(2343). SHELLS OF BEEF PALATES À LA MARINIÈRE (Coquilles de Palais de Bœuf à la Marinière).

Have some beef palates cooked and pressed as explained for à la béchamel (No. 1326), cut them in fillets of a quarter of an inch square by one inch in length. Place in a saucepan two ounces of butter, and some finely chopped shallots and mushrooms; moisten with a little white wine, add a little velouté sauce (No. 415), reduce, season to taste, then add the beef palates, heat and thicken the sauce with egg-yolks and cream. Butter well some shells (Fig. 438), besprinkle over with bread-crumbs and fill them with the above preparation, keeping them slightly dome-shaped on top. Cover with béchamel sauce (No. 409), dredge over some grated bread-crumbs and parmesan cheese, and pour melted butter over the top. Brown them nicely in a warm oven and arrange them on a napkin with green sprigs of parsley around.

(2344). SHELLS OF CHICKEN À LA SHAW (Coquilles de Poulet à la Shaw).

Cook two tender chickens, each one to weigh two pounds and a half, in a white wine mirepoix stock (No. 419), and when done strain the stock over and let get cold in this; then suppress the skin, fat and bones and cut up the meat into five-eighths inch squares. Cook the livers with the fat skimmed from the mirepoix stock and chop them up when cold; also chop up six hard-boiled eggs, the yolks and whites separately. Put the chicken meat into a sautoir with the chopped livers and eggs, season with salt, pepper and nutmeg. Place two ounces of butter in a saucepan with two ounces of flour, stir it well, then remove the saucepan from the fire and mix into it the stock from the chickens, having two gills of it; then boil it up, stirring continuously, and add a gill of cream; simmer the whole and thicken with six egg-yolks diluted with a little cream without allowing it to boil, rolling the ingredients into the sauce while tossing without using any spoon, and season properly; lastly add a glassful of sherry and half a teaspoonful of lemon juice; fill up the shells, dredge over parmesan cheese and color in a hot oven or under the salamander (Fig. 123).

(2345). SHELLS OF CHICKEN OR SWEETBREADS (Coquilles de Volaille ou de Ris de Veau).

Have either some silver or china shells (Fig. 438) or else some scallop shells; butter and dredge over with bread-crumbs; mince some braised white meat of chicken or else sweetbreads with half as many mushrooms and put it into a sautoir; mix with velouté sauce (No. 415); let all boil, then thicken with raw egg-yolks, cream and fresh butter. Fill the shells with this preparation, bestrew the tops with bread-crumbs and a little grated parmesan, and baste with melted butter; brown in a brisk oven.

(2346). SHELLS OF FISH (Coquilles de Poisson).

Cook a prepared sea bass in a court-bouillon (No. 38), then drain, suppress the skin and bones and only use the meat after shredding it well; reduce some velouté sauce (No. 415) with mushroom essence (No. 392) and the court-bouillon; season properly and thicken with egg-yolks and butter, then stir in the fish. Butter some shells (Fig. 438), besprinkle with bread-crumbs, fill them with the fish preparation, having the tops slightly dome-form; bestrew with bread-crumbs and grated parmesan, baste over with butter, then brown in the oven; serve as soon as they have attained a good color.

(2347). SHELLS OF FROGS' LEGS (Coquilles de Cuisses de Grenouilles).

Fry in butter one pound of frogs' legs without letting them acquire a color; butter some shells (Fig. 438), bread-crumb the insides, and fill the bottoms with a cream béchamel (No. 411); place on top cooked and minced mushrooms, and over this the boned frogs' legs; cover with more béchamel, make another bed of mushrooms and frogs, and finish with béchamel; dredge the tops with bread-crumbs fried in butter, set them in the oven, and when very hot and nicely browned serve at once on folded napkins.

(2348). SHELLS OF LOBSTER (Coquilles de Homard).

Kill two two-pound lobsters by plunging them into boiling water for two minutes; break off the claws, and put them into a saucepan with the bodies; cover with a court-bouillon (No. 38), and allow the liquid to boil for twenty minutes while covered; then remove the saucepan from the fire and leave the lobsters to partially cool off in this stock; drain them. Suppress the claw shells, and cut the meats up into three-sixteenths of an inch squares; lay them in a small saucepan, detach the tails from the bodies, rub the creamy parts of the latter through a sieve, and strain the lobster stock; put this on the fire to reduce to a half-glaze, and incorporate into it slowly a quart of reduced béchamel sauce (No. 409); season with a pinch of cayenne pepper; the sauce should be reduced to a proper degree and seasoned. Cut the lobster tails lengthwise in two, take out the meats, and cut them into slices; butter the insides of the shells (Fig. 438), strew over with bread-crumbs, and dress the pieces of lobster crown-shaped inside of these, alternating them with a slice of truffle; lay them in a sautoir, one very close to the other; add the dice-shaped pieces of lobster to the sauce and pour this over the contents of the shells. Besprinkle with parmesan, and color the tops, using a salamander (Fig. 123); then dress the shells on folded napkins in a circle, garnishing the center with green parsley sprigs.

(2349). SHELLS OF MUSSELS OR OYSTERS BAKED (Coquilles de Moules ou d'Huîtres au Gratin).

Suppress the black foot (the appendage) of some mussels and cut them up into two or three pieces; place these in a highly seasoned allemande sauce (No. 407); add to it chopped parsley, and fill the shells (Fig. 438) already buttered with this preparation; dust over with fried bread-crumbs, and leave them in the oven for a few minutes before serving. Oysters may be prepared exactly the same way.

(2350). OYSTERS BAKED IN THEIR SHELLS (Huîtres Gratinées dans leurs Coquilles).

Open some oysters, detach them from their shells, leaving them in the deep one; pour over a little melted butter mixed with chopped parsley, strew the tops with bread-crumbs and grated parmesan, and then range these shells very straight on a bed of salt spread over a baking-sheet; cook them for seven or eight minutes in a moderate oven, and after taking them out wipe the bottoms of the shells carefully, and lay them on napkins to serve.

(2351). OYSTERS BÉCHAMEL IN THEIR SHELLS (Huîtres Béchamel dans leurs Coquilles).

Poach and drain three dozen oysters; fry colorless in butter three shallots, moisten with white wine and the oyster liquor, and dilute with béchamel sauce (No. 409). Cook and despumate; thicken with egg-yolks, butter, and cream; season with salt, pepper and nutmeg, stirring so that the sauce thickens properly; then add the oysters to it, and with this fill the well-cleaned, deep oyster shells; sprinkle over fried bread-crumbs and butter, then brown them in the oven.

(2352). OYSTERS ROASTED AND ENGLISH STYLE IN THEIR SHELLS (Huîtres Rôties et à l'Anglaise dans leurs Coquilles).

Lay some very clean medium-sized oysters on the broiler, on the flat side of the shell; when hot, turn over and lay the hollow side to the fire until they open, then take off the flat shell and serve the oysters in the hollow one, laying a small piece of fresh butter on each.

For English style prepare the oysters as for roasted in shells, and instead of butter season them with salt, pepper, and finely chopped fresh mushrooms; add a little lean velouté sauce (No. 416) to each, bestrew with bread-crumbs fried in butter, push in the oven for a moment and serve.

(2353). OYSTERS IN THEIR SHELLS WITH FRIED BREAD (Huîtres dans leurs Coquilles Naturelles au Pain Frit).

Heat some butter in a small saucepan; mix in with it some white bread-crumbs, stir continuously and let it get a light brown color, then remove from the fire and drain. Poach and drain some oysters; lay six of their natural shells on a baking sheet having an inside perforated sheet to hold the oysters level, or cover the bottom of the pan with a bed of salt. Take up a heaping teaspoonful of the fried bread-crumbs and pour it into each shell; on top place one or two oysters and cover with a little well seasoned velouté sauce (No. 416); bestrew the surfaces with grated parmesan and on each set a small piece of butter; push the shells into a moderate oven for five or six minutes, then remove and dress in a circle on a folded napkin, with a sprig of parsley in the center.

(2354). SHELLS OF SCALLOPS, PARISIAN STYLE (Coquilles de Pétoncles à la Parisienne).

Open seven or eight large scallop shells; detach the meats as well as the white and red milts, and poach them in a little white wine; drain and cut them into dice pieces; keep this salpicon on one side. Fry in butter, chopped up onions and shallots; add raw mushrooms cut in dice shape and cook until their moisture is evaporated, then add the prepared salpicon five or six minutes later; season and thicken with a good béchamel sauce (No. 409) reduced when ready to use. Boil once more for a few minutes without ceasing to stir; it should be quite consistent, and finish it away from the fire with a pinch of cayenne pepper and a piece of fresh lobster butter (No. 580). Lift this stew up with a spoon, and with it fill the shells; cover the preparation with bread-crumbs, brush over with melted butter, and bake for ten minutes in a moderate oven. Dress the shells as soon as they are removed from the fire.

(2355). SHELLS OF SPINAL MARROW OR BRAINS (Coquilles d'Amourettes ou de Cervelles).

After the spinal marrow or brains have been prepared and cooked as explained in No. 1549, drain and cut them up in one-inch length slices, butter the interiors of either china or silver shells (Fig. 438), cover the insides with white bread raspings, fill the shells with the pieces of spinal marrow, and pour over a white Italian sauce (No. 484). Cover the tops with some well-seasoned béchamel sauce (No. 409), besprinkle with bread-crumbs and parmesan cheese, add a little butter, and brown in a hot oven. Dress them crown-shaped on a folded napkin, garnishing with sprigs of green parsley.

(2356). SHELLS OF SQUABS BAKED (Coquilles de Pigeonneaux Gratinées).

After the squabs have been plucked, singed, drawn, well cleaned and boned, divide each one into four or six pieces, according to the size of the bird, then fry these colorless in butter with minced fresh mushrooms; after they are well done, pour off the fat and replace it by allemande sauce (No. 407), adding a little finely cut up chives. Butter some shells (Fig. 438), bestrew the bottoms with a little bread-crumbs and fill them with the squabs; sprinkle more bread-crumbs over mixed with grated parmesan and brown with a salamander or in a hot oven. Instead of bread-crumbing the tops may be covered with chicken que-nelle forcemeat (No. 89) and coated with butter, then breaded and browned in the oven, or else cover the shells with a thin flat made of puff paste fragments (No. 146), egg them over twice and bake in a moderate oven.

(2357). SHELLS OF VEAL OR LAMB SWEETBREADS, À LA HARPER (Coquilles de Ris de Veau ou d'Agneau, à la Harper).

Braise unlarded sweetbreads; when cooked place them in a dish, pour over the stock and let get cold; merely cut them up into small three-sixteenths inch pieces, add to these half as much fresh mushrooms and a quarter as much unsmoked but salted red beef tongue, all cut the same size, and mix the pieces into some béchamel sauce (No. 409), seasoning with salt and pepper to taste. Butter some shells (Fig. 438), besprinkle each with bread-crumbs, fill with the above preparation and dust the tops with bread raspings and grated cheese; pour melted butter over and brown the surface to a fine color in a hot oven, then dress and serve on folded napkins.

(2358). SHELLS OF TERRAPIN WITH HAZEL-NUTS (Coquilles de Terrapène aux Noisettes).

Have a thick and well-seasoned béchamel sauce (No. 409); mix in with it four ounces of roasted hazel-nuts pounded to a pulp with a gill of sherry wine. Butter some shells, dust over with bread-crumbs, and fill the bottoms with the béchamel; over this lay some boned terrapin, sprinkle over a little fine sherry, and pour more sauce on top; throw over some bread-crumbs fried in butter and of a fine color, then set the shells in the oven, and serve when the surfaces are nicely browned.

(2359). SOUFFLÉ OF CHICKEN (Soufflé de Poulet).

Have a quarter of a pound of very white roasted chicken meat, pare it free of all sinews, fat or skin, then pound it to a pulp with an ounce of butter, a tablespoonful of béchamel sauce (No. 409) and two egg-yolks; season with salt, pepper and nutmeg and rub the whole through

FIG. 439.

a sieve; put it back into a vessel to heat, mixing in slowly two tablespoonfuls of well-drained whipped cream, then stir in two very stiffly beaten egg-whites and a teaspoonful of finely chopped truffles. Butter a soufflé pan (Fig. 182) lightly, or small paper cases (Fig. 439) stiffened in the oven; fill them up and cook in a moderate oven; it takes about twelve or fifteen

FIG. 440.

minutes to cook the soufflé in the pan; serve at once. Guests had better be kept waiting for a soufflé than to have the soufflé wait for them. It must be served immediately it leaves the oven, otherwise it loses its greatest merit, namely a beautiful appearance.

(2360). SOUFFLÉ OF CHICKEN À LA DELSART (Soufflé de Poulet à la Delsart).

Pound half a pound of the white meat of a cooked chicken with two ounces of butter, two spoonfuls of béchamel (No. 409), and two raw egg-yolks; season with salt, pepper and nutmeg. Stiffen some buttered or oiled paper cases in the oven, and ten minutes before serving incorporate into the preparation two egg-whites beaten to a stiff froth, and two tablespoonfuls of well-drained, whipped cream; fill the cases, prepared as for soufflé of chicken (No. 2359), and place them in a moderately heated oven for ten to twelve minutes, then glaze them over with a brush.

(2361). SOUFFLÉ OF FAT LIVERS WITH TRUFFLES (Soufflé de Foies-Gras aux Truffes).

Pound six ounces of fat livers with two ounces of rice thoroughly cooked in broth until per-fectly dry; add one whole egg, season and press the preparation through a sieve, putting the purée into a bowl; make it very smooth by stirring into it four spoonfuls of raw chicken quenelle force-meat (No. 89), and two well-beaten-up egg-whites. Fill with this some paper cases (Fig. 439) previously buttered and stiffened in the oven; set them in the oven for ten to twelve minutes, and glaze them with some light chicken glaze (No. 398), using a brush for this purpose.

(2362). SOUFFLÉ OF GAME À LA LUCIE (Soufflé de Gibier à la Lucie).

Pound four ounces of cooked game meat with two ounces of rice boiled in broth until dry and consistent; add two tablespoonfuls of game glaze (No. 398), two raw egg-yolks and half an ounce of melted butter, then press all through a sieve, and beat the preparation thoroughly. Ten minutes before serving mix in half an ounce of truffles cut in one-eighth inch squares, and two egg-whites beaten to a stiff froth. Butter some paper cases (Fig. 439), stiffen them in the oven, then fill them three-quarters full with the soufflé preparation, set them in the oven for about ten minutes, and when done glaze the tops with a little game glaze (No. 398) and serve without delay.

(2363). SOUFFLÉ OF LOBSTER IN CASES (Soufflé de Homard en Caisses).

Plunge a two-pound lobster into boiling water so as to kill it quickly, and when cold split it lengthwise in two, take out the meat from the half tails, cut it up and pound the pieces with two or three spoonfuls of good reduced velouté sauce (No. 415); finish with some red butter (No. 580), adding also a piece of fresh butter; press this through a sieve, and put the purée back into the mortar, and with the pestle pound it well to make it have a good, consistent body, allowing it to absorb very slowly three gills of good raw cream; season and finally add two spoonfuls of the creamy part from the bodies, a dash of cayenne pepper and two spoonfuls of whipped cream. With this preparation fill either some round buttered paper (No. 439), silver (No. 438) or porcelain cases, wiped dry and buttered; dredge over the insides with bread-crumbs and fill the cases and lay them on a baking sheet; push them into a slack oven and let the preparation cook from fifteen to twenty minutes; it should be cooked in a very hot oven, otherwise it will become black. After taking the soufflés from the oven, glaze the surfaces with a little of the same reduced velouté sauce, finish with red butter (No. 580), and serve them at once.

(2364). SOUFFLÉ OF PARTRIDGE À LA HAGGINS (Soufflé de Perdreau à la Haggins).

Pound half a pound of cold partridge meat to a pulp, add to it half an ounce of foies-gras, season with salt, pepper and nutmeg and put in four tablespoonfuls of game glaze (No. 398) and half an ounce of butter; press this through a fine sieve and place the purée in a metal basin to heat up lightly, incorporating in slowly four raw egg-yolks and four very stiffly beaten whites. When the preparation is thoroughly mixed, transfer it to some small buttered paper cases (Fig. 439), stiffened in the oven, having them three-quarters of an inch full; push them into a slack oven fifteen to twenty minutes before serving; glaze over with a brush dipped in game glaze (No. 398) and serve them instantly they leave the oven; they must not be standing. Truffles cut in eighth of an inch squares may be added to the soufflés if so desired.

(2365). SOUFFLÉ OF PHEASANT À LA ANDREW (Soufflé de Faisan à la Andrew).

Take the cooked meats from a roasted pheasant, suppressing skin, bones and sinews, pound them to a pulp with half as much cooked rice, and also one ounce of very fresh fat liver. Make an essence (No. 389) with the parings; reduce half a pint of espagnole sauce (No. 414); add it to the essence and when very thick put it with the pheasant pulp and strain the whole through a sieve into a tin basin and work well while adding some chopped truffles. Twenty-five minutes before serving heat the preparation in a bain-marie and incorporate into it seven raw egg-yolks one by one, and three ounces of fresh butter, working it in well, and then stir in five egg-whites, beaten to a very stiff froth. Butter a soufflé pan (Fig. 182), fill it half full with the preparation and push it into a slack oven; it ought to take from fifteen to twenty minutes to cook; when done, glaze over with game glaze (No. 398) and serve at once.

(2366). SOUFFLÉ OF WOODCOCKS WITH TRUFFLES (Soufflé de Bécasses aux Truffes).

Suppress all the meats from three roasted woodcocks and pound it to a pulp; fry the intestines and liver in butter, add this to the pulp and press through a sieve; dilute with a heaping spoonful of game glaze (No. 398) and remove from the fire; stir the preparation until it loses its greatest heat, then add four egg-yolks, an ounce of melted butter, an ounce of peeled truffles cut in small dice, and proper seasoning, and incorporate in slowly four beaten egg-whites, and if found necessary an ounce of boiled rice may also be added. Put this either into a buttered soufflé pan (Fig. 182) or else in buttered paper cases (Fig. 439) stiffened in the oven. If for cases of half a pint capacity, they will require fifteen minutes, but all depends upon their size.

(2367). CHICKEN LIVERS SURTOUT WITH MUSHROOMS OR IN RICE BORDER WITH CURRY (Surtout de Foies de Volaille aux Champignons ou en Bordure de Riz au Kari).

Cover the middle of a dish with a three-quarters of an inch thick layer of foies-gras forcemeat (No. 78) and poach in a slack oven. Fry some chicken livers in butter with a little blanched shallot and half as much minced mushrooms as there are livers; season with salt and pepper and dilute with Madeira sauce (No. 492). Dress these livers on the forcemeat surtout and sprinkle chopped parsley over; serve very hot.

In a Rice Border with Curry.—Make an Indian rice (No. 1872) border, dress on a hot dish and fill the center with fried chicken livers the same as the above, adding some curry powder.

(2368). WILD PIGEON SURTOUT, BAKED (Surtout de Pigeons Ramiers, au Gratin).

After the pigeons have been picked, singed and nicely cleaned, cut them lengthwise in two, then trim, removing the legs and a part of the backbone; season and fry in butter till three-quarters done, drain off the butter, cover with velouté sauce (No. 415) thickening with raw egg-yolks and a little fresh butter; leave the sautoir on the fire and roll the pigeons in until well mingled with the sauce. Spread in the middle of an oval baking dish a half-inch thick layer of godiveau (No. 84); place the pigeons on top and pour the sauce over; besprinkle with bread-crumbs and grated cheese, baste with butter and brown in a hot oven or with a salamander (Fig. 123).

(2369). BEEF TART OR PIE À LA PEREZ (Tarte de Bœuf à la Perez).

These pies are made in deep china dishes (Fig. 183), suitable to be put in the oven. Butter the bottom of the dish and garnish it with a thin layer of finely minced onions; over this put a layer of cooked potatoes cut into thin slices, and on top of the potatoes a thick layer of slices of tenderloin of beef; season with salt, pepper, nutmeg, chopped parsley, and chopped-up mushrooms; set a few whole egg-yolks here and there, then cover with another layer of onions and potatoes, both minced fine. The dish should now be quite full of the dressing, and dome-shaped on top. Roll out some cuttings of puff paste (No. 146) to an eighth of an inch in thickness; cut from it a band half an inch in width and sufficiently long to reach around the edge of the dish; wet the edge, and set the band over it, moisten and cover the whole with a rolled-out flat of the same paste an eighth of an inch in thickness; press down the paste on to the band, at the bottom of the dome, and cut away the superfluous paste all around the dish, outside the edge; then with a small knife cut grooves into the band through its thickness. Make a hole in the center of the dome in the paste, decorate around this with imitation leaves made of paste, brush it twice with beaten egg, and set the pie on a baking sheet. Cook it for an hour and a quarter in a moderate oven, and should it threaten to brown too soon cover with sheets of wet paper, and when ready to serve pour into the pie an espagnole sauce (No. 414), reduced with some clear gravy (No. 404). Set it on a dish over a folded napkin.

(2370). CHICKEN TART OR PIE À LA MANHATTAN (Tarte de Poulet à la Manhattan).

Have two young chickens, singe, draw and cut them up into six or eight pieces; lay them in a saucepan containing small blanched onions and a bunch of parsley garnished with bay leaf; moisten with stock (No. 194a), cook slowly and thicken with kneaded butter (No. 579). Fill the bottom of a deep pie dish (Fig. 183) with peeled and pressed halved tomatoes, cover with a layer of lightly parboiled fried bacon cut into three-quarters of an inch pieces; season with salt, mignonette and nutmeg, and range the chicken on top with potato balls five-eighths of an inch in diameter and boiled in salted water, also the small onions. Chop up four ounces of veal and three ounces of fat pork; season with salt, nutmeg and pepper; pound in the mortar and rub through a sieve; to this forcemeat add two tablespoonfuls of cooked fine herbs (No. 385), an ounce of bread-crumbs and one whole egg; roll this on a floured table into three-quarter inch balls and drop them here and there while putting the chicken in the dish. Moisten the edge of the dish, place on a small band made of puff paste parings half an inch wide and one-eighth of an inch thick; moisten this and cover with a flat of puff paste parings; pinch the edges together, cut away all the surplus from around the edge of the dish. egg over twice and bake in a moderate oven for half or three-quarters of an hour, then serv

(2371). CHICKEN TART OR PIE À LA RIGOLO (Tarte de Poulet à la Rigolo).

Cut up a pound and a half young chicken into four pieces, bone these and season with salt and pepper; sauté them colorless in butter with fresh mushrooms and a tablespoonful of onion, each chopped up separately; when the whole is fried add a tablespoonful of flour, mix well and moisten with stock (No. 194a); boil, skim and simmer until thoroughly cooked, then add some imitation cocks'-combs made of beef's palate and cocks' kidneys, a broiled sliced sausage having the skin removed and the gizzard cooked and cut in quarter-inch squares, seasoning with salt, pepper and chopped parsley. Make a few quenelles with the chopped chicken livers, season well and mix in some bread-crumbs and raw egg-yolk; roll this preparation into balls, three-quarters of an inch in diameter. Fill a deep pie dish (Fig. 183) with the above chicken stew, dropping the balls among it, also some small hard-boiled egg-yolk balls; finish the pie the same as pie à la Manhattan (No. 2370).

(2372). CHICKEN TART OR PIE, AUSTRALIAN STYLE (Tarte de Poulet à l'Australienne).

Singe, draw and cleanse well some young chickens, cut them up into eight pieces: two wings, two thighs, two backs and two breastbones; fry these colorless in butter, moisten with stock (No. 194a), season and cook slowly while covered; remoisten several times, then add some allemande sauce (No. 407); garnish the bottom of a pie dish (Fig. 193) with slices of fried ham, lay the chicken on top, intercalating the pieces with small hard-boiled egg-yolks, chopped-up raw mushrooms and fine herbs; pour the sauce over and cover with a layer of chicken forcemeat (No. 73). Make a flat of puff paste parings, lay it over the top, pinch the edges, egg the surface twice and decorate with puff paste leaves; bake the pie in a hot oven for thirty to forty minutes.

(2373). LAMB MINION FILLET TART OR PIE À LA MANNING (Tarte de Filets Mignons d'Agneau à la Manning).

Remove the fat and sinews from some yearling lamb fillets, wrap them up in thin slices of veal suet, and roast till rare, then cut them into escalops and range the pieces in a buttered deep pie dish (Fig. 183), intercalating the thin slices of suet with the slices of fillet. Fry in butter some cut-up shallot, add to it mushrooms and chopped parsley, and moisten with a little espagnole sauce (No. 414) and good gravy (No. 404); pour this over the fillets and cover the edge of the dish with a band of puff paste, and the top with a flat of the same rolled to an eighth of an inch thickness; stick this to the band of paste, egg the surface and cook it for one hour in a moderately heated oven. After withdrawing the pie from the fire, make an opening in the middle of the upper crust, and fill the inside with a brown Madeira sauce (No. 492) finished with mushroom essence (No. 392).

(2374). LOBSTER TART OR PIE À LA A. HÉRAULT (Tarte de Homard à la A. Hérault).

Boil two two-pound lobsters in a court-bouillon (No. 38); drain, and let get cold; detach the tails and claws; remove all the creamy parts and rub them through a fine sieve, then pick the meat from the tails and claws, and cut them into slices. Partly fry two ounces of shallot cut into one-eighth of an inch squares, with two ounces of butter; when partially fried add half a pound of chopped fresh mushrooms, and let fry together; pour in a quart of allemande sauce (No. 407), season with salt, nutmeg and cayenne, also chopped parsley, and mix well, adding the creamy parts and the pieces of lobster; transfer all this into a deep pie dish (Fig. 183), and set on the edge, slightly dampened, a narrow puff paste (No. 146) band, and over all a layer of puff paste fragments; cut it away evenly all around the outer edge, and decorate the top with leaves made of paste; pinch the edges around the pie, and egg over the surface twice, then cook it for twenty to thirty minutes in a hot oven, and serve as soon as it is done.

(2375). LEG OF MUTTON TART OR PIE, CANADIAN (Tarte de Gigot de Mouton à la Canadienne).

Butter the interior of a pie dish (Fig. 183); range on the bottom some blanched salt pork and slices of mutton from the leg; on top lay a bed of potatoes, baked in the oven, peeled and cut in slices; season each layer with salt, pepper, nutmeg, chopped parsley, and chopped onions fried in butter, and pour a little good clear gravy (No. 404) over. Wet the edges of the dish, lay on a narrow band of paste, moisten and cover the whole with a flat of puff paste fragments, decorating the top with devices of the same paste, egg it over twice, and bake in a moderate oven for an hour and a quarter.

(2376). OYSTER TART OR PIE, SMITH STYLE (Tarte aux Huîtres à la Smith).

Poach in their own liquor three dozen medium oysters, drain and remove the muscles or ligaments. Fry in two ounces of butter, four ounces of bacon cut in three-sixteenths of an inch squares, two ounces of onions cut the same size, and half a pound of peeled and seedless tomatoes cut into five-eighths of an inch pieces; add the oyster liquor, reduce the whole with a pint of velouté sauce (No. 415), and when well done and seasoned nicely, add the oysters. Place all of this into a deep pie dish (Fig. 183), and lay on the edge, after slightly wetting it, a narrow band of puff paste (No. 146) an eighth of an inch thick and half an inch wide; moisten the top of this band, and cover the whole with a layer of paste made of fragments of puff paste; cut away the extending edges, and decorate the top with bits of the paste rolled out to one-eighth of an inch in thickness; pinch the edges round the border, and egg over the surface twice, then cook the pie in a hot oven for twenty to thirty minutes, and serve on a folded napkin. Either salt or smoked bacon can be used.

(2377). PIGEON TART À LA BRITANNIA (Tarte de Pigeons à la Britannia).

Singe three clean pigeons; divide each one in two parts, beat, remove the surplus bones without boning them, then season with salt, pepper, and cayenne pepper. Cover the bottom of a pie dish (Fig. 183) with thin slices of bacon, bestrew with a spoonful of onion, and one of mushrooms both chopped separately, range the halved pigeons in the dish intermingled with more slices of bacon, and a few hard-boiled eggs cut in two; bring it to a dome. Pour a few spoonfuls of good clear gravy (No. 404) into the bottom of the dish; cover with a layer of half paste the same as for the beef pie No. 2369. Decorate the summit, egg over, and cook for an hour and a quarter in a slack oven, covering with paper should it threaten to burn.

(2378). LOIN OF PORK TART OR PIE—ENGLISH STYLE (Tarte de Longe de Porc à l'Anglaise).

Have a loin of fresh pork, bone, remove the fat and cut from it slices three-eighths of an inch thick; beat to flatten slightly, seasoning with salt, pepper and nutmeg. Butter the inside of a pie dish (Fig. 183) and lay over some thin slices of raw salted and smoked ham, seasoning with prepared red pepper (No. 168), chopped shallot and onions; on this place a bed of raw sliced potatoes, and the pieces of meat above, dropping sage leaves here and there; pour a little good cold gravy (No. 404) into the bottom of the dish; moisten the edge with a brush dipped in water, lay on it a band of paste an eighth of an inch thick and half an inch wide; wet the top of this slightly and cover the pie with a layer of foundation paste (No. 135) or puff paste parings, having it an eighth of an inch in thickness; adhere this on the band, cut away all the surplus paste from the outside and make deep marks all around with the back of a knife; egg the surface twice and cut a hole in the center. Cook this pie in a moderate oven for an hour and a quarter more or less, according to its size; this time being allowed for one containing a pound and a quarter of meat and potatoes.

(2379). RABBIT TART OR PIE WITH FINE HERBS (Tarte de Lapin aux Fines Herbes).

Suppress the skin from two good rabbits; draw and wipe well the meats; separate them at the joints, bone the shoulders and the legs, decrease the size of the backbones without boning then entirely and split each one in two. With the necks, bones and a few game parings, make a small fumet (No. 397) with white wine. Cut half a pound of bacon into small slices; put them in a sautoir with butter, and heat for five minutes while stirring, then remove with a skimmer, leaving the fat in the pan, and into this throw two spoonfuls each of onions, shallots and mushrooms; fry together for two minutes, then add the pieces of rabbit; season highly, being sparing of the salt, and besprinkle with pulverized wild thyme. Cover the bottom of a pie dish (Fig. 183) intended for the oven with a layer of the bacon; on this place the pieces of rabbit, intermingling them with the fine herbs and bacon; pour into the bottom a few spoonfuls of the prepared fumet reduced to nearly half-glaze. Wet the edges of the dish, cover it with a thin band of puff paste fragments (No. 146) or fine foundation paste (No. 135); wet this band also. Cover the whole with a flat of puff paste parings, cut off the surplus around the edge of the dish, egg over twice and cook for an hour and a quarter in a slow oven; make a hole on the top and pour in the remainder of the fumet.

(2380). VEAL TART OR PIE À LA DICKINSON (Tarte de Veau à la Dickinson).

Suppress all the fat and sinews from a kernel of veal; cut it up into thin slices, having them an inch and a half in diameter. Butter a pie dish (Fig. 183) that can go into the oven; set slices of bacon and ham on the bottom, and over these the sliced veal, alternated; season with salt, pepper and parsley; add finely cut-up potatoes, chopped shallots or onions, then continue to fill with the same until the dish is quite full and well rounded on top; pour some clear gravy (No. 404) into the bottom, lay a small band made of puff paste parings on the edge of the dish, and a flat of the same paste on top; cut away the surplus paste around the dish, decorate and egg the pie over twice; bake it in a medium oven for one hour and a half for a dish containing a quart.

(2381). TIMBALE À LA NANTAISE (Timbale à la Nantaise).

Line a timbale mold the same as for No. 2383, cook it lightly, and when removed from the oven, unmold, open on the cut end, empty it of its contents, and keep warm. Prepare a garnishing composed of a few dozen poached oysters or else crawfish tails or red shrimps (either of them shelled), or slices of cooked lobster-tail meat, four ounces of peeled truffles previously cooked in

FIG. 441.

Madeira wine, and a few dozen small salmon quenelles rolled on a floured table and poached. Range these garnishings in a sautoir and keep them well covered. Put on to reduce a few gills of good béchamel (No. 409), stir slowly into it the oyster broth, also a few spoonfuls of good court-bouillon (No. 38) reduced to a half-glaze; finish the sauce with a pinch of cayenne pepper and lobster butter (No. 580) and a handful of grated parmesan. Cover the garnishings with this sauce, set them in layers in the timbale, alternating with the remainder of the sauce; close the top with the removed lid and serve at once.

(2382). TIMBALE OF CHICKEN, PARISIAN STYLE—LARGE (Grosse Timbale de Poulet à la Parisienne).

Butter a cold oval timbale mold, decorate with fanciful cuts of truffles and cover this decoration with a layer of consistent chicken quenelle forcemeat, having it half an inch deep at the base and diminishing the thickness toward the top. Fill the inside of the timbale with a well-pared boneless chicken fricassée (No. 1861), into which mix a Toulouse garnishing (No. 766), having both thoroughly cold. Cover the top with a layer of forcemeat and place the mold in a saucepan containing boiling water, withdraw it to one side at the first boil and finish cooking the timbale in a slack oven. Let it rest for fifteen minutes after removal, then unmold and pour around a little velouté sauce (No. 415) with essence of truffles

FIG. 442.

(No. 396); serve more of this sauce separately.

(2383). TIMBALE FOR EPICURES (Timbale des Épicures).

Butter a large timbale mold (Fig. 441) slightly wider on top than on the bottom; cover the bottom with a piece of paper and line with rather thick timbale paste (No. 150). With the tip of a small knife cut all round the bottom paste (Fig. 441), following the outlines of the sides in a way not to decrease the thickness; leave the cut piece of paste in its same position, then cover the bottom and sides with buttered paper and fill the timbale with common flour; close the opening firstly with a round of paper, then with a flat of the same paste; stand it on a small baking sheet and cook for three-quarters of an hour in a slack oven. After removing it from the fire, allow to cool for a few moments, then invert it on a baking sheet to open on the cut side, and empty out the contents; take off the paper and keep the timbale for five minutes at the oven door, glaze it with a brush and fasten it on to the center of a dish, then with a cornet filled with chicken cream forcemeat (No. 75) form a garland all around the upper edge; leave the timbale in a warm heater to poach this border slightly. Place in a saucepan a garnishing composed of fine cocks'-combs, round truffles and very white and uniform mushroom heads; baste with two or three spoonfuls of good chicken stock (No. 188), cover the saucepan and keep it in a bain-marie. In another saucepan place a garnishing of cooked beef fries cut in inch and a half length slices; mix with these an equal quantity of large Italian macaroni, cooked till tender and cut into the same lengths as the fries; add also the same quantity of large fillets of cooked tongue cut likewise, and mingle these ingredients with some good béchamel (No. 409) reduced with

Fig. 443.

the mushroom broth, raw cream and melted meat glaze (No. 402). Heat the stew on a slow fire, stirring it unceasingly and not allowing the sauce to boil and incorporate into it a piece of fresh butter and a handful of parmesan. Now take the timbale from the heater, fill it up with the stew and on top dress the garnishing of the truffles, combs and mushrooms laid in the shape of a dome; cover these with two or three spoonfuls of good light velouté sauce (No. 415), and serve the timbale at once.

(2384). TIMBALE OF FILLETS OF SOLES À LA GAULOISE (Timbale de Filets de Soles à la Gauloise).

Fill the timbale paste, prepare and cook a case as explained in No. 2383. After the case is taken from the oven open it on the cut to empty. Glaze the inside with a brush, and dress it on a dish; keep it warm in a heater. Poach the fillets of sole in butter, salt and lemon juice; set them under a light weight, pare and keep them warm likewise. Add to a well-reduced allemande sauce (No. 407) some minced truffles and mushroom heads; fill the timbale with a layer of sole on top of the truffles and mushrooms, then more sole, and continue the operation until the timbale is entirely filled. Garnish around with Milanese macaroni croquettes, and the top with trussed crawfish.

Milanese Macaroni Croquettes are to be made with cooked macaroni cut into half-inch lengths and mingled with allemande sauce (No. 407), adding a salpicon of tongue, truffles and mushrooms; when cold dip in beaten eggs, then in bread-crumbs and fry in hot frying fat.

(2385). TIMBALE OF LOBSTER À LA D'AUMALE (Timbale de Homard à la d'Aumale).

After a lobster has been cooked in a court-bouillon (No. 38), drain, and lay it aside to get cold; then pick out the meat and cut it up into escalops, not having them too thick—about a pound altogether; add to these slices two medium-sized blanched oysters after suppressing the hard parts; add also half a pound of mushrooms and four ounces of truffles. Butter with unmelted butter a half spherical, plain, round or oval mold; decorate it with fanciful cuts of truffles, and keep the decoration in place with a thick pike quenelle forcemeat (No. 90) mixed with lobster coral; fill up the inside with the above preparation, and finish with more forcemeat. Poach it in a slack oven for three-quarters to one hour; unmold, and serve separately a béchamel sauce (No. 409), with lobster butter (No. 580) added to it.

(2386). TIMBALE OF PULLET (Timbale de Poularde).

Cut each of two pullets into five pieces, and five ounces of bacon into thin squares; warm these in a saucepan with some butter, then add the pieces of chicken, and fry them while tossing; season, put in the livers and three or four peeled and sliced truffles. When the chickens are partly done moisten them with a little white wine and reduce quickly; then pour the stew into a tureen. Butter a timbale mold, bestrew chopped noodles over the sides and bottom, and then line it with fine paste (No. 142); cover the sides and bottoms with veal chopped forcemeat (No. 65), finished with a few cooked fine herbs (No. 385). Pour the stew into the timbale, leaving as little empty space as possible, and covering over with a flat of the same paste; fasten this to the edge, and egg over the whole, then push the timbale into a moderate oven to cook for one hour. After removing it cut a small opening in the middle of the crust, and pour in a few spoonfuls of good half-glaze sauce (No. 413); close the opening and invert the timbale on a dish to serve.

(2387). TIMBALE OF SQUABS À LA BERCHOUX (Timbale de Pigeonneaux à la Berchoux).

Draw, singe and clean six squabs, then cut them each in four. Line a two-quart buttered timbale mold with foundation or short paste (No. 135); coat it over with a layer of chicken quenelle forcemeat (No. 89) three-sixteenths of an inch in thickness. Melt four ounces of grated fat pork in a saucepan with as much lean bacon cut into quarter-inch squares; add the squabs, and fry the whole together over a bright fire. When the squabs are nicely browned, drain off the fat and moisten with a quarter of a bottle of white wine, then reduce, add some espagnole sauce (No. 414), and season to taste, adding half a pound of small mushroom heads, and four ounces of minced truffles, then let the whole get cold. Fill up the timbale with separate layers of squabs, mushrooms, bacon, and sauce, and cover over with more quenelle forcemeat, and besides this a lid of puff paste (No. 146); cook in a moderate oven, and when the timbale is done, remove it from the fire, dress, take off the lid, and pour in some espagnole sauce (No. 414) with Madeira; serve the timbale very hot. Instead of cutting the squabs in two, they may be boned and stuffed with delicate chicken quenelle forcemeat, then laid in oval-shaped rings and braised, finishing them as for the others.

(2388). TIMBALE OF SWEETBREADS, MODERN—LARGE (Grosse Timbale de Ris de Veau à la Moderne).

Butter a large oval mold as for timbale à la Parisian (No. 2382), allowing one quart for eight persons; decorate the bottom and sides with fanciful cuts of truffles, and hold these up with a thick layer of solid chicken quenelle forcemeat (No. 89.) Cut up in half-inch squares one pound of braised, unlarded sweetbreads that have been left to cool in their stock, also as much cooked lean ham. Put four ounces of butter into a sautoir with two ounces of onion cut in small one-eighth of an inch squares, and when done without browning add four ounces of minced fresh mushrooms; when these have evaporated their moisture add the sweetbreads and ham; season and moisten with two gills of Madeira; let the latter reduce entirely, then pour in some brown sauce (No. 414) and the sweetbread braise stock; reduce once more and transfer the whole to a dish to get cold. Fill the timbale mold with this preparation; spread a half inch thick layer of forcemeat on a sheet of buttered paper, having it the same size as the timbale, turn over the sheet to fasten the forcemeat to the forcemeat in the timbale; attach it well to the top; poach the timbale by placing it in boiling water that reaches halfway up; boil this and push the timbale into a slack oven for an hour and a quarter to an hour and a half, or until the forcemeat be perfectly firm; remove the paper, unmold on a dish and pour around a Madeira sauce (No. 492), serving more of it in a sauce-boat.

(2389). TIMBALE OF YOUNG HARE (Timbale de Levraut).

Bone a young hare, cut it up into sixteen pieces, and put these into a saucepan with melted fat pork, two tablespoonfuls of chopped onions and half a pound of bacon cut in half-inch squares and blanched. Fry these meats over a good fire, season with salt and spices, and when well stiffened throw in a pound of medium-sized mushrooms turned and channeled (No. 118), also a glassful of white wine; cover the saucepan, reduce the liquid quickly and leave till cold. Butter a plain timbale mold six inches in diameter by six inches high, strew the bottom with a handful of freshly and finely cut-up noodle paste (No. 142), or else pretty pieces cut out with a column tube; apply them all over the inside surface, wetting lightly with water, then line the mold with foundation paste (No. 135), having it rolled out very thin; now cover the bottom and sides with a thin layer of chopped game forcemeat (No. 67). Fill the timbale with the hare and some game quenelles (No. 733) intermingled; cover with a layer of the same forcemeat and over this a round flat of the paste, attaching it to the lower one at the edge. Place the timbale on a small baking sheet and push it into a moderate oven to cook for one hour and a quarter; after removing from the oven, invert it on a dish, make a hole in the center and pour into the inside a brown sauce (No. 414) reduced with Madeira and game fumet (No. 397) made with the hare parings and the mushroom peelings, then strained through a tammy.

(2390). TOURTE OF PALATE OF BEEF, PARISIAN STYLE (Tourte de Palais de Bœuf à la Parisienne).

Prepare, cook and press the palates of beef as described in à la béchamel (No. 1326), then cut them in one and a half inch squares. Heat half a pound of lard, brown in it two ounces of finely chopped onions, and half a pound of chopped mushrooms; add the palates, season with salt, pepper, chopped chives and parsley; drain off the grease, and add to it half its quantity of godiveau forcemeat (No. 82) quenelles and increase the garnishing by adding an espagnole sauce (No. 414) finished with Madeira. Prepare an empty tart, ancient style (No. 174); when the tart is done, raise up the cover, remove the paper pad, and fill the interior with the above garnishing, and replace the cover before serving.

(2391). TOURTE OF CHICKEN (Tourte de Poulet).

Divide two small chickens into eight pieces each, suppressing all the bones. Melt in a sautoir three or four spoonfuls of chopped fat pork; add to it a quarter of a pound of bacon cut in large dice and fry these for four or five minutes; lift them out with a skimmer, leaving the fat in the sautoir, and into it put three spoonfuls of chopped shallot and onion; fry colorless, then add double the same quantity of chopped mushrooms, and as soon as these have evaporated their humidity, put in the chickens, a bunch of parsley and aromatic herbs; fry together and at the end of ten minutes put back the bacon, and when the meats are half cooked moisten with half a glassful of dry white wine; let reduce quickly to a glaze and pour over two or three spoonfuls of half-glaze sauce, then take out the meats and let get cold. Prepare about a pound of chicken godiveau (No. 82). Lay on a pie dish (Fig. 183) a rather thick layer of foundation paste (No. 135), having it eight inches in diameter; in the center spread a layer of the chicken godiveau six and a half inches in diameter; on this place the chickens, dressing them in a dome, and adding a few cooked mushrooms; then cover the entire dome with the remainder of the godiveau; wet the lower flat at the base of the dome and cover over with a large layer of puff paste (No. 146), press it on to the lower one and fasten the two together, decreasing the thickness, then cut very round. Wet the top layer and lay on the free surface around the dome a band of puff paste made in six turns, having it three-eighths of an inch thick; fasten the two ends, cut bias together, and wet this over; decorate the dome with fanciful cuts of paste, egg it over, as well as the bands of puff paste, and cook the tart in a moderate oven for forty minutes. After taking it out slip it on to a large dish and cut off one-third of the top of the dome to open it, and pour in a few spoonfuls of half-glaze sauce (No. 413), having more in a sauce-boat, and adding to it a few cooked mushrooms. Pigeon or rabbit tarts can be prepared the same.

(2392). TOURTE OF FILLETS OF SOLES À LA FINANCIÈRE (Tourte de Filets de Soles à la Financière).

Make a band tart the same as explained in No. 173; remove and detach it from the baking sheet, dress on a dish and keep warm. Cook five or six well-pared sole fillets in butter, having them seasoned and cut into escalops, laying them in a sautoir with sliced truffles, a few dozen poached

FIG. 444.

oysters and small fish quenelles (No. 90) molded with a small coffeespoon (No. 155), then poached; add some good lean velouté sauce (No. 416), reduced with the broth from the truffles, mushrooms and oysters. Dress this garnishing in a dome in the empty tart, ornament the surface with two sole fillets decorated with truffles, two large cooked crawfish, their tails shelled, and four large quenelles, each one having a truffle lozenge placed on the center. Between the quenelles and the fillets lay a mushroom head, turned (No. 118) and cooked very white; on top place a small round scooped-out quenelle, and on this a round peeled truffle; glaze this truffle and the fillets of sole, cover the mushrooms with a little velouté sauce and serve more of it as a separate sauce.

(2393). TURBAN OF FILLETS OF FLUKES OR SMELTS—STREAKED (Turban de Filets de Carrelets ou d'Éperlans, Bigarrés).

Raise the four fillets, peel off the skin, cut them lengthwise in two, then into slices, having them six inches long by one wide; make bias incisions on half the thickness, and set into every one a thin slice of truffle. With a fish quenelle forcemeat (No. 90) make a crown-shaped border, rounded on the top, using mold (Fig. 139); lay on it the streaked slices slanting in such a way as to cover the surfaces so that the truffles are seen on top; lay over strips of buttered paper, and cook this turban in a slack oven; drain off the butter and fill up the empty space with mushrooms, truffles and oyster kernels, cover with an allemande sauce (No. 407) reduced with cream and well buttered, and lay a garnishing of fried milts around the turban.

(2394). TURBAN OF LOBSTERS GARNISHED WITH SHELLS (Turban de Homards Garni de Coquilles).

Kill the lobsters by plunging them into boiling water for one minute; suppress the tail shells and cut up the tail meat into transversal slices a quarter of an inch thick, and dress them crown-shaped on a ring made of raw pike quenelle forcemeat (No. 90), alternating each slice with one of truffles and mushrooms; cover this crown with a velouté sauce (No. 416) well-reduced with court bouillon and wine (No. 419); dredge over with bread-crumbs and grated parmesan cheese, and besprinkle with butter; brown it in the oven and then garnish the center of the turban with a garnishing of mushrooms; pour over these a lobster sauce (No. 488) with some cayenne pepper added, and garnish around the turban with small shells filled with lobster and cream béchamel. Prepare as follows: Put into a bowl half a pound of lobster meat cut in quarter-inch squares, and the third of its quantity of cooked mushrooms cut exactly the same. Reduce a pint of béchamel sauce (No. 409) with some of the mushroom broth and cream; mix it in with the salpicon, season with nutmeg, salt and cayenne pepper, and use this preparation to fill some scallop or silver shells (Fig. 438) previously buttered and bread-crumbed; when they are all full, strew over more bread-crumbs and parmesan, besprinkle with butter, and brown them in a hot oven, or else with a red-hot shovel, or under a gas salamander (Fig. 123).

(2395). VOL-AU-VENT À LA DIEPPOISE (Vol-au-vent à la Dieppoise).

For this there must be prepared a vol-au-vent crust, as explained in No. 180; remove the cover to empty it out thoroughly, then keep it warm, or if it has been made some time beforehand just heat it in a slow oven for a few minutes. Reduce some lean velouté sauce (No. 416), then thicken it with egg-yolks, fresh butter and lemon juice, strain through a tammy and keep it in a bain-marie; add to it some cooked mussels, some fish (sole) quenelles, mushrooms and shrimps. When all is very hot, fill the crust, cover with the lid and serve.

(2396). VOL-AU-VENT À LA FINANCIÈRE (Vol-au-vent à la Financière).

Prepare a vol-au-vent crust as explained in No. 180; when cooked lift off the cover, empty

FIG. 445

out the interior and keep it warm. Prepare a garnishing of whole peeled truffles, turned and channeled mushroom heads (No. 118), cocks'-combs and quenelles, as many of one as of the other, and enough to fill the crust; put this garnishing into a sautoir and mingle in a financière sauce (No. 464). When very hot pour it into the crust, dressing the cocks'-combs in a circle, and inside of this the truffles and mushrooms, having a fine braised, larded and well-glazed sweetbread on top. The financière garnishing can be replaced by a Toulouse (No. 766) or Aquitaine (No. 640) garnishing.

(2397). VOL-AU-VENT À LA NESLE (Vol-au-vent à la Nesle).

Take some well-buttered allemande sauce (No. 407) reduced with mushroom essence (No. 392); add to it some chicken quenelles made of chicken quenelle forcemeat (No. 89) molded with a coffeespoon (No. 155), small turned and cooked mushrooms and cooked lean ham cut in three-eighth inch squares. When both the garnishing and crust are very hot fill up in layers alternated with slices of calf's brains cooked when ready to use and then well drained. Decorate the top with fine trussed crawfish, and serve.

(2398). VOL-AU-VENT, ANCIENT STYLE—LARGE (Gros Vol-au-vent à l'Ancienne).

Reduce some velouté sauce (No. 415) with sweetbread stock, and thicken it with egg-yolks; run it through a tammy, and mix in with this sauce some godiveau quenelles (No. 155, Fig. 81), medium-sized mushroom heads, cocks'-combs, slices of liver, and minced truffles. Fill the crust, as explained in à la financière (No. 2396), with this very hot garnishing, and replace the cover by small, pretty kernels of sweetbreads and trussed crawfish.

(2399). CHICKEN VOL-AU-VENT WITH MUSHROOMS—LARGE (Gros Vol-au-vent de Volaille aux Champignons).

Prepare the crust as for the financière (No. 2396), reduce some velouté sauce (No. 415) with mushroom stock, and when done thicken with raw egg-yolks diluted with a little cream, then incorporate a piece of fresh butter, pass it through a tammy, and add to this sauce some braised white of chicken free of skin, sinews, or fat, and half the same quantity of mushroom heads or cut-up mushrooms. When the crust is very hot, also the garnishing, fill and lay the cover over, then serve. The chicken may be replaced by braised sweetbreads or spring lamb, either of which should be well pared and cut in slices.

(2400) SALT CODFISH VOL-AU-VENT—LARGE (Gros Vol-au-vent de Morue Salée).

Cut some salted codfish in two-inch pieces, pare them evenly, and lay in cold water to soak for twenty-four hours, changing the water every six hours; the last change must be slightly tepid. When ready to cook put it into a saucepan containing cold water; bring this slowly to a boiling point and leave for three-quarters of an hour without allowing it to actually boil; drain, take off all the skin and bones, and then shred it in flakes; put these in a saucepan with cream béchamel sauce (No. 411). With this prepared fish fill a vol-au-vent crust the same as described in No. 180, dress it on a very hot dish, and serve.

It can also be prepared with eggs, adding to the fish hard-boiled eggs and finely chopped parsley and chives.

(2401). VOL-AU-VENT OF FROGS AND SOUBISE EGGS (Vol-au-vent de Grenouilles et d'Œufs Soubise).

Prepare the vol-au-vent crust as in No. 180. Fry colorless in a pan with butter some frogs' legs; drain, bone, and lay them in a saucepan. Boil some eggs for eight minutes to have them very hard; shell and cut lengthwise in two, then across in two; add them to the frogs' legs, and also some well-buttered soubise sauce (No. 543); butter it well, heat all very slowly, and then fill the vol-au-vent crust, placing the removed cover on top.

(2402). VOL-AU-VENT OF OYSTERS (Vol-au-vent d'Huîtres).

Prepare either one large or sufficient small vol-au-vent (No. 180). Poach a few dozen large oysters in white wine and their own liquor, and when well drained, pare and lay them in a small saucepan. On the other hand, put on to reduce two gills of good béchamel sauce (No. 409), incorporating into it slowly a part of the oyster juice, and when the sauce is considerably reduced and thick, finish it with a little cream; pour this over the oysters, and heat them in a bain-marie (Fig. 122) without allowing them to boil; at the last moment fill the vol-au-vent with this prepared garnishing, and serve very hot.

(2403). VOL-AU-VENT À LA DELMONTES—SMALL (Petits Vol-au-vent à la Delmontes).

These small vol-au-vent are prepared the same as explained in No. 180. Prepare also a brown espagnole sauce (No. 414) with Marsala wine, into which mix equal parts of cooked unsmoked beef tongue, cut in balls three-eighths of an inch in diameter with a vegetable spoon, foies-gras quenelles made with foies-gras forcemeat (No. 78) of the same size, or else replace these by marrow quenelles (No. 353) of the same diameter, small mushrooms and the cutaneous part of a calf's head cut the same size; properly heat the whole, and fill the small vol-au-vent crusts with it; on each one place a round quarter-inch in diameter slice of calf's brains breaded and fried, over this a stuffed Spanish olive (No. 695), and the whole surmounted by a ball of truffle glazed over with meat glaze.

(2404). VOL-AU-VENT À LA LUCINI—SMALL (Petits Vol-au-vent à la Lucini).

Prepare the small vol-au-vent (No. 180); when cooked take off the covers, empty out the insides and replace these covers by a game quenelle (No. 91) one inch and a half in diameter by an eighth of an inch thick; poach and bread-crumb them by dipping them in Villeroi sauce (No. 560), then rolling them in bread-crumbs, then fry to a good color. Put into a saucepan some brown sauce (No. 414) and Madeira wine; add to this some game fumet (No. 397) mixed with a garnishing composed of two-thirds of small young rabbit quenelles (No. 91) molded in a small coffeespoon (No. 155) and one-third of small turned mushroom heads (No. 118), or in case there be no small ones then cut-up others in two or four pieces. With this garnishing fill the small crusts, lay the Villeroi quenelle on top and in the center of it a round slice of truffle one inch in diameter and glaze over.

(2405). VOL-AU-VENT OF OYSTERS À LA MAINTENON—SMALL (Petits Vol-au-vent d'Huîtres à la Maintenon).

Set into a saucepan some fresh butter and lemon juice, place it over a hot fire, and add to it some fine raw oysters; after poaching and draining them cut them into pieces, return to the saucepan and season with nutmeg, pepper and salt, and then add some pike quenelles (No. 90); also some cut-up truffles and mushrooms; add a little velouté sauce (No. 415) and thicken it just when ready to serve with raw egg-yolks diluted with a little cream and fine butter. Fill the small vol-au-vent crusts with this, keeping all very warm, put on the cover and serve on a folded napkin.

(2406. VOL-AU-VENT, PARISIAN STYLE—SMALL (Petits Vol-au-vent à la Parisienne).

Have a brown (No. 414) or Madeira sauce (No. 492) and add to it some half-inch squares of veal or lamb sweetbreads, stoned olives cut in four, turned mushrooms (No. 118) and small chicken quenelles. Fill prepared small vol-au-vent crusts with this garnishing and range trussed crawfish on top, then cover.

(2407). VOL-AU-VENT OF REEDBIRDS, DIPLOMATE—SMALL (Petits Vol-au-vent de Mésanges Moustaches à la Diplomate).

With six turns of puff paste prepare eight small vol-au-vent crusts (No. 180); after taking them out of the oven detach them from the baking sheet and press on the center of the paste to enlarge the hollow space, and keep them warm. Roast two dozen reedbirds, having them rare; remove the breasts without any bones, suppress the skin and lay them in a small sautoir; mix with them an equal proportion of halved game quenelles, molded with a spoon (No. 155) and poached when wanted in salted water; also add three dozen cooked truffles trimmed into small olive shapes; mix these garnishings with a not too thin but very hot Madeira sauce (No. 492), and with this fill up the warm vol-au-vent crusts; instead of a cover close the apertures with a ring made of puff paste, and in the center have a large Spanish olive standing upright, stuffed with game baking forcemeat (No. 81) and foies-gras. Dress these vol-au-vent on a folded napkin and send them to the table at once.

(2408). VOL-AU-VENT OF SALMON TROUT À LA RÉGENCE—SMALL (Petits Vol-au-vent de Truite Saumonée à la Régence).

The only difference between bouchées and small vol-au-vent is that bouchées are filled with either a salpicon or a purée, while vol-au-vent are filled with small, distinct garnishings. Prepare eight or ten small vol-au-vent crusts (No. 180); cook them in a brisk oven; remove and detach them from the pan, impress a hollow in the center with the finger and keep them warm. Put into a small saucepan a garnishing composed of a pound of salmon-trout escalops, twelve small poached oysters, twelve mushrooms or cut up morils, twelve small fish quenelles (No. 90) rolled on a floured table and poached, also some small cut-up poached milts; cover these with a rich and very hot Normande sauce (No. 509), finishing with a piece of lobster butter (No. 580). Fill the warm vol-au-vent crusts with this garnishing, cover lightly with some of the sauce instead of a lid, and close the aperture with a pretty mushroom head, turned and very white, left in its natural state. Dress the vol-au-vent at once on folded napkins; they can also be filled with one garnishing only.

COLD SERVICE (Service Froid).

(2409). COLD DISHES (Le Froid).

The cold service is the most elegant and artistic one of the culinary art. It requires taste, skill and much study in order to learn the necessary moldings, modelings and requisite cookery. Ornaments render the socles and the pieces beautiful and coquettish; their appearance should be neat and precise; the pieces must be well defined and designed before beginning; prepare all the needed materials beforehand so that when the work has once begun there will be nothing to delay the progress. Wax flowers and leaves are very useful, therefore a good workman must learn to make them in great variety. Any ordinary cook can attain renown by studying the complicated ways of preparing cold dishes, but he must give his sole attention to this special part which helps to increase his reputation and develop his ideas, for by it he elevates his trade to a positive art. The manner of properly preparing sauces, side dishes, roasts and pastries should of course be executed with as much care as the cold. Jellies should be tasty, limpid and transparent; if they be defective, then the handsomest pieces are open to criticism. Hâtelets and jelly garnishings greatly enhance the appearance of the pieces, therefore care should be used that they are most beautiful and all croûtons cut with precision and symmetry. Cold pieces should be prepared beforehand, for they must not be hurried nor left to be finished at the last moment.

(2410). ASPIC OF COCKS'-COMBS AND KIDNEYS À LA MAZARIN (Aspic de Crêtes et de Rognons de Coqs à la Mazarin).

Braise some cocks'-combs and kidneys, and when cold drain and wipe well. Cover the combs with a white chaudfroid (No. 596), and the kidneys with a blond chaudfroid made by mixing half brown chaudfroid (No. 594) and half white chaudfroid (No. 596). Coat with jelly a plain cylindrical or channeled mold, having it rather high, and fill the bottom with the combs dressed in a ring, one overlapping the other, and cover with jelly; lay on top a garnishing of the kidneys, cover with more jelly and when this has hardened dress on some roasted chicken fillets, sliced and pared round-shaped, and covered with ravigote chaudfroid (No. 595); lay these in a circle and continue to fill up the mold, alternating the combs, kidneys and chicken; when very full let get cold and unmold on a small low socle made of stearine. Place a mandrel in the empty space in the mold, and on it a cup filled with small cases containing whole glazed truffles, and decorate around with small timbales (No. 3, Fig. 137) filled with jelly and foies-gras.

(2411). ASPIC OF FOIES-GRAS (Aspic de Foies-Gras).

Incrust a plain cylindrical mold (Fig. 150) in ice. Unmold on a small baking sheet a terrine of foies-gras; remove all the grease and keep it for one hour on ice. Cut this foies-gras into three-eighths of an inch thick slices, using a knife dipped in hot water, and then cut these slices into inch and a quarter rounds with a pastry cutter also dipped in hot water. Lift up these rounds one by one with a fork and immerse them in a brown chaudfroid sauce (No. 594), having it thin and almost cold; range them at once on a baking sheet and let this sauce get quite stiff on the ice. Cut out some rounds of cooked truffles very nearly the same diameter as the foies-gras, only have half as many; glaze them with a brush and range them at once on a baking sheet. Pour a quarter-inch thick layer of jelly into the mold, and when it has become quite hard dress on it a ring of the foies-gras rounds, the smooth side uppermost and slightly overlapping each other, but alternating every two with a round of truffle; cover this crown with cold jelly an inch and a half in thickness, and again form two more distinct crowns exactly the same as the first one in order to fill up the mold, pouring jelly between each. Keep the mold on ice for one hour or more. In order to turn it out it is only necessary to dip the mold into warm water, wipe dry, and invert it on a cold dish.

(2412). ASPIC OF FOIES-GRAS—SMALL (Petits Aspics de Foies-Gras).

On a bed of chopped-up ice lay ten timbale molds (No. 1, Fig. 137); decorate the bottoms of each with a ring of truffles filled with a piece of red tongue, and the sides with fanciful cuts

FIG. 446.

of truffles and egg-white dipped in half-set jelly to make them adhere to the cold molds, then pour into each one an eighth of an inch thickness of jelly. Unmold a terrine of foies-gras, remove from it cylindrical pieces a quarter of an inch less than the diameter of the molds and the same height; range them in the molds, finish filling up with more jelly and set them on ice for half an hour longer. Dip the timbales into hot water to facilitate the unmolding, and dress in a circle either on an inch and a quarter high foundation (Fig. 8) without the central vase, or else simply on a cold dish; fill up the inside of the circle with chopped jelly and set croûtons of jelly around.

(2413). TERRINE OF FOIES-GRAS IN ASPIC—WHOLE (Terrine Entière de Foies-Gras en Aspic).

Unmold a terrine of foies-gras; scrape it neatly with a knife on top and sides to remove all the exterior grease, and keep it on ice. Procure a mold of the same shape but an inch wider in diameter and an inch deeper; incrust it in pounded ice; decorate the bottom and sides with fanciful cuts of truffles, tongue, egg-white, and pistachios, dipping each piece into half-set jelly before fastening

FIG. 447.

them on; cover this decoration with a layer of jelly, and pour in more to lay half an inch thick in the bottom. Place the foies-gras exactly in the center and finish filling the mold with cooled-off jelly; keep on ice. Put a rice foundation bottom one inch and a half in height on a plated metal tray with a half-inch high straight edge (the rice foundation should be one inch and a half less in diameter than the tray), turn the aspic out of its mold on to the rice foundation, fastening a small basket on top secured by a skewer, and filling it with small glazed truffles. Decorate around the rice foundation with triangular jelly croûtons, as shown in the drawing.

(2414). ASPIC OF LOBSTER (Aspic de Homard).

Prepare a wooden foundation about two inches thick and furnished with a slightly raised border on the outer edge so as to uphold the entrée when dressed. The aspic mold should be chosen slightly narrower than the bottom of the dish, which is to be covered with paper. Suppress the shells from the tails and claws of two or three small cooked lobsters; cut the tails lengthways in two and also split the claw-meat in two, then put them into a vessel and season. Prepare a garnishing of carrots cut into balls with a small vegetable spoon, blanch and lay them in the vessel and with them mix gherkin balls cut the same size, small cooked Brussels sprouts, small blanched olives stuffed with anchovies, and a seasoning of salt, oil and vinegar. Incrust on ice a

Fig. 448.

dome-shaped mold wider than its height, decorate the sides and bottom with designs of hard-boiled egg-white, truffles and gherkins; coat the mold rather thickly with jelly; fill the inside with the halved lobster tail and claws, pressing the red side of the meat against the jelly; fill up the hollow space with the prepared carrot balls seasoned as for a salad and finished with mayonnaise sauce with jelly (No. 613). Let the aspic harden on ice for one hour at least. Incrust also on ice twelve small timbale molds (No. 2, Fig. 137); decorate the bottoms with rounds of truffles, the sides with small round pieces of white of egg and coat them over lightly with jelly; as soon as this is hard fill them up with lobster cream, the same as for No. 2470, and keep them for twenty-five minutes on ice. Just when ready to serve dip the dome mold into hot water, wipe it off quickly and invert the aspic on the raised-edge foundation; on top of it fasten a small lobster cream "pain" molded in a channeled mold, and against the edge of the bottom of the dish unmold the lobster cream timbales, after dipping the molds into hot water. This is to be served with a separate mayonnaise sauce (No. 606).

(2415). ASPIC OF OYSTERS (Aspic d'Huîtres).

Blanch some oysters, drain, wipe and cool; coat them over with a liberal layer of remoulade sauce (No. 628), to which liquid jelly has been added. Decorate a cylindrical mold (Fig. 150) with fanciful cuts of truffles, egg-white, gherkin and the red part of lobster, dipping each piece in half-set jelly and fastening them on to the bottom and sides of the mold; pour in a layer of jelly, having it half an inch thick, and on it dress the oysters in a circle, one overlapping the other; pour in more jelly to cover these another half inch and continue until the mold be full, then leave for several hours to become very cold; unmold and garnish around with chopped jelly and croûtons.

(2416). ASPIC OF PARTRIDGE—MINION FILLETS (Aspic de Filets Mignons de Perdreau).

Pare twelve partridge minion fillets; remove all sinews and thin skin and streak them with semicircles of truffles graduated in size; season and bend their thin ends in one direction; poach in a little butter and lemon juice; drain and when cold pare nicely. Incrust a plain cylindrical mold (Fig. 150) in ice. Decorate the sides on the top and bottom with an even chain of round pieces of truffle and red beef tongue, cut out with a tin tube an inch and a quarter in diameter; these pieces are to be dipped in half-set jelly and the red and black colors alternated, letting each chain be at an equal distance from the minions. Decorate the sides in the center as shown in Fig. 449, with the streaked fillets, dipping one at a time in half-set jelly and applying the streaked side to the mold; in order to succeed with this it will be found necessary to incline the mold on ice and turn it around as soon as the jelly hardens and the separate fillets are fastened on firmly. Coat this decoration with a thick layer of jelly and fill the mold with a partridge preparation à la Montgomery (No. 2548); leave it to cool on ice for one hour. When prepared to serve, dip the mold in hot water and invert the aspic on a bed of cold jelly on the bottom of a dish; fill the center with foies-gras balls three-quarters of an inch in size covered with brown chaudfroid (No. 594); on top

FIG. 449.

place very white cocks'-combs brushed over with jelly and surround these with a chain of small truffles dipped in jelly; keep the aspic on ice for half an hour before serving.

(2417). ASPIC OF PHEASANT (Aspic de Faisan).

Clean two young pheasants; truss them as for an entrée (No. 178), and braise white; cool off, remove the breasts (fillets) and pare into the shape of escalops one inch in diameter by three-sixteenths of an inch in thickness; cover each one with foies-gras. Pound the remainder of the meats and rub through a sieve; put the pulp in a vessel, and add to it a pint of half-glaze sauce (No. 413) prepared with truffle essence (No. 395), and a pint of strong jelly (No. 103); let this get very cold, and with it thickly cover the escalops; leave to cool on ice. Besides this make a purée with one partridge, and dilute it with white chaudfroid (No. 596); season highly, rub through a sieve, and mix in as much white jelly (No. 103) as chaudfroid. Coat a cylindrical fancy mold (No. 150) with white jelly, and incrust it very firmly in ice. On the bottom of this mold lay a bed of jelly three-quarters of an inch in thickness; on it arrange some slices of truffles one overlaying the other, each slice to be an inch in diameter and an eighth of an inch thick; on top of these place the escalops; pour on a layer of the white chaudfroid half an inch thick, and on this a row of escalops overlapping each other; cover these with more white jelly; now pour in a layer of chaudfroid, and continue the process until the mold be full; leave till very cold, then invert it on a small socle, either of stearin or carved rice (see No. 10).

(2418). ASPIC OF PULLET À LA CUSSY (Aspic de Poularde à la Cussy).

Raise the fillets from six medium chickens, weighing about two pounds each; suppress the epidermis, and remove the minion fillets, from which suppress the sinews and fine skin; pare the large fillets into half-hearts and place them in a buttered sautoir with the pointed ends lying toward the center. Make five gashes on each minion fillet and fill them in with graded scalloped rounds of truffle; roll them up crown-shaped, place them on pieces of buttered paper and with a pocket fill the center with a chicken quenelle forcemeat (No. 89) and foies-gras well-mingled, having half of each; lay on top a round piece of red beef tongue, and set these in a buttered sautoir; pour over some clarified butter and lemon juice, and cover each one with a sheet of buttered paper and let cook in a moderate oven. When cold cover the minions with half-set jelly and the large fillets with white chaudfroid sauce (No. 596); when this is cold repeat the operation and lay them on a baking sheet one beside the other without allowing them to touch; detach them by slipping a thin-bladed knife under, then pare them into half-hearts all of the same size. Decorate a plain or channeled cylindrical mold with fanciful cuts of truffles, tongue, gherkin, egg-white, or pistachios, dipping them singly into half-set jelly, and applying them symmetrically on to the bottom and sides of the very cold mold, having them only on the top and bottom, leaving the center undecorated. Coat over with jelly so as to support the decorations, then lay the minion fillets half an inch from the bottom, and at even distances from one another; fill it up with jelly half an inch above the minions, and when this is set dress on the large fillets, one overlapping the other, the pointed ends downward; then fill up with jelly and let it get perfectly hard. Have a plain dish covered with a tin bottom, and spread this with ravigote butter (No. 583) and a round of white paper over; unmold the aspic on this, and fill the center with a wooden support with a cup filled with cut-up vegetables on top, held on with a skewer. Around the bottom range chopped jelly and crusts.

(2419). ASPIC OF QUAILS—BREASTS (Aspic de Filets de Cailles).

Raise the breasts and minion fillets from three or four quails, pare and beat lightly, season and poach in butter and lemon juice, keeping them rare; cool them off under the pressure of a light weight between two buttered papers. Detach the minion fillets from the carcass and streak them with truffles; poach them also in butter and lemon juice, bending them slightly. Divide each large fillet into two pieces, pare them neatly and dip them one by one in a brown chaudfroid sauce (No. 594); range them as fast as they are done on a baking sheet to harden the sauce, then pare. Cut some croutons of very tender red beef tongue, having them the shape of the fillets, only half as many, and trim them nicely. Imbed a fancy cylindrical mold (Fig. 148) in ice; on the bottom lay a thin bed of jelly and on this dress the minion fillets, pressing them down on the sides that are streaked; cover them gradually with cold jelly to have it form a thickness of about an inch, then let it set; dress the fillets in a circle on this, laying them on their smoothest side and alternating every two with a croûton of red beef tongue; cover this circle with another layer of the jelly half an inch thick and form more circles with the fillets, proceeding as for the others. Fill the mold with cold jelly, put the mold aside on ice for an hour, and just when ready to serve invert the aspic on a bed of jelly hardened on a dish and surround it with small paper cases filled with small truffles covered with a brown chaudfroid sauce (No. 594).

(2420). ASPIC OF TONGUE À LA PICQUART (Aspic de Langue à la Picquart).

To make this aspic use a mold having four rounded top uprights without the central tube; decorate the flat part of the mold between the uprights with rounded bits of hard-boiled egg-whites and the uprights each with three rosettes, also of the egg-white; coat with a thick layer of jelly and fill each upright with tongue cut in slices three-sixteenths of inch thick, well pared and cut

FIG. 450.

round, then reconstructed as before; keep the thinnest end of the tongue at the bottom of the mold. Put a solid piece of tongue in the center of the mold to hold up the cupid. Set the mold on ice, fill it with jelly and when this is exceedingly cold unmold the aspic on a stand made in two pieces, one of which is nine inches and a half in diameter by one inch and a half high, the other eight and a quarter inches in diameter and one and a half inches high; both should be covered with montpellier butter (No. 582), besprinkled with chopped parsley. Garnish around the base of the aspic with chopped jelly and surround the upper tier with triangular croutons of clear jelly and the lower one with timbales of foies-gras made in molds (No. 3, Fig. 137); in the center of the aspic place a cupid supporting a vase filled with small glazed truffles.

(2421). ASPIC OF VEAL WITH MACÉDOINE ARTICHOKES—KERNEL (Aspic de Veau aux Artichauts Macédoine).

Braise a kernel of veal after larding the inside parts with veal udder, ham and truffles; put it in an oval mold to cool, pressing down well. Unmold, and cut it into slices. Decorate a larger mold with vegetables, coat it by pouring in some jelly and turning the mold so that the jelly covers the vegetables, then pour in more jelly to have a quarter of an inch in thickness at the bottom and lay the sliced kernel over, having reformed it to its original shape, then fill up entirely with slightly cool jelly. When perfectly cold unmold on a dish and surround the meat with chopped jelly, lay on top some artichoke bottoms filled with macédoine (No. 2650) and decorate the summit with three Bellevue hatelets (No. 2526).

(2422). ASPICS WITH SHRIMPS—SMALL (Petits Aspics aux Crevettes).

Shell one hundred shrimp tails, having them cooked very red; keep them covered in a cool place. Make a quart of good aspic jelly (No. 103). Incrust in ice ten timbale molds (No. 1, Fig. 137); decorate them with fanciful pieces of truffles or gherkins, covering the decoration with a thin layer of jelly, then pile on the shrimp tails symmetrically all around, sticking them in with the point of a larding needle after dipping them one at a time in half-set jelly. When the sides are covered, fill the hollow in the center with a bed of green asparagus; on top of the asparagus lay some jellied mayonnaise (No. 613), on this chopped mushrooms, and so on until the mold is full, finishing with mayonnaise. Keep the aspics on ice for three-quarters of an hour before unmolding and dress them on a bed of jelly on a dish to prevent them from slipping off.

(2423). VOLIÈRE GALANTINE OF PHEASANTS À LA CASIMIR PÉRIER (Volière Galantine de Faisans à la Casimir Périer).

Procure two fine English pheasants with handsome plumage, remove the skin with the feathers from the neck and upper breast, also the wings and tails, being careful not to destroy their beauty.

FIG. 451.

Fix the heads in such a way that they retain their natural appearance. Bone the pheasants, spread them open on a cloth. Prepare half a pound of peeled truffles cut in quarter-inch squares, half a pound of fat livers the same size; make a forcemeat with three-quarters of a pound of white game breasts and one pound and a quarter of pork tenderloin, also adding two pounds of fat pork. Chop the whole separately and very finely, season with galantine spices (No. 168) and pound to a pulp; press it through a sieve, afterward adding some finely chopped truffle peelings;

mix this well with the squares of truffles and fat livers, also a few pistachios. Season the pheasants, divide the forcemeat in two parts, one for each bird, and fill them with it; roll the two galantines in separate napkins, tie firmly at both ends and in the center; cook in a game stock made with parings of white meat game; when well done take them out and leave to cool off slightly; rewrap in the same napkins after cleansing them in clear water, having them six inches long; tie them up tight at the ends and leave to cool under a light weight; unwrap when cold and glaze over with a not too thick brown chaudfroid (No. 594). Ornament one end with the head, and the other with the tail, placing the wings on the sides, keeping them in position with skewers; the necks should be strongly salted and have a rather thick wire inserted in the bone of the head, then stuffed with cotton so that it resumes its original size and shape; finish with an oval piece of cardboard about three inches in length. Dress the pheasants on small oval socles from four to five inches high, these to be made of tin covered with noodle paste (No. 142), glazed and decorated, then placed on a larger socle, regarding the details for which see drawing. These tin socles can be replaced by others made either of stearin or carved rice, or else an oval pie crust the same size as the tin ones. On the edge of the socle lay small cases, each one to contain a truffle glazed over with game glaze (No. 398), or garnished with foies-gras, or else small boned birds stuffed, braised and glazed with brown chaudfroid (No. 594).

(2424). VOLIÈRE GALANTINE OF PHEASANT À LA WADDINGTON (Volière Galantine de Faisan à la Waddington).

Prepare one pheasant instead of two as described in the Casimir Périer; dress it exactly the same and stand it on an oval socle four to five inches high by seven and a half inches long and four inches wide; place this on another oval socle about six inches high, eleven and a half inches long and eight inches wide. Pick off all the meat from a young rabbit, cut it in small dice and fry them in fat pork over a brisk fire; when cold, pound and add the same quantity of grated fresh fat pork; pound all together again and season with salt, pepper, and nutmeg; press it through a sieve and mix in with the preparation a quarter as much fat pork cut in three-sixteenths of an inch squares, and then blanched, and as much truffle cut the same size. With this fill twelve timbale molds (No. 2, Fig. 137), cover with very thin slices of fat pork, and bake in a moderate oven for half an hour; remove and set aside to cool. Decorate some timbale molds (No. 1, Fig. 137), with cuts of truffles and egg-white, pour a little jelly into the bottom of each mold. Unmold the No. 2 timbales, remove all the fat from the bottoms and sides, pare nicely and then put them into the No. 1 molds, filling up with jelly; when very firm, unmold and arrange them around the small socle of the galantine exactly under the pheasant, placing a border of jelly croûtons outside.

(2425). BALLOTINES OF LAMB CUPOLA SHAPED (Ballotines d'Agneau en Forme de Coupole).

Bone two shoulders of spring lamb, remove all fat and sinews and fill them with a stuffing made with half a pound of veal, half a pound of fresh fat pork and a quarter of a pound of cooked and finely chopped ham; season with salt, pepper, nutmeg, chopped parsley and chives; mix into it some truffles, pistachios and cooked tongue, all cut into three-sixteenths of an inch dice pieces. Spread the shoulders on the table, season and put in the dressing; sew up to enclose it well, giving each a round form, then braise with very little moistening, putting them into a saucepan lined with bards of fat pork and wetting with white wine mirepoix stock (No. 419). When well done place them in oval cupola-shaped molds and let cool off under a weight; remove, wash the molds well and decorate with fanciful cuts of truffles, pistachios and tongue dipped in half-set jelly; coat the inside of the mold with a layer of white chaudfroid, return the meats as before and finish filling with jelly. Unmold when thoroughly cold and dress on long dishes on a socle of rice two inches high, the size of the cupola. Have prepared some red lambs' tongues, salted, blanched and braised for two hours in a white wine mirepoix stock (No. 419) the same as the shoulders; drain, skin and set under a weight; strain their stock over and when very cold pare them all of uniform size and oval-shaped; the size is three inches long by two wide and a quarter of an inch thick; glaze and dress around the lamb cupolas, one overlapping the other. Garnish around the dish with chopped jelly and croûtons and lay some croustades filled with a macédoine of vegetables (No. 2650) mingled with a little mayonnaise (No. 606). Stick Bellevue hatelets (No. 2526) on top of each cupola.

(2426). BALLOTINES OF QUAIL À LA TIVOLIER (Ballotines de Cailles à la Tivolier).

Remove all the meats from three young rabbits; keep the minion fillets aside and suppress the sinews from the remainder; pass the meat twice through the machine (Fig. 47), weigh and allow double the same quantity of unsalted fat pork. Chop up the pork fat, add the rabbit meat and chop together once more. Chop up also eight ounces of lean ham cooked separately and mix this in with the rabbit, seasoning with salt and spices for game galantines (No. 168). Bone twelve quails, equalize the meats, removing half of the fillets to lay them in the places that are bare of meat; spread a third of the forcemeat over the birds and on each one lay four small truffles, wrapped in udder, placing them in lengthwise; on each side of these truffles put slices of well-seasoned rabbit tenderloin, and over another third part of the forcemeat and four more truffles; lay at each end and in the center the remainder of the tenderloins and forcemeat over the whole. Close up the quails, sew and wrap them in slices of fat pork, then in a cloth; tie it firmly to keep the galantines in good shape. Line a braiziére (Fig. 134) with bards of fat pork, lay the boned quail on top with the game carcasses around; moisten with plenty of mirepoix stock (No. 419). Two hours' cooking will be quite sufficient; take off and put them under weight in molds the same shape as the ones used for ballotines of squabs à la Madison (No. 2427) and when very cold unmold and wash the same molds and decorate them with truffles and white of egg; cover the decorations with a light coating of jelly; fill them with the quails and jelly; leave on ice for two hours then turn them over and dress them on a trimmed rice socle two inches high; garnish around with chopped jelly and over this cold artichoke bottoms (No. 2501). Garnish the center with small crescents of red beef tongue glazed with jelly.

(2427). BALLOTINES OF SQUABS À LA MADISON (Ballotines de Pigeonneaux à la Madison).

Bone twelve squabs, previously singed and cleaned; season with salt and pepper. Cut into quarter-inch dice a quarter of a pound of peeled truffles, a quarter of a pound of fat pork, a quarter of a pound of fat livers, a quarter of a pound of lean ham and a quarter of a pound of pistachios; put all of these into a vessel and pour some Madeira wine over. Prepare a forcemeat with half a pound of chicken meat, half a pound of lean pork, both free of sinews, and a pound of fresh fat pork; run twice through the machine (Fig. 47), pound to a pulp and rub through

FIG. 452.

a sieve (Fig. 97). Put this forcemeat in a vessel, add to it half a pound of liver forcemeat (No. 81), and the chopped truffle peelings; mix the salpicon in with and divide it up into twelve equal parts. Lay one of these into each boned squab, inclose it neatly in the skin and lay each bird in an oval dome-shaped mold three and three-eighths inches long, two and three-eighths inches wide and one and three-quarters inches deep. Range these molds on a baking sheet, cover over with another one and cook in a slack oven for about forty-five minutes; after removing lay small boards on top of each, they to be a quarter of an inch thick, three and a quarter inches long and two and a quarter inches wide, of the same oval shape as the molds themselves. Set these aside to cool with a board over and weights on top; then unmold, clean the molds properly and decorate them with fanciful cuts of truffles; cover with a light coat of jelly and another coat of white chaudfroid (No. 596); place one of the ballotines in each, fill up with jelly and unmold again when cold; they are to be dressed on the platforms as explained later on. Place on a round dish, as shown in Fig. 452, a round-shaped stearin socle an inch and a half thick by seven and a half in diameter; fasten a slanting center support to the middle of this and on it have three metal uprights held firmly by the upraised edges of the dish. Each one of these uprights is provided with four platforms attached by movable hinges and beside has two sharp points near the edge so as to keep the ballotines in place. They are kept together by another small platform that is fastened to each upright by means of a small hook. On top lay a stearine vase garnished with cut vegetables to imitate flowers or other objects. Between each shelf at the base place a fine emptied tomato filled with seasoned macédoine (No. 2650) dressed with jellied mayonnaise (No. 613). Fill the basin of the dish with chopped jelly and clusters of truffle set at intervals, and around it set evenly cut croutons. Place on the large socle or on another dish. Have a socle made the same as represented in Fig. 453; this can be of mutton and veal fat, partly mixed with virgin wax to produce more firmness, or else it can be made of stearine. When the pieces composing the

Fig. 453.

socle, or properly speaking the body of the socle, such as the three griffons, the three shells and the stearine support, are modeled they are to be scraped the same as described in No. 56. Take a round board an inch and a half high and thirteen inches in diameter; cover it with a sheet of white paper and lay it on a large, round silver dish or tray; in the center arrange the principal parts of the socle; on the base of this socle place the three griffons and on these the three shells so they are supported by them, and the handles of the shells lie in the hollow parts of the socle intended to hold them firmly; these different parts are to be fastened with royal icing (No. 101); in the center place a stearine support an inch and a quarter high by five and a half inches in diameter; have the whole resting very straight and fastened together with royal icing (No. 101). The base of the socle can be garnished between the griffons by laying on the board some cases of larks glazed over with chaud-froid or "pains" of foies-gras or else croustades of rice filled with streaked minion fillets; on top of these lay two emptied mushrooms one and a half inches in diameter, stuffed with foies-gras, then fastened together to form balls, glazing them over with chaudfroid. The shells are to be filled with glazed truffles or crescents of tongue covered with jelly, or else substitute shells of foies-gras removed with a spoon and sprinkled over with chopped jelly. The socle is now ready to receive either a ballotine Madison or a galantine of partridge à la Clémentine (No. 2491) or any other cold piece. The advantage of using the decorated socles is that any dish can be placed on them to give a finer appearance, yet the dish can be simply laid on the table on top of a plain silver dish, if a plainer service be required.

(2428). STRIPED BASS OR SEA BASS À LA MANHATTAN (Bass Rayé ou Bass de Mer à la Manhattan).

Raise the fillets from a striped bass; remove the skin and bones, pare each one into an oval two inches by three inches, and lay them in a buttered sautoir; season with salt, pepper, and very finely chopped onion; moisten with white wine, and cook smothered in the oven; now lay them under the pressure of a light weight, pare once more, and when exceedingly cold cover entirely with jellied mayonnaise (No. 613), and return them to the ice-box. Prepare a pound of very fresh, boneless and skinless bass, put in a sautoir two tablespoonfuls of onions, and six ounces of clarified butter; first fry the onion lightly, then add the well-drained fish; season with salt, nutmeg, and cayenne pepper, and cook in a moderate oven; drain and let get cold; now suppress all the small bones from its meat and pound it well, slowly adding the stock mingled with a few spoonfuls of béchamel sauce (No. 409) reduced with mushroom essence (No. 392) until it becomes quite thick. Rub the forcemeat through a sieve, and place it in a vessel on ice to beat up well, incorporating into it a gill of jelly (No. 103); try a small part to discover whether sufficiently firm, and then add a little dissolved isinglass; thicken on ice and put in the value of a pint of unsweetened and well-drained whipped cream. Coat some No. 2 mousseline molds (Fig. 138) with jelly, dredge over chopped lobster coral, and fill with the preparation; keep them on ice, and when very hard unmold and dress in a circle one beside the other on a round or oval dish into the bottom of which a little jelly has been poured and allowed to harden; in the center dress the escalops of bass; surround with chopped jelly and croûtons; brush the fish over with almost cold jelly, and keep the dish very cold until ready to serve, sending it to the table accompanied by a fine herb mayonnaise sauce (No. 612).

(2429). BASTION À L'AMÉRICAINE (Bastion à l'Américaine).

Bone thoroughly six chickens weighing two pounds each; suppress the sinews and trim the meats evenly. To six pounds of chopped forcemeat for chicken galantines (No. 65) add one pound of lean cooked ham, well chopped, and half a pound of chopped truffle peelings; mix the whole well together with two gills of Madeira wine and one gill of brandy. Spread out the boned

FIG. 454.

chickens on the table, season with salt, pepper and nutmeg, and fill each one first with an eight-ounce layer of the forcemeat, then here and there lay two ounces of peeled, sliced truffle, a few pistachio nuts and some red beef tongue cut into quarter-inch squares, and over these spread another eight-ounce layer of forcemeat; repeat with the same quantity of truffles, tongue and pistachios and finish filling the chickens with the remainder of the forcemeat, dividing it equally between the chickens; they should all be of equal weight, about two pounds each. Enclose the stuffing well and roll them up into long, well-rounded shapes; wrap each galantine tightly in a cloth, tie it on both ends, also in the center, and place them in a saucepan with the bones, parings and a dozen calves' feet split lengthwise in two; moisten with stock (No. 194a) and boil, skim and cook slowly for two hours, then drain. Fifteen minutes later unwrap and re-enclose them again in a clean cloth, tie as before and make a loop on one end to hang them up by, and let get cold, suspended from a hook, and to the other end attach a weight to pull the cloth down and thereby pressing the galantine.   After they have been left hanging for six hours, unwrap and lay them aside in a cool place.   Have a bastion mold the same as shown in Fig. 454; it is made in two pieces, one large one and a smaller one on top; incrust it in chopped ice and decorate according to the illustration with tongue, truffles and egg-whites; imitate the door with chopped pistachios mixed with jelly and coat the decoration with a thick layer of jelly; lay it flat on a very straight table, also the tower, then unwrap the galantines, pare off the ends and put one at each end or turret, two in the center and one cut lengthwise in two and placed in the mold so that the flat side faces the door, thus making five galantines for the large mold; now place one in the tower mold and with the pieces left over fill the four cupolas surmounting the four towers; allow the molds to get thoroughly cold for six to eight hours, then unmold on a long socle and trim around with square croûtons to imitate the battlements; stick a small pointed ornament in each cupola.   The piece is now ready to serve.

(2430). PRESSED CORN BEEF (Bœuf Pressé à l'Écarlate).

Remove the bones from a piece of breast or brisket of beef weighing about twelve pounds; put it in a brine of saltpetre (No. 15).   After salting for eight days, drain and wash the meat; put it in a soup pot with plenty of water; let come to a boil, skim and leave to cook very slowly for four or five hours.   When the meat is thoroughly done, untie the string, tighten the meat in the cloth, and fasten it like a boned turkey at both ends.   Lay it under the press or a weight and as soon as the corned beef is cold undo and glaze it with some meat glaze (No. 402). Cut it in thin slices, replace as it was before cutting, garnish the dish with chopped-up jelly, or parsley sprigs, and serve.

(2431). RIBS OF BEEF À LA BOURGEOISE (Côtes de Bœuf à la Bourgeoise).

Select a three-rib piece from the thinnest end of the ribs; remove two of the bones, leaving the middle one only.   Lard the lean part of the meat with lardons (No. 1, Fig. 52) of raw, salted and unsmoked ham, season with mignonette and allspice, wrap it up in bards of bacon and tie.   Garnish the bottom of a buttered braizière (Fig. 134), with sliced onions and a carrot, a garnished bunch of parsley (No. 123), and moisten with one gill of Madeira wine, one gill of brandy, and a sufficient quantity of stock (No. 194a) to immerse the meat to three-quarters of its height. Boil, skim, and let cook for two and a half to three hours, turning the meat over and basting frequently; then remove it from the fire, and leave it in the stock to get about two-thirds cold, then take it out and lay it under a weight, and when completely cold pare it nicely into the shape of a cutlet; scrape the surface of the bone, and glaze the meat.   Set it on a dish, and garnish around with pear-shaped carrots and turnips, previously blanched and cooked in white broth with a little sugar, and reduced to a glaze.   Clarify the stock in the braizière in order to make a jelly (as explained in No. 103), garnish the dish with this jelly chopped up, and cut triangular-shaped croûtons; fasten into the meat three handsome hatelets of vegetables (No. 2526); trim the bone with a large paper frill (No. 10).

(2432). RIBS OF BEEF IN BELLEVUE (Côtes de Bœuf en Bellevue).

After the ribs of beef are prepared, cook them the same as for à la Bristed (No. 1329), adding several calves' feet.   When the meat is well cooked, remove it from the fire, strain the gravy, and clarify it.   Pare the meat well, and glaze.   Have a jelly-coated mold sufficiently large to contain this, put it in and fill the entire mold with jelly, leaving it on the ice till ready to serve.   Unmold it on a large dish, garnish around with chopped jelly, and form an outside border of oblongs or triangles of jelly.

(2433). RUMP OF BEEF À LA MODE (Pièce de Bœuf ou Pointe de Culotte à la Mode).

For this dish use a piece of beef prepared as for à la mode à la bourgeoise (No. 1340).   When nearly cold put it into an oblong mold four inches deep and four inches wide by eight inches long; lay the mold on ice.   Range some balls of braised carrots half an inch in diameter on the bottom of the mold.   Place the meat on top, covering with stock; harden and arrange over some carrots; cover with partly set jelly, and when this is cold add the rest of the meat, and when entirely cold cut in half-inch thick slices.   Range on a long dish in a straight line and garnish around with chopped jelly.

Another way is to have the meat arranged in the same mold as above, skim all the fat from the beef stock, strain it through a fine sieve and add to it as much strong jelly and a quarter bottleful of white wine; boil and cool.   With this jelly cover the slices of beef, allow to get cold, unmold and dress on a long dish, and garnish around with small carrots, cut pear-shaped; cook and let **fall** to a glaze. Then season, cool and roll in a little cold jelly; surround these with slices of gherkin. Beef à la mode can also be placed in a mold and have another larger one decorated with carrots, turnips and gherkins; protect the decoration with a heavy layer of jelly; unmold the smallest mold and place the contents in the largest or decorated one; fill up with jelly, let get cool, then unmold by dipping it in hot water; garnish around with chopped jelly, and outside of it arrange triangle or oblong jelly croûtons.

(2434). TENDERLOIN OF BEEF À LA BOUQUETIÈRE (Filet de Bœuf à la Bouquetière).

Prepare and cook a fine tenderloin, the same as described in l'Ambassade (No. 1441), only omitting the larding. Let it get cool, keeping it very straight, and when thoroughly cold trim it to a nice shape, and pour over it a brown chaudfroid sauce (No. 594); when the chaudfroid is firm cover it entirely with half-set jelly. Put the tenderloin on top of a two-tier foundation, made either of rice or hominy, the bottom one being two inches thick, the top one three-quarters of an inch, and shaped symmetrically. Fill each of thirty small paper cases with a different vegetable, or several of each kind—say three of each—such as green peas, string beans, flageolets or kidney beans, Brussels sprouts, beets, cauliflower, artichoke bottoms, mushrooms, truffles and celery, seasoned and mixed with a little mayonnaise (No. 606). Prepare fifteen roses cut from turnips, and fifteen cut from carrots, each one inch in diameter, blanched and cooked separately in white broth (No. 194a). Set a rose on the top of each and alternate the colors when decorating the upper tier with fourteen of these, and the lower one with sixteen; force some chopped jelly through a cornet or a bag between each case around the bottom and the edge, and outside of this place a row of jelly squares. Garnish the top of the tenderloin with five hatelets of vegetables (No. 2526), imitating natural flowers, the center one representing a vase decorated with small flowers.

(2435). TENDERLOIN OF BEEF À LA EVERS (Filet de Bœuf à la Evers).

This tenderloin is to be prepared and cooked exactly the same as for à la Bienvenue (No. 1445); when done, pare it nicely, and cut it into quarter of an inch thick slices; lay these in an oblong mold the same shape as the tenderloin but smaller than the one to be decorated. Reduce the gravy, add some aspic jelly (No. 103), (test the consistency of this by putting a small quantity of it in a mold on the ice, and if it should not be firm enough add some gelatine), fill in the mold containing the meat with this, and set it aside on ice to get very cold. Decorate the largest mold with pieces of tongue, pistachio nuts, and white of egg; cover the decoration with a heavy layer of jelly; unmold the one containing the meat, lay it in the center of the decorated one, and fill it in with jelly. Fill the entire center up to the inside of the dish destined for the tenderloin, edge with jelly, and when very firm unmold the tenderloin on to the center of it. Lay on each end half a nicely carved rice vase, these being filled with imitations of small truffles made of mousseline of foies-gras, and then rolled in finely chopped truffles. When cold dip them in partly cold jelly, and arrange chopped jelly all around, also oblong-shaped jelly croutons, and fasten three hatelets decorated in Bellevue (No. 2526) on the top of the meat.

(2436). TENDERLOIN OF BEEF À LA LUCULLUS (Filet de Bœuf à la Lucullus).

In order to arrange this tenderloin it will be necessary to have eight molds in two series of four each, four to be decorated and four in which the tenderloins are molded, these being an inch narrower in diameter than those to be decorated. Prepare and cook the tenderloin as explained in l'Ambassade (No. 1441); when done, cut it into slices and reshape the meat into its original form and fill the four smallest molds with it. Reduce the stock with aspic jelly (No. 103), (if necessary add some isinglass to have it very firm), pour over the meat in the molds and set on ice to get very cold. Decorate the four larger molds (see Fig. 455) intended to receive the tenderloin after they are decorated; cover the decoration with a layer of thick jelly, unmold the smaller ones, put their contents inside the larger ones and fill up with very firm jelly. After the jelly is very firm unmold the whole on a cloth, set at the bottom of the slope on each side of the bridge a strong tin square three and a half inches in width and three inches high, having rounded corners and bent in the center to form a right angle; these squares are intended to keep up the tenderloins on the inclined slope, and are most necessary; place the small molds at the ends, and set around the piece twenty-four

Fig. 455.

small croustades made of short paste (No. 135), and filled with goose livers taken from a terrine of foies-gras; around these throw some chopped jelly, making a very regular border of croutons of the same. Stick two hatelets, one at each end, and in the center put a small figure holding up a cup filled with glazed truffles.

(2437). TENDERLOIN OF BEEF À LA NOAILLES (Filet de Bœuf à la Noailles).

This tenderloin must be prepared exactly the same as for à la Bayonnaise (No. 1443); when cold trim it nicely and glaze it with meat glaze (No. 402), using a brush for the purpose. Cover it with jelly and set it on a symmetrically carved rice foundation, garnishing around with mushrooms, truffles, scallops of foies-gras and chicken mousselines made in tartlet molds. The mushrooms are to be cooked and emptied with a vegetable scoop, then filled with a foies-gras, pressed through a tammy and glazed in a white chaudfroid (No. 596). The chicken mousselines should be covered with green chaudfroid (No. 595), and scallops of foies-gras to be covered with a brown chaudfroid (No. 594), the truffles glazed. Arrange this garnishing around the tenderloin with chopped jelly and croutons of jelly, but do not decorate it with hatelets.

(2438). TENDERLOIN OF BEEF À LA VIOLETTA (Filet de Bœuf à la Violetta).

Have the tenderloin prepared and cooked the same as for à la Bayonnaise (No. 1443), and when completely cold pare it to the needed size to fit in an oblong mold, previously decorated with a variety of vegetables blanched and cooked in broth (No. 194a). Cover this decoration with a heavy coating of jelly; cut the tenderloin nine inches long by three and a half wide; trim it nicely and lay it in the center of the mold and imbed it in ice, laying it in very straight. Fill up the mold with cold melted jelly, and when it becomes quite cold and the jelly thoroughly firm, unmold it on an oval dish, and garnish around with some finely chopped jelly. Select eight equal-sized, large, ripe and very firm tomatoes; plunge them into boiling water to peel off the skins, and empty the insides through an inch and a quarter opening on the stalk end. Shred some lettuce leaves and cooked beet-root, season them with salt, pepper, oil and vinegar, and thicken the whole with a little jellied mayonnaise (No. 613), mixing in with it some whipped cream; fill the tomatoes with this, and put the covers on again; coat them over with partly cold jelly; also have eight cooked artichoke bottoms, garnish each one with asparagus tops seasoned and thickened with jellied mayonnaise (No. 613), adding to it some whipped cream. Place on top of the asparagus a small black truffle glazed with jelly; garnish around the inside of the dish with chopped jelly. Lay the prepared garnishings over, and intercalate around these a row of jelly croûtons (Fig. 457).

(2439). TENDERLOIN OF BEEF, GRENADINS ROCHAMBEAU (Filet de Bœuf, Grenadins Rochambeau).

Prepare twelve tenderloins into half-heart shapes, each one weighing four ounces; lard one third of them with larding pork, cut as represented in No. 3, Fig. 52, another third with truffles, and the last third with salted unsmoked tongue; braise them in a mirepoix stock (No. 419), and glaze, then cool and pare. Dress them in a circle on a round dish, alternating the various lardings, and fill the center with some foies-gras scooped from a terrine with a spoon; arrange chopped jelly around, surrounded by a border of jelly croutons.

(2440). TENDERLOIN OF BEEF WITH CROUSTADES MACÉDOINE (Filet de Bœuf aux Croustades Macédoine).

Prepare, lard, braise and glaze a fine tenderloin the same as for à la Bienvenue (No. 1445); put it aside to cool, keeping it very straight, then pare and glaze. Set it on a small rice foundation two and a half inches high and symmetrically carved (Fig. 9a). Garnish around with small croustades made of foundation paste (No. 135); fill these croustades with a small vegetable macédoine (No. 2650); season well and thicken with a ravigote mayonnaise (No. 612); sprinkle over some very finely chopped chervil, and garnish around the croustades with a row of chopped jelly. Decorate the top of the tenderloin with some Bellevue hatelets (No. 2526).

(2441). TENDERLOIN OF BEEF WITH VEGETABLES, MAYONNAISE (Filet de Bœuf aux Légumes, Mayonnaise).

Prepare and cook a tenderloin the same as for à la Chanzy (No. 1447), keeping it quite rare; glaze it over several times and leave till cold. The drawing that accompanies this dish will show the way to prepare the meat for a supper, or for serving at a small sideboard supper. First take an oval-shaped drum, three inches high and hollow in the center, fasten it on an oval board a quarter of an inch thick and an inch wider than the outlines of the drum; on top of this drum lay an oval wooden socle an inch and a half high and slightly curved in the center, it being two inches narrower all around than the drum itself, thus forming a shelf. Decorate all around the drum with small sticks of vegetables, such as carrots and turnips, cut out with a tin tube five-six-

FIG. 456.

teenths of an inch in diameter, and blanched separately in salted water; lay them in regular rows one over the other formed of the two distinct colors, being careful to dip each piece in half-set jelly to make it adhere to the form; when the drum is all decorated, glide it on to a long dish, the bottom being filled with jelly; keep it in a cool place at forty-two degrees temperature. Pare and cut up the tenderloin in crosswise slices, each a quarter of an inch thick, dress them on the second curved-shape form, glaze and cover over with jelly. Have a garnishing of Brussels sprouts, celery roots, and cucumbers, all of uniform size, also some green peas, all of these to be dressed in small clusters, alternating the various colors; these must be placed on the shelf between the drum and the curve; put chopped jelly in the dish around the piece. Serve mayonnaise sauce (No. 606) at the same time.

(2442). BORDERS OF DIFFERENT SHAPED JELLY CROÛTONS (Bordures de Différentes Formes en Croûtons de Gelée).

Procure very firm and very clear jelly (No. 123) cooled on tin plates two inches high; unmold when very cold on wet napkins having all the moisture squeezed out, then spread on the table without any creases whatever. The jelly can be cut into many shapes (see Figs. 457 to 465, jelly croûtons for borders). Lay them on the edge of the inside of the basin with regularity. They must be

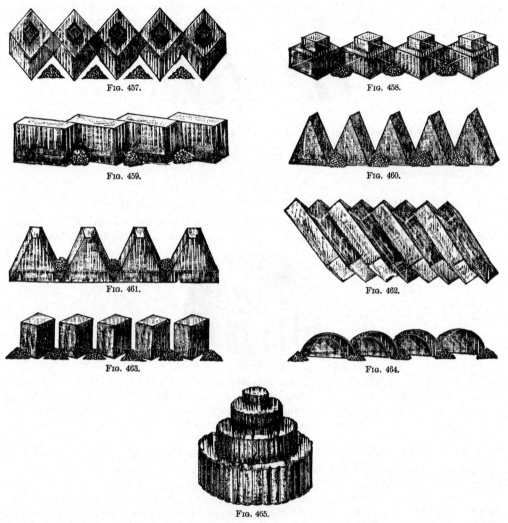

FIG. 457.   FIG. 458.

FIG. 459.   FIG. 460.

FIG. 461.   FIG. 462.

FIG. 463.   FIG. 464.

FIG. 465.

cut very evenly. The effect they produce can easily be seen on the different designs the plates offer. Round croûtons are cut with a round pastry cutter that has been well heated in **hot** water. The thickness of the croûton should be in proportion to its diameter.

(2443). VEGETABLE BORDERS (Bordures de Légumes).

Boil and cook in salted water some carrots, turnips, green peas and whole string beans; keep them all slightly firm. Cut the carrots into three-sixteenths of an inch to a quarter of an inch thick slices, according to the size of the border; lay these slices on a napkin to dry, then out half-

FIG. 466.   FIG. 467.   FIG. 468.

rings from them with a column tube and coat them with half-set jelly. Fasten them on by dipping into half-set jelly, and then placing them tastefully on the edge of the basin of a very cold **dish**; range the string beans in lozenge form between the half-rings at the base and the green **peas on** the center of the half-rings on top.

(2444). BUTTER BORDERS (Bordures en Beurre).

These borders are not very practical; they can only be made when the temperature is very low and are only mentioned in case there be no other resource available; yet they can be of great utility. The butter should be well kneaded to remove all foreign matter that it might contain; it should be

Fig. 469.

colored green or red; spread it out on sheets of paper three-sixteenths of an inch thick, then leave to cool; invert these on wet napkins, and remove the paper; cut it into rounds, rings, or triangles. Dress them on the border of a dish, alternating the colors; the dish must be kept in the refrigerator until required.

(2445). MOLDED JELLY BORDER (Bordure de Gelée Moulée).

Incrust a metal border mold, either of tinned copper or tin, on ice; decorate it with fanciful cuts, either of truffles, tongue, egg-white, pistachio nuts or vegetables, done by dipping them in half-

Fig. 470.

set jelly. When the mold is decorated, coat this decoration with a layer of jelly, done by rolling the jelly in the mold on the decoration until there is a layer sufficiently thick to protect it; fill up with jelly. When sufficiently firm unmold the border on a dish, having the basin filled with very firm jelly. The border can be filled with foies-gras, chaudfroid, etc.

(2446). LAMBS' BRAINS WITH MAYONNAISE (Cervelles d'Agneau à la Mayonnaise).

Steep six lambs' brains in fresh water for half an hour; skin them by lifting off the thin cuticle enveloping them, also the sanguineous fibers, and return them to fresh water to soak for two hours more. Place them in a saucepan with sufficient boiling water to cover, adding salt and vinegar, and let boil slowly for twenty minutes. When cold and drained, dress in a circle, placing between every brain a crouton of red lambs' tongue cut to resemble cocks'-combs; decorate all around with garnishing of eggs (No. 2513), gherkins and beets; fill the center of the circle with some green mayonnaise with fine herbs (No. 612), and surround with pretty clear jelly croutons.

(2447). CASES OF LOBSTER À LA RAVIGOTE—SMALL (Petites Caisses de Homard à la Ravigote).

Place nine or twelve small china cases two inches in diameter on ice to become thoroughly cold. Split across in two the meats taken from six cooked lobster claws, and cut these up into

Fig. 471.

small rounds, using a vegetable cutter one and a quarter inches in diameter for the purpose, and lay them in a small-sized vessel with half as many rounds of truffles cut the same size as the lobster and two or three spoonfuls of gherkins cut in slices; season with salt, a dash of cayenne pepper, oil and vinegar and let stand for fifteen minutes; drain off the seasoning; fill the cases with the preparation mixed with mayonnaise printanière, and cover the top with a layer of mayonnaise (No. 606), finished with tarragon vinegar; smooth the jelly sauce and dress the cases on a folded napkin.

(2448). CASES OF SNIPE WITH JELLY—SMALL (Petites Caisses de Bécassines à la Gelée).

This entrée should be served on a dish having its bottom covered with cooked paste (No. 131) and the outer edge decorated with an open-work border of the same; and in the center a cone-shaped support, first covered with paper then with chopped jelly. This support must have a hole through the top in order to sustain a hatelet. Bone six large snipe, stuff them with chopped forcemeat (No. 77); to this add the chopped entrails of the bird sautéd in butter and sew them up to keep the stuffing in. Maintain them in shape with a band of buttered paper. Range them in a narrow sautoir lined with fat pork and aromatic herbs, moisten with half a glassful of white wine and reduce on a brisk fire; then moisten to about their height with stock (No. 194a); season and mask over

FIG 472.

with fat pork. Boil the liquid for five minutes and then remove the saucepan to a slower fire, or to a slack oven to cook for half an hour, then let cool off in their own stock. Unwrap the snipe, pare and split them lengthwise in two, shape them properly to fit the half-heart paper cases and range the halved birds on a small baking sheet and set them aside to cool for a quarter of an hour. Now take up each half snipe, one by one, and dip them in a brown chaudfroid sauce (No. 594) thickened when required to have it quite firm; return them to the sheet and remove them separately when hard, to suppress any surplus sauce; brush them over lightly with jelly and lay each half in a half-heart-shaped case having its bottom covered with chopped jelly. Range the cases around the support, the point upward, leaning them against the border; insert a garnished hatelet into the top of the support. Surround the bottom of the dish with a chain of triangle jelly croûtons.

(2449). CASES OF THRUSHES WITH JELLY—SMALL (Petites Caisses de Grives à la Gelée).

For this entrée have a border of jelly the center being filled with a round piece of wood of the same diameter and height as the border and covered with white paper. Bone eight thrushes, spread them out on the table and season; fill them with a fine game forcemeat (No. 91), some foies-gras and truffles made into balls. Cover them with a band of paper to hold them in a round shape, then range them on the bottom of a small sautoir covered with fat pork, putting

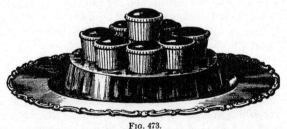

FIG. 473.

them quite close to one another; salt over and moisten to nearly their height with a good un-skimmed stock (No. 194a), and cover over with more fat pork; boil up the liquid, then withdraw the saucepan and put on the lid. Cook the boned birds for three-quarters of an hour in a slack oven; they should but simmer, as they only require to be poached, and let cool off in this same liquid. Unwrap, pare, cover by dipping each one singly into a brown chaudfroid sauce (No. 594) thickened on ice; after this sauce is cold, pare the birds and place them in round porceiain cases; dress these on the border. Garnish around the cases with jelly cut in three-sixteenths inch squares.

(2450). CÉLESTINES OF PULLET À LA TALLEYRAND (Célestines de Poularde à la Talleyrand).

Cut up into eighth of an inch squares a pound of braised and cold white pullet meat, free of fat and bones, also a quarter of a pound of peeled truffles cut in the same sized squares. With the leg meats from which the skin, bones and fat have been removed, prepare a purée and dilute it with half a pint of brown chaudfroid (No. 594); press through a tammy into a tin bowl and thicken the preparation on ice, adding to it the truffle and chicken salpicon. Cut some slices of unsmoked red beef tongue three-sixteenths of an inch thick, and these into rounds two and a quarter inches in diameter; cover one of the sides with the preparation, having it well rounded on top, smooth with a knife and let cool off on ice, then mask over with brown chaudfroid. Decorate the surfaces of these with truffles, cover with half-set jelly and dress them in a circle. Cut some medium-sized apples in two, peel and core, then lay them on a buttered baking sheet and sprinkle over with powdered sugar, and let cook for a few moments in a hot oven. When done and cold, use these apples to fill in the center of the circle; garnish around the célestines with chopped jelly and outside of this lay evenly cut jelly croutons (No. 2442).

(2451). CHAUDFROID OF CHICKEN À LA CLARA MORRIS (Chaudfroid de Poulet à la Clara Morris).

Raise the fillets from six medium two-pound chickens; remove the skin and cuticle, pare them carefully into half-hearts; salt over and lay them in a buttered sautoir in such a way that all the pointed ends are in the center; cover with clarified butter and squeeze over the juice of a lemon; place them on the fire to fry without coloring, then drain and put them under a weight to press lightly; pare them again so that they are all the same shape. Bone the second joints, keeping on half of the drumstick bones, remove the sinews and season the meats with salt, pepper and nutmeg; stuff the inside with a quenelle forcemeat (No. 89), into which mix a quarter as much foies-gras rubbed through a sieve and the same quantity of truffles, tongue and pistachios cut in three-sixteenths inch squares. Enclose the dressing well and sew the skin together to envelop it completely, then place these legs in a sautoir covered with thin slices of fat pork, moisten with mirepoix and white wine stock (No. 419), cover with buttered paper and cook them in a moderate oven. When done, drain off and place them under a weight to get cold, then cover them with either a white or brown chaudfroid sauce (No. 594). Prepare a garnishing composed of cooked channeled mushrooms (No. 118), carrot balls blanched and cooked in white broth (No. 194a), and seasoned with salt, pepper, oil, vinegar and fine herbs, and some glazed truffle balls. Dress the chaudfroid around a bread support covered with ravigote butter (No. 583), and fill in the intersections with the garnishing; around lay chopped jelly and small cases filled with asparagus tops covered with green mayonnaise with fine herbs (No. 612). On the top set a round piece of glazed truffle, and around the cases a chain of lozenge-shaped jelly croutons.

(2452). CHAUDFROID OF DOE BIRD, PLOVERS, BUSTARDS OR WOODCOCK WITH FUMET (Chaudfroid de Courlis, Pluviers, Vanneaux ou Bécasses au Fumet).

Pick, singe and clean nicely eight doe birds; draw and truss them for roasting like plovers (No. 2119); put them to roast, remove, and when cold detach the breasts, suppress the skin and cut each breast in three pieces—one breastbone and the two wings. Break up the fragments and put them in a saucepan with minced shallots and carrots, parsley, thyme and bay leaf, moisten with white wine, stock (No. 194a), and espagnole sauce (No. 414); boil, skim and simmer for thirty minutes, then strain; remove all the fat and reduce to half-glaze, adding jelly; pour this sauce into a tin basin and leave to cool on ice while stirring unceasingly until it becomes the proper consistency. Dip each one of the pieces of bird into this chaudfroid to cover with a thick layer, and when thoroughly cold brush them over with half-set jelly. Decorate a border mold with fanciful cuts of truffles and egg-whites, coat it with a thick layer of jelly, and fill with a well-seasoned macédoine (No. 2650) garnishing dressed with jellied mayonnaise (No. 613); unmold it as soon as it is cold, and fill the center with a pad of rice; on this have a sloping pyramid of rice; cover this over with thick jelly forced through a pocket. Dress the chaudfroids, leaning them against the pyramid and holding them up with sticky jelly forced through a cornet; on top insert a Bellevue hatelet (No. 2526) and place fine jelly croutons around the border; push chopped jelly into all the intersections between the chaudfroids. Proceed the same for plovers, woodcock or bustards.

(2453). CHAUDFROID OF YOUNG GUINEA FOWLS (Chaudfroid de Jeunes Pintades).

In order to dress this entrée solidly it will be found necessary to unmold a border of very smooth and hard jelly on a dish decorated at the bottom with a few fanciful cuts of truffle and egg-whites; coat over the mold and fill the inside of this border with a foundation made of wood or stearine covered over with white paper and having fastened on to its center a column-shaped wooden support; enlarge this especially toward the bottom with thick chopped-up jelly and keep the dish on ice. Truss three small, clean young guinea fowls; cook them in the pan, keeping them

Fig. 474.

quite rare and let them get partly cold in their own stock, then drain them off and carve in five pieces; remove the upper breastbones and the fillets, and lay these under a light weight till cold. Suppress also the thick second joint bone, leaving on the drumstick only; cut this much shorter, and place the legs under a weight to cool. Pare the pieces nicely, suppressing all the skin; dip them singly into a blond chaudfroid sauce (No. 596), lifting them out with a large fork, and range them at once on a baking sheet, some distance apart from each other so as to harden the sauce. Now take them off this sheet to cut away the surplus of sauce and dress them pyramidically against the support in the center of the dish, the legs underneath and the fillets and upper breast parts on top, being careful that this pyramid does not incline toward the jelly but leans against the support, which must also be covered with paper. Mask the pieces of chicken with half-set jelly laid on with a brush, and keep the dish on ice for twenty minutes before serving.

(2454). CHAUDFROID OF LARKS (Chaudfroid de Mauviettes).

Bone two dozen clean larks; spread them open on the table and season; prepare a boned game forcemeat (No. 66), season highly and add to it a few spoonfuls of liver baking forcemeat (No. 64), and some of the fried lark intestines, also a few spoonfuls of raw, chopped truffles. Use this forcemeat for filling the birds, and roll them up into balls, sew them up with coarse thread, and cook for twenty minutes in a very little good, reduced stock, and covered over with fat pork; remove from the fire and cool them off in their own stock, then drain, unwrap, and trim each one neatly, and rounded. Take them up one by one, and dip them in a brown chaudfroid (No. 594), thickened properly on ice; lay them at once on a grate, and let the sauce harden in the ice-box. Pare the larks from any excess of sauce, cover with a light layer of jelly applied with a brush, and when this has become quite cold, dress them in a pyramid form on a cold dish, and surround with more jelly.

(2455). CHAUDFROID OF PARTRIDGES À LA BÉATRICE (Chaudfroid de Perdeaux à la Béatrice).

Have four partridges picked, singed, drawn, and well cleaned; remove the legs, bone, suppress the sinews and stuff them with game quenelle forcemeat (No. 91) and cooked fine herbs (No. 385); braise and set them under a weight. Raise the fillets, and sauté them in butter without coloring; lay them under a weight also, then pare them as well as the legs into half-hearts, and cover both with brown chaudfroid (No. 594) prepared with game fumet (No. 397) extracted from the carcasses; repeat this operation until the coating of chaudfroid be of a sufficient thickness, then leave to cool, and cover over with another layer of half-set jelly. Dress all the pieces on an empty swan (No. 3597), with an opening on the top or back part of the swan, and surround with small "pains" prepared as follows: Decorate some mousseline molds (No. 2, Fig. 138) with fanciful cuts, either of truffles, tongue, or pistachios dipped in half-set jelly; coat them rather thickly with jelly, and fill with a game "pain" preparation made with game purée of the fillets and parings mixed with chaudfroid, béchamel (No. 593), and well drained, whipped cream; add a small salpicon of truffles and tongue cut in one-eighth of an inch squares, and when the molds are thoroughly cold, invert and range them around the swan; surround with chopped jelly and a border of jelly croûtons (No. 2442).

(2456). CHAUDFROID OF FILLETS OF PHEASANTS (Chaudfroid de Filets de Faisans).

This entrée is suitable to be served at a dinner or a buffet. It is dressed on a socle composed of a wooden base, having in its center a support made in tiers, the whole being covered with white paper; on the very top of this there should be a hole intended to receive a hatelet. The platform of this support is ornamented with a small overhanging border made of modeling fat or cardboard. Detach the fillets from the breasts of three large, cooked and cold pheasants, leaving the upper part of the breast—the part against the fillet adhering to the frame—then cut them up and remove, first the skin and bones, then divide each one into parts on their length, and also divide each of the fillets in three, pare them in equal shapes and sizes and cut them square on one end so as later to be able to dress them standing upright. Pound all the parings of the breast meats with as much cooked foies-gras, then rub through a sieve, season this pulp and set it in a thin iron vessel to dilute with two gills of melted game glaze (No. 398) and four to five gills of brown chaudfroid (No. 594) in such a manner that when the preparation becomes cold it acquires a certain firm consistency. After it is smooth spread it on a baking sheet in even, thin layers, cover them very lightly with cold jelly, using a brush, and range on top the eighteen fillets in a straight line,

Fig. 475.

one beside the other, pressing them down lightly; now cover them with a thin layer of the same preparation and let get thoroughly cold on ice. After removing it, cut with the tip of a small knife dipped in hot water, following the outlines of the fillets most minutely, then heat the bottom of the sheet with a wet cloth so as to be able to detach the cut-out pieces. Take them up one by one to smooth and stand them upright on another sheet on their square ends; let them get cold on ice once more for a quarter of an hour. Remove the fillets one by one and dip them into a fine flowing brown chaudfroid sauce (No. 594) in such a way that their size does not increase much, then return them to the same sheet just as they were before, (meaning upright), and let the sauce harden. With the same preparation cover the upper breast pieces, being careful that they assume their original size and shape, and smooth the surfaces nicely. When thoroughly hard dip these pieces into the same chaudfroid sauce to cover lightly and not allowing them to become misshapen. After the chaudfroid sauce is quite hard, take the fillets one by one and cut away the excess of sauce, then dress them at once upright on the lower tier, or more properly speaking on the wooden foundation (therefore around the central support); now dress the upper breast parts, also upright on the upper tier, leaning them against the support, and brush over lightly with a brush dipped in jelly both fillets and the others; surround the base with a cord of jelly pushed through a cornet so as to maintain the meats level, and also surround this base with chopped jelly, laying over a chain of small paper cases filled with truffles masked in chaudfroid. On the extreme top of the support stick a small hatelet into the hole made for the purpose. Keep the entrée cold till needed.

(2457). CHAUDFROID OF PRAIRIE HEN—GROUSE (Chaudfroid de Poule de Prairie--Tétras).

Prepare a fine garnishing composed of large cooked cocks'-combs, poached chicken kidneys, round truffles and mushroom heads; glaze the truffles with a thin layer of brown chaudfroid sauce (No. 594), the combs and kidneys remaining in their natural state glazed with half-set jelly. Cut the breasts of two cold roast pheasants into quarter of an inch thick slices, suppressing the skin;

have them well pared and of uniform size, dip each one separately in brown chaudfroid, and range them at once on a baking sheet, keeping them somewhat apart; let the sauce harden on ice. Incrust a large dome-shaped mold in ice, coat it over with an eighth of an inch thick layer of jelly, and when this is set dress on to the bottom and around the mold the prettiest pieces, intermingling them with the garnishings; fill up the mold with some half-set jelly. One hour after dip the mold in hot water, wipe dry and turn the chaudfroid over on a dish foundation covered with white paper; surround with small crimped paper cases, each one containing a small truffle dipped in brown chaudfroid. Fasten one garnished hatelet in the center of the dome, lay chopped jelly all around, and jelly croûtons around this.

(2458). CHAUDFROID OF PULLET, PLAIN (Chaudfroid de Poularde, Simple).

Draw, clean and truss two pullets of two pounds each as for an entrée (No. 178); put them into a saucepan and cover with stock (No. 194a), adding a bunch of parsley garnished with thyme and bay leaf; boil, skim and cook slowly on the side of the fire until done, then transfer them to a vessel and pour the stock over; let get partly cold and drain off to cut into pieces, first removing the two legs and from them suppressing the second joint bones, retaining only the drumstick bones to answer for holding the frill; put these legs under the pressure of a weight, then begin to cut the fillets from the breast, leaving on a piece of the bone with the breast meat; pare the whole well free of all skin and sinews; dip all the pieces into a partly cold white chaudfroid sauce (No. 596), lifting them out with a large fork to range on top of a baking sheet, or else a heavy sheet of tin, one beside the other but without touching; a grate may be used. Set on ice to harden the sauce, then remove each piece and pare, trimming off the surplus chaudfroid sauce and giving them a handsome shape. Dress in a pyramid and cover the chaudfroid with half-set jelly applied with a brush; keep on ice for twenty minutes, then trim the pinion bones and drumsticks with fancy paper frills (No. 10) and decorate the dish and chickens with chopped jelly and jelly croûtons.

(2459). CHAUDFROID OF QUAILS À LA BAUDY (Chaudfroid de Cailles à la Baudy).

This entrée is dressed on a wooden foundation covered with white paper, and bordered on the outside edge with small beads of butter forced through a cornet. It has a paper-covered support in the center two to three inches in diameter and about the same height as the quails. Singe and bone eight fresh quails, leaving on the thighs, season the insides and fill the empty space with a layer of fine galantine forcemeat (No. 66), mingled with foies-gras and truffles cut in small dice, also a piece of

Fig. 476.

raw truffle in each; all of these to be properly seasoned; cover over with another layer of the forcemeat and bring the two sides together so that the quails retain their original shape, then sew them up. Truss the thighs, and tie each bird up in a separate piece of muslin. Range the quails in a deep sautoir lined with fat pork, moisten to their height with a good stock (No. 194a) and boil up the liquid, then withdraw it to a slower fire and cook the quails for twenty to thirty minutes while covered, and let them get partly cold in their stock. Drain, unwrap, and tie them up tighter in the same cloths to keep them in shape, and when quite cold cut each one lengthwise in two; fasten the two halves together with a small wooden skewer, and cover the quails with a white chaudfroid sauce (No. 596). When the sauce becomes quite cold, stick one of the reserved legs in each half bird, and withdraw the skewer. Dress these boned quails almost upright on the foundation that is on the dish, leaning them against the support; garnish the center of this with chopped jelly, and surround the base of the bottom with small crimped paper cases filled with glazed truffles.

(2460), CHAUDFROID OF FILLETS OF REDHEAD DUCK AND VENISON (Chaudfroid de Filets de Canard Tête Rouge et de Venaison).

Raise the fillets from five redhead ducks, without the wings or minions; pare them into half-hearts; season and sauté in clarified butter, keeping them rare; then drain and cool off under a light weight between two pieces of buttered paper; remove the skin, pare them again to have all alike, and dip in a brown chaudfroid sauce (No. 594) reduced with game fumet (No. 397), properly thickened on ice; range them at some distance apart on a baking sheet to harden the sauce; decorate with ornaments of truffles dipped in jelly, and coat the whole in half-set jelly. Cut ten pieces of very red beef tongue, not too thick, but of the same shape and size as the fillets; lay a duck fillet on each piece of tongue, making it adhere, and let get cold. Dress these upright against a vegetable salad cut in small dice, and thickened with jellied mayonnaise (No. 613), then molded in a small pyramidical mold. Surround the bottom with a thick rope of jelly pushed through a pocket. On the top of the pyramid place a cluster of jelly cut in small squares.

Chaudfroid of Venison.—Cut a fillet of venison into slices; dip them in a brown chaudfroid sauce (No. 594) properly thickened on ice, then lay to cool on a baking sheet; when cold, pare and dress in a circle; glaze over with jelly, fill the center with chopped jelly, and outside with a border of jelly croûtons.

(2461), CHAUDFROID OF SNIPE IN PYRAMID (Chaudfroid de Bécassines en Buisson).

Dress this entrée on a wooden dish bottom, composed of three shelves, all to be covered with white paper. Bone fifteen to eighteen small snipe, keeping the heads and a part of the intestines aside, the latter to be cooked in melted butter and pressed through a sieve. Scald the heads, pick out the eyes, replace them with a little forcemeat and a round of truffle to imitate the original; place in the oven to poach the forcemeat. Spread the snipe out on the table, season and cover with a layer of game galantine forcemeat (No. 66). Put in the center of each one a piece of raw foies-gras and a piece of cooked truffle, cover with another layer of the forcemeat, then roll the boned snipe into ball shapes. Cover each one with a separate piece of buttered paper and range them

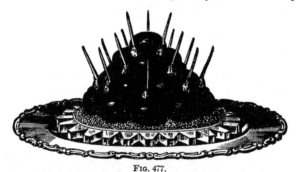

FIG. 477.

in a narrow sautoir lined with fat pork; moisten to their height with good stock (No. 194a) and cover with more of the pork, then put on the lid and let cook slowly for twenty-five minutes; leave them to cool in their own stock. Unwrap the snipe, pare and shape them properly and fill with foies-gras any crevices that may have been caused by the cooking. Pare them all alike and of a nice shape. Range them at once on a small baking sheet and put aside in a cool place for a quarter of an hour; take them up one by one and dip them in a brown chaudfroid sauce (No. 594) thickened on ice so that they are entirely covered, and return them immediately to the sheet to drain off the sauce, and keep cold for another half hour, then pare them once more of any surplus of sauce. At the last moment force some sticky chopped jelly through a pocket between the shelves, dress the snipe over, letting them form into a pyramid, and between each one dress one of the heads, and glaze it over with a brush. Push a thick rope of chopped jelly around the pyramid on the bottom of the dish and surround this with fine croûtons. Cover the snipe lightly with jelly applied with a brush, so as to render them glossy.

(2462), CHAUDFROID OF TURKEY À LA PÉRIGORD (Chaudfroid de Dinde à la Périgord).

Braise and put away to cool a fine six to eight-pound turkey; remove the fillets, free them from skin and sinews, and cut each one into six pieces, making them as long as possible; trim them all the same shape and size, and cover over one side with a thin layer of foies-gras taken from a terrine, pounded and rubbed through a sieve; let get quite cold. Prepare a chaudfroid with a quart of reduced velouté sauce (No. 415) and the braise stock, strained, skimmed and reduced to a pint, with as much aspic jelly (No. 103) added. Let the chaudfroid be cold enough to cover the meat well. Then dip the pieces one by one into it and remove them with a fork, placing one beside the other on a tray or on a grate. Let get cold, then cover them once more, exactly the same as before, and finish by covering with half-set jelly. Dress them on the bottom of a dish around a support, both the foundation and support being made of tin, having a hole in the summit and covered with noodle paste (No. 142), dried in the open air and glazed over with game glaze (No. 398). Decorate all around with small glazed truffles set in small white crimped paper cases. Insert into the top of the support a tasteful hâtelet ornamented with a fine glazed truffle and a cock's-comb.

(2463). CHICKENS ÉCARLATE À LA DERENNE (Poulets Écarlate à la Derenne).

This piece is dressed on an oval wooden bottom covered with white paper and fastened on a long dish, having in the center a slightly conical-shaped wooden support also covered with paper and a hole bored in the top to hold a hatelet. Cook in water four large calves' tongues or small red beef tongues; drain and cool under a weight. Break the breast bone of four small, singed and cleaned chickens, then remove the bone and fill up the empty space with galantine forcemeat (No. 65) mixed with truffles and cooked foies-gras cut in dice; then sew up the breast skin on the back. Truss these chickens with the legs bent under the skin, lard the tops and wrap each one in a small

FIG. 478.

piece of fine muslin without tightening them too much; cook for one hour in stock (No. 194a), but very slowly, so as not to spoil their shape, then let get very cold, drain and untruss. Detach the breasts from the back part of the chicken and cut them up in slices, then once across, keeping them in good shape, and return them to their original places. Lay the chickens on a grater, cover over with white chaudfroid sauce (No. 596), properly thickened, and let it get cold. Dress the chickens upright on the oval foundation laid on the dish, leaning them against the support and alternating each one with a tongue previously pared, skinned and cut in lengths, but returned to the original position, then glazed over with a brush. Surround the chickens on the base with a piping of chopped thick jelly pushed through a cornet and between every tongue and chicken lay a well-rounded peeled truffle cooked in white wine and glazed over with a brush. Lay all around the outside of the foundation triangular crusts of very clear jelly, and fasten a hatelet into the top garnished with jelly and a peeled truffle. It is advisable to serve this dish with a mayonnaise sauce (No. 606) in a separate sauce-boat.

(2464). CHICKEN FILLETS À LA MIREBEL (Filets de Poulet à la Mirebel).

Raise and pare twelve chicken breasts; remove the minion fillets and the skin from the larger ones as well as the pellicle covering the minions and the sinews. Streak half of the minion fillets with truffles and the other half with red beef tongue, then shape them like turbans; lay them on a buttered baking sheet and place in the oven for a few minutes to poach; remove and set under a light weight until cold. Cover with half-set jelly and fill the interiors with a purée of foies-gras pushed in through a cornet, and on top of each lay a small, very white, cooked channeled mushroom (No. 118) covered with half-set jelly. Poach the larger fillets in butter and lemon juice, lay them under a weight and pare again into half-hearts, cover over with jelly and decorate with fanciful star-shaped cuts of truffles and tongue dipped in half-set jelly. For this use a round mold two and a quarter inches in diameter, and one-eighth of an inch deep. Cut and then arrange in the pieces of truffle and tongue as shown in Fig. 479, first dipping them in half-set jelly; when this is hard, unmold and place these stars on the largest part of the fillet and cover the whole with half-cold jelly. (These stars are used for lamb cutlets, Leverrier.) Fill the basin of a dish with chopped jelly; after the large fillets are cold decorate with favor frills (No. 10) and dress them in a circle; surround with more chopped jelly and croutons, laying the minion fillets around. Cut up some lettuce hearts, season with salt, pepper, oil and vinegar, mix thoroughly, drain and place this salad in the center of the dish; serve a vinaigrette mayonnaise separately.

FIG. 479.

(2465). CHICKEN BREASTS À LA RENAISSANCE (Filets de Poulet à la Renaissance).

Pare ten chicken breasts without the minion fillets; beat them thin, then season and poach in clarified butter and the juice of a lemon laid in a sautoir, keeping them rare; drain and range them on a tray, cover with a buttered paper and set a light weight on top until they become cold. Streak the minion fillets with slices of truffles and shape them into rings; place them in a buttered sautoir and cover with buttered paper; poach in a slack oven, drain them, and when cold cover over with half-set jelly. Drain off all the butter from the pared breasts and take them up one by one with a broad fork, dip five of them into a white chaudfroid sauce (No. 596), and range them at once on a tray, keeping them slightly apart, and then put it on the ice to harden the sauce. Dissolve the remainder of the sauce in a bain-marie and add to it a purée of ravigote herbs (No. 623) pounded without any butter, but having two spoonfuls of the cold chaudfroid sauce added; strain and color with a little spinach green (No. 37). Stir this sauce on ice until of the proper thickness, and with it cover the other five fillets, the same as the first ones, and when the sauce has become cold pare off all the superfluous sauce around, then dress all these breasts in a crown-shape on a thick layer of jelly set on the dish. In the center of this crown range a pyramid of large Spanish olives stuffed with a purée of foies-gras mingled with brown chaudfroid sauce (No. 594); around dress the streaked minion fillets and in the center of each lay a small round glazed truffle.

(2466). CHICKEN BREASTS À LA GALLIER (Filets de Poulet à la Gallier).

Trim a rice socle eight inches in diameter and two inches high. Remove the sinews well from twelve chicken breasts, suppress the skin and pare nicely, then fry them white in clarified butter and lemon juice; season with salt, drain, and lay them under a light weight; trim them into half-hearts, and split them in two through their thickness; then cover one part of each with foies-gras taken from a terrine, pounded and rubbed through a sieve, and place the other part on top of this, pressing one on the other lightly and evenly. Cover half of these double fillets with a ravigote chaudfroid (No. 595), and when it is cold brush over with partly solidified jelly; decorate the others with truffles, and cover also with partly cold jelly. When cold cut away the surplus of chaudfroid and jelly and ornament the pointed ends with favor frills (No. 10). Dress the fillets in a circle on the socle, intercalating the two kinds, having first one covered with chaudfroid, then one covered with jelly; fill up the inside with some well-seasoned vegetable macédoine (No. 2650) thickened with a little jellied mayonnaise (No. 613); decorate around the socle with chopped jelly and croûtons of jelly; on top of the macédoine lay round pieces of glazed black truffle. On the edge of the socle around the fillet have a border of stuffed mushrooms covered with chaudfroid (see No. 2517).

(2467). CHICKEN FRICASSEE—CHAUDFROID (Fricassée de Poulet—Chaudfroid).

Prepare a fricassee with a good, large chicken the same as for fricassee of chicken (No. 1861), add two dozen large mushroom heads turned and channeled (No. 118). Remove the pieces of chicken singly and suppress all the skin and most of the bone, then range them on a tray; remove the mushrooms and set them aside to get cold; strain the sauce into a small saucepan without thickening it with eggs, and let get cold while stirring, incorporating into it slowly a few spoonfuls of cold jelly, then thicken it slightly on ice, stirring it the same as a chaudfroid sauce. Take up the pieces of chicken with a fork, and immerse them thoroughly in the sauce, not having it too thick; do the same with the mushrooms, and leave to drain well; dress them as quickly as each piece is done in a pyramid form on a very cold dish; cover with half-set jelly, using a brush for the purpose, and dress the mushrooms around the chickens, surrounding these with a border of jelly pushed through a cornet. Keep the dish for one-quarter of an hour in the ice-box before serving.

(2468). CHICKENS SAUTÉD À LA SHERMAN (Poulets Sautés à la Sherman).

Incrust a fancy border mold in chopped ice, having it decorated with truffles and egg-white; coat the decoration with a thick layer of jelly and fill the center with slices of tongue, mushrooms, ham and truffles; pour the sauce obtained from the chicken over, and let get cold, then mask with a thick layer of jelly to finish filling the mold; have this get quite hard. Cut up four young chickens, each weighing a pound and a half; they must be well drawn, singed and cleaned; take four pieces from each, namely, two wings and two legs, pare and sauté in butter to a fine color; drain off the butter when done and detach the glaze with a little Madeira wine and espagnole sauce (No. 414); when the whole is reduced to perfection mix in an ounce of isinglass dissolved in a little broth (No. 194a); this sauce when cold should be of the consistency of a lightly thickened chaudfroid. Take out the chickens, strain the sauce through a tammy, remove a part of it, and into it mix some unsmoked red beef tongue, mushrooms, truffles and lean cooked ham, all cut in eighth of an inch thick by one and a quarter to one and a half inches in diameter slices, adding the chicken to the remainder of the sauce. Unmold the border, and when the chicken has cooled in its sauce dress it inside the border, and finish covering with the nearly cold sauce. Garnish around with a border of jelly croûtons (No. 2442). Keep the dish in the ice-box, and cover entirely with the nearly cold jelly applied with a brush. Decorate with fancy paper frills (No. 10), then serve.

(2469). CHICKEN ROASTED WITH JELLY, CUT UP AND GARNISHED WITH TONGUE
(Poulet Rôti à la Gelée, Découpé et Garni de Langue de Bœuf).

Roasted with Jelly.—Select a fine two pound and a half to three pound chicken; it must be very tender; draw, singe and free it of all the pin feathers, then truss it to roast (No. 179); cover with a bard of thin fat pork, then roast it on the spit, basting it frequently, and when done and of a fine color, remove and let it get cold. Untruss and glaze with chicken glaze (No. 397), and surround it with chopped jelly and jelly croûtons, cut either into triangles, oblongs, lozenges, etc.

Cut up and Garnished with Salted Unsmoked Beef Tongue.—After the chicken has been cooked and is cold, the same as for the above, cut it up into five pieces, pare them nicely and glaze over. Cut from the thick part of a tongue some slices three-sixteenths of an inch in thickness; pare them into oblongs three inches long by one and three-quarters wide, and cover well with half-set jelly. Dress the chicken around an upright conical support placed in the middle of a dish, having it covered with green butter (No. 583); decorate around with chopped jelly, and over this place the oblongs of tongue in a circle, one overlapping the other. On top of the support have some ornamental piece, either a figure or a cup filled with jelly cut in squares of an eighth of an inch. This dish can be accompanied by a separate remoulade sauce (No. 624).

(2470). CREAM OF LOBSTER (Crème de Homard).

Fasten a wooden paper-covered foundation on a dish, having in its center a flat support two inches high, forming a step with a hole in the top. Decorate the bottom and interior of ten large timbale molds (No. 1, Fig. 137) with gherkins or truffles dipped in half-set jelly, coat the molds lightly with jelly, turning them around on ice. Suppress the shells from the tails and claws of

FIG. 480.

three small cooked lobsters, split the claws in two lengthwise and readjust them with half-set jelly to their original shape; keep them on ice. Cut up the tail meats and pound them with a few spoonfuls of good velouté sauce (No. 415) reduced with mushroom liquor, and mix in two spoonfuls of the creamy parts from the bodies, also a dash of cayenne pepper; pass the whole through a tammy and pour the preparation into a vessel to smooth while stirring it vigorously with a spoon; incorporate into it slowly four gills of oil, two spoonfuls of tarragon vinegar and two gills of aspic jelly (No. 103); beat the preparation on ice to thicken, then mix in at once the value of three or four gills of unsweetened whipped cream. When finished, fill the small molds with this preparation and let it harden on ice; at the last moment dip each mold separately into hot water, wipe them off quickly and invert them on the bottom of the dish around the support; cover this latter with a coat of thick chopped jelly and stick an untrimmed hatelet in the hole on top; now dress the lobster claws upright in a triangle against the hatelet, placed there with the purpose of holding them up, and fasten them on with sticky jelly; brush them over with half-set jelly and surround the base with green parsley leaves or water cress. Arrange around the dish small, even triangles of jelly, cutting off the tips, and serve with mayonnaise sauce (No. 606).

(2471). CUTLETS OF LAMB, IMPERIAL (Côtelettes d'Agneau à l'Impériale).

Trim eight to ten lamb cutlets taken from the rib near the loin of two racks, four from each rack; suppress the chine bone and fibrous skin from the rib bones, pare them, leaving only the kernel on; beat this lightly, replace the fat by lamb quenelle forcemeat (No. 92) so as to give them their original shape, season and fry on both sides in butter; when done drain on a baking sheet and cover with buttered paper, then set them under a light weight to cool; pare them once more. Put into a saucepan a few spoonfuls of tomato sauce (No. 549), strained through a tammy, and dilute it slowly with brown chaudfroid sauce (No. 594); thicken this lightly on ice, remove and dip the cutlets into it one by one, covering them entirely; range them at once on a tray and keep in a cool place to harden the sauce. Detach the cutlets from the sheet, free them of all surplus sauce and trim the handles with fancy favor frills (No. 10); dress in a circle, filling the center with whole asparagus tops seasoned with salt and pepper and dressed with jellied mayonnaise (No. 613); cover the tops of the asparagus with glazed truffles cut in slices, surround the meats with chopped jelly and place around a border of jelly croûtons.

(2472). CUTLETS OF LAMBS' KERNELS IN BELLEVUE (Côtelettes de Noix d'Agneau en Bellevue).

Pare and sauté twelve lamb cutlets; place them under a light weight and cut away the kernels; cover these with a brown chaudfroid sauce (No. 594). Decorate an aspic mold and fill it with layers of the kernels and jelly alternated and leave for two hours on ice; then unmold, dress on a dish bottom an inch and a half thick and one inch in diameter larger than the aspic and surround with chopped jelly and jelly croûtons. Place a large Bellevue hatelet (No. 2526) in the center.

(2473). CUTLETS OF LAMB WITH ASPIC (Côtelettes d'Agneau à l'Aspic).

Procure twelve cutlets cut from the covered ribs of a spring lamb and nicely pared; lard them with lardons (No. 3, Fig. 52), made of veal udder, truffles and red beef tongue. Line a sautoir with slices of fat pork, place the cutlets over and moisten with white wine mirepoix stock (No. 419); set it on the fire and at the first boil push it into the oven. When done drain and cool off under a weight, pare once more so that the lardons can be seen well. Decorate an aspic mold, range the cutlets inside of it in a circle, placing a crouton of tongue between each one, and pour in sufficient jelly to fill the mold to within a quarter from the top; after this has become firm finish filling the mold with jelly and lay it aside on ice for two hours. When prepared to serve unmold the aspic on a dish, having the basin covered with very firm jelly, or on a small, low, decorated socle. Fill the center with a blanquette of lamb sweetbreads prepared with truffles, and surround the whole with chopped jelly and croutons.

(2474). CUTLETS OF LAMBS' KERNELS WITH MAYONNAISE (Côtelettes de Noix d'Agneau à la Mayonnaise).

Fry twelve fine spring lamb chops; press them under a weight and cut out all the parts except the kernels; pare and replace the trimmings by pâte de foies-gras and dip them into a jellied mayonnaise (No. 613) so as to cover them entirely with a thick layer of it. Range some cut-up lettuce leaves on a dish, reserving the hearts for decorating; around the lettuce dress the kernels of lamb and decorate the whole with the lettuce hearts, hard-boiled eggs, anchovies, olives, etc.; surround the edge of the dish with chopped jelly and croutons of the same.

(2475). CUTLETS OF LAMB WITH TOMATOED CHAUDFROID (Côtelettes d'Agneau au Chaud-froid Tomaté).

Fry in butter a dozen fine short-handled spring-lamb cutlets; put some blond chaudfroid sauce (No. 596) into a saucepan and mix in with it a few spoonfuls of tomato purée (No. 730), so that it acquires a light red tint; thicken it by putting the saucepan on ice and moving constantly with a spoon, and when thick dip the cutlets in so as to have them well covered. Range them at once on a baking sheet slightly apart, but all on the same side, and allow the same to harden in a cool place; detach them, pare and decorate the kernels with a rosette formed of pickled gherkin and truffles dipped into half-set jelly; cover the whole with a coating of jelly, cool, then dress in a circle on a dish, having the handle bones under and the kernels on top; fill the center with chopped jelly.

(2476). CUTLETS OF LOBSTER À LA LOWERY (Côtelettes de Homard à la Lowery).

Chop up three hard-boiled eggs, the whites and yolks separately, also some pistachios. In-crust a cylindrical mold in ice; divide the bottom into six even parts with sticks of truffles dipped in half-set jelly and in one of these put the white, in another the yellow, and in a third the green; repeat, then pour over a little jelly, and when hard add sufficient to have it three-eighths of an inch thick; over this lay in a circle some lobster escalops covered with jellied mayonnaise (No. 613), one overlapping the other; pour more jelly over, and continue this process until the mold is full; leave it on ice to get thoroughly cold, invert it on a dish and surround with cutlets prepared as follows: Have some bottomless cutlet molds; lay them on sheets of oiled paper, and cover the bottom of each one with a bed of jellied mayonnaise having raw fine herbs added to it; on top place small, well-seasoned slices of lobster, also sliced truffles, and cover with a little white jellied mayonnaise (No. 613), strewing the whole with finely chopped truffles; when very cold unmold and dress them in a circle around the aspic; trim the thin ends with a fancy favor frill (No. 10), and place a border of stuffed olives (No. 695) around the cutlets, and chopped jelly and croûtons outside the whole.

(2477). CUTLETS OF PHEASANT IN CHAUDFROID (Chaudfroid de Côtelettes de Faisan).

The accompanying drawing, Fig. 481, is the model of a mold in which the cutlet preparation is hardened; this is made of thick tin, open on both ends, but it can be closed by covers that fit on the mold itself. This mold when closed measures three inches in height and two in width, it being shaped like a half-heart, but for preparing a large quantity double molds can be em-

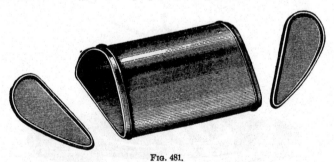

FIG. 481.

ployed, they having almost a whole heart-shape appearance; if these are used, after the prepara-tion is hardened and unmolded, it is to be cut in two through the center from the top to the bottom and each half made into a single cutlet; in this way there will be sufficient of them to dress three or four dishes. With the breast meat cut from a large cold roasted pheasant, an equal amount of cooked foies-gras, one or two gills of melted game glaze (No. 398), and two or three gills of brown chaudfroid sauce (No. 594) reduced with pheasant fumet (No. 397), make a preparation, and when smooth and of a desired consistency mix in with it a fine salpicon of cooked foies-gras and truffles, half of each; then stir it on ice to thicken sufficiently so that the truffles and livers do not fall to the bottom. Pour it into the cutlet mold, laying on ice, and wrapping the mold in a sheet of paper imbed it completely in pounded ice and keep it thus for five or six hours. At the expi-ration of this time dip the mold in warm water to unmold the preparation, and then cut it at once into two parts, from top to bottom; smooth the surfaces well and keep for a quarter of an hour on ice. After removing them, divide across in slices each three-eighths of an inch in thickness, and take these up one by one on a broad fork and dip in some brown chaudfroid sauce (No. 594) properly thickened; drain it off well and range the cutlets on a cold baking sheet slightly apart. Lay this on ice for half an hour to harden the sauce; detach the cutlets from the sheet and pare off any surplus of

Fig. 482.

sauce, and stick a pretty favor frill (No. 10) into each; dress them in a close circle on a foundation placed on a dish and covered over with paper; fill in the empty space in the circle merely with chopped jelly and surround the foundation with large croutons of jelly. Keep the dish in the ice-box until needed.

(2478). VEAL OUTLETS À L'ANACRÉON (Côtelettes de Veau à l'Anacréon).

Lard some veal cutlets cut from a rack with tongue and fat pork, a half of each; braise or poêler them while basting frequently, then lay them under a weight to reduce to five-eighths of an inch in thickness; pare neatly and cover over with cream forcemeat (No. 75), and decorate with a handsome truffle rosette; range a buttered paper on top of each and poach in a slack oven: when cold mask the surfaces with half-set jelly and dress flat in a circle, filling the center with an asparagus salad (No. 2621); surround with chopped jelly and croûtons.

(2479). OUTLETS OF WOODCOCK, PONIATOWSKI (Côtelettes de Bécasses, à la Poniatowski).

Dress this cold entrée on a wooden foundation covered with noodle paste (No. 142), fastening it on to a dish; decorate the sides of the foundation, and place a support in the center surmounted by a small fancy tin vase, both covered the same as the foundation; the top of the base is flat and closed; it is simply to be dressed with three fresh woodcock heads with feathers, and held in shape, arranged in a triangle; surround their base with chopped jelly and a chain of truffle balls.

Fig. 483.

Cut the meats of three cooked, cold woodcock into a fine montglas, put this in a saucepan with half as much cooked foies-gras, and as many truffles cut exactly like the meats; combine this montglas with some good, partly warm, succulent brown chaudfroid (No. 594), reduced with game fumet (No. 397); smooth the preparation and use it to fill twelve to fourteen tin cutlet-shaped molds brushed over with jelly; equalize the tops and leave to cool one hour on ice. Dip these cutlets in hot water, unmold on a baking sheet and smooth the surfaces once more; lift them up one by one, dip into a good brown chaudfroid sauce (No. 594) slightly thickened on ice, and return them at once to the sheet to have this sauce get thoroughly cold on ice. Surround the base of the support with a very thick layer of chopped, sticky jelly, pushed on through a pocket. At the last moment detach the cutlets from the sheet, pare neatly, fasten a small fancy favor frill (No. 10) in each, and dress them in a circle around the support on the foundation; coat with jelly so as to give them a brilliant appearance.

(2480). CUTLETS OF WOODCOCK À LA SARAH BERNHARDT (Côtelettes de Bécasses à la Sarah Bernhardt).

Take seven or eight fresh round Périgord truffles, all of equal size and very clean; peel, salt and cook them for seven or eight minutes in a little Madeira wine and leave them to cool off in this liquid. Remove all the meats from three woodcock roasted rare, keeping aside three or four of the fillets; pound the remainder of the meats with a part of the cooked intestines and three-quarters as much cooked foies-gras; season and rub through a sieve; put this purée into a vessel and beat it up for two minutes with a spoon, incorporating into it slowly four spoonfuls of good melted game glaze (No. 398) and one gill of liquid brown chaudfroid sauce (No. 594) reduced with game fumet (No. 397) and essence of truffles (No. 395); when all is well mingled add gradually to the preparation two and a half ounces of fresh butter, wiped and divided into small pats; the whole should now be very smooth without being frothy. Drain the truffles, stand them upright on a cloth to mark the tops with a tube from a column box an inch in diameter; remove this marked piece and empty the truffles out with a vegetable spoon; pound these removed pieces with as much cooked foies-gras, season the preparation and lay it in a bowl to beat up for a few moments so as to have it smooth. Prepare a montglas with half of the woodcock fillets laid aside, and an equal quantity of red beef tongue mingled with a little good reduced and thick Madeira sauce (No. 413). Moisten with a brush dipped in cold jelly a dozen tin cutlet-shaped molds, cover the bottoms and sides with the woodcock preparation, leaving an empty space in the center; fill this up with some of the cold montglas; cover with more of the preparation and smooth it at once; keep the molds for one hour on ice, then unmold them and cover with a layer of brown chaudfroid sauce (No. 594). Put a few spoonfuls of this chaudfroid sauce into a vessel, thicken it while stirring on ice and mix with it the remainder of the woodcock fillets cut in small dice and twice as much cooked foies-gras cut the same; use this preparation for stuffing the emptied truffles; range them as soon as done on a small baking sheet and close the opening with a round piece of cooked foies-gras cut out with the same tube used for marking the truffles; glaze over the whole with a brush; keep this baking sheet on ice for half an hour. Harden a thick layer of jelly on a dish and on top of it set a narrow wooden foundation covered with white paper; on this dress the truffles piled in a pyramidical form, then push chopped jelly through a cornet into all the intersections, as well as around the truffles, to maintain them in position. Around this board dress the cutlets in a circle after inserting a fancy favor frill (No. 10) into each.

(2481). LOBSTER DOME GARNISHED WITH SMALL CASES (Dôme de Homard Garni de Petites Caisses).

Pound the cooked meat of two or three lobster tails with a spoonful of prepared red pepper (No. 168), two spoonfuls of béchamel (No. 409), and a piece of lobster butter (No. 580); pass the whole through a sieve and then set it in a vessel to mix with an equal quantity of white chaudfroid sauce (No. 596) and two gills of mayonnaise (No. 606). Mix in with this preparation the claw meat cut in small dice. Incrust a dome-shaped mold wider than its height on ice; decorate the top and sides with fanciful cuts of gherkins, black truffles, lobster coral, tarragon leaves and red shrimp tails split in two, being careful to dip each separate decoration in half-set jelly. Harden a layer of jelly on the bottom of the mold, and when cold set another dome-shaped mold inside of it, having it filled with pounded ice, but half an inch narrower than the first one; pour some half-set jelly between the intersections of the two molds to fill up the empty space entirely, and as soon as this is hard remove the smaller mold, after replacing the ice by warm water. Thicken the lobster preparation on ice while stirring, and pour into it two spoonfuls of good tarragon vinegar and some blanched cut-up tarragon leaves; pour all this into the empty coated mold and let rest for one hour. Unmold the dome on to a socle of carved rice two inches high (see Fig. 9a), having it round, and surround its base with the small cases, as described herewith: Put a dozen small china cases on ice to have thoroughly cold. Split across in two the meats of four or five lobster claws; cut these same meats into small rounds with a tin tube, having them half an inch in diameter and an eighth of an inch thick; lay them in a small vessel with half the quantity of rounds of truffles and two or three spoonfuls of rounds of gherkin, all being of the same size as the lobster; season with salt, a dash of cayenne, oil and vinegar, leaving them to macerate from twelve to fifteen minutes. Drain off the seasoning and thicken it with blond chaudfroid sauce, made by mixing white and brown chaudfroid, mingled with two spoonfuls of mayonnaise (No. 606) and a pinch of chopped tarragon leaves. Fill the cases with this preparation, covering the tops with a layer of mayonnaise finished with tarragon vinegar.

(2482). DUCKLING, WITH SPANISH OLIVES (Caneton aux Olives d'Espagne).

Singe, draw and clean a duckling, then bone it from the ribs. Mix in a vessel equal quantities of liver baking forcemeat (No. 64) and chicken forcemeat (No. 73); add two spoonfuls of tomato purée (No. 730) and a large salpicon of cooked foies-gras. With this dressing fill the body and breast of the duckling where the pouch was; sew up the skin underneath, and truss it with the legs thrust inside as for an entrée (No. 178); lard over and wrap it in thin muslin, then cook slowly for one hour in some stock (No. 194a). Drain off the duckling, tighten the cloth and let get cold, after unwrapping and untrussing it; detach the breast, keeping it whole, and cut it into slices without misshaping it; then return it to its original place. Wipe the duckling well, and cut a piece from underneath so that it will stand plumb, and set it on a grate; cover it over with some excellent brown chaudfroid sauce (No. 594), finished with tomato sauce (No. 549) and reduced with Madeira wine. After this sauce has drained off well keep the duckling for ten minutes in the ice-box; remove and dress it on a thick layer of jelly that has stiffened on a dish, and surround both sides and front with a garnishing of large Spanish olives, stuffed with foies-gras and covered with brown chaudfroid sauce (No. 594).

(2483). FOIES-GRAS IN BORDER (Foies-Gras en Bordure).

Open a terrine of foies-gras; suppress all the top fat and keep on ice for two or three hours. Fill a fancy border mold (Fig. 470) with fine cold aspic jelly (No. 103), and put it on ice for one hour. Cut up the contents of the terrine with a thin steel spoon the size and shape of a tablespoon, dipping it each time into warm water; should this cutting be neatly done the pieces will each acquire the shape of the spoon, rounded lightly; lay all of these as fast as they are done on a cold baking sheet, one beside the other, repairing those that may have been broken during the process, and put them away on ice for a quarter of an hour. Just when prepared to serve dip the border mold into warm water, wipe neatly, and invert the mold on a cold dish, having a wooden or tin foundation in the center exactly the same size and covered with white paper; on this foundation dress the pieces of foies-gras pyramidically, placing the poorest looking ones underneath, and piling the remainder into a steep pyramid.

(2484). FOIES-GRAS IN CRADLE, TO BE CUT IN SLICES (Foies-Gras en Berceau, pour être Coupé en Tranches).

Prepare one pound and a half of baking forcemeat (No. 64); let this forcemeat become quite cold, then pound and rub it through a sieve. Chop up two pounds of lean veal with a pound and a quarter of fresh fat pork, and pound this to a pulp also; season and lay it in a bowl to mix with three or four raw, chopped truffles, and add liver baking forcemeat. Butter cradle-shaped molds, and cover the insides with a thin layer of the forcemeat, leaving an empty space in the center; fill up this vacancy with large strips of raw foies-gras, season and intermingle them with forcemeat and cut-up raw truffles; cover this over with more of the forcemeat and with slices of fat pork. Lay the mold on a raised-edge baking sheet containing a little water, push it into a slack oven and bake for an hour and a quarter; when removed, cool under the pressure of a slight weight. These pies are useful for cutting up in slices.

(2485a). GALANTINE OF CHICKEN (Galantine de Poulet).

Singe one large chicken, suppress the neck and drumsticks, also the pinion bones; split it in two down the back and bone it entirely. Spread the chicken out on a table, remove part of the breast meats and lay them on the skin where there is no meat. Also remove the meat from the

Fig. 484.

legs, suppress the sinews and chop them up and place in a vessel; also chop up three-quarters of a pound of lean veal and an equal amount of fresh fat pork and add it to the legs; add a quarter of a pound of blanched fat pork, cut in half-inch squares, and an equal quantity of cooked red beef tongue; add a few quartered truffles and a few peeled pistachios; season and pour over a few spoonfuls of Madeira wine. Season the inside of the chicken, fill it with the contents of the bowl, alternating with the forcemeat, then roll the boned chicken into an oblong shape, sew it up and wrap it in a cloth, tightening it well, then tie it at the two ends and in the center. Place it in a long saucepan with the broken-up bones and two or three calves' feet; moisten liberally with stock (No. 194a) and boil while skimming; cook the boned chicken slowly for an hour and a half, then drain; ten minutes later unwrap, remove the thread and wrap it up once more in the same cloth, after it has been well washed, tying it this time with five rows of string—two at the ends, one in the center, and two between; let cool off under a light weight for six hours. After it is finally unwrapped, pare and glaze with white chaudfroid sauce (No. 596) so as to be able to decorate with truffles; cool and cover with a layer of partly cold jelly, dress on a small rice or hominy socle (Fig. 9a), and surround with chopped jelly and croûtons (No. 2442) prepared with the galantine stock itself.

(2485b). TRUFFLE DECORATIONS (Ornements en Truffes).

For these decorations select large, mellow, sound black marbled truffles; cut them into thin slices a sixteenth of an inch thick, and arrange them as in shown Fig. 485. These truffle decorations are taken up with a metal needle, then dipped into half-set jelly, and applied to the object required to be decorated, the principal aim being to dispose them very regularly,

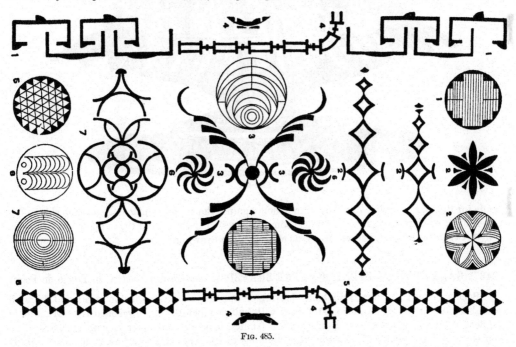

FIG. 485.

and arrange them with taste. Truffle decorations can also be made by cutting the truffles as thin as a thread with a knife, and placing them at once in Madeira wine until required for use, then drip and lay them on a napkin. With these imitate the outlines of landscapes or any other ornamentation, using them for tracing designs imitating pen or pencil drawings. When the design is finished coat over with half-set white jelly.

(2486). GALANTINE OF CHICKEN À LA D'ORLÉANS (Galantine de Poulet à la d'Orléans).

Bone two young chickens weighing two pounds each; leave on only the white meat adhering to the breasts, and suppress the leg meats; remove some of the breast meat adhering to the skin and place it where the skin is bare. These chickens when boned and stuffed should only weigh two pounds and a half each. Fill them with quenelle forcemeat (No. 89), into which mix a salpicon of truffles, pistachios, tongue and foies-gras, all cut in quarter-inch squares; let cook in a stock (No. 194a) for two hours, unwrap, wash out the cloths and rewrap them as before; hang them up by one end on a hook, and to the other end fasten a sufficiently heavy weight; leave them hanging for twelve hours; unwrap and pare them alike, then cover with an ordinary white chaudfroid (No.

596); decorate the tops with fanciful designs of truffles dipped in half-set jelly so they adhere
well to the galantines; when thoroughly fastened coat over with jelly spread over with a funnel

FIG. 486.

made for this purpose (Fig. 759), and stand them against the support; place one on each side. The
cup is filled with small truffles. Arrange some squares of jelly around the support, and chopped
jelly between the support and croûtons, as shown in the drawing.

(2487). GALANTINE OF DUCKLING, PEAR-SHAPED (Galantine de Caneton en Forme de Poire).

Bone a cleaned and singed duckling, leaving on one leg; season the inside meats and fill with
pounded galantine forcemeat (No. 65) mixed with half as much baking forcemeat (No. 81), and a
salpicon of lambs' sweetbreads, mushrooms and truffles, to be cut in quarter-inch squares, also some
cooked and cold veal udder. Restore the duckling to its original shape, sew it up, inclosing its
contents, and mold it in a bottomless mold, shaped like a pear; braise in a mirepoix stock (No. 419)
for an hour and a half in a slack oven, basting frequently. When done drain and place this mold
on a buttered baking sheet and leave it to cool under the pressure of a weight; glaze over with a
light green chaudfroid sauce (No. 595), smear one side of the galantine with a piece of wadding
that has been rubbed on very finely powdered carmine, and coat with a layer of half-set jelly; at
the end stick in either a natural or artificial pear-stalk with a few leaves around and surround, when
dished, with a border of chopped jelly and croûtons.

(2488). GALANTINE OF EEL, DECORATED (Galantine d'Anguille Décorée).

Skin a large Niagara eel, take out the middle bone, season and fill it with fish quenelle forcemeat (No. 90), mixing into it truffles and pistachios, seasoning it well. Inclose this dressing in the
eel and lay it in a well-buttered Savarin mold, baste over with white wine mirepoix stock (No. 419)
and cover with bards of fat pork. Place this mold in a low saucepan containing a little water and
push it into a slack oven; when the fish is properly done, remove and leave it to cool off in the
mold under the pressure of a light weight, then turn it out and dress on a round dish; cover over

with Cambridge butter (No. 570), decorate with cuts of truffle, the red part of a lobster, tarragon leaves and a small stalk of chervil; garnish around with quartered hard-boiled eggs (No. 2513) and fill the center with a macédoine salad (No. 2650) dressed with mayonnaise (No. 606); serve with a separate tartar sauce (No. 631).

(2489). GALANTINE OF GOSLING, MELON-SHAPED (Galantine d'Oison en Forme de Melon).

After singeing and boiling a gosling remove all its meat, spread out the skin on a buttered napkin, cut up the breast into five-eighths of an inch squares, suppress all sinews from the legs and add as much pork meat and veal meat to obtain a pound and a half in all; chop this well, then chop separately a pound of fat pork, and half a pound of beef marrow. Pound all well together and mix in with the pulp a clove of crushed and chopped garlic, some finely cut-up mushrooms, salt, spices No. 2 (No. 168), and a few egg-yolks. Lay this forcemeat on the skin and close up the napkin, giving it a round shape; tie and cook in a stock (No. 194a). Unwrap and then retighten the napkin and flatten lightly, so as to give it the shape of a melon; let cool for twenty-four hours, afterward imitate a melon by cutting eight half-inch deep grooves from top to bottom, glazing it over with white chaudfroid (No. 596) colored with yellow. Paint it with spinach green (No. 37) to imitate a cantaloup melon, and coat with layers of half-set jelly. Imitate the stalk and melon leaves with modeling fat (No. 56) and dress it on a dish, garnishing around with chopped jelly and croûtons of jelly.

(2490). GALANTINES OF GUINEA FOWL À LA LYTTON (Galantines de Pintades à la Lytton).

Bone entirely three young guinea fowls, spread them on the table, remove the thigh meats, suppress the sinews of the fillets and all the superfluous fat; cut the fillets in two on their thickness and use them to lay where the meat is lacking, then fill them with chicken quenelle forcemeat (No. 89) mingled with a salpicon of truffles, pistachios and udder, all cut in three-sixteenths inch squares and well mixed; they should, when stuffed, each weigh two pounds. Cover the entire outside with very thin slices of fat pork and wrap them up in napkins; roll all the same thickness and put on to cook in some stock (No. 194a) for one hour and a half, then drain, unwrap and wash out the napkins; wrap them up again without the fat pork and hang them on a hook, fastening a weight to the end of each one so as to have them well pressed; when very cold unwrap once more and pare again; cover them over with white chaudfroid (No. 596), decorate with black truffles, coat with jelly and dress them on a dish against an upright or sloping supporting piece, it being two inches across at the summit and six at the base by five inches in height, covered over with ravigote butter (No. 583), and strew chopped parsley over. Set a cup on top of the summit, filled with truffles. Make truffle balls with foies gras taken from a terrine, pounded and rubbed through a sieve; when very cold form this into inch and a quarter diameter balls, roll them in truffle peelings that have been finely chopped and passed through a sieve. When these imitated truffles are very cold dip them in half-set jelly and lay each one in a white paper crimped case the same size as themselves; place these also between the galantines and garnish all around with chopped jelly and jelly croûtons (No. 2442).

(2491). GALANTINES OF PARTRIDGES À LA CLÉMENTINE (Galantines de Perdreaux à la Clémentine).

Choose three nice partridges; bone and open them on the table; decrease the thickest parts of the meats to place them on the thinner spots, then season well; cover with game galantine forcemeat (No. 66) pounded and forced through a sieve. On this place lengthways some lardons (No. 1, Fig. 52) of blanched fat pork, some truffles, cooked beef tongue and foies-gras; cover with more forcemeat and repeat the operation, finishing with the forcemeat; enclose well in the partridge skin and roll up in separate cloths, tying them at both ends and in the center; the three must be of the same weight—a pound and a half apiece—and rolled to the same length. Simmer them in some stock (No. 194a) for two hours; drain and leave cool partly, then roll them up tight in a clean cloth, tie both ends and the center again and hang them up, fastening a ten-pound weight or more to the bottom of each one; leave till quite cold, then unwrap and pare to an equal size and shape; cover with white chaudfroid (No. 596); decorate with truffles and mask over with jelly, then leave to get quite cold. These galantines are to be dressed on a round dish with swan support dressed on the stearine foundation; place a galantine between each swan. Bone a partridge thoroughly, remove all the skin and sinews and cut it up in small quarter-inch pieces, fry them in oil with garlic, mignonette and cayenne, wet with good vinegar and broth and let simmer; when the meats are done and the moisture reduced add a little jelly. Prepare some pretty, red peeled tomatoes, empty them, arrange on a baking sheet, fill them with this preparation, replace the covers and when cold glaze over with half-set jelly and lay them between the galantines. Have a griffon socle prepared as for the ballotines à la Madison (see Fig. 453), place in the shells of the socle some stuffed mushroom heads (No. 2517) glazed with brown chaudfroid (No. 594). Garnish the bottom of the

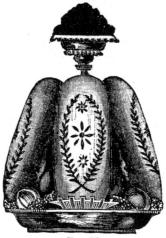

FIG. 487.

socle with cases of stuffed thrushes or larks all glazed over with blond chaudfroid; between each of these cases lay a carved hominy croustade filled with chopped jelly, with the streaked minion fillets formed into rings on the top. Finish decorating the whole with a stearine cup placed on the support, having it filled with small glazed truffles; around the base place a garland of smilax or other greens.

(2492). GALANTINES OF PARTRIDGES AND SLICED IN BELLEVUE (Galantines de Perdreaux en Tranches et en Bellevue).

Procure two or three fresh, plucked and singed partridges; bone them through the back; suppress the largest sinews from the legs and fillets, and season; remove all the meat attached to the bones and carcasses. Prepare a fine forcemeat (No. 65), pound and mix with it the chopped parings of the birds and half as much liver baking forcemeat (No. 81); pound, strain and season. Put into a bowl some strips of blanched fat pork a quarter of an inch square, mix with them some truffles and red beef tongue, cut the same. Fill the partridges with the forcemeat; reconstruct them to their original shape and sew up; wrap them in small cloths, tying them at the ends and in the center. Cook these galantines slowly for one hour and a quarter in some good unskimmed stock (No. 194a). After taking them out, remove the cloths and wrap them up once more, only much tighter, and let cool off under a light weight; finally, unwrap, pare, glaze and serve, either whole or cut up, garnished with jelly.

In Bellevue.—Have a boned partridge cooled under a weight as for the above; cut it into slices; pare them into even ovals all of the same thickness, then glaze with game glaze (No. 398) on one side only, using a brush; lay on the center of each a thin slice of truffle cut out with a column tube. Let a thin layer of clear jelly harden on a small baking tin; when stiff, range the slices on top, pressing the pieces down on the glazed side, one beside the other, then pour in between them enough cold jelly to reach as high as the slices; cool this for one hour on ice. At the last moment slit all around these slices with the heated tip of a small knife, then warm the bottom of the pan with a cloth dipped in hot water to enable the slices to be removed with the jelly attached, and dress in a circle on a cold dish. Garnish the center with chopped jelly and around with croûtons of jelly (No. 2442).

(2493). GALANTINE OF PARTRIDGE, ELIZABETH (Galantine de Perdreau Elisabeth).

Pare some quarter-inch thick slices of a boned partridge prepared as in Bellevue (No. 2492) into half-heart shapes; glaze and on each one lay a fine slice of black and well marbleized truffle, cover with jelly and dress them in a circle, filling the center with a Russian salad (No. 2645), and around with artichoke bottoms, garnished with seasoned macédoine (No. 2650).

(2494), GALANTINE OF PHEASANT À LA LORENZO (Galantine de Faisan à la Lorenzo).

Fry colorless in butter one pound of fat chicken livers; keep half of the finest ones aside. Chop up finely one pound of partridge meat and the same quantity of fat pork; season highly with salt, cayenne pepper, and nutmeg; stir well together, adding four egg-yolks and half of the liver well pounded; press the whole through a tammy and then put in an onion cut in one-eighth of an inch squares, blanched and fried colorless in butter, and some finely chopped parsley. Bone a pheasant, spread it open on the table, remove half of the thickness of the fillets, equalize the meats throughout the entire surface of the skin, then lay a third of the prepared force-meat over, on this half of the livers laid aside, and the same quantity of quartered truffles; now another layer of the forcemeat, and scatter here and there the rest of the livers and as many truffles; spread all that remains of the forcemeat, and enclose the whole well in the pheasant skin; sew and roll the galantine in a napkin; tie it firmly at both ends and in the center, and place it in a braziere with a knuckle of veal and the game carcasses, a bunch of garnished parsley (No. 123), an onion containing two cloves, and a carrot cut in four; moisten with plenty of stock (No. 194a), cook slowly for two and a half hours, then leave to cool off in the stock for one hour; unwrap and remold it once more, this time placing it under a weight. When the galantine is thoroughly cold, unwrap and pare it nicely, then cover it over with brown chaudfroid (No. 594), and decorate with cut-up truffles, pistachios, tongue, and egg-white; lay it on a small three-inch thick socle made of carved rice. Prepare sixteen larks by boning and filling them with forcemeat composed of half foies-gras forcemeat (No. 78) and half game forcemeat (No. 75) and chopped truffles; cook them in No. 3 mousseline molds, having the breasts downward; prepare the same number of streaked partridge minion fillets, form them in the shape of rings two and a quarter inches in diameter, and lay each one on a separate piece of buttered paper; fill the centers with game cream forcemeat (No. 75), and poach in a slack oven. Put some No. 1 mousseline molds on a baking sheet, having ice around; on the bottoms form an eye of egg-white and truffle, and coat the mold with brown chaudfroid (No. 594); lay the cold unmolded larks in the center and fill up with chaudfroid. Turn them out only when very cold and arrange them around the galantine with the minion fillets between. Decorate around the socle with finely chopped jelly made with the stock. Bellevue hatelets may be fastened in the top of galantine if so desired.

(2495), GALANTINE OF PHEASANT CUT UP (Galantine de Faisan Découpée).

This entrée is dressed on a wooden foundation fastened to a dish and covered with white paper, having in its center a small convex-shaped support made of tin, quite low, and covered with white paper. Singe two clean pheasants, bone the largest one by splitting it down the back, remove the meats from the legs and decrease the thickness from the breast meat; then cut this up into large shreds and lay them in a bowl, adding the breast meat of the other pheasant, pared and cut the same; also add strips of raw truffle, strips of blanched fat pork or udder, strips of foies-gras and

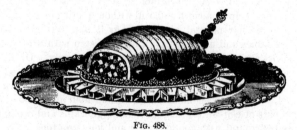

Fig. 488.

lastly a few shreds of lean cooked ham or cooked red beef tongue; season highly, pour over some Madeira wine and let macerate for one hour. Chop up the leg meats with the carcass parings and mix them with a chopped forcemeat made of game meats and lean veal and as much chopped fat pork, then season. With this chopped forcemeat and the macerated meats in the bowl prepare the boned pheasant the same as the boned pullet No. 2497, sew it up and wrap it in a cloth, then cook it for one hour and a half, cooling it off afterward under a weight. Pare the cold boned pheasant, cut it in slices and dress them one overlapping the other on the support, and glaze over lightly with a brush. Surround both sides of these slices with a few boned larks covered with brown chaudfroid (No. 594), and around these push a rope of chopped jelly through a cornet; surround the paper-covered bottom with pretty croûtons of jelly, and on one end of the galantine of pheasant stick a hatelet garnished with truffles.

(2496). GALANTINE OF PIGEONS (Galantine de Pigeons).

Bone three large, tender, clean and singed pigeons, season the inside meat and fill them with forcemeat (No. 65), mingled with a little baking forcemeat (No. 81) and a few spoonfuls of truffles cut in dice. Return them to their former shape, sew up and wrap each one in a separate piece of muslin, then cook them for one hour in a good stock; when done properly, unwrap, tighten more and let get cold under the pressure of a weight. When ready to use, take the pigeons from the cloths, glaze them over, cut in slices and dress with jelly.

(2497). GALANTINE OF PULLET OR CAPON À LA MOZART (Galantine de Poularde ou de Chapon à la Mozart).

This cold entrée can be dressed on a support slightly higher in the middle, covered with cooked paste (No. 131) and dried in the air. Singe a not too fat pullet, split it down the back, bone entirely, and season the inside. Prepare this pullet the same as a galantine of turkey à la Berger (No. 2499), and sew it up; wrap it well and cook for one hour and a half to two hours in clear, unskimmed stock (No. 194a), having the pullet bones added, and two or three boned and blanched

Fig. 489.

calves' feet, some roots, onions and aromatic herbs. When the boned pullet has cooked for a sufficient length of time, drain it off and unwrap it; wrap it up once more and reshape it, tying it very tight, and then place it to cool under the pressure of a weight. When cold, pare off the ends and cut it up into equally thick slices, and divide each of these slices into two; dress them neatly in a single row on the support; garnish around with cocks'-combs and mushrooms covered over with chaudfroid, intermingled with chopped jelly, and besides have a few small cases filled with glazed truffles.

(2498). GALANTINE OF SUCKLING PIG (Galantine de Cochon de Lait).

Prepare a suckling pig the same as for No. 1810, singe and bone it completely without piercing the skin, keeping on the four feet and removing the head. Remove the meat or fat from the different parts where there is too much. Stuff the galantine with a salpicon of truffles, one pound of red tongue mixed with pork forcemeat (No. 68) and a pound of blanched fat pork—the truffles, red tongue and fat pork cut in three-sixteenth inch squares. Season with salt, prepared red pepper (No. 168) and nutmeg; wrap it up in a cloth and roll without pulling or shortening the length of the skin and keeping the feet in their natural position. Lay it in a braziere lined with fat pork and garnish around with vegetables and uncooked pig's feet; moisten with white wine, season with salt and whole peppers, and let cook without boiling for four to five hours. Drain, cool, unwrap partly and roll up again, then tie the cloth firmly at both ends of the galantine, and hang it up with a sufficiently strong weight on the bottom. When thoroughly cold, unwrap and glaze it a dark color; put back the head, which has been blanched for half an hour and allowed to cool, and decorate the whole with fanciful cuts of egg-white, tongue, truffles, gherkins and ornamental hatelets; dress on a rice foundation and surround with chopped jelly and jelly croûtons.

(2499). GALANTINE OF TURKEY À LA BERGER—BONED TURKEY (Galantine à la Berger).

Bone a small turkey after having cut off the wings, the legs and the neck. Begin by cutting the skin down its entire length, commencing from the middle of the neck and ending at the middle of the rump, using a small thin knife and following the outlines of the rib bones; then remove the breast bone and the second joint bones, suppress the meat from the latter and chop it up finely; remove all sinews from the fillets, cut away a part of their thickness and place them where the legs were taken from. Prepare a well-seasoned chopped forcemeat (No. 65), mix well together, adding half a gill of brandy, truffle essence (No. 395) and one ounce of chopped truffles. Cut half a pound of fat pork into half-inch squares, blanch and drain; have also half a pound of unsmoked red beef tongue cut in half-inch squares, five ounces of peeled truffles cut in pieces, and three-quarters of a pound of duck or goose livers, parboiled, cold and cut in half-inch dice. With this and the forcemeat stuff the turkey, then wrap it up in a cloth and let cook in some good stock for two hours. Drain off well, take off the cloth and wrap it up again before setting under the press. When thoroughly cold unwrap, pare and cover with a white fecula

Fig. 490.

chaudfroid sauce (No. 593), and decorate with fanciful cuts of very black truffles and pistachios dipped in half-set jelly; as soon as this is quite hard, cover with half-set jelly and dress on a trimmed croûton of cooked hominy or rice. Garnish around with chopped jelly and have an outside border of jelly croûtons. Stick one Bellevue hatelet (No. 2526) in the center of the turkey, and two garnished hatelets (No. 2526) on each side.

GARNISHINGS FOR COLD DISHES (Garnitures Pour Pièces Froides).

(2500). GARNISHING OF ARTICHOKE BOTTOMS FILLED WITH MACÉDOINE (Garniture de Fonds d'Artichauts Garnis de Macédoine).

Artichoke Bottoms.—Trim some small round artichoke bottoms two inches in diameter; rub over with lemon and blanch in plenty of water; cook them in a white stock (No. 182) seasoned with salt and lemon juice, putting in also half a pound of chopped beef marrow; cover with buttered paper and boil slowly. When the bottoms are well done remove from the fire, place them into a stone bowl, cover with buttered paper and leave to cool in their liquid; wash them off in boiling water, marinate and drain. Lay each bottom on a turnip cut out to imitate the base of a vase, and fill with either macédoine salad (No. 2650) or a separate vegetable: carrots, turnips, green peas, cauliflower, string beans, asparagus tops, crawfish tails, or else a salpicon of tongue, truffles and mushrooms mixed in even parts and mingled with mayonnaise sauce (No. 606).

(2501). GARNISHING OF ARTICHOKE BOTTOMS, IMPERIAL (Garniture de Fonds d'Artichauts à l'Impériale).

Prepare and cook some artichoke bottoms as in No. 2500; they must be thick and not too broad; wipe dry and lay them on a small baking sheet; keep on ice. Prepare a cooked truffle salad, they to be cut in quarter-inch dice, small green asparagus tops and celery roots cut up the same as the truffles; season this salad with salt, oil, vinegar and mustard. Drain off this seasoning one hour later and thicken it with jellied mayonnaise (No. 613). With this preparation fill the hollow parts of the artichoke bottoms, arranging each one in a pyramid; smooth the surface and cover lightly with jellied mayonnaise, decorate with fanciful cuts of gherkins and replace on the ice for ten minutes before serving.

(2502). GARNISHING OF EGGS À LA DEVELLE (Garniture d'Œufs à la Develle).

Cut in two crossways seven or eight shelled hard-boiled eggs; use only the halves with the rounded ends and from them remove all the yolks and rub through a sieve; put this into a small vessel and add to it a little cold aspic jelly (No. 103); (scoop the whites out lightly). Pound the cooked meats of a small lobster, press through a sieve into a bowl and season with salt and a dash of cayenne; add first two spoonfuls of white chaudfroid sauce (No. 596), then some mayonnaise sauce (No. 606), and lastly a few spoonfuls of the cold jelly; stir this preparation on ice to harden, then take up sufficient of it with a spoon and fill the hollow egg-whites, smoothing the tops dome-shaped; lay them in the ice box; when cold take them in the hand one by one and dip into a chaudfroid sauce, but only on the garnished side and as far down as this begins; have the sauce hardened. Dress on jelly rings cut out with a pastry cutter, keeping the dish very cold. When the eggs are ready decorate the tops with fanciful cuts of truffles and a few small shrimp tails; dip them one by one in half-set jelly and stand them upright, each one inside of one of the jelly rings.

(2503). GARNISHING OF EGGS À LA JARDINIÈRE (Garniture d'Œufs à la Jardinière).

Divide in two crossways fifteen hard-boiled eggs; keep only the halves having the roundest end and cut these off so that they stand upright. Remove the yolks from these halves and scoop the white out lightly, then fill up the hollow with a little finely cut macédoine salad (No. 2650) dressed with mayonnaise (No. 606); smooth them into a dome and put aside on ice, then cover the dome with small carrot and gherkin balls cut in halves; brush over with half-set jelly and dress.

(2504). GARNISHING OF EGGS, JULIETTE (Garniture d'Œufs Juliette).

Fry thin slices of ham in butter without coloring; drain off the fat and place the ham under a weight; detach the glaze from the pan with a little Madeira wine, a small quantity of half-glaze (No. 400), and as much jelly (No. 103); reduce well. Pare the ham into half-hearts and cover them entirely with the sauce. Decorate a timbale mold (No. 1, Fig. 137) with pistachios and truffles; coat the decoration with a thick layer of the sauce and place in the center some small soft eggs just cooked enough to allow to peel; on these lay the ham, shredded fine, and the remainder of the sauce; when perfectly cold fill up with jelly, and as this becomes thoroughly cold invert the whole on a dish, having a layer of jelly on its bottom; surround with chopped jelly and croutons (No. 2442).

(2505). GARNISHING OF EGGS À LA JUSTINE (Garniture d'Œufs à la Justine).

Boil hard seven or eight eggs; when very cold, drain and shell. Incrust in pounded ice seven or eight tin molds the shape of half eggs, only just a little wider and higher; coat these with jelly. Cut each egg lengthways in two; take out the yolks and scoop out the whites with a vegetable spoon, leaving only a thin envelope; fill the empty inside of these half eggs with a chicken " pain " preparation (No. 2543), having it lightly buttered. Take up the stuffed eggs one by one on a wide fork passed under the flat side; dip them in a good brown chaudfroid sauce (No. 594) reduced with pheasant fumet (No. 397); drain off the sauce and let the eggs cool, then pare the surplus of it, and decorate with thin cuts of truffles and gherkins; now place a half egg in each mold, and pour cold jelly around to fill up the spaces; when cold, unmold and dress in a rosette as a garnishing.

(2506). GARNISHING OF EGGS À LA ROUENNAISE (Garniture d'Œufs à la Rouennaise).

Divide in two lengthways seven or eight shelled hard-boiled eggs; take out the yolks to pound and rub through a sieve. Harden on a small baking sheet on ice a layer of fine jelly, having it a quarter of an inch thick; from this cut out with a heated pastry cutter eight oval crusts, having them two and a quarter inches long by one and a quarter inches wide; form rings of these with a narrower pastry cutter, and detach them from the pan by warming it underneath; dress them in a rosette on a cold dish and keep it on ice. Fill the half eggs with a salpicon of cooked duckling fillets mixed with mushrooms and a brown chaudfroid sauce (No. 594) mixed with soubise sauce (No. 543); smooth the preparation into domes, and cover the eggs entirely with a thin layer of white chaudfroid sauce (No. 596). When this is quite cold, decorate the surfaces with fanciful cuts of truffles and with strings of pounded egg-yolk mixed with chaudfroid; lay one egg inside of each jelly ring.

2507). GARNISHING OF EGGS, BARREL-SHAPED (Garniture d'Œufs en Forme de Baril).

Cut off both ends of seven or eight shelled hard-boiled (eggs imitate the shape of a small barrel); empty them from top to bottom with a small tin tube, and fill up the hole with a salpicou of lobster and truffles mingled with a thick mayonnaise (No. 606); lay them on a baking sheet, and let stand on ice for half an hour. On removing them, decorate the sides with thin fillets of anchovies, dipped in half-set jelly, and cover over the top platform with a pyramid of chopped jelly.

(2508). GARNISHING OF HARD-BOILED EGGS, BASKET-SHAPED (Garniture d'Œufs Durs en Forme de Corbeille).

Cut off straight the ends of the hard-boiled egg and across through the center; take out the yolk from the upper parts, and fill them to a pointed shape with a salpicon of vegetables cut in small squares, and combined with a little mayonnaise (No. 606), or simply fill them with jelly.

FIG. 491.

(2509). GARNISHING OF HARD EGGS IN CHAUDFROID (Garniture d'Œufs Durs en Chaudfroid).

Have two oval pastry cutters—one two and a quarter inches long by one and quarter wide, and another half an inch less in diameter; cut some slices of very red cooked beef tongue three-six-teenths of an inch thick, and cut them into ovals with the largest cutter; remove the center with the smallest cutter; glaze over the rings with a brush and dress on the bottom of a cold dish. Cut lengthways in two six shelled hard-boiled eggs, take out the yolks, garnish each half with a foies-gras purée preparation, having chopped truffles added; smooth the surfaces dome-shaped. Dip the half-stuffed eggs into a brown chaudfroid sauce (No. 594), thickened to a proper consistency, and drain off the surplus, then dress a half egg into each ring. After the sauce is thoroughly cold decorate the tops with fanciful cuts of truffles, and dress.

(2510). GARNISHING OF HALVED HARD-BOILED EGGS (Garniture de Moitiés d'Œufs Durs).

Cut some hard-boiled eggs lengthwise in two even parts, and a third across on the most rounded end; try and obtain the eggs all of even size. Dress the border so that the yolks face the exterior of the dish; on top of the whites place a small lozenge of angelica, or one of very thin and very red beetroot, Which ever is used should be cut very thin. All egg borders should be dressed very regularly.

FIG. 492.

(2511). GARNISHING OF EGGS, MOSCOVITE (Garniture d'Œufs Moscovite).

Have a thin layer of aspic jelly (No. 103) three-eighths of an inch thick; harden on ice on a small baking sheet; from it cut out with a hot pastry cutter seven or eight rings sufficiently large to hold up the eggs inside of them. Cut crossways, two-thirds from the top, seven or eight shelled hard-boiled eggs; take out the yolks and pound them with a few anchovies and a piece of butter; rub this through a coarse sieve so it falls through like vermicelli, and keep cold. Scoop out the insides of the eggs lightly with a vegetable spoon, and fill them with a fine salpicon of crawfish mingled with thick tartar sauce (No. 631); leave for two minutes on ice; smooth the preparation into a dome form, and lay the eggs inside the jelly rings, to stand for a quarter of an hour longer on ice. After they are removed take up the vermicelli yolks with a fork, and cover the domes of the eggs with it.

(2512). GARNISHING OF EGGS, POLISH STYLE (Garniture d'Œufs à la Polonaise).

Cut in small dice the cooked meats of some lobster claws, add to this salpicon the same quantity of oysters poached in white wine and half as much salt, cucumber or gherkin, and beside this the white of seven or eight hard-boiled eggs, also cut up in small dice; season the salpicon with oil, vinegar and mustard, and let macerate for one hour; drain on a sieve and return it to the same vessel to combine with some mayonnaise (No. 606). Dress this preparation in a small croustade, smooth the top and decorate with the egg-yolks pounded with a little ravigote butter (No. 583) pushed through a cornet.

(2513). GARNISHING OF DECORATED QUARTERED EGGS (Garniture d'Œufs Durs en Quartiers Décorés).

FIG. 493.

Choose some hard-boiled eggs, all of uniform size; cut them across the rounded ends and then lengthwise in four even-sized quarters; dress them so that the yolks face outward. The whites may be decorated with small fanciful cuts of very black truffles, red tongue and pistachios, by dipping them into half-set jelly, and applying them tastefully on the very cold eggs (Fig. 493).

(2514). HARD-BOILED EGGS STUFFED WITH SALPICON (Œufs Durs Farcis au Salpicon).

Incorporate some rather firm jelly into a little purée of foies-gras, spread it out on a baking sheet to half an inch in thickness and leave to cool. With a pastry cutter remove from it some rounds two inches in diameter, and from these remove the center with an inch and a quarter pastry cutter. Place these rings in small shallow crimped paper cases. Cut some hard-boiled eggs in two through the center of their height, empty the interior of each half and refill them to a point with a half-inch salpicon of chicken, truffles, tongue and mushrooms, combined with a little jellied mayonnaise (No. 613); strew chopped parsley over. Lay these eggs on the rings and cover lightly with jelly.

(2515). GARNISHING OF HARD-BOILED EGGS, VASE SHAPE (Garniture d'Œufs Durs en Forme de Vase).

Cut off a third of the length of the egg; use the most rounded end for the upper part and the pointed end for the base; stick these two parts together with white chaudfroid (No. 596); take out the yolk and replace it by chopped jelly (Fig. 494).

FIG. 494.

(2516). GARNISHING OF WHOLE HARD-BOILED EGG-YOLKS (Garniture de Jaunes d'Œufs Durs Entiers).

FIG. 495.

Have some small, even-sized hard-boiled egg-yolks; stand them on rings cut from gherkins or beef tongue; lay in a circle a fillet of anchovy two-thirds the height of these yolks; besprinkle the inside of this circle with finely chopped truffles, and on top place a green pistachio nut (Fig. 495).

(2517). MUSHROOMS STUFFED AND GLAZED WITH CHAUDFROID (Champignons Farcis Glacés au Chaudfroid).

Select even-sized mushrooms about an inch in diameter; empty out the interiors and fill them up with foies-gras rubbed through a sieve. Fasten them together, two by two, to form a ball, then glaze over with brown chaudfroid (No. 594); lay them on top of a ring of cooked beef tongue and on the summit place a circle cut from hard-boiled egg-white: fill the center of this circle with a round piece of very black truffle and coat the whole with half-set jelly (Fig. 496).

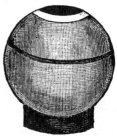

FIG. 496.

(2518). GARNISHING OF STUFFED SPANISH OLIVES (Garniture d'Olives d'Espagne Farcies).

FIG. 497.

Stone some large Spanish olives with a tin tube sufficiently large to remove the stone; pare the olives very straight at both ends and fill up the hollow space with anchovy butter (No. 569); on top of the butter lay a green pistachio nut (Fig. 497).

(2519). GARNISHING OF OYSTERS IN CROUSTADES (Garniture d'Huîtres en Croustades).

Drain and wipe some large blanched oysters; remove the muscle part and replace it by a round piece of lobster cut the same size. Make some small oval fine foundation paste croustades; cover the insides with buttered paper, fill with rice, bake and empty; fill them halfway up with cooked mushrooms, cut in three-sixteenths of an inch squares, mingled with a little well-seasoned blond chaudfroid, made by mixing a little brown chaudfroid (No. 594) with white chaudfroid (No. 596), and over these lay the oysters; put in a layer of half-set jelly, applying it with a brush, and decorate each croustade with chervil leaves; cover with more jelly.

(2520). GARNISHING OF OYSTERS WITH JELLY (Garniture d'Huîtres à la Gelée).

Open some large oysters, poach, remove the muscle and split them in two through their thickness; cover both sides with a layer of jellied mayonnaise (No. 613) and reshape them as before; then lay them slightly apart on a baking sheet; brush the surfaces several times with half-set jelly, and keep them for a few moments on ice; afterward remove by cutting away the jelly all around with a plain pastry cutter dipped in hot water; detach the oysters from the sheet, heating this underneath, then dress.

(2521). HAM DECORATED À LA GATTI (Jambon Décoré à la Gatti).

Have a ham prepared and cooked the same as for jelly (No. 2524); leave a part of the rind on the handle end, and cut it into sharp points by raising up the edge of each point on one side; glaze the ham with white chaudfroid (No. 596), all except the rind, which must be glazed with meat glaze (No. 402).

FIG. 498.

Decorate around the ham with a design of branches made of fillets of truffles and very green pistachios; decorate the top with a rosette of truffles. Place the ham on a silver dish, having two tiers covered with ravigote butter (No. 583); decorate around the dish bottom with halved eggs filled with chopped jelly, as shown in Fig. 498; surround the ham with chopped jelly, and the base with square jelly croûtons (No. 2442). Insert a piece of wood to take the place of the handle, and trim it with a fancy frill (No. 10), and a hatelet on one side.

(2522). HAM GLAZED WITH SUGAR (Jambon Glacé au Sucre).

Hams are usually purchased already salted and smoked, for the pickling only succeeds when a large quantity are done at one time. The most essential point to observe is to have them recently smoked, of a young pig of a good breed. The easiest way to cook a ham is as follows: Cut off the end handle of a ten-pound ham, shorten the loin bone, suppress a thin layer of the outside of the ham that is oversmoked, and then soak it for three hours in water; afterward place it in a large soup-pot or sauce-pan, covering with cold water; stand the vessel on the fire and bring it gradually to a boil, then drain off this water, and replace it by tepid water; add some whole spices and aromatics. It must cook about fifteen minutes for each pound, or two and a half hours in all. Take the vessel from off the fire, and leave the ham to cool in its liquid. Remove, drain thoroughly, lift off the rind, and pare nicely, keeping it a pretty shape; bestrew with fine sugar, and stand it on a baking tin; glaze to a fine color in a hot oven, remove, and when cold dress it on a bread foundation covered with ravigote butter (No. 583) and chopped parsley; surround the bottom of the dish with chopped jelly and cut-out croûtons (for these see No. 2442).

(2523). HAM TRUFFLED À LA FLORIAN (Jambon Truffé à la Florian).

In order to succeed with this dish it will be found necessary to have an oval bomb-shaped copper-tinned mold, nine and a half inches long, six and three-quarters inches wide and four inches deep. This mold must be oiled on the outside and laid on an oiled marble slab, having the opening downward; around it place an iron ring twelve inches in length, ten inches wide and five and a half inches deep; place this ring in such a way that the mold will fit exactly in its center, fill the space between the mold and the ring with plaster of Paris wetted with a little water; smooth the

Fig. 499.

top nicely and leave it to harden; turn this ring over and take out the mold. Pare a twelve-pound freshly salted smoked ham neatly, unsalt it for ten hours, and boil it in water for an hour and a half, then braise in a white wine mirepoix stock (No. 419) for three hours or more until the bones are easily detached from the meat; remove them, and pare the ham shapely, suppressing the skin and all the smoked parts, then lard it in every direction with quartered truffles and pistachios. Place this ham in the mold, the mold in the ring filled with plaster, and on the ham lay a board one inch less in diameter than the mold, and half an inch thick. Put under the press (No. 71), and when cold unmold and trim. Glaze over with pink chaudfroid, decorate with truffles and pistachios dipped in half-set jelly, cover over with jelly and lay it on a carved rice socle, having this ranged on an oval dish. Decorate the top with three hatelets, and around with chopped jelly and a border of jelly croûtons (see Fig. 461).

(2524). ENGLISH HAM WITH JELLY (Jambon Anglais à la Gelée).

If freshly salted and smoked it is unnecessary to soak it; simply wash off in warm water, pare and saw the handle bone short, then put it into a large vessel, cover with cold water and bring this

Fig. 500.

to a boil, adding aromatic herbs; close the lid and leave to boil for three hours slowly, but continuously and regularly. Remove the vessel from the fire and allow the ham to cool off in this liquor. (A ham is cooked when the meat on the handle bone becomes soft.) Drain it off, suppress the thick end bone and a part of the rind, leaving the leg end covered; pare and remove all the upper part to cut up into even slices. Lay the ham on an oval wooden board covered with white paper and fastened on a dish, dress the cut slices in a circle on top of the ham and fill the center with chopped jelly; glaze the rind and the remaining whole piece with a brush and surround the base with a string of thick jelly pushed through a pocket; dress fine triangles of jelly (No. 2442) all around; fasten a jelly-decorated hatelet in the opposite end from the handle, slanting it outward (see drawing, Fig. 501).

(2525). HAMS OF CHICKEN WITH ZAMPINO (Jambons de Poulet Garnis de Zampino).

Bone thoroughly two good chickens weighing two pounds each, leaving on only the drumstick bones; separate each one in two lengthwise, season and fill each half with galantine forcemeat (No. 65) and long shreds of cooked veal udder, also of very red beef tongue, raw foies-gras and quartered raw truffles, proceeding exactly the same as for boned chicken (No. 2485); bring the meats close together in order to sew up and wrap each of the halved boned chickens in a white cloth; cook for one hour in unskimmed white broth (No. 194a); drain the galantines and unwrap; lay on a baking sheet some bottomless molds in the shape of hams, having a slot in the thin end to allow the drumstick to pass through, place the chickens in these and let get cold under the pressure of a light weight. Pare and disengage the pinion bone. They may now be cut in slices, reconstructing them as before, and keeping in shape with a thin skewer; cover the entire surface with white chaudfroid sauce (No. 596), that has become slightly thickened on ice. After this sauce is cold cover over the hams on the drumstick end with brown chaudfroid (No. 594), imitating the real skin of a pared ham; trim each ham bone with a frill (No. 10); dress them two by two on a rice foundation, withdraw the skewers and decorate the hams with fanciful cuts of very black truffles; surround with thin slices of zampino three inches in diameter and cut in two across and dress them around the foundation, one overlapping the other. Surround with a piping of chopped jelly and some jelly croûtons.

Zampino of Modena.—Take one leg of a fresh pig about fifteen inches long, leaving the foot adhering; bone it carefully not to split the skin, turn the skin back and then remove the meat and fat; salt the skin plentifully, and leave it in brine for four to five days. After this time chop up coarsely ten pounds of lean pork meat with five pounds of beef, and mix these with five pounds of very finely chopped fresh pork rind. Season the mixture with ten ounces of salt, one ounce of crushed black pepper corns, a heavy pinch of cinnamon, a small pinch of saltpeter and one gill of red wine; mingle thoroughly. Now wash the skin in fresh water to extract all the salt, turn it over to its normal position, and fill it with the above mixture; tie it firmly at the extreme end, and enwrap with a strong inch-wide tape, beginning at the smallest end of the zampino (that is, near the foot). Lay the zampino in a large kettle, cover plentifully with cold water, and stand it on a slow fire to have the liquid almost reach boiling point; then remove the kettle to a corner of the range and let barely bubble for an hour and a half to an hour and three-quarters. Take from the fire and leave to cool in the liquid; drain and remove the tape. This zampino can be served hot with string beans as described in No. 1820.

(2526). MISCELLANEOUS COLD HATELETS, BELLEVUE VEGETABLES; CROÛTONS, CHOPPED TRANSPARENT JELLY AND STICKY CHOPPED JELLY (Hâtelets Froids Divers en Bellevue, de Légumes; de Croûtons et Gelée Hachée Transparente et de Gelée Hachée Collante).

Cold hatelets are to be prepared with plain or double white cocks'-combs enveloped in jelly, and round, black, unpeeled truffles glazed over with meat glaze (No. 402). Others are made of trussed crawfish from which the small legs have been suppressed and the body shells rubbed over with a little oil, channeled mushrooms (No. 118) coated with jelly, chicken or game quenelles (No. 91), decorated and molded in Bellevue or simply covered, or else carved vegetables blanched separately. These hatelets can also be composed of crawfish, lemons, truffles and mushrooms, having one small glazed truffle on top, a lightly oiled trussed crawfish under this truffle, and then a fine channeled glazed mushroom, having the upper part rounded, then a lemon cut into points; first one-half of the lemon, placed with the points upward, then a round piece of truffle and the other half of the lemon, the points downward, and finished with a glazed channeled mushroom, having the rounded end toward the bottom.

Lean Hatelets for Fish are composed of shrimps, crawfish, truffles, mushrooms or lemon. Cocks'-combs are not admissible for this kind of hatelets.

Bellevue Hatelets.—Prepare these hatelets as follows: Cut out with a tin tube three-fourths of an inch in diameter and an eighth of an inch in thickness, small rounds of chicken, cooked beef tongue and truffles; take pieces from the center with a smaller tin tube one-eighth of an inch

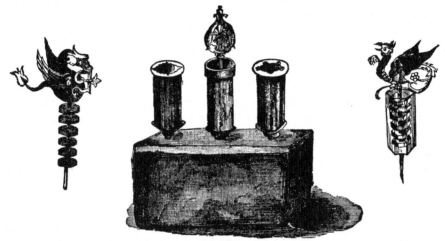

FIG. 501.

in diameter; run a hatelet through six of these rounds, beginning first by putting a small round whole truffle, then a round of chicken, tongue and truffle; begin again with another round of chicken, tongue and truffle, leaving a space between each. Cut off the upper crust of a loaf of bread, this to be six inches high; spread over the top to replace the crust a layer of butter a

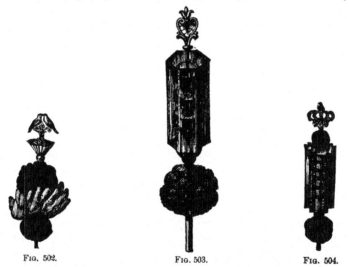

FIG. 502.   FIG. 503.   FIG. 504.

quarter of an inch thick; on top place the hatelet cases or molds (Fig. 501); run through the metal hatelets decorated with the rounds exactly in the center, stand them upright, then fill the molds with cold jelly (No. 103) and keep them in a cool place for several hours. When ready to serve the pieces unmold these hatelets and run a fine unpeeled, round and black truffle on each one, then stick them into the piece. Carrots and turnips can be substituted for the chicken and tongue.

Vegetable Hatelets.—These hatelets are composed of vegetables or roots, imitating vases of various kinds; they are turned and carved with a knife, and formed of several pieces, then filled with artificial flowers made of vegetables, such as roses, camelias, lilies, or daisies; these flowers are colored by dipping them in a solution of aniline dissolved in alcohol and diluted with water. If these flowers are well made they can imitate the natural ones most marvelously. They can be used plain, without any coloring, but this is a matter of taste.

For Chopped Transparent Jelly the fragments of jelly croûtons are generally used, chopping them on a moistened cloth with a large knife; they should be chopped sufficiently fine, still not allowing them to get thick looking; they may also be cut into small fine lengthwise strips, afterward cutting them across in small squares; in this way they are sure to remain transparent.

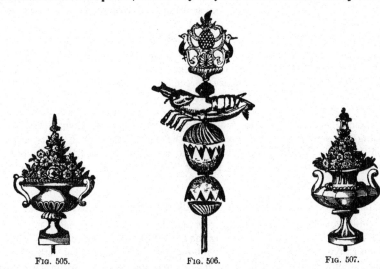

Fig. 505.   Fig. 506.   Fig. 507.

Sticky Chopped Jelly is used for pushing through a pocket or paper cornet around a cold meat piece, and is also frequently used to cover the surface of a high foundation that is to be used as a support. In order to obtain a sticky jelly, chop it up on a wet cloth, and sprinkle it over from time to time with some hot water, until it forms into a soft compact mass. This must be used at once.

(2527). KERNEL OF VEAL WITH MAYONNAISE TOMATOED SAUCE (Noix de Veau à la Sauce Mayonnaise Tomatée).

Lard thoroughly a kernel of veal with ham and fat pork, cover it with slices of udder, and then braise. Have a dome-shaped terrine or mold; put the kernel in; strain in the stock, add to it a little gelatine if not consistent enough, and when cold turn it on a dish. Remold into another mold of similar shape, but an inch larger in diameter, decorated with cuts of vegetables; fill with jelly and when cold dress it on a carved rice socle and garnish around with balls of turnips and carrots, blanched and cooked in stock (No. 194a) with a little sugar, and glazed; dress a butter border (No. 2444) or one of vegetables (No. 2443) on the edge of the dish, and serve apart a mayonnaise (No. 606) with some tomato purée (No. 730) added.

(2528). KINGFISH FILLETS À LA VALENÇAY (Filets de Kingfish à la Valençay).

Pare oblong shape and cook ten to twelve small fillets of kingfish in a sautoir with white wine court-bouillon (No. 39); drain and let cool under a weight; trim them nicely, dip them singly into a white chaudfroid sauce (No. 596), ranging them immediately on to a baking sheet to cool off the

Fig. 508.

sauce, then pare off the surplus of it. Decorate a third part of them on the smooth side with fanciful cuts of truffles or gherkins; cover them over with half-set jelly applied with a brush, and let this get cold, then dress them on an inch-high socle in pyramid form, placing the decorated ones on top. On one side fasten a hatelet garnished with shrimps. Uphold the fillets of fish on both sides with thick chopped jelly pushed through a cornet and surround, both right and left, with five or six large crawfish bodies, emptied and refilled with a salpicon of crawfish or lobster tails, combined with a salad of small vegetables dressed with mayonnaise (No. 606). Stand these bodies upright to form a half circle, and brush over with half-set jelly; surround the base of the dish with fine jelly croûtons (No. 2442), and serve with a sauce-boat of mayonnaise sauce (No. 606).

(2529). CHICKEN LEGS SHAPED AS DUCKLINGS (Cuisses de Poulet en forme de Canetons).

Cut the leg three-quarters of an inch from the joint. Remove the bones belonging to the second joint, as well as a third part of the drumsticks; stuff the legs with quenelle forcemeat (No. 89), introducing into it half as much foies-gras forcemeat (No. 78); mix in a third as much small three-sixteenths of an inch squares of tongue and mushroom, half of each, and raw fine herbs. Shape them to represent ducklings. Put in a sautoir some thin slices of fat pork and place the ducklings one beside the other. Braise, cool and pare off the under parts neatly, so that these imitated ducklings can stand plumb on their base, then glaze them with white chaudfroid (No. 596), and form the wings with crawfish claws. Make artificial eyes and form the beak by cutting the bone slanting. Surround with green parsley leaves, and serve with a bowl of ravigote sauce (No. 623).

(2530). LEG OF MUTTON À LA GARRISON (Gigot de Mouton à la Garrison).

Line a buttered saucepan with onions, carrots and slices of round of veal, slices of fat pork and ham; in the middle lay a leg of mutton having the thick loin end boned, and add a bunch of parsley garnished with thyme and bay leaf, also two boned calves' feet; moisten with stock (No. 194a), white wine and Madeira wine, a pint of each; let fall to a glaze and remoisten with stock; when it begins to boil skim and cover with a sheet of paper; push into the oven for four or five hours until the leg is thoroughly cooked, then transfer it to an oval vessel and leave till cold. Have a few dozen carrots and turnips cut in balls, also some small onions; blanch these and cook each kind separately in broth (No. 194a); when fallen to a glaze allow them to cool, thickening with a little jelly (No. 103). The leg being cold, trim it nicely, glaze over with meat glaze (No. 402), dress it in the center of a dish and surround with the jellied vegetables and jelly cut in eighth of an inch squares arranged in clusters. Decorate the leg with anchovy fillets, chervil and tarragon, dipped in half-set jelly, and surround by horseradish ribbons (No. 98). Skim the fat from the stock, add a seasoning of oil, vinegar, salt, mignonette, capers and gherkins, and serve in a sauce-boat when cold. Place on the bone the silver handle shown in Fig. 164.

(2531). LOBSTER OR SPINY LOBSTER À LA RAVIGOTE (Homard ou Langouste à la Ravigote).

Boil a lobster in a plain court-bouillon (No. 38) and let it cool off under a weight with the tail stretched out. Remove the tail meats from underneath, leaving the shell attached to the body; pare the meats on the thickest end and cut them up into slightly bias slices so as to have them somewhat wider; season and place them flat on a tinned-copper tray; decorate the tops with lobster, eggs, tarragon leaves and chervil; cover the decorations with half-set jelly and keep in a cool place. Break the shells of the large claws so as to remove the meats and divide these in two lengthwise, then brush them over with half-set aspic jelly (No. 103). Cut in dice the meats of a small boiled lobster, put the pieces in a bowl with an equal quantity of cooked truffles, a few spoonfuls of cooked mushrooms and raw gherkins; season this salpicon and stir it on ice into some thick mayonnaise (No. 606), and with it cover ten to twelve small cooked equal-sized artichoke bottoms. Turn over the lobster body and fill the empty tail with thick jelly pushed through a pocket; dress at once in its natural state, the red side uppermost, on a long dish, moistening it with half-set jelly, laid on with a brush, to prevent the lobster from slipping off. On the top of the shell, from one end to the other, push two thick strings of butter previously softened in a cloth and an inch and a quarter apart; between these strings range a bed of chopped jelly, and on top of this dress the slices of lobster, one overlapping the other. On the right and left of the head lay the jelly covered claws and around the body have chopped jelly surrounded with the garnished artichoke bottoms, and around them a border of pretty jelly croûtons (No. 2442). Serve at the same time a ravigote sauce (No. 623), having the creamy parts of the lobster added to it.

(2532). LOBSTER IN A BORDER (Homard en Bordure).

Cut into quarter-inch squares, on the bias, the tail meat of two boiled lobsters, also the claws cut into four pieces; lay them in a deep dish and season with salt, oil and vinegar. Incrust in ice a plain border mold (Fig. 139), coat the inside with clear jelly (No. 103); cut some hard-boiled eggs into four pieces, that is once lengthwise and then each half egg once across; fasten to the yolks small sprigs of green chervil dipped in jelly, and fill the border mold with these eggs; then pour into the bottom a little melted jelly; let it set, add about half an inch more, and when this begins to harden fill up the mold, and let it remain on ice until the jelly is perfectly firm; then turn the mold over on a cold dish. Fill the inside empty space as high as the jelly with a vegetable salad (No. 2650), thickened with jellied mayonnaise (No. 613); dress on top the slices of lobster, covering the whole with jellied mayonnaise; cover with more jelly, and set on top the claws dipped in jelly. A mayonnaise printanière (No. 612) should be served separately.

(2533). LOBSTER TAILS IN THEIR SHELLS (Queues de Homards dans leurs Coquilles).

Detach the bodies, claws and tails from five small cooked lobsters; open the claw shells to remove the meats. Cut the five lobster tails lengthways, both meat and shell together; remove the meats from these ten halved shells, wipe the shells neatly, and fill the bottoms with a layer of preparation made with the lobster parings, truffles and mushrooms, mingled with a little chaudfroid sauce (No. 606), and finished with a dash of cayenne pepper. Season the tail meats and cut them

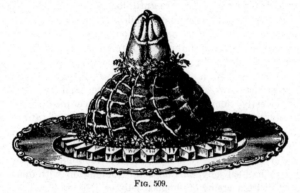

Fig. 509.

up slanting without spoiling their shape, and dip them into half-set jelly; then replace each one in its half shell, the red side uppermost, and lay them aside in a cool place. This entrée is to be dressed on a dish foundation having in the center a pyramidical support, both of which are to be covered with white paper, then with a layer of thick chopped jelly pushed through a pocket; the halved tails are to be dressed with the points upward, five on each side; the claws are to stand upright on top of the support, and surrounded by green parsley leaves. The base of the halved tails is also to be surrounded by fresh parsley, and the bottom of the dish with pretty jelly croûtons (No. 2442). As soon as the entrée is dressed place it in the ice-box until ready to serve, then send it to the table with a separate mayonnaise sauce (No. 606).

(2534). LOBSTER OR SPINY LOBSTER WITH MAYONNAISE (Homard ou Langouste à la Mayonnaise).

Cook a large lobster; drain and let get cold with the tail stretched out. Detach the large claws and divide the body lengthwise in two; remove the meats whole from each halved tail, and cut them up slanting, but without deforming them. Wipe well the empty tail shells and fill them half way with chopped jelly, then return the meats to the shells upside down so that the red part is uppermost. Suppress the black vein from the center of the bodies, also the creamy parts, and rub these through a sieve and add them to a mayonnaise sauce (No. 606). Dress the two halves of the lobster on a napkin or dish, and in the hollow space formed by the shells place a bunch of parsley leaves; on this dress the lobster claws in their shells, after suppressing half of them, and surround the lobster on the bottom of the dish with a string of chopped jelly, and around this lay either croûtons of jelly or halved hard-boiled eggs filled with a salad of vegetables (No. 2650); serve the mayonnaise sauce separately.

(2535). MOUSSELINES OF FOIES-GRAS À LA DANA (Mousselines de Foies-Gras à la Dana).

Prepare a frothy preparation with foies-gras in the following manner: Pound one pound of foies-gras taken from a terrine, pass the pulp through a sieve, season, lay it in a thin iron vessel and beat well, adding a gill of melted glaze (No. 402) and two gills of brown chaudfroid sauce (No. 594), to make the preparation of a good consistency when cold. After it has become smooth stir in slowly the equal quantity of a pint of well-drained whipped cream without sugar. Range on pounded ice fifteen quenelle molds (Fig. 76); cover the insides of these to half their height with the frothy preparation, forming a hollow in the center, and into this lay a slice of foies-gras three-sixteenths of an inch thick and cut egg-shaped; finish filling the molds with the same preparation, smooth the tops, having them perfectly flat, and then set the molds on ice for one hour. Dip them into hot water, unmold the mousselines on a cold baking sheet and cover each one with brown chaudfroid sauce (No. 594). After this has become quite cold dress the mousselines in a pyramid inside a jelly border. Garnish around the border with clear jelly cut into very small dice, and outside of this place a row of jelly croûtons (No. 2442).

(2536). MOUSSELINE OF KINGFISH À LA BRIÈRE (Mousseline de Kingfish à la Brière).

Scale two or three fresh kingfish, weighing about two pounds; suppress the head and thin tail end, the fins and gills. Put into a sautoir two soupspoonfuls of chopped onions and shallots, add half a pound of clarified butter cooked to hazelnut (No. 567) and fry the onions and shallots lightly; put in the well-wiped fish and season with salt, nutmeg, a dash of cayenne, a pinch of thyme leaves and bay leaf; fry over a brisk fire until done. Remove the skin, pour the whole into a sieve laid over a large dish, so as to be able to collect all the liquid and butter, and let this as well as the fish get cold on ice. Take all the bones out of the fish and pound the meat, adding gradually the well-strained butter and liquid, also a few spoonfuls of good béchamel sauce (No. 409) reduced with the fish stock. Press this forcemeat through a sieve and smooth it in a vessel, mixing in with it slowly a few spoonfuls of very thick jelly (No. 103); try a small part of this preparation in a small mold on ice, and if not quite firm add more dissolved jelly until perfectly thick. When cold on the ice incorporate into it slowly about one pint of very firmly whipped cream, drained and sugarless. Stir the preparation again for a few moments, then pour it into a high mold incrusted on ice, coated with jelly, and bestrew with chervil leaves; let the mousseline harden for a couple of hours and at the last moment dip the mold into hot water so as to easily unmold it on a rice foundation two inches high; fill the bottom of the dish with half-set jelly, surround the foundation with quartered hard-boiled eggs standing erect, and these with a string of chopped jelly or jelly croûtons. Serve at the same time a sauce-boat of mayonnaise (No. 606), finished with tarragon and chopped chervil.

(2537). MOUSSELINE OF LOBSTER (Mousseline de Homard).

Select a plain cylindrical mold (Fig. 150) and incrust it in pounded ice; cut some crosswise slices of large green gherkins, of equal size and thickness, lift them up with the pointed end of a larding needle, dip into half-set jelly, and then arrange them symmetrically against the sides of the mold;

Fig. 510.

coat this decoration lightly with jelly. Cut up into quarter-inch dice the claw meat of four lobsters and enclose them in a small saucepan. Pound the tail meat with two or three spoonfuls of béchamel (No. 409), pass it through a sieve and return it to the mortar to pound once more, adding three or four gills of blond chaudfroid sauce (No. 596), a few spoonfuls of jelly (No. 103) and a few drops of tarragon vinegar; season highly and set the preparation in a saucepan to thicken lightly while stirring on ice; incorporate into this five or six spoonfuls of well-drained whipped cream. After this preparation is well smoothed add to it the dice pieces of claw meat and with the whole fill up the coated mold; put on ice for one hour. Just when ready to serve dip the mold in warm water and invert the contents on a dish having a small support fastened to the center; on top of this place a hatelet garnished with fine shrimps or crawfish of graduated sizes, and serve at the same time a separate mayonnaise sauce (No. 606).

(2538). MOUSSELINE OF PHEASANTS, PRINCESS (Mousseline de Faisans, Princesse).

This cold entrée is dressed on a carved rice croustade slightly hollowed out on top to form an outspreading ledge. Incrust in chopped ice a plain pyramidical flat-top mold. Take the meat of two breasts of cooked pheasants and half a cooked foies-gras; with these make a preparation the same as for a chaudfroid of fillets of pheasants (No. 2456); before thickening it on ice put a quarter of this into a saucepan and incorporate in it two spoonfuls of black pounded truffles; thicken the two preparations separately on ice. Moisten the interior of the mold with a brush dipped in jelly, fill it to a third of its height with the white mixture, and when this is cold pour in a layer of the

FIG. 511.

black one inch deep, and on this another of the white, of the same thickness as the first, then another one of black, the same as before, and finish filling with the white; cover with a buttered white paper and leave to cool for two hours. Lastly dip the mold in hot water and turn it over to unmold on the croustade; surround the base with a row of sticky chopped jelly (No. 2526) and on this lay a chain of small, crimped paper cases, each one filled with a round of truffle. On top of the mousseline fasten a hatelet garnished with mushrooms of graduated sizes, and surround this with chopped jelly; lay around some cases the same as the lower ones, only somewhat smaller, also filled with truffles.

(2539). MOUSSELINE OF PULLET (Mousseline de Poularde).

Poach in butter four well-pared pullet fillets; when cold pound them with a third of their quantity of the very best butter; season and rub through a sieve. Put this pulp into a thin iron vessel and beat it for five minutes with a spoon to have it smooth, then incorporate slowly three gills of blond chaudfroid sauce (No. 596); try a little of this preparation on ice to rectify if necessary, and when perfect thicken it on ice, stirring in a quarter as many truffles, red beef tongue and cooked mushrooms, the whole cut in three-sixteenths of an inch dice, also the volume of a pint of well-drained whipped cream. With this preparation fill an oval mold decorated with truffles and coated with a light coating of jelly, or

FIG. 512.

else several quenelle molds, covered with half-set jelly, having used a brush for this purpose; then smooth the top nicely and keep the mold on pounded ice for one hour. At the last moment unmold the mousseline on a cold dish and surround the base with pretty jelly croûtons (No. 2442).

(2540). MOUSSELINE OF WOODCOCK (Mousseline de Bécasses).

Simply dress this on a channeled rice croustade foundation fastened on a dish. Remove some rounds of cooked truffles with a cutter, and use them to decorate symmetrically the interior sides and bottom of a plain cylindrical mold (Fig. 150) imbedded in ice, dipping them one by one in half-set jelly to be able to fasten them on, then coat over the entire inside of the mold lightly with half-set jelly. Pound the breast meats of three cooked woodcock with an equal quantity of cooked foies-gras, half as much cooked and chopped-up truffles and a very little of the cooked intestines from the birds; season and pass the whole through a sieve.　Put this pulp into a thin metal vessel and stir

FIG. 513.

into it gradually three gills of brown chaudfroid sauce (No. 594), increased with a few spoonfuls of warmed jelly (No. 103); the chaudfroid sauce should be reduced with a game fumet (No. 397) prepared with the woodcock legs and bones; thicken the preparation properly by stirring it on ice and with it fill up the mold; then harden it on ice for one hour.　When needed dip the mold in hot water, wipe dry and invert the mousseline on the rice foundation, surrounding it with a bed of chopped jelly.

(2541). TENDERLOIN OF MUTTON À LA HENRY CLAY (Filets de Mouton à la Henry Clay).

Raise the tenderloins from two saddles of mutton, and the sirloins or meats from four racks; remove the skin, pare and lard with medium lardons (No. 3, Fig. 52); season with salt, pepper, nutmeg, fine herbs and shallots.　Cover the bottom of a braziere with slices of fat pork, carrots, onions and a bunch of parsley, garnished with thyme, bay leaf and a clove; lay the fillets on top, moisten with stock (No. 194a) and Madeira wine, cover with buttered paper, then bring to a boil and set in the oven for one hour; when done lay them on a deep dish and strain the stock over; glaze and dress on a rice croustade, and garnish around with breasts of mutton in chaudfroid, prepared as follows: Braise the breasts, set them under a weight to cool, pare by removing the skin and fat, and then cut the meat into small half-hearts; cover their surfaces with foies-gras taken from a terrine, pounded and rubbed through a sieve; when cold mask them with chaudfroid made with the fillet and breast stock, and some poivrade (No. 523) added, and when cold pare and trim with fancy favors (No. 10).　Dress them in a circle, one overlapping the other, around the rice socle, and outside of the breasts place chopped jelly surrounded by jelly croutons (No. 2442) cut very regular and dressed symmetrically.　Serve at the same time a sauce-boat of printanière mayon-naise (No. 612).

(2542). SMALL "PAINS" OF CAPON WITH TARRAGON (Petits Pains de Chapon à l'Estragon).

Select some timbale molds (No. 1, Fig. 137), imbed them in chopped ice, and decorate the bottoms and sides with cut-up gherkins and blanched tarragon leaves, being careful to dip these decorations in half-set jelly when using.　Take the value of two or three gills of capon purée, and mix with it a few spoonfuls of velouté sauce (No. 415); put this into a small saucepan and dissolve gradually with a gill of good aspic jelly (No. 103) and a few spoonfuls of tarragon vinegar.　Stir this preparation on ice to thicken, and use it to fill the empty molds.　One hour later dip these timbales in warm water; unmold the timbales and dress them at once in a circle on a cold dish.　Garnish the center with chopped jelly and around with jelly croûtons.

(2543). SMALL "PAINS" OF CHICKEN À L'ÉCARLATE (Petits Pains de Volaille à l'Écarlate).

This entrée requires to be dressed on a wooden foundation fastened on a dish; cover it with white paper, and decorate its thickness with a border in relief; in the center of this foundation place a wooden support also covered, it being as high as a six-sided timbale mold about the same size as timbale No. 1, Fig. 137.　Pound the white meats of a large chicken with an equal quantity of foies-gras, both to be cooked; add two spoonfuls of velouté sauce (No. 415), season and strain through a sieve. Put this pulp into a thin metal vessel, and mix in an equal quantity of liquid blond chaudfroid (No. 596), and four spoonfuls of cooked truffles cut in small dice. Incrust the molds on ice; coat with half-set jelly, and line the sides only with narrow strips of red beef tongue, cut the same height as the molds. Thicken the preparation on ice and with it fill the lined

FIG. 514.

molds; leave to harden for one hour. When required for serving, dip the molds in hot water in order to unmold the "pains," and dress them on the foundation around the support, placing one on its summit; decorate all the tops with a large mushroom head channeled through the thickness and hollowed in the center so that it is capable of holding a small truffle ball. On the central "pain" fasten a small hatelet garnished with a truffle and cocks'-comb slightly larger than the rest.

(2544). SMALL "PAINS" OF CHICKEN À LA FREYCINET (Petits Pains de Poulet à la Freycinet).

Have a baking tin with a raised border an inch and a half high; range on it some timbale molds (No. 2, Fig. 137), and surround them with finely chopped ice: pour into the bottom of each mold some jelly to an eighth of an inch in thickness and on top set a round slice of truffle a quarter of an inch narrower than the diameter of the bottom mold; decorate the sides with fanciful cuts of truffles or egg-white dipped in half-set jelly; coat over the interior of the mold or else brush it with a layer of the jelly and fill it up with the following preparation: Pound half a pound of the white meat of a braised and cold chicken to a pulp, after removing the skin, fat and bones; add to it half a pint of velouté sauce (No. 415) well reduced with mushroom essence (No. 392) and a pint of jelly (No. 103); pass the whole through a tammy into a thin metal bowl and lay it on ice; incorporate and mix well with it the same quantity of whipped cream, drained for two hours on a sieve. Fill the molds half full and place in the center a ball of foies-gras taken from a terrine with a round five-eighths of an inch vegetable spoon dipped in hot water; finish filling up with the preparation, smooth the tops and let get thoroughly cold. Unmold the timbales and dress them in a circle on a cut-out rice socle two inches high by eight inches in diameter; place in the center of the socle a sloping support, having it three inches high and five inches in circumference at the base and two inches in circumference on the top; on this top fasten a stearine cup, filling it with very small black and glazed truffles.

(2545). "PAIN" OF GAME À LA BARTHOLDI (Pain de Gibier à la Bartholdi).

Have made beforehand a round wooden socle nine inches and a half in diameter by two and a half inches in height. At half an inch from its top have a curve two inches high in the shape of an ogive, reducing the part that rests on the dish to the diameter of eight and a half inches; also hollow it out a quarter of an inch deep on top, leaving a three-quarter-inch border all around; exactly in the center bore a half-inch hole through the entire depth. Moisten the socle lightly, and cover it over with noodle paste (No. 142), or English paste (No. 134), rolled out very thin, and let dry in the air; then glaze it over with very light meat glaze (No. 402), and decorate by applying to the glaze fancifully cut pieces of either of the pastes used or a wreath of flowers. Make one or two preparations (the cut represents only one), one white with partridge meat, and the other brown with grouse meat.

For the White Preparation.—Pound one pound of the white meat of some braised cold partridges, boned and free of fat; add to it half a pound of foies-gras, and continue to mash the two together, adding one pint of velouté sauce (No. 415) reduced with the braised stock, strained and skimmed, having added to it an ounce of well-dissolved gelatine; strain the whole through a fine sieve, and set it away to get cold in a metal vessel. Instead of gelatine half a pound of very clear jelly (No. 103) may be substituted.

For the Brown Preparation.—Proceed exactly the same as for the white, but instead of the white partridge meat and velouté sauce use grouse or prairie chicken meat and espagnole sauce (No. 414), reduced with mushroom essence (No. 392); strain through a fine sieve, and lay it aside in a metal vessel. Fry two young and tender prairie hens in butter with chopped-up fresh mushrooms; season with salt, pepper, and chopped parsley, and let them get cold. Bone and suppress the skin, pound the meat to a pulp and rub it through a sieve; mix in a few spoonfuls of game quenelle forcemeat (No. 91), and add and mingle to the whole the same quantity of truffles, tongue, liver and pistachios, all cut up in small three-sixteenths of an inch squares. Line some small mousseline molds (No. 3, Fig. 138), with very thin slices of fat pork, and fill them

Fig. 515.

up with the above preparation; arrange them on a baking sheet, one beside the other, without allowing them to touch, and bake them in a slack oven; leave them to cool off under a weight; decorate No. 2 mousseline molds, either with truffles, egg-white, or pistachios; coat with a thin layer of jelly; pour a quarter-inch thick layer of jelly in the bottom of the mold; when cold place the contents of the No. 3 mousselin molds on it, and finish filling with jelly; keep in a cool place. Incrust in chopped ice a mold made in graduated tiers. The design as represented is plain, without any decoration; if decorated, then decorate the upper edge of the sides of each tier with fanciful cuts of truffle and egg-white dipped in half-set jelly; coat over evenly the inside of the mold with jelly. Place the two preparations on ice, beat them up well and fill the bottom tier with the brown preparation; lay in the center some slices of truffle and let it get cold; then fill another tier with white preparation, using slices of foies-gras instead of truffles, and continue the same operation until the mold is all filled; then let it get quite cold, leaving it on the ice for several hours so as to harden the contents. Unmold the " pain " on to the socle, ran through the center a wooden support which must be made to hold up the subject on its summit, and decorate each tier with jelly croûtons cut into long triangles, having the pointed end cut off and dressed upright; the height of these croûtons for the lower tier dressed on the socle must be an inch and a half, then diminish the height one-eighth of an inch for each tier, so that those on the fifth tier are only one inch high; decrease their thickness and width also. Stick on top of the support a stearine figure in imitation of the statue of Liberty. Push through a cornet between all the croûtons some finely chopped jelly, and decorate the bottom of the socle as high as the basin with more chopped jelly; or surround the base with the same mousseline-shaped timbales.

(2546). "PAIN" OF GAME, DIANA (Pain de Gibier à la Diane).

This "pain" is dressed on a socle, the frieze being upheld by the trunk of a tree having many branches, these to form a support; the branches are modeled over wire, the surface of the base is covered with foliage and the frieze decorated with leaves and flowers. On top of the socle place a surtout of carved rice of similar shape, to be ten inches long by seven inches wide, or one of tin covered with noodle paste (No. 142). Have three oval molds, the largest ten inches long, by seven inches wide and two inches high, the medium-sized one eight and five-eighths inches long, and

Fig. 516.

three and a half inches high and five and a quarter inches wide; the smallest to be seven and one-eighths inches long, four and five-eighths inches wide and three inches high. Line the inside of these molds with slices of fat pork an eighth of an inch thick. Make three different preparations, one for each mold; for the largest have a young hare "pain" preparation, made as follows: Cut two pounds of young hare meat into large squares; fry in melted chopped fat pork with mushrooms, truffles and fine herbs, salt, aromatics and spices; when the hare is cooked take from the fire and set away to cool, then pound it well, adding four egg-yolks, half a pound of foies-gras from a terrine and one pound of cream panada (No. 120). After all has been well pounded and passed through a sieve, add six ounces of unsmoked cooked beef tongue, half a pound of truffles and one pound of calves' udder, all cut in three-eighths inch squares; mix thoroughly and fill the largest mold; stand it in a sautoir with boiling water and let bake in a slack oven for three hours; cool under a weight, unmold and remove the fat part from the bottom and sides, pare the "pain" neatly, smooth and set it in the ice-box. For the medium-sized mold prepare the following: Cut two pounds of prairie-hen meat in squares, fry on a brisk fire in grated fat pork and as soon as cooked remove, cool and pound well, adding the same quantity of grated fresh fat pork; pound all thoroughly together, season with salt, pepper and nutmeg. Pound eight ounces of panada and mix it slowly into the preparation, press it through a sieve and mingle into this forcemeat a quarter of a pound of truffles cut in quarter-inch squares and as much fat pork cut exactly the same. With this preparation fill the medium-sized mold, having lined it with slices of fat pork an eighth of an inch thick; stand it in a sautoir with boiling water and let cook in a slow oven for two hours and a half, then cool under a weight. Unmold the "pain," pare and smooth it and leave it in the ice-box. For the smallest mold pound thoroughly one pound of roasted pheasant, partridge or quail meat from which all bones, fat, skin and sinews have been removed, with half a pound of foies-gras from a terrine; season, strain, return to a vessel and add a pint of cold half-glaze sauce (No. 413) well reduced with essence of mushrooms (No. 392) and twelve egg-yolks. Fill the mold with this preparation, stand it in a flat saucepan containing boiling water, place it in the oven, and when poached, cool, unmold and set it in the ice-box. After cleaning the molds well apply the lozenges correctly, dipping each one in half-set cold jelly. Begin at the bottom of the mold with a lozenge of egg-white cut in half across its length, keeping the lozenges of truffles on the right and the lozenges of tongue on the left. The beauty of this decoration consists in applying and joining them nicely, putting them rather close on the bottom of the mold and a little further away toward the top to allow for the spread of the mold. Coat each mold with jelly (No. 103), having it an eighth of an inch thick at the bottom, and leave it to cool. The lozenges for the large mold are one and three-eighths inches long by three-quarters of an inch wide; for the medium size, one and a quarter inches long by one and one-sixteenth inches wide; and for the smallest, one and one-eighth inches long by five-eighths of an inch wide. Put the "pains" into these decorated molds and finish filling with cold jelly that is not set; stand them in the ice-box for six hours, then unmold the largest carefully on the rice surtout. On the largest place the next size and the smallest on top; in the center of this one place a pretty subject, and at each end of it fasten a garnished hatelet and two larger ones below on the lower "pain." Surround the base of the surtout with jelly croûtons (No. 2442).

(2547). "PAIN" OF LIVER WITH SALPICON (Pain de Foie au Salpicon).

Mince a pound and a quarter of raw calf's liver; fry it quickly in melted fat pork with aromatic herbs, parsley, thyme, bay leaf, truffle and mushroom peelings and chopped blanched shallot; remove as soon as done and leave to cool, then mix in four ounces of foies-gras parings from a terrine. Pound and return it to the mortar and add slowly one pound and a half of chopped raw veal and fat pork, the same as a galantine; pound the whole well together, press once more through a sieve and season properly. Put this preparation into a vessel and stir in a third as much truffles, cooked veal udder and cooked red beef tongue, all cut into small squares. Cover the bottom and sides of a large charlotte mold with thin slices of fat pork; put the preparation in the center and cover over with more pork; place the mold in a saucepan containing hot water to reach a third of its height; let this come to a boil, then remove to a slower fire or a slack oven. Cook the "pain" for an hour and a quarter and leave to cool for four hours; unmold, take off the pork to smooth the surfaces neatly, then glaze and decorate with fanciful cuts of gherkin, red beef tongue and truffles dipped in half-set jelly. Dress on a bread croûton covered with ravigote butter (No. 583) and decorate around with chopped jelly and croûtons (No. 2442).

(2548). "PAIN" OF PARTRIDGES À LA MONTGOMERY (Pain de Perdreaux à la Montgomery).

Cut three raw partridges in pieces as for a sautéd chicken, fry with chopped fat pork, truffles, mushrooms, fine herbs, salt, aromatics and spices; when well done, put aside to cool, remove the meat and divide in half-inch squares, then pound and add nine egg-yolks, half a pound of foies-gras, and three-quarters of a pound of flour and milk panada (No. 121); when a smooth pulp is obtained press it through a sieve and mingle in six ounces of salted, unsmoked red beef tongue, nine ounces of truffles, and fifteen ounces of udder, all to be cut into three-sixteenths inch dice. Fill a plain oval dome-shaped mold six inches long by four inches wide with the preparation; cover with fat pork, and then set it in a sautoir with a little water and cook in a slack oven for three hours; turn it out after it is thoroughly cold, remove the fat pork, smooth the surfaces and set it in a larger mold decorated with truffles, coated with a light coat of white jelly (No. 103), and another one of white chaudfroid (No. 596); finish filling the mold with jelly, and when exceedingly cold invert it on a bread support two inches high covered with lobster butter (No. 580); surround with chopped jelly, and garnish around the support with jelly croûtons and cases of thrushes prepared as follows: Bone some thrushes, keeping one leg on each that must not be boned; stuff the birds with game forcemeat (No. 91), season with salt, pepper, mushrooms, parsley and truffles, all to be finely chopped.

Fig. 517.

Then also cook some whole truffles, rounded to an inch in diameter, and when both of these are cold glaze the birds over with brown chaudfroid (No. 594), and decorate the leg with a favor frill (No. 10); lay the thrushes in oval cases, and the truffles in small round ones; arrange all of them around the support intercalating the birds and truffles.

(2549). "PAIN" OF YOUNG RABBIT (Pain de Levraut).

Suppress all the meats from a young rabbit, also the skin and sinews, and use the bones to make a game fumet (No. 397). Fry in butter the large fillets, the minion fillets and the leg meats; as soon as they are cooked take them out of the sautoir. When cold pound the leg meats finely, adding the fillets, and minion fillets then pound again with half as much cooked foies-gras, season and rub through a fine sieve. Put this pulp into a thin metal basin, and beat it for a few moments with a spoon in order to have it smooth, and incorporate into it slowly three gills of brown chaudfroid (No. 594), some game glaze (No. 398), and melted gelatine. Try a little of this preparation on ice to judge its consistency, and if not correct thicken it at once by beating it for a few moments longer on the ice, while mixing in more melted gelatine add two ounces of fresh butter broken into small bits, and when of a proper consistency stir in a few spoonfuls of cooked truffles cut in dice pieces, and an equal quantity of red beef tongue cut the same. Pour the whole into a plain cylinder mold coated over with a little half-set jelly applied with a brush, and imbed the mold on chopped ice; harden the contents for a couple of hours, then unmold it on a cold dish; surround with chopped jelly and croûtons (No. 2442).

(2550). ROAST LARDED PARTRIDGES (Perdreaux Piqués et Rôtis).

Truss two partridges after singeing, drawing and cleaning them well; lard them and roast either on the spit or in the oven. Let get cold, and when ready to use glaze them over with a brush dipped in game glaze (No. 398), and dress, either whole or cut up, on a dish and surround with jelly.

(2551). PORK LIVER PIE OR TERRINE (Pâté ou Terrine de Foies de Porc).

Terrine.—Take three pounds of the breast of fresh pork, chop it finely into a forcemeat; chop separately two pounds of pig's liver after soaking it in cold water and straining through a sieve. Put the whole into a vessel large enough to have all thoroughly mixed, add one-third of an ounce of salt for each pound and one coffeespoonful of pepper for the same quantity, prepared red pepper (No. 168), nutmeg to taste, a pinch of chopped parsley, a bay leaf, a pinch of thyme, six eggs and three and a half ounces of flour; stir the whole thoroughly until a very smooth paste is obtained. Line the bottom of one or several earthen jars, fit to be put in the oven, with slices of fat pork, then fill them with the paste; cover with another slice, having notched the fibrous parts; place it in the oven and let bake slowly. A terrine weighing four to five pounds requires three to four hours to bake. When done drain off the fat and replace it with good melted leaf lard, cover with a board and place a two-pound weight on top. After it is cold cover with a light layer of lard, and serve either in the same jar, or else cut it with a spoon.

Pie.—The above preparation can also be made into a pie by baking it in a mold, proceeding as directed in No. 2557.

(2552). ROAST PEACOCK ADORNED WITH ITS PLUMAGE (Paon Rôti et Paré de son Plumage)

Procure a young peacock with very brilliant plumage; cut off half of the rump with the tail feathers attached to it and spread them into a fan, then dry; also remove the wings with their plumage and the head with all the beautiful neck feathers as far down as the breast, including the skin; stuff the neck with wadding and insert a stiff wire in the middle to hold it in its natural position. Pick the peacock, draw, singe and free it of feathers; truss for roasting (No. 179) and stuff with a dressing made with a pound of soaked and well-pressed bread-crumbs, the same quantity of chopped beef marrow, and season with spices (No. 168), chopped shallot fried colorless in butter and raw liver chopped up finely. Cook in a moderate oven, basting over frequently with butter, and when cold dish it up on a carved rice socle; adorn it with its plumage; surround with chopped jelly and a border of jelly croûtons (No. 2442) and serve separately a cold poivrade sauce (No. 620).

(2553). PHEASANT STUFFED À LA PRINCE ORLOFF (Faisan Farci à la Prince Orloff).

Open a fresh pheasant through the back; bone it, leaving on the pinions and drumsticks, then season the meats. Take all the meat from another fresh pheasant and chop it up finely, mixing in an equal quantity of chopped fresh fat pork; season this forcemeat and add to it a quarter of its quantity of cooked foies-gras cut in large dice and as much truffles. Use this preparation to fill the boned pheasant, bring the meats together and sew it up, giving it its original form; truss and brush over with butter, then wrap it in a fine cloth, tying it well, and cook it very slowly for an hour and a quarter in good stock (No. 194a). Drain off the pheasant, untie and wrap it again in the same cloth after washing it, then let get cold. One hour before serving unwrap the pheasant, separate the back from the breast, cutting it off, then divide this in two lengthwise pieces; cut the two halves in transversal slices, reshape and put the breast back into its former place from whence it was taken. Cover the whole pheasant with a white chaudfroid sauce (No. 596) reduced with pheasant fumet (No. 397) and afterward thickened on ice. Place the pheasant on ice till needed and then decorate the pinions with paper frills (No. 10); now dress it on a small oval foundation covered over with white paper and fastened on a long dish; surround it with a thick cord of chopped jelly pushed through a pocket, and decorate the edges of the dish with jelly croûtons (No. 2442) and two clusters of medium-sized stuffed truffles.

(2554). CHICKEN PIE—TO BE CUT UP (Pâté de Poulet pour Découper).

Procure two oblong corrugated pie molds ten inches long, four inches high and four inches wide, buttered with cold butter; stand them on a sheet of buttered paper, and line with pie paste (No. 144). Bone thoroughly four tender chickens of about two and a half pounds each; suppress the fat and thigh sinews, also the minion fillets; season with No. 2 pie spices (No. 168). Put into a vessel some ham, tongue, truffles and fat pork, all cut in three-eighths of an inch squares; season and baste with Madeira wine. Prepare a forcemeat with one pound of finely chopped pork free from sinews, and one pound of fresh fat pork; mix together and chop once more; season. Cover the bottom and sides of the paste with this forcemeat, and fill the pie in alternate layers with chicken forcemeat and the salpicon, finishing the whole with forcemeat; cover with thin slices of fat pork; on top place a bay leaf and a sprig of thyme. Cover with a flat of the same paste, fasten both together, clip off the surplus paste around the edge, form and pinch a crest, and cover the whole with another flat made of puff paste parings (No. 146); egg over and cook in a slack oven for two hours. Should the crust brown too quickly, lay over a double sheet of wetted paper, and when the pie is done remove and let cool partly; fill it up with consistent jelly made from the fragments of chicken, and after the pie is thoroughly cold cut it into slices, and dress in a straight row on a cold dish surrounded by chopped jelly and croûtons (No. 2442).

(2555). DUCKLING PIE À LA ROUENNAISE (Pâté de Caneton à la Rouennaise).

Prepare two pounds of cold pie paste (No. 144), having it rather firm; let it rest for an hour and a half in a cool place. Cut off the pinions, legs and necks from two clean ducklings, bone them entirely, leave the fillets adhering to the skin, remove half the fillet through its thickness and lay on the skin that has no fillet, and detach the meat from the legs to suppress the sinews, then chop up finely; in with this mix a pound and three-quarters of boned turkey forcemeat (No. 65); pound both together for a few moments with four ounces of chopped truffles and four ounces of raw chopped ham, seasoning with No. 2 pie spices (No. 168). Place this forcemeat in a bowl and add to it a third of its volume of baked liver forcemeat (No. 64), passed through a sieve, also a few spoonfuls of cooked fine herbs (No. 385) and half a pound of blanched fat pork cut in quarter-inch squares. Prick the skin of the boned ducklings with a larding needle and fill their insides with a part of the forcemeat, placing the liver well seasoned in the center; reshape the duck to its original appearance. With the bones and parings prepare a succulent stock. Place on a small baking sheet covered with strong, well buttered paper a smooth oval hinged mold; line this mold with two-thirds of the paste and cover the bottom and sides with thin slices of fat pork; on this place a layer of the forcemeat and set one of the stuffed ducklings on the bottom, then cover over with more forcemeat and another duckling on top, finishing with the remainder of the forcemeat, having it dome-shaped on the top, then cover with thin slices of fat pork and over this place a flat of the same paste; press it down on the base of the dome and against the projecting edges of paste to fasten the two together; cut away any surplus paste close to the edges and pinch it with a pair of pincers, or else decorate the dome with fanciful cuts of the same paste; cut a small hole exactly in the center, which is intended to act as a chimney for the steam to escape. Egg over the surface and set the pie in a moderate oven; as soon as it begins to brown cover over with paper and cook for an hour and a half. An hour after the pie has been removed from the oven pour in through the opening on top a few spoonfuls of duck fumet (No. 397) reduced to a half-glaze and mixed with a little Madeira wine and jelly; close the opening with a pad of paste. Half an hour later take off the mold and let the pie cool for twelve hours before serving.

(2556). GAME PIE DRESSED À LA LESAGE (Pâté de Gibier Dressé à la Lesage).

Prepare six pounds of cold pie paste, the same being described in No. 144; after it has well rested roll out three-quarters of it to three-eighths of an inch in thickness; raise the paste with the hands several times, leaving it rest between each; place it on a sheet of buttered paper, and when it attains the height of about six inches, is rounded and properly equalized, thicker on the bottom than on the top, then pinch on the outside a row toward the right, another toward the left, and wrap several strong sheets of buttered paper around and tie with several strings. Fill the bottom and sides with bards of fat pork, and on the bottom spread a layer of forcemeat made of three pounds of pork meat, one pound of young rabbit meat, four pounds of fat pork, six ounces of prepared No. 2 pie spices (No. 168), and ten egg-yolks. Having finely chopped and pounded all these ingredients together, spread a layer in the bottom of the pie, and over it place a boned pheasant with the inside meats larded with fat pork and ham, and seasoned with salt, pepper, nutmeg, chopped parsley, chives and chopped bay leaf, and filled with some of this same forcemeat. Bone twelve woodcock and prepare them the same as the pheasant. Cut into three-sixteenth inch squares some carrots and onions; fry the onions first in butter, add the carrots and the woodcock intestines; moisten with a little broth and Madeira wine, and as soon as done (that is, when the moisture is thoroughly reduced) pound all finely and press through a sieve; let stand till cold, then mix into it some of the above forcemeat, adding eight ounces of cooked lean ham cut in one-eighth inch squares, and four ounces of chopped truffle peelings. Fill the boned woodcock, and in the center of each lay a small peeled truffle. Place eight of these birds around the pheasant, cover with more of the forcemeat, and in the center set the four remaining ones, with whole truffles laid around, also eight partridge fillets larded with lardons (No. 3, Fig. 52), and seasoned; cover with more of the forcemeat to form a dome, and on this lay thin slices of fat pork and a little thyme and bay leaf on top. Wet the edges of the pie, and lay over a cover of the rolled-out paste; fasten both together, cut the crust straight, equalize it and pinch it all around; make a chimney on the top, place several rows of noodle paste (No. 142) leaves on, and in the center arrange a noodle paste artichoke made as follows: Take a flat of paste about one-sixteenth of an inch thick, fold it in two three times, then roll it in a ball an inch and a quarter across, make two cross-shape incisions half an inch deep on the centre of the ball so as to divide it in eight parts partly open to represent an antichoke; egg over several times and bake in a moderate oven for three or four hours; leave it to cool partly, then fill the pie either with game fumet (No. 397) mixed with jelly or with chaudfroid (No. 594) made with essence of game (No. 397) or else with fresh butter and lard mixed, half and half. Filling it in this way the pie will keep much longer. It will take nearly twenty-four hours to thoroughly cool off a pie of this size.

(2557). GOOSE PIE À LA ADOLPHE HARDY—FILLETS (Pâté de Filets d'Oie à la Adolphe Hardy).

The Crust for the Pie.—Make a pie paste with three pounds of flour and one pound of butter, as described in pie paste No. 144; keep it in a cool place to rest for two hours. Have a round, plain, bottomless mold six and a half inches in diameter by six inches in height; line it with some strong buttered paper. Roll out three-quarters of the paste to a round, eighteen inches in diameter and half an inch in thickness; dredge it with flour; fold it in two, and bring the two ends toward the center in the shape of a pocket; equalize the thickness of the paste by using the rolling pin. Line the unbuttered mold with it, pressing it against the sides, and having it a little thicker toward the bottom; leave for two hours on ice, unmold and pinch it all around, beginning at the bottom and inclining the pinching toward the left, and the second row toward the right; surround the pie by another mold, a quarter of an inch wider and a quarter of an inch higher than the last one; fill the bottom and sides of the pie with sheets of buttered paper, and fill it either with rice or very dry flour; cover over with a round of paper, wet the upper edges and over the top lay a flat of the same paste; fasten the two together and cut away the paste from the border, three-quarters of an inch higher than the mold; pinch it all around and on top; cut a hole in the center, and insert therein a cardboard tube, called a chimney. Decorate the cover or dome with leaves or flowers made of thin noodle paste (No. 142), brush with egg twice, and leave for one hour in the ice-box; form a small artichoke (No. 2556) of exceedingly thin noodle paste; egg it over twice and bake it in a small noodle-paste ring. Bake the pie crust or timbale in a moderate oven for one hour, having it assume a beautiful color; as soon as done cut off the cover at the base of the dome by slipping a small thin knife between the two pastes; remove the cover, empty the inside rice and paper, and glaze the interior with a brush dipped in melted meat glaze.

Terrine of Goose Fillets.—Have half a pound of the kernel or bottom round of veal, remove the sinews, chop and pound it up finely. Chop separately a pound of fresh fat pork, mix the two together, season with pie spices (No. 168), and pound the whole, incorporating in slowly one gill of stock (No. 194a). Lard some goose fillets with medium lardons (No. 2, Fig. 52); season with salt, pepper and nutmeg. Cover the bottom and sides of a No. 3 terrine (about two quarts) with thin slices of fat pork, masking over with a layer of the above forcemeat; lay in the fillets more forcemeat and some small, whole, peeled truffles, having alternate layers, and finishing with forcemeat well rounded on top; cover with a bard of fat pork, then the lid, and cook for about an hour and a half in a slack oven; let get cold under a light pressure, leaving it on for twenty-four hours; unmold the terrine, suppress all the fat, and lay the contents inside the timbale or pie crust. Cook half a pound of leaf lard, half a pound of butter and the fat suppressed from the terrine; when clarified pass it through a strainer, leave to cool without having it set, then pour it into the pie; lay on the cover and finish filling with more of the fat. Pull out the cardboard chimney, range the paste artichoke on top, and let the pie get thoroughly cold in the ice-box for twelve hours.

(2558). HAM PIE (Pâté de Jambon).

Select a fresh, smoked ham, detach the kernel and under kernel; free these meats from their hard parts and cut them into inch and a half squares: if the meat be very salty it will require un-salting either in water or milk for a few hours before cutting up; lard each piece with a bit of truffle, passing it through from one side to the other. Melt half a pound of lard and when hot add to it the squares of ham and fry for a few moments only. Prepare a chopped forcemeat (No. 65); mix in four ounces of chopped truffle parings, pound the whole and add half a pound of lean and finely chopped cooked ham, and half a pound of fat pork cut in small three-sixteenths inch squares; season with red and white pepper, nutmeg and a little salt. Line a cold pie mold with short paste (No. 135), cover the bottom and sides of this with a layer of the prepared hash and fill the center, alternating the squares of ham with another layer of the hash; finish by giving it a dome form on top and cover with bards of fat pork; moisten the inside of the crest with a brush, then add a layer of paste; form this into a pretty crest, pinch the top and sides, egg over twice and range a puff paste (No. 146) cover over the whole, having it only a quarter of an inch thick; egg this twice also, score the entire surface and form a chimney in the center of the paste. Bake for three hours to three hours and a half. Should the pie brown too quickly cover over with strong, wetted paper. Two hours after removing it from the oven pour sufficient good jelly (No. 103) through the chimney to fill it well.

(2559). HARE PIE IN A DISH (Pâté de Lièvre dans un Plat).

Remove the meats from two young hares, keep the tenderloins and minion fillets apart and pare the remainder, suppressing all the skin and sinews; cut the meats into pieces and range them in a sautoir with half a pound of grated fat pork, the liver, the lights, and a tablespoonful of finely chopped onions; toss the whole over a brisk fire without letting it attain color, then take off to cool; chop and pound with three-quarters of a pound of grated fresh fat pork and four ounces of fresh pork tenderloins. Pare the reserved tenderloins and minion fillets, cut them in half-inch squares and add to them half a pound of peeled and cut-up truffles; season with salt and pepper and throw over a gill of Madeira wine and as much brandy. Two hours later put in the cooked meats. Line a deep pie dish, fit to go in the oven, with thin slices of fat pork, pour in the preparation and cover with a slice of the same pork, thyme and bay leaf, then lay over a foundation paste (No. 135) cover, egg it twice and bake in a moderate oven; when done allow to cool, remove both cover and pork, clean the dish, place on a folded napkin, then decorate the edges of the pie dish with a border of jelly croûtons and the center with chopped jelly.

(2560). HARE PIE WITHOUT A MOLD (Pâté de Lièvre Sans Moule).

Cut some large fillets from the back of a hare, divide them into good-sized square lardons (No. 1, Fig 52) and lay them in a vessel with as much fat pork cut exactly the same size and shape and a few raw truffles cut likewise; season highly and pour over a few spoonfuls of Madeira wine or brandy. Cut off the meats from the legs and shoulders, lay them in a frying pan with melted fat pork and an equal quantity of cut-up calf's liver; season and fry over a brisk fire; as soon as the meats are brown remove to cool; pound and rub this through a sieve, then add this forcemeat to as much chopped fresh pork, raw, pounded and seasoned highly and mixed with cooked fine herbs (No. 385). Roll out on a floured table a flat of cold pie paste (No. 144) twenty inches long by fifteen wide; spread it on a baking sheet and cover the center with a layer of the prepared forcemeat, giving it an oblong shape; then alternate the garnishing and the forcemeat, the last layer being forcemeat, and cover this with thin slices of fat pork. Moisten the edges of the paste, fold over the flaps on the sides so as to enclose the contents, roll out the ends, moisten the top and bring these ends over on the center, wet again and cover with a three-sixteenths of an inch oval flat of puff paste (No. 146), sufficiently large to cover the pie; on this flat make small openings to act as chimneys; put in pasteboard cylinders to uphold the paste. Egg over the paste and score it with the tip of a small knife. Place the pie in a moderate oven to bake, covering the top with sheets of buttered paper, and let cook for two hours. A quarter of an hour after taking it from the oven pour into the holes a few spoonfuls of game fumet (No. 397) mixed with a little Madeira wine and melted jelly (No. 103), then set it aside to cool for twelve hours before serving. This same method may be employed for the preparation of chicken, game or fish pies.

(2561). LAMB PIE—LOIN (Pâté de Longe d'Agneau).

Bone two loins and two shoulders of spring lamb; cut the loin meats into squares, lard them with larding pork and season with salt, pepper, nutmeg and spices. Chop up the shoulder meats free of all sinews and fat and add to it the same weight of fat pork, season with salt, pepper, nutmeg and spice, then pound the whole in a mortar, mixing in a little Madeira wine. Clean well and butter a pie mold, line it with ordinary pie paste (No. 144) and cover the bottom and sides with thin slices of fat pork; mask these with a layer of the forcemeat and place some slices of cooked ham on the bottom, then a layer of the forcemeat and the larded squares over, finishing with more forcemeat, having the mold quite full and rounded on the top; cover with bards of fat pork and in the center place a bay leaf and a sprig of thyme. Cover the pie with a flat of paste, having a raised edge on the border, pinch it all around and decorate the top with imitation leaves cut from puff or noodle paste and a paste artichoke (No. 2556) in the center. Egg the surfaces and cook in a medium oven, then fill up with jelly when the pie is thoroughly cold.

(2562). GOOSE LIVER PIE (Pâté de Foies-Gras).

This cold pie, as shown in Fig. 518, is intended for very large suppers. Make a preparation the same as terrine of foies-gras, cook it in a long square-shaped tin mold and let get cold under a weight; keep it for five or six hours on ice. Butter a tastefully decorated cold pie mold, lay it on a

FIG. 518.

baking sheet covered with strong buttered paper, and line it with foundation paste (No. 135) made with egg-yolks; cover the bottom and sides with buttered paper, and fill it up with common flour, then cover with another buttered paper, and close the opening on top with a flat of the same paste, fastening the two edges together; cut the top straight and pinch it prettily, then egg it over. Cook this paste for one hour and a quarter in a slack oven, so that it acquires a fine color, and as soon as it is removed open it by cutting the cover on a level with the edges and lift it off and empty out the contents; dry the inside for a few moments at a warm heater. When the crust is thoroughly cold unfasten the hinges of the mold so as to remove it, then glaze over the inside with a brush; cover the bottom with a layer of chopped jelly, and on this dress the terrine preparation cut in slices, having them in long squares of equal size and thickness; put the poorest ones at the bottom, and when this garnishing has reached nearly to the top finish filling with the prettiest slices, dressing them in a compact circle, and filling the inside of this with fine chopped jelly. Fasten the pie on a cold dish, surround the base with croûtons of jelly (No. 2442), and on top of the chopped jelly lay a fine truffle, peeled and cooked in wine.

(2563). GOOSE LIVER PIE, CUT UP (Pâté de Foies-Gras Découpé).

This entrée is dressed on a crescent-shaped support, slightly circular, and made of tin; cover it with noodle (No. 142) or cooked paste (No. 131); this support should not be fastened on the center of the dish; being of a half-circular form it should stand at one side on the edge of the hollow center so that the garnishing can be dressed inside the crescent. Prepare a chopped forcemeat for game pie (No. 67); season it highly and mix with it an equal quantity of baking liver forcemeat (No. 86), pounded and passed through a sieve. Cut into large fillets one good raw foies-gras, set them in a bowl with raw, peeled and quartered truffles; season and pour over a few spoonfuls of Madeira wine or brandy. Butter a large cradle mold, line it with thin foundation paste (No. 135), and fill the bottom and around with the prepared forcemeat; on top of this range the foies-gras, fillets and truffles; cover over with more of the forcemeat, having it slightly rounded on the top, and set over this a flat of the same paste, fastening it well on the outer edges. Make a small opening in the center of the cover, egg it over, then lay this pie on a baking sheet and push it into a moderate oven to cook for one hour and a quarter, being careful to cover the paste with a buttered paper as fast as it browns. After removing it from the fire, pour into the opening a few spoonfuls of jelly (No. 103), mixed with a little melted glaze (No. 402) and Madeira wine. Before cutting the pie into slices it must be unmolded and kept for twenty-four hours in a cool place, so that the paste is slightly softened, otherwise it will be likely to crumble when cutting. Have the slices all of equal thickness, and dress them neatly in a half circle on the support. In the empty space it has formed range a tasteful cluster of round and peeled truffles cooked in wine and glazed over; surround these truffles and the pie with a thick piping of chopped jelly forced through a cornet.

(2564). COLD STRASBURG LIVER PIE (Pâté de Foies-Gras de Strasbourg).

Line a pie mold the same as No. 2557. Prepare a forcemeat with half a pound of very fresh lean pork, and half a pound of exceedingly white and fresh lean veal, free of all sinews and fat,

Fig. 519.

and both chopped finely and separately; chop up the same weight of fat pork, and a half pound of liver; pound and pass through a sieve; pound also half a pound of cooked lean ham with some truffle peelings; rub this also through a sieve, and mix the whole together, seasoning with foies-gras spices (No. 168). Cover the bottom and sides of the pie with a thick layer of this forcemeat, place a fine well-seasoned goose liver in the center, then some peeled truffles, and cover with more forcemeat, rounding it well on top; finish the pie the same as No. 2557, baking it in a slack oven for three hours or more, according to its size; when cold fill it with butter and lard mixed together.

(2565). QUAIL PIE (Pâté de Cailles).

Prepare a forcemeat as described in No. 67, and press through a sieve; mix into it a quarter of a pound of plain foies-gras cut in quarter-inch squares; have twelve small peeled truffles. Bone twelve quails, leaving them whole; season and fill with the above forcemeat, and in the center lay one of the truffles; enclose the contents well. Butter a low pie mold, line it with foundation paste (No. 135), and cover the sides and bottom with thin slices of fat pork; over this set a layer of the forcemeat, and then a bed of the quails on the bottom; on top of these place more forcemeat containing a salpicon of fat pork and red beef tongue, mixed with an equal quantity of the forcemeat, then another bed of the quails, and finish with forcemeat raised to a dome. Cover with a thin bard of fat pork, some bay leaves, and a flat of the same paste; smooth the summit; pinch all around and on top, and decorate the dome with noodle paste leaves; egg over twice, and bake the pie for two hours and a half; cool partly and then fill with jelly (No. 103) made of quail fumet (No. 397) and Madeira wine.

(2566). SALMON PIE (Pâté de Saumon).

Cut four pounds of fresh salmon meat into large fillets; season them with salt and pepper, and put them in a vessel with two or three raw truffles also cut in fillets; pour over a little Madeira wine and leave to macerate for one hour. With some raw pike or gurnet, the salmon parings, panada, butter or veal udder and egg-yolks prepare a delicate forcemeat (No. 90), and when strained place it in a vessel to beat smooth and mix in with it a few spoonfuls of cooked fine herbs (No. 385), and the fish marinade. Butter an oblong metal pie mold selected proportionately to the quantity of fish and forcemeat, lay it on a baking sheet covered with paper and line it with cold pie paste (No. 144). Mask the bottom and sides of this paste with a layer of the forcemeat and in the hollow center dress the fillets of salmon and truffles, alternated by layers of forcemeat; the mold should be full so that when cooked there remains little or no empty space (the top layer must be of the forcemeat). Wet the edges of the paste and cover over with a flat of the same, fastening it on the edges; then cut away the paste on a level with the mold and pinch it all around. Cover the top surface above the border with a fake cover—meaning a simple layer of puff paste (No. 146) cut the same shape as the top of the pie—and in the center of this make a small opening; egg over and decorate the top with designs made with the tip of a small knife, and cook for an hour and a half in a moderate oven, being careful to cover the paste with paper as soon as it becomes dry. A quarter of an hour after the pie has been removed from the oven pour into the hole on top a few spoonfuls of good jelly (No. 103) mixed with fish essence (No. 395) and reduced to a half-glaze, also a few spoonfuls of Madeira wine. Let it get cold for ten hours. At the last moment cut the pie into slices, and dress these, one overlapping the other on a long dish, and surround with chopped jelly and jelly croûtons.

(2567). SNIPE PIE (Pâté de Bécassines).

Peel and cook some truffles in a little Madeira wine, cut them in four and season; singe and bone ten snipe, season them, and with their intestines, a few good chicken livers, some fragments of ham and aromatic herbs, prepare a baking forcemeat (No. 64). Have a chopped game forcemeat (No. 67), pound and mix with it the baking forcemeat in equal quantity, a bit of garlic, and the truffle parings; force the whole through a sieve. With some cold pie paste (No. 144) line a low-hinged bottomless mold, place it on a baking sheet over buttered paper, and cover the bottom and sides with the prepared forcemeat; in the hollow center dress the snipe, alternated with more of the chopped forcemeat and the quartered truffles; pile up the mold, cover with thin bards of fat pork, then with a layer of the same paste, fastening it on the edge of the under paste; cut it away evenly and pinch the edges; make a small hole in the top of the dome and decorate the latter with a few imitation noodle paste leaves (No. 142), then egg over both top and border. Cook the pie for an hour and a half to two hours in a moderate oven; after it has been removed pour into the hole on top some game fumet (No. 397) and finish it the same as a duckling pie (No. 2555). Let it be remembered that if all game pies, such as partridge, pheasant, reedbird, etc., have a slight bit of garlic mixed in with the forcemeat it will add greatly to the aroma, that is if it be not too predominant.

(2568). VEAL AND HAM PIE (Pâté de Veau et de Jambon).

Butter a large pie mold, line it with pie paste (No. 144), and lay it on a buttered paper, and this on a tart plate; garnish the insides with thin slices of fat pork. Fill the bottom and sides with forcemeat made with two pounds of fresh pork and veal, half of each, and two pounds of fat pork; season with salt, pepper and fine herbs; on this forcemeat lay slices of cooked lean ham, and over a layer of forcemeat; on this a layer of thick slices of kernel of veal larded with fat pork (No. 2, Fig. 53), and seasoned highly; put in more forcemeat with finely chopped lean ham; place slices of fat pork over, and a bit of thyme and bay leaf; cover with a flat of the same paste, forming a crest, pinch the edges and egg over twice; on top lay a cover of puff paste (No. 146); make a hole in the center to act as a chimney. Egg over twice; bake in a moderate oven for two hours and a half. To be well assured of its being done thrust a trussing needle through, and if it penetrates easily and comes out hot and dry, then the pie is sufficiently cooked; when cold fill with jelly.

(2569). WOODCOCK PIE (Pâté de Bécasses).

Bone six woodcocks, remove the pouches and gizzards, and fry the intestines by mixing in with them two pounds of game forcemeat (No. 67); pound and pass them through a sieve. Fry the fragments of the birds in butter with a small mirepoix of onions, carrots, thyme, bay leaf and celery root, all cut in small dice. Bone twelve larks, season and fill them with the boned turkey forcemeat mixed with their intestines previously fried in butter; press through a sieve, and season with fine spices (No. 168) and brandy. Line a pie mold with pie paste (No. 144); cover the bottom and sides with thin slices of fat pork, and at the bottom lay three of the woodcocks and six of the larks; then another bed of the forcemeat, the three other woodcocks and the six other larks; finish with more forcemeat and a bard of fat pork; wet the inside edge, cover with a flat of paste, and fasten it down; smooth the top nicely, pinch it all around and on the summit, and bake in a moderate oven; when cold fill the pie with partly cold jelly (No. 103) prepared with game fumet (No. 397).

(2570). PIG'S HEAD (Tête ou Hure de Porc).

Have a well scalded and cleaned pig's head, singe and bone without destroying the skin, beginning from underneath; fill it with layers of fine pork forcemeat (No. 68), placing on each one some lardons of fat pork (No. 1, Fig. 52), pistachios, truffles and quenelle forcemeat (No. 89), into which chopped-up ham has been mixed, and then rolled into the same sized pieces as the lardons. When the head is filled sew it up and reshape it as before, then wrap it in a cloth and cook in a stock (No. 194a) for four hours; unwrap and return it to the cloth to give it the shape of the head; unwrap once more, pare well, glaze over with meat glaze (No. 402), and dress on a low socle; put in glass eyes and place natural fangs in the mouth; decorate the head with tongue, hard-boiled egg-white and pistachios; surround with chopped jelly and a border of croûtons (No. 2442).

(2571). LARDED PULLET WITH JELLY (Poularde Piquée à la Gelée).

Break the breastbone of a not too fat pullet; fill in the breast and stomach with a large salpicon made of cooked veal udder, truffles and cooked foies-gras, mixed with a little fine galantine

FIG. 520.

forcemeat (No. 65). Cut the legs from the pullet, truss, and steep the breast for two minutes in boiling water to stiffen the meats and facilitate the larding with lardons (No. 3, Fig. 52). Cook the pullet in a little stock (No. 194a), basting over frequently; finally glaze it at the oven door. When cold untruss, detach the legs and cut each of them in two, then cut both breasts in slices and return them to their former place. Lay the pullet on a wooden foundation covered with white paper and fastened on a dish; rearrange the two pieces of each leg, thrusting a small hatelet through, in their original places, only in a contrary direction; on each pinion set a pretty favor frill (No. 10). Surround the pullet with a thick piping of chopped jelly forced through a cornet and the bottom of the dish with a row of round peeled truffles all of the same size, then cook in wine and glaze over with a brush. A mayonnaise with fine herb sauce (No. 612) can always accompany this cold piece.

(2572). PYRAMID OF CRUSTACEANS À LA ROCHELAISE AND PYRAMID OF CRAWFISH
(Buisson de Crustacés à la Rochelaise et Buisson d'Écrevisses).

To be able to dress this entrée correctly it will be found necessary to fasten a wooden foundation on a dish, having it two inches narrower than the basin of the dish itself; cover it with white paper and in the center attach a wooden support also to be covered with paper; this latter must be in the shape of a pyramid, its base measuring four and a half inches, its top two inches and

FIG. 521.

its height four inches; cover its surface with a layer of butter. This pyramid or buisson is to be composed simply of large slices of lobster tails and of red shrimps, after suppressing their beards. The shrimps are stuck into the butter on the pyramid in regular circles, but having each row lay in a contrary direction; the slices of lobster are also laid in close circles just on top of the rows of shrimps. As soon as all are dressed cover both shrimps and lobster with half-set jelly applied with a brush. In order to insure its safety it is advisable to push a thick string of sticky jelly (No. 2526) through a cornet, exactly underneath the circle of lobster slices, so as to give them a good support. The hollow formed by the upper row of shrimps can be filled in with chopped jelly or parsley leaves, or else with a crimped paper case filled with a round truffle. Surround the bottom of the dish with a chain of pretty jelly croûtons (No. 2442) cut into oblongs, having one overlap the other. Keep the buisson in a cold room and serve it with a sauce-boat of mayonnaise sauce (No. 606).

Pyramid of Crawfish.—Crawfish intended for this dish should be chosen as large as possible and cooked in a white wine court-bouillon (No. 39), then left to cool in the stock. When cold break off the small legs. Generally a buisson of shellfish is dressed on a tin step shelf made with projecting ledges, each one furnished with hooks on which the crawfish can be hung; these ledges are movable and are placed at any desired distance from each other, according to the length of the fish, but there must be no openings left between. The pyramid ought first to be fastened on to the center of a large dish and the empty space filled in with parsley leaves or water cress; surround the base with a bush of green, then fasten on the crawfish by the tails, beginning at the lower ledge. Between the edge of the dish and the pyramid dress the remainder of the crawfish, laying them down flat with the heads turned outward and the claws hanging over. This pyramid after being dressed should be laid on a large tray; have this placed in the center of the table. The green and the pronounced red of the crawfish form a pleasant contrast for the eye to rest upon.

(2573). SADDLE OF VENISON À LA HARDER (Selle de Chevreuil à la Harder).

Roast to a fine color a medium-sized saddle of venison, after having marinated it for two days, and then larded it with lardons (No. 2, Fig. 52); glaze and let stand till cold, then raise up the sirloin part and cut it in pretty slices, either bias or lengthwise. Add to some Madeira poivrade sauce (No. 620) the same quantity of jelly; reduce, despumate and pass it through a tammy; put it away on ice to cool, stirring it incessantly in the meantime until very nearly cold, then dip each slice into this chaudfroid and restore them to their respective places, reshaping the saddle as originally, and entirely cover over with the chaudfroid; then dress on a long dish. Place around on a bed of jelly some artichoke bottoms, having some garnished with small carrot balls, others with turnips, others with cauliflower, others with string beans cut lozenge-shape, and others with English green peas; all of these vegetables to be cooked separately, cooled, well seasoned and mixed with a little jellied mayonnaise (No. 613). At the ends place two fine cauliflowers boiled in salted water and butter, left to cool in their liquid, then drained properly and laid in a vessel to have a seasoning poured over of oil, tarragon vinegar, salt and pepper; baste several times with this seasoning, then drain and cover with jellied mayonnaise. Around the whole lay a pretty border of evenly cut jelly croûtons (No. 2442).

(2574). COLD SALMIS OF PARTRIDGES (Salmis Froid de Perdreaux).

Roast two partridges, cut them up, being careful to have all the pieces nicely pared, and to suppress the skin, leaving on as little bone as possible; range these when prepared on a small baking sheet and keep them in a cool place; have also a round serving dish laid aside on the ice. Prepare a salmis sauce (No. 536) with the parings and bones; strain it into a small saucepan to cool, while stirring occasionally, then incorporate into it slowly two spoonfuls of Madeira wine and several more of good cold jelly (No. 103); beat this on ice to thicken as a chaudfroid sauce. Dip each piece of game singly into this sauce to envelop thoroughly; drain and dress in a pyramid form in the center of a cold dish, reserving the choicest pieces for the top; leave the entrée on ice for another quarter of an hour. Garnish the wings and legs with paper frills (No. 10), surround the base of the pyramid with chopped jelly or croûtons of jelly (No. 2442), and small glazed truffles laid in cases.

(2575). COLD SALMIS OF QUAILS À LA BALZAC (Salmis Froid de Cailles à la Balzac).

Roast eight quails; remove the breasts and break up the legs and bones. Fry some shallots in butter, moisten with white wine and half-glaze sauce (No. 413); put in the broken-up carcasses and let simmer for twenty minutes, then strain through a sieve, and add two gelatine leaves, so as to thicken to a good consistency. Decorate some pigeon ballotine molds, the same as ballotines à la Madison (No. 2427), with fanciful cuts of egg-white and tongue; coat with jelly and lay the breasts in the center; finish filling with the cooled-off jelly; unmold the ballotines, range them in a circle on a bread socle covered with green butter (No. 583), and fill the center with chopped jelly, and around with croûtons (No. 2442).

(2576). SALMON DARNE, DECORATED (Darne de Saumon Historiée).

Cut a darne or thick five-inch slice from the middle of a large salmon after it has been scaled, emptied and cleaned. Lay it straight on the grate of a fish-kettle, salt it over liberally and let it macerate for half an hour. Boil in court-bouillon (No. 38). (It should remain at the boiling point until cooked.) Leaving it in the fish-kettle until thoroughly cold, drain off the darne, then remove the skin, wipe the fish, and cover the surfaces with a thin layer of Montpellier butter (No. 582),

Fig. 522.

softened to a proper degree. Slide the darne at once on to a wooden dish foundation covered over with white paper; smooth the butter well, and set it aside in a cool place to harden. Fill the hollow in the center of the darne with a variegated vegetable salad; decorate the top with strips of green butter alternated with mayonnaise, and decorate the sides with a fine relief wreath made of green and white butter, and ornamented with fanciful bits of gherkin, lobster and cooked truffles. Surround the base of the fish with quartered hard-boiled eggs standing upright (No. 2513), alternated with small clusters of chopped jelly or cooked green peas. Serve with a sauce-boat of mayonnaise sauce (No. 606).

(2577). SALMON SLICED AND DECORATED (Tranches de Saumon Historiées).

Take two two-inch slices from the middle of a large salmon; after cleaning them nicely lay them in salt for one hour; place them on the grate of a fish-kettle and cover profusely with cold water, adding to it a large sprig of parsley and a gill of vinegar; set the kettle on the fire, skim the liquid and at the first boil withdraw it to one side so as to have it quiver only for forty to forty-five minutes; let cool in the stock, then remove the fish with the grate and let drain for half an hour.

FIG. 523.

Trim the slices, lift off the skin, wipe neatly, lay them on a baking sheet and cover the sides with a layer of Montpellier butter (No. 582); smooth it nicely and set aside on ice to cool. Decorate the sides and tops of these slices of fish with fanciful cuts of truffles, gherkins and hard-boiled egg-whites, being careful to dip each piece into half-set jelly before applying it. Dress the two slices on a thin wooden double support covered with white paper, and in the center of the dish on both sides arrange a cluster of macédoine salad (No. 2650) dressed with mayonnaise (No. 606); on the salad lay a large cooked crawfish and surround the slices with halved hard-boiled eggs, having the yolks hidden under a round piece of truffle. On both ends of the support fasten two tasteful hatelets of red prawns, slanting them outward. Serve with the fish a separate mayonnaise sauce (No. 606).

(2578). SLICE OF SALMON WITH JELLY (Tronçon de Saumon à la Gelée).

Cut from the middle of a large clean salmon a slice ten inches long; salt it over well and lay it on the grate of a fish-kettle on the belly side; tie it down to the grate with a string to keep it in place, and cover it with cold white wine court-bouillon (No. 39); heat the liquid while skimming, and at the first boil withdraw it to one side so as to keep it quivering for one hour, then allow it to get partly cold in its own stock. Remove the fish with the grate and let

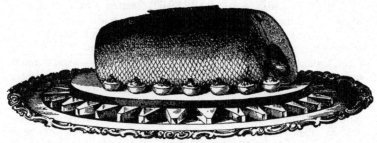

FIG. 524.

it become thoroughly cold, then leave it to drain for a couple of hours; wipe it off very cautiously, leaving the skin as entire as possible; now slide the fish on an oval wooden foundation covered with white paper and fastened on a long dish; support the slice on both sides so as to maintain it level, and cover the surface with half-set jelly applied with a brush. Surround it with small artichoke bottoms or hard eggs, à la Develle (No. 2502), fill with a vegetable salad (No. 2650), and decorate around with jelly crusts cut in triangles; serve at the same time two sauce-boats of tartar sauce (No. 631).

(2579). SALMON À LA AVELANE (Saumon à la Avelane).

Prepare and cook a salmon the same as explained à la Déstaing (No. 2580); when cold cover it with butter, then with several coats of jellied mayonnaise (No. 613). Decorate with fanciful cuts

FIG. 525.

of jelly dipped in partly cold jelly, forming a medallion as shown in drawing. Coat over with a layer of jelly (No. 103) by means of a funnel having a handle and spring stopper (Fig. 759). Place the salmon on the socle and garnish both sides with halved eggs decorated with truffles; between these place small mounds of chopped jelly.

(2580). SALMON À LA DESTAING (Saumon à la Destaing).

Have a very fresh twelve to sixteen-pound salmon; dress, that is, scrape off the scales, suppress the gills, and empty it by making an incision in the belly; wash it very clean, pare off the fins, and lay the salmon on a fish-kettle grate, on its side, the head resting toward the left; cover with cold white wine court-bouillon (No. 39) and stand the kettle on a hot fire; remove it at the first boil, and keep the liquid at boiling heat, without allowing it to boil up, for one hour for a twelve-pound salmon, and one hour and a half for a sixteen-pound one. Let it cool off in its own stock, then drain well for two hours. Remove the skin and sanguineous parts in the center so that the meat itself is entirely exposed, then slide it on a board of its own dimensions. Place a small bread croûton, shaped like the tail (a slightly lengthened triangle), at the extreme end of the tail, it being shaved down to almost nothing; fill the empty part of the fish with butter. Work some butter in a bowl and when very white, smooth and frothy, use it to cover the entire fish; have a strong straight band of paper, one inch in width, pass it over the butter several times until smooth, following the outlines of the salmon, and let get thoroughly cold; now cover it with a sufficiently thick and smooth layer of half-set red jelly, decorate this with truffles, pistachios, hard egg-white, and the red part of lobster meat; imitate the eye, mouth and gills, covering it over with more jelly. Dress it either on a socle or large dish, and surround with small shrimp aspics molded in timbale molds (No. 2, Fig. 137), decorated with eggs and truffles, filling them with a salpicon of shrimp mingled with jellied mayonnaise (No. 613), and fillets of sole, pared round. Cover with jellied mayonnaise, to which add chopped tarragon and chervil, then mask this over with jelly. Serve some mayonnaise sauce (No. 606) separately.

(2581). SALMON À LA FARRAGUT (Saumon à la Farragut).

Prepare and cook the fish as à la Destaing (No. 2580); cover with creamy white butter and let it get thoroughly cold; on the central part lay a thin band of crawfish butter (No. 573), an eighth of an inch thick by ten inches wide, so as to entirely cover this part of the fish. Decorate the top with fanciful bits of truffles, crawfish tails, anchovies and tarragon leaves; when the fish is very cold, cover it over with light red half-set jelly, and place it on its socle or dish; garnish around with sixteen small crawfish tartlets prepared as follows: Make some tartlets with fine foundation paste (No. 135), and when cold fill them either with crawfish tails or oysters, clams, etc., that have been laid in a marinade, and then cover with half-set jelly. Between these tartlets place sixteen white onions about one and three-eighths inches in diameter, from which cut off about an eighth of the stalk end, and as much from the root end; blanch for five minutes in plenty of water, then refresh and cook slightly firm in white wine court-bouillon (No. 39); drain, empty, and fill them up with Cambridge butter (No. 570), or else marinate them for two hours in oil, vinegar, salt and pepper. Place these onions on round pieces of beetroot one inch in diameter, and empty them with a half-inch tube. Cut eight more onions in three even parts across and use only the two end pieces; blanch them in salted water and vinegar, drain and fill with jellied ravigote mayonnaise, made by mixing ravigote sauce (No. 623) with jellied mayonaise (No. 613); place them over the others, and arrange small sprigs of green water cress on top. A printanière mayonnaise sauce (No. 612) is to be served separately.

(2582). SALMON À LA MODERN, ON SOCLE (Saumon à la Moderne sur Socle).

The fish, as represented in Fig. 526, is laid on its belly on a long wooden foundation covered over with white paper; the foundation with the fish is placed on a socle, and this is standing on a large tray. Every part is movable and independent, so that the piece can be easily transported. The tray is made of wood of oval form, with rounded prolongations on each end; it stands on several feet; the body of the tray is simply covered with white paper, and it has an open-work, silvered border. The socle is oval and hollow, it being made of two pieces of wood, one wider than the other, but fastened together in the center by a solid wooden support; the outlines of the socle are made of small pieces of board, or simply of strong cardboard covered with a thin layer of modeling fat (No. 56). The ornaments on the frieze and base of the socle are white and modeled in fat. The waterfall forming the frieze is made in pieces, stamped in a plaster cast, and put together, and are upheld by a tin band projecting out all around the top of the socle. The balls can also be made in plaster casts in two separate pieces, then put together. The two small socles placed on the rounded ends of the tray can be made of fat on a mandrel, or else molded in stearine;

FIG. 526.

they are movable but are held in place by a wooden peg fixed in the tray, and passing up through the base of the socle; each one of these is filled with macédoine salad (No. 2650), dressed in a pyramid and surmounted by slices of lobster. To cook the salmon whole it should be drawn through the gills, after scaling, and the inside filled with an ordinary bread stuffing (No. 61), then trussed; fasten it erect on the grate of a fish-kettle with string; cover with white wine court-bouillon (No. 39); heat up the liquid, skimming it at the first boil, and leave it on one side of the fire to quiver for an hour to an hour and a half; remove and cool partly on the grate out of the water. Untie it when cold, drain and lay it on the oval foundation, supporting it in two places on each side with wedges and supports, so as to keep it in position. These supports are hidden under sprigs of parsley leaves, then brushed over with half-set jelly. The small trout which constitute the garnishing on the front of the tray are cooked au bleu, as directed in No. 1297, well drained and laid in two symmetrical rows on a bed of chopped sticky jelly (No. 2526); they are then covered over with jelly the same as the salmon. These two rows of trout are separated by a cluster of round, peeled and cooked truffles after being covered with jelly (No. 103) or meat glaze (No. 402); this cluster of truffles may be replaced by one of red shrimps or simply by fresh parsley leaves. This dish as represented in the design is intended for a sideboard supper or a ball; it must be accompanied by four sauce-boats of mayonnaise sauce (No. 606).

(2583). SALMON À LA RÉGENCE, ON SOCLE (Saumon à la Régence sur Socle).

Arrange and cook the salmon the same as for Destaing (No. 2580); cover with a very smooth layer of white butter, then with one or two coats of jellied mayonnaise (No. 613). When cold decorate to imitate the head of the fish and ornament the surface with small truffle crescents graduated in size, or else with a large oval medallion about half the length of the salmon. Let the fish be very cold, then cover with a coating of half-set jelly; lay it on a socle and garnish around with a border of halved eggs filled with macédoine (No. 2508); between this border and the fish place lettuce hearts cut in four. Serve a well-seasoned printanière mayonnaise (No. 612) with the salmon.

(2584). SALMON À LA SEYMOUR (Saumon à la Seymour).

Have a salmon prepared and cooked the same as Destaing (No. 2580); carefully suppress the skin and the brown parts of the meat; fill the inside with butter and cover with several layers of pale pink jelly; decorate with fanciful cuts of egg-white and pistachios and garnish around with marinated lobster escalops covered with white jellied mayonnaise (No. 613), on which strew truffles, gherkins and egg-white, each of these to be chopped up separately; then mask with jelly; decorate with basket-shaped eggs (No. 2508); also have lettuce hearts cut in four and at each end place green water cress. Accompany this fish by a sauce-boat of ravigote mayonnaise sauce (No. 612).

(2585). SALMON À LA COURBET (Saumon à la Courbet).

Have the salmon already prepared and cooked the same as the Destaing (No. 2580); cover it with softened and smooth crawfish butter (No. 573) and decorate through a cornet; dredge the whole surface lightly with lobster coral chopped exceedingly fine and sifted through a sieve. Lay the fish on a socle and garnish around with lobster escalops covered with jellied mayonnaise (No. 613) and strew the surface with finely chopped truffles; between the escalops place clusters of fine large shrimp tails covered with jelly, and between each moscovite egg garnishing (No. 2511). Insert in the fish three hatelets composed of crawfish and decorated quenelles. Serve a mayonnaise cardinal sauce (No. 608) at the same time.

(2586). SALMON, RUSSIAN STYLE (Saumon à la Russe).

Prepare and cook the salmon the same as for Destaing (No. 2580); cover with white butter, then with mayonnaise (No. 606), into which stir as much slightly dissolved jelly (No. 103); cover it well through a funnel the same as explained for à la Avelane (No. 2579) and scatter over truffles, egg-white, lobster coral and parsley, all finely and separately chopped. Imitate the eyes and gills and garnish around with Polish eggs (No. 2512), and between each egg place large oysters, blanched, marinated and covered with a white chaudfroid (No. 596). Decorate the intersections with lettuce and water cress and serve with a sauce-boat of tartar sauce (No. 631).

(2587). SALMON, VENETIAN STYLE (Saumon à la Vénitienne).

Cook and prepare the salmon the same as the Destaing (No. 2580); cover it with ravigote butter (No. 583), and lay over this on its entire surface one or several beds of jellied mayonnaise (No. 613) of a light green shade; decorate with gherkins, capers, branches of chervil and tarragon leaves, imitate the eyes and gills and cover the whole with a thin layer of jelly. Dress the fish on a dish or socle and garnish around with paupiettes of smelts laid over some artichoke bottoms; between these put quartered eggs (No. 2513); intersect clusters of water cress and lettuce hearts cut in four and chopped jelly. Decorate with three hatelets, two of shrimps and one of crawfish. A green mayonnaise sauce (No. 612) accompanies this salmon.

(2588). SALMON, WITH MONTPELLIER OR CAMBRIDGE BUTTER (Saumon au Beurre de Montpellier ou au Beurre de Cambridge).

The salmon must first be prepared and cooked the same as for the Destaing (No. 2580); cover it either with Montpellier butter (No. 582), or Cambridge butter (No. 570); decorate through a cornet and in the center form a medallion; lay here and there olives, capers and sliced pickled gherkins, and garnish around with trussed crawfish, lettuce hearts, water cress and hard eggs cut as barrels (No. 2507), also oysters covered with ravigote jelly. Serve a remoulade sauce (No. 624) separately.

(2589). SLICED SHEEPSHEAD WITH JELLY (Tranches de Sheepshead à la Gelée).

Cut off two fine slices of raw sheepshead, salt over and leave to macerate for one hour. Fry in butter or oil a root and a minced onion; add root mirepoix with aromatics, parsley and a clove of garlic; moisten with white wine court-bouillon (No. 39), having plenty of it so as to cover the fish well, and boil the liquid for an hour, then strain. Put the slices of sheepshead into a deep earthen dish, suitable to be placed in the oven, cover over with the marinade stock and then with a strong paper; allow the liquid to boil up once before pushing the dish into a slack oven to cook the fish slowly for twenty minutes. After taking it out drain off the slices, remove the skin and lay them in a deep serving dish; strain the stock, lift off all the fat from the surface and mix in with it the same amount of very thick aspic jelly (No. 103) and a dash of good vinegar; pour this into the dish containing the fish and decorate the top with thin slices of lemon. After the jelly has become hard serve the fish accompanied by a sauce-boat of grated horseradish, mixed with a little good cream.

(2590). SHELLS OF CAPON WITH JELLY (Coquilles de Chapon à la Gelée).

Cut up into small dice the white meats of a capon; put them in a bowl with a third of their quantity of cooked mushrooms cut the same size; season with salt, oil and vinegar, and let macerate for half an hour, then drain off the seasoning and put the salpicon into a mayonnaise (No. 606), stirring into it two spoonfuls of gherkins likewise cut in dice pieces. With this preparation fill some shells, have the tops bomb-shaped and cover over with a thin layer of mayonnaise, then smooth the surface with a knife, decorate the top with fanciful cuts of truffles, gherkins and some beets; dress the shells on a folded napkin with sprigs of parsley in the center.

(2591). SHELLS OF PERCH OR RED SNAPPER (Coquilles de Perche ou de Red Snapper).

Cold shells are prepared with the same materials as the hot shells, using the cold meats of perch, red snapper, salmon, bass, sole, halibut, turbot, lobster or crawfish, the manner of preparation differing only. Cut the cold fish into small three-eighths of an inch dice and put them into a bowl with a third as much cooked mushrooms, as many truffles and a few spoonfuls of gherkins cut the same as the fish; season with salt, oil and vinegar and let macerate for a quarter of an hour. Drain the seasoning from the salpicon and replace it by a jellied mayonnaise (No. 613), and with this preparation fill up the shells, smoothing the surface to a dome and covering them over with a layer of the same mayonnaise; decorate the tops with details of smoked salmon, truffles, egg-white and gherkins, cut out with a column tube. Surround the base of each one of the domes with a string of chopped jelly pushed through a cornet.

(2592). SOCLES AND ORNAMENTS (Socles et Ornements).

These socles, as represented by Fig. 527-528, are made on a stand covered with modeling fat (No.

FIG. 527.

56) and cut out with a knife, then ornamented either through a cornet or else with a border of fanciful pieces stamped in a mold or molded. These two socles, although differently ornamented, are both constructed on the same principle and on the same plan.

Small socles are intended for decorating a sideboard of small dimensions; they can also be placed on a dinner table, either to figure as a center-piece—should there be no other—or at the ends of the table if there be two, but in that case it will be necessary to have the upper garnishings and decorations dressed on a dish, instead of being directly on the socle, so they can be readily

FIG. 528.

removed and handed to the guests. In either case the socles should be fastened on a large dish or tray.

Each socle stands on a solid, wooden, hollow drum that answers for a base; on top of the socle is another low-shaped drum, also made of wood and covered with white paper, having in its

FIG. 529.

center a thin wooden support forming a pyramid and arranged in such a way that it can afford a perfect support to the garnishings; this support has on its top a small platform on which can be laid any desired object or subject.

The garnishings on the first of these socles (Fig. 527) is composed of small cold chicken or partridge galantines made oval, then cut up, reconstructed and covered over with a blond chaudfroid (No. 596). They stand almost upright, leaning against the central support, but to be more assured of their safety it were advisable to inclose each galantine on the bottom with a solid wooden or cardboard shoe, the shape of a horseshoe. The galantines are decorated after they are dressed, and are then covered with half-set jelly. Exactly on top of these galantines lay a row of small paper cases filled with truffles, and fasten them against the central support. On the platform above is set a small

FIG. 530.

modeled or cast subject. The base of the small drum on which the galantines rest is surrounded by a row of round, even-sized truffles, peeled and glazed over with a brush.

The garnishings for the second socle consist of seven or eight large crimped paper cases shaped into half-hearts, pointed on one end and rounded on the other. These cases are filled with a frothy foies-gras preparation made the same as for pheasant cutlets, smoothed dome-shaped and covered with brown chaudfroid sauce (No. 594).

The figure on top represents a satyr seated on a rock, under which is laid a row of small cases containing truffles. The base of the small drum on which the garnishings repose may be decorated with small cases of truffles or with fine jelly croûtons (No. 2442).

Let it be observed that the garnishings for these socles can be modified or replaced by others.

(2593). SOLES À LA MAZAGRAN—FILLETS (Filets de Soles à la Mazagran).

This entrée is to be dressed on a wooden foundation fastened to a dish having a pyramidical

FIG. 531.

wooden support in its center, both to be covered with white paper. First prepare a small variegated macédoine salad (No. 2650); let it macerate for two hours in its seasoning, then drain it off, and dress the salad with thick mayonnaise (No. 606), and keep it on ice. Suppress the shells from the claws and tails of two lobsters simply cooked in a court-bouillon (No. 38), and left till cold; split the claws in two through their thickness, and brush over with half-set jelly, so as to be able to fasten them together again; also divide the tail meats into several slices from top to bottom, and wet each slice with half-set jelly, so as to be able to reshape them as before; keep these tails and claws on ice. Cook the fillets of three soles in a baking tin with white wine court-bouillon (No. 39), and as soon as done drain and range them on another baking tin and cover over with buttered paper; let cool off under a weight, then pare them all of the same length, not too freely, suppressing only the thin ends. Take the fillets up one by one, dip them into a white chaudfroid sauce (No. 596), reduced with a part of the stock they are cooked in, and range then once more on the same tin, keeping them a slight distance apart; cool them off on ice, and then cut away the surplus sauce. With the prepared salad, mingled with the fragments of lobster tail, cover the pyramidical support all around so as to increase its thickness, but keeping it in the same shape; smooth and cover over with a layer of jellied mayonnaise (No. 613). Against this pyramid dress the fillets of soles standing upright, one overlapping the other, and cover them with half-set jelly put on with a brush. On top of the pyramid dress the two prepared claws and tails, surround them with a thick string of chopped jelly to keep them in position and cover them as well with the half-set jelly. Place all around the bottom of the dish even-sized fine jelly croûtons (No. 2442), and keep the dish for ten minutes on ice, then serve with a separate mayonnaise sauce (No. 606).

(2594). STURGEON OR STERLET, LIVONIENNE—SMALL (Petit Esturgeon ou Sterlet Livonienne).

Clean the fish and put it in a fish-kettle to moisten with white wine court-bouillon (No. 39); boil and leave to cool off in its stock, then dress it on a dish, having carefully preserved the fish perfectly whole; let get thoroughly cold in the ice-box. Cover over with half-set jelly or else with fish-glaze (No. 399) and crawfish butter (No. 573); decorate it around with trussed crawfish, herring paupiettes (No. 789), cucumbers stuffed with vegetables, gherkins, olives, chopped jelly and croûtons. Serve a mayonnaise ravigote sauce (No. 612) at the same time.

(2595). SWEETBREADS À LA MIRABEAU (Ris de Veau à la Mirabeau).

Braise (No. 12) the sweetbreads first, and as soon as done put them in the press (Fig. 71) or under a light weight; cut them in two on their thickness; with a two inch in diameter pastry cutter cut out some round pieces, cover with blond chaudfroid (No. 596), and decorate each with a handsome rosette of very black truffles; cover over with half-set jelly, and range them on top of a macédoine salad (No. 2650), dressed with mayonnaise piled into a high dome; have a border of jelly croûtons around, and serve tartar sauce (No. 631) separately.

(2596). TERRINE OF DUCKS' LIVER À L'AQUITAINE (Terrine de Foies de Canards à l'Aquitaine).

Put two and a half pounds of fat ducks' liver in a terrine, after removing the gall, seasoned with foies-gras spices (No. 168) and larded with large fillets of raw truffles. Pound the truffle parings with five ounces of fresh chopped fat pork and six ounces of very white lean veal or pork meat, free from sinews, also chopped up finely, and four ounces of raw lean ham, adding the liver parings, salt and spices. Infuse a piece of cinnamon stick in a little Madeira wine, pass it through a sieve and mix it with the forcemeat, also six spoonfuls of cooked fine herbs (No. 385); season the whole to perfection. Cover the bottom and sides of a medium No. 3 terrine with thin bards of fat pork, lay on a bed of the prepared forcemeat and then range in the livers, pressing them closely together· mask over with a thick layer of the forcemeat and cover with a thin bard of fat pork; set on the cover and place the terrine on a small raised-edge baking pan containing a little hot water; push it into the oven to bake for an hour; remove and lay it away to cool with a light weight on top; when thoroughly cold fill it to the edge with lard and butter, melted together. This terrine is to be served either whole, by suppressing the fat, or by unmolding it on a dish without cutting it up and merely removing the fat pork and grease, or else in the terrine itself. Decorate with chopped jelly and croûtons (No. 2442).

(2597). TERRINE OF KERNEL OF HAM (Terrine de Noix de Jambon).

Raise the kernel from a fresh ham; suppress the rind and lard with large lardons (No. 1, Fig. 52), seasoned with salt, pepper, nutmeg and parsley. Put it in a vessel with carrots, minced onions, a garnished bunch of parsley (No. 123), salt, pepper and Madeira wine; let macerate for forty-eight hours in a cool place, turning it over frequently. Cover the bottom and sides of a terrine that can stand the oven with chopped forcemeat (No. 68); lay the kernel in the center, cover with more forcemeat and the whole with bards of fat pork; put on the lid and place the terrine in a deep baking tin containing water; push into a slack oven for three hours; remove, place a round of wood fitting the inside of the terrine over and a light weight on top; when cold, remove this round of wood and cover the surface with chopped jelly; then serve.

(2598). TERRINE OF HARE (Terrine de Lièvre).

Choose a fresh-skinned and clean hare, remove the fillets from the back, the minion fillets and the kidneys, reserving these apart. Take the meat from the shoulders and legs and chop it well; mix with it an equal quantity of boned turkey forcemeat (No. 65), and an equal quantity of baking forcemeat (No. 64); mix well. Pare the large fillets from the hare's back; cut them up into big squares and put into a vessel with the minion fillets and kidneys cut likewise, adding as much blanched fat pork cut the same, a few raw truffles and a piece of foies-gras; season these meats and pour over a few spoonfuls of brandy and Madeira wine, then let macerate for a few hours. Select a proper-sized cooking terrine, cover the bottom and around with thin slices of fat pork and fill it up in layers, intermingling each layer of forcemeat with a bed of the squares prepared beforehand, and finishing with forcemeat on top; cover the whole with fat pork. Set the terrine on a baking pan with a little hot water and let bake for one hour and a half to two hours in a slow oven; after removing, put it away in a cool place, with a weight laid on top, for three-quarters of an hour at least, and serve it only after twenty-four hours has elapsed; remove the fat from the top, and garnish with chopped jelly and croûtons (No. 2442).

(2599). TERRINE OF LARKS (Terrine de Mauviettes).

Bone two or three dozen larks; season, cook a part of the intestines with fat pork and then pass them through a sieve. Prepare a pound and a half of chopped galantine forcemeat (No. 66), place it in a vessel and mix in with it a few spoonfuls of cooked fine herbs (No. 385), chopped truffles and the intestine pulp. Spread the larks on the table and lay in each one a forcemeat ball. Line a terrine used for cooking and proceed to fill it exactly as described for terrine of ducks' liver à l'Aquitaine (No. 2596). Bake slowly for an hour and a quarter; let it cool, pressing it slightly half an hour after it leaves the oven; when cold garnish with jelly.

(2600). TERRINE DE NÉRAC (Terrine de Nérac).

Cut off the feet and wings from a medium-sized partridge; bone and season with allspice (No. 168); take out the liver and carefully remove the gall from it, then pound and mix it to pound again with half a pound of chopped pork forcemeat (No. 68). Cut up some cooked ham, some tongue, truffles, fat pork, and the minion fillets taken from the partridge, in quarter-inch square pieces; mix all in with the forcemeat, and with it fill the boned partridge, proceeding the same as for a boned chicken (No. 2485a). Line a terrine of the same capacity as the boned partridge (one that can be placed in the oven) with slices of fat pork; on top of this set a layer of the pork forcemeat, and then put in the partridge with the breast downward; finish filling up with truffles and more forcemeat, and lay slices of fat pork on top. Set the cover on and fasten it all around with strips of paper dipped in a flour and water paste; bake it one and a half to two hours, more or less, according to the size and thickness of the terrine. After removing and unfastening it put inside a smaller cover that can easily enter the top, to take the place of its own, and press lightly under a weight; drain off all the grease arising over the inside cover which is used for pressing it, and when the contents are perfectly cold remove the small cover and pour back the grease previously removed, and after this has cooled off cover the whole with melted lard. Return the original cover to the terrine after washing it well; fasten it on again with pasted tin foil and keep it in a cool place. When wanted for use take off all the grease, unmold, dress and garnish around with chopped jelly, or it may be served in its own terrine.

(2601). TERRINE OF PLOVERS AND LARKS (Terrine de Pluviers et Mauviettes).

Take off the fillets from eight plovers; remove their skin, lay them in a vessel and season with salt and spices, and moisten with a little brandy and Madeira. Detach and cut up the leg meats; put four ounces of fat pork in a sautoir, and when melted add the intestines without the gizzard and pouch; fry all together over a brisk fire with half a pound of chicken livers, the cut-up leg meats, and some chopped shallots and mushrooms; when this is cold pound it with an equal quantity of chopped-up fresh fat pork, and press the preparation through a sieve. Cover the bottom and sides of a terrine with thin bards of fat pork; over this a layer of forcemeat; fill the center with the skinned plover fillets; on this lay a layer of the prepared forcemeat; on this some larks boned and stuffed with game forcemeat made with a pound of game, the same of fat pork, a few truffles and pistachios, and small squares of ham; now place another layer of the forcemeat, more fillets, and so on until the terrine is quite full; all these ingredients should be well seasoned; range on top a bard of the fat pork and the cover; put it in a low saucepan containing a little water; cook in a moderate oven for an hour and a half, and when the meats are done press down lightly, and set it aside to cool. Fill the terrine with melted butter and lard, half of each, and use only when cold.

(2602). TERRINE OF PORK LIVER (Terrine de Foies de Porc).

Procure two pounds of the whitest pork liver, three pounds of fresh fat pork, four ounces of onion and one ounce of shallot, both chopped very finely and separately, four ounces together of salt, pepper, fine spices (No. 168), and a little powdered thyme, six ounces of flour, one ounce of truffles, one ounce of pistachios, and two ounces of tongue, these three latter to be chopped separately. Work the whole well together to obtain a compact paste, then divide it into three parts. Line the inside of a terrine with thin slices of fat pork, place in it one of the parts, and on it lay a bed of quarter of an inch squares of fat pork, then another one of the parts of forcemeat, another layer of fat pork squares, and on these the third or remaining part. The terrine should be filled to one inch below the edge, then covered with bards of fat pork; place a bay leaf on top, and set on the cover. Push the terrine into a moderate oven, standing on a baking sheet, and when cooked remove and lay a round of wood on it the size of the inside of the terrine; place under the press so as to press it down lightly, and leave it thus to cool for twelve hours.

(2603). TERRINE OF SNIPE (Terrine de Bécassines).

Bone two snipe, divide each one in two parts and lay them in a dish with five or six peeled and cut-up truffles, and as much cooked ham fat, or fat pork; season the meats and truffles highly and pour over a little Madeira wine. Take the meat from the leg of a hare, cut it in pieces and fry in a saucepan with double its quantity of chicken or game livers until well done, then add the birds' intestines and leave to cool; chop this up with a third as much raw and chopped fresh pork, and then season the whole; put it in a mortar to pound with the same amount of fresh fat pork previously chopped and pounded with the truffle parings; add to this forcemeat a pinch of prepared spices (No. 168). Five minutes later set it in a vessel and incorporate with it the Madeira wine used for marinating the snipe. Cover the bottom and sides of a terrine with slices of unsalted fat pork and these with a layer of the prepared forcemeat; range the pieces of snipe, truffles and ham in the center, alternated with the remainder of the forcemeat; the terrine should now be quite full. Smooth the top with a knife and cover with slices of fat pork; put on the lid and set it in a baking pan with a glassful of hot water; push it into a moderate oven to cook for an hour and a half. When the water in the pan evaporates pour in some more, and when done take it out and leave to cool partly, then set a light weight on top, and when thoroughly cold take the contents from the terrine, divide in two across, return one-half to the terrine, cut up the remaining half into oblong pieces and dress them again in a circle in the same terrine. Garnish the center with chopped jelly.

(2604). TERRINE OF WILD RABBITS (Terrine de Lapins Sauvages).

Cut off the limbs of two or three wild rabbits previously skinned, cleaned, and the meats nicely wiped; bone the four limbs and the back, cut the back fillets in pieces, also the meat from the legs, and lard them with shreds of raw ham and bits of truffles; lay them in a vessel to season with pulverized wild thyme, and pour over a few spoonfuls of brandy or Madeira wine; let macerate for two or three hours, adding a few spoonfuls of cooked fine herbs (No. 385). With the minion fillets and the nicest parings prepare a forcemeat, mix with it an equal quantity of baking forcemeat (No. 81), and to this dressing add the marinade from the meats. Cover the bottom and sides of a cooking terrine with a layer of the prepared forcemeat, then begin to fill it with the pieces of rabbit intermingled with large lardons of foies-gras and truffles, both raw, but seasoned, and alternate the forcemeat with layers of the meats; cover the top with forcemeat and thin slices of fat pork over all. Set the terrine into a deep baking pan containing hot water, and bake for one hour and a quarter to one hour and a half in a moderate oven; after it has been removed one quarter of an hour set a weight on top and allow to cool off.

(2605). TIMBALE OF PHEASANTS WITH TRUFFLES (Timbale de Faisans aux Truffes).

Remove the meat from the breast of two raw pheasants. Chop up the fleshy part of the legs with one fillet and the carcass parings, and with it mix an equal quantity of fat pork, a few raw truffles and fragments of foies-gras; pound well and pass through a sieve. Cut into large squares the remaining breast meats and lay them in a vessel with as much cut-up raw foies-gras; season highly and pour over a few spoonfuls of Madeira wine; keep this in a cool place for two hours. Butter a large dome-shaped mold, broader than it is high; line it with cold pie paste (No. 144) and cover with a layer of the forcemeat, filling the empty space with the contents of the vessel; cover the top

Fig. 532.

with a thick, well-rounded layer of the same, and then lay several slices of fat pork on all; close up the aperture of the mold with a flat of the same paste, fastening it to the edges, and in the center bore a small opening. Now lay the timbale on a small-sized baking sheet and let it cook for about an hour and a half in a slack oven; after it has been removed for a quarter of an hour pour into the hole two or three gills of brown chaudfroid (No. 594), reduced with pheasant fumet (No. 397) and Madeira wine, and let it cool for twenty-four hours before unmolding. When ready to serve invert it on the table, lift off the mold and cut from the bottom a slice about an inch thick, then begin cutting the dome into even slices, not too thick, from the top to the bottom; restore these to their original shape on the piece cut from the bottom. Dress the timbale on a wooden founda- tion attached to a dish and covered with white paper; have small holes perforated at equal distances around the edges of this foundation and into these stick a dozen small hatelets, each one being garnished with two peeled truffles, one larger than the other. On the summit of the dome insert another hatelet garnished with large truffles; surround the foundation either with handsome jelly croûtons (No. 2442), or else with slices of pie cooked in a cradle mold.

(2606). BEEF TONGUE À LA ROCHEFORT (Langue de Bœuf à la Rochefort).

Prepare and cook a tongue, as explained in red beef tongue, No. 2608; after it is cold cut away the entire center of the tongue, as in the accompanying design (Fig. 533); cut this part into slices, reconstruct and glaze it nicely with a brush dipped in partly set jelly. Set it on a plain or

Fig. 533.

carved rice foundation; ornament the ends of the tongue with fanciful cuts of truffles, egg-whites, and pistachio nuts; on the foundation place a shell made of grease, filled with slices of foies-gras, and chopped jelly sprinkled over; stick two garnished hatelets in the thick end, and at the tip of the tongue a croûton of jelly laid in tiers (Fig. 465), one on top of the other. Garnish the sides with glazed carrot balls, and the ends with chopped jelly; surround the socle with chopped jelly and croûtons of jelly cut in squares.

(2607). RED BEEF TONGUES ARCADE (Langues de Bœuf Écarlate en Arcade).

Prepare and cook the tongues in water, lay them in a mold having the shape of a tongue two and a quarter inches thick, then place them under a weight to get cool; pare, and cover them with a brown chaudfroid (No. 594) and decorate with designs of egg-white, truffles and pistachio nuts.

Fig. 534.

Mask the decoration with a partly solidified jelly, and arrange these tongues on a silver-plated support, as represented in the accompanying Fig. 534; garnish around with chopped jelly and a border of jelly croûtons.

(2608). RED BEEF TONGUES, SMOKED (Langues de Bœuf Écarlate Fumées).

Cut off the windpipes and prick the tongues with the point of a trussing needle; rub over with pulverized saltpetre, mingled with as much brown sugar, and place them in an earthen or wooden vessel between layers of white salt, with thyme, bay leaf, basil, juniper berries and cloves. Put a board over with a weight on top; turn them after three days and cover so that the air cannot enter and repeat the operation every three days during the period of twelve. To cook, place them in a stock pot after washing in several waters; cover with a sufficient quantity of water to allow them to swim, adding a bunch of parsley garnished with two carrots and two onions; boil slowly for an hour to an hour and a half until thoroughly cooked, which can be ascertained by inserting the point of a trussing needle deep into them; remove from the stock and wrap in a wet cloth; leave to cool, then dress them in a circle leaning against a croûton with the tips downward; garnish with jelly and serve.

(2609). RED BEEF TONGUES WITH JELLY (Langues de Bœuf Écarlate à la Gelée).

Cut away the fat and cartilaginous part from six beef tongues, wash and wipe them well, then prick them with a larding needle; rub each tongue over, using half an ounce of saltpetre for each one. Lay them in a bowl, covering them with a layer of salt; set a board over with a weight on top, and leave them there for twelve hours, then range them in an earthen vessel or wooden tub. Cover them with a brine prepared as follows: Have eight quarts of water and one pound or more of salt; test the brine, to see whether it be strong enough, by putting in an egg or potato, and if it floats on the surface then the brine is sufficiently strong. Boil it, adding half a pound of brown sugar, and let get cool before pouring it over the tongues; leave them in this pickle for twelve to fifteen days, setting them in a very cool place, and laying a board over with a weight on top so as to keep them continually under the brine, turning them over in it every three days; when they are to be used, place them in plenty of cold water, and set on the fire to boil for three or four hours according to their size; when done plunge them into fresh water, remove their skins, press them down under a weight, trim them nicely, then cut out the entire center of the tongue, leaving a piece underneath and at both ends; cut this square piece into thin slices, return them to their original position, then glaze the tongue with meat glaze (No. 402); dress it on a dish over a layer of bread spread with green butter (No. 583), and decorate it through a cornet with the same butter. Garnish around with chopped jelly, having a border of nicely shaped jelly croûtons (No. 2442).

(2610). CALVES' TONGUES À LA MACÉDOINE (Langues de Veau à la Macédoine).

Cook six calves' tongues, salted as the beef tongue No. 2609, in salted water for eight days, and unsalted in fresh water for six hours; when done remove and lay them to cool under a weight. After suppressing the skin, pare them rounded at the thick end, and cut the two surfaces off straight, then split each one lengthwise in two or three, brush over with meat glaze (No. 402) and cover with a little half-set jelly to give them brilliancy. Besides this prepare a vegetable macédoine with Brussels sprouts, small clusters of cauliflower, balls of potatoes and carrots, string beans sliced or cut in lozenges, asparagus tops and green peas; all of these vegetables should be blanched separately; season the salad and form it symmetrically into a pyramid on the middle of a dish. Dress the halved tongues upright in a circle around with their pointed ends upward, and surround the whole with jelly, serving a tartar sauce No. (631), or cold ravigote (No. 623) apart.

(2611). BROOK TROUT À LA CARÊME (Truites de Ruisseau à la Carême).

Scale, wash and draw the fish without opening their bellies; wrap them up in sheets of buttered paper and cook them in a white wine mirepoix stock (No. 419); when done, drain, unwrap and remove the skin carefully. Lay them in a deep dish, one beside the other, placing them very straight; strain the stock over and allow to cool off thoroughly in this, then take them from the liquor, wipe dry, dress and cover one-half with white jellied mayonnaise (No. 613), and the other half with green ravigote (No. 623) mixed with jellied mayonnaise. Decorate the tops with egg-white, truffles, anchovy fillets, gherkins and pistachios; surround with chopped jelly and croûtons, and serve a mayonnaise sauce (No. 606) at the same time.

(2612). TROUT WITH JELLY, TARTAR SAUCE (Truites à la Gelée, Sauce Tartare).

Let the fish be very fresh for it loses its best qualities when kept from the water or on ice for any length of time. Clean the fish through the gills without opening or scaling it. Lay it on the belly side on the fish grate, cover with cold and strained white wine court-bouillon (No. 39), heat the liquid and skim; at the first boil withdraw it to one side, so that it quivers

FIG. 535.

for fifteen minutes. Remove the fish with the grate, and let drain for a couple of hours, then slide it on a wooden foundation concealed by white paper and fastened on a large dish; support the fish upright, so it will not fall, and cover over with slightly reddened cold jelly; garnish the two ends with clusters of shrimps and surround the foundation with jelly croûtons (No. 2442); fill up the spaces between the fish with bunches of fresh parsley leaves or chopped jelly; serve tartar sauce (No. 631) with the fish.

(2613). TURBOT À LA RÉMOULADE (Turbot à la Rémoulade).

Place some slices of turbot cooked in a court-bouillon (No. 38), in a deep dish; pour over oil, vinegar, salt, pepper and chopped parsley. Decorate a border mold (Fig. 138), with fanciful cuts of egg-white, truffles, pistachios and red lobster meat; cover these with a thick layer of jelly (No. 103), and fill it up with shrimps dressed with jellied mayonnaise (No. 613); unmold when the border becomes very firm, and fill the center with a pad of rice, or of veal and mutton fat, half of each; lay the pieces of turbot on top, having suppressed all the bones and skin therefrom; cover the fish with remoulade sauce (No. 624), mixed with jellied mayonnaise (No. 613), and serve separately a sauce-boat of remoulade sauce.

(2614). TURKEY À LA STEVENS—STUFFED (Dinde Farcie à la Stevens).

Fry one onion in two ounces of butter with four ounces of fresh mushrooms chopped up; season with salt, nutmeg, fine pepper, parsley, thyme and bay leaf; moisten with half a pint of white wine, and set it on a slow fire to let fall to a glaze, then dilute with very thick and well-reduced allemande sauce (No. 407), strained through a tammy and cooled off. Put this into the mortar gradually with the same amount of chicken quenelle forcemeat (No. 89), and with a spoon mix in some truffles and red beef tongue, cut in three-sixteenths of an inch squares, and pistachios. Bone the breast of a young turkey, fill the empty space with the above dressing, truss it and wrap it up in several sheets of buttered paper, then put it to cook in an oval-shaped saucepan lined with bards of fat pork, and moisten to half its height with a mirepoix and white wine stock (No. 419); it requires fifteen minutes cooking for each pound of turkey when stuffed. Half an hour before serving untie the turkey and let it assume a fine color, then remove and lay it on a dish to cool off. With the stock prepare a jelly and use for making some small aspics of foies-gras (No. 2412), molded in timbale molds (No. 2, Fig. 137), and garnish around with them, placing them on chopped jelly and surround with jelly croûtons, and stick on the top three or five hatelets; trim the drumsticks with favor frills (No. 10), then serve.

(2615). TURKEY IN DAUBE À LA VERNEUIL (Dinde en Daube à la Verneuil).

After picking, singeing and drawing a large turkey, lard it with lardons (No. 2, Fig. 52), seasoned with salt, pepper, nutmeg, chives and pulverized thyme and bay leaf. Line a braziere (Fig. 134), with slices of fat pork, raw lean ham, carrots, onions, a bunch of parsley garnished with thyme and bay leaf, a clove of garlic, a gill of brandy and two split calf's feet or knuckle of veal; lay in the turkey.

Fig. 536.

Boil, skim, then set the braziere in the oven for three or four hours until perfectly cooked. Blanch and cook separately some turnip balls three-eighths of an inch in diameter, and some short sticks of carrots one inch long by three-eighths of an inch in diameter. When the turkey is cooked put it into an earthen or a tin vessel, strain the stock over and when three-quarters cooled remove the bones and skin from the meat. Mold the daube in a mold about one inch shorter and narrower than the mold to be decorated, placing in layers of turkey, calf's feet, truffles and pistachios. Decorate the larger mold, the shape of the one in Fig. 536, with the carrot sticks cut lengthwise in two and the rounded side applied to the sides of the mold, and the turnip balls also cut in two and the convex side applied; the half lozenges on top to be of turnips and the smaller lozenges above of truffles, below which place a row of small green peas. Coat the decoration and fill the bottom with jelly, and when hardened unmold the smallest mold and place it in the decorated one. Fill up with cold liquid jelly, let get thoroughly cold on ice, and when sufficiently firm unmold on a cold oval dish; garnish around with chopped jelly and triangular jelly croûtons dressed upright. On top fasten three hatelets and on the first platform range a symmetrical border of jelly squares all around.

(2616). TURKEY OR GOOSE IN DAUBE (Dindon ou Oie en Daube).

Draw a turkey cock; singe and lard it with large lardons (No. 2, Fig. 52); season with salt, pepper, nutmeg and chives, then stuff it with chicken quenelle forcemeat (No. 89), into which mix quarter-inch squares of red beef tongue and lean ham. Place the turkey in a braziere lined with slices of fat pork, carrots, minced onions, a bunch of parsley garnished with thyme, bay leaf, a clove of garlic, a gill of brandy and a split knuckle of veal. Boil, skim and simmer gently and allow to braise for three and a half to four hours. Blanch separately some carrots and small onions, both trimmed into five-eighths of an inch balls, and when the turkey is partly cooked remove it from its stock, strain the liquid, wash the saucepan, and return the turkey to it with its strained and skimmed stock; range around the carrots and onions and finish cooking the vegetables and turkey slowly. When well done, drain, untruss and lay it in an oval stone or tin vessel with the vegetables around, pour the stock (which should be sufficiently consistent to form a jelly) over and let cool off, then unmold the turkey on a long cold dish; surround the base with chopped jelly and jelly croûtons (No. 2442).

A goose in daube can be prepared the same way as the turkey.

(2617). YOUNG TURKEY BREASTS, GUSTAVE DORÉ (Filets de Dindonneau à la Gustave Doré).

Raise the breasts from two turkeys; remove the minion fillets and the skin, and sauté them in butter and lemon juice; set them separately under a weight to cool, then pare and cover over twice with white chaudfroid (No. 596), the same as for chaudfroid of turkey Périgord (No. 2462). Decorate with cuts of truffles, and cover with half-set jelly. Pare the four minion fillets, remove the light skin, and the sinews, and range them in a buttered sautoir, one beside the other, shaping them like crescents; cover over with buttered paper, and poach in a hot oven for a few moments, then cool them off and coat over with a brown chaudfroid (No. 594). Cut some slices of unsmoked red beef tongue three-sixteenths of an inch thick, and from these pare slices the same shape as the minion fillets, and cover them with jelly. Dress the turkey breasts on a cut-out rice support, and around a pad of bread covered with green butter (No. 583); decorate around this support with finely chopped jelly, and on it lay the minion fillets and tongue intercalated, and outside of the jelly place some triangular-shaped croûtons (No. 2442), cut much longer than their width. On top of the support have a vase made of vegetables, filled with small stuffed mushrooms, as explained in No. 2517.

(2618). WILD BOAR'S HEAD, DECORATED (Hure de Sanglier Décorée).

Cut off the head of a wild boar or wild pig at the neck, near the shoulders; singe and scrape carefully; when well cleaned bone it, beginning under the lower jaw, and when thoroughly boned rub it over with four ounces of salt and one of powdered saltpetre. Lay the head in a vessel with thyme, bay leaf, basil, mace, cloves, juniper berries and carrots; leave it in two days, rub it over once more and let remain six days longer; drain, open, suppress all the aromatics, remove the greater part of the meats, and cut these into half-inch squares. Have a pound of truffles in a vessel with a pound of pork minion fillet cut in half-inch pieces, the boar's tongue and a calf's tongue, both to be pickled (No. 15), cooked and cooled under a weight, then cut in three-eighths inch squares; also have a pound of blanched fat pork cut up the same size, and a quarter of a pound of green pistachios; season highly and mix these ingredients with a forcemeat prepared with two pounds of lean pork, a pound of lean veal and three pounds of fresh fat pork, the whole chopped finely and forced through a sieve. Fill the head with this preparation, close and sew up the aperture, fill the mouth with carrots so as to keep it open, cut off the ears and cook them separately in stock

(No. 194a), keeping them firm; tie the head in a cloth and boil it for five hours over a slow fire; set it to cool for half an hour, unwrap it and reshape the head as near as possible by wrapping tightly around it a linen band, beginning at the snout and finishing at the base of the head; press lightly; when entirely cool unwrap. This head may be shaped in a specially made mold, then unmolded and glazed. Reconstruct the head with imitated eyes and fangs, and glaze over the well-pared ears with meat glaze and fasten on with skewers; lay it on an oval stand made of rice, in two parts, the lower part one and a half inches high the top part one inch high; on the edge of the lower one place a wreath of oak leaves; garnish the lower tier with truffles in paper cases and the base with chopped jelly and croûtons, and ornament the head with some hatelets.

FIG. 537.

Head Cheese.—Salt a pig's head for three days in a light brine or in sea salt; cook it in remoistening (No. 189), with onion, thyme and bay leaf added. After it is done bone it entirely and cut the meat into half-inch squares. Also cut a few slices from the fatty cheek part and with them line a square tin mold. Put the squares of meat in a receptacle sufficiently large to contain them, and mix together; add four finely chopped shallots, pepper, nutmeg, a soupspoonful of chopped parsley, a glassful of good white wine and a pint of melted jelly (No. 103); mix all together. Pour all of this into the larded mold, place it in the oven and let cook slowly for half an hour. Remove and cover with a board, having a pound and a half weight on top. Cut in slices and serve cold.

(2619). WOODCOCK À LA VALÈRE (Bécasses à la Valère).

Roast six woodcocks; let them get cold, then raise the fillets from them all; suppress the skin and pare into the form of half-hearts, all the same size. Pound the remainder of the meats and the insides, from which the gizzard and pouches have been removed and to which half as much foies-gras has been added, the whole fried in butter. With this forcemeat mash the fillets on the side that adheres to the breast-bone. Put the broken bones into a saucepan with half a pint of white wine, a bay leaf and a minced shallot; let simmer slowly for half an hour, then run it through a fine sieve; add this fumet to an espagnole reduced to the consistency of a sauce, then add some jelly, cool on ice, stirring continually, and when the chaudfroid is sufficiently consistent cover the woodcock fillets; after it becomes quite cold cover with half-set jelly (No. 103), pare and dress on a dish in a circle on a nicely carved rice foundation, one and a half inches high. Lay chopped jelly around and garnish the center with some salpicon tartlets made of foundation paste (No. 135), cooked white and filled with a salpicon of game, red tongue and mushrooms, mingled with a little brown chaudfroid (No. 594). Surround with jelly croûtons of two shades alternated, brown and white—the former made of brown jelly and the latter of white.

COOKED SALADS (Salades Cuites).

(2620). DRESSINGS OR SEASONINGS FOR SALADS, TARRAGON AND CHILI VINEGAR
(Assaisonnements pour Salades, Vinaigre à l'Estragon et au Poivre de Chili).

Rémoulade Sauce, Pimentade with Tomatoes, Tarragon and Chili Vinegars.—The quantity of salad to be seasoned and the necessary proportions must be taken into consideration when using these dressings. When a salad is served no oil should ever remain at the bottom of the bowl; the quantity of oil varies according to the salad. It generally takes three to five spoonfuls of oil for one of vinegar. This can be varied according to taste. Americans do not like the taste of oil in which the taste of the olive is prominent, and therefore prefer a neutral olive oil. When a salad is prepared away from the dining-room it is better to put the salt and pepper in a bowl, dissolve them with the vinegar, add the oil and mix well; then pour this over the salad, and stir it in a common salad bowl before removing it to the one intended for the table, this being a much cleaner method. There are glass decanters for mixing the seasonings, adding to them an egg-yolk and a little mustard; shake this well, and by so doing a light mayonnaise is obtained that can be poured over the salad.

Another way is to put the salt and pepper into a spoon, add the vinegar, mix with a fork, pour it over the salad and afterward the oil, or else put the salt and pepper into the salad, stir, then add the oil, stir once more and lastly pour in the vinegar, stirring it well again.

Tarragon Vinegar.—Fill a two-quart jar two-thirds full with layers of tarragon leaves, shallots and onions; pour over some very strong vinegar and use it two months later, filtering it before doing so.

Chili Pepper Vinegar.—Put into a quart jar half its height of Chili peppers, cover with strong wine vinegar, and three months later it can be used, either with the peppers or filtered.

(2621). ASPARAGUS SALAD (Salade d'Asperges).

Cut the tender parts of asparagus into pieces of equal length and tie them in bunches, then cook them in salted water and leave them to get cold. A few minutes before serving mix them in a bowl with a third of their quantity of pared crawfish tails; season with salt and pepper. Rub through a sieve the yolks of six hard-boiled eggs, dilute this with oil and vinegar, and pour over this sauce the asparagus and crawfish, then arrange the salad symmetrically in a salad bowl and add the seasoning to it.

(2622). BAGRATION SALAD (Salade à la Bagration).

Have some very white lettuce leaves, some anchovies, marinated tunny fish, stoned olives, beetroot cut small, minced gherkins and escalops of lobster. Season the lettuce leaves and lay them at the bottom of a bowl; also season the other ingredients with a little mayonnaise (No. 606), lay them on top of the lettuce, and dredge over and around a border of chopped truffles to decorate. Place on top quartered hard-boiled eggs, in the center a pretty lettuce heart, and around this some chervil, tarragon, water cress, parsley, burnet and chives, all chopped up very fine and divided into six parts, arranging them tastefully around the lettuce heart.

(2623). BEEF SALAD WITH TOMATOES (Salade de Bœuf aux Tomates).

Scallop or trim in slices some cold boiled or braised beef, pare the pieces round-shaped, and season with salt, pepper, oil and vinegar, also very finely cut-up chervil and chives; lay all on a plate or salad bowl, giving it a dome-shape, and garnish around the salad with peeled and quartered tomatoes.

(2624). CAPON SALAD À LA MORTIMER (Salade de Chapon à la Mortimer).

Have a cold roast capon, cut off the thighs and the breasts; suppress all the skin, fat and bones. Divide the meat into slices three-sixteenths of an inch thick, and these into round pieces an inch in diameter; lay them in a deep dish, and season with salt, pepper, oil, vinegar and mustard. Now put into a salad bowl half a pound of salted cucumbers, half a pound of potatoes, a quarter of a pound of minced red radishes, a quarter of a pound of celery or celery knob, all being minced up very fine; season with salt, pepper, oil, vinegar, chopped chervil and tarragon, and mix thoroughly. Cut into eight pieces sufficient artichoke bottoms to form a border, dip the tips of each piece into finely chopped parsley. Prepare rounds of truffles one inch in diameter by one-eighth of an inch in thickness; arrange the vegetables at the bottom of a a cold dish, lay the capon on top, cover with a mayonnaise sauce (No. 606), and surround the whole with the artichoke bottoms; inside this border lay symmetrically the slices of truffles, and inside of these slices of beetroot cut smaller than the truffles, and on top of the beets smaller bits of gherkin; finish the center with a small cluster of truffles. Send this salad to the table to show the guests before removing it to stir and serve.

(2625). CHICKEN SALAD, AMERICAN STYLE—CHICKEN MAYONNAISE (Salade de Poulet à l'Américaine—Mayonnaise de Poulet).

Cook a four-pound chicken in some stock (No. 194a); the time allowed for this varies considerably, according to the age of the chicken, but the usual length of time is about two hours. When the chicken is done put it into a vessel, pour its own broth over, and let it cool therein; remove it, and begin by lifting off all the skin and white parts from the breasts; cut the meat into dice from five to six-eighths of an inch, and lay them in a bowl, seasoning with salt, pepper, oil and vinegar. Chicken salad may be prepared either with lettuce or celery, the latter being generally preferred. Choose fine white celery, wash it well, drain and cut it across in one-eighth of an inch thick pieces or else in Julienne; dry them in a cloth to absorb all the water remaining in them. Put at the bottom of a salad bowl intended for the table some salt, pepper, oil and vinegar; mustard can be added if desired; mix the seasoning in with the celery. For lettuce prepare an ordinary lettuce salad. Lay the pieces of chicken on top, and cover the whole with a layer of mayonnaise sauce (No. 606); decorate the surface with quartered hard-boiled eggs, anchovy fillets, olives, capers and beets; place some lettuce leaves around, and a fine lettuce heart in the center.

Chicken Mayonnaise.—Cut into five pieces a roasted chicken weighing two pounds and a half, remove the skin and pare nicely. Season the chicken the same as for No. 2625; two hours later toss it in the vessel with jellied mayonnaise (No. 613) and dress it pyramidically without any green salad; cover with jelly mayonnaise, and garnish around with halved eggs, olives, capers, anchovies, beetroots and chopped jelly.

(2626). MIGNON SALAD (Salade Mignonne).

Pare four heads of endive or escarole that are not too large, suppress the outer leaves, and wipe the others well without washing them; cut either of these salads across in two parts, put the upper part of the leaves in a bowl, cut up the other half into large Juliennes, and season with salt, pepper and some fine oil. Cut in medium Julienne four peeled truffles cooked in wine, season them also with salt and oil, cut up the same as the truffles two breasts of chicken cooked in butter and lemon juice without attaining a color; let them get cold and lay them on a plate. Shell four hard-boiled eggs, rub the yolks through a sieve and set this in a bowl, diluting with some mayonnaise (No. 606), a good spoonful of mustard and a dash of vinegar; add one after the other, first the truffles, then the endives, and lastly the chicken breasts, all previously drained of their seasoning. Dress the salad in a salad bowl, and decorate the top with truffles, beetroot, gherkins and lobster coral.

(2627). CHICKEN SALAD WITH VEGETABLES (Salade de Poulet aux Légumes).

Cut up a large roast chicken into eight pieces, four from the breasts and four from the legs, suppressing the pinions and carcass; remove the breast bone and the second joint bones, then cut the meats and the fillets each in two or three pieces, taking off the skin; put them in a vessel to season with salt, oil and vinegar. Prepare a macédoine salad (No. 2650), cut in small dice; for instance, carrots and turnips blanched and cooked in stock (No. 194a), also green peas and string beans boiled in salted water. After all these vegetables have been cooked and drained lay them in a bowl and season with salt, pepper, oil and vinegar; mix in some cut-up gherkins and beets, and let macerate for one hour. Drain off the seasonings and finish with mayonnaise, slightly thickened with jelly (No. 606). Dress the chicken and the vegetables in a dome-shape on a cold dish; cover this with a layer of the same mayonnaise, and decorate near the top with a row of sliced truffles; divide the dome between the truffles and the bottom into panels by means of round slices of

Fig. 538.

gherkins. Surround the base of the dome with slices of beets and potatoes, overlapping. Garnish the top with string beans.

(2628). CRAB SALAD (Salade de Crabes).

Cook some crabs as explained in bisque of crabs (No. 198); pick the meat from the shells and put it on the ice; serve when very cold, seasoned with salt, pepper, oil and vinegar; sprinkle over the whole some finely cut-up chives and chervil, also some chopped lobster or crab coral.

(2629). CRAWFISH SALAD À LA MAINTENON (Salade d'Écrevisses à la Maintenon).

In order to dress this salad in an elegant manner, and with a required solidity, it is better to fasten a wooden bottom to the dish, covering it with white paper and having on the upper outer edge a small wooden or cardboard ledge, and in the center a thin support equally covered with white paper. Detach the tails from the bodies of six or eight dozen large, cooked crawfish; suppress the tail shells and claws. Pare the meat from the tails, put it into a bowl, and season with salt, oil and vinegar; empty the crawfish bodies, and rub the insides through a sieve. Stuff about fifteen of these bodies, when well cleaned, with a salpicon composed of poached oysters and cooked truffles; mix in with it the meats from the claws, and the parings from the tails, and stir in a good

Fig. 539.

white chaudfroid sauce (No. 596). Let the preparation become firm by keeping the stuffed bodies for half an hour in the refrigerator. Cut in small quarter-inch squares some cooked and cold fillets of sole and salmon, also some anchovy and herring fillets, some marinated tunny-fish, poached eggs, potatoes and salt cucumbers; put this salpicon into a bowl, and season it with salt, oil, vinegar and mustard, then let macerate for one hour. Drain off the seasoning, and add to it a mayonnaise with jelly (No. 613). Dress it dome-shaped on the wood fastened to the dish, and let it get firm for a quarter of an hour in the ice-box; remove the dish from the ice, and cover the dome with a layer of jellied mayonnaise (No. 613). Stick in the crawfish tails one by one, with the point of a larding needle so that they lay symmetrically against the dome in two graduated rows; cover them at once with half-set jelly, and garnish the hollow of the second or top row with a bunch of green leaves or a bunch of chopped jelly. Send a sauce-boat of mayonnaise (No. 606) to the table at the same time.

(2630). CRAWFISH SALAD WITH JELLY (Salade d'Écrevisses à la Gelée).

Detach the tails from the bodies of several dozen cooked crawfish; suppress the shells from the tails and largest legs; pare the meats, season, and keep them covered. Prepare a macédoine salad (No. 2650), cut into small dice, add to it the legs and parings of shrimps, also cut in dice; season with salt, oil and vinegar, and let marinate for one hour. Select a plain border mold with a narrow cylinder, imbed it in broken ice, and decorate its sides with eggs cut in two, alternated with some small vegetable balls dipped in half-set jelly; fill up the empty space in the mold gradually with some partly cold jelly (No. 103). Drain the salad on a sieve, lay it back into the bowl and mix in with it a jellied mayonnaise (No. 613); stir it on ice for a few minutes. Unmold the border on a cold dish; place into the cylindrical space a wooden foundation of exactly the same diameter, having on the

FIG. 540.

center a light upright support, both being covered with white paper; lay the salad around this support, giving it a pyramidical shape, smooth the surfaces, and cover it with a thin layer of thick jellied mayonnaise (No. 613); keep for two minutes on ice. Stick in the crawfish tails one by one, using a larding needle for the purpose, first dipping them in half-set jelly, then fasten them to the salad in three graduated rows, each one laying in a different direction, and forming a pyramid. As soon as each row is finished coat it over with some half-set jelly to consolidate it; in the hollow of the third or top row lay a pretty lettuce heart, and serve a sauce-boat of mayonnaise sauce (No. 606) at the same time as the salad.

(2631). FISH SALADS (Salades de Poissons).

These consist principally of perch, trout, turbot and salmon. For these salads the fish must be boiled or cooked in a court-bouillon (No. 38) beforehand, so that they are cold when needed for use. They can also be made of sautéd fillets of fish; in either case the skin and bones must first be removed. Put the fish into a bowl and season it with salt, oil and vinegar; it is generally arranged shaped as a pyramid on a cold dish, alternating and upholding the pieces of fish with a mixed cooked vegetable salad (No. 2650) cut in quarter-inch dice or balls five-sixteenths of an inch in diameter. When the salad is dressed, smooth the surface, and cover it with a layer of mayonnaise with jelly (No. 613), then let it get firm for half an hour in a cold place, decorating it afterward with pieces of pickled cucumber and truffles. Surround the base with halved hard-boiled eggs, standing upright one against the other, after cutting off a quarter of their length on the round end, so as to enable them to stand erect against the salad. A row of small lettuce hearts cut in four, and simply salted, may be arranged above the eggs, and also fasten a lozenged cut of very red and thin beetroot over the cut end of the egg, on top of the yolks (Fig. 492). Instead of an egg border, one of jelly may be substituted, decorated with shrimp tails, hard-boiled eggs, crawfish and stoned olives.

(2632). FROG SALAD (Salade de Grenouilles).

Have one pound of very white medium-sized frogs, cooked in a little mushroom broth, and seasoned with salt, pepper, butter and lemon juice; when cold cut the meats into three-eighths of an inch squares, and put them in a vessel with cooked artichoke bottoms, potatoes and hard-boiled eggs, all cut the same size as the frogs; season with salt, pepper, oil and vinegar, and macerate for fifteen to twenty minutes. Drain the salad on a sieve, return it to the vessel, and dress it with a consistent mayonnaise (No. 606), finished with mustard and chopped tarragon; arrange it in a salad bowl, smoothing the top to a dome. Split some lobster claw meat in two, season and form into a rosette in the center of the salad; decorate around with truffles and gherkins, having a lettuce heart exactly in the middle.

(2633). HERRING SALAD WITH POTATOES (Salade de Harengs et Pommes de Terre).

Wash four salted herrings, soak them in milk for several hours, then drain and dry them. Remove the fillets and cut them into half-inch squares; cut into three-eighths inch squares eight ounces of cooked potatoes; add a four-ounce apple, peeled and cored, then minced very finely, half a pound of roasted veal cut in quarter-inch squares, a four-ounce pickled beetroot cut in three-sixteenths inch squares, and four ounces of salt cucumbers cut equally into quarter-inch squares. Put into a salad bowl the potatoes, herrings, apples and veal; season with oil and vinegar, a little hot water or broth (No. 194a), salt, pepper, mustard and some chopped chives, all well mixed; smooth the surface with a knife and decorate it with anchovy fillets, pickled cucumbers, beets, capers, pickled cherries and the yolks and whites of hard-boiled eggs, chopped up very fine, also some chopped parsley.

(2634). IMPERIAL SALAD (Salade Impériale).

Cut off some green asparagus tops one inch in length; cook them in salted water in an untinned copper basin; drain and lay them in a bowl, seasoning with salt, pepper, oil and vinegar. Cut some cooked truffles into large Julienne the same length as the asparagus, season them the same, and half an hour later lay them on top of a sieve to drain well, then add them to the asparagus and mingle them both with a mayonnaise sauce (No. 606), having a little mustard added.

(2635). ITALIAN SALAD (Salade Italienne).

Cook in salted water one pint of green peas, half a pint of string beans, half a pint of carrots and as much turnips, both of these pushed through a tin tube; they should be a quarter of an inch in diameter, and three-eighths of an inch long. First blanch the carrots and turnips, then cook them in broth (No. 194a) with salt and sugar, and when done drain and leave them to get cool. Put into a salad bowl the carrots, green peas, some green peppers, string beans, turnips and finely cut-up chervil, tarragon, chives and finely chopped parsley; season with salt, pepper, vinegar and oil, mixed well together. Cut some beets and potatoes in an eighth of an inch thick slices, remove some rounds from these with a vegetable cutter three-quarters of an inch in diameter, then season; set the beetroots alternated with the potatoes around the base; near the top place a row of round slices of pickles half an inch in diameter; divide the height between the potatoes and the pickles with fillets of anchovies into six panels; in the center of these place a round slice of mortadelle and on the top lay some small channeled mushrooms (No. 118).

(2636). JAPANESE SALAD (Salade Japonaise).

Cook some peeled potatoes in broth (No. 194a), cut two pounds of them in slices while still warm, and season them with salt, pepper, olive oil, vinegar, also half a pint of white wine, some chervil, chives, tarragon, shallot, parsley and burnet, all finely and separately chopped up. Cook some mussels with minced onions, branches of celery, mignonette, but no salt, adding a little vinegar and water; set them on a good fire, toss them frequently, and when done so that they open take them from the shells and cut away their foot or black appendage. Put the potatoes into a bowl with one pound of the mussels, or else very small clams may be substituted, stir them up lightly, and dress in a salad bowl, covering the surface with slices of truffles cooked in champagne. Set the salad in a cold place for one hour, and when serving it mix in the truffles.

(2637). LAMB SALAD À LA SOMER (Salade d'Agneau à la Somer).

Cut slices of braised lamb a quarter of an inch in thickness; arrange on a deep dish in straight rows over a bed of sliced cooked potatoes. Decorate the whole with some anchovy and bloater fillets, slices of pickled gherkins, capers, small pickled onions, chopped chervil and chives, salt, pepper, oil, vinegar and mustard. Garnish the dish with hard-boiled eggs (Fig. 492) and lozenge-shaped pieces of beetroot, also a few tarragon leaves. Serve without stirring, so as to avoid breaking the slices of meat.

(2638). LOBSTER OR SPINY LOBSTER SALAD, AMERICAN STYLE (Salade de Homard ou de Langouste à l'Américaine).

Cook two medium lobsters weighing three pounds each, let get cold, then break the shells and remove the meat from the tails and claws, cutting it into five-eighth inch dice; season all with salt, pepper, oil, vinegar and mustard, and let macerate for half an hour. Drain, and range them in a salad bowl over a bed of white and well-seasoned lettuce leaves; dress it dome-shaped, and cover the surface with a firm and consistent mayonnaise (No. 606); decorate with the lobster claws, hard-boiled eggs, olives, capers, beets and pickled cucumbers, laying on the extreme top a pretty white lettuce head.

(2639). MAZARIN SALAD (Salade à la Mazarin).

Boil in salted water two heads of celery knobs; let them get cold, then cut them up into fine slices, and with an inch diameter column tube (Fig. 168) remove all that it is possible to obtain, then range the pieces in a salad bowl. Cut the white ends of two celery stalks into pieces one and a half inches long, wash them well, and split them finely lengthwise; lay them in cold water for half an hour. Drain them off, and add to them the celery knob in the salad bowl, also eight ounces of cooked truffles cut into pieces the same size as the knobs. Season with salt, pepper, oil and vinegar, and mix well by tossing them in the bowl in such a way as not to break the truffles. Pound four hard-boiled egg-yolks, rub them through a sieve, add to them a tablespoonful of mustard, half a pint of oil and a little vinegar; mix this in with the celery and truffles; range it in the bowl for the table, and sprinkle over some chopped chervil, chives and tarragon.

(2640). MIRABEAU SALAD (Salade à la Mirabeau).

Have some shrimp tails, blanched oysters, truffles cooked in white wine, and potatoes baked in their skins, and cut into bits while hot, also the truffles. Season each article separately with salt, pepper, oil and vinegar; macerate them from fifteen to twenty minutes, then drain and mix them together in a bowl, and thicken with a mayonnaise sauce (No. 606), and a little tarragon mustard. Dress the salad in a salad bowl, smooth the surface, and decorate the top with some shrimp tails and truffles kept aside for this purpose.

(2641). NORWEGIAN SALAD (Salade à la Norvégienne).

For this salad have one pound of salted anchovies (sardels), soak them in cold water for two hours, and then wipe them with a cloth to remove the white skin covering them; cut off the fillets, pare the ends either on one side or the other, and split them across in two. (Herrings may be used instead of anchovies.) Cut into quarter-inch squares some boiled potatoes, boiled celery root, boiled and pickled beetroot, raw russet apples, and roasted tenderloin of beef, having half a pound of each kind, also half a pound of minced cabbage blanched for fifteen minutes, and then drained and cooled; put all these into a bowl, season highly with salt, pepper, oil and vinegar, and mix together thoroughly. Range the pieces in a salad bowl, garnish the edge and inside of the bowl with a row of well-drained pickled oysters, about three dozen in all, and cover with a jellied mayonnaise (No. 613); inside of this row of oysters make another one of olives stuffed with anchovy butter (No. 569); divide the surface in quarters, and on one quarter lay chopped hard-boiled egg-white, on the next quarter some finely chopped chervil and chives, the third quarter filled with hard-boiled egg-yolks, and the last quarter with chopped beetroot. Decorate the oysters with slightly blanched tarragon leaves dipped in jelly, and lay between each olive a thin slice of pickled cucumber, and stick in the center a finely pared bunch of white celery, previously laid in cold water to curl nicely.

(2642). OYSTER SALAD (Salade d'Huîtres).

Half-fill a salad bowl with white and finely cut lettuce leaves; place on top some pickled oysters cut in two or three pieces, and cover with a layer of mayonnaise sauce (No. 606). Decorate the top with lobster coral, beetroot, pickled cucumbers, capers, hard-boiled eggs and small pickled oyster crabs, or else use young pepper grass, two inches long, and well washed. (This cress can be sown in pots and will grow during the whole season; the smaller the plant the better and stronger is the taste.)

(2643). SALMON SALAD (Salade de Saumon).

Cook some slices of salmon; when cold separate the meat in flakes. Mince some celery very fine, place it in a salad bowl with the salmon over it; season with oil, vinegar, salt and pepper, mixed in another vessel and thrown over it. Pour over some ravigote mayonnaise sauce (No. 612), decorate the top with tarragon leaves, lobster coral, quartered hard-boiled eggs and fanciful cut of truffles.

(2644). PARISIAN SALAD (Salade Parisienne).

Cut in quarter-inch squares some artichoke bottoms, beetroots and celeriac, boiled in water, and some cooked potatoes. Lay these vegetables in a bowl with a sliced, salted and pickled cucumber; add some marinated tunny-fish, season and pour over some good sweet oil. Pass through a sieve six cooked egg-yolks, beat them with a spoonful of olive oil, a tablespoonful of mustard and tarragon vinegar. Dress the vegetables, cover them with this sauce, and decorate the top with anchovies, olives, truffles, shrimp tails and a few fanciful cuts of red beef tongue.

(2645). RUSSIAN SALAD (Salade Russe).

Lay in a salad bowl two ounces of celeriac cut in fine Julienne, four ounces of boiled and cold potatoes, cut in quarter-inch squares, four ounces of artichoke bottoms, each one divided into sixteen pieces, four ounces of well-pared roast sirloin of beef, cut in quarter-inch squares, four ounces of string-beans cut lozenge-shaped, two ounces each of chicken, ham and tongue cut into three-sixteenths of an inch squares: season with salt, pepper and vinegar. Cover the whole with a highly seasoned mayonnaise sauce (No. 606), in which some mustard is mixed, and garnish all around the outer edge with cucumbers and gherkins cut in fine slices, alternating them, and having one overlapping the other, then toward the center decorate with another row of sliced truffles, inside of these a row of beetroot, inside a row of anchovies and capers, and in the center lay a fine lettuce heart. There may be arranged outside of the cucumbers, and upright against the salad bowl, a row of thin slices of sausage.

(2646). RUSSIAN SALAD FOR LENTEN DINNERS (Salade Russe au Maigre).

Have some small quarter-inch carrot balls, small sticks of turnips, both blanched and cooked separately in water with some butter, salt and sugar, green peas and lozenge-shaped string beans, both cooked in salted water. Lay these vegetables in a salad bowl in four distinct sections, cover them over with a mayonnaise (No. 606), highly seasoned, and set on top four groups, one composed of smoked salmon, one of fillets of sole, one of salt herring, and one of egg-white, all cut into quarter-inch dice. Decorate with fillets of anchovies, sliced pickled cucumbers, capers, olives, shrimps, beetroots and truffles, and in the middle set a fine lettuce heart.

(2647). SHRIMP SALAD (Salade de Crevettes).

Skin the shrimps, already cooked in unsalted water, season them with salt, pepper, oil and vinegar, and serve them in a salad bowl on top of lettuce leaves, and sprinkle over some chopped parsley; lay a lettuce head on top, or, if preferred, when the shrimps are dressed, cover them with a mayonnaise sauce (No. 606), and instead of laying them in the salad bowl they may be set inside a border made as follows: Coat a border mold (Fig. 470) with some clear jelly (No. 103), decorate it through a cornet with lobster butter and Montpellier butter (No. 580), then fill it up with whipped jelly. Unmold and surround it with quartered hard-boiled eggs, and garnish the inside of the border with some seasoned lettuce; on top of this lay the seasoned shrimps in a pyramid, and sprinkle some chopped parsley over them; set on the summit a lettuce heart, and serve a mayonnaise sauce (No. 606) separately.

COOKED VEGETABLE SALADS (Salades de Légumes Cuits).

(2648). CARDOON OR CELERY SALAD (Salade de Cardons ou de Céleri).

Have one pound of cardoons, remove the stringy outside coat, and cut them into inch-long pieces, then cook them the same as cardoons with half-glaze (No. 2710). When done, drain and fry them in a pan with some oil, adding one clove of garlic, salt and sweet Spanish peppers, and half a gill of vinegar. Let boil up only once, then lay the cardoons in a salad bowl, pour the liquid over, stir well and serve.

(2649). CAULIFLOWER, MAYONNAISE SALAD (Salade de Choux-fleurs, Mayonnaise).

Lay some fine, white, cooked, cold and seasoned cauliflower in a spherical-shaped mold; unmold it over a salad bowl, and cover it entirely with a highly seasoned mayonnaise sauce (No. 606). Garnish it around with slices of pickled beetroot and dredge over some fine herbs and capers.

(2650). MACÉDOINE SALAD (Salade Macédoine).

Have four ounces of artichoke bottoms, four ounces of celery knob, four ounces of beetroot, four ounces of turnips all cut in quarter-inch squares, four ounces of string beans, cut lozenge-shaped, four ounces of asparagus tops and four ounces of green peas, all cooked separately in salted water, then refreshed, except the beetroots, which must be cooked whole and cut into squares afterward. Season with salt, pepper, oil and vinegar, and mix with a fine herb mayonnaise (No. 612).

(2651). OKRA AND SWEET PEPPER SALAD (Salade de Gombo et de Piments Doux).

Cut the ends and stalks from some tender, stringless okras; cook them in salted water, refresh and drain, then lay them in a salad-bowl. Throw some sweet peppers into hot fat, peel off the skins and cut them in Julienne, add them to the okras, and season with a fine herb mayonnaise (No. 612).

(2652). POTATO AND BEETROOT SALAD (Salade de Pommes de Terre et Betteraves).

Cut some cold boiled potatoes in three-sixteenths inch slices, also some cooked and pickled beetroots; remove twenty-four rounds from each of these, using a one-inch diameter vegetable cutter, and range them crown-shaped, one overlapping the other, intercalating the beets and the potatoes, both previously seasoned. Fill the hollow in the center with finely cut, seasoned lettuce, romaine or escarole, and cover with a layer of very thick mayonnaise (No. 606); decorate the summit with anchovy fillets and tarragon leaves; surround the border with quartered hard-boiled eggs.

(2653). POTATO AND HERRING SALAD (Salade de Pommes de Terre et de Harengs).

Cut in three-eighths of an inch squares, four pounds of potatoes cooked in salted water, half a pound of sour apples cut in four, peeled and minced, eight medium-sized vinegar pickles also minced, and four salted herrings boned and cut in three-eighths inch dice, previously unsalted in cold water. Put the potatoes into a bowl, season them with salt, pepper, oil and vinegar, and when the seasoning is well mixed add the apples, pickles and herrings, a tablespoonful of finely chopped onion, and four spoonfuls of pickled beetroot cut in quarter-inch squares; mix all the ingredients thoroughly, then range the salad on a dish or in a salad bowl.

(2654). HOT POTATO SALAD (Salade de Pommes de Terre Chaudes).

Cook twenty potatoes, either in water or steam, leaving on their skins; drain as soon as done, peel and cut into slices; lay them in a bowl with two or three gills of boiling broth (No. 194a) poured over, season with salt, pepper, oil and vinegar, and add two spoonfuls of finely chopped white onion. This salad can be served with roast veal, lamb or mutton.

(2655). POTATO SALAD IN BORDER WITH TRUFFLES (Salade de Pommes de Terre en Bordure aux Truffes).

For a plain potato salad put some fresh boiled and sliced potatoes into a bowl, season them with salt and pepper, oil, vinegar and chopped fine herbs.

For a Bordered Salad with Truffles, have some carrots and turnips sliced one inch long by three-quarters wide; take out pieces with a three-eighth inch column tube, and put them to cook in salted water; when done drain them, and set on the center of each piece of carrot and turnip one asparagus top an inch and three-quarters long; range them crown-shaped, intercalating the carrots and turnips, and set some chopped jelly around. Garnish the center with the potato salad dressed dome-shaped; cover the potatoes with round slices of truffle and then serve.

(2656). OYSTER PLANT SALAD (Salade de Salsifis).

Scrape two pounds of oyster plants, plunge them as soon as they are done in water acidulated with vinegar, then cut into inch long pieces. Dilute two spoonfuls of flour with two quarts of water, add to it salt and the juice of a lemon, a medium-sized onion, a bunch of parsley garnished with thyme and bay leaf; boil up the liquid, then put in the oyster plants, and let simmer until they are thoroughly cooked, then set them aside to drain and get cold, and cut each one into four pieces lengthwise. Range these in a salad bowl, season with salt, pepper, oil and vinegar, also some chopped parsley, and half an hour before serving cover with a mayonnaise sauce (No. 606).

(2657). STRING BEAN SALAD (Salade de Haricots Verts).

Have one pound of small string beans; if too large cut them lengthwise in two, and cook them in salted water in an untinned copper vessel; refresh them and drain. Put them into a salad bowl and season with salt and pepper, adding one tablespoonful of vinegar and three of oil.

(2658). WHITE BEAN SALAD (Salade de Haricots Blancs).

When the white beans are cooked the same as for No. 2701, and cold, put them in a salad bowl with a little shallot, chives and parsley, all finely chopped, and for each quart of beans add two tablespoonfuls of vinegar and six of oil, salt and pepper; stir well and serve.

RAW VEGETABLE SALADS (Salades de Légumes Crus).

(2659). CABBAGE SALAD—WHITE OR RED (Salade de Choux—Blancs ou Rouges).

Have either a very fresh white or red cabbage; suppress the outer leaves, also the hard parts and core; mince it up finely, and lay it in a bowl, sprinkle over some salt, and let macerate for one hour, then drain off its liquid and season with salt, pepper, oil and vinegar. A cabbage salad, called cold slaw, is made by shredding the cabbage as finely as possible and seasoning it with salt, pepper, oil, vinegar and tomato catsup.

(2660). CELERY SALAD AND CELERY KNOB SALAD (Salade de Céleri et Salade de Céleri Rave)

Remove the first stalks, which are generally hollow, and put the good ones into a bowl of cold water; cut each stalk into pieces one inch and a half long, then divide these pieces into lengths the same as a large Julienne; wash well, drain and dry them thoroughly; season with salt, pepper, mustard, oil and vinegar.

Celery Knob.—Choose these very tender, peel and cut them into thin round slices, set them in a bowl in layers, salting each one separately. One hour later pour off the water and season with oil, vinegar, ground pepper and mustard. Macerate for one hour in its seasoning, and then serve.

(2661). CUCUMBER SALAD, ENGLISH STYLE (Salade de Concombres à l'Anglaise).

Select the tenderest cucumbers, peel off the rind, slice the interior finely, and lay them in a dish, sprinkle over some fine salt, and let macerate for fifteen minutes; season them, after straining off the liquid, with salt, pepper, oil and vinegar, adding some chopped parsley.

English Style.—The same, only add a very finely minced onion.

(2662). CUCUMBER AND TOMATO SALAD (Salade de Concombres et Tomates).

The same as for English style, only adding very firm, finely sliced and peeled tomatoes as well as the onion.

(2663). EGGPLANT SALAD, PROVENÇAL (Salade d'Aubergines Provençale).

Peel and slice some eggplant into quarter of an inch thick slices, pare it in rounds one and a quarter inches in diameter, lay them in salt for ten minutes, then sponge them off and season with pepper, garlic, oil and vinegar; then add the same quantity of water cress and a few hard-boiled eggs.

(2664). GERMAN SALAD WITH CROÛTONS (Salade Allemande aux Croûtons).

Blanch in boiling water one pound of sauerkraut for five minutes, refresh and add to it one pound of red cabbage previously pickled in vinegar. Cut up the sauerkraut to make the pieces shorter, and lay them in a bowl with three ounces of very fine chopped onions, blanched and refreshed; add to this one ounce of grated horseradish and a tablespoonful of chopped chervil. Season with salt, pepper, six tablespoonfuls of olive oil and two of vinegar, and serve in a salad bowl with a ring of round croûtons on top made of fragments of puff-paste (No. 146), one and a quarter inches thick, cut with a round pastry-cutter, then cooked in a very slack oven.

(2665). ONION SALAD—BERMUDA (Salade d'Oignons de Bermude).

Mince the onions very finely, either with a knife or the machine, and season them with salt, pepper, oil and vinegar.

(2666). TOMATO SALAD (Salade de Tomates).

To peel tomatoes throw them into boiling water; cut them in slices across and season with salt, pepper, vinegar and a little oil; arrange them in a salad bowl.

(2667). TRUFFLE SALAD À LA GAMBETTA (Salade de Truffes à la Gambetta).

Mince six fine peeled Piedmontese truffles, weighing eight ounces, put them into a bowl with three artichoke bottoms, previously cooked and cut into eight pieces. Rub through a sieve four hard-boiled egg-yolks, lay them in a bowl with two tablespoonfuls of mustard, work well together, then incorporate three gills of oil and tarragon vinegar; rub the bottom of a salad bowl with a clove of garlic, set the truffles in, and the artichokes over; cover all with some mayonnaise (No. 607), mixing in also some tarragon, chervil, chives and parsley, all finely chopped.

GREEN SALADS (Salades Vertes).

(2668). CHICORY SALAD (Salade de Chicorée).

Select the chicory heads; having yellow hearts and very fine leaves; cut away all the green and wash the white part, drain and shake well in a napkin or wire basket to remove all the water. Season with salt, pepper, oil, vinegar, chervil and tarragon, or, instead of these herbs use a piece of bread-crust after rubbing a clove of garlic over it. This piece of bread is called a capon.

(2669). CORN SALAD OR LAMB'S LETTUCE SALAD (Salade de Mâche ou Doucette).

This salad can be mixed with monk's beard and slices of cooked beetroot. It should be well picked and all the yellow leaves removed; clean the roots, cut them off when too large, and divide the stalks into two or four parts; add cooked slices of beetroot and chopped chervil; season with salt, pepper, oil and vinegar. Monk's beard may be mixed with it, half and half.

(2670). DANDELION SALAD (Salade de Dent-de-lion).

This salad takes the place of wild chicory, especially in winter, and by growing it in cellars it can be had very white and tender. Prepare and season it the same as monk's beard (No. 2674).

(2671). ESCAROLE AND ENDIVE SALAD (Salade d'Escarolle et d'Endive).

Take the leaves when quite yellow, remove the hard parts, and split each leaf in the center its entire length; it is always preferable not to wash these salads, as the leaves can be cleaned by wiping them. Season with salt, pepper, oil, vinegar and finely chopped chervil and tarragon.

(2672). LETTUCE SALAD, PLAIN (Salade de Laitue, Simple).

Choose freshly gathered and well-filled lettuce heads, suppress the hard leaves, keeping only the yellow ones; pick them off the stalks, retaining the heart whole, the size of an egg, and cut it in four. Split each leaf through the center, wash them at once, drain, wipe and shake the salad well to extract all the water, then place it in a salad bowl, sprinkling over some chopped chervil and tarragon. Put into a bottle four egg-yolks, two spoonfuls of vinegar and eight of oil, some salt and pepper; shake the seasoning up well in the bottle, and pour it over the lettuce, stirring it until it is properly mixed.

(2673). LETTUCE AND ANCHOVY SALAD (Salade de Laitue aux Anchois).

This is made with well washed and dried lettuce by shredding it up finely; season and lay it in a salad bowl, cover with a mayonnaise sauce (No. 606), decorated with fillets and anchovies, hard-boiled yolks and whites of eggs, and some finely chopped herbs. A lettuce salad may be served garnished with hard-boiled eggs and plenty of herbs. Lettuce salad may also be seasoned with sweet or sour cream instead of oil.

(2674). MONK'S BEARD SALAD (Salade de Barbe de Capucin).

This salad is very much liked and is exceedingly wholesome. Clean it well by wiping the leaves with a towel—do not wash it; season with salt, pepper, oil and vinegar, adding a few slices of beetroot.

(2675). COS LETTUCE SALAD (Salade de Romaine).

Remove all the green leaves until the yellow ones are reached; wipe each leaf well, and split them lengthwise, then cut into two-inch long pieces, continuing as far as the heart; split it in four; place in a salad bowl and season the salad with chervil, tarragon, all finely cut, egg-yolks (one egg for two persons) and dilute with eight spoonfuls of oil and two of vinegar; add salt, pepper and green mustard; mix well when ready to serve. The egg-yolks may be suppressed.

(2676). WATER CRESS AND APPLE SALAD AND NONPAREIL [CHIFFONADE] SALAD
(Salade de Cresson aux Pommes d'Arbre et Salade Nonpareil [Chiffonade].)

Have very clean and green water-cress; season it only when ready to serve with a very little oil, salt, pepper, vinegar and some sour apples cut in slices. Pepper water-cresses are prepared the same.

Nonpareil (Chiffonade) Salad.—Place in the bottom of a bowl some seasoning composed of salt, pepper, oil and vinegar; mix well with a fork. Mince some lettuce very fine, also the same quantity of chicory and celery; dress dome-shaped in the bowl containing the seasoning. Chop up separately the whites and the yolks of two hard-boiled eggs, and cut in three-sixteenths of an inch squares the same volume of beets and potatoes. Divide the dome in four equal parts with anchovy fillets, garnish one of these parts with beets, one with the chopped egg-white, one with the chopped yolks, and the last one with the chopped potatoes; bestrew over all finely chopped truffles, parsley, lobster coral, and in the center place a nice Spanish olive.

VEGETABLES (Légumes).

(2677). ARTICHOKE BOTTOMS À LA FLORENCE (Fonds d'Artichauts à la Florence).

Prepare and cook some artichoke bottoms the same as for la Villars (No. 2682); fill the hollow in the center with minced truffles and mushrooms fried in butter, this to be drained off and the preparation mingled with well-reduced allemande sauce (No. 407); let get cold after they are filled dome form, and smooth neatly with a knife; then lay them on a buttered sheet, bestrew with bread-crumbs and grated parmesan, pour butter over and color in a hot oven. Dress them in a circle, filling the center with blanched artichoke bottoms, cut in six parts, pared and cooked in butter; pour over a buttered suprême sauce (No. 547) and send to the table.

(2678). ARTICHOKE BOTTOMS À LA JUSSIENNE (Fonds d'Artichauts à la Jussienne).

Turn some artichoke bottoms the same as mushrooms (No. 118), rub them over with lemon and cook in a seasoned white stock (No. 182), to which add pieces of marrow; drain when well done. Mince a few mushrooms, cut them into strips and fry them in butter; drain off the latter and replace it by thick béchamel sauce (No. 409); cover the artichoke bottoms with this, mask over with allemande sauce (No. 407), reduced with a little jelly (No. 103), into which mix more mushrooms and chopped truffles; allow to cool; roll them in white bread-crumbs, dip in beaten eggs, again in bread-crumbs and fry to a fine golden color; drain, wipe and arrange them on a dish in a circle, having the center filled with sliced cooked sweet potatoes, cut three-eighths of an inch thick and one and a quarter inches in diameter. Serve separately a Colbert sauce (No. 451).

(2679). ARTICHOKE BOTTOMS À LA MONTGLAS (Fonds d'Artichauts à la Montglas).

Have some artichoke bottoms prepared and cooked the same as for la Villars (No. 2682); drain and fill the hollow centers with a montglas garnishing cut in small sticks, composed of red beef tongue, truffles, mushrooms and some cooked white meat of a chicken; mingle them with a well reduced allemande sauce (No. 407), and remove from the fire at the first boil and leave till cold; then fill the artichoke bottoms, forming them bomb-shaped on top; cover with chicken quenelle forcemeat (No. 89), smooth and strew bread-crumbs and grated parmesan over the entire surface. Range them on a small baking sheet, pour plenty of clarified butter over and finish cooking in a slack oven, basting frequently.

(2680). ARTICHOKE BOTTOMS À LA MORNAY (Fonds d'Artichauts à la Mornay).

Wipe dry ten to twelve cooked artichoke bottoms, all of the same size; fill the hollow side with a foies-gras baking forcemeat (No. 81), mixed with a few spoonfuls of chopped cooked truffles; smooth the top of the preparation and cover with a layer of well-reduced Mornay sauce (No. 504); bestrew the sauce with parmesan cheese, and brown for two minutes under a salamander (Fig. 123).

(2681). ARTICHOKE BOTTOMS À LA SOUBISE (Fonds d'Artichauts à la Soubise).

Prepare a soubise purée (No. 723). Select some equal-sized cooked artichoke bottoms, drain and wipe them on a cloth; cover the hollow side with a part of the soubise purée (No. 723) and let it get cold, then over this lay a thin layer of delicate raw chicken quenelle forcemeat (No. 89); besprinkle with bread-crumbs, and brush over with butter. Range these artichoke bottoms in a sautoir with some good gravy (No. 404), and heat them well while browning slightly.

(2682). ARTICHOKE BOTTOMS À LA VILLARS (Fonds d'Artichauts à la Villars).

Procure twelve raw artichoke bottoms; when turned (Figs. 547–548) and pared blanch them in salted water and cook in white stock (No. 182), with aromatics and a little white wine, keeping them slightly firm; drain on a cloth and then cut out the bottom with a two and a quarter inch diameter tin cutter. Lay them in a sautoir, moisten with a little chicken bouillon (No. 188) and a small piece of butter. Reduce the liquid entirely. Mince some white onions, blanch them for a few minutes, fry them lightly in butter and moisten with broth (No. 194a) and cream, half of each, adding the same quantity of minced fresh mushrooms; reduce and leave to cool. Drain the artichoke bottoms, cover the hollow side with the preparation, and this with a layer of raw cream forcemeat (No. 75); strew over bread-crumbs and grated cheese, and lay them in a sautoir with a little stock (No. 194a); color in a moderate oven, and dress on a well-buttered reduced cream velouté sauce (No. 415).

(2683). ARTICHOKE BOTTOMS FRIED (Fonds d'Artichauts Frits).

Pare off the bottoms of some young, tender and stringless artichokes; after cutting away the green part divide each one in four, remove the choke and cut the leaves at half an inch from the bottom; divide each quarter in four and throw them at once into a pan of water acidulated with vinegar; drain and lay them in a vessel with salt, pepper, oil and lemon juice. Prepare a frying paste with flour, diluted with water, adding a few egg-yolks and a little olive oil; whip the whites to a stiff froth and beat them into the paste; dip each piece of artichoke into this and plunge them in hot frying fat; cook slowly, drain, wipe and salt over with salt; dress on a folded napkin with a bunch of parsley on top.

(2684). ARTICHOKE BOTTOMS STUFFED—LEAN (Fonds d'Artichauts Farcis au Maigre).

Pare eight or ten raw artichoke bottoms, blanch them in salted water and cook them in a white stock (No. 182) with aromatic herbs and a little white wine, keeping them rather hard, then drain them on a cloth. Prepare a duxelle (No. 385) composed of chopped onions, shallots, truffles and mushrooms, mingled first with a little smooth cream frangipane panada (No. 120), then with a little sauce; season the preparation and finish it with some raw egg-yolks, chopped parsley and a few spoonfuls of salted anchovy fillets cut in small dice. With this forcemeat cover the artichoke bottoms, smooth and bestrew with bread-crumbs; range them in a small deep baking dish, capable of being placed in the oven, and besprinkle lightly with oil; finish cooking in a slack oven, basting over frequently.

(2685). ARTICHOKE BOTTOMS WITH BAKED CAULIFLOWER (Fonds d'Artichauts aux Choux-Fleurs Gratinés).

Have some artichoke bottoms cooked and prepared as for la Villars (No. 2682); drain and fill the hollow centers with flowerets of cauliflower; cover with béchamel sauce (No. 409), bestrew the top with bread-crumbs and grated parmesan, baste over with butter, and range them at once on a buttered baking sheet; bake in a moderate oven and dress in a circle on a dish; pour béchamel cream sauce (No. 411) in the center, or else a brown half-glaze sauce (No. 413).

(2686). ARTICHOKE BOTTOMS WITH CREAM BÉCHAMEL, BAKED (Fonds d'Artichauts Béchamel à la Crème, au Gratin).

Drain some cooked artichoke bottoms (Fig. 546-548) on a cloth, selecting those of equal size; fill the hollow in the center with a layer of delicate chicken godiveau (No. 82); cover this with cream béchamel sauce (No. 411) and besprinkle the surface with grated parmesan, pouring some butter over. Range them at once in a sautoir, having its bottom covered with a little good gravy (No. 404); baste over with more melted butter and bake in a moderate oven for twenty minutes; they should be of a nice color. Dress in a circle on a dish and pour some cream béchamel in the center.

(2687). ARTICHOKE BOTTOMS WITH MARROW (Fonds d'Artichauts à la Moelle).

In case there be no fresh artichokes canned ones can be procured at any time of the year. Drain and range the cooked bottoms in a flat saucepan; moisten with a little good unskimmed stock (No. 194a) with white wine; heat them simply over a slow fire, but if too hard boil them until perfectly done. Soak two or three pieces of raw beef marrow, without the bone; wrap them up in fine pieces of muslin and poach for a quarter of an hour in stock (No. 194a). Just when prepared to serve drain the artichoke bottoms carefully, wipe them on a towel, and drain the pieces of marrow as well; unwrap these and let get partly cold; then cut them across in thick slices and glaze them with a brush; keep them for a few moments at the oven door, then set one slice in the hollow of each artichoke bottom; dress these on a dish, cover with a little brown sauce (No. 414) reduced with Madeira wine, not having it too consistent. For garnishing artichoke bottoms, a macédoine of vegetables (No. 680) may be substituted for the marrow, or else green peas, Parisian style (No. 2745), with which mix a quarter as much cooked chicken, using only the white part cut in three-sixteenths of an inch squares.

(2688). ARTICHOKES QUARTERED À LA COLBERT, STUFFED À LA VILLEROI, FRIED AND BRAISED (Quartiers d'Artichauts à la Colbert, Farcis à la Villeroi, Frits et Fraisés).

To prepare these artichokes the hard outside leaves must first be removed, the remaining ones shortened and the bottoms pared; then divide them in four, blanch in salted acidulated water until the choke detaches easily; throw them into cold water, drain and pare once more (see Fig. 545). They can be cooked in several ways, either sautéing in butter to finish the cooking, and adding just when ready to serve some meat glaze (No. 402), lemon juice, seasoning and chopped parsley. Or they can be cooked in a white stock (No. 182), and then served in their natural state, either by filling the space between the leaves and the bottom with chicken quenelle forcemeat (No. 89) that has had cooked fine herbs (No. 385) mingled in, then poached and covered with Villeroi sauce (No. 560), breaded and fried. Those not stuffed may also be breaded à la Villeroi and fried. They can also be braised in a sautoir lined with bards of fat pork; moisten with mirepoix stock (No. 419), and cover with more bards of fat pork. When done dress them in a vegetable dish, and have half of their stock skimmed and strained over; reduce the other half with espagnole sauce (No. 414), and when well reduced fill some hollowed-out bread-crusts (No. 51) with blanched marrow; cover with a part of this last sauce, and serve the remainder in a sauce-boat.

(2689). ARTICHOKES—WHOLE—À LA BARIGOULE (Artichauts Entiers à la Barigoule).

Pare eight medium-sized artichokes; suppress the hardest leaves from the bottom (Fig. 544)

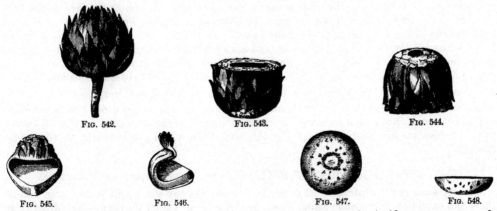

Fig. 542.   Fig. 543.   Fig. 544.

Fig. 545.   Fig. 546.   Fig. 547.   Fig. 548.

and cut the upper ones off straight on the pointed end; empty out the inside, or more properly speaking the chokes (Fig. 543), wash thoroughly and drain well, turning them upside down so as to have no water left in the inside. Pour some oil in a pan; when very hot fry the tips of the artichoke leaves in it. Should the bottoms be thin, then lay another one inside, thus having two bottoms to one artichoke. To make the dressing, chop up half a pound of fresh fat pork with half a pound of butter; add three finely chopped small shallots, a spoonful and a half of chopped parsley, salt, pepper, nutmeg, a pound of finely minced or chopped mushrooms, and a gill of Madeira wine. Have all these ingredients properly mingled, divide in eight parts, and fill the inside of the artichokes with them; cover with bards of fat pork, tie with two rows of string and lay them in a saucepan with slices of fat pork; on the bottom place carrots, onions, a bunch of parsley with thyme and bay leaf, moisten with half stock (No. 194a) and white wine; boil, skim and then cook in a moderate oven for one hour or longer, until the leaves detach easily; drain the stock, skim and reduce it with espagnole sauce (No. 414) to half-glaze, adding lemon juice. Untie the artichokes, suppress the fat pork and dress; cover lightly with a part of the sauce, serving the remainder separately.

(2690). ARTICHOKES—WHOLE—À LA RACHEL (Artichauts Entiers à la Rachel).

These proportions are for six artichokes: Pare them by removing the hardest leaves next to the stalk, suppress the green bottom part and cut off the tip of each leaf straight; empty the inside by removing all the choke (Fig. 543), wash and drain well. Cut a medium-sized onion and one shallot into small squares, fry in butter and add one pound of fresh mushrooms chopped very finely; place the saucepan on the fire and keep stirring with a spoon until the mushrooms have their moisture reduced, then add some chopped parsley and fresh bread-crumbs; season with salt, pepper and nutmeg and pour in a little béchamel (No. 409). Fill the artichokes bomb-shaped with this and lay on top one fine turned or channeled mushroom (No. 118); cover with bards of fat pork, tie with two turns of string and braise in a low saucepan lined with pieces of fat pork, moistening with white wine mirepoix stock (No. 419); drain this off when done, skim the fat and reduce to a quarter-glaze. Dress the artichokes and pour a little of the stock over. Serve separately a velouté sauce (No. 415) reduced with mushroom essence (No. 392), the rest of the stock and a little well-buttered tomato purée (No. 730); serve.

(2691). ARTICHOKES—WHOLE—BOILED, WITH WHITE OR VINAIGRETTE SAUCE (Artichauts Entiers Bouillis, à la Sauce Blanche ou à la Vinaigrette).

Select artichokes of a medium size; remove the hardest leaves from the base, pare the bottoms well, suppressing all the green part, then cut off the tips of each leaf straight (see Fig. 543). Put them into a saucepan of boiling salted water and cook until the leaves detach, then drain, remove the choke, and washing them in their own liquor range them on a napkin bottom downward to have them drain thoroughly; serve at the same time either a white sauce (No. 562) or else a vinaigrette sauce (No. 634).

Boiled and cold artichokes are served with a vinaigrette sauce.

(2692). BOILED ASPARAGUS WITH HOLLANDAISE, HOLLANDAISE MOUSSELINE OR VINAIGRETTE SAUCE (Asperges Bouillies à la Sauce Hollandaise à la Sauce Hollandaise Mousseline).

Have the asparagus freshly picked, if practicable; trim the tops, and scrape or peel the stalks; then pare them into equal lengths, and tie them in small bunches, separating the larger ones from the smaller. Fasten them well with string. Boil the asparagus in plenty of salted water in an untinned copper basin, plunging them into the liquid; cover the vessel and let cook slowly. As soon as they are done drain them on a sieve, and afterward untie the bunches on a cloth and dress them symmetrically in a pyramid on a folded napkin; carefully reserve the handsomest ones for the top. Send to the table at the same time a good Hollandaise sauce (No. 477), or else a vinaigrette sauce.

Vinaigrette.—Put into a vessel six hard-boiled egg-yolks rubbed through a sieve, smooth nicely while beating with a spoon, and incorporate slowly two gills of good oil, two spoonfuls of cold velouté sauce (No. 415), a little vinegar, mustard, pepper, chopped parsley or chervil. Serve this sauce the same time as the asparagus, or else serve them with a Hollandaise mousseline sauce (No. 477).

(2693). ASPARAGUS, COUNTESS STYLE—HEADS (Têtes d'Asperges à la Comtesse).

Scrape some green asparagus, cut them, leaving the tops two and a half inches long, and tie these into small bunches; cook in salted water, and when done cut off the strings and dress them in a pyramid; garnish around with bouchées filled with asparagus tops and mushrooms as follows: After the asparagus is cut off for the above break the remaining tender parts of the stalks, and cut them into quarter of an inch thick pieces; cook in salted water, and drain; put these into a saucepan with as much cooked mushrooms cut into quarter-inch squares, and dilute with good buttered velouté (No. 415); season properly, and fill very hot bouchées (No. 11) with it. Serve a velouté sauce apart, having it thickened at the last moment with egg-yolks, cream, a liberal piece of fresh butter and lemon juice.

(2694). ASPARAGUS IN SMALL BUNCHES—HEADS (Têtes d'Asperges en Petites Bottes).

Scrape the stalks of some medium-sized asparagus; cut them from the top end into two and a half inch lengths, and with these form small bunches, holding them together by two rings cut from a carrot about two inches in diameter; cook them in salted water. Use these small bunches for garnishing hot or cold removes, pouring a little Hollandaise sauce (No. 477) over, or else a vinaigrette sauce (No. 634), both to be well seasoned.

(2695). ASPARAGUS TOPS À LA MAINTENON (Pointes d'Asperges à la Maintenon).

Have all the asparagus of the same size, not too slender; break off the stalks at the beginning of the tender part; strip off the heads, and cut the tender part into inch lengths; put the heads aside to cook separately. Plunge the lengths into boiling salted water placed in an untinned copper pan; boil quickly, keeping them slightly hard, then wipe on a cloth, and put them into a thin sautoir with melted butter; season, heat rapidly while tossing, then remove. The asparagus can now be laid in a little velouté (No. 415) and chicken purée (No. 713). Serve the asparagus in a vegetable dish, surrounded with croûtons of bread shaped like a cock's-comb, and fried in butter, just when prepared to dish up.

(2696). ASPARAGUS TOPS FRIED À LA MIRANDA (Pointes d'Asperges Frites à la Miranda).

Bend and break off the tender part of the asparagus into one inch lengths; blanch them well in salted water; drain and dip in fine cracker dust, then in beaten egg, and finally in bread-crumbs; fry, drain, salt, and dress on a folded napkin, laying a bunch of fried green parsley on top. Serve apart a sauce made with one hard-boiled egg-yolk mingled with one raw yolk, mustard, salt and pepper; beat vigorously, stirring in a little olive oil and tarragon vinegar.

(2697). ASPARAGUS TOPS WITH CHEESE (Pointes d'Asperges au Fromage).

Scrape some medium-sized asparagus; cut them into quarter of an inch lengths, cook in salted water, keeping them slightly hard, drain and put them into a sautoir with butter, and toss for a few moments over the fire to evaporate all the moisture. Drain off the butter, season and dress on a vegetable dish; cover the surface with freshly kneaded butter, into which mix as much grated parmesan as the butter can absorb; salt, if found necessary, adding a little cayenne pepper; push into a hot oven, and serve as soon as it browns.

(2698). FRESH BEANS, WITH CREAM AND ENGLISH STYLE (Fèves Fraîches à la Crème et à l'Anglaise.)

Take freshly picked, shelled and tender beans; put them to blanch in salted water with a small bunch of savory added, then transfer them to a saucepan with hot butter; season. Fry them for two minutes on a hot fire to evaporate their moisture and thicken with a few spoonfuls of reduced béchamel (No. 409); remove from the fire and stir in a large piece of butter divided in small pats; finish with a little nutmug and serve with puff-paste croûtons around.

English Style.—Blanch some fresh green beans in salted water until the skin detaches easily, then let get cold and suppress these skins; sauté the beans in butter, season with salt, nutmeg and finely cut-up fresh savory. Transfer them to a vegetable dish and serve with thin slices of butter laid on top.

(2699). LIMA OR KIDNEY BEANS, MAÎTRE D'HÔTEL (Haricots de Lima ou Flageolets Maître d'Hôtel).

Have a pound of medium-sized, freshly picked lima beans; boil them in salted water in an untinned copper saucepan, then drain. Put four ounces of butter in a sautoir, heat it well, add the beans and sauté, seasoning with salt and chopped parsley; stir in a little velouté sauce (No. 415) and fresh butter, squeeze the juice of a lemon over, then serve.

(2700). RED BEANS, SMOTHERED (Haricots Rouges à l'Étuvée).

Steep a pound of red beans for six hours in cold water, drain, put them into a saucepan and moisten to double their height with cold water; add half a pound of blanched bacon, a carrot cut in four, and a bunch of parsley garnished with thyme and bay leaf. When the beans are three-quarters done, take out the carrots and herbs and put in one pound of small onions fried in clarified butter, also a pint of red wine; continue to boil until thoroughly done, then drain, and put them back into a sautoir and thicken with a little espagnole sauce (No. 414), seasoning with salt, pepper and chopped parsley. Dress the beans and surround them with the bacon cut up in slices. The red beans may be replaced by white or black beans.

(2701). WHITE BEANS, THICKENED MAÎTRE D'HÔTEL AND BRETONNE (Haricots Blancs Maître d'Hôtel Liée et Bretonne).

Put a pound of dry white beans to soak in cold water for six hours; place them in a saucepan and cover to three times above their height with cold water; set this on the fire and withdraw the saucepan to the side of the range at the first boil; add to it two ounces of butter, let cook, and when they crush easily under the pressure of the finger drain and transfer to another saucepan; season with salt, prepared red pepper (No. 168) and nutmeg; add a little thickened maître d'hôtel butter and chopped parsley.

Bretonne.—Add chopped onions, cooked colorless in butter, to the above, and instead of the maître d'hôtel butter substitute espagnole sauce (No. 414), finishing with chopped parsley.

(2702). BEETROOT FRITTERS À LA DICKENS; BEETROOTS WITH BUTTER AND FINE HERBS AND BEETROOTS WITH CREAM (Beignets de Betteraves à la Dickens; Betteraves au Beurre et fines Herbes et Betteraves à la Crème).

Cut some beetroots cooked as below in slices, each one an eighth of an inch thick; wipe dry and place on half of them a quarter of an inch thick layer of the following preparation: Fry two well-chopped onions colorless in butter; add four ounces of chopped mushrooms and a pinch of minced chervil, salt and pepper; on this layer place another round of beetroot, and from the whole remove rounds an inch and a half in diameter; dip these in frying batter (No. 137) and plunge into very hot frying fat, drain, wipe and dress as a garnishing around a meat remove.

With Butter and Fine Herbs.—These beets can be cooked in boiling water or by steam without suppressing the stalk or root end; select them always of a fine red; peel after they are done and cut them up into quarter-inch thick slices and from these remove rounds two to two and a half inches in diameter; lay them in saucepan with salt, pepper and a little vinegar; sauté for a few moments and serve; chopped parsley and chives can be scattered over the top.

With Cream.—After the beetroots are cooked and cut into slices, as above, simmer them in fresh cream, seasoning with salt, cayenne pepper and nutmeg; thicken just when ready to serve with egg-yolks and fresh butter.

(2703). BRUSSELS SPROUTS À LA BARONESS (Choux de Bruxelles à la Baronnè).

Clean, prepare and cook the sprouts the same as for sautéd (No. 2704); the only difference to be observed is that instead of boiling them entirely have them only three-quarters cooked. Put them into a saucepan with as many chestnuts also three-quarters cooked; moisten with fresh cream, season with salt and nutmeg, and let simmer together until done and the liquid sufficiently reduced.

(2704). BRUSSELS SPROUTS SAUTÉD (Choux de Bruxelles Sautés).

Select three pounds of the freshest and firmest Brussels sprouts, having them of as uniform size as possible; pare and plunge them into an untinned vessel full of boiling water to cook green; when done drain, refresh in cold water, drain once more, wipe and pare again. Put six ounces of butter into a sautoir and when hot add the sprouts; season with salt and shake them in the butter; sprinkle in some chopped parsley, and if so desired they can be mingled with a little velouté sauce (No. 415).

(2705). CABBAGE IN BALLOTINES—STUFFED (Choux Farcis en Ballotines).

Cut each of two clean cabbages in half, plunge them into boiling salted water and boil for fifteen minutes; then drain, refresh and press out all the water. Dampen some pieces of linen six by five inches; lay over each a thin slice of fat pork four by three inches, and on this spread a blanched cabbage leaf, mincing the heart-leaves up finely. Fry in lard four ounces of finely chopped onion, and one pound of chopped mushrooms; when the moisture has been evaporated from the latter add the minced cabbage, season with salt and pepper, then add half a pound of cooked sausage meat, and half a pound of boiled rice; thicken this preparation with a few raw egg-yolks and range it in the center of the spread-out leaves; roll each one in the shape of a sausage, then in the bards of fat pork, and lastly in the linen; tie both ends the same as a boned turkey. Lay them in a sautoir, cover with more slices of fat pork, and pour in some unskimmed broth (No. 194a), then let cook for two hours; free the stock from fat, strain it through a sieve and reduce it with as much espagnole sauce (No. 414). Unwrap the ballotines, remove the pork and dress them in the center of a dish, covering over with a third part of the sauce, and serving the remainder in a sauce-boat.

(2706). CABBAGE, PEASANT STYLE (Choux à la Paysanne).

Parboil half a cabbage for fifteen minutes, remove the core, drain and braise; when well done drain once more and suppress the hard parts; mash the remainder with a spoon, seasoning with salt, pepper and nutmeg. Have a linen bag two and a quarter inches in diameter; fill it with the seasoned cabbage and tie it firmly, pressing it down tight; lay this under a weight to get thoroughly cold, then cut it into even slices· remove the pieces of linen and dip each slice in beaten egg and then in bread-crumbs; fry in clarified butter and dress in a circle. To fill the center chop up finely the other half of the cabbage, after blanching it for ten minutes and draining very dry; put it into a saucepan with fresh butter, and fry colorless; season, moisten with broth (No. 194a), and let simmer until thoroughly done and the liquid reduced, then drain off the fat and thicken with a little velouté sauce (No. 415) and fresh butter; lay this inside the circle as described above.

(2707). RED CABBAGE À LA MONTARGIS (Choux Rouges à la Montargis).

Divide two red cabbages in four pieces, remove the core and the hard stalks from the leaves; mince finely, wash and drain. Place in a saucepan half a pound of butter, and half a pound of bacon cut in quarter-inch squares; first blanch them, then let fry in the butter, and add the cabbage, salt, pepper and nutmeg; moisten with a pint of broth (No. 194a) and a gill of brandy. Have six sour apples, peel, round and core them with a tin tube five-eighths of an inch in diameter; lay them in with the cabbage, and cover the top with a buttered paper; cook in a slow oven for two hours and a half. Just when ready to serve remove the fat and dress the cabbage in the center of a dish with the apples around, arranging a small Chipolata sausage (No. 754) between each one.

(2708). KOHL-RABIES, HOUSEKEEPER'S STYLE (Choux Raves à la Ménagère).

Cut some medium-sized kohl-rabies in four equal parts, or if very large, then in six or eight; peel and pare them into crescent olive form, obtaining about three pounds in all. Blanch these in boiling salted water, refresh and drain once more. Put six ounces of butter into a saucepan and when very hot and cooked to hazel-nut (No. 567) lay in the blanched kohl-rabies and toss them so they do not color; moisten with broth (No. 194a), let cook, reduce to a glaze and when serving dilute with a pint of béchamel sauce (No. 409), also adding three ounces of fresh butter, a very small lump at a time.

(2709). KOHL-RABIES, STUFFED (Choux Raves Farcis).

Shape them perfectly round and all of uniform size; empty out the insides and stuff them while raw, or else blanch them first in boiling salted water for a few moments; the stuffing consists of godiveau forcemeat (No. 85), having truffles, mushrooms and parsley, all chopped up, mixed in with it; range them in a sautoir lined with fat pork and moisten with a little gravy (No. 404); when done drain and strain the stock, remove all of its fat and reduce it with as much espagnole sauce (No. 414). Lay the kohl-rabies over the sauce and serve.

(2710). CARDOONS WITH HALF-GLAZE (Cardons à la Demi-glace).

Remove the large strings from a head of cardoon; cut the tenderest parts into four-inch lengths and throw them at once into cold acidulated water, then plunge them into boiling water, also acidulated with citric acid or vinegar; blanch until the downy skin detaches, rubbing with a cloth and drain to plunge at once into an abundance of cold water. Pare the cardoon, suppressing the superficial threads, and range them in a saucepan lined with fat pork; cover with more pork and moisten with unskimmed broth (No. 194a) mixed with a little white wine; add the cut-up pulp of a lemon, salt and aromatics, cover the saucepan and finish cooking very slowly. At the last moment drain them on a tammy, then on a cloth and cut them up into even lengths to dress in a pyramid on a dish, covering over with a half-glaze sauce (No. 413) reduced with Madeira wine.

Cardoons may be covered with a velouté sauce (No. 415) or else a brown sauce (No. 414), having some poached marrow cut into large dice added.

(2711). CARROTS, COLBERT (Carottes à la Colbert).

Take a few dozen small, new carrots of uniform-size, trim them pear-shaped, blanch for a few moments in salted water, drain and lay them in a saucepan with a little butter, salt, a pinch of sugar and white broth (No. 194a); cook until they fall to a glaze, and should they then not be sufficiently tender, remoisten and reduce the liquid once more; finish with a little half-glaze sauce (No. 413), butter and lemon juice.

(2712). CARROTS GLAZED OR WITH FINE HERBS (Carottes Glacées ou aux Fines Herbes).

Turn or cut out with a spoon (Fig. 91) some carrots, shaping them to resemble olives; blanch, then sauté in butter with a little sugar; moisten with broth (No. 194a) and cook slowly until reduced to a glaze, and the moistening reduced the same, in the meanwhile having the carrots done; add a little root glaze (No. 403) and then dish up in a pyramid.

For Fine Herbs add to the carrots prepared as for the above some chopped parsley and finely cut-up chives.

(2713). CARROTS, VIENNESE STYLE (Carottes à la Viennaise).

Scrape some large carrots and cut them up into balls with a vegetable spoon five-eighths of an inch in diameter; blanch them in salted water until half done, then drain, place them in a saucepan with white broth (No. 194a), salt and a very little sugar; finish cooking, letting the liquid fall to a glaze, and just when ready to serve thicken with a little well-buttered velouté sauce (No. 415), to which add lemon juice, fine herbs and meat glaze (No. 402).

(2714). CARROTS WITH CREAM (Carottes à la Crème).

Cut some carrots into inch lengths; from the red parts remove cylindricals with a round vegetable cutter five-sixteenths of an inch in diameter; blanch until half done, then drain and sauté in butter with a little sugar; moisten with white broth (No. 194a) and put on to cook; when ready to serve boil with cream and thicken with egg-yolks and fresh butter.

(2715). STUFFED CAULIFLOWER À LA BÉCHAMEL—BAKED (Choux-fleurs Farcis à la Béchamel au Gratin).

Prepare, cook and drain the cauliflower the same as for fried bread-crumbs (No. 2718); scoop out the hearts and fill them with veal godiveau (No. 85), into which mix parsley and chives, both finely chopped. Place the cauliflower stalk downward on a buttered dish and cover over with allemande sauce (No. 407), into which mix half as much cooked herbs (No. 385). Strew the top with bread-crumbs and grated parmesan, pour butter over and push into a moderate oven for ten minutes; baste at frequent intervals and color the cauliflower; remove and decorate around with heart-shaped croûtons fried in butter, then serve.

(2716). CAULIFLOWER À LA VILLEROI, FRIED AND SAUTÉD WITH FINE HERBS (Choux-fleurs à la Villeroi, Frits et Sautés aux Fines Herbes).

À la Villeroi.—This is to be cooked and drained the same as for white sauce (No. 2719), then covered with well-reduced allemande sauce (No. 407) into which mingle chopped-up fresh mushrooms and chopped parsley; **when thoroughly cold immerse in beaten eggs, then in bread-crumbs, smooth the breading and fry it a golden color**; drain, salt and dress on a folded napkin, laying a bunch of fried parsley on top.

Fried.—Have the cauliflowers cooked and well drained, then dip each piece in beaten eggs, roll in bread-crumbs and fry to a fine color.

Sautéd with Fine Herbs.—After the cauliflowers are boiled and drained the same as for the above, divide in flowerets and sauté in butter, seasoning with salt, pepper and chopped parsley.

(2717). CAULIFLOWERS WITH CHEESE—BAKED (Choux-fleurs au Fromage Gratinés).

Suppress the hard parts from some cauliflowers, divide in small flowerets and cook in salted water. When they are tender and drained range them in layers in a vegetable dish with a little reduced béchamel (No. 409); bestrew with grated parmesan and pour over some butter; give them a dome shape and cover with a layer of thick béchamel, finished with grated parmesan and butter; dredge evenly with more parmesan and color nicely in the oven for twelve minutes.

(2718). CAULIFLOWERS WITH FRIED BREAD-CRUMBS (Choux-fleurs à la Mie de Pain Frite).

Divide some cauliflowers into separate flowerets all of uniform size; pare the stalks to a point, wash and drop them into a saucepanful of hot water, then boil the liquid very slowly. When the pieces are three-quarters cooked salt the water and withdraw the saucepan to allow them to finish cooking much slower; in this way they remain firmer; drain, dress the cauliflowers and cover over with butter having fried bread-crumbs added to it.

(2719). CAULIFLOWERS, BROCCOLI, OR SEA KALE, WITH WHITE, BUTTER OR CREAM SAUCE (Choux-fleurs, Brocolis et Choux de Mer à la Sauce Blanche, au Beurre à la Crème).

For serving whole with sauces the cauliflowers should be chosen very white and close; cut off the bottom of the stalks, clean the inner parts well, removing the outer peel and leaves covering the stalk, then lay them in a well-tinned and very clean saucepan containing hot water and a little butter; remove to the side of the range to cook slowly until three-quarters done, then salt the water and finish cooking. Dress on a folded napkin, the stalk end downward, and serve apart either a white sauce (No. 562), a butter sauce (No. 440), or a cream sauce (No. 454).

Broccoli, a long-stalked cauliflower, can be prepared the same way, also sea kale; the only difference to be observed is that these must be served with slices of toast, buttered with fresh butter.

(2720). CELERY WITH BÉCHAMEL AND CROÛTONS (Céleri Béchamel aux Croûtons).

Cut into large squares, each one inch in size, the yellow stalks of a head of celery; blanch them in water, drain and place in a saucepan with a quart of white broth (No. 194a), an ounce of butter and a coffeespoonful of powdered sugar; cook so that the liquid reduces, and when the celery is done add to it a pint of béchamel sauce (No. 409), some grated nutmeg and salt. Just when serving incorporate two ounces of fresh butter; pour into a vegetable dish and garnish around with bread croûtons shaped like small hearts (Fig. 40) and fried in butter.

(2721). CELERY STALKS WITH HALF-GLAZE, ESPAGNOLE AND MARROW, OR VELOUTÉ SAUCE (Pieds de Céleri à la Demi-glace à la Sauce Espagnole à la Moelle ou au Velouté.

Suppress the outer hard stalks from eight or ten tender, but not too large celery heads; cut the remainder into four or five-inch lengths and pare the roots to a point. Wash them carefully and blanch for twenty minutes; refresh and range them in a saucepan to cover with unskimmed broth (No. 194a); lay a buttered paper or a thin slice of fat pork on the top and cook very slowly. Drain, wipe well, pare and dress them on a dish; mask over entirely with a half-glaze sauce (No. 413) reduced with Madeira wine, or else an espagnole sauce (No. 414) with marrow, or a velouté sauce (No. 415) reduced with mushroom essence (No. 392) and buttered when ready to serve.

(2722). CELERIAC MIRABEAU OR À LA VILLEROI (Céleri-rave Mirabeau ou à la Villeroi).

Mirabeau.—Peel the celeriac, cut them either into balls with a large vegetable spoon (Fig. 91) or in the shape of cloves or crescents; blanch in salted water, drain and place in a deep buttered sautoir; cover with broth (No. 194a) and finish cooking while glazing; dress and pour over some Mirabeau sauce (No. 500).

À la Villeroi.—Cut the celeriac into four pieces; pare them like cloves of garlic, having one pound in all; blanch in salted water, drain, place in a saucepan, adding half a pint of stock (No. 194a), and a little sugar; cook, drain once more, and when cold cover over with a Villeroi sauce (No. 560) with mushrooms and chopped parsley; lay on a baking sheet to cool, after which pare off the surplus sauce, dip them in eggs and bread-crumbs and fry to a fine color; dress on a folded napkin, with a bunch of parsley leaves on top.

(2723). CÈPES, PROVENÇAL STYLE (Cèpes à la Provençale).

Wash and wipe some cèpes heads after suppressing the stalks; split them in two through their thickness and fry in oil over a brisk fire, with some chopped onions, a clove of garlic and bay leaf, seasoning with salt and pepper. When their moisture has been reduced add a little reduced espagnole sauce (No. 414) and tomato sauce (No. 549); boil up once or twice and finish with chopped parsley and lemon juice. Take out the garlic and bayleaf, dish them up and surround with croûtons of bread (No. 51), fried in oil.

(2724). CÈPES BAKED WITH CREAM (Cèpes Gratinés à la Crème).

Suppress the stalks from some clean cèpes; divide the heads and salt over, flour them briskly and put them into a sautoir with hot butter, moisten with a little good raw cream, adding chopped onions and parsley and a bunch of fennel; finish cooking very slowly while covered for three-quarters of an hour, then remove with a skimmer, lay them in a bowl, and thicken the gravy with some good béchamel sauce (No. 409); let this reduce without ceasing to stir and when the sauce becomes succulent add to it the cèpes and let cook for two minutes. Pour the stew into a vegetable dish, bestrew with bread-crumbs and bake for ten minutes in a quick oven; serve the cèpes in this same dish.

(2725). CÈPES MINCED IN CROUSTADES (Cèpes Émincés en Croustades).

Trim some bread croûtons into ovals three inches long by two inches wide and half an inch thick; slit them all around an eighth of an inch from the edges and fry in clarified butter; remove the tops and empty them completely. Peel some cèpes, cut them in two through their thickness, salt over and leave them for twenty minutes, then mince them finely and fry in butter; drain this off and transfer them to a saucepan, adding some sour cream; finish cooking, then mingle in a little bechamel sauce (No. 409) and meat glaze (No. 402); add a small bit of finely cut-up green fennel and fill the croustades with this preparation; serve at once, very hot.

(2726). CÈPES STUFFED (Cèpes Farcis).

Choose cèpes of even size one inch and three-quarters to two inches in diameter, firm and fresh; remove the stalks and scoop out the heads from the stalk end with a vegetable spoon (Fig. 91), then peel and salt over; chop up the stalks and parings, mix with them some fat pork and cooked ham, both chopped, bread-crumb panada (No. 121), chopped parsley with a clove of garlic, a few raw egg-yolks, salt and pepper. A quarter of an hour after fill the hollow spaces with the prepared dressing and strew with bread-crumbs; range them in a sautoir, pour over butter or oil and cook very slowly for one hour in a slack oven, while covered; serve with their own stock, thickened with a little half-glaze sauce (No. 413) or bechamel sauce (No. 409).

(2727). CHESTNUTS WITH GRAVY (Marrons au Jus).

Remove the shells from several dozen large chestnuts, then scald so to be able to peel off the red skins; put them into a buttered flat saucepan, salt and moisten to their height with good broth (No. 194a); boil the liquid and withdraw the saucepan to a slower fire to have the chestnuts cook while remaining whole. When tender the moisture should be entirely reduced; glaze with a brush before serving.

(2728). CHICORY TIMBALES (Timbales de Chicorée).

Have some chicory prepared the same as for cream (No. 2729), strain it through a sieve; put one pound of this into a saucepan with four ounces of finely chopped cooked mushrooms, seasoning with salt, pepper and nutmeg; mix in singly four whole eggs, two yolks and lastly a gill of cream. Decorate some timbale molds (No. 2, Fig. 137), or a larger one, with fanciful cuts of truffles and tongue; fill these with the preparation and lay them in a sautoir on the fire; pour in boiling water to reach to half their height, boil and finish poaching in a slack oven; unmold and serve separately a Hungarian sauce (No. 479).

(2729). CHICORY WITH CREAM (Chicorée à la Crème).

Pick eight chicory heads, suppress all the green leaves, wash well, and cut the bottoms into a cross; plunge into boiling salted water, and let cook for twenty-five to thirty minutes; refresh, drain, press out all the moisture, and pick over carefully to remove any small straws or other impurities that may be found among the leaves, then chop up finely. Heat some butter in a saucepan, put in the chicory, and dry it over a brisk fire for ten minutes without ceasing to stir; add a heaping tablespoonful of flour, some salt, nutmeg, sugar and rich cream; when very hot and ready to serve incorporate four ounces of fresh butter. If to be served as a vegetable pour it into a vegetable dish, and surround with bread croûtons (No. 51) fried in butter.

(2730). CORN ON THE COB—BOILED (Maïs Bouilli en Tige).

Select white and close-grained corn; open the husks without tearing, and remove the silk found between these and the corn; brush over, and close up the husks, tying them at the ends, or remove them entirely from the stalk end, either way being optional, then cut the stalks off straight at both ends. Boil them in water, to which add a quarter as much milk and salt. They take about twenty to twenty-five minutes to cook. Dress in a napkin, serving butter at the same time.

(2731). CORN CUT UP, SUCCOTASH AND CORN PANCAKES (Maïs Coupé, "Succotash," et Crêpes de Maïs).

Cut-up Corn.—Boil the corn without the leaves the same as for on the cob (No. 2730); split the grains with a knife through the center their entire length; press down forcibly with the back of a knife to extract all the inside parts without the skin; season in a pan with salt, pepper and fresh butter; toss well, and serve very hot in a vegetable dish.

Succotash.—Use corn that has been cut the same as in the preceding paragraph, having as much lima beans or string beans. Sauté both corn and beans together in butter, adding salt and pepper. The succotash can be thickened with a little velouté sauce (No. 415), or béchamel sauce (No. 409).

Corn Pancakes.—The same preparation as for ordinary unsweetened pancakes, mixing in as much cut-up and chopped corn. Make pancakes a quarter of an inch thick; color well, and serve them very hot.

(2732). CUCUMBERS FRIED, BREADED ENGLISH STYLE AND FRIED À LA VILLEROI (Concombres Frits, Panés à l'Anglaise et Frits à la Villeroi).

Fried.—Cut some peeled cucumbers in slices a quarter of an inch thick by one and three-quarters inches in diameter; empty out the center seed parts with a three-quarter inch diameter tube; salt over for fifteen minutes, then drain, wipe, dip them in flour, and fry to a fine golden color in very hot frying fat.

Fried Breaded English Style.—Cut the cucumbers in two-inch lengths and then once across in the center; peel, remove the inner seeds, round the corners, and cook them in salted water. Drain, wipe, immerse in beaten eggs, bread-crumb English style, and fry to a nice color, having fennel sauce (No. 463), served apart.

Fried à la Villeroi.—Prepare and cook the cucumbers the same as the glazed ones (No. 2733), and cover with cold Villeroi sauce (No. 560); place on a baking sheet to cool; take them up with a thin knife; dip each piece in egg and bread-crumbs, fry to a good color, and dress on a folded napkin.

(2733). CUCUMBERS GLAZED (Concombres Glacés).

Split some cucumbers crosswise into two-inch pieces, having them an inch and a half in diameter, and each of these lengthways and across to obtain four quarters; peel and remove the seeds; pare them into the shape of cloves, add garlic, and cook in salted water; drain, wipe on a cloth, and put them in a thin sautoir with melted butter to reduce their humidity, then pour off the butter, and moisten with some gravy (No. 404), letting this fall to a glaze.

(2734). CUCUMBERS STUFFED (Concombres Farcis).

Peel the cucumbers and cut them in inch lengths; empty each piece with a vegetable spoon (Fig. 91), retaining a quarter of an inch at the bottom; blanch, then cook in consommé (No. 189) and drain. Fry a little onion in butter, add some chopped mushrooms, evaporate their humidity, then throw in some chopped truffles and parsley, also a little gravy (No. 404); simmer and add soaked and well-pressed bread-crumbs and raw egg-yolks. Stuff the cucumbers with this, stand them on a dish, bestrew the cucumbers with bread-crumbs and a little grated parmesan, pour over melted butter and finish cooking brown in a moderate oven. Dress in a vegetable dish on a little half-glaze sauce (No. 413).

(2735). EGGPLANT À LA DUPERRET—BROILED (Aubergines Grillées à la Duperret).

Peel some eggplants, cut them up into three-eighths of an inch thick slices, each one to be three inches in diameter; season with salt, pepper, oil and vinegar, and let marinate for two hours, then drain off and dry; baste over with oil and broil them on a slow fire; dress with maître d'hôtel butter (No. 581) poured over.

Eggplant can also be prepared by cutting it up three-quarters of an inch in thickness and three inches in diameter; score and besprinkle with fine salt; leave for one hour, then wipe dry and season with salt and black or red pepper, pour over a little oil, and turn them frequently before broiling to a fine color on a slow fire. Fry a little well-chopped shallot, mushroom and parsley in butter, season with salt and pepper, add a little espagnole sauce (No. 414), and lemon juice. Dish up the eggplant and pour the sauce over after incorporating a small piece of fresh butter.

(2736). EGGPLANT IN CASES À LA MORTON (Aubergines en Caisses à la Morton).

Butter some cases, either of paper or china; cover the bottom of each with a slice of peeled eggplant an eighth of an inch thick, and around with small bands of the same, exactly like an apple charlotte; cut up the remainder of the plant in squares, and fry them colorless in butter, then drain. Chop up as much cooked chicken meat as eggplant, and mix both together with mushrooms, truffles and chopped parsley, seasoning with salt, pepper and nutmeg, adding a very little thick allemande sauce (No. 407). With this preparation fill the cases, smooth the tops and bestrew with bread-crumbs; pour a little oil over and push into a moderate oven; when done drain off the fat, cover over with a little half-glaze sauce (No. 413) and serve.

(2737). EGGPLANT À LA ROBERTSON (Aubergines à la Robertson).

Have some peeled eggplants cut in half-inch diameter slices, sprinkle over with salt, and leave them to marinate for twenty minutes, then wipe and fry in oil over a brisk fire; color them to a light golden brown, season and drain; dress in a circle, intercalating a layer of béchamel sauce (No. 409) between each slice; fill the center of the circle with more eggplant, cooked smothered with a piece of butter, then pressed through a sieve. Cover the whole with thick béchamel, and scatter on white bread-crumbs and a little grated parmesan; pour over fresh butter and brown in a hot oven, serving as quickly as it assumes a fine color.

(2738). EGGPLANT STUFFED AND BAKED (Aubergines Farcies Gratinées).

Divide some small eggplants, each one in two, without peeling them; score and fry, then drain and empty out the center with a spoon, leaving a layer a quarter of an inch thick against the peel. Chop up the parts that have been removed, adding as much soaked and well-pressed bread-crumbs, and a clove of crushed garlic; cook the preparation for a few moments, season with salt, pepper and nutmeg, and remove from the fire until it loses its greatest heat, then finish with a few raw egg-yolks and chopped parsley. Fill the interior of the halved eggplants with this, smooth the tops and range them on a baking sheet; pour over plenty of oil and cook in a slack oven. When a fine color dress them on an espagnole sauce (No. 414) reduced with tomato sauce (No. 549) and run through a fine sieve.

(2739). EGGPLANT FRIED (Aubergines Frites).

Peel some eggplants; cut them into three-eighths of an inch slices, and from these remove round pieces two and a half inches in diameter, using a pastry cutter for the purpose; roll them in flour and then fry to a fine color, or they can be fried plain without any flour.

Another Way is to cut peeled eggplant into three-eighths of an inch slices and divide these into squares; salt over and drain for fifteen minutes on a sieve; wipe on a cloth and flour them quickly, a few at a time; drop them into very hot frying fat, and when done and of a fine color drain, salt and dress either kind on a napkin.

Breaded Eggplant.—Cut each slice a quarter of an inch thick; remove from them rounds two and a quarter inches in diameter; dip them in flour, then in beaten egg, and lastly in breadcrumbs; smooth the breading with a knife and fry to a fine color; drain and dress on a napkin.

(2740). ENDIVES OR ESCAROLES GLAZED (Endives ou Escaroles Glacées).

Wipe the endives well, cut them of an even length and range them in a flat buttered saucepan; season and baste over with butter; cook on a slow fire while covered and with no other moistening, turning them over once only. At the last moment drain off the endives; arrange them on a dish and unglaze the saucepan with a little half-glaze sauce (No. 413) or light béchamel (No. 409), then strain the sauce over.

(2741). GREEN PEAS—MANGETOUT—À LA FLEURETTE (Petits Pois Mangetout à la Fleurette).

These are prepared with "mangetout" peas, a species of very tender peas, the pods of which are eaten as well as the contents. String the threads on both sides of the pod from some "mangetout" peas after they are partly cooked; drain and put them in a saucepan with some fresh cream; let simmer until the peas are entirely cooked, and just when serving season with salt, a little sugar, finely cut-up chives and a dash of vinegar. They can be thickened with egg-yolks, cream and fresh butter just before serving.

(2742). GREEN PEAS, ENGLISH STYLE, AND PURÉE OF GREEN PEAS (Petits Pois à l'Anglaise et Purée de Pois Verts).

Boil some green peas in an untinned copper vessel containing boiling salted water and a few mint leaves; when cooked, drain and place them in a sautoir with salt, sugar and fresh butter, divided in small pats, mixing it into the peas without stirring them. Dress in a vegetable dish and lay small bits of butter on top.

Purée of Green Peas.—To obtain a purée pound the cooked and drained peas in a mortar, adding some very thick béchamel (No. 409); season with salt and sugar, press through a fine sieve, and return to the saucepan to boil; stir in some fine butter at the last moment.

(2743). GREEN PEAS, FRENCH STYLE (Petits Pois à la Française).

Put one pint of fresh-shelled green peas into a saucepan with a little cold water, stirring in a piece of butter; add salt and a bunch of parsley; cook with the lid on. When sufficiently done and the liquid reduced add a small piece of kneaded butter (No. 579); then take from the fire and finish by incorporating a large piece of butter divided in small bits. The peas should be well buttered and thickened so that the liquid be entirely absorbed.

With Sugar.—Prepare them exactly the same, only adding a pinch of powdered sugar.

(2744). GREEN PEAS, HOUSEKEEPER'S STYLE (Petits Pois à la Ménagère).

Take half a pound of lean unsmoked bacon cut in quarter-inch squares; blanch, drain and put them into a saucepan with four ounces of butter; fry the bacon colorless, then add a spoonful of flour and when this begins to brown moisten with a quart of stock (No. 194a); add three quarts of shelled fresh peas, a bunch of parsley and three green onions. When the peas are done remove the parsley and onion, drain off the stock, thicken it with a little kneaded butter (No. 579) and pass it through a sieve; put it back with the peas, boil both together again and remove from the fire; thicken with egg-yolks diluted in cream, at the same time incorporating a piece of fresh butter.

(2745). GREEN PEAS, PARISIAN STYLE—SMALL (Petits Pois fins à la Parisienne).

Cook some small green peas in a pan or small copper vessel with salted water, a large green onion and a bunch of parsley; as soon as done, take out the parsley and onion, drain through a colander without refreshing and put the peas into a sautoir with a pinch of sugar and nutmeg, thickening with a little velouté sauce (No. 415); take the peas from the fire, toss well and dress in a vegetable dish, garnishing around with puff paste croûtons.

(2746). GREEN PEAS WITH BRAISED LETTUCES (Petits Pois aux Laitues Braisées).

Blanch and braise fifteen lettuce heads; drain them to pare, fold and trim evenly; put them back into the sautoir and pour over a few spoonfuls of half-glaze (No. 400) so as to be able to heat them up. At the last moment dress them in a circle on a dish, alternating each one with a thin bread-crumb crust fried in butter and then glazed with a brush. In the hollow of the circle dress a garnishing of small green peas cooked in salted water and simply finished with a piece of fresh butter.

(2747). GREEN PEAS WITH SHREDDED LETTUCES (Petits Pois aux Laitues Ciselées).

Put a pound and a half of fresh green peas, recently shelled, into a saucepan with two tender lettuce heads shredded up coarsely, one small onion, a bunch of parsley, salt, a pinch of sugar and sufficient cold water to reach to about their height; cover the saucepan and cook for twenty to twenty-five minutes on a hot fire. Suppress the parsley and onion, thicken the liquid with a small piece of butter kneaded with flour (No. 579), and finish off the fire with a lump of fresh butter divided in small pats.

(2748). HOP STALKS OR POINTS FRIED AND WITH VIENNESE SAUCE (Pointes ou Tiges de Houblon Frites et à la Sauce Viennaise).

Select the white parts of some young hops; these should be picked from the 15th of May to the 15th of June; blanch them in boiling water with salt, drain and lay them on a dish to season with salt and lemon juice, roll in rice flour, dip them in frying batter (No. 137), not too thick, plunge into hot fat, and when done drain, salt and serve.

Viennese.—After the hops have been cooked in salted water, drain well and place them in a vegetable dish, covering over with Viennese sauce (No. 558).

(2749). JERUSALEM ARTICHOKES À LA SALAMANDER (Topinambours à la Salamandre).

Pare Jerusalem artichokes into three-quarter inch rounds, or else in the shape of a pigeon's egg; cook in salted water, drain and sauté in butter without letting attain a color. Prepare a purée by placing some peeled Jerusalem artichokes in a saucepan to boil; drain when done, and cover over with a damp cloth; dry in the oven, then press through a sieve. Return this purée to the saucepan; season with salt, nutmeg, fresh butter and egg-yolks, and form it into a border inside a dish, either pushed through a channeled socket pocket or else modeled with the hand; lay the sautéd Jerusalem artichokes in the center, strew grated parmesan over, cover with some rather thin cream béchamel sauce (No. 411), and then more parmesan; color in a brisk oven, serving it immediately after it is baked to a golden brown.

(2750). LENTILS WITH BACON (Lentilles au Petit Salé).

Soak a pound and a half of lentils for six hours, after picking and washing them in several waters; put them into a saucepan with half a pound of unsalted and blanched lean breast of bacon, some carrots, a bunch of parsley garnished with thyme and bay leaf, an onion with one clove stuck in it, pepper, nutmeg and stock (No. 194a); boil, skim, and simmer until thoroughly done, and after removing the carrots, parsley, onion and pork, drain off the stock, toss the lentils in butter, and season with salt, pepper, chopped parsley and lemon juice, or they can be sautéd with a little allemande sauce (No. 407). Dress and surround with well-pared slices of the bacon, and over this pour a little gravy (No. 404), then serve.

(2751). LETTUCES CHOPPED WITH CROÛTONS (Laitues Hachées aux Croûtons).

Pick and pare nicely some lettuce heads by removing the green leaves from the bottom of the stalk; detach all the leaves separately, and wash them in several changes of water, then blanch, refresh and drain; press down well to extract the liquid; pick over to remove all straws and other impurities that may be attached to the lettuce, then chop it up finely, and lay it in a saucepan with a piece of butter; dry over the fire, and season with salt and nutmeg, adding a pinch of flour; moisten with some clear gravy (No. 404), and then dress. Surround the lettuce with croûtons fried in butter. The gravy may be replaced by cream and the flour by velouté sauce (No. 415) or espagnole sauce (No. 414). Cos lettuce can be prepared and served the same way.

(2752). LETTUCES STUFFED AND FRIED (Laitues Farcies et Frites).

Pare and wash some lettuce heads in several changes of water, blanch them in a copper basin and cook in boiling, salted water for twenty minutes; drain, refresh and press out the liquid from each one separately. Spread them on a cloth, open the leaves, and fill each lettuce with a forcemeat ball an inch and a half in diameter, prepared as follows: Take a quarter of a pound of cooked chicken meat, the same of cooked ham, the same of cooked mushrooms, and add a pound of veal udder, a quarter of a pound of soaked and pressed-out bread-crumbs, salt, pepper, chopped parsley, minced chives and five egg-yolks, the whole to be well pounded in a mortar. Enclose the forcemeat ball in the lettuce. Wrap each of these in a slice of fat pork, braise for one hour, drain and dip in egg and bread-crumbs, either whole or cut in two, fry to a fine color, and serve with a half-glaze sauce (No. 413) apart.

(2753). LETTUCES WITH HALF-GLAZE SAUCE—STUFFED (Laitues Farcies à la Sauce Demi-Glace).

Blanch some pared and well-washed lettuces for ten to twelve minutes; drain on a sieve, and press them singly to extract all the water, then double them over and range them in a sautoir lined with fat pork; season and moisten with broth (No. 194a), cover with buttered paper and cook for one hour on a slow fire. Drain the lettuces once more, open them and stuff with veal quenelle forcemeat (No. 92), closing them up again carefully; return to a clean sautoir one beside the other and pour over a little gravy (No. 404); cook once more for twenty minutes on a slow fire, drain and shape them prettily. Dress on a dish in a circle, and cover over with a little half-glaze sauce (No. 413).

(2754). LETTUCES WITH THICKENED GRAVY—BRAISED (Laitues Braisées au Jus Lié).

Trim some lettuce heads by removing the green leaves from the stalks; pare these stalks to a point, wash the lettuces in several waters, changing it each time, and then blanch for ten minutes in a copper basin with boiling salted water; drain on a sieve, press each one separately to extract all the liquid, and fold them lengthwise in two, wrapping each one in a thin slice of fat pork tied on with a thin string. Range them in a sautoir, braise in a mirepoix stock (No. 419) and broth (No. 194a) half of each, and cover with buttered paper; let cook for one hour and a quarter on a slow fire or in the oven, being careful to baste occasionally during the operation. Drain the lettuces, dress them in a circle; strain the stock, remove its fat and reduce it well with a little espagnole sauce (No. 414); pour a third part of this over the lettuces and serve the remainder separately.

(2755). MACÉDOINE À LA MONTIGNY (Macédoine à la Montigny).

Cut carrots into small quarter-inch cylindricals, turnips into five-sixteenths inch in diameter balls, string beans into lozenges; also have small flageolet beans and peas. Blanch and cook each vegetable separately, drain, fry together colorless in butter, and mingle in a good soubise sauce (No. 543), thickening when ready to use with a little fresh butter and seasoning. Bread-crumb and egg over some small teaspoon chicken quenelles (No. 155), fry them in clarified butter, drain and range them around the dressed macédoine.

FIG. 549.

(2756). MUSHROOMS À LA RAYNAL—MOUSSERONS (Champignons Mousserons à la Raynal).

Prepare a foundation paste (No. 135) croustade, having it broad and rather high; place it on a baking sheet and fill it with a preparation made with a pound and a half of mushrooms cooked for five minutes in a little butter and broth (No. 194a); season with salt, then drain: when they are done cut them up finely and add the pieces to a chicken purée (No. 713), having it the consistency of a thick sauce, mixing in some raw egg-yolks. Push the filled croustade into the oven and let cook without browning. Have prepared a dozen mushroom heads, each one an inch and a half in diameter, suppress the stalks, scoop out the inside and chop up the fragments and stalks very fine; fry them in butter until quite dry, add lemon juice and let cool; mix this with the same quantity of chicken forcemeat (No. 86) and chopped parsley, season well and use this to fill the mushroom heads, forming them slightly rounded on top; lay them on a baking pan, scatter bread-crumbs over and pour on some butter; slip a little broth into the bottom and place in the oven for half an hour; dress these mushrooms on top of the croustade and serve.

(2757). MUSHROOMS À LA DUMAS—ORONGES (Champignons Oronges à la Dumas).

Remove the skin from some oronges; mince finely and fry in oil; when the moisture has all evaporated, season and drain in a colander. Put some fresh oil in the pan, add to it parsley and a clove of garlic and afterward the drained oronges with the addition of a little salt and cayenne pepper; dress on a baking dish, dredge over bread-crumbs to cover and push into the oven. Turn eighteen whole mushroom oronges, having them an inch and three-quarters in diameter; chop up the stalks with the removed parts from the inside. Have a sautoir on the fire, set into it a quarter of a pound of butter with as much oil; in this fry colorless four finely chopped and blanched shallots, a clove of garlic, the chopped oronges and a heaping tablespoonful of chopped parsley; when there is no more moisture, add half a pint of espagnole sauce (No. 414). Remove the garlic, stuff the whole oronges with this preparation, bestrew with bread-crumbs, pour butter over and place them in a baking pan; moisten with mushroom liquor and cook in a moderate oven for twenty minutes, and garnish the baked preparation around with these.

(2758). MUSHROOMS À LA RIVERA—MORILS (Champignons Morilles à la Rivera).

Select large-sized morils; cut off the stalks, wash well and throw them into a saucepanful of tepid water; leave to soak for half an hour, then take them up, one by one, and rub them several times through the hands, being careful not to break them and changing the water each time so as to remove all the adhering sand, then drain. Cut some lean ham into one-eighth inch dice pieces, fry in butter, add the morils and toss both together, then moisten with half a pint of good sherry and a little Malaga; season and cook slowly for half an hour. Fry some sweet Spanish peppers in oil; when done and well drained, add a little meat glaze (No. 402) and lemon juice. Dress the morils in the center of a dish and surround with the sweet peppers; bestrew with chopped parsley.

(2759). MUSHROOM CRUSTS AND WITH TRUFFLES—MOUSSERONS (Croûtes aux Champignons Mousserons et Croûtes aux Champignons Mousserons aux Truffes).

These are prepared in various ways. Flat crusts are made three inches in diameter and a quarter of an inch thick, to be covered over with butter and placed in the oven to attain a fine color. Or cut off the tops of some rolls or flutes, empty out all the crumbs, coat the inside with fresh butter and put them into the oven to color nicely. Turn and channel (No. 118) one pound of sound mushroom heads; wash them in clear water, then place in a saucepan with a small piece of butter, salt, lemon juice and a little water, boil for a few moments, keeping the vessel closed. Reduce some velouté sauce (No. 415) with this mushroom liquid, add to it the mushrooms, remove at the first boil and thicken with four egg-yolks, a little cream and fresh butter; fill or cover the crusts with this and serve at once.

For Mushroom and Truffle Crusts.—Prepare the same way, only adding minced truffles to the mushrooms; they may be colored in the oven by besprinkling the tops with bread-crumbs and cheese, pouring butter over, then set in the oven for a few moments.

(2760). MUSHROOMS SAUTÉD WITH THICKENED BUTTER AND BROILED MUSHROOMS ON TOAST—MOUSSERONS (Champignons Mousserons Sautés au Beurre Lié et Champignons Grillés).

Turn one pound of mushroom heads (No. 118); peel the stalks and cut them up into medium-sized pieces. Put some clarified butter in a sautoir, add all the mushrooms, set it on the fire and let cook with salt, lemon juice and white wine. Just when ready to serve add a little béchamel sauce (No. 409); thicken with two egg-yolks and dilute with a gill of cream.

Broiled Mushrooms on Toast.—Choose large, fully opened mushrooms, remove the stems and peel the heads, season with salt and pepper, besmear with oil or melted butter and place them in a hinged gridiron (Fig. 172). Broil on a slow fire and when cooked on one side, turn over. About ten minutes should be sufficient to cook them. Dress on toast, having the rounded sides uppermost, spread over the top partly melted maître-d'hôtel butter (No. 581) and serve hot.

(2761). MUSHROOMS SERVED UNDER A GLASS COVER AND WITH CREAM (Champignons Servis Sous Cloche en Verre et à la Crème).

Have some round slices of bread three inches in diameter and three-eighths of an inch thick. Cut off the stalks from some very fresh mushroom heads, channel (No. 118) and sauté; range these on the slices of bread (the heads downward); season with salt and pepper and lay a single slice on a dish so that each individual guest can be supplied with a separate one. Cover with a bell made either of glass or silver and push them into the oven for twenty minutes. After removing lift off the bells and cover the mushrooms with a white wine velouté sauce (No. 415) or a white wine espagnole sauce (No. 492).

Fig. 550.

Under a Glass Cover with Cream.—Fry some turned mushroom heads in butter; moisten with fresh cream, season with salt and pepper; cover and simmer until the cream becomes partially reduced. Have slices of bread prepared the same as for the above, put a slice on each plate, and on these dress the mushrooms in a pyramid form, pouring a part of their liquid over each; put on the bells and lay them to bake in a slack oven for twenty minutes, then serve with the bells still on.

(2762). MUSHROOMS STUFFED IN CASES WITH MADEIRA—MOUSSERONS (Champignons Mousserons Farcis en Caisses au Madère).

Procure twelve mushrooms, each an inch and three-quarters in diameter; remove both peel and stalks; wash and with a vegetable spoon (Fig. 91) scoop out the centers until the firm mushroom meat is reached, then wash the whole, and chop up the stalks. Have some hot butter and in it fry a little shallot, parsley and truffles, all well chopped; season with salt, pepper and nutmeg, and dilute with half a pint of well reduced allemande sauce (No. 407); fill the insides of the mushroom heads with this dressing. Prepare paper cases the same size as the mushroom heads, coat them with oil, and stiffen in the oven; into each case place a little Madeira wine, and one mushroom with the stuffed side uppermost; bestrew with bread-crumbs, pour over a little butter, and bake in the oven; when done to a fine color baste with Colbert sauce (No. 451), and serve.

(2763). OKRA OR GUMBO, GARNISHED WITH BARLEY BECHAMEL CROUSTADES (Gombo Garni de Croustades d'Orge, Bechamel).

Procure young and tender okras; cut off both ends, keeping the gumbo two inches long; blanch them in a copper pan with boiling salted water, drain and lay them in a sautoir one beside the other; moisten to their height with mirepoix stock (No. 419), let simmer until cooked and the stock reduced to a glaze; dress, cover over with well-buttered béchamel sauce (No. 409), garnishing around with barley béchamel croustades, made according to the following directions.

Barley Béchamel Croustades.—Boil some pearl barley in salted water for three hours, drain, put into a sautoir, and dilute with a well-buttered and highly seasoned sauce. Fill some hollow croustade tartlets with this, forming a cover with a round piece of savarin (No. 148) an inch and a quarter in diameter and three-eighths of an inch thick, having it buttered and glazed in the oven.

(2764). ONIONS BOILED, HOLLANDAISE OR SOUBISE SAUCE (Oignons Bouillis, Sauce Hollandaise ou Soubise).

Peel medium-sized onions, each one weighing two ounces; boil them in salted water, and when done, drain, wipe carefully, and dress them in clusters or in a row, covering over with Hollandaise sauce (No. 477) or a well-buttered soubise sauce (No. 543).

(2765). ONIONS BRAISED (Oignons Braisés).

Peel eighteen onions, weighing an ounce and a half each, being careful not to break them; cut off the stalks and roots and make a crosswise incision on the root end; sauté them in butter or fat with salt and a pinch of sugar, browning slightly; then range them in a sautoir with bards of fat pork; moisten with a little veal blond stock (No. 423), just sufficient to cover, and cook slowly while reducing the liquid. Dress in a vegetable dish and pour the stock over, or else cover with matelote sauce (No. 498), having reduced it with the stock.

(2766). ONIONS, WHITE OR BERMUDA—STUFFED (Oignons Blancs Ordinaires ou d'Espagne Farcis).

Take either common white onions or Bermudas of medium size, each weighing about three ounces; plunge those selected into boiling water for two minutes, then drain and peel off the outer skin; empty the insides with a vegetable spoon (Fig. 91), blanch for a few moments, drain and stuff them with chicken forcemeat (No. 79), incorporating as much cooked fine herbs (No. 385); bestrew the tops with bread-crumbs, pour butter over and lay them in a sautoir lined with fat pork; moisten to a third of their height with broth (No. 194a), then cook until they attain a color in a moderate oven; dress on a half-glaze sauce (No. 413) and serve.

(2767). PARSNIP CAKES FRIED IN BUTTER (Galettes de Panais Frites au Beurre).

Cut three pounds of young parsnips in six or eight pieces, according to their size, after they have been peeled and washed; boil them in water with salt and butter; when cooked drain off well, then pound and season with salt, pepper and nutmeg. Press this pulp forcibly through a sieve, incorporate a little butter, then leave to cool. Divide the preparation into two-inch diameter balls, roll these in flour, flatten to half an inch in thickness and fry in clarified butter; drain and dress on napkins with fried parsley on top.

(2768). GREEN PEPPERS STUFFED (Piments Verts Farcis).

Plunge the peppers into hot fat, leaving them in sufficiently long to be able to detach the outer skin by rubbing with a cloth; cut off the stalk ends and empty out the seeds, etc. Prepare a forcemeat with finely chopped onions and fry it in oil with as much cut-up peppers; let get cold, then mix in a quarter of a pound of cooked sausage meat (No. 68), a quarter of a pound of chopped fresh mushrooms and a little thick tomato purée (No. 730). Put the whole into a saucepan on the fire, boil, thicken with bread-crumbs and season with salt, pepper and nutmeg; when partially cold stir in four egg-yolks. Fill the peppers with this, lay them on a baking pan covered with thin slices of fat pork, pour butter over and set in a moderate oven for fifteen minutes; dress in a circle, pouring a little light half-glaze sauce (No. 413) in the center.

(2769). SWEET PEPPERS SAUTÉD (Piments Doux Sautés).

Plunge the sweet peppers in hot fat, or broil them, to be able to remove the light skin; divide each one in two, cut away the hard parts and sauté slowly in oil, cooking them at the same time; season with salt, prepared red pepper (No. 168), finely chopped shallot and parsley; dress in a vegetable dish and serve. Instead of fresh sweet peppers canned ones can be substituted, these being imported from Spain.

(2770). POTATOES, ANNA (Pommes de Terre Anna).

Select long-shaped potatoes; they must be peeled and cut into the form of a large cork; mince them finely, and soak in water for a few moments; drain and wipe on a cloth. Butter and bread the inside of a thick copper pan, having a well-fitted cover; range on the bottom and sides a thin layer of the potatoes, one overlapping the other, then fill entirely with the remaining ones in separate layers, covering each with butter free from moisture, softened by working in a napkin; mask the upper layer with the same, and close with the lid. Cook the potatoes for three-quarters of an hour in the oven; a quarter of an hour before serving take from the fire, drain off the butter and cut a cross through the potatoes yet in the sautoir, and turn each quarter over with the aid of a palette; put back the drained-off butter and return to the oven until ready, and invert on a dish to serve. These potatoes may be made in a smaller pan; in this case they should not be cut but turned over whole before putting in the oven the second time.

FIG. 551.

(2771). POTATOES BAKED (Pommes de Terre au Gratin).

Wash and brush medium-sized potatoes, wipe dry and lay them on a dish, then push into a hot oven for thirty to forty minutes; when done serve on a napkin, or else they may be steamed or boiled, then baked and peeled; cover with butter, color in the oven, and serve in a vegetable dish.

(2772). POTATOES BIARRITZ—BAKED (Pommes de Terre au Gratin à la Biarritz).

Put a pound of peeled potatoes to boil in salted water; drain as soon as done, and dry in the oven; rub through a sieve, then put this purée into a saucepan to dilute with a little clear gravy (No. 404), and add meat glaze (No. 402), two shallots prevoiusly fried in butter, chopped parsley, salt, pepper, nutmeg, a quarter of a pound of raw ham cut in three-sixteenths inch squares and four egg-yolks. Put aside the eighth part of this preparation, and dress the remainder dome-form on a baking dish; to the eighth reserved part add four egg-yolks and a little cream; beat well, and then stir in two well-whipped egg-whites; cover the dome with this, bestrew it with bread-crumbs, pour melted butter over, and set it in the oven for twenty minutes to heat and bake to a fine color.

(2773). POTATOES, BIGNON (Pommes de Terre Bignon).

Turn some raw potatoes into rounds two and one-eighth inches in diameter; make an opening in them of one and one-eighth inch, leaving a thickness of a quarter of an inch; blanch these hollow balls for a few moments in salted water, then turn them over to drain well. Prepare a forcemeat with a shallot fried colorless in butter, adding some sausage meat (No. 68), and let cook together; put in salt, pepper, bread-crumbs, chopped parsley, and a few egg-yolks, and with this preparation fill the holes in the potatoes; strew bread-crumbs over, then parmesan cheese, sprinkle over melted butter, and range them as fast as they are ready in a sautoir lined with bards of fat pork; pour more butter over, and put on the lid, then set it in an oven to finish cooking the potatoes; when done remove the cover and brown them nicely; range neatly in a vegetable dish on a little half-glaze (No. 400).

(2774). POTATOES BOILED IN THEIR SKINS OR PEELED, ENGLISH STYLE, PERSILLADE BALLS (Pommes de Terre Bouillies en Robe ou Pelées, à l'Anglaise, en Boules Persillade).

Boiled in Their Skins or Peeled.—Wash some uniform-sized potatoes; cook them either by steam or in salted water from twenty-five to thirty minutes, and when nearly done (if in salted water) drain and cover with a damp cloth; put them into the oven until all their moisture has evaporated, and serve in folded napkins, with or without skins, or in a covered vegetable dish, so they keep hot.

Boiled English Style.—Peel some raw potatoes; pare them in the shape of large olives, and put them in a saucepan with salt and water; cover and let the liquid boil until the potatoes are done, then drain off the water and cover over with a cloth. Close the saucepan and set it in the oven for a few moments to dry them well; pour a little melted salt butter over and dress in a vegetable dish.

Persillade Balls are potatoes formed into balls three-quarters of an inch to one inch in diameter with a vegetable spoon (Fig. 91), and cooked the same as the English. Serve them in a vegetable dish, pour salted butter and chopped parsley over.

(2775). POTATOES, BORDELAISE—NEW (Pommes de Terre Nouvelles à la Bordelaise).

Select small, uniform-sized new potatoes; rub the peelings off with a cloth and sauté them in lard, keeping the pan covered until done and of a fine color, then drain and sauté in butter with a little chopped shallot, a trifle of garlic, salt and fine herbs. In case there be no new potatoes, pare old ones into olive forms, wash and boil partly in salted water, then drain and finish cooking in butter the same as the new ones.

(2776). POTATOES BROILED WITH FRIED BREAD-RASPINGS (Pommes de Terre Grillées à la Chapelure Frite).

To prepare broiled potatoes boiled ones are generally used, cut in half-inch thick slices; lay them on a double-hinged broiler, salt and baste with melted butter, then place the broiler over a slow fire, and cook the potatoes to a good color; dress them in the center of a dish. Fry fresh bread-crumbs in butter, and when a fine golden brown pour over the potatoes, and serve.

(2777). POTATOES, BUSSY (Pommes de Terre Bussy).

After having the potatoes prepared the same as for the dauphine potatoes (No. 2783), and before dividing it into balls, mix in some chopped parsley. Take up some with a teaspoon, detach it with the finger, and let fall into hot frying fat; when of a good color drain dry, and dress on a folded napkin.

(2778). POTATO CAKES (Gâteaux de Pommes de Terre).

Bake eight potatoes in the oven, and when done cut them lengthwise in two, empty out entirely, and place this in a saucepan with two finely chopped shallots fried in butter, and a pound of lean meat, either of veal or lamb or dark poultry meat, chives, salt, pepper, nutmeg, two ounces of butter, six egg-yolks, and two gills of velouté sauce (No. 415). With this preparation make inch and a half diameter balls flattening them down to five-eighths of an inch in thickness; roll in beaten egg-white, then in flour, and fry in a pan with clarified butter. Dress on a folded napkin in a circle with fried parsley in the center.

(2779). POTATO CAKES WITH HAM (Galettes de Pommes de Terre au Jambon).

Lay in a saucepan one pint of mashed potatoes (No. 2798), rubbed through a sieve; mix in with it a lump of butter, a pinch of sugar, nutmeg, a handful of grated parmesan, six raw egg-yolks, two beaten whites, a little salt and four ounces of cooked and finely chopped lean ham. Heat a griddle or frying-pan, butter well the surface, take the preparation up with a spoon, and let it fall on it in rounds three inches each, keeping them slightly apart; cook them on a slow fire, turning over; when nicely colored and hardened drain and serve hot. The preparation may be let fall into three-inch diameter rings, five-sixteenths of an inch thick, filling them to the top; in this way the cakes will be more uniform than when cooked as above.

(2780). POTATOES CHOPPED WITH CREAM, AND BAKED (Pommes de Terre Hachées à la Crème et au Gratin).

Peel some boiled potatoes after they are cold; chop them up and lay in a sautoir with butter, salt, nutmeg, white pepper and cream; boil and simmer until the preparation has acquired a sufficient consistency, then serve in a vegetable dish.

Baked.—Butter the bottom of a dish, bestrew it with bread-raspings, and fill slightly bomb-shaped with chopped potatoes and cream as the above; dredge more bread-raspings over, pour on some butter, wipe the edges of the dish, and bake in a hot oven.

(2781). POTATOES, CREAM OF, BAKED (Crème de Pommes de Terre au Gratin).

Cut up some boiled potatoes the same as for duchess (No. 2785). After they have steamed take from the fire and stir in a piece of butter; work rapidly with a large fork to make a purée, but do not rub it through a sieve; season with salt, nutmeg, a pinch of sugar, and for three or four gills of the purée add four or five raw egg yolks and a handful of parmesan cheese, diluting very slowly with a gill and a half of rich, raw cream, so as to have the preparation as smooth as for a pudding; when this degree is acquired stir well on the side of the range for two minutes to heat slightly, then remove and incorporate two or three ounces of fresh butter divided in small pats. Pour the preparation at once into a small vegetable dish, lay it on a baking tin and brown the surface lightly in the oven. Eight or ten minutes will be sufficient. Serve in the same dish.

(2782). POTATO CROQUETTES, IN SURPRISE AND MAÏSIENNE (Croquettes de Pommes de Terre en Surprise et à la Maïsienne).

Obtain one pound of very hot mashed potato preparation (No. 2798), and rub it through a sieve; put it into a saucepan with two ounces of butter, work it well with salt, nutmeg and four egg-yolks; let get cold, then form it into cylindrical croquettes an inch in diameter by two and a quarter inches in length; roll them in bread crumbs, then in beaten egg and again in bread-crumbs; smooth this breading with a knife, and fry a few at a time in hot frying fat; drain and dress on a napkin.

In Surprise.—Use the same preparation as for the above; form into round croquettes instead of cylindricals, and in the center of each one insert a half-inch diameter ball of consistent chestnut purée (No. 712); bread-crumb and fry them the same as the potato croquettes.

Maïsienne Croquettes.—Have a pound of the mashed potato preparation (No. 2798), put it into a saucepan with an ounce of butter, two egg-yolks, half a pint of béchamel sauce (No. 409), and the same quantity of green corn, the grains scraped free of skin; mix well and leave till cold; with this form two and a half inch cylindrical croquettes, having them an inch and a quarter thick; roll in eggs and bread-crumbs, fry in plenty of hot frying fat, drain and serve on folded napkins.

(2783). POTATOES, DAUPHINE (Pommes de Terre Dauphine).

Bake two pounds of potatoes, cut them lengthways in two, remove sufficient pulp to obtain a pound, and mix this with a quarter as much pâte-à-chou (No. 132), eggs, a little cream, salt and nutmeg. Divide it to make inch and a half balls, lengthen them to the shape of an egg, roll in butter, then in bread-raspings, and fry in hot frying fat.

(2784). POTATOES, HALF-GLAZE (Pommes de Terre Demi-Glace).

Prepare potatoes the same as for gastronome (No. 2789), lay them in a sautoir with clarified butter, without having them previously boiled; when nearly done change into another saucepan and moisten with a little gravy (No. 404), espagnole sauce (No. 414) and meat-glaze (No. 402); cover the pan and cook so that the liquid be reduced to the consistency of a half-glaze as soon as the potatoes are finished.

(2785). POTATOES, DUCHESS (Pommes de Terre Duchesse).

The same preparation as the marchioness (No. 2797), adding a handful of grated parmesan; roll in one and three-quarter inch diameter balls, lengthen these and roll them in bread-crumbs to have them assume an oblong form two and five-eighths inches by one and three-quarter inches; flatten to the thickness of half an inch, cut off the four corners, dip them in melted butter, then in bread-crumbs and lay them on a liberally buttered baking sheet, pouring more butter over; push into a very hot oven and when of a fine color remove from the oven and serve.

(2786). POTATOES, PARISIENNE (Pommes de Terre Parisienne).

Cut them with a three-quarters of an inch diameter vegetable spoon (Fig. 91); fry slowly in plenty of hot fat and when three-quarters done drain this off and lay them in a sautoir with clarified butter, toss, season with salt, sprinkle over with chopped parsley and serve.

(2787). POTATOES FRIED AND CHANNELED (Pommes de Terre Cannelées Frites).

Put some frying fat (No. 55) in a pan provided with a wire basket (Fig. 121). Peel raw potatoes, cut them in slices with a channeled knife (Fig. 157), having each one about an inch and a half in diameter and three-sixteenths of an inch thick; throw them into cold water immediately, soak for one hour, then drain; put them into a wire basket, and plunge into the warm frying fat; then cook, keeping them at the same degree of heat, stirring about several times; when done and nicely colored, drain, wipe, salt and dress in a pyramid.

(2788). POTATO FRITTERS (Beignets de Pommes de Terre).

Imitate small eggs with potato croquette preparation (No. 2782); leave them till quite cold on ice, then cut each one lengthwise in two, thus obtaining two halves for every egg, then cut these again in two on their length; dip these separate quarters in a light frying batter (No. 137), then in hot frying fat and fry to a fine golden color. Dress on a folded napkin.

(2789). POTATOES, GASTRONOME (Pommes de Terre Gastronome).

From some raw potatoes trim cylindricals one inch in diameter by an inch and a quarter long; blanch them for ten minutes, then drain off and finish cooking in clarified butter; when done pour this butter off and add salt, lemon juice, a small quantity of meat glaze (No. 402), chopped truffles and a little Madeira wine. Range and serve in a vegetable dish.

(2790). POTATOES HOLLANDAISE WITH MELTED BUTTER OR HOLLANDAISE SAUCE
(Pommes de Terre à la Hollandaise au Beurre Fondu ou à la Sauce Hollandaise).

Cut potatoes into inch balls with a round vegetable spoon (Fig. 91); cook them in salted water, and a few moments before they are finished drain off the water and cover with a damp cloth, then lay them in the oven for a few minutes; return to a saucepan and pour over slightly melted salty butter or else use a well-buttered Hollandaise sauce (No. 477).

(2791). POTATOES, HOUSEKEEPER'S STYLE (Pommes de Terre Ménagère).

Cut a quarter of a pound of lean, unsmoked bacon into three-eighths of an inch squares; blanch and fry in butter two ounces of chopped onion; moisten with broth (No. 194a), having just sufficient to moisten, and let the bacon cook so that when done the liquid will all be reduced; add about a pound of mashed potatoes, and season with salt, pepper, nutmeg and chopped parsley.

FIG. 552.

(2792). POTATOES, JULIENNE OR STRAW (Pommes de Terre Julienne ou Pommes de Terre Paille).

Peel the potatoes and cut them in eighth of an inch slices and these into fillets. For straws the fillets are much thinner than for Julienne; fry the same as the channeled (No. 2787).

(2793). POTATOES, LONG BRANCH (Pommes de Terre Long Branch).

Cut up some peeled potatoes with the machine (Fig. 552); these pieces can be obtained several yards long. Soak them in cold water for some hours, and fry the same as channeled potatoes (No. 2787) in white fat.

(2794). POTATOES, LYONNESE (Pommes de Terre Lyonnaise).

Pare some cooked potatoes into cylinders one inch in diameter, cut them three-sixteenths of an inch thick and sauté in butter; mince finely one medium-sized onion; fry it in butter, and when nicely colored mix in the sautéd potatoes and season with salt and pepper; toss them again for a few moments, drain off the butter and dress.

(2795). POTATOES, MAÎTRE D'HÔTEL (Pommes de Terre Maître d'Hôtel).

Boil the potatoes the same as for plain boiled No. 2774; leave them to cool partly, then pare into cylindricals an inch in diameter, and these into three-sixteenths of an inch slices; place them in a saucepan having its bottom well buttered, season with salt and nutmeg, and moisten to three-quarters of their height with broth (No. 194a). Boil slowly until the liquid be reduced, then remove from the fire and stir in a few bits of butter, chopped parsley and lemon juice. They can also be prepared by using raw potatoes pared to the same size and thickness as those for the above; set them in a buttered saucepan, moisten with veal blond (No. 423), season and cook on a brisk fire in such a way as to have the liquid almost dry by the time the potatoes are done; just when serving add a few small lumps of butter, lemon juice and chopped parsley.

(2796). POTATOES, MARSHAL (Pommes de Terre Maréchal).

Mince some raw potatoes; wash and wipe well on a cloth; put them in a flat saucepan with butter; season and cook very slowly while covered, tossing them frequently; when soft beat them up and dress in layers in a vegetable dish; bestrew each of these with grated parmesan, pour melted butter over and bake for half an hour in a slack oven.

(2797). POTATOES, MARCHIONESS (Pommes de Terre Marquise).

Peel and cut up some raw potatoes; boil them in salted water, drain it off as soon as they are done and cover over with a clean cloth; let steam for a few moments in a slack oven, then remove and rub a few at a time through a sieve; put this purée into a saucepan, and for each pound stir in quickly one ounce of butter, five raw egg-yolks, salt, nutmeg, a pinch of sugar and two tablespoonfuls of good raw cream. Pour the preparation on a floured table, roll it into thick cork-shaped pieces and cut these across in ovals two inches wide, three inches long and half an inch thick; range them in a copper baking pan with hot clarified butter and brown on both sides in the oven, turning them over while cooking.

(2798). POTATOES, MASHED, IN SNOW, IN PURÉE OR BAKED (Pommes de Terre en Neige, en Purée ou au Gratin).

Boil mealy potatoes, the same as described in No. 2774; pass them through a small hand strainer (Fig. 553), or a large pressure strainer if for larger quantities (Fig. 554).

For Snow Potatoes use the purée as it leaves the strainer (Fig. 553), put it in a napkin and

FIG. 553.

FIG. 554.

form it into a ball inside of this; remove the napkin slowly to have the ball remain whole and serve in a covered vegetable dish.

In Purée.—After removing the potatoes from the strainer, put the purée in a saucepan, adding one ounce of butter for each pound, and a gill of milk; serve.

Baked Mashed Potatoes.—Lay the potatoes in a baking dish, smooth the top nicely, bestrew with bread-crumbs and parmesan, pour butter over and bake in the oven, or substitute potato croquette preparation (No. 2782); dress in the center of a baking dish in pyramid form and mark with a knife in large stripes from top to bottom; brush over with beaten eggs, baste with melted butter and brown in a not too hot oven.

(2799). POTATOES, MELLOW (Pommes de Terre Fondantes).

Prepare a few dozen small potatoes, giving them the shape of a pigeon's egg, all of uniform size; lay them in a sautoir with melted veal kidney fat, or good lard, and cook slowly while turning so that they color on all their surfaces; when done, press down slightly with a palette so as to flatten without breaking; they should now be oval-shaped. Pour off the fat from the pan and cover with butter; put in the potatoes, one beside the other, and keep them in the oven from ten to twelve minutes, to have them absorb the largest part of the butter while turning and basting; salt over and dress in a vegetable dish.

Another way is to prepare by first boiling olive-shaped potatoes, then crushing them one after the other in a cloth; place on a buttered baking sheet, pour slightly melted fresh butter over and color in a hot oven, basting at frequent intervals with the butter while cooking; dress in a vegetable dish.

(2800). POTATOES, PONT-NEUF (Pommes de Terre Pont-Neuf).

These are potatoes cut in square lardon shapes, three-eighths of an inch by two inches in length, to be fried and dressed the same as the channeled potatoes (No. 2787).

(2801). POTATOES, PROVENÇAL (Pommes de Terre à la Provençale).

Trim raw potatoes to the shape of corks, then cut them across three-sixteenths of an inch in thickness; wipe perfectly dry and sauté slowly in oil so they have plenty of time to cook, then add a little garlic and a little onion all finely chopped; salt them and finish in the oven just when serving; drain off the butter and strew over with chopped parsley and lemon juice.

(2802). POTATOES, SARAH (Pommes de Terre Sarah).

Cut some raw potatoes into corkscrew shapes with a special machine (Fig. 555); fry till half done in not too hot fat; drain and place them in a sautoir with clarified butter to finish cooking, seasoning with salt, and adding chopped parsley and lemon juice.

(2803). POTATOES, SARATOGA (Pommes de Terre Saratoga).

Mince the potatoes very finely in the machine (Fig. 556), or cut thinly with a knife; lay them in cold water for twelve hours, changing it several times, then drain and fry in very hot white lard; when finished they should be exceedingly white and dry.

FIG. 556.

FIG. 555.   ### (2804). POTATOES SAUTÉD (Pommes de Terre Sautées).

Boil some long unpeeled potatoes in salted water; remove their skins and when partly cold pare into the shape of corks, then in three-sixteenths inch slices and put them in a pan with melted butter; season and sauté over a moderate fire to have them slightly browned; bestrew with chopped parsley and serve at once.

(2805). POTATOES SAUTÉD WITH ARTICHOKE BOTTOMS AND TRUFFLES (Pommes de Terre Sautées aux Fonds d'Artichauts et aux Truffes).

Trim long potatoes, shaping them into cylinders one inch in diameter; cut them into three-sixteenths of an inch thick slices, drain and dry on a cloth; also trim small artichoke bottoms, cut them in four pieces, and pare. Heat a liberal quantity of good oil in a sautoir; put in the potatoes and artichoke bottoms, and cook while tossing to have them attain a color; drain when done, and add salt and butter; shake off of the fire until the butter dissolves, then add minced truffles cooked in Madeira wine, tossing continually in the meanwhile; serve up in a vegetable dish.

(2806). POTATOES IN THE SHAPE OF AN OMELET (Pommes de Terre en Forme d'Omelette).

Boil a few raw, peeled potatoes in salt and water; when cooked drain off the water, and let steam for five or six minutes; invert them on a clean cloth to dry all the moisture, and return them to a pan containing melted butter; fry for two minutes, then break by chopping them up with an iron palette until well crumbled, adding a little melted butter from time to time; season; brown nicely while tossing incessantly; lastly bring the potatoes to the front of the pan to have them all together, and shape the mass like a folded omelet; color it nicely, adding a little more butter, and invert it on a small long dish.

Another Way is to peel boiled cold potatoes; chop them up or else cut them in small three-sixteenths of an inch cubes; sauté them in a pan with clarified butter, season with salt and chopped parsley and let color nicely, tossing them unceasingly; bring the preparation forward to the front of the pan, assemble it together, and shape it like a folded omelet; color, adding a little more butter, and when finely browned drain off the fat and turn it over as an omelet on a long dish.

(2807). POTATO SHAVINGS (Pommes de Terre en Copeaux).

These are to be cut with a special machine (Fig. 557); they are shaped like thin spirals. Leave them soak in cold water for two hours, then drain well, and place inside a hinged double broiler to keep them apart; fry the same as the channeled potatoes (No. 2787).

(2808). POTATOES SOUFFLÉD (Pommes de Terre Soufflées).

Good souffléd potatoes can best be made by using those called Holland potatoes.

FIG. 557.

First trim the raw potatoes in ovals of equal size, two and a quarter inches long by one and a quarter wide, and then proceed to slice them lengthwise three-sixteenths of an inch in thickness. As quickly as they are cut throw them into a bowl of cold water, leaving them in for twenty-five minutes. Heat two panfuls of fat, one of fresh beef kidney suet, the other having previously been used for other purposes and therefore its strength being somewhat extracted, it should be clean and white. Wipe the sliced potatoes on a cloth, dry them thoroughly, put them in a basket and plunge them into the oldest fat, leaving them cook until they become soft, but do not let them take color. Remove and place them on a large sieve to drain and cool for a few moments, and just before serving plunge the potatoes into the fresh, hot fat, toss them, remove those that do not soufflé, also those that soufflé badly; set them to cool, and return them again to the hot fat. Should they not soufflé at the second immersion, it is useless to try again. Salt the potatoes before serving, dress around the meat, or on a napkin in a separate dish.

(2809). POTATOES IN SURPRISE (Pommes de Terre en Surprise).

Wash and brush medium-sized potatoes, wrap them in separate sheets of damp paper; range on a baking tin, and cook in a slack oven for thirty to forty minutes; remove, unwrap and make an opening on one side of each potato; empty the contents with a small spoon (Fig. 91), pound this to a pulp with fresh butter, salt, nutmeg and egg-yolks; refill the potatoes, close the aperture with the piece removed, and lay them on a buttered baking tin, having the opening uppermost. Push into a slack oven for twenty minutes, then dress on or inside of a folded napkin.

(2810). POTATO TARTLETS (Tartelettes de Pommes de Terre).

Prepare mashed potatoes the same as for duchess (No. 2785); make it rather firm with egg-yolks, butter and parmesan; with it fill some large buttered molds lined with puff paste parings (No. 146), rolled out thin; press down well, and smooth the tops. Place on a baking sheet and push in a hot oven; unmold when nicely colored and dress as a garnishing or on a folded napkin.

(2811). POTATO TIMBALE À LA PARMENTIER (Timbale de Pommes de Terre à la Parmentier).

Remove some rounds with a three-quarter inch diameter tin tube from slices of potatoes three-sixteenths of an inch thick; sauté them in butter for two minutes, then drain. Line the bottom of a buttered timbale mold with part of these rounds, and the sides with separate rows laid on flat, intercalating them in such a way that a round of potato lays between two others of the next row. Prepare a purée with a pound of potatoes boiled in salted water, drained and covered with a damp cloth, then dried in the oven; rub through a sieve and stir in two ounces of butter, one whole egg, one yolk, salt and nutmeg. Fill the timbale with this, lay the cover over and push into a moderate oven to cook for half an hour or more; when removed let stand for ten minutes, and invert on a hot dish.

(2812). POTATOES, VIENNESE (Pommes de Terre Viennoise).

To be made with the same preparation as Marchioness (No. 2797); divide it into balls, roll these on a table, covered with rice flour, to look like a Vienna loaf,—thick in the center and pointed at the ends. Imitate the gashes in the center of its length, egg over twice and cook in a hot oven. Serve on a folded napkin.

(2813). POTATOES WITH MINCED TRUFFLES (Pommes de Terre aux Truffes Émincées).

Peel raw potatoes and cut them into one-inch diameter corks, then across in three-sixteenths of an inch slices; wash, wipe well and lay them in a thin sautoir with melted butter, seasoning with salt; cover and cook in a slack oven, being careful to shake them about frequently until they are slightly browned, then add a quarter as much minced truffles cut one inch in diameter and an eighth of an inch thick; drain off the butter and baste with a small quantity of good Madeira wine, meat glaze (No. 402), and lemon juice. Pour into a vegetable dish and serve.

(2814). PUMPKIN FRIED IN SMALL STICKS (Potiron en Bâtonnets Frits).

Peel and remove the inside part of a pumpkin or marrow squash so that only the meat remains; cut two pounds of this into small sticks an inch and a half long, and three-eighths of an inch across; lay them in a vessel, strew salt over and let macerate for fifteen minutes, then drain, wipe and dip quickly in flour; plunge a few at a time into very hot fat; when cooked, drain, salt and dress on a napkin.

(2815). PURSLAIN, GREEN OR GOLDEN À LA BARBANÇON (Pourpier Vert ou Doré à la Barbançon).

Clean three pounds of the golden purslain; blanch in salted boiling water, drain and finish cooking in some good blond veal stock (No. 423), thickening with a little kneaded butter (No. 579), and adding four ounces of lean cooked ham cut in squares. Dish it up and garnish around with small tartlets prepared in the following manner: Cook some of the purslain in salted water after it has been cleaned; drain and press out all the liquid, then fry it in butter, season and add bread-crumbs and raw egg-yolks. Line some round tartlet molds with thin puff paste (No. 146), fill them with the preparation, strew over grated parmesan and cook in a moderate oven; turn them out to range around the purslain, laying between each one a small marinated purslain stalk dipped in light frying batter (No. 137) and fried to a fine color.

(2816). COS LETTUCE À LA RUDINI—STUFFED (Romaine Farcie à la Rudini).

Remove the green stalk leaves from six cos lettuces; cut each one lengthwise in two, remove the centers or hard parts, and blanch in boiling salted water; drain properly, and lay them on a cloth; suppress all the hard part from the leaves and stuff each half with veal quenelle forcemeat (No. 92), into which mix the insides of four cooked and skinned sausages, also a coffeespoonful of finely cut-up chives. Roll the romaines into muff-shapes, wrap them around with fat pork, then braise and drain; strain and reduce the stock with espagnole sauce (No. 414), and pour this over after it has been well reduced.

(2817). SALSIFY OR OYSTER PLANT À LA POULETTE, SAUTED WITH FINE HERBS OR FRIED (Salsifis ou Scorsonères à la Poulette, Sautés aux Fines Herbes ou Frits).

À la Poulette.—Scrape some oyster plants to remove their covering of brown skin, cut off the tops and thin end parts, and throw them as quickly as they are done in cold water acidulated with vinegar; divide them into two and a half inch lengths, and cook in a white stock (No. 182), into which add chopped beef kidney suet and sliced lemon pulp; let cook slowly, and when they crush under the pressure of the finger, then drain. Sauté them colorless in butter, season, drain off the fat, and put in a little velouté (No. 415); roll them in the sautoir and thicken with egg-yolks and butter, finishing with lemon juice and chopped parsley.

Sautéd With Fine Herbs.—Are first to be cooked the same as the poulette, then cut across in slices a quarter of an inch thick, and sautéd in butter, seasoning with salt, pepper, chopped parsley and lemon juice.

Fried.—Prepare the same as for the poulette, drain and season with salt, pepper, lemon juice and chopped parsley; dip them into frying batter (No. 137), and fry slowly in plenty of hot white fat; drain, salt, and dress on a folded napkin with a bunch of fried parsley on top.

(2818). SORREL WITH GRAVY (Oseille au Jus).

Pick some clean, tender sorrel leaves; wash well, changing the water. Put them into a saucepan with a little salt and water; dissolve while stirring with a spoon; throw the sorrel into a colander and when cold press it through a sieve. Put this purée with a little prepared white roux (No. 163), and cook it for a few moments while stirring; moisten with a small quantity of gravy (No. 404); reduce the purée, mixing well all the time; season and finish with a little half-glaze (No. 400).

(2819). SAUERKRAUT GARNISHED (Choucroute Garnie).

Butter the bottom of a saucepan; lay in two pounds of fresh sauerkraut washed in several waters; in the center arrange a quarter of a pound of bacon and a quarter of a pound of goose or chicken fat; moisten to its height with broth (No. 194a), and in the middle lay an eight-ounce cervelas sausage, one onion or carrot cut in four and a garnished bunch of parsley (No. 123); cover over with buttered paper and cook for two hours or more; the moistening should be reduced when the sauerkraut is done; drain off the fat, take out the bacon, sausage and vegetables, and add to the sauerkraut one gill of white wine, a piece of kneaded butter (No. 579) and three ounces of plain butter divided in small pats. Suppress the bacon rind, cut it and the sausage into slices and dress them around the sauerkraut as a garnishing; thicken the sauce with some espagnole (No. 414), and serve separately.

(2820). SPINACH WITH BÉCHAMEL SAUCE AND WITH CREAM (Épinards à la Béchamel et à la Crème).

Pick some fresh, tender spinach, using only the leaves; when well cleaned and washed in several waters plunge into boiling salted water and blanch for five or six minutes; drain, refresh and press out every particle of moisture. Chop finely and put into a saucepan with hot melted butter. Season, place the saucepan on a brisk fire for a few moments without ceasing to stir until the moistening is reduced, and finish with two spoonfuls of thick béchamel (No. 409), and another piece of butter.

With Cream.—After the spinach has been prepared as for the above, and thoroughly dried, add to it a little flour, moisten with cream and stir constantly. Just when ready to serve incorporate a piece of fresh butter, then dress and garnish around with puff paste crescents or small bouchées filled with béchamel (No. 411).

(2821). SPINACH À LA NOAILLES (Épinards à la Noailles).

Carefully pick the spinach, removing the largest stalks; wash it several times, changing the water, then blanch in an untinned copper vessel with salted water, letting it boil incessantly. When the stalks are tender enough to crush under the pressure of the finger, drain the spinach in a coarse colander, refresh and drain again; press out all the water, pick over to remove any straws or other impurities and then chop it up; force this through a coarse sieve; place the pulp in a saucepan with a piece of butter, put the saucepan on the fire, stir continuously until the moisture is evaporated, then besprinkle with flour; moisten with some thick veal blond (No. 423), adding a little meat glaze (No. 402), salt and nutmeg. A moment before serving stir in a piece of fresh butter. The flour can be replaced by some velouté sauce (No. 415).

(2822). SPINACH À LA ROUGEMONT (Épinards à la Rougemont).

Have the spinach picked and prepared the same as for à la Noailles (No. 2821). Brown a piece of butter to hazel-nut (No. 567), put in the spinach, place the pan on a hot fire, stir continually until the spinach is consistent and the moisture evaporated; season with salt and nutmeg; thicken with espagnole sauce (No. 414), a little chicken glaze (No. 398), and fresh butter; dress it in a dome-form and decorate around with small bouchées of sweetbreads, mingled with very rich and thick financière sauce (No. 464).

(2823). SPINACH, ENGLISH STYLE (Épinards à l'Anglaise).

Pick and wash the spinach in several waters; blanch it in an untinned copper vessel with boiling, salted water; drain well and cut it up without chopping; now put it into a saucepan on the fire, season with salt and pour it into a vegetable dish, cover with small bits of fresh butter, set on the cover and serve very hot.

(2824). SQUASH—MARROW—WITH PARMESAN (Citrouille au Parmesan).

Peel the squash and cut it into quarter-inch thick slices; from these remove twenty-four round pieces with an inch and a quarter diameter cutter; blanch, drain, and sauté them in butter over a brisk fire, seasoning with salt and nutmeg; dress them in a circle, one overlapping the other, on a dish that is fit to be placed in the oven. Cut as much of the squash into five-eighths of an inch squares, blanch by dropping them into boiling salted water, continuing the boiling process for fifteen minutes, then drain and fry them in butter, salt over, and lay them in the center of the circle; dredge grated parmesan cheese on top, pour on some butter, and color in a hot oven; strew chopped parsley over the surface, and when serving squeeze the juice of a lemon over the whole.

(2825). STRING BEANS À L'ALBANI (Haricots Verts à l'Albani).

String some medium-sized tender beans; cut them into lozenges, and boil in salted water placed in an untinned copper pan. Drain them off, sauté in butter, and thicken with a little velouté (No. 415) and chicken glaze (No. 398), adding the juice of a lemon. Dress, bestrew with chopped parsley, and surround with triangular croûtons (No. 51), on which lay quartered artichoke bottoms sautéd in butter, and mingled with meat glaze (No. 402) and lemon juice.

(2826). STRING BEANS À LA BOURGUIGNONNE (Haricots Verts à la Bourguignonne).

Cut two ounces of onion into squares; blanch in boiling salted water, drain, and fry colorless in butter; add to it some lean unsmoked bacon cut in three-sixteenths of an inch squares, an equal quantity of lean cooked ham cut the same and fried in butter, also two pounds of cleaned string beans; fry until the latter have evaporated their moisture, seasoning with salt; moisten with a pint of stock (No. 194a), and as much red wine, and when the beans are done and the liquid reduced add a little espagnole sauce (No. 414), butter, lemon juice, and a small pinch of finely sliced chives.

(2827). STRING BEANS À LA PETTIT (Haricots Verts à la Pettit).

Prepare and cook some string beans the same as with butter (No. 2829), but they should only be partly done; drain, wipe, and sauté them in a sautoir with butter without allowing to attain color, then pour off the butter and substitute some good sweet cream; let simmer until this is almost reduced, seasoning with salt and nutmeg. Thicken when ready to serve with a thickening of egg-yolks, cream, and a small lump of fine fresh butter.

(2828). STRING BEANS SMOTHERED (Haricots Verts Étuvés).

Choose string beans not too small but tender and fresh; cut them up and put them into a buttered sautoir, salting lightly; moisten to about their height with broth (No. 194a), cover the sauce pan, and cook the beans slowly, adding a little more broth as fast as it reduces. When the beans are done they should be dry, then baste them over with two or three spoonfuls of good thickened half-glaze sauce (No. 400); finish off the fire with some good fresh butter divided in small pats. Pour into a vegetable dish and serve.

(2829). STRING BEANS WITH BUTTER (Haricots Verts au Beurre).

If the beans be young and tender leave them whole; if large and yet tender, cut them in two or three lengthwise fillets; string and plunge the beans into boiling water in a copper pan; salt and cook them over a brisk fire without covering; keep them slightly hard; drain and throw in cold water, then spread them quickly on a cloth to wipe away all the moisture; put them at once into a vessel with fresh butter divided into small pieces, and stir them about with two forks without breaking, or else toss until the butter is dissolved; season and serve immediately.

(2830). SWEET POTATOES, BOILED AND WITH LOBSTER CORAL (Patates Bouillies et au Corail de Homard).

This tubercle originally came from the island of St. Domingo, and may be prepared in various ways.

Boiled.—Wash, cut off the ends, and lay them in a large-mesh basket; cook them by steam for twenty minutes or else in boiling water. They can be served either in their skins or peeled.

With Lobster Coral.—After the sweet potatoes are boiled, cut them into olive-shapes; lay them in a vegetable dish, pour melted butter over, and strew the top with finely chopped lobster coral.

(2831). SWEET POTATOES SOUFFLÉD AND SWEET POTATO CROQUETTES (Patates Soufflées et Croquettes de Patates).

Souffléd.—Cut them up raw into quarter-inch slices, pare them oval-shaped two and three-quarters by one and a half inches, then fry slowly in white fat to have them cook without coloring or stiffening; drain and ten minutes later throw them back into hot fat; they should puff out considerably.

Croquettes.—After the potatoes are roasted cut them lengthwise in two and empty out the insides; to this add salt, nutmeg, egg-yolks and fresh butter; mix well together, and when the preparation is thoroughly cold roll it up into inch and three-quarter diameter balls, dip them in eggs, then roll in bread-crumbs and fry to a fine golden brown; dress in a circle, having a bunch of fried parsley to decorate the center.

(2832). SWEET POTATOES ROASTED AND BROILED (Patates Rôties et Grillées).

In the Oven.—Wash and cut off both ends, pare them olive-shaped, lay them on a baking pan, cover with butter and roast in a moderate oven for about thirty minutes; when done serve inside of a folded napkin.

Broiled.—In order to have them broiled cut some steam-boiled, peeled potatoes in slices three-eighths of an inch thick, then trim olive-shaped and lay them in a double broiler; salt and coat over with melted butter and broil on a slow fire; dress them inside a folded napkin.

(2833). TOMATOES À LA BOQUILLON (Tomates à la Boquillon).

Have very plump tomatoes, plunge them into boiling water, peel off the skins and cut them into four pieces; place these in a saucepan with salt, pepper, fresh butter and sugar, cover and let cook on a brisk fire for a few moments; they are then ready to serve.

(2834). TOMATOES À LA FROSSART (Tomates à la Frossart).

From the stalk end of the tomatoes suppress with a pastry cutter a round piece an inch and a half in diameter; empty out the insides, drain and fill them with chicken forcemeat (No. 75), adding to it as much foies-gras from a terrine pressed through a sieve, truffles, mushrooms, chopped parsley, salt, pepper, nutmeg and grated parmesan. Fill the tomatoes through a pocket and bake them in a slack oven for fifteen minutes. Range them in a circle, pour Madeira sauce (No. 492) in the center and on each tomato lay a round piece of glazed truffle.

(2835). TOMATOES, PROVENÇAL STYLE—STUFFED (Tomates Farcies à la Provençale).

Tomatoes for stuffing must be selected of uniform size; cut off the tops an inch and a half in diameter, extract all the seeds, salt the insides and then drain; fill them with the following preparation: Fry some finely chopped onions in oil with a little crushed garlic and finely chopped mushrooms; when these have rendered up their moisture add chopped parsley, moisten with espagnole sauce (No. 414) and meat glaze (No. 402), season and thicken with bread-crumbs. Fill the tomatoes, range them on a baking tin, cover the tops with bread-crumbs, pour oil over and bake for half an hour in a moderate oven.

(2836). TOMATOES À LA TRÉVISE (Tomates à la Trévise).

Cut twelve medium, sound tomatoes across in two through their thickest part; extract all the liquid and lay them one beside the other on a buttered baking tin. Have a pint of good white wine mirepoix stock (No. 419), into which pour four tablespoonfuls of tomato purée (No. 730) and sufficient bread-crumbs to thicken, adding salt, pepper, a quarter of a pound of finely chopped ham and chopped parsley. Fill the halved tomatoes with this preparation, dredge bread-crumbs and grated parmesan over, pour on some oil and let brown nicely in a hot oven; dress them on top of a buttered thickened half-glaze sauce (No. 413), mixing into it more butter and lemon juice.

(2837). TOMATOES BAKED (Tomates Gratinées).

Remove the skins by plunging the tomatoes into boiling water; cut each one across in two, press out the seeds and lay them in a large frying pan with melted butter; season and reduce all their moisture. Range them in a buttered baking dish, the round parts on the bottom and scatter over cooked fine herbs, composed of shallot fried in butter with chopped mushrooms, chopped ham, parsley and bread-crumbs; pour butter or oil over and bake for fifteen minutes in a slack oven.

(2838). TOMATOES BROILED, HOT MAYONNAISE SAUCE (Tomates Grillées, à la Sauce Mayonnaise Chaude).

Throw some sound tomatoes in boiling water to remove the skin; cut them across in two, season with salt and pour oil over. Place them on a hinged double broiler and broil on a slow fire, basting frequently with oil. Dress them on a hot dish and cover with hot mayonnaise sauce (No. 433). The mayonnaise sauce may be served separately if desired.

Tomatoes are frequently served broiled without any sauce, simply cooked as above.

(2839). TOMATOES IN CASES, BAKED (Tomates en Caisses Gratinées).

Throw some tomatoes into boiling water to peel off their skins readily; cut them in two through their thickest part, press out all the liquid and seeds and fill them with a forcemeat made with cold chicken meat, cut from the legs, as much bread-crumbs and as much cooked fine herbs (No. 385) as bread; season well and stir in a few egg-yolks. Lay each half tomato in an oiled case (Fig. 439) stiffened in the oven, bestrew bread-crumbs and grated parmesan over, baste with butter and bake in a moderate oven.

(2840). TOMATOES, QUEEN STYLE (Tomates à la Reine).

Throw some small tomatoes an inch and three-quarters to two inches in diameter into boiling water; peel off the skins and open them on top, then take out the seeds, salt the insides and drain off all their water. Fill them with well-seasoned chicken cream forcemeat (No. 75), adding to it the same amount of cooked fine herbs (No. 385) and on top lay a channeled mushroom (No 118), then cover with a thin bard of fat pork. Arrange the tomatoes on a buttered baking tin and set them in a moderate oven for fifteen minutes; dress in a circle and pour in the center a well-buttered suprême sauce (No. 547), adding chopped-up truffles to it.

(2841). TOMATOES À LA GIBBONS—SAUTÉD AND FRIED (Tomates Sautées et Frites à la Gibbons).

Split the tomatoes in two through their thickness, drain off their liquid and season; sauté them in butter and oil, half of each, strew over chopped parsley and place them in the center of a dish; garnish around with fried tomatoes prepared as follows: Plunge some small tomatoes in boiling water, peel and cut them in four even parts; season with salt, pepper, oil and vinegar, dip them into frying batter (No. 137), then in hot frying fat, drain, salt and arrange them around the sautéd tomatoes.

(2842). TOMATOES STUFFED WITH FRESH MUSHROOMS (Tomates Farcies aux Champignons Frais).

Chop up some clean fresh mushrooms, fry a chopped onion, and add it to these, and continue to fry until all the moisture is evaporated, then season and remove from the fire. Bind it with a little sauce, then with an equal quantity of bread-crumbs soaked and pressed, a few raw egg-yolks, adding some chopped parsley. Select fine, sound tomatoes, smooth and round, of even size, but not too large nor too ripe; cut out a piece from the top in order to open and empty out partially, then salt and drain them for a quarter of an hour, filling them afterward with the mushroom preparation, and smoothing the tops nicely. Range the tomatoes in a small bordered baking pan, bestrew them with bread crumbs and pour over some oil; cook for three-quarters of an hour in a slow oven.

(2843). TRUFFLES IN A NAPKIN OR IN A CROUSTADE (Truffes en Serviette ou en Croustade).

Choose one pound of the finest medium-sized, round and well-marbled truffles; clean and brush over; wrap each one separately in a thin slice of fresh pork. Fry slowly in butter without coloring one ounce of raw lean ham, cut from the kernel and the sinews removed, as much carrot and the same of onions, all three to be cut in eighth of an inch pieces, one bay leaf,

Fig. 557.

thyme, a small slice of garlic and one clove. When these ingredients have been fried colorless moisten with a quarter of a bottleful of champagne or white wine and let boil, then skim and simmer for twenty minutes. Add the truffles and cook slowly for ten minutes; thicken the stock very slightly with a bit of kneaded butter (No. 579) and close the saucepan hermetically; set it in a bain-marie for half an hour. Dress the truffles in a folded napkin (Fig. 557). Butter the sauce, pass it through a tammy and serve it in a sauce-boat the same time as the truffles. These can also be dressed in a basket made of border paste (No. 131), decorated with fanciful cuts made of the same paste, or even one made of carved bread. In either case have the basket very tasteful and elegant and spread out open on the top.

(2844). TRUFFLES IN SHELLS, BAKED (Truffes en Coquilles, Gratinées).

Peel some truffles and put the parings into a saucepan with a little Madeira wine, parsley, thyme and bay leaf; let boil and leave in a bain-marie (Fig. 122) for half an hour. Cut the truffles in three-sixteenths inch slices, warm them in butter, drain this off and replace it by thick béchamel (No. 409), the above truffle essence and cream, seasoning with salt, nutmeg, prepared red pepper (No. 168) and Madeira wine, then reduce. Butter some silver shells (Fig. 438), strew over with bread-crumbs and fill with the truffles, then sprinkle over more bread-crumbs and grated parmesan; pour melted butter over and brown in a hot oven; serve. The minced truffles can be replaced by small whole ones trimmed into balls or olives.

(2845). TRUFFLES STUFFED (Truffes Farcies).

Select seven or eight large, unpeeled truffles, having them very clean, round and of equal size; put them into a narrow saucepan one beside the other and cook them for eight or ten minutes while covered, adding salt and white or Madeira wine; leave them to get partly cold in this stock. Place in a small saucepan a few spoonfuls of cooked purée of foies-gras; mingle with it a little good reduced and thickened Madeira sauce (No. 492), add some raw egg-yolks and seasoning. Drain the truffles, cut a round piece from the top, remove it and empty the insides with a vegetable spoon (Fig. 91); cut up a part of these removed pieces and add them to the foies-gras. Use this preparation to fill the truffles; close the opening with the removed cover and return them to the original saucepan with a little of their broth and a little melted glaze (No. 402); heat them for ten minutes while basting, then remove and cook the contents, while covered, for seven or eight minutes longer, off the fire. Dress them in a vegetable dish and pour over their own stock.

(2846). TRUFFLE TIMBALE À LA PÉRIGORD (Timbale de Truffes à la Périgord).

Decorate a timbale mold with fanciful cuts of noodle paste (No. 142); dampen these and line the mold with a layer of fine foundation paste (No. 135) an eighth of an inch in thickness; cover both bottom and sides of the timbale with very thin bards of fresh fat pork. Peel as many medium-sized truffles as the timbale will hold, having them black and mellow; put them to cook in a foies-gras terrine, seasoning with salt, pepper, nutmeg, sprigs of parsley, thyme and bay leaf, also some minced ham and Madeira wine; place the terrine in the oven and as soon as the liquid comes to a boil take it out and let stand till cold, leaving the truffles in with the stock. Suppress the thyme and bay leaf, drain off the stock and reduce it with a pint of financière sauce (No. 464) reduced to the consistency of a succulent sauce; transfer the truffles to the timbale, cover with a part of the sauce and lay over a flat of the same paste. Cook the timbale in a hot oven for three-quarters of an hour and serve unmolded; pour the remainder of the sauce into an aperture on top; serve at once.

(2847). TURNIPS GLAZED (Navets Glacés).

Prepare some cylindricals of turnips one inch in diameter and one and a half inches long, having them beveled on both ends; blanch these in salted water, refresh and when well drained put them into a frying pan containing very hot butter. Color and season with salt and a pinch of sugar; drain once more, then place them in a sautoir and moisten with broth (No. 194a). When cooked the liquid should be reduced to a glaze.

(2848). TURNIPS, WITH SPANISH, BÉCHAMEL OR ALLEMANDE SAUCE (Navets à la Sauce Espagnole à la sauce Béchamel ou à la sauce Allemande).

Trim some turnips into seven-eighths of an inch balls, or in the shape of crescents, olives or cloves of garlic; blanch in salted water, drain and sauté them colorless in butter, seasoning with salt and sugar; drain off the butter, lay them in a saucepan, and moisten with gravy (No. 404) and espagnole sauce (No. 414), finishing to cook quite slowly. The espagnole sauce can be replaced by béchamel sauce and cream (No. 411), or else allemande sauce (No. 407) and broth (No. 194a), finishing with chicken glaze (No. 398) and fresh butter.

(2849). TELTOW TURNIPS WITH CHESTNUTS (Navets de Teltow aux Marrons).

Scrape and throw the turnips into tepid water, then plunge into boiling salted water placed in a well-tinned saucepan; boil over a moderate fire, and when done drain and put them back into a saucepan with a piece of butter and a little sugar; toss for a few moments, and moisten with broth (No. 194a); season and thicken with a little butter, into which stir some flour slightly browned in the oven; reduce to a short sauce, then pour into a vegetable dish; spread them over to form a hollow in the center to be filled with whole chestnuts cooked in broth (No. 2727).

EGGS (Œufs).

Fig. 558.

(2850). EGGS (Œufs).

The eggs of chickens are most generally used. Boiled eggs should be moderately cooked; they are the most nourishing and easily digested; duck eggs are as nutritive as those of chickens. After these, the best are pheasant eggs, but they are very scarce. In order to discover whether an egg be fresh, hold it against the light of a candle, and if transparent without being spotted then it is fresh.

Tne white of an egg consists of one part of albumen and one part solid matter, this appearing as an envelope to the albuminous liquid, and has the appearance of white flakes, also of a fatty substance formed of olein and stearine.

The yolk is composed partly of albumen, partly of a fatty matter containing olein, and another part that is colored, besides one of a solid membranous composition.

(2851). EGGS AU MIROIR À LA JOCKEY CLUB (Œufs au Miroir à la Jockey Club).

Suppress the thin skin from one half of a white veal kidney; divide it, take out the fibrous fat, and then cut the meat into small dice. Heat some butter in a pan, put with it the kidneys, season and toss on a bright fire to have them cook rapidly, then remove with a skimmer, and set into a small vessel. Into the pan the kidneys were stewed in put two or three spoonfuls of half-glaze sauce (No. 413), and as much tomato purée (No. 730), reduce all to a third, mixing in a spoonful of Madeira wine; boil up once or twice, then take it from the fire and return the kidneys, also half as much cooked truffles cut exactly the same size as these; the sauce should be consistent. Cook six eggs au mirior on a large buttered dish, that is, baste the egg yolk with boiling butter several times while cooking in the oven; this will make them very glossy; cut them into rounds with a pastry cutter (three inches in diameter), take up with a palette, and dress in a circle on the bottom of a dish; heat the kidneys without boiling, and dress them inside the circle.

(2852). EGGS AU MIROIR À LA LULLY (Œufs au Miroir à la Lully).

Butter a large dish or baking pan; break in six eggs, pour boiling butter over the yolks, and put in a very hot oven or under a salamander (Fig. 123); when done properly cut them rounded with a pastry cutter two and a quarter to two and a half inches in diameter; take them up with a large palette and dress on a dish on slices of ham of the same dimensions, and three-sixteenths of an inch thick, and the ham on croûtons of fried bread cut the same, having taken them from the

FIG. 559.

kernel part of a good raw ham; fry them in butter in a pan, turning them over. Fill the center of this circle with a hash made of sliced and seasoned ducks' livers mingled with a little brown Madeira wine sauce (No. 492).

(2853). EGGS AU MIROIR À LA MEYERBEER (Œufs au Miroir à la Meyerbeer).

Peel off the skin from two mutton kidneys; split them lengthwise on the roundest side without separating the parts, run two small wooden skewers through each kidney, season and roll in oil, then broil for eight or ten minutes, turning them over in the meanwhile. Cook two eggs in a china dish (Fig. 567), having them glossy on top; cut them round-shaped with a two and a half inch pastry cutter and take them up with a palette and dress on a hot dish with some tomato sauce (No. 549) underneath. After removing the kidneys from the fire glaze them with a brush, pull out the skewers and divide each one in two. Dress them on both sides of the eggs, the cut side uppermost, and fill the hollow with a consistent Périgueux sauce (No. 517); serve.

(2854). EGGS AU MIROIR À LA PROVENÇAL (Œufs au Miroir à la Provençale).

Pick out three or four even-sized tomatoes, cut them through their thickest part in two, suppress the seeds and put them into a pan with some oil; season and cook on both sides until they have reduced their moisture, then take them from the pan and dress on a serving dish capable of being put in the oven; bestrew with chopped parsley mingled with a bit of garlic and a pinch of dry bread-crumbs, pour over some oil and let brown for ten minutes; remove and lay on top of each tomato one miroired egg cut round with a pastry cutter two and a quarter inches in diameter.

(2855). EGGS AU MIROIR À LA TIVOLIER (Œufs au Miroir à la Tivolier).

Toast some slices of bread cut into rounds two and a half inches across and on each one place a layer of chopped marrow; set into a hot oven. Fry raw ham cut in one-eighth inch squares in a pan with lard; drain this off and finish with butter, meat glaze (No. 402) and lemon juice. Fry some eggs in a pan; gloss by putting them in the oven and sprinkling with boiling butter; dress the marrow toasts with the ham around; pare the eggs with a two and a half inch pastry cutter, lift them up one after the other to place on top of the toast. Dress in a circle, garnish around with the tomatoes and serve with a good Madeira sauce (No. 492), sprinkling chopped parsley over the whole.

(2856). BOILED EGGS (Œufs à la Coque).

When only a few eggs are required proceed as follows: Boil some water in a saucepan, remove it from the fire, and plunge the eggs into the liquid with a skimmer, being careful not to

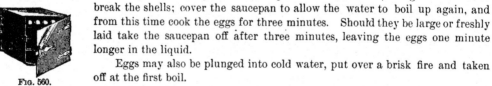

break the shells; cover the saucepan to allow the water to boil up again, and from this time cook the eggs for three minutes. Should they be large or freshly laid take the saucepan off after three minutes, leaving the eggs one minute longer in the liquid.

Eggs may also be plunged into cold water, put over a brisk fire and taken off at the first boil.

FIG. 560.

Another Way is to plunge them into boiling water and let cook for one minute after the water has boiled up again, then withdraw the vessel from the fire, and leave them in the water for five minutes. Eggs are cooked by steam in four minutes. The ordinary method is the first mentioned. However it is very difficult to tell exactly how long to boil an egg, for some like them scarcely heated through, while others prefer the whites slightly hard. Boiled eggs are generally eaten from their shells with a spoon, but many empty the contents into a glass or cup, seasoning with salt, pepper, and a little fresh butter, then mixing thoroughly. Boiled eggs should be served in folded napkins or in imitated chickens made of china.

(2857). HARD-BOILED EGGS AND AURORA (Œufs Durs et à l'Aurore).

These should not be cooked too long, still they only attain a proper degree after they have boiled ten to twelve minutes. On removing from the fire they must be thrown into cold water, and left to cool for at least fifteen minutes; drain and shell, without injuring any of the white part, which should remain intact.

Aurora.—Cut lengthwise in halves eight hard-boiled eggs; take out the yolks and divide each halved white in four parts; put these in a sautoir, season with salt, prepared red pepper (No. 168) and nutmeg, and dilute with well-reduced béchamel (No. 409), into which mix finely cut-up chives; dress this in a baking dish. Rub the yolks through a wire sieve directly over the eggs, besprinkle with salt, brush over with hazel-nut butter (No. 567), and heat for a few moments in a hot oven; serve at once. The chives may be replaced by mushrooms and truffles, both finely minced, adding to the bechamél a quarter as much soubise sauce (No. 543).

(2858). HARD-BOILED EGGS À LA BENNETT (Œufs Durs à la Bennett).

Boil eight eggs hard, the same as for Aurora (No. 2857); shell and lay them in tepid water until needed. Mince eight ounces of white onions, blanch for a few moments in salted water, drain and wipe on a cloth; lay these in a saucepan on a fire with melted butter; fry slowly while stirring until they be cooked, then season with salt, pepper and nutmeg; thicken with béchamel (No. 409), having reduced it with a little mushroom broth and melted meat-glaze (No. 402); add as much minced mushrooms as onions, and an ounce of fresh butter, and then drain the eggs, wipe and cut them crosswise, remove the yolks, press them through a sieve and mix well with the sauce. This sauce must be succulent but not too thick; strain it through a tammy. Dress the white parts in layers intercalated with the onion and the mushroom stew and pour the sauce over.

(2859). HARD-BOILED EGGS À LA BENOIST (Œufs Durs à la Benoist).

Cook six eggs, the same as for Aurora (No. 2857); shell and cut them lengthways in two; remove the yolks and rub these through a sieve. Prepare a well-reduced béchamel (No. 409) thickened with raw egg-yolks; when cold mix in the six cooked egg-yolks, as much mushrooms, and half as many truffles as mushrooms, all to be chopped up separately, and then beat in three very stiffly beaten egg-whites. Cover the bottom of a dish with a layer of veal godiveau (No. 85) with chives, having it a quarter of an inch thick; replace the egg-yolks by a little montglas and fasten the two halves together; lay these reshaped eggs over the godiveau and cover the whole with the beaten egg preparation; pour over butter, push in a moderate oven to heat the eggs well and color them nicely.

(2860). HARD-BOILED EGGS WITH NOODLES À LA CAROLLI (Œufs Durs aux Nouilles à la Carolli).

Blanch some finely shredded noodles in salted water for three minutes, drain and lay them in a saucepan with salt and nutmeg; leave to simmer for a few moments, then range them on a vegetable dish with grated parmesan strewn over. Boil eight eggs hard, the same as Aurora (No. 2857), cut them across in slices, dress them in layers over the noodles, then a layer of minced fresh mushrooms; season each one of these with salt, pepper and nutmeg and mask the surface with béchamel (No. 409) reduced with the mushroom broth, seasoned with prepared red pepper (No. 168) and well buttered. Strew the top with grated parmesan and melted butter and bake in a hot oven.

(2861). HARD-BOILED EGGS À LA GIBSON (Œufs Durs à la Gibson).

Mince some drained, blanched celery-roots; fry them colorless in butter, then cook in broth (No. 194a) with a little sugar; reduce the liquid to a glaze, add some béchamel (No. 409) and thicken with eight hard egg-yolks pounded with as much butter and then rubbed through a sieve; add also the whites of these eight eggs minced up finely and mix them together with the sauce. Butter and bread-crumb eight small silver shells (Fig. 438); fill them with the prepared eggs, strew bread-crumbs and parmesan over, baste with butter and bake in a hot oven.

(2862). HARD-BOILED EGGS À LA WASHBURN (Œufs Durs à la Washburn).

Take the whites of eight hard-boiled eggs; cut them in thin slices or in quarter-inch dice, also some cooked truffles and mushrooms; with these fill eight medium-sized shells (Fig. 438), alternating the three different ingredients; cover with some reduced soubise (No. 543). Smooth to a dome and mask this with a thin layer of chicken cream forcemeat (No. 75); dredge white bread-crumbs over all, pour on a little melted butter and bake for two minutes in the oven; serve at once.

(2863). HARD-BOILED EGG CROQUETTES (Croquettes d'Œufs Durs).

Chop twelve cold hard-boiled eggs in three-sixteenths inch squares, also half a pound of mushrooms the same size. Reduce a quart of béchamel (No. 409), season and add to it a little meat

FIG. 561.

glaze (No. 402) and chopped truffles, mix in the egg salpicon and take off at the first boil. When this preparation is cold form it into croquettes, either round, cylindrical or flat ovals; immerse them in eggs, roll in bread-crumbs and fry to a fine color; drain, salt and serve on a folded napkin with sprigs of fried parsley on top.

(2864). HARD-BOILED EGGS, NEW YORK STYLE (Œufs Durs à la New Yorkaise).

Have six eggs boiled hard, the same as for Aurora (No. 2857); shell and split them lengthwise in two; remove the yolks and pound them in a mortar with an ounce of melted butter, salt, pepper, nutmeg, two raw egg-yolks and a gill of béchamel (No. 409), beating the whole well together; then stir in half as much chicken quenelle forcemeat (No. 89). Fill the halved eggs with this preparation, rounding the tops well; range a layer of this same on the bottom of a dish, lay the stuffed eggs over, pour on some butter and dredge with parmesan cheese; push into a moderate oven to heat and brown to a fine color; pour Colbert sauce (No. 451) around and serve.

(2865). HARD-BOILED EGGS, RUSSIAN STYLE (Œufs Durs à la Russe.)

Boil six eggs hard, the same as for Aurora (No. 2857); cut them in two lengthwise, remove the yolks, and chop up separately two ounces of ham, four ounces of tongue, and four ounces of chicken, mingling all together with béchamel sauce (No. 409); pound the yolks with half as much butter. Put a bed of the chicken salpicon on a dish capable of going into the oven, range the halved egg-whites over and cover with the remainder of it; bestrew with bread-crumbs and parmesan cheese, pour over butter and bake in a moderate oven; decorate around with some round caviare canapés (No. 777) and serve.

(2866). FRIED EGGS À LA EUGÈNE ANDRÉ (Œufs Frits Eugène André).

Cut tomatoes in two through their thickness, press out and fry in oil with shallots, a little garlic and chopped parsley; finish with a little meat glaze (No. 402). Dress in a circle, filling the

FIG. 562.

center with cèpes fried in oil, with fine herbs, lemon juice and a little brown sauce (No. 414). Heat some butter in a pan and when very hot slip in the eggs broken beforehand on a plate; season the whites with salt and scald the yolks with boiling butter; when the eggs are fried, slip them over the tomatoes and cèpes and serve.

(2867). FRIED EGGS À LA MONTEBELLO (Œufs Frits à la Montebello).

Poach some eggs; when cold pare and wipe on a cloth; season and roll simply in flour then plunge them into hot frying fat, and as soon as dry and nicely colored remove with a skimmer, drain on a cloth and lay each one on a plain croûton of bread sautéd in clarified butter. Dress the eggs on a dish and cover over with Montebello sauce (No. 502).

(2868). FRIED EGGS, NEAPOLITAN STYLE, TURNED OVER (Œufs Frits des deux Cotés à la Napolitaine).

Heat either oil, lard or butter in a small, deep pan; incline it slightly, and break an egg in the liquid; cook and bring it over with a perforated spoon to have it attain a long, well-rounded shape; as soon as done drain, and cook another one the same way, until sufficient are ready, and when all are well drained lay each one on a separate croûton (No. 51). Dress in a circle, and fill the center with Neapolitan macaroni (No. 2960); pour over the eggs some tomato sauce (No. 549) reduced with espagnole sauce (No. 414) and good gravy (No. 404).

(2869). FRIED EGGS TURNED OVER—À LA SOLE (Œufs Frits des Deux Côtés—à la Sole).

Break two eggs on a plate and season: pour some clarified butter in a small pan, and when it reaches hazel-nut (No. 567), slip in the eggs carefully, and pour more butter over. When they are cooked underneath, turn them over, and a minute after slide them on a dish with the butter; baste over with a coffeespoonful of good vinegar heated in a pan.

(2870). FRIED EGGS WITH BROWN BUTTER (Œufs Frits au Beurre Noir).

Break four or five eggs into a frying pan containing some hot butter; scald the yolks with the butter, and cook until glossy; season, remove carefully with a large skimmer, and lay them on a dish. Put more butter into the pan, and when slightly brown without burning, strain it over the eggs; put a little vinegar in the frying pan, and pour it over the eggs through a strainer.

(2871). FRIED EGGS WITH CHOPPED PARSLEY (Œufs Frits au Persil haché).

Heat clarified butter in a small pan; break two very fresh eggs on a plate, season with salt, and pour them carefully in the pan; fry slowly, and then slip them on a dish, throwing over a little chopped parsley.

(2872). FRIED EGGS WITH HAM OR BACON (Œufs Frits au Jambon ou au Petit Salé).

Broil on a slow fire either some ham or bacon; put one or the other on a dish, and slip fried eggs over it.

(2873). EGGS MOLDED À LA BEDFORD—IN COCOTTES AND EGGS COCOTTES (Œufs Moulés en Cocottes à la Bedford et Œufs Cocottes).

Fig. 563.

Cover the bottoms and sides of a few cocottes, a small earthen saucepan standing on three feet, able to go in the oven (Fig. 563), with a layer of liver baking forcemeat (No. 64), thickened with a little raw forcemeat thinned with duxelle sauce (No. 461) and Madeira wine; break a fresh egg over, season the white with salt and pour a little hot butter over the top. Place these cocottes in a sautoir containing a little hot water; poach the eggs for eight to ten minutes in a slack oven, and after removing bestrew with truffles and cooked beef tongue, cut either in small dice or chopped up; dress the cocottes on a dish or on a folded napkin.

Eggs Cocottes.—Have small cocottes (Fig. 563); butter the interiors and cover the bottoms with a preparation made with a few finely chopped shallots, slightly fried in butter, to which add a few finely chopped fresh mushrooms; after these have evaporated all their moisture, add some chopped parsley, salt, pepper, nutmeg and chopped truffles. Break an egg in each cocotte, pour boiling hot melted butter over and stand the cocottes on a baking sheet; push into a medium hot oven for ten minutes, then serve.

(2874). EGGS MOLDED À LA COLBERT—IN CASES (Œufs Moulés en Caisses à la Colbert.

Butter a few china cases, covering the bottom and sides with a chopped raw truffle preparation mingled with chicken cream forcemeat (No. 75). In the hollow center of each break a fresh

Fig. 564.

egg, season the top and butter over with a brush; place the cases on a small raised-edge baking pan having hot water at the bottom, and poach them for six to eight minutes in a slack oven; after removing wipe nicely and cover the tops with a layer of Colbert sauce (No. 451).

(2875). EGGS MOLDED À L'ÉCHIQUIER—IN CASES (Œufs Moulés en Caisses à l'Échiquier).

Prepare a paste with fresh lobster butter (No. 580), an equal amount of white bread-crumbs, some chopped parsley and half as much cooked and chopped crawfish or lobster tail. With this paste cover the bottom and sides of some round china cases shaped the same as the paper cases shown in Fig. 439, leaving an empty space in the center, and into this break a fresh egg; season and cover with a little butter. Set the cases on a small baking pan containing a little hot water, push it into a slack oven and cook the eggs; pour a little velouté sauce (No. 415), over each egg, having it well buttered with lobster butter, and sprinkle chopped lobster coral over the whole.

(2876). EGGS MOLDED À LA PARISIAN, ALSO CALLED TALLEYRAND, POLIGNAC, POLISH SOYER (Œufs Moulés à la Parisienne, Dits Talleyrand, Polignac, Soyer).

Eggs à la Parisienne are molded in mousseline molds (No. 1, Fig. 138), or else in oval ones of the same size. Cut two truffles into small dice; butter eight molds, strew the insides with the truffles and into each one break a whole fresh egg, salt and baste the top with a little butter; lay the molds in a sautoir with hot water reaching to half their height, and poach in a moderate oven for eight to ten minutes; when done to perfection turn out the eggs on a dish, covering the bottom of it with a little poivrade sauce (No. 522). Instead of buttering the molds they may be wetted in the inside with melted meat glaze (No. 402) and bestrewn with chopped parsley, truffles, mushrooms or cooked red beef tongue, or else a mixture of all these.

(2877). EGGS MOLDED WITH FOIES-GRAS—IN CASES (Œufs Moulés en Caisses aux Foies-Gras).

Brush over with butter six round crimped paper cases (Fig. 439) having them three inches across at the opening, two at the bottom, and an inch and a quarter high. Rub a little pâté-de-foies-gras from a terrine through a fine sieve, and mix slowly into it some melted glaze (No. 402), and as much chicken quenelle forcemeat (No. 89) as foies-gras. Spread a layer of this on the bottom of each case, poach the forcemeat in a slack oven, and then break an egg on top of each one; scald the yolks with hot melted butter applied with a brush; season the whites with salt, and range the cases on a grate; lay this on a baking-sheet, and cook the eggs in a slow oven from eight to ten minutes, then place each case inside another paper one, having it larger and very clean, and dress on a folded napkin. The foies-gras forcemeat can be replaced by one of fish, game or chicken, with a salpicon of either shrimps, mushrooms or truffles.

(2878). ARGENTINE OMELET (Omelette à l'Argentine).

Break six fresh eggs in a bowl; season with salt and white pepper; beat with a whip or fork, and strain through a strainer into another vessel; beat again with a few bits of butter laid here and there. Set an omelet pan on a hot fire, and in it have three ounces of very hot butter; skim, then pour in the eggs all at once; stir lightly with a spoon, and when the eggs begin to thicken bring

Fig. 565.

them forward in the pan; fill the center with peeled eggplant cut in quarter-inch squares, fried in butter and thickened with a little half-glaze (No. 400). Close the omelet with a single stroke of the handle, remove the pan from the fire, and with the spoon close it entirely. Put more butter in the pan, and incline it so that it can slip under the omelet, then color it nicely, and turn it over on a dish; garnish around with an Argentine sauce (No. 429).

(2879). BACON OMELET (Omelette au Petit Salé).

For three raw eggs cut one ounce of bacon in quarter-inch thick slices; suppress the rind, and cut into small quarter-inch squares after paring off the smoked parts that cover the bacon; fry these pieces in butter, add the eggs, and finish the same as parsley omelet (No. 2903).

(2880). BEEF PALATE OR LAMB'S TROTTERS OMELET (Omelette au Palais de Bœuf ou aux Pieds d'Agneau).

Cut some beef palates or boned lamb's trotters in quarter-inch squares, and put them into a bordelaise sauce (No. 436); fill the interior of an omelet with the preparation, pouring the sauce around.

(2881). BERTINI OMELET (Omelette à la Bertini).

Prepare and cook an omelet the same as Argentine (No. 2878). Pour into a risot, thickened with parmesan, a little half-glaze (No. 400) and velouté (No. 415) and with it fill the omelet. Cut some celery hearts or roots in quarter-inch squares, blanch, cook in broth (No. 194a) and let fall to a glaze; add velouté reduced with white wine, season and pour this around the dressed omelet.

(2882). BONVALET OMELET (Omelette Bonvalet).

Fry a tablespoonful of chopped onion in butter with two ounces of chopped morils or mushrooms; add salt, pepper, nutmeg, chopped parsley, marinated tunny fish cut in quarter-inch squares, meat glaze (No. 402) and cooked ham cut in three-sixteenths of an inch pieces. With these ingredients fill an omelet, and finish it the same as an Argentine (No. 2878); pour around an espagnole sauce (No. 414) containing minced gherkins.

(2883). CHEESE OMELET—SWISS OR PARMESAN—WITH CRUSTS AND FONDUE (Omelette au Fromage de Gruyère ou au Parmesan aux Croûtes Garnies de Fondue).

Beat up eight eggs in a bowl and season; mix in four spoonfuls of fresh Swiss cheese cut up in small dice, adding two spoonfuls of grated parmesan, and also one of grated Swiss, then a piece of good butter divided in small pats. Make the omelet over a good fire, fold and turn it on to an oval dish; surround both sides with small round hollowed crusts (No. 52) filled with fondue (No. 2954).

(2884). CHICKEN LIVER OMELET (Omelette aux Foies de Volaille).

Cut some chicken livers in three-eighths of an inch squares; sauté them in butter, dilute with a little Madeira wine and half-glaze (No. 400); fill the inside of the omelet with this, and finish the same as Argentine (No. 2878), pouring the sauce around.

(2885). CLAM OMELET—HARD AND SOFT (Omelette aux Lucines Molles et Dures).

Blanch small clams; remove the hard parts and mix in well-buttered allemande sauce (No. 407); fill the inside of an Argentine omelet with this, and pour what remains of the sauce around.

(2886). CREAM OMELET—PLAIN (Omelette Nature à la Crème).

Break seven or eight eggs in a vessel, season and beat lightly, mixing in a few small pieces of butter and two spoonfuls of raw cream. Melt some fresh butter in an omelet pan, pour in the eggs, stir quickly with a large spoon and thicken properly, keeping the omelet mellow; when it detaches from the bottom bring it forward to roll over; turn it rapidly on a long dish and form it prettily, shaping the ends under so as to have them pointed; brush the surface with melted butter and throw over some chopped parsley.

(2887). DESJARDINS OMELET (Omelette à la Desjardins).

Fry in oil (for three eggs) one peeled tomato cut across in two, pressed and divided in small three-eighth inch squares, half as much minced fresh mushrooms, a little onion cut in squares and fried in butter, olives cut in eight pieces, salt, cayenne, nutmeg, chopped parsley and meat-glaze (No. 402). With this preparation fill the inside of a parsley omelet (No. 2903); decorate the top with thin anchovy fillets to imitate lozenges; fill each one of these through a cornet with solid tomatoed béarnaise sauce (No. 433), and on each point set a little bit of chopped parsley; pour around a half-glaze sauce (No. 413), finished with lemon juice and plenty of butter.

(2888). DUXELLE OR COOKED FINE HERB OMELET (Omelette à la Duxelle ou aux Fines Herbes Cuites).

Chop up some onions and shallots very small; fry them in a little grated fat pork or butter, put in some finely chopped fresh mushrooms, and when these have evaporated their moisture add some chopped parsley and two spoonfuls of chopped truffles, mixing in a little velouté sauce (No. 415). Prepare the omelet the same as the parsley and fill it with the preparation; surround each side with hollow half-round-shaped crusts (No. 52) to be filled with tomato purée (No. 730).

(2889). FINE HERB OMELET—RAW (Omelette aux Fines Herbes Crues).

Chop or cut finely some fine herbs, such as parsley, chervil, tarragon and chives; mix them in with the eggs, and finish the same as the parsley omelet, or either of these herbs may be used separately in making a chervil, tarragon or chive omelet.

(2890). FROG OMELET (Omelette aux Grenouilles).

Sauté some large frogs in butter, bone and lay the meats in a sautoir, adding well-buttered allemande sauce (No. 407) and soubise sauce (No. 543), half of each. Fill and finish an omelet the same as the parsley omelet (No. 2903), and pour around half suprême sauce (No. 547) and half soubise sauce, keeping it rather thin.

(2891). OMELET, GERMAN STYLE (Omelette à l'Allemande).

Dilute two tablespoonfuls of flour in a bowl with two whole eggs, one yolk and a gill of cream, salt, pepper and nutmeg; strain through a fine wire sieve and then add finely cut-up chives. Put four ounces of clarified butter in a pan to heat, pour in the preparation, spreading it over the entire surface of the pan; prick the omelet as fast as it swells up, and turn it over when of a fine color; add a little more butter and brown nicely on the other side before serving. With this quantity several omelets can be obtained.

(2892). GREEN OMELET WITH FINE HERBS, SPINACH, OR WITH SORREL CRUSTS (Omelette Verte aux Fines Herbes aux Croûtes d'Épinards ou d'Oseille).

Chop up parsley leaves, chervil, tarragon and clean sorrel leaves, put them into a saucer and mix in some finely shredded chives. Break eight eggs in a bowl, mix with them the chopped herbs, season and beat; melt some butter in an omelet pan, pour in the eggs and stir with a fork to thicken; as soon as the omelet detaches from the pan fold over and turn it out on a long dish; moisten the top with a brush dipped in maître-d'hôtel butter (No. 581) and surround with some hollowed-out bread-crusts filled in with a fine purée of spinach (No. 729); glaze these over also.

With Sorrel.—Chop up a full handful of sorrel leaves, free of stalks; after having them well washed and cleansed, fry in butter and mix with beaten eggs. Make an omelet the same as the above and serve without any garnishing.

(2893). HAM AND GREEN PEA OMELET (Omelette au Jambon et aux Petits Pois).

Make an omelet with three eggs the same as a parsley omelet (No. 2903), only suppressing the parsley; when done, and before folding it, put in two tablespoonfuls of lean cooked ham cut in three-sixteenths inch squares, or else only one spoonful and one of green peas cooked English style (No. 2742).

(2894). HAVANESE OMELET (Omelette Havanaise).

Chop up some chicken livers and mushrooms; fry the livers in butter, add the mushrooms and moisten with port wine and espagnole sauce (No. 414), then reduce. Cut some peeled tomatoes in two, press to extract the juice and fry them in oil, also sweet Spanish peppers. Fill the inside of an omelet with the tomatoes, the chopped liver, the sweet peppers and the mushrooms; finish the same as the Argentine (No. 2878). Surround the omelet with the peppers and pour over a little thin Colbert sauce (No. 451).

(2895). SMOKED HERRING OMELET (Omelette aux Harengs Saurs).

Pour three ounces of partly melted butter in a vessel, beat it up with a spoon, mixing in with it four egg-yolks, one after the other. When the preparation becomes frothy, add to it two small spoonfuls of flour, salt, pepper, nutmeg, and lastly three stiffly beaten egg-whites. Mix into this paste the fillets of four smoked herrings heated in the steam of boiling water until the skin is sufficiently softened to remove, then cut them into large dice, suppressing all the bones. Butter the bottom of a large frying pan with melted butter put on with a brush, and when hot pour in the preparation; cook the omelet in a slack oven, pricking it several times with a fork; brush the top with butter and slide it on a dish.

(2896). HUNTER'S OMELET (Omelette au Chasseur).

Mince some cèpes finely; fry them in oil over a hot fire with a little garlic, salt and pepper; add these to an omelet prepared as follows: Fry a little bread-crumbs or small croûtons in butter, mix them into beaten eggs seasoned with salt and pepper and make the omelet as explained for parsley omelet (No. 2903). Fill the omelet with the cèpes. Pour a hunter's sauce (No. 480) around when dressed.

(2897). KIDNEY OMELET (Omelette aux Rognons).

Use either veal or mutton kidneys; cut them up small, sauté in butter over a brisk fire, drain and put them back into the pan with half-glaze sauce (No. 413) and white wine; take out the kidneys, reduce the sauce, butter it and replace the kidneys to warm up again, then fill the inside of an omelet with the preparation, and finish it as the Argentine (No. 2878), pouring the sauce around just when ready to serve.

(2898). OMELET À LA ANDREWS (Omelette à la Andrews).

Have a chicken hash prepared as for No. 2292; with it fill a slightly cooked omelet prepared the same as an Argentine (No. 2878); invert it on a dish that may be placed in the oven. Roll some noodle paste (No. 142) out very thin; allow it to dry a little in the air, roll it on itself to facilitate mincing it finely, then boil in salted water, drain and replace it in the saucepan with milk, white pepper, salt, nutmeg and butter; let simmer for twenty minutes so that nearly all the milk is absorbed, then cover the omelet with these noodles, bestrew with bread-crumbs and parmesan cheese, sprinkle butter over and let brown in a hot oven; pour around a little bigarde sauce (No. 435).

(2899). MUSHROOM OR SWEETBREAD OMELET (Omelette aux Champignons ou aux Ris de Veau).

Cut up some mushrooms or cooked sweetbreads and place them in a sautoir with allemande sauce (No. 407), season, fill an omelet with either the mushrooms or the sweetbreads and finish by pouring the sauce around.

(2900). ONION AND HAM OMELET (Omelette aux Oignons et au Jambon).

Mince finely four ounces of white onions (new ones if in season); fry them slowly in butter or oil, stirring until they become tender and lightly colored, then add two ounces of cooked lean ham cut in one-eighth inch squares; drain off the whole. Break eight eggs in a bowl, season with salt, pepper and a little sugar; beat them up well and run through a colander, then add the onion, the ham and some chopped parsley. Heat a little butter in a pan, pour the eggs in and make the omelet over a hot fire without ceasing to stir, keeping it mellow; fold over and turn it with one stroke on a long dish; decorate with strings of tomato sauce (No. 549) put on with a brush.

(2901). OYSTER OMELET (Omelette aux Huîtres).

Blanch raw oysters in their own liquor; drain and roll in velouté sauce (No. 415) or béchamel sauce (No. 409) reduced with the oyster liquor, thickening with raw egg-yolks; dilute with a little cream and fresh butter and finish the same as an Argentine omelet (No. 2878).

(2902). OMELET WITH CAVIARE À LA STOECKEL (Omelette au Caviar à la Stoeckel)

Dilute some caviare gradually with cream béchamel (No. 411) and with it fill a chopped parsley omelet (No. 2903). Blanch a few cucumbers cut the shape of cloves of garlic, cook in white broth (No. 194a) and have them so that when done the liquid has fallen to a glaze; remoisten with sour cream sauce; place these cucumbers around the omelet.

(2903). PARSLEY OMELET (Omelette au Persil).

Parsley omelet is frequently confounded with fine herb omelet. Use only eggs, seasoning and chopped parsley. Chop up some very green fresh parsley, put it into the corner of a napkin and dip this in several waters; remove the cloth at once and squeeze out all the moisture. Break eight eggs into a vessel, add the parsley, also pepper and salt. Melt some butter in a pan, pour in the beaten eggs and set it on the open fire; move the pan rapidly with the left hand, using a stew-spoon in the right hand. When the omelet is done fold it on both ends, turn it over on to a dish and shape it prettily.

(2904). PHYSIOLOGICAL OMELET (Omelette Physiologique).

Blanch some oysters or mussels in their own liquor; drain and cut into pieces, removing the feet from the mussels and the muscles from the oysters; add as much marinated tunny fish and as much fresh smoked herring meat and carp milt cut in three-eighths of an inch dice. Fry some shallots in butter, add the oysters, milt, herring and tunny fish, all cut in three-eighths of an inch squares, also parsley, chives, chopped mushrooms, salt, pepper, nutmeg and lemon juice. Fill an omelet with this preparation, the same as an Argentine (No. 2878), and pour around a rather thin cream béchamel (No. 411).

(2905). SAUSAGE OMELET (Omelette aux Saucisses).

Sausage omelets can be made with Lubeck, Frankfort or fresh sausages. For the unsmoked ones, first broil them, then take off the skins and cut them up into small pieces. For Lubeck sausages, fry them in a pan, then cut them up. Plunge Frankfort sausages into boiling water, peel off the skin and divide the meats into small bits. Mix either of this with the uncooked omelet and finish the same as a parsley omelet (No. 2903).

(2906). SHRIMP OMELET (Omelette aux Crevettes).

Cut each shrimp in quarter-inch squares and mingle with an allemande sauce (No. 407) well buttered with lobster butter (No. 580); season, adding lemon juice, and just when ready to serve fill the omelet with the same and finish as for an Argentine omelet (No. 2878); pour the sauce around. The shrimps may be replaced by lobster or hard-shell crab meat.

(2907). SPANISH OMELET (Omelette à l'Espagnole).

This is to be prepared with a tablespoonful of chopped onion, as much peeled and cut-up green pepper, half a crushed clove of garlic and one peeled tomato cut across in two, pressed and divided into quarter-inch squares; fry the onion, garlic and the pepper colorless in oil, add the tomatoes and cover the saucepan; let simmer for fifteen minutes, seasoning with salt and pepper. Break six eggs in a bowl, beat well, season and mix in a third part of the preparation. Make a mellow omelet, fill the center with the solid remaining part and pour the sauce around the whole. Instead of mixing the tomato preparation with the eggs the omelet can be filled with it when made. Pour around a little half-glaze sauce (No. 413).

(2908). TRUFFLE OMELET (Omelette aux Truffes).

Mince some cooked peeled truffles and put them in a sautoir to mingle with either allemande sauce (No. 407) or else half-glaze sauce (No. 413) with Madeira. Fill the inside of an omelet with these truffles and pour the sauce around.

(2909). EGGS ON A DISH (Œufs sur le Plat).

There is very little difference between eggs on a dish or miroir eggs, for they are both cooked the same way, the only difference being that the first ones are served on the same dish they are

FIG. 566.

FIG. 567.

cooked in, while the miroir eggs are basted with boiling butter while cooking and cut in rounds as soon as done with a two and a half inch pastry cutter; take them up with a palette and serve on a plate or dish.

To Prepare Eggs on a Dish.—These eggs should be cooked in china egg dishes (Fig. 567); to do them properly first butter the dish with fresh or unsalted butter, break the eggs into the dish, and salt over the whites but not the yolks so as not to discolor them; set the dish on a thick, cold baking sheet and push it at once into the oven so that they receive more heat from the top than bottom; as soon as the yolks are glossy remove the dish from the oven and, if necessary, finish cooking on top, being careful not to have the whites done too much. Eggs cooked in this way are generally served on the same dish, with or without a garnishing.

(2910). EGGS ON A DISH, BERCY (Œufs sur le Plat à la Bercy).

Fry in a pan two or three sausages; pour the fat into a small egg dish (Fig. 567), leaving the sausages in the pan, then break four eggs into the dish. Pour over some melted butter, salt over the whites and cook in the range oven, leaving them in till they are glossy. Skin the sausages, cut them up and dress around the eggs, serving with a half-glaze sauce (No. 413) and tomato sauce (No. 549), reduced together and strained through a fine sieve.

(2911). EGGS ON A DISH, BIENVENUE (Œufs sur le Plat à la Bienvenue).

Lay through a pocket on the inside edge of the basin of a dish a border made of potato croquette preparation (No. 2782) softened with an egg; fill the center of this border with a bed of duxelle or cooked fine herbs (No. 385); break over some raw eggs without injuring the yolks, season with salt and pepper, and put in the center of the yolks; dredge with grated Swiss cheese, pour on some butter and cook the eggs in a hot oven. Serve as soon as removed.

(2912). EGGS ON A DISH, CONDÉ (Œufs sur le Plat à la Condé).

Through a pocket provided with a channeled socket form a border of chicken quenelle forcemeat (No. 89) and baking forcemeat (No. 81), well mixed together, laying it in the inside of the basin of the dish. Butter the bottom of this dish, season with salt and pepper, and break in a sufficiency of eggs without disturbing the yolks; strew the whites with duck's liver cut in one-eighth of an inch squares, and over the whole scatter grated parmesan cheese; pour on some butter and cook in a hot oven. Garnish around with three-quarters of an inch round chicken croquettes.

(2913). EGGS ON A DISH, CREOLE STYLE (Œufs sur le Plat à la Créole).

Fry colorless in oil one tablespoonful of chopped onions, as much finely cut-up hot pepper, a quarter of a clove of crushed garlic and a peeled tomato cut in two, pressed out, then divided into small squares; simmer, reduce, and when of a sufficient consistency add two tablespoonfuls of cooked rice, salt and cayenne pepper. With this preparation cover the bottom of a dish fit for the oven; break over the eggs carefully, keeping the yolks entire, pour on melted butter, season with salt on the white of the eggs, and in the center of the yolk put a little pepper, and cook in a moderate oven.

(2914). EGGS ON A DISH, ENGLISH STYLE (Œufs sur le Plat à l'Anglaise).

Suppress the rind from some bacon, cut it up very thin and fry in butter without browning. Break some eggs into a buttered china egg dish (Fig. 567), season the whites with a little salt only, and the yolks with a little pepper placed in the center; cook in the oven, having more heat on top than on the bottom. Serve as soon as done, surrounded with the bacon.

(2915). EGGS ON A DISH, FERMIÈRE (Œufs sur le Plat à la Fermière).

Cut the gall from one chicken liver, mince the latter and put it into a pan with butter and a spoonful of chopped onions; season and cook, but not too quickly, while turning over; remove the liver with a skimmer and put one spoonful of chopped-up mushrooms into the pan; let the moisture reduce. Place this in the bottom of an egg dish, on this the liver, break two eggs over, season, pour over some melted butter and cook in the oven.

(2916). EGGS ON A DISH, MONACO (Œufs sur le Plat à la Monaco).

Put into a sautoir one gill of tomato juice and a spoonful of melted glaze (No. 402); add a small bunch of aromatic herbs and tarragon leaves, reduce the liquid until it is the consistency of a syrup, then take out the herbs and pour the liquid into a large egg dish. Break six eggs in a dish, salt the whites, pour over some melted butter and cook in the oven until they become glossy.

(2917). EGGS ON A DISH, OMER PACHA (Œufs sur le Plat à la Omer Pacha).

Melt a little butter on a dish that can go in the oven; when heated break in twelve eggs, one beside the other, keeping the yolks whole; cook in a moderate oven for five to six minutes. Fry in butter two ounces of chopped onions and as much cut-up green peppers, add three gills of tomato sauce (No. 549) and half the quantity of half-glaze sauce (No. 413) and white wine; reduce, not having it too thick, then add bacon prepared by mincing unsmoked bacon; fry it in butter, moisten with gravy (No. 404) and Madeira wine, then cook and reduce the moistening entirely; pour this prepared sauce over the eggs or else serve in a separate sauce-boat.

(2918). EGGS ON A DISH, PLUMEREY (Œufs sur le Plat à la Plumerey).

Remove the whites from four eggs, keeping the yolks in their shells; mix with these whites half a gill of soubise (No. 723) and half a gill of tomato purée (No. 730); butter a dish plentifully and pour into it the white of eggs, soubise and tomato mixture. Lay the yolks over and cook in a slack oven, bestrewing the top with raw fine herbs. Between each yolk place a round croquette an inch in diameter, made of grated cooked ham mixed with béchamel sauce (No. 409).

(2919). EGGS ON A DISH, ROSSINI (Œufs sur le Plat à la Rossini).

Butter the bottom of a dish, break on it four eggs, being careful to keep the yolks whole. Fry some fat chicken livers cut in escalops that have been seasoned and rolled in flour; garnish around the eggs with these. Cook the eggs in a moderate oven, cover the livers with Périgueux sauce (No. 517) and serve.

(2920). EGGS ON A DISH, VENETIAN STYLE (Œufs sur le Plat à la Vénitienne).

Cut in dice pieces equal quantities of anchovy fillets, broiled and peeled sweet peppers from which the seeds have been removed and good sound tomatoes, scalded, peeled and the liquid squeezed out. Bestrew the bottom of an egg dish with these ingredients, pour over some oil and heat lightly. Break four eggs into the dish, season the whites, and cook in the oven; when removed lay the dish inside of another and serve.

(2921). EGGS ON A DISH WITH BACON (Œufs sur le Plat au Petit Salé).

Butter the dish, break in the eggs without spoiling the yolks, season and set for an instant on the fire and finish cooking in the oven; surround with slices of broiled smoked bacon.

(2922). EGGS ON A DISH WITH CÈPES (Œufs sur le Plat aux Cèpes).

Peel and chop up two or three cèpes heads; melt some butter in a large egg dish, bestrew the bottom with chopped cèpes and these with parsley; season and heat for two minutes. Break six eggs into this dish, and cook in the oven, having them glossy. Eggs can also be prepared with canned mushrooms.

(2923). EGGS ON A DISH WITH CHOPPED HAM (Œufs sur le Plat au Jambon Haché).

Butter the bottom of a small egg dish (Fig. 567), cover it with a layer of cooked and chopped lean ham and over this pour a little melted meat glaze (No. 402). Break four eggs into the dish, salt the whites, and cook in the range oven, letting them get glossy on top. They may also be prepared with boiled tongue instead of ham.

(2924). EGGS ON A DISH WITH TOMATOES (Œufs sur le Plat aux Tomates).

Scald two small partly ripe tomatoes in order to remove the skins, divide each one in two, cut them up small, salt over and drain in a sieve; sauté in butter and range them on the bottom of a small buttered egg dish (Fig. 567); break four eggs into this, salt the whites, scald the yolks and cook in the oven, glossing the tops.

(2925). POACHED EGGS À LA BOËLDIEU AND EGGS À LA BENEDICK (Œufs Pochés à la Boëldieu et Œufs à la Benedick).

Poach two or three eggs; scald two tomatoes just sufficiently to be able to peel off the skins;

Fig. 568.

drain and cut them in slices, then in dice; put the pieces in a pan with oil and sauté on a brisk fire until they have reduced their humidity without dissolving; season highly, and bestrew with chopped parsley. With these tomatoes fill two or three hollowed-out bread crusts (No. 52), and on each lay one of the poached eggs heated at the oven door, basting them over with good reduced velouté sauce (No. 415); range these crusts on separate plates.

Eggs à la Benedick.—Cut some muffins in halves crosswise, toast them without allowing to brown, then place a round of cooked ham an eighth of an inch thick and of the same diameter as the muffins on each half. Heat in a moderate oven and put a poached egg on each toast. Cover the whole with Hollandaise sauce (No. 501).

(2926). POACHED EGGS À LA BOURGUIGNONNE—BAKED (Œufs Pochés à la Bourguignonne au Gratin).

Boil water in a saucepan; add salt and a dash of vinegar. Crack six very fresh eggs and drop them slowly in a deep dish, keeping them whole; slip them into the boiling water, and when done, and found to be of a proper consistency, remove them with a skimmer, and transfer to cold water; pare each one singly. Butter thoroughly a baking dish, bestrew it with bread-crumbs and then a layer of grated parmesan; pour over butter, and lay on the eggs; mask them with a well-seasoned béchamel sauce (No. 409), sprinkle with grated parmesan and butter, and bake in a hot oven. When done strew over some chopped fine herbs and squeeze over the juice of a lemon.

(2927). POACHED EGGS À LA MIRABEAU (Œufs Pochés à la Mirabeau).

Prepare a cooked foies-gras and cut seven or eight oval-shaped slices of the same dimensions as the poached eggs; pound the parings of liver with two pounded raw peeled truffles, season and add a spoonful of raw chicken quenelle forcemeat (No. 89) and two egg-yolks; put this into a strong paper cornet and push it through to form a high string all around the upper edges of the slices of foies-gras. Range these on a small raised baking sheet, having the bottom covered with a thin layer of half-glaze sauce (No. 413) reduced with Madeira wine; keep for two minutes in a slack oven to warm the liver and poach the forcemeat. Remove and dress in a circle on a dish, placing a poached egg on each one; heat at the oven door while basting over with good velouté sauce (No. 415).

(2928). POACHED EGGS À LA VILLEROI (Œufs Pochés à la Villeroi).

Poach seven or eight eggs just sufficiently not to have the whites break; when refreshed, pared and well wiped, dip them one by one into a thick Villeroi sauce (No. 560); range as fast as they are done on a small baking sheet, slightly apart, and leave until the sauce hardens, then detach the eggs from the sheet, suppress the superfluous sauce, and roll them first in fresh bread-crumbs mingled with parmesan, then in beaten eggs; lastly plunge the eggs, one at a time, into plenty of hot frying fat to cook to a good color; drain and dress in a circle on a thin bed of chicken quenelle forcemeat (No. 89) poached on a dish to prevent the eggs from slipping off; surround each one with a string of consistent tomato purée (No. 730), mixed with béarnaise sauce (No. 433). Serve at once.

(2929). POACHED EGGS À LA WRIGHT SANFORD (Œufs Pochés à la Wright Sanford).

Blanch some straight thick vermicelli in boiling water for two minutes; drain and return them to the saucepan, adding fresh mushrooms previously minced, washed, drained, fried in butter, and moistened with a little Madeira wine and half-glaze sauce (No. 413), and reduced; season, then dress the whole in the center of a dish, and garnish around with poached eggs (No. 2931).

(2930). POACHED EGGS, MATELOTE (Œufs Pochés Matelote).

Poach some eggs the same as for poached eggs with gravy (No. 2931); prepare and fry in clarified butter some oval crusts (No. 52) measuring two and a quarter by two and three-quarter inches. Cook in butter one minced onion, add to it a bunch of parsley garnished with thyme and bay leaf, and a clove of garlic and mushroom peelings; moisten with red wine and thicken with kneaded butter (No. 579); boil all slowly for half an hour, skim and pass it through a tammy; add small cooked mushroom heads and small glazed onions. Dress the eggs on the fried crusts; range them in a circle, and pour the garnishing in the center.

(2931). POACHED EGGS WITH GRAVY (Œufs Pochés au Jus).

The eggs must be very fresh and selected of uniform size. Only a few at a time can be poached. Boil some salted water acidulated with vinegar in a saucepan; quickly crack three or four eggs, one at a time, on the edge of the saucepan; open and drop them over the water exactly in the spot where it bubbles; with a small, deep, long-shaped skimmer gather the egg together, turning it incessantly, so that it assumes a long form, then remove the pan to the side of the fire until the envelope of the yolk be sufficiently hardened not to break. The difficulty consists in giving the egg a sufficient solidity without allowing the yolks to harden, for these should remain perfectly mellow. As soon as each egg is done, lift it up delicately with the skimmer and drop it in a plentiful supply of cold water so that it hardens, then take it up very carefully, pare neatly, and return it at once into cold water. Just when ready to serve, warm the poached eggs, either in their own water that has been strained through a sieve, or on a small baking tin, in a slack oven; dress them in a vegetable dish and baste over with clear gravy (No. 404) and serve. Poached eggs are also served simply on slices of toast, without any sauce whatever.

(2932), POACHED EGGS WITH PURÉE OF CHICKEN SUPREME (Œufs Pochés à la Purée de Volaille Suprême).

Poach eight eggs, the same as for those poached with gravy (No. 2931); prepare some croustades, either of bread or paste, and fill them half full with chicken purée (No. 713), having all very hot; lay on the well-drained poached eggs, thoroughly heated at the oven door, and cover with buttered supreme sauce (No. 547).

They can also be prepared with a purée of mushrooms (No. 722), game (No. 716) or truffles (No. 731).

(2933), POACHED EGGS WITH SPINACH (Œufs Pochés aux Épinards).

After poaching the eggs the same as with gravy (No. 2931), dress them on a spinach garnishing, or else one of chicory (No. 729).

(2934), SCRAMBLED EGGS À LA COLUMBUS (Œufs Brouillés à la Colombus).

After the eggs are nearly done mix in with them some cooked lean quarter-inch squares of ham; cut some slices of raw blood pudding (No. 1772), fry them in butter over a brisk fire, then arrange them on a baking sheet and allow to cool off; bread-crumb and dip in egg, then fry to a fine color.

Fig. 569.

Also sauté some slices of beef brains over a quick fire. Dress the scrambled eggs, putting half the preparation on a dish and the brains in the center; cover these with the remainder of the eggs and surround with the fried slices of black pudding. Garnish the top with very thin half slices of sausage.

(2935), SCRAMBLED EGGS À LA DUXELLE AND WITH ANCHOVY CROUSTADES (Œufs Brouillés à la Duxelle et aux Croustades d'Anchois).

Fry in butter some chopped onions, shallots and mushrooms; mix with these a little reduced velouté sauce (No. 415). Break five or six eggs in a bowl, season, beat lightly and pour them into a saucepan, having previously buttered the bottom with one ounce of fresh butter; beat them over a slow fire with a whisk until they begin to thicken, then use a spoon, and work till smooth, incorporating about an ounce and a half more butter divided in small pats; season and throw in the fine herbs and some chopped parsley; finish with a little raw cream so as to keep them mellow. In case the eggs have to wait, then put the saucepan in a bain-marie having the water only tepid, and continue beating with the spoon. Dress the eggs in a vegetable or any deep dish, smooth the top and drop over some tomatoed half-glaze; surround with small hollow round crusts (No. 52) filled with reduced béchamel sauce (No. 409), finished with anchovy purée and a halved anchovy dressed in a ring the size of the opening on the croustade, the anchovy to be filled through a cornet with cold béarnaise sauce (No. 433), having lobster coral sprinkled over the top.

(2936). SCRAMBLED EGGS À LA JÉRÔME (Œufs Brouillés à la Jérôme.)

Cook some eggs the same as for scrambled with gravy (No. 2940), mixing in when nearly done a salpicon either of partridge, woodcock or any other seasonable game cut in three-sixteenths of an inch squares; dress, pour around the sauce and garnish with the stuffed eggs.

For the Sauce.—Prepare a game fumet (No. 397) with the fragments of game, reducing it with espagnole sauce (No. 414).

Stuffed Eggs.—Have hard-boiled eggs prepared as follows: Boil some eggs for ten minutes, throw in cold water, shell and remove the white from the pointed ends only with a tin tube half an inch in diameter; empty out the interiors with a vegetable spoon (Fig. 91) and pound this with well seasoned béarnaise sauce (No. 433), mixing in chopped-up mushrooms; fill and re-form the eggs with this stuffing, roll in flour, then in beaten eggs and bread-crumbs and fry to a fine color.

(2937). SCRAMBLED EGGS À LA MARTINEZ (Œufs Brouillés à la Martinez).

Broil four sweet Spanish peppers, selected with meaty and plump insides; suppress their skins by rubbing with a cloth, then divide each one in two; fry in butter and oil, half of each, season with salt, drain off the fat, and mix in a little meat glaze (No. 402) and chopped parsley. Scramble eight eggs, thickening over a slow fire, and when almost done mingle in some artichoke bottoms cut in quarter-inch squares, and fried in butter, and some cooked ham cut in three-sixteenths of an inch squares. Dress the whole in a vegetable dish, smooth the surface dome-shaped and pour around tomato sauce (No. 549) and half-glaze sauce (No. 413), mixed. Arrange the peppers in a circle, one overlapping the other, and serve the remainder of the sauce separately.

(2938). SCRAMBLED EGGS IN A RISOT BORDER WITH DUCKS' LIVERS (Œufs Brouillés en Bordure de Risot aux Foies de Canard).

Make a risot (No. 739), mixing in with it some cooked ducks' livers cut in quarter-inch squares. Butter a plain, round-top border mold (Fig. 138), fill it with the risot, pressing it firmly; keep warm and unmold just when ready to serve. Fill the center with scrambled eggs (No. 2940), mixing in some chopped truffles. Garnish around the eggs with small escalops of foies-gras rolled in Madeira sauce (No. 492).

(2939). SCRAMBLED EGGS WITH FINE HERBS (Œufs Brouillés aux Fines Herbes).

Have some eggs scrambled the same as with gravy (No. 2940); to avoid having lumps in them they should not be cooked excessively, and above all be well stirred; mix in one tablespoonful altogether of chopped parsley, chives and chervil. Should it be necessary to keep them any length of time before serving, then add a little good velouté sauce (No. 415). Surround with puff paste crescents baked in a slack oven.

(2940). SCRAMBLED EGGS WITH GRAVY (Œufs Brouillés au Jus).

Break six eggs in a saucepan with two ounces of butter, a gill of cream or milk, and season with salt and pepper. Lay the saucepan containing the eggs on a slow fire and stir by beating vigorously with a small wire whip (Fig. 154); as soon as they attain a consistency, remove the saucepan from the fire and continue the same process for two minutes longer; when finished pour it out on a dish and surround by bread croûtons (No. 51) fried in clarified butter. Throw over some reduced clear gravy (No. 404), mixing a little meat glaze (No. 402) into it.

(2941). SCRAMBLED EGGS WITH LOBSTER, GARNISHED WITH VILLEROI OYSTERS (Œufs Brouillés aux Homards, Garnis d'Huîtres à la Villeroi).

Add to some nearly finished scrambled eggs, prepared the same as for gravy (No. 2940), a salpicon of lobster cut in three-sixteenths of an inch dice. Dress the eggs when finished, smooth the surface and garnish around with Villeroi oysters (No. 698), or else mussels or scallops. The lobster salpicon can be replaced by one of shrimps or of crabs.

(2942). SCRAMBLED EGGS WITH MUSHROOMS (Œufs Brouillés aux Champignons).

Prepare the scrambled eggs the same as with gravy (No. 2940); when almost done mix in a salpicon of mushrooms cut in quarter-inch squares; dress and pour around a little Madeira sauce (No. 492) and surround with croûtons of bread fried in butter (No. 51).

(2943). SCRAMBLED EGGS WITH SWEETBREADS (Œufs Brouillés aux Ris de Veau).

Braise some sweetbreads and then put them under a weight to cool; cut them up in quarter-inch squares and warm in butter. Prepare some scrambled eggs the same as with gravy (No. 2940) and when nearly done add the sweetbreads and mix them in with the eggs. Dress on the center of a dish, pour around a little half-glaze sauce (No. 413) and surround with half-heart croûtons (small) of bread fried in butter (No. 51). The sweetbreads may be replaced either by unsmoked salted tongue, ham, or even thin pieces of smoked beef or squares of bacon fried in butter.

(2944). SCRAMBLED EGGS WITH SWISS AND PARMESAN CHEESE (Œufs Brouillés au Fromage de Gruyère et au Parmesan).

Beat eight eggs lightly in a bowl, pour them into a saucepan having its bottom buttered with two ounces of fresh butter; season and thicken on a slow fire while beating unceasingly, and as soon as cooked incorporate an ounce of butter and two of grated parmesan. Remove it from the fire and then pour in a little good velouté sauce (No. 415) and raw cream; finish with a few spoonfuls of Swiss cheese cut in dice and softened in cold milk. Dress the preparation in a deep dish and surround with puff-paste crescents. Scrambled eggs may be prepared with the Swiss cheese or with grated parmesan, mixing in three ounces of either. Surround with triangle-shaped bread croûtons fried in butter (No. 51).

(2945). SCRAMBLED EGGS WITH TOMATO PURÉE (Œufs Brouillés à la Purée de Tomates).

Select two or three good tomatoes; put them beside each other in a wire basket and plunge into boiling water for two minutes simply to scald and remove the skins; drain off and press through a sieve; should the purée be too thin put it on a hair sieve to drain, then warm and season it. Scramble seven or eight eggs in a saucepan the same as for scrambled with gravy (No. 2940); when properly thickened remove and mix in the prepared purée; pour the whole into a deep dish. Sprinkle over with half-glaze (No. 400), using a brush, and surround with bread croûtons (No. 51).

(2946). SCRAMBLED EGGS WITH TOMATOES AND CHIVES (Œufs Brouillés aux Tomates et à la Ciboulette).

Scald some tomatoes, peel and cut across in two, then into squares, and sauté in butter; add them to the scrambled eggs when nearly done, also some finely cut-up chives (see scrambled eggs with gravy, No. 2940).

(2947). SCRAMBLED EGGS WITH PÉRIGORD TRUFFLES (Œufs Brouillés aux Truffes du Périgord).

Cut two ounces of Périgord truffles into three-sixteenths inch squares, after they have been peeled and cooked with salt and Madeira wine; put this salpicon with a little melted meat-glaze (No. 402) into a small saucepan and set it in a bain-marie. Break four eggs in a bowl, season and beat to mix well, then pour them through a fine strainer into a saucepan, having its bottom covered with half an ounce of butter; put the saucepan on a slow fire and thicken the eggs while beating steadily with a small tinned wire whip. When almost done remove from the fire and mix in slowly about half an ounce of butter broken up small, finishing with a few spoonfuls of raw cream; add the truffles and dress in a vegetable or any other deep dish.

(2948). SCRAMBLED EGGS WITH PIEDMONT TRUFFLES (Œufs Brouillés aux Truffes du Piémont).

Prepare the scrambled eggs the same as for No. 2940, only salting them less; mix with them two spoonfuls of grated parmesan. Have two ounces of white truffles cut up into thin fillets; put the eggs in a soufflé pan (Fig. 182), make a hole in the center and in it place the truffles; pour some barely melted butter over, and on top place anchovy fillets. Cover the whole with the eggs so that the truffles are inclosed in the center; set this pan in a slack oven for a few moments and serve at once.

(2949). SOFT EGGS À LA CHIPOLATA (Œufs Mollets à la Chipolata).

As for poached eggs these must be of the freshest so as to have them well shaped, all of the same size, while cooking. Partly fresh eggs form into cavities when taken from their shells, giving them an ungainly appearance. Put the eggs into a strainer and plunge this into boiling

Fig. 570.

water; cover the vessel and allow the liquid to boil steadily for five minutes, should the eggs be large; leave them for thirty seconds in their water off the fire; then remove them from the strainer, and plunge into cold water for twelve to fifteen minutes before breaking off their shells; remove these, then return them to the cold water. Just when ready to serve heat them in salted water that must not boil; drain and dress them on hollow crusts (No. 52) and garnish around with a Chipolata garnishing (No. 657).

(2950). SOFT EGGS FOR EPICURES (Œufs Mollets des Gourmets).

Fry in clarified butter some hollowed crusts the shape of an egg (No. 52), having one for each; line the interiors with a bed of foies-gras purée, and range a hot soft egg over. Pour into a saucepan some tomato purée (No. 730), strained through a fine sieve, and incorporate, beating it in, some lobster butter (No. 580), a dash of tarragon vinegar, and a little shallot cut in one-eighth of an inch squares, and blanched. Dress the crusts (Fig. 570), and pour the sauce over.

(2951). SOFT EGGS WITH PURÉE OF SORREL (Œufs Mollets à la Purée d'Oseille).

Prepare a purée of sorrel garnishing (No. 728), finish it with a little half-glaze (No. 400), butter it well, and dress in a vegetable dish; smooth the surface, and on it arrange six soft eggs, prepared as explained in No. 2949. Baste the sorrel with half-glaze applied with a brush.

FARINACEOUS (Farineux).

(2952). RICE CROQUETTES WITH SALPICON (Croquettes de Riz au Salpicon).

Pick and wash half a pound of rice; blanch, drain and refresh; place it in a saucepan to moisten with broth (No. 194a) to three times its height; add a quarter of a pound of butter and a seasoning of salt, pepper and nutmeg. When the rice is sufficiently cooked (in twenty or thirty minutes), mix into it a salpicon weighing a quarter of a pound, composed of tongue, truffles, chicken, game and mushrooms—all to be mixed evenly after cutting in three-sixteenths of an inch squares. Leave this stand till cold, then form into round, flat, oval or oblong croquettes; dip in beaten eggs, then in bread-crumbs, and fry to a fine color. Dress on a folded napkin with fried parsley on top.

(2953). FEDELINI VERMICELLINI AU CARDINAL (Fedelini Vermicellini au Cardinal).

Have half a pound of small, straight vermicelli, one-sixteenth of an inch in diameter. Begin by plunging it in an abundance of boiling salted water for about three minutes, then drain and put it back in a saucepan with four ounces of butter divided in small lumps, and two ounces of grated parmesan, adding salt, pepper, nutmeg, béchamel sauce (No. 409), four ounces of minced mushrooms, two ounces of crawfish butter (No. 573). Have two ounces of truffles sliced sufficiently large, and an eighth of an inch thick, then fried in butter, drained and rolled in meat glaze (No. 402). Alternate the fedelini in a vegetable dish with layers of minced truffles, covering each one with grated parmesan; bestrew the top with bread-crumbs and grated cheese, pour butter over, and brown in a hot oven, or under a salamander (Fig. 123).

(2954). FONDUE WITH PIEDMONTESE TRUFFLES (Fondue aux Truffes du Piémont).

Take a pound of soft, fresh Swiss cheese and cut it up into quarter-inch squares. Break twelve egg-yolks in a bowl with two tablespoonfuls of flour; mix well together and dilute with a pint of cream, then strain through a sieve. Put the cheese into a saucepan on a slow fire with two tablespoonfuls of milk, stir it about with a spoon until it no longer forms into strings, then pour in the prepared yolks. Heat all on the fire, stirring with a spoon until it assumes the consistency of a cream (but it must not boil), then add a little butter and peeled and finely minced Piedmontese truffles. Pour the whole into a deep dish and dredge the top with finely chopped truffles.

(2955). GNOCQUIS (Gnocquis).

Put into a saucepan two gills of water, adding an ounce of butter, salt and pepper; let come to a boil, then put in a quarter of a pound of flour and an ounce and a half of grated cheese; stir the preparation for two minutes on the fire and beat in quickly three eggs, one after the other. Dredge the table with flour, pour the paste on it, divide it into small bits and rolling each one out into a string on the table, cut them so as to obtain three-eighths of an inch in diameter balls, and poach these for five minutes in boiling milk. Put an ounce of butter into a saucepan, fill it with flour and moisten with the milk the gnocquis were boiled in, then add grated parmesan cheese and the gnocquis, stir well, heat the gnocquis thoroughly and serve. Gnocquis can also be made with semolina, also with chicken quenelle forcemeat (No. 89) added to the same weight of cream cake paste (No. 132).

(2956). GNOCQUIS, ROMAN STYLE (Gnocquis à la Romaine).

Range a pound of sifted flour in a ring, form a hollow in the center and in it put salt, two ounces of butter, four ounces of mashed potatoes passed through a fine sieve, and a little hot water. Make a firm paste and divide it into small pieces to form three-fourths of an inch diameter balls; press them on a grater, throw into boiling water for fifteen minutes, then drain and serve in a soup tureen in layers alternated with parmesan cheese; pour over hazel-nut butter (No. 567) and some gravy (No. 404) reduced with espagnole sauce (No. 414) and tomato purée (No. 730).

(2957). LAZAGNETTES, PHILADELPHIA STYLE (Lazagnettes à la Philadelphie).

Blanch half a pound of lazagnettes. (These are thin bands of paste three-sixteenths of an inch wide.) Drain and put them in a saucepan to cover with some broth (No. 194a); boil and reduce this to almost nothing, then add four ounces of cooked lean ham and eight ounces of mushrooms, both to be cut in small three-sixteenths inch squares; dish in separate layers of lazagnettes and parmesan and cover with thin béchamel sauce (No. 409), into which have mixed meat-glaze (No. 402) and tomato sauce (No. 549).

(2958). MACARONI À LA BRIGNOLI (Macaroni à la Brignoli).

Braise a piece of beef by placing it in a saucepan lined with bards of fat pork, onions, carrots and a bunch of parsley; moisten with a pint of broth (No. 194a) and let fall to a glaze, then re-moisten and let fall once more to a glaze; pour in sufficient broth and white wine to reach to the height of the meat. Cook for four hours in a slack oven, strain, skim off the fat and mingle into the sauce a third as much tomato purée (No. 730). Boil some macaroni in salted water for twelve to fifteen minutes, drain and put it in a saucepan with a pint of gravy (No. 404); when this is absorbed dress two-thirds of the macaroni in layers with grated parmesan between; form a hollow in the center and in it arrange sliced truffles previously cooked in a sautoir with cocks'-combs and minced mushrooms, having them simmered with a little tomato sauce (No. 549) and half-glaze (No. 400). Cover over with more macaroni and grated parmesan, pour on a part of the prepared stock and serve the remainder in a sauce-boat.

(2959). MACARONI BAKED (Macaroni au Gratin).

Dress the macaroni, cooked as for the Parisian (No. 2961), in a buttered and bread-crumbed dish; smooth the top neatly, strew with bread-raspings and butter, and bake in a hot oven.

(2960). MACARONI, NEAPOLITAN STYLE (Macaroni à la Mode de Naples).

Line a saucepan with sliced carrots and onions, a bunch of parsley garnished with thyme and bay leaf, and on top lay a three-pound piece of rumps of beef. Into this make three holes some distance apart from each other, and each an inch in diameter; in one place some grated fat pork, in the other a little garlic and in the third hard egg, chopped and seasoned with salt, pepper and parsley. Put the meat into the saucepan with some fat, and color it on a slow fire or in the oven. Around lay a few boned calves' feet, moisten with two bottles of wine, one red and one white, and a quart of broth (No. 194a); when the beef is half-cooked, add twelve tomatoes cut in two and pressed out, and a pint of espagnole sauce (No. 414); cover the saucepan, paste on the lid with a paste made of flour and water and push it into a moderate oven for six hours; remove, skim off the fat and strain the stock. Cook a pound and a half of macaroni three-sixteenths of an inch in diameter in salted boiling water from twelve to fifteen minutes; when sufficiently done drain and range it in a large vegetable dish or soup tureen in separate layers of macaroni and grated cheese. Baste over with the beef stock and continue until it is all used, and when ready to serve stir well and send to the table, using the meat only for stock.

(2961). MACARONI, PARISIAN STYLE (Macaroni à la Parisienne).

Boil a pound of macaroni in salted water from twelve to fifteen minutes, putting it in only when the water boils. Avoid breaking it for it can always be cut the desired length after cooking. When cooked drain and return it to the saucepan, season with a little salt, pepper and nutmeg, and add half parmesan and half Swiss cheese, finishing with a little bechamel sauce (No. 409) and a large piece of butter. Toss in the saucepan, without using a spoon, and when well mingled and the cheese forms into threads then it is done. Pour it into a vegetable dish and serve.

(2962). MACARONI WITH CREAM AND TRUFFLES (Macaroni à la Crème aux Truffes).

After cooking and blanching the macaroni the same as for the Parisian, drain and lay it in a saucepan to season with salt and nutmeg; add a pint of cream and let simmer until this is reduced, then transfer it to a vegetable dish in layers, alternating each one with grated parmesan and some finely shredded truffles, finishing with the chopped truffles. Pour over melted butter and serve.

(2963). MACARONI WITH GAME PURÉE (Macaroni à la Purée de Gibier).

Pound the meats of a cooked partridge, free of skin or bones; add to it six ounces of butter and six gills of meat gravy, prepared the same as in No. 2960. Blanch the macaroni for twelve minutes, drain and dress it in layers—macaroni, grated parmesan and game purée. Serve separately a half-glaze sauce (No. 413) with essence of game (No. 389).

(2964). MACARONI MEZZANI GRANDI À LA CAVALLOTTI (Macaroni Mezzani Grandi à la Cavallotti).

Boil half a pound of this macaroni, which is a quarter of an inch in diameter. Chop up separately some cooked lean ham, some cooked cold chicken fillets and livers, mushrooms and truffles; place these ingredients in a saucepan with reduced gravy (No. 404) and finish with a few spoonfuls of tomato sauce (No. 549); keep this preparation in a bain-marie (Fig. 122). After the macaroni is cooked, drain and return it to the saucepan to mix in a gill of rich gravy; boil while stirring at times and when the gravy is all absorbed add two ounces of butter divided in small pats, also two ounces of grated parmesan. Dress the macaroni in a vegetable dish and spread a part of the sauce over; strew with parmesan, pour a little hazel-nut butter (No. 567) over and serve very hot, with the remaining gravy in a sauce-boat.

(2965). MACARONNICELLI À LA LUCINI (Macaronnicelli à la Lucini).

Boil a pound of macaronnicelli; drain and put it in a sautoir with half a pound of butter. Cut five peeled tomatoes crosswise in two; press them well and fry in butter over a brisk fire, keeping them very whole. Grate half a pound of Swiss and parmesan cheese, half of each. Chop up a medium onion, fry it in butter with four ounces of cooked lean ham and as much bacon, both cut in three-sixteenths inch squares; drain off the butter and replace it by espagnole sauce (No. 414) and meat gravy; let cook for fifteen minutes, then dress the macaronnicelli in a vegetable dish, alternating each layer with one of the grated cheese; cover the surface with the halved tomatoes and pour the sauce over the whole.

(2966). SPAGHETTI MACARONI À LA LAURENCE (Macaroni Spaghetti à la Laurence).

Cook the spaghetti in boiling water for ten minutes; drain and finish in some veal blond (No. 423) in such a way that when the paste is cooked the moistening will be entirely reduced, then dress it in a vegetable dish intercalated with layers of grated parmesan. Serve the following sauce separately: Chop up two ounces of onions, fry it in butter with six ounces of minced ham, a bunch of parsley garnished with thyme and bay leaf, mignonette, an uncrushed clove of garlic, six halved and well-pressed-out tomatoes, melted meat glaze (No. 402) and espagnole sauce (No. 414); boil together for fifteen minutes, then strain through a tammy and pour in a sauce-tureen to serve at the same time as the macaroni.

(2967). SPAGHETTI MACARONI À LA PRATI (Macaroni Spaghetti à la Prati).

Take half a pound of cold braised sweetbread escalops, one inch in diameter by three-sixteenths of an inch in thickness, and a quarter of a pound of cooked lean ham cut the same size and shape; fry both lightly in butter and moisten with some gravy (No. 404), espagnole sauce (No. 414) and Madeira wine; add two ounces of salted unsmoked tongue and one ounce of truffles. Blanch a pound of spaghetti in salted water for ten minutes, drain and put it back in the saucepan with melted glaze (No. 402), butter and a little of the gravy from the above stew; simmer and when finished cooking incorporate four ounces of grated parmesan; arrange two-thirds of this spaghetti in a circle on a dish, pour the stew in the center and cover with the remainder of the spaghetti.

(2968). SPAGHETTI MACARONI, QUEEN STYLE (Macaroni Spaghetti à la Reine).

Plunge one pound of spaghetti into boiling salted water, and when cooked drain in a colander without refreshing; return it to the saucepan with some chicken purée prepared as follows: Pound some roast chicken meat to a pulp with a pint of béchamel (No. 409); rub it through a sieve and put it in the saucepan with the spaghetti, adding salt, prepared red pepper (No. 168), nutmeg and meat glaze (No. 402). When thoroughly mixed incorporate slowly some butter and grated parmesan. Dress in a vegetable dish, scatter fine fillets of tongue and truffles over and pour on some clear half-glaze (No. 400).

(2969). SPAGHETTI MACARONI, SALVINI (Macaroni Spaghetti à la Salvini).

Cook in boiling and slightly salted water one pound of spaghetti macaroni, having it boil for twelve to fifteen minutes; drain and dress it in layers in a large vegetable dish or soup tureen, beginning with a layer of the macaroni; strew this with grated parmesan, and continue till finished. Baste over with beef gravy prepared as follows, and serve very hot: Take three pounds of rump of beef. Select a saucepan rather larger than the piece of beef, cover its bottom with bards of fat pork and sliced onions, having sufficient to conceal the bottom; lay in the meat, salt and pepper over, add a clove of garlic and a garnished bunch of parsley, cover the saucepan, put it on the fire and let fall to a glaze. When the meat is browned have two ounces of extract of tomatoes dissolved in a quart of broth (No. 194a), and add a spoonful at a time to the saucepan until the onions are well melted, then continue adding the remainder of the tomatoes and another quart of broth; cook the whole slowly for six hours.

(2970). NOODLES À LA LAUER (Nouilles à la Lauer).

Mince fine one pound of noodle paste (No. 142), rolled out to a sixteenth of an inch in thickness; cook it in boiling water for a few moments, then drain; add to it salt, pepper, nutmeg, six ounces of butter, and four ounces of grated parmesan, also a little béchamel sauce (No. 409); mix all together and serve.

(2971). NOODLES, BAKED (Nouilles au Gratin).

Butter a baking dish, lay in the same preparation as for Lauer (No. 2970), smooth nicely, and dredge over with bread-crumbs and grated parmesan; pour on melted butter, brown in a hot oven and serve.

(2972). NOODLES SAUTÉD IN BUTTER (Nouilles Sautées au Beurre).

Blanched noodles can be sautéd in butter, drained and seasoned with salt and pepper, then slightly browned in the oven.

(2973). NOODLES WITH FRIED BREAD-CRUMBS (Nouilles à la Mie de Pain Frite).

Prepare the noodles as for the Lauer (No. 2970), but instead of using six ounces of butter, have only two, and finish precisely the same. Fry a handful of bread-crumbs in butter, and when a fine color throw over the dressed noodles. It is then ready to serve.

(2974). POLENTA (Polenta).

A dried and crushed corn resembling semolina. Have a quart of water boiling in a saucepan, drop in like rain one pound and a half of polenta; boil for a few moments, adding a little salt and three ounces of butter, then stir in briskly a little grated parmesan. When cooked, pour it into mousseline molds (No. 2, Fig. 138), previously coated with meat glaze (No. 402); when the polenta is hard, unmold, or else have the molds buttered, and when the polenta is thoroughly cold unmold and cut each one into slices; spread a little melted butter and grated parmesan between each, then restore them to their respective positions; remold and place in the oven for twenty-five to thirty minutes, then unmold and serve with a cream sauce (No. 454).

(2975). RAMEKINS (Ramequins).

Pour a pint of milk into a saucepan, add to it five ounces of butter, and when this boils remove it from the fire, and stir in twelve ounces of flour; beat and dry it on the fire. Remove the saucepan from the range and then incorporate five more ounces of butter, also five ounces of grated parmesan, six whole eggs and two yolks, a pinch of pepper, two heaping tablespoonfuls of sugar and eight ounces of Swiss cheese, cut in quarter-inch squares; mix the whole well together, adding a little whipped cream. Have this paste the consistency of a pâte-à-chou, then drop it with a round spoon on a buttered pan into balls measuring an inch and a quarter in diameter; egg them over and decorate each ramekin with thin slices of Swiss cheese put on in form of a rosette. Cook in a medium oven. As soon as done take them out and detach from the pan to dress and serve at once on a folded napkin.

(2976). RAVIOLES À LA BELLINI (Ravioles à la Bellini).

Prepare some ravioles as explained in No. 158. After being blanched and drained put them in a saucepan and cover with broth (No. 194a); cook for a few minutes, then drain and dress in layers in a vegetable dish, alterating each one with grated parmesan; pour over some thickened gravy (No. 405), mixed with meat glaze (No. 402) and tomato purée (No. 730), then serve. Ravioles can also be prepared the same way, and when drained and placed in the vegetable dish pour over some melted butter, strew over grated parmesan and bake in a moderate oven for a few minutes.

(2977). RICE À LA MANHATTAN—LEAN (Riz au Maigre à la Manhattan).

Chop up two ounces of onion; fry it in butter, add a pound of rice and heat both together. When exceedingly hot moisten to three times its height (the rice one-third and the moistening two-thirds) with broth (No. 194a); let boil and cook in a slack oven for twenty minutes. Incorporate with the rice, when done, six ounces of grated parmesan. Pour two-thirds of this into a casserole or vegetable dish; make a hole in the center and fill it with shelled crawfish tails or shrimps and poached oysters, after removing their muscles, or else with mussels and minced mushrooms; pour over lean velouté sauce (No. 416) reduced with essence of mushrooms (No. 392) and chicken glaze (No. 398); mix well and cover the whole with the remainder of the rice; put in a hot oven for fifteen minutes and serve.

(2978). RICE, ORIENTAL STYLE (Riz à l'Orientale).

Wash well and drain one pound of rice, place it in a saucepan with three quarts of boiling water, cover and push it into the oven; when the rice is dry and sufficiently done pour it on a sieve. Put three-quarters of a pound of clarified butter cooked to hazel-nut (No. 567) in a saucepan, add to it the drained rice and cover with a wet cloth; place the lid on the saucepan to close it hermetically, then set it in a moderate oven for fifteen minutes. Serve the rice in a vegetable dish.

(2979). RISOT À LA FRANCATELLI (Risot à la Francatelli).

Chop up a two-ounce onion, fry it colorless in butter and add one pound of Piedmont rice, a few slices of raw smoked ham and six small chipolata sausages; moisten to double the height of the rice with broth (No. 194a), boil, put on the lid and place the saucepan in the oven for twenty minutes, then remove the ham and sausages, and incorporate four ounces of hazel-nut butter (No. 567), four ounces of grated parmesan and a very little salt and prepared red pepper (No. 168). Put two-thirds of this risot into a vegetable dish; garnish the top with a circle of escalops of sweetbreads fried in butter, and the center with the sausages, having suppressed the skin and cut them into slices: cover with the remainder of the risot. Serve separately a very thick rich sauce, into which mix some tomato paste and a little espagnole sauce (No. 414).

(2980). RISOT À LA RISTORI (Risot à la Ristori).

Prepare a risot the same as with Piedmontese truffles (No. 2981); dress half of it in a casserole or vegetable dish so as to cover the bottom and sides; in the center place a garnishing of cocks'-combs and kidneys, escaloped duck's liver and sliced truffles; cover this garnishing with espagnole sauce (No. 414) reduced with Marsala wine; mask with the remainder of the risot and this with peeled halved tomatoes pressed out and fried in oil, keeping them as whole as possible. Serve apart a little clear gravy (No. 404) and grated parmesan.

(2981). RISOT WITH PIEDMONTESE TRUFFLES (Risot aux Truffes du Piémont).

Put six ounces of butter in a saucepan; when it begins to heat add to it two ounces of chopped onion and fry for a moment, then put in a pound of unwashed but well-picked rice. When this becomes quite hot moisten to double its height with broth (No. 194a), and cook very slowly while covered for twenty minutes. When done add six ounces of butter in small lumps, and four ounces of grated parmesan, stirring them in with a large carving fork, also two tablespoonfuls of meat glaze (No. 402) or chicken glaze (No. 398). Range the risot in a casserole or vegetable dish, cover the top with two ounces of fresh white Piedmont truffles, warmed in a little butter. Serve a clear gravy (No. 404) at the same time.

(2982). SOUFFLÉ, CREAMY, WITH CHEESE (Soufflé Crémeux au Fromage).

Place twelve raw egg-yolks into a saucepan; beat them with half a pound of partly melted butter, season with pepper and nutmeg and stir the preparation on a slow fire the same as a cream, so that it thickens, without ceasing to stir, and without letting it boil; when done remove from the fire and stir in three-quarters of a pound of grated Swiss and parmesan cheese (the preparation should remain mellow); add to it first five beaten egg-whites, mixing thoroughly but gently, and then two or three spoonfuls of whipped cream. Pour this preparation in a soufflé pan (Fig. 182), lay it on a small baking sheet and cook it from eighteen to twenty minutes in a slack oven. Strew over grated parmesan before removing and serve at once.

(2983). SOUFFLÉ WITH PARMESAN CHEESE (Soufflé au Fromage Parmesan).

Have a gill of water in a saucepan, with two ounces of butter, a pinch of sugar, some whole peppers and salt; let the liquid boil, then remove and stir in a quarter of a pound of flour; thicken the paste by beating it vigorously over a slow fire until it detaches from the saucepan: pour it into a basin and let get partly cold while stirring about with a spoon. Incorporate six or seven egg-yolks, a quarter of a pound of grated parmesan and two ounces of butter divided in small pats, adding them all very slowly without ceasing to stir. At the last moment work in five beaten-up egg-whites, and lastly two or three spoonfuls of good whipped cream. With this preparation fill a buttered soufflé pan (Fig. 182) two-thirds full, lay it on a small baking sheet and cook for twenty-five minutes in a slow oven. This quantity is sufficient for eight persons.

(2984). SOUFFLÉ WITH SWISS CHEESE (Soufflé au Fromage de Gruyère).

Put a quarter of a pound of flour into a saucepan with two ounces of fecula, two ounces of butter, five ounces of grated cheese, having half Swiss and half parmesan, a pinch of pepper and some sugar; dilute slowly with a pint and a half of good milk, and stir the preparation on a slow fire to thicken; let it dry on a very low fire until it detaches from the saucepan, then remove and let get partly cold. Now incorporate a piece of butter and six or seven egg-yolks; heat it for two minutes on a slow fire without ceasing to stir. At the last moment incorporate into the preparation five or six egg-whites beaten to a froth, and a quarter of a pound of fresh Swiss cheese cut in small dice. Pour the whole into a buttered soufflé pan (Fig. 182) and lay it on a small baking sheet; place it in the oven to cook for twenty-five minutes.

(2985). SOUFFLÉS WITH SWISS AND PARMESAN CHEESE—IN CASES (Soufflés en Caisses au Fromage de Gruyère et au Fromage Parmesan).

Melt five ounces of butter in a saucepan; to it add seven raw egg-yolks; set the saucepan on the fire, and stir the preparation until it begins to thicken, then put in five ounces of parmesan cheese, and five ounces of Swiss cheese, half a teaspoonful of black pepper, a little salt, a pinch of sugar, and two beaten egg-whites, mixed in after the preparation has lost its first heat. Twenty minutes before serving incorporate five very firmly beaten whites, and use this to fill round but tered cases (Fig. 439) stiffened in the oven; cook the soufflés in a slack oven; serve promptly.

(2986). TAGLIATELLI IN CROUSTADE (Tagliatelli en Croustade).

Cook half a pound of tagliarelli (small thin bands of paste three-sixteenths of an inch wide) in salted water for a few moments; drain and put them into a sautoir to season with salt, pepper and nutmeg; add a little béchamel (No. 409), fresh butter, grated cheese and four raw egg-yolks. Butter and line a mold or ring eight inches in diameter and an inch and a half in height; fill it with the preparation, dredge the top with fresh bread-crumbs, besprinkle with butter and cook in a moderate oven; when the paste is done slip the croustade on a round dish and serve with a separate tomato sauce (No. 549) mingled with meat glaze (No. 402) and velouté (No. 415).

(2987). TIMBALE OF GNOCQUIS, À LA CHOISEUL (Timbale de Gnocquis à la Choiseul).

Prepare a paste with a pint of milk boiled with a quarter of a pound of butter; remove it at the first boil and put in a half pound of sifted flour; prepare as a pâte-à-chou (No. 132); boil for a few moments on the fire, then incorporate fourteen eggs, salt and four ounces of grated parmesan. Turn this paste over on the table and finish with sufficient flour to have it firm and solid, then roll it out into thin strings a quarter of an inch in width, and divide these into quarter-inch lengths; roll each one to the shape of a ball and plunge them into boiling water to poach for three minutes, then drain and lay them in a saucepan with grated Swiss cheese and béchamel sauce (No. 409). Line a timbale mold with thin foundation paste (No. 135), pour in the gnoquis and wet the inside upper edge; cover the timbale with a flat of the same paste, attach the edges solidly together and cook for one hour in a medium oven, remove, unmold and serve at once, dressed on a dish, with a little buttered velouté sauce (No. 415) served separately.

(2988). TIMBALE MILANESE OF MACARONI OR NOODLES (Timbale de Macaroni ou de Nouilles, Milanaise).

Butter the interior of a timbale mold; decorate the sides with slightly sweetened noodle paste (No. 142); moisten the decorations and line the whole with foundation paste (No. 135). Cut the bottom with a three-inch pastry cutter, but do not remove this round piece. Blanch some macaroni in water, drain and finish cooking in broth (No. 194a), drain once more, then cut it into three-inch lengths; season with a very little salt, pepper, grated parmesan and a liberal piece of butter. Fill the timbale with this macaroni, leaving a hollow in the center

FIG. 571.

to be filled with a garnishing composed of truffles, foies-gras, game quenelles, unsmoked red beef tongue and mushrooms, all cut an eighth of an inch thick and three quarters of an inch long; these ingredients to be mingled with half-glaze (No. 409) made of essence of game (No. 389). Close the timbale with a cover of the same paste and cook in a moderate oven. A timbale containing two quarts will require an hour and a half to cook properly; invert it immediately on a dish, remove the round that was cut, replace it and serve. Instead of macaroni, noodles or lazagnettes may be substituted, proceeding precisely the same. Send at the same time with the timbale beef à-la-mode gravy, with tomato pulp, little meat glaze (No. 402) and brown sauce (No. 414).

(2989). TIMBALE OF NOODLES À LA PEARSALL (Timbale de Nouilles à la Pearsall).

Make some noodle paste the same as for No. 142; roll it out a sixteenth of an inch thick and leave it dry slightly, then cut into very thin fillets and cook these in salted water for one minute; drain and season with salt, pepper and nutmeg, add six egg-yolks, a quarter of a pound of butter and a quarter of a pound of parmesan cheese. Garnish a timbale mold measuring five by five inches with foundation paste (No. 135), line the bottom and side with buttered paper, fill with rice, place a round of buttered paper on top, moisten the upper edge, cover over with a lid of paste and cook in a moderate oven for an hour. Unmold when cold, bread-crumb and egg over twice, mark it on the top half an inch from the edge and fry in white frying fat; remove the cover and empty out the timbale. Fry in butter one ounce of finely chopped onions with half a pound of minced mushrooms, add salt, pepper, nutmeg, meat glaze (No. 402) and tomato sauce (No. 549). Arrange the noodles in the timbale in layers separated with the mushrooms and grated parmesan. Pour over some gravy (No. 404) reduced with espagnole sauce (No. 414) and the timbale is ready to serve.

SWEET ENTREMETS.

SWEET ENTREMETS—HOT (Entremets de Douceur—Chauds).

(2990). APPLES À LA GIUDICI (Pommes à la Giudici).

Remove the cores from a dozen small pretty apples; peel them evenly and cook them in a light syrup of about twelve degrees. As soon as done, drain and place them in a vessel to cover with a hot vanilla syrup of thirty degrees. With a large vegetable spoon (Fig. 91) scoop out about thirty round balls from some large apples, blanch, drain and place them in another vessel containing a hot syrup colored with carmine. With the apple parings and a few more apples prepare some marmalade with vanilla; reduce till somewhat thick and with this fill a dozen small Savarin molds to the top, and let harden. Have a pastry cutter of the same diameter as the Savarin molds and with it cut out a dozen round pieces of cooked brioche a quarter of an inch thick; bestrew them with sugar and range on a baking sheet, then place them in the oven to glaze; mask this glazed side with currant jelly. Dress on each one the apple paste borders, having had them cooked in the Savarin molds, and fill up the hollow centers with vanilla frangipane (No. 44) mixed with a salpicon of pineapple cut in dice, and on top dress the apples that have been previously drained and covered with a layer of lightly tinted pink jelly. Dredge over with finely chopped pistachios, fill the empty spaces in the apples with vanilla frangipane and on top set a small round croquette made of chestnut purée (No. 3017). Range these dressed apples in a circle on a dish, fill the middle with the small apple balls, mixed with a few whole pistachios, the whole mingled with some apple jelly (No. 3668). Serve separately a sauce made of the apple juice thickened with a little apricot marmalade (No. 3675) and flavored with kirsch.

(2991). APPLES À LA NELSON (Pommes à la Nelson).

Prepare a semolina croquette preparation (No. 3019), pour it into a flawn mold (No. 3170) previously buttered and sugared; place this in a buttered sautoir and push it into a very slack oven to harden the preparation. Have eight fine apples, suppress the cores with a column tube, enlarge the orifices slightly and peel them very neatly; range them in a sautoir and cover with syrup, and then cook them in the oven; as soon as done drain on a grate and cover with strained peach marmalade (No. 3675). Unmold the semolina on a dish and dress the apples around the edge in a circle; fill the holes in these with marmalade, and lay on each a small round semolina croquette with a piece of angelica to represent a stalk; decorate the edge of the semolina with a wreath composed of angelica lozenges and candied cherries, and fill up the center with some of the same cherries (demi-sucre); push it into the oven for about fifteen minutes and serve with a vanilla syrup thickened with peach marmalade.

A surtout is a plain round or oval base made of semolina, etc., about three-quarters to one inch high.

(2992). APPLES BAKED (Pommes au Four).

Use a five-eighth inch tin tube from the column box to core some good russet apples without peeling them: cut off a strip of the peel all around the middle and lay the apples beside each other on a dish fit for the oven, leaving half an inch space between each one. Fill up the hole in the center of each apple with white or brown sugar, and place a little melted butter on the top of them all; pour a little hot water into the bottom of the dish and push the apples into a slack oven for about half an hour. Should the oven be too hot, cover them over with paper. Serve in the same dish they were cooked in.

(2993). APPLES, BARON DE BRISSE STYLE (Pommes à la Baron de Brisse).

Peel twelve medium-sized apples, remove the cores with a tin tube, rub them over with lemon and cook in a light syrup, being careful to keep them slightly firm; drain on a cloth. Prepare a croquette of semolina preparation (No. 3019); spread some of it on the bottom of a dish, having it half an inch thick, and pour the remainder in a pocket furnished with a channeled socket (Fig. 179) and push this out in the shape of a plait to form a border around the inside edge of the dish; range the apples in the center; fill the cavity of the apples with cream rice preparation (No. 160) and on the top of each one place a small cream rice pear-shaped croquette, containing a shred of angelica to imitate a stalk. Decorate the border between each apple with angelica lozenges and preserved cherries (demi-sucre), and fill up the center with whole marrons cooked in light syrup with vanilla, and mixed with a few spoonfuls of Smyrna raisins washed in hot water, the whole to be stirred with a little apricot marmalade. Serve separately a chestnut syrup with vanilla taken from some preserved chestnuts (No. 3689).

(2994). APPLES BROWNED (Pommes Gratinées).

Have about fifteen nice small apples; empty the centers with a half-inch in diameter column box tube; peel and pare them round, then blanch in acidulated water, keeping them whole. Drain and fill the hollow centers with frangipane cream (No. 44), finished with a whole egg. Range the apples in a baking dish, pour over some apricot and vanilla syrup, and put them for half an

FIG. 572.

hour in a slack oven, basting over frequently to finish cooking and glaze. At the last moment spread on the bottom of a vegetable dish a thick layer of vanilla cream rice (No. 160), having it very soft; remove the apples one by one with a palette knife and dress them on the rice, pressing them down slightly; close the middle hole with a half-sugared cherry, or with a round piece of greengage half an inch in diameter. Bestrew over with finely chopped and sifted almonds mixed with sugar; brush the surface lightly with butter, then brown for a few moments under a salamander (Fig. 123), or in a hot oven, until a fine color is attained, then serve at once.

(2995). APPLES IN SURPRISE (Pommes en Surprise).

Roll out sufficient puff paste parings (No. 146) to the thickness of an eighth of an inch to make eight squares of five inches each. Peel and turn eight good medium-sized russet apples to have them two and a half inches in diameter; empty out the cores with a five-eighth of an inch column tube, and on each square of paste lay one apple; brush them over with butter, besprinkle with sugar, then fill the hollow in the apple with apricot marmalade (No. 3675); wet the edges of the paste, raise it up and enclose the apples well inside, attaching it firmly on top; moisten this and lay over it a round piece of paste cut out with a channeled pastry cutter (Fig. 16). Range the apples on a baking sheet a short distance apart, egg over, and cook in a slow oven for three-quarters of an hour. Ten minutes before removing glaze them over with sugar, and lay them on a dish as soon as they are done.

(2996). APPLES, NUBIAN—MERINGUED (Pommes Meringuées à la Nubienne).

Cut in four eight fine apples; peel, core and round the angles, rub them over with lemon, and range them in a sautoir one beside the other; cover lightly with melted butter, and bestrew with vanilla sugar, then place a sheet of buttered paper over and cook in a slack oven. Butter and sugar a plain border mold (Fig. 138), fill it to the top with cream rice flavored with vanilla (No. 160), and finished with a few egg-yolks; lay it on a baking tin with water to reach to half its height, and set in a slack oven to harden. Spread a layer of the same rice on the bottom of a dish, unmold the border on this, and mask the inside with apricot marmalade (No. 3675); on this range the cooked quartered apples in a pyramid, and glaze them over with apricot marmalade (No. 3675); cover it with meringue (No. 140), shaping it like a dome over all; smooth it with a knife, and decorate the entire surface with rows of beads, having the largest at the base and decreasing at the top, made of the same, sticking a small piece of almond into each one. Dredge with sugar, and put the dish in a very slack oven to color the meringue slightly.

(2997). APPLE "PAIN" WITH VANILLA (Pain de Pommes à la Vanille).

Make a pint and a half of fine apple purée, and reduce it with half a pound of sugar. Put into a vessel six ounces of butter, beat it up to a cream, adding two egg-yolks and two whole eggs, one at a time, and then a pinch of salt; when this becomes very frothy, add to it a teaspoonful of fecula, six ounces of pulverized macaroons and the apple purée. Butter and flour a plain cylindrical mold (Fig. 150), fill it up with the preparation, and lay it in a sautoir, with water to half its height, then cook it in an oven. Just when ready to serve, unmold on a dish and send to the table with a bowlful of very fine apple purée diluted with vanilla syrup.

(2998). APPLES, PORTUGUESE (Pommes à la Portugaise).

Peel twelve medium-sized apples, remove the cores with a column tube, and cook them in a light syrup; as soon as done drain on to a cloth, wipe and brush over with a layer of apricot marmalade (No. 3675). Cut some slices of savarin, half an inch thick, and from these cut a dozen rounds with a two and a quarter inch diameter pastry cutter; cut some grooves on one of the surfaces a quarter of an inch apart to form lozenges; strew this cut side with powdered sugar, and range the slices on a baking sheet, push into the oven to glaze, and when removed mask the glazed side with currant jelly, then dress in a circle on a dish; lay an apple on each, and fill the holes in them with currant jelly; set on each a small cream rice croquette (No. 3018), made in the shape of a three-quarter inch ball. Fill the inside of the circle with stewed cherries mingled with currant and maraschino syrup, and serve separately a sauce-boat of currant sauce, made with currant jelly dissolved in a few spoonfuls of boiling syrup, and flavored with maraschino.

(2999). APPLES WITH BUTTER (Pommes au Beurre).

Cut four fine russet apples in quarters; peel and pare them, and range in a well-buttered sautoir; moisten with a few spoonfuls of twenty degree syrup, and the juice of a lemon; cover over with a well-buttered paper, and finish cooking in a slow oven. When done dress on a dish in a circle, and add to the sautoir a little apricot marmalade (No. 3675) with some Madeira wine; boil up with the lid on; strain the sauce through a tammy, and pour it over the apples.

(3000). APPLES WITH BURNT ALMONDS (Pommes au Pralin).

Cut six fine apples across in two; remove the cores with a column tube, peel and round the angles; cook them in a light syrup acidulated with lemon juice, being careful to keep them slightly firm. As soon as done drain, wipe, and cover with a layer of burnt almonds (No. 1); bestrew with sugar, place them on a buttered baking sheet, and set into an oven to color. Cut half-inch thick slices of savarin, and from these stamp out a dozen round pieces the same diameter as the apples; cover them on one side with apricot marmalade (No. 3675), and over this a layer of burnt almonds as used for the apples; dredge with sugar, range them on a baking sheet, and push into the oven. As soon as the crusts are browned lay them in a circle on a dish with an apple on top of each; fill the hollow of these with vanilla pastry cream (No. 46), and on top set a fine large preserved cherry (demi-sucre); fill the center of the circle with fresh strawberries, over which has been poured some sugar cooked to "small crack" (No. 171), and flavored with maraschino.

(3001). APRICOTS À LA JEFFERSON (Abricots à la Jefferson).

Infuse a vanilla bean in a quart of hot milk for half an hour, then take it out and set the milk on the fire; drop into it like rain six ounces of farina. Let this boil a few minutes, then remove from the hot fire to a slower one, so that it continues to cook without boiling. Then add to it six egg-yolks, two ounces of sugar, four tablespoonfuls of whipped cream, and two egg-whites beaten to a stiff froth. Butter twelve timbale molds (No. 1, Fig. 137); put into the bottom of each a ring of apricot paste and fill the interior of this ring with a round piece of angelica. Fill the molds with the above preparation and keep them in a bain-marie for twenty-five minutes, then unmold and dress in a circle on a dish. Drain some fine compotes of halved apricots, wipe them well and dress them in a dome in the center of the circle. Cover them over with the apricot syrup reduced with sugar and maraschino. Decorate the intersections of the apricots with halved, freshly skinned almonds and cherries (demi-sucre). Lay on the edge of the dish between each timbale a brandied greengage and a brandied cherry. Place the dish after it has been decorated in the oven for fifteen to twenty minutes and serve with an apricot and kirsch sauce in a sauce-boat, made as follows: Put three gills of apricot pulp into a copper pan, with as much water and half a pound of sugar; let boil up once or twice, then strain the sauce through a fine sieve and add one gill of kirsch to it.

(3002). BABA WITH MARSALA (Baba au Marsala).

Fill a buttered baba mold to half its height with a baba paste (No. 129) without any raisins; set it to rise in a rather mild temperature until the mold is nearly full, then bake it in a moderate oven. As soon as done cut it off even with the top of the mold. Unmold, and pour over a rum syrup, flavored with vanilla and orange peel; drain it well and glaze it with lemon icing (No. 102). Dress it on a very hot dish and fill up the inside of the hollow space with fruits prepared as follows, serving the surplus of them in a sauce-boat:

Preparation of Fruits.—Put in a saucepan a quarter of a pound of well-cleaned sultana raisins (No. 157), two ounces of candied orange peel, two ounces of candied green almonds and two ounces of candied pineapple, the whole to be cut in small three-sixteenths inch squares; two gills of Marsala wine, three gills of syrup at thirty-two degrees, the peel of half a lemon and the peel of half an orange; put the saucepan on the fire and take it off at the first boil.

(3003). BANANAS, CHERRY SAUCE—FRIED (Bananes Frites, Sauce aux Cerises).

Cut some bananas lengthwise in two, roll them in finely pulverized macaroons and then in flour, and fry in very hot oil until they acquire a good color; drain on a cloth, wipe and coat over with some apricot marmalade (No. 3675), laid on with a brush. Dish them up pyramidically and dredge over freshly peeled and shredded pistachio nuts. Serve a currant sauce, with cherries apart, made by putting four heaping tablespoonfuls of currant jelly in a saucepan and diluting it with a pint of syrup at thirty degrees. Stand the saucepan on the fire, let boil a few times, then strain the syrup through a fine sieve; add to it one gill of kirsch and a good handful of preserved cherries previously washed in hot water.

(3004). BISCUITS, FRASCATI (Biscuits Frascati).

Break twelve eggs, putting the yolks in one vessel and the whites in another; add to the yolks three-quarters of a pound of powdered sugar and a quarter of a pound of vanilla sugar and beat well with a whip to obtain a very light and frothy preparation. Then add to it six ounces of flour and six ounces of fecula sifted together, and afterward the stiffly beaten egg-whites; stir the preparation until perfect. Butter and flour a plain cylindrical mold (Fig. 150); fill it two-thirds full with the preparation and cook it in a slack oven. As soon as done unmold and let get cold. When cold, cut it up in transversal slices a quarter of an inch thick and cover each slice with a layer of fine vanilla cream (No. 42); dredge the surfaces with a finely chopped salpicon of pineapple and pistachios. Reconstruct the biscuit to its original shape, cover it with a layer of apricot marmalade (No. 3675) and bestrew the sides with chopped pistachios. Now place it on a dish; decorate the top with a rosette of fine candied pink and white pears cut in four and intermingle them with lozenges of angelica; brush these fruits over with a very thick syrup and surround the base with a row of apples cooked in butter, having small sticks of angelica placed between each. Fill the hollow center of the biscuit with cream rice flavored with vanilla (No. 160) and keep the biscuit warm for twenty minutes, serving it with a flavored English cream sauce.

English Cream Sauce Flavored with Vanilla.—Place in a vessel eight egg-yolks, half a pound of sugar and one ounce of starch; beat up a moment to have the mixture smooth. Stand a quart of milk on the fire in a saucepan with a split vanilla bean added to it and let boil; as soon as this occurs pour it gently over the eggs and stir all well together. Pour it all back into the saucepan, place it again on the fire and thicken the sauce without permitting it to boil, stirring continuously with a spatula, then strain through a fine sieve. The vanilla can be replaced by liquors added at the last moment.

(3005). BORDER OF RICE WITH BANANAS (Bordures de Riz aux Bananes).

Make a consistent rice cream preparation (No. 160) flavored with vanilla, and finish it with a few egg-yolks. Divide this into two portions, and into one incorporate a salpicon of chestnuts cut up small and candied pineapple cut in quarter-inch dice. Butter and sugar a plain border or savarin mold (Fig. 139), and with the rice which has no fruit cover the sides, then fill the mold with the rice and fruit, smooth the top and set this border in a sautoir with hot water reaching halfway up, and push it into a slack oven for twenty-five minutes. Unmold the border on a dish, and ornament the top with a handsome circle of angelica lozenges and candied cherries, and surround the base with preserved plums. Peel some fine bananas, cut them up into transversal slices a quarter of an inch thick, plunge them into a thick maraschino syrup, let simmer for a few moments, then drain and range them in a pyramid in the center of the border. Brush the top over with apricot marmalade (No. 3675), and dredge finely chopped pistachios over all; heat the border in the oven for twenty minutes, and serve with a sauce-boat of sauce made with apple jelly (No. 3668), diluted with a little syrup and flavored with maraschino.

(3006). BRIOCHES ST. MARK (Brioches St. Marc).

Butter twelve small timbale molds (No. 1, Fig. 137), fill them three-quarters high with brioche paste (No. 130), and leave to rise in a mild temperature, and when the molds are partly full bake them in a slow oven. After taking them out cut them off level with the tops of the molds and leave in till cold, then empty them partially and pour over the insides some syrup flavored with maraschino and almond milk (No. 4), filling them up with frangipane cream (No. 43). Cover the outsides with apricot marmalade (No. 3675) and strew the sides with green pistachios and white almonds, both chopped up finely. Ornament the tops of each brioche with a rosette composed of halved pistachios and a split cherry laid in the center. Dress them in a circle on a dish, and arrange in the center some stewed halved peaches. Cover the ornamentation on the brioches with maraschino syrup thickened with a little apricot marmalade, and dress in the intersection of the peaches some freshly shelled white split almonds, and also some candied halved cherries, then serve. Have a sauce-boat of English vanilla cream sauce (No. 3004) to accompany this entremets.

(3007). CHARLOTTE À LA DESTREY (Charlotte à la Destrey).

Butter a charlotte mold, either round or oval, this depending on the dish required for serving, and line it with fine foundation paste (No. 135), then let stand in the ice-box for half an hour. Cut eight apples in quarters, peel, core and lay them beside each other on a buttered baking sheet; besprinkle with sugar and cover with a sheet of buttered paper, then cook in the oven and when done remove and let cool off. Prepare a frangipane cream (No. 43); add to it a few spoonfuls of cream rice (No. 160) and a salpicon of fruit, such as green almonds, pears, apricots, a little orange peel cut in thin shreds and a few crushed macaroons. Fill up the charlotte in layers of cream and apples (peaches or pears may be substituted), and smooth the surface; lay the mold on a baking pan, push it into the oven and let cook for about one hour; as soon as finished remove and let rest for ten minutes before unmolding it on a dish, then cover with well-reduced apricot marmalade (No. 3675) and sprinkle highly with chopped roasted almonds; decorate the top with an angelica rosette and around the base of this with a circle of fine halved pistachios; fasten a nice cherry in the center of the rosette and all around a circle of preserved cherries (demi-sucre), cut in two and laid flat on the charlotte. Serve at the same time as this entremets a sauce-boat of English cream sauce, flavored with brandy and Madeira (No. 3004).

(3008). APPLE CHARLOTTE (Charlotte de Pommes).

Cut a few russet apples in four, peel, core and mince them up rather coarsely, then put them into a sautoir with some melted butter; stir and toss incessantly over a good fire until the moisture is reduced, then sweeten. Butter a four-inch high by four and a half inches in diameter charlotte mold, cover the bottom with a flat rosette made of long triangles of bread, an eighth of an inch thick, pointed on one end and rounded on the other, carefully dipping them as needed in clarified butter. These slices should slightly overlap each other. Remove the center with a one-inch tube and replace with a round of bread of the same size dipped in butter. Cut some one-eighth inch thick slices of bread into inch-wide strips, having them somewhat higher than the mold; dip them in clarified butter and apply them upright to the inner side of the mold, one overlapping the other, cut flush with the mold; cover the bottom and sides of the mold with part of the apples, and in the center put three spoonfuls of apricot marmalade (No. 3675); finish filling with the remainder ɓi the apples, and cover these with a round piece of bread the same size as the mold, then lay the

Fig. 573.

Fig. 574.

mold on a small baking sheet, push it into a hot oven and leave for twenty-five to thirty minutes, so that the bread becomes a fine golden color. Should it brown too fast put a metal cover on top. Invert the charlotte on a hot dish and serve it at once with an apricot and maraschino sauce poured around (see Humboldt pudding, No. 3100).

(3009). COMPIÈGNE WITH SABAYON (Compiègne au Sabayon).

Butter a dozen small timbale molds (No. 1, Fig. 137), and fill them three-quarters full with Compiègne paste (No. 3236); let rise in a mild temperature, then set them on a baking sheet, and cook in a slack oven. When done, remove and cut them off exactly level with the molds; unmold and dip them at once into a light syrup flavored with Madeira wine and vanilla; drain on a grate, and then dish them up in a circle. Prepare some rings of apricot paste of the same diameter as the top of the timbales; put them on the top of each Compiègne, place a mirabel plum in the center of each, and stick a piece of angelica into each one. Cover the Compiègnes with a Madeira sabayon, as for cabinet pudding (No. 3096), serving more of it separately.

(3010). CREAM À LA MAINTENON—FRIED (Crème Frite à la Maintenon).

Remove the outer shells from three-quarters of a pound of chestnuts; plunge them into boiling water and let boil up once or twice; then remove the saucepan from the fire, and quickly abstract the second skin; return them to a saucepan and cover with milk, adding a quarter of a vanilla stick; cook very slowly, and then press through a sieve. Put the purée into a bowl, pour over six ounces of sugar cooked to "small crack" (No. 171) and mix it into the pulp, beating it vigorously. Spread this on a sheet of buttered paper to a quarter of an inch in thickness. Prepare a pound of white and delicate apple pulp, put it in a saucepan with a pound of sugar, and reduce; then add a tablespoonful of fecula, and a gill of water; spread this over the chestnuts and smooth it to the same thickness, then let get cold. Cut it into lozenges, and cover each one with apricot marmalade (No. 3675); roll them carefully in pulverized macaroons; then dip them in beaten eggs, and afterward in bread-crumbs; smooth with the blade of a knife, and fry to a fine color in hot white frying fat; drain, wipe, and bestrew with vanilla sugar, then dress in a pyramid on a folded napkin, and serve with a separate English cream vanilla sauce (No. 3004).

(3011). CREAM OF BISCUIT WITH KIRSCH (Crème de Biscuits au Kirsch).

Put six whole eggs and four yolks into a vessel with a grain of salt and six ounces of sugar, a part of which is to be flavored with orange. (This flavored sugar is obtained by rubbing the entire surface of the fruit on a sugar loaf, and then grating the flavored part off, either with a knife or spoon.) Beat the preparation with a whip, and dilute it slowly with a quart of raw milk and four gills of raw cream. Soak four ounces of lady fingers in milk, then drain on a sieve, and put them in a bowl; dilute with the above preparation, and pass the whole through a sieve, then stir in one gill of kirsch. Butter a charlotte mold, and fill it with the preparation; set it in a saucepan containing hot water, and place it on the fire; let the water come to a boil, and keep it in this state for thirty minutes, either on the side of a slow fire or else in a slack oven. When the cream is firm to the touch in the center, take it off and and leave it for half an hour longer in the water so that it hardens, then unmold on a dish and pour over a kirsch syrup.

(3012). CREAM OF CHESTNUTS WITH CARAMEL SUGAR (Crème de Marrons au Caramel).

Cook a pound of skinned chestnuts in water with a quarter of a vanilla bean, then rub them through a sieve into a vessel, and add six whole beaten eggs and four yolks, also half a pound of sugar; dilute with a pint of raw milk, mix well, and pass the whole through a sieve. Pour into the bottom of a plain timbale mold one gill of sugar cooked to caramel: when cold butter the sides of the mold, and fill it up with the chestnut preparation; set the mold into a saucepan with hot water to half its height, leave it on the fire, and just when it reaches the boiling point cover and keep it cooking slowly, or else place it in a slack oven to maintain the liquid at the same temperature without boiling for fifty to sixty minutes, or until the preparation is firm to the touch in the center. Invert the cream on a dish, and cover it with the caramel sugar found on the bottom of the mold.

(3013). CREAM PAMELA—FRIED (Crème Frite Paméla).

Put four eggs, two yolks, four ounces of sugar and the peel of one lemon into a bowl, beat them up with a whip and dilute with a pint of milk, then run it through a sieve. Butter and sugar twelve six-sided molds, the size of timbale molds No. 2, Fig. 137, but only half as high; fill the bottoms with a layer of candied cherries cut in four, lay on these candied pineapple and angelica washed in hot water and cut in small quarter-inch squares; scatter broken macaroons over the fruit; pour on a little of the strained preparation to soak, and prevent floating to the top, then finish filling. Place these molds in a stewpan and pour in the bottom boiling water to reach to half their height; set this in a moderate oven to poach the cream, and as soon as done remove from the oven and let get cold in the water. When cold unmold them, roll in biscuit dust, dip in beaten eggs and finish by rolling in white bread-crumbs, smooth with the blade of a knife, then plunge them into hot frying fat and fry to a fine golden color, drain on a cloth and bestrew with vanilla sugar, then serve with a Bischoff sauce, made as follows:

Bischoff Sauce.—Place half a pint of white wine and as much syrup into a saucepan; boil and thicken this liquid with a spoonful of fecula diluted in a little cold water; add the peel of a lemon and the same of an orange cut in Julienne and previously blanched, also two ounces of almonds and two ounces of shredded pistachios, two ounces each of seeded Malaga and Smyrna raisins and of currants, thoroughly washed in hot water; boil a few times, then serve.

(3014). CREAM WITH APPLES (Crème aux Pommes).

Mince six peeled russet apples, fry them for a few moments in butter in a thin sautoir to soften slightly without letting them melt; sweeten moderately. Make a pint of cream of biscuit preparation (No. 3011), strain it through a fine sieve and place it in a saucepan, then heat it slightly while stirring over a slow fire. Mix the apples in with the cream and pour the whole into a deep china baking dish; cook for three-quarters of an hour in a slack oven and if deemed necessary cover over with paper. Besprinkle the surface with fine sugar a few moments before serving, then remove from the oven and serve in the same dish.

(3015). CRESCENTS OF NOODLES WITH CHERRIES (Croissants de Nouilles aux Cerises).

Cut up finely about a pound of noodles (No. 142), blanch, drain and put them into a saucepan with two gills of cream, two ounces of fresh butter, a pinch of salt, two ounces of sugar and three tablespoonfuls of brandy; set the saucepan on a slack fire and let cook slowly, being careful to stir the contents at frequent intervals until all the moisture is absorbed, then pour the preparation on two baking sheets covered with buttered paper, spreading to a layer three-eighths of an inch thick. Bake in a hot oven. Unmold as soon as done and cover one of these flats with a thick layer of reduced apricot marmalade (No. 3675); on top place the other flat, then cut into crescents, using a pastry cutter two and a half inches in diameter. Dress these crescents in a circle on a dish and fill the center with compoted cherries, serving a separate cherry and kirsch sauce (No. 3003).

(3016). CROQUETTES À LA TRIMALCION (Croquettes à la Trimalcion).

Cut twelve apples in four, peel and core them, then cut into small dice; put them into a sautoir, pour over a few spoonfuls of butter and fry, and as soon as done remove from the fire and add a tablespoonful of sugar, a pinch of cinnamon, a handful of candied cherries cut in four and two spoonfuls of apricot marmalade (No. 3675); pour this on a baking sheet to cool off. Mold this preparation into inch and a quarter balls, shape them into cylindrical croquettes an inch in diameter, roll in cracker dust, dip in beaten eggs, then roll in bread-crumbs; smooth the breading with a knife and plunge the croquettes into hot frying fat; fry till they become a light golden color, then drain on a cloth; strew over powdered sugar and dress on a napkin. Serve with a sauce-tureen of cherry sauce prepared the same as for fried bananas with cherry sauce (No. 3008).

(3017). CROQUETTES OF CHESTNUTS (Croquettes de Marrons).

Select four pounds of fine, sound chestnuts; slit them on one side and put them to roast in a large perforated pan; cover and toss at times until done. They may also be cooked by placing them on a baking sheet and then in a hot oven to roast without blackening. Skin them, removing both the skins, and picking out twenty of the finest, pound the others to a fine paste. Add, while continuing to pound, two ounces of vanilla sugar and a little raw cream. Pass this preparation through a sieve and put it into a saucepan, beating into it six egg-yolks, then dry over the fire while stirring. Pour this on a baking sheet and leave till cold, then divide it into parts and of each one make an inch and a quarter diameter ball; in the center of each insert one of the roasted chestnuts split in two; mold the croquettes to the shape of a chestnut, dip them in beaten eggs, roll in white bread-crumbs and fry in very hot clear frying fat; when done, drain and sponge, besprinkle with vanilla sugar and dress on a napkin.

(3018). CROQUETTES OF RICE WITH ORANGE, RASPBERRY SAUCE (Croquettes de Riz à l'Orange, Sauce Framboise).

Blanch half a pound of rice in plenty of water; drain and put it back into a saucepan with sufficient boiling milk to cover, then set it on the corner of the range to finish cooking while stirring it at times with a wooden spoon. As soon as the rice is consistent and dry, work into it eight egg-yolks, two ounces of butter, two ounces of orange sugar, a pinch of salt, two tablespoonfuls of whipped cream and two tablespoonfuls of candied orange peel shredded very fine. Spread this preparation on a buttered baking tin covered over with a sheet of paper and let it get cold. Divide it into balls each two inches in diameter, and draw them down on one end to give them the shape of a pear; dip in beaten eggs, then roll in white bread-crumbs and plunge them in plenty of hot fat to fry to a fine golden brown; drain. sponge, and stick a piece of angelica into the ends to imitate the stalk of a pear; besprinkle lightly with orange sugar, dress on a napkin and serve with a raspberry sauce made with a pint of raspberry juice mingled with as much boiling syrup, and Curacao, straining the whole through a fine wire sieve.

(3019). CROQUETTES OF SEMOLINA, PISTACHIO SAUCE (Croquettes de Semoule, Sauce aux Pistaches).

Boil a quart of milk, add to it half a split vanilla stick and keep it warm in a covered saucepan; take out the vanilla and place the milk on a hot fire, and at the first boil drop into it like rain six ounces of semolina, stirring the preparation continuously with a whisk, and cover the saucepan; push it into a slack oven and take it out again fifteen minutes later. Mix in with the semolina four ounces of sugar, two ounces of butter, a little salt and eight egg-yolks; stir in well with a spoon two ounces of apricot, two ounces of cherries, an ounce of pineapple and an ounce of orange peel, all cut in quarter-inch dice. Spread this on a baking sheet covered over with paper and let it get cold. Then divide it into inch and a half diameter balls; roll these in powdered macaroons, dip in beaten egg, and finally roll in white bread-crumbs; fry to a fine color, drain on a cloth, wipe and bestrew with vanilla sugar. Dress the croquettes on a napkin and serve separately an English cream sauce (No. 3004), into which has been added green pistachios shredded finely.

(3020). CROUSTADES OF VENICE, MERINGUED (Croustades de Venise Meringuées).

Line some small buttered fruit pie circles, three-quarters of an inch high and two and a quarter inches in diameter, with fine foundation paste (No. 135), or else puff paste parings (No. 146); raise an edge and pinch it; place them on a baking sheet and egg the edges of each pie over twice. Put into a vessel four spoonfuls of fecula or arrowroot, six ounces of vanilla sugar, a grain of salt, eight whole eggs and eight yolks; mix well with a whisk and dilute with a pint and a half of cream or rich milk; strain the preparation through a sieve and then pour it into a saucepan containing four ounces of fresh butter; stir on the fire until the butter is entirely melted, and with this prepara-

tion fill the small pies, then put them into a slack oven to cook without browning; when the cream
has set and the paste is cooked, remove the croustades and leave them till nearly cold. Cover the
tops with meringue, forming it into a dome; decorate this, leaving a hollow in the center and dredge
vanilla sugar over the whole; return them to a slow oven to brown to a fine light golden color,
then take them from their molds and finish decorating with apricot marmalade (No. 3675) pushed
through a cornet and some angelica and preserved cherries (demi-sucre).

For a Large Croustade.—Line a shallow hot pie mold with fine foundation paste (No. 135)
or puff paste parings (No. 146); lay it on a baking sheet and fill it up with the same preparation as
for the above; put it into a slack oven to cook for one hour. When the cream has set and the
paste is cooked take out the croustade and let get partly cold before unmolding; cover it with
meringue (No. 140), shaping it as a dome; decorate and finish the same as for the above.

(3021). GOLDEN CRUSTS (Croûtes Dorées).

Scrape off the crust from some table flutes and cut them in slices half an inch thick, then range
them one beside the other on a dish; pour over a little sweetened raw cream mixed with a few
egg-yolks. Let the crusts soak for ten to twelve minutes, basting them over with the cream, and
then take them out and extract the moisture lightly; dip them into slightly sweetened beaten
eggs, then drain and plunge them into hot frying fat a few at a time; drain as fast as they
brown nicely, and bestrew the surfaces with sugar; serve with fruit preserves or else an English
vanilla sauce (No. 3004).

(3022). CRUSTS OF PINEAPPLE, APRICOT SAUCE (Croûtes aux Ananas, Sauce d'Abricots).

Cut from cooked savarin some slices three-eighths of an inch thick; from these remove some
rounds three inches in diameter; divide these in two through the center and notch them on
their convex side. Arrange these slices shaped like cocks'-combs on a baking sheet, dredge
them over with sugar, and glaze in a brisk oven; cover them on the unglazed side with strawberry marmalade strained through a sieve, and lay on each one a fine slice of preserved pineapple; decorate the borders of the crusts reaching out beyond the pineapple with angelica lozenges
and candied cherries cut in four, then dress them on a dish in a circle, one overlapping the other.
Fill the hollow of the circle with candied fruits cut in dice, such as apricots, pears, greengages, green almonds, candied cherries, orange peel and angelica, the whole washed in warm water,
and then mingled with apricot marmalade (No. 3675) flavored with kirsch; heat the dish after
it is dressed in the oven for ten minutes. Serve an apricot kirsch sauce (No. 3001) separately.

(3023). CRUSTS WITH BANANAS À LA PANAMA (Croûtes aux Bananes à la Panama).

Slice some brioche three-quarters of an inch thick, and from them remove a dozen rounds
with a two and a quarter inch diameter pastry cutter; cut them all around a short distance from
the edges and empty out the insides; lay them on a baking sheet, besprinkle with sugar and glaze
in a quick oven; after they come from the oven cover the insides with guava jelly softened with a
little maraschino. Peel six fine very ripe bananas, cut them across in slices an eighth of an inch
thick, and plunge into a hot syrup of twenty-five degrees, flavored with maraschino, leaving them
in for five minutes only, then drain and dress dome-shaped on the crusts, covering over with very
hot apricot marmalade (No. 3675); dredge with fresh finely chopped pistachios and dress in a
circle on a dish; fill the inside of this with pineapple cut in quarter-inch squares, thrown into
the syrup in which the bananas were cooked, then brought to a boil, and mingled with some
guava jelly diluted with syrup and flavored with maraschino, serving separately a hot sauce made
with apricot marmalade, grated pineapple and maraschino.

(3024). CRUSTS WITH CHERRIES OR STRAWBERRIES À LA MICHELET (Croûtes aux Cerises ou aux Fraises à la Michelet).

Cut some slices an inch thick from a very firm kitchen loaf, using only the crumb part; from
them obtain six rounds with a two and a half inch diameter pastry cutter, and cut these rounds in
two through their diameter so as to have twelve half-rounds. Cut partly through these half-rounds
a short distance from the edge with a small kitchen knife, square the corners and plunge them into
hot clarified butter to have them assume a fine golden color. Drain them at once on a cloth, wipe
and empty out the centers. Cover the inside with apricot marmalade (No. 3675) and fill

them level to the top with rice and cream (No. 160) flavored with vanilla and finished with a few egg-yolks and then mask the tops with a heavy layer of strawberry jam, mixed with almonds and pistachios. Dress these crusts prepared in this manner in a circle on a dish and fill the center of it with stewed fresh cherries or candied cherries washed in boiling water and softened in a light syrup, then mingled with apricot marmalade and kirsch. Serve separately a sauce-boat of cherry syrup with a few spoonfuls of currant jelly added and flavored with kirsch.

(3025). CRUSTS WITH FRUITS À LA MIRABEAU (Croûtes aux Fruits à la Mirabeau).

This entremets, though simple, can be served at the most sumptuous dinners. Cut a well-pared fresh pineapple across in two; divide the largest end into two parts, and these into medium-sized slices; pare again to have them all of the same size and shape, put them into a vessel and moisten to their height with a cold syrup of twenty-eight degrees; cover with a round piece of paper, and keep them in a cool place. After six hours drain off the syrup, and adding to it a handful of powdered sugar pour it back on the fruit and operate thus twice, but should preserved pineapple be used it will require to be done four times. Bake some savarin paste (No. 148) in a large buttered savarin mold (Fig. 139), or a large cradle mold, and leave stand for twelve hours. Cut this cake straight on top, then into transversal slices of equal thickness, and cover one side of them first with a thin layer of apricot marmalade (No. 3675), then with a layer of Condé prep-

FIG. 575.

aration (No. 2), range them at once on a baking sheet, bestrew with fine sugar, glaze in a slack oven, and detach from the baking sheet as soon as glazed. Fasten a round flat of Genoese cake on a dish and on it place a ring of the same or of meringue, having it much higher than the flat itself, but not too wide (this ring is intended to uphold the slices of pineapple); brush it over with apricot marmalade, also the lower Genoese flat, and let dry in the air. Select some good, large, preserved cherries (demi-sucre), wash them in warm water, and place them in a copper vessel with some cold syrup of twenty-eight degrees. Now drain the slices of pineapple, and dress them upright in the center of the ring, one overlapping the other, and bent out slightly so they form the shape of a basket. Then fill the hollow in the inside with the well-drained cherries, dressing them in a pyramid; brush the pineapple over with some fine apricot marmalade, diluted with Madeira wine; surround the base with the slices of glazed savarin, forming them into a pretty crown, and mask the whole lightly with the marmalade. Serve with this entremets a sauce-boatful of the same marmalade diluted with syrup and Madeira wine mixed with a Julienne of candied fruits cut from orange or mandarin peel, pears and apricots, adding a spoonful of pistachios. To make this entremets more plentiful the crusts can be surrounded at their base with a row of candied green-gages, cut in two, and the stones replaced by almond paste (No. 125) flavored with vanilla.

(3026). CRUSTS WITH MADEIRA (Croûtes au Madère).

Wash in tepid water four ounces of candied citron peel, two ounces of lemon peel and two ounces of orange peel, all cut in quarter-inch squares. Put these into a saucepan with two ounces of Smyrna raisins and two ounces of currants, well picked and scalded in boiling water, then drained, and cover over the whole with boiling Madeira syrup and keep the saucepan well closed in a bain-marie until ready to serve. Make a croustade from a close and stale kitchen loaf, having it four to six inches high, and shaped like a vase. Slit the top near the edge and pass a skewer through its depth to keep it straight while cooking, then fry to a fine light golden color, drain and sponge it, remove the skewer and the slit piece on top. Scoop out a little of the inside crumbs, then fasten it on the center of a dish with a paste made of flour and egg-white. Cut slices of kitchen bread five-sixteenths of an inch in thickness and from this stamp out ovals three by two inches; brown them on both sides in clarified butter, drain and cover with apricot marmalade

(No. 3675); dress them in a circle around the croustade or else substitute slices of cooked brioche, having them the same size; lay these flat on a baking sheet, besprinkle with sugar and brown in the oven. Moisten the crusts with the syrup and arrange the fruits all around. Fill the croustade with red stewed cherries (No. 3688) and angelica and serve with a separate apricot sauce, diluted with Madeira wine. (See Humboldt pudding No. 3100.)

(3027). CRUSTS WITH PEACHES OR WITH PEARS (Croûtes aux Pêches ou aux Poires).

Put into a sautoir a dozen compoted peaches cut in halves, all of equal size; pour over some thick syrup and keep them warm. Cut from a kitchen loaf half-inch thick slices and from them take two-inch in diameter rounds, having as many as there are peaches. Color them in clarified butter, turning them over when done on one side to color on the other, then drain and cover lightly with apricot marmalade (No. 3675). Set a half peach on top of each and dress them on a dish; pour over some peach syrup mingled with a few spoonfuls of kirsch and serve more of this separately.

For Pears.—Replace the peaches by compoted pears and finish exactly the same.

(3028). CRUSTS WITH PEARS À LA DOUGLAS (Croûtes aux Poires à la Douglas).

Cut some half-inch thick slices from a kitchen loaf and form them into rounds with a plain cutter two and a half inches in diameter; remove the center of these rounds with another cutter an inch in diameter so as to make them into rings. Put two egg-yolks into a basin and dilute with a pint of good cream, adding two ounces of sugar flavored with half a grated orange peel and pass the whole through a colander over the bread rings. After they have well soaked, drain and dip them in pulverized macaroons, then in beaten eggs and lastly roll in white bread-crumbs; fry to a fine color in clarified butter; drain and mask the surface with apricot marmalade (No. 3675); throw over a pinch of powdered burnt almonds and dress in a circle on a dish; fill the center with fine pears cooked in syrup, some Malaga raisins and candied orange peel cut in small shreds and combined with apple jelly (No. 3668) and maraschino. Serve separately a sauce-boat of kirsch syrup thickened with a few spoonfuls of dissolved apple jelly and the pulp of two oranges free of their white skin and seeds.

(3029). CUPOLA À LA MADISON (Coupole à la Madison).

Butter a cupola-shaped mold and fill it three-quarters full with savarin paste (No. 148); let rise in a mild temperature, and as soon as it reaches the top of the mold push it into a slack oven to bake; when the cake is done unmold it on a grate, cool well, replace it in the mold and pare flush with the bottom; unmold again and cut an incision all around at three-quarters of its height, with a small kitchen knife, keeping its point toward the center; carefully lift off the lid and empty out the interior, leaving the sides half an inch thick; fill the empty cake with fine paper to prevent it from losing its shape; replace the lid and cover it with a very thin layer of apricot marmalade (No. 3675) and ice it with fondant (No. 58) flavored with kirsch. After this icing is well drained slip the cupola on a dish and decorate the center of the lid with a handsome rosette of angelica and candied orange peel, cut to represent crescents, arranging them alternately; place in the center a large cherry and surround the crescents with a wreath formed of angelica lozenges and candied cherries laid between. Range around the base of the cupola a circle of fine brandied greengages. Prepare a compote of pears cut in four, drain and cut them up into thin slices, adding as many preserved cherries (demi-sucre) well washed in hot water, and mingle the whole with the same quantity of white apple marmalade, reduced and flavored with kirsch. Ten minutes before serving lift off the lid from the timbale, remove the paper and fill it up with the very hot preparation; replace the lid and keep the whole hot for a few minutes; serve with a sauce-boat of apricot kirsch sauce (No. 3001).

(3030). DAMPFNOODLES WITH CREAM (Dampfnouilles à la Crème).

Put half a pound of flour into a basin and make a hollow in the center; lay in it a quarter of an ounce of compressed yeast and dissolve it slowly with two gills of warm milk, adding the flour so as to obtain a soft paste; cover it over with a cloth and leave it in a mild temperature to rise to double its volume; then incorporate into this sponge four egg-yolks, four spoonfuls of sugar and half a pound of flour added very slowly, and lastly two ounces of butter; mix well for one minute in order to give the paste a good body, then lay it in a vessel and let rise to double its volume. Work it on a floured table and roll into strings; divide each of these into pieces and shape them into balls an inch and a quarter in diameter; range these in a buttered sautoir, three-quarters of an inch apart, and leave them to rise again to double their volume. Now pour sufficient boiling vanilla-flavored milk over to have the balls swim to half their height; cover hermetically and put the sautoir in a hot oven for fifteen to eighteen minutes. Detach them from the pan, and dress in a pyramid on a dish; cover over with some English cream sauce (No. 3004) and serve more of the same separately.

(3031). STUFFED EGGS (Œufs Farcis).

Choose seven or eight large, fresh and very white eggs; saw off the top of the shell on the roundest end so as to make an opening three-quarters of an inch wide; empty the eggs into a bowl, wash the shells and leave to drain well. Beat the eggs up lightly, add to them a few spoonfuls of rich raw cream, four spoonfuls of powdered lady fingers, six or seven spoonfuls of powdered sugar, some cinnamon and a grain of salt. Butter liberally the bottom of a flat saucepan, pour in the eggs and thicken while stirring over a slow fire, the same as for scrambled eggs. When the preparation is done to perfection, mix in two or three spoonfuls of lady fingers cut up in small dice, and with this fill the shells one by one; lay each one when done into a separate egg cup; cover the opening with a small pyramid of the same cake cut small, and dress the egg cups on a dish.

(3032). EGGS WITH CREAM, MERINGUED (Œufs à la Crème Meringués).

Have seven or eight eggs in a bowl, beat them well, then run them through a sieve; add six ounces of sugar partly flavored with vanilla and eight pulverized macaroons; dilute the whole with a pint of raw cream, and stir the preparation on the fire for a few moments to warm it, then pour it at once into a soufflé saucepan (Fig. 182), or simply a buttered pie plate (Fig. 183); let it poach in a bain-marie in a slack oven, and as soon as it becomes firm take it from the water and leave stand till cold; then cover the entire surface with apricot marmalade (No. 3675). Cover over with a layer of Italian meringue (No. 140) flavored with kirsch, smooth nicely and dredge the top with pulverized macaroons; let stand for a few moments in a slack oven and glaze it with sugar.

(3033). EGGS WITH COFFEE CREAM MERINGUED (Œufs à la Crème au Café Meringués).

Break seven or eight eggs in a vessel, beat and strain through a sieve; add a grain of salt, two spoonfuls of sugar, twelve pulverized lady fingers, four gills of raw cream and one gill of very strong coffee. Stir the preparation for two minutes on the fire, then pour it into a buttered tart dish; let it set in a bain-marie or slack oven and remove as soon as firm. When nearly cold cover over with a layer of Italian meringue (No. 140) flavored with cognac, smooth nicely and besprinkle with pulverized lady fingers; poach for a few moments in a slack oven, glazing over with sugar.

(3034). FLAWN À LA MANHATTAN (Flan à la Manhattan).

Line a flawn ring (No. 3170) with sweet paste (No. 136), leaving the edges rather thick, and let it rest for half an hour in the ice-box. Then cover the paste with buttered paper and fill it up with dry rice; cook it in a hot oven and as soon as done empty it out and cover the outside border and the inside surfaces with hot and well-reduced peach marmalade (No. 3675); slide the pie on a dish; dress against the edges a circle of halved peaches; arrange in a pyramid in the center of this crown some quartered apples cooked in butter and cover the whole with strained peach marmalade; sprinkle over the entire surface some finely chopped pistachios and decorate between the peaches on the border, also on the summit of the pie, with lozenges of angelica and candied cherries. Set it for one instant in the oven to warm, then serve with a bowlful of cream vanilla sauce (No. 3004).

(3035). FLAWN AU LION D'OR (Flan au Lion d'or).

Divide some apples in eight pieces each; peel, core and cook them in butter, and when half done mingle in some apricot marmalade (No. 3675) and finish cooking. Line a flawn ring (No. 3170) with fine short paste (No. 135), raise the edges, pinch them and let the flawn stand for twenty-five minutes in the ice-box or any other cool place. Then cover the bottom and sides of the paste with buttered paper, fill up with dry rice, and cook in the oven. As soon as the crust is done, empty it out and remove the plate, then brush the surface with egg-yolks and return the crust to the oven to color. When cold mask the inside with apricot marmalade, fill in alternate layers of white and well-reduced apple marmalade, flavored with vanilla and apples cooked in butter, finishing with a layer of the apples; dredge powdered macaroons over the top and then cover with apricot marmalade and on this pour a Condé preparation (No. 2); bestrew with sugar, and glaze under a salamander (Fig. 123), then serve. Have a separate vanilla syrup mingled with apricot marmalade.

(3036). ALLIANCE FRITTERS (Beignets Alliance).

Cut six medium-sized apples in transversal slices three-eighths of an inch thick; remove the cores with a column tube, cut away the edges with a two inch in diameter vegetable cutter so as to have all the rounds of the same size; fry them in butter over a brisk fire, drain and wipe. Drain as many halves of stewed peaches as there are slices of apples, fill the hollow in the apples with apple jelly (No. 3668). Prepare a fine paste with the same quantity of dry macaroons as apple paste, and pound well together with a few spoonfuls of maraschino, and with this paste fill the center of the halved peaches, and fasten these on to the rounds of apple; cover the other side of the apple with the macaroon paste to have the whole form a ball; roll them in cracker dust, and then dip in frying batter (No. 137) and plunge into hot frying fat. When the paste has become dry and well browned, drain the fritters on to a cloth, besprinkle with sugar, and lay them on a tart dish to place in the oven in order that they may glaze. Serve separately a pineapple syrup: Put half a pint of apple pulp that has been passed through a fine sieve into a saucepan, and dilute it with three gills of syrup, boil up for one minute, and then thicken this sauce with a spoonful of fecula diluted in a little cold water; remove it at once from the fire, flavor well with kirsch, and add half a pint of pineapple cut in three-sixteenths of an inch squares; keep the sauce hot until needed.

(3037). APPLE FRITTERS AND MONTAGNARD FRITTERS—GLAZED AND UNGLAZED
(Beignets de Pommes et Beignets Montagnard—Glacés et non Glacés).

Core some apples with a column or tin tube five-eighths of an inch in diameter; peel them all around, and cut from them slices about a quarter of an inch thick; put to macerate in a little brandy and powdered sugar for one hour, tossing them about often so that they all get well covered. Dip each piece in frying batter (No. 137), and plunge into hot frying fat; when done and of a fine color, drain and dredge over with sugar, then dress on a napkin.

For Glazed Fritters.—When done place them on a baking sheet, bestrew with sugar, and glaze in a hot oven, or under a salamander (Fig. 123); serve dressed on a napkin.

For Montagnard Fritters.—After they have been cooked and glazed as above, cover the tops with a layer of currant jelly placed on with a spoon, then dress on a napkin and serve.

(3038). APPLE FRITTERS WITH PRUNELLE OR WITH KIRSCH (Beignets de Pommes à la Prunelle ou au Kirsch).

Peel some fine apples; cut them across in three pieces, remove the cores with a five-eighths of an inch diameter tin tube, and cook them partly in a syrup, then drain on a sieve. Make an apple jelly (No. 3668), and when done add to it as much peach marmalade (No. 3675); range the apples on a baking sheet and mask them several times with the jelly, having sufficient of it to leave on a thick layer. When cold remove the slices of apple with a knife and roll them in powdered macaroons, then dip in frying batter (No. 137), and plunge them into hot frying fat. As the paste becomes crisp, drain them off, wipe and brush over with a brush dipped in a sugar frosting flavored with prunelles or kirsch.

(3039). APRICOT OR PEACH FRITTERS WITH MARASCHINO (Beignets d'Abricots ou de Pêches au Marasquin).

Split a dozen fine apricots or peaches in four; remove the stones and skin, then boil up in a light syrup, but keeping them firm; drain on a cloth, wipe and fill the hollow space left by the stone with a ball of macaroon paste pounded with a little maraschino; cover over with a light layer of peach marmalade (No. 3675), roll them at once in pulverized macaroons and dip them in frying batter (No. 137), then plunge in hot frying fat and fry the fritters to a fine color; drain, wipe and dredge over with vanilla sugar and dress in a pyramid on a folded napkin. Serve separately a sauce made of purée of apricots if the fritters be of apricots, flavored with maraschino, or of peaches if the fritters are of peaches.

Another way is to peel the apricots or peaches, cut them in four, then place the pieces in a vessel with sugar, maraschino and a little vanilla syrup; one hour later drain and roll them in powdered macaroons passed through a coarse sieve. Dip the pieces in frying batter (No. 137) and immerse in hot fat, then fry to a fine color. After the paste is well fried, drain, wipe and besprinkle with vanilla sugar, then dress on a napkin and serve with the same sauce as for the above.

'3040). BRIOCHE AND CREAM FRITTERS WITH SABAYON (Beignets de Brioche à la Crème au Sabayon).

Butter a tin mold forming a box four inches wide by three inches deep and eight inches long, with a hinged cover; fill it half full with brioche paste (No. 130); let it rise in a mild temperature until the box is full, close the cover and fasten the catch, then bake it in a moderate oven. As soon as done, unmold and lay it on a wicker stand and keep it in a cool place to use only twelve hours later. Now pare and cut it up into three-eighths of an inch thick slices; cut these straight through the center so as to obtain oblong pieces three inches long by one and a half inches wide. Dilute six egg-yolks with one quart of double cream and two ounces of vanilla-flavored sugar; run the whole through a sieve and dip into it the pieces of brioche so that they soak in well; drain them off and plunge into hot frying fat, then drain again and wipe; besprinkle with powdered vanilla sugar and dress in a pyramid. Serve a sabayon with Madeira wine separately. (See cabinet pudding with sabayon, No. 3096.)

(3041). CELERIAC, PEAR AND QUARTERED APPLE FRITTERS (Beignets de Céleris-Raves de Poires et de Quartiers de Pommes).

Celeriac.—Cut some celery roots in four, pare neatly and blanch them in plenty of water, then drain and finish cooking in a twenty-two degree syrup with a gill of Madeira wine added; when done, drain, wipe dry and leave to get cold, then dip them in frying batter (No. 137), and plunge into hot fat. As soon as of a fine color and the paste is crisp, drain and wipe them off, bestrew over with sugar and serve.

Pear Fritters are prepared the same, either with small pears or quartered larger ones, blanched and cooked in syrup and kirsch. Should the pears be very ripe they may be used raw and finished exactly the same as celery fritters.

Quartered Apples.—Peel and core the apples, cook them firmly in a light syrup with maraschino, drain and fry the same as for the above; glaze with sugar, pour over some rum and serve.

(3042). CHERRY FRITTERS—FRESH OR BRANDIED (Beignets de Cerises Fraîches ou à l'Eau-de-vie).

Select some large and fine fresh cherries, remove the pits and lay the fruit in a bowl to sprinkle over with sugar, pour on a few spoonfuls of kirsch and let macerate for one hour. Then drain and thread eight of them on a silver skewer or a straw; roll these in lady finger dust and dip in frying batter (No. 137); plunge them into hot frying fat and when the paste is fried and well colored drain off the fritters on a cloth, sponge them and dredge over with vanilla sugar, then dress them in a pyramid on a folded napkin. Serve at the same time a cherry sauce made with cherry purée and flavored with kirsch.

For Brandied Cherry Fritters.—Prepare as above, using brandied cherries; besprinkle with sugar when the pits have been removed and finish as above. For the sauce, crush four ounces of sour cherries, put this into a copper pan with a pint of red Bordeaux wine, four ounces of sugar, a small piece of cinnamon and the peel of one lemon; leave to cook for a few minutes, then strain the liquid through a sieve and return it to the pan; thicken with a little fecula diluted in a small quantity of cold water and strain this sauce once more through the sieve; now add to it a heavy handful of candied cherries washed in hot water and serve.

(3043). CREAM OF RICE FRITTERS (Beignets de Crème de Riz).

Dissolve ten ounces of rice flour in a bowl with one quart of cold milk; pass this through a sieve into a saucepan, and add to it a grain of salt, three ounces of butter, two spoonfuls of sugar and the fourth part of a vanilla bean; stir over a slow fire until it comes to a boil, then continue to cook the preparation for twenty minutes on the side of the range, adding to it a little raw cream. Take out the vanilla, and pour into another saucepan, then reduce it for a few moments. When consistent take it from the fire and mix in with it three ounces of pulverized macaroons, a piece of fresh butter, and five or six well-beaten whole eggs. When the preparation has been thoroughly mingled prepare some wafer sheets, three and a half inches by two and a half; soften them between two damp napkins, and lay on the preparation run through a pocket into sticks three-quarters of an inch in diameter, having them the whole length of the leaves; roll them into cylindricals and fasten the edges firmly, or else it may be poured directly on a baking sheet without wafers, dampened with cold water, to the thickness of three-quarters of an inch, and then set aside to cool for a few hours. Divide the preparation into pieces, three-quarters of an inch wide by three and a half inches long, or an inch and a half cubes, or else in rounds measuring one and five-eighths inches in diameter by three-quarters thick; roll the fritters in pulverized macaroons, then in beaten eggs and lastly in bread-crumbs; plunge them into hot frying fat, a few at a time, and when they have attained a fine color drain and wipe, bestrew with powdered vanilla-flavored sugar and dress on a folded napkin.

(3044). MUNDANE FRITTERS (Beignets Mondains).

Prepare a cream cake paste, the same as for soufflé fritters à la Médicis (No. 3047). Cut some bands of paper three inches long by two inches wide, and butter them over. Pour the paste into a pocket furnished with a channeled socket and push through on to each paper band a string of paste to form a large S, both ends being rolled. Heat some fat made with beef kidney suet and lard in a large frying pan, and when this is hot plunge in sufficient of the fritters to cover the surface; lift off the papers as quickly as they detach from the paste and fry the fritters slowly while turning them over; when fried and of a fine color drain them on a sieve. After they become partly cold dip them one by one in a clear rum icing made with fine sugar and the liquor. Drain and place them at once on a pastry grate laid on top of a tin plate so that the icing drains off properly; when the fritters are dry dress and serve.

(3045). ORANGE FRITTERS À LA TALLEYRAND (Beignets d'Oranges à la Talleyrand).

For one-third.—Cut two oranges into six pieces, leaving on the rind, then peel them closely and remove the seeds; besprinkle with fine sugar and drain on a cloth; dip each separate piece in frying batter (No. 137), and plunge into hot fat, and when of a fine color and very crisp drain these six pieces on a baking sheet and glaze the surfaces under a salamander (Fig. 123).

For one-third.—Peel a medium-sized orange, divide it as for orange glacées with caramel and immerse them in frying batter (No. 137), plunge into very hot fat, and when they have attained a fine color drain and besprinkle with vanilla sugar.

For one-third.—Peel three oranges to the pulp and pass a knife between the sections; take off all the skin and suppressing the seeds macerate in a little prunelle and sugar; wrap two pieces of orange in a rissole made of very thin brioche paste (No. 130), having it two and a quarter inches in diameter; fold the paste over and fasten the edges together, then put to rise in a mild temperature; fry to a fine color, drain well, dry and glaze with a light flavored icing (No. 102). Dress these three kinds of fritters on a napkin, all on the same dish, but in separate groups.

(3046). SINGAPORE FRITTERS (Beignets Singapore).

Dry two dozen macaroons; break them up and mash them with some rum in order to make a consistent paste. Peel neatly a medium-sized ripe pineapple; remove the core with a column tube five-eighths of an inch in diameter and split it lengthwise in two; cut from each half, even slices, having them one-eighth of an inch thick; put these slices in a vessel, bestrew with sugar, and pour over some brandy, then let macerate for two hours. Drain, wipe, and cover one side with the macaroon and rum paste; lay another slice on top and fasten the two together so as to enclose the macaroons, then roll them in powdered cracker, and dip them in frying batter (No. 137); plunge into hot frying fat, and when the paste becomes crisp and of a fine color drain off the fritters, wipe and dredge with sugar; set them on a baking sheet, push them into a hot oven to glaze, and dress in a pyramid on a folded napkin. Serve separately a sauce made with apricot marmalade (No. 3675) diluted with the pineapple infusion and a little rum, adding some square pieces of pineapple.

(3047). SOUFFLÉD FRITTERS À LA MÉDICIS (Beignets Soufflés à la Médicis).

Put a pint of water into a saucepan with two ounces of butter, one ounce of sugar, and a grain of salt; set the saucepan on the fire and at the first boil remove it on one side and mix in quickly half a pound of sifted flour; thicken the paste over the fire, dry for a few moments, working it continually, and then take it off to have it lose its greatest heat, but continuing to stir it steadily.

Then add to it one tablespoonful of orange flower water and seven to eight eggs, breaking them in one by one. Take up a heaping teaspoonful of this paste, and push it with the finger in such a manner as to give it a round shape, then let it fall into hot frying fat; stir all the time until the fritters assume a fine golden color, then drain on to a cloth and besprinkle with vanilla-flavored sugar; glaze them in a brisk oven, and dress on a napkin. Serve separately a sauce-boatful of chocolate cream prepared as follows: Place in a saucepan three egg-yolks, two ounces of sugar, and half an ounce of fecula; beat well and dilute the preparation with half a pint of boiling milk into which has been added the fourth part of a vanilla bean; stir the whole on the fire, and as soon as it thickens pour it over an ounce of dissolved cocoa; mingle all well together, pass through a tammy and let get cold, afterward adding to it twice as much whipped cream; serve at the same time as the fritters.

(3048). SOUFFLÉD FRITTERS WITH LEMON PEEL OR WITH ROASTED HAZEL-NUTS
(Beignets Soufflés aux Zestes de Citron ou aux Noisettes Grillées).

With Lemon Peel.—Put into a small saucepan two gills of water, one ounce of butter, a pinch of sugar and a grain of salt. Stand the saucepan on the fire and remove it at the first boil, then incorporate four ounces of fine sifted flour, proceeding the same as for cream cake paste (No. 132). When the paste has become smooth beat it for a few moments on the fire to dry, then take it off and let cool partly. Then incorporate three whole eggs and two yolks, putting them in singly, also a little finely chopped lemon peel. The paste must be rather too hard than too soft. Have a deep pan; heat in it moderately some fine frying fat, half clarified butter and half lard; take it from the range to the side of the fire. Take up the paste in small quantities with a teaspoon and let it fall on a floured table; roll into balls and arrange each one as soon as done on a small smooth saucepan cover, then slip them into the hot fat, a few at a time. After the fritters are all in the fat bring the saucepan back to the hot fire so as to gradually increase the heat, being careful to toss the fritters continuously. When they are all of a fine color drain and roll each one in vanilla sugar and dress on a napkin.

With Roasted Hazel-nuts.—A pint of milk, quarter of a pound of butter, five eggs and four ounces of roasted hazel-nuts, pounded in a mortar with a little kirsch. Finish the same as the above.

(3049). STRAWBERRY FRITTERS WITH MACAROONS, GARNISHED WITH GLAZED STRAW-BERRY FRITTERS (Beignets de Fraises aux Macarons, Garnis de Beignets de Fraises Glacés).

Procure some large strawberries; cover them entirely with apricot marmalade (No. 3675) and roll them in pulverized macaroons, then dip them one by one into a light frying batter (No. 137), and plunge them immediately into very hot frying fat. When the paste has fried, and is of a fine color, drain them off, and roll in vanilla-flavored sugar; dress on a folded napkin surrounded by the strawberry fritters.

Strawberry Fritters.—These are large strawberries dipped in frying batter, and plunged into very hot frying fat, drained, wiped, and bestrewn with sugar, then glazed in the oven; dress them around the above strawberry fritters.

(3050). ROMAN TRIUMVIRATE FRITTERS (Beignets Triumvirat Romain).

This hot dessert is composed of three sorts of fritters: Stuffed greengages, stuffed pears and stuffed pineapple.

The Stuffed Greengages are made by splitting some very ripe and sound gages through the middle; separate the two parts and remove the stone; apply on the cut side a macaroon paste made by pounding macaroons to a paste with apple jelly (No. 3668) and kirsch. Give them the original shape, roll them in powdered macaroons and dip in frying batter (No. 137); plunge them into hot frying fat and when the paste is fried and of a fine color, drain and wipe; besprinkle with sugar and glaze either under a salamander (Fig. 123) or in a hot oven.

The Stuffed Pears are made by peeling some medium pears, leaving on the stalks and emptying them from the other end with a vegetable spoon (Fig. 91), removing all the seeds. Cook them in a light syrup, drain and wipe and fill the empty space with candied apricots cut in three-sixteenths inch squares and mingled with apricot marmalade (No. 3675); cork up the opening with a round piece of pear or angelica, and dip them in a frying batter (No. 137), and then in plenty of hot fat to fry to a good golden brown; drain, wipe and bestrew with vanilla sugar.

For Stuffed Pineapples.—Peel a pineapple neatly, and divide it into one-eighth of an inch slices, and each of these in four; lay them in a vessel, pour over some good brandy, and dredge with powdered sugar, leaving them to macerate for half an hour; drain, wipe, put together two by two with a layer of hazelnut paste with cooked sugar (No. 125); press down and dip in frying batter (No. 137), then in white frying fat. When the fritters are of a fine color, drain, wipe and lay them on a baking sheet, bestrew with sugar and glaze under a salamander (Fig. 123). Dress in three distinct groups on a folded napkin and serve separately a sauce made of pineapple and prunelle as follows: Mix equal parts of grated pineapple and apricot marmalade (No. 3675); put it in a saucepan on the fire and leave boil up once or twice: then dilute with as much syrup, and flavor nicely with prunelle liquor.

(3051). FRUITS À LA CREOLE (Fruits à la Créole).

Cut lengthwise in two one large, well-pared pineapple, either fresh or preserved. Divide each half into slices of even length and thickness, not having them too thin, and lay them in a flat dish to cover with a cold syrup of twenty-eight degrees; let macerate for two or three hours. Beside these split in halves five or six fine peaches, not too ripe, suppress the stones, then lay a few at a time on a large skimmer and plunge into boiling water; remove to the side of the fire and leave them until the skins detach, then throw them at once into cold water. As soon as the skins are peeled off drain and macerate them for one hour in a cold syrup of twenty-eight degrees and covered with a round piece of white paper. In case no fresh peaches can be procured use canned ones cut in two; after removing them from the can they should be wiped on a cloth and then ranged

FIG. 576.

in a china vessel and covered with a cold syrup of twenty-eight degrees, afterward with a round piece of white paper. Cook in milk three-quarters of a pound of blanched Carolina rice, keeping it consistent but tender; sweeten it well at the last moment, finishing with a little cream, fresh butter and a few egg-yolks. With this rice fill a buttered pyramidical tin mold shaped like a funnel; press down the rice and lay the mold in a narrow but deep bain-marie saucepan, and keep it hot for ten to twelve minutes. Just when prepared to serve drain the pineapples and peaches; unmold the rice on a cooked paste (No. 131) foundation, a little wider than the circumference of the mold, having it attached to the center of a dish; dress the slices of pineapple erect against the pyramid, lightly overlapping them, and dress the half peaches around the pineapple. Arange in a crown-shape on top of the pyramid a few angelica leaves cut into points and fill the center with a cluster of fine large red candied cherries. Brush the fruits over with a thick vanilla syrup and serve with a sauce-boat of apricot and maraschino sauce (No. 3001).

(3052). GRENADES WITH CHERRIES (Grenades aux Cerises).

Divide a pound and a quarter of brioche paste (No. 130) into twelve even parts; roll each one into a separate ball and lay these in bottomless oval molds, three inches long, one and three-quarters inches wide and one and three-quarters inches high; let rise until they are almost full, then cook in a hot oven; as soon as done unmold the cakes on a grate and let cool off; then pare them with a knife to give them the appearance of an egg. Put ten egg-yolks and eight ounces of sugar in a bowl and dilute with a quart of cream flavored with vanilla, then strain through a tammy. Soak the brioches in this cream, drain and roll them in pulverized macaroons; dip them in beaten eggs, roll in bread-crumbs and plunge into hot frying fat to fry to a fine color; drain, wipe and dish them up in a circle; fill the interior space with a compote of cherries with prunelle and serve separately some of the syrup from the compote.

(3053). MAZARINE WITH PINEAPPLE AND KIRSCH (Mazarine à l'Ananas et au Kirsch).

Butter a timbale mold and fill it three-quarters full with savarin paste (No. 148); let rise in a mild temperature, and when this has reached nearly to the height of the top edges lay it on a tart plate and push into a brisk oven in order to bake the cake nicely. Unmold as soon as it is done and leave stand till cold. Now pare the cake evenly and cut it into transversal slices three-eighths of an inch thick; cover each of these with a layer of pineapple marmalade flavored with kirsch, and spread over some very finely chopped pistachios; reconstruct the cake as originally and mask the outside with hot apricot marmalade (No. 3675); bestrew with a mixture of chopped pistachios and dried almonds, then slide it on a dish to keep warm. Wash at the same time in hot water four ounces of citron, two ounces of angelica, and four ounces of orange peel, all cut into thin inch-long fillets; put these in a saucepan with a quart of twenty-eight degree syrup, place it on the fire and let boil up once or twice, then withdraw the saucepan to one side, and incorporate a quarter of a pound of very fresh butter divided in small pats, stirring constantly so as to mingle the butter well with the sauce; flavor with a gill of kirsch, and serve this in a sauce-boat to accompany the mazarine.

(3054). MIRLITONS OF PEARS À LA BIENVENUE (Mirlitons de Poires à la Bienvenue).

Butter and line a dozen deep tartlet molds with fragments of puff paste (No. 146); range them on a baking sheet and keep in a cool place. Put into a basin four ounces of powdered sugar, four ounces of sifted flour and two tablespoonfuls of orange flower water; dilute with a pint and a half of cream and strain the whole through a fine sieve. Place a piece of butter the size of a half-inch ball in the bottom of each mold, and set the baking sheet at the mouth of the oven door, then fill the molds with the above preparation; dredge sugar over and push the sheet gently into a warm spot. In the meantime peel a dozen fine small Sickle pears; empty out the insides with a vegetable spoon (Fig. 91) and cook them in a light syrup; drain well and fill the insides with well-washed candied apricot cut in small squares. Lay one pear in each tartlet and cover with an apricot and kirsch sauce. Bestrew shredded pistachios over and dress in a circle on a round dish, filling up the center with compoted cherries; serve an apricot sauce with kirsch and brandy (No. 3001) apart.

(3055). MUNICH WITH PEACHES (Munich aux Pêches).

Butter twelve timbale molds (No. 1, Fig. 137); fill them half full with savarin paste (No. 148), and let rise in a mild temperature, then bake in a moderate oven. As soon as done cut them off even with the edges, unmold and dip them at once in a lemon syrup flavored with Curaçao, maraschino and kirsch. Drain on a grate, glaze with a light orange icing (No. 102), and decorate the top of each cake with a rosette of halved pistachios, having a halved candied cherry in the center. Range them in a circle on a dish, and fill up the inside with compoted peaches; serve a marmalade of peaches (No. 3675) passed through a sieve and flavored with noyau in a separate sauce-boat; see Cleveland peach pudding (No. 3102).

(3056). SMALL CÉLESTINE OMELETS (Petites Omelettes Célestine).

Make a dozen small omelets, and when done slip them on a baking sheet and cover four of them with cream frangipane (No. 44) and chopped or finely cut-up candied fruits, four with apple marmalade (No. 3675) and almonds, and four with strawberry marmalade. Fold over flat or else roll them and cut off the ends; divide each one in two and arrange them in a pyramid form on a hot dish; pour over some apricot sauce with rum, and dredge over the surface pistachios and sweet almonds cut in dice and two spoonfuls of dry currants; serve at once.

(3057). CÉLESTINE OMELET WITH WHIPPED CREAM (Omelette Célestine à la Crème Fouettée).

Break three eggs in a bowl and add to them a pinch of salt and a coffeespoonful of sugar; beat the whole well and run it through a sieve. Butter the bottom of a medium-sized frying pan with clarified butter, heat and pour it in the preparation, spreading it over the entire surface so as to obtain a mellow omelet. Put in a vessel two spoonfuls of currant jelly and dilute it with double its quantity of sweetened whipped cream, then incorporate into this two crushed macaroons; lay this cream in the center of the omelet, raise the edges to inclose it well, and invert it on a dish. Powder over with powdered sugar, and glaze with a red-hot iron. Dress on each side a spoonful of whipped cream mixed with currant jelly and crushed macaroons.

(3058). FRANGIPANE OMELET (Omelette à la Frangipane).

Prepare a frangipane cream with vanilla and almonds (No. 44). Beat up ten eggs in a vessel with a grain of salt, two tablespoonfuls of sugar and the same of melted butter; dilute the whole with a gill of cream. Make with this a dozen small omelets in a pancake pan buttered with clarified butter; after taking them from the pan, slip them on a baking tin and cover over one side with a layer of the prepared frangipane; fold them up flat and cut off the ends, bestrew with powdered sugar and glaze under a salamander (Fig. 123), then dress in a pyramid.

(3059). RUM OMELET (Omelette au Rhum).

Beat up seven or eight eggs in a bowl and add to them a grain of salt, two spoonfuls of powdered sugar and a spoonful of good rum. Warm a little butter in a pan and pour in the beaten eggs, thickening them over a brisk fire stirring with a large fork. Fold over the omelet as fast as it detaches from the pan, and invert it with one stroke on a long dish; strew its entire surface with powdered sugar and glaze it with an omelet iron heated in the fire, decorating the top any desired fashion. Serve the omelet after pouring a few spoonfuls of rum with a little syrup into the bottom of the dish and setting it on fire.

(3060). OMELET SOUFFLÉ, ANCIENT STYLE (Omelette Soufflée à l'Ancienne).

Melt half a pound of good butter and have it clarified. Put into a glazed vessel fourteen egg-yolks and ten ounces of vanilla sugar; beat the preparation the same as for lady fingers, or until it becomes frothy and light, then add to it a grain of salt, seven or eight pulverized macaroons, and lastly sixteen stiffly beaten egg-whites. Pour the melted butter into two clean omelet pans, heat and putting half the preparation into each, toss slowly to warm them both at once, having them absorb all the butter, and keep them well rounded; transfer them immediately into two deep, buttered dishes, and push into a slack but well-regulated oven; remove two minutes later and split them down through their entire depth, then return them to the oven. Twelve to fifteen minutes suffice to cook the omelets. When done and light, besprinkle liberally with powdered vanilla sugar (No. 3165), and two minutes later remove from the oven and serve immediately.

(3061). OMELET SOUFFLÉ—LIGHT (Omelette Soufflée Légère).

Put three spoonfuls of powdered sugar, four ounces of flour, a grain of salt and some lemon peel into a vessel, and dilute it first with ten egg-yolks, then with half a gill of raw cream, in order to obtain a paste the same consistency as a frying paste; incorporate into it six well-beaten whites and three-quarters of a pound of whipped cream. Have some melted butter in a large pan; when hot pour in the preparation and cook it the same as for an omelet soufflé with preserves (No. 3065); when done to perfection slip it on a sheet of paper and strew over with sugar; roll it on itself, and dress on a dish; dredge more sugar over, and glaze in the oven or under a salamander (Fig. 123).

(3062). OMELET SOUFFLÉ WITH ALMONDS (Omelette Soufflée aux Amandes).

For six persons. Beat up six egg-yolks, twelve shelled, skinned and crushed bitter almonds, and six teaspoonfuls of sugar in a bowl the same as for lady fingers; add the grated peel of a lemon and a grain of salt; as the preparation becomes light stir in delicately the beaten egg-whites, using a spoon, and cutting it with this. The mixture should now stand alone without any danger of sinking, then pour it into a long buttered plated dish, smooth the surface, shaping it like a large folded omelet, and push the dish into a well-heated but not too hot oven. As soon as the omelet begins to brown remove and split it lengthways through the center with a knife, being careful not to press too hard, then replace it in the oven and be careful to turn the dish around from time to time. Let cook for twenty-five minutes; cover with sugar before it is finished so that it can glaze, and when removed dredge over more sugar before serving.

(3063). OMELET SOUFFLÉ WITH APPLES (Omelette Soufflée aux Pommes).

Prepare an omelet soufflé preparation exactly the same as for a light omelet soufflé (No. 3061). Cut four or five good apples in quarters, peel, core and mince, then put them into a pan with warm butter, and toss on a moderate fire; besprinkle with sugar, and cook without letting them melt; then remove the pan from the fire to thicken the contents with two or three spoonfuls of apricot marmalade (No. 3675). Have four spoonfuls of clarified butter in a large frying-pan; when hot pour in the omelet preparation, heat it for two minutes, then push the pan into a slack oven to cook the omelet; when firm slip it on a large sheet of paper, then turn it over again into the pan after having buttered it once more. When done slip it on the paper again and fill it with the apples. Roll it on itself, dress on a dish, bestrew the surface with sugar, then glaze.

(3064). OMELET SOUFFLÉ WITH MACAROONS (Omelette Soufflée aux Macarons).

Stir in a bowl six egg-yolks with a grain of salt and seven ounces of powdered sugar. The whole should get quite frothy. Pound six macaroons, and shake them through a sieve; beat up six egg-whites and mix them gradually with the former preparation, also stir in the macaroon powder at the same time. Melt three ounces of butter in a pan, and when hot pour in the omelet and toss it very slowly over the fire to heat through, then double it over, and invert it on a long buttered plated dish, and finish cooking the omelet in a slack oven. A few seconds before taking it out besprinkle bountifully with powdered vanilla sugar (No. 3165) to glaze. In order to have an omelet soufflé perfect, the guest should be kept waiting.

(3065). OMELET SOUFFLÉ WITH PRESERVES (Omelette Soufflée aux Confitures).

Place in a bowl five ounces of flour with four ounces of powdered sugar; dilute with two gills of milk, strain the liquid through a sieve into a saucepan and add to it a bit of lemon peel, a grain of salt and three ounces of melted butter; stir the preparation over a slow fire to thicken and boil for two minutes without leaving it, and when it is taken from the fire remove the lemon peel and five minutes after work in six or seven egg-yolks, one at a time, without ceasing to beat; when cold stir in the beaten whites. Put into a large frying pan four or five spoonfuls of clarified butter; when hot pour in the preparation, spreading it over the entire surface, and two minutes after push it into a slack oven on a trivet; as soon as the top is firm turn the omelet over on the lid of a large saucepan covered with a sheet of paper, slide it back at once to the rebuttered pan and set it once more in the oven to finish cooking. It ought to be quite mellow. As soon as done, slip it on a sheet of paper again and fill the center with a row of preserves; fold it on itself, then invert it on a long dish with the assistance of the sheet of paper; shape it prettily, tightening the two ends, and besprinkle over with fine sugar; glaze under a salamander (Fig. 123).

(3066). OMELET SOUFFLÉ WITH VANILLA (Omelette Soufflée à la Vanille).

Place six egg-yolks in a bowl with three ounces of powdered sugar and an ounce of vanilla sugar (No. 3165); beat well with a whip until it becomes as light as for biscuits; also beat up twelve whites to a stiff froth and mix them in slowly with the others, then dress a part of this preparation in a pyramid form on a lightly buttered dish, leaving a hollow in the center; pour the remainder into a pocket furnished with a socket and decorate the surface of the omelet prettily; sugar it over and bake in a hot oven for eight or ten minutes, serving it as soon as it is done, or it may be dressed on a long dish and split lengthways through the center with the blade of a knife so as to make two pieces of it, then cook as above.

(3067). OMELET STUFFED WITH PRESERVES—GLAZED (Omelette Fourrée aux Confitures et Glacée).

Prepare a sweet omelet with seven or eight eggs; as soon as it becomes firm roll it over on itself in the pan to detach it, then bring it forward and fill it with currant jelly or apricot marmalade (No. 3675); shape it nicely, rolling it on itself lengthwise, and invert it quickly on a small long dish. Give it a pretty appearance, turning the ends under, and dredge over with powdered sugar; glaze the surface with an iron heated in the fire.

(3068). OMELET STUFFED WITH STRAWBERRIES (Omelette Fourrée aux Fraises).

Pick about forty large, ripe and very fresh strawberries; select twenty of the finest ones and cut them in four, then place them in a bowl with sugar, a piece of orange peel and two spoonfuls of rum; keep them in a cool place. Press the remainder of the strawberries through a fine sieve and put the pulp into a bowl to sweeten and also lay on ice. Break seven or eight eggs in a vessel,

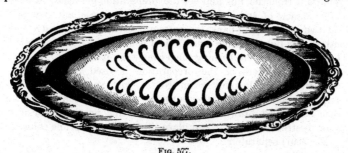

Fig. 577.

mix in two soup spoonfuls of sugar, two soup spoonfuls of good cream, a few small bits of butter and a grain of salt; beat up well. Heat some fresh butter in a pan, pour in the beaten eggs and stir with a fork until they thicken; when the omelet detaches from the pan bring it forward and fill it with the cut-up strawberries without any of the liquid and turn it over with one stroke on a long dish. Give it a pretty shape, besprinkle with powdered vanilla sugar (No. 3165), glaze with a red hot iron three-sixteenths of an inch in diameter and surround with the purée, into which should be incorporated the liquid from the quartered strawberries.

(3069). OMELET WITH FRUITS, MERINGUED (Omelette aux Fruits Meringuée).

Prepare an omelet with ten beaten eggs, a grain of salt, powdered sugar, butter and raw cream, the same as for frangipane omelet (No. 3058). With this preparation and some clarified butter cook a dozen omelets in a small frying pan and when done spread them at once on a baking sheet; brush the surfaces on one side only with apricot marmalade (No. 3675), bestrew with a fine salpicon of assorted candied fruits and roll up the omelets, cut off the ends and divide each one in two; spread them over with more marmalade and dress in a pyramid on a dish; scatter over more of the same salpicon, then cover the entire pyramid with meringue prepared as for snow eggs (No. 3163); smooth this neatly and decorate it through a cornet; dredge over powdered sugar and poach the whole in a slack oven, setting the dish on top of a thick baking tin.

(3070). OMELET WITH PURÉE OF SPINACH—SWEET (Omelette Sucrée à la Purée d'Épinards).

Blanch quickly in salt water in a copper basin a few handfuls of new spinach, having it very clean, tender and fresh—this is most important. When well drained and squeezed chop or pound and press it through a sieve. Cook some butter to hazel-nut (No. 567) in a saucepan, mix in with it three or four spoonfuls of the spinach and fry until the moisture is thoroughly evaporated, then add a handful of powdered lady fingers, a little sugar and a few spoonfuls of raw cream. Cook the whole from four to five minutes, remove and put in a bit of lemon peel and a piece of butter. Prepare a sweet omelet with seven or eight beaten eggs, and as soon as it thickens bring it to the front of the pan and fill it with the purée; fold over and invert it on a small, long dish; shape it prettily with the two ends finished in a point; bestrew with powdered sugar and glaze under a salamander (Fig. 123) or with an iron three-sixteenths of an inch in diameter heated red hot in the fire.

(3071). OMELET WITH RUSSET APPLES (Omelette aux Pommes de Reinette).

Cut three russet apples into quarters; peel, mince coarsely and put into a pan with six table-spoonfuls of melted butter; heat well without letting them dissolve. Dilute two tablespoonfuls of flour with two whole eggs and eight tablespoonfuls of raw cream; add to this two spoonfuls of powdered sugar and a grain of salt; pour the preparation over the apples, spreading them on the entire surface of the pan, then as soon as it begins to thicken prick it with a fork to dry the top. Dredge some brown sugar over the omelet and laying an inverted plate over hold it down with the right hand and turn the pan quickly so as to receive the omelet on the plate. Melt more butter in the pan and slipping the omelet into it, heat it well, rolling the pan backward and forward to glaze the sugar without allowing the omelet to adhere, then sprinkle some more of the same sugar over the top and turn it again on the plate; slip it on a dish and serve.

(3072). PANCAKES À LA DÉJAZET (Crêpes à la Déjazet).

Work nine ounces of flour with a pint of boiling milk in a saucepan until it becomes a smooth paste, then add to it at once four and a half ounces of butter, four ounces of sugar and a pinch of salt. Set the vessel on the fire and stir it with a spoon until it becomes thick and detaches from the sides, then remove it from the fire and let the preparation get cold, afterward adding to it twelve egg-yolks, four ounces of sugar, a finely chopped orange peel and ten egg-whites beaten to a stiff froth. Heat two small frying pans, the bottom of each measuring five inches across; wipe them well and butter over lightly with a brush; then pour into each one a very thin layer of the preparation and cook in a brisk oven, turning them over when half done. Drain them on to a cloth and continue until three-quarters of the preparation is used. Soak them with maraschino and cover with a layer of English coffee cream (No. 41) with vanilla added, then dress them one on top of the other, finishing with a pancake; cover the whole with the remainder of the preparation, pour over some butter and brown in a hot oven, placing another dish underneath the one they are dressed on; bestrew with sugar and glaze till they attain a fine color. Serve an apricot sauce with kirsch (No. 3001) separately.

(3073). PANCAKES À LA ROSSINI—MERINGUED (Pannequets Meringués à la Rossini).

Place in a vessel half a pound of flour, one ounce of sugar, a pinch of salt, lemon peel and two tablespoonfuls of orange flower water; beat with a whip to mix well and dilute the preparation with five gills of cream, afterward adding three ounces of melted butter. Heat two small pancake pans, wipe them nicely and brush with clarified butter; pour into each one two spoonfuls of the preparation, spreading it over well and set it on a slow fire. As soon as the pancake begins to dry turn it over quickly and a few seconds later invert it on a baking sheet; finish cooking all the preparation the same way. Cover each pancake with a layer of apricot marmalade (No. 3675) and roll them up on themselves. Spread a thick layer of pastry cream (No. 46) on the bottom of a dish, dress over the pancakes, forming them into a pyramid and cover with a layer of vanilla meringue with sugar (No. 140); decorate the summit with a rosette of the meringue pushed through a channeled socket pocket and the base with a circle of hollows; besprinkle lightly with sugar and push into a very slack oven to color the meringue, then fill the hollows with currant jelly (No. 3670) and apricot marmalade (No. 3675). A Madeira sabayon sauce (No. 3096) is to be served apart.

(3074). GERMAN PANCAKES (Crêpes à l'Allemande).

Put in a bowl six ounces of flour, eight egg-yolks, two tablespoonfuls of sugar and four table-spoonfuls of melted butter; stir the whole to obtain a smooth preparation. Dilute this with a gill and three-quarters of double cream, and add five beaten-up egg-whites and four tablespoonfuls of whipped cream. Butter lightly with clarified butter the bottom of two medium pans; heat and pour into each a thin layer of the batter, spreading it over the entire surface, and push them into a hot oven; when half done turn them over to have them cooked evenly on both sides. As soon as they are finished drain them on a cloth, bestrew with sugar and dress on a dish.

(3075). PANCAKES OF PEACH MARMALADE MACÉDOINE (Crêpes Marmelade de Pêches Macédoine).

Have four ounces of sifted flour in a basin with one ounce of sugar, a pinch of salt, two whole eggs, one egg-yolk and the finely chopped peel of a quarter of an orange; add to the whole a gill and a quarter of milk. Stir well with a whip and pour in two and a half ounces of melted butter and with this preparation make some pancakes, six inches in diameter; from them cut with a pastry-cutter rounds in the center two and a half inches in diameter and around with another cutter six inches in diameter, so as to have them all of even size. Cover with a layer of peach marmalade (No. 3675) and dress on a dish, superposing one on the other; bestrew with fine sugar and glaze under a salamander (Fig. 123), then fill the center with a macédoine of fruits cut in five-sixteenth inch squares, having them mingled with peach marmalade and maraschino. Place around a garnishing of apples cut in inch-diameter balls and cooked in syrup, and on each one of these fasten a candied cherry with a piece of angelica. Serve an apricot kirsch sauce (No. 3001) apart.

(3076). PANCAKE STICKS, ROYEAUX (Pannequets Bâtons, Royeaux).

Prepare six large pancakes as for pancakes à la Rossini (No. 3073); cut them in two and each of these pieces into oblongs, four and a half inches long by three inches wide; lay on the center of each of these a spoonful of almond cream (No. 40); fold them laterally in three so as to enclose the cream and dip them in beaten eggs; roll in bread-crumbs and plunge into very hot frying fat to have them a fine golden color, then drain, bestrew with vanilla sugar (No. 3115) and dress in a pyramid on a napkin. Serve separately an orgeat sauce thickened with a few spoonfuls of apricot marmalade. See Franklyn pudding (No. 3098).

(3077). PANCAKES WITH BROWN SUGAR—LIGHT (Crêpes Légères à la Cassonade).

Put one pound of flour into a basin; make a hollow in the center and break in the eight egg-yolks; dilute with a glassful of milk, add three spoonfuls of sugar and a grain of salt. Work in the flour slowly so as to have a smooth and light paste, then add to it three quarters of an ounce of yeast dissolved in a little warm milk and strained. Let the paste rise for two hours in a mild temperature, afterward mixing in with it five well-beaten egg-whites and one pint of whipped cream, then leave it stand for ten minutes longer. Put some clarified butter into a small sauce-pan and use it to brush over the bottom of a small frying-pan; pour in two or three spoonfuls of the pancake preparation, spreading it all over the pan, and cook in the oven. Before turning the pan-cake over cover the surface with the clarified butter; when done slip it on a baking tin, sweeten both sides with brown sugar, and when all are cooked dress and serve them very hot.

(3078). PANCAKES WITH ORANGE FLOWER WATER—LARGE (Grandes Crêpes à l'Eau de Fleur d'Oranger).

Sift twelve ounces of flour into a basin; add to it a grain of salt, and mix in six to eight eggs, one by one, beating the paste each time for three or four minutes so as to have it smooth and light; put in two spoonfuls of powdered sugar, and four spoonfuls of good olive oil; when the mix-ture is finished add two or three spoonfuls of raw cream, and as much brandy; the paste should be flowing without being liquid; cover the basin with a cloth, and let it rest for a couple of hours. Heat two omelet pans, butter them liberally with a brush dipped in clarified butter, and cover the bottom with a rather thick layer of the paste; prick it with the prong of a fork to have the liquid parts fall to the bottom. As soon as the pancake attains consistency rotate the pan vigorously to detach it from the pan, and toss it over with one stroke; butter the bottom of the pan and the top of the pancake with melted butter without ceasing to toss the pan over a slow fire so that it finishes to cook. When the pancake is properly done slide it on a round dish, having the bottom bestrewn with brown sugar, and dredge more of the same over the top; then sprinkle with a few drops of orange flower water, and on this slip the second pancake; sweeten and sprinkle it the same. Send the dish at once to the table so that they can be eaten hot while the other two are being prepared.

(3079). PANCAKES WITH PRESERVES—LIGHT (Pannequets Légers aux Confitures).

Dilute half a pound of flour with eight egg-yolks, one pint of milk, a gill of cream, and four ounces of melted clarified butter; add lemon or vanilla flavoring, a grain of salt, three grated bitter almonds, and the beaten egg-whites. Dip a brush in clarified butter, and grease over some small pancake pans; heat and pour into each one a spoonful of the preparation; spread it thinly over the entire surface of the pan, and as soon as the paste assumes a color underneath turn over on the other side. When done slip on a baking sheet, besprinkle with vanilla or lemon sugar, and dress on a dish, one on top of the other; serve with a separate plateful of preserves.

(3080). PEACHES À LA COLBERT (Pêches à la Colbert).

Plunge twelve fine peaches into boiling water for a few seconds in order to skin them easily, then split, pare and take out the kernels; put the peaches to macerate in a hot twelve-degree syrup flavored with maraschino. As soon as the fruit is tender drain on a cloth, wipe and stuff each half with rice and cream flavored with vanilla (No. 160) and finished with a few egg-yolks; place two half peaches together to resemble whole ones, then cover them with a light coating of apricot marmalade (No. 3675), roll in pulverized macaroons, dip in beaten eggs, then in white bread-crumbs and fry to a fine golden color. Cut some slices of savarin cake three-quarters of an inch thick and with a pastry cutter remove some rounds two and a half inches in diameter; slit these half an inch deep with another pastry cutter an inch and a half in diameter, inserting a small kitchen knife on the side at a quarter of an inch from the bottom and with the tip cut around to detach the center only. Lay the prepared crusts on a baking tin, besprinkle over with sugar and glaze in a hot oven. As soon as this is accomplished and they become cold fill the empty centers with a salpicon of fruits mingled with apricot marmalade; decorate the edges of each crust with twelve small sticks of angelica, each an inch long. Lay the crusts on a dish, dress the peaches on top and heat in the oven twenty minutes before serving. Have a separate apricot sauce, adding a few spoonfuls of almond milk and flavored with maraschino (No. 3001.)

(3081). CONDÉ PEACHES (Pêches Condé).

Blanch half a pound of rice; drain and replace it in the saucepan with a pint of cream and half of a vanilla stick; push the pan into a slack oven and allow it to cook for forty minutes. Re-move the rice, suppress the vanilla and put in six egg-yolks, three ounces of fresh butter, three ounces of sugar and a little salt. Butter and sugar a mold one inch high by seven inches in diameter; fill it to the top with rice and place it in a bain-marie for twenty minutes. Split in two twelve fine peaches, remove the kernels, blanch and peel off the skins, pare nicely and lay them to macerate in a hot thirty-degree vanilla syrup; one hour later drain the peaches on a cloth and wipe them well. Unmold the rice on a dish and dress the peaches over dome-shaped, cover them with apricot marmalade (No. 3675), bestrew with shredded pistachios and decorate the cavities between the peaches, and also the border of the rice, with angelica lozenges and split candied cher-ries; surround the base with small pear-shaped rice croquettes. Set the dressed dish in the oven for twenty minutes to heat well, and serve with an apricot sauce and Madeira wine diluted with vanilla syrup. (See Humboldt pudding, No. 3100.)

(3082). MERINGUED PEACHES (Pêches Meringuées).

Cook half a pound of rice in milk, proceeding the same as for rice with apples (No. 3115); finish with cream and butter. Cut six peaches in four, remove the kernels and plunge them into boiling water until the skins peel off, then drain on a cloth and cut them up into small quar-ters; besprinkle over with sugar. With the cooked rice form with a spoon any style of border, leaving a hollow in the center; inside of this dress the quartered peaches in layers, brushing them over with apricot marmalade (No. 3675) and alternating with thin layers of the rice; the whole to be covered with the rice and this with a layer of meringue (No. 140); smooth the surface, deco-rate with meringue, dredge with fine sugar and dry in a very slow oven for twenty minutes.

(3083). RICHELIEU PEACHES (Pêches à la Richelieu).

Butter some half-inch high flawn rings, having them two and a half inches in diameter; line with fine paste (No. 135), and cut it off even with the edge, then raise it up to form a crest, which must be pinched all around. Leave them in a cool place for fifteen minutes; egg over twice and prick the bottoms in several places; line the inside with buttered paper, fill up with dry rice, then cook in a hot oven and remove as soon as done; empty out and brush over the exteriors with egg-yolks and return to the oven for an instant to color the egg. Dress on a round dish and line the inside with peach marmalade (No. 3675), then fill up with frangipane cream (No. 44) into which has been mixed some crushed macaroons moistened with maraschino. Smooth the surfaces well and dress on top of each a well-drained preserved half peach the same size as the small flawns; cover over with apricot or peach marmalade and then decorate with candied cherries and fanciful cuts of angelica; fill the centers with a salpicon of pineapple, plums and pears cut in quarter-inch squares, the whole to be mixed with apricot marmalade. Keep them warm and serve separately a peach syrup with maraschino.

(3084). STEVENS PEACHES (Pêches à la Stevens).

Infuse a vanilla bean for one hour in a quart of boiling milk; take it out and return the milk to the fire; at the first boil drop into it like rain half a pound of tapioca; allow it to boil up once or twice, then finish cooking on the side of the range without allowing it to boil; add to it two ounces of sugar and four eggs, beating them in one by one. Butter some timbale molds (No. 1, Fig. 137), cover the bottoms with a ring of quince paste and fill the center of this ring with a round of greengage cut out with a cutter, then fill up the timbales with the prepared tapioca and poach in a bain-marie for thirty minutes. When firm unmold and dress in a circle on a round dish; fill the center of this circle with a compote of peaches, decorating the top with fruits. Reduce the syrup used for compoting the peaches and with it make a sauce, adding peach marmalade and maraschino.

(3085). PEARS FERRIÈRE (Poires Ferrière).

Peel some pears; hollow them with a vegetable spoon and cook in a light syrup; drain on a sieve and stuff them with powdered macaroons moistened with a little Curaçoa; cover them with a coating of fine apricot marmalade (No. 3675) and bestrew with finely chopped pistachios. Butter and sugar a surtout mold and fill it to the top with rice and cream flavored with vanilla (No. 160) and finished with a few egg-yolks; set the mold in a sautoir with water reaching to half its height and put this into a slack oven to get firm; then unmold on a dish. Dress on the edge of the rice a circle of greengages alternated with small apple-shaped rice croquettes having their stalks made of pieces of angelica; range the pears inside of this circle dressed in a pyramid, and a moment before serving push the dish in the oven to heat well; serve separately the following sauce: Take very ripe pears; peel and cut in quarters, then cook them to a compote with some thirty-degree syrup; when the fruit is well cooked strain through a fine sieve to obtain a pulp; dilute this with the syrup in which they were boiled, adding also a few spoonfuls of kirsch. Sturtout molds are made of different sizes as follows: About three inches in diameter by half an inch high, or six inches in diameter by three-quarters of an inch high.

(3086). LOMBARDE PEARS—STUFFED (Poires Farcies à la Lombarde).

Peel one dozen medium-sized pears, leave on a part of the stalk and cut them across in two at two-thirds of their height; scoop them out with a vegetable spoon (Fig. 91) and cook in a light syrup. As soon as they are done drain, wipe and stuff them with a salpicon of fruits mingled with pear marmalade and flavored with kirsch, and put them together again into their original shape. Dress a layer of rice and cream with vanilla (No. 160), finished with a few egg-yolks, on the bottom of a dish; arrange the pears in a circle on the edges of this and fill the center with some stewed apples cut into balls with a vegetable spoon, some candied cherries washed in hot water and pineapple cut in dice, the whole to be diluted with a little vanilla syrup. Serve separately a sauce made of straw-berry pulp diluted with as much syrup and flavored with maraschino.

(3087). PIE, APPLE, PEACH OR RHUBARB (Tarte aux Pommes, aux Pêches ou à la Rhubarbe).

Prepare a tart paste (No. 149). Cut into quarters six or eight very ripe apples or fine, tender peaches; range them in layers in a pie dish, besprinkle with sugar, and dress them in a dome form. Wet the edges of the dish and cover it with a band of the paste, half an inch wide by an eighth of an inch in thickness; wet this band also with a fine brush, and cover the fruits and this band with a rolled-out flat of the same paste; press it down on the base of the dome, and then on the band, so as to have the two adhere. Cut the paste even with the edge of the dish, and scallop it all around with a small knife, pressing the paste heavily with the left thumb, and cutting it at short intervals from the bottom to the top to raise the gash slightly, so that when cooking the paste will rise in relief. Brush over the top with water, and decorate with a few fanciful cuts of the same paste, then egg the surface with beaten eggs. Stand the pie on a small baking tin and push it into a slack oven to cook for forty-five minutes, then bestrew with sugar, and leave to glaze in a hot oven. Instead of egging the pie may be simply moistened with water and lightly covered with powdered sugar.

Rhubarb Pie.—Select fine tender stalks of rhubarb. Remove the leaves, wash and peel the stalks, then cut them up transversely in pieces three-quarters of an inch long; arrange these in layers in a pie dish intermingled with sugar, and cover and finish the same as the above apple or peach pies.

(3088). PIE, MARROW FRANGIPANE (Tourte Frangipane à la Moelle).

Wet an eight-inch diameter tart plate and cover with a flat made of the parings of puff paste (No. 146) an eighth of an inch thick; moisten the edges with a brush, lay all around a band of puff paste a quarter of an inch thick by three-quarters of an inch wide, and press the band down on the flat to have the two adhere, and fasten the two ends together. Put in a vessel three ounces of flour and five ounces of sugar; dilute with four eggs, dropping in one at a time, to have the whole very smooth, but in case this fails then strain through a fine wire sieve; increase the proportions of this preparation with one pint of boiling milk, and pour the whole into a saucepan to thicken on the fire; when this is accomplished remove and add two ounces of melted marrow. Leave cool, and with this fill the pie up as far as the band; over these place devices of puff paste, egg over and push the pie into a hot oven to cook it. When done, take out, sprinkle the surface with fine sugar, and return to the oven for a few moments longer, in order to have this glaze. This pie is to be served hot, as soon as removed from the oven.

(3089). MINCE PIE ("Mince Pie").

Take a tin pie plate and line it with foundation paste (No. 135); on the edge fasten a puff paste (No. 146) band three-sixteenths of an inch in thickness and three-quarters of an inch wide; fill the hollow in the plate with mincemeat (No. 117), wet the edge and cover over with a puff paste flat the same diameter, fastening it on firmly to the edges, egg the surface and trace on top some fanciful designs with the tip of a small knife; pinch all around and push in the oven to bake for an hour to an hour and a quarter. As soon as done remove to the oven door, bestrew with fine sugar and replace it in the oven for a few moments to glaze.

(3090). PINEAPPLE, CAROLINA AND WITH RICE WITH CREAM (Ananas Caroline et Ananas au Riz à la Crème).

Peel a pineapple neatly; remove the core with a column tube and split it lengthwise in two. Cut one of these halves into very small thin bands, each one being an inch and a quarter long by half an inch wide, and cut the other half into even slices an eighth of an inch thick. Put the sliced pineapple into a vessel and cover it with a cold twenty-five degree syrup, and three hours later drain off this syrup to add to it a little sugar melted in a small quantity of water, and cook it again to thirty-two degrees. Let it get cold, then flavor with a little maraschino; pour it once more over the pineapple. Two hours after drain the small bands on a cloth and wipe them carefully. Butter twelve small timbale molds (No. 1, Fig. 137), cover the bottoms with a ring cut from angelica and place a candied cherry in the center; decorate the sides with the pineapple bands overlapping each other, and fill the timbales as far as the top with rice and cream (No. 160), flavored with vanilla and finished with a few egg-yolks. Keep these timbales in a bain-marie for thirty-five minutes. Place the even slices of pineapple to drain, wipe dry and cover with a light layer of apricot marmalade (No. 3675) flavored with kirsch. Dress the unmolded timbales in the center of a round dish and range the pineapple in slices around, one overlapping the other; bestrew with finely chopped pistachios and decorate with angelica lozenges and candied cherries. Set the dish in the oven for a few moments to heat the whole and serve with the syrup used to steep the pineapple, flavored with maraschino and then strained through a fine wire sieve into a sauce-boat.

Pineapple with Rice with Cream.—Have some rice with cream (No. 160) flavored with orangé, dress it in the center of a dish and garnish around it with slices of pineapple a quarter of

FIG. 578.

an inch thick, four inches in diameter and cut in four, having prepared them as follows: Place them in a copper basin and throw over them a thirty-degree syrup and allow to infuse for an hour; drain. Pound the parings and mix them with the syrup in which the pineapples were infused; pass through a sieve and serve as a sauce.

(3091). POUPELIN (Poupelin).

Pour one pint of water into a saucepan, adding a pinch of salt, an ounce of sugar and two ounces of butter; set the saucepan on the fire and at the first boil fill up the liquid with as much flour as it can possibly absorb; then dry it on the fire, proceeding the same as a cream cake paste (No. 132). Afterward incorporate six whole eggs, one at a time, and six yolks, working the paste thoroughly. Pour this preparation into a buttered charlotte mold; cook in a slack oven, and when done unmold and allow to cool on a grate; empty the inside only, leaving a crust a quarter of an inch in thickness, and fill the empty interior with frangipane cream (No. 44), alternating with a layer of salpicon of fruits. Return it to the oven for half an hour and just when prepared to serve remove and turn it over on a dish. Serve an apricot and kirsch sauce (No. 3001) in a sauce tureen at the same time.

(3092). PUDDING À LA BENVENUTO (Pouding à la Benvenuto).

Cook five to six large pancakes and cut them up into inch-wide bands. Butter a dome-shaped cylindrical mold and line it with these bands, one overlapping the other. Put seven ounces of flour in a saucepan with one pint of boiling milk and thicken it on the fire to obtain a smooth paste; remove it at once and add to it two ounces of butter, a pinch of salt, four ounces of sugar, two ounces of grated cocoanut laid on a paper-covered baking sheet and slightly roasted in the oven, the peel of one lemon and eight raw egg-yolks; return it to the fire, stirring continuously, and as soon as the preparation attains consistency incorporate into it slowly the well-beaten whites of five eggs. With this fill up the mold, alternating it with layers of pancake parings, first covered with apple jelly (No. 3668) and then rolled up. Set the mold into a saucepan with boiling water reaching to half its height and place it on the range; when the water boils, finish cooking in a slow oven for forty-five minutes. As soon as this is accomplished take out the pudding, let it stand for five minutes, then unmold it on a dish and serve at once with a sauce-boat of orange syrup thickened with arrowroot and flavored with maraschino.

(3093). PUDDING À LA BRADLEY (Pouding à la Bradley).

Soak one pound of bread-crumbs in hot milk; extract all the moisture and place it in a saucepan, pouring over it a few spoonfuls of raw cream. Stir briskly with a spoon and add twenty-four egg-yolks, ten ounces of sugar, ten ounces of butter, a little at a time, twelve tablespoonfuls of frangipane (No. 44), a grain of salt, a grated orange peel, a pound and a quarter of Smyrna raisins and eight ounces of candied pineapple cut up in small squares, and lastly fifteen well-beaten egg-whites. With this preparation fill three-quarters full some buttered and floured pudding molds; place them in a deep baking pan containing boiling water and poach for one hour in the bain-marie in a slack oven. Serve with a Sabayon with California wine (No. 3096). This quantity is sufficient for twenty persons.

(3094). MELLOW PUDDING, APRICOT SAUCE (Pouding Moelleux, Sauce aux Abricots.)

Skin half a pound of suet and pass it twice through the machine (Fig. 47); pound it with five ounces of beef marrow and pass it through a sieve; put it into a vessel with fourteen ounces of powdered sugar and beat up for ten minutes with a spoon, then add two whole eggs and from fifteen to eighteen yolks, little by little, five ounces of white bread-crumbs soaked in hot milk and well pressed, pounded and diluted with a little raw cream and then passed through a sieve, and lastly add four or five spoonfuls of brandy, salt, grated lemon peel and one pound of candied fruits cut in quarter-inch squares and ten ounces of Smyrna raisins. Put a little of this preparation in a small timbale mold and poach it in a bain-marie to judge whether its consistency be correct. Butter some plain or cylindrical molds, flour them over and fill them three-quarters full with the preparation; place these molds in a deep baking tin with hot water and poach for one hour in a slack oven. Let stand for ten minutes and then unmold on a dish and cover with apricot and rum sauce (No. 3001). This quantity is sufficient for twenty persons.

(3095). CABINET PUDDING À LA ROYALE (Pouding Cabinet à la Royale).

Butter a square, hinged mold and fill it three-quarters full with Savarin paste (No. 148); leave it to rise in a mild temperature and when it reaches to a quarter of an inch from the top close the cover and bake in a slack oven. As soon as it is done unmold and leave set till the following day. Butter and sugar a cylindrical timbale mold. Cut up the stale Savarin cake in quarter-inch thick slices and cover one side with apricot marmalade (No. 3675); cut some of these into inch-wide bands the same height as the mold and fasten them on their uncovered side all around the inside of the mold, having them standing upright and overlapping each other; cut the remainder of the slices into dice and use them to fill up the mold in alternate layers with candied fruits also cut dice-shaped and macaroons. Put in a vessel twelve egg-yolks, two whole eggs, six ounces of sugar and two ounces of orange sugar; beat the whole together and dilute with a pint of milk and a pint of cream; pass it through a wire sieve. Pour this preparation slowly into the mold until well filled, then leave it to soak for several minutes; lay the mold in a saucepan with water reaching to half its height and cook it in a slack oven for an hour and a quarter; take it from the oven and let stand for a few moments, then unmold it on a dish and cover over with apricot marmalade. Serve with a sauce-boat of Sabayon with Marsala sauce (No. 3096).

(3096). CABINET PUDDING WITH SABAYON (Pouding Cabinet au Sabayon).

Prepare a Genoese cake mixture the same as for No. 3239; pour and spread it on a baking sheet, covered with buttered paper, in a layer half an inch thick, and bake it in a slow oven; when done, remove and invert it on a grate, lift off the paper and let get cold. Wash three-quarters of a pound of candied fruits in hot water, such as pears, apricots, plums, orange peel and cherries; cut them up into quarter-inch dice, and lay them in a vessel; mix with a few crushed macaroons, and pour a few spoonfuls of rum over the whole. Butter and sugar a plain cylindrical mold (Fig. 150), place in its bottom thin slices of the Genoese cake, overlapping each other, and scatter on top a part of the fruits and macaroons; on these lay more slices of cake, then more fruit, proceeding the same as before, and continue the operation until the mold is full. Break ten egg-yolks into a vessel, beat in four ounces of sugar, and add the grated peel of one lemon; mix with a whisk, and dilute this preparation with a quart of cream, then run the whole through a fine sieve. Pour it over the pudding, filling it well, and let it soak thoroughly for several minutes, then place it in a bain-marie and when the water has reached boiling point push it into a slack oven to cook for one hour. Unmold the pudding on a dish, cover it with Madeira Sabayon sauce, and serve more of it separately.

For the Sabayon, put half a pound of sugar and eight egg-yolks in a bain-marie, set it on the fire, and whip the preparation until it becomes frothy, then add half a pint of Madeira or other wine, and continue to whip until the sauce is very light and begins to thicken, then remove it at once from the bain-marie, and serve.

(3097). COUNTESS PUDDING (Pouding à la Comtesse).

Prepare a small biscuit preparation the same as for lady fingers (No. 3377); spread it out on a sheet of buttered paper to the thickness of three-sixteenths of an inch, and cook in a slack oven, being careful to keep it soft. As soon as done remove from the oven, take off the paper and cut the cake into four-inch wide bands down its entire length; cover each one of these bands with a layer of strawberry marmalade passed through a sieve, and roll them up into cylindricals an inch and a half in diameter; wrap them at once in paper to tighten and keep firm, and let them rest for one hour, then cut them into slices a quarter of an inch thick. Butter a dome-shaped cylindrical mold, and with the rolled slices of cake cover the interior sides, then fill the empty hollow with a Saxony soufflé pudding preparation (No. 3107); place it in a saucepan with boiling water to half its height and let come to a boil, then remove the saucepan from the fire, and push it into a slack oven. After forty minutes take it out and let cool off for a few moments, then unmold on a dish, and cover with hot apricot marmalade (No. 3675). Serve a sauceboat of Richelieu and liquor sauce made as follows: Heat a pint of thirty-degree syrup, and remove it from the fire, thicken with a little arrowroot dissolved in cold water, and add a few cherries (demi-sucre) and shredded pistachios; flavor with kirsch.

(3098). FRANKLYN PUDDING (Pouding à la Franklyn).

Put half a pound of butter into a vessel, beat it to a cream, and add to it seven egg-yolks, one at a time. When the preparation has become frothy put with it gradually six ounces of peeled and dried almonds that have been pounded and rubbed through a sieve, six ounces of sugar, six ounces of bread-crumbs, and eight ounces of candied fruits, such as candied cherries cut in two, pineapple and orange peel cut in dice, and finally six well-beaten egg-whites. Pour this preparation into a cylindrical timbale mold (Fig. 150), and place this in a sautoir with water to half its height; set it on the fire to come to a boil, then push it into a slack oven. At the expiration of forty-five minutes remove the pudding from the oven, let it rest for a few moments, then unmold it on a dish; cover it with orgeat sauce, and serve with a bowlful of the same.

The orgeat sauce is made by cooking four ounces of sugar to "small crack" (No. 171), then adding a gill of almond milk (No. 4), and boiling once. Thicken the sauce with a spoonful of fecula diluted with a little water and half a gill of rich cream.

(3099). PUDDING À LA DE FREESE (Pouding à la de Freese).

Chop up and pass through a sieve five ounces of beef marrow; place it in a vessel and beat it up to a cream with five ounces of sugar, adding singly eight egg-yolks and three whole eggs, and have the preparation very light. Then incorporate one pound of white meat taken from a chicken, pounded with two and a half gills of cream, six ounces of well-reduced apple marmalade, twelve ounces of Smyrna raisins thoroughly washed in hot water, and finally six stiffly whipped egg-whites. Pour this preparation into a dome-shaped cylindrical pudding mold, well buttered and sugared. Stand the mold in a saucepan with hot water to reach to half its height and bring to a boil, then put it into a slack oven. Take out the pudding at the end of forty-five minutes and let stand five or six minutes; then unmold it on a dish and cover with a sabayon sauce (No. 3096), well flavored with Madeira, and serve more of this sauce in a sauce-boat.

(3100). HUMBOLDT PUDDING (Pouding à la Humboldt).

Cook five or six large pancakes; cover them on one side with a layer of apricot marmalade (No. 3675) and cut them up into bands each an inch and a quarter wide and through their entire length. Butter a dome-shaped cylindrical mold and fasten the pancake bands on their uncovered side against the sides of the mold, overlapping each other. Cover the pancake parings with apricot marmalade and roll them into small rolls, then cut them in half-inch long bits. Beat eight ounces of butter to a cream, add to it, one by one, four whole eggs and two whites; when this becomes frothy, put in four ounces of sugar, then four ounces of flour and four ounces of peeled almonds dried and pounded with four ounces of sugar, afterward passed through a sieve. Mix the whole properly and lastly incorporate into it three well-beaten egg-whites. Pour this preparation into the pancake-lined mold, alternating it with layers of the small rolls previously prepared; when the mold is full set it in a bain-marie and allow the water to come to a boil on the fire, then cook it in a slack oven for forty-five minutes. As soon as the pudding is done take it out and let it stand for a few moments before unmolding it on a dish, brush it over with hot apricot marmalade and serve with a sauce-boat of apricot sauce. Place two gills of apricot marmalade in a saucepan, diluting it with two gills of syrup; set it on the fire to boil up once, then strain through a fine wire sieve and add two gills of good Madeira wine.

(3101). ITALIAN PUDDING (Pouding à l'Italienne).

Soften in boiling water half a pound of Smyrna raisins and half a pound of candied orange peel cut in small dice. Place them in a vessel with half a pound of candied cherries washed in hot water and pouring over a few spoonfuls of rum leave them to marinate for one hour. Prepare a small quantity of Genoese cake preparation (No. 3239) finished with orange and spread it on a sheet of paper in a quarter of an inch thick layer, then bake it in a hot oven. As soon as done turn it over on a table, remove the paper and cover with a layer of apricot marmalade (No. 3675), then cut it up into inch and a half in diameter round pieces. Butter and sugar a cylindrical timbale mold (Fig. 150) and lay in the bottom a circle of these pieces, overlapping each other; scatter over the marinated fruits into which have been mingled a few crushed macaroons and on top dress another circle of the cake the same as the first, then more fruits and macaroons, and continue thus until the mold is full. Put into a vessel six egg-yolks, two whole eggs and four ounces of sugar, having a part of it flavored with orange; beat the whole well to mingle properly and dilute with a pint and a half of double cream and half a gill of rum; pass this through a wire sieve and pour it slowly into the mold until full, then cook the pudding in a bain-marie in a slack oven, and just when ready to serve unmold on a dish and pour over a frothy rum sauce (No. 3103), serving more of it separately.

(3102). PEACH PUDDING À LA CLEVELAND (Pouding de Pêches à la Cleveland).

Cut twenty sound peaches in four pieces; lay them in a vessel,

FIG. 579.   FIG. 580.

sprinkle over with a handful of powdered sugar and let macerate for half an hour, tossing them about at frequent intervals. Line a dome-shaped mold wider than its height with a very thin suet pudding paste (No. 2322); fill the inside with the quartered peaches, placing them in layers and bestrewing brown sugar between each one. Cover the fruits with a round flat of the paste and fasten it solidly to the sides. Close the mold with its own lid and wrap it up in a cloth, then plunge it into boiling water and let cook for an hour and a half, having it remain at a boiling degree during the whole time. Just when ready to serve remove the mold, unwrap and invert the pudding on a dish and cover it over with a Madeira sauce with peaches, serving some of it separately. For the sauce have six to eight very ripe peaches; remove the stones, crush the fruit and adding a few spoonfuls of sugar and two gills of water let cook for a few moments. Strain this sauce through a fine wire sieve and add to it a few tablespoonfuls of maraschino.

(3103). PLUM PUDDING, ST. GEORGE (Plum Pouding St. George).

Place in a vessel one pound of beef kidney suet, very dry, free of fibers and chopped up very finely; one pound of seeded Malaga raisins; one pound of currants, cleaned and washed in plenty of water; one pound of bread-crumbs, sifted through a sieve; a

quarter of a pound of candied lemon peel chopped up very fine; one pound of powdered sugar; four tablespoonfuls of flour; a quarter of an ounce of ground cinnamon; a quarter of an ounce of nutmeg and allspice; a pint of brandy and six eggs. Mix the whole well together. Dip a strong cloth, in cold water and wring it out to extract all its moisture; spread it open on a table and butter it liberally with butter softened to the consistency of cream; dredge

Fig. 581.   Fig. 582.

over with sifted flour and shake the cloth to remove the excess of flour that has failed to adhere to the butter. Lay in the center of this cloth the above prepared mixture, form it in the shape of a ball, raise up the edges of the cloth bringing the four ends together and all around so as to enclose the preparation well, then tighten and tie firmly. Have on the fire a high saucepan filled to three-quarters of its height with water; when this boils plunge in the plum pudding and let cook for three hours, then remove it from the water. Have it stand for five minutes before cutting the string; undo the cloth carefully and invert the pudding on a hot dish; besprinkle it with sugar, pour over some brandy or rum and set it on the fire; serve immediately. Have a separate sauce-boat of frothy vanilla and rum sauce to be made as follows:

Frothy Vanilla and Rum Sauce.—Chop up half a pound of beef marrow, melt it in a bain-marie, then strain through a napkin into a bowl and whip it until it begins to froth, then add four ounces of fresh butter broken in small parts, four ounces of vanilla sugar (No. 3165) and lastly, half a gill of rum; serve.

(3104). PLUMERY PUDDING (Pouding à la Plumery).

Pound four ounces of raw beef marrow, pass it through a sieve and place it in a vessel; beat it up to a cream, adding five egg-yolks and two whole eggs, one at a time. When this preparation becomes creamy add to it four ounces of powdered almonds passed through a sieve, two ounces of cracker dust, three ounces of crushed macaroons, two ounces of bread-crumbs soaked in rum, two ounces of angelica and one ounce of orange peel, both washed in hot water and cut into quarter-inch squares. When all these ingredients have been properly mixed incorporate slowly into the whole four egg-whites beaten to a very stiff froth; pour this preparation into a cylindrical buttered and sugared mold and cook it in a bain-marie in a very slack oven. Just when prepared to serve unmold the pudding on a dish, cover it with apricot marmalade (No. 3675), and serve with a sauce-boat of apricot sauce prepared with almond milk.

Apricot Sauce with Almond Milk.—Have two gills of apricot pulp, four ounces of sugar and two gills of water placed in a saucepan; stand it on the fire and allow to cook for a few moments, then strain through a fine strainer and add one gill of almond milk (No. 4); return it to the saucepan and heat the sauce without boiling; just when prepared to serve add a tablespoonful of noyau liqueur.

(3105). RICE PUDDING À LA BAGRATION (Pouding de Riz à la Bagration).

Wash half a pound of rice; blanch it properly in plenty of water, drain and put it into a saucepan with one quart of milk and half a stick of vanilla; let it cook for forty minutes in the oven, then withdraw and suppress the vanilla; add to it three ounces of sugar, two ounces of butter, a pinch of salt, six yolks and one whole egg, mixing all well together. Stir in six ounces of candied fruits cut in quarter-inch dice, such as pears, greengages, pineapples, cherries, and lastly add three well-beaten egg-whites. Butter and sugar a dome-shaped cylindrical mold; fill it four-fifths full with the preparation and lay it in a saucepan with water to half its height; place it on the fire until the water boils, then in a slack oven to cook for fifty minutes. Remove the pudding from the fire, let it stand for five minutes, then unmold on a dish and cover with English cream vanilla sauce (No. 3004), having more of it served separately.

(3106). RICE PUDDING, FRUIT SAUCE (Pouding au Riz, Sauce aux Fruits).

Wash one pound of rice; blanch and cook in two quarts of milk and cream, half of each, proceeding the same as for rice pudding (No. 3105); when done sweeten with six ounces of sugar, finish it with a grated orange peel, a handful of chopped almonds, and two ounces of butter; remove it from the fire, and when almost cold incorporate fifteen to eighteen egg-yolks, one by one, without ceasing to beat up the preparation; add also twenty ounces of candied fruits cut in quarter-inch squares, and lastly twelve to fourteen egg-whites beaten to a stiff froth. With this fill five buttered and floured molds; place them in a deep baking-pan with hot water, and poach the puddings for nearly one hour in a slack oven. At the last moment unmold on a dish, cover them liberally with apricot and kirsch sauce (No. 3001), and serve separately a sauce-boatful of Bischoff sauce; for this see fried cream Pamela (No. 3013).

(3107). SAXONY PUDDING—SOUFFLÉD (Pouding Soufflé à la Saxonne).

Sift half a pound of flour into a saucepan and dissolve it with half a pint of boiling milk, into which has been infused half a vanilla bean; mix with this four ounces of butter and four ounces of sugar; set the saucepan on the fire and stir the mixture with a spatula until it detaches from the saucepan. Then remove it from the fire and beat in four ounces of butter and four ounces of vanilla sugar; continue to stir until it attains body, and let it lose its greatest heat, then add at once ten egg-yolks, four ounces of candied fruits cut in quarter-inch dice, and six stiffly beaten egg-whites; pour this preparation into a dome-shaped mold with a tube in the center, and cook it in a bain-marie in a slack oven for forty-five minutes. As soon as done unmold the pudding on a dish, cover it over with a little apricot marmalade (No. 3675), and serve with a separate apricot sauce with noyau (No. 3100).

(3108). SCOTCH PUDDING (Pouding à l'Écossaise).

Soften twelve ounces of beef marrow at the oven door, without letting it melt. Pass it through a strainer and lay it in a bowl to beat to a cream, adding to it one by one ten egg-yolks, two whole eggs, also a pinch of salt, then put in fourteen ounces of bread-crumbs soaked in milk, two ounces of candied cherries cut in two, four ounces of candied orange and lemon peel cut in small three-sixteenth inch squares and half a gill of rum; lastly mix in ten egg-whites, beaten to a very stiff froth. Transfer this preparation into a buttered and sugared dome-shaped mold with a tube in its center; set it into a saucepan with water reaching to half its height, and place the saucepan on the fire for the water to come to a boil, then finish cooking in the oven for forty minutes. As soon as the pudding is done unmold it on a dish and cover over with apricot marmalade (No. 3675) diluted with a little Madeira wine; serve with a sauce-boatful of sauce or punch made as follows: Put in a saucepan a gill and a half of brandy, a gill and a half of rum, a gill of vanilla syrup, the peel of a lemon and of an orange and a small bit of cinnamon. Just when ready to serve heat without boiling and then set it on the fire for a few seconds to burn out the alcohol; cover the saucepan at once to extinguish the fire, and serve.

(3109). SCHILLER PUDDING (Pouding à la Schiller).

Prepare twelve to fifteen large pancakes and with some of them line a liberally buttered cylindrical mold (Fig. 150). Cover half of the remaining pancakes with a layer of apricot marmalade (No. 3675), and the other half with frangipane cream (No. 43); roll these pancakes up separately into rolls and cut them into three-quarter inch thick slices; range these in alternate layers inside the mold with a few candied cherries washed in hot water interspersed between. Put in a vessel twelve yolks and two whole eggs, also six ounces of vanilla sugar (No. 3165); beat up well and then stir in a quart of milk. Pass it through a fine wire strainer into the mold. Lay the mold in water reaching to half its height; set it on the fire and when it comes to a boil put it into a slack oven to cook for one hour; remove, let stand and unmold on a dish; brush the pudding over with apricot marmalade and serve with a sauce-boat of English cream and vanilla sauce (No. 3004).

(3110). SPANISH PUDDING (Pouding à l'Espagnole).

Put four ounces of clarified butter into a saucepan and heat it well, then add to it eight ounces of white bread-crumbs and let it cook until it becomes a fine golden color, while stirring it from time to time with a spatula; withdraw the saucepan from the fire and dilute the preparation with a gill of milk and a gill of cream and dry it for a few moments over the fire. Add to it the peel of one lemon, a pinch of salt, a tablespoonful of rum, three ounces of sugar and six egg-yolks; stir well and lastly mix in the well-beaten whites of six eggs. Butter and sugar a dome-shaped cylindrical mold, fill it up with the preparation and place it in a saucepan with boiling water to half its height; set the saucepan on the fire to have the liquid come to a boil, then withdraw it at once and push it into a slack oven so that the pudding can cook for forty-five minutes. When this is accomplished take it out and let it stand from five to six minutes; unmold on a dish and cover with an English cream vanilla sauce (No. 3004) with rum added; serve more of the sauce apart.

(3111). TYROLEAN PUDDING (Pouding à la Tyrolienne).

Soften five ounces of beef marrow, run it through a sieve into a vessel and beat it up to a cream, adding five egg-yolks and five whole eggs, one at a time. As this becomes frothy put into it six ounces of apricot marmalade (No. 3675), six ounces of grated chocolate, six ounces of lady finger crumbs soaked in a gill and three-quarters of double cream, three ounces of Smyrna raisins well cleansed and washed in hot water, and lastly beat in six very stiff egg-whites. Butter and sugar a dome-shaped mold with a cylindrical center, fill it with the preparation and place it in a bain-marie in a saucepan; bring the water to a boil, then push it into a slack oven to cook for forty to forty-five minutes; take it from the oven and let stand for a few moments before unmolding on a dish; cover over with chocolate sauce and serve more of the same separately.

Chocolate Sauce.—Dilute two ounces of chocolate with two gills of water and a gill of vanilla syrup; let boil, then strain through a fine strainer and add one gill of rich cream.

(3112). PUDDING WITH ALMONDS—LIGHT (Pouding Léger aux Amandes).

Dissolve ten ounces of fine wheat and rice flour (half of each) in one and a half pints of almond milk (No. 4). Strain this liquid into a saucepan and add to it salt, half a pound of sugar and three ounces of butter. Cook the preparation, avoid all lumps and do not cease to stir until it detaches from the saucepan, then take it off and pour it into a vessel; incorporate with it slowly twelve egg-yolks, beating them in vigorously, and then add five ounces more butter, four ounces of

Fig. 583.

finely pounded almonds, the peel of an orange, and finally nine well-beaten egg-whites. Butter some dome-shaped pudding molds, having them wider than their height, cover the interior sides with small flat round pieces of lady fingers cut out with a cutter and fill the hollow space three-quarters full with the preparation; poach the puddings for fifty minutes in a bain-marie with the vessel covered, and before removing push them into a slack oven to dry the tops. Take them out and unmold five minutes after on a hot dish; cover them lightly with an apricot sauce made with rum (No. 3001), and in each pudding insert a small hatelet composed of three graduated rounds of candied pineapple. Serve separately an apricot sauce mingled with almond milk, the same as for Plumery pudding (No. 3104). This quantity is sufficient for ten persons.

(3113). PUDDING WITH BURNT ALMONDS—SOUFFLÉD (Pouding Soufflé aux Pralines).

Sift six ounces of rice flour in a saucepan; dissolve it with a pint of boiling milk and thicken the preparation over the fire, stirring vigorously with a wooden spoon; when it detaches from the side of the saucepan take it off and add to it one ounce of butter, four ounces of burnt almonds ground to a dust and passed through a sieve, a pinch of salt, six ounces of sugar, eight egg-yolks, two tablespoonfuls of whipped cream, and finally six very stiffly whipped egg-whites. Butter and sugar a dome-shaped cylindrical mold, fill it up in layers, alternating the preparation with slices of Savoy biscuit or lady fingers soaked in maraschino and quarters of candied apricots well washed in hot water. When the mold is full set it in a bain-marie and let the water come to a boil, then finish cooking for forty minutes in a slow oven. As soon as the pudding is unmolded on a dish cover it with apricot sauce made with almond milk (No. 4) and maraschino, serving more of it in a bowl. For this sauce see light pudding with almond milk (No. 3104).

(3114). PUDDING WITH HAZEL-NUTS—SOUFFLÉD (Pouding Soufflé aux Noisettes).

Dilute in a saucepan seven or eight spoonfuls of rice fecula with four to six gills of hazel-nut milk, prepared the same as almond milk (No. 4); add to it a grain of salt and a piece of butter; thicken the preparation over the fire, stirring it about with a spoon; after it attains the consistency of a soufflé preparation remove and add to it a quarter of a pound of vanilla sugar (No. 3165) and a quarter of a pound of butter, then ten egg-yolks, one whole egg, two spoonfuls of whipped cream and four egg-whites beaten to a stiff froth. Butter a timbale mold, fill it with the preparation laid in alternate layers with slices of biscuit cut very thin, cover over with some apricot marmalade (No. 3675), and when the mold is full set it in a saucepan containing hot water to reach to half its height, then poach for three-quarters of an hour in a bain-marie. At the last moment unmold it on a dish and cover with English cream with almonds and vanilla (No. 42), serving more of the sauce (No. 3004) separately.

(3115). RICE WITH APPLES (Riz aux Pommes).

Prepare some minced apples, the same as for an apple charlotte (No. 3008), not having them too sweet. Blanch eight ounces of picked and washed rice, drain on a sieve, refresh and put it in a saucepan with some milk; cook it slowly without stirring, keeping it slightly consistent, and lastly mix in four ounces of powdered lemon sugar, a few spoonfuls of cream and a piece of butter; remove to a much slower fire in order to allow the liquid to became entirely absorbed, then take up the rice with a spoon and place it in layers on a deep dish, alternating each one with a layer of the apples, giving the whole a dome shape, and finishing with the rice. Dredge the top with cinnamon or vanilla sugar and serve at once.

Sugar Flavored with Vanilla.--Have four ounces of vanilla beans, split them in two, chop and pound them in a mortar with a pound and a half of loaf sugar until exceedingly fine, then pass through a fine hair sieve. Keep in a hermetically closed box in a dry place until needed for use.

(3116). RISSOLES WITH PRESERVES AND WITH ALMOND CREAM (Rissoles à la Confiture et à la Crème d'Amandes).

Roll out into a square layer, an eighth of an inch in thickness, one pound of fine short paste (No. 135) or puff paste parings (No. 146); cut the edges straight and range on the top at desired distances apart small balls of any kind of thick marmalade; wet the paste to form the rissoles (No. 161), and when they are cut out press down the borders of the paste with the fingers in order to diminish its thickness, then cut the rissoles again with the same pastry cutter, so as to have them all alike, and fasten the paste together. Dip them in beaten eggs, roll in bread-crumbs and plunge into hot fat. Cook them slowly, drain and roll in vanilla sugar (No. 3165), then dress on a folded napkin.

With Almond Cream.--Prepare the rissoles the same as for the above, replacing the preserves by small balls of almond cream (No. 40) placed an inch and a half from the edges and at the same distance from one another; finish them exactly the same.

(3117). SAVARIN WITH APRICOTS (Savarin aux Abricots).

Sift one pound of flour into a warm vessel, make a leaven with a quarter of the flour and half an ounce of yeast dissolved in tepid water; cover it over with a part of the flour and let rise in a mild heat. When it has risen to double its primitive volume remove from the warm place and break it up with the hand to make the sponge, giving the paste plenty of body. Mix into it gradually eight whole eggs and six separate yolks, and working in the flour knead it vigorously for ten minutes, then add slowly half a pound of melted butter, six ounces of sugar, a grain of salt, lemon peel and lastly four spoonfuls of raw cream. Take up the paste in small parts with the hands and fill one or several buttered Savarin molds three-quarters full; let rise as high as the edges in a mild temperature, then bake the cakes in a moderate oven. As soon as they are removed moisten them with syrup infused with lemon or orange peel and any desired liqueur, then drain on a dish, cover with Madeira apricot sauce, filling the hollows with hot stewed apricots. Serve an apricot sauce with Madeira apart, the same as for Humboldt pudding (No. 3100).

(3118). SOUFFLÉ OF CHESTNUTS WITH VANILLA (Soufflé de Marrons à la Vanille).

Skin half a pound of raw chestnuts, then grate them; pound three ounces of almonds with four ounces of powdered vanilla sugar (No. 3165). Beat in a bowl four ounces of fresh butter, mixing into it six or seven egg-yolks, and when the preparation is frothy add the chestnuts, sugar and almonds, then five or six beaten whites. Pour all this into a buttered soufflé pan (Fig. 182) and cook it for three-quarters of an hour in a slack oven; glaze over with sugar before removing and serve without delay.

(3119). SOUFFLÉ OF CHOCOLATE (Soufflé au Chocolat).

Melt in a saucepan at the oven door, in a little tepid water, four ounces of grated chocolate; remove and pour it into a bowl to smooth nicely; mix into it five or six spoonfuls of vanilla sugar (No. 3165), beating it in vigorously, then add four or five spoonfuls of the following preparation: Place in a tureen two tablespoonfuls of flour, a pinch of arrowroot, two tablespoonfuls of sugar and a little salt; dilute with half a gill of milk; strain into a saucepan and add two tablespoonfuls of melted butter and a little vanilla; stir on the fire until it boils and when smooth reduce till it is consistent and detaches from the pan; take out the vanilla and let partly cool. Add eight raw egg-yolks, two ounces of melted butter, four beaten whites and three spoonfuls of whipped cream. When all these ingredients are well incorporated pour the preparation into one or two soufflé pans (Fig. 182) without filling them too high. Set the pan on a small baking sheet and bake the soufflés in a slack oven from twenty to twenty-five minutes.

(3120). SOUFFLÉS IN CASES WITH VANILLA OR ORANGE—SMALL (Petits Soufflés en Caisses à la Vanille ou à l'Orange).

Put into a vessel four spoonfuls of flour, a pinch of fecula, four spoonfuls of sugar and a grain of salt; dilute with two and a half gills of milk, then strain it into a saucepan, adding a lump of butter the size of an egg and a piece of vanilla; stir on a slow fire until it comes to a boil and when smooth reduce until it detaches easily from the saucepan, then take out the vanilla and let the preparation get almost cold before stirring in another piece of butter and five to six egg-yolks one after the other, while continuing to beat briskly; lastly add the beaten whites and three spoonfuls of whipped cream. With this mixture fill some soufflé cases (Fig. 584) two-thirds full, range them on a small baking sheet and place in a slack oven to cook for twenty minutes. Serve just as quickly as they leave the oven.

Fig. 584.   Fig. 585.

With Orange.—Instead of vanilla, flavor the soufflés with two tablespoonfuls of orange sugar (No. 3165).

(3121). SOUFFLÉ OF RICE WITH MARASCHINO (Soufflé de Riz au Marasquin).

Boil six ounces of rice in plenty of water; drain and set it in a vessel and pour a little maraschino over. Prepare a vanilla soufflé preparation (No. 3120) and after the egg-whites have been mixed in, dress it in layers in a soufflé pan (Fig. 182), alternating each one with a small part of the well-drained rice. When the soufflé pan is three-quarters full place it on a baking sheet and push it into a well heated oven; three minutes later remove to split the shape of a cross on top and return it to the oven to let cook for twenty-five minutes more, glazing it over with fresh butter. Serve as soon as it is taken from the oven, as soufflés should never be left waiting to be served.

(3122). SOUFFLÉ WITH RASPBERRIES (Soufflé aux Framboises).

Place seven ounces of rather stiff raspberry jelly in a small basin and mix slowly in with it seven ounces of powdered sugar so as to obtain a consistent preparation, then incorporate one after the other four to five unbeaten egg-whites, stirring up the whole vigorously with a whisk for twenty minutes. When this is frothy and firm color it with a few drops of vegetable carmine (No. 37) and pour it into a soufflé pan (Fig. 182) to cook for forty minutes in a very slack oven. Five minutes before removing the soufflé from the oven glaze it with sugar, set it on a hot dish and cover with a large hot dish cover; serve it immediately.

(3123). TIMBALE À LA FIGARO (Timbale à la Figaro).

Cut one pound of short paste (No. 135) into four pieces; roll them on the table into long quarter-inch thick strings and dip these strings as fast as they are done in melted clarified butter; arrange them in a spiral around the inside of a timbale mold, being careful to fasten the ends securely with beaten eggs. Leave the timbale rest for half an hour in a cool place, then fill it up in alternate layers of apples cut in quarters, cooked in butter, and masked with apricot marmalade (No. 3675) and frangipane (No. 44) with almonds. Cover over with a flat of short paste, egg the surface, and set it in the oven to cook for forty-five minutes. One moment before serving turn the timbale out on a dish, cover it with hot apricot marmalade, and strew over finely chopped pistachios and almonds, then decorate the top with rosette of angelica lozenges, having a greengage in the center; surround the base of the dome with brandied geeengages. Heat the whole for ten minutes in the oven, and serve with an apricot kirsch sauce (No. 3001).

(3124). ZEPHYR OF RICE WITH PINEAPPLE (Zéphyr de Riz à l'Ananas).

Cook half a pound of blanched rice in milk; when sweetened withdraw it to a slower fire to let attain more consistency, and then finish with a large piece of fresh butter divided in pats. Ten minutes later incorporate into it two or three spoonfuls of crushed chestnuts and six egg-yolks, one after the other, and lastly the half of five beaten whites mixed with three spoonfuls of whipped cream. Add to this preparation five to six spoonfuls of candied pineapple cut in small dice, and pour the whole into a timbale mold previously buttered and glazed with fine sugar and fecula. Lay the mold in a saucepan on a small trivet with hot water reaching to a third of its height, and boil the liquid; remove it to a much lower fire or else to a slack oven, and cook the zephyr for three-quarters of an hour. Finally unmold it on a dish and surround with small slices of preserved pineapple; cover these with vanilla syrup, and serve a sauce-boat of pineapple sauce as for Roman triumvirate fritters (No. 3050).

SWEET ENTREMETS—COLD (Entremets de Douceur—Froids).

(3125). GLAZED APPLES (Pommes Glacées).

Choose a few small, even-sized apples; empty the centers with a column tube five-eighths of an inch in diameter, peel and cook them in slightly sweetened acidulated water. In order to have them remain whole it is advisable to cook scarcely boiling, and to keep them covered.

Fig. 586.

Drain and place them in a vessel, pouring a little syrup over; leave to cool. When cold drain and cover them several times with a brush dipped in lukewarm apricot marmalade (No. 3675) so that it adheres to the apples, and cover them completely; decorate around the tops with a circle of small dots of angelica. Fill the hole in the center with candied cherries or fruit jelly, such as quince, currant or apple, or use all mingled together; arrange the apples in a pyramid on a dish.

(3126). GLAZED MARMALADE OF APPLES (Marmelade de Pommes Glacée).

Cut a few good russet apples in four, peel and put them into a saucepan with a little water; dissolve on a slow fire while covered, then pass through a sieve; return the purée to the saucepan with two-thirds as much powdered sugar and a tied bunch of lemon peel. Set the saucepan on the fire and let the marmalade reduce while stirring unceasingly with a spoon. When perfect remove the lemon peel, and after it is nearly cold pour it into a dish, smooth it dome-shaped with a knife and sprinkle fine sugar over the top; glaze this with a skewer heated in the fire, cool off and surround the base with triangles of biscuit, placing a flat rosette of the same on the summit of the apples.

(3127). FROTHY PURÉE OF APPLES (Purée de Pommes Mousseuse).

Peel six fine apples, cut them up small and cook in a covered saucepan, keeping them very white and adding four spoonfuls of water, a bit of lemon peel and two cloves. When melted press them through a fine sieve, then add seven or eight dissolved gelatine leaves, the juice of four or five lemons and eight or ten ounces of powdered sugar; beat the preparation well on ice with a whip until it whitens and becomes quite frothy, then add a salpicon of candied fruits, and pour this into a mold incrusted in chopped ice. One hour later dip the mold in hot water, unmold the contents on a cold dish and pour over a cold apple syrup flavored with lemon peel.

Apple Syrup.—This syrup is made with the liquid in which apples have been cooked and half its weight of sugar added; flavor with lemon or orange peel, boil until it attains the consistency of light jelly, then strain and cool. It is now ready to be used.

(3128). BUCKET OF WAFFLES WITH CREAM (Baquet de Gaufres à la Crème).

Prepare a waffle preparation the same as for the timbale of wafers (No. 3222); spread it in a layer on a waxed baking sheet, having it about one-sixteenth of an inch in thickness, and bake it partly, then remove from the oven and cut from it twenty-five uprights, each three-quarters of an inch wide and four inches long, and two others an inch and a half wide by five and a quarter inches long; bore a hole with a thin tube five-eighths of an inch in diameter through these two, and also cut a round bottom piece six inches in diameter. As soon as all these are cut return the sheet to the oven to finish baking the waffles; when of a fine color remove and leave to get thoroughly cold on a marble. Have a timbale mold six inches in diameter; lay the round piece on the bottom and arrange the high pieces against the sides, having the two longest and bored ones exactly opposite to each other, fastening them all on with cooked sugar. When cold unmold the bucket and encircle it with two bands of almond paste (No. 125) in imitation of hoops, having one slightly above the bottom and the other a short distance from the top; slip the bucket on a dish and when ready to serve fill it full of whipped cream flavored with vanilla.

(3129). BASKET OF NOUGAT WITH CREAM (Corbeille en Nougat à la Crème).

To prepare this dessert it requires a basket mold that opens in two or three parts; oil it over with a brush. Peel half a pound of almonds, wipe dry and mince them crossways; dry in a slack heater for twenty-four hours. Put a quarter of a pound of sugar in a copper pan with the juice of two lemons; stand it on a slow fire, stir with a wooden spoon till melted and of a nice yellow tint,

Fig. 587.

then mix in the very hot almonds; take from the fire when the almonds and sugar form one mass. Put a part of this on an oiled baking sheet, roll it out thin with the blade of a knife, and then apply it to the inside surfaces of the basket mold; close and clip off all the nougat extending beyond the edges, and when very cold unmold and trim it with the nougat rings to serve as handles. Fill it with whipped cream flavored with vanilla, having fresh strawberries mingled in; stick here and there small pieces of angelica and dress the basket on a folded napkin.

(3130). BASKETS OF ORANGES WITH JELLY (Paniers d'Oranges à la Gelée).

Select twelve even-sized oranges, cut them into basket shapes, leaving a handle on the center; empty them with a vegetable spoon (Fig. 91) and around them make a small border, scoring the peel with a knife or small punch made for this purpose (see Andalusian Sherbet, No. 2321); plunge these into boiling water for a minute; remove at once and throw them into cold water to refresh, then suppress all the inside white skin so that the jelly cannot acquire any of its bitterness. Stand them upright on a baking sheet covered with chopped ice and as soon as cold fill them with orange jelly (No. 3180), but slightly thickened and colored with a little carmine; put the sheet and its contents into the ice-box so that the jelly stiffens thoroughly. Dress on a folded napkin or on a stand and trim the handles with variegated ribbons.

(3131). CHOCOLATE BAVAROIS (Bavarois au Chocolat).

Make an English cream with a pint of milk, four egg-yolks, four ounces of sugar, and half a vanilla bean, proceeding the same as for No. 3135; as soon as finished pour it slowly over two ounces of chocolate dissolved in a few spoonfuls of water, then add one ounce of gelatine melted in a little water. As soon as the chocolate and gelatine are both well dissolved strain the whole through a fine strainer into a tin basin and set it on the ice, stirring constantly until cold, and when it begins to thicken take it off and incorporate three pints of whipped cream, having it firm and well drained. Fill a jelly mold incrusted on ice with this preparation; let the bavarois harden for two hours, and when serving dip the mold quickly into hot water and invert on a cold dish.

(3132). BAVAROIS IN SURPRISE (Bavarois en Surprise).

Coat a jelly mold incrusted in pounded ice with maraschino jelly (No. 3186), and decorate the bottom and sides with white split almonds, then coat the mold once more with a thick layer of chocolate bavarois preparation (No. 3131); as soon as this is set fill the hollow center with a vanilla bavarois, into which has been mixed a few spoonfuls of freshly peeled and cut up pistachios. Lay a round of paper over and cover with a deep lid filled with chopped ice; leave the bavarois to get thoroughly cold for an hour and a half. Just when ready to serve dip it speedily into hot water and turn it over on a cold dish. Surround the base with small Genoese cakes (No. 3307) iced with strawberry fondant (No. 3652) flavored with kirsch, and decorate with a rosette of halved pistachios.

(3133). BAVAROIS WITH MERINGUES (Bavarois aux Meringues).

Prepare a vanilla bavarois, the same as for No. 3135; pour it into a dozen oval ballotine molds and set them in the ice-box to have their contents get quite hard. When ready to serve unmold the bavarois, and range them in a circle on a dish, keeping them a slight distance apart. On either side of each one place two small meringue shells (No. 116) well scooped out and very dry.

(3134). RASPBERRY BAVAROIS (Bavarois aux Framboises).

Put into a bowl one pint of raspberry pulp strained through a tammy, dilute it with three or four gills of cold, thick syrup flavored with lemon and an equal quantity of clarified isinglass. Add to this preparation the strained juice of two oranges. Put a small part on ice to judge of its solidity (it must be rather thick than otherwise), and when perfect pour it into a small untinned copper pan, and thicken it on ice while stirring. As soon as it has acquired the consistency of a thick, smooth sauce, take it off and add to it a pint and a half of firm and well-drained whipped cream. Use this preparation to fill either a jelly mold (Fig. 149) or a plain cylindrical mold incrusted in chopped ice; cover with a piece of paper and lay on a deep cover, filling it with more chopped ice, then leave to harden for one hour. Unmold on a cold dish after dipping the mold in hot water. Various bavaroises of different fruit pulps can be prepared the same way, such as pineapple, mandarins, currants, almonds and fresh nuts. The mold may be coated on the inside with a light layer of oil of sweet almonds, thus avoiding the necessity of dipping it in hot water.

(3135). VANILLA BAVAROIS (Bavarois à la Vanille).

Boil one pint of milk with half a split vanilla bean. Whip four egg-yolks well in a basin with six ounces of sugar, dilute them with the boiling milk, and pour the whole into a saucepan to stir over a moderate fire without letting it boil. Remove the cream from the fire as soon as it thickens, take out the vanilla, and add two gelatine leaves (one ounce) previously softened in cold water.

When this is melted pass the whole through a fine wire sieve into a tin basin and leave to cool on ice. As it begins to thicken mix in about three pints of cream, whipped and drained. Fill a jelly mold (Fig. 149) incrusted on ice with this, put on it a round of paper, and then let the bavarois harden for two hours. At the last moment dip the mold in hot water, and invert it on a cold dish.

(3136). BAVAROIS WITH CHESTNUTS (Bavarois aux Marrons).

Suppress the shells from one pound of good, fresh chestnuts; put them with some water into a saucepan and let cook on a slow fire for two hours, being careful to replace the black liquid by clean boiling water. After the chestnuts are tender, drain, skin and pound them in a mortar with half a pint of syrup at twenty-five degrees, to reduce them to a fine paste, and press this paste through a sieve into a tin basin. Put four egg-yolks into a bowl and beat them up with four ounces of sugar; dilute with a pint of boiling milk into which has been added half a vanilla bean; pour this into a saucepan and place it on the fire, beating it with a whip until it begins to thicken; then remove at once and add an ounce and a half of gelatine, softened in cold water; when this is dissolved, pass the preparation through a fine wire sieve and add it to the chestnuts in the basin, putting it on pounded ice and beating well till cold. As soon as it begins to thicken incorporate into it a quart and a half of firmly whipped and drained cream; then pour it into a channeled cylindrical mold (Fig. 148) incrusted in ice. Let it harden for an hour and a half. Just when serving dip the mold quickly into hot water and invert the cream on a cold dish, surrounding the base with fine glazed chestnuts.

(3137). CREAM BISCUIT—SMALL (Petits Biscuits à la Crème).

Take some oval-shaped lady fingers and as many more shaped round like a bouchée; cover the edges with a thin layer of apricot marmalade (No. 3675); soak the oval ones lightly with maraschino and dress them in a circle on the outer edge of a deep dish; in the center of this place the round biscuits in intermingled layers after they have also been soaked in maraschino, and cover each one of these with a rather consistent English cream (No. 42) prepared with lemon peel and beaten for seven or eight minutes on ice, then mixed with a few spoonfuls of whipped cream.

(3138). BLANC-MANGE À LA SMOLENSKA (Blanc-Manger à la Smolenska).

Soften one ounce of gelatine in cold water and dissolve it in a gill of orange syrup; add to it a pint of filbert milk, made like almond milk (No. 4), substituting filberts for almonds, and strain into a tin basin. Let this preparation become cold on ice, and just as it begins to thicken incorporate about three pints of well-whipped cream. Pour this into a dome-shaped mold, cover with a sheet of paper, close hermetically with a lid, and chill in lightly salted ice. One hour will suffice for this operation. Unmold on a cold dish and serve.

(3139). STRAWBERRY BLANC-MANGE (Blanc-Manger aux Fraises).

Pound half a pound of freshly peeled almonds, a few at a time; dilute with a quart of cold milk and press the whole slowly through a napkin held by two persons, so as to extract

FIG. 588.

all the liquid thoroughly; mix into this almond milk three-quarters of a pound of powdered sugar, some lemon peel or half a split vanilla bean, and a quarter of an hour later put into the liquid fifteen clarified gelatine leaves. Strain and try a little on ice to judge of its strength. Incrust a plain cylindrical mold (Fig. 150) on ice, coat it with clear jelly mixed with strawberry or orange juice and filtered through blotting paper. Stir on ice two-thirds of the blanc-mange to thicken it slightly, using a spoon, and as soon as perfect mix in a fine salpicon of candied pine-apple; pour this into the coated mold and leave it stand for one hour. Thicken the remainder of the preparation on ice, and with it fill five small timbale molds (No. 2, Fig. 137), also incrusted on a thick bed of ice spread over the bottom of a deep sautoir. Three-quarters of an hour later empty out the centers of the small molds with a tin tube dipped in hot water; to remove these pieces it is only necessary to heat the bottom of the molds slightly; replace them on ice and fill the center with some of the same preparation mingled with strawberry juice (No. 3673); let this get hard. Unmold the small timbales and cut each one across in three parts. Dip the large mold quickly into hot water; invert on a cold dish and surround the base with the rings, then fill up the hollow with Chantilly cream (No. 50), flavored with almonds, having it dome-shaped. Surround this dome with a few large strawberries, each one cut in two and dressed flat to resemble a rosette. Serve at the same time a bowlful of strawberry purée sweetened with syrup, having it very cold.

(3140). CAROLINA BORDER WITH CHAMPAGNE (Bordure Caroline au Champagne).

Make an apricot " pain " preparation (No. 3194) a little thicker than usual, into which add the same quantity of rice cooked with cream and vanilla (No. 160), and a few spoonfuls of whipped cream (No. 50); pour it into a Savarin mold, incrusted in pounded ice. Beside this, prepare and mold a macédoine jelly with champagne the same as for No. 3179, having it in a dome the same diameter at the bottom as the hollow in the Savarin mold; put this macédoine in the ice-box to stiffen. One moment before serving unmold the border on a cold dish and in the center place a pad of Genoese cake (No. 3239), reaching three-quarters to the top; into this unmold the champagne macédoine and surround the base with a circle of croûtons made of ribboned jelly (No. 3184).

(3141). CHÂTEAU FRAMBOISÉ (Château Framboisé).

Fasten a round layer of office paste (No. 143) on a dish and on it place a charlotte mold half an inch narrower than the paste. Prepare a cream cake paste (No. 132) with five ounces of butter, three gills of water, seven ounces of flour, a spoonful of sugar, lemon peel, a grain of salt and five eggs. Put this paste into a socket pocket (Fig. 179), and put it on a baking sheet in the shape of thin even eclairs as long as the mold is high; then bake them in a slack oven until dry, then allow to cool. After the cakes are detached from the sheet, keep them warm for a few moments. When cold, open and fill them with raspberry jam (No. 3695) pushed through a cornet, and glaze over with sugar cooked to "crack" (No. 171). As this becomes cold dip one end and one side into the same sugar so as to enable them to stand upright on the layer of office paste around the mold. When the sugar is cold lift out the mold and fill the inside of the case with a raspberry bavarois preparation, the same as for No. 3134, thickened on ice, and lastly having a salpicon of candied pineapple added to it.

(3142). CHARLOTTE BENGALIAN (Charlotte Bengalienne).

Cook a flat of Genoese paste (No. 3239), having it about three-eighths of an inch thick; invert it on a sheet of paper, pare off the upper crust and divide it into two bands, each to be two and three-quarters inches wide; cut one of these bands into short uprights slightly inclined toward the right, having them half an inch wide, and the other band the same width, only inclined toward the left. Put a round piece of paper in the bottom of a charlotte mold, against its sides range a row of these uprights, inclining them according to their cut and alternating those with crusts with those without them. On this first row range a second the same way, only inclining the uprights in the opposite direction. Fill the charlotte with a banana "pain" preparation (No. 3195), and let harden in the ice-box for an hour and a half. Unmold the dessert on a dish, and just when ready to serve place a spun sugar ornament on top.

(3143). CHARLOTTE OF CALVILLE APPLES (Charlotte de Pommes de Calville).

Cut in four pieces eight or ten Calville apples; peel and cook them in a covered saucepan with a little water, very little sugar, a bit of lemon peel and half a vanilla bean. When done and all the moisture is evaporated, press them through a sieve. Cover the bottom of a charlotte mold with lady finger biscuits, or else butter biscuit for charlotte, cooked on a baking sheet covered with paper, three-eighths of an inch thick and cut up into long triangles, and form them into a rosette without any open space whatever between the pieces. From the same biscuits cut some even upright pieces three inches wide and the same height as the mold, which should be kept on ice. Pour the apple pulp into a round-bottomed pan and dilute with a gill of syrup mingled with a sheet and a half of gelatine that has been softened and dissolved. Stir the preparation on ice to thicken, and as soon as it begins to set pour in quickly two or three spoonfuls of good rum and then a quart of whipped cream. Two minutes after turn this into the charlotte mold and surround it with chopped ice, leaving it thus for one hour, and when needed unmold the charlotte on a folded napkin.

(3144). CHARLOTTE À LA METTERNICH (Charlotte à la Metternich)

Prepare a paste made by beating three whole eggs in a basin, and when creamy add half a pound of sugar, as much sifted flour, a pinch of fecula and some orange sugar (No. 3165). The paste should be quite firm. Then force it through a pocket on a buttered and floured baking sheet, having the pieces resemble lady fingers all of the same size, and bake in a moderate oven. Detach them from the sheet and cut one end off of about forty and leave till cold leaning against a support, so as to have them slightly bent on the uncut ends. Dip the cut end of each biscuit into sugar cooked to "small crack" (No. 171), drain it off and fasten the cakes upright against the thickness of a round flat of office paste; fasten each piece with cooked sugar, overlapping them slightly so that they form a pretty basket spread out open on the top. When the sugar is quite cold dress the basket on a dish and fill it with chestnut purée sweetened with vanilla sugar (No. 3165) and then mingled with whipped cream. Surround the base with candied chestnuts dipped in sugar cooked to "small crack."

(3145). CHARLOTTE RUSSE (Charlotte Russe).

Lay a round sheet of white paper at the bottom of a charlotte mold and line it all around with well-pared lady fingers (No. 3377). Boil a pint of milk with half a split vanilla bean; beat up in a vessel six egg-yolks with six ounces of sugar and dilute the preparation with the boiling milk; pour it at once into the saucepan and thicken over a moderate fire without letting it come to a boil. Then take out the vanilla and add two leaves of gelatine softened in cold water then melted in a gill of boiling water. Run the whole through a fine Chinese strainer into a vessel and leave to cool until it begins to thicken slightly. Then mix with it the volume of three pints of whipped cream and pouring it at once into the charlotte mold cover with another round of paper and place the mold on ice for an hour and a half. When ready to use invert the charlotte on a cold dish covered with a napkin, remove the upper paper and place on top a cover, made with the same paste as the lady fingers, cut the same dimension as the charlotte, icing it with a white vanilla icing (No. 102) and decorate with a handsome design of preserved fruits or with royal icing.

(3146). CHARLOTTE WITH STRAWBERRIES OR RASPBERRIES (Charlotte aux Fraises ou aux Framboises).

Cut a few large lady fingers or charlotte biscuits (No. 3377) into long triangles so as to be able to place them in the shape of a rosette in the bottom of a charlotte mold, pressing them down on their glazed side; cut out the center with a pastry cutter one and a quarter inches in diameter; replace this cut-out piece with a round of biscuit cut with the same cutter; then cut off the ends and sides of a few of the same biscuits so as to stand them upright against the sides of the mold, pressing them close to each other. Incrust the mold in ice. Strain first through a sieve and then through a tammy about two pounds of strawberries or raspberries; sweeten this pulp with some thick syrup flavored with orange peel and mixed with about two gelatine leaves or clear melted calf's foot jelly (No. 104); stir the preparation on ice and as soon as it thickens incorporate into it slowly the volume of a pint and a half of very firm, well-drained and slightly sweetened whipped cream. Fill up the mold with this and let harden for one hour on ice. At the last moment dip the mold into tepid water and invert the charlotte on a napkin.

(3147). CHESTNUTS WITH CREAM (Marrons à la Crème).

Shell a few dozen sound chestnuts; scald them in order to remove the inner skin, then cook them very slowly in milk containing a piece of vanilla bean. When done all the liquid ought to be evaporated. Rub them through a sieve to make a purée. Put this purée into a saucepan with half its weight of sugar; work the paste on a slow fire until it becomes consistent and detaches from the saucepan; leave it till partly cold, then run a little of it at a time through a coarse sieve, pressing it down with a large spoon so that it falls like vermicelli; lift it up with a palette, dress it in a circle on the bottom of a dish and in the center build a pyramid of whipped cream, sweetened and flavored with vanilla.

(3148). CORNETS OF ORANGE CREAM (Cornets, Oublies, Plaisirs de Crème à l'Orange).

Pound eight ounces of shelled and peeled almonds with eight ounces of sugar and four egg-whites to obtain a fine paste; add to it two ounces of vanilla sugar (No. 3165), two ounces of flour and eight lightly beaten egg-whites. Dress this paste on a waxed baking sheet, laying it with a table-spoonful into thin round wafers four inches in diameter, and bake them in a hot oven When of a fine golden color remove them from the oven and roll them around some tin cornet forms and leave till cold. Dress in a pyramid on a dish covered with a napkin and fill each one with whipped cream flavored with orange.

(3149). CREAM BAIN-MARIE—MOLDED (Crème au Bain-Marie Moulée).

Put into a bright copper pan two spoonfuls of powdered sugar, stir it on a slow fire until it becomes a fine yellow color, then pour it into the bottom of a low charlotte mold and let get cold. Break seven or eight eggs in a bowl with five or six yolks; beat them up for two minutes, then dilute with a quart of milk, adding ten ounces of powdered sugar and a little lemon peel. Ten minutes later strain it twice through a sieve. Butter the sides of the mold, pour the prepara-tion in, place it in a saucepan on a small trivet and pour hot water around to reach up to half the height of the mold, then bring to a boil; remove the saucepan to a slower fire, and cover it over; place some hot cinders on the saucepan lid and let poach for one hour at least without allow-ing the water to boil. Remove the saucepan and let the cream get partly cold before taking it from the water, then unmold on a dish.

(3150). MALAKOFF CREAM (Crème Malakoff).

Have eighteen to twenty ounces of Genoese cake (No. 3239) or biscuit (No. 3231) cut into not too thick slices. Cut up some candied fruits, such as apricots, greengages and pineapple, in small dice, adding whole candied cherries. With seven or eight egg-yolks, a pint of milk and ten ounces of sugar prepare an English cream (No. 42); when thick and nearly cold mix with it four spoonfuls of dissolved gelatine, strain and stir on ice to reduce it to the correct consistency (it must be very light); then mix with it five or six spoonfuls of whipped cream. Incrust a soufflé pan (Fig. 182) on ice. Soak the sliced biscuit half with rum and the other half with kirsch or Curaçoa; spread them in layers in the pan and pour the cream over; bestrew with the candied fruits, and repeat until the pan is entirely full and forms a dome on top; keep it on ice for half an hour. Cover the dome with a thin coat of apricot marmalade (No. 3675), then cover with sweetened and flavored whipped cream; decorate with the same cream, and place the pan on a napkin to serve at once.

(3151). CREAM OF RICE WITH ANGELICA (Crème de Riz à l'Angélique).

Pick and wash four ounces of good rice and cook it till tender (keeping the grains whole) with a pint and a half of milk into which has been added half a split vanilla bean; pour it at once into a basin. Put into another vessel six egg-yolks, stir in six ounces of powdered sugar, and dilute with half a pint of boiling milk; pour this into a saucepan to thicken over the fire, and then add two ounces of gelatine softened in cold water, and as soon as the gelatine is dissolved strain the whole over the rice and mix well without stirring the rice more than necessary. At the same time incorporate four ounces of angelica previously washed in hot water, cut in small three-sixteenths of an inch dice, and steeped in maraschino. Set the preparation on ice to get thoroughly cold, and as soon as it begins to thicken stir in as much whipped cream; pour the whole into a plain cylindrical mold (Fig. 150), and keep it on ice for two hours. Unmold on a cold dish, and garnish around with lady bouchées (No. 3376).

(3152). SPANISH CREAM (Crème à l'Espagnole).

Have eight egg-yolks in a vessel and mix in with them eight ounces of sugar; dilute with a quart of boiling milk, thicken on the fire, and remove at once to add to it two ounces of gelatine softened in cold water; leave it to cool off partly; now strain it into a tin basin, adding about half a pint of fine apricot marmalade (No. 3675), diluted with a gill of rum. Have this preparation thicken on ice, mixing in with it one pint of whipped cream, and then pour it immediately into a jelly mold incrusted on ice. Unmold the cream when ready, and surround the base with triangular cuts of sweet jelly (No. 106).

(3153). TUTTI-FRUTTI CREAM (Crème Tutti-Frutti).

Cut a fine salpicon of preserved fruits in three-sixteenths of an inch dice pieces, such as peaches, apricots, pears, almonds, a little angelica, and whole candied cherries (demi-sucre), if small (if large cut in two). Sprinkle a little maraschino over, and leave to marinate for one hour. Have the volume of two quarts of whipped cream, add to it a gill of strawberry pulp, into which has been mixed a little melted gelatine, place it on ice and as soon as it begins to thicken add the fruits; stir them in very slowly, and pour the whole into a cylindrical timbale mold; cover it hermetically, cement the joints well with paste, and set it on lightly salted ice, leaving it to freeze for an hour and a half. When ready dip the mold quickly into hot water, and invert the cream on a cold dish; surround the base with a circle of brandied greengages and lozenges of angelica.

(3154). CREAM WITH CHERRIES (Crème aux Cerises).

Drain on a sieve a quart of very firm whipped cream sweetened and flavored with lemon. Remove the stones from some large, black, sweet and sound cherries; stew them with powdered sugar, then leave till cold; drain their syrup into a pan and let reduce until it becomes thick. Cover the bottom of a china dish with a layer of soft macaroons broken in pieces, spread the cherries over, and mask these with another ounce of macaroons; on this dress the cream in a dome; smooth and decorate through with the cornet, and serve the syrup separately.

(3155). CREAM WITH LEMON PEEL IN POTS (Pots de Crème aux Zestes de Citron).

Fill eight small cream pots, half with cream and half with raw milk. Beat up in a bowl eight whole eggs and six more yolks, add five ounces of powdered sugar, a bit of grated lemon peel and a grain of salt; dilute slowly with the cream and milk; strain the liquid twice through a sieve and with it fill a dozen cream pots; place them in a flat saucepan with hot water reaching to half their height, and heat the water until it reaches boiling point. Then immediately remove the saucepan to a very slow fire so that the water only simmers twenty-five to thirty minutes while covered. Leave them in this until the cream becomes nearly cold, having withdrawn it from the fire. Wipe off the pots and dress them on a dish.

(3156). CROWN À LA CAMPER (Couronne à la Camper).

Coat a border mold with maraschino jelly (No. 3186); fill it with a preparation the same as for pain " of chestnut à la Béotie (No. 3196), and leave to get quite cold on ice. Unmold when very firm on an exceedingly cold dish; fill the center of the crown three-quarters full with Bar-le-duc jelly and finish filling with whipped cream flavored with maraschino, having it slightly sweetened; arrange this in a dome and decorate it through the cornet with some of the same cream; place it in an ice-box for one hour, then serve.

(3157). CROWN À LA CHOISEUL (Couronne à la Choiseul).

Cook in a plain shallow and narrow border mold some almond biscuit, the same as for No. 3229. Unmold it on a small baking sheet and let get cold. Then cover over with apricot marmalade (No. 3675) and decorate it all around with fancy cuts of candied fruits. Incrust in pounded ice another border mold more fanciful and slightly wider than the one used for the biscuit; decorate the bottom of it with candied fruits and cover this with a layer of orange jelly (No. 3180). When hard slip the biscuit into this mold upside down, and fill the empty space between the mold and the biscuit with more of the cold jelly. One hour after dip the mold in hot water and wipe and invert the dessert on a cold dish; fill the center with a pyramid of quartered oranges pared to the pulp, the pith and seeds extracted and then macerated in sugar. Dress this pyramid in layers, pouring some thick orange peel syrup between each one.

(3158). CROWN PRINTANIÈRE (Couronne Printanière).

Butter a large Savarin mold, line it with fine flawn paste (No. 135), and cut this off just level with the edge of the mold; cover over the inside with buttered paper and fill it up with cherry pips or dry rice to hold the paste in shape, and cook the crust to a fine color; empty it out as soon as done, unmold and brush over with beaten eggs, push it into a quick oven to attain a good golden color, then leave till cold. Make a fresh fruit macédoine composed of candied cherries (demi-sucre), strawberries and raspberries, quarters of well-pared oranges and a few red currants; besprinkle these fruits with powdered sugar, pour over some maraschino and let macerate for one hour. One moment before serving cover the inside of the croustade with apricot jam, and filling it level with the top with the fruits mask them with currant jelly (No. 3670) and slip it on a dish. Pile the center high with whipped cream and arrange around the crown a circle of handsome greengages and candied cherries (demi-sucre), then serve.

(3159). CUSTARD IN A DISH (Creme au Lait Dans un Plat).

Break four whole eggs in a tinned basin; add six ounces of powdered sugar; flavor either with vanilla, lemon or orange peel or else orange flower water or coffee, according to taste; whip into this one pint of boiling milk, into which has been infused the vanilla, lemon or orange peel or else coffee beans; strain all through a fine sieve, and with this preparation fill a china pie dish (Fig. 183); put it into a sautoir with a little boiling water on the bottom, and let cook in a slow oven from forty to fifty minutes; as soon as the custard is firm take it from the sautoir and leave stand to cool. When serving, a bed of whipped cream may be placed on top, flavored the same as the custard, and decorate it through a cornet.

(3160). CUSTARD OR BAIN-MARIE CREAM (Creme au Bain-Marie).

Break five whole eggs in a vessel, add three yolks, six ounces of sugar (powdered), grated lemon and orange peel and a grain of salt. Dilute with two gills of milk and two gills of cream, beat up the preparation, strain it several times through a sieve, then pour it into a soufflé pan (Fig. 182) or simply into a china pie dish (Fig. 183). Stand this vessel in a pan containing boiling water and push it in a slack oven to bake. Take it out after forty-five or fifty minutes. As soon as the cream is firm take it out and leave cool. Just when ready to serve unmold it on a cold dish, and dress over the top some whipped cream flavored with lemon.

Another way.—Have one pint of milk and one pint of raw cream, six eggs and eight yolks, half a pound of powdered sugar, one grain of salt and either some orange-flower water, zests or vanilla. Dilute with the milk and cream and strain through a sieve; put this preparation into a buttered mold in a saucepan with boiling water reaching to half its height; push it into a slack oven and when the cream is firm to the touch unmold it on a dish.

(3161). CUSTARD OR BAIN-MARIE CREAM WITH CARAMEL (Creme Bain-Marie au Caramel).

Melt half a pound of sugar in a pan with the juice of a lemon; as soon as of a light golden color pour a third part of it into the bottom of a plain timbale mold and leave to cool. Break six whole eggs in a basin, add eight yolks and beat together with half a pound of sugar; dilute with a quart of good milk and a quarter of a gill of orange flower water or vanilla and strain this preparation two or three times through a colander, and pour it into the timbale mold, then poach the cream in a bain-marie in a slack oven for an hour and a quarter; remove and cool off in the bain-marie. When ready detach it from the mold with the blade of a small knife and turn it over on a cold dish; cover with a caramel syrup made with the remainder of the caramel.

(3162). BAIN-MARIE CREAM WITH VIRGIN COFFEE (Creme Bain-Marie au Cafe Vierge).

Torrefy half a pound of coffee and when done throw it into a saucepan containing a quart of boiling milk; close hermetically and leave to infuse for half an hour. Then pass the milk through a fine sieve and add to it a gill of rich cream. Put eight yolks and six whole eggs into another vessel, beat them with half a pound of sugar and dilute with the infusion of coffee; strain this preparation two or three times through a wire sieve and then pour it into a lightly buttered and sugared timbale mold. Bake the cream for an hour and a quarter in a bain-marie in a slack oven and as soon as done remove and leave it to cool in the water of the bain-marie. When ready to serve detach it all around with the blade of a small knife, invert it on a cold dish and pour over an English cream (No. 42) prepared with coffee.

(3163). SNOW EGGS OR FLOATING ISLANDS (Oeufs a la Neige).

Prepare an English cream (No. 42) with six egg-yolks, seven ounces of sugar, a quart of milk, lemon peel and a grain of salt; strain it several times, then let get cold. Beat up five or six egg-whites to a very stiff froth and incorporate into them very delicately seven ounces of fine lemon-flavored sugar (No. 3165). Boil some water in a deep sautoir, remove it to one side, mold the beaten whites with a large spoon, as explained in No. 155, and let the preparation fall into the sautoir, retaining the shape of the spoon; turn them over carefully. As soon as these whites become hard remove them with a skimmer and drain on a cloth spread over a sieve; when cold take them up one by one to pare and dress in a pyramid on a cold dish; cover them lightly with some of the cold English cream, serving the remainder separately.

These eggs can be poached in sweetened milk flavored with vanilla instead of water, using the milk to make the sauce by adding a few egg-yolks.

(3164). SNOW EGGS MOLDED (Œufs à la Neige Moulés).

Take a cylindrical mold having wide channels; butter it with clarified butter and glaze over with sugar. Beat up five or six egg-whites to a stiff snow with a grain of salt, adding slowly to it half a pound of powdered sugar, a part of it flavored with lemon peel. With this preparation fill the glazed mold and set in a saucepanful of boiling water to reach to half its height; poach in a slack oven until it becomes firm, and lastly unmold on a dish; cover the bottom of this with a little English cream flavored with lemon (No. 42) and serve more of it separately.

(3165). TO FILTER FRUIT JUICES, TO FLAVOR SYRUPS WITH ZEST AND TO FLAVOR SUGAR WITH ZEST OR VANILLA (Pour Filtrer les Sucs de Fruits, Pour Parfumer les Sirops aux Zestes, Pour Parfumer le Sucre aux Zestes et à la Vanille).

To Filter Fruit Juices.—Orange and lemon juices are those most frequently filtered, either through a filtering paper and a glass funnel, or through unsized paper, mashed up, washed and converted into a pulp, then spread in layers on a clean sieve. To filter raspberry and currant juices in large quantities use the felt straining bag, as represented for filtering jellies (Fig. 50).

To Flavor Syrup with Zest.—Infusions are made of lemon, orange, mandarin or Seville orange peel. First peel the fruits with a small kitchen knife, being careful not to cut off any of the white part, as this is always bitter. To flavor a syrup with these peels they need only to be macerated for twenty-five minutes in a little tepid water; add this infusion with the zest to some cold syrup; after remaining in the syrup twenty-five minutes strain through a fine sieve.

To Flavor Sugar with Zest.—To flavor sugar with fruit peels, rub the fruits on a piece of loaf sugar, and at once grate off the colored damp parts of the sugar with a knife; put this on sheets of paper, and set it in the air to dry, then crush with a rolling pin and pass through a fine sieve.

To Flavor Sugar with Vanilla.—Cut the vanilla beans into small pieces, pound them with the loaf sugar, using one pound of sugar for two ounces of vanilla; sift the sugar through a fine sieve and put it away in closed glass jars.

(3166). FLAMRI OF APPLES (Flamri aux Pommes).

For this dessert employ ten ounces of sugar, one glassful of water, eight to ten apples and a small tied bunch of lemon peel. Dissolve the sugar in the water and cook it to large ball (No. 171); add half the apples peeled and minced, and boil the whole slowly for ten to twelve minutes, then put in the remainder of the peeled apples and the lemon peel. Stir around at frequent intervals, and when the sugar has again attained the same degree (the large ball), suppress the peel and pour the preparation into a dome-shaped mold dipped in cold water; keep this for twelve hours in a cool place. Unmold on a cold dish; stick on the top small fillets of almonds lightly roasted in the oven, and cover the bottom of the dish with either rum syrup or whipped cream.

(3167). FLAMRI OF CREAM (Flamri à la Crème).

Pour into a saucepan one quart of white wine and two glassfuls of water; add a bunch of aromatics and a grain of salt; let the liquid come to a boil, then incorporate into it eight ounces of good semolina; continue to cook for a quarter of an hour on the side of the range; when done sweeten with eight ounces of powdered sugar, add a piece of lemon peel and keep the preparation off the fire for ten minutes; let get cold, stirring from time to time. Incorporate slowly into this preparation about two glassfuls of good double cream, beating it vigorously on ice; pour it into a charlotte mold dipped in cold water and let get firm on ice for one hour. Unmold on a cold dish and serve with a sweetened purée of red fruits, either strawberries or raspberries.

(3168). FLAMRI OF SEMOLINA (Flamri de Semoule).

Boil two quarts of milk; incorporate slowly into it half a pound of semolina, so as to obtain a light preparation, then cook it while stirring for twelve to fifteen minutes; when creamy mix in a pound of sugar and a pinch of salt; cook again for ten minutes, then take from the fire and quickly add six to seven beaten whites with a little sugar stirred in; work the preparation with a whip so that it combines well, and put it back on the fire, while stirring steadily. Watch the preparation attentively so as to remove it at the first signs of a boil, then mix in an ounce of grated bitter almonds. Fill two or three molds to the top with this, having them simply dipped in cold water and still wet in the inside; let cool off for at least six hours in a very cold place, or in the ice-box, and unmold the contents on dishes; cover the bottoms with a sweetened raw raspberry pulp.

(3169). APPLE FLAWN—LATTICED (Flan de Pommes Grillé).

Prepare a flawn ring the same as for an apricot flawn (No. 3170); fill it with well-reduced apple marmalade (No. 3674) flavored with lemon peel. Roll out some parings of puff paste (No. 146) to a sixteenth of an inch in thickness; cut it into narrow strips or bands three-sixteenths of an inch wide. Dampen the edges of the flawn and lay over the strips, leaving a three-eighths of an inch space between each one; fasten well and cut away any surplus without stretching the paste. Moisten the first row of strips with a brush, arrange another row over slightly on the bias to form lozenges; fasten them also to the edge, having the whole form an uniform lattice work; egg twice and cook in a hot oven for one hour. After removing dust over with fine powdered sugar, and again put in the oven for a few minutes to glaze.

(3170). APRICOT, PEACH, PLUM OR NECTARINE FLAWN (Flan d'Abricots, de Pêches, de Prunes ou de Brugnons).

With some flawn paste (No. 135) line a flawn ring in the following manner: Butter the ring, roll out the paste to an eighth of an inch in thickness, and lay it in the ring so that it has the same

Fig. 589.

Fig. 590.

thickness throughout, pressing it against the sides to equalize it well. Cut off the paste a little above the height of the ring, and with this surface form a ridge, pinching it all around on top and outside. Divide some apricots in two, peel and dress them in a circle, one overlapping the other, inside the flawn; place the cracked and peeled kernels here and there among the fruit, bestrew with fine sugar and cook in a moderate oven; remove, unmold and brush over with a consistent syrup flavored with kirsch, then serve.

The apricots may be replaced by peaches, plums or nectarines, proceeding exactly the same.

(3171). CHERRY FLAWN (Flan aux Cerises).

After lining the flawn ring the same as the apricot flawn (No. 3170), fill it with fine, ripe, sour cherries, first removing the pips and arranging them so that the holes caused by the removal of these pips lie underneath; dredge with sugar, bake in a moderate oven; when done cover with currant jelly (No. 3670) diluted in a little syrup. Take the pie from the ring, leave to cool, and when serving pour over more of the currant jelly diluted as before.

(3172). FRUIT FLAWN (Flan de Fruits).

Have a flawn ring lined with flawn paste (No. 135); raise the edges to form a ridge, pinching this evenly; prick the bottom, egg the ridge twice and line the inside with buttered paper; fill with very dry rice and cook in a moderate oven. Empty and cover the bottom with fine apple marmalade (No. 3674) reduced with apricot; on top lay some white halved apples cooked in syrup and properly drained, some white compoted halved pears, strawberries, cherries, grapes or any other kind of fine green and red fruits; pour vanilla syrup over, and cover with apple jelly (No. 3668), having previously poured it in a very thin layer on a plate the same size as the flawn. To remove this jelly from the plate press a sheet of paper of larger dimensions than the plate over it, detach the jelly from the plate all around with the tip of a knife and lift the jelly by carefully raising one side of the paper. Invert this on the pie, wet the paper and lift it off without the jelly.

(3173). GOOSEBERRY FLAWN (Flan aux Groseilles Vertes).

Line some flawn rings the same as for apricot flawns (No. 3170); cut off with the tip of a small knife all the stalks and stems of some gooseberries; arrange them inside the flawn, one beside the other, very close together; bestrew plentifully with powdered sugar and cook in a hot oven. As soon as it is done remove, cool and cover with a layer of apple jelly (No. 3668) diluted in a little thick syrup.

(3174). MERINGUE FLAWN (Flan Meringué).

Line a flawn ring with flawn paste (No. 135); raise the edges and leave to repose for half an hour. Make a frangipane cream (No. 44), well flavored with vanilla; as soon as cold fill the pie with it as far as the top, then push it into a hot oven; remove when baked, cool and cover the top with a thin coating of apricot marmalade (No. 3675); cover it all with meringue (No. 140). Smooth this with a knife and decorate with some more of it pushed through a cornet; bestrew the entire surface lightly with icing sugar, set it in a slack oven to color the meringue, then decorate through a cornet with currant jully (No. 3670) or apple jelly (No. 3668), placing it inside the decorations, representing round or oval rosettes.

(3175). PEAR AND APPLE FLAWN (Flan aux Poires et aux Pommes).

Line a flawn ring the same as for apricot flawn (No. 3170); fill the bottom halfway up with fine well-reduced apple marmalade (No. 3668); over lay peeled and cored pears or apples, cut either in four or in quarter-inch slices; range them the way they are cut into a rosette on the marmalade, bestrew with sugar and cook in a hot oven. When done thoroughly, remove, brush over with apple (No. 3668) and currant jelly (No. 3670), half and half, diluted with a little syrup.

(3176). GARNISHINGS FOR COLD DESSERTS (Garnitures Pour Entremets Froids).

These are composed of compoted fruit, small cakes or frequently of cold croûtons made with blanc mange, jelly or fruit "pain" preparation. These croûtons are sometimes plain and sometimes ribboned. To make them proceed as follows: Prepare some very clear jelly and pour it on a tin sheet in an even layer three-quarters of an inch thick; place this perfectly straight in the ice-box to have the jelly harden; when quite so, dip the sheet into very hot water, and turn the jelly over on a cloth. Triangle-shaped or cube-shaped croûtons can be made by first dividing the jelly into long bands, then cutting the croûtons into any desired form. Should they be needed round or in crescents, then cut them with a pastry cutter or tin tube. To have them ribboned, pour first a layer of clear or whipped jelly on the sheet, and when hard pour a second one over, either of colored jelly tinted with carmine or a shaded "pain" preparation; as soon as this is set turn it over on a cloth and cut the same as for the above. Pretty croûtons can also be made as follows: Have twelve No. 2 or 3 mousseline molds (Fig. 138); fill six of them with carmine-tinted jelly, and leave till very cold, then invert them on a cloth and cut perpendicularly in two even parts; lay each of these in one of the twelve molds, and fill the empty space with blanc-mange preparation, and leave to harden. When this is very firm empty out the center of the timbale with a tin tube, and fill the hollow space with chocolate bavaroise (No. 3131); after the timbales become quite cold unmold and cut them perpendicularly in two. When dressing put the rounded side of the timbale turned toward the entremets.

(3177). GOOSEBERRIES WITH CREAM (Groseilles Vertes à la Crème).

Pick a few handfuls of still green but firm gooseberries; put them into a copper pan with two spoonfuls of hot water and a handful of sugar; let dissolve while tossing, and then press through a sieve; return the purée to the pan, sweeten and reduce to the consistency of a light marmalade, then pour it into a tart dish and leave till cold. Cover it with sweetened whipped cream flavored with lemon, smooth nicely, and decorate the surface with cream pushed through a cornet. The cream can be mixed in with the purée if so desired.

(3178). CALIFORNIAN PINEAPPLE JELLY (Gelée aux Ananas Californienne).

Pare neatly a ripe, medium-sized pineapple; split it in two lengthwise; remove the core and cut it into thin crosswise slices; arrange these in a dish and cover with a quart of thirty-degree syrup and one gill of cognac; let macerate for two hours. Put into a tinned basin four ounces of gelatine with a quart of water, the juice of four lemons and six oranges, also the peel of half a lemon and the same of an orange; clarify with six egg-whites, adding, just before the filtering process, all of the syrup used for marinating the pineapple. As soon as the jelly is properly filtered pour it into a vessel, cool partly on ice, and let fall on the top three pure gold leaves; mix the jelly so that the gold separates and spreads. Incrust a jelly mold on pounded ice, pour into it a layer of the gold mixed jelly and let it get hard; on this dress a crown of the prepared pineapples, drained and well wiped, and over pour a second layer of the jelly; when this is also hard range another crown of pineapple, and continue until the mold is full. Set the jelly on ice for two hours to stiffen thoroughly; unmold it on a cold dish and surround the base with a circle of the slices of pineapple, one overlapping the other.

(3179). MACÉDOINE JELLY WITH CHAMPAGNE (Gelée Macédoine au Champagne).

Prepare a macédoine of preserved or fresh fruits. They should be firm. Cut in three-eighths of an inch dice and steep in brandy. Besides this prepare two quarts of orange jelly (No. 3180) and pour it into a small bowl packed in ice; stir it continuously until almost cold, then add to it half a bottleful of champagne and continue to work it in until it attains the consistency of a thick syrup. Now put in the well-drained and wiped fruits. Keep on turning until the jelly begins to solidify, then transfer it to a jelly mold that has been incrusted on pounded ice; lay more of it over and leave for an hour and a half to set thoroughly. Unmold as for No. 3182.

(3180). ORANGE JELLY IN CUPS (Gelée d'Orange en Tasses).

Put four or five gills of sweet, clarified, liquid jelly (No. 106) into a bowl; when quite cold mix in with it the juice of three or four oranges filtered through filtering paper spread on a sieve; add two or three drops of liquid clarified carmine and incrust the vessel in chopped ice. Stir the jelly with a spoon until it is half set, then mix in with it two or three spoonfuls of candied orange peel cut in very small dice; stir again for two minutes, and with a spoon fill up some very cold small cups; keep these for twenty minutes on ice before serving.

(3181). ROSE JELLY (Gelée à la Rose).

Place a pan on the fire containing one pint of clear syrup at twenty-eight degrees; at the first boil mix in with it two handfuls of fresh, highly perfumed rose leaves, and remove from the fire to let infuse a quarter of an hour while covered. Strain the liquid through a fine sieve and mix in with it a sufficient quantity of gelatine or clarified isinglass, adding also two gills of filtered orange and lemon juice, and four or five spoonfuls of good brandy. Taste the jelly, test its consistency on ice, in a small mold, and when perfect pour it into a jelly mold and let harden for one hour on ice, then unmold on a cold dish.

(3182). RUSSIAN JELLY (Gelée à la Russe).

Make about a quart of unflavored jelly (No. 106); set it on ice to get thoroughly cold, add to it as much champagne, beating continuously until the preparation has the appearance of a cream; as soon as it begins to acquire consistency pour it at once into a jelly mold (Fig. 154) previously incrusted in slightly salted ice; set the cover on top, then cover over with salted ice. Let it freeze for half an hour, and when ready to serve dip the mold quickly in hot water, wipe it off, and invert the jelly on a cold dish.

(3183). STRAWBERRY OR RASPBERRY JELLY (Gelée aux Fraises ou aux Framboises).

Boil one quart of syrup to thirty degrees, pour it still boiling on a pound of good picked strawberries or raspberries; two hours later strain this syrup through a jelly bag. Clarify and filter four ounces of gelatine in a quart of water with six beaten whites, let cool off partly, and add to it the strawberry or raspberry syrup, and a few drops of carmine. Incrust a jelly mold (Fig. 154) on chopped ice, fill it with the jelly, and put the cover on top; cover this with ice and leave the jelly to set for two hours; when ready to use dip the mold into hot water and unmold the jelly on a cold dish.

(3184). TUNISIAN JELLY, RIBBONED (Gelée Tunisienne Rubanée).

Prepare about a quart of strawberry jelly, the same as for No. 3183, also a quart of lemon jelly into which has been added a gill of kirsch; put this last into a tin basin and beat it on ice until it becomes white. Incrust a cylindrical mold (Fig. 150) on ice; pour into its bottom a half-inch thick layer of the white jelly and let get quite hard; then on it pour a layer of the strawberry jelly of the same thickness as the other, and leave it also to harden; on this pour another one of white jelly, and continue the same until the mold is completely full, and let the whole get thoroughly hard on ice. Unmold it at the last moment.

(3185). VIOLET JELLY (Gelée aux Violettes).

Put one pint of clear syrup into a newly tinned and clean saucepan; bring it to a boil, then remove and throw in a heaping handful of fresh violets, after suppressing their stalks; let

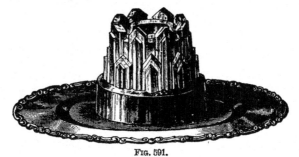

FIG. 591.

infuse for half an hour with the cover on. Strain the liquid into a glazed vessel, and mix in with it three or four spoonfuls of clarified gelatine with some orange and lemon juice. Taste the jelly, to try its consistency, and then pour it into a mold incrusted in broken ice and let set for one hour and a half, and when ready to serve dress it on a cold dish.

(3186). WINE AND LIQUOR JELLY (Gelée aux Vins et aux Liqueurs).

All wine and liquor jellies are made the same way. Prepare a sweet gelatine or fish isinglass jelly, the same as described in No. 106. As soon as this is clarified and filtered add the wine desired for flavoring the jelly, such as Madeira, Marsala, sherry, Malaga, port, etc., or any liquors such as kirsch, maraschino, noyau, Curaçoa, kümmel, etc., mixing the liquor well with the jelly, then pour into a mold previously incrusted on ice. Leave to harden on ice for an hour and a half to two hours.

(3187). JELLY WITH FRUITS AND KIRSCH (Gelée aux Fruits et au Kirsch).

Prepare about a quart of clarified gelatine with sugar, the filtered juice of four lemons, orange peels and the juice of two oranges. Try its consistency in a small mold on ice. Incrust an ornamental jelly mold (Fig. 149) or else a plain cylindrical mold (Fig. 150) on ice. Prepare a macédoine of either fresh or candied fruits, having greengages, apricots, pineapples, cherries, small quartered and peeled oranges, small balls of white apples, cooked in white syrup, and small balls of pears cooked red and also some strawberries or raspberries, currants or grapes. Candied fruits should be washed in warm water, then carefully dried, while the fresh ones should remain in their natural state. Take as much of these fruits as are necessary to fill the mold, varying the different kinds; pour the jelly into a small tin basin, mix in with it a gill of kirsch and lay it on ice, stirring it around with a clean tinned spoon until it commences to set, then put in the selected fruits, either cut up or whole. Take up this preparation with a silver soup ladle and pour it into the mold until it reaches the top, then cover over with a round sheet of paper and close with a deep cover (Fig. 146) filled with pounded ice; keep it this way for three-quarters of an hour. At the last moment dip the mold in hot water, wipe dry and invert on a cold dish. For a change, or should the jelly appear weak, the mold can be frozen with a little salted ice, but only ten or twelve minutes previous to serving.

(3188). MACARONADE (Macaronade).

Prepare a small vanilla frangipane cream (No. 44), neither too sweet nor too light; add to it an equal amount of sweet jelly (No. 106); when cold add to it a few spoonfuls of candied pineapple cut in small dice and stir on ice with a spoon until it becomes quite stiff. Cut two dozen soft macaroons in halves, dip the pieces one by one in maraschino and range them at once on a dish, leaving them until they have entirely absorbed all the liquor. Pour into the bottom of a deep dish a layer of the prepared cream; on this set a layer of the soaked macaroons; cover over with more cream and continue to alternate the cakes and cream until a high pyramid is formed, then smooth the surface and keep it for ten minutes on ice; cover the whole with a layer of well-whipped cream, drained thoroughly and flavored with vanilla, but only slightly sweetened; smooth the cream, decorate it through a cornet and serve at once.

(3189). MARSHAL NEY (Maréchal Ney).

Pound four ounces of peeled almonds with four ounces of powdered sugar and enough egg-white to have a fine paste; put this into a vessel and mix in two ounces of flour, two whole eggs and one stiffly beaten white. Push this preparation through a pocket provided with a three-eighths inch diameter socket on buttered sheets in two-inch lengths and bake them in a hot oven; remove and cool. Have four lightly oiled hexagonal tin rings ranging from five to eight inches in diameter and one and three-quarters inches high; cut the above marchpanes the same size as the sides of the hexagon; fasten these around the hexagonal rings with some sugar cooked to "small crack" (No. 171); unmold, stand one on top of the other, graduating the sizes, and fill the inside with alternate layers of vanilla bavarois (No. 3135), intercalated with small meringue shells made with fifteen egg-whites to one pound of sugar. On the top set one large meringue filled with Bavarian cream and coated with sugar cooked to "crack;" sprinkle over the sugar while hot some finely sliced pistachios.

(3190). MOSAIC WITH CREAM (Mosaïque à la Crème).

Incrust an ogive-shaped mold (Fig. 151) in ice. In this place another mold half an inch less in diameter; fill the inside mold with chopped ice; pour some kirsch jelly between the two molds so as to fill the empty space entirely, and when this gets hard remove the ice from the inside mold, replacing it with warm water, so it can be removed. Cut some Genoese cake (No. 3239) and candied fruits into large uniform squares, add a few candied cherries and with this salpicon fill the empty space in the jelly. Prepare an English vanilla cream (No. 42), cool it on ice and incorporate into it a pint and a half of whipped cream; pour this slowly over the salpicon in such a way that it falls through to the bottom, then set it away on ice for one hour; lastly, dip the mold quickly into hot water, wipe it dry and turn the jelly on a cold dish; serve it at once.

(3191). MOSCOVITE OF STRAWBERRIES (Moscovite aux Fraises).

Put one pint of clear gelatine jelly (No. 106) into a glazed vessel, having it only half as thick as usual but much sweeter. In another vessel have a pint of strawberry pulp; mixing with a grated slice of fresh pineapple, a small tied bunch of lemon or orange peel, a bit of vanilla, the juice of five or six oranges and half a pound of powdered sugar, let the whole macerate for a quarter of an hour, then strain and mix it in with the jelly. Pour this preparation into a large jelly mold furnished with a cover (Fig. 144), and let freeze for at least two hours in a pail with salted ice and saltpetre. At the last moment remove the paste from the mold, also the cover, and dip briskly in warm water; wipe and turn the jelly out on a cold dish, and surround it with a garnishing of small cakes.

(3192). MOSSAGANEM (Mossaganem).

Prepare a little cream cake paste (No. 132). Cut some round pieces of white paper four inches in diameter, and butter the edges lightly; lay the paste in a socket pocket and push it to resemble crowns on the edges of these papers, then lay them on a baking sheet; egg over the paste and bake in a slack oven. After removing the crowns detach them from the papers and let cool off; open them all around at their base, and fill them with apricot marmalade (No. 3675) pushed through a cornet, then range them in the center of a cold dish on top of each other, alternating each layer with one of frangipane cream with vanilla (No. 44), to which pounded almonds and hazel-nut butter have been added. Cover the inside of the hollow formed by the crowns with a thin layer of whipped cream sweetened and flavored with vanilla. With this same cream cover the entire outside of the cake, smooth the surface and decorate with more of the cream pushed through a cornet. At the last moment decorate the hollow with strawberries, sprinkled over with a little thick syrup and maraschino.

(3193). ORNAMENTS FOR COLD DESSERTS (Ornements d'Entremets Froids).

Uprights are generally used for cylindrical molds; they are made with a wooden base-plate, having a hole bored in the center to insert a column therein; this column must be higher than the mold and of proportionate thickness to the opening in the cylinder. It answers the purpose of supporting the dessert and all the ornamental pieces laid on top. These wooden supports are covered with gum paste and surrounded by a gum-paste edge. Cold dessert ornaments consist of hatelets, voluptes, tufts and aigrettes.

Hatelets are silver-plated skewers a quarter of an inch wide and eight inches long, pointed on one end, and fancifully decorated on the other; these hatelets are garnished with rounds of different colored fruits and finished as explained in No. 2526, using sweet jelly (No. 106) instead of aspic jelly. They can be used to decorate cold entremets. When required for ornamenting large dessert cakes they are simply garnished with fine preserved fruits.

Voluptes are scrolls of arabesque design made of cooked sugar poured in thin fillets on lightly oiled marble and then grouped together, standing upright in fours, sixes or eights, also cast in sugar.

Tufts are made of spun sugar molded in the hand into the shape of a ball. These balls are at times laid directly on the dessert or else on voluptes of cooked sugar.

Aigrettes are also made of spun sugar put together like a small sheaf; this is cut off straight at a certain height, then molded into the shape of a cone; clip it off short, invert and fasten it on the dessert, either on top of a tuft or in the center of a volupte. Spun sugar is also used for making sultanas.

(3194). "PAIN" OF APRICOTS (Pain d'Abricots).

Soften two ounces of gelatine in cold water and dissolve it in a gill of almond milk (No. 4) and a gill of syrup at thirty-two degrees; pass it at once through a fine colander into a tinned basin. Place in another vessel a pint and a half of fine apricot purée sweetened and flavored with a little kirsch; pour this purée in with the gelatine, and standing it on ice stir steadily until cold. As soon as it begins to thicken transfer it into a cylindrical jelly mold incrusted in chopped ice, keeping it thus for another hour and a half. When ready to serve unmold; surround the base with a circle of fine halved apricots covered with apricot marmalade (No. 3675) diluted with a little kirsch.

(3195). "PAIN" OF BANANAS, HAVANESE (Pain de Bananes Havanaise).

Peel eight very ripe bananas; crush the pulps and rub them through a fine sieve into a basin; add the juice of two oranges and one ounce and a half of gelatine dissolved in a gill of water, then pass the whole through a fine sieve; let it get thoroughly cold on ice and as soon as it begins to set incorporate into it the same quantity of very firm whipped cream. Have prepared a quart of clear jelly (No. 106) flavored with rum, colored with carmine, and let cool to the consistency of a thick syrup. Incrust a cylindrical jelly mold (Fig. 150) in ice, pour into the bottom a three-quarter of an inch thick layer of the banana preparation and leave it to harden; on this pour a layer of the same thickness of the rum jelly, leaving it also to harden, and over this pour another layer of the banana preparation, then another of the jelly, and so on until the mold is entirely filled, being careful that each layer is of equal thickness. Cover the top with a round piece of paper, then place on a lid with chopped ice over; leave stand for an hour and a half to two hours so that it is perfectly hard before unmolding.

(3196). "PAIN" OF CHESTNUTS À LA BÉOTIE (Pain de Marrons à la Béotie).

Incrust in ice a flat, dome-shaped mold; decorate the inner sides with fanciful cuts of assorted candied fruits, dipping each piece in half-set jelly, then coating with a layer of rather firm blanc-mange (No. 3138), having it a third of an inch thick. Cover the mold with a lid with ice on top. Put into a vessel four gills of sweet chestnut purée (No. 3136), dilute it with four spoonfuls of maraschino and a few gills of thick vanilla syrup, beat the preparation on ice to thicken and as

,oon as this occurs incorporate into it about four or five gills of good whipped cream; two minutes later add a small salpicon of candied pineapple and then pour the whole into the hollow of the

Fig. 592.

mold; replace the lid, covering it at once with more ice, and after the lapse of an hour dip the mold quickly into hot water, wipe and turn the cream on a cold dish.

(3197). PAINS" OF STRAWBERRIES WITH CREAM—SMALL (Petits Pains de Fraises à la Crème).

Decorate the sides and bottom of a dozen timbale molds (No. 1, Fig. 137) that have been on ice with fresh strawberries cut in two, being careful to dip each piece in half-set jelly before applying it; then coat them with jelly, leaving an empty space in the center and fill this with a pureé of candied pineapple mingled with some jelly and two spoonfuls of kirsch. Incrust a dome-

Fig. 593.

shaped or pyramidical mold on ice, fill it with a purée of strawberries, to which melted gelatine has been added; thicken on ice, and let it get quite hard. Fasten on a cold dish a bottom of Genoese cake (No. 3239), slightly wider than the open part of the mold; scoop it out lightly so as to permit the strawberry "pain" to stand upright inside of it, then mask it over with apricot marmalade (No. 3675). At the last moment unmold the pyramid on this and let it stand till quite cold, then cover quickly with a bavarois preparation (No. 3135) flavored with lemon peel and vanilla and thickened on ice when needed. Unmold the small "pains" and dress them at once around the cream.

(3198). PEACHES À LA LOUVOISIENNE (Pêches à la Louvoisienne).

Fill a border mold (Fig. 139) with raspberry jelly (No. 3183) tinted with a little carmine, having it rather firmer than usual. After the jelly is well set unmold the border on a cold dish and place a pad of biscuit three-quarters of an inch thick in the center. On this dress a dome of fine halved peaches and cover these with a layer of cold cream rice with vanilla (No. 160). Dress a circle of greengages around the rice and decorate the top with quartered peaches, some cherries (demi-sucre) and lozenges of angelica; surround the base with a row of croûtons made of blanc-mange (No. 3138) and red jelly alternated, each being a quarter of an inch thick.

(3199). APPLE PIE (Tarte aux Pommes).

Butter a tin plate and lay on it a flat of short paste (No. 135) an eighth of an inch thick; dampen the edges lightly and lay all around a band of puff paste three-sixteenths of an inch thick and three-quarters of an inch wide. Cut four medium apples in four; peel, suppress the cores and pips and mince them up; put them in a vessel, adding two spoonfuls of apple marmalade (No. 3674), three tablespoonfuls of sugar and a pinch of ground cinnamon; stir all together and pour them into the plate, dressing the apples in a dome form; wet the edges of the pie and cover over with a flat of puff paste (No. 146) an eighth of an inch thick and of the same diameter as the pie. Fasten both pastes together, cut away all the surplus and pinch the edges all around; egg over and trace a rosette on top with a small kitchen knife, then bake in a hot oven for three-quarters of an hour to one hour or even an hour and a quarter, according to the thickness of the apples and the heat of the oven.

(3200). COCOANUT PIE (Tarte à la Noix de Coco).

Take a deep tin pie plate and line it with foundation paste (No. 135); raise up the edges, pinch all around and leave stand for twenty minutes in a cool place. Put in a vessel four whole eggs, four ounces of sugar and the peel of one lemon; stir well together. Increase the quantity of this mixture with a pint of milk and strain through a fine strainer; spread on the bottom of the pie crust a layer of grated cocoanut and fill half full with the above preparation; push the pie cautiously into the oven, not to upset any of the liquid, keeping it very plumb, and when in the oven finish filling with more of the preparation, using a dipper for this purpose. Cook forty to fifty minutes.

(3201). CREAM PIE (Tarte à la Crème).

Line a tin pie plate with foundation paste (No. 135); raise up and pinch the edges; leave rest in a cool place, then cover the inside surface with buttered paper and fill with dry cherry pips or raw rice; partly cook the crust and empty out at once. Pour in a vessel four ounces of sugar, two and a half ounces of flour and three eggs; beat thoroughly, dilute with a pint of boiling milk, having a vanilla stick infused therein; transfer this preparation to a saucepan, thicken it over the fire and as soon as it begins to acquire consistency pour it into the crust and push into a slack oven to finish cooking.

(3202). LEMON CUSTARD PIE, VENETIAN STYLE (Tarte de Venise à la Crème au Citron).

Line a deep tin pie plate with foundation paste (No. 135), operating the same as for cocoanut pie, and let it set. Put three whole eggs and three separate yolks into a vessel, stir in three ounces of powdered sugar and an ounce of lemon sugar; dilute with a pint of milk and strain the whole through a fine strainer. Fill the pie crust three-quarters full with this, push carefully into the oven and finish filling with a dipper. Cook from forty to fifty minutes.

(3203). PUMPKIN PIE (Tarte aux Courges).

Cut one pound of very ripe pumpkin into slices; suppress the seeds and peel; cut it up into dice and put these pieces in a saucepan with some water to cook over a brisk fire; then drain and press the pulp through a sieve. Pour this into a vessel, add to it four eggs, a pinch of ginger, a pinch of cinnamon, a small pinch of nutmeg, one ounce of melted butter, a half pint of milk, and one quarter of a pound of sugar; stir well. Use this preparation for filling three-quarters full a pie plate lined the same as for a cocoanut pie (No. 3200); push it carefully into a hot oven and finish filling with a dipper. Cook forty to fifty minutes.

(3204). RHUBARB PIE AND RHUBARB WITH CREAM (Tarte à la Rhubarbe et Rhubarbe à la Crème).

Take very ripe rhubarb, suppress the leaves, peel and cut into pieces one inch long; arrange them in layers with sugar between each on a tin pie plate lined with short paste (No. 135), so as to form a dome. Moisten the edges of the paste on the plate and cover the whole with a flat of puff paste (No. 146) the same diameter as the plate, fastening it firmly to the moistened under edge, then pare off all the paste beyond the border, gash it all around with a small knife, egg the surface and trace a rosette on top with the tip of a knife. Bake in a hot oven for forty-five minutes.

Rhubarb with Cream.—Choose some very green rhubarb, suppress the leaves and hard parts near the roots, peel and cut in half-inch squares. Put one pound of this prepared rhubarb in a copper pan with a little water, a small piece of cinnamon and a sliced lemon. Put the pan on the fire, and when sufficiently cooked sweeten it according to taste. Remove from the fire, allow to cool slightly, and add a tablespoonful of cornstarch or fecula, diluted in a little cold water; put back on the fire to thicken it, take out the slices of lemon and the cinnamon. Pour the rhubarb in mousseline molds (No. 1, Fig. 138), allow to cool and unmold; or it may be served in a dish. Serve separately some sweet cream or else incorporate into it an equal quantity of whipped cream.

(3205). BOISSY PUDDING (Pouding Boissy).

Dilute four ounces of corn starch in a bowl with three gills of cold milk; on this pour a quart of boiling milk sweetened with six ounces of sugar; turn the whole into a saucepan and set it on the fire to stir until well thickened; take it off and incorporate into it quickly one gill of kirsch, the grated peel of a lemon, a salpicon of preserved fruits cut in dice, such as pears, pineapple, green almonds, and cherries cut in two, besides a few seeded Malaga raisins and six stiffly beaten fresh egg-whites. As soon as the preparation is sufficiently mixed pour it into a plain timbale mold oiled over with sweet almond oil, and leave it to harden in the ice-box for an hour and a half. When prepared to serve invert the pudding on a cold dish; cover with raspberry sauce (No. 3217), serving more of it apart.

(3206). CASTELLANE PUDDING (Pouding Castellane).

Prepare a fine purée of chestnuts, the same as for bavarois with chestnuts (No. 3136); also prepare an English vanilla cream (No. 42), with eight egg-yolks, a quart of milk, four ounces of sugar and half a split vanilla bean. As soon as the cream is done stir into it the purée of chestnuts, also two ounces of dissolved gelatine; pass the whole through a fine wire sieve into a vessel and place it on the ice to get cold, working it well until it begins to stiffen. Prepare a salpicon of chestnuts and candied pineapple cut in three-sixteenths inch dice, cherries (demi-sucre) cut in four, and macaroons also cut in four; pour a little maraschino over. Incrust a timbale mold on ice, pour into it a layer of the preparation, then the fruits and continue to alternate until the mold is full. Just when ready to serve dip the mold quickly into hot water and invert the pudding on a cold dish and pour over a syrup made of chestnuts with vanilla flavoring, into which has been added a few chestnuts cut in dice. Serve some of this syrup apart.

(3207). HARRISON PUDDING (Pouding à la Harrison).

Have some half-set sweet jelly (No. 106) and with a camel's hair brush wet the bottom and sides of a plain and very cold cylindrical mold (Fig. 150); bestrew the inside with peeled and chopped pistachios, pressing them so that they form a compact layer, then turn the mold on ice for two or three minutes; incrust it upright. Put into a small basin about three-quarters of a pound of blanc-mange preparation (No. 3138) of a proper consistency and flavored with orange peel; stir it on ice to harden, then incorporate slowly into it a pint and a half of whipped cream but slightly sweetened. Two minutes after fill up the cold mold with this in layers intermingled with macaroons soaked in kirsch; freeze the mold for one hour longer in unsalted ice, then dip it in hot water and unmold the contents on a very cold dish.

(3208). LAFAYETTE PUDDING (Pouding Lafayette).

Prepare a little meringue preparation (No. 140) with six egg-whites; divide it in two and flavor one of them with orange, having it slightly colored with a little carmine, and the other flavored with vanilla. Distribute these two preparations into small parts the size of a pigeon's egg, and poach them in milk the same as snow eggs (No. 3163); drain them at once on a cloth. Have a cupola-shaped mold incrusted in ice, pour into the bottom an English cream (No. 42) flavored with rum and mixed with a little gelatine, adding to it a few spoonfuls of whipped cream; let it get hard, then dress on it a layer of the poached eggs, alternating the two colors, and strew over some shredded pistachios; pour another layer of cream on top, then more eggs and pistachios, and so on until the mold is entirely full. Let the pudding harden in the ice-box for two hours; serve with a bowl of sweetened strawberry pulp flavored with maraschino.

(3209). MINISTERIAL PUDDING (Pouding Ministériel).

Wash in hot water one pound of cherries (demi-sucre) and lay them to marinate for one hour in a light syrup well flavored with kirsch. Make a bavarois preparation with vanilla (No. 3135), only using a little less whipped cream than usual; add to it a few tablespoonfuls of kirsch. Have a cylindrical timbale mold incrusted in ice; pour a layer of the preparation into the bottom, and on this scatter some of the cherries; when hard pour in another layer and more cherries, continuing the process until the mold is full. Then cover it with a round sheet of paper and a lid covered with ice, and leave till entirely hard. At the last moment unmold the pudding and surround the base with a circle of fine cherries (demi-sucre) previously marinated in kirsch. Serve a sauce-boat of whipped cream with vanilla and kirsch at the same time as the pudding.

(3210). RENAISSANCE PUDDING (Pouding Renaissance).

Put ten egg-yolks into a vessel, beat them well with half a pound of sugar, and dilute with a quart of boiling milk, into which a split vanilla bean has been infused; stir well, and thicken on the fire. As soon as the preparation is done remove from the range, suppress the vanilla, and add three gelatine leaves softened in cold water; beat it from time to time until the gelatine is entirely dissolved, and then pass the preparation through a fine strainer into a vessel and leave to cool slightly. Have prepared a preserved fruit macédoine cut in small dice, such as apricots, pears, plums, pineapple and cherries (demi-sucre), and pour some maraschino over. Also prepare a few chestnuts cut in quarters, and steep them in maraschino. Put a timbale mold on chopped ice, place in it a layer of the preparation and leave it to set. Then scatter the fruits and chestnuts on it; also some lady fingers soaked in maraschino; over these pour another layer of the preparation, and continue in this manner until the mold is full. Leave it on ice for an hour and a half, and just when ready to serve dip it hastily in hot water, and invert the pudding on a cold dish; pour a cold English vanilla cream sauce (No. 42) over, serving some of it separately.

(3211). VALOIS PUDDING (Pouding à la Valois).

Make a Neapolitan cake paste (No. 3250), and roll it out with a rolling pin to the thickness of an eighth of an inch; cut from this sixty rounds, each an inch in diameter; lay them on a baking sheet and cook in a brisk oven. Also have prepared at the same time a salpicon of preserved fruits composed of greengages, dates and pineapple, the whole cut in dice, and some cherries (demi-sucre). Prepare also an English cream (No. 42) with twelve egg-yolks, twelve ounces of sugar, a pint of cream and a pint of milk. As soon as finished add to it three gelatine leaves previously softened in cold water and stir the preparation until the gelatine is thoroughly dissolved. Then add to it six ounces of roasted hazel-nuts pounded with a gill of milk; pass the whole through a fine sieve into a tinned basin, and leave it on ice to cool partly. Incrust a timbale mold in chopped ice, pour on the bottom a layer of the preparation, leave it to set, and on it scatter the fruits; over this pour another layer of the cream, then on top arrange a bed of the round cakes, afterward more cream, and then more fruits, continuing the process until the mold is entirely full. Leave the pudding on ice for an hour and a half. Serve with a cold English vanilla cream sauce (No. 42).

(3212). PYRAMID OF MERINGUES (Buisson de Meringues).

Meringues make a delicious dessert. They should be small but of even size and specially of a beautiful golden color; besides they must be exceedingly dry. Select about twenty of the prettiest cold shells; use a small spoon to fill them with good whipped cream (No. 50) sweetened with vanilla sugar (No. 3165); fasten these shells, two by two together, and keep them for two hours in a cool place before dressing them in a pyramid on a napkin.

(3213). RICE MIRABEAU (Riz à la Mirabeau).

Boil three-quarters of a pound of rice in water acidulated with the juice of a few lemons, keeping the grains whole, then drain and macerate in a maraschino syrup. Prepare a fine salpicon of preserved fruits cut in dice, having pineapple, apricot, pears and citron cut up very fine, cherries divided in two and shredded pistachios; on these pour four tablespoonfuls of maraschino, four of brandy, four of Curaçoa, and four of almond milk (No. 4); leave the whole to steep for one hour; throw over two ounces of gelatine that has been dissolved in a little water. As soon as this preparation begins to thicken stir the rice into it and transfer the whole to a plain timbale mold, and let harden in the ice-box for two hours. When ready to serve unmold on a cold dish, and cover with a raspberry sauce (No. 3217).

(3214). RICE WITH APRICOTS (Riz aux Abricots).

Blanch half a pound of rice; cook it till tender in milk with vanilla and when cooked remove it from the fire, sweeten it, add raw cream and fresh butter and pour it into another saucepan to let get cold, stirring from time to time. Place the preparation on ice and incorporate slowly into it one pint of whipped cream. When well stirred in dress it in layers in a soufflé pan (Fig. 182) incrusted in ice, covering each layer with one of apricot marmalade (No. 3675); smooth it dome-shaped and decorate the summit with candied pineapple cut in pieces.

(3215). RICE WITH CREAM AND RASPBERRIES (Riz à la Crème Framboisé).

Cook about a pound of rice with cream, not having it too sweet, and finish with two gills of almond milk (No. 4). When cold set it into a small thin tin vessel and incorporate slowly about two gills of syrup, flavored with lemon peel and mingled with half as much calf's foot jelly, sweetened and clarified (No. 104). Incrust a dome-shaped mold wider than its height in lightly salted pounded ice and put in a one-inch layer of thick clear jelly with raspberry juice at the bot-

Fig. 594.

tom, and let it settle; as soon as it is hard lay another tin mold of the same shape, but narrower, on top of it, filling it up with pounded ice; pour a little of the same warm jelly between the two molds to fill up the entire vacancy and let it harden. Then remove the ice from the smaller mold and replace it by warm water so that it can be easily removed. Fill the center of the mold at once with the rice cream preparation (No. 160) thickened on ice and mixed with two spoonfuls of whipped cream and a salpicon composed of shredded pistachios, candied pineapple and half-sweetened cherries; cover the preparation with a layer of jelly and close the mold with a deep cover, on which lay pounded ice. Keep it for forty minutes longer on ice and finally remove the mold, wash it quickly in warm water and invert its contents on a cold dish. Fasten on the summit an almond paste ornament fixed on by a hatelet garnished with fruits.

(3216). RICE WITH STRAWBERRIES (Riz aux Fraises).

Wash half a pound of Carolina rice; put it into a saucepan with two quarts of water and the juice of two lemons; cook till tender, keeping the grains whole, and when done drain on a sieve, pour it into a vessel and cover with a hot syrup of twenty-eight degrees, adding some orange and lemon peel; leave till cold. At the last moment lift up the rice with a skimmer and dress it in a deep dish in layers alternated with small fresh strawberries. Pour a thick syrup over the whole.

(3217). SAUCES FOR COLD ENTREMETS (Sauces Pour Entremets Froids).

The sauces for cold desserts are cold English cream (No. 42), flavored with vanilla, lemon or orange peel or with liquor. Sweetened whipped cream also flavored with vanilla, liquors or fresh fruit juices. Fine purées of fresh fruits sweetened with icing sugar; these can also be flavored with liquors.

(3218). SUÉDOISE OF APPLES AND PEARS (Suédoise de Pommes et de Poires).

Peel as many large apples as pears and with a tin tube take from them small sticks an inch and a quarter long by five-sixteenths of an inch in diameter; cook the apple sticks in a clear syrup and the pear ones in a syrup colored with carmine, being careful to keep them all rather firm; leave to cool off in their syrup and then drain and wipe. Coat a plain timbale mold with jelly, incrust it well in ice, take up the pear and apple sticks one by one and dip them in half-set jelly, then arrange them against the sides of the mold; on the first row lay another and so on until the mold is completely lined. Then fill it with an apple "pain" preparation, made as explained in No. 3194, substituting apples for apricots, and flavor with vanilla, incorporating into it a salpicon of preserved fruits cut in dice, selecting for this purpose, pineapples, apricots, pears and cherries cut in two; let the Suédoise harden on ice for an hour and a half. When ready to serve dip the mold hastily in hot water, unmold on a cold dish and surround the base with small ribboned jelly croûtons (No. 3198).

(3219). SURPRISE OF FRUITS, FROTHY SAUCE (Surprise aux Fruits, Sauce Mousseuse).

Butter a charlotte mold and fill it three-quarters full with either baba paste (No. 129) or plain Savarin paste (No. 148); let it rise as high as the top in a mild temperature; bake the cake in a moderate oven and five minutes after it has been taken from the oven pare the top off straight, then turn it over on a pastry grate and soak it with a syrup flavored with lemon and maraschino. When the cake is thoroughly cold return it to the mold and slice off the bottom so as to be able to empty it out, leaving only a thickness of five-eighths of an inch at the top and sides; fill this hollow space with layers of small strawberries and pour over them a cooked Italian meringue (No. 140) flavored with cold burned punch. Close the opening on the cake with the removed slice and invert it on a cold dish, covering it over with a frothy sauce prepared as follows:

Frothy Sauce.—Pour into a tin basin three gills of English cream flavored either with vanilla or lemon (No. 42), having it slightly consistent and cold; beat it up vigorously for a quarter of an hour on ice and when light and frothy add two or three spoonfuls of firm and well-drained whipped cream mixed in with a spoon.

(3220). CONDÉ TART (Tarte à la Condé).

Spread a thin flat of fine foundation paste (No. 135) or half puff paste (No. 146) on a baking sheet; cut it into a round and cover the surface within an inch and a quarter from the edge with a layer of vanilla frangipane (No. 44); wet the borders of the flat and cover entirely with another thin one of fine puff paste; press the edges with the fingers and scallop out with the tip of a small knife, then cover the surface with a Condé preparation (No. 2) made of chopped almonds, powdered sugar and egg-whites; besprinkle over with fine sugar and cook the tart in a slack oven for three-quarters of an hour.

(3221). MASSILLON TIMBALES (Timbales à la Massillon).

With some icing sugar, applied with a brush, coat over the inside of a charlotte mold, having it wider than its height; line it with marchpane paste (No. 139), not too thin, then dry this for a few hours in a mild temperature, and finally apricot over the insides. Take some almond biscuit (No. 3229), some vanilla Savoy biscuit (No. 3231) and some Genoese biscuit (No. 3239) flavored with lemon and rum; cut them up in uniform dice pieces and put them in a vessel, mingling in half a pound of candied pineapple cut in small bits, and adding a few spoonfuls of light apricot marmalade (No. 3675) in such a way that the whole becomes well mixed. Fill the empty lined mold with this and pour over a bavarois cream preparation (No. 3135), mixed with a little gelatine, and keep it on ice for half an hour. Just when ready to serve unmold on a cold dish and pour slowly over the biscuit a vanilla ice cream preparation (No. 3458), mixed with a few spoonfuls of whipped cream, then close the top with a layer of massepain (No. 3392) fastening it well to the edges. Unmold the timbale on a cold dish, cover the outside with fine apricot marmalade applied with a brush, and decorate the sides and top with fanciful pieces of candied fruits prepared beforehand for this purpose. Cover the bottom of the dish with a layer of the same ice cream preparation and serve at once.

(3222). TIMBALE OF WAFFLES (Timbale de Gaufres).

Pound ten ounces of shelled and skinned almonds with one pound of sugar and sufficient egg-white to form it into a fine soft paste. Put this into a vessel and incorporate half a pound of flour; dilute with eight lightly beaten egg-yolks. With a part of this paste lay on a waxed baking sheet a band four and a half inches wide by sixteen inches long, and bake it to a fine color; as soon as done pare the edges straight and bend it around a timbale mold; fasten the two ends well with cooked sugar, and leave till cold. Add to the remainder of the paste a few spoonfuls of whipped cream, and with it arrange on waxed baking sheets about forty very thin and even waffles, each five inches in diameter, and cook them to a fine color in a brisk oven; as soon as done roll them on a small roller about a quarter of an inch in diameter. When all the waffles are cooked and rolled up dip one end of them one by one into royal icing (No. 101), then into finely chopped pistachios, and lay them on a grate and dry the icing in a heater. After this is accomplished fasten them all around the waffle timbale, close to each other, having the pistachio ends uppermost, and attach them in position with cooked sugar; set this timbale on a waffle paste foundation dredged over with pink sugar (No. 172). Decorate the base with small one-inch diameter meringues filled with bavarois cream (No. 3133). When prepared to serve slip it on a dish and fill it with a light chocolate bavarois (No. 3131).

(3223). WAFFLES BRISSELETS WITH RASPBERRY CREAM (Gaufres Brisselets à la Crème Framboisée).

Arrange one pound of sifted flour in a circle on the table; in the center place four ounces of butter. six ounces of sugar, a piece of hartshorn the size of a hazel-nut and powdered very fine. Dilute the whole with half milk and half cream to have it the consistency of a Milan paste, only slightly softer; roll out in the shape of strings and cut each one of these into small pieces, then mold them into balls three-quarters of an inch in diameter. Heat some flat round waffle irons, butter lightly with clarified butter and when hot open and place one of the balls in the center, close the irons and cook to a fine golden color on both sides; as soon as this is accomplished remove and roll them quickly around rolling pins three-quarters of an inch in diameter, and leave till cold. Just when ready to serve fill by means of a cornet with whipped cream flavored with raspberry and dress in a pyramid on a dish covered with a folded napkin.

(3224). WAFERS WITH CURAÇOA CREAM—ROLLED (Gaufres Roulées à la Crème au Curaçoa).

Have in a vessel three-quarters of a pound of sugar, six ounces of flour, six ounces of corn starch, two ounces of melted butter, ten lightly beaten egg-whites and a pint of whipped cream; make with this a smooth paste, adding a little vanilla flavoring and a few tablespoonfuls of brandy. Heat on a slow fire some flat waffle-irons, butter them with a pad dipped in clarified butter, and when hot cover one side with a spoonful of the paste; close the irons and cook the waffles on both sides; after they are done roll them on three-quarter-inch in diameter rollers; remove from these and leave till cold. Serve dressed in a pyramid on a dish covered with a napkin and fill them all by means of a cornet with whipped cream flavored with a little Curaçoa.

PASTRY (Pâtisserie).

LARGE CAKES FOR ENTREMETS (Gros Gâteaux pour Entremets).

(3225). ALMOND CAKE (Gâteau d'Amandes).

From some parings of puff paste roll out a round flat twelve inches in diameter and three-six-teenths of an inch in thickness; lay it on a slightly dampened tart plate; cover this flat with an even layer of almond cream (No. 40) a quarter of an inch thick, placed half an inch inside the border; moisten the edge lightly and cover over with another layer of the paste of the same diameter and thickness as the lower one, only making it of puff paste prepared to six turns (No. 146); press the edges well to attach the two flats together, and scallop this border with a small knife; egg the top, decorate it by making incisions in the shape of a rosette with the tip of a kitchen knife, then push the cake into a brisk oven to bake. As soon as done remove to the oven door, bestrew lightly with powdered sugar and return it again to the the oven to have the top well glazed.

(3226). ANGEL CAKE (Gâteau des Anges).

Pour twenty egg-whites into a basin and whip them till quite firm; at once add ten ounces of sugar, part of it flavored with vanilla (No. 3165), and continue whipping the whole until quite smooth, then add half a pound of flour into which has been mixed half a teaspoonful of cream of tartar and sifted several times through a sieve; mix all together lightly till smooth. With this preparation fill some angel cake molds, eight to nine inches in diameter, three-quarters full; these should be quite dry, without any buttering. Push the cakes into a very slack oven to cook for forty to fifty minutes, then take them out and keep them in their molds for two hours; now pass a small kitchen knife between the pan and the cake, knock the edges of the former gently on the table to detach the cake and turn it on a grate; pare the tops very straight, ice with royal icing (No. 101) and dress on a lace-paper-covered board or dish; after the icing is dry decorate with more of the royal icing.

(3227). BABA SYRUPED OR ICED (Baba au Sirop ou Glacé).

With some baba paste (No. 129) fill a well-buttered baba mold three-quarters full; stand this in a moderately heated place, cover and leave until the paste has reached to the upper edges of the mold, then set it on a pie plate in a slow oven to bake; this operation ought to take from an hour and a quarter to an hour and a half; as soon as baked cut away any surplus paste overreaching the top and invert the baba on a grate. Prepare a thirty-two degree hot syrup flavored with good rum; soak the baba with this, applying it with a brush, and let drain well. It can be served simply soaked with this syrup or else iced with a light layer of water icing (No. 102) or fondant (No. 58) well flavored with rum. After the icing has dried remove the baba carefully from the grate and lay it on a dish; should it be iced decorate the icing with angelica lozenges, halved cherries and cuts of orange peels, surrounding the base with a circle of marchpane in small cases; serve.

(3228). BISCUIT À LA HERNANI (Biscuit à la Hernani).

Bake a Savoy biscuit in a dome-formed mold eight inches in diameter by four inches high. Turn it out and let stand till cold, then put it back again in the mold and pare it straight; cut around the top at about two inches from the bottom a cover by means of a small knife held on a slant, to have the cut form a bevel (this is to prevent the cover falling in the biscuit), and empty it, leaving the outer crust only half an inch in thickness. Place it on a grate with its cover on and cover with reduced apricot marmalade (No. 3675), and glaze with fondant (No. 58), to which melted chocolate is added. At serving time fill the empty biscuit with whipped cream, into which mix a few chocolate pastilles, some finely shredded pistachios and a few preserved cherries cut in two. Lay the biscuit on a frolle paste (No. 136) foundation, coated with egg whites, and dredged over with white granulated sugar; slide the whole on a cold dish and surround the base with a wreath of Africans (No. 3364) glazed with chocolate.

(3229). ALMOND BISCUIT (Biscuit aux Amandes).

Beat one pound of sugar in a basin with fifteen egg-yolks, obtaining a very light mixture; add five ounces of sweet and one of bitter almonds, pounded finely with two egg-whites; continue to whip together for a few minutes longer, then add five ounces of flour, five ounces of fecula, two ounces of melted fresh butter and lastly twelve stiffly whipped egg-whites. Pour this preparation into a pound cake or "manqué" mold lined with paper, and bake in a very slow oven. Turn out the cake as soon as done, transferring it to a grate to cool; mask the surface with apricot marmalade (No. 3675) and ice with almond milk fondant (No. 58). After this icing is dry slip the cake on a round board covered with lace paper and decorate the top with royal icing. Surround the base with a circle of fine large preserved cherries and lozenges of angelica.

(3230). MOUSSELINE BISCUIT (Biscuit Mousseline).

Mix and work eight egg-yolks and two whole eggs in a basin with one pound of sugar; when quite light add two ounces of orange sugar (No. 3165) and continue to stir the preparation for a few moments longer; add four ounces of flour and four ounces of fecula and finally eight stiffly beaten egg-whites. Butter a cylindrical timbale mold, glaze it with icing sugar and fecula, half of each, then fill the mold three-quarters full with the above composition; set it in a very slack oven and let bake for an hour and a half. As soon as the biscuit is done unmold on a grate, leave to cool and afterward pare it very straight; ice over with strawberry icing (No. 102) and dress the cake on a dish. Put into a copper pan five spoonfuls of strawberry pulp and mix into it sufficient orange sugar to form a flowing paste. Heat and when quite hot pour it over five stiffly beaten egg-whites. Just when serving fill the hollow in the cylindrical mold with this preparation, dressing it in the shape of a dome; surround the base of this cream with a circle of preserved cherries and small lozenges of angelica. Arrange around the bottom of the cake some small Genoese cakes (No. 3307) iced with strawberry and cut into rectangulars.

(3231). SAVOY BISCUIT (Biscuit de Savoie).

Grease a high biscuit mold with melted prepared veal kidney suet; drain off any surplus fat by reversing the mold, then glaze with sugar icing and fecula, half of each. Pour into a vessel one pound of powdered sugar flavored with vanilla (No. 3165) and a pinch of salt, add fourteen egg-yolks one at a time and beat the whole forcibly to have it get quite frothy; whip fourteen egg-whites to a stiff froth, and put a fourth part into the yolks, also six ounces of potato fecula and six ounces of flour, the two latter to be sifted together. As soon as the whole is thoroughly combined add the remainder of the beaten whites. With this fill the mold three-quarters full and stand it on a baking pan; fix it so that the mold will not fall; place it carefully in the mildest spot in the oven. In order to bake this biscuit properly it is essential that the oven be first thoroughly heated, then allowed to fall to a mild temperature; leave it in for two and a quarter to two and a half hours. When done to perfection unmold on a grate, cool, pare very straight and dress on a dish; surround the base with a circle of lady bouchées iced with vanilla (No. 3376)

(3232). BRETON CAKE (Gâteau Breton).

Set in a basin one pound and a quarter of sugar, eighteen eggs and a small pinch of salt; beat continuously for twenty-five to thirty minutes so as to have it very light, then add six ounces of almonds, including an ounce of bitter ones, these to be pounded very finely with one egg. Continue the beating process for a few minutes longer and then mix in a pound and a half of sifted flour and finally ten ounces of melted butter. Distribute this preparation into a set of six Breton molds, having these buttered and floured; fill them up to the top and bake in a slack oven. Remove as fast as they are done, unmold on a grate, let cool and then pare very straight. Ice the smallest as well as the fourth one in size with white vanilla fondant (No. 58); the second and fifth with pink strawberry fondant and the third and sixth with chocolate fondant. Dry the icings well then dress the cakes on an office paste foundation in a pyramid, one on the other, alternating the colors and graduating the various sizes. Fill the hollow formed in the cake with Quillet cream (No. 48), and decorate with more of this pushed through a cornet. Keep the cake in a cool place until required for serving.

(3233). CROWN OF BRIOCHE (Couronne de Brioche).

Put two pounds of brioche paste (No. 130) that has been sufficiently raised and hardened on ice on a floured table, form it into a ball and lay it on a round baking sheet covered with paper; flatten it slightly with the hands and make a hole in the center, spreading out the paste so that it forms into a large ring; place it on a baking dish, equalize, egg and gash a round inside of the crown with the tip of a knife, raising the dough; push into a well-heated oven and bake for thirty-five minutes. These crowns can be made of a smaller size, two ounces each, to be served for breakfast.

(3234). LARGE BRIOCHE WITH HEAD—(Grosse Brioche à Tête).

Have a brioche paste prepared the same as described in No. 130; put this in a vessel in a cool place and let it rise to half its size again. Then work it once more and set it in the ice-box for two hours to have it harden. Butter a tin mold six and a half inches in diameter and eight inches deep; line it with paper and butter this over. Mold a four-pound round-shaped piece of the paste, put it in the mold, then mold another pound piece and roll it on the table on one side to give it a long pear-form appearance; with dampened fingers make a hole in the center of the first paste and in it insert the pointed end of the pear; leave the mold in a moderately heated place to have the paste rise to the level of the top, then egg it over twice and put in a slack oven to cook for two hours. Unmold as soon as done, allow to cool and dress on a folded napkin. In case there be no mold at hand use a cylinder of strong paper the same diameter as the mold.

(3235). CHAMOUNIX CAKE (Gâteau Chamounix).

Bake in a slack oven a small Genoese preparation (No. 3239) placed in a border mold, it having a round-shaped bottom buttered and bestrewn with chopped almonds. After it is taken from the oven, cold and pared, brush the surface over with apricot marmalade (No. 3675) and lay it on a pastry grate, then cover entirely with kirsch icing (No. 102), and when this is dry dress on a dish. Suppress the shells from about a hundred chestnuts, without touching the skins; boil them slowly in plenty of water in a covered vessel, then drain off the water, leaving them covered with a hot cloth; now quickly remove the skins; pound and rub the chestnuts through a sieve into a saucepan with three-quarters of their weight of powdered sugar added, also a small bit of vanilla; stir this well over a moderate fire until it detaches from the bottom and leave it till nearly cold, then dilute with a little light syrup and kirsch; incorporate into the mixture a few spoonfuls of well-drained whipped cream, but without weakening it, keeping it quite consistent, then stir on ice for ten minutes to harden, adding a salpicon of vari-colored fruits after it is removed. With this preparation fill up the hollow of the cake and smooth it to a dome-shape, then decorate through a cornet with whipped cream slightly sweetened and flavored with vanilla.

(3236). COMPIÈGNE CAKE (Gâteau Compiègne).

Dilute three-quarters of an ounce of compressed yeast in a vessel with one gill of warm milk; strain, return it to the vessel and incorporate five ounces of flour to make a soft leaven; put this on a floured table, mold and replace it in the vessel after cleaning it out well; cover over with a cloth and leave in a mild temperature to rise to double its size. In another vessel place three-quarters of a pound of flour, form a hole in the center and in it lay an ounce of sugar and a heavy pinch of salt (according to the saltiness of the butter), two eggs, eight yolks and six ounces of butter. Mix all well together to form into a paste, working it forcibly for a few moments in order to give it body, then add slowly one gill of rich cream; continue to work the paste until it has plenty of body, then mix in the leaven very lightly, also one pint of well-drained whipped cream. Butter a large plain cylindrical mold (Fig. 150) seven inches in diameter by seven inches high; fill it up three-quarters with the above paste and leave it in a mild temperature until quite full; stand it on a pie plate and push it carefully into a very slack oven. It should take an hour and a half to an hour and three-quarters to bake; take it out as soon as done, invert it on a grate and let cool off. Dress on a folded napkin to serve.

(3237). FLEURY CAKE (Gâteau Fleury).

Make a biscuit preparation with a pound of sugar, having two ounces of it flavored with vanilla (No. 3165), eight ounces of flour and four ounces of fecula sifted together; three-quarters of a pound of roasted and pounded filberts, twenty-two egg-yolks, six beaten whites and a grain of salt. Bake in a slack oven on a baking sheet covered with paper, having it at least half an inch thick, and when done put aside to cool for twelve hours. With seven or eight egg-yolks, some sugar, six gills of milk and a piece of vanilla, prepare an English cream (No. 42); as soon as it thickens remove and mix in a quarter of a pound of roasted chopped filberts, and pour it at once into a glazed vessel, working till cold; then strain through a tammy and return it to the saucepan to beat on a

FIG. 595.

slow fire for two minutes to have it lukewarm; remove once more and incorporate into it, without ceasing to stir, one-half pound of fresh butter divided in small pats; the cream should now be quite consistent and slightly frothy; divide it into two parts, and color one with carmine mixed with a little syrup so that it acquires a pinkish hue, leaving the other half white. Have a hexagon (six-sided) shaped cardboard pattern and with it cut three or four pieces from the prepared biscuit; split them through their thickness, mask them over with apricot marmalade (No. 3675), and reconstruct them as before; fasten these pieces on a thin Genoese bottom a third of an inch wider than the biscuit, and on this, with the remainder of the biscuit cut thin and also masked with apricot, raise an even pyramid, cut hexagonally; cover it as well as its base with a thin layer of the butter cream. Roast in the oven half a pound of filberts cut up small; when removed besprinkle with fine sugar, and when nearly cold apply them in smooth layers against the thickness of the base on which the pyramid stands, pressing them down with the blade of a knife to equalize the surface, leaving no open space whatever between. Introduce a part of the white cream into a small fancy socket pocket (Fig. 179), and push on the surfaces of the pyramid small, plain, close flowers, strictly following the divisions of the hexagon; next to these push some pink flowers, alternating the shades, in the different compartments. When the pyramid is entirely covered push a large rose on top, having the two colors mixed, then with a smaller socket surround the base of the cake with small roses made of the two colors. Keep the cake for a quarter of an hour on ice to have the cream harden superficially, and on removing slip it carefully on a napkin, and serve at once, for the buttered cream must remain hard.

(3238). FRUIT CAKE (Gâteau aux Fruits).

Proportions.—One pound and a half of butter, a pound and a half of sugar, a pound and a half of flour, twenty eggs, four pounds of seeded Malaga raisins, four pounds of Smyrna raisins, four pounds of citron, ten pounds of currants, two gills of rum, two gills of brandy, four gills of molasses, one ounce of cinnamon, half an ounce of allspice, a quarter of an ounce of mace and a quarter of an ounce of nutmeg. Beat the butter and sugar together in a tinned basin until creamy and white; adding the eggs one by one add the flour and mix perfectly, then put in the Malaga and Smyrna raisins, the currants, the finely cut-up citron and the spices; afterward the liquors and molasses; work until thoroughly mixed. For this quantity have two very strong tin molds twelve inches long at the bottom and five inches wide, with a quarter of an inch splay on each side, the depth to be six and a quarter inches. These molds must be furnished with covers closing on the outside. Butter and line them with buttered paper. Divide the preparation into two equal parts, one into each mold; cover the tops with buttered paper, put on the covers, then set both molds on a baking sheet and push into a slack oven. They take from six and a half to seven hours to bake. When partly done turn the molds upside down and finish cooking; remove from the oven, lift off the covers and arrange them one beside the other; lay blocks of wood on top, two and a quarter inches thick and of the same dimensions as the opening of the mold, or even slightly narrower, so they can enter the mold with facility. On each block lay a board and on this a sufficiently heavy weight to allow these blocks to enter entirely inside the mold, leaving it in this position for twelve hours in a cool place. Unmold the cakes carefully, wrap them in paper, and range in a hermetically closed tin box. These cakes require to be made two months beforehand, and be left tightly closed so they acquire the mellowness and flavor characteristic of their kind. When needed for use remove from the boxes, take off the paper adhering to the cakes, and cut each one into even eight crosswise slices; divide all of these on the widest side into five equal-sized pieces,

therefore obtaining forty pieces from each mold; wrap each one of these small pieces in a separate piece of waxed paper, then in tin foil, and after all are prepared put them into small cardboard boxes manufactured expressly for this purpose, they to be four and three-quarter inches long by an inch and a half wide and an inch and an eighth deep; these are the inside measurements: place on the covers, tie with a white ribbon once around their length and then around their width, forming it into a pretty

FIG. 596.　　　　　　　　　　　　　　　　　FIG. 597.

bow, which must come exactly in the center of the top of the box. For the machine for cutting these cakes see Figs. 596-597. These machines greatly facilitate the cutting. To have them very regular, according to the above proportions, put the whole cake in machine No. 596, cut it in transversal slices one after the other, pressing the cake forward on the machine for each slice that is cut. Machine No. 597 is used for dividing the first slices and to cut them very even, passing the blade of the knife between the vertical guides of the machine. If instead of small cakes in boxes a large one be desired, then put the preparation into one large round mold sixteen inches in diameter at the bottom and eighteen inches at the top or opening; it must be five and a half inches deep and furnished with a tube in the center five and a half inches at the bottom and five at the top. Cover the insides with bands of buttered paper, overlapping each other, and cook the cake the same as the preceding ones in a slack oven, leaving it in from seven to seven and a half hours. Let it get perfectly cold by placing on top a board seventeen inches in diameter, having a hole in the center five and a half inches in diameter, then press down lightly. These cakes ought to be made two months before they are needed and kept in a cool place. When required for use unmold, remove the paper and ice over with several layers of royal icing (No. 101); slide on a board covered with lace paper, and after the icing is perfectly dry decorate with more royal icing. A fine gum-paste vase can be placed in the center, filled with flowers or other ornaments.

(3239). GENOESE CAKE (Gâteau Génoise).

Butter a pound cake mold and line it with paper. Have one pound of sugar, part of it being flavored with vanilla (No. 3165), in a basin with sixteen whole eggs; whip this till light, warming the preparation over a slow fire. To have this attain a proper degree of lightness it will be necessary to whip for at least forty minutes, then mix in one pound of sifted flour, and lastly half a pound of melted butter. Fill the mold three-quarters full with this, and bake in a slack oven for an hour and a quarter. Remove, unmold on a grate and cool thoroughly. Then pare it very straight and cover with a layer of apricot marmalade (No. 3675); ice with vanilla fondant (No. 58). After the icing has dried thoroughly slip the cake on a dish and decorate either with royal icing or fanciful cuts of fruits; surround with a circle of preserved plums and cherries.

(3240). GUGELHOPFEN (Cougloff).

Butter well the inside of a baba mold having fluted sides; decorate the interior with halved almonds and keep it cool. Form a hollow in the center of four ounces of sifted flour; in it lay half an ounce of yeast, diluting it little by little with a small quantity of tepid milk; mix both flour and liquid slowly together to obtain a soft paste; gather it all up, lay it on the table and form into a ball, cutting a cross on top; place in a basin, cover with a cloth and leave in a mild temperature to have it rise to double its volume. In another vessel work ten ounces of butter with a spatula to a light cream. Lay three-quarters of a pound of flour in a circle on the table; in the center put one ounce of sugar and a little salt; dissolve these with a little water, then add four whole eggs and four separate yolks; mix the whole well and knead the paste vigorously to have it smooth with plenty of body, proceeding the same as for a baba paste; add slowly a gill and a half of good cream; continue to knead the paste until it is quite glossy, then add the butter slowly, knead once more for a few moments, put in the leaven and mingle all well together, then add four ounces of seeded Malaga raisins. As soon as all the ingredients are perfectly combined lay the paste in the mold to reach to two-thirds of its height and set it in a mild temperature until it raises to the top. Place the mold on a baking pan and bake in a slack oven for two hours; unmold on a wire grate.

(3241). HAZEL-NUT CAKE (Gâteau aux Noisettes).

Prepare a fine paste with two eggs, four ounces of almonds and four ounces of hazel-nuts, both well pounded. Put into a basin a pound and a quarter of sugar with twenty egg-yolks, beat till quite frothy, then stir in the almond and nut paste, continuing to beat for a few moments longer; mix in lightly three-quarters of a pound of flour and twenty egg-whites whipped to a stiff froth. Divide this preparation in three rings eight inches in diameter lined with paper; bake the cakes in a slow oven; turn them out as soon as done and leave cool off entirely, then mask each with a thick layer of pastry cream (No. 46) highly flavored with vanilla, adding to it a few roasted hazel-nuts pounded with a little cream. Lay one round on top of the other to form into one large cake; pare it well rounded and very uniform with a knife and cover it entirely with reduced apricot marmalade (No. 3675); ice the cake with vanilla icing (No. 102). As soon as this is hard and dry slide the cake on a dish covered with lace paper and decorate the top with a fine display of royal icing ornamentation. Surround the bottom of the cake with small lady bouchées (No. 3376) iced with white fondant (No. 58), laying each one in a small paper case.

(3242). JAMAICA CAKE (Gâteau à la Jamaïque).

Beat up a pound of sugar with fourteen egg-yolks, so as to have it frothy, then add slowly twelve beaten-up whites and at the same time one pound of sifted rice flour, then a pound of melted butter, also pouring it in slowly with some grated lemon peel, a grain of salt, six ounces of candied orange peels cut in small pieces and six ounces of small raisins. Bake this preparation in a slack oven after placing it in a buttered and floured spiral mold; when the cake is unmolded and cold apricot the surface and glaze with rum icing (No. 102). Dress on a napkin and decorate with whipped cream.

(3243). JELLY CAKE MERINGUED (Gâteau à la Gelée Meringué).

Have eight egg-yolks in a vessel with half a pound of sugar and the peel of one lemon; beat with a spatula until it becomes light and creamy, then add half a pound of flour, four ounces of melted butter and lastly eight firmly whipped egg-whites. Take some jelly cake molds eight inches in diameter and half an inch deep; butter and flour their insides and fill them to the top with the mixture, then bake in a hot oven. As soon as done unmold on grates and leave stand to cool. Place three of these cakes one on top of the other with a layer of currant jelly (No. 3670) spread between each, pare the cake round, decorate the surface with a handsome rosette of Italian meringue (No. 140) in the center, it having six to eight leaves, with an empty space in the middle; around the edges dress a continuous wreath of these rosettes, also hollow in the center. Stand the cake for two or three minutes in the oven to dry the meringue decorations, then take out and fill the cavities with apple, currant and quince jellies and apricot marmalade, alternating the different colors; set it on a lace-paper covered dish. Instead of covering the jelly cake with meringue, a piece of cardboard the same diameter as the cake, having a design of any kind cut out to form a stencil, may be used; lay it over the cake, sprinkle it entirely with finely powdered sugar, remove the cardboard carefully and the design will be found imprinted on the cake.

(3244). LADY CAKE (Gâteau des Dames).

Put fourteen ounces of butter and twenty ounces of sugar in a metal bowl and work together with the hands for fifteen or twenty minutes to have it quite frothy, then add four ounces of almonds, including a few bitter ones, pounded with a little water, and work again for a few moments. Now put in one gill of brandy or rum, twenty ounces of flour and finally twenty very stiffly whipped egg-whites. Butter a pound-cake mold, line it throughout with paper and fill it three-quarters full with the preparation; bake in a very slow oven. (Once the cake is in the oven it must not be touched until baked.) Take it out, unmold and leave to get thoroughly cold. Then ice with royal icing (No. 101) and stand it at once on a lace-paper covered board. After the icing has dried decorate the cake with more royal icing.

(3245). MANDARIN CAKE (Gâteau Mandarin).

Fasten on a dish a wooden bottom about an inch thick and cover it with white paper. Heat a medium-sized biscuit mold, grease it over with melted veal kidney suet mixed with melted butter, and turn it over to drain out all the fat, then glaze with sugar mixed with fecula. Beat up vigorously in a basin twelve egg-yolks with three-quarters of a pound of powdered sugar, having one-quarter of it grated on two mandarins, and add a grain of salt. When this preparation becomes creamy, incorporate into it ten or eleven beaten whites, and at the same time let fall into it through a sieve a pound of fine flour and fecula mixed together; carefully work without breaking, and with it fill the mold nearly to the top; surround the exterior of the top with a band of buttered paper, then lay it on a small baking sheet covered with a thick layer of hot cinders, and push it into a

FIG. 598.

moderate oven to bake for one hour, carefully turning the baking sheet around at frequent intervals. On removing the biscuit from the oven detach it from the top, inserting a small knife around the edges, and unmold on a grate, and when perfectly cold cut the bottom off straight, then let it get stale for seven or eight hours. Should the surface of the biscuit not be smooth, or else too brown, stand it upright on the grate and brush over entirely with apricot marmalade (No. 3675), then cover with raw vanilla icing (No. 102); when this is dry, cut a round piece from the cut side, about a quarter of an inch from the edge, remove this piece and empty out the biscuit as neatly as possible, not approaching the edges too closely. Cut across through the center about twelve small, fresh and sound mandarins; remove the insides neatly from the peel, keeping these as whole as possible, and lay them on one side; suppress the white pith and seeds from the fruit, and crush the pulp to rub it through a sieve; put this into a vessel and mix with it a few spoonfuls of champagne, some syrup, a small bunch of lemon peel and a few spoonfuls of calf's foot jelly (No. 104), sweetened and clarified; let infuse together for fifteen minutes. With a vegetable spoon (Fig. 91) scoop out all the white part from the halved mandarin peels, and incrust them in a thick layer of pounded, slightly salted ice, suppressing the lemon peel from the preparation; thicken it lightly while stirring on ice, and with it fill the empty peels; brush them over with jelly and keep on ice for a quarter of an hour. Open five or six oranges from the stalk end; with a tin tube empty them out entirely, suppressing all the white pith; incrust them in pounded, unsalted ice, and then fill them with clear jelly flavored with orange (No. 3180), alternated with layers of blanc-mange (No. 3138), also flavored with orange; harden both of these preparations on ice. Now fill the empty biscuit with well-drained and sweetened whipped cream flavored with Curaçoa and orange peel. Close the opening with the removed piece and dress on the center of the wooden bottom. Surround with the filled halved mandarins, and the base of the dish with the oranges cut in six, then cut off straight on one end so as to maintain them upright.

(3246). MARLY CAKE (Gâteau Marly).

Butter and glaze two dome-shaped pointed molds, seven inches high by six inches in diameter; fill them almost to the top with a lemon-flavored biscuit preparation, the same as for mandarin cakes (No. 3245), and surround the opening with a band of buttered paper; stand them upright on a raised-edge baking sheet and bake the biscuits in a slow oven for one hour. Remove and unmold on a pastry grate, and when cold cut the bottoms off straight and let get stale for the next

FIG. 599.

twelve hours. Now lay the cakes on a grate, placing them on the cut end and brush them over lightly with apricot marmalade (No. 3675), then cover one of them entirely with pink icing (No. 102) and the other with white (No. 102). Two minutes after, without letting it get dry, divide each biscuit into eight pieces from top to bottom, pointed on the tops, and when the icing is thoroughly dry take up the pieces one by one and reconstruct them into one biscuit, only being careful to alternate the colors, having first a pink piece and then a white one; empty the inside of the biscuit as neatly as possible and fill the center with St. Honoré cream (No. 49), to which pounded almonds and a little kirsch have been added, dressing it in layers alternated with cut-up macaroons soaked in rum. Invert the biscuit on a cold dish covered over with a folded napkin.

(3247). MILFOIL CAKE, POMPADOUR (Gâteau Mille-Feuilles, Pompadour).

Prepare some rounds of puff paste (No. 146) the same way and size as the milfoil with preserves (No. 3248); cover each of these with vanilla-flavored English cream (No. 42), dredging the top with a salpicon of candied fruits cut in one-eighth inch squares and macerated in kirsch. After the cake is formed, pare it round and cover with firmly beaten and well-drained whipped cream sweetened with fine vanilla sugar (No. 3165). Dress this in a dome-form on top, and decorate through a cornet with whipped cream tinted a pale pink; strew with thin green fillets of pistachios. Slip the cake on a flat two inches wider than itself and covered with strawberry icing (No. 102), sprinkled with red sugar (No. 172); surrround the base of the cake with small lady bouchées iced with strawberry (No. 3376).

(3248). MILFOIL WITH PRESERVES (Gâteau Mille-Feuilles aux Confitures).

This requires some puff paste of twelve turns (No. 146); divide it into six-ounce pieces, roll them out to three-sixteenths of an inch in thickness and cut into rounds seven inches in diameter; lay these on baking sheets slightly moistened with cold water applied with a brush; from the center of each piece remove a two-inch diameter round and leave these to rest in a cold place for half an hour; bestrew lightly with sugar, prick and bake in a slack oven. After taking them out detach from the sheets and lay them at once on grates to get cold, then stand one on top of the other intercalated with a layer either of currant jelly (No. 3670), apricot marmalade or peach marmalade (No. 3675); pare the cake neatly into a perfect round and cover with Italian meringue (No. 140) on the edges. Sprinkle over it a mixture made of equal parts of Mocha sugar (No. 3249), half of which is colored with carmine with a little syrup, chopped almonds, chopped pistachios and currants. Lay the cake on a tart dish and push into a moderate oven for a few moments to dry the meringue without coloring it, then place it on a round made of a three-eighths of an inch thickness of frolle paste (No. 136), and iced over with pink icing (No. 102), strewn with pink sugar (No. 172), it having a border of gum paste or English paste. Dress the milfoil either on a napkin or on a socle, and garnish around with small bouchées filled with currant jelly, these being called Wells of Love (No. 3338).

(3249). MOCHA CAKE (Gâteau Moka).

Deposit in a vessel half a pound of sugar, six egg-yolks and one whole egg; beat for fifteen minutes to have it light, then add six ounces of flour and two ounces of fecula sifted together, also two tablespoonfuls of brandy, six ounces of melted butter, and lastly six well-whipped egg-whites. Bake this in a buttered and paper-lined pound-cake mold; as soon as done remove, unmold on a grate and leave it there until perfectly cold. Now pare the cake very straight and cut it across in two even parts; fill it with a three-eighths of an inch thick layer of Mocha cream (No. 45); cover the top and sides with the same and decorate the surface through a channeled socket pocket (Fig. 179), using more of the cream; dredge with Mocha sugar. Leave the cake in a cool place until required for serving.

Mocha Sugar is made by pounding loaf sugar in a mortar and passing it through a six-mesh sieve cloth (No. 94).

(3250). NEAPOLITAN CAKE (Gâteau Napolitain).

Crush one pound and ten ounces of almonds with a pound and a quarter of sugar; reduce to a fine powder; pass this through a sieve. Sift on the table two pounds of flour, make a hollow in the center and in it lay the almond and sugar powder, a pound and a half of butter, a pinch of salt and four whole eggs; work the whole together just enough to form a smooth, firm paste, for if worked too much it is liable to crumble. Lay it in a vessel and leave in a cool place to rest; one hour later divide this paste into sixteen or twenty even parts and roll them to a quarter of an inch thick by six and a quarter inches in diameter; empty out the centers with a two-inch pastry cutter. Have two of the flats a little thicker and two inches wider in diameter than the others; bake on a buttered and floured baking sheet in a hot oven, and as soon as done take them out and leave to cool under the pressure of a weight; pare the large rounds eight inches in diameter and put them once more under a weight; when cold ice either with white or pink icing (No. 102); mask the small flats with well-strained and reduced apricot marmalade (No. 3675); now lay them one over the other; pare them evenly to have the cake six inches in diameter, and cover the whole with well-reduced and well-cooked apricot marmalade; place the cake on one of the large flats and over lay the second large one. Decorate around with fanciful cuts of almond gum paste and the top with a cupola of royal icing or gum paste. Ornament around the edge of the large flat with a double border of the same paste and arrange the cake on a richly decorated stand. This cake is intended for a sideboard. It can also be made with almond biscuit (No. 3229).

(3251) NOUGATINE CAKE (Gâteau Nougatine).

Make a biscuit preparation with a pound of powdered sugar, a pound of flour, six whole eggs, eighteen yolks, six beaten whites, vanilla and a grain of salt. Bake this in a slack oven in three or four smooth fruit pie circles, six or seven inches in diameter by an inch to an inch and a half high. These circles should be buttered with clarified butter and glazed with fecula. After taking them from the oven remove from the circles and leave to get thoroughly cold for twelve hours. Prepare a buttered orange cream the same as for the Fleury cake (No. 3237). Mince half a pound of sweet peeled almonds, previously dried on a sheet of paper then roasted in a pan to brown nicely. Cut the biscuits into transversal slices three-eighths of an inch thick, and taking up seven or eight of these, one by one, cover one side with a layer of the prepared cream, then put one on top of the other so as to form into a regular-shaped cake, and cover the top and sides at once with another layer of cream; now spread over the whole a layer of the roasted almonds, fastening them on with the blade of a knife, so as to equalize its thickness; besprinkle lightly with fine vanilla sugar (No. 3165), and push the cake for one minute in a hot oven, simply to have the sugar adhere to the almonds, then take out at once and when cold dress on a napkin.

(3252). PINEAPPLE CAKE (Gâteau Ananas).

Prepare a Savoy biscuit composition in the following proportions: One pound of sugar, fourteen yolks, two whole eggs, three-quarters of a pound of fecula and flour, half of each, fourteen whipped whites, and some pineapple extract. Bake a part of this in a Savarin mold seven and a quarter inches in diameter, buttered and glazed with sugar and fecula, and the remainder in a charlotte mold six inches wide by seven high. As soon as both are cooked unmold the cakes and allow to cool. Cover the one baked in the Savarin mold with apricot marmalade (No. 3675), and ice with pink fondant (No. 58) flavored with kirsch; as soon as this is dry slip it on a sweet paste (No. 136) foundation, sprinkled over with green granulated sugar; put a pad of biscuit in the center, and range it on a dish or board covered with lace paper. Pare the cake baked in the charlotte mold to the shape of a sugar loaf, then cut it into transversal slices three-eighths of an inch thick; cover all of these with a light layer of apricot marmalade, and reconstruct the cake as before; cover its entire surface with Italian meringue (No. 140) flavored with orange and slightly tinted with vegetable yellow; pour some of the same meringue in a pocket (Fig. 179) with a channeled socket and push it through to imitate the rough skin of a pineapple, forming points on the entire surface of the cake; stand it on a tart plate and push it into a slack oven to barely dry the meringue; remove it at once and allow to cool thoroughly; place it on a grate and ice over with yellow orange icing (No. 102), and when this is dry detach the pineapple cautiously from the grate and place it on top of the biscuit. Over the points of the rough pineapple form the tips with chocolate icing pushed through a cornet. Decorate the top with stalks cut from angelica dipped in sugar cooked to "crack" (No. 171) having the base of the pineapple surrounded by leaves of the same. (See pineapple, No. 3595.)

(3253). PLUM CAKE (Gâteau aux Raisins de Corinthe).

Butter a charlotte mold five and a half inches in diameter by five inches high; at the bottom lay a round piece of paper and line the sides with a band of the same. This should reach three-quarters of an inch beyond the edge and should be serrated all around. Place three-quarters of a pound of butter in a vessel with the same weight of sugar and beat together to have it creamy, then add six whole eggs, one at a time, one gill of rum, six ounces of currants cleaned and softened in hot water, three ounces of preserved cherries cut in four, three ounces of citron cut up finely, a pinch of powdered carbonate of ammonia, and lastly fourteen ounces of sifted flour. Fill the mold three-quarters full with this, and stand it on a baking plate; push it into a slack oven to bake, and when done unmold on a grate to cool thoroughly without removing the paper, then place it on a dish covered with a folded napkin and serve.

(3254). POUND CAKE (Pound Cake).

Put twelve eggs and four ounces of sugar in a basin and whip until they become quite light, warming them slightly over the fire. In a large metal vessel lay one pound of butter and three-quarters of a pound of sugar; work with the hands until creamy and light, then add gradually the prepared eggs, beating continuously, and a gill of brandy or rum, and lastly one pound of sifted flour. Butter a pound cake mold, line it with paper and pour in the preparation, having it three-quarters full, then place it in a slow oven to bake for an hour and three-quarters to two hours. Remove from the oven, unmold, and leave stand till cold, then ice it with icing flavored with rum (No. 102). After this is dry slip the cake on a board or dish and decorate with royal icing.

(3255). PUNCH CAKE, PUNCH BISCUIT, IMITATION OF BOAR'S HEAD, A BOOK OR A HAM (Gâteau Punch, Punch Biscuit, Imitation de Hure de Sanglier, d'un Livre ou d'un Jambon).

Put eight ounces of fine white apple marmalade (No. 3674) and eight ounces of sugar in a copper pan; stand this on the fire and cook for a few moments to reduce the marmalade, then remove and add a quarter of a gill of rum, a quarter of a gill of Curaçoa and eight well-beaten egg-whites. Bake a Savoy biscuit (No. 3231) in a buttered timbale mold, glazed with sugar and fecula; as soon as done, unmold, cool and cut it straight, then empty it from the bottom, leaving an inch-thick crust all around. Fill the empty cake with the above apples, lay over a round of frolle paste (No. 136) the same dimensions as the cake and invert it on a grate; ice with orange fondant (No. 58) flavored with rum and Curaçoa. After the icing has dried slide the cake on a dish, decorate with fanciful cuts of candied fruits and surround the base with a circle of greengages.

Punch Biscuit Paste—One pound of sugar, half a pound of flour, half a pound of fecula, nine ounces of melted butter, three whole eggs, eleven yolks, four whipped whites, a small glassful of rum, chopped lemon and orange peel and a grain of salt. Place the sugar in a vessel; add the yolks slowly, creaming together with a spoon, and when very light put in the butter, the rum, the whipped whites, the fecula, the sifted flour, and lastly the peels and salt.

Boar's Head—Imitation (Hure de Sanglier).—Bake thoroughly a punch biscuit in an oval mold the same size as a natural boar's head, fourteen by nine inches on the top and six inches deep, the splay to be half an inch. The next day cut the biscuit the shape of a boar's head (Fig. 537); hollow it out underneath and replace the biscuit that is removed by the same soaked in maraschino so as to make a paste, into which mix plenty of candied fruits. Lay the cake on an oval foundation the size of the head, and cover with well-cooked apricot marmalade (No. 3675), then coat the whole with cooked chocolate icing (No. 99). As soon as the icing is dry cut out the snout, leaving it partly opened, hollow out the cavities for the eyes, and on each side of the snout place two large fangs made of almond paste (No. 127) and dipped in clear dissolved gelatine. Imitate the eyes by two rounded balls of almond paste, placing a black spot in the center; mold these in a teaspoon with clarified gelatine; unmold and when cold fasten them in the cavities made to hold the eyes. Dress the cake on a foundation glazed with green fondant (No. 58). Decorate the head with fruits and transparent hatelets, ornamented with large fruits; the base should be surrounded with chopped jelly and jelly croûtons.

A Book—Imitation (Un Livre).—To be prepared the same as the boar's head with punch biscuit, the two covers and the back of the binding made of almond paste (No. 127). Empty out the center, leaving the top cover stationary. Glaze the sides of the book with orange icing, the cover with coffee icing and decorate the whole with royal icing. Fill the inside with tutti-frutti ice cream (No. 3586). This book can be laid on a socle or a cushion glazed with pink icing.

Ham—Imitation (Jambon).—As for the boar's head, prepare a punch biscuit fourteen inches long, nine inches wide and four and a half inches thick; after being cooked and thoroughly cold, trim it to the shape of a ham, then cut it through its thickness; empty it out and fill the center with a Bengalian charlotte preparation (No. 3142). Fasten the two parts together again with apricot marmalade (No. 3675) and coat it over with the same. Glaze the handle end one-third of the length of the ham with chocolate icing to imitate the rind and the other two-thirds with white prunelle icing. Stand the ham on a foundation bottom made of frolle paste (No. 136), and on the chocolate end stick a piece of pointed wood three-quarters of an inch in diameter by five inches in length; trim the end of this with a large paper rosette. Decorate the white part of the ham with almond paste (No. 127) flavored with chocolate or pistachio. Leave it to cool perfectly, then coat with jelly. Lay the ham on a small low socle (for this see ham à la Gatti, Fig. 498), and decorate around with chopped jelly and croûtons. These cakes can also be made to imitate a salmon (Fig. 521a), a swan (Fig. 723), foies-gras patty (Fig. 515), boned turkey (Fig. 479) or any other design.

(3256). QUEEN CAKE (Gâteau Reine).

Beat up a pound of butter with twelve egg-yolks, adding a pound of sugar, a little at a time, half a pound of ground almonds, half a pound of fecula and then seven beaten whites, one quart in volume of drained whipped cream, vanilla or lemon flavored, a few candied orange flowers and a grain of salt, the cream to be added lastly. Bake in a slack oven in a spiral mold glazed with sugar. After the cake is unmolded and cold cover with apricot marmalade (No. 3675) and ice with maraschino icing (No. 102). No good results can be expected unless good cream is used.

(3257). ROEDERER CAKE (Gâteau Roederer).

Pound six ounces of almonds and six ounces of pistachios with a little milk to make a fine, soft paste. Put one pound of sugar in a basin, slowly add sixteen whole eggs, and beat until very light, heating it slightly on hot embers or on a very slow fire; put in the almond paste and continue beating for a few moments longer, then mix in with a small skimmer three-quarters of a pound of rice flour and lastly half a pound of melted butter. Butter a pound cake mold, line it with paper and fill it three-quarters full with the preparation; push into a very slack oven to cook for an hour and a quarter. When done remove and invert it on a grate to cool, then detach the cake from the paper and cut it across in two; fill it with some Bavarian cream (No. 3135), into which mix three ounces of pistachios pounded with a little vanilla syrup; cover the entire cake with hot apricot marmalade (No. 3675); coat it with pistachio fondant (No. 58) and bestrew immediately with finely shredded green pistachios; let the fondant dry, then slide the cake on a lace-paper covered board or dish and surround the base with a row of small cream cakes (No. 3295), glazed with sugar cooked to "crack" (No. 171) and sprinkled with shredded pistachios.

(3258). SAND CAKE (Gâteau Sable).

Mix twelve ounces of powdered sugar and four ounces of vanilla sugar (No. 3165) in a basin with sixteen egg-yolks; beat until light, then add half a pound of flour and half a pound of fecula, sifted together, one pound of melted butter, and lastly the sixteen beaten whites; bake this in a slack oven in a pound cake or manqué mold, buttered and lined with paper, and when done to perfection take it out and invert on a grate to cool. Then cover the cake with well-reduced apricot marmalade (No. 3675) and ice over with water icing flavored with rum (No. 102). Decorate with candied fruits and dress on a dish covered with lace paper.

(3259). SAVARIN À LA VALENCE (Savarin à la Valence).

Butter a medium-sized Savarin mold, dredge the bottom with cut-up almonds and fill it half full with Savarin paste (No. 148) into which has been incorporated candied orange peel cut in the shape of small dice. Let it rise in a mild temperature until it reaches the edges, then bake in a slack oven. As soon as it is done remove from the oven, pare it even and unmold on a grate; pour some orange syrup over, cover with apricot marmalade (No. 3675) and glaze with fondant (No. 58), flavored with orange. When the icing is cold slip the Savarin on to a bottom made of office paste (No. 143) covered with green sugar (No. 172), and dress it on a dish. Decorate the top of the cake with a wreath of angelica lozenges and cherries (demi-sucre); fill the center with Chantilly cream (No. 50) flavored with orange sugar (No. 3165) and place on top a light sugar sultana (No. 3193), then serve.

(3260). SPONGE CAKE (Biscuit Léger).

Set into a basin fourteen whole eggs, two separate yolks, one pound of sugar and the peel of a lemon; beat in such a way as to have a very light composition while heating it slightly; in order to obtain the desired lightness it will be necessary to beat for at least thirty to forty minutes, then carefully mix in one pound of flour. With this fill a pound cake or "manqué" mold three-quarters full, having it buttered and glazed with sugar and fecula, half of each; bake in a slack oven. Invert the cake as soon as done on a grate, let get thoroughly cold, then bestrew with icing sugar and dress on a dish. This cake may be served plain, without icing, simply bestrewing vanilla sugar (No. 3165) over it.

(3261). ST. HONORÉ AND ST. HONORÉ SULTANA (St. Honoré et St. Honoré Sultane).

Roll out some very fine short paste (No. 135) to obtain a flat three-sixteenths of an inch in thickness and eight inches in diameter; lay it on a round baking pan dampened with water, prick it all over and with a pocket furnished with a half-inch diameter socket push flat on the edges of this a heavy string of cream cake paste (No. 132). Egg over twice and bake in a slack oven for ten to fifteen minutes. Dress on another tart plate sixteen small round cream cakes (No. 3294), three-quarters of an inch in diameter; egg over and bake them in a moderate oven, then detach from the plate by slipping a knife underneath. Peel two oranges, divide them in sections, leaving on only the fine skin covering the pulp, being careful not to break it, and range them on a grate to dry, either in the air or in a heater. Wash in hot water some candied fruits, such as cherries, apricots, angelica and pears; wipe dry and cut the apricots in four, the angelica in lozenges, the pears in four and leave the cherries whole; have also some loose green grapes, eight pieces of each kind of fruit. Cook some sugar to "crack" (No. 171); first dip in the cream cakes and arrange them on an oiled baking tin, then drain; proceed the same with the oranges, grapes, apricots, angelica, cherries, pears, etc. On the band fasten the cream cakes with sugar cooked to "crack;" on top of these place a row of quartered oranges, on each quartered orange a glazed cherry, and between each one of the sections place an angelica lozenge or one of the grapes; slip on a dish covered with lace paper. Fill the St. Honoré with St. Honoré cream (No. 49), and serve.

St. Honoré Sultana.—Replace the St. Honoré cream by a vanilla bavarois cream (No. 3135) with plenty of whipped cream, and over the fruits place a spun sugar sultana the shape of an ogive (No. 3193), and around quarters of apricots and pears, both glazed.

(3262). STRAWBERRY SHORT CAKE (Gâteau aux Fraises).

Place in a basin six ounces of butter with ten ounces of sugar; beat both well together until a creamy preparation is obtained, then add three eggs, one at a time, two gills of milk and vanilla flavoring. After the whole has been well mixed pour in a pound of sifted flour into which has been added a coffeespoonful of baking powder. Have some round flat molds seven and a half inches in diameter and the edges raised to three-eighths of an inch high; butter and flour these over, then fill them to the top with the mixture and bake in a brisk oven. Unmold on a grate as soon as they are done and leave stand till cold; cover each one of these layers of cake with a vanilla pastry cream (No. 46), and on it arrange very fine, ripe strawberries, one next to the other; bestrew with sugar and lay two of these garnished cakes one on top of the other; put on a dish and cover the cake with sweetened whipped cream (No. 50), flavored with vanilla and pushed through a pocket.

(3263). FAVART CAKE (Gâteau Favart).

Whip sixteen eggs in a basin with one pound of powdered sugar and two ounces of vanilla sugar (No. 3165); beat till very light while heating slightly, then stir in with a spoon one pound of sifted flour and later three-quarters of a pound of melted butter. Butter a hexagonal mold (Fig. 139) with clarified butter, flour it over and fill it three-quarters full with the preparation. Bake in a slow oven; when done, unmold on a grate and when thoroughly cold cover with peach marmalade (No. 3675), ice with kirsch icing (No. 102), dredging the top with chopped burnt almonds and some small one-eighth inch squares of angelica and citron.

(3264). VACHERIN CAKE WITH CREAM (Gâteau Vacherin à la Crème).

Cut three or four rounds of white paper seven inches in diameter; on the edges of these push through a socket pocket some meringue (No. 140), to form a ring an inch wide and of the same height; smooth the surfaces of the meringue on both top and sides with the blade of a knife, bestrew with fine sugar and stand each one on a board dampened with water; dry the meringue in a slack oven without letting attain color. After these rings have been removed invert them on baking sheets and replace them in the oven for ten minutes to dry the meringue that has remained

Fig. 600.

soft, then stand for twenty-four hours in a warm closet. Arrange these rings on top of each other on a layer of frolle paste (No. 136) cut exactly the same dimensions, and cover each one with meringue made of cooked sugar (No. 140), to fasten them together; mask the entire inside with a thin layer of the same meringue; smooth it quickly and dry for two hours in a warm closet. After the meringue is quite cold cover it superficially with a brush dipped in reduced apricot marmalade (No. 3675), not having it too thick; dry this in the air, then decorate the upper ring with a chain of small rings a quarter of an inch thick made of lady finger paste (No. 3377), also to be covered with the marmalade. Fill the center of these small rings with quince jelly (No. 3672) or currant jelly (No. 3670). Slip the cake on a folded napkin and at the last moment cover with whipped cream flavored with vanilla (No. 50).

(3265). VALENTINE CAKE WITH RUM (Gâteau Valentin au Rhum).

Crush one pound of almonds with one pound of sugar and three eggs; make it into a very fine paste; put it into a basin and dilute gradually with thirteen eggs and one gill of rum; beat well until perfectly light. Line a mold with very thin sweet paste (No. 136); fill it three-quarters full with the preparation and strew over some finely cut-up almonds. Bake in a very slack oven for three-quarters of an hour, then turn the cake out on a grate and allow to cool; when cold glaze with a light frosting flavored with rum. This cake can be kept for several months if wrapped in tin-foil and left in a dry cool place.

BREAKFAST CAKES (Gâteaux de Déjeuner).

(3266). BISCUITS (Biscuits).

Sift one pound of flour on a table, divide it into four parts, and take one of these to make the leaven by making a circle with the flour and diluting half an ounce of compressed yeast with a little tepid water, then mix to make a soft paste; shape this leaven into a ball and cut a cross on top; lay it in a deep vessel and cover, leaving it to rise to double its height. Make a hollow in the center of the remaining flour, lay in it two ounces of sugar, a pinch of salt, seven whole eggs and two yolks; mix well together to form a paste, working it well so that it obtains considerable body, and then incorporate three ounces of butter. As soon as the leaven is ready mix it well but lightly into the paste, then lay it in a vessel and cover to let it rise to double its volume. Afterward knead it and with it fill some tin or sheet-iron half cylindrical molds, three and a half inches in diameter by twelve inches long, and previously buttered. Leave them until the dough rises as high as the level of the edges, then set these molds in the oven so the biscuits bake all alike to a fine golden color. Unmold them as soon as they are done and cut them across in quarter-inch slices; range these on tins and push into a slack oven to brown slightly.

(3267). CINNAMON BISCUITS (Biscuits à la Canelle).

The proportion for these is one pound of flour, half an ounce of compressed yeast, four ounces of sugar and one grain of salt, seven whole eggs and two yolks. With these ingredients prepare a dough the same as for biscuits (No. 3266). As soon as it is risen properly lay it in a long, square-shaped mold four inches wide, four inches deep and twelve inches long; fill it three-quarters full and let the dough rise to the level of the edges, then bake in a moderate oven for forty minutes. As soon as done unmold and when cold cut it up into slices five-sixteenths of an inch thick by three inches long and one and a quarter inches wide. Range these on a baking tin; sprinkle the tops lightly with sugar to which has been added a little ground cinnamon; place in a slack oven and let glaze to a fine golden brown.

(3268). FLUTES OF BRIOCHE (Flûtes en Brioche).

Take some brioche paste (No. 130) hardened on ice; divide it into two-ounce pieces and roll each of these into a string on the table, having them six to seven inches long; range them at once on a baking sheet at short distances apart and egg them over twice, then cook in a hot oven, and when removed pass a knife under to detach them from the sheet.

(3269). BRIOCHES FOR BREAKFAST (Brioches Pour le Déjeuner).

Small brioches can be baked in small channeled molds or else simply laid on a baking pan. In both cases they must be rolled into balls. Have some raised brioche paste (No. 130) that has been hardened on the ice; invert it on a floured table and shape it into large rolls; cut these across into equal pieces and mold them into balls with the hands; lay them at some distance apart on tins or else each one in a separate mold; flatten down the center with a damp finger and introduce into this cavity a small piece of the same dough molded the shape of a comma; this is to form the head of the brioche. Let the dough rest for ten minutes, then egg over the brioches and bake them for twenty minutes in a brisk but not too fierce oven; after removing keep them for ten minutes at the entrance of the oven before serving.

(3270). ENGLISH BUNS AND HOT CROSS BUNS (Buns Anglaises et Cross Buns Chaudes).

Buns.—Sift a pound of flour on the table and with a fourth part of it prepare a soft leaven by forming a hollow or hole in the center and pouring in three-quarters of an ounce of yeast dissolved in a little tepid water; shape it into a ball, score a cross on top, and lay it aside till it has risen to double its size. Make a hole in the center of the remainder of the flour, place in it three ounces of sugar, half an ounce of salt, three ounces of butter and four eggs; mix these ingredients well together, incorporating the flour gradually, and adding two and a half gills of milk; continue to stir, obtaining a soft and not very consistent paste; knead this well for a few moments to let acquire a body, then put with it four ounces of currants that have been cleansed and washed several times in warm water; also add the leaven, but knead it slightly only. As soon as finished lay the paste

In a bowl, cover with a cloth and let rise in a mild temperature until it is a third larger than its original size, then turn it over on the floured table and refold it on itself two or three times; break it into pound pieces and roll these into strings three-quarters of an inch in diameter, to cut into lengths of an ounce each; mold them into balls, then roll them into oval shapes; lay them as fast as they are done on lightly buttered tins, and leave them in a mild temperature to rise; egg over and bake in a hot oven.

Hot Cross Buns.—Prepare the dough exactly as for the English buns, adding when it is finished a pinch of cinnamon and grated nutmeg; shape them into rounds instead of ovals, and egg them over once. Just when ready to put in the oven make two opposite incisions on each bun with the tip of a knife to form a cross. Bake at once in a hot oven.

(3271). BUCKWHEAT CAKES WITH BAKING POWDER (Galettes de Sarrasin à la Levure en Poudre).

This paste should be made just when ready to use, in the same proportions and in the same manner as the buckwheat cakes with yeast (No. 3272), only suppressing the yeast. When ready

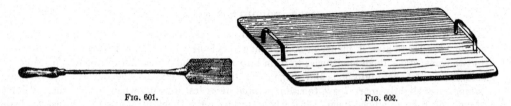

FIG. 601.   FIG. 602.

divide it into two parts, and incorporate into one of these two tablespoonfuls of baking powder; mix thoroughly and cook at once, proceeding exactly as for the others. As soon as the first part is exhausted put the same quantity of baking powder into the second part, and proceed precisely as for the first.

(3272). BUCKWHEAT CAKES WITH YEAST (Galettes de Sarrasin à la Levure).

Put a pound of buckwheat flour in a bowl with four ounces of corn flour, two ounces of sugar and a coffeespoonful of salt; dilute all these ingredients with a quart of water, beat the mixture well to have it smooth, then add three-quarters of an ounce of yeast dissolved in a little tepid water; when all has been well stirred together cover the vessel with a cloth and keep it in a temperate place until the dough has risen to double its volume, which will take at least four hours or even more; stir with a spoon and work into it two tablespoonfuls of molasses; the paste is now ready. Heat a griddle (Fig. 602), and as soon as it is sufficiently hot and smokes rub it over with a cloth and butter with clarified butter or lard; pour on enough preparation to form small cakes three and a half to four inches in diameter, and a quarter of an inch thick; in order to have them round and of equal thickness iron rings beveled on the outside are used. When the cakes are firm enough, which will take about two or three minutes, lift up the rings and turn the cakes over to finish cooking for two or three minutes longer. Dress them on a very hot covered dish and serve at once.

(3273). FLANNEL CAKES (Galettes Légères).

Place in a bowl four ounces of butter and two ounces of sugar; work well together to obtain a creamy preparation, then add four whole eggs one by one, and after the eggs are well incorporated put in eight ounces of flour and two gills of milk. Have the paste nice and smooth, and just when ready to use add a tablespoonful of baking powder mingled with an equal quantity of flour, then finish cooking and serve exactly the same as the buckwheat cakes (No. 3272).

(3274). INDIAN CAKES (Galettes Indiennes).

Have in a vessel six ounces of wheat flour and four ounces of corn flour sifted together; add one ounce of powdered sugar, a pinch of salt and one gill of milk. Mix well in order to obtain a smooth running paste, then pour in an ounce and a half of melted butter. Just when ready to cook the cakes add to the mixture a teaspoonful of baking powder, already mingled with a teaspoonful of flour, and finish exactly the same as for the buckwheat cakes (No. 3272). When cooked dish and set a cover on top, serving them immediately.

(3275). RICE CAKES (Galettes au Riz).

Put in a pan four ounces of wheat flour and four ounces of rice flour sifted together; make a hollow in the center and lay in two ounces of sugar, a pinch of salt, four eggs and one gill of milk; work the flour into the liquid and knead it in such a way as to obtain a smooth dough, then add another gill of milk and continue to work it until the paste is well mixed, then finally pour in two ounces of melted butter and also add half a pint of rice, blanched and cooked till quite soft. Just when ready to use work it well with a teaspoonful of baking powder and a teaspoonful of flour, and when sufficiently kneaded and the paste is smooth it will be ready. Finish like buckwheat cakes (No. 3272).

(3276). WHEAT CAKES (Galettes au Froment).

Mix in a bowl eight ounces of sifted flour, two ounces of sugar, two ounces of butter, a little salt, four eggs and two gills of milk; stir all well together to obtain a smooth paste. Beat one teaspoonful of flour with as much baking powder, add it to the other ingredients and when well mingled, cook and finish them the same as buckwheat cakes (No. 3272), serving them very hot.

(3277). COUQUES (Couques).

Lay a pound of brioche paste (No. 130) in a vessel, place it in the ice-box, working it from time to time to give it plenty of body; when this is firm put it on a floured table and divide it in two parts; draw them lengthwise to form into strings and cut each of these into fifteen even pieces; form all of them into balls and shape them like rolls three and a half inches long; range on a baking sheet slightly apart, leave to rise in a mild temperature and when double their volume egg over and bake in a good oven. Just when serving open them on one side and insert a little good, slightly salted butter. Send to the table very hot.

(3278). GRISSINIS WITH BUTTER (Grissinis au Beurre).

Make a hollow in the center of a pound of flour sifted on the table and in it lay half an ounce of yeast; dilute with a gill of warm water, working in slowly a little flour in order to have a soft paste; cover this with the remainder of the flour, and let rise to double the original height, then add a pinch of salt and a gill of barely tepid water; mix thoroughly to obtain a rather consistent dough, and finally add two ounces of butter; cover this over with a cloth, and leave it to rise for twenty-five minutes, then set it on a floured table and break it up into small half-ounce bits; mold these into balls, and leave them to rise for ten minutes before rolling them into strings a quarter of an inch in diameter; place them at once on lightly buttered baking tins, and leave to rise once more for ten to twelve minutes. As soon as they are ready push into a slow oven to bake to a fine golden color.

(3279). GRISSINIS WITH SUGAR (Grissinis au Sucre).

Sift a pound of flour on the table, and with a fourth part of it, half an ounce of yeast and a little warm milk make a soft leaven; place this in a deep vessel, cover over and let rise to double its height. Form a ring with the remainder of the flour; in the center put one ounce of salt, two and a half ounces of sugar, two eggs, and one gill of milk; mix all well together, incorporating the flour slowly so as to obtain a rather consistent dough; knead this for a few moments to give it body, then add two ounces of butter, and continue to knead until the butter is thoroughly worked in, finally adding the prepared leaven. Lay this dough in a vessel to rise to double its height, and then place it on a floured table and break it into pieces, having twenty-four of them to the pound; lengthen each piece into even-sized strings nine inches long, place on baking sheets, allow to rise, egg over twice, and bake in a hot oven.

(3280). OATMEAL; WHEATEN GRITS; HOMINY, BOILED (Farine d'Avoine Broyée et Bouillie; Froment Broyé Bouilli; Maïs Blanc en Semoule Bouilli).

Boiled Oatmeal.—Put two quarts of water into a saucepan; add a coffeespoonful of salt and set it on the fire; at the first boil drop in three-quarters of a pound of oatmeal, letting it fall like rain, and being careful to stir continuously with a spatula, bearing it down on the bottom of the saucepan. Remove at the first boil to the side of the range, and let it continue to bubble for twenty-five minutes, stirring it at frequent intervals with the spatula. Serve with fresh sweet cream.

Wheaten Grits, Boiled.—Wheaten grits are cooked in the same manner and in the same proportions as the oatmeal. Serve with fresh sweet cream.

Hominy.—Hominy is prepared exactly the same, using the same proportions as the oatmeal, but it only requires twenty minutes' cooking. Serve fresh sweet cream at the same time.

(3281). POLISH BLINIS (Blinis à la Polonaise).

Sift into a pan half a pound of wheat flour, a quarter of a pound of rye flour and half a pound of rice flour; make a hollow in the center. Dissolve three-quarters of an ounce of yeast with half a pint of milk, run it through a sieve into the hollow and incorporate the flour slowly, also five or six eggs and half a pound of melted butter, so as to obtain a smooth paste of the same consistency as a frying batter. Cover the pan with a cloth and keep it in a mild temperature to raise the paste to double its original height, and when this is accomplished beat in four egg-whites previously beaten to a stiff froth and also the volume of a pint of whipped cream; let this rise once more for twenty minutes. Heat twelve small tartlet molds made of tinned sheet iron, two and a half to three inches in diameter and half an inch in depth; baste them with melted butter, using a brush, and fill them half full with the paste; set them in a very hot oven, and as soon as the paste is well seized, remove and baste again with butter, using a brush; turn them over quickly, butter them on the other side and return to the oven. When done dress on a hot plate and serve at once. These are to be accompanied either with a sauce-boat of sour cream or melted butter; they can also be laid on a folded napkin, serving the cream or butter separate. Buckwheat flour may be used alone instead of the three other kinds.

(3282). ÉCHAUDÉS (Échaudés).

Arrange one pound of sifted flour in a circle on the table; in the center lay two ounces of butter, two ounces of sugar, a well-crushed piece of carbonate of ammonia the size of a hazel-nut, a pinch of salt and eight whole eggs; mix all well together, obtaining a very smooth paste, but not too firm, working it so that it attains considerable body. Flatten this paste to an inch and a half in thickness with the rolling-pin, lay it on a floured tin sheet and leave to rest for two or three hours in a cool spot. Invert this paste on a lightly floured table and cut it into pieces; roll each of these to form a string an inch and a half in diameter, then divide into three-quarter-inch lengths. Lay these cakes on their cut end on a round floured pan cover; boil water in a vessel larger than this cover; at the first boil take the water from the fire, invert the cover over and pour boiling water on this to detach the pieces of paste; return the vessel to the fire without letting the water boil, and shake it about. As soon as the pieces of paste rise to the surface remove them with a skimmer and throw into a pan of fresh water, leaving them in for twelve hours, changing the water every four hours; then drain, range then at some distance apart in hermetically closed hinged baking sheets, and bake in a hot oven for twenty to twenty-five minutes.

(3283). TOASTS, DRY, BUTTERED, DIPPED IN WATER, MILK OR CREAM (Tranches de Pain Grillées, Beurrées, Trempées Soit à l'Eau, au Lait ou à la Crème).

Dry.—Slices of bread cut from square American loaves, about three and a half inches in size by three-eighths in thickness, laid on a double broiler and toasted over a low fire, then arranged on a hot plate.

Buttered.—After the bread is toasted spread one side over with butter.

Dipped in Water, Milk or Cream.—Toast the bread, then lay the slices in a deep dish and moisten sufficiently to cover the bread with hot water, this being called dipped toast; or else with hot milk, making milk toast; or hot cream, this being called cream toast.

(3284). WAFFLES (Gaufres).

Put half a pound of butter into a vessel with four ounces of sugar and a pinch of salt; beat well with a wooden spoon to obtain a creamy mass, then break in eight whole eggs one by one, stirring unceasingly, now add a pound of flour and half a pint of milk. Put the waffle irons (Fig. 608) on the fire, heat them to a proper degree and grease over with clarified butter, then take four tablespoonfuls of the paste and stir into it a small coffeespoonful of baking powder; pour it into the waffle irons, spreading it evenly; close and cook the waffles to a fine golden color, turning the iron from time to time. As soon as the waffles are done, pare the edges, take them out and dress on a covered dish, serving them very hot.

(3285). WAFFLES WITH VANILLA—LIGHT (Gaufres Légères à la Vanille).

Beat up in a vessel half a pound of partly melted butter, and when creamy mix in slowly seven or eight egg-yolks; after the preparation becomes frothy add half a pound of flour, a pinch of sugar, a grain of salt and half an ounce of compressed yeast dissolved in two gills of milk; cover the vessel and keep it in a mild temperature. When the dough is raised work and let get cold, then incorporate into it four or five beaten egg-whites. Heat a deep waffle iron, butter it over with a brush dipped in melted butter and putting a spoonful of the paste on one side of the iron only, close and cook the waffles over a low fire, turning the iron frequently; when dry and a fine golden color take it out of the form and sprinkle fine vanilla sugar (No. 3165) over the top.

SMALL CAKES FOR ENTREMETS (Petits Gâteaux d'Entremets).

Cakes ten to a pound.

(3286). APPLE CAKE (Gâteau aux Pommes).

Prepare a frolle paste (No. 136); keep it in a cool place on ice for twenty minutes. Cut about fifteen good apples in four, peel, shred them small and cook partially, while tossing them over a brisk fire, in a pan with some butter, sugar and vanilla added, then set aside to cool. Roll out two-thirds of the paste, not too thin, four inches wide and about the length of the baking sheet on a floured table; roll it over the rolling-pin to unroll on a baking sheet and cut it away straight; surround the edges with a narrow raised rim, and put in a moderate oven to half bake and leave till quite cold. Then fill the center with the cooked apples and finish exactly the same as the gooseberry cakes (No. 3309).

(3287). APRICOTS WITH CREAM OF ALMONDS (Abricots à la Crème d'Amandes).

Line a few tartlet molds with fine foundation paste (No. 135); fill them level to the top with almond frangipane (No. 44), and lay a well-drained compoted half apricot (No. 3691) over each; bake in a moderate oven, and when done and partly cold dress an imitation apricot made of Italian meringue (No. 140) on top of each one. Place them again in the oven to dry the meringue, and then let cool. When cold glaze over with a yellow rum icing (No. 102), fasten a stalk of angelica into each, and rub each one with a little carmine on cotton to color it.

(3288). BABAS WITH RUM—SMALL (Petits Babas au Rhum).

Cut two ounces of candied fruits into small dice, such as citron, orange peel, preserved pears and a few cherries; add to them as many currants and raisins well washed in hot water, picked and cleaned. Prepare a small baba paste as described in No. 129, and when ready to mold stir in the fruits. Butter some small baba molds, fill them half full with the paste, and leave to rise; when entirely full push into a hot oven to bake; unmold as soon as done, and dip them into a hot thirty-two degree syrup well flavored with vanilla and rum (No. 102).

(3289). BISCUITS IN CASES WITH CREAM (Biscuits en Caisses à la Crème).

Choose eight fresh eggs; break the whites into a basin and the yolks into a bowl; into the latter mingle two ounces of powdered sugar flavored with grated lemon peel (No. 3165), and beat it up with a spoon until it becomes white; add a grain of salt to the whites, beating them very stiff, and mix them slowly with the yolks, sifting four ounces of good flour over the whole; lastly add a gill of well-drained whipped cream, and with this preparation fill some oblong paper cases (Fig. 548) three-quarters full; range them on a thin baking sheet, glaze the surfaces with fine sugar, and cook for twenty-five minutes in a slack oven.

(3290). BANANA BOATS (Bateaux de Bananes).

Line ten boat-shaped tartlet molds with sweet paste (No. 136), and cook them white. Peel ten small, ripe, short bananas, cut off both ends and plunge the fruit into a boiling twenty-five degree syrup; remove the pan at once from the fire, and let the bananas cool off in this syrup, then drain. Cover the insides of the unmolded boats with apricot marmalade (No. 3675), and lay in each one half a banana, the rounded surface uppermost, brushing it over several times with vanilla apple syrup; garnish both sides with apple jelly (No. 3668).

(3291). BOATS, PRINTANIER (Bateaux Printaniers).

Line a dozen boat-shaped tartlet molds with fine foundation paste (No. 135); cook them white, unmold and leave till cold, then cover the insides with apricot marmalade (No. 3675). Strain through a fine sieve the pulp of four or five sound oranges, mix in with their juice two or three spoonfuls of strawberry pulp, and two or three gills of thick syrup flavored with orange peel (No. 3165) and a little isinglass added. Stir the preparation on ice, work it well to a cream, and then mix in at once about half a pound of small, very fresh-picked strawberries; roll them well in with the above, then take some up with a spoon and fill the small boats, having them well-rounded on top; smoth this into a dome and cover with a layer of freshly made apricot marmalade (No. 3675); let this dry in the air for ten minutes, then decorate the summits quickly with a few spoonfuls of whipped cream pushed through a cornet, having it well drained and only slightly sweetened.

(3292). CANNELONS À LA CÉLESTINE (Cannelons à la Célestine).

Roll out some puff paste parings (No. 146) one-eighth of an inch thick; cut this into five-eighths of an inch wide bands, each fourteen inches long; egg them over, and roll them spirally around some cornucopia-shaped molds an inch and a half in diameter and three inches long; as they are done set on a baking sheet, then place this in a hot oven. When partly cooked dredge with powdered sugar, and finish baking; when cooked unmold and leave to get cold. When serving fill each one with whipped cream into which mix some pastry cream with vanilla (No. 46), crushed macaroons and currant jelly (No. 3670).

(3293). CASINOS (Casinos).

For these cakes take puff paste made at six turns (No. 146), having it an eighth of an inch thick; cut half of the rolled-out layer in two-inch in diameter rounds with a channeled pastry cutter (Fig. 16), and range them on a slightly dampened baking sheet, then egg over. Diviue the other half of the layer into the same number of rounds, but only an inch and a half in diameter; empty the centers of these with a pastry cutter an inch in diameter so as to form into rings, then lay them on top of the rounds; egg over lightly and decorate the surface of each one with a rosette of fine halved almonds burnt with egg-white and sugar, and then bake the cakes in a hot oven. When done fill the center holes with orange or quince jelly.

(3294). CREAM CAKES ICED WITH CHOCOLATE, VANILLA OR COFFEE (Choux à la Crème Glacés au Chocolat, à la Varille ou au Café).

On a lightly buttered baking sheet lay some small round cream cakes made of cream cake paste (No. 132) pushed through a pocket (Fig. 179); egg over and set into a medium oven to cook; detach them from the pan as soon as done, and when cold split through the sides and fill with vanilla pastry cream (No. 46) and ice over with chocolate, vanilla or coffee fondant (No. 58), the same as eclairs.

(3295). CREAM CAKES WITH BURNT ALMONDS AND GLAZED CREAM CAKES (Choux Pralinés et Choux Glacés).

Lay on a baking sheet about twelve small cream cakes (No. 3296); egg over and lay on each a small pinch of shredded or chopped almonds, and cover these with a pinch of powdered sugar; cook

FIG. 603.

FIG. 604.

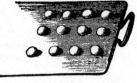

FIG. 605.

the cakes in a slack oven and when they become cold open and fill them either with apricot marmalade (No. 3675), currant (No. 3670), quince (No. 3672) or apple jelly (No. 3668), or else with Chantilly cream (No. 50) or St. Honoré cream (No. 49).

To Glaze the Cream Cakes take them up one by one and dip the upper parts into sugar cooked to "crack" (No. 171), then lay them at once on a wire grate to drain off the surplus sugar. These can also be filled with pastry cream (No. 46) flavored with vanilla, orange or orange flower water.

(3296). CREAM CAKES WITH WHIPPED CREAM OR ST. HONORÉ CREAM (Choux à la Crème Fouettée ou à la Crème St. Honoré).

With some cream cake paste (No. 132) pushed through a socket pocket dress on a lightly buttered baking sheet some small round cakes, an inch and a half in diameter; cover over with powdered sugar and leave stand for a few moments, then remove all the sugar that has failed to adhere to the paste; push into a very slack oven to cook. Detach them from the pan as soon as done and split open the side to fill with pastry cream (No. 46), or whipped cream flavored with vanilla (No. 50). They can also be filled through the top by making an opening and placing the cover on upside down. Push a small string of royal icing (No. 101) around the edge all around the opening. Dredge over some fine pink colored sugar (No. 172) and fill the insides with St. Honoré cream (No. 49) pushed in through a pocket.

(3297). CONDÉ CAKES (Gâteaux Condé).

Mix in a vessel four or five spoonfuls of chopped almonds with an equal quantity of powdered sugar; wet slowly with egg-whites so as to obtain a thin but not too flowing paste. Roll out some fragments of puff paste (No. 146) into long strips, three and a half inches wide; cover the tops with the almond preparation and cut the sides straight, then cut them across in one-inch wide pieces; take them up one at a time on the blade of a palette knife and range in straight rows on a baking sheet, slightly apart from each other. Besprinkle the cakes with fine sugar and cook in a slack oven; remove when nicely done by passing a knife under to detach from the pan.

(3298). CRESCENTS WITH PRESERVES (Croissants aux Confitures).

In order to make these crescents it is necessary to have two cutters: a round channeled pastry cutter (Fig. 16) and a smooth unchanneled pastry cutter the shape of a crescent, but much smaller than the first one. Roll out some puff paste made to eight turns (No. 146) into eighth of an inch in thickness; from this cut some channeled rounds four inches in diameter and with the same pastry cutter cut the rounds into crescent-shaped pieces. Range half of these crescents slightly apart from each other on a moist baking sheet and wet the tops over with a brush; empty out those remaining with the small and smooth crescent-shaped pastry cutter and lay them on top of those already prepared so that they cover them exactly; egg over and cook in a brisk oven without glazing. When removed press the paste on the empty part and when these crescents are cold glaze them lightly with icing (No. 102), using a brush, and press them on chopped pistachios. Fill the empty place in the crescents with apple jelly (No. 3668) or else apricot marmalade (No. 3675).

(3299). DARIOLES DUCHESS (Darioles à la Duchesse).

Have in a vessel one ounce of flour, two whole eggs, six yolks and four ounces of sugar, diluting with one pint of cream; pass the whole through a sieve and add to it six crushed macaroons. Line a dozen buttered molds (No. 1, Fig. 137) with puff paste parings (No. 146); into the bottom of each place a little finely cut-up candied fruits, fill them with the preparation and on all lay a small piece of fresh butter; sift the tops with sugar and bake in a hot oven; when the paste is well cooked, unmold on wire grates to cool.

(3300). DARIOLES WITH ORANGE FLOWER WATER (Darioles à l'eau de Fleur d'Oranger).

Line twelve buttered molds (No. 1, Fig. 137) with puff paste parings (No. 146) rolled out thin. Put into a basin one gill of flour and two ounces of sugar, dilute with two whole eggs, two tablespoonfuls of orange flower water and three gills of milk; stir well and run the preparation through a fine colander; use it to fill the molds, putting a small piece of fresh butter on the top of each. Dredge over with sugar and bake in the oven, unmolding as soon as they are done.

(3301). DARIOLES WITH VANILLA (Darioles à la Vanille).

Break three eggs in a vessel, beat and add one gill of vanilla sugar (No. 3165), as much flour, the same proportion of dried almonds and a grain of salt, diluting with three gills of good milk. Butter twelve timbale molds (No. 1, Fig. 137) and line them with puff paste parings (No. 146) and place a small piece of butter on the bottom of each, then fill with the above preparation. Lay them on a baking sheet and cook in a slack oven for half an hour; five minutes before taking out bestrew the tops with vanilla sugar and allow them to cool off before unmolding.

(3302). D'ARTOIS CAKE WITH APRICOT MARMALADE OR ALMOND CREAM (Gâteau D'Artois à la Marmelade d'Abricots ou à la Crème d'Amandes).

Roll some puff paste parings (No. 146) into a layer three-sixteenths of an inch in thickness and cut this into two bands, each three inches wide. Lay one of these bands on a baking sheet and cover the center with apricot marmalade (No. 3675) or almond cream (No. 40); moisten the edges of the paste with a brush dipped in water, then cover with the second band; pare them straight, scallop the edges and mark the band across one and a quarter inches apart with a knife; within this space place leaves formed with the tip of the blade of a small knife. Bake in a quick oven and when the cake is nearly done dredge with sugar and finish cooking and glazing. Cut it through the divided sections with a large sharp knife.

(3303). ECLAIRS, COFFEE AND CHOCOLATE CREAM (Éclairs au Café ou au Chocolat).

Put into a saucepan one pint of water, a pint of milk, half a pound of butter, two ounces of sugar and some salt; place it on the fire. When the liquid begins to boil remove the saucepan and incorporate into it a pound of sifted flour, mixing it in quickly with a spatula; return the saucepan to the fire and continue to work the paste vigorously for a few moments in order to dry and have it smooth, and when it detaches from the bottom of the saucepan take it off the fire and leave it for a second to fall below boiling heat, then incorporate into it slowly two whole eggs, stirring in well with the spatula. As these are well mixed add two more, and continue

FIG. 666.

this operation until the paste has absorbed fourteen or sixteen eggs. With this paste fill three-quarters full a linen pocket furnished with a three-eighths of an inch diameter socket (Fig. 179), and lay the eclairs through it three and a half inches long, at short distances from each other, on a lightly buttered baking sheet; egg over the tops and cook them in a slow oven. When done take them from the baking sheet and split them through the sides, either with a small knife or a pair of scissors, and fill them up with vanilla pastry cream (No. 46). Immediately dip them to half their depth into chocolate or coffee icing (No. 99) and lay them on a wire grate to drain and dry the icing. Place an instant at the oven door to gloss.

(3304). ECLAIRS, VANILLA CHANTILLY (Éclairs Chantilly à la Vanille).

Boil two gills of water in a saucepan with a grain of salt, a teaspoonful of sugar and four ounces of butter; as soon as the butter rises remove the pan from the fire and incorporate into it five ounces of flour; beat the paste with a spoon until smooth, then stir it once more over a moderate fire until it detaches from the saucepan; this is called drying; take it off and let get partly cold. Then mix into it four or five egg-yolks, one after the other, continuing to stir vigorously, and lastly add two ounces more butter. Pour the paste into a pocket (Fig. 179), having a three eighths of an inch socket, and push it on a baking sheet in regular rows of eclairs, each one three inches long and a short distance apart; egg over and cook until they become perfectly dry. After removing from the oven detach from the sheet with the blade of a thin knife. When the eclairs are cold split them through the bottom, open and fill with sweet whipped cream flavored well with vanilla (No. 50); cover the tops of the cakes with a little light apricot marmalade (No. 3675) with vanilla icing (No. 102). As soon as the cakes are iced range them on a pastry grate, and place at the entrance of the oven for a few minutes to glaze.

(3305). FRANCILLON CAKES (Gâteaux Francillon).

These are prepared with one pound of peeled sweet almonds, fourteen ounces of clarified butter kneaded with twenty ounces of vanilla sugar (No. 3165), also four and a half ounces of flour, two ounces of fecula, ten or twelve egg-yolks, seven or eight beaten whites, and a grain of salt. Pound the almonds with one egg-white, dilute with a glassful of good milk, and pass through a sieve; put the butter into a vessel, and with a spoon beat in the eggs, one at a time. When the whole is creamy mix in the sugar, the almonds, the beaten whites, and the sifted flour and fecula. Line a thin raised-edge baking sheet with sweet paste (No. 136), pour in the preparation, smooth nicely and bake in a slack oven; when unmolded and cold brush apricot marmalade (No. 3675) over the top, and cut it into small cakes without separating the pieces; ice the surface with kirsch icing (No. 102), and detach from each other only when this becomes dry, then dress.

(3306). GALETTES PUFFED AND HALF PUFFED (Galettes Feuilletées et Demi-Feuilletées).

Arrange a pound of flour in a circle on a table; in the center put a pinch of salt, two ounces of butter, and sufficient water to form a smooth but not too consistent paste; leave it for some time, then roll it out to the thickness of three-quarters of an inch; on the middle of it place three-quarters of a pound of butter, wrap it in the paste, and roll it once more; give five and a half turns to this paste, mold it into small balls weighing three ounces, then to a perfect round three-eighths of an inch in thickness; lay them on a baking sheet, egg over, trace lines on top to form a lattice work, festoon all around with a small kitchen knife, and bake in a medium oven. Half puffed galettes are made with puff paste parings (No. 146).

(3307). GENOESE CAKE—LIGHT (Génoise Légère).

Put twelve whole eggs and eight yolks into a basin with one pound of sugar, a part of it being flavored with vanilla (No. 179); beat together vigorously for twenty minutes on a slow fire, barely heating the preparation, and when well beaten and very light mix in lightly one pound of sifted flour, using a small skimmer or spoon, then half a pound of melted fresh butter added a little at a time. Butter lightly a pan twelve inches long by seven and a half wide and two inches deep; glaze it with flour and sugar, half and half, well mixed together and sifted through a sieve. Fill the pan three-quarters full with the preparation, lay it in a baking pan and place it in a slack oven to bake for forty-five to fifty minutes. As soon as the cake is done, remove and unmold it on a wire grate to get cold; afterward cover it lightly with well-reduced peach or apricot jam (No. 3675) and ice over with water icing flavored with vanilla (No. 102); place for an instant at the entrance of the oven to dry the icing; allow to cool; cut the Genoese cake into oblong pieces and serve.

This cake can also be made in a round mold and iced exactly the same, decorating the top with candied fruits; dress on a round plate ornamented with lace paper.

(3308). GENOESES WITH CREAM MERINGUED (Génoises à la Crème Meringuées).

Butter and flour some tartlet molds, fill them with Genoese preparation (No. 3307) and cook in a slack oven; unmold as soon as done and when cold hollow out the centers. Fill the cakes with a St. Honoré cream preparation (No. 49) flavored with orange; color it lightly with a little green; cover this with meringue (No. 140) laid on in beads pushed through a pocket; spread fine sugar over this and place in the oven to color the meringue.

(3309). GOOSEBERRY CAKES AND TARTS (Gâteaux et Tartes aux Groseilles Vertes).

Prepare a tart paste (No. 149) with one pound of flour, three-quarters of a pound of butter, five ounces of powdered sugar, two whole eggs, three yolks, salt and lemon flavoring. Divide this paste into two parts and roll them out separately into oblong layers not too thin; roll one of these on the pin to unroll on a large baking sheet, cutting off the four sides evenly, and edge it with a small band of the paste laid on higher, forming a border of half an inch; prick the paste. Cook this flat till it is half done in a very slack oven, not allowing it to brown, then take it out and let get cold. Fill the hollow as high up as the border with blanched gooseberries without boiling, so that they remain whole; smooth them evenly and egg over the raised border. Roll the second flat on the rolling-pin and unroll it on top of the other; press down the edges, fastening them together, and egg the surface. Lay the baking sheet on top of another and push the two into a slack oven (the second one is to prevent the half-cooked paste from burning). When the top paste is well dried remove from the fire and glaze over with a thin layer of fondant flavored with lemon (No. 58); let get cold, then cut the cake into three and a half inch wide strips and these across in such a way as to obtain oblong pieces. Round tarts may be prepared in the same way.

(3310). GORONFLOTS (Goronflots).

Butter some small tin hexagonal-shaped molds with clarified butter; fill them about three-quarters full with Savarin paste (No. 148); stand them in a mild temperature to have the paste rise as high as the edge, then cook in a moderate oven. Remove and unmold as soon as done; leave to cool and afterward dip each one in a syrup of almond milk (No. 4) with kirsch.

(3311). JEALOUSIES (Jalousies).

Roll out some puff paste parings (No. 146) to an eighth of an inch in thickness; cut this into three-inch wide bands; lay half of them on a baking sheet and mask the whole length of the center with apple marmalade (No. 3674); wet the edges and cover over with the remaining bands, scored as follows: Fold the bands in two, cut them from the folded side, this cut to be one inch long, the same as the bands for scored favors. Egg the tops, mark them across with the tip of a small knife, then bake in a hot oven. After the cakes are done bestrew with powdered sugar, return for a moment to the fire to have it melt, then divide the cakes.

(3312). ROLLED JELLY BISCUIT (Biscuit Roulé à la Gelée).

To make this cake use lady finger preparation (No. 3377), adding a little melted butter; as soon as this is mixed in pour the whole on a paper-covered baking sheet and spread it to a quarter of an inch thick layer, then bake in a hot oven; remove when done, detach from the paper and cover the surface of the cake with a layer of currant jelly (No. 3670), then roll it over on itself to form a roll; wrap this up in paper and leave to cool. When thoroughly cold undo the paper and stand the cake on a wire grate; ice it over with vanilla icing (No. 102). After this becomes very dry cut the cake into cross-wise slices, each one three-eighths of an inch thick. The rolled biscuit may also be covered with a layer of Condé almond preparation (No. 2), marking it in the places where the cake is to be sliced. Set the roll in the oven for an instant to color, then cut the cake in the marked places.

(3313). LAFAYETTE WITH RUM (Lafayette au Rhum).

Pound six ounces of almonds with six ounces of sugar to reduce to a powder. then sift it through a sieve; place this powder in a basin with six eggs and beat till light, then add one tablespoonful of rum, an ounce of flour and four ounces of melted butter. Pour the preparation into tartlet molds lined with puff paste parings (No. 146), strew the tops with sugar and bake in a hot oven. Cover the tops with a thin layer of icing flavored with rum (No. 102).

(3314). MADELEINES AND GENOESE MADELEINES (Madeleines et Madeleines Génoises).

Place in a vessel nine ounces of sugar, nine ounces of warm melted butter, seven ounces of flour, five whole eggs, four yolks, two spoonfuls of brandy, a grain of salt and some sugar flavored with lemon peel (No. 3165). Stir the ingredients well with a spoon and heat the preparation for two minutes without ceasing to stir, then fill some buttered Madeleine molds two-thirds full; bake them in a slack oven.

Genoese Madeleines are made with eighteen ounces of sugar, eighteen ounces of flour, eighteen ounces of melted butter, eight egg-yolks, eight beaten whites, some chopped lemon peel, four spoonfuls of rum and a grain of salt; fill buttered Madeleine molds, bake, finish and serve as above.

(3315). COMMERCY MADELEINES (Madeleines de Commercy).

Have in a bowl one pound of sugar, one pound of flour, ten egg-yolks and the peel of one lemon; mix well without beating and add a pound of melted butter and finally eight beaten egg-whites. Butter some long shell-shaped molds, flour over and fill three-quarters full with this preparation; strew sugar on top and bake in a medium oven. As soon as baked unmold on a wire grate and serve when cold.

(3316). MADELEINES WITH RUM (Madeleines au Rhum).

Beat half a pound of sugar with six eggs and a tablespoonful of orange flower water; when it is slightly frothy add half a pound of sifted flour and half a pound of melted butter. Butter and flour three dozen Madeleine molds and fill them three-quarters full with the preparation, strew sugar over and bake in a medium oven; unmold at once and ice with rum fondant (No. 58).

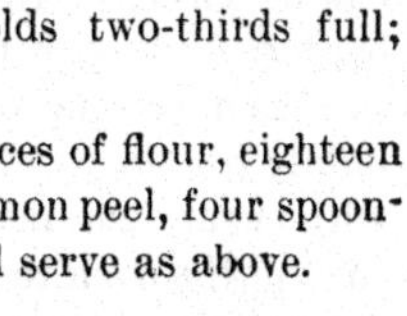

(3317). MARILLAN CAKES (Gâteaux Marillan).

Bake a baba in a flat mold having a cover, or else in a tin mold covered with another. Moisten the crust lightly with baba syrup (No. 3227) and cut it two-thirds across without detaching it at the further end; empty the crumbs

Fig. 607

out partly and fill this double crust with flavored whipped cream or else with smooth cooked Italian cream (No. 140). The top and around the base of the cake should be covered with liquid apricot marmalade (No. 3675) laid on with a brush.

(3318). MARS CAKES (Gâteaux Mars).

Roll out some foundation paste (No. 135) to an eighth of an inch in thickness; cut this into three-inch wide bands and cover these with a layer of almond cream (No. 40) mixed with as much vanilla pastry cream (No. 46); bake in a slow oven, and when done and cold mask over with a layer of meringue (No. 140), having it three-quarters of an inch thick; smooth the sides and tops well. Slit these bands across one inch and a quarter apart with the tip of a small knife and decorate each section with halved almonds or thin slices of almonds cut lengthwise and laid on symmetrically in imitation of branches, having a dry currant between each one. Cut the cakes where they have been slit, place them on a baking sheet, dredge with sugar and set into a slack oven to color the meringue; the bands may be left whole and divided where they were slit while yet hot.

(3319). NOUGAT OF APRICOTS (Nougat d'Abricots).

Make a band of brioche paste (No. 130) an eighth of an inch thick and three inches wide; raise up the edges to form a border, fill this entirely with consistent apricot marmalade (No. 3675) and bake in a moderate oven; after it is done cover the top with a layer of shredded almonds mixed with white of egg and sugar and return it to the oven to color the almonds; as soon as finished take it out and cut the cake across in inch pieces, laying them aside on a wire grate to cool.

(3320). PALMS (Palmiers).

Have some puff paste made to four turns (No. 146); give it four more, dredging each one with sugar; at the very last one roll out the paste to obtain a six-inch wide band and fold this into four on its length, making it join on to the first two that were folded, the two lateral ends being in the center, and then another fold doubling up the band. Cut this into transversal slices a quarter of an inch thick and range them on a baking sheet an inch and a half apart, laying them down flat; sift powdered sugar over and bake in a medium oven; as soon as done detach from the sheet.

(3321). PARISIAN CAKES (Gâteaux Parisiens).

Lay a band of puff paste parings (No. 146) three and a half inches wide by twelve inches long on a baking sheet; on the edges place small narrow bands of the same or else twist the edge to form a border; fill it with vanilla pastry cream (No. 46); prick the bottom and push into a hot oven. As soon as done remove the band and allow to cool. Then cover with a preparation made of very lightly beaten royal icing (No. 101) into which shredded almonds have been mixed; dredge over with sugar; cut into crosswise slices an inch and a quarter in size; place these on a baking sheet, then in the oven to color; remove and stand on a wire grate to get perfectly cold.

(3322). RICE CAKES (Gâteaux au Riz).

Line a few oval-shaped timbale molds, the size of the mold shown in No. 1, Fig. 137, with puff paste parings (No. 146); cover the bottoms with apricot marmalade (No. 3675) and fill up with a mellow rice cooked with cream (No. 160) and flavored with vanilla, finishing it with a few egg-yolks; on each place a little butter; push the cakes into the oven, and when done unmold and mask them over with a layer of apricot marmalade, or powder with icing-sugar.

(3323). ROUEN MIRLITONS (Mirlitons de Rouen).

Beat well together three eggs, two ounces of sugar, a gill of orange flower water and three gills of cream; strain the whole through a colander. Pour it into tartlet molds lined with puff paste parings (No. 146), dredge with sugar and push carefully into a hot oven to bake.

(3324). SMALL SAVARINS (Petits Savarins).

Butter some Savarin molds, dredge shredded almonds on the bottom and fill half full with Savarin paste (No. 148); let rise in a mild temperature until the molds are full, then place them in a brisk oven to bake; unmold as soon as removed and dip them in a syrup made as follows: Into five gills of thirty-two degree cold syrup, add one gill of kirsch, half a gill of maraschino, half a gill of noyau and half a gill of Curaçoa; warm this syrup and then dip in the cakes. When they are well soaked place on a wire grate to drain.

(3325). CAKES STUFFED WITH APRICOT (Gâteaux Fourrés à l'Abricot).

Roll out some puff paste parings (No. 146) to an eighth of an inch in thickness; cut it into rounds with a channeled pastry cutter (Fig. 16) two and a quarter inches in diameter. Place half these rounds on a moistened baking sheet, fill the centers with well-reduced apricot marmalade (No. 3675), wet over the borders and cover with the remaining rounds, fastening them together; egg over twice, mark a rosette on top and push into a brisk oven to bake. When the cakes are almost done sift powdered sugar over and finish cooking, allowing the sugar to melt well.

(3326). ALMONDINE TARTLETS (Tartelettes Amandines).

Have some tart paste (No. 149) and with it line some tartlet molds; prick the paste and cover the bottoms with apricot marmalade (No. 3675). Cut up finely four ounces of peeled almonds; dry them in the oven and then roast to a fine color; when cold pound with half a pound of powdered sugar, and pour this into a vessel to beat with a spoon, incorporating into it one egg-yolk and three whites, having the whole slightly creamy, then add four ounces of chopped candied peel. Fill the lined molds three-quarters full with this preparation, bestrew sugar over the tops and cook in a slack oven; glaze well with sugar before removing.

(3327). APPLE TARTLETS (Tartelettes aux Pommes).

Line two dozen hollow tartlet molds with fine short paste (No. 135); fill them to half their height with apple marmalade (No. 3674) flavored with vanilla, and on each one lay a round piece of apple cut out with a plain cutter the same diameter as the tartlet. On each slice of apple put a pinch of sugar, then cook in a hot oven. Unmold and cover each one with a thin layer of apricot marmalade (No. 3675).

Sour Apple Tartlets.—Have some deep tartlet molds and line them with short paste (No. 135), then fill three-quarters full with sour apple marmalade. Wet the edges of the tartlets and cover with a layer of the same short paste. Egg the surface and lay on each two rounds of parings of puff paste cut out with a channeled cutter and of graduating sizes; egg again and bake in a hot oven. These tartlets can be used as a garnishing for saddles of venison, etc.

Sour Apple Marmalade.—Peel and quarter some sour apples, put them in a basin, cover with water and cook on a good fire. As soon as done pour them on a sieve to drain well. Strain the pulp through a sieve into a basin, add the same weight of sugar and let reduce on the fire for a few moments. Pour into jars and leave to cool.

(3328). BORDELAISE TARTLETS (Tartelettes Bordelaises).

Pound six ounces of almonds with a pound of sugar; sift it through a sieve, then add to it a quarter of a gill of rum and seven egg-whites; beat well together; now put with it three-quarters of a pound of flour and three-quarters of a pound of melted butter and lastly fourteen very stiffly beaten egg-whites. Line scalloped tartlet molds with sweet paste (No. 136); fill them with the preparation, bestrew lightly with sugar and bake in a medium oven. Unmold as soon as done and leave till cold, then dress on top of each a rosette of Italian meringue (No. 140) flavored with vanilla; bestrew with sugar and return the cakes to the oven to color the meringue; garnish between the parts of the rosette with apricot marmalade (No. 3675), apple jelly (No. 3668) or currant jelly (No. 3670).

(3329). CHERRY TARTLETS (Tartelettes aux Cerises).

Pick the stalks and stones from a few handfuls of fine sour cherries; lay them in a basin, strew over sugar and leave to steep. Line two dozen hollow spindle-shaped tartlet molds with foundation paste (No. 135); fill with the cherries and bake in a brisk oven; unmold as soon as done and leave stand till cold, then cover with a thin layer of currant jelly (No. 3670) dissolved in a little syrup.

(3330). COLUMBIA TARTLETS (Tartelettes à la Columbia).

Pound four ounces of almonds with five ounces of sugar, afterward adding a gill and a quarter of milk; grind the whole to obtain a fine paste, put it into a vessel, add four ounces of sifted flour and four very stiffly beaten egg-whites. Line some tartlet molds with parings of puff paste (No. 146); cover the bottoms with a little apple marmalade (No. 3674), fill with the preparation and strew sugar over the tops; bake in a medium oven.

(3331). DEMONET TARTLETS (Tartelettes à la Demonet).

Line a sufficient number of tartlet molds with puff paste parings (No. 146). Put in a saucepan four ounces of sugar, four ounces of butter and half a pint of water; set it on the fire and at the first boil add half a pound of flour; dry the preparation for one second, then remove from the fire and beat in seven or eight eggs singly and a little powdered vanilla and finely chopped citron. Cover the bottom of the tartlet molds with apricot marmalade (No. 3675) and fill them with the above paste pushed through a pocket; lay two small bands of paste on top, crossing them; in each triangle place a half cherry; bake in a medium oven.

(3332). FANCHONNETTE TARTLETS MERINGUED (Tartelettes Fanchonnette Meringuées).

Lay in a vessel three ounces of sugar and one ounce of sifted flour; beat up with five egg-yolks, and dilute with five gills of milk, adding a little vanilla. Pour this into tartlet molds lined with puff paste parings (No. 146), and bake in a medium oven. After they are done cover the tops with a flat layer of meringue preparation (No. 140) and on this form a rosette or any other decoration with more meringue; sprinkle with sugar, and push in the oven for an instant to color. When cold garnish the inside of the decoration with currant jelly (No. 3670).

(3333). HÉRISSON TARTLETS (Tartelettes Hérisson).

Line some oval tartlet molds with puff paste parings (No. 146); fill them with a fanchonnette preparation (No. 3332), flavored with kirsch, and bake in a medium oven; as soon as done let get cold, then put some Italian meringue (No. 140) on top in a dome form, sticking it all over with long thin strips of almonds, sprinkling chopped almonds over all; push into a slack oven to color the almonds lightly.

(3334). PEACH TARTLETS WITH RICE (Tartelettes de Pêches au Riz).

Prepare a fine foundation paste (No. 135); line some tartlet molds, cover the bottoms with a little apple marmalade (No. 3674), and fill the molds level to the top with rice with cream flavored with vanilla (No. 160), then bake them. As soon as done unmold and lay a compoted half peach on top (No. 3691), placing a circle of meringue points all around; bestrew with sugar, and push in a slack oven in order to color the meringue lightly, and afterward cover the peaches with a light syrup.

(3335). PÈLERINE TARTLETS (Tartelettes Pèlerines).

Butter some plain tartlet molds; line them with puff paste parings (No. 146), and fill with almond cream (No. 40), and pastry cream (No. 46), half of each; cover with a flat of the same paste; cook, unmold, turn them over, and spread with a thin layer of Condé preparation (No. 2); push into the oven, bake and serve.

(3336). VALENCIA TARTLETS (Tartelettes de Valence).

Crush six ounces of almonds with six ounces of sugar and a few spoonfuls of orange flower water to make it into a paste; add to this two ounces of very finely cut-up orange peel, and five stiffly beaten egg-whites; with this preparation fill some tartlet molds lined with puff paste parings (No. 146); dredge lightly with sugar, and bake in a medium oven. Unmold as soon as done, and when cold ice the tops with orange fondant (No. 58); decorate the surfaces with a rosette made of bits of orange peel, laying a preserved cherry in the center.

(3337). VARIEGATED FRUIT TARTLETS (Tartelettes aux Fruits Variés).

Have some molds lined with fine short paste (No. 135); prick and put into the bottom a layer of apple marmalade (No. 3674), and over some halved apricots or peaches or a round slice of pear or any other cooked fruit, drained and wiped dry. Bake the tartlets in a hot oven, and after removing, unmold and leave till cold. Then cover with a thin layer of of apricot marmalade (No. 3675) diluted with a little syrup.

(3338). WELLS OF LOVE (Puits d'Amour).

Roll out some six-turn puff paste (No. 146) to the thickness of three-sixteenths of an inch; cut it out with a two-inch diameter channeled pastry cutter, and lay these rounds on a baking sheet, putting it aside in the ice-box for a few moments to set. Now egg over and mark a round in the center with a small plain cutter an inch in diameter, and bake in a hot oven. A moment before removing bestrew over with powdered sugar, and leave until this is entirely melted and glazed. Then empty them at once, and fill the hollow with currant jelly (No. 3670); strew a few chopped pistachios over, and place a fine preserved greengage (No. 3679) in the center.

TEA CAKES (Gâteaux Pour le Thé).

Forty to the Pound.

(3339). BASEL LECKERLETS (Leckerlets de Bâle).

Pour four pounds of honey into a saucepan and stand it on the range; as soon as it rises remove and leave the honey to cool. Arrange five pounds of flour in a circle on the table: in the center lay one pound of sugar, one pound of finely cut-up citron, two pounds of chopped almonds, one ounce of grated nutmeg, one ounce of ground cinnamon, half an ounce of ground cloves, two gills of kirsch, the chopped peel of two lemons, and one ounce of finely crushed carbonate of ammonia. On these ingredients pour the cold honey and mix all together, working the flour in slowly to form it into a smooth, firm paste; leave this in a cool spot to rest for two hours; then roll it with the rolling-pin into flats three-sixteenths of an inch in thickness; spread these on slightly buttered baking sheets, and bake in a hot oven. As soon as done remove and allow to cool, then ice them over with cooked icing (No. 102) flavored with orange flower water, applying it with a brush; when the icing is dry cut the flats into small cakes two and a half inches long by three-quarters of an inch wide.

(3340). BUTTER PATIENCES (Patiences au Beurre).

Beat up with a spatula half a pound of butter and half a pound of sugar with a pinch of salt to make a not too light preparation; add eight eggs, one by one, the peel of a lemon, and lastly one pound of flour, and mix well. Put this paste into a pocket (Fig. 179) furnished with a quarter-inch thick channeled socket and range it in small biscuits two and a half inches long and one inch apart on a buttered sheet, then bake in a hot oven.

(3341). CATS' TONGUES WITH BUTTER (Langues de Chat au Beurre).

Work ten ounces of butter to a cream with eight ounces of sugar and two ounces of vanilla sugar (No. 3165); add slowly eight egg-whites and finally eight ounces of flour. Range this paste on a slightly buttered baking sheet in the shape of three-inch length biscuits, keeping them at a short distance from each other; bake in a hot oven.

(3342). CATS' TONGUES WITH CREAM (Langues de Chat à la Crème).

Place in a vessel eight ounces of flour, eight ounces of powdered sugar and two ounces of vanilla sugar (No. 3165); dilute with three gills of rich cream and make a smooth paste, then add six partly whipped egg-whites. Dress this paste on a waxed baking sheet in the shape of small biscuits, each three inches long, pushing them through a quarter-inch diameter socket; bake slowly in the oven.

(3343). COCOANUT CROWNS WITH CHERRIES (Couronnes de Noix de Coco aux Cerises).

Mix together one pound of grated cocoanut, a quarter of a pound of butter, half a pound of sugar, three whole eggs and two ounces of flour; make this into a paste then leave it in the ice-box for one hour. Afterward mold this paste by hand into balls an inch in diameter, lay them on a buttered and floured baking sheet, flatten them a little, egg over, place in the center a preserved cherry and bake in a hot oven.

(3344). CROQUETS (Croquets).

Put one pound of flour on the table, make a hollow in the center and into it lay half a pound of butter, half a pound of sugar, half a pound of chopped almonds, the grated peel of a lemon, four eggs and two spoonfuls of rum; mix well to obtain a smooth paste; leave this in some cool place to rest for one hour. Then roll it into two-inch wide bands, having them three-eighths of an inch in thickness; lay them on a buttered and floured baking pan, egg over and leave rest again for half an hour in a cool place. Mark them with a fork in the shape of small lozenges. Bake them in a hot oven, brush them over with thick syrup, and after removing cut the bands across into small cakes, each one-half an inch wide.

(3345). CRUMBLED PASTE CAKES (Gâteaux en Pâte Fondante).

Mix slowly with the hands twelve ounces of butter and a pound of flour in such a way as to have it crumbling like semolina, then lay it on a table in the shape of a ring and in the center place twelve ounces of sugar, six egg-yolks, three eggs, some grated lemon peel and a grain of salt. Mingle the whole simply with the blade of a knife and incorporate this liquid into the crumbled flour; work together quickly and roll it into a ball; wrap up in a cloth and leave stand for two hours in a very cool place. Lay the paste on a floured table and divide it into small parts; roll out each of these pieces into strings four and one-half inches long; curl both extremities of each string in two spirals, bring these spirals together so as to form a sort of eye-glass imitation, arrange them gradually on a baking-sheet and let them dry for two hours. Then bake in a slack oven.

(3346). ESPAGNOLETTES (Espagnolettes).

Break five eggs in a basin, add three-quarters of a pound of sugar and beat together on a slow fire to have the whole very light, then put in the grated peel of a lemon and three-quarters of a pound of very dry sifted flour. Pour this into a pocket and with it dress the preparation on a buttered and floured baking sheet in rounds one inch in diameter; dredge the tops with coarsely chopped almonds; turn the baking sheet over quickly to remove the surplus of almonds, bestrew with sugar and bake in a very slack oven.

(3347). JAPANESE CAKES (Gâteaux Japonais).

Pound half a pound of unpeeled almonds with half a pound of sugar; pass it through a sieve, add half a pound of flour and mix the whole together. Dress this flour in a crown shape and in the center place four ounces of kneaded butter (No. 579) and three or four egg-whites; work the whole to obtain a fine smooth paste, then leave it rest for one hour in a very cold place; roll it out to an eighth of an inch in thickness and cut this into three-inch wide bands; egg these over and strew with chopped-up almonds. Range the bands two by two, one on top of the other, pressing them down lightly so they adhere together, then cut them across in small sticks three-quarters of an inch wide; lay them on buttered and floured sheets and bake in a hot oven; after removing ice over with a brush wet with rum icing (No. 102).

(3348). JUMBLES (Jumbles).

Work to a cream one pound of butter with one pound of sugar, add a little grated nutmeg and five eggs, one at a time, then a pound and a quarter of flour. Place this preparation in a pocket furnished with a channeled socket five-sixteenths of an inch in diameter and dress on a buttered sheet in the shape of one and a half inch rounds, keeping them an inch and a quarter apart, then bake in a hot oven. As soon as done remove them from the oven and when cool detach at once from the sheet.

(3349). LOZENGES (Losanges).

Arrange one pound of flour on the table, lay in the center three-quarters of a pound of butter, ten ounces of sugar, a pinch of salt, two eggs and two spoonfuls of orange flower water; mix the whole to have a smooth paste. Push this through a syringe having a scalloped plate on the end into long ribbons one and a half inches wide, and divide these into three-inch long lozenges; lay them on a buttered and floured baking sheet and leave in a cool place for half an hour, then bake in a hot oven; when cooked brush over with light gum or with a little icing sugar dissolved in milk.

(3350). MARQUIS' HATS (Chapeaux de Marquis).

Make a paste with a pound of flour, six ounces of butter, eight ounces of sugar, two whole eggs, two yolks and the peel of a lemon; leave rest in a cool place; roll it out into a flat one-eighth of an inch thick and from this cut channeled rounds two inches in diameter; egg the edges of them all and in the center lay a three-quarter-inch diameter ball made of almond paste (No. 125), incorporating into it as much crushed macaroons soaked in maraschino; lift up the edges on the three corners and fasten them together on top of the balls; egg over and leave for half an hour in a cool spot, then bake in a slack oven.

(3351). MILANESE (Milanaises).

Put four ounces of sugar in a vessel with two egg-yolks and two whole eggs; beat together for a moment to obtain a light preparation, then add two heaping spoonfuls of powdered almonds, four ounces of melted butter, four spoonfuls of finely cut-up citron and half a pound of flour, stirring together well to obtain a smooth paste; leave it in a cool place for half an hour. Roll it out with the rolling-pin to a quarter of an inch in thickness and cut this into bands, each one two and a half inches wide; brush each one with egg-yolks and trace lines on top with a fork; bestrew lightly with chopped almonds and cut them across in rectangles five-eighths of an inch thick; lay them on a buttered sheet and bake in a quick oven.

(3352). NANTES (Nantes).

Arrange a pound of flour in a circle on the table; in the center lay half a pound of sugar, half a pound of butter, three eggs and four ounces of candied orange peel and citron, chopped very finely; stir well to have a firm and smooth paste, roll it out with a rolling pin to a quarter of an inch in thickness and cut this into rounds an inch and a half in diameter; pinch the edges with a pastry pinch (Fig. 178) and lay them at once on a buttered and floured baking sheet; garnish the centers with a preparation made with an equal quantity of chopped almonds and sugar combined with a little egg-white; let rest for an instant in a cool place, then bake in a medium oven.

(3353). PALAIS DE DAMES WITH VANILLA (Palais de Dames Vanillés).

Work four ounces of butter to a cream in a vessel: add to it four ounces of sugar partly flavored with vanilla (No. 3165), then three whole eggs one by one and lastly four ounces of sifted flour. Dress this preparation by means of a pocket (Fig. 179) on a buttered and floured baking sheet and cook in a hot oven. After removing glaze over with a brush dipped in vanilla icing (No. 102).

(3354). PISTACHIO NOUGAT (Nougat de Pistaches).

Roll out some sweet paste (No. 136) to three-sixteenths of an inch in thickness; cut it into small one and a half inch diameter rounds and brush them around with egg-yolks; dredge all around on the brushed part a circle of chopped burnt almonds (No. 1), then lay them on a buttered baking sheet and leave rest for one hour in the ice-box. Bake them in a slack oven and when finished mask the centers with apricot jam (No. 3675) and lay over a round piece of preserved apricot; glaze with rum and bestrew immediately with shredded pistachios.

(3355). RIBBONS WITH ALMOND MILK (Rubans au Lait d'Amandes).

Pound six ounces of almonds with a little milk. Arrange half a pound of sifted flour in a circle on the table and in the center lay the pounded almonds, half a pound of sugar, six ounces of butter and two egg-yolks; mix all together to have it smooth. Push this paste through a syringe on a lightly floured board and form it into long pointed-edge ribbons; cut these in two-inch lengths and range them at once on a buttered and floured baking sheet; bake in a hot oven.

(3356). SCOTCH BREAD (Pain d'Écosse).

Roast four ounces of almonds and when cold pound them with half a pound of sugar to reduce to a powder and sift through a sieve. Arrange on the table in a circle half a pound of flour; in the center put the almond powder, four ounces of butter, one egg, one separate yolk and the peel of a lemon; mix well to obtain a smooth paste. Form this with the hands into small spindles two inches long; range them an inch and a half apart on a buttered and floured baking sheet, brush over twice with beaten egg-yolks and leave stand for a minute in a cool place; when ready to bake split them in two lengthwise and push into a brisk oven.

(3357). SHAVINGS (Copeaux).

Partly beat up ten egg-whites; add three-quarters of a pound of sugar, three tablespoonfuls of orange flower water, and three-quarters of a pound of flour; lay this paste through a pocket furnished with an eighth-inch diameter socket or else through a paper cornet, on a waxed baking sheet in the shape of ribbons, each four and a half inches long; bake in a brisk oven, and as soon as done detach from the sheet and roll them spirally around small rollers three-eighths of an inch in diameter, removing them as fast as they get the proper shape.

(3358). SUGAR CAKES (Gâteaux au Sucre).

Make a ring with two pounds of flour; in the center place one pound of sugar, half a pound of butter, two eggs, four yolks, three-quarters of an ounce of salaratus, a quarter of an ounce of dissolved carbonate of ammonia, the peel of a lemon and a little milk; mix all well together to have a smooth paste; lay this aside in a stone crock, and just when ready to use roll it out very thin and cut it into rounds with a two and a half inch diameter channeled pastry cutter (Fig. 16), and from the center remove small pieces with a three-quarter of an inch diameter cutter. Range these rings on a buttered sheet, and bake in a hot oven.

(3359). TROUVÈRE CAKES (Gâteaux Trouvère).

Lay a pound of flour in a circle on the table and in the center place half a pound of butter, half a pound of sugar, the peel of one orange and two eggs, also a half-inch ball of carbonate of ammonia, having it finely crushed; mix the whole carefully to obtain a smooth and fine paste, watching attentively that it does not crumble; let it rest for half an hour, then roll it to three-sixteenths of an inch in thickness; cut it into inch and a half diameter rounds with a channeled pastry cutter, range them on a baking sheet, egg over, and trace lines on top with a fork; prick the surfaces and bake in a hot oven.

(3360). TUILES (Tuiles).

Crush a pound of almonds with a pound and a quarter of sugar and six egg-whites to obtain a paste not too fine; put this into a bowl and beat well to give it body; then add eight beaten egg-whites and vanilla flavoring; mix well. Dress this preparation into flat oval macaroons on buttered and floured baking sheets; scatter shredded almonds over, bestrew lightly with powdered sugar and bake in a slack oven. As soon as done detach from the sheets, and bend each one around a wooden roller.

(3361). PARISIAN TUILES (Tuiles Parisiennes).

Beat four egg-whites to a stiff froth, add seven ounces of sugar, mixing together to form a meringue; then put in one ounce of flour and seven ounces of shredded almonds. Dress this preparation with a fork into small inch and a half diameter balls on a buttered and floured sheet: flatten them to three-eighths of an inch with a fork and bake in a slack oven. As soon as done detach and bend on a roller.

(3362). CHOCOLATE WAFFLES AND CIGARETTE WAFFLES WITH VANILLA—THIN (Gaufres Minces au Chocolat et Gaufres Cigarettes à la Vanille).

Lay six ounces of flour, four ounces of sugar, one ounce of vanilla sugar (No. 3165), and four ounces of powdered chocolate in a vessel; dilute with four egg-yolks, half a pint of double cream partly whipped and four egg-whites also partly whipped. Range this paste with a spoon on a waxed baking sheet into very thin round wafers two and a half inches in diameter and bake in a hot oven. As soon as done roll them on small wooden sticks half an inch in diameter.

Cigarette Wafers with Vanilla.—Dilute gradually six ounces of flour, an ounce and a half of sugar and half an ounce of vanilla sugar (No. 3165), with two and a half gills of milk and one egg; stir to have a smooth and flowing paste, then add an ounce of melted butter. Cook this preparation in round, flat wafer irons (Fig. 608), proceeding the same as for No. 3363. When of a fine golden color roll them on a small roller three-eighths of an inch in diameter.

(3363). WAFERS WITH ALMONDS OR HAZEL-NUTS AND WITH BRANDY—THIN (Gaufres Minces aux Amandes ou aux Noisettes et au Cognac).

Grind eight ounces of peeled sweet almonds with four egg-whites; pound them to a pulp to obtain a very fine paste, then add twelve ounces of powdered sugar, part of it flavored with vanilla (No. 3165) four ounces of flour and two egg-whites. Mix the whole well, and when the paste is quite smooth add to it four partly beaten egg-whites. Dress this paste in rounds two and a half inches in diameter with a spoon on waxed baking tins, and bake in a hot oven; when of a fine golden color remove from the tins and roll them on half-inch diameter cylinders.

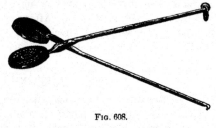

Fig. 608.

For Hazel-nut Wafers.—Substitute the same quantity of roasted nuts for the almonds.

Rolled Wafers with Brandy.—Lay twelve ounces of sifted powdered sugar in a bowl and wet it slowly with ten half-beaten egg-whites, then add six ounces of flour and six ounces of corn starch, two ounces of melted butter, and two tablespoonfuls of brandy. Mix thoroughly to a smooth paste; add a pint of milk and stir until a flowing paste is obtained. Heat two flat, round, wafer irons (Fig. 608), cover one side with a thin layer of the paste, close the irons, and cook the wafers to a fine golden color. Pare the edges as soon as they are done, then roll each one upon a small inch-diameter roll.

FANCY CAKES (Petits Fours).

Sixty to the Pound.

(3364). AFRICANS (Africains).

Make a small lady finger preparation (No. 3377); pour it in a linen bag furnished with a quarter of an inch socket, and lay the cakes on paper in the shape of small rounds an inch and a quarter in diameter; place this paper on a baking sheet, and bake the cakes in a slow oven. As soon as they are done remove them from the sheet and let get cold on the paper, then take the biscuits off, scoop them out on the flat side, and fill in the empty space with pastry cream (No. 46); fasten them together in pairs and dip them entirely in icing (No. 102) flavored with vanilla, rose, coffee or chocolate, removing them with a fork. Drain well on a wire grate, then set them at the oven door an instant to gloss.

(3365). AMARETTES (Amarettes).

Mix fifteen ounces of sweet almonds with one ounce of bitter almonds, a pound of sugar and four egg-whites, and crush to make a very fine paste; lay this in a vessel, add two more egg-whites and half a pound more sugar; stir well together until the paste is smooth. Mold it with the hands into olive shapes, and range them on a baking sheet covered with paper; leave to rest for four hours in the heater, then bake in a hot oven. After removing from the fire, and while yet hot, detach from the paper, gum over and roll them in finely chopped pistachios, then lay at once on a grate and return to the oven to dry the gum.

(3366). BARCELONNETTES (Barcelonnettes).

Pound eight ounces of almonds with a pound of sugar, four eggs and a gill of rum; make a very fine paste and put it in a vessel to add to it six egg-yolks, one at a time, beating them in until the whole becomes very light. Then sift in eight ounces of flour, mixing it in lightly, and lastly ten egg-whites whipped to a very stiff froth. Butter some small molds the shape of small channeled tartlets; glaze them over with icing sugar and fecula, half of each, and fill them three-quarters full with the preparation pushed in through a pocket; scatter chopped almonds over the tops, bestrew lightly with powdered sugar, and cook in a very slack oven; unmold as soon as done.

(3367). BIRDS' NESTS (Nids d'Oiseaux).

Put four egg-whites in a vessel and beat them up with six ounces of icing sugar to obtain a rather light icing, then add a pinch of cinnamon and a large handful of citron cut in small sticks, and some shredded almonds, having half of each. Mold this preparation with the hand into inch-diameter balls and range them on a buttered and floured baking sheet; press a small roller in the center of each to form a hollow in imitation of birds' nests; dry these for one hour in the heater and bake in a very slack oven. After removing fill the centers with apricot marmalade (No. 3675). Cover this over with thick kirsch water icing (No. 102) pushed through a cornet, and scatter over the top small candies imitating eggs, and a little green sugar (No. 172).

(3368). HAZEL-NUT BISCUITS (Biscuits aux Noisettes).

Crush twelve ounces of roasted hazel-nuts with a pound of sugar and three eggs to make a very fine paste; lay it in a basin and add half a gill of orange flower water and sixteen egg-yolks, one at a time, then beat vigorously until very creamy. Add ten ounces of flour and twelve firmly whipped egg-whites. Pour this preparation on a paper-covered baking sheet; spread it to a three-quarters of an inch thick layer and push in a slack oven to cook. Unmold the cake as soon as done on a grate and leave in a cool place for a few hours. Then pare it very straight and soak it lightly on the under side with Curaçoa; cover the top with reduced apricot marmalade (No. 3675), then cut the cake into small lozenge-shapes two inches long and dip them at once in Curaçoa fondant (No. 58); bestrew with chopped and lightly roasted hazel-nuts.

(3369). BISCUITS WITH ALMONDS—ICED (Biscuits Glacés aux Amandes).

Put a pound of sugar in a basin with eight eggs; beat until it is frothy, then add six ounces of almonds thoroughly pounded with two egg-yolks and half a gill of maraschino; continue to beat until the preparation is quite light, then add eight ounces of rice flour, mixing it in gently, and four ounces of melted butter. Pour the preparation on a baking sheet covered with paper, spreading it to a layer one inch in thickness, and place this in a slack oven. Turn the cake over on a grate and keep it in a cool place to rest until the following day. Then wet it over with a brush dipped in maraschino; cover the top with a layer of reduced apricot marmalade (No. 3675) and glaze it with white fondant (No. 58) flavored with maraschino and at once scatter chopped burnt almonds over the entire surface. After the icing is firm cut the cake into small rectangulars an inch and a half long and three-quarters of an inch wide.

(3370). CHOCOLATE CHESTNUTS (Marrons au Chocolat).

Pound together a pound of almonds and half a pound of sugar to a fine powder and pass it through a sieve; put this strained powder back in the mortar and stirring into it twelve to fourteen egg-yolks continue to pound until a fine paste is obtained, then lay it on a marble slab and incorporate six ounces of softened chocolate; leave the paste in the ice-box for one hour. Roll into strings, cut into small pieces and form these into balls three-quarters of an inch in diameter and shape them to resemble chestnuts; lay them on a paper-covered baking sheet and leave in a cool place for twelve hours. Then cook in a very hot oven and gum them over as soon as removed.

(3371). COCOANUT KISSES (Meringues Moelleuses aux Noix de Coco).

Place eight egg-whites free from yolks in a basin, whip until they become a stiff froth, then add with a small spatula one pound of sifted sugar, having part of it flavored with vanilla (No. 3165), and one pound of grated cocoanut. Wet a board thoroughly, cover it with a sheet of paper, dampen this lightly and on it range small balls of the preparation one inch in diameter, placing them slightly apart. As soon as finished bestrew with powdered sugar and push into a very slack oven to cook from eighteen to twenty minutes. After removing lift from the paper and fasten two by two together.

(3372). EXQUISITES WITH CHESTNUTS (Exquis aux Marrons).

Have ready a little firm lady finger paste (No. 3377), and with a pocket furnished with a three-eighths of an inch diameter socket dress it into small crowns an inch and a half in diameter, laying them on a sheet of paper; bake in a slack oven. When finished detach from the paper and hollow out the interiors of these crowns slightly on the flat side, then fill them up with chestnut purée; fasten together two by two, cover one side with a little apricot marmalade (No. 3675), and ice with vanilla fondant (No. 58); bestrew lightly all over with very finely chopped pistachios and with a channeled socket placed in a pocket dress in the center of each crown a rosette of Mocha cream.

(3373). FILBERT CAKES WITH RUM—SMALL (Petits Gâteaux d'Avelines au Rhum).

Roast half a pound of filberts; clean them well by removing their outer reddish skins, then pound with three-quarters of a pound of sugar, two eggs and half a gill of rum, making it into quite a fine paste; lay this in a vessel and soften it gradually with eight egg-yolks, continuing to beat until it is frothy, then add two ounces of finely shredded citron, four ounces of potato fecula, four ounces of melted butter and lastly six firmly beaten egg-whites. Pour this paste on a buttered sheet covered with paper, spread it out to half an inch in thickness and cook in a slow oven. Turn the cake over on a grate when done and leave to cool and set until the following day. Pare and cut it either in lozenges, oblongs or other shapes; steep each one slightly in Jamaica rum and ice over, dipping them into Jamaica rum fondant (No. 58); bestrew the cakes with chopped-up roasted filberts.

(3374). FANCY CAKES—SOFT (Petits Fours Moelleux).

Crush one pound of almonds with a pound and a half of sugar and five egg-whites; let this paste be very fine; lay it on a table and add a tablespoonful of strawberry essence and three more whites, and beat until it is very smooth and has attained body. Put a part of it in a channeled socket pocket and push it on a paper-covered baking sheet into small cakes shaped like an S, commas, knobs, etc. Decorate each one with a fancifully cut candied fruit or very white almonds and leave to dry in a cool place for four or five hours. Then bake in a hot oven and gum as soon as removed.

(3375). JAVANESES (Javanais).

Cook a little Genoese preparation (No. 3307) on a baking sheet, having it a quarter of an inch thick. Then divide it into two even parts; cover one of these with a layer of Quillet coffee cream (No. 48) a quarter of an inch thick and lay the other half on top, pressing it down lightly so it will adhere to the cream; cover over with apricot marmalade (No. 3675) and place the cake in the ice-box to harden the cream. Then cut it out with an oval pastry cutter two and a quarter inches long by one inch wide. Glaze these separate cakes with coffee fondant (No. 58) and in the center of each lay a pinch of lightly burnt chopped almonds.

(3376). LADY'S BOUCHÉES WITH STRAWBERRIES OR RASPBERRIES (Bouchées de Dames à la Fraise ou à la Framboise).

Make a little very firm lady finger preparation (No. 3377); lay it through a pocket on paper in small inch and a quarter rounds and bake them in a moderate oven. As soon as done and cold detach from the paper and hollow each one slightly; fill up this empty space with strawberry or raspberry marmalade (No. 3695) and fasten two together; cover with a light layer of the marmalade and glaze with raspberry fondant (No. 58).

(3377). LADY FINGERS (Biscuits à la Cuiller).

Separate the whites from twenty eggs and pour them into a basin; leave the yolks in another vessel; to these yolks add a pound of powdered sugar, part of it being flavored with vanilla (No. 3165) and beat up to make a very light preparation; then put in one pound of sifted flour and the twenty whites beaten to a stiff froth, stirring the whole lightly together. Pour a part of this preparation into a pocket (Fig. 179) furnished with a half-inch diameter socket and through it push biscuits four and a half inches in length, keeping them slightly apart and laying them on sheets of paper; bestrew with powdered sugar; put on a baking sheet and leave

FIG. 609.

stand a moment until the sugar begins to dissolve, then push it into a moderate oven. As soon as they are of a light golden color and the crust begins to harden remove at once from the oven and from the baking sheet, then range them on a table till cold.

Another Recipe is one pound of sugar, twelve eggs, half a pound of flour, a grain of salt, grated zest or a spoonful of orange flower water.

(3378). LEMON CROWNS (Couronnes au Citron).

Prepare a very fine paste with ten ounces of almonds, three-quarters of a pound of sugar, a part of it flavored with lemon (No. 3165) and five egg-whites; lay this paste on a buttered and floured baking sheet in small crowns an inch and three-quarters in diameter, pushing them through a pocket with a small three-eighths of an inch channeled socket; leave to dry in the heater for four to five hours, and when ready to cook fill the centers with frangipane cream with vanilla (No. 44); dredge over this cream with chopped almonds and cook in a hot oven. Gum over as soon as done, leave to cool and detach from the paper.

(3379). MACAROONS (Macarons).

Shell and skin one pound of almonds; pound them with two pounds of sugar, having part of it flavored with vanilla (No. 3165) and ten egg-whites; make a smooth but not too fine paste; lay it in a vessel to beat with a spatula until it acquires a body. Have a pocket provided with a half-inch diameter socket and push through it macaroons an inch in size, laying them on a paper-covered baking sheet. Moisten the surface with a slightly dampened cloth and cook in a slow oven.

(3380). ANGELICA MACAROONS (Macarons d'Angélique).

Crush one pound of almonds with a pound and a quarter of sugar and seven egg-whites; make a smooth but not too fine paste; place it in a copper basin and heat while stirring continuously with a spatula; when warm enough remove it at once from the fire to stir in five ounces of finely chopped angelica. Range this paste on a paper-covered baking sheet in small macaroon shapes an inch and a quarter in diameter; dampen the surfaces with a slightly wet cloth, powder over with sugar and bake in a slack oven.

(3381). BITTER MACAROONS (Macarons Amers).

Pound twelve ounces of sweet and four ounces of bitter almonds with two pounds of sugar and ten to twelve egg-whites; make a paste not too fine but rather soft; work this well to have it attain body, then lay it through a pocket into small oval macaroons an inch and a half long on a paper-covered baking sheet; dampen with a wet cloth and bestrew with granulated sugar; cook in a slack oven.

(3382). CHOCOLATE MACAROONS WITH NONPAREIL (Macarons au Chocolat à la Non-pareille).

With one pound of pounded almonds, two and a quarter pounds of sugar and ten egg-whites make a smooth but not too fine paste; place it in a vessel, incorporating four ounces of cocoa softened in a mild oven; mix well, adding two or three egg-whites. Dress this paste on paper through a pocket furnished with a socket into small inch-diameter balls; dampen the surfaces with a wet cloth, then cover with white nonpareil, removing the surplus that has not adhered; put the sheet of paper on a baking sheet and cook these macaroons in a slack oven.

(3383). CREAM MACAROONS IN CASES (Macarons en Caisses à la Crème).

Form a paste with one pound of pounded almonds, two pounds of sugar, one gill of good rich cream, a quarter of a gill of rum, four egg-whites and two orange peels. Put this paste into a vessel and beat it thoroughly to give it body; then add five very stiffly whipped egg whites, stirring them in gently. Have some small paper cases ready; range them one beside the other, slightly apart, on a paper-covered baking sheet; fill them three-quarters full with the preparation, letting it fall through a pocket; bestrew with powdered sugar and cook in a very slack oven.

(3384). DUTCH MACAROONS (Macarons Hollandais).

Peel one pound of almonds; pound them with two and a half pounds of icing sugar, part of it flavored with vanilla (No. 3165) and add slowly ten egg-whites to obtain a very fine paste; put it into a vessel and work to give body. Push it through a pocket on a paper-covered baking sheet into small oval macaroons one inch in length, and keep them in the heater for twelve hours, then remove and split them in two with a small kitchen knife and cook in a very slack oven.

(3385). FANCY MACAROONS (Macarons Fantaisie).

These macaroons are made with ordinary macaroon paste, the proportions being one pound of almonds, two pounds of sugar and twelve to fourteen egg-whites, preparing the paste in the manner described in Elementary Methods (No. 138). They can be made in an infinite number of designs, and among others are the following:

Angelica Macaroons.—Place the prepared paste in a pocket furnished with a socket (Fig. 179) and push through four small macaroons five-eighths of an inch in diameter in a straight line, one next to the other, fastening them all together, and decorate the entire line with a stick of angelica, then bake. Gum over after they are done, and decorate the ends with two small beads of pink icing (No. 102) made with syrup.

Clover Macaroons.—Dress three rounds the same way but place them in the form of a clover, instead of a straight line; decorate with three lozenges of angelica and then bake. Gum over as soon as they are taken from the oven and on each bead push a spot of green fondant (No. 58) through a cornet.

Orange Macaroons.—Have the same paste dressed in small, long ovals; decorate each one with two strips of candied orange peel laid on the bias; cook and gum over.

Apple Jelly Macaroons.—Make the macaroons an inch and a quarter in diameter, wet over and cook. After removing them from the oven form a hole in each with a small roller and fill this up with apple jelly (No. 3668). On top dress a bead of white icing (No. 102) pushed through a cornet.

Twin Macaroons.—Lay two small macaroons one beside the other in such a way that they adhere together. Wet over and cook. After taking them out of the oven make a hole in the center of each with a very small roller. Fill these holes with apricot marmalade (No. 3675) and cover this with a bead of pistachio fondant (No. 58).

Currant Jelly Macaroons.—Dress a small macaroon and around it form small beads of the same paste; wet and cook. Remove from the oven and make a hole in the center with a small roller and fill it up with currant jelly (No. 3670), then cover with raspberry icing (No. 102). Decorate with small beads of royal icing.

Network Macaroons.—Dress small oval-shaped macaroons, wet and cook. When done make an oval hole in the center of each and fill the hollow with apricot marmalade (No. 3675); cover this with orange fondant (No. 58) and decorate the fondant with a network of royal icing (No. 101).

Lyre Macaroons.—Push through the socket in the form of small lyres; at the base of each one range three small beads; decorate to imitate the strings with small sticks of angelica; wet and cook; gum over after taking them out of the oven.

(3386). HAZEL-NUT MACAROONS (Macarons de Noisettes).

Lay some hazel-nuts on a raised-edge baking sheet and roast them in the oven; as soon as done pour them on a large sieve, rub well to remove their skins and leave to cool. Crush three-quarters of a pound of these nuts and a quarter of a pound of almonds with two pounds of sugar and eight or ten egg-whites; make a paste the same as for plain macaroons. Put this into a vessel and stir well to give it body; then push it through a pocket on paper, dampen with a cloth and bake in a warm oven.

(3387). SOUFFLÉ MACAROONS (Macarons Soufflés).

Crush one pound of almonds with two pounds of sugar and eight egg-whites; of this make a fine paste; lay it in a vessel and work, to give it body, then mix in lightly twelve very stiffly whipped egg-whites. Push the preparation through a pocket on paper in the shape of inch and a quarter long macaroons; bestrew lightly with powdered sugar and cook in a slack oven. When done detach from the paper by wetting and fasten the macaroons together two by two with apricot marmalade (No. 3675).

(3388). STRAWBERRY MACAROONS (Macarons à la Fraise).

Pound together one pound of almonds, two pounds of sugar, five egg-whites and half a gill of strawberry spirit; make of it a plain macaroon paste; put this in a vessel and add a few drops of carmine and four very stiffly beaten egg-whites. Lay the paste through a pocket into small oval-shaped macaroons an inch and three-quarters long on a sheet of paper; dampen with a wet cloth and cook them in a slack oven; remove the paper from the baking sheet and leave the macaroons to get cold. Detach them from the paper and stick them two by two with strawberry preserves.

(3389). MADRILIANS (Madriliens).

Line some small tartlet-shaped cake molds with sweet paste (No. 136); mask the insides with well-reduced apricot marmalade (No. 3675). Pound four ounces of almonds with four ounces of sugar, two egg-yolks and a few spoonfuls of rich cream; make a soft, fine paste, add to it two ounces of orange peel cut in very small dice, and finally two whipped egg-whites. With this fill the small molds even with the top, strew crystallized sugar over and bake very slowly in a slack oven.

(3390). MAGICIANS (Magiciennes).

Prepare three pastes of different tints and flavors; have an almond paste with egg-yolks (No. 126), another paste made of pistachios the same as for pistachio lozenges (No. 3395), only keeping it a little firmer, and the third of almond paste as for ordinary fancy cakes (No. 124); into this incorporate a little softened cocoa. Roll these pastes separately to three-sixteenths of an inch in thickness and on the chocolate one spread a thin layer of well-reduced apricot marmalade (No. 3675); on top of this place the pistachio flat, cover it with more of the same marmalade and lastly put the almond flat on top. Slide this on a grate and leave it stand in a cool place for one hour to set, afterward cooking it in a hot oven; as soon as done and partly cold ice the cake with vanilla icing and divide it into small lozenges.

(3391). DEMIDOFF MARCHPANES (Massepains Demidoff).

Chop one pound of almonds finely and pass through a fine sieve; also three ounces of candied orange peel. Beat one pound of sugar with ten or eleven egg-whites and make it very light while heating gently, then add four ounces of flour, the orange peel and chopped almonds. Lay this preparation in inch and a quarter diameter rounds on a buttered and floured baking sheet; bestrew with chopped almonds, then with powdered sugar and let rest, and then bake in a very slack oven.

(3392). ORANGE MARCHPANES (Massepains à l'Orange).

Pound a pound of almonds with two and a half pounds of sugar; add twelve egg-whites, one by one; form into a smooth paste. Lay it in a vessel and continue to work until it acquires body; then add six ounces of finely chopped orange peel; mingle well and dress on buttered and floured baking sheets in the shape of oval macaroons one and a quarter inches long; bestrew with powdered sugar and cook in a slack oven; detach and fasten together two by two with apple jelly (No. 3668) flavored with orange.

(3393). SOFT MARCHPANES (Massepains Moelleux).

Crush one pound of almonds with a pound and a half of sugar, having part of it flavored with vanilla (No. 3165) and twelve to fourteen egg-yolks; make this into a fine paste. Run it through a syringe into channeled bands and decorate these at even distances with lozenges of angelica and a preserved half cherry in the center of each; leave to dry in a mild temperature until the following day, then cook in a very hot oven. Gum over when taken from the oven with gum arabic dissolved in water and cut them at once across between the decorations.

(3394). ITALIAN COFFEE MERINGUES—SMALL (Petites Meringues Italiennes au Café).

Break seven egg-whites in a basin and beat them on a slow fire with a pound of icing sugar to form into a very light and firm meringue, then add to it one good tablespoonful of coffee essence, mixing it in lightly. Lay this through a pocket on a paper-covered damp board into small meringue shapes and cook in a slack oven. As soon as done fasten them together two by two.

(3395). PISTACHIO LOZENGES (Losanges aux Pistaches).

Have two pastes ready; one made of almonds and the other of pistachio nuts, proceeding as explained herewith: Pound one pound of almonds with eighteen ounces of sugar and four or five egg-whites, obtaining a rather stiff paste; roll this out with the rolling-pin to a quarter of an inch in thickness. Besides this pound fourteen ounces of pistachio nuts with one pound of sugar and two ounces of chopped candied orange peel, using sufficient egg-whites to make a fine paste of the same consistency as a macaroon paste. Spread the pistachio layer on top of the almond one, slip it on a paper-covered baking sheet and push into a moderate oven to cook. As soon as the cake is done remove it from the fire and leave to cool partly, then spread over a coating of royal icing (No. 101), dredging the top with shredded pistachios. Cut at once into lozenges two inches long; range the cakes, one beside the other, on a baking sheet covered with paper and lay them for a few moments in the oven to dry the icing.

(3396). PISTACHIO TOURONS (Tourons aux Pistaches).

Obtain a fine firm paste with half a pound of pounded almonds, three-quarters of a pound of sugar and three or four egg-whites. Roll it out to a quarter of an inch in thickness, then cover with royal icing (No. 101), into which mix ten ounces of chopped pistachios and half a grated orange peel. Cut this paste into small sticks each two and a quarter inches long by five-eighths of an inch in width; range them on a buttered and floured baking sheet and cook in a slow oven.

(3397). QUILLETS—SMALL (Petits Quillets).

Line some small tartlet shape molds with parings of thin puff paste (No. 146), and let rest for some time. Mix three parts of cream cake paste (No. 132) with one part of pastry cream (No. 46) and with this fill the molds as far as the edges; bestrew the tops lightly with powdered sugar, then bake in a slack oven. As soon as done turn them out of the molds and leave to cool off; scoop out partially and refill with Quillet cream (No. 48). Ice the tops with vanilla fondant (No. 58).

(3398). PIGNON ROCKS WITH WHITE AND PINK ALMONDS (Rochers aux Pignons aux Amandes Blanches et Roses).

Whip eight egg-whites in a basin with a pound of icing sugar, a part to be flavored with vanilla (No. 3165); beat over a very slow fire and as soon as it begins to feel light and slightly warm take the basin from the fire and continue the beating process until perfectly light, then add one pound of pignons, mixing them in gently, or shredded almonds mixed the same. Dress the preparation with a fork into balls about an inch in diameter, lay them on waxed baking sheets and bake in a very slack oven. For the pink rocks with almonds or pignons mix in the preparation before adding the nuts one tablespoonful of spirit of raspberry and a little carmine, then finish as above.

(3399). ROCKS WITH ORANGEADE (Rochers à l'Orangeade).

Incorporate some icing sugar with three egg-whites to have a rather light icing; add to it four ounces of vanilla sugar (No. 3165) and half a pound of shredded almonds slightly roasted in the oven and a quarter of a pound of thinly sliced candied orange peel. Roll out some sweet paste (No. 136) to an eighth of an inch in thickness, divide it into small inch and a half diameter rounds and range these on a buttered baking sheet; on each one lay a ball of the above preparation an inch and a quarter in diameter and cook in a slack oven.

(3400). CHERRY STICKS (Bâtons aux Cerises).

Crush one pound of almonds with two pounds and three-quarters of icing sugar, having part of it flavored with vanilla (No. 3165) and eight to ten egg-whites; obtain a very fine paste, then spread it out three-eighths of an inch in thickness and let rest in a cool place for an hour and a half to two hours; cover the flat with a layer of the same paste, softened with more egg-white. Divide it into bands, each two and a quarter inches wide, and cut these in crosswise sticks, three eighths of an inch in width; decorate each one with four halved cherries, the cut side down, and lay them on a baking sheet covered over with paper; bake in a medium oven.

(3401). VANILLA STICKS (Bâtons à la Vanille).

Beat one pound of almonds with two pounds and three-quarters of icing sugar and a quarter of a pound of vanilla sugar (No. 3165), adding seven beaten egg-whites; obtain a very fine paste. Let it stand for a few hours in a cool place, then roll it out with the pin to three-eighths of an inch in thickness; cover the top with a layer of royal icing (No. 101). Cut this flat into bands two and a quarter inches wide, and these into sticks five-eighths of an inch long; lay them at once on a baking sheet covered with paper; cook in a very slack oven.

(3402). APRICOT TARTLETS (Tartelettes d'Abricots).

Pound one pound of almonds with three pounds of sugar, a quarter of a pound of vanilla sugar (No. 3165) and ten to twelve egg-whites; make a fine and firm paste. Roll this out with the rolling-pin to one-eighth of an inch in thickness, and with it line some small hollow tartlet molds; unmold on a baking sheet and let dry well in the heater. Fill the insides of the small tartlets with reduced apricot marmalade (No. 3675), and glaze with apricot fondant (No. 58).

(3403). STRAWBERRY TARTLETS (Tartelettes de Fraises).

Line some oval-shaped small cake molds with a thin coating of almond paste (No. 124). Crush eight ounces of pounded almonds with eight ounces of sugar, two ounces of strawberry marmalade (No. 3678), a little maraschino and two egg-whites; make this into a smooth but not too fine paste, color it slightly with carmine and incorporate five well-beaten egg-whites into which has been mixed an ounce of sugar, continuing to beat all the time. Fill the molds to the tops with this, bestrew the surfaces with powdered sugar and cook in a slow oven; unmold when done, cool off and ice over with fondant (No. 58) flavored with strawberry.

(3404). VENETIANS (Vénitiens).

Chop up a pound of almonds with a quarter of a pound of peeled, dried pistachios, and press them through a sieve (Fig. 96). Put sixteen egg-yolks into a basin with a pound and a quarter of sugar; beat till a light mixture is obtained, then add the powdered almonds, two ounces of fecula and six firmly beaten egg-whites. Turn this preparation on a baking sheet covered with paper in three-quarters of an inch thick layers and cook it in a slack oven; when done unmold on a grate, leaving it there until quite cold. Cover it with a thick layer of apricot marmalade (No. 3675) and bestrew with shredded pistachios. As soon as the apricot is hard cut the cake into rectangulars two inches long by one inch wide.

BAKERY (Boulangerie).

(3405). BREAD MAKING (Fabrication du Pain).

Although bread is considered a plain, simple food, yet it plays a very important part on the table and in the kitchen work. The preparation it requires in the kitchen, and the labor it demands, are almost innumerable, therefore I consider it necessary to give a few suggestions as to the manner of manipulating. These suggestions, of course, are only meant as a guide for the skilled practitioner, for to obtain perfect success in bread making requires both the experience and judgment of the workman, and he should always take in consideration, while performing his task, all that stands in relation to his work: The season, the weather, the temperature, the quality of the flour employed and its strength, the different kinds of flour entering into the mixture, the preparation of the dough, yeasts and ferment, the size of the bread, the quantity of either the first or second batch, the nature of the combustible for heating the oven and its capacity All these are most useful points to study and to remember, but can only be learned by practice, from whence experience arises. Both the judgment and tact must be utilized if success in bread making be desired.

(3406). NECESSARY UTENSILS FOR BREAD MAKING (Ustensiles Nécessaires à la Fabrication du Pain).

The utensils needed for bread making are few, and generally of a simple kind. *A range* for cooking the potatoes for the ferment and heating the water. *An enameled cast-iron pot* to cook the potatoes. *Two tubs*, each twenty inches in diameter and thirty inches deep—one to prepare the yeast in, the other for the ferment. *A pestle* for crushing the potatoes used to prepare the ferment. *A sieve* (Fig. 97) to strain the hop water for preparing stock yeast and common yeast. *A sieve* (Fig. 96) for sifting the flour. *A strainer* for straining the ferment. *A poker or long iron hook*, when the oven is heated by wood, to remove the embers. This is not used in the modern ovens heated with coal. *A tub* or pail to be filled with water into which the mop used for cleaning the oven is plunged. *A swab* or long stick on the end of which a heavy cloth or mop is attached. *A dipper* or tin vessel with a handle, generally holding about two quarts; it is used for measuring the water, yeast and ferment. *A scraper* or polished iron plate, four inches long by five and a half inches wide, with a handle; this is used to remove the dough adhering to the sides of the kneading trough; it is also used for cutting the dough into pieces. *Square wooden boxes*, measuring thirty inches wide by thirty-two inches long and four and a half inches deep in the inside. It is in these boxes, either simply dredged over with flour or else covered with a layer of coarse linen, that the dough rests after being cut up in all the operations succeeding the molding. *Long and narrow wooden crown boxes*, measuring in the inside sixteen inches wide by four feet ten inches long and three and a quarter inches deep. It is in these boxes, after they are covered with a layer of coarse linen, that the crowns are placed and left until ready to put in the oven. *Long strips of coarse linen* in proportionate width to the boxes they are intended for. These strips are laid in the boxes, and on these the bread rests until ready to be baked. *Two hard wood rolling-pins*, one three feet long and an inch and three-quarters in diameter; the other two feet long and five-eighths of an inch in diameter. The longest one is used to split the crowns, and the shortest to split the rolls. *Two small hard wood boards*, four inches long by thirty inches wide and half an inch thick on one end, then sloping down to scarcely nothing on the other, on the long side of the board. Cover one of these with thin flannel, to be used to remove jockos from the piece of linen, to place them on the peel, when sufficiently raised to be put in the oven; the other one remains uncovered and is used for raising the rolls from the linen when ready to cook. *A round board* half an inch thick and fifteen inches in diameter, furnished with a handle; the crowns are inverted from the linen on this to transport to the peel, just when ready to place in the oven. *Wooden and iron peels and a shovel*, one five inches wide by forty-one inches long. It is used for putting the jockos into the oven. Another of the same length and twenty inches wide is used to put all the small rolls and crowns in the oven, also to take them out, as well as the jockos. A third iron peel, seven by ten inches in length, is used for putting in and removing the molded loaves and those on tins. A shovel for coal, to be wide and quite deep. *Baking pans of Russian sheet-iron* with high sides, sixteen inches long by eight inches wide and three and a half inches deep. These pans are used for American two-pound loaves. Others, measuring twenty-four by nineteen inches wide, are intended for sweet rolls and muffins. *Sheet-iron molds with hinged covers* of two different sizes, one containing seven pounds of dough as in Fig. 610, for loaves intended for sandwiches and crusts; the other containing twelve pounds of dough, these loaves to be used for large croustades, supports and bread-crumbs. Fig. 610 mold contains seven pounds, and is twenty inches long by

Fig. 610.

five and a half wide, and five inches deep; at the bottom it is a quarter of an inch shorter and a quarter of an inch narrower than at the top. The other mold must be thirteen inches long by nine inches wide, and at the bottom a quarter of an inch shorter and a quarter of an inch narrower than at the top; that is, twelve and three-quarters by eight and three-quarters inches. The depth should be nine inches. *A kneading trough*, a large wooden case, generally thirty inches wide at the top and twenty-two inches at the bottom, twenty inches deep and eight feet long.

(3407). TO MAKE BREAD (La Fabrication du Pain).

Bread making is divided into the following operations: The preparation of the stock yeast, the yeast, the ferment, the leaven, the dough, the molding and the baking.

(3408). STOCK YEAST (Fond de Levain).

Boil five quarts of water. Put in a stone jar five ounces of flour; dilute it with a part of this boiling water, sufficient to obtain a very firm paste; put into the remainder of the water one ounce of hops; let boil for ten minutes, then remove the liquid from the fire and run it through a fine sieve into the stone jar and over the paste. Set this jar in a cool place until the liquid is only lukewarm. Then dissolve the paste with the water, and add to it four ounces of malt; cover the pot, and leave it in a rather warm temperature for forty-eight hours, where it cannot be disturbed; when this time has expired strain the liquid through a sieve into another stone jar. The stock yeast is now ready to be used.

(3409). YEAST (Levure).

All the utensils used for making yeast and leaven should be kept scrupulously clean, as also the tubs. Put fifteen quarts of water into a large pot; set it on the fire and remove it at the first boil. Lay two pounds of flour in the bottom of a tub, dilute it with a pint of boiling water and make a sufficiently hard paste. Put into the rest of the water in the pot three ounces of hops and let boil for ten minutes, then remove from the fire and strain the boiling liquid at once through a fine sieve into the tub and over the paste; set this tub in a cool place and leave it till the liquid is only lukewarm, then with the hands work the paste well into the water; add immediately one quart of barley malt and a quart of stock yeast, mixing all well together. Set the tub in a moderate temperature and leave without disturbing it while fermenting, which process will take place in eighteen to twenty hours. By attending to these elementary details with care a perfect baking will ensue. Strain the yeast through a fine sieve into another tub and set this in the icebox, or any cool place, to use as needed for the preparation of the ferment. This yeast will keep perfectly good for four days.

(3410). FERMENT (Ferment).

Wash seventeen quarts of small potatoes, put them into an enameled iron pot, pouring over sufficient cold water to cover; place the pot on the fire, and let them boil uninterruptedly until well done, then remove. Throw the potatoes into a large tub, add two and a half pounds of flour, mash well together with a pestle to reduce the whole to a smooth paste, then dilute this paste gradually with twenty-two quarts of water, either cold or barely lukewarm, according to the temperature and season; afterward add five quarts of yeast, and mix the whole well together. Cover the tub with a cloth, and set it in a moderately warm place where there is no danger of its being disturbed and leave it until fermentation takes place, which means until it rises to double its height and falls again to its normal state. The fermentation should take place in from seven to eight hours. With this quantity of ferment a barrel of flour can be used.

(3411). LEAVEN (Levain).

Sift a barrel of flour into one end of the kneading trough; into the other end strain thirty-one quarts of ferment through a colander, and work enough of the flour into it to form a dough, not too consistent; gather up this dough into a small space in the trough and keep it in position with a movable board which answers for a partition; dredge it over with flour, and cover with the lid of the trough, then leave it to rise for three hours; at the end of that time the sponge should be double its size and ready to fall again; it is then ready for the dough.

(3412). THE DOUGH (La Pâte).

Remove the supporting board and let the sponge cover a larger space in the trough; pour over it twenty-nine quarts of water and three pounds of salt dissolved in a part of the water, then mix the whole together until the sponge is well blended; then dredge over the half of the remaining flour and knead well together with the hands, giving them a vertical rotary movement, going and coming from one end to the other of the dough; it should now be rather soft and begin to acquire body. Pour the remainder of the flour in one layer over all the paste and knead it once more, but this time cutting it into small pieces with the hands and superposing these pieces at once, one on top of the other; as soon as all the flour is absorbed, then push all of the dough to one end of the trough. Cut from the whole of it a piece weighing twenty-five pounds; knead it strongly, blowing and beating it forcibly against the sides of the trough, which means to take the piece of dough by the two lateral ends, raise them to the height of the chest, stretching out the dough and bringing it down heavily against the sides of the trough in such a way as to imprison all the air possible, and give it consistency; repeat the same operation with the remainder of the paste. Superpose the pieces of dough as quickly as they are done, one on top of the other, at the other end of the trough; repeat this operation a second time, then a third and even a fourth time, until the dough has acquired the desired body, then gather it together into a small space in the trough, holding it up with the well-floured board wedged against it. Dredge over lightly with flour, cover and leave it to rise for one hour. The dough is then ready to mold.

(3413). BREAD WITH BUTTER, VARSOVIAN (Pain au Beurre à la Varsovienne).

Make a small leaven with four ounces of flour, half an ounce of yeast and sufficient warm milk to form it into a softish paste; mold it into a ball, lay in a vessel, dredge with flour, cover with a cloth and leave it in a mild temperature to raise the leaven to double its size. Sift three-quarters of a pound of flour on the table, form a hollow in the center and in it put a pinch of salt, five ounces of melted butter and half a gill of milk; make the dough of the same consistency as a brioche paste; incorporate the leaven, cutting it up to mix it well with the paste without kneading it. Lay this paste in a vessel, dredge with flour, cover with a cloth and leave it to rise in a mild temperature. Turn it over on the table when it attains twice its original size; cut it up and divide it into pieces; with each of these form a ball an inch and a half in diameter; range them on buttered baking sheets at a distance of an inch and a quarter apart and let rise to double their size; brush over with egg diluted with milk and bake in a moderate oven.

(3414). CRESCENTS WITH BUTTER—FINE (Croissants Fins au Beurre).

Make a rather firm leaven with half an ounce of yeast and six ounces of flour; let it rise in a mild temperature. Arrange twelve ounces of flour in a circle, lay a little salt in the center and moisten with a small quantity of milk, adding four ounces of butter; dilute the paste, keeping it rather firm, then add the leaven; when this is well mingled lay the paste in a vessel, cover over and leave to rise slowly, without any heat; after it is well risen cut it up on a floured table and divide it in parts the size of an inch and three-quarters diameter ball; mold each one in a round form and flatten with a roller; spread to a thin oval an eighth of an inch in thickness. With the left hand take hold of the nearest end and with the right roll the opposite end, then bring the two ends quickly together at the same time, being careful to draw the paste lightly with the left hand so as to keep the cake quite thin; this operation should be deftly and speedily performed. As soon as a band is rolled lay it on a baking sheet, ranging it in the shape of a crescent. Leave the paste to rise slowly once more, then wet with a brush dipped in water and push into a hot oven; after removing dampen the tops with fecula cooked in water to the consistency of a light syrup, applying it with a brush; this helps to give gloss to the cakes.

(3415). CROWNS (Couronnes).

For twelve crowns: Take thirty-six pounds of dough; divide it into twelve parts of three pounds each, and mold all the pieces into separate balls; flatten them to a third of their thickness. Lay these in lightly floured boxes and leave them to rise for half an hour; then remove them from the boxes and lay them on the table, one by one, to flatten out; roll over in four and finally stretch out to the shape of a roll twenty-six inches long. As soon as they are done return them to the boxes and leave them to rise for twenty-five to thirty minutes, then take one of them from its box and lay it on the table; with a wooden rolling-pin, as described in the bread-making utensils, split the dough through its whole length without separating it entirely, forming a depression along the center an eighth of an inch in thickness, separating the dough on each side, two and a half inches apart; then take up the furthest edge of the dough, and raising it, bring it forward toward yourself in such a manner as to partially envelop the other edge of the dough. Bring the two ends together and fasten so as to form a crown. Transfer this into another long box, as explained in No. 3406, covered inside with a piece of coarse linen, laying the split side underneath; continue to mold all the other balls in a like manner, then cover and leave for an hour and a half. As soon as they are sufficiently raised take the round board with a handle, as denoted in No. 3406, in the right hand, and lay it on the right of one of the first molded crowns, slanting it slightly against the crown; at the same time with the left hand take hold of the piece of linen which extends beyond the crown on its left, and with a deft stroke turn the crown over on the board without injuring its shape; transfer this crown on the board and slip it on to the peel, then push it at once into the oven. Continue the same operation for all the other crowns until they are in the oven and leave them there for thirty to thirty-five minutes.

(3416). JOCKOS—FRENCH LOAVES (Jockos).

Lay on the table a part of the dough from the trough; divide it up into pound and a half pieces each and mold them into balls as soon as they are weighed; flatten them down to a third of their thickness, and range them two inches apart in boxes previously bestrewn with flour. When a box is full sprinkle the balls lightly with flour, cover them hermetically by laying another box of the same size on top; fill this one the same as the first, and cover in a similar manner, and continue this process until there are sufficient of them. Over the last box set an empty one and let raise for twenty to twenty-five minutes; take the first ones molded, and with the hands roll and pull them out in a way to give them a cylindrical shape, twenty-two inches long; lay these on a bed of Indian meal previously spread over one end of the table, and leave them there for a few moments—sufficient time to allow the meal to adhere to the dough. Range in a box a long piece of coarse linen, the right end extending up two inches against the side of the box; lay on this piece of linen, against this side, one of the rolls of dough, putting the side the meal is on at the bottom;

raise the linen on the left side of the paste in such a manner as to form it into a fold parallel to the roll of dough, to serve as a support, so that the dough when rising does not flatten out, but stands up vertically, which helps to give the bread its round shape. Roll out another roll of dough to form a second roll, the same as the first; lay it in the meal, and then range it on the piece of linen, against the first roll; raise the linen to form a fourth fold to maintain the third roll of dough, and continue the same until the box is full. Cover it hermetically, laying another box on top, and fill it up the same way; when all the balls have been rolled out let them rest for one hour and a half to two hours, according to the temperature and season, or until they rise to a third of their original size. Now take the thin covered board, as explained in bread-making utensils, in the right hand and insert it sideways on the right of the first roll of molded dough, between the fold of linen and the dough; at the same time, with the left hand, take the end of linen on the left of the dough, and hold it so that the dough can be rolled over on this board; transport this roll of paste, and turn it over on the peel; score four slanting incisions at once on its back, using for this the tip of a small knife, and set it into the oven; continue the operation until all the jockos are in the oven, then close it up for fifteen minutes; at the expiration of this time the jockos should be baked. Begin taking out the first ones put in, and continue according to the order they were placed in the oven until all are removed.

(3417). LOAVES IN BOXES AND PANS OF TWO, SEVEN AND TWELVE POUNDS EACH
(Pains en Boîtes et en Plaques de Deux, Sept et Douze Livres Chaque).

For sixteen pan loaves, two pounds each, lay on the table thirty-two pounds of dough; cut it into sixteen pieces of two pounds each, and mold them into balls; flatten and range them in lightly floured boxes to rise for one-half hour; flatten again and lift up the four corners, fold the dough in two, and again in such a way as to form a roll or stick, eight inches long by four inches in diameter; lay these as soon as done in pans sixteen by eight inches with raised edges (No. 3406), previously greased over with lard; lay four in each, very close, one beside the other, and leave them one hour to rise, then push them into a moderate oven to bake for three-quarters of an hour; as soon as they are done remove and turn them out at once.

For seven-pound loaves to cut up for sandwiches and croûtons, and for twelve-pound loaves for large croustades and bread-crumbs, roll them out, and prepare the same as the two-pound bread, putting seven or twelve pounds of dough into each, according to the size of the mold. Butter or grease the molds, close the lids, and let rise for one hour, then push them into the mildest spot in the oven.

To bake a seven-pound loaf of bread it will take an hour and a quarter; a twelve-pound loaf takes about two hours; when done, remove from the oven and unmold.

(3418). PASTE FOR FINGER ROLLS AND SMALL ROLLS (Pâte à Petits Pains).

The ingredients are one pound of flour, two eggs, three-quarters of a gill of milk, salt, two ounces of butter, half an ounce each of sugar and yeast. Make a little leaven with a quarter of the flour and the yeast, diluting it with a little warm water; leave this in a vessel, cover and place in a temperate place so that it rises to double its height. Lay the balance of the flour on the table; make a hollow in the center and in this put a pinch of salt, the sugar and a little tepid milk, then the eggs and mix, drawing in the flour gradually and adding the rest of the tepid milk. When all is mixed bring the dough together and knead it well, striking it on the table for a few minutes (the object of this being to incorporate as much air as possible in the paste); when the paste has plenty of body add half the butter to it and continue the kneading until the butter is well worked in, then add the rest of the butter and knead again, working the paste a few minutes longer. Now put in the leaven, mixing it lightly with the dough, set into a vessel, cover with a cloth, and let it rise in a moderate temperature. As soon as this dough is sufficiently raised divide it into pieces of a pound each; roll out these into ropes half an inch in diameter, and dividing these ropes into twenty equal-sized parts give each one a round shape by rolling them on the table with the palm of the hand; roll them out to the shape of small rolls two and three-quarters inches long, pointed at both ends, and lay them on a slightly buttered baking sheet, keeping them about one inch apart, then leave them to rise in a gentle temperature. As soon as they are sufficiently raised brush them over with beaten eggs twice, and bake in a warm oven.

(3419). FINGER ROLLS (Flûtes Longues).

Sift two pounds of flour on the table, divide it into four parts and in one of the quarters form a hollow; set into it an ounce and a half of yeast, diluting with a gill and a half of lukewarm water; work the flour into the liquid in such a way as to obtain a soft leaven; mold it round shape and indent a cross on top; lay it in a vessel into which a few spoonfuls of tepid water have been deposited; cover over and let rise to double its size for twelve to fifteen minutes. During this time range the balance of the flour in a circle, and lay in the center two ounces of sugar, half an ounce of salt, two whole eggs and two and a half gills of barely warm milk; mix the ingredients together, and then incorporate gradually all of the flour; the dough must now be consistent; knead it well and cut it up with the two hands, and beat it on the table for a few moments so that it acquires body; add two ounces of butter and continue kneading for a few minutes longer. As soon as the leaven is ready mix in thoroughly with the dough but without kneading again; lay this in a basin, sprinkle over lightly with flour, cover and let rise for one hour in a mild temperature. At the expiration of that time it should have doubled its original height; knead it once more and divide it into half-pound pieces; divide each into twelve small pieces, obtaining three-quarters of an ounce in each one, then mold these into small balls and set to rise for twenty minutes, afterward rolling them out with the hand into four and a half inch lengths; range them at once on a lightly buttered baking sheet; when it is full place it in a box and close hermetically; continue to prepare and mold the remainder of the dough, and when all are done examine the first ones that were molded, and should they be sufficiently raised, or increased to a third of their original size, brush them over with beaten eggs and bake in a hot oven.

(3420). FLUTES AND SPLIT ROLLS (Flûtes et Petits Pains Fendus).

Flutes and split rolls are made with a dough slightly stiffer than for the jockos; generally both of these kind of rolls are molded at the same time. Prepare a bread dough as explained before, working it exactly the same, the only difference being it must be kept a little stiffer; let it rise for one hour; knead it again to stop the fermentation and remove it from the trough to the table. Divide it up into two and a half ounce pieces and form them into balls; range these at short distances from each other in slightly floured boxes; set the boxes one on top of the other as fast as they are filled and leave them to rise for fifteen to twenty minutes; at the expiration of this time the balls are ready to be molded into any shape desired.

For Flutes or French Rolls.—Lay on the table two of the balls of dough, beginning with those first molded; flatten them down with the palm of the hand, raise the ends of the dough and press these ends together; roll them out on the table with the hands to finish lengthening them, then lay at short distances from each other in boxes lightly dredged with white Indian meal. Continue thus until half of the balls are rolled out. Cover these boxes by setting one on top of the other and leave them to rise for twenty-five to thirty minutes.

For Split Rolls.—During the time the flutes are rising split the remainder of the balls of dough. Take six of these balls and range them on the table in rows of two and two, then with a small rolling pin, as described in the article on utensils, split two of them through at the same time; take hold of the edge of the farthest side of each piece and bring it forward; wrap it over half of the front piece so that the molding is on top and the split side underneath, then take these split rolls, one in each hand, and range them against the right side of a box that is already lined with a strip of coarse linen, laying the split side underneath; raise up the linen on the left of the rolls to form a fold which answers for a support, so that while the rolls are rising they cannot fall again. Take six more balls of dough, range them on the table two by two, the same as the first ones; split and lay them on the linen against the others, and continue this operation until all the rolls are shaped. Cover the boxes as fast as they are filled, and leave them to rise for twenty-five to thirty minutes. As soon as all the rolls are split examine the flutes to see whether they are a third larger than when molded; if so they are ready to be placed in the oven; brush them over with beaten eggs diluted in a little water, using a feather brush; take them up delicately with the hands, one by one, and lay them on the peel; cut three slanting incisions on each with the tip of a small knife and place them in the oven. As soon as they are all in, close the oven door for ten to twelve minutes, according to the degree of heat therein; when a fine golden color take them out, beginning with those first put in. By this time the rolls ought to be ready to go in the oven; take them from the linen, six at a time, turning them over on to the board, as described in the bread-making utensils, having the split sides uppermost, removing them exactly the same as the jockos; slide them on the peel, and place them in an oven not too hot: as soon as they are all in close the door for a few minutes, and when done take them out, beginning with those first put in.

(3421). SWEET ROLLS, CRESCENTS AND MUFFINS (Petits Pains au Lait et au Beurre, Croissants, Muffins).

How to Prepare the Dough.—Sift eight pounds of flour into a large wooden bowl; make a hollow in the center and lay in it three ounces of yeast; diluting with three pints of barely lukewarm water, make a soft sponge, sprinkle it over with flour and leave it to rise in a mild temperature for three hours, more or less, according to the heat, and until the sponge doubles itself, then moisten with three pints of milk into which has been dissolved half a pound of sugar and three ounces of salt, incorporating at the same time a pound and a half of butter; knead well and divide it into small pieces. As soon as it is thoroughly mixed incorporate sufficient flour to make a consistent dough and knead it well to give it plenty of body. The dough being now finished cut it into three parts.

Sweet Rolls.—Put one of these parts into a vessel, sprinkle it lightly with flour and leave it to rise for an hour and a half.

Crescents. —Take the second piece of dough, put it into a basin and incorporate four ounces of butter; work well so that it is well mixed, then leave it to rise for one hour and a half.

Muffins.—To the third and last piece add a little milk to soften and obtain a mellow dough, keeping it sufficiently firm to be able to mold with the hand on the table; take it out of the bowl, dredge the latter with flour and return the dough to it; besprinkle flour over the top, cover and 'eave it to rise, the same as the other two, for one hour and a half. At the expiration of this time the three pieces of dough should be raised to double their height. Knead them again to prevent fermentation; they are now ready to be divided and molded.

Sweet Rolls.—Begin with the sweet rolls and operate as follows: Break it into two-ounce pieces; roll these into balls and place them as fast as they are done into lightly floured boxes at short distances from each other; dredge slightly with flour, cover and leave them to rise for half an hour, then roll them over again exactly the same as before, giving them a more perfect spherical shape; range these balls as quickly as they are formed into lightly buttered baking sheets with a slight space between each, and as soon as the sheets are filled put them into boxes and cover; let them now rise from one hour to an hour and a quarter; they should be one-third larger than their original size and are then ready to be put into the oven; brush the surfaces with a feather brush dipped in beaten eggs, diluted with a little milk; with a pair of scissors make four deep incisions so as to form a cross, then push them into a slack oven and let bake for eighteen or twenty minutes.

Crescents.—Crescents are to be molded in the following manner: Lay on the table the buttered dough already prepared for these; divide it up into one ounce and a half pieces and roll them into balls; set them into the boxes as soon as done, dredge over with rye flour, cover and leave them to rise for thirty-five to forty minutes, then lay two of the first molded balls on the table one beside the other, a short distance apart, and with the roller used for rolls flatten down the two balls at once, to obtain two oval pieces, an eighth of an inch thick, leaving the two furthest sides a little thicker than the forward ones, then with the left hand hold the nearest or front one of these flats, and with the palm of the right hand roll it over on itself, beginning with the back or thick side, and bring it forward to give the shape of a shuttle, six inches long, seven-eighths of an inch in the center and one-fourth of an inch at the ends; lay them when finished on a lightly buttered baking sheet, giving them the shape of a crescent, and finish the other oval layer the same, continuing until all the balls are molded; as fast as each baking sheet is filled put them into the boxes, cover and leave for one hour to one hour and a quarter; brush over with beaten eggs diluted in a little milk and push them into a slow oven to bake for twelve to fifteen minutes.

Muffins. —Lightly butter three dozen tin muffin rings three and a half inches across and one inch high; lay them on two lightly buttered baking sheets. Place the third piece of dough—the one softened with milk—on the table, cut it into an ounce and three-quarters pieces and roll them all into balls; flatten slightly in the middle and lay them at once into the rings; when all are filled cover over with two more lightly buttered baking sheets, set a weight on top of each and leave the dough rise for three-quarters of an hour; push them gently into the oven, sheets, weights and all, being careful not to disturb them whatever; they take from twenty to twenty-five minutes to bake; turn them out of the rings as soon as they leave the oven.

(3422). CORN BREAD (Pain de Maïs).

Put four ounces of butter into a tin basin; work it to a cream with four ounces of sugar, add a pinch of salt and four eggs singly, also a gill of milk; now sift in one pound of corn flour and half a pound of ordinary flour into which has been previously added two coffeespoonfuls of baking-powder, and add another gill of milk to finish. Butter some corn-bread molds, fill them three-quarters full with the preparation, lay them on baking-sheets and set them in a hot oven to bake for twelve to fifteen minutes; unmold them as quickly as they are done and removed.

(3423). RYE BREAD, BOSTON BROWN BREAD AND GRAHAM BREAD (Pain de Seigle, Pain Brun de Boston et Pain de Graham).

The dough for rye bread is made exactly as for ordinary bread (see the article on bread dough), the only difference being that half rye and half wheat flour are used; a few caraway seeds may be added to the dough, mixing them in when the kneading process begins. When the dough is finished and sufficiently raised, cut it into two-pound pieces, turn and roll them out long-shaped and lay them in the folds of linen exactly the same as the jockos. Just when ready to put into the oven, while still on the peel, dampen the tops with water, using a brush, and cut a few slanting incisions on each one with the tip of a small knife, then set them in the oven to bake for forty-five minutes.

Boston Brown Bread.—Place in a basin two and three-quarter pounds of yellow corn meal, two pounds of white corn meal, one and three-quarter pounds of rye flour, one pound of Boston meal and an ounce of salt. Dilute these flours with one pint of New Orleans molasses, one pint of Potter molasses, one quart of ferment (No. 3410), and two quarts of water; mix all well together, making a very soft paste, then cover over and leave it in a mild temperature to raise for four hours. Then add three-quarters of an ounce of soda dissolved in a glassful of water and twelve ounces of stale bread sifted through a sieve; mingle all well together. With this paste fill three-quarters full some buttered timbale molds and leave the paste stand for one hour. Cover over and place in a very slow oven and let bake for six hours.

Graham Bread.—Put into a large vessel one and a quarter pounds of wheat flour, one and a quarter pounds of Graham flour, a coffeespoonful of salt and half a gill of molasses. Onto these ingredients pour one and a quarter pints of leaven, and one and a quarter pints of water. Mix all well together forming a dough of the same consistence as for bread; cover and leave it to raise for two hours in a mild temperature. Divide the dough into pound and a quarter pieces, mold and place each one in buttered molds; let raise again for an hour and a half to two hours, then bake in a very slack oven. Graham flour is made of the wheat ground to flour and left unsifted, consequently it contains the bran and commoner qualities than other flours.

ICES (Glaces).

(3424). ICES (Glaces).

Preliminary Remarks.—We call ice (in general) a solid body, formed naturally or artificially from a fluid substance, such as water, oil, etc., frozen to a certain degree. It can also be said to be a fluid compressed by the lowering of the temperature to zero. Therefore, ice is nothing but crystallized water, lighter than liquid water, as it floats on its surface. In alimentary language ices are compounded creams or liquors made to freeze. Many books have been written on the subject of ices, and many serious researches have been made, hence it is not our intention to enter into the various details, as they can more easily be learned by consulting these divers works. Still we have considered it our duty to recall in a few words the history of the manufacture of these perfect and delicious refreshments. By going back to the most ancient times we find, especially in southern countries, that they had learned of the benefits to be derived from cool drinks, so we suppose the use of ice was known to the Greeks and Romans, and we read that Hippocrates, the father of medicine, recognized the impropriety of its use, as well as that of snow. The Orientals partook of iced drinks, also the Persians and the Spaniards had vases called alcarazas (in French Gourgourlelles), an earthen vessel without handles, to contain and keep the water cold. Therefore, the progress made in the seventeenth century and productive of such vast improvement was but the realization of an idea discovered centuries before; this is plain, for in those days as in these, they understood the necessity of having within their reach refreshing drinks suitable for the hot seasons of the year. Doubtless they were far from possessing the resources we have at our disposal to-day as regards material, for it was only at the end of the sixteenth century that the use of ice-boxes was first invented; nevertheless, our forefathers learned how to utilize the natural means at their command. With the assistance of porous vases exposed to a brisk current of air, also to all the sunlight possible, and by wrapping them in wet cloths, a sufficient degree of cold was obtained to have the value of such a drink appreciated, while suffering from the heat of the climate. Later, the people were not satisfied by procuring a temporary cool liquid, but devised some other plan by which they could retain the cold they had thus obtained. The only way to accomplish this was to transform the liquid drinks into a solid mass—in one word freeze them. The idea was rational, but chemistry, a science so thoroughly restricted in those days, and only understood by a few privileged persons, was found to be of very little assistance. However, in one of Bacon's works (a celebrated physician and chemist of the sixteenth century), we find a sentence which reads as follows: " It is evident that salt when mixed with ice for artificial congealments increases the action of the cold." At the end of the sixteenth century, and at the beginning of the seventeenth century, all the physicians of those days devoted themselves to experimenting, and the result of their researches was as follows: " Ice and salt are the most active principles for congealing, observing at the same time that ammoniacal salt is the most effective, and will produce the quickest cooling result." Henceforth, the wonderful progress for making ices was rapid, and these wise men thought they had at last reached a degree of perfection. They froze liquors in tin and leaden boxes, by surrounding them with a powerful refrigerating mixture. These ices, called rare ices and served only in sumptuous repasts, were still very imperfect, being nothing else than blocks of solid ice, reminding one of the taste of the liquor used in their fabrication, but being so remarkably hard that the pleasure of partaking of them was overbalanced by the great difficulty in eating them. They therefore endeavored to obtain a result more satisfactory to epicures. Réamur was the first person, in the year 1734, to refer to this defect, and try to ameliorate its condition. It was observed that if any liquor or fruit juice and sugar be added to water in certain proportions and that this mixture be submitted to a sufficient degree of cold, the water would be the first to congeal, while the sugars and syrups were the last. This defect had to be overcome, therefore they found that by cooking a certain amount of sugar in water they produced a syrup which they could afterward weigh. To this syrup they could mix the juices of different fruits and freeze the preparation without any fear of the defective results they sought to obviate. This was taking a great stride toward a final success, and thereafter experience alone sufficed to teach these practitioners how to acquire the best results. Instead of leaving the mixture to refrigerate alone in order to congeal the compositions, they endeavored to find how to increase the action of the cold by giving a rotary motion, more or less rapid, to the receiver in which the operation takes place. This is why they began to employ round, elongated vessels, so much easier to manage, and to which they gave the name of sorbotières, to-day called sorbetières or freezers. The round freezer is evidently the best for working the ices, for not only does its shape facilitate the rotary movement employed, but this movement also connects with the liquid, and while keeping it continually well-mixed, it also keeps the interior sides of the freezer covered with all the particles of water, syrup or sugar, of which it is composed. These simple methods having been discovered it only remained to find the means of improving on them. It is not our intention to follow step by step all the contrivances invented for the making of ices. The most important fact was discovered that by careful manipulation a composition could be obtained not only agreeable to the taste, but easier to swallow and to relish. However, we do not intend concluding our preliminary remarks without giving some general advice on the manner of cooking sugar, on the precautions necessary to the manufacture of the frozen preparation, and also on the way to mold and unmold ice cream figures.

(3425). COMPOSITIONS FROZEN BY MACHINE (Compositions Glacées à la Machine).

Have a machine of basin or pear shape. The basin-shaped machine should be fifteen inches in diameter by fifteen inches in height and rounded at the bottom, to be provided with a tinned iron rod running through the freezer and fitting into a gear with a pivot below (see Fig. 611). Put the cover on the freezer and pack it in salted ice; remove the cover and pour into the freezer (which contains about thirty quarts), six quarts of preparation, or the fifth part of its capacity.

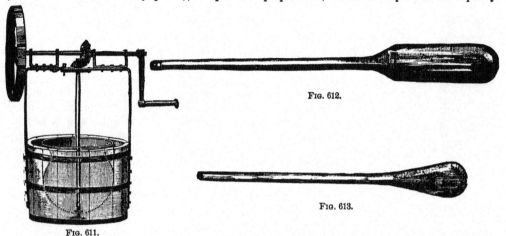

FIG. 612.

FIG. 613.

FIG. 611.

Turn the freezer by hand or by steam and detach the composition as fast as it adheres to the sides. As soon as the cream is sufficiently consistent, transfer it to a long freezer packed in salted ice (see how to pack in ice, No. 3432). Several compositions can be frozen one after the other without washing out the freezer, by beginning to freeze the composition containing the least color, and being careful to remove any particles of cream remaining after the operation is finished.

(3426). HOW TO COOK THE CREAM FOR ICES (Manière de Cuire les Crèmes pour les Glaces)

First boil the milk or cream. If with vanilla or white coffee infuse either of these into the milk or cream. Put the yolks or whites of eggs in a tinned basin of sufficient size not to have the mixture rise to over three-quarters of the height of the vessel; add sugar to the yolks or whites, beating it in well with a whisk; then add the boiling milk or cream. Set the basin on a slow fire or in a bain-marie; stir continuously with the spatula until the composition be of a sufficient thickness to cover this spatula, which will occur a few moments before it begins to boil; remove it from the fire or bain-marie and then strain through a Venice or plated copper wire sieve; stir occasionally while cooling and freeze when thoroughly cold. For cooked ice cream be careful to select only the freshest eggs and milk; the most important point to be observed in these creams is to have the eggs cooked, allowing them to proceed as far as possible without actually boiling, then pour quickly through a sieve and stir steadily until most of the heat is lost.

(3427). HOW TO FREEZE BY HAND IN A LONG COVERED FREEZER (Manière de Glacer à la Main Dans une Sorbetière Longue et Couverte).

Procure a tin freezer with a tinned copper bottom, in preference to all others, or else one of block tin; also a wooden pail deeper than the freezer; this pail, made expressly for freezing purposes, must be bored with two holes; one two inches above the bottom and another an inch and a half below the top of the freezer. Close these holes with well-fitting corks that can easily be removed. Put at the bottom of the pail a flat piece of ice about four inches thick—this is to facilitate the rotary movement of the freezer—lay the freezer exactly in the center and pack it around with ice, as described in No. 3432; now lift off the cover. pour in, to a third of its height, the prepared composition needed for freezing, turn the freezer rapidly by its handle to the right and then to the left, and as soon as the ice attaches to the sides detach it by sliding the

FIG. 614.   FIG. 615.

spatula or palette along the sides of the freezer from the top as far down as the bottom. Cover the freezer, turn and detach again and repeat the same operation until the cream is found to be of a sufficient consistency, then finish freezing and have it acquire body, while working vigorously with the spatula, giving the freezer a rotary movement at each turn with the spatula. If the cream cannot be finished without repacking the freezer, then let a little of the water run out and repack it once more.

(3428). HOW TO FREEZE BY HAND IN A WIDE, UNCOVERED FREEZER (Manière de Glacer à la Main Dans une Sorbetière Large et Découverte).

To accomplish this it will be necessary to have a wide and not very deep freezer; pack it in a pail of sufficient size to allow three inches of ice all around; add a little salted water to the ice so as to loosen the freezer before beginning the operation. The inside measurements of the pail should be sixteen inches deep and sixteen inches in diameter, so that when the freezer is packed it will be on a level with the pail. Pour two or three quarts of the composition into the freezer, put on the lid and turn it to the right and left until the movement becomes easy to perform. Lift off the cover; take hold of the edge of the freezer between the thumb and first finger and with the palm of the right hand give it a continuous rotary movement, detaching the ice as fast as it adheres to the sides, and continue the operation until

FIG. 616.

the preparation has congealed sufficiently; then transfer it to another freezer packed beforehand in ice, putting only a little in at a time; in this way it is easier to work and the ices become much finer.

(3429). MACHINE WITH LONG FREEZER (Machine avec Sorbetière Longue).

Have a machine with two or three pails and freezers of various sizes, according to requirements (for this see design, Fig. 617). Proportions for a machine containing eighteen quarts and for one containing twelve: Put the composition into the freezer packed in the pail, not having it reach above half the height of the freezer; in the center stand the detaching apparatus, intended for the purpose of detaching the cream from the sides—this turns one way and the freezer itself in the opposite direction; in this manner it detaches the cream from the sides, making it much lighter. Put the cover on the detaching apparatus and turn the freezer for ten minutes, either by steam or hand. After the cream is congealed take the spatula and detach any cream adhering to it. Should it have to remain in the same freezer, pack it once more in ice (No. 3432). Proportions for an eighteen-quart freezer: The inside pail is twenty-four inches high; diameter across the opening thirteen and a half inches; diameter across the bottom twelve inches. Either size should be made of oak an inch thick. The freezer for this pail must be nineteen and a half inches high by eight inches in diameter. For the inside measurements of a twelve-quart freezer, have the height of the pail twenty-one inches

FIG. 617.

by thirteen inches in diameter at the opening, the bottom to be eleven and a half inches. The freezer for this pail must measure eighteen and a half inches in height and seven and a half in diameter.

(3430). MANNER OF FREEZING, NEAPOLITAN STYLE (Manière de Glacer à la Napolitaine).

Have a tin freezer (sorbetière) capable of holding sixteen quarts of preparation; imbed it in salted ice, and pour into it eight quarts of composition, then turn the freezer from right to left, and as soon as it becomes easy to turn seize the edges between the thumb and first finger of the

FIG. 618.

right hand, and move it with a continuous motion. After a sufficient quantity of ice adheres, remove it with a copper spoon (Fig. 618), to detach it from bottom to top. Another tin freezer must be imbedded beforehand. Put into this second freezer the ice

taken from the first; another person must now work this ice until it becomes perfectly smooth, and then transfer it once more into a third freezer, packed in salted ice, to preserve it. Ices made this way are remarkably smooth, and can be molded at once.

(3431). HOW TO MOLD, FREEZE AND UNMOLD SMALL ICES AND LARGE ONES REPRE-
SENTING FIGURES, ETC. (Manière de Mouler, Frapper et Démouler les Petites Glaces et les Grosses Pièces Représentant des Sujets).

To mold ices representing any object or subject whatsoever calls for the greatest amount of care, otherwise a defective result will ensue. When small ices or half ices are required for molding, such as those representing flowers, fruits, etc., lay the molds on unsalted ice so they become thoroughly cold. Cover the bottom of a pail with a layer of salted ice, having a sufficient quantity of it to form a bed three inches deep; then take the mold in the left hand and in the right a copper spoon (Fig. 618, a Neapolitan spoon), this being used to take up the various ices meant for filling the molds. It should be kept continually in water so as to keep it clean, as it is used for different creams. Press down the composition without inclosing any air between the mold and the ice; in this way it can adhere to the various designs imprinted on the mold, leaving no empty space whatever between. Now, having the mold full, close it forcibly, bringing the cover down well on to it, and with the finger remove any surplus ice that may issue from the intersections of the mold. After it is pressed down stand it on a bed of prepared salted ice and over lay more of the same ice. Continue thus to mold and pack down until all the molds are finished, then cover the whole with ice and salt; leave to freeze for one hour or more, according to the composition used, the size of the mold, and also according to the humidity of the atmosphere. When it becomes a question of molding more important ices, such as figures, subjects, etc., after cooling the molds thoroughly lay them on a slightly raised bed of rice and salt, so that they can be filled cautiously and with facility, for it requires every possible precaution in order to form these figures properly. Close the mold furnished with pins. After filling it well, beginning from the bottom put on the lid and press it down forcibly, removing any surplus ice issuing from the joints, and pack the mold in plenty of salted ice (No. 3432), leaving it in as long as judged proper, a two-quart mold requiring about two hours.

To Unmold.—Take the mold out of the ice, remove any surplus ice on the outside, and the pins from the hinges, then plunge the mold thoroughly and hastily in hot water; lift off the cover and lay the fancy ice mold bottom downward on a napkin; detach all the parts quickly but cautiously from the mold so as not to deform the piece. Those of a larger size are usually dressed on colored natural ice socles; these ices may be painted over with small badger brushes dipped in vegetal colors into which a little syrup has been mixed. The base of the molds intended to stand on socles should be of ice cream and not too rich, as they support the weight of the whole piece. When packed in ice the base of the mold should always be at the bottom of the pail; cover this with a cloth, packing it down well between the ice and pail.

(3432). TO PACK SORBETIÈRES OR FREEZERS IN ICE (Pour Sangler les Sorbetières).

Salt and saltpetre are the active agents used for freezing. The quantity employed is one pound of salt for four pounds of ice, this being a proportionately active mixture for freezing the very richest cream and water ices. The salt and ice can be ranged in alternate layers or else have the whole mixed well together in a pail; in either case place ice around the freezer and pack it down well with the palette. Repeat this operation every time more salted ice is to be packed. Always pay attention that sorbetières turned by hand are to be packed lower than the edge of the pail, so that when the ice is finished the cover of the freezer may be adjusted as well as the cover on the pail. In houses where ices are being constantly made they have boxes lined with galvanized sheet-iron cylinders, and the empty space between the box and the cylinder is filled either with charcoal dust, tow or sawdust, as well as the covers;

Fig. 619.

each cylinder must be provided with a hole one inch in diameter and two inches from the bottom to allow the water to run out. In case the water should not be allowed to flow off, then it will be prudent to bore a hole half an inch in diameter, one inch lower than the height of the freezer.

(3433). FOR FREEZING WATER BOTTLES (Pour Frapper les Carafes).

Water bottles are easily frozen, only be careful to follow closely the ensuing instructions. If a handsome looking bottle is required, it must be of a spherical shape, slightly longer than its width and of ordinary thick glass; it must invariably be clean, and then filled slightly less than half full or a little lower than the circumference line of the sphere, with filtered water. Mix three-quarters of very finely chopped ice with one-quarter of rock salt; range the bottles in a box suffi-

ciently large to hold twenty, leaving an inch space between each; cover the neck of the bottle with a tinned copper cup, having a round bottom, or else with a specially made rubber cork (Fig. 620); cover entirely with salted ice, raising them all up so that the ice passes slightly underneath each bottle; neglect of this precaution will break all the bottles in the box. Pack the ice around, cover the box with a hermetically closed cover, and an hour later raise up the bottles, one by one, and give each a rotary movement to hasten the freezing; withdraw all the superfluous water above two-thirds of the height of the ball of the bottle, and leave in again for an hour and a half to finish freezing; remove the faucet that keeps the water in the box, let this run out, and besides remove the corks from the necks of the bottles; when ready to serve lift them out, wash in cold water and fill with filtered ice water.

FIG. 620.

(3434). PLAIN WATER SOCLES, COLORED (Socles d'eau Naturelle, Colorée).

Procure a box sufficiently wide and deep to contain all the molds needed for making the socles and sherbets; into it put a mixture of salt and ice equivalent to the quantity used for packing freezers; into this imbed the molds in such a way that they are not too close to one another, having all their sides well surrounded by the ice, so that when the water is poured into these molds their surfaces will be perfectly horizontal; for this examine the basket shown in Fig. 621. The mold for this basket is made in two pieces; imbed the bottom or foot in the salted ice; into it pour water colored green or blue and as the foot is to be of uniform tint fill it entirely, then leave to freeze. Now

place the upper part of the mold in salted ice, pour in water to reach halfway, having mixed a little milk into it to render it opaque. Cover the box with a raised edge sheet of zinc and fill this with more salted ice and let freeze. As soon as the whitened water is frozen fill the remainder of the mold with red water. These colored waters should be used perfectly cold and the last ones poured in only after the first ones are congealed. The colors may be varied according to the taste of the one preparing the socles and glasses. It is most important to remember that no salted water whatever must penetrate into the molds, otherwise it will melt and eat away the ice already congealed and deteriorate the beauty of these socles and glasses. The unmolding is the

FIG. 621.

same as for ices. Socles are to be dressed on folded napkins and glasses on lace papers. Ices can also be dressed on blocks of ice cut any desired size and shape. To keep these blocks together, iron rods can be procured, having on one end a sheet iron ring and on the other a nut screw to hold the whole together. These rods are to be inserted in a hole through the center of the socle formed with a tube foot in the center of the mold and held in place with butter, being careful to have it water-tight, so the liquid cannot penetrate. They can be decorated with grasses and flowers maintained by wires introduced into the water when it first begins to congeal. Blocks of all sizes can be made in square, oblong, round or oval molds, having a hollow formed in the middle; for these special molds must be procured.

(3435). ICED BISCUITS, DIPLOMATE AND HOW TO MAKE BISCUIT CASES (Biscuits Glacés à la Diplomate et Manière de Faire les Boîtes à Biscuits).

To make these biscuits use a vanilla biscuit preparation (No. 3438), or else vanilla ice cream (No. 3458) beaten in a metal bowl with as much whipped cream mixed with it. Cut candied fruits into three-sixteenths inch squares, lay them in a bowl, pour over a little kirsch and let soak while covered, adding a few crushed macaroons. Fill the cases half full with the preparation, lay a bed of the fruits and macaroons on top and then another layer of the cream, filling the cases to one-eighth of an inch below the edge of the box. Freeze the biscuits and cover with a layer of whipped cream tinted rose-pink, mixing in a pinch of ground cinnamon; return the biscuits to the freezing box and finish freezing.

Biscuit Cases.—Boxes for biscuit glacés are made with sheets of very strong paper, generally a little longer than their width, being six and a half inches long and six inches wide. In order to make these boxes take one of these sheets of paper and fold it lengthwise on itself in three even parts; again refold the two lateral parts on themselves lengthwise on the outside, thus forming a long band open in the center. These last two folds form the double lateral edges of the box. Again fold this band transversely on the open side into three parts, but in such a way that the two extreme ends exactly meet at the center of the band. Open all the folds except the two forming the outside edges of the box, and when this is done there will be found traced on the paper the various lines representing the bottom, the center and the four sides, besides four small rectangular corners which are used for closing the box. Fold each of these four rectangulars all on the inside so as to trace on each one an almost diagonal line beginning at the bottom angle of the box. Now, by following the lines of these folds, raise the lateral sides of the box, also the ends, at a straight angle with the bottom; by folding the small rectangulars at the almost diagonally traced line the result will be the angles of the box by the junction of the prolonged lines traced on the bottom of the box; then bring the two wings of each end, which are exteriorly against and in the center of the small edges, or ends, of the box. Fold outward the corners of the two ends, exceeding the edges of the box so as to form two truncated triangles; fold over these triangles on the outside against the narrow ends of the box and seal them down.

Another Way to Make Biscuit Cases.—Take a quarter of a sheet of strong white paper; cut it about twice as long as its width, so as to give it an oblong shape. Fold this paper lengthwise in three on its length, then refold the two sides on themselves on the outside so as to double them, and thus form a long, straight band, open on one side only; fold the double points of the angles inwardly again so as to have the band pointed on each end; now fold these two ends on the inner side, simply to form the fold, open the band, press the folds well and the box will be formed. The narrow sides of the band form the length of the case.

(3436). EXCELSIOR BISCUIT (Biscuit Excelsior).

FIG. 622.

Have ready a vanilla biscuit preparation (No. 3438), line a large biscuit case, the size being explained in the vanilla biscuit recipes; fill it half full with the preparation. Divide lady fingers lengthwise in two or three pieces the same length as the box; soak them in maraschino, then place in the cases over the first layer of preparation, filling with more of the same. Put them in a freezing box; freeze and ice over half their length with orange water ice (No. 3605), the other half with raspberry (No. 3607); in the center place a small size rose, molded in lemon ice (No. 3604), and on each side on the length place a lozenge of pistachio ice cream (No. 3454).

FIG. 623.

(3437). ICED BISCUITS À LA D'ORLÉANS (Biscuits Glacés à la d'Orléans).

Procure a tin box with a cover closing on the outside. The interior should measure eight inches in length, five and three-quarters in width and one and three-quarters deep. Fit the bottom of this

FIG. 624.

with twelve small cardboard cases, all together being the exact size of the bottom of the box and each half an inch high. Pour in sufficient vanilla biscuit preparation (No. 3438) to fill up the tin box to a quarter of an inch below the top, put on the cover and close the joints with butter, then pack the box in salted ice; leave it for at least an hour and a half, being careful that the water does not rise higher than the bottom of the box; take out the box, wipe, remove the cover and finish filling to the top with strawberry water

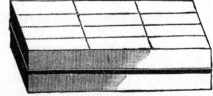

FIG. 625.

ice (No. 3607); smooth with the blade of a knife, replace the cover and fasten it once more with butter; freeze for one hour longer. Then remove both box and cover, wipe well and pass a thin knife all around the inside. Dip the bottom into hot water, unmold so that it turns over in a single block, then reverse it to have the strawberry ice on top. Divide the biscuit into twelve equal-sized parts, the exact size of the cases, and dress each one on a round piece of fancy lace paper.

(3438). ICED BISCUITS WITH VANILLA AND STRAWBERRY, MELON SHAPED (Biscuits Glacés à la Vanille et aux Fraises, et en Forme de Melon).

Put eight egg yolks in a small tinned basin with three gills of thirty-five degree syrup, four gills of rich cream and a vanilla bean split lengthwise in two; beat the whole together and when

FIG. 626.

well mingled set the basin on the fire and stir constantly with a spatula until it covers it thoroughly with a thick layer, then remove from the fire and strain the preparation through a Venice sieve. Wash the basin thoroughly and return the cream to it; lay the basin on ice, beat and when the composition is very firm incorporate therein a quart of whipped cream.* With this mixture fill some cases (Fig. 623) three-quarters full and freeze them in a freezing box (a square box furnished with movable tin shelves on the inside, they being perforated with large holes). When frozen finish filling with strawberry or any other water ice; smooth with a knife and return to the freezing box to finish freezing. The inside dimensions of large cases are four and a half inches long, two and a half wide and one and one-sixteenth deep; the medium cases measure three and a half inches long, one and seven-eighths wide and one inch deep.

Iced biscuits can also be ranged in melon-shaped molds; coat these over with strawberry water ice (No. 3607), into which mix twice as much whipped cream (No. 50), and finish filling with the above vanilla biscuit preparation; freeze and unmold on a folded napkin.

(3439). BOMB À LA CONSTANTINE (Bombe à la Constantine).

Take a special hinged mold, the same as for Fig. 627; it must have a hollow on the top, into which place a double mold filled with cotton and alcohol and set on fire when serving. The inside of the mold must be coated with chocolate ice cream, into which mix half as much whipped cream. Fill the hollow space in the inside with a preparation made as follows: Melt five ounces of sweet chocolate and five ounces of sugar in a quart of hot water; after the chocolate is all dissolved pass the whole through a fine sieve and leave to cool; pour the top off gently an hour later and reduce it to three gills. Break sixteen egg-yolks in a basin, beat with three gills of thirty-two degree syrup and three and a half gills of water and the chocolate; set this on a slow fire and stir steadily until the composition covers the spatula well, then strain through a sieve, return it to the basin, lay on ice and beat, adding half as much well-drained whipped cream (No. 50). Fill the mold quite full with this, close tightly and freeze. A two-quart bomb will require two hours' freezing. Unmold and dress on a ring of white chocolate ice cream, the proportions for making

FIG. 627.

it being three and a half gills of clarified sugar at thirty-two degrees, three and a half gills of water, sixteen egg-yolks, and eight ounces of cocoa infused in the syrup with a vanilla bean split lengthwise in two. Decorate around with Africans (No. 3364) and pistachio lady bouchées (No. 3376).

(3440). BOMB À LA TROBRIAND AND FIFTH AVENUE (Bombe à la Trobriand et à la Cinquième Avenue).

Imbed a bomb-shaped mold (Fig. 627) in ice; remove its lid and coat it perpendicularly, half with strawberry ice cream (No. 3451) and half with pistachio (No. 3454). Fill the inside with the following preparation: Pound seven ounces of filberts or sweet almonds; moisten little at a time with a pint of water and three gills of thirty-five degree syrup. Break eighteen egg-yolks in a saucepan or tinned copper basin, add the almond milk and a pint of boiling milk; set it on a slow fire and stir steadily until sufficiently cooked so that it covers the spatula; strain through a sieve,

---

* In all cases where reference is made to a given quantity of whipped cream the quantity stated should be understood as meaning when the cream is whipped and not in its liquid state.

return it to the well-cleaned basin, and add the same quantity of thoroughly drained whipped cream. Fill up the coated mold, cover with paper, put on its lid, imbed in salted ice, and if the mold contains two quarts freeze it for one hour and a half.

For Fifth Avenue Bomb.—Have the same preparation; coat the mold with strawberry ice cream only when it is frozen; dip in hot water, unmold on a napkin, and decorate with small cakes.

(3441). PRINTANIER FRUIT BOMB (Bombe aux Fruits Printanière).

Pack a bomb mold (Fig. 627) in salted ice and cover the bottom and sides with a layer of strawberry ice cream (No. 3451), having it a quarter of an inch thick; fill in the hollow with a preparation made as follows: In a tin basin have fourteen egg yolks, six gills of twenty-degree syrup, and a vanilla bean split lengthwise in two; mingle well, and set the basin on a slow fire; cook until the composition covers the spoon or spatula, then remove, strain, return it to the clean basin and set it on ice; beat thoroughly to have it light, adding one quart of firm whipped cream, drained for two hours on a sieve; mix well together and pour this preparation into the mold, filling it entirely; place over a sheet of paper and the cover; pack in salted ice, and allow one hour's freezing for each quart of cream. After the bomb is properly frozen unmold on an ice-cold dish and garnish around with a macédoine of fruits steeped in maraschino.

(3442). ROMAN BOMB (Bombe à la Romaine).

Add twelve ounces of sugar to one quart of cream; strain it through a sieve, freeze and work it briskly, adding gradually two gills of rum stirred with two ounces of sugar; incorporate two Italian meringue egg-whites (No. 140). Coat a two quart bomb-shaped mold (Fig. 627) with pineapple ice cream (No. 3451), fill it with the above, then cover, and pack it for two hours in salted ice. Take the mold from the salted ice, remove all drippings, and unmold on a folded napkin, garnishing around with strawberry lady bouchées (No. 3376).

(3443). BOMB WITH LIQUORS (Bombe aux Liqueurs).

Have twelve raw egg-yolks well beaten in a saucepan, or tinned copper basin, with four gills of thirty-two degree syrup, four gills of water and one gill of either aniseed, Curaçoa, kirsch, maraschino or mint liquors. Cook the preparation over a very slow fire; stir continuously until it covers the spatula well, then remove and pass it through a fine sieve. Wash the basin, put back the preparation and whip until firm and light, then add the same quantity of very solid whipped cream (No. 50) drained well for two hours on a hair sieve; mix together. Imbed the mold in ice, fill the inside with orange water ice if for aniseed, strawberry water ice for Curaçoa, vanilla for kirsch, pistachio for maraschino, and lemon water ice for mint. When the mold is overflowing lay on a sheet of waxed paper twice the diameter of the mold. Put on the lid, fastening it down firmly, and cover with a thick bed of salted ice; freeze for one hour and a half for two quarts. Take out the mold, dip it quickly in hot water and invert on a folded napkin; surround with a garnishing either of macaroons, small biscuit cases, small flat waffles, small cream cakes or slices of Savoy biscuit iced with prunelle.

(3444). BOMB STREAKED WITH WHITE AND BLACK COFFEE (Bombe Panachée au Café Blanc et Noir).

White Coffee.—Set into a high saucepan three gills of thirty-two degree syrup and three and a half gills of water, adding six ounces of freshly roasted coffee; cover the saucepan tightly and leave the coffee infuse in the syrup for three hours in a bain-marie. Place fourteen egg-yolks in a basin, whip them gradually with the coffee infusion and cook on a slow fire; strain the preparation when done and beat it well on ice, mixing in half as much well-drained whipped cream.

Black Coffee.—Put fourteen egg-yolks in a tinned copper basin, dilute with three gills of thirty-two degree syrup and three gills of very strong coffee, made with two ounces of ground Java, Maracaibo and Mocha; finish it exactly the same as the white coffee.

Divide a bomb mold with a tin partition to separate it perpendicularly into two compartments; put the white coffee preparation in one, remove the tin and replace it with a waffle of the same size; finish filling the mold with the black coffee preparation, having the mold quite full. Cover with paper, then with the lid and pack well in ice; leave it to freeze, allowing an hour and a half for two quarts; remove from the ice, turn it out on a folded napkin and surround with small coffee lady bouchées (No. 3376), then serve.

(3445). ICE CREAM À LA CIALDINI (Crème à la Cialdini).

Put ten egg-yolks and eight ounces of sugar in a tinned copper basin; beat up well and add a pint of boiling milk into which has been infused, for half an hour, half a vanilla bean and two ounces of ground almonds. Cook the preparation on a slow fire until it covers the spatula, adding half a pound of dissolved chocolate, a piece of Ceylon cinnamon and a tablespoonful of ground coriander seeds; let cool, then pour in one pint of cream; pass the whole through a fine sieve, freeze and incorporate a quarter as much whipped cream (No. 50), half a pound of almonds and half a pound of quartered pistachios; pack the cream in ice and salt, and it is ready to use when needed.

(3446). ANDALUSIAN ICE CREAM—WITHOUT COOKING (Crème à l'Andalouse—Sans Cuisson).

Pour in a vessel one pint of cream, one pint of orange juice, twelve ounces of sugar and half an orange peel; infuse this for one hour, then strain through a silk sieve and freeze, mixing in a little orange flower water added to a little syrup; work the ice well, pack in cracked ice and salt, and use when needed.

(3447). CARAMEL ICE CREAM (Crème au Caramel).

Put ten ounces of sugar in a copper basin with very little water, cook to caramel, then pour it on a marble to get cold; pound and return it to the basin with six egg-yolks, a quarter of a vanilla stick and a pint of boiling milk. Cook this preparation on a slow fire without boiling, remove it from the range when it covers the spatula, and when cold add a pint of cream; strain through a sieve and freeze.

(3448). COLUMBIA ICE CREAM (Crème à la Columbia).

To make this ice cream it will require two preparations: One composed of a pint of fresh cream, half a gill of maraschino and four ounces of sugar; strain through a sieve, freeze, then add another half gill of maraschino, a little at a time, one Italian meringue egg-white (No. 140), half an ounce of cherries cut in four, half an ounce of candied citron and orange peel chopped into thin shreds. The other preparation is made as follows: Grind one pound of freshly peeled pistachios with a quarter of a pound of sugar, diluting with a quart of cream. Put into a vessel twelve egg-yolks and eight ounces of sugar; mix well together, add the pistachios and a coloring of spinach green to give it a pale green hue. Set the basin on a slow fire and cook the cream without boiling, stirring continuously, and when it covers the spatula cool and put in three-quarters of a gill of orange flower water. Strain through a sieve, freeze, then mix in as much whipped cream (No. 50), two ounces of candied pineapple cut in quarter-inch squares and two ounces of angelica cut the same. Fill a Madeleine mold (Fig. 694) quite full of the two preparations divided in halves; fasten the lid on tightly, pack in salted ice and an hour after unmold on a very cold dish and bestrew with finely minced green pistachios.

(3449). CHOCOLATE AND COCOA ICE CREAM (Crème au Chocolat et au Cacao).

Dissolve in a very slack oven four ounces of unsweetened chocolate in two gills of hot water. Beat twelve egg-yolks in a tinned basin with one pound of powdered sugar and dilute the preparation with a pint and a half of boiling milk, adding the fourth part of a vanilla stick. Stir the cream on a moderate fire till nearly thick, then mix in the chocolate thoroughly dissolved with three gills of hot cream; stir well for a few moments, remove and strain twice through a sieve into a metal vessel; when cold transfer to a sorbetière to freeze.

Chocolate—Another Way.—Two pounds of fine sweet chocolate, two quarts of milk, half a vanilla bean, two pounds of sugar and twenty-four yolks; cook, let get cold and then add two quarts of fresh cream and freeze.

With Cocoa.—Boil a pint and a half of milk, add ten ounces of torrefied cocoa, and a quarter of a vanilla stick; leave to infuse for two hours. Mix five egg-yolks, ten ounces of sugar and the infusion in a tinned basin; cook over a slow fire, stirring incessantly until the preparation covers the spoon; remove, cool partly and add one pint of raw fresh cream; strain, freeze and serve, mixing in a few chocolate pastilles.

(3450). CINNAMON, GINGER OR PUMPERNICKEL RYE BREAD ICE CREAM (Glace Crème à la Canelle, au Gingembre ou au Pumpernickel Pain de Seigle).

With Cinnamon.—Infuse one ounce of cinnamon in a quart of boiling milk. Place twelve ounces of sugar in a basin with eight egg yolks; beat and add the infusion; mix so that the sugar dissolves, cook without boiling, then cool and pass through a fine sieve; freeze and mix in a few vanilla chocolate pastilles, each half an inch in diameter.

Ginger.—Substitute ginger for the cinnamon and finish the same.

Pumpernickel Rye Bread.—Grate half a pound of rye bread and pass it through a coarse sieve or colander; pour into a vessel and throw over a pint of thirty-degree syrup. Break twelve egg-yolks in a tin basin, add eight ounces of sugar, mix well with a pint of boiling milk; cook this on a slow fire without boiling, remove and when cold strain through a sieve, freeze, adding the rye bread when nearly frozen and two quarts of whipped cream (No. 50).

(3451). FRESH FRUIT ICE CREAMS—WITHOUT EGGS OR COOKING (Crème de Fruits Frais— Sans Œufs ni Cuisson).

For Strawberries, Cherries, Currants and Raspberries.—Add three pints of cream and a pint of milk to a quart of strawberry, cherry, currant or raspberry juice and two pounds of powdered sugar. Melt the sugar, strain the whole through a silk sieve and freeze.

Apricots, Peaches and Nectarines.—To be made with one pint of cream, a pint of the pulp of any of these fruits, taking those thoroughly ripe; break the kernels, peel the nuts, split them in two and infuse in a gill of syrup with the fourth part of a vanilla bean. To the cream and the fruits add ten ounces of powdered sugar and the infusion. Strain through a very fine sieve and freeze.

Pineapple.—Mix a pint of milk and twelve ounces of sugar, also a pint of pineapple juice; strain through a fine sieve and freeze. Instead of using the juice, thin slices may be cut from the pineapple, laid in a vessel and covered with a boiling syrup of thirty-two degrees; strain, cool off and freeze.

(3452). NOUGAT ICE CREAM; NOUGAT NEAPOLITAN CREAM (Crème Nougat; Crème Nougat à la Napolitaine).

Set half a pound of powdered sugar in a tinned copper pan with the juice of one lemon; place it on a slow fire, stir continuously and when melted and colored to a fine red add half a pound of unpeeled almonds and a pinch of coriander seeds; mix well. Pour this nougat on a marble and as soon as cold pound it in a mortar, moistening slowly with a pint of cream. Have ten egg-yolks in a basin with four ounces of sugar, beat well together and then add a pint of boiling milk and the crushed nougat; cook on a slow fire, stirring steadily; remove when it covers the spatula and leave till cold; into this mix a pint of cream; strain through a fine sieve and freeze.

Nougat Neapolitan Cream.—To be made with a quart of cream, fourteen ounces of sugar, twelve egg-yolks, half a pound of peeled almonds roasted to a golden brown and half an ounce of coriander seeds. Pound the almonds and corianders, wetting with two gills of cream; color with a little carmine and cook without boiling; when cold add a pint more of cream, strain and freeze.

(3453). PEACH ICE CREAM À LA HERBSTER (Crème aux Pêches à la Herbster).

Prepare a peach ice cream with two-thirds of cream and one-third of fruit pulp, adding three drops of extract of almonds; color slightly to a very pale pink and with this cream when frozen coat a pudding mold. Have some ripe peaches already peeled, stoned and cut in quarters; mince them finely and macerate in a little kirsch. Mix into the remainder of the peach ice cream half as much whipped cream (No. 50) and an equal quantity of the minced peaches; fill the mold quickly, freeze and unmold one hour later.

(3454). PISTACHIO ICE CREAM (Crème aux Pistaches).

Pound half a pound of freshly peeled pistachio nuts with two gills of cream and an ounce of candied citron peel cut up very finely. Break twelve raw egg-yolks in a tinned basin, beat with ten ounces of sugar, and moisten with a pint of boiling milk; cook on a slow fire, stirring all the time with a spatula, and when the composition is cooked add the pistachios; take from the fire, and when cold put in a pint of cream, some spinach green or vegetal green, and a little orange flower water; strain through a fine sieve and then freeze.

Pistachio Ice Cream made with Almonds.—One quart of milk, six whole eggs, a pound and a quarter of sugar, half a pound of almonds, half a gill of orange flower water, one quart of cream and vegetal coloring.

(3455). BURNT ALMOND ICE CREAM AND WITH ANGELICA (Crème Pralinée et à l'Angélique).

Crush half a pound of burnt almonds with two gills of cream; put ten egg-yolks in a basin with ten ounces of sugar, mix well together, adding the burnt almonds and a pint of boiling milk. Set the basin on a slow fire, stir constantly with a spatula until of sufficient thickness to cover the same, then put aside to cool while stirring at times to prevent a skin from forming on top; add one pint of cream, strain through a fine sieve, and freeze.

With Angelica.—After the cream is frozen add to it half as much whipped cream (No. 50) and half a pound of finely shredded angelica.

(3456). RICE ICE CREAM, PARADISE (Crème de Riz, Paradis).

Wash and blanch twelve ounces of Carolina rice; drain. Take four ounces of it and cook it thoroughly in four quarts of milk; strain through a sieve. Put thirty-two egg-yolks in a tinned basin, add two pounds and a quarter of sugar, and beat both together, then put in the rice pulp; set it on the fire and beat steadily until the preparation covers the spatula; leave stand till cold; run it through a sieve, and replace it in the basin after it has been well cleaned; lay it on ice; whip to have the mixture light, and stir in as much whipped cream. Cook the remainder of the rice in a vanilla syrup at twenty degrees; cool off, drain, add it to the composition, and freeze.

(3457). RICE ICE CREAM WITH CITRON, GARNISHED WITH TRUFFLES (Crème de Riz et au Cédrat, Garnie de Truffes).

Place eight egg-whites in a tinned basin with twelve ounces of sugar and four tablespoonfuls of rice flour; stir well together, adding a quart of boiling milk; cook without boiling on a slow fire, remove and when cold put in a pint of cream; pass through a sieve, freeze and then add half a pound of very finely shredded citron peel and half a pint of blanched rice cooked in syrup. Have it molded in a low Madeleine mold, and garnish around with imitation truffles prepared as follows:

Truffle Ice Cream.—This cream can only be made with fresh truffles. Brush over half a pound of fresh, fragrant truffles; peel, slice and infuse in a pint of boiling cream for thirty minutes. Drop twelve egg-yolks in a tinned basin with ten ounces of sugar; mix well together and then add one quart of cream, including that in which the truffles are being infused; cook the preparation without boiling, and add the truffles after pounding and passing them through a sieve. Freeze and mold in molds imitating whole truffles coated with chocolate; pack in ice. Chop up the truffle peelings very finely, mixing in a few vanilla seeds; dry in the open air, pass through a sieve and roll the unmolded imitation truffles in this powder. Use these truffles to decorate the above ice cream.

(3458). VANILLA ICE CREAMS—ITALIAN MERINGUE (Crèmes Vanille—Meringue Italienne).

Vanilla (No. 1).—Boil two quarts of milk; remove and add a large vanilla bean split in two through its length; cover the saucepan and leave infuse for fifteen minutes. Beat twelve raw egg-yolks in a vessel with one pound of powdered sugar, diluting gradually with the hot milk; strain into a tinned basin; place over a moderate fire, stirring continually until it thickens, without boiling, and pass it at once through a sieve into a glazed vessel; stir several times while cooling. Pour this composition into a spherical freezer packed in salted ice; turn the freezer around and with the spatula remove any particles of cream that may adhere against the sides. Fifteen to twenty minutes will suffice to congeal and thicken the preparation, then take it up with a spoon and lay it in a small long freezer buried in salted ice. Work it vigorously with the spatula, turning the box around on itself. Fine ices require to be well worked. Various vanilla ice creams may be prepared the same, only changing their proportions.

Vanilla Ice Cream with Milk and Cream (No. 2.)—Boil a pint of milk in which is infused half a vanilla stick. Beat in a vessel ten egg-yolks with ten ounces of sugar; finish the same as in No. 1; when the preparation is cold add one pint of fresh cream, then freeze.

Vanilla Ice Cream with Cream (No. 3).—Have a quart of boiling cream with half a vanilla bean infused therein. Whip eight egg-yolks with six ounces of sugar; pour over the cream, cook and finish as in No. 1

Vanilla Ice Cream without Cream or Milk (No. 4).—Infuse a vanilla bean in eight gills of syrup at twenty degrees. Break eighteen raw egg-yolks in a tin basin, dilute with the syrup and cook while stirring steadily over a slow fire until the mixture covers the spatula, then pass it through a sieve, leave till cold and freeze. Cook a quarter of a pound of sugar to "large ball" (No. 171), mix it slowly with two stiffly beaten egg-whites, leave stand till cold, then incorporate this meringue gradually into the ice cream.

Vanilla Snow Ice Cream, Italian Meringue and Whipped Cream (No. 5).—Beat five egg-yolks to a stiff froth; mix in slowly one pound of sugar cooked to "small ball" (No. 171) and a vanilla bean split lengthwise in two; let cool. Whip a quart of cream; when very firm drain on a sieve and mix it in lightly with the Italian meringue.

Roman Vanilla Ice Cream, Syrup and Cream (No. 6).—Put sixteen raw egg-yolks in a tinned basin; pour over eight gills of syrup at twenty degrees into which has been infused a split vanilla bean; beat well with a small whip, place it on a slow fire and continue stirring with the spatula until cooked and of a sufficient thickness to cover the spatula; remove, cool and add a quart of fresh cream before freezing.

Light Vanilla Ice Cream, Milk and Whipped Cream (No. 7).—Beat up a quart of cream; drain it on a hair sieve; add ten ounces of powdered sugar to twelve raw egg-yolks in a basin; beat and moisten with a pint of boiling milk into which has been infused a vanilla bean split down in two; set the basin on a slow fire and stir continuously until the mixture covers the spatula; then remove, strain and leave till cold. Freeze as usual and after the cream has congealed mix into it the same quantity of the whipped cream.

Vanilla Ice Cream (No. 8).—Two quarts of milk, two vanilla sticks, two and a half pounds of sugar, twenty-four egg-yolks. Cook, cool and add two quarts of cream; strain, then freeze.

(3459). VIRGIN CREAM WITH ORANGE FLOWER WATER AND NOYAU, ETC. (Crème Vierge à la Fleur d'Orange au Noyau, etc.).

Virgin creams are composed of cream, sugar and egg-whites; they are cooked the same as the egg-yolk creams and are always to be left white, either finished with orange flower water, noyau, maraschino, almond milk, lemon or hazel-nuts.

Orange Flower and Noyau.—Put twelve egg-whites in a tinned basin, add one pound of sugar, and mix thoroughly with a quart of fresh cream. Cook this preparation while stirring, being careful it does not come to a boil, then remove and beat it occasionally until cold; strain through a very fine sieve, adding half a gill of noyau liquor and a gill of orange flower water, also another gill of noyau after the ice has congealed. A quarter of its quantity of Italian meringue may be incorporated into this cream when frozen. *With Maraschino.*—Substitute two gills of maraschino for the orange flower water. *With Almond Milk.*—Six ounces of almonds, including a few bitter ones, pounded with two gills and a half of cream; stir this in when the cream is cooked and partly cold. *With Lemon.*—Infuse the peels of two lemons after the cream is cooked. *With Hazel-nuts.*—Half a pound of roasted, peeled and crushed hazel-nuts mingled with sugar and added to the cream before cooking.

(3460). WHITE COFFEE ICE CREAM (Crème au Café Blanc).

Roast very slowly, either in a roaster or in a frying pan, half a pound of good coffee beans, not having them too dark. Boil a pint of milk and pour it over the roasted coffee laid in a saucepan, cover tightly and keep it on the side of the range for half an hour. Put twenty egg-yolks in a saucepan or a tinned copper basin with twelve ounces of powdered sugar and a quarter of a vanilla stick; beat well together and dilute with three pints of milk and the infused coffee; stir this cream on a slow fire to thicken without boiling, and as soon as the preparation has attained the correct consistency transfer it to a well tinned metal vessel and stir occasionally while cooling; strain it twice, the last time through an exceedingly fine sieve. Try a small part in a freezer packed in ice to discover its consistency, and if too thin add some thirty-two degree syrup, and raw cream if too thick. Freeze by working it until firm and smooth.

Virgin Coffee Cream is prepared with egg-whites instead of yolks, exactly the same way, the proportions being, half a pound of coffee, one quart of milk, sixteen egg-whites instead of the yolks, ten ounces of sugar, a quart of cream and a quarter of a vanilla stick.

(3461). ICE CREAM WITH ALMONDS, FRESH OR DRIED NUTS (Crème d'Amandes ou de Noix Fraîches ou Sèches).

If there be any almonds or fresh nuts on hand peel to remove the skin, but should dried ones be used soak them in cold water for twelve hours, lift out and peel off their skins. Take half a pound of either fresh nuts or almonds and pound them with a pint of milk. Mix in a tinned basin ten raw egg-yolks with ten ounces of sugar, beat well together and add a pint and a half of very rich milk or fresh cream and a sixth part of a vanilla stick; stir on the fire to thicken without boiling. As soon as done remove the cream from the fire, mix in the pounded nuts, then pour into a glazed bowl to cool off while stirring occasionally; strain through a fine sieve and freeze.

For almond ice cream a few bitter almonds and a little kirsch may be added, and a little maraschino for those made of fresh nuts.

(3462). ICE CREAM WITH MARASCHINO, PRUNELLE, KIRSCH, TEA OR ALL-FLOWER (Crème au Marasquin, Prunelle, Kirsch, Thé ou Mille-Fleurs).

Place in a tinned basin twelve ounces of sugar, ten egg-yolks, the peel of one lemon and dilute with three pints of boiling milk; thicken the preparation on the fire while stirring, and as soon as done strain through a sieve into a vessel and stir occasionally till cold; freeze the same as explained in No. 3427; transfer the ice to a small long freezer to finish and when smooth and firm incorporate slowly into it a gill and a half of maraschino or one gill of kirsch or prunelle or else a gill of infused tea or highly concentrated all-flower, either of the two last named requiring the addition of a little rum. Both liqueurs and infusions should be mixed in the ice cream slowly.

(3463). ICE CREAM WITH EGGS AND BLACK COFFEE, WITHOUT EGGS, LIGHT WITH BLACK COFFEE (Crème aux Œufs et au Café Noir, Crème Sans Œufs Légère au Café Noir).

With Eggs and Black Coffee.—Prepare half a pint of very strong coffee, using Mocha, Java and Maracaibo, a pound in all, ground very finely and put into a filter (Fig. 774); moisten with a quart of boiling water and strain it entirely two or three times. Have in a tinned basin ten raw egg-yolks and eight ounces of sugar; add half a pint of boiling milk, a quarter of a vanilla bean and the infused coffee. Set the basin on a slow fire and stir until consistent enough to cover the spatula; let get cold, then add one pint of cream; pass through a fine sieve and freeze.

Without Eggs, Light with Black Coffee.—Dissolve half a pound of sugar in a quart of good cold milk; add half a pint of very strong coffee prepared the same as the above, infusing in it the fourth part of a vanilla stick; pass through a sieve and freeze. After it has been properly worked mix in as much well-drained whipped cream and at the same time half a pound of powdered sugar; stir well and pack in ice to use when needed. All light creams should be served the same day as prepared.

(3464). ICE CREAM WITH PIGNONS, BRAZILIAN NUTS, WALNUTS OR HAZEL-NUTS (Crème Glace aux Pignons, aux Noix de Brésil, aux Grosses Noix ou Noisettes).

Cook one pound of sugar slightly wetted to three hundred and thirty-eight degrees Fahrenheit or "crack" (No. 171); add half a pound of pignons or Brazilian nuts or even common walnuts or hazel-nuts; the nuts selected must be first roasted; boil once or twice in the sugar, then pour on a marble to leave till cold, when pound with a pint of cream. Break ten egg-yolks in a tinned basin, dilute with a pint of boiled milk, having already had infused in it a quarter of a vanilla stick; cook without boiling and when the preparation covers the spatula remove it from the fire, add to it the pounded nuts and cream and leave stand till cold; strain through a fine sieve and freeze as an ordinary ice cream (No. 3427).

(3465). ICE CREAM WITH ROASTED OR BOILED CHESTNUTS (Crème aux Marrons Rôtis ou Bouillis).

With Roasted Chestnuts.—Split the chestnuts on their sides, roast and skin; put them with a pound of sugar into a copper pan, adding three gills of water; cook the sugar to three hundred and thirty-eight degrees Fahrenheit, or a little above the "crack;" pour it on a marble and as soon as cold pound with a small quantity of cream; place it in a tinned basin with fifteen egg-yolks, a quart of cream and the quarter of a vanilla bean. Set the basin on a slow fire to cook the mixture without boiling and as soon as it covers the spoon remove from the fire, cool, strain and freeze.

With Boiled Chestnuts.—Suppress the hard outer shell and red inside skin from a pound of chestnuts; boil them in milk with a little vanilla, and when tender rub through a sieve. Pour this purée into a vessel and dilute with a gill of vanilla cream No. 1 (No. 3458); strain, cool and freeze, working it vigorously, and when smooth and firm mix in half as much very firm and slightly sweetened whipped cream and half a gill of maraschino.

(3466). ICE CREAM WITHOUT COOKING (Glaces sans Cuisson).

Vanilla.—Mix well together one quart of good cream, half a pound of sugar and half a stick of vanilla infused in a little milk; when the sugar has melted pass the whole through a fine silver wired sieve, and freeze either by machine or in a freezer, turning and detaching the cream with a spatula as fast as it adheres to the sides; after it has solidified finish by working with the spatula, turning the freezer by a rotary movement with this spatula. Instead of vanilla infusion extract of vanilla may be used.

Chocolate.—Boil a quart and a half of cream and with it dissolve half a pound of chocolate melted in a slack oven; add three pounds of sugar, mix well and stir in three quarts of raw cream and a little vanilla extract; strain through a fine sieve and freeze.

Orange Flower Water.—Boil one quart of milk with a quarter of a pound of sugar; dissolve two tablespoonfuls of corn starch, and stir it into the boiling milk, beating it with a whip; color to a fine green, strain through a sieve, and allow to cool. Beat one quart of cream, add six ounces of sugar and a little orange flower water; freeze and incorporate it into the above. Use this cream either for molding or dressing with a spoon.

Lemon.—One quart of cream which has had the peel of a lemon infused therein for one hour; add half a pound of sugar, strain and freeze the same as vanilla.

Coffee.—Prepare one pint of coffee, composed of four ounces of cold Mocha mixed with a pint of cream and twelve ounces of sugar; strain through a fine sieve and freeze.

Light Chocolate.—Have two ounces of chocolate melted in a pint of milk; pass through a sieve, and cool off. Mix one quart of firm whipped cream and three-quarters of a pound of sugar; freeze and add the chocolate very slowly.

(3467). FIORI DI LATTE À LA BELLINI (Fiori di Latte à la Bellini).

The fiori di latte is a light preparation composed of Italian meringue with hot syrup cooked to thirty-five degrees; add flavorings, also as much whipped, well-drained cream, sweetened when drained with a quarter of a pound of sugar for each quart of cream. The meringue and cream are to be well but lightly combined. This cream is used for filling molds the same shape as shown in Fig. 628.

Fiori di Latte à la Bellini.—Whip firmly one pint of cream and pour it on a wire sieve to drain for two hours. Cut in quarter-inch squares eight ounces of fruits, such as pineapple, cherries, orange and lemon peel, also a few shredded pistachios; lay these in a vessel, pour maraschino over and let macerate for one hour, then drain. Prepare an Italian meringue with four egg-whites beaten to a stiff froth, and a pint of hot thirty-five degree syrup; allow to cool, then mix it in with the whipped cream and well-drained fruits. Pack a two-quart mold in salted ice; cover the insides with a quarter-inch thick coating of uncooked strawberry ice cream (No. 3451); place the preparation into the empty space, letting the mold be quite full; press the cover on forcibly, imbed and freeze for one hour. Unmold by dipping it into warm water, the same as for all other ices, and invert it on a folded napkin, as shown in the drawing.

(3468). FIORI DI LATTE À LA ORLANDINI (Fiori di Latte à la Orlandini).

Whip a pint of cream, then drain on a sieve; grate the peel of a good orange on lump sugar, and scrape off the part impregnated with the peel. Make an Italian meringue preparation with five eggs (No. 140), add the sugar flavored with the peel to the sugar used for making the meringue; leave stand till cold, then incorporate gently the whipped cream without beating, and add candied citron peel cut up finely, and a little powdered vanilla. Fill a fiori di latte mold (Fig. 628), with a coating of chocolate a quarter of an inch thick, pour in the preparation, and finish the same as à la Bellini (No. 3467).

(3469). FIORI DI LATTE WITH VANILLA OR OTHER FLAVORINGS (Fiori di Latte à la Vanille ou Autres Parfums).

Beat up a pint of whipped cream; drain on a sieve. Whip five egg-whites quite stiff; cook eight ounces of sugar with half a vanilla bean to thirty-five degrees; suppress the vanilla and mix the sugar with the egg-whites, a little at a time, while stirring the meringue constantly; leave to cool on ice. Coat a fiori di latte mold with pistachio ice cream (No. 3454); pack in ice (have the coating only a quarter-inch thick); fill the center of this shell quite full, pressing down the preparation with the cover and imbed in ice, allowing one hour's freezing for each quart. Unmold on a folded napkin and serve. This ice may be prepared and finished the same way, only putting in the eighth part of a vanilla stick instead of half a one, and after the preparation is quite firm adding either maraschino, kirsch, prunelle, Curaçoa, almond milk, or concentrated orange flower water, just enough to have the preparation nicely flavored.

(3470). FIORI DI LATTE WITH VIOLETS, BURNT ALMONDS AND PISTACHIOS (Fiori di Latte à la Fleur de Violette, aux Pralines et aux Pistaches).

Cook two ounces of violet leaves in two ounces of sugar, and when this has reached "crack" (No. 171), pour it on a marble to cool, then pound and run it through a sieve. Whip a pint of cream till very firm, and drain it on a sieve. Beat five egg-whites to a stiff froth, mix into them three gills of hot thirty-five degree syrup, and cool this meringue by standing the basin on ice; mix together lightly the whipped cream, Italian meringue and violet sugar. Pack a fiori di latte mold (Fig. 628) in salted ice and line it with a coating of virgin maraschino ice cream, finishing as the Bellini (No. 3467).

FIG. 628.

Burnt Almonds and Pistachios.—The same preparation as the above; after mixing the whipped cream with the Italian meringue add two ounces of crushed burnt almonds and two ounces of shredded pistachios, also two tablespoonfuls of orange flower water. Mix well together and with this fill a mold coated with virgin orange ice cream (No. 3459). Fiori di latte can also be flavored with either chocolate, coffee, cinnamon, lemon, orange or Seville orange. Peel the three latter very finely, cut the skins up very thin or else chop them, or fruits with well-flavored juices may be substituted, etc.

(3471). MOUSSE À LA SEMIRAMIS (Mousse à la Sémiramis).

Lay a quart of well-whipped cream on a sieve to have it drain well. Pound four ounces of freshly shelled sweet almonds with half an ounce of coriander seeds and three gills of water; put this in a basin with twelve ounces of sugar; color to a pretty light red shade; add slowly and lightly the whipped cream. Imbed a high dome-shaped mold (Fig. 629) in ice, and fill with the preparation, into which add a salpicon of fruits cut in quarter-inch squares, soaked in maraschino and drained. Pack in ice, freeze for one hour

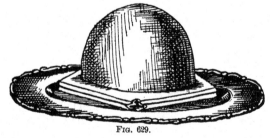

FIG. 629.

for each quart of preparation, unmold over a napkin and surround with cakes iced with kirsch or rum.

(3472). MOUSSE À LA SIRAUDIN (Mousse à la Siraudin).

Whip a quart of cream till quite firm, lay it on a sieve and when well drained mix into it eight ounces of icing sugar and a salpicon of fruits cut in squares and marinated in kirsch. Fill a high dome-shaped mold with this preparation, pack in ice, freeze an hour for each quart, and unmold on a very cold dish; cover the top with Italian cream, decorating it with fruits; freeze once more and serve.

(3473). COFFEE OR CHOCOLATE MOUSSE (Mousse au Café ou au Chocolat).

In former days they mingled milk, sugar and flavoring together, and when the preparation was beaten to a stiff froth it was lifted up with a skimmer, drained on a sieve and glasses were filled with it which were then frozen in ice-packed boxes. Now the process is different. A mousse preparation is simply cream beaten till very light, sweetened properly and flavored with natural flavors, liquors or essences.

With Coffee.—Beat a quart of cream till very light, drain it on a sieve and when thoroughly drained put it into a tin basin and mix in twelve ounces of sugar, a gill of coffee and some vanilla essence. Imbed a high-dome mold in ice, fill it with the preparation, fasten on the cover, imbed it well and freeze. It will take about one hour for each quart. Unmold the mousse on a napkin and surround with small cakes.

With Chocolate.—Dissolve two ounces of cocoa at the oven door, dilute it with two gills of twenty-six degree syrup, strain through a sieve and mix in gradually three beaten egg-whites, six ounces of sugar and a quart of well-whipped, drained cream. Pack a tall-dome mold in salted ice, fill it with the preparation, then freeze. A quart of cream takes about one hour to freeze.

(3474). FRUIT MOUSSES WITH PINEAPPLE OR OTHER FRUITS (Mousses à l'Ananas ou à d'Autres Fruits).

Strawberries, raspberries, apricots, peaches, pineapple, etc., to be used. A quart of cream must be whipped till very light; drain it on a sieve and then transfer it to a bowl; add a pound of pineapple purée and one pound of sugar, mixing both together with a little vanilla and a gill of kirsch; whip the preparation in a tin basin on ice for ten minutes to have the cream and pulp assimilate well together. Coat the inside of a high-dome mold with virgin strawberry cream (No. 3451), fill the center quite full with the preparation, and close the mold. Pack it in ice for one hour for each quart, unmold on a napkin and surround with small iced cakes. Strawberries, raspberries, apricots, peaches or other fruits may be substituted for the pineapple.

(3475). ITALIAN MOUSSE (Mousse à l'Italienne).

This mousse will require three separate preparations: One of strawberry, one of vanilla and one of pistachios; mold it in a two-quart high-dome mold (Fig. 629). Incrust the mold in salted ice, cover and leave till perfectly cold. Make the three preparations as follows:

The Strawberry.—Mix one pint of strawberry pulp with a quarter of a pound of vanilla sugar (No. 3165); beat on ice for ten minutes, and lightly add one pint of well-whipped and thoroughly drained cream.

The Vanilla.—Half a pint of whipped cream and three ounces of pounded sugar; add a little vanilla pounded and passed through a silk sieve; mix it in lightly with the mousse.

The Pistachio.—Have half a pint of very light whipped cream, three ounces of sugar, half a gill of almond milk, a little orange flower water and a small quantity of spinach green; beat the whole lightly. Fill the bottom of the mold one-third of its height and very even with the strawberry cream; on this lay exactly in the center some macaroons soaked in maraschino; freeze this for twenty minutes, then put into it another layer of the vanilla, finishing the center with soaked macaroons; the mold should now be two-thirds filled. Freeze for twenty minutes and finish with the pistachio cream. Close the mold hermetically and pack in ice for one hour and a half. Unmold on a folded napkin.

(3476). MOUSSE WITH LIQUORS (Mousse aux Liqueurs).

Whip a quart of cream until very firm, drain on a sieve and when finished return it to a basin to mix in ten ounces of sugar, and half a gill of either Curaçoa, maraschino, noyau, kirsch, aniseed, chartreuse, etc., flavoring but slightly with vanilla. Fill a dome-form mold with this, previously coated with any kind of water ice laid on in stripes.

(3477). MOUSSE WITH MACAROONS OR CHESTNUTS (Mousse aux Macarons ou Marrons).

With Macaroons.—Beat a quart of cream till very light, drain on a sieve and mix into it ten ounces of sugar; coat a high-dome mold with virgin maraschino cream and fill it in three distinct layers, alternating each one with broken macaroons soaked in kirsch; imbed in ice and freeze one hour for each quart; unmold on a napkin and surround with lady bouchées with maraschino.

With Chestnuts.—Whip one quart of cream and drain on a sieve. Prepare half a pound of chestnuts boiled in milk with a little vanilla pounded and pressed through a sieve; dilute with a pint of thirty-degree syrup and half a gill of maraschino; incorporate the whipped cream lightly into this purée; pack a mousse mold in ice, line it with a coating of ice cream made without eggs and flavored with prunelle, and fill it in three separate layers with the preparation, the same as the mousse with macaroons, only using crushed chestnuts soaked in maraschino; freeze the molds; unmold and dress on a napkin; decorate around with cream cakes garnished with apricot marmalade (No. 3675).

(3478). PARFAIT WITH NOUGAT AND WITH ALMONDS (Parfait au Nougat et aux Amandes).

Fig. 630.

Boil four gills of syrup to twenty degrees with half a vanilla bean; pour this slowly over ten egg-yolks beaten in a vessel, after removing the vanilla; whip the preparation well over the fire until it is as thick as a cream, but avoid having it boil, then remove and stir continuously until frothy and cold; now beat it again on ice to give consistency, and incorporate two quarts of well-drained whipped cream, also half a pound of almond nougat (No. 3621) crushed finely with a rolling-pin. Place the preparation in a three-quart bomb or parfait mold (Fig. 630) lined with paper, incrust in salted ice, and put on the lid, cementing the joints with butter; cover this with a thick layer of salted ice, then freeze for two hours and a half; lastly remove the mold, wash it quickly in cold water, wipe and unmold the parfait on a folded napkin; remove the paper and serve surrounded by small cakes.

With Almonds.—Have the same preparation as for the parfait with nougat. Pound half a pound of new, freshly shelled almonds with a little water, vanilla sugar (No. 3165) and noyau; when pounded to a pulp use them instead of the nougat and finish exactly the same as for the above. If the two ices are to be served in the same mold have a waffle partition the same size as the center of the mold; fill one side of it with parfait with nougat, and the other side with parfait with almonds.

(3479). EXCELLENT WITH COFFEE AND PARFAIT WITH COFFEE (Excellent au Café et Parfait au Café).

Excellent with Coffee.—Boil three pints of cream, mix in three-quarters of a pound of good freshly roasted coffee, not having it too dark; leave infuse for half an hour, being careful to keep the saucepan covered. Place sixteen egg-yolks in a tinned basin, add half a pound of sugar, stir together and cook on a slow fire, beating continuously until such a consistency is obtained that it will cover the spatula; remove the basin from the fire, leave till cold, then strain through a fine sieve; freeze in a spherical freezer and when the composition begins to congeal add half a gill of thirty-two degree vanilla syrup (No. 3165); when almost hard put in another gill of the same syrup and as much whipped and slightly sweetened cream as there is preparation. Fill some boxes, the same as illustrated in Fig. 631, and lay them on top of socles made of colored water (No. 3434). Place a spun sugar ornament on the summit.

Parfait with Coffee.—Infuse for half an hour six ounces of freshly roasted coffee and the fourth part of a vanilla bean in one pint of boiling cream; into a basin lay eight egg-yolks and a quarter of a pound of sugar, diluting with the infusion; set the basin on a slow fire, stir steadily until the mixture covers the spatula and leave till cold; pass it through a fine sieve. Clean the basin, return the preparation to it and whip on ice until quite light, adding as much whipped cream. Fill a

Fig. 631.

bomb-shaped mold (Fig. 630) with this, lay a paper over, then the cover and imbed in salted ice; freeze for one hour for one quart, two quarts requiring an hour and a half; the larger the mold the longer it will take.

(3480). PLOMBIÈRE À LA MONTESQUIEU (Plombière à la Montesquieu).

Cook half a pound of rice in plenty of water with the juice of four lemons; drain and place it in a vessel to cover with a hot thirty-two degree syrup, draining this off an hour later. Put sixteen egg-yolks in a basin with half a pound of sugar, beat both together and mix in a pint of boiling milk; cook this, without allowing it to boil, until the preparation covers the spoon, then take it

Fig. 632.

from the fire, let cool and pour in a pint of cream; pass the whole through a fine sieve and freeze; stir in the rice and a quart of well-drained whipped cream. Cut some preserved pineapple and melon in three-eighths inch squares and macerate in kirsch for two hours. Coat a plombière mold with uncooked lemon ice cream; fill the center with the rice cream, put on the cover and freeze for one hour for each quart. Unmold on a napkin and garnish around with small lady's bouchées (No. 3376) iced with coffee icing; on top and in the middle place the macerated fruits and send to the table with a sauce-boatful of prunelle sauce, made with vanilla and whipped cream, to which some prunelle has been added.

(3481). PLOMBIÈRE À LA RICHMOND (Plombière à la Richmond).

Make a Genoese biscuit preparation as herewith described: Mix in a basin one pound of powdered sugar, twelve whole eggs and a grain of salt; beat this over a slow fire, and remove to incorporate slowly one pound of sifted flour and one pound of warm melted butter, also the well-chopped peel of an orange. Take a round mold seven inches in diameter by one and a half in depth; butter and flour the interior, then fill it three-quarters full with the preparation, and bake in a slack oven; spread the remainder of the paste on a sheet of paper to a quarter of an inch in thickness, and bake this also in a hot oven. After removing the thin biscuit from the fire cut it into half rounds two inches in diameter with a channeled pastry cutter (Fig. 16); leave them to cool, coat over with apricot marmalade (No. 3675), then cover with a layer of orange sugar icing (No. 102). When the round Genoese is cooked and cold, apricot it over, and in the center, on the apricot, place a round piece of strong paper six inches in diameter, and ice the whole with rum icing (No. 102). Lay it on a grate and make an incision around the biscuit at half an inch from the edge; remove the icing and paper from the center; scoop out the cake; set it on a dish, and put it on ice until ready to serve. Imbed a plombière mold (Fig. 632) on ice; fill the bottom and sides with a coating of maraschino ice cream (No. 3462), and fill the inside with a preparation made with three-quarters of a pound of pounded roasted hazel-nuts, adding slowly a quart of cream to them; put this into a vessel with an orange peel, infuse for one hour, and strain forcibly through a fine sieve; add a gill of vanilla syrup (No. 3165) and eight ounces of sugar, freeze, then put in as much whipped cream. Mold it in layers, alternating each one with hazel-nut macaroons (No. 3386). Then unmold the plombière into the cavity of the cake, surround the base of the plombière with the above half-rounds of Genoese, and serve separately a sauce made with well-drained whipped cream flavored with kirsch, to which has been added candied apricots cut in small squares of a quarter of an inch, previously macerated in kirsch.

(3482). PLOMBIÈRE À LA ROCHAMBEAU (Plombière à la Rochambeau).

Pound half a pound of peeled almonds, but a few at a time, soaked for several hours in cold water, adding a little water at frequent intervals, then transfer from the mortar to a glazed vessel. Prepare an English cream (No. 42) with a quart of milk, half a pound of sugar, eight to ten egg-yolks and a stick of vanilla split in two; as this becomes thick pour it over the almonds and stir occasionally while cooling, then strain forcibly through a tammy and leave till thoroughly cold. Pour this cream into a deep freezer imbedded in salted ice, work it vigorously until smooth and firm—this will take forty minutes—then incorporate two or three spoonfuls of kirsch mixed with a little orange syrup. Five to six minutes later stir in a pint of sweetened whipped cream, after adding to it a few spoonfuls of the almond preparation to prevent it from granulating; work again for ten to twelve minutes. Freeze a plombière mold; coat it with nougat ice-cream (No. 3452) and at the bottom range some lady fingers soaked in prunelle; cover these with the above ice and on top of this place some preserved greengages, macerated for a quarter of an hour in kirsch and thick syrup, then drained. After the mold is full close the lid forcibly, pack it in salted ice and freeze for one hour for each quart. Unmold the plombière on a folded napkin and surround the base with small iced Genoese cakes; fill the hollow center of the plombière with some of the greengages infused in kirsch and serve separately. in a sauce tureen, whipped cream with a little kirsch added, mixing it well.

(3483). PLOMBIÈRE D'ALENÇON (Plombière d'Alençon).

Fill a plombière mold with Chantilly cream (whipped cream made with a quart of cream and a quarter of a pound of powdered sugar, both firmly whipped together); place on the cover forcibly and pack it in ice, leaving it in a quarter of an hour for each quart; remove the cover and take out the contents, leaving only a thin three-eighths of an inch coating, then fill up the inside with alternate layers of No. 1 vanilla ice-cream (No. 3458), having half as much whipped cream added to it, intermingling it with macaroons soaked in maraschino or kirsch; fill it quite full, put back the cover neatly and pack in ice, freezing one hour and a half for two quarts; unmold and garnish the hollow on top of the plombière with preserved peaches (No. 3682) and cherries, the former cut into pieces and softened in a light syrup with maraschino; place here and there a few lozenges of angelica; garnish around with various small cakes. Sauce of whipped cream flavored with noyau should be served apart.

(3484). PLOMBIÈRE, HAVANESE STYLE (Plombière à la Havanaise).

Put ten egg-yolks in a tinned basin with eight ounces of sugar; beat both well together with a whip and dilute with a pint of boiling milk; cook without boiling and when the preparation covers the spoon remove from the fire and allow to cool. Now add one pint of cream and the pulp of twelve very ripe bananas. Pass all of this through a fine sieve and freeze. Then incorporate the same quantity of whipped cream, and a gill and a half of maraschino. Coat a plombière mold with Andalusian ice cream (No. 3446); fill it quite full with the banana cream, fasten the cover on tight, pack in ice and freeze one hour for each quart; unmold and fill the hollow center in the mold with slices of raw pineapple, quartered, pared to the pulp, then macerated in maraschino. The sauce required for this is composed of apricots and maraschino.

(3485). PLOMBIÈRE WITH CHERRIES (Plombière aux Cerises).

Suppress the stalks and pips from one pound of cherries; pound and press through a sieve; into this pulp mix five gills of cold thirty-degree syrup, a few bits of lemon peel and some lemon juice; pass the preparation once more, then stir in an infusion made with a part of the crushed cherry pips and some light syrup. Bring it to twenty-two degree syrup, then freeze the whole, the same as an ordinary ice. After it becomes firm and smooth incorporate a few spoonfuls of kirsch; ten minutes later transfer three or four spoonfuls to a vessel and mix in with it six or seven gills of well-whipped rich cream, properly drained and sweetened; stir this at once into the principal preparation, but only a little at a time, to have the mixture more perfect. Beat the whole well for a few moments longer so that it attains body. Coat a plombière mold with kirsch ice cream (No. 3462), fill it full with the above, close properly and freeze. Unmold on a napkin and decorate the summit of the cupola with candied cherries that have been softened in light syrup and macerated in kirsch for one hour previously, and then well drained.

(3486). PLOMBIÈRE WITH CHESTNUTS (Plombière aux Marrons).

Pack a plombière mold in salted ice; line the bottom and sides with a thin layer of vanilla ice cream (No. 3458) and the center with chestnut cream (No. 3465), having the mold perfectly full; fasten on the cover forcibly, then freeze, allowing one hour for each quart of the plombière; unmold and range it on a folded napkin; fill the hollow in the mold with chestnuts in juice flavored with maraschino. Stick between the chestnuts lozenge shaped pieces of angelica.

(3487). BANANA PUDDING (Pouding aux Bananes).

The composition for this is one pint of banana pulp, one pint of thirty-five degree syrup and a gill of lemon juice; bring this to twenty-two degrees test, then pass it through a sieve and freeze, incorporating two Italian meringue egg-whites (No. 140). Coat a two-quart pudding mold

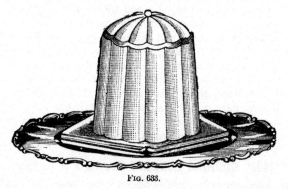

FIG. 633.

with vanilla ice cream (No. 3458); on the bottom place a layer of the banana ice, on this some slices of banana macerated for one hour in maraschino, and bestrewn with finely powdered sugar, also some biscuits soaked in Curaçoa, then another layer of banana ice, more sliced bananas and more biscuits, proceeding until the mold is thoroughly filled; freeze in salted ice for one hour and a half. Invert the pudding on a folded napkin and serve at the same time a sauce composed of whipped cream, vanilla ice cream and kirsch, the whole well mixed.

(3488). BISCUIT PUDDING (Pouding aux Biscuits).

Crumble one pound of very dry Savoy biscuit (No. 3231). Put twelve egg-yolks in a basin with six ounces of sugar; beat, add the crumbled biscuit and a quart of boiling milk; cook this on a slow fire without boiling, and when the preparation covers the spoon remove the basin from the fire, allow to cool, then strain through a sieve and freeze. Pack a two-quart pudding mold in salted ice; coat the inside with pistachio ice cream (No. 3454) and fill the center in alternate layers of the above ice, slices of biscuit soaked in maraschino, and a salpicon of fruits; continue until the mold is full, finishing the top with ice cream, then freeze for one hour for each quart. Unmold on a folded napkin and serve with a separate sauce made of vanilla ice cream beaten in a metal bowl, mixing in some rum and whipped cream.

(3489). CAVOUR PUDDING (Pouding à la Cavour).

Pick, wash and cook in an abundance of water half a pound of Piedmontese rice, leaving it boil for twenty minutes; then drain it off and place it in a vessel to macerate for two hours in a hot twenty-two degree vanilla syrup; afterward drain. Break ten raw egg-yolks in a tinned copper basin; add eight ounces of sugar and mix well, stirring in a pint of boiling milk; cook this preparation on a slow fire without boiling and without ceasing to stir until it covers the spatula, then remove; allow to cool and add to it one pint of cream and a quarter of a pound of almonds pounded with two gills of water; strain this forcibly through a sieve and freeze. Coat a two-quart pudding mold with vanilla ice cream (No. 3458), fill up the inside in distinct layers of the prepared ice cream, well-drained rice, and preserved pineapple cut in three-eighths of an inch squares. Freeze for one hour and a half in salted ice for each quart of pudding, then turn it out on a napkin and serve. Serve separately a sauce made of vanilla ice cream mingled with rum and whipped cream.

(3490). CONSTANCE PUDDING (Pouding à la Constance).

Pour a quart of cream into a vessel to stir with ten ounces of vanilla sugar (No. 3165); strain through a sieve and freeze. Prepare a salpicon of fruits, such as apricots, cherries, plums and pineapple, also have some macaroons stuffed with apricot and macerated in maraschino. Imbed a two-quart pudding mold (Fig. 633) in salted ice; coat it with a thin layer of uncooked strawberry ice cream (No. 3451) and fill it in layers composed of the above vanilla ice cream, the fruits, more vanilla ice cream and then the macaroons, continuing until perfectly full, having the last layer of ice cream; force on the cover and freeze for one hour and a half. Invert and dress on a napkin, serving separately a sauce made with vanilla ice cream (No. 3458) finished with maraschino.

(3491). DIPLOMAT PUDDING (Pouding à la Diplomate).

Prepare a salpicon of candied fruits cut in quarter-inch squares, selecting pineapple, cherries, almonds, apricots, orange peel and Smyrna raisins; pour over some hot twenty-degree syrup flavored with rum, and let all macerate for half an hour. Put in a tinned copper basin, ten egg-yolks and six ounces of sugar; beat well together and dilute with a pint of boiling milk; cook without allowing it to come to a boil, then cool off and add one pint of cream; strain through a sieve, freeze, flavor with maraschino, and mix in half as much very firm and well-drained whipped cream. Cut up some slices of Savoy biscuit (No. 3231). Take a two-quart pudding mold, incrust it in ice, line it with a layer of uncooked Andalusian ice cream (No. 3446), and on the bottom have the sliced biscuit previously soaked in rum; scatter a part of the fruit salpicon over, then place a layer of the ice cream, and continue in this way to fill the mold, finishing the top with the ice cream; set the cover on tight, pack it well in salted ice, and freeze for one hour and a half, then unmold on a napkin and serve with a sauce made of vanilla ice cream (No. 3458) flavored with rum, mixing into it half as much whipped cream (No. 50).

(3492). DUCHESS PUDDING (Pouding à la Duchesse).

Cook six very ripe peeled pears in a twelve-degree syrup; drain and rub them through a sieve; put this pulp in a vessel with two gills of syrup at thirty-five degrees, and one gill of lemon juice; strain the whole, bring it to twenty-two degrees and freeze. Cut some candied pineapple and candied cherries (half a pound of each) in quarter-inch pieces, boil them in a little thirty-degree syrup, leave to cool and drain. To the ice add two egg-whites of Italian meringue, and the well-drained fruits. Imbed a two-quart pudding mold in ice; coat the inside with a quarter of an inch layer of maraschino ice cream (No. 3462), and put in the pear ice; place the cover on, pack it well in salted ice, freeze, allowing one hour for each quart, then unmold and dress on a napkin. Accompany this pudding by a sauce prepared as follows: Put one Italian meringue egg-white in a metal bowl; stir it well with the juice of an orange and a few drops of extract of pears and a little champagne.

(3493). FLEURY PUDDING (Pouding à la Fleury).

Mix in a vessel one quart of apricot pulp, ten ounces of sugar, one gill of almond milk (No. 4) and half a gill of kirsch; bring it to twenty-two degrees of the saccharometer, then strain through a sieve and freeze; mix in half as much whipped cream. Have a two-quart pudding mold packed in ice; coat the inside with strawberry ice cream (No. 3451), and fill it in layers composed of the above prepared cream; between each layer arrange a macédoine of fresh fruits macerated in kirsch and some biscuits soaked in maraschino; let the last layer be ice cream; pack and freeze for one hour and a half; unmold and serve with a separate sauce made of strawberry ice cream, mixing into it a little kirsch and whipped cream.

(3494). IMPERIAL RICE PUDDING (Pouding de Riz à l'Impériale).

Coat a two-quart pudding mold with almond ice cream (No. 3461). Have some vanilla ice cream (No. 3458) and mix into it half as much well-drained whipped cream. In the bottom of the mold inside the coating range a layer of this vanilla cream and on it one of paradise rice (No. 3456); place over this some biscuits and macaroons steeped in maraschino, and cover with more vanilla cream, then more rice and a salpicon of fruits, finishing with vanilla cream, so that the mold be entirely full and the cover packed on tight. Imbed and freeze one hour and a half; unmold and dress on a napkin, and serve with a sauce made of apricot marmalade (No. 3675) dissolved in maraschino, stirring in some thoroughly drained whipped cream (No. 50).

(3495). NESSELRODE PUDDING WITH CANDIED CHESTNUTS (Pouding à la Nesselrode aux Marrons Confits).

Have ready a chestnut ice cream (No. 3465); mix into it a quarter as much Italian meringue (No. 140), and flavor with maraschino. Coat a two-quart pudding mold with vanilla ice cream (No. 3458); at the bottom lay a bed of the chestnut ice cream, placing a few broken candied chestnuts here and there, then another layer of chestnut cream, and continue until the mold is perfectly full, finishing with the cream; force on the cover, and freeze for an hour and a half. Unmold and dress on a napkin. Serve separately a sauce made with vanilla ice cream (No. 3458), into which mix whipped cream and maraschino.

(3496). PLUM PUDDING (Plum Pouding).

Melt half a pound of chocolate in a quart of water, add three-quarters of a pound of sugar, a little vanilla, and one quart of cold syrup at thirty degrees; strain through a sieve and freeze; now add two Italian meringue egg-whites (No. 140), some seeded Malaga and Smyrna raisins, currants, orange, lemon and citron peel cut in three-sixteenth of an inch squares, all of these previously boiled in a little twenty-two degree syrup, then drained and macerated for one hour in kirsch; drain and mix them well into the ice. Coat a two-quart pudding mold with chocolate ice cream (No. 3449); fill it with the preparation, freeze as usual and unmold an hour and a half later, on a dish without a napkin. Make the sauce of vanilla (No. 3458), whipped cream (No. 50) and rum; pour a third of the sauce on the pudding and serve the other two-thirds apart.

FIG. 634.

(3497). ROMANOFF PUDDING (Pouding à la Romanoff).

Make a chestnut cream the same as described for chestnut ice cream (No. 3465), having the chestnuts cooked with sugar. After this is frozen incorporate half the same quantity of whipped cream (No. 50). Have a two-quart pudding mold (Fig. 633) packed in salted ice, coat the interior with uncooked orange ice cream and fill the center in separate layers; first the chestnut ice cream, then lady fingers soaked in kümmel and walnuts well drained from their juice and cut lengthwise in four; have the top layer of the ice cream; cover the mold. Freeze one hour and a half, and turn it out on a napkin. Serve a separate sauce of vanilla ice cream (No. 3458) flavored with kirsch, beating it well with whipped cream.

(3498.) SERANO PUDDING (Pouding à la Serano).

Boil one quart of raspberry pulp, one pound of syrup at thirty-two degrees, one gill of lemon juice and vanilla, bringing the whole to a twenty-two degree heat, then strain through a sieve and freeze, incorporating into the ice one Italian meringue egg-white (No. 140). Have a pudding mold well packed in salted ice; coat the inside with pistachio ice cream (No. 3454). Fill up the mold in

FIG. 635.

alternate layers, having a light strawberry ice cream (No. 3451) on the bottom, then some biscuits intercalated with fruits, and over the prepared raspberry ice; continue to fill in the same order: raspberry ice, biscuits and fruits cut in small squares. Have the mold well filled, fasten the cover on tight, pack in ice and freeze for one hour for each quart; invert it on a napkin and serve with a sauce-boat of strawberry sauce mingled with maraschino and whipped cream.

(3499). SICILIAN PUDDING (Pouding à la Sicilienne).

Cut six ounces of slightly roasted almonds lengthwise in four, and six ounces of citron and four ounces of orange peel cut the same size. Coat a two-quart pudding mold with pistachio ice cream (No. 3454); mix the almonds and fruits with chocolate ice cream (No. 3449), adding a little cinnamon and one Italian meringue egg-white (No. 140); fill with this, laying in the center a little orange jelly (No. 3668). Pack in salted ice, unmolding on a napkin an hour and a half later. The sauce should be made of whipped cream (No. 50), with chocolate ice cream and brandy stirred in; serve it apart.

(3500). WADDINGTON PUDDING (Pouding à la Waddington).

Have half a pound of Smyrna raisins, a quarter of a pound of apricot paste and a quarter of a pound of orange peel; macerate these in two gills of kirsch. Have also some hazel-nut maccaroons (No. 3386) garnished with orange jelly (No. 3668) and some nougat ice cream (No. 3452). Coat a two and a half quart pudding mold with strawberry ice cream (No. 3451); on the bottom lay a bed of the nougat ice cream, over this the fruits macerated in maraschino and the marchpane, then more nougat cream and more fruits and marchpane, and nougat ice cream to finish. Close the mold, freeze and unmold two hours later. Prepare a whipped cream sauce, adding kirsch, maraschino and vanilla ice cream (No. 3458).

(3501). PUNCH AND SHERBET (Punch et Sorbet).

Punch or sherbet is served between the last entrée and the roast. Either one should be placed on the bill of fare without a separate heading, merely reading: Sherbet or punch, à la ——. The difference between sherbet and punch is that the former is a water ice into which some liquor is mixed, while punch is an ice either of water or cream mingled with a quarter as much Italian meringue and liquors; for this see Italian meringue (No. 140). Punches and sherbets are served either in medium glasses, the size usually used for Bordeaux, without any foot, but provided with a handle, or else in fancy cups, either of gum paste or of water tinted to various colors, or in many kinds made of cardboard of a basket or other shape, or in the peels of fresh

FIG. 636.

fruits. Italian meringue is mixed both in white or colored ices. The size for sherbets and punches is eight or ten from each quart.

(3502). BEATRICE PUNCH (Punch à la Béatrice).

For twelve persons take about one quart of lemon water ice (No. 3604) and add to it two drops of extract of citron. To two well-beaten egg-whites put one gill of boiling syrup at thirty-five degrees; lay aside to cool and when very cold incorporate in the ice a little good rum, a quarter of a bottleful of good champagne and four soupspoonfuls of Italian meringue (No. 140); fill with this some swans made of gum paste (No. 3624), having the top parts hollow.

(3503). BOUQUETIÈRE PUNCH (Punch à la Bouquetière).

For ten sherbets have one pint of orange water ice (No. 3605) and as much strawberry water ice (No. 3607); mix both together in a freezer with a quarter as much Italian meringue (No. 140); add one gill of maraschino and a quarter of a bottleful of champagne. Procure molds the shape of Fig. 637 and Fig. 639. The latter mold is furnished with a socket three-sixteenths of an inch in diameter in its center, a little higher than the mold. Incrust them well in salted ice and fill Fig.

FIG. 637.

FIG. 638.

FIG. 639.

637 with water whitened with milk, and Fig. 639 with reddened water; after the ice has formed on the sides to an eighth of an inch in thickness empty out the surplus water, dip the mold in hot water and unmold quickly. Place the contents of the mold (Fig. 637) in small blue cardboard boxes and fill them up with the sherbet. Unmold Fig. 639, lay on top of Fig. 637 so that the rounded part be uppermost, fasten a small bunch of natural flowers in the center and then stand them in silver-plated rings and these on silver saucers.

(3504). CHAMPAGNE PUNCH (Punch au Champagne).

Procure some imitation silver champagne pails made of cardboard or gum paste (No. 3624). Have tin molds to fit into these and incrust them in ice, filling to the top with water. As soon as this becomes frozen sufficiently thick to cover the sides to one-eighth of an inch empty out the liquid and unmold, lay these ice pails inside the cardboard ones and imitate the bottle in gum paste (No. 3624), having the surrounding ice of white rock candy; these should be laid on the cover. Pour into a small freezer one quart of pineapple water ice (No. 3606), half a gill of fine brandy, half a gill of kirsch and two gills of champagne; mix the whole and add as much Italian meringue (No. 140). When frozen fill the pails, lay on the covers and serve.

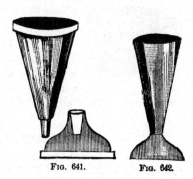

Fig. 640.

(3505). COFFEE PUNCH; GRANITE PUNCH WITH COFFEE (Punch au Café; Punch Granit au Café).

For ten persons put one quart of vanilla ice cream into a freezer and mix in with it three Italian meringue egg-whites (made with three beaten egg-whites and two gills of forty-degree syrup properly liquefied with coffee made with water). To make this coffee requires one quart of water to six ounces of coffee; add it to the cream when nearly firm so that it does not grain the punch, then put in a little brandy or kirsch.

Another way to make granite punch with coffee is to have four quarts of black coffee, one quart of cream, ten ounces of sugar, four gills of brandy and one quart of whipped cream or Italian meringue. Freeze as the above.

(3506). DOLGOROUSKI PUNCH (Punch à la Dolgorouski).

For ten persons allow one quart of peach water ice (No. 3602); beat it up well and incorporate in a third as much Italian meringue (No. 140), then mix in slowly a gill and a half of kirsch, and two gills of Cliquot champagne; with this preparation fill some natural water glasses, having the bottom of the glass red and the upper part white, made and frozen the same as American sherbet.

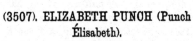

Fig. 641.   Fig. 642.

(3507). ELIZABETH PUNCH (Punch Élisabeth).

Have in a freezer one quart of strawberry (No. 3451) or currant ice cream (No. 3451), moisten it with kirsch, brandy and champagne, two gills and a half in all; whip in a quarter as much Italian meringue (No. 140) and serve this punch in imitation flower pots (Fig. 643), made in three parts, the saucer, the pot and a top. Stick two wires into the top to fasten on a small bunch of natural flowers or else a single one.

Fig. 643.

(3508). FAVORITE PUNCH (Punch à la Favorite).

Arrange in a freezer one quart of strawberry water ice (No. 3607); work it well and mix in two gills of rum, one gill of brandy and a quarter as much Italian meringue (No. 140). Prepare and pack some goblet-shaped molds in salted ice, filling them three-quarters full of water slightly whitened with milk; when frozen to one-eighth of an inch in thickness empty out, then fill the mold entirely with water tinted red; when frozen to an eighth of an inch in thickness empty and range them in small fancy blue boxes; place in a freezing box and when ready to serve fill with the strawberry punch.

Fig. 644.

(3509). IMPERIAL PUNCH (Punch à l'Impériale).

Put three gills of pineapple juice in a vessel with the juice of two lemons and the peel of one orange, also half an ounce of tea infused in a pint of water, three gills of rum, two gills of brandy, one gill of kirsch and one gill of maraschino; bring this composition to sixteen degrees, then

freeze. When frozen to an ice add half as much Italian meringue (No. 140), fill the inside of the crowns and serve. These crowns are made of gum paste, (No. 3624) having cardboard boxes fitted into the center.

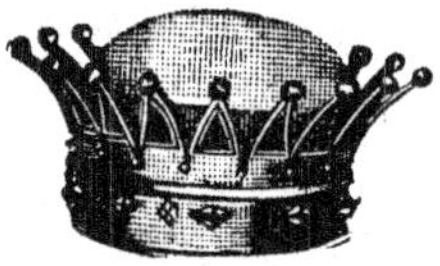

FIG. 645.

(3510). CORDIAL PUNCH—ICED (Punch Glacé aux Liqueurs).

Pour eight gills of cold twenty-eight degree syrup into a glazed vessel; mix with it a quarter of a vanilla bean, a few bits of lemon peel, a gill of lemon juice, the peel of half an orange and the juice of four oranges; let infuse for half an hour then strain; boil till it attains twenty degrees; rectify if necessary. Freeze the preparation in a freezer packed in salted ice after the usual manner, and when smooth and consistent incorporate four Italian meringue egg-whites (No. 140); beat again slowly and add two gills of liqueur or cordial, such as rum, kirsch, prunelle, maraschino, kimmel, etc. Let become consistent once more and serve.

(3511). MILK PUNCH—ICED (Punch Glacé au Lait).

This punch is not to be served the same as a liqueur punch, for it must be thoroughly frozen. Make a preparation with two quarts of milk and four ounces of sugar, strain and freeze. When three-quarters frozen mix in as much whipped cream, then add slowly one gill of rum and one gill of brandy. Use this preparation to fill some glasses, smooth the tops neatly and grate a little nutmeg over; lay them in a lightly imbedded freezing box. This milk punch can be trans-

FIG. 646.

ported quite a distance, for the ice will keep a length of time by putting the glasses in covered cardboard boxes that close hermetically.

(3512). MONTMORENCY PUNCH (Punch à la Montmorency).

Place two quarts of cherry ice cream (No. 3451) in a freezer; mix in a gill of kirsch, half a gill of noyau, half a pint of good Sauterne and a quarter as much Italian meringue (No. 140). With this punch fill some cups

FIG. 647.

made of natural ice slightly reddened.

(3513). NENUPHAR PUNCH—LILIES (Punch Nénuphar).

Place in a vessel the peel of one lemon, the peel of half an orange, half an ounce of coriander seeds and a small piece of Ceylon cinnamon, also four drops of extract of citron; set it in a heater or expose to the sun for four hours in a hermetically closed earthen vessel; afterward pass it through a filter and add a quart of syrup at thirty-two degrees. Mix the whole well and bring the composition to sixteen degrees, coloring to a light pink; strain through a very fine sieve and freeze. When the ice begins to congeal pour in three gills of kirsch and maraschino and half its volume of Italian meringue (No. 140). Use this ice for filling some gum paste Nenuphar lilies and serve at once.

(3514). PARGNY PUNCH (Punch Pargny).

Soak two gelatine leaves in cold water for half an hour, drain and dis-

FIG. 648.

solve in a quart of hot milk, afterward adding one quart of cream, half a pound of sugar, half a pint of good sherry and two gills of rum. Whip the whole well together and strain through a sieve; put it into a freezer and freeze with half as much salt as is required for ordinary ices. Add some Italian meringue (No. 140). This punch should be mellow and not hard; dress in fancy glass cups.

(3515). ROMAN PUNCH (Punch à la Romaine).

This is made with one quart of lemon water ice (No. 3604) well worked in a freezer packed in ice; add to it a little citron peel or extract; the composition should be put in a rather large freezer to allow two Italian meringue egg-whites (No. 140) to be incorporated; it should first be added slowly in small quantities, working it well with the spatula to have it acquire much lightness, then add two gills of rum and a quarter of a bottleful of champagne; work it well and detach from the sides of the freezer. The rum should be poured in gradually, as well as any kind of spirits in different punches; continue until sufficient be added to suit the taste. It is almost impossible to designate the exact quantity, that depending entirely on the quality of the ingredients composing the punch; generally the liquors are only put in just when serving. The punch should be sufficiently liquid to be drank without using spoons and as soon as served. Serve the punch in upright glasses provided with handles. This is sufficient for twelve persons.

(3516). SIBERIAN PUNCH—LALLA ROOKH (Punch à la Sibérienne—Lalla Rookh).

Siberian or Lalla Rookh punch is merely vanilla ice cream (No. 3458) worked in a freezer, mixing in with it a quarter as much Italian meringue (No. 140) and about two gills of good rum for each quart of the ice cream; with this fill plain punch glasses with handles, or cups.

(3517). SUNFLOWER PUNCH (Punch Tournesol).

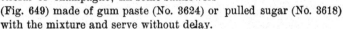

Fig. 649.

Put two quarts of pineapple water ice (No. 3606) in a freezer; work it well, adding half as much Italian meringue (No. 140), two gills of kirsch and a quarter of a bottleful of champagne; fill some sunflowers (Fig. 649) made of gum paste (No. 3624) or pulled sugar (No. 3618) with the mixture and serve without delay.

(3518). STANLEY PUNCH (Punch à la Stanley).

Fig. 650.

If for twelve guests have one quart of syrup at thirty-two degrees, the juice of four lemons, a quart of boiling water having a pound of freshly roasted coffee infused therein and half a vanilla bean; pour the infusion into the preparation, let steep together for two hours, keeping it well closed. Bring the composition to twenty-two degrees and strain through a sieve; freeze while incorporating two Italian meringue egg-whites (No. 140), one gill of kirsch and a gill of maraschino. Arrange the punch inside of a goblet beside which is a heron made of gum paste (No. 3624) surrounded by grasses.

(3519). TOSCA PUNCH (Punch à la Tosca).

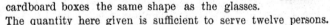

Fig. 651.

Put in a freezer packed in ice one pint of Andalusian ice cream (No. 3446) and as much almond ice cream (No. 3461); work well, adding two gills of noyau and an eighth of a bottle of champagne, also a third as much Italian meringue (No. 140). Color a delicate pink and with the preparation fill some goblets made of colorless natural water frozen to a sufficient thickness, then unmold and set in thick blue cardboard boxes the same shape as the glasses.

The quantity here given is sufficient to serve twelve persons.

(3520). TREMIÈRE PUNCH (Punch à la Tremière).

Fig. 652.

Mix in a freezer one quart of pineapple water ice (No. 3606), one pint of orange ice (No. 3605) and one pint of strawberry ice (No. 3607). When thoroughly mixed incorporate a third of its volume of Italian meringue (No. 140), three gills of kirsch and a quarter of a bottle of champagne; with this preparation fill some Tremière roses (Fig. 652) made of gum paste (No. 3624), or else they can be made of pulled sugar, and served at once.

(3521). AMERICAN SHERBET (Sorbet à l'Américaine).

Prepare some glasses of ice, using molds as shown herewith (Fig. 653), they being made in two pieces which, when unmolded, are joined together. Fill them just when ready to serve with this preparation. Have ready a water ice of one quart of water, one pound of sugar, the peel of two oranges and of one lemon, the juice of eight oranges and of six lemons; boil to attain sixteen degrees, pass through a fine sieve, then freeze, incorporating into the ice when about serving a quarter of a bottleful of American champagne mixed with two gills of kirsch and one of prunelle.

Fig. 653.

(3522). ANDALUSIAN SHERBET (Sorbet Andalouse).

Trim some fine orange peel to represent baskets (Fig. 656); scallop their borders with the punch shown in Fig. 654; decorate with narrow ribbons and freeze for one hour in a freezing box. Squeeze out the juice of four oranges and two lemons; place this in a vessel, add the peel of half an

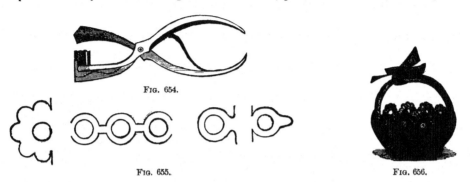

FIG. 654.

FIG. 655.

FIG. 656.

orange, two drops of extract of bitter orange and two drops of the extract of lemon; bring the composition to twenty-two degrees; strain through a fine sieve and freeze. When frozen mix in one gill of Curaçoa and as much kirsch; fill the orange peel baskets and serve at once.

(3523). CALIFORNIAN SHERBET (Sorbet Californienne).

FIG. 657.   FIG. 658.

In a vessel place four gills of syrup at thirty-five degrees, one gill of brandy, one gill of maraschino, half a bottleful of California champagne, the peel of one and the juice of three oranges, four gills of pineapple juice and the juice of twelve lemons. Reduce until it registers sixteen degrees with the saccharometer; strain through a fine wire sieve and freeze. Imbed in ice some molds as shown in Fig. 657; decorate with sprigs of fresh mint and fill with plain, colorless water; when the ice is sufficiently frozen unmold and keep them on ice until required for serving the sherbet, filling and serving them without any delay.

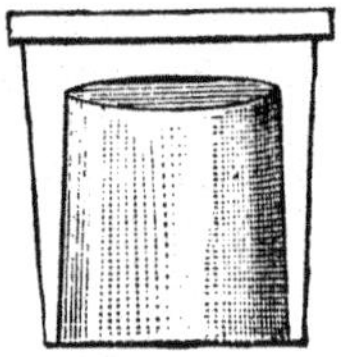

(3524). MEPHISTO SHERBET (Sorbet à la Méphisto).

Infuse for three hours in one quart of boiling syrup ten ounces of torrefied fresh cocoa and half a stick of vanilla; add the juice of four lemons and one bottleful of good white wine; bring to twenty-two degrees, then freeze; incorporate, just when ready to serve, two gills of brandy and a gill of rum; with this preparation fill a dice box and serve at once. The box and dice should be of gum paste (No. 3624) or pasteboard.

FIG. 659.

(3525). PARADISE SHERBET (Sorbet Paradis).

Prepare an orange water ice (No. 3605), into which incorporate a little carmine, kirsch and orange flower water. This is dressed in a nest with a small bird perched on its edge. The bird, the interior and the bottom should be made of gum paste (No. 3624); imitate the outside of the nest with spun sugar and the grass with fillets of angelica. Serve at once.

(3526). PARFAIT AMOUR SHERBET (Sorbet Parfait Amour).

FIG. 660.

Pour into a freezer one pint of raspberry water ice (No. 3607), one pint of orange water ice (No. 3605) and a pint of cherry water ice (No. 3602); mix thoroughly and add to them half a gill of Curaçoa, half a gill of maraschino, one gill of kirsch or one gill parfait amour cordial and half a pint of champagne just when ready to serve. Dress in tulips made of gum paste (No. 3624) or pulled sugar (No. 3618).

(3527). PÂQUERETTE SHERBET (Sorbet Pâquerette).

A light apricot ice cream (No. 3451), having one quart for ten persons; put it into an imbedded freezer and incorporate one gill of Madeira and one gill of brandy and noyau. With this sherbet fill the inside case found in the handled basket, having this trimmed with a ribbon bow. A small bunch of flowers may be fastened to it also. When prepared to serve put the case filled with the sherbet inside the basket.

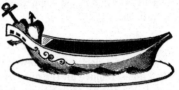

FIG. 661.

FIG. 662.

(3528). REBECCA SHERBET (Sorbet Rébecca).

Place in a freezer one quart of orange water ice (No. 3605) and one of lemon water ice (No. 3604); work both together thoroughly, mixing in a gill of kirsch and half a bottleful of champagne. This sherbet is served in small cases representing baskets, and decorated with a rich ribbon bow, or in a little well made of gum paste (No. 3624).

(3529). VENETIAN SHERBET (Sorbet à la Vénitienne).

Place in a vessel one pound of grated pineapple with a quart of twenty-degree boiling hot syrup, also half a vanilla stick. Two hours later strain forcibly through a sieve and add one gill of kirsch, one gill of brandy and a quarter of a bottleful of champagne. Serve in small gondolas (Fig. 663), made of gum paste (No. 3624).

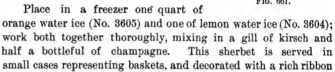

FIG. 663.

(3530). YOUNG AMERICA SHERBET (Sorbet Jeune Amérique).

Imitate a boat in gum paste (No. 3624), standing it on a thin board; fasten an American flag at the stern and fill the empty boat with the following sherbet: Place in a vessel one quart of thirty-two degree syrup, one quart of syrup of pears and currants and one gill of lemon juice, the juice of four oranges, half an orange peel and a little vanilla. Infuse for one hour, then bring it to thirty-two degrees; pass through a fine sieve and freeze. Just when prepared to serve incorporate one gill of kirsch, one gill of rum and a quarter of a bottle of champagne.

FIG. 664.

(3531). SABAYON À LA CANETTI (Sabayon à la Canetti).

Break twelve raw egg-yolks in a deep saucepan with five ounces of sugar; whip the yolks and sugar together with a wooden beater or small wire whisk, rotating either one or the other between both hands; add slowly four gills of good white wine, then a stick of vanilla, the peel of half a lemon and a little cinnamon. Place the saucepan either on a very slow fire or in a bain-marie until the preparation becomes quite frothy and firm; remove it from the fire, lay it on ice and continue the beating process. When very cold suppress the peel and vanilla and stir in one quart of whipped cream (No. 50) and half a gill of kirsch. Serve this preparation in high glasses, paper cases, or else silver souffle casseroles.

(3532). SABAYON À LA DENARI (Sabayon à la Denari).

Prepare a sabayon with Lunel wine, putting twelve egg-yolks in a deep saucepan with five ounces of sugar; beat well with the whip or whisk and slowly add four gills of Lunel wine and a stick of vanilla. Beat the preparation in a bain-marie or else over a slow fire until thoroughly frothy and firm, then remove from the fire and lay it on ice, continuing to beat until quite firm; mix in the same volume of whipped cream (No. 50) and with this preparation fill up some glasses in alternate layers of the sabayon and lady fingers soaked in maraschino, adding a few raspberries placed here and there. Cover the top with whipped cream and freeze in a freezing box, serving when well frozen.

(3533). ALCAZAR SOUFFLÉS—ICED (Soufflés Glacés à l'Alcazar).

Fill some paper cases with the following: Pour some vanilla ice cream (No. 3458) into a metal vessel; lay it on salted ice, stirring well with a spoon, mixing in as much whipped cream, finishing with macaroons and broken chestnuts infused in maraschino; with this preparation imitate the shape of some soufflés just taken from the oven. Have some pulverized macaroons sifted through a fine sieve and bestrew the soufflés with this powder; cut a gash on the side, then cover with fine powdered sugar. Color quickly in a brisk oven and then put into the freezing box; pack it on ice to freeze for one hour; serve on folded napkins.

FIG. 665.

(3534). FAVART SOUFFLÉS (Soufflés Glacés à la Favart).

Have ready a burnt almond ice cream preparation (No. 3455); when frozen mix into it as much whipped cream and with this partly fill some crimped paper cases; on top lay slices of hazelnut biscuit (No. 3241) soaked in maraschino, and strawberries in their juice macerated in kirsch; cover and shape to resemble baked soufflés; besprinkle with powdered macaroons and icing sugar; color briskly in a quick oven, then stand them on the shelves of a tin freezing box; freeze for one hour and serve.

(3535). PALMYRA SOUFFLÉ (Soufflé Glacé Palmyre).

Cook in a slack oven a few good, whole, unpeeled russet apples placed in an earthen dish; when done, remove all the pulp and rub it through a sieve. Put four gills of this into a vessel with half a pound of fine sugar flavored with vanilla, and beat on ice to give it body, then mix in a pint of whipped cream flavored with maraschino. Dress this preparation in separate layers in a soufflé dish (Fig. 182), alternating each one with a layer of almond biscuit soaked in maraschino and well-drained brandied figs; shape it like a dome, then freeze it for forty minutes in salted ice in a freezing box. After taking it out decorate the dome with sweetened and vanilla-flavored whipped cream, also candied fruits; return it to the freezing box and serve half an hour later.

(3536). SPONGADE À LA MÉDICIS (Spongade à la Médicis).

Cut up finely the peel of a citron and an orange; have also some pistachios and cherries divided in four, and pour kirsch over. Take four gills of cold syrup at thirty-five degrees, the juice of five oranges, the peel of two, the same of one lemon, one gill of vanilla syrup and two gills of egg-whites. Infuse together for half an hour, and bring the preparation to twenty-two degrees; pass it through a fine sieve. Freeze the composition by working it with a spatula to incorporate as much air as possible so as to obtain a very light ice, and then mix in the above fruits. Coat a two-quart spongade mold with raspberry ice cream (No. 3451) or water ice; fill with the preparation, press down the cover and freeze for one hour; unmold, dress on a folded napkin and surround the spongade with small cakes.

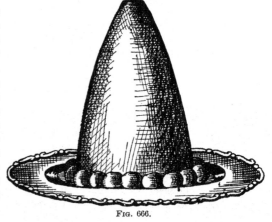

FIG. 666.

(3537). CREAM SPONGADE À LA PARÉPA (Spongade Crème à la Parépa).

Cream spongades are made by putting into a vessel four gills of fresh cream and almond milk made with five ounces of sweet and one ounce of bitter almonds; also eight egg-whites, mixing in three-quarters of a pound of sugar; beat well together, strain and freeze in medium-sized freezers; one to congeal the mixture and the other to work it. When the composition is in the first freezer, turn the latter quickly with the right hand, and as soon as the preparation adheres to the sides remove it to the second or smaller one, then work to give it body, and to incorporate plenty of air into the ice. Then add a salpicon of fruits cut in quarter-inch squares. Mold the ice in a spongade-shaped mold (Fig. 666), coated inside with pistachio cream.

(3538). ALASKA, FLORIDA (Alaska, Florida).

Prepare a very fine vanilla-flavored Savoy biscuit paste (No. 3231). Butter some plain molds two and three-quarters inches in diameter by one and a half inches in depth; dip them in fecula or flour, and fill two-thirds full with the paste. Cook, turn them out and make an incision all around the bottom; hollow out the cakes, and mask the empty space with apricot marmalade (No. 3675). Have some ice cream molds shaped as shown in Fig. 667, fill them half with uncooked banana ice cream (No. 3541), and half with uncooked vanilla ice cream (No. 3466); freeze, unmold and lay them in the hollow of the prepared biscuits; keep in a freezing box or cave. Prepare also a meringue with twelve egg-whites and one pound of sugar. A few moments before serving place each biscuit with its ice on a small lace paper, and cover

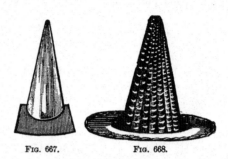

Fig. 667.   Fig. 668.

one after the other with the meringue pushed through a pocket furnished with a channeled socket, beginning at the bottom and diminishing the thickness until the top is reached; color this meringue for two minutes in a hot oven, and when a light golden brown remove and serve at once.

(3539). ALEXANDRIA (Alexandria).

Fig. 669.

Have in a tin basin ten raw egg-yolks and twelve ounces of sugar; beat both well together, diluting with a quart of boiling milk, adding the peel of one orange. Set this on a slow fire, stir and cook until the preparation covers the spatula, then leave to cool off. Add the pulp of four bananas, one pint of cream and two gills of vanilla syrup at thirty-two degrees; strain through a sieve, freeze and mix into this ice one gill of Curaçoa and half as much whipped cream. With this frozen preparation fill some crescent-shaped molds, pack in ice and freeze for half an hour. Unmold and decorate each side with lozenges of angelica and candied cherries, and stand them on whipped cream having had crushed macaroons soaked in maraschino mingled in.

(3540). ASPARAGUS (Asperges).

Cook one pound of asparagus tops in plenty of unsalted water; drain and lay them in a tinned basin with ten egg-yolks and twelve ounces of sugar; mix thoroughly, incorporating a pint of boiling milk; cook this preparation without allowing to boil, and put aside to cool, then add a pint of cream; color a third part to a pale green; strain through a sieve, and freeze the parts separately. With this ice fill some asparagus-shaped molds, the stalks or third part to be of the green ice, and the remainder white. Freeze the molds for half an hour, unmold, tie in bunches of three with a pink ribbon, and dress on napkins. Serve separately a sauce made of vanilla ice cream (No. 3458), whipped cream (No. 50) and maraschino. Asparagus can also be imitated by filling the molds with pistachio (No. 3454) and vanilla ice cream (No. 3458), and serving the same as the above.

Fig. 670.

(3541). BANANAS IN SURPRISE (Bananes en Surprise).

Fig. 671.

The proportions for eight large bananas is one quart of cream, the pulp of four bananas and one pound of sugar; press through a fine sieve and freeze. Pare and cleanse the peels nicely; freeze them in a freezer for one hour and fill with the above cream, putting inside of them a salpicon of candied fruits macerated in maraschino. Put the bananas into a freezing box well packed in ice and leave to harden for several hours. Dress on a folded napkin and serve.

(3542). BLIDAH (Blidah).

Fill a lozenge-shaped mold with cherry ice cream (No. 3451) or currant water ice (No. 3602); unmold and put it in the bottom of a Montelimar mold packed in ice; finish filling the lozenged

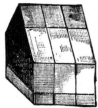

part of the mold with mandarin water ice and the rest with vanilla ice cream (No. 3458), into which mix the pulp of two oranges macerated for an hour in maraschino. Fill the molds well, force on the cover, pack and freeze for one hour; unmold and cutting in half-inch slices dress each slice on lace paper and serve. The length of the mold is eight inches long inside, the height is three and three-quarters inches and the width at its base is three and a quarter inches. The lozenge is the same length as the larger mold and its height is two inches.

FIG. 672.

(3543). CARAMEL BOUCHÉES (Bouchées au Caramel).

Lay on a sheet of paper some half-spherical rounds of lady finger paste (No. 3377), each two and a half inches in diameter; when cooked empty out the centers. Put a quarter of a pound of strawberry juice in a vessel with a pint of thirty-two degree syrup and a little vanilla; strain through a fine sieve, freeze and then mix in two Italian meringue egg-whites (No. 140) and half a pound of preserved pineapple cut in three-sixteenths inch squares and macerated in kirsch. With this ice fill the interior of the biscuits, range one on top of the other, fastening them well together;

FIG. 673.

lay them in a freezing box for one hour to congeal the ice and then dip them in sugar cooked to "crack" (No. 171). Dress these balls on rounds of waffles three inches in diameter; serve them plain or scatter over finely shredded green pistachios.

(3544). CAULIFLOWER WITH MARCHIONESS RICE (Choux-fleurs au Riz Marquise).

Blanch half a pound of rice; cook it in milk for half an hour, pass through a fine sieve and mix with it double as much hazel-nut ice cream (No. 3464). Fill a cauliflower-form mold with three pints of this preparation, keeping a cavity in the center, and fill this with the well-cooked boiled rice marinated in vanilla syrup and having added to it a salpicon of fresh fruits, macaroons and lady fingers steeped in maraschino. Close the mold after it is quite full, pack in salted ice and freeze for one hour, then unmold on a folded napkin and serve with a separate sauce-boatful of

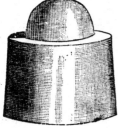

sauce prepared with vanilla ice (No. 3458) and maraschino mixed together, to which add an equal volume of whipped cream (No. 50).

(3545). CEYLON WITH COFFEE (Ceylan au Café).

Put ten egg-yolks in a tinned basin; whip in three gills of very strong coffee and bring the preparation to twenty-two degrees with a syrup gauge; set the basin on a slow fire, stir and remove when it covers the spoon, then strain through a fine sieve; return it to the cleaned basin, beat again on ice till it attains a light consistency. Coat a mold (Fig. 674) with uncooked cinnamon ice cream (No. 3450), fill the center with the coffee composition, close forcibly, pack and freeze for one hour. Unmold and dress on a folded napkin and surround with

FIG. 674.

vanilla lady bouchées (No. 3376).

(3546). CHARLOTTE CORDAY (Charlotte Corday).

Obtain some round crimped paper cases; cover the bottoms and sides with uncooked Andalusian ice cream (No. 3446) and fill the centers with biscuit glacé preparation with vanilla (No. 3438), adding a little maraschino to it; also put in some candied orange peel cut in exceedingly thin fillets;

Fig. 675.

powder the tops with pulverized macaroons and cover this with Andalusian ice cream and candied fruits. Lay them in a freezing box for an hour to finish freezing.

(3547). CORN (Maïs).

Fig. 676.

Fill tin molds, representing a medium-sized ear of corn, partly with hazel-nut ice cream (No. 3464) and partly with lemon water ice (No. 3604); in the center of each ear of corn lay pieces of lady fingers soaked in prunelle. Close the molds forcibly, pack and freeze; three-quarters of an hour after, unmold, dress on a napkin and serve with a bowlful of vanilla ice cream (No. 3458) and whipped cream (No. 50), half of each, well beaten together, adding a little kirsch.

(3548). COUNTESS LEDA ICE CREAM (Glace à la Comtesse Léda).

FIG. 677.

Coat with strawberry ice cream (No. 3451) the inside of a mold the shape of the annexed cut (Fig. 677), able to contain one quart and a half to two quarts of preparation, having previously packed it well in salted ice; fill the center with uncooked vanilla ice cream (No. 3466), into which have mixed fresh peaches cut in four and infused in maraschino, and freeze for one hour and a half. At the same time mold a swan with almond ice cream (No. 3461). At the moment of serving unmold the large form on a napkin. Surround the base with lady bouchées frosted with vanilla and strawberry frosting (No. 3376), and on the top dress the swan. Serve separately a kirsch sauce, made with vanilla ice cream (No. 3458) and whipped cream (No. 50), beaten together with a little kirsch.

(3549). DICE, DOMINOES AND CARDS (Dés, Dominos et Cartes).

Dice.—Fill some cube-shaped tin molds two inches in diameter with hazel-nut ice cream (No. 3464); in the center lay some macaroons soaked in maraschino; pack in salted ice, freeze and unmold half an hour later. Imitate the black dots of the dice with small chocolate pastilles three-sixteenths of an inch in diameter, pressing them down into the ice; put them in a freezing box to

FIG. 678.

FIG. 679.

FIG. 680.

FIG. 681.

freeze until the ice has become firm, then stand on a lace paper and cover each dice with a box of wafers cut square, being two and three-quarters inches on each side, held together with sugar cooked to "crack" (No. 171); fasten on top a quarter-inch ball of almond paste (No. 125) of four distinct colors, iced with caramel, or else a walnut emptied and filled with small candies; fasten together to enclose the candies.

Dominoes.—Have hinged tin molds two and three-eighths inches long by one and three-eighths wide and half an inch high, opening through their thickness; fill them half full with virgin maraschino cream and the other half with chocolate (No. 3449); pack in ice for half an hour, unmold, and in the center of the white side, and across from side to side, lay a strip of angelica, and on both sides of this range small dots of chocolate to imitate dominoes; form a small easel of wafers with a ledge at the base; on each side place two dominoes, making four for each guest, and over the whole stand a cover as explained for the dice.

Cards.—Procure square boxes made of pasteboard, each panel having a playing card on it. These boxes should have double boxes filling in the interior; fill this inside box with ice cream, then serve.

(3550). EGGS À LA TREMONTAINE, RED WINE SAUCE (Œufs à la Tremontaine, Sauce au Vin Rouge).

Fig. 682.

Mix some fruits previously cut dice shaped with whipped cream (No. 50); fill spherical molds of one and one-eighth inches in diameter, freeze and unmold. Coat some hinged tinned molds, the shape of an egg, containing a gill each, with pistachio ice cream (No. 3454); in the center place the spherically molded whipped cream, close and clean off the surplus, freeze, unmold and serve on a folded napkin. Serve separately a red wine sauce prepared as follows: Infuse some cinnamon and a slice of lemon in good red wine; sweeten and stand the saucepan on the fire. As soon as the wine begins to whiten thicken with fecula diluted in cold water, strain, leave stand till very cold, then serve.

(3551). ESMERALDA ICE CREAM (Glace à l'Esméralda).

Mix one pint of strawberry pulp, three pints of cream, three quarters of a one pound of sugar; strain through a fine sieve, freeze and stir in as much whipped cream (No. 50). Pound four ounces of burnt almonds with a quarter of a vanilla bean and half a gill of cream; put into a basin six egg-yolks and five ounces of sugar; dilute with half a pint of boiling milk and cook on a slow fire without boiling; cool and add a pint of cream and a little orange flower water; freeze. Stir in an ounce and a half of the finely pounded burnt almonds and an ounce and a half of shredded pistachios. Fill a pyramid-shaped mold made in two separate longitudinal divisions, half with the strawberry and the other half with the burnt almond preparation; freeze for half an hour, unmold and on top place an apricot steeped in prunelle cherries.

Fig. 683.

(3552). FRASCATI ICE CREAM (Glace Frascati).

Fill a round shallow tin mold, having flaring sides with a depression in the center, the dimensions being three inches in diameter and one inch deep, with light vanilla ice cream preparation (No. 3458); pack in ice and freeze for half an hour, unmold and put in the center some fiori di latte with kirsch (No. 3469); lay them in the freezing box to freeze, then on top of each set a macaroon soaked in maraschino; push through a pocket some very firm iced biscuit preparation, turning it around to form into a pyramid; decorate the top with candied fruits; freeze for three-quarters of an hour before serving.

Fig. 684.

(3553). FROMAGE GLACÉ (Fromage Glacé).

Have an iced mold (see Fig. 684); divide it in three parts with partitions made of tin and pack it well in salted ice. Put into a vessel three-quarters of a pound of apricot pulp, a gill and a half of raspberry juice, the juice of two oranges, three-quarters of a pound of powdered sugar and one pint of cream; strain this through a sieve and freeze, adding to it the same quantity of whipped cream (No. 50). Arrange this preparation in one of the compartments, in the other strawberry water ice (No. 3607), and in the third hazel-nut ice cream (No. 3464), adding apricots macerated in maraschino. Take the partitions out, fill up, coat well, pack the mold in salted ice, freeze for one hour, then unmold on a napkin. This preparation is rarely used nowadays.

(3554). HARLEQUIN ICE CREAM (Glace Arlequin).

This ice is molded in four triangular-shaped molds; fill one with coffee ice cream (No. 3463), another with vanilla (No. 3458), another with pistachio (No. 3454) and the fourth with strawberry ice (No. 3607). Imbed and freeze for half an hour, then unmold. Put them in a brick-shaped mold three inches square. The triangles should be two inches on one side by an inch and a half in height. The mold should be eight inches long. Place the triangles in the mold, as shown in Fig. 686, having the vanilla at the bottom, one side the strawberry, the other the pistachio and keeping the coffee on the top. Press the cover down well so no empty space remains and freeze for half an hour. Now mold some chocolate ice cream in spherical molds an inch and a quarter in diameter, freeze for half an hour and unmold the whole. Cut the brick up in slices with a special knife (Fig. 700) dipped in hot water, and place each one on a four-inch square sheet of lace paper; fasten the chocolate drops exactly on the center and put them into a freezing box for half an hour before serving. All creams that are to be

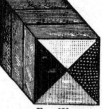

FIG. 685.　　　　FIG. 686.

cut should be laid on a small board so as to facilitate cutting and removing them, and to keep them in good shape.

(3555). JARDINIÈRE CUTLETS (Côtelettes Jardinière).

Blanch half a pound of rice, refresh and return it to the saucepan with a pint and a half of boiling cream, half a pound of sugar and the peel of half a lemon. Boil up once, push it into the oven for an hour, then remove and whip it well, adding a quart of cream; freeze and as the preparation takes body mix into it as much sweetened whipped cream as there is ice. Mold in cutlet-

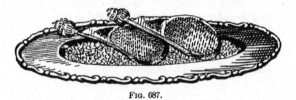

FIG. 687.

shaped molds and when thoroughly frozen turn them out and dip each one in macaroon dust sifted through a fine sieve. Dress on a salpicon of fruit macerated in maraschino and thickened with apricot marmalade (No. 3675) prepared with maraschino; trim the handles with frills (No. 10) and serve at once.

(3556). LA GRANDINA (La Grandina).

FIG. 688.

Coat some oval-shaped plaited paper cases with a part of the following ice: Whip together one pint of raspberries, the peel of one orange and the juice of three, also the juice of six lemons; tint this a beautiful pale red and boil, adding enough sugar to make a twenty-two degree syrup; strain through a fine sieve and freeze. When consistent and smooth add to it half as much whipped cream and two ounces of finely cut-up citron peel; partly fill the inside of the cases with iced chocolate biscuit preparation flavored with vanilla, into which mix pounded macaroons and a few roasted and pulverized hazel-nuts; freeze for one hour, putting the cases in a freezing box and finish filling with the raspberry ice, having it slightly bomb-shaped on top; decorate with whole cherries placed directly in the center; dredge the top with finely shredded pistachios; return to the freezing box and freeze for one hour.

(3557). LEMONS IN SURPRISE (Citrons en Surprise).

FIG. 689.

Pour a quart of fresh cream into a vessel, pound two ounces of sweet almonds and a few bitter almonds with twelve ounces of sugar; sift through a sieve and put it with the cream, adding two gills of maraschino and four ounces of candied fruits cut in quarter-inch squares; tint it to a soft pink, then freeze. With this cream fill some large lemons that have been emptied. Tie around with ribbons the same as shown in Fig. 689.

(3558). LEONA ICE CREAM (Glace Léona).

First prepare some natural ice glasses the shape of Fig. 690. (For preparing these glasses see No. 3434.) When they are all ready put them into a freezing box until serving time. Prepare some whipped cream (No. 50) flavored with maraschino and drain it on a sieve. Make an ice with half a pound of almonds, ground a few at a time, with half a pound of sugar and a pint of water, adding two gelatine leaves dissolved in two gills of water, and a gill of vanilla syrup; strain this through a fine tammy and freeze in slightly salted ice; work well with the spatula, incorporating as much whipped cream and a salpicon of assorted fruits cut in quarter-inch squares, macerated in kirsch and drained. With this ice fill some spiral-shaped molds and pack in ice. Half an hour later, just when prepared to serve, fill the glasses with the whipped cream. Unmold the ices, lay them over the cream and on top of each place a brandied cherry or one made of almond paste (No. 125); serve at once.

FIG. 690.

(3559). MACÉDOINE CROQUETTES (Croquettes Macédoine)

Mold in tins the size and shape of a medium croquette some burnt almond cream (No. 3455), ranging exactly in the center some biscuits soaked in maraschino; freeze for half an hour, then unmold and roll in pulverized macaroons sifted through a sieve. Have in an ice cream freezer all sorts of fresh or preserved fruits cut in quarter-inch squares; to them add lemon juice, maraschino and champagne; freeze with very little ice and when extremely cold drain properly and mix in whipped cream (No. 50); dress on saucers, laying the croquettes over, one or two on each saucer.

(3560). MACÉDOINE OF FRUITS AND ST. JACQUES CUPS (Macédoine de Fruits et Coupes St. Jacques).

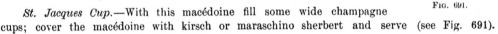

Macédoine.—Lay in a vessel one peeled banana cut in half-inch squares, one well-peeled orange having the meats lying between the intersections removed with a knife and all the seeds suppressed, a slice of pineapple half an inch thick cut in dice, four ounces of grapes, two ounces of strawberries or raspberries, four ounces of cherries, pears or peaches, half a gill of kirsch or maraschino and a little powdered sugar; mingle all together and keep it cold in a freezer with ice packed around; serve in a compote dish.

FIG. 691.

St. Jacques Cup.—With this macédoine fill some wide champagne cups; cover the macédoine with kirsch or maraschino sherbert and serve (see Fig. 691).

(3561). MADELEINE ICE CREAM (Glace Madeleine).

Decorate a Madeleine mold (Fig. 692) with candied fruits; coat the inside with vanilla ice cream (No. 3458) and fill with hazel-nut ice cream (No. 3464) into which have mingled a salpicon of fruits and whipped cream. In the very center lay a little apricot marmalade (No. 3675); pack this mold in ice and freeze for two hours; unmold on a napkin and surround with fancy cakes; serve at the same time a sauce made of whipped cream, vanilla ice cream and Curaçoa.

FIG. 692.

(3562). MADRILIAN (Madrilène).

Place in a vessel twelve raw egg-yolks and half a pound of sugar, diluting slowly with a pint of boiling milk that has just had a quarter of a vanilla stick infused therein for fifteen minutes; strain through a fine sieve. Butter some timbale molds (No. 3, Fig. 137) and fill them with the preparation; stand them in a sautoir with boiling water to reach to half their height and poach; when they are firm to the touch leave stand till cold, then unmold. Pound a quarter of a pound of sweet almonds and a few bitter ones, all freshly peeled; moisten slowly with a quart of milk and strain forcibly through a napkin; add ten ounces of sugar and a gill of kirsch, also a little vanilla syrup (No. 3165); strain, freeze, and when the ice has congealed mix in one Italian meringue egg-white (No. 140). Mold in cylindrical molds two and a half inches in diameter by two inches in height, placing the small timbale directly in the center; freeze for half an hour, then unmold and lay on lace paper; on top have a handsome brandied plum, and around this and the base set an even row of cherries cut in two.

(3563). MARVELOUS (Merveilleuse).

FIG. 693.

Break six egg-yolks in a tinned basin with twelve ounces of sugar, a quart of boiling milk, and half a pound of freshly roasted, coarsely ground coffee; set the basin on a moderate fire and stir continuously, without permitting it to boil, until the preparation will cover the spatula; strain through a fine sieve, leave till cold and freeze, adding the same quantity of sweetened whipped cream, half a pound of chopped burnt almonds, and as much candied chestnuts broken in small pieces. Put one pint of orange water ice (No. 3605) in a freezer with the same amount of burnt hazel-nut ice cream (No. 3464) and as much whipped cream. With this preparation coat some small paper cases, fill the inside with the first preparation and surround with orange flowers.

(3564). MIGNON ICE CREAM (Glace à la Mignonne).

FIG. 694.

Boil a quarter of a pound of rice in water with the juice of a lemon; put it into a vessel and pour over some vanilla syrup (No. 3165) at thirty-two degrees. Place in a freezer one pint of No. 1 vanilla ice cream (No. 3458), and the well-drained rice. With this cream fill some shell-shaped tin molds; freeze and unmold after one hour, lay in the center some fresh fruits and soaked macaroons, and cover the whole with a layer of very smooth whipped cream; decorate the top with whipped cream pushed through a cornet; freeze and serve with a sauce made of apricot marmalade (No. 3675) and kirsch.

(3565). MOKABELLE (Mokabelle).

Put into a coffee filter a quarter of a pound of ground coffee and half a vanilla stick; moisten with a pint of water to obtain a very highly concentrated extract of coffee, then add to it sufficient syrup to bring the composition to twenty-two degrees, strain through a tammy, freeze and when well congealed pour in as much whipped cream (No. 50). With this ice fill some cups, either of sugar, china or fancy pasteboard ones; return to the freezing box and freeze once more. If desired the tops can be covered with whipped cream flavored with extract of coffee and kirsch mixed together.

(3566). MONTÉLIMAR WITH HAZEL-NUT CREAM (Montélimar à la Crème aux Noisettes).

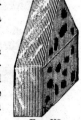

FIG. 695.

Hazel-nut Cream.—Roast a quarter of a pound of hazel-nuts; carefully remove their outer skins and pound with two gills of cream. Put in a tinned basin twelve egg-whites and ten ounces of sugar; stir to mix thoroughly, then moisten with a pint of boiling milk; set the basin on a slow fire, stir continuously, then remove from the fire when the preparation covers the spatula, add the nuts and leave stand till cool. Pour in a pint of rich sweet cream; strain through a sieve and freeze.

Montélimar.—Pound in a mortar three ounces of peeled sweet almonds with a gill of kirsch; cook ten ounces of sugar to three hundred and two degrees Fahrenheit or "small crack;" mix it slowly in a mortar with the almonds, leave till cold, then divide it into three parts; one of these color red with vegetal carmine flavored with Curaçoa, the other color green with spinach green or vegetal green flavored with orange flower water, and keep the third part white; roll them each into three-eighths of an inch thick strings. Cut some lady fingers (No. 3377) to the same size, and baste over with maraschino; pack a Montélimar mold (Fig. 695) in ice; coat it with a thin layer of the nut ice cream (No. 3461), fill it perfectly full, intermingling the various colors of almond paste and the biscuits, and close it forcibly. Two hours after unmold and cut in slices to serve.

(3567). MUFFS À LA DÉJAZET, VENUS CREAM (Manchons à la Déjazet, Crème Vénus).

Prepare the muffs according to the following description: Sift through a sieve one-quarter of a pound of sugar, place it in a vessel with four whole eggs, a quarter of a pound of flour and a little powdered vanilla; spread this on a buttered and floured baking sheet to the thickness of about one-

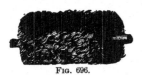

Fig. 696.

sixteenth of an inch, and bake in a brisk oven; divide this cake into bands each six and a quarter inches long by two and a half wide, roll them on a piece of rounded wood two inches in diameter, cover them with a light layer of meringue (No. 140), and over this scatter in profusion some pistachios and almonds, chopped in eighth of an inch pieces, mixing them with dried currants.

Venus Cream.—Put into a vessel one vanilla bean, as much Ceylon cinnamon broken small, a little mace and the peel of an orange; boil a quart of very fresh cream, pour it over the spices, cover and leave infuse for three hours. Break ten egg-yolks in a basin, work well with half a pound of sugar and the boiled cream, coloring it to a soft pink. Cook this preparation, let stand till cold, then strain through a fine sieve; freeze and add to this ice one quart of whipped cream. Dress each muff on a separate sheet of paper; fill the bottom with a quarter of an inch thick layer of pistachio cream (No. 3454), over this the Venus cream, and on top another one of pistachio to close the orifice. Keep in the freezing box for half an hour. When serving fasten in the center of both ends a stick of angelica.

(3568). MUSHROOMS (Champignons).

For these have some molds representing mushrooms of various sizes; fill them with maraschino ice cream (No. 3462), freeze, unmold and dip the ends or stalks in grated chocolate to imitate the roots. Dress piled high on a folded napkin.

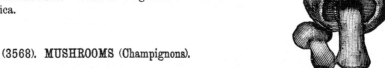

Fig. 697.

(3569). NEAPOLITAN ICE CREAM (Glace Napolitaine).

Pack in a freezer a Neapolitan mold as represented in Fig. 698; it must be made in three divisions; fill one of the round parts with vanilla ice cream (No. 3458), the other with pistachio ice cream (No. 3454), and the flat or center part with strawberry water ice (No. 3607), having the mold

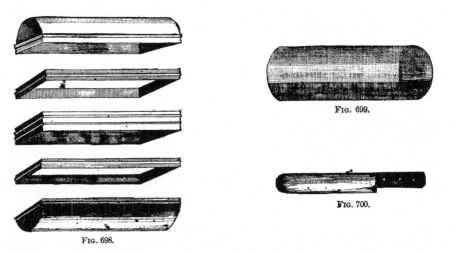

Fig. 699.

Fig. 700.

Fig. 698.

quite full so that when forcibly closed the surplus cream runs out all around, thus preventing the ice from becoming salty; pack it well in ice and let freeze for one hour; unmold on a small board and cut it into five-eighths of an inch slices with a special tinned copper or silver-plated knife so as not to blacken the ice (Fig. 700); this knife should be dipped into warm water every time a slice is cut. Dress these slices on small lace papers.

(3570). BASKET FILLED WITH ORANGES (Panier Garni d'Oranges).

The basket is of wicker furnished with an inside case; one of the handles must be trimmed with a ribbon. Fill the inside case with Andalusian ice cream (No. 3446) into which incorporate as much whipped cream (No. 50). Pare some oranges to the pulp, remove the white skin adhering to each section and marinate them in a little maraschino, sugar and kirsch; with these pieces of orange decorate the top of the cream and serve.

(3571). POSILIPO ORANGES (Oranges Posilipo).

FIG. 701.

Cut some three-inch in diameter oranges straight through the center; empty the insides entirely, scallop the edge of the peel with a machine (Fig. 654) and cut some uniform slits half an inch below this edge; run a ribbon through, tying it in a bow on one side. Have a spherical mold two and three-quarters inches in diameter and divided in three even hinged parts; fill one of these parts with strawberry ice cream (No. 3451), the other with vanilla ice cream (No. 3458) and the third with pistachio ice cream (No. 3454); equalize all these parts so that when the mold is closed there will be no more than just sufficient to fill them. Pack in ice and freeze for one hour; unmold and lay the pistachio side in the half orange; stick a piece of angelica in the top, it being run through a preserved cherry.

FIG. 702.

(3572). SEVILLE ORANGES, AND ORANGE MACEDOINE BASKETS (Oranges à la Séville et Paniers d'Oranges Macédoine).

Prepare some Seville oranges or mandarins the same as for orange Russian punch (No. 3613); after they have been emptied and are well wiped inwardly, freeze, then fill with vanilla ice cream (No. 3458) into which has been added some candied orange and citron peel cut in very thin shreds and macerated in a little maraschino, Curaçoa and kirsch. Serve, surrounding each one with green smilax. The baskets are prepared the same as the Andalusian (No. 3522), filling them with a cooked almond or hazel-nut cream (No. 3464), into which mix a macédoine of fruits; here and there on top scatter some halved pistachios and cherries.

(3573). PARISIAN ICE CREAM (Glace à la Parisienne).

Have some conical molds rounded on one end and pointed on the other (Fig. 703); fill them half with strawberry ice cream (No. 3451) and half with vanilla ice cream (No. 3458). The idea of using these molds is to avoid the necessity of using a spoon to mold the ice. On the round end lay a small macaroon soaked in maraschino; close the mold and remove any surplus ice issuing from the joints; pack in ice and freeze for an hour. On removing dress them in specially made glasses as shown in Fig. 703, and serve.

FIG. 703.

(3574). PEARS OR APPLES IN SURPRISE (Poires ou Pommes en Surprise).

Empty out the insides of the fruit, either apples, pears, oranges or others, lay them in a

FIG. 704.

FIG. 705.

freezer imbedded in ice for one hour and fill with various ices, either of cream or water. Pack in salted ice to freeze for two hours, then dress on a socle or dish with smilax.

(3575). POTATOES (Pommes de Terre).

Procure lead molds resembling medium-sized potatoes; fill them with chestnut ice cream (No. 3465) and stuff the centers with biscuits soaked in maraschino, also a salpicon of fruits. Freeze for half an hour, then unmold. Roll them in grated sweet chocolate and imitate the eyes by sticking in sticks of almonds; dress on a napkin and serve separately a sauce made of whipped cream and a little maraschino.

FIG. 706.

(3576). RIBAMBELLE (Ribambelle).

Boxes imitating the fancy boxes of the itinerant dealers of Paris. Coat the bottom and sides with nougat cream (No. 3452); fill the center with uncooked maraschino cream (No. 3462) into which incorporate half as much whipped cream (No. 50) and one ounce of small vanilla chocolate pastilles for each quart of preparation. Pack these boxes in a freezing box or cave and serve accompanied by small wafer cakes or very thin waffle cornets.

(3577). RICE À LA RISTORI (Riz à la Ristori).

Coat a dome-shaped mold with vanilla ice cream (No. 3458), range on the bottom a layer of crushed candied chestnuts, over these a bed of chocolate mousse (No. 3473), then another layer of chestnuts and apricot marmalade (No. 3675); finish filling with a light burnt almond cream (No. 3455). Have the mold quite full, forcing the cover on tightly, pack in salted ice and freeze for three-quarters of an hour. Unmold on a garnishing of thoroughly boiled rice macerated in an eighteen-degree vanilla syrup; serve a sauce-boatful of apricot maraschino sauce at the same time.

(3578). RICE WITH MARASCHINO (Riz au Marasquin).

Boil half a pound of rice in milk; when dry and soft sweeten it and two minutes after remove and put away to cool. Dilute it with a few spoonfuls of vanilla syrup (No. 3165) and three tablespoonfuls of maraschino and keep it on one side. Freeze a dome mold in pounded ice and salt for a quarter of an hour before opening it; when cold range the ice inside of it in layers, bestrewing each one with candied fruits cut in large dice. After the mold is full first close the opening with a round piece of paper larger than itself, then with its own cover, closing the joints with butter so that the salted water cannot penetrate inside; cover also with salted ice and one hour later wash the mold quickly in warm water, dry and invert the rice on a cold dish.

(3579). SICILIAN (Sicilienne).

Whip twelve raw egg-yolks in a tinned copper basin with twelve ounces of sugar and a quart of boiling milk; add three ounces of roasted coriander seeds, a piece of cinnamon and half a pound of chocolate; cook on a slow fire, allow to cool, then add a pint of cream; pass this through a sieve; freeze, and add six ounces of almonds, each one to be cut lengthwise in four, and three ounces of candied orange or lemon peel cut up very finely. Have one quart of chocolate ice cream (No. 3449) into which mix half as much whipped cream (No. 50). Line a square one-quart mold with bands of biscuit a quarter of an inch thick. At the bottom place a layer of the chocolate ice cream, over this slices of guava jelly and citron marmalade and the chocolate cream, repeating the operation until the mold is completely full. Pack in salted ice, freeze for one hour, unmold and dress.

(3580). ALGERIAN TIMBALES (Timbales à l'Algérienne).

Lay in a vessel twelve ounces of sugar, six ounces of sifted flour and six ounces of finely ground almonds and two egg-whites; mix thoroughly, then incorporate ten partly beaten egg-whites; this paste should be flowing and smooth; add four tablespoonfuls of whipped cream (No. 50). Spread this paste on a waxed baking sheet in a band nineteen inches in length by six and a half inches in width; push it into a moderate oven and when partly baked pare the edges off with a knife and finish baking; when of a fine golden color remove from the oven and range it against the interior sides of a ring six inches in diameter by six inches in height. From the same paste cut out three rounds, one eight inches in diameter and two of six and a half inches; of one of these two rounds cut out the center so as to form a ring which will serve as a cover for the timbale, the other for the bottom, and the seven-inch one is to be cut into six parts; these are intended for lining the dome-shaped mold; clip off the surplus wafer and fasten the pieces to the inside with sugar cooked to "crack" (No. 171); cover over with well-reduced apricot marmalade (No. 3675) and decorate with a green lime (chinois) on the center; around fasten on some halved cherries, dredge the whole with shredded or chopped pistachios and surround the base of the timbale with a row of nice red candied cherries.

Salpicon.—Prepare a salpicon of pineapple, cherries and almonds; macerate in a little kirsch and maraschino for one hour.

Racahout Cream.—Put six egg-yolks into a basin with two heaping tablespoonfuls of racahout and ten ounces of sugar; beat well with a whip, adding one quart of boiling milk; cook this cream until it almost boils, without allowing it to do so, then strain, cool and freeze, mixing in half as much whipped cream (No. 50). Pack two molds in ice, having covers to fasten on the outside; one cylindrical, five and a half inches in diameter and six inches high, and the other dome-shaped, four and a half inches in diameter at its base. Pour some maraschino over macaroons; place them in layers in the cylindrical mold, then racahout cream to cover, on this the fruits and more of the cream and then macaroons (No. 3379), continuing until the mold is entirely full, finishing with the cream; fit on the cover, freeze for one hour, then unmold it into the above wafer timbale; lay this timbale on a folded napkin, put on to it first the wafer ring and then the dome cover and serve.

(3581). CHATEAUBRIAND TIMBALE (Timbale Chateaubriand).

Pound finely half a pound of almonds and mix in four ounces of butter, the chopped peel of a lemon, six ounces of sifted flour, salt and three eggs; make a firm, but not too hard paste and leave it set for one hour; roll it out to three-sixteenths of an inch in thickness, and from this flat cut six pieces each six inches long by three and a half wide; lay them very straight on a baking sheet. Cut also two pieces a quarter of an inch thick, one having a diameter of seven and a quarter inches and the other nine inches; cook all these in a moderate oven and cool under weights. When very cold pare them on all sides to obtain panels six inches long and three and a quarter wide; bevel the edges on the inner long sides; cover them lightly with apricot marmalade (No. 3675) and glaze with royal icing (No. 102), white, red and chocolate. Decorate with royal icing, then fasten the panels together without attaching them to the baking sheet; decorate the joints of each panel with a small royal ice beading. Prepare the bottom piece six cornered, eight inches from end to end, and the top seven and a half inches; ice the bottom, one in white and the top one pale green; on this one stand a dome made of meringue or royal icing, and on this dome a lyre, either of royal icing or gum paste (No. 3624); decorate around the bottom with a border of pink gum paste.

FIG. 707.

Chateaubriand Cream.—Pound four ounces of almonds with half an ounce of bitter ones and two gills of cream. Put ten egg-yolks in a basin with twelve ounces of sugar, half a vanilla bean, a pint of milk and the pounded almonds; cook the preparation on a slow fire without boiling till it covers the spatula, then allow to cool; pour in a pint of fresh cream. Strain this composition through a sieve, freeze and add half as much whipped cream and four ounces of shredded pistachios as well as a salpicon of candied fruits, seedless Malaga and Smyrna raisins, having all of these macerated for one hour in kirsch. Fill a six-sided mold of the same form and size as the Chateaubriand, only half an inch smaller in diameter; pack well in ice and freeze for two hours. Unmold the ice on the largest round, place on a dish with the timbale over, then set the small round on top; decorate with the cupola or lyre; serve.

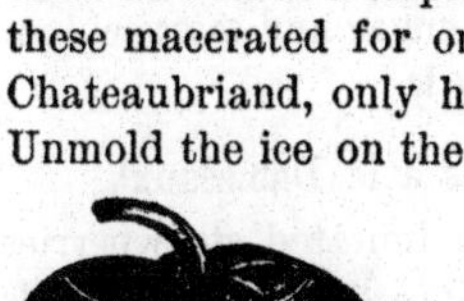

(3582). STUFFED TOMATOES (Tomates Farcies).

FIG. 708.

Mask the sides of a mold imitating a tomato with strawberry water ice (No. 3607) and in the center burnt almond ice cream (No. 3455) and a salpicon of fruits and macaroons soaked in maraschino; finish filling, close forcibly, imbed in ice and freeze for half an hour; unmold, dress in a pyramid on a napkin and serve with a bowlful of sauce made of vanilla ice cream (No. 3458), whipped cream (No. 50) and prunelle, well mixed together.

(3583). TORONCHINO PROCOPE (Toronchino Procope).

Put ten raw egg-yolks into a tin basin containing three-quarters of a pound of sugar, and half a pound of burnt almonds crushed with about a gill of cream. Set on a slow fire, stir steadily until the preparation covers the spatula, then take from the fire and let stand till cold. Now add a pint of cream and a little orange flower water, strain the whole through a sieve, freeze and use the cream to fill some plaited paper cases, scattering shredded pistachios over the tops.

(3584). TORTONI CUPS (Coupes Tortoni).

This ice requires the use of lead molds representing plain, shallow, round baskets; line them

with rather thin strawberry ice cream (No. 3451) and freeze for one hour; unmold and lay over sheets of paper placed on a tin; fill quite full and rounded on top with iced biscuit preparation (No. 3435) and put them into the freezing box. When the iced biscuit is sufficiently congealed decorate each ice cream with roses of medium size molded in raspberry, orange, lemon and pineapple water ices, one quart being sufficient for twelve flowers; fill some of the rose molds with lemon and orange, others with raspberry and pineapple. Pack in ice, freeze and unmold; lay

FIG. 709.

each one on the above biscuit preparation, it being sufficiently hard to have the rose set firmly on top of the roundest part; put them in a freezing box (Fig. 622) for half an hour and serve.

(3585). TUTTI-FRUTTI BISCUITS (Biscuits Tutti-Frutti).

Prepare a lady finger paste (No. 3377), adding a little butter; spread it in thin eighth of an inch layers on sheets of paper and bake in a brisk oven; after it has been removed punch out round pieces with a pastry cutter two and a quarter inches in diameter, also some bands seven and a half inches long by one and a half wide. Place one of the rounds at the bottom of a tin ring measuring two and three-quarters inches in diameter by an inch and a half in height; on top of this round range the band in a circle. Fill the center with two kinds of ice, one lemon water ice (No. 3604) and the other nut cream (No. 3461), both having a salpicon of fruits macerated in kirsch added to them, and freeze for one hour; unmold and range each tutti-frutti biscuit on a

FIG. 710.

lace paper of the same size. Cover entirely with a smooth coating of whipped cream and decorate with lozenges of angelica and halved cherries, placing a whole one in the center; freeze once more for half an hour and serve.

(3586). TUTTI-FRUTTI (Tutti-Frutti).

FIG. 711.

Have some very cold tutti-frutti molds (Fig. 711). Incorporate a salpicon of candied fruits, cut in three-sixteenths inch squares and marinated in kirsch, in vanilla ice cream (No. 3458). Fill the molds half full with this and the other half with orange water ice (No. 3605). Close forcibly, remove the surplus ice and freeze for half an hour. Unmold and dress on lace paper, the same diameter as the tutti-frutti, and serve.

(3587). VALENCE CUP WITH PEACHES (Coupe de Valence aux Pêches).

Prepare some Andalusian ice cream (No. 3446); mold it in a cup mold that has been imbedded in ice; freeze in ice and salt for one hour;

FIG. 712.

unmold and decorate with peeled peaches cut in four, soaked in champagne, sugar and maraschino, adding to them well-pared oranges cut in sections, having withdrawn the seeds.

(3588). VERMEIL GLOBULES À LA DAMSEAUX (Globules Vermeilles à la Damseaux).

To dress these imitated strawberries made of ice cream, it requires shells (Fig. 714), made of either nougat (No. 3621), pulled sugar (No. 3618) or clear sugar. The ends of the shells must be decorated with small flowers made of cooked sugar or gum paste. Mold half of these ices in strawberry ice cream (No.

FIG. 713.　　　　FIG. 714.

3451) and the other half in strawberry water ice (No. 3607); after all are molded pack in ice and freeze for half an hour, then unmold them; fasten an artificial stalk, surmounted with small leaves, into each one. Place them in the shells and serve at once.

(3589). WATERMELON (Pastèque).

Take a pound of the red pulp of a watermelon, the juice of four oranges and of three lemons, an orange and a lemon peel, also some syrup at twenty degrees. Bring the composition to eighteen-degree heat, strain through a sieve and freeze, adding half a gill of brandy and one quart of whipped cream (No. 50). Coat a watermelon-shaped mold with pistachio cream (No. 3454); on this place the above preparation, with strawberry water ice (No. 3607) laid in the center; pack and freeze for two hours; unmold and cut it up in four or else in two; on the red part insert imitation watermelon seeds made of chocolate. These halves or quarters can be cut in slices.

LARGE PIECES.

(3590). BACCHUS (Bacchus).

Bacchus represents wine and is the companion piece to the *well*, representing water. Molds can be purchased already made for these ices. Bacchus' barrel is of chocolate ice cream (No. 3449) and Bacchus is of virgin orange cream (No. 3459); the foot on which the barrel rests is of

FIG. 715.

pistachio ice cream (No. 3454). Mold quite full, close forcibly, having it completely filled, and freeze for an hour and a half; unmold on a water socle as represented in Fig. 715, being careful to have this piece to correspond with the other as regards its proportions.

(3591). CANTALOUP IN SURPRISE AND CANTALOUP MOLDED (Cantaloup en Surprise et Cantaloup Moulé).

In Surprise.—Take a handsome, fresh and very ripe cantaloup melon, make an opening on the top two and a half inches below the stalk, and on the bias, directing the tip of the knife toward the center; suppress all the ripe pulp from the inside, put back the cover and imbed this rind in salted ice. With the removed pulp make a melon water ice (No. 3603), color with a little red and yellow carmine to imitate the orange color of a cantaloup melon; with this fill the rind to represent the original melon, return it to the ice and freeze for two hours. When well congealed it can be cut in slices; make the seeds of almond paste (No. 3623). A macédoine of fresh fruits with champagne and lemon water ice can also be substituted for the melon ice.

Molded. — Melons may be molded in lead molds, having the shape of a melon, making the rind either of vanilla (No. 3458) or pistachio (No. 3454) and the center of orange water ice (No. 3605)

FIG. 716.

or pineapple water ice (No. 3606); pack in ice and freeze for two hours. Unmold and dress either on a water socle or folded napkin and on top of the melon range an artificial stalk and leaves.

(3592). DELICIOUS WITH HAZEL-NUTS (Délicieux aux Noisettes).

Lay half a pound of hazel-nuts taken from their shells on a baking sheet, roast in the oven, peel to suppress the red skins, then pound with two gills of cream; set this in a basin with twelve raw egg-yolks and twelve ounces of sugar; whip all together and dilute with a pint of milk which has had a quarter of a vanilla stick infused in it. Cook the preparation without boiling till it covers

FIG. 717.

the spatula well, leave stand until cold, then add a pint of fresh cream; freeze. When the cream has a proper consistency mix in two quarts of well-drained whipped cream (No. 50). Pack a two-quart mold on ice, fill it with the composition and freeze for two hours; unmold on a folded napkin, on top set a spun sugar ornament and surround with scooped-out oranges refilled with two differently tinted jellies, white and red, laid in streaks, cooled and then cut in six or eight separate parts; surround the base with small strawberries having fresh leaves attached.

(3593). FRUIT BASKET WITH DOVES (Corbeille Jardinière aux Colombes).

Make the stand representing a basket in two parts of colored water, with a hole in the center of each; when this stand has been frozen place it on the middle of an oval board thirteen inches long by nine and a half inches wide, having a half-inch diameter hole bored through the center; keep the whole firmly together and very straight with a nut-screw five to six inches long, screwing it in very tight. Have two cylindrical molds with bottoms, fill them with water and freeze; unmold and place them on the center line at one-third of the length of the stand; on each of these columns set a dove, imitating the eyes with a dry currant, and fasten a cherry-colored ribbon around his

FIG. 718.

neck; decorate all around with fruits molded in various ices and dipped in hot water to unmold; put them in the freezing box or cave and freeze; afterward color them lightly and stick into them stalks with their respective leaves. All these ice cream pieces should be dressed at the last moment and then served at a dinner table or sideboard supper.

(3594). HEN WITH CHICKS; NEST WITH EGGS (Poule Avec Poussins; Nid Garni d'Œufs).

Prepare a sponge cake stand (No. 3260) or one of wood or office paste (No. 143), eleven and a quarter inches long by eight and a quarter inches wide; cover it with coffee or chocolate icing.

FIG. 719.

Make a nest of spun sugar, on which place here and there small bits of angelica; in the center set the stand. Mold the hen in burnt almond ice cream (No. 3455), spotted over with coffee, choc-

FIG. 720.

olate, vanilla, etc.. to imitate the different shadings of the bird. Pack it in ice and freeze for one hour; unmold and dress it on the stand, surrounded with small chicks, made also of ice cream, the same as the larger one.

For the nest (Fig. 720), prepare a round nest, the same as Fig. 719, only smaller; fill with small eggs made of assorted ice cream.

(3595). PINEAPPLE IN SURPRISE AND PINEAPPLE MOLDED (Ananas en Surprise et Ananas Moulé).

In Surprise.—Suppress the stalk from a fine pineapple; empty it out entirely and pack it in ice for one hour. With the inside of the fruit make a pineapple water ice (No. 3606), mixing into it a salpicon of fresh fruits; fill the pineapple and freeze it once more; dress on a napkin and surround with small molded peaches decorated with a stalk and slightly colored over.

FIG. 721.

Molded.—They can also be molded in a pineapple-shaped mold, the top or stalk to be made of pistachio cream (No. 3454) and the pineapple in Andalusian ice cream (No. 3446), colored a reddish yellow. Cut the best pieces from a small pineapple into quarter-inch squares; steep them in kirsch and maraschino for one hour, add pieces of biscuit and macaroons, drain and with this preparation fill the inside of the pineapple. Imbed in ice and freeze for an hour and a half, unmold and dress on a water socle, serving at once.

(3596). RABBIT IN SURPRISE (Lapin en Surprise).

Rabbit or any other animal in surprise, made of spun sugar and serving for covering ices (Fig. 722). For the rabbit or hare make the ice in a half melon-shaped mold; the bear and rabbit in an

Fig. 722.

iced biscuit mold (Fig. 626). These molds can be filled with puddings, parfaits, etc., either with flavors or with fruits; pack in ice, freeze for one hour for each quart, unmold and dress; lay on top either a rabbit, hare or bear of spun sugar and serve.

[(3597). SWAN WITH REEDS AND RUSHES (Le Cygne aux Roseaux).

Have an oval bottom made of office paste (No. 143) or wood, half an inch thick, fifteen inches long and eleven wide; glaze it with royal icing (No. 101) of a soft green color and place around an inch and a half from the border a band of pistachio nougat (No. 3622) two and a half inches high, on top of this a platform of sugar cooked white to "crack" (No. 171), and the same size as the band;

FIG. 723.

garnish around the stand with reeds, rushes, etc., made of pulled sugar. Mold a swan with outstretched wings and neck in lemon virgin cream (No. 3459), the under part of the wings in coffee (No. 3460) and the body in vanilla (No. 3458); pack it in ice and freeze for two hours. Unmold and lay this swan in the center of the platform, imitating the eyes with small dry currants. This dish can be garnished all around with flowers made of ice cream placed in small paper cases.

(3598). THE HELMET (Le Casque).

The helmet shown in Fig. 724, is made in a two-quart tin mold filled with a pudding. When unmolded decorate it with halved pistachios and cover these with a thin layer of straw-

FIG. 724.

berry ice cream (No. 3451). The crest of the helmet is of vanilla, the edge resting on the socle of chocolate and the whole is dressed on a natural water socle. The feather should be made of spun sugar.

(3599). THE WELL (Le Puits).

Have a lead mold the shape of a well and fill it with light vanilla ice cream (No. 3458); this mold should have an inside one to form the hollow of the well; freeze for an hour, unmold it on a water socle dressed on a napkin and fill the inside with half a pound of rice, blanched and cooked

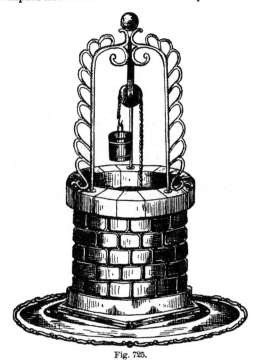

Fig. 725.

in a light twelve-degree vanilla syrup (No. 3165); drain and add a salpicon of apricots cut in small sticks and shredded pistachios; mix the whole into strawberry ice cream (No. 3451), having mixed into it the same quantity of whipped cream (No. 50) flavored with a little maraschino; the ornament on top should be made of spun sugar, fastened on to the well just when serving (see Fig. 725).

(3600). TURBAN WITH PINEAPPLE OR STRAWBERRY OR SULTANA (Turban aux Ananas ou Fraises ou Sultane).

Put one pint of apricot pulp in a vessel with two gills of almond milk (No. 4) and one gill of

FIG. 726.

maraschino; add some syrup to bring the preparation to twenty-two degrees, then strain, freeze and mix with it the same quantity of whipped cream (No. 50).   Place this preparation in a turban-shaped mold, pack in ice to freeze for one hour, then unmold and decorate around the center with some well-pared, ripe pineapple cut in four, and the hard center core suppressed; then cut up the remainder in slices, lay them it in a vessel and bestrew with sugar, pouring over some rum so that they macerate for half an hour.

Vanilla Strawberry Turban can be made by mixing in the same quantity of whipped cream (No. 50) after it is frozen; unmold and garnish the center with fresh strawberries macerated in kirsch, maraschino and a little powdered sugar. The turban can also be served plain or else trimmed with a sultana of spun sugar.

(3601). WATER ICES—HOW TO PREPARE AND FINISH THEM (Glaces à l'Eau—Manière de les Préparer et de les Finir).

The base of all water ices is the pulp or juice of fruits, with sugar syrup prepared beforehand at thirty-two degrees, or else substitute a pound and a half of sugar for each quart of water. The syrup gauge (Fig. 167) is the only arbiter for ascertaining the proper degree; they can be prepared from fourteen to twenty-four degrees. At eighteen degrees a thin ice is obtained called granite. Eighteen to nineteen degrees is an excellent degree for water ices prepared for the taste of this country, although in some climates they are made as high as twenty-four degrees. At this degree very fine and consistent ices are formed, but they are objectionably sweet and therefore not generally liked, so that water ices at eighteen to twenty degrees are considered the best — eighteen degrees with fruit pulps and twenty degrees for fruit juices, or sometimes twenty-two, according to the acidity of the fruit. The juice of three lemons make about a gill; for this quantity use two pounds and a quarter of sugar and one pint of water, obtaining a quart of syrup at thirty-degrees. To freeze the fruit preparation it requires two freezers, one of a high shape and the other semi-spherical. Before freezing the mixture in the semi-spherical freezer it must be packed in salted ice and the inside wiped out neatly, then pour in about a gill of the preparation to try its consistency, working it with a small spatula, and if found to be sufficiently congealed pour in about two quarts to freeze, setting the semi-spherical freezer in motion and detaching at times with the spatula any particles that may adhere to the sides. As soon as the ice attains a proper consistency remove and lay it in a small, long sorbetière (freezer) also imbedded in salted ice. The ice should be worked vigorously with the spatula to have it acquire body, then imbed it once more, letting all the superfluous water run out of the hole at the bottom of the pail, adding more salted ice, packing it down with a stick; cover the pail with a lid or a cloth to prevent any air from entering and keep it thus until ready for use.

(3602). FRESH FRUIT WATER ICES (Glaces à l'Eau aux Fruits Frais).

For Peaches, Apricots, Nectarines.—Select good fresh plucked fruits, yet not too ripe; split open, suppress the stalks, pith and skins; cut up finely and bestrew with vanilla sugar to hinder from blackening, then strain through a fine sieve. Put the pulp in a vessel and mix in a pint of thirty-two degree syrup for each quart, the juice of two oranges and four lemons and a bit of orange peel. Strain this preparation through a silk sieve and freeze it. As soon as the ice congeals remove with a spoon and place in a small, long freezer packed in ice; work it vigorously for ten minutes, incorporating slowly a pint of Italian meringue (No. 140) for each quart of syrup, and half a gill of kirsch or noyau; work it again ten minutes to have it smooth.

For Cherries, Pomegranates, Currants and Barberries.—A pint of fruit pulp for one quart of syrup and one gill or the juice of three lemons. If with cherries, crack the pips to extract and crush the meat and make the syrup of twenty degrees strength. For currants use the juice of two lemons; color with vegetal red, strain through a silk sieve and freeze.

(3603). GUANABANA, MELON, MEDLAR, PEAR OR PLUM WATER ICE (Glace à l'Eau à la Guanabane, au Melon, aux Nèfles, Poires ou Prunes).

Select fruits that are ripe, having them in preference a little too hard than too soft; they must be fragrant and freshly plucked. Suppress the skins or peels with a knife; press first through a sieve, then through a tammy; put the purée in a vessel, allowing for each quart one pint of cold syrup, the juice of two oranges and four lemons and the peel of half an orange infused in a gill of syrup. Stir all the ingredients well together and bring it to a twenty to twenty-two degree syrup; strain through a very fine Venice or silk sieve and pour into a semi-spherical freezer; allow it to congeal without ceasing to detach with a large spatula every particle adhering to the sides of the freezer. As soon as the ice is all congealed remove it with a spoon and transfer to a small, long freezer imbedded in salted ice to have it acquire plenty of body, and smooth while still stirring; lastly incorporate three tablespoonfuls of good rum, kirsch or prunelle, mixed with a little of the syrup and frozen preparation, being careful to incorporate it little by little; work again for a few moments, freeze once more and serve.

(3604). LEMON WATER ICE AND GRAPE FRUIT ICE (Glace à l'Eau au Citron et Glace au Poncires).

Pour into a vessel some syrup made with two and a quarter pounds of sugar and a pint of water cooked to thirty-two degrees; cool off, then add two gills or the juice of six lemons and the peel of four of the finest among them well washed and wiped; let the preparation attain twenty degrees according to the syrup gauge and infuse therein the peels, leaving them for two hours; strain through a silk sieve and freeze.

Another Way.—Proportions: Four pounds of sugar, three gills of water, the peel of fifteen lemons and the juice of twenty-five; cook to twenty degrees of the syrup gauge; infuse the peels in this for two hours; strain the whole through a silk sieve and freeze. This quantity will produce a little more than six quarts.

Grape Fruit.—Prepare this ice the same as lemon water ice, substituting grape fruit for lemons.

(3605). ORANGE WATER ICE OR WITH GELATINE (Glace à l'Eau à l'Orange et à la Gélatine).

Take one quart of syrup at thirty-two degrees, five gills of orange juice, the peel of a large orange and one gill of lemon juice. Infuse for two hours, bring it to eighteen or twenty degrees of the syrup gauge, and color with a little carmine; strain through a silk sieve and freeze.

Another Way.—Six pounds of sugar, four quarts of water, thirty oranges, using the peel of sixteen, and the juice of twelve lemons. Infuse for two hours, bring to twenty degrees, strain through a silk sieve and freeze. This will make about eight quarts.

With Gelatine.—Have one quart of water, one pound of sugar, the peel and juice of two oranges, the juice of four lemons, a sheet of gelatine weighing a quarter of an ounce, previously dissolved in a little water, then strained through a fine sieve. The ice may be flavored with extract of orange and the lemon replaced by citric acid.

(3606). PINEAPPLE WATER ICE (Glace à l'Eau à l'Ananas).

Pineapple can be prepared in two ways, either grated or pounded in a mortar or infused in a syrup.

Infused in Syrup.—Boil a quart of thirty-two degree syrup, add to it one pound of peeled pineapple cut in thin slices, also the peel of one orange; remove from the fire, cover the saucepan, and leave to cool in the syrup, adding one gill or the juice of three lemons; strain forcibly, either through a Venice sieve or a silken one; boil the mixture until it reaches twenty degrees of the syrup gauge and freeze.

Another way is to place a pound of sugar in a vessel with two quarts of water and one quart of grated or crushed pineapple; let infuse for two hours; add a leaf and a half of isinglass dissolved in half a pint of water acidulated with the juice of eight lemons or else melted citric acid; strain through a fine sieve and freeze.

Another Way.—One quart of grated pineapple, two pounds of sugar, two quarts of water, the juice of sixteen lemons or five gills. Finish the same as water ice (No. 3601).

(3607). STRAWBERRY OR RASPBERRY WATER ICE (Glace à l'Eau aux Fraises ou aux Framboises).

Small ripe wild berries are preferable to cultivated ones for these ices. Put one quart of strawberry or raspberry pulp in a basin, and dilute with a pint and a half of cold syrup at thirty degrees; add a little vanilla, the peel of an orange, the juice of two oranges and of four lemons; strain through a silk sieve. The syrup should be from twenty to twenty-two degrees.

Another Way.—Take eight pounds of powdered sugar, two quarts of fruit pulp, the juice of twenty lemons and six quarts of water; color to a light red with vegetal carmine. Bring it to twenty degrees of the syrup gauge, strain through a silk sieve and freeze.

ICED DRINKS.

(3608). ICED CHOCOLATE (Chocolat Glacé).

Dissolve a pound of sweet chocolate in a quart of water with half a bean of vanilla; when cold stir in a quart of cream, then strain through a fine sieve.

Another way is to take a pound of sweet chocolate, half a pint of water and half a vanilla bean; when the chocolate is all dissolved and cold mix into it three pints of cream and a gill of thirty-two degree syrup; strain through a sieve and put it into a freezer with lightly salted ice around, and serve in glasses.

(3609). ICED COFFEE (Café Glacé).

Black Coffee.—Iced coffee, as it is called in New York, is simply black coffee cooled in a china freezer, having lightly salted ice placed around.

Mixed Coffee.—Mixed coffee is prepared the same, only mixing the whole of the following ingredients together: One pint of milk, one gill of cream, one quart of black coffee and one gill of syrup at thirty-two degrees. Put the mixture into a china or enameled freezer with lightly salted ice around, and serve when the coffee is exceedingly cold.

Brandy Coffee.—One quart of black coffee, six ounces of sugar, one gill of brandy; to be mixed and cooled the same as the black coffee.

Iced Coffee in Sherbet.—Have one quart of black coffee mixed with one quart of cream and twelve ounces of sugar; place it in a freezer with salted ice around, detach from the sides as fast as the ice adheres, and when sufficiently cold and firm serve in glasses.

(3610). GRAMOLATES OR GRANITE WITH ORANGE (Gramolates ou Granit à l'Orange).

Put in a vessel one quart of fifteen-degree syrup, the juice and peels of three oranges; cover over and leave infuse for one hour; add the juice of four lemons and a little orange vegetal carmine; strain through a silk sieve and freeze. Peel three oranges to the pulp, remove the pulp by passing the knife near each section and lay the pieces in a bowl with a very little sugar and kirsch; steep for half an hour then add it to the ice and serve in glasses.

(3611). GRANITE IN WATER BOTTLES WITH CURRANTS, CHERRIES, POMEGRANATES, ETC. (Granits en Carafes à la Groseille, aux Cerises, Grenades, etc).

Granites are made the same as water ices, flavored with any desired fruits, the sole difference being that they must not be worked and must only attain fourteen degrees of the saccharometer; when the composition is ready pour it in water bottles having very wide necks; pack these in ice with half as much salt as for ordinary ices. Detach from the sides with a small boxwood spatula. Serve in the same decanters or else in glasses.

(3612). GRAPE FRUITS À LA MADISON (Poncires à la Madison).

The grape fruit is a species of large yellow orange, resembling the Florida orange; it is slightly bitter. Select those that are not too large, cut them across in two, empty the insides, keeping it all in a vessel, and notch the edges of the peel in points; remove the small rounds from the center and then place them to cool in a freezing-box. Prepare a mixture the same as orange punch, Russian style (No. 3613), the only difference to observe being that all the fruit juice must be used; bring to twelve degrees and let cool to a granite (No. 3611), then serve in the prepared peels.

(3613). ORANGE PUNCH, RUSSIAN STYLE—UNFROZEN COLD DRINK (Punch Orange à la Russe—Boisson Froide non Gelée).

Slit open with a tin tube an inch and a half in diameter the top of eight oranges on the side opposite to the stalk, empty them out entirely, wipe neatly and set them in low paper cases to keep them level. On the round piece removed from the orange fasten two long straws, tying them together with a ribbon passed through two holes. Put these oranges for at least two hours beforehand in a box and pack with ice and very little salt, not to freeze the rinds. Place in a freezer one pint of orange juice obtained from the pulp of the emptied oranges and strained through a fine strainer, add to it two gills of water, six ounces of sugar, a gill of rum, half a gill of kirsch, the peel of two oranges and the juice of four lemons; flavor it properly, either by adding or removing any of the ingredients; strain the whole through a very fine silk sieve and freeze with ice and a little salt. Just when ready to serve fill the oranges and serve them at once. The straws are used for drinking the contents of the orange.

Fig. 727.

CONFECTIONERY (Confiserie).

(3614). CENTER PIECES—PYRAMIDS (Pièces Montées).

Table ornaments called pyramids are used for replacing the cold pieces in the third service for French dinners. They are placed on the table at the beginning and at the dessert for a Russian dinner. The principal object is to flatter the eye of the guests by their regularity, their smoothness and their finish. To attain this end it is necessary that the subjects be chosen according to the circumstances in which the dinner is offered. Special care must be taken that they be faultlessly executed. The pieces can be selected from a number of designs, such as: Swiss cottages, temples, pavilions, towers, pagodas, mosques, fortresses, hermitages, belvederes, cabins, cascades, houses, fountains, ruins, rotundas or tents; then there are lyres, harps, helmets, boats, cornucopias, vases, baskets, hampers, beehives, trophies both military and musical, fine arts, agriculture, navigation, commerce, science, etc. A very prolific branch almost entirely overlooked is a figure representing some well-known character. Then come animals, trees and flowers, which offer an infinite number of beautiful subjects. Few workmen are capable of making these different styles of pieces, their talent being limited, for their use is confined to a very small number of houses. Therefore it would be most useful if the workman engaged in making these pieces confine himself solely to figures, as this art is certain to become fashionable in the near future. Authors of the best works on cooking and pastry only casually mention these ornamental pieces. The workman while executing them must give his entire attention and talent, for the persons before whom they are generally placed are accustomed to works of art. In case he finds it impossible to produce a perfect figure, then he had better devote himself to other kinds of work in which perfection need not be so scrupulously followed; for, after all, these pieces only serve to decorate one dinner, and consequently are very rarely preserved. Still, whatever style of work he may see fit to undertake, let him endeavor to excel and attain the pinnacle of perfection. A well-executed idea has more merit than a well-finished, but badly conceived one. The quantity of figures and subjects to select from are numerous. First, we have mythology; what a fertile theme—here a Cupid on a shell drawn by swans; Neptune among the tritons and Naïads; Bacchus; the Centaurs; the Muses; scenes from Iliad and Odyssey! How delightfully ingenuous would be a group representing Venus teaching Cupid the art of dancing: the young one in the act and the mother directing his steps; Apollo playing the flute and Jupiter benignly watching the scene, surrounded by other gods and goddesses. Then we have the history of the flood: Noah standing at the door of the Ark contemplating the ingress of all the animals into it. We can choose from the customs of different ancient and modern nations: the Normandy peasants dancing opposite to each other; a Tyrolian descending a rock carrying on his back the carcass of a chamois; an American Indian dressed in war garb burying the tomahawk; or a Tartar on horseback. Then there are scenes in ordinary life. We also choose from animated nature: birds, animals, the fox ready to attack an innocent rabbit, fish, swans on a lake surrounded by their families, birds pecking their young, and many other interesting subjects too numerous to mention.

(3615). CENTER PIECES; EXPLANATION OF VARIOUS FIGURES (Pièces Montées; Explication des Différents Sujets).

These figures as far as the letter I can be used for all pyramids, either of cooked, poured or spun sugar or of gum paste; adjust four to six pieces equally distant, and fasten them together; fill the intersections with arabesques, as in G and H, and surmount the whole with an ornament or bunch of flowers made of web sugar, the same as shown on piece K. On the projections of piece K, LLL rings of poured sugar can be placed, filling the centers with iced fruits; in the empty spaces can also be ranged sticks of poured sugar covered with fruits or small cakes, bonbons, almond paste, etc. The figures F and A show the effect that can be produced by using simpler methods. A is merely decorated with small arabesques, shown in I, in half their natural size;

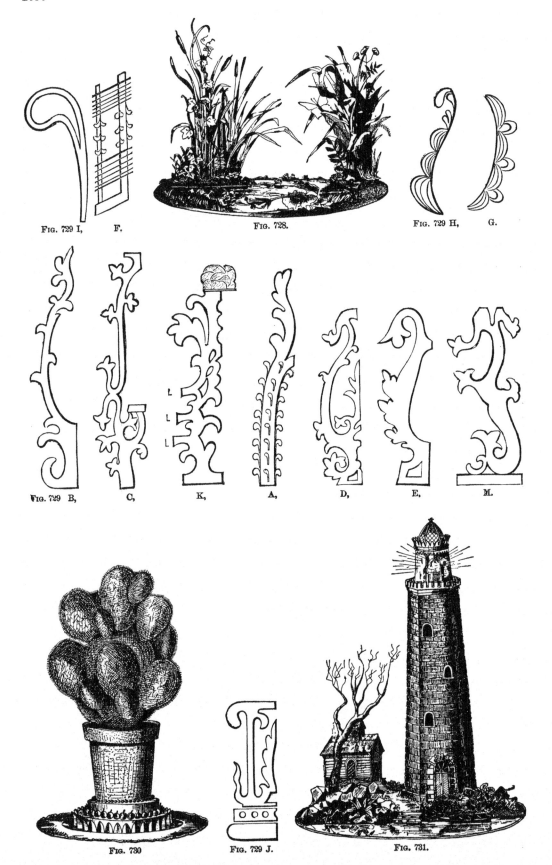

FIG. 729 I,   F.

FIG. 728.

FIG. 729 H,   G.

FIG. 729 B,   C,   K,   A,   D,   E,   M.

FIG. 730

FIG. 729 J.

FIG. 731.

on F small sticks are fastened one to the other. Fig. 728 is made of nougat; the frog to be of green pistachio nougat molded in a varnished and oiled plaster mold; the rushes are green and brown. Fig. 730 represents a cactus on a two-shelved socle made of Parisian nougat; the flower pot is of nougat containing chopped almonds and chocolate; the plant is of green pistachio nougat to imitate the cactus. The lighthouse (Fig. 731) is of gum paste; the chimney on top of the house, from whence arises the smoke, is imitated in wadding; the branches of the tree of very fine wire covered with finely cut paper to represent the leaves, and the trunk to be of gum paste or fine wire covered with silk. The staircase and the boat are of gum paste; the boat lies on a piece of looking glass. The J and M are meant for forming socles for raising the low pieces, such as the frog, etc. J is made in three pieces that can be used independently, so as to make the socle either higher or lower.

(3616). CENTER PIECES OF COOKED SUGAR (Pièces Montées en Sucre Cuit).

For cooked sugar see Elementary Methods (No. 171). It is always necessary to have sugar cooked in advance so that each time some is wanted it will not have to be prepared, especially when

only a little is to be used at a time. Have some sugar cooked to "large crack" (No. 171); when it reaches three hundred and thirty degrees add to it the juice of a quarter of a lemon and leave cook to three hundred and fifty degrees, then pour it hastily on a thick marble sufficiently large to allow it to cool, then detach and set it away in

FIG. 732.

hermetically closed tin boxes. To make web or spun sugar, first melt it slowly in a small copper pan, a little at a time, being careful it does not change color. This sugar is used for spinning sultanas, for making ornaments in spun sugar, or it can be used for Parisian nougat and even for candying fruits, reducing its degree by introducing a little syrup at thirty-two degrees or else some glucose. For spun sugar pieces lightly trace with a pencil on an unpolished and very lightly oiled marble the outlines of the design needed for reproduction; cover this tracing with a thread of firm royal icing, either large or small according to the size of the piece. Fill in between these threads of icing with melted sugar, white or colored; detach the piece from the marble before it is thoroughly cold, as then they are apt to break easily. Instead of using royal icing the tracing can be outlined with a thread of spinning sugar of a different color from that used in the inside; put all the pieces together, attaching them in four, six, or eight, and ornament them here and there, when fastened, according to taste, with candied fruits, bonbons,

FIG. 734.

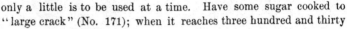

FIG. 733.

or else small cakes, almond paste, etc.; decorate with flowers or leaves made of sugar molded in oiled tin molds, dipped in sugar cooked to "crack," lightly cooled in its pan, then hung by a wire to hooks slightly apart so they cannot touch one another. Unmold as soon as they begin to cool and place on grates until ready for use. Sheaves can also be made (an imitation of sheaves of rye or wheat) in very finely drawn sugar, fastened with an imitation band prepared with the same sugar. These sheaves may be colored or white, according to the taste; the sugar should be cooked to three hundred and thirty-five degrees. Pieces may also be decorated with pulled sugar flowers.

(3617). TO KEEP SUBJECTS OR PIECES (Pour Conserver les Sujets ou Pièces Montées).

Pyramids made of spun sugar or nougat can be kept in a perfect state of preservation by standing them under a plain glass globe to protect them from the action of the air. But should it be necessary to keep them for several days, then they must certainly be placed under a glass globe fitting on to a hollow wooden stand opening on the top, having its surface bored with holes and the empty space filled in with bits of quicklime. The lime has the faculty of absorbing all the humidity of the atmosphere; in this way sugar can be kept intact for an indefinite period, especially in winter time and damp weather. Pieces made of royal icing or gum paste can also be kept for a long while if the above method be followed.

(3618). FLOWERS OF PULLED SUGAR (Fleurs en Sucre Tiré).

Among the various objects that can be made of pulled sugar must be mentioned flowers and all kinds of leaves, which with a little taste and skill can be beautifully imitated, and if this branch

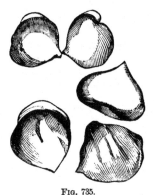

FIG. 735.

FIG. 736.

FIG. 737.

of decoration is studied it can become one of artistic merit. At the beginning learners should not undertake the task of making difficult flowers, such as roses, dahlias, or other flowers having numerous petals, but must be satisfied with more simple ones, such as apple blossoms, wild roses, poppies, pansies, etc.

Cook the sugar to "large crack" (No. 171), or 335 degrees Fahrenheit, being careful to have it very clear, transparent and grainless. Let it get cold on a marble slab. Melt a pound of this sugar in a copper pan, keeping it as white as possible. Pour a tablespoonful of the syrup on the marble, and add to it the coloring matter for the intended flowers; pound the color should it be dry; then pour over the melted sugar, and work the whole together

FIG. 739.

with a spatula, and afterward with the hand until it becomes smooth and tractable. Put this pulled sugar into a mold, or on a lightly oiled dish, and then in a heater which should register 170 degrees Fahrenheit.

It will be enough for us to explain the making of just a few kinds of flowers, in order that the work for all others may be understood. For instance, we will begin with a cluster of apple blossoms: Take from the heater a small quantity of very white pulled sugar, and dipping the finger in

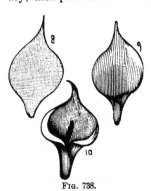

FIG. 738.

corn starch to prevent them sticking to the sugar make some petals as shown in Fig. 735, pressing it down between the thumb and first finger as thinly as possible, and detaching it with a pair of scissors as fast and as soon as it is pressed into shape, varying the shapes so that when finished they are not all alike. Use the flame of a small gas stove to keep the sugar soft; now heat the bottom of each petal over this gas flame, and adjust five of them togther to form each separate flower (Fig. 736). Make also buds and partly opened flowers. Color a little gum paste a bright yellow with a

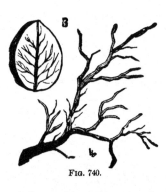

FIG. 740.

FIG. 741.

small wooden or bone tool, and form the inside. Paint the edges of the petals a pale pink, also the buds, being careful to use the coloring matter as dry as possible. Now color a little of the pulled sugar green and form the leaves the same way as the flowers, afterward pressing them on a lightly oiled plaster mold to mark the veins (Fig. 740, No. 3). Melt all the fragments of the various colored pulled sugars, and add to it some cocoa, and with it coat various lengths of wire; twist them to resemble branches of trees, and stick them together (Fig. 740, No. 4), and on it mount the flowers and buds (Fig. 741). Proceed exactly the same for all petal flowers, such as leaves, roses, violets, tulips, poppies and pansies (see Fig. 737, No. 7, for the pansies).

The bunch of apple blossoms, if well made, is most natural. For calla lilies the operation is entirely different. Leave the sugar, pulled very white, in the heater until it runs slightly. The principal object is to work it quickly. Take a small piece from the heater, the size of a walnut, and roll it with the rolling-pin on marble as thinly as possible, always using corn starch for the roller and fingers. Cut the sugar rapidly with the scissors into pieces the shape of leaves, having the bottom part pulled out lengthways; heating these over the gas, should the sugar get too cold (Fig. 738, No. 8), bend them into cornets (Fig. 738, No. 9), always while heating, and fold the edges outward (Fig. 738, No. 10). Color a little sugar a bright yellow, and make the inside of the flower. Coat it lightly with gum arabic, and roll it in powdered sugar that has already been tinted to a fine yellow.

Leaves are made the same way; roll them out with the roller, cut them into long shapes, and press on a plaster mold to mark the veins.

Mount the flowers and leaves on stalks of wire covered with green sugar (Fig. 739).

The principal thing to be observed when making any object, either of sugar or nougat, is to perform the work as speedily as possible, for the less the pulled sugar is heated at the gas flame the more beautiful and brilliant it will remain, and its glossy luster will not be marred.

Satinated Pulled Sugar.—Place three and a half pounds of lump sugar in an untinned copper pan and moistening with one quart of lukewarm water, leave soak for a few moments. Cook it on a brisk fire, skim and wash the same as for caramel and after a few boils add a heaping coffee-spoonful of cream of tartar. Let the sugar attain three hundred degrees, then pour it on to a very cold, slightly oiled marble. When sufficiently cold to allow it to be handled mass it all together and pull it slowly, then mass again with the palm of the hand; pull it again a little, just sufficient to give it a clouded appearance. Put it in the heater and use small quantities, according to the work to be done, pulling and massing to give it a brilliant surface. Never use this sugar when too hot, on the contrary work it as cold as possible so that it will not lose its brilliancy. Flowers, leaves, baskets, etc., can be made with satinated sugar.

(3619). MATERIALS FOR MAKING EASY PIECES (Matières Pour Faire les Pièces Faciles).

Macaroons, candied fruits, small cakes, bonbons, meringues or marchpanes fastened together and applied on conical-shaped molds, having their base measuring eight to ten inches in diameter, and ending in a point one inch in diameter; this style of piece is not much used nowadays except in ordinary balls or banquets. It is gum paste, nougat, royal icing and cooked sugar that the prettiest pieces are made of, and in these the true artist can be readily distinguished.

(3620). IMITATION OF NATURAL GREEN ALMONDS (Imitation d'Amandes Vertes Naturelles).

Prepare a cooked almond paste the same as explained in the Elementary Methods (No. 125); flavor it with orange flower water and tinge it to a light green color. Mold this paste into medium-sized olive shapes, split them lengthwise through the center and in the crack lay a fine white almond; mold and work the paste to have it assume the form of a natural green almond, then lay them as fast as done on a wire sieve and place in the heater to dry. When finished leave to get cold and glaze over with sugar cooked to "crack" (No. 171).

(3621). BROWN NOUGAT FOR CENTER PIECES (Nougat Brun Pour Pièces Montées).

Put into a copper pan one pound of powdered sugar and the juice of a quarter of a lemon; melt the sugar on a moderate fire, and when entirely dissolved stir in one pound of almonds, either chopped or slightly shredded; these are to be heated at the oven door, but great care must be paid that the almonds be not too hot, for should the sugar be slightly colored then the nougat would become too brown; should the almonds be too hot then have the sugar simply melted, and again, if the sugar be very hot, it is unnecessary to heat them only slightly. The best nougat for eating is made with melted sugar, but for elaborate panel pieces requiring much cutting it is better to use cooked sugar, the same as used for spinning work, without diluting with syrup. Almonds are used in the proportion of six to eight ounces for every pound of sugar. This nougat is certainly not so good for eating as the preceding, but it is much easier to work, for it cools with less rapidity and bends with more facility. It can be molded in arabesque molds made of plaster, or else pressed on to tin leaves to form moldings around different sized rings, or else around sticks to form columns. The nougat is cut out when in a flat three-sixteenths of an inch thick, or even thinner, with cardboard designs applied on, then cut away all around; these cardboards should be cut out beforehand into any shapes, such as rounds, ovals, squares, oblongs, triangles, etc.

(3622). PARISIAN, WHITE AND PISTACHIO NOUGAT (Nougat Parisien, Blanc et aux Pistaches).

Parisian.—This nougat is made of hulled almonds split lengthwise and dried in a hot closet. After dipping them in melted cooked sugar apply them in a large biscuit mold slightly oiled, the flat side of the almond lying against the inside of the mold. If a cylinder mold is used, eight inches high by six in diameter, dip the almonds in the melted sugar and then take them up one by one with a larding needle and range them on their flat side in a double reversed wreath.

White Nougat.—White nougat is made of almonds split in two through their thickness and warmed in a heater. Melt in an untinned copper pan one pound of powdered sugar with a tablespoonful of lemon juice; melt this sugar without coloring and when well dissolved mix in the halved almonds. Mold in a plain cylindrical mold, cut off even with the top, and when cold unmold on a baking sheet and decorate either with candied fruits or spun sugar.

Pistachio Nougat.—Have a pound of peeled and very dry pistachio nuts, leave them whole and warm in a heater. Melt a pound of powdered sugar on a slow fire with a tablespoonful of lemon juice; finish the same as the white. Roll both the white and pistachio nougat to a quarter of an inch thick and cut into inch and a quarter bands. This nougat is to be molded in plain and almost straight timbale molds, having just sufficient flare to allow the nougat to be unmolded; garnish the bottom of the mold with a round of pink nougat, (white nougat slightly colored with carmine); adjust the bands on the bias, alternating the white, and fasten them on the inside with bits of nougat dipped in sugar. These nougats are ornamented with fanciful designs of spun sugar. On top place a cupola of spun sugar and over an aigrette of web sugar, or any other tasteful decoration. Nougat is also made of hazel-nuts, common nuts, peanuts, Brazil nuts or butter-nuts; in fact with all kinds of almonds, and finished as explained for the others.

(3623). ALMOND PASTE CANDIED (Pâte d'Amandes au Candi).

Shell and peel fourteen ounces of sweet almonds; leave to soak in fresh water for three hours, then pound to a pulp with a little water and kirsch, half of each, just sufficient to moisten the almonds so they do not oil. Cook a pound of sugar to "crack" (No. 171), in a round bottom sugar pan, mix the almonds in with the sugar and dry them for a few moments over a slow fire.

If for chocolate almond paste add a little grated chocolate or else partly dissolved chocolate. White almond paste is colored with vegetal colorings (No. 172). Roll this paste to three-eighths of an inch in thickness and cut it up in small fanciful patterns; dry them in the heater and when sufficiently dry put them to candy (No. 3640); they can be flavored with vanilla or any other flavoring.

(3624). GUM PASTE (Pastillage.)

This is the manner of preparing gum paste used for various purposes: Have half a pound of very white Turkey gum tragacanth either in a glass vessel or a glazed one; wet the gum just sufficiently to have it covered, then close the vessel and leave it at least twelve hours or more. When the gum is quite soft and every hard particle disappears under the pressure of the finger put the gum in a heavy new towel; roll the two ends of this around two strong sticks and then twist each forcibly in a contrary direction until all the gum has passed through; lay it on a clean marble and work with the hand, incorporating half a pound of icing sugar sifted through a fine sieve, using more if the gum can absorb a larger quantity. Should the gum paste have too much consistence and recede while working, add a little water and sugar. (It is always preferable to have gum paste prepared the day before.) When it is required for making subjects, figures, dressing, draping, etc., or any other object that requires much manipulation, put a third less sugar to the above and replace it by corn starch. Should the gum paste now split it will be the result of too much body, therefore add a little water, sugar, corn starch, etc. If hard lumps be found in the gum tragacanth this is caused from it not being sufficiently or quickly worked with the sugar. For gum paste ornaments and architectural designs ordinary gum paste must be used—all sugar and no starch (only gum, icing sugar and water). Put in as much icing sugar as the gum can absorb without having too much, otherwise it will be impossible to work the paste. Should the edges of the pieces that have been cut out rise up, it is because the paste has too much body, therefore add to it a little ordinary gum paste, icing sugar and water. There must be no contraction whatever; the pieces once cut must remain as they are; dry them in the air, being careful that no dust settles on them and avoid any strong draught. With these cut-out pieces of gum paste pyramids are prepared, using cardboard models prepared in advance. They can be kept when very dry, wrapping them up carefully and placing them on edge between sheets of tissue paper and putting the pieces for each pyramid in a box to be kept in a dry place. When required for use fasten all the pieces of gum paste together with gum paste dissolved in water, having it liquid enough to force through a cornet, or else use royal icing. The paste can be colored with vegetal colorings, or gold, bronze or silver impalpable powders, after exposing the objects a few moments to steam. The gum paste may also be varnished with a varnish prepared as follows: Put a coffeespoonful of cream of tartar into a pint of milk; set it in a hot place and when the milk has soured filter and add four ounces of pulverized gum arabic, four ounces of spirits of wine and one small dissolved gelatine leaf; pour the whole into a bottle and stand it in a hot place for a few hours, then strain through a fine sieve and keep well corked in a cool spot.

(3625). MALAGA RAISINS STUFFED AND GLAZED (Raisins de Malaga Farcis et Glacés).

Split some fine Malaga raisins in two without separating the parts; remove the seeds and stuff one-third with a half-inch ball of almond paste (No. 125) colored white, another third with the same paste colored pink and the remaining third of almond paste with pistachios (No. 128); all these pastes to be prepared with cooked sugar (No. 3616); roll them into olive shapes, leaving the almond or pistachio paste show through the opening, and lay them at once on a wire sieve, then place in the heater to let get dry and glaze with sugar cooked to "crack" (No. 171).

(3626). TO SPIN SUGAR BY THROWING (Pour Filer le Sucre à la Jetée).

First have a spinner constructed as follows: On the entire surface of a round of sheet iron five inches in diameter and an eighth of an inch thick are to be riveted wire pegs an eighth of an inch in diameter and three and a half inches long, and at three-quarters of an inch apart from each other. A solid handle is fastened to the spinner. Cook in a copper pan two or three pounds of sugar to "large crack" (No. 171) or three hundred degrees Fahrenheit. As soon as done remove from the fire. Place several clean and oiled baking sheets on the floor. With the left hand take a small stick and hold it horizontally to the height of the chest or else lay it projecting over the edge of a table; with the right hand plunge the spinner into the sugar, take it out and drain off all the superfluous sugar; then, moving the instrument vigorously backward and forward over the small stick until all the sugar has run off in threads, redip the spinner into the sugar and begin the same movement again, continuing until all the sugar is spun. In case there be no spinner handy, a spoon can be used, dipping it into the cooked sugar, lifting it out and leaving all the surplus sugar drain off by moving it backward and forward the same as the spinner.

(3627). SUGAR FOR CASTING IN MOLDS (Sucre à Couler dans les Moules).

Place some lumps of sugar in a copper pan; pour over sufficient water to soak and leave till dissolved, when mix in a few drops of acetic acid and cook to 245 degrees; then remove from the fire, color a light blue with ultramarine blue and rub it against the sides of the pan with a wooden spoon to grain it. Pour it at once into molds; plaster ones are generally used for this purpose, having them properly dipped in cold water, then well drained and tied around firmly with a string so that the sugar cannot escape from the joints of the mold. After the mold is full wait until the sugar congeals on top, then break this thin crust and turn the mold upside down to empty out all the liquid sugar in order to have the subject hollow in the center. Unmold carefully, removing each piece one by one; pare them neatly and leave to cool in a dry, but not a hot place.

LARGE PIECES (Grandes Pièces).

(3628). BASKETS FILLED WITH CANDIED FRUITS, OR ICE CREAM FRUITS (Corbeilles Garnies de Fruits, ou de Fruits en Glace).

Take some ordinary nougat (No. 3621) and roll it out to a quarter of an inch in thickness; from it cut a round ten inches in diameter. Prepare twenty-one wires, each five inches long. coat them with a layer of colored pulled sugar (No. 3618) three-sixteenths of an inch thick and fasten them

FIG. 742. FIG. 743.

to the round of nougat at half an inch from the edge, leaving an inch space between each one. Have some pulled sugar, either white or colored; imitate a rope and arrange it around the base of the basket; pull some more sugar and roll it into strings a quarter of an inch thick and three feet long; make a braid of this sugar the same as a wicker basket going in and out of the wires, con-

FIG. 744.

tinuing as far as the top, finishing the whole with another rope the same as the bottom. Make the handles two and a half inches in diameter with the same sugar and pass them through rings fastened with sugar cooked to "crack (No. 171). Inside the upper part of the basket arrange a nougat foundation and cover it either with candied fruits, fresh fruits or else those made of ice cream or water ice.

(3629). PERRETTE'S BASKET (Le Panier de Perrette).

Have some nougat made of chopped almonds (No. 3621); roll it out to a quarter of an inch in thickness and cut it into an oval nine by five inches. Have sixteen pieces of wire, each six inches long; cover all of them with a three-sixteenths of an inch layer of pulled and colored sugar (No. 3618); bend each one separately while the sugar is still hot, then fasten them around the nougat oval, an inch from the border; spread the wires outward on top. Make a rope of pulled white sugar, place it around the bottom of the basket; roll some more pulled sugar into quarter-inch diameter strings and braid it around the wires, finishing the top with another braid of pulled sugar. In the

FIG. 745.

center fasten a sufficiently large handle, cover it with flowers and leaves made of pulled sugar and at one end tie a pretty satin ribbon bow three inches in width and of a color harmonizing with the basket. Put a nougat bottom inside the basket at two-thirds of its height, then fill up with chestnuts made of chestnut paste iced over with chocolate, or else ice cream in imitation of mushrooms, strawberries, etc.

(3630). BASKET WITH CHERRIES (Panier de Cerises).

To begin this basket first have an oval board ten and a half inches long by six inches wide; all around this oval bore holes a quarter of an inch in diameter and one inch apart from each other. Cut as many pieces of wire four and a half inches long as there are holes perforated in the board; straighten and envelop them in cooked sugar to form into sticks three-sixteenths

FIG. 746.

of an inch thick. After these sticks are cold dip the ends of each one separately in melted sugar and fasten them in the holes in the board. Now prepare some pulled sugar as described in No. 3618; take a little of this at a time and pull it into strings a quarter of an inch thick, and with these braid the basket as high as the top of the sticks. Pull two sticks with the same sugar, only slightly thicker than those used for braiding the basket and a little longer than half the circumference of the basket; fasten these two sticks together and twist them so as to imitate a thick rope; flatten this partly and fasten it at once on half of the edge of the basket, then pull two more sticks the same as the others, twist them the same way to obtain another thick rope, flatten it also and fasten it to the other half of the basket's edge. To make the handle pull three strings of sugar the same thickness and twenty inches long, braid them together and as soon as this is done bend the plait so as to shape the handle and when it is cold attach it to the basket. The two covers are made as follows: Pull two strings of sugar five-sixteenths of an inch thick, and bend each one so as to form a frame the shape and size of the opening of the basket, then pull more strings and while they are still hot fasten them diagonally on to these frames, and on top of these fasten others, crossing them in such a way that they form a lattice work. When these covers are finished attach them solidly against the handle of the basket. Trim around the base of the basket with a wreath of leaves, either gilded or silvered, arranging them symmetrically. Fill the basket tastefully with cherries made of almond paste (No. 125) and leaves of pulled sugar.

(3631). "BON VOYAGE" BOAT SERVED AT A FAREWELL DINNER (Bateau "Bon Voyage," Servi à l'Occasion d'un Départ).

The shell of the boat is made of brown nougat (No. 3621), molded in a plaster mold, oiled and varnished with shellac, first well dried, then oiled; the masts are made of wire covered with pulled sugar (No. 3618) of a yellowish hue; the cordage of silk, and the sails of pulled sugar exceedingly white, remelted on a slow fire, and rolled out speedily with a roller, then cut with cardboard patterns into the shape of the various sails, afterward laid on sheets of tin bent to the needed form. The waves are imitated in pulled sugar of a greenish color, and the letters on the standard are painted with gold paint. The entire boat can be made of white or colored gum paste (No. 3624), and the water

FIG. 747.

imitated with green royal icing (No. 101). This piece may be filled either with fresh or candied fruits, such as Malaga grapes stuffed with almond paste (No. 125); candied cherries or strawberries and angelica, or else instead of these have imitation flowers made of ice cream and angelica lozenges.

(3632). CHARIOT FILLED WITH LADY APPLES (Chariot Garni de Pommes d'Api).

To make the chariot the wheels must first be constructed. The hoops of the wheels are made with thick bands of nougat (No. 3621), three-quarters of an inch broad; bend these around a cylindrical mold four inches in diameter and stick the parts together with cooked sugar (No. 3616). To make the spokes of these wheels, roll out some nougat to three-eighths of an inch in thickness and then divide it into small sticks half the length of the diameter of the hoops of the wheels; when these are all cold fasten the small sticks inside the wheel with cooked sugar, having them laid at even distances apart, and fasten a small round piece of nougat in the center to imitate the naves of the wheel; now make the axles with two pieces of strong wire, each six and a half inches in length; envelop these in cooked sugar and when cold attach them firmly on the wheels. Make the bottom of the chariot with a layer of nougat twelve inches long by six wide and when this is very cold fasten it solidly on the axles. Next make the two ladders as hereby described: Roll out a band of nougat to five-sixteenths of an inch in thickness, pare it straight and even on both ends, having it twelve inches long; divide it lengthwise into four very straight sticks five-sixteenths of an inch wide; roll out some more nougat to a quarter of an inch in thickness and cut this into even sticks three and a quarter inches long; take up two of the long sticks, lay them down parallel at three and a quarter inches distance apart and between these attach diagonally a row of the small sticks slightly apart from one another, and again on these a second row also laid diagonally, but in an opposite direction, so that one row crosses the other. Having finished the first ladder, proceed to make the second. Fasten these two ladders solidly on the bottom of the chariot and against the

FIG. 748.

wheels. Make the shafts with two very thin wires enveloped in cooked sugar and when cold attach them to the front of the chariot. The socle is now to be made: Have two flats of nougat three-sixteenths of an inch thick, one for the upper part to be seventeen inches long by eleven and a half wide, and the second one for the bottom nineteen inches long by thirteen and a half inches wide; also make four nougat bands for the framework and fasten them firmly with cooked sugar; on this framework lay the second flat and fasten it also to form the socle or stand; fasten around the bottom of this socle a triple row of nougat points cut very evenly and placed symmetrically; decorate the border of the second flat with oak leaves and acorns made of sugar, and lastly construct the fence with sticks of nougat cut a quarter of an inch in thickness. Lay the chariot on this stand and fill it with small lady apples formed of gum paste (No. 3624) or grained sugar, and fasten here and there some apple leaves made of cooked sugar.

(3633). CHARIOT OF DOVES (Le Chariot des Colombes).

The body of the chariot is made and molded of white nougat (No. 3622) in a plaster mold, divided in two, well garnished with shellac and oiled; the border of the shell is made of almond paste (No. 125) and gum tragacanth cut out in a design; the wheels are of nougat or pulled sugar (No. 3618), the spokes, the ring and the axle cut out separately and fastened together with cooked sugar; the nails are imitated with royal icing (No. 101); the shafts are made of wire covered with

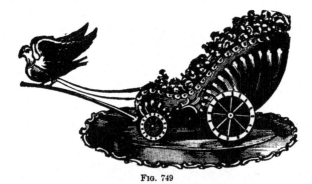

Fig. 749

nougat or pulled sugar. Stand the chariot on an oval stand of pistachio nougat (No. 3622) the size of the bottom of the dish intended for serving. Place a false nougat bottom inside the chariot, then fill it up with candied fruits iced over with caramel and angelica. This chariot can also be made of gum paste (No. 3624) and filled with candied fruits or fruits and flowers of all descriptions made in ice cream or water ice.

(3634). CHARIOT OF SWANS (Le Char des Cygnes).

This piece is made entirely of gum paste (No. 3624), the swan is molded in a two-piece plaster mold, the two halves of the swan are fastened together, the crevices filled with softened gum paste, then thoroughly dried. Wash off with a sponge and imitate the eyes and beaks with a brush.

Fig. 750.

The shell is also molded in a dry plaster mold and is decorated on the outspread parts with designs of gum paste bronzed or gilded. On the thin end of the shell stand a Cupid made of gum paste; the ring encircling the swan is of gum paste, the reins of silk and the harness of satin ribbon; the whole is made to stand on an oval bottom cut the size of the dish it is served on. The waves are made of royal icing (No. 101) tinted a pale green. Fill the chariot with iced candied fruits, candies, or else ice cream or water ices.

(3635). CORNUCOPIA, HORN OF PLENTY (Corne d'Abondance).

This cornucopia is molded in a mold the shape of Fig. 751. It is made of pulled sugar (No. 3618), remelted and rolled out with a roller—this must be done very quickly—or else it can be made of white nougat (No. 3622) decorated with royal icing (No. 101) or of gum paste (No. 3624). Fasten it on the opening side on a nougat surtout, and support the body of the cornucopia by fastening two rests molded in gum paste in a two-piece mold, and place a wire in the center of each; attach the two pieces together and let get very dry. The cornucopia is surmounted by a gum paste Cupid; the inside border of the opening of the dish is made of pulled sugar and is composed of rings, with smaller ones of a darker color placed inside of one another; bend them lightly to spread open on sheets of tin, then fasten them to the inside border of the dish with cooked sugar; between each one arrange a lozenge of glazed angelica. The opening of the cornucopia is filled with candied fruits, or else others made of chestnut or almond paste (No. 125), and glazed with sugar cooked to

FIG. 751.

"crack" (No. 171). This piece may be made of white gum paste (No. 3624) and decorated with gold reliefs, or it may be utilized by replacing the fruits with fruits imitated in cream or water ices.

(3636). THE DOSSER À LA DENIVELLE (La Hotte à la Denivelle).

Roll out some nougat (No. 3621) to a quarter of an inch in thickness, and from it cut with either a tin or oiled cardboard pattern a piece fifteen inches long by six on one end and four on the other in

FIG. 752.

width, rounding the six-inch end which is for the upper part of the dosser; also cut another piece of a semicircular shape four inches in diameter by two and a half inches in radius. Prepare eleven wires, two eight inches long, two of seven and three-quarters, two of seven and a half, two of seven and a quarter, two of seven and one of six and three-quarters inches; coat them all with colored sugar. Fasten the semi-circular bottom on the large piece at its narrowest end, near the edge; on this bottom arrange the wires, beginning with the eight-inch ones on each side beside the back of the dosser, and continuing with the others according to their various lengths, at the same time spreading them open toward the top. Coat with green sugar two more wires each nine inches long, and leave to cool. Cut out a round bottom twelve inches in diameter, then fasten the dosser on the center of it, pressing it against the two long wires to be used for a support; decorate the whole profusely with leaves and flowers made of satinated pulled sugar (No. 3618), and fill the dosser with mushrooms or strawberries made of almond paste (No. 125), also some angelica coated with sugar cooked to "crack" (No. 171). The dosser may be filled with small ices imitating flowers.

(3637). VASES OF PULLED AND DRAWN SUGAR (Vases en Sucre Filé et Tiré).

All pieces that are made of pulled and spun sugar are exceedingly useful for many reasons, as large-sized pieces can be executed at a comparatively low cost and yet be most elegant, graceful and light; besides the rapidity of the execution, they can be made to assume a great variety of shapes, and all this with very few or even no molds. The designs shown in Figs. 753 and 754,

FIG. 753.   FIG. 754.

will demonstrate the many uses to be made of pulled and spun sugar, and although they demand much skill and attention, yet they do not offer the same difficulties as gum paste. The socles or stands for these pieces may be of white nougat (No. 3622), molded and cut out, and the embellishments around the base of the vases may also be of almond paste (No. 125) glazed with caramel. The three swans seen on one of the socles are made of very white cooked sugar (320 degrees Fahrenheit), poured into slightly oiled tin molds; leave till cold, then unmold. The whole work must be mounted symmetrically, being careful that each part is firmly attached and the piece perfectly secure. For vases of white or colored cooked sugar (No. 3616) trace outlines of the designs on marble (see Fig. 733), having sixteen, twenty-four or even thirty-two pieces for each vase. Take a stick six to eight inches higher than the intended vase and coat it with cooked sugar; roll it on the marble until it becomes exceedingly smooth, leave it until cold, then fasten it vertically on to the center of the socle; adapt the traced pieces perpendicularly around this stick at equal distances apart. Prepare the flowers and leaves of pulled sugar (Figs. 735 to 741); mount them on wire stalks covered with sugar, and attach them solidly against the stick inside the top of the vase, spreading them open slightly to enlarge and to give a graceful effect to the blossoms. Decorate the base of the socle with flowers and leaves of pulled sugar. Should the pieces be very large, then it will be found advisable to mount the bouquet separately and place it in the vase when in position on the dinner table; in this case instead of having the stick higher than the vase it must be at least six inches lower, to leave room for a receptacle intended to receive the flowers, the latter to be the same shape and size as the upper portion of the vase, and to be made of nougat (No. 3622), stand this inside the vase and place the flowers tastefully within.

(3638). WHEELBARROW FILLED WITH FLOWERS ON A SOCLE (Brouette Garnie de Fleurs sur Socle).

Have ready an oval socle made of brown nougat, the same as shown in Fig. 756; decorate it with agricultural implements and leaves of pulled sugar made by hand; the rope around the base of the socle is made with two strings twisted quickly and fastened to the border and around the under base; the top tray is made of green pistachio nougat (No. 3622). On top of the entire socle arrange a wheelbarrow made in four pieces of pink or any other color of pulled sugar, rolled out to three-sixteenths of an inch in thickness, then cut out with patterns made beforehand and after the drawing; the shafts and rests are made of wire covered with pulled sugar and bent to the desired

FIG. 756.

shape. The wheel is of pulled sugar: first make a ring and place a round in the center; join the two together by small sticks of pulled sugar; between the shafts and the wheel pass a wire; fasten it on at each side with cooked sugar. The wheelbarrow is upheld and fastened with sugar cooked to "crack;" the flowers that fill the barrow and the border on top are made of pulled sugar to which a little chocolate has been added.

This piece of confectionery may be made of gum paste (No. 3624), either white or any light color; the wheelbarrow can be filled, as well as the one above, with glazed fruits or fancy ices, such as potatoes, tomatoes, mushrooms, etc., and the bottom of the socle garnished around with fruits, or fruits in cases glazed with caramel, or with small light waffles dressed in a circle, one overlapping the other.

(3639). WINDMILL (Moulin à Vent).

This pyramid, though quite an old idea, is always sure to be well received. The great variety of its details, and the figures which can be added to it, representing scenes of country life, give it an attractive appearance which can hardly be obtained in architectural pyramids. Although its execution offers no great difficulties, yet great care and exactitude must be taken in the cutting out of the different pieces of which it is composed, for there is the essential point for its successful completion. The cut is a reduction of the original, and can thus serve as a basis for its execution, either in multiplying or diminishing its dimensions, according to the desired size of the pyramid. Cut out with great precision patterns of strong cardboard, and, if to be used for nougat, oil them well. The part of the pyramid representing the walls is made of white nougat (No. 3622) with chopped almonds, rolled on the marble to about one-quarter of an inch thick, and with the help of oiled patterns cut out rapidly the windows and the doors. The roof is of nougat covered with imitation of tiles made of almond paste (No. 125) colored a light chocolate or a light brick red, rolled to a sheet one-sixteenth of an inch thick. Cut out with a tin circular cutter and then put on, beginning with the bottom layer, each layer successively overlapping the other. The large platform and the doors are of ordinary brown nougat (No. 3621), the railing of lightly colored chocolate sugar, and composed of pieces cut with a knife and stuck together with melted sugar. The windows are made of sugar boiled to three hundred and thirty degrees, very clear, rolled thin and placed in the interior.

Fig. 757.

The rustic beams are made of chocolate pulled sugar (No. 3618), the stairways of brown nougat and the wings of the mill are composed of four pieces of wire, covered and rolled in brown cooked sugar, and of white pulled sugar melted and rolled thin, and cut out with scissors. The little sticks across the wings are made of lightly colored chocolate sugar and put on about one-eighth of an inch apart. The rock or base is twelve inches high, and is composed of two wood platforms, supported by a wood framework, around which bunches of crumpled paper are put on, which is then covered with green nougat, rolled thin and garnished with herbs and plants imitated with green pulled sugar. This whole pyramid can also be made of clear sugar exclusively, boiled to three hundred and thirty-five degrees, very transparent, melted over and poured on a tracing of patterns on marble and filled in as described. Or, further yet, of gum paste (No. 3624) exclusively, in natural colors or white, taking great care, however, not to set up the pieces until each one is perfectly dry. The windows could then be imitated by thin sheets of mica or gelatine, and the base of gum paste covered with royal icing (No. 101). Or, the ambitious workman can imitate with gum paste, a miller, a bag on his shoulder, going up the stairway, or two peasants eating and drinking, or a peasant woman with children around her, and many other subjects of country life and customs.

(3639a). THE PROLIFIC TREE (L'Arbre Prodigieux).

In order to make a tree two feet in height cut the wires varying from four to fourteen inches in length. Prepare some nougat with chopped almonds (No. 3621), incorporating sufficient cocoa to color it brown; roll out enough of this to be able to cut out a piece a quarter of an inch thick, sixteen inches long and seven inches wide in the part intended for the base and slightly narrower for the top. Wrap this piece of nougat around a wooden support in imitation of the trunk of a tree and

FIG. 758.

leave to cool; coat the wires with nougat proportionately thick according to their length, and thicker on the ends that are to be attached to the trunk; bend them as soon as covered to shape them into knotty and irregular boughs, and leave to cool. Color some white nougat (No. 3622) a pistachio green, roll it out on a marble to a quarter of an inch in thickness, and from it cut a round bottom sixteen inches in diameter, then attach it to a board of the same size. At two inches from the edge fasten the trunk of the tree on solidly and decorate it with the boughs, having the heaviest attached to the trunk, and the lighter ones attached to these. Melt some cooked sugar, mix in a little cocoa and chopped almonds, and with a knife coat over the trunk and the branches to imitate the bark and the roots at the foot of the tree. Pull some dark green-colored sugar, a very little at a time, and with it form leaves as described in No. 3618; trim the branches with these, and also with cherries made of almond paste (No. 125) and glazed, or else substitute pears or little apples, or better still green almonds, but any imitated fruit can be used. Place a ladder against the tree, made of wire covered with chocolate-colored sugar, and on this stand a small image to represent a cupid stealing the fruit, and at one side another cupid receiving the picked fruit. Make these figures of gum paste (No. 3624). Make the boughs and bushes around the foot of the tree of pulled sugar (No. 3618), also the rope that surrounds it. These trees can be varied as regards both size and subject. One or more trees can be arranged on a single board without any figures or subjects.

(3640). CANDYING, COLD AND HOT (Candi à Froid et à Chaud).

Cold.—This manner of candying is specially adapted for bonbons. Put some lump sugar in a copper pan, pour over sufficient water to dissolve it, and as soon as this takes place set it on the fire to cook to thirty-five degrees; when the sugar has attained this degree take the pan from the fire and stand it in a basin or any other receptacle filled with cold water; cover the sugar with a round of paper, and leave stand till cold. Now pour it into the candy pans containing the pieces to be candied; put in a dry place in a moderate temperature and leave for twelve to eighteen hours; drain off the syrup and place the candied pieces on a grate to dry.

Hot.—This manner of candying is used specially for candying preserved fruits. Cook some syrup to thirty-six degrees; leave rest for one instant, then pour it into the candy pans, having the fruits already arranged therein; place the pan in a heater, having it moderately hot, and remove only after six or seven hours, or when the fruits are all coated.

(3641). TO CAST IN STARCH (Pour Couler à l'Amidon).

To cast in starch wooden boxes are required twenty inches long, fourteen inches wide and three inches deep. Fill these boxes with very dry starch to a quarter of an inch from the top; stir  about with a small whip to have it light, then smooth neatly with a ruler; now imprint into it with small plaster molds fastened on to a second ruler at some distance apart, burying them in the starch until the ruler touches the edges of the box. Should these small molds have a channeled surface or deeply imprinted designs, then before lifting them out of the starch rap the ruler lightly on top to have any of the starch that may adhere fall away. Care must be taken to sift the starch from time to time to rid it of any lumps or grains of sugar that may have

FIG. 759.

formed therein. To cast the sugar use a funnel in the center of which is a rod terminating in a ball that fits the outlet of the funnel accurately. This rod is moved up and down by means of a horizontal lever and a spring which are fastened to the handle of the funnel.

CANDIES (Bonbons).

(3642). BURNT ALMONDS (Pralines).

Put a pound and a half of sugar and half of a vanilla bean in a pan, dissolve it with a little water and stand it on the fire to cook to thirty-four degrees (syrup gauge), then add one pound of fine almonds; mix all together with a wooden spoon and continue to cook until the sugar reaches "crack" (No. 171), stirring the almonds steadily till the sugar granulates. Take the pan from the fire and pour both sugar and almonds into a coarse sieve to separate the almonds from the granulated sugar, return the almonds to the pan, stand it on the fire and stir constantly until the sugar covering the almonds melts away, adding from time to time a small handful of the granulated sugar. As soon as all the sugar is added and that surrounding the almonds is well dissolved, pour it immediately on to a slab, separating them from each other, and leave to cool. Put a heaping tablespoonful of dissolved gum arabic in a basin, dilute it with a little water and let it come to a boil; then add the burnt almonds and toss until entirely covered; pour at once on to a sieve and place in the heater to dry.

(3643). CHOCOLATE CREAM CARAMELS (Caramels à la Crème au Chocolat).

Melt twelve ounces of chocolate in a copper pan with a pint and a half of good cream and half a pint of fruit syrup well flavored with vanilla, then add a pound and a half of sugar. Stand the pan on a hot fire and when the liquid begins to boil stir it vigorously with a spatula until it reaches "large ball" (No. 171), then pour it on a slightly oiled marble to half an inch in thickness, securing the caramel within lightly oiled square iron rods laid in the shape of a square. This caramel takes a long while to cool; when cold remove the rulers, detach from the marble and cut it first into long bands half an inch wide, and these across in half-inch squares. As fast as the caramels are cut wrap each one in a piece of waxed paper.

(3644). VANILLA CREAM CARAMELS, OR WITH TEA OR COFFEE (Caramels à la Crème Vanillés au Thé ou au Café).

Set a pound of sugar in a copper pan to melt with three-quarters of a pint of cream, adding a split vanilla bean; stand the pan on a brisk fire and stir steadily until cooked to "large ball" (No. 171), then pour it in a square formed on the marble with slightly oiled square iron rods, having it the same thickness as the chocolate caramels. When cold cut out and wrap in waxed papers, finishing them exactly the same as the chocolates. These caramels can be flavored with tea or coffee, proceeding as for the above, only using one pound of sugar, two gills of cream and a gill and a half of infused tea or coffee.

(3645). CORDIAL CANDIES (Bonbons aux Liqueurs).

These candies are cast in starch. First prepare the boxes of starch, impressed as explained in No. 3641; put two pounds of sugar in a copper basin, dissolve with three gills of water and stand it on the fire to cook the sugar to thirty-six degrees (syrup gauge); when the sugar attains this degree add a small cordial glassful of kirsch, maraschino or any other desired cordial, to bring the syrup back to thirty-two degrees, stirring it well. Now pour this syrup into a spring funnel (Fig. 759) and cast the candies in the starch impressions; put the filled box in the heater at a moderate temperature and leave for twelve hours. They should now have formed a sufficiently thick crust to allow them to be worked; remove carefully from the starch, brush one at a time with a very soft hair brush, and lay them at once on a grate to cool, then stand this grate on a candy pan and cover the candies with a cold thirty-two degree syrup; lay a piece of paper on top to keep the candies submerged. Put this candy pan in a mild temperature and leave for six hours. Then drain off the syrup, take out the candies to arrange them on a second grate and leave to dry. Instead of crystallizing these candies they can be iced with fondant (No. 58) flavored with cordial.

(3646). DROPS (Pastilles).

These are made by mixing powdered sugar from which the icing sugar has been removed by sifting through a very fine sieve, flavored either with aromatics or fruit juices, to the consistency of a paste. They are all prepared exactly alike; those composed of fruit should be a little more liquid and a little less heated than those with aromatically flavored waters. They should all be dropped on to bright tin plates.

(3647). PEPPERMINT DROPS (Pastilles de Menthe).

Mix seven ounces of the same sugar as above with about two ounces of water, flavored with a few drops of peppermint essence, to form into a paste; heat it the same as for the strawberry drops, only warming it rather more, and finish exactly the same.

(3648). STRAWBERRY DROPS (Pastilles aux Fraises).

Place seven ounces of powdered sugar, prepared as (No. 3646), in a small copper pan having a spout, and reduce it to the consistency of a paste with about an ounce of filtered strawberry juice; color lightly with liquid carmine to give it a pink hue. Stand the pan on the fire and heat until the paste flows, stirring continuously with a small spatula; however, it must be of a consistency not to spread when dropped on the trays. To dress, hold the pan in the left hand, inclining the spout toward the tray, and in the right hand hold a small wire; with this cut the paste away from the spout as fast as it runs out, thus leaving it fall in small pieces to form into drops three-eighths of an inch in diameter and slightly apart from each other. Half an hour after they can be detached from the tray by bending it slightly and then shaking them; throw on a sieve to finish drying.

(3649). FILBERT CANDIES (Bonbons d'Avelines en Conserve).

Procure small plaster molds imitating hazel-nuts and fasten them to a ruler, then imprint them in starch. Peel six ounces of filberts and crush to form a very fine paste with a gill and a half of water. Cook a pound of sugar to "small crack" (No. 171), add the pounded nuts, stir well and cast it at once into the starch impressions; when these candies have sufficiently hardened in the starch to be able to be handled take them out, one by one, brush carefully and stand on a sieve to cool; they can afterward be dipped in cold crystallized syrup until completely coated with candy.

(3650). CHOCOLATE FONDANTS (Fondants au Chocolat).

Dissolve four ounces of chocolate with two gills of water; add half a stick of vanilla and a pound and a half of sugar; continue to cook until it reaches "small ball" (No. 171), then pour it on a marble slab and leave to cool; work to obtain a fondant, proceeding the same as for No. 58. Put a part of this in a copper pan to melt, adding a spoonful of vanilla syrup, then cast this in the starch. As soon as the candies are firm and cold take them out and brush over; melt the remainder of the fondant, softening it with vanilla syrup, and dip the candies in this.

(3651). VANILLA FONDANTS (Fondants à la Vanille).

Have some conical-shaped molds, with rounded tops, a quarter of an inch in diameter at their base and a quarter of an inch high; impress them into the starch. Put one pound of fondant (No. 58) in a sugar pan, add two tablespoonfuls of thirty-four degree syrup strongly flavored with vanilla and stand it on the fire to heat until the finger can yet be held in, then pour it into a spring funnel (Fig. 759) and run it through into the impressions in the starch; when the candies are cold and firm take them carefully from the starch, brush gently with a brush and stand them on a grate, then put away in a cold place. These can be dipped in fondant well flavored with vanilla.

(3652). FONDANTS DIPPED IN STRAWBERRY OR RASPBERRY (Fondants Trempés à la Fraise ou à la Framboise).

Put some fondant into a copper pan and heat well, dissolving it with a few spoonfuls of strawberry or raspberry juice. As soon as hot cast it through a funnel into the starch, proceeding the same as for vanilla fondant (No. 3651). When firm and cold take them carefully from the starch and dip each one in a strawberry or raspberry fondant lightly tinted with a little carmine.

(3653). CANDIES FOR MOTTOES (Bonbons pour Papillotes).

Have some small conical-shaped plaster molds, the bottoms being detruncated and rounded; they should be an inch in diameter at the bottom and one inch high. Fasten these molds on a ruler slightly apart from each other, then with this ruler imprint the molds into the starch. Put two pounds of sugar in a copper sugar basin and dissolve it with a pint and a half of water; stand this on the fire to cook to "large ball" (No. 171), being careful to remove all the scum and keep the sides of the pan clean. When the sugar has reached the proper degree let it fall to "small ball" by adding a few spoonfuls of orange flower water, then remove the pan from the fire and with a wooden spoon rub the sugar against the sides to mass it. As soon as it begins to whiten stir it well and cast it into the starch impressions, using a spring funnel (Fig. 759) for this purpose; when the box is full bestrew the candies lightly with a handful of starch and put the box in a heater for two or three hours. After the candies are hard remove them from the starch and range them on grates or on a sieve to cool thoroughly, then brush over with a camel's hair or feather brush. To wrap up these candies spread open some variegated colored motto papers, in the center of each lay a printed motto folded in four and on this one of the candies, then fold the paper all around toward the center and use a string attached to the table to enclose the candy (this is done by giving the string a turn around the motto and pulling on it, then the motto is released and will be found firmly twisted) and form a bouquet with the fringed ends of the paper.

(3654). NORTHERN JELLY CANDIES (Bonbons du Nord à la Gelée).

Fasten some plaster half-spherical or convex molds on a ruler and with it make the impressions in the starch. Prepare a pint of apple jelly the same as in No. 3668, only cooking it a little more; bring this to the ordinary degree of cooking, adding either rum, kirsch or other liquor, then cast it in the starch impressions through a spring funnel (Fig. 759). Put the boxes in a heater and leave for eight or ten hours. By this time the jelly will have formed into thin crusts sufficiently hardened to be taken out carefully and laid on a wire sieve. When cold, brush each one separately with a fine hair brush and then dip into a liquor-flavored fondant (No. 58). Instead of dipping them in the fondant they can be candied by laying them in a cold syrup, the same as for No. 3659.

(3655). NOUGAT, SOFT AND HARD (Nougat Mou et Dur).

Soft White Nougat.—Heat three pounds of white honey, cook separately three pounds of sugar to "ball" (two hundred and thirty-six degrees Fahrenheit). Whip eight egg-whites in a copper basin to a stiff froth, add the honey and the cooked sugar and continue beating the whites on a slow fire until the preparation is at "small crack" (two hundred and ninety degees Fahrenheit). This degree of heat will be recognized by taking up a small part with the tip of a knife, dipping it in cold water, and when crumbled it should fall into a powder. During this time cook three pounds of sugar to "crack" (three hundred and ten degrees Fahrenheit); mix it with the whites, adding five pounds of whole almonds and a quarter of a pound of hulled and dried pistachios. Fill some oblong tin cases with this, having them previously lined with white wafers. Pour the nougat in the case, leave to cool, then cut in slices.

Another Proportion is a pound and three-quarters of almonds, one pound of sugar, one pound of white honey, five egg-whites, a quarter of a pound of pistachios, two ounces of burnt almonds, and vanilla; finish the same as the above.

Hard White Nougat.—Four pounds of heated honey, two pounds of sugar cooked to "ball" (three hundred and twenty-six degrees Fahrenheit), two pounds cooked to "small crack" (two hundred and ninety degrees Fahrenheit), five pounds of almonds, a quarter of a pound of pistachios and five beaten egg-whites. Cut in slices when nearly cold. The same preparation as for the soft white nougat.

(3656). TORTILLONS (Tortillons).

Place one pound of loaf sugar in a copper sugar basin with sufficient water to melt, then stand it on the fire to cook to three hundred and twenty-five degrees Fahrenheit, being careful to keep the sides clean, and proceed as explained for cooking sugar (No. 171). When ready pour it on a lightly oiled marble, add at once a, few drops of peppermint essence and begin to raise up the edges, bringing them toward the center until the sugar can be handled with the hands, then begin to pull till it attains a very glossy, silvery appearance; pull again to a quarter of an inch in diameter string, and cut this quickly into small pieces an inch and a half long, bending each one immediately into the shape of a ring. The pulling, cutting and bending should be performed with despatch, before the sugar has time to cool, when it will fail to bend. The sugar may be colored either light pink or pale green just when flavoring.

(3657). TROCADEROS WITH RASPBERRY (Trocadéros à la Framboise).

Proceed the same as for Trocaderos with rum (No. 3658), using a pound and a half of sugar and a gill and a half of raspberry pulp strained through a very fine sieve and two and a half gills of rich cream. After removing from the starch and well brushed, dip in a thin royal icing (No. 101) slightly tinted with carmine and flavored with a little raspberry juice.

(3658). TROCADEROS WITH RUM (Trocadéros au Rhum).

Cook a pound and a half of sugar to "small crack" (No. 171), adding three gills of cream, and let it boil up once only; put in half a gill of rum and cast it at once in starch imprinted with small lozenge-shaped molds; set the box away in the heater for twelve hours. Now remove the candies one by one from the starch, brush carefully and range them on a grate; dip the candies in a light royal icing (No. 101) well flavored with rum.

(3659). CANDIED VIOLETS (Violettes Pralinées).

Select a pound of full-bloom violets; suppress the stalks and throw into cold water to refresh, then spread them on a towel to drain. Cook a pound and a quarter of sugar to "small ball" (No. 171), throw in the violets, remove the pan from the fire at once and stir gently to submerge them. Boil this up once and then transfer immediately to a vessel. The following day drain them on a sieve, pour the syrup back into a copper pan, add a little more sugar, and cook again to "small ball;" put in the flowers and transfer once more to the vessel to leave for another twelve hours; after this drain off again, pour this syrup back into the pan, boil it once or twice and add the violets, removing the pan at once from the fire. Stir the violets lightly in this syrup until it begins to grain, then pour the whole on sheets of paper; shake and separate the flowers carefully with the hands, and when dry pick them from the granulated sugar, arrange on a grate and leave to get cold.

PRESERVES (Conserves).

(3660). BRANDY CHERRIES (Cerises à l'Eau de Vie).

Cook two and a half pounds of sugar to "small crack" (No. 171); as soon as it reaches this degree take the pan from the fire and add slowly to it one gallon of brandy and a fourth part of a vanilla bean; leave this till cold. Cut off half of the cherry stalks, range the fruit in glass bottles and cover with the above liquid. Cork the bottles hermetically when the cherries are cold and put away in a cool place.

(3661). BRANDY FIGS (Figues à l'Eau de Vie).

Have some white even-sized figs; prick and leave them to soak for twelve hours in salted water. Parboil them properly, keeping them firm, then drain and refresh by throwing them into a plentiful supply of cold salted water and leave them to steep for two or three days; now put them in a copper pan and cover with a hot twenty-two degree syrup so that they macerate for six hours; afterward drain off this syrup, add to it more sugar and let cook to twenty-five degrees; when this is cold pour it over the figs; repeat this operation until the sugar attains thirty degrees. Drain the figs well, put them into glass jars and cover with brandy; let macerate for six weeks, then add for every quart of brandy two gills of thirty-degree syrup.

(3662). BRANDY GREENGAGES (Reines Claudes à l'Eau de Vie).

Take fine sound greengages; prick over and blanch; have them resume their former green color the same as for preserved greengages (No. 3679), and when well refreshed drain again and arrange them in glass jars, each one to contain a vanilla bean; cover with good white brandy and cork the jars hermetically; leave them thus for fifteen days. After this lapse of time drain off the brandy and add some sugar to it, allowing three pounds for each gallon of liquid; stir well together; when the sugar is dissolved pour it over the fruits; close the jars hermetically and leave them in a cool place.

(3663). BRANDY PEACHES (Pêches à l'Eau de Vie).

Let the peaches be white and sound; rub with a cloth to remove their down, prick the surfaces and lay them in cold water; drain this off and place them in a basin, covering with fresh cold water into which has been added a small piece of alum; set the basin on the fire and as soon as the liquid begins to heat stir the fruits about from time to time, and when they float on top of the liquid remove and throw them again into cold water. Drain and arrange them in one-quart glass jars, having a quarter of a vanilla stick in each, and cover with good white brandy. Close the bottles hermetically and stand them in a cool place to leave for fifteen days, and then drain off the brandy into a basin, add sugar to it, allowing three pounds for each gallon; stir well to melt the sugar, then pour this liquor over the peaches; cork the jars so no air whatever can enter and lay aside in a cool place.

(3664). CANNED CHERRIES (Cerises en Boîtes).

Suppress the stalks and pips from some fine, very ripe but sound cherries; range them at once in tin cans of a quart capacity and cover with a twenty-five degree cold syrup; put on the lids and solder tightly. Stand these cans in a large saucepanful of cold water, set it covered on the fire and boil the water for seven minutes, then remove at once from the fire and allow the cans to cool off in the liquid.

(3665). CANNED PEARS (Poires en Boîtes).

Select pears that are ripe yet firm (Sickle pears in preference); peel, turning them round, and empty with a vegetable scoop to remove all the pips, blanch and refresh. Drain as soon as they are properly cooled off and range them in tin cans each of a quart capacity; fill the can nine-tenths full with a fifteen-degree cold syrup; cover and solder. Range these cans in a large sauce-pan, immerse them in cold water, place on the fire and boil for ten minutes; remove the cans, tap a small hole in the center to allow the air to escape, solder it up immediately and boil for five minutes longer.

(3666). CANNED PINEAPPLE (Ananas en Boîtes).

Pare neatly some fine ripe pineapples; remove the hard centers with a tin tube, then split them lengthwise in two; cut across in quarter-inch thick slices and range these in tin cans of one quart capacity each. Fill the cans nine-tenths full with cold twelve-degree syrup; cover and solder, then place them in a large saucepanful of cold water so they are entirely submerged, and covering the pan stand on the fire and allow the liquid to boil for fifteen minutes. Remove the cans, punch a small hole on top to allow the air to escape and solder immediately; replace the saucepan and allow to boil five minutes more. If whole pineapples, merely cored, are used instead of slices they will require forty minutes boiling, and if not cored one hour will be found a correct time.

(3667). CELERY HEARTS, CRYSTALLIZED (Cœurs de Céleri Cristallisés).

Peel the hearts of some small celery stalks; parboil them well in acidulated water, and when very tender drain and wipe on a cloth; range them in a flat dish and cover with a cold twenty-five degree syrup. Six hours after drain off this syrup and mix in with it some sugar steeped in water and cooked to thirty degrees, adding the juice of one lemon; pour this again over the celery hearts and six hours later recommence the operation. When cold dress into a preserve dish with the syrup poured over.

(3668). APPLE AND ORANGE JELLY (Gelée de Pommes et Gelée d'Oranges).

Cut two dozen russet apples in slices, lay them in a basin with water to cover; cook tender, then pour them on a sieve to drain off the juice, collecting it in a bowl; filter this through a flannel bag and put it into the basin again with the same weight of sugar; dissolve thoroughly, mixing together with a skimmer, then set the basin on the fire and cook until the syrup coats the spatula and falls down in beads; stir continuously with the skimmer. As soon as the liquid reaches the proper degree pour it at once into stone pots or glasses previously heated; leave to cool thoroughly. Lay on the jelly a round of paper soaked in brandy, and afterward cover the glasses with strong paper or parchment.

Orange Jelly.—Remove the peel from a few nice oranges, cut it in very thin shreds, blanch them well and then drain. Pare the oranges to the pulp. Prepare some apple jelly, as explained above, and when it is nearly cooked add to it the blanched peel and the pared oranges; mix well and when cooked pour into small jars or glasses previously heated in boiling water.

(3669). CHERRY JELLY WITH KIRSCH (Gelée de Cerises au Kirsch).

Stone three pounds of cherries, pound six ounces of the kernels with one pound of currants and strain it through a sieve. Put the cherries in a copper pan on a slow fire and reduce to half, then add three pounds of sugar and one pound of the strained currant and kernel juice, and continue to cook until a drop of it placed on a flat surface will not spread; now put in half a gill of kirsch and pour at once into jars to leave in a cool place until thoroughly cold; cover with a round of paper dipped in brandy, and close the pots hermetically with their respective covers.

(3670). CURRANT JELLY AND PLAIN CURRANT JELLY; CRANBERRY JELLY (Gelée de Groseille et Gelée de Groseille Simple; Gelée de Canneberges).

Have one pound of currants free of stalks and one pound of powdered sugar; mix both together in a vessel without crusting the currants; when the sugar is dissolved pour the whole into a copper pan and stand it on the fire; after it has been boiling for five or six minutes the syrup will have cooked to the proper degree, that is, until it coats the skimmer and drops from it in beads. Now pour the fruit and syrup on to a sieve laid over a vessel fit to receive the liquid, and use this to fill jelly glasses; keep slightly warm for two hours, then leave to cool before covering the glasses with paper.

Another way is to select the currants when not too ripe; pick off all the stalks and put the fruit in a copper pan with three-quarters of their weight of powdered sugar; when this is partly melted stand the pan on a slow fire to bring the liquid to a boil while skimming; boil it once or twice only; skim well, strain through a napkin and pour into jelly glasses.

Plain.—Slightly cook ten pounds of currants with their stalks in a copper pan; pass them through a sieve having sufficiently fine meshes to prevent the seeds from passing; mix an equal weight of sugar to this juice; cook until it coats the skimmer and drops from it in beads, being careful to skim during the whole process of cooking. Fill some heated glasses or jars, and when cold cover with a round of paper soaked in brandy, then cover the top of the vessel with strong paper.

Cranberry Jelly.—Crush about two pounds of very ripe cranberries, dilute with a little water and strain the juice through a jelly bag. Pour this juice into an untinned copper pan and add a pound of sugar to each pint of liquid; let it cook on a good fire to the consistency of a jelly, following the directions found in No. 3668. As soon as it is finished pour it into small pots or glasses and leave to cool off. When the jelly is perfectly cold cover with round pieces of paper dipped in brandy, and cork up the pots or glasses to close them hermetically.

(3671). CURRANT JELLY AND CURRANT JELLY WITH APPLES (Gelée de Groseille et Gelée de Groseille aux Pommes).

Pick some not too ripe red currants from their stalks; lay them in a copper preserving pan and set this on the fire; as soon as the fruits have dissolved strain the juice forcibly through a cloth into a vessel; pour this back into the pan and add one and a half pounds of sugar for each quart of juice. When the sugar has all melted place the pan on a hot fire and cook it until the preparation dropped from the skimmer forms into a jelly, or else if a drop be placed on a flat surface it will retain the shape of a bead and not spread, being careful to stir the liquid continuously with a skimmer. As soon as the jelly is cooked pour it into stone pots or heated glasses. In order to have it fine and clear no more than two gallons should be cooked at once.

Currant Jelly with Apples.—Prepare the currant juice as above and add an equal quantity of liquid in which apples have been cooked, then finish as for the above, when a currant and apple jelly will be obtained.

(3672). QUINCE JELLY (Gelée de Coings).

Choose well-ripened, good, sound quinces; peel, cut in four, and immerse them in a basin of water. Cover the basin, place it on the fire, and cook the quinces thoroughly, then pour them on a sieve to drain off the juice, collecting it in a bowl. Filter this juice through a flannel bag, return it to the bowl, add the same weight of sugar, cook and finish the same as apple jelly.

(3673). CLEAR GRAPE JUICE AND STRAWBERRY JUICE (Jus de Raisin Clair et Jus de Fraises).

Gather the grapes when quite ripe, place them in a vessel and pound without mashing them too much, to extricate as little coloring matter as possible. Pour the whole into a thick flannel bag to filter the juice, letting it fall into a porcelain or glass receptacle. Commence the operation again, and continue to filter the juice through the bag until it flows out quite clear. After all the juice has been filtered pour it into small strong bottles (small champagne bottles), and cork with sound corks, driving them in with a mallet; tie the corks down with strings attached to the necks of the bottles, then stand them upright, slightly apart, in a deep saucepan or soup pot, and cover to the height of the bottles with cold water. Place the pot on a moderate fire, boil for ten to twelve minutes, remove and leave the bottles cool in the water, only taking them out when thoroughly cold. Cut the strings and lay the bottles down flat, keeping them in a very cool place.

Crush some very ripe strawberries and press them on a wire sieve sufficiently fine not to permit the seeds to pass through. With this juice fill some one-quart bottles, close well, tying the corks on with a string. Range these bottles in a saucepan, cover with cold water and stand it on the range. Watch the time when the water begins to boil and leave them in for only half an hour, then take the saucepan at once from the fire and leave the bottles cool off thoroughly in the liquid. When cold lift them out, wipe dry, cut the strings and lay them down, piling one on top of the other in a cool, dry place, inclining the bottles a little forward so that the juice rests against the cork.

(3674). APPLE MARMALADE OR JAM (Marmelade de Pommes).

Quarter some apples, core and cut up small; put them into a basin with the juice of several lemons and a little water; cook. As soon as done pour on a sieve to drain, pressing them through afterward. Add to this pulp three-quarters of its weight of lump sugar, and stir well together. Pour it all into a tinned copper pan and stand it on the fire to cook the marmalade until it coats the spatula and drops from it in beads; stir continuously with a spatula. As soon as it is done pour into stone pots that have been previously heated.

(3675). APRICOT OR PEACH MARMALADE OR JAM (Marmelade d'Abricots ou Marmelade de Pêches).

Split some very ripe apricots or peaches in two, suppress the kernels, mince and put them into a copper pan with a few spoonfuls of water. Melt over the fire, stirring constantly with a spatula, then strain the pulp through a sieve and weigh it. Cook three-quarters of its weight of sugar to "small crack" (No. 171); when it has attained this degree remove from the fire and pour the pulp into it, stirring vigorously; continue to cook until it coats the skimmer and the jelly drops in beads, then transfer immediately to stone pots or glasses heated beforehand. The jam must be quite cold before covering it over; keep in a cool, dry place.

Apple, Apricot, Peach, Quince and Chestnut Paste.—Prepare a purée of apples, apricots, peaches, quinces or chestnuts; add to either one of these three-quarters of a pound of sugar cooked to "small crack" (No. 171); reduce until the preparation detaches itself from the pan; spread this about one-eighth of an inch thick on sheets of tin or it may be pushed through a cornet in rounds. Put in a hot closet for two days, remove from the tins and when cut roll in coarse powdered sugar.

(3676). FIG AND ORANGE MARMALADE OR JAM (Marmelade de Figues et d'Oranges).

Select large white, ripe, but very firm figs; remove the skins and cut up the fruits; weigh, and for each pound allow seven ounces of sugar dissolved in a little water. Boil this up once or twice, put in the figs and cook until the marmalade coats the skimmer and drops from it in beads, then pour into glass jars previously heated.

Orange Marmalade.—Choose some not too ripe oranges, remove their zests with the knife shown in Fig. 156, prick them with a coarse needle and put them in a pan with boiling water; cover them over to cook until the remaining skin becomes softened, then place in an abundance of cold water for twenty-four hours. Drain, open them, suppress the seeds, and pass the orange and peel through a sieve. Cook the same weight of sugar to "ball" (No. 171) as there is orange, mix both together and cook until the marmalade falls from the skimmer in a sheet.

(3677). MELON MARMALÀDE OR JAM (Marmelade de Melon).

Suppress all the rind and seeds from the fruit and rub this through a sieve. If very sweet a quarter of a pound of sugar will suffice for each pound of pulp; reduce the marmalade in a copper pan until it covers the skimmer and drops from it in beads, then pour it into glasses.

(3678). LARGE WHITE CURRANTS, BAR-LE-DUC JELLY (Confiture de Groseilles de Bar-le-Duc).

Have one pound of large picked white currants and a pound of loaf sugar; seed the fruits, using a pointed goose quill, and lay them in a vessel. Put half a pound of the sugar into a sugar pan with two gills of water, let it soak, then cook it to "bead" (No. 171); mix in the berries, leaving their juice in the vessel, and place the pan on the side of the range; five minutes later pour both fruits and liquid into a bowl, and three hours after lay a small sieve over the sugar pan and pour the fruits and syrup into this. Mix with the syrup half of the remaining sugar, and let it melt thoroughly, then cook it until it coats the skimmer and drops from it in beads; return the currants to the syrup; give them a single boil and return the whole to the bowl. Four hours after strain the syrup into the pan again, put the rest of the sugar with it and cook once more until it coats the skimmer; now add the currants and boil the whole up once. Set the pan back on the range for five minutes, but so that the syrup does not boil. Pour the jam into small jelly glasses; let get very cold before closing with paper. A few spoonfuls of clear apple juice can be added if necessary to give more consistency to the preserve.

(3679). PRESERVED GREENGAGES (Reines-Claude Confites).

Take twenty pounds of very green and sound greengages, prick the surfaces with a large pin and throw into a panful of cold water. Fill an untinned copper pan holding ten gallons three-quarters full of water; add a heavy handful of salt, three gills of vinegar and three handfuls of spinach; stir the liquid so all the ingredients are properly mingled; drain the gages from their water and throw them into the copper pan; stand it on the fire. After the water begins to heat stir the fruits around carefully with a skimmer, and as soon as they float on the surface take them out and throw into a panful of cold water; place under a faucet and allow the water to flow over them. Prepare a twelve-degree syrup; drain the greengages properly and throw them into this, then let boil up once, pouring them afterward into shallow vessels to leave for twelve hours. Drain off the syrup, add a little sugar, and boil it again several times until it attains fourteen degrees, then throw it over the fruits and let stand again for twelve hours. Continue this operation daily until the syrup reaches thirty degrees; for the last time drain off the syrup once more, and boil it to thirty-two degrees; then put in the fruits, boil up once and transfer the whole to jars; close hermetically as soon as cold and keep in a cool, dry place.

(3680). PRESERVED LIMES (Limons Confits).

Remove the cores from the limes with a quarter-inch tin tube and leave them to soak in a pailful of water, adding a heavy handful of salt; let them remain four hours in this, then drain and throw them into a large basin of boiling water to blanch. As soon as soft take them up one by one and put into a pailful of cold water to refresh, changing it at frequent intervals. To have them turn green again, put ten quarts of water in an untinned copper pan, add two heaping handfuls of kitchen salt, half a pint of vinegar and a few handfuls of spinach; stand this vessel on the fire and boil for a few moments; drain the limes from their water and throw them into this while still in the act of boiling, allowing them to boil up several times. Take the basin from the fire and leave the fruits therein for three or four hours; they should now have assumed their natural color. Drain and plunge them into a pailful of cold water for twelve hours, changing it frequently during this time. Prepare a fifteen-degree syrup. As soon as it boils drain the limes and throw them into this, boil up once, then transfer the whole to vessels and leave in a cool place for twelve hours. The following day pour off the syrup and cook it to sixteen degrees, throw it once more over the fruits, leaving it for twelve hours; drain the syrup again, boil until it reaches twenty degrees, then pour it over the limes and leave for twelve hours longer, repeating the process every twelve hours until the syrup reaches thirty-two degrees, then pour it back into the basin and as soon as it begins to boil throw in the limes and boil up once. Transfer them immediately to their respective stone jars, cool and close hermetically.

(3681). PRESERVED ORANGE OR LEMON PEEL (Écorces d'Oranges ou de Citrons Confites).

Cut some oranges or lemons in four, remove the pulp and put the peels in a basin with water; blanch thoroughly. When they are soft to the touch take from the fire, drain and put them in a panful of cold water; leave to soak for twenty-four hours, changing the liquid from time to time, or, if possible, stand the pan under the faucet and let the water run over continuously, then drain. Range the peels in a vessel, cover with a boiling syrup at fifteen degrees and leave them in for twelve hours; at the expiration of that time drain off the syrup. boil it up to eighteen degrees, then pour it again over the peels, leaving them steep for ten or twelve hours. Repeat this operation six or seven times, gradually increasing the strength of the syrup until it reaches thirty-two degrees. The last time prepare a fresh thirty-two degree syrup. Drain the fruits from the syrup they are in and put them into this fresh one that is in the act of boiling; boil up once; remove from the fire and lay them in stone pots, covering with this last syrup; close hermetically when quite cold.

(3682). WHOLE PEACHES, PRESERVED—LARGE (Grosses Pêches Entières Confites).

The Brothers Carresa, of Nice, France, prepare boxes of preserved peaches, each one containing only four, but of extraordinary size; in the boxes are also leaves, blanched with acid; they can be arranged so exquisitely that they easily pass for fine fresh ones. Drain off the peaches one by one, wipe dry on a fine cloth, then tint their surfaces with powdered carmine dissolved in water and pounded with the finger. This first layer should only be slightly tinted, then begin again on each side of the parting division, spreading the color over well with the finger so as to represent the bright shades of a fresh peach. As soon as they are tinted place them on a dish and cover entirely with clear jelly, applying it with a brush. First dress three of these peaches in a preserve dish and lay the fourth one on top of the under triangle; surround with a few peach leaves and pour some thick syrup into the bottom of the dish, being careful not to spill any over the peaches.

(3683). CANDIED AND CRYSTALLIZED FRUITS (Fruits Confits Glacés et Cristallisés).

Apricots, green almonds, greengages, mirabelles, cherries, and in fact all preserved fruits, must first be washed in hot water to remove the sugar adhering to them, then drain and leave to dry properly. After these fruits are very dry arrange them in a single layer, one beside the other, in a candy pan having a grate on the bottom; when this first grate is full lay another one on top and fill it the same as the other, and continue thus until they reach to slightly below the edges of the candy pan. Cover the last layer of fruits with another grate, and on it lay a weight to keep the fruits submerged in the syrup. Now cook a sufficient quantity of sugar to thirty-four degrees to cover the whole of the fruit and pour it over as soon as done; put these fruits in a hot closet and leave without disturbing for twelve hours; at the end of that time drain the fruits from this syrup, lay them on dry grates and leave till very dry. A good way to judge of the thickness of the layers of candy is to put small pieces of wood reaching above the edges of the candy pan into the corners at the same time as the fruits. After a few hours take out one of these pieces of wood, drain it well and see whether it be covered with a sufficiently thick layer of candy; if the layer attached to this piece of wood be the desired thickness then certainly the fruit should be covered the same, and if not thick enough then leave the fruits in the closet for a longer time. After the lapse of a short time draw out another one of the sticks and observe it the same as the first, and continue this operation until the candy be of the desired thickness; then drain off the fruits and dry them the same as described above.

Preserved Pears.—Choose fine, sound Sickle pears in preference to others; peel them round, suppress the cores with a small vegetable spoon, and lay them at once in cold water; drain from this and blanch, taking them out one by one as soon as they rise on the surface of the boiling liquid and throw them into a panful of cold water to refresh. Drain immediately; put them into a boiling syrup at twelve degrees, leave in a cool place for twelve hours; drain the syrup, adding a little sugar to bring to fourteen degrees, pour it over the pears, and the next day draw this off, add a little sugar to bring the syrup to sixteen degrees, and continue the process daily, each time augmenting the syrup two degrees until it has reached thirty degrees; now drain off this syrup from the pears, boil it up by itself once or twice, and when it attains thirty-two degrees put in the fruit; give it one more boil and transfer the whole to jars to cool. As soon as cold close hermetically and leave in a cool, dry place.

Preserved Fruits Coated with Grained Sugar.—To coat preserved fruits with grained sugar proceed the same as for fruits with candy. Cook some sugar to "thread" (No. 171), take from the fire and with a wooden spoon spread a layer on the sides of the pan in which it has been cooked and rub it on for a few seconds with the spoon. As soon as this rubbed sugar begins to whiten mix it with the remainder of the sugar, then dip in the fruits, using a fork, and range them at once on a grate, leaving them till the sugar be dry.

Preserved and Fresh Fruits Coated with Caramel.—For preserved fruits that have to be coated with caramel, proceed first by washing them in hot water, drain and cut them into halves or quarters, or leave whole, according to necessity and to the nature of the fruits, then stick them on wires pierced into a cork and leave them to dry. When ready, cook some sugar to "large crack" (No. 171), or three hundred and forty degrees. As soon as it has attained this heat take it at once from the fire and dip in the fruits, then lay them on a marble to drain and cool; when nearly cold pull out the wires.

For Quartered Oranges.—Peel and separate in sections, leave to dry, then dip them in the sugar, using a pair of pastry pincers, and then lay them one by one on a slightly greased marble.

For Grapes.—Take them off their stalks and dip them the same way as the oranges. These fruits are used for decorating pyramids and for cases of iced fruits.

(3684). PRESERVED PINEAPPLE (Ananas Confits).

Pare some very ripe pineapples to the pulp, suppress the cores with a tin tube and cut them up into quarter-inch thick crosswise slices; throw them immediately into a panful of cold water, drain and put them into a basin of boiling water to blanch, refreshing afterward in a panful of cold water. Prepare a twelve-degree syrup, add to it the well-drained pineapple and boil up once. Now transfer to vessels to leave stand for twelve hours. At the end of this time drain off the syrup and pour it into a copper pan. Add a little sugar, boil to bring it to fourteen degrees, then add the pineapple; twelve hours later boil the syrup a little more, until it reaches sixteen degrees; pour it over the fruit and continue this same process until the syrup is at thirty degrees; when this takes place boil up several times, throw in the sliced pineapple and leave them for a few moments, then transfer the whole to jars; when cold close hermetically and keep in a cool, dry place.

(3685). PRESERVED QUINCES (Coings Confits).

Quarter some good, sound quinces; peel, core and throw them at once into cold water, then plunge them into boiling water and boil until they become quite tender. Refresh, drain and range them in wide, shallow vessels; cover with boiling syrup at fifteen degrees and keep them in a cool place for twenty to twenty-four hours; drain off the syrup, add a little sugar, boil up and let it attain two degrees more; continue the same process until it reaches thirty degrees; then drain the syrup again, add a little more sugar and boil until it reaches thirty-two degrees, then put in the fruits and boil up once. Pour into stone jars and when cold close hermetically.

(3686). STEWED APPLES WITH JELLY (Compote de Pommes à la Gelée).

Peel some fine medium-sized apples; suppress the cores with a tin tube, rub the surfaces with half a lemon and cook in a twelve-degree acidulated syrup, being careful to keep them whole. As soon as done drain and range in a tureen, cover with fresh syrup at thirty-two degrees, leaving to cool in this; keep the syrup they were cooked in for further use. Drain the apples from their syrup and dress on a compote dish; filter the syrup kept aside, add a little sugar to it and cook it to the consistency of a jelly (see apple jelly, No. 3668); leave this stand for one moment on the corner of the range, then pour it over the apples; serve when cold.

(3687). STEWED BANANAS (Compote de Bananes).

Skin some sound bananas; suppress the coarse threads and throw them immediately into boiling water; drain at once, then transfer them to a hot twenty-eight degree syrup; leave to cool in this. Drain once more, range them pyramidically in a compote dish and cover with their own syrup; they are now ready.

(3688). STEWED CHERRIES (Compote de Cerises).

Cut the stalks halfway up from a pound of fine, large, sour cherries. Boil a light syrup in a sugar pan, just having sufficient to cover the fruit, then throw in the cherries; toss them for two minutes, boiling the liquid up once only, then pour the whole into a bowl to leave till cold. Lay both syrup and fruits on a sieve placed on top of the sugar pan and take away some of the fallen syrup, pouring sufficient sugar into the remainder that when boiled again it forms a thick syrup; as this becomes almost cold add the cherries to it, take from the fire and half an hour later dress the stewed fruit.

(3689). STEWED CHESTNUTS (Compote de Marrons).

Suppress the shells from two pounds of fresh chestnuts without breaking the meats; soak them for seven or eight hours in cold water with a little citric acid added. Drain and place in a recently tinned saucepan with plenty of water, having a bag containing bran. At the first boil remove the pan to the side of the fire so that the liquid only quivers for two hours, being careful to replace at times a part of the black water by a little clean boiling water, so as to keep the chestnuts as white as possible. When tender but yet whole, drain off a few at a time to peel without getting cold, then put them at once into another saucepan with tepid syrup cooked to twelve degrees and half a stick of split vanilla; use only the whole chestnuts. Cover the saucepan and keep it on one side of the range to have the liquid hot without boiling, and two hours after drain off half the syrup, replacing it by a stronger hot one of thirty degrees; keep the chestnuts in this for one hour on the side of the fire. Drain them again delicately one by one to dress on a compote dish; strain the syrup, reduce it to twenty-eight degrees, and when cold pour it over the chestnuts.

(3690). STEWED ORANGES AND ORANGE SALADS (Compote d'Oranges et Salade d'Orange).

Cut each of four or five good oranges into six parts; pare them to the pulp, suppressing the peels and white skin, then extract the seeds. Put the oranges into a bowl and pour over a few spoonfuls of thirty-degree cold syrup flavored with orange peel and a little kirsch; half an hour after dress the fruits with the syrup poured over.

Orange Salad.—Select sweet, juicy oranges, peel them to the pulp, cut in crosswise slices, and range them in a circle in a dish; bestrew with sugar and pour rum over.

Orange and Apple Salad.—Peel some fine, sound apples, core and cut them up into thin slices, dress them in a circle on a dish with slices of orange between each piece of apple, throw powdered sugar over, and pour on some kirsch and rum.

(3691). STEWED PEACHES OR APRICOTS (Compote de Pêches ou d'Abricots).

Select very fine, sound, ripe peaches or apricots, cut them in two, peel and lay them in a twenty-eight degree boiling syrup; leave to quiver for a few moments on the side of the range, remove from the fire and put them into a tureen, leaving to cool in their own syrup; drain and dress on a compote dish, pouring the syrup over.

(3692). STEWED PEARS (Compote de Poires).

Cut some fine ripe pears in two or four, but if small keep whole; throw them into a saucepan containing cold water; blanch in hot water acidulated with the juice of a lemon; drain, range in a vessel, and cover with a boiling twenty-eight degree syrup; leave them in this until cold, then drain, dress and pour over the syrup after reducing it.

(3693). STEWED PINEAPPLE (Compote d'Ananas).

Pare neatly a fine pineapple; remove the core with a tin tube; split lengthwise in two, and cut each half in crosswise slices three-sixteenths of an inch thick. Arrange these in a vessel, and pour over some boiling thirty-two degree syrup, leaving them to marinate for two hours, then dress in a circle on a compote dish and cover with their own syrup.

(3694). STEWED PRUNES (Compote de Pruneaux).

Put a pound of fine dried prunes in a saucepan; cover with water; place on the range to boil up a few times so they can soften, then drain and cover with a twenty-eight degree syrup, adding two or three slices of lemon, a small piece of cinnamon and a quarter of a bottleful of red wine. Place the saucepan on the fire and let the whole boil slowly until the prunes are done, then leave stand till cold and serve on a compote dish.

(3695). STEWED STRAWBERRIES AND RASPBERRIES AND STRAWBERRY AND RASPBERRY JAM (Compote de Fraises et de Framboises et Marmelade de Fraises et de Framboises).

Pick some fine not too ripe strawberries or raspberries; cook some syrup to "ball," throw in the berries and pour the whole at once carefully into a vessel to leave till cold. Drain and arrange on a compote dish; pour part of the syrup over and serve.

Strawberry and Raspberry Jam.—Choose two pounds of sound, ripe strawberries or raspberries, remove the stalks and leaves. Either crush or pass them through a sieve. Have an untinned copper basin (Fig. 140), place the berries in it, reduce to half, remove the basin from the fire, then add a pound and a half of sugar cooked to "small crack" (No. 171). Put on the fire again, then stir continually until reduced sufficiently to see the bottom of the basin; now pour it in glasses or jars which have been heated; when the jam is cold cover with small rounds of paper, dipped in brandy, and close the jars or glasses hermetically and keep in a cool, dry place.

SALTED ALMONDS, CHEESES AND FRESH FRUITS (Amandes Salées, Fromages et Fruits Frais).

(3696). SALTED ALMONDS (Amandes Salées).

Select fine, whole almonds, peel and lay them on a paper-covered baking sheet. Push this into a hot oven and when roasted to a fine golden brown throw them into a basin and sprinkle with a little water, slightly thickened with gum arabic, then dredge with very fine salt through a salt box having a perforated lid. Stir the almonds from time to time until dry, then leave to cool. Hazel-nuts, walnuts, and pistachios can also be salted; these are generally dressed in crimped paper cases or small fancy boxes; they are passed around with the desert, or at the same time as the hors d'œuvre, and then left on the table during the entire length of the dinner. It is an improvement to mix these nuts and serve them together.

(3697). CHEESES (Fromages).

American, Brie, Camembert, Chester or Brighton, Cream, Briquebec, Eidam, Gorgonzola, Swiss or Gruyère, Holland, Munster, Mont-d'Or, Neufchâtel, Parmesan, Pont Leveque, Port Salut, Roquefort, Stilton, Strachino, Shedder, Gervais.
Cheese is served either after the roast, before the sweet entremets, or else with the dessert; the first is most appropriate. Cheese must be accompanied by crackers or very thin slices of toast; it should be cut in pieces or slices. At a dinner it is better to have two kinds handed to the guests, with fresh butter; serve salted almonds and nuts at the same time. Stilton must be served whole wrapped in a plaited napkin; it should be scooped out with a cheese spoon and each time it is used the vacuum should be filled with sherry wine; it must always be kept sufficiently damp to prevent cracking. Chester should be served the same as Stilton in a plaited napkin, after paring it neatly; it should also be cut with a spoon and filled each time with good Madeira wine. For Brie, Camembert, Mont-d'Or or Pont Leveque: scrape any of these cheeses and serve with a silver knife for each guest. For Roquefort and Gorgonzola carefully suppress the outer rinds and serve with silver knives; pass around at the same time some fresh butter. Strachino and Millanais are serve in a plaited napkin folded to resemble a tulip; scoop out with a cheese spoon the same as Stilton. Holland cheese should be cut in quarters or slices. Neufchâtel should be scraped and served whole. Swiss cheese, Eidam, Munster, Port Salut and Briquebec are cut in slices. They must be chosen very mellow, cleaned and served with silver knives. Gervais is a sort of fresh bondon, the paste being very fine; it must be served quite cold. It should be covered with paper, to be removed when sending to the table.

(3698). CREAM CHEESE (Fromage à la Crème).

Put two quarts of milk into a vessel and keep it in a cool place until it curdles, then pour this curdled milk on a hair sieve to drain, and pass it through the same sieve, standing over a deep vessel; add to it a little salt and half as much firmly beaten, unsweetened whipped cream. Take some heart-shaped tin molds, perforated with small holes, each mold one inch deep and three and a half inches long; line them with pieces of muslin and fill with the above; place these in the ice-box for two hours. When ready to serve invert on a plate, lift off the muslin and serve, accompanied by some thick and very cold cream.

(3699). FRESH FRUITS (Fruits Frais).

Choose ripe fruits; arrange them either in baskets, fruit stands or plates garnished with green grape leaves and fresh moss. The base must be solid so that when carried they will not be dislodged; place the handsome part of the fruit on the outer side. Early fruits are always appreciated as they foretell those that are to follow in their season. Fruits for dressing are apricots, pineapples, pears, peaches, oranges, lady apples, grapes, cherries and strawberries. In case no fresh green leaves are procurable, use artificial ones made of muslin and dipped in wax. If a pineapple is to be arranged in the center of a basket, stand it on a cardboard cylinder four inches high by three inches in diameter. All fruits to be found in New York are designated on the table for the different seasons (see page 17). Dry fruits consist of almonds, raisins, figs, dates, and innumerable others.

CHOCOLATE, COFFEES, RACAHOUT, TEAS, ETC. (Chocolat, Cafés, Racahout, Thés, Etc.

(3700). CHOCOLATE (Chocolat).

Have good, fine vanilla chocolate; dissolve it in a tin saucepan, or better still in a chocolate pan as shown in figure, using the mixer to

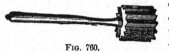

dissolve it, over a slow fire, using a pound of chocolate for a quart of water. When well dissolved strain it through a fine wire sieve and serve in a chocolate pot with a jug of hot water, and one of milk

Fig. 760.

Fig. 761.

and sugar. Some persons prefer whipped cream in their chocolate. Serve at the same time brioches, grissinis, biscuits and other fancy breads.

(3701). HOW TO MAKE COFFEE (Manière de Faire le Café).

The best-known coffee-pot is the one with a filter, of which a design is shown (Fig. 762). They

are to be had of various sizes and more or less luxurious. To obtain a limpid infusion quickly place the ground coffee in the cylinder on top of the coffee-pot, then put in the strainer on top of the coffee, press it down and pour boiling water over so that the infusion runs slowly down into the pot. While the infusion filters the coffee-pot should

be kept in a vessel containing hot water to the depth of two fingers so that the infusion attains the same degree of heat without allowing it to boil. For the sake of economy, after the infusion is made, the grounds can be boiled up once more and an infusion prepared with it to take the place of plain water, but, in order to obtain a good result, the grounds must first settle, then the water be poured off, strained and heated to boiling point. In this way less coffee can be used without deteriorating from its excellence. Use one and a half pounds of Java coffee, a pound

Fig. 762.

Fig. 763.

and a half of Maracaibo, one pound of Mocha and seven gallons of water. The best way to obtain good coffee is to make it only when required; the maxim should be "little and often." It takes three kinds of coffee to obtain a good result; for instance, Mocha for the aroma, having it only slightly roasted, Maracaibo for the color, which should be well roasted, and Java for the strength, roasted to a degree between the other two.

(3702). TURKISH COFFEE (Café à la Turque).

To be made with the same proportion of Java as Mocha, ground and passed through a very fine sieve. Put ordinary black coffee in a coffee-pot, as many cups as needed, and add for each cup a common coffeespoonful of coffee passed through a sieve, also a lump of sugar; stand it on the fire or gas stove, boil for two minutes, then take it off and pour in a little cold water to settle the coffee; let stand again for a few minutes. Serve powdered sugar with the coffee.

Fig. 764.

Fig. 765.

Fig. 766.

(3703). ARABIAN RACAHOUT (Racahout des Arabes).

Put a pint of milk into either a silver or tin saucepan. Place in a bowl two level spoonfuls of racahout, then four or five spoonfuls of cold milk; dissolve the racahout and pour it into the boiling milk; let cook for four or five minutes, stirring all the while, sweeten to taste and serve. It can also be prepared with water instead of milk.

(3704). TEA (Thé).

Black Tea for Sixty-four Cups.—One pound of black tea and four gallons of water.

Green Tea for Forty-eight Cups.—One pound of Oolong and green tea for three gallons of water.

Black Tea.—Put one ounce of black tea into a teapot; moisten it with two gills of boiling water to infuse and open the leaves and leave it thus for ten minutes, then add eight gills of boiling water. A few moments later stir with a teaspoon and let stand. Serve at the same time, sugar, cream, toast or cakes. Never allow utensils for tea-making to be used for any other purpose. The teapot should always be plunged in hot water before making the tea.

For Green and Oolong.—Use an ounce and a half instead of an ounce and prepare it with the same quantity of water.

Serve the tea on a tray covered with a cloth, accompanied by a sugar bowl, suger tongs, tea-spoons, cups and saucers, a pot of cream, boiling water, a teapot with a strainer, toast, fancy rolls, muffins, etc. For a party use the same preparation, only having the tea poured into cups.

Russian Tea for Twelve Cups, Samovar.—The samovar is a brass or silver-plated urn having a cylinder in the center, with a grating at the bottom. Lay some paper in the cylinder, over place small splints of wood, and on these some charcoal. Light it from underneath and on the cylinder arrange a pipe that is then connected to the outside or the chimney. Fill the urn with water, between the cylinder and the outside; this part of the samovar is provided with a faucet. As soon as the water boils put the samovar on the table on a silver or brass salver. A crown is fastened to the center cylinder to infuse the tea and keep it hot. Put in twelve teaspoonfuls of the very best Oolong, Formosa or any other preferred brand of tea. Pour over three teacupfuls of boiling water and allow it to draw for five minutes, keeping it hermetically closed and very hot, then add nine more cupfuls of boiling water, and even more should the tea be too strong. Gentlemen are seldom present at afternoon teas. Serve the tea in cups, but for the evening (eight o'clock), tea is then poured into glasses for the gentlemen guests. These glasses are plain, four inches high, three inches wide on top and two inches at the bottom; they are to be placed in silver or silvered glass holders, having handles; the ladies' tea is served in cups. Cream must be handed around at the same time, also very thin slices of lemon in crystal dishes, accompanied by small silver forks. Strawberry or raspberry jam, rose or currant jelly flavored with vanilla, according to taste, very thin slices of buttered bread, dry sweet tea cakes and sugar broken into pieces the size of a currant may also be served with the tea.

WINES (Vins).

(3705). WINES AND CARE OF WINES (Le Vin et les Soins qu'il Demande).

Grimod de la Reyniere has said that "No one ages at table;" he might have added, when the dinner is good and the wines are of the finest. Wine is the intellectual part of the meal and is to be served at a proper temperature in the order of the service, as will be explained further on. However, this is not an absolute rule; preference should be given to such and such a wine according to one's taste and according also to the influence it bears on one's health. This last point is easier to define for there can be no rule given regarding taste, as each individual sensation is apt to differ. Some prefer the keen savor of Bordeaux, others the delicate aroma of champagne; this one the warmth of the wines from Languedoc; another the exciting flavor of Burgundy. Tastes, for some reason or other, are formed on temperament; nature indicates and inspires in its very best way the proper method to follow for the good of our health. Sanguine temperaments feel the want of a light wine, such as champagne and Rhine wines; the phlegmatically inclined love the warmth of spirits, and the wines from Languedoc and Frontignon; gloomy dispositions crave for sweet Spanish, Italian, Roussillon and Burgundy wines; and those of a bilious nature, absorbed by the contention of their daily physical pain, require a stimulating wine such as Bordeaux. Bordeaux wine is generous, stomachic, easily digested, leaves the mouth clear and the head free, even when liberally drank. This wine can be transported to a great distance. Burgundy wine is aphrodaisical; it is extremely delicate and of a delightful aroma. Champagne wines are heady; they are limpid, light, odorous and unctuous. When champagne is frozen its effect is entirely changed; the temperature of the ice increases its tonic power and better contributes to the act of digestion, it condenses on the stomach and prevents the largest proportion from stimulating and rising to the brain. Frequently dinner parties are given when champagne alone is served. Champagne is not a natural wine, for on its preparation depends the superior qualities it is required to possess. Rhine wines are liked for the delightful mellowness of their flavor. They can support very long journeys, which instead of deteriorating only increases their value.

The Cellar.—Be very careful that the cellar is not exposed to sudden vibrations or shocks, or they will cause the lightest part of the dregs to arise, and when this mingles with the wine it produces sourness; also avoid placing any green wood in the cellar when the sap is ascending, or any vegetables, for these produce fermentation, impair the quality of the wine and prevent its preservation. Cellars should be kept very clean and at a temperature of 50 to 55 degrees Fahrenheit, without any thorough draught. In the warmest part of the cellar place the Bordeaux, and the Burgundy in the coldest.

Placing the Casks in the Cellar.—Before a cask of wine is placed in the cellar it should be thoroughly examined to see whether it be in good condition and the hoops perfectly solid. Stand the casks on wooden joists six to eight inches square, placed on bricks high enough so that a bottle can be set under the faucet; when in this position wedge each one separately with blocks of wood and be careful not to move or disturb the casks. When wines are required to be left in their barrels they should be placed sufficiently far apart to allow a free circulation between. Should the wines be of the present year the cask should be bored near the bung and the hole closed by a small plug removed from time to time so that the fermentation can be known. If, when the plug is taken out, the air comes whistling forth, then fermentation still exists; in this case remove the plug daily and at less frequent intervals as fermentation diminishes. Casks should always be refilled as quickly as they are emptied. Light wines spoil easily if their casks are not kept constantly full. The drier and more airy is the cellar the faster the barrels must be refilled. This should be done every month, and the wine used for refilling should be of exactly the same quality as that already contained therein; this alone will prevent it from deteriorating.

(3706). BOTTLING WINES (La Mise en Bouteilles).

The faucet should be partly opened to allow sufficient time for corking the bottles that have been removed. The corks should be selected perfectly sound, especially if to be kept for a long while. Dip them first in lukewarm water and force them into the bottle with a mallet or a special machine, then cut them off leaving an eighth of an inch above the bottle. Wines are bottled to have them attain the ripeness to which they are susceptible and to be able to keep them in a better condition; generally it requires two years before bottling red wines; only do so when they are found to be of a proper degree and ripeness, neither too sweet nor too sour, but of a perfect and pure flavor. White wine can be bottled earlier than red—one year to eighteen months, after it has lost its sweet taste. The clearness of a wine being one of its most essential points, an effort should be made to obtain this result; if not of a perfect limpidity, then wait a few days longer, and if not then clear it must be drawn off and transferred to another very clean cask, and clarified over again. Bottles must be rinsed carefully with lead shot or small pebbles. Bottle the wine on a clear, cold day; avoid stormy weather, and if possible select a day when the wind blows from the northeast. Bore the cask with a gimlet at an inch and a half from the inside border and stop as soon as the wine appears, then push in the opened faucet and strike it in such a way as not to disturb the dregs. The spigot must be left sufficiently open to allow enough time for filling the bottles while the corks are being put in. If required for keeping, then cover the cork and about an inch and a half of the neck of the bottle with some prepared wax, by dipping it in the heated wax and rotating the bottle until the adhering wax is cold; this coating keeps the corks from molding and from being eaten up by insects. To make this wax melt a pound of common rosin with two ounces of yellow wax and half an ounce of mutton tallow; color it with animal black, ochre, etc.; if too brittle add more tallow, and if the opposite, then more rosin. The bottles are to be stacked slightly inclined so that the wine can touch the cork at all times. The above is an abridged direction on preparing and bottling wines. The utensils needed are: one large funnel, two measures of three gallons each, a faucet for drawing off the wine and one other one, a mallet to push in the corks, a beater for the bung-hole in the cask, a pump and a felt filter, or round paper filters, for filtering the wine from the bottom of the cask.

(3707). CLARIFYING WINES (Collage des Vins).

Clarifying is not only for the purpose of rendering wines clear, but also to free them of any dissoluble matter which might precipitate later.

To Clarify Red Wines.—To clarify a cask of wine containing two hundred and twenty-five quarts, beat up partly five egg-whites with half a bottleful of wine; take out eight quarts of wine from the cask, pour in the clarifying matter and insert a stick split in four; move this about in every direction for two minutes so as to mix in the whites well, then refill the cask with the eight quarts previously extracted, and finish filling with wine or water; put back the bung. Five or six days after the wine should be clear, but in case it is not sufficiently so draw all the wine off into another very clean cask and reclarify once more the same as before, leaving it five or six days; it can then be drawn.

To Clarify White Wines.—White wines are clarified with fish isinglass. Beat with a hammer a quarter of an ounce of the isinglass, tear it to pieces, cutting it apart with a pair of scissors, then soak it for eight hours in sufficient wine to cover; when swollen, and it has absorbed all the liquid, pour over as much as before and leave it for twenty-four hours; then add half a pint of hot water; stir this about to crush, then press forcibly through a towel. Beat it with a whip, pouring a little white wine slowly over until the entire solution makes one quart of liquid. Before pouring it into the cask beat it up with three pints of white wine and finish the same as the red. The egg-whites or isinglass can be replaced by prepared powders.

(3708). DECANTING WINES AND BASKET FOR SERVING WINE (Vins Décantés et Panier à Verser le Vin).

Decanting consists of gently pouring from the bottles, inclining them slightly, any liquor that leaves a sediment; on this depends the clear appearance of an old wine. Well-decantered liquors present a beautiful limpid color through the decanter, contributing greatly to the enjoyment of drinking a glass of good wine.

Basket for Serving Wines.—In well-appointed houses the fine wines are decantered before dinner and poured into cut-glass decanters. A simpler way is to lay the bottles in a small wicker basket, fastening them in with two strings; but in order to carry out this precaution it will be absolutely necessary to have the bottle laid in the basket several hours before putting it

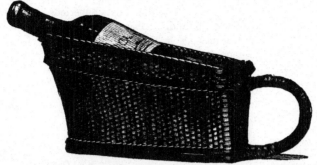

FIG. 767.

on the table, so that however little sediment the wine may contain it will settle at the bottom of the bottle. It is unnecessary to add that the basket must not be violently shaken and that the wine be poured out with the greatest care.

(3709). DELMONICO'S WINE CELLAR LIST.

Absinthe. Vermouth.

SHERRY.
From the De Renne Estate.
Duff Gordon.

Première.	G. S., 1815.	C. Old around the cape.	Peter Domecq Jerez **Med.**
Imperial.	J. S., 1815.	Peerless Cape.	1818.
Brown.	Pale Gordon.	Choice Amont'ado 1857	Montilla xxxx.
Pando.	Suarez Superior.	P. G. Old, No. 5.	Wellington, P. Domecq.
Amontillado, Dry.	Suarez Pasto.	Dry Soleras, 1828.	Jerez, 1730.
Amontillado, 1834.	Suarez Oloroso.	Solera Cape.	P. Domecq £100 Royal,
Old Mantilla.	Pale Pemartin.	Harmony.	Pale.

MADEIRA.
From the De Renne Estate.

Imperial.	L. I., 1815.	Agrella Madeira, 1818.	F. Amory Imported, 1806.
Green Seal.	Thompson's Auction.	L. C. Madeira.	Y. Amory Dom Pedro,
O. S. Y., 1820.	Old Reserve.	Thorndike A, 1809.	1791-92.
		N. G., 1798.	F. Amory, Imported, 1811.

MOSELLE.

Scharzberg Muscatel.	Brauneberger.	Scharzhofberger.	Piesporter.
Berncasteler Doctor.	Zeltinger.	Sparkling.	Josephshofer.

RHINE.

Johannisberger Red Seal.	Steinberger Cabinet.	Geisenheimer.	Rüdesheimer.
Johannisberger Gold Seal.	Steinberger Auslese.	Marcobrunner.	Rüdesheimer Berg.
Johannisberger Schloss.	Steinberger Cab. Imp'l.	Marcobrunner Aus.	Rüdesheimer Berg Aus.
Rauenthaler Berg.	Bocksbeutel.	Domdechaney.	Rüdesheimer Berg Cab.
Hochheimer.	Deidesheimer.	Laubenheimer.	
Liebfraumilch.	Assmannshauser (Red).	Niersteiner.	

HUNGARIAN.

Budai.	Tokay Imperial (White).	Somlyai (White).
Villanyi.	Tokay Cabinet (White).	Budai Crème.

BORDEAUX.
White.

Château Yquem.	Graves.	Sauterne.	Lafaurie.
Château Yquem Crème de	Haut Sauterne.	Sauterne 1re.	Latour.
Tête.	Barsac.		

BORDEAUX.

Pichon. Pontet Canet. Larose.

Château Lagrange.	Rauzan.	St. Julien.	Château Léovillé.
Batailley.	Léoville.	St. Julien Supérieur.	Château Larose.
St. Pierre.	Mouton Rothschild.	Château Couffran.	Château Margaux.
Château Langoa.	Haut Brion.	St. Estèphe.	Château Latour.
Château Pontet Canet.	Magnum Bonum.	Château de Pez.	Château Laffitte.

BURGUNDY.

Nuits.	Macon.	Clos de Vougeot.	Beaujolais.
Corton.	Macon Vieux.	Romanée.	Volnay.
Chambertin.	Pommard.	Romanée Conti.	Beaune.

BURGUNDY.

White.

Montrachet.   Chablis,
Montrachet Mousseux. Chablis Vieux.

RHONE.

Hermitage.   Côtes Rôties.
Hermitage (White).

CHAMPAGNES.

Cook's Imperial.	Pommery.	Moët, White Label.	Krug Sec, 1880.
Jules Mumm Grand Sec.	Pommery Vin Nature.	Moët, Imperial Brut.	Perrier Jouet, Special.
Deutz & Geldermann Sec.	Clicquot.	Piper Heidsieck Sec.	Heidsick Brut.
Dry Monopole.	L. Roederer.	Delbeck, Extra Dry.	Perrier Jouët, Brut.
Monopole Club, Dry.	Ruinart Brut.	Delbeck, Brut.	Mumm's Extra Dry.
Giesler.	Royal Charter.	Delmonico.	Irroy.
Giesler Brut, 1884.	Montrachet Mousseux.	Krug Sec.	Irroy Brut.

MALAGA, OLD.

PORT.

Première.	Very Old (White).	Osborn.	Sandeman's Old.

BRANDY.

Renault & Co.	Vierge.	Martell.	Private Importation.
Jules Robin & Co.	Renault, 1858.	Martell Old.	Very Old English Brandy.

WHISKEY.

Delmonico's Private Stock-Rye.	Delmonico's Private Stock-Bourbon.	Irish.
Bourbon.	Hollywood.	Irish (Powers).
Rye.	McGrath.	Old Cabinet Rye.
		Scotch.

MISCELLANEOUS.

Old Tom Gin.	Holland Gin.	Old Rum.	Very Old Jamaica Rum.

LIQUEURS.

Noyau.	Kümmel.	Bénédictine.	Curaçoa.
Prunelle de Bourgogne.	Kirsch.	Chartreuse (Yellow).	Curaçoa Sec.
Crème de Menthe.	Eckau.	Chartreuse (Green).	Anisette.
	Maraschino.		

ALES, ETC.

Scotch.   Kaiser Beer.
 Porter.   Yuengling's Tivoli Beer.
  Ginger Ale (Imported).   Milwaukee Lager.
   Beadleston & Woerz's Imperial Lager. Bass—McMullen.
    St. Louis Lager.   Bass Dog's Head.
     Ind. Coope & Co. Pale Ale. Cider, Jericho.

MINERAL WATERS.

Apollinaris.	Clysmic.	Juliushaller.	Vichy (Imported).

(3710). HOW TO FREEZE CHAMPAGNE (Manière de Frapper le Champagne).

In order to freeze champagne pounded ice and rock salt are generally used. Have a pail made of galvanized sheet iron or of wood, but the iron one is preferable, for the wine cools quicker in it. Put the bottle into a pail thirteen inches deep, seven and a half inches in diameter at the bottom and nine inches at the top; this pail must be furnished with a handle. Make a mixture of three

FIG. 768.   FIG. 769.

pounds of finely pounded ice with a pound and a half of rock salt, not too coarse; fill the pail to the top, mix well together and turn the bottle by the neck to give it a backward and forward movement from right to left. If the champagne be taken from the ice-box where it has been lying for several hours, then it will only take twelve to fourteen minutes to freeze, but if it has not been previously on ice, then it will require fifteen to eighteen minutes for the operation. Champagne can be frozen without turning it around by leaving it in the salted ice for half an hour before serving. Machines are sometimes used which simplify the work greatly; the same time is required, only the labor is less fatiguing. When finished serve in a metal silver-plated pail with salted ice around. These are to be placed either on the table or on a small side table.

(3711). APPETIZERS AND MIXED DRINKS (Apéritifs et Boissons Mélangées).

Iced drinks are those to which plenty of ice is added, then covered with a tin shaker and shaken until the contents are very cold and iced.

Cold drinks are those mixed into chopped ice with a spoon.

A glass of vermuth equals half a gill and is the glass meant in the recipes when not otherwise specified.

Five small glassfuls equal a gill.

Six dashes fill a teaspoon.

Vermuth Cocktail.—Put some fine ice into a large glass, add a glassful of Italian vermuth and one dash of Boker's bitters; mix the whole together with a spoon, strain and serve in small glasses. Another kind of vermuth cocktail is made by replacing the Italian vermuth by French vermuth, and having orange bitters instead of Boker's.

Sherry and Bitters.—Sherry into which a little bitters is mixed.

Brandy, Whiskey, Holland Gin and Tom Gin Cocktails.—Put some very finely broken ice in a large glass, add a glassful either of brandy, whiskey or Holland gin, one dash of Boker's bitters, and two dashes of sweetening (gum syrup); mix well together with a spoon, strain and serve in small glasses. Tom gin cocktail is made exactly the same, only using old Tom gin and suppressing the sweetening.

Calisaya Cocktail.—Mix in a large glass some finely chopped ice, a vermuth glassful of calisaya, one dash of orange bitters and a little vermuth; mix well, strain and serve in small glasses.

Peruvian Cocktail.—Add to some finely chopped ice in a glass, a vermuth glassful of Peruvian bitters, one dash of orange bitters and a little vermuth; mix thoroughly, strain and serve in small glasses.

Martine Cocktail.—Have some broken ice in a large glass with the third of a glassful of Tom gin and two-thirds (making a glassful in all) of vermuth, and one dash of Boker's bitters; mix well, strain and pour into small glasses.

Manhattan Cocktail.—Place some very finely broken ice in a large glass, add the third of a glassful of whiskey and two-thirds of vermuth, also one dash of Boker's bitters; mix properly, strain and serve in small glasses.

Jersey Cocktail Iced.—For three cocktails put into a vermuth glass some apple jack and two glassfuls of Italian or French vermuth, adding three dashes of Angostura bitters and finely pounded ice. Cover with a tin shaker, toss, strain and pour into small glasses.

Absinthe Cocktail Iced.—Put some finely chopped ice in a large glass, add a small glassful of absinthe, two dashes of orange bitters and two dashes of sweetening; mix properly, cover with a shaker, toss, strain and serve in small glasses.

Iced Absinthe.—Have some finely chopped ice in a large glass, add a small glassful of absinthe and water, cover with a tin shaker, toss thoroughly, strain and serve in medium-sized glasses.

Riding Club Cocktail.—Put some finely broken ice in a glass with two-thirds of a glass of Hostetter's bitters, half a teaspoonful of Horsford's acid phosphate, two dashes of French vermuth; cover with a tin shaker and toss until the cocktail is iced, then strain and pour into small glasses.

For all cocktails a piece of lemon peel is generally twisted over the cocktail.

(3712). CLARET CUP AND CLARET CUP À LA WILLARD'S.

Sweeten a pint of claret to taste, add to it one gill of maraschino or Curaçoa, one pint of soda water, a few mint leaves, fresh strawberries or raspberries and pieces of pineapple. Cucumbers or borage leaves may be added.

À la Willard's.—Crush one pound of strawberries, add four spoonfuls of powdered sugar, the juice of one lemon, a pint of whipped cream and a bottleful of soda water.

(3713). LEMONADE OR WITH SYRUP AND ORANGEADE (Limonade, Limonade au Sirop et Orangeade).

Lemonade.—Take a pint and a half of lemon juice and a pound and a half of sugar, add water to taste, add thin slices of lemon and serve very cold.

Lemonade with Syrup.—Ten gills of syrup at thirty-two degrees, one quart of lemon juice, the peel of one lemon and a quart of water; let the peel infuse, strain through a silk sieve and bring it to eleven degrees, syrup gauge (Fig. 167).

Orangeade.—Eight gills of syrup at thirty-two degrees, ten gills of lemon juice, the peel of two oranges, two and a half quarts of water, and the juice of four lemons; bring it to eleven degrees, syrup gauge, strain through a silk sieve and serve very cold.

(3714). CHAMPAGNE, CLARET AND RUM PUNCH; DESSERT DRINKS (Punch au Champagne, Bordeaux et Rhum; Boissons Pour le Dessert).

Champagne.—Three quarts of champagne wine, two quarts or bottles of Sauterne wine, three bottles of soda water, one gill of Curaçoa and fresh fruits in season.

Claret.—Four bottles of Bordeaux, one quart of water, one pound of sugar, one gill of Curaçoa and kirsch, half of each, half a gill of lemon juice and fresh fruits in season, such as cherries, strawberries, pineapple or raspberries.

Rum.—Two quarts of St. Croix rum, one pint of Jamaica rum, three pints of water, one pound of sugar, one gill of lemon juice and fresh fruits in season.

A delicious drink is currant juice, grenadine or orgeat, in large glasses, and moistened with ice cold water.

Dessert Drinks.—Fine champagne brandy, iced eckau kümmel, iced cream of peppermint (crème de menthe), Chartreuse, yellow and green, and kirsch.

Pousse Café.—The pousse café is a drink composed of four kinds of liquor of different color; that is to say, white cream of peppermint, green Chartreuse. cream of cocoa and brandy. These four liquors are poured into a glass tumbler in such a way that they remain in distinct layers, which is done by carefully pouring the above liquors, one after the other, against the side of the glass; thus the liquors flow down gently without mixing.

(3715). CLAUDIUS PUNCH AND WINE PUNCH—HOT (Punch Claudius et Punch au vin Chaud).

To one pound of Scotch oatmeal mix four quarts of boiling water; whip it in, stirring vigorously; then boil the preparation, working it steadily; add one and a half pounds of seeded Malaga raisins, the peel and juice of four lemons, a pint of good sherry wine and sufficient sugar to sweeten, a little grated nutmeg, ground cloves and cinnamon; also add a quarter of a pound of finely shredded citron, and should it be too thick then put in more boiling water, strain through a fine sieve, let cool and serve.

Wine Punch—Hot.—Put into a jar two bottles of Bordeaux wine, the juice of six oranges and the peel of three, a small stick of cinnamon, and three cloves; let the whole infuse for twelve hours, then pass through a sieve. Put the liquid in an untinned copper saucepan with six ounces of sugar; heat until it nearly reaches the boiling point and serve in punch glasses.

LAST CENTURY TABLES.

Following will be found several plates taken from works of the last century. I have thought them sufficiently interesting to publish and even to have them made use of, that is by modifying the models; for instance, replacing the colored sand beds by those of arabesques of flowers or grass; the marble statues by bronzes, the trees by graceful potted plants and the center by handsome ornamental sugar pieces. The following cuts will give a correct idea of how these tables were dressed. The center of the table was decorated with "dormants" or looking-glass platforms; on these were placed ornaments made by cutting out cardboard arabesques (see plate 1). The edges of these cardboards were trimmed with green chenille fastened on with green wax; this chenille filled up any vacant space that might occur between the cardboard and the looking-glass. The center B is decorated with a balustrade shown in the design on the top of the page. The center of this is a square flower-bed, in the middle of which a figure generally stood, and the remainder of the bed is decorated around with variegated colored sand; to meet this balustrade is a gum-paste border garnished with small fancy cakes or dried fruits. There must always be a space two feet wide left between the platform and the edge of the table. The designs A and C are decorated with beds the same as B, having also a figure in the center. In case of large tables these "dormants" or platforms were made in sections.

PLATE II.—Represents a table already dressed, taken from a work published in 1768.

PLATE III.—A table laid with the dessert, decorated with colored sand arabesques.

PLATE IV.—Represents a more modern horseshoe-shaped table; this design being frequently used for large society dinners and banquets. This form of table is very convenient, as the president is seated in the center of the rounded part and the two principal officers at the ends; on the right of the president, the most honored guest; on his left, the one next in distinction and so on, alternating from right to left for the guests or members of the society. No high center pieces or other tall ornaments should be placed before the president, merely a basket of natural flowers or one of pulled sugar flowers. On the length of the table and in the center or middle line can be placed several high pieces, candelabras, epergnes, etc., all around, sixteen inches from the edge. Arrange the plates and glassware at the usual distances, with two forks on the left, one for fish and another for the entrées; on the right have a knife, a soupspoon, a butter knife and an oyster fork, butter and salt in front, and around arrange the glasses for water, Burgundy, port, champagne, Sauterne, and sherry. The space between each place is twenty-four inches for those seated straight and twenty-two for those on the curve. Before each plate set a chair and on the plate a folded napkin containing a roll; in front a card with the number and name written on of the person who is to occupy the seat. This is a short synopsis of the manner of arranging a horseshoe-shaped table.

PLATE V.—Represents divers ornaments used for decorating a table the same as Plate I. The design D represents the palace of Circe, who metamorphized Ulysses' companions into swine. E F are statues to stand at each end; G are pedestals with vases on top; placed around the beds of sand or flowers and between each pedestal is a tree as shown in H. The looking-glass "dormant" or platform can be left undecorated. M may be used instead of the temple for a small table.

PLATE VI.—Figure No. 1 represents a border around the dormant made of gum paste; No. 2 platforms to place the dried fruits and nuts on; No. 3 flower beds; No. 4 the position for the trees; No. 5 for pedestals having grass around each one; No. 6 represents mounds of earth to stand figures on, and all the intervening empty space is to be of looking-glass, or else of sand, according to taste.

PLATE I.

PLATE II.

PLATE III.

PLATE IV.

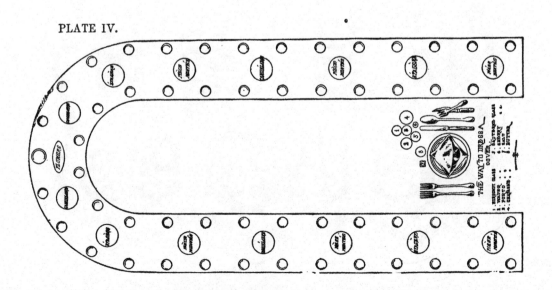

PLATE V.

PLATE VI.

I give here a series of bills of fare served by Delmonico, in 14th street and 5th avenue, and Madison square and 26th street. These are only a few among many that have been prepared, and I regret that I cannot add more, for I am sure they would please the subscribers of THE EPICUREAN. I have endeavored to select those most interesting. The bills of fare are generally and frequently very elaborate, some being engraved on sterling silver leaves; others are lithographed and are perfect masterpieces of art, the original costing several hundred dollars; others are printed on satin and others enclosed in small Russian leather books; many have been made of celluloid with relief figures, giving a very beautiful and artistic effect; they are also made of beveled-edged cards, painted by hand in water colors, either subjects or monograms being used. A bill of fare that is very much admired is two equal-sized cards having two holes in the top of each and tied together with two pretty ribbons; with these there is no necessity of having a bill of fare holder, as when opened they stand alone.

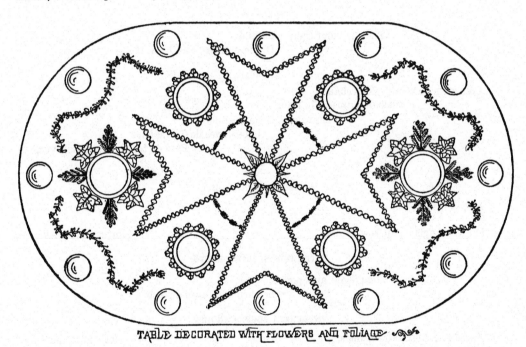

TABLE DECORATED WITH FLOWERS AND FOLIAGE

"Brillat-Savarin in his digression on taste observes that only men of wit know how to eat, while I add, that it requires a man of taste to prepare the food that pleases the men of wit."
—EVERS.

In the last dinner given by the Chamber of Commerce in the year 1893 will be found the diagram and the manner the tables were laid; the upper one is the principal table, the president and his guests being seated in the center. The other tables are placed lengthwise in front of the president's; they are classed alphabetically. Each place is designated by a number and the name of the person to occupy it. The end of each table is reserved for the members of the arrangement committee; a special table is for the press. The one numbered F is for the object of completing the seating capacity of the three hundred guests.

DÉCEMBRE, 1862.

DÎNER DE 28 COUVERTS.

Un Menu de la Série des fameux Dîners grecs.

MENU.

Huîtres.

POTAGES.

Consommé Châtelaine.

Crème de gibier à la Française.

HORS-D'ŒUVRE.

Croquettes à la Comtesse.

POISSONS.

Saumon à la Royale.   Bass à la Béchamel.

RELEVÉS.

Filet de bœuf Chateaubriand.

Dinde sauvage au Chasseur.

ENTRÉES.

Côtelettes de volaille Maréchale.

Filets de grouse à la Dauphine.

Timbales à la Parisienne.

Croustades de Terrapènes.

Pâté de foies gras en Bellevue.

———

Sorbet à l'Andalouse.

RÔTS.

Faisans Anglais piqués et truffés.   Canvas back ducks.

ENTREMETS SUCRÉS CHAUDS.

Compiègne aux poires.

Cygne surprise, sauce pistaches.

ENTREMETS SUCRÉS FROIDS.

Macédoine Alexandre Dumas.   Gelée aux fraises.

Gelée au raisin de Muscat   Pain d'abricots Montaigne.

Lait d'amandes rubané au chocolat.

Crème Portugaise,   Goronflot à l'angélique.

Charlotte Montpensier.

PIÈCES MONTÉES.

Pavillon des Colonnes.

Corbeille arabesque garnie de fruits.

Nougat Impérial.

Chaumière des Colombes.

GLACES.

Napolitaine.   Bombe à la fleur d'oranger.

Dessert.

NOVEMBRE, 1862.
MR. D. B. FEARING,
DÎNER DE 28 COUVERTS.

MENU.

Huîtres.

POTAGES.

Consommé Sévigné.   Purée de gibier.

HORS-D'ŒUVRE CHAUD.

Chartreuse à la Régence.

POISSONS.

Bass rayé, sauce aux écrevisses.

Eperlans frits, sauce Mayonnaise.

RELEVÉ.

Filet de bœuf à la Béarnaise.

ENTRÉES.

Ailes de dinde à la Léopold.

Salmis de bécasses Elisienne.

Côtelettes de cailles à la Reine.

Petits pois à l'Anglaise.

Haricots Flageolets sautés.

Fonds d'artichauts farcis.

Asperges à la sauce Hollandaise.

Punch aux liqueurs.

RÔT.

Faisans piqués et truffés.   Salade de laitue.

ENTREMETS DE DOUCEUR CHAUD.

Pouding diplomate.

Macédoine de fruits, Chateaubriand.

Glace moulée le casque Romain.   Parfait au café.

Fourteenth Street and Fifth Avenue.   *Delmonico.*

DÉCEMBRE, 1862.
MR. GIRAUD FOSTER.
DÎNER DE 16 COUVERTS.

MENU.

Huîtres.

POTAGE.

Purée de gibier.

HORS-D'ŒUVRE CHAUD.

Croquettes à la Piémontaise.

POISSON.

Filets de bass, Cambacérès.

RELEVÉ.

Selle de chevreuil, sauce venaison.

ENTRÉES.

Estomacs de dindes sauvages à la Goddard.

Suprême de faisan à l'Impériale.

Côtelettes à la Pogarski.

Petits pois à l'Anglaise.

Choux de Bruxelles.

Fonds d'artichauts farcis.

Asperges, sauce crème.

Punch au Cardinal.

RÔTS.

Cailles piquées.   Canvas back duck.

ENTREMETS SUCRÉS.

Timbale de poires Napolitaine.

Gelée au Madère.

Gâteau Savarin.

Parfait au café.

Glaces.   Biscuits glacés.

DESSERT.

Café.

Fourteenth Street and Fifth Avenue.   *Delmonica.*

BALL.

November 5, 1863, at the Academy of Music.

Russian Fleet.

Rear-Admiral Lessoffsky, Russian flagship " Alexander Weosky," 51 guns.
Captain Kopytor, Russian screw frigate " Peresvat," 48 guns.
Captain Bontakoff, Russian screw frigate " Osliaba," 33 guns.
Captain Lund (or Lurd), Russian screw sloop " Vitioz," 77 guns.
Captain Kremer, Russian screw sloop " Variag," 17 guns.

MENU.

HORS-D'ŒUVRE.

Huîtres à la poulette.   Huîtres en marinade.   Bouchées de gibier.
         Canapés de filets d'ortolans.   Snit-mitch à la Russe.

GROSSES PIÈCES.

Saumons au beurre de Montpellier.   Truites à la Régence.
    Filet de bœuf à la Mazarin.   Pâtés de canvas-back ducks.
       Galantines de cochon de lait.   Pâtés de gibier sur socles.
          Jambons de Westphalie à la moderne.   Galantines de dindes aux truffes.

ENTRÉES.

Salade de volaille à la Russe.   Canetons Rouennaise.
    Côtelette de pigeons en macédoine.   Bordures d'escalopes de homards.
       Chaudfroid de filets de faisans.   Aspics de filets de soles Victoria.
          Pain de gibier à la Royale.   Timbales à la Renaissance.
             Terrines de Nérac.   Bécassines à la Geoffroy.

RÔTS.

Cailles aux feuilles de Vignes.   Bécasses Bardées.
       Faisans Piqués.   Grouses.

ENTREMETS SUCRÉS ET DESSERTS.

Savarins au Marasquin.   Biscuits Moscovites.
    Gâteaux de mille feuilles.   Babas glacés au Rhum.
    Charlottes Sibériennes.   Charlottes, New York.
         Meringues panachées et vanillées.
    Gelées macédoine au champagne.   Pain d'abricots à la Bérisina.
    Gelées Dantzic Orientale.   Blanc manger rubané au chocolat.
    Gelées de poires à la maréchale.   Bavarois aux fraises.
    Gelées au Madère.   Biscuits glacés à la rose.
Gâteaux assortis.   Petits fours.   Compotes.   Fruits.

PIÈCES MONTÉES ET GLACÉES.

Pierre le Grand.   Washington.
    Alexandre II.   Lincoln.
       Le berceau des Palmiers.   La rotonde d'Athènes.
          La fontaine moderne.   L' Ermitage Russe.
             L'Arc de Triomphe.   Cornes jumelles d'abondance.
                Sultane à la Parisienne.   Le Pavillon des aigles.
    L'aigle Américain.   Le casque sur socle.   Pouding Nesselrode.

LA LIONNE.

Colombus.   Corbeille jardinière.   Les Dauphins.
    Diane.   Madeleine.   Mousse aux amandes.
Bombe spongade.   Citron et fraise.   Ceylan au café.   Vanille chocolat.

MAI, 1863.
DÎNER DE 18 COUVERTS.
Offert au Général McClellan par
Mr. Dunham.

MENU.

POTAGES.
Consommé Royale. Lucines.

HORS-D'ŒUVRE.
Bouchées de gibier. Bisque d'Écrevisses.

POISSONS.
Truite à la Portugaise. Soles à la Vénitienne.

RELEVÉ.
Selle d'agneau à la Périgueux.

ENTRÉES.
Caisses de ris de veau.
Salmis de bécassines.
Terrapène Maryland.
Petits pois à l'Anglaise. Haricots verts sautés.
Flageolets maître-d'Hôtel. Asperges, sauce crème.

Punch Régence.

RÔTS.
Poulets gras truffés. Pluviers dorés.

ENTREMETS SUCRÉS CHAUDS.
Beignets de pêches. Pouding aux amandes.
Crème Française aux amandes.
Macédoine de fruits. Charlotte Doria.
Gâteau Napolitain.
Glace mousse au café.
Fruits. Petits fours.
Café.

Delmonico.
Fourteenth Street and Fifth Avenue.

DÉCEMBRE, 1863.
BUFFET DE 100 COUVERTS, 20 PETITES TABLES.
LÉONARD JÉRÔME.

MENU.

CHAUD.
Consommé Royale. Huîtres Poulette. Huîtres Farcies.

FROID.
Saumon au beurre de Montpellier.
Filets de sole à la Rothschild.
Dinde en galantine.
Pâté de canvas-back. Terrine de fois-gras. Pain de gibier Royale.
Chaudfroid de côtelettes de Pigeons.
Mayonnaise de Volaille. Aspics de homards.
Faisans Anglais en Volière.
Cailles Piquées. Grouses Bardées.

ENTREMETS DE DOUCEUR.
Pain de pêches à la Louisiane.
Macédoine de fruits.
Crème Renaissance.
Bavarois aux fraises. Mille feuilles. Gâteau Breton.
Corbeille de fruits glacés. Charlotte Russe. Sultane Bayadère.

GLACES.
Casque Romain. Fruits. Christophe Colomb.
Café.

Delmonico.
Fourteenth Street and Fifth Avenue.

NOVEMBRE, 1864.
DÎNER DE 26 COUVERTS.
Offert à l'Amiral Renaud de la
Flotte Française.

MENU.

Huîtres.

POTAGES.

Crème de volaille.   Consommé Royale.

HORS-D'ŒUVRE.

Croquettes à la Victoria.

POISSONS.

Saumon à l'Impériale.   Soles farcies, sauce au champagne.

RELEVÉ.

Selle de chevreuil, sauce poivrade.

ENTRÉES.

Dindonneaux à la Toulouse.

Caisses de bécasses à la Diane.

Pâté de foies gras.

Mayonnaise de homard.

Punch à la Régence.

RÔTS.

Canvas back.   Filet de bœuf.

ENTREMETS DE LÉGUMES.

Petits pois.   Haricots verts.

Choux fleurs.   Tomates farcies.

ENTREMETS SUCRÉS CHAUDS.

Pouding Cabinet.

ENTREMETS SUCRÉS FROIDS.

Gelée macédoine.   Savarin Chantilly.

Gelée Madère.   Charlotte russe.

Blanc manger.   Meringues.

PIÈCES MONTÉES.

Le casque Romain.   Trophée maritime.

Bombe spongade, Napolitaine.

Petits fours.   Fruits.   Café

Nougat Impérial.
Chaumière des Colombes.

———

Glace Napolitaine.
Bombe fleur d'oranger.
Dessert.

FÉVRIER, 1864.
SOUPER DE 18 COUVERTS.
Offert à Mr. J. G. BENNETT, JR.

MENU.

Huîtres.
Consommé de gibier.
Coquilles d'huîtres au gratin.
Œufs pochés purée de gibier.
Filets de canvas-back, gelée de groseille.
Faisans Anglais truffés.

Punch Régence.

Truites au beurre de Montpellier.
Paté de foie en Bellevue (sur socle). Chaudfroid de perdreau.
Galantine de chapon aux truffes, sur socle.
Célestine de homard.

Gelée moscovite. Bavarois au café.
Macédoine au champagne. Gelée aux fraises.
Gâteau Berchoux. Gâteau Portugais.
Charlotte Doria.
Vase de nougat garni de fruits.
Corne d'abondance. Bombe surprise.
Glace la Lionne.
Corbeille jardinière.
Petits fours.
Fruits.
Dessert.

Delmonico.
Fourteenth Street and Fifth Avenue.

JUIN, 1864.
BUFFET POUR 150 PERSONNES.
MR. W. R. TRAVERS.

MENU.

Bisque aux Lucines.
Crème de volaille.
Coquilles de crabes moux.

Saumon au beurre de Montpellier.
Filet de bœuf macédoine à la gelée.
Galantine de poulet à la Royale.
Pain de gibier en Bellevue.
Aspics de filets de bass.
Chaudfroid de cailles.
Salade à la Russe. Salade de homard.

Mayonnaise de volaille.

Gelée aux ananas.
Bavarois aux fraises.
Crème Parisienne.
Gelée au Marasquin.
Gâteau Angélique.
Charlotte à la Doria.

Le casque Romain.
Le coquerico.
Bombe Latinville. Biscuits glacés.
Nougat Parisienne en surprise.
Sultane de raisins et oranges.

Delmonico.
Fourteenth Street and Fifth Avenue.

DINNER GIVEN BY SIR MORTON PETO,
— AT —
DELMONICO'S, OCTOBER 30, 1865.

MENU.

Barsac.

Huîtres.

POTAGES.

Xérès F. S., 1815.

Consommé Britannia.
Purée à la Derby.

HORS-D'ŒUVRE.

Cassolettes de foies-gras.   Timbales à l'écarlate.

POISSONS.

Steinberger Cabinet.

Saumon à la Rothschild.
Grenadins de bass, New York.

RELEVÉS.

Champagne Napoleon.

Chapons truffés.
Filet de bœuf à la Durham.

ENTRÉES.

Château Latour.

Faisans à la Londonderry.

Côtelettes d'agneau Primatice.
Cromesquis de volaille à la purée de marrons.
Aiguillettes de canards à la bigarade.
Rissolettes à la Pompadour.

ENTRÉES FROIDES.

Côtes Rôties.

Volière de gibier.

Ballotines d'anguilles en Bellevue.
Chaudfroid de rouges-gorges à la Bohémienne.
Buisson de ris d'agneau Pascaline.

Sorbet à la Sir Morton Peto.

RÔTIS.

Clos-Vougeot.

Selle de chevreuil, sauce au vin de Porto groseilles.
Bécasses bardées.

ENTREMETS.

Choux de Bruxelles.   Haricots Verts.
Artichauts farcis.   Petits pois.

SUCRÉS.

Tokai Impérial.

Pouding de poires à la Madison.
Louisiannais à l'ananas.

Gelée aux fruits.   Pain d'abricot à la vanille.
Moscovite fouettée.   Gelée Indienne.
Vacherin au marasquin.   Cougloff aux amandes.
Mazarin aux pêches.   Mousse à l'orange.
Caisses jardinière.   Glaces assorties.

Fruits et Desserts.

PIECES MONTÉES.

Madère Faquart.

Cascade Pÿramidale.

Corbeille arabesque.   Ruines de Poëstum.
Le Palmier.   Trophée militaire.
Corne d'abondance.   Nougat à la Parisienne.

MAI, 1865
DÎNER DE 22 COUVERTS
OFFERT AU GENERAL SHERMAN.

MENU.

Lucines.

POTAGES.

Consommé à la Royale.   Bisque aux quenelles.

HORS-D'ŒUVRE.

Cassolettes au salpicon.

RELEVÉS.

Saumon à la Parisienne.
Filet de bœuf à la Godard.

ENTRÉES.

Poulets Reine braisés à l'ivoire.
Ris de veau Victor Hugo.
Turban de filets de soles au gratin.

Épinards à la crème.
Artichauts farcis.

Haricots verts sautés.
Choux fleurs.

Punch à l'Andalouse.

Selle d'agneau, sauce menthe.
Pluviers au cresson.

ENTREMETS SUCRÉS CHAUDS.

Pouding des deux Carolines.
Bavarois aux fraises.

Gelée Californienne.
Cornets Chantilly.

PIÈCES MONTÉES.

Le vase tulipe.   Le casque moderne.

GLACES MOULÉES.

L'Aigle Américain.   Déesse de la Lionne.

Dessert.

Fourteenth Street and Fifth Avenue.

Delmonico.

MAI, 1865.
DÎNER DE 8 COUVERTS.
MR. HECKSCHER.

MENU.

Clams mignons.

POTAGE.

Consommé Rachel.

HORS-D'ŒUVRE.

Coquilles de crabes moux.

POISSON.

Saumon à la Dauphine.

RELEVÉ.

Quartier d'agneau à l'Espagnole.

ENTRÉES.

Estomacs de pigeonneaux à la Toulouse.
Croustades de bécassines au fumet.
Soufflés de volaille purée de champignons.

ENTREMETS DE LÉGUMES.

Petits pois.   Épinards.   Asperges.

Punch à l'Anglaise.

RÔTS.

Pluviers.   Filets de bœuf aux truffes.

Salade.

ENTREMETS DE DOUCEUR CHAUD.

Croûtes aux ananas Richelieu.

ENTREMETS DE DOUCEUR FROIDS.

Gelée marasquin.   Crème Parisienne.

Meringues Chantilly.

GLACES.

La poule aux œufs.   L'arbre Prodigieux.   Bombe spongade.

Dessert.

Fourteenth Street and Fifth Avenue.

Delmonico.

DINNER GIVEN BY THE CITIZENS OF NEW YORK

TO HIS EXCELLENCY

PRESIDENT JOHNSON,

In honor of his visit to the city, Wednesday, August 29, 1866.

MENU.

POTAGES.

Amontillado. Consommé Châtelaine. Bisque aux quenelles.

HORS-D'ŒUVRE.

Timbales de gibier à la Vénitienne.

POISSONS.

Hochheimerberg. Saumon Livonienne. Paupiettes de kingfish, Villeroi.

RELEVÉS.

Champagne Selle d'agneau aux concombres. Filet de bœuf à la Pocahontas.

ENTRÉES.

Suprême de volaille Dauphine.

Ballotines de pigeons Lucullus.

Chât. Margaux, '48. Filets de canetons Tyrolienne.

Côtelettes à la Maréchale.

Ris de veau Montgomery.

Boudins à la Richelieu.

Sorbet à la Dunderberg.

RÔTS.

Clos-Vougeot. Bécassines Bardées. Ortolans farcis.

ENTREMETS DE LÉGUMES.

Petits pois à l'Anglaise. Tomates farcies.
Aubergines frites. Artichauts Barigoule

ENTREMETS SUCRÉS.

Tokai Impérial. Pêches à la New York.

Abricots Siciliens.

Macédoine de fruits. Moscovites aux oranges.
Bavarois aux fraises. Gelée Californienne.
Crème aux amandes. Meringues Chantilly.
Beauséjour au Malaga. Mille feuilles Pompadour.
Gâteau soleil. Biscuits glacés aux pistaches.

FRUITS ET DESSERTS.

Madère Faquart.

PIÉCES MONTÉES.

Monument de Washington. Fontaine des Aigles.
Temple de la Liberté. Trophée National.
Casque Romain. Colonne de l'Union.
Char de la Paix. Rotonde Egyptienne.
Cassolette Sultane. Corne d'Abondance.

JUIN, 1866.
DÎNER DE 30 COUVERTS.
MR. FACHIRI.

MENU.

POTAGES.

Consommé Rachel. Purée de faisans.

HORS-D'ŒUVRE.

Bouchées de crevettes. Pieds d'agneau Villeroi.

POISSONS.

Saumon, sauce Génoise. Kingfish à la Joinville.

RELEVÉ.

Filet de bœuf, Rothschild.

ENTRÉES.

Poulets ambassadrice.
Salmis de bécasses.
Caisses de filets de pigeons. Petits pois.
Fonds d'artichauts.
Haricots verts. Choux fleurs.

Punch à la Régence.

RÔTS.

Canards (Mongrels d'Australie).
Cailles truffées.

FROID.

Pâté de foies gras. Filets de truites Historiés.

ENTREMETS SUCRÉS.

Timbale à la Madison.
Pouding à la Reine.

Gelée macédoine. Charlotte russe.
Bavarois aux fraises. Gelée Moscovite.
Fruits. Glaces moulées. Dessert.

Delmonico.
Fourteenth Street and Fifth Avenue.

OCTOBRE, 1866.
DÎNER DE 15 COUVERTS.
MR. BRADFORD,
Washington Square.

MENU.

Huîtres.

POTAGES.

Consommé à la Royale. Purée de gibier.

HORS-D'ŒUVRE.

Bouchées de terrapène.

POISSONS.

Sheepshead à la Portugaise. Kingfish à la Dieppoise.

RELEVÉ.

Filet be bœuf au Madère. Choux fleurs.

ENTRÉES.

Tomates farcies.
Cailles à la Financière. Haricots verts.
Timbales à l'Impériale. Petits pois à la Française.

Punch à l'Anglaise.

RÔTS.

Faisans garnis d'ortolans. Bécasses bardées.

ENTREMETS SUCRÉ CHAUD.

Pouding à la Royale.

ENTREMETS SUCRÉS FROIDS.

Macédoine de fruits. Charlotte russe.
Blanc manger. Gelée fouettée kirsch.
Mille feuilles Pompadour. Gâteau goronflot.
Cornes d'abondance. Croquembouche.
Glace Ceylan au café. Petits fours.
Compotes. Dessert
Fruits.

Delmonico.
Fourteenth Street and Fifth Avenue.

AVRIL, 1867.
DÎNER DE 175 COUVERTS.
En l'Honneur de Charles Dickens.

MENU.

Huîtres sur coquilles.

POTAGES.

Consommé Sévigné.　　　　　　　　　Crème d'asperges à la Dumas.

HORS-D'ŒUVRE CHAUD.

Timbales à la Dickens.

POISSONS.

Saumon à la Victoria.　　　　　　　　　Bass à l'Italienne.

Pommes de terre Nelson.

RELEVÉS.

Filet de bœuf à la Lucullus.　　　　　Laitues braisées demi-glace.
Agneau farci à la Walter Scott.　　　　Tomates à la Reine.

ENTRÉES.

Filets de brants à la Seymour.
Petits pois à l'Anglaise.
Croustades de ris de veau à la Douglas.
Quartiers d'artichauts Lyonnaise.
Epinards au velouté.
Côtelettes de grouses à la Fenimore Cooper.

ENTRÉES FROIDES.

Galantines à la Royale.
Aspics de foies-gras historiés.

INTERMÈDE.

Sorbet à l'Américaine.

RÔTS.

Bécassines.　　　　　　　　　　Poulets de grains truffés.

ENTREMETS SUCRÉS.

Pêches à la Parisienne (chaud).

Macédoine de fruits.　　　　　　　　　Moscovite à l'abricot.
Lait d'amandes rubané au chocolat.
Charlotte Doria.
Viennois glacé à l'orange.　　　　　Corbeille de biscuits Chantilly.
Gâteau Savarin au marasquin.

———

Glaces forme fruits Napolitaine.
Parfait au Café.

PIÈCES MONTÉES.

Temple de la Littérature.　　　　　　　Trophée à l'Auteur.
Pavillon international.　　　　　　　　Colonne Triomphale.
Les armes Britanniques.　　　　　　　The Stars and Stripes.
Le Monument de Washington.　　　　　La Loi du destin.

———

Fruits.　　　　　Compotes de pêches et de poires.　　　　Petits fours.
Fleurs.
Dessert.

MENU.

FÉVRIER, 1867.
DÎNER DE 14 COUVERTS.
MR. A. T. STEWART.

Huîtres.

POTAGES.

Consommé Britannia.   Crème d'asperges.

HORS-D'ŒUVRE.
Boudins à la Richelieu.

POISSON.
Bass rayé à la Chambord.   Croquettes de pommes de terre.

RELEVÉ.
Selle de mouton à l'Anglaise (gelée de groseille).
Petits pois.

ENTRÉES.
Chapons truffés à la Périgord.
Escalopes de filet de bœuf Sicilienne.
Choux de Bruxelles.   Haricots verts.

Punch à l'Impériale.

RÔT.
Cailles piquées au cresson.

ENTREMETS SUCRÉS.
Beignets à la Médicis (chaud).

PIÈCES MONTÉES.
Bavarois aux fraises.
Gelée d'orange.
Glaces asperges, sauce marasquin.
Bombe aux fruits.
Corbeille arabesque.
Le Cupidon batelier.
Paniers sultane garnis de petits fours.
Devises.   Bonbons.   Marrons surprise.
Dessert.

Fourteenth Street and Fifth Avenue.   *Delmonico.*

MENU.

NOVEMBRE, 1867.
DÎNER DE 20 COUVERTS.
MR. MURPHY.

Huîtres.

POTAGE.
Consommé à la Régence.

HORS-D'ŒUVRE.
Boudins de volaille à la Viennoise.

RELEVÉS.
Saumon à la Franklyn.   Pommes Dauphine.
Selle de mouton jardinière.

ENTRÉES.
Filets de poulet à la Patti.
Petits pois à l'Anglaise.
Salmis de bécasses au champagne.
Haricots verts.

Punch à l'Américaine.

RÔT.
Canvas-back duck.   Salade.

ENTREMETS DE DOUCEUR.
Pêches à la Richelieu.
Gelée aux ananas.   Crème Moka.
Gâteau Sicilien.   Meringue Chantilly.

PIÈCES MONTÉES.
Souvenirs Indiens.   Sultane Bayadère.
Le char des cygnes.   Nougat Parisien.
Glaces oranges Portugaise.
Biscuits Tortoni.
Dessert.

Mr. Murphy, 38 E. 39th Street.   *Servi par Delmonico*

DÉCEMBRE, 1868.

DÎNER DE 280 COUVERTS.

En l'Honneur du Professeur Morse.

MENU.

Huîtres sur coquilles.

POTAGES.

Consommé Sévigné de perdreau.

Purée d'asperges aux croûtons soufflés.

HORS-D'ŒUVRE.

Brissotins au suprême.

RELEVÉS.

Saumon à la Franklyn.   Pommes gastronome.

Escalopes de bass aux éperlans Dauphin.

Filet de bœuf aux fonds d'artichauts macédoine.

Dindonneaux à la moderne.

ENTRÉES.

Ris de veau à la Valençay.   Salmis de grouses aux truffes.

Paupiettes de poulet Vénitienne.

ENTRÉES FROIDES.

Pains de faisans Chantilly.   Galantine de pigeons à la Royale.

Homard mayonnaise en Bellevue.   Pâté de gibier Parisienne.

Sorbet Dalmatie.

RÔTS.

Canvas-back.   Cailles truffées.

ENTREMETS DE LÉGUMES.

Petits pois au beurre.   Épinards velouté.

Choux fleurs gratin.   Haricots verts sautés.

ENTREMETS DE DOUCEUR CHAUD.

Pommes à la Manhattan.

ENTREMETS DE DOUCEUR FROIDS.

Ananas à l'Orientale.   Lait d'amandes rubané.

Savarin aux fraises.   Charlotte russe, vanille ornée sucre filé.

Bavarois au cacao.   Sicilien glacé au marasquin.

Gâteau à l'angélique.   Panier de meringues.

Pièces montées.

Giace excellent au café.   Montélimar.

Fruits.   Petits fours.   Compotes.

Café.

JUIN, 1868.
DÎNER DE 200 COUVERTS.
EN L'HONNEUR DES AMBASSADEURS CHINOIS.

MENU.

POTAGE.

A la Brunoise.

HORS-D'ŒUVRE.

Bouchées à la Reine.

RELEVÉS.

Saumon à la sauce Hollandaise.
Bass rayé au gratin.
Filet de bœuf à la jardinière.
Pommes de terre Duchesse.

ENTRÉES.

Poulet sauté à la Valenciennes.

Epinards au velouté. Petits pois aux laitues.

Ris de veau braisés, sauce Madère.
Haricots verts sautés.

———

Sorbet Californienne.

RÔTS.

Brants. Salade d'escarolle.

ENTREMETS SUCRÉS.

Pouding d'ananas au Sabayon.

———

Gelée au Madère. Bavarois aux fraises.
Gâteau Savarin. Mille feuilles.

———

Glaces variées. Petits fours.
Fruits. Compotes.

PIÈCES MONTÉES.

Le Pavillon du Mandarin. Monument de Washington.
L'Arrivée du Clipper de Hong Kong, l'Enfant du Soleil.

Dessert.

OCTOBRE, 1869.
Dîner de 120 Couverts.
Les Pionniers de la Californie.

MENU.

Chablis.   Huîtres.

POTAGES.

Amontillado.   Consommé Sévigné.   Crème de gibier.

HORS-D'ŒUVRE CHAUD.

Brissotins au suprême.

RELEVÉS.

Hochheimer.   Bass à la Dieppoise.   Pommes tartelettes.
Champagne.   Filet de bœuf aux Champignons nouveaux.

ENTRÉES.

Bordeaux.   Côtelettes de volaille, sauce Périgueux.

Petits pois au beurre.

Ris de veau à la Valençay.

Épinards à l'Espagnole.

ENTRÉES FROIDES.

Galantine à la gelée.   Jambon décoré.
Salade de homard.

———

Sorbet à la Dalmatie.

RÔTS.

Champagne.   Perdreaux.   Bécasses.

ENTREMETS DE DOUCEUR.

Timbale à la Madison (chaud).

———

Gelée aux ananas.   Bavarois aux fraises.
Corbeille de meringues Chantilly.   Charlotte Parisienne.
Gâteau Sicilien.

PIÈCES MONTÉES.

L'État de l'Or.   Le Viaduc.
Le Tunnel.   Le Trophée du Commerce.
Glaces moulées.
Dessert.

AVRIL, 1869.
DÎNER DE 22 COUVERTS.
MR. SLOANE.

MENU.

Huîtres.

POTAGES.

Consommé Royale. Bisque aux quenelles.

HORS-D'ŒUVRE.

Brissotins au Suprême.

RELEVÉS.

Saumon à la Chambord. Pommes Dauphine.
Selle d'agneau aux laitues farcies.

ENTRÉES.

Pigeons à la Montmorency.
Petits pois à la Parisienne.
Chartreuse de ris de veau à la Moderne.
Côtelettes de filets de bœuf à la Russe.
Épinards à la crème.

Sorbet à la Dalmatie.

RÔTS.

Poulets de grain. Bécassines. Salade de laitue.

ENTREMETS SUCRÉS.
Poires à la condé.

Gelée Orientale. Bavarois rubané.
Gâteau baba glacé au rhum. Charlotte vanille.
Glace corbeille jardinière. Mousse café.
Pièces montées.
Fruits. Petits fours. Café.

Servi par Delmonico.

Mr. Sloane, 134 Madison Avenue.

FÉVRIER, 1869.
DÎNER DE 16 COUVERTS.
MR. L. P. MORTON.

MENU.

Huîtres sur coquilles.

POTAGES.

Consommé Sévigné. Bisque de crabes Victoria.

HORS-D'ŒUVRE CHAUD.

Rissolettes à la Pompadour.

RELEVÉS.

Bass rayé aux éperlans Diplomate. Pommes de terre Duchesse.
Selle de chevreuil Tyrolienne. Épinards au jus.

ENTRÉES.

Faisan à l'Aquitaine.
Petits pois au beurre.
Filets de poulet macédoine aux truffes.
Champignons farcis.
Quenelles de gibier, Londonderry.
Fonds d'artichauts au Suprême.

Sorbet à l'Américaine.

RÔTS.

Chapons truffés. Canvas back.

ENTREMETS DE DOUCEUR.
Timbale à la Richelieu.

Gelée d'orange Orientale. Bavarois rubané.
Gâteau Napolitain. Nougat de Provence à la crème.
Glaces excellent au café garni de Tortoni.
Asperges, sauce Marasquin.
Dessert.

Servi par Delmonico.

Mr. L. P. Morton, 987 Madison Avenue.

OCTOBRE, 1870.
DÎNER DE 50 COUVERTS.
En l'Honneur du Gouverneur Hoffman
et de Son Etat Major.

MENU.

Huîtres.

POTAGES.

Consommé Impériale.   Tortue verte au Clair.

HORS-D'ŒUVRE CHAUD.

Croquettes de ris de veau.

RELEVÉS.

Bass rayé à la Manhattan.
Filet de bœuf braisé aux champignons.

ENTRÉES.

Estomacs de poulet, sauce céleri.
Ballotines d'agneau à la Créole.
Homard farci à la Diable.

————

Sorbet au Kirsch.

————

RÔTS.

Perdreaux sauce au pain.   Grouses à la gelée de groseille.

ENTREMETS DE LÉGUMES.

Pommes de terre Duchesse.   Haricots verts à l'Anglaise.

Tomates sautées.

SUCRÉS.

Timbale Madison (chaud).

Gelée au Madère.   Charlotte Russe.
Crème Francaise aux amandes.   Corbeille meringues Chantilly.
Mille feuilles Pompadour.   Gâteau Breton.

Glace Napolitaine.

Pièces Montées.

Dessert.

MENU.

NOVEMBRE, 1870.
DÎNER DE 12 COUVERTS.
Mr. W. Astor.

Huîtres.

POTAGES.

Consommé Rachel.
Purée de gibier à la Cussy.

HORS-D'ŒUVRE.

Timbale Palermitaine.

RELEVÉS.

Saumon à la Diplomate. Pommes à la Duchesse.
Dindonneau farci aux marrons.

ENTRÉES.

Côtelettes de filet de bœuf à la Russe.
Haricots verts. Épinards au velouté.
Cailles à la Bagration.
Choux fleurs. Petits pois à l'Anglaise.
Boudins de volaille à la Viennoise.

Sorbet à l'Américaine.

RÔTS.

Canvas-back duck.
Perdreaux truffés.

ENTREMETS SUCRÉS.

Croûte aux ananas à la Florentine.

Bavarois à la vanille.
Gelée au kummel. Savarin au kirsch.
Charlotte Doria. Petits gâteaux assortis.
Caisses de fruits glacés. Excellent au café.
Glace Napolitaine.

Dessert.

Servi par Delmonico.

Mr. W. Astor, 350 Fifth Avenue.

MENU.

DÉCEMBRE, 1870.
SOUPER DE 20 COUVERTS.
Mr. Bradley.

Consommé Royale.

Rissolettes d'huîtres à la Pompadour.

Suprême de volaille aux truffes.
Petits pois.

Terrapène à la Maryland.

Volière de faisans Anglais décorés.
Pâté de gibier en croûte.

Canvas-back duck rôti. Cailles grillées.

Salade de céleri.

Gelée aux oranges. Pêches à la Condé.

Gâteau Portugais. Moscovite aux fraises.

Meringues. Gaufres Chantilly.

Glaces.
Excellent au café.

Fruits. Pièces Montées. Petits fours.

Café.

Servi par Delmonico.

Mr. Bradley, 140 West 34th Street.

DÉCEMBRE, 1871.
DÎNER DE 100 COUVERTS.
En l'Honneur de S. M. le Grand Duc Alexis.

MENU.

Huîtres.

POTAGES.

Consommé au Grand Duc.
Tortue verte au Clair.

HORS-D'ŒUVRE.
Variés.

POISSONS.

Bass rayé Portugaise garni de filets d'éperlans frits.
Saumon de Californie à la sauce Génevoise.

RELEVÉ.

Filet de bœuf à la Richelieu.

ENTRÉES.

Côtelettes de chevreuil, sauce poivrade.
Filets de perdreaux à l'Aquitaine.
Terrapène à la Maryland.

FROID.

Galantine de faisan à la Royale.
Chaudfroid de bécasses en croustades à la gelée.

———

Sorbet à la Régence.

———

RÔT.

Canvas-back duck.

ENTREMETS DE LÉGUMES.

Petits pois au beurre.   Haricots flageolets.
Artichauts à la Provençale.   Choux fleurs au gratin.

Pommes Duchesse.

ENTREMETS SUCRÉS.
Poires à la Florentine.

———

Macédoine de fruits.   Charlotte russe.
Moscovite aux abricots.   Bavarois rubané.
Gâteau mousseline.   Coupole Chantilly.
Glaces Napolitaine.   Excellent au café.

Pièces montées.
Dessert.

JANVIER, 1871.
DÎNER DE 18 COUVERTS.
MR. W. H. HURLBUT.

MENU.

Huîtres.

POTAGE.

Tortue verte au Clair.

HORS-D'ŒUVRE.

Brissotins au suprême.

POISSONS.

Pommes gastronome.

Bass rayé à la Chambord.

RELEVÉS.

Filet de bœuf aux champignons farcis.

Selle de mouton à l'Anglaise.

Épinards au velouté.

ENTRÉES.

Filets de grouse Bernardine.

Tomates sautées.

Cailles farcies Perigueux.

Petits pois au beurre.

Ris de veau macédoine.

Asperges en branches.

Sorbet en écorce.

RÔT.

Canvas-back.

Salade.

ENTREMETS SUCRÉS.

Gelée aux fruits.

Bavarois à la vanille.

Gâteau Cougloff.

Corbeille Charlotte.

Glace le Tyrolien sur socle.

Parfait au café garni de Tortoni.

Pièces montées.

Dessert.

Mr. Hurlbut, 11 West 20th Street.

Servi par Delmonico.

MARS, 1871.
DÎNER POUR 35 PERSONNES.
MR. FRANK LESLIE.

MENU.

Huîtres.

POTAGES.

Consommé Impériale.

HORS-D'ŒUVRE.

Rissolettes au salpicon.

POISSON.

Crème d'artichauts.

Truite de rivière à la Vénitienne.

Pommes gastronome.

Selle d'agneau aux tomates à la Reine.

ENTRÉES.

Paupiettes de faisan à l'Aquitaine.

Petits pois nouveaux aux laitues.

Caisses de ris de veau à la Parisienne.

Haricots verts sautés.

Asperges nouvelles en branches, sauce blanche.

Sorbet à l'Américaine.

RÔTS.

Chapons aux marrons.

Mauviettes.

ENTREMETS.

Pouding diplomate.

Gelée aux ananas.

Gâteau baba au rhum.

Glaces.

Coupole Chantilly.

Bavarois aux pêches.

Timbale de gaufres.

Excellent au café.

Pièces montées.

Dessert.

Fourteenth Street and Fifth Avenue.

Delmonico.

OCTOBRE, 1872.
SOUPER BUFFET ET ASSIS.
MR. AUGUST BELMONT

MENU.

CHAUD.

Consommé de volaille.

Huîtres à la béchamel aux truffes.

Huîtres farcies.

Croquettes homard à la Victoria.

Ragoût de Terrapène.

FROID.

Saumon, sauce ravigote vert-pré.

Filet de bœuf aux légumes.

Galantine de dinde aux truffes.

Pâté de gibier de Colmar.

Chaudfroid de grouses.

Cailles piquées à la gelée.

Salade de volaille mayonnaise.

Mayonnaise de homard.

RÔTIS CHAUDS.

Chapons.   Dindonneaux.

ENTREMETS SUCRÉS.

Gelée aux ananas.   Pain à la Reine.

Gâteau baba au rhum.   Gaufres Chantilly.

Bavarois aux fraises.   Charlotte Parisienne.

Petites glaces variées.

Pièces Montées.

Dessert.

JANVIER, 1874.
DÎNER DE 90 COUVERTS.
BULLS AND BEARS ANNUAL DINNER.

MENU.

Huîtres.

POTAGES.

Consommé Sultane.
Tortue verte au clair.

HORS-D'ŒUVRE.

Brissotins au suprême.

RELEVÉS.

Bass à la Hollandaise.
Pommes Duchesse.
Filet de bœuf aux champignons.
Laitues farcies.

ENTRÉES.

Suprême de grouse au chasseur.
Haricots verts.
Cailles braisées, sauce céleri.
Petits pois à l'Anglaise.
Ris de veau Maintenon.
Tomates sautées.

Sorbet au rhum.

RÔTIS.

Canards à tête rouge.
Chapons.

ENTREMETS SUCRÉS.

Plum pouding à l'Anglaise.
Bavarois aux fraises.
Charlotte Parisienne.
Gelée à l'Orientale.
Gâteau Savarin.

Pièces montées.
Dessert.

Fourteenth Street and Fifth Avenue.   *Delmonico.*

MAI, 1872.
DÎNER DE 72 COUVERTS.
MR. RECORDER HACKETT.

MENU.

POTAGES.

Consommé Printanier.
Queues de bœuf à l'Anglaise.

POISSONS.

Saumon à la Joinville.
Œufs d'alose grillés.
Pommes Duchesse.

RELEVÉS.

Selle d'agneau Salvandi.
Filet de bœuf aux champignons nouveaux.
Petits pois aux laitues.

ENTRÉES.

Suprême de volaille purée de truffes.
Flageolets maître-d'hôtel.
Terrapène à la Philadelphie.
Asperges en branches sauce blanche.

Sorbet Spongade au kirsch.

RÔTIS.

Chapons.
Pigeonneaux.

ENTREMETS SUCRÉS.

Pouding Bagration.
Gelée au champagne.
Gelée d'ananas Dantzic.
Corbeille de meringues.
Pain de fraises Moderne.
Gâteau Cavour.
Bavarois au lait d'amandes.
Biscuit Tortoni.
Glaces.
Tutti-frutti.
Petits fours.
Fruits.
Pièces montées.
Café.
Liqueurs.

Recorder Hackett, 72 Park Avenue.   *Servi par Delmonico,*

MARS, 1873.
DÎNER DE 12 COUVERTS.
Suivi d'un Souper de 80 Personnes.
En l'honneur du Général Grant.

MENU.

Huîtres.

POTAGES.

Consommé Pierre le Grand.   Crème d'asperges.

HORS-D'ŒUVRE.

Timbales à la Montglas.

POISSON.

Truites de rivière à la Joinville.   Pommes gastronome.

RELEVÉ.

Selle d'agneau à la Chancelière..

ENTRÉES.

Filets de canvas-back à l'Aquitaine.   Petits pois.
Grenades de volaille purée de marrons.   Haricots verts.
Aspics de foies-gras en Bellevue.
Ballotines de pigeons.

Sorbet à l'Américaine.

RÔT.

Poulets de grain truffés.

ENTREMETS DE DOUCEUR CHAUD.

Pêches à la Colbert.

ENTREMETS DE DOUCEUR FROIDS.

Gelée aux fruits Sultane.   Lait d'amandes.

Pièces montées.

Glaces moulées.

Fruits.   Dessert.

SOUPER.

CHAUD.

Consommé de volaille.   Huîtres béchamel aux truffes.
Croquettes d'huîtres Africaine.   Timbales à l'écarlate.
Truites de rivières ravigote.
Selle d'agneau de lait jardinière.
Escalopes de volaille à la Talleyrand.
Écrevisses à la Bordelaise.

FROID.

Volière de faisans Anglais.   Mayonnaise de volaille.
Salade de homard.   Aspics de foies-gras.

CHAUD.

Bécassines au cresson.   Asperges nouvelles.

ENTREMETS DE DOUCEUR CHAUDS ET DESSERTS.

Gelée d'oranges.   Bavarois rubané.
Gâteau Impérial.   Corbeille Chantilly.
Glaces: Bacchus et le puits garni de Tortoni.
Excellent au café.   Petites glaces variées.
Dessert.

FÉVRIER, 1873.
DÎNER DE 75 COUVERTS (le dîner des cygnes).
MR. LUCKMEYER.

MENU.

POTAGES.

Consommé Impériale. Bisque aux crevettes.

HORS-D'ŒUVRE.

Timbales à la Condé.

POISSONS.

Red snapper à la Vénitienne.
Paupiettes d'éperlans, sauce des gourmets.

RELEVÉ.

Filet de bœuf à l'Egyptienne.

ENTRÉES.

Côtelettes de volaille à la Sévigné.
Ailes de canvas-back, sauce bigarade.
Asperges froides en branches, sauce vinaigrette.

Sorbet de l'Ermitage en écorce.

RÔTS.

Chapons truffés. Selle de mouton.

ENTREMETS DE LÉGUMES.

Cardons à la moelle. Choux fleurs sauce crème. Petits pois au beurre.

ENTREMETS SUCRÉS.

Poires à la Richelieu.

Pain de pêches Maréchale. Gelée aux ananas. Gaufres Chantilly.
Gelée aux fruits. Coupole à l'Anglaise. Gâteaux à la Reine.
Glace délicieux aux noisettes. Biscuits Tortoni.
Petits fours. Caisses de fruits glacés. Devises, Victoria.
Bonbonnières garnies. Fruits. Bonbons surprise.
Dessert.

Fourteenth Street and Fifth Avenue. *Delmonico.*

FÉVRIER, 1873.
DÎNER DE 200 COUVERTS.
En l'Honneur du Professeur Tyndall.

MENU.

Huîtres.

POTAGES.

Consommé Marie Stuart. Bisque de homard aux quenelles.

HORS-D'ŒUVRE.

Brissotins au suprême.

POISSONS.

Rockfish à la Régence.

RELEVÉS.

Éperlans frits, sauce tartare. Pommes Dauphine.

Filet de bœuf à l'Indienne. Épinards à l'Espagnole.

ENTRÉES.

Poularde à la Lyonnaise. Petits pois à l'Anglaise.
Escalopes de grouses, sauce bigarade. Haricots verts sautés.
Côtelettes de ris de veau aux pointes d'asperges.

FROID.

Galantine de dinde. Aspic de gibier.

Sorbet à la Dalmatie.

RÔTS.

Canard à tête rouge. Salade d'escarolle. Selle de mouton.

ENTREMETS DE DOUCEUR CHAUD.

Plum pouding au sabayon.

ENTREMETS DE DOUCEUR FROIDS.

Charlotte Parisienne.
Corbeilles de meringues.

Gelée aux fruits.
Gâteau Victoria. Glaces Napolitaine.
Dessert.

Fourteenth Street and Fifth Avenue. *Delmonico.*

A BORD DU "CITY OF PEKING" DE LA PACIFIC MAIL STEAMSHIP COMPANY.

DÉJEUNER—GOÛTER—DÎNER—SOUPER.

AOÛT, 1874.   POUR 300 PERSONNES.

DÉJEUNER.

Œufs.   Omelette aux fines herbes.   Œufs au jambon.   Œufs Soubise.

Poissons.   Saumon grillé, maître-d'hôtel.   Filets de soles à la Horly.

Entrées.   Poulets frits, sauce tomate.   Côtelettes d'agneau purée de pommes.
            Rognons sautés aux champignons.   Tête de veau vinaigrette.

Froid.   Bœuf à la mode.   Galantine à la gelée.   Noix de veau piquées et glacees.

GOÛTER.

Relevé.   Selle d'agneau rôtie à l'Anglaise.

Entrées.   Poulet sauté aux pommes de terre et fonds d'artichauts.

Froid.   Sandwichs, jambon, langues, Longe de veau à la gelée.

Dessert.   Fromages, fruits, compotes, café, thé.

DÎNER.

Potages.   Consommé printanier.   Tortue verte à l'Anglaise.

Hors-d'œuvre.   Bouchées de homard.

Poissons.   Bass rayé à l'Italienne.   Salade de tomates.
            Maquereau Espagnol, sauce Colbert.   Salade de concombres.

Entrées.   Ris de veau macédoine.
            Pigeonneaux aux petits pois.
            Poulets sautés aux truffes.

Rôts.   Côtes de bœuf.   Yorkshire pudding.
            Bécasses.   Chevreuil.
            Canards.   Salade de laitue.

Entremets.   Haricots de Lima.   Maïs en feuilles.
            Petits pois au beurre.
            Pêches Condé.   Meringues Chantilly.   Glace vanille.

Dessert.   Gaufres cigarettes. Devises. Bonbons. Fruits. Fromage.
            Compotes. Petits fours.

SOUPER.

Consommé en tasses.   Crabes moux frits.

Pluviers grillés.

Froid.   Filet de bœuf.   Galantine aux truffes.

Salade de homard.

Glaces Napolitaine.

MAI, 1874.
DÎNER DE 5 COUVERTS.
OFFERT à MR. HENRI ROCHEFORT
PAR QUELQUES AMIS.

MENU.

POTAGES.
Clovisses.
Consommé châtelaine.   Bisque d'écrevisses.

HORS-D'ŒUVRE.
Timbale Palermitaine.

RELEVÉS.
Maquereau Espagnol, sauce Colbert.
Quartier d'agneau aux tomates farcies.

ENTRÉES.
Ailes de poulet à l'Orientale.
Casseroles de ris de veau truffes et champignons.

Sorbet à l'Américaine.

RÔTS.
Bécassines au cresson.   Salade de laitue.
Aspic de foies gras.

ENTREMETS DE LÉGUMES.
Artichauts à l'Italienne.   Petits pois au beurre.
Asperges, sauce crème.

ENTREMETS SUCRÉS.
Croûte aux ananas.

Glaces.   Cygne aux roseaux.
Gaufres Chantilly.   Dessert.

Fourteenth Street and Fifth Avenue.   *Delmonico.*

MAI, 1874.
DÎNER DE 6 COUVERTS.
MR. PARKER.

MENU.

Lucines (clovisses).
POTAGES.
Consommé Deslignac.   Bisque d'écrevisses.

HORS-D'ŒUVRE.
Timbales à la Renaissance.

RELEVÉS.
Kingfish au diplomate.   Pommes Duchesse.

ENTRÉES.
Selle d'agneau aux tomates Reine.
Poulets de grain à la Bagration.
Petits pois aux laitues.
Aiguillettes de canard métis Renaissance.
Artichauts à la Barigoule.

Sorbet au rhum.

RÔT.
Bécassines au cresson.

FROID.
Pâté de foies gras.   Salade de laitue.

ENTREMETS DE DOUCEUR.
Croûte aux ananas.
Gaufres de Carlsbad.   Chantilly aux fraises.
Glace mousse aux bananes.
Dessert.

Mr. Parker, 258 Madison Avenue.   *Servi par Delmonico.*

NOVEMBRE, 1875.
DÎNER DE 14 COUVERTS.
MR. WRIGHT SANFORD.

Milieu de table dormant de fleurs.

Musique.

Huîtres.

POTAGES.

Consommé Descazes.   Gombo aux crabes.

HORS-D'ŒUVRE.

Cassolettes à la Dumas.

POISSONS.

Sheepshead, sauce Hollandaise et Génevoise.
Pommes de terre croquettes.
Éperlans désossés et frits, mayonnaise printanière.

RELEVÉS.

Selle de chevreuil à la Tyrolienne.
Haricots verts sautés.

ENTRÉES.

Croustades d'escargots aux cervelles de perdreaux.
Fonds d'artichauts suprême.
Estomacs de dindonneaux Ambassadrice.
Petits pois au beurre.
Ris de veau à la Messiers.   Choux fleurs, sauce crème.

Sorbet à la Hélène.

RÔTS.

Canvas back.   Hominy sample.
Cailles en casseroles.

ENTREMETS SUCRÉS.

Timbales à la Madison.

Délicieux aux noisettes.   Ceylan au café.

Fourteenth Street and Fifth Avenue.   *Delmonico.*

MAI, 1875.
DÎNER DE 15 COUVERTS.
MR. SAM WARD.

MENU.

Clovisses.   Huîtres de Bridgeport.

POTAGES.

Consommé printanier.   Bisque d'écrevisses.

HORS-D'ŒUVRE.

Boudins à la Polonaise.

RELEVÉS.

Turban de saumon, sauce crème.
Pommes gastronome.

ENTRÉES.

Ailes de poulet Montpensier.
Petits pois.
Côtelettes de pigeonneaux Signora.
Haricots verts à la crème.

Asperges blanches, sauce Hollandaise.

Sorbet ananas au-Marasquin.

RÔTS.

Pluviers.   Bécassines.

Salade de Romaine.

Soufflés de Stilton à la Sam Ward.

Glaces aux noisettes garnies d'excellent au café en caisses.

Dessert.

Fourteenth Street and Fifth Avenue.   *Delmonico.*

JUILLET, 1876.
DÎNER DE 40 COUVERTS.
En l'Honneur du Gouverneur Tilden.

MENU.

Lucines orangées.

POTAGES.

Consommé à la Talleyrand.   Crème de pois verts, Saint Germain.

HORS-D'ŒUVRE.

Timbales à la Renaissance.

RELEVÉS.

Saumon à la Chambord.   Pommes Duchesse.

Selle d'agneau Salvandi.

ENTRÉES.

Poulets nouveaux Bagration.

Petits pois à l'Anglaise.

Côtelettes de pigeonneaux Signora.

Fonds d'artichauts sautés.

Ris de veau grillés, sauce Colbert.

Chicorée à la crème.

———

Sorbet Andalouse.

RÔT.

Bécasses.   Salade de laitue.

ENTREMETS SUCRÉS.

Croûte aux ananas à la Victoria.

———

Gelée aux fruits.   Coupole Chantilly.

Gâteau Viennois.   Gaufres de Carlsbad.

———

Glace moulée le faisan garni de biscuits Tortoni.

Excellent au café.

Petits fours.   Bonbons.   Devises.   Fruits.

DÉCEMBRE, 1877.
BUFFET POUR 100 PERSONNES.
PURIM BALL.

MENU.

CHAUD.

Bouillon.

Croquettes de volaille.

Bouchées de ris de veau.

FROID.

Galantine de dinde.

Pâté de gibier aux truffes.

Salade de légumes langues.

Mayonnaise de volaille.

Perdreaux et cailles à la gelée.

Sandwichs assortis.

DESSERT.

Gelée aux fruits.

Bavarois aux pêches.

Gâteau Mathilde.

Meringues Chantilly.

———

Glaces Napolitaine.

Biscuits glacés.

Tutti-frutti.

Mousse aux marrons.

Fruits.　　　　　　　Petit fours.

Pièces montées.

Bonbons.　　　　　　Devises.

Eug. Laperruque, Chef. Madison Square.　　　*Delmonico*

AVRIL, 1878.
Dîner de 225 Couverts.
En l'Honneur de Mr. Bayard Taylor,
Ministre des États Unis à Berlin.

MENU.

Huîtres.

POTAGES.

Consommé Washington.   Tortue verte.

HORS-D'ŒUVRE.

Brissotins à la Richelieu.

RELEVÉS.

Saumon de Kennebeck, sauce crevettes.
Pommes de terre Dauphine.
Filet de bœuf au Madère.
Tomates farcies.

ENTRÉES.

Estomacs de dinde à l'Impératrice.
Petits pois à l'Anglaise.
Escalopes d'agneau à la Chéron.
Haricots flageolets, maître-d'hôtel.
Mignons de canards, sauce bigarade.
Asperges en branches, sauce crème.
Maïs sauté au beurre.

———

Sorbet Young America.

RÔTS.

Chapons.   Pigeonneaux.

Salade de laitue.

ENTREMETS SUCRÉS.

Pouding à la Masséna.

———

Aspic de fruits.   Charlotte Russe.
Corbeille de meringues.   Pain de pêches Chantilly.
Gâteau noisettes.   Gâteau mille feuilles.
Glaces mignonne.   Dame blanche.
Fruits.   Petits fours.   Bonbons.   Devises.

Eug. Laperruque, Chef. Madison Square.   *Delmonico.*

FÉVRIER, 1879.
DÎNER DE 14 COUVERTS.
MR. W. K. VANDERBILT.

MENU.

Huîtres.

POTAGES.

Consommé Rachel.   Bisque d'écrevisses.

HORS-D'ŒUVRE.

Timbales Napolitaines.

RELEVÉS.

Escalopes de bass, Henri IV.   Pommes de terre surprise.

Selle de mouton Salvandi.

ENTRÉES.

Caisses de filets de poulet Grammont.

Choux de Bruxelles.   Petits pois à l'Anglaise.

Sauté de filets de grouses Tyrolienne.

Céleri au jus.

Terrapène à la Colombia.

———

Sorbet Aya-Pana.

RÔTS.

Canvas-back duck.   Cailles truffées.

Salade de laitue.

ENTREMETS SUCRÉS:

Pouding à la Humboldt.

———

Gelée d'orange Orientale.   Gaufres à la crème.

Blanc manger rubané.   Charlotte Victoria.

Glaces fruits en surprise.   Délicieux Impériale.

Dessert.

AOÛT, 1879.
DÎNER DE 14 COUVERTS,
Offert à Mr. Henry Irving.

MENU.

Lucines.

POTAGES.

Consommé d'Orsay. Crème d'orge Viennoise.

HORS-D'ŒUVRE.

Timbales à la Nilson.

RELEVÉS.

Maquereau Espagnol, sauce Aurore.
Pommes croquettes.
Filet de bœuf au Madère.
Tomates à la Reine.

ENTRÉES.

Suprême de volaille aux truffes.
Petits pois aux laitues.
Brochettes de ris de veau, sauce Laurent.
Maïs nouveaux sautés.

Fonds d'artichauts. Choux fleurs gratin.

Sorbet à l'Andalouse.

RÔTS.

Grouses flanquées d'ortolans. Salade de laitue.

ENTREMETS SUCRÉS.

Croûte aux ananas.

Gelée au parfait amour. Timbales au souvenir.
Glaces poires farcies. Excellent au café.
Pièces montées.
Dessert.

Delmonico.

Madison Square.

MARS, 1879.
DÎNER DE 12 COUVERTS,
Mr. H. R. Bishop.

MENU.

Huîtres.

POTAGES.

Consommé Impériale. Crème d'artichauts.

HORS-D'ŒUVRE.

Rissoles Demidoff.

RELEVÉS.

Bass à la Chambord. Pommes Duchesse.
Selle d'agneau à l'Anglaise. Pointes d'asperges.

ENTRÉES.

Filets de volaille Lorenzo.
Petits pois.
Caisses de reedbirds Périgueux.
Fonds d'artichauts aux champignons gratinés.

Sorbet Young America.

RÔTS.

Pluviers. Pigeonneaux.

Salade de laitue.

ENTREMETS SUCRÉS.

Timbale Eugénie.

GLACES.

Galée macédoine. Moscovite kummel.
Gâteau mousse orange. St. Honoré Chiboust.
Le Moulin à vent et le parfait café.
Dessert.

Delmonico.

Madison Square.

JANVIER, 1880.
DÎNER DE 32 COUVERTS.
En l'Honneur du Général Hancock.

MENU.

Huîtres.

POTAGES.

Consommé Rachel.   Purée de volaille à la Reine.

HORS-D'ŒUVRE.

Brissotins au suprême.

POISSONS.

Bass rayé aux éperlans Dauphin.
Pommes de terre Duchesse.

RELEVÉS.

Filet de bœuf aux cèpes.   Selle de mouton à l'Anglaise.
Épinards à l'Espagnole.

ENTRÉES.

Ailes de volaille à la Hongroise.
Petits pois Parisienne.
Côtelettes d'agneau maison d'Or.
Haricots panachés.
Fonds d'artichauts farcis aux champignons.

———

Terrapène en casserole à la Maryland.

———

Sorbet Montmorency.

RÔTS.

Canvas-back duck.
Cailles bardées (salade laitues).

ENTREMETS SUCRÉS.

Timbale Madison.

———

Gelée Orientale.   Gaufres Chantilly.
Glace Napolitaine.   Mousse aux bananes.
Pièces montées.

Petits fours.   Fruits.   Café.   Liqueurs.

MARS, 1880.
DÎNER DE 230 COUVERTS.
MR. DE LESSEPS.

MENU.

Huîtres sur coquilles.

POTAGES.

Consommé Sultane. Crème d'asperges Princesse.

HORS-D'ŒUVRE.
Timbales Périgordines.

RELEVÉS.

Bass rayé à la Conti. Pommes Duchesse.
Filet de bœuf à la Rossini. Tomates farcies.

ENTRÉES.

Suprême de volaille Lucullus.
Petits pois à la Française.
Côtelettes d'agneau à la Signora.
Haricots flageolets sautés.
Salmis de bécassines Lithuanienne.
Fonds d'artichauts Provençale.

ENTRÉES FROIDES.

Pain de gibier en Damier. Volière de faisans.
Aspics de foies-gras en Bellevue. Galantine de poulet aux truffes.

———

Sorbet Montmorency.

RÔTS.

Canvas-back. Pigeonneaux.
Salade de laitue.

ENTREMETS SUCRÉS.
Croûte aux ananas.

Gelée printanière. Lait d'amandes rubané.
Gaufres à la Chantilly. Gâteau Sicilien.

PIÈCES MONTÉES.

Glaces Napolitaine. Biscuits glacés.

Dessert.

MENU.

CHAUD.

Bouilion de volaille.

Huîtres à la poulette.

Coquilles de pétoncles à la Brestoise.

Dinde farcie aux marrons et aux truffes.

Croquettes de volaille.

Terrapènes.

FROID.

Filet de bœuf à la Varsovienne.

Buisson de langues à la gelée.

Galantine de chapon truffée.

Aspics de perdreaux historiés.

Volières de cailles.

Salade de volaille au céleri.

Mayonnaise de crevettes à la laitue.

Petits pains garnis de Rillettes.

Sandwichs assortis.

ENTREMETS SUCRÉS.

Gelée aux oranges.	Bavarois au café.
Charlotte Doria.	Gaufres à la crème.
Gâteau baba.	Gâteau Mathilde.

GLACES.

Petites glaces à la crème et aux fruits.

Tutti-frutti.	Parfait au café.

Biscuits glacés.

Fruits.	Petits fours.
Bonbons.	Devises.

Caisses et fruits glacés.

MENU.

MARS, 1881.
DÎNER DE 220 COUVERTS.
Offert à l'Honorable Carl Schurz.

Sauterne.   Huîtres.

POTAGES.

Amontillado Xérès.   Consommé Rachel.
Purée à la Condé.

HORS-D'ŒUVRE.

Brissotins au Suprême.

RELEVÉS.

Hochheimer Moselle.   Bass rayé, sauce Hollandaise.
Éperlans en Dauphin.
Pommes de terre Duchesse.

St. Julien Supérieur.   Filet de bœuf aux cèpes.
Epinards au velouté.

ENTRÉES.

Champagne.   Ailes de poulet à la Toulouse.
Petits pois au beurre.
Pigeonneaux à l'Allemande.
Tomates sautées.
Ris de veau purée de marrons.

Sorbet au kirsch.

Panzan, 1874, *Bourgogne.*   RÔTS.
Brants.   Selle de mouton.
Salade de laitue.

ENTREMETS SUCRÉS.

Plum pouding au sabayon.

Gelée au Madère.   Gaufres de Carlsbad.

Cigares et fleurs.   Glaces Napolitaine.   Mousse aux bananes.
Petits fours.
Fruits.   Café.   Liqueurs.

Madison Square.   *Delmonico.*

MENU.

JUIN, 1881.
DÎNER POUR 10 PERSONNES.
MR. J. F. LOUBAT.

Lucines.

POTAGES.

Consommé Sévigné.   Purée de gibier au Chasseur.

HORS-D'ŒUVRE.

Petites croustades financière.

RELEVÉS.

Saumon de Kennebeck, sauce Hollandaise.
Pommes Marquise.
Filet de bœuf à la Provençale.

ENTRÉES.

Poulet de grain à la Périgueux.   Petits pois.
Aspics de homards à la gelée.
Fondu au Parmesan.

Sorbet au Champagne.

RÔTS.

Selle d'agneau, sauce Cumberland.   Salade de Romaine.
Bécassines sur canapés.

ENTREMETS DE LÉGUMES.

Asperges en branches, sauce crème.

ENTREMETS SUCRÉS.

Timbales de fruits à la Parisienne.

GLACES.

Petites Génoises glacées.

Parfait au café.   Fruits.   Dessert.

Madison Square.   *Delmonico.*

NOVEMBRE, 1882.
BUFFET POUR 40 PERSONNES.
MR. CHARLES DANA.

MENU.

CHAUD.

Consommé de volaille.

Huîtres béchamel.   Rissolettes Pompadour.

Croquettes panachées.   Huîtres farcies.

Bouchées au financier.

FROID.

Darne de saumon à la Russe.

Filet de bœuf printanière.

Pâté de gibier aux truffes.

Ballotines de cailles en buisson.

Chaudfroid de poularde à la gelée.

Salade de homard.

Mayonnaise de volaille.

Sandwichs.

Canapés.

Rillettes.

ENTREMETS SUCRÉS FROIDS.

Gelée d'orange Orientale.   Crème bavaroise à l'abricot.

Gaufres crème.   Charlotte Parisienne.

Gâteau Viennois.   Gâteau noisettes.

Pièces Montées.

GLACES.

Napolitaine.   Merveilleuse.   Biscuit glacé.

Tutti-frutti.   Toronchino.

Devises.   Fruits.   Petits fours.

Bonbons.   Dessert.

Café.

MENU.

SEPTEMBRE, 1882.
DÎNER DE 175 COUVERTS.
En l'Honneur de l'Expédition Melville.

Haut Sauterne.	Huîtres.
	POTAGES.
Amontillado.	Consommé Andalouse.
	Crème d'artichauts.
	HORS-D'ŒUVRE.
	Timbales Périgordines.
	RELEVÉS.
Piesporter.	Aiguillettes de bass Joinville.
	Pommes de terre Anglaise.
Cliquot Sec.	Filet de bœuf Bernardi.
	ENTRÉES.
Pontet Canet.	Ailes de volaille Princere.
	Petits pois aux laitues.
	Ris de veau Napolitaine.
	Côtelettes Chateaubriand.
	Sorbet Maniniou.
	RÔT.
	Perdreaux garnis de mauviettes.
	FROID.
	Pâté de foies-gras à la gelée.
	Salade de laitue.
	ENTREMETS DE DOUCEUR CHAUD.
	Pouding Cambacérès.
Gelée aux fruits.	GLACES.
Merveilleuse.	Pièces montées.
Fruits.	Petits fours.
Café.	

Aubergines frites.

Haricots de Lima.
Maïs sautés.

Gaufres crème.
Napolitaine.
Fruits glacés.
Liqueurs.

Madison Square and Twenty-sixth Street. *Delmonico.*

MENU.

MARS, 188£.
DÎNER DE 12 COUVERTS.
MR. W. H. WICKHAM.

Chablis Vieux.	Huîtres.	
	POTAGES.	
Amontillado	Consommé Marie Stuart.	
	Tortue verte.	
	HORS-D'ŒUVRE.	
	Timbales écarlate.	
	RELEVÉS.	
Cliquot Rouge.	Alose grillée à l'Africaine.	Concombres.
	Selle d'agneau Colbert.	
	Pommes croquettes.	
	ENTRÉES.	
St. Pierre.	Ailes de poulet à la Patti.	
	Petits pois.	
	Salmis de canvas-back au vin de champagne.	
	Haricots verts.	Terrapène en casserole.
	Sorbet Andalouse.	
	RÔT.	
Château Latour.	Bécassines Anglaises.	Salade de laitue.
	Pâté de foies-gras.	
	ENTREMETS SUCRÉS.	
Champagne Roederer.	Croûte aux fruits.	
	Gelée abricotine.	Crème Carlsbad
	Pièces montées.	
	Glaces.	
Toronchino.	Milanaise.	
Fruits.	Dessert.	Café.

Madison Square and Twenty-sixth Street. *Delmonico.*

MARS, 1883.
Menu d'un Dîner Original de
14 Couverts.
Mr. Benson.

BUFFET RUSSE.

Canapés de caviar.   Olives farcies.   Céleri.

Éperlans.   Marinés radis.   Canapés d'anchois.   Olives de Lucques.

Saucisson de Lyon.   Saucisson.

Vermuth.   Sherry et bitters.   Absinthe.

———————

Johannisberg.	Huîtres.
Madère.	Bisque de Lucines (clams).
	Potage à l'oseille aux croûtons.
	Crabes d'huîtres frits. Concombres marinés.
Château Yquem.	Timbales de sheepshead à l'Ambassadrice.
	Homards grillés. Salade de tomates.
Lacrima Christi.	Vol au vent d'animelles d'agneau financière.
	Terrapène désossée à la Newberg.
Château Larose.	Filet de bœuf Brillat-Savarin.
	Croquettes de pommes de terre surprise.
	Casseroles de volaille au gourmet.
	Quenelles de pigeonneaux aux Topinambours.
Champagne Pommery.	Côtelettes d'agneau à l'Espagnole.
Champagne Perrier Jouët	Asperges nouvelles à l'huile et à la sauce Alcide.
Bourgogne Mousseux.	Champignons nouveaux sur croûtes grillées.
	Soufflés au fromage.
	Sorbet, café et kirsch en écorce de fruits variés.
Clos Vougeot.	Faisans Anglais rôtis au cresson.
	Jambon grillé. Bananes frites. Salade laitue. Mâches.
	Artichauts, sauce bavaroise.
	Pouding de fruits Sabayon Madère
	Glace cygne aux roseaux.
	Moulin à vent sur socle.
	Macédoine de fruits en bordure de Madeleine.
	Café. Liqueurs.

AVRIL, 1883.
DÎNER DE 18 COUVERTS.
MR. W. H. MORGAN.

MENU.

Huîtres.

POTAGES

Consommé Sully   Bisque de homard.

HORS-D'ŒUVRE.

Cassolettes à la Dumas.

RELEVÉS.

Truites de rivière grillées.   Concombres.

Selle d'agneau à la Florentine.

Croustades macédoine.

ENTRÉES.

Filets de poulet à la Lucullus.   Petits pois au beurre.

Quenelles de faisan Anglais à la Molière.

Asperges sauce blanche.

Sorbets Fantaisie Divers.

RÔTS.

Poulardes truffées et pigeonneaux bardés.

Aspics de foies-gras.   Salade de laitue.

ENTREMETS SUCRÉ CHAUD.

Poires à la Richelieu.

ENTREMETS SUCRÉS FROIDS.

Bavarois vanille.

Pièces montées.   Petits fours.

GLACES.

Gelée aux reines claude.

Gâteau Africain.

Fruits surprise.

Rachel historiée   Dessert.

Fruits.

Café.

Mr. Morgan, No. 7, East 26th Street.   *Servi par Delmonico.*

AOÛT, 1883.
DÎNER DE 25 COUVERTS.
MR. ELLIOTT F. SHEPARD.

MENU.

Lucines.

POTAGES.

Consommé Dumas.   Crème de choux fleurs.

HORS-D'ŒUVRE.

Bouchées financière.

POISSON.

Maquereau Espagnol marinière.   Concombres.

RELEVÉS.

Filet de bœuf Bernardi.   Haricots de Lima.

Pommes Duchesse.

ENTRÉES.

Suprême de poulet aux truffes.   Petits pois.

Salmis de pluviers aux champignons nouveaux.   Haricots verts.

Sorbet à la Royale.

RÔT.

Pigeonneaux au cresson.   Salade de Romaine.

ENTREMETS SUCRÉS.

Ananas Caroline.   Gelée Dantzick.

Bavarois vanille.

Pièces montées.

GLACES.

Fiori di latte au chocolat.   Plombière Montesquieu.

Fruits.   Dessert.

Café.

Madison Square.   *Delmonico.*

MARS, 1884.
Dîner de 150 Couverts.

"USQUE AD SUPÉROS"
L'Union des Titans
Grand repas classique et soirée Olympienne en l'honneur de notre mère la Terre.

MENU.

Chablis Vieux.   Huîtres sur coquilles de Neptune.

POTAGE.

Amontillado.   Consommé aux œufs de Léda.

HORS-D'ŒUVRE.

Céleri des Hespérides.   Olives du Mont Ida.
Timbale à la Reine Junon.

POISSON.

Rudesheimer Berg.   Bass à la Méduse Divine.

RELEVÉ.

Cliquot doux.   Filet de bœuf à l'Hercule Antique.

ENTRÉES.

St. Pierre.   Dinde aux trois Grâces.

Agneau aux sourires de Psyché.

Côtelettes à l'Harmonie des Sirènes.

Sorbet aux plaisirs Olympiens.

RÔTS.

Clos Vougeot.   Canard sauvage à la Jupiter.

Salade aux larmes d'Hébé.

LÉGUMES.

Petits pois à la Priam.   Haricots verts à l'Aurore.
Épinards à la fleur de Lotus.   Pommes à la Toison d'Or.

ENTREMETS SUCRÉS.

Croûtes d'ananas aux reflets de l'Enfer.   Gelée aux raisins de Bacchus.
Charlotte à la Phineas.   Gaufres à la Proserpine.
Pièces Montées à la Mercure.

Vieux Porto.   Glaces à la Vierge Vestale.

Petits fours à l'Ambroisie   Fruits au Mont Hélion.
Fromage à la Flore.   Café au Nectar Divin.

NOVEMBRE, 1884.
DÎNER DE 225 COUVERTS.
NEW YORK PRESS CLUB.

MENU.

POTAGES.

Consommé Souveraine
Bisque de homard.

HORS-D'ŒUVRE.

Variés.

POISSON.

Bass rayé à la Hongroise.
Pommes à la Viennoise.

RELEVÉS.

Filets de bœuf à la d'Orléans.
Tomates à la Trévise.

ENTRÉES.

Dindonneaux aux marrons.
Côtelettes de ris de veau Montebello.
Petits pois.
Haricots verts.

Sorbet à la Dalmatie.

RÔTI.

Canard à tête rouge.
Salade de laitue.

ENTREMETS SUCRÉS.

Pouding à la Humboldt.
Glaces Napolitaine.

Dessert.
Pièces montées.
Café.

Madison Square.
Delmonico

OCTOBRE, 1884.
DÎNER DE 200 COUVERTS
EN L'HONNEUR DE JAMES G. BLAINE.

MENU.

Huîtres.

POTAGES.

Consommé Victoria.
Crème de volaille Berchoux.

HORS-D'ŒUVRE.

Timbales Reynière.

POISSONS.

Kingfish Richelieu.
Éperlans frits.

RELEVÉS.

Selle de chevreuil Tyrolienne
Pommes à l'Anglaise.

ENTRÉES.

Filet de bœuf Clarendon.
Tomates Trévise.
Ailes de poulet à la Lucullus.
Ris de veau au Chancelier.
Petits pois Française.
Haricots verts.
Terrapène Marvland.

RÔT.

Sorbet a l'Impériale.

FROID.

Canvas-back duck
Galantine de poularde aux truffes.
Aspics de foies-gras.

ENTREMETS SUCRÉS.

Gelée à la prunelle.
Mazarine à l'ananas.
Charlotte Bengalienne.
Pièces montées.
Glaces Arlequin.
Soufflé aux marrons.
Petits fours.
Gâteaux.
Fruits.
Dessert.
Café.

Madison Square.
Delmonico.

MAI, 1885.
DÎNER DE 30 COUVERTS.
MR. N. L. THIEBLIN (RIGOLO).

MENU.

Chablis.   Lucines (clams).

POTAGES.

Amontillado, 1834.   Consommé Sévigné.   Tortue verte à l'Anglaise.

HORS-D'ŒUVRE.

Bressoles Chateaubriand.

POISSONS.

Scharzhofberger   Saumon grillé à la Colbert.   Concombres.
Auslese.   Aiguillettes de kingfish Marguery.   Pommes gastronome.

RELEVÉS.

Filet de bœuf à la Richelieu Moderne.
Selle d'agneau de lait aux laitues braisées.

ENTRÉES.

Rauzan.   Pâté chaud à la financière.
Ris de veau à la Théodora.

———

Sorbet a la Montmorency.

RÔTS.

Poulets reine truffés à la Périgueux.
Chambertin.   Bécassines sur canapés au cresson.

RELEVÉ.

Soufflés au fromage.

FROID.

Aspics de foies-gras historiés aux truffes.
Cliquot Doux.   Homard rémoulade à la gelée.

ENTREMETS DE LEGUMES.

Artichauts à la Duxelle   Asperges à l'Allemande.

ENTREMETS SUCRÉS.

Crème frite à l'Augusta (chaud).
Charlotte de pommes aux abricots (chaud).
Gaufres crème marasquin.   Tartelettes aux cerises.

PIÈCES MONTÉES.

Fruits frais.   Fraises   Compotes.
Fromage.   Amandes salées.   Bonbons.
Devises.   Fruits cristallisés.   Marrons rôtis.
Liqueurs.   Café

Left Menu

FÉVRIER, 1885.
DÎNER DE 240 COUVERTS.
ST. NICHOLAS SOCIETY.

MENU.

Huîtres.

POTAGES.

Consommé Adélina   Crème d'asperges.

HORS-D'ŒUVRE.

Timbales à la Reine.

POISSON.

Bass rayé Marguery.   Pommes Hollandaise.

RELEVÉ.

Filet de bœuf Piémontaise.   Tomates Trévise.

ENTRÉES.

Chapons braisés aux marrons.
Petits pois à la Française.
Ris de veau à la Béarnaise.
Haricots panachés.

Sorbet Impérial.

RÔTI.

Canvas-back ducks.   Salade de laitue.

FROID.

Pâté de foies-gras.

ENTREMETS CHAUD.

Croûtes aux ananas.

ENTREMETS FROIDS.

Oublies à la crème.   Pièces montées.
Gâteau noisettes.
Petits fours.

Glaces: Soufflés Favart.   Dessert.
Fruits.

Café.

Madison Square.   *Delmonico.*

Right Menu

FÉVRIER, 1885.
DÎNER DE 14 COUVERTS.
MR. J. B. HOUSTON.

MENU.

Huîtres.

POTAGES.

—*Crème de Tête.*

Consommé Aurélien.   Tortue verte claire.

HORS-D'ŒUVRE.

Amontillado.   Timbales Lagardère.

POISSONS.

Moët White Seal.   Red snapper, sauce Hollandaise vert-pré
Crabes d'huîtres frits.   Concombres.

RELEVÉS.

Selle d'agneau de lait à la Bernardi.
Choux de Bruxelles.

ENTRÉES.

Rauzan.   Filet de poulet à la Lucullus.
Petits pois à la Parisienne.
Terrapène à la Philadelphie

Sorbet Elisabeth.

RÔTIS.

Clos Vougeot.   Faisans Anglais piqués.
Bécassines au cresson.

Pâté de foies-gras.   Salade de laitue.

ENTREMETS SUCRÉS.

Beignets Médicis.

GLACE.

Arbre en nougat entouré de lapins et ours.

Liqueurs.   Dessert.

Madison Square.   *Delmonico.*

MENU.

Huîtres.

POTAGES.

Consommé Impériale.　　　　　　　　Bisque d'écrevisses

HORS-D'ŒUVRE.

Timbales Diplomate.

POISSON.

Saumon, sauce Hollandaise vert-pré.

Éperlans frits.　　　　　　　　Pommes Viennoise.

RELEVÉ.

Filet de bœuf Napolitaine.　　　　　　　　Haricots verts sautés.

ENTRÉES.

Ris de veau chevreuse.　　　　　　　　Tomates farcies.

Escalopes de bass à la Joinville　　　　　　　　Petits pois Française.

———

Sorbet Monthière.

———

RÔTS.

Canards à tête rouge.　　　　　　　　Salade de laitue.

Salade de crabes mavonnaise.

ENTREMETS SUCRÉS.

Pouding Impératrice.

Gelée aux mirabelles.　　　　　　　　Charlotte Parisienne.

Pièces montées.

Glace crème pralinée.　　　　　　　　Biscuits glacés.

Fruits.　　　　　　　　Dessert.

Café.

MENU.

NOVEMBRE, 1886.
DÎNER DE 16 COUVERTS.
MR. JOSEPH PULITZER.

Château Yquem. — Huîtres sur coquilles.

POTAGES.

Amontillado. — Consommé Souveraine.
Tortue verte à la Royale.

HORS-D'ŒUVRE.

Timbales Lagardère.

POISSON.

Johannisberg. — Aiguillettes de bass à la Chivry.
Concombres.

RELEVÉS.

Perrier Jouët— Spécial Magnum. — Selle de chevreuil à l'Athalin
Haricots panachés.

ENTRÉE.

St. Pierre. — Terrapène à la Baltimore en casserole.
Sorbet à l'Andalouse.

RÔT.

Romanée Conti. — Canvas back.

FROID.

Perrier Jouët. — Aspics de foies-gras historiés.
Salade de laitue.

ENTREMETS DE DOUCEUR.

Poires à la Ferrière.
Glaces de fantaisie.

Fromage. Pièces montées. Petits fours.

Cognac, Chartreuse, Kirsch, Bénédictine. Fruits. Café

Madison Square.

Delmonico.

MENU.

JANVIER, 1886.
DÎNER DE 14 COUVERTS.
MR. WARD MCALLISTER.

Potage. — Tortue verte au Clair.

Hors-d'Œuvre. — Boudins de volaille Richelieu.

Poisson. — Aiguillettes de bass au gratin.

Relevé. — Filet de bœuf Rothschild.

Entrées. — Terrapène à la Maryland.
Aspics de foies-gras en Bellevue.
Fonds d'artichauts à l'Italienne.

Sorbet au Marasquin.

Rôt. — Canvas-back duck.
Céleri mayonnaise.

Entremets Chaud. — Pommes à la Parisienne.

Glace. — Pouding Nesselrode.

Madison Square.

Delmonico

NOVEMBRE, 1887.
DÎNER DE 200 COUVERTS.
ST. ANDREWS SOCIETY.

MENU.

Huîtres.

POTAGES.

Consommé Deslignac.　　　　　　　　　Tortue verte au Clair.

HORS-D'ŒUVRE.

Timbales Reine.

POISSON.

Saumon, sauce Hollandaise vert-pré.　　　　Pommes à la Viennoise.

RELEVÉS.

Filet de bœuf aux champignons.　　　　　Choux de Bruxelles.

ENTRÉES.

Poularde à la Chevreuse.　　　　　　　Petits pois au beurre.

Caisse de ris de veau Italienne.　　　　　Haricots verts à l'Anglaise.

Haggis à l'Écossaise.

———

Sorbet Impériale.

———

RÔT.

Canards à tête rouge.　　　　　　　　Salade de laitue.

ENTREMETS DE DOUCEUR.

Pouding aux bananes.

———

Gelée aux cerises.　　　　　　　　　Charlotte Russe.

Glaces fantaisie variées.

Pièces montées.

Fruits.　　　　　　　　　　　　　Petits fours.

Café.

DÉCEMBRE, 1887.
DÎNER POUR 14 PERSONNES.
Mr. OSWALD OTTENDORFER.

MENU.

Huîtres.

POTAGES.

Consommé Mécène.   Bisque aux crevettes.

HORS-D'ŒUVRE.

Timbales Lagardère.
Truites de rivière ravigote vert-pré.
White bait frit.   Pommes Sarah.

RELEVÉS.

Concombres.
Selle d'agneau à la Colbert.   Tomates Trévise.

ENTRÉES.

Ailes de poulet à la Lucullus.
Petits pois au beurre.
Terrapène à la Maryland.
Asperges, sauce Hollandaise.

Sorbet Béatrice.

RÔTS.

Bécassines.   Pigeonneaux.

FROID.

Petits aspics de foies-gras.

ENTREMETS DE DOUCEUR.

Pommes à la Portugaise.
Pièces montées.
Glaces de fantaisie.
Marrons glacés.
Café.

Fruits.   Salade de laitue.   Petits fours.

Madison Square and Twenty-sixth Street.   Delmonico.

DÉCEMBRE, 1887.
DÎNER DE 18 COUVERTS.
Mr. LASOQUE.

MENU.

Huîtres.

POTAGES.

Consommé Bonvalet.   Bisque d'écrevisses.

HORS-D'ŒUVRE.

Timbales à la Dumas.

POISSON.

Aiguillettes de red snapper à la Masséna.
Pommes Duchesse.

RELEVÉS.

Filet de bœuf à la Bernardi.
Épinards à la crème.

ENTRÉES.

Suprême de volaille aux truffes.
Petits pois au beurre.
Terrapène Maryland Club.

Sorbet Béatrice.

RÔT.

Canvas-back duck.   Salade de laitue.

ENTREMETS DE DOUCEUR.

Gelée aux oranges.   Charlotte Doria.
Glaces fantaisie.

Fruits.   Bonbons.   Devises.
Café.

Madison Square and Twenty-sixth Street.   Delmonico.

AVRIL, 1888.
Dîner de 200 Couverts.
Ohio Society.

MENU.

Huîtres.

POTAGES.

Consommé Deslignac.　　　　　　　　　　　Crème d'asperges.

HORS-D'ŒUVRE.

Timbales à la Mentana.

POISSON.

Saumon sauce crevettes.

Pommes à l'Anglaise.

RELEVÉS.

Filet de bœuf à la Chevrelat.

Tomates farcies.

ENTRÉES.

Chapons à la Lyonnaise.

Petits pois au beurre.

Croquettes de homard à la Victoria.

———

Sorbet Régence.

RÔT.

Bécassines bardées.　　　　　　　　　　　Salade de laitue.

ENTREMETS DE DOUCEUR.

Savarin aux cerises.

Glaces Napolitaine.

Fruits.　　　　　　　　　　　　　　　Petits fours.

Café.

OCTOBRE, 1888.
DÎNER DE 29 COUVERTS.
DR. LEFFERTS.

MENU.

Lucines.

POTAGES.

Consommé Balzac. Tortue verte au Clair.

HORS-D'ŒUVRE.

Variés.

Timbales Lagardère.

POISSON.

Aiguillettes de bass Richelieu.
Pommes Viennoise.

RELEVÉS.

Selle d'agneau tardif aux fritadelles.
Céleri braisé.

ENTRÉES.

Ailes de volaille Marceau. Tomates Trévise.
Casseroles de terrapène Baltimore.

Sorbet Impériale.

RÔT.

Perdreaux garnis de mauviettes.
Salade de tomates en quartiers mayonnaise.

ENTREMETS DE DOUCEUR.

Pêches à la Condé.

Glaces fantaisie.

Café.

Fruits.

Petits fours.

NOVEMBRE, 1888.
DÎNER DE 14 COUVERTS.
MR. C. A. SEWARD.

MENU.

Huîtres.

POTAGES.

Consommé Meternich. Tortue verte au clair.

HORS-D'ŒUVRE.

Palmettes à la Perrier.

POISSON.

Aiguillettes de bass à l'Italienne. Pommes Sarah.

RELEVÉS.

Concombres.

Dinde farcie aux marrons. Haricots panachés.

ENTRÉES.

Ris de veau aux champignons nouveaux. Terrapène Newberg.

Petits pois Française.

Sorbet à la Prunelle.

RÔTS.

Canvas-back duck et cailles piquées. Salade de laitue.

Petits aspics historiés.

ENTREMETS DE DOUCEUR.

Gelée aux pistaches. Charlotte Russe.

Glaces moulées. Petits fours.

Fruits. Fromage.

Amandes salées. Marrons glacés. Fruits confits.

Bonbons. Compotes. Poires et pêches.

Café.

JANVIER, 1889.

DÎNER DE 250 COUVERTS.

Annual Dinner given by the Superintendent,
Inspectors and Captains of the
New York Police.

MENU.

POTAGES.

Consommé Rémusat.   Bisque d'écrevisses.

HORS-D'ŒUVRE.

Timbales à la Périgordine.

POISSON.

Saumon, sauce Hollandaise vert-pré.

Pommes à la Rouennaise.

RELEVÉS.

Filet de bœuf aux champignons.

Tomates au gratin.

ENTRÉES.

Dinde farcie aux marrons.   Petits pois à l'Anglaise.

Caisse de ris de veau Grammont.   Haricots panachés.

Sorbet Royale.

RÔTS.

Canvas-back duck.   Salade de laitue.

ENTREMETS DE DOUCEUR.

Pouding Schiller.

Gelée au Centerba.   Gaufres à la crème

Pièces montées.

Glaces   fantaisie.

Fruits.   Petits fours.

Café.

FÉVRIER, 1889.
DÎNER DE 21 COUVERTS.
MR. E. A. PRICE.

MENU.

Huîtres.

POTAGES.

Consommé Samaritaine. Tortue verte au Clair.

HORS-D'ŒUVRE.

Timbales Parisienne.

POISSON.

Aiguillettes de bass à la Whitney. Pommes Duchesse.

RELEVÉS.

Concombres. Selle d'antilope Tyrolienne.
Asperges sauce crème.

ENTRÉES.

Ailes de poulet à la Lucullus.
Petits pois au beurre.
Terrapène Maryland.

Sorbet Béatrice.

RÔTS.

Canvas-back duck et pigeonneaux.
Petites terrines de foies-gras.
Salade de laitue.
Pièces montées.

Gelée aux cerises. Charlotte Doria.
Glaces fantaisie.
Marrons glacés. Devises. Bonbons. Petits fours.
Amandes salées. Fromage. Café.

Madison Square and Twenty-sixth Street. Delmonico.

MARS, 1889.
DÉJEUNER DE 16 COUVERTS.
MR. COQUELIN.

MENU.

Canapés d'anchois. Caviar. Radis.
Olives. Céleri.
Huîtres.
Filets de poulet à la Génin.
Petits pois Française.
Pommes Sarah.
Asperges nouvelles, sauce Hollandaise.

Sorbet à la Russe.

Bécassines rôties au cresson.
Petites terrines de foies-gras à la gelée.
Salade de laitue.
Omelette soufflée.
Glaces: Champignons, sauce Marasquin.
Compotes.
Fruits. Petits fours.
Café.

Madison Square and Twenty-sixth Street. Delmonico.

JANVIER, 1890.
DÎNER DE 200 COUVERTS.
SECOND PANEL SHERIFF'S JURY.

MENU.

Huîtres.

POTAGES.

Consommé Bourdaloue.   Crème d'artichauts.

HORS-D'ŒUVRE.

Timbales à la Reine.

POISSON.

Saumon sauce homard.

Pommes de terre Duchesse.

RELEVÉS.

Filet de bœuf Périgueux.   Choux de Bruxelles.

ENTRÉES.

Poulet braisés à la Lyonnaise.

Ris de veau sauce tomates Andalouse.

Haricots flageolets sautés.

Sorbet Dalmatie.

RÔT.

Canvas-back ducks.

Salade de laitue.

ENTREMETS DE DOUCEUR.

Croûtes aux poires.

Pièces montées.

Glaces fantaisie.

Fruits.   Petits fours.

Café.

JANVIER, 1890.
DÎNER DE 220 COUVERTS.
HOTEL MEN'S ASSOCIATION.

MENU.

POTAGES.

Consommé St. Germain.
Bisque d'Écrevisses Dumont Durville.

HORS-D'ŒUVRE.

Petites timbales à la Soubise.

POISSONS.

Aiguillettes d'halibut à la Dugléré.

Éperlans frits.   Pommes Viennoise.

RELEVÉS.

Filet de bœuf à l'Aquitaine.
Petits pois Parisienne.

ENTRÉES.

Ailes de poulet à la Génin.
Macédoine St. Cloud.
Ris de veau purée de marrons.
Aubergines frites.

———

Sorbet Marquise.

RÔT.

Canards à tête rouge.

FROID.

Terrine de foies-gras de Strasbourg.
Salade de laitue.

ENTREMETS DE DOUCEUR.

Croûtes aux ananas.

Pièces montées.

Glaces fantaisie.

Fruits.   Petits fours.

Café.

MENU.

CHAUD.

Consommé.

Huîtres Viennoise.

Croquettes de chapon.

Bouchées aux crevettes.

Terrapène à la Maryland.

Café et thé.

FROID.

Filet de bœuf Francillon.

Galantine de poulet à l'Anglaise.

Terrine de Nérac aux truffes.

Aspic de foies-gras décoré.

Dinde en daube à l'Ancienne.

Cailles piquées rôties au cresson.

Salade de homard.

Mayonnaise de volaille.

Sandwichs.   Rillettes.   Canapés.

ENTREMETS DE DOUCEUR.

Gelée aux oranges.

Brisselets à la Chantilly.

Gâteau Madeleine.

Bavarois aux abricots.

Pièces montées.

Glaces fantaisie.   Tutti-frutti.
Montélimar.   Biscuit Diplomate.

Bonbons.   Devises.   Fruits.   Petits fours.

Dessert.

FÉVRIER, 1891.
DÎNER DE 3 COUVERTS.
MR. FRANK WORK.

MENU

Huîtres.

POTAGES.

Consommé.
Tortue au clair.

HORS-D'ŒUVRE.

Mousseline Chantilly.

POISSON.

Aiguillettes de bass aux éperlans Dauphin.
Concombres.

RELEVÉS.

Selle d'agneau de lait Colbert.
Artichauts Parmentier.

ENTRÉES.

Ailos de poulet aux truffes. Petits pois Parisienne.
Terrapène à la Baltimore.

Sorbet Impériale.

RÔT.

Canard à tête rouge. Salade de laitue.

ENTREMETS DE DOUCEUR.

Croûtes aux ananas.
Glaces de fantaisie.

Fruits. Bonbons. Devises. Petits fours.
Café.

Madison Square and Twenty-sixth Street. *Delmonico.*

JANVIER, 1891.
SOUPER ASSIS DE 50 COUVERTS.
MR. PRICE.

MENU.

Huîtres.

Consommé.

Bouchées aux champignons.

Terrapène Maryland.

Poularde Viennaise.
Petits pois Parisienne.

Côtelettes de ris de veau Moderne.

Cailles bardées rôties.

Terrine de foies-gras.
Salade de laitue.

Gelée à la prunelle.

Gaufres crème.

Pièces montées.

Glaces fantaisie.

Fruits. Devises. Petits fours.
Café.

Madison Square and Twenty-sixth Street. *Delmonico.*

NOVEMBRE, 1892.
DÎNER DE 250 COUVERTS.
Offert à l'Honorable Grover Cleveland.

MENU.

Huîtres.

POTAGES.

Consommé à la Grammont.   Bisque d'écrevisses.

HORS-D'ŒUVRE.

Timbales Renaissance.

POISSON.

Aiguillettes de bass Masséna.

Concombres.   Pommes Viennoise.

RELEVÉ.

Filet de bœuf Condé.   Tomates Trévise.

ENTRÉES.

Ailes de volaille suprême aux truffes.

Petits pois Parisienne.

Terrapène Baltimore.

Sorbet Columbus.

RÔT.

Canvas-back ducks.

FROID.

Foies-gras à la gelée.   Salade de laitue.

ENTREMETS DE DOUCEUR.

Pommes au praslin.

Pièces montées.

Glaces fantaisie.

Fruits.   Petits fours.

Café.

AVRIL, 1892.
Dîner de 200 Couverts.
Donné par la Chambre de Commerce en
l'honneur de Mr. Whitelaw Reid.

MENU.

Sherry and Bitters. Huîtres.

Haut Sauterne. POTAGES.

Consommé Berchoux.

Sherry Princesse. Tortue verte au clair.

HORS-D'ŒUVRE.

Timbales à la Dumas.

POISSON.

Diedesheimer. Saumon à la Royale.

Pommes Duchesse.

RELEVÉ.

Champagne. Filet de bœuf à la Périgueux.

Choux-fleurs au gratin.

ENTRÉES.

Ailes de poulet Montebello.

Château Lagrange. Petits pois à l'Anglaise.

Terrapène à la Baltimore.

Sorbet Impériale.

RÔT.

Beaujolais. Pluviers bardés.

FROID.

Terrine de foies-gras à la gelée. Salade.

ENTREMETS DE DOUCEUR.
Savarin aux ananas.

Gelée aux fruits. Meringues Chantilly.

Pièces montées.

Liqueurs. Glaces de fantaisie.

Fruits. Petits fours. Café.

JANVIER, 1892.
DÎNER DE 200 COUVERTS.
FIRST PANEL SHERIFF'S JURY.

MENU.

Huîtres.

POTAGES.

Consommé Deslignac.   Tortue verte claire

HORS-D'ŒUVRE.

Bouchées Chevreuse.

POISSON.

Saumon de l'Orégon, sauce Montebello.
Pommes de terre Duchesse.

RELEVÉ.

Selle de mouton Anglaise.
Épinards au velouté.

ENTRÉES.

Poulardes farcies aux truffes.
Petits pois à l'Anglaise.
Ris de veau en caisses à la Grammont.
Haricots panachés.

————

Sorbet Impériale.

RÔT.

Canards à tête rouge.

FROID.

Terrine de foies-gras de Strasbourg.
Salade de laitue.

ENTREMETS DE DOUCEUR.

Poires à la Judic.

Pièces montées.

Glaces Napolitaine.   Petits fours.

Café.

FÉVRIER, 1892.
DÎNER DE 9 COUVERTS.
GÉNÉRAL HORACE PORTER.

MENU.

Huîtres.

POTAGES.

Consommé Condorcet.   Bisque de crevettes.

HORS-D'ŒUVRE.

Variés.   Variés.

POISSON.

Bass rayé à l'Amiral.   Pommes Dauphine.

RELEVÉ.

Selle de Chevreuil Tyrolienne.

Aubergines frites.

ENTRÉES.

Filets de poulet Toulouse.   Petits pois à l'Anglaise.

Terrapène Baltimore.

———

Sorbet au Champagne.

———

RÔT.

Canard à tête rouge.   Salade de laitue.

ENTREMETS DE DOUCEUR.

Plum pouding au rhum.

Fruits.   Petits fours.

Café.

MENU

—

Huitres

Potages

Consommé, Souveraine   Tortue verte à l'anglaise

Hors d'oeuvre

Timbales, Périgourdine

Poisson

Bass rayée, Massena

Pommes de terre, fondantes

Releve

Filet de bœuf aux olives farcies

Tomates, Trévise

Entrees

Châpon à l'Amphitryon

Petits pois, parisienne

Térrapène à la Newberg

—

SORBET TULIPE

—

Rot

Canvas-back Duck   Cailles

Froid

Terrine de foie-gras

Salade de laitue

Entremets de douceur

Pommes à la Condé

Gelée aux oranges   Gaufres, Chantilly   Piéces montées

Glaces fantaisies

Fruits   Dessert   Petits fours

Café

Mardi, le 21 Novembre, 1893.   DELMONICO'S.

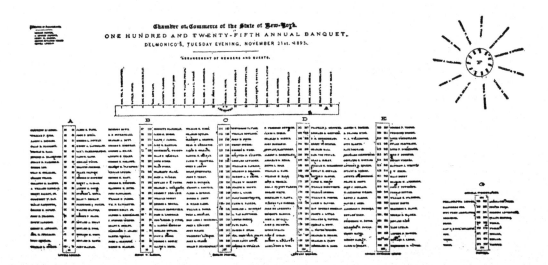

MAI, 1893.

DÎNER DE 14 COUVERTS.

Columbus Centennial Dîner en l'Honneur de
S. A. I. le Prince de Russie.

MENU.

BUFFET.

Canapés d'anchois. Caviar. Olives. Thon mariné.
Tartelettes de homard.
Lucines (clams).

POTAGES.

Consommé à la Souveraine.
Crème d'asperges.

HORS-D'ŒUVRE CHAUD.

Timbales au Prince Impérial.

POISSON.

Truites de rivière, sauce Hollandaise vert-pré.
Pommes de terre fondantes.

RELEVÉ.

Selle d'agneau aux fritadelles.
Tomates à la Reine.

ENTRÉES.

Ailes de poulet à la Lucullus. Petits pois à la Parisienne.
Champignons sous cloche.

———

Sorbet bouquetière à la Russe.

RÔT.

Pigeonneaux au cresson.

FROID.

Mousse de foies-gras en bordure.

ENTREMETS DE DOUCEUR.

Savarin aux ananas.

Glace pouding Romanoff.

Fruits. Petits fours.

Café.

Offert par Mr. F. S. Smith. *Delmonico.*

AVRIL, 1893.

Dîner de 200 Couverts.

St. George Society.

MENU.

Huîtres.

POTAGES.

Consommé Souveraine.   Crème St. Germain.

HORS-D'ŒUVRE.

Timbales à l'Écarlate.

POISSON.

Bass rayé au gratin.   Pommes de terre Viennoise.

RELEVÉ.

Baron de bœuf Yorkshire pouding.

Pommes de terre rôties.

Tomates farcies.

ENTRÉES.

Pigeonneaux à la Chevreuse.

Petits pois à l'Anglaise.

Asperges sauce crème.

———

Sorbet Régence.

———

RÔT.

Chapons.   Salade d'escarolle.

ENTREMETS DE DOUCEUR.

Plum pouding St. George.

———

Pièces montées.

Charlotte Russe.   Gelée au Madère.

Glaces fantaisie.

Fruits.   Petits fours.

Café.

NOVEMBRE, 1893.

DÎNER OFFERT PAR

Mr. L. C. Delmonico à

   Mr. Jean Charles Cazin.

MENU.

Haut Sauterne.	Huîtres.	

POTAGES.

Amontillado.	Consommé à la Daumont.	Bisque d'écrevisses.

HORS-D'ŒUVRE.

Mousseline Chantilly.

POISSONS.

Hochheimer. Aiguillettes de bass Mornay gratin.

Pommes de terre fondantes.

RELEVÉS.

Chât. Lagrange. Selle d'agneau tardif à la Colbert.

Fonds d'artichauts Florentine.

ENTRÉES.

Terrapène à la Maryland.

Vol au vent de ris de veau financière.

Petits pois à la Parisienne.

————

Sorbet " Elsinore."

RÔTS.

Chambertin. Canvas-back duck, hominy et currant gelée.

Chapons farcis aux truffes et marrons.

FROID.

Petits aspics de foies-gras.

Salade de laitue.

ENTREMETS DE DOUCEUR.

Krug Sec. Beignets Alliance, sauce abricots.

GLACES.

Cygne aux roseaux.

Liqueurs. Lapin en surprise.

Fruits.   Petits fours.

Café.

INDEX.

CPSIA information can be obtained at www.ICGtesting.com
Printed in the USA
BVOW09s0900150816

458550BV00014B/55/P